ISBN 978-0-331-51330-1
PIBN 11203631

REPORT

OF THE

POSTMASTER-GENERAL

OF THE

UNITED STATES;

BEING PART OF

THE MESSAGE AND DOCUMENTS

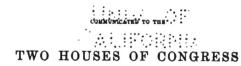

COMMUNICATED TO THE

TWO HOUSES OF CONGRESS

AT THE

BEGINNING OF THE SECOND SESSION OF THE FIFTIETH CONGRESS.

————•◆•————

WASHINGTON:
GOVERNMENT PRINTING OFFICE.
1888.

CONTENTS.

I

CONTENTS.

III

Page.

CONTENTS. **V**

REPORT

OF

THE POSTMASTER-GENERAL.

POST-OFFICE DEPARTMENT,

Washington, D. C., November 28, 1888.

SIR: I have the honor to present a report of the transactions of this Department for the fiscal year ended June 30, 1888.

As will be seen by the tabulated statements herewith submitted, the volume of business of the postal service is rapidly expanding. The average increase of business in the salary and allowance division since 1880 is 561.9 per cent., and since 1885, 108.2 per cent.

The number of postmasters appointed during the year ended June 30, 1888, was 12,288, of which 6,521 were upon resignations and commissions expired, 1,244 upon removals, 659 to fill vacancies by death, and 3,864 on establishment of new post-offices.

One thousand six hundred and forty-five post-offices were discontinued during the year, and the names and sites of 1,493 offices were changed, retaining the incumbents.

Statement of postmasters appointed during each fiscal year between June 4, 1868, and June 30, 1888, with number of post-offices in operation at the end of each fiscal year mentioned, as well as the number discontinued each year.

For the year ended June 30—	Number of post-offices established.	Number of post-offices discontinued.	Total number remaining in operation.	Appointments on resignations and commissions expired.	Appointments on removals and suspensions.	Appointments on changes of names and sites.	Appointments on deaths of postmasters.
1868	2,167	849	26,481	4,021	1,194	167	267
1869	1,653	1,028	27,106	3,994	2,691	166	230
1870	2,359	962	28,492	4,105	1,449	204	293
1871	2,407	854	30,045	4,307	1,179	178	309
1872	2,703	885	31,863	4,091	939	190	328
1873	2,462	1,081	33,244	4,802	945	193	386
1874	2,318	1,268	34,294	5,354	907	477	368
1875	2,313	1,060	35,547	6,017	974	187	380
1876	1,993	1,137	36,383	5,140	1,045	251	383
1877	1,825	863	37,345	4,800	711	215	397
1878	2,784	871	39,258	5,117	748	184	338
1879	2,676	1,079	40,855	5,627	558	187	378
1880	3,462	1,328	43,012	6,323	561	690	356
1881	2,915	1,415	44,512	6,217	958	242	421
1882	3,166	1,447	46,231	7,346	1,021	349	461
1883	3,253	1,621	47,863	7,734	705	342	468
1884	3,414	1,260	50,017	7,265	513	234	477
1885	2,121	886	51,252	6,204	810	207	412
1886	3,482	1,120	53,014	9,112	9,566	463	587
1887	3,043	1,500	55,157	6,863	2,584	482	580
1888	3,864	1,645	57,376	6,521	1,244	743	659

The total of allowances for clerk-hire, rent, fuel, light, and miscellaneous and incidental items, including furniture, advertising, and salaries of Presidential postmasters, for the year ending June 30, 1888, amounted to $11,077,498.76.

Presidential Postmasters.—The adjustment of July 1, 1888, established 97 offices in the first class, 497 in the second class, and 1,908 in the third class, making a total of Presidential offices at the date last named of 2,502.

The gross receipts which accrued at the Presidential offices for the four quarters ended March 31, 1888, amounted to $38,498,987.87, an increase of $3,322,826.13, as compared with the adjustment of July 1, 1887.

There has been an increase of $322,500 in the amount required for the salaries of Presidential postmasters over the amount required for 1887.

Review of Postmasters' Salaries.—The review of salaries under the act of March 3, 1883, as construed by the Attorney-General under date of February 13, 1884, and June 14, 1884, has been completed. The total number of claims reviewed was 68,725. Of this number 26,238 were allowed, involving the sum of $1,221,009.60 for additional compensation. Appropriations for the payment of these claims have been made by the Congress from time to time from July 7, 1884, to October 19, 1888, inclusive.

Allowances for Rent for Third-Class Offices.—The act of Congress approved July 24, 1888, authorized allowances for rent, fuel, and light for third-class post-offices, as frequently recommended by the Department. On the 1st of July, 1888, 1,908 offices were assigned to the third class, and under the operation of existing law 80 additional offices were assigned to the third class from October 1, 1888, making the total number 1,988.

The limitations of the said act, by which the maximum annual rental for an office of the third class was fixed at $300, and the maximum allowance for fuel and light at $60, should, in my opinion, be repealed, as the best interests of the service require discretionary authority in the head of the Department to fix these allowances, having regard to local needs.

Classification and Salaries of Clerks in the Larger Post-Offices.—Attention is requested to the recommendation of the First Assistant Postmaster-General regarding the classification and salaries of clerks attached to the larger post-offices. The results obtained by a commission on this subject are embodied in a report printed in the report of my immediate predecessor for the year ended June 30, 1887, at pages 177 to 182, inclusive. The subject calls for the attention of the Congress.

While the free-delivery service, with its 358 offices, has received marked legislative consideration, providing careful classification and promotion of carriers, and providing substitutes for vacations and holidays, and a limitation in the appropriation for but eight hours' service per day, at a total cost for that service during the current fiscal year of about seven millions of money, there has been provided for the cost of clerks in all the post-offices of the United States but $5,950,000. The total increase of free-delivery offices for the current year will not exceed 40.

Division of Post-Office Supplies.—This division furnishes all stationery supplies for the Post-Office Department; and stationery, wrapping paper, facing slip paper, twine, canceling, postmarking and rating stamps, canceling ink, pads, blanks, and account books to all post-offices of the first and second classes, the nine superintendents of divisions of the Railway Mail Service, and the twelve post-office inspectors in charge.

The total appropriation for wrapping-paper was $44,000; the expenditures were $43,997.55, leaving a balance unexpended of $2.45; value of inventory at close of year, $6,576.54. Twenty-five thousand four hundred and sixty reams of wrapping and facing slip paper were issued, as against 21,747 reams for the previous year, an increase of 3,713 reams, or about 17 per cent.

The appropriation for twine was $80,000; expenditures $71,175.77, leaving a balance of $8,824.23; value of inventory, $10,437.40. There was an increase of issue over the previous year of 54,252 pounds, or 7 per cent.

The appropriation for letter balances and scales was $17,000; expenditures, $16,999.92, leaving a balance of 8 cents; value of inventory, $578.41. Seven thousand one hundred and forty-seven scales were issued, as against 2,180 the previous year, an increase of 5,867, or 273 per cent. This increase was caused by the inspection of fourth-class offices, a large proportion of which were found to be without scales; and from the fact that no contracts were made the previous years for certain classes of scales, the orders for which were held up and filled from the appropriation for the year ended June 30, 1888.

The appropriation for stamps, ink, and pads was $30,000; the expenditures, $29,999.71, leaving a balance of 29 cents; the value of the inventory was $3,510.73. There was an increase in issues over the previous year of 22,363 stamps (128 per cent.), 16,110 pads (155 per cent.), and 9,004 pounds of ink (68 per cent.). The recommendation was made that a committee be appointed to investigate the question of canceling-ink. (See report of Division of Post-Office Supplies.)

The appropriation for stationery for offices of the first and second classes was $50,000; the expenditures, $49,836.73, leaving a balance of $163.27; the value of the inventory was $29,695.84. The purchases of the previous year amounted to $46,456.19, showing an excess of purchases for the present year of $3,380.54, or 7 per cent.; the inventory of the previous year amounted to $22,658.94, making the year's increase

$7,036.90, or 31 per cent. This shows a saving to the Department on this appropriation of $3,656.36.

The appropriation for stationery for the Post-Office Department was $12,000; expenditures, $9,875.72, leaving a balance of $2,124.28; the value of the inventory was $3,964.48. The amount expended the previous year was $7,514.35, showing an increase this year of $2,361.37, or 31 per cent. The inventory of the previous year amounted to $3,065.29, showing an increase of stock at the close of the present year of $899.19, or 30 per cent.

The increase of the demands for printing and binding is shown by the following figures: 66,556,830 blanks and 179,713 books were furnished by the Government Printer for the year ended June 30, 1888, as compared with 60,468,900 blanks and 112,403 books for the previous year, an increase this year of 9 per cent. in blanks and 60 per cent. in books. The recommendation is made that a branch of the Government Printing Office be established in this division, or that an appropriation of $10,000 be asked for to properly equip the stationery section of this division with presses and material for doing work required immediately. (See report.)

The recommendation is made that this division be made an independent division. (See Report.)

The Free-Delivery Service was, during the last fiscal year, extended to 169 additional places under the act of January 3, 1887, making a total of 358 free-delivery cities. The number of carriers was increased from 5,310 to 6,346, adding 1,036 to the number. The whole number of pieces of mail handled by the carriers was 2,630,861,758, against 2,234,564,656 the preceding year, showing an increase of 396,297,102 pieces, or 17.73 per cent. The percentages of increase were as follows: Letters delivered, 11.53; newspapers, etc., delivered, 25.22; letters collected, 23.19; postal-cards collected, 31.69; newspapers, etc., collected, 25. The total cost of the service was $5,422,356.38, being an increase of $803,664.29, or a percentage of 17.40 over the preceding year.

There is a largely increased estimate for the fiscal year ending June 30, 1890, called for by the eight-hour law. The Superintendent estimates that the amount required to carry out the provisions of that law will approximate about $1,462,000, of which amount $1,345,000 is for the pay of carriers, including promotions and $117,000 for incidental expenses, additional carriers, and pay of substitutes for carriers on vacation. If the law had not been enacted the appropriation required for the next fiscal year would have been about $6,538,000, whereas the estimate is $8,000,000. I append full details of this estimate, as prepared by the Superintendent of the Free Delivery System, with a statement of my allowance of $8,000,000, after careful consideration.

Independent of the eight-hour law, with the present number of offices, and the usual number of additional offices to be added annually, the annual increase would be about $500,000.

The amount of postage on local matter at these offices amounted to $7,721,689.16, an increase of $1,030,435.47 over the preceding year, being $2,299,332.80 in excess of the entire cost of the service.

Fourth-Class Post-Offices.—I have the honor to recommend a revision of the law regulating the compensation of fourth-class postmasters by which the compensation shall be permitted which was intended by the act of Congress fixing the standard. Through all reductions of postage rates the amount of postage received has furnished the standard of compensation to these officials. They number 54,874. There has been no re-adjustment of the rate of compensation in harmony with the reductions in postage rates; increased labor has been imposed by increased business resulting from lower postage, which at the same time has reduced compensation.

Efficiency and Criminal Statistics and Recommendations Thereon.—The report of the Chief Inspector shows that during the year 791 persons, officials, employés of the Department, and others, were arrested for various offenses against the postal laws and regulations. The number includes 90 postmasters, 26 assistant postmasters, 32 post-office clerks, 12 railway postal clerks, 34 letter carriers, 15 mail carriers, 9 other employés, 123 burglars of post-offices, and 380 others for various offenses—these subject to the jurisdiction of the courts of the United States. Forty-nine burglars and 23 other offenders were arrested whose cases were subject to the jurisdiction of the State courts. One hundred and seventy-one of these offenders were convicted, 35 acquitted or discharged; 510 are awaiting trial.

Attention is invited to the statement of the Chief Inspector, in his report, that the crime of burglary of post-offices is increasing at a rate to create apprehension. Six hundred and eighty-three robberies of post-offices were reported during the year, and in spite of the best efforts of the inspector's force, only 172 burglars were arrested. The Chief Inspector is of opinion that the payment of a small reward on the conviction of the guilty parties would remedy this evil to a great extent. He asks an appropriation of $10,000 for this purpose, to be expended by the direction of the Postmaster-General, and I so recommend and urge.

Cases for the Action of Inspectors.—These are classified as follows:

Class A.—Complaints of depredations upon, and all sorts of irregularities in, the domestic registered mail.

Class B.—Similar complaints in the domestic ordinary mail.

Class C.—All sorts of miscellaneous complaints and inquiries, not strictly mail depredations.

Class F.—Complaints and inquiries concerning foreign mail, both ordinary and registered.

Class A.—It is gratifying to note that in the first class there has been a marked improvement over the past year. The number of complaints received is smaller, and the percentage of ascertained loss much less.

Only 4,820 complaints were received as against 5,286 made last year, while the total number of pieces registered increased 1,042,819. The total number of losses sustained, as shown by investigation and a careful estimate, was 845, or one piece out of every 15,334 pieces handled. Last year the actual loss was 1,065, or one piece out of every 11,187. These figures show a much better service this year than last. These losses were from all causes—accidents, burnings of cars and post-offices, and other casualties, and only 213 were the result of theft by dishonest officials.

Class B.—In this class 44,917 complaints were received and 35,828 investigated. In view of the figures showing the increased number of postage-stamps sold during the year, demonstrating the great increase of mail handled, these figures show an improvement in the service. In 6,570 of these complaints investigated the claim of loss was found to be false. The letters or packages were either not mailed or were subsequently delivered.

Class C.—At the request of my predecessor an additional appropriation of $100,000 was made for the inspection service. This was done in order that the smaller post-offices, those of the fourth class, might be examined, and the postmasters instructed by a personal visit of an inspector. This had not previously been done systematically. During the past year 24,889 such offices were carefully inspected. Much good has resulted, as the Department records show. Greater promptness in making deposits and reports to the Department has resulted, and a marked increase in its receipts. The inspectors collected or caused to be deposited in the Treasury on account of cases of Class C $177,525.12.

For the good of the service in all its branches this additional appropriation of $100,000 should be renewed for the coming year.

Class F.—The total number of complaints in this class was 10,855, a considerable increase over any previous year, but it is also noticed that the number of actual losses is less in proportion to the number of complaints treated. Six thousand six hundred and eighty-three cases related to the registered mail, 3,802 to the ordinary mail, and 370 to miscellaneous complaints. Actual loss was sustained in 202 cases relating to registered matter.

The carefully prepared tables at the end of the Chief Inspector's report will prove instructive, as they show by comparison the workings of the inspection office for the past few years and its comparative cost.

The following table is a comparative statement of the work of the inspectors of the Department upon crime and fraud in and against the service for the years 1884, 1886, 1887, and 1888:

	1884.	1886.	1887.	1888.
Arrests caused by post-office inspectors	756	660	773	791
A cases made and referred to inspectors..............	4,238	4,281	5,286	4,520
B cases so referred	33,668	37,956	42,096	44,917
C cases so referred...............................	4,870	13,544	18,260	34,250
F cases treated and referred to inspectors	7,634	7,773	9,362	10,855
Total	50,410	63,554	75,009	94,842
Cases investigated and closed:				
A cases...	4,590	6,583	5,630	4,577
B cases...	28,990	58,262	42,017	45,678
C cases...	5,223	12,345	14,514	31,545
F cases...	8,391	7,173	8,774	10,044
Total	47,134	84,363	70,965	91,844
Money recovered from depredators on mails........	$18,198.81	$14,522.23	$11,548.13	$12,347.57
Money recovered from post-office employés and turned into the United States Treasury...........	26,927.11	100,991.41	242,403.72	177,525.12
Total amount recovered.........................	45,125.92	115,513.64	253,951.85	189,872.69
Total amount recovered since March 4, 1885, from postmasters on false returns *	....	....	....	604,464.10
Amount appropriated..............................	200,000.00	200,000.00	200,000.00	200,000.00
Total amount of money expended...................	197,186.00	194,953.39	197,624.63	†291,408.46
Cases on hand at end of each fiscal year.............	....	13,445	18,016	‡21,014

* See Table A as to date of appointment of such postmasters.
† Estimated.

The following is table A.

Number of orders made by the Postmaster-General from March 4, 1885, to June 30, 1888, requesting the Auditor to re-adjust the compensation of postmasters who rendered false returns of business, in order to increase their compensation, 521.

Amount the Auditor was requested to charge back, $246,624.60.

Number of orders made since March, 4, 1885, involving the accounts of postmasters for false returns, appointed prior to March 4, 1885, 449, or 87 per cent.

Number of orders made since March 4, 1885, involving the accounts of postmasters for false returns, appointed after March 4, 1885, 72, or 13 per cent.

Amount recovered by the orders involving accounts of postmasters appointed prior to March 4, 1885, $239,074.43, or 97 per cent.

Amount recovered by the orders involving accounts of postmasters appointed after March 4, 1885, $7,550.17, or 3 per cent.

Statement showing the increase in the issues of postage-stamps, stamped envelopes, newspaper wrappers, letter-sheets, and postal-cards during the year ending June 30, 1887, over the year ending June 30, 1885.

Period.	Number.	Value.
Year ending June 30, 1887	2,503,170,139	$44,619,680.65
Year ending June 30, 1885	2,142,678,890	40,460,316.04
	*360,491,249	†6,159,364.61

Number of pieces of registered matter handled during the year ending June 30, 1887 12,524,426
Number of pieces of registered matter handled during the year ending June 30, 1885 11,043,251

‡1,481,165

There has been no increase in the clerical force in the office of the Third Assistant Postmaster-General during the years 1886, 1887, and 1888.

* Or 16.8 per cent.   † Or 15.2 per cent.   ‡ Or 13.4 per cent.

Claims of Postmasters for Losses.—The report of the Assistant Attorney-General exhibits the action, with the reason therefor, upon the several claims of postmasters for losses of money-order funds, postage-stamps, stamped envelopes, newspaper wrappers, and postal-cards resulting from burglary, fire, or other unavoidable casualty, and of money-order funds lost while in transit.

During the year 534 claims were considered, 449 were allowed in whole or in part, and 86 were wholly disallowed. The allowed claims amount in the whole to $23,653.02. The amount of claims wholly disallowed is $6,442.44. The recapitulation to the accompanying report gives full details as to these losses, which are $16,947.53 less than for the previous year.

The amendment to the act of 1882, approved May 9, 1888, has opened the door for the admission of a large number of claims for "postal funds," and many were filed prior to the expiration of the fiscal year, but not early enough for action during the year.

Safety of Registered Mail.—A consideration of the following table and comparison of the results for the different years proves conclusively that the safety of the registered mail has materially and steadily improved for the past three years, and that its present treatment is one of the strongest evidences of reform in the mail service. In proof of this claim, attention is called to the fact that the number of complaints this year has decreased 466, or 8 per cent.; the number of losses has decreased from 220 to 20 per cent., while the number of pieces handled has increased 774,461, or $6\frac{1}{2}$ per cent.; and the ratio of pieces lost to pieces handled has decreased from 1 in 11,187 to 1 in 15,016—a decided improvement. It is thus shown in every respect that the registered mail is more safely handled, more accurately delivered in 1888 than in 1887 or any previous years.

TABLE B.—*Statistics relating to the domestic registered mail for the fiscal years ending June 30, 1884, 1886, 1887, and 1888.*

Fiscal year.	Complaints of loss, rifling, missent, and other depredations or accidents on or to the domestic registered mail.	Total lost each year.			Total number of letters and packages registered each year.	Total number of letters and packages handled to one piece lost.
		Ascertained by investigation.	Estimated on unfinished business.	Total.		
1884....	4,238	516	743	1,259	10,750,155	8,538
1886....	4,281	1,042	....	1,042	11,102,607	10,655
1887....	5,286	1,065	....	1,065	11,914,792	11,187
1888....	4,820	565	280	845	*12,689,253	*15,016

* Estimated on the basis of $6\frac{1}{2}$ per cent. increase over preceding year, which is probably below the actual increase.

The Volume of ordinary mail has largely increased, as shown by the increased revenue of the Department from the sale of postage-stamps. The total number of pieces handled has doubled since

1883, and the revenue on pieces handled, if at the rate of 1883 (act reducing postage), would now be upward of $70,000,000 per annum.

The Money-Order System.—The report of the Superintendent of the Money-Order System exhibits considerable increase in both the domestic and international orders, and in the postal-notes issued as well as paid.

The number of money-order offices at the close of the year was 8,241, and the number of postal-note offices 311.

The domestic orders issued numbered 9,959,207, of the aggregate amount of $119,649,064.93, while the orders paid and repaid were in excess of that sum by $94,280.27.

There were issued 6,668,006 postal-notes, amounting to $12,134,459.04 and the notes paid were only $29,577.49 less in value.

There were 759,636 orders drawn for payment in foreign countries, reaching the large total of $11,293,870.05, while 236,992 orders of the value of $4,169,675.64 were transmitted from abroad for payment in the United States.

The increase in the number of domestic orders issued was nearly 8 per cent., and in the amount thereof nearly 2 per cent. In the postal-notes issued the increase in number was nearly 6 per cent., and in amount over 3 per cent., while in the international orders the increase in the number issued was over 23 per cent., and in the amount issued nearly 25 per cent.; in the number paid and repaid nearly 7 per cent., and in the amount paid and repaid nearly 4 per cent.

It is interesting to note that the total volume of business, including domestic and international orders and postal-notes, comprised 17,386,849 issues, amounting to $143,077,394.07, and 16,816,772 payments and repayments, of the value of $136,055,662.42, an increase in issues over the preceding year of 1,231,715 transactions, or nearly 8 per cent., and an increase in amount of $4,810,378.06, or about 3½ per cent.

Notwithstanding the very large sum transmitted in the mails by money-order offices to their depositories, namely, $103,129,930.74, only 91 cases of loss were reported, amounting to $6,368.43.

It continues to be a source of gratification that the erroneous payments of money-orders bears such small ratio to the total extent of the transactions in payments. For the last year only 1 in every 161,739 orders was reported as improperly paid.

The gross revenue from the domestic business amounted to $541,272.77; from the international business, $139,159.68; and from the postal-note business, $117,885.38; a total of $798,317.83—a sum more than sufficient by $43,016.21 to meet all such expenditures as, under existing practice, are paid, for account of the money-order system, from appropriations.

This net profit of $43,016.21, the Superintendent shows, is likely to be increased somewhat during the current year by reason of a number of additional conventions, executed with foreign countries, which establish a more advantageous rate of accounting by each country to the

11843—P M G 88——II

other, such rate being fixed at one-half instead of three-fourths of 1 per cent. on the face value of the orders issued. The estimated additional annual profit from the conventions already signed to that end is over $9,500, while others in process of negotiation, if satisfactorily concluded, will result in a further profit of about $3,300 per annum.

I fully concur in the Superintendent's recommendation for the increase of the maximum amount of the international money-orders from $50 to $100, so as to make them uniform in this respect with the domestic orders. The change, it is apparent, will result in the additional advantage of reducing expenses in post-offices, on account of clerk hire, as well as in the Department on account of blank forms, by making one order take the place of two for sums from $50 to $100.

A convention for the exchange of money-orders with Denmark, a copy of which is appended to the Superintendent's report, was concluded by my predecessor to take effect January 1, 1888, so that money-order business is now transacted directly with twenty-three foreign countries.

Dead Letter Office.—There were received during the year, 6,217,876 pieces of original mail matter, an increase of 882,513 over the number received the previous year. This number was composed of the following general classes: 4,993,290 domestic mailable letters, 576,727 domestic unmailable letters; 499,881 letters, and 60,121 parcels of printed matter, samples, etc., which originated in foreign countries; 74,648 parcels of domestic third and fourth class matter of obvious value, and 22,112 registered articles.

There were restored to owners 749,515 pieces, unopened, including matter of foreign origin.

Of the number of letters opened, 20,437 were found to contain money, amounting to $35,245.38; 23,638 contained negotiable paper representing a money value of $1,343,519.52; 3,697 contained postal-notes to the value of $5,798.31; 37,619 contained receipts, paid notes, and other miscellaneous papers; 119,246 contained postage-stamps; 40,331 contained photographs. These letters were duly recorded, and 223,881, or about 91 per cent., were restored to owners.

There was deposited in the United States Treasury $8,511.44 separated from dead letters which could not be restored to owners, together with $2,023.35 realized from the annual sale of unclaimed articles.

Topographer's Report.—Referring to the report for the fiscal year ended June 30, 1888, I may state the following: The printing and delivery of the post-route sheets by the contractor were very satisfactory. Five thousand five hundred and eighty post-route maps were received during the fiscal year ended June 30, 1888; 229½ maps mounted and 340 in sheets were sold, realizing the sum of $1,885.50; 748½ maps mounted and 3,101½ in sheets were officially distributed; 489½ maps mounted and 260½ were given away. All post-route sheets becoming useless are consigned to the disbursing clerk and superintendent to be sold as waste paper. The effective force in this branch of the Department numbers 25 employés, 17 males and 8 females. In order to provide for the renewal of maps the services of an additional draughtsman will be required. Owing to the worn condition of certain of the lithographic stones, a few will have to be purchased, as set forth in the estimates.

FINANCIAL STATEMENT.

Statement of Financial Operations.—In continuation of the plan adopted in the last annual report, I present the following condensed statements of the revenue, expenditure, and cost of the postal service for the fiscal years ending June 30, 1886, 1887, and 1888, charging to the two former years whatever expenditures have been made on account thereof since their termination, and to all three their estimated liabilities, respectively, now outstanding, as well as the amounts earned by the Pacific railroad companies and credited to them on the books of the Treasury Department.

FISCAL YEAR ENDING JUNE 30, 1886.

REVENUE.

1 Ordinary postal revenue	$43,597,871.08
2. Revenue from money-order business	350,551.87
Total gross receipts	43,948,422.95
Deduct amount charged to bad debts	12,174.25
Leaves total revenue	43,936,548.70

EXPENDITURES AND LIABILITIES.

Expenditures:		
From July 1, 1885, to September 30, 1886	$50,627,553.37	
From October 1, 1886, to September 30, 1887	211,881.50	
From October 1, 1887, to September 30, 1888	12,020.34	
	50,851,455.21	
Liabilities:		
Estimated amount of outstanding indebtedness for various objects on account of the year	$286.40	
Amount due for transportation on Pacific railroads, for which no appropriation was made	251,101.61	
	251,388.01	
		51,102,843.22
Deficiency in revenue		7,166,594.52

COST OF POSTAL SERVICE.

Amount of expenditures and liabilities as above		$51,102,843.22
Amount certified to the Secretary of the Treasury for credit to Pacific railroads—		
From July 1, 1885, to September 30, 1886	$1,112,138.40	
From October 1, 1886, to September 30, 1887....	391.22	
From October 1, 1887, to September 30, 1888....	142.38	
Total amount certified...............................		1,112,672.00
Total cost of the service...............................		52,215,515.22
Excess of total cost of postal service over revenue................		8,279,266.52

FISCAL YEAR ENDING JUNE 30, 1887.

REVENUE.

1. Ordinary postal revenue..................................	48,118,273.94
2. Receipts from money-order business........................	719,335.45
Gross revenue..................................	48,837,609.39

EXPENDITURES AND LIABILITIES.

Expenditures :		
From July 1, 1886, to September 30, 1887	$52,391,677.43	
From October 1, 1887, to September 30, 1888	368,160.40	
	52,759,837.83	
Liabilities :		
Amount of outstanding liabilities for various objects on account of the year.......................	$75,000.00	
Estimated amount due for transportation on Pacific railroads, for which no appropriation was made........	300,009.87	
	375,009.87	
Total actual and estimated expenditures for the service of the year..		53,134,847.70
Deficiency in revenue...........................		4,297,238.31

COST OF POSTAL SERVICE.

Amount of actual and estimated expenditures, as shown above		53,134,847.70
Amount certified to Secretary of the Treasury by the Auditor for transportation of the mails on the Pacific railroads, and by law not charged to the appropriations for the postal service—		
From July 1, 1886, to September 30, 1887	$1,187,027.33	
From October 1, 1887, to September 30, 1888......	11,241.72	
	1,198,269.05	
Total cost of the service...............................		54,333,116.75
Excess of total cost of service over amount of revenue..............		5,495,507.36

REVENUE.

1. Ordinary postal revenue.. $51,896,858.96
2. Receipts from money-order business.............................. 798,317.83

      Gross revenue.. 52,695,176.79

EXPENDITURES AND LIABILITIES.

Expenditures:
  Amount expended to September 30, 1888, on account of the year ending June 30, 1888......... $55,795,357.84

Liabilities:
  Amount of indebtedness for various objects certified to Auditor and not yet reported for payment (partly estimated)........................... $375,000.00
  Estimated amount of indebtedness not yet reported to Auditor (railroad service)............................... 404,830.25
  Estimated amount due for transportation on Pacific railroads, for which no appropriation was made........ 307,215.75
  Estimated amount of indebtedness incurred, for which appropriation will be asked of Congress 3,000.00
                           1,090,046.00

Total actual and estimated expenditures for the service of the year.. 56,885,403.84

Estimated amount of deficiency of revenue to be supplied out of the General Treasury on account of the service of the year 4,190,227.05

COST OF POSTAL SERVICE.

Amount of actual and estimated expenditures, as shown above...... $56,885,403.84
Amount certified to the Secretary of the Treasury by the Auditor for transportation of the mails on the Pacific railroads, and by law not charged to the appropriation for the postal service................ 1,240,600.83

    Total estimated cost of the postal service for the year.......... 58,126,004.67
Deduct amount of gross revenue, as shown above.................... 52,695,176.79

Leaves excess of estimated cost of service over amount of revenue.... 5,430,827.88

Estimated Revenue for the Fiscal Years Ending June 30, 1889 and 1890.

—The increase in the ordinary revenue (excluding revenue from money-order business) for the fiscal year ended June 30, 1887, was at the rate of 10.3 per cent. over the revenue of the previous year, and the increase for the year ended June 30, 1888, was at the rate of 7.9 per cent. The receipts for the quarter ending June 30—the last quarter of the past year—were somewhat smaller than had been estimated by the Department; but this unexpected falling off in business it is thought will not continue during the present year, for special returns already received by the Department from thirty of the larger cities for the quarter ended September 30 show an increase of over 9 per cent. In estimating, therefore, for the current and coming years, it is not unreasonable to assume that an increase of 9 per cent. for each year will be maintained. Upon this basis the gross revenue for the years ending June 30, 1889 and 1890, is estimated at $57,392,576.26 and $62,508,658.12, respectively, as appears from the following statements:

FISCAL YEAR ENDING JUNE 30, 1889.

Amount of ordinary postal revenue for the fiscal year
  ending June 30, 1889................................ $51,896,858.96
Add 9 per cent. for increase........................... 4,670,717.30

Gives estimated amount of ordinary postal revenue for fiscal year
  ending June 30, 1889... $56,567,576.26
Amount of estimated revenue from money-order business........... 825,000.00

     Total estimated gross receipts for the year ending June 30, 1889. 57,392,576.26

The amount appropriated for service of this year is $60,860,233.74, or an excess over the amount of revenue estimated above of $3,467,657.48, which will be drawn from the General Treasury should the total amount appropriated be needed.

FISCAL YEAR ENDING JUNE 30, 1890.

Estimated amount of ordinary postal revenue for the
  fiscal year ending June 30, 1889 .... $56,567,576.26
Add 9 per cent. for increase........................... 5,091,081.86

Gives estimated amount of ordinary revenue for the fiscal year ending
  June 30, 1890 .... $61,658,658.12
Amount of estimated revenue from money-order business............ 850,000.00

     Total estimated gross receipts for the year ending June 30, 1890. 62,508,658.12

The probable amount of expenditure to be made in carrying on the business of the postal service for the year ending June 30, 1890, as shown by estimates submitted to the Secretary of the Treasury, is $66,812,073.02. The deficiency to be supplied from the general Treasury is, therefore, $4,303,414.90.

New Form of Quarterly Postal Account.—As a matter connected with the affairs of this office, I take pleasure in reporting that the use by postmasters of the new form of quarterly postal account and the record of postal business, adopted shortly after the commencement of the last fiscal year, has been satisfactory, both as regards the transaction of business at post-offices and the examination and audit of accounts in the office of the Auditor. I understand that fewer delinquencies as to the prompt and correct rendition of accounts by postmasters have occurred during the year than was formerly the case, and that the Auditor has been able to settle accounts with greater exactness and with fewer outstanding cases at the end of each quarter than ever before.

As time goes on the new system will probably work still more satisfactorily.

Work of Signing Drafts and Warrants.—Recommenda-
tion is made that the act of Congress of February 25, 1882, be so mod-
fied as to allow the Acting Third Assistant Postmaster-General to sign
warrants on the Treasury during the absence of the Third Assistant
Postmaster-General.

The Special-Delivery System.—The special delivery system
has met with a reasonable amount of patronage during the past fiscal
year and has, I am persuaded, been conducted by postmasters generally with increased efficiency. I present the following statement of the
year's business:

For the whole country the Auditor reports that the amount of fees
allowed in postmasters' accounts during the year for special delivery is
$109,015.64. Allowing for cases where no fees were paid, as, for exam-
ple, in cases of delivery by letter-carriers or other salaried employés of
post-offices, these figures would indicate a total of about 1,434,400
special-delivery letters received during the year at all offices, the special-
delivery stamps on which would amount to $143,440. Deducting from
this the amount allowed postmasters, and there is left a total profit to
the Government on the year's business of over $34,424.

At the letter-carrier offices, from which exact returns have been received, the business of the year will appear from the following statement:

(1) The total number of pieces of all matter received for special delivery at all the letter-carrier offices was 1,220,276, of which 899,494, or
nearly 74 per cent., came through the mails from other than the offices
of delivery, and 320,782, or 26 per cent., were of local origin.

(2) The total number of pieces delivered by the regular messengers
was 1,164,668, or over 95 per cent. of the whole, leaving 55,608, or less
than 5 per cent., as the number delivered by letter-carriers or other salaried employés, including the few where delivery was impossible.

(3) The value of the special-delivery stamps on the pieces received
was $122,027.60. The amount of special-delivery stamps sold at the
letter-carrier offices, ascertained from returns made by postmasters to
this office, aggregates $92,149.20.

(4) The average number of messengers employed during each month
of the year was 768.

(5) The average time consumed in the delivery of matter after reaching the respective offices of destination was twenty-one minutes.

Statistics in detail of the business at each of the letter-carrier offices
in existence on the 1st of July, 1888, are given in Table No. 16 of the
Third Assistant Postmaster-General's report.

The recommendation made in the last annual report concerning the
establishment of the pneumatic-tube system, or some equivalent under-

ground means of rapid transit, for special-delivery messages at a few of the prominent cities of the country, is renewed. I have received information in various ways during the year which convinces me that at least some investigation of the matter is desirable.

Division of Postage-Stamps, Stamped Envelopes, and Postal-Cards.—During the year there were issued to postmasters, through the work of this division, of the various kinds and denominations of stamped paper, 2,700,635,170 pieces, valued at $50,636,321.84, as against a total of 2,503,170,139 pieces, valued at $46,619,680.65, for the preceding year, an increase of 7.89 per cent. in number and 8.62 per cent. in value.

The several issues, by aggregates, are as follows:

	Number.	Value.
Ordinary adhesive postage-stamps	1,867,173,140	$36,291,183.00
Special-delivery stamps	1,331,790	133,179.00
Newspaper and periodical stamps	3,464,418	1,588,425.00
Postage-due stamps	10,805,572	283,914.00
Stamped envelopes, plain	186,741,600	3,634,508.44
Stamped envelopes, printed request	196,625,250	4,242,611.10
Newspaper wrappers	50,269,500	584,894.50
Letter-sheet envelopes	2,427,000	55,821.00
Postal-cards	381,797,500	3,819,835.00
Total	2,700,635,170	50,636,321.84

Postage on Second-Class Matter.—The weight of second-class matter sent in the mails during the fiscal year ended June 30, 1888, not including matter circulated free within the county of publication, was 143,662,918 pounds, or over 71,831 tons, and the amount of postage collected was $1,436,629.18. This is an increase of 13 8 per cent. as compared with the business of 1887.

The number of post-offices at which second class matter was mailed is 7,463, an increase over the previous year of 463, or 6.6 per cent. The number of new publications admitted to the mails during the year is 3,076.

Collections were made during the year to the amount of $4,954.09 from publishers and news agents for matter mailed at the second-class rate of postage which should have been charged at a higher rate. This is an increase of $1,831.72 over the amount collected for like irregularities during the preceding year.

Use of Stamped Envelopes.—The Third Assistant Postmaster-General calls attention to the increasing use of stamped envelopes—particularly of the special-request envelopes—and gives a number of reasons why they should be used, wherever practicable, in preference to adhesive postage stamps, to which I call attention.

Reduction in the Cost of Stamped Envelopes.—The present contract for supplying the Department with stamped envelopes and newspaper wrappers was made in 1886, the contract term beginning on the 1st of October of that year. The amount saved under this contract, as compared with the prices of the previous contract for the nine months ending June 30, 1887, was shown by the last annual report to be $119,488.77 ; the amount similarly saved during the fiscal year ending June 30, 1888, is $163,475.60, making a total saving since the beginning of the contract of $282,964.37. The items of saving during the past year are shown by the following table:

Quality.	Number of envelopes.	Cost under contract of—		Saving.	
		1882.	1886.	Amount.	Per cent.
First	328,048,600	$733,585.90	$594,823.09	$138,762.81	11.9
Second	12,554,100	25,738.94	18,683.06	7,055.88	27.4
Third	4,729,500	8,217.08	4,918.89	3,298.19	41.1
Circulars	83,487,500	45,927.41	37,098.33	8,829.08	19.2
Newspaper wrappers	50,269,500	49,766.80	44,237.16	5,529.64	11.1
Total	*429,089,200	863,236.13	699,760.53	163,475.60	18.*

* Four million five hundred and nine thousand and fifty envelopes, costing $8,240, were issued during the year, for which no corresponding style was issued under the contract of 1852.

Distributing Agencies for Stamped Paper.—The Third Assistant Postmaster-General reports that the distributing agencies for postage-stamps, stamped envelopes, and postal-cards, as well as the sub-agencies at Chicago and Saint Louis, have worked satisfactorily during the year.

Envelope Machine at Cincinnati Exposition.—Just prior to the close of the fiscal year arrangements were made with the stamped-envelope contractors by which one of their most improved envelope machines was erected at the Centennial Exposition of the Ohio Valley and Central States, which began on the 4th of July, 1888, at Cincinnati, Ohio, and by which it has since been operated as a part of the display made by the Post-Office Department under authority of the act of Congress approved May 28, 1888. Up to the present time, in the operation of this machine 1,408,500 first-quality stamped envelopes of the No. 4½ size have been made, 850 of which have been sent to postmasters, and the remainder of which will be disposed of in the same way. These envelopes have all been made under the same safeguards as surround the manufacture of stamped envelopes at the regular manufactory at Hartford, Conn., and of course have been or will be paid for as they are issued upon the terms of manufacture prescribed by the standing contract with the Department. I understand that the operation of this machine has proved to be a very interesting feature of the postal exhibit at the exposition.

Manufacture of Stamped Paper by the Government.—The Third Assistant Postmaster General urges that when the present contracts for the manufacture of postage-stamps, postal-cards, and stamped envelopes expire, the Government take the work into its own hands, manufacturing the articles at the Bureau of Engraving and Printing of the Treasury Department. The following provision is proposed as a part of the next Post-Office appropriation bill:

That upon the expiration of the present contracts for the manufacture of adhesive stamps and other stamped paper issued under the direction of the Post-Office Department, the work of making such stamped paper shall, if before that time considered advisable by the Postmaster-General and the Secretary of the Treasury, be performed by the Bureau of Engraving and Printing of the Treasury Department, under such regulations as the said officers shall jointly prescribe, the cost of the work to be relatively no greater than the cost under existing contracts, including the expenses of the several agencies: *Provided,* That the stamped paper hereinabove referred to shall always be supplied in sufficient quantities and kinds to meet the wants of the Post-Office Department, to be from time to time made known by the Postmaster-General or any proper official under him, and shall be turned over to that Department promptly as called for, and issued by its designated officials under methods of distribution similar to those now in operation. And payment for the stamped paper thus issued shall be made by warrants on the Treasurer of the United States in favor of the Bureau of Engraving and Printing, payable out of the appropriations now and to be hereafter made for the purpose, the bills to be rendered monthly by such Bureau, and to be regularly audited by the Sixth Auditor in the same manner as other bills for the postal service are audited: *And provided further,* That the Secretary of the Treasury is hereby authorized to provide whatever facilities are needed in the way of machinery, paper, gum, and other supplies to carry the above provision into effect.

Division of Registration.—The fees collected on registry business during the year ending June 30, 1888, amounted to $1,125,154.40, which shows an increase of $90,477.60, or 8.7 per cent. over the amount collected during the previous year. Everything considered this is a gratifying increase.

The classification and number of pieces of mail matter registered during the year are as follows:

Domestic letters	9,465,414
Domestic parcels	1,066,572
Total domestic	10,531,986
Foreign letters	674,607
Foreign parcels	44,951
Total foreign	719,558
Letters and parcels free—on Government business	2,425,625
Aggregate	13,677,169

More space and better Mechanical Arrangements needed for the Registry Division in Government Buildings.—The recommendation of the Postmaster-General in his last annual report that the Department be provided with an architect thoroughly familiar with post-office requirements to design the interior space and fixtures of post-offices, either under construction or to be leased, applies with especial force to the handling of registered matter in large post-offices. The custody and manipulation of the immense values involved and the different duties of recording, enveloping, sorting, pouching, checking, and receipting inward and outward with postal clerks, carriers, and the public, so that all transfers may be made without objectionable contact and without danger, require much planning and forethought. In but few of the new post-office buildings have the best results been obtained in the adaptation of the architect's plans to the prosecution of post-office business, so that the work has frequently to be performed with surroundings far from safe or convenient, requiring more clerical labor and involving greater delays to the service and to the public. With correct plans, based on a broad experience, far better provision could have been made without added expense in the buildings. As far as it has been possible with such means as I could command, I have endeavored to remedy some of these defects by making and devising designs for registry space and fixtures at different post-offices; but so far as concerns new post-office buildings to be erected, to say nothing of the large number of new buildings to be leased, it will be impossible for me to give any such full attention to the plans, so far as they affect the registry service, as an architect could give who had familiarized himself with the needs of the different branches of post-office work.

As showing the great importance of perfecting and improving the registry system from a Government standpoint, attention is called to table No. 15, appended to Third Assistant Postmaster General's report, which gives the Government values in the registered mail for the fiscal year as aggregating over $911,000,000.

Contrast with the Postal Service of Other Nations.—Statistics are given by the Third Assistant Postmaster-General showing that in cheapness of postage, gross revenue and expenditures, number of post-offices, extent of mail routes, mileage of mail service, and volume of mail matter transmitted, the postal system of the United States is the leading one of the world. In the amount of mail matter transmitted, the following are the statistics:

United States (year ending June 30, 1886):

Letters delivered, not including free letters on Government business...	1,769,800,000
Postal-cards delivered..	370,300,000
Newspapers and periodicals delivered (second-class matter)	1,063,100,000
Pieces of third and fourth class matter delivered (books, circulars, parcels of merchandise, etc..............................	372,900,000
Total...	3,576,100,000

(The calculations upon which the above statistics are obtained will be found in paper No. 17, appended to this report.)

Great Britain (year ending March 31, 1888):

Letters delivered, not including free letters on Government business.	1,512,260,000
Postal-cards delivered..	188,800,000
Book packets and circulars delivered	389,500,000
Newspapers delivered	152,300,000
Parcels delivered...	36,732,000
Total	2,279,532,000

Germany (year ending December 31, 1886):

Letters, not including free letters on Government business	720,497,240
Postal-cards	245,282,540
Newspapers and periodicals sent to subscribers....................	523,873,340
Miscellaneous articles of printed matter..........................	210,108,220
Samples of merchandise and parcels	116,305,050
Total	1,816,066,390

France (year ending December 31, 1886):

Letters, not including free letters on Government business........	591,451,811
Postal-cards	35,923,379
Newspapers and periodicals sent to subscribers....................	92,957,793
Miscellaneous articles of printed matter	713,962,439
Samples of merchandise and parcels...............................	28,953,858
Total...	1,463,249,280

The average number of pieces of mail matter to each inhabitant of the several countries named, taking the last census as the basis of the calculation, is now about as follows:

United States..	pieces per capita..	71
Great Britain..	do....	61
Germany	do....	41
France	do....	37

Franking Privilege.—I respectfully call attention to the several provisions of law conferring the privilege of sending mail-matter free of charge. They are as follows:

That from and after the passage of this act Senators, Representatives, and Delegates in Congress, the Secretary of the Senate, the Clerk of the House of Representatives may send and receive through the mail free all public documents printed by order of Congress; and the name of each Senator, Representative, Delegate, Secretary of the Senate, and Clerk of the House shall be written thereon with the proper designation of the office he holds, and the provisions of this section shall apply to each of the persons named herein until the first Monday of December, following the expiration of their respective terms of office. (Act of March 3, 1879, part of Sec. 1; 20 Stats., 356; P. L. and R., Sec. 409.)

That from and after the passage of this act the Congressional Record, or any part thereof, or speeches or reports therein contained, shall, under the frank of a Member of Congress or Delegate, to be written by himself, be carried in the mail free of postage under such regulations as the Postmaster-General may prescribe. (Act of March 3, 1875, part of Sec. 5; 18 Stats., 343; P. L. and R., Sec. 410.)

That seeds transmitted by the Commissioner of Agriculture or by any Member of Congress or Delegate receiving seeds for distribution from said Department, together with agricultural reports emanating from that Department, and so transmitted, shall, under such regulations as the Postmaster-General shall prescribe, pass through the mails free of charge. And the provisions of this section shall apply to ex-Members of Congress and ex-Delegates for the period of nine months after the expiration of their terms as Members and Delegates. (Act of March 3, 1875, Sec. 7; 18 Stats., 343; P. L. and R., Sec. 411.)

Pursuant to the authority above given to prescribe regulations, I find that the following have been adopted by my predecessors:

No matter can be transmitted under the franking privilege unless admissible to the mails under the provisions of chapter eleven. To entitle to free carriage the word "free" should be printed or written, and signed with the name and official designation, if any, of the person entitled to frank it, on the address face of the package, except in case of matter addressed to the persons named in the preceding section.   In the case of the Congressional Record, the name of the Senator, Member, or Delegate must be written by himself; in other cases the name may be written by any one duly deputed by him for that purpose.   A Senator, Member, or Delegate, who holds his certificate of election, is entitled to the franking privilege from the commencement of this term.

All franked matter may be forwarded like any other, but such matter, when once delivered to the addressee, can not be remailed unless properly franked again.   A bulk package of franked articles may be sent to one addressee, who, on receiving and opening the package, may place addresses on the franked articles and remail them for carriage and delivery to the respective addresses. (P. L. and R., Sec. 413.)

Where the wrappers or covers indicate that the documents are public documents. or give the name of the documents, as is generally the case, such documents, with the name and official designation of the Senator, Member, Delegate, or official written thereon, should pass free.   Such is the requirement of the statute.

Where the wrapper or covering of the document does not disclose the public character of the document, the regulation appears to be intended to require that the word "free" should appear upon the face of the package as a certification that the matter within is free.

As the statutes do not require the name of the Senator or Member to be written by himself, except in the case of Congressional Record or parts thereof, or speeches or reports therein contained, the regulation has been evidently framed to guard against the abuse of the franking privilege by others who may be deputed to use it and may exceed their authority, or by those who may forge the frank to avoid the payment of postage on matter not frankable.

As no statute provides a penalty for the unlawful placing of the name of a Senator, Member, etc., by an unauthorized person upon public documents, or upon matter not entitled to be franked, the regulation appears to have been designed for two purposes: one to require some word to be placed over the signature to bring the unlawful use of such name within the designation of forgery of a certificate for the purpose of defrauding the United States, and the other to insure uniformity in the appearance of the franking formula so as to avoid mistakes by the average intelligence of many thousand postmasters, resulting in delay to the franked matter itself.

It is possible that the regulation, in its terms, is liable to such construction as to require the word "free" to be printed or written on the face of the cover or public documents mentioned in the act of March 3, 1879, above quoted.   To avoid such construction the regulation will be made more explicit, although it was intended to guard against the abuse of the franking privilege by unauthorized persons, and to expedite the mail matter franked, rather than to qualify or place other than statutory limitations upon the rights of those entitled to use it.

In this connection I respectfully invite attention to the need for legislation which will provide penalties for the unlawful use of the names of Senators, Members, or other officials by unauthorized persons for

the purpose of sending matter frankable, and uniformity in the franking certificate.

The right to send matter in the mails under an official frank has, by
recent legislation, been considerably extended, and opportunity largely
increased for the abuse of this privilege. The placing of official names
upon public or private matter by others than the officers on whom the
right is conferred is easy, difficult of detection by postal officials, and
under present statutes not explicitly declared punishable.

If the franking privilege were abolished, and a regular yearly allowance for the purchase of postage-stamps made instead, every Senator
and Member of the House of Representatives would be placed upon an
exact equality. No one could make use of the mails beyond his own
allowance, and no unauthorized person could make use of the mails to
forward unofficial matter. Agricultural colleges, now enjoying the
franking privilege, might be furnished, through the Department of
Agriculture, with free penalty envelopes.

**The Railway Mail, Steam-boat, and Star-Route
Service.**—The report of the Second Assistant Postmaster-General
shows that the mail service on June 30, 1888, aggregated 24,869
routes, the total distance covered being 403,977 miles. The expenditure was $31,456,847, and the number of miles traveled during the
year, 287,251,056. The star service included 14,146 routes and covered
225,607 miles. Its cost for the year was $4,959,192. The mail-mes-
senger service embraced 5,906 routes and the annual cost was $883,719.
The steam-boat service comprised 127 routes and cost for the year
$438,942. The railroad service consisted of 1,995 routes and cost
$17,528,600. The railway post-office car service cost $1,996,359. The
expenditure on account of railway post-office clerks was $5,084,517.
For mail equipment $269,531 was expended. The necessary and spe-
cial facilities on trunk lines occasioned an expense of $295,987. Com-
parison with the service as it stood at the close of the previous fiscal
year shows for the entire mail service an increase of 1,107 routes, 11,102
miles, $1,650,338 in the cost, and 17,077,990 in the number of miles
traveled per annum. A decrease of .08 cent, or .72 per cent., in the
rate of cost per mile traveled and an increase of .22, or 3.32 per cent.,
in the average number of trips per week is also shown.

The star service has been materially decreased. A comparison shows
that 5,989 miles have been cut off, with a decrease of .13 cent, or 2.14
per cent., in the rate of cost per mile traveled. The mail-messenger service has 388 more routes, and it is shown the cost per mile has been decreased .03 cent, or .35 per cent. There are four more steam-boat
routes, in all 461 miles long, and the cost per mile of the service has
been decreased .28 cent, or 2.01 per cent. An increase of 168 routes
and of 12,764 miles in the railroad service is noted, and a decrease of
.12 cent, or 1.12 per cent., in the rate of cost per mile. The estimates
for the fiscal year ending June 30, 1890, are: Star service, $5,650,000;
steam-boat service, $450,000; railroad service, $19,105,537.90; railway

post-office car service, $2,260,000; for necessary and special facilities on trunk lines, $295,655.38; for railway post-office clerks, $5,676,728.74; for mail-messenger service, $1,050,000, and for mail equipments, $240,000. A comparison of these estimates with the appropriation for the current fiscal year shows for the star service an increase of $250,000; for steam-boat service no increase; for the railroad service an increase of $2,105,557.90; for necessary and special facilities on trunk lines a decrease of $332.15; for railway post-office clerks an increase of $429,938.53; for mail-messenger service an increase of $100,000; for mail equipments a decrease of $70,000. The total amount of appropriations for mail service for the current fiscal year is $3:,653,777.74. The total amount of the estimates for the next fiscal year is $34,728,942.02. This is an increase of $3,075,164.28.

Since February last, contracts have been made with the New York Central and Hudson River Railroad Company and the Lake Shore and Michigan Southern Railway Company for a fast-mail train between New York and Chicago; with the Pennsylvania Railroad Company, the Pittsburgh, Cincinnati and Saint Louis, and the Chicago, Saint Louis and Pittsburgh Railway Companies, and the Terre Haute and Indianapolis Railroad Company for a fast mail between New York and East Saint Louis. Renewals of contracts have been made with the Chicago, Burlington and Quincy Railroad Company, and the Chicago, Milwaukee and Saint Paul Railway Company for fast-mail service between Chicago and Union Pacific Transfer.

The Second Assistant Postmaster-General calls attention to the need of a general repair shop at Washington. The result of collecting the old mail-bags and bringing them to Washington for repairs has been a saving of $60,000. He recommends an appropriation of $10,000 to establish a repair shop here, not only for bags, but for locks and keys as well. Experience teaches that the ultimate saving fully justifies an outlay for a building and the necessary tools. The discovery of the extravagance heretofore existing in the repair shops led at once to a remedy of the evil, and the result is mail equipment next year will not require within $70,000 of the amount it has cost during previous fiscal years. Nearly 300,000 bags, a little damaged, had been thrown aside. These are rapidly being put into serviceable condition, and as a consequence the necessity for new bags is growing less daily.

The Second Assistant Postmaster-General again calls attention to the law regulating the compensation of railroad companies for carrying the mails, and, as in the annual reports of the two preceding years, recommends that the law should be changed so that space should be the criterion of such compensation.

Appropriation for special facilities in the Railway Mail Service.—I desire to call attention to the settled application of the appropriation made for extra facilities and to the absence of any means to improvements of the service in portions of the country and on lines equally if not more deserving than those for which special appropriations are made. These special appropriations are not sufficient for proper distribution and create an indisposition on the part of railroad companies to co-operate for the best attainable service. Dissatisfaction is natural enough when the Government pays one road more than others, and for no better or more necessary service than is expected or required from many others.

I do not venture an opinion as to whether or not the rate of compensation allowed by law is sufficiently liberal to secure for the Government adequate and the best service. It is certain that the dissatisfaction caused by extra compensation to some, and not to others, has prevented in some instances cordial co-operation with the Department to secure much-needed improvement.

The following is the settled application of appropriations for special facilities:

Statement of expenditures on account of special facilities for the fiscal year ended June 30, 1887, out of $291,000, appropriated by act approved June 30, 1886.

Number of route.	Termini.	Railroad company.	Miles.	Pay.
5005	New York to Springfield	New York, New Haven and Hartford.	136.00	$17,647.00
6011	4.35 a. m. train, between New York and Albany.	New York Central and Hudson River.	144.00	25,000.00
10006	Baltimore to Hagerstown	Western Maryland	86.60	15,804.50
10001	Philadelphia to Bay View	Philadelphia, Wilmington and Baltimore.	91.80	20,000.00
10013, 11001 (part)	Bay View to Quantico	Baltimore and Potomac	79.80	21,900.00
11001 (part)	Quantico to Richmond	Richmond, Fredericksburgh and Potomac.	81.50	17,419.26
11008	Richmond to Petersburgh	Richmond and Petersburgh	23.39	4,268.67
11009	Petersburgh to Weldon	Petersburgh	64.00	11,680.00
13002	Weldon to Wilmington	Wilmington and Weldon	162.07	29,577.77
14002	Wilmington to Florence	Wilmington, Columbia and Augusta.	110.00	20,075.00
14003	Florence to Charleston Junction.	Northeastern	95.00	17,837.50
14004	Charleston Junction to Savannah.	Charleston and Savannah	108.00	19,710.00
15009	Savannah to Jacksonville	Savannah, Florida and Western	171.50	31,298.75
10018	Jacksonville to Sanford	Jacksonville, Tampa and Key West.	126.18	17,602.10
16007	Sanford to Tampa	South Florida	116.39	16,265.49
Total				285,586.10

These are substantially the same for the current year.

It will be observed that but one New England road, the New York, New Haven and Hartford, has extra compensation, and that, with the exception of $25,000 to the New York Central and Hudson River and $15,804 to the Baltimore and Hagerstown Railroads, the entire appropriation for special facilities goes to the system whose terminals are Philadelphia and Tampa. It would seem that if extra compensation is to be given to lines south the great and growing trade between the Northwest and the new commercial South should have attention.

I submit herewith Table A, showing the routes to the South which receive extra compensation, with the average daily weight of mails carried, as compared with weights of mails carried from Chicago to New Orleans, which routes receive no such compensation. In this connection I submit, also, five tables showing the mail service and the methods of carrying to the South.

TABLE A.—*Statement of railroad service.*

Number of route.	State and terminal.	Corporate title of company carrying the mail.	Distance.	Cost per annum for transportation.	Cost per annum for R. P. O. cars.	Average weight per day.	Special facilities.	Totals.
			Miles.			*Pounds.*		
10001	Bay View (n. o.) and Philadelphia	Philadelphia, Wilmington and Baltimore R. R. Co.	91.8	$68,128.45	$9,180.00	58,491	$20,000	$97,308.45
10013	Bay View (n. o.) and Washington	Baltimore and Potomac R. R. Co	45.4	83,301.98	4,540.00	57,708	21,800	59,714.98
11001	Washington to Richmond	Richmond, Fredericksburgh and Potomac	115.90	37,537.39	13,008.00	19,325	17,419	68,864.39
11006	Richmond to Petersburgh	Richmond and Petersburgh R. R.	23.39	6,459.61	1,871.20	14,840	4,298	12,598.81
11009	Petersburgh to Weldon	Petersburgh R. R.	64.00	16,790.36	5,120.00	13,590	11,686	33,599.36
13002	Weldon to Wilmington	Wilmington and Weldon R. R.	162.07	88,522.41	12,965.60	11,291	29,577	81,065.01
14002	Wilmington to Florence	Wilmington, Columbus and Augusta R. R	110.00	20,879.10	7,150.00	6,781	20,075	48,104.10
14005	Florence to Charleston	Northeastern R. R.	102.00	21,018.12	6,630.00	8,326	17,377	44,985.12
14004	Charleston to Savannah	Savannah and Charleston Rwy	115.00	22,320.35	7,475.00	7,101	19,710	49,505.85
15009	Savannah to Jacksonville	Savannah, Florida and Western Rwy	171.50	33,725.47	11,147.50	7,442	31,298	76,170.97
10018	Jacksonville to Sanford	Jacksonville, Tampa and Key West Rwy.	129.18	20,062.39		5,186	23,027	43,089.39
10007	Sanford to Tampa	South Florida R. R	116.39	9,951.34		1,017	21,241	31,192.34
	Total		1,243.63	329,728.97	79,087.30		237,532	644,348.27
23020	Chicago to Cairo	Illinois Central R. R.	365.53	67,005.30	20,469.05	10,499	(*)	87,474.35
18001	Cairo to New Orleans	do	550.80	88,535.59	16,524.00	4,317	(*)	105,058.50
	Total		916.33	155,540.89	36,993.05			192,533.94
20020	Cincinnati to Chattanooga	Cincinnati, New Orleans and Texas Pacific Rwy	338.20	56,675.53	16,910.00	4,762	(*)	73,585.55
17015	Chattanooga to Meridian	Alabama Great Southern R. R	295.45	31,276.44		2,273	(*)	31,276.46
18016	Meridian to New Orleans	New Orleans and Northeastern R. R.	196.24	13,591.58		630		13,591.58
	Total		829.89	101,543.50	16,910.00			118,453.59
20004	Cincinnati to Louisville	Louisville and Nashville R. R.	110.10	35,896.18	6,549.00	19,548	(*)	42,408.18
20005	Louisville to Nashville	do	185.80	65,204.10	11,100.00	16,017	(*)	66,304.00
10006	Nashville to Decatur	do	122.72	16,017.19		3,350	(*)	18,047.19
17004	Decatur to Montgomery	South and North Alabama R. R.	183.28	20,184.62		2,680	(*)	20,194.25
17012	Montgomery to Mobile	Louisville and Nashville R. R.	160.57	28,067.73	9,028.50	0,146	(*)	37,994.25
17013	Mobile to New Orleans	do	141.43	25,515.38	7,071.50	5,897	(*)	32,586.88
	Total		923.10	183,465.12	33,740.00			217,225.12

* No special facilities.

11843 P M G 88——III

Chicago, Ill., to New Orleans, La. (Illinois Central Railroad).

Official designation.	Frequency of service.			Schedule.			Time in transit. South.		North.	
							Hrs.	M.	Hrs.	M.
Chicago and Centralia R. P. O.	Twice daily, once on Sundays	8.50 p. m.	5.30 a. m.	L..Chicago......A	8.00 a. m.	7.20 a. m.	9	00	10	40
		8.40 a. m.	7.00 p. m. *Express.*	A..Centralia.....L	8.50 a. m.	8.40 p. m. *Express.*				
Centralia and Cairo R. P. O.	Single daily, except Sunday	8.40 a. m.	8.50 p. m.	L..Centralia.....A	7.20 a. m.	7.20 p. m.	4	50	5	35
		1.30 a. m. *R. P. O.*	1.10 a. m.	A..Cairo........L	1.45 a. m.	2.40 p. m.				
Cairo and New Orleans R. P. O.	Single daily		1.30 a. m. *Express.*	L..Cairo........A	2.10 a. m.		22	30	20	20
			5.20 a. m.	A..Milan........L	10.23 a. m.					
			5.35 a. m.	L..Milan........A	10.22 a. m.					
			11.00 p. m.	A..New Orleans...L	5.30 p. m.					

Cincinnati, Ohio, to New Orleans, La. (Louisville and Nashville Railroad).

Official designation.	Frequency of service.			Schedule.			South.		North.	
							Hrs.	M.	Hrs.	M.
Cincinnati and Nashville R. P. O.	Double da'ly, including Sunday	8.00 p. m.	8.15 a. m. *Express.*	L..Cincinnati....A	6.35 p. m.	6.25 a. m.	11	05	10	05
		7.05 a. m.	7.40 p. m.	A..Nashville.....L	7.20 a. m. *Express.*	7.30 p. m.				
Nashville and Montgomery R. P. O.	Single daily, including Sunday	7.40 a. m.	8.25 p. m.	L..Nashville.....A	8.15 p. m.	7.05 p. m.	11	25	10	40
		7.05 p. m.	7.10 a. m.	A..Montgomery....L	7.55 p. m.	7.20 a. m.				
Montgomery and New Orleans R. P. O.	Double daily, including Sunday	7.30 p. m.	7.10 a. m.	A..Montgomery....A	8.05 a. m.	7.55 p. m.	11	40	11	00
		7.19 a. m.	7.20 p. m.	A..New Orleans...L	8.10 p. m.					

Cincinnati, Ohio, and New Orleans, La. (Cincinnati, New Orleans and Texas Pacifio Railroad).

Official designation.	Frequency of service.			Schedule.			South.		North.	
							Hrs.	M.	Hrs.	M.
Cincinnati and Chattanooga R. P. O.	Double daily, including Sunday	8.00 p. m.	7.55 a. m.	L..Cincinnati....A	6.42 p. m.	6.40 a. m.	9	40	9	42
		8.45 a. m.	8.35 p. m.	A..Chattanooga...L	9.00 a. m.	7.10 p. m.				
Chattanooga and Meridian R. P. O.	Single daily, including Sunday	8.50 a. m.	8.00 p. m.	L..Chattanooga...A	8.30 a. m.	6.30 p. m.	10	00	10	00
		10.30 p. m.	4.00 a. m.	A..Meridian......L	8.10 a. m.	5.00 a. m.				
Meridian and New Orleans R. P. O.	Single daily, including Sunday	10.55 p. m.	4.10 a. m.	L..Meridian......A	10.30 p. m.	5.00 p. m.	7	00	7	00
		6.15 a. m.	9.30 a. m.	A..New Orleans...L	5.00 a. m.	10.00 p. m.				

Chicago, Ill., to New Orleans, La., via Cincinnati, Ohio

From and to—	Distance.	Leave and arrive.	Schedule. Stations.	Schedule. Leave and arrive.
Chicago and Cincinnati, Cincinnati, Indianapolis, Saint Louis and Illinois Central Rwys.	*Miles.* 307	9.10 a. m., Monday ...... 8 p. m. Monday	L..Chicago ......A	6.50 p. m., Wednesday ... 6.50 a. m., Wednesday.
		7.15 p. m., Monday ...... 7.50 a. m., Tuesday	A..Cincinnati L	6.20 a. m., Wednesday ... 6.50 p. m., Tuesday.
Cincinnati and Chattanooga, Cincinnati, New Orleans and Texas Pacific R. R.	336	9.00 p. m., Monday ...... 7.55 a. m., Tuesday	L..Cincinnati ....A	8.40 a. m., Wednesday ... 6.42 p. m., Tuesday.
		8.45 a. m., Tuesday ..... 5.35 p. m., Tuesday	A..Chattanooga ...L	7.10 p. m., Tuesday ..... 9 a. m., Tuesday.
Chattanooga and Meridian, Alabama Great Southern.	295	8.50 a. m., Tuesday ..... 6 p. m., Tuesday	L..Chattanooga ...A	6.40 p. m., Tuesday ..... 8.30 a. m., Tuesday.
		11.30 p. m., Tuesday .... 4 a. m., Wednesday	A..Meridian L	5.10 a. m., Tuesday ..... 10.30 p. m., Monday.
Meridian and New Orleans, New Orleans and Northeastern R. R.	196	10.55 p. m., Tuesday .... 4.10 a. m., Wednesday ..	L..Meridian ......A	5 a. m., Tuesday .... 10.20 p. m., Monday.
		6.15 a. m., Wednesday ... 9.30 a. m., Wednesday ..	A..New Orleans ...L	1 p. m., Monday .... 5 p. m., Monday.
Total	1,134			

Average per hour:

	Miles.
Train 4, south	25.15
Train 2, south	30.24
Train 1, north	28.29
Train 3, north	29.97

Chicago to New Orleans via Louisville.

To and from—	Distance.	Leave and arrive.	Schedule. Stations.	Schedule. Leave and arrive.
Chicago to Louisville, Louisville, New Albany and Chicago R. R.	*Miles.* 324	8.05 p. m., Monday ...... 8.15 a. m., Monday	L..Chicago ......A	6.55 p. m., Wednesday ... 7.40 a. m., Wednesday.
		7.55 a. m., Tuesday ..... 7.40 p. m., Monday	A..Louisville ...L	7.30 a. m., Wednesday ... 7.25 p. m., Tuesday.
		1.00 p. m., Tuesday ..... 12.20 a. m., Tuesday ...	L..Louisville ...A	2.20 a. m., Wednesday ... 1.57 p. m., Tuesday.
Louisville and Nashville R. R.	811	7.40 p. m., Tuesday ..... 7.05 a. m., Tuesday	L..Nashville L	7.30 p. m., Tuesday ..... 7.20 a. m., Tuesday.
		8.25 p. m., Tuesday ..... 7.40 a. m., Tuesday	L..Nashville ....A	7.05 p. m., Tuesday ..... 6.55 a. m., Tuesday.
		7.10 a. m., Wednesday ... 7.05 p. m., Tuesday	A..Montgomery ...L	7.55 a. m., Tuesday ..... 8.15 p. m., Monday.
		7.30 a. m., Wednesday ... 7.30 p. m., Tuesday	L..Montgomery ...A	7.20 a. m., Tuesday ..... 7.55 p. m., Monday.
		7.20 p. m., Wednesday ... 7.10 a. m., Wednesday ..	A..New Orleans ..L	8.10 p. m., Monday ...... 8.05 a. m., Monday.
Total				

Average per hour:

	Miles.
Train 5, south	24.01
Train 5, south	24.18
Train 6, north	24.29
Train 4, north	23.95

Chicago, Ill., to New Orleans, La.

Route.	Distance	Leave—	Arrive—	Train No.	Speed per hour.
	Miles.				*Miles.*
Illinois Central	915 915	Chicago 8.40 a. m., Monday New Orleans 5.30 p. m., Monday	New Orleans 11 p. m., Tuesday Chicago 7.20 a. m., Wednesday	1 4	23.86 24.18

Chicago, Ill., to Cincinnati, Ohio.

Route.	Distance	Leave—	Arrive—	Train No.	Speed per hour.
Cincinnati, Indianapolis, Saint Louis and Chicago and Illinois Central Rwys.	307	Chicago 8 p. m., Monday Chicago 9.10 a. m., Monday Cincinnati 8.0 a. m., Monday Cincinnati 6.50 p. m., Monday	Cincinnati 7.30 a. m., Tuesday Cincinnati 7.15 p. m., Monday Chicago 6.50 p. m., Monday Chicago 6.50 a. m., Tuesday	2 4 1 5	26.60 30.44 29.22 25.57

Cincinnati, Ohio, to New Orleans, La.

Route.	Distance	Leave—	Arrive—	Train No.	Speed per hour.
Cincinnati, New Orleans and Texas Pacific.	8.5	Cincinnati 9 p. m., Monday Cincinnati 7.55 a. m., Monday New Orleans 5 p. m., Monday New Orleans 10 p. m., Monday	New Orleans 6 15 a. m., Wednesday New Orleans 9.30 a. m., Tuesday Cincinnati 16.42 p. m., Tuesday Cincinnati 6.40 a. m., Wednesday	5 1 2 6	24.84 32.88 31.50 25.25
Louisville and Nashville.	921	Cincinnati 8.15 a. m., Monday New Orleans 8.05 a. m., Monday New Orleans 8.10 p. m., Monday	New Orleans 7.10 a. m., Wednesday New Orleans 7.20 p. m., Tuesday Cincinnati 6 35 p. m., Tuesday Cincinnati 6.35 a. m., Wednesday	3 1 4 2	26.18 26.95 26.60 25.29

In this connection I call attention to the condition of the law, in urgent need of revision, which reposes *no authority in any official of the Government to compel the owner of a railroad to receive and carry the mails of the Republic.*

In this state of things the Government is always at a disadvantage in negotiating for improved mail facilities, and public opinion and sentiment are the only force to which the Department can now appeal to secure them.

Fast Mails.—Between Chicago and Omaha the fast mail has been made daily, instead of simply west, as before.

This connects with the fast mail between New York and Chicago at the latter place, which has also been increased to run east as well as west.

A new fast mail has been established between Portland, Oregon, and Chicago, and between Chicago and New Orleans, by way of Cincinnati, Chattanooga, and Meridian, Miss. But all these and other improvements in the mail service have been brought about by negotiations and contract in which the Government has been obliged to stipulate for special advantages to the railroads, whereas the Department should be in a position to dictate terms within the rules of fair dealing.

The increase in the Railway Mail Service has been unprecedented and far beyond the estimates for the fiscal year for which they were made. Increase has been added in the South and Southwest, whose needs in this regard had not before met with the attention which their growth and commercial importance seemed to require. The table heretofore set out furnish a showing for increased means of communication.

Foreign Mail Service.—The weight of the mails dispatched to foreign countries was as follows:

Transatlantic service, 581,130 pounds letters, 2,259,877 pounds other articles.

Transpacific and miscellaneous service, 62,483 pounds letters, 763,115 pounds other articles. Total, 643,613 pounds letters, 3,022,992 pounds other articles.

The largest quantity of mail matter was dispatched to Great Britain, 43.28 per cent. of letters and 51.22 per cent. of other articles; and the next to Germany, 21.41 per cent. of letters, and 20.27 per cent. of other articles.

The total cost of the service was $490,067.29, of which $464,910.70 was for transporting mails of United States origin. Of this amount there was paid for transatlantic service, $353,262.08; for transpacific service, $42,593.13; and for miscellaneous service, $58,553.61.

The estimates for the fiscal year ending June 30, 1890, are as follows:

Total amount, $760,000. Of this sum there will be required for transportation of mails of United States origin $613,738.97. The last mentioned sum is calculated on the basis of the following rates of annual increase:

To ports to which American vessels do not ply: Letters, 11.87 per cent.; other articles, 8.20 per cent.

To ports to which American vessels ply: Letters, 4.91 per cent.; other articles, 18.56 per cent.

Transatlantic Steam-ship Service.—The mails for Europe have been invariably assigned each month to those steamers which made the fastest time, as ascertained from an average of a number of trips as reported by the steam-ship companies.

The fastest time from New York to London via Queenstown was made by the Cunard steam-ship *Umbria*, viz, 179.7 hours.

The fastest time from New York to London via Southampton was made by the North German Lloyd steam-ship *Lahn*, viz, 188 hours.

The fastest time from New York to Havre was made by the General Transatlantic steam-ship *La Champagne*, viz, 189 hours.

Postal Convention with the Dominion of Canada.—On the 12th of January there was signed at Washington, and on the 19th of January at Ottawa, a postal convention between the United States and the Dominion of Canada, abrogating the special postal convention between the two countries of 1875.

The new convention went into operation March 1, 1888, and makes virtually one postal territory of the United States and Canada. Uniformity of postage rates had already been established, but there was still the restriction that no merchandise of any kind could be sent to Canada. This restriction has now been removed, and, with the exception of specially prohibited articles, merchandise can now be sent at fourth-class rates of postage.

Parcel Post.—Four parcel-post conventions have been concluded during the fiscal year ended June 30, 1888, viz: With Barbadoes, went into operation December 1, 1887; with the Bahamas, went into operation February 1, 1888; with British Honduras, went into operation March 1, 1888; with Mexico, went into operation July 1, 1888.

The parcel-post rates to all these countries are the same, viz, 12 cents per pound, or fraction of a pound; and, in addition to this, a charge for interior service and delivery may be collected from the addressee in the country of destination. This charge is 5 cents for each single parcel of whatever weight, and, if the weight exceed one pound, 1 cent for each four ounces or fraction thereof.

The highest charge for a parcel weighing 11 pounds sent from the United States by parcel-mail to any of the above-mentioned countries will, therefore, be $1.76 (of which the sender will have to pay $1.32 and the addressee 44 cents).

Parcel-post conventions are now pending with all the Central and South American States, and will doubtless prove a great benefit to American commerce and industry.

The Universal Postal Union.—During the year the following countries have been added to the union :

The German territories of the "New Guinea Company," of "Tago," Western Africa, of " Southwest Africa," and of the "Marshall Islands," in the Pacific, and the Regency of Tunis, north coast of Africa.

A German post-office has been established at Afia, Samoan Islands, thus making these islands virtually part of the Postal Union.

Statistics of the Postal Service in the Principal Countries of the Postal Union.—The greatest length of postal routes was possessed by the United States, viz, 410,824 miles ; next in order came Germany, France, and Russia.

The greatest number of miles of annual transportation was in the United States, viz, 252,525,293 miles ; next in order came Germany, France, and Austria.

As regards the number of articles of mail matter dispatched in the international mails, Germany takes the lead in letters, 53,151,430, and next in order came Great Britain, Austria, and the United States. The United States takes the lead in prints, 47,049,064, and next in order came Great Britain, Germany, and France.

As regards the annual postal income Germany takes the lead with $48,816,200.33 ; next comes the United States with $45,948,422, followed in order by Great Britain, France, Russia, and Austria.

As regards the annual postal expenditure the United States takes the lead with $51,018,243.79 ; next comes Germany with $42,237,084.91, followed in order by Great Britain, France, Russia, and Austria.

The greatest postal surplus was in Great Britain, viz, $12,501,850.03, and the greatest deficiency in the United States, viz, $5,069,820.85.

The largest amount of steamship subsidies was paid by France, viz, $5,154,330.61, followed by Great Britain, $3,024,334.12.

International Postal Congress of Vienna, in 1890.— The first congress was held at Berne, Switzerland, in 1873, the second at Paris, France, in 1878, and the third at Lisbon, Portugal, in 1885.

The United States were represented at all these congresses and will doubtless also be represented at the Vienna Congress, which promises to be of unusual interest, as, among the rest, the question of doing away with all transit charges will come up for discussion. An appropriation of $5,000 is asked for the expenses of the United States delegates to that congress.

Special services Maintained by Foreign Countries.— The collection service was first established by Belgium in 1842, by Germany in 1871, Switzerland in 1875, France in 1879, and Austria in 1882.

Under the regulations the post-office undertakes to collect, at certain fixed charges, bills up to a certain amount, to cash bills of exchange, and collect (in Belgium) dividend coupons of the public debt and coupons of other kinds.

The number of bills mailed for collection in Germany (in 1886) was 4,362,027 to the value of $87,550,220.66, yielding a revenue of $288,717.80 to the post-office. The number of bills mailed for collection in Belgium (in 1886) was 4,391,263 to the value of $66,949,312.34, yielding a revenue to the post-office of $178,840.40, and the number of bills mailed for collection in France (in 1883) was 5,777,541, to the value of $70,252,946.73, yielding an income to the post-office of $688,178.39.

I venture to express the hope that if the policy of subsidizing American ships for the promotion of commerce with foreign countries shall be adopted, the disbursement of the fund shall not be added to the functions of postal administration. In this connection I have the honor to quote from a communication made by me to the Committee on Post-Offices and Post-Roads of the House of Representatives on July 2, 1888. It was called out by a request for my opinion upon the provision of the bill appropriating $800,000 " to promote the purposes of a more efficient mail service between the United States and Central and South America and the West Indies by contract with American built and registered steam-ships for the transportation of the United States mails," and providing that such contract should be for a period of not less than five nor more than ten years, at a compensation not exceeding for each outward trip $1 per nautical mile:

It will hardly be claimed for this legislation that it is either demanded or required, or that it can be utilized for the benefit of the postal service merely. The resources and powers of the Department have proved entirely adequate to afford to the citizens of the United States a foreign mail service equal to, and in most cases superior to, that of any nation in the world. Nine-tenths of our foreign letter mail crosses the Atlantic, and the settled policy of the Department has been to employ the swiftest vessels from week to week for carrying the mails. The Department, at the request of prominent merchants, importers, and bankers of the United States having commercial relations with foreign countries, has endeavored to induce foreign postal administrations to adopt a similar policy to promote expedition and security in correspondence.

Under the present system, on routes other than to European ports, mails have been carried in American steam-ships at four times the rates paid for transatlantic service, although no foreign vessel has ever refused or hesitated to accept the sea postage, or one-fourth the rate paid to American bottoms. Under the present conditions the Central and South American letter mail increases at the rate of about 10 per cent. in weight a year, and the number of sailings to West Indian and Central and South American ports from the three ports of New York, New Orleans, and San Francisco increased in the fiscal year ending June 30, 1887, from 712 to 831. In addition to the compensation paid in money, all common carriers by water are greatly benefited by carrying the mail. Provision for their benefit in Brazilian ports are as follows: Mail steamers are allowed to immediately discharge their cargoes, preference being given them before any other vessel and before they have been entered at the custom-house, both on week days and on Sundays or holidays.

They may sail at any hour, day or night, after they have received the mail, and can not be detained under any pretext whatever beyond the hour fixed for sailing. Similar benefits are provided for mail steamers at other West Indian and Central and South American ports. While the Department in every case has given the preference to American ships at four times the cost of carriage on competing foreign ships as permitted by law, yet in very many cases, because of very much greater expedition or because of the absence of proper facilities in American steamers, or because of very great delays, the other ships offering have been given the business at the lower rate on the principle that the first duty of the Department to our citizens under the law was to give them the best, most expeditious, and certain mail facilities within its resources.

If there shall be superadded to the functions of postal administration that of administering a subsidy or a bounty for the promotion of American shipping interests I can readily see why, in practice, these two offices must so conflict that, so far from being of advantage to and promoter of efficient mail service, such a subsidy, with such a purpose, in the hands of the Postmaster-General must antagonize and overbear the primary object of his office, which is to give to the correspondence of our citizens the best expedition and certain transmission. If the bounty or bonus system is to be revived, it should be done without involving this Department in the complications certain to arise from administering it, and without hampering its fundamental rule of action, which is that the mails must go at all events.

While we granted aid to the Pacific railroads, with conditions imposed that the mails should be carried for a credit on the debt, yet the Department was left free to employ better or more expeditious routes in its discretion. The proposed legislation will be in effect a mandate to the Postmaster-General to contract with American-built as well as American-registered steam-ships for the transportation of the mails to the ports of Central and South America and the West Indies for a period of not less than five years and with a compensation for each outward trip of $1 per mile. There is no condition for advertisement, and indeed, unlike even the British subsidy acts, competition is not contemplated or permitted, as the contracts are to be limited to American ships, and as to these will be practically limited to those now in existence, between whom there is comparatively no competition because of the number which can be employed in the service.

In the present conditions the proposed law might as well have named the few persons to whom this money is to be paid. Even the laws (Revised Statutes sections 3976 and 4203) under which American ships might be compelled to carry the mails have been repealed (23 United States Statutes at Large, 58), and it goes without saying that the proposed legislation intends the Department to pay the maximum rate provided, i. e., $1 per nautical mile for five years, to these few persons, without troubling them with any negotiations as to terms, and, indeed, as you will observe, without even the lodgment of discretion in the Department to designate from what ports of the United States the mails shall sail. It may be said in passing that presumably the "terminal points" from which sailings will be made, if self-interest, as is usually the case, governs, will be those from which the greatest number of nautical miles may be computed, rather than from those at which the convenience and needs of the service would be suited. It may be noted also that the schedules of sailings are to be furnished by the contractors, and not by the Postmaster-General; altogether from an analysis of the proposed legislation it would seem to exclude the exercise of any power of any representative of this Government to provide for this mail service in the interest of the people, except after contract, which must be on the carriers' own terms and after the carriers have fixed the schedules according to their ideas of what the mail service should be to compel them to conform to their own expressed views and decision as to the public convenience and the public interests.

I beg you to believe that in this criticism of the bill I am not commenting unfavorably at this place upon a policy of granting bounties to American ships. I do think, however, that the carrying out of that policy should not be involved in the postal administration. Such gifts should be voted and given directly, if the Government shall determine to pursue a policy of engaging in this branch of private business. With very great respect, however, to the framers of the bill, I do seriously object to that provision of the proposed legislation which places the mail service at the mercy of any firm, individual, or corporation. While, indeed, the subsidized lines might be compelled to carry the mails if tendered, yet the Department should be independent, and should at all times be enabled to send the mails by the most expeditious routes and make use of the best facilities afforded for that purpose from among all carriers offering. The Department should be free to take advantage of all sailings, of increased facilities coming from increased business, of changes for the better wrought by time, extension of commerce, and competition, and should not be tied up for a decade to single lines of communication, unstimulated to improvement and all progress by the existence of a settled, inordinate, and certain income.

Herewith I furnish you two tables, marked "A" and "B." From them you will see that the mails of this country were carried to Central and South America and the West Indies for the fiscal year ended June 30, 1887, by foreign steamers at a cost of $7,936.27 at the single rate, and by steamers of American register at a cost of $39,381.57. The number of miles sailed by the foreign ships employed was 666,448; the miles sailed by the ships of American register employed were 546,758. It will be seen, on the plan of payment proposed, which is fixed without regard to the amount of mail carried, that the service, which cost us in the fiscal year 1887 $47,317.84, would have cost us, if paid for as proposed, $1,213.206. It is estimated that the weight of mails will be for the next fiscal year increased 20 per cent. over these figures, and from what I have before shown it will be seen that the number of sailings will be increased in about the same ratio over the figures given in Tables A and B. The total cost of the sailings under this bill, predicated upon the business of 1887, can be but an approximate standard by which to estimate the cost under a provision of $1 for every nautical mile for each outward trip.

But without regard to the cost, it is perfectly evident, from an examination of these tables and from the experience of the Department in affording the best attainable service, that "American-built ships" alone, with whom the Department can now contract under this bill, and with which it must contract for a term of years, can not perform the service absolutely essential. Heretofore, as I have said, whenever it has been possible and consistent with the best interests of the public which this Department serves, American ships have been employed to carry the mails at four times the rate paid to foreign ships; yet with this policy steadily maintained, to give proper service at all it has been necessary to employ other carriers, as shown by Schedule A. One of the most serious disadvantages from connecting the proposed subsidy with this Department will be that, even in cases where service is not furnished to certain ports by American ships at all, carriers that might be had will hardly suffer the enormous discrimination in compensation for the carriage of the mails. The conditions would certainly predispose human nature to refuse to perform the service at all.

Again, it will not commend itself to our people if, with this enormous compensation, avowedly for the carriage of the mails, frequency of transmission shall be largely curtailed, even to ports touched by American ships, as must be the case where we pay one carrier about two hundred and fifty times as much as we offer for the same service to another. In my opinion the bill would not be advantageous to the service, but the disadvantages would be positive in so far as this Department is concerned; while if it shall become a law, the Department will of course faithfully administer the fund in accordance with the spirit of the act. I feel confident that such administration will result only in a very great pecuniary benefit to a dozen individuals, at the expense and embarrassment of good service, and of inconvenience, injustice, and material injury to the great body of the people, whose money will be used in the purchase of those results.

Considering this as a subsidy pure and simple, unconnected with the postal service, it becomes a question of general policy with which this Department has nothing to do. The subject has been ably and exhaustively discussed in Congress, notably in the Thirty-fifth, Forty-fifth, Forty-sixth, and Forty-ninth. You, sir, and other distinguished members of the Post-Office Committee as at present constituted, have on the floor of the House presented the learning which the history of the subject, political economy, or the experience of legislation can teach. It has been frequently demonstrated by the experience of this and other countries that to enable one line by Government aid to carry more cheaply, and thus to destroy competition, does not promote commerce.* The most successful ocean steamship lines of the Continent—those of Hamburg and Bremen—receive no pay from the Government other than the moderate postage rates.† The British precedent is not in point and would not be even if Great Britain did not offer her mail service to the carriers of the world. " Her aims are political and not commercial. She must have constant communication with the colonies, and she has spent large sums for this object. She must have an efficient and capable transport service for the protection of those colonies."‡ The views of that Government are stated in Mr. Scudemore's report (Parl. Papers, 1867-'68 XII, 131), as follows:

" The question (mail subsidy service) can not be dealt with on commercial principles. * * * For the sake of keeping up such communication with the east as the nation requires they must set commercial principles at defiance, and cost what it may the nation must either pay them what they lose thereby or forego the communication."

Of course England may subsidize lines of ships to open up new markets for her surplus, because she freely exchanges commodities with such markets, and her policy is after establishing the commerce to steadily decrease the subsidy. If the policy of giving bounties to promote commercial relations with other countries be ever adopted again after the failures in our history, it would seem that its adoption should be deferred until closer commercial relations with those countries can be maintained, and are not antagonized by an opposing system of laws. Commerce in the very essence of its meaning is exchange. It is not to sell and never to buy. The individual or nation does not exist that will buy all one has to sell for cash with no reciprocal return in profitable exchange. Cargoes out and cargoes back are needed for the creation of a merchant marine. The cargo out will not be bought unless we buy in exchange, and it will be bought if we are willing to trade. Until these conditions come, subsidies may maintain a line so long as the subsidy lasts and then the line will go down for want of legitimate trade. If, however, the subsidy policy is to be pursued, I venture to suggest the Mexican method. When a ship arrives with a cargo the tariff tax is divided with the ship-owner, the latter taking 50 per cent. of the duty on the goods he brings in payment on account of his subsidy. The trading-ship is thus enabled to remit to the consignor, if he will employ his ship, a portion of the government duties, and thus the ship-owner is indeed enabled to promote trade with foreign countries directly. An improvement upon the Mexican method in the interest of the promotion of trade and of the building of ships to conduct it, would be to enable the owners and the builders to receive at the port of consignment in that country still a greater proportion of the duties imposed by the government upon the cargo.

In this way the Mexican ship would be enabled to get her cargo, charge a fair profit for carriage, and sell to the Mexican consumer at a price at which he could conveniently buy, take out a cargo for exchange, and repeat the process, to the cultivation of much closer commercial relations with foreign countries, and to the maintenance of Mexican shipping. Of course, the Mexican method is somewhat cumbersome, and the same end might be reached without indirection and without the payment of a subsidy by the removal or reduction of the Mexican tariff on imports.

While on the subject of closer commercial relations with South and Central America, for the promotion of which the bill under consideration is doubtless intended, I call your attention to some interesting figures.

Our total trade with Brazil for the year ended June 30, 1887, was as follows:

Total imports.. $52,955,591
Our total exports to Brazil were..................................... 8,137,794
Of the imports we imposed no tariff upon............................. 47,076,473
We did impose a tariff upon.. 5,876,703

* Mercantile marines of foreign countries, Forty-ninth Congress, Ex. Doc. No. 172.
† Forty-fifth Congress, second session, Ex. Doc. No. 38. Forty-sixth Congress, third session, House committee report No. 342.
‡ Hadley.

Our total trade with Central America for the same period was as follows:

Total imports	$7,706,978
Total exports	3,006,714
Of the imports we imposed no tariff upon	7,195,705
We did impose a tariff upon	441,916

Our total trade with Venezuela was as follows:

Total imports	8,444,967
Total exports	5,504,215
Of the imports we imposed no tariff upon	8,248,450
We did impose a tariff upon	12,786

. Our total trade with the United States of Colombia was as follows:

Total imports	4,771,303
Total exports	7,158,235
Of the imports we imposed no tariff upon	3,934,559
We did impose a tariff upon	16,594

Our total trade with the Argentine Republic was as follows:

Total imports	4,104,102
Total exports	6,364,545
Of the imports we imposed no tariff upon	3,347,936
We imposed a tariff upon	752,256

Our total trade with Chili was as follows:

Total imports	2,863,233
Total exports	2,069,138
Of the imports we imposed no tariff upon	2,634,396
We did impose a tariff upon	228,897

These illustrate the universal rule by which the limitations upon commercial relations and the carrying trade with all the countries of Central and South America may be measured. A comparison of the amount brought into the country free of tariff with what we send in exchange is instructive. It should be noted that of the Brazilian imports free of duty, the large proportion value is the item of coffee, after deducting which the lesson on exchange of trade as bearing on closer relations with all these countries is the same, and the universal one.

SPECIAL TOPICS.

Ownership by the Government of Post-office Buildings.—A bill prepared in this Department and reported favorably by the committees of both houses, but not acted upon at the last session, would provide a standard fixed by returns showing the amount of business transacted at each office, which would give the Postmaster-General the power to purchase sites and erect permanent buildings for post-office purposes. I had the honor to furnish the committees with the data showing that, in my judgment, sound business principles dictated such a policy and demonstrating that it would be a measure of economy for the Government by comparison with the present system of leasing. At the expiration of leases it is almost invariably the case that strife arises among citizens of towns over the fixing of a new site for the post-office. Real estate values are, to some extent, unsettled by such changes, and it is frequently difficult for the head of the Department to determine whether the case presented for the location has strong popular support in the interest of the general convenience of the community or whether it is not made up in the interest of mere real-estate speculation. From my experience in the matter of making new leases or of renewing old ones, I am led to present the subject to Congress with much earnestness. I am satisfied that the measure above referred to and now pending is one of the highest merit. It is known as H. R. bill No. 3319.

Postal Telegraphy.—If the correspondence of the country is to continue to be under the charge and protection of the Government, the vast and increasing volume conducted by telegraphy and the right of the great body of the people to be afforded facilities for the best and quickest transmission at rates within the means of all will press this subject upon the attention of the Congress with more and more urgency. The chief difficulties in the way are the great cost of present methods and the absence of safeguards which, according to the theory of the present mail service, should protect the privacy of correspondence. I have given the subject much consideration, and I believe that the inventive genius of this country has reached a stage in discovery in electric science when these problems may be solved. The subject is of such great importance to the people that I believe an opportunity should be given for the presentation and examination of inventions which have been informally presented to the committees of Congress the Department and the public, and that a stimulus should be given to inventors to turn their attention to the improvement of old methods. I recommend the appointment of a commission of competent and disinterested men, learned in the science, who may examine inventions and invite others, who shall be authorized to erect short experimental lines, and who shall report to the President or to Congress the result of their investigations.

A Fourth Assistant Postmaster-General.—I renew the recommendation of my immediate predecessor, as to which I have also presented an argument and information to the Congress, that this office should be created.

Salaries.—I also most earnestly recommend to the attention of the Congress all that is said by my predecessor in favor of an increase of the salaries of departmental officials at page 84 of his report. Many of these are paid not exceeding 50 per cent. of the market value of the required ability, and my views on the subject have been presented in several communications now on the files of the proper committees of the present Congress.

I can not omit to express my appreciation of the faithful services of all the officers, clerks, and employés of this Department. My relations with many of them with whom I have been brought in more constant contact have created attachments which will survive while I live, and my respect and regard for all have grown with my observation of their faithful service to the Government.

I have the honor to be, with great respect, your obedient servant,

DON M. DICKINSON,
Postmaster-General.

The PRESIDENT.

Appropriations, expenditures, and unexpended balances of appropriations for objects pertaining to the care of the Post-Office Department building, for the conduct of the departmental service, and for salaries of officers and employés of the Department for the fiscal year ended June 30, 1888.

Items.	Year ended June 30, 1888.		Balance unexpended.	
	Appropriations.	Expenditures.	Amount.	Per cent.
Stationery	$12,000.00	$9,875.72	$2,124.28	17.70
Fuel, etc	8,000.00	7,803.32	196.68	2.49
Gas	5,500.00	3,867.31	1,632.69	29.68
Plumbing and gas-fixtures	3,000.00	1,167.40	1,832.60	61.08
Telegraphing	3,500.00	2,305.60	1,194.40	30.41
Painting	3,500.00	1,956.25	1,543.75	44.10
Carpets and matting	4,000.00	2,777.87	1,222.13	30.55
Furniture	5,000.00	1,181.12	3,818.88	70.63
Keeping horses, etc	1,500.00	747.53	752.47	50.16
Hardware	1,500.00	547.76	932.24	63.48
Miscellaneous items	13,000.00	8,874.26	4,125.74	31.73
Rent:				
Topographers	1,500.00	1,500.00		
Money-order building	8,000.00	8,000.00		
Additional building for Auditor's office	4,500.00	4,500.00		
Official Postal Guides	18,000.00	16,020.70	1,979.30	10.90
Post-route maps, etc	15,000.00	14,442.78	557.22	3.71
Foreign postage	500.00	469.00	31.00	6.20
Total of items pertaining to care of building, etc	108,000.00	86,036.62	21,963.38	20.33
Salaries of officers and employés of the Post-Office Department	711,540.00	703,155.24	8,384.76	1.17
Total of all the above	819,540.00	789,191.86	30,348.14	3.45

Items.	Year ended June 30, 1887.		Balances unexpended.	
	Appropriations.	Expenditures.	Amount.	Per cent.
Stationery	$13,000.00	$7,470.02	$5,529.96	42.53
Fuel, etc	8,000.00	6,711.95	1,288.05	16.10
Gas	6,200.00	3,996.40	2,203.60	35.54
Plumbing and gas fixtures	3,000.00	1,792.23	1,207.77	40.25
Telegraphing	3,500.00	1,989.46	1,510.54	43.15
Painting	4,000.00	2,859.71	1,140.29	28.50
Carpets and matting	4,000.00	2,496.86	1,503.14	37.57
Furniture	6,000.00	2,068.58	3,931.42	65.52
Keeping horses, etc	1,500.00	1,152.80	347.20	23.51
Hardware	1,700.00	776.23	923.77	54.33
Miscellaneous items	13,000.00	8,376.76	4,623.24	35.56
Rent:				
Topographers	1,500.00	1,500.00		
Money-order building	8,000.00	8,000.00		
Additional building for Auditor's office	4,500.00	4,500.00		
Official Postal Guides	18,000.00	17,873.43	126.58	7.03
Post-route maps	15,000.00	16,631.89	539.11	3.13
Realized from sale of post-route maps	2,171.00			
Foreign postage	500.00	377.50	122.50	24.50
Total of items pertaining to care of building, etc	113,571.00	88,573.81	24,997.19	22.01
Salaries of officers and employés of the Post-Office Department	719,040.00	704,435.00	14,605.00	2.03
Total of all the above	832,611.00	793,008.81	39,602.19	4.75

Appropriations, expenditures, and unexpended balances of appropriations, etc.—Continued.

Items.	Year ended June 30, 1886.			
	Appropria-tions.	Expendi-tures.	Balances unex-pended.	
			Amount.	Per cent.
Stationery..	$9,000.00	$6,349.00	$2,651.00	29.45
Fuel, etc...	7,200.00	6,817.34	382.66	5.31
Fuel, etc., additional building............................	1,300.00	436.60	863.40	66.4
Gas..	6,600.00	4,933.11	1,666.89	25.25
Gas, additional building...................................	400.00	400.00	....	....
Plumbing and gas-fixtures..................................	4,700.00	3,634.30	1,065.70	22.6
Telegraphing...	5,000.00	2,320.79	2,679.21	53.58
Painting...	4,700.00	2,407.56	2,292.44	48.7
Carpets and matting.......................................	5,900.00	3,570.60	2,329.40	39.14
Furniture..	7,500.00	1,366.71	6,133.29	81.77
Furniture, additional building.............................	500.00	17.00	483.00	96.6
Keeping horses, etc.......................................	1,500.00	987.97	512.03	34.1
Hardware..	1,700.00	534.81	1,165.19	68.5
Miscellaneous items.......................................	13,000.00	10,897.93	2,102.07	16.16
Miscellaneous items, additional building..................	500.00	114.50	385.50	77.1
Rent, topographers..	1,500.00	1,500.00	....	....
Rent, Money-Order building................................	8,000.00	8,000.00	....	....
Rent, additional building..................................	4,500.00	4,125.00	375.00	8.3
Official Postal Guides.....................................	29,000.00	13,708.60	15,291.40	52.7
Post-route maps...	20,000.00	....	....	....
Realized from sale of post-route maps.....................	2,252.00	16,990.04	5,261.96	28.73
Foreign postage...	500.00	448.50	51.50	10.3
Free penalty envelopes....................................	3,600.00	1,533.89	2,066.11	57.3
Total of items pertaining to care of Department, etc	138,852.00	91,094.25	47,757.75	34.39
Salaries of officers and employés of Post-Office Depart-ment..	715,120.00	697,675.50	17,444.50	2.4
Total of all the above............................	853,972.00	788,769.75	65,202.25	7.63

Items.	Year ended June 30, 1885.			
	Appropria-tions.	Expendi-tures.	Balances unex-pended.	
			Amount.	Per cent.
Stationery..	$9,000.00	$8,913.30	$86.70	.96
Fuel, etc...	7,200.00	7,032.07	167.93	2.33
Fuel, etc., additional building...........................	6,600.00	3,331.94	1,268.06	19.2
Gas..				
Gas, additional building..................................				
Plumbing and gas fixtures................................	4,700.00	4,692.49	7.51	.16
Telegraphing...	5,900.00	2,880.93	3,019.07	51.1
Painting...	4,700.00	4,662.22	37.78	.8
Carpets and matting.....................................	5,900.00	5,376.61	523.39	8.8
Furniture..	7,500.00	6,340.02	1,159.98	15.4
Furniture, additional building............................				
Keeping horses, etc......................................	1,500.00	1,064.51	435.49	29
Hardware..	1,700.00	1,601.22	98.78	5.8
Miscellaneous items.....................................	13,500.00	13,500.00	....	....
Miscellaneous items, additional building.................				
Rent, topographers......................................	1,500.00	1,500.00	....	....
Rent, Money-Order building..............................	8,000.00	8,000.00	....	....
Rent, additional building.................................				
Official Postal Guides...................................	29,000.00	26,421.69	2,578.31	8.89
Post-route maps...	20,000.00	....	....	....
Realized from sales of post-route maps..................	1,219.15	21,064.25	154.90	.73
Foreign postage...				
Free penalty envelopes..................................				
Total of items pertaining to care of Department, etc.	127,019.15	118,381.23	9,537.90	7.45
Salaries of officers and employés of Post-Office Depart-ment...	696,480.00	690,267.62	6,212.38	.89
Total of all the above............................	824,399.15	808,648.87	15,750.28	1.9

Estimates of appropriations required for the service of the fiscal year ending June 30, 1890, by the Post-Office Department.

Detailed objects of expenditure, and explanations.	Estimated amount which will be required for each detailed object of expenditure.	Amount appropriated for the current fiscal year ending June 30, 1889.
UNDER THE POST-OFFICE DEPARTMENT, OUT OF THE POSTAL REVENUES.		
POSTAL SERVICE.		
Office of the Postmaster-General.		
Mail depredations and post-office inspectors and fees to United States marshals, attorneys, etc. (July 24, 1888)	$300,000.00	$200,000.00
Advertising (same act)	18,000.00	16,000.00
Miscellaneous items in the office of the Postmaster-General (same act)	1,500.00	1,500.00
Total	319,500.00	217,500.00
Office of the First Assistant Postmaster-General.		
Compensation to postmasters (same act)	13,000,000.00	12,500,000.00
Compensation to clerks in post-offices (same act)	6,550,000.00	5,950,000.00
Rent, light, and fuel for first and second class offices (same act)	600,000.00	550,000.00
Rent, light, and fuel to offices of the third class (same act)	505,080.00	450,000.00
Miscellaneous and incidental items for first and second class		
Post-offices, including furniture (same act)	110,000.00	100,000.00
Free-delivery service (same act)	8,000,000.00	7,000,000.00
Stationery in post-offices (same act)	57,500.00	55,000.00
Wrapping twine (same act)	85,000.00	80,000.00
Wrapping paper (same act)	50,000.00	45,000.00
Letter-balances, scales, and test-weights, and repairs to same (July 24, 1888)	15,000.00	15,000.00
Postmarking and rating stamps, and repairs to same, and ink and pads for stamping and canceling purposes (same act)	35,000.00	43,000.00
Packing-boxes, sawdust, paste, and hardware (submitted)	3,000.00	
Printing facing-slips, card slide-labels, blanks, and books of an urgent nature for post-offices of the first and second classes (submitted)	7,000.00	
Total	29,617,580.00	27,113,000.00
Office of the Second Assistant Postmaster-General.		
Inland mail transportation, viz: Inland transportation by star routes (July 24, 1888)	5,650,000.00	5,400,000.00
Inland transportation by steam-boat routes (same act)	470,000.00	450,000.00
Mail-messenger service (same act)	1,150,000.00	950,000.00
Mail bags and mail-bag catchers (same act)	225,000.00	285,000.00
Mail locks and keys (same act)	15,000.00	25,000.00
Inland transportation by railroad routes, of which a sum not exceeding $30,000 may be employed to pay the freight on postal-cards stamped envelopes, and stamped paper from the manufactories to post-offices and depots of distribution (same act)	19,105,557.00	17,000,000.00
Railway post-office car service (same act)	2,360,600.00	2,000,000.00
Railway post-office clerks (same act)	5,676,728.74	5,246,790.21
Necessary and special facilities on trunk-lines (same act)	205,655.38	295,987.53
Miscellaneous items (same act)	1,000.00	1,000.00
Total	34,728,942.02	31,653,777.74
Office of the Third Assistant Postmaster-General.		
Manufacture of adhesive postage and special-delivery stamps (July 24, 1888)	155,874.00	144,148.00
Pay of agent and assistants to distribute stamps, and expenses of agency (same act)	9,000.00	8,000.00
Manufacture of stamped envelopes, newspaper-wrappers, and letter-sheets (same act)	832,351.00	756,687.90
Pay of agent and assistants to distribute stamped envelopes, newspaper-wrappers, and letter-sheets, and expenses of agency (same act)	16,000.00	16,000.00
Manufacture of postal-cards (same act)	228,781.00	212,455.00
Pay of agent and assistants to distribute postal-cards and expenses of agency (same act)	7,800.00	7,800.00
Registered package, tag, official, and dead-letter envelopes (same act)	109,745.00	102,808.00
Ship, steam-boat, and way letters (same act)	2,500.00	2,500.00
Engraving, printing, and binding drafts and warrants (same act)	3,000.00	2,500.00
Miscellaneous items (same act)	1,000.00	1,000.00
Total	1,386,051.00	1,253,956.00

Estimates of appropriations required for the service of the fiscal year ending June 30, 1890, by the Post-Office Department—Continued.

Detailed objects of expenditure, and explanations.	Estimated amount which will be required for each detailed object of expenditure.	Amount appropriated for the current fiscal year ending June 30, 1889.
UNDER THE POST-OFFICE DEPARTMENT, ETC.—Continued.		
POSTAL SERVICE—continued.		
Office Superintendent Foreign Mails.		
Transportation of foreign mails (same act)	$655,000.00	$547,000.00
Balance due foreign countries (same act)	100,000.00	75,000.00
Expenses of United States delegates to Vienna Postal Congress 1890......	5,000.00	....
Total......	760,000.00	622,000.00
Total postal service...	66,812,073.02	
POSTAL REVENUE.		
Estimated amount which will be provided by the Department from its own revenue, accruing from postages and other sources, namely:		
Ordinary revenues.................... $61,658,658.12		
Net revenue from money-order business............... 850,000.00		
Total postal revenue	62,508,658.12	
DEFICIENCY IN POSTAL REVENUE.		
Leaving a deficiency in the revenue of the Post-Office Department, to be provided for out of the general treasury.		
Total postal service deficiency...................................	4,303,414.90	

THE FREE-DELIVERY SYSTEM.

The estimates, appropriations, and expenditures for this service for the past two years were as follows:

	1886-'87.	1887-'88.	Increase.
Estimates	$4,928,531.25	$5,522,500.00	$593,968.75
Appropriations	4,928,531.25	5,522,500.00	593,968.75
Expenditures	4,618,692.07	5,422,356.36	803,664.29

The large increase in expenditure for 1887-'88 over the preceding year was occasioned by the act of January 3, 1887, providing for the extension of the service, under which one hundred and sixty-nine offices were added to the system.

The appropriation for the current fiscal year is $7,000,000, $1,000,000 of which was appropriated to carry into effect the act approved May 24, 1888, entitled "An act to limit the hours that letter-carriers in cities shall be employed per day."

11843—P M G 58——IV

ESTIMATE FOR THE FISCAL YEAR COMMENCING JULY 1, 1889, AND ENDING JUNE 30, 1890.

The annual pay of carriers in service on June 30, 1889, subject to the usual changes unimportant in the aggregate, will be as follows:

3,157 carriers at $1,000 each	$3,157,000
630 carriers at $800 each	504,000
2,393 carriers at $850 each	2,034,050
2,070 carriers at $600 each	1,242,000
8,250	6,937,050

To which is to be added—

For promotions of 2,700 carriers under act of August 2, 1882	440,000
Pay of substitutes for carriers on vacation, (8,250)	206,250
Pay of substitutes for additional carriers on vacation (350)	8,750
Pay of substitutes for holidays and emergencies	3,000
Pay of post-office inspectors	15,000
Incidental expenses (of which there will be on June 30, 1889, an authorized annual charge of about $240,000)	275,000
Additional carriers (equal to 350 for a full year)	210,000
	8,095,050
Allowed	8,000,000

The increase in the amount of appropriation required for 1889-'90 is on account of the passage of the act of January 3, 1887, providing for extension of the service to additional places, which largely increases the number of offices every year, and the act of May 24, 1888, known as the "Eight-Hour Law."

In this estimate it will be seen that in addition to the amount which is required to be appropriated under existing laws, but $253,750 is for additional carriers, the extension of the service, and expenses incidental thereto.

Yours, respectfully,

J. F. BATES,
Superintendent Free-Delivery System.

Hon. A. E. STEVENSON,
First Assistant Postmaster-General.

APPENDIX.

REPORT OF THE LAW CLERK.

POST-OFFICE DEPARTMENT,
OFFICE OF LAW CLERK,
Washington, D. C., October 6, 1888.

SIR: I have the honor to submit herewith a statement of the number of post-offices and postal stations where premises were leased by the Government and in effect June 30, 1888, showing the annual rent paid and the total salary and allowances, and also showing the box-rents and commissions, surplus or deficiency, and gross receipts at each office, upon the basis of the annual re-adjustment of postmasters' salaries taking effect July 1, 1888.

Very respectfully,

J. W. NICHOL,
Law Clerk.

Hon. DON M. DICKINSON,
Postmaster-General.

Statement of post-office and postal stations where premises have been leased by the Government, showing the number leased, and annual rental paid; and also showing the salary of postmaster, total salary and allowances, box-rents and commissions, surplus or deficiency, and gross receipts at each office, upon the basis of the re-adjustment of postmasters' salaries, taking effect July 1, 1888.

No.	Office	State	Class	Post-master's salary	Term of lease From—	Term of lease To—	No. of years	Rent per annum	Fuel and light included in lease	Total salary and allowances, June 30, 1888.	Box-rents and commissions.	Surplus.	Deficiency.	Gross receipts.
1	Birmingham	Ala	2	$300	Oct. 22, 1887	Oct. 22, 1892	5	$1,900		$13,940.00	$20,508.35	$4,4685		$56,412.05
2	Selma	Ala	2	2,500	Jan. 1, 1888	Jan. 1, 1889	4	900		6,160.00	6,950.06	140.00		10,419.63
3	Hot Springs	Ark	2	2,400	Jan. 1, 1887	Jan. 1, 1892	5	1,020		8,435.00			$114.34	15,943.21
4	Marysville	Cal	2	2,000	July 1, 1886	Dec. 1, 1891	5	300		15,310.00	3,922.42	467.42		8,760.06
5	Red Bluff	Cal	3	2,100	July 1, 1887	July 1, 1892	5	1,200		4,009.20	21,325.44	6,015.44		66,149.05
6	Sacramento	Cal	1	2,100	Apr. 1, 1885	Apr. 1, 1889	5	360		3,890.00	4,009.20	119.20		9,628.24
7	Men	Cal	2	2,500	...	Aug. 1, 1889	7	2,000	Fuel and light	12,224.00	16,351.91	4,127.91		48,615.69
8		Colo	2	2,600	Feb. 1, 1888	Feb. 1, 1891	5	1		5,901.00	7,890.35	1,989.35		19,946.18
9	Eldo Springs	Colo								5,201.00	8,055.44	2,754.44		20,906.19
10	Denver	Colo	1	3,500	July 1, 1885	July 1, 1889	4	1	Fuel and light	$33,878.00	55,990.99	22,123.99		170,016.88
11	Denver*	Colo			July 1, 1884	July 1, 1889	4	600						
12	Leadville	Colo	2	2,700	Aug. 12, 1888	Aug. 12, 1888	3	1		10,881.00	11,727.59	846.59		27,321.67
13	Pueblo	Colo	2	2,600	May 1, 1887	May 1, 1892	4	1		7,276.00	8,907.35	1,631.33		22,711.30
14	Ansonia	Conn	2					800	Fuel					13,673.72
15	A ...	Conn	2	2,300	Sept. 1, 1887	Oct. 1, 1889	4	100	do	4,675.00	6,060.33	285.33		
16	Birmingham	Conn	2	2,300	Apr. 19, 1885	Apr. 19, 1889	5	900	Fuel	4,738.00	4,412.34		325.66	11,772.89
17	Meriden	Conn	2	2,700	Apr. 18, 1885	Apr. 18, 1889	5	1,100		8,228.00	13.16	2,015.16		32,766.39
18	Norwich	Conn	2	2,900	Mar. 1, 1885	Mar. 1, 1892	5	1,600	Fuel and light	8,390.00	1,060.73	1,770.73		28,970.09
19	Wallingford	Conn	2		Dec. 12, 1887	Dec. 12, 1890	3	610	Fuel	3,950.00	3,969.44	19.44		10,340.29
20	Waterbury	Conn	2	2,900	Apr. 8, 1886	Apr. 8, 1892	4	1,850	Fuel	9,935.00	12,527.99	2,592.99		34,660.04
21		dm	2	2,900	Dec. 6, 1887	Dec. 6, 1892	5	1		4,000.00	4,430.36	430.36		11,680.27
22	Aberdeen	Dak	2	2,000	Jan. 1, 1886	Jan. 1, 1890	4	900		8,300.00	8,477.85	177.85		31,253.50
23	Fargo	Dak	2	2,600	Feb. 1, 1884	Feb. 1, 1889	4	600		600	6,431.83	931.83		17,134.03
24	Sioux Falls	Dak	2	3,100	Mar. 1, 1885	Mar. 1, 1889	5	1,00	Fuel and light	16,370.00	10,061.80	561.95		38,630.18
25	Jacksonville	Fla	2	2,900	Feb. 1, 1886	Feb. 1, 1890	4	2,600		9,25.00	1	2,911.74		38,106.20
26	Augusta	Ga	2	2,500	Oct. 1, 1884	Oct. 1, 1889	4	900		5,475.00	6,416.29	943.29		38,252.47
27	Macon	Ga	2	2,900	Oct. 1, 1885	Oct. 1, 1889	4	720		9,590.00	11,241.30			28,049.93
28	Rom ...	Ga	2	2,300	Dec. 1, 1886	Dec. 1, 1890	5	1,850		21,561.12				12,155.14
29		Ga	2	3,200	Oct. 1, 1885	Oct. 1, 1890	4	648		16,620.00	23,005.41		341.05	71,711.38
30		Ga	2	2,100	Oct. 3, 1882	Oct. 1, 1888	5			800	3,505.95	543.80		9,392.81
31	Bl ...	Ill	2	2,800	Oct. 1, 1885	Oct. 1, 1891	5	1,200		11,400.00	11,943.80			36,431.84
32	Bloomington	Ill	2	2,900	May 15, 1885	May 15, 1889	5	600	Fuel	4,180.00	4,723.47	75.13		11,627.75
33	Champaign	Ill	2	2,400	July 1, 1884	Jan. 1, 1888	4	600		3,890.00	5,618.70		271.21	15,505.41
34	Danville	Ill	2	2,600	July 1, 1881	July 1, 1888	5	600		600	9,302.21			2N,136.14
35	Dixon	Ill	2	2,100	Sept. 16, 1887	Sept. 16, 1892	5	125	Fuel	3,281.00	3,781.84	500.84		9,362.47
36		Ill	2	2,800	Feb. 23, 1884	Feb. 23, 1893	5	1,500		7,480.00	10,833.02	3,248.02		32,862.82
37		Ill	2	2,400	Oct. 1, 1887	Oct. 1, 1892	5	500	Fuel and light	4,700.00	5,301.43	601.43		33,047.27
38	Evanston	Ill	2	2,300	Feb. 18, 1865	Feb. 18, 189	4	850		4,550.10	4,546.20		3.80	11,708.56

No.	Location	State										
39	Freeport	Ill					Fuel and light.			1,883.37		21,665.85
40	Galesburgh	Ill								911.21		20,803.96
41	Jacksonville	Ill								471.21		17,680.39
42	Joliet	Ill								1,007.20		21,574.23
43	Kankakee	Ill								98.91		13,161.03
44	Mattoon	Ill								54.15		8,660.73
45	Moline	Ill								1,022.29		10,868.11
46	Monmouth	Ill					Fuel and light			865.53		10,289.26
47	Ottawa	Ill								615.89		13,573.87
48	Pekin	Ill								85.89		13,323.39
49	Peoria	Ill								10,490.70		77,774.29
50	Rockford	Ind								4,220.19		42,181.48
51	Rock Island	Ind										18,425.60
52	South Chicago	Ind										10,812.75
53	Sterling	Ind								2,447.28		13,161.03
54	Streator	Ind								619.78		11,625.78
55	Crawfordsville	Ind								813.74		11,117.64
56	Elkhart	Ind								634.74		12,182.64
57	Goshen	Ind								1,712.08		11,399.61
58	La Fayette	Ind								238.89		29,676.49
59	La Porte	Ind								345.41		10,718.61
60	Logansport	Ind					Fuel and light					14,290.92
61	Madison	Ind								128.50		9,022.13
62	Muncie	Ind					Fuel and light			890.98		10,362.73
63	Peru	Ind								281.21		8,558.21
64	Richmond	Ind								1,099.73		27,051.11
65	South Bend	Ind								1,778.44		30,226.08
66	Valparaiso	Ind								416.87		8,142.01
67	Atlantic	Iowa								209.14		41,047.12
68	Burlington	Iowa									803.14	42,254.59
69	Cedar Rapids	Iowa								4,652.99		17,563.15
70	Clinton	Iowa								866.16		9,700.64
71	Creston	Iowa								119.28		39,434.50
72	Davenport	Iowa								12,632.73		100,017.78
73	Des Moines	Iowa					Fuel			11,185.72		8,282.40
74	Fort Dodge	Iowa								228.72		8,282.40
75	Iowa City	Iowa									221.61	13,499.70
76	Keokuk	Iowa								699.06		25,014.07
77	Le Mars	Iowa								817.62		9,477.78
78	Marshalltown	Iowa								548.27		18,287.64
79	Muscatine	Iowa								417.21		15,170.39
80	Ottumwa	Iowa								817.88		22,845.87
81	Sioux City	Iowa					Fuel and light			5,615.98		60,023.21
82	Vinton	Iowa								508.50		5,218.16
83	Waterloo	Iowa								318.09		11,485.43
84	Abilene	Kans								862.82		11,163.39
85	Lawrence	Kans								597.70		24,513.56

  * Addition to main room.   † Or until completion of repairs to Government building.

Statement of post-offices and postal stations where premises have been leased by the Government, etc.—Continued.

No.	Office	State	Class	Post-master's salary.	Term of lease. From—	To—	No. of years.	Rent per annum.	Fuel and light included in lease.	Total salary and allowances, June 30, 1888.	Box-rents and commissions.	Surplus.	Deficiency.	Gross receipts.
86	Leavenworth	Kans	2	$2,700	Aug. 1, 1886	Aug. 1, 1890	4	$600		$7,810 00	$9,608 12	$1,798 12		$29,756 55
87	Wellington	Kans	3	2,200	July 1, 1884	July 1, 1890	5	181		3,245 00	4,068 28	823 28		10,284 77
84	Wichita	Kans	1	3,100	Oct. 1, 1884	Oct. 1, 1891	5		Fuel and light	10,401 00	16,630 14	6,229 14		44,765 42
89	Winfield	Kans	2	2,400	Mar. 1, 1886	Mar. 1, 1892	5	900	do	4,600 00	4,892 63	292 63		13,061 66
90	Bowling Green	Ky	2	2,500	Sept. 12, 1887	Sept. 12, 1892	5	500	Fuel and light	3,550 00	3,597 36	47 36		8,519 39
91	Lexington	Ky	2	2,500	Dec. 15, 1885	Dec. 15, 1889	4	1,000		7,925 00	10,002 82	2,097 82		38,213 60
92	Newport	Ky	2	2,600	July 1, 1887	July 1, 1892	5	710		5,110 00	5,947 67	837 67		17,290 15
93	Auburn	Me	2	2,600	Apr. 1, 1887	Apr. 1, 1891	4	1,200		4,130 00	4,875 19	745 19		13,640 17
94	Augusta	Mo	1	2,600	July 1, 1886	July 1, 1891	5	1,250	Fuel	18,366 00	13,268 64		$4,997 36	41,648 05
95	Lewiston	Mo	2	3,000	July 1, 1886	July 1, 1889	3	640	Fuel and light	9,125 00	9,675 89	550 89		10,546 61
96	Waterville	Me	2	2,100	June 15, 1886	June 15, 1887	1	500		3,600 00	4,128 50	528 50		9,002 56
97	Annapolis	Md	3	2,500	Apr. 1, 1889	Apr. 1, 1891	2			3,250 00	4,023 09	773 09		11,364 72
98	*Baltimore	Md		5,000	Jan. 1, 1886	Jan. 1, 1889	3	13,000		121,689 00	168,048 29	46,359 29		536,839 31
99	Cumberland	Md	2	2,300	Apr. 1, 1887	Jan. 1, 1892	5	600		4,905 00	4,550 27	164 27		12,918 86
100	Frederick	Md	2	2,200	July 1, 1887	July 1, 1892	5	1,000	Fuel and light	4,366 00	4,550 64	850 64		11,452 58
101	Beverly	Mass	2	2,300	Apr. 1, 1887	Jan. 1, 1892	5	600	do	3,910 00	9,579 01	2,569 01		10,857 05
102	Brockton	Mass	2	2,700	Oct. 15, 1887	Oct. 15, 1892	5	1,400	Fuel	6,618 00	9,026 73	2,096 73		25,610 58
103	Fitchburg	Mass	2	2,700	Aug. 15, 1887	Aug. 15, 1891	4	1,700	Fuel and light	5,675 00	5,348 64	630 36		13,382 06
104	Greenfield	Mass	2	2,400	July 1, 1888	July 1, 1893	5	560		4,810 00	5,346 64	661 00		29,117 84
105	Haverhill	Mass	2	2,800	Nov. 1, 1887	Nov. 1, 1892	5	1,200	Fuel	8,396 00	10,257 23	3,017 23		31,118 17
106	Holyoke	Mass	2	2,900	Jan. 1, 1887	Jan. 1, 1891	4	1,65.	Fuel	7,790 00	10,919 80	2,044 80		31,967 80
107	Lawrence	Mass	1	3,400	Oct. 1, 1885	Oct. 1, 1889	4	1,815 00	do	11,815 00	17,831 93	6,016 93		54,678 23
108	Lynn	Mass	1	3,100	Oct. 1, 1887	Oct. 1, 1892	5	800		4,602 00	5,380 50	778 50		13,210 29
109	Malden	Mass	2	2,600	Oct. 1, 1887	Oct. 1, 1892	5	400	Fuel and light	3,356 00	5,713 24	2,363 24		15,999 65
110	Melrose	Mass	2	2,500	Mar. 13, 1886	Mar. 13, 1891	5	1,000	Fuel	5,765 00	6,473 15	688 15		16,805 78
111	Newburyport	Mass	2	2,500	July 1, 1887	July 1, 1892	5	673	do	8,000 39	8,007 52	2,306 39		22,21 90
112	North Adams	Mass	2	2,500	Apr. 1, 1887	Apr. 1, 1892	5	1,000	do	4,890 00	6,607 52	1,807 52		18,222 05
113	Northampton	Mass	2	2,600	July 1, 1887	July 1, 1892	5	2,100	Fuel and light	6,675 00	7,775 39	1,000 39		32,480 10
114	Pittsfield	Mass	2	2,800	Jan. 21, 1887	Jan. 21, 1892	5	625	Fuel	8,460 00	10,443 20	1,983 20		30,164 14
115	Salem	Mass	1	3,300	Oct. 1, 1887	Oct. 1, 1892	5	2,500	Fuel and light	15,830 00	28,377 49	12,547 49		89,884 98
116	South Framingham	Mass	2	2,500	July 18, 1886	July 18, 1890	4	1,250	Fuel	2,787 00	3,573 68	971 85		23,955 21
117	Springfield	Mass	1	3,300	Feb. 1, 1887	Feb. 1, 1891	4	1,200		3,176 85	5,323 00	445 82		24,661 61
118	Taunton	Mass	2	2,500	Apr. 1, 1886	Apr. 9, 1890	4	350		4,980 00	7,832 18	1,852 18		19,880 15
119	Waltham	Mass	2	2,400	Apr. 9, 1886	Apr. 9, 1890	4	1,200		5,523 00	5,459 10	238 71	540 00	14,292 58
120	Westfield	Mass	2	2,600	Mar. 1, 1885	Mar. 1, 1890	5	1,200	Fuel	7,870 00	8,108 73	1,075 19		21,474 77
121	Adrian	Mich	2	2,400	Apr. 21, 1881	Apr. 21, 1891	5			6,780 00	7,835 13	449 61		23,248 51
122	Ann Arbor	Mich	2	2,600	Apr. 1, 1885	Apr. 1, 1889	4	1,100	Fuel	7,000 00	7,489 51			22,497 72
123	Battle Creek	Mich	2	2,600	(Oct. 1, 1888	Apr. 1, 1889	5		Fuel	7,800 00	11,843 14	3,943 14		36,245 15
124	Bay City	Mich	2	2,400	Apr. 1, 1885	Apr. 1, 1880	3	800		5,190 00	5,713 75	5,14 75		14,401 07
125	East Saginaw	Mich												

127	Hillsdale	Mich
128	Ionia	Mich
129	Jackson	Mich
130	Kalamazoo	Mich
131	Lansing	Mich
132	Manistee	Mich
133	Muskegon	Mich
134	Pontiac	Mich
135	Ypsilanti	Mich
136	Duluth	Minn
137	Mankato	Minn
138	Minneapolis	Minn
139	Red Wing	Minn
140	Rochester	Minn
141	Stillwater	Minn
142	W...n	Minn
143	Meridian	Miss
144	Natchez	Miss
145	Vicksburg	Miss
146	Saint Joseph	Mo.
147	Springfield	Mo.
148	Butte City	Mont
149	Helena	Mont
150	Beatrice	Nebr.
151	Ft. ...mnt	Nebr.
152	Hastings	Nebr.
153	Nebraska City	Nebr.
154	Concord	N. H.
155	Dover	N. H.
156	Keene	N. H.
157	...ster	N. H.
158	Nashua	N. H.
159	Asbury Park	N. J.
160	Camden	N. J.
161	... Orange	N. J.
162	Elizabeth	N. J.
163	Hoboken	N. J.
164	Morristown	N. J.
165	New Brunswick	N. J.
166	Orange	N. J.
167	Paterson	N. J.
168	Plainfield	N. J.
169	...terdam	N. Y.
170	Auburn	N. Y.
171	Batavia	N. Y.
172	Bath	N. Y.
173	Binghamton	N. Y.
174	Brooklyn	N. Y.

† Rent at $3,000 from April 1, 1887.

‡ Three ... room for main ...

... dollars additional allowed for rent without a lease, for addition to main ...

Statement of post-offices and postal stations where premises have been leased by the Government, etc.—Continued.

No.	Office.	State.	Class.	Post-master's salary.	Term of lease. From—	Term of lease. To—	No. of years.	Rent per annum.	Fuel and light included in lease.	Total salary and allowances, June 30, 1888.	Box-rents and ...	Surplus.	Deficiency.	Gross receipts.
176	Cohoes	N. Y.	2	2,300	Oct. 1, 1887	Oct. 1, 1892	5	$650	Fuel and light.	$4,825.00	$3,233.37	$408.37		$8,68.06
177	Corning	N. Y.	2	2,300	Jan. 1, 1887	Mar. 1, 1892	5	975		4,375.00	4,054.46		$320.54	10,572.98
178	Cortland	N. Y.	2	2,500	Apr. 1, 1887	Apr. 1, 1892	6	700		4,706.00	662			17,550.80
179	Dansville	N. Y.	2	2,040	July 1, 1887	July 1, 1892	5	350		3,230.00	3,466.08	226.08		8,552.76
180	Dunkirk	N. Y.	2	2,300	Mar. 1, 1888	Feb. 1, 1893	5	850	Fuel and light.	3,960.00	4,469.34	489.34		12,413.22
181	Elmira	N. Y.	1	3,100	Feb. 1, 1885	Feb. 1, 1890	5	2,000	Fuel	4,290.00	4,867.64	867.64		50,277.25
182	Geneva	N. Y.	2	2,700	Feb. 1, 1885	Feb. 1, 1890	5	500		4,700.00	12,285.00			28,960.14
183	Glens Falls	N. Y.	2	2,300	Apr. 1, 1885	Apr. 1, 1890	5	800		4,570.00	8,023.38	3628		12,506.60
184	Gloversville	N. Y.	2	2,400	July 1, 1887	Apr. 1, 1890	4	60	Fuel	4,480.00	4,024.85	568		13,407.80
185	Hornellsville	N. Y.	2	2,400	July 1, 1887	July 1, 1892	5	1,200	Fuel and light.	4,020.00	4,043.48	18.48		13,200.61
186	Hudson	N. Y.	2	2,400	Nov. 15, 1887	Nov. 15, 1892	4	850		4,960.00	4,652.81	262.81		14,869.47
187	Ithaca	N. Y.	2	2,700	July 1, 1888	July 1, 1892	10	590	Fuel and light.	8,215.00	9,802.06	1,577.06		24,944.38
84	Jamestown	N. Y.	2	2,300	May 1, 1888	May 1, 1898	8	225	Fuel	8,715.00	8,118.07	1,403.07		24,025.56
149	Kingston	N. Y.	2	2,100	June 1, 1887	June 1, 1892	5	530		4,235.00	4,955.73	620.73		11,675.01
190	Leroy	N. Y.	2	2,300	July 1, 1887	Jan. 1, 1892	10	200		3,300.00	4,031.69	711.69		9,905.60
191	Little Falls	N. Y.	2	900	Apr. 1, 1884	Jan. 1, 1894	10	650	Fuel	4,16.10	4,731.04	2.01		12,168.17
192	Lockport	N. Y.	2	2,500	Apr. 1, 1887	Apr. 1, 1892	5	1,000	Fuel and light.	6,910.00	7,180.42	270.42		17,311.57
193	Middletown	N. Y.	2	2,500	Mar. 31, 1888	Mar. 31, 1893	5	940	Fuel and light.	5,700.00	6,311.80	50.30		17,067.41
194	Mount Vernon	N. Y.	2	2,700	Feb. 1, 1888	Feb. 1, 1893	5	2,100	...do	5,280.00	9,918.46	8,649.846		29,232.38
195	Newburgh	N. Y.	2	2,400	Aug. 1, 1888	Aug. 31, 1893	5	1,000	Fuel and light.	5,280.00	5,775.13	575.13		23,170.77
197	Olean	N. Y.	2	2,300	Mar. 1, 1887	Mar. 1, 1892	5	600		4,250.00	4,381.15	481.15		11,471.08
196	Oneida	N. Y.	2	280	July 1, 1887	July 1, 1892	5	700		4,290.00	963	131.15		11,020.25
199	Oneonta	N. d.	1	2,200	July 1, 1884	Oct. 1, 1891	4	5,001	Fuel	$1,964.00	92,968.98	50,+4608		10,661.89
199	Oswego	N. Y.	2	3,700	Apr. 1, 1886	Oct. 1, 1891	5	425	Fuel	6,728.22	6,728.22	1,453.22		301,985.60
200	Rochester	N. Y.	2	2,900	Oct. 1, 1886	Oct. 1, 1891	10	1,500		7,720.00	9,025.04	1,365.04		10,049.94
202	Saratoga Springs	N. Y.	2	2,500	Jan. 1, 1887	Jan. 1, 1892	5	1,000		6,100.10	7,431.87	1,331.87		27,078.70
203	Schenectady	N. Y.	2	2,500	July 1, 1886	Mar. 1, 1891	5	400		3,775.00	4,442.30	667.30		18,716.56
201	Sing Sing	N. Y.	3	2,400	Mar. 1, 1888	Mar. 1	55	4,500		25,740.00	0868	6888		34,700.25
205	Syracuse	N. Y.	1	3,200	July 1, 1887	Aug.	92	400	Fuel	71,459.88	4,359.61	369.62		134,571.67
206	Tonawanda	N. Y.	2	2,300	May 1, 1886	July 1, 1890	5	8,000		23,956.00	30,872.81	863		11,221.23
207	Utica	N. Y.	3	2,040	May 15, 1887	Jan. 1, 1892	5	900		7,575.00	7,667.90	122.90		89,171.10
208	Watertown	N. Y.	2	2,700	July 1, 1887	June 1, 1892	5	500	Fuel and light.	8,220.00	8,610.53	390.53		33,414.23
209	Waverly	N. Y.	3	2,400	Dec. 10, 1884	Nov. 10, 88	4	1,500		7,400.00	8,008.61	601		8,614.52
210	Yonkers	N. Y.	2	2,700	Sept. 1, 1884	Sept. 1, 1893	3	80		7,610.00	5,712.00	542.20		25,838.04
211	Charlotte	N. C.	2	2,400	July 1, 1885	July 1, 1889	4	1,300	Fuel	7,878.00	7,670.09	270.99		15,556.16
212	Wilmington	N. C.	2	2,600	July 18, 1885	May 16, 1890	5	1,000		7,030.00	13,925.09	6,055.09		22,864.82
213	Akron	Ohio	1	2,400	May 18, 1886	May 16, 1891	4	1,000	Fuel and light	2,980.10	10,349.53	3,299.53		43,864.22
214	...	Ohio	2	2,600	Apr. 1, 1886	Apr. 1, 1891	5	1,000	Fuel	5,400.00	6,250.72	810.72		32,270.84
215	Chillicothe	Ohio	1	1,350	Oct. 15, 1883	Oct. 15, 1893	10	2,920	Fuel	16,850.00	24,547.45	7,597.45		70,353.66

No.	Place	State			Date		Fuel							
217	Delaware	Ohio	2,300	2	Apr. 15, 1888	Apr. 15, 1889	500	4	Fuel and light	4,575.00	5,236.96	661.96		12,720.33
218	East Liverpool	Ohio	2,300	3	Oct. 1, 1885	Jan. 1, 1889	725	4	do	3,925.00	4,758.06	833.06		11,355.84
219	Elyria	Ohio	2,100	2	Feb. 11, 1886	Oct. 11, 1889	650	5		3,650.00	4,043.32	393.32		9,064.81
220	Findlay	Ohio	2,400	2	July 1, 1887	Feb. 1, 1890	650	5		4,000.00	4,944.94	944.94		15,706.50
221	Fremont	Ohio	2,200	2	July 1, 1886	Oct. 1, 1891	400	4		3,877.00	4,459.49	782.49		10,254.61
222	Hamilton	Ohio	2,500	3	July 1, 1887	July 1, 1892	600	4	Fuel and light	3,900.00	4,311.07	807		17,685.36
223	do	Ohio	2,200	2	July 1, 1885	Oct. 1, 1892	380	5		3,780.00	4,277.11	497.11		10,013.38
224	Kenton	Ohio	3,000	2	Sept. 7, 1885	Sept. 7, 1889	1	4	Fuel and light	3,021.00	3,577.54	556.54		8,290.93
225	Mansfield	Ohio	2,700	2	Apr. 1, 1886	Apr. 1, 1890	400	5		6,890.00	9,522.70	2,722.70		29,069.90
226	Marietta	Ohio	2,300	2	Jan. 1, 1886	Jan. 1, 1890	400	4		4,285.00	4,578.56	283.56		11,564.44
227	Marion	Ohio	2,200	2	July 1, 1887	July 1, 1892	1	5	Fuel and light	3,530.00	4,005.47	475.47		9,132.16
228	Massillon	Ohio	2,100	2	Sept. 20, 1888	Sept. 20, 1891	400	5		3,521.00	4,471.23	90.33		10,775.68
229	Mount Gilead	Ohio	2,300	2	Apr. 1, 1885	Apr. 1, 1892	650	4		4,894.00	4,146.06			9,854.20
230	Norwalk	Ohio	2,300	2	Oct. 1, 1885	Oct. 1, 1889	700	4		4,120.00	4,691.07			12,748.99
231	Oberlin	Ohio	2,300	2	July 1, 1888	Mar. 1, 1892	550	4		3,530.00	4,101.90			10,697.13
232	Painesville	Ohio	2,400	2	Mar. 1, 1887	Mar. 1, 1891	550	4	Fuel and light	4,310.00	5,723.30	704.63		13,274.02
233	Piqua	Ohio	2,200	2	Oct. 22, 1887	Oct. 22, 1890	275	4		3,178.00	4,096.80	581.90		12,106.18
234	Salem	Ohio	2,400	1	July 1, 1886	July 1, 1890	720	4		3,720.00	4,815.07	561.36		12,694.45
235	Springfield	Ohio	8,300	3	Aug. 1, 1885	Aug. 1, 1889	2,200	6	Fuel	13,720.00	21,049.30			66,971.33
236	Steubenville	Ohio	2,300	2	Mar. 15, 1887	Mar. 15, 1892	500	6	do	4,750.00	5,312.36			14,149.50
237	Tiffin	Ohio	2,400	2	Feb. 1, 1887	Feb. 1, 1891	500	5		4,125.00	4,226.23	100.22		11,035.25
238	Troy	Ohio	2,100	1	July 1, 1885	July 1, 1889	600	5	Fuel and light	3,700.00	4,069.30	369.30		9,452.41
239	Urbana	Ohio	2,300	2	July 1, 1887	July 1, 1891	600	4		4,013.00	4,499.30	486.30		10,613.85
240	Warren	Ohio	2,400	2	Aug. 8, 1887	Aug. 15, 1892	650	5	Fuel and light	4,100.00	4,769.88	969.88		11,606.30
241	Wooster	Ohio	2,300	2	Dec. 11, 1886	Dec. 11, 1891	600	4		4,217.00	4,321.86			11,185.97
242	Xenia	Ohio	2,700	2	Jan. 1, 1887	Jan. 1, 1892	1,200	6		4,240.00	4,160.97			17, 60.25
243	do	Ohio	2,200	1	Sept. 7, 1885	Sept. 7, 1889	900	5	Fuel and light	6,790.10	8,480.31	1,720.31		25,032.63
244	Zanesville	Ohio	2,500	3	Sept. 1, 1885	Sept. 1, 1889	500	6		7,275.00	8,453.48	2,558.48		20,055.90
245	Salem	Pa	2,700	2	Mar. 1, 1885	Mar. 1, 1889	800	4	Fuel and light	3,170.00	4,506.10	1,386.10		11,219.70
246	Allentown	Pa	2,800	2	Apr. 1, 1886	Apr. 1, 1890	1,300	5	Fuel and light	3,780.00	4,294.75	1,044.75		25,722.56
247	Altoona	Pa	2,600	2	Oct. 1, 1887	Oct. 1, 1891	900	5		3,950.00	4,765.34	1,655.14		22,852.81
248	Bethlehem	Pa	2,600	3	May 1, 1886	May 1, 1890	700	4	Fuel	4,520.00	7,111.50	215.34		12,758.81
249	Bradford	Pa	2,500	2	Nov. 16, 1887	Nov. 16, 1892	600	4	do	4,616.00	4,160.00	483.00		40,026.15
250	Chambersburg	Pa	2,600	3	Jan. 1, 1887	Jan. 1, 1888	350	5		6,165.77	1,261.73	995.77		44, 66.50
251	Chester	Pa	2,500	2	Oct. 1, 1887	Oct. 1, 1891	500	4		5,170.00	4,449.15	710.15		16, 64.64
252	Corry	Pa	2,400	2	June 1, 1885	June 1, 1892	540	5		3,780.00	3,590.47	115.47		10,257.01
253	Danville	Pa	2,600	2	Oct. 1, 1887	Oct. 1, 1892	1,100	4	Fuel	3,475.00	3,365.99			8,317.58
254	Downingtown	Pa	2,300	2	Apr. 1, 1887	Apr. 1, 1889	400	5	Fuel and light	7,401.00	7,677.03	632.03		2,847.18
255	do	Pa	2,800	2	May 1, 1885	May 1, 1892	250	4		6,925.00	14,418.71	518.71		23,494.44
256	Erie	Pa	2,300	2	July 1, 1886	July 1, 1889	975	5	Fuel	8,840.00	4,622.90	682.90		44, 06.59
257	Franklin	Pa	2,300	2	July 1, 1887	July 1, 1892	300	4	Fuel and light	4,615.00	4,657.81	162.84		10,662.43
258	Hazleton	Pa	2,500	3	Apr. 1, 1885	Apr. 1, 1891	750	4		5,050.00	4,186.26	218.26		11,057.90
259	Huntingdon	Pa	2,200	2	Mar. 1, 1886	Mar. 1, 1892		5	Fuel and light	4,360.00	6,354.40	1,344.40		17,157.18
260	do	Pa	2,500	3	July 1, 1887	July 1, 1891	2,000	6		4,090.00	3,829.15	2,861.50		38,156.28
261	Lancaster	Pa	2,200	2	Apr. 1, 1886	Apr. 1, 1891	600	5		4,360.00	5,064.31			10,715.28
262	Lock Haven	Pa	2,300	2	Jan. 1, 1887	Jan. 1, 1891	500	4		1,900.00	249.00			12,102.69
263	McKeesport	Pa	2,500	2	July 1, 1888	July 1, 1888	300	4	Fuel and light	6,400.00	6,446.18	386.18		17,810.96
264	Meadville	Pa	2,300	2	Feb. 1, 1885	Feb. 1, 1891	1,000	5	do	4,100.00	5,349.47	748.47		14,129.63
265	Norristown	Pa	2,300	2	July 1, 1888	July 1, 1891	1,000	5		4,360.00	5,257.15	907.15		11,997.04

Statement of post-offices and postal stations where premises have been leased by the Government, etc.—Continued.

No.	Office	State	Class	Post-master's salary	Term of lease From—	Term of lease To—	No. of years	Rent per annum	Fuel and light included in lease	Total salary and allowances, June 30, 1868.	Box-rents and commissions.	Surplus.	Deficiency.	Gross receipts.
269	Blairsville	Pa.	2	2,500	Apr. 1, 1885	Apr. 1, 1889	4	$850	Fuel	$5,210.00	$5,452.14	$242.14		$16,068.83
270	Reading	Pa.	1	3,100	Apr. 1, 1885	Apr. 1, 1889	4	1,300	Fuel	11,850.00	15,729.77	3,879.77		40,571.72
271	Sun.	Pa.	1	3,100	Jan. 1, 1885	Jan. 1, 1889	4	2,140	Fuel	12,608.00	16,101.74	3,493.74		40,712.39
272	Titusville	Pa.	2	2,300	July 1, 1885	May 1, 1889	4	700		5,462.00	6,298.31	836.31	$180.91	15,290.79
273	Towanda	Pa.	2	2,100	Jan. 1, 1884	Jan. 1, 1888	4	700	Fuel and light	3,900.00	3,719.03			9,192.45
274	Warren	Pa.	2	2,500	Jan. 1, 1885	Mar. 1, 1889	4	1,000	...do	6,000.00	6,965.56	1,965.56		19,501.62
275	West Chester	Pa.	2	2,400	Mar. 15, 1883	Mar. 15, 1889	5	850	Fuel	6,050.00	6,532.86	482.86		15,174.12
276	Wilkes Barre	Pa.	2	2,700	Apr. 1, 1891	Apr. 1, 1891	5	1,100	...do	8,310.00	10,720.01	2,410.01		32,966.36
277	Pawtucket	R.I.	1	2,700	Oct. 1, 1883	Oct. 1, 1889	5	1,250	Fuel	6,900.00	8,955.87	1,975.87		25,232.84
278	Bonham	Tex.	3	1,600	Jan. 1, 1886	Jan. 1, 1891	5	1	...do	1,701.00	2,181.11	480.11		4,738.78
279	Colorado	Tex.	3	2,100	Sept. 16, 1883	Sept. 16, 1889	5	1	Fuel and light.	70.00	2,137.22	435.21		4,315.73
280	Gainesville	Tex.	3	2,100	Mar. 1, 1887	Nov. 1, 1891	5	12	Light.	3,072.00	4,135.20	1,063.20		9,064.63
281	Sun.	Tex.	2	2,900	Aug. 1, 1886	Aug. 1, 1890	4	900		13,815.00	11,921.46		1,413.54	85,997.47
282	Paris	Tex.	2	2,200	Sept. 1, 1887	Sept. 1, 1892	5	240		3,740.00	4,343.91	603.91		10,540.04
283	Sherman	Tex.	2	2,400	Aug. 1, 1884	Aug. 1, 1888	5	300		4,285.00	4,840.19	555.19		13,151.23
284	Ogden	Utah	1	3,000	July 1, 1887	Nov. 1, 1891	5	720		4,920.00	5,178.84	258.84		13,253.91
285	Salt Lake City	Utah	2	2,400	July 1, 1888	Aug. 1, 1891	4	1,500		11,160.00	14,887.95	3,727.95		40,983.65
286	Brattleborough	Vt.	2	2,300	Oct. 1, 1883	Oct. 1, 1888	5	650		5,125.00	5,923.31	783.31	163.78	15,496.14
287	Montpelier	Vt.	2	2,400	Jan. 1, 1885	July 1, 1891	5	530		4,613.00	4,464.22			11,296.61
288	Lynchburgh	Va.	2	2,400	July 1, 1887	July 1, 1892	5	700		8,660.00	10,131.95	1,471.95		30,023.64
289	Staunton	Va.	2	2,200	July 1, 1886	July 1, 1891	5	400		6,158.00	6,225.00	66.00		14,497.27
290	Appleton	Wis.	2	2,200	1-8-6	Mar. 1, 1889	4	400		4,960.00	5,9x9.50	1,009.58		13,88.69
291	Beloit	Wis.	2	2,200	Jan. 1, 1885	Mar. 1, 1889	4	400		4,440.00	4,704.01	261.01		10,699.86
292	Chippewa Falls	Wis.	2	2,200	Mar. 1, 1845	Mar. 1, 1889	4	600		3,769.10	4,516.47	736.47		9,063.68
293	Eau Claire	Wis.	2	2,500	Oct. 1, 1890	Oct. 1, 1890	4	1,500	Fuel and light.	6,241.00	6,576.28	331.28		19,941.63
294	Fond du Lac	Wis.	2	2,400	Jan. 1, 1887	Jan. 1, 1890	5	1,100		6,610.00	7,235.51	635.51		17,912.41
295	Janesville	Wis.	2	2,500	Jan. 1, 1887	Jan. 1, 1892	5	1,600		8,240.00	9,953.67	1,713.07		21,623.27
296	La Crosse	Wis.	2	2,700	Jan. 1, 1886	Jan. 1, 1890	4	1,200		7,330.00	8,409.57	1,079.57		21,906.05
297	Oshkosh	Wis.	2	2,700	July 1, 1885	Jan. 1, 1889	4	1,160		7,537.00	9,154.43	1,617.41		21,358.82
298	Racine	Wis.	2	2,301	Mar. 1, 1885	Mar. 1, 1889	5	800		4,030.00	460.07	460.07		8,302.70
299	Sheboygan	Wis.	2	2,000	Jan. 1, 1888	Jan. 1, 1892	4	500	Fuel and light.	3,855.00	3,490.30	65.30		15,673.51
300	Watertown	Wis.	2	2,400	Nov. 10, 1884	Nov. 10, 1888	4	4	Light.	2,301.00	4,070.56	2,048.90	963.94	8,101.36
301	Cheyenne	Wyo.	2									1,766.56		
302	Laramie	Wyo.	2											
	Total rental at 302 post-offices							209,552						

Statement of post-offices and postal stations where premises have been leased by the Government, etc.—Continued.

STATIONS.

No.	Office.	Class.	Postmaster's salary.	Term of lease. From—	Term of lease. To—	No. of years.	Rent per annum.	Fuel and light included in lease.	Total salary and allowances.	Box-rents and commissions.	Surplus.	Deficiency.	Gross receipts.
	Baltimore, Md.	1	$5,000						$121,089.00	$168,048.29	$46,389.29		$536,539.21
1	West Baltimore			Jan. 15, 1887	Jan. 15, 1893	5	$650						
	Boston, Mass.	1	6,000						348,257.00	577,987.39	188,730.39		1,714,123.03
2	Brighton			July 1, 1887	July 1, 1892	5	575	Fuel and light.					
3	Cambridgeport			Jan. 1, 1885	Jan. 1, 1889	4	1,000	Fuel.					
4	Charlestown			Nov. 1, 1886	Nov. 1, 1891	5	800						
5	Dorchester			Aug. 1, 1885	Aug. 1, 1889	4	840						
6	East Boston			July 1, 1886	July 1, 1890	4	600						
7	Jamaica Plain			Apr. 1, 1887	Jan. 1, 1892	5	350	Fuel and light.					
8	North Cambridge			Nov. 10, 1887	Nov. 10, 1892	5	540	Do.					
9	Revere			Oct. 1, 1885	Oct. 1, 1889	4	150	Fuel.					
10	Roxbury			July 1, 1884	July 1, 1888	4	1,000	Do.					
11	Somerville			Dec. 1, 1885	Dec. 1, 1889	4	400						
12	Station A			Jan. 1, 1885	Jan. 1, 1889	4	1,050						
13	South Boston			Dec. 1, 1885	Jan. 1, 1889	4	1,000						
14	Winthrop			Sept. 1, 1887	Sept. 1, 1882	5	144						
	Brooklyn, N. Y.	1	5,000						127,090.00	175,614.05	48,524.05		578,218.18
15	Brevoort			Dec. 1, 1887	Dec. 1, 1897	10	1,700	Fuel.					
16	Greenpoint			May 1, 1886	May 1, 1891	5	720	Fuel and light.					
17	Station E			Nov. 1, 1886	Nov. 1, 1891	5	625	Do.					
18	Station S			Dec. 1, 1886	Dec. 1, 1889	4	600	Fuel.					
19	Station W			Jan. 21, 1888	Jan. 21, 1893	5	2,000						
	Chicago, Ill	1	6,000						497,000.00	735,017.87	228,017.87		2,402,103.08
20	Madison Street			May 1, 1886	May 1, 1891	5	1,115	Fuel and light.					
21	North Division			May 1, 1887	May 1, 1892	5	2,100						
22	Northwest Division			May 1, 1885	May 1, 1889	4	900	Fuel.					
23	South Division			Oct. 1, 1886	Oct. 1, 1891	5	1,300	Do.					
24	Southwest Division			Mar. 1, 1886	Mar. 1, 1890	4	1,200	Fuel and light.					
25	Stock-Yards			Nov. 15, 1886	Nov. 15, 1891	5	1,300						
26	West Division			July 1, 1884	July 1, 1888	4	1,600						
	Kansas City, Mo.	1	3,500						60,162.00	108,051.43	47,889.43		356,301.44
27	West Kansas City			June 1, 1886	June 1, 1891	5	312	Fuel.					

Statement of post-offices and postal stations where premises have been leased by the Government, etc.—Continued.

STATIONS—Continued.

No.	Office.	Class.	Post-master's salary.	Term of lease. From—	Term of lease. To—	No. of years.	Rent per annum.	Fuel and light included in lease.	Total salary and allowances.	Box-rents and commissions.	Surplus.	Deficiency.	Gross receipts.
28	New York, N. Y.	1	8,000						$1,012,434.00	$1,489,860.70	$470,426.70		$4,843,141.81
29	Station A			Feb. 1, 1884	Feb. 1, 1889	4	6,200	Fuel*					
30	Station D			Oct. 1, 1884	Oct. 1, 1889	4	4,500						
31	Station E			Jan. 1, 1885	Jan. 1, 1889	4	3,000	Fuel.					
32	Station F			May 1, 1887	Jan. 1, 1892	4	2,400	Fuel.					
33	Station G			May 1, 1888	May 1, 1893	5	2,000						
34	Station H			Jan. 1, 1887	Jan. 1, 1892	5	2,000	Fuel.					
35	Station J			Oct. 1, 1886	May 1, 1890	3½	1,500						
36	Station K			Aug. 1, 1885	Aug. 1, 1889	4	2,100						
37	Station L			May 1, 1885	May 1, 1889	4	4,500						
38	Station P			Oct. 1, 1884	Oct. 1, 1888	4	300						
39	Station R			May 1, 1885	May 1, 1889	4	300						
40	Station S			Jan. 1, 1887	Jan. 1, 1892	5	450						
	Station T												
41	Philadelphia, Pa. Station F	1	6,000	July 1, 1886	July 1, 1891	5	420		338,099.00	557,160.99	219,061.99		1,827,674.64
42	Pittsburgh, Pa.	1	3,900	June 1, 1886	June 1, 1891	5	250	Fuel and light.	76,675.00	127,315.70	50,640.70		405,809.69
43	Station B. East Liberty			Oct. 1, 1887	Oct. 1, 1892	5	400	Do.					
44	Saint Louis, Mo. Station B	1	6,000	Jan. 1, 1887	Jan. 1, 1892	5	180		186,910.00	275,819.72	88,899.72		912,652.43
45	North Saint Louis			July 1, 1886	July 1, 1890	4	420						
46	San Francisco, Cal.	1	5,000	Aug. 1, 1885	Aug. 1, 1889	4	0.000		136,689.00	181,986.77	45,297.77		570,421.56
47	Station A			Jan. 1, 1886	Jan. 1, 1890	4	120						
48	Station B. Station C			Jan. 1, 1886	Jan. 1, 1890	4	420						
49	Springfield, Mo. Station A	2	2,500	Jan. 1, 1888	Jan. 1, 1893	5	1	Fuel and light	8,181.00	7,957.05		223.95	20,871.29
50	Washington, D. C. Station C	1	5,000	July 1, 1887	July 1, 1888	1	1,000		178,070.00	106,284.59		72,785.41	344,081.23
	Total rental 50 postal stations						62,152						

* See contract.

RECAPITULATION.

	No.	Amount.
Total of post-offices	302	$269,552.00
Total of postal stations	50	62,152.00
Grand total, offices and stations	352	331,704.00

REPORT

OF THE

ASSISTANT ATTORNEY-GENERAL

FOR THE

POST-OFFICE DEPARTMENT,

UPON

CLAIMS OF POSTMASTERS UNDER THE ACT OF MARCH 17, 1882,
AND THE ACT AMENDATORY THEREOF OF MAY 9, 1888.

11843—P M G 88——1

REPORT

OF THE

ASSISTANT ATTORNEY-GENERAL FOR THE POST-OFFICE DE-PARTMENT.

POST-OFFICE DEPARTMENT,
OFFICE OF THE ASSISTANT ATTORNEY-GENERAL,
Washington, D. C., November 15, 1888.

SIR: I have the honor to report to you the action taken by the Department for the fiscal year ended June 30, 1888, under the act of Congress approved March 17, 1882, entitled "An act authorizing the Postmaster-General to adjust certain claims of postmasters for loss by fire, burglary, or other unavoidable casualty," and the act amendatory thereof approved May 9, 1888.

A list of claims allowed, with statement of the reasons for action in each particular case, is herewith respectfully submitted, marked Exhibit A.

A list of the claims disallowed is also submitted, giving reason for action in each particular case, marked Exhibit B.

The total number of claims allowed during the period from July 1, 1887, to June 30, 1888, is 449

The total amount of claims allowed for money-order funds lost or destroyed is $3,322.65

The total amount allowed for postage-stamps, stamped envelopes, newspaper wrappers, and postal-cards so lost or destroyed is 20,330.37

The losses of money-order funds, for which claims were allowed, arose as follows:

Lost in transit $855.00
Lost by fire 398.76
Lost by burglary 2,068.89

Total 3,322.65

The losses of stamps, etc., for which claims were allowed during the fiscal year, arose as follows:

Lost by fire $7,171.09
Lost by burglary 13,057.44
Lost by storm 15.31
Lost by other causes 86.53

Total 20,330.37

The number of claims wholly disallowed, withdrawn, or dismissed during the year was 86, classified as follows:

For stamps, etc.—
Lost by fire	$261.11
Lost by burglary	2,733.66
Lost by larceny	65.00
Lost by other causes	15.52
Total	3,075.29

For money-order funds:
Lost by burglary	$37.79
Lost in transit	3,083.70
Lost by fire and other causes	245.66
Total	3,367.15
Grand total	6,442.44

The reasons for disallowance, withdrawal, etc., are summarized thus:

Because not within the provisions of the statutes	6
Because not presented within the time required by statute	9
Because evidence as to fact or amount of loss was unsatisfactory	8
Because of failure to comply with instructions concerning remittances	13
Because of failure to exercise proper care for the protection of the property	22
Because withdrawn or dismissed	28
Total	86

The act of May 9, 1888, is as follows:

[PUBLIC—NO. 77

To amend an act entitled "An act authorizing the Postmaster-General to adjust certain claims of postmasters for loss by burglary, fire, or other unavoidable casualty," approved March seventeenth, eighteen hundred and eighty-two.

Be it enacted by the Senate and House of Representatives of the United States of America in Congress assembled, That the act entitled "An act authorizing the Postmaster-General to adjust certain claims of postmasters for loss by burglary, fire, or other unavoidable casualty," approved March seventeenth, eighteen hundred and eighty-two, be, and the same is hereby, amended so as to read as follows:

That the Postmaster-General be, and he is hereby, authorized to investigate all claims of postmasters for the loss of money-order funds, postal funds, postage-stamps, stamped envelopes, newspaper wrappers, and postal-cards, belonging to the United States in the hands of such postmasters, resulting from burglary, fire, or other unavoidable casualty, and if he shall determine that such loss resulted from no fault or negligence on the part of such postmasters, to pay to such postmasters, or credit them with the amount so ascertained to have been lost or destroyed, and also to credit postmasters with the amount of any remittance of money-order funds or postal funds made by them in compliance with the instructions of the Postmaster-General which shall have been lost or stolen while in transit by mail from the office of the remitting postmaster to the office designated as his depository, or after arrival at such depository office, and before the postmaster at such depository office has become responsible therefor: *Provided,* That no claim exceeding the sum of two thousand dollars shall be paid or credited until after the facts shall have been ascertained by the Postmaster-General and reported to Congress, together with his recommendation thereon, and an appropriation made therefor: *And provided further,* That this act shall not embrace any claim for losses as aforesaid, which accrued more than fifteen years prior to March seventeenth, eighteen hundred and eighty-two; and all such claims must be presented to the Postmaster-General within six months from such latter date, except claims for postal funds, which may be received, considered and allowed, if presented within six months after the passage of this act, in cases where the postmaster had, at or about the time of the loss, made report thereof to the Post-Office Department or to an inspector or special agent of the Department; and no claim for losses which may hereafter accrue shall be allowed unless presented within six months from the time the loss occurred.

SEC. 2. That it is hereby made the duty of the Postmaster-General to report his action herein to Congress annually, with his reasons therefor in each particular case.

Approved, May 9, 1888.

This act worked the following changes in the law, viz:

First. In allowing credit for money-order funds remitted for deposit, and lost after arrival at the post-office of deposit;

Second. In allowing credit for "postal funds" lost since March 17, 1867, either in transit to depositories, or by fire, burglary, or other unavoidable casualty;

Third. In removing the bar of the statute in cases arising since March 17, 1882, upon which the statute had run.

Immediately upon the passage of the act all pending and adjusted claims were examined; circular letters were prepared advising postmasters of the change in the law, copies of which were sent to all postmasters and late postmasters who had sustained losses which had been brought to the attention of this office; and the act was published in the June number of the Official Postal Guide. A summary of its provisions was also furnished the Associated Press, in order that late postmasters whose addresses were not known to this office, or who had not made formal reports of losses, or filed claims for credit or reimbursement, might be advised of their rights in the premises. The result of the efforts to bring the matter to the attention of claimants has been a large increase in the number of claims filed, the greater portion of which, however, were not received until after the expiration of the fiscal year ended June 30, 1888, and are, therefore, not included in this report.

I have the honor, sir, to be, very respectfully,

Your obedient servant,

EDWIN E. BRYANT,

Assistant Attorney-General, Post-Office Department.

The POSTMASTER GENERAL.

EXHIBIT A.—*List of claims on account of loss by fire, burglary, etc., allowed from July 1, 1887, to June 30, 1888, under acts of March 17, 1882, and May 9, 1888.*

Post-offices.	Postmasters.	Date of loss.	Cause of loss.	Amounts claimed. Stamps, etc.	Amounts claimed. M.O. funds.	Amounts allowed. Stamps, etc.	Amounts allowed. M.O. funds.
Acampo, Cal	M. A. D. Long	June 4, 1887	Burglary	$74.40		$64.63	
Adamsville, Mich	S. H. Akins	Sept. , 1887	do	20.66		20.66	$8.00
Adeline, Ill	G. R. Rummel	Feb. 25, 1888	In transit		$8.00		
Alambus Grove, Mo	T. J. Almond	Dec. 22, 1887	Burglary	44.90		43.20	
Almon, Ga	T. C. Hobbs	May 17, 1887	do	13.00		13.00	
Anchorage, Ky	J. H. Marshburn	Nov. 9, 1888	Fire	30.90		30.90	
Angola, N O	P. P. Powell	Feb. 9, 1888	do	28.98		28.98	
Angola, Tex	Henry Musador	Nov. 10, 1887	do	Not known		20.96	
Amonia, Wis	N. B. Webster	Jan. 22, 1888	do	2.50		2.50	
Amonia, Ohio	Thomas Smith	Nov. 6, 1887	Burglary	73.75		42.88	
Antioch, Tex	J. M. Lewis	Dec. 18, 1886	do	5.50		5.50	
Arba, Ind	T. J. Herndon	Feb. 2, 1888	do	11.10		11.10	
Arcadia, Fla	George A. McCoy	Mar. 8, 1888	Fire	Unknown		2.43	
Arletta, N Y	F. P. Denington	Oct. 16, 1886	Burglary	20.95		20.95	
Armstrong, Tex	John R. Kaufman	Nov. 17, 1886	Fire	38.00		38.00	
Atherton, Pa		Nov. 17, 1887	do	4.25		4.25	
Ash Grove, Mo	Huey Hay	Aug. 24, 1887	Burglary	173.00	$6.65	137.57	$30.65
Ashland, N C	S. A. Rice	Feb. 24, 1887	Fire	19.00		19.00	
Athens, Ill	E. G. Garrett	Sept. 10, 1888	do	8.61		8.61	
Auburn, Va	John R Grant	Jan. 10, 1888	do	33.00		33.00	
Avoca, Pa	L. N. Beans	Nov. 27, 1887	do	9.38		9.98	
Ball Fla, Ala	L. Mathers	Mar. 21, 1888	do	9.66		9.66	
Ballown, Pa	Margaret Davis	Dec. 24, 1887	do	20.89		20.89	
Barneville, Ohio	C. W. Hawks	Aug. 25, 1887	do	22.50		22.50	
Bath, Ga	John W. Hingeley	Feb. 14, 1888	Burglary	2.93	$69.50	2.93	69.50
Beckwith, Tenn	W. V. Thompson	July 7, 1887	Fire	10.77		10.77	
Bellair Mills, Va	Pallas Young	July 2, 1887	do	9.88		8.88	
Bellwood, Pa	R. L. Arrington	Feb. 13, 1888	do	42.94		4.10	10.00
Bentonville, Ohio	Thaddeus Stewart	July 24, 1887	Burglary	217.81	$10.00	217.84	
Berlin, Mo	John G. Bradley	Mar. 1, 1888	In transit	41.88		46.70	
Berne, Ind	Samuel Levy	Feb. 18, 1888	Burglary	Not known	38.00	80.66	780.00
Bessemer, Mich	Harvey Harruff	Sept. 10, 1887	do		178.99	6.22	115.64
Betterton, Md	E. D. Howe	June 11, 1887	do		346.91	14.12	77.91
Big Plain, Ohio	C. L. Wright	Oct. 15, 1887	Fire	Unknown		67.29	
Black, Ill	A. E. Loobbourrow	Sept. 28, 1887	do	16.12		23.42	
Black Mills, N J	Henry R. Parsload	Sept. R, 1887	Burglary	Not known		5.00	
Black River Falls, Wis	T. D. Probasco	Oct. 16, 1887	do	147.71		138.45	
Bloomfield, Ill	George W. Lewis	Sept. 23, 1886	Fire			25.70	
Bloomfield, Mo	J. L. Pflueger	Oct. 29, 1887	do	Unknown	69.23		38.23
Bloomingdale, Ill	George Croseer	Mar. 25, 1887	Burglary	4.10		4.10	
	John H. Kobusch	May 21, 1887	do				

Place	Claimant	Cause	Date			Amount
Bloomington, Nebr.	J. W. Deary	Fire	Nov. 10, 1887			64.00
Blue Creek, Ohio	H. M. Caraway	do	pt. 8, 1887			18.28
Bobbin, Tex.	James M. Stinson	do	May 8, 1886			43.00
Bolling Springs, Ala.	W. I. Fluker	do	Apr. 1867			55.83
Bolton, Vt.	Thomas R. Whalen	do	Oct. 24, 1887			4.00
Boughton, Ark.	John T. Aaron	Burglary	May 12, 1887			13.68
Bowdon, Ga.	J. W. Downs, jr	Fire	Feb. 12, 1887			29.85
Bragunna, Ga.	Miles Allertson	do	Dec. 8, 1887			17.58
Bimber, Ky.	James T. Brasher	By rats	Aug. 13, 1887			12.84
Bremen, Minn.	Wilhelmine M. Dickmann	Fire	Feb. 27, 1887			62.50
Brimfield, Ill.	G. C. Paul	Burglary	Sept. 24, 1887			53.88
Brookfield, Ga.	J. W. Bowen	do	Mar. 1887			27.78
Brooklyn, Md.	John Delamater	do	Apr. 19, 1886			28.78
Broughton, Ill.	D. A. Reeves	Fire	Jan. 17, 1888			17.00
Brownsborough, Oregon	Daniel Levi	do	Mar. 13, 1887			85.00
Brownsville, Tenn.	R. E. Brown	Burglary	July 28, 1887			211.14
Buckley, Mo.	John S. Harrison	do	Sept. 27, 1887	24.66	24.66	39.16
Bunyon, N.C.	Julia F. Elcorn	Fire	July 13, 1888			13.09
Burton, Cal	John E. Mocers	do	Mar. 14, 1888			55.00
Burrton, Kans.	G. M. Shive	Burglary	Sept. 22, 1887			13.35
Buyck, Ala	T. J. Holman	Destroyed by mice	Mar. 18, 1887			4.50
Byron, Cal	P. H. Lewis	Burglary	Dec. 14, 1887			151.96
Calico, Cal	M. E. Stacey	Fire	July 19, 1887			49.05
..., N. Y.	Gilbert Hobbs	do	Sept. 1, 1887			47.41
Camptonville, Cal	William T. Dehn	do	Nov. 17, 1887	Not known.		81.30
...eller, Ga.	Joseph D. Cobb	do	July 26, 1887			22.00
Caudo, Dak.	Charles H. Ensign	do	Mar. 22, 1887			13.85
Carlow, Mo.	A. K. ...	do	Feb. 20, 1887			68.40
Carmi, Ill.	... R. Little	Burglary	Sept. 10, 1886			41.67
Cary Station, Ill.	James Sire	Fire	Aug. 13, 1887			80.61
Carryville, Mass.	E. B. See	Burglary	Nov. 27, 1887			19.27
Oley, N.C.	L. M. Cathey	do	Nov. 25, 1887			4.50
Charlestown, W. Va.	George H. Flagg	Fire	Apr. 18, 1887			37.25
Charlie, Tex.	E. L. Taylor	Burglary	Dec. 28, 1887			27.00
Chester, Ill.	H. W. Roberts	do	Apr. 22, 1887	82.11	82.11	268.80
Churchula, Ala.	Martin L. Stevenson	do	Mar. 8, 1887	Unknown.		14.00
..., Tex.	William Still	Burglary	Oct. 9, 1887			2.10
...ten, Iowa.	John Hanrahan	Fire	Jan. 10, 1866			28.31
Clarksville, Iowa	H. A. Jolly	do	Feb. 4, 1888	Not known.		8.83
Gay Village, Ky.	John J. Elchar	Burglary	May 29, 1887	2.00		7.28
Coal Bluff, Pa.	K. F. Strain	do	Nov. 14, 1887	Not known.		2.00
... Clay, ...	Thomas Cain	do	Aug. 14, 1887	All.		4.00
Collinsville, Ohio	M. H. Richardson	Fire	Aug. 7, 1887			51.02
	J. H. Shallenbarger	do	Feb. 15, 1887			5.05

EXHIBIT A.—*List of claims on account of loss by fire, burglary, etc., allowed from July 1, 1887, to June 30, 1888, etc.*—Continued.

Post-offices.	Postmasters.	Date of loss.	Cause of loss.	Amounts claimed.		Amounts allowed.	
				Stamps, etc.	M.O. funds.	Stamps, etc.	M.O. funds.
Columbia City, Ind	Eli W. Brown	Feb. 26, 1888	Burglary		$22.41		$22.41
Columbus, Ind	G. E. Finney	Oct. 18, 1887	do		57.06		57.06
Commercial Summit, Ky	J. K. Vickers	July 14, 1887	do	$18.74		$18.74	
Conner Station, Kans	Jeptha H. Hollingsworth	July 31, 1887	Fire	70.82		70.82	
Conva, Iowa	R. A. Holland	Nov. 23, 1887	do	110.66		105.49	
Corfu, N. Y	Wilber L. Sumner	Aug. 23, 1887	In transit		20.00		20.00
Cotton Plant, Miss	R. H. Paterson	Dec. 26, 1887	Fire	All		34.15	
Cottonwood Falls, Kans	Luella P. Pugh	Oct. 20, 1887	Burglary	8.23	33.90	8.30	33.90
Craigsville, Ky	Christopher Loard	Apr. 26, 1887	do	1.80		1.80	
Crawford, N. Y	W. W. Thorn	Dec. 11, 1887	Fire	38.45		38.45	
Cresco, Mo	Uriah Jones	Apr. 12, 1887	Burglary	19.07		19.07	
Crookston, Minn	Rufus A. Lewis	July 22, 1887	do	22.00		22.00	
Cross Plains	Alex. McKinnon	July 17, 1887	do	43.00		62.83	
Cruise, Mo	W. A. Wilson	Sept. 16, 1887	In transit		160.00		160.00
Cuba, Ohio	Charles R. Gray	Feb. 7, 1888	Burglary	29.83		29.83	
Culpeper, Va	George R. Kearns	Dec. 19, 1887	do	62.89	32.90	62.89	32.90
Culver, Ind	James F. Robertson	July 3, 1887	do	317.43		317.43	
Cunningham	James Strain	Apr. 5, 1888	Fire	28.00		28.00	
Danby, Mo	D. H. Ballew	Aug. 24, 1888	do	13.75		13.75	
David City, Nebr	E. W. Porter	Sept. 10, 1887	do	5.53		5.53	
Dougherty, Tex	John W. Huffman, acting postmaster	Feb. 16, 1884	Burglary	12.47	122.21	12.47	122.21
Do Barry, Mich	F. E. Wilson	Aug. 30, 1887	Fire	*262.39		92.62	
Do Bury, Mich	F. K. De Van	Dec. 6, 1887	Burglary	27.92		20.00	
Delano, Minn	Almon Higley	May 23, 1887	Fire	83.06		83.06	
Delmar, Pa	Charles Heelon	July 10, 1887	Burglary	62.07		60.22	
Dexter, Mich	Valentine Eppel	Sept. 23, 1887	Fire	8.00	1.88	8.00	.38
Diamond Lake	Simon A. Hampton	Feb. 14, 1888	Burglary	All		7.37	
Doniphan, Nebr	M. S. Cook	May 15, 1887	Fire	194.84	122.60	194.84	122.60
Douglass, Iowa	E. B. Wright	Nov. 26, 1887	Fire	6.12		6.12	
Douglassville, Pa	W. H. Gideon	Feb. 8, 1887	do	Not known	20.70	68.00	20.70
Dresden, Mo	S. D. Hoagland	Dec. 13, 1887	do	17.00		17.00	
Eagle Mills, N. Y	George S. Reider	Oct. 22, 1887	Burglary	25.00		25.00	
Easton, Ohio	B. H. Offutt	Feb. 9, 1888	do	24.80		24.80	
Eaton, Pa	John McChesney	Sept. 23, 1887	Fire	3.75		3.75	
El Dorado, Ill	John W. Hartel	Feb. 21, 1887	Burglary	63.74		63.74	
Elba, Ky	William Elder	Dec. 1, 1887	do	67.59		65.00	
Elizabethtown, Ky	E. A. Chilton	Nov. 26, 1886	Fire	10.77		10.77	
Elkhorn, Tenn	Emily T. Helm	June 28, 1887	do	4.19		4.19	
Elkinsville, N. C	Thomas V. Burton	Apr. 16, 1887	do	24.00	20.00	24.00	20.00
Elk River, Minn	R. M. Elkins	Feb. 19, 1888	do	19.60		19.60	
	H. E. Thomas	Mar. 20, 1884	Burglary	6.00		6.00	

Place	Name	Date	Cause				
Ellinwood, Kans	William Misner	Oct. 14, 1967	do	$237.27		176.83	48.71
Elmwood, Conn	Wilbur E. Goodwin	Dec. 20, 1887	do	64.87		60.72	
Eshel, Miss	A. T. Middlebrooks	June 28, 1887	Fire	47.30		43.18	
Etna, Ill	Jacob Rains	Mar. 21, 1888	Burglary	25.65		25.65	
Eureka, La	M. L. Bennett	Apr. 2, 1886	Fire	18.50		18.50	
Fairfield, Kans	Martin E. McNemar	July 29, 1884	Burglary	46.00		46.00	
Fairmont, Nebr	S. Sawyer F.	Oct. 28, 1887	do	128.77	19.48	75.91	19.48
Fairview, Ill	W. L. Harrington	June 11, 1887	do	All	14.41	14.41	14.41
Farraville, Tex	R. Z. Powell	Aug. 29, 1887	Fire	19.71		16.63	16.63
Felicity, Ohio	O. F. Molen	Dec. 21, 1887	Burglary	71.64		19.71	
Fenton, Mo	William Longworth	Oct. 6, 1886	do	40.40		71.64	
Finleyville, Pa	John L. Lauk	Dec. 30, 1887	do	12.00		40.00	
Flag Springs, Mo	W. S. Walker	June 16, 1887	do	65.00		14.04	
Flat Woods, W. Va	Henry Wagy	Feb. 2, 1888	Fire	12.00		65.00	
Flint, Ky	J. F. Belcher	Oct. 14, 1887	do	All		17.51	
Flintville, Tenn	D. M. Mims	Nov. 27, 1887	do	9.80		18.65	
Florenville, Tex	W. C. Agee	Dec. 31, 1884	In transit	28.00	81.00	28.00	81.00
Flowery, Tenn	W. S. Morgan	Jan. 15, 1887	Burglary	$868.25		893.25	
Fort Edward, N. Y	Benjamin F. Tasker	Sept. 29, 1887	Fire	$88.22	24.72	33.28	24.72
Fort Mitchell, Va	W. H. F. Fore	Mar. 17, 1887	do	12.00		12.09	
Fort Necessity, La	W. T. Moore	Oct. 12, 1885	Burglary	31.76		31.76	
Fountain, Colo	Albert J. Benedict	Nov. 5, 1887	do	2.95		8.95	
Fountaville, Ga	J. P. Fountain	Nov. 18, 1887	Fire				
Franklin, Ill	J. M. Coons	Feb. 14, 1888	Burglary	14.90	25.77	14.90	25.78
Fulton, N. C	Robert M. Welch	June 24, 1887	do	180.25			
Galesville, Wis	Albert Tower	Oct. 13, 1887	Fire	130.25	84.81	130.25	84.81
Garfield, Wash	Harvey D. Irwin	May 29, 1887	Burglary	17.89		17.89	
Genova, Ill	John C. Strader	May 30, 1887	do	19.00		10.00	
Gentry, N. C	W. B. Gentry	Apr. 11, 1887	do				
Gentryville, Mo	D. C. Gannaway	Mar. 12, 1887	Fire	30.00	1.30	30.00	1.20
Georgeville, Mo	G. W. Akapaugh	Dec. 14, 1886	Burglary	88.22	84.08	85.22	84.08
Georgiana, Ala	John R. Scott	Nov. 8, 1887	Fire	150.00		125.00	
Gibbsborough, N. J	Josepa M. Clark	Jan. 26, 1888	do	18.50		18.50	
Gilceson, Ark	L. T. McDaniel	Jan. 20, 1887	Burglary	124.64	21.90	124.64	21.90
Gilmore, Tex	W. F. Shrum	Dec. 3, 1887	do	134.73		124.71	
Glann, N. H	Mary A. Hammond	Aug. 20, 1887	do	7.25		7.25	
Glen Garden, N. J	William W. Swarne	May 19, 1887	Fire	10.09		10.09	
Golden Lake, Ark	J. W. Rhodes	Jan. 22, 1888	do	19.02		19.02	
Goldthwaite, Tex	W. S. Marshall	Mar. 4, 1888	do	14.58		14.58	
Good Harbor, Mich	Benjamin Minaker	Apr. 2, 1887	Burglary	4.00		4.00	
Grafton, Nebr	T. P. Combs	Mar. 27, 1887	do	35.50		35.20	
Grahamton, Ky	A. M. Robinson	Jan. 16, 1888	Fire	7.02		6.21	
Grand View, Dak	Joseph J. Angus	Feb. 19, 1888	do	13.30		15.48	
Grand View, Iowa	Charles Kallenberger	June 20, 1887	Burglary	Not known			
Gray's Summit, Mo	Julius Hundhausen	Aug. 25, 1887	do		13.70		112.70
Greenfield, Mo	John Harrison	Mar. 9, 1868	Fire	7.00		7.00	
Greenhill, Mo	Melvin Toadvine	Aug. 21, 1887	do	4.00		4.00	
Greenville, Md	John H. Settle	Sept. 16, 1886	Burglary	65.60		60.60	
Greenville, Ohio	Daniel S. Hine	June 19, 1887	do				

EXHIBIT A.—List of claims on account of loss by fire, burglary, etc., allowed from July 1, 1887, to June 30, 1888, etc.—Continued.

Post-offices.	Postmasters.	Date of loss.	Cause of loss.	Amounts claimed.		Amounts allowed.	
				Stamps, etc.	M.O. funds.	Stamps, etc.	M.O. funds.
Groton, Conn.	Elisha A. Hewitt	Sept. 15, 1887	Burglary	$3.71		$3.71	
Haddam, Conn.	Andy R. Shaler	Oct. 13, 1887	...do	*35.81		35.81	
Hall Ridge, Kans	M. E. Weatherbie	Apr. 21, 1887	Cyclone	20.00		17.14	
Half Rock, Mo.	A. J. Hill	Jan. 15, 1888	Fire	58.00		54.24	
Halstead, Kans	Clement Philbrick	Dec. 27, 1887	Burglary	259.61	$95.00	259.61	$95.00
Hanford, Cal	E. Weisbaum	July 12, 1887	Fire	10.90		10.90	
Harper's Station, Ohio	John E. Galb	Apr. 17, 1888	...do	11.20		11.20	
Harris, Tenn	William H. Powers	Nov. 19, 1887	...do	11.90		11.90	
Hartmonsville, W. Va	W. J. Stump	Mar. 19, 1888	Burglary	.78		.78	
Haysville, Kans	Lewis N. Dadisman	Nov. 13, 1887	Fire	29.91		27.53	
Hegewisch, Ill	John Knippel	Nov. 18, 1887	...do	40.89		40.89	
Hellmandale, Pa	Samuel P. Hedlman	May 10, 1887	Burglary	1.85		1.85	
Henry, Tenn	B. J. Allen	Feb. 12, 1887	Fire	100.00		102.20	
Heugh, Tex	B. F. Stone	Nov. 21, 1887	...do	23.70		22.70	
Highland, Ohio	John Hanley	Feb. 16, 1888	Burglary	23.63		23.63	
Highland Center, Iowa	Daniel R. Knight	July 1, 1887	...do	31.48		31.36	
Hillsboro, Ark	T. W. Williams	Jan. 13, 1887	...do	25.85		25.85	
Hilton, N. J	C. H. Stewart	Feb. 25, 1888	...do	42.82		42.82	
Hinton, W. Va	R. S. Thompson	Aug. 14, 1887	Fire	34.56		34.56	
Hillierville, Pa	A. A. Stevens	Feb. 19, 1887	Burglary	42.35		37.64	
Holly Springs, Tex	B. Adams	Jan. 21, 1886	Fire	13.60		13.60	
Holton, Kans	Frederick Hoover	May 27, 1887	Burglary	60.88	54.75	60.88	54.75
Holton, Kans	...do	Apr. 10, 1888	Fire	114.60		114.60	
Holton, Ga	Robert E. Park	June 12, 1887	...do	5.91		5.91	
Hoosier Prairie, Ill	James Kerby	Oct. 28, 1887	Burglary	Not known.		79.43	
Hopedale, Mass	Henry L. Patrick	Oct. 28, 1887	Fire	18.91		18.91	
Hot Springs, Wash	Isaac G. McCain	Jan. 15, 1888	Fire	134.45		134.71	
Howell, Mich	Isaac W. Bush	Mar. 13, 1887	...do	13.71		13.67	
Huffman, Ind	John H. Huffman	July 9, 1887	...do	8.75		8.75	
Hurley, Wis	James A. Wood	July 3, 1887	...do	60.35		66.15	
Idel, Ark	George W. Beavers	Feb. 23, 1887	...do	Not known.		19.16	
Indianola, Tex	J. W. Hogan	Mar. 23, 1887	...do	275.21	53.00	275.21	53.00
Ithaca, Nebr	John F. Koil	Oct. 19, 1888	Burglary	42.90		42.00	
Jamesville, Minn	John Fasig	Mar. 15, 1888	Fire	1.25		1.25	
Jenisonville, Mich	J. W. Tefft	Oct. 29, 1887	Burglary	12.53		12.53	
Jesse, W. Va	Harmon W. Potter	Apr.-12, 1887	Burglary	64.89		64.89	
Kanawha Falls, W. Va	James J. Cook	Jan. 4, 1887	Fire	16.20		7.24	
Keercraville, N. C.	J. C. Watkins	Mar. 0, 1888	...do	26.07		26.07	
Kensington, Conn	W. B. Jarrett	Aug. 20, 1887	...do	12.00		12.00	
Kerrville, Tex	Royal E. Upson	Nov. 5, 1887	Burglary	23.00		14.07	
Kingston, Mass	Albert Enderlee	May 22, 1888	In transit		258.00		258.00
	Truman H. Fuller	Oct. 11, 1887	Burglary	10.20		10.20	

Place	Name	Date	Cause			
Knightsville, Ind	Scott Inge	July 12, 1887	Fire	12.70	12.70	43.00
Lake George, N.Y	John Nelson	Sept. 20, 1887	In transit	103.87	67.68	
Lake Linden, Mich	Eucharisto Brule	May 29, 1887	Fire	57.40	35.75	
Lancha Plana, Cal	J.W.D. Iler	Feb. 28, 1887	do	20.00	20.00	
Laneburgh, Ark	A.C. Lane	Feb. 15, 1886	do	80.00	79.00	
Lawrence, Tex	W.H. Phillippe	Jan. 16, 1887	do	17.67	17.67	
Lawrence, Pa	J.C. Bain	Feb. 28, 1887	do	10.14	10.14	
Lebanon, Iowa	S.K.	June 24, 1887	Burglary	106.25	106.25	
Lebanon, Ky	W.W. Wathen	Aug. 23, 1887	Fire	125.00	125.00	
Lexington, Oregon	George W. Harris	Aug. 23, 1887	do	10.00	10.00	
Liberty, Tenn	Isac Whaley	May 28, 1886	Burglary	20.58	21.64	
Liberty Hill, S.C	N.M. Richards	Oct. 19, 1887	Fire	17.29	20.58	
Lincoln, Mo	M.R. Pinkham	June 21, 1887	do		17.29	
Livermore, Iowa	W.M.	Dec. 9, 1887	Burglary	59.61	63.97	17.17
Lockbourne, Ohio	John Oly	July 8, 1887	do	27.47	27.47	
Lockwood, N.Y	George D.	May 27, 1887	do	14.91	16.91	
Loogootee, Ind	Fannie L. O'Brian	Sept. 22, 1887	do	6.00	6.00	9.75
Louisa C.H., Va	L.A. Goodwin	Jan. 6, 1886	do	102.87	71.28	
Louisville, Miss	M.A.	Oct. 28, 1886	Fire			50.00
Louisville, Nebr	Hinaa W.	Nov. 19, 1887	In transit	94.80	94.80	50.00
Lowndes, Mo	James Grisham	Apr. 30, 1887	Burglary	22.00	22.00	
Lockry, Ark	C.C. Bradley	Dec. 18, 1887	Storm	8.74	2.47	
Mesh, Mich	A.W. Norris	Dec. 28, 1887	Burglary	6.35	6.35	
Macystown, Ill		May 11, 1887	Fire	All on hand	26.70	
Magnolia, Ill	Sheeb B. Williams	July 28, 1887	Burglary	49.98	49.98	
Mann's Choice, Pa	I.S.	Dec. 1, 1887	Fire		86.59	10.00
Marlow, Ga	B.N. Shearouse	May 23, 1887	Burglary	86.59	16.29	.58
Marshall, Cal	R.L. Jennings	Oct. 27, 1887	do	16.29	44.23	
Marshall, Tex	R.D. Whitley	Feb. 27, 1887	Fire	44.23	040.83	
Martindale, N.C	Anthony Howells	Aug. 1887	do	Not known	31.00	
Massillon, Mo	M. Cobb	Dec. 27, 1887	Burglary	81.00	12.00	
Maverick, Fla	W.J. Kirk	Aug. 1887	do	12.04	5.52	
Mo	James A. Loretz	Nov. 10, 1886	Storm	5.52	4.80	
Mayflower, Ark	James S. McKean	Nov. 10, 1887	Burglary	4.40	5.52	
Fla	John Yost	Jan. 27, 1887	Fire	5.52	53.95	
Merritt's Landing, Wis	C.A. Merritt	May 1888	do	60.30	1.10	
Middlepoint, Ohio	C.E. Allen	July 8, 1887	Burglary	1.10	19.47	
do		Dec. 23, 1887	do	20.00	33.00	
Man, Tex	A.G. Seio	Jan. 1887	do	33.00	51.00	
Millville, Miss	Ida A. Blanchard	Nov. 21, 1887	Fire	51.00	5.49	6.92
Milner, Ga	W.R. Howe	Jan. 1888	Burglary	5.49	9.33	
Millston, Wis			do	9.32	14.80	
Milwaukee, Pa	Mrs B. Mills	Dec. 12, 1887	do	14.80	71.70	
Munden, Mo	Mrs Johnston	Apr. 1x, 1888	do	71.70	37.50	
Moloc, Miss	W.T.	Oct. 9, 1887	do	37.50		25.69
Montclair, N.J	William Jacobus	July 14, 1885	F.	16.00	16.30	25.69
Morrison, Colo	Patrick J. Nugent	Jan. 18, 1888	Burglary limit	149.15	42.70	10.00

* Also claimed for postal funds, $15.
† Amount claimed included damaged stamps previously credited.
‡ Also claimed for postal funds $1.50.
§ Also claimed for postal funds $7.25.
‖ Credit allowed for postal cards and stamped envelopes only. Stamps stolen left out of the safe.

Exhibit A.—*List of claims on account of loss by fire, burglary, etc., allowed from July 1, 1887, to June 30, 1888, etc.*—Continued.

Post-offices.	Postmasters.	Date of loss.	Cause of loss.	Amounts claimed.		Amounts allowed.	
				Stamps, etc.	M. O. funds.	Stamps, etc.	M. O. funds.
Morristown, Vt.	William M. Alexander	May 13, 1887	Fire	$10.69		$10.69	
Motley's Depot, Va.	J. F. Hamborough	Oct. 10, 1887	do	50.25		50.25	
Mount Jude, Ark.	Ephraim B. Greenhaw	Apr. 7, 1887	do	22.50		29.36	
Murray, N. Y.	A. H. Dusett	Jan. 4, 1887	do	Not known		19.08	
Napoleon, Mich.	Charles C. Dewey	Nov. 17, 1887	Burglary	47.82		47.82	
Nash, Tex.	Lewis Cole	Feb. 7, 1887	Fire	8.00		12.78	
Nebraska City, Nebr.	A. O. Swift	Sept. 20, 1887	Burglary	57.91	$64.00	57.91	$64.00
Neosho Falls, Cal.	Daniel Murphy	Aug. 8, 1887	Fire	*130.00		20.00	
New Albany, Miss.	H. D. Dickson	Jan. 28, 1888	Burglary	63.23	8.58	63.23	8.58
New Britton, Ind.	J. A. Smallwood	Sept. 5, 1887	Fire	10.06		10.06	
New Gronada, Pa.	C. J. McLeaser	June 23, 1887	do	Not known		6.00	
New Hamburgh, Mo.	R. S. Saunders	Apr. 27, 1887	do	20.00		86.24	
New Hope, Minn.	A. T. Wilson	Sept. 10, 1887	do	20.00		20.00	
New Moorfield, Ohio	W. G. Thorp	Dec. 28, 1886	do	10.58		10.58	
New York, Iowa	M. E. Tuohy	Nov. 19, 1882	Burglary	25.00		25.00	
Nokomis, Ill.	J. D. Biggs	Apr. 8, 1887	do	10.58		10.58	
Norcatur, Kans.	W. C. Scanland	June 2, 1887	do	38.79		38.70	
Normal, Ill.	O. C. Smith	Apr. 8, 1887	do	43.00		33.50	
North Adams, Mich.	Eli F. Armantrout	Aug. 22, 1887	Fire	38.77		38.77	
North Union, Ind.	Adolph Roblishek	Feb. 24, 1886	Burglary	1,095.60	$27.80	1,095.60	$27.80
Northville, N. Y.	Charles A. Libby	Jan. 14, 1888	Fire	73.40	96.97	73.40	96.97
North Wayne, Mo.	Dan Jones	Sept. 30, 1887	do	17.15		17.15	
North Westchester, Conn.	L. M. Nuttall	Dec. 10, 1887	Burglary	77.00	?32.93	31.70	?32.93
Nuttallburgh, W. Va.	Edwin P. Daine	Dec. 3, 1888	do	31.70		36.19	
Oak, Mich.	William W. Underhill	Sept. 12, 1887	do	36.19		70.20	
Oakdale, Wis.	J. S. Scott	Sept. 6, 1886	do	70.20		20.65	
Oconto, Kans.	R. E. Prevatt	Apr. 25, 1887	do	20.65	$14.87	51.56	14.87
Osage, Kans.	Eli Nichols	Oct. 7, 1885	Fire	51.56	5.02		5.02
Orange City, Fla.	Josie George	Dec. 12, 1887	Burglary	46.80	5.20	46.80	5.20
Orangeville Mills, Mich.	Charles Starkhouse	July 27, 1887	Fire	6.00		6.00	
Orting, Wash.	John White	Sept. 11, 1887	Burglary	Unknown		46.71	
Osage City, Kans.	George E. Saunders	Aug. 1, 1886	do	23.62	$110.01	16.28	74.26
Osage Iron Works, Mo.	S. C. Vanvliet, Jr.	Apr. 10, 1887	Fire	15.31		15.31	
Otter View, Va.	do	Nov. 6, 1887	do	10.66		10.66	
Oxford Depot, N. Y.	George W. Coburn	Oct. 13, 1887	Burglary	1.16		1.16	
Do	William Alexander	do	do	8.50		8.50	
Pacific Junction, Iowa	J. C. Collins	Aug. 31, 1887	In transit	7.00	20.00	7.00	20.00
Palestine, Ill.	W. C. Lassiter	Sept. 24, 1867	Fire	Not known		23.51	
Palmyra, Ark.	Jerome T. Stocker	Jan. 3, 1886	do	12.01		10.15	
Peedie, Tex.		Dec. 4, 18-5	Burglary	2.30		2.30	
Peston, Pa.		Oct. 30, 1887	By mice				

Office	Name	Cause	Date	Allowed on hand		
Penquite, Kans	N. B. Penquite	Fire	Mar. 12, 1887			21.27
Perpecton, N.Y.	Leslie E. Hawk	do	Sept. 17, 1887			4.07
Percival, Iowa	J. H. Williams	do	Sept. 2, 1887	8.00		8.00
Petersburgh, Ill.	Rebecca Snape	Burglary	Oct. 29, 1887	Not known		288.15
Philadelphia, Pa.	William F. Harris	do	Feb. 17, 1888	288.15		102.74
Pier post Mr., N.Y.	George F. Gardner	do	1887	102.74	23.22	28.43
Pierson,	Jay D. F. Pierson	Fire	Sept. 7, 1887	28.43		4.95
Pilgrim, Mo	Thomas W. Read	do	Mar. 28, 1887	4.95		7.53
Pit Park, Ky	R. V. Leonard	Burglary	Feb. 17, 1888	7.53	6.58	100.00
Pocahontas, Tenn	L. M. Paine	do	May 16, 1887	90.00		12.44
Point Isabel, Co.	Sue Rosson	Fire		25.00		13.31
Polkville, Miss.	Franklin T. Hodges	Burglary	Feb. 21, 1888	Not known		18.97
Port Gatland,	J. Sumner	Fire	Nov. 1884	18.97		8.00
Port Bay, Ohio.	George Vanderscheid	do	Dec. 25, 1887	8.00		11.00
Mo	Lucinda Booth	do	Feb. 13, 1888	11.00		20.41
Princeton, Miss	John Teasdale	Burglary	May 15, 1887	20.41		25.00
Pulaski, Iowa	Leonard Chandler	do	May 10, 1887	25.71		100.34
Pullett, N.O.	W. M. Hotchkiss	In transit	April 7, 1887	100.34	8.06	8.06
Radford, La.	Franklin Jackson	Fire	Feb. 2, 1888		70.00	70.00
Readington, N.J.	Wm H.	Fire	Oct. 12, 1886	Unknown		13.00
Redington, Nebr	Peter N. Williamson	Storm	July 3, 1887	13.00		7.83
Reynoldsville, Ky	Eugene E. Van Olinda	Fire	Oct. 5, 1887	5.40		5.40
Riverside, Ar.	Morton Styer	Burglary	Jan. 24, 1887	16.21		16.21
Riverside, N.J.	S. M. Jones	Fire	Dec. 8, 1887	12.04		12.04
Riverside, Ohio	Emo H. Deegins	Burglary	Nov. 4, 1887	28.67		28.67
Rockfall, Conn	E. Osmick	do	May 4, 1887	8.10		8.10
Roel ille, Ind	F. Francis	do		7.45		6.14
Do	D. S. McMullen	do	Mar. 19, 1887	17.38		4.08
	Wm E. Henkel	do	Dec. 27, 1887	5.00		4.95
	do	do	Feb. 24, 1888	7.40		7.40
Rocky River, Ko	E. P. Thompson	do	Oct. 21, 1887	67.34	68.46	67.34
Rockland, Del.	Sarah J. Ewing	do	Oct. 14, 1887	65.41		65.41
Rodgers, Tex	F. M.	do	July 16, 1887	9.05		.9.05
Rolfe, Pa	W. L. Devine	Fire	Dec. 25, 1887	63.06		63.06
Romanville, Pa.	Albert Rogers	Burglary	July 29, 1887	40.81		40.81
Roundhead, Mo.	J. W. Dunfee	Fire	Oct. 9, 1887	17.00		17.00
Rousseau, Dak	Marcel C. Rousseau	Burglary	Aug. 10, 1887	33.49		38.49
Rush er, Mo	Benjamin F. England	Fire	Apr. 2, 1887	42.00		45.40
Salem, Ohio	Frank W. Webster	Burglary	Sept. 15, 1887	12.72	47.48	12.72
Salisbury, M'd	Alfred Browning	do	Sep 1887	637.18		637.18
San Kans	G. R. Rider	Fire	Feb. 14, 1887	13.00		13.00
Kans	R. E. Harris	Burglary	Sept. 29, 1887	583.00		†110.82
ville, N.Y.	Wm Walker	In transit	Aug	240.40	67.00	240.40
Scotch Grove, Iowa	Peter Deaninger	Burglary	Sept. 13, 1887	17.82	6.44	17.52
	Sandy Shoemaker	do		30.04		30.04
Searcy, Ala.	R. J. Lee	do	Dec. 11, 1887	34.00		34.00

* Amount claimed included damaged stamps previously credited.
† Claim for money-order funds disallowed. No evidence of amount property on hand.
‡ Disallowed money-order funds; loss resulted from neglect of postmaster.
§ Also claimed for postal funds $20.12.
¶ Also claimed for postal funds $15.76.
¶ Twenty-six dollars and seventy-five ... der ... fals claimed were ... eed, and $9 had been improperly ... ten.
** Also allowed for postal ... fals 5d.
†† The greater portion of the stolen stamps was recovered.

EXHIBIT A.—*List of claims on account of loss by fire, burglary, etc., allowed from July 1, 1887, to June 30, 1888, etc.*—Continued.

Post-offices.	Postmasters.	Date of loss.	Cause of loss.	Amounts claimed.		Amounts allowed.	
				Stamps, etc.	M. O. funds.	Stamps, etc.	M. O. funds.
Sherwin Juncti n, Kans.	Charles S. Huffman	Aug. 24, 1887	Burglary	$45.00		$45.00	
Shirley Village, Mass.	Thomas L. Hazen	June 18, 1887	do	153.06	$96.79	153.34	
Sidney, Ohio	J. S. Laughlin	Aug. 7, 1887	do	185.43		185.43	
Sipe Spring, Tex	Frank K. Stamey	Mar. 30, 1887	Fire	58.31		58.81	
Skowhegan, Me	C. Davis Miller	Aug. 11, 1887	Burglary	390.00		363.00	
Slater, Mo	Samuel G. Mead	July 21, 1887	Fire	348.99		348.99	
8th Butte, Mont	W. T. Shirley	May 21, 1887	do	2.75		2.75	
South Byron N.Y.	Isaac S. Durfee	Nov. 10, 1887	Burglary	85.44		85.44	
South Fincas M, Ohio	James W. McKinney	Mar. 27, 1888	do	11.16		11.16	
South Penobscot, Me.	Elisha R. Douden	Mar. 14, 1887	Fire	8.97		8.97	
Sparta, Ill	A. Borders	Mar. 14, 1888	Burglary	702.55		702.55	$143.45
Sparta, Miss.	J. A. Wilkinson	June 15, 1887	do	15.00		15.00	
Speer, W. Va.	Henry A. Smith	Oct. 21, 1887	Fire	81.40	Not known.	81.40	162.43
Spring Lick, Ky	Squire Salesman	Apr. 20, 1887	do	6.55		6.55	
Stanley, Va	Swinfield Stanley	Apr. 17, 1887	do	18.00		18.00	
Stuincoum City, Wash.	L. R. Rigney	Nov. 20, 1887	Burglary	45.00		45.00	
Stepstone, Ky	Hiram E. Carl	Nov. 20, 1887	do	4.00		4.00	4.00
bossurgh, Pa	J. P. Hines	Apr. 21, 1887	do				
Saint Gar. Mo.	Boyle L. Ellett	Dec. 14, 1887	do	12.00		12.00	
Saint Louis Crossing, Ind	Joseph A. Newton	Nov. 10, 1887	do	7.73		7.73	
Saint Yarks, Kans.	Michael Laggart	July 30, 1887	Fire	3.75		3.27	
Strafford Mo.	W. D. Pickel	Aug. 11, 1887	Burglary	47.39		38.86	
Saches, Ga.	John C. Cannon	Feb. 18, 1887	do	1.75		1.75	
Summerfield, Mo	John H. Barnes	May 11, 1887	do	10.00	4.00	10.00	
Tappahannock, Va.	J. L. Hanley	June 27, 1887	In transit				
Tewksbury, Mass	Timothy W. Gray	Aug. 17, 1887	Burglary	7.92	90.00	7.92	90.00
Thomaston, Conn	A. K. Blakeslee	Oct. 31, 1887	do	12.11		12.11	
Thomson, Ga.	J. N. Neal	Jan. 18, 1888	Fire	3.00		3.00	
Thompson, Mo.	C. H. Vann	Feb. 17, 1887	do	143.70	17.00	140.62	17.00
Tiocralik, Mass.	Frank Santee	Aug. 1, 1887	Burglary	140.62		59.22	
Toccopola, Miss	Julia A. Evans	Nov. 26, 1887	do	100.00		7.32	
Tompkinsville, Ky	W. J. McAlister	June 25, 1887	do	7.32		11.58	
Towry, Tenn.	Thomas B. Moore	Oct. 1, 1887	Burglary	13.53		28.07	
Trenton, Tex	B. F. Hackett	Sept. 9, 1887	Fire	105.35		43.81	90.00
Troy, Iowa	M. D. L. Crawford	Oct. 12, 1887	Fire	56.00		38.88	
Tryus, Miss	Charles H. Smith	Aug. 17, 1887	Burglary	36.83		60.35	
Union City, Conn	C. A. Lindsay	May 12, 1887	Fire	60.35		16.27	
Unionville, Md	W. W. Ireland	Aug. 12, 1888	Burglary	16.27		9.87	
Unity, Ill.	E. E. Shaw	Sept. 19, 1867	Fire	9.87		1.00	
Utica Mills, Md.	R. R. Shaw			6.12			
Uxbridge, Mass.	H. S. Farnum	Aug. 17, 1887	do	6.00		5.00	

Place	Name	Kind	Date	Amount claimed	Amount allowed	
Valueti n, Mo.	R. L. Crabb	do	Jan. 20, 1887	8.33	8.33	
Valley Furnace, W. Va.	A. C. Ihmn	Fire	Sept. 24, 1887	22.00	22.00	
Valley Fort, Mo.	David R. Hardin	do	May 2, 1887	68.23	68.23	
Valleta, Cal	M. G. Lewis	do	Nov. 11, 1887	10.68	10.68	
Vallton, Wis.	L. Clemons	Burglary	Aug. 15, 1887	50.19	50.19	
Van Dyne, Wis.	W. W. Toner	do	Aug. 18, 1887	20.72	20.72	
Vienna, Ill	William A. Spann	Fire	July 1, 1887		73.40	73.40
Villa Ridge, Ill	Uriah Butler	do	May 25, 1887	22.98	22.98	
Vincennes, I wa	[ ]ulus E. Sird	do	Mar. 25, 1887	84.55	80.90	
Waddel, N.C.	John E. Grady	Fire	Aug. 3, 1887	22.17	16.00	
Waldo, Ark	C. H. Pace	do	Aug 21, 1887	12.25	12.25	
Waldron, Ind	George L. Streif	Burglary	Oct 14, 1887	80.50	80.50	
Warren ton, Va.	Isaac R. Hayard	do	Aug. 8, 1887	18.47	20.00	
Wabash, ...	L. W. Caldwell	do	Feb. 3, 1888	49.65	49.65	
Whington Center, Mo.	Lorenzo Hunsaker	Fire	Sept. 6, 1887	87.25	Not known	143.43
Waterloo, Ohio	Idas Davis	do	Dec. 19, 1886	11.56	Not known	
Waverville, ...	D. F. Hudson	do	May 20, 1887	18.96	Not known	
Wawaka, Ind	D. W. Reed	Burglary	Oct 21, 1887	88.47	88.47	
Wayne, Mich	M. M. [ ]all	do	Sept. 24, 1886	2.13	2.55	
Waynesville, Mo	Anna B. Wing	do	Nov. 15, 1887	2.25	2.25	1.73
Webb's Mills, Mo	J. R. Burchard	Fire	Dec. 3, 1887	13.82	13.88	
Webster Groves, Mo	A. A. Sutler	do	Sept. 20, 1887	8.54	8.54	
Do	John Berry	do	July 19, 1887	46.00	46.00	M
Werner, Wis	Law M. Ottofy	Burglary	Sept. 18, 1887	13.83	13.83	
West Dedham, Mass	do	do	Mar. 20, 1888	76.94	76.94	
West Cheshire, ...	Wm O. Lothrop	Fire	Aug. 31, 1887	84.62	84.62	
West Geo, N.Y	Charles H. Ellis	do	Apr. 17, 1887	19.45	19.45	
West Liberty, Ill	Edward P. Dunham	Burglary	Aug. 23, 1887	4.14	4.14	
West Middlebct, Pa.	Michael Marshall	do	Oct. 18, 1887	160.68	160.68	
West Olive, Mich	J. R. Delrohl	do	May 28, 1888	73.17	73.17	
Weston, S.C	A. Hall	do	Jan. 4, 1888	15.47	15.47	
Wetaug, Ill	Orlington Trumble	Fire	Sept. 18, 1887	180.32	180.32	
..., N.J	Robert Moody	Burglary	Aug 24, 1887	21.88	29.00	
Whiteon, N.Y.	William A. Hight	do	Aug 24, 1888	17.84	48.45	
Wiggonsville, Ohio	Gerg[ ]	Fire	Jan. 3, 1888	48.45	67.92	
Williamsport, W. Va.	John H. Mon	Burglary	Jan. 10, 1888	67.92		
Williford, Ark	J. M. Millner	do	Dec. 28, 1888	12.44	12.44	
Williston, S.C.	C. C. Marshall	Fire	May 25, 1887	6.50	6.50	
Willoughby, Ohio	T. B. Hall	do	Dec. 28, 1887	27.55	27.55	
Winchester, Ark	E. L. Ron	do	June 28, 1887	22.50	18.25	
Winnebago, Wis	John S. Ellen	Burglary	Nov. 30, 1887	85.41	Not known	161.23
Winnebago City, Minn.	T. V. Wells	Fire	Aug. 15, 1887	298.10	298.10	
	James Lewis	Fire	Dec. 1887	38.00	35.00	
	A. B. Davis	Burglary		8.63	8.63	
		Fire		207.00	207.00	77.00

Exhibit A.—*List of claims on account of loss by fire, burglary, etc., allowed from July 1, 1887, to June 30, 1888, etc.*—Continued.

Post-offices.	Postmasters.	Date of loss.	Cause of loss.	Amount claimed.		Amounts allowed.	
				Stamps, etc.	M. O. funds.	Stamps, etc.	M. O. funds.
Wise, W. Va.	J. R. Robinson	May 15, 1887	Burglary	3.00		3.00	
Wilbur, N. Y.	W. H. Brown	Dec. 14,1887	Fire	20.00		20.00	
Wolf, Ohio	Calvin J. Kinsey	Dec. 2, 1887	Burglary	18.43		18.43	
Woodville, Ky.	Isaac H. Driskell	July 31, 1887	do	92.58		92.58	
Wynnewood, Pa.	Frank P. Hunter	Apr. 1, 1887	do	6.20		6.20	
York Sulphur Springs, Pa.	A. C. Gardner	Apr. 15, 1887	do	9.17		4.69	
				20,561.86	3,726.98	20,390.97	3,822.65

RECAPITULATION.

Number of claims allowed 449

For postage-stamps, etc.	Claimed.	Allowed.
Lost by fire	$6,220.03	$7,171.09
Lost by burglary	14,462.18	13,057.44
Lost by storm	9.26	15.31
Lost by other causes	80.39	86.63
Totals	20,561.86	20,390.97

For money-order funds.	Claimed.	Allowed.
Lost by fire	$304.10	$398.76
Lost by burglary	2,567.78	2,068.89
Lost in transit	855.00	855.00
Totals	3,726.98	3,822.65

Aggregate amount claimed	$24,228.09
Aggregate amount allowed	28,653.02

EXHIBIT B.—List of claims on account of loss by fire, burglary, etc. (act of March 17, 1882), disallowed, dismissed, or withdrawn from July 1, 1887, to June 30, 1888.

Post-office	Postmasters	Date of loss	Cause of loss	Amount claimed		Reasons for disallowance, dismissal, etc.
				Stamps, etc.	M. O. funds.	
Adamsville, Tenn	James T. Combs	May 29, 1887	In transit		$203.00	Disallowed; failure to comply with regulations governing remittances.
Alton, N. H.	Herbert L. Jones	Aug. 29, 1887	Burglary		28.80	Disallowed; loss remitted from negligence of claimant.
Anson, Tex	W. McD. Bowyer	Jan. 22, 1887	In transit		10.00	Disallowed; failure to comply with regulations governing remittances.
Bellevue, Miss	William Connell	May 28, 1887	Fire	$7.75		Disallowed; credit allowed for damaged stamps covered the entire loss.
Ball's, Tex	Thomas J. Scott	June 17, 1887	In transit		78.00	Dismissed; the amount claimed has been recovered.
Bickleton, Wash	U. N. Bickle	Apr. 29, 1887	Fire	4.50		Disallowed; not received within the time required by statute.
?ld, Fla	W. D. Mendenhall	Feb. 1, 1887	Burglary	7.33		Do.
Blue Rapids, Kans	A. J. Palmer	Dec. 24, 1884	Fire	33.00		Disallowed; barred by limitation of the statute.
Bonhom m, Mo	Charles L. Boisselier	Mar. 2, 1887	Burglary	33.00		Disallowed; negligence on the part of the claimant.
Buena ??, Colo	C. B. Wilson	Dec. 20, 1886	In transit	All on hand.	225.00	Disallowed; loss occurred at depository office, not in transit.
Butler, Ga.	Walter Stewart	May 3, 1887	...do		2.00	Dismissed; loss made good by a clerk through whose negligence it occurred.
Carlisle, Ind.	Caleb A. Snapp	May 28, 1887	...do		20.00	Dismissed; money recovered and deposited.
Claresville, Va.	T. T. Gaskins	Dec. 22, 1887	Fire	15.65		Abandoned by claimant.
Clifton, ??	W. Y. Montague	Dec. 21, 1886	In transit		50.70	Dismissed; money recovered and deposited.
Concordia, Miss	W. H. Pepperell	Aug. 27, 1887	Burglary	1,345.60		Disallowed; due care not exercised by claimant.
Cowl Springs, Kans	John Wale	Oct. 18, 1887	Theft		45.00	Withdrawn by claimant.
?, Tex	J. N. Boyd	June 10, 1887	In transit		8.00	Dismissed; money recovered and deposited.
?s Plains, N. Y.	D. W. Barkley	May 10, 1887	Burglary	10.73		Disallowed; proper care not exercised to protect the stamps.
Cottonwool, Cal	William Knowlton	Oct. 2, 1887	Burglary	35.14		Disallowed; loss resulted from negligence of claimant.
?lio, Cal	Ira C. ?lle	Oct. 14, 1887	In transit		491.00	Disallowed; not presented within the time prescribed by statute.
Covington, La	Charles Heints	June 30, 1887	...do		106.00	Dismissed; money recovered and deposited.
Defiance, N. Mex	D. M. Smith	May 6, 1887	Burglary	35.00		Dismissed; loss did not result from burglary, fire, or unavoidable casualty.
Delphos, Kans	O. L. Kinsey	Jan. 25, 1887	In transit		20.00	Disallowed; failure to comply with regulations governing remittances.
Deshler, Ohio	D. D. Donnovan	July 14, 1887	...do	Not known.	74.00	Do.
East Falmouth, Mass	Herbert L. Davis	Sept. 11, 1887	Burglary			Disallowed; loss resulted from negligence of claimant.
Eastman, Ga	Eli J. Peacock	Jan. 7, 1888	In transit	131.00		Dismissed; loss made good by postmaster at office of deposit.
Do.	Robert ? ?a	Jan. 27, 1888	...do		1.00	Dismissed; money recovered and deposited.
Do.	...do	Feb. 5, 1888	...do		12.50	Do.
Ellington, Mo	Ibn ?man	July 10, 1887	Burglary	6.00		Disallowed; not presented within the time prescribed by statute.
Do.	...do	Mar. 23, 1887	...do	5.20		Disallowed; loss remitted from negligence of claimant.

Post-offices.	Postmasters.	Date of loss.	Cause of loss.	Amount claimed.		Reasons for disallowance, dismissal, etc.
				Stamps, etc.	M. O. funds.	
Ellingwood Corners, Me.	Charles F. Robinson	Sept. 14, 1887	Burglary	$70.10		Disallowed; loss resulted from negligence of claimant.
Enterprise, Pa.	Myron Dunham	Mar. 11, 1887	do	76.95		Do.
Evergreen, Ala.	P. D. Bowles	Sept. 28, 1885	Not known	15.52		Disallowed; cause of loss not shown.
Farrville, Tex	B. Z. Powell	Aug. 29, 1886	Fire		All on hand	Disallowed; loss resulted from negligence of claimant.
Ferris, Ill.	J. W. Richards.	July 15, 1887	Burglary	74.00		Disallowed; loss resulted from fault or negligence of claimant.
Garrett, Ind.	Mary Thomas	Mar. 8, 1887	In transit.		$20.00	Dismissed; money refunded by the person who stole it.
Gleadale, Colo.	J. D. Curtis	Dec. 6, 1887	Burglary	22.99		Withdrawn; the stamps supposed to have been stolen were found.
Bailey, Idaho.	J. Guy Hammer	Oct. 28, 1887	do	20.00		Disallowed; loss resulted from negligence of claimant, if at all.
Hinckley, Minn	H. B. Garton	Mar. 1, 1883	Fire	Not known		No formal claim filed; case considered as abandoned.
Houma, La.	Caroline Wagner	Feb. 2, 1888	In transit		15.00	Dismissed; money recovered and deposited.
Hunter, N. Y.	W. A. Douglass.	May 10, 1876	Burglary	55.00		Disallowed; not presented within the time prescribed by statute.
Jersey City, N. J.	John G. Gopaill.	Oct. 7, 1887	Embezzlement		200.66	Disallowed; money stolen by a clerk in the post-office.
Kanas, Utah	George B. Leonard	July 17, 1887	Burglary	60.00		Disallowed; loss not proved to have resulted from burglary.
La Fontaine, Ind	Jerome S. Hale	Mar. 15, 1887	In transit		14.00	Dismissed; loss made good by railway postal clerk.
Lake City, Mich.	F. O. Gaffney	Feb. 9, 1888	do		51.00	Disallowed; failure to comply with regulations governing remittances.
Lead Hill, Ark	James M. King	Jan. 31, 1887	do		65.00	Disallowed; failed to deposit daily, as required by section 1063, Postal Laws and Regulations of 1879.
Lexington, Ind	Patrick Storen	Apr. 2, 1887	do		25.00	Disallowed; failure to comply with regulations governing remittances.
Lovelady, Tex	John I. Moore	May 3, 1888	do		4.00	Dismissed; abandoned by claimant.
Ludlow, Miss.	F. P. Smith	Oct. 17, 1885	Burglary	13.16		Disallowed; loss resulted from negligence of claimant.
Lyle's, Pa.	Alfred Wood	Aug. 10, 1887	do	4.80		Do.
Martin, Mich	George Redpath	Feb. 10, 1888	In transit.		12.00	Disallowed; failure to comply with regulations governing remittances.
New Rockford, Dak	E. S. Miller	Dec. 27, 1887	do		20.00	Do.
North Hector, N. Y.	W. R. Welding	Nov. 15, 1887	do		40.00	Dismissed; loss made good by postmaster at Geneva, N. Y.
Ogden, Kans	Theo. Welchelbaum	Nov. 15, 1887	do		111.00	Dismissed; money recovered and deposited.
Opelousas, La.	Louis Desmarais	July 28, 1888	do		21.00	Disallowed; failure to comply with regulations governing remittances.
Ormsburgh, Mo	Charles Simmons	Nov. 4, 1887	Fire	48.32		Disallowed; not presented within the time prescribed by statute.
Osawatomie, Kans.	A. H. Hume	Feb. 22, 1887	In transit		70.00	Disallowed; evidence of remittance unsatisfactory.
Papillion, Nebr.	R. L. Carpenter	Mar. 5, 1887	Burglary	9.00		Disallowed; loss resulted from fault of claimant.
Payne, Ohio.	Daniel E. Kauffman	July 16, 1887	In transit.		104.00	Disallowed; failure to comply with instructions governing remittances.

Office	Claimant	Date	Cause of loss	Amount	Remarks
Patton's Station, Pa.	John M. Walker	Sept. 10, 1887	Fire	13.89	Disallowed; not presented within the time prescribed by statute.
Pemberville, Ohio	John H. Shroeder	Oct. 26, 1887	In transit	154.00	Dismissed; money refunded by the person who stole it.
Do.	Do.	Oct. 7, 1887	...do...	142.00	
Penrod, Ky.	H. C. Penrod	Nov. 15, 1888	...do...	257.00	
Perham, Minn.	Henry Kemper	Jan. 15, 1888	Theft		Disallowed; not within the provisions of the statute.
		Nov. 10, 1886	In transit	110.00	Dismissed; loss made good by Northern Pacific Railroad Company.
Perrysburgh, Ohio	Jas. Hayes	July 22, 1887	...do...	295.00	Dismissed; money refunded by the person who stole it.
Plashwell, Mich.	Jacob V. Rogers	Feb. 10, 1888	...do...	20.00	Dismissed; money refunded by postmaster at Grand Rapids, Mich., where it was lost.
Port ...ton, Ohio	W. W. Montgomery	Jan. 8, 1888	...do...	55.00	Dismissed; money refunded by the person who stole it.
...ter, Ill.	J. M. Firey	Feb. 13, 1888	Burglary	9.49	Disallowed; loss resulted from negligence of claimant.
...ky ...er, Ohio	E. P. Thompson	Nov. 5, 1887	...do...	2.53	Disallowed; proof of loss insufficient.
Runnels, ...	H. D. Pearce	Sept. 29, 1887	In transit	11.00	Dismissed; loss made good by postmaster at Abilene, Kans.
Rye, N. Y.	Daniel Budd	June 5, 1887	Burglary	618.83	Disallowed; loss by burglary not proved.
Saugatuck, Mich	Frank A. Winslow	Oct. 14, 1887	In transit	20.00	Disallowed; failure to comply with regulations governing remittances.
Savoy, Tex.	M. F. Smith	June 16, 1887	...do...	38.00	Dismissed; money recovered.
Seybrook, ...	Samuel H. Pratt	Sept. 16, 1887	Burglary	70.64	Disallowed; loss resulted from negligence of claimant.
Shi..., ...a., Pa.	Mary G. Black	June 20, 1887	...do...	81.26	Do.
Saint Anthony Park, Minn.	F. W. Pickard	Dec. 31, 1887	In transit	5.00	Dismissed; loss did not occur in transit.
Saint ...ph, Minn.	Jno. H. Linnemann	May 21, 1887	Burglary	111.30	Disallowed; loss resulted from negligence of claimant.
Sun, ...	T. A. Guthrie	June 4, 1887	In transit	44.00	Disallowed; failure to comply with regulations governing remittances.
...g, Tenn.	...g Myers	Nov. 12, 1887	Fire	Unknown	Disallowed; not presented within the time prescribed by statute.
Eus, Mo.	Coleman C. Ewalt	May 25, 1887	Burglary	2.00	Disallowed; loss resulted from negligence of claimant.
Trading ..., Kans	James R. Hiatt	Apr. 30, 1886	Fire	110.00	Disallowed; credit allowed for damaged stamps covered entire loss.
Win Lake, Fla.	W. F. Jackson	July 10, 1887	Burglary	0.75	Disallowed; not presented within the time prescribed by the statute.
W..., Pa.	J. C. Christian	Oct. 30, 1878	Fire	28.50	Disallowed; evidence of loss insufficient.
Warsaw, Va.	F. A. Shackleford	June 25, 1887	In transit	26.00	Disallowed; failure to comply with regulations governing remittances.
Yeagertown, Pa.	James H. Mann	Mar. 5, 1888	Burglary	17.81	Disallowed; loss resulted from negligence of claimant.
...lls				3,075.29	3,867.15

EXHIBIT B.—*List of claims on account of loss by fire, burglary, etc. (act of March 17, 1882), disallowed, dismissed, etc.*—Continued.

RECAPITULATION.

Number of claims wholly disallowed, withdrawn, or dismissed............................ 86

Amounts claimed and disallowed,, etc.:
For money-order funds:

Lost by burglary	$37.79	
Lost in transit	3,083.70	
Lost by fire and other causes..	245.66	
		$3,367.15

For stamps, and stamped paper:

Lost by burglary	$2,733.66	
Lost by fire...	261.11	
Lost by larceny..	65.00	
Lost by other causes..	15.52	
		5,075.29
Grand total..		6,442.44

Reasons for disallowance, withdrawal, etc.:

Because not within the provision of the statutes................................	6
Because not presented within the time required by statutes	9
Because evidence as to the fact or amount of loss was unsatisfactory	8
Because of failure to comply with instructions concerning remittances	13
Because of failure to exercise proper care for the protection of the property ...	22
Withdrawn or dismissed...	28
	86

REPORT

OF THE

CHIEF POST-OFFICE INSPECTOR

FOR

1888.

REPORT

OF THE

CHIEF POST-OFFICE INSPECTOR.

POST-OFFICE DEPARTMENT,
OFFICE OF CHIEF POST-OFFICE INSPECTOR,
Washington, D. C., August 18, 1888.

SIR: I have the honor to present the following report of the work of this office for the year ending June 30, 1888.

The first table, marked Exhibit A, presents the criminal statistics of the service:

EXHIBIT A.—*Statement showing number, classification, and disposition of cases of arrests made by post-office inspectors and others during the fiscal year ended June 30, 1888.*

CLASS OF OFFENDERS SUBJECT TO JURISDICTION OF THE UNITED STATES COURTS

State where arrested.	Postmasters.	Assistant postmasters.	Clerks in post-offices.	Railway post-office clerks.	Letter carriers.	Mail carriers.	Other employés.	Burglars.	Special-delivery messengers.	All others, for various offenses.	Total.
Alabama	3		1			1	1			4	10
Arizona											
Arkansas	1	2	2			3			4	10	21
California	1				1				3	4	9
Colorado		1						2	1		4
Connecticut	2	1	2		1				13		19
Dakota	1		1						1		3
Delaware							1		1		2
District of Columbia			2				2		4		8
Florida	5	2		1		2		3	3		16
Georgia	3	1			1			4	5		14
Idaho						1					1
Illinois	10	1	2		3			9	38		63
Indiana	1				1			3	11		16
Indian Territory									3		3
Iowa								1	4		5
Kansas	5	1	1	1				1	10		19
Kentucky	2		1					6	8		17
Louisiana	2	2		3	7		1	1	11		26
Maine	2	1						2	1		6
Maryland						1		4			5
Massachusetts	3		3		1				2	22	31

Exʜɪʙɪᴛ A.—*Statement showing number, classification, etc.*—Continued.

CLASS OF OFFENDERS SUBJECT TO JURISDICTION OF THE UNITED STATES COURTS—Continued.

State where arrested.	Postmasters.	Assistant postmasters.	Clerks in post-offices.	Railway post-office clerks.	Letter carriers.	Mail carriers.	Other employés.	Burglars.	Special-delivery messengers.	All others, for various offenses.	Total.
Michigan	2	1			1			7		7	18
Minnesota	4				1					3	8
Mississippi	3		1			1		4		10	19
Missouri	4	1	3		5	1		7		28	49
Montana										1	1
Nebraska	5		1							6	12
Nevada											
New Hampshire	1									1	2
New Jersey										7	7
New Mexico											
New York	1		3	1	5		1	2		36	49
North Carolina	1					1		6		12	20
Ohio	4		4	1	2		1	2		30	44
Oregon	1							1		1	3
Pennsylvania	8	3	1	1	2	1		29	1	14	60
Rhode Island								1		2	3
South Carolina	3				1			2			6
Tennessee		1	1		1	2		2		2	9
Texas	2	2	3	3		1		6		43	60
Utah	6									4	10
Vermont	1	2	1	1		1					6
Virginia		1			1			6		2	10
Washington Territory								1			1
West Virginia	3							1		4	8
Wisconsin	1	1		1						13	16
Wyoming											
Total	90	24	33	12	34	15	6	123	3	380	719

EXHIBIT A.—*Statement showing number, classification, etc.*—Continued.

DISPOSITION OF CASES SUBJECT TO JURISDICTION OF UNITED STATES COURTS.

State where arrested.	Discharged on preliminary examination.	Tried and acquitted.	Proceedings dismissed.	Escaped.	Forfeited bail.	Died awaiting trial.	Discharged by the United States grand jury.	Convicted.	Awaiting trial.	Sentence suspended.	Total.
Alabama								3	7		10
Arizona											
Arkansas	3	4						2	12		21
California								2	6		9
Colorado		1						2	1		4
Connecticut	1							8	11		19
Dakota									3		3
Delaware								2			2
District of Columbia							1	1	5	1	8
Florida	3	1						2	8	2	16
Georgia	3							1	10		14
Idaho									1		1
Illinois	2	3						30	28		63
Indiana	1							4	11		16
Indian Territory									3		3
Iowa		1				1		1	2		5
Kansas	3			1		1	1	3	11		19
Kentucky	3	2						3	9		17
Louisiana	5	1							20		26
Maine								5		1	6
Maryland	1							1	3		5
Massachusetts		1					1	2	27		31
Michigan								3	15		18
Minnesota								1	7		8
Mississippi	1			1				4	13		19
Missouri	3	2						13	28	3	49
Montana									1		1
Nebraska							2	2	8		12
Nevada											
New Hampshire									2		2
New Jersey									7		7
New Mexico											
New York	1						1	3	44		49
North Carolina	4	1		1				8	6		20
Ohio	2						1	14	27		44
Oregon	1							2			3
Pennsylvania	6	2					1	7	44		60
Rhode Island									3		3
South Carolina	2							1	3		6
Tennessee								3	6		9
Texas	2	1					6	11	40		60
Utah									10		10
Vermont								1	5		6
Virginia								5	5		10
Washington	1										1
West Virginia	1							1	6		8
Wisconsin	1							4	11		16
Wyoming											
Total	49	20		4			15	148	476	7	719

EXHIBIT A.—*Statement showing number, classification, etc.*—Continued.

SUBJECT TO JURISDICTION OF STATE COURTS.

State where arrested.	Offenders.			Disposition of cases.					Grand total in each State.
	Burglars.	All other offenders.	Total.	Convicted.	Acquitted.	Awaiting trial.	Turned over to employers.	Total.	
Alabama	4		4	4				4	14
Arizona									21
Arkansas									12
California		3	3			3		3	5
Colorado		1	1			1		1	22
Connecticut	3		3			3		3	3
Dakota									2
Delaware									8
District of Columbia	2		2			2		2	16
Florida	2		2	1		1		2	16
Georgia									1
Idaho	2	1	3	3				3	66
Illinois	3		3	3					19
Indiana									3
Indian Territory									7
Iowa	2		2	1		1		2	21
Kansas	4		4	2		2		4	19
Kentucky	2		2	1		1		2	26
Louisiana									6
Maine									5
Maryland									35
Massachusetts	3	1	4	2		2		4	31
Michigan	3		3			3		3	8
Minnesota									19
Mississippi									57
Missouri	5	3	8	1		7		8	1
Montana									12
Nebraska									
Nevada									2
New Hampshire									19
New Jersey	6	6	12	1		10	1	12	
New Mexico									
New York		5	5			3	3	5	54
North Carolina									20
Ohio	3	1	4	1		2	1	4	43
Oregon									4
Pennsylvania		1	1			1		1	61
Rhode Island									3
South Carolina									6
Tennessee	1		1	1				1	16
Texas	2		2			2		2	62
Utah									10
Vermont									6
Virginia		1	1	1				1	11
Washington									1
West Virginia	2		2	1		1		2	10
Wisconsin									16
Wyoming									
Total	49	23	72	23		44	5	72	791

EXHIBIT A¹.—*Criminal statistics as shown by the records of this office for the fiscal years ended June 30, 1883, 1884, 1885, 1886, 1887, and 1888. Classification of postal officials, employés, and others arrested in said years.*

Year.	Postmasters.	Assistant post-masters.	Clerks in post-offices.	Railway post-office clerks.	Letter-carriers.	Mail carriers.	Other employés.	Burglars.	All others for various offenses.	Total.
1883	50	26	21	14	21	32	4	68	360	596
1884	36	24	31	8	25	25	4	87	516	756
1885	64	26	35	22	12	19	5	89	266	539
1886	46	31	33	14	24	27	11	79	395	660
1887	94	24	34	11	23	23	12	132	430	773
1888	90	24	32	12	34	15	6	172	406	791

Exhibit A is a condensed statement of the arrests of offenders against the postal laws, and the action taken, as shown by the records of this service, for the past six years. The number of criminals arrested has about kept pace with the increased number of postal employés and the increase in postal business, except in the burglary of post-offices. This crime has increased to an alarming extent, and, in spite of the efforts of this office, continues to grow.

As stated in my last annual report there is no fund provided for rewards, or to pay for assistance from the local authorities to suppress this crime. I deem it my duty to again ask that you bring this matter to the attention of Congress, and request an appropriation of $10,000, to be expended under your direction in offering rewards for the arrest of criminals committing this offense. By reference to Exhibits A¹ and F, you will see that 683 post-offices were reported robbed during this fiscal year, for which only 172 arrests were made. This might seem a small number, but when it is considered that there are over 55,000 post-offices and only 100 inspectors, that the information of a robbery is usually twenty-four hours in reaching an inspector, often much longer, the burglars have time to escape. In my opinion if each postmaster, and through him the local authorities, were assured of a small reward, many more arrests would be made, and at a material saving of money to the Government.

EXHIBIT B.—*Table showing the number of recommendations made by post-office inspectors for the removal of postmasters and other employés from the postal service for violations of the postal laws and regulations, and other causes, also the number of recommendations made for the discontinuance of post-offices during the fiscal year ended June 30, 1888.*

Months when made.	Postmasters.	Assistant post-masters.	Letter-carriers.	Railway post-office clerks.	Special-delivery messengers.	Clerks in post-offices.	Discontinuance of post-offices.	Total.
July, 1887	40	3	5	......	1	......	26	75
August, 1887	40	1	5	4	......	......	33	83
September, 1887	46	......	3	......	......	......	33	82
October, 1887	63	2	......	......	2	1	41	109
November, 1887	73	1	2	1	1	......	51	129
December, 1887	66	......	4	2	......	......	50	122
January, 1888	46	1	1	1	......	......	23	72
February, 1888	63	1	6	......	......	......	30	100
March, 1888	51	......	2	2	......	......	27	82
April, 1888	59	......	9	5	......	......	32	105
May, 1888	59	1	2	8	......	1	19	85
June, 1888	57	3	3	5	......	......	26	94
Total	663	13	42	25	3	1	391	1,138

Exhibit B presents the corrective and reformative work of the inspectors. As compared with last year the increased number of recommendations is marked. This is doubtless caused by the fact that so large a number of the fourth-class offices were inspected and that we had an average of twenty-five more inspectors this year than last.

EXHIBIT C.—*Record of "A" (registered) cases referred to inspectors in previous years reported upon and closed during the fiscal year ended June 30, 1888.*

States.	O.K.	No loss. Cause of complaint.					No inclosure.	Not rifled.	Not rifled in Post-Office Dep't.	Not registered and not mailed.	Loss resulting from—				
		Improper address.	Unavoidable delay.	Carelessness.	Improper despatch.	Other causes.					Burning of post-office.	Burning of car.	Wreck of train, etc.	Estimated amount lost.	Amount recovered.
Alabama	9			1		1									
Alaska															
Arizona							2								
Arkansas	5							2							
California	4	2		1	1			2		1					
Colorado	1						1	1							
Connecticut	2				1				2					$12.00	
Dakota	2						1	2			1			$12.00	
Delaware															
District of Columbia	14					4									
Florida	2														
Georgia	1			1		1	1	2							
Idaho	1														
Illinois	7	1			2			1							
Indiana	4														
Indian Territory															
Iowa	2					1									
Kansas	7		1	1	3		1	4						77.20	
Kentucky	3			1	1			3	1		5				
Louisiana	3														
Maine															
Maryland															
Massachusetts	2		1		2			1							
Michigan	3		1	2			1								
Minnesota	1			1				1							
Mississippi	1				3		1								
Missouri	3	1		2			1	4	1						
Montana	1														
Nebraska	4			7		1	4		1						
Nevada															
New Hampshire								1							
New Jersey	1							1							
New Mexico	1						2						1	2.55	
New York	8				1		1	1							
North Carolina					1			1			1				
Ohio	5	1		1			1	2	1						
Oregon	1				1		1	1		1					
Pennsylvania	5				1			1		1					
Rhode Island					1										
South Carolina	1				1		2	1	1						
Tennessee	5			2											
Texas	4			3	1			1			1			10.00	$10.00
Utah							1	1							
Vermont								1							
Virginia	3			1	1	1	1			1					
Washington								1							
West Virginia	2				1		1	1							
Wisconsin	1			1		1	1	2							
Wyoming	1			1											
Total	121	5	3	26	20	12	23	26	7	3	8	1		101.75	10.00
				66											

EXHIBIT C.—*Record of "A" (registered) cases referred to inspectors in previous years reported upon and closed during the fiscal year ending June 30, 1888*—Continued.

States.	Chargeable to the depredations of—						Chargeable to depred'ns of—			Loss by postal employés, other causes than theft.						
	Postmaster.	Assistant postmaster.	Clerks in post-office.	Other employés.	Amount lost.	Amount recovered.	Railway post-office clerks.	Amount lost.	Amount recovered.	Accidental.	Carelessness of postmaster.	Carelessness of railway postal clerk.	Carelessness of other employés.	Other causes.	Amount lost.	Amount recovered.
Alabama		1	33	12	$583.86	$89.57					5	1	1		$52.90	$38.40
Alaska																
Arizona																
Arkansas											2		2		34.00	32.00
California			5		63.00						1				10.00	10.00
Colorado											1				.60	.60
Connecticut			1		5.00	5.00					3		1		33.50	33.50
Dakota											2				30.00	30.00
Delaware																
District of Columbia																
Florida																
Georgia			1		4.00						1	1			6.60	6.60
Idaho	1				29.78						4	1			24.05	24.05
Illinois			1		25.00	25.00									10.00	
Indiana										2					88.57	
Indian Territory										1	6	3			11.06	11.06
Iowa											1				88.10	
Kansas			1		10.00						3				88.50	20.00
Kentucky	1				100.00						2	1	2		58.50	38.50
Louisiana											1	1			14.00	14.00
Maine												1			25.00	25.00
Maryland																
Massachusetts																
Michigan				1	3.25	3.25					3	1			25.20	25.20
Minnesota				1	110.00	110.00	29	$103.75		1			1			
Mississippi			2		20.00	17.25					1	1			130.00	130.00
Missouri											4				44.50	44.50
Montana										1			1		22.50	22.00
Nebraska											3	1		1	360.23	335.23
Nevada																
New Hampshire																
New Jersey											3				106.00	
New Mexico																
New York										3	1				3.50	2.50
North Carolina											3				17.00	17.00
Ohio	1				20.00		1			2	4				33.08	33.08
Oregon			1		50.00											
Pennsylvania			1		10.00									1	5.00	5.00
Rhode Island																
South Carolina	2		5	1	21.25	21.25				1			1		11.75	11.75
Tennessee			5		86.00						1	1	1		56.50	56.50
Texas	2		5		77.00		9	218.05	$92.00							
Utah																
Vermont			2		24.00						1				9.00	9.00
Virginia				12	175.25		1	162.62								
Washington							1	23.44		1					10.00	
West Virginia										1					.50	
Wisconsin										1	3				31.51	30.00
Wyoming																
	7	1	56	29	1,417.39	262.62	41	807.89	92.00	14	59	13	11	1	1,303.05	1,095.04
			93													

Exhibit C.—*Record of "A" (registered) cases referred to inspectors in previous years, reported upon, and closed during the fiscal year ended June 30, 1888.*

States and Territories.	Loss resulting from—					Amount recovered.	Loss paid through the Post-Office Department.	Loss paid direct by outside parties.	Amount paid outside.	No recovery.	No discovery.	Total number of cases by States.
	Robbery of post-offices.	Robbery of train.	Robbery of stages, etc.	Theft.	Amount lost.							
Alabama							17			36	7	71
Alaska												
Arizona		4			$8.00					4		6
Arkansas								3	$33.00	1	2	1.
California								1	10.00	5	3	20
Colorado							1				2	6
Connecticut							5				1	11
Dakota							2			1	3	11
Delaware												
District of Columbia												18
Florida							1	1	1.60			4
Georgia							4	1	10.00	1	1	13
Idaho												2
Illinois	1				.60		1			3		18
Indiana							9	1	.51		1	15
Indian Territory			10		21.52			1	11.06	10		11
Iowa							2			1		8
Kansas	4				134.90	$90.00	8			2	1	28
Kentucky				1	2.35	2.35	2	1	9.00	6	2	20
Louisiana	1				260.00		1			1	1	6
Maine												
Maryland												
Massachusetts							5	1	10.00	18	2	6
Michigan	18						1			30	1	23
Minnesota							4			1	2	35
Mississippi	1				5.00	5.00				1	2	12
Missouri				1				4	44.50	2	2	19
Montana							1			1		3
Nebraska							1	3	333.23	1	1	23
Nevada												
New Hampshire										3		5
New Jersey										1		4
New Mexico										2	4	20
New York	1				5.00	5.00	3			1	4	10
North Carolina							4	2	6.50	2	2	20
Ohio										1	1	7
Oregon							1			1	3	10
Pennsylvania												1
Rhode Island												
South Carolina							2	3	11.75			10
Tennessee	1				25.25	25.25	4			6	1	18
Texas		5			79.00		1			21		31
Utah												2
Vermont							1			2		4
Virginia										13		21
Washington										2	2	5
West Virginia										1		5
Wisconsin	1				20.00	20.00	2	2	21.00	1	1	12
Wyoming												2
Totals	28	9	10	2	560.72	156.60	86	23	502.15	181	53	599

Exhibit C shows the result of investigation in the 599 "A" cases which were left uninvestigated at the close of the last fiscal year, and which have received attention this year. In my last report I estimated that actual loss to remitters would result in one-third of these cases, making the total loss for 1887, 1,031 cases, but investigation shows loss in 234 out of the 599 cases, changing the result to a total of 1,065 cases in which loss occurred in 1887, and from one loss in every 11,556 to one in every

11,187 of registered pieces handled. This result strengthens and confirms the correctness of my estimate of the actual losses for the years 1883, 1884, and 1885.

EXHIBIT D.—*Number and character of complaint, by States, upon which "A" cases were made up and referred to post-office inspectors for investigation during the fiscal year ended June 30, 1888.*

States and Territories.	In which contents were stated when complaint was made.	Contents not stated.	Contents stated.	Not stated.	Total.	Rifling.	Loss.	Loss from R. P. R.	Detention.	Wrong delivery.	Tampering.	Carelessness of postal employés.	Improper dispatch.	Other causes.	Total.
	Letters.		**Packages.**			**Alleged cause of complaint.**									
Alabama	75	113	1	3	192	39	131	9	2	4	3	....	3	1	193
Alaska	....	....	....	....	....	....	....	....	....	....	....	....	....	....	....
Arizona	8	11	...	5	24	7	8	5	...	...	1	....	...	3	24
Arkansas	41	68	1	4	114	31	63	11	...	1	2	....	1	5	114
California	47	51	7	8	113	36	61	10	1	4	....	....	...	1	113
Colorado	46	113	4	1	164	35	116	5	3	1	2	....	...	2	164
Connecticut	10	30	43	9	92	7	77	2	...	2	....	....	2	2	92
Dakota	32	37	1	1	71	27	32	9	...	2	....	....	...	1	71
Delaware	3	1	....	....	4	....	4	....	...	...	....	....	...	...	4
District of Columbia	19	302	2	13	336	5	319	6	3	....	....	....	...	3	336
Florida	48	43	....	2	93	43	34	5	4	3	3	....	...	1	93
Georgia	42	51	2	5	100	29	53	6	3	3	4	....	...	2	100
Idaho	11	9	...	2	22	5	7	2	1	...	2	....	1	1	22
Illinois	84	114	2	30	230	72	115	16	5	6	4	1	1	10	230
Indiana	88	46	2	....	136	74	40	7	4	5	....	1	1	2	136
Indian Territory	6	25	...	1	32	4	20	3	1	1	....	....	...	3	32
Iowa	35	34	1	5	75	20	35	12	1	....	....	....	...	1	75
Kansas	92	94	1	5	192	62	93	15	4	10	2	....	1	5	192
Kentucky	55	63	1	5	124	56	50	13	1	....	1	....	...	3	124
Louisiana	44	61	...	3	108	36	48	4	...	1	1	....	...	18	108
Maine	9	13	...	...	22	8	11	1	1	...	....	....	...	1	22
Maryland	41	31	...	1	73	37	29	3	1	...	1	....	1	1	73
Massachusetts	17	29	1	7	54	9	30	3	2	8	1	....	...	1	54
Michigan	52	43	...	3	98	31	54	7	2	3	1	....	...	...	98
Minnesota	22	28	1	1	52	23	22	1	...	3	1	....	...	2	52
Mississippi	37	60	...	7	104	39	37	19	1	1	6	....	1	...	104
Missouri	70	92	1	9	172	54	91	16	2	4	2	....	2	1	172
Montana	18	17	...	2	37	11	19	4	...	...	2	....	1	...	37
Nebraska	57	84	2	5	148	39	73	17	6	8	1	....	...	4	148
Nevada	3	6	...	....	9	2	5	2	...	...	....	....	...	...	9
New Hampshire	5	7	...	...	12	4	7	...	...	1	....	....	...	...	12
New Jersey	10	29	1	2	51	11	30	2	...	5	2	....	1	...	51
New Mexico	10	15	...	...	25	5	17	...	...	...	2	....	...	1	25
New York	78	122	44	45	280	80	178	11	2	12	2	....	2	2	289
North Carolina	42	43	...	...	85	23	40	8	1	1	1	....	...	11	85
Ohio	107	128	...	8	243	87	125	12	1	5	6	....	2	5	243
Oregon	16	25	1	3	45	12	28	1	...	2	....	....	...	2	45
Pennsylvania	98	120	4	10	232	59	142	10	5	7	2	....	2	5	232
Rhode Island	2	2	...	...	4	1	2	...	...	...	....	....	...	...	4
South Carolina	19	15	...	2	36	16	13	...	1	1	....	1	...	4	36
Tennessee	39	41	...	2	82	40	30	9	...	...	3	....	...	...	82
Texas	131	179	3	8	321	109	164	12	20	2	2	2	....	1	321
Utah	16	27	2	1	46	16	24	2	1	1	2	....	...	...	46
Vermont	3	5	...	1	9	2	5	2	...	...	....	....	...	...	9
Virginia	75	92	...	1	168	52	77	24	7	1	2	1	...	4	168
Washington	18	20	...	...	38	8	20	4	1	5	....	....	...	...	38
West Virginia	39	17	...	1	57	32	19	3	1	1	....	....	...	1	57
Wisconsin	34	28	...	2	64	22	29	4	2	...	2	....	1	4	64
Wyoming	11	10	...	1	22	10	9	1	1	...	....	....	...	1	23
Totals	1,874	2,594	128	224	4,820	1,433	2,638	318	100	120	66	6	24	115	4,820

Exhibit D shows the number and class of complaints and alleged cause of loss and detention in the domestic registered mail during this year. The 599 cases left over from last year have been accounted for in Exhibit C. The total number of complaints was 4,820. The number last year was 5,286, showing a reduction of 466 complaints.

The total number of letters and packets registered has increased from 11,914,792 in 1887 to 12,957,611 in 1888.

EXHIBIT E.—*Record of registered "A" cases referred to inspectors, investigated, and reported upon during the fiscal year ended June 30, 1888.*

States.	O.K.	No loss. Cause of complaint.						No inclosure.	Not rifled.	Not rifled in Post Office Department.	Not registered and not mailed.	Loss resulting from—			Estimated amount lost.	Amount recovered.
		Improper address.	Unavoidable delay.	Carelessness.	Improper despatch.	Other causes.						Burning of post office.	Burning of car.	Wreck of train, etc.		
Alabama	46	2	....	6	3	8	3	4	4	1	....	....	....	....	....
Alaska															
Arizona	12						1		1						
Arkansas	34	1	....	3	4	2	2	5	....		4	....			
California	56	1	1	2	5	2	1	3	2	4					
Colorado	42	2	1	5	7	58	4	9	2	4					
Connecticut	57	1	1	1	6	1	...	1	...	1	1	....	....	$10.00	.....
D.kota	26	...	1	1	1	2	2	8	2						
Delaware	2									1					
District of Columbia	248	...	2	...	1	4	...	1	...	2	1				
Florida	44	...			1	1	3	6	1	1					
Georgia	45	...	1	3	2	6	1	6	1	...	1	....	....	5.00	$5.00
Idaho	10	...		3	1	...	1								
Illinois	89	3	5	6	3	7	6	19	4	4					
Indiana	43	1	1	4	...	2	2	13	3	...	1	....	....	50.00	.....
Indian Territory	9	...		2	...		2	1..							
Iowa	37	1	...	1	...	5	4	4	1	4					
Kansas	67	1	...	1	3	6	3	7	1	1					
Kentucky	27	...	1	5	2	6	6	5	2	4	....	....	13	75.91	75.91
Louisiana	36	1	...	2	2	...	1	1	1						
Maine	10	1	1	1	...		1	1	1						
Maryland	18	...		1	1	2	...	5	2						
Massachusetts	24	...	1	1	1	4	2	...	1	1					
Michigan	32	...		6	3	...	4	4	4	1	2	....	....	30.00	.....
Minnesota	16	...		3	1	...	1	2	...	2					
Mississippi	30	2	...	2	...	2	4	5							
Missouri	63	3	1	7	2	3	6	11	4	6	1	....	....	30.00	.....
Montana	11	...	1	3	2	1	1	4	1						
Nebraska	50	1	1	9	9	13	4	8	3	2	1				
Nevada	3							1							
New Hampshire	5	...		3	...		1	...	1						
New Jersey	25	...		3	...	2	1	...	3	1	2	....	....	106.00	1.00
New Mexico	10	...		1	...	2	...		1						
New York	95	2	1	5	4	9	3	17	4	3					
North Carolina	34	1	1	1	...		2	3	1						
Ohio	64	3	1	7	8	4	5	17	1	1					
Oregon	15	...		6	2	3	1	1	1						
Pennsylvania	66	2	3	10	...	3	1	13	4	8	2	....	....	15.75	.....
Rhode Island	2	1	...		1										
South Carolina	13	...	1	1	...	1	1	2	2	2	....	1			
Tennessee	25	...			1	1	3	3	1	1					
Texas	88	2	3	4	10	9	2	16	2	3					
Utah	18	...			1	...	3								
Vermont	7	...					1								
Virginia	57	...	1	5	5	9	4	8	3	1					
Washington	11	...			...	1	1	1							
West Virginia	15	...		1	...		2	3							
Wisconsin	28	2	1	2	...	1	3	5	1						
Wyoming	7	...			2	...	2	1	...	1					
Total	1,772	34	31	125	94	175	103	233	68	65	15	1	13	325.66	84.91

459

EXHIBIT E.— *Record of registered "A" cases referred to inspectors, investigated, and reported upon during the fiscal year ended June 30, 1888—Continued.*

States and Territories.	Postmaster.	Assistant postmaster.	Clerks in post-office.	Other employés.	Amount lost.	Amount recovered.	Railway post-office clerks.	Amount lost.	Amount recovered.	Accidental.	Carelessness of postmaster.	Carelessness of railway postal clerks.	Carelessness of other employés.	Other causes.	Amount lost.	Amount recovered.
					Chargeable to the depredations of—		Chargeable to depred't'ns of—			Loss by postal employés, other causes than theft.						
Alabama	5		14	10	$218.87	$61.10	15	$253.85	$93.85	1	8	1	5	1	$97.57	$97.57
Alaska																
Arizona										1	2				46.00	46.00
Arkansas		3			100.00	100.00				1	1	1	2	1	47.80	47.80
California			1								12			1	151.60	147.10
Colorado	23				132.95					7	3	1	2	1	136.21	120.21
Connecticut										2	2		1		16.95	16.95
Dakota			6		43.00					4	3	1			144.54	138.59
Delaware																
District of Columbia											1				8.00	8.00
Florida	18				158.76	158.76				1					2.50	2.50
Georgia			3		47.26	27.26				3	9		2	4	325.42	325.42
Idaho										1			1		50.00	50.00
Illinois	4		1		110.00					6	5	3	4		697.62	596.27
Indiana	1		2		22.00	22.00				32	5		1	1	122.62	117.52
Indian Territory							5	20.00			4				39.75	39.75
Iowa							1	115.00		3	6	1			142.00	42.00
Kansas	3		13		1,143.90	492.90				19	8		1		317.06	314.56
Kentucky	2	1			78.50					5	3	2			124.85	112.85
Louisiana				3	37.00	12.00	4			5	2		2		102.45	63.60
Maine											2	1			12.25	12.25
Maryland		1		6	180.50	20.00				17	1	3			42.40	42.40
Massachusetts										1	2	1			65.50	65.50
Michigan			3		83.00	83.00				4	5	1	3		157.90	156.40
Minnesota							11	133.60		4	5		2		100.00	100.00
Mississippi		2		2	6.37	2.32				2	7		2		111.24	111.10
Missouri	2				2.85	2.85				4	11	5	3		472.17	277.04
Montana				1	30.00	30.00					10				117.70	117.70
Nebraska	3		8	1	88.75	68.00				4	1	1	1		27.75	27.75
Nevada											1				15.00	
New Hampshire																
New Jersey			1		97.50	97.50					3				43.00	43.00
New Mexico										1	3	2			150.82	150.82
New York			3	1	32.00	32.00				7	8	5	1		103.88	81.88
North Carolina			2	1	56.85	56.85				4	13	1	1		263.41	263.41
Ohio				10	1,018.00	1,018.00				14	9	5	2		272.43	272.43
Oregon										1	6	1	2	1	177.50	177.50
Pennsylvania	1		1	1	423.27	28.27				9	12	8	1		280.25	280.25
Rhode Island											1				6.00	6.00
South Carolina		1			5.00	5.00				3	1				41.83	41.83
Tennessee		1	1	1	70.00	70.00				1	3	1	7		139.00	139.00
Texas	2	10	28	1	517.89	161.39	10	855.00		2	9	22		3	595.49	561.49
Utah											3				72.00	72.00
Vermont											1	1			8.25	8.25
Virginia				6	143.00		3	82.00		4	7		2		111.60	109.99
Washington			1		15.00	15.00					6	1	2		157.93	157.93
West Virginia							3	30.19	30.19	19	3				137.51	129.54
Wisconsin										2	5	2			232.40	232.40
Wyoming										1	1				6.50	6.50
Total	64	19	98	33	4,803.22	2,491.20	52	1,439.64	124.04	195	212	73	52	9	6,465.74	5,791.05
		214														

Exhibit E.—*Record of registered "A" cases referred to inspectors, investigated, and reported upon during the fiscal year ended June 30, 1888*—Continued.

States and Territories.	Loss resulting from—						Loss paid through the Post-Office Department.	Loss paid "direct" by outside parties.	Amount paid "outside."	No recovery.	No discovery.	Total number of cases by States.
	Robbery of post-offices.	Robbery of trains.	Robbery of stages, etc.	Theft.	Amount lost.	Amount recovered.						
Alabama................	1	....	2	6	$66.53	$66.53	41	8	$58.63	20	2	148
Alaska	....	....	....	....	....	....	....	....	....	....	....	....
Arizona	....	....	6	....	74.00	....	1	1	6.00	7	....	23
Arkansas..............	....	....	27	....	217.70	149.46	20	1	2.30	19	4	95
California.............	....	....	....	....	....	....	10	2	12.40	2	7	98
Colorado	....	9	....	1	108.63	5.00	10	3	20.82	34	2	178
Connecticut	....	....	....	1	5.00	5.00	5	....	....	2	....	76
Dakota	....	....	....	....	....	....	3	3	126.50	8	....	87
Delaware	....	....	....	....	....	....	1	....	....	....	....	4
District of Columbia...	....	....	....	....	....	....	....	....	....	....	4	268
Florida	1	....	....	..	100.00	100.00	21	....	....	....	....	79
Georgia	....	....	....	4	97.90	97.90	22	3	178.63	1	1	92
Idaho.................	....	....	....	....	....	....	1	....	50.00	1	....	17
Illinois...............	10	....	....	2	853.93	208.00	11	7	702.75	17	7	188
Indiana...............	10	....	....	....	112.37	45.50	21	19	99.74	13	1	123
Indian Territory.......	2	....	....	....	7.00	7.00	5	1	3.50	5	....	26
Iowa..................	7	....	....	1	87.00	....	3	3	26.00	12	2	77
Kansas	13	....	....	1	95.00	65.00	38	4	17.00	16	7	155
Kentucky	3	....	....	1	108.00	3.00	23	....	....	6	6	93
Louisiana	10	....	....	....	5.50	....	4	1	16.10	21	1	71
Maine	....	....	....	....	....	....	3	....	....	....	....	19
Maryland	1	....	....	1	5.00	5.00	8	15	37.47	6	3	64
Massachusetts.........	....	....	....	1	1.00	1.00	5	....	....	....	4	42
Michigan	1	....	....	2	46.33	46.33	12	5	54.95	4	4	79
Minnesota	....	....	....	....	....	....	8	3	45.00	11	2	49
Mississippi............	....	....	....	8	78.34	20.00	13	1	2.35	9	8	76
Missouri..............	8	....	....	5	84.75	31.00	24	4	34.50	11	5	150
Montana..............	....	....	....	....	....	....	10	....	....	1	2	37
Nebraska..............	21	....	....	1	247.27	5.00	16	1	....	25	3	145
Nevada	....	....	....	....	....	....	....	....	....	1	....	6
New Hampshire	1	....	....	....	4.13	4.13	1	....	....	....	....	10
New Jersey............	3	....	....	....	16.50	16.50	6	2	28.50	1	2	47
New Mexico...........	....	....	....	....	....	....	2	2	140.00	....	....	18
New York	14	....	....	8	93.77	93.77	27	3	13.90	17	7	202
North Carolina........	....	....	....	1	20.00	20.00	7	18	192.41	3	3	74
Ohio	8	....	....	49	1,006.30	39.75	31	12	163.59	54	6	214
Oregon	....	....	....	....	....	....	10	1	3.00	..	4	44
Pennsylvania..........	12	....	....	2	175.47	34.43	28	5	10.25	16	4	162
Rhode Island	....	....	....	....	....	....	1	....	....	....	....	5
South Carolina	1	....	....	....	35.00	....	5	....	....	2	2	32
Tennessee	6	....	....	....	4.25	....	10	4	29.00	7	3	50
Texas.................	10	8	19	6	756.21	526.38	58	2	23.50	69	5	273
Utah	....	....	....	....	....	....	2	1	50.00	....	1	26
Vermont..............	....	....	....	....	....	....	1	1	2.37	....	....	10
Virginia..............	....	....	....	2	22.00	15.00	10	1	7.00	13	15	132
Washington...........	....	....	....	....	....	....	10	....	....	....	....	24
West Virginia	....	....	....	....	....	....	9	14	56.57	2	..	46
Wisconsin	....	....	....	....	....	....	6	2	17.00	1	3	55
Wyoming..............	....	....	....	....	....	....	1	1	5.00	....	....	15
Total	142	17	54	101	4,434.78	1,610.68	563	150	2,235.83	427	128	3,978

Exhibit E shows the result of investigation of the complaints set forth in Exhibit D. Of the total number of complaints made (4,820), 3,978 were investigated and closed, leaving for future inquiry 842 cases. The following condensed statement taken from the footings of Exhibit E shows the result of inquiry in 3,978 cases:

Total number as shown by Exhibit D 4,820
Ascertained causes of complaint:
 No loss, properly delivered 1,772
 Improper address.. 34

Ascertained causes of complaint—Continued.

Unavoidable delay	31
Careless handling	125
Wrong despatch	94
Other causes	175
No inclosure, ne loss	103
Not rifled, no loss	233
Not rifled by postal employé	68
Not registered	65

Total, no loss, no just ground for complaint	2,700
Cases in which the loss was recovered and paid to the proper owner	713

Total number of cases investigated in which no loss was sustained	3,413

Cases in which loss resulted from accidents, no blame attaching to postal officials:

From burning of post-offices	15
From burning of postal cars	1
From wrecking of postal cars	13
From other accidental causes	195
From theft by postal officials	213
From causes not ascertained	128

Number awaiting attention	842

It is shown that loss was sustained in 565 cases of the 3,978 investigated. Add to this number 280 cases, or one-third of the 842 cases outstanding (this is the basis adopted for the past five years) and we have a total loss of 845 cases out of a total number of registered articles sent for the year of 12,957,611, or one piece out of every 15,334 pieces handled. The loss last year was placed at 1,031 pieces. Investigation of the 599 cases left over showed a loss of 234 pieces (instead of 200), estimated, increasing the actual loss for last year to 1,065 pieces out of a total number of pieces registered of 11,914,792, or one piece out of every 11,187 pieces handled.

EXHIBIT F.—*Statement of complaints received and result of complaints investigated, Class B, ordinary letters.*

COMPLAINTS RECEIVED.

Where mailed.	Letters.	With inclosures.	Without inclosures.	Packages.	Post-offices robbed.	Post-offices burned.	Postal cars wrecked or burned.	Stages robbed.	Mail messengers or wagons robbed.	Pouches lost.	Pouches cut into etc.—ally or by accident, or stolen.	Total number of complaints received.
Alabama	184	135	46	95	23	8	2	2		1	2	318
Arkansas	94	77	17	28	11	11	2	3		1	4	154
California	708	503	205	388	6	15	1	3		16	1	1,138
Colorado	304	232	72	140	4	1	5	2		3	3	462
Connecticut	729	538	191	341	21	3				3	2	1,099
Delaware	94	84	10	23	5							122
Florida	212	155	57	87	11	3	2			1	3	319
Georgia	503	388	115	225	16	12	2	1		4	3	766
Illinois	2,001	1,478	523	2,088	36	18	4			7	46	4,200
Indiana	484	388	96	311	34	14	2			2	7	854
Iowa	365	290	75	236	21	12	7			2	19	652
Kansas	447	372	75	199	45	10	2	1		8	15	727
Kentucky	318	247	71	323	22	14	2	1		1	7	688
Louisiana	237	174	63	130	4	2	2	2		7	2	386
Maine	230	189	41	156	5	8				2	3	404
Maryland	515	396	119	314	10	5					3	847
Massachusetts	1,616	1,278	338	706	18	3				7	13	2,363
Michigan	584	487	97	318	23	10	1			1	4	941
Minnesota	287	233	54	179	9	7	3			4	11	500
Mississippi	117	88	20	40	6	11	1			2	7	184

EXHIBIT F.—*Statement of complaints received and result of complaints investigated, Class B, ordinary letters*—Continued.

COMPLAINTS RECEIVED—Continued.

Where mailed.	Letters.	With inclosures.	Without inclosures.	Packages.	Post-offices robbed.	Post-offices burned.	Postal cars wrecked or burned.	Stages robbed.	Mail messengers or wagons robbed.	Pouches lost.	Pouches cut intentionally or by accident, or stolen.	Total number of complaints received.
Missouri	867	686	181	918	56	17	2	....	..	10	21	1,891
Nebraska	327	279	48	148	12	7	6	....	1	3	4	508
Nevada	18	11	2	3	..	..	3	....	..	..	..	16
New Hampshire	158	137	21	64	4	3	..	....	..	1	..	231
New York	6,317	4,375	1,942	4,951	39	16	3	....	..	3	11	11,329
New Jersey	874	595	279	305	19	5	..	....	..	1*	..	1,205
North Carolina	183	129	54	50	10	11	..	1	..	7*	5	268
Ohio	1,407	1,123	284	1,098	62	15	4	....	..	6	11	2,608
Oregon	58	45	13	14	5	5	..	4	..	..	..	86
Pennsylvania	3,047	2,597	450	1,661	43	23	2	....	..	1	11	4,788
Rhode Island	183	134	49	75	5	..	..	....	..	1	1	265
South Carolina	158	127	31	60	8	4	..	....	..	1	..	231
Tennessee	319	228	91	169	9	9	3	....	..	..	1	510
Texas	364	279	85	174	25	18	8	10	3	35	8	645
Vermont	135	102	33	74	3	3	1	....	..	1	1	218
Virginia	453	351	102	131	9	9	..	....	..	4	4	610
West Virginia	144	125	19	27	13	10	..	1	..	..	3	198
Wisconsin	463	403	60	239	14	11	..	....	..	5	12	744
Alaska	1	1	..	..	..	..	..	....	..	..	..	1
Arizona	35	31	4	6	1	1	..	5	..	..	..	48
Dakota	109	82	27	53	2	8	..	....	..	3	4	179
District of Columbia	512	416	96	300	..	..	1	....	..	2	2	817
Idaho	27	19	8	9	3	..	..	1	..	..	..	40
Indian Territory	5	5	..	2	3	..	..	....	..	..	2	12
Montana	40	35	5	11	2	..	..	....	..	1	2	56
New Mexico	54	41	13	26	1	1	1	....	..	2	..	87
Utah	34	23	11	16	2	1	1	....	..	..	..	55
Washington Territory	63	41	22	22	2	4	1	....	..	..	1	93
Wyoming	26	20	6	6	..	..	..	2	..	1	4	39
	26,405	20,175	6,230	16,940	683	348	72	40	4	150	266	44,917

RESULT OF COMPLAINTS INVESTIGATED.

Where mailed.	No discovery.	No loss.	Losses chargeable to carelessness or depredation of postal employés.	Losses chargeable to accident.	Losses chargeable to persons not in the postal service.	Cases still in hands of inspectors for investigation.
Alabama	117	82	53	1	4	61
Arkansas	36	42	36	1	2	37
California	407	220	121	2	1	387
Colorado	212	143	59	3	4	41
Connecticut	266	151	342	....	6	234
Delaware	64	21	25	....	2	10
Florida	115	81	52	2	2	67
Georgia	153	186	290	2	8	127
Illinois	2,151	544	727	26	8	744
Indiana	367	124	218	1	2	212
Iowa	247	109	82	10	..	203
Kansas	128	145	193	7	1	253
Kentucky	176	142	144	1	2	223
Louisiana	15	32	300	1	2	36
Maine	205	65	91	....	4	39
Maryland	282	160	260	....	5	140
Massachusetts	704	358	830	5	20	396
Michigan	246	128	266	3	2	295
Minnesota	189	75	66	10	....	160
Mississippi	47	42	42	....	1	52
Missouri	199	288	1,092	5	6	301
Nebraska	207	160	90	8	2	41

EXHIBIT F.—*Statement of complaints received and result of complaints investigated, Class B, ordinary letters*—Continued.

RESULT OF COMPLAINTS INVESTIGATED—Continued.

Where mailed.	No discovery.	No loss.	Losses chargeable to carelessness or depredation of postal employés.	Losses chargeable to accident.	Losses chargeable to persons not in the postal service.	Cases still in hands of inspectors for investigation.
Nevada	6	2	3	....	1	4
New Hampshire	72	35	81	....	3	40
New York	2,161	1,233	5,844	2	27	2,062
New Jersey	384	145	391	....	15	270
North Carolina	94	50	67	....	8	49
Ohio	722	145	646	3	5	1,082
Oregon	42	20	2	1	5	16
Pennsylvania	1,181	651	2,413	7	70	466
Rhode Island	50	26	91	2	38	48
South Carolina	90	51	47	....	....	43
Tennessee	156	104	90	2	....	158
Texas	159	167	159	2	8	150
Vermont	64	43	89	....	1	22
Virginia	236	117	145	1	14	97
West Virginia	95	37	32	1	1	32
Wisconsin	231	106	178	7	3	219
Alaska	1	....	....	....	....	0
Arizona	17	9	7	6	1	8
Dakota	61	46	22	1	....	49
District of Columbia	273	172	237	....	....	135
Idaho	20	10	2	....	1	7
Indian Territory	....	6	3	....	1	2
Montana	25	14	....	....	2	15
New Mexico	40	26	13	....	2	6
Utah	14	8	6	....	....	27
Washington Territory	44	27	5	....	....	17
Wyoming	9	13	10	2	....	5
	12,820	6,570	16,013	125	300	9,089

Exhibit F clearly shows the complaints of all kinds, depredations on and accidents to the ordinary domestic mail and postal property for this fiscal year; also the place or State of depredation or accident. Forty-four thousand nine hundred and seventeen complaints were filed as compared with 42,096 last year. Considering the increased amount of mail handled, as indicated by increased number of stamps sold, this statement indicates a decided improvement in the service. The only exception is in the increased number of post-offices reported robbed. As heretofore stated this crime continues to increase and demands a remedy, which I have heretofore suggested, viz, the appropriation of a sum of money by Congress, to be used under your direction, for paying rewards for the arrest of post-office burglars. This appropriation was recommended by ex-Postmaster General Vilas in his last annual report. At the request of the House Committee on Post-Offices and Post-Roads, I appeared before that committee and urged the passage of this appropriation. I am under the impression that the need for this appropriation is conceded by the committee, but so far no action has been taken.

EXHIBIT G.—*Number, nature of case, and office of original reference of miscellaneous cases (Class C) referred to post-office inspectors for investigation during the fiscal year ended June 30, 1888.*

Class of cases.	First Assistant Post-master-General.	Second Assistant Post-master-General.	Third Assistant Post-master-General.	Superintendent of the Money-order system.	General Superintendent of the Railway Mail Service.	Assistant Attorney-General Post-Office Department.	Superintendent Free-Delivery system.	Law clerk Post-Office Department.	Superintendent of the Foreign Mails.	Office of Chief Post-Office Inspector.	Auditor of the Treasury, Post-Office Department.	Total number of each class.
Responsibility of sureties....	2,419	....	....	....	....	....	....	....	....	....	1	2,419
Inspection of post-offices....	6	....	89	....	....	1	....	....	....	26,297	1	26,394
Complaints and charges vs. postmasters and employes of post-offices	687	4	13	23	22	......	3	....	....	533	1	1,266
Violation of section 259 Postal Laws and Regulations of 1887..................	....	....	426	....	....	....	....	....	....	5	1	432
Establishment of post-offices and stations	42	....	....	....	....	......	1	....	....	29	......	72
Discontinuance of post-offices and stations............	27	....	....	....	....	....	....	....	....	114	......	141
Allowances for post-offices....	118	....	....	....	....	....	....	....	....	31	......	149
Location, change of site or name of post-offices........	179	....	....	....	....	....	....	....	....	39	......	218
Appointment of postmasters.	119	....	....	....	....	....	....	....	....	20	......	139
Free-delivery system	1	....	....	....	....	....	76	....	....	1	......	78
Mail-messenger service	....	10	....	....	....	....	....	....	....	56	......	66
Lease of post-offices	....	....	....	....	....	....	....	162	....	....	......	162
Routes: Establishment, discontinuance, or change of service	....	24	....	....	....	....	....	....	....	212	......	236
Routes: Charges vs. contractors, carriers, etc.	5	22	....	....	....	....	1	....	....	57	......	85
Mail-keys: Loss, etc	1	24	....	....	2	....	....	....	....	172	......	199
Charges against railway post-office clerks...........	....	....	....	....	20	....	....	....	....	22	......	42
Claims for credit by postmasters, etc...............	....	....	....	....	....	....	....	....	....	....	......	....
Collection of balance due the United States.......	....	....	....	....	....	....	..	....	....	3	31	34
Inspection of money-order business, collection of funds, forwarding statements, and instruction of postmasters..............	....	....	....	154	....	....	....	....	....	1	......	155
Wrong payment of money-orders, postal notes, etc....	....	....	....	81	....	....	....	....	....	5	......	86
Establishing money-order service..................	....	....	....	....	....	....	....	....	....	16	......	16
Discontinuance of money-order service	....	....	....	19	....	....	....	....	....	....	......	19
Postal Laws and Regulations of 1887:												
Section 380..............	7	....	4	....	4	....	....	....	....	143	......	158
Section 379..............	....	....	....	....	....	....	....	....	....	15	......	15
Section 375..............	....	....	....	....	....	....	....	....	....	2	8	10
Section 706..............	....	....	....	....	....	....	....	....	....	3	......	3
Section 1442.............	1	....	....	....	....	....	....	....	....	4	......	5
Section 1447.............	40	....	2	....	9	....	....	....	....	122	......	173
Section 1448.............	6	....	1	....	3	....	....	....	...	112	......	122
Section 1449.............	....	....	....	....	1	....	....	....	....	13	......	4
Section 1451.............	....	....	....	....	2	....	....	....	....	9	......	15
Section 1460.............	13	1	2	2	......	6	....	....	....	176	......	200
Section 1464.............	....	....	17	....	....	....	....	....	...	....	......	17
Section 1469.............	....	....	3	....	....	1	....	....	...	83	1	88
Miscellaneous investigations and complaints	211	67	98	72	43	3	9	3	....	486	30	1,022
	3,866	152	655	351	10	11	90	165	....	28,781	73	34,250

Exhibit H.—*Disposition by office of Chief Post-office Inspector of miscellaneous cases, Class C, referred to and reported upon by post-office inspectors during the fiscal year ended June 30, 1888.*

Disposition.	Number.	Disposition.	Number.
Referred to the honorable Postmaster-General	28	Referred to Superintendent Free Delivery	96
Referred to the honorable First Assistant Postmaster-General	3,868	Referred to Auditor of the Treasury for Post-Office Department	61
Referred to the honorable Second Assistant Postmaster-General	622	Placed on file in office of Chief-Post-Office-Inspector	869
Referred to the honorable Third Assistant Postmaster-General	465	Inspection reports (form 573) divided and referred to First and Third Assistant Postmaster-Generals, and	
Referred to Superintendent Money Order System	345	to Superintendent of the Money-Order System	19,581
Referred to General Superintendent Railway Mail Service	130		
Referred to Assistant Attorney-General	11	Total	26,237
Referred to the law clerk, Post-Office Department	161		

EXHIBIT I.—*Recapitulation.*

	Number.
Cases. Class C. referred to inspectors for investigation during fiscal year 1887-'88	34,250
Such cases on hand July 1, 1887, referred for investigation during previous years	5,627
Total to be accounted for	39,877
Number of such cases referred to inspectors, reported upon, and finally closed during the fiscal year 1887	26,237
Number of such cases referred to inspectors during previous years, reported upon and finally closed during the fiscal year 1887-'88	5,308
Total number of such cases closed	31,545
Number of such cases remaining in the hands of inspectors July 1, 1888 (uninvestigated)	8,332

Exhibits G, H, and I present the miscellaneous or C cases treated by this office during the past year in as comprehensive a shape as the nature and variety of the cases will permit.

A glance at the tables gives but a faint idea of the work and time required to properly report on the various subjects treated. By special request of ex-Postmaster-General Vilas Congress appropriated $100,000 in addition to the regular appropriation of $200,000 for mail depredations for the purpose of inspecting the accounts of postmasters of the fourth class, and instructing them in their duties. This class of work was commenced on July 1, 1887, and during the year the greater part of the time of this force was devoted to that special work, not, however, to the detriment or neglect of current work. Previous to 1886 no general inspection of the post-offices of the country had ever been undertaken; only such offices, generally of the higher grades, as required special examination had received this attention. In my opinion, this is the true function of an inspector, the conservator and instructor of the postal service. During 1883, 1884, and 1885 only 360 offices are reported to have been inspected; during 1886, 1,030; 1887, 4,238; and the past year 24,889. The good result to the postal service in all its branches can not be accurately estimated or intelligently stated in figures or tables.

The records of every branch of the Department plainly indicate its good results—in the promptness with which reports are sent in to the Third Assistant Postmaster-General's Office and deposits of postal funds are made; in the decrease of complaints against the conduct of postmasters in the office of the First Assistant Postmaster-General; in the saving and curtailment of expenses on mail-messenger and star-route service; the relocation of star routes in the Second Assistant Postmaster-General's Office; promptness in rendering reports and deposit of money-order funds. In the Sixth Auditor's Office a material improvement is shown in the receipts of the Department from the fourth-class offices, notably in the decreased rate per cent. of expenses to receipts from that class of offices.

There is also a marked improvement in the accuracy and safety with which the registered and ordinary mail is handled, as shown by exhibits of this report. In the prosecution of this work all offices of every grade have been inspected in Florida, Utah, Idaho, and the six New England States. In Alabama, California, Colorado, Delaware, Georgia, Illinois, Indiana, Kansas, Louisiana, Maryland, Michigan, Minnesota, Mississippi, Missouri, Nebraska, New Jersey, New York, Ohio, Oregon, Pennsylvania, Tennessee, Texas, Virginia, and Wisconsin all offices where the gross revenue or receipts amount to $10 or more per quarter have been inspected, except 6,716 offices now receiving attention, principally in Tennessee, Illinois, Indiana, Texas, and California. In Arizona, Arkansas, Dakota, Iowa, Kentucky, Montana, Nevada, North Carolina, South Carolina, Washington, West Virginia, and Wyoming this work has not been undertaken, for the reason that the appropriation for this purpose was not renewed for this fiscal year. It is proper to state that it is the intention of this office to continue this work to as great an extent as the means at its disposal will justify. It is believed that the present force can dispose of the 6,716 cases on hand and at the same time not neglect current work during the fiscal year ending June 30, 1889. The amount of money recovered from delinquent postmasters in the course of this work, and by reason of this inspection, is greater than the whole amount expended by the Department for the performance of the work. I submit for your consideration and decision the expediency of asking a renewal of this special appropriation for next year.

Note.—The amount charged to account of delinquent postmasters, under section 259, Postal Laws and Regulations, 1887, fraudulent return of stamps canceled for previous years, $205,633.37.

Amount charged as above during this fiscal year........................	$40,991.23
Amount of money-order funds collected of and caused to be deposited by delinquent postmasters..	133,138.44
Amount of postal funds collected from delinquent postmasters for other causes and paid into the Treasury..	3,395.45
Total amount so collected and caused to be deposited by inspectors for the year..	177,525.12

CLASS F.—FOREIGN CASES.

In this class are comprised all cases relating to alleged loss, delay, non-delivery, tampering, and other irregularities (including violations of customs regulations and of specific sections of the Postal Laws and Regulations) so far as concerns registered and ordinary mail matter passing between foreign countries and the United States.

These cases are subdivided into three general classes as regards the character of the complaints, and the treatment varies materially in the investigation of each class. These subdivisions consist of cases relating to registered mail matter, unregistered mail matter, and cases having reference to miscellaneous complaints against postmasters and postal employés in their handling and treatment of foreign mail.

Of class F cases there were reported to this office for investigation during the fiscal year ended June 30, 1888, 10,855. Of these 6,683 related to registered mail, 3,802 to unregistered mail, and 370 to miscellaneous complaints. Of the whole number 6,855 were reported from domestic sources, and 4,000 (approximately) were reported by foreign postal administrations.

The total number of registered cases treated of and closed during the year, in which no actual loss was sustained, was 5,690; while the number in which the loss was not accounted for, or when accounted for, no recovery could be effected, was only 246. The following tables, marked Exhibits K and L, will show between what foreign countries and what States the mail matter was passing, the character of the mail matter, and the localities chiefly affected.

EXHIBIT K.—*States and countries between which the registered mail was passing, and number of cases in which investigation determined that no loss had been sustained.*

States and Territories.	Austria.	Belgium.	Central America.	Canada.	Denmark.	France.	Germany.	Great Britain.	Hungary.	Italy.	Mexico.
Alabama				1			11	4		2	
Alaska				1							
Arizona				1			1	1			4
Arkansas	1			2			6		2	1	
California	36		3	10		9	59	83	1	32	7
Colorado	7					1	21	16		14	2
Connecticut	2			4		2	14	10	1	15	1
Dakota	4		1	6	2		7	11			
Delaware	1						3	2			
District of Columbia	2	1	2	5		2	16	12		3	5
Florida	2			4		1	3	8		3	1
Georgia	1						6	3		1	
Idaho							1	2			
Illinois	28	4		13		4	122	70	3	23	
Indiana	2			1	1		16	9	1		
Indian Territory							1			1	
Iowa	15			6			21	13			
Kansas	7		1	1			21	15			
Kentucky				1		1	5	3	1	1	1
Louisiana	8		4	6		8	9	5		15	1
Maine	2			12			1	5		5	
Maryland	4		2	1		1	16	3		2	1
Massachusetts	11			68		9	21	93	1	39	1
Michigan	9		1	8	1	3	40	20	1	5	
Minnesota	21			4		1	36	8		5	
Mississippi	1			2		1	6	2		3	
Missouri	20			8		5	47	29	3	9	6
Montana	2			1		1	10	12		1	
Nebraska	10			2	4		36	11			
Nevada				1				8		3	
New Hampshire				1				4			
New Jersey	10	1		1		3	35	25	6	14	1
New York	107	4	36	24	2	59	848	217	13	238	98
New Mexico				1			11	8			1
North Carolina				1			2	1			
Ohio	21		1	11		1	106	28	5	12	1
Oregon	7			1			7	8		4	
Pennsylvania	54	3	2	17	1	18	161	94	26	87	8
Rhode Island					2		3	11		4	
South Carolina						1	2	2	1	1	
Tennessee	2	1					3	3	1	3	
Texas	12					2	40	25	1	10	4
Utah				1	1	1	12				
Vermont							1	5			
Virginia	1	1	1			2	5	7			
Washington	7			4			7	13		1	
West Virginia	1					1	3	2		2	
Wisconsin	14	2		18			64	8		5	1
Wyoming	1							3			
Total	436	17	54	244	16	134	1,354	944	67	564	144

Exhibit K.—*States and countries between which the registered mail was passing, and number of cases in which investigation determined, etc.*—Continued.

States and Territories.	Netherlands.	Norway.	Russia.	Spain.	Sweden.	Switzerland.	South America.	United States of Colombia.	West Indies.	Miscellaneous.	Total.
Alabama											18
Alaska											2
Arizona										1	11
Arkansas						2					14
California		1	10	2	3	10	4		1	8	279
Colorado			1		1		1				64
Connecticut			6		1		3		2	1	62
Dakota		4	4		1		2				42
Delaware			1				1				8
District of Columbia		2	3	1	1	3	4			1	63
Florida			1		1			1	3	1	29
Georgia			1								12
Idaho		1	1								5
Illinois	1	4	17	1	16	7	1			1	324
Indiana		1	1	1	1		1		1	2	38
Indian Territory											2
Iowa		5	1		4	1	1		1		68
Kansas			6	1	2	4			1	1	60
Kentucky							1			1	15
Louisiana				2		1	2		6	3	70
Maine					1		2				29
Maryland		1	5				2		1		38
Massachusetts			24		6	2	5		1	4	285
Michigan	1		7		6	5					107
Minnesota		20	7		11	1					114
Mississippi		3									18
Missouri			6		2	5	2			1	143
Montana						2					29
Nebraska		1	1		2					1	68
Nevada											11
New Hampshire											5
New Jersey	2	4	7			4	4	1	1		119
New York	2	2	68	8	8	17	472	122	112	17	1,974
New Mexico		1				2					24
North Carolina											4
Ohio	1	1	13		1	7	6		8		218
Oregon			1		2					1	31
Pennsylvania	1	1	44	2	7	7	11	5	4	10	558
Rhode Island			1		2					1	27
South Carolina			1		2						10
Tennessee			1						1		16
Texas			7	3		3	1			2	111
Utah		1			2						19
Vermont						1				1	8
Virginia	2					1			1		21
Washington					2		1				35
West Virginia											9
Wisconsin	1	8	1	1	7	3			1		129
Wyoming											5
Total	11	61	247	22	91	91	527	129	140	59	5,352

EXHIBIT L.—*States and countries between which the registered mail was passing, which, after investigation, remained unaccounted for, or in which the loss or depredation was located, but no recovery effected.*

States and Territories.	Austria.	Belgium.	Canada.	Denmark.	France.	Germany.	Great Britain.	Hungary.	Italy.	Mexico.	Norway.	Russia.	Spain.	Sweden.	Switzerland.	South America.	U. S. Colombia.	Miscellaneous.	Totals.
Arizona			1																1
California			2	1	1					5		1							10
Colorado			2		1					1		1							5
Connecticut												1							1
Dakota					1							1							2
District of Columbia												1							1
Florida																1			1
Georgia					1														1
Illinois			2			3			3	4	1	3		1				1	19
Indiana			1									1							2
Iowa			1									1							2
Kansas			1		1							1							3
Kentucky					1	1													2
Louisiana						1			2					1					4
Maine			3									1							4
Maryland					1							2						1	4
Massachusetts			3			2		1				2							8
Michigan			3		8							1							12
Minnesota			3												1				4
Mississippi	2																		2
Missouri		1			2							1							4
Montana			1		1														2
Nebraska					1							2							3
New Jersey					2		1	3	1			2							9
New York	3	1	3	2	2	7		8	12			6	1		1		1	4	51
New Mexico				1															1
Ohio						3		2	2	1		1							9
Oregon						1	1												2
Pennsylvania	1		2			4	6	5	3			5		1	1				28
Tennessee										1		1							2
Texas					1					2		2							5
Utah						1													1
Washington			1			5						1							7
Wisconsin						1													1
Totals	6	2	28	1	8	42	19	8	23	17	1	37	2	3	2	1	1	6	202

In addition to the cases embraced in the foregoing table (Exhibit K), there were 338 cases of foreign origin, in which the mail matter was simply passing through the United States in transit to some other foreign country, and which were closed without loss to the persons interested; and in addition to those mentioned in Exhibit L there were 44 cases in which losses of foreign registered letters occurred in the United States by wrecks or burning of post-offices or cars, and in which the losses could not be made good or the exact origin or destination of the mail be ascertained. The table of losses, Exhibit L, may be summarized as follows:

Registered letters lost in which neither the facts or circumstances could be ascertained by investigation, ... 55
Registered letters lost for which no recovery could be made or indemnity paid .. 40
Registered letters alleged to have been rifled in transit through the mails, in which cases the depredation could not be located either in the United States or in foreign countries 75
Number of cases in which the depredation was believed to have been located, but no recovery could be made.. 9
Registered letters or packets ascertained by foreign correspondence to have been confiscated, in Russia, by reason of dutiable or unmailable nature of contents .. 23

The unregistered cases treated of in Class F and disposed of during the fiscal year are indicated on the following table, marked **Exhibit M**. The entire number is 3,824, of which 1,253 cases were closed without loss, and in 2,578 cases the losses remained unaccounted for.

EXHIBIT M.—*States and countries between which the unregistered mail was passing which became the subject of investigation, and number of cases involved.*

States and Territories.	Austria	Belgium	Central America	Canada	Denmark	France	Germany	Great Britain	Hungary	Italy	Mexico	Netherlands	Norway	Portugal	Russia	Spain	Sweden	Switzerland	South America	Turkey	U.S. Colombia	West Indies	Miscellaneous	Totals.
Alabama								2																2
Arizona								1																1
Arkansas								1																6
California	1			19	2	8	11	80		9	1			1	1							1	11	154
Colorado				14		2		20	2	1					1									41
Connecticut				16		2	4	38	1			2									1	1	2	66
Dakota	1			12		1	1	5			2					1						1		32
Delaware				2			1	3														1		8
District of Columbia	1	3		7		4	3	9	1			1										1	1	31
Florida				4			1	19																24
Georgia				4			1	6																11
Illinois	1	2		77	1	22	55	96	3	2	2	4		1		13	1			2		1	3	286
Indiana				10			6	11																31
Iowa	1	1		14	2		8	15								2								43
Kansas	1	1		16		1	5	16		1						1								42
Kentucky				9		5		7	1	1						1								24
Louisiana				5	1	8	7	10		2	3				2	1				3		8		49
Maine				14				12														2	3	31
Maryland	1			14		11	12	13	1		4			2			1	1				3		63
Massachusetts		2		98	2	21	10	119	2	1						5	1	1	3			2	5	272
Michigan	1	1		60		3	2	43		7	1					1	1					1	4	125
Minnesota				21	4		5	22			2					2						1	1	58
Mississippi				2				3																6
Missouri	1	1	2	47		9	17	82	1	3					2		2						2	119
Montana				3				5																8
Nebraska		1		3		2	4	16		1	1	1				1							2	32
Nevada				2	1																			3
New Hampshire				8			1	4																13
New Jersey	1	1		20		6	14	63		1	1					1							2	110
New Mexico				1		2		6																9
New York	19	18	5	363	3	102	164	520	2	19	20	5	8	1	14		9	17	15	7	9	72	29	1,421
North Carolina								4																6
Ohio				32		11	21	62		2		2			3		1					1	2	137
Oregon							1	8																9
Pennsylvania	2	3		57	1	20	25	184	3	3	2	2			7		1	5	2			7	5	329
Rhode Island				2		1		30																33
South Carolina	1					1		6										1						9
Tennessee				3			2	12		1														18
Texas			1	6	1	3	3	29		1	1					1							1	47
Utah				2	1			14																17
Vermont				8			4	3																15
Virginia				4		1	1	11														1	1	19
Washington							1	6									1							8
West Virginia							1	2																3
Wisconsin	1	1		17	2	4	13	14				3										1	2	58
Wyoming				1				6																7
Totals	33	37	7	1,000	20	256	406	1,597	6	39	44	25	22	1	33	2	38	32	21	11	14	105	75	3,834

The character of the mail matter embraced in the foregoing table may be stated as follows:

```
Unregistered packets.............................................  1,742
Unregistered letters containing inclosures.......................  1,476
Unregistered letters without inclosures..........................    613
                                                                   ------
                                                                    3,831
```

From this total should be deducted seven cases, regarding mail originating in foreign countries and passing through the United States to some other foreign countries, and therefore not included in the table.

The miscellaneous foreign cases, Class F, consisted of 338 cases treated and closed during the fiscal year, of a character indicated as follows:

Cases based upon complaints of United States collectors of customs of the non-payment of duty on mail matter imported from foreign countries, intended for delivery in this country 132

Complaints of the circulation of lottery circulars sent from foreign countries into the United States... 38

Complaints originating with the Superintendent of the Money-Order System, as to wrong or irregular issue and payment of foreign money-orders, etc.... 35

Miscellaneous complaints of the violation of specific sections of the postal laws by use of the mails between the United States and foreign countries, and other cases not coming under the classes previously mentioned............ 133

338

SUMMARY.

Number of F cases on hand undergoing treatment, in the hands of post-office inspectors and in the office of chief post-office inspector, on July 1, 1887... 1,940

Number of new cases reported July 1, 1887, to June 30, 1888.................... 10,855

12,795

Number of such cases completed and closed for the year....................... 10,044

Number in the hands of inspectors July 1, 1888............................... 64

Number on hand undergoing treatment in the office of chief post-office inspector, July 1, 1888 2,687

12,795

The number of foreign cases on hand at the end of the fiscal year is necessarily large, for the reason that it requires time to receive replies from foreign administrations. In some instances a month or six weeks is sufficient time in which to receive replies from abroad, but in other cases five or six months may be necessary, and some peculiar cases may even be under correspondence for as long a period as two years.

The number of communications received from foreign departments, intended for treatment by this office, and requiring translation, was approximately 4,500. The necessary translations were furnished by the office of the Superintendent of Foreign Mails.

Of the whole number of foreign cases (Class F) treated for the fiscal year, 897 were sent to inspectors for investigation and report, and 9,147 were treated by correspondence in the office of chief inspector.

EXHIBIT N.—*Statement of the receipt and disbursement of moneys collected and recovered on account of lost and rifled registered and ordinary letters for the fiscal year 1888.*

RECEIPTS.

Balance remaining over, unexpended, from the fiscal year 1887—being moneys recovered during previous fiscal years, but not disbursed for various reasons.. $550.59

Total amount collected and recovered from July 1, 1887, to and including June 30, 1888 .... 12,347.57

Total 12,898.16

DISBURSEMENTS.

In 709 A cases (registered)..$11,020.50

In 33 B cases (ordinary) 268.36

In 4 C cases (special).. 55.50

In 21 F cases (registered)..................................... 338.32

Sums covered into the United States Treasury (no proper owners found):

In 3 A cases (registered) 27.50

In 13 B cases (ordinary)................................... 174.32

In 8 special cases.. 325.43

12,209.93

Balance remaining over, unexpended, at the end of the fiscal year 1888 .... 688.23

No. 1.—*Statistics relating to the domestic registered mail, as shown by the records of this office for the fiscal years ending June 30, 1883, 1884, 1885; 1886, 1887, and 1888.*

Fiscal years.	Total complaints of loss, rifling, missent, and other depredations or accidents on or to the domestic registered mail.	Total lost each year.			Total letters and packages registered each year.	Total letters and packages handled to one piece lost.
		Ascertained by investigation.	Estimated on unfinished business.	Total.		
1883...................	4,266	418	743	1,161	10,127,121	8,722
1884...................	4,238	516	743	1,259	10,750,155	8,508
1885...................	4,912	500	743	1,243	10,531,842	8,472
1886...................	4,281	1,042	....	1,042	11,102,607	10,655
1887...................	5,286	1,065	....	1,065	11,914,792	11,187
1888...................	4,820	565	*280	845	12,967,611	15,334

* One third of cases awaiting attention (842) shows 280, the estimated loss.

Total number of complaints on the registered mail for fiscal year................................ 4,820
Total number investigated.. 3,978

Awaiting attention 842

No. 2.—*Depredatory and accidental statistics on the ordinary mail and postal property of the United States, as shown by the records of this office for the fiscal years ended June 30, 1883, 1884, 1885, 1886, 1887, and 1888.*

Year.	Number and class and cause of complaints, accidents, and losses.									Result of investigation and number unattended to each year.				
	Letters reported lost or missent.	Packages reported lost or missent.	Post-offices reported robbed.	Post-offices reported burned.	Postal cars reported wrecked or burned.	Mail trains and stages robbed.	Mail messengers reported robbed.	Pouches reported as lost, out, and stolen.	Total complaints of all kinds received.	Complaints in which no discovery was made.	Complaints in which there was no loss.	Losses chargeable to depredations and carelessness of postal employés.	Losses chargeable to accidental causes.	Complaints unattended to at the end of each year.
1883	29,908	10,310	468	200	15	19	.....	67	40,987	36,656	3,562	....	.....	.....
1884	20,377	12,078	467	278	24	23	.....	186	33,433	29,545	2,910	....	.....	.....
1885	*35,409	(*)	459	256	55	33	.....	198	36,410	....	....	....	.....	.....
1886	24,215	13,741	487	269	76	27	7	206	39,028	8,413	7,687	13,075	82	9,771
1887	24,423	16,264	620	298	81	13	18	†379	42,096	12,829	8,117	11,180	170	9,850
1888	26,405	16,940	683	348	72	40	4	†425	44,917	12,820*	6,570	16,013	425	9,089

*Consolidated.
† A large proportion of these reported losses was due to the misconnection of the railroad trains, thus delaying through registered pouches and causing immediate complaint, which, upon investigation, resulted in no loss.

Table showing amount realized from the sale of postage-stamps and the percentage of increase for the fiscal years 1885, 1886, 1887, and 1888.

Year.	Amount of sales.	Increase over previous years.
		Per cent.
1885..	$40,056,226.69	1.7
1886..	41,447,095.88	3.4
1887..	45,670,983.84	10.1
1888..	*50,000,000.00	9.0

* Estimated.

Summary of work received and performed by inspectors during the fiscal year ending June 30, 1888, and the amounts of money appropriated, expended, and recovered.

		Number and class of cases.				
		A.	B.	C.	F.	Total.
Cases on hand, June 30, 1887		599	9,850	5,627	1,940	18,016
Cases made up and referred during the year		4,820	44,917	34,250	10,855	94,842
Total number of cases to be investigated		5,419	54,767	39,877	12,795	112,858
Total number of cases investigated and closed....		4,577	45,678	31,545	10,044	91,844
Total number of cases receiving attention June 30, 1888...		842	9,089	8,332	2,751	21,014

Number of arrests caused by post-office inspectors 791

Total amount of money caused to be collected and turned into the United States Treasury $177,525.12
Total amount of money caused to be collected from depredators on the United States mails 12,347.57

Total amount caused to be collected... 189,872.69
Amount appropriated for this service.. 300,000.00
Amount expended for this service.. 290,799.66

Summary of work performed by post-office inspectors during the fiscal years 1884, 1885, 1886, 1887, and 1888, except that as regards the number of "F" (foreign) cases below stated are treated for the most part in this office.

	1884.	1885.	1886.	1887.	1888.
Arrests caused by post-office inspectors	756	539	660	773	791
A cases made and referred to inspectors	4,238	4,912	4,261	5,286	4,820
B cases so referred............	33,668	36,410	37,956	42,096	44,917
C cases so referred	4,870	6,604	13,544	18,260	34,250
F cases treated and referred to inspectors	7,634	8,343	7,773	9,362	10,855
Total.....................	50,410	56,269	63,554	75,009	94,842
Cases investigated and closed :					
A cases...................	4,590	4,550	6,583	5,680	4,577
B cases...................	28,930	31,266	58,262	42,017	45,678
C cases...................	5,223	6,404	12,345	14,514	31,545
F cases...................	8,391	8,451	7,173	8,774	10,044
Total....................	47,134	51,219	84,363	70,985	91,844
Money recovered from depredators on mails	$18,198.81	$15,203.43	$14,522.23	$11,548.13	$12,347.57
Money recovered from post-office employés and turned into the United States Treasury.....................	$26,927.11	$58,352.44	$100,991.41	$242,403.72	$177,525.21
Total amount recovered	$45,125.92	$73,555.87	$115,513.64	$253,951.85	$189,872.69
Amount appropriated........	$200,000.00	$200,000.00	$200,000.00	$200,000.00	$300,000.00
Total amount of money expended	$187,186.00	$199,239.57	$194,955.39	$197,624.63	$290,799.66
Cases on hand at end of each fiscal year...................	....	46,221	13,445	18,016	*21,014

* Of this number (21,014), 6,716 are cases of inspection of post-offices (not current work), leaving actually 14,298 cases in the hands of inspectors for investigation.

A candid consideration of Table No. 1, and comparison of the results for the different years, proves conclusively that the safety of the registered mail has materially and steadily improved for the past three years; and that its present treatment is decidedly better than heretofore. In support and proof of this claim I call attention to the fact that the number of camplaints this year has decreased 466, or 8 per cent.; the number of losses has decreased 220, or 20 per cent.; while the number of pieces handled has increased 1,042,819, or 8¾ per cent.; and the ratio of pieces lost to pieces handled has decreased from 1 in 11,187 to 1 in 15,334, a decided improvement. It is thus shown, in every respect, that the registered mail is more safely handled, more accurately delivered, in 1888 than in 1887 or previous years.

Table No. 2, compiled from the records of this office, presents the depredations and casualties to the ordinary mail and postal property for the past six years. In my opinion it fully sustains the claim of improved mail service, more definitely made in Table No. 1. Unquestionably the volume of ordinary mail has largely increased, as shown by the increased revenue of the Department from the sale of postage-stamps (see foot of Table No. 2). In 1887 the total number of complaints was 42,096; in 1888, 44,917, an increase of only 2,821, while the revenue increased $4,329,017.

Very respectfully,

WM. A. WEST,
Chief Inspector.

Hon. DON M. DICKINSON,
Postmaster-General.

REPORT

OF THE

TOPOGRAPHER OF THE POST-OFFICE DEPARTMENT

FOR

1888.

REPORT

OF THE

TOPOGRAPHER OF THE POST-OFFICE DEPARTMENT.

POST-OFFICE DEPARTMENT, TOPOGRAPHER'S OFFICE,
Washington, D. C., August 27, 1888.

SIR : Referring to the general operations carried out in the above branch of the Post-Office Department, I have the honor to submit the following report for the fiscal year ending June 30, 1888.

A. Hoen & Co., Baltimore, Md., had the contract during the year for the production of bi-monthly editions of the post-route maps. They have faithfully fulfilled the conditions of their contract as to date of delivery and finish of work. April 11, 1888, proposals were issued, inviting bids for the reproducing and furnishing so many copies of the post-route maps every two months during the fiscal year ending June 30, 1889. Two bids were received : (1) Julius Bien & Co., of New York City, $15,000; (2) A. Hoen & Co., Baltimore, Md., $15,000. In all the items referred to in the proposal both bidders are alike, with the single exception of the item referring to the printing of special railway maps; in this case Julius Bien & Co. are above A. Hoen & Co.'s bid ; the latter, being the lowest bidder, was awarded the contract for the current fiscal year. A. Hoen & Co. exceed their previous bid in the sum of $500, though the number of maps allowed to each State has not been increased. I attribute this advance to the increasing number of corrections necessary to erase from the lithographic stones, and the absense of a lively and active competition among the craft. For the past four years the competition has been chiefly confined to Julius Bien and A. Hoen. Both are practical and skilled in the matter of post-route corrections transferred to lithographic stones. Lithographers have called on me for all necessary information, carefully examined the correction sheets, but, owing to the peculiar character of the work, which consists in a series of erasures (on the stones) made month after month, they declined to bid, stating that "there was no money in the work."

The 38 lithographic stones (known as the black) now in charge of A. Hoen & Co. are the property of the Post-Office Department.

The 180 color stones in use for representing the "star service" in distinct color lines are the property of A. Hoen & Co.

During the fiscal year six editions of post-route maps are received, issued every second month. Two thousand five hundred sheets form one edition, which, when placed and arranged in the order of their respective State boundaries and junction lines (allowing each State its allotted number of maps as per schedule), produce in the aggregate 930

51

maps, showing clearly the entire postal service throughout the country, from Maine to California.

The total number of maps received during the year amount to 5,580. In order to provide against any unforeseen mishap (through fire or otherwise) to the lithographic stones, the contractor, immediately after the printing of each edition, has to deposit two copies each of twenty-five maps with the Safe Deposit and Trust Company, Baltimore, Md.; the receipt for such deposit is sent to the topographer. The chief clerk of the Post-Office Department receives a monthly report from the topographer referring to the sales of maps, as well as the general distribution of post-route maps, official and otherwise.

All post-route maps becoming obsolete and useless are delivered over to the superintendent and disbursing clerk of the Post-Office Department. All maps leaving the topographer's office, by sale or otherwise, is through written orders emanating from headquarters.

At the close of the fiscal year ending June 30, 1888, the sales of post-route maps (authorized by law) were as follows : Two hundred and thirty maps, mounted on cotton, and trimmed with strips and rollers; 340 maps furnished in sheets. The cash receipts received for the latter (570 maps) amounted during the year to the sum of $1,885.50. For the fiscal year ending June 30, 1887, 276 maps mounted, and 423 maps in sheets, were sold; cash received for the sale of 699 maps, $2,291.

Hence, comparing the cash receipts of the corresponding periods, there is a decrease of $405.50. It is respectfully suggested that, in reviewing the topographer's estimate for the production of post-route maps, renewals of lithographic stones and working material, too much reliance should not be placed in the factor, yearly derived from the sales of post-route maps. For the detailed distribution of post-route maps, I respectfully refer you to the tabular statement appended to this report.

The effective force engaged in this branch of the service number 25 employés (17 males and 8 females), and are classed as follows :

Topographer (in charge)	1
Skilled draughtsmen preparing sheets for lithographer (7 males, 1 female)	8
Projector and compiler of new maps	1
Draughtsmen engaged in drawing new maps	2
Filling in detail work on new edition of sheets (females)	4
In charge of color routes, and examiner (female)	1
Clerk in charge of records	1
Corresponding clerk (female)	1
Map-mounters	2
Office messenger	1
Watchmen	2
Charwoman	1

Eight draughtsmen are specially employed in preparing a series of correction sheets for the guidance and information of the lithographer; pending the issue of an edition, 240 sheets are interchanged between the topographer and lithographer. From day to day a graphic exhibit on said sheets is kept up of all post-offices established, changed, and discontinued, with their attendant and contiguous star routes, as well as the extension of additional and changed railway service, all of which have to be transferred to the lithographic stones for new impressions; hence the cause of the numerous erasures and re-erasures on the working surface of the stones, so that, after a period of five years, the life or usefulness of the latter is impaired.

In connection with the above duty the eight draughtsmen referred to have to correct, revise, and "bring up" 313 maps used for daily reference at the headquarters of the Department. During the year I have received (through the Postmaster-General) 929 letters emanating from the Second Auditor of the Treasury Department; these letters referred to 1,456 queries as to the shortest and most practicable mail route between two given points traveled by officers and soldiers of the U. S. Army during the years 1861 to 1865 (inclusive). Replying to these queries called for the computation (from paper) of 953,020 statute miles. The following new work has been supplied during the fiscal year ending June 30, 1888 :

Seven hundred lithographic sheets of Texas.

Five hundred lithographic sheets of Minnesota.

These 1,200 sheets show the Railway Mail Service with all necessary side connections, and were delivered to the General Superintendent of the Railway Mail Service.

One hundred lithographic sheets of central Florida.

Environs of San Francisco and Los Angeles, Cal.; the latter are laid down to an enlarged scale, and appear lithographed on their respective sheets for ready reference.

Two thousand lithographic index diagrams, showing the order in which the post-route maps are published, are attached to the price-list of maps.

The new map of Kentucky and Tennessee (in four sheets), referred to in previous yearly reports, is now in the hands of the lithographer. During the current fiscal year new maps of Texas and California will be prepared.

To insure accuracy in plotting the relative position of post-offices circular queries and location papers are daily sent to postmasters in order that they may be correctly shown. When instructed by the railway adjustment division concerning additional and changed railway service, special tracings are made of the immediate surrounding country and sent to superintendents or chief engineers, requesting that the correct course of their line or branch be plotted on the tracing and returned to topographer. In all such cases the railway officers referred to have cheerfully complied with the request, and in several instances have furnished special tracings of their surveys made under their immediate direction.

Report for the fiscal year ending June 30, 1887, referred to the condition of the maps and lithographic stones of Maine, New England, and New York States. The appropriation allowed for the current fiscal year provides for the renewals of the latter; the work is now in hands, and new maps will be issued before the close of the current year.

In my estimate for the fiscal year ending June 30, 1890, I provide for the renewals of the following maps: Illinois, Iowa, Missouri, Texas, Indian Territory, and California. To assist in the preparation of the latter, the services of an additional draughtsman will be required. The lithographic stones referred to in this report are in use since 1883, subject every second month to a series of erasures and re-erasures injurious to the working faces of the stones. In connection with the latter I respectfully direct your attention to the appended report from A. Hoen & Co., Baltimore.

I take pleasure in reporting that the employés in this office during the year have been attentive, careful, and steady in the discharge of their respective duties.

I have the honor to remain, very respectfully, your obedient servant,

DAVID ENRIGHT,
Topographer.

Hon. DON M. DICKINSON,
Postmaster-General, Washington, D. C.

Detailed statement of the distribution of post-route maps during the fiscal year ending June 30, 1888.

To whom furnished.	Mounted on cotton and trimmed with strip and rollers.	In sheets.	Fiscal year, June 30, 1887.	
			Mounted.	In sheets.
Officers and clerks of the Post-Office Department in Washington	211	14	341	5
Postmasters	226	247	165	618
The Railway Mail Service (besides special sheets, 1,200)	215	2,630	238½	1,960
Post-office inspectors	96½	10	99	3
United States Senators	57	28½	54	31
Members of the House of Representatives	149½	26	120	115
Interior Department	25	1	4	59
Treasury Department	3	....	6	39
Railway offices	58	45	27	33
The press	4	....	3	14
War Department	49	3	33	39
Miscellaneous, including Congressional committees, foreign governments, municipal and State authorities	149	157	36	57
Purchasers of maps	229½	840	276	428
Total	1,467½	3,701½	1,403½	3,396

CONDENSED STATEMENT OF THE TOPOGRAPHER'S OFFICE, POST-OFFICE DEPARTMENT, DURING THE FISCAL YEAR ENDING JUNE 30, 1888.

Number of correction sheets brought up (every two months) for lithographer. 240

Number of color sheets, showing star service (every two months), sent to lithographer . 60

Number of maps kept up in detail (monthly) for reference at the headquarters of the Department . 313

Number of post-offices established, their relative location plotted on maps thus: - - **O** . 3,454

Number of post-offices changed, their relative location plotted on maps thus: **O** . 1,376

Number of post-offices discontinued, marked on maps thus: **⊘** . 1,450

Number of star-route changes plotted on maps . 9,698

Number of railway tracings prepared in the office and sent out . 221

Number of miles of railway service extension plotted on maps . 11,873

Number of new counties established, their respective boundaries and names obtained from State records . 10

Computation of mileage distances by the shortest and most practicable mail-route between two given points traveled during the years 1861 to 1865, inclusive.

For the Second Auditor of the Treasury Department . 953,020

For the Director of the Mint . 21,758

For the War Department . 10,325

Post-route maps—epitome of distribution.

Mounted:

    Official distribution . 748½

    Complimentary distribution . 489½

    Purchasers . 229½

    Total . 1,467½

In sheets:

    Official distribution . 3,101

    Complimentary distribution . 260½

    Purchasers . 340

    Total . 3,701

Official letters sent out.

Letters to railway officers with prepared tracings inclosed . 238

Circular queries for location of post-offices sent to postmasters . 1,653

Letters replying to 1,456 queries from the Second Auditor of the Treasury Department . 929

Letters to Hoen & Co., lithographers . 173

Miscellaneous letters referring to the work . 1,496

4,158

Official letters received.

Answers from postmasters to queries in location papers........................ 869
Letters received from Second Auditor of the Treasury Department............ 929
Letters from the lithographer on the work 159
Miscellaneous letters (including returns and tracings from railway officers).... 1,715
$$\overline{3,672}$$

Establishment and changes in post-offices.

Reported from appointment office daily and entered in record (by draughtsmen), 6,280 items.

Reports of changes in service received.

Monthly reports from corresponding clerks of contract office compared by draughts-
　　men with their route books.　Total received during the year 150
Special reports from railway adjustment division of contract office, concerning
　　additional and changed railway service.　Total received during the year...... 344
Daily reports (printed bulletins).　Total received during the year 304

All of the items enumerated have been promptly transferred to the working maps, sample sheets, and to the correction sheets for the lithographer, and on 313 maps in use at headquarters of the Department.

———

BALTIMORE, MD., *July* 28, 1888.

SIR: In reply to yours of the 26th instant, we have to report as to the condition of the post-route lithographic stones, the property of the Post-Office Department, in our charge; they are in a bad state from the long use and great amount of handling they have been subjected to since 1883.　In this connection we beg to say that it is our belief that the stones have been in use longer and subjected to a greater amount of handling than any stone or stones ever used in lithography, and should be replaced by new transfers.

　　Respectfully,

　　　　　　　　　　　　　　　　　　　　A. HOEN & CO.,
　　　　　　　　　　　　　　　　　　　　　Lithographers.

Mr D. ENRIGHT,
　　Topographer, Post-Office Department.

REPORT

FIRST ASSISTANT POSTMASTER-GENERAL

FOR THE

FISCAL YEAR ENDING JUNE 30, 1888.

REPORT

OF THE

FIRST ASSISTANT POSTMASTER-GENERAL.

POST-OFFICE DEPARTMENT,
OFFICE OF THE FIRST ASSISTANT POSTMASTER-GENERAL,
Washington, D. C., November 17, 1888.

SIR: I have the honor to submit the following report of the work of this Bureau for the year ended June 30, 1888:

APPOINTMENT DIVISION.

Statement showing the number of post-offices established and discontinued, the number of postmasters appointed, and the increase or decrease as compared with the previous year.

Post-offices.	June 30, 1887.	June 30, 1888.	Increase.	Decrease.
Number of post-offices established during the year..	3,043	3,864	821	....
Number of post-offices discontinued................	1,500	1,645	145	....
Net increase over previous year.....................	1,543	2,219	676	....
Whole number of post-offices.........................	55,157	57,376	2,219	....
Number filled by appointment of the President.....	2,336	2,488	152	....
Number filled by appointment of the Postmaster-General	52,821	54,888	2,067	....

Appointments during the year.

Appointments.	June 30, 1887.	June 30, 1888.	Increase.	Decrease.
On resignations and commissions expired............	6,863	6,521	....	342
On removals..	2,584	1,244	....	1,340
On deaths of postmasters...........................	589	659	70	....
On establishment of new post-offices	3,043	3,864	821	....
Total	13,079	12,288	891	1,682

Total number of appointments during the year	12,288
Number of post-offices discontinued.......	1,645
Names and sites changed, with retention of incumbents............................	1,493
Total number of cases acted upon during the year	15,426

It will be observed from the above statement that there was an increase during the last fiscal year, both in the number of post-offices established and discontinued, as compared with the previous year, there having been 821 more post-offices established and 145 more discontinued than during the year ended June 30, 1887.

The increase in the whole number of post-offices was likewise greater than for the previous year, it having been 2,219, as against 1,543 for that ended June 30, 1887. The increase in the number of offices whose names or sites were changed during the past fiscal year largely exceeded those of the preceding year, the number having been 1,493, as compared with 696 for the year ended June 30, 1887. These changes occurred mainly in the Western States, particularly in Kansas, whose railroad facilities have been greatly increased within the last twelve months.

The increase and decrease in the number of offices, arranged by sections, States, and Territories, were as follows:

	Increase.	Decrease.	Net increase for 1888.	Net increase for previous year.
New England States.				
Maine		4		
New Hampshire		1		
Vermont	1			
Massachusetts	5			
Rhode Island	3			
Connecticut	1			
Total	10	5	5	45
Middle States and District of Columbia.				
New York	26			
New Jersey	8			
Delaware	8			
Maryland	39			
Pennsylvania	100			
District of Columbia	2			
Total	183		183	202
Southern States and Indian Territory.				
Virginia	126			
West Virginia	105			
North Carolina	158			
South Carolina	80			
Georgia	96			
Florida	43			
Alabama	106			
Mississippi	65			
Louisiana	50			
Texas	138			
Arkansas	104			
Missouri	94			
Tennessee	74			
Kentucky	126			
Indian Territory	41			
Total	1,406		1,406	785
The three States and Territories of the Pacific slope.				
Oregon	36			
California	106			
Nevada	5			
Washington	27			
Arizona	9			
Alaska	7			
Total	190		190	115
The ten States and six Territories of the West and Northwest.				
Ohio	74			
Indiana	41			
Michigan	34			
Illinois	34			
Wisconsin	12			
Iowa	32			
Minnesota	28			
Kansas	28			
Nebraska	11			
Colorado	59			
Dakota	33			
New Mexico	12			
Montana	35			
Wyoming	25			
Idaho		6		
Utah		17		
Total	458	23	435	396

There was an increase in the number of offices of one hundred or more in each of the following States during the year: North Carolina, 158; Texas, 138; Virginia, 126; Kentucky, 126; Alabama, 106; California, 106; West Virginia, 105; Arkansas, 104, and Pennsylvania, 100.

The decrease in the number of offices was as follows: In Maine, 4; in' New Hampshire, 1; in Idaho, 6, and in Utah, 17.

The following statement shows the number of States in which there were, on the 30th of June last, two thousand or more post-offices, together with the number of Presidential and money-order offices in each on that date:

States.	Whole number of post-offices.	Number of Presidential offices.	Number of money-order offices.
Pennsylvania	4,219	183	448
New York	3,274	224	531
Ohio	2,908	138	513
Virginia	2,481	35	128
Illinois	2,300	187	630
Missouri	2,268	25	130
North Carolina	2,211	79	369
Texas	2,045	78	315
Tennessee	2,044	28	229

It will be observed from the above that while Pennsylvania ranks first in the whole number of its post-offices, it is only third in the number of Presidential, and fourth in money-order offices. New York is first in the number of its Presidential offices, but second in the whole number of post-offices, and also second in its money-order offices. Illinois is first in rank in the number of money-order offices, second in the number of its Presidential offices, and fifth in the whole number of offices.

As a result of the annual adjustment of postmasters' salaries, which took effect July 1, 1888, 28 of the third class were reduced to the fourth class, and 42 offices of the fourth class were assigned to the third class, leaving 2,502 Presidential offices in operation on the first day of the present fiscal year. Divided into classes, the numbers are as follows: First, 97 ; second, 497; and third, 1,908.

The number of money-order offices in operation June 30, 1888, was 8,111, an increase of 366 over the number reported the previous year.

The number of postmasters appointed during the year was 12,288.

The total number of cases acted upon, including discontinuances and names and sites changed, with retention of incumbents, was 15,426. The number of appointments made to fill vacancies caused by deaths of postmasters was 659.

For further detailed information upon the subject of the establishment, discontinuance, and change of names and sites of post-offices and the appointment of postmasters, reference is made to tables marked A, B and C, appended to this report.

BOND DIVISION.

To this division belongs the work of recording the appointments of all postmasters, the establishment, discontinuance, and changes of names and sites of post-offices, and the preparation and transmission of the necessary letters of appointment, together with blank bonds and oaths to be executed by newly-appointed postmasters.

The aggregate of the work performed during the fiscal year ending June 30, 1886, compares favorably with that of the preceding year. The changes, contrasting one year with the other, are, in the main, so uniform as to excite no remarks.

The number of post-offices actually established during the past fiscal year was 3,501, a number never exceeded, except in the fiscal year ending June 30, 1884, and June 30, 1886, respectively. The net increase in the fiscal years ending June 30, 1885, and June 30, 1887, was 1,235 and 1,543, respectively.

The following is a statement of the operations of the bond division for the fiscal year ended June 30, 1888:

Number of Presidential cases recorded and upon which appointment papers, bonds, etc., were mailed	749
Number of cases of the fourth class recorded and upon which appointment papers, bonds, etc., were mailed	14,575
Number of appointment bonds examined, indorsed, and submitted to the Postmaster-General for approval	12,044
Number of bonds returned for correction	3,408
Number of appointment bonds filed	12,044
Number of new bonds required under the Postmaster-General's order of May 21, 1885	2,407
Number of new bonds required upon request of surety to be released	645
Number of new bonds required at the instance of the Third Assistant Postmaster-General	197
Number of new bonds required upon recommendations of post-office inspectors	165
Number of new bonds required in consequence of the extension of the money-order business	504
Number of new bonds required in consequence of the establishment of the postal-note business	278
Number of new bonds sent upon requests from postmasters	961
Total number of new bonds required	5,157
Number of new bonds received, examined, indorsed, and submitted to the Postmaster-General for acceptance	4,383
Number of new bonds reported to the Third Assistant Postmaster-General	909
Number of new bonds reported to the Auditor	4,383
Number of bonds reported to the Money-Order Office	2,731
Number of new bonds filed	4,383
Number of jackets prepared in sending new bonds	5,157
Number of commissions prepared and mailed to postmasters	12,066
Number of commissioned postmasters reported to the Auditor	12,044
Number of commissioned postmasters reported to the Third Assistant Postmaster-General	12,044
Number of commissioned postmasters reported for publication in the Postal Bulletin	12,044
Number of commissioned postmasters reported to the Money-Order Office	1,436
Number of blank designations and oaths mailed to acting postmasters	625
Number of designations and oaths of acting postmasters received, examined, indorsed, recorded, and filed	593
Number of acting postmasters reported to the Auditor	593
Number of circular letters sent on appointments, establishments, changes of names and sites, and discontinuances of post-offices	66,651
Number of circulars sent with new bonds	10,314
Number of circulars sent to appointees delinquent in the execution of their bonds	694
Number of circular letters accompanying bonds returned for correction	3,408
Number of circulars accompanying commissions sent to postmasters	12,044
Number of surety circulars sent to Chief Post-Office Inspector	2,697
Number of circulars sent to postmasters delinquent in furnishing new bonds	2,071
Number of circular letters sent notifying sureties of death of postmasters	625
Number of manuscript letters written	4,979
Number of post-office inspectors' reports on responsibility of sureties received, examined, and filed	3,023
Number of blank oaths for assistant postmasters, clerks, and employés mailed	27,112
Number of oaths of assistant postmasters, clerks, and employés received, examined, indorsed, and filed	27,179

Number of establishments, discontinuances, and changes of names and sites of post-offices reported to the Second Assistant Postmaster-General	6,548
Number of establishments, discontinuances, and changes of names and sites of post-offices reported to the Third Assistant Postmaster-General	5,585
Number of establishments, discontinuances, and changes of names and sites of post-offices reported to the equipment division	5,585
Number of new offices reported to the division of post-office supplies	3,501
Number of discontinuances reported to the Auditor	1,499
Number of entries made on the books of the division	78,076
Number of current records in use	35
Number of blank forms in use	72

DIVISION OF CORRESPONDENCE.

To this division is assigned the miscellaneous correspondence of the Department, controversies as to the proper delivery of mail, inquiries as to the construction of the postal laws and regulations, and other points of general information, correspondence in relation to which is not assigned to other offices.

This division was also charged with the classification of mail matter until September 15, 1887, when that duty was assigned to the office of the Third Assistant Postmaster-General.

The following is a summary of the work performed by this division during the fiscal year ended June 30, 1888:

Number of letters written to postmasters and private individuals involving decisions under postal laws and regulations	12,707
Number of telegrams sent in reply to communications requiring the immediate action of the Department	48
Number of newspaper and periodical publications claiming the right of admission to the mails as second-class matter examined and admitted from July 1, 1887, to September 15, 1887	645
Number of newspaper and periodical publications claiming the right of admission to the mails as second-class matter examined and rejected from July 1, 1887, to September 15, 1887	66
Amount of money collected from publishers of second-class matter for violations of law in mailing third-class matter inclosed with their publications at second-class rates, from July 1, 1887, to September 15, 1887	$393.41

The collections, amounting to $393.41, were made through the office of the Third Assistant Postmaster-General, and were the result of decisions made in this division.

The work of this division was assigned to the office of the Assistant Attorney-General for this Department by order of the Postmaster-General, dated September 15, 1888.

DIVISION OF POST-OFFICE SUPPLIES.

This division supplies offices of the fourth class with 8 ounce letter-balances, facing-slips, canceling ink, stamping-pads, post-marking, rating, and canceling stamps, thirty-eight forms of blanks, and, if the salary of the postmaster be $50 per annum or more, with twine and wrapping paper.

Offices of the third class are furnished, in addition to the above, with thirty-two forms of blanks, 4-pound scales, and, when necessary to weigh second-class matter, 62 and 240-pound scales.

Offices of the first and second classes are furnished, in addition to the above, with test weights, 600-pound scales when necessary, thirty forms of blanks pertaining to the free-delivery system, and with seventy-seven items of stationery.

The Department proper is furnished with eighty items of stationery, blanks, blank-books, labels, records, registers, etc.

WORK DONE BY DIVISION.

The number of requisitions briefed, filled, and filed for the various classes of articles furnished for the fiscal years ended June 30, 1885, June 30, 1886, June 30, 1887, and June 30, 1888, is shown by the following:

TABLE 1.

Class of articles.	1884–'85.	1885–'86.	1886–'87.	1887–'88.
Twine and wrapping paper	34,600	39,506	51,357	57,847
Marking and rating stamps	17,529	21,537	24,885	30,872
Letter balances and scales	3,728	3,170	4,122	6,464
Blanks and books	104,683	135,289	192,728	233,900
Canceling ink and pads	(*)	3,150	9,868	11,451
Stationery	2,700	3,175	4,095	4,817
Total	162,640	205,827	287,055	345,411

* No appropriation.

The number of packages, registered packages, sacks, and cases of goods sent out for the same period of time is shown by the following:

TABLE 2.

Nature of shipment.	1884–'85.	1885–'86.	1886–'87.	1887–'88.
Packages	160,000	200,000	266,563	273,729
Packages registered	585	600	1,008	3,204
Sacks	11,000	15,557	27,884	29,209
Cases	427	550	1,600	2,613
Total	171,962	216,607	297,055	308,755

The following table shows quantity of the principal contract articles furnished for the fiscal years ended June 30, 1885, June 30, 1886, June 30, 1887, and June 30, 1888. Owing to the absence of complete records prior to the year ended June 30, 1887, the comparative statement as to articles of stationery, etc., furnished is incomplete:

TABLE 3.

Articles.	1884–'85.	1885–'86.	1886–'87.	1887–'88.
Blanks	51,494,447	57,674,302	60,468,900	63,566,830
Books	87,107	125,414	112,403	179,712
Facing slips	65,146,760	120,844,680	193,091,700	311,627,520
Marking, rating, and canceling stamps	21,229	13,230	17,500	39,863
Cotton twine ....pounds..	130,000	100,000	102,700	91,732
Jute twine ....do....	500,000	500,000	500,000	736,055
Hemp twine ....do....	210,000	146,090	115,452	34,617
Letter-balances and scales	3,728	3,070	2,180	7,047
Wrapping paper ....reams..	17,313	20,837	21,747	25,400
Canceling ink ....pounds..	(*)	11,100	13,575	22,579
Inking-pads	(*)	5,475	10,411	26,530
Letter-heads and follow sheets			6,715,200	3,224,640
Card-blotter ....sheets..			80,180	93,476
Cardboard ....do....			13,309	9,875
Scratch-blocks			11,488	9,833
Slide labels			506,200	243,000
Examination cards			295,000	277,400
Envelopes			1,709,000	1,597,175
Rubber bands ....gross..			3,765	3,006
Rubber bands ....pounds..			4,552	5,653
Rubber erasers			5,287	6,277
Pens ....gross..			7,503	8,192
Pen-holders			63,828	57,033

* No appropriation.

TAELE 3—Continued.

Articles.	1884-'85.	1885-'86.	1886-'87.	1887-'88.
Lead-pencils			145,390	159,153
Writing inks ....bottles.			13,603	10,347
Mucilage ....do.			5,058	5,559
Mucilage and ink stands			5,306	6,228
Sponge-cups and paper-weights			2,750	3,334
Steel erasers and envelope knives			2,762	3,275
Shears			1,245	1,347
Rulers and folders			1,588	1,285
Carbon and semi-carbon paper..............sheets.			75,780	53,113
Rubber stamps			1,750	1,806
Press copy-books			1,075	1,108
Copying and blotting pads			1,228	1,409
Thumb-tacks			3,528	2,798
Paper-fasteners			134,000	132,506
Pen-racks			12,000	1,209
Seal papers			13,500	11,800
Sealing-wax ....pounds.			3,512	3,365
Pins ....boxes.			1,010	971
Pins ....papers.			3,774	3,397
Sponge ....pieces.			5,280	7,340

The large increase of facing slips shown as issued in the year 1887-'88 over the amount issued in the year1886-'87 (see Table 3) arises from the fact that an accurate account has been kept of the number of reams of fac-ing-slip paper sent to the larger offices of the first and second classes and to superintendents of the Railway Mail Service for the purpose of cutting into facing slips, amounting to 116,368,120 slips, which amount, added to the slips sent direct from this division, makes the amount equal to that shown in the above table. The amount given of facing slips issued in previous year represents only the amounts mailed from this division as given in itemized statement of wrapping paper in last year's report.

The amount of the more important portions of clerical labor performed for the fiscal years ended June 30, 1885, June 30, 1886, June 30, 1887, and June 30, 1888, is shown by the following table. Minor duties, though occupying considerable time of the employés, are omitted for the sake of brevity:

TABLE 4.

Work.	1884-'85.	1885-'86.	1886-'87.	1887-'88.
Entries of record:				
Wrapping paper and twine	4,300	4,506	7,999	20,168
Stamps	17,529	16,538	21,768	30,383
Scales	3,728	3,170	4,122	5,914
Ink and pads		8,150	9,868	27,022
Journals		3,744	4,095	4,817
Ledgers		8,744	4,095	4,817
Order books		1,213	1,939	2,544
Itemized accounts			18,576	19,055
Government Printing Office accounts	15,173	15,337	16,870	21,148
On sheets			30,529	24,109
Accounts kept:				
Itemized			130	132
Dollars and cents		466	489	533
Inspection reports			953	755
Orders on contractors		533	853	949
Labels and tags written	173,000	216,000	297,055	295,316
Letters written	1,842	1,950	4,087	7,729
Circular letters sent out				40,222
Receipts written	8,800	10,306	12,519	11,868
Memorandum bills filed		648	978	1,419
Duplicate bills passed		324	489	705
Books of record and press-copy books	27	33	46	55

The appropriations and expenditures for the fiscal years ended June 30, 1885, June 30, 1886, June 30, 1887, and June 30, 1888, are shown by the following, omitting cents for convenience:

TABLE 5.

	Appropriations, 1884-'85.	Expenditures, 1884-'85.	Appropriations, 1885-'86.	Expenditures, 1885-'86.	Appropriations, 1886-'87.	Expenditures, 1886-'87.	Appropriations, 1887-'88.	Expenditures, 1887-'88.
Wrapping-paper	$35, 000	$34, 997	$35, 000	$28, 916	$30, 000	$29, 971	$44, 000	$43, 997
Twine	82, 277	79, 149	85, 000	60, 632	80, 000	63, 413	80, 000	71, 175
Balances and scales	25, 000	17, 802	20, 000	1, 801	10, 000	1, 043	17, 000	16, 699
Ink, pads, and stamps	25, 000	10, 233	20, 000	12, 576	30, 000	29, 938	20, 000	29, 999
Stationery, Post-Office Department	9, 000	7, 756	12, 600	8, 590	12, 600	7, 314	12, 000	9, 873
Stationery, first and second class offices	65, 000	46, 914	65, 000	41, 030	85, 000	46, 456	50, 000	49, 836
Printing	150, 000	169, 000	178, 012	174, 055	180, 000	162, 403	278, 000	232, 580
Total	421, 277	365, 851	416, 212	336, 110	397, 600	331, 738	511, 000	454, 450

The sum of the appropriations for the fiscal year ended June 30, 1888, amounted to $511,000, and the expenditures were $454,454.58—about 89 per cent. of the appropriations. This left at the end of the fiscal year $56,545.42 unexpended, in addition to which there was on hand stock amounting as per inventory to $54,703.40.

WRAPPING-PAPER.

The appropriation of $30,000 for wrapping and facing-slip paper was practically exhausted in February, and an urgency appropriation of $14,000 was granted by Congress, making a total appropriation of $44,000 for the fiscal year. This additional appropriation was necessitated by the increased demand for facing-slip paper by postmasters and the Railway Mail Service and the additional price paid for the paper under contract. By direction of the Postmaster-General, facing-slips are being substituted for wooden tags for the purpose of addressing packages and sacks of mail matter, making an increase in the consumption of this class of paper, but with better results to the service and at a less cost to the Department. It was also found that 4 cents a ream additional had to be paid for the paper over the price paid under contract when estimates were made. From the total appropriation of $44,000 there has been expended the sum of $43,997.55 (see Table 5), leaving to the credit of the appropriation $2.45. There was on hand as per inventory of July 1, 1888, paper amounting to $6,576.54.

As shown by Table 3, there were furnished to post-offices and the Railway Mail Service 25,460 reams of wrapping and facing-slip paper, as against 21,747 reams for the previous year, an increase of 3,713 reams. Of this amount 18,031 reams were facing-slip paper, which, cut into slips, equaled 311,627,520 facing-slips (see Table 3). The same table shows that only 193,091,700 slips were furnished for the year ended June 30, 1887, which is somewhat misleading in the comparison of the amount of slips furnished for the two years, for this reason: As stated in the report for the year ended June 30, 1887, no account was kept of the number of slips cut by postmasters and the Railway Mail Service from the flat paper furnished them, whereas an accurate account has been kept this year, amounting to 116,368,120 slips, which, deducted from the 311,627,520 slips shown in Table 3, leaves 195,259,400 slips as the amount furnished direct from the Department. Of the above amount, 108,581,000 have been furnished printed to postmasters of the first and second classes, contract having been made for the printing at 4 cents per thousand. For the year ending June 30, 1889, the contract price for this work is 3¼ cents per thousand, a great reduction in price as compared with the price paid four years ago without contract—the price paid by the Department at that time ranging from 8 to 15 cents per thousand. The largely increasing demand for wrapping and facing-slip paper for the fiscal year ended June 30, 1888, as shown by Table 3, over previous years shows a large and steady increase in the demand for these papers.

It is estimated that an increase of this appropriation to $50,000 will be required to meet the demands of the service for the fiscal year ending June 30, 1890.

TWINE.

There was expended from the appropriation of $80,000 for wrapping-twine the sum of $71,175.77 (see Table 5), leaving a balance unexpended of $8,824.23. There was on hand as per inventory of July 1, 1888, twine amounting to $10,437.40. The amount of wrapping-twine issued for the fiscal year ended June 30, 1887, was 778,152 pounds (see Table 3), while the amount issued for the present year was 832,404 pounds. By the substitution of a coarse jute twine at a much less price in place of the hemp twine heretofore used, and the issue of a small jute in place of cotton twine, there has been a great saving to the Department in the expense of this item. The change was in the line of economy, and without detriment to the service.

The amount of course jute furnished for the fiscal year ended June 30, 1887, was 115,452 pounds (see Table 3), and of cotton twine 102,700 pounds, while for the present fiscal year only 34,617 pounds and 61,732 pounds, respectively, have been issued. This shows a reduction in the issue of coarse jute (called hemp in Table 3) and cotton—the expensive twines—of 121,803 pounds. The complaint made in the last report of the delay in delivery of jute twine by the contractor has been entirely overcome, a sufficient quantity being furnished and at regular stated intervals. Taking into consideration the increased demand for this twine by the natural growth of the service, it is considered prudent to increase the appropriation.

It is estimated that the sum of $85,000 will be required to meet the demands of the service for wrapping-twine for the fiscal year ending June 30, 1890.

LETTER BALANCES AND SCALES.

Table 5 shows that from the appropriation of $17,000 for letter balances and scales the sum of $16,999.92 was expended, leaving to the credit of the appropriation $0.08. Owing to the general inspection of fourth-class post-offices, ordered by the Postmaster-General, and the furnishing of the 903 scales, orders for which were held up the previous year, as no contract had been made for 8 ounce letter balances, the original appropriation of $10,000 was entirely exhausted, and an urgency appropriation of $7,000 was granted by Congress March 30, 1888, making the total appropriation for the year $17,000. There were purchased and issued during the year 7,047 letter balances and scales, and there were remaining on hand as per inventory of July 1, 1888, scales amounting in value to

$518.41. As shown by Table 3, there were issued 2,180 scales for the fiscal year ended June 30, 1887, while for the year ended June 30, 1888, 7,047 scales were required. This is an excess in issue of 5,867 scales.

A great saving has been made during the year by the issue of 4-pound scales to offices of the fourth class, in place of the 8-ounce letter balance. The custom, heretofore, has been to furnish post-offices of the fourth class, not exchange offices, with an 8-ounce balance with metric system, the scale costing $2.65. It was found that by the issue of a 4-pound scale, costing $1.56 and weighing from one-half ounce to 4 pounds, a great saving would be made, and the post-offices be better equipped, as the scale answered equally as well for a letter balance, and could also be used to weigh second-class matter. Under section 469, page 203, Postal Laws and Regulations of 1887, only post-offices whose gross receipts exceeded $400 per annum were entitled to 4-pound scales. An order was made authorizing the issue of such scales to fourth-class post-offices as seemed advisable to the First Assistant Postmaster-General, and under that order 4-pound scales were issued to fourth-class offices, as stated above, as the inspection will be completed during the coming fiscal year.

It is estimated that the demands of the service will require an appropriation of $15,000 to carry the Department through the fiscal year ending June 30, 1890.

STAMPS, INK, AND PADS.

The appropriation for stamps, ink, and pads for the fiscal year ended June 30, 1888, was $30,000, and the expenditures were $29,999.71 (see Table 5), leaving a balance of 29 cents. There were purchased and issued during the year 39,863 stamps, 26,530 pads, and 22,579 pounds of ink (see Table 3). Of these amounts there remained on hand stamps, ink, and pads amounting in value to $3,510.73, as per inventory of July 1, 1888. This was an increase of issues over the previous year of 22,363 stamps, 16,119 pads, and 9,004 pounds of ink. This large increase in the demand for these articles is accounted for, as in the case of balances and scales, by the inspection of fourth-class post-offices, a very large number of them being found poorly equipped or entirely unsupplied with the proper postmarking stamps, ink, and pads, for the postmarking of letters and canceling of postage-stamps. Owing to the large demand, the appropriation was exhausted during the early part of the fourth quarter of the fiscal year, and requisitions had to be held up until the appropriation for the fiscal year beginning July 1, 1888, became available. As the special inspection of post-offices will be practically finished during the fiscal year ending June 30, 1889, it is estimated that an appropriation of $35,000 will be required for the fiscal year ending June 30, 1890.

In this connection, I desire to call your attention to the article of canceling ink, used both for postmarking letters and canceling postage-stamps. It has long been known to the Department that unprincipled persons have made a business of collecting canceled postage-stamps, and by the use of chemicals entirely removing the cancelation, thereby rendering the stamps fit to be used again. Numerous devices for the cancellation of postage-stamps without the use of ink have been submitted to the Department, none of which would, upon test, meet the requirements of the service, either by reason of complicated machinery or of liability to destroy the contents of packages in the act of canceling stamps. Owing to the volume of letters passing through the post-offices it became a necessity to devise some instrument that would both postmark and cancel stamps at the same time. Such a device is now in use ; and the canceling ink furnished by the Department is used for both postmarking and canceling.

In response to advertisements by the Department for samples and prices for canceling ink, numerous samples have been received and submitted to chemists as to the indelibility, and to postmasters as to the practical working of the same on postmarking stamp and canceler. In no case has the chemist found an ink that was indelible that would do satisfactory work for postmarking. As a combined stamp has become a necessity in order to avoid a very large increase in the clerical force of post-offices, the indelibility of the ink used, taken with its qualities for postmarking purposes, becomes of great importance.

I would therefore recommend that a committee be appointed to thoroughly investigate the matter of a combined postmarking and canceling ink that will meet the requirements of the service ; and in case they fail to find such an ink, that they report on the feasibility of having the coloring matter in postage-stamps of such a chemical mixture that when it comes in contact with an ink of certain chemical ingredients the color of the stamp will be destroyed.

STATIONERY, FIRST AND SECOND CLASS OFFICES.

The appropriation for stationery for offices of the first and second classes for the year ended June 30, 1888, was $50,000. From this amount there has been expended $49,836.73 (see Table 5), leaving a balance to the credit of the appropriation of $163.27. Owing to the appropriation being exhausted, vouchers for the printing of facing slips and card slide labels ordered by postmasters for the second quarter of the current year 1888 had to be disallowed. During the fiscal year 1886–'87 there was expended the sum of $46,456.19, leaving stock on hand valued at $22,658.94. During the year 1887–'88 there were purchased and paid for out of this appropriation stock and miscellaneous supplies to the amount of $49,836.73, and there was on hand July 1, 1888, stock valued at $29,695.84. Comparing the amounts expended for the two years, 1886–'87 and 1887–'88, amounting to $46,456.19 and $49,836.73, respectively, it will be seen that there was expended in the year 1887–'88 $3,380.54 in excess of the amount expended the previous year, and it would seem that a greater sum was used during the year 1887–'88 than was necessary to perform the same service during the year 1886–'87 ; but by contrasting the inventories of stock on hand at the close of each year, $22,658.94 and $29,695.84, respectively, it will be seen that there was stock on hand in excess of the previous year amounting to $7,036.90, while only $3,380.54 had been expended in excess for purchases. This shows a saving to the Department of $3,656.36.

When it is taken into consideration that during the past fiscal year the nine divisions of the railway mail service, the twelve post office inspectors in charge (heretofore only partially supplied), and the thirty-five additional second-class offices established not heretofore furnished have been supplied with stationery, together with the natural growth of the service, it will be shown that a better and more extended service has been performed during the last named period, at a reduced cost to the Department. It was also found necessary to have a full stock of stationery on hand July 1, in order to fill promptly the semi-annual requisitions of postmasters of the first and second classes. By a comparison of the number of requisitions filled during the first quarter of each year, it is found that in the first quarter of the fiscal year ended

June 30, 1887, only 17 per cent. were filled, while 90 per cent. were filled during the same period this year. Taking as a basis the increase in the number of offices of the second class for the present year which have to be supplied with stationery in addition to those already furnished, and the natural growth of the service, it is estimated that it will require ·$57,500 to meet the exigencies of the service for the fiscal year ending June 30, 1890.

STATIONERY, POST-OFFICE DEPARTMENT.

The appropriation and expenditures for stationery and free penalty envelopes for the Department for the year ended June 30, 1888, were $12,000 and $9,875.72, respectively (see Table 5). leaving a balance of $2,124.28 unexpended. During the year 1886–'87 there was expended $7,514.35, and on hand June 30, 1887, supplies valued at $3,065.29. For the year 1887–'88, there was paid out of the appropriation $9,875.72, the stock on hand at the close of the year amounting to $3,964.48. By comparing the amounts expended for the two years 1886–'87 and 1887–'88, $7,514.35 and $9,875.72, and the stock on hand as shown by the inventories at the close of the same periods, $3,065.29 and $3,964.48, it will be shown that there was an increase of the expenditures this year over the fiscal year ended June 30, 1887, of $2,361.37, and also an increase of stock on hand amounting to $899.19, making an excess of expenditures over the previous year of $1,462.18 in the amount of stationery and free penalty envelopes furnished to the Department. This slight increase in the amount of supplies furnished is accounted for by the natural growth of the service.

The satisfactory showing made of expenditures from the appropriations for stationery for offices of the first and second classes and for the Post-Office Department is the result of the economical selection of the eighty-three articles issued, the advantageous contracts made for this year, the painstaking manner in which the supplies have been cared for and distributed, and the economical use of articles issued to post-offices and to the different bureaus and divisions of the Post-Office Department.

It is estimated that it will require $12,600 to meet the demands of the Post Office Department for stationery and free penalty envelopes for the fiscal year ending June 30, 1890.

PRINTING AND BINDING.

The regular appropriation for printing and binding for the fiscal year ended June 30, 1888, was $180,000. On February 13, 1888, the Government Printer notified the Department that its allotment for printing and binding was exhausted, and an urgency appropriation of $98,000 was granted by Congress March 30, 1888, making a total appropriation of $278,000 for the fiscal year. The additional appropriation was required to meet the demands for printing and binding caused by the printing of postal account-books for third and fourth class post-offices, printing a new form of quarterly postal accounts, occasioned by the change in the manner of keeping postmasters' accounts in the Sixth Auditor's Office, and to cover the amount held up by the Government Printer out of the appropriation for the year ended June 30, 1887, and transferred to and to be deducted from the appropriation for this year, amounting altogether to the sum of $47,377.92; and also to meet the demand caused by the general increase in the business of post-offices throughout the country, and to cover the Post-Office Department's proportion of the current expenses of the Government Printing-Office for the fiscal year ended June 30, 1888.

From the total appropriation of $278,000 there have been furnished by the Government Printer 69.971,183 blanks, books, etc. (see Table 3), at a cost of $232,569.98 (see Table 5), or 83.65 per cent. of the appropriation, leaving apparently an unexpended balance of $45,430.02. Requisitions amounting to $22,580.56, in addition to the amount shown above as furnished, were made upon the Government Printer before the expiration of the fiscal year, but were held up by that officer and carried to the appropriation for the fiscal year ending June 30, 1889. The amount retained for current expenses is 16.35 per cent. of the total appropriation. There was an actual increase of 6,165,240 blanks, books, etc., furnished for the year ended June 30, 1888; and if the number were added for which requisitions were made and held up by the Government Printer, a larger increase would be shown.

Great inconvenience is caused by the lack of facilities for printing blanks and forms which are required by the Department for immediate use. The Government Printer requires sixty days in which to fill all requisitions for blanks. It is almost of daily occurrence that either the Department or postmasters of the first or second classes require, at once, small blanks to meet the demands of the service arising from orders issued by the Postmaster-General, which can not be received from the Government Printer under sixty days, unless made special; and when made special, which is a serious inconvenience to him, the regular delivery of blanks is delayed, often to the great detriment of the service. For the past fiscal year 5,048 requisitions were made on the Government Printer, covering 69,971,183 blanks, books, etc. Of this amount there were 69,791,470 blanks; fully one-quarter of these were small blanks, a large proportion of which could have been printed in the Department had it been supplied with the necessary facilities, as other departments of the Government are supplied, thus saving largely in the time taken to fill requisitions, and at the same time being prepared to fill promptly orders of an urgent nature. When requisitions are filled in their regular order, as much time is required for a small quantity, say 500, of a blank needed for immediate use and which could not have been anticipated, as is required to furnish 1,000,000 blanks kept in stock, orders for which can be anticipated. I would therefore recommend that a branch of the Government Printing-Office be established in this division, or that an appropriation of $10,000 be asked for to properly equip the stationery section of this division with presses and material for doing this class of work.

It is estimated that an appropriation of $284,000 will be required to meet the demands of the service for the fiscal year ending June 30, 1890, in view of the increased demands likely to be made upon the appropriation for printing and binding from the natural growth of the service, and from the fact that the Government Printer requires about 17 per cent. of the appropriation for his current expenses.

Estimate of appropriations for fiscal year ending June 30, 1890.

Wrapping and facing-slip paper	$50,000
Wrapping twine	85,000
Letter balances and scales	15,000
Postmarking, rating, and canceling stamps, ink, and pads	35,000
Stationery, first and second class post-offices	57,500
Stationery and free penalty envelopes, Post-Office Department	12,600
Printing and binding	284,000
Total	539,100

. The present clerical force of this division consists of 21 clerks, messengers, and laborers. During the year a new and complete system has been adopted in the manner in which accounts are kept with postmasters, covering the articles issued to them out of the several appropriations for which the superintendent is held responsible, by which it is possible to tell at once the quantity and value of articles furnished to each of the 58,000 post-offices, thereby preventing duplicate orders being filled, and excessive demands being made from carelessness or otherwise, and enabling a better knowledge of the wants and requirements of the different post-offices. Receipts are required from postmasters for supplies furnished (excepting blanks); and, in the case of stationery issued to post-offices of the first and second classes, itemized receipts are furnished, thereby enabling postmasters to know at all times how their accounts stand at the Department for these articles, and preventing any claim from being afterwards made that they did not receive certain articles, as was frequently done before the adoption of this system. To handle an account for the articles representing this amount, a large increase over the last fiscal year, and consisting of thousands of tons and millions of articles, in a prompt and accurate manner, requires an amount of manual labor and clerical work that the present force will be inadequate to perform for the year ending June 30, 1890.

The lack of sufficient storage room adds greatly to the amount of clerical work and manual labor required to meet the demands made upon this division for supplies. In my report for the fiscal year ended June 30, 1887, and again under date of June 6, 1888, the matter of storage room was urgently brought to your attention. The rapidly increasing business of the postal service makes extra demands for supplies, and what a year ago seemed an urgent necessity becomes now an imperative duty. The present space is entirely inadequate to keep in hand a sufficient stock of the articles required by the postal service. Owing to this lack of room the Department is required to make orders for small quantities of the various articles contracted for, thus adding largely to the clerical work, and in case of contractors furnishing inferior supplies, owing to the limited amount of these articles enabled to be kept on hand, the inspection committee is obliged to accept the same, at a reduction, instead of rejecting them, as should be done in all cases when the supplies do not come up to the contract requirements. This course is detrimental to the service and costly to the Department. Often when contractors are delayed in their delivery of supplies, owing to the breaking of machinery or negligence in filling orders, or when railroads fail to deliver promptly, from accident or otherwise, the Department is unable to furnish postmasters with the necessary supplies to properly conduct their business and the postal service of the country is embarrassed. For nearly four years no additional storage room has been furnished, while during that time and up to June 30, 1888, 12,510 new post-offices have been established, which, taken together with the natural growth in the business of the service, have completely overrun the storage capacity of the division. Every available space is now occupied to its fullest extent, even to the corridors, and heavy articles like twine and wrapping-paper have to be piled to such a height that the lives of visitors to the Department and of employés are often endangered. Forced to adopt this course, additional help is required to perform the manual labor. Action should at once be taken to procure storage room sufficient to carry at least a three months' supply of the various articles furnished.

Taking as a basis the increased demands made upon the division for the past fiscal year (see Table 3) over those made for the fiscal year ended June 30, 1887, there will be required to properly conduct the business an additional force of four clerks and two laborers.

The division of post-office supplies differs materially from the other divisions of the Department. It furnishes the Post-Office Department, the Railway Mail Service, the twelve inspectors in charge, and the 58,000 post-offices throughout the country with the supplies which are necessary to properly conduct the business of the postal service. It represents in every respect a mercantile concern doing an annual business equal in amount to the sum expended from the several appropriations granted by Congress for this purpose, aggregating for the past fiscal year $454,454.58. Contracts have to be made yearly for the vast number of articles required to meet the demands of the service; these articles have to be ordered as required, received and inspected, and if accepted the various appropriations under which they are purchased are charged with the money valuation of the order and the contractor credited with the same, and when papers are forwarded for payment, the contractor's account has to be charged, and the business is carried on in every respect as would be required in a mercantile concern of this magnitude. It necessitates keeping in stock at all times sufficient supplies to meet the demands made by the various branches of the service that are supplied from this source. Although nominally attached to the office of the First Assistant Postmaster-General, from the very nature of the business it practically acts independently. In addition to conducting the business coming under the appropriations made to the office of the First Assistant Postmaster General, it conducts the business covered by the appropriations made to the Postmaster-General for stationery for the Post-Office Department and for printing and binding, thus virtually being under the direction of two offices.

When the Postmaster-General was authorized to establish a blank agency for the Department, June 8, 1872 (see Statutes, volume 17, page 289, section 30), appropriations were made to the amount of $132,500 (see Statutes, volume 17, pages 89 and 200) for the purchase of supplies. Since that date, by the addition of supplies required to be furnished by this division and by the natural growth of the service, the appropriations have rapidly increased, until for the past fiscal year the total amount of the appropriations for which the superintendent of the division was held accountable was $511,000, an increase of 285.66 per cent.

As an illustration showing the increase in the volume of business done by this division, reference is made to Table 1, which shows that the average yearly increase in requisitions made for wrapping-paper and twine for the fiscal years ended June 30, 1887, and June 30, 1888, was 24 per cent., and for blanks and books for the same time the increase averaged 32 per cent., while for the six items covered by that table the average increase per year was 40 per cent.

Table 2 will show that for the same period there was a yearly increase of 18 per cent. in the number of packages sent out from this division, and for the four items covered by that table an average increase of 23 per cent. per year. A much larger showing is made for the various contract articles furnished (see Table 3). For blanks furnished the yearly increase was 7½ per cent., for marking, rating, and canceling stamps 85 per cent., and for wrapping paper 11 per cent., while the yearly increase of the eleven principal articles was 44 per cent. An equally large increase in the entries of record was made (see Table 4), amounting to 63 per cent. yearly. This clearly indicates the rapid growth of the service and the increased demands made upon this division. In view of the above

11701 1ST ASST——2

facts, and of the increase of business that may naturally be expected from year to year, every endeavor should be made to facilitate the business of this division; and as it is now virtually conducted as an independent division (from force of business considerations), it should be detached from the office of the First Assistant Postmaster-General.

I therefore recommend that it be made an independent division, under the control of a superintendent with a salary of $3,000 per annum.

SALARY AND ALLOWANCE DIVISION.

As many of the accounts for the quarter ended June 30, 1888, are not closed at present, a complete statement of the transactions of this division for the fiscal year can not be furnished at this time. This data will be submitted with the estimates for the appropriations for the next fiscal year.

In order to understand clearly the operations of the division, the duties assigned to it may be briefly stated as follows:

DUTIES ASSIGNED TO THE SALARY AND ALLOWANCE DIVISION.

The most important duties are the adjustment of the salaries of Presidential postmasters, or postmasters of the first, second, and third classes; consideration of applications for allowances for clerk-hire, rent, fuel, light, furniture, miscellaneous and incidental expenditures; examination of the quarterly returns or accounts of postmasters at offices of the first and second classes before they are finally passed by the Auditor of the Treasury for the Post-Office Department; the regulation of the salaries and duties of the employés necessary for the proper transaction of the postal business in the larger post-offices; the supervision and regulation of the box-rent rates, and the deposits for keys for lock-boxes, and the management of the large and constantly increasing correspondence relative to the subject-matter stated.

In addition to the important duties as above outlined, the work of reviewing and re-adjusting the salaries of postmasters and ex-postmasters of the third, fourth, and fifth classes, under the act of Congress approved March 3, 1883, was assigned to the salary and allowance division, by verbal order of Postmaster-General Gresham, April 7, 1884. This large and important work, involving an examination and review of the records, accounts, and salaries of the postmasters of the third, fourth, and fifth classes, from 1864 to 1874, has been carried on under the supervision of the chief, as rapidly as possible consistent with accuracy and the limited clerical force at command. This work is now practically completed, as the act of Congress approved August 4, 1886, limited the presentation of original applications to January 1, 1887, and all applications made prior to the date stated have been reviewed, and all amounts found due, under the law, included in the third schedule of claims, have been transmitted to the Auditor. Detailed information relative to this work will be hereinafter stated.

The act of Congress approved March 3, 1883, which requires an annual adjustment of the salaries of Presidential postmasters to take effect at the beginning of each fiscal year (July 1), instead of a biennial adjustment, as heretofore authorized, has largely increased the duties of the salary and allowance division. The *fifth annual* adjustment of the salaries of Presidential postmasters was made upon the basis of the gross receipts accruing at the respective offices for the four quarters ended March 31, 1888.

Additional duties have also been imposed upon the division by the act of Congress approved June 29, 1886, which took effect July 1, 1886, providing that clerks doing money-order business at offices of the first and second classes shall be compensated from the allowance for clerk-hire as made by this office; and that the commissions accruing on money-order business from the date stated shall be returned as a part of the revenue of the Department.

The work of the salary and allowance division has also been further increased by the act of Congress approved July 24, 1888, which provides for allowances for rent, fuel, and light for third-class post-offices, or offices whereat the salaries of postmasters are fixed from $1,000 to $1,900 per annum. By the adjustment made in accordance with the requirements of the act of March 3, 1883, the third-class offices, July 1, 1888, numbered 1,908. These will be increased, quarterly, at the average rate of 45 offices.

The various operations of the salary and allowance division during the past year are submitted in tabulated form as follows:

Tabulated statement of the operations of the salary and allowance divisions for the fiscal year ended June 30, 1888.

Items.	Fiscal year, 1887-'88.	
	Total number.	Aggregate allowance.
Number of letters received	31,456	
Number of letters written	37,441	
Number of circular-letters sent out	28,019	
Number of allowances for clerk-hire made	5,477	
Total amount allowed for clerks in post-offices		$5,603,110.42
Number of allowances for clerk-hire declined	2,148	
Number of allowances for rent, fuel, and light made	2,142	
Total amount allowed for rent, fuel, and light		532,900.87
Number of allowances for rent, fuel, and light declined	787	
Number of allowances for miscellaneous items made	8,123	
Total amount allowed for miscellaneous items		58,551.71
Number of allowances for miscellaneous items declined	2,788	
Number of allowances for furniture made	748	
Total amount allowed for furniture		21,301.86
Number of allowances for furniture declined	919	
Number of allowances for stationery declined		
Number of allowances for advertising made	226	
Total amount for advertising allowed		10,733.90
Number of allowances for advertising declined	342	
Number of cases sent to chief post office inspector for information	459	
Number of fourth-class offices reported by the auditor, where the annual compensation of the postmaster amounts to $1,000, exclusive of money-order commissions	210	
Number of fourth-class offices assigned to the Presidential class	197	
Aggregate amount required to pay the salaries of postmasters at the above Presidential offices (197) for one year		212,900.00
Number of special adjustments of postmasters' salaries	201	
Aggregate sum required to pay the above increased salaries for one year		213,400.00
Number of postmasters' salaries reduced and discontinued	3	
Aggregate amount saved by salaries reduced and discontinued as above		4,200.00
Total number of salaries of postmasters adjusted during the year	2,746	
Aggregate amount of salaries involved in the (2,746) adjustments as above		4,420,400.00
Number of first class post-offices (salary of postmaster, $3,000 to $6,000 a year)	97	
Number of second-class post-offices (salary of postmaster, $2,000 to $2,900 a year)	497	
Number of third-class post-offices (salary of postmaster, $1,000 to $1,900 a year)	1,908	
Total number of Presidential post-offices June 30, 1888	2,502	
Total amount required for salaries, Presidential postmasters, as above (2,502), for one year		4,202,800.00
Allowances for clerk-hire reduced and discontinued	552	
Amount saved by clerk-hire reduced and discontinued		71,958.06
Allowances for rent, fuel, and light reduced and discontinued	107	
Amount saved by rent, fuel, and light reduced and discontinued		16,121.00
Number of applications for re-adjustment of postmasters' salaries under act of March 3, 1883, received and placed on file	68,725	
Number of applications under act of March 3, 18-3. received to date	68,725	
Number found below the 10 per cent. requirement of law	42,487	
Total number allowed to date	26,238	
Aggregate amount allowed for back pay of postmasters to date		1,221,000.60
Number of employés (average)	6.0	
Number of employés, review of postmasters' salaries (average)	9.5	

The number of letters received during the fiscal year ended June 30, 1888, amounted to 31,456, an increase of 1,622, or 5.4 per cent., as compared with 1887. The number of letters written amounted to 37,441, an increase of 1,873, or 5.3 per cent., as compared with the number written in 1887. Twenty-eight thousand and nineteen circular-letters were sent out, being an increase of 2,705, or 10.7 per cent., as compared with 1887.

Five thousand four hundred and seventy-seven allowances for clerk-hire were made, an increase of 740, or 15.7 per cent., as compared with 1887. The number of applications for clerk-hire declined was 2,148, a decrease of 307, or 12.5 per cent., as compared with the year 1887. These applications were declined chiefly on account of the inadequate appropriation for clerks in post-offices. A special appropriation of $100,000, as requested by the Postmaster-General, was approved by the Congress under date of March 30, 1888.

Two thousand one hundred and forty-two allowances for rent, fuel, and light were made, being an increase of 783 allowances, or 57.6 per cent. as compared with 1887. This increase was occasioned by the inadequate appropriation for rent, fuel, and light for post-offices, which required a careful revision of all the allowances for the items stated. The said allowances were reduced as far as practicable from January 1, 1888, in order to keep the expenses within the limited appropriation as fixed by the Congress. At the request of the Postmaster-General, an additional appropriation of $25,000 was made by the Congress under date of March 30, 1888, to be immediately available. With this additional appropriation, the allowances for rent, fuel, and light were again adjusted to meet the needs of the service. Seven hundred and eighty-seven applications for allowances for rent, fuel, and light were declined, being an increase of 104, or 15.2 per cent., as compared with the year 1887. This increase was occasioned, chiefly, by requests for rent, fuel, and light from postmasters at offices of the third class, who thought that authority to make allowances for the items stated at third-class offices had been granted by the Congress.

Eight thousand one hundred and twenty-five allowances for miscellaneous items were made, an increase of 1,399, or 20.8 per cent. as compared with 1887. Two thousand seven hundred and eighty-eight applications for allowances for miscellaneous items were declined, being a decrease of 343, or 11 per cent. as compared with 1887.

Seven hundred and forty-eight allowances for furniture for post-offices were made; and 919 applications for furniture was declined.

Two hundred and twenty-six allowances for advertising were made, the aggregate amount allowed being $10,733.90; and 342 applications for advertising were declined. This increase was occasioned by the circular notice to postmasters calling attention to the requirements of section 590 P. L. & R., edition of 1887, from the Superintendent of the Dead-Letter Office, under date of December 1, 1887.

Two hundred and ten post-offices of the fourth class were reported by the Auditor where the annual compensation of the postmaster amounted to $1,000 for four quarters, exclusive of money-order commissions. Of this number 197 offices were assigned to the third class; the aggregate of the salaries of the postmasters thereat making a total of $212,900, an increase of 79 offices, and $88,700 for compensation of postmasters, as compared with 1887.

The special adjustments of postmasters' salaries numbered 201, involving the aggregate amount of $213,400 for salaries of postmasters. There were three salaries of postmasters reduced or discontinued, making a saving of $4,200. The total number of salaries of Presidential postmasters adjusted during the year amounted to 2,746, and the aggregate amount involved for salaries in all the adjustments amounted to $4,420,400. Allowances for clerk-hire reduced or discontinued during the year numbered 552, making a saving of $71,958. One hundred and seven allowances for rent, fuel, and light were reduced or discontinued during the year, making a saving of $16,131.

The work of reviewing and re-adjusting the salaries of postmasters, and ex-postmasters of the third, fourth, and fifth classes, under the act of March 3, 1883, which was assigned, verbally, to the Salary and Allowance Division by Postmaster-General Gresham April 7, 1884, has been practically completed. All applications received prior to January 1, 1887, the date fixed as the limitation of presentation of claims by the act of Congress approved August 4, 1886, have been reviewed and acted upon. The total number of cases reviewed amounted to 68,725. Of this number 26,238 were allowed, involving the aggregate additional amount for compensation or back pay of postmasters of $1,221,009.69; 42,487 applications were reviewed and found to be below the 10 per cent. requirement of law, or for periods outside the dates defined by the act.

A tabulated statement is herewith respectfully submitted showing the operations of the Salary and Allowance Division for the fiscal years 1880, 1881, 1882, 1883, 1884, 1885, 1886, 1887, and 1888, with the increase of work since 1880:

Table showing volume of business transacted in the salary and allowance division, office of the First Assistant Postmaster-General, for the fiscal years ended June 30, 1880, 1881, 1882, 1883, 1884, 1885, 1886, 1887, and 1888, and increase of work since 1880.

Items.	Fiscal year ended June 30—									Increase of work of 1888 over 1880.
	1880.	1881.	1882.	1883.	1884.	1885.	1886.	1887.	1888.	
Number of letters received	4,898	4,255	8,806	10,520	17,837	21,873	24,031	29,834	31,456	26,558
Number of letters answered	5,160	4,751	7,398	10,002	21,393	28,332	30,105	35,568	37,441	32,281
Number of circular letters sent out			13,503	14,483	21,228	24,944	15,086	25,314	28,019	28,019
Number of allowances for clerk-hire, made	1,336	1,694	2,280	2,758	3,917	3,352	3,412	4,737	5,477	4,141
Number of allowances for clerk-hire declined	1,929	1,603	1,694	2,604	1,319	1,688	¹1,727	2,455	2,148	219
Number of allowances for rent, fuel, and light made	392	379	499	2,461	2,518	1,690	1,353	1,359	2,142	1,750
Number of allowances for rent, fuel, and light declined	223	144	171	622	967	507	668	683	787	564
Number of allowances for miscellaneous items made	484	703	3,177	4,970	4,551	4,709	4,983	6,726	8,125	7,641
Number of allowances for miscellaneous items declined	96	534	855	2,501	1,613	1,356	2,130	3,131	2,788	2,692
Number of allowances for furniture made	166	117	258	543	647	578	523	654	748	582
Number of allowances for furniture declined	596	337	244	915	779	595	720	907	919	323
Number of allowances for stationery made	615	635	2,628	3,239	(³)					
Number of allowances for stationery declined	19	19	918	1,128	207	50	²28			
Number of allowances for advertising made			21	368	218	222	240	207	226	226
Number of allowances for advertising declined			39	120	116	130	214	243	342	342
Number of cases referred to the chief post-office inspector	48	34	189	368	283	8	278	426	459	411

¹ Decrease.
² Transferred to division of post-office supplies.
³ Relates to stationery fiscal year ended June 30, 1883.

Table showing volume of business transacted in the salary and allowance division, office of the First Assistant Postmaster-General, etc.—Continued.

Items.	Fiscal year ending June 30—									Increase of work of 1888 over 1880.
	1880.	1881.	1882.	1883.	1884.	1885.	1886.	1887.	1888.	
Number of special adjustments, postmasters' salaries		251	238	349	328				201	201
Number of biennial adjustments, postmasters' salaries	1,764		2,012		4,875					
Number of fourth-class post-offices reported by the Auditor, where the annual compensation of the postmaster amounts to $1,000, exclusive of money-order commissions	117	152	192	298	228	44	57	118	210	93
Number of Presidential offices relegated to the fourth class			9	15	97	134	45	22	28	28
Number of fourth-class offices assigned to the third class	99	113	145	174	248	44	57	118	197	98
Number of lease cases prepared			33	176	87	(¹)				
Number of leases in operation			313	228	298	(¹)				
Number of cases of all kinds made special		117	787	378	194	181				
Discontinued rent, fuel, and light			5	22	217	110	107	76	107	107
Discontinued clerk-hire			17	217	92	720	122	1,107		
Number of Presidential post-offices	1,764	1,863	2,003	2,176	2,323	2,238	2,244	2,336	2,502	738
Number of claims for re-adjustment of postmasters' salaries, under act of March 3, 1883				6,537	26,892	16,521	11,897	11,189		
Number of railway mail allowances made		²74								
Number of employés (average)	3	3	4	5	7	³15	³13	⁴17.6	⁵15.5	

[1] Transferred to law and lease clerk.
[2] Transferred to office of the Second Assistant Postmaster-General.
[3] 8 employés on review of postmasters' salaries (1885 and 1886).
[4] 11+ employés on review of postmasters' salaries (1887).
[5] 9+ employés on review of postmasters' salaries (1888).

ADJUSTMENT OF PRESIDENTIAL POSTMASTERS' SALARIES.

The act of Congress approved March 3, 1883, provides for an annual instead of biennial adjustment of the salaries of Presidential postmasters, or postmasters at offices of the first, second, and third classes. In compliance with the requirements of this act, the fifth annual adjustment of the salaries of Presidential postmasters was made upon the basis of the gross receipts which accrued at the respective offices for the four quarters ended March 31, 1888, to take effect July 1, 1888. It should be observed that this adjustment was made, as usual, upon the gross receipts for one year, or four quarters, at the new or reduced rate of postage. The salaries of postmasters of 2,530 post-offices were reviewed. As required by law, 97 post-offices were assigned to the first class, 497 to the second class, and 1,908 to the third class. This was a net increase of 15 first-class post-offices, 61 second-class offices, and a net decrease of 63 third-class offices. Forty-two new offices (third class) were added to the Presidential list from July 1, 1888, and 28 offices (third class) were relegated to the fourth class from the same date, making the total number of Presidential offices July 1, 1888, 2,502, an increase of 166, or 7.1 per cent. as compared with the number of offices July 1, 1887.

The classification of Presidential post offices in accordance with the requirements of the act of Congress approved March 3, 1883, in effect July 1, 1888, may be concisely stated as follows:

First class:			
Total number June 30, 1888..			82
Number relegated to second class, July 1, 1888.................	1		
Number of second advanced to first, July 1, 1888..............	16		15
Net increase, first class, July 1, 1888............................		15	
Total number, first class, July 1, 1888...........................			97	97
Second class:			
Total number June 30, 1888..			436
Number of second advanced to first, July 1, 1888..............	16		
Number of second relegated to third, July 1, 1888.............	3		
Number of first relegated to second, July 1, 1888.............	1		
Number of third advanced to second, July 1, 1888.............	79		
Net increase, second class, July 1, 1888.........................		61	61
Total number, second class, July 1, 1888........................			497	497
Third class:			
Total number June 30, 1888..			1,970
Number of third advanced to second, July 1, 1888.............	79		
Number of third relegated to fourth, July 1, 1888.............	28		
Number of second relegated to third, July 1, 1888.............	3		
Number of fourth advanced to third, July 1, 1888.............	42		
Net decrease, third class, July 1, 1888...........................		62	62
Total number, third class, July 1, 1888..........................			1,908	1,908
Grand total Presidential post-offices (first, second, and third classes), July 1, 1888..				2,502

The number of offices, aggregate of salaries of postmasters, and aggregate gross receipts arranged by classes, July 1, 1888, is stated as follows:

Class.	Offices.	Aggregate of salaries.	Aggregate gross receipts.
First class...	97	$341,200	$23,816,337
Second class...	497	1,160,100	7,480,076
Third class..	1,908	2,701,500	7,202,575
Totals...	2,502	4,202,800	38,498,988

The aggregate amount required to pay the salaries of Presidential postmasters was $4,202,800, an increase of $322,500, or 8.3 per cent., as compared with the same item July 1, 1887. The aggregate of the salaries of postmasters will absorb 10.92 per cent. of the revenue of the Presidential offices, being 0.11 per cent. less than the percentage shown by the adjustment of 1887. The average amount allowed for salary of a Presidential postmaster by the adjustment of 1888, is $1,680. The grand total of gross receipts which accrued at the Presidential offices for the four quarters ended March 31, 1888, amounted to $38,498,987.80, being an increase of $3,322,826.13, or 9.4 per cent., as compared with the receipts as shown by the adjustment which took effect July 1, 1887. The grand total of the gross receipts which accrued at these offices for the four quarters ended March 31, 1888, is 74.09 per cent. of the revenue of the Department for the same period.

The several adjustments of the salaries of Presidential postmasters made in accordance with the requirements of the act of March 3, 1883, to take effect October 1, 1883, July 1, 1884, July 1, 1885, July 1, 1886, July 1, 1887, and July 1, 1888, are herewith stated, viz:

Date.	Number of Presidential offices.	Aggregate salaries of Presidential postmasters.	Average salary of Presidential postmasters.	Aggregate receipts which accrued at Presidential offices.	Per cent. of aggregate receipts absorbed for postmasters' salaries.	Per cent. of entire revenue of Department which accrued at Presidential offices.
October 1, 1883	2, 195	$3, 707, 500	$1, 689	$33, 535, 253. 95	11. 06	. 74. 28
July 1, 1884	2, 323	3, 828, 700	1, 648	33, 031, 697. 33	11. 59	74. 80
July 1, 1885	2, 233	3, 630, 600	1, 625	31, 792, 220. 55	11. 42	75. 36
July 1, 1886	2, 244	3, 685. 500	1, 642	32, 491, 551.58	11. 34	74. 07
July 1, 1887	2, 336	3, 880, 300	1, 661	35, 176, 161. 67	11. 03	74. 84
July 1, 1888	2, 502	4, 202, 800	1, 680	38, 498, 987. 80	10. 92	94. 09

A summary of the adjustments of salaries of Presidential postmasters July 1, 1887, and July 1, 1888, showing in detail the net increase of salaries, is submitted as follows:

Summary of the adjustments of the salaries of Presidential postmasters July 1, 1887, and July 1, 1888, showing in detail a comparative statement of the net increase of salaries of Presidential postmasters July 1, 1888.

Date.	No. of offices.	Salaries of postmasters.	
		Aggregate.	Net increase.
July 1, 1887	2, 336	$3, 880, 300	
July 1, 1888	2, 502	4, 202, 800	
Total increase (or gain)	166	322, 500	$322, 500
This increase ($322,500) is shown in detail as follows: Total number of first, second, and third class post-offices, whereat increases were made July 1, 1888	1, 215		
The aggregate increase, at the said offices being		154, 600	
By increase, corrected adjustments:			
West Union, Iowa		$100	
Silver Creek, N. Y.		100	
Marshall, Tex		200	
Total		400	
New offices during fiscal year:			
October 1, 1887	45	51, 000	
January 1, 1888	51	54, 100	
April 1, 1888	59	63, 900	
July 1, 1888	42	43, 900	
Total		212, 900	
Grand total		367, 900	
REDUCTIONS.			
Relegated to fourth class, July 1, 1888	28	28, 900	
By reductions at 107 Presidential offices		12, 300	
By Presidential offices discontinued:			
January 1, 1888, North Springfield, Mo		1, 700	
April 1, 1888, Astoria, N. Y.		1, 400	
April 1, 1888, Ravenswood, N. Y.		1, 100	
Total		45, 400	
By balance, net increase of salaries July 1, 1888		322, 500	322, 500
Total		367, 900	

A tabulated statement showing the number of Presidential post-offices, the aggregate of salaries of postmasters, and the aggregate gross receipts for the four quarters ended March 31, 1888, arranged by States and Territories, in alphabetical order, is respectfully submitted, as follows :

Statement showing the number of Presidential post-offices in the several States and Territories, and the aggregate salaries of the postmasters thereat, as adjusted to take effect July 1, 1888.

States and Territories.	Number of Presidential post-offices, adjustment of July 1, 1888.	Aggregate salaries of postmasters.	Aggregate receipts, four quarters ended March 31, 1888.
Alabama	20	$35, 700	$217, 864. 13
Alaska			
Arizona	4	6, 900	23, 850. 60
Arkansas	20	31, 800	134, 186. 91
California	74	127, 100	1, 229, 224. 56
Colorado	34	57, 500	375, 268. 52
Connecticut	58	103, 300	745, 367. 44
Dakota	48	72, 200	231, 801. 17
Delaware	8	12, 500	77, 882. 93
District of Columbia	1	5, 000	341, 091. 23
Florida	17	30, 700	148, 737. 88
Georgia	29	50, 800	389, 913. 06
Idaho	6	7, 900	19, 468. 93
Illinois	187	302, 400	3, 620, 119. 55
Indiana	94	157, 600	836, 265. 25
Indian Territory			
Iowa	129	208, 200	967, 833. 58
Kansas	127	202, 000	812, 731. 91
Kentucky	42	68, 500	492, 111. 42
Louisiana	12	19, 300	344, 229. 33
Maine	40	66, 400	376, 328. 10
Maryland	20	34, 200	632, 337. 44
Massachusetts	133	239, 700	3, 034, 070. 08
Michigan	124	205, 100	1, 224, 579. 97
Minnesota	57	90, 300	946, 178. 27
Mississippi	25	37, 200	122, 705. 43
Missouri	80	128, 400	1, 713, 422. 29
Montana	12	20, 400	94, 864. 91
Nebraska	78	116, 500	579, 043. 57
Nevada	7	10, 200	31, 403. 46
New Hampshire	33	53, 000	227, 650. 02
New Jersey	66	123, 800	870, 980. 63
New Mexico	9	14, 500	44, 950. 06
New York	225	400, 400	8, 125, 343. 64
North Carolina	25	41, 200	160, 639. 91
Ohio	141	255, 000	2, 403, 142. 44
Oregon	15	24, 600	152, 527. 10
Pennsylvania	183	313, 100	3, 691, 152. 27
Rhode Island	12	24, 000	310, 756. 11
South Carolina	20	30, 200	147, 165. 77
Tennessee	28	46, 900	412, 459. 15
Texas	74	120, 000*	571, 491. 81
Utah	5	9, 400	65, 673. 38
Vermont	26	43, 100	176, 849. 19
Virginia	36	61, 600	396, 470. 75
Washington	13	22, 300	95, 339. 08
West Virginia	16	26, 100	117, 752. 07
Wisconsin	83	136, 100	807, 980. 70
Wyoming	6	9, 700	36, 744. 80
Totals	2, 502	4, 202, 800	38, 498, 987. 80

Grand total gross receipts $38, 498, 897. 80
Grand total postmasters' salaries 4, 202, 800. 00
Percentage of gross receipts absorbed by salaries.. 10. 92

The grand total of gross receipts of Presidential offices for the four quarters ended March 31, 18888 amounts to 74.09 per cent. of the revenue of the Post-Office Department for the same period.

REVIEW OF SALARIES OF POSTMASTERS OF THE THIRD, FOURTH, AND FIFTH CLASSES, UNDER THE ACT OF MARCH 3, 1883.

The review of the salaries of postmasters and ex-postmasters of the third, fourth, and fifth classes, under the act of March 3, 1883, as construed by the Attorney-General of the United States, under date of February 13, 1884, and re-affirmed June 14, 1884, has been, since the report of last year (see pages 364 to 366, Report of the Postmaster-General for the fiscal year ended June 30, 1887), continued, and practically completed. Since the report mentioned was made, the second schedules of claims for the States of Ohio, Pennsylvania, Tennessee, Texas, Virginia, West Virginia, and Wisconsin, and the third schedules for all the States and Territories from Alabama to Wyoming, inclusive, have been completed and certified to the Auditor of the Treasury for the Post-Office Department. The total number of claims reviewed was 68,725. Of this number 26,238 claims have been allowed, and 42,487 claims were found below the 10 per cent. requirement of the law, or for periods outside the dates defined by the act. The total amount allowed as additional compensation, including the amount required by the series of third schedules, is $1,221,009.69. This sum exceeds the aggregate of the amounts appropriated by the Congress, to date, by $76,697.71, the several amounts appropriated by the Congress for the payment of these claims being as follows:

Under act approved July 7, 1884	$45,213.80
Under act approved March 3, 1885	178,281.23
Under act approved August 4, 1886	380,209.46
Under act approved February 1, 1888	160,286.05
Under act approved March 30, 1888	380,321.44
Total	1,144,311.98
Total amount allowed to date	1,221,009.69
Unappropriated for to date	76,697.71

A summary of the work of reviewing the salaries of postmasters and ex-postmasters of the third, fourth, and fifth classes, as required by the act of Congress approved March 3, 1883, is stated in the annual reports of the Postmaster-General for the fiscal years ended June 30, 1885, pages 217, 218, and 219; June 30, 1886, pages 155, 156, and 157, and June 30, 1887, pages 364, 365, and 366.

A tabulated statement showing the progress of the work of reviewing the said salaries from April 7, 1884, the date the said work was assigned to the salary and allowance division, to date, is herewith respectfully submitted, viz:

Statement showing progress of the work of reviewing the adjustment of the salaries of postmasters at offices of the third, fourth, and fifth classes, in compliance with the requirements of the act of March 3, 1883.

Date of schedule.	States and Territories.	No. of schedule.	Total number of cases reviewed.	No. of cases allowed.	Aggregate amount heretofore allowed postmasters.	Aggregate amount allowed under act of March 3, 1883.
1884.						
Mar. 14 } June 9 }	Alabama	1	88	38	$10,880.00	$3,392.14
11	Indiana	1	565	222	64,035.79	16,892.13
16	Iowa	1	713	175	58,905.42	14,896.54
24	Connecticut	1	261	69	31,528.79	6,157.42
24	Arizona	1	3	1	495.00	103.54
24	Dakota	1	22	1	402.50	51.85
25	Florida	1	57	10	8,709.04	2,634.06
25	Colorado	1	56	6	660.83	217.32
July 2	Kansas	1	178	69	13,251.53	3,485.93
2	Arkansas	1	26	13	3,863.11	1,566.02
5	Georgia	1	76	24	7,833.52	2,020.40
Aug. 30	California	1	156	31	13,949.29	3,422.31
30	Delaware	1	32	6	730.06	622.64
30	Illinois	1	1,722	546	164,677.33	38,747.72
30	Kentucky	1	215	70	19,482.30	5,808.25
30	Louisiana	1	75	15	7,001.56	1,947.86
30	Maine	1	497	146	20,190.73	7,657.26
30	Maryland	1	212	61	21,135.95	12,401.77
Sept. 8	Massachusetts	1	466	111	62,521.77	13,389.55
25	Michigan	1	753	224	46,180.42	10,947.89
Oct. 1	Minnesota	1	499	139	20,515.13	5,269.72
3	Mississippi	1	100	26	10,778.96	2,905.61
Nov. 12	Missouri	1	607	195	44,689.07	13,994.72
12	Nevada	1	17	7	3,868.66	943.16
13	New Mexico	1	17	4	444.19	155.45
13	Oregon	1	42	12	4,033.64	1,138.53
15	Nebraska	1	173	31	4,747.89	2,125.48
29	New Hampshire	1	375	107	22,879.67	5,409.13
Dec. 2	Montana	1	15	2	358.00	176.83
15	New Jersey	1	542	128	29,225.30	9,280.91
1885.						
Mar. 20	New York	1	3,344	1,197	306,894.56	77,059.24
23	North Carolina	1	334	110	22,893.96	4,967.40
July 13	Ohio	1	4,283	2,099	366,177.71	104,522.03
Nov. 18	Pennsylvania	1	5,139	2,514	393,414.52	111,416.51
Dec. 18	Rhode Island	1	111	30	12,523.84	3,060.46
23	South Carolina	1	182	37	13,918.90	5,986.29
31	Tennessee	1	602	149	42,164.44	10,085.52
1886.						
Jan. 8	Texas	1	373	107	29,214.61	10,764.79
9	Utah	1	147	20	1,208.00	502.60
23	Vermont	1	742	229	55,103.34	13,164.66
Mar. 6	Virginia	1	1,030	361	40,009.80	14,241.91
19	Washington	1	28	11	2,407.75	728.74
Apr. 27	West Virginia	1	736	326	45,562.79	20,007.64
May 29	Wisconsin	1	2,218	894	144,872.17	39,306.92
June 8	Wyoming	1	14	2	700.50	281.73
8	Idaho	1	13	2	401.50	85.42
Aug. 11	Alabama	2	292	121	21,231.66	6,798.85
17	Arkansas	2	240	65	10,686.91	4,371.58
Sept. 8	California	2	657	145	24,956.02	6,616.04
23	Arizona	2	4	1	50.00	16.38
23	Colorado	2	39	16	2,150.50	1,010.59
Oct. 1	Connecticut	2	545	220	56,850.60	13,742.76
13	Dakota	2	13	4	271.87	476.75
13	Delaware	2	176	66	9,890.33	2,456.65
19	Florida	2	93	16	8,487.45	2,706.66
Nov. 2	Georgia	2	388	113	16,165.37	4,873.38
3	Idaho	2	10	6	5,705.00	1,271.46
1887.						
Jan. 31	Illinois	2	2,808	1,214	203,580.26	58,197.51
Feb. 28	Indiana	2	3,025	1,530	179,963.30	57,483.03
Mar. 21	Iowa	2	1,890	840	101,882.47	28,993.32
23	Indian Territory	2	6	4	1,204.50	124.67
27	Kansas	2	429	114	17,075.86	5,330.21
Apr. 23	Kentucky	2	1,318	596	67,294.48	21,711.75
27	Maine	2	1,680	604	68,027.57	18,981.16
30	Louisiana	2	136	32	4,025.00	1,826.02
May 2	Vermont	2	299	114	17,426.10	5,106.74
4	Mississippi	2	256	74	12,414.96	4,817.37
4	Rhode Island	2	134	56	7,028.77	2,099.02
10	Maryland	2	775	334	36,269.97	10,748.69

Statement showing progress of the work of reviewing the adjustment of the salaries of postmasters at offices of the third, fourth, and fifth classes, etc.—Continued.

Date of schedule.	States and Territories.	No. of schedule.	Total number of cases reviewed.	No. of cases allowed.	Aggregate amount heretofore allowed postmasters.	Aggregate amount allowed under act of March 3, 1883.
1887.						
May 20	Massachusetts	2	1,163	400	$116,591.35	$23,724.63
31	Michigan	2	1,595	693	94,560.31	25,426.75
June 1	Montana	2	14	1	138.00	15.18
1	New Mexico	2	19	4	2,382.16	531.38
1	Washington	2	39	8	1,849.61	337.31
2	Nevada	2	45	13	4,381.98	1,365.50
2	Utah	2	97	22	1,381.00	564.60
3	South Carolina	2	94	34	5,903.12	2,325.72
4	Oregon	2	180	54	7,787.65	2,260.76
6	Nebraska	2	152	41	8,963.82	1,293.47
8	North Carolina	2	387	162	12,032.81	4,647.49
11	New Hampshire	2	579	200	36,164.08	8,202.32
17	Minnesota	2	783	292	28,263.69	9,060.08
23	New Jersey	2	792	325	37,256.41	11,918.20
29	Missouri	2	1,448	623	81,675.09	25,527.57
July 25	New York	2	3,997	1,839	242,460.29	67,929.96
Sept. 17	Ohio	2	2,906	1,166	115,993.54	33,489.21
Oct. 15	Pennsylvania	3	2,952	1,182	111,112.21	36,768.76
25	Tennessee	2	393	153	13,039.91	5,911.02
31	Texas	2	194	87	9,256.94	3,751.43
Nov. 5	Virginia	2	281	123	8,004.04	3,683.62
15	West Virginia	2	373	174	11,263.02	3,794.23
26	Wisconsin	2	573	280	28,245.40	7,119.44
1888.						
Feb. 1	Alabama	8	229	57	4,293.24	1,422.76
1	Arkansas	3	117	32	3,284.14	1,368.94
1	California	3	134	36	3,345.82	1,572.83
1	Colorado	3	16	4	138.50	49.68
1	Connecticut	3	123	52	11,354.98	2,503.56
1	Dakota	3	2			
1	Delaware	3	41	15	2,904.20	2,019.02
10	Florida	3	20	4	468.00	674.85
10	Georgia	3	125	51	4,914.98	2,937.12
10	Illinois	3	564	214	32,632.05	9,495.51
10	Indiana	3	443	182	19,292.90	6,418.75
10	Indian Territory	3	1			
10	Iowa	3	281	76	13,129.02	3,589.85
10	Kansas	3	164	26	2,404.79	1,057.50
10	Kentucky	3	155	38	4,130.41	1,173.91
10	Louisiana	3	93	14	5,864.23	2,046.27
10	Maine	3	129	29	3,233.27	919.54
10	Maryland	3	70	16	2,873.10	857.18
10	Massachusetts	3	65	19	6,910.66	1,915.13
10	Michigan	3	197	43	9,570.65	2,530.25
10	Minnesota	3	101	14	1,252.44	1,033.73
10	Mississippi	3	31	6	1,530.75	585.77
10	Missouri	3	106	30	3,766.01	1,220.25
Mar. 20	Montana	3	13	2	792.24	271.67
20	Nebraska	3	88	6	569.17	310.38
20	Nevada	3	8			
20	New Hampshire	3	34	9	1,070.36	215.46
20	New Jersey	3	60	8	936.03	529.53
20	New Mexico	3	6			
20	New York	3	327	74	13,957.86	3,427.65
20	North Carolina	3	75	8	171.75	65.54
20	Ohio	3	337	101	17,187.92	5,192.86
20	Oregon	3	28	3	504.00	137.87
20	Pennsylvania	3	1,039	219	20,453.72	6,758.05
20	Rhode Island	3	11	2	2,300.00	402.66
20	South Carolina	3	101	11	703.96	745.24
20	Tennessee	3	291	21	1,956.46	716.39
20	Texas	3	204	20	2,487.94	1,080.75
20	Utah	3	47	5	482.00	139.58
20	Vermont	3	77	10	919.25	296.91
20	Virginia	3	309	19	3,073.91	3,300.84
20	Washington	3	12	1	101.50	12.36
20	West Virginia	8	191	15	4,843.61	7,432.57
20	Wisconsin	3	42	8	2,010.05	457.70
20	Wyoming	3	3			
	Totals		68,725	26,238	4,238,717.19	1,221,009.69

Boxes are classed as call-boxes, lock-boxes. and lock-drawers. They are provided by the following methods:

(1) In Government buildings.

(2) At first and second class post-offices, the lessor by agreement in the lease often provides them.

(3) Under existing law (R. S., Sec. 4052, and Sec. 490, P. L. and R., edition of 1887) individuals may provide lock-boxes or lock-drawers for their own use, under conditions stated.

(4) In all other cases boxes must be furnished and kept in repair by the postmaster.

Boxes are provided as an accommodation to the patrons of the office, as a convenience to the postmaster, and as a source of revenue. At Presidential post-offices, or offices of the first, second, and third classes, box-rents are included in the gross receipts accruing at the offices in making the annual adjustment of salaries of Presidential postmasters, and the said postmasters, therefore, indirectly receive a part of the box-rents in the sum allowed as compensation. At fourth-class offices the box-rents, under existing law, are, practically, allowed as a part of the compensation of the postmaster.

Box-rent rates are supervised by the Department, securing thereby a greater uniformity of prices, better accommodation to the box-renters, and an increase of revenue from box-rents. This supervision of box-rent rates has improved this branch of the postal service during the past year. The revenue from box-rents would be increased if the deposit of 50 cents for each key delivered to box-renters were reduced to 25 cents for each key, as recommended last year, and as now charged for key-deposits at post-offices located in Government buildings under the control of the Treasury Department.

The regulations relative to key-deposits should be modified to conform to the recent instructions relative to key-deposits at post-offices located in public buildings under the control of the Treasury Department, fixing the deposit for each key delivered to a box-renter at 25 cents, instead of 50 cents, as heretofore required. As stated last year, I am of opinion that the reduction of the key-deposit rate from 50 cents to 25 cents will enable postmasters to rent more boxes, and thereby increase the revenue from box-rents. The modified regulations of the Treasury Department require a deposit of 25 cents for each key at the present time, while at offices in buildings leased by this Department, with box outfits covered by the lease, postmasters are required to collect a deposit of 50 cents for each key. At offices where postmasters provide their own boxes, under present regulations they are permitted to exercise their discretion in collecting a deposit for keys, and where so collected the rate is 50 cents for each key. A reduction of the amount of deposit for keys from 50 cents to the uniform rate of 25 cents for each key will improve this branch of the service, and enable postmasters to rent boxes to many would-be patrons who have heretofore refused to rent boxes where required to make a deposit of 50 cents for each key.

The key-deposit is exacted as security against the loss of keys. The fund so collected is held by the postmaster as a trust fund. When a key is lost by the renter of the box, or while he is responsible therefor, or through his fault it is broken so as to be rendered useless, or is withheld over thirty days after the box to which it belongs has been vacated, the key-deposit therefor becomes forfeited and is trans-ferred to the fund called "key-deposit forfeiture fund." This forfeiture fund is expended: (1) For the purchase of new keys to replace those lost, broken, or withheld. (2) For necessary repairs to locks. (3) For keeping the lock-boxes in serviceable condition.

Box-renters who provide their own boxes are not required to make deposits for keys furnished by themselves.

ALLOWANCES FOR RENT, FUEL, AND LIGHT FOR THIRD-CLASS OFFICES.

The recommendation heretofore made by this office that allowances for rent, fuel, and light be made at post-offices of the third class (see reports of the Postmaster-General for 1883, page 105; 1884, pages 20 and 79; 1885, pages 56 and 225; 1886, pages 48, 49, 50, 51, 158, and 159; and 1887, pages 18, 19, 132 to 151, inclusive, and 367) has been favorably considered by the Congress, act approved July 24, 1888. The text of the act is as follows:

> For rent, light, and fuel to post-offices of the third class, $450,000: *Provided,* That there shall not be allowed for the use of any third-class post-office for rent a sum in excess of $300, nor more than $60 for fuel and lights in any one year. The Post-master-General may hereafter allow rent, light, and fuel at offices of the third class in the same manner as he is now authorized to do in the case of offices of the first and second class: *Provided,* That no contract for rent for a third-class post-office shall be made for a longer period than one year, nor shall the aggregate allowance for rent made in any year exceed the amount appropriated for such purpose.

The appropriation as made by the Congress is $200,000 less than the estimates for rent, fuel, and light as made by the Department. The limitation of allowances for rent at the maximum rate of $300 a year, and fuel and light at the maximum rate of $60 a year, is not in the in-terest of good service. The Postmaster-General should have dis-cretionary authority to fix allowances for rent, fuel, and light for third-class post-offices in the same manner as he is now authorized by law to do in case of offices of the first and second classes, fixing allowances in accordance with the requirements of the service and the local conditions and surroundings of the respective offices. I therefore recommend that the limitation of allowances, as fixed by the act approved July 24, 1888, be repealed, and that the Postmaster-General be given full discretionary authority to make allowances for rent, fuel, and light for third-class post-offices.

By the adjustment of the salaries of Presidential postmasters, in ac-cordance with the requirements of the act of March 3. 1883, to take effect July 1, 1888, 1,908 offices were assigned to the third class. I sub-mit herewith a tabulated statement of these offices, arranged to exhibit the offices and grades (salary $1,000 to $1,900, inclusive) in the several States and Territories, in effect July 1, 1888, viz:

Statement showing the number of third-class post-offices in each State and Territory, arranged to exhibit the number of each grade (salary $1,000 to $1,900, inclusive) to July 1, 1888.

States and Territories.	Postmasters' salaries.										Total.
	$1,000	$1,100	$1,200	$1,300	$1,400	$1,500	$1,600	$1,700	$1,800	$1,900	
Alabama		2	*1	2	2	3	1	1	1	1	14
Alaska											
Arizona							2		1	1	4
Arkansas	1	2	3	4	1	1	1	1	1	1	16
California	5	3	11	4	4	9	8	6	4	1	55
Colorado		1	5	3		8	3	5	2		27
Connecticut	3	3	8	4	3	6	4	5	2	2	40
Dakota	2	5	11	5	3	6	4		3		39
Delaware		2	1		3				1		7
District of Columbia											
Florida			3		1	2		2	3		11
Georgia		4	2	3	4	2	2	3	1		21
Idaho		3	1	1		1		1			6
Illinois	13	16	13	18	33	23	10	15	5	4	149
Indiana	5	6	9	6	9	10	10	7	5	6	73
Indian Territory											
Iowa	7	6	19	7	19	14	13	14	3	4	106
Kansas	7	17	7	8	15	18	10	14	5	4	105
Kentucky	2	7	2	4	4	4	4	2	3		32
Louisiana	1	2	1	3	1	2				1	10
Maine	3	4	4	4	4	3	2	2	3	1	30
Maryland	1	3		4	3	1	3				15
Massachusetts	4	12	4	5	15	15	14	11	10	4	94
Michigan	7	15	9	6	14	13	11	5	11	3	94
Minnesota	4	10	7	3	7	3	6	2	4	1	47
Mississippi		5	6	2	3	1	2		1	1	21
Missouri	3	8	14	9	8	3	7	10	4	2	68
Montana				2	1	3		2			10
Nebraska	4	12	11	10	5	6	11	8	1	1	69
Nevada	1	2			1			1		1	6
New Hampshire	4	2	5		3	4	4	2	2	1	27
New Jersey		3	5	1	4	8	7	8	6	3	45
New Mexico			1	1	1	1	2	1			7
New York	8	17	18	19	14	23	26	13	11	7	156
North Carolina	1	1	4		4	4	1	2	1		18
Ohio	4	9	8	11	14	14	11	9	8	3	91
Oregon	1	1	3			2	2	3	2	1	13
Pennsylvania	10	21	17	5	19	14	17	12	15	6	136
Rhode Island		1	1	1			3	2		1	7
South Carolina	2	4	2	1		3	2	1			17
Tennessee		5	4	1	5	3	1	2			23
Texas	4	8	7	4	8	11	8	8	2	2	60
Utah			1	1		1					3
Vermont	1	3	1		6	5	1	1			18
Virginia	3	3	1	2	4	8	2	1	1	2	27
Washington	1	1	1		1	2	2	1			9
West Virginia		1	2	4	1	1	2		2		13
Wisconsin	3	11	6	10	7	10	6	7	4	3	65
Wyoming		1	1			2					4
Totals	115	241	238	177	256	272	226	187	128	68	1,90

LEGISLATION RECOMMENDED.

Allowances for rent for third-class offices.—As hereinbefore stated, I recommend that the limitations of the act of Congress approved July 24, 1888, fixing the maximum annual rental at $300, and the maximum amount for fuel and light at $60, be repealed, and the Postmaster-General be given full discretionary authority to fix the allowances for rent, fuel, and light for third-class post-offices in accordance with the best interests of the postal service, having in view the local conditions and surroundings of the respective offices.

Classification and salaries of clerks in the larger offices.—I recommend that the clerks attached to the first-class offices be classified, and that the salaries of the clerks be fixed by law. This important subject has been considered by a commission appointed by the Postmaster-General, and the result is embodied in a report printed in the Report of the Postmaster-General for the fiscal year ended June 30, 1887, pages 177 to 182, inclusive. I am of opinion that the clerks in the larger offices should be classified with compensation ranging from a minimum salary of $600 a year to a maximum salary of not exceeding $1,400 a year. This classification, with salaries as stated in even hundreds of dollars, should not include assistant postmasters, cashiers, superintendents of divisions, or other employés directly responsible to the postmasters; nor to stampers, messengers, porters, carpenters, watchmen, or laborers. The reasons for the exceptions as above stated are shown in the report of the commission, which very properly and wisely recommends compensation for clerks in accordance with their duties, responsibilities, experience, and the time required for a proper performance of their work.

On the first of January, 1888, at the 82 first-class offices there were employed a total of 4,601 clerks. By the adjustment of salaries of Presidential postmasters, made in accordance with the requirements of the act of March 3, 1883, which took effect July 1, 1888, 97 offices were assigned to the first class, making a net increase of 15 first-class offices. These additional first-class offices, with the additional clerks required for the increased service, will make a total of 5,000 clerks, in round numbers, about January 1 next.

I am of the opinion that it is in the interest of good service to classify and fix by law the compensation of the clerks attached to the first-class offices. The letter-carriers are not only classified by law, with fixed salaries, but under recent legislation their hours of duty are limited to eight hours per day. The clerks in the larger offices, who work early and late, with practically no limitation to their hours of labor, deserve consideration, and I strongly urge that some action for their relief and the improvement of the clerical service at first-class offices be taken by the Congress.

Compensation to postmasters of the fourth class.—Attention is earnestly invited to the need of legislation relative to the compensation of fourth-class postmasters. The rates of compensation as provided by the act of Congress approved March 3, 1883, are not sufficient to enable the Department to secure good service at fourth-class offices. This matter has been called to the attention of the Congress, but no measure has been provided to meet the requirements of the service.

It is respectfully suggested that the subject-matter of compensation of fourth-class postmasters be considered with a view of formulating a measure that would provide a reasonable increase of compensation to be fixed in even tens and hundreds of dollars for a specified period on the basis of the business of the respective offices for the preceding year. I am of opinion that a bill framed to include the suggestions herein made, with such additional provisions as may be deemed advisable by the Congress, will be in the interest of good service.

THE FREE-DELIVERY SYSTEM.

The fiscal year closed with 358 free-delivery offices, an increase of 169 over the number in operation June 30, 1887. The new offices established were:

Adrian, Mich.	Atlantic City, N. J.	Beaver Falls, Pa.
Alexandria, Va.	Auburn, Me.	Belleville, Ill.
Amsterdam, N. Y.	Ashland, Wis.	Bethlehem, Pa.
Annapolis, Md.	Appleton, Wis.	Birmingham, Conn.
Ann Arbor, Mich.	Abilene, Kans.	Brattleboro, Vt.
Ansonia, Conn.	Bath, Me.	Bridgeton, N. J.
Asbury Park, N. J.	Beatrice, Nebr.	Cairo, Ill.

Carlisle, Pa.
Chambersburgh, Pa.
Champaign, Ill.   .
Charleston, W. Va.
Charlotte, N. C.
Chester, Pa.
Cheyenne City, Wyo.
Clinton, Iowa.
Cohoes, N. Y.
Colorado Springs, Colo.
Columbia, S. C.
Columbus, Ga.
Corning, N. Y.
Cortland, N. Y.
Cumberland, Md.
Carthage, Mo.
Chillicothe, Ohio.
Danbury, Conn.
Danville, Ill.
Danville, Va.
Dover, N. H.
Dunkirk, N. Y.
Denison, Tex.
Delaware, Ohio.
East Orange, N. J.
Elkhart, Ind.
El Paso, Tex.
Emporia, Kans.
Englewood, Ill.
Evanston, Ill.
Flint, Mich.
Fond du Lac, Wis.
Fort Scott, Kans.
Fort Smith, Ark.
Frankfort, Ky.
Frederick, Md.
Freeport, Ill.
Fargo, Dak.
Glens Falls, N. Y.
Gloversville, N. Y.
Grand Island, Nebr.
Hamilton, Ohio.
Hastings, Nebr.
Helena, Mont.
Hornellsville, N. Y.
Hot Springs, Ark.
Hudson, N. Y.
Huron, Dak.
Hutchinson, Kans.
Huntingdon, Pa.

Hagerstown, Md.
Iowa City, Iowa.
Jackson, Miss.
Jacksonville, Ill.
Janesville, Wis.
Johnstown, Pa.
Keene, N. H.
Kansas City, Kans.
Lima, Ohio.
Little Falls, N.Y.
Logansport, Ind.
Lebanon, Pa.
Long Island City, N. Y.
Malden, Mass.
Marlborough, Mass.
Marquette, Mich.
Marshalltown, Iowa.
Meadville, Pa.
Meridian, Miss.
Middletown, Conn.
Middletown, N. Y.
Middletown, Ohio.
Moline, Ill.
Montpelier, Vt.
Muscatine, Iowa.
Muskegon, Mich.
Manistee, Mich.
Mankato, Minn.
Massillon, Ohio.
Marietta, Ohio.
McKeesport, Pa.
Nashua, N. H.
New Albany, Ind.
Newark, Ohio.
New Britain, Conn.
Newburyport, Mass.
Newcastle, Pa.
Newton, Kans.
Norristown, Pa.
North Adams, Mass.
Northampton, Mass.
New Brunswick, N. J.
Natchez, Miss.
Norwalk, Ohio.
Ogdensburgh, N. Y.
Orange, N. J.
Oskaloosa, Iowa.
Ottawa, Ill.
Ottawa, Kans.
Owego, N. Y.

Oneonta, N. Y.
Paducah, Ky.
Parkersburgh, W. Va.
Pensacola, Fla.
Piqua, Ohio.
Port Huron Mich.
Portsmouth Ohio.
Portsmouth, N. H.
Portsmouth, Va.
Pueblo, Colo.
Pekin, Ill.
Rome, Ga.
Rome, N. Y.
Saginaw, Mich.
Salem, Oregon,
San Diego, Cal.
Schenectady, N. Y.
Seattle, Wash.
Selma, Ala.
Sheboygan, Wis.
Sherman, Tex.
Shreveport, La.
Sioux Falls, Dak.
Stamford, Conn.
Staunton, Va.
Sterling, Ill.
Steubenville, Ohio.
Stillwater, Minn.
Stockton, Cal.
Streator, Ill.
Springfield, Mo.
Salem, Ohio.
Salina, Kans.
Tacoma, Wash.
Tiffin, Ohio.
Titusville, Pa.
Vicksburg, Miss. .
Vincennes, Ind.
Waltham, Mass.
Warren, Pa.
Waterloo, Iowa.
West Chester, Pa.
Westerly, R. I.
Winfield, Kans.
Woonsocket. R. I.
Wooster, Ohio.
Wellington, Kans.
Xenia. Ohio.

The number of carriers had increased from 5,310 to 6,346.

The unusually large increase in the number of new offices established was caused by the Act of Congress, approved January 3, 1887, which provides that the system may be extended to places containing a population of 10,000 within their corporate limits, according to the last general census taken by authority of State or United States law, or at any post-office which produced a gross revenue for the preceding fiscal year of not less than $10,000.

The appropriation for the service was $5,522,500. The total cost thereof was $5,422,356.36, leaving an unexpended balance of $100,143.64.

The following table gives the aggregate results of the operations of the free-delivery system for the fiscal year, and the comparison of the results with the preceding year:

Aggregate results of the free-delivery service for the fiscal year ended June 30, 1888.

Statistics of free delivery.	1887.	1888.	Increase.	Per cent.
Number of offices	189	358	169	84.12
Number of carriers	5,310	6,346	1,036	19.51
Registered letters delivered	3,706,346	4,271,105	564,759	15.23
Letters delivered	783,393,058	873,760,692	90,367,634	11.53
Postal-cards delivered	215,924,009	212,426,703	*3,507,306	*1.60
Newspapers, etc., delivered	342,361,621	428,710,933	86,349,312	25.22
Letters collected	617,016,182	760,113,963	143,097,781	23.19
Postal-cards collected	170,079,552	223,980,437	53,900,885	31.69
Newspapers, etc., collected	102,073,368	127,597,975	25,524,637	25.00
Whole number of pieces handled	2,234,564,656	2,630,861,758	396,297,102	17.72
Pieces handled per carrier	420,822	415,563	*5,250	*1.25
Total cost of service, including post-office inspectors	$4,618,692.07	$5,422,356.36	$803,664.29	17.40
Average cost per carrier	†$867.67	$852.06	*15.61	*1.79
Average cost per piece, in mills	†2.2	2.0	*.2	*9.09
Amount of postage on local matter	$6,691,253.60	$7,721,689.16	$1,030,435.47	15.39
Excess of postage on local matter over total cost of service	$2,072,561.62	$2,299,332.80	$226,771.18	10.94

* Decrease.
† Based on the aggregate, $5,407,200.16, paid carriers, and for incidental expenses, and not including $15,156.20 paid post-office inspectors.

The receipts from local postage exceeded the cost of service in 38 of the 358 offices (an increase of 8 over the previous year), as shown by the following table:

Post-offices at which the local postage exceeded the cost of the service.

Name of office.	Receipts from local postage.	Cost of carrier service.	Net gain.
Atchison, Kans	$6,652.35	$5,360.80	$1,291.55
Atlanta, Ga	19,807.32	16,852.13	2,015.19
Baltimore, Md	198,501.15	144,336.52	54,164.63
Birmingham, Ala	12,460.15	5,211.36	27,248.79
Boston, Mass	475,751.75	333,564.36	142,187.39
Brooklyn, N. Y	353,030.47	244,795.68	108,234.79
Buffalo, N. Y	85,998.82	73,498.86	12,499.96
Chicago, Ill	633,500.72	364,256.49	269,244.23
Cincinnati, Ohio	137,170.69	114,851.05	22,319.64
Denver, Colo	44,053.07	24,504.33	19,548.74
Detroit, Mich	66,899.71	60,479.94	6,419.77
Duluth, Minn	11,431.19	8,141.27	3,249.92
Elizabeth, N. J	9,493.27	8,756.63	736.64
Hartford, Conn	22,963.10	17,671.49	5,321.61
Helena, Mont	3,349.69	2,585.40	764.29
Kansas City, Mo	58,030.49	47,307.41	10,723.08
Leavenworth, Kans	10,158.40	7,189.10	2,969.30
Lexington, Ky	5,389.70	5,161.68	228.02
Lowell, Mass	23,254.13	16,455.38	6,798.75
Montgomery, Ala	7,265.96	4,587.80	2,678.16
Newark, N. J	53,219.13	42,931.29	10,287.84
New Haven, Conn	38,506.90	24,142.85	14,364.05
New Orleans, La	78,694.78	58,999.99	19,694.79
Newton, Kans	2,128.04	1,942.85	175.19
New York, N. Y	2,034,849.99	712,169.46	1,322,680.53
Omaha, Nebr	67,491.20	23,754.49	43,736.71
Philadelphia, Pa	1,184,048.90	444,864.34	739,184.56
Pittsburgh, Pa	85,966.16	62,166.38	23,799.78
Providence, R. I	46,107.80	42,789.58	3,318.22
Rochester, N. Y	49,267.80	43,421.13	5,846.67
Saint Louis, Mo	459,639.13	186,160.74	273,478.39
Saint Paul, Minn	58,674.75	48,660.40	9,014.35
San Francisco, Cal	168,329.94	114,834.17	53,495.77
Syracuse, N. Y	23,850.88	23,276.80	574.08
Topeka, Kans	10,853.14	10,085.00	768.14
Troy, N. Y	28,965.18	23,624.47	5,340.71
Wilkes Barre, Pa	12,252.82	9,326.08	2,926.74
Tacoma, Wash	2,076.57	1,810.37	266.20

The free-delivery system of the Post-Office Department was inaugurated July 1, 1863. The following table showing its growth in detail is herewith submitted:

Showing the growth of the free-delivery service from its inauguration, July 1, 1863.

Year.	Number of offices.	Number of carriers.	Cost of service.	Postage on local matter.	Excess of cost.	Excess of postage on local matter.
1863–'64	66	685	$317,063.20			
1864–'65	45	757	448,664.51			
1865–'66	46	863	589,296.41			
1866–'67	47	943	609,994.34			
1867–'68	48	1,198	995,934.59			
1868–'69	48	1,246	1,183,915.31			
1869–'70	51	1,362	1,230,079.85	$681,864.70	$548,215.15	
1870–'71	52	1,419	1,353,923.22	758,120.78	595,802.45	
1871–'72	52	1,443	1,385,965.76	907,351.93	478,613.83	
1872–'73	52	1,498	1,422,495.48	1,112,251.21	310,244.27	
1873–'74	87	2,049	1,802,696.41	1,611,481.66	191,214.75	
1874–'75	87	2,195	1,880,041.99	1,947,599.54		$67,517.55
1875–'76	87	2,269	1,981,186.51	2,065,561.73		84,375.22
1876–'77	87	2,265	1,893,619.85	2,254,597.83		360,977.98
1877–'78	87	2,275	1,824,166.96	2,452,251.51		628,084.55
1878–'79	88	2,359	1,947,706.61	2,812,523.86		864,771.14
1879–'80	104	2,688	2,363,693.14	3,068,797.14		705,104.00
1880–'81	109	2,861	2,499,911.54	3,273,630.39		773,718.85
1881–'82	112	3,115	2,623,262.74	3,816,576.09		1,193,313.35
1882–'83	154	3,680	3,173,336.51	4,195,230.52		1,021,894.01
1883–'84	150	3,890	3,504,206.52	4,777,484.87		1,274,278.35
1884–'85	178	4,358	3,985,952.55	5,281,721.10		1,295,768.55
1885–'86	181	4,841	4,312,306.70	5,839,242.97		1,526,936.27
1886–'87	189	5,310	4,618,692.07	6,691,258.69		2,072,561.62
1887–'88	358	6,346	5,422,356.36	7,721,689.16		2,299,332.80

Additional information concerning the operations of this service at every free-delivery office will be found in tabulated statement marked Table D.

Since the close of the fiscal year twenty-one additional offices have been established and a large number of applications are now pending.

The popularity of this service where it has been established, its usefulness to the people, and the great demand for its extension to additional cities prove the wisdom of its founders.

The diverse results at different offices as shown by the table, in regard to number of pieces handled, cost per piece in mills, cost of the service, disproportionate number of carriers to the population and business done, and other irregular features of the service which appear, are due to a variety of causes, among which may be mentioned the following:

The physical and geographical conditions of the territory to be served, such as streams to cross and hilly and broken ground to traverse; the amount of sparsely settled country and the number of large estates on the carriers' routes; the time of arrival and departure of mails and the quantity to be handled; the number of individual letters and pieces, and of packages of mail containing numerous letters and other matter to one address and delivered in bulk to business houses and manufacturing establishments; the failure in perhaps a majority of cases to obtain a correct count, rather than a very liberal estimate of pieces handled; the time required to make the service efficient at offices recently established; the compactness of some cities where a large business is done, and the number of dwellings in other cities more particularly occupied for residences, where a small amount only of business mail is handled.

An earnest effort is being made by the aid of competent inspectors and by correspondence to improve the service in every city.

In concluding, I desire earnestly to commend the chiefs of division and the clerks of this Bureau for faithful and efficient service.

Very respectfully,

A. E. STEVENSON,
First Assistant Postmaster-General.

Hon. DON M. DICKINSON,
Postmaster-General.

TABLE A.—*Statement showing the number of Presidential post-offices in each State and Territory June 30, 1887, and June 30, 1888, with increase and decrease; also the number of post-offices of each class, together with the number of money-order post-offices and stations by States and Territories June 30, 1888.*

States and Territories.	Presidential post-offices June 30, 1887.	Presidential post-offices June 30, 1888.	Increase.	Decrease.	Post-offices of the first class.	Post-offices of the second class.	Post-offices of the third class.	Post-offices of the fourth class.	Money-order post-offices June 30, 1888.	Money-order post-office stations June 30, 1888.
Alabama	19	20	1	...	...	4	16	1,622	100	...
Alaska	...	...	...	...	...	...	...	15	...	...
Arizona	4	4	...	...	...	1	8	152	25	...
Arkansas	17	20	3	...	...	4	16	1,336	113	...
California	65	69	4	...	4	12	53	1,135	207	8
Colorado	28	34	6	...	1	3	30	523	99	...
Connecticut	53	57	4	...	3	15	39	432	88	...
Dakota	46	50	4	...	...	8	42	1,015	144	...
Delaware	6	8	2	...	1	...	7	135	18	...
District of Columbia	1	1	...	...	1	...	...	10	1	8
Florida	17	17	...	...	1	4	12	716	84	...
Georgia	29	29	...	...	2	4	23	1,647	129	...
Idaho	5	7	2	...	...	...	7	206	27	...
Illinois	178	187	9	...	4	29	154	2,113	639	8
Indiana	87	92	5	...	1	18	73	1,887	340	...
Indian T.	...	...	...	...	...	...	...	219	9	...
Iowa	124	128	4	...	4	16	108	1,570	564	2
Kansas	110	125	15	...	1	18	106	1,696	453	1
Kentucky	39	41	2	...	1	8	32	1,936	125	...
Louisiana	12	12	...	...	1	1	10	729	71	...
Maine	38	40	2	...	3	6	31	1,007	130	...
Maryland	19	20	1	...	1	3	16	965	69	10
Massachusetts	126	133	7	...	6	28	99	695	198	16
Michigan	106	123	17	...	2	22	99	1,605	379	1
Minnesota	51	55	4	...	2	8	45	1,132	205	5
Mississippi	24	25	1	...	...	4	21	1,115	114	...
Missouri	75	79	4	...	3	7	69	2,132	369	7
Montana	11	12	1	...	...	2	10	284	39	...
Nebraska	74	79	5	...	2	6	71	987	226	...
Nevada	7	7	...	...	...	...	7	129	24	...
New Hampshire	32	35	3	...	...	6	29	480	90	...
New Jersey	64	66	2	...	3	14	49	728	98	8
New Mexico	8	9	1	...	...	2	7	318	34	...
New York	219	224	5	...	10	52	162	3,050	531	31
North Carolina	24	25	1	...	...	4	21	2,243	180	...
Ohio	136	138	2	...	6	37	95	2,770	513	7
Oregon	14	16	2	...	1	1	14	548	74	...
Pennsylvania	169	183	14	...	7	34	142	4,036	448	12
Rhode Island	11	11	...	...	1	4	6	119	23	...
South Carolina	18	20	2	...	1	2	17	996	70	...
Tennessee	26	28	2	...	3	2	23	2,016	229	...
Texas	73	78	5	...	2	11	65	1,967	315	...
Utah	5	5	...	...	...	2	3	225	41	...
Vermont	25	26	1	...	...	6	20	495	101	...
Virginia	31	35	4	...	2	6	27	2,446	128	...
Washington	13	14	1	...	...	4	10	439	44	...
West Virginia	15	15	...	...	1	2	12	1,397	70	...
Wisconsin	77	81	4	...	1	15	65	1,441	293	6
Wyoming	5	5	...	...	...	1	4	168	13	...
Total	2,336	2,488	152	...	82	436	1,970	54,888	8,111	130

TABLE B.—*Total operations of the Appointment Division of the office of the First Assistant Postmaster-General for the year ended June 30, 1888; also statement of the number of post-offices in each State and Territory June 30, 1887, and June 30, 1888, with increase or decrease.*

States and Territories.	Established.	Discontinued.	Names and sites changed.	Appointments on change of names and sites.	Resignations and commissions expired.	Removals.	Deaths.	Total number of cases.	Whole number of post-offices June 30, 1887.	Whole number of post-offices June 30, 1888.	Increase.	Decrease.
Alabama	164	58	73	37	202	16	25	538	1,536	1,642	106	....
Alaska	7	.....	.	.	2	..	...	9	8	15	7	....
Arizona	20	11	5	2	17	3	2	58	147	156	9	....
Arkansas	151	47	74	45	215	13	17	517	1,252	1,356	104	....
California	141	35	28	15	194	43	14	455	1,098	1,204	106	....
Colorado	83	24	34	21	91	13	6	251	498	557	59	....
Connecticut	7	6	2	.....	34	9	5	63	478	479	1	....
Dakota	95	62	73	39	126	25	4	385	1,032	1,065	33	....
Delaware	8	.....	1	...	15	4	1	29	135	143	8	....
District of Columbia	2	.....	2	...	3	..	...	7	9	11	2	....
Florida	83	40	19	5	118	18	8	286	690	733	43	....
Georgia	156	60	29	8	193	27	20	485	1,580	1,676	96	....
Idaho	83	39	13	7	29	12	...	158	219	213	....	6
Illinois	92	58	45	12	286	36	24	541	2,266	2,300	34	....
Indiana	78	37	12	4	309	40	13	489	1,938	1,979	41	....
Indian T	54	13	19	8	37	4	1	128	178	219	41	....
Iowa	65	33	27	17	195	31	7	358	1,666	1,698	32	....
Kansas	171	143	187	121	288	88	15	892	1,793	1,821	28	....
Kentucky	182	56	53	34	293	31	30	645	1,851	1,977	126	....
Louisiana	66	16	9	3	79	8	6	184	691	741	50	....
Maine	83	37	12	1	79	31	17	209	1,051	1,047	....	4
Maryland	50	11	5	2	103	17	9	195	946	985	89	....
Massachusetts	13	8	4	1	46	19	11	101	824	829	5	....
Michigan	69	35	46	28	193	63	21	427	1,694	1,728	34	....
Minnesota	68	40	37	23	96	30	5	276	1,159	1,187	28	....
Mississippi	105	40	12	2	134	13	18	322	1,075	1,140	65	....
Missouri	158	64	73	37	308	33	31	667	2,117	2,211	94	....
Montana	50	15	11	9	42	4	8	130	261	296	35	....
Nebraska	115	104	88	42	144	36	6	493	1,055	1,066	11	....
Nevada	12	7	1	1	18	2	2	42	131	136	5	....
New Hampshire	7	8	2	1	39	14	8	78	516	515	....	1
New Jersey	17	9	10	1	56	22	8	123	786	794	8	....
New Mexico	25	13	5	1	48	6	3	100	215	227	12	....
New York	55	29	15	2	209	88	41	437	3,248	3,274	26	....
North Carolina	211	53	71	36	195	19	20	569	2,110	2,268	158	....
Ohio	102	28	17	1	257	69	36	539	2,834	2,908	74	....
Oregon	64	28	11	7	114	19	7	243	528	564	36	....
Pennsylvania	155	55	27	7	387	87	59	770	4,119	4,219	100	....
Rhode Island	4	1	.....	...	12	5	1	23	127	130	3	....
South Carolina	109	29	39	17	75	9	12	273	906	986	80	....
Tennessee	112	38	74	39	218	21	33	496	1,970	2,044	74	....
Texas	202	64	78	29	347	83	23	747	1,907	2,045	138	....
Utah	19	36	7	3	19	43	2	126	247	230	....	17
Vermont	9	8	3	2	46	28	7	101	520	521	1	....
Virginia	166	40	49	23	200	43	36	543	2,355	2,481	126	....
Washington	43	16	23	11	62	6	6	156	426	453	27	....
West Virginia	125	20	31	24	128	20	14	338	1,307	1,412	105	....
Wisconsin	69	57	26	10	166	43	17	378	1,510	1,522	12	....
Wyoming	39	14	11	4	15	.....	.....	79	148	173	25	....
Total	3,864	1,645	1,493	743	6,521	1,244	659	15,426	55,157	57,376	2,247	28

TABLE C.—*Statement showing the number of appointments made upon resignations, commissions expired, deaths, removals, etc. at Presidential post-offices, during the fiscal year ended June 30, 1888.*

States and Territories.	Resignations.	Commissions expired.	Deaths.	Removals.	Offices becoming Presidential.	Total number of appointments.
Alabama	1		1			2
Alaska						
Arizona						
Arkansas		2			3	5
California	1	8	1		5	15
Colorado	2				7	9
Connecticut	1	5	1		4	11
Dakota	5	4			4	13
Delaware					2	2
District of Columbia		1				1
Florida	3					3
Georgia		4				4
Idaho	1				2	3
Illinois		11			9	20
Indiana	3	1	1		5	10
Indian Territory						
Iowa	4	4		3	4	15
Kansas	2	4		4	15	25
Kentucky	1	1	1		2	5
Louisiana						
Maine		3	2	1	2	8
Maryland		2			1	3
Massachusetts	1	11	1	1	6	20
Michigan	6	9	2		17	34
Minnesota	4	3			4	11
Mississippi	2	3	2			7
Missouri	5	3	3		5	16
Montana		2			1	3
Nebraska	4	3	2	1	5	15
Nevada		1				1
New Hampshire	1	1	1		3	6
New Jersey	3	5			2	10
New Mexico		1			1	2
New York	4	17	5	3	8	37
North Carolina		1				1
Ohio	5	12	3	3	2	25
Oregon	2	1			2	5
Pennsylvania	6	14	1	2	14	37
Rhode Island		1				1
South Carolina		1			2	3
Tennessee		1	2		2	5
Texas	2	10	1		5	18
Utah						
Vermont		1	1		1	3
Virginia				1	4	5
Washington	2	1			1	4
West Virginia		1	1			2
Wisconsin		3	2	1	5	11
Wyoming						
Total	71	156	34	20	155	436

TABLE D.—*Statement showing the number of carriers in service June 30, 1888, the amount*
amount of postage on local matter dur

Post-office and State.	Carriers in service June 30, 1888.	Delivered.				Collected.	
		Registered letters.	Letters.	Postal-cards.	Newspapers, etc.	Local letters.	Mail letters.
Abilene, Kans	2	185	72,311	13,418	45,704	5,750	30,339
Adrian, Mich	4	948	362,074	100,246	261,746	31,661	428,927
Akron, Ohio	9	3,234	1,072,739	233,499	748,928	80,189	1,044,925
Albany, N. Y	34	14,350	4,361,805	884,900	2,395,772	454,800	2,188,074
Alexandria, Va	4	1,344	200,178	48,827	98,538	8,794	133,992
Alleghany, Pa	21	15,732	3,088,454	734,760	1,686,027	474,722	2,445,199
Allentown, Pa	7	2,839	898,082	236,614	427,682	46,968	682,297
Altoona, Pa	8	1,570	732,851	139,626	525,051	31,331	302,952
Amsterdam, N. Y	5	867	329,762	45,691	180,639	7,703	147,645
Annapolis, Md	3	718	178,152	30,659	107,482	6,676	92,648
Ann Arbor, Mich	5	1,238	491,659	93,581	366,698	18,400	281,845
Ansonia, Conn	4	616	189,359	34,840	133,088	4,181	55,531
Appleton, Wis	4	414	120,400	21,235	99,667	2,179	58,044
Asbury Park, N.J	2	264	78,716	11,187	51,603	1,013	65,289
Ashland, Wis	5	549	171,876	64,320	97,925	9,873	96,898
Atchison, Kans	7	2,198	1,140,567	278,056	693,220	157,685	1,447,143
Atlanta, Ga	19	22,035	2,946,334	771,098	2,229,691	220,361	2,347,892
Atlantic City, N.J	4	1,654	566,468	100,420	213,287	9,032	323,602
Auburn, Me	4	762	106,802	49,759	141,526	3,171	76,195
Auburn, N. Y	10	4,280	1,292,551	253,546	792,985	84,142	763,152
Augusta, Ga	12	10,908	2,049,678	732,490	1,302,854	103,795	724,008
Augusta, Me	5	30,504	975,322	255,476	229,647	19,168	532,883
Aurora, Ill	7	2,524	705,776	143,325	590,274	49,822	532,236
Austin, Tex	7	1,990	1,150,299	254,077	912,164	35,338	473,985
Baltimore, Md	174	86,920	14,541,378	4,993,744	6,736,695	5,372,567	15,801,272
Bangor, Me	6	3,389	589,137	112,918	403,347	52,883	567,763
Bath, Me	3	2	172,604	23,024	90,357	1,550	119,297
Battle Creek, Mich	7	1,958	710,739	138,505	366,873	16,837	289,397
Bay City, Mich	8	4,513	1,092,775	258,868	918,603	96,048	643,998
Beatrice, Nebr	4	831	183,872	37,290	146,997	7,965	55,404
Beaver Falls, Pa	4	703	200,062	53,902	162,332	4,334	87,158
Belleville, Ill	5	1,305	240,206	56,972	225,782	10,251	128,151
Bethlehem, Pa	3	906	246,690	51,381	176,906	11,503	89,972
Binghamton, N. Y	9	3,857	1,183,680	249,342	689,663	68,489	536,726
Birmingham, Ala	8	2,369	742,172	96,511	252,677	33,507	450,195
Birmingham, Conn	4	1,029	360,376	56,257	212,072	20,455	156,621
Bloomington, Ill	9	7,385	1,172,903	221,206	1,091,297	56,018	575,629
Boston, Mass	333	146,891	43,819,525	11,361,769	19,531,744	20,091,151	37,692,053
Bradford, Pa	5	1,855	629,455	138,049	393,626	30,233	282,624
Brattleboro, Vt	4	2,141	225,490	54,550	181,595	18,032	219,356
Bridgeport, Conn	15	4,582	1,236,137	249,008	687,296	133,758	738,293
Bridgeton, N. J	4	496	141,629	25,117	85,619	5,392	69,018
Brockton, Mass	7	1,384	530,795	132,752	466,337	33,948	283,141
Brooklyn, N. Y	261	82,250	25,844,179	8,491,268	13,134,306	6,010,373	11,017,289
Buffalo, N. Y	81	61,290	12,930,426	2,801,784	7,078,968	2,325,075	6,666,140
Burlington, Iowa	10	4,777	1,977,225	294,371	1,848,417	173,488	1,451,943
Burlington, Vt	8	3,995	882,805	149,124	587,232	98,852	876,530
Cairo, Ill	4	8,354	344,029	77,312	121,908	37,124	457,545
Camden, N. J	17	7,409	1,273,440	384,972	947,805	173,516	641,048
Canton, Ohio	7	3,420	1,133,091	234,767	820,681	78,605	801,476
Carlisle, Pa	3	831	364,412	95,625	307,797	12,717	157,921
Carthage, Mo	2	19	30,488	5,756	24,320	2,291	38,405
Cedar Rapids, Iowa	7	1,884	527,472	114,804	430,585	16,034	247,727
Chambersburgh, Pa	3	461	138,041	25,768	85,682	4,161	80,535
Champaign, Ill	3	708	231,097	53,012	180,361	2,671	66,369
Charleston, S. C	17	16,101	1,911,571	492,355	688,109	137,827	1,276,024
Charleston, W. Va	3	1,160	136,371	21,605	64,192	8,998	99,335
Charlotte, N. C	4	1,018	183,317	35,021	89,216	975	39,693
Chattanooga, Tenn	9	12,090	1,353,478	306,326	1,036,832	78,518	682,372
Chester, Pa	5	822	334,291	74,077	180,306	23,653	178,567
Cheyenne City, Wyo	3	1,840	173,407	23,423	100,794	3,734	63,453
Chicago, Ill	401	578,641	81,577,518	9,660,131	43,268,384	21,088,848	64,991,270
Chillicothe, Ohio	4	127	45,940	9,971	39,966	1,204	18,138
Cincinnati, Ohio	127	80,339	16,141,103	4,465,344	5,789,837	2,460,778	7,779,779
Cleveland, Ohio	68	66,053	11,882,535	2,589,290	5,535,370	1,838,542	6,231,556
Clinton, Iowa	6	1,160	400,459	61,794	342,445	20,700	198,861
Cohoes, N. Y	7	460	228,085	34,124	85,587	10,135	115,915
Colorado Springs, Colo	3	500	291,459	23,145	156,873	5,963	124,540
Columbia, S. C	4	1,893	247,682	45,857	95,630	15,560	108,508
Columbus, Ga	5	1,525	296,083	101,187	153,830	22,377	270,475
Columbus, Ohio	26	15,061	5,442,286	801,211	2,877,758	382,871	3,018,410
Concord, N. H	7	3,461	814,485	102,224	459,097	48,440	405,322

of mail delivered and collected, the number of pieces handled, the cost of service, and the ing the fiscal year ended June 30, 1888.

	Collected.			Pieces handled.		Cost of service.				
	Local postal cards.	Mail postal cards.	Newspapers, etc.	Aggregate.	Per carrier.	Aggregate.	Per carrier.	Per piece in mills.	Postage on local matter.	Established.
2,644	5,903	13,523	189,867	94,934	$710 91	$355.45	3.7	$390.45	Jan. 1,1888
17,758	110,747	31,911	1,346,016	336,504	2,723.03	680.75	2.1	1,369.42	July 1,1887
42,905	180,665	445,136	11,301,273	42-,022	32,809.19	976.18	2.0	3,461.20	
270,733	457,958	272,*81	11,301,273	332,390	32,809.19	966.74	2.9	16,823.29	
2,455	45,735	12,007	552,470	138,118	1,910.25	477.56	3.4	369.29	Oct. 1,1887
289,473	467,148	237,·26	9,438,541	449,454	17,943.71	854.46	1.9	15,320.60	
16,535	187,605	48,099	2,526,721	360,960	6,174.93	8>2.13	2.4	2,083.93	
18,221	51,776	17,408	1,820,736	227,502	6,421.31	917.33	3.5	1,982.50	
4,289	18,963	10,772	746,303	149,266	3,024.52	604.90	4.0	1,201.35	July 1,1887
1,205	16,810	5,572	439,922	146,611	1,942.05	647.35	4.4	395.00	July 1,1887
9,042	53,141	16,635	1,332,259	266,478	2,679.22	535.81	2.0	1,436.69	July 1,1887
3,972	8,116	5,772	435,475	108,869	2,649.73	662.43	6.0	752.49	July 1,1887
2,151	8,197	2,216	314,503	78 6.6	1,306.94	326.73	4.1	567 69	Jan. 1,1888
1,302	13,614	5,812	228,805	114,403	1,099.61	549.80	4.2	383.49	Oct. 1,1887
5,199	11,727	4,125	462,133	92,427	1,651.15	330.23	3.5	591.58	Jan. 1,1888
108,396	297,296	196,052	4,320,613	617,230	8,360.80	765.83	1.2	6,052.36	
282,725	663,692	800,0.2	9,745,850	515,045	16,832.13	886.98	1.7	19,987.22	
4,422	65,378	7,160	1,391,732	347,933	2,795.11	748.77	2.7	565.42	July 1,1887
2,938	17,012	7,067	465,220	116,305	2,575.67	643.91	5.5	582.79	July 1,1887
37,452	129,257	122,805	3,480,373	348,037	7,692.61	769.26	2.2	2,413.97	
67,520	191,471	49,555	5,233,298	436,024	9,611.35	800.94	1.8	4,943.24	
13,459	117,924	37,265	2,211,734	442,344	4,250.85	851.97	1.9	1,376.85	
26,661	83,701	70,611	2,204,960	314,994	6,164.70	880.67	2.7	2,046.55	
32,699	78,218	48,306	2,087,165	426,738	6,456.43	9:2.34	2.1	3,218.71	
2,153,161	3,618,832	2,720,630	56,027,219	321,990	141,336.52	829.52	2.5	198,501.15	
37,907	119,577	52,370	1,909,291	323,215	4,290.01	716.50	2.2	1,976.63	
1,310	17,843	12,265	448,192	146,064	2,057.94	685 08	4.6	346.60	July 1,1887
8,204	47,087	99,040	1,058,640	236,949	4,971.50	710 08	3.0	1,113.36	
68,000	107,071	103,977	3,295,828	411,979	6,464.39	904.05	1.9	3,082.72	
3,321	14,719	8,248	487,147	121,787	1,978.60	494.65	4.0	763.34	Oct. 1,1887
4,843	20,451	8,368	537,201	134,300	2,345.85	586.46	4.3	1,151.21	July 1,1887
21,533	28,347	9 937	712,519	142,504	3,120.10	624.02	4.3	834.08	July 1,1887
5,583	19,617	3,725	604,283	201,428	1,618.40	549.46	2.7	1,069.38	Sept. 1,1887
38,435	88,768	52,633	2,911,623	323,514	6,470.39	718.93	2.2	5,165 40	
16,808	65,899	18,325	1,676,228	209,529	5,211.36	651.42	3.1	12,460.15	
5,317	27,339	19 256	860,721	215,180	2,59-.81	649 71	3.0	1,523.85	July 1,1887
37,988	223,033	202,977	3,558,894	395,377	7,781.56	861 01	2.1	2,904 46	
5,986,057	8,671,253	5,697,269	152,397,712	457,650	333,564.30	1,001.69	2.2	475,751.75	
21,472	124,880	47,831	1,669,379	333,876	4,069.11	811.82	2.4	1,774 95	
12,574	40,168	155,100	919,015	229,754	2,616.-8	629.22	2 8	880.24	July 1,1887
82,717	107,400	60,807	3,272,994	218,133	12,154.95	810.26	3.6	8,421.08	
2,075	12,298	3,542	345,146	86,297	1,475.21	368.80	4.2	436.66	Jan. 1,1888
26,848	66,015	118,413	1,659,701	237,100	6,395.03	913.43	3.1	3,804.70	
3,068,614	2,820,758	2,034,940	73,103,977	280,092	241,795.68	337.91	3.3	353,030.47	
1,616,249	1,583,536	72,410	36,787,878	441,876	73,498.86	906.65	2.0	85,998.82	
137,820	241,015	133,928	6,263,484	626,.48	8,336.50	833.65	1.3	7,224.94	
32,643	127,871	114,131	2,833,184	354,148	6,183.35	772 66	2.1	3,063.16	
16,816	102,280	24,047	1,144,409	200,102	2,609.22	652.30	2.2	1,267.13	July 1,1887
102,727	213,936	97,583	3,842,496	224,020	14,010.98	824.17	3.6	5,882 90	
71,125	203,183	242,906	3,614,236	516,319	5,947.73	855 39	1.6	2,744.06	
5,840	31,546	14,116	990,854	330,285	1,940.42	646.80	1.9	857.70	July 1,1887
1,293	8,872	1,448	112,894	56,449	671.75	335.87	6.0	216.42	Jan. 1,1888
7,180	40,887	44,492	1,440,125	205,732	5,773.10	826.14	4.0	3,001.53	
2,354	16,150	11,110	864,254	121,419	1,663.99	554.66	4.5	509.27	Sept. 1,1887
1,153	12,444	4,007	551,8 9	183,949	1,925.19	641.73	3.5	531.88	July 1,1887
166,186	276,077	162,170	5,129,979	301,587	12,396.65	725.09	2.4	7,544.33	
8,292	13,713	4,738	353,504	117,835	1,491.49	497.16	4.2	700.96	Oct. 1,1887
498	7,670	1,724	859,132	89,783	2,190.73	547.68	6.6	528.56	Sept. 1,1887
48,442	110,268	44,358	3,563,484	899,2·8	6,823.96	758.14	1.9	6,516.50	
7,660	37,994	8,567	854,933	170,987	3,331.89	666.37	3.8	2,332.06	July 1,1887
2,736	6,209	4,730	300,026	126,675	1,560.65	523.21	4.1	779.98	Sept. 1,1887
5,447,084	19,140,071	36,850,853	282,602,800	704,745	364,256.49	908.37	1.2	633,500.72	Apr. 1,1888
5*6	3,301	2,006	121,249	30,312	727.21	181.80	6.0	250.86	
1,587,840	2,126,614	1,756,126	42,187,260	332,183	114,851.05	904.82	2.7	137,170.69	
1,240,735	1,438,452	807,869	31,6.0,402	445,153	88,611 06	1,008.98	2.1	65,334.84	
6,825	35,805	9,532	1,072,650	178,775	3,330.90	555.16	3.1	1,132.58	July 1,1887
3,741	13,612	9,050	500,749	71,536	2,293.55	327 65	4.5	505.38	Oct. 1,1887
3,299	9,656	6,358	621,>81	307,294	1,613.95	517.98	2.6	1,422.52	Sept. 1,1887
11,435	40,488	12,015	669,066	167,267	2,078.15	519.54	3.1	1,002.34	Sept. 1,1887
15,552	74,889	18,047	951,963	190,791	3,134.79	626.96	3.2	943.13	July 1,1887
280,691	780,000	376 639	13,974,927	537,420	21,837.05	839.52	1.5	12,725.48	
29,133	100,567	43,589	2,006,318	295,188	5,291.76	755.07	2.5	1,985.78	

TABLE D.—*Statement showing the number of carriers in service June 30, 1888, the*

Post-office and State.	Carriers in service June 30, 1888.	Delivered.				Collected.	
		Registered letters.	Letters.	Postal-cards.	Newspapers, etc.	Local letters.	Mail letters.
Corning, N. Y	3	163	172,415	35,022	133,607	4,109	71,606
Cortland, N. Y	4	1,488	462,397	122,561	355,990	11,589	204,062
Council Bluffs, Iowa	9	4,500	1,390,223	258,949	900,930	152,622	1,182,200
Covington, Ky	10	3,064	741,390	191,482	492,317	54,473	574,556
Cumberland, Md.	4	993	166,018	36,182	136,415	2,290	42,354
Dallas, Tex	12	15,017	2,912,822	395,932	993,980	72,749	1,846,809
Danbury, Conn	5	884	274,705	46,233	238,017	7,858	94,726
Danville, Ill	4	1,539	343,553	83,465	235,890	9,271	151,165
Danville, Va.	4	557	104,182	19,973	58,228	3,115	105,079
Davenport, Iowa	10	5,679	1,702,196	290,070	971,987	96,690	964,815
Dayton, Ohio	18	13,829	2,774,613	669,467	2,077,052	280,047	1,703,887
Decatur, Ill	6	2,731	687,947	179,980	475,259	35,310	369,017
Delaware, Ohio	3	223	167,530	21,493	88,149	2,641	59,715
Denison, Tex	4	534	145,600	28,092	72,003	4,168	70,721
Denver, Colo	30	10,824	4,237,475	484,074	2,914,039	357,844	2,379,135
Des Moines, Iowa	23	12,910	2,829,252	526,530	1,359,359	176,224	1,092,201
Detroit, Mich	65	57,863	12,101,881	2,502,775	4,544,162	1,316,408	4,621,572
Dover, N. H	5	1,165	322,602	69,117	250,408	7,058	109,060
Dubuque, Iowa	10	6,037	1,110,072	212,622	798,144	71,923	1,042,851
Duluth, Minn	12	9,072	1,887,491	307,405	1,132,218	366,681	1,208,369
Dunkirk, N. Y.	4	854	293,172	80,226	199,872	11,872	127,354
Easton, Pa.	9	3,503	979,991	216,540	560,093	83,707	588,570
East Orange, N. J	6	1,058	630,063	73,442	217,319	71,632	383,039
East Saginaw, Mich	9	5,761	1,129,353	222,160	1,035,572	77,843	740,407
Eau Claire, Wis	8	1,885	534,238	91,485	472,383	57,241	561,962
Elgin, Ill	5	1,907	570,597	94,083	357,034	53,025	248,723
Elizabeth, N. J	10	3,186	1,020,088	231,608	819,088	235,432	580,728
Elkhart, Ind	4	2,394	421,930	81,736	228,9 4	11,343	264,906
Elmira, N. Y.	9	9,555	1,582,747	270,195	725,105	65,044	527,081
El Paso, Tex	3	1,409	194,737	16,620	100,6 45	16,353	225,534
Emporia, Kans	5	1,556	332,255	71,123	273,196	13,516	127,241
Englewood, Ill	8	1,070	790,385	172,113	354,370	24,816	222,356
Erie, Pa	14	2,974	2,367,822	476,445	1,944,271	214,193	1,139,980
Evanston, Ill	3	618	292,811	44,374	167,922	11,063	66,436
Evansville, Ind	14	16,013	1,976,358	705,131	1,677,394	204,000	1,457,396
Fall River, Mass	12	2,501	1,885,194	146,102	1,058,571	119,761	772,651
Fargo, Dak	4	607	101,208	13,033	59,683	9,850	103,176
Fitchburgh, Mass	6	2,383	628,816	124,410	436,121	76,910	394,400
Flint, Mich	4	1,404	330,970	68,691	221,916	7,640	129,006
Fond du Lac, Wis	6	1,538	385,664	69,450	232,732	13,542	159,677
Fort Scott, Kans	5	2,720	650,452	87,109	293,082	44,118	445,299
Fort Smith, Ark	4	1,746	259,126	31,644	120,202	9,820	153,339
Fort Wayne, Ind	12	6,797	1,753,012	337,819	1,205,2 7	77,354	627,996
Fort Worth, Tex	7	5,910	722,869	112,000	347,279	27,077	307,512
Frankfort, Ky	3	1,030	212,945	54,375	88,475	17,353	213,004
Frederick, Md	3	403	123,335	25,418	59,736	3,208	103,205
Freeport, Ill	4	1,253	488,225	90,093	307,805	13,109	210,710
Galesburgh, Ill	6	6,541	690,419	105,257	407,372	32,795	485,945
Galveston, Tex	11	9,139	2,248,867	253,467	843,373	84,856	1,805,777
Glens Falls, N. Y.	4	756	183,973	32,008	132,021	13,448	178,637
Gloversville, N. Y.	4	628	254,415	49,475	181,631	4,757	52,113
Gloucester, Mass	6	971	437,262	82,281	269,380	34,748	197,408
Grand Isla d, Nebr.	4	441	160,148	24,340	118,157	3,335	48,876
Grand Rapids, Mich	22	13,038	3,696,000	813,517	1,851,654	503,451	2,269,268
Hagerstown, Md	3	140	49,638	9,713	28,094	870	20,423
Hamilton, Ohio	6	1,273	368,019	91,719	206,309	18,112	221,775
Hannibal, Mo	5	2,649	539,056	133,149	551,754	75,116	423,311
Harrisburg, Pa.	12	3,978	1,025,084	295,675	909,071	55,359	547,392
Hartford, Conn	21	12,523	1,777,574	349,858	1,104,906	216,290	840,827
Hastings, Nebr	4	60	226,594	41,276	135,007	8,165	110,561
Haverhill, Mass	9	2,016	1,191,588	241,743	793,839	85,981	744,297
Helena, Mont	4	1,419	189,061	20,957	118,587	20,210	104,735
Hoboken, N. J	8	4,448	918,980	269,071	344,535	90,537	452,010
Holyoke, Mass	8	2,302	774,126	132,283	562,507	90,743	448,134
Hornellsville, N. Y.	5	734	297,427	61,278	200,690	7,981	133,194
Hot Springs, Ark	4	1,179	261,140	26,391	134,002	2,560	135,094
Houston, Tex	9	7,407	1,072,155	221,310	506,721	58,109	728,325
Hudson, N. Y	4	995	227,871	45,252	118,002	15,459	141,857
Huntingdon, Pa	2	264	107,785	21,136	67,896	7,203	74,128
Huron, Dak	2	1,042	112,848	17,127	73,264	4,456	88,647
Hutchinson, Kans	3	670	304,649	30,606	148,296	20,748	192,291
Indianapolis, Ind	40	33,930	6,570,115	1,285,633	2,909,517	442,432	3,204,302
Iowa City, Iowa	3	500	233,079	50,333	175,412	4,874	65,605

amount of mail delivered and collected, the number of pieces handled, etc.—Continued.

	Collected.			Pieces handled.		Cost of service.			Postage on local mat. t.r.	Established.
Local postal cards.	Mail postal cards.	Newspapers, etc.	Aggregate.	Per carrier.	Aggregate.	Per carrier.	Per piece in mills.			
1, 707	15, 059	5, 527	439, 217	146, 405	$1, 886. 43	$628. 81	4. 3	$963. 09	July 1, 1887
7, 283	50, 401	14, 850	1, 230, 601	310, 200	2, 568. 87	842. 22	2. 1	903. 53	July 1, 1887
83, 957	227, 445	300, 619	4, 501, 447	500, 161	7, 054. 98	783. 89	1. 5	4, 583. 00	
35, 641	139, 100	128, 904	2, 380, 907	238, 091	7, 915. 78	791. 58	3. 3	1, 830. 00	
800	8, 004	2, 605	395, 682	98, 920	2, 672. 53	668. 13	6. 7	718. 04	July 1, 1887
38, 288	292, 673	130, 276	6, 698, 348	558, 190	10, 660. 11	888. 34	1. 6	4, 472. 30	
2, 066	13, 812	9, 864	698, 165	137, 633	3, 383. 70	676. 74	4. 9	1, 878. 87	July 1, 1887
4, 342	42, 855	25, 102	896, 632	224, 163	2, 671. 99	668. 00	3. 0	1, 086. 54	July 1, 1887
1, 896	18, 502	7, 475	318, 977	79. 744	1, 978. 30	494. 57	6. 2	429. 21	Oct. 1, 1887
88, 608	191, 618	203, 978	4, 695, 621	489, 562	8, 042. 27	804. 23	1. 7	5, 263. 77	
21, 597	421, 225	664, 511	8, 817, 226	489, 846	13, 718. 57	762. 11	1. 5	12, 228. 00	
12, 322	98, 765	358, 150	2, 199, 509	306, 585	4, 358. 02	723. 00	1. 9	1, 719. 91	
1, 996	11, 146	3, 491	355, 814	118, 60	900. 92	300. 31	2. 5	260. 16	Jan. 1, 1888
3, 367	13, 500	3, 240	341, 225	85, 306	1, 368. 62	342. 15	4. 0	231. 14	Jan. 1, 1888
237, 314	376, 584	294, 837	11, 273, 126	375, 737	24, 504. 33	816. 81	2. 1	44, 033. 07	
71, 401	215, 8.8	173, 973	6, 457, 678	247. 725	16, 865, 76	733. 29	2. 6	7, 618. 18	
935, 514	1, 283, 057	666, 330	28, 069, 562	431, 839	60, 479. 94	930. 46	2. 1	66, 899. 71	
4, 077	17, 847	21, 586	803, 010	160, 602	3, 363. 62	672. 72	4. 1	738. 47	July 1, 1887
52, 502	147, 401	99, 427	3, 541, 071	354, 107	9, 093. 49	909. 35	2. 5	3, 348. 90	
157, 879	280, 153	97, 276	5, 446, 544	453, 879	8, 141. 27	678. 44	1. 4	11, 431. 19	
3, 530	20, 148	24, 053	761, 581	190, 395	1, 927. 83	481. 96	2. 5	423. 74	Sept. 1, 1887
51, 508	162, 849	38, 777	2, 685, 598	298, 400	6, 672. 50	741. 39	2. 5	2, 716. 76	
15, 595	52, 016	256, 259	1, 700, 425	283, 404	3, 311. 20	551. 86	1. 9	2, 742. 03	July 1, 1887
25, 900	119, 650	123, 954	3, 480, 059	386, 673	8, 251. 24	916. 80	2. 3	3, 565. 69	
21, 982	79, 977	183, 911	2, 005, 064	250, 633	5, 296. 25	662. 03	2. 6	1, 426. 94	
19, 551	58, 286	21, 540	1, 424, 796	284, 967	4, 229. 68	545. 93	2. 9	2, 462. 68	
156, 354	137, 497	147, 864	3, 322, 445	3.2, 214	8, 756. 63	875. 66	2. 3	9, 491. 27	
10, 510	39, 797	11, 483	1, 074, 125	268, 531	2, 805. 98	701. 49	2. 6	648. 59	July 1, 1887
44, 965	82, 743	69, 690	3, 387, 125	376, 316	7, 958. 94	844 33	2. 3	5, 753. 12	
11, 344	21, 807	12, 514	600, 953	300, 318	2, 691. 36	697. 12	3. 4	635 61	July 1, 1887
5, 762	23, 582	10, 904	881, 165	176, 233	3, 289. 12	657. 82	3. 7	1, 165. 59	July 1, 1887
24, 198	44, 409	27, 643	1, 661, 390	207, 074	4, 653. 03	581. 63	2. 8	1, 358. 90	July 1, 1887
163, 264	256, 159	130, 498	6, 704, 611	478, 901	12, 256. 63	9. 5. 47	1. 8	8, 851. 05	
4, 579	12, 251	5, 202	605, 315	201, 772	1, 823. 71	607. 90	3. 0	1, 804. 99	July 1, 1887
271, 247	361, 314	259, 770	6, 828, 723	487, 766	11, 500. 37	821. 45	1. 6	8, 831. 07	
98, 821	175, 097	96, 879	4, 055, 757	337, 980	10, 542. 28	878. 69	2. 6	6, 358. 65	
3, 043	11, 196	7, 196	308, 046	77, 011	1, 214. 13	303. 53	3. 9	512. 39	Jan. 1, 1588
47, 135	106, 130	101, 490	1, 917, 875	319, 646	4, 906. 08	817. 68	2. 5	3, 149. 45	
8, 165	30, 384	13, 592	8, 66, 794	161, 360	2, 082. 29	416. 46	2. 5	847. 25	Sept. 1, 1887
4, 972	20, 578	8, 037	9,6, 190	151, 032	2, 840. 47	473. 41	3. 1	1, 270. 37	July 1, 1847
28, 543	50, 275	22, 398	1, 624, 016	324, 811	3, 446. 34	689. 27	2. 1	1, 734. 52	July 1, 1887
6, 281	26, 400	7, 559	616, 117	154, 029	2, 285. 65	571. 41	3. 7	388. 63	Sept. 1, 1887
42, 400	134, 490	74, 827	4, 239, 912	354, 993	10, 131. 52	844. 29	2. 3	5, 032. 70	
18, 569	41, 227	29, 750	1, 612, 163	230, 313	6, 353. 13	907. 59	3. 9	1, 618. 87	
8, 670	37, 806	16, 568	650, 246	216, 749	2, 051. 80	683. 93	3. 1	619. 37	July 1, 1887
2, 135	27, 568	6, 315	351, 323	117, 108	1, 958. 22	652. 74	5. 5	492. 46	July 1, 1887
7, 252	38, 605	16, 920	1, 143, 972	285, 993	2, 648. 98	662. 25	2. 3	1, 119. 81	July 1, 1887
24, 987	251, 314	127, 238	2, 131, 868	355, 311	5, 142. 98	857. 16	2. 4	1, 291. 36	
72, 632	555, 375	225, 451	6, 178, 457	561, 078	9, 478. 06	861. 64	1. 5	3, 218 08	
5, 996	35, 979	31, 034	613, 814	153, 458	2, 190. 34	547. 58	3. 5	637. 39	Sept. 1, 1887
2, 246	8, 440	3, 569	537, 714	130, 428	1 9.2. 40	495. 61	3. 5	1, 020. 66	Oct. 1, 1847
17, 157	37, 728	309, 729	1, 386, 604	231, 111	5, 550 89	926. 15	4. 0	2, 262 82	
3, 124	10, 266	970	366, 677	92, 419	2, 073. 02	518. 25	5. 6	775. 75	Oct. 1, 1887
264, 119	671, 157	275, 985	10, 358, 249	470, 829	19, 287. 96	876. 73	1. 8	17, 970. 08	
428	3, 462	883	113, 651	37, 884	715. 53	238. 53	6. 3	206. 84	Jan. 1, 1888
11, 271	43, 953	28, 673	991, 050	165, 175	3, 517. 68	589. 61	2. 5	818. 68	July 1, 1887
44, 066	146, 126	177, 333	2, 691, 960	418, 392	3, 260. 06	652. 01	1. 5	2, 287. 40	
37, 374	145, 153	78, 617	3, 097, 728	258, 144	7, 465. 59	622. 13	2. 4	6, 064. 14	
112, 303	140, 709	109, 808	4, 644, 802	222, 183	17, 671. 49	811. 50	3. 8	22, 993. 10	
8, 055	17, 269	4, 897	549, 943	137, 486	2, 380. 94	582. 74	4. 2	870. 75	Sept. 1, 1887
68, 014	137, 555	72, 460	3, 335, 493	370, 610	7, 120. 08	791. 12	2. 1	4, 221. 39	
4, 123	7, 983	7, 984	474, 633	118, 658	2, 585. 40	646. 34	5. 2	3, 349. 69	July 1, 1877
121, 686	132, 459	28, 324	2, 362, 030	295, 250	6, 708. 93	838. 62	2. 8	3, 301. 51	
27, 197	66, 517	61, 176	2, 165, 074	270, 634	6, 433. 64	804. 20	3. 0	5, 106. 51	
4, 890	27, 478	20, 948	754, 618	150, 924	2, 662. 83	532. 57	3. 5	893. 8	July 1, 1887
1, 399	10, 301	8, 527	580, 382	145, 083	2, 240. 80	560. 20	3. 8	408. 07	Sept. 1, 1887
29, 670	157, 525	67, 552	2, 938, 724	326, 525	8, 620. 23	958. 47	2. 8	2, 418 76	
4, 562	21, 531	7, 326	581, 316	145, 326	1, 898. 71	474. 68	3. 2	853. 51	Oct. 1, 1887
1, 221	11, 914	55, 591	347, 142	173, 571	731. 65	365. 82	2. 1	229. 10	Jan. 1, 1888
1, 562	11, 126	20, 372	325, 449	162, 724	1, 173. 23	58 6. 61	3. 6	716. 73	Sept. 1, 1887
7, 327	24, 543	45, 554	774, 064	254, 028	1, 799. 91	466. 64	1. 8	811. 93	Oct. 1, 1887
308, 371	838, 172	246, 013	15, 839, 683	393, 992	38, 047. 48	95.. 19	2. 3	22, 257. 40	
1, 508	11, 944	4, 028	546, 743	182, 248	1, 504. 56	502. 85	2. 7	555. 18	Oct. 1, 1887

TABLE D.—*Statement showing the number of carriers in service June 30, 1888, the*

Post-office and State.	Carriers in service June 30, 1888.	Delivered.				Collected.	
		Registered letters.	Letters.	Postal-cards.	Newspapers, etc.	Local letters.	Mail letters.
Jackson, Mich	8	3,181	1,439,915	275,271	1,389,183	160,948	806,881
Jackson, Miss	3	2,204	191,784	35,550	168,264	5,639	186,384
Jacksonville, Fla	8	11,885	1,134,175	173,555	388,566	66,473	1,061,606
Jacksonville, Ill	5	1,989	520,994	97,235	473,589	29,691	325,866
Jamestown, N. Y	6	1,624	608,922	125,305	451,182	32,912	330,839
Janesville, Wis	4	712	290,561	51,797	164,842	5,405	83,236
Jersey City, N. J	43	10,739	3,074,062	819,410	1,542,538	417,229	1,828,787
Johnstown, Pa	7	1,990	431,796	88,951	331,543	34,971	385,863
Joliet, Ill	8	1,778	598,723	116,707	437,480	37,244	265,903
Kalamazoo, Mich	7	4,178	988,171	218,811	501,050	26,020	366,636
Kansas City, Kans	8	1,0-0	430,828	76,123	248,055	20,330	581,350
Kansas City, Mo	52	54,397	16,419,530	3,150,488	6,081,353	2,226,533	11,250,992
Keene, N. H	3	248	77,510	19,579	88,609	2,423	41,897
Keokuk, Iowa	7	5,779	1,123,607	284,658	613,375	87,226	442,117
Knoxville, Tenn	8	12,090	838,111	148,449	539,705	41,000	437,515
La Crosse, Wis	9	12,564	890,634	166,521	652,604	41,851	509,0.0
La Fayette, Ind	9	3,901	950,714	248,120	890,472	64,551	650,379
Lancaster, Pa	11	3,885	974,967	178,409	618,675	34,042	290,631
Lansing, Mich	6	1,681	513,487	124,536	489,311	21,029	292,218
Lawrence, Kans	6	4,981	849,964	151,564	694,519	60,336	693,605
Lawrence, Mass	14	2,392	1,536,723	213,940	1,244,677	110,300	1,137,973
Leadville, Colo	4	315	640,605	29,028	314,591	24,839	230,414
Leavenworth, Kans	8	9,361	939,550	198,280	722,967	142,683	814,743
Lebanon, Pa	4	278	141,003	29,102	77,674	12,290	73,646
Lewiston, Me	6	2,011	481,091	104,703	382,824	10,964	253,448
Lexington, Ky	7	3,150	831,369	199,495	409,816	49,699	466,255
Lima, Ohio	5	851	342,424	84,598	171,034	11,558	126,366
Lincoln, Nebr	11	2,779	1,831,419	348,102	1,289,799	115,972	1,061,549
Little Falls, N. Y	4	747	258,136	56,096	101,917	14,190	114,037
Little Rock, Ark	9	6,846	1,090,091	220,612	733,590	96,089	869,241
Lockport, N. Y	6	2,189	614,824	134,598	518,254	47,687	527,916
Logansport, Ind	5	1,640	436,842	98,002	278,770	19,238	242,506
Long Island City, N. Y	5	182	65,501	12,602	24,860	2,808	32,399
Los Angeles, Cal	26	4,798	2,224,104	391,501	1,167,179	198,217	1,995,870
Louisville, Ky	52	61,678	7,450,342	2,025,344	3,529,806	787,636	4,236,247
Lowell, Mass	19	4,655	1,790,633	369,542	1,268,984	118,476	883,126
Lynchburgh, Va	7	3,563	462,304	97,585	252,950	12,525	286,097
Lynn, Mass	17	2,246	1,792,993	407,870	1,142,073	122,840	947,723
Macon, Ga	10	10,981	1,191,306	319,789	484,043	53,073	896,514
Madison, Wis	6	3,730	602,171	123,796	526,393	66,391	385,548
Malden, Mass	7	864	591,942	99,602	361,628	8,874	130,470
Manchester, N. H	13	4,900	1,156,245	223,719	797,846	29,251	438,023
Manistee, Mich	4	294	120,435	22,211	104,891	3,008	52,603
Mankato, Minn	3	293	100,667	17,164	80,371	2,756	34,576
Mansfield, Ohio	6	2,776	821,448	204,309	514,934	52,830	672,611
Marietta, Ohio	3	80	15,461	3,408	12,306	665	16,095
Marlborough, Mass	4	542	353,429	69,003	319,875	35,526	177,562
Marquette, Mich	3	1,188	219,946	25,534	123,901	16,233	150,597
Marshalltown, Iowa	4	1,549	483,434	88,134	295,028	22,680	174,566
Massillon, Ohio	3	95	54,492	11,848	47,373	1,000	12,794
McKeesport, Pa	4	205	72,301	13,703	36,492	4,110	28,741
Meadville, Pa	4	1,077	346,543	84,091	243,019	32,617	246,199
Memphis, Tenn	18	42,452	3,136,032	531,707	1,109,768	152,137	1,375,407
Meriden, Conn	7	1,508	500,110	88,291	406,489	10,457	97,405
Meridian, Miss	4	1,163	130,459	18,603	81,067	3,065	72,298
Middletown, Conn	4	583	186,959	31,107	121,168	7,587	98,322
Middletown, N. Y	4	771	390,430	63,857	287,353	18,153	190,988
Middletown, Ohio	2	284	185,620	33,676	71,356	4,849	111,163
Milwaukee, Wis	58	48,772	9,994,202	1,940,284	3,925,649	1,330,877	6,262,079
Minneapolis, Minn	53	30,612	8,182,315	1,190,673	4,703,617	1,361,711	4,216,178
Mobile, Ala	9	6,050	736,450	134,911	829,636	51,521	526,217
Moline, Ill	4	645	233,082	43,532	208,689	12,402	144,191
Montgomery, Ala	5	1,341	404,598	51,240	310,105	98,690	772,319
Montpelier, Vt	3	621	138,292	23,253	90,612	3,625	101,944
Muscatine, Iowa	3	482	164,983	31,976	109,095	5,300	138,583
Muskegon, Mich	6	1,703	506,006	109,645	332,118	39,189	282,150
Nashua, N. H	6	1,314	493,320	99,044	338,955	17,120	196,063
Nashville, Tenn	19	39,126	3,179,766	634,201	2,113,377	267,471	2,167,892
Natchez, Miss	4	454	51,238	5,667	28,886	1,322	32,451
New Albany, Ind	6	1,587	396,089	95,194	198,651	10,162	205,936
Newark, N. J	52	26,949	5,944,434	2,041,289	2,485,057	914,549	2,601,731
Newark, Ohio	4	2,066	456,978	118,493	249,104	11,427	180,007
New Bedford, Mass	12	3,049	1,572,451	278,739	1,137,062	104,224	1,138,994

amount of mail delivered and collected, the number of pieces handled, etc.—Continued.

Collected.			Pieces handled.		Cost of service.				
Local postal cards.	Mail postal cards.	Newspapers, etc.	Aggregate.	Per carrier.	Aggregate.	Per carrier.	Per piece in mills.	Postage on local matter.	Established.
95, 046	196, 265	132, 696	4, 499, 376	562, 422	$6, 898. 48	$562. 31	1. 5	$6, 006. 94	
5, 607	34, 528	15, 159	649, 119	216. 373	1, 979. 10	659. 70	3. 0	289. 07	July 1, 1887
58, 977	186, 330	129, 666	3, 231, 233	403, 904	6, 994. 21	874. 28	2. 1	3, 205. 02	July 1, 1887
24, 774	69, 170	40, 458	1, 583, 766	316, 753	3, 302. 54	672. 51	2. 1	1, 033. 85	July 1, 1887
16, 886	65, 481	30, 128	1, 603, 281	277, 213	4, 796. 78	799. 46	2. 9	1, 919. 20	
2, 951	17. 829	8, 382	625, 715	156. 429	2, 128. 3.	532. 09	3. 4	706. 04	Oct. 1, 1887
308, 191	428. 699	266, 333	8, 753, 9r8	20 t, 581	40, 195. 85	934. 79	4. 5	13, 842. 28	
17, 8s3	49, 842	40, 659	1, 364, 498	194, 785	4, 685. 93	609. 42	4. 4	1, 654. 93	July 1, 1887
15, 600	39, 563	38, 798	1, 551, 858	193, 982	5, 923. 98	740. 50	3. 8	2, 460. 06	
15, 889	90, 108	52, 921	2, 209, 784	324, 255	6, 099. 77	871. 39	2. 7	2, 088. 88	
13, 212	73, 377	77, 763	1, 522, 118	190, 267	4, 014. 44	501. 81	2. 6	1, 400. 39	July 1, 1887
1, 252, 611	1, 625, 154	1, 435, 942	43, 515, 001	84s, 4 3	47, 307. 41	949. 76	1. 1	58, 030 49	
1, 720	5, 346	4, 402	239, 734	79 518	1, 006. 09	3 45. 36	4. 2	420. 35	Jan. 1 , 1888
47, 008	145, 125	40, 833	2, 833, 728	404, 814	6, 253. 41	893. 34	2. 2	3, 580. 50	
18, 417	68 955	27, 853	2, 152, 075	269, 009	7, 460. 56	936. 57	3. 4	2, 741. 90	
18, 471	136, 309	240, 609	2, 708, 616	300, 961	7, 787. 91	865. 32	2. 4	2, 698. 01	
47, 547	220, 707	211, 282	3, 287, 763	365, 307	8, 033. 50	872. 61	2. 4	2, 421. 09	
30, 109	93, 204	44, 784	2, 268, 706	206, 246	9, 072. 48	824. 77	4. 0	2, 753. 27	
21, 743	75, 649	173, 164	1, 712, 771	285, 462	5, 479. 79	913. 30	1. 2	1, 474. 19	
74, 557	77, 765	32, 737	2, 640, 031	440, 0 5	5, 182. 09	8s3. 68	1. 9	2, 131. 20	
71, 325	144, 916	103, 127	4, 564, 173	326, 012	10, 972. 58	783. 74	2. 4	5, 064. 78	
14. 103	20, 291	23, 709	1, 997, 945	324, 484	3, 435. 22	858. 81	2. 6	857. 03	
198, 813	122, 728	110, 087	3, 569, 202	407, 400	7, 1 9. 10	898. 64	2. 2	10, 158. 40	
2, 974	16, 291	4, 339	357, 587	80, 397	1, 370. 06	342. 51	3. 5	1, 188. 74	Jan. 1, 1888
10, 609	50, 041	44, 985	1, 340, 876	223, 446	4, 367. 99	728. 00	3. 2	1, 078. 33	
30, 915	117, 903	37, 383	2, 236, 025	319, 432	5, 161. 68	737. 38	2. 3	5, 380. 70	
6, 746	20, 753	6, 787	771, 117	154, 223	3, 354. 46	670 89	4. 3	1, 495. 94	July 1, 1887
70, 136	250, 436	93, 7r6	5, 063, 978	460, 362	9, 420. 01	s54. 18	1. 8	6, 483. 11	
4, 802	24, 496	6, 471	640, 892	160, 223	2, 671. 13	667. 78	4. 1	1, 005. 10	July 1, 1887
74, 581	157, 482	61, 589	3, 310, 121	283, 791	7, 006. 16	778. 46	2. 1	4, 928. 82	
22, 978	88, 354	226, 385	2, 183, 165	361, 841	4, 788. 70	798. 12	2. 2	1, 862. 22	
9, 190	72, 455	18, 551	1, 178, 114	235, 622	3, 321. 18	664. 24	2. 9	652. 22	July 1, 1887
1, 907	7, 249	2, 486	153, 300	30, 602	1, 064. 45	212. 80	6. 9	108. 38	Apr. 1, 1888
139, 011	174, 461	274, 890	6, 468, 031	218, 770	16, 451. 29	632. 74	2. 5	13, 311. 38	
536, 055	9s7, 914	512, 868	20, 128, 019	387, 077	47, 860. 68	920. 40	2. 3	40, 303. 12	
92, 088	146, 714	87, 291	4, 761, 509	250, 606	16, 455. 30	865. 0 :	3. 4	23, 254. 13	
10, 079	52, 505	25, 162	1, 202, 860	171, 847	5, 829. 97	832. 71	4. 8	2, 315. 11	
113, 233	186, 318	101, 071	4, 817, 267	283, 369	14, 369. 81	845. 28	3. 0	7, 392. 70	
46, 170	191, 674	52, 706	3, 246, 256	314, 626	8, 748. 27	874. 83	2. 7	1, 721. 63	
21, 884	96, 869	46, 545	1, 963, 331	327, 222	5, 024. 01	848. 00	2. 5	1, 876. 69	
8, 917	31, 811	16, 799	1, 250, 847	178, 692	3, 565. 03	504. 99	2. 8	1, 255. 91	Sept. 1, 1887
29, 555	71, 253	38, 696	2, 791, 494	214, 724	10, 053. 30	773. 33	3. 6	2, 484 56	
1, 921	5, 691	1, 615	312, 759	78, 190	1, 314. 73	328. 68	4. 2	303. 58	Jan. 1, 1888
1, 603	6, 206	1, 537	245, 173	81, 724	1, 073. 12	357. 71	4. 3	626. 22	Jan. 1, 1888
25, 343	158, 086	101, 838	2, 554, 245	425, 709	5, 119. 96	853. 33	2. 0	1, 593. 96	
630	4, 621	538	53, 864	17, 955	447. 88	149. 23	8. 3	70. 89	Apr. 1, 1888
22, 856	36, 674	16, 198	1, 031, 755	257, 939	2, 735. 13	683. 7s	2. 6	1, 390. 73	July 1, 1887
5, 735	15, 746	14, 533	573, 413	191, 138	1, 573. 47	524. 49	2. 7	801. 45	Oct. 1, 1887
11, 078	38, 383	14, 748	1, 130, 500	228, 625	2, 505. 07	6r6. 27	2. 2	1, 148. 52	July 1, 1887
538	2, 236	759	131, 235	43, 745	1, 023. 28	341. 09	7. 8	207. 04	Feb. 1, 1888
8s5	4. 8s3	1, 164	162, 484	40, 621	836. 70	209. 17	5. 1	299. 24	Apr. 1, 1888
13, 103	69, 774	13, 742	1, 052, 165	263, 041	2, 5s8. 24	647. 06	2. 4	1, 625. 37	July 1, 1887
141, 257	245, 011	128, 264	6, 862, 035	381, 224	15, 799. 92	877. 77	2. 3	8, 430. 39	
7, 538	14, 164	9, 138	1, 135, 103	182, 158	6, 295. 45	899. 35	5. 5	3, 982. 98	
3, 893	7, 991	2, 799	321, 278	80, 319	2, 558. 29	639. 57	7. 9	706. 94	July 1, 1887
4, 107	15, 663	7, 117	472, 600	118, 150	2, 633. 33	658. 33	5. 5	1, 768. 02	July 1, 1887
9, 145	51, 283	17, 844	1, 029, 824	257, 456	1, 895. 47	473. 87	1. 8	1, 091. 31	Oct. 1, 1887
1, 193	38, 184	2, 295	2 448, 620	224, 910	1, 3 9. 43	664. 71	3. 0	414. 40	July 1, 1887
846, 737	1, 554, 3e7	510, 300	6, 412, 377	455, 9s6	55, 316. 07	953. 72	2. 0	41, 455. 60	
514, 745	701, 768	928, 303	21, 809, 902	411, 508	50, 944. 85	961. 22	2. 3	39, 789. 53	
45, 252	111, 079	124, 068	2, 556, 184	284, 020	7, 344. 51	816. 06	2. 8	2, 555. 19	
6, 868	18, 678	29, 955	691, 042	172, 760	2, 753. 31	688. 33	4. 1	528. 75	July 1, 1887
76, 674	236, 275	46, 439	1, 997, 581	399, 516	4, 5s7. 80	917. 56	2. 3	7, 265. 98	
1, 548	16, 519	12, 381	38s, 791	129, 598	1, 810. 16	603. 39	4. 6	437. 33	July 1, 1887
5, 422	35, 608	12, 874	564, 323	141, 081	2, 683. 93	670. 98	5. 0	893. 02	July 1, 1887
10. 714	39, 771	22, 211	1, 343, 567	223, 928	3, 918. 81	653. 13	2. 9	2, 214 55	July 1, 1887
9, 035	36, 658	31, 018	1, 222, 527	203, 754	3, 853. 34	642. 22	3. 1	1, 401. 55	July 1, 1887
162, 808	359, 096	368, 162	9, 291, 889	489, 049	16, 213. 92	853. 36	1. 7	10, 329. 91	
176	3, 172	1, 2 9	124, 635	31, 159	1, 210. 52	302. 63	9. 7	117. 82	Jan. 1, 1888
5, 720	40, 196	14, 094	867, 668	144, 611	4, 042. 52	677. 09	4. 6	660. 31	July 1, 1887
760, 222	635, 418	334, 409	15, 764, 149	303, 157	42, 931. 29	825. 60	2. 7	53, 219. 13	
6, 206	39, 006	28, 167	1, 091, 454	272, 864	2, 543. 27	635. 82	2. 3	666. 94	July 1, 1887
71, 673	154 224	81, 387	4, 541, 803	378, 484	10, 753. 64	896. 14	2. 3	3, 940. 14.	

TABLE D.—*Statement showing the number of carriers in service June 30, 1888, the*

Post-office and State.	Carriers in service June 30, 1888.	Delivered.				Collected.	
		Registered letters.	Letters.	Postal-cards.	Newspapers, etc.	Local letters.	Mail letters.
New Britain, Conn	6	722	252, 377	44, 917	237, 644	5, 823	66, 915
New Brunswick, N. J	6	347	292, 345	30, 587	79, 361	13, 106	56, 296
Newburgh, N. Y	9	2, 302	796, 445	118, 727	523, 724	54, 077	559, 544
Newburyport, Mass	5	604	228, 359	42, 909	171, 614	5, 492	101, 339
New Castle, Pa	5	1, 410	298, 596	71, 973	182, 395	14, 434	114, 487
New Haven, Conn	27	13, 377	3, 413, 280	715, 411	2, 697, 102	394, 479	1, 346, 751
New Orleans, La	66	49, 674	7, 950, 435	2, 329, 543	4, 752, 685	2, 330, 519	6, 599, 279
Newport, Ky	6	1, 225	428, 272	83, 008	323, 972	15, 636	177, 526
Newport, R. I	10	2, 295	1, 775, 871	282, 543	694, 444	189, 078	492, 015
Newton, Kans	4	829	324, 927	64, 842	250, 850	19, 202	204, 015
New York, N. Y	768	858, 155	113, 558, 847	32, 741, 278	34, 568, 955	49, 004, 915	75, 415, 862
Norfolk Va	13	7, 303	1, 336, 288	351, 380	717, 116	138, 083	1, 109, 047
Norristown, Pa	5	833	297, 824	65, 444	185, 260	13, 572	147, 497
North Adams, Mass	4	533	255, 657	49, 866	150, 273	9, 016	79, 864
Northampton, Mass	4	339	190, 503	34, 974	118, 706	3, 411	65, 187
Norwalk, Ohio	3	106	45, 329	11, 273	45, 171	964	15, 309
Norwich, Conn	8	1, 467	566, 047	71, 584	486, 452	58, 284	310, 787
Oakland, Cal	21	4, 977	2, 153, 702	445, 693	1, 306, 533	390, 240	1, 524, 697
Ogdensburgh, N. Y	5	1, 799	371, 354	88, 308	308, 502	27, 415	371, 136
Omaha, Nebr	34	17, 182	10, 119, 850	2, 533, 855	9, 552, 226	2, 066, 057	5, 062, 290
Oneonta, N. Y	3	118	54, 319	9, 584	36, 446	673	14, 749
Orange, N. J	5	453	350, 031	45, 079	116, 993	11, 975	94, 064
Oshkosh, Wis	8	3, 187	893, 518	155, 375	684, 761	18, 296	315, 172
Oskaloosa, Iowa	3	631	141, 491	33, 849	117, 240	6, 934	93, 087
Oswego, N. Y	8	2, 786	818, 694	152, 099	426, 499	47, 593	433, 241
Ottawa, Ill	4	1, 242	407, 807	80, 101	276, 721	15, 833	177, 725
Ottawa, Kans	3	608	244, 818	26, 402	231, 912	3, 175	52, 804
Ottumwa, Iowa	7	2, 035	727, 456	158, 497	563, 679	74, 568	488, 221
Owego, N. Y	3	681	256, 927	44, 424	145, 294	11, 454	169, 811
Paducah, Ky	5	3, 255	233, 973	47, 539	110, 437	6, 992	203, 130
Parkersburgh, W. Va	3	730	153, 477	22, 995	85, 302	5, 907	103, 914
Paterson, N. J	16	4, 281	1, 641, 164	312, 064	1, 683, 070	162, 787	561, 313
Pawtucket, R. I	7	1, 163	1, 066, 236	211, 297	592, 785	55, 587	338, 267
Pekin, Ill	3	228	108, 220	24, 049	63, 148	10, 787	130, 975
Pensacola, Fla	4	653	104, 449	15, 338	55, 093	7, 350	96, 054
Peoria, Ill	13	7, 284	1, 643, 366	375, 552	987, 966	149, 413	1, 498, 644
Petersburgh, Va	7	6, 423	706, 901	120, 593	510, 435	51, 693	580, 428
Philadelphia, Pa	513	218, 807	94, 318, 920	34, 823, 050	32, 504, 030	48, 075, 810	55, 561, 570
Piqua, Ohio	3	829	193, 748	32, 050	136, 894	4, 008	113, 874
Pittsburgh, Pa	72	39, 208	10, 205, 437	2, 072, 180	3, 535, 364	2, 278, 219	5, 253, 418
Pittsfield, Mass	5	1, 094	404, 389	93, 625	320, 971	21, 269	160, 125
Port Huron, Mich	4	2, 844	394, 053	70, 451	300, 446	25, 709	297, 708
Portland, Me	16	33, 306	2, 487, 106	561, 575	1, 246, 362	175, 882	1, 738, 922
Portland, Oregon	10	10, 050	1, 269, 481	123, 101	716, 405	141, 213	1, 513, 280
Portsmouth, N. H	4	687	258, 819	44, 794	156, 975	7, 637	148, 519
Portsmouth, Ohio	4	835	208, 149	40, 535	203, 326	8, 117	161, 002
Portsmouth, Va	4	1, 101	179, 042	39, 082	98, 773	6, 632	103, 551
Pottsville, Pa	5	1, 843	465, 890	99, 935	495, 863	32, 424	347, 018
Poughkeepsie, N. Y	7	3, 000	815, 499	153, 400	424, 489	52, 176	402, 521
Providence, R. I	42	12, 232	4, 456, 603	972, 013	2, 741, 634	965, 003	2, 727, 306
Pueblo, Colo	7	2, 082	504, 558	63, 295	379, 907	46, 581	415, 344
Quincy, Ill	8	8, 300	1, 570, 372	438, 027	1, 024, 289	43, 551	619, 736
Racine, Wis	8	2, 745	784, 915	184, 713	520, 701	22, 738	398, 083
Raleigh, N. C	4	1, 575	190, 673	38, 763	157, 717	6, 885	90, 765
Reading, Pa	16	5, 153	1, 956, 899	483, 570	1, 028, 568	187, 201	841, 733
Richmond, Ind	8	4, 246	1, 099, 456	310, 503	730, 252	57, 324	472, 604
Richmond, Va	26	26, 252	2, 864, 330	715, 419	1, 160, 766	403, 412	1, 524, 967
Rochester, N. Y	48	47, 891	7, 981, 129	2, 046, 735	7, 917, 420	1, 521, 287	4, 787, 190
Rockford, Ill	10	11, 630	1, 160, 500	254, 597	948, 030	41, 795	813, 514
Rock Island, Ill	5	1, 207	362, 804	68, 563	300, 842	21, 790	225, 923
Rome, Ga	3	471	114, 618	19, 499	58, 680	8, 598	89, 703
Rome, N. Y	5	1, 225	459, 714	87, 814	266, 547	25, 495	203, 297
Rutland, Vt	5	2, 463	686, 289	87, 718	352, 834	71, 620	622, 291
Sacramento, Cal	11	3, 805	821, 172	164, 214	384, 307	33, 418	472, 260
Saginaw, Mich	5	302	814, 568	57, 124	227, 268	21, 291	149, 178
Saint Joseph, Mo	15	11, 501	2, 288, 369	500, 823	1, 381, 283	246, 737	1, 296, 255
Saint Louis, Mo	192	194, 267	40, 772, 563	12, 208, 597	14, 933, 053	10, 551, 070	16, 524, 787
Saint Paul, Minn	53	41, 541	11, 186, 516	2, 408, 820	6, 253, 078	1, 633, 949	7, 012, 233
Salem, Mass	10	1, 920	732, 810	194, 307	512, 221	44, 388	335, 304
Salem, Ohio	2	234	67, 464	17, 531	57, 234	1, 727	21, 277
Salem, Oregon	2	905	105, 518	14, 275	103, 227	3, 938	78, 914
Salina, Kans	3	5	46, 933	8, 912	39, 478	540	15, 311
Salt Lake City, Utah	7	5, 028	818, 905	95, 503	620, 320	83, 9565	55, 428

amount of mail delivered and collected, the number of pieces handled, etc.—Continued.

Collected.			Pieces handled.		Cost of service.			Postage on local matter.	Established.
Local postal cards.	Mail postal cards.	Newspapers, etc.	Aggregate.	Per carrier.	Aggregate.	Per carrier.	Per piece in mills.		
2,384	9,634	4,044	634,460	104,077	$3,322.41	$553.73	5.3	$1,767.31	July 1,1887
4,942	12,470	2,219	401,633	60,942	1,901.88	316.98	4.7	1,926 04	Jan. 1,1888
21,893	84,111	122,262	2,203,085	248.121	5,954.70	661.52	2.6	3,198.38	
4,224	17,491	10,763	582,986	116,597	3,291.87	658 37	5.6	1,500.80	July 1,1887
6,492	23,158	7,068	720,413	144,082	2,445.91	489.18	3.4	1,0.0 48	Oct. 1,1387
252,464	259,478	297,472	9,432,874	343,306	24,142.85	894.18	2.5	38,508.90	
1,868,210	1,738,928	1,258,321	28,848,596	437,676	58,999.99	894.94	2.0	78,694.78	
11,630	40,335	15,510	1,097,114	182,852	4,822.15	803.69	4.4	808 87	
46,174	76,533	42,998	3,592,556	359,256	8,587.18	858.72	2.4	4,986 39	
17,308	24,901	9,606	916,630	229,158	1,942.85	485.71	2.1	2,128.04	Sept. 1,1887
15,244,948	18,822,358	15,452,731	355,672,049	463,115	712,169.46	927 30	2.0	2,034,849 99	
100,962	282,652	87,352	4,110,163	316,166	10,243.15	787.93	2.5	7,428.63	
5,845	32,667	10,522	739,464	151,293	3,232.52	646.50	4.2	1,167.71	July 1,1887
5,127	12,663	6,509	569,450	142,363	2,202.55	550.51	3.9	1,476 11	Sept. 1,1887
2,386	8,603	4,607	428,778	107,191	2,163.27	540.82	5.0	1,550.40	July 1,1887
601	4,121	2,422	125,300	41,707	569.10	189 70	4.5	77.24	Mar. 1,1888
14,861	43,745	48,067	1,601,294	200,162	5,956.16	744.52	3.7	3,703.24	
276,839	318,946	280,592	6,704,150	310,245	16,916.80	805 56	2.5	12,100.87	
10,442	67,423	56,364	1,304,778	260,576	3,004 65	600.93	2.3	919.24	July 1,1887
1,215,469	1,773,759	637,680	33,078,168	972,887	28,754.49	608 63	0.7	67,491.20	
251	2,805	814	110,739	30,913	537.63	179.21	4.5	124.20	Apr. 1,1888
6,201	13,622	5,915	649,333	120,867	2,910.72	582 14	4.4	1,453.74	Sept. 1,1887
- 15,298	35,776	118,791	2,240,166	280,021	6,920.78	865.10	3.0	1,962.39	
6,210	18,015	5,898	423,325	141,108	1,737.50	579.17	4.1	654.63	Sept. 1,1887
33,506	82,041	87,992	2,081,301	290,545	6,961.84	870.23	3.3	1,780 02	
5,794	25,132	10,902	1,001,317	250,317	2,615.63	658.91	2.6	1,099.99	July 1,1887
3,101	10,530	3,698	577,138	192,379	1,541 16	5 0.39	2.6	681.92	Oct. 1,1887
44,427	135,453	46,943	2,241,279	320,183	5,256.81	750.97	2.	2,591.26	
6,622	35,867	18,583	689,661	229,884	1,847.99	629.33	2.7	649.64	Jnly 1,1887
7,294	38,551	16,111	667,282	1,3,456	3,140.22	628.04	4 5	2-8.53	July 1,1887
2,337	22,3 0	114,487	402,459	134,153	1,928.18	642.73	4.7	1,070.25	July 1,1887
121,913	136,857	29,736	4,743,205	290,450	11,550.20	721.89	2.4	7,217.40	
34,976	58,923	18,836	2,386,074	340,865	5,818.90	815.56	2.4	3,500 67	
7,034	22,636	38,602	405,684	135,227	1,035.09	345.33	2 5	360.68	Jan. 1,1888
5,048	8,744	1,484	303,215	75,804	2,629.12	657.28	8.6	824.42	July 1,1887
119,064	887,950	81,515	5,352,774	411,752	11,247.37	865.18	2 1	5,818 51	
26,539	103,838	33,093	2,142,005	304,601	5,365.33	766.4-	2.4	1,717 02	
22,253,070	19,202,130	18,576,150	325,333,5 7	634,598	444,864.34	867.18	1.3	1,184,048.90	
2,668	71,912	48,557	504,537	198,170	1,884.51	627.81	3.0	448.00	July 1,1887
999,584	1,435,504	695,229	26,514,231	307,420	62,106.36	861.42	2.3	85,966.16	
8,708	28,500	20,828	1,059,580	211,918	4,389.89	877.98	4.1	2,526.23	
12,093	62,353	108,504	1,274,185	318,546	2,086.35	521.59	1.6	1,046.98	Sept. 1,1887
104,116	308,195	221,394	6,874,858	420,670	13,488.16	843 01	1.9	9,953 01	
67,598	196,125	102,976	4,140,319	414,032	9,505.33	950.53	2.3	6,666.00	
5,068	22,435	12,967	654,901	163,725	2,608.55	652.14	4.0	739.70	July 1,1887
4,762	31,487	10,141	608,354	107,080	2,625.01	656.23	4 0	559.51	July 1,1887
5,353	21,601	8,172	465,310	116,328	2,443 47	608.81	5.2	513.45	July 1,1887
23,736	78,010	145,831	1,690,550	338,110	3,924.12	788.42	2 3	1,302 33	
52,032	69,556	43,474	2,018,167	248,310	4,946.46	706.67	2.4	3,917.15	
362,792	456,226	300,278	12,904,087	309,383	42,799.58	1,018.80	3 3	46,107.80	July 1,1887
37,366	43,042	34,653	1,526,829	218,118	4,469.86	638.55	2.9	2,961.34	
56,911	154,941	42,812	4,000,961	363,723	10,449.37	949.04	2.6	3,279.19	
15,847	107,376	29,699	2,066,617	258,327	7,002.88	875 36	3.3	1,616 68	
4,884	19,562	7,551	518,375	129,594	3,507.30	876.82	6.7	1,206.17	
109,309	262,099	98,926	4,943,449	308,966	12,402.61	775.16	2.5	8,565.36	
24,702	114,496	114,057	2,027,925	385,991	7,197.46	899.68	2.4	2,322.95	
277,843	380,041	113,068	7,466,188	247,161	22,521.58	866.21	3 0	11,548.57	
106,111	443,939	562,231	25,413,933	529,457	43,421.13	901.61	1.7	49,267 80	
22,051	217,527	471,565	3,941,299	394,121	8,568.79	856.88	2.1	3,793.28	
6,412	47,262	26,539	1,061,042	212,208	3,758.89	751.78	3 5	1,271.07	
2,219	15,642	2,896	412,186	104,062	1,070.17	356.72	3.4	632.38	Jan. 1,1888
10,864	42,407	16,443	1,113,838	222,768	3,414.32	682.86	3 0	1,301.29	July 1,1887
54,995	109,914	115,707	2,083,761	416,752	4,242.61	848 52	2.0	2,083.18	
34,189	45,739	41,261	1,948,865	174,354	8,136.44	739.68	4 1	2,604.45	
5,935	19,898	11,158	816,740	163,148	3,082.56	616.51	3.7	1,575.59	July 1,1887
169,998	388,336	239,092	6,492,724	432,848	13,358.41	890.56	2.0	12,3.5.96	
5,715,989	2,479,896	6,845,866	110,246,118	574,199	186,160.74	909.58	1.6	450,639.13	
912,929	1,162,966	1,026,851	31,639,176	529,457	49,660 40	936 99	1.5	58,674 75	
35,651	68,872	39,495	2,023,775	202,375	8,473.35	847.33	4.1	4,256.09	
1,774	6,032	1,174	174,467		553.64	276.82	3.1	209.92	Mar. 1,1888
1,769	8,037	25,144	339,817	168,823	1,253.43	626.77	3 6	404.56	July 1,1887
4 6	2,382	1,898	115,945	38,648	946.65	328.86	8.5	409.65	Feb. 1,1888
46,008	94,775	70,001	2,395,5 0	342,217	6,234.93	890.70	2.6	4,190.26	

TABLE D.—*Statement showing the number of carriers in service June 30, 1888, the*

Post-office and State.	Carriers in service June 30, 1888	Delivered.				Collected.	
		Registered letters.	Letters.	Postal-cards.	Newspapers, etc.	Local letters.	Mail letters.
San Antonio, Tex.........	9	5,829	747,457	56,748	512,927	34,238	482,238
San Diego, Cal..........	5	808	428,674	17,578	138,096	5,374	157,421
Sandusky, Ohio..........	6	1,161	419,557	113,253	426,779	22,944	221,158
San Francisco, Cal.......	126	103,897	23,210,987	5,838,928	9,495,589	6,511,443	15,182,680
San José, Cal	7	2,101	727,563	101,562	676,240	37,909	409,787
Saratoga Springs, N.Y...	6	3,052	1,105,480	158,293	578,381	52,262	793,256
Savannah, Ga...........	13	9,214	1,668,309	390,893	595,160	178,335	1,247,550
Schenectady, N.Y........	6	704	282,165	43,988	206,568	9,437	107,037
Scranton, Pa...........	21	5,864	1,484,603	283,330	1,042,548	215,945	768,400
Seattle, Wash..........	5	4,785	370,226	24,936	228,607	25,701	304,893
Sedalia, Mo............	7	3,575	843,093	202,452	681,631	53,481	485,885
Selma, Ala............	3	440	101,971	17,975	63,958	9,780	55,540
Sheboygan, Wis	4	601	180,388	36,624	173,587	3,936	58,095
Sherman, Tex...........	4	1,168	202,071	38,191	104,254	4,278	130,547
Shreveport, La..........	4	1,141	188,276	12,089	39,329	1,994	72,038
Sioux City, Iowa........	8	2,409	667,888	89,028	47,636	51,179	613,048
Sioux Falls, Dak........	3	1,171	277,592	47,032	171,858	10,665	140,081
South Bend, Ind........	8	6,591	1,205,189	171,148	900,453	56,454	1,077,157
Springfield, Ill.........	10	5,470	1,499,326	413,084	1,071,511	129,238	1,012,824
Springfield, Mass........	15	5,980	1,965,617	394,294	1,117,238	172,469	1,059,624
Springfield, Mo.........	7	483	143,519	22,788	83,403	7,203	126,822
Springfield, Ohio........	12	19,734	1,615,817	442,511	882,384	50,941	686,455
Stamford, Conn.........	4	667	252,612	36,787	135,954	9,276	64,132
Staunton, Va...........	4	791	142,034	28,342	90,055	13,867	183,552
Sterling, Ill	3	510	259,156	56,972	168,404	5,813	98,843
Steubenville, Ohio.......	5	1,390	350,527	77,505	251,935	12,344	193,124
Stillwater, Minn........	6	1,207	478,356	97,398	229,748	70,365	433,186
Stockton, Cal..........	5	779	225,376	27,436	139,843	17,136	225,306
Streator, Ill	5	724	205,715	54,457	148,543	9,057	104,167
Syracuse, N.Y..........	30	14,906	4,905,917	1,155,936	2,303,570	472,848	2,037,504
Tacoma, Wash..........	4	1,219	325,421	34,241	217,230	64,197	314,438
Taunton, Mass..........	8	1,357	770,885	157,530	647,214	82,986	401,689
Terre Haute, Ind........	11	9,209	1,790,212	510,128	1,602,045	132,585	1,459,074
Tiffin, Ohio...........	3	810	240,077	62,672	222,069	7,796	126,472
Titusville, Pa..........	4	174	66,452	15,566	38,204	2,609	31,078
Toledo, Ohio...........	26	16,502	3,410,913	683,071	1,601,081	218,731	1,922,423
Topeka, Kans...........	12	13,348	3,410,541	776,953	1,508,114	359,037	1,399,802
Trenton, N.J...........	16	4,021	1,240,780	243,892	799,396	163,250	687,414
Troy, N.Y............	29	10,806	3,532,328	796,779	1,517,544	980,616	2,076,948
Utica, N.Y............	19	11,689	2,542,939	447,880	1,169,844	215,894	1,436,151
Vicksburg, Miss........	6	4,661	201,300	29,672	85,508	7,202	165,647
Vincennes, Ind.........	4	1,039	589,975	162,841	251,737	24,997	502,447
Waltham, Mass.........	6	406	703,318	103,000	266,505	49,601	246,154
Warren, Pa............	3	626	200,178	46,916	158,529	13,241	76,432
Washington, D.C........	92	46,609	9,098,673	1,842,508	5,661,343	1,603,726	6,698,671
Waterbury, Conn........	7	1,407	563,156	98,762	369,179	34,069	246,727
Waterloo, Iowa.........	3	1,194	238,918	45,823	194,221	11,325	200,825
Watertown, N.Y.........	7	3,089	743,677	115,760	426,699	33,397	357,194
Wellington, Kans........	3	773	174,366	32,545	137,575	3,717	88,747
West Chester, Pa	3	406	179,432	37,706	100,673	10,611	141,770
Westerly, R.I..........	4	523	118,651	17,820	122,419	5,149	54,622
Wheeling, W.Va........	11	10,270	1,294,179	313,169	744,590	104,563	1,176,822
Wichita, Kans..........	11	4,746	1,672,644	96,712	959,877	72,386	1,194,012
Wilkes Barre, Pa........	12	2,695	1,340,303	301,675	1,096,951	193,147	857,615
Williamsport, Pa........	9	4,773	1,001,343	176,901	590,324	81,033	720,385
Wilmington, Del........	17	5,894	1,813,655	422,068	837,108	153,661	812,344
Wilmington, N.C........	6	3,186	710,908	141,102	737,059	28,965	584,406
Winfield, Kans.........	4	1,148	323,552	63,055	273,431	16,360	172,133
Winona, Minn.........	6	1,908	427,750	80,114	427,776	14,794	252,877
Woonsocket, R.I	6	847	267,709	52,169	227,068	15,358	131,141
Wooster, Ohio..........	3	1,719	366,483	97,887	29,976	11,727	217,238
Worcester, Mass.........	23	5,191	2,115,180	536,933	1,447,467	199,966	816,756
Xenia, Ohio...........	3	513	217,019	50,118	148,784	5,970	57,672
Yonkers, N.Y..........	9	978	1,434,466	172,814	602,400	157,785	551,777
York, Pa............	8	2,46	550,404	142,962	420,267	19,335	229,826
Youngstown, Ohio........	7	3,088	795,232	176,617	418,291	43,392	380,664
Zanesville, Ohio........	8	4,283	924,978	223,592	556,528	65,616	563,183
Total	6,346	4,271,103	873,760,692	212,426,703	428,710,933	215,293,097	544,820,866

amount of mail delivered and collected, the number of pieces handled, etc.—Continued.

Collected.			Pieces handled.		Cost of service.			Postage on local matter.	Established.
Local postal cards.	Mail postal cards.	Newspapers, etc.	Aggregate.	Per carrier.	Aggregate.	Per carrier.	Per piece in mills.		
24,926	45,985	36,509	1,046,857	216,317	$8,325.44	$925.05	4.2	$3,521.62	
3,276	6,567	14,708	772,502	154,500	2,470.45	494.09	3.2	2,888.66	Oct 1,1887
23,976	57,451	14,300	1,390,541	216,763	4,947.11	824.52	3.8	1,056.66	
3,140,470	1,852,440	2,631,299	67,967,480	539,424	114,834.17	911.38	1.7	168,329.94	
35,274	40,100	126,639	2,217,195	316,742	6,709.12	958.45	3.0	4,198.09	
83,154	94,036	75,923	2,891,940	481,990	5,477.77	912.96	1.9	2,475.94	
138,970	300,970	109,270	4,639,271	356,868	9,927.95	764.69	2.1	9,567.29	
3,012	16,323	10,949	680,273	113,379	2,940.68	490.11	4.3	1,165.74	Oct. 1,1887
154,998	126,927	72,204	4,155,929	197,901	17,075.20	813.10	4.1	16,103.46	
14,143	21,495	84,229	974,917	195,783	2,261.08	452.62	2.3	1,981.31	Sept. 1,1887
42,450	115,417	61,639	2,430,643	348,520	6,155.52	879.36	2.5	1,681.22	
1,558	8,559	2,380	202,103	87,387	1,651.22	550.41	6.3	1,222.31	Oct. 1,1887
1,610	8,634	3,425	409,910	117,477	2,139.86	534.06	4.5	523.36	Sept. 1,1887
4,58	20,584	15,703	521,344	130,346	2,672.86	668.22	5.1	505.66	July 1,1887
2,333	8,464	3,411	225,075	50,269	2,065.93	516.48	9.1	759.05	Sept. 1,1887
28,865	118,547	101,904	2,146,504	208,313	6,167.12	770.89	2.8	4,578.17	
6,867	22,611	9,591	686,908	228,969	1,955.71	651.90	2.8	534.36	July 1,1887
26,415	118,988	49,356	3,611,751	451,219	7,057.63	880.95	1.9	1,540.19	
75,971	248,217	447,152	4,942,701	490,279	8,443.00	844.30	1.7	3,502.66	
74,146	223,045	140,745	5,153,158	343,551	11,663.97	777.60	2.2	10,939.03	
3,238	18,171	4,190	409,817	58,545	2,271.61	324.52	5.5	873.33	Jan. 1,1888
31,014	189,765	140,076	4,024,697	335,725	9,972.73	831.06	2.4	4,269.21	
2,783	9,364	3,258	514,833	128,708	2,320.09	580.02	4.5	2,110.19	July 1,1887
7,766	57,421	15,416	539,244	134,811	2,618.74	634.68	4.8	872.15	July 1,1887
3,005	18,701	5,250	616,684	205,551	1,658.81	552.27	2.6	577.74	Sept. 1,1887
6,147	49,544	25,515	968,631	193,606	3,235.72	647.14	3.3	1,657.12	July 1,1887
32,408	54,208	48,277	1,445,153	240,859	3,234.38	539.06	2.2	2,343.11	Sept. 1,1887
8,209	15,227	2,752	680,964	136,193	3,052.60	610.52	4.4	1,244.55	July 1,1887
5,072	19,509	4,259	611,413	128,2?9	2,400.45	480.09	3.7	792.52	Sept. 1,1887
308,242	493,171	237,618	12,017,712	400,590	23,276.80	775.89	1.9	23,830.88	
25,169	34,744	29,056	1,015,915	261,479	1,810.37	452.09	1.7	2,076.57	Nov. 1,1887
59,910	89,445	52,733	2,262,809	282,856	6,904.11	863.01	3.0	6,053.95	
118,850	611,431	609,401	6,884,935	623,009	9,905.03	900.46	1.4	4,020.32	
3,971	27,743	15,276	700,880	235,629	1,970.39	656.79	2.7	601.02	July 1,1887
1,510	5,436	2,021	160,050	40,762	703.41	175.85	4.3	195.63	April 1,1888
135,946	478,701	209,339	8,676,707	333,720	22,606.97	869.50	2.5	15,764.49	
292,875	3.27,586	116,411	8,194,707	682,892	10,083.00	840.42	1.2	10,851.14	
96,226	145,289	59,553	3,439,824	214,989	12,441.94	777.62	3.6	10,727.09	
657,486	605,007	502,516	10,680,120	308,280	23,621.47	814.64	2.2	28,965.18	
90,684	271,175	170,730	6,356,906	354,577	15,173.67	794.61	2.3	9,082.52	
5,390	20,426	11,011	540,817	88,468	3,711.60	618.60	7.0	772.92	July 1,1887
15,064	124,602	75,111	1,747,813	436,953	2,270.69	567.07	1.3	767.60	July 1,1887
28,482	36,065	20,111	1,452,762	242,127	3,481.72	580.29	2.4	2,552.70	July 1,1887
3,164	13,245	13,014	524,442	174,814	1,500.56	500.19	2.8	1,057.80	July 1,1887
899,806	1,039,069	1,058,580	27,919,015	305,794	87,469.37	910.29	3.1	63,023.33	
12,644	29,312	12,544	1,361,710	194,534	5,284.08	751.95	3.8	4,760.17	
5,209	35,284	16,968	748,963	248,655	1,957.73	652.58	2.6	905.85	July 1,1887
11,260	66,976	79,568	1,817,720	262,531	5,630.94	804.42	3.0	1,884.82	
4,029	14,950	4,281	469,093	153,061	1,990.45	660.15	4.3	431.47	July 1,1887
6,383	32,350	16,068	525,345	175,115	1,964.21	654.74	3.7	1,045.10	July 1,1887
2,210	7,387	4,223	233,040	83,260	2,609.66	674.92	8.0	652.74	July 1,1887
50,835	231,479	164,173	4,109,080	372,644	9,222.45	838.40	2.2	3,788.23	
52,190	106,519	90,642	4,249,708	486,337	7,868.81	715.35	1.8	4,339.67	
89,108	192,076	98,002	4,172,574	347,714	9,326.09	777.17	2.2	12,252.82	
28,211	142,389	69,932	2,819,351	313,261	7,293.83	810.43	2.2	3,725.69	
76,223	170,101	54,607	4,307,791	256,924	13,476.82	782.75	3.8	7,441.82	
24,379	114,371	14,019	2,358,467	393,078	5,481.76	910.29	2.3	1,973.60	
10,558	82,619	19,973	964,829	241,207	2,748.33	687.08	2.8	853.66	July 1,1887
9,732	41,689	22,044	1,278,756	213,126	5,105.25	850.87	4.0	2,405.26	
6,195	20,387	7,210	728,004	121,347	3,863.50	643.91	5.3	1,306.24	July 1,1887
6,342	48,173	35,773	1,078,318	359,439	1,880.86	6.29.95	1.2	650.19	July 1,1887
112,639	167,392	80,504	5,482,025	238,349	17,431.06	757.87	3.1	12,590.00	
2,112	13,313	3,965	400,466	166,488	1,988.41	662.81	4.0	905.54	July 1,1887
56,075	88,552	67,712	3,189,559	348,173	7,986.87	847.43	2.5	6,459.73	
8,595	52,239	29,003	1,415,034	181,880	6,868.28	858.53	4.7	1,915.73	
77,768	71,331	36,949	2,004,332	286,190	6,031.18	861.60	3.0	2,682.07	
41,861	253,291	54,365	2,689,499	336,187	5,034.74	629.34	1.8	2,264.58	
98,453,544	130,526,893	127,597,925	2,630,861,758	415,563	$5,407,200.16	.....	2.?	$7,721,689.16	

REPORT

OF THE

SECOND ASSISTANT POSTMASTER-GENERAL

FOR

1888.

107

REPORT

SECOND ASSISTANT POSTMASTER-GENERAL.

POST-OFFICE DEPARTMENT,
OFFICE OF SECOND ASSISTANT POSTMASTER-GENERAL,
Washington, D. C., November 10, 1888.

SIR: The annual rate of expenditure for inland mail transportation on June 30, 1888, was:

For 14,146 star routes, aggregating 225,607.53 miles in length........	$4,959,192.00¼
For 5,906 mail messenger routes. aggregating 4,645.05 miles in length..	883,718.67
For 1¼7 steam-boat routes, aggregating 11,059.49 miles in length....	438,942.27
For 1,995 railroad routes, aggregating 143,713.32 miles in length.....	17,528,599.80
For railway post-office car service...................................	1,996,359.35
For railway post-office clerks...................................	5,084,517.00
For mail equipments...................................	269,530.73½
For necessary and special facilities on trunk lines...................	295,967.53
Total...................................	31,456,847.35¼

Comparison with the report for June 30, 1887, shows:

For the star service, an increase of 286 routes, a decrease of 5,988.75 miles in length of routes, and a decrease of $140,311.42¾ in the annual rate of expenditure.

The number of miles traveled per annum was 83,683,998.99, at a cost of 5.92 cents per mile, a decrease of 575,285.28 in the number of miles traveled per annum, and a decrease of 0.13 cent in the rate of cost per mile.

In the regulation wagon service (included in the star service) there were 30 routes, aggregating 397.47 miles in length, the annual rate of expenditure was $404,796.74, the number of miles traveled per annum, 1,514,136.29; the rate of cost per mile, 26.73 cents; an increase of 9.72 miles in length of routes, an increase of $532 in the annual rate of expenditure, an increase of 94,914.16 in the number of miles traveled per annum, and a decrease of 1.75 cents in the rate of cost per mile.

For the mail messenger service, an increase of 388 routes, an increase of 344.41 miles in length of routes, and an increase of $54,170.06 in the annual rate of expenditure.

The number of miles traveled per annum was 10,595,355.22, at a cost of 8.34 cents per mile; an increase of 693,549.61 in the number of miles traveled per annum, and a decrease of 0.03 cent in the rate of cost per mile.

In the special office service there were 2,695 routes, aggregating 18,952.56 miles in length, an increase of 261 in the number of routes, and an increase of 3,520.70 miles in the length of routes.

The number of miles traveled per annum (estimated on a basis of 2.16 trips per week for each route) was 4,269,882.24, an increase (over the estimate for June 30, 1887) of 1,060,055.36 in the number of miles traveled per annum.

For the steam-boat service, an increase of four routes, an increase of 461.37 miles in the length of routes, and an increase of $5,753.09 in the annual rate of expenditure.

The number of miles traveled per annum was 3,216,035.98, at a cost of 13.64 cents per mile, an increase of 103,752.66 in the number of miles traveled per annum, and a decrease of 0.28 cent in the rate of cost per mile.

For the railroad service, an increase of 168 routes, an increase of 12,764.51 miles in the length of routes, and an increase of $1,353,908.58 in the annual rate of expenditure for transportation.

The number of miles traveled per annum was 185,485,783.33, at a cost of 9.45 cents per mile for transportation, an increase of 15,795,917.48 in the number of miles traveled per annum, and a decrease of 0.08 cent in the rate of cost per mile for transportation.

For the railway post-office car service, an increase of $114,778.85 in the annual rate of expenditure.

The annual rate of expenditure for the railroad service (including the railway post-office car service), was $19,524,959.15, an increase of $1,468,687.43.

The rate of cost per mile traveled for railroad service (including the cost for railway post-office car service), was 10.52 cents, a decrease of 0.12 cent in the rate of cost per mile.

For railway post-office clerks, an increase of $257,051 in the annual rate of expenditure.

For mail equipments, a decrease of $5,383.09½ in the annual rate of expenditure.

For necessary and special facilities on trunk lines, an increase of $10,401.43 in the annual rate of expenditure.

The sums actually disbursed appear in the Auditor's report.

The number of contracts drawn in duplicate during the year was 4,454, a decrease of 912 from the number for the preceding year.

CONDENSED STATEMENT OF WHOLE MAIL SERVICE.

A condensed statement of the whole service for the fiscal year ended June 30, 1888, shows that the total number of routes in operation on that date was 24,869, being an increase over the previous year of 1,107 routes, or 4.65 per cent ; that the length of these routes aggregated a mileage of 403,976.95, being a net increase in mileage of 11,102.24, the percentage of increase in length of routes being 2.82; that the number of miles traveled during the year was 287,251,055.76, being an increase of 17,077.989.83 miles of travel, equivalent to an increase of 6.32 per cent. in miles traveled; that the cost per mile traveled was 10.95 cents, being a decrease of 0.72 per cent. in the cost per mile traveled from the previous year; that the annual rate of cost of this service on the same day, to wit, June 30, 1888, was $31,456,847.35¾, being a total increase over the previous fiscal year of $1,650,338.48¾, or 5.53 per cent. in the annual rate of expenditure.

Comparison of the star and steam-boat service for the year ended June 30, 1888, with the annual average of said service for the eight years next preceding develops the following results:

TABLE 1.—*Comparison of star and steam-boat service.*

	Star service.			Steam-boat service.		
	Miles traveled.	Rate of expenditure.	Cost per mile.	Miles traveled.	Rate of expenditure.	Cost per mile.
			Cents			*Cents.*
Average for years 1880 to 1887, inclusive.	80, 271, 915	$5, 691, 080	7. 09	4, 051, 527	$607 651	15. 00
For year ended June 30, 1888.............	83, 683, 999	4, 959, 292	5. 92	8, 210, 036	4.8, 942	13. 54
Increase (per cent.)......................	4. 25	......	......	20. 62	....	......
Decrease (per cent.)......................	....	12. 86	15. 09	....	27. 76	9. 06

TABLE 2.—*Percentage of increase and decrease in estimates for inland transportation.*

Statement showing the percentage of increase or decrease in the estimates of cost for in and mail service for the years 1881 to 1890, inclusive, as compared with the appropriation for the year preceding each of them.

Appropriation.		Estimate.		Percentage of increase or decrease.	
Year.	Amount.	Year.	Amount.	Increase.	Decrease.
1880.................	$20, 845, 000. 00	1881................	$24, 125, 000. 00	15. 73	....
1881.................	23, 326. 000. 00	1882................	25, 715, 032. 00	10. 24	....
1882.................	24, 376 052. 00	1883................	25, 738, 000. 00	5. 59	....
1883.................	20, 067, 000. 00	1884................	25, 494, 120. 00	....	2 20
1884.................	24, 387, 120. 00	1885................	27, 441, 505. 00	12. 52	....
1885.................	26, 401, 000. 00	1886................	30, 294, 260. 50	14. 74	....
1886.................	28, 510, 000. 00	1887................	30, 363, 733. 64	6. 50	....
1887.................	30, 100, 432. 00	1888................	30, 137, 750. 15	. 12	....
1888.................	30, 137, 750. 15	1889................	31, 816, 682. 74	5. 58	....
1889.................	31, 653, 777. 74	1890................	34, 878, 942. 02	10. 18	....

The first of the above tables (1) shows a decrease in the rate of expenditure for the star service of 12.86 per cent. and in the cost per mile of 15.09 per cent. ; in the steam-boat service a decrease in the rate of expenditure of 27.76 per cent., and in the cost per mile of service of 9.06 per cent., while there has been an increase in the number of routes in both classes of service.

STAR SERVICE.

The annual rate of expenditure for this class of service, including regulation wagon service, on June 30, 1888, was $4,959,192.00¼.

The number of routes was 14,146, of an aggregate length of 225,607.53 miles, and an annual travel of 83,683,098.99 miles.

The cost per mile traveled was 5.92 cents.

The average number of trips per week was 3.56.

A comparison with the last annual report shows, for the fiscal year ended June 30, 1888, an increase of 286 routes, a decrease of 5,988.75 miles in the length of routes, a decrease of $140,341.42¾ in the annual rate of expenditure, a decrease of 575,285.28 in the number of miles traveled per annum, a decrease of 0.13 cent in the rate of cost per mile traveled, and an increase of .07 in the average number of trips per week.

The appropriation for the last fiscal year was $5,400,000.

The sum actually expended was $5,015,178.22, leaving an unexpended balance of $384,821.78.

The annual rate of expenditure for service on July 1, 1888, under contracts made during the last fiscal year for the performance of star service rom July 1, 1888, to June 30, 1892, in the second contract section, embracing the States t North Carolina, South Carolina, Georgia, Florida, Alabama, Mississippi, Tennessee, and Kentucky, was $569,-746.21, a decrease from the annual rate of expenditure for service in the same States on June 30, 1888, of $4,201.42 ; representing a saving of $16,805.68 for the ensuing contract term of four years from July 1, 1888.

The total number of star routes in operation on June 30, 1888, was 14,146 ; on July 1, 1888, 14,923, an increase of 777.

The annual rate of expenditure for all the star service in operation was—

July 1, 1888.. $5,040,172.14¼
August 31, 1888 .... 5,134,636.94¼
September 30, 1888.. 5,151,802.08¼

The appropriation for the current fiscal year is $5,400,000, the sum estimated as necessary for the current fiscal year is $5,400,000.

The amount estimated as necessary for the fiscal year ending June 30, 1890, is $5,750,000, being $350,000, or 6.48 per cent., more than the appropriation for the current year.

REGULATION WAGON SERVICE.

This service is performed in cities in wagons of a uniform character prescribed by the Department, and is a most important and necessary arm of the service for the dispatch and transfer of the mails in the great centers of business and population. It is awarded by contract, as star-route service, and is estimated for in the appropriation for that service, and paid out of that appropriation.

The statement following shows the cities in which it has been established, and the annual rate of expenditure therefor:

Annual rate of expenditure for the regulation-wagon, mail-messenger, mail-station, and transfer service in operation June 30, 1888.

Place.	Amount.	Place.	Amount.
Baltimore, Md..........................	$8,875.20	New Orleans, La	$4,696.00
Boston, Mass..........................	34,960.00	New York, N. Y	165,000.00
Brooklyn, N. Y........................	16,800.00	Omaha, Nebr........................	2,995.00
Buffalo, N. Y	4,900.00	Philadelphia, Pa	27,200.00
Burlington, Iowa......................	1,298.00	Pittsburgh, Pa.......................	6,880.00
Charleston, S. C......................	2,390.00	Providence, R. I	2,800.00
Chattanooga, Tenn....................	1,400.00	Richmond, Va	2,690.00
Chicago, Ill	34,000.00	Saint Louis, Mo	14,945.00
Cincinnati, Ohio......................	14,749.40	Saint Paul, Minn	2,950.00
Cleveland, Ohio.......................	5,290.40	San Francisco, Cal	8,000.00
Detroit, Mich	5,380.00	Savannah, Ga	2,496.00
Kansas City, Mo	4,945.00	Toledo, Ohio	4,880.00
Knoxville, Tenn.......................	1,497.00	Washington, D. C....................	9,876.54
Louisville, Ky........................	5,800.00	Wilmington, N. C....................	890.00
Memphis, Tenn	4,000.00		
Nashville, Tenn	2,792.00	Total.........................	404,796.74

STEAM-BOAT SERVICE.

The annual rate of expenditure for this class of service on June 30, 1888, was $438,942.27.

The number of routes was 127, of an aggregate length of 11,058.49 miles, and an annual travel of 3,216,035.98 miles. The cost per mile traveled was 13.64 cents.   The average number of trips per week was 2.79.

A comparison with the last annual report shows, for the fiscal year ended June 30, 1888, an increase of four routes, an increase of 461.37 miles in length of routes, an increase of $5,753.09 in the annual rate of expenditure, an increase of 103,752.66 in the number of miles traveled per annum, a decrease of .28 cent in the rate of cost per mile traveled, and a decrease of .03 in the average number of trips per week.

The appropriation for the last fiscal year was $450,000; the sum actually expended was $409,872.56, leaving an unexpended balance of $40,127.44

The annual rate of expenditure for service on July 1, 1888, under contracts made during the last fiscal year for the performance of steam-boat service, from July 1, 1888, to June 30, 1892, in the second contract section, embracing the States of North Carolina, South Carolina, Georgia; Florida, Alabama, Mississippi, Tennessee, and Kentucky, was $134,963.25, a decrease from the annual rate of expenditure for service in the same States on June 30, 1888, of $299.35; representing a saving of $1,197.40 for the ensuing contract term of four years from July 1, 1888.

The total number of steam-boat routes in operation on June 30, 1888, was 127, and on July 1, 1888, the same number.

The annual rate of expenditure for all of the steam-boat service in operation was—

July 1, 1888	$446,119.92
August 31, 1888	453,725.87
September 30, 1888	456,653.52

The appropriation for the current fiscal year is $450,000.

The sum estimated as necessary for the current fiscal year is $475,000.

The amount estimated as necessary for the fiscal year ending June 30, 1890, is $500,000, being $50,000, or 11.11 per cent., more than the appropriation for the current year.

MAIL-MESSENGER SERVICE.

The annual rate of expenditure for this class of service on June 30, 1888, was $883,718.67; the number of routes was 5,906, of an aggregate length of 4,645.05 miles, and an annual travel of 10,595,355.22 miles. The cost per mile traveled was 8.34 cents.   The average number of trips per week was 21.93.

A comparison with the last annual report shows, for the fiscal year ended June 30, 1888, an increase of 383 routes, an increase of 344.41 miles in length of routes, an increase of $54,170.06 in the annual rate of expenditure, an increase of 693,549.61 in the number of miles traveled per annum, a decrease of .03 cent in the rate of cost per mile traveled, and a decrease of .20 in the average number of trips per week.

The appropriation for the last fiscal year was $900,000.   The sum actually expended was $851,709.39, leaving an unexpended balance of $48,290.61.

The number of routes in operation on June 30, 1888, was 5,906 ; on July 1, 1888, 5,908; an increase of 2.

The annual rate of expenditure for all service in operation was—

July 1, 1888	$883,942.67
August 31, 1888	896,959.54
September 30, 1888	901,251.31

11843—P M G 88——8

The appropriation for the current fiscal year is $950,000. The sum estimated as necessary for the current fiscal year is $950,000.

The amount estimated as necessary for the fiscal year ending June 30, 1890, is $1,050,000; being $100,000, or 10.52 per cent. more than the appropriation for the current year.

RAILROAD MAIL SERVICE.

Increase in length of railroads over which the mails were carried during each of the years from 1882 to 1888, inclusive; also, showing the number of miles of railroad service on which the pay was unadjusted on June 30, of each of said years.

Year.	Increase in length of route.	Unadjusted service, June 30.	Year.	Increase in length of routes.	Unadjusted service, June 30.
	Miles.	*Miles.*		*Miles.*	*Miles.*
1882	8,994	8,449	1886	2,901.00	1,563.00
1883	9,645	7,234	1887	7,015.81	4,195.59
1884	6,952	9,026	1888	12,764.51	6,723.31
1885	3,872	2,945			

The following table shows the average rate of cost per mile per annum based upon the aggregate length of routes for the years therein mentioned.

Year.	Length of routes.	Annual rate of expenditure for transportation.	Average rate per mile per annum.	Year.	Length of routes.	Annual rate of expenditure for transportation.	Average rate per mile per annum.
	Miles.				*Miles.*		
1880....	85,320	$9,237,945	$108.27	1885....	121,032	$14,758,495	$121.95
1881....	91,569	10,249,261	111.92	1886....	123,933	15,520,191	125.23
1882....	100,563	11,297,333	112.34	1887....	130,945	16,174,691	123.52
1883....	110,208	12,288,790	111.50	1888....	143,713	17,528,600	121.96
1884....	117,160	13,273,606	113.29				

Length of routes, and annual rate of expenditure for transportation and railway post-office cars combined, showing increase and percentage of increase for the years 1880 to 1888, inclusive.

Year.	Length of routes.	Increase in length of routes.		Annual rate of expenditure.	Increase in annual rate of expenditure.	
	Miles.	*Miles.*	*Per cent.*			*Per cent.*
1880.......	85,320	5,329	6.66	$10,408,986	$931,396	9.73
1881.......	91,569	6,249	7.32	11,613,868	1,114,382	10.61
1882.......	100,563	8,994	9.82	12,758,154	1,139,816	9.81
1883.......	110,208	9,645	9.59	13,887,800	1,134,616	8.89
1884.......	117,160	6,952	6.30	15,012,603	1,124,803	8.09
1885.......	121,032	5,872	3.30	16,627,983	1,615,380	10.76
1886.......	123,933	2,901	2.39	17,336,512	708,529	4.20
1887.......	130,949	7,016	5.66	18,056,272	719,760	4.15
1888.......	143,713	12,764	9.74	19,524,959	1,468,687	8.13

Statement showing in what States the largest part of the increase in length of routes during the year ended June 30, 1888, took place, with an estimate of the increase in annual rate of expenditure for said service.

States.	Increase in number of routes.	Increase in length of routes.	Estimated increase in the annual rate of expenditure on account of this new service.
		Miles.	
Kansas	20	2,157.56	$129,453.60
Nebraska	15	1,317.98	79,041.60
Texas	9	1,244.58	74,674.80
Dakota	9	1,122.16	67,929.60
Illinois	8	919.23	55,153.20
Colorado	7	550.41	33,024.60
Wisconsin	1	542.38	32,542.80
Iowa	5	493.98	29,638.80
Indian Territory	2	371.20	22,272.00
Michigan	8	320.51	19,230.60
Arkansas	5	282.57	16,954.20
California	6	266.36	15,981.60
Georgia	3	245.15	14,709.00
Minnesota	2	230.15	13,809.00
Missouri	6	220.62	13,237.20
Montana	5	200.69	12,041.40
Total	111	10,484.90	629,094.00

RAILWAY POST-OFFICE CAR SERVICE.

Annual rate of expenditure, with increase or decrease and percentage of increase or decrease, for the years 1880 to 1888, inclusive.

Year.	Annual rate of expenditure.	Increase or decrease in annual rate of expenditure.		Percentage of increase or decrease.	
		Increase.	Decrease.	Increase.	Decrease.
1880	$1,261,041				
1881	1,364,107	$103,066		8.17	
1882	1,455,851	91,744		6.73	
1883	1,599,001	143,150		9.83	
1884	1,738,997	139,996		8.76	
1885	1,869,488	130,491		7.50	
1886	1,816,321		$53,167		2.84
1887	1,881,580	65,259		3.59	
1888	1,996,359	114,779		6.10	

ESTIMATES FOR RAILWAY POST-OFFICE CAR SERVICE AND FOR RAILWAY POST-OFFICE CLERKS, FOR THE FISCAL YEAR ENDING JUNE 30, 1890.

The appropriation for the railway post-office car service for the year ending June 30, 1889, was $2,000,000. The estimate for the fiscal year ending June 30, 1890, exclusive of the amount to accrue to the Pacific railroads, is $2,260,000, being an increase of $260,000, or 13 per cent. over the appropriation for the current fiscal year. For railway post-office clerks the appropriation for the current fiscal year is $5,246,790.21. The estimate for the fiscal year ending June 30, 1890, is $5,676,728.74, being an increase of $429,938.53, or 8.19 per cent. over the appropriation for the current fiscal year. The increase in these two branches of the service has been rendered necessary not only by the great extension of railroad mail transportation, hereinafter mentioned, but by the large increase in the weight of the mails carried, the necessity for greatly increased facilities for distributing the mails in transit, especially in the Northern and Western States, and the additions which have been made to the lines of fast mail.

For a more particular statement of the reasons of these increased estimates I refer to the report of the General Superintendent of the Railway Mail Service.

MISCELLANEOUS.

Amount of appropriation for the current year	$1,000.00
Amount expended during current year	294.50
Balance unexpended	$705.50
Estimate for next fiscal year ending June 30, 1890	1,000.00

SPECIAL FACILITIES.

The appropriation for special facilities on trunk lines for the fiscal year ending June 30, 1889, is $295,987.53, and the current expenditure on account of this fund is as follows:

Number of route.	Termini.	Railroad company.	Miles.	Pay.
5005	New York—Springfield.	New York, New Haven and Hartford.	136	$17,647.06
6011	4.35 a. m. train	New York Central and Hudson River.	144	25,000.00
10001	Philadelphia—Bay View.	Philadelphia, Wilmington and Baltimore.	91.80	20,000.00
10012, 11001 (part)	Bay View—Quantico	Baltimore and Potomac	79.80	21,900.00
11001 (part)	Quantico—Richmond	Richmond, Fredericksburgh and Potomac.	81.50	17,419.26
11008	Richmond — Petersburgh.	Richmond and Petersburgh	23.39	4,268.67
11009	Petersburgh—Weldon	Petersburgh	64	11,680.00
13002	Weldon—Wilmington	Wilmington and Weldon	162.07	29,541.27
14002	Wilmington—Florence	Wilmington, Columbia and Augusta.	110	20,075.00
14005	Florence to Charleston Junction.	Northeastern	95	17,337.50
14004	Charleston Junction to Savannah.	Charleston and Savannah	108	19,710.00
15009	Savannah to Jacksonville.	Savannah, Florida and Western	171.50	31,309.70
10006	Baltimore to Hagerstown.	Western Maryland	86.60	15,804.50
16018, 16007	Jacksonville to Tampa.	Jacksonville, Tampa and Key West and South Florida.	242.57	43,962.42
Total				295,655.38

I recommend an appropriation of the above total amount, $295,655.38, for a continuance of this important service for the next fiscal year.

Attention is invited to the tables accompanying this report for full details respecting railroad service.

Table C shows the railroad service in operation on the 30th of June, 1888.

Table H shows the re-adjustment of the rates of pay per mile on railroad routes in States and Territories in which the contract term expired June 30, 1888, and also on certain new routes in other States and Territories; the re-adjustment of the rates based upon returns of the weight of mail, and the speed at which they are conveyed, the accommodations for railway post-office clerks, and the number of trips per week, in accordance with the acts of March 3, 1873, July 13, 1876, and June 17, 1878.

Table I shows the rate of pay per annum for the use of railway post-office cars for the fiscal years ended June 30, 1887, and June 30, 1888, and the increase or decrease of 1888, as compared with 1887, and the reasons therefor.

Table K is a statement of expenditures on account of special facilities for the fiscal year ended June 30, 1888, out of $295,987.53 appropriated by the act approved March 3, 1887.

Table L shows the number of miles of railroad mail service ordered from July 1, 1887, to June 30, 1888.

Table M gives statistics of mileage, increase in mileage, and annual transportation, and cost of the railroad service from 1836 to June 30, 1888.

ESTIMATES FOR RAILWAY MAIL TRANSPORTATION FOR FISCAL YEAR ENDING JUNE 30, 1890.

In my letter of estimates I have placed the appropriation required for railroad mail transportation for the fiscal year ending June 30, 1890, at $19,105,557.90. This is a large increase upon the estimates for last year for this branch of the service, the increase being $2,105,557.90, or 12.38 per cent. The grounds for this increased estimate are given in my letter of estimates, and they are briefly these: The increase in the length of routes of new service for the next fiscal year has been estimated by me at 7,000 miles, and it is not believed from present information that it is likely to exceed that amount.   It is true that during the past fiscal year the increase in miles of railroad mail transportation was 12,764.51, but that was an unprecedented, and, I may say, phenomenal increase in that branch of the service, not to be anticipated for any one year for sometime to come.   The source of the increase in the cost of this serv-·ice is rather to be looked for in the large increase in the weight of the mails carried, and the consequent increase in the rate of cost therefor and the extension of the fast mail service.   The section to be weighed next year, and in which the railroad service is to be adjusted for four years beginning on the 1st of July, 1889, is the eastern section, embracing the New England States and the States of New York, New Jersey, Pennsylvania, Delaware, Maryland, Virginia, and West Vir-ginia, and the District of Columbia.

This section embraces some of the great trunk lines on which the largest weights of mails are carried.   The weighing of the mails in the second section, embracing the Southern States and the States of Ohio, Indiana, and Michigan, last year, resulted in an increase in the rate of cost of 18.75 per cent. in those States.   The character of the service, particularly in the States of Ohio and Indiana is similar to the character of the service in the States of New York, New Jersey,.and Pennsylvania, and the increase in the weight of mails carried in the former States furnishes an appproximate criterion by which to gauge the probable increase in the weight of mails in the latter-named States.   As it was 18.75 per cent. in the second section, it is safe to conclude that it will be larger in the first therefore, and I put that increase at 21 per cent.   I have therefore placed the estimates in this service for the next fiscal year at the sum above named, to wit, $19,105,557.90.

The increase in the mileage of railway post-office car service was 9,701.61.   The expansion of this important branch of the service is also without a parallel in any one year since its establishment.

These increases were ordered in response to the demands and requirements of the public, whose business and commercial interests were thereby greatly promoted, and in discharging that great obligation which the Department is under to furnish the people the best mail facilities and to supply the highest grade of service attainable.

FAST MAIL.

Several most important lines of fast mail have been established.   The fast mail between Chicago and Omaha has been made daily, and now runs both ways, instead of simply west, as before.

This fast mail connects with the fast mail between New York and Chicago at Chicago, which has also been increased to run east as well as west.

A fast mail has been established between Portland, Oregon, and Chicago, and between Chicago and New Orleans, via Cincinnati, Chattanooga, and Meridian, Miss.

It will thus be seen that every part of our country has been made to share in the benefits of this fast mail service, and a wider and more liberal policy in its distribution has characterized the administration of this Department during the last fiscal year.

North, South, East, and West have been dealt with in this regard with an equal and impartial hand. The fast mail along the Atlantic coast from Portland, Me., to Havana, Cuba, via New York, Baltimore, Washington, and Key West, which has been established for many years, needed no additional facilities to augment its present general efficiency.

These improvements may be briefly summed up as having effected a reduction in the transit of the mails between New York and the Pacific coast, both east and west, one full day, and between Chicago, via Cincinnati and Chattanooga, and New Orleans and all points south to eight hours, or the equivalent to a full commercial day.

The advantage to the business community of this reduction in time of transit of the mails is incalculable, and the increase in rate of cost by which it has been accomplished is not at all disproportionate to, but is entirely justified by, the results achieved and the benefits which will accrue to the public. For a full and detailed statement of these improvements in the service I refer to the report of the General Superintendent of the Railway Mail Service, herewith transmitted.

Before leaving this subject I invite your attention to the recommendations submitted in the report of the General Superintendent of the Railway Mail Service for increased appropriations for additional clerical force for his office and also for an increase in the salaries of the clerks in the Railway Mail Service who are charged with conducting the examination of postal clerks.

I think the salaries of the last-named clerks should be increased to $1,500 per annum, and that a sum not exceeding $300 per annum for each of these clerks should be appropriated to meet the expenses which they are obliged to incur while traveling for the purpose of conducting examinations and other work incumbent upon them.

The amount asked for is moderate and is justified by the responsible and laborious duties which they discharge. Some provision should certainly be made to indemnify them for expenses incurred by them while traveling on business of the Department.

I also concur in the recommendation of the General Superintendent of the Railway Mail Service for the appointment of a chief clerk to the General Superintendent of the Railway Mail Service at such salary as should be deemed just and reasonable.

INCREASES IN STAR SERVICE.

I have also asked for an increase in the appropriation for star service amounting to $350,000.

The extension of railroad construction has enabled the Department to dispense with many long lines of this branch of the service, especially in the Western States and Territories, and to replace them with the superior facilities which railroad transportation furnishes; but while doing this, this great extension of the railroad system of our country has contributed to spread and build up the populations in those regions of the country to such an extent as to very greatly augment the demand not only for new and short lines of star service, but for a great increase of frequency in the number of trips, thus entailing very considerable and additional expenditure.

MAIL MESSENGER SERVICE.

The mail messenger service, which is a complement and an outgrowth of the railroad mail service, and which necessarily increases in proportion to the extension of railroad mail transportation, has been so largely augmented during the last year as to render an increased appropriation necessary. The amount of this increase I have placed at $100,000. This estimate of increase is justified by the rapid extension of railroad construction, the growth of the population, and the requirements and demands of an intelligent, enterprising, and commercial people.

DIVISION OF INSPECTION.

The gross amount of fines and deductions from postal contractors and others during the year ended June 30, 1888, was		$354,139.85
The amount of remissions on deductions on account of satisfactory explanation was	$77,205.10	
The amount of remissions of fines was	19,710.03	
Making total remissions of fines and deductions..................		96,915.13
Leaving the net amount of fines and deductions for the fiscal year ended June 30, 1888		257,224.72

The above amounts are classed as follows:

Deductions and fines, railroad service.......................	$279,874.47	
Deductions and fines, star service..........................	44,685.02	
Deductions and fines, steam-boat service...................	22,124.02	
Deductions and fines, mail messengers......................	2,909.08	
Deductions and fines, postal clerks	4,547.26	
Total deductions and fines		$354,139.85
Remissions, railroad service..............................	87,162.72	
Remissions, star service.................................	7,610.83	
Remissions, steam-boat service...........................	1,749.16	
Remissions, mail messengers	254.74	
Remissions, postal clerks	137.68	
Total remissions		96,915.13
Leaving net amount of fines and deductions for the fiscal year ended June 30, 1888		257,224.72

MAIL EQUIPMENTS.

Appended herewith is a tabular statement (O) of the number, description, prices, and costs of all mail bags and mail catchers purchased and put into service during the last fiscal year ended June 30, 1888, and a tabular statement (P) of all mail locks purchased or repaired for service during the same period; also a tabular statement (N) of all contracts for mail equipments in operation on June 30, 1888.

The total cost of mail bags and mail catchers, with their appurtenances and repairs, during the year ended June 30, 1888, was $247,030.19, against a cost for the same items during the previous fiscal year ended June 30, 1887, of $255,483.63.

The appropriation for these items for the last fiscal year was $275,000.

The total number of new mail bags purchased and put into service during the year was 196,300, of which number 24,300 were locked mail bags of various kinds and sizes, used chiefly for letters and registered mail matter; 172,000 were tied bags, used for mail matter of the second, third, and fourth class, when not registered.

The balance of the appropriation shown to have been unexpended ($27,969.80½, statement O) resulted from a new system pursued in the repair shops, whereby an increased force does more repairing, and from the amount reserved out of the appropriation for disbursements to postmasters for expenses necessarily incurred, and paid by them for repairs of mail bags, the cost of which is contingent and variable and can not be definitely and accurately ascertained until some time after the end of the fiscal year, when all postmasters' accounts shall have been settled by the Auditor of the Post-Office Department.

The total cost of mail catchers, and brackets for same, was $1,300. The total cost of mail locks and keys, and repairs of the same, was $22,500.54; the appropriation being $23,000.

After careful consideration the amount needed for the necessary equipments for the year ending June 30, 1890, is estimated as follows:

For mail bags and catchers and repairs. $225,000
For mail locks and repairs 15,000

Being a reduction of $70,000 on the estimates for these articles for the current fiscal year. The total number of mail locks and keys on hand and in the service on June 30, 1888, was as follows:

Mail-bag locks.. 263,003
Street letter-box locks 47.374

        Total number of locks................................... 310,377
                                                                   ==========
Keys to mail-bag locks... 67,416
Keys to street letter-box locks....................................   6,487

        Total number of mail keys................................ 73,903

The number of mail bags in the service, estimated by adding the number of bags bought during the fiscal year to the number reported in service at the close of the fiscal year 1886–'87, and then deducting the condemned reported by the repair shops, and from the remainder subtracting 10 per cent. for bags destroyed by fire, robbery, or other accidents, is as follows:

Locked mail bags of every kind 170,972
Tied mail sacks of every kind..................................... 624,850

Shortly after the appointment of the new chief of the mail equipment division the discovery was made by him that in the post-offices in the cities of Washington and New York a very large amount of bags and sacks had been suffered to accumulate for want of repairs and which could be used in the service to good advantage.

After an investigation it was discovered that from 250,000 to 300,000 bags, jute, canvas, and leather, had been allowed to thus accumulate in those two offices.

These repair shops had been placed, by the regulations of the Department, under the charge of the postmasters of those respective places, who submitted monthly reports of the condition of those shops, the amount of bags received, the number repaired, and the cost of such repair.

It is plain from the results of this investigation that for some years proper attention had not been given to this surplus stock of damaged mail bags.

By an order issued by you the repair shop in the city of Washington was placed under my immediate direction, and a general order was passed instructing that all the bags to be repaired should be sent to that office for such repair.

The working force of the repair shop in the city of Washington was, from time to time, increased until it now numbers ninety-one persons.

All this accumulated stock in New York and elsewhere was sent to this repair shop in the city of Washington. The result has been a saving of at least $60,000 per annum.

No requisitions for new jute bags, sacks or leather bags have been issued from this office since last February, and none for leather sacks since last December, and the service has been amply supplied out of this surplus damaged stock, which has been put in good and service-able repair.

In view of these results I have to recommend that a permanent repair shop be established in the city of Washington under the direction of the chief of the mail equipment division of this office, and that all the bags and sacks damaged shall be sent to the city of Washington for re-pair.

I further recommend that in connection with this shop for repairing sacks and bags there shall also be established a shop for repairing mail locks and keys. The economy achieved, as above stated, by the repair of all damaged mail bags and sacks in the city of Washington justifies the opinion that a great saving will be effected to the Government by repairing its own locks and keys.

To this end I recommend a special appropriation of $10,000 to enable the Postmaster-General to make a permanent lease of some place in the city of Washington to furnish and equip it with the tools, imple-ments, and machinery and other material which may be necessary to repair mail bags and sacks and mail locks and keys.

It is believed that a place in every way adapted for this purpose at a rent certainly not exceeding $5,000 a year can be secured.

As the saving effected already in repairing mail bags and sacks has resulted in a decreased estimate for mail equipments for the next fiscal year of $70,000, it will be seen that the expenditure of this sum is jus-tified.

I append a table showing the quantity of the sacks and bags repaired in the Washington repair shop since May 1, 1888. The work done there has enabled the Department, as I have heretofore observed, to keep the service abundantly supplied with these articles of mail equip-ment without making a single requisition for any new sacks or bags, canvas or leather, since it has been under my charge.

Before closing this part of my report it is proper to mention that under your instructions I renewed the contracts for another period of four years with the contractors for the supply thereof, for inside street let-ter-box locks, general iron locks and the repair of the general iron locks, and also for furnishing street letter-box locks. But in doing so, and under your instructions, I availed myself of the stipulations in these con-tracts authorizing the Postmaster-General, in his discretion, to extend such contracts for another period of four years.

Inside street letter-box locks are hereafter to be furnished for 80 cents each, instead of 85 cents each, being a reduction of 6 per cent.

General iron locks are hereafter to be furnished at 45 cents each, instead of 52 cents each, being a reduction of 13½ per cent.

The repairing of these general iron locks is to be done at 33 cents each, instead of 35 cents each, being a reduction of 6 per cent.

An agreement has also been entered into with the same contractors for furnishing the service with street letter-box locks for a term of four years, beginning September 1, 1888, and terminating September 1, 1892. These locks, which cost $1.25 each, will be furnished for the said con-tract term for 50 cents each, being a reduction in the cost of this article of mail equipment of 60 per cent.

Before the expiration of these contracts and the renewal of them, as above stated, the question as to the advisability of advertising for en-tirely new locks and keys was fully considered by this office. As the service requires that all locks and keys shall be the same, and as it was estimated that the replacing of the general mail lock with key attached would cost about $150,000, it was deemed in the line of a proper and wise economy to continue these locks in the service for another period of four years, to use the opportunity above stated for a reduction in the cost thereof.

The stock of these articles of mail equipment on hand being very large, and the number of new locks and keys which would be required in the service would not, it was estimated, exceed 10,000, and the mail locks in present use being generally in good order and very serviceable, it was deemed to be in the line of economy to renew these contracts for another period of four years.   If my recommendation for the establishment of a shop for the repair of these locks be carried out the cost of this article of mail equipment for the next four years will be compara- tively small.

The number of pouches and sacks at the Washington, D. C., repair shop from May 1 to October 1, 1888, was as follows :

Jute sacks	214, 381
Leather pouches	20, 236
Catcher pouches	5, 021
Horse bags	680
Registered pouches	451
Inner registered sacks	1, 113
Total	241, 882

PROPOSED CHANGE IN THE BASIS OF PAY OF RAILROAD COMPANIES FOR MAIL TRANSPORTATION.

Before closing this report I desire to again call your attention to the necessity of a revision of the present method of compensating railroads for mail transportation.   In my report of 1886 I had the honor to sub- mit a full and detailed report on this subject and to suggest a change in the basis of pay by which space occupied, instead of weight of mails carried, should be the standard and criterion of compensation.

The reasons for this opinion are given in that report fully and ex- haustively, and it is not necessary to repeat them here.

In my last annual report I called attention to this subject.   The large increase in the estimates submitted to meet the expenses of rail- road mail transportation for the fiscal year ending June 30, 1890, fur- nishes an additional reason, if any were needed, for again inviting your attention and the attention of Congress to this most important subject. It becomes more and more apparent every year that the present method is what I declared it to be two years ago, in my report of 1886, cumber- some, inequitable, and unsatisfactory, and ill-adapted to the present condition of the service.   Under the present system of adjustment the Department is sometimes paying for what it does not get and gets some- times what it does not pay for.

I am more than ever convinced, the more reflection I give to this subject, that when a reform takes place, as it must take place sooner or later, in the method or basis of pay to railroads for mail transporta- tion, it will be on the lines suggested by me in my report of 1886, and referred to in my last annual report, and in which I followed, with im- portant modifications, it is true, as to the additional payment for in- creased speed and frequency, the conclusion which has been reached by those who have preceded me in this most important field of investi- gation, namely, that the only proper and just basis of pay to railroads for mail service is the amount of space occupied by the mails in transit, and not their weight. It is not claimed, it is proper to add, for this proposed method of adjustment of railroad compensation that it will prevent a steady increase in the absolute cost of this service proportionate to its steady and uniform increase throughout the country, but it is confidently believed that the proposed system, substituting space for weight as the gauge or basis of pay, will enable the Department to keep the annual rate of that increase in cost within more reasonable and economical limits than it is possible to do under the existing system, and that it can be more easily adjusted to the changes that are daily taking place in the distribution of the mails and establish a more equitable proportion between the service rendered and the compensation given.

In conclusion I desire to express my acknowledgments to the chief clerk, the heads of the various divisions, and to the clerical force generally of this office for the faithful and efficient manner in which they have discharged their duties.

Very respectfully,

A. LEO KNOTT,
Second Assistant Postmaster-General.

Hon. DON M. DICKINSON,
Postmaster-General.

ADDENDUM.

Exhibit 1.—Statement of business disposed of during the fiscal year.
Table A.—Shows annual rate of expenditure, appropriation, and estimates.
Table B.—Shows length of routes, annual rate of expenditure, and number of miles traveled per annum, in star, steam-boat, and railroad service.
Table C.—Statement of railroad service.
Table D.—Statement of steam-boat service.
Table E.—Statement of increase and decrease in star, steam-boat, and railroad service.
Table F.—Statement of deductions, fines, and remissions.
Table G.—Statement of inland mail service, with increase and decrease and percentages of increase and decrease for fiscal year.
Table H.—Statement of weight of mails, speed and accomodations for mails, and R. P. O. clerks, and re-adjustment of pay on railroad routes, with an index.
Table I.—Statement of the annual rate of expenditure for R. P. O. cars, showing increase and decrease since last annual report.
Table K.—Statement of expenditures for necessary and special facilities on trunk lines.
Table L.—Statement of railroad service established since last annual report.
Table M.—Statement of railroad service from 1836 to June 30, 1888, showing increase and decrease in length of routes.
Table N.—Statement of all contracts for mail equipments and for use of patents.
Table O.—Statement of expenditures for certain mail equipments.
Table P.—Statement of expenditures for mail locks and keys.

EXHIBIT 1.—*Statement showing the amount of current business disposed of during the year ended June 30, 1888, in the office of the Second Assistant Postmaster-General.*

Nature of work done.	Contract division.	Division of inspection.	Railway adjustment division.	Division of mail equipment.	Total.
Accounts examined	14, 111			2, 164	16, 275
Applications involving changes in service received and considered	4, 114				4, 114
Briefs involving changes in service prepared	4, 114				4, 114
Cases of fines, deductions, and remissions made up		15, 259			15, 259
Calculations made	197, 710	114, 296	264, 800		576, 806
Certificates prepared	152				152
Circulars and circular letters sent out	149, 243	192, 451	14, 106	32, 988	388, 787
Circulars sent out (mail messenger)	20, 037				20, 037
Contracts prepared (in duplicate)	4, 454				4, 454
Contracts reported to Congress	4, 454				4, 454
Day-book entries	22, 689		1, 957	51, 296	75, 942
Day-book entries (mail messenger)	3, 425				3, 425
Distance circulars received and entered	5, 163		770		5, 933
Key chains examined and tested				4, 500	4, 500
Letters received	147, 108	43, 978	4, 071	38, 830	233, 987
Letters recorded	16, 871			477	17, 348
Letters recorded (mail messenger)	1, 383				1, 383
Letters written	20, 017	19, 944	3, 540	477	43, 978
Letters written (mail messenger)	1, 383				1, 383
Locks sent out				110, 882	110, 882
Mail-bag cord-fasteners examined and tested				126, 393	126, 393
Mail-bag cord-fasteners sent out				184, 000	184, 000
Mail-bag label-cases examined and tested				16, 500	16, 500
Mail-bag label-cases sent out				34, 000	34, 000
Mail keys, in registered letters, sent out				8, 484	8, 484
Mail locks and keys examined and tested				137, 928	137, 928
Orders arranged, numbered, and recorded on Journal	21, 548				21, 548
Orders entered on reports for Congress	5, 539	15, 259			20, 798
Orders made upon present or new service	21, 949		1, 957		23, 906
Orders made (mail messenger)	3, 425				3, 425
Orders recorded upon present or new service	26, 390	21, 052	1, 957		49, 399
Orders recorded (mail messenger)	3, 425				3, 425
Orders reported (in quadruple—by type-writer)	21, 153				21, 153

EXHIBIT 1.—*Statement showing the amount of current business disposed of during the year ended June 30, 1888, etc.*—Continued.

Nature of work done.	Contract division.	Division of inspection.	Railway adjustment division.	Division of mail equipment.	Total.
Pamphlet advertisements sent out	30,000				30,000
Postmasters' reports received and examined		452,284			452,284
Proposals indorsed, examined, and recorded (bulletin-board)	3,165				3,165
Proposals indorsed, examined, and recorded (general and miscellaneous advertisements)	96,599				'96,599
Proposals indorsed, examined, and recorded (mail messenger)	14,290				14,290
Proposals sent out	225,225				225,225
Routes advertised (bulletin-board)	585				585
Routes advertised (general and miscellaneous advertisements)	4,443				4,443
Routes advertised (mail messenger)	2,858				2,858
Tables and statements prepared	263			100	363
Telegrams	663				663
Volumes of Route Registers completed	33		9		42
Volumes of Route Registers completed (mail messenger)	3				3
Weight returns computed and adjusted			662		662

A.—Inland mail service, June 30, 1888.

Items.	Annual rate of expenditure for 1887.	Annual rate of expenditure for 1888.	Percentage of increase or decrease in annual rate of expenditure for 1888 as to annual rate of expenditure for 1887.		Appropriation for 1889.	Percentage of increase or decrease in appropriation for 1889 as to annual rate of expenditure for 1888.		Estimate for 1890.	Percentage of increase or decrease in estimate for 1890 as to appropriation for 1889.	
			Increase.	Decrease.		Increase.	Decrease.		Increase.	Decrease.
Inland transportation, star routes	$5,090,533.43	$4,939,192.00¼		2.75	$5,400,000.00	8.86		$4,750,000.00	6.48	
Inland transportation, steam-boat routes	433,189.18	438,842.27	1.32		450,000.00	2.51		500,000.00	11.11	
Inland transportation, railroad routes	16,174,691.22	17,528,569.80	8.37		17,000,000.00		3.01	19,105,537.90	12.38	
Railway post-office car service	1,861,580.50	1,906,359.35	6.10		2,000,000.00	00.18		2,280,000.00	13.00	
Necessary and special facilities on trunk lines										
Railway post-office clerks	285,598.10	295,987.53	3.64		285,987.53	3.19		295,655.88		0.11
Mail messenger service	4,837,468.00	5,064,517.00	5.32		5,246,790.21	7.50		5,676,728.74	8.19	
Mail locks and keys	829,548.61	863,718.67	6.63		850,000.00	1.10		1,050,000.00	10.62	
Mail bags and mail-bag catchers	19,522.00	22,500.54	15.25		25,000.00	15.87		15,000.00		40.00
Miscellaneous items in the office of the Second Assistant Postmaster-General	255,891.83	247,030.19		3.27	285,000.00			225,000.00		21.05
	166.90	294.50	76.45		1,000,000.00	239.55		1,000,000.00		
Total					31,663,777.74			34,878,912.02	10.18	

B.—*Table of star, steam-boat, and rail*

[The entire service on each route is included in the amount opposite the State

States and Territories.	Total length of routes.	Length of routes and annual rate of expenditure in each class of service.					
		Star.		Steam-boat.		Railroad.	
		Length.	Annual rate of expenditure.	Length.	Annual rate of expenditure.	Length.	Annual rate of expenditure for transportation.
	Miles.	*Miles.*	*Dollars.*	*Miles.*	*Dollars.*	*Miles.*	*Dollars.*
Maine	5,280.71	3,692.51	91,806.61	384.12	5,894.50	1,204.08	142,429.79
New Hampshire	2,104.37	1,150.15	34,086.35	147.50	3,325.00	806.72	84,717.93
Vermont	2,299.18	1,432.87	39,925.62	....	....	866.31	165,647.05
Massachusetts	3,269.81	1,172.20	80,341.50	89	12,063.50	2,008.61	238,073.29
Rhode Island	523.08	195.34	12,166.26	83	13,107.56	244.74	29,900.47
Connecticut	1,916.75	800.02	33,010.40	....	....	1,116.73	229,858.53
New York	14,239.15	7,549.98	352,128.78	220.50	11,096.17	6,468.72	1,132,636.01
New Jersey	2,658.12	939.07	35,792.92	....	....	1,719.05	264,807.04
Pennsylvania	15,358.75	9,103.15	290,437.88	....	....	6,255.60	832,968.13
Delaware	556.06	239.53	8,293.06	....	....	318.53	28,813.76
Maryland	4,832.15	2,276.89	83,739.41	1,119.50	13,518.36	1,436.76	324,922.63
Virginia	13,152.56	9,404.16	168,320.42	737.25	36,021.62	3,011.15	404,815.21
West Virginia	7,649.75	6,821	97,103.03	....	....	828.75	84,484.78
North Carolina	12,836.61	10,346.52	135,320.64	425	12,683.00	2,065.09	170,973.39
South Carolina	5,837.83	4,039.64	60,485.63	99.50	2,214.00	1,698.69	149,674.06
Georgia	10,973.47	6,961.61	101,902.60	12	600.00	3,999.86	858,409.76
Florida	5,390.63	2,647.95	50,384.37	867.87	79,636.03	1,874.81	117,990.54
Alabama	11,934.71	8,844.69	143,449.65	747.50	9,350.00	2,342.52	229,659.02
Mississippi	9,337.10	6,015.35	100,271.49	476	5,900.00	2,845.75	254,199.89
Tennessee	10,143.71	8,780.54	141,912.37	....	....	1,363.17	139,156.25
Kentucky	11,278.68	8,102.34	140,220.88	674	24,879.57	2,502.34	319,486.78
Ohio	16,193.04	6,208.89	169,411.80½	127.75	9,000.00	9,766.40	1,240,556.78
Indiana	9,317.89	4,471.67	91,085.38	....	....	4,846.23	649,437.46
Illinois	13,599.68	4,226.24	126,332.93	....	....	9,373.44	1,152,853.60
Michigan	10,441.46	4,661.33	108,362.52	203	5,176.00	5,577.13	514,820.73
Wisconsin	10,027.86	4,868.59	94,445.29	85	410.00	5,074.27	554,786.00
Minnesota	11,153.34	4,422.98	72,507.96	....	....	6,730.41	902,809.66
Iowa	12,607.29	4,367.33	87,389.65	....	....	8,240.57	863,504.63
Missouri	17,305.23	10,360.58	188,994.27	173	7,000.00	6,751.65	1,067,361.48
Arkansas	9,467.95	7,574.70	116,029.60	700	44,500.00	1,193.25	78,352.01
Louisiana	6,219.75	3,901	71,626.34	1,084.25	42,240.00	1,144.50	93,059.62
Texas	21,274.42	12,995.38	238,525.12	39	576.33	8,240.04	704,149.76
Indian Ter.	2,698.21	2,250.89	32,869.46	....	....	447.32	18,649.65
Kansas	15,604.81	7,272.87	115,729.20	....	....	8,331.94	700,249.54
Nebraska	10,936.46	5,365.90	85,539.02	....	....	5,570.56	806,526.08
Dakota	9,238.55	6,191.50	116,115.51	....	....	3,047.05	165,797.77
Montana	3,332.03	3,051.25	84,562.92	....	....	280.78	13,654.97
Wyoming	2,490.15	1,815.25	54,345.60	....	....	674.90	86,964.52
Colorado	6,630.09	3,548.92	115,282.29	....	....	3,081.17	302,528.05
New Mexico	3,794.58	2,603	63,952.90	....	....	1,191.58	103,277.86
Arizona	3,093.34	2,427	81,003.92	....	....	666.34	86,061.55
Utah	2,985.42	1,769.75	50,091.44	....	....	1,215.67	113,801.88
Idaho	2,726.99	2,523.25	85,443.69	....	....	203.74	9,947.18
Washington	4,612.68	2,381.23	51,988.45	955.75	54,701.99	1,275.70	152,877.74
Oregon	6,008.01	4,699.50	121,701.83	154.50	11,074.64	1,154.01	123,170.93
Nevada	3,139.56	2,544.50	67,217.07	403.50	16,944.00	595.06	34,436.62
California	12,663.76	8,198.62	240,676.61	403.50	16,944.00	4,061.64	608,979.82
Alaska	1,240	190	861.25	1,050	18,000.00	....	....
Totals	380,379.34	225,607.53	4,959,192.00½	11,058.49	438,942.27	143,713.32	17,528,569.30
Mail-messenger service	....	....	....	....	....	....	....
Railway post-office clerks	....	....	....	....	....	....	....
Mail equipments	....	....	....	....	....	....	....
Necessary and special facilities on trunk-lines	....	....	....	....	....	....	....
Aggregate	....	....	....	....	....	....	....

road mail service in operation June 30, 1888.

under which the route is numbered, though the route may extend into other States.]

Length of routes and annual rate of expenditure in each class of service.		Number of miles traveled per annum.				Total annual rate of expenditure.
Railroad.						
Annual rate of expenditure for railway post-office cars.	Total annual rate of expenditure for railroad service.	Star service.	Steam-boat service.	Railroad service.	Total.	
Dollars.	*Dollars.*	*Miles.*	*Miles.*	*Miles.*	*Miles.*	*Dollars.*
16, 671. 50	159, 101. 29	2, 017, 699. 44	88, 944. 96	1, 538, 583. 07	3, 645, 227. 47	256, 802. 40
2, 651. 00	87, 368. 93	689, 598	35, 438	1, 448, 998. 33	2, 174, 034. 33	124, 780. 28
7, 233. 00	112, 880. 05	886, 008. 76		1, 439, 362. 37	2, 325, 371. 13	152, 805. 67
40, 645. 25	376, 718. 54	1, 007, 608. 68	69, 805. 66	5, 463, 082. 04	6, 540, 502. 38	471, 153. 63
3, 090. 00	33, 050. 47	160, 992. 68	56, 922. 66	685, 302. 19	903, 217. 53	57, 324. 29
25, 297. 50	255, 156. 03	592, 708. 48		3, 001, 925. 05	3, 594, 633. 53	288, 166. 43
193, 306. 40	1, 325, 944. 41	4, 757, 759. 17	102, 787. 36	14, 529, 590. 12	19, 390, 136. 65	1, 738, 169. 36
38, 628. 25	303, 415. 29	610, 040. 08		4, 550, 064. 97	5, 160, 105. 05	339, 228. 21
96, 071. 50	931, 039. 63	4, 965, 905. 12		11, 805, 589. 84	16, 771, 494. 96	1, 211, 477. 51
	28, 812. 76	136, 440. 72		371, 608. 70	508, 049. 42	27, 106. 84
58, 450. 85	283, 972. 48	1, 368, 814. 88	313, 061. 66	3, 547, 712. 97	5, 229, 589. 51	480, 631. 25
74, 551. 20	479, 366. 41	3, 958, 869. 05	312, 900	4, 207, 008. 17	8, 478, 867. 22	683, 708. 45
8, 360. 00	92, 844. 78	2, 024, 036. 36		1, 218, 500. 51	3, 242, 545. 87	184, 947. 81
12, 985. 60	183, 938. 99	3, 094, 288. 27	143, 000	1, 683, 598. 08	4, 920, 886. 35	331, 942. 63
21, 255. 00	170, 929. 06	1, 175, 754. 84	35, 182	1, 799, 309. 19	3, 010, 246. 03	233, 628. 09
52, 100. 50	410, 510. 26	1, 992, 819. 83	14, 976	4, 316, 090. 12	6, 323, 885. 95	513, 012. 86
	117, 990. 54	739, 700	282, 074	1, 495, 347. 65	2, 515, 121. 65	248, 010. 94
29, 410. 50	250, 069. 52	2, 502, 900. 44	137, 202	2, 537, 592	5, 267, 695. 44	402, 869. 17
16, 524. 98	270, 722. 89	1, 716, 809	62, 244	2, 090, 294. 42	3, 878, 347. 42	376, 895. 38
12, 108. 50	151, 264. 75	2, 886, 183. 49		1, 640, 251. 35	4, 526, 434. 84	293, 177. 19
42, 714. 50	362, 201. 28	2, 871, 600. 14	295, 776	3, 532, 881. 52	6, 700, 257. 06	527, 901. 73
390, 308. 95	2, 339, 864. 73	3, 087, 780. 94	100, 152	15, 470, 758. 40	18, 658, 691. 34	2, 518, 276. 53½
100, 595. 20	750, 032. 66	1, 917, 990. 60		6, 998, 052. 77	8, 916, 043. 37	841, 118. 04
188, 291. 80	1, 370, 945. 40	1, 937, 027		13, 150, 903. 78	15, 087, 930. 78	1, 497, 278. 33
18, 581. 50	532, 852. 23	1, 861, 690. 13	58, 916	7, 838, 631. 90	9, 759, 288. 03	646, 390. 75
59, 129. 45	613, 916. 05	1, 715, 599	6, 630	6, 893, 109. 04	8, 615, 329. 04	708, 771. 34
45, 394. 25	948, 203. 91	1, 170, 849. 55		7, 044, 581. 48	8, 215, 431. 03	920, 711. 87
95, 717. 80	979, 222. 43	1, 604, 151. 28		8, 966, 499. 05	10, 660, 650. 33	1, 066, 612. 08
132, 840. 20	1, 200, 201. 68	3, 904, 192. 65	53, 976	9, 756, 860. 83	13, 715, 029. 48	1, 396, 195. 95
	78, 352. 01	2, 342, 697. 04	192, 140	1, 032, 099. 53	3, 566, 936. 57	238, 881. 61
	93, 069. 62	1, 178, 567	267, 089. 68	1, 160, 732. 67	2, 615, 389. 35	206, 925. 96
	704, 149. 76	4, 520, 433. 76	12, 168	7, 084, 887. 99	11, 617, 439. 75	943, 251. 21
	18, 649. 65	644, 802. 08		325, 683. 94	970, 486. 02	51, 519. 11
66, 958. 90	787, 205. 44	2, 589, 174		7, 990, 756. 66	10, 579, 930. 66	882, 934. 64
86, 469. 25	894, 995. 33	1, 542, 724. 27		4, 792, 370. 66	6, 335, 094. 93	980, 534. 35
	165, 797. 77	1, 748, 027		2, 115, 294. 91	3, 863, 321. 91	281, 913. 28
	13, 654. 97	1, 000, 993. 50		197, 010. 92	1, 198, 004. 42	98, 217. 89
	86, 964. 52	626, 017		478, 519. 64	1, 106, 536. 64	141, 310. 12
	302, 528. 05	1, 125, 649. 22		2, 985, 080. 82	4, 110, 730. 04	417, 810. 34
	103, 277. 86	764, 622. 50		858, 573. 64	1, 623, 196. 14	187, 230. 76
	86, 061. 55	746, 349		478, 490. 92	1, 224, 839. 92	167, 065. 47
	113, 801. 88	641, 757. 76		884, 907. 30	1, 526, 665. 06	163, 893. 32
	9, 947. 18	900, 331. 68		129, 326. 90	1, 029, 658. 58	95, 390. 87
	132, 877. 74	623, 657. 52	315, 224	916, 083. 93	1, 854, 965. 45	239, 588. 18
	128, 170. 93	1, 393, 245. 50	84, 552	820, 714. 01	2, 298, 511. 51	260, 947. 40
	34, 436. 62	612, 820		292, 014. 40	904, 834. 40	101, 653. 69
58, 088. 00	687, 067. 82	3, 139, 371. 58	124, 384	3, 905, 187. 58	7, 168, 943. 16	934, 688. 43
		4, 940	50, 400		55, 340	18, 861. 25
1, 996, 359. 35	19, 524, 959. 15	83, 683, 998. 99	3, 216, 035. 98	185, 485, 783. 33	272, 385, 818. 30	24, 923, 093. 42½
						883, 718. 67
						5, 084, 517. 00
						269, 580. 73½
						295, 987. 53
						31, 456, 847. 35½

C.—Railroad service as in operation on the 30th of June, 1868.

Number of route.	State and termini.	Corporate title of company carrying the mail.	Distance.	Average number of trips per week over whole route.	Annual pay for transportation.	Annual pay for railway post-office cars.	Total annual pay.	Cost per mile for transportation.	Cost per mile for railway post-office cars.	Remarks.
			Miles.		Dollars.	Dollars.	Dollars.	Dollars.	Dollars.	
	MAINE.									
1	Boundary Line (n. o.) and Presque Isle.	New Brunswick Rwy	30.51	12	1,408.64		1,408.64	46.17		
2	Newport and Dexter	Maine Central R. R.	14.92	12	752.71		752.71	50.45		
3	Farmington and Brunswick	do	67.65	12	5,379.03		5,379.03	79.52		
4	Belfast and Burnham Village	do	33.29	10.43	2,277.03		2,277.03	68.40		
5	Portland and Skowhegan	do	102.93	11.19	11,083.64		11,083.64	107.72		
6	Portland and Bangor	do	138	11.09	52,284.74		52,284.74	278.73	100.00	
7	Portland, Me., and Norton Mills, Vt.	Grand Trunk Rwy. Company of Canada.	165.73	11.16	20,971.47		20,971.47	126.54		
8	Portland, Me., and Rochester, N. H.	Portland and Rochester R. R.	55	15	6,912.95		6,912.95	125.69		
9	Milo Junction (n. o.) and Katahdin Iron Works.	Bangor and Piscataquis R. R.	18.90	6	807.97		807.97	42.75		
10	Portland, Me., and Fabyan House, N. H.	Portland and Ogdensburg R. R.	89.99	18.09	8,848.71		8,848.71	98.33		
11	Brunswick and Bath	Maine Central R. R.	9.17	28	1,262.34		1,262.34	137.66		
12	Bangor and Vanceborough	do	114.86	12	21,567.53	2,871.50	24,379.03	187.25	25.00	
13	Bangor and Bucksport	do	20.55	12	1,458.43		1,458.43	70.97		
14	Oldtown and Greenville	Bangor and Piscataquis R. R.	78.07	6	5,273.62		5,273.62	67.55		
15	Woolwich and Rockland	Knox and Lincoln R. R.	49.11	12	5,574.59		5,574.59	109.44		
16	Houlton and New Brunswick Line (n. o.).	New Brunswick Rwy.	4	12	196.36		196.36	49.09		
17	Calais and Princeton	St. Croix and Penobscot R. R.	21.28	6	909.72		909.72	42.75		
18	Oakland and North Anson	Somerset Rwy	23.77	6	1,432.29		1,432.29	55.56		
19	Mechanic Falls and Gilbertville	Rumford Falls and Buckfield R. R.	27.45	17.57	1,525.07		1,525.07	55.56		
20	Farmington and Phillips	Sandy River R. R.	18.25	12	780.18		780.18	42.75		
21	Lewiston and South Auburn	Grand Trunk Rwy. Company of Canada.	5.97	9	255.21		255.21	42.75		
22	Bridgton Junction (n. o.) and Bridgton.	Bridgton and Saco River R.R.	16.30	12	724.69		724.69	44.46		
23	......and Monson.	Monson R. R.	6.16	12	263.34		263.34	42.75		
24	Bangor and Bar Harbor	Maine Central R. R.	50.45	12	3,623.81		3,623.81	71.82		
25	Strong Station (n. o.) and Kingfield	Franklin and Megantic R.R.	16.19	6	640.37		640.37	43.75		
26	Hartland and Pittsfield	Sebasticook and Moosehead R. R.	8.58	13	278.70		278.70	32.49		

No.	Termini	Company	Miles	Trips	Amount	Extra	Total	Rate	Spl.	Remarks
27	Kennebunk Port and Kennebunk Station (n. o.).	Boston and Maine R. R.								Pay not fixed.
28	Kittery Junction (n. o.) and York Beach.	York Harbor and Beach R. R.	4.67	11.83	6					Do.
			1,204.08		163,429.79	16,671.50	159,101.29			
	NEW HAMPSHIRE.									
1001	Concord and Nashua	Concord R. R. Corporation.	84.28	40.00	8,999.50	907.00	9,716.50	243.83		
1002	Concord and Portsmouth	......do......	59.16	10.14	4,653.52		4,653.52	72.65	25.00	
1003	Manchester and North Weare	......do......	19.95	12	852.98		852.98	42.75		
1004	Hookset and Pittsfield	......do......	20.85	12	1,113.85		1,113.85	54.72		
1005	West Stewartstown and Coos	Upper Coos R. R.	21.23	6						
1006	Groveton Junction (n. o.) and Concord.	Boston and Lowell R. R. Corporation.	145.88	29.30	21,329.11		21,329.11	145.21		
1007	Fabyan House, N. H., and South Lunenburgh, Vt.	......do......	24.26	18.01	1,709.96		1,709.96	70.11		
1008	Concord, N. H., and White River Junction, Vt.	......do......	69.76	23.22	13,062.56	1,744.06	14,906.56	187.25	25.00	
1009	Concord and Claremont Junction (n. o.).	......do......	56.92	12.20	3,455.61		3,455.61	60.71		
1010	Contoocook and Peterborough	......do......	32.72	16.66	1,650.72		1,650.72	80.45		
1011	Nashua and Keene	Worcester, Nashua and Rochester R. R.	55.81	13.66	4,771.75		4,771.75	85.60		
1012	Rochester, N. H., and Worcester, Mass.	Boston and Maine R. R.	93.04	11.93	12,270.61		12,270.61	129.11		
1013	Dover and Alton Bay	......do......	28.43	15.85	1,822.57		1,822.57	64.13		
1014	Conway Junction (n. o.), Me., and North Conway, N. H.	......do......	71.81	8.63	6,282.55		6,282.55	87.21		
1015	Wolfboro Junction and Wolfborough.	......do......	12.14	12	518.98		518.98	42.75		
1016	Portsmouth and Dover	......do......	11.62	16.69	496.75		496.75	42.75		
1017	Vacant.									
1018	Whitefield Junction (n. o.) and Meadows.	Whitefield and Jefferson R. R.	8.50	6	363.87		363.87	42.75		
1019	Vacant.									
1020	Franklin and Bristol	Boston and Lowell R. R. Corporation.	-13.13	6	561.30		561.30	42.75		
1021	Rollingsford (n. o.) and Great Falls.	Boston and Maine R. R.	2.68	24	121.45		121.45	45.33	25.00	
1022	Plymouth and North Woodstock.	Boston and Lowell R. R. Corporation.	21.06	8.13	900.31		900.31	42.75		
			806.72		84,717.93	2,651.00	87,368.93			
	VERMONT.									
2001	Readsboro, Vt., and Hoosac Tunnel Station (n. o.), Mass.	Hoosac Tunnel and Wilmington R. R.	11.30	6	468.07		468.07	42.75		
2002	Windsor, Vt., and Rouse's Point, N. Y.	Central Vermont R. R.	158.77	29.56	27,829.20	3,365.75	31,194.95	176.28	25.00	R. P. O. 134.69 miles, Windsor and Saint Albans.
2003	Bellows Falls and Essex Junction.	......do......	127.97	18.20	20,132.24		20,132.24	187.33	25.00	
2004	Bellows Falls and Windsor.	Sullivan County R. R.	25.50	21	4,295.22	637.50	4,932.72	168.44	25.00	
2005	Brattleborough and Bellows Falls.	Vermont Valley R. R. Co. of 1871.	24.04	21	4,069.73	601.00	4,670.73	108.29	25.00	

C.—*Railroad service as in operation on the 30th of June, 1868—Continued.*

Number of route.	State and termini.	Corporate title of company carrying the mail.	Distance.	Average number of trips per week over whole route.	Annual pay for transportation.	Annual pay for railway post-office cars.	Total annual pay.	Cost per mile for transportation.	Cost per mile for railway post-office cars.	Remarks.
			Miles.		*Dollars.*	*Dollars.*	*Dollars.*	*Dollars.*	*Dollars.*	
	VERMONT—continued.									
2006	Saint Albans and Canada Line (n. o.).	Central Vermont R. R.	17.33	18.50	1,660.25		1,660.25	92.94		R. P. O. 106.15 miles, Newport and White River Junction.
2007	Saint Albans and Richford.	Missisquoi Valley R. R.	28.79	6	1,747.84		1,747.84	60.71		
2008	Leicester Junction, Vt., and Addison Junction, N. Y.	Central Vermont R. R.	15.63	6	668.18		668.18	42.75		
9009	Richford and Newport.	Southeastern Rwy., W. C. Van Horne, Wm. Farrell, and Wm. Blodgett, trustees.	31.57	12	2,726.88		2,726.88	86.36		
2010	White River Junction and Derby Line.	Connecticut and Passumpsic Rivers R. R.	115.29	22	16,560.25	2,628.75	19,189.00	143.64	25.00	
2011	South Lunenburgh and Swanton	Boston and Lowell R. R. Corporation.	118.56	6.89	8,514.97		8,514.97	71.82		
2012	Wells River and Montpelier	Montpelier and Wells River R. R.	38.85	16.48	2,790.20		2,790.20	71.83		
2013	White River Junction and Woodstock.	Woodstock R. R.	14.44	12	642.00		642.00	44.46		
2014	Burlington and Cambridge Junction	Burlington and Lamoille R. R.	34.40	12	2,088.42		2,088.42	60.71		
2015	Rutland and Bennington (n. o.) and	Bennington and Rutland Rwy.	57.82	20.51	8,948.22		8,948.22	154.78		
2016	Brattleborou South London-derry.	Central Vermont R. R.	36.40	6	1,898.62		1,898.62	52.16		
2017	Montpelier Junction (n. o.) and Barre.	...do...	7.63	18	832.74		832.74	43.61		
2018	North Bennington and State Line (n. o.).	Bennington and Rutland Rwy.	2.02	24	319.52		319.52	158.18		
			866.31		105,647.05	7,233.00	112,880.05			
	MASSACHUSETTS.									
2001	Boston, Mass., and Portland, Me.	Boston and Maine R. R.	109.35	42.78	40,202.52	10,925.00	51,127.52	367.65	100.00	
2002	Boston and East Saugus.	...do...	10.74	24.93	459.13		459.13	42.75		
2003	Boston and Rockport.	...do...	39.69	28	1,697.39		1,697.39	70.97		
2004	Salem and Marblehead.	...do...	3.99	18	170.57		170.57	42.75		
2005	Salem and Lawrence.	...do...	23.33	18.78	954.60		954.60	42.75		
2006	Franklin, Mass., and Valley Falls, R. I.	New York and New England R. R.	14.46	18	618.16		618.16	42.75		

For 86.63 miles to Springfield. For 102.66 miles resi-due.

No.	Stations	Railroad							Notes
3007	Salisbury and Amesbury	Boston and Maine R. R.	4.40	21		538.01	538.01	53.01	
3008	Wenham Depot and Essex	do	5.45	12		232.98	232.98	42.96	
3009	Lynn and Marblehead	do	6.88	16.16		480.98	480.98	67.55	
3010	Wakefield and Peabody	do	8.09	12		345.81	345.81	42.75	
3011	Boston, Mass., and Portland, Me.	do	116.33	84.45		10,365.70	19,365.70	166.73	
3012	Boston and Medford	do	5.81	24		227.60	227.60	42.75	
3013	Georgetown and Haverhill	do	7.91	16.07		312.50	312.50	42.75	
3014	Wakefield Junction (n. o.) and Newburyport	do	80.80	21		2,264.72	2,264.72	73.53	
3015	Newton Junction, N. H., and Merrimac, Mass.	do	4.86	18		207.83	207.83	42.75	25.00
3016	Boston, Mass., and Nashua, N. H.	Boston and Lowell R. R. Corporation.	89.85	69.71	996.25	10,890.94	11,797.10	271.04	
3017	Lowell and Lawrence	do	14.68	21		601.92	601.92	42.75	
3018	Winchester and North Woburn	do	4.56	24.8		198.86	198.86	43.61	
3019	Somerville Station (n. o.) and North Billerica.	do	19.70	21.43		842.17	842.17	42.75	
3020	Ayer and Lowell	Fitchburg R. R.	17.03	18		1,266.86	1,266.86	74.89	
3021	Boston and Greenfield	do	105.40	12		10,736.15	10,736.15	167.21	
3022	Greenfield and North Adams	do	37.35	19		6,003.63	6,003.63	160.15	
3023	South Acton and Marlborough	do	12.71	28		611.91	611.91	59.45	
3024	Ayer, Mass., and Greenfield, N. H.	do	23.96	12		1,556.92	1,556.92	64.98	{ 175.00 / 75.60
3025	Boston, Mass., and Albany, N. Y.	Boston and Albany R. R.	201.29	34.63	24,959.75	115,653.18	140,612.93	574.56	
3026	Grafton Depot (n. o.) and Millbury	do	4.46	12		190.66	193.66	42.75	
3027	Auburndale Station (n. o.) and Newton Lower Falls.	do	2.09	21		89.34	89.34	42.75	
3028	South Framingham and Milford	do	12.96	24		771.50	771.50	62.42	
3029	Pittsfield and North Adams	do	21.41	21		1,812.35	1,812.35	84.65	
3030	Palmer and Winchendon	do	50.18	14.88		2,789.00	2,789.00	53.68	
3031	North Brookfield and East Brookfield.	do	4.62	27		193.23	193.23	42.75	
3032	Natick and Saxonville	New York and New England R.R.	3.94	12		188.43	188.43	42.75	
3033	Cook Street Station (n. o.) and Bellingham.	do	22.61	12.00		1,006.57	1,000.57	44.46	
3034	North Grafton Station (n. o.) and Grafton.	Grafton Center R. R.	8	80		128.25	128.25	42.75	
3035	Boston, Mass., and Providence, R. I	Boston and Providence R. R.	44	56.81	2,200.00	10,608.84	12,808.84	241.11	50.00
3036	Boston and Dedham	do	9.75	26.30		583.54	583.51	59.85	
3037	Canton Junction (n. o.) and Stoughton.	do	4	24		171.00	171.00	42.75	
3038	Boston and South Braintree	Old Colony R. R.	11.36	134.72		2,476.83	2,476.83	218.03	
3039	South Braintree Junction (n. o.), Mass., and Newport, R.I.	do	61.25	22.24		7,803.25	7,863.25	127.40	
3040	Whitman and Bridgewater	do	8.18	10.18		347.55	347.55	42.75	
3041	Middleborough and Provincetown.	do	80.80	12		11,805.84	11,805.84	138.60	
3042	Nantucket and Siasconset	Nantucket R. R.	11.52	12		492.48	492.48	42.75	
3043	Attleborough and Middleborough	Old Colony R. R.	22	14.73		940.50	910.50	42.75	
3044	South Braintree and Fall River	do	35.17	33.22		2,766.47	2,766.47	78.60	
3045	Buzzard's Bay and Wood's Holl	do	17.83	12		1,143.43	1,143.43	64.13	

C.—Railroad service as in operation on the 30th of June, 1888—Continued.

Number of route.	State and termini.	Corporate title of company carrying the mail.	Distance.	Average number of trips per week over whole route.	Annual pay for transportation.	Annual pay for railway post-office cars.	Total annual pay.	Cost per mile for transportation.	Cost per mile for railway post-office cars.	Remarks.
	MASSACHUSETTS—continued.		*Miles.*		*Dollars.*	*Dollars.*	*Dollars.*	*Dollars.*	*Dollars.*	
3046	South Braintree and Plymouth	Old Colony R. R.	26.52	19.21	1,836.77		1,836.77	69.26		
3047	Sterling Junction and Pratt's Junction.	...do...	4.58	18	260.19		260.19	58.87		
3048	Yarmouth Junction (n. o.) and Hyannis.	...do	3.64	12	151.83		151.83	42.75		
3049	South Framingham and Lowell.	...do	29.44	12	3,671.81		3,671.81	121.41		
3050	Fairhaven and West Wareham.	...do	14.50	12	738.61		738.61	50.45		
3051	New Bedford and Fitchburg.	...do	93.64	23.92	9,297.21		9,297.21	99.18		
3052	East Thompson, Conn., and Southbridge, Mass.	New York and New England R. R.	18	13.02	846.54		846.54	47.03		
3053	Greenfield and Turner's Falls.	Fitchburg R. R.	4.87	19.70	216.53		216.53	44.48		
3054	New Bedford and Fall River.	Old Colony R. R.	14.85	18	634.88		634.88	42.75		
3055	Fitchburg, Mass., and Bellows Falls, Vt.	Cheshire R. R.	64.00	18	9,500.07		9,500.07	147.06		
3056	South Vernon Junction (n. o.), Mass., and Keene, N. H.	Connecticut River R. R.	23.93	12	1,677.73		1,677.73	70.11		
3057	Worcester and Winchendon.	Fitchburg R. R.	37.67	16.31	3,882.01		3,882.01	89.78		
3058	Winchendon, Mass., and Peterborough, N. H.	Cheshire R. R.	16.58	9.50	708.79		708.79	42.75		
3059	Milford and Bellingham	New York and New England R. R.	4.93	24	210.75		210.75	42.75		
3060	Milford and Ashland		11.85	12	506.58		506.58	42.75		
3061	Attleborough and North Attleborough.	Boston and Providence R. R.	4.08	18	283.62		283.62	65.84		
3062	Brattleborough, Vt., and New London, Conn.	Central Vermont R. R.	121.90	21.60	13,389.81	257.25	13,646.56	110.30	25.00	R. P. O., 10.29 miles, Brattleborough and South Vernon Junction (n. o.).
3063	Lawrence, Mass., and Manchester, N. H.	Manchester and Lawrence R. R.	27.07	18	2,314.48		2,314.48	88.50		
3064	Braintree Junction (n. o.) and Kingston Station (n. o.).	Old Colony R. R.	13.20	21.03	1,872.10		1,872.10	68.14		
3065	Atlantic and West Quincy.	...do	3.67	16	156.89		156.89	42.75		
3066	Spencer and South Spencer (n. o.).	Spencer R. R.	2.18	24	93.06		93.06	43.61		
3067	Springfield and South Vernon Junction (n. o.).	Connecticut River R. R.	51.88	36.30	9,698.91	1,267.00	10,965.91	183.39	25.00	

Pay not fixed.

No.		Railroad								Pay not fixed.
3068	Springfield and Athol	Boston and Albany R. R.	47.30	6	2,748.61		2,748.61	57.29		
3069	Holyoke and Westfield	New Haven and Northampton Company.	11.30	12	478.30		478.30	42.75		
3070	Ashburnham Depot and Ashburnham.	Fitchburg R. R.	2.63	21	112.00		112.00	42.75		
3071	Van Deusen and State Line.	Housatonic R. R.	11.12	8.36	475.38		475.38	42.75		
3072	Boston and Waltham	Fitchburg R. R.	11.65	29.41	472.38		472.38	42.75		
3073	Readville and Dedham	Boston and Providence R. R.	2.22	26.39	132.86		132.86	59.85		
3074	Boston and Cook Street Station (n.o.)	Boston and Albany R. R.	9.14	35.75	670.92		670.92	74.39		
3075	Bellingham and Franklin.	New York and New England R. R.	5.97	33	229.56		229.56	42.75		
3076	North Abington and Hanover.	Hanover Branch R. R.	8.25	13.12	363.97		363.97	42.75		
3077	Vacant.									
3078	Boston and Winthrop	Boston, Revere Beach and Lynn R. R.	5	6						
			2,008.61		338,073.29	40,645.25	578,718.54			
	RHODE ISLAND.									
4001	Providence, R. I., and Worcester, Mass.	...e and Worcester R. R.	43.93	35.85	5,031.91		5,031.91	114.57		
4002	Providence, R. I., and Groton, Conn.	New (M., Providence and Boston R. R.	61.80	43.06	15,640.34	8,060.00	18,730.24	253.08	50.00	
4003	Providence, R. I., and Willimantic, Conn.	New York and New England R. R.	58.61	19.26	4,660.66		4,660.66	78.53		
4004	Providence and Bristol.	Providence, Warren and Bristol R. R.	15.35	21	1,063.14		1,063.14	69.26		
4005	Warren, R. I., and Fall River, Mass.	Fall River, Warren and Providence R. R.	9.14	18	445.48		445.48	48.74		
4006	Providence and Pascoag	Providence and Springfield R. R.	23.17	13	1,624.44		1,624.44	70.11		
4007	Kingston Depot (n.o.) and Narragansett Pier.	Narragansett Pier R. R.	8.50	16.60	421.51		421.51	49.59		
4008	Auburn and Hope.	New York, Providence and Boston R. R.	10.62	12	490.32		490.32	46.17		
4009	Wood River Junction (n.o.) and Hope Valley.	Wood River Branch R. R.	5.93	18	253.50		253.50	42.75		
4010	Auburn and Warwick.	New York, Providence and Boston R. R.	7.70	13	329.17		329.17	43.75		
			244.74		29,960.47	8,060.00	33,050.47			
	CONNECTICUT.									
5001	Norwich, Conn., and Worcester, Mass.	New York and New England R. R.	59.66	24.83	5,868.33		5,868.33	98.33		
5002	New Britain and Berlin Junction (n.o.).	New York, New Haven and Hartford R. R.	3	18	128.25		128.25	42.75		

C.—Railroad service as in operation on the 30th of June, 1888—Continued.

Number of route	State and termini	Corporate title of company carrying the mail	Distance.	Average number of trips per week over whole route.	Annual pay for transportation.	Annual pay for railway post-office cars.	Total annual pay.	Cost per mile for transportation.	Cost per mile for railway post-office cars.	Remarks.
			Miles.		*Dollars.*	*Dollars.*	*Dollars.*	*Dollars.*	*Dollars.*	
	CONNECTICUT—continued.									
5003	Middletown and Berlin Depot (n. o.)	New York, New Haven and Hartford R. R.	10.99	24	498.06	....	498.06	45.82	....	
5004	New Haven and New London	....do....	51.78	34	13,326.10	2,589.00	15,915.10	257.36	50	
5005	New York, N. Y., and Springfield, Mass.	....do....	138	80.36	109,865.28	22,708.50	132,563.78	807.98	{190.00 / 140.00}	For 73.37 miles to New Haven. For 62.63 miles residue.
5006	Waterbury and Watertown	Naugatuck R. R.	6.42	12	285.43	....	285.43	44.46	....	
5007	Boston, Mass., and Hopewell Junction, N. Y.	New York and New England R. R.	214.94	17.81	36,764.74	....	36,764.74	171.00	....	
5008	Vernon and Melrose	....do....	13.15	11.06	562.16	....	562.16	42.75	....	
5009	New Canaan and Stamford	New York, New Haven and Hartford R. R.	8.25	24	366.79	....	366.79	44.46	....	
5010	New Haven, Conn., and Williamsburg, Mass.	New Haven and Northampton Company	85.53	19.06	9,213.06	....	9,213.06	107.78	....	
5011	Bridgeport and Winsted	Naugatuck R. R.	62.29	21.63	7,562.62	....	7,562.62	121.41	....	
5012	Bridgeport, Conn., and Pittsfield, Mass.	Housatonic R. R.	110.55	12.84	12,382.70	....	12,382.70	112.01	....	
5013	South Norwalk and Danbury	Danbury and Norwalk R. R.	23.80	31	2,441.65	....	2,441.65	103.46	....	
5014	New Haven and Willimantic	New York, New Haven and Hartford R. R.	54.66	15.84	8,131.76	....	8,131.76	148.77	....	
5015	Hartford and Saybrook Point	....do....	46.09	19.65	5,950.67	....	5,950.67	129.11	....	
5016	Hartford, Conn., and Springfield, Mass.	New York and New England R. R.	32.60	12	2,090.63	....	2,090.63	64.13	....	
5017	New Haven and Ansonia	New Haven and Derby R. R.	13.27	24	884.97	....	884.97	66.69	....	
5018	Hartford, Conn., and Rhinecliff, N. Y.	Hartford and Connecticut Western R. R.	110.75	13	9,943.13	....	9,943.13	89.78	....	
5019	Litchfield and Hawleyville	Shepaug, Litchfield and Northern R. R.	32.96	12	1,635.47	....	1,635.47	49.59	....	
5020	Turnerville and Colchester	New York, New Haven and Hartford R. R.	4.20	18	179.55	....	179.55	42.75	....	
5021	Farmington Station (n. o.) and New Hartford.	New Haven and Northampton Company	14.87	18	810.99	....	810.99	54.43	....	
5022	Danbury and Brookfield Junction (n. o.)	Housatonic R. R.	6.30	18	269.32	....	269.32	42.75	....	
5023	Branchville and Ridgefield	Danbury and Norwalk R. R.	4.36	18	186.89	....	186.89	42.75	....	
5024	Bethel and Hawleyville	....do....	6.08	6	291.11	....	291.11	47.88	....	

No.	Route	Railroad	1,116.78	4.90	24	209.47	25,297.50	265,156.03	209.47	42.75	80.00 / 40.00	Remarks
5025	Windsor Locks and Suffield	New York, New Haven and Hartford R. R.										
	NEW YORK.											
6001	New York and Dunkirk	New York, Lake Erie and Western R. R.	459.55	29.86		114,940.68	31,628.40	144,969.08		248.61	{80.00 / 40.00	For 321.16 miles to Hornellsville. For 128.39 miles residue.
6002	Tallman and Sparkill	do	13.11	7.17		560.45		560.45		42.75		
6003	Buffalo and Suspension Bridge	do	25.69	28		2,757.68		2,757.68		107.73		
6004	Newburgh and Greycourt (n.o.)	do	19.09	29.93		1,887.46		1,887.46		72.68		
6005	Rochester and Corning	do	94.97	25		11,043.11		11,043.11		116.28		
6006	Dansville and Attica	do	65.18	12.70		5,740.40		5,740.40		88.07		
6007	Dresden and Penn Yan	Fall Brook Coal Company	6.28	12.70		268.47		268.47		42.75		
6008	Buffalo and Hornellsville	New York, Lake Erie and Western R. R.	92.35	28.14		16,502.94		16,502.94		178.70		
6009	Goshen and Montgomery	do	10.65	12		701.19		701.19		65.84		
6010	Goshen and Pine Island	do	12.00	13		516.84		516.84		42.75		
6011	New York and Buffalo	New York Central and Hudson River R. R.	443	90.23		523,783.36	157,520.00	681,303.36		1,185.03	{370.00 / 330.00	For 291.5 miles to Syracuse. For 150.5 miles residue.
6012	Troy and Schenectady	do	22.12	18		1,645.50		1,645.50		74.39		
6013	Syracuse and Rochester	do	104	28.00		16,806.40	4,100.00	20,906.40		161.60	40.00	
6014	Canandaigua and Tonawanda	do	85.62	6		3,925.61		3,925.61		45.32		
6015	.... ction (n.o.)		12.56	24		1,046.27		1,046.27		84.65		
6016	Buffalo and Lewiston	The New York and Northern Rwy.	39.48	62.50		6,276.29		6,276.29		212.90		
6017	New York (155th street) and Brewster.		54.62	6		3,035.77		3,035.77		55.08		
6018	Rochester and Niagara Falls	New York Central and Hudson River R. R.	78.88	29.50		11,747.18		11,747.18		153.90		
6019	Dunkirk, N.Y., and Titusville, Pa.	Dunkirk, Allegheny Valley and Pittsburgh R. R.	91.28	12		6,243.85		6,243.85		68.40		
6020	Albany Junction (n.o.) and Troy	Delaware and Hudson Canal Company.	5.81	30		538.49		538.49		92.34		
6021	Vacant.											
6022	New York and Chatham	New York Central and Hudson River R. R.	130.98	18.12		13,775.16		13,775.16		105.17		
6023	Golden's Bridge and Mahopac	Delaware and Hudson Canal Company.	7.50	6		320.62		320.62		42.75		
6024	EagleBridge, N.Y., and Rutland, Vt.		62.58	13.67		5,053.66		5,053.66		80.87		
6025	Schenectady and Ballston	do	15.20	21		649.80		649.80		42.75		
6026	Albany and	do	188.75	18.87		31,653.48		31,653.48		108.29		
6027	Albany and Cherry Valley	do	22.58	12		996.92		996.92		42.61		
6028	Albany and Binghamton	do	143.22	22.70		18,491.13		18,491.13		128.11		
6029	Plattsburg and Au Sable Forks	do	23.62	6		1,005.48		1,005.48		42.75		
6030	Quaker Street and Schenectady	do	15.40	18		660.91		660.91		42.75		
6031	Ninevoh Junction (n.o.), N.Y., and Jefferson Junction (n.o.), Pa.	do	21.70	6		1,001.88		1,001.88		16.17		
6032	Fort Edward and Lake George	do	15.95	19.93		1,077.42		1,077.42		67.55		
6033	West Chazy and Rouse's Point	do	14.78	12		2,236.80		2,236.80		151.34		
6034	Oswego and Richland	Rome, Watertown and Ogdensburg R. R.	29.02	20.33		2,530.83		2,530.83		87.21		

C.—*Railroad service as in operation on the 30th of June, 1888*—Continued.

Number of route.	State and termini.	Corporate title of company carrying the mail.	Distance.	Average number of trips per week over whole route.	Annual pay for transportation.	Annual pay for railway post-office cars.	Total annual pay.	Cost per mile for transportation.	Cost per mile for railway post-office cars.	Remarks.
	NEW YORK—continued.		*Miles.*		*Dollars.*	*Dollars.*	*Dollars.*	*Dollars.*	*Dollars.*	
6035	Watertown and Cape Vincent	Rome, Watertown and Ogdensburg R. R.	25.77	12	1,888.22		1,888.22	53.87		
6036	Rome and Ogdensburgh	do	142.27	19.31	18,732.69		18,732.69	131.67		
6037	Syracuse and Pulaski	do	38.61	15	2,806.17		2,806.17	72.68		
6038	Oswego and Suspension Bridge	do	151.13	12	14,213.77		14,213.77	94.05		
6039	Watertown and Sackett's Harbor	Utica and Black River R. R.	12.59	12	535.23		535.23	42.75		
6040	Chenango Forks and Norwich	Delaware Lackawanna and Western R. R.	36.81	13.50	2,617.57		2,617.57	86.36		
6041	Utica and Norwich	do	53.99	25.62	5,170.06		5,170.06	95.78		
6042	Oswego and Ithaca	do	35.11	12	2,401.53		2,401.53	68.40		
6043	Richfield Junction (n. o.) and Richfield Springs	do	22.05	15	1,414.70		1,414.70	64.13		
6044	Mineola and Locust Valley	Long Island R. R	11.57	12	524.35		524.35	45.25		
6045	Long Island City and Greenport	do	95.23	21.99	10,503.98		10,503.98	110.30		
6046	Hicksville and Port Jefferson	do	33.95	12	2,467.43		2,467.43	72.68		
6047	Conesus Lake Junction (n. o.) and Lakeville.	Conesus Lake R. R.	1.90	12	81.22		81.22	42.75		
6048	Oswego and Cornwall Station (n. o.).	New York, Ontario and Western Rwy.	274.20	11	19,663.04		19,663.04	71.82		
6049	Wellsville, N. Y., and Eldred, Pa.	Bradford, Eldred and Cuba R. R.	33.18	6	1,758.87		1,758.87	53.01		
6050	Walton and Delhi	New York, Ontario and Western Rwy.	17.29	9	783.56		783.56	45.32		
6051	Clinton and Rome	do	13.19	12	563.87		563.87	42.75		
6052	Moira and Brandon	Northern Adirondack R. R	34.81	12	531.38		531.38	42.75		Pay not fixed on 22.58 miles.
6053	Rouse's Point and Ogdensburgh	Ogdensburgh and Lake Champlain R. R.	119.16	12	12,124.58		12,124.58	101.75		
6054	Chatham, N. Y., and Bennington, Vt.	New York, Rutland and Montreal Rwy.	57.60	13.85	3,053.37		3,053.37	53.01		
6055	Schoharie and Middleburgh	Middleburgh and Schoharie R. R.	5.95	18	254.36		254.36	42.75		
6056	Schoharie Junction (n. o.) and Schoharie.	Schoharie Valley R. R.	4.50	18	260.11		260.11	55.56		
6057	Utica and Randallsville	New York, Ontario and Western Rwy.	31.30	13.8	2,321.96		2,321.96	70.97		

No.									
6058	Buffalo, N. Y., and Emporium, Pa.	Buffalo, New York and Philadelphia R.R.	121.87		12.84	12,867.61		12,867.61	106.02
6059	Olean and Angelica	Lackawanna and Pittsburgh R. R.	40.60		17.15	1,729.40		1,729.49	42.75
6060	Skaneateles Junction (n. o.) and Skaneateles.	Skaneateles R. R.	5.18		21	248.61		248.61	47.03
6061	Buffalo, N. Y., and Corry, Pa.	Buffalo, New York and Philadelphia R.R.	94.12		19	9,254.81		9,254.81	98.33
6062	New York (foot Whitehall street) and Mariner's Harbor.	Staten Island Rapid Transit R. R.	9.78		27	1,003.42		1,003.42	102.60
6063	Canandaigua and Elmira.	Northern Central Rwy.	69.99		18	9,335.26		9,335.26	133.38
6064	Syracuse and Oswego.	Delaware, Lackawanna and Western R. R.	35.02		19.94	4,781.62		4,781.62	134.34
6065	Syracuse and Binghamton.	Syracuse, Binghamton and New York R.R.	80.30		12.88	9,866.53		9,866.53	122.12
6066	Rouse's Point and Canada Line (n. o.).	New York and Saint Lawrence R. R.	1.71		12.5	226.85		226.85	38.51
6067	Troy, N.Y., and North Adams, Mass.	Fitchburg R. R.	48.15		27.42	9,190.78		9,190.78	190.67
6068	Saint George (n. o.) and Tottenville	Staten Island Rapid Transit R. R.	15.28		18.75	770.87		770.87	50.45
6069	Hudson and Chatham.	Boston and Albany R. R.	17.96		18	767.79		767.79	43.75
6070	Silver Springs and Perry.	Silver Lake Rwy.	7.31		15	312.50		312.50	41.75
6071	Syracuse and Earlville.	Syracuse, Chenango and New York Rwy.	44.30		18	2,348.34		2,348.34	53.01
6072	Lyons, N.Y., and Sayre, Pa.	Geneva, Ithaca and Sayre R.R.	92.58		10.77	7,292.34		7,292.34	78.66
6073	Rondout and Hobart.	Ulster and Delaware R.R.	78.36		12	7,369.75		7,369.75	94.05
6074	Vail's Gate Junction (n. o.) and Newburgh Junction (n. o.).	New York, Ontario and Western R. R.	12.00		21.48	571.03		571.03	45.92
6075	Elmira and Cortland.	Elmira, Cortland and Northern R.R.	70.91		7.21	5,820.29		5,820.29	82.08
6076	Freeville and Auburn	Southern Central R. R.	39.46		6	1,686.91		1,686.91	42.75
6077	Saratoga Springs and Schuylerville.	Boston, Hoosac Tunnel and Western Ry.	13.02		12	556.60		556.60	42.75
6078	Port Jervis and Monticello.	Port Jervis, Monticello and New York R. R.	24.70		6	1,055.92		1,055.92	42.75
6079	Poughkeepsie and Boston Corner.	Poughkeepsie, Hartford and Boston R. R.	38.11		6	1,629.30		1,629.30	42.75
6080	Canastota and Cortland.	Elmira, Cortland and Northern R.R.	40.27		10.23	00.06		00.06	82.08
6081	Fonda and Northville.	Fonda, Johnstown and Gloversville R.R.	27.03		14.23	2,056.98		2,056.98	76.10
6082	Johnsonville and Greenwich.	Greenwich and Johnsonville Rwy.	15.34		18	655.78		655.78	42.75
6083	Montgomery and Kingston, N.Y.	Wallkill Valley R. R.	34.12		6	2,013.08		2,013.08	59.00
6084	Sayre, Pa., and North Fair Haven, N.Y.	Southern Central R. R.	118.11		17.28	8,786.30		8,786.30	74.39
6085	Dutchess Junction and Millerton.	Newburgh, Dutchess and Connecticut R. R.	57.90		6.4	3,520.57		3,520.57	60.71
6086	Cooperstown and Cooperstown Junction (n. o.).	Cooperstown and Susquehanna Valley R.R.	16.5		27.4	931.09		931.09	56.43
6087	Utica and Watertown.	Utica and Black River R.R.	91.77		27.68	13,024.91		13,024.91	141.91
6088	Carthage and Ogdensburgh.	do	64.77		12	6,328.91		6,328.91	104.31

C.—*Railroad service as in operation on the 30th of June, 1883*—Continued.

Number of route.	State and termini.	Corporate title of company carrying the mail.	Distance.	Average number of trips per week over whole route.	Annual pay for transportation.	Annual pay for railway post-office cars.	Total annual pay.	Cost per mile for transportation.	Cost per mile for railway post-office cars.	Remarks.
	NEW YORK—continued.		*Miles.*		*Dollars.*	*Dollars.*	*Dollars.*	*Dollars.*	*Dollars.*	
6089	Cayuga and Ithaca	Geneva, Ithaca and Sayre R. R.	38.97	6	2,232.59		2,232.59	57.29		
6090	Sodus Point and Stanley	Northern Central Rwy	33.5	10.47	1,432.12		1,432.12	42.75		
6091	Buffalo and Jamestown	New York, Lake Erie and Western R. R.	69.24	13.6	5,150.76		5,150.76	74.39		
6092	Middletown and Pine Bush	...do	13.74	6	587.88		587.88	42.75		
6093	Long Island City and Sag Harbor	Long Island R. R	100.15	17.03	9,076.59		9,076.59	90.63		
6094	Long Island City and Whitestone	...do	11.36	34.68	757.59		757.59	66.69		
6095	Saratoga Springs and North Creek	Adirondack Rwy	58.72	6	4,518.50		4,518.50	76.95		
6096	Bath and Hammondsport	Bath and Hammondsport R. R. (Allen Wood, lessee).	9.4	18	442.08		442.08	47.03		
6097	Silver Lake Junction (n. o.) and Silver Springs.	Buffalo, Rochester and Pittsburgh R. R.	1.14	15	54.58		54.58	47.88		
6098	Whitehall and Castleton	Delaware and Hudson Canal Company.	14.85	15.5	1,177.84		1,177.84	82.08		
6099	Crown Point and Hammondville	Crown Point Iron Co.'s R. R.	11.95	6	510.86		510.86	42.75		
6100	Valley Stream and Far Rockaway.	Long Island R. R	5.25	12	224.43		224.43	42.75		
6101	Sidney Plains and New Berlin	New York, Ontario and Western Rwy.	25.08	6	1,072.17		1,072.17	42.75		
6102	Rochester and Salamanca	Rochester and Pittsburgh R. R.	109.23	18	7,752.05		7,752.05	70.97		
6103	Corning and Geneva	Fall Brook Coal Company	57.76	10.73	5,096.92		5,096.92	88.07		
6104	New City and Nanuet Junction (n. o.).	New Jersey and New York R. R.	4.59	12	196.22		196.22	42.75		
6105	Plattsburgh and Lyon Mountain	Chateaugay R. R.	34.67	12	1,482.14		1,482.14	42.75		
6106	Albany and Troy	New York Central and Hudson River R. R.	7.5	66	1,410.75		1,410.75	188.10		
6107	Mechanicsville and Reynolds	Boston, Hoosac Tunnel and Western Rwy.	4.86	12	425.59		425.59	87.21		
6108	Vacant.									
6109	New Rochelle and Harlem River	New York, New Haven and Hartford R. R.	12.18	30	1,617.80		1,617.80	133.38		
6110	De Kalb Junction and Norwood	Rome, Watertown and Ogdensburg R. R.	25.43	18	2,244.02		2,244.02	88.07		
6111	Mineola and Hempstead	Long Island R. R	2.8	18	119.70		119.70	42.75		
6112	Stewart Junction (n. o.) and Babylon	...do	21.21	12	997.50		997.50	47.03		

No.	Terminals	Railroad	Miles					Rate	Notes
6113	Summitville and Ellenville....	New York, Ontario and Western Rwy.							
6114	Clove Branch Junction and Clove Valley	Clove Branch R.R.	8.55	19	387.48	387.48		46.52	
6115	Theresa Junction (n. o.) and Clayton	Utica and Black River R.R.	8.1		346.27	346.27		42.75	
6116	Hoosac Junction (n. o.) and Slate Line (n. o.).	Fitchburg R. R.	16.25	12	708.08	708.08		43.61	
6116			6.01	24	797.22	797.22		138.18	
6117	Mapor Junction (n. o.) and Eastport Junction (n. o.).	Long Island R.R.	5.5	6	235.12	235.12		42.75	
6118	Fhoenicia and . . . . . Clove and Catskill		16.11	6	800.97	800.97		53.01	
6119	Herkimer and Poland	Herkimer, Newport and Poland Narrow Gauge Rwy.	17.06	12	743.98	743.98		43.61	
6120	Whitestone Junction (n. o.) and Thomaston.	Long Island R.R.	7.07	13.3	360.00	350.00		49.60	
6121	Mechanicville and Schuylerville Junction (n. o.).	Boston, Hoosac Tunnel and Western Rwy.	15.18	13	648.94	648.94		42.75	
6122	Addison, N.Y., and Galeton, Pa.	Addison and Northern Pennsylvania Rwy.	47.24	9.42	3,191.06	3,191.06		67.55	
6123	Rochester and Hinsdale	Buffalo, New York and Philadelphia R.R.	100.02	6	5,302.06	5,302.06		53.01	
6124	Brooklyn and Jamaica	Long Island R.	9.18	22.86	375.00	375.00		40.85	
6125	Hopewell Junction and Wicopee Junction (n. o.).	New York and England R. R.	11.23	6	168.45	168.45		15.00	
6155	Buffalo (Erie street) and Black Rock (n. o.) (N. Y. C. and H. R. R. R. station).	Grand Trunk Railway Company of Can	4.59	6	196.22	196.22		42.75	
6127	Bradford Junction (n. o.), N. Y., and Punxsutawney, Pa.	Rochester and burgh R.	120.94	6	6,204.22	6,204.22		51.30	
6128	Hart's Corners and Willard	Geneva, Ithaca and Sayre R. R.	5.75	16	245.81	245.81		42.75	
6129	New York (foot 42d street) and Albany.	New York Central and Hudson River R. R.	142.27	25.05	14,596.90	14,596.90		102.60	
6130	Buffalo (Exchange Street station) and Ashford Junction (n. o.).	Rochester and Pittsburgh R. R.	49.28	6	2,865.13	2,865.13		58.14	
6131	Kaaterskill Junction (n. o.) and Kaaterskill.	Kaaterskill R. R.	7.4	12	816.35	816.35		42.75	
6132	Lyon Mountain and Saranac Lake..	Chateaugay R. R.	39.06	6	1,025.65	1,025.65		50.45	
6133	Hatfield and Norwood	Rome, Watertown and Ogdensburg R. R.	13.54	12	463.06	463.06		34.20	
6134	Harrisville and Carthage	Carthage and Adirondack Rwy.	21.71	6	649.78	649.78		29.98	
6135	Jamestown and Mayville	Chautauqua Lake Rwy.	22.25	6					Pay not fixed on 12.33 miles.
6136	Windsor Beach (n. o.) and Rochester.	Rome, Watertown and Ogdensburg R. R.	8.30	12.6	652.87	652.87		78.06	Pay not fixed.
			6,468.72		1,132,636.01	193,308.40	1,325,944.41		
	NEW JERSEY.								
7001	New York, N. Y., and Easton, Pa ..	Central R. R. Co. of New Jersey.	73.94	30.59	10,937.20	10,937.20		147.92	
7002	Somerville and Flemington	do	16.01	15	698.19	698.19		43.61	

C.—*Railroad service as in operation on the 30th of June, 1889*—Continued.

Number of route.	State and terminl.	Corporate title of company carrying the mail.	Distance.	Average number of trips per week over whole route.	Annual pay for transportation.	Annual pay for railway post-office cars.	Total annual pay.	Cost per mile for transportation.	Cost per mile for railway post-office cars.	Remarks.
			Miles.		*Dollars.*	*Dollars.*	*Dollars.*	*Dollars.*	*Dollars.*	
	NEW JERSEY—continued.									
7003	Elizabethport (n. o.) and Bayhead Junction (n. o.)	Central R. R. Co. of New Jersey.	50.19	38.65	8,539.83		8,539.83	170.15		
7004	New York, N. Y., and Philadelphia, Pa.	Pennsylvania R. R.	90.89	172.14	143,143.56	38,628.25	181,771.81	1,574.91	425.00	
7005	Camden and Monmouth Junction	do	53.68	18.36	4,497.94		4,497.94	83.79		
7006	Camden and Hightstown	do	50.77	11.91	3,290.03		3,290.03	64.98		
7007	Burlington and Lumberton	do	10.43	12	445.45		445.45	42.75		
7008	Trenton and Manunka Chunk (n.o.)	do	67.98	16.47	6,028.77		6,028.77	88.98		
7009	Lambertville and Flemington	do	12.46	15	533.66		533.66	42.75		
7010	East Millstone and New Brunswick	do	8.56	15	365.94		365.94	42.75		
7011	Rocky Hill and Monmouth Junction	do	6.72	12	287.28		287.28	42.75		
7012	Kinkora and Jullustown	do	9.87	12	421.94		421.94	42.75		
7013	Hoboken, N. J., and Easton, Pa.	Delaware, Lackawanna and Western R. R.	84.24	29.67	13,244.28		13,244.28	145.35		
7014	Dover and Chester	do	14.05	12	600.68		600.68	42.75		
7015	Philadelphia, Pa., and Atlantic City, N. J.	Camden and Atlantic R. R.	56.53	12	4,478.28		4,478.28	75.24		
7016	Hopping (n. o.) and Atlantic Highlands	Central R. R. Co. of New Jersey.	8.10	15	123.53		123.53	42.75		
7017	Jersey City, N. J., and Nyack, N. Y.	Northern R. R. Co. of New Jersey.	28.50	24	1,931.25		1,931.25	67.65		
7018	Easton, Pa., and Metuchen Station	Lehigh Valley R. R.	54.30	29	7,644.53		7,644.53	141.08		
7019	Newfield and Atlantic City (n. o.), N. J.	West Jersey R. R.	34.71	11.01	1,483.85		1,483.85	42.75		
7020	Pleasantville and Somers Point	do	7.31	6	312.50		312.50	42.75		
7021	Elmer and Salem	do	17.35	16.78	756.68		756.68	43.61		
7022	Woodbury and Riddleton Junction (n. o.).	do	22.21	16.81	1,082.51		1,082.51	48.74		
7023	Jamesburgh and Sea Girt (n. o.)	Pennsylvania R.R.	27.43	14.48	1,735.49		1,735.49	63.27		
7024	Jersey City, N.J., and Haverstraw, N.Y.	New Jersey and New York R.R.	41.66	18	2,134.06		2,134.06	54.72		Pay not fixed on 2.66 miles.
7025	Waterloo and Franklin Furnace	Delaware, Lackawanna and Western R.R.	23.40	18.23	1,225.23		1,225.23	52.16		
7026	Highlands and Whiting	Central R. R. Co. of New Jersey.	42.23	16.07	2,599.06		2,599.06	61.56		

Pay not fixed on 4.10 miles.

No.	Route	Railroad					
7027	Newark and Mont Clair.	Delaware, Lackawanna and Western R.R.	6.60	12	855.54		855.54	53.87
7028 7029	Hoboken and Denville. Whiting and Atsion.	...do Central R. R. Co. of New Jersey	34.30 24.47	25.86 9	4,909.54 1,046.00		4,909.54 1,046.00	140.22 42.75
7030	Newark and Paterson	...do	11.37	12	486.07		486.07	42.75
7031	Atsion and Bridgeton	New York, Lake Erie and Western R.R. Central R. R. Co. of New Jer- sey.	37.81	9	1,616.37		1,616.37	42.75
7032 7033	Whiting and Tuckerton. Bridgeton and Port Norris.	Tuckerton R. R. and ' Mo River R.R. Cumberland and ' Mo River R.R.	29.70 21.30	12 32	1,447.57 965.31		1,447.57 965.31	48.74 45.32
7034	Jersey City, N.J., and Greenwood Lake, N.Y.	New York and Greenwood Lake Rwy.	51.46	10.33	2,375.90		2,375.90	44.17
7035	Atco Junction (n.o.) and Glassborough.	Williamstown and Delaware River R.R.	17.71	12	757.10		757.10	42.75
7036	Summit and Bernardsville.	Delaware, and ... R.R.	14.68	12	627.57		627.57	42.75
7037	Jersey City, N.J., and Middletown, N.Y.	New York, Susquehanna and Western R.R.	88.40	16.40	6,878.40		6,878.40	77.81
7038 7039 7040	Rahway and Perth Amboy Woodbury and Penn's Grove High Bridge and Rockaway	Pennsylvania R.R. Delaware River R. R. Cal R. R. Co. of New Jersey	7.58 20.87 30.76	27 15	466.18 895.46 1,314.90		466.18 895.46 1,314.90	60.71 42.75 42.75
7041 7042 7043 7044 7045	Camden and Cape May Beach Haven and Manahawkin Keyport and Freehold Trenton and Trenton Junction Haddonfield and Medford	West Jersey R. R. Pennsylvania R. R. Freehold and New York Bay R.R. Philadelphia and Reading R.R. Camden and ... R. R.	89.19 12.03 14.99 4.28 12.23	21.18 12 20.24 12 6	7,097.92 949.71 781.87 88.97 809.50		7,097.92 949.71 781.87 88.97 809.50	84.36 29.07 52.16 42.75 42.75
7046 7047 7048	Bordentown and Trenton Jamesburgh and South Amboy Branchville Junction (n.o.) and Branchville.	Pennsylvania R. R. ...do Delaware, Lackawanna and Western R.R.	6.68 13.63 6.37	20 12 15	317.13 1,072.13 272.31		317.13 1,072.13 272.31	52.16 78.86 42.75
7049	Eatontown and Port Monmouth	Central R. R. Co. of New Jer- sey.	9.47	12.81	550.58		550.58	58.14
7050 7051 7052	Manchester and Barnegat Glassborough and Bridgeton Greycourt (n.o.), N. Y., and Belvi- dere, N.J.	West Jersey R.R. Lehigh and Hudson River Rwy.	22.24 20.20 63.36	16.17 18 6.97	950.76 1,623.47 2,925.33		950.76 1,623.47 2,925.33	43.75 80.37 44.17
7053 7054	Princeton Junction and Princeton Whiting and Bayhead Junction (n.o.)	Pennsylvania R. R. ...do	3.44 28.89	39 8.62	197.07 1,235.64		197.07 1,235.64	57.29 42.75
7055	Rutherford Junction (n.o.) and Ridgewood Junction (n.o.)	New York, Lake Erie and Western R.R.	9.96	12.50	1,365.28		1,365.28	186.90
7056	Barnegat City and Barnegat City Junction (n.o.)	Pennsylvania R. R.	8.94	12	183.44		183.44	20.52
7057 7058	Manunuskin and Hetslerville Kays, N.J., and Stroudsburgh, Pa.	West Jersey R.R. New York, Susquehanna and Western R. R.	9.10 47.83	10.21 6	241.15 2,045.58		241.15 2,045.58	28.50 42.75
7059	Delaware and Columbia Junction (n. o.).	...do	3.16	6	125.09		3.509	42.75

C.—Railroad service as in operation on the 30th of June, 1888—Continued.

Number of route.	State and termini.	Corporate title of company carrying the mail.	Distance. (Miles.)	Average number of trips per week over whole route.	Annual pay for transportation. (Dollars.)	Annual pay for railway post-office cars. (Dollars.)	Total annual pay. (Dollars.)	Cost per mile for transportation. (Dollars.)	Cost per mile for railway post-office cars. (Dollars.)	Remarks.
	NEW JERSEY—continued.									
7060	Sea Isle Junction (m. o.) and Sea Isle City.	West Jersey R. R	5.06	12	217.17		217.17			
7061	Angleses Junction (n. o.) and Angleses.	Angleses R. R	5.25	12	224.43		224.43	42.75		
7062	Vacant.									
7063	Whiting an irmingham o.) and	Pennsylvania R. R.	18.75	12	801.56		801.56	42.75		
7064	Evansville o.) and Vincentown.	...do	3.04	12	129.96		129.96	42.75		
			1,719.05		264,807.04	38,628.25	303,435.29			
	P PA.									
8001	Philadelphia Pittsburgh	Pennsylvania R. R.	352.90	70.13	387,120.71	97,047.50	484,168.21	1,096.97	275.00	
8002	Philadelphia Pottsville.	Philadelphia and Reading R. R.	93.1	35.95	13,850.48		13,860.48	148.77		
8003	Philadelphia West Chester.	Philadelphia, Wilmington and Baltimore R. R.	27.81	35.41	3,376.41		3,376.41	121.41		
8004	Philadelphia Bethlehem.	Philadelphia and Reading R. R.	56.01	46.88	9,625.87		9,625.87	171.86		
8005	Philadelphia.	...do	16.21	18	1,053.32		1,053.32	64.98		
8006	Sunbury and Williamsport	Pennsylvania R. R.	40.96	24.50	7,949.92	1,024.00	8,973.92	194.09	25.00	
8007	Bridgeport and Exton	Philadelphia and Reading R. R.	16.93	7.33	651.46		651.46	88.48		
8008	Chester, Pa., and Port Deposit, Md	Philadelphia, Wilmington and Baltimore R. R.	58.74	15.16	4,871.89		4,871.89	62.94		
8009	Honesdale and Lackawaxen	New York, Lake Erie and Western R. R.	24.94	12	1,407.36		1,407.36	56.43		
8010	Easton, Pa., and Waverly, N. Y.	Lehigh Valley R. B.	205.57	28.49	30,582.64		30,582.64	148.77		
8011	Penn Haven Junction (n. o.) and Mount Carmel.	...do	45.79	15	2,506.63		2,506.63	54.72		
8012	Hazle Creek Bridge (n. o.) and Audenried.	...do	8.52	6	864.23		864.23	42.75		
8013	Pottsville and Herndon.	Philadelphia and Reading R. R.	78.06	10.37	5,139.47		5,139.47	65.84		
8014	Port Clinton and Williamsport.	Pennsylvania R. R.	122.07	9.3	6,679.57		6,679.57	54.72		
8015	Sunbury and Sugarloaf.	Lehigh Valley R. R.	44.41	6	2,012.66		2,012.66	45.32		
8016	Penn Haven Junction (n. o.) and Sugarloaf.	Lehigh Valley R. R.	23.0	20.88	1,654.59		1,654.59	70.11		
8017	Scranton and Northumberland.	Delaware, Lackawanna and Western R. R.	80.48	24	8,394.96		8,394.96	104.31		

No.	Between what points	Name of railroad	Miles		Amount	Amount		Remarks
8018	Scranton and C boundale	Delaware and Hudson Canal Company	17.43	24	1,402.45	1,402.45	60.37	
8019	Binghamton, Y., and Washington, N. J.	Delaware, Lackawanna and Western R. R.	140.5	22.41	19,220.40	19,220.40	130.80	
8020	Elmira, N. Y., Hoytville, Pa	New York, Lake Erie and Western R. R.	64.94	10.55	4,386.09	4,386.09	67.55	
8021	Williamsport, and Elmira, N. Y.	Northern Central Rwy	78.81	18	11,253.27	11,253.27	142.79	
8022	Williamsport, Erie	Pennsylvania R. R.	248.75	18.56	25,810.31	25,810.31	101.75	
8023	Sunbury and Mount Carmel	Northern Central Rwy	27.47	18	1,244.94	1,244.94	45.82	
8024	Bradford, Pa., and Carrollton, N. Y.	New York, Lake Erie and Western R. R.	11.58	18	920.84	920.84	79.53	
8025	Irvine and Corry	...delphia R. R.	96.13	21.31	8,378.09	8,378.09	88.07	
8026	Strasburgh and Leaman Place	Strasburgh R. R., Isaac Pfenegar, lessee	5.25	6	224.43	224.43	42.75	
8027	Lancaster and Middletown	Pennsylvania R. R.	30.98	22.23	2,542.83	2,542.83	82.08	
8028	Harrisburgh and Auburn	Philadelphia and Reading R.R.	59.05	10.82	2,594.38	2,594.38	42.75	
8029	Stewartstown and New Freedom	Stewartstown R. R.	7.63	12	327.03	327.03	42.75	
8030	Harrisburgh, Pa., and Martinsburgh, W. Va.	Cumberland Valley R. R.	94.87	22.44	11,994.21	11,994.21	125.09	
8031	Columbia and Sinking Spring	Reading and Columbia R. R.	39.73	16.53	2,309.90	2,309.90	68.14	
8032	Columbia, Pa., and Frederick, Md.	Pennsylvania R. R.	69.8	17.52	4,563.71	4,563.71	65.84	
8033	Berlin Junction (n. o.) and East Berlin	Berlin Branch R. R.	7.23		309.08	309.08	43.75	
8034	Huntingdon and Mount Dallas Station (n. o.)	Huntingdon and Broad Top Mountain R. R. and Coal Co.	45.15	12	3,204.29	3,204.29	70.97	
8035	Tyrone and Curwinsville	Pennsylvania R. R.	47.48	18	3,613.23	3,613.23	76.10	
8036	Altoona and Henrietta	do	57.92	16.28	1,699.63	1,699.63	57.29	
8037	Cresson and Ebensburgh	do	11.59	15	585.11	585.11	44.17	
8038	Tyrone and Lock Haven	do	65.26	18	3,826.61	3,826.61	69.26	
8039	Blairsville and Allegheny	do	67.84	12	5,104.28	5,104.28	75.24	
8040	Pittsburgh, Pa., and Wheeling, W. Va.	Baltimore and Ohio R. R.	70.41	12	4,965.61	4,965.61	68.09	
8041	Pittsburgh and Oil City	Allegheny Valley R. R.	132.61	19	18,255.09	18,255.09	137.96	
8042	Branch Junction and Indiana	Pennsylvania R. R.	19.25	18.75	1,882.53	1,882.53	71.82	
8043	Meadville and Oil City	New York, Lake Erie and Western R. R.	86.67	18	2,441.52	2,441.52	66.09	
8044	Erie and Kenwood (n. o.)	Pennsylvania Company	119.20	12	10,491.81	10,491.81	96.33	
8045	Oil City, Pa., and Ashtabula, Ohio	Lake Shore and Michigan Southern Rwy.	88.46	10.78	5,748.13	5,748.13	64.96	
8046	Bethlehem and Bangor	Lehigh and Lackawanna R R	31.48	12	1,345.78	1,345.78	42.75	
8047	Downingtown and New Holland	Pennsylvania R. R.	28.29	18	1,402.90	1,402.90	49.69	
8048	West Chester and Phœnixville	do	18.43	16.72	787.88	787.88	42.75	
8049	Lewistown Junction (n. o.) and Milroy		12.94	12	553.18	553.18	43.75	
8050	Pottsville and Frackville	Philadelphia and Reading R. R.	11.55	13.85	469.76	469.76	42.75	
8051	Greenville and Butler	Shenango and Allegheny R. R.	58.25	8.9	3,287.61	3,287.61	56.43	
8052	Carlisle and Pine Grove Furnace	South Mountain Railway and Mining Co.	18.97	10.91	1,086.79	1,086.79	57.29	
8053	Freeport and Butler	Pennsylvania R. R.	21.96	12	1,428.91	1,428.91	64.08	
8054	Wilmington, Del., and Reading, Pa	Wilmington and Northern R.R.	71.9	9	3,258.50	3,258.50	45.32	

Pay not fixed on 12.5 miles.

C.—*Railroad service as in operation on the 30th of June, 1868—Continued.*

Number of route.	State and termini.	Corporate title of company carrying the mail.	Distance.	Average number of trips per week over whole route.	Annual pay for transportation.	Annual pay for railway post-office cars.	Total annual pay.	Cost per mile for transportation.	Cost per mile for railway post-office cars.	Remarks
	PENNSYLVANIA—continued.		*Miles.*		*Dollars.*	*Dollars.*	*Dollars.*	*Dollars.*	*Dollars.*	
8855	Pittsburgh and Washington	Pittsburgh, Cincinnati and Saint Louis Rwy.	32.9	24	2,192.90		2,192.90	95.76		
8856	Perkiomen Junction (n. o.), Emaus	Perkiomen R. R.	37.83	7.78	1,917.59		1,917.59	51.30		
8857	Pottstown and Tarto's	Philadelphia and Reading R. R.	13.22	11.95	565.15		565.15	42.75		
8858	Jeddo and Freeland	Lehigh Valley R. R.	2.47	18	105.59		105.59	42.75		
8859	Lebanon and Tower City	Philadelphia and Reading R. R.	43.49	9.78	1,806.59		1,806.59	41.61		
8860	Towanda and Bernice	Pennsylvania and New York Canal and R. R. Co.	23.66	12	1,012.32		1,012.32	42.75		
8861	Schuylkill Haven and Glen Carbon	Philadelphia and Reading R. R.	13.64	10.12	563.11		563.11	42.75		
8862	Topton and Kutztown	do	5.06	24	216.51		216.51	42.75		
8863	Pittsburgh, Pa., and Cumberland, Md.	Baltimore and Ohio R. R.	149.58	18.63	21,741.45		21,741.45	145.35		
8864	Carbondale and Susquehanna	New York, Lake Erie and Western R. R.	39.51	6	1,756.61		1,756.61	44.46		
8865	Corning, N. Y., and Antrim, Pa.	Fall Brook Coal Co.	51	13.23	5,278.46		5,278.46	102.46		
8866	Phœnixville and Urwhland	Philadelphia and Reading R. R.	11.23	10.04	482.32		482.32	42.74		
8867	Lewisburgh and Bellefonte	Pennsylvania R. R.	66.23	11.15	3,227.56		3,227.56	48.74		
8868	Bloomfield and Titusville	Buffalo, New York and Philadelphia R. R.	10.49	6	448.44		448.44	42.75		
8869	Towanda and Barclay	Towanda Coal Co.	17.85	6	763.08		763.08	42.75		
8870	Rockwood and Johnstown	Baltimore and Ohio R. R.	43.69	18	2,043.47		2,043.47	45.83		
8871	South Penn Junction (n. o.) and Richmond Furnace	Cumberland Valley R. R.	19.38	9.49	977.72		977.72	50.45		
8872	Mount Dallas Station (n. o.), Pa., and Cumberland, Md.	Pennsylvania R. R.	45.39	12	2,594.86		2,594.86	57.20		
8873	Allentown and Harrisburgh	Philadelphia and Reading R. R.	90.40	30.56	12,135.29		12,135.29	134.24		
8874	Conshohocken and Plarrtown	do	7.19	6	307.57		307.57	42.76		
8875	Lansdale and Doylestown		16.71	20.09	714.34		714.34	42.60		
8876	Reednam Furnace and Pittstown	Allegheny Valley R. R.	100.91	12	7,424.43		7,424.43	67.55		
8877	Chambersburgh and Wayne-borough.	Mont Alto R. R.	22.18	12	1,081.03		1,081.03	48.74		
8878	Tunkhannock and Montrose	Montrose Rwy.	29.11	6	1,244.45		1,244.45	42.75		
8879	Wilkes-Barre and Scranton	Delaware and Hudson Canal Co.	19.32	12	825.92		825.92	42.75		
8880	Mechanicsburgh and Dillsburgh	Cumberland Valley R. R.	8.84	12	415.74		415.74	47.03		
8881	Pittsburgh and West Brownsville	Pennsylvania R. R.	51.42	18	4,513.50		4,513.50	82.14		

No.	Location	Railroad					
8082	Valley Junction (n. o.), Pa., and Melrose, Md.	Western Maryland R. R.	11.49		677.91	677.91	50.00
8083	Bellefonte and Snow Shoe	Pennsylvania R. R.	21.83	12	923.23	923.23	42.75
8084	Hollidaysburgh and Williamsburgh	do	14.26	15	617.16	617.16	45.33
8085	Mount Union and Robertsdale	East Broad Top R. R. and Coal Co.	30.06	10.30	1,285.06	1,285.06	42.75
8086	Mount Jewett and Callery	Pittsburgh and Western R. R.	1.88	8.90	7,255.97	7,255.97	52.16
8087	Bellwood and Irvona	Bell's Gap R. R.	25.62	12	1,065.25	1,065.25	42.75
8088	Alaska (n. o.) and Mount Carmel	Philadelphia and Reading R.R.	1.95	12	83.36	83.36	42.75
8089	Reading and Slatington	do	44.13	12	1,866.65	1,866.65	42.75
8090	Berlin and Garrett	Pittsburg and Ohio R. R.	8.43		560.38	560.38	42.75
8091	Larrabee and Clermont	Buffalo, New York and Phila. R. R.	23.30	8.5	1,067.72	1,067.72	47.88
8092	York and Peach Bottom	York and Peach Plan Rwy.	40.59	6	2,012.85	2,012.85	49.59
8093	Larwenham and Sligo	Alleg'ny Val'y R. R.	10.70	6	461.27	461.27	42.75
8094	Oxford and Peter's Creek	Peach Bottom R. R.	19.12	8.35	817.88	817.88	42.75
8095	Pittsburgh and Castle Shannon	Castle Shannon R. R.	6.02	6	257.35	257.35	42.75
8096	New Castle and Stoneborough	Buffalo, New York and Phila-delphia R. R.	33.33	12	1,842.81	1,842.81	52.16
8097	White Haven and Upper Lehigh	Central R. R. Company of New Jersey	8.80	12	376.20	376.20	42.75
8098	Norristown and Lansdale	Stony Creek R. R.	10.80	9	461.70	461.70	42.75
8099	Osceola Mills and Madera	Pennsylvania R. R.	14.64	15	659.78	659.78	44.46
8100	Tamaqua and Mauch Chunk	Central R. R. Company of New Jersey	16.22	15.75	711.71	711.71	43.61
8101	Wilkes-Barre and Wie.	do	12.40	6	532.66	532.66	42.75
8102	Hanover Slon and Gettysburgh	Western Maryland R.R.	29.92	16.79	2,124.13	2,124.13	76.97
8103	Mrgs, Pa., and Boundbrook N. J.	Philadelphia and Reading R.R.	49.27	15.12	2,443.39	2,443.39	49.59
8104	Greensburgh and Fairchance	Pennsylvania R. R.	44.72	18.00	3,441.30	3,441.30	76.93
8105	Sheffield and Einlain	Tionesta Valley R.R.	12.78	6	544.30	544.30	42.75
8106	Millersburgh and Williamstown	Northern Central Rwy.	21.04	10.26	935.43	935.43	44.46
8107	Meadville and e Mie.	Meadville and Linesville Rwy.	21.10	14.34	920.17	920.17	43.61
8108	Mrs. Slon (n. o.) and Selin's Grove Junction (n. o.)	Pennsylvania R. R.	44.06	6.18	1,906.66	1,906.66	42.75
8109	Ington Station (n. o.) and Bready-ville	Northeast Pennsylvania R. R.	9.83	12	420.23	420.23	42.75
8110	Hartley Hall and Me.	Williamsport and North Branch R. R.	27.16	16.33	1,207.53	1,207.53	44.46
8111	Manor Station and Claridge	Pennsylvania R. R.	4.31	12	184.25	184.25	42.75
8112	Jersey Shore and Gazzam	Beech Creek R. R.	116.01	6	5,000.00	5,000.00	8.62
8113	Tyrone and Renovo	Pennsylvania R. R.	25.61	12	1,094.82	1,094.82	42.75
8114	Washington and Waynesburgh	Waynesburg and Washing-ton R. R.	22.73	12	1,906.58	1,906.58	64.13
8115	Bangor Junction (n. o.), Pa., and Brainards, N. J.	Bangor and Portland Rwy.	4.57	24	214.92	214.92	47.08
8116	Honesdale and Carbondale	Delaware and Hudson Canal Co.	17.48	12	747.27	747.27	42.75
8117	Philadelphia (Third and Berks streets station) and Newtown.	Philadelphia, Newtown and New York R. R.	23.28	18	1,214.28	1,214.28	52.16
8118	Latrobe and Ligonier	Ligonier Valley R. R.	10.90	12	461.70	461.70	42.75

C.—Railroad service as in operation on the 30th of June, 1888—Continued.

Number of route.	State and termini.	Corporate title of company carrying the mail.	Distance.	Average number of trips per week over whole route.	Annual pay for transportation.	Annual pay for railway post-office cars.	Total annual pay.	Cost per mile for transportation.	Cost per mile for railway post-office cars.	Remarks.
	PENNSYLVANIA—continued.		Miles.		Dollars.	Dollars.	Dollars.	Dollars.	Dollars.	
8119	Shenandoah and Mahanoy Plane....	Philadelphia and Reading R. R.	6.92	15	295.83		295.83	42.75		
8120	Birkin and Goss Run Junction (n. o.)	Pennsylvania R. R.	1.04	12	44.46		44.46	42.75		
8121	Pa., and Olean, N. Y.	Buffalo, New York and Philadelphia R. R.	23.68	14.10	1,012.83		1,012.83	42.75		
8122	Summit City and Bradford	....do....	8.97	6	383.46		383.46	43.01		
8123	Pittsburgh, Pa., and Youngstown, Ohio.	Pittsburgh and Lake Erie R. R.	63.83	26.45	9,906.09		9,906.09	150.48		
8124	Columbia, Pa., and Port Deposit, Md.	Pennsylvania R. B.	39.62	6	1,727.83		1,727.83	43.61		
8125	Allegheny and New Castle	Pittsburgh and Western R. R.	61.08	13.45	4,278.81		4,278.81	70.11		
8126	D. and M Junction (n. o.) and Shippensburgh.	Harrisburg and Potomac R. R.	28.82	11.82	1,232.05		1,232.05	42.75		
8127	Montour Junction (n. o.) and Imperial.	Montour R. B.	11	12	470.25		470.25	42.75		
8128	Portland and Nazareth	Bangor and Portland Rwy	26.14	18.93	1,117.48		1,117.48	42.75		
8129	Irwin and Buckburn	Penn Gas Coal Co.'s Youghioghony R. R.	8.53	6	364.65		364.65	42.75		
8130	Daguscahonda and Dagus Mines.	Northwestern Mining and Exchange Co.	6.01	12	256.92		256.92	42.75		
8131	Landenburgh and Pomeroy	Pennsylvania R. R.	18.54	6	792.58		792.58	42.75		
8132	Bradford and Smethport.	Bradford, Bordell and Kinzua R. R.	26.18	6	1,141.70		1,141.70	43.61		
8133	Kinzua Junction (n. o.) and Eldred.	....do....	14.25	6	792.01		792.01	55.58		
8134	Lumber Yard (n o) and Eccrvale.	Lehigh Valley R. R.	6.23	12	266.33		266.33	43.75		
8135	Tunnel and Eckley.	....do....	1.20	6	51.30		51.30	42.75		
8136	Blossburgh and Morris Run.	New York, Lake Erie and Western R. R.	3.76	6	160.74		160.74	42.75		
8137	Junction and Quarryville.	Reading and Columbia R. R.	23.50	14.31	1,024.83		1,024.83	43.61		
8138	Saxton and Dudley.	Huntingdon and Broad Top Mountain R. R. and Coal Co.	6.18	6	264.19		264.19	42.73		
8139	Lawrenceville and Harrison Valley.	Fall Brook Coal Co	32.43	8.26	1,385.95		1,385.95	42.75		
8140	Hollidayaburgh Junction (n. o.) and Mary.	Pennsylvania R. R.	3.06	12	130.81		130.81	42.75		
8141	Broad Ford and Mount Pleasant.	Baltimore and Ohio R. R.	10.38	6	443.74		443.74	42.75		
8142	Fall Brook and Blossburgh.	Fall Brook Coal Co	7.61	6	326.61		326.61	42.75		
8143	Negley and Verona.	Allegheny Valley R. R.	5.42	9	115.87		115.87	21.88		

No.	Stations	Railroad								Remarks
8144	Port Allegheny and Coudersport	Coudersport and Port Allegany R. R.	17.57	13	751.11		751.11	42.75	42.75	
8145	Mercersburgh Junction (n. o.) and Mercersburgh	Cumberland Valley R. R.	2.64	13	142.21		142.21	53.87		
8146	West Brownsville and Uniontown	Pennsylvania R. R.	18.90	0	993.70		993.70	42.75	42.75	
8147	Clarion Junction (n. o.) and Clarendon	Pittsburgh and Western R.R	6.42	18	274.45		274.45	42.75	42.75	
8148	North Clarendon and Cherry Grove	Warren and Farnsworth Valley R. R.	10.47	13	447.59		447.59	42.75	42.75	
8149	Lebanon and Cornwall	Cornwall R. R.	6.25	12	287.18		287.18	42.75	42.75	
8150	Williamsport and Stokesdale Junction (n. o.)	Fall Brook Coal Co	78.52	13	6,042.11		6,042.11	76.95	76.95	
8151	Youngwood Station (n. o.) and United	Pennsylvania R. R.	11.09	0	474.09		474.09	42.75	42.75	
8152	Branchton and Hilliard's	Shenango and Allegheny R. R.	10.47	0	447.59		447.59	42.75	42.75	
8153	Sunbury and Lewisburgh	Philadelphia and Reading R. R.	9.85	7.81	899.71		899.71	42.75	42.75	
8154	Cornwall and Conewago (n. o.)	Cornwall and Lebanon R. R.	16.96	0	725.04		725.04	42.75	42.75	
8155	Hunter's Run and Gettysburgh	Gettysburg and Harrisburg R. R.	22.79	12	1,578.43		1,578.43	69.20	69.20	
8156	New Castle Junction (n. o.) and New Castle	Pittsburgh and Lake Erie R. R.	3.05	29.5	166.99		166.99	54.72	54.72	
8157	Springfield Junction (n. o.) and Mines	Pennsylvania R. R.	8.20	0	350.55		350.55	42.75	42.75	
8158	Park Place and Mahanoy City	Lehigh Valley R. R.	3.27	0	178.34		178.34	53.01	53.01	
8159	Pittsburgh and Lake Erie R. R.	Pittsburgh and Lake Erie R. R.	59.51	0	3,002.27		3,002.27	50.45	50.45	
8160	Philadelphia and Chestnut Hill Railroad Station (n. o.)	Pennsylvania R. R.	11.96	87	780.96		780.96	65.84	65.84	
8161	Holmesburg Junction (n. o.) and Bustleton Railroad Station (n. o.)	do	4.04	12	172.71		172.71	42.75	42.75	
8162	Springfield Station (n. o.) and Saint Peter's	Wilmington and Northern R. R.	7.90	12	299.25		299.25	42.75	42.75	
8163	Roaring Spring and Ore Hill	Pennsylvania R. R.	3.86	0	143.64		143.64	42.75	42.75	
8164	Warren, Pa., and Salamanca, N. Y.	Buffalo, New York and Philadelphia R. R.	42.19	0	1,000.00		1,000.00	22.70	22.70	
8165	Iveona and Punxsutawney	Bell's Gap R. R.	83.47	12	1,631.33		1,631.33	48.74	48.74	
8166	Turbotville and Watsontown	Wilkes Barre and Western R'y.	6.58	0	153.99		153.99	20.53	20.53	
8167	Keating and Karthaus	Pennsylvania R. R.	22.17	0	454.92		454.92	20.62	20.62	
8168	Coalport and Cresson	New York Short and Clearfield County and R.R	24.50	0	568.01		568.01	23.09	23.09	
8169	Hazleton and New Boston	Lehigh Valley R. R.	18.06	21.98	849.35		849.35	47.08	47.08	
8170	Luzerne and Alderson	Pennsylvania and New York and R. R. Co.	14.06	8.99	300.60		300.60	21.38	21.38	
8171	Forest House and Austin	Sinnemahoning Valley R. R.	9.19	0	243.62		243.62	26.51	26.51	
8172	Benton and Bloomsburgh	Bloomsburg and Sullivan R. R.	20.68	12	777.98		777.98	37.62	37.62	
8173	Silver Brook and Silver Brook Junction (n. o.)	Lehigh Valley R. R.	2.81	0	53.55		53.55	20.52	20.52	
8174	Wilkes-Barre and Rock Glen Junction (n. o.)	Pennsylvania R. R.	39.58	15	1,759.72		1,759.72	44.46	44.46	
8175	New Boston and Potterville	do	10.21	0	480.07		480.07	47.02	47.02	
8176	Goff and Donohoe Station (n. o.)	do	4.29	0						Pay not fixed.
8177	Wampum and Rock Point	Pennsylvania Company	3.52	0						Do.
			6,255.60		832,966.13	98,071.50	931,039.63			

C.—*Railroad service as in operation on the 30th of June, 1883—Continued.*

Number of route.	State and terminal.	Corporate title of company carrying the mail.	Distance.	Average number of trips per week over whole route.	Annual pay for transportation.	Annual pay for railway post-office cars.	Total annual pay.	Cost per mile f'r transportation.	Cost per mile for railway post-office cars.	Remarks.
	DELAWARE.		*Miles.*		*Dollars.*	*Dollars.*	*Dollars.*	*Dollars.*	*Dollars.*	
9501	Wilmington and Delmar........	Philadelphia, Wilmington and Baltimore R. R.	97.12	20.00	14,780.69	....	14,780.69	152.19	....	
9502	Delmar, Del., and Crisfield, Md..	New York, Philadelphia and Norfolk R. R.	38.23	9	4,118.51	....	4,118.51	107.73	....	
9503	Clayton, Del., and Oxford, Md......	Philadelphia, Wilmington and Baltimore R. R.	54.70	8.41	3,460.86	....	3,460.86	63.27	....	
9504	Georgetown and Lewes..........	Delaware, Maryland and Virginia R. R.	16.02	6	684.85	....	684.85	42.75	....	
9505	Wilmington, Del., and Landenburgh, Pa.	Baltimore and Philadelphia R. R.	19.48	6	832.77	....	832.77	42.75	....	
9506	Harrington, Del., and Franklin City, Va.	Delaware, Maryland and Virginia R. R.	80.30	6	4,394.01	....	4,394.01	54.72	....	
9507	Newark and Delaware City....	Philadelphia, Wilmington and Baltimore R. R.	12.68	9.71	542.07	....	542.07	42.75	....	
			318.53		28,812.76		28,812.76			
	MARYLAND.									
10001	Bay View (n. o.), Md., and Philadelphia, Pa.	Philadelphia, Wilmington and Baltimore R. R.	91.50	74.48	68,128.45	9,180.00	77,308.45	742.14	100.00	
10002	Baltimore, Md., and Sunbury, Pa..	Northern Central Rwy	138.01	22.53	82,922.28	3,450.25	86,372.53	238.55	25.00	
10003	Baltimore, Md., and Bellaire, Ohio.	Baltimore and Ohio R. B.	399.39	30.75	137,186.94	39,115.60	176,302.54	351.41	{129.00 / 40.00}	For 223.75 miles, Baltimore and Grafton. For 96.64 miles, Grafton and Bellaire.
10004	Amby and Frederick...	do	3.85	37	230.06	....	230.06	67.55	....	
10005	Weverton and Hagerstown...	do	24.56	15	1,365.04	....	1,365.58	55.58	....	
10006	Baltimore and Williamsport..	Western Maryland R. B.	93.14	15.41	14,015.70	2,165.00	16,180.70	150.48	25 00	For 86.6 miles, to Hagerstown.
10007	Annapolis and Annapolis Junction.	Annapolis, Washington and Baltimore R. R.	21.08	21.14	1,423.95	....	1,423.95	67.53	....	
10008	Cambridge, Md., and Seaford, Del.	Philadelphia, Wilmington and Baltimore R. R.	33.64	6	1,725.73	....	1,725.73	51.30	....	
10009	Salisbury and Ocean City.......	Wicomico and Pocomoke R. R.	31.05	12	1,327.38	....	1,327.38	42.75	....	

No.	Termini	Railroad	Miles	No.	Amount	Additional	Total	Rate	
10010	Townsend, Del., and Centreville, Md.	Philadelphia, Wilmington and Baltimore R. R.	35.28	12	1,029.43		1,029.43	54.73	
10011	Cumberland, Md., and Piedmont, W. Va.	Cumberland and Pennsylvania R. R.	33.79	12	1,963.61		1,963.61	50.00	
10012	Clayton, Del., and Chestertown, Md.	Baltimore and Delaware Bay R. R., Fred. Gerker, lessee.	31.11	6	2,048.38		2,048.38	65.84	
10013	Bay View (n. o.), Md., and Washington, D. C.	Baltimore and Potomac R. R.	45.4	73.07	33,361.96	4,560.00	37,844.96	732.50	100.00
10014	Bowie and Pope's Creek	do	49.01	6	2,252.70		2,252.70	46.17	
10015	Peninsula Junction, Md., and Cape Charles, Va.	New York, Philadelphia and Norfolk R. R.	73.52	6	6,706.04		6,706.04	91.49	
10016	Vacant								
10017	Baltimore, Md., and Harper's Ferry, W. Va.	Baltimore and Ohio R. R.	81.13	19.28	6,242.95		6,242.95	74.96	
10018	Lake Roland and Stevenson	Northern Central Rwy.	5.51	9	212.02		212.02	38.48	
10019	Emmitsburgh and Rocky Ridge	Emmitsburgh R. R.	6.94	8	295.68		295.68	42.75	
10020	Valley Junction (n. o.), Pa., and Glyndon, Md.	Western Maryland R. R.	20.33	12	1,544.35		1,544.35	76.10	
10021	Edgemont, Md., and Chambersburgh, Pa.	Baltimore and Ohio R. R.	21.98	12	987.50		987.50	42.75	
10022	Baltimore and Brooklyn	Baltimore and Ohio R. R.	7	10.39	290.25		290.25	42.75	
10023	Perryville and Port Deposit	Pennsylvania R. R.	4.49	12	222.85		222.85	49.50	
10024	Baltimore, Md., and Delta, Pa.	Maryland Central R. R.	45.58	12	2,416.19		2,416.19	53.01	
10025	Brandywine and Mechanicsville	Washington and Potomac R. R.	20.3	6	885.28		685.28	42.61	
10026	Saint Agnes Station (n. o.), and Catonsville.	Baltimore and Potomac R. R.	3.93	12	168.00		168.00	42.75	
10027	Philadelphia, Pa., and Baltimore, Md.	Baltimore and Ohio R. R.	98.00	6	4,104.00		4,104.00	42.75	
10028	Baltimore and Annapolis	Annapolis and Baltimore Short Line R. R.	28.22	9	989.11		989.11	35.06	
			1,436.76		324,022.63	58,450.85	385,372.48		
	VIRGINIA.								
11001	Washington, D. C., and Richmond, Va.	Richmond, Fredericksburgh and Potomac R. R.	115.90	20	37,557.39	13,908.00	51,465.39	224.05	120.00
11002	Alexandria and Lynchburgh	Richmond and Danville R. R.	166.40	18.50	57,477.88	19,132.00	76,612.88	245.42	115.00
11003	Manassas and Strasburgh	do	62.93	6	4,869.19		4,046.19	64.98	
11004	Alexandria and Round Hill	do	50.63	13.02	3,276.51		3,276.51	66.89	
11005	Newport News, Va., and Huntington, W. Va.	Chesapeake and Ohio Rwy.	486.18		58,970.99		58,970.99	118.85	
11006	Richmond and North Danville	Richmond and Danville R. R.	140.71	14	17,445.22		17,445.22	123.96	
11007	Richmond and West Point	Richmond and West Point R. R.	38.72	10	2,284.48		2,284.48	59.00	
11008	Richmond and Petersburgh	Richmond and Petersburgh R. R.	23.59	32	6,459.61	1,671.20	8,330.81	278.17	90.00
11009	Petersburgh, Va., and Weldon, N. C.	Petersburgh R. R.	64.00	17	16,799.36	5,120.00	21,919.36	262.49	80.00
11010	Petersburgh and City Point	Norfolk and Western R. R.	10.47	6	447.59		447.59	42.75	80.00
11011	Petersburgh and Norfolk	do	82.18	13	7,793.70		7,793.70	94.91	
11012	Petersburgh and Lynchburgh	do	122.70	7	9,730.24		9,730.24	78.00	
11013	Lynchburgh, Va., and Roanoke, Va., and Bristol, Tenn.	do	54.24 / 150.16	14	37,671.63	8,864.00	44,438.85	183.93	25.00 / 50.00

C.—*Railroad service as in operation on the 30th of June, 1888*—Continued.

Number of route.	State and terminal.	Corporate title of company carrying the mail.	Distance.	Average number of trips per week over whole route.	Annual pay for transportation.	Annual pay for railway post-office cars.	Total annual pay.	Cost per mile for transportation.	Cost per mile for railway post-office cars.	Remarks.
	VIRGINIA—continued.		*Miles.*		*Dollars.*	*Dollars.*	*Dollars.*	*Dollars.*	*Dollars.*	
11014	Glade Spring and Saltville...........	Norfolk and Western R.R.	9.65	6	412.53		412.53	42.75		
11015	Portsmouth, Va., and Weldon, N.C.	Seaboard and Roanoke R.R.	78.96	12	6,550.60		6,550.60	82.94		
11016	Lynchburgh and Danville Junction. (b.o.)	Richmond and Danville R.R.	65.72	14	18,205.75	5,914.80	24,120.55	277.02	90.90	
11017	Bermuda Hundred and Winterpock.	City Point R'wy.	29.61	6	978.46		978.46	34.20		
11018	Washington, D.C., and Alexandria, Va.	Alexandria and Washington R.R.	7.42	45	562.05	863.90	3,435.38	347.99	115.00	
11019	Sutherlin, Va., and Milton, N.C.	Richmond and Danville R.R.	7.26	12	310.96		310.96	42.75		
11020	Fredericksburgh and Orange C.H.	Potomac, Fredericksburgh and Piedmont R.R.	39		1,667.25		1,667.25	42.75		
11021	Hagerstown, Md., and Roanoke, Va.	Shenandoah Valley R.R.	229.80	14	32,804.84	5,995.00	38,799.64	188.80	25.00	
11022	Elba and Rocky Mount.	Richmond and Danville R.R.	67.47	6	1,601.84		1,601.84	82.75		
11023	Richmond and Lynchburgh.	Richmond and Danville R.R.	147.07	18	13,197.96		13,197.96	82.94		
11024	Owl Run and Warrenton.	...and Allegheny R.R.	9.43	14	411.70		411.35	44.48		
11025	Orange C.H. and Gordonsville.	...do........	9.25	6	402.70		402.70	42.75		
11026	Norfolk, Va., and Edenton, N.C.	Norfolk Southern R.R.	75.07	12	5,584.45		5,584.45	74.39		
11027	Clifton Forge and Lynchburgh.	Richmond and Allegheny R.R.	84.90	12	5,183.85		5,183.85	61.56		
11028	Danville and Stuart.	Danville and New River R.R.	76.52	12	3,271.23		3,271.23	42.75		
11029	Balcony Falls and Lexington.	Richmond and Allegheny R.R.	23.12	14	1,021.74		1,021.74	46.17		
11030	Suffolk, Va., and Amboy, N.C.	Suffolk and Carolina R.R.	79.96	6	1,024.97		1,024.97	25.05		
11031	Newport News and Fortress Monroe.	Chesapeake and Ohio R'wy.	10.75	13	707.78		707.78	65.84		
11032	Keyville and Clarksville.	Richmond and Danville R.R.	55.78		1,378.38		1,378.38	40.61		Pay not fixed on 24.15 miles.
11033	New River Depot and Pocahontas.	Norfolk and Western R.R.	73.69	6	4,168.33		4,168.33	56.43		36.00 miles Waverley Station to Belifield at $23.09 per mile.
11034	Claremont to Belifield.	Atlantic and Danville R'wy.	55.10	6	1,635.90		1,635.90	42.75		
11035	Norfolk and Virginia Beach.	Norfolk and Virginia Beach R.R. and Improvement Co.	18.80	6	803.70		803.70	42.75		
11036	Emporia, Va., and Margaretsville, N.C.	Meherrin Valley R'wy.	18.77	6	802.41		802.41	42.75		
11037	Suffolk and Whaleyville.	Suffolk Lumber Co. R.R.	12.17	6	563.01		563.01	42.75		
11038	North Danville, Va., and Charlotte, N.C.	Richmond and Danville R.R.	143.21	14	38,815.63	12,888.90	51,704.53	171.04	90.00	
920	Pulaski City and Ivanhoe Furnace.	Norfolk and Western R.R.	22.23	6	666.22		666.22	29.07		Pay not fixed on 8.13 miles.

No.	Terminal points	Railroad	Length of route	Trips				Rate	Remarks
			82.51 3,011.18		1,029.61 404,815.21	74,651.50	1,029.61 479,300.41	81.64	
11940	Bristol, Tenn., and Estillville, Va	South Atlantic and Ohio R. R......							
	WEST VIRGINIA.								
12001	Harper's Ferry, W. Va., and Lexington, Va.	Baltimore and Ohio R. R......	165.54	14.53	15,285.96		15,285.96	92.34	
12002	Grafton and Parkersburgh........	do	104.50	21.15	30,134.20	8,969.00	30,134.20	874.40	
12003	Volcano Junction and Volcano...	Laurel Fork and Sand Hill R.R.	7.03	12	300.10		300.10	42.25	80.00
12004	Pennsborough and Ritchie C. H...	Pennsboro and Harrisville, Ritchie County, Rwy.	9.09	13	388.59		388.59	42.75	
12005	Wheeling Junction (n. e.) and Wheeling.	Pittsburgh, Cincinnati and Saint Louis Rwy.	24	24	1,785.36		1,785.36	74.89	
12006	Clarksburgh and Weston........	Clarksburgh, Weston and Glenville R. R. and Transportation Company.	57.07	18	3,060.02		3,060.02	76.10	
12007	Piedmont and Mineville........	West Virginia Central and Pittsburgh Rwy.	13.33	8	559.85		559.85	42.75	
12008	Winifrede Junction (n. o.) and Winifrede.	Winifrede R. R...........	4.64	7	194.06		194.06	42.75	
12-09	Shaw and Davis........	West Virginia Central and Pittsburgh Rwy.	43.82	12	1,856.70		1,856.70	42.75	
12010	Charleston, W. Va., and Columbus, Hocking Valley and Toledo Junction (n. o.), Ohio.	Ohio Central R. R......	50.70	6.30	2,807.60		2,807.60	47.08	
12011	Weston and Buckhannon........	Weston and Buckhannon R. R.	16.29	12	724.25		724.25	44.46	
12012	Grafton and Belington........	Grafton and Greenbrier R. R.	43	42	2,046.66		2,046.66	48.73	
12013	Grafton and Point Pleasant......	Ohio River R. R.....	172.29	18.05	12,982.99		12,982.99	75.26	
12014	Green Spring and Romney......	Baltimore and Ohio R. R......	16.64	12	711.86		711.86	42.76	
12015	Romney Junction (n. o.) and Wheeling.	do	4	50	584.84		584.84	145.21	
12016	Bino Stone Junction (n. o.) and Duhring.	Norfolk and Western R.R.	7.83	8	140.22		140.22	42.75	
12017	Morgantown and Fairmount.....	Baltimore and Ohio R. R......	25.95	12	1,176.05		1,176.05	45.32	
12018	Piedmont, W. Va., and Cumberland, Md.	West Virginia Central and Pittsburgh Rwy.	28.87	6	1,658.67		1,658.67	57.28	
12020	Point Pleasant and Huntington...	Ohio River R. R.........	43.32	6					Pay not fixed miles.
12021	Tunnelton and Kingwood......	Kingwood Rwy........	10.95	6					Pay not fixed. Do.
			823.75		84,484.78	8,969.00	92,844.78		
	NORTH CAROLINA.								
13001	Raleigh and Weldon........	Raleigh and Gaston R. R.....	97.78	12	9,865.02		9,865.02	100.89	
13002	Weldon and Wilmington......	Wilmington and Weldon R. R.	162.07	17.5	38,522.41	12,945.60	51,488.01	237.60	80.00
13003	Wilmington and Charlotte.....	Carolina Central R. R......	188.53	6	12,089.78		12,089.78	64.13	
13004	Goldsborough and Greensborough.	Richmond and Danville R. R.	129.89	7	11,771.93		11,771.93	90.63	
13005	Goldsborough and Morehead City.	Atlantic and North Carolina R. R.	94.05	6	6,031.43		6,031.43	64.13	

C.—Railroad service as in operation on the 30th of June, 1888—Continued.

Number of route.	State and termini.	Corporate title of company carrying the mail.	Distance.	Average number of trips per week over whole route.	Annual pay for transportation.	Annual pay for railway post-office cars.	Total annual pay.	Cost per mile for transportation.	Cost per mile for railway post-office cars.	Remarks.
			Miles.		Dollars.	Dollars.	Dollars.	Dollars.	Dollars.	
	NORTH CAROLINA—continued.									
13006	Salisbury and Kinsel (n. o.)	Richmond and Danville R. R.	188.43	6	19,959.74		19,959.74	106.88		6.18 miles, Hot Springs to Kinsel (n.o.) at $77.81 per mile.
13007	Charlotte, N. C., and Augusta, Ga.	do	192.58	10.00	24,861.43		24,861.43	129.11		
13008	Charlotte and Rutherfordton	Carolina Central R. R.	55.53	6	4,907.31		4,907.31	67.29 63.27		
13009	Charlotte and Taylorsville	Richmond and Danville R. R.	65.60	6	3,824.36		3,824.36	58.00		10.96 miles, Statesville to Taylorsville, at $56.43 per mile.
13010	Raleigh and Hamlet	Raleigh and Augusta Air Line R. R.	98.90	6	7,782.27		7,782.27	78.66		
13011	Bennettsville, S. C., and Mount Airy, N. C.	Cape Fear and Yadkin Valley R. R.	225.06	6	11,005.92		11,005.92	53.16		54.79 miles, Greensborough to Pilot Mountain, at $53.61 per mile. Pay not fixed on 14.93 miles.
13012	Greensborough and Winston	Richmond and Danville R. R.	29.10	12	2,199.46		2,199.46	75.24		
13013	Jamesville and Washington	Jamesville and Washington R. R., William Bissell, lessee.	22.57	6	964.96		964.96	42.75		
13014	Oxford and Henderson	Oxford and Henderson R. R., A. H. Williams, lessee.	14.20	6	607.05		607.05	42.75		
13015	Rocky Mount and Tarborough	Wilmington and Weldon R. R.	17.80	7	1,060.20		1,060.20	59.00		
13016	Abbeville Junction (n. o.) and Jarret.	Richmond and Danville R. R.	98.95	6	4,905.93		4,905.93	49.59		
13017	Alma and Plainview	Alma and Little Rock R. R.	12.88	6	550.63		550.63	42.75		
13018	University Station and Chapel Hill.	Richmond and Danville R. R.	11.16	6	477.09		477.09	42.75		
13019	Halifax and Scotland Neck	Wilmington and Weldon R. R.	21.47	6	997.76		997.76	42.75		
13020	Tarborough and Williamston	Albemarle and Raleigh R. R.	33.67	7	1,438.58		1,438.58	42.75		
13021	Vacant									
13022	Danville, Mocksville and Southwestern Junction (n. o.) and Leaksville.	Danville, Mocksville and Southwestern R. R.	7.97	6	240.71		240.71	42.75		
13023	Hickory and Lenoir	Charlotte, Columbia and Augusta R. R.	20.51	6	876.90		876.90	42.75		

No.	Termini	Railroad	Miles	Trips	Amount		Total	Rate	Extra	Remarks
13024	Chadbourn, N.C., and Conway, S.C.	Wilmington, Chadbourn and Conwayboro R.R.	39.17	6	1,210.08		1,210.08	42.75		25.84 miles, Mount Tabor to Conway, at $24.80 per mile.
13025	Louisburgh and	Raleigh and Gaston R.R.	10.40	6	444.00		414.00	42.75		
13026	Warren Plains and Warrenton	Warrenton R.R.	3.13	12	133.90		133.90	42.75		
13027	Wilson and Fayetteville	Wilmington and Weldon R.R.	74.02	6	2,341.09		2,341.09	31.64		
13028	Rocky Mountain Spring Hope	do	19.12	6	441.47		441.47	23.00		
13029	Moncure and Pittsborough	Pittsboro R.R.	12.81	12	347.26		347.26	28.21		
13030	Warsaw and Clinton (n.o.) and Mill	Wilmington and Weldon R.R.	13.11	12	560.45		560.45	42.75		
13031	Factory Junction (n.o.) and Millboro.	Cape Fear and Yadkin Valley Rwy.	9.55	6	195.96		195.96	20.52		
13032	Hamilton and Tarboro, h	Hamilton R.R. and Lumber Co.	20.05	6	423.73		423.73	20.52		
13033	Boykins Va., and Boxobel, N.C.	Roanoke and Tar River R.R.	28.92	6						Pay not fixed.
13034	Hamlet and Gibson Station	Raleigh and Augusta Air Line R.R.	10.50	6						Do.
13035	Wilmington and Wrightsville	Wilmington Seacoast R.R.	9.24	6						Do.
			2,065.00		170,973.39	12,065.60	183,038.99			
	SOUTH CAROLINA.									
14001	Columbia and Greenville	Richmond and Danville R.R.	144.82	6	10,982.75		10,982.75	76.10		
14002	{ Columbia and Florence / Florence, S.C., and Wilmington N.C.	Wilmington, Columbia and Augusta R.R.	53 / 110	14	34,633.38	7,180	43,783.38	189.81 / 189.81		
14003	Columbia and Charleston	South ... Rwy	131.50	15.2	13,529.85		13,529.85	105.17		
14004	Charleston, S.C., and Savannah, Ga.	Charleston and Savannah Rwy.	115	14	22,520.85	7,475.00	29,705.86	194.00		
14005	Charleston and Florence	Northeastern R.R.	102	14	21,018.12	6,690.00	27,648.12	206.00	65.00	
14006	Florence and Cheraw	Cheraw and Darlington R.R.	40.82	7	2,094.06		2,094.06	51.30	65.00	
14007	Chester, S.C., and Hickory, N.C.	Charlotte, Columbia and Augusta R.R.	85.62	6	4,052.18		4,052.18	51.30	65.00	Pay between Newton and Hickory, 9.25 miles, at $14.58 per mile.
14008	Alston and Spartanburgh	Richmond and Danville R.R.	68.39	6	8,216.38		8,216.38	47.08		
14009	... and ...ville	do	11.93	14	510.00		510.00	42.75		
14010	Port Royal, S.C., and Augusta, Ga.	Port Royal and Augusta R.R.	110.77	14	6,061.33		6,061.33	54.72		
14011	Spartanburgh, S.C., and Asheville, N.C.	Richmond and Danville R.R.	72.27	6	8,588.86		8,588.86	48.50		
14012	Newberry and Laurens	do	31.78	6	1,385.92		1,385.92	43.61		
14013	...er and Lancaster	do	29.47	6	1,259.84		1,259.84	42.75		
14014	Cheraw, S.C., and Wadesborough, N.C.	Cheraw and Salisbury R.R.	26.09	7	1,312.70		1,312.70	50.43		
14015	Lane's and Sumter	Central R. R. Co. of S.C.	49	7	1,710.00		1,710.00	42.75		
14016	Belton and ...Wil	Richmond and ... R.R.	43.92	7	2,625.61		2,625.61	59.85		
14017	Branchville, S.C., and Augusta, Ga.	Seh Carolina Rwy	76.43	21.95	5,816.32		5,816.32	78.10		
14018	Kingsville and ...len	do	38.28	13	1,079.22		1,079.22	42.75		
14019	Blackville and Barnwell	Rail Rwy	8.64	12	412.11		412.11	42.75		
14020	Lane's ...gtown	Georgetown and Lane's R.R.	39.20	7	1,675.90		1,675.90	42.75		
14021	Greenwood and Spartanburgh	Port Royal and Western Carolina Rwy.	56.20	7	3,622.46		3,622.46	54.72		

C.—*Railroad service as in operation on the 30th of June, 1888—Continued.*

Number of route.	State and termini.	Corporate title of company carrying the mail.	Distance.	Average number of trips per week over whole route.	Annual pay for transportation.	Annual pay for railway post-office cars.	Total annual pay.	Cost per mile of transportation.	Cost per mile for railway post-office cars.	Remarks.
	SOUTH CAROLINA—continued.		*Miles.*		*Dollars.*	*Dollars.*	*Dollars.*	*Dollars.*	*Dollars.*	
14022	Elloree and Pregnalls.	Eutawlle R. R.	33.78	6	837.74		837.74	24.80		
14023	McCormick and Anderson.	Port Royal and Western Carolina Rwy.	59	6	1,465.20		1,465.20	24.80		
14024	Laurens and Greenville.	do	36.85	6						Pay not fixed.
14025	Green Pond and Walterborough	Green Pond, Walterborough and Branchville R. R.	12.87	6.50						Do.
14026	Blackville and Salley.	Blackville, Alston and Newberry R. R.	18.14	6	1,134.24		1,134.24	30.78		Do.
14027	Camden and Lancaster.	Charleston, Cincinnati and Chicago R. R.	41.50	6	432.69		432.69	35.06		Do.
14028	Ravenels and Young's Island.	Charleston and Savannah Rwy.	5.70	6						
14029	Atkins and Bishopville.	Bishopville R. R.	15.79	6						
			1,668.60		160,674.06	21,255.00	170,929.06			
	GEORGIA.									
15001	Atlanta, Ga., and Air-line Junction (n. o.) N.C.	Richmond and Danville R. R.	268.03	14	58,896.91	24,122.70	83,019.61	218.74	90.00	
15002	Atlanta, Ga., and Chattanooga, Tenn.	Western and Atlantic R. R.	138.47	21	28,177.58	12,463.30	40,636.56	203.49	90.00	
15003	Atlanta and West Point.	Atlanta and West Point R. R.	87.36	21	17,254.47	4,368.00	21,622.47	197.61	50.00	
15004	Augusta and Atlanta.	Georgia R. R.	171.59	14	33,768.93		33,768.93	138.51		
15005	Millen and Augusta.	Central R. R. and Banking Co.	54.51	7	8,635.27		8,635.27	66.69		
15006	Washington and Barnett.	Georgia R. R.	18.56	14	794.29		794.29	42.75		
15007	Union Point and Athens.	do	40.48	7	2,319.09		2,319.09	57.29		
15008	Kingston and Rome.	Rome R. R.	20.28	21	1,057.80		1,057.80	52.16		
15009	Savannah, Ga., and Jacksonville, Fla.	Savannah, Florida and Western Rwy.	171.50	14	33,725.47	11,147.50	44,872.97	198.65	65.00	
15010	Savannah and Macon.	Central R. R. and Banking Co.	191.43	14	24,878.23		24,878.23	129.96		
15011	Macon and Columbus.	Southwestern R. R.	101.04	7	6,738.35		6,738.35	66.69		
15012	Macon and Atlanta.	Central R. R. and Banking Co.	102.83	14	17,754.93		17,754.93	171.00		
15013	Rome and Brunswick.	East Tennessee, Virginia and Georgia Rwy.	350.80	7	24,160.39		24,160.39	70.97		Pay between Austel and Atlanta, 18.81 miles, at $30.78 per mile.

No.	Termini	Railroad	Distance	Trips	Amount	Amount		Rate
15014	Gordon and Eatonton	Central R. R. and Banking Co.	88.53	6	1,647.15	1,647.15		42.75
15015	Tennille an d Wrightsville	Wrightsville and Tennille R. R.	14.50	6	705.87	705.87		42.75
15016	Macon, Ga., and Eufaula, Ala.	Southwestern R. R.	144.57	7	12,607.94	12,607.94		87.21
15017	Fort Valley and Perry	do	12.90	6	549.76	549.76		58.07
15018	Waycross and Albany	Savannah, Florida and Western Rwy.	163.11	12.49	14,365.69	14,365.69		
15019	Barnesville and Thomaston	Central R. R. and Banking Co.	16.63	12	706.65	706.65		42.75
15020	Carterville, Ga., and Pell City, Ala.	Central R. R. and Banking Co. of East and West R. R. Co. of Ala.	117.36	6	5,042.11	5,042.11		42.75
15021	Camak and Macon	Georgia R. R.	78.59	14	5,846.31	5,846.31		74.39
15022	Griffin and Carrollton	Savannah, Griffin and North Alabama R. R.	60.87	6	2,652.73	2,652.73		43.61
15023	Brunswick and Albany	Brunswick and Western R. R.	171.78	7	7,782.80	7,782.80		45.32
15024	Columbus and Greenville	Columbus and Rome Rwy.	50.53	6	2,165.28	2,165.28		42.75
15025	Athens and Belton	Richmond and Danville R. R.	39.59	12	2,200.41	2,200.41		55.58
15026	Toccoa and Elberton	do	51.45	14	2,190.48	2,190.48		42.75
15027	Sandersville and Tennille	Sandersville and Tennille R. R.	3.50	12	149.62	149.62		42.75
15028	Wadley and Louisville	Louisville and Wadley R. R.	10.62	6	454.00	454.00		42.75
15029	Hartwell and Bowersville	Richmond and Danville R. R.	10.15	6	433.91	433.91		42.75
15030	Marietta, Ga., and Murphy, N. C	Marietta and North Georgia R. R.	109.05	6	4,288.14	4,288.14		39.33
15031	Thomasville and Bainbridge	Savannah, Florida and Western Rwy.	56.99	7	2,972.88	2,972.88		30.97
15032	Savanee and Lawrenceville	Richmond and Danville R. R.	10.43	6	445.88	445.88		42.75
15033	Talbotton and Bostick (n.o.)	Talbotton R. R.	7.20	12	307.80	307.80		42.75
15034	Gainesville and Social Circle	Gainesville, Jefferson and Southern R. R.	53.37	6	3,234.54	3,234.54		42.75
15035	Roswell Junction (n.o.) and Roswell	Richmond and Danville R. R.	10.87	6	464.69	464.69		42.75
15036	Dupont, Ga., and Gainesville, Fla.	Savannah, Florida and Western Rwy.	112.37	13	6,730.40	6,730.40		54.43
15037	Augusta, Ga., and Greenwood, S. C.	Port Royal and Western Carolina Rwy.	68.90	13	3,096.61	3,096.61		44.46
15038	Cochran and Hawkinsville	East Tennessee, Virginia and Georgia Rwy.	10.39	7	444.17	444.17		42.75
15039	Smithville and Albany	Southwestern R. R.	24.08	6	1,585.42	1,585.42		65.84
15040	Albany and Blakely	do	50.19	18	2,145.63	2,145.63		42.75
15041	Cuthbert and Fort Gaines	do	22.53	13	963.08	963.08		42.75
15043	Atlanta, Ga., and Coalburgh, Ala.	Georgia Pacific Rwy.	175.76		10,276.82	10,276.82		58.14
15043	Belton and Tallulah	Richmond and Danville R. R.	33.22		1,067.58	1,067.58		43.75
15044	Climax, Ga., and Chattahoochee, Fla.	Savannah, Florida and Western Rwy.	52.17	7	2,778.20	2,778.20		86.36
15045	Belmont and Jefferson	Gainesville, Jefferson and Southern R. R.	13.51	6	577.55	577.55		42.75
15046	Sylvania and Rocky Ford	Sylvania R. R.	14.99	7	640.82	640.82		42.75
15047	Americus and Buena Vista	Buena Vista and Ellaville R.R	29.63	6	1,266.68	1,266.68		42.75
15048	Augusta and Sandersville	Augusta, Gibson and Sandersville R. R.	81.05	6	3,464.71	3,464.71		30.78
15049	Wrightsville and Dublin	Wrightsville and Tennille R.R	18.56	6	826.19	826.19		42.75

7.90 miles, Broken Ar-row to Pell City, at $46.17 per mile.

Pay between Belton and Rabun Gap Junction (n.o.), 1½ miles, at $15 per mile.

C.—*Railroad service as in operation on the 30th of June, 1888—Continued.*

Number of route.	State and termini.	Corporate title of company carrying the mail.	Distance.	Average number of trips per week over whole route.	Annual pay for transportation.	Annual pay for railway post-office cars.	Total annual pay.	Cost per mile for transportation.	Cost per mile for railway post-office cars.	Remarks.
			Miles.		*Dollars.*	*Dollars.*	*Dollars.*	*Dollars.*	*Dollars.*	
	GEORGIA—continued.									
15050	Americus and Louvale	American, Preston and Lumpkin R. R.	48.46	6	2,013.77		2,013.77	42.75		9.89 miles, Lumpkin to Louvale, at $28.77 per mile.
15051	Columbus and McDonough	Georgia, Midland and Gulf R. R. (operated by the Ga. Midland Construction Co.)	100.00	6	3,093.90		3,093.90	30.53		64.49 miles, Shiloh to McDonough, at $44.46 per mile.
15052	Macon and Madison	Covington and Macon R. R.	72.61	6	1,369.31		1,369.31	29.93		Pay not fixed on 27.16 miles.
15053	Midville and Swainsborough	Midville and Swainsborough R. R. (owned and operated by Jesse Thompson & Co.)	18.42	6	488.31		488.31	26.61		
15054	Americus and Abbeville	American, Preston and Lumpkin R. R.	61.95	6	2,277.89		2,277.89	36.77		
15055	Rogers and Summit	Rogers and Summit R. R.	20.00	6	410.40		410.40	20.52		Pay not fixed.
15056	Atlanta and Zebulon	Atlanta and Florida Rwy.	51.26	6						
			2,999.96		356,499.76	52,100.50	410,516.26			
	FLORIDA.									
16001	Fernandina and Cedar Keys	Florida Railway and Navigation Company.	155.15	6.92	10,824.81		10,824.81	69.77		All land grant.
16002	Lake City and River Junction	...do...	155.87	7	9,381.81		9,381.81	60.19		Do.
16003	Pensacola, Fla., and Flomaton, Ala.	Louisville and Nashville R. R.	44.84	14	3,097.99		3,097.99	69.00		Do.
16004	Jacksonville, Tampa and Key West Junction (n. c.) and New Smyrna	Blue Springs, Orange City and Atlantic Rwy.	28.09	6	848.48		848.48	31.63		
16005	Pensacola and Millview	Pensacola and Perdido R. R.	10.25	7	438.18		438.18	42.75		
16006	Jacksonville and Lake City	Florida Railway and Navigation Company.	60.33	7	4,125.88		4,125.88	68.40		Do.
16007	Sanford and Tampa	South Florida R. R.	116.39	7.01	9,951.34		9,951.34	85.50		
16008	Astor and Leesburgh	Saint John's and Lake Eustis Rwy.	56.75	6	2,814.23		2,814.23	49.60		
16009	Hart's Road and Jacksonville	Florida Railway and Navigation Company.	23.27	13	994.79		994.79	42.75		
16010	Sanford and Orlando	Sanford and Indian River R.R.	17.63	6	753.66		753.66	42.75		Land grant.
	Waldo and Wildwood	Florida Railway and Navigation Company.	72.50					63.61		Not land grant.
16011	Wildwood and Tavares	Florida Railway and Navigation Company.	21.95	6	6,357.18		6,357.18	79.52		

No.	Termini	Railway company							All land grant
16012 16013	Palatka and Gainesville .... Tallahassee and Saint Mark's	Florida Southern Rwy .... Florida Railway and Navigation Company.	49.77 21.59	7.22 3	2,996.00 655.16	2,996.00 655.16	....	52.16 20.93	....
16014 16015 16016	Rochelle and Fort Mason.......... Pensacola and River Junction...... Jacksonville and Saint Augustine.	Florida Southern R. R. .... Pensacola and Atlantic R. R. ...... Jacksonville, Saint Augustine and Halifax River Rwy.	86.81 161.52 36.90	6 7 14	7,379.50 11,380.09 2,234.12	7,379.50 11,380.09 2,234.12	....	85.50 70.46 60.71	....
16017	Micanopy Junction (n. o.) and Micanopy	Florida Southern Rwy.	4.11	6	175.70	175.70	......	42.75	......
16018 16019	Jacksonville and Sanford.......... Wildwood and Plant City..........	Jacksonville, Tampa and Key West Rwy. Florida Railway and Navigation Company.	55.21 69.97 68.86	}10 6	20,062.39 537.74	20,062.39 537.74	....	{141.93 172.71 34.20	All land grant. 9.98 miles, Pensacola to Macomb, at $17.78 per mile. Pay not fixed on 48 14 miles.
16020	De Land Landing (n.o.) and De Land	Jacksonville, Tampa and Key West Rwy.	5.30	6	228.57	228.57	......	42.75	......
16021 16022	Wahneta and Bartow.............. Tavares and Orlando..............	South Florida R. R. .... Tavares, Orlando and Atlantic R. R.	17.53 52.95	6 6	749.40 2,225.77	749.40 2,225.77	....	42.75 67.55	....
16023 16024 16025 16026 16027	Leesburgh and Brooksville........ Pemberton and Bartow............ Enterprise Junction (n. o.) and Titusville. Bartow and Punta Gorda.......... Saint Augustine and Palatka......	Florida Southern Rwy. .... South Florida R. R. .... Jacksonville, Tampa and Key West Rwy. Florida Southern R. R. .... Saint Augustine and Palatka Rwy.	46.68 57.85 40.43 75.30 26.71	6 6 6 6 6	2,957.34 3,460.53 3,730.37 3,862.58 543.08	2,957.34 3,460.53 3,730.37 3,862.58 543.08	....	72.64 59.85 67.55 51.90 20.53	....
16028 16029	Sanford and Tavares.............. Monroe (n. o.) and Tarpon Springs	Sanford and Lake Eustis R.R. Orange Belt Rwy.	23.65 116.20	6 6	981.92 2,114.53	981.92 2,114.53	....	23.07 19.53	19.16 miles, Oakland to Mascotte, at $44.46 per mile. Pay not fixed on 64.94 miles.
16030 16031 16032	Jacksonville and Pablo Beach...... Palatka and Daytona.............. Lake City and Fort White..........	Jacksonville and Atlantic R. R Saint John's and Halifax R. R Savannah, Florida and Western Rwy.	17.43 54.15 21.93	6 6 6	358.08 2,037.12 463.64	358.08 2,037.12 463.64	....	20.53 37.03 21.37	....
16033	Ocala and Dunnellon..............	Silver Springs, Ocala and Gulf R. R.	25.43	6	739.25	739.25	......	29.07	80.00
			1,874.81		117,900.64	117,900.64			
ALABAMA.									
17001	Montgomery, Ala., and West Point, Ga.	Western Rwy. Co. of Alabama	86.21	14	16,457.66	16,457.66	4,310.50	199.67	80.00
17002 17003 17004 17005	......do .... Montgomery and Selma.......... Montgomery and Eufaula.......... Montgomery and Decatur.......... Memphis, Tenn., and Chattanooga, Tenn.	Montgomery and Eufaula R. R. South and North Alabama R. R. Memphis and Charleston R. R.	51.23 80.49 183.28 311.99	7 7 14 7.75	4,380.16 6,400.56 20,184.69 36,843.36	4,380.16 6,400.56 20,184.69 36,843.36	....	85.30 79.52 110.18 120.63	All land grant. Pay between Stevenson, Ala., and Chattanooga, Tenn., 58 miles, at $1,000 per annum.

C.—Railroad service as in operation on the 30th of June, 1888—Continued.

Number of route.	State and terminal.	Corporate title of company carrying the mail.	Distance.	Average number of trips per week over whole route.	Annual pay for transportation.	Annual pay for railway post-office cars.	Total annual pay.	Cost per mile for transportation.	Cost per mile for railway post-office cars.	Remarks.
			Miles.		Dollars.	Dollars.	Dollars.	Dollars.	Dollars.	
	ALABAMA—continued.									
17006	Selma and Akron Junction	Cincinnati, Selma and Mobile Rwy.	67.76	7	3,660.23		3,660.23	53.67		
17007	Opelika, Ala., and Columbus, Ga.	Columbus and Western Rwy.	29.53	13	2,297.72		2,297.72	77.81		All land grant.
17008	Columbus, Ga., and Troy, Ala.	Mobile and Girard R.R.	85.70	13	5,054.39		5,054.39	59.00		
17009	Selma, Ala., and Meridian, Miss.	East Tennessee, Virginia and Georgia Rwy.	114.34	7	8,201.71		8,201.71	71.82		
17010	Selma and Patona (n. o.), Patona (n. o.), Ala., and Cleveland, Tenn.	do	156 / 108.92	12	24,779.61		24,779.61	84.83 / 106.02		Land grant. Not land grant.
17011	Vacant.									
17012	Mobile and Flomaton	Louisville and Nashville R.R.	61.14 / 112.43	14	28,667.75	9,028.50	37,696.25	182.97 / 146.37	50.00	Not land grant. Land grant.
17013	Flomaton and Montgomery	do	141.43	14	25,515.88	7,071.50	32,588.88	180.41	50.00	Land grant.
17014	Mobile, Ala., and New Orleans, La. Opelika and Roanoke.	East Alabama Rwy.	38.88	6	1,771.67		1,771.67	43.75	50.00	17.19 miles, Buffalo to Roanoke, at $47.88 per mile.
17015	Chattanooga and Wauhatchie, Tenn. Wauhatchie, Tenn., Meridian, Miss.	Alabama Great Southern R.R.	5.95 / 299.10	14	31,276.46		31,276.46	131.67 / 101.33		Not land grant. Land grant. Pay not fixed on 26.57 miles.
17016	Opelika and Childersburg.	Columbus and Western Rwy.	86.72	6	2,674.26		2,674.26	44.46		
17017	Selma and Pineapple Station (n. o.)	Louisville and Nashville R.R.	47.50	6	2,206.92		2,206.92	46.17		
17018	Dolomite and Wheeling Station (n. o.)	Woodward Iron Co.	4.50	6	106.70		106.70	23.23		
17019	Chehaw (n. o.) and Tuskegee	Tuskegee R.R.	6	6	256.50		256.50	42.75		
17020	Atalla and Gadsden	Tennessee and Coosa R.R.	5.90	6	252.22		252.22	42.75		
17021	Eufaula and Clayton	Eufaula and Clayton R.R.	21.53	3	920.40		920.40	42.75		
17022	Selma and Martin's Station	Birmingham, Selma and New Orleans Rwy.	21	3	628.53		628.53	29.93		
17023	Birmingham and Pratt Mines	Tennessee Coal, Iron and R.R. Co.	6.74	12	288.13		288.13	43.75		
17024	Elmore and Wetumpka	South and North Alabama R.R.	6.92	7	295.83		295.83	42.75		
17025	Tuscumbia and Florence	Memphis and Charleston R.R.	6.29	7	268.59		268.59	42.75		
17026	Flomaton and Repton	Louisville and Nashville R.R.	29.87	8	536.46		536.46	17.96		
17027	Montgomery and Pataburgh	Montgomery Southern Rwy.	40	6	1,154.74		1,154.74	23.94		12.50 miles, Argus to Pataburgh, at $23.23 per mile.
17028	Woodstock and Blockton	Cahaba Coal Mining Co.	8.67	12	291.99		291.99	33.67	33.67	

No.	Route	Railroad	Miles							Remarks
17029	Anniston and Sylacauga	Anniston and Atlantic R. R.	53.96	6			2,167.23	3,167.23	42.75	7.84 miles, Sycamore to Sylacauga, at $23.23 per mile.
17030	Talladega and Renfroe	Talladega and Coosa Valley R.R	25.12	6	1,131.88	1,131.88		1,131.88	42.75	10.96 miles, Renfroe to Pell City, at $46.17 per mile.
17031	Shelby Iron Works and Junction Station (n. o.),	Shelby Iron Co	6	6	188.54	188.54		188.54	28.09	
17032	Elora, Tenn., and Huntsville, Ala	Nashville, Chattanooga and Saint Louis Rwy.	27.62	6	873.63	873.63		873.63	31.63	
			2,842.52		229,660.02	250,069.52	20,410.50			
	MISSISSIPPI.								30.00	
16001	New Orleans, La., and Cairo, Ill.	Illinois Central R. R.	550.80	14	88,535.59	105,059.59	16,524.00		160.74	Not land grant.
16002	Memphis, Tenn., and Grenada, Miss.	Mississippi and Tennessee R. R.	102.34	7	7,963.07	7,963.07			77.61	
16003	Vicksburg and Meridian	Vicksburg and Meridian R. R	45.48	7	13,105.70	13,105.70			107.73	Land grant.
16004	Jackson and Meridian	Mobile and Ohio R. R.	95.21	7	29,343.91	29,343.91			88.19	All land grant.
16005	Mobile, Ala. and Cairo, Ill.	Georgia Pacific Rwy.	493.89	7	3,246.57	3,246.57			79.84	Pay not fixed on 33.96 miles.
16006	Columbus, Miss., and Coalburgh, Ala.		114.85	6					42.75	
16006	Glendale and Eagle's Nest	Mobile and Northwestern R.	21.00	9	448.76	448.76			21.37	
16007	Muldon and Aberdeen	Mobile and Ohio R. R.	9.50	7	422.87	422.87			44.46	7.65 miles, Cotton Plant to New Albany, at $27.63 per mile.
16008	Middleton, Tenn., and New Albany, Miss.	Ship Island, Ripley and Kentucky R R	44.00	6	2,183.80	2,183.80			52.16	
16009	Durant and Aberdeen	Illinois Central R. R.	108.20	7.23	5,648.92	5,648.92			52.16	
16010	Natchez and Jackson	Natchez, Jackson and Columbus R. R.	99.45	7	10,033.51	10,033.51			100.89	
16011	Greenville and Stoneville	Georgia Pacific Rwy	7.07	8	327.89	327.89			43.75	
16012	Greenwood and Pete	Illinois Central R. R.	18.12	3	971.83	971.83			20.53	
16013	Stoneville and Johnsonville	Georgia Pacific Rwy	29.54	8	614.76	614.76			20.80	
16014	Artesia and Columbus		13.55	7	728.94	728.94			53.87	
16015	Artesia and Starkville	Mobile and Ohio R. R.	11.90	7	535.57	535.57			45.17	
16016	Meridian, Miss., and New Orleans.	New Orleans and Northwestern R. R.	193.24	6	13,591.58	13,591.58			69.26	
	LA.									
16017	Vacant									
16018	Jackson and Shrwood	Illinois Central R. R.	94.83	6	6,083.97	6,083.97			61.56	
16019	La, Tenn., and New Orleans,	Louisville, New Orleans and Texas Rwy.	455.60	6	41,291.02	41,291.02			90.63	
16020	Leland, Miss., and Arkansas City, Ark.	...do	24.16	7	1,611.23	1,611.23			66.69	
16021	Memphis, Tenn., and Birmingham, Ala.	Kansas City, Memphis and Birmingham R. R.	251.20	6.16	15,166.13	15,166.13			43.61	205.23 miles, Holly Springs to Birmingham, at $44.12 per mile.
16022	Wilmiski Junction (n. o.) and Glen Allan.	Louisville, New Orleans and Texas Rwy.	24.91	7.57	1,512.06	1,512.06			44.46	

C.—*Railroad service as in operation on the 30th of June, 1888*—Continued.

Number of route.	State and terminal.	Corporate title of company carrying the mail.	Distance. (Miles.)	Average number of trips per week over whole route.	Annual pay for transportation. (Dollars.)	Annual pay for railway post-office cars. (Dollars.)	Total annual pay. (Dollars.)	Cost per mile for transportation. (Dollars.)	Cost per mile for railway post-office cars. (Dollars.)	Remarks.
	MISSISSIPPI—continued.									
18023	Durant and Tchula	Illinois Central R. R.	27.41	6	1,429.70		1,429.70	53.16		
			2,845.75		254,190.89	16,524.00	270,733.89			
	TENNESSEE.									
18001	Nashville and Lebanon	Nashville, Chattanooga and Saint Louis Rwy.	31.52	12	1,886.47		1,886.47	59.85		
18002	Bristol and Chattanooga	East Tennessee, Virginia and Georgia Rwy.	242.17	15.18	45,346.33	12,108.50	57,454.83	187.25	50.00	
18003	Rogersville and Bull's Gap	Rogersville and Jefferson R. R.	16.42	6	701.95		701.95	42.75		
18004	Nashville and Chattanooga	Nashville, Chattanooga and Saint Louis Rwy.	151.00	20	25,176.23		25,176.23	166.73		
18005	Fayetteville and Decherd	do	40.41	6	1,727.52		1,727.52	42.75		
18006	Nashville, Tenn., and Decatur, Ala.	Louisville and Nashville R. R.	122.78	14	18,847.19		18,847.19	147.06		
18007	Nashville, Tenn., and Hickman, Ky.	Nashville, Chattanooga and Saint Louis Rwy.	170.11	17.01	17,930.46		17,930.46	105.17		
18068	Knoxville and Jellico	East Tennessee, Virginia and Georgia Rwy.	65.63	7	5,106.67		5,106.67	77.81		
18009	Morristown and Kinsell (n. o.)	do	42.39	7	3,276.17		3,276.17	77.81		
18010	Tracy City and Cowan	Nashville, Chattanooga and Saint Louis Rwy.	20.25	7	865.08		865.08	42.75		
18011	Ooltewah, Tenn., and Cohutta, Ga.	East Tennessee, Virginia and Georgia Rwy.	11.85	6	820.73		820.73	69.26		
18012	Inman, Tenn., and Bridgeport, Ala.	Nashville, Chattanooga and Saint Louis Rwy.	24.84	6	1,061.90		1,061.90	42.75		
18013	Tullahoma and Sparta	do	62.07	6	3,678.03		3,678.03	49.59		
18014	Knoxville and Maryville	Knoxville and Augusta R. R.	17.78	6	760.09		760.09	42.75		
18015	Columbia and Fayetteville	Nashville, Chattanooga and Saint Louis Rwy.	48.87	6	2,089.19		2,089.19	42.75		
18016	Dickson and Ætna	Nashville and Tuscaloosa R. R.	44.38	6	1,401.01		1,401.01	31.64		
18017	Columbia and Saint Joseph	Nashville and Florence R. R.	56.74	6	2,425.63		2,425.63	42.75		
18018	Johnson City, Tenn., and Cranberry, N.C.	East Tennessee and Western North Carolina R. R.	33.50	6	1,444.96		1,444.96	43.76		
18019	Moscow and Somerville	Memphis and Charleston R. R.	13.49	6	576.69		576.69	42.75		

	Route	Railroad							Remarks
19920	Wartrace and Shelbyville....	Nashville, Chattanooga and Saint Louis Rwy.	8.36	15	365.98		365.98	46.17	
19921	Spring City and Balta.....	Tennessee Central R. R.	8.19	6	350.13		350.13	42.75	
19922	Keithley and Oliver Springs.	Walden's Ridge R. R.	16.74	6	715.63		715.63	42.75	
19923	Vacant.								
19924	Clarkville, Tenn., and Princeton, Ky.	Louisville and Nashville R. R.	57.53	6	1,694.73		1,694.73	28.23	27.83 miles, Newstead to Princeton, at $30.78 per mile.
19925	Victoria and Dunlap........	Nashville, Chattanooga and Saint Louis Rwy.	19.14	6	589.93		589.93	28.21	
19926	Gallatin, Tenn., and Scottsville, Ky.	Chesapeake and Nashville Rwy.	85.87	6	1,698.96		1,698.96	47.03	
			1,363.17		139,154.25	12,106.50	151,284.75		
	KENTUCKY.								
20001	Elkton and Guthrie........	Louisville and Nashville R. R.	11.95	6.54	510.96		510.96	42.75	
20002	Covington and Lexington...	Kentucky Central R. R.	94.85	18	13,270.96		13,270.96	134.24	
20003	La Grange and Lexington......	Louisville and Nashville R. R.	67.44	19	6,468.05		6,468.05	95.76	
20004	Cincinnati, Ohio, and Louisville, Ky.	Louisville and Nashville R. R.	110.10	25.21	42,406.18	6,560.00	35,866.18	325.78	60.00
20005	Louisville, Ky., and Nashville, Tenn.	do	185.00	23.8	66,394.00	11,100.00	55,294.00	298.40	60.00
20006	Truscelton and Springfield.....	do	37.29	6	1,785.13		1,785.13	42.75	
20007	Lebanon Junction, Ky., and Jellico, Tenn.	do	170.97	14	16,811.48		16,811.48	98.33	
20008	Bowling Green, Ky., and Memphis, Tenn.	do	263.15	14	52,434.73	7,894.50	52,434.73	199.22	30.00
20009	Louisville, Ky., and Memphis, Tenn.	Chesapeake, Ohio and Southwestern R. R.	389.40	9.9	32,296.83		32,296.83	82.94	
20010	Elizabethtown and Cecilian.	do	6.37	12	272.31		272.31	42.75	
20011	Glasgow Junction and Glasgow...	Louisville and Nashville R. R.	11.66	6	565.11		565.11	53.01	
24012	Anchorage and Shelbyville...	do	18.48	12	1,027.11		1,027.11	55.58	
20013	Willard and Greenup....	Eastern Kentucky R. R.	24.31	7.65	1,466.75		1,466.75	42.75	
20014	Owensborough and Adairville	Owensborough and Nashville R. R.	65.90	9.95	5,288.00		5,288.00	61.86	
20015	Maysville and Paris.....	Kentucky Central R. R.	50.17	13	3,774.79		3,774.79	75.24	
20016	Lexington, Ky., and Huntington, W. Va.	Chesapeake and Ohio Rwy.	140.30	13	13,785.86		13,785.86	98.33	
20017	Cincinnati Junction (n. o.) and Sax.	Louisville and Nashville R. R.	4.50	17	1,353.10	270.00	1,353.10	296.09	60.00
20018	Richmond and Livingston.....	Kentucky Central R. R.	34.62	6	1,565.50		1,565.50	42.75	
20019	Johnson Junction and Hillsborough.	Cincinnati and Southeastern R. R.	16.90	9.81	722.47		722.47	42.75	
20020	Cincinnati, Ohio, and Chattanooga, Tenn.	Cincinnati, New Orleans and Texas Pacific Rwy.	338.20	16.84	73,585.55	16,910.00	56,675.55	167.58	50.00
20021	Harrodsburgh and Harroosburgh Junction (n.o.).	Southwestern R. R.	5.44	18	251.16		251.16	46.17	
20022	Mount Sterling and Cornwell......	Kentucky and South Atlantic R. R.	18.75	6	801.56		801.56	42.75	
20023	Louisville and Prospect.	Louisville and Nashville R. R.	11.00	6	470.25		470.25	42.75	R. P. O. cars on 100 miles only. 18.65 miles, Bardstown to Springfield, at $52.01 per mile. Pay not fixed on 0.71 miles.
20024	Lebanon and Greensburgh	do	31.90	6	1,466.30		1,466.30	44.17	

C.—*Railroad service as in operation on the 30th of June, 1888—Continued.*

Number of route.	State and termini.	Corporate title of company carrying the mail.	Distance.	Average number of trips per week over whole route.	Annual pay for transportation.	Annual pay for railway post-office cars.	Total annual pay.	Cost per mile for transportation.	Cost per mile for railway post-office cars.	Remarks.
			Miles.		*Dollars.*	*Dollars.*	*Dollars.*	*Dollars.*	*Dollars.*	
	KENTUCKY—continued.									
20025	Vanest.									
20026	Shelbyville and Bloomfield.	Louisville and Nashville R. R.	27.75	12	1,186.31		1,186.31	42.75		
20027	Ashland and Richardson.	Chattard Rwy.	50.26	9	2,386.43		2,386.43	47.63		
20028	King's Mountain Station and Yo-semite.	Cincinnati and Green River Rwy.	11.43	9.73	488.20		488.20	42.75		
20029	Midway and Versailles.	Versailles and Midway Rwy.	7.58	21	337.00		337.00	44.46		
20030	Richmond Junction (n. o.) and Richmond.	Kentucky Central R. R.	34.21	9	1,701.43		1,701.43	49.50		
20031	Madisonville and Providence.	Louisville and Nashville R. R.	16.70	9	713.92		713.92	42.75		
20032	Paris and Richmond.	Kentucky Central R. R.	40.84	13.42	2,686.90		2,686.90	65.84		
20033	Dodge and Clay City.	Kentucky Union Rwy.	14.75	6	630.56		630.56	42.75		
20034	Henderson and Princeton.	Ohio Valley Rwy.	93.86	6	4,782.42		4,782.42	42.75		44.35 miles, Commercial Point to Princeton, at $68.27 per mile.
20035	Morganfield and Uniontown.	......do......	13.31	12	329.96		329.96	24.79		
20036	Glasgow Junction and Mammoth Cave.	Louisville and Nashville R. R.	8.51	14	263.72		263.72	21.94		
20037	Corbin and Pineville.	......do......	31.43	6						Pay not fixed.
20038	Elizabethtown and Hodgenville.	Hodgenville and Elizabeth-town R. R.	11.70	6						Do.
			2,562.34		319,486.78	42,714.50	362,201.28			
	OHIO.									
21001	{ Bellaire and Newark. { Newark and Columbus.	Central Ohio R. R.	105.47	20.54	22,297.34	4,218.80	27,516.14	194.94 / 82.34	40.00	
21002	Pittsburgh, Pa., and Chicago, Ill.	Pennsylvania Company.	468.20	30	170,134.51	23,410.00	193,544.51	363.38	50.00	
21003	Pittsburgh, Pa., and Bellaire, Ohio.	......do......	94.90	21.05	16,130.22		16,130.22	170.15		
21004	Hudson and Columbus.	Cleveland, Akron and Columbus Rwy.	143.15	15.07	11,417.49		11,417.49	78.66		
21005	Cleveland, Ohio, and Pymatuning, Pa. (n. o.)	New York, Lake Erie and Western R. R.	80.25	24.07	12,984.54		12,984.54	153.90		
2,006	Cleveland and Wellsville.	Pennsylvania Company.	101.29	19.9	20,957.91		20,957.91	206.91		Pay not fixed on 4.68 miles.
21007	Elyria and Millbury.	Lake Shore and Michigan Southern Rwy.	74.90	27.28	34,453.25	10,486.00	44,939.25	459.99	140.00	

No.	Route	Railroad					
21008	Bayard and New Philadelphia	Pennsylvania Company	32.41	6	2,078.45		2,078.45	64.13	
21009	Cleveland and Sherrodsville	Cleveland and Canton R. R.	103.24	13.98	4,015.97		4,015.97	65.58	
21010	Sandusky and Chicago		28	17.85	19,515.10	8,551.60	19,515.10	62.34	40.00
21011	Xenia and Dayton	Baltimore and Ohio R. R.	48.79	19	1,605.89		1,605.89	130.67	
			16.77					65.76	
21012	Springfield and Sandusky	Pittsburgh, Cincinnati and Saint Louis Rwy.	131.35	13.17	11,567.99		11,567.99	88.07	
21013	Columbus and Delaware	Cincinnati, Sandusky and Cleveland R. R.	25.51	20	3,293.59		3,293.59	129.11	
21014	Columbus and Cincinnati	Cleveland, Columbus, Cincinnati and Indianapolis Rwy.	120.05	28.55	43,529.53	12,005.00	43,529.53	362.59	100.00
21015	Columbus Ohio, and Indianapolis, Ind.	Pittsburgh, Cincinnati and Saint Louis Rwy.	188.55	21.55	134,933.92	42,428.75	134,933.92	715.64	225.00
21016	Galion, Ohio, and Indianapolis, Ind.	Chicago, Saint Louis and Pittsburgh R. R.	204.97	21.31	36,818.20	5,101.75	36,818.20	130.41	25.00
21017	Blanchester and Hillsborough	Cleveland, Columbus, Cincinnati and Indianapolis Rwy.	21	12	1,274.91		1,274.91	60.71	
21018	Portsmouth and Hamden Junction	Cincinnati, Washington and Baltimore R. R.	56	12	2,968.56		2,968.56	53.01	
21019	Toledo, Ohio, and La Fayette, Ind. La Fayette, Ind., and Decatur, Ill. Decatur, Ill., and Quincy, Ill.	do.	204.70	14.14	112,515.32	28,851.80	112,515.32	227.69	50.00 90.00 40.00
			117.40						
			151.37						
21020	Ohio, and Bloomington,	Wabash, Saint Louis and Pacific Rwy.	379.88	8.68	25,011.29		25,011.29	65.84	
21021	Carey and Findlay	Lake Erie and Western Rwy.	18	6	684.00		684.00	42.75	
21022	Dayton, Ohio, and Union City, Ind.	Cincinnati, Sandusky and Cleveland R. R.	47.32	12	2,680.04		2,680.04	55.00	
21023	Dayton and Toledo	Dayton and Union R. R.	142.28	12.55	22,521.95		22,521.95	158.18	
21024	Hamilton, Ohio, and Indianapolis, Ind.	Dayton and Michigan R. R.	96.83	15.5	8,109.19		8,109.19	81.23	
21025	Hamilton, Ohio, and Richmond, Ind.	Cincinnati, Hamilton and Indianapolis R. R.	45.00	19	5,008.41		5,008.41	111.15	
21026	Cincinnati and Dayton	Cincinnati, Richmond and Chicago R. R.	59.38	37.28	10,509.66		10,509.66	170.99	
21027	Xenia and Springfield	Cincinnati, Hamilton and Dayton R. R.	19.99	21	905.94		905.94	46.32	
21028	Cincinnati, Ohio, and Parkersburgh, W. Va.	Pittsburgh, Cincinnati and Saint Louis Rwy.	195.15	30	74,082.84	15,612.00	74,082.84	878.62	80.00
21029	Morrow and Dresden	Cincinnati, Washington and Baltimore R. R.	148.73	12	11,190.44		11,190.44	75.24	
21030	Dayton, Ohio, and Richmond, Ind.	Cincinnati and Muskingum Valley Rwy.	43.13	12.5	3,602.11		3,602.11	83.50	
21031	Harrison, Ohio, and Hagerstown, Ind	Pittsburgh, Cincinnati and Saint Louis Rwy.	63.08	8.4	3,565.98	62,361.25	3,565.98	55.58	325.00
21032	Columbus, Ohio, and Pittsburgh, Pa.	White Water R. R.	191.55	33.50	180,590.91		180,590.91	941.38	
21033	Columbus and Springfield	Pittsburgh, Cincinnati and Saint Louis Rwy.	46.03	12.50	4,407.83		4,407.83	95.76	
21034	Salamanca, N. Y., and Dayton, Ohio.	Indiana, Bloomington and Western Rwy.	389.21	20.9	49,916.18		49,916.18	128.25	
21035	Youngstown, Ohio, and Mahoning-town, Pa.	New York, Lake Erie and Western R. R.	18.40	9	786.60		786.60	42.75	
		Pennsylvania Company							

C.—*Railroad service as in operation on the 30th of June, 1878*—Continued.

Number of route	State and termini	Corporate title of company carrying the mail	Distance.	Average number of trips per week over whole route.	Annual pay for transportation.	Annual pay for railway post-office cars.	Total annual pay.	Cost per mile for transportation.	Cost per mile for railway post-office cars.	Remarks.
	OHIO—continued.		*Miles.*		*Dollars.*	*Dollars.*	*Dollars.*	*Dollars.*	*Dollars.*	
21036	Columbus and Athens	Columbus, Hocking Valley and Toledo Rwy.	77.44	18	7,018.38		7,018.38	90.63		
21037	Niles and New Lisbon	New York, Lake Erie and Western R. R.	34.85	12	1,758.18		1,758.18	50.45		
21038	Newark and Shawnee	Baltimore and Ohio R. R.	43.67	12	2,814.94		2,814.94	58.01		
21039	Delphos and Dayton	Dayton, Fort Wayne and Chicago Rwy.	92.35	5	5,906.25		5,906.25	63.97		
21040	Marietta and Zear Station	Cleveland and Marietta Rwy.	105.72	9.54	7,653.72		7,653.72	72.68		
21041	Lorain and Bridgeport	Cleveland, Lorain and Wheeling R. R.	158.41	9.94	12,325.58		12,325.58	77.81		
21042	Cleveland and Gallion; Gallion and Cincinnati	Cleveland, Columbus, Cincinnati and Indianapolis Rwy.	98.00 / 164.00	27.68 / 12	64,623.23	14,230.00	78,853.23	284.20	75.00 / 50.00	
21043	Mansfield and Toledo	Pennsylvania Company	98.20	12	5,085.80		5,085.80	59.00		Pay not fixed on 16.21 miles.
21044	Ashtabula and Youngstown		98.96	7.01	2,623.60		2,623.60	44.45		
21045	Toledo, Ohio, and Elkhart, Ind.	Lake Shore and Michigan Southern Rwy.	133.80	23.54	58,916.15	25,422.00	84,338.15	440.33	190.00	
21046	Painesville and Youngstown	Pittsburgh and Western Rwy.	61.98	6	2,074.29		2,074.29	45.32		
21047	Chicago, Ohio, and Chicago, Ill.	Baltimore and Ohio R. R.	271	20	43,877.59	10,840.00	54,717.59	189.29	40.00	
21048	Morgan Junction and Cumberland	Cincinnati, Wheeling and New York R. R.	17.70	9.53	754.67		754.67	42.75		
21049	Marietta, Ohio, and Parkersburgh, W. Va.	Cincinnati, Washington and Baltimore R. R.	15.06	17.50	1,121.90		1,121.90	74.39		
21050	Deshler and McComb	McComb, Deshler and Toledo R. R.	10.28	6	439.47		439.47	42.75		
21051	Columbus and Coal Grove	Scioto Valley Rwy.	132	13	16,265.36		16,265.36	123.98		
21052	Cincinnati and Portsmouth	Ohio and Northwestern R. R.	108	7.92	6,835.16		6,835.16	63.10		
21053	Columbus and Toledo	Columbus, Hocking Valley and Toledo R'wy.	124.57	18	9,579.78		9,579.78	76.10		
21054	Dayton and Ironton	Dayton, Fort Wayne and Chicago Rwy.	169.19	6	7,382.87		7,382.87	42.75		
21055	Toledo and Thurston	Toledo and Ohio Central Rwy	147.87	6.73	8,091.44		8,091.44	51.72		
21056	Saint Clairsville and Steel	Bellaire and Saint Clairsville Rwy.	7.28	12	311.22		311.22	42.75		
21057	Springfield, Ohio, and Indianapolis, Ind.	Indiana, Bloomington and Western Rwy.	189.51	19.50	13,859.47		13,859.47	95.76		

No.	Termini	Railroad	Miles					Remarks
21059	Wellston and Springfield	Ohio Southern R. R.	116.89	7.25	5,591.39	5,591.39	47.08	
21060	Junction with Cincinnati, Hamilton, and Dayton R. R. (n. o.) and Mount Healthy.	Cincinnati Northwestern Rwy	7.06	12	302.67	302.67	42.75	
31060	Columbia and Georgetown							
21061	Cincinnati, Georgetown and Portsmouth R. R.		42.17	12	2,848.58	2,848.58	07.55	
21062	Toledo and Delphos	Toledo, Saint Louis and Kansas City R. R.	74.10	0	4,668.31	4,668.31	63.97	
21063	Andover and Youngstown	Lake Shore and Michigan Southern Rwy.	38.84	12	2,656.05	2,656.05	68.40	
21064	Bellaire and Zanesville	Bellaire, Zanesville and Cincinnati Rwy.	112.57	8.29	5,101.67	5,101.67	45.82	
21065	Vacant.							
	Delphos, Ohio, and Kokomo, Ind.	Toledo, Saint Louis and Kansas City R. R.	108.02	0	4,967.28	4,967.28	46.17	
21066	Hillsborough and Sardinia	Ohio and Northwestern R. R.	19.50	6	867.81	867.81	45.53	Pay not fixed on 35.30 miles.
21067	Bergholz and Phalanx Station (n. o.)	Lake Erie, Alliance and Southern Rwy.	61.90	12	1,115.77	1,115.77	42.76	
21068	Columbus and Corning	Toledo and Ohio Central Rwy.	66.05	12	4,291.92	4,291.92	64.98	
21069	Thurston and Redfield	Columbus and Eastern R. R.	32.76	0	1,443.22	1,443.22	42.75	
21070	Tontogany and Bowling Green	Bowling Green R. R.	5.94	18	253.98	253.98	42.75	
21071	Valley Junction (n. o.) and Harrison	Cincinnati, Indianapolis, Saint Louis and Chicago Rwy.	7.40	12	512.81	512.81	70.11	
21072	Edison and Mount Gilead	Cleveland, Columbus, Cincinnati and Indianapolis Rwy.	2.40	18	102.60	102.60	42.75	
21073	Cleveland and Zoar Station	Valley Rwy.	76.12	10.92	5,532.40	5,532.40	72.98	
21074	Logan and Pomeroy	Columbus, Hocking Valley and Toledo Rwy.	53.71	12	6,790.76	6,790.76	81.23	
21075	Alvordton and Carlisle	Cincinnati, Jackson and Mackinaw R. R.	162.59	0	4,175.37	4,175.37	42.75	Pay not fixed on 64.92 miles.
21076	Akron, Ohio, and Mahoningtown, Pa.	Pittsburgh and Western R. R. Co., lessee of Pittsburgh, Cleveland and Toledo R. R.	78.10	0	4,607.90	4,607.90	59.00	
21077	Nelsonville and New Straitsville	Columbus, Hocking Valley and Toledo Rwy.	19.94	12	852.43	852.43	42.75	
21078	Cincinnati and Dodds	Northern Rwy.	36.20	10.92	3,631.01	3,631.01	72.08	
21079	Solon and Chagrin Falls	Chagrin Falls & Southern R. R.	5.57	18	247.64	247.64	44.46	10.00 miles, Zoar Station to Bowerston, at $925.40 per mile.
21080	Toledo and Bowerston	Wheeling and Lake Erie R. R.	171.66	6.84	10,560.34	10,560.34	60.71	
21081	Delphos and Carey	Cleveland and Western R. R.	56.60	0	2,419.65	2,419.65	42.75	
21082	Saint Mary's and Minster	Lake Erie and Western Rwy.	10.66	0	480.00	480.00	42.75	
21083	Means and Cadiz	Pittsburgh, Cincinnati and Saint Louis Rwy.	8.11	15	395.38	395.38	48.74	
21084	Logan and New Straitsville	Columbus, Hocking Valley and Toledo Rwy.	13.89	12	684.01	684.01	49.59	
21085	Vacant.	Pennsylvania Company	27.93	6	1,194.00	1,194.00	42.75	Pay not fixed on 11.06 miles.
21086	Alliance and Niles							
21087	Akron and Norwalk	Wheeling and Lake Erie R. R.	13.67	12	584.39	584.39	42.75	
21088	Corning and Gallipolis	Oh o Central R. R.	71.93	0	2,528.44	2,528.44	44.46	

C.—*Railroad service as in operation on the 30th of June, 1883*—Continued.

Number of route.	State and termini.	Corporate title of company carrying the mail.	Distance.	Average number of trips per week over whole route.	Annual pay for transportation.	Annual pay for railway post-office cars.	Total annual pay.	Cost per mile for transportation.	Cost per mile for railway post-office cars.	Remarks.
	OHIO—continued.		*Miles.*		*Dollars.*	*Dollars.*	*Dollars.*	*Dollars.*	*Dollars.*	
21089	Cleveland, Ohio, and Chicago, Ill.	New York, Chicago and Saint Louis R. R.	339.07	6.83	23,463.96		23,463.96	69.20		
21090	Marion, Ohio, and Chicago Junction (n.o.), Ind.	Chicago and Atlantic R. R.	249.95	6	13,962.22		13,962.22	55.58		
21091	Toledo and Findlay	Toledo, Columbus and Southern Ry.	44.02	6	1,881.98		1,881.98	42.75		
21092	Canton and Coshocton	Cleveland and Canton R. R.	54.73	6	2,714.06		2,714.06	49.59		Pay not fixed on 11.23 miles.
21093	New Gallilee, Pa., and New Lisbon, Ohio.	Pittsburgh, Marion and Chicago Rwy.	25.33	6	903.20		903.20	42.75		
21094	Columbus and Midland City	Columbus and Cincinnati Midland R. R.	72.73	12	4,160.70		4,160.70	57.20		
21095	Buffalo, N. Y., and Cleveland, Ohio. Cleveland and Elyra. Elyra and Millbury. Millbury and Toledo. Toledo, Ohio, and Elkhart, Ind. Elkhart, Ind., and Chicago, Ill.	Lake Shore and Michigan Southern Rwy.	188.20 25.50 79.30 8.00 142.70 101.80	87.41	462,164.40	142,805.00	604,969.40	853.88 855.88 855.88 855.88 855.88	380.00 365.00 215.00 140.00 380.00	7.83 miles, Big Run to Amsville, at 625.00 per mile. Pay not fixed on 4.57 miles.
21096	Marietta and Sharpsburgh	Marietta Mineral Rwy.	36.50	6	1,368.68		1,368.68	42.75		
21097	Saint Clairsville and Barton	The Saint Clairsville Company operating Saint Clairsville and Northern Rwy.	4.85	6	185.96		185.96	42.75		
21098	Ashtabula and Harbor	Ashtabula Street R. R., J. N. Stewart, proprietor.	4.00	6	171.00		171.00	42.75		
21099	Adelphi and Kingston	John Karshner, general manager Cincinnati, Hocking Valley and Huntington Rwy.	11.17	6	343.81		343.81	30.78		
21100	Zanesville and Waterford	Zanesville and Ohio River Rwy.	54.65	6	1,681.50		1,681.50	59.00		Pay not fixed on 28.16 miles.
21101	Danbury and Point Marblehead	Lakeside and Marblehead R. R.	8.00	12	342.00		342.00	42.75		

No.	Route	Railroad						Pay not fixed.
			84.14	9,766.40	1,040,555.78	399,308.95	2,339,864.73	
21109	Killbuck and Tridway ...	Cleveland, Akron and Columbus Rwy.						
	INDIANA.							
22001	Indianapolis and Vincennes ...	Pennsylvania Company ...	118.21	9.64	8,489.84	16,737.75	8,489.84	71.82	225.00
22002	Indianapolis and Terre Haute ...	Terre Haute and Indianapolis R.R.	74.39	83	50,565.11		67,302.86	679.73	225.00
22003	Indianapolis, Ind., and Cincinnati, Ohio.	Cincinnati, Indianapolis, Saint Louis and Chicago R.R.	111.40	83.05	34,669.91	10,926.00	44,666.91	311.22	90.00
22004	Indianapolis and Michigan City	Lake Erie and Western R.R.	161.62	16.54	13,128.39		13,128.39	81.23	
22005	Indianapolis and La Fayette	Cincinnati, Indianapolis Saint Louis and Chicago R.R.	64.79	21.66	22,435.48	5,831.10	23,266.58	346.28	90.00
22006	Columbus and Madison	Pennsylvania Company	45.75	12	8,520.46		8,520.46	76.95	
2.007	Jeffersonville and Indianapolis	...do	108.84	26.03	10,844.08		10,844.08	154.76	
2.008	Louisville Junction(n.o.) and Michigan City.	Louisville, New Albany and Chicago Rwy.	293.63	11.15	24,603.25		24,603.25	83.79	
22009	Richmond, Ind., and Chicago, Ill.	Chicago, Saint Louis and Pittsburgh R.R.	225.16	14.09	21,176.29		21,176.29	94.05	
22010	Cincinnati, Ohio, and East Saint Louis, Ill.	Ohio and Mississippi Rwy. ...	338.20	20.4	106,702.10	23,674.00	129,376.10	315.50	70.00
22011	Cambridge City and Columbus.	Pennsylvania Company	68.58	6	2,935.46		2,935.46	46.17	
2.012	Evansville and Terre Haute.	Evansville and Terre Haute R.R.	109.71	17.03	14,727.47		14,727.47	134.24	
22013	Terre Haute and South Bend.	Terre Haute and Indianapolis R.R.	186.49	6	10,842.52		10,842.52	58.14	
22014	State Line (n. o.) and Logansport.	Pittsburgh, Cincinnati and Saint Louis Rwy.	61.19	12	6,644.62		6,644.62	108.59	
22015	North Vernon and Rushville.	Cincinnati, Indianapolis, Saint Louis and Chicago R.R.	45.50	6	1,945.12		1,945.12	42.75	
22016	Fairland and Martinsville.	Fairland, Franklin and Martionsville R.R.	38.35	6	1,639.46		1,639.46	42.75	
22017	Bradford, Ohio, and Logansport, Ind.	Pittsburgh, Cincinnati and Saint Louis Rwy.	114.29	6	7,426.56		7,426.56	64.98	
22018	Indianapolis, Ind., and Peoria, Ill.	Indiana, Bloomington and Western Rwy.	213.02	15.09	29,505.40		29,505.40	138.51	
22019	Louisville, Ky., and North Vernon, Ind.	Ohio and Mississippi Rwy. ...	54.86	27	8,021.08		8,021.08	146.21	
22020	Fort Wayne and Connersville ...	Fort Wayne, Cincinnati and Louisville R.R.	109.54	7.35	6,275.54		6,275.54	57.29	
22021	Richmond and Fort Wayne.	Grand Rapids and Indiana R.R.	92.73	12	6,501.38		6,501.30	70.11	
22022	Anderson, Ind., and Benton Harbor, Mich.	Cincinnati, Wabash and Michigan Rwy.	164.68	7.08	10,700.90		10,700.00	64.98	
22023	Oakland City, Ind., and Mount Vernon, Ill.	Louisville, Evansville and Saint Louis Rwy.	88.56	13	4,619.28		4,619.28	52.16	
22024	Terre Haute, Ind., and Danville, Ill.	Chicago and Eastern Illinois R.R.	56.48	19	6,229.74		6,229.74	110.30	

C.—Railroad service as in operation on the 30th of June, 1889—Continued.

Number of route.	State and termini.	Corporate title of company carrying the mail.	Distance.	Average number of trips per week over whole route.	Annual pay for transportation.	Annual pay for railway post-office cars.	Total annual pay.	Cost per mile for transportation.	Cost per mile for railway post-office cars.	Remarks.
			Miles.		Dollars.	Dollars.	Dollars.	Dollars.	Dollars.	
	INDIANA—continued.									
22025	Indianapolis and Terre Haute......	Indianapolis and Saint Louis Rwy.	73.29	12.78	7,707.90		7,707.90	105.17		
22026	Worthington and Evansville......	Evansville and Indianapolis R. R.	57.70 / 40.69	6	4,757.72		4,757.72	42.75 / 56.43		
22027	Detroit, Mich., and Logansport, Ind	James P. Joy, Thomas H. Hubbard, Ossian D. Ashley, and Edgar T. Welles, purchasing committee of the bondholders of the Wabash, Saint Louis and Pacific Rwy. Co.	204.96	11.46	13,278.31		13,278.31	64.96		
22028	Lacrosse and Attica......	Chicago and Indiana Coal Rwy.	53.40	6	2,408.53		2,408.53	42.75	90.00	Pay not fixed on 27.08 miles.
22029	La Fayette, Ind., and Kankakee, Ill.	Cincinnati, La Fayette and Chicago R. R.	75.70	14.8	25,272.16	6,821.10	32,093.26	353.45		
22030	Terre Haute and Worthington......	Evansville and Indianapolis R. R.	40.98	6	1,821.97		1,821.97	44.44		
22031 22032	Attica and Brazil ...... Evansville and Jasper	Chicago and Indiana Coal Rwy Louisville, Evansville and Saint Louis Rwy.	63.42 55.13	12 18	3,199.52 3,676.62		3,199.52 3,676.62	50.45 66.69		
22033	Frankfort and Kokomo......	Toledo, Saint Louis and Kansas City R. R.	25.70	6	1,098.67		1,098.67	42.75		
22034	Bockport and Bockport Junction (n. o.).	Louisville, Evansville and Saint Louis Rwy.	16.20	18	775.66		775.66	47.88		
22035	New Salisbury and Corydon......	Louisville, New Albany and Corydon R. R.	8.39	6	358.57		358.57	42.76		
22036 22037	Britts City and Bedford ...... Anderson and Ladoga......	Bedford and Bloomfield R. R. Midland Rwy.	41.47 65.87	6 6	1,772.84 853.29		1,772.84 853.29	42.75 42.75		Pay not fixed on 45.91 miles.
22038	Indianapolis, Ind., and Chicago, Ill.	Louisville, New Albany and Chicago Rwy.	184.06	9.85	13,123.55		13,123.55	76.10		Pay between Hammond and Chicago, 20.70 miles, at $33.35 per mile.
22039	Fort Branch and Mount Vernon......	Evansville and Terre Haute R. R.	38.73	7.05	1,656.56		1,656.56	42.75		
22040	Vacant.									

No.	Route								Remarks
22911	Stewartsville and New Harmony	7.34	12	813.78		813.78	42.75		
22912	New Castle and Rushville	24.89	6	1,191.73		1,191.73	47.88		
22913	Terre Haute, Ind., and East Saint Louis, Ill.	190.13	18.85	18,045.23		18,045.23	84.91		
22914	Terre Haute, Ind., and East Saint Louis, Ill.	166.69	29.97	108,315.16	87,565.25	145,520.41	649.80	225.00	
22915	Lawrenceburgh Junction (n.o.), and Lawrenceburgh.	2.46	26	134.61		134.61	54.72		
22916	Frankfort, Ind., and East Saint Louis, R. R. Station (n.o.), Ill. Toledo, Saint Louis and Kansas City R. R. The H. Hub-	243.86	6	10,417.32		10,417.32	42.75		
22917	Attica and Corington, James C. Joy, Owen D. Ashley, and Edgar T. Welles, purchasing Committee of the .... ers of the Wabash, Saint Louis and Pacific Rwy. Co.	14.91	6	637.40		637.40	42.75		
22918	Louisville, Ky., and Oakland City, Ind., Evansville and Saint Louis Rwy.	90.55	18.53	7,319.91		7,319.91	73.53		
22919	Greensburgh and Columbus, St. Hope and Greens- bugh R. R.	25.90	8.76	1,149.97		1,149.97	42.75		
22950	Vacant.								Pay not fixed.
22951	Orleans and French Lick, French Lick Springs Rwy.	18.76	6						Do.
22952	Kerobeval and Cannelton, Louisville, Evansville and Saint Louis Rwy.	22.50	6						Do.
22953	Brazil and Saline City, Evansville and Indianapolis R. R.	12.31	6						
		4,846.22		649,437.46	100,595.20	750,032.66			
	ILLINOIS.								
2201	Chicago, Ill., and Milwaukee, Wis., Chicago and Northwestern Rwy.	85.40	22.90	18,181.66	2,135.00	20,316.66	213.90	25.00	
2202	Chicago and Freeport ......do	121.30	24.60	20,742.90	4,832.00	25,594.30	171.00	40.00	
993	Chicago, Ill., and Union Pacific Transfer (n.o.), Iowa. ......do	488.90	20.22	111,036.98	28,321.00	139,357.98	202.83 / 254.79	65.00 / 50.00 / 75.00	270.50 miles land grant, Cedar Rapids to U. P. Transfer (n.o.) R. P. O. 965 for 219.40 miles; $50 for 248.10 miles; and $75 for 21.40 miles.
2204	Elgin, Ill., and Lake Geneva, Wis.	43.79	16.87	1,981.56		1,964.56	45.22		
2205	Rock Island and East Saint Louis, Chicago, Burlington and Quincy R. R.	247.71	15.52	33,405.43		33,405.43	130.83		

C.—*Railroad service as in operation on the 30th of June, 1888—Continued.*

Number of route.	State and terminal.	Corporate title of company carrying the mail.	Distance.	Average number of trips per week over whole route.	Annual pay for transportation.	Annual pay for railway post-office cars.	Total annual pay.	Cost per mile for transportation.	Cost per mile for railway post-office cars.	Remarks.
	ILLINOIS—continued.		*Miles.*		*Dollars.*	*Dollars.*	*Dollars.*	*Dollars.*	*Dollars.*	
22006	Sidell and Olney	Chicago and Ohio River R. R.	86.31	6	3,281.20		3,321.20	38.48		R. P. O., $315 per mile for $7.50 miles; $290 per mile for 125.10 miles; and $250 per mile for 43.30 miles.
22007	Chicago, Ill., and Burlington, Iowa	Chicago, Burlington and Quincy R. R.	206.00	37.50	175,250.38	58,948.00	234,198.38	850.73	{315.00 / 290.00 / 250.00}	
22008	Rushville and Yates City	do	63.27	8.98	5,193.20		5,193.20	82.08		
22009	Peoria and Rio	do	66.10	19.19	7,742.96		7,742.96	117.14		
22010	Galesburg and Quincy	do	100.61	20	26,063.03		26,063.03	259.07		
22011	Burlington and Quincy	do	72.42	6	5,077.36	6,398.65	5,077.36	70.11	65.00	
22012	Streator and Aurora	do	60.97	12	6,307.95		6,307.95	108.48		
22013	Mendota and Fulton	do	64.82	14.00	3,824.38		3,824.38	59.00		
22014	Sterling and Shabbona	do	47.97	7.31	2,091.97		2,091.97	43.61		
22015	Chicago, Ill., and Davenport, Iowa	Chicago, Rock Island and Pacific Rwy.	182.63	21.83	45,127.87	11,870.95	56,998.82	247.10	65.00	
22016	Bureau and Peoria	Chicago and Alton R. R.	47.13	12	5,883.23		5,883.23	124.83		
22017	Chicago and East Saint Louis	do	281.10	10.02	77,389.64	22,488.00	99,877.64	275.31	80.00	
22018	Bloomington and Roodhouse	do	111.28	15.80	11,035.75		11,035.75	99.18		
22019	Washington and Dwight	do	70.12	7.61	3,477.25		3,477.25	46.59		
22020	Chicago and Cairo	Illinois Central R. R.	365.53	10.40	57,003.39	30,469.05	87,474.35	188.31	{140.00 / 50.00 / 23.00}	All land grant. R. P. O., $140 per mile for 55.87 miles; $50 per mile for 106.33 miles; and $23 per mile for 113.43 miles.
22021	Dubuque, Iowa, and Centralia, Ill.	do	343.27	14.82	45,078.21	4,834.15	49,912.36	131.23	{65.00 / 25.00}	All land grant. R. P. O., $65 per mile for 69.56 miles, and $25 per mile for 12.61 miles.
22022	Joliet, Ill., and Lake Station, Ind	Michigan Central R. R.	45.15	6	1,312.51		1,312.51	29.07		
22023	Decatur and East Saint Louis	Wabash, Saint Louis and Pacific Rwy.	113.66	20	23,376.35	5,682.00	34,059.35	249.08	50.00	
22024	Peoria, Ill., and Evansville, Ind	Peoria, Decatur and Evansville Rwy.	250.56	12	19,290.59		19,290.59	76.93		

No.	Route	Railway						
22025	Hannibal, Mo., and Bluffs, Ill	Wb. Saint Louis and Pacific Rwy.	50.36	18	5,166.93		5,166.93	102.00	
22026	Effingham, Ill., and Switz City, Ind	Indiana and Illinois Southern R.R.	90.07	6	3,888.96		3,888.96	42.75	
22027	State Line (n.o.) and Warsaw	Chicago, Peoria and Western Rwy.	229.20	12.75	25,475.58		25,475.58	111.15	
22028	Mound Junction and Mound City	Illinois Central R.R.	2.96	12	68.34		68.34	22.09	
22029	Champaign and Havana		101.64	6.91	5,966.78		5,966.78	59.00	
22030	East Saint Louis and El Dorado	Saint Louis, Alton and Terre Haute R.R.	121.65	14.18	15,706.23		15,706.23	129.11	
22031	Belleville and O'Fallon	Louisville and Nashville R.R.	6.80	9	145.38		145.38	21.38	
22032	East Saint Louis, Ill., and Nashville, Tenn.	do	318.78	15.13	50,150.46		50,150.46	157.32	
22033	Beardstown and Shawneetown	Ohio and Mississippi Rwy.	229.06	12	13,318.71		13,318.71	58.11	
22034	Springfield and Gilman	Illinois Central R.R.	112.71	12	7,323.59		7,323.59	64.98	
22035	Chicago, Ill., and Milwaukee, Wis.	Chicago, Milwaukee and Saint Paul Rwy.	85.98	37.68	60,354.52	17,196.00	60,354.52	70.96	200.00
22036	Aurora and Forreston	Chicago and Iowa R.R.	81.60	12	14,951.28		14,951.28	179.55	
22037	Vincennes, Ind., and Saint Francisville, Ill.	Anthony J. Thomas and Charles Edward Tracy, receivers of the Cairo Division of the Wabash, Saint Louis and Pacific Rwy.	10.88	13	567.50	2,940.00	567.50	52.18	25.00
22038	Peoria and Jacksonville	Chicago, Peoria and Saint Louis Rwy.	84.26	13	5,835.84		5,835.84	62.26	
22039	Carbondale and Grand Tower	Grand Tower and Carbondale R.R.	26.80	13	1,090.87		1,090.87	41.04	
22040	Peoria and Rock Island	Rock Island and Peoria Rwy	81.82	12	8,243.59		8,243.59	98.78	
22041	Quincy, Ill., and Hannibal, Mo.	Chicago, Burlington and Quincy R. R.	18.18	10.07	1,341.70		1,341.70	70.11	
22042	Chicago and Danville	Chicago and Eastern Illinois R.R.	124.68	22.77	17,995.83		17,995.83	141.93	
22043	Streator and Fairbury	Wabash, Saint Louis and Pacific Rwy.	32.05	9.68	981.09		981.09	29.07	
22044	Danville and Tuscola	Chicago and Eastern Illinois R. R.	56.49	8.79	2,257.70		2,257.70	45.81	
22045	Marion and Harrison Station (n.o.)	Saint Louis, Alton and Terre Haute R.R.	27.21	8.47	1,163.22		1,163.22	42.75	
22046	Jacksonville and Drivers	Wabash, Saint Louis and Pacific Rwy.	130.91	11.20	7,611.10		7,611.10	68.14	
22047	Chester and Tamaroa	Wabash, Chester and Western R. R.	42.90	11.76	2,861.00		2,861.00	66.69	
22048	Terre Haute, Ind., and Peoria, Ill.	Terre Haute and Peoria R.R.	177.60	6	10,021.96		10,021.96	58.43	
22049	Springfield and Havana	Chicago, Peoria and Saint Louis Rwy.	44.25	7.75	2,195.60		2,195.60	43.23	
22050	Danville and Cairo	Anthony J. Thomas and Charles Edward Tracy, receivers of the Cairo Division of the Wabash, Saint Louis and Pacific Rwy.	261.06	12.21	17,855.82		17,855.82	68.40	

C.—Railroad service as in operation on the 30th of June, 1888—Continued.

Number of route.	State and terminal.	Corporate title of company carrying the mail.	Distance.	Average number of trips per week over whole route.	Annual pay for transportation.	Annual pay for railway post-office cars.	Total annual pay.	Cost per mile for transportation.	Cost per mile for railway post-office cars.	Remarks.
	ILLINOIS—continued.		Miles.		Dollars.	Dollars.	Dollars.	Dollars.	Dollars.	
23051	Ancona and Pekin	Chicago, Santa Fé and California Rwy.	57.50	6	2,902.55		2,902.55	48.74		
23052	Courtland and Sycamore	Chicago and Northwestern Rwy.	4.94	9	101.36		101.36	20.52		
23053	East Saint Louis and Cairo	Mobile and Ohio R. R.	153.54	8.14	11,552.34		11,552.34	75.24		
23054	Chicago and Lanark Junction (n. o.)	Chicago, Milwaukee and Saint Paul Rwy.	116.60	17.60	23,027.82	3,915.00	26,942.82	202.64	25.00	
23055	Decatur, Ill., and Indianapolis, Ind.	Indianapolis, Decatur and Springfield Rwy.	154.26	13	16,467.30		16,467.30	104.88		
23056	Geneva and Aurora	Chicago and Northwestern Rwy.	10.31	30	573.02		573.02	55.58		
23057	Rochelle and Rockford	Chicago and Iowa R. R.	27.72	6	1,019.26		1,019.26	36.77		
23058	West Lebanon, Ind., and Le Roy, Ill	Illinois Central R. R.	74.99	6	2,949.35		2,949.35	39.33		
23059	Rock Island and Cable	Rock Island and Peoria Rwy.	27.35	6	935.37		935.37	34.20		
23060	Barnett and Kampsville	Litchfield, Carrollton and Western R. R.	52.42	8.61	2,151.31		2,151.31	41.04		
23061	Alton Junction (n. o.) and Chicago and Alton Junction (n. o.).	Indianapolis and Saint Louis Rwy.	4.20	12	158.00		158.00	37.62		
23062	Kankakee and Bloomington	Illinois Central R. R	86.38	7.95	3,249.61		3,249.61	37.62		
23063	Shumway and Effingham	Wabash, Saint Louis and Pacific Rwy.	9.24	6	537.21		537.21	58.14		
23064	Kempton and Kankakee Junction (n. o.).	Illinois Central R. R.	43.01	6	1,470.94		1,470.94	34.20		
23065	Sidney and Champaign	Wabash, Saint Louis and Pacific Rwy.	12.29	6	357.27		357.27	29.07		
23066	Chicago and Altamont	do	215.84	10.95	19,192.49		19,192.49	88.92		
23067	Havana and Galesburgh	Fulton County Narrow Gauge Rwy.	60.45	6	2,842.96		2,842.96	47.63		
23068	Peoria, Ill., and Oskaloosa, Iowa	Central Iowa Rwy.	191.20	6	9,323.96		9,323.96	48.74		
23069	Kankakee and Seneca	Kankakee and Seneca R. R.	43.56	6	1,154.77		1,154.77	26.51		
23070	Galva and Gladstone	Chicago, Burlington and Quincy R. R.	74.54	12	5,035.17		5,035.17	67.55		
23071	Aurora and Turner	do	13.01	6	323.64		323.64	24.80		
23072	Elmwood and Buda	do	44.98	6	2,692.05		2,692.05	59.45		
23073	Oregon, Ill., and Saint Paul, Minn.	Chicago, Burlington and Northern R. R.	833.31	11.14	27,074.77		27,074.77	81.23		

22074 22075	Varna and Lacon .... Mayville and Pittsfield	Chicago and Alton R. R. ..... Wabash, Saint Louis and Pacific Rwy.	10.66 6.90	12 19	291.96 337.21		291.96 337.21	21.90 40.50
22076	La Harpe, Ill., and Burlington, Iowa	Toledo, Peoria and Western Rwy.	20.10	12	670.33		670.33	33.35
22077 22078 22079	White Heath and Decatur ...... McLeansborough and Shawneetown Fall Creek, Ill., and Louisiana, Mo.	Illinois Central R. R. .... Louisville and ... Mo. R. R Chicago, Burlington and Quincy R. R.	31.98 41.22 32.10	6 6 6	1,613.39 1,586.14 1,390.88		1,613.39 1,586.14 1,390.88	50.45 38.46 43.61
22080	Wellington and Cleara Park	Chicago and Eastern Illinois R. R.	12.72	6	890.70		890.70	29.93
22081	Clayton, Ill., and Keokuk, Iowa ...	Wabash, Saint Louis and Pacific Rwy.	43.09	13	2,726.30		2,726.30	63.27
22082	Streator, Ill., and Knox, Ind.	Indiana, Ills. and Iowa R. R.	119.82	6	3,175.23		3,175.23	28.50
22083	Springfield and Grafton	Saint Louis and Gfral Illinois R. R.	85.30	12	4,081.16		4,081.16	47.88
22084	Sterling and Barstow	Chicago, Burlington and Quincy R. R.	40.75	13.62	2,264.88		2,264.88	55.58
22085	Murphysborough and Pickneyville	Saint Louis, Alton and Terre Haute R. R.	23.33	6.62	957.46		957.46	41.04
22086 22087	Buckingham and Clarke City ...... Caledonia and Spring Valley	Illinois Central R. R. .... Chicago and Northwestern Rwy.	9.77 86.20	6 6.72	199.45 3,611.78		199.45 3,611.78	20.52 41.90
22058	East Saint Louis and Belleville ...	East Saint Louis R. R. and Gl Co.	15.85	6	387.47		387.47	23.94
22089	Chicago, Ill., and Rugby Junction (n. o.).	Wisconsin and Minnesota R. R.	117.00	13	12,568.08		12,568.08	106.81
22090	Savanna and Fulton	Chicago, Burlington and Northern R. R.	18.57	13	1,047.90		1,047.90	55.43
22091	Galewood (n. o.) and Dunning......	Chicago, Milwaukee and Saint Paul Rwy.	2.60	12	57.45		57.45	29.52
22092	Galena and Galena Junction (n. o.)	Chicago, Burlington and Northern R. R.	3.79	13	77.77		77.77	30.52
22093 22094	Springfield and Litchfield .... Geneva and Saint Charles	Saint Louis and Chicago Rwy. Chicago and Northwestern Rwy.	45.64 3.21	6 21	2,185.24 128.24		2,185.24 128.24	47.88 39.33
22095	Chicago, Ill., and Dubuque, Iowa...	Chicago, Saint Paul and Kansas City Rwy.	167.33	6				Pay not fixed.
22096	Rockford and Rockton	Chicago, Milwaukee and Saint Paul Rwy.	16.37	15	1,805.44		1,805.44	110.29
22097	Marion and Parker City (n. o.)......	Saint Louis, Alton and Terre Haute R. R.	15.34	6	814.77		814.77	29.52
22098	Chicago, Ill., and Kansas City, Mo	Chicago, Santa Fé and California Rwy.	454.82	6				Do.
22099	Rondout and Libertyville	Chicago, Milwaukee and Saint Paul Rwy.	3.28	6	72.91		72.91	33.28
22100	Millstadt Junction (n. o.) and Millstadt.	Mobile and Ohio R. B	7	6				Do.
			9,373.44		1,183,658.60	188,291.80	1,370,945.40	

Number of route.	State and termini.	Corporate title of company carrying the mail.	Distance. (Miles.)	Average number of trips per week over whole route.	Annual pay for transportation. (Dollars.)	Annual pay for railway post-office cars. (Dollars.)	Total annual pay. (Dollars.)	Cost per mile for transportation. (Dollars.)	Cost per mile for railway post-office cars. (Dollars.)	Remarks.
	MICHIGAN.									
24001	Toledo, Ohio, and Detroit, Mich...	Lake Shore and Michigan Southern Rwy.	64.90	23	10,709.79		10,709.79	165.02		
24002	Monroe and Adrian...	do	34.90	14.15	2,478.85		2,478.85	70.97		
24003	Adrian and Jackson...	do	47.41	12	4,418.61		4,418.61	93.20		
24004	White Pigeon and Grand Rapids.	do	96.32	12	11,364.79		11,364.79	117.99		
24005	Jonesville and Lansing...	do	61.04	9.71	3,214.98		3,214.98	52.67		
24006	Detroit, Mich., and Chicago, Ill	Michigan Central R. R.	255.10	34.84	84,341.13	18,681.50	102,872.93	295.83	65.00	All land grant.
24007	Kalamazoo and South Haven.	do	40.18	12	1,820.95		1,820.95	45.23		
24008	Jackson and Niles...	do	104.30	3. 7	8,115.58		8,115.58	77.81		
24009	Jackson and Bay City...	do ...A...	114.81	12.78	10,267.31		10,267.31	103.46 / 62.77		{ Land grant, Lansing to Bay City, 77.36 miles.
24010	Jackson and Grand Rapids.	do	94.72	25	11,905.35		11,905.35	125.69 / 42.75		
24011	Slocum Junction (n. o.) and Grosse Isle.	do	2.36	6	100.89		100.89	42.75		
24012	Niles, Mich., and South Bend, Ind.	do	12.43	9	531.38		531.38	42.75		
24013	Detroit and Mackinaw City...	do	290.22	12.36	31,866.74		31,866.74	125.69 / 100.55		{ Land grant, Bay City to Mackinaw City, 182.22 miles.
24014	Saginaw and Caro...	do	34.04	14.00	1,629.83		1,629.83	47.88		
24015	Monroe and Ludington...	Flint and Pere Marquette R. R.	254.41	16.87	30,123.06		30,123.06	109.44 / 136.90		{ Land grant, Flint to Ludington, 171.06 miles.
24016	Ionia and Big Rapids...	Detroit, Lansing and Northern R. R.	68.09	10.44	5,472.30		5,472.30	80.37		
24017	Detroit and Howard City...	do	160.72	17.28	20,750.55		20,750.55	129.11		
29028	Fort Wayne, Ind., and Mackinaw City, Mich.	Grand Rapids and Indiana R. R.	368.90	15.91	86,434.88		86,434.88	96.45 / 120.56		{ Land grant, Fort Wayne to Petoskey, 332.48 miles.
24019	Toledo, Ohio, and Allegan, Mich...	Michigan and Ohio R. R...	156.92	6.67	6,135.11		6,135.11	43.61		
24020	Toledo, Ohio, and Emery, Mich...	Toledo, Ann Arbor and Grand Trunk Rwy.	52.00	10.51	2,801.24		2,801.24	53.87 / 12.83		{ Toledo to Dundee, 23 miles, at $12.83 per mile.
24021	Grand Rapids, Mich., and La Crosse, Ind.	Chicago and West Michigan Rwy.	154.54	15.64	18,631.34		18,631.34	120.56		

$29.92 per mile for 34.96 miles extension from Iron River to Watersmeet.

No.	Termini	Name of railway					
24022	Big Rapids and Holland	...do......	91.00	14.48	7,090.71	7,090.71	77.81
24023	Allegan and Holland	...do......	24.64	6	1,254.63	1,254.63	51.30
24024	Ypsilanti and Hillsdale	Lake Shore and Michigan Southern Rwy.	63.14	6	3,291.01	3,294.64	53.01
24025	Zion and East Saginaw	Port Huron and Northwestern Rwy.	78.85	12	3,640.50	3,640.50	46.17
24026	Grand Rapids and Baldwin	Chicago and West Michigan Rwy.	73.96	9.78	4,744.33	47,744.83	64.13
24027	Detroit and Grand Haven	Detroit, Grand Haven and Milwaukee Rwy.	189.96	22.90	26,905.87	26,905.87	142.70
24028	Detroit and Fort Gratiot	Chicago, Detroit and Canada Grand Trunk Junction R. R.	60.84	18.93	8,114.83	8,114.83	133.86
24029	Jackson, Mich., and Fort Wayne, Ind.	Lake Shore and Michigan Southern Rwy.	96.39	12.76	6,966.12	6,966.12	70.11
24030	East Saginaw and Ithaca	Saginaw Valley and Saint Louis R. R.	43.98	12.94	2,987.78	2,987.78	64.98
24031	Fort Howard, Wis., and Ishpeming, Mich.	Chicago and Northwestern Rwy.	178.45	8.69	19,394.95	19,394.95	108.08
24032	Powers and Crystal Falls	...do......	57.95	14	3,220.86	3,220.86	55.58
24033	Lenox and Jackson	Michigan Air Line Rwy.	106.58	7.76	5,882.05	5,882.05	64.72
24034	Walton and Traverse City	Traverse City R. R.	29.27	12	1,707.02	1,707.02	64.96
24035	Toledo, Ohio, and Detroit, Mich.	Michigan Central R. R.	59.50	28	10,438.16	10,438.16	175.28
24036	Trenton, Mich., and Fayette, Ohio.	Lake Shore and Michigan Southern Rwy.	68.40	7.57	3,090.88	3,090.88	45.32
24037	Saint Clair and Richmond	Michigan, Midland and Canada R. R.	16	12	766.06	766.06	47.98
24038	Iron River Junction (n. o.) and Watersmeet.	Chicago and Northwestern Rwy.	54.76	7	1,892.57	1,892.57	42.75
24039	Fort Gratiot, Mich., and Chicago, Ill.	Chicago and Grand Trunk Rwy.	338.46	12.16	26,044.49	26,044.49	76.95
24040	Marquette and Houghton	Marquette, Houghton and Ontonagon R. R.	95.93	6.90	5,708.79	5,708.79	59.51
24041	Alma and Howard City	Detroit, Lansing and Northern R. R.	42.73	12	2,557.39	2,557.39	50.85
24042	Fort Huron and Port Austin	Port Huron and Northwestern Rwy.	87.71	11.41	5,849.37	5,849.37	66.09
24043	Coleman and Mount Pleasant	Flint and Pere Marquette R. R.	15.04	12	642.96	642.96	43.75
24044	Harrison Junction (n. o.) and Meredith.	...do......	29.65	8.97	1,267.53	1,267.53	43.76
24045	Manistee Junction (n. o.) and Manistee.	...do......	27.13	15	2,203.76	2,203.76	81.23
24046	Mears and Hart	Chicago and West Michigan Rwy.	4.15	9	177.41	177.41	43.75
24047	Flint and Fostoria	Flint and Pere Marquette R. R.	24.46	6	1,045.66	1,045.66	43.75
24048	East Saginaw and Bay City	...do......	13.21	25	1,288.93	1,288.93	98.33
24049	Detroit and Bay City Crossing (n. o.) and Saginaw.	...do......	3.76	19	183.26	183.26	43.74

Number of route.	State and termini.	Corporate title of company carrying the mail.	Distance.	Average number of trips per week over whole route.	Annual pay for transportation.	Annual pay for railway post-office cars.	Total annual pay.	Cost per mile for transportation.	Cost per mile for railway post-office cars.	Remarks
			Miles.		*Dollars.*	*Dollars.*	*Dollars.*	*Dollars.*	*Dollars.*	
	MICHOAN—continued.									Pay not fixed.
24050	Missaukee Junction (n. o.) and Jennings.	Grand Rapids and Indiana R.R.	8.05	6						
24051	Point Saint Ignace (n. o.) and Marquette.	Duluth, South Shore and Atlantic Rwy.	151.37	6	6,471.06		6,471.06	42.75		
24052	Pestwater and Muskegon	Chicago and West Michigan Rwy.	45.13	11.02	2,701.03		2,701.03	60.86		
24053	Humboldt and Republic	Marquette, Houghton and Ontonagon R. R.	8.70	6	371.92		371.92	42.75		
24054	East Saginaw and Bad Axe	Saginaw, Tuscola and Huron R. R.	68.23	10.08	3,092.18		3,092.18	45.32		
24055	Grand Rapids and Muskegon	Muskegon, Grand Rapids and Indiana R.R.	39.50	6	2,938.01		2,938.01	74.88		
24056	Petoskey and Harbor Springs	Bayview, Little Traverse and Mackinaw R. R.	8.35	18	356.96		356.96	42.75		
24057	Alger and Alpena	Detroit, Bay City and Alpena R. R.	104.50	6	7,326.49		7,326.49	70.11		
24058	Narenta Station (n. o.) and Metropolitan.	Chicago and Northwestern Rwy.	35.01	6	1,496.67		1,496.67	42.75		
24059	Milton Junction (n. o.) and Copley	Grand Rapids and Indiana R.R.	14.18	16.79	606.19		606.19	42.75		
24060	Port Huron and Almont	Port Huron and Northwestern Rwy.	34.62	12	1,534.75		1,534.75	44.46		
24061	Palm Station and Sand Beach	do	18.83	12	804.98		804.98	42.75		
24062	Milwaukee Junction (n. o.) and West Detroit.	Chicago, Detroit and Canada Grand Trunk Junction R. R.	4.61	3	197.07		197.07	42.75		
24063	Lawton and Hartford	Paw Paw and Toledo and South Haven R. R.	20.31	10.02	868.97		868.97	42.75		
24064	Pontiac and Caseville	Pontiac, Oxford and Port Austin R. R.	100.73	6	4,565.08		4,565.08	45.32		
24065	Emery and Mount Pleasant	Toledo, Ann Arbor and North Michigan Rwy.	116.23	12.85	8,745.14		8,745.14	75.24		
24066	Cadillac and Lake City	Wellington W. Cummer, owner and manager of the Cadillac and Northeastern R. R.	13.65	12	568.53		568.53	42.75		
24067	Houghton and Calumet	Mineral Range R. R.	15.52	12	782.98		782.98	50.45		
24068	Hancock and Red Jacket	Hancock and Calumet R. R.	14.74	12	428.49		428.49	29.07		

24069 24070	Junction (n. o.) and Lake Linden Howard City and Grand Rapids.	......do.......... Detroit, Lansing and Northern R. R.	3.23 34.48	18 6	143.60 141.38		143.60 141.98	44.46 4.70	Lap service over route 24018. Pay not fixed.
24071 24072	Bessemer, Mich., and Mellen, Wis. Sault de St. Marie and Sault Junction (n. o.)	Penokee R. R............ Duluth, South Shore and Atlantic Rwy.	33.72 47.90	6 12		3,269.52	3,269.52	68.40 25.65	Do.
24073 24074	Pinconning and Gladwin............ Rodney and Chippewa Lake......	Michigan Central R. R. Detroit, Lansing and Northern R. R.	28.28 6.91	6 6	725.38		725.38		Do.
24075 24076	Vacant. Ashley and Muskegon............	Toledo, Saginaw and Muskegon Rwy.	96.24	6	4,069.77		4,069.77	48.73	
24077	Kalamazoo and Hastings............	Kalamazoo and Hastings Construction Co. (Limited), operating the Chicago, Kalamazoo and Saginaw Rwy.	31.08	6					Do.
	WISCONSIN.		5,577.18		514,320.73	18,531.50	532,852.23		
25001	Milwaukee, Wis., and North McGregor, Iowa.	Chicago, Milwaukee and Saint Paul Rwy.	195.98	15.52	32,172.07	4,899.50	37,061.57	25.00 164.16	
25002	Milwaukee and La Crosse	......do............	198.42	33.23	113,661.89	32,102.75	145,787.64	572.85	R. P. O., $175 per mile for $3.59 miles, Milwaukee to Portage; $150 per mile for 104.83 miles, Portage to La Crosse.
25003 25004 25005 25006 25007 25008	Milwaukee and Berlin.......... Milton Junction and Shullsburgh. Watertown and Madison....... Horicon and Portage........... Rush Lake and Winneconne ..... Oshkosh and Ripon.............	......do............ ......do............ ......do............ ......do............ ......do............ ......do............	97.22 75.50 38.97 52.24 14.84 20.40	12 11.40 12 7.27 6 12	10,639.75 8,391.07 3,765.28 4,064.79 444.16 1,779.08		10,639.75 8,391.07 3,765.28 4,064.79 444.16 1,779.08	{175.00 150.00 109.44 84.65 96.62 77.81 29.98 87.21	
25009	Chicago, Ill., and Fort Howard, Wis.	Chicago and Northwestern Rwy.	242.47	22.23	45,291.67	12,206.80	57,498.47	{197.51 158.00	65.77 miles land grant, Fond du Lac to Fort Howard. R. P. O., $80 per mile for 62.70 miles, Chicago to Harvard; $45 per mile for 179.77 miles, Harvard to Fort Howard.
25010	Caledonia, Ill., and Winona Junction (n. o.).	......do............	189.55	16.58	37,438.02	7,582.00	45,020.02	80.00 40.00 197.51	
25011	Kenosha, Wis., and Rockford, Ill.	......do............	73.71	11.16	7,438.60	600.00	8,038.60	40.00 100.99	R. P. O., Harvard to Caledonia, 15 miles.
25012 25013	Milwaukee and Fond du Lac ...... Vacant.	......do............	64.12	19	11,677.53		11,677.53	40.00 182.12	

Number of route.	State and termini.	Corporate title of company carrying the mail.	Distance.	Average number of trips per week over whole route.	Annual pay for transportation.	Annual pay for railway post-office cars.	Total annual pay.	Cost per mile for transportation.	Cost per mile for railway post-office cars.	Remarks.
			Miles.		Dollars.	Dollars.	Dollars.	Dollars.	Dollars.	
	WISCONSIN—continued.									
25014	Winona, Minn., and La Crosse, Wis	Chicago and Northwestern Rwy.	33.86	17.07	6,021.66	1,188.40	7,210.06	177.84	46.00	R. P. O. Winona to Winona Junction (n. o.), 20.71 miles. All land grant.
25015	Stevens Point and Portage	Wisconsin Central R. R.	74.13	6	4,563.44		4,563.44	61.56		
25016	Milwaukee and Republic	Milwaukee and Northern R. R.	256.04	11.77	22,109.05		22,109.05	86.35		{Milwaukee to Schlei-singerville, 32.99 miles, at $35 91 per mile. 187.25 miles land grant, Stevens Point to Ashland
25017	Milwaukee and Ashland	Wisconsin Central R. R	345.84	16.19	32,512.40		32,512.40	35.91 / 113.72 / 90.97		
25018	Milwaukee and Two Rivers	Milwaukee, Lake Shore and Western Rwy.	84.96	18.91	11,622.52		11,622.52	136.80		
25019	Sheboygan and Princeton	Chicago and Northwestern Rwy.	78.22	9.82	5,283.18		5,283.18	66.69		
25020	Warren, Ill., and Mineral Point, Iowa.	Chicago, Milwaukee and Saint Paul Rwy.	32.94	12	2,816.37		2,816.37	85.50		
25021	Calamine and Platteville	do	18.74	18	897.27		897.27	47.88		All land grant.
25022	New Lisbon and Necedah	do	13.09	18	559.59		559.59	42.75		
25023	Madison and Portage	do	38.40	6	2,048.64		2,048.64	53.35		R. P. O. Lanark Junction (n. o.) to Savanna 22 miles.
25024	Racine, Wis., and Rock Island, Ill.	do	197.85	10.25	25,882.73	550.00	26,432.73	130.83	25.00	
25025	Galena, Ill., and Woodman, Wis.	Chicago and Northwestern Rwy.	76.29	8.24	5,414.30		5,414.30	70.97		
25026	Eau Claire and Abbotsford	Wisconsin and Minnesota R.R.	66.39	19	6,982.23		6,982.23	165.17		
25027	Fort Howard, Wis., and Winona, Minn.	Green Bay, Winona and Saint Paul R. R.	214.88	6	14,515.14		14,515.14	67.55		
25028	Hudson and Bayfield	Chicago, Saint Paul, Minneapolis and Omaha Rwy.	181.11	13.27	13,255.44		13,255.44	73.19		All land grant.
25029	Lone Rock and Richland Centre	Chicago, Milwaukee and Saint Paul Rwy.	16.33	13	907.02		907.02	55.58		
25030	Elroy, Wis., and Saint Paul, Minn.	Chicago, Saint Paul, Minneapolis and Omaha Rwy.	198.00	26.26	22,332.18		22,332.18	113.54		Do.
25031	Tomah and Tomahawk	Chicago, Milwaukee and Saint Paul Rwy.	131.06	6	7,757.99		7,757.99	71.82		Pay not fixed on 23.04 miles.

No.	Between	Railway							All land grant.	Land grant, Superior Junction to Superior, 63 miles.
25033	Ashland Junction (n.o.) and Ashland	Chicago, Saint Paul, Minneapolis and Omaha Rwy.	4.63	13	294.51	294.51	291.51	63.61	......	
25033	River Falls Junction (n.o.) and Ellsworth	do	25.76	9	1,211.40	1,211.40	1,211.49	47.03	......	
25034	Sparta and Viroqua	Chicago, Milwaukee and Saint Paul Rwy.	35.76	6	2,017.93	2,017.93	2,017.93	56.43	......	
25035	Fond du Lac and Iron Ridge	do	28.72	12	1,031.33	1,031.33	1,031.33	35.91	......	
25036	Janesville and Beloit	do	15.72	12	443.61	443.61	443.61	28.23	......	
25037	Merrillon and Neillsville	Chicago, Saint Paul, Minneapolis and Omaha Rwy.	15.43	16.5	672.90	672.90	672.90	43.61	......	
25038	Milwaukee and Montfort	Chicago and Northwestern Rwy.	146.37	11.06	14,142.26	14,142.26	14,142.26	96.62	......	
25039	Mazo Manie, and Prairie du Sac	Chicago, Milwaukee and Saint Paul Rwy.	10.23	12	485.81	485.81	485.81	47.03	......	
25040	Hilbert and Appleton	Milwaukee and Northern R.R	21.94	9	750.34	750.34	750.34	34.20	......	
25041	Elkhorn and Eagle	Chicago, Milwaukee and Saint Paul Rwy.	17.56	6	360.33	360.33	360.33	20.52	......	
25042	Lancaster Junction (n.o.) and Lancaster.	Chicago and Northwestern Rwy.	12.28	12	1,061.49	1,061.49	1,061.49	88.07	......	
25043	Ipswitch and Platteville	do	4.38	12	153.56	153.56	153.56	35.06	......	
25044	Brodhead and New Glarus	Chicago, Milwaukee and Saint Paul Rwy.	22.90	12	861.49	861.49	861.49	37.62	......	
25045	Monico and Rhinelander	Milwaukee, Lake Shore and Western Rwy.	14.64	12	413.14	413.14	413.14	28.22	......	
25046	Oshkosh and Hortonville	do	23.77	9	853.58	853.58	853.58	35.91	......	
25047	Wabasha, Minn. and Eau Claire, Wis.	Chicago, Milwaukee and Saint Paul Rwy.	49.27	9.12	3,538.57	3,538.57	3,538.57	71.82	......	
25048	Eau Claire and Chicago Junction (n.o.).	Chicago, Saint Paul, Minneapolis and Omaha Rwy.	81.85	7.44	6,578.28	6,578.28	6,578.28	80.37	......	
25049	Manitowoc and Wausau	Milwaukee, Lake Shore and Western Rwy.	133.61	17.79	15,764.64	15,764.64	15,764.64	117.99	......	
25050	Eland and Watersmeet	do	105.46	14.16	10,552.21	10,552.21	10,552.21	100.04	......	
25051	Superior Junction (n.o.), Wis., and Duluth, Minn.	Chicago, Saint Paul, Minneapolis and Omaha Rwy.	70.83	13	4,132.30	4,132.30	4,132.90	56.77 / 70.97	......	
25052	Afton and Janesville	Chicago and Northwestern Rwy.	6.69	24.03	251.67	251.67	251.67	37.62	......	
25053	Red Cedar Junction (n.o.) and Menomonee.	Chicago, Milwaukee and Saint Paul Rwy.	14.38	6	812.28	812.28	812.28	49.50	......	
25054	Trempealeau and Galesville	Chicago and Northwestern Rwy.	8.23	15	295.53	295.53	295.53	35.91	......	
25055	Brandon and Markesan	Chicago, Milwaukee and Saint Paul Rwy.	11.91	6	386.95	386.95	386.95	32.49	......	
25056	Dexterville Junction (n.o.) and Vesper.	Wisconsin, Pittsville and Superior Rwy.	20.87	7.53	517.57	517.57	517.57	24.80	......	
25057	Menominee, Mich., and Colvitz, Wis.	Milwaukee and Northern R.R.	22.90	13	765.71	765.71	765.71	33.35	......	
25058	Clintonville and Oconto	Milwaukee, Lake Shore and Western Rwy.	56.75	12	2,765.99	2,765.99	2,765.99	48.74	......	

C.—*Railroad service as in operation on the 30th of June, 1888*—Continued.

Number of route.	State and terminal.	Corporate title of company carrying the mail.	Distance.	Average number of trips per week over whole route.	Annual pay for transportation.	Annual pay for railway post-office cars.	Total annual pay.	Cost per mile for transportation.	Cost per mile for railway post-office.	Remarks.
			Miles.		*Dollars.*	*Dollars.*	*Dollars.*	*Dollars.*	*Dollars.*	
	WISCONSIN—continued.									
25059	Minneapolis, Minn., and Sault de St. Marie, Mich.	Minneapolis, Sault Ste. Marie and Atlantic Rwy.	492.19	6	1,254.18	....	1,254.18	27.35	....	Pay not fixed on 78.51 miles, Turtle Lake to Minneapolis, and on 373.84 miles, Brace to Sault de St. Marie.
25060	Antigo and Malcolm	Milwaukee, Lake Shore and Western Rwy.	13.37	6	274.35	....	274.35	20.52	....	
25061	Chippewa Falls, Wis., and Saint Paul, Minn.	Minnesota, Saint Croix and Wisconsin R. R.	104.63	13	10,556.12	....	10,556.12	104.89	....	
25062	Needah Junction (n.o.) and Needah	Chicago and Northwestern Rwy.	16.48	9.30	338.16	....	338.16	20.52	....	
25063	Watermeet, Mich., and Ashland, Wis.	Milwaukee, Lake Shore and Western Rwy.	98.42	7	8,331.25	....	8,331.25	84.65	....	
25064	Jamesville and Evansville	Chicago and Northwestern Rwy.	16.75	12	2,649.51	....	2,649.51	158.18	....	
25065	Dexterville and Hogan	Wisconsin, Pittsville and Superior Rwy. Company, lessee of the Milwaukee, Dexterville and Northern Rwy.	15.72	6	....	....	....	....	....	Pay not fixed.
25066	Chelsea and Rib Lake	Wisconsin Central R. R.	6.35	6	....	....	....	....	....	Do.
			5,074.27		554,786.60	59,129.45	613,916.05			
	MINNESOTA.									
26001	Saint Paul, Minn., and Missoula, Mont.	Northern Pacific R. R.	1,280.02	8.73	248,015.94	11,902.50	260,518.44	238.40 / 191.53	25.00	1,297.62 miles land grant, Saint Paul to Minneapolis, and Wadab to Missoula, and R. P. O. Saint Paul to Mandan, 476.10 miles.
26002	Vacant.									
26003	Vacant.									
26004	Saint Cloud and Saint Vincent	Saint Paul, Minneapolis and Manitoba Rwy.	314.85	9.73	41,132.00	....	41,132.00	130.64	....	All land grant.

No.	Route	Railway							Remarks
25032	Ashland Junction (n. o.) and Ashland	Chicago, Saint Paul, Minneapolis and Omaha Rwy.	4.63	13	294.51		294.51	63.61	All land grant.
25033	River Falls Junction (n. o.) and Ellsworth.	do	25.76	9	1,211.40		1,211.49	47.03	
25034	Sparta and Viroqua	Chicago, Milwaukee and Saint Paul Rwy.	35.76	6	2,017.93		2,017.93	56.43	
25035	Fond du Lac and Iron Ridge	do	28.72	12	1,031.33		1,031.33	35.91	
25036	Janesville and Beloit	do	15.72	12	443.61		443.61	28.22	
25037	Merrillon and Neillsville	Chicago, Saint Paul, Minneapolis and Omaha Rwy.	15.43	16.5	672.90		672.90	43.61	
25038	Milwaukee and Montfort	Chicago and Northwestern Rwy.	146.37	11.06	14,142.26		14,142.26	96.62	
25039	Mazo Manie and Prairie du Sac	Chicago, Milwaukee and Saint Paul Rwy.	10.33	12	485.81		485.81	47.03	
25040	Hilbert and Appleton	Milwaukee and Northern R.R.	21.94	9	750.34		750.34	34.20	
25041	Elkhorn and Eagle	Chicago, Milwaukee and Saint Paul Rwy.	17.56	6	360.33		360.33	20.52	
25042	Lancaster Junction (n. o.) and Lancaster.	Chicago and Northwestern Rwy.	12.28	12	1,081.49		1,081.49	88.07	
25043	Ipswitch and Platteville	do	4.38	12	153.56		153.56	35.06	
25044	Brodhead and New Glarus	Chicago, Milwaukee and Saint Paul Rwy.	22.90	12	861.49		861.49	37.62	
25045	Monico and Rhinelander	Milwaukee, Lake Shore and Western Rwy.	14.64	12	413.14		413.14	28.22	
25046	Oshkosh and Hortonville	do	23.77	9	853.58		853.58	35.91	
25047	Wabasha, Minn. and Eau Claire, Wis.	Chicago, Milwaukee and Saint Paul Rwy.	49.27	9.12	3,538.57		3,538.57	71.82	
25048	Eau Claire and Chicago Junction (n. o.).	Chicago, Saint Paul, Minneapolis and Omaha Rwy.	81.85	7.44	6,578.29		6,578.29	80.37	
25049	Manitowoc and Wausau	Milwaukee, Lake Shore and Western Rwy.	133.61	17.70	15,764.64		15,764.64	117.99	
25050	Eland and Waternmeet	do	165.46	14.16	10,552.21		10,552.21	100.04	
25051	Superior Junction (n. o.), Wis., and Duluth, Minn.	Chicago, Saint Paul, Minneapolis and Omaha Rwy.	70.83	13	4,132.90		4,132.20	56.77 / 70.97	Land grant, Superior Junction to Superior, 63 miles.
25052	Afton and Janesville	Chicago and Northwestern Rwy.	6.69	24.05	251.67		251.67	37.03	
25053	Red Cedar Junction (n. o.) and Menomonee.	Chicago, Milwaukee and Saint Paul Rwy.	16.38	6	812.28		812.28	49.50	
25054	Trempealeau and Galesville	Chicago and Northwestern Rwy.	8.23	15	295.53		295.53	35.91	
25055	Brandon and Markesan	Chicago, Milwaukee and Saint Paul Rwy.	11.91	6	386.95		386.95	32.49	
25056	Dexterville Junction (n. o.) and Vesper.	Wisconsin, Pittsville and Superior Rwy.	20.87	7.53	517.57		517.57	24.80	
25057	Menominee, Mich., and Crivitz, Wis.	Milwaukee and Northern R. R. and	22.98	12	785.71		785.71	33.35	
25058	Clintonville and Oconto	M	54.75	12	2,785.99		2,785.99	48.74	

Number of route.	State and termini.	Corporate title of company carrying the mail.	Distance.	Average number of trips per week over whole route.	Annual pay for transportation.	Annual pay for railway post-office cars.	Total annual pay.	Cost per mile for transportation.	Cost per mile for railway post-office cars.	Remarks.
	MINNESOTA—continued.		Miles		Dollars.	Dollars.	Dollars.	Dollars.	Dollars	
26035	Junction (n. o.) and Boundary Line (n. o.).	Saint Paul, Minneapolis and Manitoba Rwy.	2.15	7	294.12		294.12	136.80		
26036	North Pacific Junction and Cloquet.	Saint Paul and Duluth R. R.	6.67	6	188.22		188.22	28.22		
26037	Minneapolis and Cologne.	Chicago, Milwaukee and Saint Paul Rwy.	33.16	13	5,160.02		5,160.02	155.61		
26038	Minneapolis and Birch Cooley.	Minneapolis and Saint Louis Rwy.	100.99	6	8,461.95		8,461.95	83.79		
26039	Crookston, Minn., and Devil's Lake, Dak.	Saint Paul, Minneapolis and Manitoba Rwy.	114.55	8	11,067.82		11,067.82	96.62		
26040	Minneapolis and Saint Cloud.	....do....	66.30	13	12,414.67		12,414.67	187.25		
26041	Vacant.									
26042	Wadena, Minn., and Milnor, Dak.	Northern Pacific, Fergus and Black Hills R. R.	119.31	6	5,815.16		5,815.16	48.74		
26043	Fergus Falls and Pelican Rapids.	Saint Paul, Minneapolis and Manitoba Rwy.	23.58	6	786.39		786.39	33.35		
26044	Mendota and Minneapolis.	Chicago, Milwaukee and Saint Paul Rwy.	10.17	13	521.72		521.72	51.30		All land grant.
26045	Hastings and Stillwater.	....do....	28.12	19	1,228.42		1,228.42	47.03		
26046	Little Falls and Morris.	Little Falls and Dakota R. R.	88.31	6	3,926.26		3,926.26	44.46		
26047	Sauk Centre and Eagle Bend.	Saint Paul, Minneapolis and Manitoba Rwy.	36.91	6	1,262.32		1,262.32	34.20		
26048	Mankato and Red Wing.	Minneapolis and Saint Louis Rwy.	95.16	6	3,999.17		3,999.17	59.85		Pay not fixed on 28.34 miles extension from Waterville to Mankato.
26049	Saint Cloud and Hinckley.	Saint Paul, Minneapolis and Manitoba Rwy.	65.24	6	1,575.66		1,575.66	23.09		
26050	Crookston and Saint Hilaire.	....do....	28.30	4	580.71		580.71	20.52		
26051	Rush City, Minn., and Grantsburgh, Wis.	Saint Paul and Duluth R. B.	17.17	6	395.45		395.45	23.09		
26052	Moorhead and Halstad.	Saint Paul, Minneapolis and Manitoba Rwy.	34.51	4	845.84		845.84	24.80		
26053	Birch Cooley, Minn., and Watertown, Dak.	Wisconsin, Minnesota and Pacific Rwy.	123.39	6	8,545.90		8,545.90	69.20		
26054	Duluth and Tower.	Duluth and Iron Range R. R.	96.27	6	2,963.19		2,963.19	30.78		

No.	Route	Railroad	Miles							Remarks
26055	Saint Paul and Lyle	Minnesota and Northwestern R.R.	109.51	17 48	11,968.05		11,968.05		109.44	
26056	Glencoe and Hutchinson	Chicago, Milwaukee and Saint Paul Rwy.	14.24	12	547.95		547.36		38.48	
26057	Saint Cloud and Willmar	Saint Paul, Minneapolis and Manitoba Rwy.	56.69	6	3,061.27		3,061.27		52.16	
26058	Minneapolis, Minn., and Fairmount, Dak.	Minneapolis and Pacific Rwy.	192.30	6	9,207.32		9,207.32		47.88	
26059	Elk River and Milaca	Saint Paul, Minneapolis and Manitoba Rwy.	33.12	6	877.68		877.68		26.50	
26060	Hutchinson Junction (n.o.) and Hutchinson	do	53.40	6						Pay not fixed.
26061	Winnipeg Junction, Minn., and Pembina, Dak.	Northern Pacific R.R.	200.15	6						Do.
26062	Saint Paul and Cardigan Junction (n.o.).	Minneapolis, Sault Ste. Marie and Atlantic Rwy.	8	6						Do.
			6,730.41		802,899.66	45,394.25	842,203.91			
	IOWA.									
27001	Burlington, Iowa, and Albert Lea, Minn.	Burlington, Cedar Rapids and Northern Rwy.	252.70	16.24	37,811.50		37,811.50		149.63	
27002	Cedar Rapids and Decorah	do	122.21	6	8,350.16		8,350.16		68.40	
27003	Cedar Rapids, Iowa, and Watertown, Dak.	do	390.56	9.52	33,520.90		33,520.90		15.39 / 88.07	Service to Vinton, 23.10 miles, at $15.59 per mile.
27004	Muscatine and What Cheer	do	76.02	6.93	4,978.76		4,978.76		64.98	
27005	Burlington and Union Pacific Transfer (n.o.)	Chicago, Burlington and Quincy R.R.	294.00	16.66	151,279.24	73,500.00	234,779.24	250.00	506.84 / 633.56	276.10 miles land grant, Burlington to Pacific Junction
27006	Charlton, Iowa, and Grant City, Mo.	do	63.91	9.69	7,949.48		7,949.48		84.65	
27007	Creston, Iowa, and Hopkins, Mo.	Chicago, Burlington and Kansas City Rwy.	44.27	13	5,904.73		5,904.73		133.38	
27008	Burlington, Iowa, and Carrollton, Mo.		230.57	6	17,539.72		17,539.72		79.52	
27009	Villisca, Iowa, and Burlington Junction, Mo.	Chicago, Burlington and Quincy R.R.	37.54	6	2,471.63		2,471.63		65.81	
27010	Albia, Iowa, and Lyle, Minn.	Central Iowa Rwy.	198.71	13	22,426.41		22,426.41		112.98	
27011	Keokuk and Burlington	Chicago, Burlington and Quincy R.R.	43.26	13	6,916.84		6,916.84		159.89	
27012	Clinton, Iowa, and Lacrosse, Wis.	Chicago, Milwaukee and Saint Paul Rwy.	181.79	15.19	23,485.40	2,482.50	27,917.90	25.00	141.93 / 112.54	10.79 miles land grant, from near Dubuque south to Tété des Morts Creek. R.P.O., 96.90 miles, Sabula to McGregor
27013	Stanwood and Tipton	Chicago and Northwestern Rwy.	8.94	12	344.01		344.01		38.48	

C.—Railroad service as in operation on the 30th of June, 1888—Continued.

Number of route.	State and termini.	Corporate title of company carrying the mail.	Distance. (Miles.)	Average number of trips per week over whole route.	Annual pay for transportation. (Dollars.)	Annual pay for railway post-office cars. (Dollars.)	Total annual pay. (Dollars.)	Cost per mile for transportation. (Dollars.)	Cost per mile for railway post-office cars. (Dollars.)	Remarks.
	IOWA—continued.									
27014	Davenport and Union Pacific Transfer (n. o.).	Chicago, Rock Island and Pacific Rwy.	317.97	19.01	46,541.26	16,708.05	63,249.31	146.37	63.90 / 50.00	All land grant. R. P. O., $965 per mile for 53.97 miles, Davenport to Iowa City, and $50 per mile resid'ue.
27015	Des Moines and Indianola	do	22.54	12.78	1,580.27		1,580.27	70.11		
27016	Washington and Knoxville	do	78.78	12.07	5,725.73		5,725.73	72.08		
27017	Davenport, Iowa, and Leavenworth, Kans.	do	338.77	14.85	48,081.62		48,081.62	141.93		
27018	Davenport and Maquoketa	Chicago, Milwaukee and Saint Paul Rwy.	43.97	7.74	2,143.09		2,143.09	48.74		
27019	Keokuk and Des Moines	Chicago, Rock Island and Pacific Rwy.	163.04	12	14,916.52		14,916.52	91.49		
27020	Farley and Cedar Rapids	Chicago, Milwaukee and Saint Paul Rwy.	57.87	9.07	4,354.13		4,354.13	75.24		All land grant.
27021	Dubuque and Sioux City	Illinois Central R. R.	327.70	12.43	40,792.09		40,792.09	124.48		
27022	Waterloo, Iowa, and Lyle, Minn	do	82.12	12	7,653.58		7,653.58	93.20		
27023	Beula and Elkader	Chicago, Milwaukee and Saint Paul Rwy.	19.52	6	767.72		767.72	39.33		
27024	Clinton and Anamosa	Chicago and Northwestern Rwy.	72.07	6	4,276.87		4,276.87	47.88 / 59.85		3.05 m..es land grant, Clinton to Lyons. 210.56 miles land grant, Calmar to Sheldon Junction.
27025	Calmar, Iowa, and Running Water, Dak.	Chicago, Milwaukee and Saint Paul Rwy.	250.06	10.92	45,543.59		45,543.59	116.23 / 147.92		
27026	Conover and Decorah	do	9.51	18	780.58		780.58	82.08		
27027	Davenport and Calmar	do	165.73	7.12	15,446.03		15,446.03	93.20		
27028	Savanna and Union Pacific Transfer (n. o.).	do	352.37	13.06	46,396.55	85.50	46,482.05	131.67	25.00	R. P. O., Savanna to Sabula, 3.43 miles. R.P.O., $50 per mile for 6.15 miles, Missouri Valley to California, $25 per mile for 70.12 miles, residue.
27029	Missouri Valley and Sioux City	Sioux City and Pacific R. R.	76.27	17.99	14,803.24	2,080.50	16,883.74	194.09	50.00 / 25.00	

No.	Route	Railroad	Miles	Trips					Remarks
29055	Saint Paul and Lyle	Minnesota and Northwestern R. R.	109.51	17 43	11,968.05		11,968.03	109.44	Pay not fixed.
29056	Glencoe and Hutchinson	Chicago, Milwaukee and Saint Paul R'wy.	14.24	12	547.95		547.25	38.48	Do.
29057	Saint Cloud and Willmar	Saint Paul, Minneapolis and Manitoba Rwy.	58.69	6	3,061.27		3,061.27	52.16	Do.
29058	Minneapolis, Minn., and Fairmount, Dak.	Minneapolis and Pacific Rwy.	192.30	6	9,207.32		9,207.32	47.88	
29059	Elk River and Milaca	Saint Paul, Minneapolis and Manitoba Rwy.	33.12	6	877.68		877.68	28.50	
29060	Hutchinson Junction (n. o.) and Hutchinson.	do	53.40	*					
29061	Winnipeg Junction, Minn., and Pembina, Dak.	Northern Pacific R. R.	200.15	6					
29062	Saint Paul and Cardigan Junction (n. o.).	Minneapolis, Sault Ste. Marie and Atlantic Rwy.	8	6					
			6,730.41		802,899.06	45,394.25	843,203.91		
	IOWA.								
27001	Burlington, Iowa, and Albert Lea, Minn.	Burlington, Cedar Rapids and Northern Rwy.	252.70	16.24	37,811.50		37,811.50	149.63	Service to Vinton, 23.10 miles, at $15.39 per mile.
27002	Cedar Rapids and Decorah	do	122.21	6	8,359.16		8,359.16	68.40	
27003	Cedar Rapids, Iowa, and Watertown, Dak.	do	399.68	9.52	33,520.90		33,520.90	15.39 / 88.07	
27004	Muscatine and What Cheer	do	76.03	6.93	4,978.76		4,978.76	64.98	
27005	Burlington and Union Pacific Transfer (n. o.).	Chicago, Burlington and Quincy R. R.	294.00	16.66	151,779.24	73,500.00	224,779.24	500.84 / 633.56	276.10 miles land grant, Burlington to Pacific Junction
27006	Chariton, Iowa, and Grant City, Mo.	do	93.91	9.69	7,949.48		7,949.48	84.65	$250.00
27007	Creston, Iowa, and Hopkins, Mo.	do	44.27	13	5,904.73		5,904.73	133.38	
27008	Burlington, Iowa, and Carrollton, Mo.	Chicago, Burlington and Kansas City Rwy.	220.57	6	17,539.72		17,539.72	79.52	
27009	Villisca, Iowa, and Burlington Junction, Mo.	Chicago, Burlington and Quincy R. R.	37.54	6	2,471.63		2,471.63	65.81	
27010	Albia, Iowa, and Lyle, Minn.	Central Iowa Rwy.	198.71	13	22,426.41		22,426.41	112.98	
27011	Keokuk and Burlington	Chicago, Burlington and Quincy R. R.	43.26	13	6,916.84		6,916.84	159.80	
27012	Clinton, Iowa, and Lacrosse, Wis.	Chicago, Milwaukee and Saint Paul Rwy.	181.79	15.19	25,465.40	2,452.50	27,917.90	141.93 / 112.54	$25.00 — 10.78 miles land grant, from near Dubuque south to Tété des Morts Creek. R. P. O., 96.90 miles, Sabula to McGregor
27013	Stanwood and Tipton	Chicago and Northwestern Rwy.	8.94	12	844.01		844.01	38.48	

Number of route.	State and terminal.	Corporate title of company carrying the mail.	Distance.	Average number of trips per week over whole route.	Annual pay for transportation.	Annual pay for railway post-office cars.	Total annual pay.	Cost per mile for transportation.	Cost per mile for railway post-office cars.	Remarks.
	IOWA—continued.		*Miles.*		*Dollars.*	*Dollars.*	*Dollars.*	*Dollars.*	*Dollars.*	
27059	Menlo and Guthrie Centre	Chicago, Rock Island and Pacific Rwy.	14.96	12	652.40		652.40	43.61		
27060	Harvey and Des Moines	Wabash Western Rwy.	43.52	6	2,716.51		2,716.51	62.42		
27061	Bethany Junc. (n. o.), Iowa, and Albany, Mo.	Chicago, Burlington and Quincy R. R.	46.12	13	3,943.28		3,943.28	85.50		
27062	Mount Zion and Keosauqua	Chicago, Rock Island and Pacific Rwy.	4.97	12	169.97		169.97	34.20		
27063	Arcoa and Carson	Fort Madison and Northwestern Rwy.	17.79	12	775.82		775.82	43.61		Pay not fixed on 3.44 miles extension from Birmingham to Collett.
27064	Fort Madison and Collett	do	45.12	6	1,068.06		1,068.06	25.65		
27065	Thornburgh and Monkenuna	Burlington, Cedar Rapids and Northern Rwy.	16.33	6	781.88		781.88	47.88		
27066	Jewell and Wall Lake Junc. (n. o.)	Chicago and Northwestern Rwy.	73.50	6	6,032.88		6,032.88	82.06		
27067	Van Wert and Shenandoah	Humeston and Shenandoah R. R.	96.77	6	6,784.54		6,784.54	70.11		
27068	Newburgh and State Centre	Central Iowa Rwy.	27.00	6	623.43		623.43	23.09		
27069	Hudson and Oelwein	Chicago, Saint Paul and Kansas City Rwy.	35.92	13	2,364.61		2,364.61	65.83		
27070	Eagle Grove, Iowa, and Iroquois, Dak.	Chicago and Northwestern Rwy.	271.67	7.65	30,894.31		30,894.31	113.72		
27071	Carroll and Kirkman	do	35.07	12	1,829.25		1,829.25	52.16		
27072	Clinton and Elmira (n. o.)	Burlington, Cedar Rapids and Northern Rwy.	69.53	6	3,032.20		3,032.20	43.61		
27073	Pacific Junc., Iowa, and Plattsmouth, Nebr.	Chicago, Burlington and Quincy R. R.	5.64	27	1,038.90	141.00	1,179.90	160.89 208.62	25.00	(3.30 miles land grant; Pacific June, to East Plattsmouth (n. o.).
27074	Red Oak, Iowa, and Nebraska City, Nebr.	do	53.67	7.57	4,634.94		4,634.94	86.36		
27075	Webster City and Lehigh	Webster City and Southwestern Rwy.	17.83	6	411.00		411.00	23.09		
27076	Summerset and Winterset	Chicago, Rock Island and Pacific Rwy.	27.70	12	1,871.13		1,871.13	67.55		
27077	California, Iowa, and Fremont, Nebr	Sioux City and Pacific R. R.	32.01	13	5,864.23	800.25	6,164.48	167.50	25.00	

No.	Termini	Railroad company							Remarks
27078	Hampton and Belmond	Central Iowa Rwy	22.96	0	810.40		810.40	22.23	
27079	Marshalltown and Story City	do	39.14	0	1,104.53		1,104.53	28.22	
27080	Manning and Audubon	Chicago and Northwestern Rwy	17.95	12	874.88		874.88	48.74	
27081	Des Moines and Boone	Saint Louis, Des Moines and Northern Rwy	43.06	0	2,208.97		2,208.97	51.30	
27083	Winfield and Oskaloosa	Burlington and Western Rwy	71.35	7.77	3,721.61		3,721.61	52.18	
27083	Clarinda and Northborough	Quincy, Burlington and Southern R. R.	18.90	0	995.58		995.58	53.61	
27084	Des Moines, Iowa, and Cainsville, Mo.	Des Moines, Osceola and Southern R. R.	112.13	0	4,218.33		4,218.33	37.62	
27085	Lake Park, Iowa, and Worthington, Minn.	Burlington, Cedar Rapids and Northern Rwy.	18.80	0	819.86		819.86	43.61	
27086	Vacant.								
27087	Tara and Ruthven	Des Moines and Fort Dodge R. R.	55.40	0	3,565.15		3,565.15	63.27	
27088	Eldora Junction and Alden	Chicago, Iowa and Dakota Rwy.	26.42	7.20	971.46		971.46	38.77	
27089	Sac City and Moville	Chicago and Northwestern Rwy.	67.41	11.18	4,322.32		4,322.32	64.12	
27090	Wilton Junction and Muscatine	Chicago, Rock Island and Pacific Rwy.	12.75	15	719.48		719.48	58.43	
27091	Near Sharon and Newton	Central Iowa Rwy.	33.80	0	1,206.57		1,206.57	35.91	
27092	Indianola and Avon Junction (n. o.)	Chicago, Burlington and Quincy R. R.	14.47	13	965.00		965.00	66.09	
27093	Relay (n. o.) and Albia	Centerville, Moravia and Albia R. R.	24.53	0	798.97		798.97	32.49	
27094	Waverly Junc. (n. o.) and Waverly	Burlington, Cedar Rapids and Northern Rwy.	0.00	12	138.54		138.54	23.09	
27095	Hayfield, Minn., and Dubuque, Iowa	Minnesota and Northwestern R. R.	172.68	6.51	14,322.07		14,322.07	82.94	
27096	Spencer and Spirit Lake	Chicago, Milwaukee and Saint Paul Rwy.	21.99	12	808.57		808.57	38.77	
27097	Mason City, and Fort Dodge	Mason City and Fort Dodge R. R.	72.05	0	3,497.63		3,497.63	47.88	
27098	Sioux City and Manilla	Chicago, Milwaukee and Saint Paul Rwy.	90.70	13	10,546.59		10,546.59	116.28	
27099	Cherokee and Onawa		61.18	0					Pay not fixed.
27100	Cherokee, Iowa, and Sioux Falls, Dak.	Cherokee and Dakota R. R.	97.07	0					Do.
27101	Cedar Rapids and Manchester	Illinois Central R. R.	42.58	0					Do.
27102	Union Pacific Transfer (n. o.) and Broadway Depot in Council Bluffs.	Union Pacific Rwy	1.76	0					Do.
			8,240.57	23.63	863,504.63	95,717.80	970,222.43	{490.33 / 624.15} {150.00	
	MISSOURI.								
28001	Saint Louis, Mo., and Atchison, Kans.	Missouri Pacific Rwy	330.17	23.63	201,468.10	42,468.00	243,956.10		36.75 miles land grant, Saint Louis to Pacific. R. P. O. $160 per mile for 283.12 miles, Saint Louis to Kansas City.

Number of route.	State and termini.	Corporate title of company carrying the mail.	Distance.	Average number of trips per week over whole route.	Annual pay for transportation.	Annual pay for railway post-office cars.	Total annual pay.	Cost per mile for transportation.	Cost per mile for railway post-office cars.	Remarks.
	MISSOURI—continued.		*Miles.*		*Dollars.*	*Dollars.*	*Dollars.*	*Dollars.*	*Dollars.*	
28002	Saint Louis and Bismarck	Saint Louis, Iron Mountain and Southern Rwy.	75.33	40.03	23,637.80	4,806.45	28,534.25	313.79	65.00	
28003	Saint Louis, Mo., and Vinita, Ind. T.	Saint Louis and San Francisco Rwy.	359.70	12.57	56,343.40	14,105.00	70,448.40	156.04	50.00	Allland grant. R. P. O. Saint Louis to Monett, 282.10 miles.
28004	Saint Louis and Kansas City	Wabash Western Rwy.	277.46	23.12	60,020.14	13,873.00	73,893.14	216.32	50.00	Allland grant. R. P. O. Quincy to Cameron, 171.24 miles.
28005	Quincy, Ill., and Saint Joseph, Mo.	Hannibal and Saint Joseph R. R.	207.55	18.95	38,612.60	11,130.60	49,743.20	188.04	65.00	
28006	Kansas City, Mo., and Union Pacific Transfer (n. o.) Iowa.	Kansas City, Saint Joseph and Council Bluffs R.R.	201.22	24.32	45,763.46	5,030.50	50,793.96	227.43	25.00	
28007	Moberly, Mo. and Ottumwa, Iowa.	Wabash Western Rwy	131.54	13	17,544.80		17,544.80	133.38		
28008	Versailles and Boonville	Missouri Pacific Rwy	44.25	9.43	2,724.03		2,724.03	61.56		
28009	Centralia and Columbia	Wabash Western Rwy	22.14	14	1,438.65		1,438.65	64.98		
28010	Kansas City and Cameron	Hannibal and Saint Joseph R. R.	55.06	20	13,291.65	3,580.20	15,871.85	233.16	65.00	
28011	Sedalia, Mo., and Denison, Tex.	Missouri Pacific Rwy.	433.13	14	105,491.62	10,828.25	116,319.87	194.99 / 246.24	25.00	{23.60 miles land grant, Parsons to Chetopa.
28012	Saint Joseph and Henry	Saint Joseph and Saint Louis R.R.	73.48	13	6,533.84		6,533.84	88.92		
28013	Brunswick and Pattonsburgh	Wabash Western Rwy.	78.99	13	10,258.71		10,258.71	128.25		
28014	Hannibal and Sedalia	Missouri Pacific Rwy.	143.85	17.38	21,816.43		21,816.43	152.19		
28015	Keokuk, Iowa, and Van Wert, Iowa	Keokuk and Western R. R.	149.32	8.67	9,681.46		9,681.46	58.14		
28016	Raymore Junction (n. o.), Mo., and Olathe, Kans.	Kansas City, Clinton and Springfield Rwy.	28.50	11.21	1,427.55		1,427.55	63.87		
28017	Springfield, Mo., and Memphis, Tenn.	Kansas City, Fort Scott and Memphis R. R.	285.40	15.55	34,162.88		34,162.88	119.70		
290 8	Mount Pleasant, Iowa, and Saint Peter's, Mo.	Saint Louis, Keokuk and Northwestern R. R.	189.27	11.12	28,481.34		28,481.34	150.46		
28019	Quincy, Ill., and Trenton, Mo.	Quincy, Omaha and Kansas City Rwy.	137.53	6	9,760.50		9,760.50	70.97		
28020	Pierce City, Mo., and Halstead, Kans.	Saint Louis and San Francisco Rwy.	242.97	14	27,268.61		27,268.61	119.70 / 47.88		{$47.88 per mile for 25.27 miles, Wichita to Halstead.
28021	Mexico and Cedar City	Chicago and Alton R. R.	50.34	6	2,840.68		2,840.68	56.43		

No.	Termini	Railroad							Remarks
982	East Saint Louis, Ill., and Kansas City, Mo		321.00	20.78	43,814.96		42,814.96	133.38	
28023	Cuba Station (n. o.) and Salem	Saint Louis and San Francisco Rwy	40.41	0	1,694.07		1,694.07	40.19	
28024	Holden, Mo., and Paola, Kans	Missouri Pacific Rwy	54.47	11.18	6,520.05		6,520.05	119.70	
28025	Slater and Glasgow	Wabash Western Rwy	15.81	6	361.45		361.45	22.23	
9826	..., Mo., and Texarkana, Ark	Missouri Pacific Rwy	414.28	16.08	95,018.46	26,928.20	121,917.06	217.51 / 271.80	$65.00 {324 miles land grant, Poplar Bluff to Texarkana.
28027	..., Ill., and Poplar Bluff, Mo	Saint Louis, Iron Mountain and Southern R. R.	74.87	7	3,635.68		3,635.68	48.56	
28028	Saint Joseph and Hopkins	Kansas City, Saint Joseph and Council Bluffs R. R.	59.80	13	7,771.80		7,771.80	129.90	
28029	Hannibal and Gilmore	Saint Louis and Hannibal Rwy.	98.41	11.30	5,836.99		5,836.99	67.55	
28030	Saint Joseph, Mo., and Atchison, Kans.	Hannibal and Saint Joseph R. R.	22.19	14	2,675.22		2,675.22	120.56	
28031	Saint Louis and Florissant	Saint Louis, Cable and Western Rwy.	15.65	6	361.35		361.35	23.09	
28032	Atchison, Kans., and Atchison Junction, Mo.	Chicago, Rock Island and Pacific Rwy.	29.24	8.48	2,100.01		2,100.01	71.82	
28033	Independence and Sedalia	Missouri Pacific Rwy.	89.22	14	7,094.77		7,094.77	79.52	
28034	Bismarck, Mo., and Columbia, Ky.	Saint Louis, Iron Mountain and Southern Rwy.	121.34	14	11,931.36		11,931.36	98.33	
28035	Neelyville and Doniphan	...do	20.04	6	855.71		855.71	42.75	
28036	Fort Scott, Kans., and Springfield,	Kansas City, Fort Scott and Memphis R. R.	104.32	14	14,360.60		14,360.60	137.66	
28037	Saint Joseph and Albany	Chicago, Burlington and Quincy R. R.	49.63	13	4,455.78		4,455.78	89.78	
28038	North Springfield and Bolivar	Saint Louis and San Francisco Rwy.	40.05	7	1,849.10		1,849.10	46.17	
28039	Monett, Mo., and Fort Smith, Ark.	...do	133.44	7	13,805.70		13,805.70	103.46	
28040	Pleasant Hill and Joplin	Missouri Pacific Rwy.	133.47	14.53	16,547.61		16,547.61	123.96	
28041	Miami, Kans., and Carbon Centre, Mo.	Kansas City, Fort Scott and Memphis R. R.	24.05	6.2	994.76		994.76	37.62	
28042	Sedalia and Warsaw	Missouri Pacific Rwy.	43.16	6	2,066.50		2,066.50	47.88	
28043	Summitville and Bonne Terre	Saint-Joe Railway	13.20	19	417.64		417.64	31.64	
28044	Bigelow and Burlington Junction	Kansas City, Saint Joseph and Council Bluffs R. R.	32.12	6	1,840.15		1,840.15	57.29	
28045	Cape Girardeau and Chaonia	Cape Girardeau Southwestern Rwy.	58.51	8.04	2,447.91		2,447.91	47.03	Pay not fixed on 6.46 miles, Wappapello to Chaonia.
28046	Corning, Mo., and Northborough, Iowa.	Kansas City, Saint Joseph and Council Bluffs R. R.	27.74	0	1,375.62		1,375.62	49.59	
9847	Jefferson City and Bagnell	Missouri Pacific Rwy.	45.71	6	2,110.43		2,110.43	48.17	
9848	Allenville and Jackson	Saint Louis, Iron Mountain and Southern Rwy.	16.80	6	560.28		560.28	83.35	
28049	Mineral point and Potosi	...do	4.43	13	132.56		132.56	29.98	
28050	Palmyra and Hannibal	Hannibal and Saint Joseph R. R.	15.58	20	852.53		852.53	54.72	

Number of route.	State and termini.	Corporate title of company carrying the mail.	Distance.	Average number of trips per week over whole route.	Annual pay for transportation.	Annual pay for railway post-office cars.	Total annual pay.	Cost per mile for transportation.	Cost per mile for railway post-office cars.	Remarks.
	MISSOURI—continued.		*Miles.*		*Dollars.*	*Dollars.*	*Dollars.*	*Dollars.*	*Dollars.*	
28051	Bird's Point, Mo., and Texarkana, Ark.	Saint Louis, Arkansas and Texas Rwy. Co. in Arkansas and Missouri.	417.92	7	32,518.35		32,518.35	77.81		
28052	Paw Paw (n.o.) and New Madrid..	do	6.95	13	297.54		297.54	42.75		
28053	North Springfield and Chadwick.	Saint Louis and San Francisco Rwy.	36.63	7	1,558.82		1,558.82	43.61		
28054	Oronogo and Galena	do	12.44	15.97	1,306.18		1,306.18	71.82		
28055	Clinton and Brownington.......	Kansas City and Southern Rwy.	43.40	6	1,203.55		1,203.55	26.51		
28056	Raymore Junction (n.o) and Ash Grove.	Kansas City, Clinton and Springfield Rwy.	129.30	7	6,637.70		6,637.70	51.30		
28057	Altamont (n.o.) and Rushville.	Saint Joseph and Iowa R.R.	65.68	13	7,412.64		7,412.64	112.96		Pay not fixed.
28058	Nevada, Mo., and Chetopa, Kans	Nevada and Minden Rwy.	77.88	7	5,491.65		5,491.65	70.97		
28059	Marshall and Myrick Station (b.o.).	Missouri Pacific Rwy.	47.82	6						
28060	Cameron and Kansas City	Chicago, Rock Island and Pacific Rwy.	55.06	13	470.76		470.76	8.55		
28061	Pattonsburgh, Mo., and Council Bluffs, Iowa.	Omaha and Saint Louis Rwy.	144.61	7	14,342.41		14,342.41	99.18		
28062	Saint Louis and Union.........	Saint Louis, Kansas City and Colorado R.R.	59.91	6	1,997.99		1,997.99	33.35		
28063	Greenfield and Watkins........	Greenfield and Northern R.R.	3.46	14	130.16		130.16	37.62		
28064	Napier (n.o.), Mo., and Rulo "Y." (n.o.) Nebr.	Burlington and Missouri River R.R. Co. in Nebraska.	11.07	6						Do.
28065	Brownwood and Bollinger's Mills.	Cape Girardeau Southwestern Rwy.	8.68	6						Do.
28096	Union depot, Saint Louis, Mo., and termini of all railroads at East Saint Louis, Ill.	Saint Louis Union Railroad and the Tunnel Railroad Company of Saint Louis, Mo.			25,000.00		25,000.00			
			6,751.65		1,067,361.48	132,840.30	1,200,201.68			
	ARKANSAS.									
29001	Memphis, Tenn., and Little Rock, Ark.	Memphis and Little Rock R.R.	135	14	15,066.00		15,066.00	115.00		All land grant.
29002	Helena and Clarendon......	Arkansas Midland R.R.	49.77	6	2,084.91		2,084.91	42.75		

No.	Termini	Name of railroad						
29003	Little Rock Fort Smith	Little Rock and Fort Smith Rwy.	166	7	11,719.08	11,719.08	60.76	All land grant
29004	Trippe and Warren	Saint Louis, Iron Mountain and Southern Rwy.	40.25	0	2,278.87	2,278.87	46.17	
29005	Malvern and Hot Springs	Hot Springs R. R.	23.40	14	2,106.67	2,106.67	82.01	
29006	Brinkley and Jacksonport	Batesville and Brinkley R. R.	57.39	6	2,564.47	2,564.47	42.75	
			3.51	} 7.38			31.61	
2967	Little Rock and Arkansas City	Saint Louis, Iron Mountain and Southern Rwy.	113.75		8,753.06	8,753.06	74.90	
29008	Forrest City and Helena	do	44.65	7	2,901.35	2,901.35	64.99	
29009	Nashville and Hope	Arkansas and Louisiana Rwy.	27.58	14	1,624.27	1,624.27	59.00	
29010	Gurdon and Camden	Saint Louis, Iron Mountain and Southern Rwy.	37.07	0	1,643.13	1,643.13	44.46	
29011	Searcy and Kensett	Searcy and West Point R. R.	4.76	21	232.00	232.00	48.74	
29012	Knobel and Forrest City	Saint Louis, Iron Mountain and Southern Rwy.	97.76	2.50	6,519.61	6,519.61	06.09	
29013	Seligman and Eureka Springs	Eureka Springs Rwy.	20.82	14	1,459.69	1,459.69	70.11	
29014	Newport and Cushman	Saint Louis, Iron Mountain and Southern Rwy.	40.57	7	2,046.35	2,046.35	50.44	
29015	McNeil and Magnolia	Saint Louis, Arkansas and Texas Rwy. Co. in Arkansas and Missouri.	6.72	7	287.28	287.28	42.75	
29016	Varner and Cummins	Varner Branch R. R., Urquhart & Green, lessees.	5.75	0	245.81	245.81	42.75	
29017	Smithton and Okolona	Southwestern Arkansas and Indian Territory R. R.	14.58	0	623.29	623.29	42.75	
29018	Rogers and Bentonville	Bentonville R. R.	7.05	13	307.45	307.45	43.61	
29019	Fort Smith, Ark., and Paris, Tex	Saint Louis and San Francisco Rwy.	166.93	7	12,132.54	12,132.54	71.82	
29020	Pine Bluff and English	Pine Bluff, Monroe and New Orleans Rwy.	34.42	0	934.17	934.17	25.05	
29021	Fayetteville and Saint Paul	Saint Louis and San Francisco Rwy.	35.56	0	1,686.49	1,686.49	47.00	
29022	Arkadelphia and Dalark	Ultima, Thule, Arkadelphia and Mississippi Rwy.	11.43	6	234.54	234.54	20.52	
29023	Bald Knob and Augusta	Saint Louis, Iron Mountain and Southern Rwy.	14.05	0	360.38	360.38	25.05	
29024	Jenson and Mansfield	Saint Louis and San Francisco Rwy.	18.23	0				Pay not fixed
			1,193.25		78,352.01	78,352.01		
	LOUISIANA.							
30001	Vacant.							
30002	New Orleans and Cheneyville	Texas and Pacific Rwy.	171.54	14	17,747.53	17,747.53	103.46	Land Grant. Not land grant.
30003	New Orleans and Morgan City	Morgan's Louisiana and Texas R. R. and Steamship Co.	183.52	} 11.95	26,958.66	26,958.66	111.49	
			128.92				139.27	
30004	Schriever and Houma	do	25.80	14	652.36	652.36	42.75	
30005	Vidalia and Troyville	Natchez, Red River and Texas R. R.		0	1,094.40	1,094.40	43.75	

Number of route.	State and termini.	Corporate title of company carrying the mail.	Distance.	Average number of trips per week over whole route.	Annual pay for transportation.	Annual pay for railway post-office cars.	Total annual pay.	Cost per mile for transportation.	Cost per mile for railway post-office cars.	Remarks.
			Miles.		Dollars.	Dollars.	Dollars.	Dollars.	Dollars.	
	LOUISIANA—continued.									
30006	Clinton and Port Hudson........	Louisville, New Orleans and Texas Rwy. Co., lessee (linton and Port Hudson R. R.	22.10	4 20	944.77	....	944.77	42.75	....	Pay based on service not less than 6 round trips per week.
30007	Bayou Sarah and Woodville....	West Feliciana R. R.	28.29	4	1,123.89	....	1,123.89	42.75	....	Do.
30008	Vicksburg, Miss., and Shreveport, La.	Vicksburg, Shreveport and Pacific R. R.	172.66	7	11,100.31	....	11,100.31	64.29	....	All land grant.
30009	Schriever and Thibodeaux....	Morgan's Louisiana and Texas R. R. and Steamship Co.	5.77	14	246.66	....	246.66	42.75	....	
30010	La Fayette, La., and Orange, Tex.	Louisiana Western R. R.	113.25	7	15,689.99	....	15,689.99	137.68	....	
30011	Shreveport and Cheneyville	Texas and Pacific Rwy.	156.57	14	14,457.67	....	14,457.67	92.34	....	
30012	Cedes and Saint Martinville	Morgan's Louisiana and Texas R. R. and Steamship Co.	7.06	14	301.81	....	301.81	42.75	....	
30013	Baton Rouge Junction (n. o.) and Baton Rouge.	Texas and Pacific Rwy.	9.50	7	406.12	....	406.12	42.75	....	
30014	New Orleans and Covington...	East Louisiana R. R.	59.50	6	651.93	....	651.93	42.75	....	Pay not fixed.
30015	Baldwin Station (n. o.) and Louisa...	Morgan's Louisiana and Texas R. R. and Steamship Co.	15.25	7	....	....	....	42.75	....	
30016	Shreveport and Logansport...	Shreveport and Houston Rwy.	41.72	6	1,783.53	....	1,783.53	42.75	....	Do.
30017	Cypress and Natchitoches....	Natchitoches R. R.	11.62	6	....	....	....	....	....	Do.
30018	Gibsland and Homer......	Louisiana North and South Rwy.	19.63	6	....	....	....	....	....	Do.
30019	Galveston, Ark., and Shreveport, La.	Saint Louis, Arkansas and Texas Rwy. Co. in Arkansas and Missouri.	61.04	6	93,060.62	....	93,060.62	....	....	
			1,144.50		93,060.62		93,060.62			
	TEXAS.									
31001	Houston and Galveston......	International and Great Northern R. R.	51.40	21	6,855.73	....	6,855.73	133.38	....	
31002	Houston and San Antonio....	Galveston, Harrisburgh and San Antonio Rwy.	218.01	7	26,841.39	....	26,841.39	123.12	....	
31003	Houston and Denison......	Houston and Texas Central Rwy.	837.09	14	54,473.74	....	54,473.74	161.60	....	
31004	Hempstead and Austin......	......do......	115.16	14	9,354.44	....	9,354.44	81.23	....	

No.	Between	Railroad	Length of route	No. of trips	Amount	Amount	Pay per mile	Remarks
31005	Bremond and Albany	do	230.89	7.77	17,570.72	17,570.72	74.10	
31006	Longview and Houston	International and Great Northern R. R.	253.45	7	33,133.55	33,133.55	161.98	
31007	Palestine and Laredo	do	415.80	8.96	53,326.35	53,326.35	128.25 / 42.75	
31008	Houston and Columbia	do	Nl / 19.39	0	2,180.25	2,180.25	137.22	
31009	Shreveport, La., and State Line (n. o.), Tex., and State Line (n. o.), Tex., and El Paso	Texas and Pacific Rwy	515.42	10.58	125,012.87	125,012.87	150.08	Land grant. 91.50 miles. Sierra Blanca to El Paso, at $61.23 per mile.
31010	Texarkana, Ark. and Marshall, Tex.	do	69.64	14	15,838.23	15,838.23	237.43	
31011	Whitesborough, Tex., and Texarkana, Ark.	do	173.44	7	16,905.19	16,905.19	97.47	
31012	Houston and Orange	Texas and New Orleans R. R.	106.33	7	14,637.38	14,637.38	137.96	
31013	Jefferson and McKinney	Missouri, Kansas and Texas Rwy.	155.46	6	8,906.30	8,906.30	57.29	
31014	Columbus and La Grange	Galveston, Harrisburgh and San Antonio Rwy.	31.60	8	1,404.93	1,404.93	44.46	
31015	Henderson and Overton	International and Great Northern R. R.	17.01	7	756.26	756.26	44.46	
31016	Corpus Christi and Laredo	Mexican National Rwy. Co., lessee Texas Mexican Rwy.	161.60	6	8,981.72	8,981.72	55.56	
31017	Denison and Mineola	Missouri, Kansas and Texas Rwy.	103.19	7	7,490.84	7,490.84	72.68	
31018	Brownsville and Isabel	Rio Grande R. R.	23.16	7	980.09	980.09	42.75	Pay based on service of not less than 6 round trips per week.
31019	Port Lavaca and Cuero	Gulf, Western Texas and Pacific Rwy.	65.49	4.71	2,419.92	2,419.92	43.61	Do.
31020	Houston and Sealy	John W. Smith, receiver Texas Western Rwy.	52.87	3	2,290.19	2,290.19	42.75	
31021	Waxahachie and Garrett (n. o.)	Central Texas and Northwestern R. R.	12.90	14	736.15	736.15	59.85	
31022	Denison and Henrietta	Missouri, Kansas and Texas Rwy.	111.32	14	6,280.65	6,280.65	153.90	Pay not fixed on 70.51 miles.
31023	Houston and Logansport	Houston East and West Texas Rwy.	192.70	7	9,555.99	9,555.99	49.59	
31024	Navasota and Conroe	Gulf, Colorado and Santa Fé Rwy.	43.95	7	1,878.86	1,878.86	42.75	
31025	Texarkana, Ark., and Gatesville, Tex.	Saint Louis, Arkansas and Texas Rwy. Co. in Texas.	305.39	7	20,629.10	20,629.10	67.56	
31026	Georgetown and Round Rock	International and Great Northern R. R.	10.32	14	502.99	502.99	48.74	
31027	Galveston and Fort Worth	Gulf, Colorado and Santa Fé Rwy.	346.87	7.58	35,568.96	35,568.96	102.60	
31028	Whitesborough and Taylor	Missouri, Kansas and Texas Rwy.	234.05	12.94	36,621.90	36,621.90	156.47	
31029	Beaumont and Rockland	Sabine and East Texas Rwy.	75.85	6	3,242.58	3,242.58	42.75	
31030	Dallas and Denton	Missouri, Kansas and Texas Rwy.	88.07	21	5,969.17	5,969.17	157.82	
31031	Dallas and Kemp	Texas Trunk R. R.	49.38	6	2,110.99	2,110.99	42.75	
31032	Mineola and Troup	International and Great Northern R. R.	44.54	7	3,503.51	3,503.51	78.06	

C.—Railroad service as in operation on the 30th of June, 1888—Continued.

Number of route.	State and terminal.	Corporate title of company carrying the mail.	Distance.	Average number of trips per week over whole route.	Annual pay for transportation.	Annual pay for railway post-office cars.	Total annual pay.	Cost per mile for transportation.	Cost per mile for railway post-office cars.	Remarks.
			Miles.		Dollars.	Dollars.	Dollars.	Dollars.	Dollars.	
	LOUISIANA—continued.									
30006	Clinton and Port Hudson	Louisville, New Orleans and Texas Rwy. Co., lessee Clinton and Port Hudson R. R.	23.10	4.20	944.77		944.77	42.75		Pay based on service not less than 6 round trips per week.
30007	Bayou Sarah and Woodville	West Feliciana R. R.	26.29	4	1,123.89		1,123.89	42.75		Do.
30008	Vicksburg, Miss., and Shreveport, La.	Vicksburg, Shreveport and Pacific R. R.	172.66	7	11,100.81		11,100.81	64.29		All land grant
30009	Schriever and Thibodeaux	Morgan's Louisiana and Texas R. R. and Steamship Co.	5.77	14	246.66		246.66	42.75		
30010	La Fayette, La., and Orange, Tex.	Louisiana Western R. R.	113.25	7	15,589.99		15,589.99	137.66		
30011	Shreveport and Cheneyville	Texas and Pacific Rwy.	156.97	14	14,457.67		14,457.67	92.34		
30012	Cades and Saint Martinsville	Morgan's Louisiana and Texas R. R. and Steamship Co.	7.06	14	301.81		301.81	42.75		
30013	Baton Rouge Junction (n. o.) and Baton Rouge.	Texas and Pacific Rwy.	9.50	7	406.12		406.12	42.75		Pay not fixed.
30014	New Orleans and Covington	East Louisiana R. R.	59.50	6?	651.93		651.93	42.75		
30015	Baldwin Station (n. o.) and Louisa	Morgan's Louisiana and Texas R. R. and Steamship Co.	15.25	7				42.75		
30016	Shreveport and Logansport	Shreveport and Houston Rwy	41.72	7	1,783.53		1,783.53			Do.
30017	Cypress and Natchitoches	Natchitoches R. B.	11.62	6						Do.
30018	Gibsland and Homer	Louisiana North and South	19.63	6						Do.
30019	Galveston, Ark., and Shreveport, La.	Saint Louis, Arkansas and Texas Rwy. Co. in Arkansas and Missouri.	61.04	6						
			1,144.50		93,059.62		93,059.62			
	TEXAS.									
31001	Houston and Galveston	International and Great Northern R. R.	51.40	21	6,655.73		6,655.73	129.38		
31002	Houston and San Antonio	Galveston, Harrisburgh and San Antonio Rwy.	218.01	7	26,841.39		26,841.39	123.12		
31003	Houston and Denison	Houston and Texas Central Rwy.	337.39	14	54,473.74		54,473.74	161.60		
31004	Hempstead and Austin	...do...	115.16	14	9,354.44		9,354.44	81.23		

No.	Termini	Name of road	Length of route	Trips per week						Remarks
31051	Coleman Junction (n. o.) and Coleman.	...do...	6.25	6		187.00	187.16	29.93		
31052	Fort Worth and Waxahachie	Fort Worth and New Orleans Rwy.	41.88	6		1,698.00	1,898.00	45.32		
31053	Dallas and Honey Grove	Gulf, Colorado and Santa Fé Rwy.	80.71	6		2,898.29	2,898.29	35.91		
31054	Fort Worth, Tex., and Purcell, Ind. T.	...do...	170.68	9.66		13,568.48	13,568.48	79.52		
31055	Greenville and Dallas	Dallas and Greenville Rwy.	54.84	6		2,476.28	2,476.28	45.32		
31056	Taylor and La Grange	Taylor, Bastrop and Houston Rwy.	70.02	7		3,472.29	3,472.29	40.50		
31057	Kennedy and Wallis Station	San Antonio and Aransas Pass Rwy.	133.02	6		7,733.78	7,733.78	58.14		
31058	San Antonio and Kerrville	...do...	71.75	6		4,601.32	4,601.32	64.13		
31059	Ladonia and Paris	Gulf, Colorado and Santa Fé Rwy.	30.16	14		1,983.43	1,983.43	63.81		
31060	Mount Pleasant and Sherman	Saint Louis, Arkansas and Texas Rwy.	110.10	7		6,777.75	6,777.75	81.56		Pay not fixed on 20.05 miles.
31061	Fort Worth and Granbury	Fort Worth and Rio Grande Rwy.	41.35	6		1,503.27	1,863.27	43.61		Pay not fixed.
31062	San Marcos and West Point	San Antonio and Aransas Pass Rwy.	50.20	6		773.34	773.34	25.65		
31063	Yoakum and West Point	Taylor, Bastrop and Houston Rwy.	17.12	6						Do.
31064	Corsicana and Hillsborough	Saint Louis, Arkansas and Texas Rwy. Co. in Texas.	42	6						
31065	Texline (n. o.) Tex., and Pueblo, Colo.	Denver, Texas and Fort Worth R. R.	228.51	6						Pay not fixed. Lap service Trinidad to Pueblo, 61.21 miles.
31066	Panhandle and Washburn	Fort Worth and Denver City Rwy.	18.18	6						Pay not fixed.
31067	Commerce and Fort Worth	Saint Louis, Arkansas and Texas Rwy. Co. in Texas.	98.31	6						Do.
			8,240.04			784,149.76	784,149.76			
	INDIAN TERRITORY.									
32001	Atoka and Lehigh	Missouri, Kansas and Texas Rwy.	8.11	6		346.70	246.70	42.75		
32002	Vinita and Red Fork	Saint Louis and San Francisco Rwy.	68.01	7		2,325.94	2,325.94	34.20		
32003	Arkansas City, Kans., and Purcell, Ind. T.	Southern Kansas Rwy.	154	7		7,565.96	7,565.96	48.74		All land grant.
32204	Kiowa, Kans., and Panhandle, Tex.	...do...	217.20	7		8,471.05	8,471.05	50.43		Pay not fixed on 49.29 miles.
			447.32			18,649.65	18,649.65			
	KANSAS.									
33001	Kansas City, Mo., and Denver, Colo.	Union Pacific Rwy.	641.02	10.94	16,025.50	115,095.14	131,120.64	179.55		
33002	Lawrence and Leavenworth	...do...	34.95	7		2,121.81	2,121.81	66.71		
33003	Atchison and Waterville	Central Branch Union Pacific R. R.	100.28	7		14,401.34	14,401.34	143.64	25.00	

C.—Railroad service as in operation on the 30th of June, 1888—Continued.

Number of route.	State and termini.	Corporate title of company carrying the mail.	Distance.	Average number of trips per week over whole route.	Annual pay for transportation.	Annual pay for railway post-office cars.	Total annual pay.	Cost per mile for transportation.	Cost per mile for railway post-office cars.	Remarks.
	KANSAS—continued.		Miles.		Dollars.	Dollars.	Dollars.	Dollars.	Dollars.	
33004	Lawrence and Coffeyville	Southern Rwy	141.87	10.82	15,718.19		15,718.19	110.80		Land grant.
33005	Cherryvale and Hunnewell	do	131.53	7.30	15,069.39		15,069.39	114.57		
33006	Kansas City, Mo., and Ottawa, Kans	do	58.80	13	9,753.15		9,753.15	165.87		
33007	Saint Joseph, Mo., and Grand Island, Nebr.	Saint Joseph and Grand Island R.R.	{ 227.82 { 25.07 }	13	19,851.71		19,851.71	{ 78.90 { 95.76 }		{ Land grant Saint Joseph to Hastings, 227.82 miles.
33008	Kansas City, Mo., and Webb City, Mo.	Kansas City, Fort Scott and Memphis R.R.	181.71	10.76	24,062.02		24,062.02	132.53		
33009	Junction City and Parsons	Missouri Pacific Rwy	157.15	7	9,781.01		9,781.01	62.24		Land grant.
33010	Atchison, Kans, South Pueblo, (n.o.) Colo.	Atchison, Topeka and Santa Fé R.R.	{ 470.41 { 150.04 }	16.03	127,362.44	45,580.00	172,942.44	{ 193.57 { 241.97 }	80.00	{ Land grant Atchison to State line (n.o.), 470.41 miles. R.P.O. Topeka to South Pueblo (n.o.) only, 590.75 miles.
33011	Newton and Arkansas City	do	78.81	8.41	7,412.08		7,412.08	94.05		
33012	Atchison, Kans., and Columbus, Nebr.	Burlington and Missouri River R.R. (in Nebraska).	220.48	8.62	29,597.23		29,597.23	134.24		
33013	Leavenworth and Miltonvale	Kansas Central R.R.	166.18	6	11,082.54		11,082.54	66.69		
33014	Lawrence and Carbondale	Lawrence, Emporia and Southwestern R.R.	33.75	6						
33015	Junction City and Concordia	Junction City and Fort Kearney Rwy.	70.77	12.36	6,474.74		6,474.74	91.49		
33016	Topeka, Kans., and Kansas City, Mo.	Atchison, Topeka and Santa Fé R.R.	66.88	14	21,043.12	5,350.40	26,393.52	314.64	80.00	
33017	Florence and Winfield	do	75.03	9	3,207.53		3,207.53	42.75		
33018	Vacant.									
33019	Ottawa and Burlington	Southern Kansas Rwy	47.04	8.16	2,493.59		2,493.59	53.01		
33020	Girard, Kans., and Joplin, Mo.	Saint Louis and San Francisco Rwy	38.77	7	1,780.01		1,780.01	46.17		Pay not fixed
33021	Waterville and Washington	Central Branch Union Pacific R.R.	20.99	8.83	2,476.59		2,476.59	119.70		
33022	Greenleaf and Concordia	do	43.19	7	5,982.24		5,982.24	138.51		
33023	Emporia and Howard	Atchison, Topeka and Santa Fé R.R.	77.65	12	3,717.87		3,717.87	47.88		

No.	Station	Railroad	Miles			Amount		Amount			Notes
33024	Cherryvale and Arcadia	Kansas City, Fort Scott and Memphis R. R.	72.97	7		4,800.57		4,800.57		64.96	
33025	Solomon City and Beloit	Solomon R. R.	57.86	13		4,601.02		4,601.02		70.32	
33026	Concordia and Lemora	Central Branch Union Pacific R. R.	18.70	7		14,824.25		14,824.25		106.88	
33027	Yuma and Warwick	do	30.98	7		1,318.28		1,318.28		42.75	
33028	Salina and McPherson	Salina and Southwestern Rwy.	38.78	7		1,572.34		1,572.34		41.75	
33029	Downs and Alton	Central Branch Elon Pacific R. R.	24.05			1,583.45		1,583.45		65.84	
33030	Florence and Ellenwood	Atchison, Topeka and Santa Fé R. R.	99.01	8		6,857.43		6,857.43		69.26	
33031	Panola and Le Roy Junction (n. o.)	Missouri Pacific Rwy.	61.56	7		4,528.50		4,528.50		72.53	
33032	Jamestown and Burr Oak	Central Branch Union Pacific R. R.	33.86	7		1,881.93		1,881.93		55.58	
33033	Osawatomie and Ottawa	Missouri Pacific Rwy.	21.42	7		915.70		915.70		42.75	
33034	Burlingame and Manhattan	Man, Alma and Burlingame Rwy.	57.27	8		3,378.93		3,378.93		59.00	
33035	Wellington and Kiowa	Southern Kansas Rwy.	69.33	7		5,631.67		5,631.67		81.23	
33036	Fort Scott and Anthony	Saint Louis, Fort Scott and Wita R. R.	214.48	7		15,776.71		15,776.71		73.53	
33037	Mulvane and Caldwell	Atchison, Topeka and Santa Fé R. R.	38.33	6		2,883.94		2,883.94		75.21	
33038	Leavenworth and Meriden Junction (n. o.)	Leavenworth, Topeka and Western Ry.	47.07	6		2,012.24		2,012.24		42.75	
33039	Girard and Pittsburgh	Southern Kansas Rwy.	54.80	6		1,766.14		1,766.14		42.75	Pay not fixed on 13.53 miles.
33040	Atchison and Omaha	Missouri Pacific Rwy.	166.42	13		16,220.95		16,220.95		97.47	
33041	Ottawa and Emporia	Southern Kansas Rwy.	56.85	6		2,576.44		2,576.44		15.32	
33042	Wichita and Kingman	Wita and Western R. R.	46.10	12		3,626.22		3,626.22		78.66	
33043	Weir City Junction (n. o.) and Weir	Kansas City, Fort Scott and Gulf R. R.	3.90	14		166.72		166.72		42.75	
33044	Lawrenceburgh and Belleville	Junction City and Fort Kearney Rwy.	17.13	7		732.30		732.30		42.75	
33045	Butler, Mo., and Le Roy, Kans	Saint Louis and Emporia R. R.	78.83	7		3,025.43		3,025.43		47.03	
33046	El Dorado and McPherson	Saint Louis, Fort Scott and Wichita R. R.	62.17	7		2,172.68		2,172.68		35.06	
33047	Alton and Stockton	Rooks County R. R.	19.07	7		1,125.13		1,125.13		59.00	
33048	Attica and Medicine Lodge	Southern Kansas Rwy.	21.76	7		1,525.59		1,525.59		70.11	
33049	Beaumont and Bluff	Saint Louis and San Francisco Rwy.	106.14	7		5,980.48		5,980.48		54.43	
33050	Council Grove and Salina	Topeka, Salina and Western Rwy.	72.22	7		4,754.96		4,754.96		65.84	Pay not fixed on 15.50 miles.
33051	Wichita and Hutchinson	Wichita and Colorado Rwy.	47.28	11.63		2,545.89		2,545.89		53.87	
33052	Hutchinson and Kimley	Chicago, Kansas and Western R. R.	94.20	6		4,751.40		4,751.40		66.43	
33053	Independence and Cedar Vale	do	56.12	7		2,639.31		2,639.31		47.03	
33054	Manhattan and Maryville	Manhattan and Blue Valley R. R.	55.61	7		3,092.46		3,092.46		55.58	
33055	Quenemo and Osage City	Chicago, Kansas and Western R. R.	20.60	12		596.84		596.84		29.07	

C.—*Railroad service as in operation on the 30th of June, 1888*—Continued.

Number of route.	State and termini.	Corporate title of company carrying the mail.	Distance.	Average number of trips per week over whole route.	Annual pay for transportation.	Annual pay for railway post-office cars.	Total annual pay.	Cost per mile for transportation.	Cost per mile for railway post-office cars.	Remarks.
			Miles.		Dollars.	Dollars.	Dollars.	Dollars.	Dollars.	
	KANSAS—continued.									
33056	Chetopa and Belle Plaine	Denver, Memphis and Atlantic Rwy.	146.20	7	5,183.17		5,183.17	86.14		Pay not fixed on 57.03 miles.
33057	Salina and Luray	Salina, Lincoln and Western Rwy.	67.07	9.69	3,670.07		3,670.07	54.72		
33058	Belle Plaine and Larned	Denver, Memphis and Atlantic Rwy.	128.87	7	2,557.81		2,557.81	46.17		Pay not fixed on 73.27 miles.
33059	Great Bend and Scott	Chicago, Kansas and Western R. R.	121.12	7	8,077.49		8,077.49	66.69		
33060	Topeka and Fort Scott	Kansas, Nebraska and Dakota Rwy.	130.79	7	4,869.14		4,869.14	36.77		
33061	Larned and Jetmore	Chicago, Kansas and Western R. R.	46.84	7	2,082.50		2,082.50	44.46		
33062	Kingman and Mullinville	Kingman, Pratt and Western R. R.	75.73	13	5,114.89		5,114.89	67.54		
33063	Le Roy and Dearing	Verdigris Valley, Independence and Western R. R.	81.26	14	4,591.60		4,591.60	66.69		Pay not fixed on 12.41 miles.
33064	Howard and Moline	Kansas City, Emporia and Southern Rwy.	8.76	6	411.98		411.98	47.03		
33065	Little River and Hollyrood	Chicago, Kansas and Western R. R.	27.15	6	1,021.38		1,021.38	37.63		
33066	Chanute and Longton	do	45.13	7	4,167.30		4,167.30	92.34		
33067	Ottawa and Council Grove	Council Grove, Osage City and Ottawa R. R.	71.34	7	4,635.67		4,635.67	64.98		
33068	Mulvane and Englewood	Chicago, Kansas and Western R. R.	166.79	7	11,468.42		11,468.42	68.40		
33069	Benedict and Madison	do	45.65	6	1,405.10		1,405.10	30.78		Pay not fixed.
33070	Salina and McCracken	Kansas and Colorado R. R.	128.25	6						Do.
33071	Holsington and Great Bend	do	10.34	6						Do.
33072	Colony and Neosho Falls	Chicago, Kansas and Western R. R.	12.17	6	301.09		301.09	24.79		
33073	Anthony and Kiowa	Saint Louis, Fort Scott and Wichita R. R.	30.43	6						Do.
33074	Hutchinson and Geneseo	Salina, Sterling and El Paso Rwy.	41.84	6						Do.
33075	Saint Joseph, Mo., and Liberal, Kans	Chicago, Kansas and Nebraska Rwy.	434.14	14.10	26,220.25		26,220.25	88.06		Pay not fixed on 135.25 miles.

No.	Termini	Railroad	Length (miles)	No. trips	Amount	Amount	Amount	Pay	Extra pay	Remarks
33976	Horton, Kans., and Nelson, Nebr	...do...	167.26	7	12,298.61		12,298.61	73.53		Pay not fixed.
33977	Bazaar and Barnard	...do...	132.18	6						Do.
33978	Sidell and Peru	Le Roy and Caney Valley Air Line R. R.	62.91	6						
33979	Kansas City, Mo., and Seneca, Kans	Kansas City, Wyandotte and Northwestern R. R.	118.75	7	6,294.93		6,294.93	53.01		
33980	Burlington and Gridley	Chicago, Kansas and Western R. R.	11.32	6	232.28		232.28	20.52		Do.
33981	Olcott and Iuka	Kansas Southwestern Rwy.	20.29	0						
33982	Burlington and Caldwell	Chicago, Kansas and Nebraska Rwy.	122.73	14	9,944.17		9,944.17	80.27		
33983	Coffeyville and Kincaid	Kansas City and Pacific R. R.	85.59	7	2,455.89		2,455.89	33.35		Pay not fixed on 11.95 miles. Pay not fixed.
33984	McCracken, Kans., and Towner, &c.	Denver, Mis and Atlantic Rwy.	141.35	6						
33985	Oakley and Colby	Oakley and Colby Rwy.	22.12	6	945.63		945.63	42.75		Do.
33986	Geneseo and Kanopolis	Kanopolis and Kansas Central Rwy.	14.76	6						
33987	Wichita and Ellsworth	Saint Louis and San Francisco Rwy.	106.01	7	3,920.04		3,920.04	36.77		Do.
33988	Keystone and Concordia	Chicago, Kansas and Western R. R.	41.02	6						Do.
33989	Belleville and McFarland	Chicago, Kansas and Nebraska Rwy.	104.78	6						Do.
33990	Le Roy and Madison	La...te R. R.	29.98	6						Do. Do.
33991	Kansas City, Mo., and Paola, Kans	Kansas City and Southwestern Rwy.	54.09	6						
33992	Bucklin and Dodge City	Chicago, Kansas and Nebraska Rwy.	21.55	6						Do.
33993	Dexter and Arkansas City	Grouse ...tk Rwy.	26.26	6						Do
			8,331.94		700,240.54	66,955.90	787,205.44			
	NEBRASKA.									
34001	Union Pacific Transfer (n. o.), Iowa, and Ogden City, Utah.	Union Pacific Rwy.	293.03 / 741.21	9.58	423,572.99	66,363.50	488,936.49	409.55	100.00 / 50.00 / 50.00	From Plattsmouth to Ashland covered by Route 34039.
34002	Ashland and Hastings.	Burlington and Missouri River R. R. (in Nebraska).	121.98	14.58	24,300.85	6,099.00	30,399.85	198.22	50.00	
34003	Omaha and Covington.	Chicago, Saint Paul, Minneapolis and... Rwy.	121.74	10.74	11,762.51		11,762.51	96.62		
34004	Omaha and Oreopolis Junction (n. o.)	Omaha and Southwestern R. R. Rwy.	16.00	27	2,611.51	415.00	3,026.51	157.32	25.00	
34005	Nemaha City and York	Omaha and Southwestern R. R. ...	127.41	6	11,748.55		11,748.55	85.56		
34006	Crete and Beatrice	...Saint Paul, Minneapolis and Omaha Rwy.	30.57	15.5	3,816.05		3,816.05	124.83		
34007	Coburn Junction (n. o.) and Ponca.	...olis and Omaha Rwy.	16.44	6	702.81		702.81	42.75		
34008	Valley and Stromsburgh.	...sha and Republican Valley R. R.	90.42	6.41	6,339.34		6,339.34	70.11		
34009	Hastings, Nebr., and Denver, Colo.	Republican Valley R. R.	387.37	12.59	57,629.08	6,599.00	64,228.03	148.77	50.00	R. P. O. only between Hastings and McCook, 131.96 miles.

C.—Railroad service as in operation on the 30th of June, 1888—Continued.

Number of route.	State and termini.	Corporate title of company carrying the mail.	Distance.	Average number of trips per week over whole route.	Annual pay for transportation.	Annual pay for railway post-office cars.	Total annual pay.	Cost per mile for transportation.	Cost per mile for railway post-office cars.	Remarks.
	NEBRASKA—continued.		Miles.		Dollars.	Dollars.	Dollars.	Dollars.	Dollars.	
34010	Fremont, Nebr., and Rapid City, Dak	Fremont, Elkhorn and Missouri Valley R. R.	510.25	7.43	75,476.18	5,321.00	80,797.18	147.92	25.00	R. P. O. only between Fremont and Long Pine, 212.84 miles.
34011	York and Central City	Republican Valley R. R.	42.00	6	3,016.44		3,016.44	71.82		
34012	Columbus and Norfolk	Omaha, ?, and Black Hills R. R.	50.68	7.09	3,076.78		3,076.78	60.71		
34013	Lincoln and Marysville	? and Republican Valley R. R.	78.48	7	5,636.43		5,636.43	71.82		
34014	Valparaiso and Lincoln	do	20.59	13	1,760.44		1,760.44	85.50		
34015	Grand Island and Ord	do	62.44	12	4,644.91		4,644.91	74.39		
34016	Beatrice and Red Cloud	? Valley R. R.	120.25	14.14	17,170.49		17,170.49	142.79		
34017	Oconnee and Albion	Omaha, Niobrara and Black Hills R. R.	34.17	6	1,986.64		1,986.64	58.14		
34018	Norfolk Junc. (n. o.) and Creighton	Fremont, Elkhorn and Missouri Valley R. R.	42.53	6	2,145.63		2,145.63	50.45		
34019	Nemaha City and Beatrice	Republican Valley R. R.	67.90	6	4,470.53		4,470.53	65.84		
34020	Wymore and Table Rock	do	40.87	13	6,185.26		6,185.26	151.24		
34021	Emerson and Norfolk	Chicago, Saint Paul, Minneapolis and Omaha Rwy.	47.09	6	2,335.19		2,335.19	45.59		
34022	Wakefield and Hartington	do	33.94	6	1,450.93		1,450.93	42.75		
34023	Vacant.									
34024	Chester and Hebron	Nebraska and Colors of R. R. Omaha, Niobrara and Black Hills R. R.	12.20	12	521.55		521.55	42.75		
34025	Genoa and Cedar Rapids	? and Colorado R. R.	30.71	6	1,312.85		1,312.85	42.75		
34026	De Witt and Superior	Republican Valley R. R.	85.52	6	5,118.37		5,118.37	59.85		
34027	Aurora and Grand Island	Chicago, Nebraska and Kansas R. R.	19.36	6	1,894.40		1,894.40	94.91		
34028	Odell and Concordia	do	72.29	6	4,697.40		4,697.40	64.98		
34029	Hastings and Oxford	Republican Riley R. R. Burlington and Missouri River R. R. (in ?	108.26	11.62	17,443.64		17,443.64	164.16		
34030	Kenesaw and Kearney		24.57	7	1,344.47		1,344.47	54.72		
34031	Holdredge and Elwood	Nebraska and Endo R. R.	28.72	6	1,227.78		1,227.78	42.75		
34032	Republican City and Oberlin	Republican Valley and Kansas and Burlington and Kansas and ? Burn R. R.	78.73	6	5,587.46		5,587.46	70.97		

No.	Between	Railroad	Length (miles)	Trips	Amount	Extra	Total	Rate		Remarks
34033	Saint Paul and Loop City	Oban and Republican Valley R. R.	39.50	6	2,132.71		2,132.71	53.87		
34034	Fairmont and Hebron	Burlington and Missouri River R. R. (in Nebraska).	36.45	6	1,962.21		1,932.21	53.01		
34035	Chadron, Nebr., and Douglas, Wyo	Fremont, Elkhorn and Missouri Valley R. R.	140.38	6	522.46		8,522.46	60.71		
34036	Grand Island and Alliance	Grand Island and Wyoming Central R. R.	270.25	6	7,088.47		7,088.47	79.52		Pay not fixed on 170.42 miles.
34037	Fremont and Lincoln	Fremont, Elkhorn and Missouri Valley R. R.	52.97	6	2,717.36		2,717.36	51.30		
34038 / 34039	Omaha and Ashland / Plattsmouth and Ashland	Omaha and North Platte R. R. / Burlington and Missouri River R. R. (in Nebr.)	31.20 / 31.37	6 / 14.58	5,441.90 / 5,632.48	1,560.00 / 111.75	7,001.90 / 5,744.23	174.42 / 179.55	50.00 / 25.00	R. P. O. only between Plattsmouth and Oreapolis Junction, 4.17 miles.
34040 / 34041	Weeping Water and Lincoln / Scribner and Oakdale	Missouri Pacific Rwy. / Fremont, Elkhorn and Missouri Valley R. R.	35.11 / 115.73	6 / 6	1,621.02 / 8,313.35		1,621.02 / 8,313.35	46.17 / 70.97		
34042	Elwood, Nebr., and Sterling, Colo	Nebraska and Colorado R. R.	202.60	6	1,894.68		1,894.68	42.75		Pay not fixed on 158.34 miles.
34043 / 34044	Edgar and Holdrege / Aurora and Hastings	do. / Burlington and Missouri River R. R. (in Nebraska).	61.11 / 29.84	6 / 6	3,328.75 / 791.05		3,328.75 / 791.05	41.04 / 29.51		
34045 / 34046	Fairfield and Stromsburgh / Oicuns and Blakeman	Kansas City and Omaha R. R / Burlington and Missouri River R. R. (in Nebraska).	65.49 / 93.57	6 / 6	2,799.69 / 6,454.70		2,799.69 / 6,454.70	42.75 / 67.54		
34047 / 34048 / 34049	Weeping Water and Nebraska City / Nebraska City and Auburn / Central City and Arcadia	Missouri Pacific Rwy. / Nebraska Southern Rwy. / Burlington and Missouri River R. R. (in Nebraska).	24.87 / 24.89 / 71.07	6 / 6 / 6	3,827.83		3,827.83	53.86		Pay not fixed. Do.
080	Fairbury, Nebr., and Phillipsburgh, Kans.	Burlington and Missouri River R. R. (in Nebraska), and Nebraska Rwy.	162.77	7	1,170.75		7,170.75	55.57		Pay not fixed on 33.73 miles.
34051	Omaha and Arlington	Fremont, Elkhorn and Missouri Valley R. R.	28.69	13	3,237.05		3,237.05	112.86		
34052	Platte River Junction (n. o.) and Hastings	do.	119.98	7	7,685.42		7,685.42	64.12		
34053 / 34054	Fairfield and Alma / Fairbury and McCool Junction	Kansas City and Omaha R. R. / Saint Joseph and Grand Island R. R.	57.79 / 50.62	6 / 6	3,602.90 / 2,250.56		3,602.90 / 2,250.56	41.04 / 44.46		
34055	Palmer and Burwell	Burlington and Missouri River R. R. (in Nebraska).	69.38	6	3,203.27		3,203.27	46.17		
34056	Linwood and Geneva	Fremont, Elkhorn and Missouri Valley R. R.	77.53	6	4,971.23		4,971.23	64.12		
34057 / 34058	Ashland and Schuyler / Boelus and Nantasket	Omaha and North Platte R. R. / Omaha and Republican Valley R. R.	50.71 / 9.74	6 / 6	2,167.85		2,167.85	42.75		Pay not fixed.
			5,570.56		800,526.08	86,469.25	894,995.33			
	DAKOTA.									
35001	Sioux City, Iowa, and Mitchell, Dak	Chicago, Milwaukee and Saint Paul Rwy.	138.18	9.59	10,751.78		10,751.78	77.81		

C.—*Railroad service as in operation on the 30th of June, 1888—Continued.*

Number of route.	State and termini.	Corporate title of company carrying the mail.	Distance.	Average number of trips per week over whole route.	Annual pay for transportation.	Annual pay for railway post-office cars.	Total annual pay.	Cost per mile for transportation.	Cost per mile for railway post-office cars.	Remarks.
	DAKOTA—continued.		*Miles.*		*Dollars.*	*Dollars.*	*Dollars.*	*Dollars.*	*Dollars.*	
35002	Marion and Chamberlain	Chicago, Milwaukee and Saint Paul Rwy.	111.65	12	14,415.13		14,415.13	129.11		Pay based on a service of not less than six round trips per week.
35003	Breckenridge and Hope	Saint Paul, Minneapolis and Manitoba Rwy.	93.25	5.04	7,016.13		7,016.13	75.24		
35004	Vacant.									
35005	Fargo and Neche	do	157.94	6	15,654.57		15,654.57	99.18		
35006	Everest and Langdon	do	155.22	6	10,748.98		10,748.98	69.25		
35007	Flandreau and Sioux Falls	Chicago, Milwaukee and Saint Paul Rwy.	39.31	6	2,252.06		2,252.06	57.29		
35008	Egan and Woonsocket	do	85.30	6	8,022.46		8,022.46	94.05		
35009	Millbank and Wilmot	do	17.26	6	737.86		737.86	42.75		
35010	Huron and Columbia	Dakota Central Rwy	97.26	7	7,235.17		7,235.17	74.39		
35011	Vacant.									
35012	Ashton and Edgeley	Chicago, Milwaukee and Saint Paul Rwy.	96.81	6.30	7,697.36		7,697.36	78.51		
35013	Ripon and Portland Junction (n. o.)	Saint Paul, Minneapolis and Manitoba Rwy.	41.41	6	2,514.00		2,514.00	60.71		
35014	Brookings and Watertown	Dakota Central Rwy.	48.21	12	2,184.87		2,184.87	45.23		
35015	Fargo and Edgeley	Fargo and Southwestern R. R.	110.00	6	5,047.24		5,047.24	57.29		Pay not fixed on 21.90 miles.
35016	Jamestown and Minnewaukon	Jamestown and Northern R. R.	99.25	6	4,475.49		4,475.49	49.59		
35017	Mitchell and Ashton	Chicago, Milwaukee and Saint Paul Rwy.	96.10	7	10,435.49		10,435.49	108.59		
35018	Sanborn and Cooperstown	Sanborn, Cooperstown and Turtle Mountain R. R.	36.35	6	1,553.96		1,553.96	42.75		
35019	Fargo and Ortonville	Chicago, Milwaukee and Saint Paul Rwy.	119.52	6	7,357.65		7,357.65	61.56		
35020	Jamestown and La Moure	James River Valley R. R	48.87	6	2,089.19		2,089.19	42.75		
35021	Centreville and Yankton	Chicago and Northwestern Rwy.	29.39	13	1,382.21		1,382.21	47.03		
35022	Andover and Harlem	Chicago, Milwaukee and Saint Paul Rwy.	55.70	6	2,003.40		2,003.40	35.91		
35023	Columbia and Oakes	Chicago and Northwestern Rwy.	39.30	6	3,565.55		3,565.55	91.49		
35024	Redfield and Gettysburgh	do	75.31	6	4,700.09		4,700.09	62.41		

No.	Route	Railway						Remarks
35925	Tripp and Armour	Chicago, Milwaukee and Saint Paul Rwy.	20.23	6	691.56	691.56	34.30	Pay not fixed.
35026	Devil's Lake, Dak., and Great Falls, Mont.	Saint Paul, Minneapolis and Manitoba Rwy.	987.82	6				
35027	Tintah Junction (n. o.), Minn., and Aberdeen, Dak.	do	119.31	7	9,090.35	9,090.35	81.23	
35028	Valley Junction (n. o.) and Oakes	James River Valley R. R.	15.21	7	936.32	936.32	61.56	
35029	Roscoe and Orient	Chicago, Milwaukee and Saint Paul Rwy.	41.73	6	2,069.39	2,069.39	49.50	
35030	Rugby and Bottineau	Saint Paul, Minneapolis and Manitoba Rwy.	88.10		1,237.86	1,237.86	82.49	
35031	Rutland and Ellendale	Chicago, Milwaukee and Saint Paul Rwy.	49.73	7	1,657.99	1,657.99	83.34	Pay not fixed on 7.96 miles.
35032	Roscoe and Eureka	do	26.70	6	528.65	528.65	28.21	
35033	Madison and Bristol	Minneapolis and Pacific Rwy.	103.39	6	5,834.29	5,834.29	56.43	
35034	Fairmount and Oakes	Chicago and Northwestern Rwy.	72.64	6	4,285.03	4,285.03	58.99	
35035	Doland and Groton		38.21	6	1,073.60	1,073.60	27.98	
35036	Salem and Mitchell	Chicago, Saint Paul, Minneapolis and Omaha Rwy.	33.10	7	1,556.36	1,556.36	47.02	
35037	Rapid City and Whitewood	Fremont, Elkhorn and Missouri Valley R. R.	37.27	7	4,365.43	4,365.43	117.13	
			3,047.05		165,797.77	165,797.77		
	MONTANA.							
36001	Silver Bow and Garrison	Utah Northern Rwy.	44.90	7	3,724.00	3,724.00	82.94	
36002	Helena and Wickes	Helena and Jefferson County R. R.	28.06	7	1,139.71	1,139.71	42.75	
36003	Stuart and Anaconda	Montana Rwy.	8.63	7	364.65	364.65	42.75	
36004	Drummond and Phillipsburgh	Northern Pacific R. R.	26.47	7	1,222.11	1,222.11	46.17	
36005	Helena and Great Falls	Montana Central Rwy.	99.14	7	7,294.50	7,294.50	72.67	
36006	Jefferson City and Basin	Northern Pacific R. R.	28.38	6				
36007	Clough Junction (n. o.) and Basin	do	12.97	6				
36008	Missoula and Victor	Missoula and Bitter Root Valley R. R.	35.75	6				
			280.78		13,654.97	13,654.97		
	WYOMING.							
37001	Granger, Wyo., and Huntington, Oregon.	Oregon Short Line Rwy.	541.34	7	81,000.70	81,000.70	149.03	Pay not fixed. Do. Do.
37002	Cheyenne City and Ura	Cheyenne and Northern Rwy.	103.26	6	4,590.93	4,590.93	44.46	
37003	Douglas and Glenrock	Fremont, Elkhorn and Missouri Valley R. R.	30.30	6	1,372.89	1,372.89	45.31	
			674.90		86,964.52	86,964.52		
	COLORADO.							
38001	Denver and El Moro	Denver and Rio Grande R. R.	200.94	16.38	29,370.99	29,370.99	141.93	
38002	Brighton and Boulder	Denver and Boulder Valley R. R.	26.12	7	1,346.38	1,346.38	47.68	

C.—Railroad service as in operation on the 30th of June, 1888—Continued.

Number of route.	State and termini.	Corporate title of company carrying the mail.	Distance.	Average number of trips per week over whole route.	Annual pay for transportation.	Annual pay for railway post-office cars.	Total annual pay.	Cost per mile for transportation.	Cost per mile for railway post-office cars.	Remarks.
	COLORADO—continued.		Miles.		Dollars.	Dollars.	Dollars.	Dollars.	Dollars.	Pay is based upon a service of not less than six round trips per week.
38003	Denver and Fort Collins.	Colorado Central R. R.	74.71	12.68	7,920.76		7,920.76	106.02		
38004	Cucharas and Espanola.	Denver and Rio Grande R. R.	200.99	5.08	14,951.64		14,951.64	74.89		
38005	Denver and Leadville.	Denver, South Park and Pacific R. R.	150.74	11.61	13,275.67		13,275.67	88.07		
38006	La Junta, Colo., and Deming, N. Mex.	Atchison, Topeka and Santa Fé R. R.	678.05	7	95,056.84		95,056.84	164.16		
38007	Denver, Colo., and Cheyenne, Wyo.	Union Pacific Rwy	107.39	14.73	11,936.39		11,936.39	111.15		
38008	Vacant.									
38009	Poncho Springs and Monarch.	Denver and Rio Grande R. R.	16.09	6	697.84		697.84	42.75		
38010	Cañon City and West Cliff.	...do	33.22	6	1,576.44		1,576.44	47.60		
38011	Alamosa and Del Norte.	...do	31.86	6	1,388.97		1,388.97	43.61		
38012	Salida and State Line (n. o.).	...do	244.51	7.40	26,551.34		26,551.34	108.59		
38013	Vacant.									
38014	Schwander's Station (n. o.) and Castleton.	Denver, South Park and Pacific R. R.	83.83	7	4,377.78		4,377.78	52.16		
38015	Mears and Villa Grove.	Denver and Rio Grande R. R.	20.16	6	861.84		861.84	42.75		
38016	Gunnison and Crested Butte.	...do	28.62	6	1,223.50		1,223.50	42.75		
38017	Julesburgh and La Salle.	Colorado Central R. R.	150.96	14	12,948.93		12,948.93	53.70		
38018	Leadville and Aspen.	Denver and Rio Grande R. R.	137.52	7	12,254.95		12,254.95	88.92		
38019	South Pueblo (n. o.) and Leadville.		161.32	16.20	22,307.31		22,307.31	137.66		
38020	Argo Junction (n. o.) and Silver Plume.	Colorado Central R. R.	51.96	12.33	4,087.16		4,087.16	78.66		
38021	Forks Creek and Central City.	...do	11.47	14	588.41		588.41	51.30		
38022	Bear Creek Junction (n. o.) and Morrison.	Denver, South Park and Pacific R. R.	9.55	7	408.26		408.26	42.75		
38023	Denver and Pueblo.	Denver, Texas and Gulf R. R.	126.48	7	7,029.75		7,029.75	55.68		
38024	Garo and London.	Denver, South Park and Pacific R. R.	15.57	7	665.61		665.61	42.75		
38025	Manitou Junction (n. o.) and Colorado Springs.	Denver, Texas and Gulf R. R.	9.92	14	424.08		424.08	42.75		
38026	Dickey Station (n. o.) and Dillon.	Denver, South Park and Pacific R. R.	2.94	7	125.68		125.68	42.75		

No.	Route	Railroad	Length	No.	Amount	Amount	Rate	Remarks
38927	Greeley and Stout	Greeley, Salt Lake and Pacific Rwy.	39.17	6.63	2,311.03	2,311.03	59.00	Pay not fixed. Do.
38928	Denver and Lyons	Denver, Utah and Pacific R. R.	44.97	6	1,922.46	1,922.46	42.75	
38929	Boulder and Sunset	Greeley, Salt Lake and Pacific Rwy.	13.05	6	557.88	557.88	43.75	
38930	Colorado Springs Station (n. o.) and Manitou Station (n. o.)	Denver and Rio Grande R. R.	5.40	14	240.08	240.08	44.46	
38931	Como and Buena Vista	Denver, South Park and Pacific R. R.	48.39	9.94	2,937.14	2,937.14	60.71	
38932	Como and King	do	3.48	6	71.40	71.40	20.52	
38933	El Moro and Trinidad	Denver and Rio Grande R. R.	4.48	14	233.63	233.63	52.15	
38934	Colorado Springs and Leadville	Colorado Midland Rwy	133.05	7	7,621.10	7,621.10	57.28	
38935	Denver and Pueblo	Atchison, Topeka and Santa Fé R. R.	117.40	15.86	15,666.81	15,666.81	133.38	
38936	Towner and Pueblo	Pueblo and State Line R. R.	150.76	6				
38937	Montrose and Ouray	Denver and Rio Grande R. R.	36.38	6				
			3,081.71		302,528.05	302,528.05		
NEW MEXICO.								
39001	Lamy and Santa Fé	Atchison, Topeka and Santa Fé R. R.	19.19	14	1,132.21	1,132.21	59.00	
39002	Antonito, Colo., and Silverton, Colo.	Denver and Rio Grande R. R.	217.05	6	16,140.34	16,140.34	74.59	Land grant.
39003	Albuquerque, N. Mex., and Needles, Cal.	Atlantic and Pacific R. R.	574.96	7	61,734.21	61,734.21	107.39	
39004	Rincon, N. Mex., and El Paso, Tex.	Atchison, Topeka and Santa Fé R. R.	77.20	7	6,931.01	6,931.01	89.78	
39005	Deming, N. Mex., and El Paso, Tex.	Central Pacific R. R. Co. (lessee Southern Pacific R. R. of New Mexico).	88.70	7	11,375.77	11,375.77	128.25	
39006	Deming and Silver City	Silver City, Deming and Pacific R. R.	47.86	7	2,537.05	2,537.05	53.01	
39007	Las Vegas and Las Vegas Hot Springs.	Atchison, Topeka and Santa Fé R. R.	6.45	21	275.73	275.73	41.75	
39008	Nutt Station (n. o.) and Lake Valley.	do	13.25	7	566.43	566.43	42.75	
39009	San Antonio and Carthage	do	9.61	7	400.58	400.58	44.46	
39010	Socorro and Magdalena	do	27.65	7	1,182.03	1,182.03	42.75	
39011	Espanola and Santa Fé.	Texas, Santa Fé and Northern R. R.	28.86	6	986.50	986.50	25.65	
39012	Lordsburgh, N. Mex., and Clifton, Ariz.	Arizona and New Mexico Rwy.	71.51	6				Pay not fixed.
			1,191.58		103,277.96	103,277.96		
ARIZONA.								
40091	Yuma, Ariz., and Deming, N. Mex.	Central Pacific R. R. Co. (lessee Southern Pacific R. R. of Arizona).	467.18	7	74,295.63	74,295.63	159.08	
40092	Benson and Nogales.	New Mexico and Arizona R. R.	88.50	7	5,145.39	5,145.39	58.14	

C.—*Railroad service as in operation on the 30th of June, 1888—Continued.*

Number of route.	State and termini.	Corporate title of company carrying the mail.	Distance.	Average number of trips per week over whole route.	Annual pay for transportation.	Annual pay for railway post-office cars.	Total annual pay.	Cost per mile for transportation.	Cost per mile for railway post-office cars.	Remarks.
			Miles.		*Dollars.*	*Dollars.*	*Dollars.*	*Dollars*	*Dollars.*	
	ARIZONA—continued.									
40003	Seligman and Prescott.	Prescott and Arizona R. R.	74.68	6	4,417.92		4,417.92	59.00		
40004	Maricopa Junction (n. o.) and Phenix.	Maricopa and Phoenix R. R.	35.78	7	2,202.61		2,202.61	61.56		
			696.84		86,061.55		86,061.55			
	UTAH.									
41001	Ogden City and Frisco	Utah Central Rwy	281.05	7	21,915.18		21,915.18	77.81		
41002	State Line (n. o.) and Ogden City	Denver and Rio Grande Western Rwy	313.83	7	27,638.12		27,638.12	88.07		
41003	Ogden City and Butte City	Utah Northern Rwy	416.95	7.11	54,999.80		54,999.80	131.67		Pay not fixed on 7.55 miles.
41004	Bingham Junction (n. o.) and Bingham Canyon.	Denver and Rio Grande Western Rwy.	17.33	7	740.85		740.85	42.75		
41005	Salt Lake City and Stockton	Utah and Nevada Rwy	40.50	6	1,731.37		1,731.37	42.75		
41006	Bingham Junction (n. o.) and Alta	Denver and Rio Grande Western Rwy.	18.32	6	783.18		783.18	42.75		
41007	Vacant.									
41008	Echo City and Park City	Echo and Park City R. R.	28.29	10.5	1,451.27		1,451.27	51.30		
41009	Colton and Scofield	Denver and Rio Grande Western Rwy.	17.40	5	743.85		743.85	42.75		
41010	Nephi and Moroni	San Pete Valley Rwy	27.16	6	1,579.08		1,579.08	58.14		
41011	Lehi Junction and Silver City	Salt Lake and Western Rwy	54.25	6	2,319.18		2,319.18	42.75		
			1,215.67		113,801.88		113,801.88			
	IDAHO.									
42001	Shoshone and Ketchum	Oregon Short Line Rwy	70.01	6	4,010.87		4,010.87	57.29		
42002	Hauser and Coeur d'Alene	Spokane Falls and Idaho R. R.	13.98	6	415.42		415.42	29.93		
42003	Coeur d'Alene and Burke	Coeur d'Alene Rwy and Navigation Co.	99.16	6	4,229.63		4,229.63	46.17		
42004	Nampa and Boise City	Idaho Central Rwy	29.69	7	1,291.26		1,291.26	62.41		
			203.74		9,947.18		9,947.18			

No.	Termini	Railroad	Distance	Rate	Amount	Amount	Rate per mile	Land grant
	WASHINGTON TERRITORY.							
43001	Portland, Oreg., and Tacoma, Wash. Terr.	Northern Pacific R. R.	146.66	7	16,752.97	16,752.97	114.23	
43002	Seattle and Newcastle	Columbia and Puget Sound R. R.	18.25	9.72	822.93	822.93	42.75	
43003	Olympia and Tenino	Olympia and Chehalis Valley R. R.	15.84	7	853.30	853.30	53.87	
43004	Walla Walla and Wallula	Walla Walla and Columbia River R. R.	32.06	7	2,933.16	2,933.16	91.49	
43005	Tacoma and Carbonado	Northern Pacific R. R.	53.89	8.28	1,159.03	1,159.03	84.20	Do.
43006	Colfax and Moscow	Columbia and Palouse R. R.	117.30	6	6,812.82	6,812.82	58.14	
43007	Renton and Black Diamond	Columbia and Puget Sound R. R.	18.50	6	458.80	458.80	24.80	
43008	Walla Walla and Dayton	Oregon Rwy. and Navigation R. R.	38.54	7	2,965.65	2,965.65	76.96	
43009	Wallula, Wash. Terr. and Missoula, Mont.	Northern Pacific R. R.	418.61	7	64,562.58	64,562.58	153.90	Do.
43010	Bolles Junction (n. o.) and Riparia.	Oregon Rwy. and Navigation Co.	31.80	7	1,359.45	1,359.45	42.75	
43011	Pasco and Melrose	Northern Pacific R. R.	233.61	7	27,164.17	27,164.17	116.28	Do.
43012	Black River Junction (n. o.) and Stuck	Puget Sound Shore R. R.	13.50	7	577.12	577.12	42.75	
43013	Stuck and Puyallup Junction (n. o.) and	Northern Pacific and Puget Sound Shore R. R.	7.50	7	320.62	320.62	42.75	
43014	Starbuck and Pomeroy	Oregon Rwy. and Navigation Co.	29.53	6	1,489.78	1,489.78	50.45	
43015	Marshall and Belmont	Spokane and Palouse Rwy.	42.97	6	1,359.13	1,359.13	81.63	
43016	Colfax and Farmington	Columbia and Palouse R. R.	27.81	6	927.18	927.18	33.34	
43017	Walla Walla, Wash. Terr., and Pendleton, Oregon.	Oregon Rwy. and Navigation Co.	47.43	7	2,352.05	2,352.05	49.59	
			1,275.70		132,877.74	132,877.74		
	OREGON.							
44001	Portland and Ashland	Oregon and California R. R.	342.58	7.41	37,491.95	37,491.95	109.44	
44002	Portland and Corvallis	....do	97.78	6	6,772.24	6,772.24	69.26	
44003	Umatilla and Huntington	Oregon Rwy. and Navigation Co.	218.04	7	29,063.17	29,063.17	133.36	
44004	Vacant.							
44005	Portland, Oregon, and Wallula, Wash. Terr.	....do	214.76	7	41,498.07	41,498.07	193.22	
44006	Albany and Yaquina	Oregon Pacific R. R.	85.16	6	4,223.08	4,223.08	49.59	
44007	Portland and Coburg	Oregonian Rwy. Co. (Limited) Line.	123.38	6	6,857.46	6,857.46	55.58	
44008	Dundee Junction (n. o.) and Airlie.	....do	52.60	6	3,024.04	3,024.04	38.48	
44009	Sheridan Junction (n. o.) and Sheridan.	....do	7.21	12	231.92	231.92	30.78	
44010	Albany Station (n. o.) and Lebanon Station (n. o.).	Oregon and California R. R.	12.50	6				Pay not fixed.
			1,154.01		128,170.98	128,170.98		

C.—*Railroad service as in operation on the 30th of June, 1888*—Continued.

Number of route.	State and termini.	Corporate title of company carrying the mail	Distance.	Average number of trips per week over whole route.	Annual pay for transportation.	Annual pay for railway post-office car.	Total annual pay.	Cost per mile for transportation.	Cost per mile for railway post-office car.	Remarks.
	NEVADA.		*Miles.*		*Dollars.*	*Dollars.*	*Dollars.*	*Dollars.*	*Dollars.*	
45001	Virginia City and Reno.	Virginia and Truckee R. R.	53.08	7	4,850.28		4,850.28	91.49		Pay is based upon service of not less than six round trips per week.
45002	Palisade and Eureka.	Eureka and Palisade R. R.	90.88	3	5,283.75		5,283.75	58.14		Do.
45003	Battle Mountain and Austin.	Nevada Central R'y	93.15	3	8,962.16		8,962.16	42.75		Do.
45004	Mound House, Nev., and Keeler, Cal.	Carson and Colorado R. B.	293.00	5.07	17,035.02		17,035.02	58.14		
45005	Reno, Nev., and Long Valley, Cal.	Nevada and California R. B.	57.15	6	2,825.92		2,825.92	63.41		Pay not fixed on 11.87 miles.
45006	Belleville Junction (n. o.) and Candelaria.	Carson and Colorado R. B.	7.80	7	453.49		453.49	58.14		
			595.06		34,486.62		34,486.62			
	CALIFORNIA.									
46001	San Francisco, Cal., and Ogden City, Utah.	Central Pacific R. R.	{45.40 {788.77	9.76	292,418.19	42,843.50	335,261.70	850.56	{75.00 {50.00	
46002	San Francisco and Soledad.	Southern Pacific R. R.	142.98	12	12,811.00		12,811.00	89.60		Land grant.
46003	Roseville, Cal., and Ashland, Oregon	Central Pacific R. R.	322.30	11.18	50,308.71	1,168.50	51,477.21	155.61	25.00	R. P. U. only on 46.74 miles.
46004	Petaluma and Lakeville.	San Francisco and North Pacific R. R.	7.55	6	321.90		321.90	42.75		
46005	Sacramento City and Placerville.	Sacramento and Placerville R. R.	60.75	8.81	3,199.83		3,199.83	63.84		
46006	Suisun City and Napa Junction.	California Pacific R. R.	13.08	13	592.78		592.78	45.32		
46007	Woodland and Grafton.	...do	9.22	7	424.06		424.08	42.75		
46008	Vallejo Junction (n. o.) and Calistoga	Northern California R. B.	43.58	13	3,074.43		3,074.43	70.11		
46009	Marysville and Oroville.	Central Pacific R. R.	27.50	12	1,316.70		1,316.70	47.88		
46010	Lathrop and Goshen.	Central Pacific and North Pacific R. R.	146.39	13	25,032.69		25,032.44	171.00		
46011	San Francisco and Cloverdale.	San Francisco and North Pacific R. R.	84.95	13	9,951.04	3,059.75	9,951.04	117.14	25.00	Pay not fixed on 12.15 miles.
46012	Stockton and Milton.	Stockton and Copperopolis R. R.	30.00	9	1,775.31		1,775.31	59.00		
46013	San Pedro and Los Angeles.	Southern Pacific R. R.	26.46	7	1,131.16		1,131.16	42.75		

No.	Termini	Railroad	491.76	7.27	60,679.88	6,068.50	60,949.38	123.90	25.00	Remarks
48014	Goshen, Cal., and Yuma, Ariz									R. P. O. only between Goshen and Los Angeles, 242.78 miles. Land grant.
48015	Elmira and Madison	Vaca Valley and Clear Lake R. R.	27.51	6.9	1,189.71		1,189.71	43.61		
48016	San Francisco and Ingram's	North Pacific Coast R. R.	87.00	9.3	4,984.23		4,984.23	57.29		
48017	Los Angeles and Santa Ana	Central Pacific R. R. Company (lessee Los Angeles and San Diego R. R.).	35.00	6	2,404.78		2,404.78	67.55		
48018	Visalia and Goshen	Visalia R. R.	7.98	19	392.85		392.95	51.30		
48019	Colfax and Nevada City	Nevada County Narrow Gauge R. R.	22.77	14	1,557.46		1,557.46	68.40		
48020	Los Angeles and Santa Monica	Los Angeles and Independence R. R.	19.77	7	845.16		845.16	42.76		
48021	Santa Cruz and Pajaro	Santa Cruz R. R.	22.07	7	943.49		943.49	42.75		
48022	Davisville and Tehama	Central Pacific R. R. Company (lessee Northern Rwy.)	111.64	7.59	14,986.55	2,791.00	17,777.55	134.24	25.00	
48023	Galt and Ione	Amador Branch Rwy.	27.85	7	1,452.65		1,452.65	52.16		
48024	West Oakland Station (n. o.) and Berkeley	Central Pacific R. R. Company (lessee Berkeley Branch R. R.).	5.30	16	226.77		226.77	43.61		
48025	San Anselmo (n. o.) and San Quentin	North Pacific Coast R. R.	6.00	19	256.50		256.50	42.75		
48026	San Francisco and Alameda	Central Pacific R. R.	11.26	20.60	560.61		500.61	44.46		
48027	Fulton and Guerneville	San Francisco and North Pacific R. R.	16.04	7	685.71		685.71	42.75		
48028	San Francisco and Sacramento	Central Pacific R. R.	140.55	11.50	17,425.38		17,425.38	123.98		
48029	Niles and San José	Central Pacific R. R.	18.30	13	923.23		923.23	64.45		
48030	Monterey and Castroville	Monterey R. R.	16.40	6	712.64		712.64	42.75		
48031	San Francisco and Santa Cruz	South Pacific Coast R. R.	81.10	13.8	6,323.91		6,323.91	78.10		
48032	Port Costa and Lathrop	Central Pacific R. R. Company (lessee San Pablo R.R.).	62.23	13	10,641.33	1,655.75	12,197.08	171.00	25.00	
48033	Citrus Station (n. o.) and Riverside	California Southern R. R	2.79	28	243.05		243.05	64.12		
48034	Gilroy and Tres Pinos	Southern Pacific R. R	20.64	10	733.95		733.95	35.56		
48035	Peters and Oakdale	Stockton and Copperopolis R. R.	19.22	6	821.65		821.65	42.75		
48036	Vacant.									
48037	National City and Barstow	California Southern R. R	212.69	7	17,457.59		17,457.59	82.98		Land grant.
48038	Goshen and Huron	Southern Pacific R. R.	40.56	7	1,497.88		1,497.88	36.93		Land grant.
48039	Sonoma Landing (n. o.) and Glen Ellen.	Sonoma Valley R. R.	21.47	7	917.84		917.84	42.75		
48040	San Luis Obispo and Los Olivos.	Pacific Coast Rwy	57.30	6	3,327.40		3,327.40	49.59		
48041	San Luis Obispo and Port Harford	do	12.30	9	521.55		521.55	43.75		Do.
48042	Mojave and Needles	Atlantic and Pacific R. R.	240.72	7	23,544.82		23,544.82	97.81		
48043	Lodi and Valley Springs	San Joaquin and Sierra Nevada R. R.	28.81	7	1,650.42		1,650.42	61.56		
48044	Eureka and Hydesville	Eel River and Eureka R. R	28.70	7	1,897.99		1,897.99	59.85		
48045	Felton and Boulder Creek	South Pacific Coast R. R.	8.14	12	847.98		847.98	42.75		Covered by 48053.
48046	Vacant									
48047	do									
48048	Colusa and Sites	Colusa and Lake R. R	21.95	7	674.69		674.69	26.78		
48049	Campbell and New Almaden	South Pacific Coast R. B.	13.96	13	582.90		582.90	28.22		

C.—*Railroad service as in operation on the 30th of June 1888*—Continued.

Number of route.	State and terminal.	Corporate title of company carrying the mail.	Distance.	Average number of trips per week over whole route.	Annual pay for transportation.	Annual pay for railway post-office cars.	Total annual pay.	Cost per mile for transportation.	Cost per mile for railway post-office cars.	Remarks.
	CALIFORNIA—continued.		*Miles.*		*Dollars.*	*Dollars.*	*Dollars.*	*Dollars.*	*Dollars.*	
46050	Soledad and Templeton	Southern Pacific R. R.	78.78	7	5,966.15		5,966.15	75.10		
46051	Saugus Station (n.o.) and Santa Barbara.	do	78.80	14	7,411.14		7,411.14	94.05		
46052	Arcata Wharf (n.o.) and Blue Lake	Arcata and Mad River R. R	10.80	6	335.27		335.27	31.63		Pay not fixed.
46053	San Bernardino and Los Angeles	California Central Rw'y	63.13	22.10	11,388.64		11,388.64	180.40		Do.
46054	Escondo and Raymond	Southern Pacific R. R.	21.30	7	437.07		437.07	20.52		Do.
46055	Riverside and Capistrano	California Central Rw'y	59.94	7						Do.
46056	San Bernardino and Lugonia	do	9.25	6						
46057	Oceanside and Escondido	do	22.77	6						
46058	Los Angeles and Port Ballona	do	18.07	6						
			4,061.64		608,978.82	58,088.00	667,067.82			

D.—*Steam-boat service in operation on the 30th of June, 1888.*

No. of route.	State and terminal.	Name of contractor.	Annual pay.	Length of route.	Trips per week.	Remarks.
				Miles.		
	MAINE.					
85	Bangor to Deer Isle	Bangor and Bar Harbor Steam-boat Co	$168.00	50	*3	During season of navigation, from about May 1 to November 30, 1888. $2 per round trip.
87	Portland to Cousin's Island	Horace B. Townsend	290.00	9	†2	For 9 months, from April 1 to December 31.
90	Middle Dam to Errol, N. H.	Charles A. J. Farrar	437.50	9	6	For 5 months, from May 1 to September 30.
91	Andover to Upper Dam	do	50.00	24	6	For 4 months; from June 1 to September 30.
92	Bemis to Indian Rock	Fred. C. Barker	275.00	15	6	For 4 months; from May 25 to September 30.
93	Rangeley to Indian Rock	Frank C. Hewey	200.00	8	6	For 4 months; from June 1 to September 30.
94	Greenville to Kineo	Lemuel Nichols	470.00	20	3	Six times a week from May 16 to November 15, and three times a week (* *) from November 16 to May 15.
95	Chebeague Island to Portland	George F. West	600.00	16	6	For 2½ months.
96	Bath to Booth Bay / Wiscasset to Booth Bay	Eastern Steam-boat Co / do	1,000.00	15 / 15½	12 / 6	For 5½ months. / For 4 months.
97	Vinal Haven to Rockland	Moses Webster	1,064.00	15	12	For 4 months.
98	Portland to Eastport	Frank W. Aiken	850.00	180	1	For 8 months.
100	Eastport to Lubec	J. R. Pligg	490.00	3	6	
			5,894.50	384½		
	NEW HAMPSHIRE.					
1097	Lakeside to Camp Carthon, Me.	Androscoggin Lakes Transportation Co	500.00	71½	6	For 5 months; from June 1 to October 31.
1098	Lakeside to Wentworth's Location	Charles A. J. Farrar	525.00	17	6	For 6 months; from May 1 to October 31.
1099	The Weirs to Wolfborough	Winnipiseogee Steam-boat Co	700.00	29	6	For 4½ months; from June 1 to October 28.
1100	Alton Bay to Centre Harbor	Boston and Maine Railroad Co	1,000.00	20	3	From June 21 to October 31.
			2,825.00	147½		
	MASSACHUSETTS.					
2004	Wood's Holl to Nantucket	Nantucket and Cape Cod Steam-boat Co	7,875.00	37	12	For 6 months; from May 1 to October 31.
3095	New Bedford to Nonquit	George A. Bourne	350.00	6	13	For 6 months; from November 1 to April 30.
3099	New Bedford to Cuttyhunk	Samuel C. Hart	1,388.50	16	1	For 3 months; from June 11 to September 24. For 9 months, from September 15 to June 14.
3100	New Bedford to Edgartown	New Bedford, Vineyard and Nantucket Steam-boat Co	2,600.00	31	19	The year round on 31 miles. Additional from June 26 to September 10 on 25 miles.
			12,963.50	89		

* For 4 months. † For 3 months.

D.—*Steam-boat service in operation on the 30th of June, 1888*—Continued.

No. of route.	State and terminl.	Name of contractor.	Annual pay.	Length of route.	Trips per week.	Remarks.
	RHODE ISLAND.			*Miles.*		
4095	Watch Hill to Railroad Station (n. o.) at Stonington, Conn.	Henry L. Ripley	$165.00	5	12	For 2½ months; from July 1 to September 20.
4099	Block Island to Newport	George W. Conley and Martin V. Ball	3,095.00	30	8	For 8 months; from June 16 to September 1½. For 9 months; from September 16 to June 1½.
4100	Newport to Providence	do		30	8	For 8 months; from June 16 to September 1½. For 5 months; from June 1 to October 31.
	Newport to Wickford Junction (n. o.)	Newport and Wickford Railroad and Steam-boat Co.	8,847.56	18	25 / 18	For 7 months; from November 1 to May 31.
			12,107.56			
	NEW YORK.					
6979	Canandaigua to Naples	James McKechnie	500.00	20½	6	From April 1 to December 10 of each year.
6980	Penn Yan to Hammondsport	Crooked Lake Navigation Co	190.00	24	6	From March 15 to December 15 of each year.
6982	Sag Harbor to New London	Rilas F. Morgan	3,000.00	40	6	From March 15 to November 30 of each year.
6983	Brooklyn to Jersey City	Brooklyn Annex Co	2,000.00	3	36	
6984	Lake George to Fort Ticonderoga	Champlain Transportation Co	1,328.38	4½		From June 1 to October 30 of each year, pay being $275 per month.
6985	Geneva to Watkins	Seneca Lake Steam Navigation Co	2,213.94	43½	6	During season of navigation.
6986	Plattsburgh to Burlington	Champlain Transportation Co	1,060.00	25	6	From July 1 to August 31 of each year.
7520	Mayville to Jamestown	Buffalo, New York and Philadelphia Railroad Co.	750.00	21½	12	
			11,096.17	224½		
	MARYLAND.					
10087	Piney Point, Md., to Washington, D. C.	Potomac Steam-boat Co	400.00	90	3	June 1 to September 30 of each year.
10088	Baltimore to Salisbury	Maryland Steam-boat Co	900.00	140	1	January 1 to February 28.
10091	Washington, D. C., to Colonial Beach, Va.	J. B. Colegrove	450.00	6½	3	March 1 to December 31. June 1 to September 30.
10093	Baltimore to Queenstown	Chester River Steam-boat Co	350.00	33	3	Or 6 times a week if trips are made by steamer. June 1 to September 15.
10094	Baltimore to Chestertown	Wm. C. Eliason	400.00	30½	3	115 miles, May 1 to December 31.
10095	Baltimore to Wilson's Wharf, (n. o.)	Eastern Shore Steam-boat Co	3,000.00	33½	2 / 1	124½ miles, May 1 to December 31. 115 miles, January 1 to April 30.
10096	Baltimore to Saint Michael's	H. C. Dodson	395.00	63½	3	124½ miles, January 1 to April 30.
10097	Washington, D. C., to Glymont, Md.	Thos. Adams	2,180.00	30½	6	

No.	Route	Contractor	Amount	Miles	Trips
10098	Baltimore to Benedict	Henry Williams	1,800.00	117½	2
10099	Baltimore to Fitchett's, Va.	Maryland Steam-boat Co.	1,703.98	211½	2
10100	Baltimore to Cambridge	Choptank Steam-boat Co.	1,470.00	90½	6
			13,518.96	1,110½	
	VIRGINIA.				
11093	Norfolk to Thompson's Wharf	Old Dominion Steam-ship Co	900.00	70	8
11094	Norfolk to Cape Charles	New York, Philadelphia and Norfolk R.R.	10,971.62	88	7
11095	Newport News to Norfolk	J. B. Colsgrove	3,200.00	14	14
11096	Franklin City to Chincoteague Island and.	Old Dominion Steam-ship Co	750.00	7	6
11097	Norfolk, Va., to Baltimore, Md.	Baltimore Steam Packet Co	12,000.00	184	3
11099	Norfolk to Richmond	Virginia Steam-boat Co	3,500.00	138½	3
11100	Fredericksburgh, Va., to Baltimore, Md.	Henry Williams	5,800.00	289	3
			96,021.62	737½	
	NORTH CAROLINA.				
13094	Edenton to Williamston	Roanoke, Norfolk and Baltimore Steam-boat Co.	3,000.00	51	6
13095	Elizabeth City to Fairfield	M. K. King	2,750.00	109	3
13097	Edenton to Franklin	Albemarle Steam Navigation Co.	3,500.00	97	8
13098	Plymouth to Windsor	C. T. Hardin	883.00	28	6
13099	Wilmington to Southport	John W. Harper	1,100.00	25	6
13100	Wilmington to Fayetteville	Samuel W. Skinner	1,450.00	112	3
			12,683.00	425	
	SOUTH CAROLINA.				
14097	Georgetown to Bucksville	A. A. Springs	652.00	49	3
14099	Charleston to Moultrieville	W. M. Bird	962.00	7½	14
14100	Charleston to Edisto Island	Carl Berlin	600.00	43	2
			2,214.00	99½	
	GEORGIA.				
15100	Brunswick to Saint Simon's Mills	Urbanus Dart	600.00	12	12
	FLORIDA.				
16073	Titusville to Melbourne	Indian River Steam-boat Co.	2,850.00	43	6
16074	Melbourne to Jupiter	do	3,800.00	88	3
16075	Cleveland to Meyers	Wellington M. White	1,600.00	80	3
16080	Palatka to Drayton Island	George W. Beach and John W. Miller	2,500.00	40	6

D.—Steam-boat service in operation on the 30th of June, 1888—Continued.

No. of route.	State and termini.	Name of contractor.	Annual pay.	Length of route.	Trips per week.	Remarks.
			Dollars.	*Miles.*		
	FLORIDA—continued.					
16063	Tampa to Havana, Cuba	Henry B. Plant	58,393.28	386	3	For 6 months.
16065	Jacksonville to Orange Dale	J. B. Colegrove	1,650.00	38½	3	For 6 months.
16087	Fernandina to Oakwell, Ga	John Richardson	1,797.75	50	6	On 15 miles.
16096	Chattahoochee to Apalachicola	G. D. Owens	5,500.00	144	3	On 85 miles.
16097	Jacksonville to Fort George	J. B. Colegrove	1,560.00	23½	6	
			70,698.08	367½		
	ALABAMA.					
17097	Mobile to Selma	John Quill	1,850.00	313½	3	
17098	Mobile to Demopolis	Frank S. Stone	2,375.00	254	1	For 6 months.
17099	Mobile to Point Clear	Peter Burke	2,375.00	26	7	For 6 months.
17100	Rome to Gadsden	John J. Seay	2,750.00	155	3	
			9,350.00	747½		
	MISSISSIPPI.					
18098	English Lookout, La., to Gainesville, Miss.	John Poitevent and J. A. Favre	1,500.00	24½	6	
18099	Vicksburg to Paionia	E. C. Carroll	2,000.00	186	1	
18100	Vicksburg to Greenwood	do	2,400.00	285½	1	
			5,900.00	476		
	KENTUCKY.					
20095	Paducah to Florence, Ala	The Evansville, Paducah and Tennessee River Packet Company.	3,000.00	300	3	
20097	Louisville to Evansville, Ind	William W. Hite	10,900.00	187	6	
20099	Evansville, Ind., to Paducah, Ky	William H. Caldwell	10,872.87	137	6	
20100	Paducah to Cairo, Ill	do	1,099.00	50	6	
			24,872.57	674		

No.	Route	Contractor	Amount	Miles	No.	Remarks
21206	OHIO. Portsmouth to Cincinnati	Cincinnati, Portsmouth, Big Sandy and Pomeroy Packet Co.	9,000.00	65½, 62½	9	
			9,000.00	127¼	4	
24095	MICHIGAN. Harbor Springs to Saint James	Charles W. Caskey	1,964.00	81	3	April 1 to November 30 each year, at $15 per round trip.
24096	Manistee to Milwaukee	Flint and Pere Marquette R. R. Co.	1,430.00	122	6	During season of navigation, at $10 per round trip.
24097	Charlevoix to East Jordan	Morris J. Stockman and John Mason	312.00	17	6	
24098	Mackinaw City to Mackinac (Island)	J. B. Colegrove	1,776.00	13	6	May 15 to November 15 each year, at $2 per round trip.
			5,176.00	203		
25099	WISCONSIN. Milwaukee to Grand Haven	Detroit, Grand Haven and Milwaukee Railway Co.	410.00	85	6	May 15 to June 30, 1888, at $10 per round trip.
28099	MISSOURI. Cairo, Ill. to Elmot, Ark.	Theodore C. Zeigler	7,000.00	178	3	
29093	ARKANSAS. Memphis to Friar's Point	James Lee, jr.	7,500.00	128	3	
29096	Arkansas City to Vicksburg	E. S. Merkel	15,000.00	204½	3	
29097	Memphis to Arkansas City	John D. Adams	14,000.00	252½	3	
29099	Memphis to Gold Dust	James Lee, sr.	8,000.00	115	3	
			44,500.00	700		
30091	LOUISIANA. New Orleans to Vicksburg	Thomas P. Leathers	1,000.00	395½	1	
30092	Natchez to Vicksburg	Joseph N. Carpenter	8,900.00	112½	3	
30093	Natchez to Bayou Sara	Louis A. Jauf	8,975.00	102½	3	
30094	Baton Rouge to Bayou Sara	Planters and Merchants' Packet Co.	4,500.00	41	4	
30095	Troyville to Tooley's	H. D. Vaughan	950.00	59	3	
30096	Lake Charles to Cameron	A. H. Wait	2,925.00	55	2	
30097	New Orleans to Fort Vincent	M. B. Munoy	3,592.00	93½	2	
30098	New Orleans to Grand Isle	John F. Kraas	800.00	89	1	For 8 months. For 4 months.
30100	New Orleans to Port Eads	Charles P. Truslow	7,800.00	83, 41, 12	8, 1	
			43,240.00	1,084½		

D.—*Steam-boat service in operation on the 30th of June, 1888—Continued.*

No. of route.	State and termini.	Name of contractor.	Annual pay.	Length of route.	Trips per week.	Remarks.
			Dollars.	*Miles.*		
	TEXAS.					
31190	Houston to Bay View	Leon F. Allien	576.33	89	3	
	WASHINGTON TERRITORY.					
43078	Portland, Oregon, to Vancouver	Oregon Railway and Navigation Co	500.00	18	6	
43079	Portland, Oregon, to Cascades	...do	2,000.00	65½	3	
43080	Seattle to Seattle	Rufus M. Creswell	995.00	27½	2	
43081	Seattle to Blakely	James Nugent	500.00	8	6	
43062	Port Gamble to Skokomish	H. N. Warren	828.32	18	1	
4964	Oysterville to Willapa	...do	2,847.00	46	5	
43065	Montesano to Laidlaw	George W. Emerson	3,083.53	19	6	
43066	Cosmopolis to Markham	H. N. Warren	691.00	15	3	
43067	Tacoma to Tacoma	C. O. Lorenz	494.00	85	1	
43068	...do	Edward Miller	539.00	21	1	
43069	Seattle to Juniata	Jay Clinton O'Connor	600.00	18	6	
43090	Hoquiam to Damon	James B. Kirkaldie	400.00	15	1	
43051	Seattle to Mount Vernon	George W. Gove	2,500.00	74½	3	
43052	Seattle to Snohomish	Charles H. Low	1,000.00	53	6	
43066	Port Townsend to Neah Bay	James Morgan	5,407.00	104	2	
43065	Sehome to Blaine	H. N. Warren	316.68	36	1	
43098	Port Townsend to Sehome	J. C. Brittain	7,575.45	181½	3	
43096	Seattle to Whatcom	Oregon Railway and Navigation Co	5,000.00	181½	6	
43099	Seattle to Port Townsend	George S. Jacobs	18,139.42	128	6	
43100	Port Townsend to Irondale	C. C. McCoy	420.00	6½	6	
			54,701.99	965½		
	OREGON.					
44096	Myrtle Point to Bandon	Fred. Jarvis	1,474.64	24½	6	
44100	Portland to Astoria	Oregon Railway and Navigation Co	9,600.00	93	6	
				38	3	
			11,074.64	154½		

	CALIFORNIA.					
44096	Tahoe to Tahoe......*	J. A. Tolman	4,000. 00	26½	......	Six times a week from May 1 to October 31, twice a week the residue of the year.
46097	Eureka to Arcata Wharf	M. V. Nichols	944.00	8	12	
46098	San Francisco to Eureka	Pacific Coast Steam-ship Co	6,000.00	240	1	
46099	San Francisco to Sacramento	C. J. Wilder	6,000.00	119	6	
			16,944.00	409½		
	ALASKA.					
47100	Port Townsend, Wash., to Sitka, Alaska.	Pacific Coast Steam-ship Co	18,000.00	1,069	......	Two trips a month.

E.—*Increase and decrease in star, steam-boat, and*

States and Territories.	STAR.						STEAM-BOAT.	
	Length of routes.		Annual rate of expenditure.		Number of miles traveled per annum.		Length of routes.	
	Increase.	Decrease.	Increase.	Decrease.	Increase.	Decrease.	Increase.	Decrease.
	Miles.	Miles.	Dollars.	Dollars.	Miles.	Miles.	Miles.	Miles.
Maine	8.96		902.67		19,317.21		49.99	
New Hampshire		72.36		791.13		30,889.72	71.50	
Vermont	2.66	42.70		232.18		10,341.89		
Massachusetts	2.66		1,000.53		17,342.78			
Rhode Island		.51	16.16		197.08			
Connecticut	8.12		344.97		6,685.38			
New York	6.98		4,344.52		62,287.32			
New Jersey	7.58		992.41		16,577.67			
Pennsylvania	12.02		5,931.58		101,956.92			
Delaware	4.25		264.31		4,053.92			
Maryland	23.63		2,028.04		47,112.40		78.00	
Virginia	156.93		5,465.63		134,183.39		70.00	
West Virginia	234.80		5,995.53		119,796.98			
North Carolina		171.94		1,243.60		40,055.85		
South Carolina	93.70		1,610.80		48,314.64			
Georgia	22.14		614.10		3,975.05			
Florida		191.31		2,562.59		28,024.31	130.00	
Alabama		85.31		2,810.04		60,524.56	4.50	
Mississippi	72.49		2,357.07		35,455.82			133.75
Tennessee		12.57	449.24		11,480.74			
Kentucky		82.19	1,675.05		47,167.51		300.00	
Ohio	14.55		404.85½		87,437.18			92.75
Indiana		18.78		6,515.09		78,174.21		
Illinois		270.49		11,260.59		83,621.85		
Michigan		78.08		13,723.10		88,891.80		75.00
Wisconsin		162.00		9,377.04		85,396.25	85.00	
Minnesota		196.74		12,087.20		13,080.82		
Iowa		486.88		12,319.57		72,826.22		
Missouri		42.87		14,033.63	203,294.79			
Arkansas	77.47		1,580.11		65,755.48		5.75	
Louisiana	117.62			1.57	20,182.00		.50	
Texas		381.38		11,847.21		114,988.02		
Indian Territory		513.96		7,203.32		124,407.92		
Kansas		1,944.33		23,252.43		631,384.50		
Nebraska		475.63		8,187.20		101,504.00		
Dakota		655.69		8,346.48		185,094.00		
Montana		430.50		12,549.73		188,706.00		
Wyoming		94.00		50.87		6,877.00		
Colorado	37.42			4,028.58	6,466.56			
New Mexico	44.25		37.95		4,235.00			
Arizona		76.00		4,653.77		57,190.00		
Utah		127.75		5,149.89		64,712.24		
Idaho		226.50		5,038.77		90,196.32		
Washington	6.58		2,380.08		22,576.32			30.37
Oregon	128.00		8,414.88		70,885.50			
Nevada		49.50		4,340.27		40,040.00		
California		189.95		5,575.45		57,644.85		2.00
Alaska		66.25			380.00			
Total	1,090.61	7,079.96	46,826.30½	187,169.73	1,343,152.95	1,918,438.23	795.24	333.37
Increase							461.37	
Decrease		5,988.75		160,341.42½		575,285.28		

railroad service during the year ended June 30, 1888.

STEAM-BOAT.				RAILROAD.					
Annual rate of expenditure.		Number of miles traveled per annum.		Length of routes.		Annual rate of expenditure.		Number of miles traveled per annum.	
Increase.	Decrease.	Increase.	Decrease.	Increase.	Decrease.	Increase.	Decrease.	Increase.	Decrease.
Dollars.	Dollars.	Miles.	Miles.	Miles.	Miles.	Dollars.	Dollars.	Miles.	Miles.
385.50		11,906.96		16.00		278.76		9,984.00	
675.00		20,858.00		21.23				13,247.51	
						4,220.50			.01
			.01	10.95		1,800.33		12,150.10	
						366.79		15,443.99	
			3,899.30	45.43		771.81		29,621.27	
				9.30		416.07		18,471.53	
				178.05		7,345.75		234,876.96	
903.36		6,864.00		124.22		5,093.11		86,317.91	
800.00		21,840.00		79.28		2,735.49		49,470.72	
				106.33		2,701.69		56,349.92	
				185.66		7,122.44		112,395.42	
				79.13		433.69		50,020.35	
				245.15		8,511.02		152,973.59	
11,387.03		53,040.00		174.60		5,344.01		108,956.39	
	150.00	936.00		102.43		3,368.44		64,205.70	
				174.20		10,895.97		114,580.82	
3,000.00	3,000.00	62,400.00	27,820.00	73.82	47.56	2,480.52	7,877.02	45,406.47	114,617.28
	5,400.00		57,876.00	183.61		79,951.54		146,980.50	
				83.77		34,087.92		271,215.91	
				919.22		211,657.67		2,228,335.20	
416.00	1,418.00	6,630.00	1,690.00	320.51		14,296.82		233,530.14	
				542.38		79,714.47		1,338,046.99	
				230.15		104,334.60		1,085,613.17	
	2,547.48			493.98		190,204.00		1,282,010.47	
		1,794.00		220.62		203,222.81		1,603,317.41	
	200.00		2,928.99	282.57		15,909.34		195,461.98	
				151.79				94,716.96	
				1,244.58		36,161.78		977,859.11	
				371.20		15,977.01		270,978.00	
				2,157.56		129,136.70		2,108,969.91	
				1,317.36		101,323.68		911,840.30	
				1,122.16		46,055.01		722,786.23	
				200.69		8,426.61		135,545.22	
				138.56		5,963.82		83,341.44	
				550.41		33,762.10		492,313.03	
				35.78	3.90	6,620.53	226.74	26,119.40	2,433.61
	4,906.34	3,094.00		119.85		5,530.89		76,979.54	
				172.43		26,660.27		137,388.55	
				12.50		990.40		7,800.00	
	236.00		2,496.00	57.15		2,825.92		35,661.60	
6,650.00		11,600.00		266.36		51,100.95		258,995.27	
23,610.80	17,857.80	200,462.90	96,710.30	12,815.97	51.46	1,476,791.19	8,103.76	15,912,968.88	117,050.90
5,753.09		103,752.66		12,764.51		1,468,687.43		15,795,917.48	

E.—*Increase and decrease in star, steam-boat, and*

States and Territories.	STAR.						STEAM-BOAT.	
	Length of routes.		Annual rate of expenditure.		Number of miles traveled per annum.		Length of routes.	
	Increase.	Decrease.	Increase.	Decrease.	Increase.	Decrease.	Increase.	Decrease.
	Miles.	*Miles.*	*Dollars.*	*Dollars.*	*Miles.*	*Miles.*	*Miles.*	*Miles.*
Maine	8.36		902.67		19,817.21		49.99	
New Hampshire		72.36		791.13		30,889.72	71.50	
Vermont		42.70		232.18		10,341.89		
Massachusetts	3.66		1,000.53		17,342.78			
Rhode Island		.51	16.16		197.08			
Connecticut	8.13		344.97		6,685.38			
New York	6.98		4,344.52		62,287.32			
New Jersey	7.58		992.41		16,577.67			
Pennsylvania	12.02		5,936.58		101,956.92			
Delaware	4.29		264.81		4,053.92			
Maryland	83.63		2,028.04		47,113.40		78.00	
Virginia	156.93		5,465.63		134,133.38		70.00	
West Virginia	234.80		5,995.53		119,796.98			
North Carolina		171.94		1,243.60		40,055.85		
South Carolina	93.76		1,616.80		48,314.64			
Georgia	22.14		614.10		3,975.05			
Florida		191.31		2,562.59		28,024.31	130.00	
Alabama		85.31		2,810.04		60,524.56	4.50	
Mississippi	72.49		2,357.07		35,455.82			123.75
Tennessee		13.57	449.24		11,480.74			
Kentucky		82.19	1,675.05		47,167.51		300.00	
Ohio	14.55		404.85½		87,437.18			92.75
Indiana		13.78		6,515.09	78,174.21			
Illinois		270.49		11,260.59	83,621.85			
Michigan		78.08		13,723.10	84,891.80			75.00
Wisconsin		162.00		9,877.04	85,896.25		85.00	
Minnesota		196.74		12,087.20		13,080.82		
Iowa		486.88		12,319.57		72,826.22		
Missouri		42.87		14,033.63	203,294.79			
Arkansas	77.47		1,530.11		65,755.48		5.75	
Louisiana	117.62		1.57		20,182.00		.50	
Texas		381.33		11,847.91	114,933.02			
Indian Territory		518.36		7,263.32	124,407.92			
Kansas		1,944.38		28,252.43	631,384.50			
Nebraska		475.62		3,167.20	101,804.00			
Dakota		655.69		8,846.48	185,094.00			
Montana		430.50		12,549.73	188,706.00			
Wyoming		94.00		50.87	6,877.00			
Colorado	37.42		4,028.58		5,466.56			
New Mexico	44.25		37.95		4,235.00			
Arizona		76.00		4,653.77	57,190.00			
Utah		127.75		5,149.89	64,712.24			
Idaho		226.50		5,038.77	90,196.82			
Washington	6.58		2,380.08		22,576.32			30.37
Oregon	128.00		8,414.88		70,885.50			
Nevada		49.50		4,340.27	40,040.00			
California		189.95		5,575.45	57,644.85			2.00
Alaska				66.25		380.00		
Total	1,090.61	7,079.36	46,828.30½	187,169.73	1,343,152.95	1,918,438.23	795.24	333.87
Increase							461.37	
Decrease		5,988.75		140,341.42½		875,285.28		

F.—Division of Inspection, Contract Bureau.—Deductions, fines, and remissions year ending June 30, 1888.

States and Territories.	STAR ROUTES.				RAILROAD ROUTES.				STEAM-BOAT ROUTES.				TOTALS FOR THE YEAR.			
	Deductions.	Remissions.	Fines.	Remissions.	Deductions.	Remissions.	Fines.	Remissions.	Deductions.	Remissions.	Fines.	Remissions.	Deductions.	Remissions.	Fines.	Remissions.
Alabama	$2,032.19	$321.47	$1,230.31	$65.62	$1,214.13	$765.96	$130.82	$977.42	$227.50				$3,573.82	$1,067.43	$1,375.63	$1,043.04
Alaska	908.97	33.13	263.02	115.00	582.87	378.96	85.00	43.50	1,125.00		$15.00		1,125.00	83.13	248.02	153.00
Arizona	79.80	146.61	14.64	5.00	1,060.76	418.62		64.46	1,019.82	$24.03			2,461.66	548.10		
Arkansas	1,166.67	2,327.64	45.00	105.00	2,350.89	626.00	343.00						1,190.56	433.28	60.00	60.48
California	1,643.12	84.66	180.00		1,090.25	1,058.92	126.00	64.46	18.16	18.16			3,476.72	972.80	471.00	169.48
Colorado	421.10	102.06	162.50		1,040.44	370.78	5.00						2,133.87	1,143.00	236.50	1.00
Connecticut	945.35	112.35	4.00	9.50	6,455.13	5,696.20							3,452.35	472.70	9.00	
Dakota	30.07	11.20	123.00		64.00	64.00							7,404.48	6,207.55	123.00	9.50
Delaware	788.23	119.60			7.08								94.76	63.59		
Florida	1,516.02	89.64	99.89	12.00	3,436.25	1,961.90	284.00	364.77	4,782.09	1,250.00	151.00	$5.00	5,568.40	1,369.50	250.80	17.00
Georgia	1,560.07	18.66	744.01	67.06	48.89	33.18					5.00		4,062.30	2,074.96	958.01	431.33
Idaho	653.72	299.86	83.00	5.00	24,875.53	4,098.13	1,426.00	2,608.99					608.96	51.87	58.00	5.00
Illinois	179.61	8.84	77.00	150.00	10,938.13	4,113.83	635.00	537.16					35,429.25	4,325.66	1,507.10	2,623.99
Indiana	690.86	4.91	111.00	4.00									11,117.84	4,122.17	746.00	541.16
Indian T.	46.00	14.01	14.61										46.00	14.01	14.61	
Iowa	750.86	62.33	61.00	10.00	5,059.72	5,238.35	59.00	238.57					8,810.58	5,520.56	100.00	848.77
Kansas	1,017.61	21.36	61.17	61.17	4,559.78	1,473.67	1,138.61	812.24	6.02	6.02	199.88	119.72	5,577.27	1,494.97	1,190.78	814.94
Kentucky	571.89	8.16	222.61	2.00	6,171.43	1,861.09	639.00	3,901.79	176.49	176.49	3.00		9,227.41	1,866.77	1,052.89	4,128.52
Louisiana	1,097.60	163.17	184.79	2.00	591.99		3.00						1,791.20	248.70	243.50	2.00
Maryland	354.66	51.46	137.60	2.50	687.33	130.11		11.00	50.79				2,784.74	232.28	137.79	15.50
Massachusetts	381.22	23.47	68.84	12.00	9,028.25	421.27	520.00	54.17	627.38		12.00		10,597.56	474.72	660.60	64.77
Michigan	402.79	397.05	116.94		1,230.80	201.70	1,100.00	16.21	1,216.73				3,819.87	262.71	137.79	16.21
Minnesota	1,891.81	359.66	28.56	35.00	2,968.00	961.34	522.34	280.75	18.94				3,419.49	1,089.82	1,188.66	65.75
Mississippi	1,328.92	44.27	125.82	2.00	22,187.83	313.46	22.00	217.89	2,383.84				25,792.64	258.59	227.94	200.00
Missouri	1,035.87		132.01	1.00	745.78	337.14	778.00	1,220.20	842.11				2,916.81	666.88	549.34	219.89
Montana	2,034.93	290.16	58.00	3.00	13,837.06	2,516.09			1,828.00		68.68		10,082.62	2,561.26	147.62	1,231.20
Nebraska		51.46	44.73	2.00		34.73							4,252.79	220.01	983.64	2.00
Nevada	385.65	45.96	5.00		3,480.29	2,076.36	5,813.00	8.00					4,252.79	2,127.82	5,857.78	10.00
New Hampshire	381.82	69.74	28.75		8,731.84		2.00	4.15					1,117.50	45.83	7.00	
New Jersey	459.32	113.89	32.50		403.83	114.65	45.00						8,304.75	2,325.50	184.50	78.75
New Mexico	811.43	69.62	32.50		3,874.94	2,812.18	46.00	8.00					3,760.13	757.33	45.70	75.50
New York	2,848.32	549.18	454.38	2.66	3,729.70	1,727.80	85.00						25,100.41	3,961.90	5,428.29	8.00
North Carolina	1,044.28	72.85	119.00	2.00	33,558.43	3,422.99	4,972.00	50.35	24.47		65.00	45.00	41,187.53	1,628.07	177.00	59.85
Ohio	144.40		194.00		368.25	588.87	2.00	4,522.00			21.49		2,821.10	790.00	85.00	47.00
Oregon	595.06	61.46	78.00		648.14	1,644.14	7.00	6,225.23	1,205.49	16.31		45.00	41,187.53	1,028.12	4,828.26	225.23
Pennsylvania	1,367.74	249.41	1,013.49	14.75	17,313.56	1,036.71	1,866.00		848.82				18,701.30	1,286.12	2,911.49	31.00

F.—*Division of Inspection, Contract Bureau.—Deductions, fines, and remissions year ending June 30, 1888—Continued.*

States and Territories.	STAR ROUTES.				RAILROAD ROUTES.				STEAM-BOAT ROUTES.				TOTALS FOR THE YEAR.			
	Deductions.	Remissions.	Fines.	Remissions.	Deductions.	Remissions.	Fines.	Remissions.	Deductions.	Remissions.	Fines.	Remissions.	Deductions.	Remissions.	Fines.	Remissions.
Rhode Island	$26.12	$42.22	$9.50		$42.78	$29.55	$4.00	$3.00	$74.88				$143.78	$29.55	$4.50	$63.00
South Carolina	354.35	120.25	76.00		141.36	53.54	198.00	221.72	14.43				465.61	125.76	80.00	226.72
Tennessee	784.90	365.71	333.00	$18.00	1,234.87	968.66	968.00	812.16		$7.31			2,965.66	475.74	831.00	827.16
Texas	2,672.96	4.12	948.85	15.00	16,644.92	1,411.65							19,333.26	1,773.84	1,184.86	
Utah	276.18	18.00	39.00		850.07	775.72	75.00	66.36					1,126.25	981.81	85.50	66.36
Vermont	538.00	90.61	27.75		790.94	191.30	378.00	27.00					1,328.94	981.81	102.75	43.00
Virginia	702.68	14.82	204.82	9.00	2,023.17	1,698.82			1,192.22	87.58	$7.00	$1.00	3,918.06	1,751.22	588.30	
Washington	444.11	10.88	33.00		1,333.97	2,308.26	28.00		2,142.79	87.94	164.50		3,920.87	2,874.58	234.00	
West Virginia	455.74	12.96	64.00		27.14		40.00						483.88	12.96	113.00	
Wisconsin	381.68	22.28	100.63		3,269.79	1,331.27	233.00	137.07					3,651.47	1,253.55	321.63	137.67
Wyoming	376.10	7.18	26.50		442.60	110.94							818.70	118.07	26.50	
Total	34,949.94	7,062.61	7,735.68	548.62	252,833.70	68,177.44	27,050.77	18,965.28	21,396.52	1,578.43	727.50		170,731	311,169.56	513,0835	19,704.08

RECAPITULATION.

	Deductions.	Remissions on deductions.	Fines.	Remissions on fines.
Railroads	$252,833.70	$68,177.44	$27,050.77	$18,965.28
Steam-boats	21,396.32	1,578.43	1,578.43	170.78
Star routes	34,949.94	7,062.81	7,735.68	548.62
Mail messengers	4,514.33	242.74	884.75	6.00
Postal clerks		137.68		
Total	318,321.15	77,205.10	35,908.70	19,710.08
Net	241,026.05		16,198.07	

of in- crease `e of` `e.`	Numbe miles tra per ann
l ease.	
	Mile
2. 75	83, 683, 9
......	10, 505, 3
....	3, 216, 0
......	185, 485, 7
......	4, 269, 8
......	....
1. 95	....
......	....
......	287, 251, 0
......	287, 251, 0
3. 00	82, 169, 8
......	1, 514, 1
2. 75	83, 683, 9
......	185, 485, 7
......	....
......	185, 485, 7

F.—*Division of Inspection, Contract Bureau.—Deductions, fines, and remissions year ending June 30, 1888—Continued.*

States and Territories.	STAR ROUTES.			RAILROAD ROUTES.				STEAM-BOAT ROUTES.				TOTALS FOR THE YEAR.			
	Deductions.	Fines.	Remissions.	Deductions.	Remissions.	Fines.	Remissions.	Deductions.	Remissions.	Fines.	Remissions.	Deductions.	Remissions.	Fines.	Remissions.
Rhode Island	$25.12	$9.50		$42.78	$29.55	$4.00	$3.00	$74.83				$148.73	$29.55	$9.50	$3.00
South Carolina	354.85	75.00		141.26	53.54	198.00	231.72					495.61	125.76	381.00	239.72
Tennessee	784.90	833.00	$18.00	1,334.87	968.65	968.00	812.16		$7.31			2,983.69	476.74	381.00	827.16
Texas	3,673.36	348.86	15.00	16,464.92	1,411.66			14.43				19,233.28	1,773.87	1,156.96	
Utah	276.18	38.50		850.07	776.72	75.00						1,126.25	1,773.84	98.50	
Vermont	538.00	27.75		790.94	191.20	378.50	66.36					1,325.94	361.81	102.75	66.36
Virginia	702.68	14.82	9.00	2,023.17	1,698.52	378.00	27.00	1,192.23	37.58	$7.00	$1.00	3,918.08	1,751.22	569.50	43.00
Washington	444.11	10.88		1,333.97	2,306.28	29.00		2,142.79	57.94	164.50		3,920.87	2,374.58	224.00	
West Virginia	456.74	12.98		27.14		42.00						483.88	12.98	113.00	
Wisconsin	381.68	100.63		3,209.79	1,231.27	232.00	187.67					3,651.47	1,253.55	383.63	187.67
Wyoming	376.10	26.50		442.00	118.94							818.70	118.97	26.50	
Total	38,949.34	7,062.81	548.03	252,823.70	68,177.44	27,060.77	18,985.52	21,393.82	178.72	727.50		311,160.56	76,818.63	35,513.95	19,704.03

RECAPITULATION.

	Deductions.	Remissions on deductions.	Fines.	Remissions on fines.
Railroads	$252,823.70	$68,177.44	$27,060.77	$18,985.52
Steam-boats	21,393.82	1,578.43	727.50	170.72
Star routes	38,949.34	7,062.81	7,735.66	548.02
Mail messengers	2,514.33	248.74	7,394.75	6.90
Postal clerks	4,547.36	137.08		
Total	318,221.16	77,205.10	35,908.70	19,716.08
Net	241,026.05		16,188.67	

of in-crease e of fe.	Numbe miles tra per ann
rease.	
2. 75	*Mile* 83, 683, 9
......	10, 595, 3
......	3, 216, 0
......	185, 485, 7
......	4, 269, 8
......	......
1. 95	......
......	......
......	287, 251, 0
......	287, 251, 0
3. 00	82, 169, 8
......	1, 514, 1
2. 75	83, 683, 9
......	185, 485, 7
......	......
......	185, 485, 7

E.—*Table showing the re adjustment of the rates of pay per mile on railroad routes in States routes in other States and Territories ; the re-adjustment of the rates based upon returns mails and railway post-office clerks, and the number of trips per week, in accordance*

[Abbreviations: r. p. o., railway post-office;

Index order.	State.	Number of route.	Termini.	Corporate title of company carrying the mail.	Length of route.	Average weight of whole distance per day.	Miles per hour.	Size, etc., of mail car or apartment.
					Miles	*Lbs.*		*Feet and inches.*
1	Ohio ..	21095	Buffalo, N. Y., Chicago, Ill.	Lake Shore and Michigan Southern Rwy.	540. 26	9d, 761	..	See parts ....
pt.	Ohio ..	21095	Buffalo, Cleveland	....do	183. 26	....		r. p. o., 49.5 by 9, 1 L.; 50 by 9, 1 L.; 60 by 9, 5 l.
pt.	Ohio ..	21095	Cleveland, Elyria	....do	25. 06	....		r. p. o., 49.5 by 9, 1 L.; 50 by 9, 1 l.; 60 by 9, 5 l.; apt., 17.8 by 9, 1 l.
pt.	Ohio ..	21095	Elyria, Millbury	....do	79. 77	....		r. p. o., 49.5 by 9, ½ l.; 45 by 9, ·1 L. (40 ft. auth.); 50 by 9, ½ l.; 60 by 9.4½ L
pt.	Ohio ..	21095	Millbury, Toledo	....do	8. 07	....		r. p. o., 49.5 by 9, 1 L.; 45 by 9, 1 l. (40 ft. auth.); 50 by 9, 1 l.; 60 by 9, 5 l.
pt.	Ohio ..	21095	Toledo, Elkhart	....do ...._	142. 90	......		r. p. o., 49.5 by 9, ½ l.; 50 by 9, ½ l.; 60 by 9, 2 l.; apt., 20 by 9, 1 l.; 15 by 9, 1 l., Hillsdale to Jonesville, and 1 l. White Pigeon to Elkhart.
pt.	Ohio ..	21095	Elkhart, Chicago......	....do	101. 20	......		r. p. o., 49.5 by 9, 1 l.; 50 by 9, 1 l.; 60 by 9, 5 l.
2	Ohio ;..	21032	Pittsburgh, Pa., Columbus, Ohio.	Pittsburgh, Cincinnati and Saint Louis Rwy.	193. 8:	34, 201	32	r. p. o., 60 by 8.6, 6 L.; 40 by 8.6, 1 l.; apt., 19 by 9.9, 2 L., to Putnam, 8 5 m., and 1 l., thence to Steubenville, 34 8 m.
3	Ohio ..	21032	Columbus, Ohio, Pittsburgh, Pa.	....do	191. 8:	77, 139		r. p. o., 60 by 8 6, 61.; 40 by 8 6, 1 l.; apt., 19 by 9.9, 1½ l., between Pittsburgh and Steubenville.
4	Ohio ..	21015	Columbus, Ohio, Indianapolis, Ind.	Chicago, Saint Louis and Pittsburgh R. R.	189. 66	64, 409	30	r. p. o., 60 by 8.6, 4 l.; 40 by 8.6, 1 l.
5	Ind ...	22002	Indianapolis, Terre Haute.	Terre Haute and Indianapolis R. R.	74. 39	61, 121	30	r. p. o., 60 by 8.6, 4 l.; 40 by 8 6, 1 L.; apt., 16 by 9.2, 2 l.
6	Ind ...	22044	Terre Haute, Ind., East Saint Louis, Ill.	....do	167. 75	58, 026	30	r. p. o., 60 by 8.6, 4 l.; 40 by 8.6, 1 l.; apt., 16 by 9.2, 1 l.
7	Ohio ..	21015	Columbus, Indianapolis.	Chicago, Saint Louis and Pittsburgh R. R.	188. 53	55, 968	3:	r. p. o, 60 by 8 6, 4 l.; 40 by 8.6, 1 l.
8	Ind ...	22002	Indianapolis. Terre Haute.	Terre Haute and Indianapolis R. R.	74. 39	52, 624	32	r. p. o., 60 by 8.6, 4 l.; 40 by 8.6, 1 L.; apt., 16 by 9.2, 1 l.
9	Ind ...	22044	Terre Haute, Ind., East Saint Louis, Ill.	....do	166. 69	49, 829	:32	r. p. o., 60 by 8.6, 4 l.; 40 by 8.6, 1 l.; apt., 16 by 9.2, 1 l.
10	Ohio ..	21045	Toledo, Ohio, Elkhart, Ind.	Lake Shore and Michigan Southern Rwy.	133. 97	46, 485	29	r. p. o., 49 5 by 9, ½ L.; 50 by 9 ½ L.; 60 by 9, 3 l.

and Territories in which the contract term expired June 30, 1888, and also on certain new of the weight of the mails, the speed with which they are conveyed, the accommodations for with the acts of March 3, 1873, July 12, 1876, and June 17, 1878.

apt., apartment; l.. line or lines; m., miles.]

Average trips per week.	Pay per mile per annum for transportation.	Pay per mile per annum for r. p. o. cars.	Former pay per mile per annum for transportation.	Former pay per mile per annum for r. p. o. cars.	Amount of annual pay for transportation.	Amount of annual pay for r. p. o. cars.	Former amount of annual pay for transportation.	Former amount of annual pay for r. p. o. cars.	Date of adjustment or re-adjustment.	Remarks.
	Dollars	Dolls.	Dolls.	Dolls	Dollars.	Dollars	Dollars.	Dollars.	1888.	
35.49	1,173.00	......	855.86	......	633,757.39	148,772.25	462,161.40	142,905.00	July 1	Weighed 30 days from Mar. 19, 1888. 0.26 m. increase.
......	......	330.00	......	......	......	......	......	......	......	Part.
......	......	355.00	......	......	......	......	......	......	......	Do.
......	......	290.00	......	......	......	......	......	......	......	Do.
......	......	355.00	......	......	......	......	......	......	......	Do.
......	......	140.00	......	......	......	......	......	......	......	Do.
......	......	330.00	......	......	......	......	......	......	......	Do.
30.43	1,017.45	325.00	941.36	325.00	197,232.68	63,001.25	180,599.91	62,351.25	July 1	Weighed 30 days from Mar. 19, 1888 2 m. increase.
31.80	941.36	325.00	776.34	275.00	180,599.91	62,351.25	148,940.83	52,758.75	1887 Mar. 13	Weighed 30 days from Mar. 30, 1887.
21.36	805.41	225.00	715.64	225.00	152,754.06	42,673.50	134,933.92	42,423.75	1888 July 1	Weighed 30 days from Mar. 19, 1888. 1.11 m. increase.
33.00	770.35	225.00	679.73	225.00	57,306.33	16,737.75	50,565.11	16,737.75	July 1	Weighed 30 days from Mar. 19, 18-8.
29.30	737.01	225.00	649.80	225.00	123,633.42	37,743.75	108,315.16	37,505.23	July 1 1887	Weighed 30 days from Mar. 19, 1888. 1.06 m. increase.
21.55	715.64	225.00	572.00	175.00	134,933.92	42,423.75	107,850.60	32,996.25	Mar. 13	Weighed 30 days from Mar. 30, 1887.
33.00	679.73	225.00	554.04	175.00	50,565.11	16,737.75	41,215.03	13,018.25	Mar. 13	Do.
29.97	649.80	225.00	526.68	175.00	108,315.16	37,505.25	87,792.28	29,170.75	Mar. 13	Do.
25.50	613.80	190-00	440.33	190.00	82,242.84	25,454.30	58,916.15	25,422.00	1888. July 1	Weighed 30 days from Mar. 19 1888. 0.17 m. increase.

H.—*Table showing the ré-adjustment of the rates of pay per mile on railroad routes in*

Index order.	State.	Number of route.	Termini.	Corporate title of company carrying the mail.	Length of route.	Average weight of mails, whole distance per day.	Miles per hour.	Size, etc., of mail car or apartment.
					Miles.	*Lbs.*		*Feet and inches.*
11	Ohio ..	21002	Pittsburgh, Pa., Chicago, Ill.	Pennsylvania Co.....	468. 20	27, 731	30	r. p. o., 60 by 9, 1 l.; apt. (av.) 17 by 9, 1 l. and 1 l addl between Pittsburgh and Kenwood Junc. (n. o.)
12	Ohio ..	21028	Cincinnati, Ohio, Parkersburgh, W. Va.	Cincinnati, Washington and Baltimore R. R.	195. 30	27, 445	31	r. p. o., 50.2 by 9, 2 l.; apt., 19 by 9.3, 2 l. Cincinnati to Midland City, 1 l. Chillicothe to Parkersburgh.
13	Ind ...	22005	Indianapolis, La Fayette.	Cincinnati, Indianapolis, Saint Louis and Chicago Rwy.	64. 91	26, 749	35	r. p. o., 60 by 9.3, 1 l., 50 by 9.1, 1 l.,
14	Cal...	46001	San Francisco, Cal., Ogden City, Utah.	Central Pacific R. R..	834. 17	25, 702	23	r p o., 55.1 by 9.5, 1 L; 55.1 by 9.5 (40 ft. authorized), 1 l. addit'l between San Francisco and Port Costa, 32.17 m , and between Sacramento and Davisville, 13.23 m.
15	Ind ...	22029	La Fayette,Ind.,Kankakee, Ill.	Cincinnati, LaFayette and Chicago R. R.	79. 79	25, 021	35	r. p. o., 60 by 9.3, 1 l.; 50 by 9 1, 1 l.
16	Ohio ..	21014	Columbus, Cincinnati	Pittsburgh, Cincinnati and Saint Louis Rwy.	120. 29	24, 079	31	r. p. o., 60 by 8.6, 2 l.; apt. ,18 by 9.
17	Ind ...	22003	Indianapolis, Ind., Cincinnati, Ohio.	Cincinnati. Indianapolis, Saint Louis and Chicago Rwy.	111. 40	23, 584	35	r. p. o., 60 by 9.1 ; 1 l.; 50 by 9.3, 1 l
18	Ohio ..	21014	Columbus, Cincinnati	Pittsburgh, Cincinnati and Saint Louis Rwy.	120. 05	22, 930	34	r p o., 60 by 8.6 2 l.; apt., 18 by 9, 1 l.
19	Ky....	20004	Cincinnati, Ohio, Louisville, Ky.	Louisville and Nashville R. R.	110. 10	22, 829	26	r. p. o., 49.11 by 9, 2 l. (15 feet authorized); apt., 14 9 by 9, ½ l.
20	Ky....	20017	Cincinnati Junction (n o.) L.and N.Junction (n. o.).	....do	4. 50	21, 318	27	r. p. o , 49 10 by 9, 2 l (45 ft. authorized).
21	Ga	15001	Atlanta, Ga., Charlotte, N. C.	Richmond and Danville R. R.	268. 24	19, 494	27	r. p. o., 60 by 9, 1 l.; 50 by 9, 1 l.
22	Ohio ..	21042	Cleveland, Cincinnati	Cleveland, Columbus, Cincinnati and Indianapolis Rwy.	241. 92	19, 359	30	r. p. o., 40.4 by 9.3, 3 l. to Galion, 2 l. residue; apt., 16 8 by 9.4, 1 l. to Grafton.
23	Ind ...	22010	Cincinnati, Ohio, East Saint Louis, Ill.	Ohio and Mississippi Rwy.	338. 14	19, 316	32	r. p. o., 50 by 9, 2 l...
24	Ky....	20005	Louisville, Ky., Nashville, Tenn.	Louisville and Nashville R. R.	186. 14	18, 913	27	r. p. o., 49.11 by 9, 2 l. (45 ft. auth'd); apt., 14.9 by 9, 1 l., and 3 l. addl'l Louisville to Trunnelton; 2 l. addl'l Trunnelton to Lebanon Junction.
25	Mich..	24006	Detroit, Mich., Chicago, Ill.	Michigan Central R. R.	285. 50	17, 799	30	r. p. o., 44 by 9, 1 l. (40 ft. auth'd); 50 by 9, 1 l.; apt.,18.6 by 8.11, 3 l. to Wayne Junc. 17.60 m ; 16.9 by 9, 2 l. thence to Jackson, 53.10 m.
26	Ohio ..	21007	Elyria, Millbury	Lake Shore and Michigan Southern Rwy.	75. 01	17, 168	..	r. p. o., 60 by 9, ½ l.; 50 by 9, ½ l.; 49.5 by 9, ½ l.; apt., 17.8 by 9, ½ l.

States and Territories in which the contract term expired June 30, 1888, etc.—Continued.

Average trips per week.	Pay per mile per annum for transportation.	Pay per mile per annum for r. p. o. cars.	Former pay per mile per annum for transportation.	Former pay per mile per annum r. p. o. cars.	Amount of annual pay for transportation.	Amount of annual pay for r. p. o. cars.	Former amount of annual pay for transportation.	Former amount of annual pay for r. p. o. car.	Date of adjustment or re-adjustment.	Remarks.
	Dolls	*Dolls*	*Dolls.*	*Dolls.*	*Dollars*	*Dollars.*	*Dollars.*	*Dollars.*	1888.	
20 69	413 8.	50.00	363.38	50.00	193,750.52	23,410.00	170,134.51	23,410.00	July 1	Weighed 30 days from Mar. 19, 1888.
24.12	410.40	80.00	379.62	80.00	60,151.12	15,624.00	74,682.84	15,612.00	July 1	Weighed 30 days from Mar. 19, 1888. 0.15 m. increase.
22.00	402.7.	90.00	346.28	90.00	26,139.25	5,841.90	22,435.48	5,831.10	July 1	Weighed 30 days from Mar. 19, 1888. 0.12 m. increase.
17.14	391.50	75.00	350.55	75.80	326,652.63	42,843.50	292,418.29	42,843.50	1887. Oct. 25	Weighed 20 days from Oct. 25, 1887. r.p.o. on 788.77 m. at $50 per m.
14.77	384.75	90.0	333.45	90.00	29,160.20	6,821.10	25,272.16	6,821.10	1888. July 1	Weighed 30 days from March 19, 1888.
29.59	374.49	100.0	362.52	100.00	45,047.40	12,629.00	43,520.52	12,005.00	July 1	Weighed 30 days from March 19, 1888. 0 24 m. increase.
8 06	369.36	90.00	311.22	90.00	41,146.70	10,026.00	34,669.91	10,026.00	July 1	Weighed 30 days from March 19, 1888.
8.55	362.50	100.00	334.31	100.00	43,520.52	12,005.00	40,123.91	12,005.00	1887. Mar. 13	Weighed 30 days from March 30, 1887.
24.48	360.81	60.00	325.76	66.00	39,725.18	6,540.00	35,866.18	6,540.00	1888. July 1	Weighed 30 days from Feb. 20, 1848. r.p.o. cars on 109 m. only.
14 00	344.56	60.00	296.69	66.00	1,550.52	270.00	1.335.10	270.00	July 1	Weighed 30 days from Feb. 20, 1888.
14.68	325.75	90.00	219.74	90.00	87,379.18	24,141.60	57,896.91	24,122.70	July 1	Weighed 30 days from Feb. 20, 1888. 0.21 m. increase.
29.70	324.04	75.00	264.20	75.00	78,391.75	14,089.50	64,623.32	14,230.00	July 1	Weighed 30 days from March 19.1888. 162.18 m. Galion to Cincinnati, $50 per m. for r. p. o. cars, formerly 164 m. 2 68 m. decrease.
28.04	323.19	70.00	315.50	70.00	109,283.46	23,669.80	106,702.10	23,674.00	July 1	Weighed 30 days from March 19, 1888. 0.06 m decrease.
24.05	318.91	60.00	296.40	60.00	59,361.90	11,168.40	55,294.00	11,100.00	July 1	Weighed 30 days from Feb. 20, 1888, 1.14 m. increase.
34.85	306.94	65.00	295.83	65.00	87,631.37	18,557.50	84,341.13	18,531.50	July 1	Weighed 30 days from March 19, 1888. 0.40 m. increase.
22	300.96	65.00	459.09	140.00	22,575.00	4,875.65	34,453.25	10,486.00	July 1	Weighed 30 days from Mar. 19, 1888. 0.11 m. increase.

H.—*Table showing the re-adjustment of the rates of pay per mile on railroad routes in*

Index order.	State.	Number of route.	Termini.	Corporate title of company carrying the mail.	Length of route.	Average weight of mails, whole distance per day.	Miles per hour	Size, etc., of mail car or apartment.
					Miles.	*Lbs.*		*Feet and inches.*
27	N. C ..	13002	Weldon, Wilmington.	Wilmington and Weldon R. R.	161.87	15,606	32	r. p. o., 50 by 8.9, 2 l...
28	Ga	15002	Atlanta, Ga., Chattanooga, Tenn.	Western and Atlantic R. R.	138.34	15,022	26	r. p. o., 49 4 by 9.8, 1 l.; 41.10 by 8.8, 1 l. (50 ft. and 40 ft. auth.)
29	Ohio ..	21019	Toledo, Ohio, Quincy, Ill.	Wabash, Saint Louis and Pacific Rwy.	474.25	13,486	36	r. p. o., 1 l., 60 ft., Toledo to La Fayette, 203 10 m.; 1 l., 60 ft.; and 1 l. 50 ft.; La Fayette to Decatur, 119.80 m.; 1 l., 50 ft.; Decatur to Quincy, 151.35 m.; apt. (av.) 35.6 by 9.4, 1 l. to La Fayette and 1 l. between Bement and Decatur.
3	Ga	15003	Atlanta, West Point .	Atlanta and West Point R. R.	87.36	12,988	29	r. p. o., 50 by 9 4, 2 l. (40 ft. authorized).
31	S. C ...	14005	Charleston, Florence.	Northeastern R. R ...	102.44	12,824	42	r. p. o., 49.9 by 8 10, 1 l.; 41 7 by 9.4, 1 l. (50 and 40 ft. auth); apt. (av.), 18.3 by 8.6, 1 l.
32	Ala ...	17001	Montgomery, West Point.	Western Railway Company of Alabama.	86.60	12,295	29	r. p. o., 50 by 9 4, 2 l. (40 ft. authorized).
33	Ga	15009	Savannah, Ga., Jacksonville, Fla.	Savannah, Florida and Western Rwy.	171.56	12,098	28	r. p. o., 49.9 by 8.1, 1 l.; 41.7 by 9.4, 1 l. (50 ft. and 40 ft. auth.)
34	Ky....	20020	Cincinnati, Ohio, Chattanooga, Tenn.	Cincinnati, New Orleans and Texas Pacific Rwy.	338.70	11,234	31	r. p. o., 52.7 by 9.4, 2 l. (40 feet authorized).
35	S. C ...	14004	Charleston, S. C., Savannah, Ga.	Charleston and Savannah Rwy.	115	11,078	24	r. p. o., 49.9 by 8 2, 1 l.; 41.7 by 9.4, 1 l. (50 ft. and 40 ft. auth.)
36	Ohio...	21006	Cleveland, Wellsville	Pennsylvania Co	101.35	11.044	30	19.10 by 9, 4 l. to Hudson, 25.8 m., 3 l. res.
37	Ala ...	17012	Mobile, Montgomery	Louisville and Nashville R. R.	179.34	10,408	30	r. p. o., 49.4 by 9.2, 2 l. (40 ft. authorized).
37a	Ala ...	17013	Mobile, Ala., New Orleans, La.	....do	140.06	9,750	32	r. p. o., 49.4 by 9.2, 2 l. (40 ft. authorized).
28	Ky	20008	Bowling Green, Ky., Memphis, Tenn.	....do	262.70	9,518	22	r. p. o., 44.10 by 9.7, 1 l. (45 ft. authorized).
39	Ohio ..	21001	Bellaire, Columbus...	Baltimore and Ohio R. R.	137.67	9,294	30	r. p. o., 51.3 by 8.8, 1 l. between Bellaire and Newark, 103.82 m ; apt. 20 by 8.9, 11 . Newark to Columbus.
40	Ohio ..	21026	Cincinnati, Dayton...	Cincinnati, Hamilton and Dayton R. R.	58.38	8,951	31	r. p. o., 40 by —, 1 l., auth. June 16, 1888 ; apt. 20 by 9.4, 2 l.
41	Ohio ..	21010	Sandusky, Newark...	Baltimore and Ohio R. R.	116.86	8,719	30	r. p. o., 51.5 by 8.8, 1 l. between Chicago and Newark, Ohio, 88.04 m.; apt., 20 by 8.9, 1 l.

States and Territories in which the contract term expired June 30, 1888, etc.—Continued.

Average trips per week.	Pay per mile per annum for transportation.	Pay per mile per annum for r. p. o. cars.	Former pay per mile per annum for transportation.	Former pay per mile per annum for r. p. o. cars.	Amount of annual pay for transportation.	Amount of annual pay for r. p. o. cars.	Former amount of annual pay for transportation.	Former amount of annual pay for r. p. o. cars.	Date of adjustment or re-adjustment.	Remarks.
	Dolls	Dolls	Dolls	Dolls	Dollars.	Dollars	Dollars.	Dollars	1888.	
16.03	283.86	80.00	237.69	80.00	43,948.41	12,949.60	38,522.41	12,965.60	July 1	Weighed 30 days from Feb. 20, 1888. 0.20 m. decrease.
21	277.87	90.00	203.49	90.00	38,440.53	12,450.60	28,177.26	12,462.30	July 1	Weighed 30 days from Feb. 20, 1888. 0.13 m. decrease.
19.39	261.63	50.00	237.69	50.00	124,078.02	26,991.0:	112,515.32	26,851.80	July 1	Weighed 30 days from Mar. 19, 1888. 0.88 m. increase. r. p. o. 117.40 m., La Fayette to Decatur, at $90 per m.; 151.27 m., Decatur to Quincy, at $40 per m.
21	235.64	50.00	197.51	50.00	22,832.71	4,368.00	17,254.47	4,368.00	July 1	Weighed 30 days from Feb. 20, 1888.
21	253.93	65.00	206.06	65.00	26,012.5-	6,658.60	21,018.12	6,061.33	July 1	Weighed 30 days from Feb. 20. 1888. 0.44 m. increase.
21	246.80	50.00	190.67	50.00	21,546.8	4,330.00	16,437.60	4,310.50	July 1	Weighed 30 days from Feb. 20, 1888. 0.39 m. increase.
21	246.24	65.00	196.65	65.00	42,244.93	11,151.40	33,725.47	11,147.50	July 1	Weighed 30 days from Feb. 20, 1888. 0 06 m. increase.
25.05	236.83	50.00	167.58	50.00	80,214.32	16,935.00	56,675.55	16,910.00	July 1	Weighed 30 days from Feb. 20, 1888. 0.50 m. increase.
21	235.12	65.00	194.09	65.00	27,038.80	7,475.00	22,320.35	7,475.00	July 1	Weighed 30 days from Feb. 20, 1888.
24.19	235.12	....	206.91	....	23,829.41	....	20,937.91	....	July 1	Weighed 30 days from Mar. 19, 1888. 0.06 m. increase.
14	228.28	50.00	182.97	50.00	35,485.18	8,967.00	28,667.75	9,028.50	July 1	Weighed 30 days from Feb. 20. 1888. 119 46 m., Flomaton to Montgomery, land grant, at $182.62 per m.; formerly 119.43 m. at $146.37 per m. 1.23 m. decrease.
17.58	221.44	50.00	180.41	50.00	31,014.88	7,003.00	25,515.38	7,071.50	July 1	Weighed 30 days from Feb. 20, 1888. 1.37 m. decrease.
16.11	218.88	30.00	199.22	30.00	57,499.77	7,881.00	52,424.73	7,894.50	July 1	Weighed 30 days from Feb. 20, 1888. 0.45 m. decrease.
25.90	216.31	40.00	194.94	40.00	29,779.39	4,152.80	23,297.34	4,218.80	July 1	Weighed 30 days from Mar. 19, 1888. 0.80 m. decrease; 33 m., Newark to Columbus, formerly at $82.94 per m.
44.88	212.89	23.00	176.99	....	12,428.51	1,459.50	10,509.66	....	July 1	Weighed 30 days from Mar. 19, 1868. 1 m. decrease.
19.30	210.33	40.00	190.67	40.00	24,579.16	3,521.60	19,515.10	3,551.60	July 1	Weighed 30 days from Mar. 19, 1888. 0.07 m. increase. 28 m. Sandusky to Chicago, Ohio, formerly at $92.34 per m.

H.—*Table showing the re-adjustment of the rates of pay per mile on railroad routes in*

Index order.	State.	Number of route.	Termini.	Corporate title of company carrying the mail.	Length of route.	Average weight of mails, whole distance per day.	Miles per hour.	Size, etc., of mail-car or apartment.
					Miles.	*Lbs.*		*Feet and inches.*
42	S. C ...	14002	Columbia, S. C., Wilmington, N. C.	Wilmington, Columbia and Augusta R. R.	193.17	8,064	28	r. p. o., 49.9 by 8.10.1 l.; 44.6 by 9, 1 l, between Florence and Wilmington, 110 40 m. (30 ft. and 40 ft. auth.); apt. 34 by 13.2, 1 l., between Columbia and Florence 82 77 m., and 24 by 8 8 between Columbia and Sumter 42 77 m.
43	Ga....	15012	Macon. Atlanta......	Central R. R. and Banking Co.	103.91	8,120	28	24.8 by 9.2, 21 ....
44	Mich..	24035	Toledo, Ohio, Detroit, Mich.	Michigan Central R. R.	59.30	7,322	30	12 by 8.8, 11 ....
45	Ohio ..	21047	Chicago, Ohio, Chicago, Ill.	Baltimore and Ohio R. R.	271.28	6,904	30	r. p. o., 51.5 by 8.8, 11.
46	Ohio ..	21023	Dayton, Toledo......	Dayton and Michigan R. R.	142.38	6,648	25	r. p. o., 40 by —, 1 l. auth. June 16, 1888; apt. 20 by 9.4, 1 1.
47	Tenn..	19004	Nashville, Chattanooga.	Nashville, Chattanooga and St. Louis Rwy.	151	6,608	30	20 by 9.3. 21 ....
48	Oregon	44005	Portland, Oregon, Wallulah, Wash. Ter.	Oregon Rwy. and Navigation Co.	214.73	6,382	26	24.10 by 9.1, 11 ......
49	Fla ...	16018	Jacksonville, Sanford.	Jacksonville, Tampa and Key West Rwy.	125.30	6,418	26	27.4 by 9.4, 21 ....
50	Ohio ..	21003	Pittsburgh, Pa., Bellaire, Ohio.	Pennsylvania Co.	94.79	5,936	30	19.10 by 9.1, 21.......
51	Cal ...	46053	San Bernardino, Los Angeles.	California Central Rwy.	63.13	5,916	20	(av.) 17.4 by 9.3, 2 1..
52	Tenn..	19002	Bristol, Chattanooga.	East Tennessee, Virginia and Georgia Rwy.	242.79	5,833	28	r. p. o.,40 by 8.10, 2 l,; apt. 20 1 by 8 6, 1 l. betw. Morristown and Knoxville; 18 by 7 2 1 l. betw. Ooltewah and Chattanooga.
53	Ohio..	21013	Columbus, Delaware.	Cleveland, Columbus, Cincinnati and Indianapolis Rwy.	25.48	5,662	30	10.8 by 8.3, 1 1.
54	Tenn .	19006	Nashville, Tenn., Decatur, Ala.	Louisville and Nashville R. R.	121.66	5,601	28	14 9 by 9, 11. and 1 addl. l. betw. Nashville and Columbia. 47.1 miles ; r.p.o., 40 by —, 1 l.
55	Ohio ..	21005	Cleveland, Ohio, Sharpeville, Pa.	New York, Lake Erie and Western R. R.	83.60	5,596	30	20 by 7, 2 l. to Youngstown, 66.50 m. ; 1 l. residue.
56	Miss..	18001	New Orleans, La., Cairo, Ill.	Illinois Central R. R.	550.11	5,177	24	r. p. o., 45 by 9.3, 11.
57	Mich..	24001	Toledo, Ohio, Detroit, Mich.	Lake Shore and Michigan Southern Rwy.	64.97	4,869	28	36 by 9.4, 2 1. to Monroe, 24.48 m. ; 1 l. residue.
58	Wyo ...	37001	Granger, Wyo., Huntington, Oregon.	Oregon Short Line Rwy.	541.34	4,793	..	50.8 by 9.3 (r. p. o. cars not auth.).

States and Territories in which the contract term expired June 30, 1888, *etc.*—Continued.

Average trips per week.	Pay per mile per annum for transportation.	Pay per mile per annum for r. p. o. cars.	Former pay per mile per annum for transp. r'lation.	Former pay per mile per annum for r. p. o. cars.	Amount of annual pay for transportation.	Amount of annual pay for r. p. o. cars.	Former amount of annual pay for transportation.	Former amount of annual pay for r. p. o. cars.	Date of adjustment or re-adjustment	Remarks.
	Dolls	Dolls.	Dolls.	Dolls.	Dollars.	Dollars.	Dollars.	Dollars.	1888.	
15.54	209.47	65.00	189.81	65.00	46,463.31	7,176.00	36,633.33	7,150.00	July 1	Weighed 30 days from Feb. 20, 1888. r. p. o. cars between Florence and Wilmington 110.40 m.; formerly 110 m.; 0.17 m. increase.
28	204.84	......	171.00	......	21,232.96	....	17,754.93	....	July 1	Weighed 30 days from Feb. 20, 1888. 0.06 m. decrease.
13	195.79	......	175.28	......	11,610.34	....	10,429.16	....	July 1	Weighed 30 days from Mar 19, 1888. 0.20 m. decrease.
20	190.66	40.00	169.29	40.00	51,722.24	10,851.20	45,877.59	10,840.00	July 1	Weighed 30 days from Mar. 19, 1888. 0.28 m. increase.
21.55	183.10	25.00	158.18	......	26,781.67	3,559.50	22,521.66	....	July 1	Weighed 30 days from Mar. 19, 1888.
21	188.10	......	166.73	......	28,403.10	....	25,176.23	....	July 1	Weighed 30 days from Feb. 20, 1888.
14	185.54	......	193.23	......	39,846.57	....	41,496.07	....	1887. Oct. 25	Weighed 30 days from Oct. 25, 1887.
20	185.53	......	141.93	......	23,246.90	....	20,062.39	....	1888. July 1	Weighed 30 days from Feb. 20, 1888. 0.88 m. decrease. 69.97 m. Palatka to Sanford, formerly at $172.71 per m.
25.60	180.40	......	170.15	......	17,100.11	....	16,130.22	....	July 1	Weighed 30 days from Mar. 19, 1888. 0.01 m. decrease.
22.10	180.40				11,888.64				Mar 23	Weighed 20 days from Mar. 23, 1888. 41.04 m. San Bernardino to Duarte from July 4, 1887; 22.09 m. ext. Duarte to Los Angeles from Mar. 23, 1888.
15.54	179.55	50.00	187.25	50.00	43,592.94	12,139.50	45,346.33	12 108.50	July 1	Weighed 30 days from Feb. 20, 1888. 0.62 m. increase.
29.50	177.84	......	129.11	......	4,531.36	....	3,293.59	....	July 1	Weighed 30 days from Mar. 19, 1888. 0.03 m. decrease.
16.30	176.96	25.00	147.06	......	21,531.38	3,041.50	18,047.19	....	July 1	Weighed 30 days from Feb. 20, 1888. 1.06 m. decrease.
42.02	176.96	......	153.90	......	14,795.52	....	12,984.54	....	July 1	Weighed 30 days from Mar. 19, 1888. 0.77 m. decrease.
15.39	172.71	30.00	160.74	30.00	95,009.49	16,503.30	88,535.59	16,524.00	July 1	Weighed 30 days from Feb. 20, 1888. 0.69 m. decrease.
23.26	168.43	......	165.02	......	10,942.89	....	10,709.79	....	July 1	Weighed 30 days from Mar. 19, 1888. 0.07 m. increase.
7	167.56	......	149.63	......	90,717.73	....	81,000.70	....	1887. Oct. 25	Weighed 30 days from Oct. 25, 1887.

H.—*Table showing the re-adjustment of the rates of pay per mile on railroad routes in*

Index order.	State.	Number of route.	Termini.	Corporate title of company carrying the mail.	Length of route.	Average weight of mails, whole distance per day.	Miles per hour.	Size, etc., of mail car or apartment.
					Miles.	*Lbs*		*Feet and inches*
59	Ohio ..	21016	Gall n, Ohio, Indianapolis, Ind.	Cleveland, Columbus, Cincinnati and Indianapolis Rwy.	204. 09	4,084	30	r. p. o., 39.0 by 9.1, 1 1
60	Ala ..	17015	Chattanooga, Tenn., Meridian, Miss.	Alabama Great Southern R. R.	295. 60	4,586	25	r. p. o., 45.6 by 8.6, 11 (not auth.).
61	Ind ...	22007	Jeffersonville, Indianapolis.	Pennsylvania Company.	108. 84	4,395	40	19 2 by 9.2, 2 1.
62	Ind ...	22008	Louisville Junction (n. o), Ky., Chicago, Ill.	Louisville, New Albany and Chicago Rwy.	322. 40	4,314	31	r. p. o., 40 by —, 1 1 ; apt. 20 by 9.3, 2 1.
63	Ind ...	22019	Louisville, Ky., North Vernon, Ind.	Ohio and Mississippi Rwy.	57. 45	4,047	30	17.7 by 9.4, 1 1 ....
64	Cal....	46003	Roseville, Cal., Ashland, Oregon.	Central Pacific R. R..	323. 30	3,975	17	r. p. o., 55 1 by 9.5 '40 feet auth.), 1 1. between Tehama and Redding. 46 74 m. ; apt. (av.), 28.5 by 8.11, 1 1.
65	Mich..	24028	Detroit, Fort Gratiot.	Chicago, Detroit and Canada Grand Trunk Junction R. R.	58. 97	3,954	26	22.4 by 9.4, 1 1 ....
66	Mich..	24010	Jackson, Grand Rapids.	Michigan Central R. R.	94. 68	3,922	26	16.10 by 8.5, 1 1 ......
67	Ga	15010	Savannah, Macon	Central R. R. and Banking Co.	191. 57	3,664	28	24.8 by 9.2, 1 1........
68	Ga	15004	Augusta, Atlanta	Georgia R. R	171. 59	3,618	25	20.2 by 8.9, 2 1........
69	Ala ...	17005	Memphis, Chattanooga, Tenn.	Memphis and Charleston R. R.	311. 39	3,600	29	20 by 8.9, 1 1 ....
70	Mich..	24013	Detroit, Mackinaw City.	Michigan Central R. R.	291. 29	3,549	90	15.6 by 9, 1 1 ....
71	Oreg..	44003	Umatilla, Huntington.	Oregon Rwy. and Navigation Co.	218. 04	3,461	25	24.10 by 9.1, 1 1.......
72	Ind ...	22018	Indianapolis, Ind., Peoria, Ill.	Ohio, Indiana and Western Rwy.	212. 41	3,439	25	21.8 by 8.7, 2 1........
73	Fla ...	16007	Sanford, Tampa	South Florida R. R ...	115. 59	3,309	22	27.4 by 9.3, 2 1...... .
74	Ind ...	22012	Evansville, Terre Haute.	Evansville and Terre Haute R. R.	109. 71	3,118	30	(av.) 30.9 by 8.7, 1 1..

States and Territories in which the contract term expired June 30, 1888, etc.—Continued.

Average trips per week.	Pay per mile per annum for transportation.	Pay per mile per annum for r. p. o. cars.	Former pay per mile per annum for transportation.	Former pay per mile per annum r. p. o. cars.	Amount of annual pay for transportation.	Amount of annual pay for r. p. o. cars.	Former amount of annual pay for transportation.	Former amount of annual pay for r. p. o. cars.	Date of adjustment or re-adjustment.	Remarks.
	Dolls.	Dolls.	Dolls.	Dolls.	Dollars.	Dollars.	Dollars.	Dollars.	1888.	
23.47	165.87	25.00	180.41	25.00	33,852.40	5,102.25	36,816.26	5,101.75	July 1	Weighed 30 days from Mar. 19, 1888. 0.01 m. increase
14.22	165.01	......	131.67	......	39,210.65	....	31,276.46	....	July 1	Weighed 30 days from Feb. 20, 1888. 0.15 m. increase. 289.80 m. Waubatchie to Meridian land-grant at $133 per m.; formerly 269.50 m. at $105.38 per m.
23	161.59	......	154.76	......	17,587.45	....	16,844.08	....	July 1	Weighed 30 days from Mar. 19, 1888.
13	160.74	25.00	83.79	......	51,822.57	8,060.00	24,603.25	....	July 1	Weighed 30 days from Mar. 19, 1888. r. p. o. 1 line from Aug. 5, 1888.
28	157.32	......	146.21	......	9,038.03	....	8,021.08	....	July 1	Weighed 30 days from Mar. 19, 1888.
11.18	155.61	25.00	99.18	25.00	50,308.71	1,163.50	18,889.82	1,168.50	Mar. 19	Weighed 30 days from Mar. 19, 1888. 26.27 m. ext. Bayles to Upper Soda Springs Station (n. o.), from Dec. 15, 1886; 30.90 m. ext. Upper Soda Springs Station (n. o.) to Edgewood from Mar. 21, 1887; 39 m. ext. Edgewood to Henley from May 16, 1887; 36.67 m. ext. Henley to Ashland from Dec. 29, 1887. r. p. o. on 46.74 m. only.
13	155.61	......	133.28	......	9,176.32	....	8,114.83	....	July 1	Weighed 30 days from Mar. 19, 1888. 1.87 m. decrease.
13	155.61	......	125.69	......	14,733.15	....	11,905.35	....	July 1	Weighed 30 days from Mar. 19, 1888. 0.04 m. decrease.
14	151.33	......	129.96	......	28,990.28	....	24,878.23	....	July 1	Weighed 30 days from Feb. 20, 1888. 0.14 m. increase.
21	150.48	......	138.51	......	25,820.86	....	23,766.93	....	July 1	Weighed 30 days from Feb. 20, 1888.
14.75	150.48	......	130.82	......	42,601.58	....	36,843.36	....	July 1	Weighed 30 days from Feb. 20, 1888 0.00 m. decrease. 38 m., Stevenson to Chattanooga, lap service, at $38.47 per m.; formerly $1.000 per annum for lap service.
12.75	149.62	......	125.69	......	38,126.87	....	31,896.74	....	July 1	Weighed 30 days from Mar. 19, 1888. 1.07 m. increase. 182.39 m. land grant at $119 69 per m.; formerly $100 55 per m.
7	148.77	......	133.38	......	32,437.81	....	29,062.17	....	1887. Oct. 25	Weighed 30 days from Oct. 25, 1887.
19	147.91	......	138.51	......	31,417.56	....	29,505.40	....	1888. July 1	Weighed 30 days from Mar. 19, 1888. 0.61 m. decrease
13	146.20	......	85.50	......	16,899.25	....	9,951.34	....	July 1	Weighed 30 days from Feb. 20, 1888. 0.8 m. decrease.
18	143.64	......	134.04	......	15,758.74	....	14,727.47	....	July 1	Weighed 30 days from Mar. 19, 1888.

H.—*Table showing the re-adjustment of the rates of pay per mile on railroad routes in*

Index order.	State.	Number of route.	Termini.	Corporate title of company carrying the mail.	Length of route.	Average weight of mails, whole distance per day.	Miles per hour.	Size, etc., of mail-car or apartment.
					Miles	*Lbs.*		*Feet and inches.*
75	Mich .	24017	Detroit, Howard City.	Detroit, Lansing and Northern R. R.	160.68	3,040	25	20 by 8.10, 1 1 ... .
76	Mich .	24027	Detroit, Grand Haven	Detroit, Grand Haven and Milwaukee Rwy.	188.44	3,017	25	22.2 by 8.6, 1 1........
77	Mich .	24015	Monroe, Ludington ..	Flint and Pere Marquette R. R.	254.41	2,941	23	22 2 by 8.11, 2 1, Wayne to East Saginaw ; 1 1, res.
78	Mo ...	28064	Napier (n. o.), Mo., Rulo "Y" (n. o.), Nebr.	Burlington and Missouri River R. R. Co. (in Nebraska).	11.7	2,704	24	21 by 8.10............
79	Mich..	24021	Grand Rapids, Mich., La Crosse, Ind.	Chicago and West Michigan Rwy.	154.18	2,609	19	15 by 9, 1 1..........
80	Ky....	20002	Covington, Lexington.	Kentucky Central R. R.	98.92	2,694	29	13 by 8.10, 2 1. Covington to Paris, 7s.36m.; no clerk residue.
81	Ga ...	15016	Macon, Ga., Eufaula, Ala.	Southwestern R. R ...	144.59	2,645	25	26.4 by 9. 1 1........
82	N. C ..	13007	Charlotte, N. C., Augusta, Ga.	Richmond and Danville R. R.	192.00	2,642	22	22.7 by 9, 1 1........
83	Ga	15039	Smithville, Albany ..	Southwestern R. R ...	24.12	2,587	23	15.2 by 8.4, 1 1.......
84	Ohio ..	21030	Dayton, Ohio, Richmond, Ind.	Pittsburgh, Cincinnati, and St. Louis Rwy.	42.08	2,581	30	20 by 8.2, 1 1. ......
85	Mich..	24018	Fort Wayne, Ind., Mackinaw City, Mich.	Grand Rapids and Indiana R. R.	360.26	2,542	25	22 by 8.10, 1 1 ....
86	Ohio ..	21051	Columbus, Coal Grove	Scioto Valley Rwy...	132.45	2,496	27	15 by 8.11, 2 1........
87	Ohio ..	21034	Salamanca, N. Y., Dayton, Ohio.	New York, Lake Erie and Western R. R.	388.82	2,429	30	20 by 7, 1 1............
88	Tenn..	19007	Nashville, Tenn., Hickman, Ky.	Nashville, Chattanooga and St. Louis Rwy.	171.10	2,421	25	18.8 by 9.2, 1 1 ....
89	Utah..	41003	Ogden City, Butte City.	Utah and Northern Rwy.	416.95	2,408	22	r. p. o. (av.) 46 by 8. 1 1 (not anth.), apt. 16 6 by 7.6, 1 1, between Silver Bow and Butte City, 7.96 m.
90	Colo...	38035	Denver, Pueblo	Atchison, Topeka and Santa Fé R. R.	117.46	2,384	27	no apt ....
91	Ky....	20007	Lebanon Junction, Ky., Jellico, Tenn.	Louisville and Nashville R. R.	171.44	2,362	23	14.9 by 9, 2 1. ....
92	Mich..	24004	White Pigeon, Grand Rapids.	Lake Shore and Michigan Southern Rwy.	96.35	2,362	26	(av.) 15 by 9, 2 1 ......
93	Ala ...	17004	Montgomery, Decatur.	South and north Ala. R. R.	183.86	4,645	28	r. p. o., 40 by —, 1 1.; apt. 14.9 by 9 —, 1 1.
94	Ohio ..	21033	Columbus, Springfield.	Cincinnati, Sandusky, and Cleveland R. R.	46.03	2,351	20	20 by 8.9 —, 1 1.......

States and Territories in which the contract term expired June 30, 1888, etc.—Continued.

Average trips per week	Pay per mile per annum for transportation.	Pay per mile per annum for r. p. o. cars.	Former pay per mile per annum for transportation.	Former pay per mile per annum for r. p. o. cars.	Amount of annual pay for transportation.	Amount of annual pay for r. p. o. cars.	Former amount of annual pay for transportation.	Former amount of annual pay for r. p. o. cars.	Date of adjustment or re-adjustment.	Remarks.
	Dolls.	Dolls.	Dolls.	Dolls.	Dollars.	Dollars.	Dollars.	Dollars.	1888.	
7.41	142.78	......	129.11	......	22,941.89	....	20,750.55	....	July 1	Weighed 30 days from Mar 19, 1888. 0.04 m. decrease.
6	141.93		142.79		26,745.28		26,995.87		July 1	Weighed 30 days from Mar. 19, 1888. 0 62 m. decrease.
17.63	141.07		136.80		31,064.01		30,123.06		July 1	Weighed 30 days from Mar. 19, 188d 171 06 m. land grant at $112.86 per m.; formoly $109.44 per m.
7	137.65				1,610.50				Jan. 7	Weighed 30 days from May 27, 1888.
11.25	137.65		120.56		21,222.87		18,631.34		July 1	Weighed 30 days from Mar. 19, 1888, 0.36 m. decrease.
15.80	137.65		134.24		18,616.33		13,270.96		July 1	Weighed 30 days from Feb. 20, 1888, 0.06 m. increase.
18.04	136.80		87.21		19,779.91		12,607.94		July 1	Weighed 30 days from Feb. 20, 1888. 0.02 m. increase.
10.08	136.80		129.11		26,265.60		24,861.42	.. ....	July 1	Weighed 30 days from Feb. 20, 1888. 0.56 m. decrease.
31	135.94		65.84		8,278.87		1,585.42		July 1	Weighed 30 days from Feb. 20, 1888. 0.04 m. increase.
30	135.94		85.50		5,720.35		3,602.11		July 1	Weighed 30 days from Mar. 19, 1888. 0.05 m. decrease.
10.01	135.94		120.56		41,129.06		36,434.38		July 1	Weighed 30 days from Mar. 19, 1888. 0.36 m. increase. $33.51 m. land grant, at $108.75 per m.; formaly $06.45 per m.
19	135.09		123.98		17,892.67		16,365.36		July 1	Weighed 30 days from Mar. 19, 1888. 0.45 m. increase.
31.05	134.23		128.25		52,191.30		49,916.18		July 1	Weighed 30 days from Mar. 19, 1888. 0.39 m. decrease.
14	134.23		105.17		22,966.75		17,890.46		July 1	Weighed 30 days from Feb. 20, 1888. 0.99 m. increase.
7.01	133.38		131.67		55,612.79		54,899.80		1887. Oct. 28	Weighed 30 days from Oct. 25, 1887.
15.86	133.38				15,666.81				Dec. 14	Weighed 30 days from Apr. 10, 1888. New.
15.31	133.38		98.33		22,866.66		16,811.48		1888. July 1	Weighed 30 days from Feb. 20, 1888. 0.47 m. increase.
12	133.38		117.99		12,851.16		11,364.79		July 1	Weighed 30 days from Mar. 19, 1888. 0.04 m. increase.
14	132.69	25.0	110.13		24,396.88	4,596.50	20,184.62		July 1	Weighed 30 days from Feb. 20, 1888. 0.58 m. increase land grant. r. p. o. cars auth. June 8, 1888.
22	132.52		95.76		6,099.89		4,407.83		July 1	Weighed 30 days from Mar. 19, 1888.

H.—*Table showing the re-adjustment of the rates of pay per mile on railroad routes in*

Index order.	State.	Number of route.	Termini.	Corporate title of company carrying the mail.	Length of route.	Average weight of mails, whole distance per day.	Miles per hour.	Size, etc., of mail-car or apartment.
					Miles.	*Lbs.*		*Feet and inches.*
95	Ind ...	22024	Terre Haute, Ind., Danville, Ill.	Chicago and Eastern Illinois R. R.	55.43	2,305	27	25 by 9.2, 1 l.........
96	Ohio ..	21025	Hamilton, Ohio, Richmond, Ind.	Cincinnati, Richmond and Chicago R. R.	44.36	2,262	30	12.6 by 9.3, 1 l.........
97	Ohio ..	21011	Xenia, Dayton	Pittsburgh, Cincinnati and St. Louis Rwy.	16.73	2,229	30	20 by 8.2, 1 l ......
98	Miss ..	18003	Vicksburg, Meridian.	Vicksburg and Meridian R. R.	140.70	2,207	24	40.3 by 9, 1 l ....
99	Ind ...	22009	Richmond, Ind., Chicago, Ill.	Chicago, St. Louis and Pittsburgh R. R.	226.43	2,185	30	19.1 by 8.10, 1 l .....
100	S. C ..	14003	Columbia, Charleston	South Carolina Rwy..	131.04	2,182	13	18 by 8.11, 1 l. and 1 l. add'l between Branchville and Charleston, 69 m.
101	Mich..	24009	Jackson, Bay City ...	Michigan Central R. R.	115.36	2,126	23	16.8 by 8.10, 1 line ...
102	Ga.....	15012	Atlanta, Ga., Birmingham, Ala.	Georgia Pacific Rwy.	167.88	2,071	25	27.4 by 8.6, 1 l ......
103	Ind ...	22017	Bradford, Logansport	Chicago, St. Louis and Pittsburgh R. R.	114.65	2,020	30	11.8 by 9, 1 l.........
104	Ky ...	20016	Lexington, Ky., Huntington, W. Va.	Newport News and Mississippi Valley Co.	140.05	1,992	21	19.5 by 8.10, 1 l ......
105	Ind ...	22023	Indianapolis, Terre Haute.	Indianapolis and St. Louis Rwy.	73.39	1,971	30	39.6 by 9.1, 1 l ......
106	Mich..	24031	Fort Howard, Wis., Ishpeming, Mich.	Chicago and Northwestern Rwy.	80.08	4,029	24	36 by 10, 1 l ....
107	Mich..	24039	Fort Gratiot, Mich., Chicago, Ill.	Chicago and Grand Trunk Rwy.	327.56	1,937	24	20 by 8.6, 1 l.........
108	Ohio ..	21024	Hamilton, Ohio, Indianapolis, Ind.	Cincinnati, Hamilton and Indianapolis R. R.	100.13	1,925	33	20 by 9.3, 2 l.........
109	N. C ..	13004	Goldsborough, Greensborough.	Richmond and Danville R. R.	130.05	1,924	20	20 by 8 9, 1 l.........
110	Ky ...	20003	Louisville, Ky., Memphis, Tenn.	Newport News and Mississippi Valley Co.	392.00	1,834	24	15 3 by 9, 1 l.........
111	Dak ...	35037	Rapid City, Whitewood.	Fremont, Elkhorn and Missouri Valley R. R.	37.27	1,741	21	24 by 9.3, 1 l.........
112	Wash. Ter.	43011	Pasco, Melrose.	Northern Pacific R. R.	233.61	3,209	20	24.6 by 9, 1 l.........
113	Iowa..	27098	Sioux City, Manilla ..	Chicago, Milwaukee and St. Paul Rwy.	90.70	1,727	26	20.8 by 8.11, 1 l.......
114	Ala ...	17003	Montgomery, Eufaula	Montgomery and Eufaula Rwy.	80.57	1,667	27	26.4 by 9, 1 l...........

States and Territories in which the contract term expired June 30, 1888, etc.—Continued.

Average trips per week.	Pay per mile per annum for transportation.	Pay per mile per annum for r. p. o. cars.	Former pay per mile per annum for transportation.	Former pay per mile per annum for r. p. o. cars.	Amount of annual pay for transportation.	Amount of annual pay for r. p. o. cars.	Former amount of annual pay for transportation.	Former amount of annual pay for r. p. o. cars.	Date of adjustment or re-adjustment.	Remarks.
	Dolls	*Dolls*	*Dolls.*	*Dolls.*	*Dollars.*	*Dollars.*	*Dollars.*	*Dollars*	1888.	
19	132. 52	......	110. 30	......	7, 345. 58	....	6, 229. 74	......	July 1	Weighed 30 days from Mar. 19, 1888. 1.05 m. decrease.
19	131. 67	....	111. 15	......	5, 840. 88	....	5, 008. 41	......	July 1	Weighed 30 days from Mar. 19, 1888. 0.70 m. decrease.
28	130. 81	......	95. 76	......	2, 188. 45	....	1, 605. 89	......	July 1	Weighed 30 days from Mar. 19, 1888. 0.04 m. decrease.
7	130. 81	......	107. 73	......	15, 912. 32	....	13, 105. 70	....	July 1	Weighed 30 days from Feb. 20, 1888. 0.01 m. increase. 95.21 m. Jackson to Meridian; land grant, at $104.54 per m.; formerly $86.19 per m.
14. 08	130. 81	......	94. 05	......	29, 619. 30	....	21, 176. 29	....	July 1	Weighed 30 days from Mar. 19, 1888. 1.27 m. increase.
23. 46	130. 81	......	105. 17	......	17, 141. 34	....	13, 829. 85	....	July 1	Weighed 30 days from Feb. 20, 1888. 0.46 m. decrease.
6. 80	129. 96	......	103. 46	......	12, 956. 37	....	10, 267. 31	....	July 1	Weighed 30 days from Mar. 19, 1888. 0.55 m. increase. 78.30 m. land grant, at $103.96 per m.; formerly $82.77 per m.
14	129. 10	......	58. 14	......	21, 873. 30	....	10, 276. 38	....	July 1	Weighed 30 days from Feb. 20, 1888.
16	128. 25	......	64. 98	......	14, 703. 86	....	7, 426. 56	......	July 1	Weighed 30 days from Mar. 19, 1888. 0.36 m. increase.
18. 36	127. 39	......	98. 33	......	17, 840. 96	....	13, 785. 86	......	July 1	Weighed 30 days from Feb. 20, 1888. 0.05 m. decrease.
24	126. 54	......	103. 17	......	9, 286. 77	....	7, 707. 90	......	July 1	Weighed 30 days from Mar. 19, 1888. 0.10 m. increase.
13. 28	125. 17	......	108. 08	......	22, 540. 61	....	19, 394. 95	......	July 1	Weighed 30 days from Mar. 19, 1888. 0.63 m. increase. All land grant.
13	124. 83	......	76. 95	......	42, 137. 61	....	26, 044. 49	....	July 1	Weighed 30 days from Mar. 19, 1888. 0.90 m. decrease.
16. 50	124. 83	......	81. 23	......	12, 499. 22	....	8, 109. 19	......	July 1	Weighed 30 days from Mar. 19, 1888. 0 30 m. increase.
13	124. 83	......	90. 63	......	16, 231. 14	....	11, 771. 93	......	July 1	Weighed 30 days from Feb. 20, 1888. 0.16 m. increase
14. 15	120. 55	......	82. 94	......	47, 255. 60	....	32, 296. 83	......	July 1	Weighed 30 days from Feb. 20, 1888. 2.60 m. increase.
7	117. 13	......	......	......	4, 365. 43	....			Feb. 20	Weighed 30 days from Mar. 19, 1888. New.
7	116. 26	......	40. 36	......	27, 164. 17	....	5, 142. 26	......	Mar. 19	Weighed 30 days from Mar. 19, 1888. 24.80 m. ext., Ellensburgh to Cle Elum, from May 2, 1887; 81.40 m. ext., Cle Elum to Melrose, from Oct. 3, 1887. Land grant.
13	116. 26	......	116. 26	......	10, 546. 50	....	10, 546. 50	....	1887. Oct. 10	Weighed 30 days from Apr. 30, 1888.
17. 04	112. 71	......	79. 52	......	9, 161. 61	....	6, 400. 56	....	1888. July 1	Weighed 30 days from Feb. 20, 1888. 0 08 m. increase.

H.—*Table showing the re-adjustment of the rates of pay per mile on railroad routes in*

Index order.	State.	Number of route.	Termini.	Corporate title of company carrying the mail.	Length of route.	Average weight of mails whole distance per day.	Miles per hour.	Size, etc., of mail-car or apartment.
					Miles.	*Lbs.*		*Feet and inches.*
115	Nebr..	34051	Omaha, Arlington....	Fremont, Elkhorn and Missouri Valley R. R.	28.69	1,652	27	20 by 9.3, 1 l.........
116	Ky....	20003	La Grange, Lexington	Louisville and Nashville R. R.	67.37	1,646	20	14.6 by 9, 1 l..........
117	Ala ...	17002	Montgomery, Selma..	Western Rwy. Co. of Ala.	51.29	1,635	14	12.5 by 6.9, 1 l........
118	Miss ..	18019	Memphis, Tenn., New Orleans, La.	Louisville, New Orleans and Texas Rwy.	455.60	1,632	26	15.5 by 9, 1 l.........
119	Ill	23096	Rockford, Rockton...	Chicago, Milwaukee and St. Paul Rwy.	16.37	1,595	20	20.2 by 9.4, 1 l........
120	Miss ..	18016	Meridian, Miss., New Orleans, La.	New Orleans and Northeastern R. R.	196.30	1,593	31	16 by 7.3, 1 l.........
121	Ind ...	22043	Terre Haute, Ind., East St. Louis, Ill.	Indianapolis and St. Louis Rwy.	189.65	1,569	30	39.6 by 9.1, 1 l........
122	Ind ...	22048	Louisville, Ky., Oakland City, Ind.	Louisville, Evansville and St. Louis Rwy.	99.29	1,567	25	14 by 9.6, 1 l........
123	Wash. Ter.	43005	Tacoma, Carbonado ..	Northern Pacific R. R.	83.89	2,374	15	24.6 by 9.1, 1 l. to Melrose 25.15 m. No clerk residue.
124	Mich..	24057	Alger, Alpena........	Detroit, Bay City and Alpena R. R.	105.34	1,486	17	13 by 7, 1 l............
125	Ohio ..	21036	Columbus, Athens ...	Columbus, Hocking Valley and Toledo Rwy.	77.90	1,469	23	15.8 by 9.4, 21 ....
126	Ga	15018	Way Cross, Albany ..	Savannah, Florida and Western Rwy.	163.06	1,468	28	18.4 by 9.3, 1 l........
127	N. C ..	13001	Raleigh, Weldon	Raleigh and Gaston R. R.	97.28	1,449	26	12.2 by 8.6, 1 l........
128	S. C...	14017	Branchville, S. C., Augusta, Ga.	South Carolina Rwy..	75.62	1,436	26	18 by 8.11, 1 l ....
129	Mich..	24020	Toledo, Ohio, Mt. Pleasant, Mich.	Toledo, Ann Arbor and North Michigan Rwy.	170.99	1,421	23	16.8 by 9.5, 1 l........
130	N. C ..	13006	Salisbury, Kinsel (n. o.).	Richmond and Danville R. R.	185.48	1,410	26	20 1 by 8.6, 1 l.; 6.10 by 6.4, 1 l., between Asheville and Asheville Junction (n. o.) 1.10 m.
131	Ind ...	22004	Indianapolis, Michigan City.	Lake Erie and Western R. R.	161.77	1,382	28	14.6 by 9.3, 1 l........
132	Ky....	20032	Paris, Richmond.....	Kentucky Central Rwy.	89.75	1,356	24	14 by 9, 1 l..........
133	Ohio .	21004	Hudson, Columbus ...	Cleveland, Akron and Columbus Rwy.	145.41	1,355	28	15 by 8.7, 1 l........
134	Fla....	16011	Waldo, Tavares......	Florida Rwy. and Navigation Company.	96.85	1,344	20	22.9 by 8.9, 21 ....

States and Territories in which the contract term expired June 30, 1888, etc.—Continued.

Average trips per week.	Pay per mile per annum for transportation.	Pay per mile per annum for r. o. cars.	Former pay per mile per annum for transportation.	Former pay per mile per annum for r. p. o. cars.	Amount of annual pay for transportation.	Amount of annual pay for r. p. o. cars.	Former amount of annual pay for transportation.	Former amount of annual pay for r. p. o. cars.	Date of adjustment or re-adjustment.	Remarks.
	Dolls.	*Dolls.*	*Dolls.*	*Dolls.*	*Dollars.*	*Dollars.*	*Dollars.*	*Dollars.*	1888.	
13	112. 86				3, 237. 96				Jan. 16	Weighed 30 days from Mar. 19, 1888. New.
19	112. 86		95. 76		7, 803. 87		6, 456. 05		July 1	Weighed 30 days from Feb. 20, 1888. 0.07 m. decrease.
20	112. 00		85. 50		5, 734. 40		4, 380. 16		July 1	Weighed 30 days from Feb. 20, 1888. 0.03 m. increase.
14	112. 00		90. 63		51, 027. 20		41, 291. 02		July 1	Weighed 30 days from Feb. 20, 1888.
15	110. 29		110. 29		1, 805. 44		1, 805. 44		1887. Dec. 5	Weighed 30 days from Mar. 19, 1888.
14	110. 29		69. 26		21, 649. 92		13, 591. 58		1888. July 1	Weighed 30 days from Feb. 20, 1888. 0.06 m. increase.
26. 95	109. 44		94. 91		20, 755. 39		18, 045. 23		July 1	Weighed 30 days from Mar. 19, 1888. 0.48 m. decrease.
18. 52	109. 44		78. 53		10, 866. 29		7, 819. 91		July 1	Weighed 30 days from Mar. 19, 1888. 0.26 m. increase.
10. 76	106. 70		34. 20		3, 616. 06		1, 159. 03		Mar. 19	Weighed 30 days from Mar. 19, 1888. Land grant.
6	106. 02		70. 11		11, 168. 14		7, 326. 49		July 1	Weighed 30 days from Mar. 19, 1888. 0.84 m. increase.
18	105. 16		90. 63		8, 191. 96		7, 018. 30		July 1	Weighed 30 days from Mar. 19, 1888. 0.46 m. increase.
21	105. 16		88. 07		17, 147. 38		14, 365. 09		July 1	Weighed 30 days from Feb. 20, 1888 0.03 m. decrease.
12	104. 31		100. 89		10, 147. 27		9, 865. 02		July 1	Weighed 30 days from Feb. 20, 1888. 0.50 m. decrease.
20	103. 45		76. 10		7, 822. 88		5, 816. 32		July 1	Weighed 30 days from Feb. 20, 1888. 0.81 m. decrease.
7. 61	103. 45		53. 87		17, 688. 91		2, 801. 24		July 1	Weighed 30 days from Mar. 19, 1888. Route formerly from Toledo, Ohio, to Emory, Mich. Extended to Mt. Pleasant covering route 24065 from July 1, 1888.
8. 66	102. 60		106. 88		19, 030. 24		19, 478. 88		July 1	Weighed 30 days from Feb. 20, 1888. 6.18 m. Hot Springs to Kinzel (n. o.) formerly at $77.81 per m. 2.03 m. decrease.
17. 87	101. 74		81. 23		16, 458. 47		13, 128. 39		July 1	Weighed 30 days from Mar. 19, 1888. 0.15 m. increase.
15. 50	100. 08		65. 84		3, 976. 19		2, 688. 90		July 1	Weighed 30 days from Feb. 20, 1888. 1.09 m. decrease.
22. 40	100. 03		78. 66		14, 545. 36		11, 417. 49		July 1	Weighed 30 days from Mar. 19, 1888. 0.26 m. increase.
13. 00	100. 03		79. 52		8, 237. 18		6, 357. 18		July 1	Weighed 30 days from Feb. 20, 1888. 2.4 m. increase. 72.5 m. Waldo and Wildwood, L. G., at $80.03 per m.; formerly $63.61 per m.

H.—*Table showing the re-adjustment of the rates of pay per mile on railroad routes in*

Index order.	State.	Number of route.	Termini.	Corporate title of company carrying the mail.	Length of route.	Average weight of mails, whole distance per day.	Miles per hour.	Size, etc., of mail-car or apartment.
					Miles.	*Lbs.*		*Feet and inches.*
135	Mich..	24048	East Saginaw, Bay City.	Flint and Pere Marquette R. R.	13.24	1,339	18	....
136	Miss ..	18010	Natchez, Jackson....	Natchez, Jackson and Columbus R. R.	99.54	1,326	19	12.3 by .8, 1 1........
137	Miss..	18002	Memphis, Tenn., Grenada, Miss.	Illinois Central R. R..	100.37	1,302	25	28.4 by 9.2, 1 1........
138	Ga....	15023	Brunswick, Albany.	Brunswick and Western R. R.	171.78	1,292	20	14.6 by 7, 1 1.........
139	Ohio ..	21057	Springfield, Ohio, Indianapolis, Ind.	Ohio, Indiana and Western Rwy.	139.51	1,258	29	22.2 by 8.7, 1 1........
140	Nebr..	34047	Weeping Water, Nebraska City.	Missouri Pacific Rwy.	24.87	1,236	23	16.4 by 6.9, 1 1........
141	Fla ...	16012	Palatka, Gainesville..	Florida Southern Rwy.	50.12	1,230	17	16.2 by 7.6, 1 L to Rochelle, 39.93 m.; no apt. residue.
142	Mich..	24003	Adrian, Jackson.....	Lake Shore and Michigan Southern Rwy.	47.26	1,210	25	11.3 by 8.10, 1 1........
143	Cal....	46051	Saugus Station (n. o.), Santa Barbara.	Southern Pacific R. R.	78.80	1,201	20	18 by 8.11, 1 1 ....
144	Ohio ..	21012	Springfield, Sandusky	Cincinnati, Sandusky and Cleveland R. R.	130.20	1,162	30	(av.) 14.10 by 8.9, 1 L
145	N.C...	13012	Greensborough, Winston.	Richmond and Danville R. R.	29.09	1,150	19	8 by 6, 2 1.............
146	Fla....	16014	Rochelle, Fort Mason.	Florida Southern Rwy.	80.76	1,141	18	16.2 by 7.6, 1 1 ....
147	Kans..	33070	Salina, McCracken...	Kansas and Colorado R. R.	126.25	1,141	25	20.4 by 7.3, 1 1........
148	Ind....	22014	State Line (n. o.), Logansport.	Chicago, St. Louis and Pittsburg R. R.	61.27	1,139	30	31.9 by 8 9, 1 1........
149	Ind....	22021	Richmond, Fort Wayne.	Grand Rapids and Indiana R. R.	92.66	1,136	26	20 by 8.10, 1 1........
150	Ohio...	21074	Logan, Pomeroy.....	Columbus, Hocking Valley and Toledo Rwy.	83.76	1,112	22	15.11 by 9.4, 2 1......
151	Colo...	38018	Leadville, Aspen.....	Denver and Rio Grande R. R.	137.82	1,097	29	15.1 by 6.10, 1 1......
152	Nebr .	34048	Nebraska City, Auburn.	Nebraska Southern Rwy.	22.89	1,081	26	16.4 by 6.9, 1 1........
153	Mich..	24022	Big Rapids, Holland.	Chicago and West Michigan Rwy.	91.63	1,079	21	15 by 9, 1 1..........
154	Kans..	33075	Saint Joseph, Mo., Pratt, Kans.	Chicago, Kansas and Nebraska Rwy.	296.89	1,070	24	16.6 by 7.8, 21. to Horton, 40.60 m.; 1 line residue, 258.29 m.

States and Territories in which the contract term expired June 30, 1888, etc.—Continued.

Average trips per week.	Pay per mile per annum for transportation.	Pay per mile per annum for r.p.o. cars.	Former pay per mile per annum for transportation.	Former pay per mile per annum for r. p. o. cars.	Amount of annual pay for transportation.	Amount of annual pay for r. p. o. cars.	Former amount of annual pay for transportation.	Former amount of annual pay for r. p. o. cars.	Date of adjustment or re-adjustment.	Remarks.
	Dolls.	Dolls.	Dolls.	Dolls.	Dollars.	Dollars.	Dollars.	Dollars.	1888.	
7.00	99.18	......	98.33	......	1,313.14	....	1,298.93	....	July 1	Weighed 30 days from Mar. 19, 1888. 0.03 m. increase.
8.01	99.18	......	100.89	......	9,872.37	....	10,033.51	....	July 1	Weighed 30 days from February 20, 1888. 0.09 m. increase.
7	98.32	......	77.81	......	9,868.37	....	7,963.07	....	July 1	Weighed 30 days from February 20, 1888. 1.97 m. decrease.
11.61	97.47	......	45.32	......	16,743.39	....	7,782.80	....	July 1	Weighed 30 days from February 20, 1888. 0.05 m. increase.
19.56	95.76	......	95.76	......	13,359.47	....	13,359.47	....	July 1	Weighed 30 days from March 19, 1888.
14	94.90	......			2,960.16				1887. Nov. 27	Weighed 30 days from March 28, 1888. New.
7.21	94.90	......	52.16	......	4,756.38	....	2,596.00	....	1888. July 1	Weighed 30 days from February 20, 1888. 0.35 m. increase.
12	94.05	......	93.20	......	4,444.80	....	4,418.61	....	July 1	Weighed 30 days from March 19, 1888. 0.15 m. decrease.
14	94.05	......			7,411.14				1887. July 1	Weighed 30 days from March 19, 1888. New.
16.11	92.34	......	83.07	......	12,022.66	....	11,567.99	....	1888. July 1	Weighed 30 days from March 19, 1888. 1.15 m. decrease.
13	91.48	......	75.24	......	2,661.15	....	2,189.48	......:...	July 1	Weighed 30 days from Feb. 20, 1888 0.01 m. decrease.
7.08	91.48	......	85.50	......	7,337.92	....	7,379.50	....	July 1	Weighed 30 days from Feb. 20, 1888. 5.55 m. decrease.
7	91.48	......			11,549.35				1887. May 9	Weighed 30 days from Mar. 19, 1888. New.
12	90.63	......	108.59	......	5,552.90	....	6,644.62	....	1888. July 1	Weighed 30 days from Mar. 19, 1888. 0.08 m. increase.
12	90.63	......	70.11	......	6,397.77	....	6,501.90	....	July 1	Weighed 30 days from Mar. 19, 1888. 0.07 m. decrease.
12	89.77	......	81.23	......	7,519.13	....	6,799.76	....	July 1	Weighed 30 days from Mar. 19, 1888. 0.05 m. increase.
7	88.92	......	42.75	......	12,254.95	....	1,214.10	....	Apr. 1	Weighed 30 days from Apr. 1, 1888. 68.68 m. ext. Red Cliff to Glenwood Springs from Oct. 28, 1887; 40.74 m. ext. Glenwood Springs to Aspen from Dec. 15, 1887.
14	86.92	......	......		2,035.37				1887. Nov. 27	Weighed 30 days from Mar. 28, 1888. New.
8.75	88.06	......	77.81	......	8,068.93	....	7,080.71	....	1888. July 1	Weighed 30 days from Mar. 19, 1888. 0.03 m. increase.
14.10	88.06	......	......		26,320.25				1887. Oct. 17	Weighed 30 days from Mar. 19, 1888. 126.45 m., Saint Joseph, Mo., to Alma, Kans., from July 1, 1887; 45.29 m. ext. Alma to Herington from July 20, 1887; 127.15 m. ext. Herington to Pratt from Oct. 17, 1887.

II.—*Table showing the re-adjustment of the rates of pay per mile on railroad routes in*

Index order.	State.	Number of route.	Termini.	Corporate title of company carrying the mail.	Length of route.	Average weight of mails, whole distance per day.	Miles per hour.	Size, etc., of mail-car or apartment.
					Miles.	*Lbs.*		*Feet and inches.*
155	Ohio ..	21041	Loralu, Bridgeport ..	Cleveland, Lorain and Wheeling R. R.	156. 13	1, 057	23	16 by 8.8, 1 l. Grafton to Bridgeport, 142.33 m.
156	Mich..	24008	Jackson, Niles	Michigan Central R. R.	104. 25	1, 057	25	18 by 10, 1 l ....
157	Ind ...	22054	Butler, Logansport...	Wabash Western Rwy.	94. 01	1, 044	23	17.10 by 9.2, 1 l ....
158	Ohio ..	21029	Morrow, Dresden ...	Cincinnati and Muskingum Valley Rwy.	148. 61	1, 042	29	19.1 by 8.10, 2 l ......
159	Tenn..	19008	Knoxville, Jellico ...	East Tennessee, Virginia, and Georgia Rwy.	65. 51	1, 039	24	15 by 9.4, 1 l..........
160	Ohio ..	21094	Columbus, Midland City.	Columbus and Cincinnati Midland R. R.	72. 22	1, 036	30	18.6 by 8.10, 2 l.......
161	Ind ...	22027	Detroit, Mich., Butler, Ind.	Wabash, St. Louis and Pacific Rwy.	115	1, 035	34	17.10 by 9.2, 1 l.......
162	Wis...	25016	Milwaukee, Wis., Republic, Mich.	Milwaukee and Northern R. R.	256. 04	1, 028	24	....
163	Ga	15013	Rome, Brunswick	East Tennessee, Virginia and Georgia Rwy.	352. 03	1, 026	23	25 by 10, 1 l ......
164	Ohio ..	21019	Marietta, Ohio, Parkersburgh, W. Va.	Cincinnati, Washington and Baltimore R. R.	14. 06	1, 021	20	....
165	Ohio ..	21068	Columbus, Corning ..	Toledo and Ohio Central Rwy.	66. 27	1, 019	25	20.6 by 9.1, 2 l........
166	Fla...	16016	Jacksonville, Saint Augustine.	Jacksonville, St. Augustine and Halifax River Rwy.	37. 71	1, 008	24	no apt ....
167	Ohio ..	21053	Columbus, Toledo	Columbus, Hocking Valley and Toledo Rwy.	124. 85	1, 004	25	(av.) 13.11 by 8.5, 11..
168	Mich..	24045	Manistee Junction (n. o), Manistee.	Flint and Pere Marquette R. R.	27. 12	1, 002	24	22.2 by 8.11, 1 l.......
169	Ala ...	17010	Selma, Ala., Cleveland, Tenn.	East Tennessee, Virginia and Georgia Rwy.	263. 92	1, 002	23	16.4 by 8.5, 1 l., and 1 l. add'l between Cohutta and Rome, 53.24 m.
170	Ohio ..	21071	Valley Junction (n. o.), Harrison.	Cincinnati, Indianapolis, St. Louis and Chicago Rwy.	7. 75	990	35	12 by 7, 1 l ....
171	Fla ...	16006	Jacksonville, Lake City.	Florida Rwy. and Navigation Co.	60. 26	1, 449	21	13.7 by 6.8, 1 l., and 1 l. add'l to Baldwin, 19 miles.
172	Ga	15044	Climax, Ga., Chattahoochee, Fla.	Savannah, Florida and Western Rwy.	32. 17	957	29	19.4 by 9.2, 1 l ......
173	Ohio ..	21027	Xenia, Springfield....	Pittsburgh, Cincinnati and St. Louis Rwy.	20. 07	957	30	20 by 8.2, 1 l ....
174	Tenn.	19009	Morristown, Kinzel (n. o.).	East Tennessee, Virginia and Georgia Rwy.	43. 50	955	26	20.1 by 8.6, 1 l ......
175	Ala...	17007	Opelika, Columbus ...	Columbus and Western Rwy.	29. 58	949	25	12.9 by 6.9, 1 l ......
176	Ind ...	22038	Indianapolis, Michigan City.	Louisville, New Albany and Chicago Rwy.	155. 18	947	57	14.9 by 3, 1 l ....

States and Territories in which the contract term expired June 30, 1888, etc.—Continued.

Average trips per week.	Pay per mile per annum for transportation.	Pay per mile per annum for r. p. o. cars.	Former pay per mile per annum for transportation.	Former pay per mile per annum for r. p. o. cars.	Amount of annual pay for transportation.	Amount of annual pay for r. p. o. cars.	Former amount of annual pay for transportation.	Former amount of annual pay for r. p. o. cars.	Date of adjustment or re-adjustment.	Remarks.
	Dolls.	Dolls.	Dolls.	Dolls.	Dollars.	Dollars.	Dollars.	Dollars.	1888.	
10. 47	87. 21	......	77. 81	......	13, 790. 51	....	12, 325. 88	....	July 1	Weighed 30 days from Mar. 19, 1888. 0.28 m. decrease.
9. 7	87. 21	......	77. 81	......	9, 091. 64	....	8, 115. 58	....	July 1	Weighed 30 days from Mar. 19, 1888. 0.95 m. decrease.
13. 75	87. 21	......	64. 98	......	8, 196. 61	....	....	....	July 1	Weighed 30 days from Mar. 19, 1888. Formerly part of 22027.
12. 50	87. 21	......	75. 24	......	2, 960. 27	....	11, 190. 44	....	July 1	Weighed 30 days from Mar. 19, 1888. 0.12 m. decrease.
7	86. 35	......	77. 81	......	5, 656. 78	....	5, 106. 67	....	July 1	Weighed 30 days from Feb. 20, 1888. 0.12 m. decrease.
21	86. 35	... ..	57. 29	......	6, 296. 19	....	4, 166. 70	....	July 1	Weighed 30 days from Mar. 19, 1888. 0.51 m. decrease.
13	86. 35	......	64. 98	......	9, 990. 25	....	13, 279. 31	....	July 1	Weighed 30 days from Mar. 19, 1888.
11. 77	86. 35	......	86. 35	......	22, 109. 05	....	22, 109. 05	....	Feb. 27	Weighed 30 days from Mar. 19, 1888.
14	86. 35	......	70. 97	......	29, 119. 57	....	24, 160. 39	....	July 1	Weighed 30 days from Feb. 20, 1888. 17.80 m. Austell to Atlanta lap service at $14.54 per m.; formerly 18.31 m. at $30.78 per m. 1.23 m. increase.
21	86. 35	......	74. 39	......	1, 214. 08	....	1, 121. 80	....	July 1	Weighed 30 days from Mar. 19, 1888. 1.02 m. decrease.
10. 70	85. 50	......	64. 98	......	5, 666. 08	....	4, 291. 92	....	July 1	Weighed 30 days from Mar. 19, 1888. 0 23 m. increase.
20	85. 50	......	60. 71	......	3, 224. 20	....	2, 234. 12	....	July 1	Weighed 30 days from Feb. 20, 1888. 0.91 m. increase.
19	85. 50	......	76. 10	......	10, 674. 67	....	9, 479. 78	....	July 1	Weighed 30 days from Mar. 19, 1888. 0.28 m. increase.
12	85. 50	......	81. 23	......	2, 318. 76	....	2, 203. 76	....	July 1	Weighed 30 days from Mar. 19, 1888. 0.01 m. decrease.
15. 21	85. 50	......	106. 02	......	19, 807. 56	....	24, 779. 61	....	July 1	Weighed 30 days from Feb. 20, 1888. 1 m. decrease. 156 m. Selma to Patona (n. o.) land grant at $68.40 per m.; formerly $84.82 per mile.
12	84. 64	......	70. 11	......	655. 90	....	518. 81	....	July 1	Weighed 30 days from Mar. 19, 1888. 0.35 m. increase.
17. 43	83. 44	......	68. 40	......	5, 028. 09	....	4, 125. 88	....	July 1	Weighed 30 days from Feb. 20, 1888. 0.06 m. decrease. Land grant.
7	82. 93	......	86. 36	......	2, 667. 85	....	2, 778. 20	....	July 1	Weighed 30 days from Feb. 20, 1888.
16. 50	82. 93	......	45. 32	......	1, 604. 40	....	905. 94	....	July 1	Weighed 30 days from Mar. 19, 1888. 0.08 m. increase.
14	82. 93	......	77. 81	......	3, 607. 45	....	3, 376. 17	....	July 1	Weighed 30 days from Feb. 20, 1888. 0.11 m. increase.
14	82. 93	......	77. 81	......	2, 453. 06	....	2, 297. 72	....	July 1	Weighed 30 days from Feb. 20, 1888. 0.05 m. increase.
12. 51	82. 93	......	76. 10	......	12, 869. 07	....	13, 123. 55	....	July 1	Weighed 30 days from Mar. 19, 1888. Formerly part of 22008.

II.—*Table showing the re-adjustment of the rates of pay per mile on railroad routes in*

Index order.	State.	Number of route.	Termini.	Corporate title of company carrying the mail.	Length of route.	Average weight of mails, whole distance per day.	Miles per hour.	Size, etc., of mail car or apartment.
					Miles.	*Lbs.*		*Feet and inches.*
177	Ohio	21083	Means, Cadiz	Pittsburgh, Cincinnati and St. Louis Rwy.	8.12	941	15	....
178	Miss	18004	Mobile, Ala., Cairo, Ill.	Mobile and Ohio R. R.	495.57	1,466	19	22.6 by 10, 1 l ....
179	Ind	22006	Columbus, Madison	Pennsylvania Company.	45.58	932	35	19.2 by 9.2, 2 l .. ...
180	Mich	24016	Ionia, Big Rapids	Detroit, Lansing and Northern R. R.	68.08	928	24	20 by 8.10, 1 l.
181	S. C.	14001	Columbia, Greenville	Richmond and Danville R. R.	144.33	908	20	19.6 by 9,1 l. whole route; 13.8 by 8.10, 1 l. Columbus to Alston, 25.10 m.; 8.3 by 6.7, 1 l. Columbus to Newberry, 46.70 m.; 13.10 by 8.6, 1 l. Belton to Greenville, 26.50 m.
182	Dak	35027	Tintah Junction (n. o.), Minn., Aberdeen, Dak.	St. Paul, Minneapolis and Manitoba Rwy.	119.31	902	27	16 by 8.10, 1 l.
183	Iowa	27047	Cedar Rapids, Iowa, Kansas City, Mo.	Chicago, Milwaukee and St. Paul Rwy.	390.63	896	25	26 by 9.3, 1 l.
184	Ohio	21055	Toledo, Thurston	Toledo and Ohio Central Rwy.	148.13	887	25	20.6 by 9.1, 1 l........
185	Kans	33082	Herington, Caldwell	Chicago, Kansas and Western R. R.	123.73	885	24	16.6 by 7 8, 1 l........
186	Ohio	21080	Toledo, Bowerston	Wheeling and Lake Erie Rwy.	175.62	883	27	(av.) 16.9 by 8.1, 1 l, to Zoar Station, 153.7 m.
187	Tex	31054	Fort Worth, Tex., Purcell, Ind. Ter.	Gulf, Colorado and Santa Fé Rwy.	170.63	861	26	20.4 by 9.2, 1 l........
188	Ohio	21052	Batavia Junction (n. o.), Portsmouth.	Ohio and Northwestern R. R.	98.02	865	25	12 by 8.6, 1 l.........
189	Dak	35012	Ashton, Edgeley	Chicago, Milwaukee and St. Paul Rwy.	96.81	861	22	20.1 by 9.1, 1 l, to Aberdeen, 82.74 m. No clk. res.
190	Ind	22023	Oakland City, Ind., Mount Vernon, Ill.	Louisville, Evansville and St. Louis Rwy.	88.63	858	26	14 by 9.6, 1 l.........
191	N. Y.	6136	Windsor Beach (n. o), Rochester.	Rome, Watertown and Ogdensburg R. R.	8.3	851	23	No apt ....

States and Territories in which the contract term expired June 30, 1888, etc.—Continued.

Average trips per week.	Pay per mile per annum for transportation.	Pay per mile per annum for r.p.o. cars.	Former pay per mile per annum for transportation.	Former pay per mile per annum for r.p.o. cars.	Amount of annual pay for transportation.	Amount of annual pay for r.p.o. cars.	Former amount of annual pay for transportation.	Former amount of annual pay for r.p.o. cars.	Date of adjustment or re-adjustment.	Remarks.
	Dolls.	Dolls.	Dolls.	Dolls.	Dollars.	Dollars.	Dollars.	Dollars.	1888.	
21	82.93		48.74		673.39		396.28		July 1	Weighed 30 days from Mar. 19, 1888. 0.01 m. increase.
7	82.08		79.34		40,676.38		39,349.91		July 1	Weighed 30 days from Feb. 20, 1888. 0.32 m. decrease. Land grant.
12	82.08		76.95		3,741.20		3,520.46		July 1	Weighed 30 days from Mar. 19, 1886. 0.17 m. decrease.
12	82.08		80.37		5,588.00		5,472.39		July 1	Weighed 30 days from Mar. 19, 1888. 0.01 m. decrease.
10.21	81.22		76.10		11,722.48		10,962.75		July 1	Weighed 30 days from Feb. 20, 1888. 0.1 lm. increase.
7	81.22				9,690.35				1887. June 18	Weighed 30 days from Apr. 15, 1888. New.
6	80.37		59.00		24,160.02		5,370.77		1888. Mar. 19	Weighed 30 days from Mar. 19, 1888. From Jan. 30, 1888, on 209.58 m. ext. from Ottumwa, Iowa, to Kansas City, Mo
6.75	80.37		54.72		11,905.20		8,091.44		July 1	Weighed 30 days from Mar. 19, 1888. 0.26 m. increase.
14	80.37				9,944.17				1887. Nov. 28	Weighed 30 days from Mar. 19, 1888. 74.35 m. Herington to Wichita from Oct. 24.1887; 49.38 m. ext. Wichita to Caldwell from Nov. 28, 1887.
6.06	80.37		60.71		14,114.57		10,550.34		1888. July 1	Weighed 30 days from Mar. 19, 1888. 3.94 m. increase. 16.60 m. Zoar Station to Bow-erston formerly at $68.40 per m.
9.66	79.52		79.52		13,568.48		5,160.84		1887. Sept. 12	Weighed 30 days from Feb. 20, 1888. 105.73 m. ext. Gainesville to Purcell from Sept. 12, 1887.
12	79.51		63.27		7,793.57		6,883.16		1888. July 1	Weighed 30 days from Mar. 19, 1888. 0.68 m. decrease.
6.30	79.51		82.08		7,697.36		5,770.22		Mar. 19	Weighed 30 days from Mar. 19, 1888. 26.34 m. ext. Ellendale to Edgeley from July 25, 1887.
14	78.66		52.16		6,971.63		4,619.28		July 1	Weighed 30 days from Mar. 19, 1888. 0.07 m. increase.
12.6	78.66				652.57				1887. Oct. 3	Weighed 30 days from Mar. 19, 1888. New.

H.—*Table showing the re-adjustment of the rates of pay per mile on railroad routes in*

Index order.	State.	Number of route.	Termini.	Corporate title of company carrying the mail.	Length of route.	Average weight of mails, whole distance per day.	Miles per hour.	Size, etc., of mail-car or apartment.
					Miles.	*Lbs.*		*Feet and inches.*
192	N. C ..	13003	Wilmington, Charlotte.	Carolina Central R. R.	188.07	844	15	16 by 9, 1 1............
193	Ga....	15031	Thomasville, Bainbridge.	Savannah, Florida and Western Rwy.	87.97	844	22	19.4 by 9.2, 1 1. between Thomasville and Climax, 28.72 m.
194	Mich .	24026	Grand Rapids, Baldwin.	Chicago and West Michigan Rwy.	74.90	838	20	12 by 8 9, 1 1..........
195	..do ...	24031	Point Saint Ignace (n. o.), Marquette.	Duluth, South Shore and Atlantic Rwy.	151	829	21	....
196	Ohio ..	21040	Marietta, Valley Junction (n.o.).	Cleveland and Marietta Rwy.	106	807	24	19.2 by 6.9, 1 1........
197	Ky ...	20015	Maysville, Paris	Kentucky Central Rwy.	50.29	805	21	12 by 8.9, 1 1 ....
198	Miss..	18020	Leland, Miss., Arkansas City, Ark.	Louisville, New Orleans and Texas Rwy.	24.44	802	10	17.9 by 8.4, 1 1. and 1 1. addl. between Leland and Wilzinski, 7 22 m.
199	Ohio ..	21073	Cleveland, Zoar Station.	Valley Rwy..........	75.97	800	25	19.6 by 9, 1 1..........
200	Minn .	26061	Winnipeg Junction, Minn., Pembina, Dak.	Northern Pacific R. R.	200.13	799	25	(av.) 23 by 8.11, 1 1....
201	Ohio ..	21090	Marion, Chicago Junction (n.o.).	Chicago and Atlantic Rwy.	250.70	783	30	18.3 by 8.4, 1 1.......
202	..do ...	21089	Cleveland, Ohio, Chicago, Ill.	New York, Chicago and Saint Louis R. R.	339.33	781	25	20 by 9.2, 1 1..........
203	Fla ...	16025	Enterprise Junction (n. o.), Titusville.	Jacksonville, Tampa and Key West Rwy.	40.69	780	10	1 line ....
204	Mich..	24042	Port Huron, Port Austin.	Port Huron and Northwestern Rwy.	87.96	777	20	16.6 by 7.6, 1 1.......
205	Kans..	33084	McCracken, Kans., Towner, Colo.	Denver, Memphis and Atlantic Rwy.	141.35	768	27	20.4 by 7.3, 1 1........
206	Ind ...	22022	Anderson, Ind., Benton Harbor, Mich.	Cincinnati, Wabash and Michigan Rwy.	165.09	767	35	16.2 by 8.8, 1 1 ....
207	Ga....	15006	Mellen, Augusta.....	Central R. R. and Banking Co.	55.43	762	26	24.6 by 9, 1 1..........
208	Ohio ..	21060	Columbia, Georgetown.	Cincinnati, Georgetown and Portsmouth R. R.	42.17	760	18	19.6 by 7.6 ....
209	Ind ...	22001	Indianapolis, Vincennes.	Pennsylvania Company.	117.26	754	25	20 by 9, 1 1..........
210	Mich..	24055	Grand Rapids, Muskegon.	Muskegon, Grand Rapids and Indiana R. R.	40.73	748	30	....
211	Fla....	16023	Leesburgh, Brooksville.	Florida Southern Rwy.	40.46	745	20	16.2 by 7.6, 1 1. to Pemberton, 29.96 m. No apt. residue.
212	Ohio ..	21043	Mansfield, Toledo	Pennsylvania Company.	86.25	745	29	20 by 8.11, 1 1......

States and Territories in which the contract term expired June 30, 1888, etc.—Continued.

Average trips per week.	Pay per mile per annum for transportation.	Pay per mile per annum for r. p. o. cars.	Former pay per mile per annum for transportation.	Former pay per mile per annum for r. p. o. cars.	Amount of annual pay for transportation.	Amount of annual pay for r. p. o. cars.	Former amount of annual pay for transportation.	Former amount of annual pay for r. o. cars.	Date of adjustment or re-adjustment.	Remarks.
	Dolls.	*Dolls.*	*Dolls.*	*Dolls.*	*Dollars.*	*Dollars.*	*Dollars.*	*Dollars.*	1888.	
6	78. 66	......	64. 13	......	14, 793. 58	....	12, 089. 78	....	July 1	Weighed 30 days from Feb. 20, 1888. 9.45 m. decrease.
8. 70	78. 60	......	80. 37	......	2, 986. 72	....	2, 972. 88	....	July 1	Weighed 30 days from Feb. 20, 1888. 0.98 m. increase.
6	77. 80	......	64. 13	......	5, 834. 22	....	4, 744. 33	....	July 1	Weighed 30 days from Mar. 19, 1888. 1.01 m. increase.
7	77. 80	......	42. 75	......	11. 747. 80	....	6, 471. 06	....	July 1	Weighed 30 days from Mar. 19, 1888. 0.37 m. decrease.
12	76. 95	......	72. 68	......	8, 156. 70	....	7, 683. 72	....	July 1	Weighed 30 days from Mar. 19, 1888.
12	76. 95	......	75. 24	......	3, 869. 81	....	3, 774. 79	....	July 1	Weighed 30 days from Feb. 20, 1888. 0.12 m. increase.
12. 31	76. 95	......	66. 69	......	1, 880. 65	....	1, 611. 23	....	July 1	Weighed 30 days from Feb. 20, 1888. 0.28 m. increase.
15. 50	76. 95	......	72. 68	......	5, 845. 89	....	5. 532. 40	....	July 1	Weighed 30 days from Mar. 19, 1888. 0.15 m. decrease.
7	76. 09	......	......	......	15, 229. 40	....	....	....	Jan. 2	Weighed 30 days from Mar. 19, 1888. From Oct. 3, 1887, on 106.66 m., Winnipeg Junc. to Grand Forks; from Jan. 2, 1888, on 93 49 m. ext. Grand Forks to Pembina.
14. 80	76. 09	......	55. 58	......	19, 075. 76	....	13, 892. 22	....	July 1	Weighed 30 days from Mar. 19, 1888. 0 75 m. increase.
6. 82	76. 09	......	69. 20	......	25, 819. 61	....	23, 483. 98	....	July 1	Weighed 30 days from Mar. 19, 1888. 0.26 m. increase.
12. 68	76. 09	......	67. 55	......	3, 096. 10	....	2, 730. 37	....	July 1	Weighed 30 days from Feb. 20, 1888. 0.27 m. increase.
12	75. 24	......	66. 69	......	6, 619. 61	....	5, 849. 87	....	July 1	Weighed 30 days from Mar. 19, 1888. 0.27 m. increase.
7	75. 24	......	......	......	10, 635. 16	....	....	....	Mar. 1	Weighed 30 days from Mar. 19, 1888. 126.06 m., McCracken to Horace, Kans. from Dec. 5, 1887; 15.29 m. ext. Horace, Kans. to Towner, Colo., from Mar. 1, 1888.
12	75. 24	......	64. 98	......	12, 421. 37	....	10, 700. 90	....	July 1	Weighed 30 days from Mar. 19, 1888. 0.41 m. increase.
21	75. 24	......	66. 69	......	4, 172. 05	....	3, 635. 27	....	July 1	Weighed 30 days from Feb. 20, 1888. 0.94 m. increase.
12	75. 24	......	67. 55	......	3, 172. 87	....	2, 848. 58	....	July 1	Weighed 30 days from Mar. 19, 1888.
12	74. 38	......	71. 82	......	8, 721. 79	....	8, 489. 84	....	July 1	Weighed 30 days from Mar. 19, 1888. 0.95 m. decrease.
6	74. 38	......	74. 38	......	3, 029. 49	....	2, 938. 01	....	July 1	Weighed 30 days from Mar. 19, 1888. 1.23 m. increase.
6	74. 38	......	72. 68	......	3, 009. 41	....	2, 957. 34	....	July 1	Weighed 30 days from Feb. 20, 1888. 0 23 m. decrease.
21	74. 38	......	59. 09	......	6, 415. 27	....	5, 085. 80	....	July 1	Weighed 30 days from Mar. 19, 1888. 0.05 m. increase.

H.— *Table showing the re-adjustment of the rates of pay per mile on railroad routes in*

Index order.	State.	Number of route.	Termini.	Corporate title of company carrying the mail.	Length of route.	Average weight of mails, whole distance per day.	Miles per hour.	Size, etc., of mail-car or apartment.
					Miles.	*Lbs.*		*Feet and inches.*
213	Mich..	24052	Pentwater, Muskegon.	Chicago and West Michigan Rwy.	44.96	741	17	11 by 8.9, 1 l ....
214	Mich..	24032	Powers, Crystal Falls.	Chicago and Northwestern Rwy.	57.75	740	23	25.5 by 8.7, 1 l. from Powers to Florence, 41.75 m.
215	Ohio ..	21031	Harrison, Ohio, Beeson's, Ind.	White Water R. R...	48.92	739	23	12 by 7.7, 1 l.........
216	Kans..	33076	Horton, Kans., Nelson, Nebr.	Chicago, Kansas and Nebraska Rwy.	167.26	739	24	16.6 by 7.8, 1 l.........
217	Mich..	24034	Walton, Traverse City.	Traverse City R. R...	26.22	724	17	....
218	Fla ...	16003	Pensacola, Fla., Flomaton, Ala.	Louisville and Nashville R. R.	43.43	1,148	21	14 by 9.1, 1 l.........
219	Ind ...	22032	Evansville, Jasper...	Louisville, Evansville and Saint Louis Ry.	54.36	717	25	14 by 9.3, 1 l ....
220	Wis...	25031	Tomah, Tomahawk..	Chicago, Milwaukee and Saint Paul Rwy.	131.06	702	23	23.1 by 9.5, 1 l. Tomah to Merrill, 107.62 m.
221	Mont .	36095	Helena, Great Falls..	Montana Central Rwy	99.14	701	17	24 by 8.4, 1 l.........
222	Fla ...	16015	Pensacola, River Junction.	Pensacola and Atlantic R. R.	161.20	1,124	22	13 by 6.10, 1 l.........
223	Ohio ..	21092	Canton, Coshecton...	Cleveland and Canton R. R.	56.05	697	22	12.10 by 7.8, 1 l......
224	Mich..	24029	Jackson, Mich., Fort Wayne, Ind.	Lake Shore and Michigan Southern Rwy.	100.40	689	24	16.10 by 9, 1 l.........
225	Mich..	24030	East Saginaw, Ithaca.	Saginaw Valley and Saint Louis R. R.	45.96	686	23	15.7 by 8.9, 1 l to Saint Louis, 35.06 m.
226	Ark...	29019	Fort Smith, Ark., Paris, Tex.	Saint Louis and San Francisco Rwy.	168.93	686	24	22.6 by 7.4, 1 l.........
227	Fla ...	16022	Tavares, Orlando	Tavares, Orlando and Atlantic R. R.	33.55	686	30	22.9 by 8.9, 1 l.........
228	N. C ...	13010	Raleigh, Hamlet	Raleigh and Augusta Air Line R. R.	97.52	686	20	13.6 by 6.6, 1 l.........
229	Ohio ..	21020	Sandusky, Ohio, Bloomington, Ill.	Lake Erie and Western Rwy.	377.63	661	28	17.3 by 9, 1 l ....
230	Mich..	24041	Alma, Howard City..	Detroit, Lansing, and Northern R. R.	42.90	681	23	15.7 by 8.9, 1 l.........
231	Ga	15036	Dupont, Ga., Gainesville, Fla.	Savannah, Florida, and Western Rwy.	119.31	680	25	18.9 by 3, 1 l ....
232	Nebr..	34041	Scribner, Oakdale....	Fremont, Elkhorn and Missouri Valley R. R.	115.73	674	24	14.4 by 9.4, 1 l.......

States and Territories in which the contract term expired June 30, 1888, etc.—Continued.

Average trips per week.	Pay per mile per annum for transportation.	Pay per mile per annum for r. p. o. cars.	Former pay per mile per annum for transportation.	Former pay per mile per annum for r. p. o. cars.	Amount of annual pay for transportation.	Amount of annual pay for r. p. o. cars.	Former amount of annual pay for transportation.	Former amount of annual pay for r. p. o. cars.	Date of adjustment or re-adjustment.	Remarks.
	Dolls.	Dolls.	Dolls.	Dolls.	Dollars.	Dollars.	Dollars.	Dollars.	1888.	
6	74. 38		59. 85		3, 344. 12		2, 701. 03		July 1	Weighed 30 days from Mar. 19, 1888. 0.17 m. decrease.
14	74. 38		55. 58		4, 295. 44		3, 220. 86		July 1	Weighed 30 days from Mar. 19, 1888. 0.20 m. decrease.
6	73. 53		55. 58		3, 597. 08		3, 505. 96		July 1 1887	Weighed 30 days from Mar. 19, 1888.
7	73. 53				12, 296. 61				Sept. 26	Weighed 30 days from Mar. 19, 1888. 160. 77 m. Horton, Kans., to Nora, Nebr., from July 1, 1887 ; 6.49 m. ext. Nora to Ne.son, from Sept. 26, 1887.
6	73. 53		64. 98		1, 927. 95		1, 707. 02		1888 July 1	Weighed 30 days from Mar. 19, 1888. 0 05. m. decrease.
21	73. 18		69. 09		3, 178. 20		3, 097. 99		July 1	Weighed 30 days from Feb. 20, 1888. 1.41 m. decrease. Land-grant.
19. 76	72. 67		66. 69		3, 950. 84		3, 676. 62		July 1	Weighed 30 days from Mar. 19, 1888. 0.77 m. increase.
6	72. 67		71. 82		9, 524. 12		7, 757. 99		Apr '16	Weighed 30 days from Apr. 16, 1888. From Dec. 26, 1887, on 23.04 m. exten. from Merrill to Tomahawk.
7	72. 67				7, 204. 50				Jan. 16	Weighed 30 days from Mar. 19, 1888. New.
14	72. 50		70. 46		11, 687. 00		11, 380. 69		July 1	Weighed 90 days from Feb. 20, 1888. 0 32 m. decrease. Land-grant.
15	71. 82		49. 59		4, 025. 51		2, 714. 06		July 1	Weighed 30 days from Mar. 19, 1888. 1.32 m. increase.
12	71. 82		70. 11		7, 210. 72		6, 896. 12		July 1	Weighed 30 days from Mar. 19, 1888. 2.01 m. increase.
6. 45	71. 82		64. 96		3, 300. 84		2, 967. 78		July 1	Weighed 30 days from Mar. 19, 1888. 0.02 m. decrease.
7	71. 82				12, 132. 64				1887. Oct. 31	Weighed 30 days from Feb. 20, 1888. 13.97 m. Fort Smith to Jenson from May 2, 1887 ; 154.96 m. Jenson to Paris from Oct. 31, 1887.
13	71. 82		67. 55		2, 409. 56		2, 225. 77		1888. July 1	Weighed 30 days from Feb. 20, 1888. 0.60 m. increase.
6	71. 82		78. 06		7, 003. 88		7, 782. 27		July 1	Weighed 30 days from Feb. 20, 1888. 0.78 m. decrease.
13. 22	71. 82		65. 84		27, 121. 38		25, 011. 29		July 1	Weighed 30 days from Mar. 19, 1888. 2.23 m. decrease.
12.	71. 82		59. 85		3, 081. 07		2, 557. 39		July 1	Weighed 30 days from Mar. 19, 1888. 0.17 m. increase.
7	71. 82		56. 43		8, 568. 84		6, 730. 40		July 1	Weighed 30 days from Feb. 20, 1888. 0.01 m. increase.
6	70 97		41. 90		8, 213. 35		2, 686. 20		Mar. 19	Weighed 30 days from Mar. 19, 1888. 51.62 m. ext. Lindsay to Oakdale from July 25, 1887.

H.—*Table showing the re-adjustment of the rates of pay per mile on railroad routes in*

Index order	State.	Number of route.	Termini.	Corporate title of company carrying the mail.	Length of route.	Average weight of mails, whole distance per day.	Miles per hour.	Size, etc., of mail-car or apartment.
					Miles.	*Lbs.*		*Feet and inches.*
233	Fla....	16024	Pemberton, Bartow..	South Florida R. R...	57.39	666	15	21.2 by 7.9, 1 l ....
234	Ind ...	22020	Fort Wayne, Beeson.	Fort Wayne, Cincinnati and Louisville R. R.	102.96	661	26	12 by 7.7, 1 l ....
235	Ga	15025	Athens, Lula	Richmond and Danville R. R.	39.58	655	22	11.3 by 7.1, 1 l ....
236	Dak ...	35006	Everest, Langdon....	St. Paul, Minneapolis and Manitoba Rwy.	155.22	637	16	22 by 8.11, 1 l, to Larimore. No clerk residue.
237	N. C ..	13005	Goldsborough, Morehead City.	Atlantic and North Carolina R. R.	93.91	625	16	10.6 by 8.1, 1 l ....
238	Tenn ..	19001	Nashville, Lebanon ..	Nashville, Chattanooga and St. Louis Rwy.	31.52	620	20	17.4 by 7.4, 2 l ....
239	Mich ..	24040	Marquette, Houghton	Duluth, South Shore and Atlantic Rwy.	94.82	1,036	19	12 by 7.2, 1 l ....
240	Ind ...	22011	Cambridge City, Columbus.	Pennsylvania Company.	63.73	614	31	19.2 by 9.2, 2 l ....
241	Mich ..	24072	Sault de Ste. Marie, Sault Junction.	Duluth, South Shore and Atlantic Rwy.	47.80	612	20	....
242	Mich ..	24033	Lenox, Jackson	Michigan Air Line Rwy.	106.47	611	16	24 by 8.4, 1 l...........
243	N. C...	13015	Rocky Mount, Tarborough.	Wilmington and Weldon R. R.	17.97	609	15	7 by 6.8, 1 l ....
244	Miss ..	18005	Columbus, Miss., Birmingham, Ala.	Georgia Pacific Rwy.	124.83	607	19	15.3 by 8.10, 1 l ....
245	Kans..	33068	Mulvane, Englewood.	Chicago, Kansas and Western R. R.	166.79	607	23	12.8 by 8.4, 1 l ....
246	Kans..	33056	Chetopa, Belle Plaine.	Denver, Memphis and Atlantic Rwy.	146.20	605	21	16.4 by 6.8, 1 l. to Peru, 60.90 m.; 2 l. thence to Sedan, 5.30 m.; 1 l. residue, 80 m.
247	Ala ...	17009	Selma, Ala., Meridian, Miss.	East Tennessee, Virginia and Georgia Rwy.	110.76	605	23	16.5 by 8.7, 1 l........
248	Fla ...	16002	Lake City, River Junction.	Florida Rwy. and Navigation Co.	151.87	993	21	13.7 by 6.8, 1 l........
249	Ga	15011	Macon, Columbus....	Southwestern R. R...	101.05	599	23	15.3 by 9.8, 1 l........

States and Territories in which the contract term expired June 30, 1888, etc.—Continued.

Average trips per week.	Pay per mile per annum for transportation.	Pay per mile per annum for r. p. o. cars.	Former pay per mile per annum for transportation.	Former pay per mile per annum for r. p. o. cars.	Amount of annual pay for transportation.	Amount of annual pay for r. p. o. cars.	Former amount of annual pay for transportation.	Former amount of annual pay for r. p. o. cars.	Date of adjustment or re-adjustment.	Remarks.
	Dolls	*Dolls.*	*Dolls.*	*Dolls.*	*Dollars.*	*Dollars.*	*Dollars.*	*Dollars.*	1888.	
6	70.96	......	50.85	......	4,072.39	....	3,460.52	....	July 1	Weighed 30 days from Feb. 20, 1888. 0.43 m. decrease.
7.43	70.96	......	57.29	......	7,306.04	....	6,275.54	....	July 1	Weighed 30 days from Mar. 19, 1888.
12	70.11	......	55.58	......	2,774.95	....	2,200.41	....	July 1	Weighed 30 days from Feb. 20, 1888. 0.01 m. decrease.
6	69.25	......	59.85	......	10,748.98	....	6,925.24	....	Apr. 16	Weighed 30 days from Apr. 16, 1888. 80.51 m. extension Park River to Langdon, from Dec. 5, 1887.
6	69.25	......	64.13	......	6,503.26	....	6,031.42	....	July 1	Weighed 30 days from Feb. 20, 1888. 0.14 m. decrease.
12	69.25	......	59.85	......	2,182.76	....	1,886.47	....	July 1	Weighed 30 days from Feb. 20, 1888.
7.75	69.08	......	59.51	......	6,550.16	....	5,708.79	....	July 1	Weighed 30 days from Mar. 19, 1888. 1.11 m. decrease. All land grant.
12	68.40	......	46.17	......	4,359.13	....	2,985.48	....	July 1	Weighed 30 days from Mar. 19, 1888. 0.15 m. increase.
12	68.40	......	68.40	......	3,269.52	....	3,269.52	....	Jan. 9	Weighed 30 days from Apr. 21, 1888.
6.80	68.40	......	54.72	......	7,282.54	....	5,832.05	....	July 1	Weighed 30 days from Mar. 19, 1888. 0.11 m. decrease.
7	68.40	......	59.00	......	1,229.14	....	1,050.20	....	July 1	Weighed 30 days from Feb. 20, 1888. 0.17 m. increase.
7	68.40	......	42.75	......	8,538.37	....	5,906.59	....	July 1	Weighed 30 days from Feb. 20, 1888. 38.86 m. ext. York to Coalburgh from June 6, 1887.
7	68.40	......		......	11,408.42	....			Mar. 1	Weighed 30 days from Mar. 19, 1888 51.67 m. Mulvane to Spivey from Mar. 28, 1887; 100 m. ext. Spivey to Ashland from Oct. 17, 1887; 15.12 m. ext. Ashland to Englewood fro Mar. 1, 1888. New.
7.03	68.40	......	58.14	......	10,000.08	....	5,182.17		Mar. 19	Weighed 30 days from Mar. 19, 1888. 36.08 m. ext. Cedar Vale to Winfield from Nov. 7, 1887; 20.97 m. ext. Winfield to Belle Plaine from Nov. 10, 1887.
7	68.40	......	71.82	......	7,575.96	....	8,204.71	....	July 1	Weighed 30 days from Feb. 20, 1888. 3.48 m. decrease.
13.50	67.71	......	60.19	......	10,283.11	....	9,381.81	. ...	July 1	Weighed 30 days from Feb. 20, 1888. 4 m. decrease. Land grant.
14	67.55	......	66.60	......	6,825.92	....	6,738.35	....	July 1	Weighed 30 days from Feb. 20, 1888. 0.01 m increase.

H.—*Table showing the re-adjustment of the rates of pay per mile on railroad routes in*

Index order.	State.	Number of route.	Termini.	Corporate title of company carrying the mail.	Length of route.	Average weight of mails whole distance per day.	Miles per hour.	Size, etc., of mail-car or apartment.
					Miles.	*Lbs.*		*Feet and inches.*
250	Kans .	33062	Kingman, Mullinville	Kingman, Pratt and Western R. R.	75. 73	592	25	17 by 7, 1 l ....
251	Ind ...	22013	Terra Haute, South Bend.	Terre Haute and Indianapolis R. R.	185. 56	590	26	16.9 by 9.2, 1 l ....
252	Ky....	20014	Owensborough, Adairville.	Owensborough and Nashville R. R.	85. 65	589	21	8.4 by 8.6, 1 l. Owensborough to Russellville, 72.08 m. No clerk residue.
253	Nebr .	34046	Orleans, Nebr., Blakeman, Kans.	Burlington and Missouri River R. R. (in Nebraska).	95. 57	586	20	13.11 by 7.7, 1 l ....
254	S. C...	14008	Alston, Spartanburgh	Richmond and Danville R. R.	68. 58	584	21	13.6 by 8.8, 1 l........
255	Mich .	24019	Toledo, Ohio, Allegan, Mich.	Cincinnati, Jackson and Mackinaw R. R.	156. 92	582	23	(av.) 11.9 by 6.9, 1 l..
256	Ga....	15021	Camak, Macon	Georgia R. R........	78. 59	578	15	15.6 by 8.4, 1 l ....
257	Kans .	33059	Great Bend, Scott....	Chicago, Kansas and Western R. R.	121. 12	574	23	20.8 by 9.3, 1 l........
258	S. C...	14011	Spartanburgh, S. C., Asheville, N. C.	Richmond and Danville R. R.	71. 92	569	17	13.6 by 8.8, 1 l........
259	Ohio .	21009	Cleveland, Sherrodaville.	Cleveland and Canton R. R.	110. 52	566	20	20 by 7.8, 1 l ....
260	Ohio ..	21017	Blanchester, Hillsborough.	Cincinnati, Washington and Baltimore R. R.	21. 92	564	19	....
261	Ohio ..	21008	Bayard, New Philadelphia.	Pennsylvania Company.	32. 33	561	20	14.6 by 8.6, 2 l........
262	N. C ..	13008	Charlotte, Rutherfordton.	Carolina Central R. R.	81. 80	559	12	16 by 9, 1 l ....
263	Ill	23095	Chicago, Ill., Dubuque, Iowa.	Chicago, St. Paul and Kansas City Rwy.	167. 33	557	25	15.7 by 8.8, 1 l. to Byron, 83.76 m.
264	Mich..	24002	Monroe, Adrian	Lake Shore and Michigan Southern Rwy.	34. 96	550	26	10 by 6, 1 l ....
265	Fla ...	16026	Bartow, Trabue......	Florida Southern Rwy.	75. 4	546	15	16.2 by 7.6, 1 l........
266	Tex...	31059	Ladonia, Paris	Gulf, Colorado and Santa Fé Rwy.	30. 16	546	20	15.6 by 9, 1 l ....

States and Territories in which the contract term expired June 30, 1888, etc.—Continued.

Average trips per week.	Pay per mile per annum for transportation.	Pay per mile per annum for r. p. o. cars.	Former pay per mile per annum for transportation.	Former pay per mile per annum for r. p. o. cars.	Amount of annual pay for transportation.	Amount of annual pay for r. p. o. cars.	Former amount of annual pay for transportation.	Former amount of annual pay for r. p. o. cars.	Date of adjustment or re-adjustment.	Remarks.
	Dolls.	*Dolls.*	*Dolls.*	*Dolls.*	*Dollars.*	*Dollars.*	*Dollars.*	*Dollars.*	1888.	
13	67.54	......	64.98	......	5,114.80	....	2,892.90	....	Mar. 19	Weighed 30 days from Mar. 19, 1888. 21.24 m. ext. Cullison to Greensburgh from Aug. 8, 1887; 9.97 m. ext. Greensburgh to Mullinville from Mar. 19, 1888.
12	67.54	......	58.14	......	12,532.72	....	10,842.52	....	July 1	Weighed 30 days from Mar. 19, 1888. 0.93 m. decrease.
9.32	67.54	......	61.56	......	5,784.80	....	5,288.00	....	July 1	Weighed 30 days from Feb. 20, 1888. 0.25 m. decrease.
6	67.54				6,454.79				1887. Dec. 5	Weighed 30 days from Apr. 30, 1888. New.
7	67.54	......	47.03	......	4,631.89	....	3,216.38	....	1888. July 1	Weighed 30 days from Feb. 20. 1888. 0.19 m. increase.
7.47	67.54	......	43.61	......	9,615.85	....	6,125.11	....	July 1	Weighed 30 days from Mar. 19, 1888. 23 m. lap service at $24.80 per m., formerly $12.83 per m.
12	66.69	......	74.39	......	5,241.16	....	5,846.31	....	July 1	Weighed 30 days from Feb. 20, 1888.
7	66.69	.....	55.58	......	8,077.49	....	3,636.59	....	Mar. 19	Weighed 30 days from Mar. 19, 1888. 55.69 m. ext. Ness City to Scott from Sept. 10, 1887.
7	66.69	......	49.59	......	4,796.34	....	3,583.86	....	July 1	Weighed 30 days from Feb. 20, 1888. 0.35 m. decrease.
11.68	66.69	......	55.58	......	7,370.57	....	6,015.97	....	July 1	Weighed 30 days from Mar. 19, 1888. 2.29 m. increase.
12	66.69	......	60.71	......	1,461.84	....	1,274.91	....	July 1	Weighed 30 days from Mar. 19, 1888. 0.92 m. increase.
12	66.69	......	64.13	......	2,156.08	....	2,078.45	....	July 1	Weighed 30 days from Mar. 19, 1888. 0.08 m. decrease.
6	65.83	......	57.29	......	5,384.89	....	4,907.31	....	July 1	Weighed 30 days from Feb. 20, 1888. 27.28 m. Shelby to Rutherfordton, formerly at $63.27 per m. 1.01 m. decrease.
6	65.83				6,292.68				1887. Oct. 3	Weighed 30 days from Mar. 19, 1888. Pay fixed for service from Chicago to German Valley, 95.59 m. Not weighed on residue.
12	65.83	......	70.97	......	2,301.41	....	2,476.85	....	1888. July 1	Weighed 30 days from Mar. 19, 1888. 0.06 m. increase.
6	65.83	......	51.30	......	4,963.58	....	3,962.88	....	July 1	Weighed 30 days from Feb. 20, 1888. 0.1 m. increase.
14	65.83				1,985.43				1887. July 1	Weighed 30 days from Feb. 20, 1888. New.

II.—*Table showing the re-adjustment of the rates of pay per mile on railroad routes in*

Index order.	State.	Number of route.	Termini.	Corporate title of company carrying the mail.	Length of route.	Average weight of mails, whole distance per day.	Miles per hour.	Size, etc., of mail car or apartment.
					Miles.	*Lbs.*		*Feet and inches.*
267	Iowa..	27069	Hudson, Oelwein	Chicago, St. Paul and Kansas City Rwy.	35.92	545	25	15.7 by 8.8, 1 1........
268	Miss..	18018	Jackson, Greenwood.	Illinois Central R. R..	100.46	540	21	11.9 by 7.8, 1 1 ....
269	Mich..	24037	St. Clair, Lenox	Michigan Central R. R	16.06	530	19	....
270	Ga	15037	Augusta, Ga., Greenwood, S. C.	Port Royal and Western Carolina Rwy.	68.22	520	21	10 by 8, 1 1...........
271	Fla ...	16001	Fernandina, C e d a r Keys.	Florida R w y. and Navigation Co.	155.84	883	20	16.9 by 7.8 (av.), 1 1..
272	Tex ...	31058	San Antonio, K e r r-ville.	San A n t o n i o and Aransas Pass Rwy.	71.75	519	15	7 by 9, 1 1............
273	Iowa..	27089	Sac City, Moville.....	Chicago and Northwestern Rwy.	67.41	517	23	12.2 by 7.5, 1 1 ....
274	Ohio ..	21061	Toledo, Delphos	Toledo, St. Louis and Kansas City R. R.	74.11	515	25	20.2 by 8, 1 1........
275	Nebr..	34056	Linwood, Geneva	Fremont, Elkhorn and Missouri Valley R. R.	77.53	510	28	29 by 9.3, 1 1.........
276	Miss..	18021	Memphis, Tenn., Birmingham, Ala.	Kansas City, Memphis and Birmingham R. R.	251.60	510	23	27.10 by 10.10, 1 1 ....
277	Mich..	24025	Zion, East Saginaw ..	Port Huron and Northwestern Rwy.	79.10	506	24	11 by 6, 1 1...........
278	Ind ...	22033	Frankfort, Kokomo..	Toledo, St. Louis and Kansas City R. R.	25.77	506	24	20.2 by 8, 1 1 ....
279	Nebr..	34052	Platte River Junction (n. o.), Hastings.	Fremont, Elkhorn and Missouri Valley R. R.	119.96	506	27	29 by 9.3, 1 1... ....
280	S. C ...	14018	Kingsville, Camden ..	South Carolina Rwy..	39.03	499	22	20 by 8.2, 2 1........
281	Ky....	20034	Henderson, Princeton.	Ohio Valley Rwy	89.88	493	24	10 by 8.11, 1 1........
282	Mich..	24067	Houghton, Calumet ..	Mineral Range R. R..	15.85	487	17	....
283	Idaho .	42004	Nampa, Boisé City ...	Idaho Central Rwy ..	20.69	487	20	no apt ....

States and Territories in which the contract term expired June 30, 1888, etc.—Continued.

Average trips per week.	Pay per mile per annum for transportation.	Pay per mile per annum for r. p. o. cars.	Former pay per mile per annum for transportation.	Former pay per mile per annum for r. p. o. cars.	Amount of annual pay for transportation.	Amount of annual pay for r. p. o. cars.	Former amount of annual pay for transportation.	Former amount of annual pay for r. p. o. cars.	Date of adjustment or re-adjustment.	Remarks.
	Dolls.	Dolls.	Dolls.	Dolls.	Dollars.	Dollars.	Dollars.	Dollars.	1888.	
13	65.83	......	65.83	.....	2,364.61		2,364.61	....	Mar. 19	Weighed 30 days from Mar. 19, 1888. From Oct. 3, 1887, on 26.74 m. ext. from Waterloo to Oelwein.
6	65.83	......	61.56	......	6,613.26	....	6,083.97	....	July 1	Weighed 30 days from Feb. 20, 1888. 1.63 m. increase.
6	64.98	......	47.88	......	1,043.57	....	766.08	....	July 1	Weighed 30 days from Mar. 19, 1888. 0.06 m. increase.
7	64.98	......	44.46	......	4,432.93	....	3,036.32	....	July 1	Weighed 30 days from Feb. 20, 1888. 0.08 m. decrease.
7.64	64.29	......	69.77	......	10,018.95	....	10,824.81	....	July 1	Weighed 30 days from Feb. 20, 1888. 0 69 m. increase. Land grant.
6	64.13	......	......		4,601.32				Oct. 3	Weighed 30 days from Feb. 20, 1888. 34.36 m. San Antonio to Boerne from Apr. 1, 1887; 37.39 m. ext. Boerne to Kerrville from Oct. 3. 1887.
11.18	64.12	......	63.27	......	4,322.32		3,687.37	....	Mar. 19	Weighed 30 days from Mar. 19, 1888. From Oct. 24, 1887, on 9.13 m. ext. Kingsley to Moville.
8.37	64.12	......	63.27	......	4,751.93		,688.31	....	July 1	Weighed 30 days from Mar. 19, 1888. 0.01 m. increase.
6	64.12				4,971.22				Feb. 20	Weighed 30 days from Mar. 19, 1888. New.
6.16	64.12	......	43.61	......	16,132.59		15,166.13	....	July 1	Weighed 30 days from Feb. 20, 1888. 0.40 m. increase. 33.24 m. ext. Holly Springs to New Albany from Feb. 28, 1887; 25.88 m. ext. New Albany to Tupelo from May 30, 1887; 146 21 m. ext. Tupelo to Birmingham from Nov. 21, 1887.
12	64.12	......	66.17	......	5,071.89		3,640.50	..	July 1	Weighed 30 days from Mar. 19, 1888. 0.25 m. increase.
6	64.12	......	42.75	......	1,652.37		1,098.67	....	July 1	Weighed 30 days from Mar. 19, 1888. 0.07 m. increase.
7	64.12	......	......		7,685.42				Feb. 1	Weighed 30 days from Mar. 19, 1888. New.
12	63.27	......	42.75	......	2,469.42		1,679.22	...	July 1	Weighed 30 days from Feb. 20 1888. 0.25 m. decrease.
6	63.27	......	42.75	......	5,686.70	....	4,752.42	....	July 1	Weighed 30 days from Feb. 20, 1888. 19 31 m. ext. Commercial Point to Marion from June 13, 1887; 25.04 m. ext. Marion to Princeton from Nov. 21, 1887.
12.5	62.41	......	50.45	......	989.19		782.98	....	July 1	Weighed 30 days from Mar. 19, 1888. 0.33 m. increase.
7	62.41	......	......		1,291.26	....		....	1887. Oct. 3	Weighed 30 days from Mar. 19, 1888. New.

H.—*Table showing the re-adjustment of the rates of pay per mile on railroad routes in*

Index order.	State.	Number of route.	Termini.	Corporate title of company carrying the mail.	Length of route.	Average weight of mails, whole distance per day.	Miles per hour.	Size, etc., of mail car or apartment.
					Miles.	*Lbs.*		*Feet and inches.*
284	Tenn..	19013	Tullahoma, Sparta ...	Nashville, Chattanooga and St. Louis Rwy.	61.11	487	20	11.10 by 9, 1 1 ....
285	Kans..	33074	Hutchinson, Geneseo.	Salina, Sterling and El Paso Rwy.	41.84	483	25	16.6 by 8.8, 1 1 ....
286	Dak...	35024	Redfield, Gettysourgh	Chicago and Northwestern Rwy.	75.31	483	17	16.6 by 7, 1 1 ....
287	Miss..	18009	Durant, Aberdeen....	Illinois Central R. R .	108.63	482	21	14.9 by 7.3, 1 1 ....
288	Nev...	45005	Reno, Nev., Camp Ham (n. o.), Cal.	Nevada and California R. R.	45.28	479	12	no apt ....
289	S. C...	14006	Florence, Cheraw	Cheraw and Darlington R. R.	40.78	476	19	12.6 by 8.5, 1 1 ....
290	Ind ...	22026	Worthington, Evansville.	Evansville and Indianapolis R. R.	98.10	469	25	(av.) 15.5 by 8.10, 1 1 .
291	Cal....	46043	Lodi, Valley Springs .	San Joaquin and Sierra Nevada R. R.	26.81	468	18	no apt ....
292	Ky....	20012	Anchorage, Shelbyville.	Louisville and Nashville R. R.	18.44	468	21	10 by 8.5, 1 1 ....
293	Tex...	31060	Mount Pleasant, Sherman.	St. Louis, Arkansas and Texas Rwy.	110.10	467	20	23.6 by 8, 1 1........
294	Dak...	35028	Valley Junction (n. o.), Oakes.	James River Valley R. R.	15.21	467	20	17.6 by 9, 1 1 ....
295	S. C...	14015	Lane's, Sumter.......	Central R. R. Co. of S. C.	49.69	465	33	24 by 8 8, 1 1.... .....
296	Ariz ..	40004	Maricopa Junction (n. o.), Phœnix.	Maricopa and Phœnix R. R.	35.78	464	19	no apt ....
297	Miss ..	18014	Artesia, Columbus ...	Mobile and Ohio R. R.	14.61	463	20	15.3 by 8.10, 1 1 ......
298	Fla ...	16031	Palatka, Daytona....	St. John's and Halifax R. R.	54.84	462	18	no apt ....
299	Ala ...	17006	Selma, Akron Junction.	Cincinnati, Selma and Mobile Rwy.	67.69	460	22	12.5 by 6.9, 1 1 ....
300	Colo ..	38036	Towner, Pueblo......	Pueblo and State Line R. R.	150.76	458	27	20.4 by 7.3, 1 1 ....
301	Kans .	33086	Geneseo, Kanopolis ..	Kanopolis and Kansas Central Rwy.	14.76	458	25	16.6 by 8.8, 1 1 ....
302	Kans .	33058	Belle Plaine, Larned .	Denver, Memphis and Atlantic Rwy.	128.67	457	25	16.4 by 6.8, 1 1 ....
303	Ala ...	17017	Selma, Pine Apple Station (n. o.).	Louisville and Nashville R. R.	46.40	457	13	7.9 by 6.4, 1 1 ....
304	Ohio ..	21065	Delphos, Ohio, Kokomo, Ind.	Toledo, St. Louis and Kansas City R. R.	108.24	456	25	20.2 by 8, 1 1 ....

States and Territories in which the contract term expired June 30, 1888, etc.—Continued.

Average trips per week.	Pay per mile per annum for transportation.	Pay per mile per annum for r.p.o. cars.	Former pay per mile per annum for transportation.	Former pay per mile per annum r.p.o. cars.	Amount of annual pay for transportation.	Amount of annual pay for r.p.o. cars.	Former amount of annual pay for transportation.	Former amount of annual pay for r.p.o. cars.	Date of adjustment or re-adjustment.	Remarks.
	Dolls.	Dolls.	Dolls	Dolls.	Dollars.	Dollars.	Dollars.	Dollars.	1888.	
7	62.41	......	49.59	......	3,813.87	....	3,078.03	....	July 1	Weighed 30 days from Feb. 20, 1888. 0.96 m. decrease.
14	62.41	......	......		2,611.23				1887. June 20	Weighed 30 days from Mar. 19, 1888. New.
6	62.41	......	37.62	......	4,700.09	....	1,226.78	....	1888. Mar. 19	Weighed 30 days from Mar. 19, 1888. 42.70 m. ext., Faulkton to Gettysburgh, from Nov. 28, 1887.
7	62.41	......	52.16	......	6,779.59	....	5,648.92	....	July 1	Weighed 30 days from Feb. 20, 1888. 0.53 m. increase.
6	62.41	......	......	......	2,825.92	....	....		Mar. 1	Weighed 30 days from Mar. 19, 1888. New.
6	62.41	......	51.30	......	2,545.07	....	2,094.06	....	July 1	Weighed 30 days from Feb. 20, 1888. 0.04 m. decrease.
8.42	61.56	......	56.43	......	6,039.03	....	4,757.72	....	July 1	Weighed 30 days from Mar. 19, 1888. 0.20 m. decrease. 57.79 m., Washington to Evansville, formerly at $42.75 per m.
7	61.56	......	64.98	......	1,650.42	....	1,488.69	....	Mar. 19	Weighed 30 days from Mar. 19, 1888. 3.90 m. ext., Burson to Valley Springs, from Oct. 3, 1887.
18	61.56	......	55.58	......	1,137.62	....	1,027.11	....	July 1	Weighed 30 days from Feb. 20, 1888.
7	61.56	......	......	......	6,777.75	....	....		1887. Sept. 12	Weighed 30 days from Feb. 20, 1888. New.
7	61.56	......	......	......	936.32	....	....		June 20	Weighed 30 days from Dec. 12, 1887. New.
14	61.56	......	42.75	......	2,504.87	....	1,710.00	....	1888. July 1	Weighed 30 days from Feb. 20, 1888. 0.69 m. increase.
7	61.56	......	......	......	2,202.61	....	....		1887. Sept. 15	Weighed 30 days from Feb. 20, 1888. New.
21	60.70	......	53.87	......	886.82	....	729.94	....	1888. July 1	Weighed 30 days from Feb. 20, 1888. 1.06 m. increase.
6	60.70	......	37.62	......	8,292.36	....	2,037.12	....	July 1	Weighed 30 days from Feb. 20, 1888. 0.09 m. increase.
7	60.70	......	53.87	......	4,108.78	....	3,650.23	....	July 1	Weighed 30 days from Feb. 20, 1888. 0.07 m. decrease.
7	60.70	......	......	......	9,151.13	....	....		Mar. 1	Weighed 30 days from Mar. 19, 1888. New.
7	60.70	......	......	......	895.93	....	....		Feb. 20	Weighed 30 days from Mar. 28, 1888. New.
7	60.70	......	46.17	......	7,810.26	....	2,557.81	....	Mar. 19	Weighed 30 days from Mar. 19, 1888. 36.50 m. ext., Kingman to Stafford, from June 20, 1887; 36.77 m. ext., Stafford to Larned, from Nov. 10, 1887.
6	60.70	......	46.17	......	2,816.4:	....	2,206.92	....	July 1	Weighed 30 days from Feb. 20, 1888. 1.40 m. decrease.
6	59.85	......	46.17	......	6,478.16	....	4,967.28	....	July 1	Weighed 30 days from Mar. 19, 1888. 0.23 m. increase.

H.—*Table showing the re-adjustment of the rates of pay per mile on railroad routes in*

Index order.	State.	Number of route.	Termini.	Corporate title of company carrying the mail.	Length of route.	Average weight of mails, whole distance per day.	Miles per hour.	Size, etc., of mail-car or apartment.
					Miles.	*Lbs.*		*Feet and inches.*
305	Dak ..	35026	Devil's Lake, Dak., Great Falls, Mont.	St. Paul, Minneapolis and Manitoba Rwy.	667.82	441	22	24.6 by 9.4, 1 1 ....
306	Mont..	36006	Jefferson City, Basin.	Northern Pacific R. R.	26.36	441	18	23.7 by 8.10, 1 1 ......
307	Ariz ..	40003	Seligman, Prescott...	Prescott and Arizona Central Rwy.	74.88	439	20	no apt ... .
308	Tenn..	19011	Ooltewah, Tenn., Cohutta, Ga.	East Tennessee, Virginia and Georgia Rwy.	11.54	436	29	25 by 10, 1 1..........
309	Dak...	35034	Fairmount, Oakes....	Minneapolis and Pacific Rwy.	72.64	435	25	16.6 by 7.3, 1 1 ....
310	Ill	23046	Jacksonville, Drivers.	Jacksonville Southeastern Rwy.	130.91	425	28	13 by 7.7, 1 1 to Centralia, 113.32 m.
311	S. C ...	14016	Belton, Walhalla.....	Richmond and Danville R. R.	44.33	425	18	13.8 by 8.10, 1 1 ......
312	Tex...	31057	Kennedy, Wallis.....	San Antonio and Aransas Pass Rwy.	133.02	425	22	14 by 9, 1 1...........
313	Ohio ..	21063	Bellaire, Zanesville...	Bellaire, Zanesville, and Cincinnati Rwy.	112.46	424	16	(av.) 11.4 by 6.9, 1 1 ..
314	Kans..	33073	Anthony, Kioba......	St. Louis, Fort Scott and Wichita R. R.	30.43	422	25	18.6 by 6.10, 1 1 ......
315	Ohio ..	21018	Portsmouth, Hamden Junction.	Cincinnati, Washington and Baltimore R. R.	56.35	421	20	14.7 by 8.1, 1 1 ....
316	Ala ...	17008	Columbus, Ga., Troy, Ala.	Mobile and Girard R. R	85.66	709	24	15.3 by 9, 1 1., and 1 1. addl. betw. Columbus and Union Springs, 55.48 m.
317	Ind ...	22030	Terre Haute, Worthington.	Evansville and Indianapolis R. R.	40.91	414	25	(av.) 15.5 by 8.10, 1 1.
318	W. Va.	12019	Piedmont, W. Va., Cumberland, Md.	West Virginia, Central and Pittsburgh Rwy.	28.87	412	20	8.6 by 7, 1 1 ....
319	Ohio ..	21075	Alvordton, Carlisle...	Cincinnati, Jackson and Mackinaw R. R.	162.59	411	23	14.2 by 7.3, 1 1. Bryan to Carlisle, 146.99 m.

States and Territories in which the contract term expired June 30, 1888, etc.—Continued.

Average trips per week.	Pay per mile per annum for transportation.	Pay per mile per annum for r. p. o. cars.	Former pay per mile per annum for transportation.	Former pay per mile per annum for r. p. o. cars.	Amount of annual pay for transportation.	Amount of annual pay for r. p. o. cars.	Former amount of annual pay for transportation.	Former amount of annual pay for r. p. o. cars.	Date of adjustment or re-adjustment.	Remarks.
	Dolls.	Dolls.	Dolls.	Dolls.	Dollars.	Dollars.	Dollars.	Dollars.		
6	59.85	......	......		39,969.02	......	......	......	1837. Dec. 15	Weighed 30 days from May 5, 1888. 76.34 m. Devil's Lake to Towner, Dak., from Apr. 25, 1887; 41.84 m. ext. Towner to Minot, Dak., from May 18, 1887; 549.64 m. ext. Minot to Great Falls, Mont., from Dec. 15, 1887.
7	59.85	......	......	......	1,577.64	......	......	......	1888. Mar. 7	Weighed 30 days from Mar. 19, 1888. New.
7	59.00	......	......	......	4,417.92	......	......	......	1887. Apr. 25	Weighed 30 days from Dec. 1, 1887. New.
14	58.99	......	69.26	......	630.74	......	820.73	......	1888. July 1	Weighed 30 days from Feb. 20, 1888. 0.31 m. decrease.
6	58.99	......	......	......	4,285.03	......	......	......	Jan. 10	Weighed 30 days from Apr. 10, 1888. 92.27 m. Fairmount to Monango from Dec. 5, 1887. Route curtailed 24.63 m. to end at Oakes from Jan. 10, 1888.
11.20	58.14	......	65.84	......	7,611.10	......	7,460.98	......	Mar. 19	Weighed 30 days from Mar. 19, 1888. 17.93 m. exten. Centralia to Drivers from Mar. 12, 1888.
6	58.14	......	59.85	......	2,577.34	......	2,628.61	......	July 1	Weighed 30 days from Feb. 20, 1888. 0.41 m. increase.
6	58.14	......	32.49	......	7,733.78	......	6,639.79	......	Feb. 20	Weighed 30 days from Feb. 22, 1888. 33.95 m. ext. Cuero to Hallettsville from June 20, 1887; 56.42 m. ext. Hallettsville to Wallis from Oct. 3, 1887.
8.24	58.14	......	45.32	......	6,538.42	......	5,101.67	......	July 1	Weighed 30 days from Mar. 19, 1888. 0.11 m. decrease.
14	58.14	......	......	......	1,769.20	......	......	......	1887. June 20	Weighed 30 days from Mar. 19, 1888. New.
12	58.14	......	53.01	......	3,276.18	......	2,968.56	......	1888. July 1	Weighed 30 days from Mar. 19, 1888. 0.35 m. increase.
13	58.13	......	59.00	......	4,978.83	......	5,056.30	......	July 1	Weighed 30 days from Feb. 20, 1888. 0.05 m. decrease. Land-grant.
6	57.28	......	44.46	......	2,343.32	......	1,821.97	......	July 1	Weighed 30 days from Mar. 19, 1888. 0.07 m. decrease.
6	57.28	......	......	......	1,653.67	......	......	......	1887. Sept. 5	Weighed 30 days from Feb. 20, 1888. New.
6	57.28	......	42.75	......	9,313.15	......	4,175.37	......	1888. July 1	Weighed 30 days from Mar. 19, 1888. 13.07 m. ext. West Manchester to West Alexandria from Apr. 18, 1887; 16.65 m. ext. West Alexandria to Carlisle from Aug. 22, 1887; 19.71 m. ext. Cecil to Bryan from Oct. 10, 1887; 15.49 m. ext. Bryan to Alvordton from Jan. 16, 1888,

H.—*Table showing the re-adjustment of the rates of pay per mile on railroad routes in*

Index order.	State.	Number of route.	Termini.	Corporate title of company carrying the mail.	Length of route.	Average weight of mails, whole distance per day.	Miles per hour.	Size, etc., of mail-car or apartment.
					Miles.	*Lbs.*		*Feet and inches.*
320	Ohio ..	21037	Niles, New Lisbon ...	New York, Lake Erie and Western R. R.	34.01	409	25	20 by 7, 1 1..........
321	Ga ...	15007	Union Point, Athens.	Georgia R. R........	40.48	408	18	10.6 by 6.3, 1 1 ......
322	Ohio ..	21069	Columbus, Zanesville	Columbus and Eastern R. R.	68.66	406	30	12.6 by 7.4, 1 1 ......
323	S. C ...	14010	Port Royal, S. C., Augusta, Ga.	Port Royal and Western Carolina Rwy.	112.99	405	15	10.4 by 6.8, 1 1 ....
324	Colo ..	38034	Colorado Springs, Leadville.	Colorado Midland Rwy.	133.05	405	19	20.4 by 9.2, 1 1 ......
325	Mich..	24064	Pontiac, Caseville....	Pontiac, Oxford and Port Austin R. R.	100.91	403	20	12 by 7, 1 1.... ......
326	Kans..	33049	Beaumont, Bluff......	St. Louis and San Francisco Rwy.	106.14	403	23	12 by 6.6, 1 1 ....
327	Dak...	35033	Madison, Bristol	Chicago, Milwaukee and St. Paul Rwy.	103.39	400	25	15.8 by 7.2, 1 1.......
328	N. C...	13023	Hickory, Lenoir......	Richmond and Danville R. R.	20.51	396	17	14.10 by 7.2, 1 1 ......
329	Ohio ..	21062	Andover, Youngstown	Lake Shore and Michigan Southern Rwy.	39.2	394	26	17.4 by 9, 1 1 ......
330	Ky...	20018	Richmond, Livingston.	Kentucky Central Rwy.	36.94	394	10	14 by 9, 1 1............
331	N. C...	13009	Charlotte, Taylorsville.	Richmond and Danville R. R.	65.13	394	18	9.10 by 7.4, 1 1 ....
332	Ky....	20027	Ashland, Richardson.	Chattaroi Rwy.......	50.24	391	20	15.3 by 8.10, 1 1 ......
333	Mich..	24007	Kalamazoo, South Haven.	Michigan Central R. R.	40.09	389	18	11.1 by 7, 1 1.........
334	Ind ...	22045	Lawrenceburgh Junction (n. o.), Lawrenceburgh.	Cincinnati, Indianapolis, St. Louis and Chicago Rwy.	2.50	386	20	no apt..............
335	S. C ...	14007	Chester, S. C., Hickory, N. C.	Richmond and Danville R. R.	89.91	386	17	9.10 by 7.2, 1 1 ......
336	Ky....	20011	Glasgow Junction, Glasgow.	Louisville and Nashville R. R.	11.03	385	20	no apt ....

States and Territories in which the contract term expired June 30, 1888, *etc.*—Continued.

Average trips per week.	Pay per mile per annum for transportation.	Pay per mile per annum for r. p. o. cars.	Former pay per mile per annum for transportation.	Former pay per mile per annum for r. p. o. cars.	Amount of annual pay for transportation.	Amount of annual pay for r.p.o. cars.	Former amount of annual pay for transportation.	Former amount of annual pay for r. p. o. cars.	Date of adjustment or re-adjustment.	Remarks.
	Dolls.	Dolls.	Dolls.	Dolls.	Dollars.	Dollars.	Dollars.	Dollars.	1888.	
12	57.28	......	50.45	......	1,948.09	....	1,758.18	....	July 1	Weighed 30 days from Mar. 19, 1888. 0.84 m. decrease.
21	57.28	......	57.29	......	2,318.69	... .	2,319.09	....	July 1	Weighed 30 days from Feb. 20, 1888.
9.33	57.28	......	42.75	......	2,754.39	....	1,443.23	.. ..	July 1	Weighed 30 days from Mar. 19, 1888. 30.55 m. ext. Columbus to Thurston from July 1, 1888; ext. Fultonham to Zanesville from July 1, 1888. Lap Shepherds to Thurston, 25.10 m. at $17.95 per m. and Newton to Zanesville, 4.76 m. at $17.10 per m.
8.32	57.28	......	54.72	......	6,472.06	....	6,061.33	....	July 1	Weighed 30 days from Feb. 20, 1888. 2.22 m. increase.
7	57.28	......	......		7,621.10	....	....	....	1887. Oct. 18	Weighed 30 days from Mar. 19, 1888. New.
6	57.28	......	45.32	......	5,780.12	....	4,563.08	....	1888. July 1	Weighed 30 days from Mar. 19, 1888. 0.18 m. increase.
7	56.43	......	44.46	......	5,989.48	:........	4,072.98	....	Mar. 19	Weighed 30 days from Mar. 19, 1888. 14.53 m. ext. Caldwell to Bluff from June 1, 1887.
6	56.43	......	....		5,834.29	....	....	....	1887. Oct. 17	Weighed 30 days from Mar. 19, 1888. New.
6	56.43	......	42.75	......	1,157.37	....	876.80	....	1888. July 1	Weighed 30 days from Feb. 20, 1888.
12	56.43	......	68.40	......	2,212.05	....	2,656.65	....	July 1	Weighed 30 days from Mar. 19, 1888. 0.36 m. increase.
6	56.43	......	42.75	......	2,084.52	....	1,565.50	...., ...	July 1	Weighed 30 days from Feb. 20, 1888. 0.32 m. increase.
6	56.43	......	59.00	......	3,675.28	....	3,824.30	....	July 1	Weighed 30 days from Feb. 20, 1888. 19.98 m. ext. Statesville to Taylorsville from Jan. 2, 1888. 0.56 m. decrease.
6	55.57	......	47.03	......	2,791.82	....	2,368.43	....	July 1	Weighed 30 days from Feb. 20, 1888. 0.12 m. decrease.
12	55.57	......	45.32	......	2,227.80	....	1,820.95	....	July 1	Weighed 30 days from Mar. 19, 1888. 0.09 m. decrease.
18.50	55.57	......	54.72	......	138.92	....	134.61	....	July 1	Weighed 30 days from Mar. 19, 1888. 0 04 m. increase.
6	55.57	......	51.30	......	4,599.06	....	4,052.18	....	July 1	Weighed 30 days from Feb. 20, 1888. 4.29 m. increase. 9.25 m. Newton to Hickory lap service on route 13006, formerly at $14.50 per m. Lap service from July 1, 1888, 10.10 m. at $16 24 per mile.
10	55.57	......	53.01	......	612.93	....	583.11	....	July 1	Weighed 30 days from Feb. 20, 1888. 0.03 m. increase.

H.—*Table showing the re-adjustment of the rates of pay per mile on railroad routes in*

Index order.	State.	Number of route.	Termini.	Corporate title of company carrying the mail.	Length of route.	Average weight of mails, whole distance per day.	Miles per hour.	Size, etc., of mail-car or apartment.
					Miles.	*Lbs.*		*Feet and inches.*
337	Kans .	33077	Bazaar, Keystone ..	Chicago, Kansas and Western R. R.	89.22	385	20	11.1 by 6.1, 1 l., between Strong and Keystone, 76.62 m. No apt. residue, 12.60 m.
338	Nebr..	34050	Fairbury, Nebr., Phillipsburgh, Kans.	Chicago, Kansas and Nebraska Rwy.	129.04	382	23	14.6 by 7.2, 1 l........
339	Ohio ..	21076	Akron, Ohio, Mahoningtown, Pa.	Pittsburgh and Western Rwy.	78.27	380	30	19.9 by 8.7 ....
340	Mich..	24023	Allegan, Holland. ..	Chicago and West Michigan Rwy.	24.61	379	22	9.6 by 6.8, 1 l.........
341	Ala ...	17016	Opelika, Goodwater..	Columbus and Western Rwy.	60.26	377	25	12.9 by 6.9, 1 l........
342	Tenn..	19005	Fayetteville, Decherd	Nashville, Chattanooga and St. Louis Rwy	40.41	374	20	8.9 by 6.8, 1 l ....
343	Ky....	20024	Lebanon, Greensburgh.	Louisville and Nashville R. R.	32.27	373	13	14.9 by 8.6, 1 l........
344	Ohio ..	21068	Corning, Gallipolis...	Kanawha and Ohio Rwy.	74.60	371	28	20 by 9, 1 l............
345	Kans..	33057	Salina, Luray	Salina, Lincoln and Western Rwy	67.07	370	16	6 by 7, 1 l.............
346	N. C ..	13020	Tarborough, Williamston.	Albemarle and Raleigh R. R.	33.53	369	15	7 by 6.8, 1 l ....
347	Mich..	24005	Jonesville, Lansing..	Lake Shore and Michigan Southern Rwy.	60.95	587	26	15 by 9.4, 1 l ....
348	Minn .	26048	Mankato, Red Wing..	Minneapolis and St. Louis Rwy.	95.16	360	25	9 by 8.10, 11..........
349	Nebr..	34049	Central City, Arcadia.	Burlington and Missouri River R. R. (in Nebr.).	71.07	358	25	11 by 7.1, 1 l ....
350	Mich..	24024	Ypsilanti, Hillsdale..	Lake Shore and Michigan Southern Rwy.	61.51	356	24	8.8 by 6.9, 1 l ....
351	N. C ..	13011	Bennettsville, S. C., Pilot Mountain N. C.	Cape Fear and Yadkin Valley Rwy.	208.26	355	20	20 by 9, 1 l............
352	Ky....	20006	Trunnelton, Springfield.	Louisville and Nashville R. R.	36.58	354	19	9 by 8, 1 l ....

States and Territories in which the contract term expired June 30, 1888, etc.—Continued.

Average trips per week.	Pay per mile per annum for transportation.	Pay per mile per annum for r. p. o. cars.	Former pay per mile per annum for transportation.	Former pay per mile per annum for r. p. o. cars.	Amount of annual pay for transportation.	Amount of annual pay for r. p. o. cars.	Former amount of annual pay for transportation.	Former amount of annual pay for r. p. o. cars.	Date of adjustment or re-adjustment.	Remarks.
	Dolls.	Dolls.	Dolls.	Dolls.	Dollars.	Dollars.	Dollars.	Dollars.	1888.	
6.90	55.57	......	......	......	4,957.95	......	......	......	Feb. 29	Weighed 30 days from May 21, 1888. 64.96 m. Cottonwood Falls to Abilene from Aug. 8, 1887; 10.44 m. ext. Cottonwood Falls to Bazaar, and 13.82 m. ext. Abilene to Keystone from Feb. 20, 1888.
7	55.57	......	......	......	7,170.75	......	......	......	Jan. 16	Weighed 30 days from Mar. 19, 1888. New.
6.71	55.57	......	59.00	......	4,349.46	......	4,607.90	......	July 1	Weighed 30 days from Mar. 19, 1888. 0.17 m. increase.
12	54.72	......	51.30	......	1,346.65	......	1,264.03	......	July 1	Weighed 30 days from Mar. 19, 1888. 0.03 m. decrease.
7	54.72	......	44.46	......	3,297.42	......	2,674.42	......	July 1	Weighed 30 days from Feb. 20, 1888. 0.11 m. increase.
6	54.72	......	42.75	......	2,211.23	......	1,727.52	......	July 1	Weighed 30 days from Feb. 20, 1888.
6	54.72	......	46.17	......	1,765.81	......	1,468.20	......	July 1	Weighed 30 days from Feb. 20, 1888. 0.47 m. increase.
6	54.72	......	44.46	......	4,087.03	......	2,528.44	......	July 1	Weighed 30 days from Mar. 26, 1888. 15.06 m. ext. Middleport Junction (n. o.) to Gallipolis from Mar. 19, 1888.
9.60	54.72	......	52.16	......	8,670.07	......	1,884.01	......	Mar. 19	Weighed 30 days from Mar. 19, 1888. 30.95 m. ext. Lincoln to Luray from Dec. 28, 1887.
7	54.72	......	42.75	......	1,834.76	......	1,439.38	......	July 1	Weighed 30 days from Feb. 20, 1888. 0.14 m. decrease.
7.41	54.03	......	52.67	......	3,203.12	......	3,214.98	......	July 1	Weighed 30 days from Mar. 19, 1888. 0.09 m. decrease. All land grants.
7.75	53.86	......	59.86	......	5,125.31	......	3,999.17	......	Apr. 30	Weighed 30 days from Apr. 30, 1888. From Aug. 20, 1887, on 28.34 m. ext. Waterville to Mankato.
6	53.86	......	......	......	3,827.83	......	......	......	1887. Dec. 28	Weighed 30 days from Apr. 30, 1888. New.
6	53.86	......	53.01	......	3,312.92	......	3,294.04	......	1888. July 1	Weighed 30 days from Mar. 19, 1888. 0.63 m. decrease.
6.18	53.01	......	52.16	......	11,089.86	......	11,006.92	......	July 1	Weighed 30 days from Feb. 20, 1888. 29.43 m. ext. Greensboro to Walnut Cove, from June 13, 1887; 18.04 m. ext. Walnut Cove to Dalton, from Sept. 26, 1887; 7.32 m. ext. Dalton to Pilot Mountain, from Dec. 5, 1887. 1.87 m. decrease.
12	53.01	......	42.75	......	1,939.10	......	1,755.13	......	July 1	Weighed 30 days from Mar. 19, 1888. 19.36 m. ext. Bardstown to Springfield from Mar. 12, 1889.

H.—*Table showing the re-adjustment of the rates of pay per mile on railroad routes in*

Index order.	State.	Number of route.	Termini.	Corporate title of company carrying the mail.	Length of route.	Average weight of mails, whole distance per day.	Miles per hour.	Size, etc., of mail car or apartment.
					Miles.	*Lbs.*		*Feet and inches.*
254	Mich .	24014	Saginaw, Caro........	Michigan Central R. R.	36.85	351	20	....
255	S. C ...	14014	Cheraw, S. C., Wadesborough, N. C.	Cheraw and Salisbury R. R.	26.30	349	19	12, 6 by 8, 5, 1 1 ....
256	Kans..	33079	Kansas City, Mo., Seneca, Kans.	Kansas City, Wyandotte and Northwestern R. R.	118.75	346	22	19 by 6, 2, 11..........
257	S. C ...	14021	Greenwood, Spartanburgh.	Port Royal and Western Carolina Rwy.	66.20	344	21	10 by 8, 11 ....
258	Ohio ..	21058	Wellston, Springfield	Ohio Southern R. R.	118.48	343	20	11.9 by 7, 1 1 ....
259	Ind ...	22028	La Crosse, Attica ...	Chicago and Indiana Coal Rwy. Co.	83.93	343	15	14 by 7.4. 1 1 ....
260	Colo .	38033	El Moro, Trinidad....	Denver and Rio Grande R. R.	4.48	340	26	no apt ....
261	Ohio ..	21078	Cincinnati, Dodds....	Cincinnati, Lebanon and Northern Rwy.	37.60	337	20	(av.) 37.5 by 7.7, 1 1 ..
262	Tenn..	19020	Watrace, Shelbyville.	Nashville, Chattanooga and St. Louis Rwy.	8.36	334	16	no apt ....
263	Ky ...	20021	Harrodsburgh, Harrodsburgh June.(n.o.)	Southwestern R. R...	5.44	333	15	no apt ....
264	Ohio ..	21044	Ashtabula, Ohio, Mahoningtown, Pa.	Pennsylvania Co.....	78.81	329	25	20 by 9, 1 1 ....
265	Ohio ..	21100	Zanesville, Waterford	Zanesville and Ohio River Rwy.	54.65	329	20	15 by 8.3, 1 1 ....
266	Ala ...	17020	Attalla, Gadsden.....	Tennessee and Coosa R. R.	5.90	323	15	no apt ....
267	Indian Ter.	32004	Kiowa, Kans., Miami, Tex.	Southern Kansas Rwy	167.91	318	15	....do................
268	Ga ..	15015	Tennille, Wrightsville.	Wrightsville and Tennille R. R.	16.74	315	13	9 by 8, 1 1 ....
269	Ky ...	20026	Midway, Versailles ..	Versailles and Midway Rwy.	8.32	314	25	no apt ....
270	Ark...	29014	Newport, Cushman ..	St. Louis, Iron Mountain and Southern Rwy.	40.57	313	12	13.9 by 9.3, 11 ....
271	N. C ..	13016	Asheville Junction (n o.), Jarrett's.	Richmond and Danville R. R.	98.94	312	15	6.10 by 6.4, 1 1 ....
272	Ohio ..	21022	Dayton, Ohio, Union City, Ind.	Dayton and Union R. R	47.37	312	25	11 by 7.6, 1 1 ....

States and Territories in which the contract term expired June 30, 1888, etc.—Continued.

Average trips per week.	Pay per mile per annum for transportation.	Pay per mile per annum for r. p. o. cars.	Former pay per mile per annum for transportation.	Former pay per mile per annum for r. p. o. cars.	Amount of annual pay for transportation.	Amount of annual pay for r. p. o. cars.	Former amount of annual pay for transportation.	Former amount of annual pay for r. p. o. cars.	Date of adjustment or readjustment.	Remarks.
	Dolls.	Dolls.	Dolls.	Dolls.	Dollars.	Dollars.	Dollars.	Dollars.	1888.	
14.23	53.01	......	47.88	......	1,900.40	....	1,629.83	....	July 1	Weighed 30 days from Mar. 19, 1888. 1.8J m. increase.
6	53.01	......	50.45	......	1,394.16	....	1,312.70	....	July 1	Weighed 30 days from Feb. 20, 1888. 0.28 m. increase.
7.00	53.01	......	......	......	6,294.93	....	....	....	Apr. 2	Weighed 30 days from Mar. 26, 1888. 80.15 m., Kansas City, Kans., to Tongamoxie from Aug. 22, 1887; 86.57 m. ext., Tongamoxie to Seneca, from Mar. 5, 1888; 2.03 m. ext., Kansas City, Kans., to Kansas City, Mo., from Apr. 2, 1888.
7	53.01	......	54.72	......	3,509.26	....	3,622.46	....	July 1	Weighed 30 days from Feb. 20, 1888.
9.11	52.15	......	47.03	......	6,178.73	....	5,591.39	....	July 1	Weighed 30 days from Mar. 19, 1888. 0.41 m. decrease.
6	52.15	......	42.75	......	4,376.94	....	3,819.70	....	July 1	Weighed 30 days from Mar. 19, 1888. 27.06 m. ext., Fair Oaks to La Crosse, from Feb. 20, 1888. 0.53 m. increase.
14	52.15	......	......	......	233.63	....	....	....	1887. Oct. 10	Weighed 20 days from Apr. 19, 1888. New.
10.73	52.15	......	72.08	......	1,960.84	....	2,631.01	....	1888. July 1	Weighed 30 days from Mar. 19, 1888. 1.40 m. increase.
12	52.15	......	46.17	......	435.97	....	385.96	....	July 1	Weighed 30 days from Feb. 20, 1888.
18	52.15	......	46.17	......	283.69	....	251.16	....	July 1	Weighed 20 days from Feb. 20, 1888.
9.39	51.30	......	44.46	......	4,042.93	....	2,683.60	....	July 1	Weighed 30 days from Mar. 19, 1888.
8.89	51.30	......	59.00	......	2,863.54	....	1,681.50	....	July 1	Weighed 30 days from Mar. 19, 1888. 9.75 m. ext., McConnellville to Stockport from Sept. 5, 1887; 16.40 m. ext., Stockport to Waterford from Mar. 19, 1888.
14	51.30	......	42.75	......	302.67	....	252.22	....	July 1	Weighed 30 days from Feb. 20, 1888.
7	50.45	......	......	......	8,471.05	....	....	....	1887. Dec. 5	Weighed 30 days from Feb. 20, 1888. New.
6	50.44	......	42.75	......	844.30	....	705.37	....	1888. July 1	Weighed 30 days from Feb. 20, 1888. 0.24 m. increase.
24	50.44	......	44.46	......	419.66	....	317.00	....	July 1	Weighed 30 days from Feb. 20, 1888. 0.74 m. increase.
6.73	50.44	......	51.30	......	2,046.35	....	1,485.13	....	Feb. 20	Weighed 30 days from Feb. 20, 1888. 11.62 m. ext. Batesville to Cushman, from Nov. 7, 1887.
6	50.44	......	49.59	......	4,990.53	....	4,906.93	....	July 1	Weighed 30 days from Feb. 28, 1888. 0.01 m. decrease.
16.33	50.44	......	55.58	......	2,389.34	....	2,630.04	....	July 1	Weighed 30 days from Mar. 19, 1888. 0.05 m. increase.

H.—*Table showing the re-adjustment of the rates of pay per mile on railroad routes in*

Index order.	State.	Number of route.	Termini.	Corporate title of company carrying the mail.	Length of route.	Average weight of mails, whole distance per day. Miles per hour.	Size, etc., of mail car or apartment.
					Miles.	*Lbs.*	*Feet and inches.*
373	Kans..	33028	Keystone, Concordia.	Chicago, Kansas and Western R. R.	41. 02	310 20	11.6 by 6.1, 1 1 ....
374	Mich..	24075	Grosvenor (n. o.), Mich., Fayette, Ohio	Lake Shore and Michigan Southern Rwy.	25. 57	310 22	12 by 6.7, 1 1 ....
375	Ind ...	22031	Attica, Brazil	Chicago and Indiana Coal Rwy.	62. 32	306 15	14 by 7.4, 1 1 ....
376	Oregon	44006	Albany, Yaquina	Oregon Pacific R. R .	85. 16	306 20	no apt ....
377	Tex...	31056	Taylor, La Grange...	Taylor, Bastrop and Houston Rwy.	70. 02	306 17	16.3 by 6.9, 1 1........
378	Wash. Ter.	43017	Walla Walla, Wash. Pendleton, Oregon.	Oregon Rwy. and Navigation Co.	47. 43	303 15	no apt ....
379	Dak ..	35029	Roscoe, Orient	Chicago, Milwaukee and St. Paul Rwy.	41. 73	299 14	13.7 by 7, 1 1 ....
380	Mich..	24036	Trenton, Corbus Junction (n. o.).	Lake Shore and Michigan Southern Rwy.	37. 23	293 28	13 by 7, 1 1 ....:..
381	Ga	15040	Albany, Blakely	Southwestern R. R...	50. 38	297 14	15.2 by 8.4, 1 1........
382	Cal ...	46040	San Luis Obispo, Los Olivos Station (n.o.)	Pacific Coast Rwy...	67. 30	296 15	17.10 by 6, 1 1........
383	Pa ...	8165	Irvona, Punxsutawney.	Bell's Gap R. R	33. 47	291 18	7.1 by 6.10, 1 1 ....
384	Indian Ter.	32003	Arkansas City, Ark., Purcell, Ind. Ter.	Southern Kansas Rwy	154	287 30	no apt ....
385	Mich..	24076	Ashley, Muskegon ..	Toledo, Saginaw and Muskegon Rwy.	96. 24	293 16	8.3 by 6.10, 1 1 ....
386	Ohio ..	21039	Delphos, Dayton	Dayton, Fort Wayne and Chicago R. R.	95. 43	293 16	11.8 by 7.6, 1 1.......
387	W. Va.	12912	Grafton, Belington...	Grafton and Greenbrier R. R.	42	292 15	10.2 by 6.6, 1 1.......
388	Mich..	24043	Coleman, Mount Pleasant.	Flint and Pere Marquette R. R.	15. 03	230 15	....
389	Ind ...	22034	Rockport, Rockport Junction (n. o.).	Louisville, Evansville and St. Louis Rwy.	16. 35	289 20	no apt ....
390	Me....	28	Kittery Junction (n. o.), York Beach.	York Harbor and Beach R. R.	11. 33	289 22	....do.................
391	Ga	15026	Toccoa, Elberton.....	Richmond and Danville R. R.	50. 62	286 14	10 by 4.6, 1 1.........
392	Ohio ..	21091	Toledo, Findlay......	Toledo, Columbus and Southern Rwy.	44. 02	285 30	11.6 by 8.5, 1 1.......

States and Territories in which the contract term expired June 30, 1888, etc.—Continued.

Average trips per week.	Pay per mile per annum for transportation.	Pay per mile per annum for r. p. o. cars.	Former pay per mile per annum for transportation.	Former pay per mile per annum for r. p. o. cars.	Amount of annual pay for transportation.	Amount of annual pay for r. p. o. cars.	Former amount of annual pay for transportation.	Former amount of annual pay for r. p. o. cars.	Date of adjustment or re-adjustment.	Remarks.
	Dolls.	Dolls.	Dolls.	Dolls.	Dollars.	Dollars.	Dollars.	Dollars.	1888.	
7	50. 44	......	......	......	2, 069. 04	......	......	......	Mar. 5	Weighed 30 days from May 21, 1888. New.
12	50. 44	......	45. 32	......	1, 289. 75	......	......	......	July 1	Formerly part of route 24036.
6	49. 59	......	50. 45	......	3, 090. 44	......	3, 199. 53	......	July 1	Weighed 30 days from Mar. 19, 1888. 1. 10 m. decrease.
6	49. 59	......	44. 46	......	4, 223. 06	......	3, 232. 68	......	Mar. 19	Weighed 30 days from Mar. 19, 1888. 12. 45 m. ext. from Corvallis to Albany, from May 2, 1887.
7	49. 59	......	41. 04	......	3, 472. 29	......	3, 169. 78	......	Feb. 20	Weighed 30 days from Feb. 20, 1888. 34. 64 m. ext. Bastrop to La Grange, from Dec. 5, 1887.
									1887.	
7	49. 59	......	......	......	2, 352. 05	......	......	......	Aug. 25	Weighed 30 days from Mar. 19, 1888. New.
6	49. 59	......	......	......	2, 069. 39	......	......	......	July 25	Weighed 30 days from Mar. 19, 1888. New.
									1888.	
6	49. 59	......	45. 32	......	1, 846. 23	......	3, 009. 88	......	July 1	Weighed 30 days from Mar. 19, 1888. The termini formerly were Trenton, Mich., and Fayette, Ohio.
6	49. 59	......	42. 75	......	2, 498. 34	......	2, 145. 62	......	July 1	Weighed 30 days from Feb. 20, 1888. 0. 19 m. increase.
6	49. 59	......	48. 74	......	3, 337. 40	......	2, 685. 57	......	Mar. 19	Weighed 30 days from Mar. 19, 1888. 12. 20 m. ext. Los Alamos to Los Olivos Station (n. o.), from Jan. 16, 1888.
12	48. 74	......	23. 09	......	1, 631. 32	......	370. 59	......	Mar. 19	Weighed 30 days from Mar. 19, 1888. 17. 42 m. ext. from Mahaffey to Punxsutawney from Mar. 5, 1888.
									1887.	
7	48. 74	......	......	......	7, 505. 96	......	......	......	Sept. 12	Weighed 30 days from Feb. 20, 1888. New.
									1888.	
6	48. 73	......	45. 73	......	4, 680. 77	......	4, 689. 77	......	Mar. 13	Weighed 30 days from Mar. 19, 1888.
6	48. 73	......	63. 27	......	4, 650. 30	......	5, 906. 25	......	July 1	Weighed 30 days from Mar. 19, 1888. 2. 08 m. increase.
6	48. 73	......	42. 75	......	2, 046. 66	......	1, 026. 00	......	Feb. 20	Weighed 30 days from Feb. 20, 1888. 18 m. ext. Philippi to Belington from Aug. 21, 1887.
6	48. 73	......	42. 75	......	732. 41	......	612. 96	......	July 1	Weighed 30 days from Mar. 19, 1888. 0.01 m. decrease.
19	48. 73	......	47. 88	......	796. 73	......	775. 65	......	July 1	Weighed 30 days from Mar. 19, 1888. 0.15 m. increase.
12	48. 73	......	......	......	552. 11	......	......	......	Jan. 16	Weighed 30 days from July 2, 1888. New.
6	48. 73	......	42. 75	......	2, 466. 71	......	2, 199. 48	......	July 1	Weighed 30 days from Feb. 20, 1888. 0.83 m. decrease.
12	48. 73	......	42. 75	......	2, 145. 09	......	1, 881. 86	......	July 1	Weighed 30 days from Mar. 19, 1888.

H.—*Table showing the re-adjustment of the rates of pay per mile on railroad routes in*

Index order.	State.	Number of route.	Termini.	Corporate title of company carrying the mail.	Length of route.	Average weight of mails whole distance per day.	Miles per hour.	Size, etc., of mail-car or apartment.
					Miles.	*Lbs.*		*Feet and inches.*
392a	Kans..	33045	Butler, Mo., Le Roy, Kans.	St. Louis and Emporia R. R.	79.83	285	20	16.4 by 6.10, 1 l.......
393	Ga ...	15030	Marietta, Ga., Murphy, N. C.	Marietta and North Georgia R. R.	110	284	17	8 by 6, 1 l............
394	Ill ..	23093	Springfield, Litchfield	St. Louis and Chicago Rwy.	45.64	282	25	20.6 by 9.2, 1 l........
395	Ohio ..	21084	Logan, New Straitsville.	Columbus, Hocking Valley and Toledo Rwy.	12.74	282	25	8.4 by 6.7, 1½ l........
396	Ga	15049	Wrightsville, Dublin.	Wrightsville and Tennille R. R.	20.09	279	13	9 by 8, 1 l............
397	Iowa..	27097	Mason City, Fort Dodge.	Mason City and Fort Dodge R. R.	73.05	276	25	11.6 by 7.1, 1 l........
398	Ohio ..	21046	Painesville, Youngstown.	Pittsburgh and Western Rwy.	61.70	274	30	r. p. o.,47.3 by 8.11, 1 l. (not auth.).
399	Ala ...	17014	Opelika, Roanoke	East Alabama Rwy ..	39.38	274	17	12.2 by 7, 1 l...........
400	Fla ...	16020	De Land Junction (n. o.), De Land.	St. John's and De Land Rwy.	4.10	273	24	no apt ....
401	Tenn .	19017	Columbia, Saint Joseph.	Nashville and Florence R. R.	57.31	273	22	14.3 by 8.6, 1 l........
402	Tenn .	19003	Rogersville, Bull's Gap.	Tennessee and Ohio Rwy.	16.73	272	16	5.6 by 6.2, 1 l.........
403	N. C .	13014	Oxford, Henderson ...	Oxford and Henderson R. R.	13.50	272	20	no apt ....
404	Miss ..	18007	Muldon, Aberdeen ...	Mobile and Ohio R. R.	9.46	272	13	.. do.............
405	Pa ...	8169	Hazleton, New Boston.	Lehigh Valley........	18.06	265	23	8 by 6.6, 1 l ....
406	Ten ...	19026	Gallatin, Tenn., Scottsville, Ky.	Chesapeake and Nashville Rwy.	35.87	262	12	10.6 by 8.6, 1 l ....
407	Ark...	29021	Fayetteville, Saint Paul.	St. Louis and San Francisco Rwy.	35.86	261	10	no apt ....
408	S. C ...	14020	Lanes, Georgetown ..	Georgetown and Western R. R.	36	267	20	....do.......
409	Mich...	24060	Port Huron, Almont .	Port Huron and Northwestern Rwy.	34.50	267	19	....
410	Ga	15006	Washington, Barnett	Georgia R. R.........	18.58	265	16	no apt ....
411	Ga	15022	Griffin, Carrollton....	Savannah, Griffin and North Ala R. R.	60.37	284	13	14.6 by 5.9, 1 l........
412	Pa ...	8175	New Boston, Pottsville.	Pennsylvania R. R ...	10.21	263	23	8 by 6.6, 1 l............
413	Dak...	35026	Salem, Mitchell......	Chicago, St. Paul, Minneapolis and Omaha Rwy.	33.10	262	20	no apt.............

States and Territories in which the contract term expired June 30, 1888, etc.—Continued.

Average trips per week.	Pay per mile per annum for transportation.	Pay per mile per annum for r. p. o. cars.	Former pay per mile per annum for transportation.	Former pay per mile per annum for r. p. o. cars.	Amount of annual pay for transportation.	Amount of annual pay for r. p. o. cars.	Former amount of annual pay for transportation.	Former amount of annual pay for r. p. o. cars.	Date of adjustment or re-adjustment.	Remarks.
	Dolls.	*Dolls.*	*Dolls.*	*Dolls.*	*Dollars.*	*Dollars.*	*Dollars.*	*Dollars*	1888.	
7	48.73	......	47.03	......	3,890.11	....	3,780.74	....	Mar. 19	Weighed 30 days from Mar. 19, 1888. 15.50 m. ext. Colony to Le Roy from June 6, 1887.
6	48.73	......	39.33	......	5,360.30	....	4,288.14	....	July 1	Weighed 30 days from Feb. 20, 1888. 0.97 m. increase.
6	47.88	......	47.88	......	2,185.24	....	2,185.24	....	1887. July 1	Weighed 30 days from Mar. 19, 1888.
9	47.88	......	49.59	......	609.99	....	664.01	....	1888. July 1	Weighed 30 days from Mar. 19, 1888. 0.65 m. decrease.
6	47.88	......	42.75	......	961.90	....	836.19	....	July 1	Weighed 30 days from Feb. 20, 1888. 0.53 m. increase.
6	47.88	......	47.88	......	3,497.63	....	3,497.63	....	June 6	Weighed 30 days from Mar. 19, 1888.
12	47.88	......	45.32	......	2,413.75	....	2,074.29	....	July 1	Weighed 30 days from Mar. 19, 1888. 0.28 m. decrease. 16 21 m. Warren to Youngstown, lap service, at $14.54 per m.
6	47.88	......	42.75	......	1,885.51	....	1,771.67	....	July 1	Weighed 30 days from Feb. 20, 1888. 17.19 m. ext. Buffalo to Roanoke, from Feb. 15, 1888.
19	47.88	......	42.75	......	196.30	....	226.57	....	July 1	Weighed 30 days from Feb. 20, 1888. 1.2 m. decrease.
6	47.88	......	42.75	......	2,744.00	....	2,425.63	....	July 1	Weighed 30 days from Feb. 20, 1888.
6	47.88	......	42.75	......	801.03	....	701.95	....	July 1	Weighed 30 days from Feb. 20, 1888. 0.31 m. increase.
6	47.88	......	42.75	......	646.38	....	607.05	....	July 1	Weighed 30 days from Feb. 20, 1888. 0.70 m. decrease.
14	47.88	......	44.46	......	452.94	....	422.37	....	July 1	Weighed 30 days from Feb. 20, 1888. 0.04 m. decrease.
21.86	47.03	......			849.35	....	....	....	Mar. 1	Weighed 30 days from Mar. 19, 1884. 9.21 m. Hazleton and Lofty, from Oct. 14, 1887; 8 85 m. ext. Lofty to New Boston, Mar. 1, 1888.
6	47.03	......	47.03	......	1,686.96	....	1,686.96	....	Jan. 2	Weighed 30 days from Feb. 20, 1888. New.
7	47.03	......	......	......	1,686.49	....	....	....	Apr. 2	Weighed 30 days from Feb. 20, 1888. 37.15 m. from Aug. 22, 1887, to Apr. 1, 1888.
14	47.02	......	42.75	......	1,692.72	....	1,675.80	....	July 1	Weighed 30 days from Feb. 20, 1888. 3.20 m. decrease.
6	47.02	......	44.46	......	1,632.19	....	1,534.75	....	July 1	Weighed 30 days from Mar. 19, 1888. 0.02 m. decrease.
14	47.02	......	42.75	......	873.63	....	794.29	....	July 1	Weighed 30 days from Feb. 20, 1888.
6	47.02	......	43.61	......	2,838.59	....	2,632.73	....	July 1	Weighed 30 days from Feb. 20, 1888.
24	47.02	......			480.07	....	....	....	Mar. 1	Weighed 30 days from Mar. 19, 1888. New.
7	47.02	......			1,556.36	....	....	....	Feb. 20	Weighed 30 days from Mar. 19, 1888. New.

H.—*Table showing the re-adjustment of the rates of pay per mile on railroad routes in*

Index order.	State.	Number of route.	Termini.	Corporate title of company carrying the mail.	Length of route.	Average weight of mails, whole distance per day.	Miles per hour.	Size, etc., of mail car or apartment.
					Miles.	*Lbs.*		*Feet and inches.*
414	Ohio ..	21038	Newark, Shawnee-town.	Baltimore and Ohio R. R.	44.04	261	25	16.1 by 8.6, 1 l........
415	Ga	15008	Kingston, Rome	Rome R. R	19.20	261	20	no apt.............
416	Mich..	24049	Saginaw City Junction (n. o.), Saginaw.	Flint and Pere Marquette R. R.	3.75	260	14	....
417	Idaho .	42003	Cœur d'Alene, Wallace.	Cœur d'Alene Railway and Navigation Co.	91.61	255	12	no apt............
418	Ohio..	21054	Dayton, Ironton......	Dayton, Fort Wayne and Chicago Rwy.	109.65	258	20	12.8 by 9.2, 1 l........
419	Ga	15020	Cartersville, Ga., Pell City, Ala.	East and West R. R. Co. of Alabama.	118.55	258	15	7.6 by 7.6, 1 l.........
420	Ga	15024	Columbus, Greenville	Columbus and Rome Rwy.	50.78	258	14	10.7 by 7.1, 1 l........
421	Ala ...	17030	Talladega, Pell City..	Talladega and Coosa Valley R. R.	25.96	236	20	7.4 by 5.3, 1 l.........
422	Mont..	36004	Drummond, Phillipsburgh.	Northern Pacific R. R.	26.47	253	15	no apt ....
423	Ohio ..	21081	Delphos, Carey.......	Cleveland and Western R. R.	56.78	252	16	apt. 7.9 by 5.8, 1 l ...
424	Nebr..	34055	Palmer, Burwell......	Burlington and Missouri River R. R. (in Nebraska).	69.38	252	23	9 by 6.7, 1 l ....
425	Ohio ..	21056	Saint Clairsville, Steel	Bellaire and St. Clairsville Rwy.	7.56	248	18	....
426	Ohio ..	21072	Edison, Mount Gilead	Cleveland, Columbus, Cincinnati and Indianapolis Rwy.	2.38	248	12	....
427	La	30017	Cypress, Natchitoches	Natchitoches R. R ...	11.62	243	15	no apt ....
428	Tenn .	19016	Dickson, Aetna	Nashville, Chattanooga and St. Louis Rwy.	43.72	241	12	7 by 6.6, 1 l ....
429	Wyo ..	37003	Douglas, Glen Rock..	Fremont, Elkhorn and Missouri Valley R. R.	30.30	240	17	14 by 9.3, 1 l ....
430	S. C...	14013	Chester, Lancaster...	Richmond and Danville R. R.	29.47	238	11	(av.), 9.10 by 7.2, 1 l .
431	Ill	23044	Danville, Tuscola	Chicago and Eastern Illinois R. R.	50.49	236	20	....
432	Mich..	24054	East Saginaw, Bad Axe,	Saginaw, Tuscola and Huron R. R.	68.23	236	22	7 by 6, 1 l............

States and Territories in which the contract term expired June 30, 1888, etc.—Continued.

Average trips per week.	Pay per mile per annum for transportation.	Pay per mile per annum for r. p. o. cars.	Former pay per mile per annum for transportation.	Former pay per mile per annum for r. p. o. cars.	Amount of annual pay for transportation.	Amount of annual pay for r. p. o. cars.	Former amount of annual pay for transportation.	Former amount of annual pay for r. p. o. cars.	Date of adjustment or re-adjustment.	Remarks.
	Dolls.	Dolls.	Dolls.	Dolls.	Dollars.	Dollars.	Dollars.	Dollars.	1888.	
12	47.02	......	53.01	......	2,070.76	....	2,314.94	....	July 1	Weighed 30 days from Mar. 19,1888. 0.37 m. increase.
14	47.02		52.16		902.78	....	1,057.80	....	July 1	Weighed 30 days from Feb. 20, 1888. 1.06 m. decrease.
7	47.02		48.74		176.32	....	188.26	....	July 1	Weighed 30 days from Mar. 19, 1888. 6 01 m. decrease. Initial point was formerly called Detroit and Bay City Crossing.
6	46.17				4,229.63				1887. Oct. 17	Weighed 30 days from Mar. 19, 1888. 81.90 m. Cœur d'Alene to Wardner from July 20, 1887; 9.71 m. ext. Wardner to Wallace from Oct. 17, 1887.
12	46.17		42.75		7,832.74	....	7,232.87	....	1888. July 1	Weighed 30 days from Mar. 19, 1888. 0.46 m. increase.
6	46.17		42.75		5,473.45	....	5,042.11	....	July 1	Weighed 30 days from Feb. 20, 1888. 1.19 m. increase. 7.36 m. ext. Broken Arrow to Pell City from Jan. 2, 1888.
6	46.17		42.75		2,344.51	....	2,165.28	....	July 1	Weighed 30 days from Feb. 20, 1888. 0.13 m. increase.
12	46.17		42.75		1,198.57	....	1,131.88	....	July 1	Weighed 30 days from Feb. 20, 1888. 0.84 m. increase. 16.94 m. ext. Renfroe to Pell City from Dec. 19, 1887.
7	46.17				1,222.11				Jan. 2	Weighed 30 days from Mar. 19, 1888. New.
6	46.17		42.75		2,621.53	....	2,419.65	....	July 1	Weighed 30 days from Mar. 19, 1888. 0.18 m. increase.
6	46.17				3,203.27	....			Feb. 20	Weighed 30 days from Apr. 30, 1888. New.
21	46.17		42.75		349.04	....	311.22	....	July 1	Weighed 30 days from Mar. 19, 1888. 0.22 m. increase.
18	46.17		42.75		109.88	....	102.60	....	July 1	Weighed 30 days from Mar. 19, 1888. 0.02 m. decrease.
14	45.31				526.50				Feb. 20	Weighed 30 days from Aug 1, 1888. New.
6	45.31		31.64		1,980.95		1,491.01	....	July 1	Weighed 30 days from Feb. 20, 1888. 0 56 m. decrease.
6	45.31				1,372.89				Feb. 20	Weighed 30 days from Mar. 19,1888. New.
6	45.31		42.75		1,335.28		1,259.84		July 1	Weighed 30 days from Feb 20, 1888.
8.79	45.31		36.77		2,287.70		868.50	....	Mar. 19	Weighed 30 days from Mar. 19, 1888. 26.87 m. ext. Sidell to Tuscola from Dec. 5,1887.
12	45.31		45.32		3,091.50		3,092.18		July 1	Weighed 30 days from Mar. 19, 1888.

H.—*Table showing the re-adjustment of the rates of pay per mile on railroad routes in*

Index order.	State.	Number of route.	Termini.	Corporate title of company carrying the mail.	Length of route.	Average weight of mails, whole distance per day.	Miles per hour.	Size, etc., of mail-car or apartment.
					Miles.	*Lbs.*		*Feet and inches.*
433	Kans..	33061	Larned, Jetmore	Chicago, Kansas and Western R. R.	46.84	235	19	25 by 9.2, 1 l ....
434	Ga ...	15051	Columbus, McDonough.	Georgia, Midland and Gulf R. R.	99.20	234	21	13.9 by 6.6, 1 l. to Griffin, 80 m.; no apt. rea.
435	Pa	8174	Wilkes-Barre, Rock Glen Junction (n. o.).	Pennsylvania R. R...	39.58	234	23	8.6 by 8.4, 1 l ....
436	Ohio ..	21093	New Galilee, Pa., New Lisbon, Ohio.	Pittsburgh, Marion and Chicago Rwy.	25.94	234	15	13 by 6.3, 1 l........
437	Mich..	24069	Junction (n. o.), Lake Linden.	Hancock and Calumet R. R.	3.85	231	17	....
438	Miss ..	18022	Wilzinski Junction (n. o.), Glen Allan.	Louisville, New Orleans and Texas Rwy.	34.34	231	12	5.8 by 7, 1 l.........
439	Ala ...	17025	Tuscumbia, Florence.	Memphis and Charleston R. R.	5.63	230	12	no apt ....
440	Fla ...	16029	Monroe, Mascotte....	Orange Belt Rwy	51.27	230	16	13.5 by 7.6, 1 l to Clermont. 41.75 m. No apt. rea.
441	N.C ..	13013	Jamesville, Washington.	Jamesville and Washington R. R.	22.57	220	12	no apt ....
442	Nebr .	34054	Fairbury, McCool Junction.	St. Joseph and Grand Island R. R.	56.62	228	..	12.2 by 7.6, 1 l........
443	Pa ...	8099	Osceola Mills, Madera.	Pennsylvania R. R ...	14.84	227	16	no apt ....
444	Kans	33078	Sidell, Peru	Le Roy and Caney Valley Air Line R. R.	52.91	227	20	16.4 by 6.8, 1 l........
445	Wyo..	37002	Cheyenne City, Uva..	Cheyenne and Northern Rwy.	103.96	226	21	no apt ....
446	Fla ...	16028	Sanford, Tavares.....	Jacksonville, Tampa and Key West Rwy.	29.95	226	22	....do ....
447	Ga ...	15043	Cornelia, Tallulah....	Blue Ridge and Atlantic R. R.	21.13	226	19	9.7 by 8.7, 1 l........
448	Ohio..	21070	Tontogany, Bowling Green.	Bowling Green and Toledo R. R.	6.42	224	30	....
449	Tex ..	31061	Fort Worth, Granbury.	Fort Worth and Rio Grande Rwy.	41.35	221	13	no apt ....
450	Mass..	3018	Winchester, North Woburn.	Boston and Lowell R. R. Corporation.	4.56	219	19	....do ....

States and Territories in which the contract term expired June 30, 1888, *etc.*—Continued.

Average trips per week.	Pay per mile per annum for transportation.	Pay per mile per annum for r.p.o. cars.	Former pay per mile per annum for transportation.	Former pay per mile per annum for r. p. o. cars.	Amount of annual pay for transportation.	Amount of annual pay for r. p. o. cars.	Former amount of annual pay for transportation.	Former amount of annual pay for r. p. o. cars.	Date of adjustment or re-adjustment.	Remarks.
	Dolls.	Dolls.	Dolls.	Dolls.	Dollars.	Dollars.	Dollars.	Dollars.	1888.	
7	44.46	......	22.23	......	2,082.50	....	536.18	....	Mar. 19	Weighed 30 days from Mar. 19, 1888. 22.72 m. ext. Burdett to Jetmore from Nov. 7, 1887.
6	44.46	......	20.52	......	4,410.43	....	3,603.30	....	July 1	Weighed 30 days from Feb. 20, 1888. 29.10 m. ext. Shiloh to Concord from July 1, 1887; 16.50 m. ext. Concord to Griffin from Aug. 1, 1887; 19 20 m. ext. Griffin to McDonough from Oct. 31, 1887. 0.80 m. decrease.
15	44.46	......			1,759.72	....			Mar. 1	Weighed 30 days from Mar. 19, 1888. New.
7.22	44.46	......	42.75	......	1,153.29	....	603.20	....	July 1	Weighed 30 days from Mar. 19, 1888. 0.61 m. increase.
18.5	44.46	......	44.46	......	148.94	....	143.60	....	July 1	Weighed 30 days from Mar.19, 1888. 0.12 m. increase.
7.57	44.46	......			1,526.75	....			July 1	Weighed 30 days from Feb. 20, 1888. 0.33 m. increase. 34.01 m. from Mar. 7, 1887.
6	44.46	......	42.75	......	250.30	....	268.89	....	July 1	Weighed 30 days from Feb. 20, 1888. 0.66 m. decrease.
6	44.46	......	39.33	......	2,279.46	....	2,114.33	....	uly 1	Weighed 30 days from Feb. 20, 1888. 9.65 m. ext. Oakland to Clermont from Sept. 26, 1887; 9.51 m. ext. Clermont to Mascotte from Dec. 19, 1887.
6	44.46	......	42.75	......	1,003.46	....	964.86	....	July 1	Weighed 30 days from Feb. 20, 1888.
6	44.46	......			2,250.56	....			Feb. 20	Weighed 30 days from Mar 19, 1888. New.
15	44.46	......	42.75	......	659.78	....	386.46	....	Mar. 19	Weighed 30 days from Mar. 19, 1888. 5.8 m. ext. from Ramey to Madera from Oct. 31, 1887.
7	44.46	......			2,352.37	....			1887. Aug. 8	Weighed 30 days from Mar. 19, 1888. New.
6	44.46	......			4,590.93	....			Dec. 23	Weighed 30 days from Mar. 19, 1888. New.
6	44.46	......	29.07	......	1,331.57	....	861.72	....	1888. July 1	Weighed 30 days from Feb. 20, 1888. 0.3 m. increase.
7	44.46	......	42.75	......	939.43	....	1,087.58	....	July 1	Weighed 30 days from Feb. 20, 1888.
21	44.46	......	42.75	......	285.43	....	253.93	....	July 1	Weighed 30 days from Mar. 19, 1888. 0.48 m. increase.
6	43.61	......			1,803.27	....			1887. Nov. 21	Weighed 30 days from Feb. 20, 1888. New.
24.8	43.61	......	47.88	......	198.86	....	131.95	....	1888 Mar. 19	Weighed 30 days from Mar. 19, 1888. 2.18 m. ext. from Woburn to North Woburn from Aug. 16, 1887.

H.—*Table showing the re-adjustment of the rates of pay per mile on railroad routes in*

Index order.	State.	Number of route.	Termini.	Corporate title of company carrying the mail.	Length of route.	Average weight of mails whole distance, per day.	Miles per hour.	Size, etc., of mail-car or apartment.
					Miles.	*Lbs.*		*Feet and inches.*
451	S. C...	14022	Elloree, Pregnalls....	Eutawville R. R......	35.22	212	14	8.3 by 6.3, 2 l ......
452	Ohio ..	21067	Bergholtz, Phalanx Station (n. o.).	Lake Erie, Alliance and Southern Rwy.	60.80	223	20	8 by 6, 1 l............
453	Iowa..	27099	Cherokee, Onawa	Cherokee and Dakota R. R.	61.18	222	20	....
454	Ky....	20026	Shelbyville, Bloomfield.	Louisville and Nashville R. R.	27.75	220	22	10 by 5.8, 1 l.........
455	Miss ..	18015	Artesia, Starkville...	Mobile and Ohio R. R.	11.52	219	13	no apt ....
456	Ind ..	22035	New Salisbury, Corydon.	Louisville, New Albany and Corydon R. R.	8.57	215	18	....do................
457	Ky....	20030	Richmond Junction (n. o.), Richmond.	Kentucky Central Rwy.	34.91	212	13	8 by 6.7, 1 l..........
458	Ind ...	22056	Jeffersonville, Watson.	Ohio and Mississippi Rwy.	7.50	211	30	no apt ....
459	Tenn .	19010	Tracy City, Cowan...	Nashville, Chattanooga and St. Louis Rwy.	20.03	210	20	12 by 6.8, 1 l ....
460	Nebr..	34045	Fairfield, Stromsburgh.	Kansas City and Omaha R. R.	65.49	210	..	13.5 by 6.6, 1 l ....
461	Nebr..	34057	Ashland, Schuyler ...	Omaha and North Platte R. R.	50.71	209	25	8.6 by 7.4, 1 l.......
462	Mich..	24061	Palm Station, Sand Beach.	Port Huron and Northwestern Rwy.	18.93	208	15	....
463	Ohio ..	21079	Solon, Chagrin Falls..	Chagrin Falls and Southern R. R.	5.57	207	12	....
464	Ga	15014	Gordon, Eatonton....	Milledgeville and Eatonton R. R.	38.48	205	14	15.2 by 8.9, 1 l........
465	N. C...	13030	Warsaw, Clinton....	Wilmington and Weldon R. R.	13.11	202	20	no apt ....
466	Kans..	33085	Oakley, Colby........	Oakley and Colby Rwy.	22.12	202	14	....
467	Ohio ..	21021	Carey, Findlay........	Cincinnati, Sandusky and Cleveland R. R.	15.50	198	22	....
468	Ind ...	22046	Frankfort, Ind., and East St. Louis Station (n. o.) Ill.	Toledo, St. Louis and Kansas City R. R.	244.55	197	15	8 by 5.8, 1 l..........
469	Ga	15034	Gainesville, Social Circle.	Gainesville, Jefferson and Southern R. R.	52.29	197	18	6.4 by 5.4, 11. ....
470	Md ...	10027	Philadelphia, Pa., Baltimore, Md.	Baltimore and Ohio R. R.	96	197	24	17.9 by 8.5, 1 l.......
471	S. C...	14024	Laurens, Greenville..	Port Royal and Western Carolina Rwy.	37.48	196	18	7.6 by 6.7, 1 l ....
472	Mich..	24016	Mears, Hart.........	Chicago and West Michigan Rwy.	4.15	193	16	....
473	Ohio ..	21086	Alliance, Niles.......	Pennsylvania Company.	27.93	191	30	....
474	Tenn..	19014	Knoxville, Maryville.	Knoxville and Augusta R. R.	18.49	191	16	8.10 by 7.6, 1 l........

States and Territories in which the contract term expired June 30, 1888, etc.—Continued.

Average trips per week.	Pay per mile per annum for transportation.	Pay per mile per annum for r. p. o. cars.	Former pay per mile per annum for transportation.	Former pay per mile per annum for r. p. o. cars.	Amount of annual pay for transportation.	Amount of annual pay for r. p. o. cars.	Former amount of annual pay for transportation.	Former amount of annual pay for r. p. o. cars.	Date of adjustment or re-adjustment.	Remarks.
	Dolls.	Dolls.	Dolls.	Dolls.	Dollars.	Dollars.	Dollars.	Dollars.	1888.	
12	43.61		24.80		1,535.94		837.74		July 1	Weighed 30 days from Feb. 20, 1888. 1.44 m. increase.
8.6	43.60		42.75		2,650.88		1,115.77		July 1	Weighed 30 days from Mar. 19, 1888. From Feb. 20, 1888, on 35.80 m. ext. Alliance to Bergholtz. 1.10 m. decrease.
6	43.60				2,667.44				Feb. 27	Weighed 30 days from Mar. 19, 1888. New.
12	43.60		42.75		1,209.90		1,186.31		July 1	Weighed 30 days from Feb. 20, 1888.
20.77	43.60		46.17		502.27		535.57		July 1	Weighed 30 days from Feb. 20, 1888. 0.08 m. decrease.
18	43.60		42.75		373.65		358.67		July 1	Weighed 30 days from Mar. 19, 1888. 0.18 m. increase.
6	42.60		49.50		1,522.07		1,701.43		July 1	Weighed 30 days from Feb. 20, 1888. 0.60 m. increase.
18.50	42.75	146.21			320.62				July 1	Weighed 30 days from Mar. 19, 1888. Formerly part of route 22019.
13	42.75		42.75		856.28		865.68		July 1	Weighed 30 days from Feb. 20, 1888. 0.22 m. decrease.
6	42.75				2,799.69				1887. Aug. 22	Weighed 30 days from Mar. 19, 1888. New.
6	42.75				2,167.85				Feb. 20	Weighed 30 days from Apr. 30, 1888. New.
6	42.75		42.75		809.25		804.98		1888. July 1	Weighed 30 days from Mar. 19, 1888. 0.10 m. increase.
24	42.75		44.46		238.11		247.64		July 1	Weighed 30 days from Mar. 19, 1888.
6	42.75		42.75		1,645.02		1,647.15		July 1	Weighed 30 days from Feb. 20, 1888. 0.05 m. decrease.
12	42.75				560.45				July 1	Weighed 30 days from Feb. 20, 1888.
6	42.75				945.63				1887. Dec. 28	Weighed 30 days from Mar. 19, 1888. New.
13	42.75		42.75		662.62		684.00		1888. July 1	Weighed 30 days from Mar. 19, 1888. 0 50 m. decrease.
6	42.75		42.75		10,454.51		10,417.32		July 1	Weighed 30 days from Mar. 19, 1888. 0 87 m. increase.
7.15	42.75		42.75		2,235.39		2,234.54		July 1	Weighed 30 days from Feb. 20, 1888. 0.02 m. increase.
6	42.75				4,104.00				1887. July 1	Weighed 30 days from Mar. 19, 1888. New.
7	42.75		30.78		1,602.27		1,134.20		1888. July 1	Weighed 30 days from Feb. 20, 1888, 0.63 m. increase.
6	42.75		42.75		177.41		177.41		July 1	Weighed 30 days from Mar. 19, 1888, 0.33 m. decrease.
9.05	42.75		42.75		1,194.00				July 1	Weighed 30 days from Mar. 19, 1888.
6	42.75		42.75		790.44		760.09		July 1	Weighed 30 days from Feb. 20, 1888. 0.71 m. increase.

H.—*Table showing the re-adjustment of the rates of pay per mile on railroad routes in*

Index order.	State.	Number of route.	Termini.	Corporate title of company carrying the mail.	Length of route.	Average weight of mails, whole distance per day.	Miles per hour.	Size, etc., of mail car or apartment.
					Miles.	*Lbs.*		*Feet and inches.*
475	Tenn .	19015	Columbia, Fayetteville.	Nashville, Chattanooga and St. Louis Rwy.	48.87	190	12	7.5 by 5, 1 1.........
476	Nebr..	34033	Fairfield, Alma	Kansas City and Omaha R. R.	87.79	190	25	13.5 by 6.6, 1 1.......
477	N. C .	13027	Wilson, Fayetteville	Wilmington and Weldon, R. R.	74.58	189	21	10 by 7, 1 1.........
478	Wis...	25059	Minneapolis, Minn., Sault de Ste. Marie, Mich.	Minneapolis, St. Paul and Sault Ste. Marie Rwy.	406.19	188	25	12 by 7.3, 1 1. to Brace, 122.35 m.
479	Ind ...	22039	Fort Branch, Mount Vernon.	Evansville and Terre Haute R. R.	38.75	187	20	9.9 by 6.3, 1 1.........
480	Ga....	15027	Sandersville, Tennille	Sandersville and Tennille R. R.	3.29	185	15	no apt ....
481	Tenn .	19018	Johnson City, Tenn., Cranberry, N. C.	East Tennessee and Western North Carolina R. R.	34.19	183	12	10.8 by 5.6, 1 1.......
482	K5 ...	20001	Elkton, Guthrie	Louisville and Nashville R. R.	12.07	183	15	no apt ....
483	Ill ...	23094	Geneva, Saint Charles	Chicago and Northwestern Rwy.	3.21	182	12	....
484	S. C...	14019	Blackville, Barnwell.	Barnwell Rwy	9.41	182	14	no apt ....
485	Ga....	15048	Augusta, Sandersville	Augusta, Gibson and Sandersville R. R.	81.41	181	15	8 by 6, 1 1.............
486	Ind ...	22041	Stewartsville, New Harmony.	Peoria, Decatur and Evansville Rwy.	7.42	180	12	no apt ....
487	Ind ...	22016	Fairland, Martinsville.	Cincinnati, Indianapolis, St. Louis and Chicago Rwy.	37.85	180	20	12 by 7, 1 1.........
488	Ga....	15038	Cochran, Hawkinsville.	East Tennessee, Virginia and Georgia Rwy.	10.52	179	14	no apt ....
489	Fla ...	16021	Wahneta, Bartow....	South Florida R. R..	17.67	179	18	....do ....
490	N. Y..	6135	Jamestown, Mayville.	Chautauqua Lake Rwy.	23.25	179	22	....do..............
491	Ga	15052	Macon, Monticello...	Covington and Macon R. R.	45.45	178	15	12.4 by 8.8, 1 1.....
492	Ind ...	22037	Anderson, Ladoga...	Midland Rwy	65.87	177	15	15 by 8.4, 1 1.........
493	Ohio ..	21096	Marietta, Sharpsburgh.	Marietta, Columbus and Northern R. R.	36.50	177	20	8.5 by 6.11, 1 1.......
494	Mich..	24003	Lawton, Hartford....	Toledo and South Haven R. R.	20.20	176	14	....

States and Territories in which the contract term expired June 30, 1888, etc.—Continued.

Average trips per week.	Pay per mile per annum for transportation.	Pay per mile per annum for r. p. o. cars.	Former pay per mile per annum for transportation.	Former pay per mile per annum for r. p. o. cars.	Amount of annual pay for transportation.	Amount of annual pay for r. p. o. cars.	Former amount of annual pay for transportation.	Former amount of annual pay for r. p. o. cars.	Date of adjustment or re-adjustment.	Remarks.
	Dolls.	*Dolls.*	*Dolls.*	*Dolls.*	*Dollars.*	*Dollars.*	*Dollars.*	*Dollars.*	1888.	
6	42.75	......	42.75	......	2,089.19	....	2,089.19	....	July 1	Weighed 30 days from Feb. 20, 1888.
6	42.75	......	41.04	......	3,753.02	....	3,602.90	....	July 1	Weighed 30 days from Mar. 19, 1888. New from Feb. 20, 1888.
6	42.75	......	31.64	......	3,188.29	....	2,341.99	....	July 1	Weighed 30 days from Feb. 20, 1888. 0.56 m. increase.
6.56	42.75	......	27.36	......	21,212.12	....	1,254.18	....	July 1	Weighed 30 days from June 5, 1888. From Dec. 5, 1887, on 76.51 m. ext. Turtle Lake to Minneapolis: from Mar. 5, 1888, on 373.84 m. ext. Bruce to Sault de Ste. Marie.
6	42.75	......	42.75	......	1,656.56	....	1,656.56	....	July 1	Weighed 30 days from Mar. 19, 1888.
6	42.75	......	42.75	......	140.64	....	140.62	....	July 1	Weighed 30 days from Feb. 20, 1888. 0.21 m. decrease.
6	42.75	......	42.75	......	1,461.62	....	1,444.95	....	July 1	Weighed 30 days from Feb. 20, 1888. 0.09 m. increase.
12	42.75	......	42.75	......	515.99	....	510.86	....	July 1	Weighed 30 days from Feb. 20, 1888. 0.12 m. increase.
21	42.75	......	39.33	......	137.22	....	126.24	....	July 1	Weighed 30 days from Mar. 19, 1888.
14	42.75	......	42.75	......	402.27	....	412.11	....	July 1	Weighed 30 days from Feb. 20, 1888. 0.23 m. decrease.
6	42.75	......	30.78	......	2,480.27	....	2,494.71	....	July 1	Weighed 30 days from Feb. 20, 1888. 0.36 m. increase.
12	42.75	......	42.75	......	317.20	....	313.78	....	July 1	Weighed 30 days from Mar. 19, 1888. 0.08 m. increase.
6	42.75	......	42.75	......	1,618.08	....	1,632.46	....	July 1	Weighed 30 days from Mar. 19, 1888. 0.50 m. decrease.
12	42.75	......	42.75	......	449.73	....	444.17	....	July 1	Weighed 30 days from Feb. 20, 1888. 0.13 m. increase.
19	42.75	......	42.75	......	755.39	....	749.40	....	July 1	Weighed 30 days from Feb. 20, 1888. 0.14 m. increase.
12	42.75	......	39.33	......	993.96	....	914.42	....	July 1	Weighed 30 days from June 1, 1888. New from Oct. 12, 1887.
6	42.75	......	29.93	......	1,942.98	....	1,360.31	....	July 1	Weighed 30 days from Feb. 20, 1888.
6	42.75	......	42.75	......	2,815.94	....	2,619.44	....	July 1	Weighed 30 days from Mar. 19, 1888. 25.78 m. ext., Noblesville to Lebanon from Aug. 12, 1887; 20.13 m. ext., Lebanon to Ladoga, from Jan. 9, 1888.
6	42.75	......	42.75	......	1,560.37	....	1,308.63	....	July 1	Weighed 30 days from Mar. 19, 1888. 7.33 m. Big Run to Amesville formerly at $35.06 per m. 4.57 m. ext., Amesville to Sharpsburgh, from Oct. 3, 1887.
6	42.75	......	42.75	......	863.55	....	863.97	....	July 1	Weighed 30 days from Mar. 19, 1888. 0.01 m. decrease.

H.—Table showing the re-adjustment of the rates of pay per mile on railroad routes in

Index order.	State.	Number of route.	Termini.	Corporate title of company carrying the mail.	Length of route.	Average weight of mails, whole distance per day.	Miles per hour.	Size, etc., of mail car or apartment.
					Miles.	*Lbs.*		*Feet and inches.*
495	S. C ...	14012	Newberry, Laurens.	Richmond and Danville R. R.	31.76	174	15	8.3 by 6.7, 1 l.........
496	Pa	8172	Benton, Bloomsburgh	Bloomsburgh and Sullivan R. R.	20.68	171	17	no apt ....
496a	Mo....	28063	Greenfield, Watkins	Greenfield and Northern R. R.	8.46	171	20	....do...............
497	Ohio ..	21066	Hillsborough, Sardinia.	Ohio and Northwestern R. R.	19.42	170	20	....
498	Wis ..	25044	Brodhead, New Glarus.	Chicago, Milwaukee and St. Paul Rwy.	22.90	169	12	....
499	Mich..	24056	Petoskey, Harbor Springs.	Grand Rapids and Indiana R. R.	8.20	169	25	....
500	Ga	15019	Barneville, Thomaston.	Upson County R. R. ..	16.35	167	16	no apt ....
501	Miss ..	18008	Middleton, Tenn.; New Albany, Miss.	Ship Island, Ripley and Kentucky R. R.	43.94	166	13	8.6 by 6.1, 1 l.........
502	Fla....	16009	Hart's Road, Jacksonville.	Florida Rwy. and Navigation Co.	25.41	165	25	no apt ....
503	Kans..	33087	Wichita, Ellsworth..	St. Louis and San Francisco Rwy.	106.61	164	19	12 by 6.6, 1 l.........
504	S. C ...	14009	Hodges, Abbeville...	Richmond and Danville R. R.	11.85	162	14	no apt ....
505	Ohio ..	21082	St. Mary's, Minster...	Lake Erie and Western Rwy.	10.23	161	20	....
506	Ga	15050	Abbeville, Louvale ..	Americus, Preston and Lumpkin R. R.	110.08	161	14	7.3 by 4.5, 1 l.........
507	N. C ..	13019	Halifax, Scotland Neck.	Wilmington and Weldon R. R.	19.64	157	14	no apt ....
508	Ala ...	17024	Elmore, Wetumpka..	South and North Alabama R. R.	6.91	156	13	no apt ....
50	Mich..	24068	Hancock, Red Jacket.	Hancock and Calumet R. R.	15.67	154	17	....
51	Mich..	24044	Clare, Meredith......	Flint and Pere Marquette R. R.	32.06	154	20	....
511	N. C ..	13018	University Station, Chapel Hill.	Richmond and Danville R. R.	11.33	152	11	no apt...............
512	S. C ...	14025	Green Pond, Walterborough.	Green Pond, Walterborough and Branchville R. R.	12.37	150	12	....do...............
513	W. Va.	12021	Tunnelton, Kingwood	Kingwood Rwy	10.95	150	11	....do ....
514	Mass..	3042	Nantucket, Siasconset.	Nantucket R. R	11.52	149	14	....do ....

States and Territories in which the contract term expired June 30, 1888, etc.—Continued.

Average trips per week.	Pay per mile per annum for transportation.	Pay per mile per annum for r.p.o. cars.	Former pay per mile per annum for transportation.	Former pay per mile per annum for r.p.o. cars.	Amount of annual pay for transportation.	Amount of annual pay for r.p.o. cars.	Former amount of annual pay for transportation.	Former amount of annual pay for r.p.o. cars.	Date of adjustment or re-adjustment.	Remarks.
	Dolls.	*Dolls.*	*Dolls.*	*Dolls.*	*Dollars.*	*Dollars.*	*Dollars.*	*Dollars.*	1888.	
6	42.75		43.61		1,357.74		1,385.92		July 1	Weighed 30 days from Feb. 20, 1888. 0.02 m. decrease.
12	42.75		37.62		884.07		777.98		July 1	Weighed 30 days from Mar. 19, 1888. New from Jan. 28, 1888.
14	42.75		37.62		147.91		130.16		July 1	Weighed 30 days from Feb. 20, 1888.
12	42.75		45.32		830.20		887.81		July 1	Weighed 30 days from Mar.19,1888. 0.17 m. increase.
12	42.75		31.64		978.97		861.49		July 1	Weighed 30 days from Mar. 19, 1888. From Oct. 24, 1887, on 15.28 m. ext. from Albany to New Glarus.
12	42.75		42.75		350.55		356.96		July 1	Weighed 30 days from Mar. 19, 1888. 0.15 m. decrease.
12	42.75		42.75		696.96		706.65		July 1	Weighed 30 days from Feb. 20, 1888. 0.18 m. decrease.
6	42.75		52.16		1,878.43		2,183.80		July 1	Weighed 30 days from Feb. 20, 1888. 0.06 m. decrease. 7.65 m. ext. Cotton Plant to New Albany from Aug. 8, 1887.
13	42.75		42.75		1,086.27		994.79		July 1	Weighed 30 days from Feb. 20, 1888. 2.14 m. increase.
7	42.75		36.77		4,557.57		3,920.04		July 1	Weighed 30 days from Mar. 19, 1888. New from Mar. 5, 1888.
6	42.75		42.75		506.58		510.00		July 1	Weighed 30 days from Feb. 20, 1888. 0.08 m. decrease.
9	42.75		42.75		437.33		430.06		July 1	Weighed 30 days from Mar. 19, 1888. 0.17 m. increase.
7	42.75		42.75		4,705.92		4,291.66		July 1	Weighed 30 days from Feb. 20, 1888. 0.33 m. decrease. 9.68 m.ext. Lumpkin to Louvale from July 1, 1887.
6	42.75		42.75		839.61		897.75		July 1	Weighed 30 days from Feb. 20, 1888. 1.36 m. decrease.
14	42.75		42.75		295.40		295.83		July 1	Weighed 30 days from Feb. 20, 1888. 0.01 m. decrease.
9.60	42.75		29.07		669.89		428.49		July 1	Weighed 30 days from Mar. 19, 1888. 0.93 m. increase.
6	42.75		42.75		1,370.56		1,267.53		July 1	Weighed 30 days from Mar. 19, 1888. 2.41 m. increase. Initial point formerly was Harrison Junction (n. o.).
6	42.75		42.75		484.35		477.09		July 1	Weighed 30 days from Feb. 20, 1888. 0.17 m. increase.
6.50	42.75		35.06		528.81		433.69		July 1	Weighed 30 days from Feb. 20, 1888. Service began April 8, 1887.
12	42.75		35.05		468.11		383.79		July 1	Weighed 30 days from Sept. 3, 1888. New from Mar. 5, 1888.
12	2.75				492.48				1887. July 1	Weighed 30 days from Aug. 15, 1887. New.

H.—*Table showing the re-adjustment of the rates of pay per mile on railroad routes in*

Index order.	State.	Number of route.	Termini.	Corporate title of company carrying the mail.	Length of route.	Average weight of mails, whole distance per day.	Miles per hour.	Size, etc., of mail-car or apartments.
					Miles.	*Lbs.*		*Feet and inches.*
515	Md ..	10028	Baltimore, Annapolis.	Annapolis and Baltimore Short Line R. R	28.22	148	24	no apt ....
516	Ind...	22051	Orleans, French Lick	Orleans, West Baden, and French Lick Springs Rwy.	18.76	146	18	....do...............
517	N. Y ..	6133	Hatfield, Norwood...	Rome, Watertown, and Ogdensburg R. R.	13.54	144	21	....do...............
518	Ala ...	17019	Chehaw, Tuskegee...	Tuskegee R. R	6.00	143	12	....do...............
519	Iowa ..	27057	Dows, Forest City....	Burlington, Cedar Rapids and Northern Rwy.	48.88	142	14	
520	Ind ...	22015	North Vernon, Rushville.	Cincinnati, Indianapolis, St. Louis and Chicago Rwy.	46.37	142	20	12 by 7, 1 l..........
521	Ky....	20013	Willard, Greenup....	Eastern Kentucky Rwy.	34.31	142	20	10 by 4.8, 1 l........
522	Dak...	35031	Rutland, Ellendale...	St. Paul, Minneapolis and Manitoba Rwy.	40.73	141	16	no apt ....
523	Mo...	29062	St. Louis, Union......	St. Louis, Kansas City and Colorado R. R.	59.91	140	20	12.7 by 7.3, 1 l.......
524	Ind ...	22049	Greensburgh, Columbus.	Cincinnati, Indianapolis, St. Louis and Chicago Rwy.	26.80	140	25	no apt ....
525	Ohio ..	21099	Adelphi, Kingston...	Cincinnati, Hocking Valley and Huntington Rwy.	10.99	140	15	....
526	Wash Ter.	48016	Colfax, Farmington..	Columbia and Palouse R. R.	27.81	140	15	no apt ....
527	Ohio ..	21077	Nelsonville, New Straitsville.	Columbus, Hocking Valley and Toledo Rwy.	19.80	137	23	8.4 by 6.7, 1¼ l........
528	Kans..	33083	Coffeyville, Morantown.	Kansas City and Pacific R. R.	73.64	136	20	12 by 7, 1 l...........
529	Kans..	33081	Olcott, Iuka..........	Kansas Southwestern R. R.	20.29	135	20	no apt ....
530	Ky....	20033	Dodge, Clay City.....	Kentucky Union Rwy.	14.82	134	18	....do...............
531	Ala ...	17021	Eufaula, Clayton.....	Eufaula and Clayton R. R.	21.48	134	16	....do...............
532	Ga....	15041	Cuthbert, Fort Gaines	Southwestern R. R...	22.41	133	18	....do...............
533	Ind ...	22030	Switz City, Bedford ..	Louisville, New Albany and Chicago Rwy.	41.53	132	10	6 by 5, 1 l ....
534	Dak...	35030	Rugby, Bottineau	St. Paul, Minneapolis and Manitoba Rwy.	38.10	132	16	no apt ....
535	Ky....	20019	Johnson's Junction, Hillsborough.	Cincinnati and Southeastern Rwy.	16.91	131	12	....do...............
536	Mich..	24059	Orono, Copley........	Grand Rapids and Indiana R. R.	14.62	130	13	....
537	S. C ...	14023	McCormick, Anderson.	Port Royal and Western Carolina Rwy.	59.46	129	18	8.4 by 6, 1 l..........
538	Ga....	15082	Suwanee, Lawrenceville.	Richmond and Danville R. R.	9.96	129	15	no apt ....

States and Territories in which the contract term expired June 30, 1888, etc.—Continued.

Average trips per week.	Pay per mile per annum for transportation.	Pay per mile per annum for r. p. o. cars.	Former pay per mile per annum for transportation.	Former pay per mile per annum for r. p. o. cars.	Amount of annual pay for transportation.	Amount of annual pay for r. p. o. cars.	Former amount of annual pay for transportation.	Former amount of annual pay for r. p. o. cars.	Date of adjustment or re-adjustment.	Remarks.
	Dolls.	*Dolls.*	*Dolls.*	*Dolls.*	*Dollars.*	*Dollars.*	*Dollars.*	*Dollars.*	1888.	
9	42.75	......	35.05	......	1,206.40	......	989.11	....	July 1	Weighed 30 days from Mar. 19, 1888. New from Dec. 5, 1887.
12	42.75	......	32.40	......	801.99	......	641.59	....	July 1	Weighed 30 days from Mar. 19, 1888. New from Aug. 1, 1887.
12	42.75	......	34.20	......	578.88	......	463.06	....	July 1	Weighed 30 days from Aug. 2, 1887. New from Mar. 14, 1887.
14	42.75	......	42.75	......	256.50	......	256.50	....	July 1	Weighed 30 days from Feb. 20, 1888.
6	42.75	......	34.20	......	2,083.76	......	1,671.01	....	Mar. 19	Weighed 30 days from Mar. 19, 1888. From Dec. 5, 1887, on 15.87 m. ext. from Garner to Forest City.
6	42.75	......	42.75	......	1,962.31	......	1,945.12	....	July 1	Weighed 30 days from Mar. 19, 1888. 0.87 m. increase.
6.84	42.75	......	42.75	......	1,466.75	......	1,466.75	....	July 1	Weighed 30 days from Feb. 20, 1888.
7	42.75	......	33.34	......	2,125.95	......	1,657.99	....	July 1	Weighed 30 days from Apr. 16, 1888. New from Aug. 25, 1887.
7.20	42.75	......	33.35	......	2,561.15	......	1,997.99	....	July 1	Weighed 30 days from Dec. 7, 1887.
8.78	42.75	......	42.75	......	1,149.54	......	1,149.97	....	July 1	Weighed 30 days from Mar. 19, 1888. 0.01 m. decrease.
12	42.75	....	30.78	......	469.82	......	343.81	....	July 1	Weighed 30 days from Mar. 19, 1888. 0.18 m. decrease.
6	42.75	......	33.34	......	1,188.87	......	927.18	....	July 1	Weighed 30 days from Mar. 19, 1888. New from July 1, 1887.
9	42.75	......	42.75	.....	846.45	......	852.43	....	July 1	Weighed 30 days from Mar. 19, 1888. 0.14 m. decrease.
7	42.75	......	33.35	......	3,148.11	......	2,455.89	....	July 1	Weighed 30 days from Mar. 19, 1888. New from Oct. 24, 1887.
7	42.75	......	32.49	......	867.39	......	659.22	....	July 1	Weighed 30 days from Mar. 19, 1888. New from Oct. 3, 1887.
9	42.75	......	42.75	......	633.55	......	630.56	....	July 1	Weighed 30 days from Feb. 20, 1888. 0.07 m. increase.
6	42.75	......	42.75	......	918.27	......	920.40	....	July 1	Weighed 30 days from Feb. 20, 1888. 0.05 m. decrease.
6	42.75	......	42.75	......	1,000.77	......	998.08	....	July 1	Weighed 30 days from Feb. 20, 1888. 0.18 m. increase.
6	42.75	......	42.75	......	1,775.40	......	1,772.84	....	July 1	Weighed 30 days from Mar. 19, 1888. 0.06 m. increase.
6	42.75	......			1,628.77	......	1,237.86	....	July 1	Weighed 30 days from Apr. 16, 1888. New from Aug. 8, 1887.
10.23	42.75	......	42.75	......	722.90	......	722.47	....	July 1	Weighed 30 days from Feb. 20, 1888. 0.01 m. increase.
6	42.75	......	42.75	......	625.00	......	606.19	....	July 1	Weighed 30 days from Mar. 19, 1888. 0.44 m. increase.
7	42.75	......	24.80	......	2,541.91	......	1,463.20	....	July 1	Weighed 30 days from Feb. 20, 1888. 0.46 m. increase.
6	42.75	......	42.75	......	425.79	......	415.88	....	July 1	Weighed 30 days from Feb. 20, 1888. 0.47 m. decrease.

H.—*Table showing the re-adjustment of the rates of pay per mile on railroad routes in*

Index order.	State.	Number of route.	Termini.	Corporate title of company carrying the mail.	Length of route.	Average weight of mails whole distance per day.	Miles per hour.	Size, etc. of mail-car or apartment.
					Miles.	*Lbs.*		*Feet and inches.*
539	Fla ...	16004	J. T. and K. W. Junction (n. o.), New Smyrna.	Atlantic and Western R. R.	26. 09	129	9	no apt ....
540	N. C ..	13025	Louisburgh, Franklinton.	Louisburgh R. R	10. 34	128	16	.......do........
541	Va	11040	Bristol, Tenn., Estillville, Va.	South Atlantic and Ohio R. R.	32. 51	126	20	.......do........
542	Cal....	46352	Arcata Wharf (n. o.), Blue Lake.	Arcata and Mad River R. R.	10. 60	128	8	.......do........
543	Wash. Ter.	43015	Marshall, Belmont ...	Spokane and Palouse Rwy.	42. 97	127	15	.......do........
544	Ala ...	17032	Elora, Tenn , Huntsville, Ala.	Nashville, Chattanooga and St. Louis Rwy.	27. 62	125	20	.......do........
545	N. C ..	13026	Warren Plains, Warrenton.	Warrenton R. R	3. 13	124	20	.......do........
546	Miss ..	18023	Durant, Tchula	Illinois Central R. R..	26. 57	123	12	.......do........
547	Kans..	33069	Benedict, Madison ...	Chicago, Kansas and Western R. R.	45. 65	122	12	7.6 by 8.6, 1 l ....
548	Fla ...	16008	Astor, Lane Park....	Florida Southern Rwy	34. 53	120	17	7.4 by 5.5, 1 l. to Eustis, 27 m. No apt. residue.
549	Tenn..	19024	Clarksville, Tenn., Princeton, Ky.	Louisville and Nashville R. R.	57. 53	119	17	9.10 by 8, 1 l..........
550	Ky....	20022	Mount Sterling, Cornwell.	Kentucky and South Atlantic R. R.	18. 70	118	12	no apt ....
551	Cal ...	46048	Colusa, Sites.........	Colusa and Lake R. R	21. 92	118	20	....do................
552	Ind ...	22042	New Castle, Rushville	Fort Wayne, Cincinnati and Louisville R. R.	24. 85	116	24	12 by 7.7, 1 l ......
553	Ga....	15028	Wadley, Louisville ..	Louisville and Wadley R. R.	10. 42	115	12	no apt...............
554	Ala...	17029	Anniston, Sylacauga.	Anniston and Atlantic R. R.	53. 96	115	15	....do........
555	Mass..	3078	Boston, Winthrop....	Boston, Revere Beach and Lynn R. R.	5	115	12	....
556	Mich..	24038	Iron River Junction (n. o.), Watersmeet.	Chicago and Northwestern Rwy.	54. 79	112	27	....

States and Territories in which the contract term expired June 30, 1888, etc.—Continued.

Average trips per week.	Pay per mile per annum for transportation.	Pay per mile per annum for r. p. o. cars.	Former pay per mile per annum for transportation.	Former pay per mile per annum for r. p. o. cars.	Amount of annual pay for transportation.	Amount of annual pay for r. p. o. cars.	Former amount of annual pay for transportation.	Former amount of annual pay for r. p. o. cars.	Date of adjustment or re-adjustment.	Remarks.
	Dolls.	*Dolls.*	*Dolls.*	*Dolls.*	*Dollars.*	*Dollars.*	*Dollars.*	*Dollars.*	1888.	
6	42.75	......	31.63	......	1,200.84	....	888.48	....	July 1	Weighed 30 days from Feb. 20, 1888. New from May 23, 1887.
12	42.75	......	42.75	......	442.02	....	444.60	....	July 1	Weighed 30 days from Feb. 20, 1888. 0.06 m. decrease.
6	42.75	......	31.64	......	1,389.80	....	1,028.61	....	July 1	Weighed 30 days from Feb. 20, 1888. New from Sept. 12, 1887.
6	42.75	......	31.63	......	453.15	....	335.27	....	July 1	Weighed 30 days from Mar. 19, 1888. New from July 1, 1887.
6	42.75	......		......	1,836.96	....	1,359.13	....	July 1	Weighed 30 days from Mar. 19, 1888. 27.18 m. Marshall to Rosalia from May 23, 1887; 15.79 m. ext. Rosalia to Belmont from Aug. 25, 1887.
6	42.75	......	31.63	......	1,180.75	....	873.62	....	July 1	Weighed 30 days from Feb. 20, 1888. New from Jan. 2, 1888.
12	42.75	......	42.75	......	133.80	....	133.80	....	July 1	Weighed 30 days from Feb. 20, 1888.
7	42.75	......	52.16	......	1,185.86	....	1,429.70	....	July 1	Weighed 30 days from Feb. 20, 1888. 0.84 m. decrease.
6	42.75	......	30.78	......	1,951.53	....	1,405.10	....	July 1	Weighed 30 days from Mar. 19, 1888. 10.96 m. Benedict to Coyville from Apr. 25, 1887; 34.67 m. ext. Coyville to Madison from Dec. 5, 1887. New.
6.78	42.75	......	49.50	......	2,729.16	....	2,814.23	....	July 1	Weighed 30 days from Feb. 20, 1888. 7.09 m. increase. Route curtailed to end at Lane Park from Sept. 17, 1888.
6	42.75	......	28.22	......	2,459.40	....	1,694.73	....	July 1	Weighed 30 days from Feb. 20, 1888. 27.83 m. ext. Newstead to Princeton from Feb. 13, 1888.
6	42.75	......	42.75	......	799.42	....	801.56	....	July 1	Weighed 30 days from Feb. 20, 1888. 0 05 m. decrease.
7	42.75	......	36.77	......	937.08	....	353.35	....	July 1	Weighed 30 days from Mar. 19, 1888. 12.31 m. ext. Colusa Junction to Sites from June 6, 1887.
6	42.75	......	47.88	......	1,062.33	....	1,191.73	....	July 1	Weighed 30 days from Mar. 19, 1888. 0.04 m. decrease.
6	42.75	......	42.75	......	445.45	....	454.00	....	July 1	Weighed 30 days from Feb. 20, 1888. 0.20 m. decrease.
12	42.75	......	42.75	......	2,306.79	....	2,167.22	....	July 1	Weighed 30 days from Feb. 20, 1888. 0.60 m. increase.
18	42.75	......	29.92	......	213.75	....	149.60	....	July 1	Weighed 30 days from June 1, 1888. New from Aug. 10, 1887.
7	42.75	......	42.75	......	2,342.27	....	1,892.57	....	July 1	Weighed 30 days from Mar. 19, 1888. 0.03 m. increase. former pay per m $29.92 on extension from Iron River to Watersmeet.

H.—*Table showing the re-adjustment of the rates of pay per mile on railroad routes in*

Index order.	State.	Number of route.	Termini.	Corporate title of company carrying the mail.	Length of route.	Average weight of mails, whole distance per day.	Miles per hour.	Size, etc., of mail-car or apartment.
					Miles.	*Lbs.*		*Feet and inches.*
557	N. J..	7042	Beach Haven, Manhawkin.	Pennsylvania R. R...	12. 03	111	24	no apt.............
558	Va....	11089	Pulaski City, Foster Falls.	Norfolk and Western R. R.	23. 95	111	20	....do.................
559	Ga....	15046	Sylvania, Rocky Ford	Sylvania R. R........	14. 97	109	10	....do.................
560	Mich..	24047	Flint, Fostoria	Flint and Pere Marquette R. R.	24. 45	109	15	....
561	Ga....	15017	Fort Valley, Perry ...	Southwestern R. R...	12. 98	108	15	no apt ....
562	Fla ...	16083	Ocala, Dunnellon.....	Silver Springs, Ocala and Gulf R. R.	25. 43	106	13	....do.................
563	Ala ...	17027	Montgomery, Pataburgh.	Montgomery and Florida Rwy.	46	105	10	....do.................
564	Tenn .	19012	Dunlap, Tenn., Bridgeport, Ala.	Nashville, Chattanooga and Saint Louis Rwy.	38. 06	104	20	8 by 6, 11 ....
565	Ga....	15029	Hartwell, Bowersville.	Richmond and Danville R. R.	10. 22	104	10	no apt ....
566	Dak ..	35032	Roscoe, Hillsview....	Chicago, Milwaukee and Saint Paul Rwy.	18. 74	103	12	....do.................
567	N. C ..	13029	Moncure, Pittsborough.	Pittsboro R. R	12. 31	102	16	....do.................
568	Ga....	15033	Talbotton, Bostick (n. o.).	Talbotton R. R.......	7. 04	101	14	....do.................
569	Ohio ..	21059	Junction with C., H. and D. R. R. (n. o.), Mount Healthy.	Cincinnati Northwestern Rwy.	7. 07	100	18	
570	Dak ..	35035	Doland, Groton.......	Chicago and Northwestern Rwy.	39. 24	98	18	no apt ....
571	Fla ...	16010	Sanford, Oviedo	Sanford and Indian River R. R.	17. 36	97	14	....do.................
572	Mo....	28055	East Lynne, Brownington.	Kansas City and Southern Rwy.	45. 40	96	20	7.8 by 7, 11 ....
573	Pa	8171	Forest House, Austin	Sinnamahoning Valley R. R.	9. 19	95	13	no apt ....
574	Ga....	15047	Americus, Buena Vista.	Buena Vista and Ellaville R. R.	29. 79	94	14	....do.................
575	Ala ...	17023	Birmingham, Pratt Mines.	Tennessee Coal, Iron and R. R. Co.	6. 80	94	6	....do.................
576	Minn .	26059	Elk River, Milaca....	St. Paul, Minneapolis and Manitoba Rwy.	33. 12	93	16	....do.................
577	Mich..	24012	Niles, Mich., South Bend, Ind.	Michigan Central R. R.	12. 12	93	18	....do.................

States and Territories in which the contract term expired June 30, 1888, etc.—Continued.

Average trips per week.	Pay per mile per annum for transportation.	Pay per mile per annum for r. p. o. car.	Former pay per mile per annum for transportation.	Former pay per mile per annum for r. p. o. cars.	Amount of annual pay for transportation.	Amount of annual pay for r. p. o. cars.	Former amount of annual pay for transportation.	Former amount of annual pay for r. p. o. car.	Date of adjustment or re-adjustment.	Remarks.
	Dolls.	Dolls.	Dolls.	Dolls.	Dollars.	Dollars.	Dollars.	Dollars.	1888.	
12	42.75		29.07		514.28		349.71		July 1	Weighed 30 days from Aug. 2, 1887. New from June 6, 1887.
6	42.75		29.07		1,023.86		696.22		July 1	Weighed 30 days from Feb. 20, 1888. New from June 20, 1887.
12	42.75		42.73		639.96		640.82		July 1	Weighed 30 days from Feb. 20, 1888. 0.02 m. decrease.
6	42.75		42.75		1,045.23		1,045.66		July 1	Weighed 30 days from Mar. 19, 1888. 0.01 m. decrease.
6	42.75		42.75		554.89		549.76		July 1	Weighed 30 days from Feb. 20, 1888. 0.12 m. increase.
6	42.75		29.07		1,087.13		739.25		July 1	Weighed 30 days from Feb. 20, 1888. New from Dec. 12, 1887.
6	42.75		23.94		1,966.50		1,154.74		July 1	Weighed 30 days from Feb. 20, 1888. 15 m. ext. Argus to Live Oak, from Sept. 26, 1887. Route curtailed to end at Pateburgh from Apr. 9, 1888.
6.92	42.75		42.75		1,637.06		1,061.90		July 1	Weighed 30 days from Feb. 20, 1888.
6	42.75		42.75		436.90		433.90		July 1	Weighed 30 days from Feb. 20, 1888. 0.07 m. increase.
6	42.75		28.21		801.13		528.65		July 1	Weighed 30 days from Mar. 19, 1888. New from Oct. 3, 1887.
12	42.75		28.21		826.25		847.26		July 1	Weighed 30 days from Feb. 20, 1888. From May 16, 1887, at $28.21 per m.
6	42.75		42.75		300.96		307.80		July 1	Weighed 30 days from Feb. 20, 1888. 0.16 m. decrease.
12	42.75		42.75		302.24		302.67		July 1	Weighed 30 days from Mar. 19, 1888. 0.01 m. decrease.
6	42.75		27.36		1,677.51		1,073.60		July 1	Weighed 30 days from Mar. 19, 1888. New from Dec. 15, 1887.
6	42.75		42.75		742.14		753.66		July 1	Weighed 30 days from Feb. 20, 1888. 0.27 m. decrease.
6	42.75		26.51		1,940.85		1,208.55		Jan. 23	Weighed 30 days from Jan. 23, 1888. 34.03 m. ext. Clinton to East Lynne, from July 15, 1887.
6	42.75		26.51		392.87		243.62		July 1	Weighed from Mar. 30, 1888. New from Jan. 16, 1888. Curtailed to end at Austin from Mar. 1, 1888, decreasing distance 3.07 m.
6	42.75		42.75		1,273.52		1,266.68		July 1	Weighed 30 days from Feb. 20, 1888. 0.16 m. increase.
12	42.75		42.75		290.70		288.12		July 1	Weighed 30 days from Feb. 20, 1888. 0.06 m. increase.
6	42.75		26.50		1,415.88		877.68		July 1	Weighed 30 days from Apr. 16, 1888.
6	42.75		42.75		518.13		531.38		July 1	Weighed 30 days from Mar. 19, 1888. 0.31 m. decrease.

II.—Table showing the re-adjustment of the rates of pay per mile on railroad routes in

Index order	State	Number of route	Termini.	Corporate title of company carrying the mail.	Length of route.	Average weight of mails whole distance per day.	Miles per hour.	Size, etc., of mail-car or apartment.
					Miles.	*Lbs.*		*Feet and inches.*
578	Ga ..	15053	Midville, Swainsborough.	Midville and Swainsborough R. R.	18.42	93	12	no apt................
579	Ill ...	23082	Streator, Ill., Knox, Ind.	Indiana, Illinois and Iowa R. R.	119.82	92	15	14.7 by 7.1, 11 ....
580	N. J...	7057	Manumuskin, Heislerville.	West Jersey R. R ...	9.10	92	17	no apt ....
581	Kans..	33071	Hoisington, Great Bend.	Kansas and Colorado R. R.	10.34	92	20	....do ....
582	Ohio .	21087	Huron, Norwalk....	Wheeling and Lake Erie Rwy.	14.63	90	16	....do ....
583	Ohio .	21048	Morgan Junction, Cumberland.	Cinn., Wheeling and New York R. R.	17.70	90	16	....do ....
584	Mich..	24053	Humboldt, Republic .	Duluth, South Shore and Atlantic Rwy.	8.61	90	20	....do ....
585	Ark...	29020	Pine Bluff, English ..	Pine Bluff, Monroe and New Orleans Rwy.	36.42	89	10	....do ....
586	Tex...	31062	Yoakum, Flatonia...	San Antonio and Aransas Pass Rwy.	30.15	89	13	....do ....
587	Ohio ..	21098	Ashtabula, Harbor..	Ashtabula Street R. R.	4.01	88	6	....do ....
588	Ark...	29023	Bald Knob, Augusta.	St. Louis, Iron Mountain and Southern Rwy.	14.05	87	10	....do ....
589	Va	11030	Suffolk, Va., Amboy, N. C.	Suffolk and Carolina R. R.	39.96	87	18	.... o ....
590	Mich.	24073	Pinconning, Gladwin.	Mich. Central R. R ..	26.28	87	16	... do ....
591	Fla ...	16017	Micanopy Junction (n. o.), Micanopy.	Florida Southern Rwy	3.86	86	8	....do ....
592	Ohio ..	21101	Danbury, Point Marblehead.	Lakeside and Marblehead R. R.	8.00	86	..	....do ....
593	Ga ..	15045	Bellmont, Jefferson ..	Gainesville, Jefferson and Southern R.R.	13.34	85	13	....do ....
594	Ky....	20035	Morganfield, Uniontown.	Ohio Valley Rwy....	13.31	83	19	....do ....
595	N. C ..	13021	Chadbourn, N. C., Conway, S. C.	Wilmington, Chadbourn and Conway R. R.	39.17	83	13	....do ....
596	Ind ..	22052	Kercheval, Cannelton.	Louisville, Evansville and St. Louis Rwy.	22.50	82	20	....do ....
597	Ala .	17031	Shelby Iron Works, Junction Station (n. o).	Shelby Iron Co......	6.67	82	16	....do . ...
598	Ky ..	20028	Kings Mountain Station, Yosemite.	Cinn. and Green River Rwy.	11.76	80	15	....do ....,

States and Territories in which the contract term expired June 30, 1888, etc.—Continued.

Average trips per week.	Pay per mile per annum for transportation.	Pay per mile per annum for r.p.o. cars.	Former pay per mile per annum for transportation.	Former pay per mile per annum for r. p. o. cars.	Amount of annual pay for transportation.	Amount of annual pay for r. p. o. cars.	Former amount of annual pay for transportation.	Former amount of annual pay for r. p. o. cars.	Date of adjustment or re-adjustment.	Remarks.
	Dolls.	Dolls.	Dolls.	Dolls.	Dollars.	Dollars.	Dollars.	Dollars.	1888.	
6	42.75	......	25.51	......	787.65	....	488.31	....	July 1	Weighed 30 days from Feb. 20, 1888. New from May 2, 1887.
6	42.75	......	26.50	......	5,122.30	....	3,175.23	....	Mar. 19	Weighed 30 days from Mar. 19, 1888. 9.41 m. ext. North Judson to Knox from Nov. 7, 1887.
10.21	42.75	......	26.50	......	389.02	....	241.15	....	July 1	Weighed 30 days from Mar. 19, 1888. New from Jan. 2, 1888.
7	42.75	......	26.50	......	442.03	....	274.01	....	July 1	Weighed 30 days from Mar. 19, 1888. New from May 9, 1887.
12	42.75	......	42.75	......	604.05	....	584.39	....	July 1	Weighed 30 days from Mar. 19, 1888. 0.46 m. increase.
9	42.75	......	42.75	......	756.67	....	756.67	....	July 1	Weighed 30 days from Mar. 19, 1888.
6	42.75	......	42.75	......	868.07	....	871.92	....	July 1	Weighed 30 days from Mar. 19, 1888. 0.09 m. decrease.
6	42.75	......	25.65	......	1,556.96	....	934.17	....	July 1	Weighed 30 days from Feb. 20, 1888. New from July 18, 1887.
6	42.75	......	25.65	......	1,288.91	....	773.34	....	July 1	Weighed 30 days from Feb. 20, 1888. New from Jan. 16, 1888.
18	42.75	......	42.75	......	171.42	....	171.00	....	July 1	Weighed 30 days from Mar. 19, 1888. 0.01 m. increase.
6	42.75	......	25.65	......	600.63	....	360.28	....	July 1	Weighed 30 days from Feb. 20, 1888. New from Nov. 28, 1887.
6	42.75	......	25.65	......	1,708.29	....	1,024.97	....	July 1	Weighed 30 days from Mar. 19, 1888. 25 m. Suffolk to Sunbury from Apr. 25, 1887; 14.96 m. ext. Sunbury to Amboy from Mar. 12, 1888.
6	42.75	......	25.65	......	1,206.97	....	725.38	....	July 1	Weighed 30 days from Mar. 19, 1888.
6	42.75	......	42.75	......	165.01	....	175.70	....	July 1	Weighed 30 days from Feb. 20, 1888. 0.25 m. decrease.
12	42.75	......	42.75	......	342.00	....	342.00	....	July 1	Weighed 30 days from Mar. 19, 1888.
6	42.75	......	42.75	......	579.28	....	577.55	....	July 1	Weighed 30 days from Feb. 20, 1888. 0.17 m. decrease.
12	42.75	......	24.79	......	569.00	....	329.95	....	July 1	Weighed 30 days from Feb. 20, 1888. New from July 25, 1887.
6	42.75	......	42.75	......	1,674.51	....	1,210.68	....	July 1	Weighed 30 days from Feb. 20, 1888. 7 m. ext. Mount Tabor to Loris from May 14, 1887; 18.84 m. ext. Loris to Conway from Jan. 23, 1888, at $24.79 per m.
12	42.75	......	24.79	......	961.87	....	557.77	....	July 1	Weighed 30 days from Mar. 19, 1888. New from Feb. 20, 1888.
12	42.75	......	23.09	......	285.14	....	138.54	....	July 1	Weighed 30 days from Feb. 20, 1888. 0.67 m. increase.
6	42.75	......	42.75	......	502.74	....	488.20	....	July 1	Weighed 30 days from Feb. 20, 1888. 0.84 m. increase.

H.—*Table showing the re-adjustment of the rates of pay per mile on railroad routes in*

Index order.	State.	Number of route.	Termini.	Corporate title of company carrying the mail.	Length of route.	Average weight of mails, whole distance per day.	Miles per hour.	Size, etc., of mail-car or apartment.
					Miles.	*Lbs.*		*Feet and inches.*
509	Ohio ..	21101	Danbury, Point Marblehead.	Lakeside and Marblehead R. R.	8.00	80	..	no apt ....
600	Kans..	32072	Colony, Neosho Falls	Chicago, Kansas and Western R.R.	12.17	80	20	....do ....
601	Mich .	24066	Cadillac, Lake City ..	Cadillac and Northeastern R.R.	13.65	80	18	....do ....
602	Mich .	24058	Narenta Station (n. o.), Metropolitan.	Chicago and Northwestern Rwy.	34.90	76	15	....do ....
603	Mich .	24062	Milwaukee Junction (n. o.), West Detroit.	Chicago, Detroit and Canada Grand Trunk Junction R. R.	4.64	76	13	....do ....
604	Ky....	20036	Glasgow Junc., Mammoth Cave.	Louisville and Nashville R. R.	8.51	75	18	....do ....
605	Tenn .	19019	Moscow, Somerville..	Memphis and Charleston R. R.	13.57	74	15	....do ....
606	Ky ..	20031	Madisonville, Providence.	Louisville and Nashville R. R.	16.67	72	16	....do ....
907	Pa	8168	Coalport, Cresson	Cresson, Clearfield County and New York Short Route R.R.	24.6	72	15	....
608	N. C ..	13017	Alma, Plainview	Alma and Little Rock R. R.	12.30	71	10	no apt ....
609	N. C ..	13028	Rocky Mount, Pine View.	Wilmington and Weldon R. R.	19.12	71	16	....do ....
610	Ohio..	21102	Killbuck, Warsaw	Cleveland, Akron and Columbus Rwy.	18.62	70	28	....
611	Fla ...	16027	Saint Augustine, Palatka.	St. Augustine and Palatka Rwy.	24.9	69	15	no apt.............
612	Ohio ..	21097	Saint Clairsville, Barton.	St. Clairsville Company, operating St. Clairsville and Northern Rwy.	4.36	68	15	....
613	Ga	15035	Roswell Junction (n. o.), Roswell.	Richmond and Danville R. R.	10.69	62	15	no apt.............
614	Miss .	18013	Stoneville, Johnsonville.	Georgia Pacific Rwy.	20.44	69	12	....do ....
615	Ala ...	17018	Dolomite, Wheeling Station (n. o.).	Woodward Iron Company.	4.60	65	4	....do ....
616	Minn .	26060	Hutchinson Junction (n. o.), Hutchinson.	St. Paul, Minneapolis and Manitoba Rwy.	53.40	64	24	....
617	Ill	23099	Rondout, Libertyville.	Chicago, Milwaukee and St. Paul Rwy.	8.28	63	12	....

States and Territories in which the contract term expired June 30, 1888, etc.—Continued.

Average trips per week.	Pay per mile per annum for transportation.	Pay per mile per annum for r. p. o. cars.	Former pay per mile per annum for transportation.	Former pay per mile per annum for r. o. cars.	Amount of annual pay for transportation.	Amount of annual pay for r. p. o. cars.	Former amount of annual pay for transportation.	Former amount of annual pay for r. p. o. cars.	Date of adjustment or re-adjustment.	Remarks.
	Dolls.	Dolls.	Dolls.	Dolls.	Dollars.	Dollars.	Dollars.	Dollars.	1888.	
12	42.75	......	24.80	......	342.00	....	210.80	....	Mar. 6	Weighed 30 days from Nov. 2, 1887. From Aug. 23, 1887, to Mar. 5, 1888, distance was 8.50 miles. New.
20	42.75	......	24.79	......	520.26	....	301.69	....	July 1	Weighed 30 days from Mar. 19, 1888. New.
12	42.75	......	42.75	......	583.53	....	583.53	....	July 1	Weighed 30 days from Mar. 19, 1888.
6	42.75	......	42.75	......	1,491.97	....	1,496.67	....	July 1	Weighed 30 days from Mar. 19, 1888. 0.11 m. decrease.
6	42.75	......	42.75	......	196.36	....	197.07	....	July 1	Weighed 30 days from Mar. 19, 1888. 0.03 m. increase.
14	42.75	......	23.94	......	363.80	....	203.72	....	July 1	Weighed 30 days from Feb. 20, 1888. New from Jan. 2, 1888.
6	42.75	......	42.75	......	580.11	....	576.69	....	July 1	Weighed 30 days from Feb. 20, 1888. 0.08 m. increase.
6	42.75	......	42.75	......	712.64	....	713.92	....	July 1	Weighed 30 days from Feb. 20, 1888. 0.9? m. decrease.
6	42.75	......	23.09	......	1,051.65	....	566.01	....	July 1	Weighed 30 days from Mar. 19, 1888. New from Aug. 1, 1887.
6	42.75	......	42.75	......	525.82	....	550.62	....	July 1	Weighed 30 days from Feb. 20, 1888. 0.58 m. decrease.
6	42.75	......	23.09	......	817.58	....	441.47	....	July 1	Weighed 30 days from Feb. 20, 1888. 10.73 m. Rocky Mount to Nashville, from May 2, 1887, at $23.09 per m.; 8.40 m. ext., Nashville to Pine View, from Jan. 9, 1888, at $23.09 per m.
10.32	42.75	......	23.08	......	796.00	....	429.74	....	July 1	Weighed 30 days from Mar. 19, 1888. New from Mar. 12, 1888.
12	42.75	......	20.52	......	1,064.47	....	548.08	....	July 1	Weighed 30 days from Feb. 20, 1888. 1.81 m. decrease.
14	42.75	......	42.75	......	186.39	....	185.96	....	July 1	Weighed 30 days from Mar. 19, 1888. 0.01 m. increase.
6	42.75	......	42.75	......	456.99	....	464.69	....	July 1	Weighed 30 days from Feb. 20, 1888. 0.18 m. decrease.
6	42.75	......	29.93	......	873.81	....	614.76	....	July 1	Weighed 30 days from Feb. 20, 1888. 0.10 m. decrease.
6.52	42.75	......	22.23	......	196.65	....	106.70	....	July 1	Weighed 30 days from Feb. 20, 1888. 0.20 m. decrease. New from June 1, 1886.
6	42.75	......	22.23	......	2,382.85	....	1,187.08	....	July 1	Weighed 30 days from Apr. 16, 1888.
6	42.75	......	22.23	......	140.22	....	72.91	....	July 1	Weighed 30 days from Mar. 19, 1888.

H.—*Table showing the re-adjustment of the rates of pay per mile on railroad routes in*

Index order.	State.	Number of route.	Termini.	Corporate title of company carrying the mail.	Length of route.	Average weight of mail, whole distance, per day.	Miles per hour.	Size, etc., of mail car or apartment.
					Miles.	*Lbs.*		*Feet and inches.*
618	Miss..	18006	Glendale, Eagle's Nest.	Louisville, New Orleans and Texas Rwy.	19.62	61	10	no apt...............
619	Ala ...	17028	Woodstock, Blockton	Cahaba Coal Mining Co.	9.16	60	17	....do...............
620	Ala ...	17022	Selma, Martin's Station.	Birmingham, Selma and New Orleans Rwy.	20.32	57	14	....do...............
621	Pa	8170	Luzerne, Alderson...	Pennsylvania and New York Canal and R.R. Co.	14.06	57	20	....do...............
622	Ky....	20810	Elizabethtown, Cecilian.	Newport News and Mississippi Valley Co.	6.22	56	15	....do...............
623	Fla ...	16632	Lake City, Fort White	Savannah, Florida and Western Rwy.	21.93	56	15	....do...............
624	Ky ...	20023	Louisville, Prospect.	Louisville and Nashville R.R.	11.03	55	11	....do...............
625	Ind ...	22847	Attica, Covington....	Wabash, St. Louis and Pacific Rwy.	15.78	54	15	....do...............
626	Ohio ..	21085	Fultonham, Redfield.	Columbus and Eastern R.R.	7.11	54	30	....
627	N.J ..	7056	Barnegat City, Barnegat City Junction (n.o.).	Pennsylvania R.R ..	8.94	53	22	no apt...............
628	Ill	23097	Marion, Parker City (n.o.).	St. Louis, Alton and Terre Haute R.R..	15.34	52	17	....
629	N.C...	18082	Hamilton, Tarborough.	Hamilton R.R. and Lumber Co.	20.65	50	10	no apt...............
630	Kans..	33080	Burlington, Gridley..	Chicago, Kansas and Western R.R.	11.32	50	25	....do...............
631	Mich..	24074	Rodney, Chippewa Lake.	Detroit, Lansing and Northern R.R.	5.91	48	10	....
632	Ill	23092	Galena, Galena Junction (n.o.).	Chicago, Burlington and Northern R.R.	3.79	47	15	....
633	Pa	8167	Keating, Karthaus...	Pennsylvania R.R...	22.17	47	18	no apt...............
634	Cal...	46054	Berenda, Raymond...	Southern Pacific R.R.	31.30	47	17	....do...............
635	Tenn..	19022	Keathley, Oliver Springs.	East Tennessee, Virginia and Georgia Rwy.	16.74	46	18	....do...............
636	Fla ...	16030	Jacksonville, Pablo Beach.	Jacksonville and Atlantic R.R.	17.38	45	21	....do...............

States and Territories in which the contract term expired June 30, 1888, *etc.*—Continued.

Average trips per week.	Pay per mile per annum for transportation.	Pay per mile per annum for r. p. o. cars.	Former pay per mile per annum for transportation.	Former pay per mile per annum for r. p. o. cars.	Amount of annual pay for transportation.	Amount of annual pay for r. p. o. cars.	Former amount of annual pay for transportation.	Former amount of annual pay for r. p. o. cars.	Date of adjustment or re-adjustment.	Remarks.
	Dolls.	Dolls.	Dolls.	Dolls.	Dollars.	Dollars.	Dollars.	Dollars.	1888.	
7	42.75	......	21.37	......	838.75		448.76	......	July 1	Weighed 30 days from Feb. 20, 1888. 1.38 m. decrease. 8.30 m. Glendale to Lula from May 9, 1857; 10.48 m. ext. Lula to Jonestown from June 13, 1887; 2.22 m. ext. Jonestown to Eagle's Nest from Nov. 21, 1887.
12	42.75	......	......	......	391.59		291.99	......	July 1	Weighed 30 days from Feb. 20, 1888. Former pay was by agreement with company. 0.49 m. increase.
4	42.75	......	29.93	......	868.68		628.53	......	July 1	Weighed 30 days from Feb. 20, 1888. Pay based on a service of not less than six round trips per week. 0.68 m. decrease.
8.99	42.75	......	21.38	......	601.06		300.60	......	July 1	Weighed 30 days from Mar. 19, 1888. New from Nov. 14, 1887.
12	42.75	......	42.75	......	265.90		272.31	......	July 1	Weighed 30 days from Feb. 20, 1888. 0.15 m. decrease.
12	42.75	......	21.37	......	937.50		468.64	......	July 1	Weighed 30 days from Feb. 20, 1888. New from Oct. 10, 1887.
8.18	42.75	......	42.75	......	471.53		470.25	......	July 1	Weighed 30 days from Feb. 20, 1888. 0.03 m. increase.
12	42.75	......	42.75	......	674.59		637.40	......	July 1	Weighed 30 days from Mar. 19, 1888. 0.87 m. increase.
9	42.75	......	42.75	......	303.95		......	......	......	Formerly part of Route 21069.
12	42.75	......	20.52	......	382.18		183.44	......	July 1	Weighed 30 days from Aug. 2, 1887. New from June 13, 1887.
6	42.75	......	20.52	......	655.78		314.77	......	July 1	Weighed 30 days from March 19, 1888.
6	42.75	......	20.52	......	882.78		423.73	......	July 1	Weighed 30 days from Feb. 20, 1888. From Feb. 13, 1888, at $20.52 per mile.
6	42.75	......	20.52	......	483.93		232.28	......	July 1	Weighed 30 days from Mar. 19, 1888. New from Aug. 25, 1887.
6	42.75	......	20.52	......	252.65		121.27	......	July 1	Weighed 30 days from Mar. 19, 1888.
12	42.75	......	20.52	......	162.02		77.77	......	July 1	Weighed 30 days from Mar. 19, 1888. From May 30, 1887, to June 30, 1888, at $20.52 per m.
6	42.75	......	20.52	......	947.76		454.92	......	July 1	Weighed 30 days from Sept. 2, 1887. New from June 6, 1887.
7	42.75	......	20.52	......	910.57		437.07	......	July 1	Weighed 30 days from Mar. 19, 1888. New from July 11, 1887
6	42.75	......	42.75	......	715.63		715.63	......	July 1	Weighed 30 days from Feb. 20, 1888.
6	42.75	......	20.52	......	742.99		358.68	......	July 1	Weighed 30 days from Feb. 20, 1888. 0.1 m decrease.

H.—Table showing the re-adjustment of the rates of pay per mile on railroad routes in

Index order.	State.	Number of route.	Termini.	Corporate title of company carrying the mail.	Length of route.	Average weight of mails, whole distance per day.	Miles per hour.	Size, etc., of mail-car or apartment.
					Miles.	*Lbs.*		*Feet and inches.*
637	Ohio ..	21050	Deshler, McComb....	Columbus, Findlay and Northern Rwy.	10.17	44	15	....
638	Tenn..	19021	Spring City, Balta....	Tennessee Central R. R.	9.32	42	12	no apt ....
639	Ark...	26022	Arkadelphia, Dalark.	Ultima Thule, Arkadelphia and Mississippi Rwy.	11.43	40	9	....do ....
640	Ill......	23091	Galewood (n. o.), Dunning.	Chicago, Milwaukee and St. Paul Rwy.	2.80	37	12	....
641	Pa....	8173	Silver Brook, Silver Brook Junction (n. o.).	Lehigh Valley R. R ..	2.61	35	12	no apt ....
642	Fla ...	16005	Pensacola, Millview..	Pensacola and Perdido R. R.	10.50	34	8	....do ....
643	Ga....	15055	Rogers, Summit......	Rogers and Summit R. R.	20.00	31	16	....do ....
644	Miss..	18011	Greenville, Stoneville	Georgia Pacific Rwy.	9.60	27	9	....do ....
645	Mich..	24050	Missaukee Junction (n. o.), Jennings.	Grand Rapids and Indiana R. R.	8.04	27	14	....do ....
646	Tenn..	19025	Victoria, Inman......	Nashville, Chattanooga and St. Louis Rwy.	5.68	25	12	....do ....
647	Miss ..	18012	Greenwood, Peete....	Illinois Central R. R .	18.12	25	11	....do ....
648	Mich..	24011	Slocum Junction (n.o.), Grosse Isle.	Michigan Central R.R.	2.41	25	15	... do ....
649	Colo ..	38032	Como, King	Denver, South Park and Pacific R. R.	3.48	24	8	....do ....
650	Ala ...	17026	Flomaton, Repton....	Louisville and Nashville R. R.	30.15	21	12	....do ....
651	Fla....	16013	Tallahassee, St. Marks.	Florida Rwy. and Navigation Co.	22.03	18	13	....do ....
652	Wis...	25065	Dexterville, Hogan...	Wisconsin, Pittsville and Superior Rwy.	15.72	17	12	... do ....
653	Ind ...	22055	Beesons, Hagerstown	White Water R. R ..	14.15	14	23	....do ....
654	N.C...	13031	Factory Junction (n. o.), Millboro.	Cape Fear and Yadkin Valley Rwy.	9.55	14	15	....do ....
655	N.C...	13022	D. M. and S. W. Junction (n. o.), Va., Leaksville, N. C.	Danville, Mocksville and Southwestern R. R.	8.21	37	15	...do ....

States and Territories in which the contract term expired June 30, 1888, etc.—Continued.

Average trips per week.	Pay per mile per annum for transportation.	Pay per mile per annum for r.p.o. cars.	Former pay per mile per annum for transportation.	Former pay per mile per annum for r.o. cars.	Amount of annual pay for transportation.	Amount of annual pay for r.p.o. cars.	Former amount of annual pay for transportation.	Former amount of annual pay for r.p.o. cars.	Date of adjustment or re-adjustment.	Remarks.
	Dolls.	*Dolls.*	*Dolls.*	*Dolls.*	*Dollars.*	*Dollars.*	*Dollars.*	*Dollars.*	1888.	
6	42.75	......	42.75	......	434.76	....	439.47	....	July 1	Weighed 30 days from Mar. 19, 1888. 0.11 m. decrease.
6	42.75	......	42.75	......	396.43	....	350.13	....	July 1	Weighed 30 days from Feb. 20, 1888. 1.13 m. increase.
6	42.75	......	20.52	......	486.63	....	234.54	....	July 1	Weighed 30 days from Feb. 20, 1888. New from Oct. 30, 1887.
12	42.75	......	20.52	......	119.70	....	57.45	....	July 1	Weighed 30 days from Mar. 19, 1888. From May 16, 1887, to June 30, 1888, at $20.52 per m.
6	42.75	......	20.52	......	111.57	....	53.55	....	July 1	Weighed 30 days from Mar. 19, 1888. New from Feb. 1, 1888.
6	42.75	......	42.75	......	448.87	....	438.18	....	July 1	Weighed 30 days from Feb. 20, 1888. 0.25 m. increase.
6	42.75	......	20.52	......	855.00	....	410.40	....	July 1	Weighed 30 days from Feb. 20, 1888. New from Nov. 7, 1887.
6	42.75	......	42.75	......	410.40	....	327.89	....	July 1	Weighed 30 days from Feb. 20, 1888. 1.93 m. increase.
6	42.75	......	20.52	......	343.71	....	165.18	....	July 1	Weighed 30 days from Mar. 19, 1888. 0.01 m. decrease.
5	42.75	......	28.21	......	242.88	....	589.98	....	July 1	Weighed 30 days from Feb. 20, 1888. 4.73 m. Victoria to Whitewell from Sept. 19, 1887; 14.41 m. ext. Whitewell to Dunlap from Feb. 20, 1888. Formerly part of route 19012.
6	42.75	......	20.52	......	774.63	....	371.82	....	July 1	Weighed 30 days from Feb. 20, 1888. New from Dec. 19, 1887.
6	42.75	......	42.75	......	103.02	....	100.80	....	July 1	Weighed 30 days from Mar. 19, 1888. 0.05 m. decrease.
6	42.75	......	20.52	......	148.77	....	71.40	....	July 1	Weighed 30 days from Mar. 19, 1888. New from Oct. 3, 1887.
3	42.75	......	17.96	......	1,288.91	....	536.46	....	July 1	Weighed 30 days from Feb. 20, 1888. 0.28 m. increase. Pay based on a service of not less than six round trips per week.
3	42.75	......	29.93	......	941.78	....	655.10	....	July 1	Weighed 30 days from Feb. 20, 1888. 0.14 m. increase. Pay based on a service of not less than six round trips per week.
6	42.75	......	20.52	......	672.03	....	322.57	....	July 1	Weighed 30 days from June 25, 1888.
6	42.75	......	55.56	......	604.91	....	....	....	July 1	Weighed 30 days from Mar. 19, 1884. Formerly part of 2103 1.
6	42.75	......	20.52	......	408.26	....	195.96	....	July 1	Weighed 30 days from Feb. 20, 1888. New from Feb. 6, 1888.
6	42.75	......	42.75	......	350.97	....	348.71	....	July 1	Weighed 30 days from Feb. 20, 1888. 0.24 m. increase.

REPORT OF THE POSTMASTER-GENERAL.

H.—*Table showing the re-adjustment of the rates of pay per mile on railroad routes in*

Index order.	State.	Number of route.	Termini.	Corporate title of company carrying the mail.	Length of route.	Average weight of mails whole distance per day.	Miles per hour.	Size, etc., of mail-car or apartment.
					Miles.	*Lbs.*		*Feet and inches.*
656	Cal....	46038	Goshen, Huron.......	Southern Pacific R. R.	40.56	259	22	no apt..............
657	Ga	15054	Americus, Abbeville .	Americus, Preston and Lumpkin R. R..	61.95	161	14	7.3 by 4.5 11. ....
658	Fla....	16019	Wildwood, Massacre.	Florida Railway and Navigation Co.	22.66	97	24	no apt ....
659	Ala ...	17029	Anniston, Sylacauga.	Anniston and Atlantic R. R.	53.36	103	15	....do.................
660	Mich..	24070	Howard City, Grand Rapids.	Detroit, Lansing and Northern R. R.	34.48	369	31	....do.................
			Total					
			Increase over former amount of pay by re-adjustment					

States and Territories in which the contract term expired June 30, 1888, etc.—Continued.

Average trips per week.	Pay per mile per annum for transportation.	Pay per mile per annum for r. p. o. cars.	Former pay per mile per annum for transportation.	Former pay per mile per annum for r. p. o. cars.	Amount of annual pay for transportation.	Amount of annual pay for r. p. o. cars.	Former amount of annual pay for transportation.	Former amount of annual pay for r. p. o. cars.	Date of adjustment or re-adjustment.	Remarks.
	Dolls.	Dolls.	Dolls.	Dolls.	Dollars.	Dollars.	Dollars.	Dollars.	1888.	
7	36.93	......	36.25	......	1,497.88	....	774.66	....	Mar. 19	Weighed 30 days from Mar. 19, 1888. 19.19 m. ext. Lemoore to Huron from May 10, 1887. Land grant.
7.	36.77	......	......	......	2,277.89	....	....	....	1887. Oct. 31	Weighed for 30 days from Feb. 20, 1888. 25.70 m. Americus to Gum Creek from July 1, 1887; 36.25 m. Gum Creek to Abbeville from Oct. 31, 1887. Consolidated with route 15050 from July 1, 1888.
6	34.20	......	34.20	......	774.97	....	537.74	....	1888. July 1	Weighed 30 days from Feb. 20, 1888. 0.01 m. increase. 9.99 m., Panasoffkee to Massacre, formerly at $17.78 per mile. Land grant.
6	28.22	......	42.75	......	2,167.22	......	1,945.98	....	1887. May 16	Weighed 30 days from Nov. 2, 1887. 7.86 m ext. Sycamore to Sylacauga from May 16, 1887.
6	4.10	......	4.10	......	141.36	....	141.36	......	1888. July 1	Weighed 30 days from Mar. 19, 1888. Lap service over route 24018.
	.....	.....	.....	.....	7,594,225.79 5,975,410.38	....	5,975,410.38			
	.....	.....	.....	.....	1,618,815.41					

Index to Table H.

Title.	Order.	No. of route.
Alabama Great Southern R. R	60	17015
Albemarle and Raleigh R. R	346	13020
Alma and Little Rock R. R	608	13017
America, Preston and Lumpkin R. R.	506	13050
Do	657	15054
Annapolis and Baltimore Short Line R. R	315	10028
Anniston and Atlantic R. R	854	17029
Do	650	17029
Arcata and Mad River R. R	542	46052
Ashtabula Street R. R	587	21098
Atchison, Topeka and Santa Fé R. R ..	90	13035
Atlanta and West Point R. R	80	15003
Atlantic and North Carolina R. R	237	13005
Atlantic and Western R. R	539	16004
Augusta, Gibson and Sandersville R. R.	485	15048
Baltimore and Ohio R. R	470	10027
Do	39	21001
Do	41	21010
Do	414	21038
Do	45	21047
Barnwell Rwy	484	14019
Bellaire, Zanesville and Cincinnati Rwy.	313	21063
Bellaire and St. Clairsville Rwy	425	21056
Bell's Gap R. R	383	8165
Birmingham, Selma and New Orleans R. R.	620	17022
Bloomsburg and Sullivan R. R	496	8172
Blue Ridge and Atlantic R. R	447	15043
Boston and Lowell R. R. Corporation	450	3018
Boston, Revere Beach and Lynn R. R.	555	3078
Bowling Green and Toledo R. R	448	21070
Brunswick and Western R. R	138	15023
Buena Vista and Ellaville R. R	674	15047
Burlington, Cedar Rapids and Northern Rwy	519	27057
Burlington and Missouri River R. R. (in Nebraska)	78	28064
Do	253	34046
Do	349	34049
Do	424	34055
Cadillac and Northeastern R. R	601	24066
Cahaba Coal Mining Co	619	17028
California Central Rwy	51	46053
Cape Fear and Yadkin Valley Rwy	351	13011
Do	654	13001
Carolina Central R. R	192	13003
Do	262	13008
Central Pacific R. R	14	46001
Do	64	46003
Central R. R. and Banking Co	207	15003
Do	67	15010
Do	43	15012
Central R. R. of South Carolina	205	14015
Chagrin Falls and Southern R. R	463	21079
Charleston and Savannah Rwy	35	14004
Chattaroi Rwy	332	20027
Chautauqua Lake Rwy	490	6135
Cheraw and Darlington R. R	289	14006
Cheraw and Salisbury R. R	355	14014
Cherokee and Dakota R. R	453	27099
Chesapeake and Nashville Rwy	406	19026
Cheyenne and Northern Rwy	445	37002
Chicago and Atlantic Rwy	201	21090
Chicago and Eastern Illinois R. R	95	22024
Do	431	23044
Chicago and Grand Trunk Rwy	107	24039
Chicago and Indiana Coal Rwy	359	22028
Do	375	22031
Chicago and Northwestern Rwy	483	23094
Do	106	24031
Do	214	24032
Do	556	24038
Do	602	24058
Do	272	27060
Do	296	35024
Chicago and Northwestern Rwy	570	35035
Chicago and West Michigan Rwy	79	24021
Do	153	24022
Do	340	24023
Do	194	24026
Do	472	24046
Do	213	24052
Chicago, Burlington and Northern R. R.	632	23092
Chicago, Detroit and Canada Grand Trunk Junction R. R	65	24028
Do	603	24002
Chicago, Kansas and Nebraska Rwy ..	154	36075
Do	216	33076
Do	185	33082
Do	338	34050
Chicago, Kansas and Western Rwy	257	33059
Do	433	33061
Do	245	33068
Do	547	33069
Do	600	33072
Do	185	33082
Do	337	33077
Do	630	33080
Do	373	33088
Chicago, Milwaukee and St. Paul Rwy.	640	23001
Do	119	23006
Do	617	23009
Do	230	25031
Do	498	25044
Do	183	27047
Do	118	27098
Do	189	35012
Do	379	35029
Do	566	35032
Do	327	35033
Chicago, St. Louis and Pittsburgh R. R.	7	21015
Do	4	21015
Do	99	23009
Do	148	22014
Do	102	22017
Chicago, St. Paul and Kansas City Rwy.	263	22095
Do	367	27069
Chicago, St. Paul, Minneapolis and Omaha Rwy	413	35036
Cincinnati and Green River Rwy	566	20028
Cincinnati and Muskingum Valley Rwy.	156	21029
Cincinnati and Southeastern Rwy	535	20019
Cincinnati, Georgetown and Portsmouth R. R	206	21060
Cincinnati, Hamilton and Dayton R. R.	40	21026
Cincinnati, Hamilton and Indianapolis R. R	106	21024
Cincinnati, Hocking Valley and Huntington Rwy	525	21099
Cincinnati, Indianapolis, St. Louis and Chicago Rwy	170	21071
Do	17	22003
Do	13	22005
Do	530	22015
Do	487	22016
Do	334	22045
Do	524	22049
Cincinnati, Jackson and Mackinaw R. R.	319	21075
Do	255	24019
Cincinnati, La Fayette and Chicago Rwy	15	22029
Cincinnati, Lebanon and Northern R. R.	361	21078
Cincinnati, New Orleans and Texas Pacific Rwy	34	20029
Cincinnati Northwestern Rwy	291	21059
Cincinnati, Richmond and Chicago R. R.	96	21025
Cincinnati, Sandusky and Cleveland R. R	144	21012
Do	467	21021
Do	94	21022
Cincinnati, Selma and Mobile Rwy	290	17006

Index to Table H—Continued.

Title.	Order.	No. of route.	Title.	Order.	No. of route.
Cincinnati, Wabash and Michigan Rwy.	208	22022	East Tennessee, Virginia and Georgia Rwy.	306	19011
Cincinnati, Washington and Baltimore R. R	260	21017	Do.	635	19022
Do.	315	21018	Eufaula and Clayton R. R.	531	17021
Do.	12	21028	Eutawville R. R.	451	14022
Do.	164	21049	Evansville and Indianapolis R. R	290	22026
Cincinnati, Wheeling and New York R. R.	583	21048	Do.	317	22080
Cleveland, Akron and Columbus Rwy.	183	21004	Evansville and Terre Haute R. R.	74	22012
Do.	610	21102	Do.	479	22039
Cleveland and Canton R. R	259	21009	Flint and Pere Marquette R. R	77	24015
Do.	223	21092	Do.	388	24042
Cleveland and Marietta Rwy	196	21040	Do.	510	24044
Cleveland and Western R. R	423	21081	Do.	168	24045
Cleveland, Columbus, Cincinnati and Indianapolis Rwy	53	21013	Do.	560	24047
Do.	59	21016	Do.	135	24048
Do.	22	21042	Do.	416	24049
Do.	426	21072	Florida Rwy. and Navigation Co	271	16001
Cleveland, Lorain and Wheeling R. R.	155	21041	Do.	248	16002
Cœur d'Alene Rwy. and Navigation Co.	417	42003	Do.	171	16006
Colorado Midland Rwy	324	38034	Do.	502	16009
Columbia and Palouse R. R.	526	43016	Do.	134	16011
Columbus and Cincinnati Midland R. R.	160	21094	Do.	651	16013
Columbus and Eastern R. R.	323	21069	Do.	658	16019
Do.	226	21085	Florida Southern Rwy.	548	16008
Columbus and Rome R. R	420	15024	Do.	141	16012
Columbus and Western Rwy	175	17007	Do.	146	16014
Do.	341	17016	Do.	591	16017
Columbus, Findlay and Northern R. R.	637	21050	Do.	211	16023
Columbus, Hocking Valley and Toledo Rwy.	125	21036	Do.	265	16026
Do.	167	21053	Fort Wayne, Cincinnati and Louisville R. R.	234	22090
Do.	150	21074	Fort Worth and Rio Grande Rwy.	449	31061
Do.	527	21077	Do.	232	34041
Do.	395	21084	Do.	115	34051
Colusa and Lake R. R.	551	46048	Fremont, Elkhorn and Missouri Valley R. R.	279	34052
Covington and Macon R. R	491	15052	Do.	275	34056
Cresson, Clearfield County and New York Short Route R. R.	607	8168	Do.	111	35037
Danville, Mockville and Southwestern R. R.	655	13022	Do.	429	37003
Dayton and Michigan R. R.	48	21023	Gainesville, Jefferson and Southern R. R.	469	15034
Dayton and Union R. R	372	21022	Do.	503	15045
Dayton, Fort Wayne and Chicago Rwy.	386	21039	Georgetown and Western R. R	408	14020
Do.	418	21054	Georgia R. R	68	15004
Denver and Rio Grande R. R	151	38018	Do.	410	15006
Do.	360	38023	Do.	321	15007
Denver, Memphis and Atlantic Rwy ..	246	33056	Do.	256	15021
Do.	302	33058	Georgia Midland and Gulf R. R.	434	15051
Do.	205	33084	Georgia Pacific Rwy.	102	15042
Denver, South Park and Pacific R. R.	649	38032	Do.	244	18005
Denver, Bay City and Alpena R. R....	124	24057	Do.	644	18011
Detroit, Grand Haven and Milwaukee Rwy	76	24027	Do.	614	18013
Detroit, Lansing and Northern R. R ..	180	24016	Grafton and Greenbrier R. R.	387	12012
Do.	75	24017	Grand Rapids and Indiana R. R	149	22021
Do.	230	24041	Do.	85	24018
Do.	660	24070	Do.	645	24050
Do.	631	24074	Do.	499	24056
Duluth, South Shore and Atlantic Rwy.	239	24040	Do.	536	24059
Do.	195	24051	Greenfield and Northern R. R	496a	28063
Do.	584	24053	Green Pond, Walterboro and Branchville R. R.	512	14023
Do.	241	24072	Gulf, Colorado and Santa Fé Rwy	187	31054
East Alabama R. R.	399	17014	Do.	266	31059
East and West R. R. of Alabama.	419	15020	Hamilton R. R. and Lumber Co	629	13032
Eastern Kentucky Rwy	521	20013	Hancock and Calumet R. R.	502	24068
East Tennessee and Western North Carolina R. R.	481	19018	Idaho Central Rwy	437	24069
East Tennessee, Virginia and Georgia Rwy.	163	15013	Illinois Central R. R	283	42004
Do.	488	15038	Do.	56	18001
Do.	247	17009	Do.	137	18002
Do.	169	17010	Do.	287	18009
Do.	52	19002	Do.	647	18012
Do.	159	19008	Do.	268	18018
Do.	174	19009	Do.	546	18023
			Indiana, Illinois and Iowa R. R.	579	22082
			Indianapolis and St. Louis Rwy	195	22025
			Do.	131	22043

Index to Table H—Continued.

Index to Table H—Continued.

Title.	Order.	No. of route.	Title.	Order.	No. of route.
Natches, Jackson and Columbus R. R..	136	18010	Pittsburgh, Cincinnati and St. Louis Rwy	2	21032
Natchitoches R. R...	427	30017	Do	3	21032
Nebraska Southern Rwy	152	34048	Do	177	21063
Nevada and California R. R.	284	45005	Do		
New Orleans and Northeastern R. R ..	120	18016	Pittsburgh, Marion and Chicago Rwy.	436	21063
Newport News and Mississippi Valley Co	110	20009	Pontiac, Oxford and Port Austin R. R.	325	21061
			Port Huron and Northwestern Rwy ..	277	24025
Do	622	20010	Do	204	24042
Do	104	20016	Do	409	24060
New York. Chicago and St. Louis Rwy.	202	21089	Port Royal and Western Carolina Rwy.	323	14010
New York, Lake Erie and Western R.R.	53	21005	Do	357	14021
Do	87	2'034	Do	537	14023
Do	320	21037	Do	471	14024
Norfolk and Western R. R.	538	11039	Do	270	15037
Northeastern R. R	31	14005	Prescott and Arizona Central Rwy	307	40003
Northern Pacific R. R	200	26061	Pueblo and State Line R. R.	300	38036
Do	4:2	36004	Raleigh and Augusta Air Line R. R .	228	13010
Do	306	36006	Raleigh and Gaston R. R	127	13001
Do	123	43005	Richmond and Danville R. R	109	13004
Do	112	43011	Do	130	13006
Oakley and Colby Rwy	466	33085	Do	82	13007
Ohio and Mississippi Rwy	23	22010	Do	331	13009
Do	63	22019	Do	145	13012
Do	458	22050	Do	371	13016
Ohio and Northwestern R. R	188	21052	Do	511	13018
Do	497	21066	Do	328	13022
Ohio, Indiana and Western Rwy	189	21057	Do	181	14001
Do	72	22018	Do	335	14007
Ohio Southern R. R	358	21058	Do	254	14008
Ohio Valley Rwy	281	20034	Do	504	14009
Do	594	20035	Do	258	14011
Omaha and North Platte R. R	461	34057	Do	495	14012
Orange Belt Rwy	440	160::9	Do	430	14013
Oregon Pacific R. R	376	44006	Do	811	14016
Oregon Rwy. and Navigation Co	378	43017	Do	21	15001
Do	71	44003	Do	235	15025
Do	48	44005	Do	391	15026
Oregon Short Line Rwy	58	37001	Do	565	15029
Orleans, West Baden, and French Lick Springs Rwy	516	22051	Do	538	15032
			Do	613	15035
Owensboro and Nashville R. R.	252	30014	Rogers and Summit R. R	643	15055
Oxford and Henderson R. R	403	13014	Rogersville and Jefferson R. R. (See		
Pacific Coast Rwy	382	46040	Tennessee and Ohio Rwy.)		
Pennsylvania and New York Canal and R. R. Co	621	8170	Rome R. R	415	15008
Pennsylvania Company	11	21002	Rome. Watertown and Ogdensburg R. R.	517	6132
Do	50	21003	Do	191	6136
Do	36	21006	Saginaw, Tuscola and Huron R. R.	432	24054
Do	261	21008	Saginaw Valley and St. Louis R. R.	225	24030
Do	212	21043	St. Augustine and Palatka Rwy	611	16027
Do	364	21044	St. Clairsville Co	612	21097
Do	473	21086	St. John's and Deland Rwy	400	16020
Do	209	22001	St. John's and Halifax R. R	298	16031
Do	179	22006	St. Joseph and Grand Island R. R.	442	34054
Do	61	22007	St. Louis, Alton and Terre Haute R. R.	628	23097
Do	240	22011	St. Louis and Chicago Rwy	394	23093
Pennsylvania R. R.	557	7042	St. Louis and Emporia R. R.	392a	33045
Do	627	7056	St. Louis and San Francisco Rwy	236	29019
Do	443	8099	Do	407	29021
Do	633	8167	Do	326	33049
Do	435	8174	Do	563	33087
Do	412	8175	St. Louis, Arkansas and Texas Rwy ..	293	31060
Pensacola and Atlantic R. R	222	16015	St. Louis, Fort Scott and Wichita R. R.	314	33073
Pensacola and Perdido R. R	642	16005	St. Louis, Iron Mountain and Southern Rwy	370	29014
Peoria, Decatur and Evansville Rwy ..	486	22041	Do	588	29023
Pine Bluff, Monroe and New Orleans Rwy	585	29020	St. Louis, Kansas City and Colorado R. R.	528	29062
Pittsboro R. R	567	13029	St. Paul, Minneapolis and Manitoba Rwy	576	26050
Pittsburgh and Western Rwy	398	21046	Do	616	26060
Do	339	21070	Do	296	35006
Pittsburgh, Cincinnati and St. Louis Rwy	97	21011	Do	805	35026
Do	16	21014	Do	182	35027
Do	18	21014	Do	584	35030
Do	173	21027	Do	522	35031
Do	84	21030	Salina, Lincoln and Western Rwy	345	33057

Index to Table H.—Continued.

Title.	Order.	No. of route.	Title.	Order.	No. of route.
Salina, Sterling and El Paso Rwy	285	23074	Terre Haute and Indianapolis R. R.	9	22044
San Antonio and Aransas Pass Rwy	312	31057	Toledo and Ohio Central Rwy	184	21055
Do	272	31058	Do	165	21068
Do	566	31062	Toledo and South Haven R. R.	494	24063
Sandersville and Tennille R. R.	480	15027	Toledo, Ann Arbor and North Michigan Rwy	129	24020
Sanford and Indian River R. R.	571	16010			
San Joaquin and Sierra Nevada R. R.	291	46043	Toledo, Columbus and Southern Rwy	392	21091
Savannah, Florida and Western Rwy	83	15009	Toledo, Saginaw and Muskegon Rwy	385	24076
Do	126	15018	Toledo, St. Louis and Kansas City R. R	274	21061
Do	231	15036	Do	304	21065
Do	172	15044	Do	278	22032
Do	623	16082	Do	468	22046
Savannah, Griffin and North Alabama R. R.	411	15022	Traverse City R. R.	217	24034
			Tuskegee R. R.	518	17019
Scioto Valley Rwy	80	21051	Ultima Thule, Arkadelphia and Mississippi Rwy	639	29032
Shelby Iron Co	597	17031			
Ship Island, Ripley and Kentucky R. R.	501	18008	Upson County R. R.	500	15019
Silver Springs, Ocala and Gulf R. R.	562	16033	Utah and Northern Rwy	88	41003
Simmahoning Valley R. R.	573	8171	Valley Rwy	199	21073
South and North Alabama R. R.	93	17004	Versailles and Midway Rwy	369	20439
Do	506	17024	Vicksburg and Meridian R. R.	98	18003
South Atlantic and Ohio R. R.	541	11040	Wabash, St. Louis and Pacific Rwy	29	21019
South Carolina Rwy	100	14003	Do	161	22027
Do	128	14017	Do	625	23047
Do	280	14018	Wabash Western Rwy	157	22054
Southern Kansas Rwy	384	32003	Warrenton R. R.	545	13026
Do	367	32004	Western and Atlantic R. R.	28	15002
Southern Pacific R. R.	656	46068	Western Rwy. of Alabama	82	17001
Do	143	46051	Do	117	17002
Do	634	46054	West Jersey R. R.	580	7057
South Florida R. R.	73	16007	West Virginia Central and Pittsburgh Rwy	318	12019
Do	489	16021			
Do	233	16024	Wheeling and Lake Erie Rwy	186	21089
Southwestern R. R.	249	15011	Do	582	21087
Do	81	15016	White Water R. R.	215	21031
Do	561	15017	Do	653	22055
Do	83	15039	Wilmington and Weldon R. R.	27	13002
Do	381	15040	Do	243	13015
Do	532	15041	Do	507	13019
Do	363	20021	Do	477	13027
Spokane and Palouse Rwy	543	43015	Do	609	13028
Suffolk and Carolina R. R.	589	11030	Do	465	13030
Sylvania R. R.	559	15046	Wilmington, Chadbourn and Conway R. R.	595	13024
Talbotton R. R.	568	15033			
Talladega and Coosa Valley R. R.	421	17030	Wilmington, Columbia and Augusta R. R.	42	14002
Tavares, Orlando and Atlantic R. R.	227	16023			
Taylor, Bastrop and Houston Rwy	377	31056	Wisconsin, Pittsville and Superior Rwy. Co., lessee of the Milwaukee, Dexterville and Northern Rwy	652	25065
Tennessee and Coosa R. R.	369	17020			
Tennessee and Ohio Rwy	402	19043			
Tennessee Central R. R.	638	19021	Woodward Iron Co	615	17018
Tennessee Coal and Iron Co	575	17023	Wrightsville and Tennille R. R.	368	15015
Terre Haute and Indianapolis R. R.	5	22002	Do	396	15049
Do	8	22002	York Harbor and Beach R. R.	390	28
Do	251	22013	Zanesville and Ohio River Rwy	385	21100
Do	6	22044			

I.—*Table showing the rate of pay per annum for the use of railway post-office cars for the as compared with 1887,*

No. of route.	State and termini.	Corporate title of company.	June 30, 1887.		
			Length of route.	Pay per annum.	Pay per mile.
	MAINE.		*Miles.*	*Dollars.*	*Dollars.*
6	Portland and Bangor	Maine Central R. R	138.00	13,800.00	100.00
12	Bangor and Vanceborough ...	......do	114.86	2,871.50	25.00
	NEW HAMPSHIRE.				
1001	Concord and Nashua..........	Concord R. R. Corporation ...	36.28	907.00	25.00
1008	Concord and White River Junction.	Boston and Lowell R. R. Corporation.	69.76	1,744.00	25.00
	VERMONT.				
2002	Windsor and Rouse's Point...	Central Vermont R. R	·158.77	....	....
Part.	Windsor and Saint Albans....	......do	120.50	3,012.50	25.00
2004	Bellows Falls and Windsor...	Sullivan County R. R	....	....	....
2005	Brattleborough and Bellows Falls.	Vermont Valley R. R. Co. of 1871.	....	....	....
2010	White River Junction and Derby Line.	Connecticut and Passumpsic Rivers R. R.	....	....	....
Part.	Newport and White River Junction.	......do	....	....	....
	MASSACHUSETTS.				
3001	Boston and Portland	Boston and Maine R. R........	109.35	10,935.00	100.00
3016	Boston and Nashua..........	Boston and Lowell R. R. Corporation.	39.85	996.25	25.00
3025	Boston and Albany	Boston and Albany R. R......	201.29		
Part.	Boston and Springfield	......do	98.63	} 24,959.75	{ 175.00
Part.	Springfield and Albany.......	......do	102.66		{ 75.00
3035	Boston and Providence	Boston and Providence R. R..	44.00	2,200.00	50.00
3062	Brattleborough, Vt., and New London, Conn.	Central Vermont R. R	....	....	....
Part.	Brattleborough and South Vernon Junction (n. o.).	......do	....	....	....
3067	Springfield and South Vernon Junction (n. o.).	Connecticut River R. R.......	....	....	....
	RHODE ISLAND.				
· 4002	Providence and Groton	New York, Providence and Boston R. R.	61.80	3,090.00	50.00
	CONNECTICUT.				
5004	New Haven and New London.	New York, New Haven and Hartford R. R.	51.78	2,589.00	50.00
5005	New York and Springfield....	......do	136.00	....	{ 190.00
Part.	New York and New Haven....	......do	73.37	} 22,708.50	{ 140.00
Part.	New Haven and Springfield...	......do	62.63		
	NEW YORK.				
6001	New York and Dunkirk	New York, Lake Erie and Western R. R.	459.55	....	....
Part.	New York and Hornellsville...	......do	331.16	} 21,628.40	{ 90.00
Part.	Hornellsville and Dunkirk....	......do	128.39		{ 40.00
6011	New York and Buffalo.......	New York Central and Hudson River R. R.	442.00	....	....
Part.	New York and Syracuse	......do	291.50	} 157,520.00	{ 370.00
Part.	Syracuse and Buffalo	......do	150.50		{ 330.00
6013	Syracuse and Rochester	......do	104.00	4,160.00	40.00 ·

fiscal years ending June 30, 1887, and June 30, 1888, and the increase or decrease of 1888 and the reasons therefor.

June 30, 1888.			Increase per annum of 1888.	Decrease per annum of 1888.	Number of lines and authorized length of cars, June 30, 1888.	Remarks.
Length of route.	Pay per annum.	Pay per mile.				
Miles.	*Dollars.*	*Dollars.*	*Dollars.*	*Dollars.*		
138.00	13,800.00	100.00	....	....	2 lines 60 feet...	
114.86	2,871.50	25.00	....	....	1 line 40 feet....	
36.28	907.00	25.00	....	....	1 line 40 feet....	
69.76	1,744.00	25.00	....	....	1 line 40 feet....	
158.77	....	....	....	....		
134.63	3,365.75	25.00	3.3.23	...?......	1 line 40 feet...	1 line 40 feet R. P. O. cars established Oct. 12, 1887, between Windsor and White River Junction, 14.13 miles.
25.50	637.50	25.00	637.50	....	1 line 40 feet ..	Established Oct. 12, 1887.
24.04	601.00	25.00	601.00	....	1 line 40 feet...	Do.
115.29	....	....	....	....	....	
105.15	2,628.75	25.00	2,628.75	....	1 line 40 feet ...	Do.
109.35	10,935.00	100.00	....	....	2 lines 60 feet ...	
39.85	996.25	25.00	....	....	1 line 40 feet....	
201.29	....	....	....	....	3 lines 55 feet, and 1 line 40 feet (45 feet reported).	
98.63	{ 24,959.75	{ 175.00	....	....	1 line 55 feet, and 1 line 40 feet (45 feet reported).	
102.66		{ 75.00	....	....		
44.00	2,200.00	50.00	....	....	1 line 55 feet	
121.39	....	....	....	....		
10.29	257.25	25.00	257.25	....	1 line 40 feet	Established October 12, 1887.
51.88	1,297.00	25.00	1,297.00	....	1 line 40 feet....	Do.
61.80	3,090.00	50.00	....	....	1 line 55 feet	
51.78	2,589.00	50.00	.. ..	...:....	1 line 55 feet	
136.00	....	{ 190.00	....	....	3 lines 55 feet and 1 line 50 feet (55 feet reported).	
75.37	} 22,708.50		....	....	2 lines 55 feet and 1 line 50 feet (55 feet reported).	
62.63		{ 140.00	....	....		
459.55	....	....	....	....		
231.16	} 31,628.40	{ 80.00	....	....	2 lines 50 feet ...	
128.39		{ 40.00	....	....	1 line 50 feet	
442.00	....	....	....	....		
291.50	{157,530.00	{ 370.00	....	....	5 lines 60 feet, and 3 lines 50 feet.	
150.50		{ 330.00	....	....	5 lines 60 feet, and 2 lines 50 feet.	
104.00	4,160.00	40.00	....	....	1 line 50 feet	

I.—*Table showing the rate of pay per annum for the use of railway post-office*

No. of route.	State and termini.	Corporate title of company.	June 30, 1887.		
			Length of route.	Pay per annum.	Pay per mile.
	NEW JERSEY.		*Miles.*	*Dollars.*	*Dollars.*
7004	New York and Philadelphia..	Pennsylvania R. R............	90.89	38,628.25	425.00
	PENNSYLVANIA.				
8001	Philadelphia and Pittsburgh..	Pennsylvania R. R............	352.90	97,047.50	275.00
8006	Sunbury and Williamsport ...	.....do	40.96	1,024.00	25.00
	MARYLAND.				
10001	Bay View (n. o.) and Philadelphia.	Philadelphia, Wilmington and Baltimore R. R.	91.80	9,180.00	100.00
10002	Baltimore and Sunbury.......	Northern Central Rwy	138.01	3,450.25	25.00
10003	Baltimore and Bellaire.......	Baltimore and Ohio R. R.....	390.39		
Part.	Baltimore and Grafton.......	.....do	293.75	39,115.60	120.00
Part.	Grafton and Bellaire..........	.....do	96.64		40.00
10006	Baltimore and Williamsport..	Western Maryland R. R......	93.14		
Part.	Baltimore and Hagerstown ...	.....do	86.60	2,165.00	25.00
10013	Bay View (n. o.) and Washington.	Baltimore and Potomac R. R..	45.40	4,540.00	100.00
	VIRGINIA.				
11001	Washington and Richmond ...	Richmond, Fredericksburgh and Potomac R. R.	115.90	13,908.00	120.00
11002	Alexandria and Lynchburgh..	Richmond and Danville R. R	166.40	19,136.00	115.00
11008	Richmond and Petersburgh ..	Richmond and Petersburgh R. R.	23.39	1,871.20	80.00
11009	Petersburgh and Weldon.....	Petersburgh R. R............	64.00	5,120.00	80.00
11013	Lynchburgh and Roanoke, Roanoke and Bristol.	Norfolk and Western R. R..	54.24 / 150.16	8,864.00	25.00 / 50.00
11016	Lynchburgh and Danville Junction (n. o)	Richmond and Danville R. R..	65.72	5,914.80	90.00
11018	Washington and Alexandria	Alexandria and Washington R. R.	7.42	853.30	115.00
11021	Hagerstown and Roanoke....	Shenandoah Valley R. R	239.80	5,995.00	25.00
11038	North Danville and Charlotte.	Richmond and Danville R. R	143.21	12,888.90	90.00
	WEST VIRGINIA.				
12002	Grafton and Parkersburgh ...	Baltimore and Ohio R. R	104.50	8,360.00	80.00
	NORTH CAROLINA.				
13002	Weldon and Wilmington......	Wilmington and Weldon R. R.	162.07	12,965.60	80.00
	SOUTH CAROLINA.				
14002 Part.	Florence and Wilmington..	Wilmington, Columbia and Augusta R. R.	110.00	7,150.00	65.00
14004	Charleston and Savannah.....	Charleston and Savannah Rwy	115.00	7,475.00	65.00
14005	Charleston and Florence......	Northeastern R. R............	102.00	6,630.00	65.00
	GEORGIA.				
15001	Atlanta and Air-Line Junction (n. o.).	Richmond and Danville R. R..	268.03	24,122.70	90.00
15002	Atlanta and Chattanooga....	Western and Atlantic R. R...	138.47	12,462.30	90.00
15003	Atlanta and West Point.......	Atlanta and West Point R R.	87.36	4,368.00	50.00
15009	Savannah and Jacksonville...	Savannah, Florida and Western Rwy.	171.50	11,147.50	65.00
	ALABAMA.				
17001	Montgomery and West Point .	Western Rwy. Co. of Alabama	86.21	4,310.50	50.00
17012	Mobile and Montgomery......	Louisville and Nashville R. R.	180.57	9,028.50	50.00
17013	Mobile and New Orleans......	.....do	141.43	7,071.50	50.00
	MISSISSIPPI.				
18001	New Orleans and Cairo.......	Illinois Central R. R	550.80	16,524.00	30.00

cars for the fiscal year ending June 30, 1887, *and June* 30, 1888, *etc.*—Continued.

June 30, 1888.			Increase per annum of 1888.	Decrease per annum of 1888.	Number of lines and authorised length of cars, June 30, 1888.	Remarks.
Length of route.	Pay per annum.	Pay per mile.				
Miles.	*Dollars.*	*Dollars.*	*Dollars.*	*Dollars.*		
90. 89	38, 628. 25	425. 00			8 lines 60 feet, and 1 line 40 feet.	
353. 90	97, 047. 50	275. 00			5 lines 60 feet, and 1 line 40 feet.	
40. 96	1, 024. 00	25. 00			1 line 40 feet ...	
91. 80	9, 180. 00	100. 00			2 lines 60 feet (3 lines reported).	
138. 01	3, 450. 25	25. 00			1 line 40 feet	
390. 99						
293. 75	39, 115. 60	120. 00			3 lines 50 feet ...	
96. 64		40. 00			1 line 50 feet ...	
93. 14						
86. 60	2, 165. 00	25. 00			1 line 40 feet ...	
45. 40	4, 540. 00	100. 00			2 lines 60 feet (3 lines reported).	
115. 90	13, 908. 00	120. 00			3 lines 50 feet...	
166. 40	19, 136. 00	115. 00			1 line 60 feet; 1 line 50 feet; 1 line 40 feet.	
23. 39	1, 871. 20	80. 00			2 lines 50 feet...	
64. 00	5, 120. 00	80. 00			2 lines 50 feet...	
54. 24	8, 884. 00	25. 00			1 line 40 feet....	
150. 16		50. 00			2 lines 40 feet...	
65. 72	5, 914. 80	90. 00			1 line 60 feet; 1 line 50 feet.	
7. 42	853. 30	115. 00			1 line 60 feet; 1 line 50 feet; 1 line 40 feet.	
239. 80	5, 995. 00	25. 00			1 line 40 feet...	
143. 21	12, 888. 90	90. 00			1 line 60 feet; 1 line 40 feet.	
104. 50	8, 360. 00	80. 00			2 lines 50 feet ...	
162. 07	12, 965. 60	80. 00			2 lines 50 feet...	
110. 00	7, 150. 00	65. 00			1 line 50 feet; 1 line 40 feet.	
115. 00	7, 475. 00	65. 00			1 line 50 feet; 1 line 40 feet.	
102. 00	6, 630. 00	65. 00			1 line 50 feet; 1 line 40 feet.	
268. 03	24, 122. 70	90. 00			1 line 60 feet; 1 line 50 feet.	
138. 47	12, 462. 30	90. 00			1 line 50 feet; 2 lines 40 feet.	
87. 36	4, 368. 00	50. 00			2 lines 40 feet...	
171. 50	11, 147. 50	65. 00			1 line 50 feet; 1 line 40 feet.	
86. 21	4, 310. 50	50. 00			2 lines 40 feet...	
180. 57	9, 028. 50	50. 00			2 lines 40 feet...	
141. 43	7, 071. 50	50. 00			2 lines 40 feet...	
550. 80	16, 524. 00	30. 00			1 line 45 feet....	

I.—*Table showing the rate of pay per annum for the use of railway post-office*

No. of route.	State and termini.	Corporate title of company.	June 30, 1887.		
			Length of route.	Pay per annum.	Pay per mile.
			Miles.	*Dollars.*	*Dollars.*
	TENNESSEE.				
19002	Bristol and Chattanooga......	East Tennessee, Virginia and Georgia Rwy.	242. 17	12, 1t8. 50	50. 00
	KENTUCKY.				
20004	Cincinnati and Louisville....	Louisville and Nashville R. R.	109. 00	6, 540. 00	60. 00
20005	Louisville and Nashville......	......do	185. 00	11, 100. 00	60. 00
20008	Bowling Green and Memphis..	......do	263. 15	7, 894. 50	30. 00
20017	Cincinnati Junction (D. o.) and Sax.	......do	4. 50	270. 00	60. 00
20029	Cincinnati, Ohio, and Chatta- nooga, Tenn.	Cincinnati, New Orleans and Texas Pacific Rwy.	338. 20	8, 455. 00	25. 00
	OHIO.				
21001 Part.	} Bellaire and Newark........	Central Ohio R. R	105. 47	4, 218. 89	40. 00
21002	Pittsburgh and Chicago......	Pennsylvania Co..............	468. 20	23, 410. 00	50. 00
21007	Elyria and Millbury..........	Lake Shore and Michigan Southern Rwy.	74. 90	10, 486. 00	140. 00
21010 Part.	} Chicago and Newark	Baltimore and Ohio R. R.....	88. 79	3, 551. 80	40. 00
21014	Columbus and Cincinnati....	Pittsburgh, Cincinnati and St. Louis Rwy.	120. 05	12, 005. 00	100. 00
21015	Columbus and Indianapolis...	Chicago, St. Louis and Pitts- burgh R. R.	188. 55	32, 996. 25	175. 00
21016	Galion and Indianapolis......	Cleveland, Columbus, Cincin- nati and Indianapolis Rwy.	204. 07	5, 101. 75	25. 00
21019	{ Toledo and La Fayette.... La Fayette and Decatur... Decatur and Quincy...... }	Wabash, St. Louis and Paci- fic Rwy.	{ 204. 70 117. 40 151. 27	} 26, 851. 80	{ 56. 00 90. 00 40. 00
21028	Cincinnati and Parkersburgh	Cincinnati, Washington and Baltimore R. R.	195. 15	15, 612. 00	80. 00
21032	Columbus and Pittsburgh....	Pittsburgh, Cincinnati and St. Louis Rwy.	191. 85	52, 758. 75	275. 00
21042	{ Cleveland and Galion...... Galion and Indianapolis... }	Cleveland, Columbus, Cincin- nati and Indianapolis Rwy.	{ 80. 00 164. 80	} 14, 230. 00	{ 75. 00 50. 00
21045	Toledo and Elkhart..........	Lake Shore and Michigan Southern Rwy.	133. 80	25, 422. 00	190. 00
21047	Chicago, Ohio, and Chicago, Ill.	Baltimore and Ohio R. R	271. 00	10, 840. 00	40. 00
21095	{ Buffalo and Cleveland.....		[183. 20		[330. 00
	Cleveland and Elyria......		25. 50.		355. 00
	Elyria and Millbury.......	Lake Shore and Michigan Southern Rwy.	79. 30	} 142,805.00	215. 00
	Millbury and Toledo		8. 00		355. 00
	Toledo and Elkhart........		142. 70		140. 00
	Elkhart and Chicago...... }		[101. 30		[330. 00
	INDIANA.				
22002	Indianapolis and Terre Haute	Terre Haute and Indianapolis R. R.	74. 39	13, 018. 25	175. 00
22003	Indianapolis and Cincinnati..	Cincinnati, Indianapolis. St. Louis and Chicago R. R.	111. 40	10, 026. 00	90. 00
22005	Indianapolis and La Fayette..	......do	64. 79	5, 831. 10	90. 00
22010	Cincinnati and East Saint Louis.	Ohio and Mississippi Rwy....	338. 20	23, 674. 00	70. 00
22025	Indianapolis and Terre Haute.	Indianapolis and St. Louis R. R.	73. 29	1, 832. 25	25. 00
22029	La Fayette and Kankakee...	Cincinnati, La Fayette and Chicago R. R.	72. 75	6, 547. 50	90. 00
22043	Terre Haute and East Saint Louis.	Indianapolis and St. Louis Rwy.	190. 13	4, 753. 25	25. 00
22044	Terre Haute and East Saint Louis.	Terre Haute and Indianapolis R. R.	166. 69	29, 170. 75	175. 00

cars for the fiscal year ending June 30, 1887, and June 30, 1889, etc.—Continued.

June 30, 1888.			Increase per annum of 1888	Decrease per annum of 1888	Number of lines and authorized length of cars, June 30, 1888.	Remarks.
Length of route.	Pay per annum.	Pay per mile.				
Miles.	*Dollars.*	*Dollars.*	*Dollars.*	*Dollars.*		
242.17	12,108.50	50.00	....	....	2 lines 40 feet ..	
109.00	6,540.00	60.00			2 lines 45 feet..	
185.00	11,100.00	60.00			2 lines 45 feet..	
263.15	7,894.50	30.00			1 line 45 feet...	
4.50	270.00	60.00			2 lines 45 feet...	
338.20	16,910.00	50.00	8,455.00		2 lines 40 feet....	1 line 40 feet cars established February 1, 1888.
105.47	4,218.80	40.00			1 line 50 feet....	
468.20	23,410.00	50.00			1 line 60 feet....	
74.90	10,486.00	140.00			2 lines 60 ft.; 1 line 50 ft.	
88.79	3,551.60	40.00			1 line 50 feet...	
120.05	12,005.00	100.00			2 lines 60 feet...	
188.55	42,423.75	225.00	9,427.50		4 lines 60 ft.; 1 line 40 ft.	1 line 60 feet cars established March 13, 1887.
204.07	5,101.75	25.00			1 line 40 feet...	
204.70 117.40 151.27 }	26,851.90	{ 50.00 90.00 40.00 }	{		1 line 60 feet .. 1 line 60 ft.; 1 line 50 ft. 1 line 50 feet ...	
195.15	15,612.00	80.00			2 lines 50 feet...	
191.85	62,351.25	325.00	9,592.50		6 lines 60 ft.; 1 line 40 ft.	1 line 60 feet cars established March 13, 1887.
80.00 164.60 133.60 }	14,230.00 25,422.00	75.00 50.00 190.00			3 lines 40 feet... 2 lines 40 feet... 3 lines 60 ft. ; 1 line 50 feet.	
271.00	10,840.00	40.00			1 line 50 feet....	
183.20		330.00			2 lines 50 ft.; 5 lines 60 feet.	
25.50		335.00			1 line 40 ft.; 2 lines 50 ft.; 5 lines 60 feet.	
79.30	142,805.00	215.00			1 line 40 ft.; 1 line 50 ft.; 3 lines 60 feet.	
8.00		355.00			1 line 40 ft.; 2 lines 50 ft.; 5 lines 60 feet.	
142.70		140.00			1 line 50 ft.; 2 lines 60 feet.	
101.30		330.00			2 lines 50 ft.; 5 lines 60 feet.	
74.39	16,737.75	225.00	3,719.50		4 lines 60 feet; 1 line 40 feet.	1 line 60 feet cars established March 13, 1887.
111.40	10,026.00	90.00			1 line 60 feet; 1 line 50 feet.	
64.79	5,831.10	90.00			1 line 60 feet; 1 line 50 feet.	
338.20	23,674.00	70.00			1 line 50 feet; 1 line 45 feet.	
....	....	....	....	1,832.25	....	1 line 40 feet cars discontinued from July 10, 1888. Increase in distance.
75.79	6,821.10	90.00	273.60		1 line 60 feet; 1 line 50 feet.	
....				4,753.25		1 line 40 feet cars discontinued from July 10, 1888.
166.69	37,505.25	225.00	8,334.50		4 lines 60 feet; 1 line 40 feet.	1 line 60 feet cars established March 13, 1888.

I.—Table showing the rate of pay per annum for the use of railway post-office

No. of route.	State and termini.	Corporate title of company.	June 30, 1887.		
			Length of route.	Pay per annum.	Pay per mile.
	ILLINOIS.		*Miles.*	*Dollars.*	*Dollars.*
23001	Chicago, Ill., and Milwaukee, Wis.	Chicago and Northwestern Rwy.	85. 37	2, 134. 25	25. 00
23002	Chicago and Freeport...........	.....do	121. 39	4, 855. 60	40. 00
23003	Chicago, Ill., and Union Pacific Transfer (n. o), Iowa.	......lo	490. 14	23, 296. 80	.....
Part.	Chicago and Cedar Rapids....	.....do	216. 32	....	65. 00
Part.	Cedar Rapids and Missouri Valley.	.....do	251. 02	....	50. 00
Part.	Missouri Valley and Council Bluffs.	.....do	21. 40	....	75. 00
Part.	Council Bluffs and Union Pacific Transfer (n o.).	.....do	1. 40	....	50. 00
23007	Chicago, Ill., and Burlington, Iowa.	Chicago, Burlington and Quincy R. R.	206. 00	48, 645. 00	....
Part.	Chicago and Aurora	.....do	37. 00	....	265. 00
Part.	Aurora and Galesburgh	.....do	126. 00	....	240. 00
Part.	Galesburgh and Burlington...	.....do	43. 00	....	200. 00
23010	Galesburgh and Quincy.......	.....do	101. 09	6, 570. 85	65. 00
23015	Chicago, Ill., and Davenport, Iowa.	Chicago, Rock Island and Pacific Rwy.	182. 92	11, 889. 80	65. 00
23017	Chicago and East Saint Louis	Chicago and Alton R. R	281. 17	22, 493. 60	80. 00
23020	Chicago and Cairo...........	Illinois Central R. R	365. 53	20, 469. 05	....
Part.	Chicago and Kankakee......	.....do	55. 87	....	140. 00
Part.	Kankakee and Centralia......	......do	196. 23	....	50. 00
Part.	Centralia and Cairo..........	......do	113. 43	....	25. 00
23021	Dubuque, Iowa, and Centralia, Ill.	......do	345. 14	4, 884. 15	....
Part.	Dubuque and Freeport.......	......do	69. 56	....	65. 00
Part.	Freeport and Forreston	......do	12. 51	....	25. 00
23023	Decatur and East Saint Louis..	Wabash, Saint Louis and Pacific Rwy.	113. 44	5, 672. 00	50. 00
23035	Chicago, Ill., and Milwaukee, Wis.	Chicago, Milwaukee and Saint Paul Rwy.	86. 18	15, 081. 50	175. 00
23036	Aurora and Forreston	Chicago and Iowa R. R.	81. 57	2, 03). 25	25. 00
23054	Chicago and Lanark Junction (n. o.).	Chicago, Milwaukee and Saint Paul Rwy.	116. 50	2, 912. 50	25. 00
	MICHIGAN.				
24006	Detroit, Mich., and Chicago, Ill.	Michigan Central R. R........	285. 10	18, 531. 50	65. 00
	WISCONSIN.				
25001	Milwaukee, Wis., and North McGregor, Iowa.	Chicago, Milwaukee and Saint Paul Rwy.	....	....	....
25002	Milwaukee and La Crosse	.....do	197. 95	32, 019. 50	....
Part.	Milwaukee and Portage	.....do	93. 08	....	175. 00
Part.	Portage and La Crosse.......	.....do	104. 87	....	150. 00
25009	Chicago, Ill., and Fort Howard, Wis.	Chicago and Northwestern Rwy.	242. 70	12, 216. 00	....
Part.	Chicago and Harvard........	.....do	62. 70	....	80. 00
Part.	Harvard and Fort Howard....	.....do	180. 00	....	40. 00
25010	Caledonia, Ill., and Winona Junction (n. o.), Wis.	.....do	189. 52	7, 580. 80	40. 00
25011	Kenosha, Wis., and Rockford, Ill.	.....do	72. 40	....	....
Part.	Harvard and Caledonia......	.... do	14. 80	592. 00	40. 00
25014	Winona, Minn., and La Crosse, Wis.	.... do	34. 07	....	....
Part.	Winona and Winona Junction (n. o.).	.... do	29. 82	1, 192. 80	40. 00
25024	Racine, Wis., and Rock Island, Ill.	Chicago, Milwaukee and Saint Paul Rwy.	197. 91	....	....
Part.	Lanark Junction (n. o.) and Savanna, Ill.	.....do	22. 00	550. 00	25. 00

cars for the fiscal years ending June 30, 1887, and June 30, 1888, etc.—Continued.

June 30, 1888.			Increase per annum of 1888.	Decrease per annum of 1888.	Number of lines and authorised length of cars, June 30, 1888.	Remarks.
Length of route.	Pay per annum.	Pay per mile.				
Miles.	*Dollars.*	*Dollars.*	*Dollars.*	*Dollars.*		
85.40	2,135.00	25.00	0.75	....	1 line 40 feet ...	Increase in distance.
121.30	4,862.00	40.00	....	3.60	1 line 50 feet....	Decrease in distance.
488.90	26,321.00	....	34.20	....	....	Increase in distance.
219.40	....	65.00	....	....	1 line 50 feet; 1 line 40 feet.	
247.70	....	50.00	....	....	2 lines 40 feet ...	
21.40	....	75.00	....	....	2 lines 40 feet ...	
1.40	....	50.00	....	....	2 lines 40 feet ...	
206.00	·66,948.00	....	10,303.00	....	....	Establishment of an additional line of 60 feet cars over whole line from May 13, 1888.
37.60	....	315.00	....	....	5 lines 60 feet; 1 line 50 feet; 1 line 40 feet.	
125.10	....	290.00	....	....	5 lines 60 feet; 1 line 50 feet.	
43.30	....	250.00	....	....	5 lines 60 feet ...	
100.61	6,536.65	65.00	....	31.20	1 line 50 feet; 1 line 40 feet.	Decrease in distance.
182.63	11,870.95	65.00	....	18.85	1 line 50 feet; 1 line 40 feet.	Do.
281.10	22,488.00	80.00	....	5.60	2 lines 50 feet ...	Do.
365.53	20,469.05					
55.87	....	140.00	....	....	2 lines 40 feet; 1 line 50 feet; 1 line 60 feet.	
196.23	....	50.00	....	....	2 lines 40 feet ...	
113.43	....	25.00	....	....	1 line 40 feet	
343.27	4,834.15		....	....	....	
69.56	....	65.00	....	....	1 line 40 feet; 1 line 50 feet.	
12.51	....	25.00	....	....	1 line 40 feet	
113.86	5,683.00	50.00	11.00	....	1 line 60 feet	Increase in distance.
55.98	17,196.00	200.00	2,114.50	....	3 lines 60 feet; 2 lines 40 feet.	Establishment of an additional line of 40 feet cars from October 1, 1887.
81.80	2,040.00	25.00	0.75	....	1 line 40 feet....	Increase in distance.
116.60	2,915.00	25.00	2.50	....	1 line 40 feet....	Do.
285.10	18,531.50	65.00	....	....	1 line 50 feet; 1 line 40 feet.	
195.98	4,899.50	25.00	4,899.50	....	1 line 40 feet	1 line of 40 feet cars established from October 1, 1887.
196.42	32,702.75	....	83.25	....	....	Change in distance.
93.59	....	175.00	....	....	3 lines 60 feet; 1 line 40 feet.	
104.58	....	150.00	....	....	3 lines 60 feet ..	
242.47	12,206.80	....	....	9.20	....	Do.
62.70	....	80.00	....	....	2 lines 50 feet ...	
179.77	....	40.00	....	....	1 line 50 feet	
180.55	7,562.00	40.00	1.20	....	1 line 50 feet	Do.
72.71	....		....	....	....	
15.00	600.00	40.00	8.00	....	1 line 50 feet	Do.
33.86	....					
29.71	1,188.40	40.00	....	4.40	1 line 50 feet	Do.
197.85	....		....	....	....	
22.00	550.00	25.00	....	....	1 line 40 feet	Do.

I.—*Table showing the rate of pay per annum for the use of railway post-office*

No. of route.	State and termini.	Corporate title of company.	June 30, 1887.		
			Length of route.	Pay per annum.	Pay per mile.
	MINNESOTA.		*Miles.*	*Dollars.*	*Dollars.*
26001	Saint Paul, Minn., and Missoula, Mont.	Northern Pacific R. R......	....	....	....
Part.	Saint Paul and Mandan, Minn.	......do	476.25	11,906.25	25.00
26006	Saint Paul and Breckenridge.	Saint Paul, Minneapolis and Manitoba Rwy.	216.12	5,403,00	25.00
26013	Minneapolis, Minn., and La Crosse, Wis.	Chicago, Milwaukee and Saint Paul Rwy.	142.57	21,385.50	150.00
26025	Saint Paul, Minn., and Sioux City, Iowa.	Chicago, Saint Paul, Minneapolis and Omaha Rwy.	269.65	6,741.25	25.00
	IOWA.				
27005	Burlington and Union Pacific Transfer (n. o.).	Chicago, Burlington and Quincy R. R.	291.00	58,200.00	200.00
27012	Clinton, Iowa, and La Crosse, Wis.	Chicago, Milwaukee and Saint Paul Rwy.	....	....	....
Part.	Sabula and McGregor	......do	96.60	2,415.00	25.00
27014	Davenport and Union Pacific Transfer (n. o.).	Chicago, Rock Island and Pacific Rwy.	317.95	16,706.75	....
Part.	Davenport and Iowa City.....	......do	53.95	....	65.00
Part.	Iowa City and Union Pacific Transfer (n. o.).	......do	264.00	....	50.00
27028	Savanna, Ill., and Union Pacific Transfer (n. o.).	Chicago, Milwaukee and Saint Paul Rwy.	351.18		
Part.	Savanna, Ill., and Sabula, Iowa.	......do	2.74	68.50	25.00
27029	Missouri Valley and Sioux City	Sioux City and Pacific R. R...	76.18	1,904.50	25.00
Part.	Missouri Valley and California		....	....	....
27073	Pacific Junction, Iowa, and Plattsmouth, Nebr.	Chicago, Burlington and Quincy R. R.	6.89	172.25	25.00
27077	California, Iowa, and Fremont, Nebr.	Sioux City and Pacific R. R...	....	....	....
	MISSOURI.				
28001	Saint Louis, Mo., and Atchison, Kans.	Missouri Pacific Rwy........	331.20	30,732.50	....
Part.	Saint Louis and Kansas City.	......do	283.45	....	100.00
Part.	Kansas City, Mo., and Atchison, Kans.	......do	47.75	....	50.00
28002	Saint Louis and Bismarck....	Saint Louis, Iron Mountain and Southern Rwy.	75.28	4,893.20	65.00
28003	Saint Louis, Mo., and Vinita, Ind. Terr.	Saint Louis and San Francisco Rwy.	360.81		
Part.	Saint Louis and Pierce City ..	......do	287.20	14,360.00	50.00
Part.	Saint Louis and Monett.......	......do	....	....	....
28004	Saint Louis and Kansas City..	Wabash Western Rwy.......	277.20	13,860.00	50.00
28005	Quincy, Ill., and Saint Joseph, Mo.	Hannibal and Saint Joseph R. R.	207.79		
Part.	Quincy, Ill., and Cameron. Mo	......do	171.51	11,148.15	65.00
28006	Kansas City, Mo., and Union Pacific Transfer (n. o.), Iowa	Kansas City, Saint Joseph and Council Bluffs R. R.	....	....	....
28010	Kansas City and Cameron....	Hannibal and Saint Joseph R. R.	54.98	3,572.70	65.00
28011	Sedalia, Mo., and Denison. Tex	Missouri Pacific Rwy........	431.46	10,786.50	25.00
28014	Hannibal and Sedalia........	......do	142.63	3,565.75	25.00
28026	Bismarck, Mo., and Texarkana, Ark.	......do	414.03	26,923.00	65.00
	KANSAS.				
33001	Kansas City, Mo., and Denver, Colo.	Union Pacific Rwy...........	....	....	....
Part. 33010	Topeka, Kans., and South Pueblo, Colo.	Atchison, Topeka and Santa Fé R. R.	569.75	45,580.00	80.00
33016	Topeka, Kans., and Kansas City, Mo.	......do	66.88	5,350.40	80.00

cars for the fiscal years ending June 30, 1887, and June 30, 1888, etc.—Continued.

June 30, 1888.			Increase per annum of 1888.	Decrease per annum of 1888.	Number of lines and authorized length of cars, June 30, 1888.	Remarks.
Length of route.	Pay per annum.	Pay per mile.				
Miles.	Dollars.	Dollars.	Dollars.	Dollars.		
476.10	11,992.50	25.00	....	3.75	1 line 40 feet....	Change in distance.
214.58	5,364.50	25.00	....	38.50	1 line 40 feet....	Do.
142.55	21,382.50	150.00	....	3.00	3 lines 60 feet...	Do.
269.79	6,744.75	25.00	3.50	....	1 line 40 feet....	Do.
294.00	73,500.00	250.00	15,300.00	....	5 lines 60 feet...	Increase in distance and an additional line of 60 feet cars from May 13, 1888.
96.90	2,422.50	25.00	7.50	....	1 line 40 feet....	Change in distance
317.97	16,708.05	....	1.30	....		Do.
53.97	....	65.00	....	....	1 line 50 feet; 1 line 40 feet.	
264.00	....	50.00	....	....	1 line 50 feet...	
353.97	....					
3.42	85.50	25.00	17.00	....	1 line 40 feet....	Do.
76.27	2,060.50	25.00	156.00	....	1 line 40 feet....	
6.15	....	50.00	....	....	2 lines 40 feet...	An additional line of 40 feet cars from Sept. 18, 1887.
5.64	141.00	25.00	....	31.25	1 line 40 feet...	Change in distance.
32.01	800.25	25.00	800.25	....	1 line 40 feet ..	Establishment of a line of 40 feet cars from Sept. 18, 1887.
330.17	42,468.00	....	11,735.50	....	....	Establishment of an additional line of 60 feet cars between Saint Louis and Kansas City from April 1, 1887, and discontinuance of the line of 60 feet cars between Kansas City and Atchison from June 6, 1888.
283.12	....	150.00	....	..	3 lines 60 feet ..	
75.33	4,896.45	65.00	3.25	....	1 line 50 feet; 1 line 40 feet.	Change in distance.
359.70	....	....			....	
282.10	14,105.00	50.00	....	255.00	2 lines 40 feet...	{Curtailment of service to end at Monett from October 2, 1887.
277.46	13,873.00	50.00	13.00	....	2 lines 40 feet...	Change in distance.
207.55						
171.24	11,130.60	65.00	....	17.55	1 line 50 feet; 1 line 40 feet.	Do.
201.23	5,030.50	25.00	5,030.50	....	1 line 40 feet ..	Establishment of a line of 40 feet cars from March 8, 1888.
55.08	3,580.20	65.00	6.50	....	1 line 50 feet; 1 line 40 feet.	Change in distance.
433.13	10,828.25	25.00	41.75	....	1 line 40 feet ..	Do.
....	....	....		3,565.75	....	Discontinued from January 24, 1888.
414.28	26,928.20	65.00	5.20	....	1 line 50 feet; 1 line 40 feet.	Change in distance.
641.02	16,025.50	25.00	16,025.50	....	1 line 40 feet....	R. P. O. re-established January 27, 1887.
569.75	45,580.00	80.00	....	....	2 lines 50 feet ..	
66.88	5,350.40	80.00	....	....	2 lines 50 feet...	

I.—*Table showing the rate of pay per annum for the use of railway post-office*

No. of route.	State and termini.	Corporate title of company.	June 30, 1887.		
			Length of route.	Pay per annum.	Pay per mile.
	NEBRASKA.		*Miles.*	*Dollars.*	*Dollars.*
34001	Union Pacific Transfer (n. o.), Iowa, and North Platte, Nebr. North Platte, Nebr., and Ogden City, Utah.	Union Pacific Rwy	{ 293. 03 741. 21	{ 59, 037. 75	{ 75. 00 50. 00
34002	Plattsmouth and Ashland	Burlington and Missouri River R. R. (in Nebraska).	121. 96	6, 099. 00	50. 00
34004	Omaha and Oreopolis Junction (n. o.).	Omaha and Southwestern R. R	....	....	....
Part 34009	Hastings and McCook	Republican Valley R. R.......	131. 96	6, 599. 00	50. 00
Part 34010	Fremont and Long Pine	Fremont, Elkhorn and Missouri Valley R. R.	}	....	....
34038	Omaha and Ashland..........	Omaha and North Platte R. R	31. 20	780. 00	25. 00
34039	Plattsmouth and Oreopolis Junction (n. o.). Oreopolis Junction (n. o.), and Ashland.	Burlington and Missouri River R. R. (in Nebraska).	{ 31. 37	{ 784. 25	{ 25. 00
	CALIFORNIA.				
46001	San Francisco, Cal , and Ogden City, Utah.	Central Pacific R. R..........	{ 45. 40 788. 77	} 42, 843. 50	{ 75. 00 50. 00
Part 46003	Tehama and Redding	.......do	46. 74	1, 168. 50	25. 00
46010	Lathrop and Goshen..........	......do	146. 39	3, 659. 75	25. 00
Part 46014	Goshen and Los Angeles	Southern Pacific R. R........	242. 78	6, 069. 50	25. 00
46022	Davisville and Tehama.	Central Pacific R. R. Co. (lessee Northern Rwy).	111. 64	2, 791. 00	25. 00
46032	Port Costa and Lathrop	Central Pacific R. R. Co. (lessee San Pablo R. R.).	62. 23	1, 555. 75	25. 00
	Total	....	....	1,881,580.50	......
	Net increase..............				

RECAPITULATION.

Number of lines of 40-feet cars 120
Number of lines of 45-feet cars 8
Number of lines of 50-feet cars 76
Number of lines of 55-feet cars 14
Number of lines of 60-feet cars 105

Total number of lines authorized.. 323

cars for the fiscal year ending June, 30, 1887, and June 30, 1888, etc.—Continued.

June 30, 1888.			Increase per annum of 1888.	Decrease per annum of 1888.	Number of lines and authorized length of cars, June 30, 1888.	Remarks
Length of route	Pay per annum.	Pay per mile.				
Miles.	*Dollars.*	*Dollars.*	*Dollars.*	*Dollars.*		
293.03	⎫ 66,363.50	⎰ 100.00	7,325.75	....	1 line 60 feet; 2 lines 40 feet.	
741.21	⎬	50.00	....	....	1 line 60 feet ..	
121.98	6,099.00	50.00	....	....	2 lines 40 feet...	
16.60	415.00	25.00	415.00	....	1 line 40 feet ...	R. P. O re-established November 27, 1887.
131.98	6,599.00	50.00	....	....	2 lines 40 feet...	
212.84	5,321.00	25.00	5,321.00	....	1 line 40 feet ..	⎰ R. P. O. established September 18, 1887.
31.20	1,560.00	50.00	780.00	....	2 lines 40 feet..	One additional line of 40 feet R. P. O. cars from November 27, 1887.
4.47	111.75	25.00	....	....	1 line 40 feet ...	R. P. O. service discontinued between Oreopolis Junction (n. o.) and Ashland November 27, 1887.
....	....	....	....	672.50	....	
45.40	⎫ 42,843.50	⎰ 75.00	....	....	1 line 55 feet; 1 line 40 feet (55 feet reported).	
786.77	⎬	50.00	....	....	1 line 55 feet....	
46.74	1,168.50	25.00	....	....	⎰1 line 40 feet (55 feet reported).	
146.39	3,659.75	25.00	....	....	1 line 40 feet (55 feet reported).	
242.78	6,069.50	25.00	....	....	⎰1 line 40 feet (55 feet reported).	
111.64	2,791.00	25.00	....	....	1 line 40 feet (55 feet reported).	
62.23	1,555.75	25.00	....	....	1 line 40 feet (55 feet reported).	
....	1,996,359.35 / 1,881,580.50	....	126,024.50 / 11,245.65	11,245.65		
....	114,778.85	....	114,778.85			

K.—*Statement of expenditures on account of special facilities for the fiscal year ended June 30, 1888, out of $295,957.53 appropriated by act approved March 3, 1887.*

Number of route.	Termini.	Railroad company.	Miles.	Pay per. annum.
5003..............	New York, N. Y., to Spring-field, Mass.	New York, New Haven and Hartford.	136.00	$17,647.06
6011 (part).......	4.35 a. m. train, New York to Albany.	New York Central and Hudson River.	144 00	25,000.00
10006 (part)......	Baltimore to Hagerstown.....	Western Maryland	86.60	15,804.50
10001..............	Philadelphia, Pa., to Bay View (n. o), Md.	Philadelphia, Wilmington and Baltimore.	91.80	20,000.00
10013..............	Bay View (n. o.), Md., to Washington, D. C.			
11001 (part)	Washington, D. C., to Quantico (n. o.), Va	Baltimore and Potomac.......	79.80	21,900.00
11001 (part)......	Quantico (n. o) to Richmond..	Richmond, Fredericksburgh and Potomac.	81.50	17,419.23
11008	Richmond to Petersburgh	Richmond and Petersburgh ..	23.39	4,268.67
11009..............	Petersburgh to Weldon.......	Petersburgh	64.00	11,680.00
13002	Weldon to Wilmington	Wilmington and Weldon......	162.07	29,577.77
14002 (part).....	Wilmington to Florence	Wilmington, Columbia and Augusta.	110.00	20,075.00
14005 (part)......	Florence to Charleston Junction (n. o.).	Northeastern	95.00	17,337.50
14004 (part)	Charleston Junction (n. o.) to Savannah.	Charleston and Savannah.....	108.00	19,710.00
15009..............	Savannah to Jacksonville.....	Savannah, Florida and Western	171.50	31,298.75
16018..............	Jacksonville to Sanford	Jacksonville, Tampa and Key West.	126.18	23,027.83
16007..............	Sanford to Tampa	South Florida	116.39	21,241.17
Total	....	....	....	255,987.53

L.—*Statement showing miles of railroad service ordered from July 1, 1887, to June 30, 1888.*

No. of route.	State.	Termini.	Character of service.	Title of company.	Miles.	Date of commencement.
27	Maine	Kennebunk Port and Kennebunk Station (n. o.)	New	Boston and Maine R. R.	4.67	Aug. 10, 1887
28	...do	York Beach and Kittery Junction (n. o.)	..do	York Harbor and Beach R. R.	11.33	Jan. 10, 1864
1065	New Hampshire	West Stewartstown and Coos	..do	Upper Coos R. R.	21.23	Mar. 10, 1888
	Vermont	None.				
3042	Massachusetts	Nantucket and Sisaconset	New	Nantucket R. R.	11.12	July 1, 1887
3078	...do	Boston and Winthrop	..do	Boston, Revere Beach and Lynn R. R.	5.00	Aug. 10, 1887
2018	...do	Winchester and Woburn—North Woburn	Ext.	Boston and Lowell R. R. Corporation	2.18	Aug. 16, 1887
	Rhode Island	None.				
	Connecticut	Do.				
6135	New York	Jamestown and Mayville	New	Chautauqua Lake Rwy	22.25	Oct. 12, 1887
6136	...do	Windsor Beach (n. o.) and Rochester	..do	Rome, Watertown and Ogdensburg R. R.	8.30	Oct. 3, 1887
6132	...do	Inman and Saranac Lake	Ext.	Chateaugay R. R.	19.33	Jan. 2, 1888
6052	...do	Saint Regis Falls and Brandon	..do	Northern Adirondack R. R.	22.38	Apr. 23, 1888
7057	New Jersey	Manumuskin and Heislerville	New	West Jersey R. R.	10.67	Jan. 2, 1888
7045	...do	Haddonfield and Marlton—Medford	Ext.	Camden and Atlantic R. R.	4.99	June 1, 1888
7024	...do	Jersey City and Garnerville—Havenstraw	..do	New Jersey and New York R. R.	2.86	Jan. 1, 1888
8108	Pennsylvania	Coalport and Cresson	New	Cresson, Clearfield County and New York Short Route R. R.	24.6	Aug. 1, 1887
8151	...do	Youngwood Station and United	Embrace Monmouth.	Pennsylvania R. R.	2.25	July 1, 1887
8169	...do	Hackleton and Lofty	New	Lehigh Valley R. R.	9.21	Oct. 14, 1887
8400	...do	Osceola Mills and Ramey—Madera	Ext.	Pennsylvania R. R.	8	Oct. 31, 1887
8170	...do	Luzerne and Alderson (n. o.)	New	Pennsylvania and New York Canal and R. R.	14.06	Nov. 14, 1887
8171	...do	Forest House and Costella	..do	Sinnemahoning Valley R. R.	12.28	Jan. 16, 1888
8872	...do	Denton and Bloomsburgh, Pa.	..do	Bloomsburgh and Sullivan R. R.	29.66	Jan. 28, 1888
8173	...do	Silver Brook and Silver Brook Junction (n. o.)	..do	Lehigh Valley R. R.	2.01	Feb. 1, 1888
8169	...do	Hackleton and Lofty. Ext. New Boston	Ext.	..do	8.85	Mar. 1, 1888
8174	...do	Wilkes Barre and Rock Glen Junction (n. o.)	New	Pennsylvania R. R.	39.56	Mar. 1, 1888
8175	...do	New Boston and Pottsville	..do	..do	16.21	Mar. 1, 1888
8165	...do	Ireona and Mahaffey. Ext. Punxsutawney.	Ext.	Bell's Gap R. R.	17.42	Mar. 6, 1888
8176	...do	Goff and Iconedon Station (n. o.)	..do	Pennsylvania R. R.	4.29	Apr. 16, 1888
8179	...do	Wampun Junction (n. o.) and Kenwood Junction (n. o.)	..do	..do	12.50	Apr. 16, 1888
	Delaware	None.				
10027	Maryland	Philadelphia and Baltimore	New	Baltimore and Ohio R. R.	96.00	July 1, 1887
10028	...do	Baltimore and Annapolis	..do	Annapolis and Baltimore Short Line R. R.	28.22	Dec. 5, 1887
11040	Virginia	Bristol, Tenn. and Latilville, Va.	..do	South Atlantic and Ohio R. R.	32.51	Sept. 21, 1887
11039	...do	Sunbury and Amboy, N. C.	Ext.	Suffolk and Carolina Rwy	14.06	Mar. 12, 1888
11032	...do	Foster Falls and Austinville	..do	Norfolk and Western R. R.	6.46	Apr. 16, 1888
11032	...do	C	..do	Richmond and Danville R. R.	24.15	June 13, 1888
11039	...do		..do	Norfolk and Western R. R.	3.23	June 25, 1888
12013	West Virginia	Phillippi and Belington	New	Grafton and Green Brier R. R.	18.00	Aug. 27, 1887
12019	...do	Piedmont and Cumberland	..do	West Virginia Central and Pittsburgh Rwy	28.87	Sept. 5, 1887
12020	...do	Point Pleasant and C. and O. Junction (n. o.)	New	Ohio River R. R.	40.82	Feb. 20, 1888
12020	...do	C. and O. Junction (n. o.) and Huntington	Ext.	..do	8.06	Feb. 20, 1888

L.—*Statement showing miles of railroad service ordered from July 1, 1887, to June 30, 1888—Continued.*

No. of route.	State.	Termini.	Character of service.	Title of company.	Miles.	Date of commencement.
12921	West Virginia	Tunnelton and Good	New.	Kingwood Rwy	10.95	Mar. 5, 1888
12916	do	Bramwell and Freemans	Ext.	Norfolk and Western R. R.	0.84	Mar. 8, 1888
12916	do	Freemans and Duhring	do		4.55	May 21, 1888
13030	North Carolina	Warsaw and 4th	New.	Wilmington and Weldon R. R.	13.11	July 1, 1887
13011	do	Mint Cove and Dunn	Ext.	Cape Fear and Yadkin Valley Rwy	13.01	Sept. 28, 1887
13409	do	Dalton and Pilot Mountain	do		7.83	Dec. 5, 1887
13028	do	Statesville and Taylorsville	do	Charlotte, Columbia and Augusta R. R.	19.98	Jan. 2, 1888
13024	do	Nashville and Rue View	do	Wilmington and Weldon R. R.	8.40	Jan. 9, 1888
13031	do	Loris and Conway	New.	Wilmington, Chadbourn and Conway R. R.	18.84	Jan. 23, 1888
13032	do	Factory and Millboro	do	Cape Fear and Yadkin Valley Rwy	9.55	Feb. 6, 1888
13023	do	Hamilton and Tarborough	do	Hamilton R. R. and Lumber Co.	20.65	Feb. 18, 1888
13031	do	Boykins, Va., and Nixonville, N. C.		Roanoke and Tar River R. R.	9.35	Mar. 8, 1888
13035	do	Hamlet and Gibson Station	Ext.	Raleigh and Augusta Air Line R. R.	10.50	Mar. 12, 1888
13011	do	Pilot Mountain and Bliss	New.	Cape Fear and Yadkin Valley Rwy	6.84	May 7, 1888
13011	do	Wilmington and Wrightsville	Ext.	Wilmington Sea Coast R. R.	9.24	June 15, 1888
14026	South Carolina	Bee and Mount Airy	New.	Cape Fear and Yadkin Valley Rwy	6.50	June 15, 1888
14027	do	Camden and Bee		Blackville, Alston and Newberry R. R.	16.14	Mar. 12, 1888
14028	do	Ravenels and Younges Island	do	Charleston, Cincinnati and Chicago R. R.	41.50	June 4, 1888
14029	do	Atkins and Bishopville	do	Charleston and Savannah Rwy	5.70	June 16, 1888
15050	Georgia	Smithville and Lumpkin. Ext. Hannah Lee	Ext.	Bishopville R. R.	15.79	June 25, 1888
15051	do	Americus and Gum Creek	New.	Americus, Preston and Lumpkin R. R.	9.98	July 1, 1887
15051	do	Columbus and Shiloh. Ext. Concord	do	Georgia Midland and Gulf R. R.	23.70	July 1, 1887
15051	do	Sun and Borough. Ext. Griffin	Ext.		29.10	July 1, 1887
15034	do	Gum Creek and Abbeville	do	Americus, Preston and Lumpkin R. R.	16.60	Aug. 1, 1887
15034	do	Rogers and Summit	New.	Rogers and Summit R. R.	36.25	Oct. 21, 1887
150.10	do	Broken Arrow and Poll City	Ext.	East and West R. R. Co. of Alabama	20.00	Oct. 7, 1887
15047	do	New route to begin at Americus	Restoring	Buena Vista and Ellaville R. R.	7.80	Jan. 2, 1888
15056	do	Atta and Zebulon	New.	Atlanta and Florida Rwy	8.00	Nov. 29, 1887
15052	do	Mio and Man	Ext.	Covington and Macon R. R.	51.28	May 14, 1888
16029	Florida	Oakland and Clermont	do	Orange Belt Rwy	27.18	June 11, 1888
16032	do	Lake City and Fort White	New.	Savannah, Florida and Western Rwy	9.65	Sept. 28, 1887
16033	do	dela and Dunnellon	do	Silver Spring, Ocala and Gulf R. R.	21.93	Oct. 10, 1887
16029	do	Gala and Oak	do	Orange Belt Rwy	23.43	Dec. 12, 1887
16029	do	Mio and Tarpon Springs	do		9.61	Dec. 19, 1887
16019	do	Massacre and Plant City	do	Florida Rwy. and Navigation Co	66.62	Apr. 10, 1888
17027	Alabama	Argus and Oak	do	Montgomery and Southern Rwy	43.14	May 31, 1888
17020	do	Renfroe and Poll City	New.	Talladega and Coosa Valley Rwy	13.00	Sept. 19, 1887
17032	do	Ebury Trace and Wesville, Ala.	Ext.	Nashville, Chattanooga and St. Louis Rwy	27.63	Dec. 19, 1887
17016	do	Buffalo and Roanoke		East Alabama Rwy	17.19	Jan. 3, 1888
17016	do	Goodwater and Sylacauga	do	Columbus and Western Rwy	14.85	Feb. 1, 1888
17016	Mississippi	Sylacauga and Wedurgh	do		9.72	Mar. 25, 1888
198		Middleton and off Gon Plant. Ext. New Albany	do	Ship Island, Ripley and Kentucky R. R.	7.65	Aug. 8, 1887

No.	State	Type	Route	Railway	Amount	Date
19891	do	do	Tupelo, Miss., and Birmingham, Ala.	Kansas City, Memphis and Birmingham R. R.	140.21	Nov. 21, 1887
19896	do	do	Jonestown and Eagle's Nest	Mobile and Northwestern R. R.	2.22	Dec. 17, 1887
19012	Tennessee	M.	Greenwood and Presto	Illinois Central R. R.	18.13	Jan. 19, 1887
19025	do	do		Nashville, Chattanooga and St. Louis Rwy	4.72	Sept. 19, 1887
19026	do	do		Chesapeake and Nashville Rwy	25.87	Jan. 2, 1888
19024	do	Ext.		Louisville and Nashville R. R.	27.83	Feb. 1, 1888
190.5	do	M.		Nashville, Chattanooga and St. Louis Rwy	14.41	Feb. 11, 1887
	Kentucky			Ohio Valley Rwy	13.11	Nov. 21, 1887
20034	do	New		do	24.04	Jan. 25, 1887
20035	do	Ext.	Glasgow Junction and Mammoth Cave	Louisville and Nashville R. R.	6.81	Mar. 3, 1888
20036	do	Ext.	Bardstown and Springfield	do	10.38	Mar. 12, 1888
20037	do	Ext.	Corbin and Barboursville	do	10.74	Mar. 19, 1888
398	do	New	Barboursville and Pineville	do	14.60	June 7, 1888
21093	do	Ext.	Elizabethtown and Hodgensville	Hodgensville and Elizabethtown R. R.	11.70	Aug. 16, 1887
21101	Ohio	do	Hogen and New Lisbon	Pittsburgh, Marion and Chicago Rwy	11.23	Aug. 22, 1887
21075	do	do	Danbury and Point Marblehead	Lakeside and Marblehead R. R.	8.50	Sept. 6, 1887
21100	do	Ext.	West Alexandria and Carlisle	Cincinnati and Ohio River Rwy	10.05	Aug. 22, 1887
21090	do	do	McConnelsville and Stockport	Zanesville, Jackson and Mackinaw R. R.	9.75	Oct. 3, 1887
615	do	do	Cecil and Bryan	Cincinnati, Jackson and Mackinaw R. R.	19.71	Oct. 3, 1887
21067	do	New	Ameville and Sharpsburgh	Marietta Mineral Rwy	4.67	Jan. 10, 1888
21102	do	Ext.	Bryan and Alvordton	Cincinnati, Jackson, and Mackinaw R. R.	33.49	Feb. 6, 1888
21110	do	New	Alliance and Bergholz	Lake Erie, Alliance and Southern Rwy	33.50	Mar. 12, 1888
21065	do	Ext.	Killbuck and Warsaw	Cleveland, Akron and Columbus Rwy	18.63	Mar. 19, 1888
21058	do	do	Stockport and Waterford	Zanesville and Ohio River Rwy	16.40	Mar. 19, 1888
21688	do	do	Warren and Youngstown	Pittsburgh and Western Rwy	4.84	May 1, 1888
21103	do	do	Sharpeville and Pymatuning (n. o.)	New York, Lake Erie and Western R. R.	11.10	May 19, 1888
22051	do	do	Columbus, Hocking Valley and Toledo Junction (n. o.) and Point Pleasant Junction (n. o.).	Ohio Central R. R.		Mar. 19, 1888
22037	do	do	Extended to Gallipolis	do	3.98	Mar. 19, 1888
22047	do	New	Warsaw and Trinway	Cleveland, Akron and Columbus Rwy	15.52	June 23, 1888
22028	Indiana	Ext.	Orleans and French Lick	Orleans, West Baden and French Lick Springs Rwy	18.76	Aug. 1, 1887
22029	do	do	Noblesville and Lebanon	Midland Rwy	25.78	Aug. 22, 1887
22033	do	New	Lebanon and Ladoga	*	20.13	Feb. 9, 1888
22040	do	do	Fair Oaks and La Cross	do	22.50	Feb. 21, 1888
22004	Illinois	New	Kercheval and Cannelton	Chicago and Indiana Coal Rwy	3.04	Mar. 24, 1888
22095	do	do	Add to length of route	Louisville, Evansville and St. Louis Rwy	12.31	Apr. 23, 1888
22082	do	do	Brazil and Saline City	Cincinnati, La Fayette and Chicago R. R	13.69	July 1, 1887
394	do	New	Bates and Grafton. Ext. Springfield	Evansville and Indianapolis R. R.	45.61	July 25, 1887
22060	do	New	Springfield and Litchfield	St. Louis and Central Illinois R. R.	3.21	Aug. 22, 1887
22097	do	do	Geneva and Saint Charles	St. Louis and Chicago Rwy	101.39	Oct. 7, 1887
22098	do	do	Chicago and Dunbar (n. o.)	Chicago and Northwestern Rwy	9.41	Nov. 7, 1887
22046	do	Ext.	Streator, Ill., and North Judson, Ind. Ext. Knox, Ind.	Chicago, St. Paul and Kansas City	28.87	Dec. 5, 1887
395	do	New	Danville and Sidell. Ext. to Tuscola	Indiana, Illinois and Iowa R. R.	18.84	Feb. 4, 1887
22096	do	do	Rockford and Rockton	Chicago and Eastern Illinois R. R.	288.82	Feb. 6, 1888
	do	do	Marion and Parker City (n. o.)	Chicago, Milwaukee and St. Paul Rwy	3.28	Feb. 27, 1888
	do	do	Chicago, Ill., and Fort Madison, Iowa	Chicago, Santa Fé and California Rwy	11.59	Mar. 12, 1888
	do	Ext.	Rondout and Libertyville, Ill.	Chicago, Milwaukee and St. Paul Rwy	65.94	Apr. 3, 1888
	do	New	Jacksonville and Centralia. Ext. Drivers	Jacksonville Southeastern Rwy	7.00	Apr. 20, 1888
	do	Ext.	Chicago, Ill., and Fort Madison, Iowa. Ext. Kansas City, Mo.	Chicago, Santa Fé and California Rwy	218.00	May 22, 1884

L.—*Statement showing miles of railroad service ordered from July 1, 1887, to June 30, 1884—Continued.*

No. of route.	State.	Termini.	Character of service.	Title of company.	Miles.	Date of commencement.
24070	Michigan	Howard City and Grand Rapids	New	Detroit, Lansing and Northern R. R.	34.07	Aug. 1, 1887
24050	do	Missaukee Junction (n. o.) and Jennings	do	Grand Rapids and Indiana R. R.	8.05	Sept.
24071	do	Bessemer, Mich. and Mellen, Wis.	do	Penokee R. R	31.72	Oct. 10, 1887
938	do	Iron River Junction (n. o.) and Iron River. Ext. Watersmeet	Ext.	...go and Northwest.Rwy.	34.95	Oct. 24, 1887
942	do	Sault de Ste. Marie and Sault Junction (n. o.), Mich.	New	Duluth, ...	47.80	Jan.
24673	do	Pinconning and Gladwin	do	Michigan Central R. R.	28.28	Feb.
24674	do	Rodney and Chippewa Lake	do	Detroit, Lansing and ...ern R. R.	6.91	Feb. 6, 1888
949	do	Ashley and Muskegon. Ext. New Glarus	Ext.	Toledo, Saginaw and ...on Rwy.	96.24	Mar. 12, 1887
3844	Wi...sin	Broadhead and Albany	New	Chicago, Milwaukee and St. Paul Rwy	15.28	Oct. 24, 1887
2913	do	Dresser Junction (n. o.) and Sault Croix Falls	Ext.	Minneapolis, Salt Ste. ...rie and Atlantic Rwy.	4.28	Oct. 5, 1887
25059	do	Turtle Lake and Bruce. Ext. Turtle Lake to Minneapolis	Ext.	...go, ...kee and St. Paul Rwy	76.51	Dec. 5, 1887
25031	do	Tomah and Merrill. Ext Tomahawk	do	...go, ...kee and St. Paul Rwy	23.04	Dec. 28, 1887
5966	do	Chelsea and Rib Lake	New	Wisconsin Central R. R.	6.35	Feb. 27, 1888
5959	do	Minneapolis, Minn., and Bruce, Wis. Ext Sault de Ste. Marie	Ext.	Minneapolis, Sault de Ste. Marie and Atlantic Rwy.	373.84	Mar. 5, 1888
25016	Minnesota	Milwaukee and Iron Mountain. Ext. Republic	do	Milwaukee and ... R. R.	46.74	Feb. 27, 1888
26048	do	Waterville and Red Wing. Ext. Waterville to Mankato	Ext.	Minneapolis and St. Louis Rwy	28.34	Aug. 25, 1887
592	do	Wabasha and Zumbrota. Ext. Wabashato West Wabasha(n.o.)	do	..., Milwaukee and St. Paul Rwy	0.98	July 1, 1887
26061	do	Winnipeg Junction, Minn. Grand Forks, Dak.	New	Northern Pacific R. R.	106.66	Oct. 1, 1887
26062	do	Winnipeg Junction and Grand Forks, Dak. Ext. Pembina, Dak.	Ext.	...	93.49	Oct. 2, 1888
	do	Saint Paul and Cardigan Junction (n. o.)	New	Minneapolis, Sault Ste. Marie and Atlantic Rwy.	8.00	Apr. 16, 1888
2999	Iowa	Hudson and Waterloo. Ext Oelwein	Ext.	Chicago, Saint Paul and Kansas City Rwy.	24.74	Oct. 8, 1887
2998	do	Sioux City and Mann Ill.	Ext.	Chicago, Milwaukee and St. Paul Rwy.	90.70	Oct. 10, 1887
789	do	Sac City and Kingsley. Ext. Moville	Ext.	Chicago and Northwest. Rwy	9.13	Oct. 24, 1887
27057	do	Downs and Garner. Ext. Forest City	do	Burlington, Cedar Rapids and Northern Rwy.	115.87	Dec. 5, 1887
27047	do	Cedar Rapids and Ottumwa. Ext. Kansas City, Mo.	do	Chicago, Milwaukee and St. Paul Rwy	209.58	Jan. 30, 1888
2710	do	Cherokee and Onawa	New	Cherokee and Dakota R. R.	61.18	Feb. 5, 1888
27100	do	Cherokee and Sioux Falls, Dak	do	do	97.07	Apr. 2, 1888
27101	do	Cedar Rapids and Manchester	do	Illinois ...l R. R., lessee of Cedar Rapids ...	42.58	Apr. 30, 1888
27102	do	U. P. Transfer (n. o.) and Broadway Depot, Council Bluffs	do	Union Pacific Rwy ... R. R.	1.76	June 25, 1887
27003	Missouri	Saint Louis and Union	do	St. Louis, Kansas City and Colorado R. R	59.91	July 15, 1887
2855	do	Clinton and Bloomington. Ext. Clinton to East Lynne	Ext.	... City and Southern Rwy.	34.03	July 16, 1887
27053	do	Greenfield and Watkins	New	... and Northern R. R	8.46	Aug 1, 1887
284	Ne...	Napier (n. o.), Mo., and Rulo Y (n. o.), Nebr.	do	...on and ... River R. R. Co. (in Nebraska).	11.7	Jan. 7, 1888
2865	do	Brownwood and Bollinger Mills (n. o.)	do	Cape ... Rwy	8.63	Apr. 2, 1888
2259	do	Marshall and Myrick Station (n. o.)	do	Missouri Pacific Rwy.	47.82	June 11, 1888
845	do	Cape Girardeau and Wappapello. Ext. Chaonia	Ext.	... Ohio Rwy	6.46	June 18, 1888
2920	Arkansas	Pine Bluff and English	New	Pine Bluff, Monroe and New Orleans Rwy.	36.42	July 18, 1887
29021	do	Fayetteville and Saint Paul	do	St. Louis and San Francisco Rwy	37.15	Aug. 22, 1887
29019	do	Jenson, Ark., and Paris, Tex	Ext.	do	134.96	Oct. 31, 1887

No.	State	Type	Route	Railway	Rate	Date
29914	do	do	Batesville and Cushman	St. Louis, Iron Mountain and Southern Rwy	11.62	Nov. 7, 1887
29922	do	New	Arkadelphia and Delark	Ultima Thule, Arkadelphia and Mississippi Rwy.	11.43	Oct. 31, 1887
29923	Louisiana	do	Dahl Knob and Augusta	St. Louis, Iron Mountain and Southern Rwy	14.05	Nov. 23, 1888
2891	do	do	Jenson and Mansfield	St. Louis and San Francisco Rwy	18.23	Mar. 12, 1888
2911	do	do	Cypress and Natchitoches	Natchitoches R. R.	11.63	Feb. 20, 1888
30017	do	do	Gibsland and Homer	Louisiana North and South Rwy	18.83	Apr. 14, 1888
30018	do	do	New Orleans and Covington	East Louisiana R. R.	59.50	May 14, 1888
29814	do	do	Galveston, Ark., and Shreveport, La.	St. Louis, Arkansas and Texas Rwy. in Ark. and Mo.	61.04	June 25, 1888
31022	Texas	Ext	Denison and Gainsville. Ext Henrietta	Missouri, Kansas and Texas Rwy	70.51	July 1, 1887
31050	do	New	Falls and Paris	Gulf, Colorado and Santa Fé Rwy	80.16	July 1, 1887
854	do	New	Gainsville, Tex., and Purcell, Ind. Ter.	do	165.73	Sept. 12, 1887
2891	do	Ext	Mount Pleasant and Sherman	St. Louis, Arkansas and Texas Rwy	110.10	Sept. 12, 1887
30057	do	do	Hallettsville and Wallis	San Antonio and Aransas Pass Rwy	56.42	Oct. 3, 1887
31058	do	New	Beeton and Kerrville	do	87.99	Oct. 8, 1887
31037	do	New	Quanah and Clarendon	Fort Worth and Denver City Rwy.	85.88	Oct. 10, 1887
31081	do	Ext	Fort Worth and Granbury	Ft. Worth and Rio Grande Rwy	41.35	Nov. 21, 1887
31056	do	Ext	Bastrop and La Grange	Taylor, Bastrop and Houston Rwy	34.64	Dec. 16, 1888
31052	do	New	Yoakum and Fla ??	San Antonio and Aransas Pass Rwy	30.15	Feb. 20, 1888
31048	do	Ext	Win and Beckville	Galveston, Sabine and St. Louis Rwy	7.70	Mar. 19, 1888
31061	do	Ext	San Macos and Lockhart	Taylor, Bastrop and Houston Rwy	17.12	Apr. 2, 1888
3162	do	Ext	Flat ?? and West Point	San Antonio and Aransas Pass Rwy	20.05	May 7, 1888
31064	do	New	Corsicana and Hillsborough	St. Louis, Arkansas and Texas Rwy, Co., in Texas.	42.00	May 7, 1888
31048	do	Ext	Beckville and Carthage	Galveston, Sabine and Saint Louis Rwy	9.59	May 7, 1888
31037	do	do	Clarendon and Texline (n.o)	Ft. Worth and Denver City Rwy	174.20	June 4, 1888
3196	do	New	Texline (n.o.), Tex., and Pueblo, Colo.	Denver, Texas and Fort Worth R. R.	228.51	June 4, 1888
31035	do	do	Panhandle and Washburn	Ft. Worth and Denver City Rwy	16.18	June ?, 1888
31067	do	Ext	Cleburne and Weatherford	Gulf, Colorado and Santa Fé Rwy	39.68	June 9, 1888
		New	Commerce and Fort Worth	St. Louis, Arkansas and Santa Fé Rwy. Co., in Texas.	88.31	June 25, 1888
32903	Indian Territory	New	Arkansas City, Kans., and Purcell, Ind. Ter.	Southern Kansas Rwy	154.00	Sept. 12, 1887
32904	do	do	Kiowa, Kans., and Miami, Ter.	do	167.91	Dec. 9, 1887
33075	Kansas	Ext	Miami and Panhandle	do	40.36	Apr. 1, 1887
33075	do	New	Saint Joseph, Mo., and Alma, Kans.	Chicago, Kansas and Nebraska Rwy	128.43	July 1, 1887
33077	do	Ext	Horton, Kans., and Nora, Nebr.	do	160.77	July 20, 1887
33078	do	do	Saint Joseph, Mo., and Alma, Kans. Ext. Herington, Kans.	Kingman, Pratt and Western R. R.	45.29	Aug. 8, 1887
33079	do	do	Kingman and Cullison. Ext. Greensburgh.	Chicago, Kansas and Western R. R.	21.24	Aug. 9, 1887
	do	New	Cottonwood Falls and Abilene.	Le Roy and Caney Valley Air Line R. R.	64.96	Aug. 22, 1887
	do	do	Slidell and Fern. Ext Herington, Kans.	Kansas City, Wyandotte and Northwestern R. R.	52.91	
	do	do	Wyandotte and Tonganoxie		80.15	
380	do	Ext	Burlington and Gridley	Chicago, Kansas and Western R. R.	11.32	Aug. 25, 1887
33059	do	do	Great Bend and Ness City. Ext to Scott	Chicago, Kansas and Nebraska Rwy	45.69	Sept. 10, 1887
820	do	do	Horton, Kans., and Nora, Nebr. Ext. Nelson, Nebr.	Kansas Southwestern Rwy	6.49	Sept. 24, 1887
33081	do	New	Olcott and Inka	Chicago, Kansas and Nebraska Rwy	20.29	Oct. 3, 1887
33075	do	do	Saint Joseph, Mo., and Herington, Kans. Ext. Pratt, Kans.	Chicago, Kansas and Nebraska Rwy	127.16	Oct. 17, 1887
33063	do	do	Malvane and Spivey. Ext. Ashland	Chicago, Kansas and Western R. R.	100.00	Oct. 17, 1887
33068	do	do	Herington and Wichita	Chicago, Kansas and Nebraska Rwy	74.35	Oct. 24, 1887
33050	do	New	Chetopa and Cedar	Denver, Memphis and Atlantic Rwy	38.08	Nov. 7, 1887
881	do	Ext	Larned and Bartlett. Ext Jetmore ... Bell	Chicago, Kansas and Western R. R.	22.72	Nov. 7, 1887

I.—*Statement showing miles of railroad service ordered from July 1, 1887, to June 30, 1888—Continued.*

No. of route.	State.	Termini.	Character of service.	Title of company.	Miles.	Date of commencement.
33056	Kansas	Chetopa and Winfield. Ext Belle Plain	Ext	Denver, Memphis and Atlantic Rwy	29.97	Nov. 10, 1887
33058	do	Belle Plain and Stafford. Ext Larned	do	do	72.64	Nov. 10, 1887
33063	do	Coffeyville and Morantown	New	Kansas City and Pacific R. R.	72.64	Oct. 24, 1887
33062	do	Herington and Wichita. Ext Caldwell	Ext	Chicago, Kansas and Nebraska Rwy	49.36	Nov. 29, 1887
33061	do	McCracken and Horace	Ext	Denver, Memphis and Atlantic Rwy	126.66	Dec. 5, 1887
33069	do	Benedict and Coyville. Ext Madison	New	Chicago, Kansas and Western R. R.	34.67	Dec. 29, 1887
33065	do	Oakley and Colby	New	Oakley and Colby Rwy / Western R. R.	22.12	Dec. 29, 1887
33057	do	Salina and Lincoln. Ext Lura	Ext	Salina, Lincoln and Western Rwy	39.93	Dec. 28, 1887
33077	do	Cottonwood Falls and Abilene. Ext Cottonwood Falls—Bazaar. Ext Abilene to Keystone.	do	Chicago, Kansas and Western R. R.	24.26	Feb. 29, 1868
33066	do	Geneseo and Kanopolis	New	Kanopolis and Kansas Central Rwy	14.70	Feb. 1, 1888
33084	do	McCracken and Horace. Ext Towner Station (n. o.)	Ext	Denver, Memphis and Atlantic Rwy	14.29	Mar. 1, 1888
33068	do	Mulvane and Ashland. Ext Englewood.	do	Chicago, Kansas and Western R. R.	14.12	Mar. 1, 1888
33067	do	Wichita and Ellsworth	New	St. Louis and San Francisco Rwy	106.61	Mar. 5, 1888
33079	do	Kansas City, Kans, and Tonganoxie. Ext Seneca	Ext	Kansas City, Wyandotte and Northern R. R.	80.67	Mar. 5, 1888
33088	do	Keystone and Concordia	Ext	Chicago, Kansas and Western R. R.	41.92	Mar. 10, 1888
33082	do	Kingman and Greensburgh. Ext Mullinville	Ext	Kingman, Pratt and Western R. R.	9.97	Mar. 19, 1888
33077	do	Bazaar and Keystone. Ext Nnurod	do	do	42.06	Apr. 2, 1888
33013	do	Girard and Chanute. Ext Girard to Pittsburgh.	do	Southern Kansas Rwy	11.52	Apr. 2, 1888
33014	do	Lawrence and Carbondale.	Ext	Lawrence, Emporia and Southwestern Rwy	23.75	Apr. 9, 1888
33069	do	Belleville and McFarland.	New	Chicago, Kansas and Nebraska Rwy	164.76	Apr. 2, 1888
33070	do	Kansas City, Kans, and Seneca. Ext Kansas City, Mo.	Ext	Kansas City, Wyandotte and Northwestern R. R.	2.02	Apr. 2, 1888
33075	do	Saint Joseph, Mo., and Pratt, Kans. Ext Liberal, Kans.	do	Chicago, Kansas and Nebraska Rwy	135.25	May 1, 1888
33069	do	Le Roy and Madison	New	Interstate R. R.	29.96	May 10, 1888
33083	do	Coffeyville and Morantown. Ext Kincaid	Ext	Kansas City and Pacific R. R.	11.95	May 10, 1888
33091	do	Kansas City, Mo., and Paola, Kans.	Ext	Kansas City and Southwestern Rwy	84.09	May 14, 1888
33092	do	Bucklin and Dodge City.	do	Chicago, Kansas and Nebraska Rwy	26.25	May 21, 1888
33096	do	Dexter and Arkansas City. Ext Dearing	do	Gronau Creek Rwy	16.41	June 10, 1888
33096	do	Le Roy and Independence.	Ext	Verdigrese Valley, Independence and Western R. R.		
34041	Nebraska	Scribner and Lindsay. Ext Oakdale	do	Fremont, Elkhorn and Missouri Valley R. R.	51.62	July 25, 1887
34045	do	Fairfield and Stromsburg.	New	Kansas City and Omaha R. R.	61.49	Aug. 22, 1887
34042	do	Elwood and Curtis. Ext Grant	New	Nebraska and Colorado R. R.	71.74	Oct. 17, 1887
34047	do	Orleans, Nebr., and Blakeman, Kans	New	Burlington and Missouri River R. R. (in Nebr.)	68.12	Dec. 5, 1887
34048	do	Weeping Water and Nebraska City	do	Missouri Pacific Rwy	24.87	Nov. 27, 1887
34049	do	Nebraska City and Auburn.	do	Nebraska Southern Rwy	22.89	Nov. 28, 1887
34040	do	Central City and Arcadia.	do	Burlington and Missouri River R. R. (in Nebr.)	71.97	Dec. 28, 1887
34050	do	Fairbury, Nebr., and Phillipsburgh, Kans	do	Chicago, Kansas and Nebraska Rwy	129.04	Jan. 16, 1888
34051	do	Omaha and Arlington.	do	Fremont, Elkhorn and Missouri Valley R.	28.09	Jan. 16, 1888
34052	do	Platt River Junction (n. o.) and Hastings.	do	do	110.80	Feb. 1, 1888
34053	do	Fairfield and Alma	do	Kansas City and Omaha R. R.	87.70	Feb. 20, 1888

No.	State	Kind	Termini	Railway	Amount	Date
34054	do	do	Fairbury and McCool Junction	St. Joseph and Grand Island R. R.	30.62	Feb. 20, 1888
34055	do	do	Palmer and Burwell	Burlington and Missouri River R. R. (in Nebr).	60.28	Feb. 20, 1888
34050	do	do	Linwood and Geneva	Fremont, Elkhorn and Missouri Valley R. R.	77.53	Feb. 20, 1888
34057	do	do	Ashland and Schuyler	Omaha and Oki Platte R. R.	50.71	Feb. 20, 1888
34058	do	do	Grand Island and Anselmo. Ext. Whitman	Old Island and Wyoming Central R. R.	64.28	Feb. 20, 1888
34030	do	Ext.	Doctus and Nantasket	Omaha and Republican Valley Rwy	9.74	Apr. 10, 1888
34060	do	Ext.	Fairbury, Nebr. and Phillipsburgh, Kans. Ext. Norton, Kans	Chicago, Kansas and Nebraska Rwy	33.78	May 1888
34042	do	do	Grand Island and Whitman. Ext. Alliance	Grand Island and Wyoming Central R. R.	72.14	May 10, 1888
34043	Mo.	do	Elwood and Grant. Ext. Sterling Mo.	Nebraska and Colorado R. R.	86.00	May 1888
35029	do	New.	Roscoe and Menton, Dak.	Chicago, Milwaukee and St. Paul Rwy	41.73	July 25, 1887
35012	do	Ext.	Ashton and Ellendale. Ext. Edgeley	do	26.51	July 25, 1887
35080	do	New.	Rugby and Bottineau	St. Paul, Minneapolis and Manitoba Rwy	38.10	July 8, 1887
35081	do	do	Rutland and Ellendale	do	40.73	Aug. 25, 1887
35002	do	do	Roscoe and Hillview	Chicago, Milwaukee and St. Paul Rwy	18.74	Oct. 3, 1887
35003	do	do	Madison and Bristol	do	103.89	Oct. 1887
35024	do	Ext.	Redfield and Faulkton. Ext Gettysburgh	Chicago and Northwestern Rwy	42.70	Nov. 28, 1887
35004	do	do	Everest and Park River. Ext. Langdon	St. Paul, Minneapolis and Manitoba Rwy	30.51	Dec. 1887
35025	New	do	Fairmont and Monango. Ext Great Falls, Mont.	Minneapolis and Pacific Rwy	36.27	Dec. 5, 1887
35005	do	do	Devil's Lake and Minot	St. Paul, Minneapolis and Manitoba Rwy	349.64	Dec. 15, 1887
35035	New	do	Doland and Groton	Chicago and Northwestern Rwy	30.24	Dec. 1887
35016	do	do	Salem and Mitchell	Chicago, St. Paul, Minneapolis and Omaha Rwy	33.10	Feb. 1888
35028	Ext.	do	Rapid City and Whitewood	Fremont, Elkhorn and Missouri Valley R. R.	37.27	Feb. 1888
35015	do	do	Fargo and La Moure. Ext. Edgeley	Chicago, Milwaukee and St. Paul Rwy	21.90	May 10, 1888
35012	do	Ext.	Roscoe and Hillview. Ext. Eureka	Fargo and Northwestern R. R.	7.98	June 1888
38004	New	do	Drummond and Philipsburgh	Northern Pacific R. R.	26.47	Jan. 2, 1888
38005	Montana.	do	Helena and Great Falls	Montana Central Rwy	99.14	Jan. 10, 1888
38006	do	do	Jefferson City and Basin	Northern Pacific R. R.	28.26	Mar. 7, 1888
38007	do	do	Clough Junction (n. o.) and Marysville	do	12.97	Mar. 20, 1888
36008	Wyoming	do	Missoula and Victor	Missoula and Bitter Root Valley R. R.	35.75	May 10, 1888
37003	Colorado.	do	Chico and King	Fremont, Elkhorn and Missouri Valley R. R.	30.30	May 1888
38023	do	do	El Chico and Trinidad	Denver, South Park and Pacific R. R.	2.48	Oct. 3, 1887
38033	do	do	Chico Springs and Leadville	Denver and Rio Grande R. R.	4.48	Feb. 10, 1887
38034	do	Ext.	Mia (n. o.) and Redcliffe. Ext.	Colorado Midland Rwy	133.05	Oct. 17, 1887
38018	do	do	Mia (n. o.) and Glenwood Spring. Ext Aspen.	Denver and Rio Grande R. R.	48.68	Oct. 28, 1887
38025	do	do	Denver and Red. Glo.	Denver and Rio Grande R. R.	40.72	Dec. 16, 1887
38018	New	do	Mia (u. o.) and Aspen. Change terminus from Mia to Leadville.	Atchison, Topeka and Santa Fé R. R.	117.44	Nov. 27, 1887
				Denver and Rio Grande R. R.	0.56	
38036	do	New	Towner Station (n. o.) and Pueblo	Pueblo and State Line R. R.	150.76	Mar. 1, 1888
38037	Arizona Ter	do	Chico and Ouray	Denver and Rio Grande R. R.	84.88	Apr. 2, 1888
40004	Utah.	do	Maricopa Junction (n. o.) and Phoenix	Maricopa and Phoenix R. R.	35.78	Sept. 15, 1887
42004	Idaho.	do	Coeur d'Alene and Wardner	Coeur d'Alene Rwy. and Navigation Co.	81.90	July 20, 1887
42004	do	do	Algo and Boise City	Idaho Central Rwy	30.69	Oct. 3, 1887
42003	do	Ext.	Coeur d'Aleno and Wardner. Ext. Wallace	Coeur d'Alene Rwy. and Navigation Co	9.71	Oct. 17, 1887
42005	do	do	Coeur d'Aleno and Mo. Ext. Mo.		7.85	May 1888
42016	Washington Ter	New	Walla Walla, Wash. Ter. and Pendleton, Oregon	Columbia and Palouse R. R.	27.81	July 1, 1888
42015	do	New	Marshall and Mo. Ext. Belmont.	Oregon Rwy. and Navigation Co	47.43	Aug. 25, 1887
43017	do	do	Pasco and Cle Elum. Ext Mol no.	Spokane and Palouse Rwy	15.70	Aug. 25, 1887
43011	do	Ext.		Northern Pacific R. R.	81.40	Oct. 3, 1887

L.—*Statement showing miles of railroad service ordered from July 1, 1887, to June 30, 1888—Continued.*

No of route.	State.	Terminal.	Character of service.	Title of company.	Miles.	Date of commencement.
44910	Oregon	Albany Station (n. o.) and Lebanon Station (n. o.)	New	Oregon and California R. R.	12.50	Apr. 9, 1888
45005	Nevada	Reno, Nev., and Camp Ham Station (n. o.), Cal.	do	Nevada and California R. R.	45.28	Mar. 1, 1888
45006	...do	Reno, Nev., and Camp Ham Station (n. o.), Cal. Ext. Long Valley, Cal.	Ext.	...do	11.57	June 26, 1886
46051	California	Saugus Station (n. o.) and Santa Barbara	New	Southern Pacific R. R.	78.88	July 1, 1887
46052	...do	Arcata Wharf (n. o.) and Blue Lake	...do	Arcata and Mad River R. R.	16.00	July 1, 1887
46053	...do	San Bernardino and Duarte	...do	California Central Rwy	41.64	July 4, 1887
46054	...do	Berendo and Raymond	...do	Southern Pacific R. R.	31.38	July 11, 1887
46043	...do	Lodi and Burson. Ext. Valley Springs	Ext.	San Joaquin and Sierra Nevada R. R.	2.00	Oct. 3, 1887
46002	...do	Roseville and Hepley. Ext. Ashland, Oregon	do	Central Pacific R. R.	28.57	Dec. 20, 1887
46055	...do	Riverside and Santa Ana	New	California Central Rwy	37.90	Dec. 19, 1887
46040	...do	San Luis Obispo and Los Alamos. Ext. Los Olivos Station	Ext.	Pacific Coast Rwy	12.20	Jan. 10, 1888
46053	...do	San Bernardino and Duarte. Ext. Los Angeles, covering route 46046. (n. o.)	do	California Central Rwy	22.09	Mar. 23, 1888
46056	...do	San Bernardino and Lugonia	New	do	9.25	Apr. 9, 1888
46057	...do	Oceanside and Escondido	do	do	22.77	Apr. 9, 1888
46058	...do	Los Angeles and Port Ballona	do	do	18.07	May 1, 1888
46005	...do	Sacramento City and Shingle Spring. Ext. Placerville	Ext.	Sacramento and Placerville R. R.	12.15	June 15, 1888
46053	...do	Riverside and Santa Ana. Ext. Capistrano	do	California Central Rwy	21.95	Apr. 9, 1888

M.—*Statistics of mileage, increase in mileage, annual transportation, and cost of the railroad service from 1836 to June 30, 1888.*

Date.	Length of routes.	Annual transportation.	Cost per annum.	Increase in length of routes.	Decrease in length of routes.
	Miles.	*Miles.*		*Miles.*	*Miles.*
June 30, 1836		*1,878,296			
June 30, 1837	974	*1,793,024	*$307,444		
June 30, 1838		*2,356,852	*494,123		
June 30, 1839		*3,396,055	*520,602		
June 30, 1840		*3,889,053	*595,353		
June 30, 1841		*3,946,450	*585,843		
June 30, 1842	3,091	*4,424,262	482,568	2,117	
June 30, 1843		*5,692,402	*733,687		
Nov. 4, 1843	3,714	(*)	531,752	622	
June 30, 1844		*5,747,355	*802,006		
June 30, 1845		*6,484,592	*843,430		
Oct. 31, 1845	4,092	(*)	587,760		
June 30, 1846		*7,781,828	*870,570		
Nov. 1, 1846	4,402		587,769	310	
June 30, 1847		4,170,403	597,475		
Nov. 1, 1847	4,735		597,923	333	
June 30, 1848		4,327,400	584,192		
Oct. 1, 1848	4,957		587,204	222	
June 30, 1849	5,497	4,861,177	635,740	540	
June 30, 1850	6,886	6,524,593	818,227	1,389	
June 30, 1851	8,255	8,364,503	985,019	1,369	
June 30, 1852	10,146	11,083,768	1,275,520	1,891	
June 30, 1853	12,415	12,986,705	1,601,329	2,269	
June 30, 1854	14,440	15,433,389	1,758,619	2,025	
June 30, 1855	18,333	19,902,469	2,073,089	3,893	
June 30, 1856	20,323	21,809,296	2,310,389	1,990	
June 30, 1857	22,530	24,267,944	2,559,817	2,207	
June 30, 1858	24,431	25,763,452	2,828,301	1,901	
June 30, 1859	26,010	27,268,384	3,243,974	1,579	
June 30, 1860	27,129	27,653,749	3,349,662	1,119	
May 31, 1861	16,886	15,701,093	†978,910		6,886
June 30, 1861	22,018	23,116,823	2,543,709	1,775	
June 30, 1862	21,338	22,777,219	2,498,115		689
June 30, 1863	22,152	22,871,558	2,538,517	814	
June 30, 1864	22,616	23,301,942	2,567,044	464	
June 30, 1865	23,401	24,087,568	2,707,421	785	
June 30, 1866	32,092	30,609,467	3,301,592	‡8,691	
June 30, 1867	34,015	32,437,900	3,812,600	1,923	
June 30, 1868	36,018	34,886,178	4,177,126	2,003	
June 30, 1869	39,537	41,899,284	4,723,680	3,519	
June 30, 1870	43,727	47,551,970	5,128,901	4,190	
June 30, 1871	49,834	55,857,048	5,734,979	6,107	
June 30, 1872	57,911	62,491,749	6,502,771	8,077	
June 30, 1873	63,457	65,621,445	7,257,190	5,546	
June 30, 1874	67,734	72,460,545	9,118,190	4,277	
June 30, 1875	70,083	75,154,910	9,216,518	2,349	
June 30, 1876	72,348	77,741,172	9,543,184	2,265	
June 30, 1877	74,546	85,358,710	§9,653,936	2,198	
June 30, 1878	77,120	92,120,305	9,546,595	2,574	
June 30, 1879	79,991	93,092,992	‖9,067,590	2,871	
June 30, 1880	85,320	96,497,463	10,408,986	5,329	
June 30, 1881	91,569	103,521,229	11,613,368	6,249	
June 30, 1882	100,563	113,995,918	12,733,184	8,994	
June 30, 1883	110,208	129,198,641	13,847,800	9,645	
June 30, 1884	117,160	142,541,392	15,012,603	6,952	
June 30, 1885	121,032	151,910,845	16,637,983	3,872	
June 30, 1886	123,933	165,699,389	17,336,512	2,901	
June 30, 1887	130,949	169,689,866	18,056,272	7,016	
June 30, 1888	143,713	185,485,783	19,524,959	12,764	

* Railroad and steam-boat service combined; no separate report.
† Decrease caused by the discontinuance of service in the Southern States.
‡ Increase attributable in part to the resumption of service in the Southern States.
§ Decrease in cost caused by reductions in the rates of pay under act of July 12, 1876.
‖ Decrease in cost caused by reductions in the rates of pay under act of June 17, 1878.

N.—*Statement of all contracts made, or in operation, for mail-bags, mail-catchers, mail-bag label-cases, use of patents, and mail locks and keys during the fiscal year ending June 30, 1888.*

Articles contracted for.	Name of contractor.	Residence.	Term of contract.	Contract price.					
				Size No. 0.	Size No. 1.	Size No. 2.	Size No. 3.	Size No. 4.	Size No. 5.
Cotton-canvas mail-sacks*	John Boyle	New York, N. Y.	Four years from April 1, 1885	$0.95	$0.89	$0.71	$0.29½		
Registered foreign mail-sacks*	do	do	do	.77	.48	.22½	.15		
Jute-canvas mail-sacks*	Lewis S. Samuel	do	do		.46½	.46½	.11½		
Leather horse mail-bags*	Perkins, Campbell & Co.	Cincinnati, Ohio	do		6.83	4.90	3.75		
Leather mail-pouches*	John E. Quinn	Toledo, Ohio	do			5.30	6.40	$2.90	$2.34
Through registered mail-pouches*	Francis H. Smith	New York, N. Y.	do	5.84	5.84	4.17		.69	
Inner registered mail-sacks	John Boyle	do	do	1.29½	1.29½	.83½	.67		
Corn mail-sacks*	Lewis S. Samuel	do	do						
Mail-catcher pouches*	John Boyle	Brooklyn, N. Y.	One year from February 1, 1888						$9.64½
Mail-bag label cases (iron)‡	The Wm Lang Co	do	do						3.44
Mail-bag label cases (brass)‡	Eugene Beebe, jr.	Montgomery, Ala.	One year from July 1, 1887						.64½
Mail-bag catchers‡	do	do	One year from February 1, 1888						12.00
Brackets for catchers‡	The Smith & Egge Manufacturing Company,	Bridgeport, Conn.							1.10
Mail-bag cord-fasteners and label-holders‡	D. K. Sickles, V. Hodges and A. L. Pitney.	Washington, D. C.	Determinable at any time by the Postmaster-General.						.30
Use of patent.									97.32
Do	John Boyle.	New York, N. Y.	Four, eight, or twelve years from September 1, 1880, at option of Postmaster-General						.96
General mail-locks†	The Smith & Egge Manufacturing Company.	Bridgeport, Conn.	do						.10
Keys to same†	do	do	do						.32
Through mail-locks†	do	do	do						.06
Keys to same†	do	do	do						.75
City-mail service locks†	do	do	do						.12
Keys to same†	do	do	do						.34
Street letter-box locks (inside)†	do	Oxford, N. C	do						.60
Keys to same†	W. F. Beasley		Four, eight, or twelve years from January 1, 1881, at option of Postmaster-General.						.86
Through registered mail-locks†									.15
									1.50
Keys to same†	do	Bridgeport, Conn.	From May 26, 1888						.25
Street letter-box locks (outside)	The Smith & Egge Manufacturing Company.	do	do						.50
Repaired letter-box locks (outside).	do	do	do						.30
Repaired locks (iron)	do								.32

PLACES OF DELIVERY.

*Boston, New York, Philadelphia, Washington, Cincinnati, Chicago, and Saint Louis.   †Washington, D. C.

O.—*Statement of the number, description, prices, and cost of mail-bags, mail-catchers, etc., purchased, and put into service during the fiscal year ending June 30, 1888.*

No.	Article.	Size.	Price.	Itemized cost.	Aggregate cost.
5,000	Leather mail-pouches	No. 2	$5.29	$26,450.00	
5,000	......do	No. 3	4.09	20,450.00	
5,000	......do	No. 4	2.98	14,900.00	
15,000					$61,800.00
800	Leather horse mail-bags	No. 1	5.33	4,264.00	
700	......do	No. 2	4.39	3,073.00	
300	......do	No. 3	3.70	1,110.00	
1,800					8,447.00
1,000	Through registered pouches	No. 1	5.84	5,840.00	
500	......do	No. 2	4.47	2,235.00	
	Royalty on same		.10	150.00	
1,500					8,225.00
6,000	Mail-catcher pouches		3.41	20,460.00	
	Royalty on same		.10	600.00	
					21,060.00
144,000	Jute-canvas sacks	No. 1	.48½	70,470.00	
10,000	......do	No. 2	.43½	4,393.75	
15,000	......do	No. 3	.12½	1,940.62½	
169,000					76,804.37½
2,000	Cotton-canvas sacks	No. 3	.23½	470.00	
1,000	Foreign registered-sacks	No. 1	.43	430.00	
100,000	Mail-bag cord-fasteners		.087	8,700.00	
	Royalty on same		.05	5,000.00	
					13,700.00
16,000	Mail-bag label-cases (iron)		.0442	707.20	
400	Mail-catchers		3.10	1,240.00	
200	Brackets for same		.30	60.00	
					1,300.00
	Total cost of mail-bags, etc				192,943.57½
	Cost of repairing mail-bags				54,086.62
	Grand total				247,030.19
	Unexpended balance of appropriation				27,969.81
	Appropriation				275,000.00

P.—*Statement of mail locks and keys purchased and repaired, and of the expense incurred on account thereof, during the year ending June 30, 1888.*

Quantity.	Description.	Price.	Cost.	Aggregate.
25,000	Iron mail-locks	$0.52	$13,000.00	
100	Inside box mail-locks	.85	85.00	
5,000	Street letter-box locks (repaired)	.35	1,750.00	
10,000	Street letter-box locks (new)	.47	4,700.00	
6,138	Iron mail-locks (repaired)	.33	2,025.54	
				$21,560.54
500	Mail-key chains (No. 1)	.28	140.00	
4,000	Mail-key chains (No. 2)	.20	800.00	
				940.00
				22,500.54
	Unexpended balance			499.46
	Appropriation			23,000.00

REPORT

OF THE

GENERAL SUPERINTENDENT

OF

RAILWAY MAIL SERVICE

FOR THE

FISCAL YEAR ENDED JUNE 30, 1888.

REPORT

GENERAL SUPERINTENDENT OF RAILWAY MAIL SERVICE.

POST-OFFICE DEPARTMENT,
OFFICE OF GENERAL SUPERINTENDNET OF
RAILWAY MAIL SERVICE,
Washington, D. C., November 1, 1888.

SIR: I have the honor to present to you herewith the annual report
of the operations of the Railway Mail Service for the fiscal year ended
June 30, 1888, which may be summarized as follows: Up to the close of
the fiscal year ended June 30, 1888, service had been authorized by the
Department upon 143,713.42 miles of railroad. Postal clerks were employed in the distribution of the mail on 126,310.73 miles; service on
the remainder, namely, 17,402.69 miles, being performed by closed
pouches. On the same date there were in operation 41 inland steam-
boat lines, aggregating 5,972.80 miles, on which postal clerks were employed.

There were employed in handling and separating the mails while in
transit on railroad routes 4,641, and on steam-boat routes 54 railway
postal clerks, making a total of 4,695 men.

While in the performance of their duty the postal clerks on railroads
traveled (in crews) 122,031,104 miles, and those employed on steamboats 1,767,649 miles.

While so traveling they distributed 6,528,772,060 pieces of ordinary
mail matter, and receipted for, recorded, protected, and properly distrib-
16,001,059 registered packages and cases and 1,103,083 through-registered pouches and inner-registered sacks.

During the year 12,764.42 miles of new railroad service have been
added, being an increase of 9.74 per cent. The lines on which service
was performed by clerks show an increase of 9,701.61 miles, or 8.32 per
cent. Lines supplied by closed pouches were increased from 14,350.05
miles at the close of the fiscal year 1887 to 17,402.59 miles on June 30,
1888, being an increase of 3,052.54 miles, or 21.27 per cent. The annual
mileage of this class of service for 1887 was 14,489,613 miles; for 1888
17,436,819 miles, an increase of 2,947,206 miles, or 20.34 per cent.; and
the number of pouches exchanged daily increased from 11,714 for the
year 1887 to 13,059 at the close of 1888, being a daily increase of 1,345,
or 11.48 per cent.

Compared with 1887 the number of clerks employed on steam-boat
lines decreased from 57 to 54, and the length of routes increased from
5,864.89 miles to 5,972.80, being an increase of 107.91 miles, or 1.84 per

331

cent.; while the number of miles run by clerks dropped from 1,868,747 miles in 1887 to 1,767,649 in 1888, being a decrease of 101,098 miles, or 5.41 per cent.

The total number of clerks in the service at the close of the fiscal year ended June 30, 1887, was 4,851; on June 30, 1888, 5,094, being an increase of 243, or 5.01 per cent.

The following exhibit shows the nature of service, the number of clerks engaged in each class of work, and the increase over 1887:

Fiscal year ended—	Employed on railroad lines.	Employed on steamboat lines.	Detailed to transfer service.	Detailed to office duty.	Total.
June 30, 1888	4,641	54	219	180	5,094
June 30, 1887	4,403	57	218	173	4,851
Increase	238	*3	1	7	243

* Decrease.

During the year ended June 30, 1887, 5,851,394,057 pieces of all classes of mail matter were handled, and 1,734,617 errors checked, showing that .99.971 per cent. of all mail handled was correctly distributed, or, in other words, of every 3,374 pieces handled, 3,373 were correctly dispatched and 1 incorrectly. In 1888 the number of pieces handled was 6,545,876,202, and the number of errors checked 1,765,821, being a correct distribution of .99.973 per cent. of all mail handled, or one error to every 3,707 pieces.

The increase in the number of pieces of ordinary mail handled was 8.76 per cent., while the increase in the number of errors was but 1.79 per cent.

As will be seen by table K^x., facilities for the handling of mail in transit have been increased since June 30, 1887, on 19,145 miles of railway post-office routes. These betterments include new railway post-office lines established or extended, additional trips over old lines, together with the miles of routes covered by full railway post-office car service on lines where apartment car service was in operation at the close of the previous fiscal year.

Division.	Comprising the States of—	Miles.
First	New England	451.40
Second	New York, New Jersey, Pennsylvania, Delaware, and the Peninsula of Maryland and Virginia	369.51
Third	Maryland (excluding the eastern shore), part of Virginia, West Virginia, North Carolina, and the District of Columbia	412.52
Fourth	South Carolina, Georgia, Florida, Alabama, Mississippi, and Louisiana	1,413.52
Fifth	Ohio, Indiana, Kentucky, and Tennessee	3,237.37
Sixth	Wisconsin, Illinois, Iowa, Nebraska, Minnesota, Upper Peninsula of Michigan, and the Territories of Dakota and Wyoming	5,169.73
Seventh	Missouri, Kansas, Arkansas, Texas, Colorado, and the Territories of Indian and New Mexico	7,179.48
Eighth	California, Nevada, Oregon, and the Territories of Alaska, Idaho, Montana, Utah, and Washington	799.59
Ninth	Through mails, New York to Chicago, via Buffalo, Suspension Bridge, Toledo and Detroit; the lines of the Lake Shore and Michigan Southern Railroad, and the Lower Peninsula of Michigan	112.73
	Total	19,145.85

CASE EXAMINATIONS.

A marked improvement is shown this year in the record of case examinations of the permanent railway postal clerks, the average per cent. of cards correctly distributed having increased from 87.50 in 1887 to 90.50 in 1888.

The subjoined table is inserted to show the record of case examinations of permanent clerks made during the year under review, compared with similar examinations held during 1887 :

Division.	Examinations.	Cards handled.	Cards correct.	Cards incorrect.	Cards not known.	Average per cent. correct.
First	705	444, 240	439, 744	4. 482	14	98. 09
Second	1, 088	1, 534, 224	1, 182, 912	107, 982	243, 330	77. 10
Third	443	561, 395	490, 691	36, 280	34, 419	87. 40
Fourth	882	683, 419	658, 746	21, 661	3, 012	96. 39
Fifth	983	1, 145, 801	1, 105, 195	39, 100	1, 506	96. 46
Sixth	837	1, 154, 418	1, 064, 642	50, 313	39, 463	92. 22
Seventh	2, 011	1, 320, 668	1, 235, 686	76, 081	8, 901	93. 57
Eighth	272	110, 032	101, 899	3, 005	5, 128	92. 60
Ninth	588	963, 707	886, 473	53, 372	23, 862	91. 98
Total for 1888	7, 809	7, 917, 904	7, 165, 988	392, 276	359, 635	90. 50
Total for 1887	6. 577	6, 517, 650	5, 703, 176	337, 240	477, 234	87. 50
Increase	1, 232	1, 400, 254	1, 462, 812	55, 036	*117, 599	3. 00

* Decrease.

Statement of case examinations of probationary railway postal clerks for the fiscal year ended June 30, 1888.

Division.	Probationary appointees.	Examinations.	Cards handled.	Cards correct.	Cards incorrect.	Cards not known.	Average per cent. correct.	Probationers who received permanent appointments.	Average per cent. correct during probation made by those permanently appointed.	Dropped during probation including those permitted to resign.	Probationary appointees who failed to pass final examination.
First	71	144	102, 927	92, 075	9, 502	1, 350	89. 46	48	92. 97	14	19. 72
Second	319	1, 043	636, 564	388, 080	58, 919	189, 656	60. 96	130	65. 97	88	27. 58
Third	64	343	258, 237	194, 707	23, 751	39, 779	75. 39	45	79. 24	21	32. 81
Fourth	95	220	136, 214	124, 544	11, 384	286	91. 43	35	96. 65	22	23. 15
Fifth	179	657	553, 886	528, 087	23, 353	2, 603	95. 34	160	96. 18	15	8. 37
Sixth	270	949	1, 018 873	769, 811	80, 586	108, 476	73. 55	217	80. 80	64	23. 71
Seventh	294	1, 379	763, 995	633, 696	73, 615	56, 684	82. 95	141	87. 57	53	18. 63
Eighth	52	371	169, 735	145, 764	8, 580	15, 391	85. 87	34	91. 16	17	32. 69
Ninth	109	527	451, 919	347, 200	41, 470	63, 249	76. 82	26	82. 26	20	18. 34
Total 1888	1, 453	5, 633	4, 092, 350	3, 223, 964	331, 160	537, 474	78. 78	836	85. 87	314	21. 51
Total 1887	1, 449	4, 482	3, 630, 858	2, 944, 239	307, 055	319, 564	81. 09	778	85. 34	341	23. 53
Increase	4	1, 151	461, 492	279, 725	*25, 895	217, 910	*2. 31	58	. 53	*27	*2. 02

* Decrease.

It may not be out of place to explain here that the reason why the average per cent. of cards correctly handled by probationers approaches so near to the percentage attained by the permanent clerks each year is owing to the fact that while the former have many examinations on a small number of offices the latter, who are required to make a much wider distribution, have many more cards to handle at each examination.

The above tables show that the clerks holding permanent appoint ments increased their percentage of cards correctly handled from 87.50 in 1887 to 90.50 in 1888, and there was an increase from 85.34 in 1887 to 85.87 in 1888, shown in the record made by probationary clerks who received permanent appointments during the year.

The average number of cards handled at each examination by each probationary clerk during the year ended June 30, 1888, was 726, and the average number handled by each permanent clerk was 1,014.

In 1887 950,613 through registered pouches (including inner-registered sacks) were handled by postal clerks, and in 1888 1,103,083, being an increase of 152,470 pieces, or 16.03 per cent., while the registered pack ages and cases handled increased from 15,752,569 in 1887 to 16,001,059 in 1888, being an increase of 248,490 pieces, or 1.57 per cent.

For many years past postal-cards and stamped envelopes, issued to post-masters for sale to the public, have been forwarded from the manufacto-ries as registered matter through railway post-offices to the post-offices ordering them. In order to relieve postal clerks of the care and handling of these heavy cases of supplies and allow sufficient room on several of the more important railway post-office lines for the storage and distribution of the legitimate mail, Congress, at its last session, granted authority to the honorable Postmaster General to forward a portion of this bulky matter by freight lines to depots of distribution. This measure, so far as the postal-cards are concerned, was put into operation early in the current year by the establishment of distributing depots at Chicago, Ill., and Saint Louis, Mo., to which points postal-cards, to meet the de-mand in certain Western and Southwestern States, are now forwarded by the car-load as freight, thereby relieving the main railway post-office lines between New York and Chicago and New York and Saint Louis of the handling of much of this matter and allowing room and time for the storage, separation, and distribution of the ordinary and registered mails, as well as in saving to the Government a considerable sum of money.

MAIL FOR CITY DELIVERY.

In addition to the number of letters, etc., distributed during the year, there were separated for city delivery 143,091,750 pieces of letter and 19,575 pieces of paper mail.

The number of pieces of this matter has decreased somewhat from the number reported last year, owing, mainly, to changes of schedules, which resulted in the arrival of railway post-offices at destination at earlier hours, thereby allowing the post-office, through which the mail is to be delivered, to make its own distribution in time for the first carrier delivery.

The following is a comparative statement of city letters distributed by railway post-offices:

Year ended—	Packages distributed.	Incorrect slips.	Errors.	Letters distributed.	Papers distributed.
June 30, 1887	1,966,858	6,117	18,705	147,537,232	22,882
June 30, 1888	1,907,890	11,342	23,559	143,091,750	19,575
Decrease	58,968	*5,225	*4,854	4,445,482	3,307

*Increase.

CASUALTIES.

The casualties during 1887–'88 were more numerous than for any preceding fiscal year, there having been 248 accidents to trains upon which postal clerks were employed. In the wrecks on lines 4 clerks were killed, 63 seriously and 45 slightly injured. Sixty-four were so severely injured as to require the employment of acting clerks to keep up their runs. The sum of $9,022.48 was paid such acting clerks during the fiscal year for the services rendered by them. Acting clerks had also to be provided for 12 postal clerks who were injured in 1886–'87 and not able to resume service at the commencement of the fiscal year; the amount paid by the Department during the year on account of the casualties in 1886–'87 being $2,840.64.

INSURANCE.

In view of the fact that no action has ever been taken by Congress in reference to providing for the care of clerks permanently injured in this service, and those dependent upon them in case of death, which humane action has so often been recommended by the Department, I am led to believe that there are insurmountable objections on the part of the people's representatives to the creation of anything of the nature of a civil pension roll, and it would therefore seem to be useless for me to renew the recommendations of my predecessors. I believe, however, that some steps should be taken in the direction of affording aid to the families of those who may be killed while in the discharge of their duties, and beg to invite your attention to the following outlines of a plan for relief in such cases which, I think, will commend itself to every railway postal clerk, and which, I trust, may meet with the sanction of Congress.

For the purpose of insuring the lives of railway postal clerks while in the actual performance of duty, there shall be deducted from the pay of each and every railway postal clerk the sum of 10 cents per month, which sum shall be withheld by the paying office upon the payment of monthly salaries; and the total amount accrued from this source shall be passed quarterly to the credit of an account to be known as "The railway postal clerk's insurance fund," by the proper accounting officer of the Treasury of the United States. Upon the death of a railway postal clerk from injuries received while in the actual performance of his duties as such, provided his death occurs within the period of one year from the date of injury, there shall be paid to his heir, or heirs, out of such fund the sum of $1,000, by United States Treasury warrant; that a committee of three, consisting of the General Superintendent and two division superintendents of the railway mail service, be authorized to pass upon the evidence of death, etc., and upon whose joint certificate payment by warrant is to be based.

Before any plan of this character can be carried into effect it will, of course, be necessary to obtain the consent of all who are to be affected thereby, and as it is desirable to have the consent of every railway postal clerk borne on the roll of the Department, it is suggested, as an inducement to those clerks who are detailed to office duty and do not run the risk attending travel in R. P. O. cars, to enter into this arrangement, that, in the event of the death of any one of the latter class from injury or natural causes during their term of service, a sum equal to one-third of the amount to be allowed in cases of death resulting from accidents on the line be paid in the same manner as is prescribed for that class of cases.

Under this plan of insurance it will be noticed (1) that the Government is not called upon to contribute to the fund; (2) that the amount deducted from the pay of the clerks for the fund need not be drawn from the Treasury by paying offices; (3) that the security is ample; (4) that the rate of assessment is merely nominal, and (5) that the creation of any additional offices for the supervision or management of the fund will be unnecessary.

REGISTERED PACKAGES, ETC.

In the matter of handling registered matter in transit, I desire to call attention to the necessity for the employment of registry clerks in certain railway post-office lines running between the more important commercial centers of the country, who should be required to take charge of the registered matter that may be received on their trains, and become solely responsible for its safety and proper disposition; thereby relieving the clerk in charge so that he may have sufficient time to see that his subordinates properly perform their duties, and that the ordinary mail is properly pouched and dispatched. Under existing arrangements, and owing to the enormous quantity of ordinary mail delivered to the larger railway post-offices on each trip, the clerk in charge, into whose custody registered matter is placed, can not give such an examination to each separate piece of this valuable matter as is required by the Department and which it should receive when the transfer is made.

These clerks in charge are now compelled, on account of the limited time allowed for the exchange of mails at stations, to give receipts for packages, pouches, and cases of this matter, representing large amounts in value, which they have no time to verify or even cursorily examine until their trains are miles away from the place of transfer. The number of pieces delivered is, of course, counted upon delivery; but while the total number delivered may be correct, there can be no certainty on the part of the receiving clerk that he gave receipts for the same numbered packages as it is claimed were delivered to him, or that this mail is moving to destination in the right direction. The Chief Post-Office Inspector, in a letter to this office concerning the custom of receipting for through-registered pouches without checking or verifying the lists, says:

This reprehensible practice * * * is against the regulations, good administration, honest treatment of the patrons of the mails; subjects good clerks to suspicion and totally prevents the object and theory of the registry system.

With this opinion I fully concur and believe that the evils referred to can be remedied by the appointment of registry clerks, whose runs could be so arranged as to lap over several miles of the route, thereby giving sufficient time to enable a hand-to-hand delivery to be made, and a descriptive list of the articles turned over to be exchanged and checked. These clerks would be required to perform all and every duty in connection with the registered mail to insure its safety while in the custody of this service, and would render unnecessary the detention of the mail at any point en route, for the purpose of verification. I regret that, owing to the condition of the current appropriation, this plan can not be put into operation at once. I have, however, entered, in my estimates for the fiscal year ending June 30, 1890, submitted herewith, an item to cover the expense of employing additional railway postal clerks for the performance of this special service, which I trust will meet with the approval of Congress.

IMPROVEMENTS.

The improvements in this service during the past fiscal year and up to date have been more extensive than perhaps during any previous year in its history. A noticeable feature in the improvements is that they have been more general and distributed over a greater area of country than has heretofore been found practicable, embracing New England, the Southern and Middle States, the transcontinental service between Chicago and San Francisco, and also the northwestern section traversed by the Northern Pacific Railroad.

Following are brief statements of the new service ordered, with date of establishment, chronologically arranged:

September 20, 1887.—A line of 40-foot postal cars was authorized between Chicago, Ill., and North McGregor, Iowa, this new service taking up and discontinuing the old apartment car line between Milwaukee and Prairie du Chien, Wis., and establishing a through railway post-office line of 40-foot cars the whole distance between Chicago and North McGregor, thereby furnishing an additional and independent line between Chicago and Milwaukee, and securing to the old line between Milwaukee and Prairie du Chien a greatly improved service by the additional space afforded for the proper and speedy distribution of the mails, and greatly enhancing its importance to the country local to it by the extension to Chicago, thereby affording the country dependent upon the entire line all possible facilities for direct communication with that important business center.

December 20, 1887.—New service was on this date ordered between Ashland, Oregon, and Henley, Cal., thereby opening a new line between Portland, Oregon, and Sacramento, Cal. The establishment of this new service followed immediately the completion of the Oregon and California Railroad, and resulted in an advance in delivery of twenty-four hours of all ordinary mails passing between Portland and Sacramento, and in the advance of valuable registered mails from two to three days, as previous to the opening of the through line all registered mails were forwarded via Ogden, Utah, and the Green River and Huntington railway post office.

This is looked upon by the Department as one of the most important pieces of new service established during the present fiscal year, as the advantages above detailed fully indicate.

A further slight change in this railway post-office has been made by extending it to San Francisco, so that the railway post-office cars now run direct to and from Portland and San Francisco.

January 1, 1888.—An important change in the service, affecting New England, was the change of schedule on the Boston and Albany Railroad, to leave Boston at 6.30 p. m. instead of 6 p. m., and connect at Albany at 1.35 a. m. with the fast mail leaving New York at 9 p. m., thereby affording an opportunity for a more complete close of the p. m. business mails and connections from Boston.

January 17, 1888.—Under this date an order was issued establishing a line of 40-foot postal cars between Cincinnati, Ohio, and Chattanooga, Tenn. This additional space became absolutely essential to meet the demands of the public servable by or dependent upon this railway post-office for the transmission of the mails from and to Cincinnati and Chattanooga via the Cincinnati, New Orleans and Texas Pacific Railroad; but the demands were not satisfied until long after the Department fully realized the needs in the premises, because of more urgent demands elsewhere and insufficient appropriation. These 40-foot cars were placed on the new fast through run, and the apartment cars formerly used were placed on a later train, thereby providing an additional line for local and intermediate service, which was not possible with previous facilities.

February 14, 1888.—An order was issued substituting a line of 50-foot postal cars between Pacific Junction, Iowa, and McCook, Nebr., for the line of 40-foot cars before in operation, and establishing a 40-foot line between Kansas City, Mo., and Oxford, Nebr., for the apartment cars previously in use on this line.

The above increase in space was an absolute necessity to complete the establishment of a through R. P. O. line between Chicago and Denver via Omaha, Nebr., and between Saint Louis and Denver via Kansas City, Mo., and the Burlington and Missouri River Railroad system, to constitute a through direct line to run in connection with the fast mail between Chicago and Omaha. This new service affords improved facilities for the satisfactory and expeditious handling of the mails for the country traversed by the above line, and one that fully compensates the Department for the expense incurred, by insuring to the public the more rapid transmission of its mails.

March 3, 1888.—Arrangements were completed between the Department and the Chicago, Burlington and Quincy Railroad Company for increasing the fast-mail service between Chicago, Ill., and Council Bluffs, Iowa, from six to seven times a week, so as to make the service between those points daily, Sundays included, instead of daily except Sundays, as was the schedule previous to the change. This change affected the trains moving in both directions, east and west. The benefits of this new service are very far-reaching in their effects, being equally advantageous to Boston, New York, and other points in the east as to Chicago and vicinity. Previous to this change there was no through direct connection for points west of Chicago via the fast mail for such mails as accumulated for dispatch on Fridays from Boston, New York, and the east for the Pacific coast; but now, the service being daily, there is no interruption or delay to the regular course of transmission.

Prior to the date above mentioned there was no fast-mail service east from Council Bluffs, although the Department had the privilege of utilizing the fastest trains in operation between San Francisco and Council Bluffs. But from the latter point east no special provision existed for advancing the mails delivered at Council Bluffs from the west. In connection, however, with the increase of the service west-bound from daily except Sundays, to daily, Sundays included, arrangements were also completed with the Chicago, Burlington and Quincy Railroad for a fast mail east-bound between Council Bluffs and Chicago, taking up at the former point the through fast connection from San Francisco in the p. m. and delivering the same at Chicago in the early a. m. of the following day. This fast mail had the effect of reducing the transit time one full day between the Pacific coast and Chicago stand-point, securing the arrival at Chicago on Fridays at 7.50 a. m. of the mails dispatched from San Francisco the previous Monday at 3 p. m., instead of arriving at Chicago, as by previous schedule, Saturday at 6.55 a. m.

March 30, 1888.—It seems proper in this place to mention that facilities for exchanging mails with Mexico have been greatly improved during the past year by the completion of the Mexican International Railroad between Eagle Pass, Tex. (Piedras Negras, Mexico), and Torreon, Mexico. This line was completed about the 1st of March last, and immediately upon official notification of the same a general order was issued March 30, 1888, directing the dispatch of all foreign closed mails for the City of Mexico, and also the domestic accumulation destined for the interior of Mexico, to be dispatched via Eagle Pass. By this change an advance of one full day is secured to all mails from New York and the Northern, Middle, and Southern States to the City of Mexico. Under the former schedule of dispatch via El Paso. Tex., the transit time from New York to the City of Mexico was as follows:

Leave New York 4.30 a. m. Monday; arrive Mexico City 7.15 a. m. following Monday.

The present schedule is: Leave New York 4.30 a. m. Monday; arrive Mexico City 7.15 a. m. Sunday.

A net gain of one full day from New York and the East to Mexico City, and a similar gain is also made for correspondence from Mexico City destined for New York and the East.

May 6, 1888.—A line of 60-foot postal cars was ordered in lieu of the 50-foot cars then in use on the R. P. O. line between Washington, D. C., and Charlotte, N. C. This is the north end of the trunk line between Washington, D. C., and New Orleans, La. The increased space has long been needed to admit of the correct handling and distribution of the heavy mails passing over this line to and from New York and New Orleans.

May 27, 1888.—An important item is the improved service via the Chicago and Louisville R. P. O. (Louisville, New Albany and Chicago R. R.). Frequent demands were made for an earlier dispatch from Louisville in the a. m. of mails for the South via the Louisville and Nashville road, but a compliance with these demands had always been impracticable for the reason that no sufficient quantity of mail was available for dispatch in the early a. m. from Louisville, owing to the schedules between Chicago and Cincinnati, the hour of arrival at Louisville being about 9 a. m. This was too late to justify the expense of a fast train from that point south. Now, however, the fast train is had, leaving Chicago at 8.30 p. m., and arriving at Louisville at 6.29 a. m., and leaving Louisville at 6.50 a. m., and arriving at Nashville at 12.20 p. m., Montgomery 9.45 p. m., and New Orleans 7.55 following a. m. This is a very advantageous arrangement of schedule, as it places the p. m. Chicago mails in Louisville for first carrier delivery the following morning, and delivers the Louisville morning papers same day of publication, for all points south of Louisville to Montgomery, Ala., reaching New Orleans the next morning at 7.55, instead of next night at 7.20, as by the old schedule; reaching Montgomery at 9.45 p. m., instead of 7.10 following a m., by old schedule; reaching Nashville at 12.20 p. m., instead of 7.40 p. m., and advances the connections for southern Texas from twelve to twenty-four hours, by making the connection at New Orleans in the a. m., by the new schedule, instead of in the p. m., as was the case by the old schedule.

May 29, 1888.—A new schedule was put into operation between Portland, Oregon, and Chicago, Ill., via the Northern Pacific and the Chicago, Minneapolis and Saint Paul railroads. Previous to the introduction of this new schedule the transit time east-bound between Portland and Chicago was five days three hours and thirty minutes, but by the introduction of the new schedule the time was reduced one full day, so as to leave Portland at 11 a. m. Monday and arrive at Chicago 7 a. m. Friday, instead of leaving Portland at 11.55 p. m. Monday, and arriving at Chicago at 7 a. m. Saturday, under the old schedule. This is a very important improvement because of the commercial relationship existing between Chicago and all points via the Northern Pacific road, even to Portland, and furnishes a fast mail service east and west, between Chicago and Portland, which fully meets all reasonable demands for the expeditious transmission of the mails. The present schedule between these points is three days thirteen hours west, and three days twenty hours east.

June 1, 1888.—Growing out of the improved service between Chicago and Louisville, an order was issued June 1, 1888, for a line of 40-foot postal cars to run between Nashville, Tenn., and Montgomery, Ala., in lieu of the line of apartment cars at that time in operation. The gradual natural increase in the volume of mail going forward via the R. P. O. from Cincinnati, Ohio, to New Orleans, La., via the Louisville and Nashville trunk-line system, together with the new connection from Chicago via the Louisville, New Albany and Chicago Railroad to Louisville, resulted in a volume of mail of such proportions that it was found absolutely necessary to furnish increased space and facilities to meet the requirements of storage and distribution in order to fully secure all the advantages of lateral connections between Nashville and Montgomery and beyond.

June 3, 1888.—Taking effect this date an important change was made in the schedule of the trains between New York and Boston via the New York, New Haven and Hartford and Boston and Albany Railroads (Boston, Springfield and New York R. P. O.), so as to leave New York at 11 p. m. instead of 10.30 p. m., and arriving at Boston at 6.01 instead of 6.20 a. m., thereby shortening the time east-bound 49 minutes; and to leave Boston at 11.01 instead of 10.31 p. m., and arrive at New York at 6 instead of 6.25 a. m., decreasing the transit time between Boston and New York 55 minutes.

This is one of the most important changes made for many years for the transmission of the heavy mails from and to New England and New York. The later dispatch from New York insures the heavy and important connection from the southwest via the Pennsylvania Railroad and the south via the Washington and Jacksonville and Washington and New Orleans railway post-offices, which two latter connections reached New York at 9.15 p. m. Heretofore (as above stated in connection with the Pennsylvania arrival at Jersey City) the important connections from Jacksonville and New Orleans were frequently missed for New England at New York because of slight delay in the arrival at Jersey City. This, however, by the new schedule leaving New York at 11 p. m., is entirely overcome. The arrival at Boston and New York at an earlier hour than heretofore insures all connections previously made, and makes some additional connections which, under the old schedule, it was impossible to make. The later departure from Boston admits of a sure and complete dispatch from that point of mails from all sections of northern New England destined for New York and points in the West, Southwest, and South.

These expedited trains between Boston and New York meet a want that has long been felt, as the Department has frequently been petitioned by the business communities of Boston and the East to afford some facilities for a later dispatch from Boston and an earlier arrival at New York; also for a later departure from New York and an earlier arrival at Boston, with a view to expediting the important commercial mails between the two cities. These demands the Department has heretofore been unable to satisfy, for the reason that it would involve compensation for special facilities.

June 16, 1888.—A line of 40-foot postal cars was ordered under this date between Cincinnati and Toledo, Ohio, via the Cincinnati, Hamilton and Dayton and Dayton and Michigan Railroads. It had been apparent to the Department for a long time that the needs of this route demanded greater space and facilities for the proper distribution and dispatch of local mails and connections at the two important terminal offices, and the failure to furnish increased facilities before has deprived the public dependent upon this line of postal conveniences which they were justly entitled to expect.

June 24, 1888.—A schedule change was made by the roads constituting the Boston, Providence and New York R. P. O., between Boston, Mass., and New York, N. Y., via Providence, R. I., so as to leave New York at 11.31 instead of 11.01 p. m. and arrive at Boston at 7 instead of 6.50, a gain of twenty minutes; to leave Boston at 11.30 instead of 11 p. m. and arrive at New York the following a. m., the time of the old schedule.

While this change is a move in the direction of improvement, the advantages resulting are rather local to the country directly dependent upon this R. P. O. for its mail supply. The bulk of the mail between Boston and New York is moved via the Boston, Springfield and New York R. P. O., because of its superior facilities as to equipment and space; and further, because it is not liable to obstructions by ferries and otherwise which frequently interfere with the movement on schedule time of trains via the Boston, Providence and New York line.

July 15, 1888.—Specially improved facilities for the movement of mails via the Detroit and Grand Rapids R. P. O. were secured by a change of schedule so as to leave Detroit at 3.45 a. m. and reach Grand Rapids at 10 a. m., instead of leaving Detroit at 7.30 a. m. and reaching Grand Rapids at 3.15 p. m. This change, to leave Detroit at 3.45 a. m., is one that for a long time has been badly needed in order to place the early a. m. Detroit mails and connections at that point throughout the lower peninsula of Michigan before a late hour in the day. The new schedule advances mail for all points between Detroit and Grand Rapids from four to six hours, and in addition secures connection at Jackson for all points on the Bay City and Jackson line, reaching Lansing at 8.20 a. m. and Saginaw at 10.50 a. m. In fact, it advances mail for all points in central, southern and western Michigan, and even to Fort Wayne, Ind.

September 15, 1888.—Under this date service was ordered between Des Moines, Iowa, and Saint Joseph, Mo., via the Chicago, Saint Paul and Kansas City Railroad, completing the line between Saint Paul, Minn., and Saint Joseph, Mo., via the system of road above mentioned. This is a very important new service and affords greatly improved facilities via Des Moines, Iowa, for the transmission of the important mails accumulating in the north Minnesota country for the Southwest to Saint Joseph and Kansas City, Mo., and connections at these points.

September 21, 1888.—A single daily line of 40-foot postal cars was ordered on the Alabama and Great Southern Railroad (Chattanooga and Meridian R. P. O.). This increase in space followed as a necessity upon the improved service via the Cincinnati, New Orleans and Texas Pacific before described, as by the improved facilities between Cincinnati and Chattanooga a considerably increased quantity of mails was diverted to the latter line because it was found a more expeditious transmission of mails from a Cincinnati stand-point could be attained for the

Mississippi and Louisiana country, including New Orleans, via the Alabama and Great Southern as a direct connection, and consequently increased space on the Chattanooga and Meridian was found necessary to handle in a proper manner the additional volume of mail to be distributed. It should be remembered that this line in connection with the Cincinnati and Chattanooga run constitutes the shortest trunk line between Cincinnati and New Orleans, running via Chattanooga, Tenn., and Meridian, Miss., and thence via the New Orleans and Northeastern Railroad to New Orleans.

September 22, 1888.—An order was issued for a line of 40 foot postal cars between Atlanta and Way Cross, Ga. This additional space was found necessary to afford proper facilities for the distribution of the increased volume of mail going forward from Atlanta and connections from that point for Florida and southeastern Georgia. This increase in volume was largely due to the fact that gradually the channel for the transmission of mails from Chicago to Florida has been fixed via Louisville, Ky., Chattanooga, Tenn., and Atlanta, Ga.

October 1, 1888.—Taking effect October 1, a further addition to the fast-mail service of the country was made by changing the schedule of the line between Saint Louis, Mo., and New York, N. Y., via the Pennsylvania Railroad.

For more than a year the Department has had a fast mail via the Pennsylvania Railroad, leaving New York at 7.40 p. m., and reaching Saint Louis at 2.45 a. m., second morning, connecting at the latter point with the fast mail via the Missouri Pacific Railroad, leaving Saint Louis at 3 a. m. By experience it was found that this service was far from satisfactory; first, because the important a. m. connections from Pittsburgh, Pa., could not be secured, and, secondly, because the margin for connection at Saint Louis being so small, the heavy mails from the East for the Southwest were frequently delayed from twelve to twenty-four hours at Saint Louis, owing to some slight delay preventing the Pennsylvania train from reaching that city in time to connect the 3 a. m. train departing. To remove these two causes of complaint the new schedule by the Pennsylvania road leaves New York at the same hour as formerly, 7.40 p. m., but reaches Pittsburgh at 8.30 a. m., instead of 9.30, as was the case under the old schedule. By this arrival one hour earlier a forenoon carrier delivery is secured at Pittsburgh and all the important connections from that point for Pennsylvania and Ohio are made, which under the old schedule it was impossible to do.

It has been the effort of the Department for some years to secure to the people of Pittsburgh the advantages which they were justly entitled to, and which they now have, of an earlier a. m. arrival of the important business mails from New York and Philadelphia; and from reports received I am convinced that the recent change fully meets the desires of the people of that city.

Under this schedule the train reaches Saint Louis at 1.45 a. m., leaving a margin of one hour and fifteen minutes in which to make the connection with the Missouri Pacific departing at 3 o'clock a. m. Previous to the introduction of this schedule the connection at Saint Louis was very frequently missed with the fast mail departing, but since it went into effect not a single failure has occurred, and I am confident that the connection at that point between the fast mail from the East and the fast mail departing for the West may be considered secure, except for unavoidable causes.

The putting into effect of this new schedule was only a part of the scheme for the improvement of the facilities between Saint Louis and

New York. Heretofore, while there was a fast mail west, the Department has had no facilities for the expeditious transmission of the important mails from the Southwest to the East via this line. Now, however, taking effect October 8, 1888, a fast train is had, leaving Saint Louis at 8.10 a. m., reaching Philadelphia at 1.25 p. m. and New York at 4 p. m. the following day, instead of leaving Saint Louis at 7.30 a. m. and reaching Philadelphia at 6.50 and New York at 9.40 the following evening.

This is by far the most important change that has been made on the Pennsylvania Railroad in recent years, as it admits of the a. m. dispatch of mails from Saint Louis being delivered in the early p. m. of the following day at Philadelphia and a full carrier and box delivery at New York. Under the old schedule neither of these deliveries could be made until the following a. m., showing a gain of one full business day by the introduction of this fast mail. The system of separating the city mails by the clerks in the cars is also a very advantageous feature of this new Saint Louis and New York run, so that the city carrier delivery is made at Philadelphia and New York immediately upon the arrival of the train, thus avoiding the delay necessary to make the separation at the post-offices before furnishing the mail to the carriers for delivery.

The important p. m. connections at Philadelphia and New York are entirely secured by the new schedule, while under the old one the arrival at Philadelphia was too late for mail to be utilized until the next day, either for local delivery or connections; and the connections at New York for the New England country at 10.30 p. m. were frequently broken because of the time required to make the transfer between Jersey City and the Grand Central Depot. So that the slightest delay in the arrival at Jersey City would result in a failure to connect the departing trains for Boston and the East. Frequent efforts had been made by the Department to overcome this difficulty, but it was always found impossible, for the reason that no arrangements could be made with the Pennsylvania Company to arrive at Jersey City earlier than 9.30 p. m., nor could any satisfactory arrangement be made with the companies running the New England trains to delay their departures from New York. The new fast mail, however, overcomes this difficulty entirely and insures the connection at New York for New England, the importance of which can not be overestimated, as it involves all the mails from the Southwest via Saint Louis and the accumulation between Saint Louis and New York for the New England country, both of which are very important and heavy mails.

October 11, 1888.—In order to fully secure the advantages of the improved service west of Chicago for the East, arrangements were completed taking effect October 11, 1888, with the New York Central and Hudson River and the Lake Shore and Michigan Southern Railroads between New York and Chicago for a daily fast mail east-bound, to leave Chicago at 8.30 a. m. and reach New York at 12.30 p. m. next day, being twenty-seven hours between Chicago and New York.

This last-mentioned fast service is one of the most important improvements yet made in the east-bound mail facilities, the advantages of which to commercial and other correspondence it is hardly possible to estimate too highly. At Chicago this fast mail receives connection from the fast mail arriving from San Francisco via the Central and Union Pacific roads, and also from Portland, Oregon, via the Northern Pacific and Chicago, Milwaukee and Saint Paul roads, thus constituting a fast mail from the Pacific to the Atlantic coast, resulting in a saving of one full day for all correspondence from the Pacific Coast States for all points in the East. Previous to the establishment of this fast mail east-bound between Chicago and New York, the a. m. dispatch of Monday from Chicago did not reach New York until 7 p. m. Tuesday, instead of 12.30 noon as at present. The arrival at 7 p. m. via the old schedule rendered the mail unavailable at New York until the next day. This was a very serious delay to commercial correspondence and mercantile paper, the latter being thereby deprived of treatment at the banks and clearing-house until the next day. Under the present schedule, however, arriving at 12.30 p. m., ample time remains for treatment day of receipt. And then, too, the fact should not be lost sight of that the intermediate country partakes of the advantages of this fast service equally with the terminal points.

The advantages of the fast mail are further increased by having a separation of city mails made on the cars by the postal clerks, so that immediately upon the arrival of the car at New York the mail is properly separated for immediate carrier delivery without necessitating the delay in the post-office which was formerly required to make the separation. This is a very important item, as on the arrival in the late p. m., by the system above described, an opportunity is had for a carrier delivery the same day, while if the mail had to be separated at the office the separation would not in many cases be completed until too late to secure the last carrier delivery.

In connection with this new fast mail service between Chicago and New York, an order was issued authorizing a line of 60-foot postal cars in lieu of the 50-foot cars that were in use on the former run which the fast mail east was intended to replace. These new cars will be constructed and fitted with all the latest improvements contributing to the expeditious distribution of the mails and are, in many respects, better adapted to the general purposes for which they are used, including comfort and ease for the clerks engaged in the trying and laborious work incident to the handling and distribution of mails on the cars. If the newly constructed cars prove entirely satisfactory, it is agreed by the railroad companies that all the remaining cars on this line shall be reconstructed and fitted with such improvements as the experience of the Department shall determine best adapted to secure the fullest possible results to the public.

Under the present arrangements for the transmission of the mails between San Francisco and New York, the schedule is as follows: Leave New York, 9 p. m. Monday, arrive San Francisco, 8.15 a. m. Sunday. Leave San Francisco 9 a. m. Monday, arrive New York 12.30 p. m. Saturday.

There are two other trains between these points, but the two first mentioned are the trains upon which the mails are forwarded, as they are the most expeditious.

In connection with this trans-continental service it will appear clear that no further improvement is possible with the facilities at the command of the Department, and when it is considered that the distance covered is over 3,340 miles it does not appear that any further improvement could be reasonably expected.

PRINTING.

Printing offices have been in operation during the year at the head-quarters of the first, fourth, fifth, sixth, seventh, eighth, and ninth divisions of the service, and in the office of the General Superintendent. These offices have furnished such printed matter as was required for immediate use by the divisions in which they are located.

The subjoined table shows the output of the several printing offices during the year:

Division.	General orders.			Facing slips.		
	No. of forms.	No. of ems set.	No. of impressions.	No. of forms.	No. of slips on a form.	No. of slips printed.
Office of General Superintendent*	141	752,000	20,700	367	12	3,145,080
First division	206	956,062	61,291	165	8	6,514,580
Fourth division	179	537,845	37,363	806	12	9,621,000
Fifth division	168	671,600	49,725	1,364	9 & 15	16,907,500
Sixth division	130	953,740	146,100	818	4,8 & 16	10,476,000
Seventh division	98	859,234	39,500	233	4,5,10 & 12	2,305,000
Eighth division	89	408,000	25,887	614	5,6 & 12	3,531,750
Ninth division	212	1,014,420	16,952	811	6 & 10	10,052,500
Total	1,168	6,152,901	397,460	4,678		62,646,600

Division.	Circulars.			Other job work.		
	No. of forms.	No. of ems set.	No. of impressions.	No. of forms.	No. of ems set.	No. of impressions.
Office of General Superintendent*..	65	206,300	43,440	135	205,690	64,670
First division				180	212,984	58,790
Fourth division	14	46,831	2,540	75	76,450	54,127
Fifth division				60	38,534	263,450
Sixth division	14	21,600	6,705	744	418,556	178,126
Seventh division	3	12,584	1,750	94	450,822	53,600
Eighth division	15	42,000	3,880	252	1,435,800	108,808
Ninth division				586	827,564	356,778
Total	111	328,715	58,315	2,126	3,666,319	1,138,349

*Government owns plant.

NOTE.—For the office of General Superintendent the following was performed on the Daily Bulletin: Number of forms, 365; number of ems set, 4,197,300; number of impressions, 346,330.

At division headquarters the work was done by men appointed as railway post-office clerks and detailed as printers, with the understanding that they were to furnish, at their own expense, certain presses, paper-cutters, type, etc., necessary to do the work required of them. The amount paid these printers for services rendered during the fiscal year ended June 30, 1888, was $13,350, and the postal clerks detailed to operate the printing-office plant owned by the Government, and located in the basement of the Department building, received $4,300.

ASSISTANT GENERAL SUPERINTENDENT.

This service has assumed such large proportions during the past few years that the employment of an Assistant General Superintendent of the Railway Mail Service should be provided for by law, as such an officer would be of great service to this office in the transaction of the business of the executive branch of the service.

Prior to 1884 the duties of an Assistant General Superintendent were performed by a post-office inspector-in-charge, who was detailed to this office for the purpose, but by the promotion of the incumbent to the position of General Superintendent in that year the vacancy thereby created was filled by the appointment of an inspector-in-charge, who was needed elsewhere by the Department. This office thus lost the services of an assistant to the General Superintendent.

For the reasons stated above an Assistant General Superintendent should be provided, and I have the honor to recommend that the sum of $3,000 be included in your estimates for the fiscal year ending June 30, 1890, for that purpose.

CHIEF CLERK.

Attention is invited to the fact that a chief clerk has never been provided by law for this office. Up to the month of April, 1884, such an officer was employed at a salary of $2,200 per annum and charged to the clerical force of the Washington city post-office; but under a subsequent ruling of the Department, based upon the ground that the detail was not warranted by law, the place was abolished, and since then the duties appertaining to it have been performed for a portion of the time by a $1,400 clerk detailed for the purpose, and later by an assistant superintendent, whose compensation is $1,600 per annum. In view of the fact that the duties and responsibilities of this position have increased with (and in the same ratio) as the railway mail service throughout the country, a much larger salary should be paid this officer for the services rendered by him, and the position should be placed on an equality with all other chief clerks of the Post-Office Department as to grade and rate of compensation.

I would, therefore, recommend that the sum of $2,000 be inserted in your estimate for the fiscal year ending June 30, 1890, for one chief clerk for the office of General Superintendent of the Railway Mail Service. The following table will show the increase in service since the above-mentioned reductions in force and pay were made:

Fiscal year ended.	Miles of railroad over which mails were carried.	Annual transportation of mails by railroads.	Length of railway post-office lines.	Annual miles of service by railway post-office lines.	Number of railway postal clerks.	Number of pieces of mail matter handled by railway postal clerks.	Number of post-offices in the United States.
June 30, 1888	143,713	185,485,783	126,310	122,031,104	5,094	6,545,876,202	57,376
June 30, 1884........	117,160	142,541,392	102,140	92,640,099	3,963	4,536,697,326	50,017
Increase	26,553	42,944,591	24,170	29,391,005	1,131	2,009,178,876	7,359
Increase per cent...	+22.6	+30.1	+23.6	+31.7	+28.5	+44.2	14.7

CHIEF CLERKS.

Another matter to which I desire to invite particular attention is the apparent injustice to which chief clerks of the several divisions are subjected in being required to pay their traveling expenses while on the road in the performance of duty. To these officers is committed the immediate supervision of all the details of the service within certain territorial limits, with headquarters at designated places where many railway post-office lines terminate, and from which others may be easily reached, and, to quote from the Annual Report of my immediate predecessor for the fiscal year ended June 30, 1887:

"Their duties are to examine the men under their charge; to see that they perform all the duties required of them properly and thoroughly; that the schemes of distribution furnished them are kept corrected and that all orders issued by the General Superintendent and division superintendents are obeyed. All irregularities, insubordination, inefficiency, and lax morality occurring ou routes under their charge must be reported to their division superintendents at once. In the performance of these duties the chief clerk must travel a great deal, and for his expenses while on the road he is not re-imbursed, as is done in the case of other Government officers, but must pay them out of his salary of $1,400. This is not only unjust to these men but also a detriment to the service; for, in many instances where a personal inspection should be made, the chief clerk endeavors to settle the matter by correspondence rather than reduce his salary by incurring the increased expenditure incident to such inspection. In other words, the more useful the chief clerk makes himself by traveling about inspecting lines, examining, instructing, and encouraging the men, the greater will be his expenses, and, consequently, the less his salary. * * * The best men in the service being selected for these positions, they are, as a rule, possessed of more than the average amount of executive ability; and, from their apprenticeship on the road, are well versed in the distribution and dispatch of mail. They certainly earn more money than is now paid them."

From an investigation of this matter, I am convinced that the salaries received by these officers for the services rendered is entirely inadequate, and tuat the zeal and skill manifested by them in the performance of their onerous and exacting duties during the past year would command a much higher rate of pay in any other branch of the public service. I would, therefore, earnestly renew, in substance, the recommendation of my predecessor that the law approved July 31, 1872, entitled "An act to designate, classify and fix the salaries of persons in the railway mail service," be so amended as to authorize the payment of these chief clerks at the rate of $1,500 per annum, being an increase of $100 each, and in addition thereto that their actual expenses, while traveling on the business of the Department, to an amount not to exceed $300 in any fiscal year, be paid out of the appropriation for the transportation of the mails.

SPECIAL FACILITIES.

There are no changes of importance to report this year in reference to the running of mail trains on lines where special facilities are paid for by the Department.

The appropriation for that purpose for the fiscal year ending June 30, 1889, is $295,655.38, and the current expenditure on account of this fund is as follows:

Number of route.	Termini.	Railroad company.	Miles.	Pay.
5005..............	New York—Springfield.......	New York, New Haven and Hartford.	136.00	$17,647.06
6011..............	4.35 a. m train	New York Central and Hudson River.	144.00	25,000.00
10001.............	Philadelphia—Bay View......	Philadelphia, Wilmington and Baltimore.	91.80	20,000.00
10013 } part ...... / 11001 }	Bay View—Quantico	Baltimore and Potomac.......	79.80	21,900.00
11001 part........	Quantico—Richmond	Richmond, Fredericksburgh and Potomac.	81.50	17,419.26
11008.............	Richmond to Petersburgh	Richmond and Petersburgh ..	23.39	4,268.67
11009.............	Petersburgh to Weldon.......	Petersburgh	64.00	11,680.00
13002.............	Weldon to Wilmington.......	Wilmington and Weldon	161.87	29,541.27
14002.............	Wilmington to Florence	Wilmington, Columbia and Augusta	110.00	20,075.00
14005.............	Florence to Charleston Junction.	Northeastern	95.00	17,337.50
14004.............	Charleston Junction to Savannah.	Charleston and Savannah....	108.00	19,710.00
15009.............	Savannah to Jacksonville	Savannah, Florida and Western.	171.55	31,309.70
10006.............	Baltimore to Hagerstown.....	Western Maryland	86.60	15,804.50
16018, 16007.......	Jacksonville to Tampa	Jacksonville, Tampa and Key West, and South Florida.	240.89	43,962.42
Total				295,655.38

As is well understood, the annual appropriations for special facilities on trunk lines secure very important results in expedition to the mails which could not be otherwise obtained; and, believing that it is the desire of Congress to have these fast mail trains continued, I have the honor to recommend that, for the fiscal year ending June 30, 1890, the sum of $295,655.38 be appropriated for extra and special facilities on trunk lines, this sum being about the same as the amount appropriated for the current fiscal year, which is $295,987.53.

ESTIMATES AND EXPENDITURES.

The amount appropriated for railway post-office car service, exclusive of the gross amount accrued to Pacific roads for the fiscal year ended June 30, 1888, was...$1,934,560.00
Amount expended.. 1,822,964.37

Leaving an unexpended balance of 111,595.63
Add to the above expenditure the amount accrued to Pacific roads..... 128,237.62
And we have the total cost for railway post-office cars during the year. 1,951,201.99

Compared with 1887, this is an increase of $111,434.86. or 6.05 per cent.

The following tabular statement shows in concise form the growth of this branch of the service from July 1, 1879, to June 30, 1888:

Fiscal year ended June 30—	Amount of appropriation.	Amount expended.	Expenditures.		Per cent.		Gross amount accrued to Pacific railroads.
			Increase.	Decrease.	Increase.	Decrease.	
1880	$1,250,000.00	$1,141,545.19	....	....	....	....	$91,851.15
1881	1,366,000.00	1,268,221.50	$126,676.31	....	11.09	....	110,181.23
1882	1,426,000.00	1,317,242.23	49,020.73	....	3.86	....	124,373.66
1883	1,526,000.00	1,483,086.85	165,844.62	....	12.59	....	131,690.17
1884	1,575,000.00	1,585,597.29	102,510.44	....	6.89	....	135,790.20
1885	1,625,000.00	1,716,437.13	130,839.84	....	8.25	....	134,342.92
1886	1,705,026.00	1,692,025.30	....	$24,411.83	......	1.42	123,873.80
1887	1,808,000.00	1,713,391.92	21,366.62	....	1.26	....	126,875.21
1888	1,934,560.00	1,822,964.37	109,572.45	....	6.38	....	128,237.62
	14,275,586.00	13,740,511.78	705,831.01	24,411.83	50.32	....	
Decrease........	....	....	....	....	1.42	....	
					48.90		
Average per cent. per year...	....	....	....	....	6.98	*	

No separate appropriation made for 1879.

From the above it will be seen that, excluding amounts accrued to the subsidized Pacific roads and branches (which are not paid from this appropriation), the average annual increase for the last seven years (1886 not included) is 6.98 per cent. In making up this average increase 1886 was excluded for the reason that the apparent decrease in that year was owing entirely to the discontinuance of payment for apartment cars less than 40 feet in length.

The annual *rate* of cost of railway post-office car lines (exclusive of the amounts to be credited the subsidized Pacific lines) on July 1, 1888, was $1,858,958.60. From July 1 up to and including October 27, 1888, additional lines aggregating $109,017.45 have been authorized by the Department, and it is apparent from carefully prepared data that during the current fiscal year additional lines costing $130,800.45 will be needed. If these are authorized the annual *rate* of cost on July 1, 1889, will be $2,098,776.50. There are also recommendations on file from division superintendents for additional service amounting to $143,336.70, which will increase the aggregate for the new fiscal year to $2,242,113.20. As there are good reasons for believing that the expansion of this service is likely to continue during the coming year I do not think it advisable to place the estimate below $2,260,000, and I have the honor to recommend that the sum of $2,260,000 be appropriated for railway post-office car lines, *exclusive of lines on the subsidized Pacific roads*, for the fiscal year ending June 30, 1890.

While the amount called for is somewhat in excess of the average increase for previous years, the phenomenal growth of the service in the Western, Southern, and Southwestern States of late, which the Department now finds itself unable to keep pace with in the matter of postal-car service (for want of sufficient appropriation), would seem to imperatively demand that the full amount estimated for should be appropriated for the railway post-office car service.

On the 30th of June, 1887, there were 4,851 railway postal clerks in the service; and on June 30, 1888, there were 5,094, being an increase of 243, or 5.01 per cent. The amount paid for salaries during the former period was $4,694,561.75; during the latter $4,981,365.93, being an increase of $286,804.18, or 6.11 per cent. The amount appropriated for salaries of postal clerks for the fiscal year ending June 30, 1888, was $4,990,240.62, and the expenditures amounted to $4,981,365.93, leaving an unexpended balance of $8,874.69. The annual rate of expenditures for salaries of railway postal clerks was, on July 1, 1888, $5,084,517, and the appropriation for the fiscal year ending June 30, 1889, is $5,246,790.21, leaving a margin of $162,273.21 for extensions of service, additional help on lines where mails are getting heavier, and the promotion of clerks who were serving as probationers at the beginning of the fiscal year.

The following table shows the per cent. of increase in expenditures on account of salaries of railway postal clerks for the period from October 1, 1886, to June 30, 1888, by quarters:

Quarter ending—	Expenditure	Increase.	
		Amount.	Per cent.
September 30, 1886	$1,145,999.67		
December 31, 1886	1,160,202.92	$14,203.25	1.24
March 31, 1887	1,182,510.39	22,307.47	1.92
June 30, 1887	1,205,818.77	23,338.38	1.98
September 30, 1887	1,219,994.52	14,145.75	1.17
December 31, 1887	1,232,965.62	12,971.10	1.07
March 31, 1888	1,254,111.01	21,145.39	1.72
June 30, 1888	1,274,294.78	20,183.77	1.61
			10.71
Average quarterly increase			1.53

SUMMARY.

Quarter.	Amount.	Quarter.	Amount.
Third quarter, 1886	$1,145,999.67	Third quarter, 1887	$1,219,994.52
Fourth quarter, 1886	1,160,202.92	Fourth quarter, 1887	1,232,965.62
First quarter, 1887	1,182,510.39	First quarter, 1888	1,254,111.01
Second quarter, 1887	1,205,848.77	Second quarter, 1888	1,274,294.78
Total	4,694,561.75	Total	4,981,365.93

Increase 1888 over 1887, $286,804.18, or 6.11 per cent.

Taking the average quarterly increase of 1.53 per cent. and applying it to the fiscal year ending June 30, 1889, we have the following:

Amount expended quarter ended June 30, 1888 .... $1,274,294.78

Estimate third quarter, 1888 .... 1,293,791.49
Estimate fourth quarter, 1888 .... 1,313,586.49
Estimate first quarter, 1889 .... 1,333,084.36
Estimate second quarter, 1889 .... 1,354,089.73

Total 5,295,152.07

This is $48,361.86 in excess of the amount appropriated.

Assuming that the expenditure for the quarter ending June 30, 1889, will be $1,354,089.73, and applying the average quarterly increase of

1.53 per cent., we have the following as the probable cost for the fiscal year ending June 30, 1890:

Third quarter, 1889	$1,374,807.30
Fourth quarter, 1889	1,395,841.85
First quarter, 1890	1,417,198.23
Second quarter, 1890	1,438,»81.36
Total	5,626,728.74
Add for pay of additional railway postal clerks to handle registered matter	50,000.00
	5,676,728.74

Excluding the amount of the estimate for railway postal clerks to handle registered matter, this is an increase of $379,938.53, or 7.24 per cent. over the appropriation for the current fiscal year (in which a deficiency is likely to be created), and the data above given warrants the belief that the service can not be properly performed for a less sum; and I, therefore, have the honor to recommend that this amount of $5,676,728.74 be appropriated for the payment of salaries of railway postal clerks for the fiscal year ending June 30, 1890.

COMMENDATION.

In concluding this report I desire to acknowledge the deep obligations I am under to division superintendents and chief clerks for the aid they have afforded this office in carrying into effect the improvements inaugurated during the year, and for the energy and ability displayed by them in effecting needed changes in the service. Each of these and their subordinates, and those connected with this office, are entitled to a full measure of praise and commendation for the prompt and cheerful manner with which they have met all demands upon them for the performance of extra service, and for the fidelity and zeal with which they have performed the duties assigned them.

I have the honor to be, very respectfully. your obedient servant,
W. L. BANCROFT,
General Superintendent.

Hon. A. LEO KNOTT,
Second Assistant Postmaster-General.

TABLE A³.—*Statement of railway post-offices*

Designation of railway post-office. (Lines upon which railway post-office cars are paid for, in *italics*.)	Division	Distance run by clerks, register to register.	Initial and terminal stations, running from east to west, north to south, or northwest to southeast (with abbreviated title of railroad company).	Number of route.	Miles of route for which railroad is paid.
		Miles.			
Abbeville and Louvale, Ga.....	4	109.79	Americus, Abbeville, Ga. (Amer., Pres. and Lum. R. R.).	15054	61.95
			Americus, Louvale, Ga. (Amer. Pres. and Lum. R. R.).	15050	48.46
Aberdeen and Durant, Miss ..	4	108.30	Aberdeen, Durant, Miss. (Ill. Cent.)	18009	108.30
Aberdeen and Orient, Dak	6	83.04	Aberdeen, Roscoe, Dak. (Chi., Mil. and St. Paul).	¹26016 (part)	41.60
			Roscoe, Orient, Dak. (Chi., Mil. and St. Paul).	35029	41.73
Addison, N. Y., and Galeton, Pa	2	46.56	Addison, N. Y., and Galeton, Pa. (Add. and Pa.).	6122	47.24
Adrian, Mich., and Fayette, Ohio¹.	9	33.26	Adrian, Grosvenor, Mich. (L. S. and M. S.).	²21095 (part)	(⁴)
			Grosvenor, Mich., Fayette, Ohio (L. S. and M. S.).	³24036 (part)	24.83
Albany and Binghamton, N. Y.	2	143.21	Albany, N. Y., Binghamton, N. Y. (D. and H.C. Co.).	6028	143.22
Albany, Kingston, and New York, N. Y.	2	146.23	Albany, N. Y., New York, N. Y. (West Shore).	6129	162.27
Albany and New York, N. Y.⁸.	2	145.35	Albany, N. Y., New York, N. Y. (N. Y. C. and H. R.).	6011 (part)	(⁹)
Albany and Thomasville, Ga..	4	¹¹58.92	Albany, Thomasville, Ga. (S. F. and W. Rwy.).	15018 ¹⁰(pa't)	58.92
Albert Lea, Minn., and Burlington, Iowa.	6	253.14	Albert Lea, Minn., Burlington, Iowa (Burl., C. Rap. and Northern).	27001	252.70
Albuquerque, N. Mex., and El Paso, Tex.	7	254.39	Albuquerque, Rincon, N. Mex. (A., T. and S. F.).	¹²38006 (part)	177.14
			Rincon, N. Mex., El Paso, Tex. (A., T. and S. F.).	39004	77.20
Albuquerque N. Mex., and Los Angeles, Cal.	8	868.66	Albuquerque, N. Mex., Needles, Cal. (Atlantic and Pacific R. R.).	39003	574.86
			Needles, Barstow, Cal. (Atlantic and Pacific).	¹⁴46042 (part)	169.42
			Barstow, San Bernardino, Cal. (Cal. Southern).	4603 (part)	81.00
			San Bernardino, Los Angeles, Cal. (Central Pacific).	46853	63.13
Allentown and Harrisburg, Pa.	2	91.84	Allentown, Pa., Harrisburg, Pa. (P. and R.).	8073	90.40
Allentown and Pawling, Pa....	2	44.18	Allentown, Pa., Emaus Junction, Pa. (P. and R.).	8073 (part)	(¹⁵)
			Emaus Junction, Pa., Pawling, Pa. (Perkiommen).	8056	37.38
Alpena and Alger, Mich	9	104.50	Alpena, Alger, Mich. (D., B., C. and A.)...	24057	104.50
Alton Bay and Dover, N. H ..	1	28.42	Alton Bay, Dover, N. H. (Bos. and Me.) ..	1013	28.42
Anderson and Ladoga, Ind¹⁹...	5	64.70	Anderson, Ladoga, Ind. (Midland)	22037	65.87
Anderson and McCormick, S.C.	4	59.00	Anderson, McCormick, S. C (P. R. and W. C. Rwy.).	14023	59.00
Annapolis Junction and Annapolis, Md.	3	21.09	Annapolis Junction, Annapolis, Md. (Annap., Wash. and Balto.).	10007	21.08
Antonito, Colo., and Santa Fé, N. Mex.	7	130.00	Antonito, Colo., Espanola, N. Mex. (D. and R. G.).	¹⁷38004 (part)	91.47
			Espanola, Santa Fé, N. Mex. (T., S. F. and N.).	39011	38.95

¹ Balance of route covered by Hastings and Cologne, Minn., R. P. O. (56.51 miles), St. Paul, Minn., and Mitchell, Dak., R. P. O. (256.34 miles), and by Roscoe and Bowdle, Dak., pouch service (15.29 miles). See Table C⁵.
² In reserve.
³ Runs over route 21095, Adrian to Grosvenor, Mich. (7.60 miles).
⁴ Shown in report of New York and Chicago R. P. O.
⁵ Balance of route (43.57 miles), covered by Trenton and Adrian R. P. O.
⁶ One helper. Albany and Maryland (70 miles).
⁷ Double daily service, except Sunday.

⁸ Short run, New York and Rochester, R. P. O.
⁹ 143 miles, covered by New York and Chicago R. P. O.
¹⁰ Clerks accounted for on New York and Rochester R. P. O.
¹¹ 104.19 miles shown as Waycross and Chattahoochee R. P. O.
¹² Short run, Cedar Falls to Burlington, Iowa (157.08 miles).
¹³ 348.09 miles of route 38006, between La Junta, Colo., and Albuquerque, N. Mex., covered by La Junta, Colo., and Albuquerque, N. Mex., R. P. O., and 53.82 miles between Rincon and

in operation in the United States on June 30, 1888.

Average weight of mail whole distance per day.	Date of last re-adjustment.	Average speed per hour (train numbers taken from division schedules).				Number of round trips with clerks per week.	Annual miles of service with clerks.	Average miles run daily by crews.	Number of mail cars, or cars in which are mail apartments.	Inside dimensions of cars or apartments (railway post-office cars in black figures).		Number of crews.	Number of clerks to crew.	Number of clerks appointed to line.
		Train No. outward.	Av'ge speed (miles).	Train No. inward.	Av'ge speed (miles).					Length	Width			
Lbs.										*Ft. In.*	*Ft. In.*			
		2 14.4		1 13.4		6	68,928	109.79	1	5 1	4 9	1	1	2
									1	7 3	3 9			
161	July 1, 1888	2 13.3		1 15.7										
482	July 1, 1888	23 20.9		24 19.8		7	79,275	108.30	2	14 9	7 3	2	1	2
2,377	July 1, 1887	9 22.70		8 22.70		6	52,149	166.08	1	13 0	7 7	1	1	1
299	July 1, 1888	15 13.91		14 16.69										
582	July 1, 1885	1 16.14		4 16.38		6	29,240	98.12	1	12 0	7 0	1	1	1
									[21]1	12 0	7 0			
69,142	July 1, 1883	144 13.29		143 6.51		6 }	20,887	66.52	1	12	6 7	1	1	1
240	July 1, 1884	144 13.72		143 12.66		6								
2,087	July 1, 1885	1 25.62		2 25.62		6	89,936	95.47	2	20 0	9 0	3	1	[14]4
									[4]1	15 0	9 0			
1,403	July 1, 1885	66 30.24		65 28.74		6	91,832	146.23	1	21 0	9 0	2	1	4
		62 29.22		61 24.72		6	[9]91,832		1	21 0	9 0	2	1	
									[12]2	21 0	9 0			
99,901	July 1, 1885	24 28.08		27 29.04		6	91,280	145.35	1	17 0	8 7	2	2	([16])
									1	20 0	8 7			
1,674	July 1, 1884	6 23.2		5 23.2		7	43,129	117.84	1	14 4	8 7	1	1	1
3,804	July 1, 1887	2 26.17		1 25.27		6	158,972	126.57	2	26 6	9 1	4	2	10
		4 15.13		3 24.70		6	98,646	157.08	2	17 6	9 1	[16]2	1	
4,546	July 1, 1886	3 25.50		4 18.80		7	186,213	127.20	([14])	....		4	1	4
1,101	July 1, 1886	3 23.40		4 23.40		7								
2,428	July 1, 1886	1 20.45		2 19.82		7	650,499	222.16	5	21 3	9 3	8	1	12
									2	21 0	9 3			
1,873	July 1, 1886	1 22.58		2 18.21										
927	July 1, 1886	1 24.54		2 23.47										
5,916	June 21, 1888	1 15.39		2 25.76										
		63 28.05		50 26.52		6	39,546	126.26	1	16 0	9 3	1		
2,443	July 1, 1885	10 18.06		9 25.62		6	57,675	122.45	1	14 0	8 6	1	1	3
		6 23.94		3 23.94		6	[9]57,675	....	1	14 0	8 6	1	1	
									[12]1	14 0	8 6			
2,443	July 1, 1885	10 24.54		5 24.54		6	27,745	88.36	1	8 0	6 2	1	1	1
									1	8 6	6 4			
329	July 1, 1885	10 23.10		5 22.62		6	....		1	8 4	6 0	([17])	([17])	([17])
655	Mar. 30, 1887	1 26.25		2 24.70		6	65,626	104.50	1	13 1	17 1	2	1	2
655	Mar. 30, 1887	54 23.65		19 21.00		6	17,847	113.68	1	11 1	6 7	1	1	1
		122 28.00		75 24.00		6	17,847		[16]1	9 5	6 7			
177	July 1, 1888	1 14.61		6 17.57		6	29,484	129.40	1	15 0	8 4	1	1	1
81	Oct. 15, 1886	90 17.8		89 16.7		6	37,052	118.00	1	8 4	6 0	1	1	1
583	July 1, 1885	4 20.50		1 25.60		6	13,245	42.18	[20]3	6 6	8 9	1	1	1
748	July 1, 1886	473 15.90		473 15.90		6	81,640	130.00	2	13 5	7 5	2	1	2
									[21]1	16 0	8 11			
89	Feb. 21, 1887	2 17.20		1 17.20		6								

Deming, N. Mex., by Rincon and Silver City, N. Mex., R. P. O.

[14] Cars shown under La Junta, Colo., and Albuquerque, N. Mex., R. P. O.

[15] 71.30 miles of route 46042 closed pouch service. See Table C³. Balance of route 46037, 131 69 miles, covered by San Bernardino and National City R. P. O.; double daily service between San Bernardino and Los Angeles; clerk makes six round trips per week; three helpers between Albuquerque and Winslow average daily 190.46 miles.

[16] 4.50 miles covered by Allentown and Harrisburg R. P. O.

[17] Clerks shown on route 8073.

[18] Reserve car.

[19] R. P. O. service established on this line September 5, 1887, between Anderson and Lebanon, Ind., 45 74 miles; January 9, 1888, service extended to Ladoga, Ind. Increase 20.13 miles.

[20] One in reserve.

[21] 109.52 miles of route 38004, between Cucharas and Antonito, Colo., covered by Pueblo and Silverton, Colo., R. P. O.

TABLE A⁵.—*Statement of railway post-offices in operation*

Designation of railway post-office. (Lines upon which railway post-office cars are paid for, in *italics*.)	Division.	Distance run by clerks, register to register.	Initial and terminal stations, running from east to west, north to south, or northwest to southeast (with abbreviated title of railroad company).	Number of route.	Miles of route for which railroad is paid.
		Miles.			
Arcadia and Cherry Vale, Kans.	7	71. 37	Cherry Vale, Arcadia, Kans. (K. C., Ft. S. and M.).	33024	73. 97
			Weir City Junction (n. o.), Weir, Kans. (K. C., Ft. S. and M.).	²33043	3 90
Arkansas City and Warren, Ark.	7	56. 60	Arkansas City, Trippe, Ark. (St. L., I. M. and S.).	29007 (part)	(³) °
			Trippe, Warren, Ark. (St. L., I. M. and S.).	29004	49. 25
Asheville and Jarretts, N. C ...	3	101. 33	Asheville, Asheville Junction (n. o.), N. C. (Rich. and Dan.).	13005 (part)	(⁴)
			Asheville Junction (n. o.), Jarretts, N. C. (Rich. and Dan.).	13016	96. 95
Ashland and Abbotsford, Wis..	6	133. 70	Ashland, Abbotsford, Wis. (Wisconsin Central).	⁵25017 (part)	133. 10
Ashland and Milwaukee, Wis..	6	480. 69	Ashland, Wis., Watersweet, Mich. (Mil., L. S. and West.).	25063	98. 42
			Watersweet, Mich., Eland, Wis. (Mil., L. S. and West.).	25050	105. 48
			Eland, Manitowoc, Wis. (Mil., L. S. and West.).	⁸25049 (part)	110. 60
			Manitowoc, Milwaukee, Wis. (Mil., L. S. and West.).	¹¹25018 (past)	77. 63
Ashland, Wis., and Saint Paul, Minn.	6	184. 22	Ashland, Ashland Junction, Wis. (Chi., St. P., Minn. and Om.).	25032	4. 63
			Ashland Junction, Hudson, Wis. (Chi., St. P., Minn. and Om.).	¹²25028 (part)	159. 96
			Hudson, Wis., Saint Paul, Minn. (Chi., St. P., Minn. and Om.).	25030 (part)	(¹²)
Ashland and Richardson, Ky ..	5	50. 42	Ashland, Richardson, Ky. (Chattaroi)......	20027	50. 36
Asheville, N. C., and Columbia, S. C.	4	164. 00	Asheville, N. C., Spartanburgh, S. C. (R. and D. R. R.).	14011	72. 27
			Spartanburgh, Alston, S. C. (R. and D. R. R.)	14008	68. 39
			Alston, Columbia, S. C. (R. and D. R. R.) ...	14001	(¹⁴)
Ashley and Muskegon, Mich. ¹⁵	9	96. 24	Ashley and Muskegon, Mich. (T., S. and M.)	24076	96. 24
Ashtabula, Ohio, and New Castle, Pa.	5	81. 25	Ashtabula, Youngstown, Ohio (Pa. Co.).....	21044	60. 36
			Youngstown, Ohio, Mahoningtown, Pa. (Pa. Co.).	21035	18. 40
			Mahoningtown, New Castle, Pa. (Pa. Co.)..	8044 (part)	(¹⁷)
Ashtabula and Youngstown, Ohio.¹⁸	9	64. 70	Ashtabula, Andover, Ohio (L. S. and M. S.).	8045 (part)	(¹⁹)
			Andover, Youngstown, Ohio (L. S. and M. S.).	21062	38. 84
Astor and Leesburgh, Fla.....	4	40. 90	Astor, Fort Mason, Fla. (Fla. So. Rwy.).....	²⁰16008 (part)	27. 20
			Fort Mason, Leesburgh, Fla. (Fla. So. R. R.)	²¹16014 (part)	13. 60
Atchison and Lenora, Kans. ²².	7	294. 52	Atchison, Waterville, Kans. (C. Bch. U. P.).	33003	100. 26
			Waterville, Greenleaf, Kans. (C. Bch. U. P.)	²³33021 (part)	13. 11
			Greenleaf, Concordia, Kans. (C. Bch. U. P.).	33022	43. 19
			Concordia, Lenora, Kans. (C. Bch. U. P.)....	33026	138. 70

¹ Clerk is relieved every third week by the additional clerk of Fort Scott, Kans., and Webb City, Mo., R. P. O., who alternates between this line, Fort Scott, Kans., and Webb City, Mo., R. P. O., and Yates Centre and Sedan, Kans., R. P. O.
² Clerk doubles route 33043 twice each round trip.
³ Distance over route 29007 (7.30 miles) covered by Fort Smith, Ark., and Leland, Miss., R. P. O.
⁴ One mile, covered by the Salisbury and Knoxville R. P. O.
⁵ Balance of route covered by Chicago, Ill., Abbotsford, Wis., and Minneapolis, Minn., R. P. O. (185. 54 miles) and by Milwaukee and Rugby Junction, Wis., pouch service (27.30 miles). (See Table C⁰.)
⁶ Reserve.

⁷ North Division, Ashland to Appleton, Wis.
⁸ One of these cars in reserve. There is double daily R. P. O. service between Appleton and Antigo, Wis.
⁹ Balance of route (23.01 miles) covered by Eland and Wausau, Wis., pouch service. (See Table C⁰.)
¹⁰ South Division, Antigo to Milwaukee, Wis.
¹¹ Balance of route (17.33 miles) covered by Two Rivers and Manitowoc, Wis., pouch service. (See Table C⁰.)
¹² Balance of route (21.91 miles) covered by Bayfield and Ashland Junction, Wis., pouch service. (See Table C⁰.)
¹³ Distance (19.60 miles) covered by Saint Paul, Minn., and Elroy, Wis., R. P. O.

in the United States on June 30, 1888—Continued.

Average weight of mail whole distance per day.	Date of last re-adjustment.	Average speed per hour (train numbers taken from division schedules).				Number of round trips with clerks per week.	Annual miles of service with clerks.	Average miles run daily by crews.	Number of mail cars, or cars in which are mail apartments.	Inside dimensions of cars or apartments (railway post-office cars in black figures).		Number of crews.	Number of clerks to crew.	Number of clerks appointed to line.
		Train No. outward.	Av'ge speed (miles).	Train No. inward.	Av'ge speed (miles).					Length.	Width.			
Lbs.										*Ft. In.*	*Ft. In.*			
524	July 1, 1886	15	21.10	16	22.40	7	59,563	[1]120.64	1	25 0	9 1½	[1]1	1	1
86	May 15, 1884	15	19.50	16	18.80	7								
802	July 1, 1886	958	9.66	957	12.54	6	35,545	113.20	1	17 8	6 8	1	1	1
250	July 1, 1886	958	11.21	957	9.74	6								
1,410	July 1, 1888	18	12.00	17	12.00	6	63,635	101.33	1	8 2	3 4	2	1	2
312	July 1, 1888	18	11.00	17	10.60				1	6 10	6 4			
1,669	July 1, 1887	6	21.00	5	21.57	6	83,964	133.70	1	30 0	9 4	2	1	2
993	July 1, 1887	6	22.28	5	27.46	6	170,935	136.09	[6]1	14 10	7 7	[7]4	1	7
									3	22 5	9 6			
1,351	July 1, 1887	6	27.51	5	22.60	......	......	......	[7]2	24 8	9 4			
1,775	July 1, 1887	4	26.23	1	23.60	6	130,938	139.00	......	......	......	[10]3	1	
2,640	July 1, 1887	4	25.76	1	25.76									
861	July 1, 1887	61	25.60	62	25.80	6	115,690	122.81	1	24 7	9 3	3	1	3
1,142	July 1, 1887	61	23.95	62	22.04	......	......	......	1	22 0	9 4			
3,000	July 1, 1887	61	19.63	62	21.18									
263	July 1, 1884	42	12.23	43	10.78	6	31,564	100.84	1	15 0	8 10	1	1	
560	July 1, 1888	55	21.00	54	21.00	7	120,048	109.30	1	13 10	8 6	3	1	3
									1	14 6	9 7			
584	July 1, 1888	......	20.5	......	21.5									
908	July 1, 1888	......	23.2	......	25.00									
......	....	1	21.13	2	20.90	6	60,439	192.48	1	8 3	6 10	2	1	2
329	July 1, 1888	24	24.96	23	24.46	6	51,025	81.25	1	20 0	9 0	2	1	2
									[16]1	15 0	9 0			
211	July 1, 1884	24	16.23	23	12.84	6								
1,305	July 1, 1885	24	28.80	23	28.80	6								
529	July 1, 1885	10	15.47	5	24.50	6 }	40,632	129.40	1	17 4	9 0	1	1	1
394	July 1, 1888	10	17.67	5	27.03	6 }								
305	Feb. 15, 1886	31	11.00	32	8.4	6	25,685	81.80	1	7 4	5 5	1	1	1
1,141	July 1, 1888	31	10.00	32	11.7									
3,138	July 1, 1886	403	21.71	404	23.99	6	[22]131,478	[23]139.57	2	22 6	9 1	3	1	[24]11
		401	22.33	402	24.24	7	215,589	147.26	1	29 4	9 4	4	2	
1,805	July 1, 1886	403	21.71	404	23.99	6	......	......	1	20 0	9 0			
		401	22.33	402	24.24	7	....	......	1	20 0	8 9			
2,735	July 1, 1886	403	26.02	404	23.94	6								
		401	21.59	402	28.94	7								
1,516	July 1, 1886	403	21.28	404	23.13	6								
		401	21.03	402	21.67	7								

[14] 25 miles shown as Greenville and Columbia R. P. O.

[15] Order March 2, 1888, establishing R. P. O. service to commence March 12, 1888.

[16] In reserve.

[17] Covered by lines in the second division, 2.40 miles.

[18] Runs on route 8045, Ashtabula to Andover, Ohio (24.50 miles).

[19] Shown in report of Oil City and Ashtabula R. P. O. In connection with Oil City and Ashtabula R. P. O. gives double service between Ashtabula and Andover, Ohio, daily, except Sunday.

[20] 2 miles, Eustis to Fort Mason; double daily 25 miles, Eustis to Leesburgh, reported in Table C²; closed pouches.

[21] 72.71 miles shown as Palatka and Punta Gorda R. P. O.

[22] Double daily service between Atchison and Downs.

[23] Clerks on trains 403 and 404 run only to Downs, Kans. (209.36 miles).

[24] The clerk appointed to Downs and Stockton, Kans., R. P. O., also performs service on this line, acting as second clerk on trains 401 and 402; these clerks leave Atchison and Lenora car every day at Downs, and perform service on Downs and Stockton, Kans., R. P. O.; 1 helper on trains 403 and 404 between Atchison, Kans., and meeting point (78.55 miles).

[25] 7.58 miles of route 13021, between Washington and Greenleaf, Kans., covered by closed-pouch service. (See Table C².)

TABLE A⁸.—*Statement of railway post-offices in operation*

Designation of railway post-office. (Lines upon which railway post-office cars are paid for, in *italics*.)	Division.	Distance run by clerks, register to register.	Initial and terminal stations, running from east to west, north to south, or northwest to southeast (with abbreviated title of railroad company).	Number of route.	Miles of route for which railroad is paid.
		Miles.			
Atchison and Topeka, Kans...	7	51. 11	Atchison, Topeka, Kans. (A , T. and S. F.)	133010 (Pa..¹)	50. 70
Atchison Junction, Mo., and Atchison, Kans.	7	20. 24	Atchison Junction, Mo., Atchison, Kans. (C., R. I. and P.).	28032	20. 24
Athens and Union Point, Ga...	4	40. 48	Athens, Union Point. Ga. (Ga. R. R)	15007	40. 48
Athol and Springfield, Mass ..	1	48. 34	Athol, Springfield, Mass. (Bos. and Alb'y).	3068	47. 89
Atlanta, Ga., and Artesia, Miss	4	167. 63	Atlanta, Ga., Coalburgh, Ala., (Ga. P. R. R.)	15042	176. 76
Eastern Division	(⁴)	.. ....	Coalburgh, Ala., Columbus, Miss. (Ga. Pac. R. R.).	18005	114. 85
Western Division...........	(⁵)	138. 24	Columbus, Miss , Artesia, Miss. (Mob. and Ohio R. R.).	18014	13. 53
Atlanta and Brunswick, Ga ..	4	278. 00	Atlanta, Brunswick, Ga. (E. T. V. and G. R. R.).	15013 (²part)	277. 75
Atlanta and Macon, Ga..... ..	4	103. 83	Atlanta, Macon, Ga. (Cen. R. R)	15012	103. 83
Atlanta, Ga., and Montgomery, Ala.	4	175. 68	Atlanta, West Point, Ga. (A. and W. Pt. R. R).	15003	87. 36
			West Point, Ga., Montgomery, Ala. (West R. R. of Ala.).	17001	86. 21
Atlanta and Savannah, Ga	4	294. 08	Atlanta, Macon, Ga. (Cen. R. R.)....	15012	(¹²)
			Macon, Savannah, Ga. (Cen. R. R.)	15010	191. 43
Atlanta and Zebulon, Ga	4	51. 26	Atlanta, Zebulon, Ga. (Atlanta and Fla. R R).	15056	51. 26
Attica and Medicine Lodge, Kans.	7	21. 76	Attica, Medicine Lodge, Kans. (So. Kans.)..	33048	21. 76
Auburn and Freeville, N. Y....	2	39. 41	Auburn, Freeville, N. Y. (L. V.)..........	6076	39. 46
Auburn and Harrisburg, Pa...	2	59. 84	Auburn, Harrisburg, Pa.(P. and R.)......	8028	59. 05
Auburn and Lincoln, Nebr.....	6	76. 84	Auburn, Weeping Water, Nebr. (Mo. Pacific).	¹⁴33040 (part)	43. 01
			Weeping Water, Lincoln, Nebr. (Mo. Pacific).	34040	35. 11
Augusta and Atlanta, Ga	4	171. 59	Augusta, Atlanta, Ga., Ga. R. R	15004	171. 59
Augusta and Millen, Ga.......	4	53. 51	Augusta, Millen, Ga. (Cen. R. R.)..........	15005	54. 51
Augusta and Portland, Me ...	1	63. 39	Augusta, Portland, Me. (Me. Cen.)	150 (part)	(²⁰)
Augusta, Ga., and Port Royal, S. C.	4	112. 52	Augusta, Ga., Port Royal, S. C. (Cen. R. R. of Ga.).	14010	110. 77
Augusta and Sandersville, Ga..	4	81. 05	Augusta, Sandersville, Ga. (Aug , Gib. and Sand. R. R. ;.	15048	81. 05
Aurora and Arcadia, Nebr	6	90. 73	Aurora, Central City, Nebr. (Rep. Valley)..	²¹34011 (part)	19. 25
			Central City, Arcadia, Nebr. (B. and M. R. in Nebr.).	34049	71. 07
Austin, Minn., and Mason City, Iowa.	6	40. 74	Austin, Minn., Mason City, Iowa (Chi., Mil. and St. Paul).	26012	41. 33
Babylon and New York, N. Y²².	2	37. 36	Babylon, Long Island City, N. Y. (L. I.)....	6093 (part)	(²⁹)
Bad Axe and East Saginaw, Mich.	9	68. 23	Bad Axe, East Saginaw, Mich. (S.T. and H)	24054	68. 23
Baldwin and Grand Rapids, Mich.	9	74. 70	Baldwin, Grand Rapids, Mich. (C. and W. M.).	24026	73. 98

¹ 569.75 miles of route 33010 between Topeka, Kans., and South Pueblo (n. o.), Colo., covered by Kansas City, Mo., and Pueblo, Colo., R. P. O. Leavenworth and Topeka, Kans., R. P. O. also runs over route 33010 between Meriden Junction (n. o.) and Topeka, Kans. (10.20 miles).
² Service on this line is performed by helpers on Trenton, Mo., and Leavenworth, Kans., R. P. O.

³ Reserve car.
⁴ Line divided at Birmingham, Ala.
⁵ Eastern Division.
⁶ Western Division.
⁷ One transfer clerk, Birmingham, Ala.
⁸ 73.05 miles shown as the Chattanooga, Rome and Atlanta R. P. O.: 1 reserve car.
⁹ One detailed to office of superintendent fourth division ; 1 transfer clerk, Macon, Ga.
¹⁰ Paid for as 40-foot cars.

in the *United States on June* 30, 1888—Continued.

Average weight of mail whole distance per day.	Date of last re-adjustment.	Average speed per hour (train numbers taken from division schedules).				Number of round trips with clerks per week.	Annual miles of service with clerks.	Average miles run daily by crews.	Number of mail cars, or cars in which are mail apartments.	Inside dimensions of cars or apartments (railway post-office cars in black figures.)		Number of crews.	Number of clerks to crew.	Number of clerks appointed to line.
		Train No. outward.	Av' gespeed (miles).	Train No. inward.	Av' gespeed (miles).					Length.	Width.			
Lbs.										Ft. In.	Ft. In.			
11,653	July 1, 1886	101 25.60		102 25.60		7	37,413	102.22	1	21 0	9 3¼	1	1	1
693	July 1, 1887	51 25.17		52 25.17		6	18,363	(²)	1	8 8	6 11	(²)		
408	July 1, 1888	52 13.8		53 13.8		6	25,421	80.96	1	10 6	6 3	1	1	1
404	July 1, 1885	475 23.30		472 21.23		6	30,357	96.68	1	10 11	6 4	1	1	1
									*1	9 0	6 4			
2,071	July 1, 1888	50 24		51 23.2		7								
607	July 1, 1888	52 20		53 20		....	*122,705	......	*4	15 3	8 10	5	1	6
463	July 1, 1888	52 20		53 20			*101,191	......	1	39 6	8 6	...	..	(⁷)
1,026	July 1, 1888	15 24.1		16 22.6		7	203,496	111.2	*4	25 0	9 2	5	1	5
									1	18 0	9 2			
5,013	July 1, 1884	12 34.2		11 25.2		6	65,205	103.8	1	24 0	9 0	2	1	*4
12,088	July 1, 1888	50 30.3		51 30.7		14	257,195	140.54	4	50 0	9 4	5	2	13
		52 25.4		53 31.2					(¹⁰)					(¹¹)
12,295	July 1, 1888	50 30.3		51 30.7										
		52 25.4		53 31.2										
5,013	July 1, 1884	2 28.7		1 28.7		7	215,276	147.04	3	24 8	9 2	4	1	6
									4	24 6	9 0			(¹³)
3,664	July 1, 1888	8 29.2		1 29.0					(¹⁴)					
		1 13.3		2 13.8		6	32,191	102.52	1	8 3	6 10	1	1	1
......	......													
657	July 1, 1886	461 17.42		464 16.72		7	15,928	(¹⁸)	1	11 1	6 1	1	1	(¹⁶)
145	July 1, 1885	81 12.12		82 12.12		6	24,749	78.82	1	7 2	6 6	1	1	1
163	July 1, 1885	20 27.16		6 29.92		6	37,579	119.68	1	8 0	6 8	1	1	1
1,285	July 1, 1886	359 23.43		300 24.60		7	56,247	153.68	1	16 4	6 9	1	1	1
252	Feb. 14, 1887	359 23.33		360 23.33										
3,618	July 1, 1888	1 24.4		2 22.8		14	251,206	114.39	1	25 5	8 6	6	1	7
		3 22.8		4 28.8					1	24 6	8 7			(¹⁷)
									1*2	15 0	9 0			
762	July 1, 1888	70 25.5		71 26.5		6	33,604	107.02	1	24 6	9 0	1	1	1
15,122	July 1, 1885	44 25.86		25 23.43		6	39,809	110.92	1	15 0	6 9	1	1	1
405	July 1, 1888	63 20.4		64 20.4		7	82,365	112.52	2	10 4	6 8	2	1	2
181	July 1, 1888	2 14.08		3 14.08		6	50,899	162.10	1	8 0	6 0	1	1	1
693	July 1, 1886	49 20.72		50 25.33		6	56,978	181.46	1	11 0	7 1	1	1	1
356	July 1, 1888	49 23.69		50 25.81										
529	July 1, 1887	12 28.92		11 28.92		6	25,584	81.48	1	14 8	7 5¼	1	1	1
1,121	Aug 25, 1885	14 25.74		33 24.11		6	23,462	74.72	1	12 4	6 0	1	1	(²⁴)
									1	10 3½	5 8			
241	Mar. 30, 1887	1 21.77		4 21.20		6	42,848	130.46	1	7 0	6 0	1	1	1
505	July 1, 1884	46 24.13		45 20.76		0	46,912	149.40	1	8 0	9 0	1	1	1

[11] One detailed to office of superintendent fourth division; 2 detailed as printers for fourth division.
[12] Reported as Atlanta and Macon R. P. O.
[13] One transfer clerk Savannah, Ga.; 1 helper.
[14] Five reserve cars.
[15] Service on this line is performed by clerks on Newton and Kiowa, Kans., R. P. O.
[16] Balance of route (123.41 miles) covered by Omaha, Nebr., and Atchison, Kans. R. P. O.
[17] Transfer clerk, Augusta, Ga.
* Night line.

[19] Balance of route covered by Bangor, Bos., R. P. O. (75.06) miles. This clerk runs in connection with Skowhegan and Portland R. P. clerk.
[20] Covered by Bangor, Bos., R. P. O. (62.94) miles.
[21] Balance of route (22.75 miles) covered by Nebraska City and Whitman, Nebr., R. P. O.
[22] Short run, Sag Harbor and New York R. P. O.
[23] 37 miles covered by Sag Harbor and New York R. P. O.
[24] Clerk accounted for on Sag Harbor and New York R. P. O.

TABLE A*.—*Statement of railway post-offices in operation*

Designation of railway post-office. Lines upon which railway post-office cars are paid for, in *italics*.)	Division.	Distance run by clerks, register to register.	Initial and terminal stations, running from east to west, north to south, or northwest to southeast (with abbreviated title of railroad company).	Number of route.	Miles of route for which railroad is paid.
		Miles.			
Baltimore, Md., and Bristol, Tenn.	3	477.57	Baltimore, Hagerstown, Md. (Western Md.).	10006 (part)	(¹)
			Hagerstown, Md., Roanoke, Va. (Shen. Valley).	11021	239.80
			Roanoke, Va., Bristol, Tenn. (Norfolk and Western).	11013 (part)	(²)
Baltimore, Md., and Grafton, W. Va.	3	294.86	Baltimore, Md., Grafton, W. Va. (Balto. and Ohio).	10003 (part)	293.75
Baltimore, Md., and Lexington, Va.	3	258.32	Baltimore, Md., Harper's Ferry, W. Va. (Balto. and Ohio).	10003 (part)	(³)
			Harper's Ferry, W. Va., Lexington, Va. (Balto. and Ohio).	12001	165.54
Baltimore, Md., and Martinsburgh, W. Va.	3	101.32	Baltimore, Saint Denis, Md. (Balto. and Ohio).	10003 (part)	(¹²)
			Saint Denis, Washington Junction (n. o.), Md. (Balto. and Ohio).	10017 (part)	(¹³)
			Washington Junction (n. o.), Md., Martinsburgh, W. Va. (Balto. and Ohio).	10003 (part)	(¹⁴)
Baltimore, Md., and Washington, D. C.	3	43.37	Baltimore, Md., Washington, D. C. (Balto. and Potomac).	10013 (part)	(¹⁵)
Baltimore and Williamsport, Md.	3	94.12	Baltimore, Williamsport, Md. (Western Md.).	10006	93.14
Baltimore, Md., and Winchester, Va.	3	114.48	Baltimore, Md., Harper's Ferry, W. Va. (Balto. and Ohio).	10017	81.13
			Harper's Ferry, W. Va., Winchester, Va. (Balto. and Ohio).	12001 (part)	(¹⁶)
Bangor and Bucksport, Me....	1	19.24	Bangor, Bucksport, Me. (Me. Cen.)	13	20.55
Bangor and Bar Harbor, Me...	1	51.00	Bangor, Bar Harbor, Me. (Me. Cen.)	24	50.45
Bangor, Me., and Boston, Mass.	1	245.90	Bangor, Portland, Me. (Me. Cen.)	6	138.00
			Portland, Me., Boston, Mass. (Bos. and Me.).	3001	109.35
Batavia, and Buffalo, N. Y.....	2	47.39	Batavia, Tonawanda, N.Y. (N. Y. C. and H. R.).	6014 (part)	¹⁷36.00
			Tonawanda, Buffalo, N. Y. (N. Y. C. and H. R.).	6016 (part)	(¹²)
Bath and Lewiston, Me........	1	28.47	Bath, Brunswick, Me. (Me. Cen.)	11	(¹⁸)
			Brunswick, Lewiston, Me. (Me. Cen.).....	¹⁸3 (part)	15.03
Bayard and New Philadelphia, Ohio.	5	32.34	Bayard, New Philadelphia, Ohio (Pa. Co.).	21008	32.41

[1] 86.60 miles covered by the Baltimore and Williamsport R. P. O.

[2] This line is in two divisions; 6 clerks performing daily service in the eastern division, Baltimore, Md., to Roanoke, Va. (326.93 miles), with two helpers, daily, except Sunday, between Baltimore, Md., and White Post, Va. (135.80 miles), and 4 clerks performing daily service between Roanoke, Va., and Bristol, Tenn. (150 64 miles).

[3] 150.60 miles covered by the Lynchburgh and Bristol R. P. O.

[4] 96.25 miles covered by the Grafton and Chicago and Grafton and Wheeling R. P. O.'s.

[5] Owned by O. and M. R. R. Co.; 1 in reserve.

[6] 1 chief clerk and 4 transfer clerks at Baltimore, Md.; 2 transfer clerks Washington, D. C.; 2 transfer clerks Cumberland, Md.; 4 detailed to office general superintendent R. M. S.: 1 janitor dormitory Washington, D. C.; 3 detailed to Post-Office Department. Third clerks on train 5 run as helpers in the Baltimore and Lexington R. P. O. between Washington, D. C., and Washington Junction (n. o.), Md., daily except Sunday.

[7] Cars on this line in use between Baltimore, Md., and Saint Louis, Mo.; 1 in reserve.

[8] See Grafton and Chicago R. P. O.

[9] 95 miles, Baltimore, Md., via Washington, D C., to Harper's Ferry, W. Va., covered by the Baltimore and Grafton R. P. O.

[10] 1 in reserve.

[11] 1 helper, Staunton to Winchester, Va., 94 miles.

[12] 9 miles covered by the Baltimore and Lexington R. P. O. Clerks on this line alternately, for 3 days, relieve clerk in the Baltimore and Winchester R. P. O. every 6 days, making runs of all clerks on both lines 6 days on and 3 days off duty.

in the United States on June 30, 1888—Continued.

Average weight of mail whole distance per day.	Date of last re-adjustment.	Average speed per hour (train numbers taken from division schedules).				Number of round trips with clerks per week.	Annual miles of service with clerks.	Average miles run daily by crews.	Number of mail cars, or cars in which are mail apartments.	Inside dimensions of cars or apartments (railway post-office cars in black figures).		Number of crews.	Number of clerks to crew.	Number of clerks appointed to line.
		Train No. outward.	Av'ge speed (miles).	Train No. inward.	Av'ge speed (miles).					Length.	Width.			
Lbs.										*Ft. In.*	*Ft. In.*			
3,576	July 1, 1885	1	28.55	10	29.69	7	349,581	119.39	2	44 6	9 0	6	1	[12]12
2,612	July 1, 1885	3	24.97	2	24.75				1	40 2	8 9			
6,222	July 1, 1885	1	27.77	2	28.66	.....	....	....	2	40 0	8 10	2	2	
21,912	July 1, 1885	1	30.92	6	33.57	7	215,838	147.43	[15]5	50 2	9 0	4	2	[16]49
		3	30.49	4	31.33	7	215,838	....	7	52 2	9 1	4	3	
		5	33.26	2	32.94	7	215,838	....	(3)			4	3	
21,912	July 1, 1885	9	30.00	10	28.50	6	162,225	129.16	[17]3	21 0	9 0	4	1	[15]15
1,176	July 1, 1885	409	22.71	410	19.05									
21,912	July 1, 1885	63	31.13	66	20.76	6	63,629	101.82	1	18 0	9 0	2	1	2
813	July 1, 1885	63	25.56	66	18.86									
21,912	July 1, 1885	63	26.74	66	26.74									
57,708	July 1, 1885	57	27.03	52	22.83	6	27,236	86.74	[20]4	14 7	8 7	1	1	1
2,576	July 1, 1885	17	21.07	8	24.05	6	59,107	94.12	2	19 6	8 2	2	1	2
									[16]1	10 6	8 2			
813	July 1, 1885	69	24.30	70	24.30	6	71,893	228.96	1	21 0	8 2	1	1	[17]1
1,176	July 1, 1885	469	27.04	470	29.53									
676	July 1, 1885	101	16.11	100	16.11	6	12,082	76.96	1	16 2	6 10	1	1	1
		105	15.45	106	15.03	6	12,082	....						
699	July 1, 1885	115	17.80	114	15.13	6	32,028	102.00	[19]2	16 0	6 7	1	1	1
15,122	July 1, 1885	64	24.83	9	26.43	6	154,425	122.95	1	60 0	9 1	4	4	[20]37
		2	23.41	71	21.85	7	179,998	....	1	60 0	9 1	4	3	
29,409	July 1, 1885	61	28.87	9	24.08	6	....	....	1	60 0	9 1			
		2	24.99	71	27.07	7			1	60 0	9 1			
									[21]1	40 0	9 0			
241	July 1, 1885	01	15.96	02	12.30	6	29,761	94.78	1	6 0	6 0	1	1	1
8,979	July 1, 1885	70	14.64	02	16.50	6	....	....	(24)			(24)		
2,697	July 1, 1887	57	26.10	62	26.10	6	17,879	113.88	1	15 6	7 5	1	1	1
		65	28.99	74	26.10	6	17,879	....	[21]1	16 0	7 3			
870	July 1, 1885	55	18.00	62	18.00									
		65	19.18	74	18.00									
561	July 1, 1888	51	22.88	52	11.11	6	20,309	129.36	1	14 6	8 8	1	1	1
		53	16.20	54	21.80	[37]6	20,309							

[13] 59.75 miles covered by the Baltimore and Winchester R. P. O.

[14] 31.25 miles covered by the Baltimore and Grafton R. P. O.

[15] 41.70 miles covered by the New York and Washington R. P. O.

[16] In reserve.

[17] This clerk runs 6 days on and 3 off, being relieved by clerks in the Baltimore and Martinsburgh R. P. O.

[18] 32 miles covered by the Baltimore and Lexington R. P. O.

[19] One of these cars is reserve.

[20] 1 clerk detailed as chief clerk, Portland, Me.; 1 clerk detailed as assistant to chief clerk, Portland, Me.; 1 clerk detailed to superintendent's office; 2 clerks detailed as transfer clerks (one at Bangor and one at Portland,

Me.); 4 clerks as short stops (2 on day and 2 on night train) between Portland and Boston (108.80 miles).

[21] Reserve car.

[22] 50.62 miles covered by Canandaigua and Batavia R. P. O.

[23] 11 miles covered by Suspension Bridge and Buffalo R. P. O.

[24] Cars and clerks shown on route No. 6014.

[25] Covered by Rockland and Portland R. P. O. (9.17 miles).

[26] Balance of route covered by Farmington and Lewiston R. P. O. (36.20 miles), and closed-pouch service between Leeds Junction and Lewiston (16.32 miles). (See Table C*.)

[27] Clerk makes two round trips daily, except Sunday.

[28] 3 cars in reserve.

TABLE A⁴.—*Statement of railway post-offices in operation*

Designation of railway post-office. (Lines upon which railway post-office cars are paid for, in *italics*.)	Division.	Distance run by clerks, register to register.	Initial and terminal stations, running from east to west, north to south, or northwest to southeast (with abbreviated title of railroad company).	Number of route.	Miles of route for which railroad is paid.
		Miles.			
Bay City, Wayne, and Detroit, Mich.[1]	9	121.41	Bay City, East Saginaw, Mich. (F. and P. M.).	24048	13.21
			East Saginaw, Wayne, Mich. (F. and P. M.).	24015 (part)	(²)
			Wayne, Detroit, Mich. (Mich. Cent.)......	24006 (part)	(⁴)
Bay City and Jackson, Mich⁵..	9	115.00	Bay City, Jackson, Mich. (Mich. Cent.)...	24009	114.81
Beardstown and Shawneetown, Ill.	6	228.35	Beardstown, Shawneetown, Ill. (Ohio and Miss.).	23033	229.06
Beatrice, Nebr., and Manhattan, Kans.⁶	7	93.68	Beatrice, Nebr., Marysville, Kans. (U. P.).	⁷34013 (part)	38.26
			Marysville, Manhattan, Kans. (U. P.)	33051	55.64
Beaumont and Bluff, Kans. ...	7	106.14	Beaumont, Bluff, Kans. (St. L. and S. F.)..	33049	106.14
Bedford and Switz City, Ind⁸ ..	5	41.54	Switz City, Bedford, Ind. (Bed. and Bloom.).	22936	41.47
Belfast and Burnham, Me	1	33.95	Belfast, Burnham, Me. (Me. Cen.)	4	33.29
Bellaire and Zanesville, Ohio...	5	112.74	Bellaire, Zanesville, Ohio (Bell., Zanes. and Cin.).	21063	112.57
Belle Plaine and Muchakinock, Iowa.	6	62.90	Belle Plaine, Muchakinock, Iowa (Chic. and No. West.).	27049	64.68
Bellevue and Cascade, Iowa ...	6	36.32	Bellevue, Cascade, Iowa (Chic., Mil. and St. Paul).	27053	36.40
Bellwood and Punxsutawney, Pa.	2	58.30	Bellwood, Irvona, Pa. (Bell's Gap)	8087	25.62
			Irvona, Punxsutawney, Pa. (Bell's Gap)....	8165	33.47
Beloit and Solomon City, Kans.	7	57.86	Beloit, Solomon City, Kans. (U. P.)	33025	57.86
Belvidere. N. J., and Philadelphia, Pa.	2	102.54	Manunka Chunk, Trenton, N. J. (Penna.)..	7008	67.89
			Trenton, N. J., Philadelphia, Pa. (Penna.)..	7004 (part)	(¹²)
Bement and Effingham, Ill	6	62.26	Bement, Shumway, Ill. (Wab., St. L. and Pac.).	¹⁵23060 (part)	52.50
			Shumway, Effingham, Ill. (Wab., St. L. and Pac.).	23063	9.24
Bennington, Vt., and Chatham, N. Y.	2	57.79	Bennington, Vt., Chatham, N. Y. (N. Y., R. and M.).	6054	57.60
Benson and Nogales, Ariz.....	8	88.50	Benson, Nogales, Ariz. (New Mexico and Arizona R R.).	40002	88.50
Benton Harbor, Mich., and Anderson, Ind.	5	164.48	Benton Harbor, Mich., Anderson, Ind. (Cin., Wab. and Mich.).	22022	164.68
Berlin and Salisbury, Md......	2	23.86	Berlin, Salisbury, Md. (Wico. and Poco.)..	10009 (part)	¹⁷23.86
Bethany Junction, Iowa, and Grant City, Mo.	6	44.28	Bethany Junction (n. o.), Iowa, Grant City, Mo. (Chi. and Burl. and Qcy.).	¹⁸27000 (part)	44.23
Bethlehem and Philadelphia, Pa.	2	¹⁹57.60	Bethlehem, Philadelphia, Pa. (P. and R.).	5004	56.01
Big Rapids and Detroit, Mich²¹	9	190.70	Big Rapids, Ionia, Mich. (D. L. and N.)....	24016	68.09
			Ionia, Detroit, Mich. (D. L. and N.).......	24017 (part)	(²⁰)
Big Rapids and Holland, Mich²⁴	9	91.00	Big Rapids, Holland, Mich. (C. and W. M.)..	24022	91.00

Runs on route 24015, East Saginaw to Wayne, Mich. (90.50 miles), and, in connection with Ludington and Toledo R. P. O., gives double service between those points daily, except Sunday; also runs on route 24006, Wayne to Detroit, Mich. (18.16 miles).

² Shown in report of Ludington and Toledo R. P. O.
³ Clerks appointed to Ludington and Toledo R. P. O.
⁴ Shown in report of Detroit and Chicago R. P. O.
⁵ Double service daily, except Sunday.
⁶ Reported last year as Marysville and Manhattan, Kans., R. P. O ; increased distance, 38.02 miles.

⁷ 40.22 miles of route 34013, between Beatrice and Lincoln, Nebr., covered by Omaha and Beatrice, Nebr., R. P. O.
⁸ Prior to September 20, 1887, this R. P. O. was known as the Switz City and Bedford R. P. O.
⁹ One car in reserve.
¹⁰ Reserve car.
¹¹ In reserve.
¹² Cars and clerks shown on route 8087.
¹³ 34.01 miles covered by New York and Washington R. P. O.
¹⁴ Cars and clerks shown on route 7008.
¹⁵ Balance of route covered by Chicago, Decatur

in the United States on June 30, 1888—Continued.

Average weight of mail whole distance per day.	Date of last re-adjustment.	Average speed per hour (train numbers taken from division schedules).				Number of round trips with clerks per week.	Annual miles of service with clerks.	Average miles run daily by crews.	Number of mail cars, or cars in which are mail apartments.	Inside dimensions of cars or apartments (railway post-office cars in black figures).		Number of crews.	Number of clerks to crew.	Number of clerks appointed to line.
		Train No. outward.	Av'ge speed (miles).	Train No. inward.	Av'ge speed (miles).					Length.	Width.			
Lbs.										*Ft. In.*	*Ft. In.*			
1, 300	July 1, 1884	405	24. 82	403	24. 82	6	} 76. 245	121. 41	1	22 2	8 11	2	1	(?)
2, 653	July 1, 1884	5	27. 75	2	28. 19	6								
16, 713	July 1, 1884	42	27. 00	33	27. 00	6								
1, 423	July 1, 1884	72	25. 38	73	22. 84	6	72, 220 } 115. 00		1	16 8	8 10	} 4	1	4
		74	22. 84	71	24. 04	6	72, 220		1	17 0	8 11			
417	July 1, 1887	20	19. 25	21	20. 31	6	143, 404	114. 17	1	14 0	9 0	4	1	4
		22	16. 14	23	17. 41	...	....		1	16 4	9 4			
									1	15 0	9 0			
									1	16 8	9 3			
682	July 1, 1886	242	22. 82	241	21. 07	7	68, 574	93. 68	1	15 2	7 5	2	1	2
387	Dec. 1, 1886	242	22. 96	241	19. 68	7								
403	July 1, 1888	3	22. 04	4	23. 51	7	77, 694	106. 14	1	12 1	7 4	2	1	2
132	July 1, 1888	62	9. 22	61	9. 05	6	26, 007	93. 08	2	5 4	4 10	1	1	1
612	July 1, 1885	86	22. 06	87	17. 20	6	21, 320	135. 80	1	17 5	7 7	1	1	1
		88	14. 70	80	22. 00	6	21, 320	......	14 1	12 0	7 0			
424	July 1, 1888	1	15. 34	2	15. 17	6	70, 801	112. 74	3	12 0	7 8	2	1	2
329	July 1, 1887	101	23. 42	102	20. 34	6	39, 501	125. 80	1	12 2	7 5	1	1	1
159	July 1, 1887	25	10. 00	26	10. 29	6	22, 809	72. 64	1	8 6	6 6	1	1	1
......	....	7	18. 48	16	17. 04	6	36, 612	116. 60	1	7 2	6 0	1	1	1
									11 1	7 2	6 0			
291	July 1, 1888	7	17. 18	16	18. 24	6	....		(17)			(12)		
164	July 1, 1883	262	24. 59	261	24. 59	7	42, 354	115. 72	1	18 0	8 11	1	1	1
									11 1	17 6½	7 11			
1, 031	July 1, 1885	573	28. 62	554	28. 02	6	64, 395	205. 08	1	15 6	8 3	1	1	1
136, 401	July 1, 1885	49	21. 66	54	24. 54	6	....		(14)			(14)		
1, 085	July 1, 1887	85	22. 50	84	22. 50	6	39, 099	124. 52	1	11 5	6 8½	1	1	1
418	July 1, 1887	85	21. 25	84	21. 25									
354	July 1, 1885	4	18. 54	5	22. 32	6	36, 292	115. 58	1	14 0	7 0	1	1	1
420	July 1, 1886	1	11. 25	2	12. 29	7	64, 782	88. 50	14 3	20 0	9 2	2	1	2
767	July 1, 1888	2	26. 92	1	25. 68	6	103, 243	164. 48	1	12 6	9 0	2	1	2
133	July 1, 1885	2	14. 31	3	15. 00	6	14, 984	47. 72	1	9 8	4 1	1	1	1
991	July 1, 1887	47	10. 00	48	11. 23	6	27, 806	88. 56	1	11 3½	8 10	1	1	1
5, 094	July 1, 1885	308	24. 09	301	27. 48	6	36, 173	114. 87	2	15 0	7 6	1	2	3
		310	28. 09	315	24. 68	6	36, 022		1	12 0	7 6	1		
		314	28. 09	......		3	18, 011	....	11 1	15 4	7 6			
889	July 1, 1884	4	27. 00	7	23. 14	6	119, 760	127. 13	2	20 0	8 10	3	1	24 4
2, 107	July 1, 1884	6	25. 41	5	24. 16	6								
821	July 1, 1884	28	13. 92	21	15. 51	6	57, 148	91. 00	1	15 0	9 0	2	1	2

Ill., and Saint Louis, Mo., R.P.O. (152.80 miles), and between Shumway and Altamont (10 5¼ miles), by closed pouches. (See Table C°.)

16 1 reserve car.

17 7.19 miles covered by closed pouch service. (See Table C°.)

18 Balance of route (49.68 miles) covered by Des Moines, Iowa, and Saint Joseph, Mo., R. P. O.

19 Distance on trains 308 and 315—57.90 miles. Distance on trains 301, 310, and 314—57.36 miles.

20 Triple daily service outward and double daily service inward, except Sunday.

21 Runs on route 24017 Ionia to Detroit, Mich.

(122.73 miles), and, with Howard City and Detroit R. P. O., gives double service between these points daily except Sunday.

22 Shown in report of Howard City and Detroit R. P. O.

23 One clerk assigned as helper between Detroit and Howell, Mich., in the Howard City and Detroit R. P. O.

24 In connection with Muskegon and Allegan R. P. O. gives double service between Muskegon and Holland, Mich. (35.50 miles), daily except Sunday.

TABLE A*.—*Statement of railway post-offices in operation*

Designation of railway post-office. (Lines upon which railway post-office cars are paid for, in *italics*.)	Division	Distance run by clerks, register to register.	Initial and terminal stations, running from east to west, north to south, or northwest to southeast (with abbreviated title of railroad company).	Number of route.	Miles of route for which railroad is paid.
		Miles.			
Binghamton, and New York, N. Y.	2	208.70	Binghamton, N. Y., Washington, N. J. (D., L. and W.).	8019	140.50
			Washington, Denville, N. J. (D., L. and W.).	7013 (part)	(7)
			Denville, Hoboken, N. J. (D., L. and W.).	7028	34.30
Birmingham, Ala., and Memphis, Tenn.	4	251.20	Birmingham, Ala., Memphis, Tenn. (K. C., Mem. and Birm. R. R.).	18021	251.20
Bloomington and Roodhouse, Ill.	6	110.75	Bloomington, Roodhouse, Ill. (Chicago and Alton.).	23018	111.28
Bluffs, Ill., and Hannibal, Mo..	6	50.01	Bluffs, Ill., Hannibal, Mo. (Wabash)	23025	50.36
Bolivar and Springfield, Mo.⁶..	7	40.05	Bolivar, North Springfield, Mo. (St. L. and S.F.).	28038	40.05
Boone and Des Moines, Iowa..	6	43.30	Boone, Des Moines, Iowa (St. L., D. M. and North.).	27681	43.06
Boonville and Versailles, Mo.⁷.	7	44.25	Boonville, Versailles, Mo. (Mo. Pac.).......	28808	44.25
Boston, Mass., and Albany, N.Y.	1	208.26	Boston, Mass., Albany, N. Y. (Bos. and Alb.)	3025	201.39
Boston, Mass., and Albany, N. Y. (short run).	1	99.44	Boston, Springfield, Mass. (Bos. and Alb.).	¹²3025 (part)	(¹¹)
Boston, Clinton, and Fitchburgh, Mass.	1	62.49	Boston, South Framingham, Mass. (Bos. and Alb.).	¹³3095 (par	(¹⁴)
			South Framingham, Fitchburgh, Mass. (Old Colony).	¹⁶3 1 (part)	40.47
Boston, Mass., and Greenville, N. H.	1	60.33	Boston, Ayer, Mass. (Fitch.)	¹⁶3021 (part)	(¹⁷)
			Ayer, Mass., Greenville, N. H. (Fitch.) . ..	3024	23.96
Boston, Mass., and Hopewell Junction, N. Y.	1	215.23	Boston, Mass., Hopewell Junction, N. Y. (N. Y. and N. Eng.).	5007	214.04
Boston, Mass., and Hopewell Junction, N. Y. (short run).	1	118.30	Boston, Mass., Hartford, Conn. (N. Y. and N. Eng.).	¹⁹5007 (part)	(²⁰)
Boston, Mass., Nashua and Keene, N. H.	1	96.22	Boston, Mass., Nashua, N. H. (Bos. and Low. Div. B. and Me.).	3016	(²²)
			Nashua, Keene, N. H. (Bos. and Low. Div. B. and M.).	1011	55.81
Boston, Mass., Providence, R. I., and New York, N. Y.	1	233.07	Boston, Mass., Providence, R. I. (Old Col. Prov. Div.).	3035	44.00
			Providence, R. I., Groton, Conn. (N. Y., Prov. and Bos.).	4002	61.80
			New London, New Haven, Conn. (N. Y., N. H. and Hart.).	5004	51.78
			New Haven, Conn., New York, N. Y. (N. Y., N. H. and Hart.).	²⁴5005 (part)	(²⁵)
Boston, Mass., and New York, N. Y. (short run).	1	135.73	Springfield, Mass., New York, N. Y. (N. Y., N. H. and Hart.).	5005	(²⁶)

¹ In reserve.
² 81 miles covered by New York, Dover and Easton R. P. O.
³ Cars and clerks shown on route No. 8019.
⁴ 1 reserve car.
⁵ Whole cars, one in reserve.
⁶ Reported last year as Bolivar and North Springfield, Mo.; increased distance, .62 of a mile.
⁷ Double daily service between Boonville and Tipton, Mo. (25.00 miles).
⁸ 1 clerk detailed as chief clerk; 2 clerks detailed to superintendent's office; 6 clerks on short run, between Boston and Springfield (99.44 miles).
⁹ Reserve car.
¹⁰ Balance of route covered by Boston and Albany R. P. O. (102.66 miles).
¹¹ Covered by Boston and Albany R P. O. (96.63 miles).
¹² Shown in column 17, Boston and Albany R. P. O.
¹³ Balance of route covered by Boston and Albany R. P. O. (180.06 miles).
¹⁴ Covered by Boston and Albany R. P. O. (21.21 miles).
¹⁵ Balance of route covered by Lowell and Taunton R. P. O. (32.26 miles), and closed-pouch service between Taunton and New Bedford (20.91 miles). (See table C*.)
¹⁶ Balance of route covered by Boston and Troy R. P. O. (09.33 miles).
¹⁷ Covered by Boston and Troy R. P. O. (36.07 miles).
¹⁸ On the a. m. run west there are two clerks to Bristol, Conn., the second clerk stopping there, and returning with Boston and Hopewell Junction short run east next morning; 6 clerks on Boston and Hopewell Junction short

in the United States on June 30, 1888—Continued.

Average weight of mail whole distance per day.	Date of last re-adjustment.	Average speed per hour (train numbers taken from division schedules).				Number of round trips with clerks per week	Annual miles of service with clerks.	Average miles run daily by crew.	Number of mail cars, or cars in which are mail apartments.	Inside dimensions of cars or apartments (railway post-office cars in black figures).		Number of crews.	Number of clerks to crew.	Number of clerks appointed to line.
		Train No. outward.	Av'ge speed (miles).	Train No. inward.	Av'ge speed (miles).					Length.	Width.			
Lbs.										*Ft. In.*	*Ft. In.*			
2,604	July 1, 1885	2	27.00	1	26.08	6	131,064	139.13	2 [11]	20 0	9 0	3	2	6
3,229	July 1, 1885	2	29.52	1	28.17	6	....	....	(7)	20 0	9 0	(3)		
2,897	July 1, 1885	2	27.42	1	25.40	6			(3)			(3)		
510	July 1, 1888	1	23.09	2	24.05	6	157,753	125.60	43 3	27 10	9 10	4	1	4
1,233	July 1, 1887	6	23.67	5	26.12	6	69,551	110.75	22	40 0	9 1	2	1	2
1,417	July 1, 1887	43	22.25	42	25.02	6	31,406	100.02	1	27 5	8 7½	1	1	1
257	July 1, 1886	46	14.70	45	14.70	6	25,151	80.10	1	12 1	7 4	1	1	1
4,306	July 1, 1887	2	21.53	1	19.08	6	27,192	86.60	1	8 4	5 10	1	1	1
467	July 1, 1887	182	11.92	181	11.43	6	27,789	*138.50	1	8 4	6 5	1	1	1
		184	11.57	183	20.00	6	*15,700							
42,810	July 1, 1885	1	25.26	12	25.80	6	127,641	101.62	1	45 1	8 9	4	3	*37
									1	45 1	8 6			
		111	28.20	6	33.03	6½	138,210	......	*1	56 7	8 9	4	4	
										27 10	8 7			
42,810	July 1, 1885	109	23.67	24	26.30	6	62,448	99.44	1	27 7	8 7	2	3	(12)
42,810	July 1, 1888	7	32.62	735	23.13	6	39,243	124.98	1	14 0	6 0	1	1	1
									*1	14 0	6 0			
1,330	July 1, 1885	7	28.18	735	29.30									
6,568	July 1, 1885	122	24.04	451	16.22	6	37,887	120.66	1	16 0	8 2	1	1	1
									*1	8 9	6 3			
521	July 1, 1885	122	23.53	451	23.53									
5,042	July 1, 1885	1	27.72	2	28.15	6	135,164	107.61	1	18 2	8 11	4	1	*12
									1	21 8	9 3			
5,042	July 1, 1835	5	25.59	6	29.32	6	74,292	118.30	1	18 2	8 11	2	(21)	(21)
										17 4	9 0			
14,362	July 1, 1885	53	29.79	236	29.79	6	60,426	96.22	1	14 2	7 0	2	1	2
									*1	13 5	6 10			
1,012	July 1, 1885	53	33.77	236	23.94									
11,597	July 1, 1888	A	33.00	82	33.00	7	170,607	116.58	2	55 0	8 8	4	4	*21
12,702	July 1, 1888	A	24.67	82	29.53									
13,103	July 1, 1885	A	33.97	82	29.12									
64,611	July 1, 1885	A	31.38	82	30.51									
64,611	July 1, 1885	205	29.08	6	25.13	6	85,238	105.48	2	55 4	8 7	4	4	(27)

run, 2 on a. m. east from Hartford, Conn., and one short stop between Boston and Willimantic; 1 clerk on p. m. west, the clerk in charge doubles the road every day; every other week off. The second clerk's run two-thirds of the time, daily average 100.02 miles; 1 clerk detailed as transfer clerk Hartford, Conn.; one clerk detailed as transfer clerk at Boston, Mass.

19 Balance of route covered by Boston and Hopewell Junction R. P. O. (97.54 miles).

20 Covered by Boston and Hopewell Junction R. P. O. (117.30 miles).

21 Shown in column 17, Boston and Hopewell Junction R. P. O.

22 Covered by Saint Albans and Boston R. P. O. (39.85 miles).

23 1 clerk detailed as transfer clerk at Providence, R. I.; 1 clerk detailed as transfer clerk at New London, Conn.; 1 clerk detailed as transfer clerk at Saybrook Junction, Conn.; 2 clerks as short-stops between New York and Saybrook; daily average, 105 miles.

24 Balance of route covered by Boston, Springfield and New York R. P. O. (62.77 miles). These clerks register at depot at New York, N. Y.

25 Covered by Boston, Springfield and New York R. P. O. (73.23 miles).

26 Covered by Boston, Springfield and New York R. P. O. (136 miles). These clerks register at depot at Springfield, Mass., and New York. N. Y.

27 Shown in column 17, Boston, Springfield and New York R. P. O.

TABLE A⁵.—*Statement of railway post-offices in operation*

Designation of railway post-office. (Lines upon which railway post-office cars are paid for, in *italics*.)	Division.	Distance run by clerks, register to register.	Initial and terminal stations, running from east to west, north to south, or northwest to southeast (with abbreviated title of railroad company).	Number of route.	Miles of route for which railroad is paid.
		Miles.			
Boston and Springfield, Mass., and New York, N. Y.	1	235.17	Boston, Springfield, Mass. (Bos. and Alb.)..	3025 ²(part)	(¹)
			Springfield, Mass., New York, N. Y. (N. Y., N. H. and Hart.).	5005	136.00
Boston, Mass., and Troy, N. Y..	1	191.04	Boston, Greenfield, Mass. (Fitch.).........	3021	103.40
			Greenfield, North Adams, Mass. (Fitch.)..	3022	37.35
			North Adams, Mass., Troy, N. Y. (Fitch.)..	6067	48.15
Boston and Wellfleet, Mass....	1	106.56	Boston, South Braintree, Mass. (Old Col.)...	3038	11.36
			South Braintree, Middleborough, Mass. (Old Col.).	3039 ⁹(part)	23.09
			Middleborough, Wellfleet, Mass. (Old Col.).	3041 ¹⁰part	71.94
Boston Corners, and Poughkeepsie, N. Y.	2	38.06	Boston Corners, Poughkeepsie, N. Y. (N. Y. and Mass.).	6079	88.11
Boundary Line (n. o.) and Presque Isle, Me.	1	39.00	Andover, N. B., Presque Isle, Me. (New Bruns.).	1	30.51
Boundary Line and Saint Paul Minn.	6	391.80	Boundary Line (n.o.) Junction (n.o.), Minn. (St. P., Minn. and Man.).	26035	2.15
			Saint Vincent, Saint Cloud, Minn. (St. P., Minn. and Man.).	26004	314.85
			Saint Cloud, Minneapolis, Minn. (St. P., Minn. and Man.).	26040	66.30
			Minneapolis, Saint Paul, Minn. (St. P., Minn. and Man.).	26006 (part)	(¹⁴)
Bound Brook, N. J., and Philadelphia, Pa.	2	59.96	Bound Brook, N. J., Jenkintown, Pa. (P. and R.).	8103	49.27
			Jenkintown, Philadelphia, Pa. (P. and R.)..	8004 (part)	(¹⁵)
Bowie and Pope's Creek, Md...	3	49.14	Bowie, Pope's Creek, Md. (Balto. and Pot.).	10014	49.01
Bowling Green, Ky., and Memphis, Tenn.	5	263.57	Bowling Green, Ky., Memphis, Tenn. (Louis. and Nash.).	20098	261.15
Branch Junction and Pittsburgh, Pa.	2	70.85	Branch Junction, Blairville, Pa. (Penna.).	8042 (part)	(¹⁸)
			Blairville, Allegheny, Pa. (Penna.)	8039	67.84
Branchville and Waterloo, N. J.	2	22.02	Branchville, Branchville Junction, N. J. (Sussex).	7048	6.37
			Branchville Junction, Waterloo, N. J. (Sussex).	7025 (part)	²⁰14.86
Brattleborough, Vt., and Palmer, Mass.	1	56.33	Brattleborough, Vt., Palmer, Mass. (New Lon. North'n Div., Cent. Vt.).	3962 ²²part	56.28
Breckenridge, Minn., and Aberdeen, Dak.	6	136.78	Breckenridge,. Tintah Junction (n. o.), Minn. (St. P., Minn. and Man.).	26006 (part)	(²⁴)
			Tintah Junction (n. o.), Minn., Aberdeen, Dak. (St. P., Minn. and Man.).	35027	119.31
Bremond and Albany, Tex.....	7	230.89	Bremond, Albany, Tex. (H. and T. C)	31005	230.83
Brewster, and New York, N. Y.	2	62.19	Brewster, New York, N. Y. (N. Y. and Nor.).	6017	54.62

¹ Covered by Boston and Albany R. P. O. (98.63 miles).

² 16 clerks on Boston and New York short run. (See column remarks, and columns 15 and 16 that line.) Two clerks detailed as chief clerks, Boston, Mass.; 1 clerk detailed as chief clerk New York, N. Y.; 6 clerks detailed to superintendent's office; 7 clerks detailed as transfer clerks (1 at New Haven, Conn., 2 at Springfield, Mass., 1 at Hartford, Conn., 1 at Worcester, Mass., 2 at Boston, Mass.).

³ Balance of route covered by Boston and Albany R. P. O. (102.66 miles).

⁴ 4.30 p. m. messengers, no apartment; mail worked in baggage-car.

⁵ Reserve car; 1 acting clerk detailed to transfer duty at Hartford, Conn., vice J. Dundee, injured.

⁶ 1 clerk detailed as transfer clerk, Boston, Mass.; 2 clerks as short-stops between Troy, N. Y., and Shelburne Falls, Mass.; daily average, 71.67 miles.

⁷ Reserve cars.

⁸ 2 clerks detailed as transfer clerks, Boston, Mass.

⁹ Balance of route covered by closed-pouch service between Middleborough and Newport (38.16 miles). (See table C⁹.)

¹⁰ Balance of route covered by closed-pouch service Wellfleet and Provincetown (14.36 miles). (See Table C⁹.) 1 acting clerk as helper, additional.

in the United States on June 30, 1888—Continued.

Average weight of mail whole distance per day.	Date of last re-adjustment.	Train No. outward.	Av'ge speed (miles).	Train No. inward.	Av'ge speed (miles).	Number of round trips with clerks per week.	Annual miles of service with clerks.	Average miles run daily by crews.	Number of mail cars, or cars in which are mail apartments.	Length.	Width.	Number of crews.	Number of clerks to crew.	Number of clerks appointed to line.
Lbs.										*Ft. In.*	*Ft. In.*			
11,507	July 1, 1885	3	32. 87	14	36. 75	6	147, 687	117. 58	1	55 0	8 8	4	6	284
		75	39. 71	48	39. 71	} 14	344, 288	....	1 {	54 6	8 8	4	1	
		63	34. 00	80	34. 00				1	55 0 (4)	8 8	4	0	
64, 611	July 1, 1885	3	34. 38	14	36. 35				1	55 0	8 8			.
		75	39. 34	48	39. 32									
		63	33. 51	80	33. 78	.....	....	....	1	54 6	8 8			
									81	60 0	8 0			
6, 568	July 1, 1885	54	23. 20	32	30. 10	6	119, 973	95. 52	1	30 0	8 3	4	2	819
		34	29. 05	35	27. 30	6	119, 973	....	1	17 0	8 8	4	2	
4, 302	July 1, 1885	54	25. 89	32	31. 78	....	....	....	1	31 11	8 8			
		34	28. 15	35	32. 23	....	....	....	1	16 11	8 5			
									1	17 6	8 5			
6, 909	July 1, 1885	54	26. 11	33	27. 45	....	....	....	{ 1	15 10	8 9			
		34	26. 00	35	29. 61	....	....	....	{ 1	15 0	8 6			
									1	18 0	6 6			
9, 471	July 1, 1885	47	28. 14	86	35. 55	6	66, 920	106. 56	1	20 6	9 2	2	2	810
		133	33. 78	190	28. 14	6	66, 920	....	1	20 6	9 2	2	2	
1, 963	July 1, 1885	47	24. 73	86	32. 98	....	....	....						
		133	33. 78	190	27. 16	....	....	....	71	21 5	8 7			
2, 627	July 1, 1885	47	25. 20	86	23. 92									
		139	26. 60	190	22. 08									
190	July 1, 1885	3	20. 76	4	20. 76	0	23, 902	76. 12	1	9 0	6 11	1	1	1
									111	7 5	6 10			
26	Apr. 6, 1886	51	29. 25	52	28. 53	7	24, 492	78. 00	1	24 0	10 0	1	1	1
									1	20 0	10 0			
2, 636	July 1, 1887	4	21. 49	3	22. 64	7	286, 797	130. 60	3	24 7	9 1	6	1	128
4, 496	July 1, 1887	4	21. 49	3	22. 64	....	....	....	121	22 2	8 11			
6, 586	July 1, 1887	4	27. 43	3	24. 86									
4, 937	July 1, 1887	4	18. 31	3	18. 31									
297	July 1, 1885	572	20. 10	557	26. 58	6	37, 655	119. 92	1	13 9	6 4	1	1	1
									111	13 0	8 6			
5, 094	July 1, 1885	572	21. 60	557	20. 88	6	....	....	(16)			(16)		
256	July 1, 1885	195	11. 23	196	12. 16	6	30, 960	98. 28	1	9 7	8 9	1	1	1
7, 963	July 1, 1884	103	22. 23	102	22. 23	7	192, 933	131. 79	2	45 0	9 0	4	2	179
699	July 1, 1885	3	16. 80	2	21. 00	6	44, 500	141. 70	1	15 0	8 6	1	1	1
760	July 1, 1885	3	16. 26	2	23. 10	6			(19)			(19)		
188	July 1, 1885	204	19. 08	201	19. 08	6	13, 829	69. 40	1	5 4	6 10	1	1	1
236	July 1, 1885	204	21. 22	201	22. 26	6			1	5 6	6 10			
		200	25. 26	209	30. 42	0	217, 963	....	1	5 8	8 10	(22)		
1, 587	July 1, 1885	44	23. 77	33	25. 38	6	35, 375	112. 06	1	10 6	6 5	1	1	1
4, 937	July 1, 1887	42	19. 00	41	20. 88	0	85, 898	136. 78	1	16 0	9 3	2	1	2
902	July 1, 1888	71	26. 94	72	26. 94									
706	July 1, 1886	33	14. 20	84	14. 57	257	26154, 255	105. 31	3	17 8	9 4	4	1	4
									111	14 0	8 10			
380	July 1, 1885	12	19. 50	1	20. 73	6	39, 055	124. 38	1	8 4	6 10	2	1	2
		6	21. 80	7	21. 70	6	39, 055							

11 In reserve.
12 One clerk detailed to transfer duty at St. Paul, Minn., one helper between St. Paul and Minneapolis, and in depot at St. Paul, Minn., daily.
13 Reserve.
14 Distance (10.68 miles) covered by Neche, Dak., and St. Paul, Minn., R. P. O.
15 10.10 miles covered by Bethlehem and Philadelphia R. P. O.
16 Cars and clerks shown on route No. 8163.
17 One clerk detailed to transfer duty at Milan, Tenn.
18 2.80 miles covered by Indiana and Branch Junction R. P. O.
19 Cars and clerks shown on route No. 8042.

20 8.63 miles covered by closed-pouch service. (See Table C².)
21 Short run between Newton and Waterloo, 12.65 miles.
22 Clerks shown on route No. 7048.
23 Balance of route covered by Palmer and New London R. P. O. (65.11 miles).
24 Distance (17.40 miles) covered by Neche, Dak., and St. Paul, Minn.. R. P. O.
25 Service performed daily between Bremond and Walnut, Tex. (89 m.), and daily except Sunday between Walnut and Albany, Tex. (141.89 m.).
26 Last year's service was but tri-weekly between Walnut and Albany, Tex.
27 Double daily service except Sunday.

TABLE A*.—*Statement of railway post-offices in operation*

Designation of railway post-office. (Lines upon which railway post-office cars are paid for, in *italics*.)	Division.	Distance run by clerks, register to register.	Initial and terminal stations, running from east to west, north to south, or northwest to southeast (with abbreviated title of railroad company).	Number of route.	Miles of route for which railroad is paid.
		Miles.			
Bristol and Chattanooga, Tenn.	3	242.37	Bristol, Chattanooga, Tenn. (East Tenn., Va. and Ga.).	19002	242.17
Bristol and Madison, Dak......	6	103.34	Bristol, Madison, Dak. (Chic., Mil. and St. Paul).	35034	103.39
Bruce, Wis., and Minneapolis, Minn.	6	122.27	Bruce, Wis., Minneapolis, Minn. (Minn., Sault de Ste. Marie and Atl.).	*25059 (part)	122.27
Brunswick and Albany, Ga ...	4	171.73	Brunswick, Albany, Ga. (B. and W. R. R.).	15023	171.73
Bryan and Carlisle, Ohio*	5	147.51	Bryan, Carlisle, Ohio(Cin., Wab. and Mack.).	*21075 (part)	146.19
Buda and Yates City, Ill	6	48.35	Buda, Elmwood, Ill. (Chi., Bur. and Qcy.)..	23072	44.98
			Elmwood, Yates City, Ill. (Chi., Bur. and Qcy.).	23009 (part)	(*)
Buffalo, N. Y., and Emporium, Pa.	2	121.55	Buffalo, N. Y., Emporium, Pa. (W. N. Y. and Pa.).	6058	121.37
Buffalo, N. Y., and Pittsburgh, Pa.	2	273.10	Buffalo, N. Y., Corry, Pa. (W.N.Y. and Pa.).	6061	94.12
			Corry, Oil City, Pa. (W. N. Y. and Pa.).....	8025 (part)	1245.60
			Oil City, Pittsburgh, Pa. (A. V.)............	8041	132.61
Buffalo and West, N. Y	2	49.56	Buffalo, West. N. Y. (B., R. and P.)....	6130	49.28
Buffalo, N. Y., and Youngstown, Ohio.	2	196.79	Buffalo. Jamestown, N. Y. (N. Y., L. E. and W.).	6091	69.24
			Jamestown, N. Y., and Pymatuning, Pa. (N. Y., L. E. and W.).	21034 (part)	16100.46
			Pymatuning, Pa., and Youngstown, Ohio (N. Y., L. E. and W.).	21005 (part)	1722.50
		1834.08	Salamanca, Jamestown, N. Y. (N. Y., L. E. and W.).	21034 (part)	1934.06
Bureau and Peoria, Ill	6	47.03	Bureau, Peoria, Ill. (Chi., R. Isl'd and Pac.).	23016	47.13
Burlington, Iowa, and Carrollton, Mo.	6	220.57	Burlington, Iowa, Carrollton, Mo. (Chi., Bur. and K. City).	27008	220.57
Burlington and Council Bluffs, Iowa.	6	294.00	Burlington, Union Pacific Transfer, Iowa (Chi., Bur. and Qcy.).	27005	294.00
Burlington and Oskaloosa, Iowa.	6	105.00	Burlington, Winfield, Iowa (Burl. and No. West.).	2327035 (part)	34.09
			Winfield, Oskaloosa, Iowa (Burl. and Western).	27082	71.35
Burlington, Iowa, and Quincy, Ill.	6	72.00	Burlington, Iowa, Quincy, Ill. (Chi., Burl. and Qcy.).	23011	72.42
Burlington, Iowa, and Saint Louis, Mo.	6	214.19	Burlington, Keokuk, Iowa (Chi., Burl. and Qcy.).	27011	43.26
			Keokuk, Iowa, Saint Peters, Mo. (St. L., Keo. and No. West.).	2328018 (part)	138.41
			Saint Peters, Saint Louis, Mo. (Wabash Western).	28004 (part)	(28)
Burnet and Austin, Tex.	7	60.72	Burnet, Austin, Tex. (A. and N. W.).......	31038	60.72
Butler and Freeport, Pa........	2	21.46	Butler, Freeport, Pa. (Penna.).	8053	21.99

[1] Owned by East Tenn., Va. and Ga. R.R. Co., 1 in reserve. (See Lynchburgh and Bristol R. P. O. Cars on that line run through to Chattanooga, Tenn.)

[2] Balance of route (373.92 miles) Sault de Ste. Marie, Mich., to Bruce, Wis., covered by closed pouches. (See Table C*.)

[3] Reserve.

[4] Reserved cars.

[5] One transfer clerk, Waycross, Ga.; 1 transfer clerk, Albany, Ga.

[6] This line was formerly the Crill and West Alexandria R. P. O., 110.74 miles. August 22, 1887, service was extended to Carlisle, Ohio; increased distance 16.65 miles. October 10, 1887,

service was extended to Bryan, Ohio; increased distance 19.71 miles.

[7] Balance of route, between Bryan and Alvordton, Ohio, covered by closed pouches, 16.40 miles. (See Table C*.)

[8] Distance (2 miles) covered by Peoria and Galesburgh, Ill., R. P. O.

[9] Larabee and Clermont clerk alternates with Dunkirk and Titusville clerk as a helper between Buffalo and Larabee.

[10] In reserve.

[11] Two helpers between Buffalo and Oil City.

[12] 49.53 miles covered by Salamanca and Oil City R. P. O.

in the United States on June 30, 1888—Continued.

Average weight of mail whole distance per day.	Date of last re-adjustment.	Average speed per hour (train numbers taken from division schedules). Train No. outward.	Av'ge speed (miles).	Train No. inward.	Av'ge speed (miles).	Number of round trips with clerks per week.	Annual miles of service with clerks.	Average miles run daily by crews.	Number of mail cars, or cars in which are mail apartments.	Inside dimensions of cars or apartments (railway post-office cars in black figures). Length.	Width.	Number of crews.	Number of clerks to crews.	Number of clerks appointed to line.
Lbs.										*Ft. In.*	*Ft. In.*			
5,833	July 1, 1888	1	24.80	2	26.72	7	177,415	121.18	[1]3	40 0	8 10	4	2	16
		8	30.22	4	29.01	7	177,415							
400	July 1, 1888	16	25.75	15	25.75	6	64,838	103.34	1	15 8	7 2	2	1	2
188	Aug. 7, 1888	85	17.98	84	17.47	6	76,785	122.27	2	12 0	7 3	2	1	2
									[8]1	16 6	7 8			
238	July 1, 1884	1	21.40	2	19.50	7	125,706	114.48	2	14 6	7 0	3	1	5
									[4]1	13 0	7 0	....	....	(5)
									[4]1	12 0	6 3			
411	July 1, 1888	3	24.51	2	24.51	6	87,714	147.51	2	14 2	7 5	2	1	2
440	July 1, 1887	51	29.98	52	26.99	6	80,864	96.70	1	13 8¼	7 0½	1	1	1
1,759	July 1, 1887	51	18.00	52	18.00									
1,492	July 1, 1885	2	24.72	3	23.52	6	[9]76,833	121.55	1	19 6	9 11	2	1	2
									[10]1	20 0	9 00			
1,800	July 1, 1885	2	26.02	1	29.58	6	171,507	136.55	2	18 0	8 8	4	1	[11]6
									1	19 6	8 8			
1,069	July 1, 1885	2	22.24	1	22.80	.....	....	....	[10]1	15 6	8 8	(12)		
2,690	July 1, 1885	2	24.86	1	25.20	.....	....	....	(13)	....	....	(13)		
416	July 1, 1885	9	25.85	12	25.85	6	31,124	99.12	1	15 0	9 0	1	1	1
									[10]1	15 0	9 0			
740	July 1, 1885	109	25.17	12	25.96	6	184,653	129.07	2	29 0	9 6	3	2	[14]6
2,049	July 1, 1884	8	24.20	112	24.20	7	....	....	(16)	....	....	(16)		
3,814	July 1, 1884	3	23.17	112	21.18	7	....	....	(16)	....	....	(16)		
2,040	July 1, 1884	3	21.89	112	22.10	7	24,947	....	(16)	....	....	(16)		
1,920	July 1, 1887	1	28.20	2	28.20	6	29,535	94.06	1	20 0	9 4	1	1	1
864	July 1, 1887	1	22.05	2	22.05	6	138,518	110.28	[8]1	23 11½	9 0¼	4	1	4
									1	18 9	9 4½			
									1	14 6	7 7			
3,731	Mar. 11, 1884	7	31.22	4	23.68	7	215,208	147.00	(20)	....	....	4	[21]5	[22]23
				8	32.96									
		5	21.51	6	23.83	7	215,208	147.00	.....	....	....	4	3	
407	July 1, 1887	1	22.11	2	22.14	6	65,940	105.00	2	11 8	5 10	2	1	2
334	July 1, 1887	1	22.11	2	22.14									
654	July 1, 1887	181	21.60	182	22.74	6	45,216	144.00	1	13 3¾	7 2	1	1	1
									[1]1	22 7	8 9½			
4,231	July 1, 1887	71	24.71	74	25.97	6	134,511	107.10	2	23 11½	9 0½	4	1	[24]6
3,563	July 1, 1887	1	21.87	2	21.58									
9,316	July 1, 1887	18	24.15	17	25.76									
701	July 1, 1886	1	14.29	2	14.81	6	38,132	121.44	1	8 10	7 10	1	1	1
									[10]1	8 10	7 10			
526	July 1, 1885	71	25.24	10	23.40	6	13,477	85.84	1	5 3	8 7	1	1	1
		13	22.58	72	20.11	6	[27]13,477							

[13] Cars and clerks shown on route No. 6061.

[14] One clerk runs from Buffalo to Jamestown and one from Salamanca to Jamestown—both between Jamestown and Youngstown. No service Sunday Buffalo to Jamestown.

[15] 29.70 miles covered by closed-pouch service. (See table C°.)

[16] Cars and clerks shown on route No. 6091.

[17] Balance of route (66.75 miles) covered by Cleveland, Youngstown and Pittsburgh R. P. O.

[18] Salamanca to Jamestown.

[19] 224 58 miles covered by Leavittsburgh and Cincinnati R. P. O.

[20] Cars run through between Chicago, Ill., and Union Pacific Transfer, Iowa. (See Chicago, Ill., and Burlington, Iowa, R. P. O.)

[21] Three clerks east on train No. 4; two clerks east on train No. 8.

[22] One clerk detailed as assistant to chief clerk at Burlington, Iowa.

[23] Balance of route, Winfield to Washington, Iowa (18.57 miles), covered by closed pouches. (See table C°.)

[24] One helper between Burlington and Keokuk, Iowa, and one helper between Winfield and Saint Louis, Mo.

[25] Balance of route (50 86 miles) covered by Mount Pleasant and Keokuk, Iowa, R. P. O.

[26] Distance (32.20 miles) covered by Saint Louis, Moberly, and Kansas City, Mo., R. P. O.

[27] Double daily service except Sunday.

TABLE A⁰.—*Statement of railway post-offices in operation*

Designation of railway post-office. (Lines upon which railway post offices cars are paid for, in *italics*.)	Division.	Distance run by clerks, register to register.	Initial and terminal stations, running from east to west, north to south, or northwest to southeast (with abbreviated title of railroad company).	Number of route.	Miles of route for which railroad is paid.
		Miles.			
Butler and Madison, Kans[1]....	7	109. 81	Butler, Mo., Le Roy, Kans. (St. L. and E.)..	33045	79. 83
			Le Roy, Madison, Kans. (Interstate)	33090	29. 96
Butte City, Mont., and Ogden, Utah.[2]	8	416. 95	Ogden, Utah. Butte City, Mont. (Utah and Northern R. R.).	41003	416. 95
Cadillac, Mich., and Fort Wayne, Ind.[3]	9	240. 76	Cadillac, Mich., Fort Wayne, Ind. (G. R. and I.).	24018 (part)	[4]143. 23
Cairo, Ill., and Mobile, Ala.[4]....	4 (8) (9)	.... 260. 15 233. 15	Cairo, Ill., Mobile, Ala. (M. and O. R. R.).	18004	495. 89
Cairo, Ill., and New Orleans, La.[12]	4 (8) (7)	.... 368. 46 184. 12	Cairo, Ill., New Orleans, La. (Ill. Cent. R. R.).	18001	560. 80
Cairo, Ill., and Poplar Bluff, Mo.	7	74. 87	Cairo, Ill., Poplar Bluff, Mo. (St. L., I.M. and S.).	28027	74. 87
Cairo, Ill., and Texarkana, Ark[18]	7	[17]422. 47	Bird's Point, Mo., Texarkana, Ark. (St. L., Ark. and Tex.).	28051	417. 92
Caledonia and Spring Valley, Ill.	6	85. 74	Caledonia, Spring Valley, Ill. (Chic. and No. West.).	23087	86. 20
Calistoga and Vallejo Junction (p. o.), Cal.	8	43. 83	Vallejo, Calistoga, Cal. (Cal. Pacific R. R.)..	46008	43. 83
Calmar, Iowa, and Chamberlain, Dak.	6	399. 02	Calmar, Iowa, Marion, Dak. (Chic., Mil. and St. Paul).	[16]27025 (part)	287. 64
			Marion, Chamberlain, Dak. (Chic., Mil. and St. Paul).	35002	111. 65
Calmar and Davenport, Iowa ..	6	165. 70	Calmar, Davenport, Iowa (Chic., Mil., and St. Paul).	27037	165. 73
Camak and Macon, Ga	4	78. 50	Camak, Macon, Ga. (Georgia R. R.)	15021	78. 50
Cambridge City and Madison, Ind.	5	108. 81	Cambridge City, Columbus, Ind. (Penna. Co.).[28]	22011	63. 58
			Columbus, Madison, Ind. (Penna Co)	22006	45. 75
Cambridge Junction and Burlington, Vt.	1	34. 47	Cambridge Junction, Burlington, Vt. (Burl. and Lam.).	2014	34. 40
Cameron and Atchison, Mo....	7	57. 44	Cameron, Saint Joseph, Mo. (H. and St. J.).	[27]28005 (part)	36. 71
			Saint Joseph, Mo., Atchison, Kans. (H. and St. J.).	28030	22. 19
Canandaigua and Batavia, N. Y.	2	50. 17	Canandaigua and Batavia, N. Y. (N. Y. C. and H. R.)	6014 (part)	[18]50. 62
Canandaigua and Elmira, N. Y.	2	69. 1[7]	Canandaigua and Elmira, N. Y. (Nor. Cent.).	6003	69. 99
Canastota and Elmira, N. Y...	2	118. 76	Canastota, Cortland, N. Y. (E., C. and N.)..	6080	49. 27
			Cortland, Elmira, N. Y. (E., C. and N.). .	6075	70. 91
Canton and Mechanic Falls, Me.	1	25. 52	Canton. Mechanic Falls, Me. (Rum. Falls and Buck).	[25]19 (part)	25. 52

[1] Reported last year as Butler, Mo., and Le Roy, Kans.; increased distance 29.98 miles.
[2] One reserve car. This line is narrow gauge Ogden, Utah, to Pocatello, Idaho, and standard gauge Pocatello, Idaho, to Butte City, Mont.
[3] In connection with the Grand Rapids and Cincinnati and Mackinaw City and Grand Rapids R. P. O's give double service between Cadillac, Mich., and Fort Wayne, Ind. (240 miles), daily except Sunday.
[4] Balance of route (225.07 miles) covered by Mackinaw City and Grand Rapids R. P. O.
[5] Clerks appointed to Mackinaw City and Fort Wayne R. P. O. (See Mackinaw City and Grand Rapids R. P. O.)
[6] Line divided at West Point, Miss.
[7] Four helpers as second clerks.
[8] Northern division.

[9] Southern division.
[10] 2 helpers: 1 transfer clerk Corinth, Miss.
[11] One reserve car.
[12] Paid for as 40-foot cars, 2 reserve.
[13] Line divided at Jackson, Miss.
[14] One chief clerk, New Orleans, La.; 1 transfer clerk, Jackson, Miss.; 1 transfer clerk, Jackson, Tenn.; 1 helper, South division.
[15] In reserve.
[16] This line is divided at Pine Bluff, Ark., into Cairo, Ill., and Pine Bluff, Ark., division (270.71 miles), and Pine Bluff and Texarkana, Ark., division (151.76 miles).
[17] Clerks register at Cairo, Ill., 3 miles from Bird's Point, Mo.
[18] Cars run from Cairo, Ill., to Gatesville, Tex., over Cairo, Ill., and Texarkana, Ark., and Texarkana, Ark., and Gatesville, Tex., R. P. O's.

in the United States on June 30, 1888—Continued.

Average weight of mail whole distance per day.	Date of last re-adjustment.	Average speed per hour (train numbers taken from division schedules).				Number of round trips with clerks per week.	Annual miles of service with clerks.	Average miles run daily by crews.	Number of mail cars, or cars in which are mail apartments.	Inside dimensions of cars or apartments (railway post-office cars in black figures).		Number of crews.	Number of clerks to crew.	Number of clerks appointed to line.
Lbs.		Train No. outward.	Av'ge speed (miles).	Train No. inward.	Av'ge speed (miles).					Length. Ft. In.	Width. Ft. In.			
285	July 1, 1888	241 21.88		342 20.51		7	80,381	109.81	2	16 4	6 10	2	1	2
		343 12.64		344 11.78		7								
2,406	Aug.15,1886	601 24.03		602 18.01		7	305,207	138.96	11½ / 3	40 0 / 52 0	7 5½ / 8 11	6	1	6
1,831	July 1,1884	8 19.72		7 17.56		6	151,197	120.38	2	22 0	8 10	4	1	(8)
1,406	July 1,1888	5 19.6		6 19.2		7	*190,426 / *170,665	130.08 / 116.15	2 / 3 {(11)(12)}	21 6 / 22 5	8 9 / 9 0	4 / 4	[2] 1	15 / (16)
5,177	July 1,1888	1 26.2		4 26.2		7	*269,712 / *134,775	122.82 / 122.75	3/1/1/1 {13(1)}	45 0/50 0/48 6/56 9	9 3/9 2/9 5/9 2	6 / 3	3 / 1	25 / (14)
452	July 1, 1887	801 18.01		802 17.29		7	54,805	74.87	1 / 13(1)	15 9 / 14 2	9 3 / 9 6	2	1	2
828	July 1, 1887	1 19.51		2 19.90		7	198,160 / 111,088	135.35 / 101.17 13(3)	5/3/2	24 5/22 0/23 6	9 0/9 3/8 0	4 / 3	1	7
196	July 1, 1887	137 22.93		138 19.85		6	53,844	171.48	13(2)	12 0	7 5	1	1	1
646	July 1, 1886	25 21.94 / 27 21.07		26 21.40 / 28 21.94		12	55,113	175.52	1	10 0	8 10	1	1	1
3,402	July 1, 1887	3 21.02		2 22.23		6	125,851	100.20	2	26 2	9 3	3(4)	2	13(5)
2,061	July 1, 1886	1 22.96		4 22.11		7	145,390	132.41	2	26 2	9 3	3(3)	1	
1,183	July 1, 1887	2 19.68		1 22.09		6	104,059	110.46	1 / 1	20 0 / 20 0	9 1 / 8 9	3	1	3
753	July 1, 1884	33 15.2		32 15.3		6	49,354	157.18	1	15 6	8 4	1	1	1
614	July 1, 1888	106 23.84 / 104 26.31		105 23.84 / 107 23.84		12(12)	120,033	145.08	2	19 0	8 10	3	1	3
932	July 1, 1888	106 22.87 / 104 22.87		105 22.87 / 107 22.87		12								
462	July 1, 1885	90 21.93		90 22.66		6	21,647	68.94	1 / 1(1)	8 9 / 6 10	7 0 / 6 9	1	1	1
10,773	July 1, 1887	63 26.99		64 25.28		7	42,046	124.44(23)	1	15 4	8 8	1	1	1
1,835	July 1, 1887	63 21.20		64 23.10		7								
241	July 1, 1885	5 25.06		2 26.16		6	31,507	100.34	2	5 9	6 0	1	1	1
2,367	July 1, 1885	10 27.66		9 28.62		6	43,439	98.87(30)	1/1/1/1 13(1)	14 8/15 0/15 1½/15 0	8 7/8 7/8 7/8 7	1	1	1
931	July 1, 1885	4 26.87		1 24.80		6	74,581	118.76	2 / 13(1)	16 0 / 14 6	9 0 / 9 0	2	1	2
932	July 1, 1885	4 27.44		1 25.62		6			(21)			(21)		
388	July 1, 1885	3 23.55		4 21.87		6	16,026	51 04	1	10 0	6 9	1	1	1

[19] One in reserve.
[20] Balance of route (62.42 miles) covered by Marion and Running Water, Dak., R. P. O.
[21] East division, Calmar to Sanborn, Iowa.
[22] Two helpers on west division between Sanborn, Iowa, and Marion, Dak.
[23] West division, Sanborn, Iowa, to Chamberlain, Dak.
[24] Prior to December 2, 1887, 6 trips per week between Cambridge City and Madison (109.03 miles) and 6 trips per week between Columbus and Madison (45.59 miles). Thus making double daily service, except Sunday, between Columbus and Madison, Ind.
[25] Double daily service, except Sunday, over entire route.

[26] Reserve car.
[27] 170.84 miles of route 28005 between Quincy, Ill., and Cameron, Mo., covered by Quincy, Ill., and Kansas City, Mo., R. P. O.
[28] Clerk on this line alternates with 1 clerk on Quincy and Kansas City line between Brookfield, Mo., and Atchison, Kans., acting as helper to Quincy and Kansas City line between Brookfield and Cameron, Mo (67 miles).
[29] 36 miles covered by Batavia and Buffalo R. P. O.
[30] Clerk alternates with Elm and Williamsport clerk.
[31] Cars and clerks shown on route No. 6080.
[32] Balance of route covered by closed-pouch service between Canton and Gilbertville (1.93 miles). (See Table C⁹.)

TABLE A⁶.—*Statement of railway post-offices in operation*

Designation of railway post-office. (Lines upon which railway post-office cars are paid for, in *italics*.)	Division.	Distance run by clerks, register to register.	Initial and terminal stations, running from east to west, north to south, or northwest to southeast (with abbreviated title of railroad company).	Number of route.	Miles of route for which railroad is paid.
		Miles.			
Canton and Sherodsville, Ohio	5	48.44	Canton, Sherodsville, Ohio (Cleve. and Canton)	¹21009 (part)	48.24
Cape Girardeau and Chaonia, Mo.³	7	56.47	Cape Girardeau, Chaonia, Mo. (C. G. and S. W).	28045	56.51
Carbondale and Scranton, Pa ..	2	17.46	Carbondale, Scranton, Pa. (D. and H. C. Co).	8018	17.45
Carey and Delphos, Ohio	5	56.48	Carey, Delphos, Ohio (Cleve. and West.) ..	21081	56.60
Carlisle and Gettysburgh, Pa .	2	32.34	Carlisle, Hunter's Run, Pa. (Gettys. and Harris.)	8052 (part)	⁶10.00
			Hunter's Run, Gettysburgh, Pa. (Gettys. and Harris.).	8153	22.79
Carroll and Moville, Iowa......	6	160.80	Carroll, Maple River, Iowa (Chi. and No. West.).	28003 (part)	(⁸)
			Maple River, Wall Lake, Iowa (Chi. and No. West.).	⁸270.8 (part)	16.70
			Wall Lake, Sac City, Iowa (Chi. and No. West).	27050	14.13
			Sac City, Moville, Iowa (Chi. and No. West.)	27089	67.41
Cartersville, Ga., and Talladega, Ala. ·	4	142.48	Cartersville, Ga., Pell City, Ala. (E. and W. R. R. of Ala).	15020	117.36
			Pell City, Talladega, Ala. (T. and C.V. R. R)	17030	25.12
Caseville and Pontiac, Mich ...	9	100.73	Caseville, Pontiac, Mich. (P.O. and Pt. A.)	21064	100.73
Cayuga and Ithaca, N. Y.......	2	39.11	Cayuga, Ithaca, N. Y. (G., I. and S.)	6689	38.97
Cedar Rapids and Council Bluffs, Iowa.	6	270.77	Cedar Rapids, Union Pacific Transfer, Iowa (Chi and N. West.).	¹²23903 (part)	270.50
Cedar Rapids, Iowa, and Kansas City, Mo.	6	301.51	Cedar Rapids, Iowa, Kansas City, Mo. (Chi., Mil. and St. P.)	27047	300.61
Cedar Rapids, Iowa, and Watertown, Dak.	6	400.33	Cedar Rapids, Iowa, Watertown, Dak. (Burl., C. Rap. and North.).	27003	399.68
Centralia and Cairo, Ill.	6	112.79	Centralia, Cairo, Ill. (Ill. Cent.)	¹²23020 (part)	113.43
Chadron, Nebr., and Glenrock, Wyo.	6	169.88	Chadron, Nebr., Douglas, Wyo. (Fre., Elk. and Mo. Vall.).	34035	140.38
			Douglas, Glenrock, Wyo. (Fre., Elk. and Mo. Vall.).	37003	30.30
Chambersburgh and Richmond Furnace, Pa.	2	31.85	Chambersburgh and South Penn. Junction, Pa. (Cum. Val.)	8030 (part)	(¹⁰)
			South Penn. Junction and Richmond Furnace, Pa. (Cum. Val.).	807i	19.38
			Mercersburgh Junction and Mercersburgh, Pa. (Cum. Val.)	8145	2.64
Champaign and Havana, Ill.....	6	101.07	Champaign, Havana, Ill. (Illinois Cent'l)...	23029	101.64
Chanute and Longton, Kans ...	7	63.86	Chanute, Cherry Vale, Kans.(So. Kans.)...	33004 (part)	(²¹)
			Cherry Vale, Longton, Kans.(So. Kans)...	53005 (part)	(²²)
Charleston, S. C., and Augusta, Ga.	4	139.22	Charleston, Branchville, S. C. (S. C. R. R.)..	³¹14003 (part)	62.79
			Branchville, S. C., Augusta, Ga. (S C. R. R.)	14017	76.43
Charlotte, N. C., and Atlanta, Ga.	4	268.22	Charlotte, N. C., Atlanta, Ga. (Rich. and Dan. R. R)	15001	268.03
Charlotte, N. C., and Augusta, Ga.	4	192.00	Charlotte, N. C., Augusta, Ga. (Rich. and Dan. R. R.)	13007	192.56

¹ Balance of line 60 miles, shown on Cleveland and Coshocton R. P. O.
² 1 car in reserve.
³ Reported last year as Cape Girardeau and Wappapello, Mo.; increased distance, 6.46 miles.
⁴ In reserve.
⁵ Triple daily service except Sunday.
⁶ 8.97 miles covered by closed pouch service. See Table C⁶.
⁷ Cars and clerks shown on route No. 8052.
⁸ Distance (4.27 miles) covered by Cedar Rapids and Council Bluffs, Iowa, R. P. O.

⁹ Balance of route (64.57 miles) covered by Des Moines and Sioux City, Iowa, R. P. O.
¹⁰ One car held in reserve.
¹¹ Balance of route (219.40 miles) covered by Chicago. Ill., and Cedar Rapids Iowa. R. P. O.
¹² Cars run through from Chicago, Ill., to Union Pacific Transfer, covering Chicago, Ill., and Cedar Rapids, Iowa, and Cedar Rapids and Council Bluffs Iowa, R. P. O.
¹³ Two clerks detailed to transfer duty at Council Bluffs, Iowa.
¹⁴ One of each of these cars in reserve.

in the United States on June 30, 1888—Continued.

Average weight of mail whole distance per day.	Date of last readjustment.	Train No. outward	Av'ge speed (miles).	Train No. inward.	Av'ge speed (miles).	Number of round trips with clerks per week.	Annual miles of service with clerks.	Average miles run daily by crews.	Number of mail cars, or cars in which are mail apartments.	Length		Width		Number of crews.	Number of clerks to crew.	Number of clerks appointed to line.
Lbs.										*Ft. In*		*Ft. In*				
566	July 1, 1888	91	20.38	38	20.67	6	30,420	96.88	*2	19	6	6	0	1	1	1
269	July 1, 1887	1	14.32	2	16.02	7	42,800	116.94	1	12	0	6	10	1	1	1
										15	0	7	0			
891	July 1, 1885	6	21.07	5	21.07	6	10,965	104.76	1	10	3½	6	9½	1	1	1
		10	23.77	9	22.26	6	*10,965		1	10	6	6	7½			
		14	21.07	13	21.07	6	10,965									
252	July 1, 1888	1	12.58	2	12.81	6	35,438	112.80	1	6	8	7	9	1	1	1
413	July 1, 1885	3	26.08	6	18.75	6	20,319	64.68	1	9	9	6	6½	1	1	1
620	July 1, 1885	3	22.05	6	18.72	6	....	......	(7)	....				(7)		
12,894	July 1, 1887	15	31.50	16	31.50	6	63,392	100.80	1	12	2	7	5	2	1	2
1,163	July 1, 1887	15	21.32	16	27.08											
821	July 1, 1887	15	23.14	16	23.16											
517	June 8, 1888	15	20.97	16	24.90											
146	July 21, 1884	1	15.4	2	13.7	6	89,477	142.48	1	7	2	7	0	2	1	2
									1	7	11	8	0			
256	July 1, 1888	1	16.6	2	16.6				1	7	4	5	3			
241	July 1, 1884	2	21.82	1	30	6	63,250	201.46	*2	12	0	7	0	1	1	1
408	July 1, 1885	15	24.16	8	24.70	6	24,561	78.22	1	10	4	7	0	1	1	1
									4	15	0	9	8			
12,894	July 1, 1887	5	23.02	6	22.54	7	196,203	135.38	(12)	....				4	2	1318
		3	23.69	4	24.04	7	196,203	135.38						4	2	
896	June 14, 1888	1	24.04	2	22.54	6	188,348	120.60	2	26	0	9	3	5	1	5
1,076	July 1, 1887	61	24.78	62	24.83	6	251,407	103.66	14 3	19	10	9	1	14 4	1	14 8
		63	23.57	64	26.86	....	....	128.67	14 2	22	0	9	1	17 3	1	
		71	23.57	72	26.86											
10,499	July 1, 1887	5	23.38	2	20.24	6	70,832	112.70	1		4½	9		2	2	4
461	Oct. 1, 1886	91	16.19	92	16.10	6	106,685	169.88	3	14	0	9	3	2	1	2
		91	16.19	92	16.19											
....	....															
1,942	July 1, 1885	41	21.30	42	23.66	6	19,688	62.70	1	8	8	8	0	1	1	1
319	July 1, 1885	41	23.73	42	15.50	6	....	......	(20)	....				(20)		
358	July 1, 1885	41	26.40	42	15.84	6	....	......	(20)	....				(20)		
436	July 1, 1887	1	21.26	2	22.44	6	63,472	101.07	1	9	9	6	11½	2	1	2
									1	9	5½	6	10½			
436	July 1, 1887	209	20.93	210	20.93	7	46,746	127.72	1	22	1	9	1	1	1	(22)
1,691	July 1, 1886	209	20.42	210	20.42	7										
2,182	July 1, 1888	1	30	2	30	14	203,818	139.22	5	18	0	8	11	4	1	4
		3	38	4	38	....	....	......	(23)							
1,436	July 1, 1888	1	27.5	2	27.3											
		3	27.5	4	26.8											
19,694	July 1, 1888	50	27.5	51	27.4	14	392,674	134.11	(24)	....				8	2	22
		52	27.3	53	28.1											(27)
2,642	July 1, 1888	52	23.4	53	21.9	7	140,544	128	2	27	7	9	0	3	1	3

15 East division, Cedar Rapids to Estherville, Iowa.
16 One clerk detailed to transfer duty at Cedar Rapids, Iowa.
17 West division, Estherville, Iowa, to Watertown, Dak.
18 Balance of route (232.10 miles) covered by Chicago and Centralia, Ill., R. P. O.
19 7.10 miles covered by Harrisburgh and Martinsburgh R. P. O.
20 Cars and clerks shown on route No. 8030.
21 29.30 miles, distance on route 33004 covered by Kansas City, Mo., and Wellington, Kans., R. P. O.
22 Clerk is appointed to Kansas City, Mo., and Wellington, Kans., R. P. O.
23 33.90 miles distance on route 33005 covered by Kansas City, Mo., and Wellington, Kans., R. P. O.
24 68.71 miles shown as Columbia and Branchville R. P. O.
25 These cars also used by the Columbia and Branchville R. P. O.
26 See Washington and Charlotte R. P. O.
27 1 chief clerk fourth division; 1 detailed to office superintendent fourth division; 4 helpers.

TABLE A⁵.—*Statement of railway post-offices in operation*

Designation of railway post-office. (Lines upon which railway post-office cars are paid for, in *italics*.)	Division.	Distance run by clerks, register to register.	Initial and terminal stations, running from east to west, north to south, or northwest to southeast (with abbreviated title of railroad company.)	Number of route.	Miles of route for which railroad is paid.
		Miles.			
Chatham, N. Y.,[4] and New York, N. Y.	2	130.44	Chatham, N. Y., and New York, N. Y. (N. Y. C. and H. R.).	6022	130.98
Chattanooga, Tenn., and Atlanta, Ga.	4	138.55	Chattanooga, Tenn., Atlanta, Ga. (West and Atlantic R. R.).	15002	138.47
Chattanooga and Memphis, Tenn.	5	310.77	Chattanooga, Memphis, Tenn. (Memphis and Charleston).	17005	311.99
Chattanooga, Tenn., and Meridian, Miss.	4	295.71	Chattanooga, Tenn., Meridian, Miss. (A. G. S. R. R.).	17015	295.45
Chattanooga, Tenn., Rome and Atlanta, Ga.	4	153.00	Chattanooga, Ooltewah, Tenn. (E. T., V. and Ga. R. R.).	19002	(?)
			Ooltewah, Tenn., Cohutta, Ga. (E. T., V. and Ga. R. R.).	19011	11.86
			Cohutta, Rome, Ga. (E. T., V. and Ga. R. R.).	17010	(¹⁰)
			Rome, Atlanta, Ga. (E. T., V. and Ga. R. R.).	15012 (part)	¹¹73.05
Cheneyville and La Fayette, La.	4	66.20	Cheneyville, La Fayette, La. (South Pacific R. R.).	30003 (part)	¹²63.20
Chetopa and Larned, Kans[14]...	7	275.88	Chetopa, Belle Plaine, Kans. (D., M. and A.).	¹⁴²33058	146.20
			Larned, Belle Plaine, Kans. (D., M. and A.).	33058	128.67
Cheyenne, Wyo., and Denver, Colo.	7	107.39	Cheyenne, Wyo., Denver, Colo. (U. P.).....	¹⁶³38007	107.39
Chicago, Ill., Abbotsford, Wis., and Minneapolis, Minn.	6	473.50	Chicago, Ill., Rugby Jct., Wis. (Wis. Central).	23089	117.60
			Rugby Jct., Abbotsford, Wis. (Wis. Central).	¹⁹²25017 (part)	185.51
			Abbotsford, Chippewa Falls, Wis. (Wis. Central).	²¹²25020 (part)	53.10
			Chippewa Falls, Wis., St. Paul, Minn. (Wis. Central).	25061	104.63
			St. Paul, Minneapolis, Minn. (St. Paul, Minn. and Minn.).	26006 (part)	(²³)
Chicago, Ill., and Burlington, Iowa.	6	207.50	Chicago, Ill., Burlington, Iowa (Chi., Burl. and Qcy.).	23007	206.00
Chicago, Ill., and Cedar Rapids, Iowa.	6	220.40	Chicago, Ill., Cedar Rapids, Iowa (Chi. and No. West.).	²⁶²23003 (part)	219.40
Chicago and Centralia, Ill	6	252.96	Chicago, Centralia, Ill. (Illinois Central) .	²⁶²23020 (part)	252.10

¹ Double daily service except Sunday.
² In reserve.
³ Cars on trains 1, 2, 11, and 20 paid for as 40 feet cars.
⁴ One chief clerk Atlanta, Ga.; 2 detailed to office superintendent 4th division; 2 transfer clerks Atlanta.
⁵ One reserve car.
⁶ One clerk detailed to transfer duty at Chattanooga, Tenn.; 1 clerk detailed to transfer duty at Grand Junction, Tenn.; 2 clerks detailed to transfer duty at Memphis, Tenn.
⁷ No pay for car-service.
⁸ One reserve.
⁹ 15.20 miles reported as Brist. and Chatt. R. P. O.
¹⁰ 55.5 miles reported as Cleve. and Selma R. P. O.
¹¹ 277.75 miles reported as Atlanta and Brunswick R. P. O.

¹² Two reserve cars.
¹³ 149.94 miles reported as New Orleans and Houston R. P. O.
¹⁴ Reported last year as Belle Plaine and Stafford, Kans., R. P. O.; increased distance, 131.96 miles.
¹⁵ Holden, Mo., and Coffeyville, Kans., R. P. O.; also runs over 5.33 miles of route 33056, between Deering and Coffeyville, Kans., and Yates Center and Sedan, Kans., R. P. O., over 5.66 miles of same route between Peru and Sedan, Kans.
¹⁶ Julesburg and Denver, Colo., R. P. O. also runs over 46.92 miles of route 38007 between La Salle (n. o.) and Denver, Colo.
¹⁷ East Division, Chicago, Ill., to Neenah, Wis.
¹⁸ Two helpers on west division, between Neenah and Chippewa Falls, Wis.

in the United States on June 30, 1888—Continued.

Average weight of mail whole distance per day.	Date of last readjustment.	Average speed per hour (train numbers taken from division schedules).				Number of round trips with clerks per week.	Annual miles of service with clerks.	Average miles run daily by crew.	Number of mail cars, or cars in which are mail apartments.	Inside dimensions of cars or apartments (railway post-office cars in black figures).		Number of crews.	Number of clerks to crew.	Number of clerks appointed to line.
		Train No. outward.	Av'ge speed (miles).	Train No. inward.	Av'ge speed (miles).					Length.	Width.			
Lbs.										*Ft. In.*	*Ft. In.*			
1,469	July 1, 1885	18	29.31	25	27.83	6	81,916	104.35	1	20	8.4	8	1	8
		34	27.94	13	19.81	6	81,916	......	1	20	8 4	2	1	
									2	20	8 4			
15,022	July 1, 1888	1	26.8	2	25.5	21	304,257	118.76	5	50	9	5	3	24
		3	26.7	4	24.2	......			5	50	9	2	3	(4)
		11	26.6	20	27.4	......			2	41 10	8 10			
3,600	July 1, 1888	3	25.13	4	26.35	7	237,484	124.31	3	20 0	9 0	5	1	19
4,588	July 1, 1888	5	21.1	6	21.1	7	216,495	147.85	2	45 6	8 6	4	2	8
									1	42 10	9 2			
5,833	July 1, 1888	13	25.5	14	25.5	6	96,084	153.00	4	25 0	9 0	2	1	2
436	July 1, 1888	......							(12)					
1,002	July 1, 1888													
1,026	July 1, 1888													
2,814	July 1, 1886	51	24.	50	20	7	44,066	120.40	2	18 0	9 0	1	1	1
605	July 1, 1888	483	20.17	484	20.50	7	200,480	136.94	2	16 4	6 10	4	1	4
457	July 1, 1888	483	24.10	484	24.74	7								
1,615	July 1, 1886	302	25.27	301	26.20	7	78,609	107.39	1	24 2	9 4	2	1	2
									1	24 1	9 4			
1,501	July 1, 1887	9	25.80	4	27.00	6	297,358	134.76	2	30 6	9 4	173	1	139
1,669	July 1, 1887	9	25.80	4	27.00	......	......	143.18	2	30 0	9 4	24	1	
1,465	July 1, 1887	1	26.52	2	25.74	......	......		3	21 2	9 4			
1,374	July 1, 1887	1	26.52	2	25.74									
4,937	July 1, 1887	1	24.16	2	24.16									
54,621	Mar. 11, 1884	5	25.75	6	30.90	7	151,890	103.75	3	60 0	9 3½	44	4	50
		7	36.90	8	34.33	7	151,890	103.75	6	60 0	9 3½	34	6	
									7	60 0	9 3½			
									2	60 5½	9 3½			
12,894	July 1, 1887	3	25.29	4	27.22	7	161,333	110.20	3	50 0	9 5	44	3	29
		5	35.96	6	24.55	7	161,333	110.20	2	50 0	9 5	34	3	
									2	60 0	9 5			
10,499	July 1, 1887	1	24.39	2	22.40	6	158,859	126.48	3	44 4½	9 0	44	3	32
		3	28.00	4	23.63	7	185,166	......	2	41 4½	9 0	34	3	

19 Balance of route covered by Ashland and Abbotsford, Wis., R. P. O. (183.10 miles), and between Milwaukee and Rugby Jct, Wis (27.30 miles), by closed pouches. See Table C².

20 West Division, Neenah, Wis., to Minneapolis, Minn.

21 Balance of route (11 29 miles) between Chippewa Falls and Eau Claire, Wis., covered by closed pouches. See Table C².

22 Reserve.

23 Distance (10 66 miles) covered by Neche, Dak., and St. Paul, Minn., R. P. O.

24 Day line

25 One clerk detailed as chief clerk at Burlington, Iowa; 4 clerks detailed to transfer duty at Chicago, Ill.; 2 at Burlington, Iowa, and 1 at Galesburgh, Ill.; 2 helpers on fast mail between Chicago and Galesburgh, and deadhead back.

26 Fast mail.

27 Storage cars; 1 in reserve.

28 Balance of route (270.80 miles) covered by Cedar Rapids and Council Bluffs, Iowa, R. P. O.

29 Three clerks detailed to clerical duty at office of superintendent; 2 helpers between Chicago. Ill., and Stanwood, Iowa, on train No. 5, and deadhead back on train No. 4.

30 One of each of these cars in reserve.

31 Night line.

32 Balance of route (113.48 miles) covered by Centralia and Cairo, Ill., R. P. O.

33 Two helpers on day line between Chicago and Champaign, Ill.; 5 clerks detailed to transfer duty at Chicago, Ill., and 1 at Grand Crossing. Ill.; 2 clerks detailed as printers at office of superintendent, Chicago; 1 clerk detailed as stenographer at office of superintendent, Chicago, and 1 clerk detailed in charge of dormitory at Chicago, Ill.

TABLE A^a.—*Statement of railway post-offices in operation*

Designation of railway post-office. (Lines upon which railway post-office cars are paid for, in *italics*.)	Divisions.	Distance run by clerks, register to register.	Initial and terminal stations, running from east to west, north to south, or northwest to southeast (with abbreviated title of railroad company).	Number of route.	Miles of route for which railroad is paid.
		Miles.			
Chicago, Ill., and Cincinnati, Ohio.	5	307.16	Chicago, Kankakee, Ill. (Illinois Central) .	23020 (part)	(¹)
			Kankakee, Ill., La Fayette, Ind. (Cin., La Fay. and Chi.).	220.9	75.79
			La Fayette, Indianapolis, Ind. (Cin., Ind., St. Louis and Chi.).	22005	64.79
			Indianapolis, Ind., Cincinnati, Ohio (Cin., Ind., St. Louis and Chi.).	22003	111.40
Chicago, Decatur, Ill., and Saint Louis, Mo.	6	286.80	Chicago, Bement, Ill. (Wabash)...........	⁴²23066 (part)	152.80
			Bement, Decatur, Ill. (Wabash)............	21019 (part)	(⁴)
			Decatur, Ill., Saint Louis, Mo. (Wabash) ..	23023	117.66
Chicago, Dunbar, Ill., and Dubuque, Iowa.	6	168.28	Chicago, Ill., Dubuque, Iowa (Chi., St. P., and Kans. City).	23005	167.33
Chicago, Forreston, Ill., and Dubuque, Iowa.	6	200.04	Chicago, Aurora, Ill. (Chi., Bur. and Qcy.)	23007 (part)	(⁹)
			Aurora, Forreston, Ill. (Chic. and Iowa) .	73038	(¹⁰)
			Forreston, Ill., Dubuque, Iowa (Illinois Central).	2J021 (part)	(¹¹)
Chicago, Freeport, Ill., and Dubuque, Iowa.	6	189.72	Chicago, Freeport, Ill. (Chic. and Nor. West.).	2J002	121.90
			Freeport, Ill., Dubuque, Iowa (Illinois Central).	23021 (part)	(¹²)
Chicago, Ill., and Fort Madison, Iowa.	6	237.44	Chicago, Ill., Fort Madison, Iowa (Chic., S. Fé., and Cal.).	¹⁵23098 (part)	236.82
Chicago, Ill., and Louisville, Ky.	5	324.38	Chicago, Ill., Monon, Ind. (Louis., Nash. and Chat.).	¹⁶22038 (part)	88.52
			Monon, Ind., Louisville Junct., No. Ind. (Louis., N. A. and Chic.).	¹⁷22008 (part)	233.80
. *Chicago, Ill., McGregor, Iowa, and St. Paul, Minn.*	6	450.63	Chicago, Kittridge, Ill. (Chi., Mil. and St. Paul).	23054	(²⁰)
			Kittridge, Savanna, Ill. (Chi., Mil. and St. Paul).	25024 (p rt)	(²⁴)
			Savanna, Ill., Sabula Jct., Iowa (Chi., Mil. and St. Paul).	27028 (part)	(²⁵)
			Sabula Jct., McGregor, Iowa (Chi., Mil. and St. Paul).	²⁷27012 (part)	²⁶43.60
			McGregor, Iowa, St. Paul, Minn. (Chic., Mil. and St. Paul).	26009	212.21
Chicago, Ill., and Minneapolis, Minn.	6	423.15	Chicago, Ill., Milwaukee, Wis. (Chi., Mil. and St. P.).	23035	85.98
			Milwaukee, La Crosse, Wis. (Chi., Mil. and St. P.).	25002	193.42
			La Crosse, Wis., Minneapolis, Minn. (Chi., Mil. and St. P.).	26013	142.55

¹ Covered by lines of the Sixth Division (55.87 miles).
² Day line; 4 crews, 4 clerks to a crew.
³ Night line; 4 crews, 6 clerks to a crew.
⁴ One car in reserve.
⁵ Balance of route covered by Bement and Effingham, Ill., R. P. O (52.50 miles), and between Shumway and Altamont, Ill. (10.54 miles), by closed pouches. (See Table C⁴.)
⁶ Distance (19.50 miles) covered by La Fayette, Ind., and Quincy, Ill., R. P. O.
⁷ 1 clerk detailed to transfer duty at East Saint Louis, Ill.
⁸ Reserve.
⁹ Distance (37 miles) covered by Chicago, Ill., and Burlington, Iowa, R. P. O.
¹⁰ Distance (81.00 miles) covered by Forreston and Aurora, Ill., R. P. O.
¹¹ Distance (82.07 miles) covered by Dubuque, Iowa, and Mendota, Ill., R. P. O.
¹² 1 clerk detailed to transfer duty and 1 to clerical duty at office of superintendent, Chicago, Ill.

¹³ Distance (68.80 miles) covered by Dubuque Iowa, and Mendota, Ill., R. P. O.
¹⁴ 1 clerk detailed to transfer duty at Dubuque, Iowa, 1 clerk detailed as porter at office of superintendent, Chicago, Ill.
¹⁵ Balance of route (218 miles) covered by Fort Madison, Iowa, and Kansas City, Mo., R. P. O.
¹⁶ Balance of route covered by Chicago and Monon and Cincinnati R. P. O. (93.56 miles).
¹⁷ Day line.
¹⁸ Night line.
¹⁹ Balance of route covered by Michigan Cl'y and Monon R. P. O. (59 57 miles)
²⁰ Distance (116.60 miles) covered by Chicago, Savanna, Ill., and Cedar Rapids, Iowa, R. P. O.
²¹ Railway post-office cars paid for between Chicago, Ill., and McGregor, Iowa.
²² East Division, Chicago, Ill., to McGregor, Iowa.
²³ Two helpers on West Division, between McGregor, Iowa, and Austin, Minn.
²⁴ Distance (22 miles) covered by Racine, Wis., and Rock Island, Ill., R. P. O.

in the United States on June 30, 1888—Continued.

Average weight of mail whole distance per day.	Date of last readjustment.	Average speed per hour (train numbers taken from division schedules).				Number of round trips with clerks per week.	Annual miles of service with clerks.	Average miles run daily by crews.	Number of mail cars, or cars in where are mail apartments.	Inside dimensions of cars or apartments (railway post-office cars in black figures).		Number of crews.	Number of clerks to crew.	Number of clerks appointed to line.
		Train No. outward.	Av. speed (miles).	Train No. inward.	Av'g speed (miles).					Length.	Width.			
Lbs										Ft. in.	Ft. in.			
10,499	July 1, 1887	4	27.93	1	28.90	6	192,896	153.58	2	60 0	9 5	24	4	40
		2	25.78	3	23.04	7	224,841	......	43	50 0	9 0	24	6	
25,021	July 1, 1888	4	32.95	1	31.14	8								
		2	28.42	3	26.29	7								
26,749	July 1, 1888	4	31.86	1	27.18	6								
		2	27.77	3	28.81	7								
23,584	July 1, 1888	4	31.86	1	32.60	6								
		2	32.28	3	30.86	7								
1,085	July 1, 1887	5	26.61	4	23.54	6	180,110	143.40	41	25 7	9 2	4	1	75
11,242	July 1, 1884	5	34.41	4	30.79				2	25 6	9 2½			
12,340	July 1, 1887	5	26.54	4	28.75									
537	July 25, 1888	6	24.60	5	24.58	6	105,680	112.19	2	19 9	7 5	3	1	3
54,621	Mar. 11, 1884	31	23.37	12	23.43	6	125,625	182.36	2	40 1½	8 9½	3	2	128
5,877	July 1, 1887	7	27.66	2	25.47									
4,579	July 1, 1887	6	22.36	3	22.88									
5,603	July 1, 1887	49	24.20	50	24.27	6	119,144	126.48	2	50 0	9 6	3	3	411
4,579	July 1, 1887	2	25.87	1	27.60									
......	......	5	22.93	6	22.93	6	149,112	118.72	2	26 3	9 4	4	1	4
947	July 1, 1888	5	27.66	6	28.74	6	203,711	162.19	2	14 0	9 2	174	1	8
		3	29.50	4	26.28	7	237,446	......	2	20 0	9 2	184	1	
4,314	July 1, 1888	5	30.86	6	32.32	6								
		3	33.47	4	30.33	7								
8,012	July 1, 1887	3	27.43	2	25.91	6	149,527	119.05	21 1	49 3	9 3	174	2	214
2,231	July 1, 1887	3	29.33	2	29.27				21 1	4 1	8 10	24	1	
2,249	July 1, 1887	3	12.80	2	9.60				1	24 0	9 3			
2,982	July 1, 1887	3	29.18	2	21.13				1	23 6½	9 3			
2,720	July 1, 1887	3	22.06	2	22.51	6	133,468	106.26						
43,949	Mar.13,1884	55	34.40	8	31.27	7	309,746	141.05	3	60 1	9 3	296	4	882
		1	34.40	2	31.27	7	309,746	141.05	3	60 1	9 3	176	4	
		8	30.03	6	32.25	6	111,784	118.94	1	50 1	9 3	213	3	
									1	49 3	9 3			
35.167	Mar. 9, 1884	55	36.00 & 44	19.80					24	60 6	9 3			
		1	29.70	56	36.00				21	59 3	9 3			
		3	28.28	6	33.00									
		5	28.28	6	33.00	6	124,608	198.42	1	20 10	9 1	22	1	
28,860	Mar. 9, 1884	55	30.00	2	25.52				1	20 9	8 9			
		1	27.14	56	30.53									

24 West Division, McGregor, Iowa, to St. Paul, Minn.

25 Distance (3.20 miles) covered by Chicago, Savanna, Ill., and Cedar Rapids, Iowa, R. P. O.

27 Balance of route covered by La Crosse, Wis., and Dubuque, Iowa, R. P. O. (121.73 miles), and between Sabula Jct., and Clinton, Iowa (16 46 miles), covered by closed pouches. See Table C².

28 Balance of distance (53.10 miles) covered by La Crosse, Wis., and Dubuque, Iowa, R. P. O.

29 Fast mail.

30 Four helpers between Chicago, Ill., and Watertown, Wis., west on train No. 53, and east on train No. 56 and No 2, daily.
Two helpers between Chicago, Ill., and Watertown, Wis., west on train No. 53, and deadhead east.
Two helpers between Chicago, Ill., and Oconomowoc, Wis., west on train No. 3 and east on train No. 2.
Two helpers between Chicago, Ill., and Mil-

waukee, Wis., north with Chicago, Ill., and North McGregor, Iowa, R. P. O., and south with Milwaukee, Wis., and Chicago, Ill., R. P. O. train No. 10. Two helpers between Chicago, Ill., and Milwaukee, Wis., north with Chicago, Ill., and North McGregor, Iowa, R. P. O., and south on train No 6. Two clerks distribute letter mail on trains No. 55 and No. 1 for city delivery at Minneapolis, Minn.; one clerk distributes letter mail on train No. 55 for city delivery at Saint Paul, Minn.; one clerk detailed to transfer duty at Chicago, Ill.; one at Milwaukee, Wis.; one at La Crosse, Wis., and one at Minneapolis, Minn. One clerk detailed as chief clerk at Chicago, Ill., one at Milwaukee, Wis., and one at Saint Paul, Minn. One clerk detailed as assistant to chief clerk at Saint Paul, Minn.

31 Short run; Chicago, Ill., to Portage, Wis.

32 Storage cars.

33 Short run; Milwaukee to La Crosse, Wis.

TABLE Aª.—*Statement of railway post-offices in operation*

Designation of railway post-office. (Lines upon which railway post-office cars are paid for, in *italics*.)	Division.	Distance run by clerks, register to register.	Initial and terminal stations, running from east to west, north to south, or northwest to southeast (with abbreviated title of railroad company).	Number of route.	Miles of route for which railroad is paid.
		Miles.			
Chicago, Ill., Monon, Ind., and Cincinnati, Ohio.[1]	5	309.64	Chicago, Ill., Monon, Ind. (Louis., New Alb. and Chic.).	22038 (part)	(²)
			Monon, Ind., Indianapolis, Ind. (Louis., New Alb. and Chic.).	22038 (part)	95.56
			Indianapolis, Ind., Hamilton, Ohio (Cin., Ham. and Ind.).	21024	99.83
			Hamilton, Cincinnati, Ohio (Cin., Ham. and Day.).	21026 (part)	(⁴)
Chicago, Ill., and North McGregor, Iowa.	6	281.00	Chicago, Ill., Milwaukee, Wis. (Chi., Mil. and St. P.).	23035	(⁵)
			Milwaukee, Wis., North McGregor, Iowa (Chi., Mil. and St. P.).	25001	195.98
Chicago and Quincy, Ill.	6	263.50	Chicago, Galesburgh, Ill. (Chi., Bur. and Qcy.).	23007 (part)	(⁹)
			Galesburgh, Quincy, Ill. (Chi., Bur. and Qcy.).	23010	100.61
Chicago, Ill., Richmond, Ind., and Cincinnati, Ohio.	5	295.71	Chicago, Ill., Richmond, Ind. (Chi., St. Lou., and Pitts.).	22009	225.16
			Richmond, Ind., Hamilton, Ohio (Cin., Rich. and Chic.).	21025	45.00
			Hamilton, Cincinnati, Ohio (Cin., Ham. and Day.).	21026 (part)	(¹⁴)
Chicago, Ill., and Saint Louis, Mo.	6	284.70	Chicago, Ill., Saint Louis, Mo. (Chicago and Alton).	23017	281.10
Chicago, Savanna, Ill., and Cedar Rapids, Iowa.	6	223.44	Chicago, Kittridge, Ill. (Chi., Mil. and St. P.).	23054	116.60
			Kittridge, Savanna, Ill. (Chi., Mil. and St. P.).	25024 (part)	(²⁰)
			Savanna, Ill., Marion, Iowa (Chi., Mil. and St. P.).	²¹27028 (part)	89.90
			Marion, Cedar Rapids, Iowa (Chi., Mil. and St. P.).	27020 (part)	(²²)
Chicago and Streator, Ill.	6	97.70	Chicago, Aurora, Ill. (Chi., Bur. and Qcy.).	24017 (part)	(²²)
			Aurora, Streator, Ill. (Chi., Bur. and Qcy.).	23012	60.97
Chicago, Ill., and Terre Haute, Ind.	6	186.02	Chicago, Danville, Ill. (Chi. and East. Ill.).	23042	124.68
			Danville, Ill., Terre Haute, Ind. (Chi. and East. Ill.).	22024	56.48
Chicago, Ill., and West Liberty, Iowa.	6	221.52	Chicago, Ill., Davenport, Iowa (Chi., R. Isl'd and Pac.).	23015	182.63
			Davenport, West Liberty, Iowa (Chi., R. Isl'd and Pac.).	²⁴27014 (part)	38.87
Chicago, Ill., and Winona, Minn.	6	297.70	Chicago, Harvard, Ill. (Chi. and No. West.).	25009 (part)	(²⁵)
			Harvard, Caledonia, Ill. (Chi. and No. West.).	25011 (part)	(²⁶)
			Caledonia, Ill., Winona Jct., Wis. (Chi. and No. West.).	25010	189.55
			Winona Jct., Wis., Winona, Minn. (Chi. and No. West.).	²⁵25014 (part)	29.72
			Janesville, Evansville, Wis. (Chi. and No. West.).	²⁶25064 (part)	16.75

[1] This line was formerly the Michigan City, Monon and Indianapolis, and Cincinnati, Hamilton and Indianapolis R. P. O.'s. December 15, 1887, run of clerks on Michigan City, Monon and Indian polis R. P. O was curtailed to end at Monon, Ind., and is now known as the Michigan City and Monon R. P. O.; distance 56 57 miles. (See that line.) Run of clerks on Cincinnati Hamilton and Indianapolis trains 8 and 31 was extended to begin at Chicago.

[2] Covered by Chicago and Louisville R. P. O. (88.52 miles.) Four clerks run daily, except Sunday, over whole route, acting as helpers to Chicago and Louisville day line between Chicago, Ill., and Monon, Ind. One clerk runs daily, except Sunday, on trains 37 and 38, between Cincinnati, Hamilton and Indianapolis (see that line), thus making double daily service, except Sunday, between Cincinnati, Hamilton, and Indianapolis

[4] Covered by Toledo and Cincinnati R. P. O. (25 40 miles.)

[5] Distance (85 98 miles) covered by Chicago, Ill., and Minneapolis, Minn., R. P. O.

[6] One reserve.

[7] Two helpers between Waukesha, Wis., and North McGregor, Iowa; one clerk detailed to transfer duty at Prairie du Chien, Wis.

[8] Distance (163 miles) covered by Chicago, Ill., and Burlington, Iowa, R. P. O.

[9] Two of these cars in reserve.

[10] Through run.

[11] Two helpers on a through run between Chicago and Galesburgh, Ill.

[12] Short run; Galesburgh to Quincy, Ill.

[13] One car in reserve.

[14] Covered by Toledo and Cincinnati R. P. O. (25.40 miles.)

In the United States on June 30, 1888—Continued.

Average weight of mail (whole distance per day)	Date of last readjustment.	Train No. outward.	Av'ge speed (miles).	Train No. inward.	Av'ge speed (miles).	Number of round trips with clerks per week.	Annual miles of service with clerks.	Average miles run daily by crews.	Number of mail cars or cars in which are mail apartments.	Length.	Width.	Number of crews.	Number of clerks to crew.	Number of clerks appointed to line.
Lbs.										Ft. In.	Ft. In.			
947	July 1, 1888	5	27.66	6	26.74	6								
947	July 1, 1888	11	24.92	12	27.43	6	186,000	174.02	2 / 2	20 0 / 19 9	11 0 / 9 2	4	1	[16]5
1,925	July 1, 1888	31	31.52	8	31.52	6								
8,951	July 1, 1888	31	33.86	8	40.48	6								
43,949	Mar.13,1884	9	28.66	56	28.66	6	176,468	140.50	[*]2	49 3	9 3	4	2	[17]11
......	....	1	24	4	18.80	6			1	50 1	9 3			
54,621	Mar.11,1884	17	26.79	8	34.32	7	192,882	131.75	3	[*]54 10	8 9¼	10[6]	5	[11]22
13,263	July 1, 1887	8 / 1	24.49 / 24	4 / 2	23.53 / 27.91	.... / 7	73,200	100	2	51 4½ / 44 11	8 9¼ / 8 9¼	12[2]	5	
2,185	July 1, 1888	2	28.14	1	28.80	6	185,706	147.85	[12]8	20 0	9 0	4	1	4
2,262	July 1, 1888	2	30.03	1	27.60	6								
8,951	July 1, 1888	2	30.48	1	29.28	6								
14,834	July 1, 1887	2 / 4	27.19 / 27.19	1 / 3	26.14 / 24.80	6 / 7	178,791 / 208,400	142.35 / 142.35	2 / 2 / 12[2]	60 0 / 60 0 / 44 5	9 4 / 9 4 / 9 1	15[4] / 17[4]	3 / 3	[16]32
8,012	July 1, 1887	1	27.43	4	27.43	6	146,600	116.72	1	24 6	9 4	4	1	[19]7
2,231	July 1, 1887	1	29.33	4	29.16	....			1	24 0	9 3			
2,249	July 1, 1887	1	24.00	4	25.71									
768	July 1, 1887	13	21.60	12	21.60									
54,621	Mar.11,1884	13	24.67	14	27.75	6	61,355	97.70	1	27 3½	8 9¼	2	1	2
1,420 / 2,984 / 801	July 1, 1887 / July 1, 1887 / July 1, 1887	81 / 1 / 1	27.72 / 24.90 / 24.00	82 / 2 / 2	26.14 / 24.90 / 27.67	.... / 6 /	113,052	120.01	[31]1 / 2 / [13]1	35 5 / 25 0 / 17 3	8 9¼ / 9 2 / 6 3	3	1	3
12,153	July 1, 1887	1	25.76	2	28.07	7	162,152	110.76	[32]2 / [37]2 / [33]3	50 0 / 49 4 / 50 0	9 4 / 9 4 / 9 4	15[4]	3	[30]26
6,186	July 1, 1887	3	26.00	4	24.89	7	162,152	110.76				17[4]	3	
7,499 / 1,376	July 1, 1887 / July 1, 1887	107 / 113 / 1	26.87 / 26.87 / 24.50	114 / 110 / 2	26.87 / 25.94 / 23.07	7 / 6	217,916 / 186,935	148.85 / 148.85	2 / 2	50 0 / 50 0	9 5 / 9 5	4 / 4	2 / 2	16
7,507	July 1, 1887	1 / 7	23.45 / 23.45	2 / 6	21.87 / 22.64									
5,660	July 1, 1887	1 / 3	24.76 / 27.02	2 / 4	20.32 / 26.96									
4,139	July 1, 1887	7	25.12	6	25.12									

15 Day line.
16 Two helpers on night line between Chicago and Bloomington, Ill. Three clerks detailed to office superintendent and three to transfer duty at Chicago, Ill.
17 Night line.
18 Reserve.
19 Two helpers between Kirkland, Ill., and Cedar Rapids, Iowa; one clerk detailed in charge of label-room at office superintendent, Chicago, Ill.
20 Distance (22 miles) covered by Racine, Wis., and Rock Island, Ill., R. P. O.
21 Balance of route (262.47 miles) covered by Marion and Council Bluffs, Iowa, R. P. O.
22 Distance (5.40 miles) covered by Farley and Cedar Rapids, Iowa, R. P. O.
23 Distance (37 miles) covered by Chicago, Ill., and Burlington, Iowa, R. P. O.
24 Whole car; reserve.
25 Cars run through between Chicago, Ill., and U. P. Transfer, Iowa, covering West Liberty and Council Bluffs, Iowa, R. P. O.
26 One clerk detailed as chief clerk at Des Moines, Iowa; one clerk detailed to through register run between Chicago, Ill., and U. P. Transfer. Iowa.
27 One in reserve.
28 Balance of route (270.10 miles) covered by West Liberty and Council Bluffs, Iowa, R. P. O.
29 Distance (62.70 miles) covered by Ft. Howard, Wis., and Chicago, Ill., R. P. O.
30 Distance (15 miles) covered by Kenosha, Wis., and Rockford, Ill., R. P. O.
31 Balance of route (4.11 miles) Winona Junction, to La Crosse, Wis, covered by closed pouches. (See Table C*.)
32 Night line runs between Chicago, Ill, and Janesville, Wis., over route 25009; thence to Evansville over route 25064; thence to Winona, Minn, over routes 25010 and 25014.

TABLE A*.—*Statement of railway post-offices in operation*

Designation of railway post-office. (Lines upon which railway post-office cars are paid for, in *italics*.)	Division.	Distance run by clerks, register to register.	Initial and terminal stations, running from east to west, north to south, or northwest to southeast (with abbreviated title of railroad company).	Number of route.	Miles of route for which railroad is paid.
		Miles.			
Childersburgh, Ala., and Columbus, Ga.	4	116.12	Childersburgh, Opelika, Ala. (Col. and West. R. R.).	17016	86.72
			Opelika. Ala., Columbus, Ga. (Col. and West. R. R).	17007	29.53
Cincinnati, Ohio, and Chattanooga, Tenn.[1]	5	339.53	Cincinnati, Ohio, Chattanooga, Tenn. (Cin., N. O., Tex. Pacific).	20020	338.20
Cincinnati, Hamilton, Ohio, and Indianapolis, Ind.	5	125.41	Cincinnati, Hamilton, Ohio (Cin., Ham. and Day.).	21025	([6])
			Hamilton, Ohio, Indianapolis, Ind. (Cin., Ham. and Ind).	21024	([5])
Cincinnati, Ohio, and Junction City, Ky.	5	122.56	Cincinnati, Ohio, Junction City, Ky. (C., N. O. and T. P.).	20020 (part)	([7])
Cincinnati, Ohio, and Livingston, Ky.	5	155.54	Covington, Paris, Ky. (Ky. Cent.)..........	20002 (part)	79.36
			Paris, Richmond, Ky. (Ky. Cent.)	20032	40.84
			Richmond, Livingston, Ky. (Ky. Cent.) ...	20 + 8	36.62
Cincinnati, Ohio, and Louisville, Ky.	5	111.32	Cincinnati, Ohio, Louisville, Ky. (Louis. and Nash.)	20004	([12])
Cincinnati, Ohio, and Nashville, Tenn.	5	303.60	Cincinnati, Ohio, Louisville, Ky. (Louis. and Nash.)	20004	110.10
			Cincinnati Junction (n. o.), Sax, Ky. (Louis. and Nash.)	20017	4.50
			Louisville, Ky., Nashville, Tenn. (Louis. and Nash.)	20005	185.00
Cincinnati, Ohio, North Vernon, Ind., and Louisville, Ky.	5	131.50	Cincinnati, Ohio, North Vernon, Ind. (Ohio and Miss.).	22010 (part)	([17])
			North Vernon, Ind., Louisville, Ky. (Ohio and Miss.).	22019	54.86
Cincinnati, Ohio, and Saint Louis, Mo.	5	341.56	Cincinnati, Ohio, East Saint Louis, Ill. (Ohio and Miss.).	22010	338.20
Claremont, N. H., and Boston, Mass.	1	129.84	Claremont, Concord, N. H. (Bost. and Me. Low. Syst.)	1009 (part)	54.90
			Concord, Nashua, N. H. (Concord)	1001	([32])
			Nashua, N. H., Boston, Mass. (Bost. and Me. Low. Syst.)	3016	([33])
Clarendon and Fort Worth, Tex.[36]	7	278.92	Clarendon, Fort Worth, Tex. (Ft. W. and D. C.).	31037 (part)	278.87
Clarinda, Iowa, and Corning, Mo.	6	46.36	Clarinda, Northborough, Iowa (Chi., Burl. and Qcy.).	27083	18.80
			Northborough, Iowa, Corning, Mo. (K. C., St. Jo. and C Bl.).	23046	27.74
Clarksburgh and Weston, W. Va.	3	26.05	Clarksburgh, Weston, W. Va. (Clarks., Weston, and Glenv.).	12006	27.07

[1] Full R. P. O. service of 40 feet cars placed on day trains of this line February 1, 1888; previous to this time full R. P. O. service on night trains; mail apartment service on day trains May 3, 1888; additional service established on trains 3 and 4 between Cincinnati, Ohio, and Junction City, Ky.; in mail apartment cars, distance, 122.56 miles.

[2] One clerk detailed to duty in office superintendent Fifth Division; one clerk detailed to transfer duty at Junction City, Ky.

[3] Two cars in reserve; one clerk in apartment car between Cincinnati, Ohio, and Junction City, Ky. (See that line.)

[4] Covered by Chicago, Monon and Cincinnati R. P. O. 99 83 miles.

[5] This is short run of Chicago, Monon and Cincinnati R. P. O.; clerks hold an appointment, and are shown with that line. (See that line.)

[6] Covered by Toledo and Cincinnati R. P. O. 25.40 miles.

[7] Covered by Cincinnati and Chattanooga R. P. O.

[8] Mail apartment service in addition to Cincinnati and Chattanooga R. P. O. established on trains 3 and 4 on this line May 3, 1884.

[9] Clerk holds appointment on Cincinnati and Chattanooga R. P. O. and is shown with that line.

[10] Closed-pouch service on route 20002 between Paris and Lexington, Ky., 19.36 miles. (See Table C*.)

[11] One car in reserve.

[12] Covered by Cincinnati and Nashville R. P. O. 110.10 miles.

[13] Clerks act as helpers to Cincinnati and Nashville; day line on south trips, running north in apartment cars daily on train 8. Clerks are appointed to Cincinnati and Nashville R. P. O., and are shown with that line.

[14] Day line.

[15] Two clerks run south from Cincinnati, Ohio, to Louisville, Ky., with day line, and north in apartment car on train 8, commencing May 20, 1888. Apartment car service on this line between Cincinnati, Ohio, and Nashville, Tenn., on trains 5 and 2 performed as follows: Four clerks run between Cincinnati, Ohio, and Nashville, Tenn., on these trains. Fourth clerks of night line perform service on train 5, Cincinnati, Ohio, to Nashville, assisting local clerk through. Second clerk of Cincinnati and Nashville night line performs service on train 2, Nashville, Tenn., to Cincinnati, Ohio, by assisting local clerk Nashville, Tenn , to Cincinnati, Ohio. Previous to May 20, 1888,

in the United States on June 30, 1888—Continued.

Average weight of mail whole distance per day.	Date of last re-adjustment.	Average speed per hour (train numbers taken from division schedules).				Number of round trips with clerks per week.	Annual miles of service with clerks.	Average miles run daily by crews.	Number of mail cars, or cars in which are mail apartments.	Inside dimensions of cars or apartments (railway post-office cars in black figures).		Number of crews.	Number of clerks to crew.	Number of clerks appointed to line.
		Train No. outward.	Av'ge speed (miles).	Train No. inward.	Av'ge speed (miles).					Length.	Width.			
Lbs.										*Ft. In.*	*Ft. In.*			
377	July 1, 1888	61	23.00	62	26.08	7	84,999	116.12	1	12 10	9 1	2	1	2
949	July 1, 1888	61	24.01	62	24.07									
4,762	July 1, 1884	1	34.99	2	34.87	7	248,530	169.76		50 0	9 2	4	2	*19
		5	.7.42	6	29 40	7	248,536	....	3	40 0	9 2	4	2	
2,362	July 1, 1888	38	29.06	37	33.27	6	78,757	250.82	....	....		1	1	(4)
1,923	July 1, 1888	38	27.99	37	30.48	6								
4,762	July 1, 1884	*3	23.94	4	24.06	6	12,501	245.12	1	....		1	1	(*)
2,694	July 1, 1888	2	25.06	3	30.72	6	97,679	103.69	113	14 0	9 8	3	1	3
717	July 1, 1888	2	17.50	3	21.30	6								
141	Apr.15, 1884	2	9.78	3	6.66	6								
19,548	July 1, 1884	....	....	8	25.08	7	81,486	111.32	1	15 0	9 6	2	1	(18)
19,548	July 1, 1884	1	27.64	4	28.14	7	222,235	151.80	4	50 0	9 6	144	3	141
		3	28.14	6	27.52	7	222,235	....		45 0	9 6	144	4	
16,822	July 1, 1884	1	22.50	4	22,50	7								
		3	18.00	6	22.50	7								
18,913	July 1, 1888	1	26.88	4	30.83	7								
		3	28.62	6	30.83	7								
19,316	July 1, 1888	1	31.9.	18	30.36	6	82,582	131.50	141	17 7	9 4	2	1	142
4,047	July 1, 1888	101	26.94	18	29.94	6								
19,316	July 1, 1888	1	32.46	2	32.22	7	250.022	170.78	(30)	50 0	9 4	144	4	139
		5	30.24	4	28.62	7	250,022	....				144	5	
452	July 1, 1885	12	21.43	73	20.35	6	68,971	129.84	2	14 2	7 0	2	1	2
									1	15 0	7 0			
11,723	Aug.5, 1885	12	19.99	73	24.13	....			142 2	13 0	6 6			
14,963	July 1, 1885	12	23.83	73	27.08	'								
944	July 1, 1886	1	22.46	2	21.60	7	204,169	139.46	{ 4 / 1 / 1 / 2 }	18 6 / 24 8 / 24 8 / 16 10	7 3 / 9 3 / 9 3 / 9 3	4	1	5
349	July 1, 1887	87	25.06	88	25.06	6	29,114	92.72	1	22 0	9 2	1	1	1
305	July 1, 1887	16	28.02	15	22.41									
887	July 1, 1885	4	13.47	1	13.13	6	16,359	52.10	1	10 0	6 0	1	1	1

local clerks ran between Louisville, Ky., and Nashville. Tenn., on trains 5 and 6 (see Lou. and Nash R. P. O.). One clerk detailed as chief clerk at Louisville. Ky ; one clerk detailed as assistant chief clerk at Louisville, Ky.; two clerks detailed to transfer duty at Louisville, Ky.; one clerk detailed to transfer duty at Bowling Green, Ky.; one clerk detailed to transfer duty at Nashville, Tenn.; one clerk detailed to clerical duty in office superintendent of Fifth Division.

16 Night line.

17 Covered by Cincinnati and Saint Louis R. P. O. 72.80 miles.

18 Mail apartment on this line runs only between North Vernon, Ind., and Louisville, Ky.

19 These clerks act as helpers to Cincinnati and Saint Louis, train 1, between Cincinnati, Ohio, and North Vernon, Ind., on west trips; on east trips they perform no service between North Vernon, Ind., and Cincinnati, Ohio.

20 Thirteen cars on line between Baltimore, Md., and Saint Louis, Mo. (See Baltimore and Graiton R. P. O. for full equipment of line in Third Division report.)

21 Two clerks detailed to duty in office of superin-

tendent Fifth Division ; one clerk detailed to transfer duty at Vincennes, Ind.

22 Balance of route covered by closed-pouch service between Claremont and Claremont Junction 2.02 miles. (See Table C.)

23 Covered by Saint Albans and Boston R. P. O. 36 28.

24 Reserve car.

25 Covered by Saint Albans and Boston R. P. O. 39.85 miles. Claremont and Lowell R. P. O. to April 15, 1888. Claremont and Boston R. P. O. from April 16, 18-8.

26 Reported last year as Quanah and Fort Worth, Tex.; increased distance, 85 98 miles.

27 174.25 miles of route 31037, between Clarendon and Texline (n. o.), Tex., covered by Texline (n. o.) and Clarendon ponch service.

28 Cars run from Fort Worth, Tex., to Denver, Colo., over Clarendon and Fort Worth, Tex., R. P. O., Texline (n. o.) and Clarendon, Tex., R. R., Pueblo, Colo., and Texline (n. o.) R. R., and Denver and Pueblo, Colo., R. P. O.

29 One helper between Fort Worth and Bowie, Tex. (68 miles.)

30 In reserve.

TABLE A*.—*Statement of railway post-offices in operation*

Designation of railway post-office. (Lines upon which railway post-office cars are paid for, in *italics*.)	Division.	Distance run by clerks, register to register.	Initial and terminal stations, running from east to west, north to south, or northwest to southeast (with abbreviated title of railroad company).	Number of route.	Miles of route for which railroad is paid.
		Miles.			
Clayton, Del., and Chestertown, Md.	2	32.71	Clayton, Del., and Chestertown, Md. (B. and D. B.).	10012	31.11
Clayton, Del., and Easton, Md.	2	44.52	Clayton, Del., and Easton, Md. (P., W. and B.).	9503 (part)	[1]44.08
Cleveland and Cincinnati, Ohio.	5	244.66	Cleveland, Cincinnati, Ohio (Cleve., Col., Cin and Ind.).	21042	244.60
Cleveland and Coshocton, Ohio.	5	115.55	Cleveland, Canton, Ohio (Cleve. and Canton).	[2]21009 (part)	60.00
			Canton, Coshocton, Ohio (Cleve. and Canton).	21092	54.73
Cleveland, Ohio, Fort Wayne, Ind., and Chicago, Ill	9	340.50	Cleveland, Ohio, Fort Wayne, Ind., Chicago, Ill. (N. Y. C. and St. L.).	21089	339.07
Cleveland, Hudson, and Columbus, Ohio.	5	171.19	Cleveland, Hudson, Ohio (Pa. Co.).	21006 (part)	(²)
			Hudson, Columbus, Ohio (Cleve., Akron and Col.).	31004	145.15
Cleveland, Ohio, and Indianapolis, Ind.	5	283.00	Cleveland. Galion, Ohio (Cleve., Col., Cin. and Ind.).	21042 (part)	(²)
			Galion, Ohio, Indianapolis, Ind. (Cleve., Col., Cin. and Ind.).	21016	204.07
Cleveland and New Lisbon, Ohio.	5	91.75	Cleveland, Niles, Ohio (New York, L. E. and West.).	21005 (part)	(¹⁵)
			Niles, New Lisbon, Ohio (New York., L. E. and West.).	21037	34.85
Cleveland, Ohio, and Pittsburgh, Pa.	5	149.90	Cleveland, Wellsville, Ohio (Pa. Co.)......	21006	101.29
			Wellsville, Ohio, Pittsburgh, Pa. (Pa. Co.)..	[13]21003 (part)	48.20
Cleveland, Tenn., and Selma, Ala.	4	264.05	Cleveland, Tenn., Selma, Ala. (E. Tenn. Va. and Ga. R. R.	17010	264.92
Cleveland and Toledo, Ohio	9	113.37	Cleveland, Toledo, Ohio (L. S. and M. S.)...	21095 (part)	(¹⁵)
Cleveland, Ohio, and Wheeling, W. Va.	5	168.50	Elyria, Millbury, Ohio (L. S. and M. S.)	21007 (part)	(¹⁶)
			Cleveland, Grafton, Ohio (Cleve., Col., Cin. and Ind.).	21012 (part)	(¹⁹)
			Grafton, Bridgeport, Ohio (Cleve., Lor. and Wheel.).	[16]21C41 (part)	142.06
Cleveland, Youngstown, Ohio, and Pittsburgh, Pa.	5	136.77	Cleveland, Youngstown, Ohio (New York, L. E. and West.).	[11]21003 (part)	66.75
			Youngstown, Ohio, Pittsburgh, Pa. (Pitts. and Lake Erie).	8123	65.88
Cleveland and Zoar Station, Ohio.	5	76.39	Cleveland, Zoar Station, Ohio (Valley).....	21073	76.12
Clinton and Anamosa, Iowa ..	6	71.90	Clinton, Anamosa, Iowa (Chi. and No. West.)	27024	72.07
Clinton and Iowa City, Iowa ..	6	78.41	Clinton, Elmira (n. o.), Iowa (Bur., C. R. and North.).	27072	69.53
			Elmira (n. o.), Iowa City, Iowa (Bur., C. R. and North.).	[24]27048 (part)	8.90
Cloverdale and San Francisco, Cal.	8	85.46	San Francisco. Cloverdale, Cal. (S. F. and North Pacific R. R.).	46011	84.95
Colmesneil and Trinity, Tex ..	7	66.81	Colmesneil, Trinity, Tex. (I. and G. N.)...	31046	66.81
Colorado Springs and Leadville, Colo.[26]	7	133.05	Colorado Springs, Leadville, Colo. (Colo. Mid.).	38034	133.05

[1] 10.62 miles covered by closed-pouch service. (See Table C*.)

[2] Day line.

[3] 2 clerks act as helpers between Cleveland and Delaware day line on trip south and Delaware and Crestline, Ohio, on trip north. (See Cleve. and Ind. R. P. O.) 2 clerks detailed to clerical duty in office superintendent fifth division. 1 clerk detailed as chief clerk at Columbus, Ohio.

[4] Night line. Balance of route shown on Canton and Sherodsville R. P. O. (48.24 miles). 1 car in reserve. 2 cars held in reserve. Covered by Cleveland and Pittsburgh R. P. O. (26.10 miles).

[9] Covered by Cleveland and Cincinnati R. P. O. (80 miles). Cleveland and Cincinnati R. P. O. helpers assist in car of this R. P. O. on north trips between Crestline and Cleveland, Ohio.

[10] Covered by Cleveland, Youngstown and Pittsburgh R. P. O. (58.25 miles).

[11] Clerks act as helpers to Cleveland, Youngstown and Pittsburgh R. P. O. between Cleveland and Niles, on trains 65 and 72, daily, except Sunday.

[12] Three helpers on trains 37 and 42, running over whole line.

[13] Balance of route covered by Wellsville and Bellaire R. P. O.; distance 46.59 miles.

[14] Cars also used by Selma and Meridian R. P. O. Two reserve cars.

In the United States on June 30, 1888—Continued.

Average weight of mail whole distance per day.	Date of last re-adjustment.	Average speed per hour (train numbers taken from division schedules).				Number of round trips with clerks per week.	Annual miles of service with clerks.	Average miles run daily by crews.	Number of mail cars, or cars in which are mail apartments.	Inside dimensions of cars or apartments (railway post-office cars in black figures).		Number of crews.	Number of clerks to crew.	Number of clerks appointed to line.
		Train No. outward.	Av'ge speed (miles).	Train No. inward.	Av'ge speed (miles).					Length.	Width.			
Lbs.										*Ft. In.*	*Ft. In.*			
546	July 1, 1885	2	15.09	1	15.09	6	20,542	65.42	1	8 3	5 7	1	1	1
497	July 1, 1885	21	18.02	280	25.20	6	27,959	89.04	1	10 10	6 6	1	1	1
19,359	July 1, 1888	8	28.80	12	33.36	7	179,091	122.23	5	40 0	9 3	24	2	25
		9	23.40	8	25.74	7	179,091					44	3	
566	July 1, 1888	7	24	20	25.71	6	72,565	115.55	2	14 2	7 9	2	1	2
697	July 1, 1888	7	22.80	20	21.90	6								
781	July 1, 1888	3	24.80	4	25.11	6	213,834	170	4	20 0	9 0	4	1	4
11,044	July 1, 1888	2	29.88	3	24	6	107,507	114.12	4	15 0	8 6	3	1	3
1,355	July 1, 1888	2	27.66	3	27.90	6								
19,359	July 1, 1888	3	28.20	2	24.61	7	207,156	141.50	8	40 0	8 11	4	2	8
4,684	July 1, 1888	3	26.41	2	25.26	7								
5,598	July 1, 1888	72	29.13	69	23.28	6	57,619	91.75	1	6 6	6 6	2	1	2
409	July 1, 1888	72	24.60	69	23.22	6								
11,044	July 1, 1888	36	22.92	35	22.50	6	93,760	99.53	4	19 8	9 1	9	1	12
		38	27	37	24.80	6	93,780	....	1	20 2	8 11			
		42	22.50	41	22.14	7	109,288							
5,936	July 1, 1888	36	22.24	35	23.15	6								
		38	22.24	37	25.14	6								
		42	24.10	41	27.28	7								
1,002	July 1, 1888	3	23.9	4	23.4	7	193,284	132.03	14	14 6	8 6	4	1	4
									14	12 1	7 6			
									14	22 6	9 4			
98,761	July 1, 1888	16 21 & 29	25.70	24	27.80	6	71,196	113.37	17	45 0	9 0			
17,168	July 1, 1888	25	32.28	22	30.07	6	67,696	107.80	1	20 0	9 0	4	1	(18)
19,359	July 1, 1888	1	23.22	4	25.10	6	105,818	84.25	2	16 8	9 4	4	1	4
1,057	July 1, 1888	1	22.38	4	23.10	6								
5,598	July 1, 1888	64	26.70	67	23.58	7	100,116	109.41	4	18 2	9 2	25	1	5
		72	32.04	69	26.28	7	100,116							
3,575	July 1, 1885	64	28.60	67	24.66	7								
		72	29.28	69	28.20	7								
800	July 1, 1888	1	25.37	10	26.94	6	47,973	76.29	2	19 6	9 0	2	1	2
445	July 1, 1887	41	22.76	42	23.12	6	45,090	71.80	2	12 2	7 5	2	1	2
223	July 1, 1887	41	19.40	40	26.07	6	49,241	156.82	1	13 8	9 1	1	1	1
928	July 1, 1887	41	26.70	40	21.96	....	....	....	1	11 11	9 4			
1,754	July 1, 1886	1	26.97	12	24.27	7	62,557	85.46	2	19 3	8 11	2	1	2
164	July 1, 1886	680	12.61	679	12.42	7	48,905	133.62	1	23 3	9 5	1	1	1
405	July 1, 1886	1	19.57	2	20.82	7	97,393	133.05	2	20 4	9 2	2	1	2
									2	20 4	9 2			

---

14 Shown in report of New York and Chicago R. P. O.

15 This R. P. O. runs on train 21 from Cleveland to Elyria, Ohio; thence over route 21047 on train 29 to Toledo, Ohio, daily, except Sunday and Monday. Monday this R. P. O. runs to Toledo on train 21 via Norwalk, Ohio, over route 21095.

17 This car used as an apartment car.

18 Clerks appointed to the New York and Chicago R. P. O.

19 Covered by Cleveland and Cincinnati R. P. O. (25.10 miles).

20 Balance of route between Loraine and Grafton, Ohio (16.35 miles), covered by closed-pouch service. (See Table O¹.)

21 Balance of route covered by lines of the second division (23.50 miles).

22 Clerks of Cleveland and New Lisbon R. P. O. act as helpers to this R. P. O. on trains 69 and 72, Cleveland to Niles (56.25 miles), daily, except Sunday.

23 Clerks make two round trips daily.

24 Balance of route, Iowa City to Iowa Junction, Iowa (11.90 miles), covered by closed pouches. (See Table C¹.)

25 Reserve.

26 New service; not reported last year.

27 In reserve.

TABLE A°.—*Statement of railway post-offices in operation*

Designation of railway post-office. (Lines upon which railway post-office cars are paid for, in *italics.*)	Division.	Distance run by clerks, register to register.	Initial and terminal stations, running from east to west, north to south, or northwest to southeast (with abbreviated title of railroad company).	Number of route.	Miles of route for which railroad is paid.
		Miles.			
Columbia and Branchville, S. C.	4	68.00	Columbia, Branchville, S. C. (S.C.).......	14003 (part)	¹68.71
Columbia and Fayetteville, Tenn.	5	48.96	Columbia, Fayetteville, Tenn. (Nash., Chatt. and St. Louis).	19015	48.87
Columbia, Pa., and Perryville, Md.	2	43.88	Columbia, Pa., Port Deposit, Md. (Penna.).	8124	39.62
			Port Deposit, Perryville, Md. (Penna.) ...	10023	4.49
Columbia, Sumter, and Charleston, S. C.	4	136.00	Columbia, Sumter, S. C. (W., C. and A. R. R.).	14002	(⁵)
			Sumter, Lanes, S. C. (Cent. R. R. of S. C.)..	14015	40
			Lanes, Charleston, S. C. (N. E. R. R. of S. C).	14005	(⁶)
Columbus and Albion, Nebr ...	6	43.45	Columbus, Oconee, Nebr. (Om., Nio. and Blk. Hills).	34012 (part)	(⁷)
			Oconee, Albion, Nebr. (Om., Nio., and Blk. Hills).	34017	34.17
Columbus, Ohio, and Ashland, Ky.	5	134.14	Columbus, Coal Grove, Ohio (Scioto Valley)	21051	132
Columbus, Nebr., and Atchison, Kans.	6	220.50	Columbus, Nebr., Atchison, Kans. (B. and M. in Nebr).	33012	220.48
Columbus and Athens, Ohio...	5	77.66	Columbus, Athens, Ohio (Col., Hoc. Val. and Tol.).	21036	77.44
Columbus, Ohio, and Charleston, W. Va. ¹⁰	5	197.52	Columbus, Corning, Ohio (Tol. and Ohio Cent.).	21068	66.05
			Corning, Gallipolis, Ohio (Ohio Cent)	21068	71.93
			C., H. V. and T. Junction (n. o.), Charleston, W. Va. (Ohio Cent.)	12010	59.70
Columbus and Cincinnati, Ohio.	5	121.13	Columbus, Cincinnati, Ohio (Pitts., Cinn. and Saint Louis).	21014	(¹¹)
Columbus, Midland City, and Cincinnati, Ohio.	5	117.85	Columbus, Midland City, Ohio (Col. and Cinn. Mid.).	21094	72.73
			Midland City, Cincinnati, Ohio (Cinn., Wash. and Balto).	21028 (part)	(¹²)
Columbus, Springfield, Ohio, and Indianapolis, Ind.	5	185.39	Columbus, Springfield, Ohio (Cinn., Sand. and Cleve.).	21033	46.03
			Springfield, Ohio, Indianapolis, Ind. (Ind., Bloom. and West.).	21057	139.51
Commerce and Fort Worth, Tex.¹⁴	7	96.31	Commerce, Fort. Worth, Tex. (St. L., Ark. and Tex.).	³¹067	96.31
Concordia and Junction City, Kans.	7	70.77	Concordia, Junction City, Kans. (U. P.) ...	33015	70.77
Concordia and Strong, Kans.¹⁴	7	117.44	Concordia, Keystone, Kans. (C., K. and W.).	33088	41.02
			Keystone, Strong, Kans. (C., K. and W.)..	¹⁵33077 (part)	76.40
Conroe and Somerville (n. o.), Tex.¹⁶	7	70.93	Conroe, Navasota, Tex. (G., C. and S. F.)...	31024	43.95
			Navasota, Somerville (n. o.), Tex. (G., C. and S. F.).	31030	27.20
Corpus Christi and Laredo, Tex.	7	161.60	Corpus Christi, Laredo, Tex. (Mex. Nat.)...	31016	161.60
Corsicana and Hillsborough, Tex.¹⁴	7	42.00	Corsicana, Hillsborough, Tex. (St. L., Ark. and Tex.).	31064	42
*Council Bluffs, Iowa, and Kansas City, Mo.*¹⁷	7	¹⁸196.50	U. P. transfer (n. o.), Iowa, Kansas City, Mo. (K. C., St. J. and C. B.).	28006	201.22

¹ 62.79 miles shown as Charleston and Augusta R. P. O.
² 1 transfer clerk Columbia, including one acting clerk additional.
³ In reserve.
⁴ Cars a d clerks shown on route No. 8124.
⁵ Reported as Florence and Augusta R. P. O.
⁶ Reported as Wilmington and Jacksonville R. P. O.
⁷ Distance (9.10 miles) covered by Norfolk and Columbus, Nebr., R. P. O.
⁸ Clerks make two round trips daily, except Sunday.

⁹ One car in reserve.
¹⁰ Previous to April 5, 1888, this line was a part of the Toledo and Charleston R. P. O. The R. P. O. service on this line between Thurston and Corning is in addition to Toledo and Corning R. P. O. (See that line.)
¹¹ Covered by Pittsburgh and Cincinnati R. P. O. (120.29 mil. s)
¹² Clerks on this line are appointed to the Pittsburgh and Cincinnati R. P. O., and are shown with that line.
¹³ Covered by Grafton and Cincinnati R. P. O. (45 miles).

in the United States on June 30, 1888—Continued.

Average weight of mail whole distance per day.	Date of last re-adjustment.	Average speed per hour (train numbers taken from division schedule).				Number of round trips with clerks per week.	Annual miles of service with clerks.	Average miles run daily by crews.	Number of mail cars, or cars in which are mail apartments.	Inside dimensions of cars or apartments (railway post-office cars in black figures).		Number of crews.	Number of clerks to crew.	Number of clerks appointed to line.
		Train No. outward.	Av'ge speed (miles).	Train No. inward.	Av'ge speed (miles).					Length.	Width.			
Lbs.										*Ft. In.*	*Ft. In.*			
2,182	July 1, 1888	50 16.7		51 18.1		14	99,552	136	......			2	1	¹⁴
		52 16.7		53 13										
190	July 1, 1888	2 12.22		1 12.22		6	30,747	97.93	1	6 6	4 6	1	1	1
216	July 1, 1885	20 18.71		23 20.67		6	27,557	87.76	1	8 2	6 4	1	1	1
									1	8 2	6 4			
306	July 1, 1885	20 20.71		23 19.24		6			(⁴)			(⁴)		
8,664	July 1, 1888	53 32.4		52 36		7	99,552	136	1	27 6	8 0	2	1	2
465	July 1, 1888	.... 32.4		 36										
12,811	July 1, 1888	.... 32.4		 36										
450	July 1, 1886	69 27.30		70 21.84		6	27,286	86.90	1	13 1	6 8	1	1	1
422	July 1, 1886	69 25.65		70 25.65										
2,496	July 1, 1888	4 23.64		5 26.94		¹⁶6	84,240	134.14	¹⁶5	15 0	8 11	4	1	4
		6 23.28		3 22.82		6	84,240							
1,641	Jan.15,1885	72 25.68		71 22.73		6	138,474	110.25	2	19 8	8 8	4	1	4
1,469	July 1, 1888	1 23.82		3 23.82		¹⁶6	48,770	103.55	¹⁶4	15 9	9 4	3	1	3
		2 23.82		4 24 18		6	48,770							
1,019	July 1, 1888	10 23.34		9 23.34		6	29,628	131.68	1	20 0	9 5	3	1	3
									¹⁶2	15 0	10 0			
371	July 1, 1888	10 20.64		9 19.26		6								
270	Feb.15,1886	10 15.24		9 18.12		6								
24,079	July 1, 1888	1 30.70		12 30.70		6	76,070	121.13	¹⁶2	18 0	9 0	2	1	(¹⁸)
1,036	July 1, 1888	103 29.04		108 33.10		¹⁶6	74,010	157.13	3	18 6	8 10	3	1	3
		101 33.10		104 23.88		6	74,010							
27,445	July 1, 1878	103 30		108 30		⁸6								
		101 30		104 24.06		6								
2,351	July 1, 1888	5 30.66		4 26.52		6	116,425	92.69	2	23 0	8 2	4	1	4
1,258	July 1, 1888	5 28.80		4 25.14		6								
......	......	87 9.26		86 8.84		7	71,963	98.31	2	23 6	8 0	2	1	2
1,156	July 1, 1886	252 24.18		231 25.67		7	51,804	141.54	1	15 2	7 5	1	1	1
310	July 1, 1888	302 21.10		301 24.52		7	85,966	117.44	1	11 1	6 1	2	1	2
									¹⁶2	11 1	6 1			
385	July 1, 1888	302 21.34		301 22.34		7								
107	July 1, 1886	26 8.80		27 9.61		7	51,920	70.93	1	13 0	9 0	2	1	2
110	July 1, 1886	26 11.28		27 13.00		7	......		¹1	11 3½	6 10½			
383	July 1, 1886	2 12.88		1 12.96		6	101,485	107.73	2	12 0	6 0	3	1	3
......	......	91 12.83		92 12.83		7	30,744	84	1	23 6	8 0	1	1	1
10,352	July 1, 1887	2 26.20		1 27.10		7	143,838	131	2	44 3	9 2	3	2	14
		4 22.69		3 22.25		7	143,838	131	2	22 0	9 2	3	2	

¹⁴ New service; not reported last year.

¹⁵ 43 18 miles of route 33077, between Keystone and Barnard, Kans., covered by Keystone and Barnard, Kans., R. P. O., and 12.60 miles, between Strong and Bazaar, covered by closed-pouch service. (See Table C².)

¹⁶ Reported last year as Montgomery and Somerville (n. o.), Tex.; increased distance, 15.93 miles.

¹⁷ Double daily service: full postal car service on trains 1 and 2, and mail-apartment service on trains 3 and 4. Last year there was only mail-apartment service on all trains.

¹⁸ Clerks do not run over branches of route 28006 from Winthrop Junction to East Atchison (1.10 miles), and from Payne to Eastport, Iowa (3.62 miles). Two helpers, one on each line. from Kansas City to Saint Joseph, Mo. (67 miles).

TABLE A⁸.—*Statement of railway post-offices in operation*

Designation of railway post-office. (Lines upon which railway post-office cars are paid for, in *italics*).	Division.	Distance run by clerks, register to register.	Initial and terminal stations, running from east to west, north to south, or northwest to southeast (with abbreviated title of railroad company).	Number of route.	Miles of route for which railroad is paid.
		Miles.			
Council Bluffs, Iowa, and Moberly, Mo.	7	263.53	Council Bluffs, Iowa, Pattensburgh, Mo. (O. and St. L.).	28061	144.61
			Pattensburgh, Brunswick, Mo. .(Wab West.).	28013	79.99
			Brunswick, Moberly, Mo. (Wab. West.) ...	28004 (part)	(¹)
Covington and Norfolk, Nebr..	6	73.96	Covington, Emerson, Nebr. (C., St. P., Minn and Om).	34093 (part)	(²)
			Emerson, Norfolk, Nebr. (C., St. P., Minn. and Om).	34021	47.09
Creighton and Norfolk, Nebr..	6	44.20	Creighton Norfolk, Nebr. (Fre., Elk. and Mo. Vall.).	34015	42.53
Crestline, Ohio, and Chicago, Ill.	5	286.15	Crestline, Ohio, Chicago, Ill. (Penna. Co.).	31092 (part)	(³)
Creston and Cumberland, Iowa	6	50.34	Creston, Cumberland, Iowa (Chi., Bur. and Qcy.).	27041	47.29
Creston, Iowa, and Saint Joseph, Mo.	7	103.88	Creston, Iowa, Hopkins, Mo. (C., B. and Q.).	27007	44.27
			Hopkins, Saint Joseph, Mo. (K. C., St. J. and C. B.).	28028	56.90
Crookston, Minn., and Minot, Dak.	6	231.62	Crookston, Minn., Devil's Lake, Dak. (St. P., Minn. and Man.).	26639	114.55
			Devil's Lake, Minot, Dak. (St. P., Minn. and Man.).	*35026 (part)	117.66
Cranberry, N. C., and Johnson City, Tenn.	3	34.11	Cranberry, N C., Johnson City, Tenn. (E. Tenn. and Western N. C.).	19018	34.19
Cuba and Salem, Mo...........	7	40.96	Cuba Junction (B. o.), Salem, Mo. (St. L. and S. F.).	28023	40.41
Cumberland, Md., and Davis, W. Va.	3	85.10	Cumberland, Md., Piedmont, W.Va. (West Va. Central).	12019	26.87
			Piedmont, Shaw, W. Va. (West Va. Central).	12007	*11.33
			Shaw, Davis, W. Va. (West Va. Central).	12009	45.82
Cumberland, Md., and Piedmont, W. Va.	3	33.73	Cumberland, Md., Piedmont, W.Va. (Cumb. and Pa.).	10011	33.79
Cumberland, Md., and Pittsburgh, Pa.	3	150.73	Cumberland, Md., Pittsburgh, Pa. (Balto. and Ohio)	8063	149.58
Curwensville and Tyrone, Pa.	2	47.45	Curwensville, Tyrone, Pa. (Penna.)	8035	47.48
Dallas and Kemp, Tex	7	49.38	Dallas, Kemp, Tex. (Texas Trunk)	31081	49.38
Dallas and Weatherford, Tex.¹¹.	7	93.78	Dallas, Weatherford, Tex. (G. C. and S.F.).	31085	98.78
Danbury and South Norwalk, Conn.	1	23.61	Danbury. So. Norwalk, Conn. (Dan. and Nor. Div. Hous.).	5013	23.60
Dansville and Buffalo, N. Y ...	2	95.98	Dansville, Attica, N. Y. (N. Y., L. E., and W.).	6006	65.18
			Attica, Buffalo, N. Y. (N. Y., L. E. and W.).	6008 (part)	(¹⁴)
Danville and Cairo, Ill.........	6	259.03	Danville, Cairo, Ill. (Cairo, Vinc. and Chi.).	33050	261.05
Danville and Stuart, Va........	3	76.16	Danville, Stuart, Va. (Danv. and New River.)	11028	76.52
Danville and Tuscola, Ill	6	51.10	Danville, Tuscola, Ill. (Chi. and East., Ill	23044	50.49
Davenport, Iowa, and Atchison, Kans.	6	337.35	Davenport, Iowa, Altamont, Mo. (Chi., R. Isl'd and Pac).	¹⁷27017 (part)	262.55
			Altamont, Rushville, Mo. (Chi., R.Isl'd and Pac).	28057	65.66
			Rushville, Mo., Atchison, Kans. (Chi., R. Isl'd. and Pac.).	28032 (part)	(¹⁹)

¹ 33.90 miles distance on route 28004, covered by Saint Louis, Moberly, and Kansas City, Mo , R. P. O.

² In reserve.

³ Distance (27 miles) covered by Sioux City, Iowa, and Omaha, Nebr., R. P. O.

⁴ Reserve.

⁵ Covered by Pittsburgh and Chicago R. P. O., 279.50 miles.

⁶ Clerks are appointed to the Pittsburgh and Chicago R. P. O , and are shown with that line.

⁷ One helper out of Saint Joseph runs through three days in the week.

⁸ Balance of route, Minot, Dak., to Great Falls, Mont (550.14 miles), covered by closed pouches. (See Table C⁸.)

⁹ Balance of route (2 miles) covered by closed pouch service. (See Table C⁸.)

in the United States on June 30, 1888—Continued.

Average weight of mail whole distance per day.	Date of last re-adjust-ment.	Average speed per hour (train num-bers taken from di-vision schedules).				Number of round trips with clerks per week.	Annual miles of service with clerks.	Average miles run daily by crews.	Number of mail cars, or cars in which are mail apartments.	Inside dimen-sions of cars or apartments (railway post-office cars in black figures).		Number of crews.	Number of clerks to crew.	Number of clerks ap-pointed to line.
		Train No. outward.	Av'ge speed (miles).	Train No. inward.	Av'ge speed (miles).					Length.	Width.			
Lbs.										*Ft. In.*	*Ft. In.*			
1,330	July 1, 1887	8	23.34	7	24.29	7	192,904	131.75	1	25 8	9 3	4	1	4
2,012	July 1, 1887	8	30.04	7	29.05	7	....	......	1	18 9	9 2½			
9,016	July 1, 1887	8	29.25	7	30.39	7	....	......	2 1	25 6½	9 3			
1,260	July 1, 18▪6	11	21.60	12	23.82	6	46,447	147.92	2 1	19 6½	9 2½			
									1	9 0	7 9½			
300	July 1, 1886	11	23.54	12	22.24		....	......	4 1	11 9	9 4	1	1	1
310	July 1, 1886	8	14.58	81	13.09	6	27,757	88.40	1	11 7	9 4			
27,731	July 1, 1888	1	26.04	12	27.30	6	175,934	149.07	3	10 0	7 6	1	1	1
334	July 1, 1887	71	18.91	72	19.56	6	81,613	190.68	1	24 0	9 0	4	2	(6)
2,370	July 1, 1887	63	30.99	64	29.33	6	65,237	103.88	4 1	11 11	6 9	1	1	1
									1	10 1	6 11			
2,166	July 1, 1887	12	27.78	11	25.83	6	....	......		22 0	9 2	2	1	73
1,367	July 1, 1887	71	20.09	72	18.72	6	145,457	115.81	1	24 7	9 1	4	1	4
441	July 1, 1888	71	18.52	72	21.33	....	....	......	1	24 6	9 0			
									4 1	17 1	8 11			
183	July 1, 1888	2	10.46	1	8.33	6	21,421	68.22	1	10 8	5 6	1	1	1
188	July 1, 1887	51	15.04	52	15.04	6	25,723	81.92	1	10 0	7 0	1	1	1
412	July 1, 1888	1	19.24	4	20.37	6	53,443	170.29	1	8 6	7 0	1	1	1
......		1	16.99	4	18.37									
......		1	18.32	4	17.96									
433	July 1, 1885	2	17.41	1	18.18	6	42,365	134.92	1	10 4	8 0	1	1	1
		4	17.11	3	17.41	6			91	10 0	8 9			
3,200	July 1, 1885	5	27.72	6	30.04	6	94,658	100.48	2	18 2	8 10	3	1	164
735	July 1, 1885	3	18.72	2	18.36	6	29,799	94.90	1	15 0	8 7	1	1	1
69	July 1, 1886	2	14.11	1	13.17	6	31,011	98.76	1	8 0	8 0	1	1	1
395	July 1, 1886	16/ 23}	20.73 {	15/ 34}	16.48 {		68,647	93.78	1	13 10	9 0	2	1	2
									3 1	13 0	9 0			
									2 1	10 6	7 0			
1435	July 1, 1885	5	23.56	8	23.17	6	14,827	94.44	1	11 2	6 0	1	1	1
		15	24.81	18	23.17	6	14,827	......	15 1	10 5	5 9			
1078	July 1, 1885	117	26.07	118	23.41	6	60,275	13127.42	1	14 6	8 0	1	1	1
5787	July 1, 1885	117	23.94	118	23.94	6	....	......	(12)	....	....	(12)		
613	July 1, 1887	1	22.21	2	25.05	6	162,671	129.51	1	19 6	7 9	4	1	165
									1	18 10	7 6			
									4 1	18 0	7 6			
									4 1	13 0	6 10			
193	July 1, 1885	2	14.01	1	14.07	6	47,828	152.32	1	8 6	4 10	1		1
236	July 1, 1888	73	18.93	70	18.38	6	32,090	102.20	1	12 0	7 0	1	1	1
3,017	July 1, 1887	5	24.00	6	23.66	7	246,940	168.67	18 1	41 4	9 4	4	2	8
1,655	July 1, 1887	5	24.00	6	23.30	....	....	......	18 1	39 4	9 4			
693	July 1, 1887	5	20.00	6	18.01									

10 One helper between Pittsburgh and Connells-ville, 57.98 miles; daily (except Saturday and Sunday).
11 Reported last year as Dallas and Cleburne, Tex.; increased distance, 39.68 miles.
12 Reserve car.
13 Clerk alternates with Rochester and Elmira clerks.
14 81.18 miles covered by Hornellsville and Buffalo R. P. O.
15 Cars and clerks shown on route 6006.
16 One clerk detailed to transfer duty at Danville, Ill.
17 Balance of route (69.22 miles) covered by Tren-ton, Mo., and Leavenworth, Kans., R. P. O.
18 Whole cars.
19 Distance (15 miles) covered by Atchison Junc-tion, Mo., and Atchison, Kans., R. P. O.

TABLE A⁵.—*Statement of railway post-offices in operation*

Designation of railway post-offices. (Lines upon which railway post-office cars are paid for, in *italics*.)	Division.	Distance run by clerks, register to register.	Initial and terminal stations, running from east to west, north to south, or northwest to southeast (with abbreviated title of railroad company).	Number of route.	Miles of route for which railroad is paid.
		Miles.			
Dayton and Ironton, Ohio......	5	168.79	Dayton, Ironton, Ohio (Day., Ft. W. and Chic.).	¹21054 (part)	169.19
Dayton, Wash., and Umatilla, Oregon.	8	97.85	Walla Walla, Dayton, Wash. (O. R. and N. Co.).	43008	38.54
			Walla Walla, Wallula, Wash. (Walla Walla and Colo. River R. R.).	42004	32.06
			Umatilla, Oreg., Wallula, Wash. (O. R. and N. Co.).	²44005 (part)	27.29
Decherd and Fayetteville, Tenn.	5	46.28	Decherd,Fayetteville, Tenn. (Nash., Chatt. and St. Louis).	19005	40.41
Decorah and Cedar Rapids, Iowa.	6	122.06	Decorah, Cedar Rapids, Iowa (Bur., C. Rap. and North.).	27002	122.21
Delaware and Columbus, Ohio .	5	25.61	Delaware, Columbus, Ohio (Cleve., Col., Cin. and Ind.).	21013	25.51
Delphos and Dayton, Ohio......	5	96.94	Delphos, Dayton, Ohio (Day., Ft. W. and Chic.).	21039	93.35
Delta, Pa., and Baltimore, Md..	3	47.83	Delta, Pa., Baltimore, Md. (Md. Central) ...	10024	45.56
Deming, N. Mex., and Los Angeles, Cal.	8	715.96	Yuma, Aris., Deming, N. Mex. (Southern Pacific).	40061	467.18
			Los Angeles, Cal., Yuma, Aris. (Southern Pacific).	46014 (part)	248.70
Denison and Houston, Tex	7	337.09	Denison, Houston, Tex. (H. and T. C.).....	³31003	337.09
Denison and San Antonio, Tex.	7	376.63	Denison, Whitesborough, Tex. (Mo. Pac.)..	⁴31022 (part)	25.48
			Whitesborough, Taylor, Tex. (Mo. Pac.)...	⁵31028 (part)	234.05
			Taylor, San Antonio, Tex. (L and G. N.)..	31007 (part)	(⁷)
Denison and Troup, Tex	7	147.51	Denison, Mineola, Tex. (Mo. Pac.)..........	31017	103.19
			Mineola, Troup, Tex. (L and G. N.)........	31032	44.54
Denver and Georgetown, Colo .	7	51.10	Denver, Argo Junction (n. o.), Colo. (Colo. Cent.).	38003 (part)	(¹⁰)
			Argo Junction (n. o.), Georgetown, Colo. (Colo. Cent.).	¹⁰38029 (part)	47.50
Denver and Leadville, Colo ...	7	150.74	Denver, Leadville, Colo. (D., S. P. and P.)...	38005	150.74
Denver, Colo., and Ogden, Utah	7	772.56	Denver, Pueblo, Colo. (D. and R. G.)..:....	38001 (part)	(¹³)
			Pueblo, Salida, Colo. (D. and R. G.).........	38019 (part)	(¹⁴)
			Salida, State Line (n. o.), Colo. (D. and R. G.)..	39012	244.51
			State Line (n. o.), Colo., Ogden, Utah (D. and R. G. W.).	41062	313.82
Denver and Pueblo, Colo.......	7	¹²126.48	Denver, Pueblo, Colo. (D., T. and G.).......	38028	126.48
Denver, Pueblo, and Leadville, Colo.	7	278.52	Denver, Pueblo, Colo. (D. and R. G.).......	¹⁶38001 (part)	120.14
			Pueblo, Leadville, Colo. (D. and R. G.).....	¹⁶38019	161.32
Des Moines and Albia, Iowa ...	6	68.46	Des Moines, Albia, Iowa (Chi., Bur. and Qcy.).	27083	68.81
Des Moines, Iowa, and Cainesville, Mo.	6	116.55	Des Moines, Iowa, Cainesville, Mo. (D. M., Osc. and South.).	27064	112.13
Des Moines and Harvey, Iowa.	6	44.74	Des Moines, Harvey, Iowa (Wabash, Western).	27060	43.52
Des Moines and Keokuk, Iowa	6	163.06	Des Moines, Keokuk, Iowa (Chi., R. Isl'd and Pac.).	27019	163.04

¹ Previous to June 5, 1888, R. P. O. did not run over that part of route between Ironton Junction (n. o.), and Wellston, Ohio, 3 miles. Service performed by closed pouches. (See Table C².)

² 187.56 miles of route 44005 covered by Huntington and Portland R. P. O. Reported last year as Dayton and Wallula extended to Umatilla September 16, from October 3, 1887. One reserve car.

³ 1 acting clerk as helper.

⁴ 1 clerk detailed as assistant chief clerk, Dallas, Tex.

⁵ In reserve.

⁶ 35.84 miles, balance of route 31022, covered by Henrietta and Dallas, Tex., R. P. O.

⁷ 4 helpers between Denison and Taylor, Tex. (258.50 miles.)

⁸ Henrietta and Dallas, Tex., R. P. O.; also runs over 35.70 miles of route 31028, between Whitesborough and Denton, Tex.

⁹ 116.50 miles covered by route 31007 covered by Palestine and Laredo, Tex., R. P. O.

¹⁰ 3.20 miles distance on route 38003, covered by Greeley and Denver, Colo., R. P. O.

in the United States on June 30, 1888—Continued.

Average weight of mail whole distance per day.	Date of last re-adjustment.	Average speed per hour (train numbers taken from division schedules).				Number of round trips with clerks per week.	Annual miles of service with clerks.	Average miles run daily by crews.	Number of mail cars, or cars in which are mail apartments.	Inside dimensions of cars or apartments (railway post-office cars in black figures).		Number of crews.	Number of clerks to crew.	Number of clerks appointed to line.
		Train No outward.	Av'ge speed (miles).	Train No. inward.	Av'ge speed (miles).					Length.	Width.			
Lbs.										*Ft. In.*	*Ft. In.*			
865	July 1, 1888	1	21.14	2	21.36	6	102.520	112.53	2	11 0	8 4	3	1	3
819	July 1, 1886	1	26.57	2	26.21	7	71,626	97.80	2	21 8	8 10	2	1	2
487	June 25,1888	1	22.11	2	25.04									
6,382	Aug.15,1888	1	25.66	2	25.90									
374	July 1, 1888	141	18.65	140	20.40	6	25,296	80.56	1	8 0	6 6	1	1	1
614	July 1, 1887	52	24.44	51	22.91	6	76,653	122.06	2	13 8	9 1	2	1	2
5,662	July 1, 1888	3	30.61	2	31.61	6	16,063	51.22	1	10 2	8 4	1	1	1
293	July 1, 1888	23	8.76	22	8.70	6	60,313	96.04	2	10 0	7 0	2	1	2
345	July 1, 1885	17	15.68	4	16.14	6	30,037	95.66	1	8 0	5 8	1	1	1
4,208	July 1, 1886	19	21.88	20	24.20	7	524,083	178.99	7	27 0	9 5½	8	1	[13]8
3,880	July 1, 1886	19	18.79	20	23.47									
4,393	July 1, 1886	2	27.04	1	25.04	7	246,750	134.84	3	22 0	9 0	5	2	[13]11
									[b]3	22 0	9 0			
3,852	July 1, 1886	507	23.15	504	24.27	7	275,693	125.54	2	22 0	9 6	6	1	[17]10
									1	22 2	9 2			
4,603	July 1, 1886	507	20.76	504	20.98	7	....	....	[b]1	21 9	9 7			
2,030	July 1, 1886	653	21.86	654	24.53	7			1	22 0	9 0			
715	July 1, 1886	601	21.26	602	21.26	7	107,977	147.51	1	22 2	9 1	2	1	2
853	July 1, 1886	657	24.26	658	25.37	7	....	....	1	22 2	9 2			
1,496	July 1, 1886	381	15.00	382	25.00	7	37,405	102.20	1	14 11	7 6	1	1	1
842	July 1, 1886	381	14.18	382	14.71	7			[b]1	16 1	7 5			
1,070	July 1, 1886	401	15.07	402	15.46	7	110,342	100.49	2	15 3	7 7	3	1	[18]4
									1	16 3	7 5			
									[b]1	14 0	7 6			
2,975	July 1, 1886	7	26.11	8	24.76	7	565,514	193.14	2	18 5	7 5	8	1	8
									1	16 0	7 5			
2,714	July 1, 1886	7	25.30	8	25.30	7	....	....	1	18 4	7 5			
									1	19 8	7 5			
1,558	July 1, 1886	7	20.48	8	19.04	7	....	....	[b]2	16 0	8 11			
1,107	July 1, 1886	7	24.21	8	23.29	7								
389	July 1, 1886	1	25.39	2	25.91	7	92,583	126.48	([15])	....		2	1	2
2,975	July 1, 1886	1	26.11	2	26.11	7	203,877	139.26	2	16 0	7 5	4	1	4
									[b]1	16 0	7 5			
2,714	July 1, 1886	1	22.80	2	34.58	7								
1,968	July 1, 1887	32	26.32	31	26.32	7	50,112	68.46	1	17 5	9 0	2	1	2
171	July 1, 1887	1	16.40	2	17.23	6	73,193	116.55	1	8 0	5 2	2	1	2
									1	6 5	5 7½			
485	July 1, 1887	8	26.11	7	22.70	7	32,749	89.48	([16])	....		1	1	1
1,152	July 1, 1887	52	21.50	53	24.15	6	102,414	108.72	3	16 6	9 0	3	1	3

[11] 4.46 miles of route 38020, between Georgetown and Silver Plume, Colo., covered by closed-pouch service. (See Table C².)

[12] 1 clerk detailed to transfer service, Denver, Colo.

[13] 120.14 miles distance on route 38001 covered by Denver, Pueblo and Leadville, Colo., R.P.O.

[14] 96.90 miles distance on route 38019 covered by Denver, Pueblo and Leadville, Colo., R.P.O.

[15] Cars shown under Clarendon and Fort Worth, Tex., R.P.O.

[16] 49.70 miles of route 38001, between Pueblo and Cucharas, Colo., covered by Pueblo and Silverton, Colo., R.P.O., and 87.10 miles, between Cucharas and El Moro, Colo., covered by pouch service. (See Table C².)

[17] Denver, Colo., and Ogden, Utah, R.P.O. also runs over route 38001, between Denver and Pueblo, Colo. (120.14 miles), and over route 38019 between Pueblo and Salida, Colo. (97 miles).

[18] Cars run through between Des Moines, Iowa, and Moberly, Mo. (See Ottumwa, Iowa, and Moberly, Mo., R.P.O.)

TABLE A³.—*Statement of railway post-offices in operation*

Designation of railway post-office. (Lines upon which railway post-office cars are paid for, in *italics*.)	Division.	Distance run by clerks, register to register.	Initial and terminal stations, running from east to west, north to south, or northwest to southeast (with abbreviated title of railroad company).	Number of route.	Miles of route for which railroad is paid.
Des Moines, Iowa, and St. Joseph, Mo.	6	*Miles.* 200.06	Des Moines, Avon, Iowa (Chi., Burl. and Qcy.).	27033 (part)	(¹)
			Avon, Indianola, Iowa (Chi., Burl. and Qcy.).	27092	14.47
			Indianola, Chariton, Iowa (Chi., Burl. and Qcy.).	27042	34.05
			Chariton, Bethany Junction, Iowa (Chi., Burl. and Qcy.).	*27006 (part)	42.68
			Bethany Junction, Iowa, Albany, Mo. (Chi., Burl. and Qcy.).	27061	46.12
			Albany, St. Joseph, Mo. (Chi., Burl. and Qcy.).	28037	43.63
Des Moines and Sioux City, Iowa.	6	238.64	Des Moines, Jewell, Iowa (Chi. and No. West.).	27030	80.02
			Jewell, Wall Lake Junction, Iowa (Chi. and No. West.).	27066	73.50
			Wall Lake Junction, Onawa, Iowa (Chi. and No. West.).	*27028 (part)	64.57
			Onawa, Sioux City, Iowa (S. City and Pac.).	27029 (part)	(²)
Des Moines and Winterset, Iowa.	6	42.90	Des Moines, Summerset Junction, Iowa (Chi., R. Isl'd and Pac.).	*27015 (part)	16.07
			Summerset Junction, Winterset, Iowa (Chi., R. Isl'd and Pac.).	27076	27.70
Detroit, Mich., and Chicago, Ill. ⁷	9	286.09	Detroit, Mich., Chicago, Ill. (Mich. Cent.).	24006	285.10
Detroit and Grand Haven, Mich.	9	188.94	Detroit, Grand Haven, Mich. (D. G. H. and M.).	24027	189.06
Detroit and Grand Rapids, Mich.¹²	9	170.65	Detroit, Jackson, Mich. (Mich. Cent.)......	24006 (part)	(¹⁴)
			Jackson, Grand Rapids, Mich. (Mich. Cent.).	24010	94.72
Detroit, Mich., and Logansport, Ind.¹⁴	9	204.36	Detroit, Mich., Logansport, Ind. (W., St. L. and P.).	22027	204.36
Detroit, Three Rivers, Mich., and Chicago, Ill.	9	274.49	Detroit, Jackson, Mich. (Mich. Cent.)......	24006 (part)	(¹⁴)
			Jackson, Niles, Mich. (Mich. Cent.)	24008	104.30
			Niles, Mich., Chicago, Ill. (Mich. Cent.)	24006 (part)	(¹⁴)
Detroit, Mich., and Toledo, Ohio (day line).	9	60.50	Detroit, Mich., Toledo, Ohio (Mich. Cent.)..	24035	59.50
Detroit, Mich., and Toledo, Ohio (night line).	9	65.90	Detroit, Mich., Toledo, Ohio (L.S. and M.S.).	24001	64.96
DeWitt and Superior, Nebr....	6	85.75	DeWitt, Superior, Nebr. (Nebr. and Colo.)..	34026	85.52
Dickson and Ætna, Tenn.......	5	43.79	Dickson, Ætna, Tenn. (Nash. and Tus.)....	19016	44.28
Dodds and Cincinnati, Ohio	5	36.75	Dodds, Cincinnati, Ohio (Cin., Leb. and North.).	21078	36.20
Downingtown and New Holland, Pa.	2	28.28	Downingtown and New Holland, Pa. (Penna.).	8047	28.29
Downs and Stockton, Kans....	7	42.32	Downs, Alton, Kans. (Cen. Bch. U. P.)....	33029	24.05
			Alton, Stockton, Kans. (Rooks Co.)........	33047	19.07
Dresden and Cincinnati, Ohio..	5	185.47	Dresden, Morrow, Ohio (Cin. and Musk. Val.).	21029	148.73
			Morrow, Cincinnati, Ohio (Pitts., Cin. and St. Louis).	21014	(²⁵)

¹ Distance (7.50 miles) covered by Des Moines and Albia, Iowa, R. P. O.

² One helper between Bethany Junction, Iowa, and Saint Joseph, Mo., 95 miles.

³ Balance of route (44.23) covered by Bethany Junction and Grant City, Mo., R. P. O.

⁴ Balance of route (16.70 miles) covered by Carroll and Moville, Iowa, R. P. O.

⁵ Distance (37.20 miles) covered by Sioux City and Missouri Valley, Iowa, R. P. O.

⁶ Balance of route, Summerset Junction to Indianola, Iowa (6.47 miles) covered by closed pouches. (See Table C⁴.)

Double service trains 2 and 3 daily, except Sunday; trains 9 and 16 daily.

⁸ 1 car held in reserve.

⁹ 4 clerks detailed to the Detroit, Three Rivers, and Chicago R. P. O.; 2 clerks detailed as transfer clerks at Detroit, Mich.; 1 clerk detailed as transfer clerk at Jackson, Mich.; 1 clerk detailed as transfer clerk at Michigan City, Ind.; 2 clerks assigned as helpers between Detroit and Battle Creek, Mich., on trains 9 and 16; 2 clerks assigned as helpers on trains 2 and 3, between Chicago, Ill., and Kalamazoo, Mich.; 1 clerk detailed as chief clerk at Detroit, Mich.

¹⁰ 1 car held in reserve.

¹¹ 1 clerk detailed as transfer clerk, Detroit, Mich.;

in the United States on June 30, 1888—Continued.

Average weight of mail whole distance per day.	Date of last re-adjustment.	Train No. outward.	Av'ge speed (miles).	Train No. inward.	Av'ge speed (miles).	Number of round trips with clerks per week.	Annual miles of service with clerks.	Average miles run daily by crews.	Number of mail cars, or cars in which are mail apartments.	Length.	Width.	Number of crews.	Number of clerks to crew.	Number of clerks appointed to line.
Lbs.										Ft. In.	Ft. In.			
1,968	July 1,1887	41	22.50	42	22.50	6	125,637	100.03	1	22 8	8 9½	4	1	²5
1,959	July 1,1887	41	24.80	42	28.94	....	....	....	1	20 0½	9 1			
1,997	July 1,1887	41	22.67	42	22.67									
991	July 1,1887	41	27.10	42	22.08									
1,017	July 1,1887	41	30.74	42	23.06									
1,110	July 1,1887	41	24.81	42	24.81									
2,398	July 1,1887	54	22.50	57	21.18	6	149,866	119.32	1	24 2	7 3	4	1	4
934	July 1,1887	13	26.00	12	28.45	....	....	....	1	24 0	9 3			
1,163	July 1,1887	13	23.48	12	22.79									
7,209	July 1,1887	9	29.76	10	29.76									
643	July 1,1887	33	18.54	34	21.43	6	26,941	85.80	1	9 0	7 0	1	1	1
599	July 1,1887	33	24.44	34	19.55									
16,713	July 1,1884	3	30.05	2	20.28	6	180,041	122.86	¹³3	45 0	10 0	4	2	³37
		9	30.05	16	30.59	7	209,857	143.31	8	51	10 0	4	4	
3,038	July 1,1884	3	22.91	6	23.87	6	116,654	94.47	10	22 8	9 1	4	1	¹¹8
		12¹	35.29	12⁸	34.92	6	98,910	157.50		23 1	9 0	2	1	
16,713	July 1,1884	15	26.72	14	33.64	6	} 107,168	113.76 {		15 6	10 0	3	1	}
1,958	July 1,1884	107	30.45	102	34.14	6			1	15 6	10 0	....	...	5
		105	29.19	104	32.19	6	59,484	94.72	1	16 10	8 5	2	1	
1,035	July 1,1888	51	28.43	52	24.60	6	128,838	136.24	2	17 10	9 2	3	1	3
16,713	July 1,1884	11	28.75	4	26.72	6	....	....	1	18 0	9 0			
834	July 1,1884	61	26.97	62	28.20	6	} 172,380	137.24	1	18 0	9 0	} 4	1	(¹⁸)
16,713	July 1,1884	11	25.29	4	25.63	6								
543	July 1.1884	301	32.34	306	30.94	6	37,994	121.00	1	12 1	8 8	1	1	1
4,634	July 1,1884	¹⁷101	27.81	130	12.68	6	37,994	131.80	1	36 0	9 4	1	1	1
441	Mar.30,1887	97	24.43	98	34.43	6	53,851	171.50	1	12 0	9 0	1	1	1
241	July 1,1888	61	10.26	62	10.85	6	27,500	87.58	1	6 6	7 0	1	1	1
337	July 1,1888	8	18.10	1	18.10	6	23,079	73.50	¹²2	8 0	6 0	1	1	1
303	July 1,1885	253	8.27	250	15.01	6	17,760	56.56	1	6 6	6 5	1	1	1
543	July 1,1886	411	23.39	412	22.91	7	30,978	(¹⁹)	1	22 6	9 1	¹⁹1	1	1
432	July 1,1886	411	22.38	412	22.86	7								
1,042	July 1,1888	11	29.75	12	26.34	6	116,475	133.61	3	18 0	8 0	5	1	5
24,079	July 1,1888	7	27.90	6	27.18	²⁰6	93,296							
		11	20.76	12	22.92	6	......	......	²²4	18 11	8 9			

1 clerk detailed as helper between Detroit and Durand, Mich. (67 miles).

¹² Clerks on trains 1 and 8 run only between Detroit and Grand Rapids, Mich. (157.50 miles), giving, in connection with trains 3 and 6, double service between these points daily, except Sunday.

¹³ Double service between Jackson and Grand Rapids, Mich. (94.72 miles), daily, except Sunday.

¹⁴ Shown in report of Detroit and Chicago R. P. O.

¹⁵ Order July 21, 1887, extending run to end at Logansport, Ind., increase distance 16.49 miles.

¹⁶ Clerks appointed to Detroit and Chicago R. P. O.

¹⁷ On trips eastward this clerk takes charge of registered matter. Local service performed by the day line.

¹⁸ One car in reserve.

¹⁹ Service on this line is performed by Downs and Stockton, clerk in connection with three clerks of the Atchison and Lenora, Kans., R. P. O.

²⁰ Clerks make 12 round trips per week between Dresden and Morrow; 6 trips reside.

²¹ Covered by Pittsburgh and Cincinnati R. P. O., 36.30 miles.

²² Two cars in reserve.

TABLE A*.—*Statement of railway post-offices in operation*

Designation of railway post-office. (Lines upon which railway post-office cars are paid for, in *italics*.)	Division.	Distance run by clerks, register to register.	Initial and terminal stations, running from east to west, north to south, or northwest to southeast (with abbreviated title of railroad company).	Number of route.	Miles of route for which railroad is paid.
		Miles.			
Driftwood, Pa., and Red Bank Furnace, Pa.	2	109.96	Driftwood, Pa., Red Bank Furnace, Pa. (A. V.)	8076	109.91
Dubuque, Iowa, and Mendota, Ill.	6	132.39	Dubuque, Iowa, Mendota, Ill. (Ill. Cent.)..	*26021 (part)	131.79
Dubuque and Sioux City, Iowa	6	327.64	Dubuque, Sioux City, Iowa (Illinois Central)	27021	327.70
Duluth and Brainerd, Minn....	6	114.67	Duluth, Brainerd, Minn. (North. Pac.)	26011	114.29
Duluth, Minn., and Eau Claire, Wis.	6	160.80	Duluth, Minn., Superior Junction, Wis. (C., St. P., Minn. and Om.).	25051	70.83
			Superior Junction, Chicago Junction, Wis. (C., St. P., Minn. and Om.).	25028 (part)	(*)
			Chicago Junction, Eau Claire, Wis. (C., St. P., Minn. and Om.).	25048	81.85
Duluth and St. Paul, Minn	6	151.83	Duluth, St. Paul, Minn. (St. Paul and Dul.).	26007	151.83
Dundee Junction (n. o.) and Airlie, Oregon.[8]	8	52.86	Dundee Junction, Airlie, Oregon (Oreg. Rwy. Co. Limited Line).	44008	52.60
Dunkirk, N. Y., and Titusville, Pa.	2	91.41	Dunkirk, N. Y., and Titusville, Pa. (D., A. V. and P.).	6019	91.28
Dunlap, Tenn., and Bridgeport, Ala.[11]	5	50.03	Dunlap, Victoria, Tenn. (Nash., Chatt. and St. Louis).	19025	19.14
			Victoria, Tenn., Bridgeport, Ala. (Nash., Chatt. and St. Louis).	[13]19012	19.53
Du Pont, Ga., and Gainesville, Fla.	4	119.27	Du Pont, Ga., Gainesville, Fla. (S. F. and W. Rwy.).	15036	119.27
Dwight and Washington, Ill...	6	70.13	Dwight, Washington, Ill. (Chi. and Alton).	23019	70.12
East Lynne and Brownington, Mo.[16]	7	45.40	East Lynne, Brownington, Mo. (K. C. and S.).	28053	45.40
Easton and Hazleton, Pa.).[16]...	2	69.18	Easton, Pa., Penn Haven Junction, Pa. (L. V.).	8010 (part)	(*[17])
			Penn Haven Junction, Pa., Hazleton, Pa. (L. V.).	8016 (part)	[21]14.80
East Saginaw and Howard City, Mich.	9	81.51	East Saginaw, Alma, Mich. (D., L. and N.).	[22]24030 (part)	38.78
			Alma, Howard City, Mich. (D., L. and N.)..	24041	42.73
East Saginaw and Port Huron, Mich.[23]	9	92.06	East Saginaw, Zion, Mich. (Pt. H. and N. W.).	24025	78.85
			Zion, Port Huron, Mich. (Pt. H. and N. W).	24043 (part)	(*[26])
Eatonton and Gordon, Ga......	4	38.73	Eatonton, Gordon, Ga. (Cent. R. R. of Ga.).	15014	38.53
Eau Claire, Wis., and Wabasha, Minn.	6	49.40	Eau Claire, Wis., Wabasha, Minn. (Chi., Mil. and St. P.).	25047	49.27
Edgar and Curtis, Nebr	6	154.30	Edgar, Holdrege, Nebr. (Nebr. and Colo.) .	34043	81.11
			Holdrege, Elwood, Nebr. (Nebr. and Colo.) .	34031	28.72
			Elwood, Curtis, Nebr. (Nebr. and Colo.)....	[29]34042 (part)	44.32

[1] In reserve.
[2] Balance of route (211.48 miles) covered by Mendota and Centralia, Ill., R. P. O.
[3] One helper between Freeport and Mendota, Ill.
[4] Day line.
[5] Night line.
[6] Two helpers on day line between Dubuque and Ackley, Iowa; two helpers on night line between Dubuque and Ackley, Iowa; one clerk detailed to transfer duty at Sioux City, Iowa.
[7] Reserve.
[8] Distance (8.20 miles) covered by Ashland, Wis., Saint Paul, Minn., R. P. O.
[9] R. P. O. service established June 20; commenced July 1, 1887.

[10] Clerk alternates with Larabee and Clermont clerk in Buffalo and Emporium R. P. O., as helper.
[11] September 19, 1887, Inman and Bridgeport R.P.O. curtailed to end at Cheekville, Tenn., decrease in distance 0.57 mile. February 20, 1888, Cheekville and Bridgeport R. P. O. extended to Dunlap, Tenn.; increase, 14.41 miles.
[12] Balance of route Inman to Victoria, Tenn., 5.30 miles, covered by closed pouches.
[13] Commencing April 9, 1888, clerks make extra trips on trains 81 and 82 between Bridgeport, Ala., and Jasper, Tenn.; distance, 12 miles.
[14] One car in reserve.
[15] New service; not reported last year.

In the United States on June 30, 1888—Continued.

Average weight of mail whole distance per day.	Date of last re-adjust-ment.	Train No. outward.	Av'ge speed (miles).	Train No. inward.	Av'ge speed (miles).	Number of round trips with clerks per week.	Annual miles of service with clerks.	Average miles run daily by crews.	Number of mail cars, or cars in which are mail apartments.	Length.	Width.	Number of crews.	Number of clerks to crew.	Number of clerks appointed to line.
Lbs.										*Ft. In.*	*Ft. In.*			
584	July 1, 1885	2	18.85	1	19.75	6	69,067	109.98	1	17 6	8 9	2	1	2
									1	18 0	8 10			
									1¹	14 8	8 5			
4,579	July 1, 1887	5	22.29	4	24.75	6	83,141	132.39	1	27 6	9 0	2	●1	²3
3,922	July 1, 1887	4	22.81	3	23.36	6	205,758	131.05	2	35 4	9 0	⁴5	1	⁶15
		2	23.08	1	24.52	6	205,758	131.95	3	30 0	9 0	⁴5	1	
									1	30 4	9 0			
									⁷1	30 2	9 0			
477	July 1, 1887	7	22.80	8	20.00	6	72,012	229.34	1	22 0	7 2	1	1	1
									⁷1	17 6	9 4			
666	July 1, 1887	91	25.00	92	24.28	6	100,962	160.80	2	22 2	9 4	2	1	2
1,142	July 1, 1887	91	9.84	92	9.84									
886	July 1, 1887	91	22.32	92	25.84									
1,883	July 1, 1887	2	20.70	1	21.69	6	95,349	101.22	2	22 0	8 6	3	1	3
									⁷1	23 0	9 4			
....	....	1	10.01	2	9.83	6	83,196	105.72	2	21 0	7 6	1	1	1
605	July 1, 1885	1	21.93	4	24.37	6	57,405	106.80	1	15 6	6 6	¹⁰2	1	2
									1	13 0	7			
25	July 1, 1888	80	19.14	83	15.31	6	20,139	100.06	¹⁴2	8 0	6 0	1	1	1
104	July 1, 1888	80	19.53	83	16.80	6								
		82	14.40	81	16.86	¹³6								
1,313	July 1, 1888	59	23.6	60	23.4	7	87,305	119.27	1	18 0	9 3	2	1	2
307	July 1, 1887	122	23.37	121	23.37	6	44,041	140.26	1	13 10	9 5	1	1	1
96	Apr. 17, 1888	2	20.64	1	14.64	6	28,511	90.80	1	10 0	6 8¼	1	1	1
									1	7 0	6 9			
3,459	July 1, 1885	¹⁰2	25.93	7	23.71	6	43,445	97.96	1	13 1	10 0	2	1	¹⁹5
		18	23.58	3	23.71	6	43,445	......	1	13 9	10 0			
		6	24.81	21	28.14	6	²⁰28,574	......	1	15 0	10 0	2	1	
645	July 1, 1885	2	22.20	7	17.76	6	....	......	1	14 7½	10 0			
		18	21.65	3	17.76	6	....	......	1	21 10	10 0			
									1¹	14 9½	10 0			
527	July 1, 1884	17	24.12	20	22.92	6	} 51,188	108.68	1	20 0	8 10			
443	July 1, 1884	13	24.34	20	26.90	6								
248	July 1, 1884	5	24.68	8	23.12	6			²²1	8 9	5 7	²⁴1	1	1
575	July 1, 1884	5	21.82	8	18.00	6	57,814	138.09	1	11 0	6 0	1	1	²⁷2
154	July 1, 1884	22	14.6	21	14.6	6	24,322	77.46	1	15 2	8 9	1	1	1
682	July 1, 1887	4	22.61	3	22.61	6	31,023	98.80	1	18 5	9 1	1	1	1
195	Feb. 21, 1887	101	15.45	102	15.95	6	96,900	154.30	1	9 0	8 3	2	1	2
122	July 1, 1886	151	29.20	152	28.25	....	......	......	1	14 0	9 0			
211	Feb. 21, 1887	151	29.20	152	28.25	....	......	......		14 0	7 0			

16 Short run, New York and Elmira R. P. O.

17 52.50 miles covered by New York and Elmira R. P. O.

18 Service performed in New York and Elmira R. P. O.

19 One helper, Easton and Hazleton.

20 Double daily service except Sunday, and an additional run to Mauch Chunk and return (45.50 miles).

21 8.80 miles covered by Hazleton and Sunbury R. P. O.

22 Remainder of route (7.20 miles), Alma to Ithaca, Mich., covered by closed-pouch service. (See Table C⁴.)

23 One car held in reserve.

24 One clerk appointed to the Ludington and Toledo R. P. O. alternates between this line and the Manistee and East Saginaw R. P. O.

25 Runs on route 24042, Zion to Port Huron, Mich. (12.75 miles).

26 Shown in report of Port Austin and Port Huron R. P. O

27 One clerk alternates between the East Saginaw and Port Huron, Fort Gratiot and Detroit, and Port Austin and Port Huron R. P. O's.

28 Balance of route (158.34 miles) covered by Curtis, Nebr., and Sterling, Colo., closed pouch service. (See Table C⁵.)

29 One in reserve.

TABLE A².—*Statement of railway post-offices in operation*

Designation of railway post-office. (Lines upon which railway post-office cars are paid for, in *italics*.)	Division	Distance run by clerks, register to register.	Initial and terminal stations, running from east to west, north to south, or northwest to southeast (with abbreviated title of railroad company).	Number of route.	Miles of route for which railroad is paid.
		Miles.			
Egan, Dak., and Sioux City, Iowa.	6	125.98	Egan, Sioux Falls, Dak. (Chi., Mil. and St. P.).	¹35007 (part)	54.91
			Sioux Falls, Elk Point, Dak. (Chi., Mil. and St. P.).	27034	70.61
			Elk Point, Dak., Sioux City, Iowa (Chi., Mil. and St. P.).	35001 (part)	(²)
Elba and Rocky Mount, Va.....	3	37.26	Elba, Rocky Mount. Va. (Rich. and Dan.).	11022	37.47
Elloree and Pregnalls, S. C	4	32.78	Elloree, Pregnalls, S. C., (Eutawville R. R.).	14022	33.75
Ellsworth and Wichita, Kans⁴..	7	106.61	Ellsworth, Wichita, Kans. (St. L. and S. F.).	33087	106.61
Elmira, N. Y., and Blossburgh, Pa.	2	52.41	Elmira, N. Y., Blossburgh, Pa. (N. Y., L. E. and W.).	8028 (part)	⁶49.35
Elmira, N. Y., and Wilkes Barre, Pa.⁶	2	124.13	Elmira, Waverly, N. Y. (N. Y., L. E. and W.).	6001 (part)	(⁷)
			Waverly N. Y., Wilkes Barre, Pa. (L. V.)..	8010 (part)	(¹¹)
Elmira, N. Y., and Williamsport, Pa.	2	79.13	Elmira, N. Y., Williamsport, Pa. (N. C.)...	8021	78.81
Emporia and Moline, Kans	7	85.31	Emporia, Howard, Kans. (A., T. and S. F.).	33032	77.65
			Howard, Moline, Kans. (K. C., E. and S.)..	33064	8.76
Erie and Pittsburgh, Pa.......	2	148.00	Erie, Kenwood, Pa. (E. and P.)............	8044	119.29
			Kenwood, Pittsburgh, Pa. (P., F. W. and C.)..	21002 (part)	(¹⁵)
Essex Junction, Vt., and Boston, Mass.	,1	241.86	Essex Junction, Bellows Falls, Vt. (Ct. Ver.).	2003	127.97
			Bellows Falls, Vt., Fitchburg, Mass. (Cheshire.)	3055	64.60
			Fitchburg, Boston, Mass. (Fitch.)..........	¹²3021 (part)	(²²)
Evansville, Ind., and Providence, Ky.²¹	5	75.48	Evansville, Ind., Madisonville, Ky. (Louis. and Nash.).	22032 (part)	(²²)
			Madisonville, Providence, Ky. (Louis. and Nash.).	20031	16.70
Fairbury, Nebr., and Norton, Kans.⁷	7	162.77	Fairbury, Nebr., Norton, Kans. (C., K. and N.).	34050	162.77
Fairland and Martinsville, Ind.	5	37.83	Fairland, Martinsville, Ind. (Fair., Frank and Martins.).	22016	38.35
Fairmont and Chester, Nebr ..	6	48.00	Fairmont, Hebron, Nebr. (B. and M. R., in Nebr.).	34034	36.45
			Hebron, Chester, Nebr. (Nebr. and Colo.).	34034	12.20
Fargo, Dak., Barnesville and St. Paul, Minn.	6	243.38	Fargo, Dak., Barnesville, Minn. (St. P., Minn. and Man.).	26005 (part)	(²⁴)
			Barnesville, St. Cloud, Minn. (St. P., Minn. and Man.).	26004 (part)	(²⁵)
			St. Cloud, Minneapolis, Minn. (St. P., Minn. and Man.).	26040 (part)	(²⁶)
			Minneapolis, St. Paul, Minn. (St. P., Minn. and Man.).	26006 (part)	(²⁷)
Fargo and La Moure, Dak.....	6	88.15	Fargo, La Moure, Dak. (North. Pac.).......	²⁸35015 (part)	88.10
Fargo and Minnewaukon, Dak.	6	183.25	Fargo, Jamestown, Dak. (North. Pac.)....	26001 (part)	(²⁹)
			Jamestown, Minnewaukon, Dak. (North. Pac.).	35016	90.25
Farley and Cedar Rapids, Iowa	6	57.81	Farley, Cedar Rapids, Iowa (Chi., Mil. and St. Paul).	27020	57.87

¹ Balance of route (4.60 miles) covered by La Crosse, Wis., and Woonsocket, Dak., R. P. O.
² Distance (20.82 miles) covered by Manilla, Iowa, and Mitchell, Dak., R. P. O.
³ Reserve.
⁴ New service; not reported last year.
⁵ Clerks run in the order of two weeks on and one off. One clerk alternates between this line and the Wichita and Kanopolis, Kans., R. P. O.
⁶ 15.59 miles covered by closed-pouch service. (See Table C².)
⁷ Double daily service except Sunday, between Tioga Junction and Lawrenceville, 3.20 miles.

⁸ Short run New York and Elmira. R. P. O.
⁹ 17.54 miles covered by New York and Dunkirk R. P. O.
¹⁰ Cars and clerks shown in New York and Elmira R. P. O.
¹¹ 105 miles covered by New York and Elmira R. P. O.
¹² In reserve.
¹³ Clerk alternates with Canandaigua and Elmira clerk.
¹⁴ One clerk detailed as transfer clerk at Erie, Pa.
¹⁵ 28.35 miles covered by Pittsburgh and Chicago R. P. O.

in the United States on June 30, 1888—Continued.

Average weight of mail whole distance per day.	Date of last re-adjust-must.	Average speed per hour (train numbers taken from division schedules).				Number of round trips with clerks per week.	Annual miles of service with clerks.	Average miles run daily by crews.	Number of mail cars, or cars in which are mail apartments.	Inside dimensions of cars or apartments (railway post-office cars in black figures).		Number of crews.	Number of clerks crew.	Number of clerks appointed to line.
		Train No. outward.	Av'ge speed (miles).	Train No. inward.	Av'ge speed (miles).					Length.	Width.			
Lbs.										Ft. In.	Ft. In.			
404	July 1, 1886	2	27.22	1	26.18	6	78,738	125.38	1	20 0	9 3	2	1	2
998	July 1, 1887	2	26.48	1	27.33	....			1	16 0	6 11			
838	Mar. 30, 1887	4	24.96	1	24.96	....			*1	20 3	9 2	a		
128	July 1, 1885	50	12.33	51	10.57		23,399	74.52	1	5 3	5 1	1	1	1
212	July 1, 1888	4	14	1	16.2	12	42,377	134.96	1	8 3	6 3	1	1	1
		2	12.7	3	18.2									
164	July 1, 1888	2	23.13	1	23.13	7	78,039	139.20	1	12 1	7 4	2	1	2
588	July 1, 1885	103	19.05	106	20.55	6	732,913	104.82	1	15 9	6 7	1	1	1
12,297	July 1, 1885	9	32.88	30	26.31	6	77,954	248.26	(16)	....	....	1	1	(16)
3459	July 1, 1885	9	34.05	30	24.70	6			(16)	....	....	(16)		
3039	July 1, 1885	6	27.92	3	25.66	6	49,694	98.87	2	15 0	8 6	2	1	192
									*1	15 0	8 6			
281	July 1, 1886	271	21.09	272	23.23	7	62,447	170.62	1	11 1	6 1	1	1	1
265	Feb. 21, 1887	271	16.20	272	10.80	7								
1,305	July 1, 1885	24	24.24	21	25.09	6	92,944	96.66	2	17 3	9 0	3	1	144
									1	20 0	9 6			
23,000	July 1, 1885	24	22.68	21	22.68	6			1	20 7	9 0			(16)
4,099	July 1, 1885	53	24.72	82	24.72	6	151,888	120.93	1	23 9	6 10	4	2	179
									1	24 2	6 10			
3,374	July 1, 1885	53	28.87	82	28.23				192	24 0	6 10			
6,568	July 1, 1885	53	31.32	82	31.99									
4,071	July 1, 1887	69	23.28	70	22.96	6	9,510	150.96	2	11 0	7 0	1	1	1
		69	9.54	70	9.38	6			*1	8 0	5 6			
382	July 1, 1888	9	22.91	10	22.91	7	119,148	106.51	2	14 6	7 2	3	1	3
180	July 1, 1888	41	11.22	40	9.96	6	23,757	75.66	1	12 6	7 0	1	1	1
353	Mar. 30, 1887	105	17.08	106	20.83	6	30,144	96.00	1	8 6	7 4	1	1	1
159	July 1, 1887	105	19.78	106	24.40									
2,863	July 1, 1887	2	26.77	1	29.45	6	152,902	121.69	2	24 7	9 3	4	1	4
4,496	July 1, 1887	2	23.32	1	23.96				*1	24 6	9 4			
6,586	July 1, 1887	2	26.82	1	26.82									
4,937	July 1, 1887	2	25.63	1	18.31									
408	July 1, 1886	33	21.19	34	20.55	6	55,358	176.30	1	17 6	7 7	1	1	1
	....	3	23.25	4	21.88	6	115,081	133.16	1	24 6	9 1	2	1	3
	....	53	21.23	54	22.10	....			1	24 0	8 10			
408	July 1, 1886	20	19.29	19	18.28	6	36,304	115.62	1	18 1	7 7	1	1	1

[16] Clerk shown on route 9044.
[17] One clerk detailed as transfer clerk, Rutland, Vt.
[18] Reserve cars.
[19] Balance of route covered by Boston and Troy R. P. O., 55.80 miles.
[20] Covered by Boston and Troy R. P. O., 49.60 miles.
[21] R. P. O. service established April 19, 1888.
[22] Covered by Nashville and St. Louis R. P. O. (58.29 miles).
[23] 1 car in reserve.
[24] Distance (24.54 miles) covered by Neche, Dak., and St. Paul, Minn., R. P. O.
[25] Distance (143.79 miles) covered by Boundary Line and St. Paul, Minn., R. P. O.
[26] Distance (64.81 miles) covered by Boundary Line and St. Paul, Minn., R. P. O.
[27] Distance (10.68 miles) covered by Neche, Dak., and St. Paul, Minn., R. P. O
[28] Balance of route, La Moure to Edgeley, Dak. (21.90 miles), covered by closed-pouch service (See Table C*.)
[29] Distance (93 miles) covered by St. Paul, Minn., and Mandan, Dak., R. P. O.

TABLE A⁸.—*Statement of railway post-offices in operation*

Designation of railway post-office. (Lines upon which railway post-office cars are paid for, in *italics*.)	Division.	Distance run by clerks, register to register.	Initial and terminal stations. running from east to west, north to south, or northwest to southeast (with abbreviated title of railroad company).	Number of route.	Miles of route for which railroad is paid.
		Miles.			
Farmington and Lewiston, Me.	1	47.12	Farmington, Leeds Junction, Me. (Me. Cen.).	¹3 (part)	26.30
			Leeds Junction, Lewiston, Me. (Me. Cen.)..	²5 (part)	(³)
Fernandina and Orlando, Fla...	4	210.05	Fernandina, Waldo, Fla. (F. R. and N. Co.).	16001 (part)	⁴84.15
			Waldo, Tavares, Fla. (F. R. and N. Co.) ..	16011	94.45
			Tavares, Orlando, Fla. (T. O. and A. R. R.)	16022	32.95
Flomaton, Ala., and Pensacola, Fla.	4	44.84	Flomaton, Ala., Pensacola, Fla. (Louis. and Nash. R. R.).	18003	44.84
Florence and Arkansas City, Kans.⁶	7	87.49	Florence, Winfield, Kans. (A., T. and S. F.)	33017	75.03
			Winfield, Arkansas City, Kans. (A., T. and S. F.).	33011 (part)	(⁷)
Florence, S. C., and Augusta, Ga.	4	164.37	Florence, Columbia, S. C. (W. C. and A. R. R.).	14002 (part)	⁸63
			Columbia, S. C., Augusta, Ga. (Rich. and Dan. R. R.).	13007	(⁹)
Florence and Ellinwood, Kans .	7	99.01	Florence, Ellinwood, Kans. (A., T. and S. F.).	33030	99.01
Fonda and Des Moines, Iowa ..	6	115.17	Fonda, Des Moines, Iowa (Wabash Western).	27046	115.11
Fond du Lac and Milwaukee, Wis.	6	64.18	Fond du Lac, Milwaukee, Wis. (Chi. and No. West.).	25012	64.12
Forreston and Aurora, Ill......	6	81.58	Forreston, Aurora, Ill. (Chi. and Iowa)	23036	81.60
Fort Branch and Mt. Vernon, Ind.	5	39.37	Fort Branch, Mt. Vernon, Ind. (Evans. and T. H.).	23039	38.75
Fort Gratiot, Mich., and Chicago, Ill.	9	337.73	Fort Gratiot, Mich., Chicago, Ill. (C. and G. T.).	24039	338.46
Fort Gratiot and Detroit, Mich	9	61.34	Fort Gratiot, Detroit, Mich. (Grand Trunk)	24028	60.84
Fort Howard, Wis., and Chicago, Ill.	6	243.33	Fort Howard, Wis., Chicago, Ill. (Chi. and No. West.).	25009	242.47
Fort Howard, Wis., and Winona, Minn.	6	215.40	Ft. Howard, Wis., Winona, Minn. (G. Bay, Win. and St. P.).	25027	214.88
Fort Madison, Iowa, and Kansas City, Mo.¹⁷	7	218.27	Fort Madison, Iowa, Kansas City, Mo. (C., S. F. and C.).	¹⁸23098 (part)	218
Fort Scott and Kiowa, Kans ...	7	243.87	Fort Scott, Anthony, Kans. (Ft. S., W. and W.)	23036	214.48
			Anthony, Kiowa, Kans. (Ft. S., W. and W.).	33073	30.43
Fort Scott, Kans., and Webb City, Mo.¹⁹	7	83.32	Fort Scott, Kans., Webb City, Mo. (K. C., Ft. S. and M.).	¹⁹23008 (part)	82.90
Fort Smith, Ark., and Leland, Miss.²²	7	305.70	Fort Smith, Little Rock, Ark. (St. L., I. M. and S.).	29003	168
			Little Rock, Arkansas City, Ark. (St. L., I. M. and S.).	²⁴29007	112.75
			Arkansas City, Ark., Leland, Miss. (L., N. O. and T.).	18020	24.16
Fort Smith and Mansfield, Ark.¹⁷	7	32.32	Fort Smith, Jenson, Ark. (St. L. and S. F.).	29019 (part)	(²⁵)
			Jenson, Mansfield, Ark. (St. L. and S. F.).	29024	18.23
Fort Wayne, Ind., and Cincinnati, O.	5	178.81	Ft. Wayne, Beeson's, Ind. (Ft. W., Cin. and Lou.).	²⁷22020 (part)	104.94
			Beeson's, Harrison, Ind. (White Water)....	²⁸21031 (part)	48.91
			Harrison, Ind., Valley Junction, Ohio (Cin. Ind., St. L. and Chi.).	21071	7.40
			Valley Junction, Cincinnati, Ohio (Cin. Ind., St. L. and Chi.).	22003 (part)	(²⁹)

¹ Balance of route covered by Bath and Lewiston R. P. O. (15.03 miles), and closed-pouch service between Leeds Junction and Lewiston (16.32 miles). (See Table C⁸.)

² Balance of route covered by Skowhegan and Portland R. P. O. (92.27 miles).

³ Covered by Skowhegan and Portland R. P. O. (10 66 miles.)

⁴ 71 miles reported as Waldo and Cedar Keys R. P. O.

⁵ 1 reserve car.

⁶ Reported last year as Florence and Winfield, Kans.; increased distance, 12.46 miles.

⁷ 13.18 miles, distance on route 33011, covered by Newton, Kans., and Gainesville, Tex., R. P. O.

⁸ 110 miles shown as Wilmington and Jacksonville R. P. O.

⁹ Reported as Charlotte and Augusta R. P. O.

¹⁰ In reserve.

¹¹ Reserve.

¹² 1 car held in reserve.

¹³ 1 clerk runs as helper between Fort Gratiot and Battle Creek, Mich. (159.73 miles.)

¹⁴ This clerk has relief every fourth week by clerk appointed to the East Saginaw and Pt. Huron R. P. O.

¹⁵ Two clerks detailed to register transfer duty at Chicago, Ill.

¹⁶ One in reserve.

¹⁷ New service; not reported last year.

¹⁸ 236.82 miles of route 23098, between Chicago. Ill., and Fort Madison, Iowa, covered by Chicago, Ill., and Fort Madison, Iowa, R. P. O.

in the United States on June 30, 1888—Continued.

Average weight of mail whole distance per day.	Date of last re-adjustment.	Average speed per hour (train numbers taken from division schedules).				Number of round trips with clerks per week.	Annual miles of service with clerks.	Average miles run daily by crews.	Number of mail cars, or cars in which are mail apartments.	Inside dimensions of cars or apartments (railway post-office cars in black figures).		Number of crews.	Number of clerks to crew.	Number of clerks apointed to line.
		Train No. outward.	Av'ge speed (miles).	Train No. inward.	Av'ge speed (miles).					Length.	Width.			
Lbs.										*Ft. In.*	*Ft. In.*			
870	July 1, 1885	56	19. 27	67	20. 54	6	29, 591	94. 24	1	14 6	6 6	1	1	1
1, 521	Feb. 11, 1885	56	14. 92	67	11. 67									
883	July 1, 1888	7	19. 3	8	20	7	153, 756	105. 02	2	22 0	8 9	4	1	4
1, 344	July 1, 1888	7	21. 5	8	25. 1									
593	Oct. 15, 1885	7	27. 6	8	26. 6									
1, 038	July 1, 1884	5	14. 4	6	17. 3	6	28, 159	80. 68	1 2 1	14 0 10 0	9 2 9 0	1	1	1
211	Mar. 30, 1887	425	21. 67	426	21. 67	7	64, 043	174. 98	1	12 0	7 3½	1	1	1
1, 201	July 1, 1886	425	19. 20	426	19. 20	7								
8, 664	July 1, 1888	50	23. 1	51	23	7	120, 318	109. 58	1 1	34 0 20 4	9 2 9 1	3	1	3
2, 642	July 1, 1888	50	23. 1	51	23. 1									
624	July 1, 1886	334	19. 09	337	23. 22	7	72, 475	90. 01	1 16 1	13 4½ 13 0	5 3½ 7 7	2	1	2
435	July 1, 1887	2	19. 19	1	17. 97	6	72, 326	115. 17	2 11 1	14 1 15 6	7 10 7 9	2	1	2
6, 119	July 1, 1887	6	29. 54	5	28. 44	6	46, 305	128. 36	1	12 8	9 2	1	1	1
5, 877	July 1, 1887	10	25. 50	1	25. 11	6	51, 232	81. 58	2	8 0	9 0	2	1	2
187	July 1, 1888	27	12. 92	28	12. 92	6	24, 724	78. 74	1	6 0	9 6	1	1	1
811	July 1, 1884	4	29. 56	1	24. 97	6	212, 094	168. 86	12 3	20 0	8 8	4	1	14 5
....	July 1, 1887	4 106	25. 18 23. 05	1 105	26. 11 23. 23	6 6	38, 52? 152, 811	92. 01 121. 66	1 2	23 0 50 0	9 0 9 5	1 4	1 2	14 1 15 10
7, 499														
590	July 1, 1887	1	19. 68	2	19. 68	6	135, 271	107. 79	16 4	17 3	7 4	3	1	3
....		3	20. 37	4	19. 38	7	159, 774	145. 51	2 16 2	26 3 23 7½	9 4 8 11	3	1	3
722	July 1, 1886	453	23. 08	454	21. 68	7	178, 513	121. 94	2	20 6½	7 3	4	1	4
422	July 1, 1886	453	23. 56	454	24. 10	7								
2, 333	July 1, 1885	13	23. 60	14	22. 57	7	60, 990	120. 64	1	14 0	9 0½	12	1	2
1, 048	July 1, 1886	941	19. 47	942	19. 29	7	122, 978	112. 60	2	18 0	8 9	3	1	7
							100, 796	91. 80	2	17 0	9 5	3		
802	July 1, 1886	951	19. 83	952	18. 78	7			16 1	14 0	7 2			
578	July 1, 1886	15	11. 50	16	8. 69	7								
686	Oct. 31, 1887	57	24	56	24	7	23, 658	64. 64	(26)	....	....	1	1	1
....	July 1, 1888	57 1	23. 88 23. 52	56 2	23. 88 23. 04	7 6	112, 293	119. 21	3	11 9	7 6	3	1	3
661														
739	July 1, 1888	1	24. 45	2	24. 45	6								
990	July 1, 1888	1	27. 72	2	16. 50	6								
23, 584	July 1, 1888	1	16. 62	2	25. 92	6								

19 Reported last year as Fort Scott, Kans., and Joplin, Mo.; increased distance, 6.55 miles.

20 96.81 miles of route 33008, between Kansas City, Mo., and Fort Scott, Kans., covered by Kansas City, Mo., and Memphis, Tenn., R. P. O.

21 One clerk alternates between this line, Arcadia and Cherry Vale, Kans., and Yates Center and Sedan, Kans., R. P. O.

22 This line is divided at Little Rock, Ark., into two divisions: Little Rock and Fort Smith, Ark. (168.90 miles) and Little Rock, Ark., and Leland, Miss. (137.70 miles).

23 One helper between Little Rock and Atkins, Ark. (63.60 miles).

24 Arkansas City and Warren, Ark., R. P. O., also runs over 7.30 miles of route 29007, between Arkansas City and Trippe, Ark.

25 13.90 miles distance on route 29019 covered by Monett, Mo., and Paris, Tex., R. P. O.

26 Mails distributed in baggage car.

27 No mail carried over route 22020 between Beeson's and Connersville, Ind.; distance, 8.60 miles.

28 Closed-pouch service between Hagerstown and Cambridge City (7.17 miles). (See Table C3). No mail carried over route 31031 between Cambridge City and Beeson's, Ind., 7 miles.

29 Covered by Chicago and Cincinnati R. P. O. (17.70 miles).

TABLE A.—*Statement of railway post-offices in operation*

Designation of railway post-office. (Lines upon which railway post-office cars are paid for, in *italics*.)	Division.	Distance run by clerks, register to register.	Initial and terminal stations, running from east to west, north to south, or northwest to southeast (with abbreviated title of railroad company).	Number of route.	Miles of route for which railroad is paid.
		Miles.			
Fort Worth and Guide, Tex ...	7	53.78	Fort Worth, Waxahachie, Tex. (Ft. W. and N.O.).	31052	41.86
			Waxahachie, Guide, Tex. (C.T. and N.W.).	31021	12.30
Frankfort, Ind., and St. Louis, Mo.	5	246.07	Frankfort, Ind., East St. Louis, Ill. (Tol., Cin., and St. Louis).	22046	243.66
Fredericksburgh and Orange C.H., Va.	3	38.92	Fredericksburgh, Orange C.H., Va. (Pot., Fred. and Piedmont).	11020	39.00
Fremont and Lincoln, Nebr....	6	52.67	Fremont, Lincoln, Nebr. (Fre., Elk. and Mo. Vall.).	34037	52.97
Gainesville and Galveston, Tex.	7	411.65	Gainesville, Fort Worth, Tex. (G., C. and S.F.).	²31054 (part)	64.90
			Fort Worth, Galveston, Tex. (G., C. and S.F.).	31027	346.87
Gainesville and Social Circle, Ga.	4	52.27	Gainesville, Social Circle, Ga. (Gaine., Jeff. and South R.R.)	15034	52.27
Galesburgh and Havana, Ill..	6	62.03	Galesburgh, Havana, Ill. (Fulton Co., N.G.)	22067	60.45
Galva, Ill., and Burlington, Iowa.	6	85.15	Galva, Gladstone, Ill. (Chi., Bur. and Qcy.).	23070	74.54
			Gladstone, Ill., Burlington, Iowa (Chi., Bur. and Qcy.).	23007 (part)	(⁷)
Garrison and Butte City, Mont.	8	52.14	Silver Bow, Garrison, Mont. (Montana Union).	36001	44.90
			Silver Bow, Butte City, Mont. (Utah Northern).	41003 (part)	(⁸)
Geneva, N.Y., and Williamsport, Pa.	2	172.29	Geneva, Corning, N.Y. (F.B. Coal Co.)......	6103	57.76
			Corning, N.Y., and Stokesdale Junction, Pa. (F.B. Coal Co.).	8065 (part)	⁹35.20
			Stokesdale Junction, Pa., and Williamsport, Pa. (F.B. Coal Co.).	8150	78.52
Georgetown and Cincinnati, Ohio.	5	47.86	Georgetown, Columbia, Ohio (Cin., Geo. and Ports.).	21060	42.17
			Columbia, Cincinnati, Ohio (Pitta., Cin. and St. Louis).	21014 (part)	(¹¹)
Georgetown, Del., and Franklin City, Va.	2	56.26	Georgetown, Del., Franklin City, Va., (P. W. and B.).	9506 (part)	¹²53.21
Gilman and Springfield, Ill	6	112.77	Gilman, Springfield, Ill. (Illinois Central)..	23034	112.71
Girard and Galena, Kans	7	47.68	Girard, Kans., Joplin, Mo. (St. L. and S.F.).	33020	38.77
			Joplin, Mo., Galena, Kans. (St. L. and S.F.).	28054 (part)	¹⁴.928
Glyndon, Md., and Gettysburgh, Pa.	2	51.42	Gettysburgh, Valley Junction, Pa. (W. Md.).	8102 (part)	¹⁵23.90
			Valley Junction, Intersection, Pa. (W. Md.).	8082 (part)	¹⁷7.70
			Intersection, Pa., Glyndon, Md. (W. Md.) .	10020	20.32
Goldsborough and Greensborough, N.C.	3	130.01	Goldsborough, Greensborough, N.C., (Rich. and Dan.).	13004	129.89
Goldsborough and Moorehead City, N.C.	3	94.93	Goldsborough, Moorehead City, N.C. (Atlantic and N.C.).	13005	94.05
Grafton and Belington, W. Va.	3	41.84	Grafton, Belington, W. Va. (Grafton and Greenbrier).	12012	42.00

¹ One car in reserve.
² 105.78 miles of route 31054 covered by Newton, Kans., and Gainesville, Tex., R.P.O.
³ Cars run from Galveston, Tex., to Newton, Kans., over Gainesville and Galveston, Tex., R.P.O. and Newton, Kans., and Gainesville, Tex., R.P.O.
⁴ One helper between Fort Worth and Clifton, Tex. (75.40 miles).
⁵ In reserve.
⁶ Reserve.
⁷ Distance (9.40 miles) covered by Chicago, Ill., and Burlington, Iowa, R.P.O.
⁸ Route 41003, Silver Bow to Butte City (7 miles), covered by Butte City, Mont., and Ogden, Utah, R.P.O.
⁹ 15.80 miles covered by closed-pouch service. (See Table C².)

in the United States on June 30, 1888—Continued.

Average weight of mail whole distance per day.	Date of last re-adjustment.	Average speed per hour (train numbers taken from division schedules).				Number of round trips with clerks per week.	Annual miles of service with clerks.	Average miles run daily by crews.	Number of mail cars, or cars in which are mail apartments.	Inside dimensions of cars or apartments (railway post-office cars in black figures).		Number of crews.	Number of clerks to crew.	Number of clerks appointed to line.
		Train No. outward	Av'ge speed (miles).	Train No. inward	Av'ge speed (miles).					Length.	Width.			
Lbs.										*Ft. In.*	*Ft. In.*			
244	Oct. 18, 1886	44	23.09	43	23.09	7	39,367	107.56	2	17 6	8 10	1	1	1
		44	24	44	24.00	7								
197	July 1, 1888	1&11	10.14	2&12	9.60	7	154,532	123.03	2	12 0	5 8	4	1	4
									13	8 0	6 0			
211	July 1, 1885	1	13.81	2	13.81	6	24,442	77.84	1	7 0	7 4	1	1	1
324	Jan. 17, 1887	43	25.42	42	26.48	6	33,076	105.34	2	20 0	9 3	1	1	1
861	Sept. 12, 1887	2	27.17	1	24.21	7	301,328	137.22	35	20 2½	9 0	6	1	47
									53	20 2½	9 0			
		2	25	1	25.39	7								
197	July 1, 1888	2	13	1	13	6	32,825	104.54	1	6 4	5 4	1	1	1
267	July 1, 1887	1	18.13	2	19.60	6	38,955	124.06	1	6 0	6 0	1	1	1
									61	6 11	6 0			
587	July 1, 1887	141	26.31	142	26.62	6	53,474	170.30	1	11 0	6 11	1	1	1
		141	22.56	142	20.83									
941	July 1, 1886	1	19.18	2	30.96	7	38,166	104.28	1	8 0	7 6	1	1	1
2,408	Aug. 15, 1888	1	21	2	24.70									
1,066	July 1, 1885	1	25.66	6	23.89	6	108,198	114.86	2	15 0	9 0	3	1	3
									61	15 0	9 0			
1,423	July 1, 1885	1	18.36	6	22.23	6			(10)			(10)		
805	July 1, 1885	1	20.04	6	25.46	6			(10)			(10)		
760	July 1, 1888	3	17.44	4	16.98	6	30,056	95.72	121	10 4	7 5	1	1	1
24,079	July 1, 1888	3	14.10	4	14.10	6								
374	Feb. 11, 1886	401	26.16	412	26.37	6	35,331	112.52	1	10 0	6 10	1	1	1
531	July 1, 1887	1	22.54	2	23.32	6	70,819	112.77	1	13 10	7 5	2	1	2
									1	11 8	7 5			
		26	18.94	25	18.94	7	34,902	95.36	1	12 1	7 6	1	1	1
		27	21.60	28	18.60	7								
671	July 1, 1885	61	22.18	62	20.86	6	32,292	102.84	1	17 4	7 5	1		2
										16 8	8 3			
		69	22.54	70	21.84	6	1032,292		52	17 0	8 8	1	1	
431	July 1, 1885	61	25.56	62	22.40	6			(18)			(18)		
		69	27.34	70	25.47	6								
7,090	July 1, 1885	61	25.56	62	22.40	6			(15)			(16)		
		69	27.34	70	25.47	6								
1,924	July 1, 1888	50	21.61	51	19.01	7	95,167	130.51	2	20 0	8 9	2	1	2
									51	19 4	9 0			
625	July 1, 1888	51	20.16	50	19.54	6	59,616	94.93	1	10 6	8 1	2	1	2
									61	11 1	8 6			
292	July 1, 1888	1	11.11	2	11.72	6	26,276	83.63	1	10 2	6 0	1	1	1

[10] Cars and clerks shown on route No. 6103.
[11] Covered by Pittsburgh and Cincinnati R. P. O. 4.70 miles.
[12] Car dropped and received at Columbia, Ohio. No local work performed between Columbia and Cincinnati, O.
[13] 25.09 miles covered by Harrington and Lewes, R. P. O.
[14] 10.16 miles of route 28054, between Oronogo and Joplin, Mo., covered by closed-pouch service. (See Table C².)
[15] 6.63 miles covered by closed-pouch service. (See Table C².)
[16] Double daily service, except Sunday.
[17] 3.79 miles covered by closed-pouch service. (See Table C².)
[18] Cars and clerks shown on route No. 8102.

TABLE A².—*Statement of railway post-offices in operation*

Designation of railway post-office. (Lines upon which railway post-office cars are paid for, in *italics*.)	Division.	Distance run by clerks, register to register.	Initial and terminal stations, running from east to west, north to south, or northwest to southeast (with abbreviated title of railroad company.)	Number of route.	Miles of route for which railroad is paid.
		Miles.			
Grafton, W. Va., and Chicago, Ill.[1]	5	200.99	Grafton, W. Va., Bellaire, Ohio (Balto. and Ohio).	[²10003 (part)	1.39
Eastern division[5]			Bellaire, Newark, Ohio (Cent. Ohio)	⁴21001 (part)	104.62
Western division[7]	5	359.80	Newark, Chicago, Ohio (Balto. and Ohio) ..	21010 (part)	(⁸)
			Chicago, Ohio, Chicago, Ill., (Balto. and Ohio)	21047	271
Grafton, W. Va., and Cincinnati, Ohio.	5	300.16	Grafton, Parkersburgh, W. Va. (Balto. and Ohio-)	12002	(⁹)
			Parkersburgh, W. Va., Cincinnati, Ohio (Cin., Wash. and Balto.)	21028	195.15
Grafton and Parkersburgh, W. Va.	3	104.54	Grafton, Parkersburgh, W. Va. (Balto. and Ohio.)	12002	104.50
Grafton and Wheeling, W. Va..	3	99.44	Grafton, Benwood Junction (n. o.), W. Va. (Balt. and Ohio.)	10003 (part)	95.25
			Benwood Junction (n. o.), Wheeling, W. Va. (Balt. and Ohio.)	12015	4
Grand Rapids, Mich., and Cincinnati, Ohio.[14]	5	303.76	Grand Rapids, Mich., Fort Wayne, Ind. (Grand Rap. and Ind.)	24018 (part)	(¹⁶)
			Fort Wayne, Richmond, Ind. (Grand Rap. and Ind.)	22021	92.73
			Richmond, Ind., Hamilton, Ohio (Cin., Rich. and Ohio.)	21025	(¹⁷)
			Hamilton, Cincinnati, Ohio (Cin., Ham. and Day.)	21026 (part)	(¹⁸)
Grand Rapids, Mich., and Elkhart, Ind.[19]	9	115.02	Grand Rapids, White Pigeon, Mich. (L., S. and M. S.)	24004	96.32
			White Pigeon, Mich., Elkhart, Ind. (L., S. and M. S.)	21695 (part)	(²⁰)
Grand Rapids, Mich., and La Crosse, Ind.	9	154.54	Grand Rapids, Mich., La Crosse, Ind. (C. and W. M.)	24021	154.54
Great Bend and Scott, Kans[²³] ..	7	121.12	Great Bend, Scott, Kan. (C., K. and W.)	33059	121.12
Great Falls and Helena, Mont.	6	99.14	Great Falls, Helena, Mont. (Mont. Cent.)	36005	99.14
Greeley and Denver, Colo.[24]	7	98.43	Greeley, Fort Collins, Colo. (G., S. L. and P.)	38027 (part)	²⁵24.03
			Fort Collins, Denver, Colo. (Colo. Cent.)	38002	²⁶74.71
Greenport and New York, N. Y.	2	98.60	Greenport, Long Island City, N. Y. (L. I.).	6045	95.23
Green River, Wyo., and Huntington, Oreg.	6	571.22	Green River, Granger, Wyo. (Union Pac.)	34001 (part)	(²⁹)
			Granger, Wyo., Huntington, Oreg. (Oreg. Short Line.)	37001	541.34
Greensborough and Winston, N. C.	3	29.10	Greensborough, Winston, N. C. (Rich. and Dan.)	13012	29.09
Greenup and Willard, Ky.	5	36.96	Greenup, Willard, Ky. (East Ky.)	20013	34.31
Greenville and Bangor, Me.	1	91.03	Greenville, Oldtown, Me. (Bang. and Pis.).	16	78.07
			Oldtown, Bangor, Me. (Me. Cen.)	³²12 (part)	(³³)
Greenville, Pa., and Butler, Pa.	2	58.87	Greenville, Pa., Butler, Pa. (P. S. and L. E.)	6051	58.25

[1] This line is in two divisions, dividing at Newark, Ohio.

[2] For balance of route, Grafton to Benwood Junction (n. o.) 95.25 miles, see Third Division.

[3] 1 car in reserve.

[4] 1 clerk detailed to transfer duty at Newark, Ohio. 1 clerk detailed to transfer duty at Shelby, Ohio.

[5] Eastern Division, Grafton, W. Va., to Newark, Ohio, postal car running of trains 5 and 6 between Baltimore, Md., and Newark, Ohio, seven times per week.

[6] Closed pouch service between Newark and Columbus, Ohio (33.85 miles). (See table C².)

[7] Western Division, Newark, Ohio, to Chicago, Ill., postal car running on trains 9 and 10 six times per week; cars lying over on west trips 3 hours and on east trips 2 hours and 30 minutes at Newark, Ohio. This R. P. O., together with Sandusky and Wheeling, and Grafton and Wheeling R. P. O's forms double daily service between Grafton, W. Va., and Chicago, Ohio.

[8] Covered by Sandusky and Wheeling R. P. O. (88.79 miles).

[9] Covered by lines of Third Division (104.50 miles).

[10] 13 cars on line between Baltimore, Md. and Saint Louis, Mo. (See Baltimore and Grafton R. P. O. Third Division Report for full equipment of line)

[11] Day line.

[12] Four clerks running in apartment cars between Cincinnati, Ohio, and Parkersburgh, W. Va., and Parkersburgh, W. Va., and Chillicothe, Ohio, on trips west act as helpers to day line Chillicothe to Cincinnati, Ohio; second clerks on day line run east to Chillicothe in mail apartment with Parkersburgh and Cincinnati R. P. O. as helpers ; 4 clerks detailed to transfer duty at Cincinnati, Ohio ; 2 clerks detailed to clerical duty in office superintendent Fifth Division.

in the United States on June 30, 1888—Continued.

Average weight of mail whole distance per day.	Date of last re-adjustment.	Average speed per hour (train numbers taken from division schedules).				Number of round trips with clerks per week.	Annual miles of service with clerks.	Average miles run daily by crews.	Number of mail cars, or cars in which are mail apartments.	Inside dimensions of cars or apartments (railway post-office cars in black figures).		Number of crews.	Number of clerks to crew.	Number of clerks appointed to line.
		Train No. outward.	Av'ge speed (miles).	Train No. inward.	Av'ge speed (miles).					Length.	Width.			
Lbs.										*Ft. In.*	*Ft. In.*			
21,912	July 1,1885	5	29.43	6	25.98	7	146,685	100.19	²⁴	51 ·0	8 10	4	2	⁴18
9,294	July 1,1888	5	34.87	6	31.85	7								
8,719	July 1,1888	9	24.18	10	26.63	6	225,954	179.90	2	51 0	8 10	4	2	
6,904	July 1,1888	9	28.14	10	23.40	6								
24,107	July 1,1884	3	31.35	4	29.88	7	219,717	150.08	(¹⁶)	50 0	9 4	11⁴	2	12³4
		1	33	2	33.89	7	219,717	....	....			12⁴	3	
27,445	July 1,1888	3	24.65	4	24.65	7								
		1	31.22	2	31.22	7								
24,107	July 1,1884	681	24.50	646	23.80	6	65,651	104.54	1	20 8	8 9	2	1	·2
21,912	July 1,1885	3	24.84	4	24.84	7	72,790	99.44	1	17 10	8 3	2	1	2
....	....	3	9.60	4	9.60									
1,831	July 1,1884	2	26.34	3	25.20	6	190,761	151.38	²8	20 0	8 11	4	1	¹⁴4
1,136	July 1,1888	2	24.18	3	26.46	6								
2,262	July 1,1888	2	30	3	27.60	6								
8,951	July 1,1888	2	30.48	3	29.32	6								
1,760	July 1,1884	1	24.70	4	25.25	6	72,233	115.02	1	15 0	9 2			
		3	26.43	2	24.70	6	72,233	115.02	1	15 0	9 0	}		
96,761	July 1,1888	1	28.77	4	28.05	6	(²¹)		(²¹)			4	1	4
		3	28.05	2	28.05	6	(²¹)							
1,629	July 1,1884	4,16	20.65	1,19	17.18	6	97,051	103.62	2	15 0	9 0	3	1	3
574	July 1,1888	573	20.69	574	20.58	7	88,660	121.12	2	9 11½	6 11½	2	1	2
									²⁰1	13 4½	5 3½			
....	....	1	17	2	16.53	6	62,280	99.14	2	24 0	8 4	2	1	2
434	July 1,1886	343	29.40	344	29.40	7	72,051	98.43	1	25 11	8 10	2	1	2
									²⁹1	13 8	8 11			
1,496	July 1,1886	362	21.55	361	22.12	7								
1,582	Aug.25,1885	22	29.28	23	29.28	6	61,921	128.99	1	17 10	8 10	2	1	²⁷4
		34	28.17	9	27.51	6	²⁸61,921	....	1	17	6 4	1	1	
27,325	July 1,1886	501	28.06	502	22.80	7	418,133	163.20	³⁰4	50 8	9 4	7	1	7
4,798	July 1,1888	501	30.07	502	28.24									
1,150	July 1,1888	6	14.58	5	13.01	7	21,301	108.10	1	8 0	6 9	1	1	1
		8	14.64	7	18.18	6	18,275							
126	July 1,1884	3	13.72	4	13.45	6	22,646	72.12	1	10 0	4 8	1	1	1
506	July 1,1885	4	18.73	1	19,53	6	57,166	182.06	1	18 0	7 0	1	1	1
									³¹1	10 0	9 0			
6,509	Feb.11,1885	4	16.80	1	16.80									
893	July 1,1885	3	22.07	2	24.36	6	36,970	117.74	1	13 0	7 0		1	1
									1	13 11	6 11			

¹²Night line.
¹⁴This R. P. O., in connection with Cadillac and Ft. Wayne R. P. O., Ninth Division, forms double daily service between Grand Rapids, Mich., and Ft. Wayne, Ind.
¹⁵Covered by lines of the Ninth Division, 142.78 miles.
¹⁶These clerks do no local work between Richmond, Ind., and Cincinnati, Ohio, running in cars of the Chicago, Richmond and Cincinnati R. P. O in both directions as helpers.
¹⁷Covered by Chicago, Richmond and Cincinnati R. P.O., 45 06 miles.
¹⁸Covered by Toledo and Cincinnati R. P. O., 25.40 miles.
¹⁹Double daily service except Sundays.
²⁰Shown in report of New York and Chicago R.P.O.
²¹Reported on Route 24004.
²²Reported last year as Great Bend and Ness City, Kan.; increased distance 55.69 miles.

²³In reserve.
²⁴Reported last year as La Salle (n. o.) and Denver, Colo.; decreased distance per 21.07 miles.
²⁵15.14 miles of route 38027, between Fort Collins and Stout, Colo., covered by closed pouch service. (See Table C².)
²⁶Denver and Georgetown, Colo., R. P. O., also runs over 3.20 miles of route 38003 between Denver and Argo Junction (n. o.), Colo.
²⁷1 clerk detailed to carry registers into N. Y. P. O. and for duty in lobby of N. Y. P. O.
²⁸Double daily service except Sunday.
²⁹Distance (30.40 miles) covered by Omaha and Ogden R. P. O.
³⁰Whole cars.
³¹Reserve car.
³²Balance of route (102.26 miles) covered by Vanceborough and Bangor R. P. O.
³³Covered by Vanceborough and Bangor R. P. O. (12.60) miles.

TABLE Aᵃ.—*Statement of railway post-offices in operation*

Designation of railway post-office. (Lines upon which railway post-office cars are paid for, in *italics*.)	Division.	Distance run by clerks, register to register.	Initial and terminal stations, running from east to west, north to south, or northwest to southeast (with abbreviated title of railroad company).	Number of route.	Miles of route for which railroad is paid.
		Miles.			
Greenville and Columbia, S. C.	4	144.09	Greenville, Columbia, S. C. (R. and D. R. R.).	14001	144.32
Greenville and Columbus, Ga..	4	51.77	Greenville, Columbus, Ga. (Columbus and Rome R. R.).	15024	50.65
Greenville and Dallas, Tex....	7	54.64	Greenville, Dallas, Tex. (D. and G.)	31055	54.64
Greenville and Laurens, S. C..	4	36.85	Greenville, Laurens, S. C. (P. R. and W. C. R. R.).	14024	36.85
Greenville and Walhalla, S. C..	4	70.16	Greenville, Belton, S. C. (R. and D. R. R.). Belton, Walhalla, S. C. (R. and D. R. R.)..	14001 14016	(²) 43.92
Greenwood and Jackson, Miss..	4	96.83	Greenwood, Jackson, Miss. (Ill. Cent. R. R.)	18018	96.83
Greenwood Lake and New York, N. Y.	2	45.63	Sterling Forest, N. Y., and Jersey City, N. J. (N. Y. and G. L.).	7034	³45.63
Greycourt, N. Y., and Belvidere, N. J.	2	63.36	Greycourt, N. Y., and Belvidere, N. J. (L. and H. R.).	7052	63.36
Griffin and Carrollton, Ga.....	4	60.37	Griffin, Carrollton, Ga. (Cent. R. R.)	15022	60.37
Griffin and Columbus, Ga	4	80.80	Griffin, Columbus, Ga. (G. Mid. R. R.)	15051	⁵99.80
Gurdon and Camden, Ark	7	37.07	Gurdon, Camden, Ark. (St. L., L. M. and S.).	29010 (part)	37.07
Hagerstown and Weverton, Md.	3	24.52	Hagerstown, Weverton, Md. (Balto. and Ohio).	10005	24.56
Hamden and Portsmouth, Ohio.	5	56.37	Hamden Junction, Portsmouth, Ohio (Cin., Wash. and Balto.).	21018	56
Hannibal and Gilmore, Mo	7	86.41	Hannibal, Gilmore, Mo. (St. L. and H.).	28029	86.41
Hannibal and Sedalia, Mo.⁶	7	143.35	Hannibal, Sedalia, Mo. (Mo. Pac.).	28014	143.35
Harrington and Lewes, Del....	2	40.79	Harrington, Georgetown, Del. (P. W. and B.)	9506 (part)	⁸25.09
			Georgetown, Lewes, Del. (P. W. and B.)....	9504	16.02
Harrisburg, Pa., and Baltimore, Md.¹⁰	2	86.22	Harrisburg Pa., Baltimore, Md. (Nor. Cent.)¹⁰	10002 (part)	(¹¹)
Harrisburg, Pa., and Martinsburgh, W. Va.	2	94.79	Harrisburg, Pa., Martinsburgh, W. Va. (Cum. Val.).	8030	94.87
Hartford, Conn., and Millerton, N. Y.	1	70.96	Hartford, Conn., Millerton, N. Y. (Hart. and Conn. West.).	¹⁵5018 (part)	70.93
Hartford and Saybrook, Conn.	1	45.36	Hartford, Saybrook, Conn. (Valley Div. N. Y., N. H. and Hart.)	¹⁶5015 (part)	44.43
Hastings and Cologne, Minn...	6	55.88	Hastings, Cologne, Minn. (Chi., Mil. and St. P.).	¹⁷26010 (part)	56.51
Havana and Springfield, Ill ...	6	48.12	Havana, Springfield, Ill. (Jack. and So. E.).	23049	48.25
Haverstraw and New York, N. Y.	2	43.41	Haverstraw, N. Y., Jersey City, N. J. (N. J. and N. Y.).	7024	39
Hayfield, Minn., and Dubuque, Iowa.	6	172.70	Hayfield, Minn., Dubuque, Iowa (Chi., St. P. and K. C.).	27095	172.68
Hays, N. J., and Stroudsburgh, Pa.	2	47.90	Hays, N. J., Stroudsburgh, Pa. (N. Y. S. and W.).	7058	47.85
Hazleton and Sunbury, Pa.....	2	52.32	Hazleton, Sugar Loaf, Pa. (L. V.)..........	8016 (part)	¹⁸8.80
			Sugar Loaf, Sunbury, Pa. (Penna.)........	8015	44.41
Helena and Basin, Mont	6	47.70	Helena, Jefferson City, Mont. (North. Pac.)	²⁰26002 (part)	23.08
			Jefferson City, Basin, Mont. (North. Pac.).	26005	26.36
Helena and Clarendon, Ark....	7	48.77	Helena, Clarendon, Ark. (Ark. Mid.).......	29002	48.77

¹ Reserve car.
² Reported as Greenville and Columbia R. P. O.
³ 5.83 miles covered by closed-pouch service. (See Table C⁵.)
⁴ In reserve.
⁵ 19.20 miles closed-pouch service, McDonough and Griffin. (See Table C⁵.)
⁶ New service; last year service on this line was performed by Hannibal, Mo., and Denison, Tex., R. P. O., which has been curtailed to begin at Sedalia, Mo.

⁷ One clerk detailed to transfer service, Hannibal, Mo.; 1 helper every day except Monday between Hannibal and Moberly, Mo. (70.71 miles).
⁸ 55.21 miles covered by Georgetown and Franklin City R. P. O.
⁹ Clerk shown on route No. 9506.
¹⁰ Short run of Williamsport and Baltimore R. P. O.
¹¹ 84.60 miles covered by Williamsport and Baltimore R. P. O.

in the United States on June 30, 1888—Continued.

Average weight of mail whole distance per day.	Date of last re-adjustment.	Average speed per hour (train numbers taken from division schedules).				Number of round trips with clerks per week.	Annual miles of service with clerks.	Average miles run daily by crews.	Number of mail cars, or cars in which are mail apartments.	Inside dimensions of cars or apartments (railway post-office cars in black figures).		Number of crews.	Number of clerks to crew.	Number of clerks appointed to line.
		Train No. outward.	Av'ge speed (miles).	Train No. inward.	Av'ge speed (miles).					Length.	Width.			
Lbs.										*Ft. In.*	*Ft. In.*			
908	July 1, 1888	52	21	53	21.70	6	90,488	96.06	2	19 6	9 0	3	1	3
137	Feb. 23, 1885	72	14.60	71	15.80	6	32,511	103.54	1	11 9	6 9	1	1	1
									11	9 4	7 4			
315	Mar. 1, 1887	603	19.87	604	20.54	7	39,996	109.28	1	13 1	7 1	1	1	1
196	July 1, 1888	96	17.40	97	25	6	23,141	73.70	1	7 7	6 8	1	1	1
908	July 1, 1888	54	18.50	55	18.80	6	44,060	140.32	1	13 8	8 10	1	1	1
425	July 1, 1888	53	14.10	52	14.16									
540	July 1, 1888	11	20.90	12	20.90	6	62,065	98.87	2	14 7	7 2	2	1	2
255	July 1, 1885	34	13.89	7	16.10	6	28,656	91.26	2	10 0	7 0	1	1	1
257	July 1, 1885	5	18.10	4	11.34	6	39,790	126.72	1	13 2	6 6	1	1	1
									41	13 2	6 6			
215	July 1, 1884	29	15	30	15	6	37,912	120.74	1	14 6	5 9	1	1	1
		50	28.30	51	27.50	6	50,742	101.60	2	13 9	6 8	1	1	1
224	July 1, 1886	935	6.74	936	6.74	6	23,280	74.14	1	9 5	9 4	1	1	1
389	July 1, 1884	348	15.28	305	24.2	6	15,309	98.08	1	7 0	4 0	1	1	1
		366	24.20	347	18.15		15,399	....	1	9 0	8 0			
421	July 1, 1888	55	18.98	50	19.41	6	35,400	112.74	1	13 1	7 4	1	1	1
596	July 1, 1887	1	24.69	2	25.41	6	54,265	86.41	2	15 0	7 0	2	1	2
3,731	July 1, 1887	501	20.58	506	22.19	7	104,932	95.57	3	21 10	9 5	3	1	5
									3	21 10	9 4			
371	Feb. 11, 1885	301	25.95	312	28.40	6	25,616	81.58	1	11 10	6 7	1	1	1
121	Feb. 11, 1885	301	30.03	312	32.04	6	54,146	86.22	1	11 9	6 8	(*)	(*)	(*)
11,371	July 1, 1885	12	23.07	11	23.60	6			1	20 0	9 0	2		2
									41	20 0	9 0			
									12?	15 0	8 7			
1,042	July 1, 1885	9	24.80	6	22.72	6	59,528	136.14	1	15 0	8 7	3	1	124
		1	24.80	14	25.27	6	1450,528	....	1	23 10	8 8			
									42	23 10	8 8			
										15 6	8 4½			
1,101	July 1, 1885	7	23.72	10	23.59	6	44,562	141.02	1	13 0	6 0	1	1	2
		13	24	14	24.70	6	44,562	....	1	13 0	6 0	1	1	
									1	12 0	6 0			
2,679	July 1, 1885	703	25.83	706	27.16	6	28,488	90.72	1	11 6	7 0	1	1	2
		709	26.89	712	27.16	6	28,488	....	1	10 0	6 9	1	1	
									11	10 0	7 0			
2,377	July 1, 1887	5	22.60	6	21.20	6	35,092	111.76	1	10 5	6 10	1	1	1
245	July 1, 1887	17	19.30	18	19.96	6	30,219	96.24	1	11 0	6 6	1	1	1
		18	20.03	1	20.19	6	27,261	80.82	1	6 0	8 0	1	1	1
									41	6 8	8 0			
941	July 1, 1887	5	30.03	6	26.23	6	108,455	115.13	2	19 9	7 5	3	1	3
180	July 1, 1885	1	20.23	12	13.74	6	30,081	95.80	1	11 9	6 9	1	1	1
645	July 1, 1885	407	28.69	408	26.30	6	33,039	104.64	1	10 0	6 6	1	1	1
242	July 1, 1885	14	28.69	13	26.30	6	....	....	(19)			(19)		
		71	17.60 {7 72}	72	10.50	7	34,916	95.40	1	23 7	8 10	1	1	1
441	July 1, 1888	71	14.38	72	13.18	6	30,628	97.54	1	14 8	6 10	1	1	1
1,052	July 1, 1887	1	10.11	2	10.67									

[12] In repair shop.
[13] One helper Harrisburg and Shippensburgh.
[14] Double daily service except Sunday.
[15] Balance of route (39 82 miles) covered by State Line and Rhinecliff R. P. O. (Second Division).
[16] Balance of route (1 66 miles) covered by closed pouch service between Saybrook and Saybrook Point.
[17] Balance of route covered by Saint Paul, Minn., and Mitchell, Dak., R. P. O. (256.34 miles); Aber-

deen and Orient, Dak., R. P. O. (41.80 miles) and between Roscoe and Bowdle, Dak. (15.29 miles), covered by closed pouches. (See Table C°)
[18] 14.50 miles covered by Easton and Hazleton R. P. O.
[19] Cars and clerks shown on route No. 8016.
[20] Balance of route, Jefferson City to Wickes, Mont. (4.50 miles), covered by closed pouches. (See Table C°.)

TABLE A⁰.—*Statement of railway post-offices in operation*

Designation of railway post-office. (Lines upon which railway post-office cars are paid for, in *italics*.)	Division.	Distance run by clerks, register to register.	Initial and terminal stations, running from east to west, north to south, or northwest to southeast (with abbreviated title of railroad company).	Number of route.	Miles of route for which railroad is paid.
		Miles.			
Helena, Mont., and Portland, Oregon.	8	932.36	Helena, Missoula, Mont. (Northern Pacific).	[1]26001 (part)	124.30
			Missoula, Mont., Pasco, Wash. (Northern Pacific).	43009 (part)	402.50
			Pasco, Melrose, Wash. (Northern Pacific).	43011	233.61
			Melrose, Tacoma, Wash. (Northern Pacific).	43005 (part)	25.29
			Tacoma, Wash., Portland, Oregon (Northern Pacific).	43001	146.66
Hempstead and Austin, Tex.	7	115.16	Hempstead, Austin, Tex. (H. and T. C.)....	31004	115.16
Henderson and Princeton, Ky.[2]	5	89.73	Henderson, Princeton, Ky. (Ohio Valley)...	20034	89.88
Henrietta and Dallas, Tex.[3]....	7	159.23	Henrietta, Whitesborough, Tex. (Mo. Pac.).	431022 (part)	85.84
			Whitesborough, Denton, Tex. (Mo. Pac.)..	31028 (part)	(4)
			Denton, Dallas, Tex. (Mo. Pac.)............	31030	38.07
Henry and Saint Joseph, Mo.[6].	7	73.48	Henry, Saint Joseph, Mo. (St. J., St. L. and S. F.)	26012	73.48
Herington and Dodge City, Kans.[7]	7	203.19	Herington, Bucklin, Kans. (C., K. and N.)..	[8]33075 (part)	176.40
			Bucklin, Dodge City, Kans. (C., K. and N.).	53092	26.55
Heron Lake and Pipestone, Minn.	6	55.33	Heron Lake, Pipestone, Minn. (Chi., St. P., Minn. and Om.).	26028	55.45
Holden, Mo., and Coffeyville, Kans.[11]	7	201.58	Holden, Mo., Paola, Kans. (Mo. Pac.).......	28024	54.47
			Paola, Le Roy Junction (n. o.), Kans. (Mo. Pac.).	[12]33031	61.56
			Le Roy, Dearing, Kans. (V., V., I. and A.)..	[12]33063	81.26
			Dearing, Coffeyville, Kans. (D., M. and A.).	33056 (part)	(14)
Horicon and Portage, Wis.....	6	53.17	Horicon, Portage, Wis. (Chi., Mil. and St. P.)	25006	52.24
Hornellsville and Buffalo, N. Y.	2	92.61	Buffalo, Hornellsville, N. Y. (N. Y., L. E. and W.).	6008	92.35
Houston and Eagle Pass, Tex.[16]	7	386.70	Houston, San Antonio, Tex. (G., H. and S. A.)	31002	218.01
			San Antonio, Spofford, Tex. (G., H. and S. A.).	[18]31039 (part)	134.03
			Spofford, Eagle Pass, Tex. (G., H. and S. A.).	31043	34.66
Houston and Galveston, Tex.[6].	7	51.40	Houston, Galveston, Tex. (G., H. and N.)..	31001	51.40
Howard City and Detroit, Mich.[20]	9	161.22	Howard City, Detroit, Mich. (D., L. and N.).	24017	160.72
Humeston and Shenandoah, Iowa.	6	113.91	Humeston, Van Wert, Iowa (Keo and West.).	[22]26015 (part)	17.82
			Van Wert, Shenandoah, Iowa (Hum. and Shen).	27067	96.77
Huntingdon, Pa., and Cumberland, Md.	2	90.69	Huntingdon, Mt. Dallas Sta., Pa. (H. and B. T. M.).	8034	45.15
			Mt. Dallas Sta., Pa., Cumberland, Md. (Penna.).	8072	45.29
Huntington, W. Va., and Lexington, Ky.	5	139.93	Huntington, W. Va., Lexington, Ky. (Chesa. and Ohio).	20016	140.20

[1] Balance of route 26001 reported in sixth division. 16.50 miles of route 43009, Pasco to Wallula, closed-pouch service. (See Table C⁰.) Balance of route 43005, 8.00 miles closed-pouch service. Course of R. P. O. changed Sept. 16, 1887, covering 76.2 miles of route 43011 and 25.7 miles of route 43005, over which no R. P. O. service was heretofore performed. Discontinuing Pasco and Cle-Elum and Tacoma and Portland R. P. O.'s. Line divided at Spokane Falls—east division, 6 clerks, 389.16 miles; west division, 543.20 miles. One chief clerk at Portland, and 1 chief clerk Helena, Mont.
[2] This line was formerly the Henderson and Marion R. P. O. November 21, 1887, service extended to Princeton, Ky.; increased distance 25.04 miles.

[3] Reported last year as Denton and Dallas, Tex. increased distance, 121.16 miles.
[4] 25.48 miles of route 31022, between Denison and Whitesborough, Tex., covered by Denison and San Antonio, Tex., R. P. O.
[5] 35.70 miles distance on route 31028 covered by Denison and San Antonio, Tex., R. P. O.
[6] Double daily service.
[7] New service; not reported last year.
[8] 172.24 miles of route 33075, between Saint Joseph, Mo., and Herington, Kans., covered by Saint Joseph, Mo., and Caldwell, Kans., R. P. O. and 85.50 miles of same route, between Bucklin and Liberal, Kans., by Pratt and Liberal, Kans., R. P. O.
[9] In reserve.
[10] Reserve.

in the United States on June 30, 1888—Continued.

Average weight of mail whole distance per day.	Date of last re-adjustment.	Train No. outward	Av'ge speed (miles).	Train No. inward	Av'ge speed (miles).	Number of round trips with clerks per week	Annual miles of service with clerks.	Average miles run daily by crews.	Number of mail cars, or cars in which are mail apartments.	Length	Width	Number of crew.	Number of clerks to crews.	Number of clerks appointed to line.
Lbs.										Ft. In.	Ft. In.			
10,412	July 1,1885	1	27.31	2	24.51	7	682,488	129.72	6	24 6	9 1	6	1	17
7,068	July 1,1886	1	29.67	2	25.83	....		120.68	....	....	....	9		
3,209	June 27,1886	1	22.57	2	20.58									
2,374	July 5,1888	1	18.73	2	18.73									
3,023	July 1,1886	1	23.09	2	23.09									
911	July 1,1887	21	23.29	22	24.59	7	84,297	115.16	2	14 0	8 10	2	1	2
493	July 1,1888	3	23.94	4	24.52	6	50,282	179.46	1	10 0	8 11	1	1	1
3,852	July 1,1886	542	19.39	541	18.96	7	116,556	159.23	2	16 5	6 11	2	1	2
4,003	July 1,1886	551	22.81	552	21.51	7								
4,078	July 1,1886	551	20.44	552	19.58	7								
1,083	July 1,1887	1	24.30	2	25.05	7	*53,787	146.96	1	12 0	9 0	1	1	2
		3	23.52	4	23.52	7	*53,787	146.96	1	12 0	9 0	1	1	
1,070	July 1,1888	21	24.33	22	24.50	7	148,735	135.46	2	14 6	7 2	3	1	3
									*)	14 6	7 2			
....		21	25.50	22	28.40	7								
135	July 1,1887	39	10.63	40	10.63	7	34,747	110.66	1	9 0	7 5	1	1	1
									10)	21 11	9 4			
1,812	July 1,1887	223	22.12	224	21.94	7	147,557	134.39	2	16 4	6 10	3	1	3
726	July 1,1886	221	21.70	222	21.22	7								
573	Feb.21,1887	221	22.54	222	21.52	7								
605	July 1,1888	222	21.32	221	22.32	7								
827	July 1,1887	7	26.12	6	26.12	6	33,391	106.34	1	15 7	8 9	1	1	1
									10)	11 1	7 11			
5,787	July 1,1885	19	30.87	8	32.68	6	58,159	92.61	1	15 0	9 0	2	1	107
									1	15 0	10 0			
									1	14 6	8 0			
1,882	July 1,1886	18	25.93	17	24.11	7	159,583	145.34	(17)	....	....	3	1	107
1,218	July 1,1886	20	26.02	19	28.56	7	123,481	112.46	....			3	1	
		1	20	2	16.83	7								
2,388	July 1,1886	661	21.63	662	23.15	7	*87,625	102.80	1	20 8	9 2	1	1	2
		655	26.18	656	21.15	7	*37,625	102.80	1	22 2	9 2	1	1	
									*)	16 7	9 1			
2,107	July 1,1884	10	26.40	1	27.93	6	101,246	161.22	1	20 0	8 10	2	1	(26)
									11					2
419	July 1,1887	1	23.76	4	26.73	....	71,535	113.01	2	23 0	9 0	2	1	2
653	July 1,1887	1	22.77	4	23.41	....								
676	July 1,1885	1	22.65	2	21.62	6	56,953	90.69	1	15 0	8 0	2	1	2
414	July 1,1885	1	23.58	2	22.64	6	....		(22)	....	....	(22)		
1,992	July 1,1888	1	22.98	2	26.22	6	87,876	139.93	*43	19 7	8 10	2	1	2

11 Reported last year at Holden, Mo., and Independence, Kans.; increased distance, 18.07 miles.
12 Kansas City, Mo., Salina, Kans., and Pueblo, Colo., R. P. O., also runs over 7.20 miles of route 33031, between Paola and Osawatomie, Kans.
13 Yates Center and Sedan, Kans., R P O, also runs over 17.55 miles of route 33063, between Yates Center and Sidell, Kans.
14 5.33 miles, distance on route 33056, covered by Chetopa and Larned, Kans., R. P. O.
15 Four clerks detailed as transfer clerks at Buffalo, N. Y., and one clerk as assistant to chief clerk at Buffalo, N. Y.
16 Reported last year as Houston and Del Rio, Tex.; decreased distance, 3.53 miles. This line is divided at San Antonio, Tex., into two divisions—Houston and San Antonio, Tex. (218.61 miles), and San Antonio and Eagle Pass, Tex. (168.69 miles).

17 Cars on this line shown under New Orleans, La., and Houston, Tex., R. P. O.
18 One helper between Houston and Columbus Tex. (69 miles).
19 500 25 miles of route 31039, between Snofford and El Paso, Tex., covered by closed-pouch service. (See Table C*.)
20 In connection with the Big Rapids and Detroit R. P. O. gives double service between Detroit and Ionia, Mich. (122.73 miles), daily, except Sunday. One clerk appointed to the Big Rapids and Detroit R. P. O. runs as helper on the two lines between Detroit and Ionia.
21 Held in reserve.
22 Balance of route (131.50 miles) covered by Keokuk and Humeston, Iowa, R. P. O.
23 Cars and clerks shown on route No. 8934.
24 1 car in reserve.

TABLE A². - *Statement of railway post-offices in operation*

Designation of railway post-office. (Lines upon which railway post-office cars are paid for, in *italics*).	Division.	Distance run by clerks, register to register.	Initial and terminal stations, running from east to west, north to south, or northwest to southeast (with abbreviated title of railroad company).	Number of route.	Miles of route for which railroad is paid.
		Miles.			
Huntington and Portland, Oreg. [1]	8	405. 60	Umatilla, Huntington, Oreg. (Oreg. Rwy. and Navigation Co.).	44003	218. 04
			Umatilla, Portland, Oreg. (Oreg. Rwy. and Navigation Co.).	44005 (part)	187. 56
Hutchinson and Kinsley, Kans.	7	84. 20	Hutchinson, Kinsley, Kans. (C., K. and W.)	33052	84. 20
Independence and Cedar Vale, Kans. [2]	7	56. 12	Independence, Cedar Vale, Kans. (C , K. and W.).	33053	56. 12
Indiana and Branch Junction, Pa.	2	19. 20	Indiana Branch Junction, Pa. (Penna.).......	8012	19. 25
Indianapolis, Ind., and .Decatur, Ill.	5	153. 40	Indianapolis, Ind., Decatur. Ill. (Ind., Bloom. and West.).	23055	154. 26
Indianapolis, Ind., and Louisville, Ky.	5	111. 21	Indianapolis, Jeffersonville, Ind. (Penna. Co.).	22007	108. 84
Indianapolis, Ind., and Peoria, Ill.	5	212. 42	Indianapolis, Ind., Peoria, Ill. (Ind., Bloom and West.).	22018	213. 02
Indianapolis, Ind., and Saint Louis, Mo. [11]	5	265. 30	Indianapolis, Terre Haute, Ind. (Ind. and St. Louis).	22023	73. 29
			Terre Haute. Ind., East St. Louis, Ill (Ind. and St. Louis).	22013	190. 13
Indianapolis and Terre Haute. Ind.	5	72. 50	Indianapolis, Terre Haute, Ind. (Ter. H. and Ind.).	22002	([13])
Indianapolis, Ind., Vandalia, Ill., and Saint Louis, Mo.	5	240. 80	Indianapolis, Terre Haute, Ind. (Terre Haute and Ind.).	22002	([16])
			Terre Haute, Ind., East Saint Louis, Ill (Terre Haute and Ind.).	22044	([17])
Indianapolis and Vincennes. Ind.	5	116. 70	Indianapolis, Vincennes, Ind. (Penna Co.)..	22001	118. 21
Ingrams and San Francisco, Cal	8	87. 25	Ingrams, San Francisco, Cal. (Northern Pacific Coast R. R).	46016	87. 00
Iron Mountain, Mich., and Milwaukee, Wis	6	209. 94	Iron Mountain, Mich., Milwaukee, Wis., (Mil. and North.).	[19]25016 (part)	209. 04
Ishpeming. Mich., and Fort Howard Wis.	6	179. 50	Ishpeming, Mich., Fort Howard, Wis (Chi. and No. West).	24031	179. 45
Ithaca and Owego, N. Y	2	35. 00	Ithaca, N. Y., Owego, N. Y. (D. L. and W.)	0042	35. 11
Jackson and Adrian, Mich. ...	9	47 55	Jackson, Adrian, Mich., (L. S. and M. S.)...	24003	47. 41
Jackson and Hillsdale. Mich., and Fort Wayne, Ind.	9	99. 26	Jackson, Mich., Ft. Wayne, Ind. (L. S. and M. S.).	24029	98. 59
Jackson and Natchez, Miss ..	4	99. 55	Jackson, Natchez, Miss. (N, T. and Col. Rwy.).	18010	99. 45
Jacksonport and Brinkley, Ark.	7	60. 90	Jacksonport, Brinkley, Ark. (B. and B) ...	29006	60. 90
Jacksonville and Mount Vernon, Ill.	6	134. 59	Jacksonville, Drivers, Ill. (Jack. So. East)..	23046	130. 91
			Drivers, Mount Vernon, Ill. (Louis. and Nash.).	23032 (part)	([20])
Jacksonville and Pensacola, Fla.	4	207. 50	Jacksonville, Lake City, Fla. (F. R. and N. Co.).	16006	60. 32
		161. 89	Lake City, River Junct., Fla. (F. R. and N. Co).	16002 [21](part)	151. 87
	28	....	River Junct. Pensacola, Fla (P. and A. R. R.).	16015	161. 52
Jacksonville and Tampa, Fla ...	4	241. 54	Jacksonville, Sanford, Fla. (J. T. and E. W. Rwy).	16018	126. 18
			Sanford, Tampa, Fla. (South Fla. R. R.)...	16007	116. 39

[1] This line reported as Umatilla and Huntington last year. Extended from Umatilla to Portland September 16, commencing October 3, 1887. Owing to change of Helena and Portland R. P. O.; one city distributor for Portland ; daily average, 176 6 mil 's.

[2] Reported last year as Chanute and Cedar Vale, Kans.; decreased distance, '8 88 miles.

[3] Double daily service, except Sunday.

[4] One car in reserve.

[5] Two cars in reserve.

[6] Day line.

[7] Two helpers on day and night line between Indianapolis and Seymour, Ind. (58.91 miles) ; clerks run to Louisville, Ky.

[8] Night line.

[9] Four helpers on night line running through between Indianapolis, Ind , and Peoria, Ill.

[10] Night line. Service placed on night trains of this line December 8, 1887.

[11] July 10, 1887, department discontinued paying for R P O. service to be performed in apartment cars.

[12] Two helpers between Indianapolis, Ind , and Mattoon, Ill., distance 168.70 miles.

[13] Covered by Pittsburgh and St. Louis R. P. O. 74 30 miles

[14] This clerk holds an appointment on the Pittsburgh and St Louis R. P. O. and is shown with that line.

[16] Covered by Pittsburgh and Saint Louis R. P. O., distance 94.39 miles.

in the United States on June 30, 1888—Continued.

Average weight of mail whole distance per day.	Date of last re-adjustment.	Average speed per hour (train numbers taken from division schedules).				Number of round trips with clerks per week.	Annual miles of service with clerks.	Average miles run daily by crews.	Number of mail cars, or cars in which are mail apartments.	Inside dimensions of cars, or apartments (railway post-office cars in black figures).		Number of crews.	Number of clerks to crew.	Number of clerks appointed to line.
		Train No. outward.	Av'g'e speed (miles).	Train No. inward.	Av'g'e speed (miles).					Length.	Width.			
Lbs.										*Ft. In.*	*Ft. In.*			
3,461	Aug.15,1888	3	23.19	4	24.09	7	296,899	162.24	3	24 10	9 1	5	1	6
6,382	Aug.15,1888	3	26.60	4	23.16									
395	Oct.11,1886	341	22.46	342	22.46	7	61,634	168.40	1	20 0	9 1	1	1	1
264	Apr.25,1887	261	20.96	262	20.96	7	41,080	112.24	1	18 1	8 5½	1	1	1
699	July 1,1885	80 / 84	19.20 / 19.86	81 / 87	5.26 / 19.20	6 / 6	12,058 / *12,058	76.80	1	15 0	8 0	1	1	1
1,512	July 1,1885	1	29.47	2	28.44	6	96,335	102.27	*3	21 0	3 9	3	1	3
4,395	July 1,1888	2 / 10	33.60 / 36.26	8 / 1	32.40 / 35.34	7	81,406 / 81,406	111.21	*4	19 0	9 0	*2 / 2	1	*6
3,430	July 1,1888	1 / 3	34.54 / 25.80	2 / 4	24.12 / 25.80	6 / 7	123,400 / 57,517	106.21	*6	23 0	8 3	*4 / 10½	2	*12
1,971	July 1,1888	9	26.94	8	27.84	6	166,608	132.65	*3	40 0	9 0	*4	1	12₆
1,569	July 1,1888	9	24.18	8	23.22	6								
61,121	July 1,1888	3	26.34	4	26.34	6	45,530	145.00	*2	15 6	8 10	1	1	(14)
61,121	July 1,1888	5	27.54	2	33.54	6	151,222	120.40	*3	19 10	9 0	4	1	(15)
56,036	July 1,1888	5	24.28	2	25.64	6								
754	July 1,1888	5	25.33	8	26.40	6	73,288	116.70	*4	19 0	9 0	2	1	2
414	July 1,1886	11	16.89	8	16.41	6	54,793	87.25	2	9 0	5 6	2	1	2
1,028	June 23,1888	4 / 2	23.75 / 26.08	5 / 1	21.11 / 26.59	6	131,842	139.96	3	33 4½	9 4	,3	1	3
2,529	July 1,1884	2	23.93	1	23.16	7	131,394	119.66	19 2 / 19 1 / 1	36 0 / 35 4 / 7 8	9 5 / 9 3 / 6 9	3	1	*5
601	July 1,1885	8	23.32	9	23.32	6	21,980	70.00	2 / 1 / 21 1	7 10 / 11 2 / 7 10	6 8 / 8 10 / 6 8	1	1	1
1,190	July 1,1884	115	24.00	116	25.55	6	29,861	95.10	1	16 10	9 0	1	1	1
652	July 1,1884	156	25.00	157	23.53	6	62,335	99.26	1			2	1	2
1,326	July 1,1888	2	19.4	1	19.7	6	62,517	99.55	1 / 1	13 8 / 10 10	7 10 / 7 6	2	1	2
129	Jan.17,1887	2	15.31	1	14.39	6	38,245	121.80	1	12 0	6 0	1	1	1
425	July 1,1888	5	22.26	4	20.42	6	84,522	134.59	.1	13 0	6 6	2	1	2
2,253	Feb.15,1886	5	22.26	4	20.42				23 1	12 0	7 4			
1,011	July 1,1884	1	23.2	2	23.3	7	24 151,890	103.75	23 3	13 0	6 10	6	1	27 7
765	July 1,1884	1	23.2	2	23.3		25 118,357	161.69	25 3	14 0	9 0			
1,070	July 1,1884	2	27.2	1	25.8	6								
5,186	Apr.16,1886	27 / 13	30.6 / 27.4	14 / 6	25 / 26.6	7	176,807	127.90	3 / 1	27 4 / 33 3	9 4 / 9 2	6	1	8
1,017	Apr.1,1885	27 / 13	25.5 / 11.2	14 / 78	28.7 / 14	(29) / 6	104,147							(30)

16 These clerks are appointed to the Pittsburgh and Saint Louis R. P. O., and are shown with that line. Four clerks on West Division Pittsburgh and Saint Louis day line act as helpers between East Saint Louis, Ill., and Indianapolis, Ind., on east trips.
17 Covered by Pittsburgh and Saint Louis R. P. O., distance 166.69 miles.
18 Balance of route Republic to Iron Mountain, Mich. (47 miles), covered by closed pouches. (See Table C*.)
19 One in reserve. Whole cars.
20 Two helpers between Escanawba Mich., and Fort Howard, Wis.
21 In reserve.

22 Distance (7.60 miles) covered by Nashville, Tenn., and St. Louis, Mo., R. P. O.
23 Reserve.
24 Eastern Div.
25 Two reserve cars.
26 One helper, West Div. Line divided at River Junction.
27 Four miles reported in Table C*. Monticello and Drifton, closed pouches.
28 Western Div.
29 Short run six times per week. Jacksonville to Kissimmee (165.84 miles). Clerks alternate on long and short run.
30 Two helpers.

TABLE A*.—*Statement of railway post-offices in operation*

Designation of railway post-office. (Lines upon which railway post-office cars are paid for, in *italics*.)	Division.	Distance run by clerks, register to register.	Initial and terminal stations, running from east to west, north to south, or northwest to southeast (with abbreviated title of railroad company).	Number of route.	Miles of route for which railroad is paid.
		Miles.			
Jamestown and Oakes, Dak ...	6	69.81	Jamestown. La Moure, Dak. (North Pac.).	35020	48.87
			La Moure, Valley Junction, Dak. (North Pac.).	35015 (part)	(¹)
			Valley Junction, Oakes, Dak. (North Pac.).	35028	15.21
Jefferson and McKinney, Tex .	7	155.46	Jefferson, McKinney, Tex. (Mo. Pac.).....	31013	155.46
Jefferson City and Bagnell, Mo.	7	45.71	Jefferson City, Bagnell, Mo. (Mo. Pac.)....	28047	45.71
Johnstown and Rockwood, Pa .	2	45.71	Johnstown, Rockwood, Pa. (B. and O.).....	8070	45.09
Julesburg and Denver, Colo ...	7	197.88	Julesburg, La Salle (n. o.), Colo. (Colo. Cent.).	38017	150.96
			La Salle (n. o.), Denver, Colo. (Den. Pac)...	380 7 (part)	(²)
Junction City and Parsons, Kans.	7	157.15	Junction City, Parsons, Kans. (Mo. Pac.)..	38009	157.15
Kalamazoo and South Haven, Mich.	9	40.20	Kalamazoo, South Haven, Mich. (Mich. Cent.)	34007	40.18
Kane and Callery, Pa	2	126.87	Kane, Callery, Pa. (P. and W.).............	8086 (part)	*126.87
Kankakee and Kankakee Junction, Ill.	6	71.52	Kankakee, Kempton, Ill. (Ill. Cent.)	*29062 (part)	28.27
			Kempton, Kankakee Junction, Ill. (Ill. Cent.).	29064	43.01
Kankakee and Seneca, Ill......	6	43.30	Kankakee, Seneca, Ill. (Kank. and Sen)....	29069	43.56
Kansas City, Mo., and Denver, Colo.	7	641.02	Kansas City, Mo., Denver, Colo. (U. P.) ...	33001	641.02
Kansas City and Joplin, Mo.⁵..	7	169.25	Kansas City, Pleasant Hill, Mo. (Mo. Pac.).	28001 (part)	(³)
			Pleasant Hill, Joplin, Mo. (Mo. Pac.).......	28040	123.47
Kansas City, Mo., and Memphis, Tenn.¹⁰	7	487.20	Kansas City, Mo., Fort Scott, Kans. (K. C., Ft. S. and M.).	¹²33008 (part)	96.58
			Fort Scott, Kans., Springfield, Mo. (K. C., Ft. S. and M.).	29038	104.32
			Springfield, Mo., Memphis, Tenn. (K. C., Ft. S. and M.).	29017	286.40
Kansas City, Mo., and Oxford, Nebr.	6	363.66	Kansas City, Napier, Mo. (K. C., St. Jo. and C. Bl.).	28006 (part)	(¹⁴)
			Napier, Mo., Rulo "Y," Nebr. (B. and M. R. in Nebr.).	29064	11.70
			Rulo "Y," Table Rock, Nebr. (B. and M. R. in Nebr.).	33012 (part)	(¹⁶)
			Table Rock, Wymore, Nebr. (B. and M. R. in Nebr.).	34020	(¹⁷)
			Wymore, Red Cloud, Nebr. (B. and M. R. in Nebr.).	34016 (part)	(¹⁸)
			Red Cloud, Oxford, Nebr. (B. and M. R. in Nebr.).	34029 (part)	(¹⁹)

¹ Distance (5.30 miles) covered by Fargo and La Moure, Dak., R. P. O.

² Distance on route 38007 (46 92 miles) covered by Cheyenne, Wyo., and Denver, Colo., R. P. O.

³ 12.24 miles covered by closed-pouch service. (See Table C⁴.)

⁴ In reserve.

⁵ Balance of route (58.11 miles) covered by Kempton and Bloomington, Ill., R. P. O.

⁶ Mail apartment service between Kansas City, Mo., and Wallace, Kans, (4.20.40 miles), in addition to postal-car service (see trains 203 and 204), making double daily service between those points.

⁷ 2 helpers, one on each line, between Kansas City, Mo., and Saint Mary's, Kans. (99 99 miles), six days each week, and between Kansas City, Mo., and Wamego, Kans. (104 miles), five days each week; one clerk detailed as chief clerk at union depot, Saint Louis, Mo.; one clerk detailed as assistant chief clerk, Kansas City, Mo.; one clerk detailed as assistant chief clerk, Denver, Colo.; one clerk on this line is an acting clerk additional.

⁸ This line is divided at Nevada, Mo., into two divisions—Kansas City and Nevada, Mo., (104.91 miles), and Nevada and Joplin, Mo. (65.34 miles), clerks in charge alternating and performing service on both divisions.

in the United States on June 30, 1888—Continued.

Average weight of mail whole distance per day.	Date of last re-adjustment.	Train No. outward.	Av'g speed (miles).	Train No. inward.	Av'g speed (miles).	Number of round trips with clerks per week.	Annual miles of service with clerks.	Average miles run daily by crews.	Number of mail cars, or cars in which are mail apartments.	Length.	Width.	Number of crews.	Number of clerks to crew.	Number of clerks appointed to line.
Lbs.										*Ft. In.*	*Ft. In.*			
90	July 1, 1886	62	24.43	61	23.46	6	43,526	138.62	1	17 3	9 1	1	1	1
583	July 1, 1886	62	24.40	61	21.20									
467	July 1, 1888	62	22.82	61	22.82	7	113,797	103.64	1	16 5	6 11	3	1	8
412	July 1, 1886	621	14.70	622	14.70				1	14 2	5 9			
									1	11 5	5 7			
231	July 1, 1887	153	12.29	154	11.74	6	28,706	91.42	1	10 5	7 5	1	1	1
216	July 1, 1885	92	22.85	93	22.85	6	28,706	91.42	1	18 0	8 6	1	1	1
962	July 1, 1886	308	32.38	307	27.89	7	144,848	131.92	2	12 2	6 6	3	1	3
1,615	July 1, 1886	308	27.62	307	27.62	7								
824	July 1, 1886	523	20.71	526	20.05	7	115,034	101.77	1	20 7	7 6	3	1	3
									1	20 6	7 5			
241	July 1, 1884	123	26.33	122	24.95	6	25,246	80.40	1	11 1	7 0	1	1	1
341	July 1, 1885	17	16.19	18	17.37	6	79,674	126.87	2	13 3	7 0	2	1	2
									4 2 {	13 . 4	7 7			
										6 6	8 6			
171	July 1, 1887	1	25.32	2	25.32	6	44,914	143.04	1	14 7	7 0	1	1	1
146	July 1, 1887	1	23.44	2	23.89									
95	July 1, 1887	71	11.34	72	13.05	6	27,192	86.60	1	17 2	9 4	1	1	1
5,861	July 1, 1886	201	30.08	202	30.43	7	469,237	213.67	3	45 4	9 4	6	2	†26
									1	45 6	9 10			
		203	28.62	204	28.00	7	307,733	168.16	1	24 9	8 10	5	2	
									2	24 1	9 4			
47,461	July 1, 1887	302	21.92	301	22.00	7	123,891	112.83	1	40 11	8 11	3	1	105
1,902	July 1, 1887	301	24.98	302	24.96	7			11					
		305	22.01	306	23.29	7								
2,333	July 1, 1886	3	30.40	4	27.22	7	13356,696	194.92	1	25 0	9 1½	5	2	16
									2	25 2	9 0			
		1	24.70	2	23.75	7	13148,825	135.09	1	18 '1½	8 10½	3	2	
									1	25 2	9 0			
2,687	July 1, 1887	3	28.91	4	24.64	7			2	18 1½	8 10½			
		1	24.88	2	23.90	7								
1,818	July 1, 1887	3	23.23	4	20.22	7			1	25 0	9 1½			
10,352	July 1, 1887	3	23.88	10	23.88	7	266,199	181.83	2	21 0	8 10	4	1	146
2,704	Aug. 3, 1888	39	20.05	40	17.55									
1,641	July 15, 1885	39	33.25	40	31.04									
3,627	July 1, 1886	39	27.86	40	35.03									
3,030	July 1, 1886	39	27.85	40	32.45									
4,566	July 1, 1886	39	20.00	40	25.91									

9 34.03 miles, distance on route 28001, covered by Saint Louis and Kansas City, Mo., R. P. O.

10 2 helpers between Kansas City and Nevada, Mo. (103 32 miles), who also perform service on Nevada, Mo., and Chetopa, Kans., line, alternating with the clerk appointed to that R. P. O.

11 Baggage-car.

12 Double daily service between Kansas City and Springfield, Mo. (204.63 miles); trains 1 and 2 between Kansas City and Springfield and 3 and 4 between Kansas City and Memphis.

13 83.13 miles of route 83008, between Fort Scott, Kans., and Webb City, Mo., covered by Fort Scott, Kans., and Webb City, Mo., R. P. O.

14 Distance (101.50 miles) covered by Council Bluffs, Iowa, and Kansas City, Mo., R. P. O.

15 Two helpers between Kansas City, Mo., and Pawnee City, Nebr.

16 Distance (38 80 miles) covered by Columbus, Nebr., and Atchison, Kans., R. P. O.

17 Distance (40 87 miles) covered by Kansas City, Mo., and Red Cloud, Nebr., R. P. O

18 Distance (108.18 miles) covered by Kansas City, Mo., and Red Cloud, Nebr., R. P. O.

19 Distance (64.78 miles) covered by Omaha and McCook, Nebr., R. P. O.

TABLE A*.—*Statement of railway post-offices in operation*

Designation of railway post-office. (Lines upon which railway post-office cars are paid for, in *italics*.)	Division.	Distance run by clerks, register to register.	Initial and terminal stations, running from east to west, north to south, or northwest to southeast (with abbreviated title of railroad company).	Number of route.	Miles of route for which railroad is paid.
		Miles.			
Kansas City, Mo., and Pueblo, Colo.[1]	7	....			....
Eastern Division[2]		368.64	Kansas City, Mo., Topeka, Kans. (A., T. and S. F.).	33016	66.88
			Topeka, Kans., Pueblo, Colo. (A., T. and S. F.).	[4]33010 (part)	302.00
Western Division[6]		267.91			267.75
Kansas City, Mo., and Red Cloud, Nebr.	6	278.92	Kansas City, Winthrop Junction, Mo. (K. C., St. Jo. & C. Bl.).	28006 (part)	(7)
			Winthrop Junction, Mo., Atchison, Kans. (K. C., St. Jo. & C. Bl.).	28006 (part)	(9)
			Atchison, Kans., Table Rock, Nebr. (B. & M. R. in Nebr.).	33012 (part)	(10)
			Table Rock, Wymore, Nebr. (B. & M. R. in Nebr.).	34020	40.87
			Wymore, Red Cloud, Nebr. (B. & M. R. in Nebr.).	[11]34016 (part)	108.18
Kansas City, Mo., and Seneca, Kans.[13]	7	117.64	Kansas City, Mo., Seneca, Kans. (K. C., W. and N. W.).	33079	118.75
Kansas City, Mo., Salina, Kans., and Pueblo, Colo.[15]	7	[13]301.77	Kansas City, Mo., Paola, Kans. (K. C. and S. W.).	33091	54.09
		[13]339.06	Paola, Osawatomie, Kans. (Mo. Pac.)	33031 (part)	(16)
			Osawatomie, Ottawa, Kans. (Mo. Pac.)	33033	21.42
			Ottawa, Council Grove, Kans. (C. G., O. C. and O.).	33067	71.34
			Council Grove, Salina, Kans. (T., S. and W.)	33050	72.22
			Salina, McCracken, Kans. (Kans. and Colo.)	33070	126.25
			McCracken, Kans., Towner, Colo. (D., M. and A.).	33084	141.35
			Towner, Pueblo, Colo., (P. and S. Line.) ..	38036	150.76
Kansas City, Mo., and Wellington, Kans.[17]	7	270.09	Kansas City, Mo., Ottawa, Kans. (So. Kans.)	33006	58.80
			Ottawa, Cherry Vale, Kans. (So. Kans.) ...	[20]33001 (part)	97.80
			Cherry Vale, Wellington, Kans. (So. Kans.) ..	[21]33005 (part)	113.41
			Chanute, Longton, Kans. (C. K. and W.) ...	33066	45.13
Keene, N. H., and South Vernon (n. o.), Vt.	1	24.35	Keene, N. H., South Vernon (n. o.), Vt. (Conn. Riv.)	3056	23.93
Kempton and Bloomington, Ill..	6	57.77	Kempton, Bloomington, Ill. (Illinois Central).	[22]23062 (part)	58.11
Kenedy and Corpus Christi, Tex.[23]	7	89.00	Kenedy, Corpus Christi, Tex. (S. A. and A. P.).	[24]31033 (part)	88.50
Kenosha, Wis., and Rockford, Ill.	6	73.42	Kenosha, Wis., Rockford, Ill. (Chi. & No. West.).	25011	73.71
Keokuk and Humeston, Iowa..	6	132.05	Keokuk, Humeston, Iowa (Keo. & West.) ...	[26]28015 (part)	131.50
Keokuk, Iowa, and Clayton, Ill.	6	43.09	Keokuk, Iowa, Clayton, Ill. (Wabash)	23081	43.09
Ketchum and Shoshone, Idaho.	8	70.34	Ketchum, Shoshone, Idaho (Oregon Short Line).	42001	70.01

[1] Double daily service. This line is in two divisions, dividing at Dodge City, Kans.

[2] Two helpers between Kansas City, Mo., and Newton, Kans. (301.10 miles).

[3] Kansas City, Mo., to Dodge City, Kans.

[4] 50.70 miles of route 33010, between Atchison and Topeka, Kans., covered by Atchison and Topeka, Kans., R. P. O.

[5] In reserve.

[6] Dodge City, Kans., to Pueblo, Colo.

[7] Distance (48.10 miles) covered by Council Bluffs, Iowa, and Kansas City, Mo., R. P. O.

[8] Whole cars.

[9] Distance (2.10 miles) covered by Cameron, Mo., and Atchison, Kans., R. P. O.

[10] Distance (82.53 miles) covered by Columbus, Nebr., and Atchison, Kans., R. P. O.

[11] Balance of route (12.07 miles) covered by Lincoln, Nebr., and Concordia, Kans., R. P. O.

[12] New service; not reported last year.

[13] This line is in two divisions, dividing at Hoisington, Kans. Kansas City, Mo., and Hoisington, Kans., division, 301.77 miles; Hoisington, Kans., and Pueblo, Colo., division, 339.06 miles.

[14] 1 helper between Kansas City, Mo., and Ottawa, Kans. (81.80 miles).

[15] Reported last year as Osawatomie and McCracken, Kans.; increased distance, 353.05 miles.

[16] 7.20 miles distance on route 33031, covered by Holden, Mo. and Coffeyville, Kans., R. P. O.

in the United States on June 30. 1888—Continued.

Average weight of mail whole distance per da.	Date of last re-adjustment.	Average speed per hour (train numbers taken from division schedules).				Number of run d trips with clerks per week.	Annual miles of service with clerks.	Average miles run daily by crews.	Number of mail cars or cars in which are mail apartments.	Inside dimensions of cars or apartments (railway post-office cars in black figures).		Number of crews.	Number of clerks to crew.	Number of clerks appointed to line.
		Train No. outward.	Av'ge speed (miles).	Train No. inward.	Av'ge speed (miles).					Length.	Width.			
Lbs.										Ft. In.	Ft. In.			
18,512	July 1, 1886	5	24.18	8	26.60	7	¹269,844	184.82	4	50 0	9 3½	4	4	
		7	26.60	4	26.60	7	289,844	184.32	4	50	9 3½			
11,653	July 1, 1886	5	28.44	6,8	24.88	7	....		⁵1	50 0	9 3½			
		7	22.68	4	23.07	7								
							¹106,110	178.61				3	2	
							196,110	178.61)				3	2	
10,352	July 1, 1887	7	32.00	8	27.43	7	204,169	139.46	*2	35 2	8 9	4	1	4
10,352	July 1, 1887	7	8.40	8	8.40									
1,641	July 15, 1883	18	29.13	16	31.93									
3,627	July 1, 1886	15	28.82	16	28.82									
3,020	July 1, 1886	15	28.22	16	31.66									
346	July 1, 1888	1	23.91	2	23.34	7	86,112	117.64	1	28 6	7 2½	2	1	2
									⁵1	12 1	7 2½			
		221	21.56	221	23.96	7	220,896	159.39	2	20 5	7 5	4	1	¹⁸9
		222		222										
726	July 1, 1886	221	28.80	222	28.80	7	248,192	169.53	1	20 5	7 6	4	1	
									1	19 9	7 2			
200	July 1, 1886	201	28.02	202	28.02	7								
5.9	Mar.14, 1887	201	20.14	202	21.17	7	....		⁵1	16 4	6 10			
549	Mar.30, 1887	201	26.29	202	26.24	7								
1,141	July 1, 1888	201	25.41	202	27.29	7								
768	July 1, 1888	201	36.42	202	30.97	7								
458	July 1, 1888	201	28.11	201	27.31	7								
4,648	July 1, 1886	201	24.23	202	23.36	7	197,706	135.05	2	21 0	9 3½	4	1	¹⁸14
		203	26.31	204	25.40	7	¹⁹183,871	¹⁹125.60	2	21 0	9 3½	4	2	
2,740	July 1, 1886	201	22.59	202	22.18	7								
		203	24.64	204	23.46	7	....		*4	21 0	9 3½			
1,691	July 1, 1886	201	20.60	202	18.84	7								
		203	20.52	204	20.73	7								
1,174	Feb.21, 1887	203	23.56	204	23.07	7	15,292	97.40	1	8 10	7 0	1	1	1
645	July 1, 1885	18	24.00	3	24.00	6	15,292							
		32	26.17	23	24.00	6								
171	July 1, 1887	9	11.05	8	25.77	6	36,279	115.54	2	15 0	7 2½	1	1	1
837	July 1, 1886	5	19.56	4	19.95	6	55,892	178	2	14 0	9 0	1	1	1
1,376	July 1, 1887	91	12.82	92	12.82	6	46,107	146.84	1	13 6	7 6	1	1	1
									*1	13 8	7 6			
419	July 1, 1887	5	23.30	6	22.08	6	82,927	132.05	2	10 8	7 0	2	1	2
									1	15 11½	8 10			
									1	16 8½	8 11			
491	July 1, 1887	442	23.45	443	21.54	6	27,060	86.18	1	17 7	8 7½	1	1	1
407	July 1, 1886	521	17.28	522	17.50	6	44,174	140.68	1	10 2	6 8	1	1	1

¹⁷ Double daily service.

¹⁸ 1 helper on trains 201 and 202 between Kansas City, Mo., and Garnett, Kans. (83 miles); 1 clerk performs service on trains 209 and 210, Chanute and Longton (via Cherry Vale), Kans., R. P. O.

¹⁹ Night-line clerks leave main line at Chanute, Kans., and run over route 33066 to Longton, Kans. Distance, from register to register, 251 10 miles.

²⁰ 27.39 miles of route 33004, between Lawrence and Ottawa, Kans., covered by Lawrence and Gridley, Kans., R. P. O., and 16.68 miles, between Cherry Vale and Coffeyville, Kans., by closed pouch service. (See Table C⁷.)

²¹ 18 12 miles of route 33005, between Wellington and Hunnewell, Kans., covered by closed-pouch service. (See Table C³.)

²² Balance of route (28.27 miles) covered by Kankakee and Kankakee Junction, Ill., R. P. O.

²³ Reported last year as San Antonio and Corpus Christi, Tex.; decreased distance, 67.06 miles.

²⁴ 67 56 miles of route 31033, between I. and G. N. R. R., San Antonio and Kenedy, Tex., covered by Wallis Station and San Antonio, Tex., R. P. O.

²⁵ Reserve.

²⁶ Balance of route (17.82 miles) covered by Hampton and Shenandoah, Iowa, R. P. O.

TABLE A⁶.—*Statement of railway post-offices in operation*

Designation of railway post-office. (Lines upon which railway post-office cars are paid for, in *italics*.)	Division.	Distance run by clerks, register to register.	Initial and terminal stations, running from east to west, north to south, or northwest to southeast (with abbreviated title of railroad company).	Number of route.	Miles of route for which railroad is paid.
		Miles.			
Keystone and Barnard, Kans¹..	7	43.23	Keystone, Barnard, Kans. (C., K. and W.).	*33077 (part)	43.18
Keysville, Va., and Oxford, N. C.	3	55.86	Keysville, Va., Oxford, N. C. (Rich. and Dan.).	11032	55.78
Killbuck and Trinway, Ohio²...	5	34.14	Killbuck, Trinway, Ohio (Cleve., Ak. and Col.).	21102	34.14
Kinkaid and Coffeyville, Kans¹.	7	85.59	Kinkaid, Coffeyville, Kans. (K., C. and P.).	23083	85.59
Kingston and Goshen, N. Y....	2	44.26	Kingston, Montgomery, N Y. (Walkill Valley).	6083	34.12
			Montgomery, Goshen, N.Y. (N.Y., L. E. and W.).	6009	10.65
Knobel and Helena, Ark	7	140.65	Knobel, Forrest City, Ark. (St. L., I. M. and S.).	29012	97.78
			Forrest City, Helena, Ark. (St. L., I. M. and S.).	29008	44.65
Knox, Ind., and Streator, Ill....	6	119.65	Knox, Ind., Streator, Ill. (Ind., Ill. and Iowa).	23082	119.82
Knoxville and Maryville, Tenn.	3	17.78	Knoxville, Maryville, Tenn. (Knoxv. and Augusta.)	19014	17.78
La Cro se and Brasil, Ind⁷	5	145.65	La Crosse, Attica, Ind. (Chic. and Ind. Coal).	22026	83.40
			Attica, Brazil, Ind. (Chic. and Ind. Coal)....	22031	63.42
La Crosse, Wis., and Dubuque, Iowa.	6	122.47	La Crosse, Wis., Dubuque, Iowa (Chi., Mil. and St. P.).	*27012 (part)	121.73
La Crosse, Wis., and Woonsocket, Dak.	6	400.45	La Crosse, Wis., Flandreau, Dak. (Chi., Mil. and St. P.).	26023	311.29
			Flandreau, Egan, Dak. (Chi., Mil. and St. P.).	¹⁰35007 (part)	4.40
			Egan, Woonsocket, Dak. (Chi., Mil. and St. P.).	35008	85.30
La Fayette, Ind., and Quincy, Ill.	6	271.00	La Fayette, Ind., Quincy, Ill. (Wabash)	¹¹21019 (part)	268.67
La Junta, Colo., and Albuquerque, N. Mex.	7	348.22	La Junta, Colo., Albuquerque. N. Mex. (A., T. and S. F.).	¹²38006 (part)	348.09
Lake Crystal, Minn., and Eagle Grove, Iowa.	6	110.48	Lake Crystal, Elmore, Minn. (Chi., St. P., Minn. and Om.).	26029	44.15
			Elmore, Minn., Eagle Grove, Iowa (Chi. and No. West.).	¹²27052 (part)	66.30
Lake Geneva, Wis., and Elgin, Ill.	6	44.15	Lake Geneva, Wis., Elgin, Ill. (Chi. and No. West.).	23004	43.79
Lake Station, Ind., and Joliet, Ill.	6	45.68	Lake Station, Ind., Joliet, Ill. (Mich. Central.)	23022	45.15
Lancaster, N. H., and Boston, Mass.	1	212.03	Lancaster, Concord, N. H. (Bos. and Me., Low. Sys.).	¹⁰1C06 (part)	136.30
			Concord, Nashua, N. H. (Con.)	1001	(²⁰)
			Nashua, N. H., Boston, Mass. (Bos. and Me., Low. Sys.).	3016	(²⁰)
Lancaster, Pa., and Frederick, Md.	2	81.67	Lancaster, Columbia, Pa. (Penna.)..........	8027 (part)	(²⁰)
			Columbia, Pa., and Frederick, Md. (Penna.)..	8032	69.30
Lancaster and Kingville, S. C..	4	80.53	Lancaster, Camden, S. C. (C. C. and C., R. R.)	14027	41.50
			Camden, Kingville, S C. (S. C. R. R.)....	14018	39.28

¹ New service; not reported last year.
² 76.40 miles of route 33077, between Keystone and Strong, Kans., covered by Concordia and Strong, Kans., R. P. O., and 12.60 miles, between Strong and Bazaar, Kans, covered by closed pouch service (See Table C⁴.)
³ R. P. O. service established June 25, 1884.
⁴ Clerk runs only between Coffeyville and Parsons on Sunday (31.27 miles).
⁵ In reserve.
⁶ Cars and clerks shown on route No. 6083
⁷ Fair Oaks and Brasil R. P. O. extended to La Crosse, Ind., Feb. 20, 1888; increase in distance 27.00 miles.
⁸ Balance of route covered by Chicago, Ill., Mc-Gregor, Iowa, and Saint Paul, Minn.. R. P. O. (43 60 miles), and between Sabula Junction and Clinton, Iowa (16.46 miles), by closed pouches (See Table C⁴.)
⁹ Short run, La Crosse, Wis., to Jackson, Minn., 215.54 miles.
¹⁰ Balance of route (34 91 miles) covered by Egan, Dak , and Sioux City, Iowa, R. P. O.
¹¹ Balance of route (201.70 miles) covered by Toledo, Ohio, and La Fayette, Ind. R P.O.
¹² 1 clerk detailed as chief clerk at Quincy, Ill.; 1 to clerical duty at office of superintendent, Chicago, Ill.; 1 to transfer duty at Decatur, Ill., and 9 to transfer duty at Quincy, Ill.

In the United States on June 30, 1888—Continued.

Average weight of mail whole distance per day.	Date of last re-adjustment.	Average speed per hour (train numbers taken from division schedules).				Number of round trips with clerks per week.	Annual miles of service with clerks.	Average miles run daily by crews.	Number of mail cars, or cars in which are mail apartments.	Inside dimensions of cars or apartments (railway post-office cars in black figures).		Number of crews.	Number of clerks to crew.	Number of clerks appointed to line.
		Train No. outward.	Av'ge speed (miles).	Train No. inward.	Av'ge speed (miles).					Length.	Width.			
Lbs.										*Ft. In.*	*Ft. In.*			
383	July 1, 1888	321	22.55	322	21.55	7	31,644	86.48	1	7 5	6 2	1	1	1
216	July 1, 1885	50	13.82	51	13.27	6	35,080	111.72	1	12 0	8 0	1	1	1
70	July 1, 1888	38	24	3	22.50	6	440	68.28	1	15 0	9 0	1	1	1
136	July 1, 1888	1	15.05	2	14.49	7	457,003	155.66	1	12 0	7 0	1	1	1
									5 1	12 0	7 0			
435	July 1, 1885	4	27.29	1	27.29	6	27,795	88.52	2	18 2	8 10	1	1	1
									1	18 0	7 6			
547	July 1, 1883	4	30.42	1	35.49	6	....	....	(9)	....	....	(9)		
570	July 1, 1887	901	20.15	902	20.48	7	102,956	93.77	2	14 6	8 11	3	1	3
525	July 1, 1886	901	18.93	902	18.28	7								
92	June 28, 1888	1	11.94	2	11.41	6	75,140	119.65	1	15 0	7 4	2	1	2
									1	14 2	6 11			
191	July 1, 1888	1	10.70	2	10.70	6	11,166	35.56	1	8 10	7 8	1	1	1
343	July 1, 1888	1	14.76	2	14.82	6	80,764	145.65	2	14 0	7 3	2	1	2
306	July 1, 1888	1	18.12	2	16.20	6								
2,982	July 1, 1887	6	24.34	5	21.17	6	76,911	122.47	1	22 0	9 4	2	1	2
									1	20 0	9 4			
2,119	July 1, 1887	1	22.28	4	20.22	6	251,482	133.48	1	26 0	9 3	6	1	9
		3	30.07	2	29.73	6	135,330	143.89	2	15 9	7 6	3	1	
404	July 1, 1886	1	26.40	4	20.31				1	23 1	9 3			
1,204	July 1, 1886	1	28.33	4	24.87		....	....	1	21 1	9 4			
11,242	July 1, 1884	45	21.44	44	26.36	6	170,188	135.50	3	50 0	9 2	4	3	17
4,546	July 1, 1886	1	20.68	2	20.47	7	254,897	139.29	1 49	21 0	9 3½	5	1	7
									2 1	21 0	9 3½			
									5 1	13 4½	5 3½			
521	July 1, 1887	13	25.23	14	25.23	6	69,381	110.48	1	11 9	9 4	2	1	2
		10	25.66	9	22.10				1	12 2	7 5			
									17 1	13 6	7 2			
									17 1	8 9	7 5			
246	July 1, 1887	60	25.02	59	24.98	6	27,726	88.30	19 2	12 2	7 5	1	1	1
107	July 1, 1887	141	24.54	144	25.71	6	28,687	91.36	1	11 1	7 0	1	1	1
3,263	July 1, 1885	54	20.50	29	21.01	6	110,174	100.01	1	27 6	9 0	3	2	7
									1	25 6	8 6			
11,733	July 1, 1885	54	32.30	29	23.32									
14,366	July 1, 1885	54	29.07	29	27.08									
938	July 1, 1885	85	24.20	82	25.92	6	51,280	81.67	1	15 0	8 6	2	1	2
512	July 1, 1885	4	21.88	1	18.90	6	....	....	(24)	....	....	(24)		
		102	23.7	101	21.7	6	50,572	161.06	1	20 0	8 0	1	1	1
499	July 1, 1888	102	28.0	101	28.0									

[13] 77.14 miles of route 38006, between Albuquerque and Rincon, N. Mex., covered by Albuquerque, N. Mex., and El Paso, Tex., R. P. O., and 53.82 miles between Rincon and Deming, N. Mex., covered by Rincon and Silver City, N Mex., R. P. O.

[14] Cars are run between Kansas City, Mo., and El Paso, Tex.

[15] 1 helper between La Junta and Thatcher, Colo. (45.10 miles), and 1 clerk detailed to transfer service, La Junta, Colo.

[16] Balance of route (98.34 miles) covered by Tama and Hawarden, Iowa, R. P. O.

[17] Reserve.

[18] One in reserve.

[19] Balance of route (9.58 miles) covered by closed-pouch service between Lancaster and Groveton Junction. (See table Ce).

[20] One clerk detailed as transfer clerk, Manchester, N. H.

[21] Covered by Saint Albans and Boston R. P. O. (36.28 miles).

[22] Covered by Saint Albans and Boston R. P. O. (39.85 miles). Lancaster and Boston R. P. O. to November 30, 1887; Lancaster and Concord R. P. O. from December 1, 1887; Lancaster and Boston R. P. O. from May 28, 1888.

[23] 18.10 miles covered by Lancaster and Harrisburg R. P. O.

[24] Cars and clerks shown on route No. 5027.

TABLE A°.—*Statement of railway post-offices in operation*

Designation of railway post-office. (Lines upon which railway post-office cars are paid for, in *italics*.)	Division.	Distance run by clerks, register to register.	Initial and terminal stations, running from east to west, north to south, or northwest to southeast (with abbreviated title of railroad company).	Number of route.	Miles of route for which railroad is paid.
		Miles.			
Lancaster and Harrisburg, Pa	2	40. 87	Lancaster, Middletown, Pa. (Penna.)......	8027	30. 96
			Middletown, Harrisburgh, Pa. (Penna.) ...	8001	(1)
Langdon and Larimore, Dak..	6	76. 19	Langdon, Larimore, Dak. (St. P., Minn. and Man.)	*35006 (part)	76. 19
Lansing and Hillsdale, Mich.4..	9	65. 68	Lansing. Jonesville, Mich. (L. S. and M..S)..	24005	61. 04
			Jonesville, Hillsdale, Mich. (L. S. and M. S).	21095 (part)	(5)
Larabee and Clermont, Pa....	2	*22. 16	Larabee, Clermont, Pa. (W. N. Y. and Pa.).	8091	22. 30
Larimore, Dak., and Breckenridge, Minn.	6	131. 40	Larimore, Everest, Dak. (St. P., Minn. and Man.)	*35006 (part)	79. 53
			Portland Junction, Ripon, Dak. (St. P., Minn. and Man.)	35012	41. 41.
			Ripon, Dak., Breckenridge, Minn. (St. P., Minn. and Man.)	*85003 (part)	63. 41
Larned and Jetmore, Kans.9...	7	46. 84	Larned, Jetmore, Kans. (C., K. and W.)....	33061	46. 84
Laurens and Columbia, S. C....	4	79. 92	Laurens, Newberry, S. C. (It. and D. R. R.).	14012	31. 78
			Newberry, Columbia, S. C. (R. and D. R. R.).	14001	(10)
Lawrence and Gridley, Kans.11	7	83. 67	Lawrence, Ottawa, Kans. (So. Kans.)........	1923004 (part)	27. 39
			Ottawa, Burlington, Kans. (So. Kans.).....	33019	47. 04.
			Burlington, Gridley, Kans. (So. Kans.).....	33080	11. 32
Leadville, Aspen, Colo.9...	7	137. 82	Leadville, Aspen, Colo. (D. and R. G.)	38018	137. 82
Leavenworth and Lawrence, Kans.	7	34. 95	Leavenworth, Lawrence, Kans (U.P.).....	33002	34. 95
Leavenworth and Miltonvale, Kans.	7	166. 18	Leavenworth, Miltonville, Kans. (K.C.)...	33013	166. 18
Leavenworth and Topeka, Kans.	7	57. 68	Leavenworth. Meriden Junction (n. o.), Kans. (L., T. and S. W.).	33038	47. 07
			Meriden Junction (n. o.), Topeka, Kans. (A., T. and S. F.).	33010 (part)	(12)
Leavittsburgh and Cincinnati, Ohio.16	5	281. 19	Leavittsburgh, Dayton, Ohio (N. Y., L. E. and W.).	1721034 (part)	224. 58
			Dayton, Cincinnati, Ohio (Cleve., Col., Cinn. and Ind.).	21042 (part)	(20)
Lebanon and Greensburgh, Ky.	5	31. 83	Lebanon, Greensburgh, Ky. (Louis. and Nash.).	20024	31. 80
Lebanon and Nashville, Tenn..	5	31. 66	Lebanon, Nashville, Tenn. (Nash., Chatt. and St. Louis).	19001	31. 52
Leland and Glen Allan, Miss..	4	41	Leland, Wilzinski, Miss. (L., N. O. and T. R. R.).	18020	(22)
			Wilzinski, Glen Allan, Miss. (L., N. O. and T. R. R.).	18022	34. 01
Lenoir, N. C., and Lancaster, S. C.	4	138. 25	Lenoir, Hickory, N. C. (R. and D. R. R.).	13023	20. 51
			Hickory, N. C., Chester, S. C. (R. and D. R. R.).	14007	85. 62
			Chester, Lancaster, S. C. (R. and D. R. R.)	14013	29. 47
Lenox and Jackson, Mich	9	106. 68	Lenox, Jackson, Mich. (Grand Trunk)	24633	106. 58
Lexington and Louisville, Ky.	5	94. 72	Lexington, La Grange, Ky. (Louis. and Nash.).	20003	67. 44
			La Grange, Louisville, Ky. (Louis. and Nash.).	20004 (part)	(24)

In the United States on June 30, 1888—Continued.

Average weight of mail whole distance per day.	Date of last readjustment.	Average speed per hour (train numbers taken from division schedules)				Number of round trips with clerks per week.	Annual miles of service with clerks.	Average miles run daily by crews.	Number of mail cars, or cars in which are mail apartments.	Inside dimensions of cars or apartments (railway post-office cars in black figures).		Number of crews.	Number of clerks to crew.	Number of clerks appointed to line.
		Train No. outward.	Av'ge speed (miles).	Train No. inward.	Av'ge speed (miles.)					Length.	Width.			
Lbs.										*Ft. in.*	*Ft. in.*			
938	July 1, 1885	72	23.35	73	22.70	6	25,666	81.74		15 0	8 7	1	1	*1
......	....	72	23.30	73	21.60	6	......	......	(?)				(2)	
627	July 1, 1888	82	11.87	81	12.19	6	47,847	152.38	1	16 0	9 3	1	1	1
832	July 1, 1884	152	25.71	155	24.87	6 }	41,247	131.36	1	15 0	9 4	1	1	1
98,761	July 1, 1888	152	23.45	155	25.80	6 }								
273	July 1, 1885	26	15.10	25	13.70	6	*13,916	146.88	1	8 7	6 8	1	1	1
627	July 1, 1888	48	16.74	47	17.34	6	82,519	131.40	1	22 2	8 11	2	1	2
453	July 1, 1886	48	18.40	47	18.40									
763	July 1, 1886	48	18.28	47	19.32									
235	July 1, 1888	361	19.82	362	21.29	7	34,287	93.68	1	21 0	9 3½	1	1	1
174	July 1, 1884	4	13.29	3	13.80	6	50,189	159.82	1	8 3	6 7	1	1	1
904	July 1, 18x8	4	21.82	3	15.40									
2,740	July 1, 1886	207	20.38	208	20.38	6	52,545	83.67	1	20 2½	8 10	2	1	2
									1	20 0	8 10			
351	July 1, 1886	207	21.81	208	20 72	6								
50	July 1, 1888	207	24.72	208	20.60	6								
1,097	July 1, 1888	3	19.77	4	18.26	7	100,884	137.82	2	15 1½	7 6	2	1	2
456	July 1, 1886	231	21.52	232	21.52	7	25,583	69.90	1	12 0	9 1	1	1	1
576	July 1, 1886	15291	20.90	15292	19.18	6	104,861	110.79	1	15 5	7 6	3	1	3
		15293	10.69	15294	13.58	6	......	......	1	19 10	6 4			
									14]1	15 5	7 6			
139	July 1, 1886	131	23.05	132	23.05	7	42,222	115.36	1	7 0	6 0	1	1.	1
									14]1	7 0	6 0			
11,653	July 1, 1887	131	20.40	132	20.40	7								
2,429	July 1, 1888	5	29.64	4	30.62	6	174,217	140.59	14]3	18 6	9 0	4	1	14]4
19,359	July 1, 1888	5	26.88	4	31.14	6								
255	July 1, 1884	79	12.72	78	12.72	6	20,002	63.70	1	7 6	7 6	1	1.	1
620	July 1, 1888	150	21.24	151	19.92	6	19,882	120.64	1	17 3	7 2	1	1	1
		152	9.79	153	14.82	21]6	19,882							
802	July 1, 1888	22	11.06	21	11.05	6	25,748	82	1	5 9	7 1	1	1	1
231	July 1, 1888	22	13.60	21	13.60									
396	July 1, 1888	52	16.60	53	18.20	6								
386	July 1, 1888	52	18.40	53	16.90	.....	86,821	92.16	1	7 2	6 6	3	1.	3
									1	13 2	7 2			
238	July 1, 1888	52	17.80	53	17.80									
373	July 1, 1884	2	21.77	3	21.22	6	66,995	22]106.66	1	24 0	6 4	2	1	2
		8	11.67		7 10		......	......	1	17 10	7 4			
1,243	July 1, 1884	21	25.74	18	23.88	6	59,484	94.72	1	14 9	9 6	2	1	2
19,543	July 1, 1884	21	28.38	18	18.36	6								

* and Garrison, and 293 and 294 between Garrison and Miltonvale, Kans.

14 In reserve.

15 10.20 miles, distance on route 33010, covered by Atchison and Topeka, Kans., R. P. O.

16 This line was formerly the Kentucky and Cincinnati R. P. O., August 22, 1887; run of clerks was extended to Leavittsburgh, Ohio, increasing distance 27 miles.

17 Balance of route covered by lines of the Second Division 164.24 miles.

18 1 car in reserve.

19 These clerks do no local work between Dayton and Cincinnati, Ohio, running in cars of Cleveland and Cincinnati day line on north trips as helpers.

20 Covered by Cleveland and Cincinnati R. P. O., 56 miles.

21 Clerk makes two round trips daily, except Sunday.

22 Reported as Fort Smith and Leland R. P. O.

23 This line is divided at Pontiac. One clerk runs from Lenox to Pontiac and return, a distance of 70 miles daily, except Sunday. One clerk runs from Pontiac to Jackson, Mich., and return, a distance of 141.50 miles daily, except Sunday.

24 Covered by Cincinnati and Nashville R. P. O. (27.40 miles).

TABLE A⁶.—*Statement of railway post-offices in operation*

Designation of railway post-office. (Lines upon which railway post-office cars are paid for, in *italics*.)	Division.	Distance run by clerks, register to register.	Initial and terminal stations, running from east to west, north to south, or northwest to southeast (with abbreviated title of railroad company).	Number of route.	Miles of route for which railroad is paid.
		Miles.			
Lincoln and Alma, Nebr........	6	224.81	Lincoln, Valparaiso, Nebr. (Om. and Rep. Vall.).	34014	20.50
			Valparaiso, Stromsburgh, Nebr. (Om. and Rep. Vall.).	¹34008 (part)	52.80
			Stromburgh, Fairfield, Nebr. (Kan. City and Om.).	34045	65.49
			Fairfield, Alma, Nebr. (Kan. City and Om.).	34053	87.79
Lincoln, Nebr., and Concordia, Kans.	6	143.12	Lincoln, Crete, Nebr. (B. and M. R. in Nebr.)	34002 (part)	(⁷)
			Crete, Beatrice, Nebr. (B. and M. R. in Nebr.)	34006	30.57
			Beatrice, Odell, Nebr. (B. and M. R. in Nebr.)	²34016	⁴12.07
			Odell, Nebr., Concordia, Kans. (B. and M. R. in Nebr.).	34028	72.29
Linwood and Geneva, Nebr....	6	77.41	Linwood, Geneva, Nebr. (Fre., Elk. and Mo. Vall.).	34056	77.53
Litchfield and Bethel, Conn...	1	39.03	Litchfield, Hawleyville, Conn. (Shep., Litch and Northern).	5019	32.96
			Hawleyville, Bethel, Conn. (Dan. Nor. Div. N. Y., N. H. and Hart.).	5024	6.06
Litchfield and Kampsville, Ill.	6	58.68	Litchfield, Barnett, Ill. (Jack. and So. East)	23046 (part)	(⁵)
			Barnett, Kampsville, Ill. (Jack. and So. East.	23060	52.42
Little Falls and Morris, Minn..	6	88.33	Little Falls, Morris, Minn. (North. Pac.)....	26046	88.31
Lock Haven and Harrisburg, Pa.	2	118.63	Lock Haven, Williamsport, Pa. (Penna.)....	8022 (part)	(⁶)
			Williamsport, Sunbury, Pa. (Penna.)......	8006	(⁷)
			Sunbury, Harrisburg, Pa. (N. C.).........	10002 (part)	(¹¹)
Lock Haven and Tyrone, Pa...	2	60.46 (¹²)	Lock Haven, Tyrone, Pa. (Penna.)........	8038	55.25
			Bellefonte, Milesburgh, Pa. (Penna.).....	8083 (part)	¹²2.70
Logan and Nelsonville, Ohio...	5	32.76	Logan, New Straitsville, Ohio (Col., H. V. and Tol.).	21084	13.39
			New Straitsville, Nelsonville, Ohio (Col. H. V. and Tol).	21077	19.94
Logan and Pomeroy, Ohio.....	5	83.71	Logan, Pomeroy, Ohio (Col., H. V. and Tol.).	21074	83.71
Logansport, Ind., and Columbus, Ohio.	5	196.71	Logansport, Ind., Bradford, Ohio (Pitts., Cin. and St. Lou.).	22017	114.29
			Bradford, Columbus, Ohio (Chic., St. Lou. and Pitts.).	21015 (part)	(¹³)
Logansport, Ind., and Keokuk, Iowa.	6	283.02	Logansport, State Line, Ind. (Chic., St. L. and Pitts.).	22014	61,19
			State Line, Ind., Keokuk, Iowa (Tol , Peo. and West.).	²¹23027 (part)	222.83
Los Angeles and Santa Ana, Cal.²⁸	8	35.60	Los Angeles, Santa Ana, Cal. (Southern Pacific).	46017	35.60
Los Angeles and Santa Barbara, Cal ²⁴	8	111.20	Sangus Station (n. o.), Santa Barbara, Cal. (Southern Pacific).	46051	78.80
			Los Angeles, Sangus Station (n. o), Cal. (Southern Pacific.)	46014 (part)	243.06

¹ Balance of route (37.62 miles) covered by Omaha and Beatrice, Nebr., R. P. O.
² Distance (20.1 miles) covered by Omaha and McCook, Nebr., R. P. O.
³ Balance of route (108.18 miles) covered by Kansas City, Mo., and Red Cloud, Nebr., R. P. O.
⁴ Difference in distance (9 miles) covered by Kansas City, Mo., and Red Cloud, Nebr. R. P. O.
⁵ Distance (6.50 miles) covered by Jacksonville and Mount Vernon, Ill., R. P. O.

⁶ 24.50 miles covered by Williamsport and Erie R. P. O.
⁷ Two helpers.
⁸ Double daily service except Sunday.
⁹ 40 96 miles covered by Williamsport and Baltimore R. P. O.
¹⁰ Cars and clerks shown on route No. 8022.
¹¹ 53.20 miles covered by Williamsport and Baltimore R. P. O.
¹² R. P. O. runs in and out of Bellefonte.

in the United States on June 30, 1888—Continued.

Average weight of mail whole distance per day.	Date of last readjustment.	Average speed per hour (train numbers taken from division schedules).				Number of round trips with clerks per week.	Annual miles of service with clerks.	Average miles run daily by crews.	Number of mail cars, or cars in which are mail apartments.	Inside dimensions of cars or apartments (railway post-office cars in black figures).		Number of crews.	Number of clerks to crew.	Number of clerks appointed to line.
		Train No. outward	Av'ge speed (miles).	Train No. inward	Av'ge speed (miles).					Length.	Width.			
Lbs.										Ft. In.	Ft. In.			
1,009	July 1, 1886	48	27.45	47	27.45	6	141,180	149.87	1	12 2	7 6	3	1	3
646	July 1, 1886	40	26.4.	59	21.85				1	13 5	6 6			
210	July 1, 1888	{13½ 48}	21.83	{14½ 47½}	23.11									
190	July 1, 1858	48	25.08	47	26.33									
7,641	July 1, 1886	89	26.66	90	37.50	6	89,879	143.12	2	14 0	9 0	2	1	2
1,939	July 1, 1886	89	28.22	90	30.57									
3,020	July 1, 1886	89	9.58	90	21.00									
....	....	89	24.09	90	25.51									
510	July 1, 1888	51	28.19	52	27.36	6	48,613	154.82	1	22 0	9 3	1	1	1
296	July 1, 1885	5	11.06	6	21.45	6	24,510	78.06	1	6 4	6 6	1	1	1
277	July 1, 1885	5	7.20	6	18.94									
549	July 1, 1887	14	19.50	13	19.48	6	36,851	117.36	1	12 0	7 2¾	1	1	1
190	July 1, 1887	14	12.83	13	15.42									
205	July 1, 1887	35	20.00	32	20.79	6	55,471	176.66	1	25 9	8 10½	1	1	1
1,363	July 1, 1885	14	26.72	1	28.26	6	74,500	118.63	1	20 0	9 7	2	1	[18]
		6	26.72	15	24.50	6	[23]4,500	....	1	20 0	9 7	2	1	
7,227	July 1, 1885	14	24.57	1	27.30	6	....	....	1	20 0	7 7			
		6	23.40	15	34.12	6			([16])			([16])		
11,371	July 1, 1885	14	29.01	1	30.39	6	....	....	([16])			([16])		
		6	30.39	15	30.99	6			([14])			([16])		
624	July 1, 1885	53	20.49	50	21.33	6	37,969	120.92	1	15 0	8 0	1	1	1
82	July 1, 1885	53	20.49	50	21.33	6	....	....	([14])			([14])		
282	July 1, 1888	9	22.92	8	22.92	6	20,573	65.52	[16]3	16 0	9 3	1	1	1
187	July 1, 1888	9	24.96	8	25.50	6								
1,112	July 1, 1888	1	20.34	2	23.36	6 [146]	52,570	111.61	2	16 4	9 6	3	1	3
2,020	July 1, 1888	12	29.40	1	27.96	6	52,570 124,790	132.47	[17]5	11 2	7 6	3	1	[18]6
55,968	Dec. 8, 1887	12	27.18	1	34.20	6								
1,351	July 1, 1884	105	27.72	104	27.11	6	177,736	114.34	1	32 0	8 9	[10]3	2	8
1,607	July 1, 1887	5	26.12	4	25.61	....	....	....	[20]2	32 4	8 9			
		3	24.17	2	25.54	....	....	111.50	1	28 2	8 8	[19]2	1	
598	July 1, 1886	9	27.38	12	27.38			26,059	71.20	1	8 4	6 11	1	1	1
1,201	June 20, 1888	41	22.07	42	19.60	7	81,398	111.20	1	15 10	9 0	2	1	2
3,880	July 1, 1886	27	23.14	28	24.00	7	....	....	1	15 0	9 0			
									1	25 6	9 0			

[13] 19.13 miles covered by closed pouch service. (See table C[c].)
[14] Cars and clerks shown on route No. 8038.
[15] 1 car in reserve.
[16] Clerk makes two round trips daily except Sunday.
[17] 3 cars in reserve.
[18] Clerks run in car of Pittsburgh and Saint Louis R. P. O. train, 1 between Columbus and Bradford, Ohio, as helper.
[19] Covered by Pittsburgh and Saint Louis R. P. O. (84.71 miles).
[20] East division, Logansport, Ind., to Peoria, Ill.
[21] Balance of route (6.37 miles), between Keokuk, Iowa, Warsaw, Ill., covered by closed pouches. (See table C[c].)
[22] One of these in reserve.
[23] West division, Peoria, Ill., to Keokuk, Iowa.
[24] New R. P. O. service established July 1, 1887, additional to San Francisco and Los Angeles R. P. O. Sangus Station to Los Angeles, Route 46014, covered by Deming and Los Angeles R. P. O. (248.70 miles).

TABLE A³.—*Statement of railway post-offices in operation*

Designation of railway post-office. (Lines upon which railway post-office cars are paid for, in *italics*.)	Division.	Distance run by clerks, register to register.	Initial and terminal stations, running from east to west, north to south, or northwest to southeast (with abbreviated title of railroad company).	Number of route.	Miles of route for which railroad is paid.
		Miles.			
Louisville and Bloomfield, Ky..	5	58.05	Louisville, Anchorage, Ky. (Louis. and Nash.).	20004 (part)	(¹)
			Anchorage, Shelbyville, Ky. (Louis. and Nash.).	20012	18.48
			Shelbyville, Bloomfield, Ky. (Louis. and Nash.).	20026	27.75
Louisville, Ky., Huntingburgh and Evansville, Ind.²	5	124.46	Louisville, Ky., Huntingburgh, Ind. (Louis., Evans. and St. L.).	22048 (part)	(³)
			Huntingburg, Evansville, Ind. (Louis., Evans. and St. L.)	²22032 (part)	47.39
Louisville, Ky., and Knoxville, Tenn.	5	267.51	Louisville, Lebanon Junction, Ky. (Louis. and Nash.).	20005 (part)	(⁴)
			Lebanon Junction, Ky., Jellico, Tenn. (Louis. and Nash.).	20007	170.97
			Jellico, Knoxville, Tenn. (E. Tenn., Va. and Ga.).	19008	65.63
Louisville, Ky., and Nashville, Tenn.	5	187.92	Louisville, Ky., Nashville, Tenn. (Louis. and Nash.).	20005	(¹⁰)
Louisville and Paducah, Ky ...	5	227.26	Louisville, Paducah, Ky. (Chesa., Ohio and S. W.).	¹³20009	223.30
Louisville, Ky., and Saint Louis, Mo.¹⁵	5	267.25	Louisville, Ky., Oakland City, Ind. (Lou., Evans. and St. L.).	22048	99.55
			Oakland City, Ind., Mount Vernon, Ill. (Lou., Evans. and St. L.).	22023	88.56
			Mount Vernon, East Saint Louis, Ill. (Louis. and Nash.).	23032 (part)	(¹⁶)
Louisville and Springfield, Ky.¹⁷	5	69.75	Louisville, Trunnelton, Ky. (Louis. and Nash.).	20005 (part)	(¹⁸)
			Trunnelton, Springfield, Ky. (Louis. and Nash.).	20006	37.29
Loup City and Grand Island, Nebr.	6	61.20	Loup City, Saint Paul, Nebr. (Om. and Rep. Vall.).	34033	39.59
			Saint Paul, Grand Island, Nebr. (Om. and Rep. Vall.).	34015 (part)	(¹⁹)
Lowell and Ayer, Mass.......	1	16.98	Lowell, Ayer, Mass. (Bos. and Me., Low. Syst.).	3020	17.03
Lowell and Taunton, Mass	1	62.01	Lowell, South Framingham, Mass (Old Col.).	3049	29.44
			South Framingham, Taunton, Mass. (Old Col.).	²⁰3051	32.26
Ludington, Mich., and Toledo, Ohio.	9	278.59	Ludington, Monroe, Mich. (F. and P. M.)...	²⁴24015	254.41
			Monroe, Mich., Toledo, Ohio (L., S. and M. S.).	24001 (part)	(²⁶)
Lula and Athens, Ga	4	38.59	Lula, Athens, Ga. (R. and D. R. R.)	15025	39.59
Lynchburgh, Va., and Bristol, Tenn.	3	204.48	Lynchburgh, Va., Bristol, Tenn. (Norfolk and Western).	11013	204.40

¹ Covered by Cincinnati and Nashville R. P. O. (12 miles).

² This line was formerly the Jasper and Evansville R. P. O. February 28, 1888, run of clerks extended to Louisville, Ky.; increase in distance, 66.84 miles.

³ Covered by Louisville and Saint Louis R. P. O. (74.90 miles).

⁴ Clerks act as helpers to Louisville and Saint Louis R. P. O., train 1, between Louisville, Ky., and Huntingburgh, Ind.

⁵ Balance of route covered by closed-pouch service between Jasper and Huntingburgh, Ind.; distance, 6.97 miles. (See Table C⁷.)

⁶ Covered by Cincinnati and Nashville R. P. O. (29.60 miles).

⁷ Day line.

⁸ Night line.

⁹ Clerks on day line run on trains 23 and 24 between Louisville, Ky., and Jellico, Tenn., dis-

tance, 201.87 miles. Clerks on night line run on trains 25 and 26 over whole line; this making double service between Louisville, Ky., and Jellico, Tenn.

¹⁰ Covered by Cincinnati and Nashville R. P. O. (185 miles.)

¹¹ Prior to September 25, 1887, clerks run daily; on and after that date daily, except Sunday. May 20, 1888, daily service restored and clerks run through between Cincinnati and Nashville in apartment cars. (See that line.)

¹² Clerks are appointed to Cincinnati and Nashville R. P. O., and are shown with that line.

¹³ Remainder of route shown on Paducah and Memphis R. P. O. (166.10 miles).

¹⁴ This also includes cars on Paducah and Memphis R. P. O. All cars running through between Louisville, Ky., and Memphis, Tenn.

¹⁵ Louisville, Huntingburgh and Evansville R.P.O. clerks run in car of this R. P. O. on train 1

in the United States on June 30, 1888—Continued.

Average weight of mail whole distance per day.	Date of last re-adjustment.	Average speed per hour (train numbers taken from division schedules).				Number of round trips with clerks per week.	Annual miles of service with clerks.	Average miles run daily by crews.	Number of mail cars, or cars in which are mail apartments.	Inside dimensions of cars or apartments (railway post-office cars in black figures).		Number of crews.	Number of clerks to crews.	Number of clerks appointed to line.
		Train No. outward.	Av'ge speed (miles).	Train No. inward.	Av'ge speed (miles).					Length.	Width.			
Lbs.										Ft. In.	Ft. In.			
19,504	July 1,1884	54	18.00	53	14.40	6	36,455	116.10	1	10 0	7 0	1	1	1
391	July 1,1884	54	10.56	53	9.24	6								
201	July 1,1884	54	12.33	53	13.87	6								
1,567	July 1,1888	11	28.96	6	19.98	6	49,885	124.46	3	14 1	7 5	2	1	42
707	July 1,1888	11	16.25	6	24.72	6			1	14 0	9 6			
18,913	July 1,1888	23	23.64	24	25.38	7	147,769	134.11	2	18 0	9 0	3	1	7
		25	29.60	26	29.60	7	195,817	......	2	15 0	10 0	4	1	
2,362	July 1,1888	23	20.70	24	23.28	7								
		25	20.89	26	26.30	7								
1,039	July 1,1888	25	24.61	26	24.61	7								
18,913	July 1,1888	5	35.82	2	36.36	117	134,496	125.26	2 / 2	1 8 / 18 0	9 6 / 9 2	4	1	(12)
1,834	July 1,1888	1	23.40	2	24.81	7	166,354	113.63	146 / 1	15 3 / 14 0	9 1 / 10 6	4	1	4
									2	14 10	9 0			
									2	14 8	9 2			
1,567	July 1,1888	1	22.74	2	24.68	7	195,627	133.62	2	14 0	9 4	4	1	4
858	July 1,1888	1	27.67	2	28.80	7								
717	July 1,1888	-1	24.10	2	26.16	7								
18,913	July 1,1888	41	19.44	42	22.00	6	29,714	121.50	1	16 0	6 6	1	1	1
354	July 1,1888	41	19.14	42	19.14	6								
360	Mar.30,1887	84	22.63	83	25.01	6	38,433	122.40	1	17 3	6 10	1	1	1
749	Mar.30,1887	82	25.92	81	24.92	6								
745	July 1,1885	403	25.47	406	22.22	6	10,663	67.92	1	11 2	1 0	1	1	1
		409	22.63	410	25.47	6	10,663							
1,841	July 1,1885	819	30.60	20	25.46	6	38,942	124.02	1	13 2	6 2	1	1	2
		831	30.60	370	28.11	6	38,942	......	1	12 0	7 0	1	1	
1,330	July 1,1885	819	29.77	20	25.46	....	....	......	1	14 0	7 0			
		831	25.80	370	22.77	....			211	15 0	8 6			
2,653	July 1,1884	3	24.51	4	24.01	6								
4,631	July 1,1884	109	29.40	110	24.50	6	174,955	139.29	823	22 2	8 11	4	1	249
658	July 1,1888	50	23.4	53	23.4	6	24,234	77.18	1	11 3	7 00	1	1	1
6,222	July 1,1885	3	27.50	4	29.49	7	149,679	102.24	5 / 340	0 / 40 0	8 10	4	2	710

between Louisville, Ky., and Huntingburgh, Ind, as helpers; distance, 74 90 miles.

16 Covered by Nashville and Saint Louis R. P. O., (76 29 miles).

17 Louisville and Bardstown R. P. O. extended to Springfield, Ky., March 12, 1888; increase in distance, 19 36 miles.

18 Covered by Cincinnati and Nashville R. P. O., (22 miles)

19 Distance (21.60 miles) covered by Ord and Grand Island, Nebr., R. P. O.

20 Balance of route covered by Boston, Clinton and Fitchburg R P. O. (40 47 miles) and closed-pouch service (20 91 miles) between Taunton and New Bedford. (See Table C'.)

21 Reserve car.

22 Runs over route 24001, Monroe, Mich., to Toledo, Ohio (24 47 miles), in connection with the Manistee and East Saginaw, and Bay City, Wayne and Detroit R. P. O.'s, gives double service between Manistee Junction and Wayne, Mich. (210.33 miles), daily except Sunday.

23 One car held in reserve.

24 Two clerks detailed to the Bay City, Wayne and Detroit R. P. O. Three clerks detailed to the Manistee and East Saginaw R. P. O. One of these clerks alternates between the Manistee and East Saginaw and East Saginaw and Howard City R. P. O's.

25 Shown in report of Detroit and Toledo R. P. O. night line.

26 Two in reserve.

27 Two transfer clerks, Lynchburgh, Va.; cars owned by the Norfolk and Western Railroad Company.

TABLE A°.—*Statement of railway post-offices in operation*

Designation of railway post-office. (Lines upon which railway post-office cars are paid for, in *italics*).	Division.	Distance run by clerks, register to register.	Initial and terminal stations, running from east to west, north to south, or northwest to southeast (with abbreviated title of railroad company).	Number of route.	Miles of route for which rail cost is paid.
		Miles.			
Lynchburgh and Pocahontas, Va.	3	171. 95	Lynchburgh, New River Depot, Va. (Norfolk and Western).	11013	(¹)
			New River Depot, Pocahontas, Va. (Norfolk and Western).	11033	73. 69
Lyons, N. Y., and Sayre, Pa.,....	2	92. 22	Lyons, N. Y., Sayre, Pa. (G. L and S.)	6072	92. 58
McCook, Nebr., and Denver, Colo.	6	255, 53	McCook, Nebr., Denver, Colo. (B. and M. R. in Nebr.).	²34009 (part)	255. 30
McCool Junction and Fairbury Nebr.	6	50. 61	McCool Junction, Fairbury, Nebr. (K. City & Omaha).	34054	50. 62
McFarland and Belleville, Kans.⁴	7	104. 78	McFarland, Belleville, Kans. (C. K. and N.).	33089	104. 78
McLeansborough and Shawneetown, Ill.	6	41. 22	McLeansborough, Shawneetown, Ill. (Louis. and Nash.).	23078	41. 22
McPherson and El Dorado, Kans.	7	62. 17	McPherson, El Dorado, Kans. (Ft. S., W. and W.)	33046	62. 17
Mackinaw City and Detroit, Mich.	9	291. 23	Mackinaw City, Detroit, Mich. (Mich. Cent.).	}24012	290. 22
Mackinaw City and Grand Rapids, Mich.⁸	9	226. 30	Mackinaw City, Grand Rapids, Mich. (G. R. and I.).	°24018 (part)	225. 07
Macon, Ga., and Montgomery, Ala.	4	224. 51	Macon, Ga., Eufaula, Ala. (S. W. R. R.)..	15016	144. 57
			Eufaula, Montgomery, Ala. (M. and E. R. R.).	17003	80. 49
Macon, Ga., and Union Springs, Ala.	4	156. 25	Macon, Columbus, Ga. (South West R. R.)..	15011	101. 04
			Columbus, Ga., Union Springs, Ala., (M. and G. R. R.).	¹²17008 (part)	55. 70
Madison and Benedict, Kans⁴..	7	45. 65	Madison, Benedict, Kans. (C., K. and W.)..	33069	45. 65
Madison and Macon, Ga........	4	72. 61	Madison, Macon, Ga. (C. and M. R. R.)....	15052	72. 61
Manchester, N. H., Lawrence and Boston, Mass.	1	53. 85	Manchester, N. H., Lawrence, Mass. (Man. & Law. Div. Conc.).	3063	27. 07
			Lawrence, Boston, Mass. (Bos., Me.)......	¹⁶9011 (part)	(¹⁶)
Manchester and Peterborough, N. H.	1	63. 37	Manchester, Concord, N. H. (Con)	¹⁷1001 (part)	(¹⁸)
			Concord, Contoocook, N. H. (Bos., Me., Low. Syst.).	¹⁹1009 (part)	(²⁰)
			Contoocook, Peterborough, N. H. (Bos., Me., Low. Syst.).	1010	32. 72
Mandan, Dak., and Helena, Mont.	6	681. 23	Mandan, Dak., Helena, Mont. (North. Pac.).	²¹26001 (part)	679. 10
Manhattan and Burlingame, Kans.	7	57. 27	Manhattan, Burlingame, Kans. (M., A. and B.).	33034	57. 27
Manilla, Iowa, and Mitchell, Dak.	6	228. 25	Manilla, Sioux City, Iowa (Chi., Mil. and St. P.).	27098	90. 70
			Sioux City, Iowa, Mitchell, Dak. (Chi., Mil. and St. P.).	35001	138. 18
Manistee and East Saginaw, Mich.²⁴	9	148. 13	Manistee, Manistee Junction, Mich. (F. and P. M.).	24045	27. 13
			Manistee Junction, East Saginaw, Mich. (F. and P. M.).	24015 (part)	(²⁵)

¹ 96.50 miles covered by the Lynchburgh and Bristol R. P. O.
² In reserve.
³ Balance of route (132. 07 miles) covered by Pacific Junction, Iowa, and McCook, Nebr., R. P. O.
⁴ New service; not reported last year.
⁵ Trains 202 and 205 carry a R. P. O. between Bay City and Detroit, Mich., and in connection with trains 206 and 201 give double service daily, except Sunday, between these points (108 miles), R. P. O. of trains 202 and 205 perform daily service
⁶ In connection with the Cadillac and Fort Wayne and Grand Rapids and Cincinnati R. P. O.'s gives double service between Cadillac, Mich., and Fort Wayne, ⁷nd (240 miles) daily except Sunday,

⁷ Balance of route (143. 23 miles) covered by the Cadillac and Fort Wayne R. P. O.
⁸ One car held in reserve.
⁹ One clerk assigned as chief clerk at Grand Rapids, Mich. One clerk assigned as transfer clerk at Grand Rapids, Mich. Four clerks assigned to the Cadillac and Fort Wayne R. P. O. One acting clerk employed.
¹⁰ 1 reserve car.
¹¹ 2 helpers.
¹² Cars also used by Montgomery and Troy R. P. O. 2 reserve cars.
¹³ 30 miles shown as Montgomery and Troy R. P. O.
¹⁴ No clerks on trains 1 and 2 Sundays.
¹⁵ Balance of route covered by Portland and Boston R. P. O. (89. 33 miles). These clerks double the road between Manchester, N. H., and Lawrence, Mass.

in the United States on June 30, 1888—Continued.

Average weight of mail whole distance per day.	Date of last re-adjustment.	Average speed per hour (train numbers taken from division schedules).				Number of round trips with clerks per week.	Annual miles of service with clerks.	Average miles run daily by crews.	Number of mail cars, or cars in which are mail apartments.	Inside dimensions of cars or apartments (railway post-office cars in black figures).		Number of crews.	Number of clerks to crew.	Number of clerks appointed to line.
		Train No. outward.	Av'ge speed (miles).	Train No. inward.	Av'ge speed (miles).					Length.	Width.			
Lbs.										*Ft. In.*	*Ft. In.*			
6,222	July 1, 1888	5	24.12	6	21.07	6	107,985	171.95	2 / [2]1	18 3 / 15 6	8 7 / 8 6	2	1	2
......	....	23	22.61	23	21.95									
848	July 1, 1885	109	26.34	102	29.11	6	57,914	92.22	1 / [2]1	15 9½ / 15 9½	8 8½ / 8 8½	2	1	2
3,479	July 1, 1886	3	27.32	4	31.22	7	187,048	170.35	2	14 0	7 0	3	1	3
228	July 1, 1888	20	11.68	19	12.14	6	31,783	101.22	1	13 2	7 6	1	1	1
......	....	13	26.56	14	24.49	7	76,699	104.78	1	14 6	7 2	2	1	2
173	July 1, 1887	81	14.12	80	10.93	6	25,886	82.44	1	8 0	6 2	1	1	1
149	Mar. 30, 1887	468	15.40	467	15.40	7	45,508	124.34	1	10 5	7 2	1	1	1
1,957	July 1, 1884	92}/206	21.61	91}/201	23.20	6	182,892	145.61	1}/1	15 0	9 0	6	1	6
		[2]202	27.00	[2]205	27.00	7	79,056	108.00	1					
1,831	July 1, 1884	6	23.40	5	22.62	6	142,116	113.15	[9]3	22 0	8 10	4	1	[9]10
1,049	July 1, 1884	3	24.90	4	22.30	7	104,341	112.25	[10]3	26 4	9 0	4	1	[11]6
1,667	July 1, 1884	3	26.60	4	25.50									
599	July 1, 1888	55	25.50	56	25.00	[14]13	212,500	156.25	[12]3	22 10	9 1	4	1	4
		1	26.00	2	23.50	......	....	....	1	12 10	9 1			
709	July 1, 1888	55	27.50	56	27.50	......	....	....	1	15 3	8 9			
		1	27.50	2	27.50	......	....	....	1	13 6	9 0			
122	July 1, 1888	273	12.63	274	12.63	6	28,668	91.30	1	23 0	8 6	1	1	1
178	July 1, 1888	2	19.30	1	20.00	6	45,599	145.22	1	12 4	8 8	1	1	1
1,013	July 1, 1885	37	21.66	34	24.37	6	83,817	80.37	2	10 0	7 0	2	1	2
		89	20.52	36	24.00	6	16,654							
4,739	July 1, 1885	39	26.12	34	24.54	0								
11,733	July 1, 1885	75	28.41	12	17.41	6	39,796	126.74	1 / 1	9 0 / 10 0	7 0 / 7 0	1	1	1
452	July 1, 1885	75	15.94	12	21.63									
311	July 1, 1885	75	19.81	12	14.86									
11,448	July 1, 1887	1	27.72	2	27.43	7	498,660	136.25	[22]9 / [21]1	24 6 / 23 7	9 1 / 8 10	10	1	10
430	July 1, 1886	154	14.39	153	14.10	6	35,966	114.54	1	9 11½	6 11	1	1	1
1,727	June 21, 1888	1	27.00	4	27.69	6	143,341	152.16	2	26 0	9 3	3	1	3
838	Mar. 30, 1887	1	23.65	4	24.00	......	....	....	1	20 8	8 10			
901	July 1, 1884	705	24.42	706	24.42	6}	93,026	98.75	2	22 2	8 11	3	1	([36])
2,653	July 1, 1884	5	23.30	6	21.25	6}								

[16] Covered by Portland and Boston R. P. O. (27 miles).

[17] Balance of route covered by Saint Albans and Boston R. P. O. (18.02 miles).

[18] Covered by Saint Albans and Boston R. P. O. (18.26 miles).

[19] Balance of route covered by Claremont and Boston R. P. O. (42.93 miles), and closed-pouch service (1.02 miles) between Claremont and Claremont Junction. (See Table C².) This clerk runs in the same car with Claremont and Boston clerk between Concord and Manchester, N. H.

[20] Covered by Claremont and Boston R. P. O. (11.97 miles).

[21] Balance of route (600.9% miles) covered by Saint Paul, Minn., and Mandan, Dak., and Helena, Mont., and Portland, Oregon, R. P. O.'s.

[22] Cars run through between Mandan, Dak., and Portland, Oregon, covering Helena, Mont., and Portland, Oregon, R. P. O.

[23] Reserve.

[24] Runs on route 24615, Manistee Junction to East Saginaw, Mich. (119.83 miles), and in connection with Bay City, Wayne and Detroit and Ludington and Toledo R. P. O.'s gives double service between Manistee Junction and Wayne, Mich. (210.33 miles), daily, except Sunday.

[25] Shown in report of Ludington and Toledo R.P.O.

[26] Clerks appointed to Ludington and Toledo R. P. O.

TABLE A*.—*Statement of railway post-offices in operation*

Designation of railway post-office. (Lines upon which railway post office cars are paid for, in *italics*.)	Division.	Distance run by clerks, register to register.	Initial and terminal stations, running from east to west, north to south, or northwest to southeast (with abbreviated title of railroad company).	Number of route.	Miles of route for which railroad is paid.
		Miles.			
Mankato and Wells, Minn.....	6	38.26	Mankato, Wells, Minn. (Chi., Mil. and St. P.).	26024	38.30
Maquoketa and Davenport, Iowa.	6	43.85	Maquoketa, Davenport, Iowa (Chi., Mil. and St. P.).	27018	43.97
Marietta and Sharpsburgh, Ohio.[1]	5	34.96	Marietta, Sharpsburgh, Ohio (Mar. Mineral).	21096	34.50
Marion, Ohio, and Chicago, Ill.	5	276.12	Marion, Ohio, Chicago Junction (n. o.) Ind. (Chicago and Atlantic).	*21090 (part)	249.95
Marion and Council Bluffs, Iowa.	6	261.90	Marion. U. P. Transfer, Iowa (Chi., Mil. and St. P.).	*27028 (part)	262.47
Marion and Running Water, Dak.	6	62.72	Marion, Running Water, Dak. (Chi., Mil. and St. P.).	*27025 (part)	62.42
Marquette and Houghton, Mich.	6	95.20	Marquette, Houghton, Mich. (Dul., S. S. and Atl.).	24040	95.93
Marshalltown and Stony City, Iowa.	6	39.55	Marshalltown, Stony City, Iowa (Central Iowa).	27079	39.14
Mason City and Albia, Iowa...	6	169.55	Mason City, Albia, Iowa (Central Iowa) ...	*27010 (part)	170.21
Mason City and Fort Dodge, Iowa.	6	73.05	Mason City, Fort Dodge, Iowa (Mason City and Ft. Dodge).	27097	73.05
Maysville, Paris, Ky., and Cincinnati, Ohio.	5	130.32	Maysville, Paris, Ky. (Ky. Cent.)..........	20315	50.17
			Paris, Covington, Ky. (Ky. Cent.).........	20002 (part)	(*)
Meadville and Oil City, Pa.....	2	36.62	Meadville, Pa.,. Oil City, Pa. (N. Y., P. and O.).	8043	36.67
Memphis, Tenn., and Grenada, Miss.	4	101.60	Memphis, Tenn., Grenada, Miss. (Miss. and Tenn. R. R.).	18002	102.34
Memphis, Tenn., and Little Rock, Ark.	7	136.00	Memphis, Tenn., Little Rock, Ark. (M. and L. R.).	29001	135.00
Memphis, Tenn., and New Orleans, La.	4	....	Memphis, Tenn., New Orleans, La. (L., N. O. and T. Rwy.).	18019	455.60
	[11]	221.46	....	....	....
	[12]	235.06	....	....	....
Mendota and Centralia, Ill.....	6	211.99	Mendota, Centralia, Ill. (Illinois Central) ..	1*23021 (part)	211.48
Mendota and Fulton, Ill	6	65.26	Mendota, Fulton, Ill. (Chi., Bur. and Qcy.).	23013	64.82
Meridian, Miss., and New Orleans, La.	4	196.24	Meridian, Miss., New Orleans, La. (N. O. and N. E. R. R.	18016	196.24
Meridian and Vicksburg, Miss.	4	140.70	Meridian, Vicksburg, Miss. (V. and M. R. R.)	18003	140.69
Merrill and Tomah, Wis	6	107.50	Merrill, Tomah, Wis. (Chi., Mil. and St. P.).	1*25031 (part)	108.07
Mexico and Cedar City, Mo....	7	50.34	Mexico, Cedar City, Mo. (C. and A.).......	28021	50.34
Michigan City and Indianapolis, Ind.	5	161.18	Michigan City, Indianapolis, Ind. (Lake Erie and West.).	22004	161.62
Michigan City and Monon, Ind.[10]	5	59.77	Michigan City, Monon, Ind. (Lou., N. A. and C.).	2*22008 (part)	59.57
Middleton, Tenn., and New Albany, Miss.	4	44.00	Middleton, Tenn., New Albany, Miss. (Ills. Cent'l.)	18008	44.00
Middletown and New York, N. Y.	2	89.78	Middletown, N. Y., and Jersey City, N. J. (N. Y., S. and W.).	7037	88.40
Millerton and Dutchess Junction, N. Y.	2	57.97	Millerton, Dutchess Junction, N. Y. (N., D. and C.).	6085	57.99
Milton and Stockton, Cal	5	30.09	Milton, Stockton, Cal. (Stockton, Copperopolis R. R.).	46012	30.09

[1] Marietta and Amesville R. P. O. extended to Sharpsburgh, Ohio, October 3, 1887; increase in distance, 4.57 miles.
[2] Balance of line (20.70 miles) not paid for by Department.
[3] Balance of route (89.90 miles) covered by Chicago, Savanna, Ill., and Cedar Rapids, Iowa, R. P. O.
[4] Balance of route (287.64 miles) covered by Calmar, Iowa, and Chamberlain, Dak., R. P. O.
[5] 1 of these cars in reserve.
[6] Reserve.
[7] Balance of route (28.50 miles) covered by Lyle, Minn., and Mason City, Iowa, closed-pouch service. (See Table C*.)
[8] 2 helpers between Chapin and Albia, Iowa.
[9] Covered by Cincinnati and Livingston R. P. O., 79.36 miles.
[10] In reserve.
[11] Northern division.
[12] Southern division; line divided at Vicksburg Miss.

in the United States on June 30, 1888—Continued.

Average weight of mail whole distance per day.	Date of last re-adjust-ment.	Train No. outward.	Av'ge speed (miles).	Train No. inward.	Av'ge speed (miles).	Number of round trips with clerks per week.	Annual miles of service with clerks.	Average miles run daily by crews.	Number of mail cars, or cars in which are mail apartments.	Length.	Width.	Number of crews.	Number of clerks to crew.	Number of clerks appointed to line.
Lbs.										Ft. In.	Ft. In.			
254	July 1, 1887	24	22.80	21	22.80	6	24,027	76.52	1	13 9	7 1¼	1	1	1
291	July 1, 1887	24	22	23	21.87	6	27,538	87.70	1	14 10	7 6	1	.1	1
177	July 1, 1888	4	16.85	1	16.27	6	21,244	69.92	1	8 6	6 8	1	1	1
783	July 1, 1888	1	24.54	10	24.38	6	169,635	135.06	2	18 6	8 6	4	1	4
2,249	July 1, 1887	3	23.12	2	18.04	6	184,473	130.95	1 / 1	26 0 / 28 7	9 3 / 9 3	4	1	4
3,402	July 1, 1887	41	15.40	40	20.81	6	39,388	125.44	1	12 1	7 2	1	1	1
743	Apr. 16, 1884	3	19.18	2	19.18	7	69,686	95.20	[13]3 / [6]1	12 0 / 14 0	7 2 / 6 9	2	1	2
165	July 1, 1887	35	13.05	36	10.40	6	24,837	79.10	1 / [6]1	7 0 / 10 0	7 0 / 7 3	1	1	1
1,652	July 1, 1887	2	22.92	1	21.25	6	106,477	113.03	[6]2 / 1	22 0 / 22 0	9 6 / 8 11	3	1	[6]5
276	June 20, 1888	1	24.35	2	20.86	6	45,875	146.10	1	11 6	7 1	1	1	1
762	July 1, 1884	10	21.60	11	21.60	6	81,841	130.32	1 / 1	12 6 / 11 7	9 1 / 9 5	2	1	2
2,694	July 1, 1888	10	24.41	11	25.08	6								
827	July 1, 1884	93	25.84	94	24.40	6	22,907	73.24	1	16 0	7 0	1	1	1
1,302	July 1, 1888	2	25	1	25.5	7	74,371	101.60	1 / 1	12 2 / 16 0	9 2 / 9 2	2	1	2
8,194	July 1, 1886	3	20.52	2	18.23	7	99,552	90.67	2 / [16]1	22 10 / 17 0	8 9 / 7 8	3	1	3
1,633	July 1, 1888													
------	------------	7	24.7	8	24.3	7	[11]162,108	110.73						
------	------------	3	23.6	4	25.3	.....	[15]172,068	117.53	6	15 5	9 0	9	1	10
		5	24.6	6	24.6	6	[15]55,766	177.60						
4,579	July 1, 1887	3	22.21	2	24.82	6	133,129	105.99	2 / [6]1	27 6 / 27 1	9 0 / 9 0	4	1	[16]9
435	July 1, 1887	95	22.68	96	21.13	6	40,983	130.52	1	8 0	8 6½	1	1	1
1,593	July 1, 1888	5	26.5	6	26.5	7	143,647	130.83	2	16 0	7 4	3	1	[14]4
2,207	July 1, 1888	1	24.7	2	23.6	6	102,992	93.80	[17]2 / 1	42 2 / 40 3	9 4 / 9 5	3	1	3
702	Aug. 3, 1888	2	26.88	1	25.29	6	67,510	107.50	1 / 1	23 1 / 25 0	9 5 / 9 5	2	1	2
397	July 1, 1887	138	16.67	137	14.23	6	31,614	100.68	1 / [18]1	17 6 / 25 8	9 0 / 8 9	1	1	1
1,382	July 1, 1888	11	22.26	10	22.02	6	101,221	107.45	[19]3	14 4	9 0	3	1	3
4,314	July 1, 1888	11	24.60	12	26.46	6	20,441	119.54	1	14 0	9 3	1	1	1
166	July 1, 1888	1	12.2	2	12.2	6	27,632	88	1	8 5	6 0	1	1	1
825	July 1, 1885	18	16.57	25	16.83	6	56,382	134.36	1 / 1 / [16]1	12 6 / 11 6 / 14 5	6 9 / 6 9 / 5 6	[22]2	1	2
459	July 1, 1885	51	20.58	54	19.75	6	36,405	115.94	1	12 0	6 0	1	1	1
433	July 1, 1896	5	23.65	8	28.65	6	18,897	60.18	[19]1 / 1	12 0 / 10 0	6 6 / 8 9	1	1	1

[13] Short run on trains 5 and 6 between New Orleans and Baton Rouge (88.8 miles); 1 detailed to chief clerk's office, New Orleans.
[14] Balance of route (131.79 miles) covered by Dubuque, Iowa, and Mendota, Ill., R. P. O.
[15] 3 helpers between Mendota and Pana, Ill.; 1 clerk detailed to clerical duty at office of superintendent, Chicago, Ill.; 1 clerk detailed to transfer duty at Bloomington, Ill.
[16] 1 transfer clerk, Meridian, Miss.
[17] No pay for car service. Cars also used by Vicksburg and Shreveport R. P. O. 1 reserve car.

[18] Balance of route (22.99 miles) covered by Tomahawk and Merrill closed-pouch service. (See Table C⁶.)
[19] One car in reserve.
[20] This was formerly the Michigan City, Monon, and Indianapolis R. P. O. December 15, 1887, run of clerks curtailed to end at Monon, Ind.
[21] Balance of route covered by Chicago and Louisville R. P. O., 233.80 miles.
[22] Relieved every fourth week by the Port Jervis and New York clerk.

TABLE A².—*Statement of railway post-offices in operation*

Designation of railway post-office. (Lines upon which railway post-office cars are paid for, in *italics*.)	Division.	Distance run by clerks, register to register.	Initial and terminal stations running from east to west, north to south, or northwest to southeast (with abbreviated title of railroad company).	Number of route.	Miles of route for which railroad is paid.
		Miles.			
Milwaukee, Wis., and Chicago, Ill.	6	86.14	Milwaukee, Wis., Chicago, Ill. (Chi. and No. West.).	23001	85.40
Milwaukee and Lancaster, Wis.	6	168.40	Milwaukee, Montfort, Wis. (Chi. and No. West.).	25038	146.37
			Montfort, Lancaster Junction, Wis. (Chi. and No. West.).	²25025 (part)	10.00
			Lancaster Junction, Lancaster, Wis. (Chi. and No. West.).	25042	12.28
Minneapolis, Minn., Hayfield and Waterloo, Iowa.	6	202.32	Minneapolis, Saint Paul, Minn. (St. P., Minn. and Man.).	26006 (part)	(⁴)
			Saint Paul, Lyle, Minn. (Chi., St.'P. and K. C.).	26055	109.51
			Lyle, Minn., Waterloo, Iowa (Illinois Central).	27022	82.12
Minneapolis, Minn., and Oakes, Dak.	6	265.13	Minneapolis, Minn., Fairmount, Dak. (Minn. and Pac.).	26058	192.30
			Fairmount, Oakes, Dak. (Minn. and Pac.)...	35034	72.64
Minneapolis, Minn., and Oregon, Ill.	6	344.27	Minneapolis, Saint Paul, Minn. (St. P., Minn. and Man.).	26006 (part)	(⁴)
			Saint Paul, Minn., Oregon, Ill. (Chi., Bur. and North.)	23073	333.31
Missouri Valley, Iowa, and Whitewood, Dak.	6	584.70	Missouri Valley, California, Iowa (S. City and Pac.).	27029 (part)	(⁷)
			California, Iowa, Fremont, Nebr. (S. City and Pac.).	27077	32.01
			Fremont, Nebr., Rapid City, Dak. (Fre., Elk. and Mo. Vall.).	34010	510.25
			Rapid City, Whitewood, Dak. (Fre., Elk. and Mo. Vall.).	35037	37.27
Monett, Mo., and Paris, Tex.¹⁰..	7	302.07	Monett, Mo., Fort Smith, Ark. (St. L. and S. F.).	28039	133.44
			Fort Smith, Ark., Paris, Tex., (St. L. and S. F.).	¹³29019	168.93
Monett, Mo., and Vinita, Ind. T.¹⁴	7	77.74	Monett, Mo., Vinita, Ind. T. (St. L. and S. F.).	¹⁴28003 (part)	¹⁴72.80
Monmouth Junction and Manasquan, N. J.	2	33.18	Monmouth Junction, Jamesburgh, N. J. (Penna.).	7005 (part)	¹⁷6.10
			Jamesburgh, Sea Girt, N. J. (Penna.)	7023	27.43
Monroe and Adrian, Mich..	9	34.29	Monroe, Adrian, Mich. (L. S. and M. S.) ...	24002	34.90
Monroe Junction and Tarpon Springs, Fla.	4	116.20	Monroe Junction (n. o.), Tarpon Springs, Fla. (Orange Belt Rwy.).	16029	116.20
Montandon and Bellefonte Pa.	2	67.63 ²³1.64	Lewisburgh, Bellefonte, Pa. (Penna.)	3067	66.22
Montgomery and Akron Junction, Ala.	4	113.15	Montgomery, Selma, Ala.(W. Rwy. of Ala.)	17032	51.23
			Selma, Akron Junction, Ala. (C. S. and M. R. R.).	17006	67.76
Montgomery, Ala., and New Orleans, La.	4	321.85	Montgomery, Mobile, Ala. (L. and N. R. R.).	17012	180.57
			Mobile, Ala., New Orleans, La. (L. and N. R. R.).	17013	141.43
Montgomery and Troy, Ala....	4	70.83	Montgomery, Union Springs, Ala. (M. and E. R. R.).	17003	(²⁵)
			Union Springs, Troy, Ala. (M. and G. R. R.).	²⁵17008 (part)	30.00

¹ One clerk detailed to transfer duty at Milwaukee, Wis.

² Balance of route covered by Montfort, Wis., and Galena, Ill., R. P. O. (47.76 miles), and between Woodman and Lancaster Junction, Wis. (18.53 miles), by closed pouches. (See Table C⁴.)

³ One in reserve.

⁴ Distance (10.68 miles) covered by Neche, Dak., and Saint Paul, Minn., R. P. O.

⁵ One of these cars in reserve.

⁶ Reserve.

⁷ Distance (5.90 miles) covered by Sioux City and Missouri Valley, Iowa, R. P. O.

⁸ East Division, Missouri Valley, Iowa, to Long Pine, Nebr.

⁹ West Division, Long Pine, Nebr.,to Whitewood, Dak.; one car in reserve.

¹⁰ Reported last year as Pierce City, Mo., and Fort Smith, Ark.; increased distance, 162.19 miles.

¹¹ Double daily service between Monett, Mo., and Fort Smith, Ark. (133.44 miles); last year service was but single daily.

¹² One helper on trains 3 and 4 between Monett, Mo., and Springdale, Ark. (60.70 miles).

¹³ Fort Smith and Mansfield, Ark., R. P. O. also runs over 13.90 miles of route 29019 between Fort Smith and Jenson, Ark.

in the United States on June 30, 1888—Continued.

Average weight of mail whole distance per day.	Date of last re-adjustment.	Average speed per hour (train numbers taken from division schedules).				Number of round trips with clerks per week.	Annual miles of service with clerks.	Average miles run daily by crews.	Number of mail cars, or cars in which are mail apartments.	Inside dimensions of cars or apartments (railway post-office cars in black figures).		Number of crews.	Number of clerks to crew.	Number of clerks appointed to line.
		Train No. outward.	Av'ge speed (miles).	Train No. inward.	Av'ge speed (miles).					Length.	Width.			
Lbs.										*Ft. In.*	*Ft. In.*			
8,988	July 1, 1887	4	28.46	9	28.46	6	54,096	86.14	1	50 0	9 5	2	1	4
		10	28.46	5	31.05	6	54,096	86.14	1	50 0	9 5	2	1	
1,276	July 1, 1887	101	23.36	100	25.03	6	105,756	112.26	1	24 2	7 3	2	1	14
602	July 1, 1887	101	20.00	100	16.22	....	....	....	*2	24 0	9 3			
1,073	July 1, 1887	101	18.42	100	16.37									
4,937	July 1, 1887	1	18.31	4	18.31	6	127,057	134.88	2	24 6	9 1	3	1	3
1,502	July 1, 1887	1	27.38	4	25.77									
1,194	July 1, 1887	15	20.48	16	20.56									
....		65	20.21	66	21.33	6	166,501	132.56	2	16 5	7 2	4	1	4
435	July 1, 1888	65	22.35	66	23.47									
4,937	July 1, 1887	2	21.36	1	21.36	6	216,201	137.71	*4	25 6	8 11½	5	1	5
910	July 1, 1887	2	28.96	1	27.37	....			*2	14 6	7 6			
7,009	July 1, 1887	3	23.60	4	27.23	7	428,000	125.75	*2	50 0	9 3	*4	2	13
4,814	July 1, 1887	3	22.60	4	21.33	....	....	133.28	*3	24 0	9 3	*5	1	
3,438	Mar.30, 1887	3	22.17	4	22.50	....	....		1	20 0	9 3			
1,741	July 1, 1888	3	20.80	4	20.80									
1,430	July 1, 1887	1	23.85	2	23.85	7	11221,115	151.04	2	20 6	7 6	4	1	197
686	July 1, 1887	3	21.61	4	21.61	7	11197,678	133.44	2	20 6	7 6	2	1	
	Oct.31, 1887	1	24.06	2	24.06	7								
7,234	July 1, 1887	3	21.23	4	23.91	7	56,906	155.48	1	18 0	7 4	1	1	1
909	July 1, 1885	380	26.14	387	36.60	6	1820,837	66.36	1	15 0	9 3	1	1	1
438	July 1, 1885	380	28.37	387	36.54	6	....	....	(19)	10 0	6 0	19)	1	1
674	July 1, 1884	101	24.90	102	26.56	6	21,534	68.58	1	14 6	7 5	1	1	
230	July 1, 1886	9	12.2	10	12.8	6	72,973	116.20	2	13 6	7 5	2	1	202
291	Apr. 1, 1886	103	20.13	112	20.13	6	42,472	138.54	1	15 0	8 4	1	1	1
		22103	3.93	112	9.84	6	1,030							
		101	9.84	102	9.84	6								
1,635	July 1, 1888	8	14.4	7	14.4	6	2371,058	113.15	1	12 0	6 9	2	1	2
460	July 1, 1888	8	14.8	7	14.1				1	10 6	5 3			
10,408	July 1, 1888	1	28.08	4	27.05	14	471,188	160.92	4	49 4	9 2	8	2	17
		3	33.03	2	33.09	....	....		*1	50 0	9 0	....	...	(28)
9,750	July 1, 1888	1	27.04	4	28.07									
		3	32.20	2	33.20									
1,007	July 1, 1888	56	26.80	55	23.60	6	44,481	141.66	(27)	....		1	1	1
709	July 1, 1888	56	20.00	55	20.00									

14 Reported last year as Pierce City, Mo., and Vinita, Ind. T.; increased distance, 4.08 miles.

15 Balance of route covered by Saint Louis, Mo.,and Halstead, Kans., R. P. O.

16 Distance between Pierce City, Mo., and Vinita, Ind. T.; that portion of route between Monette and Pierce City, Mo., covered by Saint Louis, Mo., and Halstead, Kans., R.P.O.

17 47.58 miles covered by the South Amboy and Philadelphia R. P. O

18 Clerk runs to Trenton in the a. m.

19 Cars and clerks shown on route 7005.

20 Including 1 acting additional clerk.

21 One reserve car.

22 Short run between Montandon and Lewisburgh.

23 Double daily service, except Sunday, between Montandon and Lewisburgh.

24 Paid for as 40 foot cars.

25 One transfer clerk, Montgomery, Ala.

26 Reported as Macon and Montgomery R. P. O.

27 See Macon and Union Springs R. P. O.

28 55.7 miles reported as Macon and Union Springs R. P. O.

TABLE A*.—*Statement of railway post-offices in operation*

Designation of railway post-office. (Lines upon which railway post-office cars are paid for, in *italics*).	Division.	Distance run by clerks, register to register.	Initial and terminal stations, running from east to west, north to south, or northwest to southeast (with abbreviated title of railroad company).	Number of route.	Miles of route for which railroad is paid.
		Miles.			
Montfort, Wis., and Galena, Ill.	6	56.08	Montfort, Ipswich, Wis. (Chi. and No. West.).	¹25023 (part)	21.50
			Ipswich, Plattville, Wis. (Chi. and No. West.).	25043	4.38
			Ipswich, Wis., Galena, Ill. (Chi. and No. West.).	¹25025 (part)	26.26
Montrose and Tunkhannock, Pa.	2	29.16	Montrose, Tunkhannock, Pa. (Montrose).	8078	29.11
Morgantown and Fairmont, W. Va.	3	25.88	Morgantown, Fairmont, W. Va. (Balto. and Ohio).	12017	25.95
Moscow, Idaho, and Connell, Wash.	8	117.30	Moscow, Idaho, Connell, Wash. (Columbia and Palouse R. R.).	43006	117.30
Mound House, Nev., and Keeler, Cal.⁴	8	160.72	Mound House, Nev., Keeler, Cal. (Carson and Colo. R. R.).	45004	293.00
		141.00	Belleville Junction (n.o.), Candelaria, Nev. (Carson and Colo. R. R.).	45006	7.80
Mount Airy, N. C., and Bennettsville, S. C.	3	224.84	Mount Airy, N. C., Bennettsville, S. C. (Cape Fear and Yad. Val.).	13011	225.06
Mount Carmel and Sunbury, Pa.	2	27.47	Mount Carmel, Sunbury, Pa. (Nor. Cent.)..	8023	27.47
Mount Pleasant and Keokuk, Iowa.	6	50.40	Mount Pleasant, Keokuk, Iowa (St. L., Keo. and N. W.).	⁵28018 (part)	50.86
Mount Pleasant and Sherman, Tex.⁶	7	110.10	Mount Pleasant, Sherman, Tex. (St. L., Ark. and Tex.).	31060	110.10
Mount Pleasant, Mich., and Toledo, Ohio.	9	171.82	Mount Pleasant, Emory, Mich. (T., A. A. and N. M.).	24065	116.23
			Emory, Mich., Toledo, Ohio (T., A. A. and N. M.).	24026 (part)	52.00
Mulvane and Englewood, Kans.⁷	7	166.79	Mulvane, Englewood, Kans. (C., K. and W.).	33068	166.79
Murphy, N. C., and Marietta, Ga.	4	109.02	Murphy, N. C., Marietta, Ga. (M. and N. G. R. R.).	15030	109.02
Muscatine and Montezuma, Iowa.	6	96.87	Muscatine, What Cheer, Iowa (Bur., C. Rap. and North.).	27004	76.62
			Thornburgh, Montezuma, Iowa (Bur., C. Rap. and North.).	27065	16.33
Muskegon and Allegan, Mich..	9	60.06	Holland, Allegan, Mich. (C. and W. M.)	24023 (part)	⁹24.64
			Muskegon, Holland, Mich. (C. and W. M.).	24022	(¹⁰)
Nashville and Chattanooga, Tenn.	5	151.55	Nashville, Chattanooga, Tenn. (Nash., Chatt. and St. Louis).	19004	151.00
Nashville, Tenn., and Hickman. Ky.	5	169.58	Nashville, Tenn., Hickman, Ky. (Nash., Chatt. and St. Louis).	19007	170.11
Nashville and Hope, Ark.¹⁴....	7	27.53	Nashville, Hope, Ark. (Ark. and La.)......	29009	27.53
Nashville, Tenn., and Montgomery, Ala.	5	306.14	Nashville, Tenn., Decatur, Ala. (Louis. and Nash.).	19006	122.72
			Decatur, Montgomery, Ala. (Louis. and Nash.).	17004	183.28
Nashville and Saint Joseph, Tenn.¹⁹	5	103.89	Nashville, Columbia, Tenn. (Louis. and Nash.).	19006 (part)	(²⁰)
			Columbia, Saint Joseph, Tenn. (Nash. and Florence).	19017	56.74
Nashville, Tenn., and Saint Louis, Mo.	5	321.58	Nashville, Tenn., East Saint Louis, Ill. (Louis. and Nash.).	23032	318.76

¹ Balance of route covered by Milwaukee and Montfort, Wis., R. P. O. (10 miles) and between Woodman and Lancaster Junction, Wis. (18 53 miles), by closed pouches. (See Table C*.)
² One in reserve.
³ In reserve.
⁴ Three clerks perform daily service Mound House to Belleville Junction, 152 miles, and embrace route 45006, 7.80 miles. One clerk makes three round trips per week; Belleville Junction, Nev., to Keeler, Cal., 141 miles, and is relieved every thirty days.

⁵ Balance of route (138.41 miles) covered by Burlington, Iowa, and Saint Louis, Mo., R. P. O.
⁶ New service; not reported last year.
⁷ Reported last year as Mulvane and Spivey, Kans.; increased distance, 115.12 miles.
⁸ Reserve.
⁹ Runs on route 24022, Muskegon to Holland, Mich. (35.50 miles), and in connection with Big Rapids and Holland R. P. O.; gives double service between these points daily, except Sunday.
¹⁰ Shown in report of Big Rapids and Holland R. P. O.

in the United States on June 30, 1888—Continued.

Average weight of mail whole distance per day.	Date of last re-adjustment.	Average speed per hour (train numbers taken from division schedules).				Number of round trips with clerks per week.	Annual miles of service with clerks.	Average miles run daily by crews.	Number of mail cars, or cars in which are mail apartments.	Inside dimensions of cars or apartments (railway post-office cars in black figures).		Number of crews.	Number of clerks to crew.	Number of clerks appointed to line.
		Train No. outward.	Av'ge speed (miles).	Train No. inward.	Av'ge speed (miles).					Length.	Width.			
Lbs.										*Ft. In.*	*Ft. In.*			
662	July 1, 1887	120	18.43	121	23.45	6	35,218	112.16	[22]2	12 2	7 3	1	1	1
151	July 1, 1887	120	15.46	121	21.02									
662	July 1, 1887	120	23.87	121	24.24									
158	July 1, 1885	2	17.49	3	13.14	6	18,312	58.32	1	6 0	6 8	1	1	1
									[21]1	4 0	6 2			
245	Mar. 15, 1886	703	17.00	700	17.00	6	16,253	51.76	1	17 8	8 7	1	1	1
400	July 1, 1886	19	11.50	20	11.73	6	73,664	117.30	2	18 4	9 1	2	1	2
426	July 1, 1886	1	14.47	2	13.11	7	117,647	107.14	3	10 9	8 8	4	1	4
425	July 1, 1886	3	11.70	4	11.70	3	43,992	141.00						
355	July 1, 1888	2	15.42	1	16.87	6	141,190	112.42	2	20 0	9 1	4	1	4
									[21]1	11 0	8 2			
244	July 1, 1885	1	20.59	6	21.97	6	17,251	55.66	1	14 8	8 10	1	1	1
									1	12 10	6 3			
									(?)	14 8	8 5			
									2	24 6	8 2			
3,563	July 1, 1887	15	12.00	16	11.30	6	31,651	100.80	1	9 10	6 8	1	1	1
467	July 1, 1888	81	19.43	80	20.00	7	80,593	110.10	2	23 6	8 0	2	1	2
760	Mar. 30, 1887	3	24.80	2	23.72	6	} 107,903	114.54	2	16 5	9 2	3	1	3
364	July 1, 1884	3	27.41	2	23.04	6								
607	July 1, 1888	457	20.13	454	20.75	7	122,090	166.79	2	14 5	9 2½	2	1	2
									[21]1	12 0	7 7			
179	Apr. 13, 1887	2	16.5	1	16.50	6	68,465	109.02	1	9 0	6 0	2	1	2
									1	8 0	5 6			
526	July 1, 1887	32	21.89	31	24.20	6	60,834	96.87	1	12 0	8 9	2	1	2
282	July 1, 1887	32	21.77	31	21.77	.....	....	......	[21]1	19 10	9 1			
322	July 1, 1884	26	23.09	23	25.09	6	} 37,718	120.12	1	9 6	6 8	1	1	1
821	July 1, 1884	26	24.92	23	26.60	6								
6,608	July 1, 1888	1	38.32	2	27.06	7	110,935	121.24	[11]5	20 0	9 0	5	1	5
		3	29.76	6	30.20	[13]6	95,173							
2,421	July 1, 1888	51	22.80	52	23.16	6	106,496	113.05	2	15 6	9 0	3	1	[11]4
436	July 1, 1886	1	14.21	2	11.56	7	[14]20,152	110.12	1	8 10	6 1	1	1	1
		3	16.46	4	11.56	7	[14]20,152							
5,601	July 1, 1888	3	25.83	6	26.22	7	224,094	153.07	[16]6	20 0	9 0	[16]4	2	[17]11
		1	28.86	4	27.30	7	30,002	......	......	......	......	[16]4	1	
4,645	July 1, 1888	3	22.66	6	24.99	7								
		1	28.56	4	28.92	7								
5,601	July 1, 1888	5	23.72	8	18.97	6	59,346	103.89	1	15 7	8 10	2	1	2
273	July 1, 1888	5	18.91	8	20.04	6								
4,071	July 1, 1887	52	25.32	51	26.34	7	235,397	16.79	4	18 0	9 6	[21]4	1	[22]14
		54	24.96	53	27.12	7	235,397	......	1	16 0	9 6	[21]4	2	
		[24]56	21.36	55	24.61	6	22,099							

[11] One car in reserve.
[12] Double service over whole line; trains 1 and 2 daily; 5 and 6 daily, except Sunday.
[13] One helper between Nashville and McKenzie, Tenn. (116.70 miles), 4 days in a week—Mondays, Wednesdays, Thursdays, and Fridays.
[14] Double daily service; last year there was but single daily service on this line.
[15] Two cars in reserve.
[16] Day line, 4 helpers running through.
[17] One additional clerk not yet appointed.
[18] May 13, 1888, apartment-car service established on night trains of this line.

[19] Run of clerks on Columbia and Saint Joseph R. P. O. extended to Nashville, Tenn., Sept. 13, 1887; increase in distance, 47 miles.
[20] Covered by Nashville and Montgomery R. P. O. (47.44 miles).
[21] Day line.
[22] Two helpers on day line running between Nashville and Evansville, Ind; 4 helpers on night line running through.
[23] Night line.
[24] January 23, 1888, additional R. P. O. service placed on trains 55 and 56 between Nashville, Tenn., and Hopkinsville, Ky., to be performed by night-line helpers; distance, 80.07 miles.

TABLE A².—*Statement of railway post-offices in operation*

Designation of railway post-office. (Lines upon which railway post-office cars are paid for, in *italics*.)	Division.	Distance run by clerks, register to register.	Initial and terminal stations, running from east to west, north to south, or northwest to southeast (with abbreviated title of railroad company).	Number of route.	Miles of route for which railroad is paid.
		Miles.			
Nebraska City and Beatrice, Nebr.	6	95.24	Nebraska City, Nemeha City, Nebr. (Nebraska.)	[1]34005 (part)	27.56
			Nemeha City, Beatrice, Nebr. (Rep. Valley.)	34019	67.90
Nebraska City and Whitman, Nebr.	6	348.06	Nebraska City, York, Nebr. (Nebraska) ..	[2]34005 (part)	109.85
			York, Aurora, Nebr. (Rep. Valley)	[4]34011 (part)	22.75
			Aurora, Grand Island, Nebr. (Rep. Valley).	34027	19.96
			Grand Island, Whitman, Nebr. (Gr. Isl. and Wyo. Cent.)	[6]34036 (part)	198.65
Neche, Dakota, and St. Paul, Minn.	6	425.76	Neche, Fargo, Dak. (St. P., Minn. and Man.)	35005	157.84
			Fargo, Dak., Breckenridge, Minn. (St. P., Minn. and Man.).	26005	53.41
			Breckenridge, St. Paul, Minn. (St. P., Minn. and Man.).	26006	214.58
Nevada, Mo., and Chetopa, Kans.	7	77.38	Nevada, Mo., Chetopa, Kans. (N. and M.)...	28058	77.38
Newark and Shawnee, Ohio	5	43.20	Newark, Shawnee, Ohio (Balto. and Ohio)..	21088	43.67
New Berlin and Sidney, N. Y ..	2	25.16	New Berlin, Sidney, N. Y. (N. Y., O. and W.).	6101	25.08
Newburyport and Boston, Mass.	1	40.63	Newburyport, Wakefield, Mass. (Bos. and Me.).	3014	30.80
			Wakefield, Boston, Mass. (Bos. and Me.)..	[13]2011 (part)	([14])
New Castle and North Vernon, Ind.	5	69.99	New Castle, Rushville, Ind. (Ft. W., Cin. and Lou.).	22042	24.39
			Rushville, North Vernon, Ind. (Cin., Ind., St. Lou. and Chic.).	22015	45.50
New Galilee, Pa., and New Lisbon, Ohio.[15]	5	25.17	New Galilee, Pa., New Lisbon, Ohio (Pgh., Mar. and Chic.).	21093	25.33
New Hartford and Farmington, Conn.	1	14.30	New Hartford, Farmington, Conn. (N. Y., N. H., New Hart. Br.)	5621	14.37
New Haven, Conn., and New York, N. Y.	1	77.05	New Haven, Conn., New York, N. Y. (N. Y., N. H. and Hart).	[16]45005 (part)	([17])
New London and New Haven, Conn.	1	51.81	New London, New Haven, Conn. (N. Y., N. H. and Hart.).	5004	([20])
New Orleans, La., and Houston, Texas.	4	362.74	New Orleans, La Fayette, La. (South. Pac. R. R).	30003 (part)	140.94 ([21])
			La Fayette, La., Orange, Tex. (South. Pac. R. R.).	30010	113.25
			Orange, Houston, Tex. (South. Pacific R. R.).	31012	106.33
New Orleans, La., and Marshall, Texas.	4	369.37	New Orleans, Cheneyville, La. (Tex. Pac. R. R.).	30002	171.54
			Cheneyville, Shreveport, La. (Tex Pac.)...	30011	156.57
			Shreveport, La., Marshall, Tex. (Tex. Pacific).	31009 [22](pa't)	40.44
Newport and Cushman, Ark.[23]	7	40.57	Newport, Cushman, Ark. (St. L., I. M. and S.).	29014	40.57

[1] Balance of route (109.85 miles) covered by Nebraska City and Whitman, Nebr., R. P. O.
[2] Balance of route (27.56 miles) covered by Nebraska City and Beatrice, Nebr., R. P. O.
[3] One in reserve.
[4] Balance of route (19.25 miles) covered by Aurora and Arcadia, Nebr., R. P. O.
[5] Balance of route (71.60 miles) covered by Whitman and Alliance, Nebr., closed pouch service. (See Table C⁶.)
[6] Railway post-office cars paid for between Saint Paul and Barnesville, Minn.
[7] Through run.
[8] Three helpers between Breckenridge and Saint Paul, Minn., on through run.
[9] Reserve.
[10] Short run between Saint Paul and Morris, Minn., 158.16 miles.
[11] Clerk appointed to this line also acts as helper to Kansas City and Joplin, Mo. R. P. O. between Kansas City and Nevada, Mo. (103.32 miles).
[12] Two clerks appointed to Kansas City and Joplin, Mo., R. P. O. also perform service on this line.

*in the United States on June 30, 1888—*Continued.

Average weight of mail whole distance per day.	Date of last readjustment.	Train No. outward.	Av'ge speed (miles).	Train No. inward.	Av'ge speed (miles).	Number of round trips with clerks per week.	Annual miles of service with clerks.	Average miles run daily by crews.	Number of mail cars, or cars in which are mail apartments.	Length.	Width.	Number of crews.	Number of clerks to crew.	Number of clerks appointed to line.
Lbs.										*Ft. In.*	*Ft. In.*			
1,018	**July 1, 1886**	109	19.12	110	22.58	6	59,810	95.24	1	18 2	8 8	2	1	2
540	July 1, 1886	109	19.23	110	16.82	...	....	....	1	14 0	7 0			
1,018	July 1, 1886	41	21.88	42	23.44	6	218,581	139.22	[13]3	21 0	8 10	5	1	5
693	July 1, 1886	41	24.22	42	28.43	...			1	18 2	8 8			
1,231	July 1, 1886	41	27.07	42	23.13									
878	M'h 30,1887	41	14.82	42	15.16									
1,322	**July 1, 1886**	10	21.52	9	22.54	7	311,636	141.92	[14]3	40 0	8 9	[17]6	1	[18]11
2,863	**July 1, 1887**	10	21.36	9	21.36									
4,937	**July 1, 1887**	10	25.23	9	23.00									
		8	25.28	7	24.69	6	99,337	158.18	[19]1	15 10	8 10	[19]2	1	
									1	24 7	9 3			
									1	24 6	9 4			
677	**July 1, 1887**	321	23.38	322	24.68	7	56,642	[11]120.47	1	16 4	6 10	3	1	[21]21
261	July 1, 1888	104	24.96	103	24.90	6	27,126	86.46	1	10 0	8 6	1	1	1
191	July 1, 1885	24	**14.38**	25	41.56	6	15,800	50.32	1	14	6 10	1	1	1
721	July 1, 1885	13	26.14	68	26.14	6	25,515	81.26	1	12 0	8 6	2	1	2
		71	26.14	118	23.16	6	25,515							
4,739	**July 1, 1885**	13	18.99	68	17.80									
		71	18.99	118	17.26									
110	**July 1, 1888**	1	29.82	2	29.82	6	43,954	139.98	1	12 0	7 6	1	1	1
									1	10 6	9 4			
142	**July 1, 1888**	1	16.80	2	17.49	6								
234	July 1, 1888	7	11.28	4	14.76	6	7,752	50.34	1	13 0	7 6	1	1	1
128	**July 1, 1885**	631	24.00	650	24.00	6	8,980	57.20	1	10 0	6 6	1	1	1
		637	21.00	636	24.00		8,980							
64,611	**July 1, 1885**	23	27.45	52	27.12	6	48,387	115.56	1	16 4	6 10	1	1	[15]2
									[15]1	15 6	6 6			
13,103	July 1, 1885	405	26.50	404	26.50	6	32,536	103.62	1	15 0	6 2	1	1	[2]13
		75	33.97	44	33.97	6	32,536		1	12 11	6 4	1	1	
2,814	**July 1, 1886**	18	26,6	17	25	14	**531,051**	145.10	4	22 6	9 0	10	1	11
		20	23.2	19	23.6				4	22 9	9 2	...		(1)
2,714	July 1, 1886	18	28,6	17	26	...	....	....	3	24 3	9 2			
		20	21.9	19	24.4				(23)					
2,714	July 1, 1886	18	26	17	25.5									
		20	23.7	19	25.5									
1,436	**July 1, 1886**	51	22.6	52	22.9	7	270,378	123.12	[24]4	18 0	7 1	6	1	6
1,161	**July 1, 1886**	51	25.4	52	25									
....		51	26.5	52	26.5									
313	**July 1, 1888**	921	10.98	922	11.59	7	29,697	81.14	1	14 5	7 7	1	1	1

[13] Balance of route covered by Portland and Boston R. P. O. (106.33 miles).
[14] Covered by Portland and Boston R. P. O. (10 miles).
[15] R. P. O. service established on this line January 4, 1888.
[16] Balance of route covered by Boston, Springfield, and New York, R. P. O. (62.77 miles).
[17] Covered by Boston, Springfield, and New York, R. P. O. (73.23 miles).
[18] One clerk detailed as transfer clerk at New Haven, Conn.
[19] Reserve car.
[20] Covered by Boston, Providence, and New York, R. P. O. (51.78 miles).
[21] One clerk detailed as transfer clerk at New London, Conn.
[22] 60.20 miles reported as Cheneyville and La Fayette, R. P. O.
[23] Cars also used by San Antonio and Houston, R. P. O.; three reserve cars; one helper.
[24] One reserve car.
[25] 794.28 miles reported as Texar. and El Paso, R. P. O.
[26] Reported last year as Newport and Batesville, Ark.; increased distance, 11.63 miles.

TABLE A⁹.—*Statement of railway post-offices in operation*

Designation of railway post-office. (Lines upon which railway post-office cars are paid for, in *italics*.)	Division.	Distance run by clerks, register to register.	Initial and terminal stations, running from east to west, north to south, or northwest to southeast (with abbreviated title of railroad company).	Number of route.	Miles of route for which railroad is paid.
Newport, Vt., and Springfield, Mass.	1	*Miles.* 229.60	Newport, White Riv. Junction Vt. (Conn. and Pass.).	[1]2010 (part)	105.15
			White Riv. Junction, Windsor, Vt. (Cen. Vt.).	[2]2002 (part)	14.00
			Windsor, Bellows Falls, Vt. (Sul. Co.)	2004	25.50
			Bellows Falls, Brattleborough , Vt. (Ver. Valley).	2005	24.04
			Brattleborough, So. Vernon, Vt. (n. o.)(Cen. Vt.).	[3]3063 (part)	([9])
			So. Vernon, Vt. (n. o.), Springfield, Mass. (Conn. Riv.).	3067	51.88
Newport, Vt., and Springfield, Mass. (short run).	1	124.39	White River Junction, Windsor, Vt. (Cen. Vt.).	[7]2002 (part)	([9])
			Windsor, Bellows Falls, Vt. (Sul. Co.)	2004	([10])
			Bellows Falls, Brattleborough, Vt. (Ver. Valley).	2005	([11])
			Brattleborough, South Vernon, Vt. (n. o.), (Cen. Vt.).	[12]3062 (part)	([13])
			South Vernon, Vt. (n. o.), Springfield, Mass. (Conn. Riv.).	3067	([14])
Newton, Kans., and Gainesville, Tex.[17]	7	338.61	Newton, Arkansas City, Kans. (A., T. and S. F.).	[15]33011 (part)	78.81
			Arkansas City, Kans., Purcell, Ind. T. (So. Kans.).	32003	154.60
			Purcell, Ind. T., Gainesville, Tex. (G., C. and S. F.).	[18]31054 (part)	105.73
Newton and Kiowa, Kans.[19] ...	7	127.85	Newton, Mulvane, Kans. (A., T. and S. F.).	33011 (part)	([20])
			Mulvane, Wellington, Kans. (A., T. and S. F.).	[15]33037 (part)	16.41
			Wellington, Kiowa, Kans. (So. Kans.).	33035	69.32
New York, N. Y., and Chicago, Ill. This line is divided into three divisions, as follows:		....	....	....	......
East Division.—New York, and Syracuse, N. Y.	9	289.50	New York, Syracuse, N. Y. (N. Y. C. and H. R.).	6011 (part)	289.50

[1] Balance of route (10.14 miles) covered by closed-pouch service between Newport and Derby Line. (See Table C⁹.)

[2] Two clerks on Newport and Springfield short run (124.39) miles; 2 clerks as short stops between Springfield, Mass., and Brattleborough, Vt.; daily average 120 miles (one on day and one on short run); 1 clerk detailed as transfer clerk White Riv. Junction, Vt.

[3] Balance of route covered by Saint Albans and Boston R. P. O. (120.50 miles), and by Saint Albans and Ogdensburgh R. P. O. (Second Division) (24.27 miles).

[4] Reserve cars

[5] Balance of route (65.11 miles) covered by Palmer and New London R. P. O. and 46 miles by Brattleborough and Palmer R. P. O. (Richford and Springfield R. P. O. to Apr. 15, 1888); Newport and Springfield R. P. O. from Apr. 16, 1888.)

[6] Covered by Brattleborough and Palmer R. P. O. (10.28 miles.

[7] Balance of route (120.50 miles) covered by Saint Albans and Boston R. P. O. and by Saint Albans and Ogdensburgh R. P. O. (second division), 24.27 miles.

[8] Covered by Newport and Springfield R. P. O. (14 miles).

[9] Shown in column 17, Newport and Springfield R. P. O.

[10] Covered by Newport and Springfield R. P. O. (25.50 miles).

[11] Covered by Newport and Springfield R. P. Q. (24.04 miles).

[12] Balance of route (65.11 miles) covered by Palmer and New London R. P. O., and 46 miles by Brattleborough and R. P. O.

[13] Covered by Brattleborough and Palmer R. P. O. (10.28 miles.)

[14] Covered by Newport and Springfield R. P. O. (51.88 miles).

[15] Florence and Arkansas City, Kans., R. P. O. also runs over 13.18 miles of route 33011, between Winfield and Arkansas City, Kans. Newton and Kiowa, Kans., R. P. O., runs over 42.81 miles of route 33011, between Newton and Mulvane, Kans.

[16] Cars shown under Gainesville and Galveston, Tex., R. P. O.

[17] New service; that portion of line between Newton and Arkansas City, Kans., reported last year as Newton and Arkansas City, Kans.

[18] 64.90 miles of route 31054, between Gainesville and Fort Worth, Tex., covered by Gainesville and Galveston, Tex., R. P. O.

in the United States on June 30, 1888—Continued.

Average weight of mail whole distance per day.	Date of last re-adjustment.	Train No. outward.	Av'ge speed (miles).	Train No. inward.	Av'ge speed (miles).	Number of round-trips with clerks per week.	Annual miles of service with clerks.	Average miles run daily by crews.	Number of mail cars, or cars in which are mail apartments.	Length.	Width.	Number of crews.	Number of clerks to crew.	Number of clerks appointed to line.
Lbs.										*Ft. In.*	*Ft. In.*			
3,128	Aug. 5,1885	4	23.36	3	22.13	6	144,188	114.80	1	41 6	9 0	4	2	[32]21
		15	24.26	33	23.36	6	150,753	......	1	18 0	6 8	4		
5,453	July 1,1885	4	24.00	3	24.00				1	41 4	9 0			
		15	27.99	33	27.99				1	18 6	6 8			
4,861	July 1,1885	4	28.36	3	28.36									
		15	34.65	33	26.89				41	21 2	6 9			
4,919	July 1,1885	4	28.80	3	26.17				41	21 8	6 4			
		15	31.99	33	30.63				41	18 4	6 9			
1,587	July 1,1885	4	22.21	3	21.42									
		15	33.83	33	30									
6,514	July 1,1885	4	24.99	3	24.58									
		15	34.48	33	31.57									
5,453	July 1,1885	15	15.27	23	27.99	6	78,116	124.89	1	26 0	6 0	2	1	(⁷)
4,861	July 1,1885	15	25.99	23	25.99									
4,919	July 1,1885	15	28.80	23	26.17									
1,587	July 1,1885	15	22.21	23	13.83									
6,514	July 1,1885	15	23.07	23	34.99									
1,201	July 1,1886	403	21.39	408	22.89	7	247,863	169.31	(¹⁶)	....		4	1	4
287	Sept.12,1887	403	27.58	408	30.10	7								
861	Sept.12,1887	2	25.47	1	26.03	7								
1,201	July 1,1886	407	20.53	408	33.23	7	98,586	[25]99.74	2 / [21]1	21 0 / 20 6¼	9 3½ / 9 4½	[21]2	[22]2	3
767	July 1,1886	437	17.76	438	21.72	7								
		447	22.80	448	21.57	7		(²⁴)	....					[25]345 (²⁶)
99.901	July 1,1885	21	32.57	12	32.57	7	211.914	144.75	[27]4	60 0	9 0	4	[28] 8
		23	28.10		......	6	181.806	124.12	1	60 0	9 0	4	7 2
				2	31.66				2	60 0	9 0	(²⁹)	(³⁰)
									2	60 0	9 0		(³¹)
		11	33.83		......				1	50 0	9 0		(³²)
						7	211.914	144.75	1	49 5	9 0		
				16	31.11				1	60 0	9 0	4	12
									1	50 0	9 0		
									1	49 5	9 0		

[19] Reported last year as Newton and Caldwell, Kans.; increased distance 47.31 miles.

[20] 42.81 miles distance on route 33011, covered by Newton, Kans., and Gainesville, Tex., R. P. O.

[21] Clerks run in the order of two weeks on and one off, and separate at Attica, Kans., one going through to Kiowa and the other performing service on Attica and Medicine Lodge, Kans. R. P. O.

[22] In reserve.

[23] 21.92 miles of route 33037 between Wellington and Caldwell, Kans., covered by closed-pouch service. (See Table C⁴.)

[24] The total equipment of this line is as follows: 24 cars, 60 feet by 9 feet; 6 cars, 50 feet by 9 feet; 6 cars, 49 feet 5 inches by 9 feet. Eight of these cars are held in reserve. The figures in the body of the report show the number and dimensions of cars upon each train upon each contract route.

[25] Clerks are detailed as follows: 1 as chief clerk, Grand Central Depot, N. Y.; 1 as chief clerk, Syracuse, N. Y.; 2 in the office of chief clerk, R. M. S., Syracuse, N. Y.; 2 as transfer clerks, Union Depot, Cleveland, Ohio; 1 as transfer clerk, N. Y., P. and O. depot, Cleveland, Ohio; 2 as transfer clerks, Toledo, Ohio; 1 as trans-

fer clerk, Elkhart, Ind.; 3 to R. M. S. printing office, Cleveland, Ohio; 7 to the office of superintendent R. M. S., Cleveland, Ohio; 4 to Cleveland and Toledo R. P. O.; 8 to Toledo and Chicago R. P. O.; and 5 to office of the General Superintendent R. M. S., Washington, D. C.

[26] There is one vacancy on the line, one acting clerk employed as additional.

[27] Two cars on each train.

[28] Eight clerks assigned as helpers on train 21 outward, between New York and Fonda, N. Y., 183.94 miles. Two clerks assigned as helpers on train 21 outward and 2 inward, between Utica and Buffalo, N. Y. (208.50 miles).

[29] Two clerks assigned as helpers on train 23 outward and train 16 inward, between Albany and Syracuse, N. Y. (147.50 miles).

[30] Four clerks assigned as helpers on train 9 inward and train 2 inward, between Albany and Syracuse, N. Y. (147.50 miles).

[31] One clerk assigned as helper on train 11 outward, between New York and Albany, N. Y. (142.68 miles).

[32] Two clerks assigned as helpers on train 11 outward and train 16 inward, between Albany and Syracuse, N. Y. (147.50 miles).

TABLE A².—*Statement of railway post-offices in operation*

Designation of railway post-offices. (Lines upon which railway post-office cars are paid for, in *italics*.)	Division.	Distance run by clerks, register to register.	Initial and terminal stations, running from east to west, north to south, or northwest to southeast (with abbreviated title of railroad company).	Number of route.	Miles of route for which railroad is paid.
Middle Division.—Syracuse, N. Y., and Cleveland, Ohio.	9	*Miles.* 336.26	Syracuse, Buffalo, N. Y. (N. Y. C. and H. R.)	6011 (part)	152.40
			Buffalo, N. Y., Cleveland, Ohio (L. S. and M. S.).	21095 (part)	183.20
West Division.—Cleveland, Ohio, and Chicago, Ill.¹³	9	¹²356.61	Cleveland, Ohio, Chicago, Ill. (L. S. and M. S.).	21095 (part)	356.80
			Elyria, Milbury, Ohio (L. S. and M. S.)	21007	74.90
			Toledo, Ohio, Elkhart, Ind. (L. S. and M. S.).	21045	133.80
New York, N. Y., Dover, N. J., and Easton, Pa.	2	86.87	Hoboken, N. J., Easton, Pa. (D. L. and W.).	7013	84.24
New York and Dunkirk, N. Y. ..	2	461.38	New York, Dunkirk, N. Y. (N. Y. L. E. and W.)	6001	450.55
New York and Elmira, N. Y. ...	2	303.56	Waverly, Elmira, N. Y. (N. Y. L. E. and W.)	6001 (part)	(²⁴)
			Easton, Pa., Waverly, N. Y. (L. V.)	8010	205.57
			Metuchen, N. J., Easton, Pa. (L. V.)	7018	54.20
			New York, N. Y., Metuchen, N. J. (Pa.)	7004 (part)	(²⁷)
New York, N. Y., and Hackettstown, N. J.²⁸	2	62.79	New York, N. Y., Hackettstown, N. J. (D. L. and W.).	7013 (part)	(²⁸)

¹ 2 cars on each train.

² 2 clerks assigned as helpers on train 21 outward, and 2 inward, between Utica and Buffalo, N. Y., 208.50 miles.

³ One clerk assigned as helper on train 11 outward, between Syracuse and Buffalo, N. Y., 152.40 miles.

⁴ Four clerks assigned as helpers on train 11 outward and 8 inward, between Syracuse, N. Y., and Cleveland, Ohio, 336.26 miles.

⁵ Shown on route 6011, Middle Division.

⁶ Four clerks assigned as helpers on train 1 outward and train 8 inward, between Buffalo, N. Y., and Cleveland, Ohio, 183.76 miles.

⁷ Two clerks assigned as helpers on train 3 outward and train 12 inward, between Buffalo, N. Y., and Cleveland, Ohio, 183 76 miles.

⁸ Four clerks assigned as helpers on train 11 outward and 8 inward, between Buffalo, N. Y., and Toledo, Ohio, 306.56 miles.

⁹ One clerk assigned as helper on train 11 outward, between Buffalo, N. Y., and Cleveland, Ohio, 183.20 miles.

¹⁰ Three clerks assigned as helpers on train 1 outward and 2 inward, between Toledo, Ohio, and Chicago, Ill., 235.10 miles.

¹¹ Two clerks assigned as helpers on train 3 outward and train 2 inward, between Cleveland and Tol do, Ohio, 112.80 miles.

¹² This is the distance by route 21095. The distance from Cleveland, Ohio, to Chicago, Ill. vis route 21095, Cleveland to Elyria, Ohio, thence over route 21007 to Millbury, Ohio, thence over route 21095 to Toledo, Ohio, thence over route 21045 to Elkhart, Ind., and thence over route 21095 to Chicago, Ill., is 344.55 miles.

¹³ Routes 21095, 21007, and 21045 constitute the main line of the Lake Shore and Michigan Southern Railway between Buffalo, N. Y., and Chicago, Ill.

¹⁴ Two clerks assigned as helpers on train 3 out-

in the United States on June 30, 1888—Continued.

Average weight of mail whole distance per day.	Date of last re-adjustment.	Average speed per hour (train numbers taken from division schedules).				Number of round trips with clerks per week.	Annual miles of service with clerks.	Average miles run daily by crews.	Number of mail cars, or cars in which are mail apartments.	Inside dimensions of cars or apartments (railway post-office cars in black figures).		Number of crews.	Number of clerks to crew.	Number of clerks appointed to line.
		Train No. outward.	Av'ge speed (miles).	Train No. inward.	Av'ge speed (miles).					Length.	Width.			
Lbs.										*Ft. In.*	*Ft. In.*			
99.901	July 1, 1885	21, 23 and 3	27.03 27.43	12	34.04	7 6	246.142 211.171	163.13 144.17	1 1 2 1 1	60 0 60 0 60 0 50 0 50 0	9 0 9 0 9 0 9 0 9 0	4 4	27 8 (2)	
		11	39.11						1 1 1 1	60 0 49 5 60 0 49 0	9 0 9 0 9 0 9 0		(3, 4)	
				16	30.04	7	246.142	163.13	1 1	60 0 49 5	9 0 9 0	4	8	
96.761	July 1, 1888	1 3	40.66 31.37	12 2	34.36 33.27	7 6	(5) (5)		1 2 4	60 0 60 0 60 0	9 0 9 0 9 0	6 (6)	(6) (7) (7)	
		11	39.21						2 1 1	60 0 50 0 49 5	9 0 9 0 9 0	6	(8) (4)	
				8	30.50	7	(8)		1 1	60 0 49 5	9 0 9 0		(8)	
96.761	*July 1, 1888	1 3	36.32 26.77	12 2	23.66 27.12	7 6	257.351 218.481	176.12 149.16	1 2 4	60 0 60 0 60 0	9 0 9 0 9 0	4 4	16 5 11 6 14, 10	
		11	31.97						2 1 1 1 1	60 0 50 0 49 5 60 0 50 0	9 0 9 0 9 0 9 0 9 0	4	(9) 9	
17.168	July 1, 1888	(15)		8	27.78 27.56	(16)	(17)	175.03 256.240		1 1	49 5 60 0	9 0 9 0		15	
46.485	July 1, 1888	1 3	40.02 28.08	(16) 2	30.20	(17) 6	(17) (17)		1 4 1	49 5 60 0 60 0	9 0 9 0 9 0	15 15	(10) 20, 13	
		(15)		8	30.78	(16)	(17)		1 1	50 0 49 5	9 0 9 0	15		
3,229	July 1, 1885	13	24.55	14	23.68	6	54,554	115,82	2 22	13 0 13 0	8 10 8 4	2	1	16 3
12,297	July 1, 1885	9 3	28.22 28.53	8 12	33.71 29.54	6 7	208,892 337,730	158.80	2 2	50 0 50 0	9 0 9 0	4 4	3 3	24 48
12,297	July 1, 1885	2	40.47	5	32.88	6	190,648	151.79	2 22	23 4 20 0	9 10½ 10 0	4	1	26 7
3,459 2,958 136,401	July 1, 1885 July 1, 1885 July 1, 1885	2 2 2	25.53 41.16 27.10	5 5 5	26.35 42.22 31.44	6 6 6			(28) (28) (28)			(28) (28) (28)		
3,229	July 1, 1885	17	23.69	22	25.11	6	39.432	83.72	1	12 9	8 11	1	1	(32)

ward and 2 inward, between Cleveland and Wauseon, Ohio, 146 miles.

[14] The opposite train (11) runs outward on route 21095, from Cleveland, Ohio, to Chicago, Ill., 356.60 miles.

[15] Seven trips inward.

[16] Shown on route 21095, Western Division.

[17] The opposite train (12) runs inward on route 21095 from Elkhart, Ind., to Toledo, Ohio, 142.70 miles.

[18] Seven trips outward.

[20] Alternates with New York and Hackettstown clerk.

[21] One clerk New York and Hackettstown R. P. O.

[22] In reserve.

[23] Trains 9 and 8 run daily, except Sunday, between New York and Hornellsville (332.63 miles).

[24] Three helpers, Hornellsville to Binghamton; 4 helpers, Hornellsville to Susquehanna; 1 clerk, chief clerk of line; 4 clerks detailed to super-

intendent's office; 1 clerk, transfer clerk at Elmira; 1 clerk, transfer clerk at Binghamton; 1 clerk, transfer clerk at Dunkirk; 1 clerk, transfer clerk at Jersey City; 2 clerks Port Jervis and New York R. P. O.

[25] On Western Division, Hornellsville to Dunkirk.

[26] 17.54 miles covered by N. Y. and Dunkirk R. P. O.

[27] One clerk to transfer duty at Easton, Pa.; 1 clerk as helper; 1 clerk to Elmira and Wilkes Barre R. P. O.

[28] Cars and clerks shown on route No. 6001.

[29] 26.20 miles covered by N. Y. and Washington R. P. O.

[30] Short run, New York, Dover, and Easton R. P. O.

[31] 60.20 miles covered by New York, Dover, and Easton R. P. O.

[32] Clerk shown on New York, Dover, and Easton R. P. O.

TABLE A*.—*Statement of railway post-offices in operation*

Designation of railway post-office. (Lines upon which railway post-office cars are paid for, in *italics*.)	Division.	Distance run by clerks, register to register.	Initial and terminal stations, running from east to west, north to south, or northwest to southeast (with abbreviated title of railroad company).	Number of route.	Miles of route for which railroad is paid.
New York, N. Y., and Philadelphia, Pa.[1]	2	*Miles.* 91.82	New York, N. Y., Philadelphia, Pa. (Penna.)	7004	(?)
New York, N. Y., and Pittsburgh, Pa.	2	443.20	New York, N. Y., Philadelphia, Pa. (Penna.)	7004	(?)
			Philadelphia, Pittsburgh, Pa. (Penna.)......	8001	352.90
New York, N. Y., and Point Pleasant, N. J.	2	60.64	New York, N. Y., Elizabethport, N. J. (N. Y. and L. B.).	7001 (part)	(14)
			Elizabethport, Point Pleasant, N. J; (N. Y. and L. B.).[16]	7003 (part)	49.19
New York and Rochester, N. Y.	2	397.12	New York, Syracuse, N. Y. (N. Y. C. and H. R.).	6011 (part)	(19)
			Syracuse, Rochester, N. Y. (N. Y. C, and H. R.).	6013	104.00
New York and Saint George, N. Y.	2	5.90	New York, Saint George, N. Y. (S. I. R. T. Co.).	6062 (part)	**5.90
New York, N. Y., Somerville, N. J., and Easton, Pa.	2	75.09	New York, N. Y., Easton, Pa. (Cent. of N. J.).	7001	73.94
New York, N. Y., and Washington, D. C.	2	227.85	New York, N. Y., Philadelphia, Pa. (Penna.).	7004	90.89
			Philadelphia, Pa., Bay View, Md. (P., W. and B.).	10001	91.80
			Bay View, Md., Washington, D. C. (B. and P.).	10013	45.40

[1] Short run New York and Pittsburgh R. P. O.
[2] 90.60 miles covered by New York and Washington R. P. O.
[3] Runs on New York and Washington R. P. O.
[4] Clerks accounted for in New York and Pittsburgh R. P. O.
[5] In reserve.
[6] Train 27 becomes train 13 at Philadelphia.
[7] Crews run as follows: On train No. 27, 6 crews of 8 each, through to Pittsburgh, and return on train No. 8 to Harrisburg, where they lie over till next day and bring to New York train No. 4 with 3 clerks; train No. 6 with 5 clerks. On train No. 7, 6 crews of 13 each through to Pittsburgh, returning on train No. 10, 5 clerks; train No. 4, 2 clerks, train No. 6, 6 clerks, to Harrisburg, where they lie over till next day and bring in to New York train No. 8 with 8 clerks and train No. 10 with 5 clerks.
[8] 2 helpers on trains 3 and 10; 6 clerks on Philadelphia and Harrisburg R. P. O.; 3 clerks on New York and Philadelphia R. P. O.; 1 clerk detailed

to general superintendent's office; 1 clerk detailed as chief clerk of line; 2 clerks detailed in superintendent's office; 2 clerks as assistants to chief clerk, 1 clerk, janitor dormitory, Harrisburg; 1 clerk, janitor dormitory, Philadelphia; 6 clerks as transfer clerks, Philadelphia; 4 clerks as transfer clerks, Harrisburg; 4 clerks as transfer clerks, Pittsburgh; 1 clerk as transfer clerk, Lancaster. The total equipment of this line from New York to Saint Louis is as follows: Penna. R. R., 17 cars, 60 feet by 8 feet 7 inches; Penna. R. R., 3 cars, 40 feet by 8 feet 7 inches; P. O. and St. L. R. R., 5 cars, 60 feet by 8 feet 7 inches; C, St. L. and P. R. R., 5 cars, 60 feet by 8 feet 7 inches; C., St. L. and P. R. R., 3 cars, 40 feet by 8 feet 7 inches; Little Miami R. E., 2 cars, 60 feet by 8 feet 7 inches; Vandalia Line, 5 cars, 60 feet by 8 feet 7 inches; Vandalia Line, 2 cars, 40 feet by 8 feet 7 inches
* On Sundays, leaves New York on train No 9, runs to Philadelphia; west of Philadelphia runs on train No. 7.

in the United States on June 30, 1888—Continued.

Average weight of mail whole distance per day.	Date of last re-adjustment.	Average speed per hour (train numbers taken from division schedules). Train No. outward.	Av'ge speed (miles).	Train No. inward.	Av'ge speed (miles).	Number of round trips with clerks per week.	Annual miles of service with clerks.	Average miles run daily by crews.	Number of mail cars, or cars in which are mail apartments.	Inside dimensions of cars or apartments (railway post-office cars in black figures). Length.	Width.	Number of crews.	Number of clerks to crew.	Number of clerks appointed to line.
Lbs.										*Ft. In.*	*Ft. In.*			
136,401	July 1, 1885	[9]15	34.86	74	39.34	6	57,663	122.42	1	15 0	8 7¾	2	1	(4)
		99	31.84	34	36.72	6	57,663	....	1	15 0	8 7¾	1	1	
									[5]4	15 0	8 7¾			
136,401	July 1, 1885	[9]27	38.82	.....	.....	3½	324,422	145.96	2	60 0	8 7	[7]6	8	[8]164
				8	38.01	3½	....	....	2	60 0	8 7			
									3	60 0	8 7			
		[9]7	35.07	.....	.....	3½	324,422	....	1	40 0	8 7			
				10	36.24	3½	....	....	1	60 0	8 7	6	13	
				4	36.24	3½	162,211	....	1	60 0	8 7			
				6	37.48	3½	162,211	....	1	60 0	8 7			
91,679	July 1, 1885	[11]13	26.13	8	31.50	7	....	....	(10)	....	....	(10)		
		[12]7	31.36	10	28.60	7	....	....	(10)	....	....	(10)		
				[12]4	29.41	3½	....	....	(10)	....	....	(10)		
				6	34.14	3½	....	....	(10)	....	....	(10)		
		[11]3	25.98	.....	.....	3	78,186	....	1	20 0	9 0	2	1	(10)
				[12]14	28.28	3	41,448	....	1	15 0	9 0	2	1	(10)
									[6]1	19 9	8 8			
									[12]13	60 0	8 7			
									[13]1	40 0	8 7			
									[6]12	60 0	8 7			
									[6]5	40 0	8 7			
3,412	July 1, 1885	302	19.87	313	20.20	6	38,082	121.28	1	40 8	8 10	1	1	[14]4
		306	21.20	319	22.71	6	38,082	....	1	16 0	7 0	1	1	
		318	22.71	307	25.44	6	38,082	....	1	16 7	7 0	1	1	
4,999	July 1, 1885	302	17.05	313	25.66	6	....	(17)	[6]1	14 0	7 0	....	....	(18)
		306	25.66	319	25.22	6	....	(17)	(18)	....	....	....	....	(18)
		318	27.58	307	26.82	6	....	(17)	(18)	....	....	....	....	(18)
99,901	July 1, 1885	21	32.57	26	34.17	[20]6½	270,041	148.70	2	50 0	9 0	6	3	[21]52
4,373	July 1, 1885	19	21.15	6	26.55	6	....	....	2	50 0	9 0			
1,403	July 1, 1886	1	14.16	2	14.16	6	3,705	47.20	(22)	6 0	7 0	1	1	1
		3	14.16	4	14.16	6	3,705	....	(22)	6	7 0			
		5	14.16	6	14.16	6	[22]3,705	....	(22)	6 0	7 0			
		7	14.16	8	14.16	6	3,705	....	(22)	6 0	7 0			
3,412	July 1, 1885	2	23.68	5	26.50	6	47,157	100.12	2	15 0	8 0	2	1	3
		48	25.30	15	26.50	6	[24]47,157	....	[6]1	15 7	7 4	1	1	
136,401	July 1, 1885	27	38.82	[25]14	36.35	6½	154,938	113.92	2	60 0	8 7	4	4	[26]77
		[25]15	34.86	40	33.01	6½	154,938	....	2	60 0	8 7	4	3	
		23	28.99	58	30.29	7	166,786	....	2	60 0	8 7	4	[27]5	
58,491	July 1, 1885	27	33.99	[25]14	37.46	6½	(28)	....	(10)	....	....	(10)		
		[25]15	32.87	40	27.96	6½	(28)	....	(10)	....	....	(10)		
		23	26.22	58	25.60	7	(28)	....	(10)	....	....	(10)		
57,706	July 1, 1885	27	37.31	[25]14	37.20	6½	....	....	(10)	....	....	(10)		
		[25]15	36.06	40	34.92	6½	....	....	(10)	....	....	(10)		
		23	23.68	58	25.93	7	....	....	(10)	....	....	(10)		
									[6]1	60 0	8 7			

[10] Cars and clerks shown on route No. 7004.
[11] Service between Harrisburg and Pittsburgh only.
[12] Service between Harrisburg and Altoona only.
[13] In use west of Pittsburgh.
[14] 10.60 miles covered by New York, Somerville, and Easton R. P. O.
[15] One helper; one acting clerk.
[16] 1 mile covered by Point Pleasant and Philadelphia R. P. O.
[17] Triple daily service except Sunday.
[18] Cars and clerks shown on route No. 7001.
[19] 290.50 miles covered by New York and Chicago R. P. O.
[20] Train No. 21 runs to Syracuse on Sunday.
[21] Four helpers; 4 clerks on Albany and New York R. P. O.; 5 clerks detailed to superintendent's office; 1 clerk, janitor, dormitory, New York; 1 clerk on Buffalo and Suspension Bridge R. P. O.; 6 clerks to transfer duty at New York, N. Y.; 5 clerks to transfer duty at Albany, N. Y.; 3 clerks to transfer duty at Rochester, N. Y.; 2 clerks to transfer duty at Troy, N. Y.; 2 clerks to transfer duty at Syracuse, N. Y.; 1 clerk to transfer duty at Castleton, N. Y.
[22] 3.88 miles covered by closed-pouch service. (See Table C[a].)
[23] This service is by steam-boat fitted with mail apartment and four trips are made daily.
[24] Double daily service except Sunday.
[25] Trains 14 and 15 do not run Sundays.
[26] 11 helpers; 1 chief clerk of line; 1 chief clerk Superintendent's office; 1 chief clerk chief examiner; 3 clerks detailed to General Superintendent's office; 5 clerks detailed to Superintendent's office; 7 clerks detailed for transfer duty at Jersey City.
[27] One clerk from each crew detailed to run north on train No. 78 in baggage-car and works New York City mail only.
[28] Triple daily service except Sundays; on Sundays, double service.

TABLE A².—*Statement of railway post-offices in operation*

Designation of railway post-office. (Lines upon which railway post-office cars are paid for, in *italics*.)	Division.	Distance run by clerks, register to register.	Initial and terminal stations, running from east to west, north to south, or northwest to southeast (with abbreviated title of railroad company).	Number of route.	Miles of route for which railroad is paid.
		Miles.			
Nineveh, N. Y., and Carbondale, Pa.	2	57.56	Nineveh, N. Y.; and Jefferson Junction, Pa. (D. and H. C. Co.)	6031	21.70
			Jefferson Junction, Pa., and Carbondale, Pa. (N. Y., L. E. and W.).	8064 (part)	²35.71
Nordmont, Pa., and Hartley Hall, Pa.	2	27.16	Nordmont, Pa., and Hartley Hall, Pa. (W'msport & N. Branch).	8110	27.16
Norfolk and Columbus, Nebr..	6	50.64	Norfolk, Columbus, Nebr. (Om., Nio. and B. Hills).	34012	50.68
Norfolk, Va., and Edenton, N. C.	3	75.25	Norfolk, Va., Edenton, N. C. (Norfolk Southern).	11026	75.07
Norfolk and Lynchburgh, Va..	3	205.22	Norfolk, Petersburgh, Va. (Norfolk and Western).	11011	82.18
			Petersburgh, Lynchburgh, Va. (Norfolk and Western).	11012	123.7
Norfolk, Newport News, and Richmond, Va.⁴	3	91.32	Norfolk, Richmond, Va. (C. and O. Rwy., and O. D. S. B. Co.).	11005 (part)	91.32
Norfolk, Va., and Raleigh, N. C.	3	179.02	Portsmouth, Va., Weldon, N. C. (Seaboard and Roanoke).	11015	78.98
			Weldon, Raleigh, N. C. (Raleigh and Gaston).	13001	97.78
North Adams and Pittsfield, Mass.	1	21.43	North Adams, Pittsfield, Mass. (Bos. and Alb'y).	3029	21.41
No. Anson and Portland, Me..	1	104.17	No. Anson, Oakland, Me. (Som.)	18	25.77
			Oakland, Portland, Me. (Me. Cen.)	⁵5 (part)	(⁶)
No. Conway, N. H., and Boston, Mass.	1	189.37	No. Conway, N. H., Conway Jct. (n. o.) (Bos. and Maine).	1014	71.81
			Conway Jct. (n. o.), Boston, Mass. (Bos. and Maine).	⁵3001 (part)	(⁷)
North Creek and Saratoga, N. Y.	2	58.25	North Creek, Saratoga, N. Y. (Adirondack).	6095	58.72
North Fair Haven, N. Y., and Sayre, Pa.	2	118.11	North Fair Haven, N. Y., Sayre, Pa. (L. V.)	6084	118.11
Northville and Fonda, N. Y....	2	26.79	Northville, Fonda, N. Y. (F., J. and G.)....	6081	27.08
Norwood and Rome, N. Y......	2	146.92	Norwood, De Kalb Junc., N. Y. (R., W. and O.).	6110	25.48
			De Kalb Junc., Rome, N. Y. (R., W. and O.)	6036 (part)	¹²²²2.72
Nyack and New York, N. Y...	2	.29.35	Nyack, New York, N. Y. (Nor. of N. J.)...	7017	28.59
Oakes, Dak., and Hawarden, Iowa.	6	280.67	Oakes, Columbia, Dak. (Chi. and No. West.)	35023	39.30
			Columbia, Huron, Dak. (Chi. and No. West.).	35010	97.26
			Huron, Iroquois, Dak. (Chi. and No. West.).	26031 (part)	(¹⁶)
			Iroquois, Dak., Hawarden, Iowa (Chi. and No. West.).	¹⁵27070 (part)	126.37
Oconto and Clintonville, Wis...	6	56.75	Oconto, Clintonville, Wis. (Mil., L. S. and West.).	25058	56.73
Oelwein and Des Moines, Iowa.	6	132.28	Oelwein, Hudson, Iowa (Chi., St. P. and Kan. City).	27069	35.92
			Hudson, Des Moines, Iowa (Chi., St. P. and Kan. City).	¹²27056 (part)	96.72
Ogden and Salt Lake, Utah¹²..	8	38.73	Ogden, Salt Lake, Utah (Utah Central R. R.).	41001 (part)	37.50
Ogden, Utah, and San Francisco, Cal.	8	534.65	Ogden, Utah, San Francisco, Cal. (Central Pacific R. R.).	46001	534.17

In reserve.

² 3.80 miles covered by closed pouch service. (See Table C².)
³ Cars and clerks shown on route No. 6031.
⁴ 12 miles of this service performed by steam-boat, Norfolk to Newport News, Va.
⁵ Balance of route (25.13 miles) covered by Skowhegan and Portland, R. P. O.
⁶ Covered by Skowhegan and Portland R. P. O. (77.80 miles.)
⁷ Shown in column 9, Skowhegan and Portland R. P. O.

These clerks run between Oakland and Portland with Skowhegan and Portland clerks as assistants.
⁸ Balance of route (41.95 miles) covered by Bangor & Boston R. P. O.
⁹ Covered by Bangor and Boston R. P. O. (67.40 miles.
¹⁰ Reserve car.
¹¹ Short run between Auburn, N. Y., and Sayre, Pa.
¹² Double daily service, except Sunday.
¹³ 19.55 miles covered by closed pouch service. (See Table C².)

in the United States on June 30, 1888—Continued.

Average weight of mail whole distance per day.	Date of last readjustment.	Average speed per hour (train numbers taken from division schedules).				Number of round trips with clerks per week.	Annual miles of service with clerks.	Average miles run daily by crews.	Number of mail cars, or cars in which are mail apartments.	Inside dimensions of cars or apartments (railway post-office cars in black figures).		Number of crews.	Number of clerks to crew.	Number of clerks assigned to line.
		Train No. outward.	Av'ge speed (miles).	Train No. inward.	Av'ge speed (miles).					Length	Width			
Lbs.										*Ft. In.*	*Ft. In.*			
250	July 1, 1885	2	27.70	1	28.30	6	36,148	115.12	1	10 0	6 8	1	1	1
									1]	8 11	6 7			
231	July 1, 1885	2	25.50	1	25.50	6	....	....	(²)			(²)		
3,450	July 1, 1885	1	12.53	4	11.89	6	17,056	54.32	1	8 0	6 0	1	1	1
460	July 1, 1886	66	26.44	67	22.59	6	31,802	101.28	1	15 2	7 5	1	1	1
745	July 1, 1885	2	22.76	1	22.76	6	47,257	75.25	²]	12 0	6 9	2	1	2
1,226	July 1, 1885	3	28.14	2	30.27	7	150,221	102.61	1	19 8	9 5	4	1	4
857	July 1, 1885	3	22.99	2	27.23				1	15 9	8 2			
1,781	July 1, 1885	1	27.30	2	29	6	57,349	91.32	1	21 8	8 9	2	1	2
957	July 1, 1885	47	18.49	48	21.43	6	112,425	119.34	2	13 2	8 6	3	1	3
									1	12 2	8 9			
1,449	July 1, 1888	2	24.25	1	24.25		13,458	85.72	1	9 6	6 0	1	1	1
985	July 1, 1885	481	25.12	486	25.12	6	13,458							
		489	25.12	492	25.12	6								
1,521	July 1, 1885	2	23.07	1	22.72	6	65,418	104.17	1	14 0	6 10	2	1	2
1,521	July 1, 1885	2	(?)	1	(?)									
1,052	July 1, 1885	44	21.33	9	21.33	6	87,524	120.38	2	19 6	8 6	3	2	6
		48	22.72	57	22.72	6	25,622							
23,499	July 1, 1888	44	24.50	9	15.75		....	....	10]	24 6	8 11			
		48	31.50	57	34.50									
808	July 1, 1885	6	21.18	1	21.18	6	36,581	116.50	1	12 0	6 6	1	1	1
754	July 1, 1885	15	23.62	8	22.40	6	74,173	136.56	1	12 1	6 9	2	1	3
		7	14.25	2	25.38	6	[11]54,473	....	1	13 8	6 7	1	1	
									[1]	11 3	6 3			
783	July 1, 1885	1	17.60	2	19.36	6	16,824	107.16	1	8 0	6 0	1	1	1
		5	20.60	6	20.87	6	[12]16,824	....	1	11 7	7 0			
									[1]	13 9	8 7			
1,073	July 1, 1885	6	27.79	1	25.48	6	92,266	146.44	1	20 6	6 3	3	1	3
									1]	24 6	7 2			
2,258	July 1, 1885	6	26.77	1	24.54	6	....	....	(14)			(14)		
598	July 1, 1885	202	21.42	205	19.16	6	19,060	121.40	1	9 0	7 0	1	1	1
		216	21.17	215	20.23	6	[12]19,060	....	1]	6 9	7 0			
1,156	Feb.10, 1887	22	29.25	21	26	7	205,450	140.33	2	24 7	9 3	4	1	[15]5
749	July 1, 1886	22	29.04	21	27.66									
2,327	July 1, 1887	42	27,15	41	27.15									
1,673	July 1, 1887	42	28.04	41	27.04									
296	July 1, 1887	24	25.22	25	10.47	6	35,639	113.50	1	14 0	7 8	1	1	1
549	June 20, 1888	5	25.35	6	23.95	6	83,072	132.28	2	15 6	8 9	2	1	2
612	July 1, 1887	5	23.97	6	25.04									
21,862	July 1, 1886	1	31.25	6	31.25	14	56,701	154.92	1	14 2	8 8	1	1	1
25,702	Aug. 15, 1888	1	20.85	2	22.27	7	310,964	166.93	7	55 11½	9 5½	10	2	[20]37
		13	23.20	14	27.57	7	66,385	90.69	1	21 4	8 10			

[14] Cars and clerks shown on route No. 6110.

[15] One helper between Parker, Dak., and Hawarden, Iowa.

[16] Distance (18.10 miles) covered by Tracy, Minn., and Pierre, Dak., R. P. O.

[17] Balance of route (145.30 miles) covered by Tama and Hawarden, Iowa, R. P. O.

[18] Balance of route, Cedar Falls to Hudson, Iowa (10.59 miles), covered by closed pouches. (See Table C².)

[19] Double daily service, 105 miles of route covered by Salt Lake and Juab R. P. O.; balance of route (139.15 miles), Juab to Frisco, closed pouch service. (See Table C².)

[20] One chief clerk, Ogden, Utah; one chief clerk, Los Angeles, Cal.; one chief clerk and five clerks office of superintendent; one transfer clerk, Oakland Pier, Cal.; two clerks, short run, San Francisco to Sacramento via Benicia, 90.69; four city distributors for San Francisco, daily average, 237.72 miles; two helpers at Ogden, Utah, average 175 miles daily.

TABLE Aª.—*Statement of railway post-offices*

Designation of railway post-office. (Lines upon which railway post-office cars are paid for, in *italics*.)	Division.	Distance run by clerks, register to register.	Initial and terminal stations, running from east to west, north to south, or northwest to southeast (with abbreviated title of railroad company).	Number of route.	Miles of route for which railroad is paid.
		Miles.			
Ogdensburgh and Utica, N.Y..	2	134.78	Ogdensburgh and Carthage, N.Y. (R., W. and O.).	6088	60.77
			Carthage and Utica, N.Y. (R., W. and O.).	6087 (part)	(²)
Oil City, Pa., and Ashtabula, Ohio.⁵	9	88.10	Oil City, Pa., Ashtabula, Ohio (L.S. and M.S.).	8045	88.46
Olathe, Kans., and Ash Grove, Mo.	7	155.89	Olathe, Kans., Raymore Junction (n.o.), Mo. (K.C., C. and S.).	28016	26.50
			Raymore Junction (n.o.), Ash Grove, Mo. (K.C., C. and S.).	28056	129.39
Omaha and Beatrice, Nebr.	6	122.94	Omaha, Valley, Nebr. (Union Pac.)	34001 (part)	(⁷)
			Valley, Valparaiso, Nebr. (Union Pac.)	⁸34008 (part)	37.62
			Valparaiso, Lincoln, Nebr. (Om. and Rep. Vall.)	34014	(⁹)
			Lincoln, Beatrice, Nebr. (Om. and Rep. Vall.)	¹⁰34013 (part)	40.22
Omaha and Hastings, Nebr.	6	163.96	Omaha, Arlington, Nebr. (Fre., Elk. and Mo. Vall.)	34051	28.69
			Arlington, Fremont, Nebr. (Fre., Elk. and Mo. Vall.)	34010 (part)	(¹²)
			Fremont, Platte River Jc., Nebr. (Fre., Elk. and Mo. Vall.)	34037	(¹²)
			Platte River Jc., Hastings, Nebr. (Fre., Elk. and Mo. Vall.)	34052	119.96
Omaha, Nebr., and Kansas City, Mo.¹⁴	7	216.65	Omaha, Weeping Water, Nebr. (Mo. Pac.).	¹⁵33040 (part)	39.74
			Weeping Water, Nebraska City, Nebr. (Mo. Pac.).	34047	24.87
			Nebraska City, Auburn, Nebr. (Mo. Pac.).	34048	22.89
			Auburn, Nebr., Acthison, Kans. (Mo.Pac.).	¹⁵33040 (part)	83.67
			Atchison, Kans., Kansas City, Mo. (Mo. Pac.).	¹⁵28001 (part)	47.17
Omaha and McCook, Nebr.	6	312.58	Omaha, Ashland, Nebr. (B. and M.R. in Nebr.).	34038	31.20
			Ashland, Hasting, Nebr. (B. and M.R. in Nebr.).	34002	121.98
			Hastings, Oxford, Nebr. (B. and M.R. in Nebr.).	34029	106.26
			Oxford, McCook, Nebr. (B. and M.R. in Nebr.).	34009 (part)	(¹⁶)
Omaha, Nebr., and Ogden Utah.	6	1,035.30	U.P. Transfer, Iowa, Ogden, Utah (Union Pac.).	34001	1,034.24
Oneida and New York, N.Y.	2	270.33	Oneida, Cornwall Station, N.Y. (N.Y., O and W.).	6048 (part)	¹⁹216.30
			Cornwall Station, New York, N.Y. (West Shore).	6129	(²⁰)
Ord and Grand Island, Nebr.	6	62.40	Ord, Grand Island, Nebr. (Union Pac.)	34015	62.44
Orleans, Nebr., and Beakeman, Kans.	6	95.56	Orleans, Nebr., Beakeman, Kans. B. and M.R. in Nebr.).	34046	95.57
Oshkosh and Milwaukee, Wis.	6	104.90	Oshkosh, Ripon, Wis. (Chi., Mil. and St. Paul.).	25008	20.40
			Ripon, Milwaukee, Wis. (Chi., Mil. and St. Paul.).	²²25003 (part)	84.50

¹ One clerk Watertown and Utica R. P. O.
² 74.34 miles covered by Watertown and Utica R. P. O.
³ In reserve.
⁴ Clerk shown on route No 6088.
⁵ One helper
⁶ In connection with the Ashtabula and Youngstown R. P. O.; gives double service between Andover and Ashtabula, Ohio (24.50 miles), daily except Sunday.
⁷ Distance (31.80 miles) covered by Omaha, Nebr., and Ogden, Utah, R. P. O.
⁸ Balance of route (52.80 miles) covered by Lincoln and Alma, Nebr., R. P. O.

⁹ Distance (20.59 miles) covered by Lincoln and Alma, Nebr., R. P. O.
¹⁰ Balance of route (38.26 miles) covered by Beatrice, Nebr., and Manhattan, Kans., R. P. O.
¹¹ One car in reserve.
¹² Distance (7.9 miles) covered by Missouri Valley, Iowa and Whitewood, Dak., R. P. O.
¹³ Distance (7 miles) covered by Fremont and Lincoln, Nebr., R. P. O
¹⁴ Reported last year as Omaha, Nebr., and Atchison, Kans.; increased distance, 47.17 miles.
¹⁵ 43.01 miles of route 33040, between Weeping Water and Auburn, Nebr., covered by Auburn and Lincoln, Nebr., R. P. O.

in operation in the United States June 30, 1888—Continued.

Average weight of mail whole distance per day.	Date of last re-adjustment.	Average speed per hour (train numbers taken from division schedules).				Number of round trips with clerks per week.	Annual miles of service with clerks.	Average miles run daily by crews.	Number of mail cars, or cars in which are mail apartments.	Inside dimensions of cars or apartments (railway post-office cars in black figures).		Number of crews.	Number of clerks to crew.	Number of clerks appointed to line.
		Train No. outward.	Av'ge speed (miles).	Train No. inward.	Av'ge speed (miles).					Length.	Width.			
Lbs.										*Ft. In.*	*Ft. In.*			
1,458	July 1, 1885	206	23.52	201	24.30	6	84,642	151.14	1 / 1	20 0 / 20 0	6 6 / 7 2	2	1	14
2,964	July 1, 1885	206	24.78	201	26.23	6	....	......	1	20 0	7 2			
629	July 1, 1885	1	24.88	2	24.30	6	55,327	88.10	2	18 0	6 0	2	1	2
359	July 1, 1887	19	24.15	20	22.07	7	114,111	103.93	2 / 1	25 1½ / 25 1½	8 11½ / 8 11½	3	1	3
330	July 1, 1887	19	23.45	20	22.83	7								
23,990	Apr. 1, 1884	7	25.15	8	27.85	7	97,312	132.94	2	15 2	7 5	2	1	2
646	July 1, 1886	41	26.55	44	28.21									
1,009	July 1, 1886	41	27.45	44	24.71									
682	July 1, 1886	41	28.39	44	26.81									
1,652	July 1, 1888	31	21.52	32	21.52	7	120,018	163.96	11 3	20 0	9 3	2	1	2
3,438	Mar. 30, 1887	31	23.70	32	23.70									
324	Jan. 17, 1887	31	26.25	32	26.25									
506	July 1, 1888	31	26.15	32	25.23									
1,285	July 1, 1886	4	20.21	3	21.71	7	158,588	144.43	1 / 1	20 5 / 20 5	7 5 / 7 5	3	1	14
1,236	July 1, 1888	4	24.50	3	19.60	7	....		1	20 5	7 0			
1,081	July 1, 1886	4	23.88	3	26.28	7								
1,285	July 1, 1886	4	22.81	3	22.81	7								
47,461	July 1, 1887	4	23.45	3	22.55	7								
5,377	Jan. 5, 1887	5	29.25	6	30.60	7	228,808	156.29	2	40 0	9 0	4	2	9
		1	29.14	2	27.82									
7,641	July 1, 1886	5	21.06	6	22.02	7	111,044	303.60	....			12 1	1	
		1	33.03	2	35.44									
....	....	5 & 15	15.84	6 & 16	20.11									
3,479	July 1, 1886	16	29.51	16	36.06									
23,990	Apr. 1, 1884	1	23.00	2	22.36	7	757,839	172.10	5	60 1	8 11	36	3	48
		3	29.20	4	30.73	7	214,673	146.63	3	55 5	8 11	24	3	
		7	23.73	8	20.15	7	214,673	146.63	2	50 8	8 11	24	1	
								230.07	1	60 11	8 11	19	1	
									7	59 5	8 11			
529	July 1, 1885	2	25.69	1	25.89	6	169,767	135.16	2	15 4	7 4	4	1	
1,403	July 1, 1885	2	30.00	1	26.15	6	....		1	15 4	7 4	27		
749	Mar. 30, 1887	86	14.60	85	13.78	6	39,187	124.80	1	15 2	7 5	1	1	1
586	July 1, 1888	141	26.00	142	20.36	6	60,011	191.12	1	15 11	7 7	1	1	1
1,155	July 1, 1887	2	24.00	3	24.00	6	65,877	104.90	1	20 11	9 3½	2	1	2
1,565	July 1, 1887	2	25.84	3	25.20									

[footnotes:]
16 One helper between Kansas City, Mo., and Hiawatha, Kans. (86.60 miles), daily except Monday.
17 Balance of route 28001 (283 miles) covered by Saint Louis and Kansas City, Mo., R. P. O.
18 Short run, Omaha to Hastings, Nebr.
19 Distance (54.10 miles) covered by Pacific Junction, Iowa, and McCook, Nebr., R. P. O.
20 Short run, Omaha, Nebr., to Cheyenne, Wyo.
21 Two helpers on trains 7 and 8 between Omaha and Silver Creek, Nebr., one clerk detailed to transfer duty at Omaha, Nebr., and one clerk detailed as chief clerk at Omaha, Nebr.,

and one clerk detailed as assistant to chief clerk at Omaha, Nebr.
22 Short run, Omaha to North Platte, Nebr.
23 Reserve.
24 Through run.
25 57 90 miles covered by Oswego and Oneida R. P. O.
26 52.30 miles covered by Albany, Kingston and New York R. P. O.
27 Cars and clerks shown on route 6048.
28 Balance of route (12.72 miles) covered by closed pouches. (See Ripon and Berlin, Wis., Table C.)

TABLE A².—*Statement of railway post-offices in operation*

Designation of railway post-office. (Lines upon which railway post-office cars are paid for, in *italics*.)	Division	Distance run by clerks, register to register.	Initial and terminal stations, running from east to west, north to south, or northwest to southeast (with abbreviated title of railroad company).	Number of route.	Miles of route for which railroad is paid.
		Miles.			
Oswego and Binghamton, N. Y.	2	115.90	Oswego, Syracuse, N. Y. (D., L. and W.)....	6064	35.62
			Syracuse, Binghamton, N.Y.(S.B.and N.Y.)	6065	80.30
Oswego and Oneida, N. Y	2	58.33	Oswego, Oneida, N. Y. (N. Y., O. and W.)...	6045 (part)	⁴57.90
Oswego and Suspension Bridge, N. Y.⁵	2	151.19	Oswego, Suspension Bridge, N. Y. (R. W. and O.).	6088	(⁶)
Ottawa and Emporia, Kans	7	56.85	Ottawa, Emporia, Kans. (So. Kans.) ....;	33041	56.85
Ottumwa, Iowa, and Moberly, Mo.⁸	7	131.54	Ottumwa, Iowa, Moberly, Mo.(Wab.West.)	28007	131.54
Owensboro and Russellville, Ky.	5	72.71	Owensboro, Russellville, Ky. (Owens. and Nash.).	¹⁰20014 (part)	72.40
Pacific Junction, Iowa, and Mc-Cook, Nebr.	6	399.42	Pacific Junction, Iowa, Plattsmouth, Nebr. (B. and M. R. in Nebr.).	27073	5.64
			Plattsmouth, Oreopolis Junction, Nebr. (B. and M. R. in Nebr.).	34039 (part)	(¹¹)
			Oreopolis Junction, Omaha, Nebr. (B. and M. R. in Nebr.).	34004	16.60
			Omaha, Ashland, Nebr. (B. and M. R. in Nebr.).	34038	(¹²)
			Ashland, Hastings, Nebr. (B. and M. R. in Nebr.).	34002	(¹³)
			Hastings, McCook, Nebr. (B. and M. R. in Nebr.).	¹⁴34009 (part)	132.07
Pacific Junction, Iowa, and Schuyler, Nebr.	6	86.07	Pacific Junction, Iowa, Plattsmouth, Nebr. (B. and M. R. in Nebr.).	27073	(¹⁵)
			Plattsmouth, Ashland, Nebr. (B. and M. R. in Nebr.).	34039	31.37
			Ashland, Schuyler, Nebr. (B. and M. R. in Nebr.).	34057	50.71
Paducah, Ky., and Memphis, Tenn.	5	167.26	Paducah, Ky., Memphis, Tenn. (Chesa., Ohio and So. West.);.	¹⁶20009 (part)	166.10
Painesville and Youngstown, Ohio.¹⁸	5	61.27	Painesville, Youngstown, Ohio (Paines. and Youngs.)	21046	61.98
Palatka and Punta Gorda, Fla.¹⁹	4	²⁰134.86	Palatka, Rochelle, Fla. (Fla. South. Rwy.).	³¹16012 (part)	40.07
			Rochelle, Leesburgh, Fla. (Fla. South. Rwy.).	²¹16014 (part)	72.71
			Leesburgh, Pemberton, Fla. (Fla. South. Rwy.).	²⁴16023 (part)	30.19
		²⁴57.82	Pemberton, Bartow, Fla. (South Fla. R. R.).	16024	57.82
		²⁶75.30	Bartow, Punta Gorda, Fla. (Fla. South. Rwy.).	16026	75.30
Palestine and Laredo, Tex.²⁸...	7	418.25	Palestine, Laredo, Tex. (I. and G. N.)	²⁷31007	415.80
Palmer and Burwell, Nebr.....	6	69.38	Palmer, Burwell, Nebr. (B. and M. R. in Nebr.).	34055	69.38
Palmer, Mass., and New London, Conn.	1	65.30	Palmer, Mass., New London, Conn. (N. L. N. Div. Ct. Ver.).	²⁹3062 (part)	65.11
Paris and Dallas, Tex.²⁰........	7	98.57	Paris, Ladonia, Tex. (G. C. and S. F.)	³¹1059	30.16
			Ladonia, Dallas, Tex. (G. C. and S. F.)	³¹²31063 (part)	68.41

¹ Double daily service, except Sunday.
² In reserve.
³ Cars and clerks shown on route No. 6064.
⁴ 216.30 miles covered by Oneida and New York R. P. O.
⁵ Short line Richland and Niagara Falls R. P. O.
⁶ 151.13 miles covered by Richland and Niagara Falls R. P. O.
⁷ Clerks accounted for in Richland and Niagara Falls R. P. O.
⁸ Double daily service; Sunday single daily.
⁹ Cars also run over Des Moines and Harvey, Iowa, R. P. O.
¹⁰ Balance of route covered by closed pouches, 13.50 miles. . (See Table Cⁿ.)

¹¹ Distance (4.30 miles) covered by Pacific Junction, Iowa, and Schuyler, Nebr., R. P. O.
¹² Distance (31.20 miles) covered by Omaha and McCook, Nebr., R. P. O.
¹³ Distance (121.98 miles) covered by Omaha and McCook, Nebr., R. P. O.
¹⁴ Balance of route (255.30 miles) covered by McCook, Nebr., and Denver, Colo., R. P. O.
¹⁵ Distance (5.64 miles) covered by Pacific Junction, Iowa, and McCook, Nebr.. R. P. O.
¹⁶ Balance of route covered by Louisville and Paducah R. P. O., 223.30 miles.
¹⁷ For full equipment of line see Louisville and Paducah R. P. O.; all cars running through between Louisville, Ky., and Memphis, Tenn.

in the United States on June 30, 1888—Continued.

Average weight of mail whole distance per day.	Date of last re-adjustment.	Average speed per hour (train numbers taken from division schedules).				Number of round trips with clerks per week.	Annual miles of service with clerks.	Average miles run daily by crews.	Number of mail cars, or cars in which are mail apartments.	Inside dimensions of cars or apartments (railway post-office cars in black figures).		Number of crews.	Number of clerks to crew.	Number of clerks appointed to line.
		Train No. outward.	Av'ge speed.	Train No. inward.	Av'ge speed.					Length.	Width.			
Lbs.										*Ft. In.*	*Ft. In.*			
2,428	July 1, 1885	4	30.52	3	30.52	6	72,408	115.30	2	18 0	6 0	2	1	4
		2	30.52	9	30.52	6	²72,408	....	²1	15 7	7 4	2	1	
1,880	July 1, 1885	4	34.41	3	33.22	6	....	....	(²)	....	....	(²)		
		2	25.36	9	31.08	6								
698	July 1, 1885	42	27.79	41	23.16	6	36,631	116.66	1	15 0	6 11	1	1	1
1,291	July 1, 1885	104	24.18	117	26.29	6	94,947	151.19	1	12 0	7 0	2	1	(²)
									²1	11 3	7 0			
243	July 1, 1886	99	12.58	100	10.78	6	35,702	113.70	1	11 1	6 1	1	1	1
									²1	12 0	7 7			
2,367	July 1, 1887	2	19.67	3	22.47	²6	82,607	131.54	²3	19 0	9 2½	2	1	4
		8	24.21	7	22.78	7	96,287	131.54	²1	10 3	7 3½	2	1	
472	July 1, 1884	1	19.74	2	20.22	6	45,662	145.42	1	10 0	7 5	1	1	1
8,556	July 1, 1887	3	30.00	4	20	7	226,495	154.71	2	40 0	9 0	4	3	12
5,860	Jan. 5, 1887	3	25.80	4	25.80									
......	....	3	24.90	4	33.20									
5,377	Jan. 5, 1887	3	25.86	4	30.60									
7,641	July 1, 1886	3	25.49	4	22.02									
843	July 1, 1886	3	26.20	4	23.82									
8,556	July 1, 1887	7	20	8	20	6	54,052	172.14	1	8 6	7 4	1	1	1
5,800	Jan. 5, 1887	7	24.56	8	28.31									
209	July 1, 1888	7	23.76	8	24.95									
1,834	July 1, 1888	7	25.56	8	25.56	6	122,434	111.51	(¹⁷)	....	....	3	1	3
274	July 1, 1888	15	21.24	23	20.88	6	31,856	122.54	1	11 4	6 9	1	1	1
333	July 1, 1884	3	21.6	20	24.6	6								
1,141	July 1, 1888	3	20.3	20	18.4	......	²⁰84,692	134.86	2	16 3	7 6	4	1	4
706	Oct. 21, 1885	3	22.4	20	23	....	....	....	1	24 4	7 9			
									1	18 1	7 10			
450	Feb. 23, 1887	19	14.8	20	14.8		²⁴36,310	115.64	1	9 6	6 4			
......	....	19	15.2	20	15.2		²⁴47,288	150.6						
2,036	July 1, 1886	651	22.56	652	22.41	7	²⁶192,811	131.36	1	22 2	9 2	4	1	²⁸8
		651	19.21	652	18.63	7	²⁶113,848	103.09	1	21 2	8 10	3	1	
									1	21 1	9 4			
									1	21 0	9 2			
									²1	23 8	9 5			
252	July 1, 1888	53	14.24	54	14.24	6	43,570	138.76	1	9 0	6 7	1	1	1
1,587	July 1, 1888	14	24.37	9	25.15	6	41,008	130.60	1	10 3	6 5	1	1	1
546	July 1, 1888	18	14.31	17	17.66	7	72,153	98.57	1	13 6	9 0	2	1	2
......	....	18	20.15	17	18.74	7								

¹⁸ Painesville and Warren R. P. O. extended to Youngstown, Ohio, March 23, 1888, increasing distance 16.21 miles.

¹⁹ Line divided at Pemberton and at Bartow.

²⁰ First division.

²¹ 9.70 miles, Rochelle to Gainesville. (See Table C².)

²² 13.60 miles shown as Astor and Leesburgh R. P. O.
10.50 miles, Pemberton to Brooksville. (See Table C².)

²⁴ Second division.

²⁵ Third division.

²⁶ This line is divided at San Antonio, Tex., into two divisions, Palestine and San Antonio,

Tex. (262.72 miles), and San Antonio and Laredo, Tex. (155.53 miles).

²⁷ Denison and San Antonio, Tex., R. P. O. also runs over 116.50 miles of route 31607, between Taylor and San Antonio, Tex.

²⁸ 1 helper between Taylor and Austin, Tex. (36.20 miles).

²⁹ Balance of route (56.28 miles) covered by Brattleboro and Palmer R. P. O.

³⁰ Reported last year as Honey Grove and Dallas, Tex.; increased distance 17.86 miles.

³¹ 12.30 miles of route 31053, between Ladonia and Honey Grove, Tex., covered by closed-pouch service. (See Table C².)

TABLE A°.—*Statement of railway post-offices in operation*

Designation of railway post-office. (Lines upon which railway post-office cars are paid for, in *italics*.)	Division	Distance run by clerks, register to register.	Initial and terminal stations, running from east to west, north to south, or northwest to southeast (with abbreviated title of railroad company).	Number of route.	Miles of route for which railroad is paid.
		Miles.			
Parkersburgh, W. Va., and Cincinnati, Ohio.	5	196.50	Parkersburgh, W. Va., Cincinnati, Ohio (Cinn., Wash. and Balto.).	21028	(¹)
Pembina, Dak., and Winnipeg Junction, Minn.	6	199.61	Pembina, Dak., Winnipeg Junction, Minn. (North Pac.).	26061	200.15
Peninsular Junction, Md., and Cape Charles, Va.	2	73.51	Peninsular Junction, Md., Cape Charles, Va. (N. Y., P. and N.).	10015	73.32
Penn Haven and Mount Carmel, Pa.	2	45.78	Penn Haven, Mount Carmel, Pa. (L. V) ...	8011	45.79
		*6.00	Park Place, Mahanoy City, Pa. (L. V.) ...•	8158	3.27
Pentwater and Muskegon, Mich.	9	45.13	Pentwater, Muskegon, Mich. (C. and W. M.).	24052	45.13
Peoria, Ill., and Evansville, Ind.	6	250.10	Peoria, Ill., Evansville, Ind. (Peo., Dec. and Evans.).	23024	250.56
Peoria and Galesburgh, Ill.....	6	52.80	Peoria, Galesburgh, Ill., (Chi., Bur. and Qcy.).	*23009 (part)	52.83
Peoria and Jacksonville, Ill...	6	84.50	Peoria, Jacksonville, Ill., (Jack. and So. East).	23038	84.26
Peoria, Ill., and Oskaloosa, Iowa.	6	190.82	Peoria, Ill., Oskaloosa, Iowa (Central Iowa).	23068	191.30
Peterborough, N. H., and Worcester, Mass.	1	53.80	Peterborough, N. H., Winchendon, Mass. (Ches.)	3058	16.58
			Winchendon, Worcester, Mass. (Wor. Div. Fitch.)	3057	37.67
Phalanx Station and Bergholz, Ohio.¹¹	5	60.96	Phalanx Station, Bergholz, Ohio (L., E. All. and Sou.).	21067	61.90
Philadelphia, Pa., Aiken, and Baltimore, Md.	2	96.00	Philadelphia, Pa., and Baltimore, Md. (B. and O.).	10027	96.00
Philadelphia, Pa., Atlantic City, N. J.	2	60.76	Philadelphia, Pa., Atlantic City, N. J. (O. and A.).	7015	59.52
Philadelphia, Pa., Baltimore, Md.	2	96.04	Philadelphia, Pa., Bay View, Md. (P., W. and B.).	13601	(¹²)
			Bay View, Baltimore, Md. (B. and P.)	10012 (part)	(¹⁴)
Philadelphia, Pa., Cape May, N. J.	2	83.60	Camden, Cape May, N. J. (West Jersey)....	7041	82.19
Philadelphia, Pa., Crisfield, Md.	2	162.92	Philadelphia, Pa., Delaware Junction, Del., (P., W. and B.).	10001 (part)	(¹⁵)
			Delaware Junction, Delmar, Del. (P., W. and B.).	9501	97.12
			Delmar, Del., and Crisfield, Md. (N. Y., P. and N.).	9502	38.23
Philadelphia, Pa., and Dover, Del.²¹	2	75.22	Philadelphia, Pa., and Delaware Junction, Del. (P., W. and B.)	10001 (part)	(²⁰)
			Delaware Junction, Dover, Del. (P., W. and B.).	9501 (part)	(²⁴)
Philadelphia, Pa., and Harrisburg, Pa.²⁶	2	106.55	Philadelphia, Harrisburgh, Pa. (Pa.)	8001 (part)	(²⁶)

¹ Covered by Grafton and Cincinnati R. P.O. (193.15 miles).
² One car in reserve.
³ Clerks are appointed to Grafton and Cincinnati R. P. O., and are shown with that line. Run in mail apartment-car between Cincinnati, Ohio, and Parkersburgh, W. Va., on east trips and Parkersburgh, W. Va., and Chillicothe, Ohio, on west trips. On west trips act as helpers to Grafton and Cincinnati R. P. O. day line, Chillicothe to Cincinnati, Ohio. Second clerks of Grafton and Cincinnati day line act as helpers to Parkersburgh and Cincinnati clerks, Cincinnati to Chillicothe.

⁴ In reserve.
⁵ On train No. 3 the R. P. O. runs in and out of Mahanoy City, a distance of 3 miles.
⁶ Cars and clerks shown on route No. 8011.
⁷ Balance of route (13.27 miles) covered by closed pouches. (See Galesburgh and Rio, Ill., Table C°.)
⁸ Reserve.
⁹ These cars are also used by the Winchendon, and Worcester R. P. O. (See column remarks, that line.)
¹⁰ Reserve cars.
¹¹ Phalanx Station and Alliance R. P. O. extended

In the United States on June 30, 1888—Continued.

Average weight of mail whole distance per day.	Date of last re-adjustment.	Average speed per hour (train numbers taken from division schedules).				Number of round trips with clerks per week.	Annual miles of service with clerks.	Average miles run daily by crews.	Number of mail cars, or cars in which are mail apartments.	Inside dimensions of cars or apartments (railway post-office cars in black figures).		Number of crews.	Number of clerks to crew.	Number of clerks assigned to line.
		Train No. outward.	Av'ge speed (miles).	Train No. inward.	Av'ge speed (miles).					Length.	Width.			
Lbs.										*Ft. In.*	*Ft. In.*			
27,445	July 1, 1888	5	22.44	6	22.74	6	123,402	98.25	[2]3	19 0	9 3	4	1	(²)
799	Aug. 25, 1888	54	22.11	51	21.05	7	146,114	133.07	1 1	22 3½ 22 4	8 10 8 10	3	1	3
1,155	July 1, 1885	1	24.50	12	26.73	6	46,164	147	1	8 6	6 8	1	1	1
374	July 1, 1885	2	21.97	3	23.89	6	28,750	98.30	1 [4]1	12 10 24 6	6 3 8 2	1	1	1
345	July 1, 1885	(⁵)	.....	3	23.89	6	3,768		(⁹)	....	....	(⁶)		
443	July 1, 1884	22	17.03	27	18.21	6	28,342	90.26	1	11 0	8 9	1	1	1
801	July 1, 1887	2	22.40	1	24.39	6	157,063	125.05	[2]3	20 0	9 2	4	1	4
1,759	July 1, 1887	6	29.71	5	28.37	6	33,158	105.60	1	19 4½	8 11½	1	1	1
620	July 1, 1887	3	24.56	2	23.00	6	53,066	84.50	1 [2]1	22 0 13 0	9 0 7 7	2	1	2
287	July 1, 1887	3	22.35	4	21.11	6	119,835	127.21	1 1	10 0 10 0	7 3 6 4	3	1	3
203	July 1, 1885	37	13.33	500	17.45	6	33,786	107.60	1 [9]1	16 0 10 5	6 6 6 10	1	1	1
1,104	July 1, 1885	37	23.36	500	17.34	.....	....		[9]1 [10]1 [10]1	10 7 8 3 7 11	7 1 7 0 6 11			
223	July 1, 1888	2	14.52	1	19.56	6	24,055	121.96	[2]2 [2]1	6 0 5 0	8 0 6 0	1	1	1
197	July 1, 1888	49	24	42	22.58	6	60,288	96	[2]2	17 9	8 5	2	1	2
769	July 1, 1885	255 267	26.04 28.26	260 252	25.14 29.16	6 6	38,157 [13]38,157	121.52	1 1 [4]1	19 0 15 0 8 0	6 8 8 2 6 6	1 1	1 1	2
58,491	July 1, 1885	[14]27	42.01	24	27.22	6	61,569	98.04	1 1	20 0 20 0	8 0 8 0	2	1	2
57,708	July 1, 1885	[14]27	42.01	24	27.22	6	....		[4]1	20 0	8 0	(¹⁶)		
1,025	July 1, 1885	5	32.35	20	32.35	6	52,501	167.20	2 1	15 0 15 0	8 6 8 4	1	1	[17]3
		11	27.40	8	27.87	6	[12]52,501	......	1 [4]1	8 0 11 10	8 6 7 0	1	1	
58,491	July 1, 1888	1	24.38	12	25.20	6	102,314	108.62	1 1	24 6 20 0	8 4 8 4	3	1	[19]6
3,711	July 1, 1885	1	27.10	12	27.74	6	....		(²⁰)	....	....	(²⁰)		
1,534	July 1, 1885	1	15.81	12	15.84	6	....		(²⁰)	....	....	(²⁰)		
58,491	July 1, 1885	39	24.25	24	22.20	6	47,238	150.44	[4]3 1	20 0 16 0	8 0 6 8	1	1	(²²)
3,711	July 1, 1885	39	30.51	22	22.88	6	....		(²⁰)	....	....	(²⁰)		
91,679	July 1, 1885	77 71	35.52 32.78	14 70	31.18 31.96	6 6	66,913 [1]66,913	106.55	1 1 [4]1	20 0 15 0 19 9	9 0 9 0 8 8	2 2	2 1	(²⁷)

to Bergholz, Ohio, February 20, 1888; increased distance, 35.80 miles.
[12] Double daily service except Sunday.
[13] 91.90 miles covered by N. Y. and Washington R. P. O.
[14] In N. Y. and Washington R. P. O.
[15] 4 miles covered by N. Y. and Washington R. P. O.
[16] Clerks shown on route 10001.
[17] One clerk detailed as transfer clerk at Camden, N. J.
[18] 25.20 miles covered by N. Y. and Washington R. P. O.
[19] One clerk detailed as examiner and instructor at

Phila., Pa.; 1 clerk to Phila. and Dover R. P. O.; 1 helper.
[20] Cars and clerks shown on route 10001.
[21] Short run, Philadelphia and Crisfield R. P. O.
[22] 25.20 miles covered by New York and Washington R. P. O.
[23] Clerk accounted for on Philadelphia and Crisfield R. P. O.
[24] 45.77 miles covered by Philadelphia and Crisfield R. P. O.
[25] Short run, New York and Pittsburg R. P. O.
[26] 105.20 miles covered by New York and Pittsburgh R. P. O.
[27] Clerks accounted for in the New York and Pittsburg R. P. O.

TABLE A^a—*Statement of railway post-offices in operation*

Designation of railway post-office. (Lines upon which railway post-office cars are paid for, in *italics*.)	Division.	Distance run by clerks, register to register.	Initial and terminal stations, running from east to west, north to south, or northwest to southeast (with abbreviated title of railroad company).	Number of route.	Miles of route for which railroad is paid.
		Miles.			
Philadelphia, Pa., and Port Deposit, Md.	2	68.80	Philadelphia and Wawa, Pa. (P., W. and B.).	8002 (part)	(¹)
			Wawa, Pa., and Port Deposit, Md. (P., W. and B.).	8005 (part)	²51.57
Philadelphia, Pa., and Port Norris, N. J.	2	59.14	Camden and Glassborough, N. J. (West Jersey).	7041 (part)	(⁶)
			Glassborough and Bridgeton, N. J. (West Jersey).	7051	20.29
			Bridgeton and Port Norris, N. J. (C. and M. R.).	7033	21.30
Philadelphia and West Chester, Pa.	2	28.50	Philadelphia and West Chester, Pa. (P., W. and B.).	8003	27.81
Pinkneyville and Marion, Ills..	6	52.82	Pinkneyville, Murphysborough, Ills. (St. L., A. and T. Haute).	23085	28.33
			Harrison Sta., Marion, Ills. (St. L., A. and T. Haute).	23045	27.21
Pittsburgh, Pa., and Akron, O.	5	136.72	Allegheny, New Castle Junction, Pa. (Pitts. and West.).	⁹8125 (part)	58.10
			New Castle Junction, Mahoningtown, Pa. (Pitts. and Lake Erie).	8125 (part)	(¹⁰)
			Mahoningtown, Pa., Akron, Ohio. (Pitts., Cleve. and Tol.).	21076	78.10
Pittsburgh and Chanute, Kans.¹¹	7	54.89	Pittsburgh, Chanute, Kans. (So. Kans.)....	33039	54.89
Pittsburgh, Pa., and Chicago., Ill.¹²	5	188.95	Pittsburgh, Pa., Chicago, Ill. (Penna. Co.).	21002	188.70
Eastern Division.............			......	......	......
Western Division¹⁴.............	5	280.15			272.50
Pittsburgh, Pa., and Cincinnati, Ohio.¹⁵	5	313.74	Pittsburgh, Pa., Columbus, Ohio (Pitts., Cin. and St. Lou.).	21032	(¹⁶)
			Columbus, Cincinnati, Ohio (Pitts, Cin. and St. Lou.).	21014	120.29
Pittsburgh, Pa., and Crestline, Ohio	5	188.95	Pittsburgh, Pa., Crestline, Ohio (Penna. Co.).	21002 (part)	(²¹)
Pittsburgh and Fairchance, Pa.	2	75.84	Southwest Junction and Pittsburgh, Pa., (Penna.).	8001 (part)	(²²)
			Southwest Junction and Fairchance, Pa. (Penna.).	8104	44.72
Pittsburgh and New Haven, Pa.	2	60.12	Pittsburgh and New Haven, Pa. (P. and L. E.).	8159	59.51
Pittsburgh, Pa., and St. Louis, Mo., Eastern Division ²⁵	5	312.80	Pittsburgh, Pa., Columbus, Ohio (Pitts. Cin. and St. Louis).	21032	191.85

¹ 18.13 miles covered by Philadelphia and Westchester R. P. O.
² Double daily service except Sunday.
³ 7.17 miles covered by closed pouch service. (See Table C³.)
⁴ Cars and clerks shown on route No. 8003.
⁵ In reserve.
⁶ 17.64 miles covered by Philadelphia and Cape May R. P. O.
⁷ Trains 61 and 66 run between Philadelphia and Bridgeton only.
⁸ Cars and clerks shown on route No. 7041.
⁹ Balance of route, New Castle Junction to New Castle, Pa. (2.93 miles) covered by closed pouches. (See Table C³.)
¹⁰ Covered by Cleveland, Youngstown and Pittsburgh R. P. O., .60 miles; in reserve.
¹¹ Reported last year as Girard and Chanute, Kans.; increased distance, 13.53 miles.
¹² This line is in two divisions, dividing at Crestline, Ohio. East division Pittsburgh, Pa., to Crestline, Ohio.
¹³ 4 clerks and 2 helpers in apartment cars between Pittsburgh and Crestline. Helper running between Pittsburgh, Pa., and Or-

ville, Ohio, 124 miles; 4 clerks and 4 helpers in apartment cars between Crestline, Ohio, and Chicago, Ill. Helper running over whole line; 1 clerk detailed as chief clerk at Crestline, Ohio; 2 clerks detailed to transfer duty at Crestline, Ohio; 1 clerk detailed to transfer duty at Fort Wayne, Ind.; 1 clerk detailed to transfer duty at Mansfield, Ohio; 1 car in reserve.
¹⁴ West division Crestline to Chicago, Ill.
¹⁵ The day line of this R. P. O. runs west and the day and night lines run east between Pittsburgh, Pa., and Columbus, Ohio, on same train but in separate cars, as the Pittsburgh and Saint Louis R. P. O.
¹⁶ Covered by the Pittsburgh and Saint Louis R. P. O., 191.85 miles.
¹⁷ Cars all run through between New York, N. Y., Cincinnati, Ohio, Saint Louis, Mo. For full equipment of line see New York and Pittsburgh R. P. O. in 2d division report.
¹⁸ Day line.
¹⁹ 2 clerks in apartment cars between Columbus and Cincinnati, Ohio; 5 clerks detailed to clerical duty in office superintendent 5th division; 2 clerks detailed as printers in office superin-

in the United States on June 30, 1888—Continued.

Average weight of mail whole distance per day.	Date of last re-adjustment.	Average speed per hour (train numbers taken from division schedules).				Number of round trips with clerks per week.	Annual miles of service with clerks.	Average miles run daily by crews.	Number of mail cars or cars in which are mail apartments.	Inside dimensions of cars or apartments (railway post-office cars in black figures).		Number of crews.	Number of clerks in crew.	Number of clerks appointed to line.
		Train No. outward.	Av'ge speed (miles).	Train No. inward.	Av'ge speed (miles).					Length.	Width.			
Lbs.										*Ft. In.*	*Ft. In.*			
1,850	July 1, 1885	5	24.72	46	23.64	6	43,106	137.60	1	14 8	8 0	1	1	2
		33	27.19	28	26.51	6	²43,106	......	1	8 9	6 6	1	1	
945	July 1, 1885	5	22.41	46	21.04	6	......	......	(⁴)			(⁴)		
		33	21.48	28	18.38	6	......	......	⁵1	10 0	6 0			
1,025	July 1, 1885	63	25.52	64	22.70	6	37,140	98.86	1	14 9	8 0	1	1	2
		⁷61	18.56	⁷66	19.20	6	⁷24,932	......	1	14 9	8 0	1	1	
897	July 1, 1885	63	10.72	64	21.40	6	......	......	1	8 0	7 0			
		⁷61	25.24	⁷66	24.80	6	......	......	(⁸)			(⁸)		
240	July 1, 1885	63	20	64	24.55	6	......	......	⁸1	8 0	6 6			
......	......	7	20.11	22	21.64	6	17,898	114.00	1	10 0	6 6	1	1	1
		31	18	52	22.20	6	²17,898	......						
193	July 1, 1887	2	10.62	22	23.36	6	33,171	105.64	1	18 6	9 3	1	1	1
201	July 1, 1887	21	10.40	22	20.25	......	......	......	⁵1	11 4	7 3			
659	July 1, 1885	2	23.28	5	14.40	6	85,609	136.32	2	18 9	8 8	2	1	2
									1	10 0	6 6			
3,575	July 1, 1885	2	5.10	5	4.50	6	......	......						
380	July 1, 1888	2	26.58	5	25.32	6	......	......						
98	July 1, 1886	242	21.64	241	22.36	6	34,471	109.78	1	12 0	7 7	1	1	1
27,731	July 1, 1888	3	24.61	4	22.02	7	138,311	125.97		60 0	9 2	3	3	¹¹40
......	......	7	30.54	4	24.66	7	205,070	140.07	......	......		4	3	
84,201	July 1, 1888	7	34.86	6	29.88	7	229,658	156.87	(¹⁷)	......		18 ½	4	¹⁸40
		5	28.74	2	30.72	7	229,658	......				²9 ½	3	
24,079	July 1, 1888	9	32.82	6	32.10	7	......	......						
		5	28.32	2	32.82	7	......	......						
27,731	July 1, 1888	7	25.15	10	22.64	6	118,661	94.47	2	20 0	9 0	4	1	(²²)
91,679	July 1, 1885	42	29.62	47	26.32	6	47,628	151.68	1	14 10	8 6	1	1	1
841	July 1, 1885	42	20.79	47	21.81	6	......	......	(²⁴)			(²⁴)		
317	July 1, 1885	4	20.61	13	22.54	6	37,755	120.24	1	9 6	6 4	1	1	1
77,139	Dec. 8, 1887	7	34.86	6	29.88	7	228,970	²¹56.40	(²⁶)	......		27 ½	9	²⁸143
		1	30.72	2	30.72	7	228,970	......				²9 ½	3	

[20] tendent 5th division; 1 clerk detailed to transfer duty at Columbus, Ohio; 2 helpers running on night line between Cincinnati and Newark, Ohio, working Cincinnati City mail.
[20] Night line.
[21] Covered by Pittsburgh and Chicago R. P. O., 188.70 miles.
[22] Clerks are appointed to Pittsburgh and Chicago R. P. O. and are shown with that line; 2 helpers between Pittsburgh, Pa., and Orrville, Ohio, 124 miles.
[23] 31.60 miles covered by New York and Pittsburgh R. P. O.
[24] Cars and clerks shown on route No. 8001.
[25] This line in two divisions, dividing at Richmond, Ind.
[26] Letter and paper cars are 60 feet long, and storage cars are 40 feet long. Cars on this line all run through between New York, N. Y., Cincinnati, O., Saint Louis, Mo. For full equipment of line see New York and Pittsburgh R. P. O. in Second Division.
[27] East Division, day line, 4 crews, 9 clerks.
[28] Clerks of Logansport and Columbus R. P. O. run west on train 1 in car of this R.

P. O. as helpers between Columbus and Bradford. Four clerks of West Division day line, act as helpers to Indianapolis, Vandalia and Saint Louis R. P. O. on train 2, Saint Louis, Mo., to Indianapolis, Ind., 2 helpers on West Division, day line, 4 days in week running through; 4 clerks on Indianapolis, Vandalia and Saint Louis R. P. O.; 1 clerk on Indianapolis and Terre Haute R. P. O.; 1 clerk detailed as chief clerk at Indianapolis; 2 clerks detailed as assistant chief clerks at Indianapolis, Ind.; 1 clerk detailed as chief clerk at Pittsburgh, Pa.; 2 clerks detailed to transfer duty at Columbus, Ohio; 5 clerks detailed to transfer duty at Indianapolis, Ind.; 1 clerk detailed to transfer duty at Richmond, Ind., 1 clerk detailed to transfer duty at Terre Haute, Ind.; 2 porters on trains 6 and 7, between Pittsburgh, Pa., and Columbus, Ohio; 1 porter on trains 6 and 7 between Pittsburgh, Pa., and Trinway, Ohio; 2 porters on trains 5 and 2 between Pittsburgh, Pa., and Columbus, Ohio; 2 porters on trains 1 and 8 and 7 and 12, between Richmond and Brasil, Ind.
[29] East Division, night line, 4 crews, 7 clerks.

TABLE A*.—*Statement of railway post-offices in operation*

Designation of railway post-office. (Lines upon which railway post-office cars are paid for, in *italics*.)	Division.	Distance run by clerks, register to register.	Initial and terminal stations, running from east to west, north to south, or northwest to southeast (with abbreviated title of railroad company).	Number of route.	Miles of route for which railroad is paid.
		Miles.			
Pittsburgh, Pa., and St. Louis, Mo.—Eastern Division.	..	....	Columbus, O., Indianapolis, Ind. (Chic., St. Louis and Pitts.).	21015	189. 66
Western Division	5	309. 00	Indianapolis, Terre Haute, Ind. (T. H. and Ind.).	22002	74. 39
			Terre Haute, Ind., East Saint Louis, Ill. (T. H. and Ind.).	22044	165. 69
Pittsburgh, Pa., Steubenville, O., and Wheeling, W. Va.	5	69. 04	Pittsburgh, Pa., Steubenville, O. (P. C. and St. L.).	21032 (part)	(³)
			Steubenville, O., Wheeling, W. Va. (P. C. and St. L.).	12005	24. 00
Pittsburgh and Washington, Pa.	2	31. 62	Pittsburgh, Mansfield Valley, Pa. (P. C. and St. L.).	21032 (part)	(⁶)
			Mansfield Valley, Washington, Pa. (P. C. and St. L.).	8055	22. 90
Pittsburgh and West Brownsville, Pa.	2	54. 34	Pittsburgh, West Brownsville, Pa. (Penn'a.).	8081	54. 42
Pittsburgh, Pa., and Wheeling, W. Va.	2	72. 08	Pittsburgh, Pa., Wheeling, W. Va. (B. and O.).	8040	70. 41
Pittsfield, Mass., and Bridgeport, Conn.	1	110. 49	Pittsfield, Mass., Bridgeport, Conn. (Hous.).	5012	110. 55
Pittsfield and Hooksett, N. H .	1	20. 35	Pittsfield, Hooksett, N. H. (Conn.)	1004	20. 35
Placerville and Sacramento, Cal⁹	8	64. 25	Placerville, Sacramento, Cal. (Sacramento Val. R. R.).	46005	63. 75
Plattsburgh and Saranac Lake, N. Y.	2	72. 82	Plattsburgh, Lyon Mountain, N. Y. (Chateangay.)	6105	34. 67
			Lyon Mountain, Saranac Lake, N. Y. (Chateangay.)	6132	39. 66
Plymouth and Concord, N. H ..	1	51. 40	Plymouth, Concord, N. H. (Bos. and Low.).	¹²1006 (part)	(¹¹)
Point Pleasant, N. J., and Philadelphia, Pa.	2	71. 86	Camden, Birmingham, N. J. (Penn'a)	7006 (part)	¹⁴23. 64
			Birmingham, Whiting, N. J. (Penn'a.).....	7063	18. 75
			Whiting, Bay Head Junc., N. J. (Penn'a.) ..	7054	28. 89
			Bay Head Junc., Point Pleasant, N. J. (Penn'a.).	7003 (part)	¹⁴1. 00
Portage and Madison, Wis	6	40. 51	Portage, Madison, Wis. (Chi., Mil. and St. Paul).	25023	38. 40
Port Austin and Port Huron, Mich.	9	87. 71	Pt. Austin, Port Huron, Mich. (Pt. H. and N. W.).	24042	87. 71
Port Harford and Las Olivas, Cal.¹⁰	8	79. 50	San Luis Obispo, Las Olivas, Cal. (Pacific Coast R. R.).	46040	67. 30
			San Luis Obispo, Port Harford, Cal.(Pacific Coast Rwy).	46041	12. 20
Port Jefferson and Long Island City, N. Y.	2	46. 75	Port Jefferson, Hicksville, N. Y. (L. I.)....	6046	33. 96
			Hicksville, Jamaica, N. Y. (L. I.)	6045 (part)	(²¹)
Port Jervis and New York, N. Y.²⁴	2	87. 77	Port Jervis, New York, N. Y. (N. Y., L. E. and W.).	6001 (part)	(²⁵)
Portland, Me., and Boston, Mass.	1	116. 70	Portland, Me., Boston, Mass. (Bos. and Me.).	3011	116. 33
Portland and Coburg, Oregon .	8	123. 38	Portland, Coburg, Oregon (Oreg. Rwy. Co., limited line).	44007	123. 38
Portland and Corvallis, Oregon	8	97. 99	Portland, Corvallis, Oregon (Oreg. and Cal. R. R.).	44002	97. 78

¹ West Division, day line, 4 crews, 7 clerks.
² West Division, night line, 4 crews, 6 clerks.
³ Covered by Pittsburgh and Saint Louis R. P. O. 43.40 miles.
⁴ 8.50 miles covered by Pittsburgh and Saint Louis R. P. O.
⁵ Double daily service, except Sunday.
⁶ Cars and clerks shown on route No. 21032.
⁷ One clerk detailed as transfer clerk, Bridgeport, Conn.
⁸ Reserve car.

⁹ Reported last year as Shingle Springs and Sacramento. Service extended May 25, commenced June 15, 1888.
¹⁰ Cars and clerks shown on route No. 6105.
¹¹ Covered by Lancaster and Boston R. P. O., 51.34 miles.
¹² Balance of route covered by Lancaster and Boston R. P. O. (84.96 miles) and closed-pouch service between Lancaster and Groveton Junction, 9.58 miles. (See Table C*.)
¹³ Reserve cars.

in the United States on June 30, 1888—Continued.

Average weight of mail whole distance per day.	Date of last re-adjustment.	Train No. outward.	Avg'e speed (miles).	Train No. inward.	Avg'e speed (miles).	Number of round trips with clerks per week.	Annual miles of service with clerks.	Average miles run daily by crews.	Number of mail cars, or cars in which are mail apartments.	Length (Ft. In.)	Width (Ft. In.)	Number of crews.	Number of clerks to crew.	Number of clerks appointed to line.
Lbs. 64409	July 1, 1888	7	36.72	6	28.44	7								
		1	31.61	8	30.78	7								
61121	July 1, 1888	7	37.19	12	23.28	7	226,188	154.50	......	......	......	14	7	
		1	33.60	8	30.78	7	226,188	......				24	6	
58026	July 1, 1888	7	35.10	12	28.56	7								
		1	31.02	8	26.16	7								
84201	July 1, 1888	13	20.04	14	19.32	6	43,357	138.06	1	19 0	9 0	1	1	1
752	July 1, 1885	209	19.20	210	18.36	6								
61656	July 1, 1885	21	21.07	22	17.24	6	19,857	126.48	1	15 0	9 0	1	1	1
		27	18.06	32	18.97	6	*19,857							
1179	May 1, 1884	21	21.07	22	17.24	6	......	......	(9)	......	......	(9)		
		27	18.06	32	18.97	6								
953	July 1, 1885	4	19.75	9	19.75	6	34,126	106.68	1	15 0	8 8	1	1	1
560	July 1, 1885	7	22.17	8	22.17	6	45,266	144.16	1	17 2	8 11	1	1	1
1,663	July 1, 1885	8	26.93	11	28.08	7	80,878	110.49	2	14 7	6 0	2	1	75
		14	28.00	21	17.34	7	69,388	......	1	14 7	6 0	2		
									8] 1	14 7	6 0			
										14 7	6 0			
372	July 1, 1885	65	15.00	64	16.89	6	12,779	40.70	1	8 0	7 0	1	1	1
557	July 1, 1886	1	19.40	2	19.92	6	40,349	128.50	1	6 6	6 0	1	1	1
......	......	1	18.88	4	15.88	6	45,731	145.64	1	16 4	5 10	1	1	1
......	......	1	15.88	4	15.88	6			(10)			(10)		
3,263	July 1, 1885	52	24.52	55	24.52	6	32,279	102.80	2	10 0	7 0	1	1	1
									12] 1	6 8	6 1			
									13] 1	10 0	6 10			
									1	15 0	8 0			
......	......	397	33.16	396	22.57	6	45,128	143.72	1	15 0	8 0	1	1	1
......	......	307	33.16	396	22.57	6	......	......	(15)	......	......	(15)		(15)
......	......	397	33.16	396	22.57	6								
......	......	397	33.16	396	22.57	6								
563	July 1, 1887	46	25.33	47	22.80	6	25,440	81.02	1	13 3	7 8	1	1	1
571	July 1, 1884	3	21.75	2	20.63	6	55,082	131.56	1	16 6	7 6	1	1	171
									16] 1	10 0	6 6			
290	June 21, 1888	3	21.03	4	21.03	6	49,926	159.00	1	10 0	7 6	1	1	1
......	......	3	18.30	4	20.91	6								
716	Aug. 25, 1885	18	28.56	15	25.00	6	29,987	191.00	1	15 0	5 7	1	1	1
		32	25.00	31	27.80	6	22,608	......	1	15 6	7 7			
1,467	July 1, 1885	18	28.56	15	25.00	6			23] 1	12 0	6 0	(23)		
		32	25.00	31	27.80	6								
12,297	July 1, 1885	15	27.71	16	29.26	6	55,120	133.74	1	16 6	6 10	1	1	(24)
		19	15.95	6	26.07	6	*55,120	......	1	20 8	9 2	1	1	
4,739	July 1, 1885	70	25.20	7	23.20	6	73,287	116.70	1	25 4	9 0	2	3	10
		122	25.66	75	26.65	6	73,287	......	1	25 6	9 2	2	2	
									12]	25 0	8 6			
										25 0	8 6			
387	Mar. 28, 1887	7	12.33	8	12.03	6	77,483	123.38	2	18 0	7 6	2	1	2
630	July 1, 1886	1	21.27	2	21.97	6	61,538	97.99	2	10 0	8 10	2	1	2

14 2 miles covered by closed-pouch service. (See Table C*.)
15 Cars and clerks shown on route No. 7006.
16 49.19 miles covered by New York and Point Pleasant R. P. O.
17 This clerk has relief every fourth week.
18 One car held in reserve.
19 New R. P. O. service established January 25, 1888.
20 Service between Jamaica and Port Jefferson on trains 18 and 15, and between Westbury and Port Jefferson on trains 32 and 31.

21 11.25 miles covered by Greenport and New York R. P. O.
22 In reserve.
23 Clerks shown on route No. 6046.
24 Short run New York and Dunkirk R. P. O.
25 87.79 miles covered by New York and Dunkirk R. P. O.
26 Clerks accounted for in New York and Dunkirk R. P. O.

TABLE A⁵.—*Statement of railway post-offices in operation*

Designation of railway post-office. (Lines upon which railway post-office cars are paid for, in *italics*).	Division.	Distance run by clerks, register to register.	Initial and terminal stations running from east to west, north to south, or northwest to southeast (with abbreviated title of railroad company).	Number of route.	Miles of route for which railroad is paid.
		Miles.			
Portland, Me., and Island Pond, Vt.	1	149.78	Portland, Me., Island Pond, Vt. (Grand Trunk).	[1]7 (part)	149.71
Portland, Me., and Island Pond, Vt., short run.	1	92.16	Portland, Me., Gorham, N. H. (Grand Trunk).	47 (part)	(3)
Portland, and Nazareth, Pa.....	2	26.64	Portland and Nazareth, Pa. (Bang. and Port.).	8126	26.14
Portland, Me., and Rochester, N. H.	1	52.74	Portland, Me., and Rochester, N. H. (Port. and Roch.).	46 (part)	(3)
Portland, Oregon, and Sacramento, Cal.	8	684.54	Portland, Ashland, Oregon (Oreg. and Cal. R. R.).	24001	342.56
			Ashland, Oregon; Roseville, Cal. (Cal. and Oreg. R. R.).	46003	323.30
			Roseville, Sacramento, Cal. (Central Pacific).	46001 (part)	(12)
Portland, Me., and Swanton, Vt.	1	232.90	Portland, Me., Fabyan House, N. H. (Port. and Ogd.).	10	89.99
			Fabyan House, N. H., South Lunenburgh, Vt. (Bos. and Low.).	1007	24.26
			South Lunenburgh, Swanton, Vt. (St. J. and L. Cham. Br., B. and Low.).	2011	118.56
Portland, Me., and Swanton, Vt., short run.	1	72.87	Portland, Me., Bartlett, N. H. (Port. and Ogd.).	1410 (part)	(16)
Portland, Me., and Worcester, Mass.	1	147.34	Portland, Me., Rochester, N. H. (Port. and Roch.).	8	55.00
			Rochester, N. H., Worcester, Mass. (B. and Me., Wor., N. Port. Div.).	1012	95.04
Portland, Me., and Worcester, Mass., short run.	1	46.76	Nashua, N. H., Worcester, Mass. (B. and Me., Wor., N. Port. Div.).	191012 (part)	(70)
Portsmouth and Cincinnati, Ohio.	5	107.58	Portsmouth, Cincinnati, Ohio (Ohio and Northwest).	21052	106.00
Portsmouth and Concord, N. H.	1	59.25	Portsmouth, Concord, N. H. (Concord)....	1002	59.16
Portsmouth and Manchester, N. H.	1	41.53	Portsmouth, Manchester, N. H. (Concord).	221002 (part)	(24)
Pottsville and Philadelphia, Pa.	2	94.13	Pottsville, Philadelphia, Pa. (P. and R.)....	8002	93.10
Pottsville, Tamaqua, and Herndon, Pa.	2	78.74	Pottsville, Herndon, Pa. (P. and R.)	8013	78.06
Powers, Mich., and Florence, Wis.	6	42.00	Powers, Mich., Florence, Wis., (Chi. and No. West.).	2924032 (part)	41.74
Pratt and Liberal, Kans. 31	7	136.23	Pratt, Liberal, Kans. (C., K. and N.).......	3233075 (part)	3385.50
Princeton, Ky., and Clarksville, Tenn. 34	5	57.71	Princeton, Ky., Clarksville, Tenn. (Louis. and Nash.).	19024	57.53

¹ Balance of route covered by closed-pouch service between Island Pond and Norton's Mills (16.02 miles). (See Table C⁵.)

²² 3 clerks as helpers; 2 clerks on Portland and Island Pond, short run (92.16 miles).

³ Reserve car.

⁴ Balance of route covered by Portland and Island Pond R. P. O. (57.72 miles), and closed-pouch service between Island Pond and Norton's Mills (16.02 miles). (See Table C⁵.)

⁵ Covered by Portland and Island Pond R. P. O. (91.92 miles).

⁶ Shown in column 17, Portland and Island Pond R. P. O.

⁷ In reserve.

⁸ Balance of route (2.50 miles) not covered.

⁹ Covered by Portland and Worcester R. P. O. (52.50 miles).

¹⁰ This clerk runs from Rochester to Portland, with Portland and Worcester clerk as assistant.

¹¹ Shown in column 17, Portland and Worcester R. P. O.

¹² Six clerks run from Portland to Ashland; 4 clerks Ashland, Oregon, to Red Bluff, Cal.; 2 clerks Red Bluff to Sacramento, Cal.; 2 helpers at Portland, Oregon; average daily, 158 miles. Reported last year as Portland and Ashland. 132.40 miles of route 46003, not heretofore covered by R. P. O. service, extended. Route 46001 covered by Ogden and San Francisco R. P. O.

¹³ One clerk on short run between Portland and Bartlett (72.87 miles).

¹⁴ Reserve cars.

¹⁵ Balance of route covered by Portland and Swanton R. P. O. (17.99 miles).

¹⁶ Covered by Portland and Swanton R. P. O. (72 miles).

¹⁷ Shown in column 17, Portland and Swanton R. P. O.

¹⁸ One clerk on Portland and Worcester short run

In the United States on June 30, 1888—Continued.

Average weight of mail whole distance per day.	Date of last re-adjustment.	Average speed per hour (train numbers taken from division schedules).				Number of round trips with clerks per week.	Annual miles of service with clerks.	Average miles run daily by crews.	Number of mail cars or cars in which are mail apartments.	Inside dimensions of cars or apartments (railway post-office cars in black figures).		Number of crews.	Number of clerks to crew.	Number of clerks appointed to line.
		Train No. outward.	Av'ge speed (miles).	Train No. inward.	Av'ge speed (miles).					Length.	Width.			
Lbs.										*Ft. In.*	*Ft. In.*			
1,963	July 1,1885	2	21.83	1	25.22	6	94,061	99.85	1	20 0	7 4	3	1	²⁷
									1	21 6	7 6			
									³¹	22 4	7 8			
1,963	July 1,1885	4	29.67	5	25.53	6	57,876	92.16	2	15 9	7 6	2	1	(⁸)
211	July 1,1885	2	17.76	5	16.82	6	16,730	53.28	1	7 1	8 9	1	1	1
									⁷1	6 0	6 8			
									⁷1	9 0	6 6			
1,941	July 1,1885	2	24.00	(¹⁰)	(¹⁰)	3	16,560	105.48	1	15 0	9 0	1	1	(¹¹)
21,802	July 1,1886	1	21.01	2	20.10	7	501,063	114.09	3	25 0	8 10	12	1	¹²14
									2	36 0	9 5½			
									2	20 0	8 0			
3,973	June 25,1888	15	18.75	16	18.68	.....	....							
25,702	Aug.15,1888	11	21.88	12	27.11									
1,319	July 1,1885	2	22.40	71	22.28	6	146,261	116.45	2	13 0	6 8	4	1	¹²5
									14¹	13 8	6 8			
									14¹	15 0	6 6			
651	Jan.20,1886	2	20.59	71	23.38	.....	....							
696	July 1,1885	2	19.99	71	21.13									
1,319	July 1,1885	4	21.60	1	22.15	6	45,762	145.74	1	10 0	6 0	1	1	(¹⁷)
1,941	July 1,1885	4	27.12	3	27.12	6	92,529	96.22	1	15 0	8 0	3	2	¹⁸8
									1	15 6	8 10			
2,103	July 1,1885	4	18.73	3	27.33									
2,103	July 1,1885	4	20.46	7	22.06	6	29,365	93.52	1	18 0	6 10	1	1	(²¹)
									²1	14 6	8 8			
865	July 1,1888	63	22.32	60	22.32	6	67,560	107.58	1	19 6	8 7	2	1	2
847	July 1,1885	50	18.97	9	21.93	6	37,209	118.50	1	13 0	6 8	1	1	²²2
847	July 1,1885	43	22.71	51	23.14	6	26,074	83.04	1	13 0	7 0	1	1	(²³)
3,447	July 1,1885	2	29.72	3	27.54	6	59,114	141.19	1	14 8	8 7	1	2	²⁴6
		4	29.72	21	22.59	6	²⁷59,114	......	1	15 3	8 7	1	1	
		6	21.50	5	24.55	6	59,114	......	1	15 3	8 7	2	1	
									⁷1	15 3	8 7			
540	July 1,1885	1	18.52	4	17.30	6	49,449	136.38	1	14 10	8 8	2	1	2
		3	19.40	2	18.80	6	²⁵36,198	......	1	14 9	8 6			
									⁷1	14 6	8 6			
									1	10 6	6 8			
396	July 1,1887	8	25.20	5	25.18	7	30,744	84.00	²⁵1	35 5	8 7	1	1	1
1,070	July 1,1888	23	25.94	24	25.94	7	99,713	136.22	2	16 6	7 8	2	1	2
119	July 1,1888	1	19.74	2	19.74	6	13,273	115.42	1	10 0	9 0	1	1	1

(46.76 miles). One clerk on Portland and Rochester R. P. O. (52.74 miles). The Portland and Rochester clerk runs from Rochester to Portland, with Portland and Worcester clerk as assistant.

¹⁹ Balance of route covered by Portland and Worcester R. P. O. (48.47 miles).

²⁰ Covered by Portland and Worcester R. P. O. (46.57 miles).

²¹ Shown in column 17, Portland and Worcester R. P. O.

²² 1 clerk on Portsmouth and Manchester R. P. O. (41.52 miles).

²³ Balance of route (17.76 miles) covered by Portsmouth and Concord R. P. O.

²⁴ Covered by Portsmouth and Concord R. P. O. (41.40 miles).

²⁵ Shown in column 17 Portsmouth and Concord R. P. O.

²⁶ One clerk detailed as transfer clerk at Reading, Pa.

²⁷ Triple daily service except Sunday.

²⁸ Trains 2 and 3 run only between Pottsville and Shamokin. Double daily service except Sunday.

²⁹ Balance of route (16.21 miles) covered by closed pouches. (See Florence, Wis., and Crystal Falls, Mich., Table C'.)

³⁰ Whole car.

³¹ New service; not reported last year.

³² 172.24 miles of route 33075, between Saint Joseph, Mo., and Herington, Kans., covered by Saint Joseph, Mo., and Caldwell, Kans., R. P. O., and 176.40 miles between Herington and Bucklin, Kans., covered by Herington and Dodge City, Kans., R. P. O.

³³ Represents distance between Bucklin and Liberal; 49.90 miles between Pratt and Bucklin covered by Herington and Dodge City, Kans., R. P. O.

³⁴ R. P. O. service established on this line February 18, 1888.

TABLE A⁵.—*Statement of railway post-offices in operation*

Designation of railway post-office. (Lines upon which railway post-office cars are paid for, in *italics.*)	Division.	Distance run by clerks, register to register.	Initial and terminal stations, running from east to west, north to south, or northwest to southeast (with abbreviated title of railroad company).	Number of route.	Miles of route for which railroad is paid.
		Miles.			
Providence, R. I., and New London, Conn.	1	65.24	Providence, R. I., Gröton, Conn. (N. Y., Prov. and Bos.).	4002	(¹)
Providence and Pascoag, R. I..	1	23.75	Providence, Pascoag, R. I. (Prov. and Spring.).	4006	23.17
Providence, R. I., and Willimantic, Conn.	1	59.04	Providence, R. I., Willimantic, Conn. (N. Y. and N. Eng.).	4003	58.61
Pueblo and Silverton, Colo.....	7	376.55	Pueblo, Cucharas, Colo. (D. and R. G.)	³38001 (part)	49.70
			Cucharas, Antonito, Colo. (D. and R. G.) ...	⁶38004 (part)	109.52
			Antonito, Silverton, Colo. (D. and R. G)...	39002	217.05
Quincy, Ill., and Kansas City, Mo.⁵	7	225.92	Quincy, Ill., Cameron, Mo. (H. and St. Jo.)..	⁹28005 (part)	170.84
			Cameron, Kansas City, Mo. (H. and St. J.)..	28010	55.08
Quincy, Ill., and Louisiana, Mo.	6	44.96	Quincy, Fall Creek, Ill. (Chi., Bur. and Qcy.)	¹⁰23041 (part)	13.10
			Fall Creek, Ill., Hannibal, Mo. (Chi., Bur. and Qcy.).	23079	32.10
Quincy, Ill., and Trenton, Mo ..	7	137.10	Quincy, Ill., Trenton, Mo. (Q., O. and K. C.).	28019	137.53
Racine, Wis., and Rock Island, Ill.	6	197.88	Racine, Wis., Rock Island, Ill. (Chi., Mil. and St. P.).	25024	197.85
Raleigh and Gibson's Station, N. C.	3	108.80	Raleigh, Hamlet, N. C. (Ral. and Aug. Air Line).	13010	98.30
			Hamlet, Gibson's Station, N. C. (Ral. and Aug. Air Line).	13034	10.50
Reading, Pa., and Quarryville, Pa.	2	57.50	Reading, Pa., Sinking Springs, Pa. (P. and R.).	8073 (part)	(¹⁸)
			Sinking Springs, Junction, Pa. (P. and R.).	8031 (part)	¹⁸28.00
			Junction, Quarryville, Pa. (L. and Q.)	8137	23.50
Reading, Pa., and Wilmington, Del.	2	74.07	Reading, Pa., Wilmington, Del. (W. and N.)	8054	71.90
Red Bank, N. J., and Bridgeton, N. J.	2	95.20	Red Bank and Eatontown, N. J. (N. J. Southern).	7049 (part)	¹⁰2.89
			Eatontown and Whiting, N. J. (N. J. Southern).	7026 (part)	¹⁹30.41
			Whiting and Atsion, N. J. (N. J. Southern).	7029	24.47
			Atsion and Bridgeton, N. J	7031	37.81
Redding and Sacramento, Cal.	8	171.41	Tehama, Davisville, Cal. (Central Pacific).	46022 (part)	111.64
			Redding, Tehama, Cal. (Central Pacific)...	46003	(²¹)
			Davisville, Sacramento, Cal. (Central Pacific).	46001 (part)	(²¹)
Redfield and Gettysburgh, Dak.	6	75.84	Redfield, Gettysburgh, Dak. (Chi. and No. West.).	35024	75.31
Red Oak. Iowa, and Nebraska City, Nebr.	6	53.69	Red Oak. Iowa, Nebraska City, Nebr. (Chi., Bur. and Qcy.).	27074	53.67
Red Wing and Mankato, Minn.	6	94.62	Red Wing and Mankato, Minn. (Minn. and St. Louis).	26048	95.16

¹ Covered by Boston, Providence and New York R. P. O. (61.80 miles).
² Reserve car.
³ 120.14 miles of route 38001 between Denver and Pueblo, Colo., covered by Denver, Pueblo, and Leadville, Colo., R. P. O., and 37.10 miles between Cucharas and El Moro, Colo., covered by closed-pouch service. (See Table C'.)
⁴ Trains between Pueblo and Alamosa (130.84 miles) seven times a week, and between Alamosa and Silverton (245.71 miles) six times a week.
⁵ 1 clerk detailed to transfer service, Pueblo, Colo.

⁶ 91.17 miles of route 38004, between Antonito, Colo., and Espanola, N. Mex., covered by Antonito, Colo., and Santa Fé, N. Mex, R.P.O.
⁷ In reserve.
⁸ Double daily service.
⁹ 86.71 miles of route 28005 between Cameron and Saint Joseph, Mo., covered by Cameron, Mo., and Atchison, Kans., R. P. O.
¹⁰ Cars on day line belong to C., B., and Q. Railway. (See Chicago and Quincy, Ill.)
¹¹ 1 helper out of Quincy, Ill., and 1 helper on day line between Brookfield and Cameron, Mo., (67 miles); the latter helper alternating be-

in the United States on June 30, 1888—Continued.

Average weight of mail whole distance per day.	Date of last re-adjustment.	Average speed per hour (train numbers taken from division schedules).				Number of round trips with clerks per week.	Annual miles of service with clerks.	Average miles run daily by crews.	Number of mail cars, or cars in which are mail apartments.	Inside dimensions of cars or apartments (railway post-office cars in black figures).		Number of crews.	Number of clerks to crew.	Number of clerks assigned to line.
		Train No. outward.	Av'ge speed (miles).	Train No. inward.	Av'ge speed (miles).					Length.	Width.			
Lbs.										Ft. In.	Ft. In.			
12,702	July 1, 1885	6	26.07	11	25.25	6	40,971	130.48	1	16 3	6 11	1	1	2
		24	24.46	15	30.10	6	40,971	....	1	15 10	6 10	1	1	
									²1	15 10	6 6			
658	July 1, 1885	53	19.43	54	19.71	6	14,915	95.00	1	6 9	6 5	1	1	1
		57	18.39	56	21.22	6	14,915	....	1	6 4	5 2			
5,042	July 1, 1885	7	25.99	4	25.06	6	37,077	118.06	²1 1	14 2	6 8	1	1	1
2,975	July 1, 1886	33	22.69	34	28.55	7	⁴250,081	125.51	2	13 8½	7 5	6	1	⁷7
									1	15 1½	7 6			
748	July 1, 1886	33	19.04	34	18.62	7	....	....	1	13 8½	7 6			
		413	......	414	......	....			²1	13 8½	7 5			
745	July 1, 1886	413	15.86	414	16.35	6								
		483		484										
10,773	July 1, 1887	3	22.06	4	23.88	7	⁸165,373	112.96	(¹⁶)	....	....	4	2	¹¹18
9,956	July 1, 1886	¹²1	23.88	¹²²4	24.15	7	165,373	112.96	1	30 1½	9 1½	4	2	
		3	20.68	4	21.32	7	....	....	1	40 4	9 2			
		15	27.50	¹⁵²2	23.61	7			²1	40 4	9 2			
643	July 1, 1887	209	26.20	208	18.05	6	28,235	89.92	1	12 0	6 11	1	1	1
214	July 1, 1887	209	15.24	208	11.64	....	....	....	¹⁴1	11 0	6 11			
668	July 1, 1887	1	20.68	2	21.23	6	86,099	137.10	1	16 7	7 9	2	1	2
									⁷1	34 3	7 4			
2,231	July 1, 1887	1, 53	19.06	2, 52	18.76	6	124,268	98.94	1	26 0½	9 3	4	1	4
									1	24 0	9 3			
686	July 1, 1888	1	20.78	2	22.81	6	68,326	108.80	1	13 6	6 6	2	1	2
		1	13.33	2	13.33									
2,444	July 1, 1885	9	30	2	30	6	86,110	115.00	2	12 0	8 11	1	1	1
									⁷1	9 0	6 7			
									1	7 6	6 7			
417	July 1, 1885	9	19.53	2	18.06	6	....	....	(¹⁷)	....	....	(¹⁷)		
219	July 1, 1885	9	9.46	2	16.57	6	....	....	(¹⁷)	....	....	(¹⁹)		
237	July 1, 1885	10	19.32	3	20.19	6	46,516	148.14	1	7 6	6 6	1	1	1
									⁷1	6 3	5 7			
425	July 1, 1885	312	17.34	313	21.67	6	59,786	190.40	1	8 3	6 9	1	1	1
									⁷1	8 3	6 9			
471	July 1, 1885	312	28.50	313	30.41	6	....	....	(²⁰)	....	....	(²⁰)		
119	July 1, 1885	312	31.23	313	31.23	6	....	....	(²⁰)	....	....	(²⁰)		
70	July 1, 1885	312	24.12	313	22.02	6	....	....	(²⁰)	....	....	(²⁰)		
		17	27.59	18	27.59	7	125,472	114.27	²¹ 2	55 ½	9 5½	3	1	3
3,973	June 25, 1888	17	25.20	18	25.20	6								
25,702	Aug. 15, 1888	19	20.46	20	26.46									
483	July 1, 1888	39	16.36	40	16.66	6	47,627	151.68	1	16 6	7 0	1	1	1
1,034	July 1, 1887	91	23.55	92	23.55	6	33,717	107.38	1	15 4	8 10	1	1	1
360	Aug. 3, 1888	22	22.90	21	23.50	6	59,421	180.24	1	8 10	9 0	1	1	1

tween Brookfield, Mo., and Atchison, Kans., with clerk on Cameron, Mo., and Atchison, Kans., R. P. O.

¹² Clerks run west on train 15 Sunday night and east on train 16 Saturday night.

¹³ Balance of route (6.08 miles) covered by closed pouches. (See Fall Creek, Ill., and Hannibal, Mo., Table Cᶜ.)

¹⁴ Reserve.

¹⁵ 6 miles covered by Allentown and Harrisburg R. P. O.

¹⁶ 11.73 miles covered by closed-pouch service. (See Table Cᶜ.)

¹⁷ Cars and clerks shown on route No. 8073.

¹⁸ 6.58 miles covered by closed-pouch service. (See Table Cᶜ.)

¹⁹ 11.81 miles covered by closed-pouch service. (See Table Cᶜ.)

²⁰ Cars and clerks shown on route No. 7049.

²¹ 46.54 miles of route 46003 covered by Portland, Oregon, and Sacramento, Cal., R. P. O.; 13.23 miles of route 46001. Davisville to Sacramento, shown on Ogden, Utah, and San Francisco, Cal., R. P. O.; 40-foot cars authorized.

TABLE A*.—*Statement of railway post-offices in operation*

Designation of railway post-office. (Lines upon which railway post-office cars are paid for, in *italics*.)	Division.	Distance run by clerks, register to register.	Initial and terminal stations, running from east to west, north to south, or northwest to southeast (with abbreviated title of railroad company).	Number of route.	Miles of route for which railroad is paid.
		Miles.			
Reno and Preston, Minn	6	57.70	Reno, Preston, Minn. (Chi., Mil. and St. Paul).	26032	57.66
Reno and Virginia City, Nev	8	53.08	Reno, Virginia City, Nev. (Virginia and Truckee R. R.).	45001	53.08
Republican City, Nebr., and Oberlin, Kans.	6	78.87	Republican City, Nebr., Oberlin, Kans. (B. and M. R. in Nebr.).	34032	78.73
Richford and Saint Albans, Vt.	1	28.91	Richford, Saint Albans, Vt. (Miss. Val'y)..	2007	28.79
Richland and Niagara Falls, N.Y.	2	181.40	Richland, Oswego, N.Y. (R. W. and O.)....	6034	29.02
			Oswego, Suspension Bridge, N.Y. (R. W. and O.).	6038	151.18
			Suspension Bridge, Niagara Falls, N.Y. (N.Y., C. and H. R.).	6016 (part)	(³)
Richland and Syracuse, N.Y.	2	42.33	Richland, Pulaski, N.Y. (R. W. and O.)....	6034 (part)	(⁴)
			Pulaski, Syracuse, N.Y. (R. W. and O.) ...	6037	38.61
Richmond and Danville, Va.	3	141.08	Richmond, Danville, Va. (Rich. and Dan.)	11006	140.71
Richmond, Va., and Huntington, W. Va. [6]	3	420.70	Richmond, Va., Huntington W. Va	11005 (part)	419.05
Richmond, Lynchburgh, and Clifton Forge, Va.	3	230.55	Richmond, Lynchburgh, Va. (Rich. and Alleghany).	11023	147.07
			Lynchburgh, Clifton Forge, Va. (Rich. and Alleghany).	11027	84.20
Richmond and Stanford, Ky.	5	35.57	Richmond, Stanford, Ky. (Ky. Cent.).......	20030	34.31
Ridgway, and Erie Pa. [8]	2	119.48	Ridgway and Erie, Pa. (Penna.)............	8022 (part)	(⁹)
Rincon and Silver City, N. Mex. [11]	7	101.12	Rincon, Deming, N. Mex.(A., T. and S.F.).	¹⁷38006 (part)	53.82
			Deming, Silver City, N. Mex. (A., T. and S. F.)	39006	47.86
Roanoke and Opelika, Ala.	4	39.38	Roanoke, Opelika, Ala. (E. Ala. Rwy.) ...	17014	39.38
Rochester and Elmira, N.Y.	2	112.50	Rochester and Corning, N.Y. (N.Y., L. E. and W.).	6005	94.97
			Corning and Elmira, N.Y. (N.Y., L. E. and W).	6001 (part)	(¹⁴)
Rochester and Olean, N.Y.	2	108.23	Rochester and Hinsdale, N.Y. (W. N. Y. and Pa.).	6123	100.02
			Hinsdale and Olean, N.Y. (W. N. Y. and Pa.).	6058 (part)	(¹⁸)
Rochester, N.Y., and Punxsutawney, Pa.	2	230.98	Rochester, N.Y., Bradford Junc., Pa. (B., R. and P.)	6102 (part)	¹⁸107.90
			Bradford Junc., N.Y., Punxsutawney, Pa. (B., R. and P.)	6127	118.70
Rochester and Suspenpension Bridge, N.Y.	2	74.89	Rochester and Suspension Bridge, N.Y. (N.Y.C. and H. R.)	6018 (part)	²¹74.52
Rockaway and High Bridge, N.J.	2	30.57	Rockaway and High Bridge, N.J. (Cent. of N.J.).	7040	30.76

[1] 2 clerks on Suspension Bridge and Oswego R. P. O.
[2] Cars and clerks shown on route No 6034.
[3] 1.80 miles covered by Suspension Bridge and Buffalo R. P. O.
[4] 4.30 miles covered by Richland and Niagara Falls R. P. O.
[5] One in reserve.
[6] This line is in two divisions, 8 clerks performing double daily (except Sunday) service Richmond to Clifton Forge, Va. (193.31 miles), and 4 clerks performing single daily service on trains 5 and 6 Clifton Forge, Va., to Huntington W. Va. (227.39 miles.) Clerks on eastern division, trains 5 and 6, run as helpers on same trains between Clifton Forge, Va., and White Sulphur Springs, W. Va. Two acting clerks employed as additional men performing service as helpers on trains 1 and 2 between Pendleton and Clifton Forge, Va. (127.78 miles). Service on trains 5 and 6 Richmond to Clifton Forge, Va., during summer season only.
[7] One car in reserve.
[8] Short run, Williamsport and Erie R. P. O.
[9] 119.48 miles covered by Williamsport and Erie R. P. O.
[10] Clerks accounted for on Williamsport and Erie R. P. O.

in the *United States on June* 30, 1888.—Continued.

Average weight of mail whole distance per day.	Date of last readjustment.	Average speed per hour (train numbers taken from division schedules).				Number of round trips with clerks per week.	Annual miles of service with clerks.	Average miles run daily by crew.	Number of mail cars, or cars in which are mail apartments.	Inside dimensions of cars or apartments (railway post-office cars in black figures).		Number of crews.	Number of clerks to crew.	Number of clerks assigned to line.
		Train No. outward.	Av'ge speed (miles).	Train No. inward.	Av'ge speed (miles).					Length.	Width.			
Lbs.										*Ft. In.*	*Ft. In.*			
160	July 1, 1887	37	18.92	38	16.68	6	36,235	115.40	1	9 6	5 5	1	1	1
1,152	July 1, 1887	1	21.23	2	21.66	7	38,855	106.16	1	18 11	8 5½	1	1	1
675	July 1, 1886	121	24.00	122	24.00	6	49,530	157.74	1	18 4	8 10	1	1	1
458	July 1, 1885	2	22.39	3	22.39	6	18,155	57.82	1	8 4	6 10	1	1	1
1,040	July 1, 1885	110	29.02	113	29.02	6	113,919	120.93	2	23 10	6 10	3	1	15
1,201	July 1, 1885	110	23.56	113	23.56	6	....	....	(?)	....	....	(?)		
8,979	July 1, 1885	110	10.80	113	10.80	6	....	....	(?)			(?)		
1,040	July 1, 1885	128	25.80	123	25.80	6	26,563	84.66	1	8 6	6 6	1	1	1
708	July 1, 1885	128	23.16	123	27.25	6	....	....	(?)			(?)		
1,904	July 1, 1885	50	27.21	51	25.18	7	103,271	94.05	*3	41 2	8 10	3	1	3
1,781	July 1, 1885	1	21.54	2	22.60	6	121,399	140.23	1	18 8	9 1	12	1	12
									1	18 9	8 11			
		5	21.12	6	19.47	7	287,848	....	1	18 7	8 0			
									2	20 4	8 11			
									1	20 0	8 0			
942	July 1, 1885	1	28.60	2	25.13	6	144,785	115.27	*3	16 0	8 0	4	1	4
467	July 1, 1885	1	22.34	2	24.50	6									
299	July 1, 1885	6	9.78	1	9.38	6	22,338	71.14	*2	8 0	6 7	1	1	1
1,381	July 1, 1885	17	23.50	18	26.55	6	75,033	119.48	1	15 0	8 0	2	1	(16)
4,546	July 1, 1886	621	25.72	622	24.65	7	74,020	101.12	{1	13 5	9 4¼	2	1	2
									{1	13 4½	5 3¼			
....	....	621	23.75	622	19.63	7								
274	July 1, 1888	66	14.20	65	15.60	6	24,730	78.76	1	12 2	7 0	1	1	1
1,738	July 1, 1885	102	27.79	107	26.50	6	1*70,750	138.99	1	20 6	9 2	2	1	2
....	....	102	29.14	107	29.14	6			(13)			(13)		
350	July 1, 1885	30	21.43	35	19.88	6	67,968	108.23	2	15 6	8 9	2	1	2
1,492	July 1, 1885	30	21.43	35	19.88	6	....	....	(17)	....	....	(17)		
668	July 1, 1885	1	28.51	4	27.54	6	145,055	114.16	2	15 0	9 0	4	1	4
821	July 1, 1885	1	19.14	4	18.73	6	....	....	(19)	....	....	(19)		
3,851	July 1, 1885	11	27.94	10	24.50	6	47,031	98.85	*02 2	15 0	9 0	2	1	*24
		21	26.30	26	24.50		22*47,031	....	1	21 0	8 4	1	1	
									20*1	21 0	8 4			
83	July 1, 1885	5	23.21	4	24.45	6	19,198	61.14	1	7 6	6 9	1	1	1

[11] Reported last year as Rincon and Deming, N. Mex.; increased distance, 46.59 miles.

[12] 348.09 miles of route 38006, between La Junta, Colo., and Albuquerque, N. Mex, covered by La Junta, Colo., and Albuquerque, N. Mex., R. P. O. and 177.14 miles between Albuquerque and Rincon, N. Mex., by Albuquerque, N. Mex., and El Paso, Tex., R. P. O.

[13] Alternates with Danville and Buffalo clerk.

[14] 17 miles covered by New York and Dunkirk R. S. O.

[15] Cars and clerks shown on route No. 6005.

[16] 6.96 miles covered by Buffalo and Emporium R. P. O.

[17] Cars and clerks shown on route No. 6123.

[18] 1.33 miles covered by closed-pouch service. (See Table C*.)

[19] Cars and clerks shown on route No. 6102.

[20] In reserve.

[21] 1.80 miles covered by closed-pouch service. (See Table C*.)

[22] 1 clerk detailed as transfer clerk at Suspension Bridge, N. Y.

[23] Double daily service, except Sunday.

[24] 4 miles covered by closed-pouch service. (See Table C*.)

TABLE A².—*Statement of railway post-offices in operation*

Designation of railway post-office. (Line upon which railway post-office cars are paid for, in *italics*).	Division.	Distance run by clerks, register to register.	Initial and terminal stations, running from east to west, north to south, or northwest to southeast (with abbreviated title of railroad company).	Number of route.	Miles of route for which railroad is paid.
		Miles.			
Rockford, Ill., and Mineral Point, Wis.	6	115.69	Rockford, Rockton, Ill. (Chi., Mil. and St. Paul).	23096	16.37
			Rockton, Ill., Beloit, Wis. (Chi., Mil. and St. Paul).	25024 (part)	(¹)
			Beloit, Janesville, Wis. (Chi., Mil. and St. Paul).	25036	15.72
			Janesville, Gratiot, Wis. (Chi., Mil. and St. Paul).	³25004	55.80
			Gratiot, Mineral Point, Wis. (Chi., Mil. and St. Paul).	⁴25020 (part)	25.79
Rock Island and Peoria, Ill....	6	92.20	Rock Island, Peoria, Ill. (R. Island and Peoria).	23040	91.82
Rock Island, Ill., and St. Louis, Mo.	6	248.99	Rock Island, Ill., St. Louis, Mo. (Chi., Bur. and Qcy.).	23005	247.71
Rockland and Beaumont, Tex.	7	73.52	Rockland, Beaumont, Tex. (S. and E. T.).	31029	75.85
Rockland and Portland, Me....	1	88.42	Rockland, Woolwich, Me. (Knox and Lin.).	15	49.11
			Bath, Brunswick, Me. (Me. Cen.)..........	11	9.17
			Brunswick, Portland, Me. (Me. Cen.)......	⁷6 (part)	(⁸)
Rogersville and Bull's Gap, Tenn.	3	16.27	Rogersville, Bull's Gap, Tenn. (Tenn. and Ohio).	19003	16.42
Rondout and Stamford, N. Y...	2	74.36	Rondout and Stamford, N. Y. (Ula. and Del.).	6073 (part)	⁹74.36
Rosenberg and Cuero, Tex....	7	120.29	Rosenberg, Victoria, Tex. (N. Y., T. and M. P).	31036	92.60
			Victoria, Cuero, Tex. (G., W. T. and P)....	¹²31019 (part)	28.29
Rouse's Point and Albany, N. Y.	2	113.90	Rouse's Point and West Chazy, N. Y. (D. and H. C. Co.).	6033	14.78
			West Chazy and Albany, N. Y. (D. and H. C. Co.).	6026 (part)	¹⁴177
		101.55	Rutland and Castleton, Vt. (D. and. H. C. Co.).	6024 (part)	(¹⁵)
			Castleton, Vt., and Whitehall, N. Y. (D. and H. C. Co.).	6098	14.35
Ruthven and Des Moines, Iowa.	6	137.59	Ruthven, Tara, Iowa (Des M. and Ft. Dodge).	27087	55.46
			Tara, Des Moines, Iowa, (Des. M. and Ft. Dodge).	27031	82.91
Rutland and Bennington, Vt., and Troy, N. Y.	1	85.19	Rutland, North Bennington, Vt. (Benn. and Rut.).	¹⁷2015 (part)	52.75
			North Bennington, Vt., State Line (Benn. and Rut.).	2018	2.02
			State Line, Hoosac Junction, N. Y.(Fitch).	6116 (part)	5.04
			Hoosac Junction, Troy, N. Y. (Fitch)	¹⁸6067 (part)	(¹⁹)
Rutland, Vt., and Troy, N. Y..	2	85.84	Rutland, Vt., Eagle Bridge, N. Y. (D. and H. C. Co.).	6024	62.88
			Eagle Bridge, Troy, N. Y., (Fitchburg)....	6067 (part)	(²⁰)
Sacramento and San Francisco, Cal.	8	140.90	Sacramento, San Francisco, Cal., Central Pacific).	46028	140.55
Sag Harbor and New York, N. Y.	2	100.75	Sag Harbor, N. Y., and Long Island City, N. Y. (L. I.).	6093	100.15

¹ Distance (3.40 miles) covered by Racine, Wis., and Rock Island, Ill., R. P. O.
² Reserve.
³ Balance of route (19.70 miles) covered by closed pouches. (See Milton Junct and Janesville, Wis., and Gratiot and Shullsburgh, Wis., Table Cᵃ.)
⁴ Balance of route (7.15 miles) covered by closed pouches. (See Gratiot, Wis., and Warren, Ill.. Table Cᵃ.)
⁵ Short run.
⁶ Reserve cars.

⁷ Balance of route covered by Bangor and Boston R. P. O. (108.90) miles.
⁸ Covered by Bangor and Boston R. P. O. (29.10 miles).
⁹ 4 miles covered by closed-pouch service. (See Table Cᵃ.)
¹⁰ Double daily service except Sunday.
¹¹ In reserve.
¹²,²⁷.20 miles of route 31019 between Victoria and Port Lavaca, Tex., covered by closed-pouch service. (See Table Cᵃ.)

in the United States on June 30, 1888—Continued.

Average weight of mail whole distance per day.	Date of last re-adjustment.	Average speed per hour (train numbers taken from division schedules).				Number of round trips with clerks per week.	Annual miles of service with clerks.	Average miles run daily by crews.	Number of mail cars, or cars in which are mail apartments.	Inside dimensions of cars or apartments (railway post-office cars in black figures).		Number of crews.	Number of clerks to crews.	Number of clerks appointed to line.
		Train No. outward.	Av'ge speed (miles).	Train No. inward.	Av'ge speed (miles).					Length.	Width.			
Lbs.										Ft. In.	Ft. In.			
1,595	June 22,1888	40	27.43	35	26	6	72,653	115.69	1	20 2	9 4	2	1	2
2,231	July 1, 1887	40	20.40	35	22.66	....	....	....	*1	16 9	7 5			
....	....	40	25.85	35	25.81									
981	July 1, 1887	1	26.57	18	26.64									
1,015	July 1, 1887	1	25.77	18	26.32									
1,104	July 1, 1887	4	27.30	1	26.00	6	57,901	92.20	1	16 2	9 0	2	1	2
									*1	15 6	9 0			
2,223	July 1, 1887	2	23.62	1	22.64	7	182,260	124.49	2	19 0	8 10	4	1	4
									*1	19 6	8 10			
145	July 1, 1886	103	13.36	104	16.33	7	53,817	147.04	1	11 0	7 0	1	1	1
1,578	July 1, 1885	2	21.45	68	21.77	6	55,527	117.90	1	16 0	6 8	2	1	3
		4	22.61	54	21	6	*36,913	78.37	1	16 0	6 8	1	1	
2,697	July 1, 1885	2	26.10	68	26.10									
		4	21.12	54	26.10				*1	13 0	6 7			
15,122	July 1, 1883	2	23.28	68	23.28	....	....	....	*1	16 0	6 7			
272	July 1, 1888	1	8.53	2	8.53	6	10,218	32.54	1	5 6	6 2	1	1	1
1,003	July 1, 1885	3	18.59	10	19.39	6	46,698	109.69	1	20 0	6 8	2	1	3
		9	18.59	6	19.82	6	1046,698	......	1	20 0	6 8	1	1	
									111	20 0	6 8			
737	July 1, 1886	152	20.44	151	20.86	7	88,052	120.29	2	14 6	9 0	2	1	2
217	July 1, 1886	152	21.05	151	19.86	7								
3,365	July 1, 1885	4	30.60	3	29.56	6	15135,303	108.26	1	21 0	7 0	2	1	6
									111	21 0	7 0			
4,939	July 1, 1885	4	18.43	3	15.17	6	....	......	(15)	....	......	(15)		
883	July 1, 1885	6	27.83	1	25.60	6	....	......	1	20 0	8 10	2	2	
929	July 1, 1885	6	31.88	1	28.70	6	....	......	(15)	....	......	(15)		
489	July 1, 1887	54	17.84	53	20	6	86,406	137.59	2	16 6	9 0	2	1	2
1,161	July 1, 1887	54	22.13	53	25.54									
3,892	July 1, 1885	104	28.57	7	27.87	6	53,499	85.19	1	22 3	7 2	2	1	2
4,129	July 1, 1885	104	36.99	7	27.75									
4,137	July 1, 1885	104	18.90	7	21.60									
6,909	July 1, 1885	104	23.37	7	24.51									
883	July 1, 1885	54	23.58	53	25.11	6	53,908	85.84	1	16 0	6 11	2	1	2
......	....	54	25.08	53	25.08	6	....	......	(21)	....	......	(21)		
1,904	July 1, 1886	25	25.78	26	22.48	7	103,139	93.93	2	17 10	8 11	3	1	3
1,121	July 1, 1888	20 25		23 25		6	63,271	100.75	1	14 8	6 8	4	1	226
		56 25		27	21.14	6	2263,271	......	1	20 0	8 8			
									111	12 4	6 0			

13 This R. P. O. is in two divisions: Rouse's Point to Whitehall, and Albany, N. Y., to Rutland, Vt.

14 11.75 miles covered by closed-pouch service. (See Table Cᶜ.)

15 Cars and clerks shown on routes Nos. 6024 and 6033.

16 10.87 miles covered by Rutland and Troy R. P. O.

17 Balance of route covered by closed-pouch service between North Bennington and Bennington, Vt. (5.07 miles). (See table Cᶜ.)

18 Balance of route (22.82 miles) covered by Boston and Troy R. P. O.

19 Covered by Boston and Troy R. P. O. (25.33 miles).

20 23 miles covered by Boston and Troy R. P. O.

21 Cars and clerks shown on route No. 6024.

22 One clerk detailed for transfer duty at Long Island City, N. Y.; 1 clerk on Babylon and New York R. P. O.

23 Double daily service except Sunday.

TABLE A[a].—*Statement of railway post-offices in operation*

Designation of railway post-office. (Lines upon which railway post-office cars are paid for, in *italics*).	Division.	Distance run by clerks, register to register.	Initial and terminal stations, running from east to west, north to south, or northwest to southeast (with abbreviated title of railroad company).	Number of route.	Miles of route for which railroad is paid.
Saint Albans, Vt., and Boston, Mass.	1	*Miles.* 265.40	Saint Albans, White River Junction, Vt., (Cen. Vt.).	[1]2002 (part)	120.50
			White River Junction, Vt., Concord, N. H. (Bos. Low.).	1008	69.76
			Concord, Nashua, N. H. (Con.)	1001	36.28
			Nashua, N. H., Boston, Mass. (Bos. Low.).	3016	39.85
Saint Albans, Vt., and Ogdensburgh, N. Y.	2	143.15	Saint Albans, Vt., and Rouse's Point, N.Y. (Cen. Vert.).	2002	[4]24.27
			Rouse's Point and Ogdensburgh, N. Y. (O. and L. C.).	6052	[5]119.16
Saint Albans, Vt., and Troy, N. Y.	1	194.69	Saint Albans, Essex Jct., Vt. (Cen. Vt.)...	[6]2002 (part)	[7]
			Essex Jct., Rutland, Vt. (Cen. Vt.)	[8]2003 (part)	[11]
			Rutland, No. Bennington, Vt. (Benn. and Rut.).	[12]2015 (part)	[14]
			No. Bennington, Vt., State Line (Benn. and Rut.).	2018	[15]
			State Line, Hoosac Jct., N. Y. (Fitch.)	6116	[16]
			Hoosac Jct., Troy, N. Y. (Fitch.)...........	[17]6067 (part)	[18]
Saint Cloud and Willmar, Minn.	6	56.61	Saint Cloud, Willmar, Minn. (St. P., Minn. and Man.).	26057	56.69
Saint Joseph, Mo., and Caldwell, Kans.[19]	7	295.55	Saint Joseph, Mo., Herington, Kans. (C. K. and N.).	[20]33075 (part)	172.24
			Herington, Caldwell, Kans. (C., K. and N.).	33082	123.73
Saint Joseph, Mo., and Grand Island, Nebr.	7	252.54	Saint Joseph, Mo., Grand Island, Nebr. (St. J. and G. I.).	33007	252.39
Saint Joseph, Mo., and Nelson, Nebr.[19]	7	208.43	Saint Joseph, Mo., Horton, Kans. (C. K. and N.).	33075 (part)	[20]
			Horton, Kans., Nelson, Nebr. (C. K. and N.).	33076	167.26
Saint Louis, Mo., and Cairo, Ill.	6	153.60	Saint Louis, Mo., Cairo, Ill. (Mobile and Ohio).	23053	153.54
Saint Louis, Mo., and Columbus, Ky.	7	195.65	Saint Louis, Bismarok, Mo. (St. L., I., M. and S.).	28002	[24]
			Bismarck, Mo., Columbus, Ky. (St. L., I., M. and S.).	28034	191.34
Saint Louis, Mo., and Eldorado, Ill.	6	124.50	Saint Louis, Mo., Eldorado, Ill. (St. L., Alton and T. H.).	23030	121.65
Saint Louis, Mo., and Halstead, Kans.[27]	7	530.14	Saint Louis, Pierce City, Mo. (St. L. and S. F.).	[26]28003 (part)	286.90
			Pierce City, Mo., Halstead, Kans. (St. L. and S. F.).	28020	242.97

[1] Balance of route covered by Newport and Springfield R. P. O. (14 miles), and Saint Albans and Ogdensburgh R. P. O. (Second Division), (24.27 miles)

[2] 1 clerk detailed as chief clerk, Boston, Mass.; 2 clerks detailed to superintendent's office; 2 clerks detailed as transfer clerks (one at Saint Albans, Vt., and one at Concord, N. H.).

[3] Reserve cars.

[4] 14 miles covered by Newport and Springfield R. P. O.

[5] 120.50 miles covered by Saint Albans and Boston R. P. O.

[6] Cars and clerks shown on route No. 2002.

[7] In reserve.

[8] Balance of route covered by Saint Albans and Boston R. P. O. (95.73 miles); Newport and Springfield R. P. O. (14 miles), and Saint Albans and Ogdensburgh R. P. O. (Second Division) (24.27 miles).

Covered by Saint Albans and Boston R. P. O. (24.77 miles).

[10] Balance of route covered by Essex Jct. and Boston R. P. O. (52.77 miles).

[11] Covered by Essex Jct. and Boston R. P. O. (75.20 miles).

[12] Reserve car.

[13] Balance of route covered by closed-pouch service between No Bennington and Bennington (5.07 miles). (See Table C[c]).

[14] Covered by Rutland, Bennington and Troy R. P. O. (52.75 miles).

[15] Covered by Rutland, Bennington and Troy R. P. O. (2.02 miles).

[16] Covered by Rutland, Bennington and Troy R. P. O. (5.04 miles).

[17] Balance of route covered by Boston and Troy.

[18] Covered by Boston and Troy R. P. O. (25.33 miles).

[19] New service; not reported last year.

[20] 176.40 miles of route 33075 between Herrington and Bucklin, Kans., covered by Herington

in the United States on June 30, 1888—Continued.

Average weight of mail whole distance per day.	Date of last re-adjustment.	Average speed per hour (train numbers taken from division schedules).				Number of round trips with clerks per week.	Annual miles of service with clerks.	Average miles run daily by crew.	Number of mail cars, or cars in which are mail apartments.	Inside dimensions of cars or apartments (railway post-office cars in black figures).		Number of crews.	Number of clerks in crew.	Number of clerks appointed to line.
		Train No. outward.	Av'gespeed (miles).	Train No. inward.	Av'gespeed (miles).					Length.	Width.			
Lbs.										Ft. In.	Ft. In.			
5,453	July 1, 1885	53	25.81	29	28.92	6	166,671	132.70	1	0 9 4		4	2	²21
		67	28.35	285	27.28	6	166,671	....	1	34 4 6 11		4	2	
6,579	Feb.11, 1885	53	26.02	29	33.31	......	....	......	1	50 0 9 5				
		67	28.71	285	23.79	......	....	......	1	35 1 6 3				
11,733	July 1, 1885	53	42.30	29	23.32									
		67	32.30	285	32.30		....	......	²1	4 9 4				
14,363	July 1, 1885	53	31.78	29	27.08	......	....	......	²1	42 2 8 8				
		67	28.04	285	31.78									
5,453	July 1, 1885	50	32.36	63	26.47	6	89,898	143.15	2	20 0 6 3		2	1	2
1,381	July 1, 1887	50	27.50	63	26.47	6	....	......	(⁴)			(⁴)		
5,453	July 1, 1885	63	33.02	15	33.02	6	115,985	123.12	⁷1	24 0 6 6		3	1	3
									1	22 0 7 9				
									1	21 9 7 2				
4,090	July 1, 1885	63	24.45	15	24.45				¹⁴⁷1	23 0 7 9				
3,892	Feb.11, 1885	63	29.57	15	34.03									
4,129	July 1, 1885	63	36.99	15	27.75									
4,137	July 1, 1885	63	13.74	15	14.40									
6,909	July 1, 1885	63	28.67	15	26.20									
235	July 1, 1887	5	23.20	6	25.78	6	36,807	117.22	1	17 1 8 11		1	1	1
1,070	July 1, 1888	1	23.38	2	24.77	7	216,343	147.78	2	16 6 7 8		4	1	4
									⁷1	14 6 7 2				
885	July 1, 1888	1	23.31	2	25.02	7								
1,251	July 1, 1886	3	23.68	4	23.97	6	158,595	126.27	2	20 0 9 3		4	1	²⁵5
									⁷1	20 0 9 3				
1,070	July 1, 1885	5	20.30	6	18.09	7	152,571	138.95	2	16 6 7 8		3	1	3
									⁷1	16 6 7 8				
739	July 1, 1888	5	24.63	6	22.41	7								
769	July 1, 1887	1	20.40	2	20.57	6	96,461	102.40	²⁹3	21 6 8 10		3	7	3
18,426	July 1, 1887	757	18.83	758	20.09	7	143,216	130.43	2	18 8 9 3		3	1	²⁴4
									⁷1	24 10 8 11				
1,302	July 1, 1887	757	22.99	758	18.83	7								
2,106	July 1, 1887	1	25.74	6	25.74	6	78,186	124.50	1	24 0 9 0		2	1	²⁹3
		19	12.05	20	12.55	....			1	14 2 5 6				
7,234	July 1, 1887	1	24.19	2	26.23	7	206,512	141.06	2	49 10 9 0		4	2	³⁰25
		3	25.61	4	25.59	7	206,512	141.06	2	49 10 9 0		4	2	
1,804	July 1, 1887	1	20.97	2	23.41	7	³⁰164,034	112.05	2	20 6 7 6		4	1	
		3	23.97	4	23.23	7	181,551	124.01	1	22 6 7 6		4	1	
									1	20 6 7 6				
									⁷1	49 10 9 0				

and Dodge City, Kans., R. P. O., and 85.50 miles between Bucklin and Liberal, Kans., covered by Pratt and Liberal, Kans., R. P. O. Saint Joseph, Mo., and Nelson, Nebr., R. P. O. also runs over route 33075 between Saint Joseph, Mo., and Horton, Kans. (41.54 miles).

²¹ 1 clerk detailed to transfer service at Saint Joseph, Mo.

²² 41.54 miles, distance on route 33075 covered by Saint Joseph, Mo., and Caldwell, Kans., R. P. O.

²³ 1 car in reserve.

²⁴ 74.82 miles distance on route 28002 covered by Saint Louis, Mo., and Texarkana, Ark., R. P. O.

²⁵ 1 helper between Saint Louis and Bismarck, Mo. (74.82 miles.)

²⁶ 1 helper between Saint Louis, Mo., and Duquoin, Ill.

²⁷ This line is divided at Monett, Mo., into two divisions—Saint Louis and Monett, Mo. (282.12 miles), and Monett, Mo. and Halstead, Kans. (248.02 miles). Double daily postal-car service between Saint Louis and Monett., Mo (282 miles), and double daily mail-apartment service between Monett, Mo., and Wichita, Kans. (222.60 miles); single daily mail-apartment service between Wichita and Halstead, Kans. (25.10 miles). Last year mail-apartment service was but single daily between Pierce City, Mo., and Halstead, Kans.

²⁸ 72.80 miles of route 28003 between Pierce City, Mo., and Vinita. Ind. Ter., covered by Monett, Mo., and Vinita, Ind. Ter., R. P. O.

²⁹ 1 clerk detailed as chief clerk at large.

³⁰ Trains 1 and 2 run to Wichita, Kans., only; distance from Monett (including terminals) 224.09 miles.

TABLE A[a].—*Statement of railway post-offices in operation*

Designation of railway post-office. (Lines upon which railway post-office cars are paid for, in *italics*.)	Division.	Distance run by clerks, register to register.	Initial and terminal stations, running from east to west, north to south, or northwest to southeast (with abbreviated title of railroad company).	Number of route.	Miles of route for which railroad is paid.
		Miles.			
Saint Louis and Kansas City, Mo. [1]	7	283.00	Saint Louis, Kansas City, Mo. (Mo. Pac.)...	[2,3]28001 (part)	283.00
Saint Louis, Louisiana and Kansas City, Mo.	7	[7]323.39	East Saint Louis, Ill., Kansas City, Mo. (C. and A.).	28022	321.00
Saint Louis, Moberly and Kansas City Mo. [10]	7	276.80	Saint Louis, Kansas City, Mo. (Wab. West.)	[11]28004	277.46
Saint Louis, Mo., and Texarkana, Ark. [14]	7	491.72	Saint Louis, Bismarck, Mo. (St. L., I. M. and S.).	[12]28002	75.33
			Bismarck, Mo., Texarkana, Ark. (St. L., I. M. and S.).	28026	414.28
Saint Louis and Union, Mo. [20]..	7	59.91	Saint Louis, Union, Mo., (St. L., K. C. and C.).	28062	59.91
Saint Paul, Minn., and Council Bluffs, Iowa.	6	368.67	Saint Paul, Minn., Sioux City, Iowa (Chi., St. P., Minn. and Om.).	26025	269.79
			Sioux City, Missouri Valley, Iowa (S. C. and Pac.).	27029	(25)
			Missouri Valley, U. P. Transfer, Iowa (Chi. and No. West.).	23008 (part.)	(26)
Saint Paul, Minn., and Des Moines, Iowa.	6	310.00	Saint Paul, Minn., Angus, Iowa (Minn. and St. Louis).	26021	275.30
			Angus, Des Moines, Iowa (Des M. and Ft. Dodge).	27031 (part.)	(28)
Saint Paul, Minn., and Elroy, Wis.	6	197.08	Saint Paul, Minn., Elroy, Wis. (Chi., St. P., Minn. and Om.).	25030	196.69
Saint Paul, Minn., and Mandan, Dak.	6	477.00	Saint Paul, Minn., Mandan, Dak. (North. Pac.).	[29]26001 (part)	476.00
Saint Paul, Minn., and Mitchell, Dak.	6	426.99	Saint Paul, Minneapolis, Minn. (Chi., Mil. and St. Paul).	26013 (part)	(32)
			Minneapolis, Cologne, Minn. (Chi., Mil. and St. Paul).	26037	33.16
			Cologne, Minn., Aberdeen, Dak. (Chi., Mil. and St. Paul).	[36]26010 (part)	256.34
			Aberdeen, Ashton, Dak. (Chi., Mil. and St. Paul).	[37]35012 (part)	32.69
			Ashton, Mitchell, Dak. (Chi., Mil. and St. Paul).	35017	96.10

[1] Reported last year as Saint Louis, Mo. and Atchison, Kans.; decreased distance, 47.17 miles. Service three times daily westward and twice daily eastward.

[2] 47.17 miles of route 28001, between Kansas City, Mo., and Atchison, Kans., covered by Omaha, Nebr., and Kansas City, Mo., R. P. O.

[3] Sedalia and Kansas City, Mo., R. P. O., also runs over 10.38 miles of route 28001, between Independence and Kansas City, Mo.; Kansas City and Joplin, Mo., R. P. O., also runs over 34.63 miles of route 28001, between Kansas City and Pleasant Hill, Mo.

[4] Clerks and cars on train 7 return from Kansas City to Saint Louis on train 4.

[5] Six helpers on train 7 between Saint Louis and Kansas City, Mo., three out of Saint Louis each morning; 4 helpers on trains 3 and 4 between Saint Louis and Kansas City, Mo.; 1 helper on trains 1 and 6 to meeting point, daily except Monday and Tuesday; 8 clerks detailed to office Superintendent; 2 clerks detailed as chief clerks at large; 1 clerk detailed as chief clerk, Denver, Colo.; 1 clerk detailed as chief clerk, Kansas City, Mo.; 1 clerk detailed to office chief clerk, Kansas City, Mo.; 4 clerks detailed to transfer service, Saint Louis, Mo.; 2 clerks detailed to transfer service, Atchison, Kans.; 1 clerk detailed to transfer service, Kansas City, Mo.; 4 clerks on this line are acting clerks additional.

[6] In reserve.

[7] Clerks register at Union Depot, Saint Louis, Mo.

[8] Trains 41 and 42 between Saint Louis, Mo., and Roodhouse, Ill., and 47 and 48 between Roodhouse, Ill., and Kansas City, Mo.

[9] Two helpers between Saint Louis and Bowling Green, Mo. (119.40 miles).

[10] Double daily service.

[11] Council Bluffs, Iowa, and Moberly, Mo., R. P. O. also runs over 38.90 miles of route 28004 between Brunswick and Moberly, Mo.

[12] One helper on trains 11 and 12 between Saint Louis and Mexico, Mo. (110 miles); 2 helpers on trains 7 and 8 between Saint Louis and Moberly, Mo. (148 miles); 2 clerks detailed to office Superintendent; 1 clerk detailed to transfer service, Kansas City, Mo.

[13] Trains 7 and 8 between Saint Louis and Moberly, Mo., and 5 and 4 between Moberly and Kansas City, Mo.

in the United States on June 30, 1888—Continued.

Average weight of mail whole distance per day.	Date of last re-adjustment.	Average speed per hour (train numbers taken from division schedules).				Number of round trips with clerks per week.	Annual miles of service with clerks.	Average miles run daily by crews.	Number of mail cars, or cars in which are mail apartments.	Inside dimensions of cars or apartments (railway post-office cars in black figures).		Number of crews.	Number of clerks to crew.	Number of clerks assigned to line.
		Train No. outward.	Av'ge speed (miles).	Train No. inward.	Av'ge speed (miles).					Length.	Width.			
Lbs.										*Ft. In.*	*Ft. In.*			
47,461	July 1, 1887	4 7	35. 38	....	....	4 7	103, 578	141. 50	4	60 0	9 3½	4	5	6 79
		1	29. 30	6	24. 09	7	207, 156	141. 50	3	59 11	9 3	4	4	
		3	26. 13	4	27. 61	7	207, 156	141. 50	2	59 11	9 3	4	4	
									1	60 0	9 3½			
									2	59 11	9 3			
2,362	July 1, 1887	41 &	26. 29	42 &	26. 40	7	236, 721	161. 70	2	40 0	9 1	4	1	6
		48		47					1	40 0	9 1			
9,316	July 1, 1887	11	24. 60	12	24. 80	7	202, 618	184. 53	2	55 0	9 3	3	2	20
		5		4					2	55 0	9 3	4	2	
		17 &	27. 93	18 &	28. 16	7	202, 618	138. 40	1	55 0	9 3			
18,426	July 1, 1887	751	23. 75	752	23. 17	7	359, 939	138. 40	4	55 0	9 4	710	3	46
		755	25. 79	754	24. 45	7	359, 939	116. 58	4	49 4	9 4	175	2	
14,457	July 1, 1887	751	23. 01	752	21. 07	7								
		755	27. 30	754	21. 80	7			1	55 0	9 4			
									1	49 4	9 4			
140	Jan. 24, 1888	13	19. 80	14	16. 59	7	43, 854	119. 82	1	13 8	7 3	1	1	1
7,158	July 1, 1887	1	24. 83	2	25. 27	7	269, 866	147. 47	1	50 0	9 0	5	2	14
		3	23. 40	4	24. 45	6	169, 830	135. 21	1	49 6	8 9			
7,209	July 1, 1887	8	26. 82	7	27. 64				3	24 0	9 2½	4	1	
12,804	July 1, 1887	9	29. 33	12	29. 33									
1,963	July 1, 1887	2	23. 91	1	23. 91	6	194, 680	155. 00	2	15 0	9 4	4	1	6
		6	28. 47	5	25. 93	7	88, 608	121. 05	1	25 0	9 4	2	1	
1,161	July 1, 1887	2	28. 50	1	28. 50	....			1	19 9	9 4			
3,000	July 1, 1887	2	26. 56	3	26. 56	7	144, 262	98. 54	1	27 3	9 1½	4	1	5
									1	24 2	8 9¼			
11,448	July 1, 1887	1	27. 60	2	27. 20	7	349, 164	150. 00	5	50 0¼	9 3	6	3	23
		5	24. 62	4	23. 74	6	174, 019	138. 55	2	24 6	9 1	4	1	
28,360	Mar. 9, 1884	3	20. 00	2	20. 00	7	312. 556	149. 16	1	26 2	9 3	4	1	6
....	....	3	24. 75	2	24. 75	....	....	128. 67	1	26 1	9 4	2	1	
2,377	July 1, 1887	3	26. 03	2	25. 60	....	....	....	1	20 10	9 1			
861	July 1, 1888	3	27. 85	2	28. 67									
....	....	3	27. 34	2	27. 28									

14 Double daily service. This line is divided at Little Rock, Ark., into two divisions—Saint Louis, Mo., and Little Rock, Ark. (346 miles), and Little Rock and Texarkana, Ark. (145.74 miles).
15 Saint Louis, Mo., and Columbus, Ky., R. P. O. also runs over route 28002.
16 Daily average of North Division crews.
17 Five crews on each line on North Division and 5 crews on both lines on South Division.
18 Four helpers between Saint Louis, Mo., and Walnut Ridge, Ark. (225 miles), 2 on each line; 1 clerk detailed as chief clerk, Little Rock, Ark.; 1 clerk detailed to office Superintendent.
19 Daily average of South Division crews.
20 New service; not reported last year.
21 Short run between Saint Paul, Minn., and Sioux City, Iowa, 270.43 miles.
22 Distance (76.27 miles) covered by Sioux City and Missouri Valley, Iowa, R. P. O.
23 Distance (22.08 miles) covered by Cedar Rapids and Council Bluffs, Iowa, R. P. O.
24 One helper on trains 5 and 6, between Chaska and Albert Lea, Minn.; one clerk detailed as assistant to chief clerk at Des Moines, Iowa.
25 Short run between Saint Paul and Albert Lea, Minn. (121.05 miles).

26 Distance (38 miles) covered by Ruthven and Des Moines, Iowa, R. P. O.
27 Reserve.
28 One helper between Augusta and Elroy, Wis.
29 Balance of route (804.02 miles) covered by Mandan, Dak., and Helena, Mont., and Helena, Mont., and Portland, Oregon, R. P. O.
30 One reserve.
31 One clerk detailed to transfer duty at Saint Paul, Minn.
32 Short run between Saint Paul, Minn., and Fargo, Dak. (277.10 miles).
33 Distance (10 miles) covered by Chicago, Ill., and Minneapolis, Minn., R. P. O.
34 East Division, Saint Paul, Minn., to Aberdeen, Dak.
35 West Division, Aberdeen to Mitchell, Dak.
36 Balance of route covered by Hastings and Cologne, Minn., R. P. O. (56.51 miles); Aberdeen and Orient, Dak., R. P. O. (41.60 miles), and between Roscoe and Bowdle, Dak. (15.29 miles), by closed pouches. See Table C.
37 Balance of route (64.12 miles) covered by closed pouches. (See Edgeley and Aberdeen, Dak., Table Cᶜ.)

TABLE A⁸.—*Statement of railway post-offices in operation*

Designation of railway post-office. (Lines upon which railway post-office cars are paid for, in *italics*.)	Division.	Distance run by clerks, register to register.	Initial and terminal stations, running from east to west, north to south, or northwest to southeast (with abbreviated title of railroad company).	Number of route.	Miles of route for which railroad is paid.
		Miles.			
Saint Paul, Ortonville, Minn., and Fargo, Dak.	6	307.32	Saint Paul, Minneapolis, Minn. (Chi., Mil. and St. Paul).	26013 (part)	(¹)
			Minneapolis, Cologne, Minn. (Chi, Mil. and St. Paul).	26037	(²)
			Cologne, Ortonville, Minn. (Chi., Mil. and St. Paul).	26010 (part)	(³)
			Ortonville, Minn., Fargo, Dak. (Chi. Mil. and St. Paul).	35019	119.52
Saint Paul, Minn., and Watertown, Dak.	6	226.23	Saint Paul, Minneapolis, Minn. (Minn. and St. Louis).	26021 (part)	(⁵)
			Minneapolis, Birch Cooley, Minn. (Minn. and St. Louis).	26038	100.99
			Birch Cooley, Minn., Watertown, Dak. (Minn. and St. Louis).	26053	123.39
Salamanca, N. Y., and Oil City, Pa.	2	97.69	Salamanca, N. Y., Warren, Pa. (W. N. Y. and Pa).	8164	42.19
			Warren, Irvine, Pa. (W. N. Y. and Pa)..	8022 (part)	(⁷)
			Irvine, Oil City, Pa. (W. N. Y. and Pa.) ...	8025 (part)	⁸49.53
Salina and Luray, Kans.¹⁰......	7	67.07	Salina, Luray, Kans. (S. L and W.)......	33957	67.07
Salina and McPherson, Kans...	7	36.78	Salina, McPherson, Kans. (S. and SW.)....	33028	36.78
Salisbury, N. C., and Knoxville, Tenn.	3	273.73	Salisbury, N. C., Kinzel (n. o.), Tenn. (Rich. and Dan.).	13006	188.43
			Kinzel (n. o.), Morristown, Tenn. (E. Tenn., Va. and Ga.).	19009	43.39
			Morristown, Knoxville, Tenn. (E. Tenn., Va. and Ga.).	19002 (part)	(¹²)
Salt Lake and Juab, Utah......	8	105.03	Salt Lake, Juab, Utah (Utah Central).....	41001 (part)	¹³105.00
San Antonio and Kerville, Tex.¹⁴	7	71.75	Kerville, San Antonio, Tex. (S. A. and A. P.).	31058	71.75
San Bernardino and National City, Cal.	8	132.81	San Bernardino, National City, Cal. (Cal. Southern R. R.).	46037 (part)	¹⁵131.69
Sandusky, Ohio, and Bloomington, Ill.¹⁶	5	379.94	Sandusky, Ohio, Bloomington, Ill. (Lake E. and West.).	21020	379.88
Sandusky and Springfield, Ohio.	5	130.84	Sandusky, Springfield, Ohio (Cin., Sand. and Cleve.).	21012	131.35
Sandusky, Ohio, and Wheeling, W. Va.¹⁹	5	225.78	Sandusky, Newark, Ohio (Balto. and Ohio).	21010	116.79
			Newark, Bellaire, Ohio (Cent. Ohio)	²²21001 (part)	(²³)
			Bellaire, Ohio, Benwood Junction, W. Va. (Balto. and Ohio).	10003	(²⁴)
			Benwood Junction, Wheeling, W. Va. (Balto. and Ohio).	12015	(²⁵)
San Francisco and Los Angeles, Cal.	8	482.71	San Francisco, Port Costa, Cal. (Central Pacific).	46001 (part)	(²⁶)
			Port Costa, Lathrop, Cal. (Southern Pacific).	46032	62.23
			Lathrop, Goshen, Cal. (Southern Pacific).	46010	146.39
			Goshen, Los Angeles, Cal. (Southern Pacific).	46014 (part)	(²⁸)

¹ Distance (10 miles) covered by Chicago, Ill., and Minneapolis, Minn., R. P. O.
² Distance (23.18 miles) covered by Saint Paul, Minn., and Mitchell, Dak., R. P. O.
³ Distance (146.50 miles) covered by Saint Paul, Minn., and Mitchell, Dak., R. P. O.
⁴ Reserve.
⁵ Distance (10.70 miles) covered by Saint Paul, Minn., and Des Moines, Iowa, R. P. O.
⁶ In reserve.
⁷ 5.90 miles covered by Williamsport and Erie R. P. O.
⁸ Cars and clerks shown on route No. 8164.
⁹ 45.60 miles covered by Buffalo and Pittsburgh, R. P. O.

¹⁰ Reported last year as Salina and Lincoln, Kans.; increased distance, 30.95 miles.
¹¹ 1 helper between Salisbury and Hickory, N. C. (58 miles), daily, except Monday.
¹² 41.50 miles covered by the Bristol and Chattanooga R. P. O.
¹³ 37.50 miles of route shown on Ogden and Salt Lake R. P. O. Balance of route (139 15 miles) covered by closed-pouch service. (See Table C', Juab and Frisco.)
¹⁴ New service; not reported last year.
¹⁵ 81 miles of route covered by Albuquerque and Los Angeles R. P. O. Extended from Colton July 28, 1887. Reported last year as Colton and National City.

in the United States on June 30, 1888—Continued.

Average weight of mail while distance per day.	Date of last re-adjustment.	Average speed per hour (train numbers taken from division schedules).				Number of round trips with clerks per week.	Annual miles of service with clerks.	Average miles run daily by crews.	Number of mail cars, or cars in which are mail apartments.	Inside dimensions of cars or apartments (railway post-office cars in black figures).		Number of crews.	Number of clerks to crew.	Number of clerks appointed to line.
		Train No. outward.	Av'ge speed (miles).	Train No. inward.	Av'ge speed (miles).					Length.	Width.			
Lbs.										*Ft. In.*	*Ft. In.*			
26,360	Mar. 9, 1884	1	20.00	4	20.00	6	102,997	153.66	1	25 0	9 3	4	1	4
......	....	1	24.75	4	24.75	......	......	......	1	20 9	8.8			
2,877	July 1, 1887	1	23.75	4	26.24	......	......	......	*1	16 6	6 6			
......	....	101	25.97	104	26.44									
1,963	July 1, 1887	14	20.00	13	20.00	6	148,352	118.11	2	20 0	9 0	4	1	4
976	July 1, 1887	14	22.31	13	21.91	......			*1	15 0	9 3			
639	July 1, 1887	14	26.35	13	26.83									
629	July 1, 1887	29	21.00	28	23.01	6	61,349	97.69	2	14 0	8 6	2	1	2
									*1	16 0	8 6			
379	June 8, 1897	29	17.70	28	17.70	6	......	......	(²)	......		(²)		
1,383	July 1, 1885	29	25.80	28	25.80	6	......	......	(²)	......		(²)		
870	July 1, 1888	277	11.61	278	11.27	6	42,120	67.07	1	5 10	7 2¼	2	1	2
									1	6 1½	7 0			
157	July 1, 1896	271	23.67	272	25.00	7	26,923	73.56	1	10 4½	9 0	1	1	1
1,410	July 1, 1888	52	26.54	53	23.37	7	200,370	136.86	1	20 1	8 6	4	1	[11]5
									1	19 11	8 11			
955	July 1, 1888	43	27.10	44	27.10	......			1	20 2	8 5			
5,833	July 1, 1888	43	31.35	44	31.35									
834	July 1, 1884	3	23.07	4	23.07	7	76,882	105.03	2	20 2	8 5	2	1	2
519	Oct. 3, 1887	6	14.60	5	14.84	6	45,059	143.50	1	7 4	9 4	1	1	1
927	July 1, 1886	5	21.69	6	21.07	7	97,217	132.81	2	11. 0	8 2	2	1	2
681	July 1, 1888	1	24.78	4	24.78	6	238,602	126.65	[17]7	14 0	7 8	6	1	[17]7
1,162	July 1, 1888	3	28.62	4	27.12	6	82,168	87.23	1	15 2	9 0	3	1	3
									1	14 6	9 0			
8,719	July 1, 1888	8	25.44	7	21.90	7	165,271	112.89	[20]3	20 0	9 0	4	2	[11]8
9,294	July 1, 1888	8	19.93	7	28.80	7								
21,912	July 1, 1885	8	8.34	7	11.92	7								
3,288	July 1, 1885	8	5.28	7	5.28	7								
25,702	Aug.15,1888	17	22.97	18	23.82	14	706,687	148.52	8	55 1½	9 5¼	13	1	15
		19	22.97	20	21.73									
5,068	July 1, 1886	17	28.28	18	28.28									
		19	28.28	20	27.41									
5,007	July 1, 1886	17	27.50	18	27.44									
		19	27.86	20	23.94									
3,889	July 1, 1886	17	19.51	18	18.13									
		19	18.36	20	19.81									

[16] This line is in two divisions, dividing at La Fayette, Ind.

[17] 3 cars in reserve.

[18] 4 clerks and 1 helper on East Division, helper running between Sandusky and Lima, Ohio, 19.10 miles; 2 clerks on West Division, running between La Fayette and Bloomington.

[19] Prior to Sept. 20, 1887, this line was known as Sandusky, Newark and Wheeling R. P. O.

[20] 1 car in reserve.

[21] 4 helpers running over whole line.

[22] Balance of route, Newark to Columbus, covered by closed pouches. (See Table C².)

[23] Covered by Grafton and Chicago R. P. O., 104.62 miles.

[24] Distance shown on Grafton and Chicago R. P. O. 1.39 miles; balance covered by lines of Third Division.

[25] Covered by lines in Third Division, 4 miles.

[26] 32 17 miles of route 46001 covered by Ogden and San Francisco R. P. O.; 243.06 miles of route 46014 covered by Deming and Los Angeles R. P. O.; forty-feet cars authorized and are run on trains 17 and 18; apartments on trains 19 and 20 and run to Deming, N. Mex.; cars shown on Deming and Los Angeles R. P. O.; 7 clerks on trains 19 and 18; 6 clerks on trains 17 and 20, 2 helpers on trains 17 and 20; average, daily 129.28 miles.

TABLE A⁸.—*Statement of railway post-offices in operation*

Designation of railway post-offices. (Lines upon which railway post-office cars are paid for, in *italics*.)	Division.	Distance run by clerks, register to register.	Initial and terminal stations, running from east to west, north to south, or northwest to southeast (with abbreviated title of railroad company).	Number of route.	Miles of route for which railroad is paid.
		Miles.			
San Francisco and Santa Cruz, Cal.	8	83.85	San Francisco, Santa Cruz, Cal. (South Pacific Coast Rwy.).	46031	83.10
San Francisco and Templeton, Cal.	8	223.34	San Francisco, Soledad, Cal. (Southern Pacific).	46002	142.96
			Soledad, Templeton, Cal. (Southern Pacific)	46050	78.78
Scottsville, Ky., and Gallatin, Tenn.²	5	35.94	Scottsville, Ky., Gallatin, Tenn. (Chesa. and Nash.).	19026	35.87
Scribner and Oakdale, Nebr ...	6	115.73	Scribner, Oakdale, Nebr. (Fre., Elk. and Mo. Vall.).	34041	115.73
Scranton and Northumberland, Pa.	2	80.48	Scranton, Northumberland, Pa. (D., L. and W.).	8017	80.48
Seaford, Del., and Cambridge, Md.	2	33.64	Seaford, Del., Cambridge, Md. (P., W. and B.).	10068	33.64
*Sedalia, Mo., and Denison, Tex.*⁵	7	433.13	Sedalia, Mo., Denison, Tex. (Mo. Pac.)	28011	433.13
Sedalia and Kansas City, Mo..	7	99.35	Sedalia, Independence, Mo. (Mo. Pac.)....	28033	89.22
			Independence, Kansas City, Mo. (Mo. Pac.)	28001 (part)	(¹⁰)
Sedalia and Warsaw, Mo	7	43.16	Sedalia, Warsaw, Mo. (Mo. Pac.)	28042	43.16
Selma, Ala., and Meridian, Miss.	4	111.28	Selma, Meridian, Miss. (E. T., V. and Ga. R. R.).	17009	114.34
Selma and Pine Apple, Ala. ...	4	47.79	Selma, Pine Apple, Ala. (L. and N. R. R.).	17017	47.80
Shabbona and Sterling, Ill.....	6	47.97	Shabbona, Sterling, Ill. (Chi., Bur. and Q'cy.).	23014	47.97
Sheboygan and Princeton, Wis.	6	79.22	Sheboygan, Princeton, Wis. (Chi. and No. West.).	25019	79.22
Shreveport, La., and Houston, Tex.	7	234.36	Shreveport, Logansport, La. (S. and H.)...	30016	41.72
			Logansport, La., Houston, Tex. (H., E. and W. T.).	31023	192.70
Sidell and Olney, Ills	6	86.31	Sidell, Olney, Ill. (Dan., Olney and O. Riv.).	23006	86.31
Sioux City and Missouri Valley, Iowa.	6	76.10	Sioux City, Missouri Valley, Iowa (S. City and Pac.).	27029	76.27
Sioux City, Iowa, and Omaha, Nebr.	6	124.06	Covington, Omaha, Nebr.(Chi., St. P.,Minn. and Om.).	34003	121.74
Skowhegan and Portland, Me..	1	103.00	Skowhegan, Portland, Me. (Me. Cen.).....	5	102.93
Slatington and Reading, Pa ...	2	43.63	Slatington, Reading, Pa. (P. and R.).......	8089	44.12
Smithville and Blakely, Ga....	4	73.54	Smithville, Albany, Ga. (S. W. R. R.)......	15039	24.06
			Albany, Blakely, Ga. (S. W. R. R.)........	15040	50.19
Sodus Point and Stanley, N. Y.	2	34.03	Sodus Point, Stanley, N. Y. (Nor. Centl.) .	6090	33.50
South Amboy, N. J., and Philadelphia, Pa.	2	62.92	South Amboy, Jamesburgh, N. J. (Penna.).	7047	12.63
			Jamesburgh, Camden, N. J. (Penna.)	7006 (part)	¹⁴47.58
South Bend and Terre Haute, Ind.	5	184.30	South Bend, Terre Haute, Ind. (Terre H. and Ind.).	22013	186.49
South Londonderry and Brattleboro, Vt.	1	36.47	South Londonderry, Brattleboro, Vt. (Cen. Vt.).	2016	36.40
Sparta and Tullahoma, Tenn...	5	61.02	Sparta,Tullahoma,Tenn.(Nash., Chatt. and St. Lou.).	19013	62.07
Sparta and Virogua, Wis	6	35.65	Sparta, Virogua, Wis. (Chi., Mil. and St. P.)	25034	35.76
Spartanburgh, S. C., and Augusta, Ga.	4	134.79	Spartanburgh, Greenwood, S. C. (P. R. and W. C. Rwy.).	14021	66.20
			Greenwood, S. C., Augusta, Ga. (P. R. and W. C. Rwy.).	15037	68.30
Springfield and Chadwick, Mo¹⁹	7	35.63	North Springfield (Station A), Chadwick, Mo. (St. L. and S. F.).	28053	35.63

¹ One reserve car; train changes number at Castroville.
² R. P. O. service established January 20, 1888.
³ Double daily service except Sunday.
⁴ In reserve.
⁵ Reported last year as Hannibal, Mo., and Denison, Tex.; decreased distance 141.96 miles.
⁶ Double daily service.
⁷ Service on both lines is performed in five cars,

same being run in the order of first in first out.
⁸ Three helpers on trains 507 and 506 between Sedalia, Mo., and Chotean, Ind. Ter. (244.70 miles) ; 1 clerk detailed as chief clerk, Dallas, Tex.; 1 clerk detailed to transfer service, Sedalia, Mo.
⁹ Three crews perform service on all trains.
¹⁰ 10.38 miles, distance on route No. 28001, covered by Saint Louis and Kansas City, Mo., R. P. O.

in the United States on June 30, 1888—Continued.

Average weight of mail whole distance per day.	Date of last re-adjustment.	Train No. outward.	Av'ge speed (miles).	Train No. inward.	Av'ge speed (miles).	Number of round trips with clerks per week.	Annual miles of service with clerks.	Average miles run daily by crews.	Number of mail car, or cars in which are mail apartments.	Length	Width	Number of crews.	Number of clerks to crew.	Number of clerks appointed to line.
Lbs.										*Ft. In.*	*Ft. In.*			
792	July 1, 1886	7	24.08	8	20.77	6	52,344	166.70	1	11 0	7 6	1	1	1
1,622	July 1, 1886	7	30.55	8	27.08	7	163,485	148.89	[13]	17 0	9 9	3	1	3
		63	30.18	62	31.02									
792	Mar. 7, 1887	63	30.86	62	25.71									
262	July 1, 1888	2	11.92	1	12.78	6	10,063	71.88	1	10 6	6 6	1	1	1
674	July 1, 1888	71	24.64	72	24.21	6	72,678	115.73	2	14 0	9 3	2	1	2
1,449	July 1, 1885	1	25.14	8	24.14	6	50,541	107.30	1	20 6	9 4	2	1	3
		5	25.41	2	24.'14	6	*50,541	....	1	16 2	8 3	1	1	
									41	20 6	9 4			
322	July 1, 1885	501	18.35	512	16.82	6	21,126	67.28	1	10 0	6 0	1		1
12,093	July 1, 1887	501	22.30	506	23.09	7	*317,051	144.38	[13]	50 9	9 2	6	2	*35
		507	22.79	504	22.59	7	317,051	144.38	[12]	50 9	9 1	6	3	
									41	50 9	9 1			
878	July 1, 1887	193	23.39	194	23.70	7	*72,724	*132.47	1	19 9	7 3	3	1	3
		191	23.21	192	24.28	7	72,724	....	1	19 9	7 3			
47,461	July 1, 1887	193	19.44	194	15.57	7								
		191	20.76	192	20.76	7								
277	July 1, 1887	523	12.16	524	12.09	6	27,104	86.32	1	9 3	5 10	1	1	2
605	July 1, 1888	3	24.5	4	22.4	7	81,456	111.28	(11)	....	....	2	1	2
457	July. 1, 1888	49	14.1	50	15	6	30,012	95.58	1	7 9	6 4	1	1	1
576	July 1, 1887	79	23.98	78	23.94	6	30,125	95.94	1	7 8	6 11	1	1	1
									13	12 0	6 7½			
1,383	July 1, 1885	63	19.80	62	20.05	6	49,750	79.22	1	12 8	8 0	2	1	2
174	July 1, 1886	2	18.43	1	19.51	7	171,478	117.13	[18] { 1	14 0	7 6	4	1	4
									1	13 4	7 5			
297	July 1, 1886	2	16.23	1	16.77	7	....	....	1	13 8	7 5			
....	....	1	10	2	10	6	54,202	86.31	2	8 0	7 0	2	1	2
7,209	July 1, 1887	2	26.82	1	27.63	7	55,705	76.10	1	17 9	9 3	2	1	2
587	July 1, 1883	1	23.05	2	23.80	6	77,909	124.06	2	22 2	9 4	2	1	2
1,521	Feb. 11, 1885	12	23.55	13	25	6	64,684	110.92	1	44 0	8 10	2	1	2
									1	42 0	8 9			
									14 1	41 0	8 8			
207	July 1, 1885	2	26.65	3	26.81	6	27,400	87.26	1	8 0	6 8	1	1	1
2,587	July 1, 1888	43	21.8	44	23.5	6	46,183	147.08	1	15 2	8 4	1	1	1
297	July 1, 1888	43	14.1	44	14.1									
127	July 1, 1885	26	25.51	23	17.00	6	21,371	68.06	1	16 0	8 0	1	1	1
852	July 1, 1888	315	24.20	318	24.04	6	39,514	125.84	1	15 0	8 6	1	1	2
		339	24.78	306	28.20	6	*39,514	....	1	15 0	9 3	1		
969	July 1, 1885	315	26.92	318	21.79	6			(16)	....	....	(16)		
		339	25.48	306	21.15	6								
519	July 1, 1888	53	24.60	52	25.80	6	115,740	122.87	3	16 0	9 3	3	1	3
									41	11 0	7 2			
325	Aug. 5, 1885	1	12.34	2	12.34	6	22,903	72.94	1	8 5	5 6	1	1	1
									17 1	10 2	5 8			
487	July 1, 1888	72	20.28	71	19.20	6	38,321	122.04	1	11 0	8 0	1	1	1
397	July 1, 1887	53	24.70	52	24.70	6	22,388	71.30	1	11 10	7 6	1	1	1
344	July 1, 1888	68	24.3	67	21.9	7	98,615	134.72	1	11 1	8 9	2	1	2
									1	12 0	8 6			
									1	10 4	7 0			
520	July 1, 1888	68	20.8	67	20.8	....	....	....	(19)	....	....			
219	July 1, 1887	43	11.77	44	10.32	7	26,081	71.26	1	12 6	9 1	1	1	1

[11] See Cleveland and Selma R. P. O.
[12] Reserve.
[13] One car is held in reserve alternately each day in Houston, Tex.
[14] Reserve car; the North Anson and Portland clerk runs between Oakland and Portland with Skowhegan and Portland clerk as assistant; the Augusta and Portland clerk runs in connection with this R. P. O.

[15] 6.10 miles covered by Monmouth Junction and Manasquan R. P. O.
[16] Cars, 1; clerks shown on route No. 7047.
[17] Reserve car.
[18] 1 reserve car.
[19] Reported last year as North Springfield and Chadwick, Mo.

TABLE A⁸.—*Statement of railway post-offices in operation*

Designation of railway post-office. (Lines upon which railway post-office cars are paid for, in *italics*.)	Division.	Distance run by clerks, register to register.	Initial and terminal stations, running from east to west, north to south, or northwest to southeast (with abbreviated title of railroad company).	Number of route.	Miles of route for which railroad is paid.
		Miles.			
Springfield and Grafton, Ill....	6	85.30	Springfield, Grafton, Ill. (St. L. and Cent. Ill.)	23063	85.30
Springfield, Mass., and Hartford, Conn.	1	32.29	Springfield, Mass., and Hartford, Conn. (N. and N. Eng.).	5016	32.60
Springfield and Litchfield, Ill..	6	45.52	Springfield, Litchfield, Ill. (Chi. and St. Louis).	23093	45.64
Springfield and Richmond, Ind.²	5	77.40	Springfield, Xenia, Ohio (Pitts., Cin. and St. Louis).	21027	19.99
			Xenia, Dayton, Ohio (Pitts., Cin. and St. Louis).	21011	16.77
			Dayton, Ohio, Richmond, Ind. (Pitts., Cin. and St. Louis).	21030	42.13
Springfield and Wellston, Ohio.	5	118.43	Springfield, Wellston, Ohio (Ohio Sou.)	21058	118.89
State Line and Rhinecliff, N.Y.	2	42.53	State Line, Rhinecliff, N.Y. (H. and C. W.).	5018 (part)	³39.82
Sterling and Rock Island, Ill...	6	52.43	Sterling. Barstow, Ill. (Chi., Bur. and Qcy.)	23064	40.75
			Barstow, Rock Island, Ill. (Chi., Bur. and Qcy.).	23005 (part)	(⁵)
Stevens Point and Portage, Wis.	6	73.84	Stevens Point, Portage, Wis. (Wis. Cent.).	25015	74.13
Stoneboro and New Castle, Pa.	2	36.49	Stoneboro, New Castle, Pa. (W.N. Y. and Pa.).	8096	35.33
Streator and Fairbury, Ill	6	31.98	Streator, Fairbury, Ill. (Wabash)..........	28043	32.05
Streator and Pekin, Ill.........	6	65.06	Streator, Ancona, Ill. (Chi., S. Fé and Cal.).	23098 (part)	(⁶)
			Ancona, Pekin, Ill. (Chi., S. Fé and Cal.)...	23051	57.50
Sumner and Hampton, Iowa...	6	65.33	Sumner, Hampton, Iowa (Chi., St. P. and K. City).	27051	64.08
Sunbury and Lewistown, Pa...	2	51.12	Sunbury, Selins Grove Junction, Pa. (Nor. Cent.).	10002 (part)	(⁷)
			Selins Grove Junction, Lewistown, Pa. (Pa.).	8108	44.60
Suspension Bridge and Buffalo, N.Y.	2	24.25	Suspension Bridge, Buffalo, N.Y. (N.Y. C. and H. R.).	6016 (part)	⁸24.73
Switz City, Ind., and Effingham, Ill.	6	90.56	Switz City, Ind., Effingham, Ill. (Ind. and Ill. So.).	23026	90.97
Syracuse, Auburn, and Rochester, N.Y.	2	104.71	Syracuse, Rochester, N.Y. (N.Y. C. and H. R.).	6013	(¹²)
Syracuse and Earlville, N.Y..	2	43.66	Syracuse, Earlville, N.Y. (S., O. and N. Y.).	6071	44.30
Tama and Hawarden, Iowa ...	6	243.34	Tama, Eagle Grove, Iowa (Chi. and No. West.).	¹⁴27052 (part)	98.34
			Eagle Grove, Hawarden, Iowa (Chi. and No. West.).	¹⁴27070	145.30
Tamaroa and Chester, Ill......	6	42.79	Tamaroa, Chester, Ill. (Tam., Ches. and Western).	23047	42.90
Taylor and La Grange, Texas¹⁰.	7	70.02	Taylor, La Grange, Texas (T., B. and H.)..	31056	70.02
Taylorsville and Charlotte, N. C.	3	65.69	Taylorsville Charlotte, N. C. (Rich. and Dan.)	13009	65.69
Temple and Ballinger, Tex....	7	191.41	Temple Ballinger, Tex. (G., C. and S. F.)..	31049	191.41
Tennille and Dublin, Ga.......	4	35.25	Tennille, Wrightsville, Ga. (W. and T. R. R.).	15015	16.50
			Wrightsville, Dublin, Ga. (W. and D. R. R.).	15049	19.56
Terre Haute and Evansville, Ind.	5	110.41	Terre Haute, Evansville, Ind. (Evans. and Terre H.).	22012	109.71
Terre Haute, Ind. and Peoria, Ill.	6	176.90	Terre Haute, Ind., Peoria, Ill. (Ill. Mid.)..	23048	177.60

¹ Reserve.
² Run of clerk on Xenia and Richmond R. P. O. extended to Springfield, Ohio, April 5, 1888, increasing distance 19.99 miles.
³ 70.93 miles covered by Hartford and Millerton R. P. O.
⁴ In reserve.
⁵ Distance (11.60 miles) covered by Rock Island, Ill., and Saint Louis, Mo., R. P. O.

⁶ Distance (6.10 miles) covered by Chicago, Ill., and Fort Madison, Iowa, R. P. O.
⁷ 4.90 miles covered by Williamsport and Baltimore R. P. O.
⁸ Cars and clerks shown on route No. 10002.
⁹ 4.75 covered by closed-pouch service. (See Table C⁸.)
¹⁰ Service performed in baggage-car.

in the United States on June 30, 1888—Continued.

Average weight of mail whole distance per day.	Date of last re-adjustment.	Average speed per hour (train numbers taken from division schedules).				Number of round trips with clerks per week.	Annual miles of service with clerks.	Average miles run daily by crew.	Number of mail cars, or cars in which are mail apartments.	Inside dimensions of cars or apartments (railway post-office cars in black figures).		Number of crews.	Number of clerks to crew.	Number of clerks assigned to line.
		Train No. outward.	A'ge speed (miles).	Train No. inward.	A'ge speed (miles).					Length.	Width.			
Lbs.										Ft. In.	Ft. In.			
272	July 1, 1887	1	13. 60	4	13. 60	6	53, 568	85. 30	1	11 0	6 10	2	1	2
511	July 1, 1885	141	22. 23	142	22. 23	6	20, 278	129. 16	1	11 0	6 6	1	1	1
		143	22. 23	144	22. 23	6	20, 278							
282	May 17, 1886	1	25. 71	2	25. 71	6	28, 586	91. 04	1	20 6	9 2	1	1	1
									11	19 11	8 10½			
957	July 1, 1888	7	23. 94	6	21. 78	6	39, 501	154. 80	1	20 0	9 0	1	1	1
2, 229	July 1, 1888	7	22. 38	6	20. 10	6								
2, 581	July 1, 1888	7	28. 07	6	25. 26	6								
343	July 1, 1888	2	20. 64	1	19. 82	6	74, 374	115. 43	1	12 0	7 0	2	1	2
									1	8 10	8 0			
1, 101	July 1, 1885	9	16. 25	8	14. 80	6	26, 709	85. 06	1	10 6	6 0	1	1	1
									41	10 6	6 6			
382	July 1, 1887	36	20. 49	35	24. 00	6	32, 926	101. 86	1	11 4	6 7½	1	1	1
2, 233	July 1, 1887	21	17. 40	22	19. 89				11	12 0	6 7½			
810	July 1, 1887	50	22. 78	49	24. 33	6	46, 371	147. 68	1	20 8	9 5	1	1	1
									12	15 0	7 8			
833	July 1, 1885	1	21. 25	2	18. 30	6	22, 916	72. 98	1	15 0	8 6	1	1	1
106	July 1, 1887	251	18. 30	252	18. 28	6	20, 083	63. 96	1	12 2½	7 7½	1	1	1
		101	24. 40	102	18. 30		40, 857	130. 12	1	26 8	9 4	1	1	1
		101	24. 43	102	24. 43									
436	July 1, 1887	24	11. 64	23	14. 22	6	41, 027	130. 66	1	13 5	7 7	1	1	1
11, 378	July 1, 1885	3	24. 50	2	24. 50	6	32, 103	102. 24	1	6 2	6 2	1	1	1
169	July 1, 1885	3	22. 45	2	24. 77	6			(9)			(9)		
8, 079	July 1, 1885	16	27. 00	19	27. 00	6	15, 292	97. 40	(10)			1	1	(11)
		54	29. 67	51	29. 67	6	12 15, 292							
211	July 1, 1887	1	14. 60	2	14. 51	6	56, 884	181. 16	1	17 0	7 7½	1	1	1
4, 375	July 1, 1885	11	23. 70	14	23. 27	6	65. 758	104. 71	1	19 10	8 10	2	2	4
848	July 1, 1885	1	24. 94	6	24. 94	6	27, 418	87. 32	1	9 1	8 6	1	1	1
									41	9 1	8 6			
1, 338	July 1, 1887	5	22. 61	6	21. 78	6	152, 817	121. 67	2	24 0	9 3	4	1	4
1, 673	July 1, 1887	5	27. 19	6	26. 36									
568	July 1, 1887	2	15. 27	3	18. 00	6	26, 872	85. 58	1	14 0	6 0	1	1	1
306	July 1, 1888	571	8. 73	572	8. 73	7	51, 255	70. 02	2	16 5	6 11	2	1	17 1
394	July 1, 1888	18	17. 90	17	17. 51	6	41, 253	131. 38	1	9 10	7 4	1	1	1
632	July 1, 1886	11	22. 06	12	22. 93	7	140, 112	127. 61	2	13 6	9 0	3	1	3
									41	11 3½	6 10½			
53	May 1, 1885	3	13. 00	4	13. 50	6	22, 137	70. 50	1	8 0	9 0	1	1	1
279	July 1, 1888	3	13. 00	4	13. 50									
3, 118	July 1, 1888	1	25. 32	2	27. 43	6	69, 337	147. 21	182	16 0	9 0	3	1	18 4
		3	24. 54	4	27. 43	20 7	17, 886		1	24 0	8 4			
399	July 1, 1887	1	21. 45	2	22. 12	6	111, 093	117. 93	3	17 9	7 2	3	1	17 4

11 Clerk accounted for in New York and Rochester R. P. O.
12 Double daily service except Sunday.
13 104 miles covered by New York and Rochester R. P. O.
14 Balance of route (66.30 miles) covered by Lake Crystal, Minn., and Eagle Grove, Iowa, R. P. O.
15 Balance of route (126.37 miles) covered by Oakes, Dak., and Hawarden, Iowa, R. P. O.

16 New service; not reported last year.
17 1 acting clerk additional.
18 1 car in reserve.
19 1 clerk detailed to transfer duty at Evansville, Ind.
20 Service established on night trains April 11, 1888.
21 1 clerk detailed to transfer duty at Peoria, Ill.

TABLE A⁹.—*Statement of railway post-offices in operation*

Designation of railway post-offices. (Lines upon which railway post-office cars are paid for, if *italics*.)	Division.	Distance run by clerks, register to register.	Initial and terminal stations, running from east to west, north to south, or northwest to southeast (with abbreviated title of railroad company).	Number of route.	Miles of route for which railroad is paid.
		Miles.			
Terre Haute, Worthington, and Evansville, Ind.	5	139. 51	Terre Haute, Worthington, Ind. (Evans. and Ind.).	22030	40. 98
			Worthington, Evansville, Ind. (Evans. and Ind.).	22026	98. 30
Texarkana, Ark., and El Paso, Tex.[1]	7	869. 22	Texarkana, Ark., Marshall, Tex. (Tex. and Pac.).	⁸31010	69. 64
			Marshall, El Paso, Tex. (Tex. and Pac.).	⁴31009 (part)	794. 28
Texarkana, Ark., and Gatesville, Tex.[2]	7	305. 39	Texarkana, Ark., Gatesville, Tex. (St. L., Ark. and Tex).	31025	305. 39
Texarkana, Ark., and Houston, Tex.	7	330. 49	Texarkana, Ark., Marshall, Tex. (Tex. and Pac.).	31010	(⁵)
			Marshall, Longview, Tex. (Tex. and Pac.)..	31009 (part)	(¹²)
			Longview, Houston, Tex. (I. and G. N.)....	31006	233. 45
Texarkana, Ark., and Whitesborough, Tex.	7	173. 74	Texarkana, Ark., Whitesborough, Tex. (Tex. and Pac.).	31011	173. 44
Titusville and Sanford, Fla....	4	47.00	Titusville, Enterprise Junction (n. o.), Fla.	16025	40. 42
			Enterprise Junction (n. o.), Sanford, Fla ...	16018	(¹³)
Toccoa and Elberton, Ga.......	4	51. 45	Toccoa, Elberton, Ga. (R. and D. R. R.)...	15026	51. 45
Toledo, Ohio, and Allegan, Mich.	9	157.42	Toledo, Ohio, Allegan, Mich. (C., J. and M.)	24019	156. 92
Toledo, Ohio, and Chicago, Ill..	9	244. 99	Toledo, Ohio, Chicago, Ill. (L. S. and M. S.)	21095 (part)	(¹⁶)
Toledo and Cincinnati, Ohio....	5	203. 27	Toledo, Dayton, Ohio (Day. and Mich.)....	21023	142. 38
			Dayton, Cincinnati, Ohio (Cin., Ham. and Day.).	21026	59. 38
Toledo and Columbus, Ohio....	5	125. 59	Toledo, Columbus, Ohio (Cols., H. V. and Tol).	21053	124. 57
Toledo and Corning, Ohio ²¹....	5	185. 09	Toledo, Thurston, Ohio (Tol. and Ohio Cent.).	21055	147. 87
			Thurston, Corning, Ohio (Tol. and Ohio Cent.).	²²21068 (part)	36. 47
Toledo and Findlay, Ohio......	5	45. 87	Toledo, Findlay, Ohio (Tol., Col. and Sou.).	21091	44. 02
Toledo, Ohio, and Frankfort, Ind.	5	207. 17	Toledo, Delphos, Ohio (Tol., St. Lou. and K. C.).	21061	74. 10
			Delphos, Ohio, Kokomo, Ind. (Tol., St. Lou. and K. C.).	21065	108. 02
			Kokomo, Frankfort, Ind. (Tol., St. Lou. and K. C.).	22033	25. 70
Topeka and Fort Scott, Kans..	7	130. 79	Topeka, Fort Scott, Kans. (K., N. and D.)	33060	130. 79
Toledo, Ohio, and La Fayette, Ind.	5	204. 56	Toledo, Ohio, La Fayette, Ind. (Wab., St. Lou. and Pac.).	21019 (part)	(³⁶)
Toledo and Mansfield, Ohio....	5	87. 16	Toledo, Mansfield, Ohio (Penna. Co.).......	21043	86. 20
Toledo and Marietta, Ohio....	5	263. 25	Toledo, Zoar Station, Ohio (Wheel. and Lake Erie).	²⁷21080 (part)	155. 06
			Zoar Station, Marietta, Ohio (Cleve. and Mar.).	21040	105. 72

[1] Service on trains 3 and 4 between Texarkana, Ark., and El Paso, Tex., and on 1 and 2 between Texarkana, Ark. and Fort Worth, Tex., making double daily service between Texarkana, Ark., and Fort Worth, Tex. (254.17 miles). Runs of clerks on trains 3 and 4 divided at Dallas, Tex., East Division, Texarkana, Ark., to Dallas, Tex., 221.83 miles, and West Division, Dallas to El Paso, Tex., 647.39 miles.

[2] Texarkana, Ark., and Houston, Tex., R. P. O., also runs over route 31010 and 23.50 miles of route 31009 between Marshall and Longview, Tex.

[3] Daily average of Texarkana, Ark., and Dallas, Tex., line.

[4] Three helpers on trains 3 and 4 between Texarkana, Ark., and Dallas, Tex. (221.83 miles), and two between Dallas and Cisco, Tex. (147 miles.).

[5] Daily average of Dallas and El Paso, Tex., line.

[6] 40.44 miles, balance of route 31009, between Shreveport, La., and Marshall, Tex., covered by New Orleans, La., and Marshall, Tex., R. P. O.

[7] Trains 3 and 4 between Texarkana, Ark., and Sierra Blanca, Tex., and 131 and 132 between Sierra Blanca and El Paso, Tex.

[8] Daily average of Texarkana, Ark., and Fort Worth, Tex., line.

[9] Reported last year as Texarkana, Ark., and Waco, Tex.; increased distance, 46.64 miles.

[10] Cars shown under Cairo, Ill., and Texarkana, Ark., R. P. O.

in the United States on June 30, 1888—Continued.

Average weight of mail whole distance per day.	Date of last re-adjustment.	Average speed per hour (train numbers taken from division schedules).				Number of round trips with clerks per week.	Annual miles of service with clerks.	Average miles run daily by crews.	Number of mail cars, or cars in which are mail apartments.	Inside dimensions of cars or apartments (railway post-office cars in black figures).		Number of crews.	Number of clerks to crew.	Number of clerks appointed to line.
		Train No. outward.	Av'g speed (miles).	Train No. inward.	Av'g speed (miles).					Length.	Width.			
Lbs.										Ft. In.	Ft. In.			
414	July 1, 1888	9	22.32	10	18.85	6	87,612	139.51	1	8 4	6 4	2	1	2
									1	14 3	9 0			
460	July 1, 1888	9	15.78	10	20.58	6								
10,345	July 1, 1886	3	20.71	4	22.25	7	[11]636,269	[11]110.92	6	21 6	9 4	4	1	[12]21
		1	21.17	2	23.37	7	[11]186,052	[11]161.85	2	21 6	9 4	8	1	
4,211	July 1, 1886	[7]3	22.45	[7]4	21.53	7	....	[8]127.09				4	1	
		[7]132	34.60	[7]131	34.60	7								
		1	30.87	2	22.87	7								
599	July 1, 1886	1	19.87	2	20.31	7	223,545	152.69	([13])	....		4	1	4
10,345	July 1, 1886	5	21.86	6	21.17	7	341,919	132.20	1	21 0	8 10	5	1	5
									1	21 0	9 1			
4,211	July 1, 1886	5	25.80	6	25.80	7								
2,978	July 1, 1886	655	23.20	656	21.93	7								
1,291	July 1, 1886	31	21.40	32	22.57	7	127,178	115.83	2	18 0	7 0	3	1	[18]8
									[14]1	18 0	7 0			
580	Mar.22,1886	100	17.6	103	17.6	6	29,516	94	1	13 3	7 4	1	1	1
2,990	Feb.11,1885	100	17.6	103	17.6	6								
296	July 1, 1888	1	13.3	2	13.6	6	32,310	102.9	1	10 0	4 6	1	1	1
214	Mar.20,1884	2	24.63	1	25.64	6	98,800	157.42	2	10 8	6 4	2	1	2
										12 10	7 2			
98,761	July 1, 1885	25	27.36	22	25.24	6	153,854	122.49	2	20 0	9 2	4	2	([17])
6,648	July 1, 1888	25	24.78	8	25.14	[16]6	127,654	101.63	3	20 0	9 3	4	2	[18]16
		1	25.80	28	25.14	[16]7	143,794	....				4	2	
8,951	July 1, 1888	25	27.60	8	32.34	6								
		1	27.60	28	26.40	7								
1,004	July 1, 1888	4	27.12	3	26.22	6	78,871	125.59	1	15 0	9 8	2	1	2
									1	12 0	7 6			
									3	15 0	9 3			
887	July 1, 1888	2	24.30	1	23.04	6	176,990	123.39	[22]5	20 0	9 4	3	1	3
1,919	July 1, 1888	2	21.88	1	21.88	6								
285	July 1, 1888	2	20.40	1	20.40	6	28,806	91.74	1	9 2	8 0	1	1	1
									[14]1	9 2	6 5			
515	July 1, 1888	1	23.40	2	25.38	6	130,103	103.58	2	20 0	8 6	4	1	4
									[14]1	12 0	5 6			
450	July 1, 1888	1	24	2	25.80	6								
506	July 1, 1888	1	30.42	2	26.58	6								
162	Feb.10, 1887	281	20.58	282	19.21	7	95,738	130.79	2	8 5	7 0	2	1	2
13,486	July 1, 1888	41	31.50	46	32.88	6	128,464	102.28	3	36 0	9 4	4	1	([25])
745	July 1, 1888	12	27.96	1	27.96	6	54,736	87.16	[26]2	20 0	8 7	2	1	2
883	July 1, 1888	5	24.48	6	24.84	6	165,321	131.62	[26]3	15 7	8 10	4	1	4
807	July 1, 1888	3	22.26	2	20.40	6								

[11] Distance on route 31010 covered by Texarkana, Ark., and El Paso, Tex., R. P. O.
[12] 23.50 miles distance on route 31009, covered by Texarkana, Ark., and El Paso, Tex., R. P. O.
[13] 1 clerk detailed to office chief clerk, Dallas, Tex.; 1 clerk on this line is an acting clerk additional.
[14] In reserve.
[15] Reported as Jacksonville and Tampa R. P. O.
[16] Shown in report of New York and Chicago R. P. O.
[17] Clerks appointed to the New York and Chicago R. P. O.
[18] Day line.
[19] 4 helpers on day line running over whole line; 4 helpers on night line running over whole line.

[20] Night line.
[21] April 5, 1888, Toledo and Charleston R. P. O. was curtailed to end at Corning, Ohio.
[22] 3 cars in reserve.
[23] Balance of route (29.56 miles) covered by Zanesville and Columbus R. P. O.
[24] Covered by Toledo and St. Louis R. P. O. (204.70 miles).
[25] These clerks are appointed to Toledo and St. Louis R. P. O. and are shown with that line; 1 car in reserve.
[26] 1 car in reserve.
[27] Closed-pouch service between Zoar Station and Bowerstown, Ohio (16.60 miles). (See Table C[a].)

TABLE A*—*Statement of railway post-offices in operation*

Designation of railway post-office. (Lines upon which railway post-office cars are paid for, in *italics*.)	Division.	Distance run by clerks, register to register.	Initial and terminal stations, running from east to west, north to south, or northwest to southeast (with abbreviated title of railroad company).	Number of route.	Miles of route for which railroad is paid.
		Miles.			
Toledo, Ohio, and Saint Louis, Mo. [1]	5	437.79	Toledo, Ohio, Decatur, Ill. (Wab., St. Lou. and Pgh.).	21019 (part)	*204.70
			Decatur, East St. Louis, Ill. (Wab., St. Lou. and Pgh.).	23023	(*)
Towanda and Bernice, Pa. ...	2	30.72	Towanda, Bernice, Pa. (S. L. and S.)	8060	22.68
Tower City and Lebanon, Pa ..	2	42.26	Tower City, Lebanon. Pa. (P. and R.)	8059	43.49
Townsend, Del., and Centreville, Md.	2	35.21	Townsend, Delaware, Centreville, Md. (P. W. and B.).	10010	35.26
Tracy, Minn., and Pierre, Dak.	6	255.69	Tracy, Minn., Pierre, Dak. (Chi. and No. West).	26031	255.69
Tracy, Minn., and Redfield, Dak.	6	164.14	Tracy, Minn., Redfield, Dak. (Chi. and No. West.).	*26014 (part)	164.14
Tracy City and Cowan, Tenn..	3	20.21	Tracy City, Cowan, Tenn. (Nash., Chat. and St. Louis).	19010	20.25
Trenton and Adrian, Mich. [18] ...	9	49.60	Trenton, Corbus, Mich. (L. S. and M. S.)..	1124086 (part)	43.57
			Corbus, Adrian, Mich. (L. S. and M. S.)....	24002 (part)	(13)
Trenton, Mo., and Leavenworth, Kans. [13]	7	103.56	Trenton, Mo., Leavenworth, Kans. (C., R. I. and P.).	1427017 (part)	69.22
Turkey River and West Union, Iowa.	6	58.34	Turkey River, West Union, Iowa (Chi., Mil. and St. P.).	27039	58.03
Tyler and Lufkin, Tex	7	89.61	Tyler, Lufkin, Tex. (K. and G. S. L.)	31044	89.61
Union City, Ind., and Dayton, Ohio.	5	47.45	Union City, Ind., Dayton, Ohio (Day. and Union).	21022	47.32
Utica and Binghamton, N. Y ..	2	95.70	Utica, Norwich, N. Y. (D. L. and W.).....	6041	53.99
			Norwich, Chenango Forks, N. Y. (D. L. and W.).	6040	30.31
			Chenango Forks, Binghamton, N. Y. (S. B. and N. Y.).	6065 (part)	(19)
Utica and Randallsville, N. Y..	2	31.47	Utica, N. Y. (N. Y., O. and W.)	6057	31.30
Vanceborough and Bangor, Me	1	114.44	Vanceborough, Bangor, Me. (Me. Cen.) ...	12	114.86
Vicksburg, Miss., and Shreveport, La.	4	172.60	Vicksburg, Miss., Shreveport, La..........	30008	172.66
Villisca, Iowa, and Bigelow, Mo.	6	69.24	Villisca, Iowa, Burlington Jct., Mo. (Chi. Bur. and Qcy.).	27009	37.54
			Burlington Jct., Bigelow, Mo. (K. C., St. Jo. and C. Bl.).	28044	32.12
Wabasha and Zumbrota, Minn	6	59.20	West Wabasha, Zumbrota, Minn. (Chi. Mil. and St. P.).	26022	60.29
Wadena, Fergus Falls, Minn...	6	53.36	Wadena, Fergus Falls, Minn. (North Pac.).	3426042 (part)	51.95
Wadesborough, N. C., and Lanes, S. C.	4	114.40	Wadesborough, N. C., Cheraw, S. C. (Ch. and Sal's. R. R.).	14014	26.02
			Cheraw, Florence, S. C. (Ch. and F. R. R.)...	14006	46.82
			Florence, Lanes, S. C. (N. E. R. R. of S. C.) ..	14005	(35)

[1] This line, together with Toledo and La Fayette, La Fayette and Quincy, and Chicago and Decatur, and Saint Louis R. P. O's, form double daily service between Toledo and Saint Louis, Mo.

[2] This is the distance from Toledo, Ohio, to La Fayette, Ind. Whole of route 21019 is Toledo, Ohio, to Quincy, Ill.. 472.37 miles. Toledo and Saint Louis R. P. O. runs over this route between Toledo, Ohio, and Decatur, Ill., 322 10 miles, but only that part of contract route between Toledo, Ohio, and La Fayette, Ind.; distance, 204.70 miles, is shown by this division; balance, 266.62 miles, La Fayette to Quincy, Ill., is covered by La Fayette and Quincy R. P. O. (See Sixth Division Report).

[3] Night line only.

[4] 1 car in reserve.

[5] 1 clerk detailed as chief clerk at Toledo, Ohio; 1 clerk detailed to transfer duty at Fort Wayne, Ind.; 1 clerk detailed to transfer duty at La Fayette, Ind.; 4 clerks in apartment cars between Toledo, Ohio, and La Fayette, Ind.; 2 clerks act as helpers three days in the week each between Toledo, Ohio, and Attica, Ind.; distance 224.50 miles.

[6] Covered by lines of the Sixth Division, 113.66 miles.

[7] Whole car.

[8] Two helpers between Tracy, Minn., and Huron, Dak.

[9] Balance of route (91.23 miles) covered by Winona and Tracy, Minn., R. P. O.

in the United States on June 30, 1888—Continued.

Average weight of mail whole distance per day.	Date of last re-adjustment.	Train No. outward.	Av'ge speed (miles).	Train No. inward.	Av'ge speed (miles).	Number of round trips with clerks per week.	Annual miles of service with clerks.	Average miles run daily by crews.	Number of mail cars, or cars in which are mail apartments.	Inside dimensions of cars or apartments (railway post-office cars in black figures).		Number of crews.	Number of clerks to crew.	Number of clerks appointed to line.
										Length.	Width.			
Lbs.										*Ft. in.*	*Ft. in.*			
13, 480	July 1, 1888	43	19.02	42	19.56	[17]7	320, 462	145.93	[18]3	60 0	9 8	6	5	[10]39
......	....	43	31.02	42	30.72	7								
[10]6	July 1, 1885	11	19.40	14	19.40	6	19, 292	61.44	1	7 11	8 8	1	1	1
218	July 1, 1885	9	18.92	10	25.35	6	26, 539	84.52	1	8 3	6 4	1	1	1
369	July 1, 1885	23	14.08	180	25.76	6	22, 112	70.42	1	11 10	6 8	1	1	1
2, 327	July 1, 1887	1	23.18	2	22.66	7	187, 165	127.84	[12]1	36 0	9 5	4	1	[13]6
										24 0	9 3			
2, 385	Mar. 30, 1887	1, 33	22.62	2, 34	21.60	6	103, 080	109.43	1	14 6	7 6	3	1	3
										16 6	7 0			
										12 0	6 8			
210	July 1, 1888	122	16.20	121	16.20	6	12, 692	40.42	1	12 0	6 8	1	1	1
240	July 1, 1886	121	28.80	120	29.59	6 }	31, 149	99.20	1	13 0	7 0	1	1	1
674	July 1, 1884	121	31.64	120	24.00	6 }								
3, 017	July 1, 1887	11	22.73	12	22.34	7	75, 806	103.56	1	22 4	9 3	2	1	[14]4
454	July 1, 1887	29	18.21	20	16.57	6	36, 637	116.68	1	15 2	7 5	1	1	1
									[16]1	16 8	7 6			
213	July 1, 1886	101	16.88	102	18.65	7	65, 595	89.61	1	16 0	6 4	2	1	2
										16 0	6 4			
312	July 1, 1888	2	27.04	3	27.04	6	29, 799	94.90	[17]1	16 0	6 4	1	1	1
									1	11 8	7 4			
1, 242	July 1, 1885	14	27.00	3	27.00	6	60, 100	100.89	1	16 2	6 10	[19]2	1	2
									[17]1	17 0	8 4			
1, 036	July 1, 1885	14	27.55	3	25.61	6	......	......	(20)	......	(20)			
1, 880	July 1, 1885	14	28.20	3	33.81	6	......	......	(20)	......	(20)			
676	July 1, 1885	2	22.21	13	23.80	6	19, 763	[21]100.89	1	11 11	7 0	1	1	1
		14	24.17	1	24.50	6	[22]15, 179	......	1	12 6	7 2			
6, 599	July 1, 1887	64	24.01	71	25.35	6	71, 868	114.44	2	40 0	9 0	2	2	8
		2	24.45	19	23.60	6	71, 868	......	1	20 0	8 6	2	2	
									1	28 0	9 6			
882	July 1, 1886	1	18.6	2	18.6	7	127, 363	116.00	(23)	......		3	1	3
555	July 1, 1887	81	24.66	82	22.68	6	43, 482	138.48	1	17 5	9 0	1	1	1
308	July 1, 1883	14	24.00	13	21.33	6								
310	July 1, 1887	1	17.56	2	18.46	6	37, 177	118.40	1	10 5	6 7	1	1	1
289	July 1, 1887	33	20.80	34	20.00	6	83, 510	106.72	1	23 9	8 11	1	1	1
349	July 1, 1888	65	16.4	64	15.8	6	71, 843	114.4	1	12 6	8 5	2	1	2
476	July 1, 1888	65	22.9	64	23.00									
12, 822	July 1, 1888	63	29.2	64	30.7									

10 Runs on route 24002, Corbus to Adrian, Mich. (12.80 miles).

11 Balance of route (24.83 miles) covered by Adrian and Fayette R. P. O.

12 Shown in report of Monroe and Adrian R. P. O.

13 Trenton, Mo., and Leavenworth, Kans., R. P. O. is additional to Davenport, Iowa, and Atchison, Kans., R. P. O., between Trenton and Altamont (n. o.), Mo. (33.40 miles).

14 269.55 miles of route 27017, between Davenport, Iowa, and Altamont (n. o.), Mo., covered by Davenport, Iowa, and Atchison, Kans., R. P. O.

1 Two helpers between Trenton and Atchison Junction, Mo. (80.80 miles.) These helpers also perform service on Atchison Junction, Mo., and Atchison, Kans., R. P. O.

16 Reserve.

17 In reserve.

18 Alternates with Utica and Randallsville clerk.

19 11.27 miles covered by Oswego and Binghamton R. P. O.

20 Cars and clerks shown on route No. 6041.

21 Alternates with Utica and Binghamton clerk.

22 On trains 1 and 14 the clerk does not run beyond Bouckville (24. 17 miles); double daily service, except Sunday.

23 See Meridian and Vicksburg, R. P. O.

24 Balance of route (67.36 miles) covered by closed pouches. (See Fergus Falls, Minn., and Milnor, Dak., Table C*.)

25 Reported as Wilmington and Jacksonville R. P. O.

TABLE A⁹.—*Statement of railway post-offices in operation*

Designation of railway post-office. (Lines upon which railway post-office cars are paid for, in *italics*.	Division.	Distance run by clerks, register to register.	Initial and terminal stations, running from east to west, north to south, or northwest to southeast (with abbreviated title of railroad company).	Number of route.	Miles of route for which railroad is paid.
		Miles.			
Waldo and Cedar Keys, Fla....	4	71.00	Waldo, Cedar Keys, Fla. (F. R. and N. C.)..	16001	71.00 [¹(part)]
Wallis and San Antonio, Tex.².	7	200.58	Wallis Station, Kenedy, Tex. (S. A. and A. P.).	31057	133.02
			Kenedy Depot, I. and G. N. R. R., San Antonio, Tex. (S. A. and A. P.).	²³31033 (part)	67.56
Washington, D. C., and Charlotte, N. C.	3	382.04	Washington, D. C., Alexandria, Va. (Alex. and Wash.).	11018	7.42
			Alexandria, Lynchburgh, Va. (Rich. and Dan.).	11002	166.40
			Lynchburgh, Danville Junction (n. o.), Va. (Rich. and Dan.).	11016	65.72
			Danville Junction (n. o.), Charlotte, N. C. (Rich. and Dan.)	11038	143.21
Washington, D. C., and Charlotte, N. C. (short run).	3	172.98	Washington, D. C., Alexandria, Va. (Alex. and Wash.).	11018	(⁵)
			Alexandria, Lynchburgh, Va. (Rich. and Dan.).	11002	(⁶)
Washington and Knoxville, Iowa.	6	77.94	Washington, Knoxville, Iowa (Chi., R. Isl'd and Pac.).	27016	78.78
Washington, D. C., and Round Hill, Va.	3	53.35	Washington, D. C., Alexandria Junction, (n. o.) Va., (Alex. and Wash.).	11018, (part)	(⁹)
			Alexandria Junction (n. o.), Round Hill, Va. (Rich. and Dan.).	11004 (part)	48.40
Washington, D. C., and Strasburgh, Va.	3	93.55	Washington, D. C., Alexandria, Va. (Alex. and Wash.).	11018 (part)	(¹¹)
			Alexandria, Manassas, Va. (Rich. and Dan.).	11002 (part)	(¹²)
			Manassas, Strasburgh, Va. (Rich. and Dan.).	11003	62.93
Washington, D. C., and Wilmington, N. C.	3	362.38	Washington, D. C., Richmond, Va. (A. and W., and R., F. and P.)	11001	115.90
			Richmond, Petersburgh, Va. (R. and P.) ..	11008	23.39
			Petersburgh, Va., Weldon, N. C. (Petersburgh).	11009	64.00
			Weldon, Wilmington, N. C. (W. and W.)..	13002	162.07
Washington, D. C., and Wilmington, N. C. (short run).	3	116.93	Washington, D. C., Richmond, Va. (A. and W., and R., F. and P.).	11001	(¹⁴)
Watertown and Madison, Wis.	6	38.97	Watertown, Madison, Wis. (Chi. Mil. and St. Paul.).	25005	38.97
Watertown and Utica, N. Y.¹⁰..	2	91.93	Watertown, Utica, N. Y. (R., W. and O.) .	6087	91.77
Waycross, Ga., and Chattahoochee, Fla.	4	164.21	Waycross, Thomasville, Ga. (S. F. and W. Rwy.).	²¹15018 (part)	104.19
			Thomasville, Climax, Ga. (S. F. and W. Rwy.).	²²15031 (part)	27.59
			Climax, Ga., Chattahoochee, Fla. (S. F. and W. Rwy.).	15044	32.17
Wells River and Montpelier, Vt.	1	38.64	Wells River, Montpelier, Vt. (Mont. W. Riv.).	2012	38.85
Wellsville and Bellaire, Ohio²³.	5	46.96	Wellsville, Bellaire, Ohio (Penna. Co.).....	²⁴21003 (part).	46.59

¹ 84.15 miles reported as Fernandina and Orlando R. P. O.

² New service; that portion of line between Kenedy and San Antonio, Tex., reported last year under head of San Antonio and Corpus Christi, Tex., R. P. O.

³ 88.50 miles of route 31033, between Kenedy and Corpus Christi, Tex., covered by Kenedy and Corpus Christi, Tex., R. P. O.

2 of each in reserve.
chief clerk as examiner; 3 detailed to office superintendent third division; 1 transfer clerk, Charlottesville, Va.; 3 to short run, Washington, D. C., to Lynchburgh, Va.; 4 helpers on trains 52 and 53, Washington, D. C., to Charlottesville, Va., daily (113.42 miles).

⁶ 7.42 miles covered by the Washington and Charlotte R. P. O.

⁷ Washington and Charlotte short run. Clerks shown on that line.

⁸ 166.40 miles covered by the Washington and Charlotte R. P. O.

⁹ 4.80 miles covered by the Washington and Charlotte R. P. O.

¹⁰ 1 in reserve.

¹¹ 7.42 miles covered by the Washington and Charlotte R. P. O.

¹² 25.60 miles covered by the Washington and Charlotte R. P. O.

¹³ 1 chief clerk, office superintendent third division; 1 chief clerk Washington, D. C.; 5 detailed to office of General Superintendent R.

in the United States on June 30, 1888—Continued.

Average weight of mail whole distance per day.	Date of last re-adjust-ment.	Average speed per hour (train numbers taken from division schedules).				Number of round trips with clerks per week.	Annual miles of service with clerks.	Average miles run daily by crews.	Number of mail cars, or cars in which are mail apartments.	Inside dimensions of cars or apartments (railway post-office cars in black figures).		Number of crews.	Number of clerks to crew.	Number of clerks appointed to line.
		Train No. outward.	Av'ge speed (miles).	Train No. inward.	Av'ge speed (miles).					Length.	Width.			
Lbs.										*Ft. In.*	*Ft. In.*			
1, 046	July 1, 1884	21	16. 9	22	15. 2	7	51, 972	142	1	9 10	6 10	1	1	1
425	Feb.22, 1888	2	21. 68	1	21. 68	7	146, 825	133. 72	2	14 0	9 0	3	1	3
837	July 1, 1886	2	25. 74	1	25. 74	7								
21, 616	July 1, 1885	50	17. 12	53	22. 02	7	279, 658	121. 34	46	50 0	8 9	6	3	448
		52	17. 80	51	22. 02	7	279, 653	....	46	60 0	9 0	6	3	
21, 333	July 1, 1885	50	28. 00	53	29. 24									
		52	29. 24	51	25. 94									
14, 964	July 1, 1887	50	24. 31	53	26. 89									
		52	23. 10	51	25. 48									
14, 436	July 1, 1885	50	28. 00	58	30. 00									
		52	30. 98	51	29. 65									
21, 616	July 1, 1885	58	17. 80	59	22. 02	7	126, 621	115. 33	2	41 2	8 10	3	1	(7)
21, 338	July 1, 1885	58	27. 23	59	27. 75									
703	July 1, 1887	5	23. 40	6	21. 27	6	48, 946	155. 88	1	22 6	9 4	1	1	1
21, 616	July 1, 1885	141	19. 12	142	19. 12	6	33, 503	106. 70	102	16 0	6 2	1	1	1
573	July 1, 1885	141	21. 71	142	19. 40									
21, 606	July 1, 1885	56	16. 32	57	22. 66	6	58, 749	93. 55	1	12 9	6 9	2	1	2
21, 308	July 1, 1885	56	27. 92	57	21. 94									
528	July 1, 1885	56	22. 86	57	23. 31									
19, 326	July 1, 1885	23	24. 92	78	26. 89	7	265, 262	144. 95	8	50 0	8 9	5	2	1844
		27	30. 00	14	28. 99	7	265, 262	....				5	2	
14, 840	July 1, 1885	23	28. 93	78	28. 75									
		27	35. 38	14	32. 18									
13, 596	July 1, 1885	23	31. 01	78	28. 14									
		27	34. 85	14	30. 67									
15, 606	July 1, 1888	23	28. 90	78	28. 47									
		27	38. 42	14	36. 54									
19, 326	July 1, 1885	15	24. 40	(15)	.....	146	36, 716	116. 98	(17)	....	....	2	2	(17)
1, 267	July 1, 1887	23	21. 11	24	29. 23	6	24, 473	155. 88	1	11 0	7 6	1	1	101
		27	21. 71	28	26. 82	6	24, 473							
1, 074	July 1, 1885	202	26. 51	205	24. 51	6	57, 732	151. 14	1	20 0	7 2	1	1	(20)
1, 074	July 1, 1884	7	31. 5	8	32. 00	7	120, 201	109. 47	1	27 4	9 2	3	1	2
									1	17 4	9 2			
884	July 1, 1884	7	27. 00	8	29. 00									
957	July 1, 1888	7	24. 9	8	30. 00									
697	July 1, 1885	56	24. 12	1	25. 46	6	24, 266	77. 28	1	12 0	6 7	1	1	1
5, 936	July 1, 1888	53	21. 60	38	21. 60	346	47, 358	93. 72	2	19 9	8 11	2	1	2
		37	22. 38	40	23. 30	346	11, 902							

M. S. ; 2 to office superintendent third division ; 2 transfer clerks, Washington, D. C. ; 1 transfer clerk Richmond, Va. ; 4 helpers on trains 23 and 78 Washington, D. C., to Richmond, Va., daily, (116.93 miles) ; 4 helpers on trains 27 and 14, 2 to Richmond and 2 to Peters-burgh, Va. (140.32 miles) ; 4 to short run, Washington, D. C., to Richmond, Va.

[14] 116.93 miles shown on through run.
[15] Clerks on train 15 return to Washington on train 14 daily, except Sunday.
[16] Half trips.
[17] Short run of Washington and Wilmington R. P. O. cars and clerks shown on that line.
[18] Clerk doubles the route twice daily each way.

[19] Short run, Ogdensburgh and Utica R. P. O.
[20] Clerk accounted for on Ogdensburgh and Utica R. P. O.
[21] 58.92 miles reported as Albany and Thomasville R. P. O.
[22] 9.40 miles, Climax to Bainbridge, closed pouches. (See Table C.º)
[23] February 4, 1888, the run of Pittsburgh and Bellaire R. P. O. clerks was curtailed to end at Wellsville, Ohio.
[24] Balance of route (48.20 miles) covered by Cleveland and Pittsburgh R. P. O. (See that line.)
[25] Clerks make two round trips daily, except Sunday.

TABLE A⁰.—*Statement of railway post-offices in operation*

Designation of railway post-office. (Lines upon which railway post-office cars are paid for, in *italics*.)	Division	Distance run by clerks, register to register.	Initial and terminal stations, running from east to west, north to south, or northwest to southeast (with abbreviated title of railroad company).	Number of route.	Miles of route for which railroad is paid.
		Miles.			
Wellsville, N. Y., and Bradford, Pa.	2	56.65	Wellsville, N. Y., Eldred, Pa. (B., E. and C.).	6049	32.18
			Eldred, Kinsua Junc., Pa. (B., B and K.).	8133	14.25
			Kinsua Junc., Bradford, Pa. (B., B. and K.).	8132 (part)	³10.34
West Lebanon, Ind., and Rantoul, Ill.	6	41.82	West Lebanon, Ind., Rantoul, Ill. (Ill. Central).	⁴29058 (part)	41.82
West Liberty and Council Bluffs, Iowa.	6	279.96	West Liberty, U. P. Transfer, Iowa (Chi., R. Isl'd and Pac.).	⁵27014 (part)	279.10
West Point and Richmond, Va..	3	39.07	West Point, Richmond, Va. (Rich. and Dan).	11007	38.72
West Point and Yoakum, Tex¹⁰.	7	50.20	West Point, Yoakum, Tex. (S. A. and A. P.).	31062	50.20
West Winstead and Bridgeport, Conn.	1	62.22	Winsted, Bridgeport, Conn. (Naugatuck) ..	5011	62.29
Wheeling and Huntington, W. Va.	3	216.97	Wheeling, Point Pleasant, W. Va. (Ohio River).	12013	172.29
			Point Pleasant, Huntington, W. Va. (Ohio River).	12020	43.32
White Heath and Decatur, Ill..	6	29.70	White Heath, Decatur, Ill. (Ill. Central).	29077	31.96
Whiting, N. J., and Tuckerton, N. J.	2	29.48	Whiting, N. J., and Tuckerton, N. J. (Tuckerton).	7032	29.70
Wichita and Kanopolis, Kans.¹²	7	102.19	Wichita, Hutchinson, Kans. (W. and C.)....	33051	47.26
			Hutchinson, Geneseo, Kans. (S., S. and El P.).	33074	41.84
			Geneseo, Kanopolis, Kans. (K. and K. C.)..	33086	14.76
Wichita and Mullinville, Kans.¹⁷	7	121.58	Wichita, Kingman, Kans. (W. and W.)	33042	46.10
			Kingman, Mullinville, Kans. (K., P. & W.).	33063	75.73
Wilkes Barre and Pottsville, Pa.	2	81.30	Wilkes Barre, Rock Glen Junction, Pa. (Pa.)	8174	39.58
			Rock Glen Junction, Sugar Loaf, Pa. (Pa.).	8015 (part)	(¹⁵)
			Sugar Loaf, Hazleton, Pa. (L. V.)	8016 (part)	(¹⁶)
			Hazleton, New Boston, Pa. (L. V.).........	8169	18.06
			New Boston, Pottsville, Pa. (Pa.)	8175	10.21
Williamsburgh, Mass., and New Haven, Conn.	1	85.59	Williamsburgh, Mass., New Haven, Conn. (Northampton Div. N. Y., N. H. and Hart.).	5010	85.52
Williamsport, Pa., and Baltimore, Md.	2	179.83	Williamsport, Sunbury, Pa. (N. C.)	8006	40.96
			Sunbury, Pa., Baltimore, Md. (N. C.).......	10002	138.01
Williamsport and Erie, Pa.....	2	349.68	Williamsport, Erie, Pa. (Penna.)	8022	348.75
Williamsport and Gassam, Pa .	2	141.34	Williamsport, Jersey Shore, Pa. (Beech Creek).	8150 (part)	(³⁴)
			Jersey Shore, Gassam, Pa. (Beech Creek)..	8112	116.01
Williamsport and Port Clinton, Pa.	2	121.77	Williamsport, Port Clinton, Pa. (P. and R.).	8014	122.07
Williamston and Rocky Mount, N. C.	3	50.46	Williamston, Tarborough, N. C. (Albe. and Raleigh).	12020	32.67
			Tarborough, Rocky Mount., N. C. (Wilm. and Weldon).	12015	17.80
Willimantic and New Haven, Conn.	1	54.69	Willimantic, New Haven, Conn. (N. Y., N. H. and Hart.) (A'r Line Div.)	3614	34.00

¹ In reserve.
² Cars and clerks shown on route No. 6049.
³ 15.84 miles covered by closed-pouch service. (See Table C⁰.).
⁴ Balance of route (33.17 miles) covered by closed pouches. (See Rantoul and Le Roy,,Ill., Table C⁰.).
⁵ Balance of route (88.87 miles) covered by Chicago, Ill. and West Liberty, Iowa, R. P. O.
⁶ Cars run through between Chicago, Ill., and U.

P. Transfer, Iowa. (See Chicago, Ill., and West Liberty, Iowa, R. P. O.
⁷ Day line.
⁸ 1 clerk detailed to transfer duty at Des Moines, Iowa.
⁹ Night line.
¹⁰ New service; not reported last year.
¹¹ 1 clerk detailed on relief on this line, New Haven and New York R. P. O.
¹² Reserve car.

in the United States on June 30, 1888—Continued.

Average weight of mail whole distance per day.	Date of last re-adjustment.	Average speed per hour (train numbers taken from division schedules).				Number of round trips with clerks per week.	Annual miles of service with clerks.	Average miles run daily by crews.	Number of mail cars, or cars in which are mail apartments.	Inside dimensions of cars or apartments (railway post-office cars in black figures).		Number of crews.	Number of clerks to crew.	Number of clerks appointed to line.
		Train No. outward.	Av'ge speed (miles).	Train No. inward.	Av'ge speed (miles).					Length.	Width.			
Lbs.										Ft. In.	Ft. In.			
344	July 1, 1885	2	17.31	3	18.10	6	35,576	113.30	1 [1]	9 10 / 9 7	6 11 / 6 11	1	1	1
389	July 1, 1885	2	17.10	3	19.00	6	......	......	([2])	......	......	([2])		
220	July 1, 1885	2	17.72	3	15.51	6			([2])			([2])		
183	July 1, 1887	1	10.70	2	9.65	6	26,263	83.64	1 / 1	21 8 / 17 9	8 11 / 9 0	1	1	1
6,186	July 1, 1887	3 / 1	23.25 / 24.26	4 / 2	24.61 / 26.00	7 / 7	204,491 / 204,491	139.68 / 139.68	([5])			[7]4 / [4]4	2 / 2	[4]17
438	July 1, 1885	50	22.98	51	24.18	6	24,536	78.14	1	10 6	6 8	1	1	1
89	July 1, 1888	31	13.09	32	13.09	6	31,526	100.46	1	10 2	7 2	1	1	1
1,857	July 1, 1885	305 / 315	23.29 / 23.89	310 / 316	24.05 / 23.59	6 / 6	39,074 / 39,074	96.33 /	1 / 1	15 1 / 15 1	6 10 / 6 10	1	1	[11]3
......	......	1	22.43	4	22.93	6	135,880	108.18	[12]1 / 2 / [1]1	15 4 / 15 9 / 5 10	6 9 / 8 6 / 5 3	4	1	[12]6
......	......	1	23.88	4	22.43									
315	July 1, 1887	3	12.40	4	13.78	6	18,651	59.40	1	10 4	6 10½	1	1	1
292	July 1, 1885	12 / 20	27.63 / 27.63	9 / 17	28.07 / 28.07	6 / 6	[14]18,513 / 18,513	117.92	1	3 0	6 11	1	1	1
359	Nov. 5, 1886	463	23.36	461	23.60	7	74,803	[16]139.20	1	16 7	8 10	[16]1	1	1
483	July 1, 1888	463	22.12	464	23.00	7								
458	July 1, 1888	463	18.64	464	18.64	7	76,352	121.58	1	16 6	7 6	2	1	2
843	July 1, 1886	1	24.78	4	24.37	6								
592	July 1, 1888	1	17.06	4	21.20	6								
234	July 1, 1888	434	24.99	401	25.81	6	51,056	162.60	1	8 0	6 6	1	1	1
242	July 1, 1885	434	24.00	401	23.50	6			([19])			([19])		
645	July 1, 1885	434	24.00	401	23.50	6			([19])			([19])		
265	July 1, 1888	434	18.06	401	21.67	6			([19])			([19])		
263	July 1, 1888	434	17.50	401	22.68	6			([19])			([19])		
1,599	July 1, 1885	651 / 655	25.67 / 26.48	626 / 624	26.59 / 28.75	6 / 6	53,750 / 53,750	114.12 /	1 / 1 / 1 / [12]1	15 4 / 14 10 / 9 9 / 10 6	6 7 / 6 10 / 6 7 / 6 8	3	1	3
1,388	July 1, 1885	4	28.91	3	24.58	6	112,933	119.89	2	40 0	8 4	3	4	[21]14
11,371	July 1, 1885	4	24.71	3	23.65	6			([22]) / [2]1	40 0	8 4	([22])		
1,383	July 1, 1885	3	32.01	4	24.90	6	156,799	124.84	2 / 1 / 1	20 0 / 20 0 / 15 0	10 0 / 10 0 / 9 0	4	1	[23]6
803	July 1, 1885	17	20.16	18	21.06	6	88,762	141.34	[1]1 / [1]1	7 6 / 7 6	6 6 / 6 6	2	1	2
132	July 1, 1885	17	19.17	18	21.41	6	76,472	121.77	([25])			([25])		
376	July 1, 1885	4	21.61	1	22.34	6			[2]1 / [1]1	15 0 / 15 0	8 4 / 8 4	2	1	2
369	July 1, 1888	22	15.83	21	19.80	7	31,689	100.92	1	7 0	6 8	1	1	1
609	July 1, 1888	22	14.50	21	15.67									
3,481	July 1, 1885	507	28.17	500	27.00	6	34,345	109.38	1	10 8	6 10	1	1	1

[13] 2 helpers, Wheeling to Letart, W. Va., 144 miles.
[14] Double daily service except Sunday.
[15] Reported last year as Wichita and Geneseo, Kans.; increased distance 14.47 miles.
[16] Clerk alternates with 1 clerk of the Ellsworth and Wichita, Kans., R. P. O
[17] Reported last year as Wichita and Cullison, Kans.; increased distance 31.17 miles.
[18] 6 miles covered by Hazleton and Sunbury R. P. O.

[19] Cars and clerks shown on route No. 8174.
[20] 8 miles covered by Hazleton and Sunbury R. P. O.
[21] 1 clerk detailed as transfer clerk at Williamsport, Pa.; 1 helper.
[22] Cars and clerks shown on route No. 8006.
[23] 2 clerks on Ridgway and Erie R. P. O.
[24] 15.80 miles covered by Geneva and Williamsport R. P. O.
[25] Cars and clerks shown on route No. 8150.

TABLE A⁹.—*Statement of railway post-offices in operation*

Designation of railway post-office. (Lines upon which railway post-office cars are paid for, in *italics*.)	Division	Distance run by clerks, register to register.	Initial and terminal stations, running from east to west, north to south, or northwest to southeast (with abbreviated title of railroad company).	Number of route.	Miles of route for which railroad is paid.
		Miles.			
Wilmington, N. C., and Jacksonville, Fla.	4	494.14	Wilmington, N. C., Florence, S. C. (W., C. and A. R. R.).	¹14002 (part)	110
			Florence, Charleston, S. C. (N. E. R. R. of S. C.).	14005	102
			Charleston, S. C., Savannah, Ga. (C. and S. R. R.).	14004	115
			Savannah, Ga., Jacksonville, Fla. (S. F. and W. Ry.).	15009	171.50
Wilmington, Del., and Landenburgh, Pa.	2	20.38	Wilmington, Del., and Landenburgh, Pa. (B. and O.).	9505	19.48
Wilmington and Rutherfordton, N. C.	3	268.70	Wilmington, Charlotte, N. C. (Car. Central).	13003	188.52
			Charlotte, Rutherfordton, N. C. (Car. Central).	13008	82.81
Wilson and Fayetteville, N. C.	3	74.44	Wilson, Fayetteville, N. C. (Wilm. and Weldon).	13027	74.02
Winchendon and Palmer, Mass.	1	49.94	Winchendon, Palmer, Mass. (Bos. and Alby.).	3030	50.18
Winchendon and Worcester, Mass.	1	38.05	Winchendon, Worcester, Mass. (Wor. Div. Fitch.).	3057	(⁸)
Winona and Tracy, Minn	6	229.43	Winona, Saint Peter, Minn. (Win. and St. Peter).	26015	139.81
			Saint Peter, Tracy, Minn. (Win. and St. Peter).	¹⁴26014 (part)	91.23
Worcester, Mass., and Norwich, Conn.	1	59.72	Worcester, Mass., Norwich, Conn. (N. Y. and N. Eng.).	5001	59.68
Worcester, Mass., and Providence, R. I.	1	44.14	Worcester, Mass., Providence, R. I. (Prov., Nor. Div. N. Y., Prov. and Bos.).	4001	43.92
Worthington, Minn., and Sioux Falls, Dak.	6	62.50	Worthington, Minn., Sioux Falls, Dak. (Chi., St. P., Minn. and Om.).	26020 (part)	¹⁴⁵61.95
Yates Center and Sedan, Kans¹⁹	7	76.70	Yates Center, Sidell, Kans. (V. V., L and W.).	33063 (part)	(¹⁹)
			Sidell, Peru, Kans. (L. and C. V. A. L.)	33078 (part)	52.91
			Peru, Sedan, Kans. (D., M and A.)	33056 (part)	(²¹)
Yates City and Rushville, Ill.	6	63.95	Yates City, Rushville, Ill. (Chi., Bur. and Q'cy).	23008	63.27
York and Peach Bottom, Pa.	2	40.67	York and Peach Bottom, Pa. (Y. and P. B.)	8092	40.59
Ypsilanti and Hillsdale, Mich.	9	62.14	Ypsilanti, Hillsdale, Mich. (L., S. & M. S.)	24024	62.14
Zanesville and Columbus, Ohio.	5	68.55	Zanesville, Darlington (n. o.), Ohio (Cin. and Musk. Val.).	21029 (part)	(²⁸)
			Darlington (n. o.), Fultonham, Ohio (Cols. and East.).		(²⁸)
			Fultonham, Thurston, Ohio (Cols. and East.).	²⁸21069 (part)	27.64
			Thurston, Columbus, Ohio (Tol. and Ohio Cent.).	21068 (part)	(²⁸)
Zanesville and Waterford, Ohio²⁸	5	51.70	Zanesville, Waterford, Ohio (Zanes. and Ohio River).	21100	54.65

¹ 53 miles reported as Florence and Augusta R. P. O.
² Paid for as one line of 50-foot cars, and one line of 40-foot cars; 6 reserve cars.
³ West India Fast Mail on trains Nos. 27 and 14; clerks run through; 50-foot cars.
⁴ 1 chief clerk, Charleston; 1 detailed to chief clerk's office, Charleston; 1 transfer clerk, Charleston; 1 transfer clerk, Yemassee; 1 transfer clerk, Jacksonville; 3 helpers.
⁵ Trains 15, 23, and 78, clerks run between Wilmington and Charleston.
⁶ Trains 13, 6, and 66, clerks run between Charleston and Jacksonville.
⁷ In reserve.

⁸ One reserve car.
⁹ Covered by Peterborough and Worcester R. P. O. (27.67 miles).
¹⁰ The cars used on this line are also used on Peterborough and Worcester R. P. O. (shown in column 14 of that line).
¹¹ 1 clerk detailed as transfer clerk at Worcester, Mass.
¹² Whole cars.
¹³ Two helpers between Winona and Havana, Minn.
¹⁴ Balance of route (164.14 miles) covered by Tracy, Minn., and Redfield, Dak., R. P. O.
¹⁵ Reserve cars.

in the United States on June 30, 1888—Continued.

Average weight of mail whole distance per day.	Date of last re-adjustment.	Average speed per hour (train numbers taken from division schedule).				Number of round trips with clerks per week.	Annual miles of service with clerks.	Average miles run daily by crews.	Number of mail cars, or cars in which are mail apartments.	Inside dimensions of cars or apartments (railway post-office cars in black figures).		Number of crews.	Number of clerks to crew.	Number of clerks appointed to line.
		Train No. outward.	A'ge speed (miles).	Train No. inward.	A'ge speed (miles).					Length.	Width.			
Lbs.										Ft. In.	Ft. In.			
8,864	July 1, 1888	27 34.8 / 15 31.4		14 31.4 / 78 27.5		7	³361,801	164.71	⁷8	49 9	8 10	6	4	⁴39
12,823	July 1, 1888	27 31.9 / 23 30		14 31.9 / 7d 30		7	⁵156,318	142.36	3	44 6	9 0			
11,078	July 1, 1888	27 36 / 19 23		14 30.9 / 66 27		....	....	....	3	41 7	9 4	7	1	
12,098	July 1, 1888	27 35.1 / 13 24.5		12 38.1 / 6 24.5		7	⁶211,428	144.40	1	42 6	9 5			
72	July 1, 1885	125 20.38		128 18.81		6	12,799	40.76	1 / ⁷1	7 6 / 7 6	6 10 / 6 10	1	1	1
844	July 1, 1888	1 32.58		2 22.66		6	168,743	179.13	2 / 1	16 9 / 14 3	9 0 / 9 0	4	1	4
559	July 1, 1888													
189	July 1, 1888	51 20.50		50 21.13		6	46,747	148.88	1	10 0	7 0	1	1	1
390	July 1, 1885	460 15.68		453 24.10		6	31,362	99.88	⁸2	10 0	6 0	1	1	1
1,104	July 1, 1885	505 22.88		508 25.22		6	22,895	76.10	(¹⁰)	....		1	1	¹¹2
5,064	July 1, 1887	3 22.54		4 22.24		6	144,082	114.71	¹²2	35 4	9 5	4	1	¹³6
2,385	July 1, 1887	3 25.40		4 27.30										
1,313	July 1, 1885	5 20.66		6 22.08		6	37,504	119.44	1	12 2	7 0	1	1	1
1,692	July 1, 1885	8 26.04 / 36 22.63		7 22.63 / 33 26.04		6 / 6	27,720 / 27,720	88.28 /	1 / 1 / 14 1 / 14 1	16 4 / 16 4 / 14 6 / 14 6	6 8 / 6 8 / 6 8 / 6 6	1 / 1	1 / 1	2
462	July 1, 1887	19 20.91		20 20.36		6	39,250	125	1 / 17 1	14 4 / 13 1	7 5 / 7 4	1	1	1
573	Feb. 21, 1887	481 22.52		482 22.52		7	56,064	¹⁶120.64	2	16 4	6 10	²⁰1	1	1
227	July 1, 1888	481 19.25		482 21.26		7								
605	July 1, 1888	481 20		482 20		7								
922	July 1, 1887	53 21.09		54 24.39		6	40,160	127.90	1	19 4	8 10	1	1	1
302	July 1, 1885	5 15.25		2 24.40		G	25,541	81.34	1 / 7 1	14 0 / 8 6	7 6 / 7 0	1	1	1
351	July 1, 1884	153 23.65		154 24.44		6	39,024	124.28	1 / 1	8 8 / 13 6	6 9 / 6 8	1	1	1
1,042	July 1, 1888	51 28.20		54 22.20		6	43,049	137.10	2	13 6	6 8	1	1	1
......	....	51 26.20		54 25.98		6								
406	July 1, 1888	51 28.80		54 25.86		6								
1,019	July 1, 1888	51 24.66		54 25.28		6						*'		
329	July 1, 1888	73 21.84		70 20.40		6	25,378	103.40	²³3	14 0	6 0	1	1	1

16 Balance of route (39.62 miles) covered by closed pouches. (See Sioux Falls and Salem, Dak., Table C°.)

17 Reserve.

18 New service; not reported last year.

19 17.55 miles distance on route 33063 covered by Holden, Mo., and Coffeyville, Kans., R. P. O.

20 Clerk is relieved every third week by the additional clerk of Fort Scott, Kans., and Webb City, Mo., R. P. O., who alternates between this line, Fort Scott, Kans., and Webb City, Mo., R. P. O., and Arcadia and Cherry Vale, Kans., R. P. O.

21 5.66 miles distance on route 33056 covered by Chetopa and Larned, Kans., R. P. O.

22 Covered by Dresden and Cincinnati R. P. O. (4.70 miles).

23 Distance 6.50 miles, contract route not yet established by Department.

24 Balance of route, Fultonham to Redfield, Ohio (6.12 miles), covered by closed pouches. (See Table C°.)

25 Covered by Columbus and Charleston R. P. O. (29.58 miles). (See that line.)

26 Zanesville and McConnelsville R. P. O. extended to Stockport, Ohio, September 5, 1887 (increase in distance 9.75 miles); March 19, 1888, Zanesville and Stockport R. P. O. extended to Waterford, Ohio (increased in distance 16.40 miles).

27 2 cars in reserve.

TABLE A⁰.—*Statement of railway post-offices in operation*

RECAPITULATION.

Division.	Number of railway post-office lines.	Number of crews.	Number of railway clerks at work on lines.	Whole number of railway postal clerks appointed to railway lines.	Distance in miles run by clerks from register to register.	Miles of railroad route paid for by Department over which clerks run.
First	73	187	363	407	7,188.20	5,075.62
Second	162	330	572	662	14,662.64	13,126.93
Third	53	156	246	281	7,190.93	6,283.00
Fourth	85	246	392	365	12,704.85	12,190.09
Fifth	137	422	767	825	20,873.19	16,696.15
Sixth	240	680	1,047	1,117	37,311.09	34,576.37
Seventh	161	485	714	745	26,291.05	25,356.68
Eighth	33	122	148	159	7,849.39	7,697.62
Ninth	48	153	452	487	7,297.30	6,303.27
Total	992	2,781	4,641	*5,048	141,368.64	126,310.73
Total as per report for fiscal year ended June 30, 1887	913	2,610	4,403	4,798	130,958.53	116,609.12
Increase	79	171	238	250	10,410.11	9,701.61

* Including 8 vacancies existing on June 30, 1888.

Total miles of railroad route (including distances from depots to post-offices) 141,368.64
Total miles of railroad routes over which railway postal clerks run 126,310.73
Total miles of railroad routes upon which there is no railroad service by clerks 17,402.69
Total annual miles of service by railway postal clerks (by crews) 122,031,104
Total annual miles of railway service of trains carrying express mail and closed pouches 17,436,519

in the United States June 30, 1888—Continued.

RECAPITULATION.

Annual miles of service performed by crews.	Number of cars and apartments.					Total number of letters and pieces of ordinary mail matter handled exclusive of mail separated for city delivery.	Total number of registered packages and cases handled.	Total number of through registered pouches, including inner registered sacks handled.
	Whole cars in use.	Whole cars in reserve.	Apartments in use.	Apartments in reserve.	Total cars and apartments.			
6,466,425	24	5	118	51	198	458,176,620	1,137,771	84,748
12,477,735	41	22	258	104	420	740,668,260	2,067,510	145,981
6,146,679	89	9	71	16	185	825,984,260	1,011,787	98,419
10,884,125	28	9	151	29	217	491,049,220	1,564,777	97,691
17,378,024	34	6	244	59	343	1,155,579,850	2,213,045	184,739
28,522,047	111	19	353	72	554	1,360,621,930	3,374,016	144,685
22,624,508	45	11	286	72	414	1,128,396,010	2,218,067	177,982
10,867,561	12	....	76	3	91	228,651,970	888,551	34,730
6,664,005	32	10	70	10	122	639,628,810	894,085	139,108
122,031,104	366	91	1,616	416	3,489	6,528,772,060	16,001,659	1,108,083
107,067,643	342	90	1,476	297	2,305	5,834,690,875	15,752,569	950,613
14,963,461	24	1	140	19	184	694,081,185	248,490	152,470

Average annual distance run by postal clerks (by crews)................................ 43,880
Total number of letters, pieces of ordinary mail, registered packages, through registered pouches, and inner registered sacks handled 6,545,876,202
Total number of errors in distribution 1,765,821
Average annual number of errors made by each postal clerk............................ 376
Average daily miles run by each postal clerk at work on line 132.09

TABLE B^b.—*Statement of steam-boat mail service, with postal clerks, in operation*

Railway mail service designation.	Division.	Number of route.	Contract designation, termini of route.	Contractor.	Miles of route.
Arkansas City, Ark., and Vicksburg, Miss.	4	29096	Arkansas City, Ark., Vicksburg, Miss.	....	198. 75
Baltimore and Benedict, Md.	3	10098	Baltimore, Benedict, Md..	Henry Williams...........	123
Baltimore and Crisfield, Md.	3	10094	Baltimore, Wilson's Wharf, Md.	Eastern Shore Steam-boat Company.	238. 50
Baltimore, Md., and Fitchett's, Va.	3	11099	Baltimore, Md., Fitchett's, Va.	Maryland Steam-boat Company.	188
Baltimore, Md., and Fredericksburgh, Va.	3	11100	Fredericksburgh, Va., Baltimore, Md.	Henry Williams	293. 50
Baltimore, Md., and Norfolk, Va.	3	11096	Baltimore, Md., Norfolk, Va.	Baltimore Steam Packet Company.	200
Baltimore and Salisbury, Md.	3	10068	Baltimore, Salisbury, Md.	Maryland Steam-boat Company.	140
Bayou Sara and Baton Rouge, La.	4	30095	Bayou Sara, Baton Rouge, La.	....	32
Cairo, Ill., and Elmot, Ark.	7	29099	Cairo, Ill., Elmot, Ark....	John A. Scudder...........	173
Cape Charles and Norfolk, Va.	2	11094	Cape Charles, Norfolk, Va.	New York, Philadelphia, and Norfolk R. R. Co.	38
Demopolis and Mobile, Ala.	4	17098	Demopolis, Mobile, Ala ...	....	240
Evansville, Ind., and Paducah, Ky.	5	20099	Evansville, Ind., Paducah, Ky. (Ohio River).	F. Hopkins	150. 41
Faisonia and Vicksburg, Miss.	4	18099	Faisonia, Vicksburg, Miss.	....	299
Franklin, Va., and Edenton, N. C.	3	13097	Edenton, N. C., Franklin, Va.	Albemarle Steam Navigation Company.	108
Gallipolis, Ohio, and Huntington, W. Va.	3	21150	Gallipolis, Ohio, Huntington, W. Va.	William Bay...............	45. 50
Geneva and Watkins, N. Y.	2	6985	Geneva, Watkins, N. Y...	Seneca Lake Steam Navigation Company.	43. 50

in the United States at any time during the year ended June 30, 1888.

Annual miles of service.	Number of round trips with clerks per week.	Number of steam-boats on lines.	Dimensions of mail apartments.		Number of crews.	Number of clerks to crew.	Average miles run daily by crew.	Number of clerks appointed to line.	Remarks—Connections with railway post-offices, etc.
			Length, feet and inches.	Width, feet and inches.					
62,407	3	2	8 8	7 8	2	1	85.87	2	Clerks run between Greenville and Vicksburg, Miss. Closed pouches between Arkansas City and Greenville, Miss. Connects at Greenville with Leland and Glen Allen R. P. O.
25,584	2	1	13 0	5 0	1	1	123	1	Connects lines centering at Baltimore, Md.
71,280	6	2	9 0	10 0	3	1	75.66	3	Connects lines centering at Baltimore, Md. Service on this route is performed between Baltimore and Crisfield (115 miles) 6 times a week and twice a week the residue of the route (123.50 miles) from May 1 to December 31, and twice a week to Crisfield, and once a week the residue of the route from January 1 to April 5 of each year.
39,104	2	1	10 0	3 0	1	1	188	1	Connects lines centering at Baltimore, Md.
85,280	2	1	9 8	7 6	2	1	293.50	2	Connects lines centering at Baltimore, Md., and with the Washington and Wilmington, and Fredericksburgh and Orange C. H. R. P. O's., at Fredericksburgh, Va. One additional trip per week between Baltimore, Md., and Tappahannock, Va. (233 miles).
125,600	6	1 1	10 6 10 0	7 0 6 0	2	1	200	2	Connects lines centering at Baltimore, Md., and Norfolk, Va.
43,680	3	1	6 2	10 3	1	1	140	1	Connects lines centering at Baltimore, Md., and at Salisbury, Md., with Philadelphia and Crisfield R. P. O.
20,096	6	1	8 0	4 0	1	1	64	1	Connects at Baton Rouge with Memphis and New Orleans R. P. O., and New Orleans and Mobile R. P. O.
53,976	3	5	8 4	7 0	2	1	86.50	2	Connects at Cairo, Ill., with Cairo, Ill., and Poplar Bluff, Mo., R. P. O.; Cairo, Ill., and Texarkana, Ark., R. P. O.; Cairo, Ill., and Mobile, Ala., R. P. O.; Cairo, Ill., and New Orleans, La., R. P. O.; Centralia and Cairo, Ill., R. P. O.; Saint Louis, Mo., and Cairo, Ill., R. P. O.; Danville and Cairo, Ill., R. P. O., and Paducah, Ky., and Cairo, Ill., R. P. O. (river line) at Columbus, Ky., with Saint Louis, Mo., and Columbus, Ky., R. P. O.; at Hickman, Ky., with Nashville, Tenn., and Hickman, Ky., R. P. O., and at Elmot, Ark., with Goldaust and Memphis R. P. O. (river line).
2*,816	7	1	7 6	6 3	1	1	76	1	Connects Peninsula Junction and Cape Charles R. P. O., Norfolk and Lynchburgh R. P. O., Norfolk and Raleigh R. P. O., Norfolk and Edenton R. P. O., Norfolk and Richmond R. P. O., Norfolk, Newport News, and Richmond R. P. O.
24,960	1	1	6 0	5 0	1	1	76	1	Connects at Demopolis with Selma and Meridian R. P. O.
94,457	6	*3	9 2	6 4	2	1	150.41	2	¹Makes all connections at Evansville, Ind., Shawneetown, Ill., and Paducah, Ky.; also at Henderson, Ind., with Henderson and Princeton, and Nashville and St. Louis R. P. O's.; at Mt. Vernon, Ind., with Nashville and St. Louis, and Ft. Branch and Mt. Vernon R. P. O's. ²One boat in reserve.
1,806	1	1	(¹)	....	(²)		70	1	¹Mail carried in cabin. ²Nominal salary, officer of the boat. Connects with lines at Vicksburg.
33,696	3	1	8 2	6 9	1	1	108	1	Connects Norfolk and Edenton R. P. O. at Edenton, N. C., and Norfolk and Raleigh R. P. O. at Franklin, Va.
....			....	....				....	This line discontinued January 1, 1888, service being taken up by the extension of the Wheeling and Point Pleasant R. P. O. to Huntington, W. Va.
27,318	6	1 1 1 1	8 0 7 10 7 06 6 0	8 0 7 0 5 0 4 08	1	2	87	2	Connects Syracuse, Auburn and Rochester R. P. O., Canandaigua and Elmira R. P. O., New York and Rochester R. P. O., Geneva and Williamsport R. P. O., Lyon and Sayre R. P. O.

TABLE B[b].—*Statement of steam-boat mail service, with postal clerks, in operation*

Railway mail service designation.	Division.	Number of route.	Contract designation, termini of route.	Contractor.	Miles of route.
Golddust and Memphis, Tenn.	7	29099	Golddust, Memphis, Tenn.	James Lee..................	106. 50
Greenwood and Vicksburg, Miss.	4	18100	Greenwood, Vicksburg, Miss.	....	242. 00
Jamestown and Mayville, N. Y.	2	7520	Jamestown, Mayville, N. Y.	Chautauqua Lake Steamboat Company.	21. 00
Johnsonville, Tenn., and Waterloo, Ala.	5	19097	Johnsonville, Tenn., Waterloo, Ala. (Tennessee River).	W. G. Brown..............	148. 00
Louisville, Ky., and Evansville, Ind.	5	20097	Louisville, Ky., Evansville, Ind. (Ohio River).	W. C. Hite	217. 62
McConnellsville and Marietta, Ohio.	5	21147	McConnellsville, Marietta, Ohio (Muskingum River).	K. M. Armstrong..........	46. 39
Melbourne and Jupiter, Fla.	4	16074	Melbourne, Jupiter, Fla...		86. 00
Memphis, Tenn., and Arkansas City, Ark.	4	29097	Memphis, Tenn., Arkansas City, Ark.		252. 50
Memphis, Tenn., and Friar's Point, Miss.	4	29098	Memphis, Tenn., Friar's Point, Miss.		111. 00
Natchez, Miss., and Bayou Sara, La.	4	30092	Natchez, Miss., Bayou Sara, La.		110. 00
New Orleans and Port Eads, La.	4	30100	New Orleans, Port Eads, La.	....	128. 00
New Orleans and Port Vincent, La.	4	30097	New Orleans, Port Vincent.	....	105. 00
Norfolk and Richmond, Va.	3	11089	Norfolk, Richmond, Va...	Virginia Steam-boat Company.	150. 00
Palatka and Drayton Island, Fla.	4	16080	Palatka, Drayton Island, Fla.		40. 00
Paducah, Ky., and Cairo, Ill.	5	20100	Paducah, Ky., Cairo, Ill. (Ohio River).	F. Hopkins	50. 86
Paducah, Ky., and Florence, Ala.	5	*20095	Paducah, Ky., Florence, Ala. (Tennessee River).	H. M. Sweetser..........	300. 00
Portland and Astoria, Oregon.	8	44100	Portland, Astoria, Oregon.	Oregon Railway and Navigation Company.	120. 00

in the United States at any time during the year ended June 30, 1888—Continued.

Annual miles of service.	Number of round trips with clerks per week.	Number of steam-boats on line.	Dimensions of mail apartments.		Number of crews.	Number of clerks to crew.	Average miles run daily by crews.	Number of clerks appointed to line.	Remarks—Connections with railway post-offices, etc.
			Length, feet and inches.	Width, feet and inches.					
33,228	3	1	7 0	6 0	1	1	106.50	1	Connects at Elmot, Ark., with Cairo, Ill., and Elmot, Ark., R. P. O. (river line); at Memphis, Tenn., with Chattanooga and Memphis, Tenn., R.P.O.; Bowling Green, Ky., and Memphis, Tenn., R. P. O.; Paducah, Ky., and Memphis, Tenn., R. P. O.; Kansas City, Mo., and Memphis, Tenn., R. P. O.; Memphis, Tenn., and Little Rock, Ark., R.P.O.; Memphis, Tenn., and Grenada, Miss., R. P. O.; Memphis, Tenn., and New Orleans, La., R. P. O.; Birmingham, Ala., and Memphis, Tenn., R. P. O.; Memphis, Tenn., and Arkansas City, Ark., R. P. O. (river line), and Memphis, Tenn., and Friar's Point, Miss., R. P. O. (river line.)
25,248	1	1	(¹)	....	(²)	....	80.50	1	¹ Mail carried in cabin. ² Nominal salary; officer of the boat. Connects at Greenwood with Green, and Jackson R. P. O.
4,396	¹12	1 1 1	12 01- 7 08 5 07	9 07 5 02 5 06	(²)	(²)	84.00	(²)	¹ Service for 2 months only. ² One-acting clerk additional. Connects Buffalo and Youngstown R. P. O. and Buffalo and Pittsburgh R. P. O.
3,848	2	4	5 6	5 6	4	1	25.00	4	Connected at Johnsonville, Tenn., with Nashville and Hickman R. P. O. R. P. O. service discontinued August 15, 1887. Nominal salaries; officers of boat.
136,665	6	3	9 3	6 2	3	1	145.08	3	Makes all connections at Louisville, Ky., and Evansville, Ind.; at West Point, Ky., with Louisville and Paducah R. P. O.; at Rockport, Ind., with branch of Louisville, Evansville and Saint Louis Railroad; at Owensborough, Ky., with Owensborough and Russellville R. P. O.
3,526	6	1 1	8 0 6 0	5 6 6 0	1	1	92.78	1	This line discontinued August 13, 1887, service being taken up by Zanesville and Waterford R. P. O. (See Table A⁴.)
27,004	3	1	7 4	4 0	1	1	86.00	1	Connects at Melbourne with Titusville and Melbourne R. P. O.
52,520	2	1	6 0	6 0	1	1	108.33	1	Connects with lines at Memphis, and Fort Smith and Leland R. P. O. at Arkansas City.
34,854	3	1	7 9	6 6	1	1	110.00	1	
34,540	3	1	7 9	6 6	1	1	110.00	1	Connects at Bayou Sara with Bayou Sara and Baton Rouge R. P. O.; at Natchez with Jackson and Natchez R. P. O.
62,288	6	2	6 0	8 0	2	1	99.50	2	79 miles, New Orleans to Buras, La., 6 times per week; 37 miles, Buras to Port Eads, La., 3 times per week; 12 miles side supply, Pilot Town, La., 1 time per week.
21,840	2	1	(¹)	....	(²)	....	70.00	1	¹ Mail carried in cabin. ² Nominal salary to officer of the boat.
47,112	3	1	9 8	3 2	1	1	150.00	1	Connects at Norfolk and Richmond, Va., with lines centering at those points.
25,120	6	1	(¹)	....	1	1	80.00	1	¹ Mails carried in the cabin.
31,940	6	1	6 0	6 0	1	1	101.72	1	Makes all connections at Paducah, Ky., and Cairo, Ill.
21,800	2	²4	5 6	5 6	2	1	100.00	²2	¹ Connects at Paducah with all lines; at Danville, Tenn., with Bowling Green and Memphis R. P. O.; at Johnsonville, Tenn., with Nashville and Hickman R. P. O.; at Florence, Ala., with branch of Memphis and Charleston Railroad. ² Service established February 25, 1888. ³ Two boats in reserve. ⁴ Nominal salaries; officers of boats.
51,496 3,952	6	2	14 0 8 0	6 6 8 2	2	1	101.00	2	82 miles of route six times per week. Additional offices supplied three times per week; increases distance 28 miles. Connects at Portland with Helena and Portland, Huntington and Portland, Portland and Coburg and Portland and Corvallis R. P. O's.

TABLE B[b].—*Statement of steam-boat mail service, with postal clerks, in operation*

Railway mail service designation.	Division.	Number of route.	Contract designation, termini of route.	Contractor.	Miles of route.
Portsmouth and Cincinnati, Ohio.[1]	5	21149	Portsmouth, Cincinnati, Ohio (Ohio River).	Cincinnati, Portsmouth, Big Sandy, and Pomeroy Packet Company.	128.66
Port Townsend and Seattle, Wash.	8	43099	Seattle, Port Townsend, Wash.	Washington Steam-boat and Transportation Company.	60
Rome, Ga., and Gadsden, Ala.	4	17100	Rome, Ga., Gadsden, Ala.	....	155
Sehome and Port Townsend, Wash.	8	43097	Port Townsend, Sehome, Wash.	J. C. Brittain..............	140.50
Selma and Mobile, Ala....	4	17097	Selma, Mobile, Ala		308
Ticonderoga and Lake George, N. Y.	2	6984	Ticonderoga, Lake George N. Y.	Champlain Transportation Company.	40
Titusville and Melbourne, Fla.	4	16073	Titusville and Melbourne, Fla.		43
Vicksburg and Natchez, Miss.	4	30091	Vicksburg and Natchez, Miss.	....	100
Vicksburg, Miss., and New Orleans, La.	4	30096	Vicksburg, New Orleans, La.		408
Whatcom and Seattle, Wash.	8	43098	Seattle, Whatcom, Wash..	Oregon Railway and Navigation Company.	128

RECAPITULATION.

Division.	Number of lines.	Total number of crews.	Total number of clerks.	Miles of route run by clerks.	Annual miles run by crews.	Number of mail apartments.
First						
Second.............................	4	3	3	142.50	69,800	10
Third..............................	9	12	12	1,486.50	471,336	10
Fourth	17	20	20	2,768.25	610,095	20
Fifth	5	10	10	817.55	352,814	13
Sixth						
Seventh	2	3	3	279.50	87,204	6
Eighth.............................	4	6	6	448.50	176,900	6
Ninth..............................						
Total	41	54	54	5,972.80	1,767,649	65
Total as per report for the fiscal year ended June 30, 1887.	41	56	57	6,864.59	1,868,747	71
Decrease.........................	....	2	3	*107.91	101,098	6

* Increase.

Total miles of route 5,972.80
Total annual miles of service.. 1,767,649
Average annual distance run by crews 36,074

in the United States at any time during the year ended June 30, 1888—Continued.

Annual miles of service.	Number of round trips with clerks per week.	Number of steam-boats on line.	Dimensions of mail apartments.		Number of crews.	Number of clerks to crew.	Average miles run daily by crews.	Number of clerks appointed to line.	Remarks.—Connections with railway-post offices, etc.
			Length, feet and inches.	Width, feet and inches.					
60,578	6	1 1	8 0 6 6	6 0 6 3	2	1	97.08	¹2	¹ Makes all connections at Portsmouth, Ohio, Maysville, Ky., and Cincinnati, Ohio. ² One clerk makes three round trips per week between Portsmouth and Cincinnati; and one clerk three round trips per week between Maysville, Ky., and Cincinnati, Ohio (65.50 miles), also three round trips per week between Portsmouth and Cincinnati by closed pouch.
37,680	6	2	14 0	7 0	2	1	60	2	Connects at Port Townsend with steamers for Victoria, B. C., and Sehome and Port Townsend R. P. O.; at Seattle with Whatcom and Seattle R. P. O.
22,240	2	1	7 0	5 0	1	1	103.33	1	Connects at Rome with Cleveland and Selma R. P. O. and Chattanooga, Rome, and Atlanta R. P. O.
43,836	3	1	7 10	7 0	1	1	140.50	1	Connects at Port Townsend with Port Townsend and Seattle R. P. O.
64,064	2	2.	6 0	6 0	2	1	102.66	2	Connects at Selma with Cleveland and Selma R. P. O.; Montgomery and Akron Junc. R. P. O.; Selma and Meridian R. P. O., and lines at Mobile.
9,770	¹6	2	9 6	6 2	(²)	(²)	80	(²)	¹ Service for 4½ months only. ² One acting clerk additional connects Rouse's Point and Albany R. P. O.
27,004	6	1	7 0	6 0	1	1	84	1	Connects at Titusville with Titusville and Sanford R. P. O.
31,400	3	1	8 6	8 6	1	1	100	1	
42,704	1	1	(¹)	....	²1	....	136	1	¹ Mail carried in cabin. ² Officer of boat, nominal salary.
39,936	3	1	12 6	5 6	1	1	128	1	Connects at Seattle with Port Townsend and Seattle R. P. O.

TABLE C⁵.—*Statement of mail service performed in closed pouches upon railroads and parts*
June

Initial and terminal stations running east to west, north to south, and northwest to southeast.	Division.	Number of route.	Contract designation, termini of route.	Corporate title of company.
Aberdeen and Muldon, Miss...	4	18007	Muldon, Aberdeen, Miss....	Mobile and Ohio R. R.......
Adelphi and Kingston, Ohio...	5	21099	Adelphi, Kingston, Ohio ...	Cincinnati, Hocking Valley and Huntington.
Alameda and San Francisco, Cal.	8	46026	San Francisco, Alameda, Cal.	Central Pacific R. R ....
Alamosa and Del Norte, Colo..	7	38011	Alamosa, Del Norte, Colo...	Denver and Rio Grande .....'
Albany and Yaquina, Oregon .	8	44006	Albany, Yaquina, Oregon ..	Oregon Pacific..............
Albia and Centreville, Iowa...	6	27093	Albia, Relay (n. o.), Iowa...	Centreville, Moravia and Albia.
		28015 (part)	Relay (n. o.), Centreville, Iowa.	Keokuk and Western.
Alden and Eldora Junction, Iowa.	6	27088	Eldora Junction, Alden, Iowa.	Chicago, Iowa and Dakota..
Alderson and Luzerne, Pa.....	2	8170	Luzerne, Alderson, Pa......	Pennsylvania and New York Canal and R. R.
Alma and Ithaca, Mich........	9	24030 (part)	East Saginaw, Ithaca, Mich.	Detroit, Lansing and Northern.
Alma and Plainview, N. C.....	3	13017	Alma, Plainview, N. C......	Alma and Little Rock ......
Alta and Bingham Junction, (n. o.) Utah.	8	41006	Bingham Junction, Alta, Utah.	Denver and Rio Grande Rwy.
Alton Junction and Alton, Ill.	5	28061	Alton Junction (n. o.) and Chicago and Alton Junction (n. o.), Ill.	Indianapolis and Saint Louis.
Altoona and Henrietta, Pa	2	8036	Altoona, Henrietta, Pa	Pennsylvania..............
Alvordton and Bryan, Ohio ...	5	¹21075 (part)	Alvordton, Carlisle, Ohio..	Cincinnati, Jackson and Mackinaw.
Americus and Buena Vista, Ga.	4	15047	Americus, Buena Vista, Ga.	Buena Vista R. R............
Amesbury and East Salisbury, Mass.	1	3007	East Salisbury, Amesbury, Mass.	Boston and Maine R. R.....
¹ Anderson and Lebanon........	5	22037	Anderson, Lebanon, Ind	Midland ....
Anglesea Junction and Anglesea, N. J.	2	7061	Anglesea Junction, Anglesea, N. J.	Anglesea ....
Angelica and Olean, N. Y......	2	6059	Olean, Angelica, N. Y.......	Lackawanna and Pittston..
Anniston and Sylacauga, Ala .	4	17029	Anniston, Sylacauga, Ala ..	Anniston and Atlantic R. R.

of railroads over which no railway post-offices run, in operation during the fiscal year ended 30, 1888.

Miles of route.	Annual miles of service.	Number of round trips per week.	Number of pouches exchanged daily.	Date of last re-adjustment.	Average weight of mail whole distance daily.	Remarks.
					Pounds.	
9.50	13,908	14	4	July 1, 1888	272	
11.17	7,015	6	12	July 1, 1888	140	
11.26	25,533	7	24	July 1, 1886	231	Seven round trips per week between Oakland Pier (n. o.) and Alameda (7.79 miles); 31 trips inward between Alameda and San Francisco. San Francisco, Oakland, and Alameda exchange by local trains over route 46031. Pouches returned via this route.
31.85	20,002	6	16	July 1, 1886	219	Connects at Alamosa, Colo., with Pueblo and Silverton, Colo., R. P. O.
85.16	53,480	6	49	June 25, 1888	306	Exchanges made with initial and terminal offices; connects with Portland and Corvallis R. P. O. at Corvallis, and Portland, Oregon, and Sacramento, Cal., R. P. O. at Albany, Oregon.
24.53	15,325	6	16	July 1, 1887	121	Supplied by initial and terminal offices. Connects at Albia, Iowa, with Burlington and Council Bluffs, Iowa, and with Mason City and Albia, Iowa, R. P. O's., and at Centreville, Iowa, with Davenport, Iowa, and Atchison, Kans., and with Keokuk and Humeston, Iowa, R. P. O's.
(¹)						¹ Distance (2 miles) covered by Keokuk and Humeston, Iowa, R. P. O. (See Table A¹.)
26.42	33,183	12	14	July 1, 1887	103	Supplied by Eldora, Iowa, and by Tama and Hawarden, Iowa, R. P. O. Connects at Eldora, Iowa, with Mason City and Albia, Iowa, R. P. O., and at Iowa Falls, Iowa, with Dubuque and Sioux City, Iowa, and with Cedar Rapids, Iowa and Watertown, Dak., R. P. O's.
14.06	17,650	12	12	July 1, 1888	57	
7.20	9,043	12	6	July 1, 1884	527	Connects at Alma, Mich., with the East Saginaw and Howard City R. P. O. Balance of route (38.78 miles) covered by East Saginaw and Howard City R. P. O.
12.68	8,068	6	4	July 1, 1888	71	Connects Wilmington and Rutherfordton R. P. O. at Alma.
18.32	13,410	7	4	....	....	Supplied by Salt Lake City. Connects at Bingham Junction, Utah, with Denver, Colo., and Ogden, Utah, R. P. O.
4.20	5,275	12	4	July 1, 1887	169	
27.92	52,601	18	40	July 1, 1885	407	
16.40	4,723	6	12	July 1, 1888	411	¹ For balance of route, distance 146.19 miles, see Bryan and Carlisle R. P. O., Table A¹, route 21,075. Bryan to Carlisle extended to Alvordton, January 16, 1888, increasing distance 16.40 miles. R. P. O. service not extended. Service between Alvordton and Bryan, Ohio, performed by closed pouches.
29.63	18,607	6	8	July 1, 1888	94	Route changed to begin at Americus, omitting Andersonville.
4.49	11,278	24	21	July 1, 1885	353	Amesbury exchanges pouches with Salisbury, Newburyport, Boston, Bangor and Boston R. P. O., Boston and North Conway R. P. O., and Newburyport and Boston R. P. O.
....	2,854	6	18	July 1, 1888	177	¹ This was formerly the Anderson and Noblesville R. R., distance 19.96 miles. August 22, 1887, service extended to Lebanon, Ind., increasing distance 25.78 miles. September 5, 1887, R. P. O. service established and is now known as the Anderson and Ladoga, R. P. O. (See table A¹.)
5.25	3,297	6	6	July 1, 1885	79	
40.69	51,107	12	26	July 1, 1885	130	
53.36	52,349	16	16	July 1, 1888	103	¹ 12 trips per week between Anneston and dega.

TABLE C^c.—*Statement of mail service performed in closed pouches upon railroads and*

Initial and terminal stations running east to west, north to south, and northwest to southeast.	Division.	Number of route.	Contract designation, termini of route.	Corporate title of company.
Ansonia and New Haven, Conn.	1	5017	New Haven, Ansonia, Conn.	New Haven and Derby R. R.
Arcata Wharf (n. o.) and Blue Lake, Cal.	8	46052	Arcata Wharf and Blue Lake, Cal.	Arcata and Blue Lake R.R.
Artesia and Starkeville, Miss .	4	18015	Artesia, Starkeville, Miss...	Mobile and Ohio R. R.......
Ashburnham and Ashburnham Depot, Mass.	1	3070	Ashburnham, Ashburnham Depot, Mass.	Ashburnham R. R ....
Ashland and Milford, Mass ...	1	3060	Milford, Ashland, Mass.....	Hopkinton R. R..............
Atco Junction and Glassborough, N. J.	2	7035	Atco Junction, Glassborough, N. J.	Williamstown ....
Atkins and Bishopville, S. C .	4	14029	Atkins, Bishopville, S. C ...	Bishopville R. R............
Atlantic and Griswold, Iowa ..	6	27054	Atlantic, Griswold, Iowa	Chicago, Rock Island and Pacific.
Atlantic and West Quincy, Mass.	1	3065	Atlantic, West Quincy, Mass	Old Colony R. R ....
Atlantic Highlands and Hopping, N. J.	2	7016	Hopping (n. o.), Atlantic Highlands, N. J.	Central R. R. of New Jersey.
Atoka and Lehigh, Ind. T	7	32001	Atoka, Lehigh, Ind. Ter....	Missouri Pacific............
Attica and Covington, Ind	5	22047	Attica, Covington, Ind	Wabash, St. Louis and Pacific.
Auburn and Hope, R. I........	1	4C08	Auburn, Hope, R. I	New York, Providence and Boston R. R.
Auburn and Warwick, R. I....	1	4010	Auburn, Warwick, R. I.	New York, Providence and Boston R. R.
Auburndale Station (n. o.) and Newton Lower Falls, Mass.	1	3027	Auburndale Stat. (n. o.) and Newton Lower Falls, Mass.	Boston and Albany R. R ....
Audubon and Atlantic, Iowa..	6	27044	Atlantic, Audubon, Iowa ...	Chicago, Rock Island and Pacific.
Augusta and Bald Knob, Ark.	7	29023	Bald Knob, Augusta, Ark...	Saint Louis, Iron Mountain and Southern.
Aurora and Hastings, Nebr ...	6	34044	Aurora, Hastings, Nebr.....	Burlington and Missouri River in Nebraska.
Avoca and Carson, Iowa	6	27063	Avoca, Carson, Iowa........	Chicago, Rock Island and Pacific.
Balcony Falls and Lexington, Va.	3	11029	Balcony Falls, Lexington, Va.	Richmond and Alleghany...
Baldwin and Louisa, La	4	30015	Baldwin, Louisa, La	Morgan's La. and Texas R.R.
Ballston and Schenectady, N.Y.	2	6025	Schenectady, Ballston, N. Y.	Del. and Hud. Canal Co ....
Baltimore and Annapolis, Md..	3	10028	Baltimore, Annapolis, Md..	Annapolis and Baltimore Short Line.
Baltimore and Brooklyn, Md..	3	10022	Baltimore, Brooklyn, Md..	Baltimore and Ohio ....
Bangor and Bethlehem, Pa ..	2	8046	Bethlehem, Bangor, Pa ...	Central R. R. of New Jersey.
Bangor Junction, Pa., and Brainards, N. J.	2	8115	Bangor Junction, Pa., Brainards, N. J.	Bangor and Portland ....
Barnegat City and Barnegat City Junction, N. J.	2	7056	Barnegat City, Barnegat City Junction, N. J.	Pennsylvania...............

parts of railroads over which no railway post-offices run, in operation, etc.—Continued.

Miles of route.	Annual miles of service.	Number of round trips per week.	Number of pouches exchanged daily.	Date of last re-adjustment.	Average weight of mail whole distance daily.	Remarks.
					Pounds.	
13.27	33,334	24	52	July 1, 1885	565	New Haven exchanges pouches with Ansonia, Birmingham, Derby, Orange, Tyler City, Waterbury, Seymour, and West Winsted and Bridgeport R. P. O's. Boston, Springfield, and New York R. P. O. exchanges with Ansonia, Birmingham, and Derby.
19.60	7,759	7	6	June 21, 1888	128	Supplied by Eureka, Cal. New service established from June 15, 1887, from July 1.
11.60	25,473	21	16	July 1, 1888	219	
2.62	4,936	18	10	July 1, 1885	123	Ashburnham exchanges pouches with Boston, Boston and Troy R. P. O., and Essex Junction and Boston R. P. O.
11.85	14,884	12	16	July 1, 1885	75	Ashland exchanges pouches with Hayden Row and Hopkinton; Boston exchanges pouches with Milford and Hopkinton.
17.71	22,244	12	16	July 1, 1885	87	
15.79	9,916	6	6			
15.22	19,116	12	16	July 1, 1887	207	Supplied by initial and terminal offices and by West Liberty and Council Bluffs, Iowa, R. P. O. Connects at Griswold, Iowa, with Griswold and Red Oak, Iowa, pouch service.
3.67	4,609	12	12	July 1, 1885	90	Boston exchanges pouches with East Milton and West Quincy. Extra round trip daily to East Milton.
3.10	2,920	15	6	Apr. 26, 1886	75	
8.11	10,186	12	6	July 1, 1886	32	Connects at Atoka, Ind. Ter., with Sedalia, Mo., and Denison, Tex., R. P. O.
14.91	18,727	12	8	July 1, 1888	54	
10.62	13,338	12	20	July 1, 1885	252	Providence, R. I., exchanges pouches with Howard, Pontiac, Phenix, Fiskdale, and Hope.
7.70	9,671	12	4	May 1, 1885	55	Providence exchanges pouches with Warwick.
2.09	3,937	18	10	July 1, 1885	104	Newton Lower Falls exchanges pouches with Auburndale and Boston.
26.06	34,279	12	32	July 1, 1887	277	Supplied by initial and terminal offices and by West Liberty and Council Bluffs, Iowa, R. P. O. Connects at Audubon, Iowa, with Manning and Audubon, Iowa, pouch service, and at Atlantic, Iowa, with Atlantic and Griswold, Iowa, pouch service.
14.05	20,569	14	8	July 1, 1888	87	New service; not reported last year. Connects at Bald Knob, Ark., with Saint Louis, Mo., and Texarkana, Ark., R. P. O.
29.84	18,739	6	8	Mar. 7, 1887	96	Supplied by initial and terminal offices. Connects at Hastings, Nebr., with Omaha and McCook, Nebr., Saint Joseph, Mo., and Grand Island, Nebr., and Omaha and Hastings, Nebr., R. P. O., and at Aurora and Arcadia, Nebr., R. P. O., and with Nebraska City and Whitman, Nebr., R.P.O.
17.97	22,570	12	22	July 1, 1887	219	Supplied by initial and terminal offices and by West Liberty and Council Bluffs, Iowa, R. P. O. Connects at Carson, Iowa, with Carson and Hastings, Iowa, pouch service, and at Harlan, Iowa, with Harlan and Avoca, Iowa, pouch service.
22.13	27,795	12	31	July 1, 1885	251	Connects Richmond, Lynchburgh and Clifton Forge R. P. O. at Balcony Falls and Baltimore and Lexington R. P. O. at Lexington.
15.25	9,577	6	4	July 1, 1886	25	
15.20	28,750	18	16	July 1, 1885	194	
28.22	17,722	6	28	July 1, 1888	148	Connects lines centering at Annapolis and Baltimore, Md.
7.00	8,792	12	4	Aug. 2, 1886	49	Connects lines centering at Baltimore, Md.
81.48	39,539	12	16			
4.57	11,480	24	12			
8.94	11,229	12	6	July 1, 1888	53	

TABLE C^c.—*Statement of mail service performed in closed pouches upon railroads and*

Initial and terminal stations running east to west, north to south, and northwest to southeast.	Division.	Number of route.	Contract designation, termini of route.	Corporate title of company.
Barnesville and Thomaston, Ga.	4	15010	Barnesville, Thomaston, Ga.	Central R. R. of Georgia....
Barstow and Mojave, Cal.....:	8	46042 (part)	Mojave, Barstow, Cal.......	Atlantic and Pacific R. R...
Barton and Saint Clairsville, Ohio.	5	21097	Saint Clairsville, Barton, Ohio.	Saint Clairsville and Northern.
Bartos and Pottstown, Pa......	2	8057	Pottstown, Bartos, Pa......	Philadelphia and Reading ..
Baton Rouge Junction and Baton Rouge, La.	4	30013	Baton Rouge Junction (n. o.), Baton Rouge, La.	Texas and Pacific R. R .....
Battle Mountain and Austin, Nev.	8	45003	Battle Mountain, Austin, Nev.	Nevada Central R. R ......
Bayfield and Ashland Junction, Wis.	6	'25028 (part)	Hudson, Bayfield, Wis......	Chicago, Saint Paul, Minn., and Omaha.
Bear Creek Junction (n. o.) and Morrison, Colo.	7	38022	Bear Creek Junction (n. o.), Morrison, Colo.	Denver, South Park and Pacific.
Beaumont and Sabine Pass, Tex.	7	31045	Beaumont, Sabine Pass, Tex.	Sabine and East Texas .....
Belleville and East Saint Louis, Ill.	6	23088	East Saint Louis, Belleville, Ill.	Illinois and Saint Louis.....
Belleville and Lawrenceburgh, Kans.	7	33044	Lawrenceburgh, Belleville, Kans.	Junction City and Fort Kearney.
Belmont and Jefferson, Ga	4	15045	Belmont, Jefferson, Ga	Gainesville, Jefferson and Southern R. R.
Benore and Tyrone, Pa	2	8113	Tyrone, Benore, Pa	Pennsylvania ....
Benton and Bloomsburgh, Pa..	2	8172	Benton, Bloomsburgh, Pa..	Bloomsburgh and Sullivan..
Berkeley and West Oakland, Cal.	8	46024	West Oakland, Berkeley, Cal.	Central Pacific R. R ....
Berlin and Garrett, Pa	2	8090	Berlin, Garrett, Pa..........	Baltimore and Ohio .... ..
Bermuda Hundred and, Winterpock, Va.	3	11017	Bermuda Hundréd, Winterpock, Va.	Brightbope Railway ....
Bessemer, Mich., and Mellen, Wis.	6	24071	Bessemer, Mich., Mellen, Wis.	Wisconsin Central ....
Beulah and Elkader, Iowa. ...	6	27023	Beulah, Elkader, Iowa......	Chicago, Milwaukee and Saint Paul.
Bingham Junction and Bingham Canyon, Utah.	8	41004	Bingham Junction, Bingham Canyon, Utah.	Denver and Rio Grande Rwy.
Birmingham and Pratt Mines, Ala.	4	17023	Birmingham, Pratt Mines, Ala.	Tennessee Coal, Iron and R. R. Co.
Black River Junction (n. o.) and Stuck, Wash.	8	43012	Black River Junction, Stuck, Wash.	Puget Sound Shore R. R....
Black Rock and Buffalo, N. Y .	2	6126	Buffalo, Black Rock, N. Y...	N. Y. C. and H. R. R. R......
Blackville and Barnwell, S. C..	4	14019	Blackville, Barnwell........	South Carolina R. R ....
Blanchester and Hillsborough, Ohio.	5	21017	Blanchester and Hillsborough, Ohio.	Cin'ti, Washington and Baltimore.
Bloomfield and Titusville, Pa..	2	8068	Bloomfield. Titusville, Pa...	Westn. New York and Penna.
Blossburgh and Hoytville, Pa..	2	8020 (part)	Elmira, N. Y., Hoytville, Pa.	N. Y., L. E. and W ....
Blue Springs (n. o.) and New Smyrna, Fla.	4	16004	J T. and K. W. Junct. (n. o.), New Smyrna, Fla.	Blue Spring, Orange City and Atlantic R. R.
Blue Stone Junction (n. o.) and Duhring, W. Va.	3	12016	Blue Stone Junction (n. o.) During, W. Va.	Norfolk and Western.......
Boelus and Nantasket, Nebr...	6	34058	Boelus, Nantaskct, Nebr	Omaha, Niobrara and Blk. Hills.

parts of railroads over which no railway post-offices run, in operation, etc.—Continued.

Miles of route.	Annual miles of service.	Number of round trips per week.	Number of pouches exchanged daily.	Date of last re-adjustment.	Average weight of mail whole distance daily.	Remarks.
					Pounds.	
16.53	20,762	12	12	July 1, 1884	149	
71.30	52,192	7	12	July 1, 1886	1,873	Including sacks. Connects at Mojave with San Francisco and Los Angeles R. P. O., and at Barstow, with Albuquerque, N. Mex., and Los Angeles R. P. O. Balance of route covered by Albuquerque and Los Angeles R. P. O. (See Table A^a.)
4.35	5,464	12	8	July 1, 1888	68	
13.22	20,755	15	20	July 1, 1885	169	
9.50	6,934	7	4	July 1, 1886	106	
93.15	29,063	3	6	July 1, 1886	194	Connects at Battle Mountain, Nev., with Ogden, Utah, and San Francisco R. P. O.
21.21	26,639	12	6	July 1, 1887	1,142	¹Balance of route covered by Ashland, Wis., and Saint Paul, Minn., R. P. O. (See Table A^a.) Connects at Ashland Junction (n. o.), Wis., with Ashland, Wis., and Saint Paul, Minn., R. P. O.
9.55	9,969	(¹)	4	July 1, 1886	81	¹Trains 13 times a week east, and 7 times a week west bound. Trains run into Denver, Colo., direct from Morrison, Colo.
31.21	9,738	3	2	July 1, 1886	43	Connects at Beaumont, Tex., with Rockland and Beaumont, Tex., and New Orleans, La., and Houston, Tex., R. P. O.
15.35	11,236	7	2	July 1, 1887	79	Supplied by Saint Louis, Mo., and by transfer clerk at East Saint Louis, Ill. Connects with lines centering at East Saint Louis, Ill.
17.13	23,297	13	10	July 1, 1886	157	Connects at Belleville, Kans., with McFarland and Belleville, Kans., and Fairbury, Nebr., and Norton, Kans., R. P. O's. Trains run from Belleville to Concordia, Kans., and there connect with Atchison and Lenora, Kans., R. P. O.; Lincoln, Nebr., and Concordia, Kans., R. P. O., and Concordia and Junction City, Kans., R. P. O.
13.51	8,484	6	4	July 1, 1888	85	
25.61	32,166	12	20	July 1, 1885	92	
20.68	25,974	12	6	July 1, 1888	171	
5.20	14,803	25	20	July 1, 1886	220	Connects with Ogden, Utah, and San Francisco, Cal., R. P. O. Berkeley exchanges with Alameda, Oakland, and San Francisco.
8.43	10,537	12	4	July 1, 1885	20	Connects Washington and Wilmington R. P. O. at Cheater.
28.61	17,967	6	6	July 1, 1885	20	
33.72	21,176	6	14	....	....	Supplied by initial and terminal offices and by Ashland and Abbottsford, Wis., R. P. O. Connects at Bessemer, Mich., with Ashland and Milwaukee, Wis., R. P. O.
19.52	12,258	6	20	July 1, 1887	182	Supplied by initial and terminal offices and by Chicago, Ill., McGregor, Iowa, and Saint Paul, Minn., R. P. O.
17.33	12,686	7	4	....	....	Supplied by Salt Lake City, Utah.
6.74	8,465	12	4	July 1, 1888	94	
13.50	19,764	14	80	July 1, 1886	104	Pouches for Seattle, Tacoma, Wash., and Portland, Oregon, and exchanges with Helena, Mont., and Portland, Oregon, R. P. O., carried over this route.
4.59	8,648	18	¹16	July 1, 1885	180	¹Including sacks.
9.64	12,107	12	4	July 1, 1888	182	
21.00	26,376	12	26	July 1, 1888	564	
10.49	6,588	6	14	July 1, 1885	54	
¹15.59	9,791	6	6	July 1, 1885	588	¹Balance of route (49.35 miles) covered by Elmira and Blossburgh R. P. O. (See Table A^a.)
28.09	17,640	6	8	July 1, 1888	129	
7.83	4,917	6	6	Feb. 23, 1886	87	Connects Lynchburgh and Pocahontas R. P. O. at Blue Stone Junction (n. o.).
9.74	6,116	6	4	....	....	Supplied by Loup City and Grand Island, Nebr., R. P. O.

TABLE C^c.—*Statement of mail service performed in closed pouches upon railroads and*

Initial and terminal stations running east to west, north to south, and northwest to southeast.	Division.	Number of route.	Contract designation, termini of route.	Corporate title of company.
Boisé City and Nampa, Idaho .	8	42004	Nampa, Boisé City, Idaho ...	Idaho Central Rwy ....
Bonne Terre and Summit, Mo	7	28043	Summit, Bonne Terre, Mo..	Saint Joe and Desloge......
Boston and Cook Street Station (n. o.), Mass.	1	3074	Boston, Cook Street Station (n. o.), Mass.	Boston and Albany R. R....
Boston and Dedham, Mass....	1	3036	Boston, Dedham, Mass......	Old Colony R. R., Providence Division.
Boston and Waltham, Mass....	1	3072	Boston, Waltham, Mass	Fitchburgh R. R ....
Boston and Winthrop, Mass...	1	3078	Boston, Winthrop, Mass....	Boston, Revere Beach and Lynn R. R. Co.
Boulder and Sunset, Colo......	7	38029	Boulder, Sunset, Colo......	Greeley, Salt Lake and Pacific.
Boulder Creek and Felton, Cal.	8	46045	Felton, Boulder Creek, Cal..	South Pacific Coast Rwy ....
Bowling Green and Tontogany, Ohio.	5	21070	Tontogany, Bowling Green, Ohio.	Bowling Green ....
Boykins, Va., and Roxobel, N. C.	3	13033	Boykins, Va., Roxobel, N. C.	Roanoke and Tar River.....
Bradford Junction and Salamanca, N. Y.	2	6102 (part)	Rochester, Salamanca, N. Y.	Buffalo, Rochester, and Pittsburgh.
Braintree Junction (n. o.) and Kingston Station (n. o.), Mass.	1	3064	Braintree Junction (n. o.), Kingston Station (n. o.), Mass.	Old Colony R. R ....
Brandon and Markesan, Wis ..	6	25055	Brandon, Markesan, Wis....	Chicago, Milwaukee and St. Paul.
Brandywine and Mechanicsville, Md.	3	10025	Brandywine, Mechanicsville, Md.	Washington and Potomac ..
Brazil and Saline City, Ind ...	5	22053	Brazil, Saline City, Ind......	Evansville and Indianapolis.
Breadysville and Abington Station, Pa.	2	8109	Abington Station, Breadysville, Pa.	Philadelphia and Reading ..
Bridgeport and Exton, Pa.....	2	8007	Bridgeport, Exton, Pa	......do ....
Bridgeton and Bridgeton Junction (n. o.), Me.	1	22	Bridgeton Junction (n. o.) and Bridgeton, Me.	Bridgeton and Saco River R. R.
Brighton and Boulder, Colo...	7	38002	Brighton, Boulder, Colo	Denver and Boulder Valley.
Brisbin and Goss Run Junction, Pa.	2	8120	Brisbin, Goss Run Junction, Pa.	Pennsylvania................
Bristol, Tenn , and Estillville, Va.	3	11040	Bristol, Tenn., Estillville, Va.	South Atlantic and Ohio....
Bristol and Franklin, N. H ...	1	1020	Franklin and Bristol, N. H..	Boston and Maine R. R., Lowell system Northern R. R.
Brookfield Junction (n. o.) and Danbury, Conn.	1	5022	Danbury, Brookfield Junction (n. o.), Conn.	Housatonic R. R............
Brownwood and Bollinger's Mills, Mo.	7	28005	Brownwood, Bollinger's Mills, Mo.	Cape Girardeau and Southwestern.

parts of railroads over which no railway post-offices run, in operation, etc.—Continued.

Miles of route.	Annual miles of service.	Number of round trips per week.	Number of pouches exchanged daily.	Date of last re-adjustment.	Average weight of mail whole distance daily.	Remarks.
					Pounds.	
20.69	28,138	13	8	June 28, 1888	487	Connects at Nampa, Idaho with Green River, Wyo., and Huntington, Oregon, R. P. O. New service established Sept. 14, 1887.
13.20	33,158	24	8	July 1, 1887	128	Connects at Summit, Mo., with Saint Louis, Mo., and Columbus, Ky., R. P. O., and Saint Louis, Mo., and Texarkana, Ark., R. P. O.
9.14	11,490	12	32	July 1, 1885	747	Boston exchanges pouches with Brookline, Chestnut Hill, Newton Centre, Newton Highlands, with additional round trip to Newton Centre, and five additional trips to Brookline.
9.75	18,369	18	26	July 1, 1885	449	Boston exchanges pouches with Jamaica Plain, Roslindale, West Roxbury, and Dedham.
11.05	20,818	18	13	July 1, 1885	197	Waltham exchanges pouches with Watertown, Boston ; Boston, Springfield and New York R. P. O., and Bangor and Boston R. P. O.; Boston exchanges pouches with Watertown.
5	9,420	18	6	July 1, 1888	115	Boston exchanges pouches with Winthrop, from August 10, 1887.
13.05	8,195	6	14	July 1, 1886	116	Connects at Boulder, Colo., with Greeley and Denver, Colo., R. P. O.
8.14	11,070	13	8	July 1, 1886	.66	Connects with San Francisco and Santa Cruz R. P. O.
5.94	11,191	18	8	July 1, 1888	224	
28.92	18,162	6	36	....	....	Connects Norfolk and Raleigh R. P. O. at Boykins.
¹1.33	1,670	12	6	July 1, 1885	668	¹ Balance of route (107.90 miles) covered by Rochester and Punxsutawney R. P. O. (See Table A°).
32.20	40,443	12	88	July 1, 1885	416	Boston exchanges pouches with East Braintree, Weymouth, North, East, and South Weymouth, Hingham, Nantasket, Hull, Cohasset, Scituate, Scituate Centre, North Scituate, Beechwood, Egypt, Greenbush, Sea View, Marshfield, East and Centre Marshfield, Castlecove, Brant Rock, Duxbury, South Duxbury, and Island Creek. One additional round trip daily from Braintree Junction to Hingham.
11.91	7,479	6	12	July 1, 1887	131	Supplied by Brandon, Wis., and by Oshkosh and Milwaukee, Wis., R. P. O.
20.30	12,748	6	22	July 1, 1885	220	Connects Bowie and Pope's Creek R. P. O. at Brandywine.
12.31	1,477	6	6	....	....	Railroad service established April 23, 1888.
9.83	12,346	12	14	July 1, 1885	190	
16.93	21,264	12	20	July 1, 1885	58	
16.30	20,473	12	16	July 1, 1885	224	Portland and Swanton R. P. O. exchanges pouches with Sandy Creek, Bridgeton, North Bridgeton, and Harrison. Portland and Swanton R. P. O. S. R. exchanges pouches with Sandy Creek, Bridgeton, North Bridgeton, and Harrison.
28.12	20,584	7	18	July 1, 1886	274	Trains run from Denver, Colo.; connects at Boulder, Colo., with Greeley and Denver, Colo., R. P. O., and at Erie and Canfield, Colo., with Lyons and Denver, Colo., pouch service.
1.04	653	6	2	July 1, 1886	51	
32.51	20,410	6	8	July 1, 1888	128	Connects lines centering at Bristol, Tenn.
13.13	8,246	6	22	July 1, 1885	142	Bristol exchanges pouches with Hill, Franklin, Franklin Falls, Concord, Saint Albans, and Boston R. P. O., and Claremont and Boston R. P. O. Hill exchanges pouches with Franklin Falls, Concord, Saint Albans, and Boston R. P. O., and Claremont and Boston R. P. O.
6.30	15,825	24	8	July 1, 1885	109	Danbury exchanges pouches with Pittsfield and Bridgeport, R. P. O.
8.63	5,420	6	4	....	....	New service; not reported last year; connects at Brownwood, Mo., with Cape Girardeau and Chaonia, Mo., R. P. O.

TABLE C*c*.—*Statement of mail service performed in closed pouches upon railroads and*

Initial and terminal stations running east to west, north to south, and northwest to southeast.	Division.	Number of route.	Contract designation, termini of route.	Corporate title of company.
Buena Vista and Gunnison,[1] Colo.	7	*38014 (part)	Schwander's Station (n. o.), Castleton, Colo.	Denver, South Park and Pacific.
Burke and Cœur d'Alene, Idaho.	8	42008	Cœur d'Alene, Burke, Idaho.	Cœur d'Alene Rwy. and Navigation Co.
Burlington and Lumberton, N. J.	2	7007	Burlington, Lumberton, N. J.	Penna. (Amboy Div) ......
Bustleton R. R. Station and Holmesburgh Junction, Pa.	2	8161	Holmesburgh Junction, Bustleton R. R. Station.	Pennsylvania...............
Buzzard's Bay and Wood's Holl, Mass.	1	9045	Buzzard's Bay, Wood's Holl, Mass.	Old Colony R. R.............
Cades and Saint Martinsville, La.	4	30012	Cades, Saint Martinsville, La.	Morgan's La. and Texas R. R.
Calais and Princeton, Me......	1	17	Calais, Princeton, Me	St. Croix and Penobscot R. R.
Calamine and Plattville, Wis..	6	25021	Calamine, Plattville, Wis...	Chicago, Milwaukee and St. Paul.
Calumet and Houghton, Mich.	6	24067	Houghton, Calumet, Mich..	Mineral Range ....
Cameron and Kansas City, Mo.	7	28060	Cameron, Kansas City, Mo..	Chicago, Rock Island and Pacific.
Campbell and New Almaden, Cal.	8	46049	Campbell, New Almaden, Cal.	South Pacific Coast Rwy ...
Canada Line and Rouse's Point, N. Y.	2	6066	Rouse's Point, Canada Line, N. Y.	Grand Trunk...............
Canada Line (n. o.) and Saint Albans, Vt.	1	2006	Saint Albans, Vt., Canada Line (n. o.).	Central Vermont R. R ....
Cañon City and West Cliff, Colo.	7	38010	Cañon City, West Cliff, Colo.	Denver and Rio Grande.....
Canton Junction (n. o.) and Stoughton, Mass.	1	3027	Cañton Junction (n. o.) and Stoughton, Mass.	Old Colony R. R. (Providence Division.)
Cape Vincent and Watertown, N. Y.	2	6035	Watertown, Cape Vincent, N. Y.	Rome, Watertown, and Ogdensburgh.
Carbon Centre, Mo., and Miami, Kans.	7	26,041	Miami, Kans., Carbon Centre, Mo.	Kansas City, Fort Scott, and Memphis.
Carbondale and Grand Tower, Ill.	6	22,069	Carbondale, Grand Tower, Ill.	Grand Tower and Carbondale.

parts of railroads over which no railway post-offices run, in operation, etc.—Continued.

Miles of route.	Annual miles of service.	Number of round trips per week.	Number of pouches exchanged daily.	Date of last re-adjustment.	Average weight of mail whole distance daily.	Remarks.
					Pounds.	
20.55	15,043	7	8	....	....	¹Last year there was R. P. O. service over route 38014 between Schwander's Station (n.o.) and Gunnison, Colo., which was discontinued September 27, 1887. Trains ran from Buena Vista to Schwander's Station (n. o.), Colo., over 3.90 miles of route 38031. ²14.92 miles of route 38014 between Castleton and Gunnison, Colo., covered by Castleton and Gunnison, Colo., pouch service. Service and pay on this route between Saint Elmo and Gunnison, Colo., was suspended from January 1 to June 30, 1888. Connects at Buena Vista, Colo., with Denver, Pueblo and Leadville R. P. O., Colorado Springs and Leadville R. P. O., and Como and Buena Vista, Colo., pouch service, and at Gunnison, Colo., with Denver, Colo., and Ogden, Utah, R. P. O., Crested Butte and Gunnison, Colo., and Castleton and Gunnison, Colo., pouch service.
99.16	72,585	7	26	June 27,1886	258	Supplied by Helena, Mont., and Portland, Oregon, R. P. O., and Spokane Falls, Wash., and exchanges made with initial and terminal offices. New service, established July 8, 1887.
10.42	13,068	12	4	July 1, 1885	102	
4.04	6,943	15	6	July 1, 1885	42	
17.88	22,394	12	26	July 1, 1885	514	Boston and Wellfleet R. P. O. exchanges pouches with Monument Beach, Pocasset, Cataumet, North Falmouth, West Falmouth, East Falmouth, Wood's Holl, Cottage City, Edgartown, Waqnoit, Vineyard Haven, Nantucket, and Siasconset.
7.06	16,385	14	4	July 1, 1886	88	
21.28	13,364	6	8	July 1, 1885	46	Calais exchanges pouches with Baring, Princeton, and Milltown. Princeton exchanges pouches with Baring.
18.74	23,527	12	16	July 1, 1887	282	Supplied by initial and terminal offices and by Rockford, Ill., and Mineral Point, Wis., R. P. O. Connects at Plattville, Wis., with Montfort, Wis., and Galena, Ill., R. P. O.
15.52	19,483	12	16	Apr. 15, 1886	318	Supplied by Houghton, Mich., and by Marquette and Houghton, Mich., R. P. O.
55.06	74,882	13	14	July 1, 1887	3,017	Quincy, Ill., and Kansas City, Mo., R. P. O. runs over same track between Cameron and Kansas City, Mo. Trains over this route carry closed mails between Kansas City, Mo., and lines centering there, and Davenport, Iowa, and Atchison, Kans., and Trenton, Mo., and Leavenworth, Kans., R. P. O's.
12.86	8,076	6	6	July 12, 1886	108	Including sacks. Supplied by San José. Connects with San Francisco and Santa Cruz R. P. O. at Campbell.
1.71	2,148	12	¹20	July 1, 1886	2,729	¹All sacks.
17.33	10,868	6	8	July 1, 1885	542	Saint Albans and Boston R. P. O. exchanges pouches with Highgate Springs, Vt., and Montreal. P. Q.
33.52	21,051	6	10	July 1, 1886	264	Connects at Cañon City, Colo., with Denver, Pueblo, and Leadville, Colo., R. P. O., and Denver, Colo., and Ogden, Utah, R. P. O.
4.00	10,043	24	10	July 1, 1886	138	Stoughton exchanges pouches with Boston, Mass., and Providence, R. I.
25.77	16,134	12	26	July 1, 1885	364	
24.65	15,103	6	30	July 1, 1887	171	Connects at Rich Hill, Mo., with Kansas City and Joplin, Mo., R. P. O., and at Miami, Kans., with Kansas City, Mo., and Memphis, Tenn., R. P. O.
26.90	33,661	12	10	July 1, 1887	192	Supplied by Carbondale, Ill., and by Centralia and Cairo, Ill., R. P. O.; connects at Murphysborough, Ill., with Saint Louis, Mo., and Cairo, Ill., and with Pinkneyville and Marion, Ill., R. P. O's.

TABLE C^c.—*Statement of mail service performed in closed pouches upon railroads and*

Initial and terminal stations running east to west, north to south, and northwest to southeast.	Division.	Number of route.	Contract designation, termini of route.	Corporate title of company.
Cardigan Junction and Saint Paul, Minn.	6	26062	Saint Paul, Cardigan Junction (n. c.), Minn.	Minn., Sault de Ste. Marie and Atl.
Carey and Findlay, Ohio........	5	21021	Carey, Findlay, Ohio........	Cincinnati, Sandusky and Cleveland.
Caro and Saginaw, Mich........	9	24614	Saginaw, Caro, Mich	Michigan Central............
Carroll and Kirkman, Iowa....	6	27071	Carroll, Kirkman, Iowa	Chicago and Northwestern..
C rrollton, N. Y., and Bradford, Pa.	2	8024	Bradford, Pa., Carrollton, N. Y.	New York, Lake Erie and Western.
Carson and Hastings, Iowa.....	6	27058	Hastings, Carson, Iowa	Chicago, Burlington and Quincy.
Carthage and San Antonio, N. Mex.	7	39009	San Antonio, Carthage, N. Mex.	Atchison, Topeka and Santa Fé.
Castleton and Gunnison, Colo..	7	¹38014 (part)	Schwander's Station (n. c.), Castleton, Colo.	Denver, South Park and Pacific.
Castroville and Monterey, Cal.	8	46030	Monterey, Castroville, Cal...	Southern Pacific Co.........
Cedar Falls and Hudson, Iowa.	6	²27056 (part)	Des Moines, Cedar Falls, Iowa.	Chicago, St. Paul and Kansas City.
Centralia and Columbia, Mo...	7	28009	Centralia, Columbia, Mo	Wabash Western............
Centreville and Yankton, Dak.	6	35021	Centreville, Yankton, Dak ..	Chicago and Northwestern..
Chadbourn, N. C., and Conway, S. C.	3	13024	Chadbourn, N. C., Conway, S. C.	Wilmington, Chadbourn and Conwayborough.
Chagrin Falls and Solon, Ohio.	5	21079	Solon, Chagrin Falls, Ohio..	Chagrin Falls and Southern.
Chambersburgh, Pa., and Edgemont, Md.	2	10021	Edgemont, Md., Chambersburgh, Pa.	Western Maryland ....
Chambersburgh and Waynesborough, Pa.	2	8077	Chambersburgh, Waynesborough, Pa.	Mont Alto ....
Chatham and Hudson, N. Y....	2	6ⁿ69	Hudson, Chatham, N. Y.....	Boston and Albany ....
Chehaw and Tuskegee, Ala ...	4	17019	Chehaw, Tuskegee, Ala.....	Tuskegee R. R.............
Cherokee and Onawa, Iowa ..	6	27099	Cherokee, Onawa, Iowa	Illinois Central ....

parts of railroads over which no railway post-offices run, in operation, etc.—Continued.

Miles of route.	Annual miles of service.	Number of round trips per week.	Number of pouches exchanged daily.	Date of last re-adjustment.	Average weight of mail whole distance daily.	Remarks.
					Pounds.	
8	10,068	12	4	....	....	Connects Bruce, Wis., and Minneapolis, Minn., R. P. O. with St. Paul, Minn., and lines centering there.
16	20,006	12	14	July 1, 1888	196	
34.04	42,754	12	45	July 1, 1884	281	At Vassar, Mich., connects East Saginaw and Port Huron and Mackinac City and Detroit R. P. O's. At East Saginaw, Mich., connects Bay City, Wayne, and Detroit, East Saginaw and Howard City, Ludington and Toledo and Manistee and East Saginaw R. P. O's. At Saginaw, Mich., connects Bay City and Jackson R. P. O.
35.07	44,048	12	28	July 1, 1887	335	Supplied by Carroll and Manning, Iowa, and by Cedar Rapids and Council Bluffs, Iowa, R. P. O. Connects at Carroll, Iowa, with Carroll and Moville, Iowa, R. P. O., and at Manning, Iowa, with Marion and Council Bluffs, Iowa, R. P. O., and with Manning and Audubon, Iowa, pouch service.
11.58	32,725	27	30	July 1, 1885	879	
16.24	20,397	12	6	July 1, 1886	879	Supplied by initial and terminal offices and by Burlington and Council Bluffs, Iowa, R. P. O.; connects at Carson, Iowa, with Avoca and Carson, Iowa, pouch service, and at Hastings, Iowa, with Hastings and Sidney, Iowa, pouch service.
9.01	6,595	7	6	July 1, 1887	145	Connects at San Antonio, N. Mex., with Albuquerque, N. Mex., and El Paso, Tex., R. P. O.
14.92	9,370	6	2	May 26, 1884	385	[1]20.55 miles of route 38014, between Schwander's Station (n. o.) and Saint Elmo, Colo., covered by Buena Vista and Gunnison, Colo., pouch service. Service and pay on this route between Saint Elmo and Gunnison, Colo., was suspended from January 1 to June 30, 1888. Connects at Gunnison, Colo., with Denver, Colo., and Ogden, Utah, R. P. O.; Crested Butte and Gunnison, Colo., and Buena Vista and Gunnison, Colo., pouch service.
16.67	23,671	13	12	July 1, 1886	169	Connects at Castroville with San Francisco and Santa Cruz R. P. O.; Monterey and Pacific Grove exchange with San Francisco.
10.59	13,301	12	4	....	....	Balance of route covered by Oelwein and Des Moines, Iowa, R. P. O. (See Table A[1].) Connects Oelwein and Des Moines, Iowa, R. P. O. with Cedar Falls, Iowa.
22.14	32,413	14	22	July 1, 1887	524	Connects at Centralia, Mo., with Saint Louis, Moberly, and Kansas City, Mo., R. P. O., and Saint Louis, Louisiana and Kansas City R. P. O.
29.39	43,027	14	12	July 1, 1886	271	Supplied by Yankton, Dak., and by Oakes, Dak., and Hawarden, Iowa, R. P. O.; connects at Yankton, Dak., with Manilla, Iowa, and Mitchell, Dak., R. P. O.
39.17	24,599	6	12	July 1, 1888	83	Connects Wilmington and Jacksonville R. P. O. at Chadbourn.
5.57	13,992	24	12	July 1, 1888	207	
21.93	41,316	18	36	July 1, 1885	110	
22.18	27,858	12	16	July 1, 1885	292	
17.96	28,197	15	16	July 1, 1885	133	
6.00	7,536	12	8	July 1, 1888	143	
61.18	38,421	6	32	Aug. 3, 1888	222	Supplied by initial and terminal offices. Connects at Cherokee, Iowa, with Dubuque and Sioux City, Iowa, R. P. O., and with Cherokee, Iowa, and Sioux Falls, Dak., pouch service. Connects at Correctionville, Iowa, with Carroll and Moville, Iowa, R. P. O., and at Onawa, Iowa, with Sioux City and Missouri Valley, Iowa, R. P. O.

TABLE C°.—*Statement of mail service performed in closed pouches upon railroads and*

Initial and terminal stations running east to west, north to south, and northwest to southeast.	Division.	Number of route.	Contract designation, termini of route.	Corporate title of compa n
Cherokee, Iowa, and Sioux Falls, Dak.	6	27100	Cherokee, Iowa, Sioux Falls, Dak.	Illinois Central ....
Cherry Vale and Coffeyville, Kans.	7	¹33004 (part)	Cherry Vale, Coffeyville, Kans.	Southern Kansas ....
Cherry Valley and Cobleskill, N. Y.	2	6027	Cobleskill, Cherry Valley, N. Y.	Delaware and Hudson Canal Co.
Citrus Station (n. o.) and Riverside, Cal.	8	46033	Citrus Station, Riverside, Cal.	California Southern R. R ...
Claremont and Belfield, Va....	3	11034	Claremont, Belfield, Va.....	Atlantic and Danville ......
Chippewa Falls and Eau Claire, Wis.	6	¹25026 (part)	Abbotaford, Eau Claire, Wis.	Wisconsin Central..........
Claremont and Claremont Junction, N. H. (n. o.).	1	1009 (part)	Concord, Claremont Junction, N. H. (n. o.).	Boston and Maine R. R. (Lowell System).
Clarion Junction and Clarion, Pa.	2	8147	Clarion Junction, Clarion, Pa.	Pittsburgh and Western....
Clarke City and Buckingham, Ill.	6	23686	Buckingham, Clarke City, Ill.	Illinois Central ....
Clarksville, Tenn., and Princeton, Ky.	5	19024	Clarksville, Tenn., Princeton, Ky.	Louisville and Nashville....
Clifton, Ariz., and Lordsburg, N. Mex.	8	39012	Lordsburg, N. Mex., Clifton, Ariz.	Arizona and New Mexico R. R.
Climax and Bainbridge, Ga....	4	¹15031 (part)	Thomasville, Bainbridge, Ga.	Savannah, Fla., and Western R. R.
Clinton and Port Hudson, La..	4	30006	Clinton, Port Hudson, La...	Louisiana, New Orleans and Texas R. R.
Cloquet and Northern Pacific Junction, Minn.	6	26036	Junction, Cloquet, Minn....	Saint Paul and Duluth ....

parts of railroads over which no railway post-offices run, in operation, etc.—Continued.

Miles of route.	Annual miles of service.	Number of round trips per week.	Number of pouches exchanged daily.	Date of last readjustment.	Average weight of mail whole distance daily.	Remarks.
					Miles.	
97.07	60,960	6	38	....	....	Supplied by initial and terminal offices. Connects at Cherokee, Iowa, with Dubuque and Sioux City, Iowa, R. P. O., and with Cherokee and Onawa, Iowa, pouch service; at Sheldon, Iowa, with Saint Paul, Minn., and Council Bluffs, Iowa, and with Calmar, Iowa, and Chamberlain, Dak., R. P. O's.; at Rock Rapids, Iowa, with Luverne, Minn., and Doon, Iowa, pouch service, and at Sioux Falls, Dak., with all lines centering at that point.
16.68	22,685	12	14	July 1,1886	2,740	[1] 27.39 miles of route 33004, between Lawrence and Ottawa, Kans., covered by Lawrence and Gridley, Kans., R. P. O., and 97.80 miles between Ottawa and Cherry Vale, Kans., covered by Kansas City, Mo., and Wellington, Kans., R. P. O. Connects at Cherry Vale, Kans., with Kansas City, Mo., and Wellington, Kans., R. P. O.; Arcadia and Cherry Vale, Kans., R. P. O.; Saint Louis, Mo., and Halstead, Kans., R. P. O., and Chanute and Longton, Kans., R. P. O. Connects at Coffeyville, Kans., with Chetopa and Larned, Kans., R. P. O.; Holden, Mo., and Coffeyville, Kans., R. P. O., and Kincaid and Coffeyville, Kans., R. P. O
22.86	28,712	12	16	July 1,1885	220	
3.79	11,097	28	34	Jan. 25,1887	502	Connects at Citrus Station with San Bernardino and National City R. P. O. Riverside exchanges with Deming, N. Mex., and Los Angeles, Cal., and Albuquerque, N. Mex., and Los Angeles, Cal., R. P. O's; also Colton, San Bernardino, and Los Angeles, Cal., pouches for offices Riverside to Capistrano carried over this line.
55.10	34,603	6	6	Sept. 15,1886	73	Connects Norfolk and Lynchburgh R. P. O. at Waverly Station and Washington and Wilmington R. P. O. at Belfield.
11.29	14,186	12	8	July 1,1887	1,465	[1] Balance of route covered by Chicago, Ill., Abbotaford, Wis., and Minneapolis, Minn., R. P. O. (See Table A*.) Connects at Eau Claire, Wis., with Saint Paul, Minn., and Elroy, Wis., and with Duluth and Eau Claire, Wis., R. P. O. Also with Eau Claire, Wis., and Wabash, Minn., R. P. O.
2.02	6,342	30	20	July 1,1885	452	Balance of route, 54.90 miles, covered by R. P. O. service. (See Table A*.) Claremont exchanges pouches with West Claremont, Newport, and Springfield R. P. O., Newport and Springfield R. P. O. & R., and New York. Newport exchanges pouches with Newport and Springfield R. P. O., Newport and Springfield R. P. O. & R. Claremont and Boston R. P. O. exchanges with Boston and Troy R. P. O. and Newport and Springfield R. P. O.
6.43	16,127	24	10	July 1,1885	185	
9.72	6,104	6	2	July 1,1887	15	Supplied by Buckingham, Ill., and by Kankakee and Kankakee Junction, Ill., R. P. O.
....	12,099	6	24	July 1,1888	119	Clarksville and Newstead R. R. (29.70 miles), extended to Princeton, Ky., February 13, 1888, increasing distance 27.83 miles; February 18, 1888, R. P. O. service established. (See Table A*.)
71.51	44,908	6	8	....	....	Connects at Lordsburgh with Deming, N. Mex., and Los Angeles, Cal., R. P. O.; supplied by initial and terminal offices.
[2] 9.40	11,806	12	4	July 1,1884	881	[1] 127.59 miles of route reported as Waycross and Chattahoochee R. P. O. (See Table A*.)
22.10	7,536	[3] 6	4	July 1,1886	65	[3] 3 round trips per week, only, between Ethel and Port Hudson.
6.67	4,188	6	2	....	....	Supplied by Northern Pacific Junction and by Duluth and Saint Paul, Minn., R. P. O.; connects at Northern Pacific Junction with Duluth and Brainerd, Minn., R. P. O.

TABLE C^c.—*Statement of mail service performed in closed pouches upon railroads and*

Initial and terminal stations running east to west, north to south, and northwest to southeast.	Division.	Number of route.	Contract designation termini of route.	Corporate title of company.
Clove Valley and Clove Branch Junction, N. Y.	2	6114	Clove Branch Junction, Clove Valley, N. Y.	Newburgh, Dutchess and Connecticut.
Coburn Junction and Ponca, Nebr.	6	34007	Coburn Junction and Ponca, Nebr.	Chicago, Saint Paul, Minn., and Omaha.
Coalport and Cresson, Pa	2	8168	Coalport, Cresson, Pa	Clearfield County and New York Short Route.
Cochran and Hawkinsville, Ga.	4	15038	Cochran, Hawkinsville, Ga .	East Tennessee, Virginia and Georgia R. R.
Colby and Oakley, Kans.	7	33085	Colby, Oakley, Kans	Oakley and Colby............
Coleman Junction (n. o.) and Coleman, Tex.	7	31051	Coleman Junction (n. o.), Coleman, Tex.	Gulf, Colorado and Santa Fé.
Coleman and Mount Pleasant, Mich.	9	24043	Coleman, Mount Pleasant, Mich.	Flint and Pere Marquette ..
Colorado Springs and Manitou Springs, Colo.	7	38080	Colorado Springs Station (n. o.), Manitou Springs, Colo.	Denver and Rio Grande.....
Colton and Scofield, Utah......	8	41009	Colton, Scofield, Utah	Denver and Rio Grande Rwy.
Colony and Neosho Falls, Kans.	7	33072	Colony, Neosho Falls, Kans.	Chicago, Kansas and Western.
Columbia Junction and Delaware Station, N. J.	2	7059	Delaware Station, Columbia Junction, N. J.	New York, Susquehanna and Western.
Columbus and La Grange, Tex.	7	31014	Columbus, La Grange, Tex.	Galveston, Harrisburgh and San Antonio.
Colusa and Sites, Cal..........	8	46048	Colusa, Sites, Cal	Colusa and Lake R. R ......
Como and Buena Vista, Colo'..	7	38031	Como, Buena Vista, Colo ...	Denver, South Park and Pacific.
Como and King, Colo	7	38032	Como, King, Colo.............	Denver, South Park and Pacific.
Conesus Lake Junction and Lakeville, N. Y.	2	6047	Conesus Lake Junction, Lakeville, N. Y.	Conesus Lake................
Cook Street Station (n. o.) and Bellingham, Mass.	1	9683	Cook Street Station (n. o.) Bellingham, Mass.	New York and New England R. R.
Cooperstown and Cooperstown Junction, N. Y.	2	6086	Cooperstown, Cooperstown Junction, N. Y.	Cooperstown and O. Valley.
Cooperstown and Sanborn, Dak.	6	35013	Sanborn, Cooperstown, Dak.	Sanborn, Cooperstown and Turtle Mountain.
Copley and Milton Junction (n. o.), Mich.	9	24059	Copley, Milton Junction (n. o.), Mich	Grand Rapids and Indiana .

parts of railroads over which no railway post-offices run, in operation, etc.—Continued.

Miles of route.	Annual miles of service.	Number of round trips per week.	Number of pouches exchanged daily.	Date of last re-adjustment.	Average weight of mail whole distance daily.	Remarks.
8.10	5,087	6	6	July 1, 1885	*Pounds.* 44	
16.44	10,324	6	8	July 1, 1886	194	Supplied by Sioux City, Iowa. Connects at Coburn Junction, Nebr., with Sioux City, Iowa, and Omaha, Nebr., and with Covington and Norfolk, Nebr., R. P. O.'s.
24.60	15,448	6	10	July 1, 1888	72	
10.39	13,049	12	4	July 1, 1888	179	
22.12	13,391	6	4	July 1, 1888	202	New service; not reported last year. Connects at Oakley, Kans., with Kansas City, Mo., and Denver, Colo., R. P. O.
6.25	4,575	7	4	Aug. 16, 1886	113	Connects at Coleman Junction (n. o.) Tex., with Temple and Ballinger, Tex., R. P. O.
15.04	18,890	12	16	July 1, 1884	210	Connects at Coleman, Mich., with Ludington and Toledo and Manistee and East Saginaw R. P. O's. Connects at Mount Pleasant, Mich., with the Mount Pleasant and Toledo R. P. O.
5.40	15,811	28	12	July 1, 1886	235	Connects at Colorado Springs, Colo., with Denver, Colo., and Ogden, Utah, R. P. O.; Denver, Pueblo, and Leadville, Colo., R. P. O., and Colorado Springs and Leadville, Colo., R. P. O. Connects at Colorado City and Manitou Springs, Colo., with Colorado Springs and Leadville, Colo., R. P. O.
17.40	10,927	6	4	July 1, 1886	19	Connects at Colton with Denver, Colo., and Ogden, Utah, R. P. O.
12.17	7,643	6	10	July 1, 1888	80	Connects at Colony, Kans., with Kansas City, Mo., and Wellington, Kans., R. P. O., and Butler, Mo., and Madison, Kans. R. P. O. Connects at Neosho Falls, Kans., with Junction City, and Parsons, Kans., R. P. O.
3.16	1,984	6	2	July 1, 1885	1,978	
31.60	19,845	6	10	July 1, 1886	233	Connects at Columbus, Tex., with Houston and Eagle Pass, Tex., R. P. O.
21.92	16,045	7	12	June 27, 1888	118	Connects at Colusa Junction with Redding and Sacramento R. P. O.
48.38	²38,196	7	20	....	....	¹Last year there was R. P. O. service over this route, which was discontinued September 27, 1887. ²Buena Vista and Gunnison, Colo., trains double 3.80 miles of route 38031 each day. Connects at Como, Colo., with Denver and Leadville, Colo., R. P. O., and Como and King, Colo., pouch service, and at Buena Vista, Colo., with Denver, Pueblo, and Leadville, Colo., R. P. O.; Colorado Springs and Leadville, Colo., R. P. O. and Buena Vista and Gunnison, Colo., pouch service. Connects at Garo, Colo., with Garo and London, Colo., pouch service.
3.48	2,185	6	2	July 1, 1888	24	New service; not reported last year. Connects at Como, Colo., with Denver and Leadville, Colo., R. P. O., and Como and Buena Vista, Colo., pouch service.
1.90	2,386	12	4	July 1, 1885	54	
22.64	14,217	6	42	July 1, 1885	252	Boston exchanges pouches with Newton, Upper Falls, Highlandville, Needham, Charles River Village, Dover, Millis, Medway, West Medway, Caryville, North Bellingham, and Bellingham, with additional round trip to North Bellingham.
16.50	20,724	12	22	July 1, 1885	395	
36.35	22,828	6	16	July 1, 1886	115	Supplied by initial and terminal offices. Connects at Sanborn, Dak., with Saint Paul, Minn., and Mandan, Dak., R. P. O.
14.18	17,810	12	14	Oct. 15, 1885	102	At Milton Junction (n. o.) connects Cadillac and Fort Wayne and Mackinaw City and Grand Rapids R. P. O's.

Table C*c*.—*Statement of mail service performed in closed pouches upon railroads and*

Initial and terminal stations running east to west, north to south, and northwest to southeast.	Division.	Number of route.	Contract designation, termini of route.	Corporate title of company.
[1]Corbin and Pineville, Ky......	5	20027	Corbin, Pineville, Ky........	Louisville and Nashville....
Cornwall and Conewago, Pa...	2	8154	Cornwall, Conewago, Pa	Cornwall and Lebanon......
Cornwell and Mt. Sterling, Ky.	5	20022	Mt. Sterling, Cornwell, Ky..	Coal Road Construction Co.
Cortland and Sycamore, Ill....	6	23052	Cortland, Sycamore, Ill.....	Chicago and Northwestern.
Coudersport and Port Allegheny, Pa.	2	8144	Port Allegheny, Coudersport, Pa.	Coudersport and Port Allegheny.
[1]Covington and Snoddy's Mills, Ind.	5	22040	Covington, Snoddy's Mills, Ind.	Chicago and Eastern Illinois.
Cresson and Ebensburgh, Pa...	2	8037	Cresson, Ebensburgh, Pa...	Pennsylvania............ ..
Crested Butte and Gunnison, Colo.	7	38016	Gunnison, Crested Butte, Colo.	Denver and Rio Grande.....
Crown Point and Hammondsville, N. Y.	2	6099	Crown Point, Hammondsville, N. Y.	Crown Point Iron Company.
Cucharas and El Moro, Colo...	7	[1]38001 (part)	Denver, El Moro, Colo......	Denver and Rio Grande ....
Cummins and Varner, Ark....	7	29016	Varner, Cummins, Ark.....	Varner Branch ....
Curtis, Nebr., and Sterling, Colo.	6	[1]34042 (part)	Elwood, Nebr., Sterling, Colo.	Nebraska and Colorado.....
Cuthbert and Fort Gaines, Ga.	4	15041	Cuthbert. Fort Gaines, Ga..	Southwestern R. R.........
Daguscahonda and Dagus Mines, Pa.	2	8139	Daguscahonda, Dagus Mines, Pa.	Daguscahonda ....
Dalark and Arkadelphia, Ark.	7	29022	Arkadelphia, Dalark, Ark ..	Ultima Thule, Arkadelphia and Mississippi.
[1]Danbury and Point Marblehead, Ohio.	5	21101	Danbury, Point Marblehead, Ohio.	Lakeside and Marblehead..
Danville, Va., and Leaksville, N. C.	3	13022	Danville, Mocksville, Southwestern Junction (n. o.), Va., Leaksville, N. C.	Danville, Mocksville and Southwestern.
Decorah and Connover, Iowa..	6	27026	Connover, Decorah, Iowa ...	Chicago, Milwaukee and Saint Paul.
DeLand Landing (n. o.) and DeLand, Fla.	4	16020	DeLand Landing (n. o.) DeLand, Fla.	DeLand and St. Johns River Rwy.
Delhi and Walton, N. Y	2	6050	Walton, Delhi, N. Y.........	New York, Ontario and Western.
Denver and Pueblo, Colo......	7	38035	Denver, Pueblo, Colo........	Atchison, Topeka and Santa Fe.

parts of railroads over which no railway post-offices run, in operation, etc.—Continued.

Miles of route.	Annual miles of service.	Number of round trips per week.	Number of pouches exchanged daily.	Date of last re-adjustment.	Average weight of mail whole distance daily.	Remarks.
31.43	4,071	6	12	....	*Pounds.*	[1] Service established March 19, 1888, between Corbin and Barbourville, Ky., distance 16.74 miles. May 21, 1888, service extended to Pineville, Ky., increasing distance 14.69 miles.
16.96	20,422	12	12	July 1, 1885	43	
18.75	11,775	6	4	July 1, 1884	97	
4.94	6,204	12	6	July 1, 1887	32	Supplied by Cortland, Ill., and by Chicago, Ill., and Cedar Rapids, Iowa, R. P. O. Connects at Sycamore, Ill., with Caledonia and Spring Valley, Ill., R. P. O.
17.57	22,068	12	8	July 1, 1885	205	
....	4,954	6	2	July 1, 1884	37	[1] April 30, 1888, service discontinued.
11.59	21,836	18	10	July 1, 1885	255	
28.62	17,973	6	10	July 1, 1886	160	Connects at Gunnison, Colo., with Denver, Colo., and Ogden, Utah, R. P. O., and Castleton and Gunnison, Colo., pouch service, and Buena Vista and Gunnison, Colo., pouch service.
11.95	15,109	12	8	July 1, 1885	43	
37.10	27,157	7	4	July 1, 1886	2,975	[1] 120.14 miles of route 380*1, between Denver and Pueblo, Colo., covered by Denver, Pueblo and Leadville, Colo., R. P. O., and 49.70 miles, between Pueblo and Cucharas, Colo., by Pueblo and Silverton, Colo., R. P. O. (See Table A*.) Connects at Cucharas, Colo., with Pueblo and Silverton, Colo., R. P. O., and at El Moro, Colo., with La Junta, Colo., and Albuquerque, N. Mex., R. P. O., and Pueblo, Colo., and Texline (n. o.), Tex., pouch service.
5.75	7,222	12	4	July 1, 1886	32	Connects at Varner, Ark., with Fort Smith, Ark., and Leland, Miss., R. P. O.
158.34	115,905	7	44	....	....	[1] Balance of route (44.32 miles) covered by Edgar and Curtis, Nebr., R. P. O. (See Table A*.) Supplied by Sterling. Colo., and by Edgar and Curtis, Nebr., R. P. O. Connects at Sterling, Colo., with Julesburgh and Denver, Colo., R. P. O.
23.23	14,588	6	4	July 1, 1888	133	
6.01	7,549	12	4	July 1, 1885	65	
11.43	8,347	7	2	July 1, 1888	40	New service; not reported last year. Connects at Arkadelphia, Ark., with Saint Louis, Mo., and Texarkana, Ark., R. P. O.
8	8,640	12	12	July 1, 1888	86	[1] Service established August 22, 1887.
7.97	5,005	6	10	July 1, 1880	37	Supplied by closed pouches from Danville, Va.
9.51	11,944	12	10	July 1, 1887	935	Supplied by Connover, Iowa, and by Chicago, Ill., McGregor, Iowa, and Saint Paul, Minn., R. P. O. Connects at Decorah, Iowa, with Decorah and Cedar Rapids, Iowa, R. P. O.
5.30	9,952	18	8	July 1, 1888	273	
17.29	27,145	15	20	July 1, 1885	236	
117.46	226,203	[1]21	24	July 1, 1888	2,384	[1] 14 round trips over entire route and 7 round trips between Colorado Springs and Denver, Colo. (74.10 miles). New service; not reported last year. Makes Denver, Colo., and Pueblo, Colo., connections. Connects at Castle Rock, Colo., with Denver, Pueblo and Leadville, Colo., R. P. O., and Denver, Colo., and Ogden, Utah, R. P. O., and at Colorado Springs, Colo., with Denver, Pueblo and Leadville, Colo., R. P. O., Denver, Colo., and Ogden, Utah, R. P. O., Colorado Springs and Leadville, Colo., R. P. O., and Colorado Springs and Manitou Springs, Colo., pouch service.

TABLE C°.—*Statement of mail service performed in closed pouches upon railroads and*

Initial and terminal stations running east to west, north to south, and northwest to southeast.	Division.	Number of route.	Contract designation, termini of route.	Corporate title of company.
Derby Line and Newport, Vt..	1	2010 (part)	White River Junction, Derby Line, Vt.	Boston and Maine R. R., Lowell system.
Deshler and McComb, Ohio....	5	21050	Deshler, McComb, Ohio	McComb, Deshler, and Toledo.
Dexter and Arkansas City, Kans.	7	33092	Dexter, Arkansas City, Kans.	Grouse Creek...............
Dexter and Newport, Me.......	1	2	Newport, Dexter, Me........	Maine Central R. R.........
Dexterville and Hogan, Wis ..	6	25065	Dexterville, Hogan, Wis....	Wisconsin, Pittsfield, and Superior.
Dillon and Dickey, Colo.......	7	38026	Dickey Station (n. o.), Dillon, Colo.	Denver, South Park and Pacific.
Dillsburgh and Mechanicsburgh Junction and Shippensburgh, Pa.	2	8126	Dillsburgh, Mechanicsburgh Junction, and Shippensburgh, Pa.	Harrisburgh and Potomac..
Dodge and Clay City, Ky......	5	20023	Dodge, Clay City, Ky	Kentucky Union ....
Dolomite and Wheeling, Ala ..	4	17018	Dolomite, Wheeling Station (n. o.), Ala.	Woodward Iron Co.........
Dover and Chester, N. J.......	2	7014	Dover, Chester, N. J........	Del., Lack. and West. (M. and E. div.).
Dover and Portsmouth, N. H..	1	1015	Portsmouth, Dover, N. H...	Boston and Maine R. R.....
Doylestown and Lansdale, Pa.	2	8075	Lansdale, Doylestown, Pa..	Philadelphia and Reading ..
Dresden and Penn Yan, N. Y.	2	6007	Dresden, Penn Yan, N. Y..	Fall Brook................
Dudley and Saxton, Pa........	2	8138	Saxton, Dudley, Pa........	Hunt. and Broad Top.......
Durant and Tchula, Miss	4	18023	Durant, Tchula, Miss......	Illinois Central R. R ......
Drummond and Phillipsburgh, Mont.	8	36004	Drummond, Phillipsburgh, Mont.	Northern Pacific R. R ......
Eagle and Elkhorn, Wis	6	25041	Elkhorn, Eagle, Wis........	Chicago, Milwaukee, and Saint Paul.
Eagle Bend and Sauk Centre, Minn.	6	26047	Sauk Centre, Eagle Bend, Minn.	Saint Paul, Minn., and Manitoba.
East Berlin and Berlin, Pa	2	8033	Berlin, East Berlin, Pa	Western Maryland ....
East Las Vegas and Las Vegas Hot Springs, N. Mex.	7	39007	Las Vegas, Las Vegas Hot Springs, N. Mex.	Atchison, Topeka, and Santa Fé.
Easton and Oxford, Md........	2	9503 (part)	Easton, Oxford. Md	P. W. and B. (Del. Div).....
East Saugus and Boston, Mass	1	3002	Boston, East Saugus, Mass..	Boston and Maine R. R .....
Ebervale and Lumber Yard, Pa.	2	8134	Lumber Yard, Ebervale, Pa.	Lehigh Valley ....
Echo and Belton, Tex	7	31041	Echo, Belton, Tex...........	Missouri Pacific ....
Echo and Park City, Utah.....	8	41008	Echo, Park City, Utah	Echo and Park City R. R ...
Eckley and Tunnel, Pa........	2	8135	Tunnel, Eckley, Pa	Lehigh Valley ....

parts of railroads over which no railway post-offices run, in operation, etc.—Continued.

Miles of route.	Annual miles of service.	Number of round trips per week.	Number of pouches exchanged daily.	Date of last re-adjustment.	Average weight of mail whole distance daily.	Remarks.
					Miles.	
10.14	6,368	6	28	Aug. 5, 1885	3,128	Balance of route (105.15 miles) covered by R. P. O. service. (See Table A°.) Newport and Springfield R. P. O. daily line exchanges pouches with Derby Line, North Derby, Beebe Plain, Montreal, Quebec, Stanstead, Stanstead and Sherbrooke R. P. O.'s. Newport and Springfield R. P. O. night line exchanges pouches with Derby Line and Beebe Plain. Newport exchanges pouches with North Derby, Derby Line, Beebe Plain, and Lenoxville.
10.28	12,912	12	10	July 1, 1888	44	
26.26	19,222	7	4	....	......	New service; not reported last year. Connects at Dexter, Kans., with Chetopa and Larned, Kans., R. P. O., and at Arkansas City, Kans., with Beaumont and Bluffs, Kans., R. P. O., Florence and Arkansas City, Kans., R. P. O., and Newton, Kan., and Gainesville, Tex., R. P. O.
14.92	18,738	12	20	July 1, 1886	318	Bangor and Boston R. P. O. day line exchanges pouches with Corinna, Cambridge, Dexter, and Dover. Dexter exchanges pouches with Corinna and Newport exchanges pouches with Corinna.
15.72	9,872	6	4	Aug. 25, 1888	17	Supplied by Dexterville, Wis.; connects at Dexterville, Wis., with Fort Howard, Wis., and Winona, Minn., R. P. O., and with Dexterville Junction and Vesper, Wis., closed-pouch service.
2.94	1,846	6	2	July 1, 1886	43	Connects at Dickey Station (n. o.), Colo., with Denver and Leadville, Colo., R. P. O.
28.82	36,197	12	26	July 1, 1886	178	
14.75	9,263	6	20	Mar. 15, 1886	97	
4.80	8,014	6	2	July 1, 1888	65	
14.05	17,647	12	10	July 1, 1885	165	
11.62	14,594	12	10	July 1, 1885	125	Dover exchanges pouches with Dover Point, Portsmouth, Bangor, and Boston R. P. O., and Boston with one additional trip from Portsmouth to Dover, daily.
10.71	36,992	83	22	July 1, 1885	564	
6.28	7,888	12	12	Aug. 26, 1885	65	
6.18	3,881	6	4	July 1, 1885	96	
27.41	17,213	6	8	July 1, 1888	123	
26.47	19,376	7	12	July 1, 1888	253	New service. Established December 16, 1887. Connects at Drummond with Helena, Mont., and Portland, Oregon, R. P. O.
17.56	11,027	6	16	July 1, 1887	47	Supplied by initial and terminal offices. Connects with Eagle, Wis., with Chicago, Ill., and North McGregor, Iowa, R. P. O., and at Elkhorn, Wis., with Racine, Wis., and Rock Island, Ill., R. P. O.
36.91	23,179	6	18	July 1, 1887	146	Supplied by Sauk Centre, Minn. Connects at Sauk Centre, Minn., with Fargo, Dak., Barnesville and Saint Paul, Minn., and with Little Falls and Morris, Minn., R. P. O.
7.23	4,540	6	4	July 1, 1885	76	[1]Trains 21 times a week westward and 14 times a week eastward. Connects at East Las Vegas, New Mex., with La Junta, Colo., and Albuquerque, N. Mex., R. P. O.
6.45	11,804	(¹)	10	July 1, 1886	103	
[1]10.62	6,669	9	6	July 1, 1885	497	[1]Balance of route (44.08 miles) covered by Clayton and Easton R. P. O. (See Table A°).
10.74	13,489	12	28	July 1, 1885	199	Boston exchanges pouches with Linden, Cliftondale, Saugus, and East Saugus.
6.23	6,811	9	12	July 1, 1885	169	
7.06	10,336	14	10	July 1, 1886	246	Connects at Echo, Tex., with Denison and San Antonio, Tex., R. P. O., and at Belton, Tex., with Temple and Ballinger, Tex., R. P. O.
28.29	61,417	14	14	July 1, 1886	324	Park City exchanges with Ogden and Salt Lake City R. P. O. Connects at Echo with Omaha, Nebr., and Ogden, Utah, R. P. O.
1.20	754	6	5	July 1, 1885	87	

TABLE C^c.—*Statement of mail service performed in closed pouches upon railroads and*

Initial and terminal stations running east to west, north to south, and northwest to southeast.	Division.	Number of route.	Contract designation, termini of route.	Corporate title of company.
Edgeley and Aberdeen, Dak ...	6	¹35012 (part)	Ashton, Edgeley, Dak......	Chicago, Milwaukee and Saint Paul.
Eland and Wausau, Wis......	6	¹25049 (part)	Manitowoc, Wausau, Wis..	Milwaukee, Lake Shore and Western.
Elizabethtown and Cecelian, Ky.	5	20010	Elizabethtown, Cecelian, Ky.	Chesapeake, Ohio and Southwest.
Elkton and Guthrie, Ky.......	5	20001	Elkton, Guthrie, Ky........	Louisville and Nashville....
Ellenville and Summitville, N. Y.	2	6113	Summitville, Ellenville, N. Y.	N. Y., Ont. and West ....
Ellsworth, Minn., and Sioux Falls, Dak.	6	27037	Ellsworth, Minn., Sioux Falls, Dak.	Burlington, Cedar Rapids and Northern.
Elmer and Salem, N. J........	2	7021	Elmer, Salem, N. J.........	West Jersey.................
El Moro and Trinidad, Colo ...	7	38033	El Moro, Trinidad, Colo	Denver and Rio Grande.....
¹ Elora, Tenn., and Huntsville, Ala.	5	17032	Huntsville, Ala., Elora, Tenn.	Nash., Chatt. and St. Louis.
El Paso, Tex., and Deming, N. Mex.	7	39005	Deming, N. Mex., El Paso, Tex.	Southern Pacific...........
Emmitsburgh and Rocky Ridge, Md.	3	10019	Emmittsburgh, Rocky Ridge, Md.	Emmittsburgh...............
English and Pine Bluff, Ark...	7	29020	Pine Bluff, English, Ark	Pine Bluff, Monroe and New Orleans.
Escondida and Oceanside, Cal.	8	46057	Oceanside, Escondida, Cal...	California Central Rwy.....
Essex and Wenham Depot, Mass.	1	3008	Wenham Depot, Essex, Mass	Boston and Maine R. R.....
Eufaula and Clayton, Ala.....	4	17021	Eufaula, Clayton, Ala......	Eufaula and Clayton........
Eureka and Hydesville, Cal...	8	46044	Eureka, Hydesville, Cal....	Eel River and Eureka R. R.
Eureka and Roscoe, Dak......	6	35032	Roscoe, Eureka, Dak.......	Chicago, Milwaukee and Saint Paul.
Eustis and Leesburgh, Fla	4	16008 (part)¹	Astor, Leesburgh, Fla......	Florida Southern R. R.......
Ewensville and Vincentown, N. J.	2	7064	Ewansville, Vincentown, N. J.	Penna. (Amboy Div.).......
Factory Junction (n. o.) and Millboro, N. C.	3	13031	Factory Junction (n. o.), Millboro, N. C.	Cape Fear and Yadkin Valley.
Fall Brook and Blossburgh, Pa.	2	8142	Fall Brook, Blossburgh, Pa.	Fall Brook Coal Company ..
Fall Creek, Ill., and Hannibal, Mo.	6	¹23041 (part)	Quincy Ill, Hannibal, Mo...	Chicago, Burlington and Quincy.
Farmington and Colfax, Wash.	8	43016	Colfax, Farmington, Wash..	Colfax and Palouse R. R....

parts of railroads over which no railway post-offices run, in operation, etc.—Continued.

Miles of route.	Annual miles of service.	Number of round trips per week.	Number of pouches exchanged daily.	Date of last re-adjustment.	Average weight of mail whole distance daily.	Remarks.
					Pounds.	
64.12	46,936	7	22	July 1, 1888	861	¹Balance of route covered by Saint Paul, Minn., and Mitchell, Dak., R. P. O. Connects at Edgeley, Dak., with La Moure and Edgeley, Dak., pouch service; at Ellendale, Dak., with Rutland and Ellendale, Dak., pouch service, and at Aberdeen, Dak., with all lines centering there.
23.01	28,900	12	22	July 1, 1887	1,775	¹Balance of route covered by Ashland and Milwaukee, Wis., R. P. O. (See Table A¹.) Supplied by Wausau, Wis., and by Ashland and Milwaukee, Wis., R. P. O. Connects at Wausau, Wis., with Merrill and Tomah, Wis., R. P. O.
6.37	4,000	6	6			
11.95	15,009	12	12	Mar. 16, 1885	98	
8.55	13,423	15	10	July 1, 1885	245	
42.83	26,897	6	20	July 1, 1887	235	Supplied by Sioux Falls, Dak., and by Cedar Rapids, Iowa, and Watertown, Dak., R. P. O. Connects at Rock Rapids, Iowa, with Cherokee, Iowa, and Sioux Falls, Dak., and with Luverne, Minn., and Doon, Iowa, pouch service, and at Sioux Falls, Dak., with all lines centering there.
17.35	27,240	15	14	July 1, 1885	213	New service; not reported last year.
4.48	3,279	7	2	July 1, 1888	340	Connects at El Moro and Trinidad, Colo., with La Junta, Colo., and Albuquerque, N. Mex., R. P. O., and Pueblo and Texline (n. o.), Tex., pouch service; also at El Moro, Colo., with Cucharas and El Moro, Colo., pouch service.
27.02	8,617	6	20	....	....	Service established January 2, 1888.
88.70	64,928	7	12	July 1, 1886	959	Makes all El Paso, Tex., connections and connects at Deming, N. Mex., with Deming, N. Mex., and Los Angeles, Cal., R. P. O. and Rincon and Silver City, N. Mex., R. P. O.
6.94	13,075	18	15	July 1, 1885	203	Connects Baltimore and Bristol and Baltimore and Williamsport R. P. O's at Rock Ridge.
36.42	22,872	6	12	July 1, 1888	89	New service; not reported last year. Connects at Pine Bluff, Ark., with Cairo, Ill., and Texarkana, Ark., R. P. O., and Fort Smith, Ark., and Leland, Miss., R. P. O. Connects at Rob Roy, Ark., with Cairo, Ill., and Texarkana, Ark., R. P. O.
22.77	33,335	14	12	....	....	Connects at Oceanside with San Bernardino and National City R. P. O. New service; established March 19, 1888.
5.45	6,845	12	4	July 1, 1885	80	Essex exchanges pouches with Bangor and Boston R. P. O. and Boston.
21.53	13,520	6	4	July 1, 1888	134	Supplied by initial and terminal offices.
26.70	33,535	12	24	July 1, 1886	444	Supplied by Roscoe, Dak., and by Aberdeen and Orient, Dak., R. P. O. Connects at Roscoe, Dak., with Roscoe and Bowdle, Dak., pouch service.
20.70	16,767	6	12	July 1, 1888	103	
29.55	18,357	6	12	Feb. 15, 1886	305	¹ 27.20 miles reported as Astor and Leesburg R. P. O. in Table A¹.
3.04	3,818	12	4	July 1, 1885	57	
9.55	5,997	6	2	July 1, 1888	14	Connects Mount Airy and Bennettsville R. P. O. at Factory Junction (n. o.).
7.64	4,798	6	4	Aug. 2, 1886	42	¹Balance of route covered by Quincy, Ill., and Louisiana, Mo., R. P. O. (See Table A¹.) Connects at Quincy, Ill., with LaFayette, Ind., and Quincy, Ill., and with Chicago and Quincy, Ill., R. P. O's, and at Hannibal, Mo., with Hannibal and Sedalia, Mo., R. P. O.
6.08	4,450	7	12	July 1, 1887	643	
27.81	20,357	7	18	June 25, 1888	140	Established June 15, 1887, from July 1. New service, supplied by initial and terminal offices. Connects at Colfax with Moscow, Idaho, and Connell, Wash., R. P. O.

TABLE C^c.—*Statement of mail service performed in closed pouches upon railroads and*

Initial and terminal stations running east to west, north to south, and northwest to southeast.	Division.	Number of route.	Contract designation, termini of route.	Corporate title of company.
Farmington and Phillips, Me..	1	20	Farmington, Phillips, Me ..	Sandy River R. R............
Fayetteville and Saint Paul, Ark.	7	29021	Fayetteville, Saint Paul, Ark.	Saint Louis and San Francisco.
Fergus Falls, Minn., and Milnor, Dak.	6	¹26042 (part)	Wadena, Minn., Milnor, Dak	Northern Pacific............
Flemington and Lambertville, N. J.	2	7009	Lambertville, Flemington, N. J.	Pennsylvania...............
Flomaton and Repton, Ala	4	17026	Flomaton, Repton, Ala......	Louisville and Nashville R. R.
Florence, Wis., and Crystal Falls, Mich.	6	¹24032 (part)	Powers, Crystal Falls, Mich.	Chicago and Northwestern..
Florence and Tuscumbia, Ala.	4	17025	Florence, Tuscumbia, Ala...	Memphis and Charleston R. R.
Flourtown and Conshohocken, Pa.	2	5074	Conshohocken, Flourtown, Pa.	Philadelphia and Reading ..
Fond du Lac and Iron Ridge, Wis.	6	25035	Fond du Lac, Iron Ridge, Wis.	Chicago, Milwaukee and St. Paul.
Forest City and Dows, Iowa...	6	27057	Dows, Forest City, Iowa....	Burlington, Cedar Rapids and Northern.
Forest House and Austin, Pa.	2	8171	Forest House, Austin, Pa...	Sinnamahoning............
Forks Creek and Central City, Colo.	7	38021	Forks Creek, Central City, Colo.	Colorado Central ....
Fort Collins and Stout, Colo...	7	¹38027 (part)	Greeley, Stout, Colo.........	Greeley, Salt Lake and Pacific.
Fort Madison and Collett, Iowa.	6	27064	Fort Madison, Collett, Iowa.	Fort Madison and Northwestern.
Fort Valley and Perry, Ga....	4	15017	Fort Valley, Perry, Ga	Southwestern R. R ....
Fort Worth and Granbury, Tex.	7	31061	Fort Worth, Granbury, Tex.	Fort Worth and Rio Grande.
Fostoria and Flint, Mich.......	9	24047	Fostoria, Flint, Mich........	Flint and Pere Marquette..
Frackville and Pottsville, Pa..	2	8050	Pottsville, Frackville, Pa...	Philadelphia and Reading..

parts of railroads over which no railway post-offices run, in operation, etc.—Continued.

Miles of route.	Annual miles of service.	Number of round trips per week.	Number of pouches exchanged daily.	Date of last re-adjustment.	Average weight of mail whole distance daily.	Remarks.
					Pounds.	
18.25	22,922	12	46	July 1, 1885	179	Farmington and Lewiston R. P. O. exchange with Strong, Fairbanks, Phillips, West Freeman, Salem, and Kingfield. Phillips exchanges with Strong and Fairbanks. Strong with Fairbanks, West Freeman, Salem, and Kingfield. Salem with Kingfield and West Freeman.
35.36	26,250	7	30	Apr. 2, 1888	261	New service; not reported last year. Connects at Fayetteville, Ark., with Monett, Mo., and Paris, Tex., R.P.O.
67.36	49,307	6	26	July 1, 1887	289	[1] Balance of route covered by Wadena and Fergus Falls, Minn., R.P.O. (See Table A².) Supplied by Wahpeton and Milnor, Dak., and by Wadena and Fergus Falls, Minn., R.P.O. Connects at Breckenridge, Minn., with Larimore, Dak., and Breckenridge, Minn.; Breckenridge, Minn., and Aberdeen, Dak.; and with Neche, Dak., and Saint Paul, Minn., R. P. O's.
12.46	23,475	18	22	July 1, 1885	179	
29.37	9,379	3	3	July 1, 1888	21	[1] Balance of route covered by Powers, Mich., and Florence, Wis., R. P. O. (See Table A².) Supplied by Florence, Wis., and by Powers, Mich., and Florence, Wis., R. P. O. Connects at Iron River Junction, Mich., with Iron River Junction and Watersmeet, Mich., pouch service.
16.21	22,045	12	14	July 1, 1884	286	
6.29	7,900	12	4	July 1, 1888	230	
7.19	4,515	6	6	July 1, 1885	40	
28.72	36,072	12	24	July 1, 1887	154	Supplied by Fond du Lac, Wis., and by Oshkosh and Milwaukee, Wis., R. P. O. Connects at Fond du Lac, Wis., with Chicago, Ill., Abbotsford, Wis., and Minneapolis, Minn.; Fort Howard, Wis., and Chicago, Ill.; Fond du Lac and Milwaukee, Wis.; and Sheboygan and Princeton, Wis., R. P. O.'s.
48.86	30,634	6	18	July 1, 1888	142	Supplied by initial and terminal offices, and by Cedar Rapids, Iowa, and Watertown, Dak., R. P. O. Connects at Forest City, Iowa, with Saint Paul, Minn., and Des Moines, Iowa, R. P. O.; at Garner, Iowa, with Calmar, Iowa, and Chamberlain, Dak., R. P. O.; and at Belmond, Iowa, with Mason City and Fort Dodge, Iowa, R. P. O., and with Hamilton and Belmond, Iowa, pouch service.
9.19	5,771	6	6	July 1, 1888	95	Connects at Forks Creek, Colo., with Denver and Georgetown, Colo., R. P. O,
11.47	16,792	14	10	July 1, 1886	328	
15.14	9,508	6	2	July 1, 1886	434	[1] 24.03 miles of route 38027, between Greeley and Fort Collins, Colo., covered by Greeley and Denver, Colo., R. P. O. (See Table A².) Connects at Fort Collins, Colo., with Greeley and Denver Colo., R. P. O.
45.12	28,335	6	22	July 1, 1887	88	Supplied by initial and terminal offices; connects at Fort Madison, Iowa, with Burlington, Iowa, and Carrollton, Mo.; Burlington, Iowa, and St. Louis, Mo.; Chicago, Ill., and Fort Madison, Iowa, and with Fort Madison, Iowa, and Kansas City, Mo., R. P. O's.
12.86	16,152	12	8	July 1, 1884	95	New service; not reported last year. Supplied by Fort Worth, Tex., Denison, and San Antonio, Tex., R. P. O. and Texarkana, Ark., and El Paso, Tex., R. P. O.
41.35	25,968	6	6	Nov. 21, 1887	221	
24.46	15,361	6	16	July 1, 1884	84	At Otter Lake, Mich., connects Mackinaw City and Detroit R. P. O. At Flint, Mich., connects Bay City, Wayne, and Detroit; Fort Gratiot and Chicago, and Ludington and Toledo R. P. O's.
11.55	21,760	18	16	July 1, 1885	125	

TABLE C⁰.—*Statement of mail service performed in closed pouches upon railroads and*

Initial and terminal stations running east to west, north to south, and northwest to southeast.	Division.	Number of route.	Contract designation, termini of route.	Corporate title of company.
Franklin and Bellingham, Mass.	1	3075	Bellingham, Franklin, Mass.	New York and New England R. R. (Milford Branch).
Franklin, Mass., and Valley Falls, R. I.	1	3006	Franklin, Mass., Valley Falls, R. I.	New York and New England R. R.
Franklin Furnace and Branchville Junction, N. J.	2	7025 (part)	Waterloo, Franklin Furnace, N. J.	Del., Lack. and West........
Frederick and Araby, Md	3	10004	Araby, Frederick, Md	Baltimore and Ohio ....
Freeland and Jeddo, Pa	2	8058	Jeddo, Freeland, Pa.........	Lehigh Valley ....
Fulton and Guerneville, Cal...	8	40027	Fulton, Guerneville, Cal	San Francisco and North Pacific R. R.
Fultonham and Redfield, Ohio¹.	5	21069 (part.)	Thurston, Redfield, Ohio....	Columbus and Eastern......
Gadsden and Attalla, Ala	4	17020	Attalla, Gadsden, Ala........	East Ala. Rwy ....
Galena and Galena Junction, Ill	6	23092	Galena, Galena Junction (n. o.), Ill.	Chicago, Burlington and Northern.
Galesburgh and Rio, Ill	6	¹23009 (part)	Peoria, Rio, Ill	Chicago, Burlington and Quincy.
Galesville and Trempealeau, Wis.	6	25054	Trempealeau, Galesville, Wis.	Chicago and Northwestern..
Galewood and Dunning, Ill....	6	23091	Galewood, Dunning, Ill.....	Chicago, Milwaukee and St. Paul.
Galveston, Ark., and Shreveport, La.	7	30019	Lewisville, Ark., Shreveport, La.	Saint Louis, Arkansas and Texas.
Garo and London, Colo........	7	38024	Garo, London, Colo	Denver, South Park and Pacific.
Geneva and Aurora, Ill........	6	23056	Geneva, Aurora, Ill	Chicago and North Western
Genoa and Cedar Rapids, Nebr.	6	34025	Genoa, Cedar Rapids, Nebr .	Omaha, Niobrara and Black Hills.
Georgetown and Haverhill, Mass.	1	3013	Georgetown, Haverhill, Mass	Boston and Maine R. R ....,.
Georgetown and Round Rock, Tex.	7	31026	Georgetown, Round Rock, Tex.	International and Great Northern.
Georgetown and Silver Plume Colo.	7	¹38020 (part)	Argo Junction (n. o.) Silver Plume, Colo.	Colorado Central...........
Gilbertville and Mechanic's Falls, Me.	1	10	Mechanic's Falls, Gilbertville, Me.	Rumford Falls and Buckfield R. R.
Gilroy and Tres Pinos, Cal ..	8	46034	Gilroy, Tres Pinos, Cal.....	South Pacific Company.....
Glade Spring and Saltville, Va.	3	11014	Glade Spring, Saltville, Va...	Norfolk and Western.......
Glasgow Junction and Glasgow, Ky.	1	20011	Glasgow Junction, Glasgow, Ky.	Louisville and Nashville....
Glen Carbon and Schuylkill Haven, Pa.	2	8061	Schuylkill Haven, Glen Carbon, Pa.	Philadelphia and Reading ..

parts of railroads over which no railway post-offices run, in operation, etc.—Continued.

Miles of route.	Annual miles of service.	Number of round trips per week.	Number of pouches exchanged daily.	Date of last re-adjustment.	Average weight of mail whole distance daily.	Remarks.
					Pounds.	
5.37	10,117	18	10	July 1, 1885	125	Milford exchanges with Providence, R. I., and Boston and Hopewell Junction R. P. O.
14.46	18,162	12	34	July 1, 1885	143	Boston exchanges with South Attleborough. Providence exchanges with Abbot Run, Arnold's Mills, Diamond Hill, South Attleborough, West Wrenthaw, Sheldonville, and Milford. Boston and Hopewell Junction R. P. O. exchange with Sheldonville and West Wrenthaw.
¹8.63	10,839	12	8	July 1, 1885	336	¹Balance of route (14.86 miles) covered by Franklin Furnace and Waterloo R. P. O. (See Table A⁴.)
3.85	17,327	43	31	July 1, 1885	583	Connects Baltimore and Martinaburgh and Baltimore and Winchester R. P. O's at Araby, and Lancaster and Frederick R. P. O. at Frederick.
2.47	1,552	6	4	July 1, 1885	161	Connects at Fulton with Cloverdale and San Francisco R. P. O.
16.04	11,741	7	8	July 1, 1886	76	
6.12	7,687	12	8			¹Balance of route between Thurston and Fultonham (27.64 miles) covered by the Zanesville and Columbus R. P. O. (See Table A⁴.)
5.90	7,410	12	8	July 1, 1888	323	Connects Minneapolis, Minn., and Oregon, Ill., R. P. O. with Galena, Ill.
3.79	4,790	12	4	May 23, 1888	47	
1327	16,627	12	12	July 1, 1887	1,759	¹Balance of route covered by Peoria and Galesburgh, Ill., R. P. O. (See table A⁴.) Supplied by Galesburgh, Ill., and by Rock Island, Ill., and Saint Louis, Mo., R. P. O. Connects at Galesburgh, Ill., with all lines centering there.
	10,337	12	4	July 1, 1887	154	Supplied by Trempealeau, Wis., and by Chicago, Ill., and Winona, Minn., R. P. O.
823 380	3,517	12	4	May 16, 1887	37	Supplied by Chicago, Ill.
6104	44,681	7	10			New service; not reported last year. Connects at Galveston, Ark. with Cairo, Ill., and Texarkana, Ark., R. P. O., and at Shreveport, La., with New Orleans, La., and Marshall, Tex., R. P. O., Shreveport, La., and Houston, Tex., R. P. O., and Vicksburg, Miss., and Shreveport, La., R. P. O.
13.57	11,397	7	14	July 1, 1886	171	Supplied by Denver and Leadville, Colo., R. P. O., and Garo, Colo.
16.31	32,373	30	86	July 1, 1887	391	Supplied by initial and terminal offices. Connects at Geneva, Ill., with Chicago, Ill., and Cedar Rapids, Iowa, R. P. O., and with Saint Charles and Geneva, Ill., pouch service. Connects at Aurora, Ill., with all lines centering there.
30.71	19,286	6	16	July 1, 1886	146	Supplied by Genoa, Nebr., and by Columbus and Albion, Nebr., R. P. O.
7.31	4,500	6	4	July 1, 1885	65	South Groveland exchanges with Haverhill and Newburyport and Boston R. P. O. Newburyport and Boston R. P. O. exchanges with Portland and Boston R. P. O. via Haverhill.
10.32	15,108	14	14	July 1, 1886	285	Connects at Round Rock, Tex., with Palestine and Laredo, Tex., R. P. O., and Denison and San Antonio, Tex., R. P. O.
4.46	6,060	13	4	July 1, 1886	842	¹47.50 miles of route 38030, between Argo Junction (n. o.) and Georgetown, Colo., covered by Denver and Georgetown, Colo., R. P. O. (See Table A⁴.) Connects at Georgetown, Colo., with Denver and Georgetown, Colo., R. P. O.
1.93	1,212	6	2	July 1, 1885	388	Gilbertville exchanges pouches with Canton and Mechanic's Falls R. P. O.
20.04	15,108	7	12	July 1, 1886	232	Connects at Gilroy with San Francisco and Templeton R. P. O.; Hollister and Tres Pinos exchange with San Francisco.
9.65	6,060	6	2	July 1, 1885	64	Connects Baltimore and Bristol and Lynchburgh and Bristol R. P. O's at Glade Spring.
11.00	14,960	13	8	July 1, 1886	406	
18.64	17,182	12	24	July 1, 1885	123	

TABLE Cᶜ.—*Statement of mail service performed in closed pouches upon railroads and*

Initial and terminal stations running east to west, north to south, and northwest to southeast.	Division.	Number of route.	Contract designation, termini of route.	Corporate title of company.
Glencoe and Hutchinson, Minn.	6	26056	Glencoe, Hutchinson, Minn.	Chicago, Milwaukee and Saint Paul.
Glendale and Eagle's Nest, Minn.	4	18006	Glendale, Eagle's Nest, Miss.	Mobile and Northwestern R. R.
Glen Ellen and Sonoma Landing (n. o.), Cal.	8	46039	Sonoma Landing, Glen Ellen, Cal.	Sonoma Valley R. R ....
Goffand and Donohoe Station (n. o.), Pa.	2	8176	Goffand, Donohoe Station, Pa.	Pennsylvania ....
Goshen and Huron, Cal	8	46038	Goshen, Huron, Cal	Southern Pacific Co ....
Goshen and Pine Island, N. Y.	2	6010	Goshen, Pine Island, N. Y..	N. Y., L. E. and W.......
Graiton and Woodland, Cal...	8	46007	Woodland, Grafton, Cal	California Pacific R. R......
Grand Rapids and Muskegon, Mich.	9	24055	Grand Rapids, Muskegon, Mich.	Muskegon, Grand Rapids and Indiana.
Grantsburgh, Wis., and Rush City, Minn.	6	26951	Rush City, Minn., Grantsburgh, Wis.	St. Paul and Duluth.........
Gratiot and Shullsburgh, Wis.	6	¹25004 (part)	Milton Junction, Shullsburgh, Wis.	Chicago, Milwaukee and St. Paul.
Gratiot, Wis., and Warren, Ill.	6	¹25020 (part)	Warren, Ill., Mineral Point, Wis.	Chicago, Milwaukee and St. Paul.
Great Falls and Rollingsford (n. o.), N. H.	1	1021	Rollingsford (n. o.) and Great Falls, N. H.	Boston and Maine R. R......
Greensburgh and Columbus, Ind.	5	22,049	Greensburgh, Columbus, Ind.	Columbus, Hope and Greensburgh.
Greenfield and Watkins, Mo..	7	26,063	Greenfield, Watkins, Mo....	Greenfield and Northern....
Green Spring and Romney, W. Va.	3	12,014	Green Spring, Romney, W. Va.	Baltimore and Ohio.........
Greenwich and Johnsonville, N. Y.	2	6,062	Johnsonville, Greenwich, N. Y.	Greenwich and Johnsonville.
Greenwood Lake and Sterling Forest, N. Y.	2	7034 (part)	Jersey City, N. J., Greenwood Lake, N. Y.	New York and Greenwood Lake.
Grinnell and Montezuma, Iowa.	6	27032	Grinnell, Montezuma, Iowa.	Central Iowa ....
Griswold and Red Oak, Iowa ..	6	27055	Red Oak, Griswold, Iowa.....	Chicago, Burlington and Quincy.

parts of railroads over which no railway post-offices run, in operation, etc.—Continued.

Miles of route.	Annual miles of service.	Number of round trips per week.	Number of pouches exchanged daily.	Date of last re-adjustment.	Average weight of mail whole distance daily.	Remarks.
					Pounds.	
14.24	17,885	12	4	Dec. 1,1886	178	Supplied by Glencoe, Minn., and by Saint Paul, Ortonville, Minn., and Fargo, Dak., R. P. O.
21.00	13,188	6	8	July 1,1888	61	
21.47	15,716	7	6	July 1,1886	88	Supplied by San Francisco.
4.29	5,388	12	4			
46.56	59,390	14	26	June 26,1888	259	Connects at Goshen with San Francisco and Los Angeles R. P. O. Goshen and Tulare exchange with Hanford, Lemoore, Armona, and Huron.
12.09	15,185	12	12	July 1,1885	101	Connects at Woodland with Redding and Sacramento R. P. O. Supplied also by Sacramento and Woodland P. O's.
9.92	7,261	7	8	July 1,1886	65	
39.50	74,418	18	32	....	....	At Grand Rapids, Mich., connects Baldwin and Grand Rapids, Cadillac and Fort Wayne, Detroit and Grand Haven, Detroit and Grand Rapids, East Saginaw and Howard City, Grand Rapids and Cincinnati, Grand Rapids and Elkhart, Grand Rapids and La Crosse, and Mackinaw City and Grand Rapids R. P. O's. At Muskegon connects the Big Rapids and Holland, Muskegon and Allegan, and Pentwater and Muskegon R. P. O's.
17.17	10,782	6	6	July 1,1887	73	Supplied by Rush City, Minn., and by Duluth and Saint Paul, Minn., R. P. O.
11.79	14,808	12	8	July 1,1887	981	[1] Balance of route covered by Rockford, Ill., and Mineral Point, Wis., R. P. O. (see Table A³), and by Milton Junction and Janesville, Wis., pouch service. Supplied by Gratiot, Wis., and by Rockford, Ill., and Mineral Point, Wis., R. P. O. Connects at Gratiot, Wis., with Gratiot, Wis., and Warren, Ill., pouch service.
7.15	4,490	6	14	July 1,1887	1,015	[1] Balance of route covered by Rockford, Ill., and Mineral Point, Wis., R. P.O. Supplied by Warren, Ill., and by Rockford, Ill., and Mineral Point, Wis., R. P. O. Connects at Gratiot, Wis., with Gratiot and Shullsburgh, Wis., pouch service, and at Warren, Ill., with Chicago, Ill., and Dubuque, Iowa, and Dubuque, Iowa, and Mendota, Ill., R. P. O's.
2.66	6,732	24	25	July 1,1885	247	Portland and Boston R. P. O. exchanges pouches with Great Falls, Berwick, and North Conway and Boston R. P. O. Great Falls exchanges with Dover, Portsmouth, and Manchester R. P.O. and Boston.
26.90	33,796	12	28	July 1,1888	140	
2.46	5,065	14	8	Apr. 20,1888	171	New service; not reported last year. Connects at Watkins, Mo., with Kansas City, Mo., and Memphis, Tenn., R. P. O.
16.64	20,900	12	8	July 1,1885	108	Connects Baltimore and Grafton R. P. O. at Green Spring.
15.34	28,901	18	20	July 1,1885	180	
¹5.83	3,661	6	6	July 1,1885	255	[1] Balance of route (45.63 miles) covered by Greenwood Lake and New York R. P. O. (See Table A³.)
17.49	21,967	12	10	July 1,1887	209	Supplied by initial and terminal offices. Connects at Grinnell, Iowa, with West Liberty and Council Bluffs, Iowa, and with Mason City and Albia, Iowa, R. P. O's, and at Montezuma, Iowa, with Muscatine and Montezuma, Iowa, R. P. O.
18.81	23,625	12	16	July 1,1887	210	Supplied by initial and terminal offices and by Burlington and Council Bluffs, Iowa, R. P. O. Connects at Griswold, Iowa, with Atlantic and Griswold, Iowa, pouch service, and at Red Oak, Iowa, with Red Oak, Iowa, and Nebraska City, Nebr., R. P. O.

TABLE C^c.—*Statement of mail service performed in closed pouches upon railroads and*

Initial and terminal stations running east to west, north to south, and northwest to southeast.	Division.	Number of route.	Contract designation, termini of route.	Corporate title of company.
Grosse Isle and Slocum Junction (n. o.) Mich.	9	24011	Grosse Isle, Slocum Junction (n. o.), Mich.	Michigan Central ....
Groton and Doland Dak	6	35035	Duland, Groton, Dak	Chicago and Northwestern
Groveton Junction and Lancaster, N. H.	1	1006 (part)	Groveton Junction, Concord, N. H.	Boston and Maine R. R. (Lowell System).
Guthrie Centre and Menlo, Iowa.	6	27050	Menlo, Guthrie Centre, Iowa.	Chicago, Rock Island, and Pacific.
Hagerstown, Ind , and Cambridge City, Ohio.	5	21031 (part)	Harrison, Ohio, Hagerstown, Ind.	White Water...............
Halifax and Scotland Neck, N. C.	3	13019	Halifax, Scotland Neck, N. C.	Wilmington and Weldon....
Halstad and Moorhead, Minn .	6	26052	Moorhead, Halstad, Minn ..	Saint Paul, Minn., and Manitoba.
Hamilton and Tarborough, N. C.	3	13032	Hamilton, Tarborough, N. C.	Hamilton Railway and Lumber Company.
Hammondsport and Bath, N. Y.	2	6096	Bath, Hammondsport, N. Y.	Bath and Hammondsport...
Hampton and Belmond, Iowa .	6	27078	Hampton, Belmond, Iowa ..	Central Iowa...............
Hanover Junction and Valley Junction, Pa.	2	8102 (part)	Hanover Junction, Gettysburgh, Pa.	Western Maryland ....
Harbor and Ashtabula, Ohio .	5	21098	Ashtabula Harbor, Ohio....	Ashtabula Street...........
Harbor Springs and Petosky, Mich.	9	24056	Harbor Springs, Petoskey, Mich.	Grand Rapids and Indiana .
Harlan and Avoca, Iowa	6	27045	Avoca, Harlan, Iowa........	Chicago, Rock Island and Pacific.
Harlem and Andover, Dak ...	6	35022	Andover, Harlem, Dak......	Chicago, Milwaukee and St. Paul.
Harrisville and Carthage, N. Y	2	6134	Harrisville, Carthage, N. Y.	Carthage and Adirondack ..
Harrodsburgh Junction and Harrodsburgh, Ky.	5	20031	Harrodsburgh, Harrodsburgh Junction, Ky.	Southwestern ....
Hartington and Wakefield, Nebr.	6	34022	Wakefield, Hartington, Nebr.	Chicago, St. Paul, Minn., and Omaha.
Hart and Mears, Mich.........	9	24046	Hart, Mears, Mich	Chicago and West Michigan.
Hartland and Pittsfield, Me ...	1	26	Hartland, Pittsfield, Me.....	Sebasticook and Moosehead R. R.
Hart's Road and Jacksonville, Fla.	4	16009	Hart's Road, Jacksonville, Fla.	Fla. Rwy. and Nav. Co......
Hartwell and Bowersville, Ga.	4	15029	Hartwell, Bowersville, Ga ..	Rich. and Danville R. R .....
Harwood and Gonzales, Tex ..	7	31040	Harwood, Gonzales, Tex ..	Galveston, Harrisburgh and San Antonio.
Hastings and Sidney, Iowa....	6	27043	Hastings, Sidney, Iowa	Chicago, Burlington and Quincy.
Hatfield and Norwood, N. Y...	2	6133	Hatfield, Norwood, N. Y	Rome, Wat. and Ogdensburgh.

parts of railroads over which no railway post-offices run, in operation, etc.—Continued.

Miles of route.	Annual miles of service.	Number of round trips per week.	Number of pouches exchanged daily.	Date of last re-adjustment.	Average weight of mail whole distance daily.	Remarks.
					Pounds.	
2.36	1,482	6	2	July 1, 1884	27	At Slocum Junction (n.o.), Mich., connects with Detroit and Toledo R.P.O., day line.
39.24	24,642	6	20	July 1, 1888	98	Supplied by initial and terminal offices.
0.58	12,032	12	22	July 1, 1885	3,263	Connects at Groton, Dak., with Saint Paul, Minn., and Mitchell, Dak., R.P.O., and at Doland, Dak., with Tracy, Minn., and Redfield, Dak., R.P.O. Balance of route (136.30 miles) covered by R.P.O. service. (See Table A*). Lancaster and Boston R.P.O. exchanges pouches with Northumberland Groveton, and Portland and Island Pond R.P.O.; this R.P.O. exchanges with Northumberland and Lancaster, Lancaster exchanges with Northumberland and Groveton.
14.96	18,789	12	28	July 1, 1887	214	Supplied by Stuart, Iowa, and by West Liberty and Council Bluffs, Iowa, R.P.O.
7.17	4,503	6	2	July 1, 1888	739	Fort Wayne and Cincinnati R.P.O. runs over this route between Harrison, Ohio, and Beesons, Ind. (see Table A*), distance 48.91 miles. No service between Beesons and Cambridge City, Ind., 7 miles.
21.00	13,188	6	16	July 1, 1888	157	Connects Washington and Wilmington R.P.O. at Halifax.
34.51	14,356	4	10	July 1, 1887	84	Supplied by Moorhead, Minn. Connects at Moorhead, Minn., with Neche, Dak., and Saint Paul, Minn., and with Saint Paul, Minn., and Mandan, Dak., R.P.O's.
20.65	12,968	6	12	July 1, 1888	50	Connects Williamston and Rocky Mount R.P.O. at Tarborough, N.C.
9.40	17,710	18	12	July 1, 1885	260	
22.96	14,419	6	12	July 1, 1887	67	Supplied by initial and terminal offices. Connects at Hampton, Iowa, with Mason City and Albia, Iowa, and with Sumner and Hampton, Iowa, R. P. O's. Connects at Belmond, Iowa, with Mason City and Fort Dodge, Iowa, R. P. O., and with Forest City and Dows, Iowa, pouch service.
¹6.63	8,327	12	8	July 1, 1885	671	¹ Balance of route (23.30 miles) covered by Glyndon and Gettysburgh R.P.O. (See Table A*.)
4.00	7,952	19	6	July 1, 1888	88	Service performed on street cars.
8.35	10,487	12	11	July 1, 1884	53	At Petosky, Mich., connects Mackinaw City and Grand Rapids R.P.O.
14.35	18,023	12	20	July 1, 1887	236	Supplied by Avoca, Iowa; connects at that point with West Liberty and Council Bluffs, Iowa, R. P. O., and with Avoca and Carson, Iowa, pouch service.
55.79	35,036	6	26	Mar. 24, 1887	155	Supplied by Andover, Dak.; connects at that point with Saint Paul., Minn., and Mitchell, Dak., R. P. O.
21.71	18,624	6	6			
5.44	13,665	24	16	July 1, 1884	249	
33.94	21,314	6	22	July 1, 1886	152	Supplied by initial and terminal offices and by Covington and Norfolk, Nebr., R.P.O.
4.15	2,606	6	8	July 1, 1884	70	At Mears, Mich., connects Pentwater and Muskegon R.P.O.
8.58	10,776	12	22			Pittsfield exchanges pouches with Bangor and Boston R. P. O., West Palmyra and Hartland. West Palmyra exchanges with Pittsfield. Hartland exchanges with West Palmyra, Pittsfield, and Bangor and Boston R. P. O.
23.27	45,144	19	14	July 1, 1884	141	
10.15	12,748	12	4	July 1, 1888	104	
12.62	18,476	14	6	July 1, 1886	206	Connects at Harwood, Tex., with Houston and Eagle Pass, Tex., R.P.O.
22.14	13,904	6	10	July 1, 1887	139	Supplied by Hastings, Iowa, and by Burlington and Council Bluffs, Iowa, R.P.O. Connects at Hastings, Iowa, with Carson and Hastings, Iowa, pouch service.
13.54	17,006	12	21	July 1, 1888	144	

TABLE C^c.—*Statement of mail service performed in closed pouches upon railroads and*

Initial and terminal stations running east to west, north to south, and northwest to southeast.	Division.	Number of route.	Contract designation, termini of route.	Corporate title of company.
Hauser and Cœur d'Alene, Idaho.	8	42002	Hauser, Cœur d'Alene, Idaho.	Spokane Falls and Ida. R. R.
Hayt's Corners and Willard, N. Y.	2	6128	Hayt's Corners, Willard, N. Y.	Geneva, Ithaca and Sayre...
Hazle Creek Bridge and Audenried, Pa.	2	8012	Hazle Creek Bridge, Audenried, Pa.	Lehigh Valley ....
Henderson and Overton, Tex ..	7	31015	Henderson, Overton, Tex ...	International and Great Northern.
Henderson and Oxford, N. C...	8	13014	Oxford, Henderson, N. C	Oxford and Henderson......
Highlands and Branchport Junction, N. J.	2	7026 (part)	Highlands, Whiting, N. J ..	Central R. R. of New Jersey
Hilbert and Appleton. Wis....	6	25040	Hilbert, Appleton, Wis	Milwaukee and Northern...
Hillard's and Branchton Junction, Pa.	2	8152	Branchton Junction, Hillard's, Pa.	Pittsburgh, Shenango and Lake Erie.
Hillsborough and Sardinia, Ohio	5	21066	Hillsborough, Sardinia, Ohio.	Ohio and Northwestern.....
Hinckley and Saint Cloud, Minn.	6	26049	Saint Cloud, Hinckley, Minn.	Saint Paul, Minn., and Manitoba.
Hodges and Abbeville, S. C...	4	14009	Hodges, Abbeville, S. C	Richmond and Danville R.R.
¹Hogdensville and Elizabethtown, Ky.	5	20038	Elizabethtown, Hogdensville, Ky.	Hogdensville and Elizabethtown.
Hoisington and Great Bend, Kans.	7	33071	Hoisington Station, Great Bend., Kans.	Kansas and Colorado.......
Hollidaysburgh Junction (n.o.) and Newry, Pa.	2	8140	Hollidaysburgh Junction, Newry, Pa.	Pennsylvania..............
Holyoke and Westfield, Mass..	1	3069	Holyoke, Westfield, Mass ..	New Haven and Northampton R. R.
Homer and Gibsland, La......	4	30018	Gibsland, Homer, La	Louisiana North and South Rwy.
Honesdale and Carbondale, Pa..	2	8116	Honesdale, Carbondale, Pa..	Delaware and Hudson Canal Co.
Honesdale and Lackawaxen, Pa.	2	8009	Honesdale, Lackawaxen, Pa.	New York, Lake Erie and Western.
Honey Grove and Ladonia, Tex..	7	¹31053 (part)	Dallas, Honey Grove, Tex..	Gulf, Colorado and Santa Fé.
Hope and Ripon, Dak..........	6	¹35003 (part)	Breckenridge, Minn., Hope, Dak.	Saint Paul, Minn., and Manitoba.
Hope Valley and Wood River Junction (n. o.), R. I.	1	4009	Wood River Junction (n. o.), Hope Valley R. R.	Wood River Branch R. R...
Hopewell Junction and Wicopee Junction, N. Y.	2	6125	Hopewell Junction, Wicopee Junction, N. Y.	New York and New England.

parts of railroads over which no railway post-offices run, in operation, etc.—Continued.

Miles of route.	Annual miles of service.	Number of round trips per week.	Number of pouches exchanged daily.	Date of last re-adjustment.	Average weight of mail whole distance daily.	Remarks.
					Pounds.	
13.38	10,160	7	6	Mar. 14, 1887	112	Connects at Hauser with Helena and Portland R. P. O.
5.75	12,639	21	13	July 1, 1885	124	
8.52	10,701	12	12	July 1, 1885	132	
17.01	12,451	7	10	July 1, 1886	229	Connects at Overton, Tex., with Texarkana, Ark., and Houston, Tex., R. P. O.
14.20	8,017	6	12	July 1, 1888	272	Connects Norfolk and Raleigh R. P. O. at Henderson.
¹7.91	14,902	²21	24	July 1, 1886	471	¹ Balance of route (30.41 miles) covered by Red Bank and Bridgeton R. P. O. (see Table A³), and no service 3.90 miles, Branchport Junction and Eatontown. ² Twenty-one times a week for 3 months and 12 times a week for 9 months, from Highlands to Branchport Junction.
21.94	27,556	12	12	July 1, 1887	144	Supplied by Appleton, Wis., and by Iron Mountain, Mich., and Milwaukee, Wis., R. P. O. Connects at Menasha, Wis., with Fort Howard, Wis., and Chicago, Ill., R. P. O. Connects at Appleton, Wis., with Ashland and Milwaukee, Wis., R. P. O.
10.47	12,150	12	14	July 1, 1888	63	
19.50	12,303	6	22	July 1, 1888	170	Supplied by initial and terminal offices. Connects at Hinckley, Minn., with Duluth and Saint Paul, Minn., R. P. O.; at Saint Cloud, Minn., with Fargo, Dak., Barnesville and Saint Paul, Minn., R. P. O., and with Saint Cloud and Willmar, Minn., R. P. O., and at Milacca, Minn., with Milacca and Elk River, Minn., pouch service.
68.24	42,854	6	26	July 1, 1887	70	
11.98	14,984	12	4	July 1, 1888	162	
11.70	491	6	2			¹ Service established June 7, 1888.
10.34	15,138	14	10	July 1, 1888	92	Connects at Great Bend, Kans., with Kansas City, Mo., and Pueblo, Colo., R. P. O. and Great Bend and Scott, Kans., R. P. O. Connects at Hoisington, Kans., with Kansas City, Mo., Salina, Kans., and Pueblo, Colo., R. P. O.
3.06	3,813	12	10	July 1, 1885	124	
11.20	14,067	12	8	July 1, 1885	101	Holyoke exchanges with Westfield and Williamsburgh and New Haven R. P. O.
10.03	12,328	6	4			
17.48	38,421	21	30	July 1, 1885	205	
24.94	45,906	15	36	July 1, 1885	401	
12.30	18,007	14	4			¹ 68.41 miles of route 31053, between Ladonia and Dallas, Tex., covered by Paris and Dallas, Tex., R. P. O. (See Table A¹.) Connects at Honey Grove, Tex., with Texarkana, Ark., and Whitesborough, Tex., R. P. O., and at Ladonia, Tex., with Paris and Dallas, Tex., R. P. O. Last year there was R. P. O. service between Honey Grove and Ladonia, Tex.
29.87	9,319	3	16	July 1, 1886	763	¹ Balance of route covered by Larimore, Dak., and Breckenridge, Minn., R. P. O. (See Table A³) Supplied by Ripon, Dak., and by Larimore, Dak., and Breckinridge, Minn., R. P. O.
5.93	11,172	18	10	July 1, 1885	150	Providence and New London R. P. O. exchanges pouches with Woodville and Hope Valley.
11.23	10,579	9	8	July 1, 1885	1,051	

TABLE C^c.—*Statement of mail service performed in closed pouches upon railroads and*

Initial and terminal stations running east to west, north to south, and northwest to southeast.	Division.	Number of route.	Contract designation, termini of route.	Corporate title of company.
Hortonville and Oshkosh, Wis.	6	25046	Oshkosh, Hortonville, Wis..	Milwaukee, Lake Shore and Western.
Houlton, Me., and New Brunswick Line (n. o.).	1	16	Houlton, Me., New Brunswick Line (n. o.).	New Brunswick R. R.
Houston and Alvin, Tex.	7	31047	Houston, Alvin, Tex	Gulf, Colorado and Santa Fé
Houston and Columbia, Tex...	7	31003	Houston, Columbia, Tex	International and Great Northern.
Houston and Sealy, Tex.	7	31020	Houston, Sealy, Tex	Texas Western
Howard City and Grand Rapids, Mich.	9	24070	Howard City, Grand Rapids, Mich.	Detroit, Lansing and Northern.
Humboldt and Republic, Mich.	6	24053	Humboldt, Republic, Mich .	Duluth, South Shore and Atlantic.
Hunter and Phœnicia, N. Y...	2	6118	Phœnicia, Hunter, N. Y....	Stony Clove and Catskill ...
Hunter's Run and Pine Grove Furnace, Pa.	2	8052 (part)	Carlisle, Pine Grove Furnace, Pa.	Gettysburgh and Harrisburgh.
Huntsville and Phelps, Tex ...	7	31034	Phelps, Huntsville, Tex	International and Great Northern.
Huron and Norwalk, Ohio......	5	21057	Huron, Norwalk, Ohio......	Wheeling and Lake Erie....
Hutchinson Junction and Hutchinson, Minn.	6	26060	Hutchinson Junction (n. o.), Hutchinson, Minn.	Saint Paul, Minneapolis and Manitoba.
Inman and Victoria, Tenn.....	5	¹19012 (part)	Inman, Tenn., Bridgeport, Ala.	Nash., Chatt. and Saint Louis.
Intersection, Pa., and Melrose, Md.	2	8082 (part)	Valley Junction, [Pa., Melrose, Md.	Western Maryland
Ione and Galt, Cal.	8	46023	Galt, Ione, Cal.	Central Pacific R. R
Iowa City and Iowa Junction, Iowa.	6	²27048 (part)	Elmira (n. o.), Iowa Junction (n. o.), Iowa.	Burlington, Cedar Rapids and Northern.
Iron River Junction and Watersmeet, Mich.	6	24038	Iron River Junction (n. o.), Watersmeet, Mich.	Chicago and Northwestern .
Ironton Junction (n. o.) and Wellston, Ohio.	5	¹21054 (part)	Dayton, Ironton, Ohio	Dayton, Ft. W. and Chic ....

parts of railroads over which no railway post-offices run, in operation, etc.—Continued.

Miles of route.	Annual miles of service.	Number of round trips per week.	Number of pouches exchanged daily.	Date of last re-adjustment.	Average weight of mail whole distance daily.	Remarks.
					Pounds.	
23.77	29,855	12	14	July 1, 1887	156	Supplied by Oshkosh, Wis., and by Ashland and Milwaukee, Wis., R. P. O. Connects at Crete, Wis., with Chicago, Ill., Abbotsford, Wis., and Minneapolis, Minn., R. P. O., and at Oshkosh, Wis., with Fort Howard, Wis., and Chicago, Ill., and with Oshkosh and Milwaukee, Wis., R. P. O.
4.00	5,024	12	18	Apr. 15, 1886	206	Houlton exchanges with Vanceborough and Bangor R. P. O., Calais, Caribou, Presque Isle, Fort Fairfield, Saint Andrew's, and Vanceborough and Andover R. P. O.
23.71	43,389	(1)	8	July 1, 1886	447	1 Trains 21 times a week southward and 14 times a week northward. Makes Houston, Tex., connections and connects at Alvin, Tex., with Gainesville and Galveston, Tex., R. P. O.
51.00	15,912	3	20	July 1, 1886	139	Makes Houston, Tex., connections.
52.87	16,495	3	7	July 1, 1886	46	Makes Houston, Tex., connections and connects at Sealy, Tex., with Gainesville and Galveston, Tex., R. P. O.
34.07	19,283	6	15	....	....	Order July 11, 1887, establishing this service from August 1, 1887. At Grand Rapids, Mich., connects Baldwin and Grand Rapids, Cadillac and Fort Wayne, Detroit and Grand Haven, Detroit and Grand Rapids, East Saginaw and Howard City, Grand Rapids and Cincinnati, Grand Rapids and Elkhart, Grand Rapids and La Crosse, and Mackinac City and Grand Rapids R. P. O's. At Howard City, Mich., connects East Saginaw and Howard City, Howard City and Detroit, and Mackinac City and Grand Rapids R. P. Os.
8.70	10,927	12	4	July 1, 1884	60	Supplied by Humboldt, Mich., and by Marquette and Houghton, Mich., R. P. O.
15.11	18,778	12	8	July 1, 1884	60	
18.97	11,266	12	8	July 1, 1886	213	1 Balance of route (10 miles) covered by Carlisle and Gettysburgh R. P. O. (See Table A.)
8.38	12,268	14	6	July 1, 1886	213	Connects at Phelps, Tex., with Texarkana, Ark., and Houston, Tex., R. P. O.
13.67	17,170	12	8	July 1, 1888	90	
53.40	33,535	6	28	July 1, 1888	64	Supplied by Minneapolis, Minn. Connects at Hutchinson Junction, Minn., with Neche, Dak., and Saint Paul, Minn., R. P. O., and at Hutchinson, Minn., with Glencoe and Hutchinson, Minn., pouch service.
846.59	321,407		350			
5.31	2,613	6	2	July 1, 1888	104	1 Balance of route (19.53 miles) covered by Dunlap and Bridgeport, R. P. O. (See Table A.) September 19, 1887, Inman and Bridgeport R. P. O. changed to run to Cheekville, Tenn., leaving closed-pouch service between Inman and Victoria, Tenn. February 20, 1888, run extended to Dunlap, Tenn.
3.79	2,373	6	4	July 1, 1885	331	1 Balance of route (10 miles) covered by Glyndon and Gettysburgh R. P. O. (See Table A.)
27.85	20,386	7	22	....	....	Connects at Galt with Sacramento and San Francisco R. P. O.
11.90	7,473	6	10	....	....	1 Balance of route covered by Clinton and Iowa City, Iowa, R. P. O. Connects at Iowa City, Iowa, with West Liberty and Council Bluffs, Iowa, R. P. O., and at Iowa Junction with Muscatine and Montezuma, Iowa, R. P. O.
54.76	34,389	6	8	July 1, 1884	88	Supplied by Florence, Wis., and Watersmeet, Mich. Connects at Iron River Junction, Mich., with Florence, Wis., and Crystal Falls, Mich., pouch service, and at Watersmeet, Mich., with Ashland and Milwaukee, Wis., R. P. O.
....	1,746	6	4	July 1, 1888	258	1 Balance of route covered by Dayton and Ironton R. P. O., 166.19 miles. (See Table A.) June 5, 1888, R. P. O. run over this part of the route, thereby discontinuing this closed-pouch service; distance, 3 miles.

TABLE C°.—*Statement of mail service performed in closed pouches upon railroads and*

Initial and terminal stations running east to west, north to south, and northwest to southeast.	Division.	Number of route.	Contract designation, termini of route.	Corporate title of company.
Irwin and Blackburn. Pa	2	8129	Irwin, Blackburn, Pa	Youghiogheny.................
Isabel and Brownsville, Tex ..	7	31018	Brownsville, Isabel, Tex	Rio Grande...................
Jackson and Allenville, Mo ...	7	28048	Allenville, Jackson, Mo.....	Saint Louis, Iron Mountain and Southern.
Jacksonville and Pablo Beach, Fla.	4	16030	Jacksonville, Pablo Beach, Fla.	Jacksonville and Atlantic R. R.
Jacksonville and Saint Augustine, Fla.	4	16016	Jacksonville, Saint Augustine, Fla.	Jacksonville, Saint Augustine and Halifax River R.R.
Jamaica and Brooklyn, N. Y .	2	6124	Brooklyn, Jamaica, N. Y	Long Island ....
Jamestown and Burr Oak, Kans.	7	33032	Jamestown, Burr Oak, Kans.	Central Branch Union Pacific.
Jamesville and Washington, N. C.	3	13013	Jamesville, Washington, N. C.	Jamesville and Washington.
Janesville and Afton, Wis.....	6	25052	Afton, Janesville, Wis......	Chicago and North Western.
Jasper and Huntingburgh, Ind.	5	¹22032 (part)	Evansville, Jasper, Ind.....	Louisville, Evansville and St. Louis.
Jefferson City and Wickes, Mont.	6	¹36006 (part)	Helena, Wickes, Mont......	Northern Pacific........,----
Jefferson Junction and Susquehanna, Pa.	2	8064 (part)	Carbondale, Susquehanna, Pa.	N. Y., L. E. and W...........
Jeffersonville and New Albany, Ind. ¹	5	22007 (part)	Jeffersonville, Indianapolis, Ind.	Pennsylvania................
Johnson Junction (n. o.) and Hillsborough, Ky.	5	20019	Johnson Junction (n. o.) and Hillsborough, Ky.	Cincinnati and Southeastern
Johnsonville and Stoneville, Miss.	4	18013	Stoneville, Johnsonville, Miss.	Georgia Pacific Rwy........
Juab and Frisco, Utah	8	41001 (part)	Juab, Frisco, Utah	Utah Central R. R...........
Junction and Columbia, Pa....	2	8031 (part)	Columbia, Sinking Spring, Pa.	Philadelphia and Reading ..
Junction and Mound City, Ill.	6	23028	Junction, Mound City, Ill...	Illinois Central.............
Kaaterskill and Kaaterskill Junction, N. Y.	2	6131	Kaaterskill Junction, Kaaterskill, N. Y.	Kaaterskill ....
Kalamazoo and Hastings, Mich.	9	24077	Kalamazoo, Hastings, Mich.	Chicago, Kalamazoo and Saginaw.
Katahdin Iron Works and Milo Junction (n. o.), Me.	1	9	Milo Junction (n. o.), Katahdin Iron Works, Me.	Bangor and Katahdin Iron Works R. R.
Keating and Karthus, Pa......	2	8167	Keating, Karthus, Pa	Pennsylvania................
Keneeaw and Kearney, Nebr..	6	34090	Keneeaw, Kearney, Nebr....	Burlington and Missouri River in Nebraska.
Kennebunk Port and Kennebunk Station (n.o.), Me.	1	27	Kennebunk Port, Kennebunk Station (n. o.), Me.	Boston and Maine R. R .....

parts of railroads over which no railway post-offices run, in operation, etc.—Continued.

Miles of route.	Annual miles of service.	Number of round trips per week.	Number of pouches exchanged daily.	Date of last re-adjustment.	Average weight of mail whole distance daily.	Remarks.
					Pounds.	
8.58	5,357	6	4	July 1, 1885	31	Isabel and Brownsville, Tex., exchange pouches.
24.16	16,953	7	2	July 1, 1886	26	Connects at Allenville, Mo , with Saint Louis, Mo.,
16.80	21,191	12	18	July 1, 1887	139	and Columbus, Ky., R. P. O.
17.48	21,954	12	6	Feb. 4, 1887	44	
36.80	76,965	20	12	July 1, 1888	1,008	
9.18	19,217	20	[1]12	July 1, 1886	381	[1] Average number.
33.86	42,528	12	30	July 1, 1886	381	Connects at Jamestown, Kans., with Atchison and Lenora, Kans., R. P. O., and at Mankato, Kans., with Fairburgh, Nebr., and Norton, Kans , R.P.O.
22.57	14,174	6	14	July 1, 1888	230	Connects Norfolk and Edenton R. P. O. at James ville by boat between Jamesville and Edenton.
6.69	12,604	18	10	July 1, 1887	168	Connects Chicago and Winona R P. O. with Janes ville, Wis.
6.97	2,963	12	12	July 1, 1888	717	[1] Balance of route (47 39 miles) covered by Louis ville, Huntingburgh and Evansville R. P. O. (See Table A[*].) February 28, 1888, run of clerks on Jasper and Evansville R. P. O. was extended to Louisville, Ky., leaving closed-pouch service be tween Jasper and Huntingburgh, Ind.
4.50	3,294	7	4	July 1, 1888	441	[1] Balance of route covered by Helena and Basin, Mont., R. P. O. (See Table A[*].) Supplied by Jefferson City, Mont., and by Helena and Basin, Mont. R. P. O.
[1]3.80	2,386	6	2	July 1, 1885	231	[1] Balance of route (35.71 miles) covered by Nineveh and Carbondale R. P. O. (See Table A[*].)
....	749	24	16	July 1, 1888	4,395	[1] Balance of route (107.72 miles) covered by Indian apolis and Louisville R. P. O. (See Table A[*].) July 21, 1887, route curtailed to end at Jefferson ville, Ind.; decrease in distance, 5.20 miles, and service discontinued.
16.90	18,149	[1]6	10	July 1, 1884	111	[1] Six round trips per week over whole route, and twelve additional round trips per week between Johnson Junction and Flemingsburgh; distance 6 miles.
26.54	12,899	6	2	July 1, 1888	68	
139.15	101,858	7	12	July 1, 1886	837	Balance of route covered by Ogden and Salt Lake and Salt Lake and Juab R. P. O.
[1]11.73	14,733	12	8	July 1, 1885	417	[1] Balance of route (28 miles) covered by Reading and Quarryville R. P. O. (See Table A[*].)
2.96	1,859	6	2	July 1, 1887	73	Connects Centralia and Cairo, Ill., R. P. O., with Mound City, Ill.
7.40	9,294	[1]12	12	July 1, 1885	154	[1] Service only three months in the year.
31.08	2,673	6	10	....	....	Order April 16, 1888, establishing this service to commence May 1, 1888. At Kalamazoo connects the Cadillac and Fort Wayne, Detroit and Chi cago, Grand Rapids and Elkhart, Grand Rapids and Cincinnati, and Kalamazoo and South Haven R. P. O's. At Hastings, Mich., connects Detroit and Grand Rapids R. P. O.
18.90	11,869	6	12	July 1, 1885	50	Greenville and Bangor R. P. O. exchanges pouches with Brownville and Katahdin Iron Works. Brownville exchanges with Milo; Katahdin Iron Works exchanges with Brownville and Milo. Extra round trip daily from Milo Junction to Brownville.
22.17	13,922	6	6	June 6, 1887	47	Supplied by initial and terminal offices, and by Omaha and McCook, Nebr., R. P O. Connects at Kearney, Nebr., with Omaha, Nebr., and Ogden, Utah, R. P. O.
24.57	17,985	7	16	July 1, 1886	369	
4.67	2,576	6	16	....	....	From August 10, 1887. Kennebunk Port exchanges pouches with Portland and Boston R. P. O's. and Kennebunk. Kennebunk Beach exchanges with Portland and Boston R. P. O.

Table C⁴.—*Statement of mail service performed in closed pouches upon railroads and*

Initial and terminal stations running east to west, north to south, and northwest to southeast.	Division.	Number of route.	Contract designation, termini of route.	Corporate title of company.
Kercheval and Cannelton, Ind.	5	22052	Kercheval, Cannelton, Ind ..	Louisville, Evansville and Saint Louis.
Kensett and Searcy, Ark......	7	29011	Searcy, Kensett, Ark........	Searcy and West Point. ....
Keokuk, Iowa, and Warsaw, Ill.	6	¹23027 (part)	State Line (n. o.), Warsaw, Ill.	Toledo, Peoria and Western.
Keyport and Freehold, N. J....	2	7043	Keyport, Freehold, N. J....	Freehold and New York....
Killbuck and Warsaw, Ohio...	5	21102	Killbuck, Trinway, Ohio...	Cleveland, Akron and Columbus.
Kingfield and Strong Station (n. o.), Me.	1	25	Strong Station (n. o.), Kingfield Me.	Franklin and Megantic R. R.
Kingston and Rome, Ga.......	4	15006	Kingston, Rome, Ga	Rome R. R..................
Kingston Depot and Narragansett Pier, R. I.	1	4007	Kingston Depot, Narragansett Pier, R. I.	Narragansett Pier R. R.....
Kingsville and Yosemite, Ky..	5	20028	Kingsville, Yosemite, Ky ...	Cincinnati and Green River.
Kingwood and Tunnelton, W. Va.	3	12021	Tunnelton, Kingwood, W. Va.	Kingwood Railway ....
Kinkora and Juliustown, N. J.	2	7012	Kinkora, Juliustown, N. J...	Pennsylvania..............
Kinzua Junction and Smethport, Pa.	2	8132 (part)	Bradford, Smethport, Pa	Brad., B. and K ....
Kiowa, Kans., and Panhandle, Tex.	7	22004	Kiowa, Kans., Panhandle, Tex.	Southern Kansas ....
Kittery Junction (n. o.) and York Beach, Me.	1	28	Kittery Junction (n. o.), York Beach, Me.	York Harbor and Beach R. R.
La Harpe, Ill., and Burlington, Iowa.	6	23076	La Harpe, Ill., Burlington, Iowa.	Toledo, Peoria and Western.
Lake City and Cadillac, Mich.	9	24066	Lake City, Cadillac, Mich ..	Cadillac and Northeastern..
Lake City and Fort White, Fla.	4	16032	Lake City and Fort White, Fla.	Savannah, Florida, and Western R. R.
Lake George and Fort Edward, N. Y.	2	6032	Fort Edward, Lake George, N. Y.	Delaware and Hudson Canal Company.
Lake Linden and Junction, Mich.	6	24069	Junction (n. o.), Lake Linden, Mich.	Hancock and Calumet ......
Lake Park, Iowa, and Worthington, Minn.	6	27085	Lake Park, Iowa, Worthington, Minn.	Burlington, Cedar Rapids and Northern.
Lake Roland and Stevenson, Md.	3	10018	Lake Roland, Stevenson, Md.	Northern Central...........
La Moure and Edgeley, Dak...	6	¹35015 (part)	Fargo, Edgeley, Dak........	Northern Pacific...........

parts of railroads over which no railway post-offices run, in operation, etc.—Continued.

Miles of route.	Annual miles of service.	Number of round trips per week.	Number of pouches exchanged daily.	Date of last re-adjustment.	Average weight of mail whole distance daily.	Remarks.
					Pounds.	
22.50	10,260	12	22	July 1, 1888	82	Service established February 20, 1888.
4.76	10,453	21	10	July 1, 1886	286	Connects at Kensett, Ark., with Saint Louis, Mo., and Texarkana, Ark., R. P. O.
6.37	8,000	12	6	July 1, 1887	1,607	[1] Balance of route covered by Logansport, Ind., and Keokuk, Iowa, R. P. O. Supplied by Keokuk, Iowa, and by Logansport, Ind., and Keokuk, Iowa, R. P. O.
14.99	47,069	30	36	July 1, 1885	334	Service established March 12, 1888; distance, 18.62 miles. June 25, 1888, service extended to Trinway, Ohio, increasing distance 15.52 miles, and R. P. O. service established. (See Table A[a].)
....	6,763	12	12	July 1, 1858	70	
15.19	9,530	6	22	July 1, 1885	65	Farmington and Lewiston R. P. O. exchange pouches with West Freeman, Salem, and Kingfield. Farmington exchanges with Freeman, Salem, and Kingfield. Salem exchanges with Strong and West Freeman. Kingfield exchanges with Salem and Strong.
20.23	29,688	14	6	July 1, 1888	261	Providence and New London R. P. O. exchange pouches with Narragansett Pier, Gould, Peandale, Rocky Brook, and Wakefield. Narragansett Pier exchanges with Boston, Providence, and New York R. P. O. and Providence.
8.50	16,014	18	29	July 1, 1885	298	
11.42	7,172	6	8	July 1, 1884	83	Connects Baltimore and Grafton R. P. O. at Tunnelton.
10.95	6,877	6	6	....	....	
9.87	12,397	12	12	July 1, 1885	125	[1] Balance of route (10.34 miles) covered by Wellsville and Bradford R. P. O. (See Table A[a].) New service; not reported last year.
[1]15.84	19,895	12	20	July 7, 1885	125	
217.20	158,990	7	40	Dec. 5, 1887	....	Supplied by Kiowa, Kans., and Newton and Kiowa, Kans., R. P. O. Connects at Panhandle, Tex., with Panhandle and Washburn, Tex., pouch service.
11.33	3,262	6	20	....	....	From January 16, 1888. Bangor and Boston R. P. O. exchanges pouches with York, York Beach, York Village, Kittery, and Cape Neddick. Kittery Depot exchanges with Bangor and Boston R. P. O. and North Conway and Boston R. P. O. and with Kittery Point.
20.10	25,255	12	10	July 1, 1887	141	Supplied by Burlington, Iowa, and by Logansport, Ind., and Keokuk, Iowa, R. P. O. Connects at Burlington, Iowa, with all lines centering there.
13.65	17,144	12	4	Feb. 1, 1886	82	At Cadillac, Mich., connects Cadillac and Fort Wayne, and Mackinaw City and Grand Rapids, Mich., R. P. O's.
21.93	27,544	12	6	July 1, 1888	56	
15.95	52,083	[1]30	[2]6.8	July 1, 1886	584	[1] 12 round trips for 9 months, and 30 round trips for 3 months, per week. [2] 44 pouches daily for 9 months, and 68 pouches daily for 3 months.
3.23	6,521	19	14	Sept. 10, 1886	225	Supplied by Houghton and Calumet, Mich., and by Marquette and Houghton, Mich. R. P. O. Connects at Junction, (n. o.), Mich. with Calumet and Houghton, Mich., pouch service.
18.80	11,806	6	10	July 1, 1887	216	Supplied by Worthington, Minn., and by Cedar Rapids, Iowa, and Watertown, Dak., R. P. O. Connects at Worthington, Minn. with Saint Paul, Minn., and Council Bluffs, Iowa, and with Worthington, Minn., and Sioux Falls, Dak. R. P. O's.
5.51	3,460	6	4	July 1, 1885	33	Supplied by closed pouches from Baltimore, Md.
21.90	13,753	6	6	July 1, 1886	408	[1] Balance of route covered by Fargo and La Moure, Dak., R. P. O. (See Table A[a].) Supplied by initial and terminal offices and by Fargo and La Moure, Dak., R. P. O. Connects at Edgely, Dak., with Edgely and Aberdeen, Dak., pouch service, and at La Moure, Dak., with Jamestown and Oakes, Dak., R. P. O.

TABLE C*c*.—*Statement of mail service performed in closed pouches upon railroads and*

Initial and terminal stations running east to west, north to south, and northwest to southeast.	Division.	Number of route.	Contract designation, termini of route.	Corporate title of company.
Lanes and Georgetown, S. C...	4	14020	Lanes and Georgetown, S. C.	Georgetown and Lanes R. R.
Lansdale and Norristown, Pa..	2	8098	Norristown, Lansdale, Pa...	Stony Creek................
Latrobe and Ligonier, Pa......	2	8118	Latrobe, Ligonier, Pa.......	Ligonier Valley............
Lawrence and Carbondale, Kans.	7	33014	Lawrence, Carbondale, Kans.	Lawrence, Emporia and Southwestern.
Lawrence and Lowell, Mass...	1	3017	Lowell, Lawrence, Mass....	Boston and Maine R. R. (Lowell system).
Lawrence and Salem, Mass....	1	3005	Salem, Lawrence, Mass	Boston and Maine R. R .....
Lawrenceburgh Junction (n. o.) and Lawrenceburgh, Ind.	5	22045	Lawrenceburgh Junction (n. o.), Lawrenceburgh, Ind.	Cin., Ind., St. Louis and Chicago.
Lawrenceville and Harrison Valley, Pa.	2	8139	Lawrenceville, Harrison Valley, Pa.	Fall Brook Coal Co ....
Lawton and Hartford, Mich ...	9	24063	Lawton, Hartford, Mich.....	Toledo and South Haven ...
Leaman Place and Strasburgh, Pa.	2	8026	Strasburgh, Leaman Place, Pa.	Strasburgh ....
Lebanon Station and Albany Junction (n. o.), Oregon.	8	44010	Albany Station (n. o.), Lebanon Station (n. o.), Oregon.	Oregon and California R. R..
Lebanon and Cornwall, Pa	2	8149	Lebanon, Cornwall, Pa	Cornwall ....
Leeds Junction (n. o.) and Lewiston, Me.	1	3 (part)	Farmington, Brunswick, Me	Maine Central R. R ....
Lehi and Silver City, Utah	8	41011	Lehi, Silver City, Utah	Salt Lake and Western R. R.
Leicester Junction, Vt., and Addison Junction (n. o.), N. Y.	1	2008	Leicester Junction, Vt., and Addison Junction (n. o.), N. Y.	Central Vermont R. R ......
Lewisburgh and Sunbury, Pa..	2	8153	Sunbury, Lewisburgh, Pa..	Philadelphia and Reading ..
Lewiston and South Auburn, Me.	1	21	Lewiston, South Auburn, Me.	Grand Trunk R. R..........
Lewiston and Suspension Bridge, N. Y.	2	6016 (part)	Buffalo, Lewiston, N. Y	N. Y. C. and H. R............
Little River and Hollyrood, Kans.	7	33005	Little River, Hollyrood, Kans.	Chicago, Kansas and Western.
Lockhart and San Marcos, Tex.	7	31063	San Marcos, Lockhart, Tex..	Taylor, Bastrop and Houston.
Lockport Junction (n. o.) and Tonawanda, N. Y.	2	6015	Tonawanda, Lockport Junction (n. o.) N. Y.	N. Y. C. and H. R. ....
Locust Valley and Mineola, N. Y.	2	6044	Mineola, Locust Valley, N. Y.	Long Island ....
Long Valley, Cal., and Reno, Nev.	8	45005	Reno, Nev., Long Valley. Cal.	Nevada and California R. R.
Longview and Carthage, Tex..	7	31048	Longview, Carthage, Tex...	Galveston, Sabine and Saint Louis.

parts of railroads over which no railway post-offices run, in operation, etc.—Continued.

Miles of route.	Annual miles of service.	Number of round trips per week.	Number of pouches exchanged daily.	Date of last re-adjustment.	Average weight of mail whole distance daily.	Remarks.
					Pounds.	
39.20	24,617	6	6	July 1, 1888	267	
16.80	10,674	9	13	July 1, 1885	127	
10.80	13,585	12	8	July 1, 1886	103	
33.75	21,195	6	16	....	....	Not reported last year; service on this route restored by order of March 17, 1888. Supplied by initial and terminal offices. Connects at Richland, Kans., with Topeka and Fort Scott, Kans., R. P. O.
14.06	26,527	18	14	July 1, 1885	127	Turksbury exchanges ponches with Boston. Lowell, and Saint Albans and Boston R. P. O. Lowell with Lawrence and Portland and Boston R. P. O.
22.33	28,046	12	41	July 1, 1885	133	Salem exchanges with Peabody, Danvers, Topesfield, Danversport, Asylum Station, Middleton, Lawrence, and Manchester, Lawrence, and Boston R. P. O.; Portland and Boston R. P. O. Peabody with Boston and Manchester, Lawrence and Boston R. P. O., with additional round trip daily from Salem to Peabody.
2.46	4,890	¹19	8	July 1, 1888	386	¹One round trip daily and two round trips daily, except Sunday.
32.42	40,720	12	22	July 1, 1886	129	
20.21	25,384	12	14	July 1, 1884	136	At Lawton connects Detroit and Chicago R. P. O. At Hartford, Mich., connects Grand Rapids and La Crosse R. P. O.
5.25	6,594	12	4	July 1, 1886	56	
12.50	18,300	14	10	....	....	Connects at Albany Junction with Portland, Oregon, and Sacramento, Cal., R. P. O.; at Tallmon with Portland and Coburg R. P. O.
6.25	5,867	9	12	July 1, 1885	76	
16.32	20,498	12	18	July 1, 1885	870	Balance of route (51.33 miles) supplied by R. P. O. service. (See Table A⁵.) Farmington and Lewiston R. P. O. exchanges with Sabattus, Wilton. Livermore Falls, Farmington, and West Farmington. Bangor and Boston R. P. O. exchanges with Sabattus, Wilton, Farmington, and Wes-Farmington; Lewiston with Sabattus
54.25	34,069	6	6	July 1, 1886	50	
15.63	9,816	6	20	July 1, 1885	83	Connects at Lehi with Salt Lake and Juab R. P. O. Essex Junction and Boston R. P. O. exchanges with Whiting, East Shoreham, North Orwell, Larabee Point and Ticonderoga. North Orwell with Ticonderoga. Rutland, Bennington and Troy R. P. O. exchanges with East Shoreham and North Orwell.
9.35	11,744	12	10	July 1, 1885	50	
5.97	7,498	12	8	July 1, 1885	137	Portland and Island Pond R. P. O., long and short runs, exchanges with Lewiston and Auburn.
4.75	4,474	9	7	July 1, 1885	8,979	Balance of route (24.73 miles) covered by Suspension Bridge and Buffalo R. P. O. (See Table A⁵.)
27.15	19,874	7	28	Feb. 21, 1887	168	Connects at Little River, Kans., with Florence and Ellinwood, Kans., R. P. O.; at Geneseo, Kans., with Kansas City, Mo., Salina Kans., and Pueblo, Colo., R. P. O., and Wichita and Kanopolis, Kans., R. P. O.; at Lorraine, Kans., with Ellsworth and Wichita, Kans., R. P. O.
17.12	25,064	14	10	....	....	New service, not reported last year, connects at San Marcos, Tex., with Denison and San Antonio Tex., R. P. O.
12.36	34,929	27	¹40	July 1, 1885	981	¹Including sacks.
11.57	14,532	12	32	Aug. 25, 1885	244	
57.15	35,890	6	6	June 16, 1888	479	Connects at Reno, Nev., with Ogden, Utah, and San Francisco, Cal., R. P. O. Supplied by Reno, Nev. New service established February 16 and extended June 6, 1888.
36.90	29,134	7	20	Jan. 24, 1887	24	Reported last year as Longview and Tatum, Tex., increased distance 17.29 miles. Connects at Longview, Tex., with Texarkana, Ark., and El Paso, Tex., R. P. O. and Texarkana, Ark., and Houston, Tex., R. P. O.

TABLE C^c.—*Statement of mail service performed in closed pouches upon railroads and*

Initial and terminal stations running east to west, north to south, and northwest to southeast.	Division.	Number of route.	Contract designation, termini of route.	Corporate title of company.
Lorain and Grafton, Ohio......	5	¹21041 (part)	Lorain, Bridgeport, Ohio ...	Cleveland, Lorain and Wheeling.
Los Angeles and Port Ballona, Cal	8	46058	Los Angeles, Port Ballona, Cal.	Southern Pacific Co.........
Los Angeles and San Pedro, Cal.	8	46013	San Pedro, Los Angeles, Cal.	Southern Pacific Co.........
Los Angeles and Santa Monica, Cal.	8	46020	Los Angeles, Santa Monica, Cal.	Los Angeles and Independence R. R.
Louisburgh and Franklinton, N. C.	3	13025	Louisburgh, Franklinton, N. C.	Raleigh and Gaston.........
Louisville and Prospect (n. o.), Ky.	5	20023	Louisville, Prospect (n. o.), Ky.	Louisville and Nashville ...
Louisville and Wadley, Ga ...	4	15028	Wadley, Louisville, Ga.....	Louisville and Wadley R. R.
Lugonia and San Bernardino, Cal.	8	46056	San Bernardino, Lugonia, Cal.	California Central Rwy.....
Luverne, Minn., and Doon, Iowa.	6	26030	Luverne, Minn., Doon, Iowa.	Chicago, Saint Paul, Minn., and Omaha.
Lyle, Minn., and Mason City, Iowa.	6	¹27010 (part)	Albia, Iowa, Lyle, Minn....	Central Iowa ....
Lyons and Denver, Colo.......	7	38028	Denver, Lyons, Colo........	Denver, Utah and Pacific...
McDonough and Griffin, Ga....	4	¹15051 (part)	Columbus, McDonough, Ga.	Georgia Midland R. R ......
McNeil and Magnolia, Ark....	7	29015	McNeil, Magnolia, Ark.....	Saint Louis, Arkansas and Texas.
Madison and Elmira, Cal......	8	46015	Elmira, Madison, Cal........	Vaca Valley and Clear Lake R. R.
Madisonville and Providence, Ky.	5	20031	Madisonville, Providence, Ky.	Louisville and Nashville....
Mahopac and Golden's Bridge, N. Y.	2	6023	Golden's Bridge, Mahopac, N. Y.	N. Y. C. and H. R. (Harlem Div.).
Malcolm and Antigo, Wis....	6	25060	Antigo, Malcolm, Wis.......	Milwaukee, Lake Shore and Western.
Malvern and Hot Springs, Ark.	7	29005	Malvern, Hot Springs, Ark .	Hot Springs ....
Mammoth Cave and Glasgow Junction, Ky.¹	5	20036	Glasgow Junction, Mammoth Cave, Ky.	Louisville and Nashville....
Manahawkin and Beach Haven, N. J.	6	7042	Beach Haven, Manahawkin N. J.	Pennsylvania..............
Manchester and Barnegat, N. J.	2	7050	Manchester, Barnegat, N. J.	Central R. R. of New Jersey.
Manchester and Cedar Rapids, Iowa.	6	27101	Cedar Rapids, Manchester, Iowa.	Illinois Central ....
Manchester and North Weare, N. H.	1	1033	Manchester, North Weare, N. H.	Concord R. R...............

parts of railroads over which no railway post-offices run, in operation, etc.—Continued.

Miles of route.	Annual miles of service.	Number of round trips per week.	Number of pouches exchanged daily.	Date of last readjustment.	Average weight of mail whole distance daily.	Remarks.
					Pounds.	
16.35	20,536	12	16	July 1, 1888	1,057	[1] Balance of route (142.06 miles) covered by Cleveland and Wheeling R. P. O. (See Table A².).
18.07	26,454	14	4	....	....	New service established April 12, 1888, supplied by Los Angeles.
26.46	38,737	14	14	July 1, 1886	158	Connects at Los Angeles with Deming, N. Mex., and Los Angeles, Cal., San Francisco and Los Angeles, Albuquerque, N. Mex., and Los Angeles R. P. O's. Supplied by Los Angeles.
19.77	28,943	14	6	July 1, 1886	70	Connects at Los Angeles with Deming, N. Mex., and Los Angeles, Cal., San Francisco and Los Angeles and Albuquerque and Los Angeles R. P. O's. Supplied by Los Angeles.
19.40	13,662	12	4	July 1, 1888	128	Connects Norfolk and Raleigh R. P. O. at Franklinton.
11.00	6,908	6	8	July 1, 1884	41	
10.62	13,338	12	6	July 1, 1884	131	
9.25	13,542	14	6	....	....	New service established March 17, 1888. Connects at San Bernardino with Albuquerque, N. Mex., and Los Angeles, Cal., and San Bernardino and National City R. P. O.
28.31	17,770	6	10	July 1, 1887	114	Supplied by Luverne, Minn., and by Worthington, Minn., and Sioux Falls, Dak.. R. P. O. Connects at Rock Rapids, Iowa, with Ellsworth, Minn., and Sioux Falls, Dak., and with Cherokee, Iowa, and Sioux Falls, Dak., pouch service.
28.50	38,760	13	16	July 1, 1887	1,652	[1] Balance of route covered by Mason City and Albia, Iowa, R. P. O. (See Table A².) Connects at Lyle, Minn., with Minneapolis, Hayfield, Minn., and Waterloo, Iowa, R. P. O.; at Manly, Iowa, with Albert Lea, Minn., and Burlington, Iowa, R. P. O., and at Mason City, Iowa, with Mason City and Albia, Iowa, Calmar, Iowa, and Chamberlain, Dak., Mason City and Fort Dodge, Iowa, and Austin, Minn., and Mason City, Iowa, R. P. O's.
44.97	28,241	6	14	July 1, 1886	85	Makes Denver, Colo., connections and connects at Longmont, Colo., with Greeley and Denver, Colo., R. P. O., and at Erie and Canfield, Colo, with Brighton and Boulder, Colo., pouch service.
19.20	12,057	6	6	July 1, 1888	224	[1] 80.80 miles of this route reported as Griffin and Columbus R. F. O. in Table A².
6.72	9,838	14	6	July 1, 1886	130	Connects at McNeil, Ark., with Cairo, Ill., and Texarkana, Ark., R. P. O.
27.51	34,552	12	18	July 1, 1886	223	Connects at Elmira with Ogden, Utah, and San Francisco, Cal.
....	8,383	6	6	....	....	[1] April 19, 1888, R. P. O. service established between Evansville, Ind., and Providence, Ky., covering this route. (See Table A².)
7.50	9,420	12	8	July 1, 1885	48	
13.37	8,396	6	4	July 1, 1887	35	Supplied by Antigo, Wis. Connects at that point with Ashland and Milwaukee, Wis., R. P. O.
25.40	55,778	21	18	July 1, 1886	959	Connects at Malvern, Ark., with Saint Louis, Mo., Texarkana, Ark., R. P. O.
8.51	5,736	13	6	....	....	*Service established January 2, 1888.
12.03	11,110	12	6	July 1, 1888	111	
22.24	58,783	21	24	July 1, 1885	188	
42.58	26,740	6	24	....	....	Supplied by initial and terminal offices. Connects at Manchester, Iowa, with Dubuque and Sioux City, Iowa, R. P. O., and at Cedar Rapids, Iowa, with lines centering at that city.
19.95	12,528	6	22	July 1, 1885	177	Supplied by Manchester and Saint Albans and Boston R. P. O.

TABLE C^c.—*Statement of mail service performed in closed pouches upon railroads and*

Initial and terminal stations running east to west, north to south, and northwest to southeast.	Division.	Number of route.	Contract designation, termini of route.	Corporate title of company.
Manitou Junction (n. o.) and Colorado Springs, Colo.	7	38025	Manitou Junction (n. o.), Colorado Springs, Colo....	Denver, Texas and Gulf....
Mankato Junction and Mankato, Minn.	6	26019	Mankato Junction (n. o.), Mankato, Minn.	Chicago and Northwestern.
Manning and Audubon, Iowa.	6	27080	Manning, Audubon, Iowa...	Chicago and Northwestern.
Manor Junction and Eastport Junction, N. Y.	2	6117	Manor Junction, Eastport Junction, N. Y.	Long Island ....
Manor Station and Claridge, Pa.	2	8111	Manor Station, Claridge, Pa.	Pennsylvania ....
Manumuskin and Heislerville, N. J.	2	7057	Manumuskin, Heislerville, N. J.	West Jersey.................
Marblehead and Lynn, Mass ..	1	3009	Lynn, Marblehead, Mass ..	Boston and Maine R. R. .....
Marblehead and Salem, Mass..	1	3004	Marblehead, Salem, Mass ..	Boston and Maine R. R. .....
Marietta, Ohio, and Parkersburgh, W. Va.	5	21049	Marietta, Ohio, Parkersburgh, W. Va.	Marietta and Parkersburgh.
Margarettsville, N.C., and Emporia, Va.	3	11036	Emporia, Va., Margarettsville, N. C.	Meherrin Valley.............
Marion and Parker City, Ill....	6	23097	Marion, Parker City, Ill....	Saint Louis, Alton and Terre Haute.
Marshall and Myrick Station (n. o.), Mo.	7 / 2	28059	Marshall, Myrick Station (n. o.), Mo.	Missouri Pacific.............
Marshall and Belmont, Wash..	8	43015	Marshall, Belmont, Wash ..	Spokane and Palouse Rwy. Co.
Mauch Chunk and Tamaqua, Pa.	2	8100	Tamaqua, Mauch Chunk, Pa.	Central R. R. of New Jersey
Mayville and Jamestown, N. Y.	2	6135	Jamestown, Mayville, N. Y.	Chautauqua Lake.............
Marysville and Clough Junction (n. o.), Mont.	8	36007	Clough Junction, Marysville, Mont.	Northern Pacific R. R ......
Maysville and Pittsfield, Ill ...	6	23075	Maysville, Pittsfield, Ill	Wabash ....
Meadows and Whitefield Junction (n. o.), N. H.	1	1018	Whitefield Junction (n. o), Meadows, N. H.	Whitefield and Jefferson R. R
Meadville and Lineville, Pa	2	8107	Meadville, Lineville, Pa	Pennsylvania...............
Mears (n. o.) and Villa Grove, Colo.	7	38015	Mears (n. o.), Villa Grove, Colo.	Denver and Rio Grande ....
Mechanicsburgh and Dillsburgh, Pa.	2	8080	Mechanicsburgh, Dillsburgh, Pa.	Cumberland Valley.........
Means and Cadiz, Ohio........	5	21083	Means, Cadiz, Ohio.........	Pittsburgh, Cin. and St. Louis
Mechanicsville and Reynolds, N. Y.	2	6107	Mechanicsville, Reynolds, N. Y.	Fitchburgh ....
Medford and Boston, Mass ..	1	3012	Boston, Medford, Mass......	Boston and Maine R. R. .....
Medford and Haddonfield, N.J.	2	7045	Haddonfield, Medford, N. J.	Camden and Atlantic........
Melrose and Carbonado, Wash.	8	43005 (part)	Tacoma Carbonado, Wash..	Northern Pacific R. R ....

parts of railroads over which no railway post-offices run, in operation, etc.—Continued.

Miles of route.	Annual miles of service.	Number of round trips per week.	Number of pouches exchanged daily.	Date of last re-adjustment.	Average weight of mail whole distance daily.	Remarks.
					Pounds.	
9.02	14,523	14	4	July 1, 1886	63	Last year service on this route was covered by Denver and Pueblo, Colo., R. P. O. Connects at Manitou Junction (n. o.), Colo., with Denver and Pueblo, Colo., R. P. O., and at Colorado Springs, Colo., with Denver, Colo., and Ogden, Utah, R. P. O., Denver, Pueblo, and Leadville, Colo., R. P. O., Colorado Springs and Leadville, Colo., R. P. O., and Colorado Springs and Manitou Springs, Colo., pouch service.
4.09	11,125	26	6	July 1, 1887	250	Connects Winona and Tracy, Minn., R. P. O., with Mankato, Minn.
17.95	22,545	12	16	July 1, 1887	287	Supplied by Carroll and Manning, Iowa, and by Cedar Rapids and Council Bluffs, Iowa, R. P. O. Connects at Manning, Iowa, with Marion and Council Bluffs, Iowa, R. P. O., and with Carroll and Kirkman, Iowa, pouch service. Connects at Audubon, Iowa, with Audubon and Atlantic, Iowa, pouch service.
5.50	3,454	6	12	Aug. 25, 1886	72	
4.31	5,413	12	6	Apr. 12, 1886	69	
9.10	11,430	12	20	July 1, 1888	92	
6.28	12,020	18	6	July 1, 1885	588	Marblehead exchanges pouches with Lynn and Boston via Lynn.
3.99	7,517	18	13	July 1, 1888	167	Marblehead exchanges with Salem and Bangor and Boston R. P. O., and Boston via Salem, and with Lynn via Salem.
15.06	33,116	21	34	July 1, 1888	1,021	
18.77	11,788	6	10	....	....	Connects Washington and Wilmington R. P. O. at Emporia, and Norfolk and Raleigh R. P. O. at Margaretteville.
15.34	19,267	12	8	May 17, 1888	52	Supplied by Marion, Ill.. and by Pinkneyville and Marion, Ill., R. P. O. Connects at Parker City, Ill., with Danville and Cairo, Ill., R. P. O.
47.82	30,031	6	14	....	....	New service; not reported last year. Trains run to Lexington, Mo., and there connect with Sedalia and Kansas City, Mo., R. P. O. Connects at Marshall, Mo., with Saint Louis, Louisiana, and Kansas City, Mo. R. P. O.
42.97	26,985	6	8	June 30, 1888	127	Connects at Marshall with Helena, Mont., and Portland, Oregon, R. P. O. Spangle, Rosalia, Oakdale, and Belmont exchange with Spokane Falls.
16.32	36,872	21	30	July 1, 1885	221	
22.25	21,902	9	14	July 1, 1888	179	
12.97	9,494	7	4	....	....	New service established March 7, 1888. Connects at Clough Junction with Helena, Mont., and Portland, Oregon, R. P. O.
6.80	18,496	26	6	July 1, 1887	304	Supplied by Bluffs, Ill., and Hannibal, Mo., and La Fayette, Ind., and Quincy, Ill.. R. P. O's.
8.50	5,338	6	12	July 1, 1885	74	Supplied by Lancaster and Boston R. P. O., and Whitefield.
21.10	39,752	18	14	July 1, 1885	221	
20.16	14,757	7	12	July 1, 1886	150	Trains run from Salida, Colo., and there connect with Denver, Colo., and Ogden, Utah. R. P. O., and Denver, Pueblo, and Leadville, Colo., R. P. O.
8.84	11,103	12	12	July 1, 1885	263	
8.11	10,186	12	12	July 1, 1888	941	
4.88	6,129	¹12	4	....	....	¹ Fifteen times per week between Saratoga Junction and Mechanicsville; six times per week over whole route.
5.31	13,339	24	14	July 1, 1885	200	Boston exchanges with Glenwood and Medford.
12.23	26,883	21	14	July 1, 1885	45	
8.60	10,802	12	4½	July 5, 1888	2,374	Connects at Melrose with Helena, Mont., and Portland, Oregon, R. P. O. Balance of route covered by that line. (See Table A*.)

TABLE C^c.—*Statement of mail service performed in closed pouches upon railroads and*

Initial and terminal stations running east to west, north to south, and northwest to southeast.	Division.	Number of route.	Contract designation, termini of route.	Corporate title of company.
Melrose and Vernon, Conn	1	5008	Vernon, Melrose, Conn	New York and New England R. R.
Menominee, Mich., and Crivity, Wis.	6	25057	Menominee, Mich., Crivity, Wis.	Milwaukee and Northern...
Menomonee and Hunt, Wis ...	6	25053	Red Cedar Junction (n. o.), Menomonee, Wis.	Chicago, Milwaukee, and Saint Paul.
Meredith and Harrison Junction (n. o.), Mich.	9	24044	Meredith, Harrison Junction (n. o.), Mich.	Flint and Pere Marquette..
Micanopy Junction (n. o.) and Micanopy, Fla.	4	16017	Micanopy Junction (n. o.), Micanopy. Fla.	Florida Southern R. R ......
Middleborough and Attleborough, Mass.	1	3043	Attleborough, Middleborough, Mass.	Old Colony R. R ....
Middleborough and Fall River, Mass.	1	3039 (part)	South Braintree Junction (n. o.), Mass., Newport, R. I.	Old Colony R. R ....
Middletown and Berlin Depot (n. o.), Conn.	1	5003	Middletown, Berlin Depot (n. o.), Conn.	New York, New Haven and Hartford R. R.
Midville and Swainsborough, Ga.	4	15053	Midville, Swainsborough, Ga.	Midville and Swainsborough R. R.
Midway and Versailles, Ky ...	5	20020	Midway, Versailles, Ky ...	Versailles and Midway ....
Milaca and Elk River, Minn ..	6	26059	Elk River, Milaca, Minn ...	Saint Paul, Minneapolis and Manitoba.
Milford and Ashland, Mass...	1	3060	Milford, Ashland, Mass ...	New York and New England R. R. (Milford Branch).
Milford and Bellingham, Mass.	1	3059	Milford, Bellingham, Mass	......do ....
Millbury and Grafton Depot (n. o.), Mass.	1	3026	Grafton Depot (n. o.), Millbury, Mass.	Boston and Albany R. R....
Millstadt and Millstadt Junction, Ill.	6	23100	Millstadt Junction, (n. o.), Millstadt, Ill.	Mobile and Ohio............
Milroy and Lewistown Junction, Pa.	2	8049	Lewistown Junction, Milroy, Pa.	Pennsylvania ....
Milton Junction and Janesville, Wis.	6	25004 (part)	Milton Junction, Shullsburgh, Wis.	Chicago, Milwaukee and St. Paul.
Milwaukee and Rugby Junction, Wis.	6	25017 (part)	Milwaukee, Ashland, Wis...	Wisconsin Central..........

parts of railroads over which no railway post-offices run, in operation, etc.—Continued.

Miles of route.	Annual miles of service.	Number of round trips per week.	Number of pouches exchanged daily.	Date of last re-adjustment.	Average weight of mail whole distance daily.	Remarks.
					Pounds.	
13.15	16,516	12	29	July 1, 1885	109	Springfield and Hartford R. P. O. and Boston and Hopewell Junction R. P. O. exchanges with Ellington and Rockville. Hartford with Vernon Centre and Rockville.
22.96	28,837	12	14	July 1, 1887	141	Supplied by Menominee, Mich., and by Iron Mountain, Mich., and Milwaukee, Wis., R. P. O. Connects at Menominee, Mich., with Ishpeming, Mich., and Fort Howard, Wis., R. P. O.
16.38	10,286	6	12	July 1, 1887	303	Supplied by Menomonee, Wis., and by Eau Claire, Wis., and Wabasha, Minn., R. P. O. Connects at Menomonee, Wis., with Saint Paul, Minn., and Elroy, Wis., R. P. O.
29.65	37,240	12	18	May 1, 1884	85	At Clare, Mich., connects Ludington and Toledo and Manistee and East Saginaw R. P. O's. Order February 24, 1888, stating service on this route from Clare, Mich., instead of Harrison Junction (n. o.), commencing July 1, 1888.
4.11	5,162	12	4	Mar. 11,1884	48	
22	27,632	12	29	July 1, 1885	40	Taunton exchanges with Middleborough, East Taunton, Boston, and Wellfleet R. P. O's; Barrowsville. Attleborough, Boston, Providence, and Boston, Providence, and New York R. P. O's.
38.16	47,928	12	40	July 1, 1885	1,083	Balance of route (23.09 miles) covered by R. P. O. service. (See Table A².) Newport exchanges with Boston, Providence, and New York R. P. O., Boston and Wellfleet R. P. O., Boston, Springfield, and New York R. P. O., and Fall River. Taunton with Myrick's and Tiverton. Additional trip from Newport to Fall River.
10.99	24,156	21	27	July 1, 1885	246	Supplied by Boston, Springfield, and New York R. P. O., Boston and New York R. P. O., short run, Boston and Hartford.
18.42	11,568	6	6	July 1, 1888	93	
7.58	14,281	18	14	Oct. 21,1885	229	
33.12	20,799	6	12	July 1,1888	93	Supplied by initial and terminal offices. Connects at Milaca, Minn., with Hinckley and Saint Cloud, Minn., pouch service, and at Elk River, Minn., with Saint Paul, Minn., and Mandan, Dak., R. P. O.
11.85	14,884	12	12			Ashland exchanges with Boston, Springfield, and New York R. P. O.
4.93	9,288	18	10	July 1, 1885	95	Milford exchanges with Franklin, Providence, and Boston and Hopewell Junction R. P. O.
4.46	5,602	12	4	July 1, 1885	57	Millbury exchanges with Boston and Albany R. P. O. and Boston.
7.00	8,792	12	4			Supplied by Saint Louis, Mo., and Cairo, Ill., R. P. O.
12.04	16,253	12	12	July 1, 1885	116	
7.91	9,935	12	16	July 1, 1887	981	[1] Balance of route covered by Gratiot and Shullsburgh, Wis., pouch service, and by Rockford, Ill., and Mineral Point, Wis., R. P. O. (See Table A².) Connects Janesville, Wis., and Rockford, Ill., and Mineral Point, Wis., R. P. O., with Chicago, Ill., and North McGregor, Iowa, R. P. O.
27.30	54,272	19	26	July 1, 1887	1,069	[1] Balance of route covered by Chicago, Ill., Abbotsford, Wis., and Minneapolis, Minn., and Ashland and Abbotsford, Wis., R. P. O's. (See Table A².) Connects at Milwaukee, Wis., with all lines centering at that city and at Rugby Junction, Wis., with Chicago, Ill., Abbotsford, Wis., and Minneapolis, Minn., R. P. O.

TABLE C*c*.—*Statement of mail service performed in closed pouches upon railroads and*

Initial and terminal stations running east to west, north to south, and northwest to southeast.	Division.	Number of route.	Contract designation, termini of route.	Corporate title of company.
Milwaukee Junction (n. o.), and West Detroit, Mich.	9	24062	Milwaukee Junction (n. o.), Detroit Junction, Mich.	Grand Trunk...............
Mineral Point and Potosi, Mo.	7	28049	Mineral Point, Potosi, Mo...	Saint Louis, Iron Mountain and Southern.
Minneapolis and Mendota, Minn.	6	26044	Mendota, Minneapolis, Minn.	Chicago, Milwaukee and Saint Paul.
Mineola and Hempstead, N. Y. Minot, Dak., and Great Falls, Mont.	2 6	6111 ¹35026 (part)	Mineola, Hempstead, N. Y .. Devil's Lake, Dak., Great Falls, Mont.	Long Island .... Saint Paul, Minn., and Manitoba.
Missaukee Junction (n.o.) and Jennings, Mich.	9	24050	Missaukee Junction (n. o.), Jennings, Mich.	Grand Rapids and Indiana..
Missoula and Victor, Mont	8	38008	Missoula, Victor, Mont.....	Missoula and Bitter Root Valey R. R.
Moira and Brandon, N. Y......	2	6052	Moira, Saint Regis Falls, N. Y.	Northern Adirondack......
Moncure and Pittsborough, N. C.	3	13029	Moncure, Pittsborough, N. C.	Pittsborough ....
Monico and Rhinelander, Wis.	6	25045	Monico, Rhinelander, Wis..	Milwaukee, Lake Shore and Western.
Monmouth Junction and Rocky Hill, N. J.	2	7011	Rocky Hill, Monmouth Junction, N. J.	Pennsylvania..............
Monson and Monson Junction(n. o.), Me.	1	* 23	Monson Junction (n. o.), Monson, Me.	Monson R. R...............
Montclair and Newark, N. J...	2	7027	Newark, Montclair, N. J....	Delaware, Lackawanna and Western.
Montgomery and Patsburg, Ala.	4	17027	Montgomery, Patsburg, Ala.	Montgomery and Southern Rwy.
Monticello and Drifton, Fla ...	4	¹16002 (part)	Lake City, River Junction.	Florida Rwy and Nav. Co...
Monticello and Port Jervis, N. Y.	2	6078	Port Jervis, Monticello, N. Y.	Port Jervis, Monticello and New York.
Montour Junction and Imperial, Pa.	2	8127	Montour Junction, Imperial, Pa.	Montour....................
Montpelier Junction (n o.) and Barre, Vt.	1	2017	Montpelier Junction (n. o) and Barre, Vt.	Central Vermont R. R ......
Montrose and Ouray, Colo....	7	38037	Montrose, Ouray, Colo	Denver and Rio Grande ...
Mooers and West Chazy, N. Y	2	6026 (part)	Albany, Mooers, N. Y	Delaware and Hudson Canal Company.
Morganfield and Uniontown, Ky.¹	5	20035	Morganfield, Uniontown, Ky	Ohio Valley...............
Morgan Junction and Cumberland, Ohio.	5	21048	Morgan Junction, Cumberland, Ohio.	Cintl, Wheeling and N. Y ..
Morris and Brown's Valley, Minn.	6	26034	Morris, Brown's Valley, Minn	Saint Paul, Minn., and Manitoba.

parts of railroads over which no railway post-offices run, in operation, etc.—Continued.

Miles of route.	Annual miles of service.	Number of round trips per week.	Number of pouches exchanged daily.	Date of last re-adjustment.	Average weight of mail whole distance daily.	Remarks.
4.61	2,895	6	12	July 1, 1884	*Pounds.* 58	At Milwaukee Junction (n. o.), Mich., connects Detroit and Grand Haven and Fort Gratiot and Detroit, R. P. O's.
						At West Detroit, Mich., connects Bay City, Wayne and Detroit, Big Rapids and Detroit, Detroit and Chicago, Detroit, Three Rivers and Chicago, Detroit and Grand Rapids, Detroit and Toledo, Howard City, and Detroit and Mackinaw City and Detroit R. P. O's.
4.43	11,128	24	8	July 1, 1887	116	Connects at Mineral Point, Mo., with Saint Louis, Mo., and Columbus, Ky., R. P. O., and Saint Louis, Mo., and Texarkana, Ark., R. P. O.
10.17	12,773	12	6	July 1, 1887	501	Supplied by Minneapolis and Saint Paul, Minn., connects at Mendota, Minn., with Chicago, Ill., McGregor, Iowa, and Saint Paul, Minn., R. P. O., and at Minneapolis, Minn., with lines centering at that city.
2.80	1,758	6	2	Aug. 25, 1885	161	[1] Balance of route covered by Crookston, Minn., and Minot, Dak., R. P. O. (See table A⁰.)
550.14	345,488	6	36	....	....	Supplied by Great Falls, Mont., and Minot, Dak., and by Crookston, Minn., and Minot, Dak., and Great Falls and Helena, Mont., R. P. O's.
8.05	4,057	6	4	....	....	Order August 11, 1887, establishing this service, to commence September 1, 1887.
						At Missaukee Junction, connects Cadillac and Fort Wayne, and Mackinaw City and Grand Rapids R. P. O's.
35.75	26,109	7	8	....	....	New service, established April 12, 1888. Connects at Missoula with Helena, Mont., and Portland, Oregon, R. P. O.
34.81	43,721	12	12	Mar. 15, 1886	90	
12.31	15,461	12	8	July 1, 1888	102	Connects Raleigh and Gibson's Station R. P. O. at Moncure.
14.64	9,194	6	2	July 1, 1887	101	Connects Ashland and Milwaukee, Wis., R. P. O. with Rhinelander, Wis. Connects at Rhinelander, Wis., with Sault de Ste. Marie, Mich., and Bruce, Wis., pouch service.
6.72	8,440	12	12	July 1, 1885	116	
6.16	7,737	12	4	July 1, 1885	63	Monson exchanges pouches with Greenville and Bangor R. P. O.
6.60	17,270	25	28	July 1, 1883	338	
46.00	28,888	6	22	July 1, 1888	105	
4.00	5,024	12	4	July 1, 1884	765	[1] 151.87 miles reported as Jacksonville and Pensacola R. P. O., in Table A⁰.
24.70	31,023	12	20	July 1, 1885	206	
11.00	13,816	12	12	July 1, 1885	121	
7.63	14,374	18	10	Aug. 5, 1885	215	Barre exchanges with Montpelier and Saint Albans and Boston R. P. O.
36.36	26,676	7	20	....	....	New service, not reported last year. Connects at Montrose, Colo., with Denver.
[1]11.75	11,069	9	6	July 1, 1885	4,939	[1] Balance of route (177 miles) covered by Rouse's Point and Albany R. P. O. (See Table A⁰.)
13.31	15,653	12	6	July 1, 1888	83	[1] Service established July 25, 1887.
17.70	11,116	6	18	July 1, 1888	90	
47.23	29,580	6	22	July 1, 1887	227	Supplied by initial and terminal offices. Connects at Morris, Minn., with Neche, Dak., and Saint Paul, Minn., and with Little Falls and Morris, Minn., R. P. O. Connects at Graceville, Minn., with Saint Paul, Ortonville, Minn., and Fargo, Dak., R. P. O.

TABLE C*c*.—*Statement of mail service performed in closed pouches upon railroads and*

Initial and terminal stations running east to west, north to south, and northwest to southeast.	Division.	Number of route.	Contract designation, termini of route.	Corporate title of company.
Morris Run and Bloasburgh, Pa.	2	8136	Blossburgh, Morris Run, Pa.	Fall Brook Coal Company ..
Mount Carmel and Alaska, Pa.	2	8088	Alaska, Mount Carmel, Pa..	Philadelphia and Reading ..
Mount Gilead and Edison, Ohio	5	21072	Edison, Mount Gilead, Ohio.	Cleveland, Columbus, Cincinnati and Indianapolis.
Mount Healthy and Cincinnati, Hamilton and Dayton R. R. Junction (n. o.).	5	21059	Junction with Cincinnati, Hamilton and Dayton R. R. to Mount Healthy, Ohio.	Cincinnati and Northwestern.
Mount Jewett and Kane, Pa ..	2	8086 (part)	Mount Jewett, Callery, Pa..	Pittsburgh and Western....
Mount Pleasant and Broad Ford, Pa.	2	8141	Broad Ford, Mount Pleasant, Pa.	Baltimore and Ohio.........
Mount Union and Robertsdale, Pa.	2	f085	Mount Union, Robertsdale, Pa.	East Broad Top ....
Mount Zion and Keosauqua, Iowa.	6	27062	Mount Zion, Keosauqua, Iowa.	Chicago, Rock Island and Pacific.
Nantucket and Siasconset, Mass.	1	3042	Nantucket, Siasconset, Mass.	Nantucket R. R. ....
Narenta Station and Metropolitan, Mich.	6	24058	Narenta Station, Metropolitan, Mich.	Chicago and Northwestern .
Natchitoches and Cypress, La.	4	30017	Cypress, Natchitoches, La ..	Natchitoches R. R ....
Necedah and Necedah Junction, Wis.	6	25062	Necedah Junction, Necedah, Wis.	Princeton and Western.....
Necedah and New Lisbon, Wis.	6	25022	New Lisbon, Necedah, Wis.	Chicago, Milwaukee and St. Paul.
Neelysville and Doniphan, Mo.	7	28035	Neelysville, Doniphan, Mo..	Saint Louis, Iron Mountain and Southern.
Nephi and Moroni, Utah	8	41010	Nephi, Moroni, Utah........	San Pete Valley Rwy.......
Nevada City and Colfax, Cal ..	8	46019	Colfax, Nevada City, Cal....	Nevada Co. Narrow Gauge Railroad.
Newark and Columbus, Ohio..	5	'21001 (part)	Bellaire, Columbus, Ohio....	Central, Ohio ....
Newark and Delaware City, Del.	2	9507	Newark, Delaware City, Del.	Philadelphia, Wilmington and Baltimore.
New Bedford and Fall River, Mass.	1	3054	New Bedford, Fall River, Mass.	Old Colony R. R ....
New Britain and Berlin Junction (n. o.), Conn.	1	5002	New Britain, Berlin Junction (n. o.), Conn.	New York, New Haven and Hartford R. R.
New Brunswick and East Millstone, N. J.	2	7010	East Millstone, New Brunswick, N. J.	Pennsylvania ....
Newburgh and Greycourt, N. Y.	2	6004	Newburgh, Greycourt, N. Y.	New York, Lake Erie and Western.
Newburgh and State Centre, Iowa.	6	27068	Newburgh, State Centre, Iowa.	Central Iowa ....
Newburgh Junction and Vail's Gate Junction, N. Y.	2	6074	Vail's Gate Junction, Newburgh Junction, N. Y.	New York, Lake Erie and Western.
New Canaan and Stamford, Conn.	1	5009	New Canaan, Stamford, Conn	New York, New Haven and Hartford R. R.
New Castle and New Castle Junction (n. o.), Pa.	5	'8125 (part)	Allegheny, New Castle, Pa..	Pittsburgh and Western....
New Castle and New Castle Junction (n. o), Pa.	2	8156	New Castle Junction (n. o.), New Castle, Pa.	Pittsburgh and Lake Erie ..
New City and Nanuet Junction, N. Y.	2	6104	New City, Nanuet Junction, N. Y.	New Jersey and New York ..
Newfield and Atlantic City, N. J.	2	7019	Newfield, Atlantic City, N.J.	West Jersey ....
New Galilee, Pa., and New Lisbon, Ohio.¹	5	21093	New Galilee, Pa., New Lisbon, Ohio.	Pitts., Marion and Chicago..

parts of railroads over which no railway post-offices run, in operation, etc.—Continued.

Miles of route.	Annual miles of service.	Number of round trips per week.	Number of pouches exchanged daily.	Date of last re-adjustment.	Average weight of mail whole distance daily.	Remarks.
					Pounds.	
3.76	4,723	12	4	July 1, 1885	62	
1.96	4,809	24	8	Feb. 11, 1885	80	
2.40	4,522	18	10	July 1, 1888	248	
7.08	8,892	12	8	July 1, 1888	100	
¹12.24	15,373	12	8	July 1, 1885	341	¹ Balance of route (126.87 miles) covered by Kane and Callery R. P. O. (See Table A⁵.)
10.38	6,519	6	18	July 1, 1885	54	
30.06	37,755	12	22	July 1, 1885	113	
4.97	6,242	12	8	July 1, 1887	114	Supplied by Mount Zion, Iowa, and by Des Moines and Keokuk, Iowa, R. P. O.
11.52	7,235	6	4	July 1, 1888	149	Siasconset exchanges pouches with Nantucket and Boston and Wellfleet R. P. O.
35.01	21,986	6	12	July 1, 1884	41	Supplied by Escanaba, Mich., and by Ishpeming, Mich., and Fort Howard, Wis., R. P. O.
11.62	14,595	12	4	Feb. 20, 1888	343	
16.48	10,349	6	4	July 1, 1887	25	Supplied by Necedah, Wis., and by Saint Paul, Minn., and Elroy, Wis., R. P. O.; connects at Necedah, Wis., with Necedah and New Lisbon, Wis., pouch service.
13.09	24,661	18	10	July 1, 1887	200	Supplied by New Lisbon, Wis., and by Chicago, Ill., and Minneapolis, Minn., R. P. O. Connects at Necedah, Wis., with Necedah Junction and Necedah, Wis., pouch service.
20.04	12,585	6	23	July 1, 1887	207	Connects at Neelysville, Mo., with Saint Louis, Mo., and Texarkana, Ark., R. P. O.
27.16	17,056	6	6	July 1, 1886	427	Connects at Nephi with Salt Lake and Juab R. P. O.
22.77	33,335	14	24	July 1, 1886	601	Connects at Colfax with Ogden, Utah, and San Francisco, Cal., R. P. O. Supplied, also, by Sacramento.
33.85	49,556	14	24	July 1, 1888	9,294	¹ Balance of route covered by Grafton and Chicago R. P. O., 104.62 miles. (See Table A⁵.)
12.68	27,871	21	12	July 1, 1885	89	
14.85	27,978	18	6	July 1, 1885	66	New Bedford exchanges with Fall River.
2.00	5,652	18	6	July 1, 1883	75	New Britain exchanges with Boston, Springfield, and New York R. P. O. day run, and New York and Boston R. P. O. short run.
8.56	10,741	12	8	July 1, 1885	75	
19.09	41,960	21	38	July 1, 1885	718	
27.00	16,936	6	18	July 1, 1887	73	Supplied by Grinnell and State Centre, Iowa. Connects at Newburgh, Iowa, with Mason City and Albia, Iowa, R. P. O.; at Capron, Iowa, with Marion and Council Bluffs, Iowa, R. P. O., and at State Centre, Iowa, with Cedar Rapids and Council Bluffs, Iowa, R. P. O.
12.60	23,738	15	28	July 1, 1885	227	
8.25	15,543	18	22	....	....	Supplied by Springdale, Boston and New York R. P. O. (a. r.) and New Haven and New York R. P. O.
2.93	3,680	12	6	July 1, 1885	650	¹ Balance of route (58.10 miles) covered by Pittsburgh and Akron R. P. O. (See Table A⁵.)
3.05	4,788	15	6	July 1, 1885	370	
4.59	5,765	12	12			
34.71	65,394	18	38	July 1, 1885	72	
....	7,253	6	16	July 1, 1888	234	¹ New Galilee and Rogers R. R. (14.11 miles) extended to New Lisbon, Ohio, August 15, 1887, increasing distance 11.22 miles. R. P. O. service established January 4, 1888.

TABLE C^c.—*Statement of mail service performed in closed pouches upon railroads and*

Initial and terminal stations running east to west, north to south, and northwest to southeast.	Division.	Number of route.	Contract designation, termini of route.	Corporate title of company.
New Glarus and Brodhead, Wis.	6	25044	Brodhead, New Glarus, Wis.	Chicago, Milwaukee and St. Paul.
New Madrid and Paw Paw (n. o.), Mo.	7	28052	Paw Paw (n. o.), New Madrid, Mo.	Saint Louis, Arkansas and Texas.
New Orleans and Covington, La.	4	30014	New Orleans, Covington, La.	East Louisiana R. R........
Newport News and Fortress Monroe, Va.	3	11031	Newport News, Fortress Monroe, Va.	Chesapeake and Ohio.......
New Rochelle and Harlem River, N. Y.	2	6109	New Rochelle, Harlem River, N. Y.	New York, New Haven and Hartford.
New Salisbury and Corydon, Ind.	5	22035	New Salisbury, Corydon, Ind.	Louisville, New Albany and Chicago.
New Sharon and Newton, Iowa.	6	27091	New Sharon, Newton, Iowa.	Central Iowa ....
Newton and Monroe, Iowa....	6	27036	Newton, Monroe, Iowa.......	Chicago, Rock Island and Pacific.
Newton Junction, N. H., and Merrimac, Mass.	1	3015	Newton Junction, N. H., Merrimac, Mass.	Boston and Maine R. R.....
Newtown and Philadelphia, Pa.	2	8117	Philadelphia, Newtown, Pa	Philadelphia, Newtown and New York.
Neillsville and Merrillon, Wis.	6	25037	Merrillon, Neillsville, Wis..	Chicago, St. Paul, Minn. and Omaha.
Niles and Alliance, Ohio.......	5	21086	Alliance, Niles, Ohio........	Pennsylvania................
Niles and San José, Cal........	8	46029	Niles, San José, Cal.........	Central Pacific R. R ....
Niles, Mich., and South Bend, Ind.	9	24012	Niles, Mich., South Bend, Ind.	Michigan Central...........
Norfolk and Virginia Beach, Va.	3	11035	Norfolk, Virginia Beach, Va.	Norfolk and Virginia Beach.
Norristown and Philadelphia, Pa.	2	8005	Philadelphia, Norristown, Pa.	Philadelphia and Reading ..
North Abington and Hanover, Mass.	1	3076	North Abington, Hanover, Mass.	Old Colony R. R ....
North Attleborough and Attleborough, Mass.	1	3061	Attleborough, North Attleborough, Mass.	Old Colony R. R. (Providence Division).
North Bennington and Bennington, Vt.	1	2015 (part)	Rutland, Bennington, Vt....	Bennington and Rutland R. R.
North Billerica and Somerville Station (n. o.), Mass.	1	3019	Somerville Station (n. o.), North Billerica, Mass.	Boston and Maine R. R. (Lowell System).
North Brookfield and East Brookfield, Mass.	1	3031	North Brookfield, East Brookfield, Mass.	Boston and Albany R. R...
North Clarendon and Cherry Grove, Pa.	2	8148	North Clarendon, Cherry Grove, Pa.	Warren and Farnsworth Valley.
North Grafton Station (n. o.) and Grafton, Mass.	1	3034	North Grafton Station (n. o.), Grafton, Mass.	Grafton and Upton R. R....

parts of railroads over which no railway post-offices run, in operation, etc.—Continued.

Miles of route.	Annual miles of service.	Number of round trips per week.	Number of pouches exchanged daily.	Date of last re-adjustment.	Average weight of mail whole distance daily.	Remarks.
					Pounds.	
22.90	28,762	12	22	July 1,1888	169	Supplied by Brodhead, Wis., and by Rockford, Ill., and Mineral Point, Wis., R. P. O.
6.96	9,466	13	4	July 1,1887	283	Connects at Paw Paw (n. o.), Mo., with Cairo, Ill., and Texarkana, Ark., R. P. O., and at New Madrid, Mo., with Cairo, Ill., and Elmot, Ark., R.P.O. river line.
56.50	37,366	6	6			
10.75	20,253	18	16	July 1,1885	546	Connects Norfolk, Newport News and Richmond R. P. O. at Newport News and Cape Charles, and Norfolk R. P. O. at Fortress Monroe.
12.13	26,662	21	31	July 1,1885	2,407	
8.39	10,538	12	8	July 1,1888	215	
33.60	21,101	6	28	July 1,1887	154	Supplied by initial and terminal offices, and by Mason City and Albia, Iowa, R. P. O. Connects at Newton, Iowa, with West Liberty and Council Bluffs, Iowa, R. P. O., and with Newton and Monroe, Iowa, pouch service.
18.13	22,771	12	14	July 1,1887	119	Supplied by initial and terminal offices. Connects at Newton, Iowa, with West Liberty and Council Bluffs, Iowa, R. P. O. and with New Sharon and Newton, Iowa, pouch service. Connects at Monroe, Iowa, with Des Moines and Keokuk, Iowa, R. P. O.
4.85	9,137	18	10	July 1,1885	126	Portland and Boston R. P. O. exchanges with Merrimac and Newton; Boston with Merrimac.
23.26	58,479	24	48	July 1,1885	332	
15.43	19,380	12	8	July 1,1887	215	Supplied by Merrillon, Wis., and St. Paul, Minn., and Elroy, Wis., R. P. O. Connects at Merrillon, Wis., with Fort Howard, Wis., and Winona, Minn., R. P. O.
27.93	35,080	12	26	July 1,1888	191	
18.30	51,679	27	30	July 1,1886	312	Connects at Niles with Sacramento and San Francisco R.P.O. Supplied also by closed pouch from Oakland and San Francisco.
12.43	15,612	12	10	July 1,1884	98	At Niles, Mich., connects Benton Harbor and Anderson, Detroit and Chicago, and Detroit, Three Rivers and Chicago R. P. O's. At South Bend, Ind., connects Fort Gratiot and Chicago, New York and Chicago, Toledo and Chicago, and South Bend and Terre Haute R. P. O's.
18.80	23,613	12	10	July 1,1885	57	Connects lines centering at Norfolk, Va.
16.21	93,316	55	158	July 1,1885	534	1 Including sacks.
8.28	10,400	12	18	July 1,1885	129	Supplied by initial and terminal offices, and Rockland, West Hanover, South Hanover, Hanover, and Boston.
4.06	8,968	21	18	July 1,1886	542	Supplied by initial and terminal offices, and Boston, Providence, Attleborough Falls, and Plainville.
5.07	19,104	36	26	Feb. 11,1885	3,892	Balance of route (82.75 miles) covered by R. P. O. service. (See Table A*.) Supplied by initial and terminal offices, and Rutland, Albany and Troy, Boston and Troy R. P. O's, and Essex Junction and Boston, Rutland, Bennington and Troy, and Saint Albans and North Bennington R. P. O's.
19.70	24,943	12	24	July 1,1886	198	Boston exchanges with Arlington, Arlington Heights, Bedford, Lexington, East Lexington, South Billerica, Billerica, and North Billerica, with one additional round trip daily to Lexington.
4.52	12,773	27	12	July 1,1885	199	Supplied by initial and terminal offices and Boston and Albany R. P. O.
10.47	13,151	12	4	July 1,1885	74	
3.00	9,420	30	24	Aug. 5,1885	193	Supplied by initial and terminal offices and Worcester, Boston, Springfield and New York R. P. O., and Boston and Albany R. P. O.

TABLE Cᶜ.—*Statement of mail service performed in closed pouches upon railroads and*

Initial and terminal stations running east to west, north to south, and northwest to southeast.	Division.	Number of route.	Contract designation, termini of route.	Corporate title of company.
North Woodstock and Plymouth, N. H.	1	1022	Plymouth, North Woodstock, N. H.	Boston and Maine R. R. (Lowell system).
Norton's Mills and Island Pond, Vt.	1	7 (part)	Portland, Me., Norton's Mills, Vt.	Grand Trunk R. R..........
Nutt (n. o.) and Lake Valley, N. Mex.	7	39008	Nutt Station (n. o.), Lake Valley, N. Mex.	Atchison, Topeka and Santa Fé.
Ocala and Dunnellon, Fla.....	4	16033	Ocala, Dunnellon, Fla......	Silver Springs, Ocala and Gulf R. R.
Ocean City and Berlin, Md....	2	10009 (part)	Salisbury, Ocean City, Md..	Wicomico and Pocomoke...
O'Fallen Depot and Belleville, Ill.	6	23031	Belleville, O'Fallen Depot, Ill.	Louisville and Nashville...
Ogdensburgh and De Kalb Junction, N. Y.	2	6036 (part)	Rome, Ogdensburgh, N. Y...	Rome, Watertown and Ogdensburgh.
Olcott and Iuka, Kans..........	7	33081	Olcott, Iuka, Kans	Kansas Southwestern.......
Olean, N. Y., and Bradford, Pa.	2	8121	Bradford, Pa., Olean, N. Y ..	West. New York and Penn..
Oliver Springs and Keathley, Tenn.	5	19022	Keathley, Oliver Springs, Tenn.	Walden's Ridge ....
Olympia and Tenino, Wash ...	8	43003	Tenino, Olympia, Wash	Olympia and Chehalis Valley R. R.
Orange C. H. and Gordonsville, Va.	3	11025	Orange C. H., Gordonsville, Va.	Richmond and Danville.....
Orleans and French Lick, Ind.	5	22051	Orleans, French Lick, Ind ..	Orleans, West Baden, and French Lick Springs.
Oronogo and Joplin, Mo.......	7	¹28054 (part)	Oronogo, Mo., Galena, Kans.	Saint Louis and San Francisco.
Oroville and Marysville, Cal ..	8	46009	Marysville, Oroville, Cal ..	California Northern R. R ...
Osceola Mills and Madera, Pa.	2	8099	Osceola Mills, Ramey, Pa...	Pennsylvania ....
Owl Run and Warrenton, Va..	3	11024	Owl Run, Warrenton, Va...	Richmond and Danville.....
Oxford and Peters Creek, Pa..	2	8094	Oxford, Peters Creek, Pa...	Peach Bottom ....
Palatka and Daytona, Fla	4	16031	Palatka, Datona, Fla	Saint John's and Halifax ...
Palmyra Junction and Hannibal, Mo.	7	28050	Palmyra, Hannibal, Mo.....	Hannibal and Saint Joseph .
Palisades and Eureka, Nev....	8	45002	Palisades, Eureka, Nev.....	Eureka and Palisades R. R..
Panhandle and Washburn, Tex.	7	31066	Panhandle, Washburn, Tex.	Fort Worth and Denver City.
Paris and Lexington, Ky.......	5	20002 (part)	Covington, Lexington, Ky..	Kentucky Central ....

parts of railroads over which no railway post-offices run, in operation, etc.—Continued.

Miles of route.	Annual miles of service.	Number of round trips per week.	Number of pouches exchanged daily.	Date of last re-adjustment.	Average weight of mail whole distance daily.	Remarks.
					Pounds.	
21.06	13,226	6	28	July 1, 1885	117	Lancaster and Boston exchange pouches with Blair, Campton, West Campton, Campton Village, West Thornton, Woodstock, and North Woodstock. Plymouth exchanges with Campton Village and West Campton.
16.02	20,121	12	16	July 1, 1885	1,963	Island Pond exchanges with Norton's Mills, Newport, Newport and Springfield R. P. O., Montreal and Canadian R. P. O. Portland and Island Pond R. P. O. exchanges with Montreal and the Canadian R. P. O.
13.25	9,699	7	6	July 1, 1886	153	Connects at Nutt Station (n. o.), N. Mex., with Rincon and Silver City, N. Mex., R. P. O.
25.43	15,970	6	14	July 1, 1888	106	
7.19	4,515	6	2	July 1, 1885	133	Balance of route (23.86 miles) covered by Berlin and Salisbury R. P. O. (See Table A*.)
7.34	4,609	6	4	July 1, 1887	58	Supplied by Belleville, Ill., and by Cincinnati, Ohio, and Saint Louis, Mo., R. P. O.; connects at Belleville, Ill., with Nashville, Tenn., and Saint Louis, Mo., Louisville, Ky., and Saint Louis, Mo., and with Saint Louis, Mo., and El Dorado, Ill., R. P. O's, and with Belleville and East Saint Louis, Ill., pouch service.
19.55	36,833	18	14	July 1, 1885	2,258	Balance of route (122.72 miles) covered by Norwood and Rome R. P. O. (See Table A*)
20.29	14,852	7	14	July 1, 1888	135	New service; not reported last year. Connects at Olcott, Kans., with Chetopa and Larned, Kans., R. P. O., and at Preston, Kans., with Herington and Dodge City, Kans., R. P. O.
23.68	44,613	18	24	July 1, 1885	136	
16.74	10,513	6	4	July 1, 1888	46	
15.84	9,948	6	12	July 1, 1886	357	Connects at Tenino with Helena, Mont., and Portland, Oregon, R. P. O.; Portland and Olympia also exchange by express train.
9.42	19,719	20	23	July 1, 1885	80	Connects Fredericksburgh and Orange C. H. and Washington and Charlotte R. P. O's at Orange C. H., and Richmond and Clifton Forge R. P. O. at Gordonsville.
18.76	14,483	6	24	July 1, 1888	146	Service established August 1, 1887. During summer season, from June 10 to October 2, six additional round trips per week over entire route.
10.16	14,874	14	8	July 1, 1887	681	9.28 miles of route 28054, between Joplin, Mo. and Galena, Kans., covered by Girard and Galena, Kans., R. P. O. (See table A*.) Connects at Oronogo, Mo., with Saint Louis, Mo. and Halstead, Kans., R. P. O. At Joplin, Mo., with Kansas City and Joplin, Mo., R. P. O.; Fort Scott, Kans., and Webb City, Mo., R. P. O., and Girard and Galena, Kans., R. P. O.
27.50	40,200	14	10	July 1, 1886	272	Connects at Marysville with Portland, Oregon, and Sacramento, Cal., R. P. O.
14.84	23,299	15	20	July 1, 1888	227	
9.25	20,313	21	29	July 1, 1885	233	Connects Washington and Charlotte R. P. O. at Owl Run.
19.12	12,007	6	20	July 1, 1885	93	
54.15	34,906	6	8	Mar. 17, 1887	170	
15.58	32,593	20	16	....	....	Makes Hannibal, Mo., connections and connects at Palmyra, Mo., with Quincy, Ill., and Kansas City, Mo., R. P. O.
90.88	28,355	3	14	July 1, 1886	208	Including Sacks. Connects at Palisades, Nev., with Ogden, Utah, and San Francisco, Cal., R. P. O. Mail carried by stage alternate days.
16.18	11,844	7	4	....	....	New service; not reported last year. Connects at Panhandle, Tex., with Kiowa, Kans., and Panhandle, Tex., pouch service, and at Washburn, Tex., with Texline (n. o.) and Clarendon, Tex., pouch service.
19.36	38,488	19	20	July 1, 1884	2,460	Balance of route (79.36 miles) covered by Cincinnati and Lexington and Maysville, Paris and Cincinnati R. P. O's. (See Table A*.)

TABLE C^c.—*Statement of mail service performed in closed pouches upon railroads and*

Initial and terminal stations running east to west, north to south, and northwest to southeast.	Division.	Number of route.	Contract designation, termini of route.	Corporate title of company.
Pasco and Wallula, Wash.....	8	43009 (part)	Wallula, Wash., Missoula, Mont.	Northern Pacific R. R ......
Paterson and Newark, N. J...	2	7030	Newark, Paterson, N. J	New York, Lake Erie and Western.
Peete and Greenwood, Miss...	4	18012	Greenwood, Peete, Miss.....	Illinois Central R. R ....
Pelican Rapids and Fergus Falls, Minn.	6	26043	Fergus Falls, Pelican Rapids, Minn.	Saint Paul, Minn. and Manitoba.
Pemberton and Brooksville, Fla.	4	16023 (part)	Leesburgh, Brooksville, Fla.	Florida Southern Rwy ......
Pennsborough and Ritchie C. H., W. Va.	3	12004	Pennsborough, Ritchie C. H., W. Va.	Pennsborough. Harrisville, and Ritchie County.
Pensacola and Millview, Fla..	4	16005	Pensacola, Millview, Fla...	Pensacola and Perdido R. R.
Perry and Silver Springs, N. Y.	2	6070	Silver Springs, Perry, N. Y.	Silver Lake.................
Petaluma and Lakeville, Cal..	8	45004	Petaluma, Lakeville, Cal....	San Francisco and North. Pacific R. R.
Peters and Oakdale, Cal.......	8	46035	Peters, Oakdale, Cal........	Stockton and Copperopolis R. R.
Petersburgh and City Point, Va.	3	11010	Petersburgh, City Point, Va.	Norfolk and Western.......
Philadelphia and Chestnut Hill R. R. Station, Pa.	2	8160	Philadelphia, Chestnut Hill R. R. Station, Pa.	Philadelphia, Germantown and C. H.
Phœnix and Maricopa, Ariz...	8	40004	Maricopa, Phœnix, Ariz	Maricopa and Phœnix R. R.
Phœnixville and Uwchland, Pa.	2	8066	Phœnixville, Uwchland, Pa.	Philadelphia and Reading ..
Phœnixville and West Chester, Pa.	2	8048	West Chester, Phœnixville, Pa.	Pennsylvania.................
Pinconning and Gladwin, Mich	9	24073	Pinconning, Gladwin, Mich .	Michigan Central...........
Pine Bush and Middletown, N. Y.	2	6092	Middletown, Pine Bush, N. Y	N. Y., L. E. and W. (Middletown and Crawford Branch).
Pittsburgh and Castle Shannon, Pa.	2	8095	Pittsburgh, Castle Shannon, Pa.	Pitts. and Castle Shannon ..
Plainview and Chatfield, Minn.	6	26018	Chatfield, Plainview, Minn .	Winona and Saint Peter ....
Plattsburgh and Au Sable, N. Y.	2	6029	Plattsburgh, Au Sable, N. Y.	Del. and Hud. Canal Co .....
Pleasantville and Somers Point, N. J.	2	7020	Pleasantville, Somers Point, N. J.	West Jersey.................
Poland and Herkimer, N. Y...	2	6119	Herkimer, Poland, N. Y....	Herk., Newport and Poland.
Pomeroy and Landenburgh, Pa	2	8131	Landenburgh, Pomeroy, Pa..	Pennsylvania.................
Pomeroy and Starbuck, Wash	8	43014	Starbuck, Pomeroy, Wash ..	Oreg. Rwy. and Navig. Co ...
Poncho Springs and Monarch, Colo.	7	38009	Poncho Springs, Monarch, Colo.	Denver and Rio Grande.....
Port Huron and Almont, Mich.	9	24060	Port Huron, Almont, Mich..	Port Huron and Northwestern.
Port Monmouth and Red Bank, N. J.	2	7049 (part.)	Eatontown, Port Monmouth, N. J.	Central R. R. of New Jersey.
Prairie du Sac and Maso Manie, Wis.	6	25039	Maso Manie, Prairie du Sac, Wis.	Chicago, Milwaukee and St. Paul.
Pratt's Junction and Sterling Junction, Mass.	1	8047	Sterling Junction, Pratt's Junction, Mass.	Old Colony R. R ....

parts of railroads over which no railway post-offices run, in operation, etc.—Continued.

Miles of route.	Annual miles of service.	Number of round trips per week.	Number of pouches exchanged daily.	Date of last re-adjustment.	Average weight of mail whole distance daily.	Remarks.
					Pounds.	
16.50	12,078	7	32	....	....	Mail connected for the Dayton and Umatilla, Huntington and Portland, from the Helena and Portland, west bound, and sent from those R. P. O's to the Helena and Portland R.P.O., east bound, over this route. Balance of route covered by Helena and Portland R. P. O. (See Table Aᵇ.)
11.37	21,421	18	26	July 1, 1885	120	
18.12	11,379	6	4	July 1, 1888	25	
23.58	14,808	6	10	July 1, 1887	141	Supplied by Fergus Falls, Minn. Connects at Fergus Falls, Minn., with Fargo, Dak., Barnesville and Saint Paul, Minn., and with Wadena and Fergus Falls, Minn., R. P. O's, and with Fergus Falls, Minn., and Milnor, Dak., pouch service.
10.50	6,594	7	2	Oct. 21, 1885	106	¹ 30.19 miles reported as the Palatka and Punta Gorda R. P. O. in Table Aᵇ.
9.09	11,417	12	6	....	....	Connects Grafton and Parkersburgh and Grafton and Cincinnati R. P. O's at Pennsborough.
10.25	6,437	6	2	July 1, 1884	24	
7.31	9,181	12	10	July 1, 1885	196	
7.53	4,729	6	4	July 1, 1886	28	Connects at Petaluma with Cloverdale and San Francisco R. P. O.
19.29	24,140	12	6	July 1, 1886	93	Connects at Peters with Milton and Stockton R. P. O. Supplied by Stockton office.
10.47	6,575	6	2	July 1, 1885	34	Connects Norfolk and Lynchburgh and Washington and Wilmington R. P. O's at Petersburgh, and Norfolk and Richmond R. P. O. at City Point.
11.86	45,930	37	¹38	July 1, 1883	548	¹ Including sacks.
35.78	26,191	7	8	Apr. 20, 1888	464	Connects at Maricopa with Deming, N. Mex., and Los Angeles, Cal., R. P. O.
11.28	14,168	12	22	July 1, 1885	112	
18.43	23,148	12	30	July 1, 1885	175	
28.28	7,183	6	6	....	....	Order January 14, 1888, establishing service on this route to commence February 6, 1888.
13.74	17,657	12	12	July 1, 1885	110	At Pinconning, Mich., connects Mackinaw City and Detroit R. P. O.
6.02	3,781	6	4	July 1, 1885	63	
28.73	54,127	18	38	....	....	Supplied by Eyota, Minn., and by Winona and Tracy, Minn., R. P. O.
23.52	14,771	6	10	July 1, 1885	179	
7.31	9,181	12	12	July 1, 1885	40	
17.06	21,427	12	12	July 1, 1885	219	
18.54	11,643	6	6	July 1, 1885	49	
29.53	18,445	6	8	Sept. 1, 1886	312	Supplied by Dayton, Wash., and Umatilla, Oregon, R. P. O.
16.09	10,105	6	18	July 1, 1886	106	Trains run from Salida, Colo., and there connect with Denver, Colo., and Ogden, Utah, R. P. O. and Denver, Pueblo and Leadville, Colo., R. P. O.
34.52	43,357	12	28	July 1, 1884	235	At Port Huron, Mich., connects East Saginaw and Port Huron, Fort Gratiot and Chicago, Fort Gratiot and Detroit, and Port Huron and Port Austin R. P. O's.
¹6.58	4,132	6	8	July 1, 1885	425	¹ Balance of route (2.89 miles) covered by Red Bank and Bridgeton R. P. O. (See Table Aᵇ.)
10.33	12,974	12	16	July 1, 1887	265	Supplied by Mazo Manie, Wis., and by Chicago, Ill., and North McGregor, Iowa, R. P. O.
4.83	9,099	18	23	July 1, 1885	356	Portland and Worcester R. P. O., and Portland and Worcester R. P. O., short run, exchange with Sterling, Pratt's Junction, Leominster, and Fitchburg. Fitchburg with Worcester and Boston and Springfield and New York R. P. O.

TABLE C⁶.—*Statement of mail service performed in closed pouches upon railroads and*

Initial and terminal stations running east to west, north to south, and northwest to southeast.	Division.	Number of route.	Contract designation, termini of route.	Corporate title of company.
Princeton and Princeton Junction, N. J.	2	7053	Princeton Junction, Princeton, N. J.	Pennsylvania................
Providence and Bristol, R. I...	1	4004	Providence, Bristol, R. I	Providence, Warren and Bristol R. R.
Pueblo, Colo., and Texline (n. o.), Tex.	7	31065	Texline (n. o.), Tex., Pueblo, Colo.	Denver, Texas and Fort Worth.
Pulaski City and Ivanhoe Furnace, Va.	3	11039	Pulaski City, Ivanhoe Furnace, Va.	Norfolk and Western.......
Pymatuning, Pa., and Leavittsburgh, Ohio.	2	21034 (part)	Salamanca, Dayton, Ohio....	New York, Lake Erie and Western.
Quenemo and Osage City, Kans.	7	33055	Quenemo, Osage City, Kans	Chicago, Kansas and Western.
Rahway and Perth Amboy, N.J.	2	7038	Rahway, Perth Amboy, N.J.	Pennsylvania,................
Rantoul and Le Roy, Ill........	6	103058 (part)	West Lebanon, Ind., Le Roy, Ill.	Illinois Central ....
Ravenels and Young's Island, S. C.	4	14028	Ravenels, Young's Island, S. C.	Charleston and Savannah R. R.
Raymond and Berjendo, Cal.	8	46034	Berjendo, Raymond, Cal....	Southern Pacific Co........
Readville and Dedham, Mass..	1	3073	Readville, Dedham, Mass..	Old Colony R. R. (Providence Division).
Readsborough, Vt., and Hoosac Tunnel Station (n. o.), Mass.	1	2001	Readsborough, Vt., Hoosac Tunnel Station (n. o.), Mass.	Deerfield River R. R ....
Red Jacket and Hancock, Mich.	6	24068	Hancock, Red Jacket, Mich.	Hancock and Calumet ......
Renton and Black Diamond, Wash.	8	43007	Renton, Black Diamond, Wash.	Columbia and Puget Sound R. R.
Republic and Iron Mountain, Mich.	6	125016 (part)	Milwaukee, Wis., Republic, Mich.	Milwaukee and Northern...
Rib Lake and Chelsea, Wis ...	6	25066	Chelsea, Rib Lake, Wis	Wisconsin Central..........
Richfield Junction and Richfield Springs, N. Y.	2	0043	Richfield Junction, Richfield Springs, N. Y.	Delaware, Lackawanna and Western.
Richland Centre and Lone Rock, Wis.	6	25029	Lone Rock, Richland Centre, Wis.	Chicago, Milwaukee and Saint Paul.
Ridgefield and Branchville, Conn.	1	5023	Branchville, Ridgefield, Conn.	Danbury and Norwalk R. R

parts of railroads over which no railway post-offices run, in operation, etc.—Continued.

Miles of route.	Annual miles of service.	Number of round trips per week.	Number of pouches exchanged daily.	Date of last re-adjustment.	Average weight of mail whole distance daily.	Remarks.
					Pounds.	
3.44	17,283	48	¹36	July 1, 1885	410	¹ Including sacks.
15.35	28,919	18	53	July 1, 1885	629	Providence exchanges pouches with Barrington Centre, Riverside, Warren, Fall River, Nyatt's Point, Drownville, Bristol, and Newport. Bristol with Warren. Boston, Providence, and New York R. P. O. exchanges with Bristol and Warren. Fall River with Providence and New London R. P. O., Boston, Springfield, and New York R. P. O., and Warren.
228.51	167,269	7	52	....	....	New service; not reported last year. Makes Pueblo, Colo., connections, and connects at El Moro and Trinidad, Colo., with La Junta, Colo., and Albuquerque, N. Mex., R. P. O., and at Texline (n. o.), Tex., with Texline (n. o.), Tex., and Clarendon, Tex., pouch service.
32.23	20,240	6	12	July 1, 1888	111	
¹29.70	55,955	18	24	July 1, 1884	2,040	¹ Balance of route (134.54 miles) covered by Buffalo and Youngstown R. P. O. (see Table A².) and by Leavittsburgh and Cincinnati R. P. O. (See Table A²., Fifth Division).
20.60	25,874	12	22	Aug. 15, 1886	107	Connects at Quenemo, Kans., with Ottawa and Emporia, Kans., R. P. O., and Topeka and Fort Scott, Kans., R. P. O.; at Lyndon, Kans., with Kansas City, Mo., Salina, Kans., and Pueblo, Colo., R. P. O., and at Osage City, Kans., with Kansas City, Mo., and Pueblo, Colo., R. P. O., and Kansas City, Mo., Salina, Kans., and Pueblo, Colo., R. P. O.
7.58	19,041	24	10	July 1, 1885	458	
33.17	20,830	6	28	....	....	¹ Balance of route covered by West Lebanon, Ind., and Rantoul, Ill., R. P. O (See Table A².) Supplied by Rantoul, Howard, and Le Roy, Ill. Connects at Rantoul, Ill., with Chicago and Centralia, Ill., R. P. O., at Howard, Ill., with Chicago, Decatur, Ill., and Saint Louis, Mo., R. P. O., and at Le Roy, Ill., with Indianapolis, Ind., and Peoria, Ill., R. P. O.
5.70	5,369	9	4	....	....	Two trips outward, one trip inward, daily.
21.30	15,592	7	4	June 30, 1888	47	New service established June 25, 1887, from July 11. Connects at Bernendo with San Francisco and Los Angeles R. P. O.
2.22	3,483	15	8	....	....	Boston exchanges with Dedham and Walnut Hill; Dedham with Walnut Hill.
11.30	7,000	6	6	Mar. 1, 1886	46	Readsborough exchanges pouches with Boston and Troy R. P. O., Sherman, Vt., and Monroe Bridge, Mass.
14.74	9,256	6	2	Sept. 10, 1886	108	Supplied by initial and terminal offices. Connects at Junction (n. o.), Mich., with Lake Linden and Junction, Mich., pouch service, and at Hancock, Mich., with Calumet and Houghton, Mich., pouch service.
18.50	13,542	7	18	July 1, 1886	85	Including sacks. Supplied by Helena and Portland R. P. O., and exchanges mail with Seattle. Connects at Renton with Seattle and New Castle R. R.
47.00	29,436	6	8	June 23, 1888	1,028	¹ Balance of route covered by Iron Mountain, Mich., and Milwaukee, Wis., R. P. O. (See Table A².) Supplied by initial and terminal offices and by Iron Mountain, Mich., and Milwaukee, Wis., R. P. O. Connects at Republic, Mich., with Humboldt and Republic, Mich., pouch service.
6.35	3,987	6	2	....	....	Supplied by Chelsea, Wis., and by Ashland and Abbottsford, Wis., R. P. O.
22.06	27,707	12	40	July 1, 1885	509	
16.23	20,510	12	24	July 1, 1887	387	Supplied by Lone Rock, Wis., and by Chicago, Ill., and North McGregor, Iowa, R. P. O.
4.36	8,214	18	6	July 1, 1885	113	Ridgefield exchanges pouches with Danbury and South Norwalk R. P. O.

TABLE C^c.—*Statement of mail service performed in closed pouches upon railroads and*

Initial and terminal stations running east to west, north to south, and northwest to southeast.	Division.	Number of route.	Contract designation, termini of route.	Corporate title of company.
Ridgewood Junction and Rutherford Junction, N. J.	2	7055	Rutherford Junction, Ridgewood Junction, N. J.	New York, Lake Erie and Western.
Riparia and Bolles Junction (n. o.), Wash.	8	43010	Bolles Junction, Riparia, Wash.	Oregon Railway and Navigation Company.
Ripon and Berlin, Wis	6	*25008 (part)	Milwaukee, Berlin, Wis.....	Chicago, Milwaukee and St. Paul.
River Falls Junction and Ellsworth, Wis.	6	25033	River Falls Junction (n. o.), Ellsworth, Wis.	Chicago, St. Paul, Minn., and Omaha.
Riverside and Capistrano, Cal..	8	46055	Riverside, Capistrano, Cal..	California Central Rwy.....
Roaring Springs and Ore Hill, Pa.	2	8163	Roaring Springs, Ore Hill, Pa.	Pennsylvania..............
Roberts and Guide, Tex.......	7	31042	Guide, Roberts, Tex...	Houston and Texas Central
Rochelle and Gainesville, Fla..	4	¹16012 (part)	Palatka, Gainesville, Fla....	Florida Southern Rwy......
Rockford and Rochelle, Ill.....	6	23057	Rochelle, Rockford, Ill......	Chicago and Iowa...........
Rock Island and Cable, Ill....	6	23059	Rock Island, Cable, Ill......	Rock Island and Mercer Co
Rockport and Salem, Mass	1	3003	Salem, Rockport, Mass	Boston and Maine R. R .....
Rockport Junction (n. o.) and Rockport, Ind.	5	22034	Rockport, Rockport Junction, (n. o.) Ind.	Louis., Evans. and St. Louis.
Rocky Mount and Spring Hope, N. C.	3	13028	Rocky Mount, Spring Hope, N. C.	Wilmington and Weldon.
Rodney and Chippewa Lake, Mich.	9	24074	Rodney, Chippewa Lake, Mich.	Detroit, Lansing, and Northern.
Rogers and Bentonville, Ark...	7	29018	Rogers, Bentonville, Ark....	Bentonville...............
Rogers and Summit, Ga.......	4	15055	Rogers, Summit, Ga	Rogers and Summit R. R ...
Rome and Clinton, N. Y.......	2	6051	Clinton, Rome, N. Y	New York, Ontario and Western.
Rondout and Libertyville, Ill..	6	23099	Rondout, Libertyville, Ill...	Chicago, Milwaukee and St. Paul.
Roscoe and Bowdle, Dak......	6	¹26010 (part)	Hastings, Minn., Bowdle, Dak.	......do ....

parts of railroads over which no railway post-offices run, in operation, etc.—Continued.

Miles of route.	Annual miles of service.	Number of round trips per week.	Number of pouches exchanged daily.	Date of last re-adjustment.	Average weight of mail whole distance daily.	Remarks.
					Pounds.	
9.98	9,501	9	12			
31.80	19,970	6	12	....	....	Connects at Bolles Junction with Dayton, Wash., and Umatilla, Oregon, R.P.O., and supplied by that line.
12.72	15,976	12	14	July 1, 1887	1,565	[1] Balance of route covered by Oshkosh and Milwaukee, Wis., R. P. O. (See Table A*.) Supplied by Ripon, Wis., and by Oshkosh and Milwaukee, Wis., R. P. O. Connects at Ripon, Wis., with Sheboygan and Princeton, Wis., R. P. O., and at Rush Lake, Wis., with Winneconne and Rush Lake, Wis., pouch service.
25.76	32,354	12	16	July 1, 1887	262	Supplied by Hudson, Wis. Connects at River Falls Junction, Wis., with St. Paul, Minn., and Elroy, Wis., R. P. O.
59.94	43,876	7	14	....	....	New service; established December 12, 1887; extended March 21, 1888; supplied by Riverside.
3.36	2,110	6	2	July 1, 1885	46	
52.13	32,738	6	20	July 1, 1886	775	Connects at Terrell, Tex, with Texarkana, Ark., and El Paso, Tex., R. P. O.; at Kaufman, Tex. with Dallas and Kemp, Tex., R. P. O.; and a. Guide, Tex., with Fort Worth and Guide, Tex.[t] R. P. O., and Denison and Houston, Tex., R. P. O.
9.70	12,183	12	6	July 1, 1884	333	[1] 40.07 miles reported as Palatka and Punta Gorda, R. P. O., Table A*.
27.72	34,816	12	18	July 1, 1887	163	Supplied by initial and terminal offices, and by Forreston and Aurora, Ill., R. P. O. Connects at Rockford, Ill., with Kenosha, Wis., and Rockford, Ill.; Chicago, Freeport, Ill., and Dubuque, Iowa, and with Rockford, Ill., and Mineral Point, Wis., R. P. O's. Connects at Holcomb, Ill., with Chicago, Dunbar, Ill., and Dubuque, Iowa, R. P. O.; at Davis Junction, Ill., with Chicago, Savanna, Ill., and Cedar Rapids, Iowa, R. P. O.; and at Rochelle, Ill., with Chicago, Ill., and Cedar Rapids, Iowa, R. P. O.
27.35	17,176	6	16	July 1, 1887	147	Supplied by Rock Island, Ill. Connects with all lines centering at that city.
19.69	24,731	12	68	July 1, 1885	667	Boston exchanges pouches with Rockport, Gloucester, Magnolia, Manchester, Beverly Farms, and Pride's Crossing. Salem exchanges with Rockport, Gloucester, Magnolia, Pride's Crossing, Manchester, and Beverly Farms. Gloucester with Rockport, Magnolia, Manchester, Bangor, and Boston R. P. O. and Boston, Springfield, and New York R. P. O. Manchester with Bangor and Boston R. P. O. Two additional round trips daily from Salem to Gloucester.
16.20	30,521	18	16	July 1, 1888	289	
19.12	12,007	6	4	July 1, 1888	71	Connects Washington and Wilmington R. P. O. at Rocky Mount.
5.91	1,347	6	2	....	....	Order February 9, 1888, establishing service on this route to commence February 20, 1888. At Rodney connects the Big Rapids and Detroit R. P. O.
7.05	10,321	14	6	July 1, 1886	217	Connects at Rogers. Ark., with Monett, Mo., and Paris, Tex., R. P. O.
20.00	12,560	6	8	July 1, 1888	81	
13.19	16,567	12	28	July 1, 1885	139	
3.28	2,060	6	4	July 1, 1888	68	Supplied by Rondout, Ill., and by Chicago, Ill., and Minneapolis, Minn., R. P. O.
15.29	11,192	7	8	July 1, 1887	2,377	[1] Balance of route covered by Hastings and Cologne, Minn., Saint Paul, Minn., and Mitchell, Dak., and Aberdeen and Orient, Dak., R. P. O's. (See Table A*.) Supplied by Roscoe, Dak., and by Aberdeen and Orient. Dak., R. P. O. Connects at Roscoe, Dak., with Eureka and Roscoe Dak., pouch service.

TABLE C^c.—*Statement of mail service performed in closed pouches upon railroads and*

Initial and terminal stations running east to west, north to south, and northwest to southeast.	Division.	Number of route.	Contract designation, termini of route.	Corporate title of company.
Roswell and Chamblee, Ga....	4	15035	Roswell Junction (n. o.), Roswell, Ga.	Richmond and Danville R. R.
Rugby and Bottineau, Dak....	6	35030	Rugby, Bottineau, Dak.....	St. Paul, Minn. and Manitoba.
Russellville and Adairsville, Ky.	5	¹20014 (pa't)	Owensborough, Adairsville, Ky.	Owensborough and Nashville
Rutland and Ellendale, Dak...	6	35031	Rutland, Ellendale, Dak.....	St. Paul, Minn. and Manitoba
Sabula and Clinton, Iowa......	6	¹27012 (part)	Clinton, Iowa, La Crosse, Wis.	Chicago, Milwaukee and St. Paul.
Saginaw City Junction (n. o.) and Saginaw, Mich.	9	24049	Detroit, Bay City Crossing, Saginaw, Mich.	Flint and Pere Marquette ..
Saint Agnes Station and Catonsville, Md.	3	10026	Saint Agnes Station, Catonsville, Md.	Baltimore and Potomac....
Saint Augustine and Palatka, Fla.	4	16027	Saint Augustine, Palatka, Fla.	Saint Augustine and Palatka R. R.
Saint Charles and Geneva, Ill .	6	23094	Geneva, Saint Charles, Ill ..	Chicago and Northwestern .
Saint Clair and Lenox, Mich.	9	24037	Saint Clair, Richmond, Mich.	Michigan Central..........
Saint Clairsville and Steele, Ohio.	5	21056	Saint Clairsville, Steele, Ohio	Bellaire and Saint Clairsville
Saint George and Mariner's Harbor, N. Y.	2	6062 (part)	New York, Mariner's Harbor, N. Y.	Staten Island R. T. Co ......
Saint George and Tottenville, N. Y.	2	6068	Saint George, Tottenville, N. Y.	Staten Island R. T. Co ......
Saint Hilaire and Crookston, Minn.	6	26050	Crookston, Saint Hilaire, Minn.	Saint Paul, Minn. and Manitoba.
Saint Ignace and Marquette, Mich.	9	24051	Saint Ignace, Marquette, Mich.	Duluth, South Shore and Atlantic.
Saint Louis and Florisant, Mo.	7	28031	Saint Louis, Florisant, Mo..	St. Louis Cable and Western,
Saint Mary's and Minster, Ohio.	5	21082	Saint Mary's, Minster, Ohio.	Lake Erie and Western....
Saint Peter's and Springfield Station, Pa.	2	8162	Springfield Station, Saint Peters, Pa.	Wilmington and Northern..
Salisbury and Glasgow, Mo ...	7	28023	Salisbury, Glasgow, Mo	Wabash Western ....
Salley and Blackville, S. C.....	4	14026	Blackville, Salley, S. C	Blackville, Alston and Newberry R. R.
Salt Lake and Stockton, Utah.	8	41005	Salt Lake, Stockton, Utah ..	Utah and Nevada Rwy.....
San Anselmo and San Quentin, Cal.	8	46025	San Anselmo, San Quentin, Cal.	North Pacific Coast R. R....
Sand Beach and Palm Station, Mich.	9	24061	Sand Beach, Palm Station, Mich.	Port Huron and Northwestern.
Sandersville and Tennile, Ga..	4	15027	Sandersville, Tennile, Ga....	Sandersville and Tennile R. R.
Sanford and Oviedo, Fla.......		16010	Sanford, Oviedo, Fla	Sanford and Indian River R. R.

parts of railroads over which no railway post-offices run, in operation, etc.—Continued.

Miles of route.	Annual miles of service.	Number of round trips per week.	Number of pouches exchanged daily.	Date of last re-adjustment.	Average weight of mail whole distance daily.	Remarks.
					Pounds	
10.87	6,826	6	4	July 1,1858	62	
38.10	23,927	6	12	July 1,1888	132	Supplied by Rugby, Dak., and by Crookston, Minn., and Minot. Dak., R. P. O.
13.50	8,478	6	8	July 1,1884	472	[1]Balance of route (72 40 miles) covered by the Owensborough and Russellville R. P.O. (See Table A*.)
49.73	31,230	6	24	July 1,1888	141	Supplied by Ellendale, Dak., and by Breckenridge, Minn., and Aberdeen, Dak., R. P. O. Connects at Ludden, Dak., with Oakes, Dak., and Hawarden, Iowa, R. P. O., and at Ellendale, Dak., with Edgeley and Aberdeen, Dak., pouch service.
16.46	31,010	18	14	July 1,1887	2,962	[1]Balance of route covered by Chicago, Ill., McGregor, Iowa, and Saint Paul, Minn., and by La Crosse, Wis., and Dubuque, Iowa, R. P. O's. (See Table A*.)
						Supplied by Chicago, Savanna, Ill., and Cedar Rapids, Iowa, and by Chicago, Ill., McGregor, Iowa, and Saint Paul, Minn., R. P. O's. Connects at Clinton, Iowa, with Clinton and Iowa City, Iowa, Clinton and Anamosa, Iowa, Mendota and Fulton, Ill., and with Chicago, Ill., and Cedar Rapids, Iowa, R. P. O's.
3.76	10,626	26	11	July 1,1884	286	At Detroit and Bay City Crossing connects Bay City, Wayne, and Detroit and Ludington, and Toledo R. P. O.
3.93	4,936	12	4	Aug. 1,1885	84	At Saginaw connects Bay City and Jackson, and East Saginaw and Howard City R. P. O's.
26.71	39,103	14	10	Aug. 23,1886	50	Supplied by closed pouches from Baltimore, Md.
3.21	8,063	24	10	May 28,1888	182	Supplied by Geneva, Ill., and by Chicago, Ill., and Cedar Rapids, Iowa R. P. O. Connects at Saint Charles, Ill., with Chicago, Dunbar, Ill., and Dubuque, Iowa R. P. O., and at Geneva, Ill., with Geneva and Aurora, Ill., pouch service.
16.00	20,096	12	12	July 1,1884	274	At Lenox, Mich., connects Fort Gratiot and Detroit R. P. O. and Lenox and Jackson R. P. O.
7.28	13,716	18	14	July 1,1888	248	
[1]3.88	12,183	30	60	July 1,1886	1,403	[1]Balance of route (5 90 miles) covered by Saint George and New York R. P. O. (See Table A*.)
15.28	47,979	30	32	Sept. 3,1886	311	
28.30	11,772	4	4	July 1,1887	54	Supplied by Crookston, Minn. Connects at that point with Boundary Line and Saint Paul, Minn., and with Crookston, Minn., and Minot, Dak., R. P. O's.
151.37	95,060	6	69	July 1, 1884	157	At Saint Ignace, Mich., connects the Mackinaw City and Detroit and Mackinaw City and Grand Rapids R. P. O.'s. At Marquette, Mich., connects the Marquette and Houghton R. P. O.
15.65	10,642	(1)	6	July 1, 1887	71	[1] Trains seven times a week outward and six times a week inward. All offices on line exchange pouches with Saint Louis, Mo.
10.06	12,635	12	8	July 1, 1888	101	
7.00	8,792	12	8	July 1, 1885	46	
15.81	9,920	6	14	July 1, 1887	65	Connects at Salisbury, Mo., with Saint Louis, Moberly, and Kansas City, Mo., R. P. O., and at Glasgow, Mo., with Saint Louis, Louisiana, and Kansas City, Mo., R. P. O.
16.14	10,133	6	6			
40.50	25,434	6	10	July 1,1886	131	Supplied by Salt Lake.
6.00	11,928	19	16	July 1,1886	139	Connects at San Anselmo with Ingrams and San Francisco R. P. O. San Rafael and San Quentin exchange with San Francisco.
18.83	23,650	12	12	July 1,1884	163	At Palm Station connects with the Port Austin and Port Huron R. P. O.
3.50	4,396	12	8	July 1,1884	167	
17.63	11,071	6	4	Mar.14,1887	112	

TABLE C^c.—*Statement of mail service performed in closed pouches upon railroads and*

Initial and terminal stations running east to west. north to south, and northwest to southeast.	Division.	Number of route.	Contract designation, termini of route.	Corporate title of company.
Sanford and Tavares, Fla	4	16028	Sanford, Tavares, Fla	Sandford and Lake Eustis R. R.
Santa Cruz and Pajaro, Cal ...	8	46021	Santa Cruz, Pajaro, Cal....	Santa Cruz R. R.............
Santa Fé and Lamy, N. Mex..	7	39001	Lamy, Santa Fé, N. Mex ...	Atchison, Topeka and Santa Fé.
Sault de Ste. Marie, Mich., and Bruce, Wis.	6	¹25059 (part)	Minneapolis, Minn., Sault de Ste. Marie, Mich.	Minneapolis, Sault de Ste. Marie and Atlantic.
Sault de Ste. Marie and Sault Junction, Mich.	6	24072	Sault de Ste. Marie, Sault Junction, Mich.	Duluth, South Shore and Atlantic.
Savanna and Fulton, Ill.......	6	23090	Savanna, Fulton, Ill	Chicago, Burlington and Northern.
Saxonville and Natick, Mass..	1	3032	Natick, Saxonville, Mass....	Boston and Albany R. R....
Saybrook Junction and Saybrook Point, Conn.	1	5015 (part)	Hartford, Saybrook Point, Conn.	Hartford and Conn. Valley R. R.
Schenectady and Quaker Street, N. Y.	2	6030	Quaker Street, Schenectady, N. Y.	Del. Hud. Canal Co.........
Schoharie and Middleburgh, N. Y.	2	6055	Schoharie, Middleburgh, N. Y.	Schoharie and Middleburgh.
Schoharie Junction and Schoharie, N. Y.	2	6056	Schoharie Junction, Schoharie, N. Y.	Schoharie Valley...........
Schriever and Houma, La.....	4	30004	Schriever, Houma, La.......	Morgan's La. and Tex. R. R.
Schriever and Thibodeaux, La.	4	30009	Schriever, Thibodeaux, La..	Morgan's La. and Tex. R. R.
Schuylerville and Saratoga Springs, N. Y.	2	6077	Saratoga Springs, Schuylerville, N. Y.	Fitchburg ....
Schuylerville Junction and Mechanicsville, N. Y.	2	6121	Mechan csville, Schuylerville Junction, N. Y.	Fitchburg ....
Scranton and Wilkes-Barre, Pa.	2	8079	Wilkes-Barre, Scranton, Pa.	Del. and Hud. Canal Co.....
Sea Isle Junction and Sea Isle City, N. J.	2	7060	Sea Isle Junction, Sea Isle City, N. J.	West Jersey.................
Seattle and New Castle, Wash.	8	43002	Seattle, New Castle, Wash..	Columbia and Puget Sound R. R.
Seligman, Mo., and Eureka Springs, Ark.	7	29013	Seligman, Mo., Eureka Springs, Ark.	Eureka Springs ....
Seligman and Prescott, Ariz..	8	40003	Seligman, Prescott, Ariz ...	Prescott and Arizona R. R..
Selma and Martin's, Ala	4	17022	Selma, Martin's Station, Ala.	Birmingham, Selma and New Orleans R. R.
Shaw and Mineville, W. Va ...	3	12007 (part)	Piedmont, Mineville, W. Va.	West Virginia Central......
Shelby and Junction Station (n. o.), Ala.	4	17031	Shelby, Junction Station (n. o.), Ala.	Shelby Iron Co ....
Sheridan Junction (n. o.) and Sheridan, Oregon.	8	44009	Sheridan Junction, Sheridan, Oregon.	Oreg. R. R. Co. Limited Line
Sheffield and Eulalia, Pa	2	8105	Sheffield, Eulalia, Pa........	Tionesta Valley ....
Shenandoah and Mahanoy Plane, Pa.	2	8119	Shenandoah, Mahanoy Plane, Pa.	Philadelphia and Reading ..
Shumway and Altamont, Ill...	6	¹23066 (part)	Chicago, Altamont, Ill	Wabash ....

parts of railroads over which no railway post-offices run, in operation, etc.—Continued.

Miles of route.	Annual miles of service.	Number of round trips per week.	Number of pouches ex changed daily.	Date of last re-adjustment.	Average weight of mail whole distance daily.	Remarks.
					Pounds.	
29.65	18,620	6	12	July 1, 1888	226	
22.07	30,015	13	16	July 1, 1886	134	Connects at Pajaro with San Francisco and Templeton R. P. O. Watsonville exchanges with all offices on line in addition to supply by R. P. O.
19.19	28,094	14	6	July 1, 1886	433	Connects at Santa Fé, N. Mex., with Antonito, Colo., and Santa Fé, N. Mex., R. P. O., and at Lamy, N. Mex., with La Junta, Colo., and Albuquerque, N. Mex., R. P. O.
373.92	234,821	6	56	Aug. 7, 1888	188	¹ Balance of route covered by Bruce, Wis., and Minneapolis, Minn., R. P. O. (See Table A⁴.) Supplied by Sault de Ste, Marie, Gladstone, Mich., and by Bruce, Wis., and Minneapolis, Minn., R. P. O. Connects at Gladstone Station, Mich., with Ishpeming, Mich., and Fort Howard, Wis., R. P. O. and at Rhinelander, Wis., with Monico and Rhinelander, Wis., pouch service.
47.80	69,979	14	8	....	....	Supplied by Saint Ignace, Mich., and Marquette, Mich. Connects at Sault Junction, Mich., with Saint Ignace and Marquette, Mich., pouch service.
18.57	25,255	13	12	July 1, 1887	395	Connects Minneapolis, Minn., and Oregon, Ill., R. P. O. with Fulton, Ill., and lines centering there.
3.94	4,949	12	4	July 1, 1885	63	Supplied by initial and terminal offices.
1.66	3,127	18	12	July 1, 1885	63	Balance of route (44.43 miles) covered by R. P. O. service. (See Table A⁴.) Saybrook Point exchanges with Hartford and Saybrook R. P. O. and New London and New Haven R. P. O.
15.46	29,127	18	16	July 1, 1885	113	
5.95	11,210	18	8	July 1, 1885	210	
4.50	8,478	18	12	July 1, 1885	389	
15.26	22,340	14	8	July 1, 1886	149	
5.77	8,447	14	6	July 1, 1886	209	
13.02	24,530	18	18	July 1, 1885	112	
15.18	19,066	12	12	July 1, 1885	126	
19.32	30,332	15	50	July 1, 1885	126	
5.08	6,381	12	10	July 1, 1885	43	
19.25	28,182	14	104	July 1, 1886	126	Mail for offices located on routes 43012 and 43013 exchanges with Seattle. The exchange between Tacoma and Seattle and Seattle and Portland, including those for the Helena and Portland R. P. O., pass over this route between Seattle and Black River Junction
20.82	30,480	14	22	July 1, 1886	640	Connects at Seligman, Mo., with Monett, Mo., and Paris, Tex., R. P. O.
74.88	54,612	7	14	Feb. 28, 1888	439	Connects at Seligman with Albuquerque, N. Mex., and Los Angeles, Cal., R. P. O.
21.00	13,188	6	6	July 1, 1888	57	
2.00	1,777	6	4	July 1, 1885	124	Connects Cumberland and Davis R. P. O. at Shaw.
6.00	7,536	12	4	July 1, 1888	82	
7.21	9,056	12	4	Mar. 28, 1887	119	Connects at Sheridan Junction with Dundee Junction and Airlie R. P. O.
12.73	15,969	12	12	July 1, 1885	70	
6.92	15,210	21	10	July 1, 1885	205	
10.54	6,619	6	4	July 1, 1887	1,085	¹ Balance of route covered by Chicago, Decatur, Ill., and Saint Louis, Mo., and by Bement and Effingham, Ill., R. P. O's. (See Table A⁴.) Supplied by Bement and Effingham, Ill., R. P. O. Connects at Altamont, Ill., with Beardstown and Shawneetown, Ill., and with Pittsburgh. Pa., and Saint Louis, Mo., R. P. O's.

TABLE C^c.—*Statement of mail service performed in closed pouches upon railroads and*

Initial and terminal stations running east to west, north to south, and northwest to southeast.	Division.	Number of route.	Contract designation, termini of route.	Corporate title of company.
Silver Brook Junction and Silver Brook, Pa.	2	8173	Silver Brook, Silver Brook Junction, Pa.	Lehigh Valley..............
Silver Lake Junction (n. o.) and Silver Springs, N. Y.	2	6097	Silver Lake Junction (n. o.), Silver Springs, N. Y.	Silver Lake.................
Sidney and Champaign, Ill	6	23065	Sidney, Champaign, Ill	Wabash ....
Sioux Falls and Mitchell, Dak.	6	'26020 (part)	Worthington, Minn., Salem, Dak.	Chicago, Saint Paul, Minn. and Omaha.
		35036	Salem, Mitchell, Dak	do ....
Skaneateles Junction and Skaneateles, N. Y.	2	6060	Skaneateles Junction, Skaneateles, N. Y.	Skaneateles..................
Sleepy Eye and Redwood Falls, Minn.	6	26016	Sleepy Eye, Redwood Falls, Minn	Chicago and Northwestern .
Sligo and Lawsonham, Pa	2	8093	Lawsonham, Sligo, Pa	Allegheny Valley..........
Smithton and Okolona, Ark...	7	29017	Smithton, Okolona, Ark....	Southwestern Ark. and Indian Ter.
Snow Shoe and Milesburgh, Pa.	2	8083 (part)	Bellefonte, Snow Shoe, Pa..	Pennsylvania................
Socorro and Magdalena, N. Mex.	7	39010	Socorro, Magdalena, N. Mex.	Atchison, Topeka and Santa Fé
Somerset Junction and Indianola, Iowa.	6	'27015 (part)	Des Moines, Indianola, Iowa.	Chicago, Rock Island and Pacific.
Somerville and Flemington, N. J.	2	7002	Somerville, Flemington, N.J.	Central R. R. of N. J........
Somerville and Moscow, Tenn.	5	19019	Moscow, Somerville, Tenn ..	Memphis and Charleston ...
South Acton Depot (n. o.) and Marlborough, Mass.	1	3023	South Acton Depot (n. o.), Marlborough, Mass.	Fitchburg R. R ....
South Braintree and Fall River, Mass.	1	3044	South Braintree, Fall River, Mass.	Old Colony R. R ....
South Braintree and Plymouth, Mass.	1	3046	South Braintree, Plymouth, Mass.	Old Colony R. R ....
Southbridge, Mass., and East Thompson, Conn.	1	9052	East Thompson and Southbridge, Mass.	New York and New England R. R.

parts of railroads over which no railway post-offices run, in operation, etc.—Continued.

Miles of route.	Annual miles of service.	Number of round trips per week.	Number of pouches exchanged daily.	Date of last re-adjustment.	Average weight of mail whole distance daily.	Remarks.
					Pounds.	
2.61	1,639	6	2	July 1, 1888	35	
1.14	1,432	12	16	Aug. 9, 1886	276	
12.29	15,436	12	8	July 1, 1887	108	Supplied by initial and terminal offices. Connects at Sidney, Ill., with La Fayette, Ind., and Quincy, Ill., R. P. O., and at Champaign, Ill., with Champaign and Havana. Ill., and Indianapolis, Ind., and Peoria, Ill., R. P. O's.
39.62	96,899	13	38	July 1, 1887	462	[1]Balance of the route covered by Worthington, Minn., and Sioux Falls, Dak., R. P. O. (See Table A[a].)
33.10						Supplied by Sioux Falls, Salem, and Mitchell, Dak., and by Worthington, Minn., and Sioux Falls, Dak., R. P. O. Connects at Salem, Dak., with Oakes, Dak., and Hawarden, Iowa, R. P. O., and at Mitchell, Dak., with Calmar, Iowa, and Chamberlain, Dak.; Manilla, Iowa, and Mitchell, Dak., and with Saint Paul, Minn., and Mitchell, Dak., R. P. O's.
5.18	1,312	24	18	July 1, 1885	268	
26.67	33,497	12	12	July 1, 1887	210	Supplied by Sleepy Eye, Minn., and by Winona and Tracy, Minn., R. P. O. Connects at Redwood Falls, Minn., with Saint Paul, Minn., and Watertown, Dak., R. P. O.
10.79	6,776	6	6	July 1, 1885	42	Connects at Smithton, Ark., with Saint Louis, Mo., and Texarkana, Ark., R. P. O.
14.58	18,312	12	4	July 1, 1886	41	
[1]19.13	24,027	12	10	July 1, 1885	82	[1]Balance of route (2.70 miles) covered by Lock Haven and Tyrone R. P. O. (See Table A[a].)
27.65	20,240	7	4	July 1, 1886	110	Connects at Socorro, N. Mex., with Albuquerque, N. Mex., and El Paso, Tex., R. P. O.
6.47	16,252	24	16	July 1, 1887	643	[1]Balance of route covered by Des Moines and Winterset, Iowa, R. P. O. (See Table A[a].) Supplied by Des Moines and Winterset, Iowa, R. P. O. Connects at Indianola, Iowa, with Des Moines, Iowa, and Saint Joseph, Mo., R. P. O.
16.01	30,163	18	24	July 1, 1885	212	
13.40	8,472	6	6	July 1, 1888	74	
12.71	35,918	27	26	Dec. 8, 1886	316	Boston exchanges pouches with Maynard, Hudson, Rock Bottom, Boston, and Troy R. P. O.; and Essex Junction and Boston R. P. O. exchanges with Maynard, Hudson, Rock Bottom, and Marlborough; Maynard with Boston and Greenville R. P. O.
35.17	88,357	24	87	July 1, 1885	847	Boston exchanges pouches with Randolph, North Stoughton, North Easton, South Easton, Easton, North Raynham, Taunton, Dighton, North Dighton, Fall River, and Somerset. Taunton exchanges with Berkley, North Dighton, Dighton, Somerset, and Fall River. Fall River exchanges with Steep Brook, Somerset, Dighton, North Dighton, Middleborough, Boston, and Welfleet R. P. O. and Lowell and Taunton R. P. O.
26.52	49,964	18	71	July 1, 1885	629	Boston exchanges pouches with South Weymouth, Rockland, Hanover, West Hanover, South Hanover, Abington, Whitman, South Abington Station, East Bridgewater, Hanson, South Hanson, Halifax, Silver Lake, Kingston, and Plymouth.
18.00	22,608	12	84	July 1, 1885	267	Boston and Hopewell Junction R. P. O. exchange with Globe Village, Quinebaug, Southbridge, Webster, West Dudley; Boston with Globe Village, West Dudley, Southbridge, and Webster; Quinebaug with Webster.

TABLE C^c.—*Statement of mail service performed in closed pouches upon railroads and*

Initial and terminal stations running east to west, north to south, and northwest to southeast.	Division.	Number of route.	Contract designation, termini of route.	Corporate title of company.
South Framingham and Milford, Mass.	1	3028	South Framingham and Milford, Mass.	Boston and Albany R. R ....
Sparkill and Tallman, N. Y	2	6002	Tallman, Sparkill, N. Y	N. Y., L. E. and W ....
Spencer and South Spencer (n. o.), Mass.	1	3066	Spencer, South Spencer (n. o.), Mass.	Boston and Albany R. R ....
Spirit Lake and Spencer, Iowa.	6	27096	Spencer, Spirit Lake, Iowa..	Chicago, Milwaukee and Saint Paul.
Spofford and El Paso, Tex.....	7	¹31099 (part)	San Antonio, El Paso, Tex ..	Galveston, Harrisburgh and San Antonio.
Spring City and Balta, Tenn...	5	19021	Spring City, Balta, Tenn ...	Tennesse Central ....
Springfield and Xenia, Ohio¹ ..	5	21027	Xenia, Springfield, Ohio.....	Pitts., Cin'ti and St. Louis..
Springfield Junction and Mines, Pa.	2	8157	Springfield Junction, Mines, Pa.	Pennsylvania ....
Stamford and Hobart, N. Y....	2	6073 (part)	Rondout, Hobart, N. Y	Ulster and Delaware........
Stanwood and Tipton, Iowa....	6	27013	Stanwood, Tipton, Iowa.....	Chicago and Northwestern..
State Line and Van Deusen, Mass.	1	3071	Van Dusen, State Line, Mass	Housatonic R. R ....
Stewart Junction and Babylon, N. Y.	2	6112	Stewart Junction, Babylon, N. Y.	Long Island ....
Stewartstown and New Freedom, Pa.	2	8029	Stewartstown, New Freedom, Pa.	Stewartstown..............
Stewartsville and New Harmony, Ind.	5	22041	Stewartsville, New Harmony, Ind.	Peoria, Decatur and Evans..
Stillwater and Hastings, Minn.	6	26045	Hastings, Stillwater, Minn.	Chicago, Milwaukee and St. Paul.
Stillwater and Minneapolis, Minn.	6	26008	Minneapolis, Stillwater, Minn.	Saint Paul and Duluth......
Stillwater and Stillwater Junction, Minn.	6	26027	Stillwater Junction (n. o.), Stillwater, Minn.	Chicago, Saint Paul, Minn., and Omaha.
Stokesdale Junction and Antrim, Pa.	2	8065 (part)	Corning, N. Y., Antrim, Pa.	Fall Brook Coal Co.........
Stoneville and Greenville, Miss.	4	18011	Greenville, Stoneville, Miss.	Georgia Pacific Rwy........

parts of railroads over which no railway post-offices run, in operation, etc.—Continued.

Miles of route.	Annual miles of service.	Number of round trips per week.	Number of pouches exchanged daily.	Date of last re-adjustment.	Average weight of mail whole distance daily.	Remarks.
					Pounds.	
12.36	23,292	18	46	July 1, 1885	478	South Framingham exchanges with East Holliston, Holliston, Metcalf, Braggville, and Milford; Holliston with Boston and Boston and Albany R. P. O.; Milford with Boston, Holliston, Worcester, Boston and Albany R. P. O.; Boston, Clinton, and Fitchburg R. P. O.; Boston, Springfield, and New York R. P. O., and Lowell and Taunton R. P. O.
13.11	16,456	12	20	July 1, 1885	114	
2.18	5,476	24	8	....	....	Spencer with Boston and Albany R. P. O.
21.90	27,619	12	16	....	....	Supplied by initial and terminal offices, and by Calmar, Iowa, and Chamberlain, Dak., R. P. O. Connects at Spirit Lake, Iowa, with Cedar Rapids, Iowa, and Watertown, Dak., R. P. O.
500.25	366,183	7	106	July 1, 1886	1,218	R eported last year as Del Rio and El Paso, Tex. [1] 134.03 miles of route 31039, between San Antonio and Spofford, Tex., covered by Houston and Eagle Pass, Tex., R. P. O. Makes El Paso, Tex., connections, and connects at Spofford. Tex., with Houston and Eagle Pass, Tex., R. P. O.
8.19	5,143	6	6	July 1, 1888	42	[1] Run of clerk on Xenia and Richmond R. P. O. extended to Springfield, Ohio, April 5, 1888, and closed-pouch service discontinued on Xenia and Springfield R. R., distance 19.99 miles. (See Springfield and Richmond R. P. O., Table A*.)
....	31,864	20	22	July 1, 1888	957	
8.20	5,150	6	4	July 1, 1885	37	
[1]4.00	5,024	12	4	July 1, 1885	1,202	[1] Balance of route (74.36 miles) covered by Rondout and Stamford R. P. O. (See Table A*.)
8.94	11,228	12	10	July 1, 1887	177	Supplied by Chicago, Ill., and Cedar Rapids, Iowa, R. P. O. Connects at Tipton, Iowa, with Clinton and Iowa City, Iowa, R. P. O.
11.12	6,963	6	12	July 1, 1886	192	Pittsfield and Bridgeport R. P. O. exchange with Rockdale Mills, West Stockbridge, State Line, Albany, Boston, and Albany R. P. O., and New York and Chicago R. P. O.
21.21	26,640	12	12	Feb. 1, 1886	140	
7.65	9,608	12	8	July 1, 1884	29	
7.34	9,219	12	10	July 1, 1888	180	
26.12	38,239	14	24	July 1, 1887	270	Supplied by initial and terminal offices. Connects at Stillwater, Minn., with Stillwater and Minneapolis, Minn., and Stillwater and Stillwater Junction, Minn., pouch service. Connects at Hastings, Minn., with Hastings and Cologne, Minn., and with Chicago, Ill., and Minneapolis, Minn., R. P. O's.
29.39	36,914	12	12	July 1, 1887	199	Connects at Stillwater, Minn., with Stillwater and Hastings, Minn., and with Stillwater and Stillwater Junction, Minn., pouch service; at White Bear Lake, Minn., with Duluth and Saint Paul, Minn., R. P. O., and at Minneapolis, Minn., with all lines centering at that city.
3.59	14,274	28	16	July 1, 1887	336	Connects at Stillwater, Minn., with Stillwater and Hastings, Minn., and with Stillwater and Minneapolis, Minn., pouch service. Connects at Stillwater Junction, Minn., with Saint Paul, Minn., and Elroy, Wis., R. P. O.
[1]15.90	13,884	9	28	July 1, 1886	158	[1] Balance of route (35.20 miles) covered by Geneva and Williamsport R. P. O. (See Table A*.)
7.67	5,614	7	4	July 1, 1888	27	

TABLE C^r.—*Statement of mail service performed in closed pouches upon railroads and*

Initial and terminal stations running east to west, north to south, and northwest to southeast.	Division.	Number of route.	Contract designation, termini of route.	Corporate title of company.
Strong and Bazaar, Kans......	7	¹33077 (part)	Bazaar, Barnard, Kans.....	Chicago, Kansas and Western.
Stuart and Anaconda, Mont...	8	36003	Stuart, Anaconda, Mont....	Montana Rwy ....
Stuck and Puyallup Junction (n. o.), Wash.	8	43013	Stuck, Puyallup Junction, Wash.	Nor. Pac. and Puget Sound Shore R. R.
Suffield and Windsor Locks, Conn.	1	5025	Windsor Locks, Suffield, Conn.	New York, New Haven and Hartford R. R.
Suffolk, Va., and Amboy, N. C.	3	11030	Suffolk, Va., Amboy, N. C...	Suffolk and Carolina ....
Suffolk and Whaleyville, Va...	3	11037	Suffolk, Whaleyville, Va....	Suffolk Lumber Company's R. R.
Suisun and Napa Junction, Cal.	8	46006	Suisun, Napa Junction, Cal..	California Pacific R. R......
Summit and Bernardsville, N. J.	2	7036	Summit, Bernardsville, N. J.	Del., Lack. and Western....
Summit City and Bradford, Pa.	2	8122	Summit City, Bradford, Pa..	Buff., N. Y. and Phila ......
Suspension Bridge and Buffalo, N. Y.	2	6003	Buffalo, Suspension Bridge, N. Y.	N. Y., L. E. and W ....
Suspension Bridge and Niagara Falls, N. Y.	2	6018 (part)	Rochester, Niagara Falls, N. Y.	N. Y. C. and H. R ....
Sutherlin, Va., and Milton, N. C.	3	11019	Sutherlin, Va., Milton, N. C.	Richmond and Danville ....
Suwanee and Lawrenceville, Ga.	4	15032	Suwanee, Lawrenceville, Ga.	Richmond and Danville R. R.
Sylvania and Rocky Ford, Ga.	4	15046	Sylvania, Rocky Ford, Ga ..	Sylvania R. R ....
Talbotton and Paschal, Ga	4	15033	Talbotton, Bostick (n. o.), Ga.	Talbotton R. R...............
Tallahassee and Saint Marks, Fla.	4	16013	Tallahassee, Saint Marks, Fla.	Fla. Rwy. and Nav. Co.....
Tallulah Falls and Cornelia, Ga.	4	15043	Belton, Tallulah Falls, Ga..	Richmond and Danville R. R.
Taunton and New Bedford, Mass.	1	3051 (part)	New Bedford, Fitchburg, Mass.	Old Colony R. R ....
Taylor's Falls and Wyoming, Minn.	6	26033	Wyoming, Taylor's Falls, Minn.	Saint Paul and Duluth......
Texline (n. o.) and Clarendon, Tex.	7	¹31037 (part)	Fort Worth, Texline (n.o.), Tex.	Fort Worth and Denver City.
Theresa Junction and Clayton, N. Y.	2	6115	Theresa Junction, Clayton, N. Y.	Rome, Wat. and Ogdens ....
Thomaston and Whitestone Junction, N. Y.	2	6120	Whitestone Junction, Thomaston, N. Y.	Long Island.................
Tomahawk and Merrill, Wis..	6	¹25031 (part)	Tomah, Tomahawk, Wis...	Chicago, Milwaukee and St. Paul.
Topton and Kutztown, Pa	2	8062	Topton, Kutztown, Pa.......	Philadelphia and Reading...

parts of railroads over which no railway post offices run, in operation, etc.—Continued.

Miles of route.	Annual miles of service.	Number of round trips per week.	Number of pouches exchanged daily.	Date of last re-adjustment.	Average weight of mail whole distance daily.	Remarks.
					Pounds.	
12.60	7,913	6	10	July 1, 1888	385	New service; not reported last year. [1] 76.40 miles of route 33077, between Keystone and Strong, Kans., covered by Concordia and Strong, Kans., R. P. O., and 43.13 miles, between Keystone and Barnard, Kans., covered by Keystone and Barnard, Kans., R. P. O. (See Table A*.) Connects at Strong, Kans., with Concordia and Strong, Kans. R. P. O. and Kansas City, Mo., and Pueblo, Colo , R. P. O.
8.53	18,732	21	4	July 1, 1886	158	Connects with Butte City, Mont., and Ogden, Utah, R. P. O.
7.50	10,980	14	64	July 1, 1886	118	Connects at Stuck with Black River Junction and Stuck R. R., and at Puyallup Junction with the Helena, Mont., and Portland, Oregon, R. P. O.
4.90	12,308	24	8	July 1, 1885	156	Suffield exchanges with Windsor Locks; Hartford and Boston, Springfield and New York R. P. O.
39.96	25,095	6	18	July 1, 1888	87	Supplied by closed pouches from Suffolk, Va.
13.17	8,271	6	2	July 1, 1886	244	Do.
13.06	19,149	14	8	July 1, 1886	244	Connects at Suisun with Ogden, Utah, and San Francisco, Cal., R. P. O., and at Napa Junction with Calistoga and Vallejo Junction R. P. O.
14.68	18,438	12	27	July 1, 1885	199	
8.97	14,073	15	20	July 1, 1885	79	
25.69	56,466	21	[1]37	July 1, 1885	1,522	[1] Including closed Canada mail.
[1]1.80	3,391	18	14	July 1, 1885	3,851	[1] Balance of route (74.33 miles) covered by Rochester and Niagara Falls R. P. O. (See Table A*.)
7.26	9,119	12	8	July 1, 1885	109	Connects Richmond and Danville R. P. O. at Sutherlin.
10.43	6,550	6	4	July 1, 1888	129	
14.99	9,414	6	6	July 1, 1888	109	
7.20	5,270	7	4	July 1, 1888	101	
21.89	13,746	6	4	July 1, 1884	15	
33.23	30,834	14	12	July 1, 1888	226	Service on this route is performed between Cornelia and Tallulah Falls (21.13 miles) by closed pouches; 12.10 miles covered by the Charleston and Atlanta R. P. O.
20.91	52,426	24	41	July 1, 1885	1,330	Balance of route (72 73 miles) covered by R. P. O. service. (See Table A*.) New Bedford exchanges with Taunton, East Freetown, Providence, Boston, Providence and New York R. P. O., Boston, Springfield and New York R. P. O., New York, Boston and Wellfleet R. P. O., and Lowell and Taunton R. P. O.; Taunton with Freetown and Myrick's.
20.78	26,099	12	28	July 1, 1887	425	Supplied by initial and terminal offices. Connects at Wyoming, Minn., with Duluth and Saint Paul, Minn., R. P. O.
174.25	127,551	7	50	....	....	New service; not reported last year. [1] 278.87 miles of route 31037, between Clarendon and Fort Worth, Tex., covered by Clarendon and Fort Worth, Tex., R. P. O. (See Table A*.) Connects at Texline (n.o.), Tex., with Pueblo, Colo., and Texline (n. o.), Tex., pouch service; at Washburn, Tex , with Panhandle and Washburn, Tex., pouch service, and at Clarendon, Tex., with Clarendon and Fort Worth, Tex., R. P. O.
16.25	35,718	12	36	July 1, 1885	218	
7.07	8,880	12	80	Aug. 25, 1885	299	
22.99	14,437	6	8	Aug. 3, 1888	702	[1] Balance of route covered by Merrill and Tomah, Wis., R. P. O. (See Table A*.) Supplied by Merrill, Wis., and by Merrill and Tomah, Wis., R. P. O.
5.06	12,671	24	8	July 1, 1885	138	

TABLE C^c.—*Statement of mail service performed in closed pouches upon railroads and*

Initial and terminal stations running east to west, north to south, and northwest to southeast.	Division.	Number of route.	Contract designation, termini of route.	Corporate title of company.
Towanda and Barclay, Pa.....	2	8069	Towanda, Barclay, Pa.......	Barclay......................
Tower and Duluth, Minn......	6	26054	Duluth, Tower, Minn	Duluth and Iron Range.....
Traverse City and Walton, Mich.	9	24034	Walton, Traverse City, Mich	Grand Rapids and Indiana..
Trenton and Bordentown, N. J.	2	7046	Bordentown, Trenton, N. J..	Pennsylvania...............
Trenton Junction and Trenton, N. J.	2	7044	Trenton, Trenton Junction, N. J.	Central R. R. of N. J........
Tripp and Armour, Dak.......	6	35025	Tripp, Armour, Dak	Chicago, Milwaukee and St. Paul.
Troy and Albany, N. Y........	2	6106	Albany, Troy, N. Y........	N. Y. C. and H. R ....
Troy and Albany Junction, N. Y.	2	6020	Albany Junction, Troy, N. Y.	Del. and Hud. Canal Co ....
Troy and Schenectady, N. Y...	2	6012	Troy, Schenectady, N. Y	N. Y. C. and H. R ....
Turbotville and Watsontown, Pa.	2	8166	Turbotville, Watsontown, Pa.	Wilkes-Barre and Western.
Turner and Aurora, Ill	6	23071	Aurora, Turner, Ill	Chicago, Burlington, and Quincy.
Turnerville and Colchester, Conn.	1	5020	Turnerville, Colchester, Conn.	New York, New Haven and Hartford R. R.
Turner's Falls and Greenfield, Mass.	1	3053	Greenfield, Turner's Falls, Mass.	Fitchburg R. R.............
Two Rivers and Manitowoc, Wis.	6	¹25018 (part)	Milwaukee, Two Rivers, Wis.	Milwaukee, Lake Shore and Western.
U. P. Transfer, Broadway Depot, Council Bluffs, Iowa.	6	27102	U. P. Transfer, Council Bluffs, Iowa.	Union Pacific...............
University Station and Chapel Hill, N. C.	3	13018	University Station, Chapel Hill, N. C.	Richmond and Danville.....
Uva and Cheyenne, Wyo ...	6	37002	Cheyenne, Uva, Wyo........	Union Pacific...............
Valley Springs and Lodi, Cal..	8	46043	Lodi, Valley Springs, Cal...	San Joaquin and Sierra Nevada R. R.
Valley Stream and Far Rockaway, N. Y.	2	6100	Valley Stream, Far Rockaway, N. Y.	Long Island ....
Varna and Lacon, Ill..........	6	23074	Varna, Lacon, Ill...........	Chicago and Alton..........
Verona and Negley, Pa........	2	8143	Negley, Verona, Pa.........	Allegheny Valley...........
Vesper and Dexterville Junction, Wis.	6	25056	Dexterville Junction, Vesper, Wis.	Wisconsin, Pittsfield and Superior.
Victoria and Port Lavaca, Tex.	7	¹31019 (part)	Port Lavaca, Cuero, Tex....	Gulf, Western Texas and Pacific.
Vidalia and Troyville, La	4	30005	Vidalia, Troyville, La.......	Natchez, Red River and Texas R. R.
Vincennes, Ind., and Saint Francisville, Ill.	6	23037	Vincennes, Ind., Saint Francisville, Ill.	Cairo, Vincennes and Chicago.
Vinita and Red Fork, Ind. T ...	7	32002	Vinita, Red Fork, Ind. T	Saint Louis and San Francisco.
Visalia and Goshen, Cal	8	46018	Visalia, Goshen, Cal.........	Visalia R. R.................
Volcano Junction and Volcano, W. Va.	3	12003	Volcano Junction, Volcano, W. Va.	Laurel Fork and Sand Hill..
Wahneta and Bartow, Fla	4	16021	Wahneta, Bartow, Fla	South Florida R. R..........
Wakefield and Peabody, Mass.	1	3010	Wakefield, Peabody, Mass .	Boston and Maine R. R .....

parts of railroads over which no railway post-offices run, in operation, etc.—Continued.

Miles of route.	Annual miles of service.	Number of round trips per week.	Number of pouches exchanged daily.	Date of last re-adjustment.	Average weight of mail whole distance daily.	Remarks.
					Pounds.	
17. 85	11, 210	6	10	July 1, 1885	76	
96. 27	60, 457	6	4	July 1, 1887	119	Supplied by Duluth, Minn. Connects with all lines centering at that point.
26. 27	49, 492	18	36	July 1, 1884	520	At Walton, Mich., connects with Mackinaw City and Grand Rapids R. P. O.
0. 06	22, 909	36	14	July 1, 1885	343	
4. 28	8, 064	18	10	July 1, 1885	84	
20. 23	12, 704	6	8	Mar. 23, 1887	142	Supplied by Manilla and Mitchell R. P. O.
7. 50	70, 650	[1]90	[2]365	July 1, 1885	1, 161	[1] Three round trips on Sunday. [2] Including sacks.
5. 81	36, 487	60	[1]160	July 1, 1885	1, 161	[1] Including sacks.
22. 12	48, 620	21	[1]98	July 1, 1885	747	[1] Including sacks.
6. 53	4, 101	6	4			
13. 01	8, 170	6	10	July 1, 1887	85	Supplied by Aurora, Ill. Connects at Turner, Ill., with Chicago, Freeport, Ill., and Dubuque, Iowa, R. P. O., and at Aurora, Ill., with all lines centering there.
4. 20	10, 550	24	12	July 1, 1885	128	Colchester exchanges with Turnerville, New Haven, Willimantic, and Willimantic and New Haven, R. P. O.
4. 87	9, 175	18	24	July 1, 1885	231	Turner's Falls exchanges with Greenfield, Newport, and Springfield R. P. O., and Boston and Troy R. P. O. Greenfield with Montague City.
7. 33	9, 206	12	8	July 1, 1887	2, 640	[1] Balance of route covered by Ashland and Milwaukee, Wis., R. P. O. (See Table A[a].) Supplied by Manitowoc, Wis., and by Ashland and Milwaukee, Wis., R. P. O.
1. 76	3, 498	19	6			Carries local exchanges between Omaha, Nebr., and Council Bluffs, Iowa.
11. 16	14, 017	12	8	July 1, 1888	152	Connects Goldsborough and Greensborough R. P. O. at University Station.
103. 26	64, 847	6	20			Supplied by Cheyenne, Wyo. Connects at that point with Omaha, Nebr., and Ogden, Utah, and with Cheyenne, Wyo., and Denver, Colo., R. P. O's.
26. 81	19, 625	7	30	June 21, 1888	468	Connects at Lodi with Sacramento and San Francisco R. P. O. Supplied also by Lodi.
5. 25	6, 594	12	20	Aug. 25, 1885	134	
10. 66	13, 389	12	8	July 1, 1887	82	Supplied by Dwight and Washington, Ill., R. P. O.
5. 42	5, 106	4				
20. 87	13, 106	6	14	July 1, 1887	82	Supplied by Dexterville, Wis., and by Merrill and Tomah, Wis., R. P. O. Connects at Dexterville, Wis., with Fort Howard, Wis., and Winona, Minn., R. P. O., and with Dexterville and Hogan, Wis., pouch service.
27. 20	8, 486	3	4	July 1, 1886	217	[1]28.29 miles of route 31019 between Victoria and Cuero, Tex., covered by Rosenberg and Cuero, Tex., R. P. O. (See Table A[a].) Connects at Victoria, Tex., with Rosenberg and Cuero, Tex., R. P. O.
25. 60	16, 076	6	4	Apr. 19, 1886	12	
16. 88	13, 665	12	8	July 1, 1887	234	Connects Danville and Cairo, Ill., R. P. O. with Vincennes, Ind., and lines centering there.
68. 01	49, 783	7	26	July 1, 1886	168	Connects at Vinita. Ind. T., with Sedalia, Mo., and Denison, Tex., R. P. O., and Monett, Mo., and Vinita, Ind. T., R. P. O.
7. 66	20, 039	25	16	July 1, 1886	324	Connects at Goshen with San Francisco and Los Angeles R. P. O., and Goshen and Huron R. P. . Visalia exchanges with Hanford, Lemoore, and Tulare.
7. 09	8, 817	12	4	July 1, 1885	48	Connects Grafton and Cincinnati and Grafton and Parkersburgh R. P. O's at Volcano Junction.
17. 53	23, 840	12	10	Feb. 16, 1885	171	Newburyport and Boston R. P. O. exchanges with Lynnfield and Peabody; Boston with Lynnfield and Peabody.
8. 09	10, 161	12	8	July 1, 1885	60	

TABLE C°.—*Statement of mail service performed in closed pouches upon railroads and*

Initial and terminal stations running east to west, north to south, and northwest to southeast.	Division.	Number of route.	Contract designation, termini of route.	Corporate title of company.
Walla Walla, Wash., and Pendleton, Oregon.	8	43017	Walla Walla, Wash., Pendleton, Oregon.	Oreg. Rw'y and Navig. Co ..
Walterborough and Green Pond, S. C.	4	14025	Green Pond, Walterborough, S. C.	Green Pond, Walter. and Branchville R. R.
Wampum and Rock Point, Pa.	2	8177	Wampum, Rock Point, Pa ..	Penn's Company.............
Warren, R. L., and Fall River, Mass.	1	4005	Warren, R. L., Fall River, Mass.	Providence, Warren, and Bristol R. R.
Warren Plains and Warrenton, N. C.	3	13026	Warren Plains, Warrenton, N. C.	Warrenton ....
Warsaw and Clinton, N. C.....	3	13030	Warsaw, Clinton, N. C.	Wilmington and Weldon ...
Wartrace and Shelbyville, Tenn.	5	19020	Wartrace, Shelbyville, Tenn	Nashville, Chat. and St. Louis.
Warwick and Yuma, Kans....	7	33027	Yuma, Warwick, Kans.....	Central Branch U. P........
Washington and Barnett, Ga..	4	15006	Washington, Barnett, Ga ...	Georgia R. R...............
Washington and Greenleaf, Kans.	7	¹33021 (part)	Waterville, Washington, Kans.	Central Branch U. P........
Washington and Waynesburgh, Pa.	2	8114	Washington, Waynesburgh, Pa.	Waynesburgh and Washington.
Watertown and Brookings, Dak.	6	35014	Brookings, Watertown, Dak.	Chicago and North Western.
Watertown and Sackett's Harbor, N. Y.	2	6039	Watertown, Sackett's Harbor, N. Y.	Rome, Wat. and Ogdens.....
Watertown and Waterbury, Conn.	1	5006	Waterbury, Watertown, Conn.	Naugatuck, R. R. ....
Waukon Junction and Waukon, Iowa.	6	27040	Waukon Junction, Waukon, Iowa.	Chicago, Milwaukee and St. Paul.
Waverly and Waverly Junction, Iowa.	6	27,094	Waverly Junction, Waverly, Iowa.	Burlington, Cedar Rapids and Northern.
Wawa and Chester, Pa	2	8,008 (part)	Chester, Pa., Port Deposit, Md.	Phila., Wilm. and Balto.....
Webster City and Lehigh, Iowa	6	27,075	Webster City, Lehigh, Iowa.	Webster City and Southwestern.
Wellfleet and Provincetown, Mass.	1	3,041 (part)	Middleborough and Provincetown, Mass.	Old Colony R. R.............
Wellington and Caldwell, Kans.	7	¹33037 (part)	Mulvane, Caldwell, Kans....	Atchison, Topeka, and Santa Fé.
Wellington and Cissna Park, Ill.	6	22090	Wellington, Cissna Park, Ill.	Chicago and Eastern Ill.....

parts of railroads over which no railway post-offices run, in operation, etc.—Continued.

Miles of route.	Annual miles of service.	Number of round trips per week.	Number of pouches exchanged daily.	Date of last re-adjustment.	Average weight of mail whole distance daily.	Remarks.
					Pounds.	
47.43	34,719	7	14	June 25, 1888	303	Connects at Walla Walla with Dayton, Wash., and Umatilla, Oregon, R. P. O., and at Pendleton, with the Huntington and Portland R. P. O. New service established August 8, 1887.
12.37	16,823	13	8	July 1, 1888	150	
3.52	2,211	6	2	July 1, 1885	290	Fall River exchanges with Warren, Providence, Providence and New London R. P. O., and Boston, Springfield, and New York R. P. O.
9.14	17,220	18	10			
3.13	3,981	12	8	July 1, 1888	124	Connects Norfolk and Raleigh R. P. O. at Warren Plains.
13.11	16,466	12	14	July 1, 1888	202	Connects Washington and Wilmington R. P. O. at Warsaw.
8.36	10,500	12	12	July 1, 1888	334	
30.86	22,590	7	24	July 1, 1886	201	Connects at Warwick, Kans., with Kansas City, Mo., and Red Cloud, Nebr., R. P. O.; at Scandia, Kans., with Fairburg, Nebr., and Norton, Kans., R. P. O., and at Yuma, Kans., with Atchison and Lenora, Kans., R. P. O.
13.58	27,200	14	12	July 1, 1888	265	[1] 13.11 miles of route 33021, between Waterville and Greenleaf, Kans., covered by Atchison and Lenora, Kans., R. P. O. (See Table A[a].) Connects at Washington, Kans., with Lincoln Nebr., and Concordia, Kans., R. P. O., and at Greenleaf, Kans., with Atchison and Lenora, Kans., R. P. O.
7.58	9,520	12	8	July 1, 1886	1,805	
29.73	37,341	12	18	July 1, 1885	563	
48.21	30,276	6	22	July 1, 1886	242	Supplied by Watertown, Dak., and by Tracy, Minn., and Pierre, Dak., R. P. O. Connects at Watertown, Dak., with Tracy, Minn., and Redfield, Dak., R. P. O.
12.52	15,725	12	6	July 1, 1885	157	
6.42	8,064	12	16	July 1, 1885	235	West Winsted and Bridgeport R. P. O., and Waterbury exchanges with Watertown and Oakville.
23.05	14,475	6	8	July 1, 1887	170	Supplied by La Crosse, Wis., and Dubuque, Iowa, R. P. O.
6.00	7,586	12	6	July 1, 1887	71	Supplied by Albert Lea, Minn., and Burlington, Iowa, R. P. O. Connects at Waverly, Iowa, with Sumner and Hampton, Iowa, and with Minneapolis, Hayfield, Minn, and Waterloo, Iowa, R.P.O's.
[1] 7.17	11,257	15	18	July 1, 1885	945	[1] Balance of route (51.57 miles) covered by Philadelphia and Port Deposit R. P. O. (See Table A[a].)
17.83	11,197	6	6	July 1, 1887	71	Supplied by Webster City, Iowa. Connects at that point with Dubuque and Sioux City, Iowa, and with Tama and Hawarden, Iowa, R. P. O's.
14.36	18.036	12	16	July 1, 1885	2,627	Balance of route (71.94 miles) covered by R. P. O. service. (See Table A[a].) Boston and Wellfleet R. P. O. exchanges with Truro, North Truro, South Truro, and Provincetown. Wellfleet exchanges with Provincetown.
21.92	48,136	21	8	July 1, 1886	767	[1] 16.41 miles of route 33037 between Mulvane and Wellington, Kans., carried by Newton and Kiowa, Kans., R. P. O. (See Table A[a].) Connects at Wellington, Kans., with Kansas City, Mo., and Wellington, Kans., R. P. O.; Newton and Kiowa, Kans., R. P. O.; Saint Joseph, Mo., and Caldwell, Kans., R. P. O., and Wellington and Hunnewell, Kans., pouch service. Connects at Perth, Corbin, and Caldwell, Kans., with Saint Joseph, Mo., and Caldwell, Kans., R. P. O., and at Caldwell, Kans., with Beaumont and Bluff, Kans., R. P. O.
12.72	7,988	6	14	July 1, 1887	117	Supplied by Wellington, Ill. Connects at that point with Chicago, Ill., and Terre Haute, Ind., R. P. O.

TABLE C°.—*Statement of mail service performed in closed pouches upon railroads and*

Initial and terminal stations running east to west, north to south, and northwest to southeast.	Division.	Number of route.	Contract designation, termini of route.	Corporate title of company.
Wellington and Hunnewell, Kans.	7	¹23005 (part)	Cherry Vale, Hunnewell, Kans.	Southern Kansas............
West Brownsville and Uniontown, Pa.	2	8146	West Brownsville, Uniontown, Pa.	Pennsylvania..............
Weston and Buckhannon, W. Va.	3	12011	Weston, Buckhannon, W. Va.	Weston and Buckhannon...
West Stewartstown and Coos, N. H.	1	1005	West Stewartstown, Coos, N. H.	Upper Coos R. R............
West Wareham and Fairhaven, Mass.	1	3050	Fairhaven, West Wareham, Mass.	Old Colony R. R............
Wetumpka and Elmore, Ala...	4	17024	Elmore, Wetumpka Ala ...	Louisville and Nashville R. R.
White Haven and Upper Lehigh, Pa.	2	8097	White Haven, Upper Lehigh, Pa.	Cent. R. R. of N. J..........
White River Junction and Woodstock, Vt.	1	3013	White River Junction, Woodstock, Vt.	Woodstock R. R.............
Whitestone and Long Island City, N. Y.	2	6094	Long Island City, Whitestone, N. Y.	Long Island ....
Whitman and Alliance, Nebr.	6	¹34,036 (part)	Grand Island, Alliance, Nebr.	Burlington and Missouri River in Nebr.
Whitman and Bridgewater, Mass.	1	3040	Whitman, Bridgwater, Mass.	Old Colony R. R ....
Wildwood and Plant City, Fla.	4	16019	Wildwood, Plant City, Fla..	Fla. Railway and Nav. Co...
Wilkes Barre and Wanamie, Pa.	2	8101	Wilkes Barre, Wanamie, Pa.	Cent. R. R. of N. J ....
Williamsburgh and Hollidaysburgh, Pa.	2	8084	Hollidaysburgh, Williamsburgh, Pa.	Pennsylvania.............
Williamstown and Millersburgh, Pa.	2	8106	Millersburgh, Williamstown, Pa.	Northern Central...........
Wilmot and Millbank, Dak....	6	35009	Millbank, Wilmot, Dak	Chicago, Milwaukee and Saint Paul.
Wilton Junction and Muscatine, Iowa.	6	27090	Wilton Junction, Muscatine, Iowa.	Chicago, Rock Island and Pacific.
Winchester and North Woburn, Mass.	1	3018	Winchester, North Woburn, Mass.	Boston and Maine R. R. (Lowell system.)
Windsor Beach (n. o.) and Rochester, N. Y.	2	6136	Windsor Beach, Rochester, N. Y.	Rome, Wat. and Ogdens....
Wilmington and Wrightsville, N. C.	3	13035	Wilmington, Wrightsville, N. C.	Wilmington Sea Coast......
Winfield and Washington, Iowa.		¹27035 (part)	Burlington, Washington, Iowa.	Burlington and Northwestern.
Winifrede Junction and Winifrede, W. Va.	3	12008	Winifrede Junction, Winifrede, W. Va.	Winifrede ....

parts of railroads over which no railway post-offices run, in operation, etc.—Continued.

Miles of route.	Annual miles of service.	Number of round trips per week.	Number of pouches exchanged daily.	Date of last re-adjustment.	Average weight of mail whole distance daily.	Remarks.
					Pounds.	
18.12	18,264	7	12	July 1, 1886	1,691	[1]113.41 miles of route 23005 between Cherry Vale and Wellington, Kans., covered by Kansas City, Mo., and Wellington, Kans., R. P. O. (See Table A[a].) Connects at Wellington, Kans., with Kansas City, Mo., and Wellington, Kans., R. P. O.; Newton and Kiowa, Kans., R. P. O.; Saint Joseph, Mo., and Caldwell, Kans., R. P. O., and Wellington and Caldwell, Kans., pouch service. Connects at South Haven, Kans., with Beaumont and Bluff Kans., R. P. O.
18.80	22,613	12	22	July 1, 1885	76	
16.29	20,460	12	17	July 1, 1885	76	Connects Clarksburgh and Weston R. P. O. at Weston.
21.23	7,598	6	12	....	......	New service established March 19, 18+8 (89 days). Supplied by Portland and Island Pond R. P. O's.
15.59	19,581	12	33	July 1, 1885	215	New Bedford exchanges pouches with Rochester, Marion, Mattapoisett, West Wareham, and Boston, Providence, and New York R. P. O. Boston and Wellfleet R. P. O. exchanges with Fairhaven, Marion, Mattapoisett, Nantucket, and New Bedford.
6.92	8,692	12	6	July 1, 1888	156	
8.80	11,053	12	10	July 1, 1885	65	
14.44	18,337	12	20	July 1, 1885	231	White River Junction exchanges pouches with Quechee, Taftsville, and Woodstock. Taftsville exchanges with Quechee and Woodstock. Quechee with Woodstock.
11.36	35,670	30	45	Aug. 25, 1885	572	
71.60	44,965	6	12	July 1, 1886	1,231	[1] Balance of route covered by Nebraska City and Whitman, Nebr., R. P. O. (See Table A[a].) Supplied by Whitman, Nebr., and by Nebraska City and Whitman, Nebr., R. P. O.
8.13	10,211	12	6	....	......	East Bridgewater exchanges pouches with Boston and Boston and Wellfleet R. P. O.
63.66	39,978	6	20	Aug. 16, 1886	67	
12.46	15,650	12	18	July 1, 1885	69	
14.28	22,420	15	18	July 1, 1885	237	
21.04	26,426	12	30	July 1, 1885	226	
17.26	10,839	6	4	July 1, 1886	90	Supplied by Millbank, Dak. Connects at that point with Saint Paul, Minn., and Mitchell, Dak. R. P. O.
12.75	16,014	12	8	July 1, 1887	398	Connects at Wilton Junction, Iowa, with Chicago, Ill., and West Liberty, Iowa, R. P. O., and at Muscatine, Iowa, with Davenport, Iowa, and Atchison, Kans., and with Muscatine and Montezuma, Iowa, R. P. O's.
4.56	5,727	12	16	July 1, 1888	219	Supplied by Boston, Woburn, and Boston, Nashua, and Keene R. P. O. Twenty-four additional times per week outward and thirty additional times per week inward, between Woburn and Winchester.
8.30	26,062	30	[1]44	July 1, 1888	851	[1] Including sacks.
9.24	6,764	7	2	....	......	Connects lines centering at Wilmington, N. C.
18.57	11,662	6	14	July 1, 1887	407	[1] Balance of route covered by Burlington and Oskaloosa, Iowa, R. P. O. (See Table A[a].) Supplied by Washington, Iowa, and by Burlington and Oskaloosa, Iowa, R. P. O. Connects at Washington, Iowa, with Davenport, Iowa, and Atchison, Kans., R. P. O.
4.54	2,351	6	4	July 1, 1885	36	Connects Richmond and Huntington R. P. O. at Winifrede Junction.

TABLE C^c.—*Statement of mail service performed in closed pouches upon railroads and*

Initial and terminal stations running east to west, north to south, and northwest to southeast.	Division.	Number of route.	Contract designation, termini of route.	Corporate title of company.
Winneconne and Rush Lake, Wis.	6	25007	Rush Lake, Winneconne, Wis.	Chicago, Milwaukee and St. Paul.
Winona Junction and La Crosse, Wis.	6	¹25014 (part)	Winona, Minn., La Crosse, Wis.	Chicago and Northwestern.
Wolfborough and Wolfborough Junction, N. H.	1	7015	Wolfborough Junction, Wolfborough, N. H.	Boston and Maine R. R......
Woodbury and Penn's Grove, N. J.	2	7039	Woodbury, Penn's Grove, N. J.	Delaware River..............
Woodbury and Riddleton Junction, N.J.	2	7022	Woodbury, Riddleton Junction, N. J.	West Jersey.................
Woodman and Lancaster Junction, Wis.	6	¹25025 (part)	Galena, Ill., Woodman, Wis.	Chicago and Northwestern.
Woodstock and Blockton, Ala.	4	17025	Woodstock, Blockton, Ala..	Cahaba Coal Mining Company.
Woodville, Miss., and Bayou Sara, La.	4	30007	Bayou Sara, La., Woodville, Miss.	West Feliciana R. R........
Yarmouth Junction (n. o.) and Hyannis, Mass.	1	3048	Yarmouth Junction (n. o.), Hyannis, Mass.	Old Colony R. R............
Youngwood Station and United, Pa.	2	8151	Youngwood Station, United, Pa.	Pennsylvania..............
Zoar Station and Bowerston, Ohio.	5	¹21080 (part)	Toledo, Bowerston, Ohio	Wheeling and Lake Erie....
Zumbrota and Rochester, Minn	6	26017	Rochester, Zumbrota, Minn.	Winona and St. Peter.......

RECAPITULATION.

Division.	Number of routes.	Miles of route.	Annual miles of service.	Number of pouches exchanged daily.
First	105	1,122.96	1,555,256	2,123
Second	214	2,612.36	3,995,027	3,968
Third	46	723.57	620,709	512
Fourth	78	1,437.92	1,264,668	525
Fifth	60	751.30	834,957	850
Sixth	164	4,827.77	4,050,658	2,278
Seventh	98	3,270.51	2,754,153	1,291
Eighth	70	2,068.23	1,790,441	1,099
Ninth	25	587.97	567,950	413
Total	860	17,402.59	17,436,819	13,059
Total as per report for the fiscal year ended June 30, 1887............................	795	14,350.05	14,489,613	11,714
Increase	65	3,052.54	2,947,206	1,345

parts of railroads over which no railway post-offices run, in operation, etc.—Continued.

Miles of route.	Annual miles of service.	Number of round trips per week.	Number of pouches exchanged daily.	Date of last re-adjustment.	Average weight of mail whole distance daily.	Remarks.
					Pounds.	
14. 84	9, 319	6	12	July 1, 1885	36	Supplied by Ripon, Wis., and by Oshkosh and Milwaukee, Wis., R. P. O.; connects at Rush Lake, Wis., with Ripon and Berlin, Wis., pouch service.
4. 14	11, 261	26	8	July 1, 1887	113	¹ Balance of route covered by Chicago, Ill., and Winona, Minn., R. P. O. Connects Chicago, Ill., and Winona, Minn., R. P. O. with La Crosse, Wis., and lines centering at that city.
12. 14	15, 248	12	10	July 1, 1885	141	Wolfborough exchanges pouches with East Wolfborough and Boston. North Conway and Boston R. P. O. exchanges pouches with Wolfborough and East Wolfborough. Wolfborough exchanges pouches with Wolfborough Junction.
20. 97	39, 597	18	32	July 1, 1885	183	
22. 21	48, 904	21	96	July 1, 1885	286	
18. 53	11, 686	13	16	July 1, 1885	236	¹ Balance of route covered by Montfort, Wis., and Galena, Ill., and by Milwaukee and Lancaster, Wis., R. P. O's. (See Table A⁵.) Connects at Woodman, Wis., with Chicago, Ill., and North McGregor, Iowa, R. P. O.
8. 67	10, 889	12	4	July 1, 1888	60	
26. 29	10, 936	4	4	July 1, 1886	24	
3. 54	4, 446	12	6	July 1, 1888	80	Boston and Wellfleet R. P. O. exchange pouches with Hyannis and Hyannisport.
11. 09	10, 447	9	12	July 1, 1885	80	
16. 60	14, 632	6	32	July 1, 1888	863	¹ Balance of route (155.08 miles) covered by the Toledo and Marietta R. P. O. (See Table A⁵.) Six additional round trips per week between Bowerston and Sherodsville (6.70 miles).
31. 44	40, 393	18	22	July 1, 1887	173	Supplied by initial and terminal offices. Connects at Zumbrota, Minn., with Wabasha and Zumbrota, Minn., R. P. O., and at Rochester, Minn., with Winona and Tracy, Minn., R. P. O.

TABLE D⁴.—*Comparative statement of the railway mail service 1830 to 1888.*

Fiscal year ending June 30—	Miles of railroad in the United States.	Miles of railroad upon which mail was carried.	Miles of annual transportation of mail by railroads.	Annual cost of railroad mail transportation.	Average annual cost per mile of railroad mail transportation.	Number of employés of railway mail service.	Annual expenditure for all employés of the railway mail service.
1830	23						
1831	95						
1832	229						
1833	380						
1834	633	78					
1835	1,098						
1836	1,273		*1,878,296				
1837	1,497	974	*1,793,024	*$307,444	$0.1714		
1838	1,913		*2,413,080	*410,488	.1701		
1839	2,302		*2,396,055	*520,602	.1532		
1840	2,818		*3,880,053	*595,853	.1530		
1841	3,535		*3,946,450	*585,843	.1484		
1842	4,026	3,091	*4,424,262	432,568	.0977		†$22,987.00
1843	4,185		*5,692,402	*733,687	.1288		†28,965.00
1844	4,877	3,714	*5,747,855	531,752	.0925		†29,744.60
1845	4,633		*6,484,592	*843,430	.1306	43	†37,513.00
1846	4,930	4,092	*7,781,828	*870,570	.1118		†42,406.00
1847	5,598	4,402	4,170,403	597,475	.1432	186	†46,153.00
1848	5,996	4,735	4,327,400	584,192	.1349		†54,063.00
1849	7,365	5,497	4,861,177	635,740	.1307		†61,512.60
1850	9,021	6,886	6,524,593	818,227	.1254		†107,042.00
1851	10,982	8,255	8,364,503	985,019	.1177	148	†145,897.00
1852	12,908	10,146	11,082,768	1,275,520	.1150	185	†196,966.00
1853	15,360	12,415	12,986,705	1,601,829	.1283	235	176,722.00
1854	16,720	14,440	15,436,389	1,758,610	.1139	257	197,090.00
1855	18,374	18,333	19,202,469	2,073,089	.1079	348	254,498.00
1856	22,016	20,822	21,809,296	2,310,389	.1059	394	287,187.00
1857	24,503	22,530	24,267,944	2,550,847	.1054	451	339,388.00
1858	26,968	24,431	25,763,452	2,828,301	.1097	491	392,739.00
1859	28,789	26,010	27,263,584	3,243,974	.1190	548	429,175.00
1860	30,635	27,129	27,053,749	3,349,662	.1211	582	405,819.00
1861	31,286	†22,018	†23,116,822	†2,843,709	.1100	†427	†314,179.00
1862	32,170	†21,338	†22,777,219	†2,496,115	.1096	†474	†295,823.00
1863	32,908	†22,152	†22,871,558	†2,528,517	.1109	†525	†324,524.00
1864	35,085	†22,616	†23,301,942	†2,567,044	.1101	†572	†352,701.00
1865	36,801	†23,401	†24,087,568	†2,707,421	.1123	†612	†342,071.00
1866	39,250	32,092	30,609,467	3,391,592	.1108	702	542,401.00
1867	42,229	34,015	32,437,900	3,812,600	.1175	827	729,680.00
1868	42,229	36,018	34,886,178	4,177,126	.1197	995	839,975.00
1869	46,844	39,537	41,399,284	4,723,680	.1141	1,129	973,560.00
1870	52,914	43,727	47,551,970	5,128,901	.1078	1,106	1,109,140.00
1871	60,288	49,834	55,557,048	5,724,979	.1030	1,382	1,441,020.00
1872	66,171	57,911	62,491,749	6,502,771	.1040	1,547	1,709,546.00
1873	70,278	63,457	65,621,445	7,257,196	.1105	1,895	1,958,876.00
1874	72,383	67,734	72,460,545	8,587,063	.1185	2,175	2,186,330.00
1875	74,096	70,083	75,154,910	9,216,518	.1226	2,342	2,410,490.00
1876	76,808	72,348	77,741,172	9,543,134	.1227	2,415	2,504,140.00
1877	79,089	74,546	85,856,710	8,053,936	.1060	2,500	2,484,846.00
1878	81,776	77,120	92,120,395	9,566,595	.1038	2,608	2,579,013.00
1879	86,497	79,991	95,098,993	9,792,589	.1051	2,609	2,624,890.00
1880	93,671	85,320	96,497,463	10,648,966	.1103	2,946	2,850,990.00
1881	104,813	91,569	103,521,229	11,963,117	.1155	3,177	3,104,861.00
1882	113,329	100,563	113,995,318	13,127,715	.1151	3,570	3,486,779.00
1883	120,552	110,208	129,196,541	13,887,80)	.1075	3,855	3,688,022.00
1884	125,150	117,100	142,541,392	15,012,603	.1053	3,963	3,972,071.00
1885	128,067	121,032	151,912,140	16,627,983	.1095	4,387	4,346,209.51
1886	137,986	123,933	165,699,389	15,495,191	.1045	4,573	4,516,525.54
1887	149,913	130,949	169,689,865	16,174,691	.1064	4,851	4,694,561.75
1888	(§)	143,713	185,485,783	17,528,599	.1052	5,094	4,981,365.93

* Including steam-boat service; no separate report.
† Including mail-messenger service.
‡ Service suspended in Southern States.
§ This column is taken from Poor's Manual, and is made up at the end of the calendar year. The other columns represent the state of the service at the close of each fiscal year.

The figures in columns in reference to transportation are taken from the reports of the Second Assistant Postmaster-General.

TABLE E°.—*Statement of mail distributed en route on the cars by railway postal clerks during the fiscal year ended June 30, 1888 (exclusive of mail separated for city delivery).*

Division.	Number of letter packages distributed.	Whole number of letters distributed.	Number of sacks of second, third, and fourth class matter distributed.	Whole number of pieces of second, third, and fourth class matter distributed.	Whole number of letters and pieces of other matter distributed.	Number of packages and cars of registered matter distributed.	Number of through registered pouches handled.	Number of inner registered sacks.
First	7,492,783	299,711,320	1,056,422	158,403,300	458,174,620	1,137,771	53,161	31,587
Second	11,371,209	454,848,360	1,905,568	285,824,000	740,683,200	2,607,510	123,977	22,0?4
Third	4,854,319	194,172,710	878,744	131,811,600	325,964,360	1,041,787	67,859	23,7?0
Fourth	7,152,079	285,263,120	1,371,774	205,766,100	491,049,220	1,564,777	70,479	27,2?2
Fifth	16,843,492	673,739,680	3,212,268	481,840,200	1,155,579,880	2,213,015	168,298	16,411
Sixth	20,317,342	812,693,680	3,652,835	547,928,250	1,360,621,930	3,374,916	110,560	34,119
Seventh	17,111,364	684,454,560	2,969,623	443,943,450	1,128,398,010	2,218,067	91,604	8,5??
Eighth	3,653,428	146,137,120	550,099	83,514,830	228,651,970	888,551	24,937	9,79?
Ninth	9,496,951	379,878,160	1,731,671	259,750,650	639,628,810	804,685	130,822	8,29?
Total	98,272,969	3,930,918,760	17,319,022	2,597,853,300	6,528,772,060	16,001,030	841,593	261,4??
Total as per report for the fiscal year ended June 30,1887	90,266,660	3,614,221,825	14,803,127	2,220,469,050	5,834,000,875	15,752,560	816,112	134,501
Increase	8,006,309	316,696,935	2,515,895	377,384,250	694,681,185	248,490	25,481	1,6,???

The percentage of increase in number of pieces of—

Ordinary mail matter handled, 1888 over 1887, was... 8.76+

Ordinary mail matter handled, 1887 over 1886, was... 9.47+

Registered matter handled, 1888 over 1887, was .... 2.31+

Registered matter handled, 1887 over 1886, was .... 2.32+

TABLE F¹.—*Statement of errors made by postal clerks during fiscal year ended June 30, 1888.*

Division.	Incorrect slips returned.	Errors on incorrect slips.	Missent.					Misdirected.			Errors charged against postal clerks.	Errors charged against post-masters.
			Letter packages.	Pouches.	Sacks.	Registered packages.	Registered pouches and inner registered sacks.	Letter packages.	Pouches.	Sacks.		
First	18,136	31,683	1,929	725	174	73	11	66	64	26	27,615	35,90?
Second	55,428	107,525	1,862	1,344	378	179	34	216	74	78	96,780	97,?48
Third	45,816	105,955	541	67	47	33	5	102	15	36	119,100	68,013
Fourth	83,200	178,909	1,128	251	126	83	11	177	13	62	310,080	110,714
Fifth	132,482	365,117	3,112	373	279	62	6	541	115	356	342,288	170,5??
Sixth	146,079	369,816	3,788	969	400	29	....	836	125	349	638,424	112,7??
Seventh	128,868	358,908	2,417	1,000	917	311	37	658	101	347	617,077	1,1,7??
Eighth	10,844	19,118	193	7	3	4	....	86	12	4	61,053	29,2??
Ninth	79,858	228,790	1,735	1,122	322	19	....	237	28	169	84,181	74,9?0
Total	700,711	1,765,821	16,705	5,858	2,646	793	104	2,919	547	1,427	2,296,604	8?4,990
Total as per report for fiscal year ended June 30, 1887	697,513	1,734,617	17,498	6,016	2,685	971	105	2,894	653	1,277	2,257,014	616,365
Increase	3,198	31,204	*793	*158	*39	*178	*1	25	*106	150	39,590	208,625

* Decrease.

Number of letters and pieces of other mail distributed during the fiscal year ended June 30, 1888 6,545,876,302

Number of errors made in the distribution of the same 1,765,821

Number of letters and pieces of other mail matter distributed to each error, 1888 3,706

Number of letters and pieces of other mail matter distributed to each error, 1887 3,878

Percentage of correct distribution, 1888 .... .99.973

Percentage of correct distribution, 1887 .... .99.971

TABLE G.—*Statement of errors in the distribution and forwarding of mails by post-offices during the fiscal year ended June 30, 1888.*

Post-offices	Class	Division	No. of incorrect slips returned	No. of errors on incorrect slips	Missent — No. of letter packages	No. of pouches	No. of registered packages	No. of registered pouches	No. of inner registered sacks	No. of sacks	Misdirected — No. of letter packages	No. of pouches	No. of registered packages	No. of registered pouches	No. of inner registered sacks	No. of sacks	Errors checked — Against railway postal clerks	Against post-offices
Aberdeen, Dak	3	6	18	64	1						2						1	
Aberdeen, Miss	3	4	10	63														
Abilene, Kans	2	7	348	961	4						8						1	405	47
Abingdon, Va	3	3	34	38									1				9	13
Adrian, Mich	3	9	197	274							1						93	2
Aiken, S. C	3	4	64	142	1													
Akron, Ohio	2	5	504	1,022	14	1	2				7	4					3	308	724
Alameda, Cal	3	8	8	9							4							
Albany, Ga	3	4	17	72														
Albany, N. Y	1	2	1,306	2,173	26		1		1		12	9					2	188	131
Albany, Oregon	3	8	181	378	1						3						1,263	295
Albion, Mich	3	9	10	26								8						
Albuquerque, N. Mex	2	7	58	88	1		1				1						374	40
Alexandria, Va	2	3	98	107	1												85	125
Allegheny, Pa	1	2	711	1,184	22	1					6						1	151	281
Annapolis, Md	3	3	129	185	3	1	1				4						320	150
Anniston, Ala	3	4	105	295	5					1	1							
Ann Arbor, Mich	3	9	108	231	1												400	95
Anderson, S. C	3	4	25	82	1													
Anderson, Ind	3	5	28	34														
Anaconda, Mont	3	8	19	37														
Amsterdam, N. Y	2	2	210	273	2		1				2	1					321	265
Amherst, Mass	2	1	11	12			1										14	12
Amesbury, Mass	2	1	4	4	1												1	
Altoona, Pa	2	2	293	443	10		1										179	363
Alton, Ill	2	6	47	88							2							
Alpena, Mich	2	9	26	46	1							1					71	63
Alliance, Ohio	3	5	4	7							1							
Allentown, Pa	2	2	19	26													26	16
Ansonia, Conn	2	1	51	125							2	1					169	168
Appleton, Wis	2	6	248	527	11		1				1	2					201	147
Atchison, Kans	2	7	558	963	5	1					7						1,241	38
Athens, Ga	3	4	74	137													1	
Atlanta, Ga	1	4	5,320	10,102	81	3					3	25	5				8	2,349	675
Atlantic, Iowa	2	6	19	30	1						2	2					28
Atlantic City, N. J	2	2	56	69													115	80
Attica, Ind	3	5	40	52													45	192
Asbury Park, N. J	2	2	41	53	2							1					42	63
Ashland, Ohio	3	5	28	176	1												1	
Ashland, Ky	3	5			1		1											
Ashland, Oregon	3	8	1	1														
Ashland, Wis	2	6	17	43	1													
Ashtabula, Ohio	3	5	49	75	1		4				1						4	49
Asheville, N. C	2	3	138	243	1						1						502	125
Aspen, Colo	3	7	38	100	1												373	305
Astoria, Oregon	3	8	15	41													4	
Auburn, Cal	3	8	10	15	1	1												
Auburn, Me	2	1	48	85	2						2	1	1				11	47
Auburn, N. Y	2	2	331	528	5						2						773	409
Augusta, Ga	2	4	809	1,363	1		1				4	1					1	391	305
Augusta, Me	1	1	318	533	3						2						2	184	71
Aurora, Ill	2	6	93	138							6						75	1
Aurora, Ind	3	5	20	43	3													2
Austin, Tex	2	7	1,105	2,126	17	3	1				14	2					5	1,164	12
Baker City, Oregon	3	8	33	36							1							4
Bakersfield, Cal	3	8	13	60							2							
Baltimore, Md	1	3	2,834	4,219	54	2					2	8	2				6	957	570
Bangor, Me	1	1	107	168							4			1				29
Bainbridge, Ga	3	4																
Bartow, Fla	3	4	7	11								1						
Batavia, N. Y	2	2	92	223	1												19	96
Bath, Me	2	1	35	40	1						2						51	123
Bath, N. Y	2	1	14	15							2						2	2
Baton Rouge, La	2	4	370	622	7	1						1						

Table G6.—*Statement of errors in the distribution and forwarding of mails, etc.*—Cont'd.

Post-offices.	Class.	Division.	No. of incorrect slips returned.	No. of errors on incorrect slips.	Missent. No. of letter packages.	No. of pouches.	No. of registered packages.	No. of registered pouches.	No. of inner registered sacks.	No. of sacks.	Misdirected. No. of letter packages.	No. of pouches.	No. of registered packages.	No. of registered pouches.	No. of inner registered sacks.	No. of sacks.	Errors checked— Against railway postal clerks.	Against post-offices.
Battle Creek, Mich	2	9	47	84		4											1	
Bay City, Mich	2	9	167	281	2													
Beatrice, Nebr	2	6	59	118	2						1						739	274
Beaufort, S. C	3	4	11	28														
Beaver Falls, Pa	2	2	10?	184	7												83	24
Bel Air, Md	3	3	3	3														
Bellaire, Ohio	2	5	115	181	1	1					3						3	7
Bellefontaine, Ohio	3	5	17	49														
Belleville, Ill	2	6	59	153	2						1	1					11	
Beloit, Wis	2	6	69	134							2	1						
Benicia, Cal	3	8	12	16													3	
Benton Harbor, Mich	3	9	9	10														
Berkeley, Cal	3	8	19	65														
Berryville, Va	3	3	28	68													5	12
Bethlehem, Pa	2	2	27	37	1						2						12	7
Beverly, Mass	2	1	52	72							1						235	209
Biddeford, Me	2	1	120	192													269	133
Big Rapids, Mich	2	9	42	86							1							
Billings, Mont	3	8	62	94	1						5							
Binghamton, N. Y	1	2	194	418	6	3					6						65	13
Birmingham, Ala	2	4	3,806	7,530	22	3					10	17	1			2	4,328	283
Birmingham, Conn	2	1	47	62														
Bloomington, Ill	2	6	607	1,962	22						12	4			1			83
Bodie, Cal	3	8	9	15	2													
Boise City, Idaho	3	8	54	83													8	
Bolivar, Ohio	4	5																
Boston, Mass	1	1	11,572	21,643	327	8	25				7	114	7		1	25	1,652	3,089
Bowling Green, Ky	2	5	38	56							1						17	381
Bowling Green, Ohio	3	5	31	65							1						1	12
Bozeman, Mont	3	8	29	64														
Bradford, Pa	2	2	131	219	4	1					1	4					417	462
Brattleborough, Vt	2	1	40	119	2		1				2						204	218
Brazil, Ind	3	5	124	215			1					1					132	774
Bridgeport, Conn	1	1	403	693	13	1					14	4				2	561	291
Bridgeton, N. J	2	2	57	81													65	5J
Brockport, N. Y	2	2	8	9														
Brockton, Mass	2	1	44	61							3						43	99
Brooklyn, N. Y	1	2	5,184	7,553	51	1					2	35	1			4	3,280	11,323
Brunswick, Ga	2	4	64	199	2													
Bryan, Ohio	3	9	10	13													265	
Bucyrus, Ohio	3	5	18	34							2							
Buffalo, N. Y	1	2	1,067	2,508	62	1	8	1			12	6	1			7	118	211
Burlington, Iowa	1	6	115	166	2						2						257	14
Burlington, Vt	2	1	126	1,095	1						3	1			1		121	43
Butte City, Mont	2	8	109	133													43	
Cadillac, Mich	3	9		22													65	9
Cambridge, Ohio	3	5	93	205			1				1						93	111
Cairo, Ill	2	6	57	107	2												8	18
Camden, N. J	2	2	61	66	1						1	3					18	70
Camden, S. C	3	4	5	6														
Canandaigua, N. Y	2	2	45	68													45	46
Canton, Ohio	2	5	261	522	12	1	4				7	3						
Canton, Miss	3	4	20	40	1													
Carlisle, Pa	2	2	211	339	6						2	1				2	1	
Carson City, Nev	3	8	14	15													23	
Cartersville, Ga	3	4	3	6														
Carthage, Mo	2	7	91	198							1						301	171
Catskill, N. Y	2	2	34	31	1	1					1						71	113
Cedar Rapids, Iowa	2	6	650	2,040	25		8				9	1					114	
Chambersburgh, Pa	2	2	148	245	6	1					1						390	64
Champaign, Ill	2	6	39	81	6						1	3					112	17
Charleston, S. C	1	4	940	1,480	10	2	1				1					1	1,410	941
Charleston, W. Va	2	3	72	86													184	191
Charlestown, W. Va	3	3	41	56													20	24
Charlotte, N. C	3	3	420	883	8	5					3	3	2			1	714	179

TABLE G⁸.—*Statement of errors in the distribution and forwarding of mails, etc.*—Cont'd.

Post-offices.	Class.	Division.	No. of incorrect slips returned.	No. of errors on incorrect slips.	Missent.						Misdirected.						Errors checked—	
					No. of letter packages.	No. of pouches.	No. of registered packages.	No. of registered pouches.	No. of inner registered sacks.	No. of sacks.	No. of letter packages.	No. of pouches.	No. of registered packages.	No. of registered pouches.	No. of inner registered sacks.	No. of sacks.	Against railway postal clerks.	Against post-offices.
Charlotte, Mich..........	2	9	23	52	1						1						88	38
Chattanooga, Tenn........	1	5	1,196	2,393	11	1				4	4					4	1,254	2,37
Charlottesville, Va.......	3	3	298	687	5												341	80
Cheboygan, Mich..........	3	9	53	78							1							
Cheney, Wash	3	8	7	18														
Chester, Pa..............	2	2	205	298	7		1				1						1,041	708
Chester, S.C	3	4	35	117														
Cheyenne, Wyo...........	2	6	321	692	1						2						1,022	224
Chicago, Ill.............	1	6	22,135	30,967	24						51							
Chico, Cal..............	3	8	2	2							1							
Chillicothe, Ohio........	2	5	103	162	4	1					1	6					43	51
Chippewa Falls, Wis......	2	6	18	40														
Cincinnati, Ohio.........	1	5	5,971	10,003	91	4				4	71	1				12	14,700	13,238
Clarksburgh, W. Va.......	3	3	55	84	1												65	712
Clarksville, Tenn	2	5	1	1								1						2
Clay Centre, Kans	2	7	18	62											1		19	19
Cleveland, Ohio..........	1	5	2,599	3,857	49	1	2			1	21					10	73	332
Cleveland, Tenn	3	5	6	8													13	16
Clinton, Iowa............	2	6	110	233	12						1					1	59	74
Clinton, Mass............	2	1	14	28													9	4
Cohoes, N.Y.............	2	2	100	143							1						187	109
Coldwater, Mich..........	2	9	231	399							2	1					1,955	31
Colorado Springs, Colo....	2	7	201	448	1			1	1		1						2,316	335
Colton, Cal..............	3	8	17	60							1						8	
Columbia, Mo............	2	7	6	3	.2								1				16	
Columbia, S.C	3	4	93	118												3	505	208
Columbia, Tenn	3	5	62	100													36	187
Columbia City, Ind.......	3	5	26	105							1							46
Columbus, Ind...........	2	5	81	144	1	5					3							
Columbus, Ga	2	4	454	723		2					2						814	358
Columbus, Kans	2	7	156	296							3						309	20
Columbus, Miss..........	3	4	105	177														
Columbus, Ohio..........	1	5	1,410	2,238	30	1					10	4				12	265	618
Colusa, Cal.............	3	8	9	13						2							168	107
Concord, N.H	2	1	80	39	2	1					1						9	126
Concord, N.C	3	3	11	24													136	70
Connersville, Ind	3	5	11	23														3
Corinth, Miss	3	4	30	62														
Corning, N.Y............	2	2	52	72							1							1
Corry, Pa...............	2	2	111	190	2	4					6	2					126	52
Cortland, N.Y	2	2	107	252													38	
Coshocton, Ohio..........	3	5	4	10		1					1							
Corvallis, Oregon.........	3	8	24	46														
Crawfordsville, Ind	2	5	251	593	9						1					1	20	63
Council Bluffs, Iowa	2	6	201	344							3	1					406	168
Covington, Ky	2	5	358	499	4	1					4					1	219	509
Creston, Iowa............	2	6	315	573	7						1	1					1,973	115
Culpepper, Va	3	3	3	5														
Cumberland, Md	2	3	40	100	3												109	69
Cuyahoga Falls, Ohio......	3	5	13	49	1													54
Dallas, Tex..............	1	7	775	1,638	8		7		2	1	9	2			1	1	752	11
Dalton, Ga..............	3	4	6	20														
Danbury, Conn	2	1	39	45							1						6	3
Danville, Ky............	3	5	13	24							1							
Danville, Ill............	2	6	64	100							1						763	151
Danville, Ind...........	3	5	107	208							5							
Danville, Pa............	2	2	20	53							1						7	7
Danville, Va............	2	3	595	1,090	6						3						826	277
Dansville, N.Y	2	2	5	11							1							
Darlington, S.C..........	3	4	35	121														
Davenport, Iowa.........	1	6	249	521	14						5	1				1	135	1
Dayton, Ohio............	1	5	774	1,174	9	2					19					2	149	321
Decatur, Ala	3	4	77	164	23													
Decatur, Ill.............	2	6	194	416	8						2	1				2	3,147	1,374
Deer Lodge City, Mont....	3	8	24	43														

TABLE G⁸.—*Statement of errors in the distribution and forwarding of mails, etc.*—Cont'd.

Post-offices.	Class.	Division.	No. of incorrect slips returned.	No. of errors on incorrect slips.	Missent.						Misdirected.						Errors checked—	
					No. of letter packages.	No. of pouches.	No. of registered packages.	No. of registered pouches.	No. of inner registered sacks.	No. of sacks.	No. of letter packages.	No. of pouches.	No. of registered packages.	No. of registered pouches.	No. of inner registered sacks.	No. of sacks.	Against railway postal clerks.	Against post-offices.
Defiance, Ohio	3	5	5	7			4											
De Land, Fla	3	4	15	35														
Delaware, Ohio	2	5	189	316	1													
Delphos, Ohio	3	5	5												1			
Dennison, Ohio	4	5	3	7	2													
Denison, Texas	2	7	83	194		2					3	1					366	31
Denver, Colo	1	7	2,902	4,576	80	11	2	1		4	40	7				2	853	1,026
Des Moines, Iowa	1	6	1,532	4,482	92	1				1	10	7				4	710	71
Detroit, Mich	1	9	2,405	4,480	43		3				14	1				12	240	65
Dillon, Mont	3	8	37	57							1							
Dixon, Cal	3	8	9	9														
Dixon, Ill	2	6	57	131	17						1						60	
Dodge City, Kans	2	7	80	130		1					1						179	103
Dover, N. H	2	1	12	19													1	1
Dubuque, Iowa	1	6	302	484	6	3					1						456	323
Duluth, Minn	2	6	444	1,014	2						2							1
Dunkirk, N. Y	2	2	42	51													100	51
Durham, N. C	3	3	46	122													112	37
Eagle Rock, Idaho	3	8	20	38							1							
East Liverpool, Ohio	2	5	68	147							6						23	55
Easton, Pa	2	2	49	97	3	2					1	3					30	87
East Orange, N. J	2	2	43	72							3	4					207	31
East Portland, Oregon	3	8	381	775													207	31
East Saginaw, Mich	2	9	236	388	7	1	1				2						138	29
Eau Claire, Wis	2	6	92	162												1	217	114
Elgin, Ill	2	6	516	868												1	1	
Elizabeth, N. J	2	2	54	57	1	1					1	1					152	151
Ellensburgh, Wash	3	8	9	13														
Elizabeth City, N. C	3	3	6	9														
Elkhart, Ind	2	5	145	280		1					2						3	
Elkton, Md	3	3																
Ellicott City, Md	3	3	9	10													17	8
Elmira, N. Y	2	7	357	517	2						3							1
El Paso, Tex	2	7	68	97							3						369	20
Elyria, Ohio	2	5	72	124	1						2							
Emmitsburgh, Md	3	3	2	3														
Emporia, Kans	2	7	63	96												1	162	105
Englewood, Ill	2	0	295	410													1,648	579
Erie, Pa	1	2	274	482	10						6	2				1	2,275	278
Eufaula, Ala	3	4	10	31														
Eugene City, Oregon	3	8	214	366	5												355	43
Eureka, Cal	2	8	31	62		1											29	
Eureka, Nev	3	8	9	13							3							
Evanston, Ill	2	6	54	98							3						61	10
Evansville, Ind	2	5	331	547	11		1				7					4	305	1,419
Fairbury, Nebr	2	6			1	1		1									30	
Fairmount, W. Va	3	3	1	2													20	7
Fall River, Mass	2	1	80	90	5		1				2							
Fargo, Dak	2	6	29	100													3	
Faribault, Minn	2	6	41	133	1						1						213	105
Farmville, Va	3	3	17	21													1	
Fayetteville, N. C	3	3	35	48													132	58
Fernandina, Fla	3	4	157	289	1				1									
Findlay, Ohio	2	5	85	109	3						1						27	82
Fitchburgh, Mass	2	1	40	69	3		1										137	
Flint, Mich	2	9	79	122	3													
Florence, Ala	3	4	8	12														
Florence, S. C	3	4	39	76	2													
Fond du Lac, Wis	2	6	12	22														
Fortress Monroe, Va	3	3	28	80	1													
Fort Benton, Mont	3	8	5	6							1							
Fort Dodge, Iowa	2	6	33	65							1							
Fort Gratiot, Mich	3	9	9	21							7							
Fort Scott, Kans	2	7	153	228		1					1	2	2			4	948	256
Fort Smith, Ark	2	7	287	685	2	1		1									576	271

TABLE G6.—*Statement of errors in the distribution and forwarding of mails, etc.—Cont'd.*

Post-offices.	Class.	Division.	No. of incorrect slips returned.	No. of errors on incorrect slips.	Missent. No. of letter packages.	No. of pouches.	No. of registered packages.	No. of registered pouches.	No. of inner registered sacks.	No. of sacks.	Misdirected. No. of letter packages.	No. of pouches.	No. of registered packages.	No. of registered pouches.	No. of inner registered sacks.	No. of sacks.	Errors checked— Against railway postal clerks.	Against post-offices.
Fort Wayne, Ind	2	5	138	266	15						1	1						3
Fort Worth, Tex	2	7	303	580	6	1	1		1	2	3					1	361	29
Fostoria, Ohio	3	5	59	147	3	2					2							
Frankfort, Ind	3	5	24	51	2												11	139
Frankfort, Ky	2	5	332	789													11	80
Franklin, Ind	3	5	20	60														
Franklin, Ky	3	5	82	132													31	169
Franklin, Pa	2	2	188	424	4	1											257	118
Franklin, Tenn	3	5	102	173							1						373	889
Frederick, Md	2	3	32	75	1											1	91	75
Fredericksburgh, Va	3	3	48	75	1												119	53
Fredonia, N. Y	2	2	198	550	1						8						205	113
Freeport, Ill	2	6	21	65		1											194	12
Fremont, Nebr	2	6	57	79													143	37
Fremont, Ohio	2	5	22	56	1							1						
Fresno City, Cal	3	8	55	77	3						2	2						
Frostburgh, Md	3	3															4	2
Fullerton, Nebr	2	6	1	2														
Gadsden, Ala	3	4	57	60														
Gainesville, Fla	3	4	71	148														
Gainesville, Ga	3	4	14	83														
Gainesville, Tex	2	7	165	428	2						2		1				828	
Galesburgh, Ill	2	6	212	500	1						2					2	212	89
Gallatin, Tenn	3	5	37	96	7													
Galveston, Tex	1	7	857	1,238	2		1			8						8	1,022	512
Garden City, Kans	2	7	110	151													99	100
Geneva, N. Y	2	2	163	212					1		1						472	99
Georgetown, S. C	3	4	113	180	4													
Glasgow, Ky	5	5	16	25						1								
Glen Allen, Va	3	3	6	22													48	25
Glens Falls, N. Y	2	2	29	30	1												20	
Gloucester, Mass	2	1	51	140	2						2						193	131
Gloversville, N. Y	2	2	64	77													140	113
Goldsborough, N.C	3	3	52	70													299	70
Gordonsville, Va	3	3	12	29													8	
Grafton, W. Va	3	3	1	1														22
Grand Forks, Dak	2	6	27	69	1						1						42	38
Grand Haven, Mich	3	9	19	28	2												77	66
Grand Rapids, Mich	1	9	505	1,074	3						7	1				2	121	13
Grass Valley, Cal	3	8	29	42							2	2					51	
Green Bay, Wis	2	6	39	56														
Greenfield, Ind	3	5	63	336														
Greenfield, Mass	2	1	30	85	1											1	6	10
Greensborough, N.C	3	3	96	266	7											1	501	68
Greensburgh, Ind	3	5	115	214	4						2		2				4	26
Greenville, Mich	3	9	29	48									3				41	13
Greenville, Miss	3	4	31	68														
Greenville, S. C	2	4	64	111							1	1					550	103
Greenville, Ohio	3	5	27	39	1		1				2							
Grenada, Miss	3	4	2	23		1												
Griffin, Ga	3	4	49	97							1							
Hagerstown, Md	2	3	306	572	3		2						1				484	184
Hamilton, Ohio	2	5	141	226	3						5	1					263	383
Hammond, Ind	5	5	56	72							2						4	149
Hampton, Va	3	3	53	140	1						1	1					32	34
Hanford, Cal	3	8	19	35													16	
Hannibal, Mo	2	7	206	522	5				1								1	110
Harrisburg, Pa	1	2	529	802	42						8	8					20	137
Harrisonburgh, Va	3	3	40	70							1						134	126
Harrodsburgh, Ky	3	5	84	105			1				1	1					1	83
Hartford, Conn	1	1	785	1,310	20				3	1	8	1				2	1,757	2,704
Hastings, Nebr	2	6	155	600	14	3					3					8		
Havre de Grace, Md	3	3	4	14														
Haverhill, Mass	2	1	120	197	2						6	5					486	767
Hazleton, Pa	2	2	8	14													81	17

TABLE G8.—*Statement of errors in the distribution and forwarding of mails, etc.*—Cont'd.

Post-offices.	Class.	Division.	No. of incorrect slips returned.	No. of errors on incorrect slips.	Missent.						Misdirected.						Errors checked—	
					No. of letter packages.	No. of pouches.	No. of registered packages.	No. of registered pouches.	No. of inner registered sacks.	No. of sacks.	No. of letter packages.	No. of pouches.	No. of registered packages.	No. of registered pouches.	No. of inner registered sacks.	No. of sacks.	Against railway postal clerks.	Against post offices.
Healdsburgh, Cal	3	8	3	7			1										8	10
Helena, Mont	2	8	65	114	1												9	10
Henderson, Ky	3	5	71	99							1						37	188
Henderson, N.C	3	3	23	47													138	54
Hillsborough, Ohio	3	5	97	193	2							1				1	85	148
Hillsdale, Mich	2	9	28	43							1							7
Hoboken, N.J	2	2	27	30	2												92	98
Hollister, Cal	3	8	2	2														
Holly Springs, Miss	3	4	6	53														
Holyoke, Mass	2	1	151	219	2						3	3					219	225
Hopkinsville, Ky	3	5	129	245													258	381
Hornellsville, N.Y	2	2	30	62							1						2	18
Hot Springs, Ark	2	7	431	602	2							3					2,708	215
Houston, Tex	2	7	284	560	8	1					2					2	430	46
Hudson, Mich	3	9	14	40													19	
Hudson, N.Y	2	2	62	124													29	43
Huntingdon, Pa	2	2	35	91	1						1						1	
Huntington, Ind	3	5	8	10	1						1					1		
Huntington, W.Va	3	3	157	298	1												45	53
Huntsville, Ala	3	4	115	305														
Huron, Dak	2	6	78	155							1						405	96
Hutchinson, Kans	2	7	44	54	1						1					1	6	21
Hyde Park, Mass	2	1	16	9	1												61	34
Indianapolis, Ind	1	5	1,978	5,379	70	3			1	18	1				41		85	1208
Ionia, Mich	2	9	36	75	1	4					1							11
Iowa City, Iowa	2	6	102	406	1	5					1					1	1	
Ironton, Ohio	2	5	24	47							1							
Ithaca, N.Y	2	2	114	237	2						1						119	16
Jackson, Mich	2	9	357	588	4	1					2						13	35
Jackson, Miss	2	4	274	703	1						1							
Jacksonville, Fla	2	4	755	995	1	1					1						429	206
Jacksonville, Ill	2	6	93	203	5						2						250	48
Jacksonville, Oregon	3	8	5	10														
Jamestown, N.Y	2	2	54	102							1						43	109
Janesville, Wis	2	6	23	44	8												170	
Jefferson City, Mo	2	7	95	147	3						1						1,287	345
Jeffersonville, Ind	3	5	41	83	2													
Jersey City, N.J	1	2	625	1,187	10	3						7				1	194	98
Johnstown, N.Y	2	2	52	77							2						34	20
Johnstown, Pa	2	2	288	39?	2	1					1						1,012	691
Joliet, Ill	2	6	336	791	9	1					5						456	127
Kalamazoo, Mich	2	9	213	484	6						6					1		89
Kankakee, Ill	2	6	52	217	7												197	
Kansas City, Kans	2	7	469	951	8	1					2	1				2	1,019	550
Kansas City, Mo	1	7	11,560	24,088	364	8	26		1	10	128	7			25		14,888	7,760
Kearney, Nebr	2	6	54	123	6												155	16
Keene, N.H	2	1	22	27							1							53
Kent, Ohio	3	5	7	10														7
Keokuk, Iowa	2	6	77	179	1	1					1					1		
Key West, Fla	3	4	182	490		2					1						23	8
Kingston, N.Y	2	2	32	49		1					1	1					97	22
Kinston, N.C	3	3	4	4													20	316
Knightstown, Ind	3	5	35	81	1												20	157
Knoxville, Tenn	2	4	1,314	2,641	2						15						92	157
Kokomo, Ind	3	5	6	13							2						25	408
Kosciusko, Miss	3	4	8	16														
La Crosse, Wis	2	6	29	53	1	1					1					1	109	20
La Fayette, Ind	2	5	244	513	3	1	1				2	2				6		
Lake Charles, La	3	4	5	17														
Lancaster, Ohio	3	5	5															
Lancaster, Pa	2	2	428	902	24	1					2	1				1	189	476
Lansing, Mich	2	9	148	217	2						5					1	16	
Lapeer, Mich	3	9											1					
La Porte, Ind	2	5	39	62	1						4							

Table G6.—*Statement of errors in the distribution and forwarding of mails, etc.*—Cont'd.

Post-offices.	Class.	Division.	No. of incorrect slips returned.	No. of errors on incorrect slips.	Missent. No. of letter packages.	No. of pouches.	No. of registered packages.	No. of registered pouches.	No. of inner registered sacks.	No. of sacks.	Misdirected. No. of letter packages.	No. of pouches.	No. of registered packages.	No. of registered pouches.	No. of inner registered sacks.	No. of sacks.	Errors checked— Against railway postal clerks.	Against post-offices.
Las Vegas, N. Mex	3	7	112	242	5		14		2							1	3,586	1C4
Lawrence, Kans	2	7	1,012	1,950	2						5						470	177
Lawrence, Mass	2	1	56	71							3						12	157
Lawrenceburgh, Ind	3	5	241	472		1					2						202	601
Leadville, Colo	2	7	705	1,051	5	4					2						3,087	2,097
Leavenworth, Kans	2	7	590	1,133	2	1				1	14					6	151	110
Lebanon, Ky	3	5	47	120							4		1				79	179
Lebanon, Ohio	3	6	45	100	2						4					2		
Lebanon, Pa	2	2	271	450							1						331	46
Leesburgh, Fla	3	4																
Leesburgh, Va	3	3																
Le Mars, Iowa	2	6	22	96	1						2							
Le Roy, N. Y	2	2	11	19													1	2
Lewiston, Me	2	1	37	98													21	94
Lexington, Ky	2	5	202	362	3	1					1	1					1	
Lexington, Va	3	3	90	126							2						84	50
Liberty, Va	3	3	167	285													725	349
Lima, Ohio	2	5	141	235	3						1						53	97
Lincoln, Ill	2	6	7	7														
Lincoln, Nebr	1	6	650	1,304						1	2						627	141
Little Falls, N. Y	2	2	65	103	10						2						282	41
Little Rock, Ark	2	7	803	1,404	7	4	8		1	2	8	3				3	391	152
Livingston, Mont	3	8	14	15							1							
Lock Haven, Pa	2	2	69	108							1						195	61
Lockport, N. Y	2	2	120	80									1				105	80
Logan, Utah	3	8	6	18													24	201
Logansport, Ind	2	5	41	51														
Los Angeles, Cal	1	8	1,892	2,449	8						11	1					3,145	1,536
Louisville, Ky	1	5	3,710	6,924	40	10				8	14	2				6		
Lowell, Mass	1	1	161	292	12	2					7	1				1	152	73
Ludington, Mich	3	9	6	6														
Lynchburgh, Va	2	3	538	926	6	2					1						703	320
Lynn, Mass	1	1	197	500							2						172	296
McKeesport, Pa	2	2	69	145	3						1						16	20
Macon, Ga	2	4	947	1,256	19						8	2					712	601
Madison, Ind	2	5	47	79														
Madison, Wis	2	6	82	126													105	11
Madisonville, Ky	3	5	22	51														106
Malden, Mass	2	1	25	105							1						1	4
Malone, N. Y	2	2	36	44													112	98
Manchester, N. H	2	1	119	345	2						2					1	127	284
Mankato, Minn	2	6	42	63	2						1		1				106	38
Manistee, Mich	2	9	66	108													299	106
Mansfield, Ohio	2	5	80	159		1										1	1	30
Marion, S. C	3	4	11	36														
Marietta, Ga	3	4	71	141													27	161
Marietta, Ohio	2	5	71	92	2						4						165	1
Marquette, Mich	2	6	63	96	2												10	4
Marshall, Mich	2	9	21	24													226	22
Marshalltown, Iowa	2	6	57	154	2						1							
Martin, Tenn	4	5					4										8	4
Martinez, Cal	3	8	15	21	1		4											
Martinsburgh, W. Va	3	3	12	17														39
Martinsville, Ind	3	5	18	28														
Marysville, Cal	2	8	32	59	1												6	
Massillon, Ohio	2	5	4	4	1								1					
Mattoon, Ill	2	6	74	203														
Maysville, Ky	2	5	113	139							1						31	19
Meadville, Pa	2	2	43	95	1											2	31	49
Medina, Ohio	3	5	71	211							2					2	169	481
Melrose, Mass	2	1	5	9													7	5
Memphis, Tenn	1	5	894	1,873														2
Merced, Cal	3	8	55	101	2	1					3	2					49	
Meriden, Conn	2	1	257	579	3						4						298	328
Meridian, Miss	2	4	187	243							1						121	

Table G⁶.—*Statement of errors in the distribution and forwarding of mails, etc.*—Cont'd.

Post-offices.	Class	Division	No. of incorrect slips returned.	No. of errors on incorrect slips.	Missent.						Misdirected.						Errors checked—	
					No. of letter packages.	No. of pouches.	No. of registered packages.	No. of registered pouches.	No. of inner registered sacks.	No. of sacks.	No. of letter packages.	No. of pouches.	No. of registered packages.	No. of registered pouches.	No. of inner registered sacks.	No. of sacks.	Against railway postal clerks.	Against post-offices.
Michigan City, Ind	3	5	13	24														3
Middletown, Conn	2	1	50	119	3													
Middletown, N.Y.	2	2	72	92		2											52	12
Middletown, Ohio	2	5	99	308								8					165	488
Milford, Mass	2	1	5	17			3											
Miles City, Mont	3	8	5	5														
Milwaukee, Wis	1	6	2,290	3,582	12						22	3				2	1,652	1,657
Minneapolis, Minn	1	6	1,729	3,930	28	2	1	1		4	30	2						
Missoula, Mont	3	8	38	67							1							
Mitchell, Dak	2	6	49	77	4			1				1					308	503
Moberly, Mo	2	7	17	9	5	2					2					1	3	3
Mobile, Ala	2	4	659	1,189	11	2			1		11					16	13	22
Modesto, Cal	3	8	32	64			1										74	36
Molino, Ill	2	6	31	72							1	1					59	21
Monmouth, Ill	2	6	84	171	5		1				1							
Monroe, Mich	3	9	75	153	1												1,091	279
Monterey, Cal	3	8	23	36													53	
Montgomery, Ala	2	4	645	994	5	1	4										519	51
Montpelier, Vt	2	1	22	45	2						2	1					107	103
Morgantown, W. Va	3	3																
Morristown, N.J.	2	2	11	33							1						65	10
Moundsville, W. Va	3	3	5	8													.	
Mount Pleasant, Iowa	2	6	30	58	1													10
Mount Sterling, Ky	3	5	23	48							4							
Mount Vernon, N.Y.	2	2	9	23													173	817
Mount Vernon, Ohio	2	5	37	77							2						160	770
Muncie, Ind	2	5	13	35														
Marlborough, Mass	2	1	32	59							2						389	302
Muscatine, Iowa	2	6	115	233	1						1						77	20
Muskegon, Mich	2	9	38	47							1						350	45
Napa City, Cal	2	8	10	11													133	44
Nashua, N.H.	2	1	22	30													12	5
Nashville, Tenn	1	5	4,071	10,041	19					1	8	1				4	603	704
Natchez, Miss	2	4	12	435							1						135	46
National Stock Yards, Ill.	2	6	119	372							1						70	
Nebraska City, Nebr.	2	6	114	277	9				1	1	1						1,246	8
Nevada City, Cal	3	8	141	235	6												197	188
Newark, N.J.	1	2	2,079	3,968	19	26				6	17	2				1	149	140
Newark, Ohio	2	5	173	351	15	2					2	1					1	217
New Albany, Ind	2	5	172	261	11						2						56	979
New Bedford, Mass	1	1	147	290	4		1				6						213	451
New Berne, N.C.	3	3	30	47													283	90
Newberry, S.C.	3	4	30	39														
New Britain, Conn	2	1	60	68								1						99
New Brunswick, N.J.	2	2	102	185	1						2						9	99
Newburgh, N.Y.	2	2	41	50	2												221	419
Newburyport, Mass	2	1	44	92								3					19	19
New Castle, Ind	3	5	4	26	1												30	95
New Castle, Pa	2	2	50	82													34	6
New Haven, Conn	1	1	478	1,115	20						10					2	534	93
New London, Conn	2	1	34	55	2						1						10	12
New Orleans, La.	1	4	6,564	10,585	97	2	1				33	1				19	98	72
Newport, Ky	2	5	188	307	9												32	24
Newport, R.I.	2	1	20	316	1						3						44	20
Newport News, Va	3	3	66	87							1						3	20
New Ross, Ind	4	5	5	9													20	39
Newton, Kans	2	7	165	280		1	4		1								36	19
Newton, Mass	2	1	54	77							3						66	65
New York, N.Y.	1	2	68,001	148,755	479	0	8	1			14	397	5			75	18,901	2,030
Nicholasville, Ky	3	5	86	33														
Niles, Mich	3	9	9	20							1						3	
North Adams, Mass	2	1	109	206	1		2										135	195
Norfolk, Va	1	3	446	612	3						1	2	1				500	391
Northampton, Mass	2	1	24	44	3						1						7	
Northfield, Conn	2	1	6	20													33	26

Table G⁶.—*Statement of errors in the distribution and forwarding of mails, etc.*—Cont'd.

Post-offices.	Class.	Division.	No. of incorrect slips returned.	No. of errors on incorrect slips.	Missent.						Misdirected.						Errors checked—	
					No. of letter packages.	No. of pouches.	No. of registered packages.	No. of registered pouches.	No. of inner registered sacks.	No. of sacks.	No. of letter packages.	No. of pouches.	No. of registered packages.	No. of registered pouches.	No. of inner registered sacks.	No. of sacks.	Against railway postal clerks.	Against post-offices.
North Manchester, Ind	3	5	30	65														1
North Yakima, Wash	3	8	18	27		1												
Norristown, Pa	2	2																
Norwalk, Conn	2	1	47	60	1		1						3				14	8
Norwalk, Ohio	2	5	60	97									3				213	972
Norwich, Conn	2	1	39	45	1								2				36	12
Norwich, N. Y	2	2	22	71														
Oakland, Cal	1	8	478	760	4		1						5				352	224
Oak Park, Ill	2	6	1	1														
Ocala, Fla	3	4	117	364	1													
Ogden, Utah	2	8	109	171													74	4
Ogdensburgh, N. Y	2	2	55	77													1	
Oil City, Pa	2	2	25	33	7	2							1	1			13	16
Olean, N. Y	2	2	59	97													22	17
Olympia, Wash	3	8	111	183	5								2				658	164
Omaha, Nebr	1	6	2,005	4,225	18				2	10	2					4	1,543	1,846
Oneida, N. Y	2	2	54	93	1						2					2	36	24
Oneonta, N. Y	2	2	47	56							1						125	69
Opelika, Ala	3	4	58	81														
Orange, N. J	2	2	22	24							1						5	14
Orangeburgh, S. C	3	4	25	34														
Oregon City, Oregon	3	8	108	198							1						297	18
Orlando, Fla	3	4	80	179				1								1	238	37
Oroville, Cal	3	8	34	92													16	
Oskaloosa, Iowa	2	6	158	443	21						1	4	1				1,134	101
Oshkosh, Wis	2	6	65	108		3							2				7	25
Ottawa, Ill	2	6	92	58	2												118	79
Ottumwa, Iowa	2	6	201	449	11		3										280	115
Ottawa, Kans	2	7	82	185							1						77	24
Oswego, N. Y	2	2	68	123		2					1							
Owego, N. Y	2	2	44	71							1							
Owensborough, Ky	3	5	83	136													94	1,517
Oxford, N. C	3	3	4	9														
Paducah, Ky	2	5	206	376	4								3	1			50	229
Painesville, Ohio	2	5	137	313	3												90	829
Palatka, Fla	2	4	273	379	13												755	196
Palestine, Tex	2	7	43	103				1									183	4
Paris, Tex	2	7	35	136	1	2											153	3
Park City, Utah	3	8	91	172													7	
Parkersburgh, W. Va	2	3	88	169	7											1	60	42
Parsons, Kans	2	7	26	29		5											236	49
Pasadena, Cal	2	8	291	467												1	968	173
Paterson, N. J	2	2	26	47		2					1	2					13	28
Pawtucket, R. I	2	1	77	103	1		1										332	127
Peekskill, N. Y	2	2	6	7	1												36	24
Pekin, Ill	2	6	72	146	2								2				127	63
Pendleton, Oregon	3	8	67	136	3												92	12
Penn Yan, N. Y	2	2	14	30													1,120	316
Pensacola, Fla	2	4	369	537							1	1					7,401	299
Peoria, Ill	1	6	825	1,628	12								1	7			4	12
Peru, Ind	2	5	51	104	1												30	8
Petaluma, Cal	3	8	2	2													133	54
Petersburgh, Va	2	3	101	258	1								1				10	
Petoskey, Mich	3	9	10	10													741	455
Philadelphia, Pa	1	2	12,404	29,010	143	18			1	16	77	6				44		
Phœnix, Ariz	3	8	27	39														2
Piedmont, W. Va	3	3															479	18
Pine Bluff, Ark	2	7	142	252	1						1						96	760
Piqua, Ohio	2	5	142	331												6	6,037	2,310
Pittsburgh, Pa	1	2	3,902	5,470	89	4	1			2	26						121	134
Pittsfield, Mass	2	1	89	202	8	1	4				3						29	184
Pittston, Pa	2	2	25	54								2					251	219
Placerville, Cal	3	8	13	45													245	369
Plainfield, N. J	2	2	31	42													8	22
Plattsburgh, N. Y	2	2	96	112	1	4				1	1	1	1			1		

TABLE G⁸.—*Statement of errors in the distribution and forwarding of mails, etc.*—Cont'd.

Post-offices.	Class.	Division.	No. of incorrect slips returned.	No. of errors on incorrect slips.	Missent. No. of letter packages.	No. of pouches.	No. of registered packages.	No. of registered pouches.	No. of inner registered sacks.	No. of sacks.	Misdirected. No. of letter packages.	No. of pouches.	No. of registered packages.	No. of registered pouches.	No. of inner registered sacks.	No. of sacks.	Errors Checked— Against railway postal clerks.	Against post-offices.
Plymouth, Mass	2	1	53	60													455	423
Pomona, Cal	3	8	43	133														
Pontiac, Mich	2	9	62	116													18	17
Portland, Ind	3	6	22	168	1													
Portland, Mo	1	1	943	1,612	31		20			1	10					1	484	470
Portland, Oregon	1	8	266	346	2						4						75	
Port Deposit, Md	3	3																
Port Huron, Mich	2	9	55	92													24	1
Port Jervis, N. Y	2	2	22	25							1						1	8
Port Townsend, Wash	3	8	69	110	1												75	22
Portsmouth, N. H	2	1	34	49													28	83
Portsmouth, Ohio	2	5	49	90													14	53
Portsmouth, Va	8	3	54	67							1						82	100
Pottstown, Pa	2	2	12	55													27	25
Pottsville, Pa	2	2	7	7							1						3	3
Poughkeepsie, N. Y	2	2	197	631	2						3	1				2	174	23
Princeton, Ind	3	5	1	1	2												19	
Princeton, N. J	2	2	37	47	5		1										10	
Providence, R. I	1	1	572	935	19	5	1				6	5				2	174	320
Provo City, Utah	3	8	26	50														
Pueblo, Colo	2	7	852	1,677	10		15		2		7	1				1	721	418
Pulaski, Tenn	3	5	34	61													102	180
Quincy, Ill	1	6	350	584	33	1					5	1					177	10
Racine, Wis	2	0	184	292												2	378	
Raleigh, N. C	2	3	307	504	2		2										216	100
Rapid City, Dak	2	6	2	6														
Reading, Pa	1	2	143	233	2								1				8	45
Red Bluff, Cal	3	8	2	2														
Rod Wing, Minn	2	6	135	283							3						88	41
Reidsville, N. C	3	3	134	246												1	719	140
Reno, Nev	3	8	33	52	5												17	
Rensselaer, Ind	3	5	6	8			1											104
Richmond, Ind	2	6	205	386	4													104
Richmond, Va	1	3	1,629	2,954	49	6					7	23	3			2	687	472
Rising Sun, Ind	4	5	33	48													30	177
Riverside, Cal	3	8	72	99	2												7	
Roanoke, Va	2	3	260	431	2		2				1						191	49
Rochester, Minn	2	6	20	29													13	
Rochester, N. Y	1	2	2,332	4,031	54	1				1	29	3				6	442	120
Rockford, Ill	1	6	510	861	2						1					1	1,520	331
Rock Island, Ill	2	6	123	378	1						1						46	19
Rockland, Me	2	1	24	36													29	35
Rome, Ga	2	4	214	249							1						483	115
Rome, N. Y	2	2	69	234			2				1						20	4
Rondout, N. Y	2	2	7	11		1					1						1	185
Roseburgh, Oregon	3	8	11	18		1												
Rushville, Ind	3	5	80	167													17	67
Rutland, Vt	2	1	141	229	8	1					5					1	74	68
Sacramento, Cal	1	8	331	462	7						7						376	170
Saint Albans, Vt	2	1	11	12	1						2						6	5
Saint Augustine, Fla	3	4	752	1,311							2							
Saint Cloud, Minn	2	6	12	14							1							
Saint Helena, Cal	3	8	5	5														
Saint Johnsbury, Vt	2	1	2	2	2		2										84	11
Saint Joseph, Mo	1	7	2,987	7,941	27	4			1	2	11	1				7	954	331
Saint Louis, Mo	1	7	6,181	10,549	41		4	1		2	39					19	2,780	87
Saint Paul, Minn	1	6	3,028	7,311	56	7				13	59	6				6		
Saginaw, Mich	2	9	91	168	10						1	1					63	
Salem, Mass	2	1	273	383	7		1				2					1	69	303
Salem, N. C	3	3	8	28	1												222	51
Salem, Ohio	2	5	36	69									1					
Salem, Oregon	2	8	74	137							2						25	2
Salem, Va	3	3	20	85							2						2	
Salina, Kans	2	7	95	160	6	2	8		1	1	1						71	52
Salinas, Cal	3	8	1	2														

Table Gs.—*Statement of errors in the distribution and forwarding of mails, etc.—Cont'd.*

Post-offices.	Class.	Division.	No. of incorrect slips returned.	No. of errors on incorrect slips.	Missent.						Misdirected.						Errors checked—	
					No. of letter packages.	No. of pouches.	No. of registered packages.	No. of registered pouches.	No. of inner registered sacks.	No. of sacks.	No. of letter packages.	No. of pouches.	No. of registered packages.	No. of registered pouches.	No. of inner registered sacks.	No. of sacks.	Against railway postal clerks.	Against post-offices.
Salisbury, N. C	3	3	81	112							1						110	54
Salt Lake City, Utah	2	8	266	402	7		2				1						240	325
San Antonio, Tex	2	7	363	831	10	2					3						1,179	43
San Bernardino, Cal	2	8	126	290							1						23	3
San Buenaventura, Cal	3	8	19	37							1							
San Diego, Cal	2	8	628	995	1						3					2	846	79
Sandusky, Ohio	2	5	205	322	1						2							
Sanford, Fla	3	4	15	17														
San Francisco, Cal	1	8	5,024	10,042	99	1	1			5	37					5	407	142
San José, Cal	2	8	125	167	2		4				6						7	
San Luis Obispo, Cal	3	8	1	6														
Santa Ana, Cal	3	8	86	254													236	41
Santa Barbara, Cal	3	8	57	122							1						90	22
Santa Clara, Cal	3	8	3	4														
Santa Cruz, Cal	3	8	12	16													46	17
San Rafael, Cal	3	8	10	24		2												
Saratoga Springs, N. Y	2	2	224	323	6					1	2						236	266
Savannah, Ga	1	4	2,403	4,531		7	4	2			13	1				1	768	115
Schenectady, N. Y	2	2	61	80							1						26	15
Scranton, Pa	1	2	196	318	10	4					2	1					15	58
Seattle, Wash	2	8	452	782	4						10						1,250	506
Sedalia, Mo	2	7	388	615	1	6		2			3	1			2		22	6
Selma, Ala	2	4	640	968	12						2					1	2,523	117
Seneca Falls, N. Y	2	2	61	154							1						36	3
Shelbyville, Ind	3	5	3	5														
Shelbyville, Ky	3	5	2	4	1													
Shelbyville, Tenn	3	5	15	41													14	51
Sherman, Tex	2	7	304	872	6						3	2					35	14
Shreveport, La	2	4	301	1,087						1	2				1			
Sidney, Ohio	2	5	36	65							1							
Sing Sing, N. Y	2	2	28	59													12	10
Sioux City, Iowa	2	6	1,463	4,394	24	2				5	19	1			2			
Sioux Falls, Dak	2	6	119	299	4	1					3	2						
South Bend, Ind	2	5	164	276														
South Framingham, Mass	2	1															6	2
South Norwalk, Conn	2	1	12	13							1							
Spartanburgh, S. C	3	4	248	358	12	1					1							
Sprague, Wash	3	8	3	4														
Spokane Falls, Wash	2	8	216	281							1						78	
Springfield, Ill	2	6	295	700	11		1			2	7	1					4,835	174
Springfield, Mass	1	1	113	281	11	1	1				1	5			5		198	142
Springfield, Mo	2	7	427	877	5	6	5		1		2				1		2,154	807
Springfield, Ohio	1	5	468	1,272													178	272
Stamford, Conn	2	1	78	100	2		1				1	2					11	13
Statesville, N. C	3	3	229	833							3						454	100
Staunton, Va	2	3	362	532	8	1					2	1					930	317
Sterling, Ill	2	6	4	13	1												47	7
Steubenville, Ohio	2	5	60	116													40	96
Stillwater, Minn	2	6	288	644	1													
Stockton, Cal	2	8	52	61							1						7	
Streator, Ill	2	6	47	100	1						5						56	15
Suffolk, Va	3	3	160	292		1											519	98
Sumter, S. C	3	4	74	100														
Syracuse, N. Y	1	2	713	1,143	6						5	1					68	320
Tacoma, Wash	2	8	291	391	4						4						252	208
Tampa, Fla	3	4	44	82														
Tarborough, N. C	3	3	1	3													23	14
Taunton, Mass	2	1	54	81	1						1	1					30	76
Terre Haute, Ind	2	5	536	1,196	8	1	1				9				21		114	753
The Dalles, Oregon	3	8	91	114							1						7	27
Thomasville, Ga	3	4	21	29														
Tiffin, Ohio	2	5	3	7	5													
Titusville, Pa	2	2	122	196	8	2	1				2						201	108
Toledo, Ohio	2	5	780	1,346	15	2					11	3			4		90	330
Tonawanda, N. Y	2	2	52	187	2						1							

TABLE G⁸.—*Statement of errors in the distribution and forwarding of mails, etc.*—Cont'd.

Post-offices.	Class.	Division.	No. of incorrect slips returned.	No. of errors on incorrect slips.	Missent. No. of letter packages.	No. of pouches.	No. of registered packages.	No. of registered pouches.	No. of inner registered sacks.	No. of sacks.	Misdirected. No. of letter packages.	No. of pouches.	No. of registered packages.	No. of registered pouches.	No. of inner registered sacks.	No. of sacks.	Errors checked— Against railway postal clerks.	Against post-offices.
Topeka, Kans	1	7	1,629	4,008	10	2					12	1				1	2,445	1,11?
Towanda, Pa	2	2	18	46	2	2						2					6	5
Traverse City, Mich	3	9	28	36							1						1	70
Trenton, N. J	1	2	316	448	5						10						25	12
Troy, Tenn	7	5	23	74														16
Troy, N. Y	1	2	610	991	4	2					12	3				3	376	4
Troy, Ohio	2	5	29	44	3						2	1					173	205
Tucson, Ariz	2	8	13	55	1												18	
Tulare, Cal	3	8	20	29							2						37	4
Tuscaloosa, Ala	3	4	41	63														
Tuscumbia, Ala	3	4	21	35														
University of Virginia, Va	3	3	33	60	1												122	56
Upper Sandusky, Ohio	3	5	9	17							1							
Urbana, Ohio	2	5	24	38														70
Utica, N. Y	1	2	200	301				1			2						42	105
Vallejo, Cal	2	8	16	23													15	31
Vacaville, Cal	3	8	12	21	2						1						25	26
Valparaiso, Ind	2	5	37	126							4	1						
Vancouver, Wash	3	8	53	134							1						66	13
Vicksburg, Miss	2	4	77	282	11	1					2						91	148
Vincennes, Ind	2	5	139	251							1						1	106
Virginia City, Nev	3	8	20	44							1							
Visalia, Cal	3	8	14	16			1				1						6	10
Waco, Texas	2	7	308	771	6	2					1	3				1	289	10
Walla Walla, Wash	2	8	45	80							2						2	117
Wallingford, Conn	2	1	62	440											1		230	71
Waltham, Mass	2	1	91	130	4						2						5	9
Wapakoneta, Ohio	3	5	14	41	1													6
Warren, Pa	2	2	19	84	4	2	1			1	1					1		
Warrenton, Va	3	3	4	6														
Warsaw, Ind	3	5	16	75	1													
Washington, D. C	1	3	7,435	12,252	142	3				6	38	4				6	7,036	4,773
Washington, Ind	3	5	72	101	14							3				2	15	144
Washington, N. J	2	2	73	208							6						42	25
Washington, N. C	3	3	19	52	1						1						307	222
Washington, Pa	2	2	221	415	1	2					8	3				2	636	338
Waterbury, Conn	2	1	347	566	8		1				6						287	349
Waterloo, Iowa	2	6	214	407	5						5						218	28
Watertown, N. Y	2	2	243	377		1		1		3	1	3					158	55
Watertown, Wis	2	6	1	1														
Waterville, Me	2	1	2	2													3	21
Waukesha, Wis	2	6	50	86								1					1	
Waverly, N. Y	2	2	1	1													1	
Wellington, Kans	2	7	90	189	1												200	65
Wellsburgh, W. Va	3	3	16	32													21	9
West Bay City, Mich	3	9	1	1														
West Chester, Pa	2	2	62	128							1						24	18
Westerly, R. I	2	1	8	9	3													3
Westerville, Ohio	3	5	43	83														91
Westfield, Mass	2	1	70	109	4	1						2					191	112
West New Brighton, N. Y	2	2															56	309
Weston, W. Va	3	3	10	12													442	72
West Point, Miss	3	4	33	100														
Wheeling, W. Va	1	3	380	740	4	1					5	1					2,196	871
Wichita, Kans	2	7	1,111	2,720	1	4	2		3		12				2		247	91
Wilkes Barre, Pa	2	2	25	29							1						11	15
Williamsport, Pa	2	2	170	344	4						1					1	289	110
Willimantic, Conn	2	1	9	10	1						1						9	22
Wilmington, N. C	2	3	181	301	1	1	1										358	124
Wilmington, Del	1	2	371	486	15	4					4	2					30	129
Wilson, N. C	3	3	68	177	1						3						13	15
Winchester, Ky	3	5	13	18	1													
Winchester, Va	3	3	48	95														
Winfield, Kans	2	7	163	291							2						910	111
Winona, Minn	2	6	130	295	1	1				1							66	2

TABLE G⁴.—*Statement of errors in the distribution and forwarding of mails, etc.*—Cont'd.

Post-offices.	Class.	Division.	No. of incorrect slips returned.	No. of errors on incorrect slips.	Missent.						Misdirected.						Errors checked—	
					No. of letter packages.	No. of pouches.	No. of registered packages.	No. of registered pouches.	No. of inner registered sacks.	No. of sacks.	No. of letter packages.	No. of pouches.	No. of registered packages.	No. of registered pouches.	No. of inner registered sacks.	No. of sacks.	Against railway postal clerks.	Against post-offices.
Winston, N. C	3	3	100	184	...	...	...	...	...	...	...	...	...	...	...	...	177	57
Woodland, Cal	3	3	83	107	...	2	...	...	...	...	1	...	...	...	...	...	115	56
Woodstock, Va	3	3	116	181	...	...	...	...	...	...	...	...	...	...	...	...	669	170
Woonsocket, R. I	2	1	14	18	5	...	...	...	...	...	...	...	...	...	...	...	24	27
Worcester, Mass	1	1	554	786	14	7	...	...	...	...	1	...	...	...	...	1	100	179
Wytheville, Va	3	3	9	6	...	...	...	...	...	...	3	2	...	...	...	...	11	10
Xenia, Ohio	2	5	47	90	...	1	...	1	...	...	...	3	...	...	...	4	2	55
Yankton, Dak	2	6	198	508	6	...	1	...	...	...	2	...	...	...	...	...	1,665	13
Yonkers, N. Y	2	2	69	356	2	...	7	...	...	...	2	...	...	...	...	...	27	65
York, Pa	2	2	197	368	3	...	...	...	...	...	1	...	...	...	...	...	339	187
Youngstown, Ohio	2	5	114	170	...	...	...	...	...	...	1	...	...	...	...	...		
Ypsilanti, Mich	2	9	90	68	...	...	...	...	...	...	...	...	...	...	...	...	6	...
Yreka, Cal	3	3	1	1	...	...	...	...	...	...	...	...	...	...	...	...		
Zanesville, Ohio	2	5	276	498	5	...	...	...	1	3	8	2	...	...	...	1	63	241
All other offices		1	3,628	3,849	152	14	58	...	3	1	75	26	...	...	...	1	6,201	5,485
Do	3–4	2	10,325	20,222	281	273	142	...	1	2	243	93	...	...	...	25	20,279	11,896
Do		4	3	1,701	4,965	12	3	2	...	...	...	6	2	...	...	...	6	172	98
Do	3–4	4	2,833	5,365	52	...	...	...	...	...	16	...	...	...	...	...		
Do		6	9,361	24,153	386	35	56	...	...	7	157	64	...	...	...	16	10,404	5,631
Do	3–4	7	11,344	32,596	300	79	139	3	16	32	98	77	...	...	1	15	947	527
Do		8	1,626	3,339	63	16	37	3	...	5	35	11	...	...	...	1		
Do		9	1,552	4,387	53	25	13	...	...	...	23	14	...	...	...	2	1,866	445

RECAPITULATION.

Division.	Incorrect slips returned.	Errors on incorrect slips.	Missent.						Misdirected.						Errors checked—	
			Letter packages.	Pouches.	Registered packages.	Registered pouches.	Inner registered sacks.	Sacks.	Letter packages.	Pouches.	Registered packages.	Registered pouches.	Inner registered sacks.	Sacks.	Against railway postal clerks.	Against postmasters.
First	23,920	46,344	722	42	127	...	7	10	342	76	...	2	1	50	17,896	10,782
Second	120,004	247,668	1,495	379	170	2	5	48	1,013	187	1	...	...	188	64,975	39,706
Third	20,575	36,741	333	28	10	...	...	18	108	23	...	...	...	24	24,360	12,763
Fourth	32,285	56,667	407	23	13	4	2	22	151	15	...	...	...	55	15,541	4,915
Fifth	36,347	69,144	554	40	39	...	...	22	349	60	...	...	...	149	21,929	38,328
Sixth	56,295	110,372	978	65	76	3	...	44	496	117	...	...	6	63	39,580	9,557
Seventh	51,643	96,278	974	147	243	5	39	69	453	121	...	...	...	106	64,813	34,306
Eighth	15,274	27,300	244	22	41	...	...	14	162	23	...	...	...	12	18,972	5,672
Ninth	7,060	14,384	141	31	21	...	...	...	71	24	...	...	...	18	7,436	1,490
Total	363,356	706,898	5,849	777	740	17	53	247	3,147	646	1	3	7	665	274,057	156,818
Total as per report for fiscal year ended June 30, 1887.	341,712	669,034	6,627	684	874	27	26	194	2,888	754	1	7	7	621	248,947	97,814
Increase.	21,644	37,864	*778	93	*134	*10	27	53	259	*108	...	*5	...	44	25,110	59,004

*Decrease.

TABLE H².—*Statement of case examinations of permanent railway postal clerks for the fiscal year ended June 30, 1888.*

Division.	Examinations.	Cards handled.	Cards correct.	Cards incorrect.	Cards not known.	Average per cent. correct.	Highest individual per cent. correct.	Lowest individual per cent. correct.
First...............	705	444, 240	439, 744	4, 482	14	98.90	100	81.60
Second............	1, 088	1, 534, 224	1, 182, 912	107, 982	243, 830	77.10	100	01.76
Third.............	443	561, 395	490, 691	36, 280	34, 419	87.40	100	16.11
Fourth............	882	683, 419	658, 746	21, 661	3, 012	96.99	100	71.11
Fifth	963	1, 145, 801	1, 105, 195	39, 100	1, 506	96.46	100	14.42
Sixth	837	1, 154, 418	1, 064, 642	50, 313	39, 463	92.22	100	4.00
Seventh	2, 011	1, 320, 668	1, 235, 686	76, 081	8, 901	93.57	100	5.03
Eighth............	272	110, 032	101, 899	3, 005	5, 128	92.60	100	36.66
Ninth.............	588	963, 707	886, 473	53, 372	23, 862	91.98	100	14.44
Total	7, 809	7, 917, 904	7, 155, 988	392, 276	359, 635	90.50	100	1.76
Total as per report for fiscal year ended June 30, 1887..............	6, 577	6, 517, 650	5, 703, 176	337, 240	477, 234	87.50	100	1.14
Increase.....	1, 232	1, 400, 254	1, 452, 812	55, 036	°117, 599	3.00	....	....

°Decrease.

TABLE II.—*Statement of case examinations of railway postal clerks during probation for the fiscal year ended June 30, 1888.*

Division	Probationary appointees.	Examinations.	Cards handled.	Cards correct.	Cards incorrect.	Cards not known.	Average per cent. correct.	Probationers who received permanent appointments.	Average per cent. correct during probation made by those permanently appointed.	Dropped during probation, including those permitted to resign.	Per cent. of probationary appointees who failed to pass final examination.	Average per cent. cards correct of those dropped.	Highest individual per cent. correct.	Lowest individual per cent. correct.	Per cent. correct required for permanent appointment.
First	71	144	109,927	92,075	9,502	1,350	80.46	48	82.97	14	19.72	60.84	99.85	35.83	90.00
Second	319	1,043	696,864	588,060	68,919	189,658	60.96	139	65.97	68	27.58	38.74	99.97	04.67	90.00
Third	64	343	258,327	194,707	53,751	39,779	75.58	45	78.54	21	12.81	30.51	99.97	07.21	90.00
Fourth	95	520	193,214	175,544	11,384	286	91.43	35	94.65	12	23.15	74.21	100.00	33.50	90.00
Fifth	170	667	653,886	558,871	23,353	2,606	95.34	160	94.18	15	8.37	71.37	100.00	02.53	90.00
Sixth	270	949	1,018,673	789,811	98,588	163,476	75.55	217	80.99	64	23.11	44.68	100.00	01.10	90.00
Seventh	294	1,270	763,995	635,696	73,615	55,684	82.95	141	87.57	53	18.03	61.54	100.00	01.10	90.00
Eighth	62	371	199,735	144,754	8,598	15,391	85.87	34	91.16	17	32.69	72.74	99.88	26.60	90.00
Ninth	108	527	451,919	347,390	41,470	63,249	78.82	28	82.28	20	18.34	53.71	99.97	05.91	90.00
Total	1,453	5,633	4,092,350	3,223,994	381,160	537,474	78.78	836	85.87	314	21.51	56.39	100.00	1.00	90.00
Total as per report for the fiscal year ended June 30, 1887	1,449	4,482	3,630,858	2,944,239	367,055	319,564	81.09	778	85.34	341	23.53	62.22	100.00	0.02	90.00
Increase	4	1,151	461,482	279,725	*35,865	217,910	*2.31	68	0.53	*27	*2.02	*5.83	......	0.98	......

* Decrease.

TABLE K⁴.—Statement of new railroad service established and service extended during the fiscal year ended June 30, 1888.

FIRST DIVISION.

New service.	Corporate title of company.	Distance.	Date of order for commencement of railroad service.	Remarks.
		Miles.		
Nantucket to Siasconset, Mass	Nantucket	11.52	July 1, 1887	New service.
Boston to Winthrop, Mass	Bos., Rev. Beach and Lynn	5	Aug. 10, 1887	Do.
Kennebunkport to Kennebunk Station (n.o.)	Bos. and Maine	4.67	Aug. 10, 1887	Do.
Winchester to North Woburn, Mass	Bos. and Low	2.18	Aug. 16, 1887	Extension of route 3018.
Kittery Junction to York Beach, Me	York Harbor and Beach	11.83	Jan. 10, 1888	New service.
West Stewartstown to Coos, N. H	Upper Coos	21.23	Mar. 19, 1888	Do.

SECOND DIVISION.

New service.	Corporate title of company.	Distance.	Date of order for commencement of railroad service.	Remarks.
Benton to Bloomsburgh, Pa	Bloomsburgh and Sullivan	20.68	July 12, 1888	Established.
Coalport to Cresson, Pa	Cresson, Clearfield Co. and N. Y. Short Line	24.60	July 9, 1887	Do.
Forest House to Austin, Pa	Sinnamahoning	9.19	Jan. 10, 1888	Established to Costello; curtailed February 17, 1888.
Goff to Donahoe, Pa	Pennsylvania	4.29	Apr. 16, 1888	Established.
Jamestown to Mayville, N. Y	Chautauqua Lake	23.25	Sept. 21, 1887	Do.
Lazerne to Alderson, Pa	Penn. and N. Y. Canal and R. R. Co	14.00	Oct. 25, 1887	Do.
Manumuskin to Heislerville, N. J	West Jersey	9.10	Dec. 10, 1887	Do.
Mailton to Medford, N. J	Camden and Atlantic	4.98	May 25, 1888	Haddonfield and Marlton extended.
Ramey to Madera, Pa	Pennsylvania	5.80	Oct. 21, 1887	Osceola Mills and Ramey extended.
Saint Regis Falls to Brandon, N. Y	Northern Adirondack	22.38	Apr. 16, 1888	Moira and Saint Regis Falls extended.
Silver Brook to Silver Brook Junction, Pa	Lehigh Valley	2.61	Jan. 16, 1888	Established.
Wampum to Rock Point, Pa	Pennsylvania Company	3.53	Apr. 12, 1888	Do.
Windsor Beach to Rochester, N. Y	Rome, Watertown and Ogdensburgh	8.30	Sept. 30, 1887	Do.

THIRD DIVISION.

New service.	Corporate title of company.	Distance.	Date of order for commencement of railroad service.	Remarks.
Warsaw to Clinton, N. C	Wilmington and Weldon R. R	12.11	July 1, 1887	New R. R. service.
Phillipi to Bolington, W. Va	Grafton and Greenbrier R. R	18.00	Aug. 22, 1887	Do.
Bristol, Tenn., to Zollville, Va		12.51	Sept. 12, 1887	Do.
Walnut Cove to Dalton, N. C	Cape Fear and Yadkin Valley R. R	18.04	Sept. 28, 1887	Do.
Baltimore to Annapolis, Md	Annapolis and Baltimore Short Line R. R	28.22	Dec. 6, 1887	Do.
Nashville to Pine View, N. C	Wilmington and Weldon R. R	8.40	Jan. 2, 1888	Do.
Loris to Conway, S. C	Wilmington, Chadbourn and Conwayborough R. R.	18.81	Jan. 21, 1888	R. R. service, Chadbourn, N. C., to Loris, S. C., extended to Conway, S. C.

TABLE K².—*Statement of new railroad service established and service extended during the fiscal year ended June 30, 1888*—Continued.

THIRD DIVISION—Continued.

New service.	Corporate title of company.	Distance.	Date of order for commencement of railroad service.	Remarks.
		Miles.		
Factory Junction (n. o.) to Millborough, N. C.	Cape Fear and Yadkin Valley R. R.	9.55	Feb. 6, 1888	New R. R. tne.
Hamilton to Tarborough, N. C.	Hamilton R. R. and Lumber Co.	20.65	Feb. 15, 1888	Do.
Tunnelton to Kingwood, W. Va.	Kingwood Railway	10.25	Mar. 5, 1888	Do.
Bramwell to Freeman's, W. Va.	Norfolk and Western R. R.	.64	Mar. 8, 1888	Do.
Hamlet to Gibson's Station, N. C.	Raleigh and Augusta Air Line R. R.	10.50	Mar. 12, 1888	Do.
Sunbury	Suffolk and Carolina R. R.	14.90	Mar. 12, 1888	R. R. service, Suffk, Va., to Sunbury, N.C., extended to day, N. C.
Boykin's, Va., to Roxobel, N. C.	Roanoke and Tar River R. R.	28.92	Mar. 19, 1888	New R. R. service.
Foster's Falls to Austinville, Va.	Norfolk and Western	6.00	Apr. 16, 1888	R. R. service, Pulaski City to r's Falls, Va., ex-, ille, Va.
Wilmington to Wrightsville, N. C.	Wilmington Sea Coast R. R.	9.24	June 11, 1888	New R. R. tne.

FOURTH DIVISON.

New service.	Corporate title of company.	Distance.	Date of order for commencement of railroad service.	Remarks.
Argus to Patsburg, Ala.	Montgomery and Southern Rwy	12.50	Sept. 12, 1887	Route 17027 uled to Live Oak, curtailed at Patsburg, March 30, 18.
Talladega to Pell City, Ala.	Talladega and Coosa Valley R. R.	16.98	Dec. 12, 1887	New tne.
Broken Arrow to Pell City, Ala.	East and West of Ala. R. R	7.30	Dec.	Route 5420 extended.
Buffalo to Roanoke, Ala.	East Ala. R. R.	17.19	Feb. 3, 1888	Route 17014 extended.
Good Water to Sylacauga, Ala.	Columbus and Western R. R.	16.85	Feb. 21, 1888	Route 17016 extended.
Sylacauga to Childersburgh, Ala.		9.72	June 2, 1888	
Oakland to Clermont, Fla.		3.66	Sept. 13, 1887	
Clermont to Mascotte, Fla.	Orange Belt R. R.	9.61	Dec. 9, 1887	Route 16029 ded.
Mascotte to Tarpon Springs, Fla.		64.94	Dec. 9, 1887	
Lake City to Fort White, Fla.	Sah. Fla. and Western R. R.	21.93	Sept. 28, 1887	New service.
Ocala to Dunnellon, Fla.	Silver Springs, Ocala and Gulf R. R.	23.43	Nov. 28, 1887	Do.
Mascotte to Plant City, Fla.	Florida Rwf. and Navigation Co. R. R.	43.14	May 17, 1887	Route 10019 extended.
Lumpkin to Louvale, Ga.	Americus, Preston and Lumpkin R. R.	9.66	June 22, 1887	Route 11650 extended.
Americus to Gum Creek, Ga.	do	23.70	June 22, 1887	New service.
Gum Creek to Abberville, Ga.	do	24.25	Oct. 19, 1887	Do.
Atlanta to Zebulon, Ga.	Atlanta and Florida R. R.	51.28	Apr. 28, 1888	Do.
Monticello to Madison, Ga.	...ington and Macon R. R.	27.16	May 31, 1888	Do.
Cypress to Natchitoches, La.	Natchitoches R. R.	11.62	Feb. 20, 1888	Do.
New Orleans to Covington, La.	East ...lana R. R.	60.50	Apr. 28, 1888	Do.
Cotton Plant to New Albany Miss	Ship Island, Ripley and Kentucky R. R	7.65	Aug. 1, 1887	Route 18008 extended.

Route	Railroad	Miles	Date	Remarks
Jonestown to Eagle Nest, Miss.	Mobile and North Western R. R.	2.22	Nov. 8, 1887	Route 18006 extended.
Tupelo, Miss., to Birmingham, Ala.	Kansas City, Memphis and Birmingham R. R.	104.99	Nov. 8, 1887	Route 16021 extended.
Greenwood to Peoto, Miss.	Illinois Central R. R.	18.12	Dec. 19, 1887	New service.
Blackville to Salley, S.C.	Blackville, Alston and Newberry R. R	16.14	Mar. 12, 1888	Do.
Camden to Lancaster, S C.	Cheraw and Chester R. R	41.50	June 4, 1888	Do.
Ravenels to Young's Island, S.C.	Charleston and Savannah R. R.	5.70	June 8, 1888	Do.
Atkins to Bishopville, S. C.	Bishopville R. R	15.59	June 18, 1888	Do.
Shiloh to Concord, Ga.	Georgia Midland R. R.	29.10	June 22, 1887	Route 15051 extended.
Concord to Griffin, Ga.		16.50	July 22, 1887	
Griffin to McDonough, Ga.		10.20	Oct. 19, 1887	New service.
Rogers to Summit, Ga.	Rogers and Summit R. R.	20.00	Oct. 19, 1887	New service.
Americus to Buena Vista, Ga.	Buena Vista and Ellaville R. R	3.00	Feb. 23, 1888	Route 15017 changed to begin at Americus, Ga., instead of Andersonville; increase in distance 3 miles.

FIFTH DIVISION.

Route	Railroad	Miles	Date	Remarks
Orleans to French Lick, Ind	Orleans, West Baden and French Lick Springs Rwy.	18.76	Aug. 1, 1887	New railroad. Formerly star-route service.
Morrasfield to Uniontown, Ky.	Ohio Valley Rwy.	13.31	Aug. 1, 1887	Do.
New Gallice, Pa., to New Lisbon, Ohio.	Pittsburgh, Marion and Chicago Rwy.	11.22	Aug. 15, 1887	New Gallice and Rogers service extended.
Danbury to Point Marblehead, Ohio	Lakeside and Marblehead R R	8.50	Aug. 22, 1887	New railroad. Formerly star-route service.
Anderson to Ladoga, Ind	Midland Rwy	25.78	Aug. 22, 1887	Anderson and Noblesville service (19.96 miles) extended to Lebanon, Ind.
Alvordton to Carlisle, Ohio	Cincinnati, Jackson and Mackinaw R. R	20.12	Jan. 9, 1888	January 9, 1888, extended to Ladoga, Ind., making whole distance 65.67 miles.
		16.65	Aug. 22, 1887	August 22, 1887, Cecil and West Alexandria route, distance 110.74 miles, extended to Carlisle, Ohio; increased distance 16 05 miles.
		19.71	Oct. 10, 1887	October 3, 1887, extended to Bryan, Ohio; increased distance 19 71 miles.
		15.49	Jan. 16, 1888	January 16, 1888, extended to Alvordton, Ohio; increased distance 15.49 miles, making whole distance 162 59 miles.
Zanesville to Waterford, Ohio	Zanesville and Ohio River Rwy.	0.75	Sept. 5, 1887	September 5, 1887, Zanesville and McConnelsville service, 28.50 miles, extended to Stockport, Ohio; increased distance 9.75 miles.
		16.40	Mar. 9, 1888	March 19, 1888, Zanesville and Stockport service extended to Waterford, Ohio; increased distance, 16.40 miles, making whole distance 54.65 miles.
Dunlap, Tenn., to Bridgeport, Ala.	Nashville, Chattanooga and St. Louis Rwy.	4.73	Sept. 19, 1887	September 19, 1887, R. R. service extended from Victoria to Cheekville.
		11.41	Feb. 20, 1888	February 20, 1888, R. R. service extended from Cheekville to Dunlap, Tenn., 11.11 miles.
Marietta to Sharpsburgh, Ohio	Marietta Mineral Rwy.	4.57	Oct. 3, 1887	Marietta and Amesville service extended.
Henderson to Princeton, Ky	Ohio Valley Rwy.	25.04	Nov. 21, 1887	Henderson and Marion service extended.
Gallatin, Tenn., to Scottsville, Ky.	Chesapeake and Nashville Rwy.	35.87	Jan. 2, 1888	New railroad. Formerly star-route service.
Elora, Tenn., to Huntsville, Ala.	Nashville, Chattanooga and St. Louis Rwy.	27.02	Jan. 2, 1888	Do.
Glasgow Junction to Mammoth Cave, Ky.	Louisville and Nashville R. R.	8.51	Jan. 2, 1888	Do.

TABLE K¹.—*Statement of new railroad service established and service extended during the fiscal year ended June 30, 1888*—Continued.

FIFTH DIVISION—Continued.

New service.	Corporate title of company.	Distance.	Date of order for commencement of railroad service.	Remarks.
		Miles.		
Princeton, Ky., to Clarksville, Tenn.	Louisville and Nashville R. R.	27.83	Feb. 13, 1888	Newstead, Ky., and Clarksville, Tenn., service extended.
Lacrosse to Brazil, Ind.	Chicago and Indiana Coal Rwy.	27.06	Feb. 20, 1888	Fair Oaks and Brazil service extended.
Phalanx Station to Bergholz, Ohio.	Lake Erie, Alliance and Southern Rwy.	35.90	Feb. 20, 1888	Phalanx Station and Alliance service extended.
Kercheval to Cannelton, Ind.	Louisville, Evansville and St. Louis R. R.	32.50	Feb. 20, 1888	New railroad. Formerly star-route service.
Louisville to Springfield, Ky.	Louisville and Nashville R. R.	19.26	Mar. 12, 1888	March 12, 1888, Louisville and Bardstown service extended.
Killbuck to Trinway, Ohio	Cleveland, Akron and Columbus Rwy.	18.62	Mar. 12, 1888	March 12, 1888, R. R. service established between Killbuck and Warsaw, Ohio, distance 18.62 miles. New railroad; formerly no direct service.
Painesville to Youngstown, Ohio	Pittsburgh and Western Rwy.	13.52	June 25, 1888	June 25, 1888, service extended to Trinway, Ohio.
Cleveland, Ohio, to Fymaining (n. o.), Pa.	New York, Lake Erie and Western R. R.	16.21	Mar. 19, 1888	Painesville and Warren, Ohio, service extended.
		4.88	May 1, 1888	Route 21005 extended from Sharpsville to Fymaining (n. o.), Pa.
Brazil to Saline City, Ind.	Evansville and Indianapolis R. R.	12.31	Apr. 25, 1888	New railroad.
Corbin to Pineville, Ky.	Louisville and Nashville R. R.	18.74	Mar. 19, 1888	March 19, 1888, railroad service established between Corbin and Barbourville, Ky., distance 16.74 miles. New railroad. Formerly star-route service.
Elizabethport to Hodgensville, Ky.	Hodgensville and Elizabethtown R. R.	14.60	May 21, 1888	May 21, 1888, extended to Pineville, Ky.
		11.76	June 7, 1888	New railroad. Formerly star-route service.
Corning to Gallipolis, Ohio.	Ohio Central R. R.	16.06	Mar. 19, 1888	Railroad service of route 21068, Corning and C., H. V. and T. Junction (n. o.), Ohio (Columbus and Charleston R. P. O.), extended to Gallipolis, Ohio, making lap service on connection with route 21074, Logan and Pomeroy R. P. O.

SIXTH DIVISION.

New service.	Corporate title of company.	Distance.	Date of order for commencement of railroad service.	Remarks.
Roscoe to Orient, Dak.	Chicago, Milwaukee and St. Paul	41.73	July 25, 1887	
Springfield to Litchfield, Ill.	St. Louis and Chicago	45.64	July 25, 1887	
Ellendale to Edgeley, Dak.	Chicago, Milwaukee and St. Paul	28.84	July 25, 1887	
Lindsay to Oakdale, Nebr.	Fremont, Elkhorn and Mo. Valley	35.62	July 25, 1887	
Bagby to Bottineau, Dak.	St. Paul, Minneapolis and Manitoba	88.10	Aug. 1, 1887	
Fairfield to Stromsburgh, Nebr.	Kansas City and Omaha	65.49	Aug. 22, 1887	
Waterville to Mankato, Minn.	Minneapolis and St. Louis	28.24	Aug. 25, 1887	

Route	Railroad	Amount	Date
Rutland to Ellendale, Dak	St. Paul, Minneapolis and Manitoba	49.73	Aug. 25, 1887
Geneva to Saint Charles, Ill	Chicago and Northwestern	3.21	Aug. 22, 1887
Chicago to Dunbar (n. o.), Ill	Chicago, St. Paul and Kansas City	101.89	Oct. 3, 1887
Waterloo to Oelwein, Iowa	do.	98.74	Oct. 3, 1887
Winnipeg Junction, Minn., to Grand Forks, Dak	Northern Pacific	108.86	Oct. 3, 1887
Roscoe to Hillsview, Dak	Chicago, Milwaukee and St. Paul	18.74	Oct. 10, 1887
Manilla to Sioux City, Iowa	do	55.72	Oct. 10, 1887
Bessemer, Mich., to Molien, Wis	Wisconsin Central	103.30	Oct. 17, 1887
Madison to Bristol, Dak	Chicago, Milwaukee and St. Paul	44.83	Oct. 17, 1887
Curtis to Grant, Nebr	Burlington and Mo. River in Nebr	9.13	Oct. 24, 1887
Kingsley to Moville, Iowa	Chicago and Northwestern	8.95	Oct. 24, 1887
Iron River to Watersmeet, Mich	do	11.28	Oct. 24, 1887
Albany to New Glarus, Wis	Chicago, Milwaukee and St. Paul	9.41	Nov. 1, 1887
North Judson to Knox, Ind	Indiana, Illinois and Iowa	42.70	Nov. 28, 1887
Faulkton to Gettysburgh, Dak	Chicago and Northwestern	18.87	Dec. 5, 1887
Rockford to Rockton, Ill	Chicago, Milwaukee and St. Paul	88.44	Dec. 5, 1887
Orleans, Nebr., to Blakeman, Kans	Burlington, and Mo. River in Nebr	78.51	Dec. 5, 1887
Turtle Lake, Wis., to Minneapolis, Minn	Minneapolis, Sault de Ste Marie and Atl	11.87	Dec. 5, 1887
Sidell to Tuscola, Ill	Chicago and Eastern Illinois	11.87	Dec. 5, 1887
Garner to Forrest City, Iowa	Burlington, Cedar Rapids and Northern	72.64	Dec. 5, 1887
Park River to Langdon, Dak	Minneapolis and Pacific	549.84	Dec. 15, 1887
Fairmount, Minn., to Oakes, Dak	St. Paul, Minneapolis and Manitoba	39.24	Dec. 15, 1887
Minot, Dak., to Great Falls, Mont	Chicago and Northwestern	70.70	Dec. 23, 1887
Doland to Groton, Dak	Chicago, Milwaukee and St. Paul	103.26	Dec. 23, 1887
Merrill to Toonabawk, Wis	Chicago and Northwestern	70.97	Jan. 7, 1888
Cheyenne to Uva, Wyo	Cheyenne and Northern	93.49	Jan. 16, 1888
Central City to Arcadia, Nebr	Burlington and Mo. River in Nebr	11.70	Jan. 16, 1888
Grand Forks to Pembina, Dak	Northern Pacific	47.80	Jan. 30, 1888
Napier, Mo., to Kato "Y," Nebr	Burlington and Mo. River in Nebr	97.95	Jan. 30, 1888
Sault de Ste Marie to Sault Junction, Mich	Duluth, South Shore and Atlantic	28.09	Feb. 1, 1888
Helena to Great Falls, Mont	Montana Central	209.58	Feb. 6, 1888
Omaha to Arlington, Nebr	Fremont, Elkhorn and Mo. Valley	119.86	Feb. 10, 1888
Ottumwa, Iowa, to Kansas City, Mo	Chicago, Milwaukee and St. Paul	15.34	Feb. 20, 1888
Platte River Junction (n. o.) to Hastings, Nebr	Fremont, Elkhorn and Mo. Valley	88.80	Feb. 20, 1888
Marion to Parker City (n. o.), Ill	St. Louis, Alton and Terre Haute	41.30	Feb. 20, 1888
Douglas to Gisborough, Wyo	Fremont, Elkhorn and Mo. Valley	187.00	Feb. 20, 1888
Chicago to Joliet, Ill	Chicago, Santa Fé and California	57.79	Feb. 20, 1888
Ancona, Ill, to Fort Madison, Iowa	do	58.62	Feb. 20, 1888
Fairfield to Alma, Nebr	Kansas City and Omaha	69.38	Feb. 20, 1888
Fairbury to McCool Junction, Nebr	St. Joseph and Grand Island	77.58	Feb. 27, 1888
Palmer to Burwell, Nebr	Burlington and Mo. River in Nebr	83.10	Feb. 27, 1888
Linwood to Geneva, Nebr	Fremont, Elkhorn and Mo. Valley	60.71	Feb. 27, 1888
Salem to Mitchell, Dak	Chicago, St. Paul, Minn., and Omaha	37.27	Feb. 27, 1888
Ashland to Schuyler, Nebr	Omaha and North Platte	98.28	Feb. 27, 1888
Rapid City to Whitewood, Dak	Fremont, Elkhorn and Mo. Valley	61.18	Feb. 27, 1888
Anselmo to Whitman, Nebr	Burlington and Mo. River in Nebr	6.35	Feb. 27, 1888
Cherokee to Onawa, Iowa	Cherokee and Dakota	3.28	Feb. 27, 1888
Chelsea to Elbi Lake, Wis	Wisconsin Central	44.72	Mar. 5, 1888
Roselen to Libertyville, Ill	Chicago, Milwaukee and St. Paul		
Iron Mountain to Republic, Mich	Milwaukee and Northern		
Bruce, Wis., to Sault de Ste Marie, Mich	Minneapolis, Sault de Ste Marie and Atl	373.84	

TABLE Kt.—*Statement of new railroad service established and service extended during the fiscal year ended June 30, 1888—Continued.*

SIXTH DIVISION—Continued.

New service.	Corporate title of company.	Distance.	Date of order for commencement of railroad service.	Remarks.
... Cit ...		*Miles.*		
... to	Northern Pacific	28.38	Mar. 7, 1888	
Cherokee, Iowa, to Sioux Falls, Dak.	Jacksonville and Southwestern	17.59	Mar. 12, 1888	
Dunbar (n. o.), Ill., to Dubuque, Iowa.	Cherokee and Dakota	97.07	Apr. 2, 1888	
Beatse to Nantasket, Nebr.	Chicago, St. Paul and Kansas City	65.94	Apr. 9, 1888	
Saint Paul to Cardigan Junction (n. o.), Minn.	Omaha and Republican Valley	9.74	Apr. 16, 1888	
Millstadt Junction (n. o.) to Millstadt, Ill.	Minn. Sault de Ste. Marie and Atl.	8.00	Apr. 16, 1888	
Cedar Rapids to Mane	Mobile and Ohio	7.00	Apr. 30, 1888	
Whitman to ... Dak.	Illinois Central	42.58	Apr. 30, 1888	
La Monte to ...	Grand Island and Wyoming	72.14	May 10, 1888	
Grant, Nebr.	Fargo and Southwestern	21.90	May 10, 1888	
Hillsview to ... Colo.	Burlington and Mo. River in Nebr.	86.60	May 14, 1888	
Union Pacific transfer to Broadway depot at Council Bluffs, Iowa.	Chicago, Milwaukee and St. Paul	7.98	June 1, 1888	
	Union Pacific	1.76	June 4, 1888	

SEVENTH DIVISION.

New service.	Corporate title of company.	Distance.	Date of order for commencement of railroad service.	Remarks.
Arkadelphia to Dalark, Ark.	Ultima Thule, Arkadelphia and Mississippi	11.43	Oct. 31, 1888	Route 29922 established.
Abilene to Keystone, Kans.	Chicago, Kansas and Western	13.82	Feb. 20, 1888	Extension of route 33077.
Alma to Herington, Kans.	Nebraska	45.59	July 20, 1887	Extension of route 33075.
Arkansas City, Kans., to Purcell, Ind. Ter.	Southern Kansas	154.00	Sept. 12, 1887	Route 32003 established.
Ashland to Englewood, Kans.	...do ... Western	15.13	Mar. 1, 1888	Extension of route 32008.
Bald Knob to Augusta, Ark.	Saint Louis, Iron Mountain and Southern	16.05	Mar. 28, 1887	Route 29923 established.
Bastrop to La Grange, Tex.	Taylor, Bastrop and Houston	34.64	Dec. 5, 1887	Extension of route 31056.
Batesville to Cushman, Ark.	Saint Louis, Iron Mountain and Southern	11.63	Nov. 7, 1887	Extension of route 29014.
Beckville to Carthage, Tex.	Galveston, Sabine and Saint Louis	9.59	May 7, 1888	Extension of route 31048.
Belleville to McFarland, Kans.		104.78	Apr. 9, 1888	Route 33089 established.
Beerne to Kerrville, Tex.		37.59	Oct. 3, 1887	Extension of route 31068.
Brownwood to Bollinger's Mill, Mo.	Cape Girardeau Southwestern	8.63	Apr. 2, 1888	Route 29505 established.
Anelin in Dodge City, Kans.	Chicago, Kansas and Nebraska	29.55	May 22, 1888	Route 32092 established.
Burdett to Jetmore, Kans.	Chicago, Kansas and Western	22.72	Nov. 7, 1887	Extension of route 33061.
Burlington to Gridley, Kans.	... do	11.82	Aug. 25, 1887	Route 32080 established.
Cedar Vale to Winfield, Kans.	Denver, Memphis and Atlantic	38.08	Nov. 7, 1887	Extension of route 33056.
Claredon to Texline (n. o.), Tex.	Fort Worth and Denver City	174.20	June 4, 1888	Extension of route 31057.
Cleburne to Weatherford, Tex.	Gulf, Colorado and Santa Fé	38.68	June 4, 1888	Extension of route 31035.

		Railroad	Miles	Date	Remarks
Clinton to East L...... Mo......		Kansas City and Southern	24.63	July 15, 1887	Extension of route 29055
		Kansas City and Pacific	73.04	Oct. 24, 1887	Route 33962 established
		Colorado Midland	123.85	Oct. 17, 1887	Route 31057 established
		Saint Louis, Arkansas and Texas	98.31	June 25, 1888	Route 31067 established
		Denver, South Park and Pacific	3.45	Oct. 8, 1887	Route 31064 established
		Saint Louis, Arkansas and Texas	42.00	May 6, 1888	Route 33077 established
		Chicago, Kansas and Western	64.96	Aug. 8, 1887	Extension of route 33077
		do	10.44	Feb. 20, 1888	Extension of route 3306A
	Mo	do	84.67	Dec. 5, 1887	Extension of route 33062
		Kingman, Pratt and Western	21.24	Aug. 8, 1887	Route 38035 established
		Atchison, Topeka and Santa Fé	117.43	Dec. 14, 1887	Route 33098 established
		Grouse Creek	28.20	May 21, 1888	Route 38033 established
		Denver and Rio Grande	4.48	Oct. 10, 1887	Route 34050 established
		Chicago, Kansas and Nebraska	129.04	Jan. 16, 1888	Route 29021 established
		Saint Louis and San Francisco	16.28	Aug. 22, 1887	Extension of route 31062
		San Antonio and Aransas Pass	20.95	May 28, 1888	Extension of route 22068
	Ind. Ter	Chicago, Santa Fé and California	218.00	May 7, 1888	Route 31001 established
		Fort Worth and Rio Grande	41.81	July 1, 1887	Extension of route 31063
		Missouri Kansas and Texas	70.01	Sept. 12, 1887	Route 31064 established
		Gulf, Colorado and Santa Fé	64.90	Feb. 20, 1888	Route 33036 established
		Kanopolis and Kansas Central	14.76	Apr. 2, 1888	Extension of route 33039
	Colo	Southern Kansas	13.53	Dec. 15, 1887	Extension of route 3301B
	Kans	Denver and Rio Grande	40.74	Mar. 19, 1888	Extension of route 33062
		Kingman, Pratt and Western	9.97	Dec. 3, 1887	Extension of route 31057
		San Antonio and Aransas Pass	58.42	Oct. 17, 1887	Extension of route 33075
	tion (n. o.), Colo	Chicago, Kansas and Nebraska	127.15	Oct. 24, 1887	Route 33062 established
		Denver, Memphis and Atlantic	74.35	Mar. 1, 1888	Extension of route 33064
		Chicago, Kansas and Nebraska	15.29	July 1, 1887	Route 33078 established
		Verdigris Valley, Independence and Western	160.77	June 10, 1888	Extension of route 33063
		Saint Louis and San Francisco	12.41	Mar. 12, 1888	Route 29024 established
		do	18.20	Oct. 31, 1887	Route 29016 established
	to Kansas City, Mo	Kansas City, Wyandotte and Northwestern	154.96	Apr. 2, 1888	Extension of route 33070
		Kansas City and Southwestern	2.03	May 14, 1888	Extension of route 33079
		Chicago, Kansas and Western	64.00	Mar. 6, 1888	Route 33091 established
		do	41.02	Mar. 26, 1888	Route 33086 established
	Kans	Southern Kansas	42.96	Dec. 1, 1887	Extension of route 33077
		Gulf, Colorado and Santa Fé	167.91	July 1, 1887	Route 32004 established
		Lawrence, Emporia and Southwestern	30.10	Apr. 2, 1888	Route 31059 established
Le Roy to Madison, Kans		Interstate	33.75	May 10, 1888	Service on route 31014 restored.
Lewisville (Galveston), Ark., to Shreveport, La		Saint Louis, Arkansas and Texas	29.98	June 25, 1888	Route 33060 established
Lincoln to Luray, Kans		Salina, Lincoln and Western	61.04	Dec. 28, 1887	Route 30019 established
McCracken to Horace, Kans		Denver, Memphis and Atlantic	30.95	Dec. 6, 1887	Extension of route 33057
Marshall to Myrick Station (n. o.), Mo		Missouri Pacific	131.05	June 11, 1888	Route 33084 established
Miami to Panhandle, Tex		Southern Kansas	47.82	Apr. 9, 1888	Route 28039 established
Morantown to Kincaid, Kans		Denver and Rio Grande	38.29	Apr. 2, 1888	Extension of route 33004
Nebraska City to Auburn, Nebr		Saint Louis, Arkansas and Texas	110.10	Sept. 12, 1887	Route 28057 established
Ness City to Scott, Kans		Kansas City and Pacific	11.95	May 10, 1888	Route 31060 established
Norn to Nelson, Nebr		Nebraska Southern	22.89	Nov. 27, 1888	Extension of route 33083
Chicago, Kansas and Western		Chicago, Kansas and Western	55.60	Sept. 10, 1887	Route 34048 established
Chicago, Kansas and Nebraska		Chicago, Kansas and Nebraska	6.49	Sept. 26, 1887	Extension of route 33059
Oakley to Colby, Kans		Oakley and Colby	22.12	Dec. 24, 1887	Route 33085 established

TABLE K⁴.—Statement of new railroad service established and service extended during the fiscal year ended June 30, 1888—Continued.

SEVENTH DIVISION—Continued.

New service	Corporate title of company	Distance.	Date of order for commencement of railroad service.	Remarks.
		Miles.		
Olcott to Iuka, Kans.	Kansas Southwestern	20.29	Oct. 3, 1887	Route 33061 established.
Panhandle to Washburn, Tex.	Fort Worth and Denver City	16.18	June 4, 1888	Route 31005 established.
Phillipsburgh to Norton, Kans.	Chicago, Kansas and Nebraska	33.75	May 1, 1888	Extension of route 34000.
Pine Bluff to English, Ark.	Pine Bluff, Monroe and New Orleans	28.62	May 18, 1887	Route 29022 established.
Pratt to Liberal, Kans.	Chicago, Kansas and Nebraska	125.25	May 1, 1888	Route 33090 established.
Quanah to Clarendon, Tex.	Fort Worth and Denver City	46.88	Oct. 10, 1887	Extension of route 31097.
Red Cliff to Glenwood Springs, Colo.	Denver and Rio Grande	63.68	Oct. 28, 1887	Extension of route 33072.
Saint Joseph, Mo., to Alma, Kans.	Chicago, Kansas and Nebraska	128.45	July 1, 1887	Route 33075 established.
Saint Louis to Union, Mo.	Saint Louis, Kansas City and Colorado	59.91	July 25, 1887	Route 29002 established.
San Marcos to Lockhart, Tex.	Taylor, Bastrop and Houston	17.12	Mar. 19, 1888	Route 31063 established.
Sidell to Fern, Kans.	Le Roy and Caney Valley Air Line	52.81	Aug. 8, 1887	Route 33078 established.
Spivey to Ashland, Kans.	Chicago, Kansas and Western	100.00	Oct. 17, 1887	Extension of route 33068.
Stafford to Larned, Kans.	Denver, Memphis and Atlantic	34.77	Nov. 10, 1887	Extension of route 33068.
Tatum to Beckville, Tex.	Galveston, Sabine and Saint Louis	7.70	Feb. 20, 1888	Extension of route 31043.
Texline (n. o.), Tex., to Pueblo, Colo	Denver, Texas and Forth Worth	225.51	June 4, 1888	Route 31065 established.
Tonganoxie to Seneca, Kans.	Kansas City, Wyandotte and Northwestern	66.57	Mar. 1, 1888	Extension of route 33079.
Wappapello to Chaonia, Mo.	Pueblo and State Line	159.76	Mar.	Route 33036 established.
Weeping Water to Nebraska City, Nebr.	Cape Girardeau Southwestern	4.46	June 18, 1888	Extension of route 29046.
Wichita to Caldwell, Kans.	Missouri Pacific	24.67	Nov. 27, 1887	Route 34047 established.
Wichita to Ellsworth, Kans.	Chicago, Kansas and Nebraska	49.38	Nov. 28, 1887	Extension of route 33082.
Winfield to Belle Plaine, Kans.	Saint Louis and San Francisco	109.61	Mar. 6, 1888	Route 33087 established.
Wyandotte (Kansas City) to Tonganoxie, Kans.	Denver, Memphis and Atlantic	20.97	Nov. 10, 1887	Extension of route 33058.
Yoakum to Flatonia, Tex.	Kansas City, Wyandotte and Northwestern	30.39	Aug. 22, 1887	Route 33070 established.
	San Antonio and Aransas Pass	50.15	Jan. 16, 1888	Route 31062 established.

EIGHTH DIVISION.

New service	Corporate title of company	Distance.	Date of order for commencement of railroad service.	Remarks.
Arcata Wharf (n. o.) to Blue Lake, Cal.	Arcata and Blue Lake R. R.	10.00	June 15, 1887	New service.
Albany Junction (n. o.) to Lebanon Station (n. o.), Oregon.	Oregon and California R. R.	12.50	Mar. 20, 1888	Do.
Berenda to Raymond, Cal.	Southern Pacific Co.	21.30	June 25, 1887	Do.
Burson to Valley Springs, Cal.	San Joaquin and Sierra, Nev. R. R.	8.90	Sept. 10, 1887	Route 46043 extended.
Camp Ham (n. o.) to Long Valley, Cal.	Nev. and California R. R.	11.87	June 6, 1888	Route 46005, Reno, Nev., to Camp Ham (n. o.), Cal, extended.

Cle Elum to Melrose, Wash.	Northern Pacific R. R.	81.40	June 23, 1887	Route 43011 extended.
Coeur d'Alene to Wardner, Idaho.	Coeur d'Alene Rwy. and Nav. Co.	81.90	July 8, 1887	New service.
Colfax to Farmington. Wash.	Columbia and Palouse R. R.	27.81	June 15, 1887	Do.
Drummond to Phillipsburgh, Mont	Northern Pacific R. R.	13.97	Mar. 7, 1888	Do.
Clough Junction (n. o.) to Marysville, Mont	do	20.47	Dec. 16, 1887	Do.
Henley, Cal., to Ashland, Oregon.	Central Pacific R. R.	38.67	Nov. 30, 1887	Route 46002, Roseville to Henley, Cal., extended to Ashland, Oregon.
Los Alamos to Los Olivos, Cal	Pacific Coast Rwy.	12.20	Dec. 29, 1887	Route 46040 extended.
Los Angeles to Port Ballona, Cal.	California Central R. R.	18.07	Apr. 12, 1888	New service.
Maricopa Junction to Phenix, Ariz.	Maricopa and Phenix R. R.	35.78	Sept. 1, 1887	Do.
Missoula to Victor. Mont	Missoula and Bitter Root Valley R. R.	35.75	Apr. 12, 1888	Do.
Nampa to Boisé City, Idaho.	Idaho Central Rwy.	20.69	Sept. 14, 1887	Do.
Oceanside to Escondido, Cal.	California Central R. R.	22.77	Mar. 19, 1888	Do.
Reno, Nev., to Camp Ham (n. o.), Cal	Nevada and California R. R.	45.28	Feb. 16, 1888	Do.
Rosalia to Belmont, Wash.	Spokane and Palouse Rwy. Co.	15.79	Aug. 8, 1887	Route 43015 extended.
Riverside to Santa Ana, Cal	California Central Rwy.	27.99	Dec. 12, 1887	New service.
Santa Ana to Capistrano, Cal.	do	21.95	Mar. 21, 1888	Route 46055 extended.
San Bernardino to Ingroam, Cal	do	9.25	Mar. 17, 1888	New service.
San Bernardino to Duarte, Cal.	do	41.04	June 22, 1887	New service. Order of July 14 extends this route to Los Angeles, covering and discontinuing route 46044.
Saugus Station (n. o.) to Santa Barbara, Cal	Southern Pacific Co.	78.90	June 11, 1887	New service.
Shingle Springs to Placerville, Cal.	Sacramento Valley R. R.	12.15	May 25, 1888	Route 46005 extended.
Walla Walla, Wash., to Pendleton, Oregon.	Oregon Rwy. and Nav. Co	47.48	Aug. 3, 1887	New service.
Wardner to Wallace. Idaho.	Coeur d'Alene Rwy. and Nav. Co.	9.71	Oct. 3, 1887	Route 42003 extended.
Wallace to Burke, Idaho.	do	7.65	Apr. 3, 1888	Do.

NINTH DIVISION.

Howard City to Grand Rapids, Mich.	Muskegon, Grand Rapids and Indiana	34.07	July 11, 1887	New service.
Kalamazoo to Hastings, Mich.	Chicago, Kalamazoo and Saginaw	31.08	Apr. 16, 1888	Do.
Missaukee Junction (n. o.) to Jennings, Mich.	Grand Rapids and Indiana	8.65	Aug. 11, 1887	Do.
Pinconning to Gladwin, Mich.	Michigan Central	28.28	Jan. 14, 1888	Do.
Rodney to Chippewa Lake, Mich	Detroit, Lansing and Northern	5.91	Feb. 19, 1888	Do.

TABLE LI.—*Statement of new railway post-office service established and service extended during the fiscal year ended June 30, 1888.*

FIRST DIVISION.

New service.	Corporate title of company.	Distance.	Date of order for commencement of railway post-office service.	Remarks.
		Miles.		
Claremont to Boston, Mass	Boston, Lowell and Concord	25.34	Apr. 16, 1888	Extension of Claremont and Lowell R. P. O. to Boston.
Lancaster to Boston, Mass	do	75.10	May 28, 1888	Extension of Lancaster and Concord R. P. O. to Boston.
Boston, Springfield, Mass., to New York, N. Y.	Boston and Albany, and N. Y., N. H. and Hartford.	284.63	June 20, 1888	Additional 60-foot R. P. O. car line authorized.
Portland, Me., to Boston, Mass	Boston and Maine	116.83	May 15, 1888	Forty-foot R. P. O. car line authorized.

SECOND DIVISION.

New service.	Corporate title of company.	Distance.	Date of order for commencement of railway post-office service.	Remarks.
Bellwood to Punxsutawney, Pa	Belle Gap R. R. Co. and Clearf. and Jeff. Rwy.	58.90	Feb. 24, 1888	New service.
Haverstraw to New York, N. Y.	New Jersey and N. Y. R. R. Co.	.53	Mar. 12, 1888	Extension of Stony Point and N. Y. R. P. O. to Haverstraw. The distance (.53) is net increase in mileage on branch between Garnerville and Haverstraw, over service on branch between Garnerville and Stony Point. (Discontinued.)
Lancaster to Harrisburg, Pa	Penn's R. R. (Phila. Div.).	40.87	June 8, 1888	New service commenced June 30.
Philadelphia, Pa., Aiken to Baltimore, Md	Balto. and Ohio R. R. (Phila. Div.).	98.00	June 21, 1887	Service commenced July 6, 1887. Title changed from Phila. Upland and Balto.
Chateaugay to Saranac Lake, N. Y.	Chateaugay R. R.	72.82	Jan. 16, 1888	New service.
Point Pleasant, N. J., to Philadelphia, Pa.	Penn's R. R. (Amboy Div.)	10.09	June 13, 1888	Extension of Hightstown and Philadelphia. The distance (10.09 miles) is the net increase in mileage over service as performed, between Hightstown and Philadelphia (52.17 miles), between Point Pleasant and Philadelphia (71.86 miles).
Wilkes Barre to Potsville, Pa	Penn's R. R. (Sunbury and Schuylk. Div's.) and Lehigh Valley R. R. (Mahanoy Div.).	81.90	Feb. 24, 1888	New service.

THIRD DIVISION.

New service.	Corporate title of company.	Distance.	Date of order for commencement of railway post-office service.	Remarks.
Lovely Mount to Lynchburgh, Va	Norfolk and Western R. R	95.60	Aug. 1, 1887	Lovely Mount and Pocahontas R. P. O. extended to Lynchburgh.
Piedmont, W. Va., to Cumberland, Md	West Virginia Central and Pittsburgh Rwy.	28.87	Sept. 6, 1887	New service, and Piedmont and Davis R. P. O. extended to Cumberland.

Grafton to Belington, W. Va.	Grafton and Belington R. R.	42.00	Sept. 7, 1887	Grafton and Belington R. P. O. established.
Greensborough to Dalton, N. C.	Cape Fear and Yadkin Valley R. R.	47.47	Oct. 6, 1887	Greensborough and Dalton R. P. O. established.
Dalton to Pilot Mountain, N. C.	do	7.82	Dec. 5, 1887	New service and Greensborough and Dalton R. P. O. extended to Pilot Mountain.
Statesville to Taylorsville, N. C.	Richmond and Danville R. R.	19.98	Jan. 2, 1888	New service, and Statesville and Charlotte R. P. O. extended to Taylorsville.
Point Pleasant to Huntington, W. Va.	Ohio River R. R.	43.83	Feb. 20, 1888	New service from Point Pleasant to C. and O. Junction, and Wheeling and Point Pleasant R. P. O. extended to Huntington.
Morristown to Knoxville, Tenn.	East Tennessee, Virginia and Georgia R. R.	42.23	Feb. 18, 1888	Salisbury and Morristown R. P. O. extended to Knoxville.
Pilot Mountain to Bliss, N. C.	Cape Fear and Yadkin Valley R. R.	8.34	May 7, 1888	New service, and Greensborough and Pilot Mountain R. P. O. extended to Bliss.
Hamlet to Gibson's Station, N. C.	Raleigh and Augusta Air Line R. R.	10.50	June 11, 1888	Raleigh and Hamlet R. P. O. extended to Gibson's Station.
Greensborough to Bliss, N. C.	Cape Fear and Yadkin Valley R. R.	60.30	do	Greensborough and Bennettsville R. P. O. extended to Bliss, taking up and discontinuing the Greensborough and Bliss R. P. O.
Bliss to Mount Airy, N. C.	do	6.59	June 15, 1888	Bliss and Bennettsville R. P. O. extended to Mount Airy.

FOURTH DIVISION.

Abbeville to Zontralc, Ga.	Americus, Preston and Lumpkin R. R.	109.79	Nov. 11, 1887	New service.
Atlanta to Zebulon, Ga.	Atlanta and Florida R. R.	51.20	May 10, 1888	Do.
Tupelo, Miss. to Birmingham, Ala.	Kans. City, Mem. and Birm. R. R.	146.21	Nov. 30, 1887	Memphis and Tupelo R. P. O. extended.
Broken Arrow to Pell City, Ala.	East and West of Ala. R. R.	7.30	Dec. 27, 1887	Cartersville and Broken Arrow R. P. O. extended.
Pell City to Talladega, Ala.	Talladega and Coosa Valley R. R.	32.42	Dec. 28, 1887	
Augusta, Ga. to Branchville, S. C.	South Carolina R. R.	62.79	May 29, 1888	Service increased to double daily.
Cleveland, Tenn. to Rome, Ga.	E. Tenn. Va. and Georgia R. R.	56.45	Oct 15, 1887	Rome and Selma R. P. O. extended.
Goodwater, Ala. to Sylacauga, Ala.	Columbus and Western R. R.	16.85	Mar. 15, 1888	Goodwater and Columbus R. P. O. extended.
Childersburgh to Sylacauga, Ala.	do	9.73	June 19 1888	Service increased to double daily.
Columbia to Branchville, S. C.	South Carolina R. R.	68.71	May 29, 1888	New service.
Elbore to Fregnalls, S. C.	Entawville R. R.	33.78	Mar. 23, 1888	Eolton and Walhalla R. P. O. extended, making double daily service Eolton to Greenville, S. C.
Dalton to Greenville, S. C.	Richmond and Danville R. R.	28.82	Nov. 15, 1887	
Sanford to Tampa, Fla.	Richmond and South Fla. R. R.	115.00	Feb. 4, 1888	Double daily service on Jacksonville and Tampa R. P. O. Sanford to Tampa. Summer schedule double daily only to Kissimmee, 40 miles.
Camden to Lancaster, S. C.	Charleston, Cin. and Chicago R. R.	41.50	May 21, 1888	Camden and Kingville R. P. O. extended.
Macon to Columbus, Ga.	Southwestern R. R.	101.04	May 10, 1888	Service on night trains, making double daily.
Macon to Fort Valley, Ga.	do	29.00	Sept. 22, 1887	Fort Valley and Troy R. P. O. extended.
Gribin to Columbus, Ga.	Georgia Midland R. R.	80.80	Aug. 12, 1887	New service.
Monticello to Madison, Ga.	Covington and Macon R. R.	27.16	June 1, 1888	Monticello and Macon R. P. O. extended.
Cotton Plant to New Albany, Miss.	Ship Island, Ripley and Kentucky R. R.	7.65	Aug. 3, 1887	Middleton and Cotton Plant R. P. O. extended.
Oakland to Clermont, Fla.	Orange Belt R.	9.65	Sept. 10, 1888	Monroe and Oakland R. P. O. extended.
Clermont to Tarpon Springs, Fla.	do	74.45	May 19, 1888	
New Orleans to Baton Rouge, La.	Louis., New Orleans and Texas R. R.	88.80	Apr. 28, 1888	Additional service, trains 5 and 6, Memphis and New Orleans R. P. O.

TABLE L.—*Statement of new railway post-office service established and service extended during the fiscal year ended June 30, 1888—Continued.*

FOURTH DIVISION—Continued.

New service.	Corporate title of company.	Distance.	Date of order for commencement of railway post-office service.	Remarks.
		Miles.		
Roanoke to Opelika, Ala.	East Alabama	39.38	Feb. 24, 1888	New service.
Florence to Lanes, S.C.	Northeastern of S.C.	48.50	Jan. 23, 1888	Wadesborough and Florence R. P. O. extended. Additional service, Florence to Lanes.
Titusville to Melbourne, Fla.	Jack, Tampa and Key West	43.00	Aug. 9, 1887	New service on river.
Melbourne to Jupiter, Fla.	do	86.00	July 11, 1887	Do.
FIFTH DIVISION.				
Bryan to Carlisle, Ohio	Cincinnati, Jackson and Mackinaw R. R.	16.65	Aug. 22, 1887	Cecil and West Alexandria R. P. O. (distance 110.77 miles) extended to Carlisle, Ohio; increase distance 16.65 miles.
		19.71	Oct. 10, 1887	Oct. 10, 1887, extended to Bryan, Ohio; increase distance 19.71 miles, making whole distance 147.13 miles.
Anderson to Ladoga, Ind	Midland Railway	65.87	Sept. 5, 1887	Sept. 5, 1887, R. P. O. service placed on this route between Anderson and Lebanon, Ind. (45.74 miles), on account of unsatisfactory service performed by closed pouches. Extended to Ladoga, Ind., Jan. 9, 1888, increase distance 20.13 miles.
Zanesville to Waterford, Ohio	Zanesville and Ohio River Railway	9.75	...do	Sept. 5, 1887, Zanesville and McConnelsville R. P. O. (distance 28.50 miles) extended to Stockport, Ohio; distance 9.75 miles.
		16.40	Mar. 19, 1888	Mar. 19, 1888, Zanesville and Stockport R. P. O. extended to Waterford, Ohio; increase distance 16.40 miles, making whole distance 64.65 miles.
Nashville to Saint Joseph, Tenn	Louisville and Nashville Railroad	47.00	Sept. 13, 1887	Columbia and St. Joseph R. P. O. extended to Nashville, Tenn., making R. P. O. service in addition to Nashville and Montgomery R. P. O. between Nashville and Columbia, Tenn.
			Sept. 19, 1887	Sept. 19, 1887, Inman and Bridgeport R. P. O. changed to run to Chickville, Tenn.; decrease in distance .57 miles, leaving closed pouch service between Inman and Victoria.
Dunlap, Tenn., to Bridgeport, Ala	Nashville, Chattanooga and St. Louis Railway	14.41	Feb. 20, 1888	Chickville and Bridgeport R. P. O. extended to Dunlap, Tenn.; increase distance 14.41 miles, making whole distance 38.40 miles.

Route	Railway	Miles	Date	Remarks
Marietta to Sharpsburgh, Ohio	Marietta and Mineral Railway	4.57	Oct. 3, 1887	Marietta and Amsville R. P. O. extended.
Henderson to Princeton, Ky.	Ohio Valley Railway	25.04	Nov. 21, 1887	Henderson and Marion R. P. O. extended.
Indianapolis, Ind., to Peoria, Ill	Indianapolis, Bloomington and Western Ry.	213.42	Dec. 8, 1887	Apartment car service established on night trains.
Pittsburgh, Pa., to Saint Louis, Mo.	Pitts., Cin. and St. Louis, Chic., St. Louis and Pitts., Vandalia Rwys.	621.48	Mar. 13, 1887	Additional daily line of 60-feet R. P. O. car established December 9, 1887, from March 13, 1887.
New Galilee, Pa., to New Lisbon, Ohio	Pittsburgh, Marion and Chicago Railway	25.33	Jan. 4, 1888	New R. P. O. service; satisfactory service not performed by closed pouch service.
Gallatin, Tenn., to Scottsville, Ky.	Chesapeake and Nashville Railway	35.87	Jan. 20, 1888	New R. P. O. service; satisfactory service not performed by closed ponchies.
Nashville, Tenn., to Saint Louis, Mo	Louisville and Nashville Railroad	71.30	Jan. 23, 1888	Additional R. P. O. service to Nashville and Saint Louis; R. P. O. established between Nashville, Tenn., and Hopkinsville, Ky.
Cincinnati, Ohio, to Chattanooga, Tenn	Cincinnati, New Orleans and Texas Pacific Ry	338.20	Feb. 1, 1888	Single daily line of R. P. O. cars (40 feet) established on day trains to meet the demands of the service on this line.
Princeton, Ky., to Clarksville, Tenn	Louisville and Nashville Railroad	57.53	Feb. 18, 1888	New R. P. O. service; service not satisfactorily performed by closed pouches.
Lacrosse to Brazil, Ind	Chicago and Indiana Coal Railway	27.06	Feb. 20, 1888	Fair Oaks and Brazil R. P. O. extended.
Phalanx Station to Bergholtz, Ohio	Lake Erie, Alliance and Southern Railway	35.90	...do	Phalanx Station and Alliance R. P. O. extended.
Louisville, Ky., to Huntingburgh and Evansville, Ind.	Louisville, Evansville and St. Louis Railway	68.84	Feb. 24, 1888	Jasper and Evansville R. P. O. extended from Huntingburgh, Ind. to Louisville, Ky.; service between Jasper and Huntingburgh to be performed by closed pouches.
Paducah, Ky., to Florence, Ala.	River service	300.00	Mar. 3, 1888	To satisfactorily perform service on steam boats on Tennessee River.
Louisville to Springfield, Ky.	Louisville and Nashville Railroad	18.05	Mar. 12, 1888	Louisville and Bardstown R. P. O. extended.
Painesville to Youngstown, Ohio	Pittsburgh and Western Railroad	16.21	Mar. 23, 1888	Painesville and Warren R. P. O. extended.
Springfield, Ohio, to Richmond, Ind	Pittsburgh, Cincinnati and St. Louis R.R.	10.99	Apr. 6, 1888	Xenia and Richmond R. P. O. service extended to Springfield, so as to have R. P. O. between Xenia and Springfield.
Evansville, Ind., to Providence, Ky	Louisville and Nashville Railroad	78.73	Apr. 19, 1888	Established to provide needed R. P. O. service. This is in addition to Nashville and Saint Louis R. P. O. between Evansville, Ind., and Earlington, Ky.
Terre Haute to Evansville, Ind.	Evansville and Terre Haute Railroad	110.41	Apr. 11, 1888	Service in apartment cars established on night trains.
Cincinnati, Ohio, to Chattanooga, Tenn	Cincinnati, New Orleans and Texas Pacific Railway.	117.80	May 3, 1888	Additional R. P. O. service to Cincinnati and Chattanooga; R. P. O. established between Cincinnati, Ohio, and Junction City, Ky., in apartment car.
Nashville, Tenn., to Montgomery, Ala	Louisville and Nashville Railroad	306.05	May 12, 1888	Additional service (mail apartment) placed on night trains of this line and a line of 45-feet postal cars placed on day trains.
Toledo to Cincinnati, Ohio	Dayton and Michigan and Cin., Ham. and Day, R. R's.	201.76	June 18, 1888	Single daily line of 40-feet postal cars established on night trains of this line.
Chicago, Ill., to Louisville, Ky	Louisville, New Albany and Chicago R. R	322.40	June 21, 1888	Do.
Killbuck to Trinway, Ohio	Cleveland, Akron and Columbus Railway	34.14	June 25, 1888	New R. P. O. service; service not satisfactorily performed by closed pouches.

TABLE L'.—*Statement of new railway post-office service established and service extended during the fiscal year ended June 30, 1888—Continued.*

SIXTH DIVISION.

New service.	Corporate title of company.	Distance.	Date of order for commencement of railway post-office service.	Remarks.
		Miles.		
Breckenridge, Minn., to Aberdeen, Dak	St. Paul, Minneapolis and Manitoba	138.83	July 7, 1887	Breckenridge and Aberdeen R. P. O. established.
Aberdeen to Orient, Dak	Chicago, Milwaukee and St. Paul	83.04	Oct. 25, 1887	Aberdeen and Orient R. P. O. established.
Springfield to Litchfield, Ill	St. Louis and Chicago	45.64	July 18, 1887	Springfield and Litchfield R. P. O. established.
Lindsay to Oakdale, Nebr	Fremont, Elkhorn and Mo. Valley	56.62	July 25, 1887	Scribner and Lindsay R. P. O. established.
Stromsburgh to Fairfield, Nebr	Kansas City and Omaha	65.49	Aug. 22, 1887	Stromsburgh and Fairfield R. P. O. established.
Waterville to Mankato, Minn	Minneapolis and St. Louis	28.34	Aug. 25, 1887	Red Wing an
to Minneapolis, Minn	Chicago, St. Paul and Kansas City	10.44	Sept. 1, 1887	Saint Paul, Hayfield and Waterloo R. P. O. extended.
Chicago to Dunlap (b. e.) Ill	do	101.39	Oct. 3, 1887	Chicago and Freeport R. P. O. established.
Hudson to Delavan, Iowa	do	26.74		Cedar Falls and Des Moines R. P. O. changed and extended
Winnipeg Junction, Minn., to Grand Forks, Dak.	Northern Pacific	100.86	do	Grand Forks and Winnipeg Junction R. P. O. established.
Chicago, Ill., to Milwaukee, Wis	Chicago, Milwaukee and St. Paul	85.00	Oct. 1, 1887	Milwaukee and Prairie du Chien R. P. O. extended.
Manilla to Sioux City, Iowa	do	90.70	Oct. 15, 1887	Sioux City and Mitchell R. P. O. extended
Bristol to Madison, Dak	do	103.39	Oct. 17, 1887	Bristol and Madison R. P. O. established.
Kingsley to Moville, Iowa	Chicago and Northwestern	9.13	Oct. 24, 1887	Carroll and Kingsley R. P. O. extended.
North Judson to Knox, Ind	Indiana, Illinois and Iowa	9.41	Nov. 7, 1887	North Judson and Streator R. P. O. extended.
Towner to Minot, Dak	St. Paul, Minneapolis and Manitoba	41.84	do	Crookston and Towner R. P. O. extended.
Redfield to Gettysburgh, Dak	Chicago and Northwestern	75.84	Nov. 28, 1887	Redfield and Gettysburgh R. P. O. established.
Janeville, Wis., to Rockford, Ill	Chicago, Milwaukee and St. Paul	25.03	Dec. 5, 1887	Milton and Mineral Point changed and extended.
Orleans, Nebr., to Brakeman, Kans	Burlington and Mo. River in Nebr	95.44	do	Orleans and Brakeman R. P. O. established.
Bruce, Wis., to Minneapolis, Minn	Minneapolis, Sault de Ste. Marie and Atl.	122.27	Dec. 8, 1887	Bruce and Minneapolis R. P. O. established.
Sidell to Tuscola, Ill	Chicago and Eastern Illinois	26.87	Dec. 5, 1887	Danville and Olney R. P. O. curtailed, and Danville and Tuscola R. P. O. established.
Langdon to Larimore, Dak	St. Paul, Minneapolis and Manitoba	76.19	do	Langdon and Larimore R. P. O. established.
Fairmount, Minn., to Oakes, Dak	Minneapolis and Pacific	72.64	Dec. 21, 1887	Fairmount and Minneapolis R. P. O. extended.
Auburn to Weeping Water, Nebr	Missouri Pacific	41.00	Nov. 28, 1887	Weeping Water and Lincoln R. P. O. extended.
Aurora to Arcadia, Nebr	Burlington and Mo. River in Nebr	90.73	Jan. 1, 1888	Aurora and Arcadia R. P. O. extended.
Grand Forks to Pembina, Dak	Northern Pacific	92.49	Jan. 7, 1888	Grand Forks and Winnipeg Junct. R. P. O. extended.
Napier, Mo., to Rulo "Y", Nebr	Burlington and Mo. River in Nebr	11.70	do	Kansas City and Oxford R. P. O. changed to run via Saint Joseph, Mo., and Rulo, Nebr.
Kansas City, Mo., to Table Rock, Nebr	do	132.75	do	Crete and Red Cloud R. P. O. changed to begin at Kansas City.
Great Falls to Helena, Mont	Montana Central	97.95	Jan. 16, 1888	Great Falls and Helena R. P. O. established.
Omaha to Hastings, Nebr	Fremont, Elkhorn and Mo. Valley	161.96	Feb. 1, 1888	Omaha and Hastings R. P. O. established.
Ottumwa, Iowa, to Kansas City, Mo	Chicago, Milwaukee and St. Paul	209.58	Jan. 30, 1888	Cedar Rapids and Ottumwa R. P. O. extended.
Douglass to Glenrock, Wyo	Fremont, Elkhorn and Mo. Valley	30.30	Mar. 7, 1888	Chadron and Douglass R. P. O. extended.

Ancona, Ill., to Fort Madison, Iowa	Chicago, Santa Fé, and California	187.00	Feb. 20, 1888	Chicago and Pekin R. P. O. changed to end at Fort Madison.
Streator to Ancona, Ill.	...do	6.10	...do	Streator and Pekin R. P. O.
McCool Junction to Alma, Nebr	Kansas City and ...dia	128.61	M. 1, 1888	McCool Junction and Alma R. P. O. established.
McCool Junction to Fairbury, Nebr.	St. Joseph and Grand ...ald	50.62	Feb. 20, 1888	McCool Junction and Fairbury R. P. O. established.
Palmer to Burwell, Nebr.	Burlington and Mo. River in Nebr	69.38	...do	Palmer and Burwell R. P. O. established.
Linwood to Geneva, Nebr	Fremont, Elkhorn and Mo. Valley	77.53	...do	Linwood and Geneva R. P. O. established.
Nebr	Burlington and Mo. River in Nebr	98.07	Apr. 6, 1888	...er R. P. O. established.
	...dort, Elkhorn and Mo. ...Eley	117.27	Feb. 20, 1888	Pacific Junction and ...ber R. P. O. extended.
	...ign and Mo. River in Nebr	117.93	Apr. 3, 1888	Missouri Valley and Rapid City R. P. O. extended.
Iowa	Northern ...do	47.70	Apr. 2, 1888	Nebraska City and ...ern Dow R. P. O. ...all.
	...ago, St. Paul and Kansas City	65.94	Apr. 9, 1888	Hicknon and Kanaas R. P. O. established.
Ind.	Union I ...fic	20.59	Apr. 20, 1888	Elo and Freeport R. P. O. changed and extended.
	Jacksonville and South Eastern	21.99	June 88	...all Junct. and Alma R. P. O. ...all to Lincoln.
	Northern Pacific	93.00	Mar. 29, 88	Jacksonville and Centralia R. P. O. extended.
	Mo. ...y	189.00	Apr. 30, 1886	Fargo and Minnewatan R. P. O. established.
	...do Mo. and St. Paul	10.00	May 788	Ortonville and Mitchell R. P. O. extended.
	...do Chicago, Burlington and Northern	47.00	May 25, 1888	Minneapolis and ...ago R. P. O. ...ded.
		206.00	Feb. 14, 1888	60-foot R. P. O. car line authorized.
		294.00	...do	Do.
Omaha, Nebr., to Ogden, Utah		311.87	May 8, 1881	50-foot R. P. O. car line authorized. ...thized.
Chicago, Ill., to North McGregor, Iowa		262.03	Sept. 9, 1887	40-foot R. P. O. car line authorized.
Mendota to Centralia, Ill.		212.88	June 27, 1888	40-foot R. P. O. car line authorized.

SEVENTH DIVISION.

Abilene to Concordia, Kans.	Chicago, Kansas and Western	54.84	Mar. 14, 1888	Abilene and Cottonwood Falls, Kans., R. P. O. extended to ...igin at Concordia, Kans.
Abileno to Cottonwood Falls, Kans.	...do	64.96	Aug. 8, 1887	Abilene and ...ter ...roi ...dils, Kans., R. P. O. established.
Alma to Herington, Kans.	Chicago, Kansas and Nebraska	45.39	July 20, 1887	Saint Joseph, Mo., and ...len, Kans., R. P. O. extended.
Arkansas City, Kans., to Purcell, Ind. T.	Southern Kansas	154.00	Feb. 25, 1888	Purcell, Ind. T., and ...Gile, Tex., R. P. O. extended.
Ashland to Engl.wood. Kans	Chicago, Kansas and Western	15.12	Mar. 1, 88	Mulvane and Ashland, Kans., R. P. O. ...all.
Atchison to Iowa s, Kans	Central Branch U. P.	209.38	July 19, 1887	Downs and ...ain, Kans., R. P. O. extended.
Batesville to Cushman, Ark	Saint Louis, Iron Mountain and Southern	11.63	Nov. 15, 1887	...ert and Batesville, ...o., R. P. O. extended.
Burlington to Gridley, Kans	Southern Kansas	9.27	Apr. 20, 1888	Lawrence and Burlington, Kans., R. P. O. extended.
Cedar Vale to Belle Plaine, Kans.	Denver, Memphis and Atlantic	51.91	Apr. 19, 1888	Belle Plaine and Burlington, Kans., R. P. O. extended.
Clarendon to Quanah, Tex.	Fort Worth and Denver City	81.88	Feb. 14, 1888	...igh and Fort Worth, Tex., R. P. O. ...all.
Cleburne to Weatherford, Tex.	Gulf, Colorado and Santa Fé	39.66	June 2888	...ille and Cleburne, Tex., R. P. O. extended.
Colorado Springs to Leadville, Colo.	Colorado Midland	133.05	Oct. 17, 1887	Colorado Springs and Ladville, Clo., H. P. O. established.
Commerce to Fort Worth, Tex.	Saint Louis, Arkansas and Texas	98.31	June 25, 1888	...rce and Fort Worth, Tex., R. P. O. established.
Coarse to Montgomery, Tex.	Gulf, Colorado and Santa Fé	15.93	June 5, 1888	...ery and Somerville (m o), Tex., R. P. O. extended.
Corsicana to Hillsborough, Tex.	Saint Louis, Arkansas and Texas	42.00	May 31, 1888	Corsicana and Hillsborough, Tex., R. P. O. established.

TABLE L.—*Statement of new railway post-office service established and service extended during the fiscal year ended June 30, 1888*—Continued.

SEVENTH DIVISION—Continued.

New service.	Corporate title of company.	Distance.	Date of order for commencement of railway post-office service.	Remarks.
		Miles.		
Cottonwood Falls to Bazaar, Kans	Chicago, Kansas and Western	10.44	Mar. 14, 1888	Abilene and Cottonwood Falls, Kans., R. P. O. extended to end at Bazaar, Kans.; Concordia and Bazaar R. P. O. afterward curtailed to end at Strong, Kans.; decreased distance, 12.80 miles.
Callison to Greensburgh, Kans	Kingman, Pratt and Western	21.24	Aug. 8, 1887	Wichita and Callison, Kans., R. P. O. extended.
Deming to Silver City, N. Mex	Atchison, Topeka and Santa Fé	46.59	Sept. 24, 1887	Rincon and Deming, N. Mex., R. P. O. extended.
East Lynne to Brownington, Mo	Kansas City and Southern	45.40	July 25, 1887	East Lynne and Deming, Mo., R. P. O. established.
Ellis to Wallace, Kans	Union Pacific	117.90	Apr. 17, 1888	Double daily service extended on Kansas City, Mo., and Denver, Colo. R. P. O.
Ellsworth to Wichita, Kans	Saint Louis and San Francisco	108.61	Mar. 5, 1888	Ellsworth and Wichita, Kans., R. P. O. established.
Fairbury, Nebr., to Phillipsburgh, Kans	Chicago, Kansas and Nebraska	129.04	Jun. 7, 1888	Fairbury, Nebr., and Phillipsburgh, Kans., R. P. O. established.
Fort Madison,Iowa, to Kansas City, Mo	Chicago, Santa Fé and California	218.27	May 28, 1888	Fort Madison, Iowa, and Kansas City, Mo., R. P. O. established.
Fort Smith to Mansfield, Ark	Saint Louis and San Francisco	32.23	Apr. 18, 1888	Fort Smith and Mansfield, Ark., R. P. O. established.
Fort Smith, Ark., to Paris, Tex	....do	154.96	Jan. 10, 1888	Monett, Mo., and Fort Smith, Ark., K. P. O. extended.
Geneseo to Kanopolis, Kans	Kanopolis and Kansas Central	14.47	Feb. 20, 1888	Wichita and Geneseo, Kans., R. P. O. extended.
Glenwood Springs to Aspen, Colo	Denver and Rio Grande	42.84	Dec. 15, 1887	Leadville and Glenwood Springs, Colo., R. P. O. extended.
Greensburgh to Mullinville, Kans	Kingman, Pratt and Western	9.93	Mar. 19, 1888	Wichita and Greensburgh, Kans., R. P. O. extended.
Halletsville to Kenedy Junction, Tex	San Antonio and Aransas Pass	76.90	July 19, 1887	Halletsville and Kenedy Junction, Tex., R. P. O. established.
Hebron to Nora, Nebr	Chicago, Kansas and Nebraska	21.90	July 15, 1887	Saint Joseph, Mo., and Hebron, Nebr., R. P. O. extended.
Henrietta to Denton, Tex	Missouri Pacific	121.16	July 1, 1887	Denton and Dallas, Tex., R. P. O. extended.
Herington to Pratt, Kans	Chicago, Kansas and Nebraska	127.15	Oct. 17, 1887	Herington and Pratt, Kans., R. P. O. established.
Herington to Wichita, Kans	....do	74.35	Oct. 24, 1887	Saint Joseph, Mo., and Herington, Kans., R. P. O. extended.
Horace, Kans., to Pueblo, Colo	Denver, Memphis and Atlantic, and Pueblo and State Line.	165.00	Mar. 1, 1888	Oswatomie and Horace, Kans., R. P. O. extended.
Independence to Coffeyville, Kans	Verdigris Valley, Independence and Western, and Denver, Memphis and Atlantic.	18.07	June 10, 1888	Holden, Mo., and Independence, Kans., R. P. O. extended.
Joplin to Webb City, Mo	Kansas City, Fort Scott and Memphis	6.55	Mar. 29, 1888	Fort Scott, Kans., and Joplin, Mo., R. P. O. extended.
Kansas City, Kans., to Kansas City, Mo	Kansas City, Wyandotte and Northwestern	7.88	Apr. 2, 1888	Kansas City and Seneca, Kans., R. P. O. extended.
Kansas City to Seneca, Kans	....do	116.06	Apr. 7, 1888	Kansas City and Seneca, Kans., R. P. O. established.
Kansas City, Mo., to Osawatomie, Kans	Kansas City and Southwestern and Missouri Pacific.	61.88	May 14, 1888	Osawatomie, Kans., and Pueblo, Colo., R. P. O. extended.

Route	Railroad		Date	Remarks
Keystone to Barnard, Kans	Chicago, Kansas and Western	43.33	Mar. 26, 1888	Keystone and Barnard, Kans., R. P. O. established.
Kincaid to Morantown, Kans	Kansas City and Pacific	11.95	May 10, 1888	Morantown and Coffeyville, Kans., R. P.O. extended.
Larned to Jetmore, Kans	Chicago, Kansas and Western	44.34	Nov. 8, 1887	Larned and Jetmore, Kans, R. P. O. established.
Leadville to Glenwood Springs, Colo	Denver and Rio Grande	91.98	Nov. 15, 1887	Leadville and Glenwood Springs, Colo., R-P. O. established.
Le Roy to Madison, Kans	Interstate	30.98	May 10, 1888	Butler, Mo., and Le Roy, Kans, T. P. O. extended.
Lincoln to Luray, Kans	Salina, Lincoln and Western	30.95	Dec. 31, 1887	Salina and Lincoln Kans. R. P. O. extended.
McCracken to Horace, Kans	Denver, Memphis and Atlantic	125.57	Dec. 5, 1887	and McCracken Kans., R.P.O. extended.
McFarland to Belleville, Kans	Chicago, Kansas and Western	104.78	Apr. 9, 1888	McFarland and Belleville Kans., R. P.O. established.
Madison to Beatrice, Kans	Chicago, Kansas and Western	45.65	Dec. 1888	Madison and Beatrice, Kans., R. P. O. established.
Marysville, Kans, to Beatrice, Nebr	Union Pacific	38.02	July 1887	Marysville and Manhattan, Kan., R. P. O. extended, and Omaha, etc., and Beatrice, Kans, R.P.O. curtailed.
Monett, Mo., to Wichita, Kans	Saint Louis and San Francisco	222.00	pt. 20, 1888	Double daily service established between Monett and Wichita.
Mount Pleasant to Sherman, Tex	Saint Louis, Arkansas and Texas	110.10	Sept 12, 1887	Mount Pleasant and Sherman, Tex R. P. O. established.
Morantown to Coffeyville, Kans	Kansas City and Pacific	73.64	Oct. 24, 1887	Morantown Coffeyville Kans., R.P. O. established.
Nashville to Hope, Ark	Arkansas and Louisiana	27.53	July 5, 1887	Double daily used on Nashville and Hope, Ark., R.P.O.
Ness City to Scott, Kans	Kansas, Kansas and Western	63.60	Aug. 24, 1887	Great End and Ness City, Kans., R.P.O extended.
Nora to Nelson, Nebr	Chicago, Kansas and Nebraska	6.40	Sept 28, 1887	Saint Joseph, Mo. and Nora, Nebr., R. P. O. extended.
Paris to Ladonia, Tex	Gulf, Colorado and Santa Fé	98.16	July 1, 1887	Honey Grove and Tex., P. T. P.O. curtailed to Ladonia and extended to Paris, Tex.
Phillipsburgh to Norton, Kans	Chicago, Kansas and Nebraska	83.73	May 1, 1888	Fairbury, Nebr., and Phillipsburgh, Kans., R. P. O. extended.
Pittsburgh to Girard, Kans	Southern Kansas	13.53	Apr. 2, 1888	Girard and Chanute, Kans., R. P. O. extended.
Pratt to Dodge City, Kans	Chicago, Kansas and Nebraska	74.04	May 25, 1888	Herington and Pratt, Kans., R.P.O. extended.
Pratt to Liberal, Kans	Chicago, Kansas and Nebraska	134.22	May 4, 1888	Pratt and Liberal, Kans., R.P.O. established.
Purcell, Ind T., to Gainesville, Tex	Gulf, Colorado and Santa Fé	105.73	Sept. 12, 1887	Purcell, Ind. T., and Gainesville, Tex., R. P. O. established.
Saint Louis to Tuton, Mo	Saint Louis, Kansas City and Colorado	59.91	July 25, 1887	Saint Louis and Union, Mo., R. P. O. established.
Saint Joseph, Mo., to Alma, Kans	Chicago, Kansas and Nebraska	128.45	July 1, 1887	Saint Joseph, Mo., and Alma, Kans., R. P. O. established.
Saint Joseph, Mo., to Hebron, Nebr	Chicago, Kansas and Nebraska	180.74	...do......	Saint Joseph, Mo., and Hebron, Nebr., R. P. O. established.
San Antonio to Kerrville, Tex	San Antonio and Aransas Pass	71.75	Oct. 4, 1887	San Antonio and Kerrville, Tex., R. P. O. established.
Sidell to Sedan, Kans	Le Roy and Caney Valley Air Line and Denver, Memphis and Atlantic	58.62	Jan. 13, 1888	Sidell and Sedan, Kans., R. P.O.
Spivey to Ashland, Kans	Chicago, Kansas and Western	100.00	Oct. 17, 1887	Mulvane and Spivey, Kans., R. P. O. extended.
Spofford to Eagle Pass, Tex	Galveston, Harrisburgh and San Antonio	84.66	May 15, 1888	Houston and Del En, Tex., R. P. Overhauled to Spofford, and extended to Eagle Pass, Tex.
Stafford to Larned, Kans	Denver, Memphis and Atlantic	38.77	Nov. 10, 1887	Bello and Stafford, Kans., R. P. O. extended.
Taylor to La Grange, Tex	Taylor, Bastrop and Houston	70.02	Dec. 6, 1887	Taylor and La Grange, Tex., R. P. O.
Waco to Gatesville, Tex	Saint Louis, Arkansas and Texas	44.04	May 31, 1888	Texarkana, and Waco, Tex., R. P. O.
Wallis to Halletsville, Tex	San Antonio and Aransas Pass	56.42	Oct. 3, 1887	Halletsville and Kenedy Jt tion, Tex., R.P.O. extended.
Wappapello to Chaonia, Mo	Cape Girardeau Southwestern	8.46	June 18, 1888	Cape Girardeau and Wappaello, Mo., R. P. O. extended.
Weeping Water to Auburn, Nebr. (via Nebraska City)	Missouri Pacific	47.76	Dec. 1, 1887	Route of Omaha and Kansas City clerks changed to include this service.
West Point to Yoakum Tex	San Antonio and Aransas Pass	50.30	Apr. 17, 1888	West Point and Yoakum, Tex. R. P. O. established.

TABLE LI.—*Statement of new railway post-office service established and service extended during the fiscal year ended June 30, 1888—Continued.*

SEVENTH DIVISION—Continued.

New service.	Corporate title of company.	Distance.	Date of order for commencement of railway post-office service.	Remarks.
		Miles.		
Wichita to Caldwell, Kans.	Chicago, Kansas and Nebraska	49.98	Nov. 28, 1887	Saint Joseph, Mo., and Wichita, Kans., R. P. O. extended.
Yates Center to Sidell, Kans.	Verdigris Valley, Independence and Western	18.05	Feb. 18, 1888	Sidell and Sedan, Kans. R. P. O. extended.
Sedalia, Mo., to Denison, Tex		453.13	Nov. 2, 1887	Additional line of 40 foot cars authorized.
Council Bluffs, Iowa, to Kansas City, Mo		201.22	Dec. 12, 1887	40-foot R. P. O. car line authorized.
Kansas City, Mo., to Oxford, Nebr		208.19	Feb. 14, 1888	40-foot R. P. O. car line authorized.
Kansas City, Mo., to Denver, Col		641.02	Oct. 12, 1887	40-foot R. P. O. car line authorized.
Saint Louis and Kansas City, Mo		284.15	Sept. 13, 1888	Additional 60 foot line of R. P. O. cars authorized.

EIGHTH DIVISION.

New service.	Corporate title of company.	Distance.	Date of order.	Remarks.
Ashland, Oregon, to Delta, Cal	Central Pacific Co	132.40	Jan. 7, 1888	Portland and Ashland, Oregon, extended to Sacramento, Cal. New service between Ashland and Delta.
Barstow to Los Angeles, Cal	Cal. Southr. and Cal. Central	72.09	June 25, 1887	Albuquerque and Mojave extended to Los Angeles. The R. P. O. was reported in Table A by Seventh Division last year. The increase in R. P. O. service was not reported.
Cle Elum to Tacoma, Wash	Northern Pacific	101.09	Sept. 16, 1887	Helena, Mont., and Portland, Oregon, changed to cover part of routes 43605 and 43611, over which no R. P. O. service was performed.
Colton to San Bernardino, Cal	Cal Southern R. R	3.99	July 28, 1887	Colton and National City R. P. O. extended to San Bernardino.
Dundee Junction (n. o.) to Alrlie, Oregon	Oregon Rwy. Co., Limited Line	52.60	June 20, 1888	Service commenced July 1, 1887.
Los Angeles to Santa Barbara, Cal	Southern Pacific Co	109.00	July 11, 1887	New service Saugus Station to Los Angeles, 32.4 miles additional to San Francisco and Los Angeles.
Port Harford to Los Olivos, Cal	Pacific Coast Rwy	79.50	Jan. 25, 1888	New R. P. O. service.
Shingle Springs to Placerville, Cal	Sacramento Valley R. R	12.15	May 25, 1888	Shingle Springs and Sacramento extended.

NINTH DIVISION.

New service.	Corporate title of company.	Distance.	Date of order.	Remarks.
Ashley to Muskegon, Mich	Toledo, Saginaw and Muskegon	96.24	Mar. 2, 1888	New service.
Detroit, Mich., to Logansport, Ind	Wabash Western	16.49	July 21, 1887	Extending service from Denver to Logansport, Ind.

TABLE M^m.—*Statement of annual salaries of railway postal clerks, by classes, on June 30, 1888.*

Class.	Annual salary.	Number of railway postal clerks.	Aggregate annual salary.	Class.	Annual salary.	Number of railway postal clerks.	Aggregate annual salary.
Fifth	$1,400	67	$93,800	First	$660	2	$1,320
Fifth	1,300	566	735,800	First	650	3	1,950
Fourth	1,150	693	796,950	First	640	3	1,920
Third	1,000	2,034	2,034,000	First	630	1	630
Second	900	800	720,000	First	610	2	1,220
Second	890	6	5,340	First	600	54	32,400
Second	880	10	8,800	First	580	2	1,160
Second	870	13	11,310	First	570	2	1,140
Second	860	17	14,620	First	560	1	560
Second	850	8	6,800	First	540	1	540
Second	840	10	8,400	First	530	1	530
Second	830	2	1,660	First	520	2	1,040
Second	820	7	5,740	First	510	3	1,530
Second	810	10	8,100	First	500	5	2,500
First	800	618	494,400	First	480	3	1,440
First	790	6	4,740	First	420	3	1,260
First	780	5	3,900	First	410	2	820
First	770	7	5,390	First	400	1	400
First	760	8	6,080	First	370	1	370
First	750	5	3,750	First	360	1	360
First	740	5	3,700	First	320	1	320
First	730	4	2,920	First	300	11	3,300
First	720	30	21,600	First	240	1	240
First	710	6	4,260	First	150	2	300
First	700	23	16,100	First	100	2	200
First	690	3	2,070	First	12	6	72
First	680	6	4,080	First	1	5	5
First	670	4	2,680	Total		5,094	5,064,517

Statement of miles traveled by railway postal clerks in the performance of duty during the fiscal year ended June 30, 1888.

FIRST DIVISION.

Railway post-office.	Distance from register to register.	No. of round trips per week.	No. of clerks at work on line.	Annual distance traveled by clerks.	Average annual distance traveled by clerks.	Remarks.
	Miles.			*Miles.*	*Miles.*	
Alton Bay and Dover	28.42	12	1	35,694	35,694	
Athol and Springfield	48.34	6	1	30,357	30,357	
Augusta and Portland	68.39	6	1	(¹)	(¹)	This clerk runs in connection with Skowhegan and Portland R. P. O. The 3 clerks performing the service of the two R. P. O's. ¹ Shown in columns 5 and 6, Skowhegan and Portland R. O.
Bangor and Bar Harbor	51.00	6	1	32,028	32,028	
Bangor and Boston:						
Night run	245.90	7	12	539,996	44,999	
Day run	245.90	6	16	617,700	38,606	
Short stops	108.80	....	4	136,652	34,163	Short stops between Portland and Boston.
Bangor and Bucksport	19.24	12	1	24,164	24,164	
Bath and Lewiston	28.47	12	1	35,758	35,758	
Belfast and Burnham	33.95	12	1	42,640	42,640	
Boston and Albany:						
Day run	203.25	6	12	382,923	31,910	
Night run	203.25	6½	16	595,116	37,194	
Short run	99.44	6	4	124,896	31,224	
Helpers	99.44	....	2	62,448	31,224	Between Boston and Springfield.

Statement of miles traveled by railway postal clerks, etc.—Continued.

FIRST DIVISION—Continued.

Railway post-office.	Distance from register to register.	No. of round trips per week.	No. of clerks at work on line.	Annual distance traveled by clerks.	Average annual distance traveled by clerks.	Remarks.
	Miles.			*Miles.*	*Miles.*	
Boston, Clinton and Fitchburg.	62.49	6	1	39,243	39,243	
Boston and Greenville.........	60.32	6	1	37,837	37,837	
Boston and Hopewell Junction.	215.23	6	4	135,164	33,791	
Boston and Hopewell Junction:						
Short run	118.30	6	2	74,292	37,146	These clerks run between Boston
Second clerks..............	153.43	....	3	96,200	32,067	and Bristol, two-thirds time.
Short stop	86.13	....	1	36,002	36,002	Between Boston and Williman-tic, 4 days in the week.
Boston, Nashua and Keene...	96.22	6	2	60,426	30,213	
Boston, Providence and New York.	233.07	7	16	682,429	42,651	
Boston, Providence and New York.	105.35	....	2	76,116	38,558	Short stops between New York and Saybrook.
Boston, Springfield and New York:						
Day	235.17	6	24	886,120	36,921	
Night	235.17	7	24	1,032,866	43,036	
Messengers...............	235.17	7	4	172,144	43,036	
Short run	135.73	6	12	261,427	21,785	
Short stops ....,......	(¹)	....	4	140,980	35,245	¹There are 12 clerks on this line who run one way a day, and 4 clerks as short stops who double the road between New York and Springfield, 135.73 miles, 3 days, and New York and Wallingford, 85.73 miles, 3 days. The Sunday run between New York and New Haven is divided among the 16 men (73.23 miles).
Boston and Troy:						
A. m.................	191.04	6	8	289,946	29,993	
P. m	191.04	6	8	239,946	29,993	
Short stops ....,...	71.67	....	2	45,008	22,504	Between Troy and Shelburne Falls, from June 14, 1888.
Boston and Wellfleet:						
A. m.................	106.56	6	4	133,839	33,459	1 acting clerk additional, 1,476 miles.
P. m.................	106.56	6	4	133,839	33,459	
Boundary Line and Presque Isle	39.00	6	1	24,492	24,492	
Brattleborough and Palmer....	56.33	6	1	35,375	35,375	
Cambridge Junction and Burlington.	34.47	6	1	21,647	21,647	
Canton and Mechanic Falls....	25.52	6	1	16,026	16,026	
Claremont and Boston	129.84	6	2	68,971	34,485	Claremont and Lowell to Apr. 15, 1888; Claremont and Boston from Apr. 16, 1888.
Danbury and South Norwalk ..	23.61	12	1	29,654	29,654	
Essex Junction and Boston....	241.86	6	8	303,776	37,972	
Farmington and Lewiston	47.12	6	1	29,591	29,591	
Greenville and Bangor.........	91.03	6	1	57,166	57,166	
Hartford and Millerton	70.96	12	2	89,125	44,562	
Hartford and Saybrook	45.36	12	2	56,972	28,486	
Keene and South Vernon	24.35	12	1	30,584	30,584	
Lancaster and Boston...........	212.03	6	6	201,265	35,898	Lancaster and Boston to Nov. 30, 1887; Lancaster and Concord from Dec. 1, 1887; Lancaster and Boston from May 28, 1888.
Litchfield and Bethel	39.03	6	1	24,510	24,510	
Lowell and Ayer.............	16.98	12	1	21,326	21,326	
Lowell and Taunton	62.01	12	2	77,884	38,942	
Manchester, Lawrence and Boston.	53.85	12	2	50,471	25,236	Double service between Manchester and Lawrence.
Manchester and Peterborough.	63.37	6	1	39,796	39,796	
New Hartford and Farmington.	14.90	12	1	17,960	17,960	
New Haven and New York....	77.05	6	1	48,387	36,290	This clerk is relieved every fourth week by West Winsted and Bridgeport clerk.
New London and New Haven..	51.81	12	2	65,072	32,536	
Newburyport and Boston.....:	40.63	12	2	51,030	25,515	

Statement of miles traveled by railway postal clerks, etc.—Continued.

FIRST DIVISION—Continued.

Railway post-office.	Distance from register to register.	No. of round trips per week.	No. of clerks at work on line.	Annual distance traveled by clerks.	Average annual distance traveled by clerks.	Remarks.
Newport and Springfield:	*Miles.*			*Miles.*	*Miles.*	
Day	229.60	6	8	288,377	36,047	
Night	229.60	6	8	319,506	39,938	Line curtailed to begin at Newport from Apr. 16, 1888, inclusive.
Short run	124.39	6	2	78,117	39,058	
Short stops	120.00	....	2	{ 37,680	37,680	Day run, runs all the time.
				31,400	31,400	Short run, 5 days in the week.
North Adams and Pittsfield	21.43	12	1	26,916	26,916	
North Anson and Portland	104.17	6	2	65,418	32,709	These clerks run between Oakland and Portland, with Skowhegan and Portland clerks as assistants.
North Conway and Boston	139.37	¹12	6	226,054	37,675	¹ Double service between Wolfboro Junction and Portsmouth.
Palmer and New London	65.30	6	1	41,008	41,008	
Peterborough and Worcester	53.80	6	1	33,786	33,786	
Pittsfield and Bridgeport	110.49	13	4	150,266	37,566	One round trip Sundays.
Pittsfield and Hooksett	20.35	6	1	12,779	12,779	
Plymouth and Concord	51.40	6	1	32,279	32,279	
Portland and Boston:						
A. m	116.70	6	6	219,862	36,643	
P. m	116.70	6	4	146,575	36,643	
Portland and Island Pond	140.78	6	{ 3	94,061	31,353	¹ Helpers.
			{ ¹2	94,061	47,030	
Portland and Island Pond (short run).	92.16	6	2	57,876	28,938	
Portland and Rochester	52.74	3	1	33,120	33,120	Clerk appointed to Portland and Worcester R. P. O., and runs as assistant with that R. P. O. from Rochester to Portland.
Portland and Swanton	232.90	6	4	146,261	36,565	
Portland and Swanton (short run).	72.87	6	1	45,762	45,762	
Portland and Worcester	147.34	6	6	185,059	30,843	
Portland and Worcester (short run).	46.76	6	1	29,365	29,365	
Portsmouth and Concord	59.25	6	1	37,209	37,209	
Portsmouth and Manchester	41.52	6	1	26,074	26,074	
Providence and New London	65.24	12	2	81,942	40,971	
Providence and Pascoag	23.75	12	1	29,830	29,830	
Providence and Willimantic	59.04	6	1	37,077	37,077	
Richford and Saint Albans	28.91	6	1	18,155	18,155	
Rockland and Portland	88.42	6	3	92,441	30,813	Double service between Rockland and Brunswick.
Rutland, Bennington and Troy.	85.19	6	2	53,499	26,749	
Saint Albans and Boston:						
Day	265.40	6	8	333,342	41,667	
Night	265.40	6	8	333,342	41,667	
Saint Albans and Troy	184.69	6	3	115,985	38,661	
Skowhegan and Portland	103.00	6	2	104,492	34,831	These clerks run in connection with Augusta and Portland R. P. O., the three clerks performing service of the two R. P. O's.
South Londonderry and Brattleborough.	36.47	6	1	22,903	22,903	
Springfield and Hartford	32.29	12	1	40,556	40,556	
Vanceborough and Bangor:						
Day	114.44	6	4	143,736	35,934	
Night	114.44	6	4	143,736	35,934	
Wells River and Montpelier	38.64	6	1	24,206	24,206	
West Winsted and Bridgeport.	62.22	12	3	78,149	26,049	One of these clerks relieves the New Haven and New York clerk every fourth week.
Williamsburgh and New Haven	85.59	12	3	107,500	35,833	
Willimantic and New Haven	54.69	6	1	34,345	34,345	
Winchendon and Palmer	49.94	6	1	31,362	31,362	
Winchendon and Worcester	38.05	6	1	23,895	23,895	
Worcester and Norwich	59.72	6	1	37,504	37,504	
Worcester and Providence	44.14	12	2	55,440	27,720	

Statement of miles traveled by railway postal clerks, etc.—Continued.

SECOND DIVISION.

Railway post-office.	Distance from register to register.	No. of round trips per week.	No. of clerks at work on line.	Annual distance traveled by clerks.	Average annual distance traveled by clerks.	Remarks.
	Miles.			*Miles.*	*Miles.*	
Addison and Galeton	46.56	6	1	29,240	29,240	
Albany and Binghamton	148.21	6	4	133,896	33,474	1 helper Albany and Maryland, 70 miles.
Albany and New York	145.35	6	6	228,200	38,033	2 helpers one way; they return in New York and Rochester R.P.O.
Albany, Kingston and New York.	146.23	12	4	183,664	45,916	
Allentown and Harrisburg	91.84	12	3	115,350	38,450	
Allentown and Pawling	44.18	6	1	27,745	27,745	
Auburn and Freeville	39.41	6	1	24,749	24,749	
Auburn and Harrisburgh	59.94	6	1	37,579	37,579	
Babylon and New York........	37.96	6	1	37,501	37,501	Clerk alternates with Sag Harbor and New York clerk.
Batavia and Buffalo	47.39	6	1	29,761	29,761	
Bellwood and Punxsutawney.....	58.30	6	1	36,612	36,612	
Belvidere and Philadelphia....	102.54	6	1	64,395	64,395	
Bennington and Chatham......	57.79	6	1	36,292	36,292	
Berlin and Salisbury.........	23.86	6	1	14,984	14,984	
Bethlehem and Philadelphia...	57.60	15	3	108,217	36,072	Triple daily service outward and double inward.
Binghamton and New York....	208.70	6	6	262,127	43,688	
Boston Corners and Poughkeepsie.	38.06	6	1	23,902	23,902	
Bound Brook and Philadelphia.	59.96	6	1	37,655	37,655	
Branch Junction and Pittsburgh.	70.86	6	1	44,500	44,500	
Branchville and Waterloo	22.02	12	1	21,792	21,792	6 of these trips are between Newton and Waterloo, 12.68 miles.
Brewster and New York.......	62.19	12	2	78,110	39,055	
Buffalo and Emporium	121.55	6	2	76,333	38,166	
Buffalo and Pittsburgh	278.10	6	6	254,717	42,453	2 helpers Oil City and Pittsburgh, 132.50 miles.
Buffalo and West	49.56	6	1	31,124	31,124	
Buffalo and Youngstown.......	227.87	7	6	250,770	41,795	1 clerk runs between Buffalo and Jamestown and 1 between Salamanca and Jamestown, both between Jamestown and Youngstown. No service on Sunday between Buffalo and Jamestown.
Butler and Freeport	21.46	12	1	26,954	26,954	
Canandaigua and Batavia......	50.17	6	1	31,507	31,507	
Canandaigua and Elmira..... ..	66.17	6	1	31,047	31,047	Clerk alternates with Elmira and Williamsport clerk.
Carbondale and Scranton	17.46	18	1	32,895	32,895	
Carlisle and Gettysburgh......	32.34	6	1	20,310	20,310	
Cayuga and Ithaca	39.11	6	1	24,561	24,561	
Chambersburgh and Richmond Furnace.	31.35	6	1	19,688	19,688	
Chatham and New York.......	130.44	12	5	163,832	32,766	
Canastota and Elmira	118.76	6	2	74,581	37,290	
Clayton and Chestertown......	32.71	6	1	20,542	20,542	
Clayton and Easton..........	44.52	6	1	27,959	27,959	
Columbia and Perryville......	43.88	6	1	27,557	27,557	
Curwensville and Tyrone......	47.45	6	1	29,799	29,799	
Dansville and Buffalo.........	95.98	6	1	43,641	43,641	Clerk alternates with Rochester and Elmira clerk.
Downingtown and New Holland.	28.28	6	1	17,760	17,760	
Driftwood and Red Bank Furnace.	109.98	6	2	69,067	34,583	
Dunkirk and Titusville........	91.41	6	2	80,466	40,233	Clerk alternates with Larabee and Clermont clerk on the Buffalo and Emporium R. P. O. as helper between Buffalo and Clermont.
Easton and Hazleton...........	69.18	18	5	153,797	30,759	6 of these trips, Easton to Mauch Chunk, 45.50 miles.
Elmira and Bloesburgh	52.41	6	1	32,913	32,913	
Elmira and Wilkesbarre.......	124.13	6	1	77,954	77,954	

SECOND DIVISION—Continued.

Railway post-office.	Distance from register to register.	No. of round trips per week.	No. of clerks at work on line.	Annual distance traveled by clerks.	Average annual distance traveled by clerks.	Remarks.
	Miles.			*Miles.*	*Miles.*	
Elmira and Williamsport	79.13	6	2	62,094	31,047	Clerk alternates with Canandaigua and Elmira clerk.
Erie and Pittsburgh	148.00	6	3	92,944	30,981	
Geneva and Williamsport	172.29	6	3	108,198	36,066	
Georgetown and Franklin City.	56.26	6	1	35,331	35,331	
Glyndon and Gettysburgh	51.42	12	2	64,584	32,292	
Greenport and New York	98.60	12	4	123,842	30,960	1 clerk performs no service on road, but carries registers from New York post office to Long Island City, and also works in lobby of New York post-office
Greenville and Butler	58.87	6	1	36,970	36,970	
Greenwood Lake and New York.	45.63	6	1	28,656	28,656	
Greycourt and Belvidere	63.36	6	1	39,790	39,790	
Harrington and Lewes..........	40.79	6	1	25,616	25,616	
Harrisburg and Baltimore.....	86.22	6	2	54,146	27,073	
Harrisburg and Martinsburgh.	94.79	12	4	170,552	42,638	1 helper Harrisburg and Shippensburgh, 41 miles.
Haverstraw and New York ...	43.41	6	1	27,261	27,261	
Hasleton and Sunbury........	52.32	6	1	33,039	33,039	
Hornellsville and Buffalo	92.61	6	2	58,159	29,079	
Huntingdon and Cumberland ..	90.69	6	2	56,953	28,476	
Indiana and Branch Junction..	19.20	12	1	24,116	24,116	
Ithaca and Owego	35.00	6	1	21,980	21,980	
Johnstown and Rockwood ...	45.71	6	1	28,706	28,706	
Kane and Callery	126.87	6	2	79,674	39,837	
Kays and Stroudsburgh........	47.90	6	1	30,081	30,081	
Kingston and Goshen..........	44.26	6	1	27,795	27,795	
Lancaster and Harrisburg.....	40.87	6	1	25,666	25,666	
Lancaster and Frederick.......	81.67	6	2	51,289	25,644	
Larabee and Clermont	22.16	6	1	46,120	46,120	Clerk alternates with Dunkirk and Titusville clerk as helper in Buffalo and Emporium R. P. O. between Buffalo and Clermont.
Lock Haven and Harrisburg...	118.63	12	6	297,999	49,666	
Lock Haven and Tyrone........	60.46	6	1	37,969	37,969	
Lyons and Sayre...............	92.22	6	2	57.914	28,957	
Meadville and Oil City	36.62	6	1	22,997	22,997	
Middletown and New York....	89.78	6	2	83,942	41,971	Alternates with Port Jervis, N. Y., clerk.
Millerton and Dutchess Junction.	57.97	6	1	36,406	36,405	
Monmouth Junction and Manasquan.	33.18	6	1	20,837	20,837	
Montandon and Bellefonte. ..	69.27	6	1	43,502	43,502	
Montrose and Tunkhannock...	29.16	6	1	18,312	18,312	
Mount Carmel and Sunbury ...	27.47	6	1	17,251	17,251	
New Berlin and Sidney........	25.16	6	1	15,800	15,800	
New York and Dunkirk:						
East division................	332.63	13	31	1,532,716	49,442	4 helpers Hornellsville and Susquehanna; 3 helpers Hornellsville and Binghamton.
West division.............	128.75	7	6	262,735	47,122	
New York and Elmira	303.58	6	5	233,070	46,614	1 helper Elmira and Laceyville.
New York and Hackettstown .	62.79	6	1	26,288	26,288	Clerk relieved every third week by New York, Dover, and Easton clerk.
New York and Philadelphia...	91.82	12	3	115,320	38,440	
New York and Pittsburgh.....	443.20	27	132	7,052,180	53,425	3 of these trips between Pittsburgh and Harrisburg, 249 miles; 3 of these trips between Altoona and Harrisburg, 132 miles.
New York and Point Pleasant.	60.64	18	4	161,974	40,493	1 helper and 1 additional clerk.
New York and Rochester......	397.12	6½	20	934,059	46,702	
New York and Saint George...	5.90	24	1	14,820	14,820	•
New York and Washington:	} 227.85					
Fast mail		{ 6½	21	798,563	38,027	5 helpers.
Day line		6½	12	464,814	38,734	
Night line		7	26	1,042,412	40,098	6 helpers.

Statement of miles traveled by railway postal clerks, etc.—Continued.

SECOND DIVISION—Continued.

Railway post-office.	Distance from register to register.	No. of round trips per week.	No. of clerks at work on line.	Annual distance traveled by clerks.	Average annual distance traveled by clerks.	Remarks.
	Miles.			*Miles.*	*Miles.*	
New York, Dover and Easton..	86.87	6	2	67,708	33,854	1 clerk relieves New York and Hackettstown every third week.
New York, Somerville and Easton.	75.09	12	3	94,314	31,438	
Nineveh and Carbondale	57.56	6	1	36,148	36,148	
Nordmont and Hartley Hall ...	27.16	6	1	17,056	17,056	
North Creek and Saratoga	58.25	6	1	36,581	36,581	
North Fair Haven and Sayre ..	118.11	12	3	128,646	42,882	6 of these trips between Auburn and Sayre, 86.74 miles.
Northville and Fonda..........	26.79	12	1	33,648	33,648	
Norwood and Rome.............	146.92	6	3	137,946	45,982	
Nyack and New York	30.35	12	1	38,150	38,120	
Ogdensburgh and Utica.........	134.78	6	3	137,866	49,955	1 helper Utica and Castorland, 66 miles. Clerk alternates with Watertown and Utica Clerk.
Oneida and New York.........	270.33	6	4	169,767	42,442	
Oswego and Binghampton......	115.30	12	4	144,816	36,204	
Oswego and Oneida............	58.33	6	1	36,631	36,631	
Oswego and Suspension Bridge.	151.19	6	2	94,947	47,473	
Peninsular Junction and Cape Charles.	73.51	6	1	46,164	46,164	
Penn Haven and Mount Carmel.	51.78	6	1	32,518	32,518	
Philadelphia and Atlantic City.	60.76	12	2	76,314	38,157	
Philadelphia and Baltimore...	98.04	6	2	61,569	30,784	
Philadelphia and Cape May...	83.60	12	2	105,002	52,501	
Philadelphia and Crisfield	162.92	6	4	142,506	35,626	1 helper Philadelphia and Clayton.
Philadelphia and Dover........	75.22	6	1	47,238	47,238	
Philadelphia and Harrisburg ..	166.55	12	6	200,739	33,456	
Philadelphia and Port Deposit.	98.80	12	2	86,212	43,106	
Philadelphia and Port Norris..	59.14	12	2	62,072	31,036	6 of these trips between Philadelphia and Bridgeton.
Philadelphia and West Chester.	28.50	12	1	35,796	35,796	
Philadelphia, Aiken and Baltimore.	96.00	6	2	60,288	30,144	
Pittsburgh and Fairchance....	75.84	6	1	47,628	47,628	
Pittsburgh and New Haven....	60.12	6	1	37,755	37,775	
Pittsburgh and Washington...	31.62	12	1	39,714	39,714	
Pittsburgh and West Brownsville.	54.34	6	1	34,126	34,126	
Pittsburgh and Wheeling......	72.08	6	1	45,266	45,266	
Plattsburgh and Saranac Lake.	72.83	6	1	45,731	45,731	
Point Pleasant and Philadelphia.	71.86	6	1	45,128	45,128	
Port Jefferson and Long Island City.	46.75	12	1	52,595	52,595	6 of these trips between Port Jefferson and Westbury; 6 of these trips between Port Jefferson and Jamaica.
Port Jervis and New York.....	87.77	12	2	82,680	41,340	Clerk relieved every third week by Middletown and New York clerk.
Portland and Nazareth	26.64	6	1	16,730	16,730	
Pottsville and Philadelphia....	94.13	18	5	236,456	47,291	
Pottsville, Tamaqua and Herndon.	78.74	12	2	85,647	42,823	6 of these trips are between Pottsville and Shamokin, 57.64 miles.
Reading and Quarryville.......	57.50	6	1	36,110	36,110	
Reading and Wilmington.......	74.07	6	1	46,516	46,516	
Red Bank and Bridgeton.......	95.20	6	1	59,786	59,786	
Richland and Niagara Falls....	181.40	6	3	113,919	37,973	
Richland and Syracuse.........	42.33	6	1	26,583	26,583	
Ridgway and Erie	119.48	6	2	75,033	37,516	
Rochester and Elmira..........	112.50	6	2	87,284	43,642	Clerk alternates with Dansville and Buffalo clerk.
Rochester and Olean..........	108.23	6	2	67,968	33,984	
Rochester and Punxsutawney ..	230.98	6	4	145,055	36,264	
Rochester and Suspension Bridge.	74.89	12	3	94,062	31,354	
Rockaway and High Bridge ...	30.57	6	1	19,198	19,198	
Rondout and Stamford	74.86	12	3	103,328	34,443	
Rouse's Point and Albany (Rouse's Point division).	113.90	6	2	71,529	35,764	Between Rouse's Point and Whitehall.

Statement of miles traveled by railway postal clerks, etc.—Continued.

SECOND DIVISION—Continued.

Railway post-office.	Distance from register to register.	No. of round trips per week.	No. of clerks at work on line.	Annual distance traveled by clerks.	Average annual distance traveled by clerks.	Remarks.
	Miles.			*Miles.*	*Miles.*	
Rouse's Point and Albany (Rutland division).	101.55	6	4	127,547	31,886	Between Albany, N. Y., and Rutland, Vt.
Rutland and Troy	85.84	6	2	53,908	26,954	
Sag Harbor and New York	100.75	12	4	144,217	36,054	1 helper runs 50.50 miles daily; clerks alternate with Babylon and New York.
Saint Albans and Ogdensburgh.	143.15	6	2	89,898	44,949	
Salamanca and Oil City	97.69	6	2	61,349	30,674	
Scranton and Northumberland	80.48	12	3	101,082	33,694	
Seaford and Cambridge	33.64	6	1	21,126	21,126	
Slatington and Reading........	43.63	6	1	27,400	27,400	
Sodus Point and Stanley........	34.03	6	1	21,371	21,371	
South Amboy and Philadelphia.	62.92	12	2	79,028	39,514	
State Line and Rhinecliff	42.53	6	1	26,709	26,709	
Stoneboro and New Castle	36.49	6	1	22,916	22,916	
Sunbury and Lewistown........	51.12	6	1	32,103	32,103	
Suspension Bridge and Buffalo	24.35	12	1	30,584	30,584	
Syracuse and Earlville.	43.66	6	1	27,418	27,418	
Syracuse, Auburn and Rochester.	104.71	6	4	131,516	32,879	
Towanda and Bernice	30.72	6	1	19,292	19,292	
Tower City and Lebanon	42.26	6	1	26,539	26,539	
Townsend and Centreville. ...	35.21	6	1	22,112	22,112	
Utica and Binghamton.........	95.70	6	2	63,360	31,680	Clerk alternates with Utica and Randallsville clerk.
Utica and Randallsville.... ..	81.47	12	1	31,680	31,680	Clerk alternates with Utica and Binghamton clerk; 6 of these trips between Utica and Bouckville, 24.17 miles.
Watertown and Utica	91.93	6	1	45,556	45,556	Clerk alternates with Ogdensburgh and Utica clerk.
Wellsville and Bradford	56.65	6	1	35,576	35,576	
Whiting and Tuckerton	29.48	12	1	37,027	37,027	
Wilkesbarre and Potteville....	81.30	6	1	51,056	51,056	
Williamsport and Baltimore...	179.83	6	13	510,137	39,241	1 helper, Harrisburg and Williamsport.
Williamsport and Erie.........	249.68	6	4	156,799	39,199	
Williamsport and Gazzam	141.34	6	2	88,762	44,381	
Williamsport and Port Clinton.	121.77	6	2	76,472	38,236	
Wilmington and Landenburgh.	29.38	6	1	12,799	12,799	
York and Peach Bottom	40.67	6	1	25,541	25,541	

THIRD DIVISION.

Railway post-office.	Distance from register to register.	No. of round trips per week.	No. of clerks at work on line.	Annual distance traveled by clerks.	Average annual distance traveled by clerks.	Remarks.
Annapolis Junction and Annapolis.	21.09	6	1	13,245	13,245	
Asheville and Jarrett's	101.33	6	2	63,635	31,817	
Baltimore and Bristol..........	477.57	7	12	545,300	45,441	2 helpers perform daily (except Sunday) service, Baltimore, Md., to White Post, Va., 135.80 miles. West division, 2 clerks to crew.
Baltimore and Grafton	294.86	21	32	1,726,704	53,959	
Baltimore and Lexington	258.32	6	5	224,397	44,879	1 helper Staunton to Stephenson, Va., 99 miles.
Baltimore and Martinsburgh ..	101.32	6	2	63,629	31,814	
Baltimore and Washington	43.37	6	1	27,236	27,236	
Baltimore and Williamsport ...	94.12	6	2	59,107	29,553	
Baltimore and Winchester.....	114.48	6	1	71,893	23,962	Clerk relieved every 6 days by clerks in the Baltimore and Martinsburgh R. P. O.
Bowie and Pope's Creek.......	49.14	6	1	30,860	30,860	
Bristol and Chattanooga.......	242.37	14	16	709,680	44,353	
Clarksburgh and Weston......	26.06	6	1	16,350	16,350	
Cranberry and Johnson City ..	34.11	6	1	21,421	21,421	
Cumberland and Davis	85.10	6	1	51,443	53,443	
Cumberland and Piedmont	33.73	12	1	42,365	42,365	
Cumberland and Pittsburgh...	150.73	6	4	130,956	32,739	1 helper Pittsburgh to Connellsville, Pa., 57.80 miles.

Statement of miles traveled by railway postal clerks, etc.—Continued.

THIRD DIVISION.

Railway post-office.	Distance from register to register.	No. of round trips per week.	No. of clerks at work on line.	Annual distance traveled by clerks.	Average annual distance traveled by clerks.	Remarks.
	Miles.			*Miles.*	*Miles.*	
Danville and Stuart............	76.16	6	1	47,828	47,828	
Delta and Baltimore...........	47.83	6	1	30,037	30,037	
Elba and Rocky Mount........	37.26	6	1	23,399	23,399	
Fredericksburgh and Orange Court-House.	38.92	6	1	24,442	24,442	
Goldsborough and Greensborough.	130.01	7	2	95,167	47,583	
Goldsborough and Morehead City.	94.93	6	2	59,616	29,898	
Grafton and Bolington.........	41.84	6	1	26,276	26,276	
Grafton and Parkersburgh	104.54	6	2	65,651	65,651	
Grafton and Wheeling.........	99.44	7	2	72,790	36,395	
Greensborough and Winston ...	29.10	13	1	39,576	39,576	
Hagerstown and Weverton	24.52	12	1	30,798	30,798	
Keysville and Oxford	55.86	6	1	35,080	35,080	
Knoxville and Maryville.......	17.78	6	1	11,166	11,166	
Lynchburgh and Bristol . ..	204.48	7	8	299,358	37,419	
Lynchburgh and Pocahontas ..	171.95	6	2	107,985	53,992	
Morgantown and Fairmont ...	25.88	6	1	16,253	16,253	
Mount Airy and Bennettsville.	224.84	6	4	141,199	35,299	
Norfolk and Edenton	75.25	6	2	47,257	23,628	
Norfolk and Lynchburgh	205.22	7	4	150,221	37,555	
Norfolk, Newport News, and Richmond.	91.32	6	2	57,349	28,674	
Norfolk and Raleigh...........	179.02	6	3	112,425	37,475	
Raleigh and Gibson's Station ..	108.80	6	2	68,326	34,163	
Richmond and Danville........	141.08	7	3	103,271	34,423	
Richmond and Huntington	420.70	12	¹14	516,848	36,917	¹ Including 2 acting clerks additional performing service as helpers on trains 1 and 2, Pendleton to Clifton Forge, Va., 137.78 miles. Double daily (except Sunday) service Richmond to Clifton Forge, Va., 193.31 miles. Clerks on night line run through to White Sulphur Springs, W. Va.; whole distance 226.87 miles. West division, service daily, 227.39 miles.
Richmond, Lynchburgh, and Clifton Forge.	230.55	6	4	144,785	36,198	
Rogersville and Bull's Gap ...	16.27	6	1	10,218	10,218	
Salisbury and Knoxville.......	273.73	7	5	236,794	47,358	1 helper Salisbury to Hickory, 58 miles.
Taylorsville and Charlotte.....	65.69	6	1	41,253	41,253	
Washington and Charlotte.....	382.04	14	40	1,843,965	46,099	4 helpers Washington, D. C., to Charlottesville, Va., 112.42 miles.
Washington and Charlotte (short run).	172.98	7	3	126,621	42,207	
Washington and Round Hill ..	53.35	6	1	33,503	33,503	
Washington and Strasburg ...	93.55	6	2	58,749	29,374	
Washington and Wilmington...	382.38	14	28	1,420,540	50,733	6 helpers Washington, D. C., to Richmond, Va., 116.93 miles. 2 Washington, D. C., to Petersburgh, Va., 140.32 miles.
Washington and Wilmington (short run).	116.93	6	4	146,864	36,716	
West Point and Richmond	39.07	6	1	24,536	24,536	
Wheeling and Huntington.....	216.37	6	6	236,312	40,214	2 helpers Wheeling to Letart, W. Va., 144 miles.
Williamston and Rocky Mount	50.46	7	1	31,689	31,689	
Wilmington and Rutherfordton	268.70	6	4	168,743	42,185	
Wilson and Fayetteville	74.44	6	1	46,747	46,747	

Statement of miles of route traveled by railway postal clerks, etc.—Continued.

FOURTH DIVISION.

Railway post-office.	Distance from register to register.	No. of round trips per week.	No. of clerks at work on line.	Annual distance traveled by clerks.	Average annual distance traveled by clerks.	Remarks.
	Miles.			*Miles.*	*Miles.*	
Abbeville and Louvale	109.79	6	2	68,928	34,464	
Aberdeen and Durant	108.30	7	3	79,275	39,637	
Albany and Thomasville.......	58.92	7	.1	43,129	43,129	
Anderson and McCormick....	59.00	6	1	37,052	37,052	
Arkansas City and Vicksburg..	171.74	3	2	62,407	31,208	River service; R.P. clerks Greenville to Vicksburg.
Asheville and Columbia	164.00	7	3	120,048	40,016	
Astor and Leesburgh.........	40.90	6	1	25,685	25,685	
Athens and Union Point.......	40.48	6	1	25,421	25,421	
Atlanta and Artesia:						
Eastern division	167.63	7	3	122,705	40,901	Atlanta and Birmingham.
Western division	138.24	7	2	101,191	50,595	Birmingham and Artesia.
Atlanta and Brunswick........	278.00	7	5	203,496	40,849	
Atlanta and Macon...........	103.83	6	2	65,205	32,603	
Atlanta and Montgomery......	175.68	14	10	514,391	51,439	
Atlanta and Savannah........	294.08	7	4	215,278	53,819	
Helper..................	43.00	6	1	27,004	27,004	Atlanta and Griffin.
Atlanta and Zebulon	51.26	6	1	32,191	32,191	
Augusta and Atlanta	171.59	14	6	251,206	41,867	
Augusta and Millen	53.51	6	1	33,604	33,604	
Augusta and Port Royal.......	112.52	7	2	82,365	41,183	
Augusta and Sandersville......	81.05	6	1	50,899	50,899	
Bayou Sara and Baton Rouge..	32.00	6	1	20,096	20,096	River service.
Birmingham and Memphis....	251.20	6	4	157,753	39,438	
Brunswick and Albany........	171.73	7	3	125,706	41,902	
Cairo and Mobile:						
Northern division	260.15	7	8	380,852	47,606	Cairo and West Point.
Southern division	233.15	7	4	170,665	42,666	West Point and Mobile.
Helpers southern division...	144.00	7	2	105,408	52,704	Tupelo and Meridian.
Cairo and New Orleans:						
Northern division.........	368.46	7	18	809,136	44,952	Cairo and Jackson, Miss.
Southern division.........	184.12	7	3	134,775	44,925	Jackson, Miss., and New Orleans.
Helper southern division ..	53.00	7	1	38,796	38,796	Hammond and New Orleans.
Camak and Macon............	78.59	6	1	49,354	49,354	
Cartersville and Talladega.....	142.48	6	2	89,477	44,738	
Charleston and Augusta.......	139.22	14	4	203,818	50,954	
Charlotte and Atlanta........	268.22	14	16	785,348	49,084	
Day-line helpers...........	201.00	6	2	126,229	63,114	Atlanta and Cowpens.
Night-line helpers	226.00	6	2	141,928	70,964	Atlanta and Grover.
Charlotte and Augusta	192.00	7	3	140,544	46,848	
Chattanooga and Atlanta:						
First and second clerks....	138.55	21	14	608,511	43,465	
Third clerks...............		14	5	202,837	40,567	No third clerks on trains 2 and 3.
Chattanooga and Meridian.....	295.71	7	8	432,990	54,124	
Chattanooga, Rome, and Atlanta.	153.00	6	2	96,084	48,042	
Cheneyville and La Fayette ...	60.20	7	1	44,066	44,066	
Childersburg and Columbus ...	116.12	7	2	84,999	42,499	
Cleveland and Selma...........	264.05	7	4	193,284	48,321	
Columbia and Branchville	68.00	14	2	99,552	49,776	
Columbia, Sumter, and Charleston.	136.00	7	2	99,552	49,776	
Demopolis and Mobile	240.00	1	1	24,960	24,960	River service.
Du Pont and Gainesville.......	119.27	7	2	87,305	43,652	
Eatonton and Gordon	38.73	6	1	24,322	24,322	
Elloree and Pregnalls.........	33.78	6	1	42,377	42,377	
Fasonia and Vicksburg........	209.00	1	1	21,806	21,806	River service.
Fernandina and Orlando.......	210.05	7	4	153,756	38,439	
Flomaton and Pensacola.......	44.84	6	1	28,159	28,159	
Florence and Augusta........	164.87	7	3	120,318	40,106	
Gainesville and Social Circle ..	52.27	6	1	32,825	32,825	
Greenville and Columbia	144.09	6	3	90,488	30,162	
Greenville and Columbus	51.77	6	1	32,511	32,511	
Greenville and Laurens.......	36.85	6	1	23,141	23,141	
Greenville and Walhalla.......	70.16	6	1	44,060	44,060	
Greenwood and Jackson	98.83	6	2	62,865	31,032	
Greenwood and Vicksburg	242.00	1	1	25,248	25,248	River service.
Griffin and Carrollton..........	60.37	6	1	37,912	37,912	
Griffin and Columbus..........	80.80	6	1	50,742	50,742	
Jackson and Natches..........	99.55	6	2	62,517	31,258	

Statement of miles of route traveled by railway postal clerks, etc.—Continued.

FOURTH DIVISION—Continued.

Railway post-office.	Distance from register to register.	No. of round trips per week.	No. of clerks at work on line.	Annual distance traveled by clerks.	Average annual distance traveled by clerks.	Remarks.
	Miles.			*Miles.*	*Miles.*	
Jacksonville and Pensacola:						
Eastern division............	207.50	7	4	151,890	37,972	Jacksonville and River Junct.
Western division	161.69	7	2	118,357	59,178	River Junct. and Pensacola.
Helper western division ...	80.00	7	1	58,560	58,560	De Funak and Pensacola.
Jacksonville and Tampa......	241.54	7	6	176,807	} 46,824	Clerks alternate on long and short run.
Short run to Kissimmee ...	165.84	6	....	104,147		
Helpers....................	147.04	7	2	107,633	53,816	Jacksonville and Orlando.
Lancaster and Kingville......	80.53	6	1	50,572	50,572	
Laurens and Columbia........	79.92	6	1	50,189	50,189	
Leland and Glen Allan	41.00	6	1	25,748	25,748	
Lenoir and Lancaster........	138.25	6	3	86,820	28,940	
Lula and Athens	38.59	6	1	24,234	24,234	
Macon and Montgomery.......	224.51	7	4	164,134	41,033	
Helper	140.30	7	2	102,699	51,349	Smithville and Montgomery.
Macon and Union Springs	156.25	13	4	212,500	53,126	
Madison and Macon	72.61	6	1	45,599	45,599	
Melbourne and Jupiter	86.00	3	1	27,004	27,004	River service.
Memphis and Arkansas City ..	252.50	2	1	52,520	52,520	Do.
Memphis and Friar's Point...	111.00	3	1	34,854	34,854	Do.
Memphis and Grenada........	101.60	7	2	74,371	37,185	
Memphis and New Orleans:						
Northern division	221.46	7	4	162,108	40,527	Memphis and Vicksburg.
Southern division.........	235.06	7	4	172,063	43,015	Vicksburg and New Orleans.
Short run	88.80	6	1	55,706	55,766	New Orleans and Baton Rouge; additional service.
Meridian and New Orleans	196.24	7	3	143,647	47,882	
Meridian and Vicksburg.......	140.70	7	3	102,992	34,330	
Middleton and New Albany ...	44.00	6	1	27,632	27,632	
Montgomery and Akron Junct.	113.15	6	2	71,058	35,529	
Montgomery and New Orleans.	321.85	14	16	942,376	58,898	
Montgomery and Troy.........	70.83	6	1	44,481	44,481	
Monroe and Tarpon Springs ...	116.20	6	2	72,973	36,486	
Murphy and Marietta.........	109.02	6	2	68,465	34,232	
Natchez and Bayou Sara.......	110.00	3	1	34,540	34,540	River service.
New Orleans and Houston.....	362.74	14	10	531,051	53,105	
Helper.....................	40.00	7	1	29,280	29,280	New Orleans and Raceland.
New Orleans and Marshall.....	369.37	7	6	270,378	45,063	
New Orleans and Port Eads....	128.00	¹6	2	62,288	31,144	¹ River service, irregular. See Table B⁴.
New Orleans and Port Vincent.	105.00	2	1	21,840	21,840	River service.
Palatka and Drayton Island ...	40.00	6	1	25,120	25,120	Do.
Palatka and Punta Gorda:						
First division..............	134.86	6	2	84,692	42,346	Palatka to Pemberton.
Second division.............	57.82	6	1	36,310	36,310	Pemberton to Bartow.
Third division..............	75.30	6	1	47,288	47,288	Bartow to Punta Gorda.
Roanoke and Opelika.........	39.38	6	1	24,730	24,730	
Rome and Gadsden	155.00	2	1	32,240	32,240	River service.
Selma and Meridian	111.28	7	2	81,456	40,728	
Selma and Pine Apple........	47.79	6	1	30,012	30,012	
Selma and Mobile.............	308.00	2	2	64,064	32,032	Do.
Smithville and Blakely.......	73.54	6	1	46,183	46,183	
Spartanburg and Augusta.....	134.72	7	2	96,615	49,307	
Tennille and Dublin	35.25	6	1	22,137	22,137	
Titusville and Melbourne.....	43.00	6	1	27,004	27,004	Do.
Titusville and Sanford........	47.00	6	1	29,516	29,516	
Toccoa and Elberton..........	51.45	6	1	32,310	32,310	
Vicksburg and Natchez.......	100.00	3	1	31,400	31,400	Do.
Vicksburg and New Orleans...	408.00	1	1	42,704	42,704	Do.
Vicksburg and Shreveport.....	172.60	7	3	126,343	42,114	
Wadesborough and Lanes......	114.40	6	2	71,843	35,921	
Waldo and Cedar Keys	71.00	6	1	51,972	51,972	
Waycross and Chattahoochee..	164.21	7	3	120,201	40,067	
Wilmington and Jacksonville:						
"West India mail," trains 27 and 14.	494.14	7	24	1,447,204	60,300	Wilmington and Jacksonville.
Northern division, trains 15 and 78.	213.54	7	3	156,311	52,104	Wilmington and Charleston.
Southern division, trains 35 and 66.	144.40	7	4	211,438	52,859	Charleston and Jacksonville.
Southern division helpers..	171.05	7	3	125,208	41,736	Savannah and Jacksonville.

Statement of miles traveled by railway postal clerks, etc.—Continued.

FIFTH DIVISION.

Railway post-office.	Distance from register to register.	No. of round trips per week.	No. of clerks at work on line.	Annual distance traveled by clerks.	Average annual distance traveled by clerks.	Remarks.
	Miles.			*Miles.*	*Miles.*	
Anderson and Ladoga, Ind.....	64.70	6	1	29,484	29,484	
Ashland and Richardson, Ky ..	50.42	6	1	31,664	31,664	
Ashtabula, Ohio, and New Castle, Pa.	81.25	6	2	51,025	25,513	
Bayard and New Philadelphia, Ohio.	32.34	12	1	40,618	40,618	Clerks make two round trips daily, except Sunday.
Bedford and Switz City, Ind ...	41.54	6	1	26,007	26,007	
Bellaire and Zanesville, Ohio...	112.74	6	2	70,801	35,401	
Benton Harbor, Mich., and Anderson, Ind.	164.48	6	2	103,293	51,647	
Bowling Green, Ky., and Memphis, Tenn.	263.57	7	8	385,866	48,233	
Bryan and Carlisle, Ohio.......	147.51	6	2	87,714	43,857	
Cambridge City and Madison, Ind.	168.81	12	3	120,033	40,011	Do.
Canton and Sherodsville, Ohio .	48.44	6	1	30,420	30,420	
Carey and Delphos, Ohio.......	56.43	6	1	35,438	35,438	
Chattanooga and Memphis, Tenn.	310.77	7	5	227,484	45,497	
Chicago, Ill., and Cincinnati, Ohio:						
Day line	307.16	6	16	771,584	48,224	
Night line	....	7	24	1,349,040	56,210	
Chicago, Ill., and Louisville, Ky.:						
Day line	324.38	6	4	203,711	50,928	
Night line	....	7	4	237,446	59,362	
Chicago, Ill., Monon, Ind., and Cincinnati, Ohio.	309.64	6	4	186,000	46,500	
Cincinnati, Hamilton, Ohio, and Indianapolis, Ind.	125.41	6	1	78,757	78,757	Short run of the Chicago, Monon and Cincinnati.
Chicago, Ill., Richmond, Ind., and Cincinnati, Ohio.	295.71	6	4	185,706	46,427	
Cincinnati, Ohio, and Chattanooga, Tenn. :						
Day line	339.53	7	8	497,072	62,134	
Night line		7	8	497,072	62,134	
Cincinnati, Ohio, and Junction City, Ky.	122.56	6	1	12,501	12,501	Short run of Cincinnati and Chattanooga R. P. O. R. P. O. service established May 3, 1883.
Cincinnati, Ohio, and Livingston, Ky.	155.54	6	3	97,679	32,560	
Cincinnati, Ohio, and Nashville, Tenn.:						
Day line	303.60	7	12	666,708	55,559	
Night line	....	7	16	888,944	55,550	
Cincinnati, Ohio, and Louisville, Ky.	111.82	7	2	81,486	40,743	Short run of Cincinnati and Nashville R. P. O.
Louisville, Ky., and Nashville, Tenn.	187.92	7	4	134,496	33,624	Do.
Cincinnati, Ohio, and Saint Louis, Mo. :						
Day line	341.56	7	16	1,000,080	62,505	
Night line	....	7	20	1,250,100	62,505	
Cincinnati, Ohio, North Vernon, Ind., and Louisville, Ky.	131.50	6	2	82,582	41,291	
Cleveland and Cincinnati, Ohio:						
Day line	244.66	7	10	429,713	42,971	
Night line	....	7	12	537,276	44,773	
Cleveland and Coshocton, Ohio.	115.55	6	2	72,565	36,283	
Cleveland, Ohio, and Indianapolis, Ind.	283.00	7	8	414,312	51,789	
Cleveland and New Lisbon, Ohio.	91.75	6	2	57,619	28,810	
Cleveland, Ohio, and Pittsburgh, Pa.	149.30	19	12	406,092	33,841	Trains 35, 36, 37, and 38 daily, except Sunday; trains 41 and 42 daily.
Cleveland, Ohio, and Wheeling, W. Va.	168.50	6	4	105,818	26,455	
Cleveland and Zoar Station, Ohio.	76.39	6	2	47,973	23,987	

Statement of miles traveled by railway postal clerks, etc.—Continued.

FIFTH DIVISION—Continued.

Railway post-office.	Distance from register to register.	No. of round trips per week.	No. of clerks at work on line.	Annual distance traveled by clerks.	Average annual distance traveled by clerks.	Remarks.
	Miles.			*Miles.*	*Miles.*	
Cleveland, Hudson and Columbus, Ohio.	171.19	6	3	107,507	35,836	
Cleveland, Youngstown, Ohio, and Pittsburgh, Pa.	136.77	14	5	290,232	40,046	Clerks make two round trips daily.
Columbia and Fayetteville, Tenn.	48.96	6	1	30,747	30,747	
Columbus, Ohio, and Ashland, Ky.	134.14	12	4	168,480	42,120	Clerks make two round trips daily, except Sunday.
Columbus and Athens, Ohio ...	77.66	12	3	97,540	29,180	Do.
Columbus, Ohio, and Charleston, W. Va.	197.52	6	3	29,628	9,876	Previous to April 5, 1888, this line was a part of Toledo and Charleston R. P. O.
Columbus, Midland City and Cincinnati, Ohio.	117.85	12	3	148,020	49,340	Clerks make two round trips daily, except Sunday.
Columbus, Springfield, Ohio, and Indianapolis, Ind.	185.39	6	4	116,425	29,106	
Dayton and Ironton, Ohio	168.79	6	3	102,520	34,173	
Delaware and Columbus, Ohio .	25.61	6	1	16,083	16,083	
Decherd and Fayetteville, Tenn.	40.28	6	1	25,296	25,296	
Delphos and Dayton, Ohio	96.04	6	2	60,313	30,157	
Dickson and Ætna, Tenn	43.79	6	1	27,500	27,500	
Dodds and Cincinnati, Ohio ...	36.75	6	1	23,079	23,079	
Dresden and Cincinnati, Ohio..	185.47	6	3	116,475	38,825	3 clerks run between Dresden and Cincinnati, Ohio.
Do.......................	....	6	2	93,296	46,648	2 clerks run between Dresden and Morrow, Ohio.
Dunlap, Tenn., and Bridgeport, Ala.	50.03	6	1	20,139	20,139	
Evansville, Ind., and Paducah, Ky.	150.41	6	2	94,457	47,229	River service.
Evansville, Ind., and Providence, Ky.	75.48	6	1	9,510	9,510	R. P. O. service established April 19, 1888.
Fairland and Martinsville, Ind.	37.83	6	1	23,757	23,757	
Fort Branch and Mount Vernon, Ind.	39.37	6	1	24,724	24,724	
Fort Wayne, Ind., and Cincinnati, Ohio.	178.81	6	3	112,293	37,431	
Frankfort, Ind., and Saint Louis, Mo.	246.07	6	4	154,532	38,633	
Georgetown and Cincinnati, Ohio.	47.86	6	1	30,056	30,056	
Grafton, W. Va., and Chicago, Ill.:						
Eastern division	200.39	7	8	293,368	36,671	
Western division	359.80	6	8	451,912	56,489	
Grafton, W. Va., and Cincinnati, Ohio:						
Day line	300.16	7	12	659,148	54,929	
Night line	....	7	12	659,148	54,929	
Parkersburgh, W. Va., and Cincinnati, Ohio.	196.50	6	4	123,402	30,851	Short run of Grafton and Cincinnati R. P. O.
Grand Rapids, Mich., and Cincinnati, Ohio.	303.76	6	4	190,761	47,690	
Greenup and Willard, Ky. ...	36.06	6	1	22,646	22,646	
Hamden and Portsmouth, Ohio.	56.37	6	1	35,400	35,400	
Henderson and Princeton, Ky.	89.73	6	1	50,282	50,282	Formerly the Henderson and Marion R. P. O. Nov. 2, 1887, service extended to Princeton, Ky.
Huntington, W. Va., and Lexington, Ky.	139.93	6	2	87,876	43,938	
Indianapolis, Ind., and Decatur, Ill.	153.40	6	3	96,335	32,112	
Indianapolis, Ind., and Louisville, Ky.:						
Day line...................	111.21	7	3	81,406	27,135	
Night line	....	7	3	81,406	27,135	
Indianapolis, Ind., and Peoria, Ill.:						
Day line	212.42	6	4	133,400	33,350	
Night line	....	7	3	175,040	21,880	Established Dec. 8, 1887.

Statement of miles traveled by railway postal clerks, etc.—Continued.

FIFTH DIVISION—Continued.

Railway post-office.	Distance from register to register.	No. of round trips per week.	No. of clerks at work on line.	Annual distance traveled by clerks.	Average annual distance traveled by clerks.	Remarks.
	Miles.			*Miles.*	*Miles.*	
Indianapolis and Vincennes, Ind.	116.70	6	2	73,288	36,644	
Indianapolis, Ind., and Saint Louis, Mo.	265.30	6	6	272,552.	45,425	
Johnsonville, Tenn., and Waterloo, Ala.	....	...	....	3,848	....	River service; discontinued Aug. 15, 1887.
Killbuck and Trinway, Ohio ...	34.14	6	1	410	410	Service established June 25, 1888.
La Crosse and Brazil, Ind	145.65	6	2	80,764	40,382	
Lexington and Louisville, Ky ..	94.72	6	2	59,484	29,742	
Leavittsburgh and Cincinnati, Ohio.	281.19	6	4	174,217	43,554	
Lebanon and Greensburgh, Ky.	31.85	6	1	20,002	20,002	
Lebanon and Nashville, Tenn..	31.66	12	1	39,764	39,764	Clerks make two round trips daily, except Sunday.
Logan and Nelsonville, Ohio ...	32.76	6	1	20,573	20,573	
Logan and Pomeroy, Ohio	83.71	12	3	105,140	35,047	Do.
Logansport, Ind., and Columbus, Ohio.	198.71	6	3	124,790	41,597	
Louisville and Springfield, Ky.	60.75	6	1	29,714	29,714	
Louisville and Bloomfield, Ky..	58.05	6	1	36,455	36,455	
Louisville, Ky., and Evansville, Ind.	217.62	6	3	136,665	45,555	River service.
Louisville, Ky., and Knoxville, Tenn.:						
Day line	267.51	7	3	147,769	49,256	Runs between Louisville, Ky., and Jellico, Tenn.
Night line	....	7	4	105,817	48,954	Runs through.
Louisville, Ky., and Saint Louis, Mo.	267.25	7	4	195,627	48,907	
Louisville and Paducah, Ky....	227.26	7	4	166,354	41,589	
Louisville, Ky., Huntingburgh and Evansville, Ind.	124.40	6	2	49,885	24,943	
Marietta and Sharpsburgh, Ohio	34.96	6	1	21,244	21,244	
Marion, Ohio, and Chicago, Ill.	270.12	6	4	169,635	42,409	
McConnellsville and Marietta, Ohio.	....	...	....	3,526	....	River service; discontinued Aug. 13, 1887.
Maysville, Paris, Ky., and Cincinnati, Ohio.	130.32	6	2	81,841	40,921	
Michigan City and Indianapolis, Ind.	161.18	6	3	101,221	33,740	
Michigan City and Monon, Ind.	59.77	6	1	20,441	20,441	Service established Dec. 15, 1887.
Nashville and Chattanooga, Tenn.:						
Trains 1 and 2, daily	151.55	7	3	110,985	36,978	
Trains 5 and 6, daily, except Sunday.	....	6	2	95,173	47,587	
Nashville, Tenn., and Hickman, Ky.	169.58	6	4	155,044	38,761	
Nashville, Tenn., and Montgomery, Ala.:						
Day line...................	306.14	7	8	448,192	56,024	
Night line	....	7	3	30,002	10,000	Service established May 13, 1888.
Nashville and Saint Joseph, Tenn.	103.89	6	2	59,346	29,673	
Nashville, Tenn., and Saint Louis, Mo.:						
Day line	321.53	7	6	335,174	55,862	
Night line	....	7	8	470,792	58,849	
Nashville and Hopkinsville, Tenn.	....	6	....	22,099	....	Short run of Nashville and Saint Louis R.P.O.; service performed by second clerks of night line; established Jan. 23, 1888.
Newark and Shawnee, Ohio....	43.20	6	1	27,130	27,130	
New Castle and North Vernon, Ind.	69.99	6	1	43,954	43,954	
New Galilee, Pa., and New Lisbon, Ohio.	25.17	6	1	7,752	7,752	R. P. O. service established Jan 4, 1888.
Owensborough and Russellville, Ky.	72.71	6	1	45,662	45,662	
Princeton, Ky., and Clarksville, Tenn.	57.71	6	1	13,273	13,273	
Paducah, Ky., and Cairo, Ill....	50.86	6	1	31,940	31,940	River service.

Statement of miles traveled by railway postal clerks, etc.—Continued.

FIFTH DIVISION—Continued.

Railway post-office.	Distance from register to register.	No. of round trips per week.	No. of clerks at work on line.	Annual distance traveled by clerks.	Average annual distance traveled by clerks.	Remarks.
	Miles.			*Miles.*	*Miles.*	
Paducah, Ky., and Florence, Ala.	300.00	2	2	21,800	10,900	River service.
Paducah, Ky., and Memphis, Tenn.	167.26	6	3	122,434	40,811	
Painesville and Youngstown, Ohio.	61.27	6	1	31,856	31,856	
Phalanx Station and Berghols, Ohio.	60.98	6	1	24,055	24,055	
Pittsburgh, Pa., Steubenville, Ohio, and Wheeling, W. Va.	69.04	6	1	43,357	43,357	
Pittsburgh, Pa., and Chicago, Ill.:						
Eastern division...........	188.95	7	9	414,936	46,104	
Western division	280.15	7	12	615,204	51,267	
Pittsburgh, Pa., and Crestline, Ohio.	188.95	6	6	196,533	32,755	Short run of Pittsburgh and Chicago R. P. O.
Crestline, Ohio, and Chicago, Ill.	280.15	6	8	351,872	43,984	Do.
Pittsburgh, Pa., and Cincinnati, Ohio:						
Day line..................	313.74	7	16	918,624	57,414	
Night line		7	14	800,525	57,180	
Columbus and Cincinnati, Ohio.	121.13	6	2	76,070	38,035	Short run of Pittsburgh and Cincinnati R. P. O.
Portsmouth and Cincinnati, Ohio.	107.58	6	2	67,560	33,780	
Pittsburgh, Pa., and Saint Louis, Mo.:						
East division (day line) ..	312.80	7	39	2,251,910	57,742	
East division (night line) ...		7	30	1,744,052	58,135	
West division (day line) ...	309.00	7	31	1,734,733	55,960	
West division (night line)..		7	25	1,380,021	55,201	
Indianapolis, Ind., Vandalia, Ill., and Saint Louis., Mo.	240.80	6	4	151,222	37,806	Short run of Pittsburgh and Saint Louis R. P. O.
Indianapolis and Terre Haute, Ind.	72.50	6	1	45,530	45,530	Do.
Pittsburgh, Pa., and Akron, Ohio.	136.32	6	2	85,609	42,805	
Portsmouth and Cincinnati, Ohio.	128.66	6	2	60,578	30,289	River service.
Richmond and Stanford, Ky ...	35.57	6	1	22,338	22,338	
Sandusky, Ohio, and Bloomington, Ill.	379.94	6	7	306,019	43,717	
Sandusky and Springfield, Ohio	130.84	6	3	82,168	27,389	
Sandusky, Ohio, and Wheeling, W. Va.	225.78	7	8	330,544	41,318	
Scottsville, Ky., and Gallatin, Tenn.	35.94	6	1	10,063	10,063	R. P. O. service established Jan. 20, 1888.
South Bend and Terre Haute, Ind.	184.30	6	3	115,740	38,580	
Sparta and Tullahoma, Tenn ..	61.02	6	1	38,321	38,321	
Springfield, Ohio, and Richmond, Ind.	77.40	6	1	39,501	39,501	
Springfield and Wellston, Ohio	118.43	6	2	74,374	37,187	
Terre Haute and Evansville, Ind. (day line).	110.41	6	3	69,337	29,074	Clerks alternate from day to night trains. Service established on night trains Apr. 11, 1888.
		7	....	17,886		
Terre Haute, Washington and Evansville, Ind.	139.51	6	2	87,612	43,806	
Toledo and Corning, Ohio	185.09	6	3	176,990	58,997	
Toledo and Cincinnati, Ohio:						
Day line..................	203.27	6	8	255,320	31,915	
Night line		7	8	297,584	37,198	
Toledo and Columbus, Ohio....	125.59	6	2	78,871	39,436	
Toledo and Findlay, Ohio......	45.87	6	1	28,806	28,806	
Toledo, Ohio, and Frankfort, Ind.	207.17	6	4	130,103	32,526	
Toledo and Mansfield, Ohio ...	87.16	6	2	54,736	27,368	
Toledo and Marietta, Ohio	263.25	6	4	165,321	41,330	
Toledo, Ohio, and Saint Louis, Mo.	437.79	7	32	1,672,344	52,261	

Statement of miles traveled by railway postal clerks, etc.—Continued.

FIFTH DIVISION—Continued.

Railway post-office.	Distance from register to register.	No. of round trips per week.	No. of clerks at work on line.	Annual distance traveled by clerk.	Average annual distance traveled by clerk.	Remarks.
	Miles.			*Miles.*	*Miles.*	
Toledo, Ohio, and Lafayette, Ind.	204.56	6	4	128,464	32,116	Short run of Toledo and Saint Louis R. P. O.
Tracy City and Cowan, Tenn ..	20.21	6	1	12,692	12,692	
Union City, Ind., and Dayton, Ohio.	47.45	6	1	29,799	29,799	
Wellsville and Bellaire, Ohio ..	46.86	12	2	59,260	29,630	Clerks make two round trips daily, except Sunday.
Zanesville and Columbus, Ohio.	68.55	6	1	43,049	43,049	
Zanesville and Waterford, Ohio.	51.70	6	1	25,378	25,378	

SIXTH DIVISION.

Aberdeen and Orient..........	83.04	6	1	52,149	52,149	
Albert Lea and Burlington:						
Through run...............	253.14	6	8	317,944	39,743	
Short run, Cedar Falls to Burlington.	159.08	6	2	98,646	49,226	
Ashland and Abbotsford.......	133.70	6	2	71,403	35,701	
Ashland and Milwaukee:						
North division, Ashland to Appleton.	272.19	6	4	170,935	42,734	
South division, Antigo to Milwaukee.	208.50	6	3	130,938	43,646	
Ashland and Saint Paul.......	184.22	6	3	115,690	38,563	
Auburn and Lincoln...........	76.84	7	1	56,247	56,247	
Aurora and Arcadia..........	90.73	6	1	56,978	56,978	
Austin and Mason City.......	40.74	6	1	25,584	25,584	
Beardstown and Shawneetown.	228.35	6	4	143,404	35,851	
Belle Plaine and Muchakinook.	62.90	6	1	39,501	39,501	
Bellevue and Cascade..........	36.32	6	1	22,809	22,809	
Bement and Effingham	62.26	6	1	39,099	39,099	
Bethany Junction and Grant City.	44.28	6	1	27,808	27,808	
Bloomington and Roodhouse...	110.75	6	2	69,551	34,775	
Bluffs and Hannibal, Mo.......	50.01	6	1	31,406	31,406	
Boone and Des Moines.........	43.30	6	1	27,192	27,192	
Boundary Line and Saint Paul.	391.80	7	8	294,615	36,827	1 helper runs 7, 18 miles.
Breckenridge and Aberdeen ...	136.78	6	2	85,898	42,949	
Bristol and Madison	103.84	6	2	64,898	32,449	
Bruce and Minneapolis	122.27	6	2	76,785	38,392	
Buda and Yates City	48.35	6	1	30,364	30,364	
Bureau and Peoria.............	47.03	6	1	29,535	29,535	
Burlington and Carrollton	220.57	6	4	138,518	34,629	
Burlington and Council Bluffs:						
Fast mail and train 4.......	294.00	7	20	1,076,040	53,902	
Trains 5 and 6...............	294.00	7	12	645,624	53,802	
Burlington and Oskaloosa......	105.00	6	2	65,940	32,970	
Burlington and Quincy	72.00	6	1	45,216	45,216	
Burlington and Saint Louis....	214.19	6	6	191,633	31,939	2 helpers run 57,122 miles.
Caledonia and Spring Valley...	85.74	6	1	53,844	53,844	
Calmar and Chamberlain:						
East division, Calmar to Sanborn, Iowa.	200.40	6	8	251,702	31,463	
West division, Sanborn to Chamberlain.	196.62	7	5	209,074	41,815	2 helpers run 63,684 miles.
Calmar and Davenport.........	165.70	6	3	104,059	34,686	
Carroll and Moville............	100.80	6	2	63,302	31,651	
Cedar Rapids and Council Bluffs:						
Day line	270.77	7	8	396,408	49,551	
Night line	270.77	7	8	396,406	49,551	
Cedar Rapids and Kansas City.	301.51	6	5	189,348	37,869	
Cedar Rapids and Watertown:						
East division, Cedar Rapids to Estherville.	207.32	6	4	130,197	32,549	
West division, Estherville to Watertown.	193.01	6	3	121,210	40,403	
Centralia and Cairo............	112.79	6	4	141,664	35,416	
Chadron and Glen Rock........	169.88	6	2	106,685	53,342	

Statement of miles traveled by railway postal clerks, etc.—Continued.

SIXTH DIVISION—Continued.

Railway post-office.	Distance from register to register.	No. of round trips per week.	No. of clerks at work on lines.	Annual distance traveled by clerks.	Average annual distance traveled by clerks.	Remarks.
	Miles.			*Miles.*	*Miles.*	
Champaign and Havana........	101.07	6	2	63,472	31,736	
Chicago, Abbotsford and Minneapolis:						
East division, Chicago to Neenah.	187.15	6	3	117,530	39,177	
West division, Neenah to Minneapolis.	286.35	6	6	287,153	47,859	2 helpers run 107,325 miles.
Chicago and Burlington:						
Day line....................	207.50	7	16	451,890	37,972	
Fast mail..................	207.50	7	26	1,030,290	39,626	2 helpers run 113,950 miles
Chicago and Cedar Rapids:						
Day line	220.40	7	12	488,999	40,333	
Night line	220.40	7	14	622,932	44,495	2 helpers run 138,933 miles
Chicago and Centralia:						
Day line	252.96	6	10	397,913	39,791	2 helpers run 80,195 miles.
Night line	252.96	7	12	555,496	46,291	
Chicago, Decatur and Saint Louis.	286.80	6	4	180,110	45,027	
Chicago, Dunbar and Dubuque.	168.28	6	3	105,680	35,227	
Chicago and Fort Madison. ...	237.44	6	2	149,112	37,278	
Chicago, Forreston and Dubuque.	200.04	6	6	251,250	41,875	
Chicago, Freeport and Dubuque	189.72	6	9	357,432	39,715	
Chicago, McGregor and Saint Paul:						
East division, Chicago to McGregor.	238.10	6	8	299,054	37,382	
West division, McGregor to Saint Paul.	212.53	6	6	202,987	33,831	2 helpers run 69,519 miles.
Chicago and Minneapolis:						
Fast mail..................	423.15	7	32	1,710,268	55,164	6 helpers and 2 city distributers run 471,284 miles.
Trains 1 and 2..............	423.15	7	29	1,434,166	49,454	4 helpers and 1 city distributer run 195,182 miles.
Short run, Chicago to Portage.	178.00	6	11	408,451	37,132	2 helpers run 73,099 miles.
Short run, Milwaukee to La Crosse.	196.42	6	2	176,458	88,234	
Chicago and North McGregor	281.00	6	10	461,517	46,152	2 helpers run 108,581 miles.
Chicago and Quincy...........	263.50	7	22	1,083,360	49,243	2 helpers run 118,950 miles.
Short run, Galesburgh to Quincy.	100.00	7	10	360,000	36,600	
Chicago and Saint Louis:						
Day line ....; ...	284.70	6	12	536,373	44,698	
Night line	284.70	7	14	717,798	51,271	2 helpers run 92,596 miles.
Chicago, Savanna and Cedar Rapids.	233.44	6	6	250,596	41,766	2 helpers run 104,996 miles.
Chicago and Streator	97.70	6	2	61,355	30,677	
Chicago and Terre Haute......	180.02	6	3	113,052	37,684	
Chicago and West Liberty:						
Day line..................	221.52	7	12	486,456	40,538	
Night line.................	221.52	7	12	486,456	40,538	
Chicago and Winona:						
Day line	297.70	7	8	435,832	54,479	
Night line	297.70	6	8	373,910	46,739	
Clarinda and Corning.........	46.36	6	1	29,114	29,114	
Clinton and Anamosa	71.80	6	2	45,090	22,545	
Clinton and Iowa City........	78.41	6	1	49,241	49,241	
Columbus and Albion.........	43.45	6	1	27,286	27,286	
Columbus and Atchison	220.50	8	4	138,474	34,618	
Covington and Norfolk	73.96	6	1	46,447	46,447	
Creighton and Norfolk........	44.20	6	1	27,757	27,757	
Creston and Cumberland	50.34	6	1	31,618	31,618	
Crookston and Minot	231.62	6	4	145,457	36,364	
Danville and Cairo	259.03	6	4	162,671	40,668	
Danville and Tuscola	51.10	6	1	32,090	32,098	
Davenport and Atchison	337.35	7	8	493,880	61,735	
Decorah and Cedar Rapids ...	122.06	6	2	76,653	38,326	
Des Moines and Albia	68.46	7	2	50,112	25,056	
Des Moines and Cainesville....	116.55	6	2	73,193	36,596	
Des Moines and Harvey	44.74	7	1	32,749	32,749	
Des Moines and Keokuk.......	163.08	6	3	102,414	34,138	

Statement of miles traveled by railway postal clerks, etc.—Continued.

SIXTH DIVISION—Continued.

Railway post-office.	Distance from register to register.	No. of round trips per week.	No. of clerks at work on lines.	Annual distance traveled by clerks.	Average annual distance traveled by clerks.	Remarks.
	Miles.			*Miles.*	*Miles.*	
Des Moines and Saint Joseph..	200.06	6	5	165,045	37,009	1 helper runs 59,408 miles.
Des Moines and Sioux City....	238.64	6	4	149,866	37,466	
Des Moines and Winterset.......	42.90	6	1	26,941	26,941	
DeWitt and Superior..........	85.75	6	1	53,651	53,851	
Dubuque and Mendota	132.39	6	3	123,012	41,004	1 helper runs 39,871 miles.
Dubuque and Sioux City:						
Day line	327.64	6	7	288,654	41,236	2 helpers run 82,806 miles.
Night line	327.64	6	7	288,654	41,236	2 helpers run 82,896 miles.
Duluth and Brainerd	114.67	6	1	72,012	72,012	
Duluth and Eau Claire	160.80	6	2	100,982	50,491	
Duluth and Saint Paul.........	151.83	6	3	95,349	31,783	
Dwight and Washington	70.18	6	1	44,041	44,041	
Eau Claire and Wabasha	49.40	6	1	31,023	31,023	
Edgar and Curtis..............	154.30	6	2	96,900	48,450	
Egan and Sioux City	125.38	6	2	78,788	39,369	
Fairmont and Chester.........	48.00	6	1	30,144	30,144	
Fargo, Barneeville and Saint Paul.	243.38	6	4	152,902	38,225	
Fargo and La Moure	88.15	6	1	55,358	55,358	
Fargo and Minnewaukon.......	183.25	6	3	115,081	38,360	
Farley and Cedar Rapids.......	57.81	6	1	83,604	38,304	
Fonda and Des Moines	115.17	6	2	72,326	36,163	
Fond du Lac and Milwaukee ..	64.18	6	1	40,305	40,305	
Forreston and Aurora	81.58	6	2	51,232	25,616	
Fort Howard and Chicago	243.33	6	8	305,622	38,203	
Fort Howard and Winona	215.40	6	3	135,271	45,090	
Fremont and Lincoln	52.67	6	1	33,076	33,076	
Galesburgh and Havana.......	62.03	6	1	38,955	38,955	
Galva and Burlington........	85.15	6	1	53,474	53,474	
Gilman and Springfield	112.77	6	2	70,819	35,409	
Great Falls and Helena........	99.14	6	2	62,260	31,130	
Green River and Huntington..	571.22	7	7	418,133	59,733	
Hastings and Cologne	55.88	6	1	35,092	35,092	
Havana and Springfield........	48.12	6	1	30,219	30,219	
Hayfield and Dubuque.........	172.70	6	3	108,455	36,152	
Helena and Basin..............	47.70	7	1	34,916	34,916	
Heron Lake and Pipeston......	55.33	6	1	34,747	34,747	
Horicon and Portage...........	53.17	6	1	33,391	33,391	
Humeston and Shenandoah....	113.91	6	2	71,535	35,767	
Iron Mountain and Milwaukee.	209.94	6	3	131,842	43,947	
Ishpeming and Fort Howard ..	179.50	7	5	215,500	43,100	2 helpers run 84,166 miles.
Jacksonville and Mount Vernon	134.59	6	2	84,522	42,261	
Jamestown and Oakes	69.31	6	1	43,526	43,526	
Kankakee and Kankakee Junction.	71.52	6	1	44,914	44,914	
Kankakee and Seneca	43.30	6	1	27,192	27,192	
Kansas City and Oxford	363.66	7	6	377,990	62,998	2 helpers run 111.791 miles.
Kansas City and Red Cloud ...	278.92	7	4	204,169	51,042	
Kempton and Bloomington	57.77	6	1	36,279	36,279	
Kenosha and Rockford........	73.42	6	1	46,107	46,107	
Keokuk and Humestown	132.05	6	2	82,927	41,463	
Keokuk and Clayton	43.09	6	1	27,000	27,060	
Knox and Streator.............	119.65	6	2	75,140	37,570	
La Crosse and Dubuque.........	122.47	6	2	76,911	38,455	
La Crosse and Woonsocket:						
Through run................	400.45	6	6	251,482	41,914	
Short run, La Crosse to Jackson.	215.54	6	3	135,359	45,119	
La Fayette and Quincy........	271.00	6	12	510,564	42,547	
Lake Crystal and Eagle Grove.	110.48	6	2	69,381	34,690	
Lake Geneva and Elgin.........	44.15	6	1	27,726	27,726	
Lake Station and Joliet........	45.68	6	1	28,687	28,687	
Langdon and Larimore	76.19	6	1	47,847	47,847	
Larimore and Breckenridge....	181.40	6	2	82,519	41,259	
Lincoln and Alma	224.81	6	3	141,180	47,060	
Lincoln and Concordia.........	143.12	6	2	89,879	44,939	
Linwood and Geneva	77.41	6	1	48,613	48,613	
Litchfield and Kampsville	58.68	6	1	36,851	36,851	
Little Falls and Morris	88.33	6	1	55,471	55,471	
Logansport and Keokuk:						
East division, Logansport to Peoria.	171.52	6	6	215,429	35,905	

Statement of miles traveled by railway postal clerks, etc.—Continued.

SIXTH DIVISION—Continued.

Railway post-office.	Distance from register to register.	No. of round trips per week.	No. of clerks at work on line.	Annual distance traveled by clerks.	Average annual distance traveled by clerks.	Remarks.
	Miles.			*Miles.*	*Miles.*	
Logansport and Keokuk:						
West division, Peoria to Keokuk.	111.50	6	2	70,022	35,011	
Loup City and Grand Island...	61.20	6	1	38,433	38,433	
McCook and Denver............	255.53	7	3	187,048	62,349	
McCool Junction and Fairbury	50.61	6	1	31,783	31,783	
McLeansborough and Shawnee-town.	41.22	6	1	25,886	25,886	
Mandan and Helena	681.23	7	10	498,660	49,866	
Manilla and Mitchell	228.25	6	3	143,341	37,780	
Mankato and Wells	38.26	6	1	24,027	24,027	
Maquoketa and Davenport	43.85	6	1	27,538	27,538	
Marion and Council Bluffs.....	261.90	6	4	164,473	41,118	
Marion and Running Water...	62.72	6	1	39,388	39,388	
Marshalltown and Story City..	39.55	6	1	24,837	24,837	
Marquette and Houghton.......	95.20	7	2	69,686	34,843	
Mason City and Albia	169.55	6	5	190,440	38,088	2 helpers run 83,963 miles.
Mason City and Fort Dodge...	73.05	6	1	45,875	45,875	
Mendota and Centralia	211.99	6	7	228,503	32,643	3 helpers run 95,374 miles.
Mendota and Fulton..........	65.26	6	1	40,983	40,983	
Merrill and Tomah	107.50	6	2	67,510	33,755	
Milwaukee and Chicago	86.14	12	4	108,192	27,048	
Milwaukee and Lancaster	168.40	6	3	105,755	35,252	
Minneapolis, Hayfield and Waterloo.	202.32	6	3	127,057	42,352	
Minneapolis and Oakes	265.13	6	4	166,501	41,625	
Minneapolis and Oregon	344.27	6	5	216,201	43,240	
Missouri Valley and Whitewood:						
East division, Missouri Valley to Long Pine.	251.50	7	8	368,196	46,024	
West division, Long Pine to Whitewood.	333.20	7	5	243,902	48,780	
Montfort and Galena	56.08	6	1	35,218	35,218	
Mount Pleasant and Keokuk ..	50.40	6	1	31,651	31,651	
Muscatine and Montezuma	96.87	6	2	60,834	30,417	
Nebraska City and Beatrice ...	95.24	6	2	59,810	29,905	
Nebraska City and Whitman ..	348.06	6	5	218,581	43,716	
Neche and Saint Paul:						
Through run	425.76	7	9	468,728	52,081	3 helpers run 157,072 miles.
Short run, Saint Paul to Morris.	158.18	6	2	99,337	49,668	
Norfolk and Columbus........	50.64	6	1	31,802	31,802	
Oakes and Hawarden	260.60	7	5	227,066	45,413	1 helper runs 96,307 miles.
Oconto and Clintonville	56.75	6	1	35,639	35,639	
Oelwein and Des Moines.......	132.23	6	2	83,072	41,536	
Omaha and Beatrice	132.94	7	2	97,312	48,656	
Omaha and Hastings	163.96	7	2	120,018	60,009	
Omaha and McCook:						
Through run	312.58	7	8	457,616	57,202	
Short run, Omaha to Hastings.	151.70	7	1	111,044	111,044	
Omaha and Ogden:						
Through run on trains Nos. 1 and 2.	1,035.30	7	9	757,839	84,204	
Short run, Omaha to Cheyenne, on trains Nos. 1 and 2.	518.00	7	18	1,137,528	63,196	
Short run, Omaha to North Platte, on trains Nos. 3 and 4.	293.27	7	12	644,019	53,668	
Short run, Omaha to North Platte, on trains Nos. 7 and 8.	293.27	7	6	294,534	49,089	2 helpers run 79,861 miles.
Ord and Grand Island.........	62.40	6	1	39,187	39,187	
Orleans and Blakeman	95.56	6	1	60,011	60,011	
Oshkosh and Milwaukee.......	104.90	6	2	65,877	32,938	
Pacific Junction and McCook..	309.42	7	12	679,485	56,624	
Pacific Junction and Schuyler.	86.07	6	1	54,052	54,052	
Palmer and Burwell	69.38	6	1	43,570	43,570	
Pembina and Winnipeg Junction.	199.61	7	3	146,114	48,705	

Statement of miles traveled by railway postal clerks, etc.—Continued.

SIXTH DIVISION.—Continued.

Railway post-office.	Distance from register to register.	No. of round trips per week.	No. of clerks at work on line.	Annual distance traveled by clerks.	Average annual distance traveled by clerks.	Remarks.
Peoria and Evansville..	250. 10	6	4	157, 063	39, 268	
Peoria and Galesburgh	52. 80	6	1	33, 158	33, 158	
Peoria and Jacksonville	84. 50	6	2	53, 066	26, 533	
Peoria and Oskaloosa..........	190. 82	6	3	119, 835	30, 945	
Pinkneyville and Marion......	52. 82	6	1	33, 171	33, 171	
Portage and Madison..........	40. 51	6	1	25, 440	25, 440	
Powers and Florence...........	42. 00	7	1	30, 744	30, 744	
Quincy and Louisiana.........	44. 96	6	1	28, 235	28, 235	
Racine and Rock Island.......	197. 88	6	4	124, 68	31, 067	
Redfield and Gettysburgh	75. 84	6	1	47, 627	47, 627	
Red Oak and Nebraska City...	53. 69	6	1	33, 717	33, 717	
Red Wing and Mankato........	94. 62	6	1	50, 421	50, 421	
Reno and Preston.............	37. 70	6	1	36, 235	36, 235	
Republican City and Oberlin ..	78. 87	6	1	49, 530	49, 530	
Rockford and Mineral Point...	115. 69	6	2	72, 653	36, 326	
Rock Island and Saint Louis...	248. 99	7	4	182, 260	45, 565	
Rock Island and Peoria........	92. 20	6	2	57, 901	28, 950	
Ruthven and Des Moines......	137. 59	6	2	86, 406	43, 203	
Saint Cloud and Willmar.......	58. 61	6	1	36, 807	36, 807	
Saint Louis and Cairo.........	153. 60	6	3	96, 461	32, 154	
Saint Louis and Eldorado......	124. 50	6	3	122, 648	40, 883	
Saint Paul and Mandan:						
Through run...............	447. 00	7	18	1, 047, 492	58, 194	
Short run, Saint Paul to Fargo.	277. 10	6	4	174, 019	43, 505	
Saint Paul and Council Bluffs:						
Through run...............	368. 67	7	10	539, 732	53, 973	
Short run, Saint Paul to Sioux City.	270. 43	6	4	169, 830	42, 457	
Saint Paul and Des Moines:						
Through run...............	310. 00	6	4	194, 680	48, 670	
Short run, Saint Paul to Albert Lea.	121. 05	7	3	151, 047	50, 349	1 helper runs 62,439 miles.
Saint Paul and Elroy	197. 08	7	5	207, 580	41, 516	1 helper runs 63.318 miles.
Saint Paul and Mitchell	426. 99	7	6	312, 556	52, 092	
Saint Paul, Ortonville and Fargo.	307. 32	6	4	192, 997	48, 249	
Saint Paul and Watertown.....	236. 23	6	4	148, 352	37, 088	
Scribner and Oakdale..........	115. 73	6	2	72, 678	36, 339	
Shabbona and Sterling........	47. 97	6	1	30, 125	30, 125	
Sheboygan and Princeton......	79. 22	6	2	49, 750	24, 875	
Sidell and Olney	86. 31	6	2	54, 202	27, 101	
Sioux City and Missouri Valley.	76. 10	7	2	55, 705	27, 852	
Sioux City and Omaha.........	124. 06	6	2	77, 909	38, 955	
Sparta and Virogua...........	35. 65	6	1	22, 388	22, 388	
Springfield and Grafton.......	85. 30	6	2	53, 568	26, 784	
Springfield and Litchfield......	45. 52	6	1	28, 586	28, 586	
Sterling and Rock Island	52. 43	6	1	32, 926	32, 926	
Stevens' Point and Portage....	73. 84	6	1	46, 371	46, 371	
Streator and Fairbury	31. 98	6	1	20, 083	20, 083	
Streator and Pekin	65. 06	6	1	40, 857	40, 857	
Sumner and Hampton	65. 33	6	1	41, 027	41, 027	
Swits City and Effingham......	90. 58	6	1	56, 884	56, 884	
Tama and Hawarden	243. 34	6	4	152, 817	38, 204	
Tamaroa and Chester..........	42. 79	6	1	26, 872	26, 872	
Terre Haute and Peoria	176. 90	6	3	111, 093	37, 031	
Tracy and Pierre	255. 69	7	6	287, 009	47, 835	2 helpers run 99,844 miles.
Tracy and Redfield	164. 14	6	8	103, 080	34, 360	
Turkey River and West Union..	58. 84	6	1	36, 637	36, 637	
Villisca and Bigelow..........	69. 24	6	1	43, 482	43, 482	
Wabasha and Zumbrota.......	59. 20	6	1	37, 177	37, 177	
Wadena and Fergus Falls......	53. 86	6	1	33, 510	33, 510	
Washington and Knoxville	77. 94	6	1	48, 946	48, 946	
Watertown and Madison	38. 97	12	1	48, 946	48, 946	
West Lebanon and Rantoul....	41. 82	6	1	26, 263	26, 263	
West Liberty and Council Bluffs:						
Day line	279. 36	7	8	408, 982	51, 123	
Night line	279. 36	7	8	408, 982	51, 123	
White Heath and Decatur	29. 70	6	1	18, 651	18, 651	
Winona and Tracy............	229. 43	6	6	197, 462	32, 910	2 helpers run 53,280 miles.
Worthington and Sioux Falls ..	62. 50	6	1	39, 250	32, 250	
Yates City and Rushville......	63. 95	6	1	40, 160	40, 160	

Statement of miles traveled by railway postal clerks, etc.—Continued.

SEVENTH DIVISION.

Railway post-office.	Distance from register to register.	No. of round trips per week.	No. of clerks at work on line.	Annual distance traveled by clerks.	Average annual distance traveled by clerks.	Remarks.
	Miles.			*Miles.*	*Miles.*	
Albuquerque, N. Mex. and El Paso, Tex.	254.39	7	4	186,213	46,553	
Antonito, Colo., and Santa Fé, N. Mex.	130.00	6	2	81,640	40,820	
Arcadia and Cherry Vale, Kans.	81.37	7	1	59,563	34,143	4 clerks performed all service on this line, Fort Scott, Kans., and Webb City, Mo. R. P. O., and Yates Center and Sedan, Kans., R. P. O.
Arkansas City and Warren, Ark.	56.60	6	1	35,545	35,545	
Atchison and Lenora, Kans:						
Day line	209.36	6	4	180,807	45,202	1 helper runs 49,329 miles.
Night line	294.52	7	4	212,643	53,161	From July 6, 1887.
Night line (helpers' run).	250.32	7	4	180,731	45,183	Helpers run from Atchison to Stockton, Kans., over Atchison and Lenora R. P. O., to Downs, and thence over Downs and Stockton R. P. O.
Atchison and Topeka, Kans.	51.11	7	1	37,413	37,413	
Beatrice, Nebr., and Manhattan, Kans.	93.68	7	2	66,672	33,336	Marysville and Manhattan, Kans., R. P. O. extended to begin at Beatrice, Nebr., July 26, 1887; increase, 38.04 miles.
Beaumont and Bluff, Kans.	106.14	7	2	77,694	38,847	
Beloit and Solomon City, Kans.	57.86	7	1	42,354	42,354	
Bolivar and Springfield, Mo.	40.05	6	1	25,151	25,151	
Boonville and Versailles, Mo.	44.25	6	1	27,789	43,489	
Boonville and Versailles, Mo., (short run).	25.00	6	....	15,700	....	
Bremond and Albany, Tex.	230.89	7	4	153,687	38,422	7 round trips per week between Bremond and Walnut (89 miles) and 6 between Walnut and Albany, Tex. (141.89 miles). From June 1, 1888, but 3 round trips per week between Walnut and Albany.
Burnet and Austin, Tex.	60.72	6	1	38,132	38,132	
Butler, Mo., and Madison, Kans.	109.81	7	2	61,553	30,777	Butler, Mo., and Le Roy, Kans., R. P. O. extended to Madison, Kans., May 10, 1888; increase 29.98 miles.
Cairo, Ill., and Elmot. Ark	173.00	3	2	53,976	26,988	River service.
Cairo, Ill. and Poplar Bluff, Mo.	74.87	7	2	54,805	27,403	
Cairo, Ill., and Texarkana, Ark.:						
Cairo to Pine Bluff	270.71	7	4	198,160	49,540	
Pine Bluff to Texarkana	151.76	7	3	111,088	37,029	
Cape Girardeau and Chaonia, Mo.	58.47	7	1	38,239	38,239	Cape Girardeau and Wappapello, Mo., R. P. O. extended June 18, 1888, to Chaonia, Mo.; increase 6.46 miles.
Chanute and Longton, Kans.	63.86	7	1	61,077	61,077	Chanute and Wellington R. P. O. (124.30 miles) established Oct. 22, 1887, to June 15, 1888; Chanute and Longton (via Cherry Vale) R. P. O. June 16 to 30, 1888.
Chetopa and Larned, Kans.	273.88	7	4	142,437	35,609	Belle Plaine and Stafford, Kans., R. P. O. extended Nov. 10, 1887; increase 181.98 miles.
Cheyenne, Wyo., and Denver, Colo.	107.39	7	2	78,609	39,305	
Clarendon and Fort Worth, Tex.	278.92	7	5	211,349	42,270	Quanah and Fort Worth R. P. O. extended Mar. 5, 1888, to begin at Clarendon; increase 85.88 miles; 1 helper runs 49,776 miles.
Colmesneil and Trinity, Tex.	66.81	7	1	48,905	48,905	
Colorado Springs and Leadville, Colo.	133.05	7	2	68,654	34,327	Established Oct. 17, 1887.
Commerce and Fort Worth, Tex.	98.31	7	2	1,180	590	Established June 25, 1888.

Statement of miles traveled by railway postal clerks, etc.—Continued.

SEVENTH DIVISION—Continued.

Railway post-office.	Distance from register to register.	No. of round trips per week.	No. of clerks at work on line.	Annual distance traveled by clerk.	Average annual distance traveled by clerk.	Remarks.
	Miles.			*Miles.*	*Miles.*	
Como and Gunnison, Colo......	121. 60	7	(¹)	¹16, 051	8, 026	¹ Service discontinued Sept. 4, 1887, and clerks transferred to other lines.
Concordia and Strong, Kans...	117. 44	7	2	54, 438	27, 219	Abilene and Cottonwood Falls R. P. O. (64.96 miles) established Aug. 8, 1887; extended Feb. 20, 1888, to Keystone and Bazaar R. P. O. (89.65 miles) ; extended Mar. 21, 1888, to Concordia and Bazaar R. P. O. (130.24 miles); curtailed to Concordia and Strong R. P. O. (117.44 miles) June 17, 1888.
Concordia and Junction City, Kans.	70. 77	7	1	51, 804	51, 804	
Conroe and Somerville (n. o.), Tex.	70. 93	7	2	34, 731	17, 366	Montgomery and Somerville R. P. O. (55 miles daily except Sunday) extended June 25, 1888.
Corpus Christi and Laredo, Tex.	161. 60	6	3	101, 485	33, 828	
Corsicana and Hillsborough, Tex	42. 00	7	1	2, 268	2, 268	Established June 4, 1888.
Council Bluffs, Iowa, and Kansas City, Mo.:						
Day line	196. 50	7	7	322, 512	46, 075	1 helper, run 34,840 miles.
Night line	196. 50	7	7	322, 512	46, 075	Do.
Council Bluffs, Iowa, and Moberly, Mo.	263. 53	7	4	192, 904	48, 226	
Creston, Iowa, and Saint Joseph, Mo.	103. 88	6	3	97, 648	32, 549	1 helper, run 32,411 miles.
Cuba and Salem, Mo..........	40. 96	6	1	25, 722	25, 722	
Dallas and Weatherford, Tex..	93. 78	7	2	39, 212	19, 606	Dallas and Cleburne R. P. O. extended June 4, 1888; increase 39.68 miles.
Dallas and Kemp, Tex........	49. 38	6	1	31, 011	31, 011	
Denison and Houston, Tex	337. 09	7	10	433, 500	49, 350	
Denison and San Antonio, Tex.	376. 63	7	10	468, 215	46, 822	4 helpers run 192,522 miles.
Denison and Trup, Tex.......	147. 51	7	2	107, 977	53, 989	
Denver and Georgetown, Colo..	51. 10	7	1	37, 405	37, 405	
Denver and Leadville, Colo....	150. 74	7	3	110, 342	36, 781	
Denver, Colo., and Ogden, Utah.	772. 56	7	8	565, 514	70, 689	
Denver, Pueblo, and Leadville, Colo.	278. 52	7	4	203, 877	50, 969	
Denver and Pueblo, Colo	126. 48	7	2	92, 583	46, 292	
East Lynne and Brownington, Mo.	45. 40	6	1	25, 878	25, 878	Established Aug. 3, 1887.
Ellsworth and Wichita, Kans..	106. 61	7	2	25, 160	31, 064	Established Mar. 5, 1888; 3 clerks performed all service on this line and Wichita and Kanopolis, the two lines being operated in connection with each other.
Emporia and Moline, Kans	85. 31	7	1	62, 447	62, 447	
Fairbury, Nebr., and Norton, Kans.	162. 77	7	3	47, 282	15, 761	Fairbury and Phillipsburgh R. P. O. established Jan. 16, 1888; extended Apr. 30, 1888; increase 33.73 miles.
Florence and Ellinwood, Kans.	99. 01	7	2	72, 475	36, 238	
Florence and Arkansas City, Kans.	87. 43	7	1	43, 816	43, 816	Florence and Winfield R. P. O. (75.03 miles) from July 1, 1887, to Mar. 31, 1888, and Florence and Arkansas City R. P. O. from June 17 to 30, 1888. Distance traveled Apr. 1 to June 16, 1888, shown under Newton and Gainesville R. P. O.
Fort Madison, Iowa, and Kansas City, Mo.	218. 27	7	3	14, 842	4, 947	Established May 28, 1888.
Fort Scott and Kiowa, Kans...	243. 87	7	4	178, 513	44, 628	
Fort Scott, Kans., and Webb City, Mo.	83. 32	7	2	57, 309	34, 143	Fort Scott and Joplin R. P. O. extended Apr. 7, 1888, to Webb City; increase 6.55 miles. 4 clerks performed all service on this line, Arcadia and Cherry Vale and Yates Center and Sedan R. P. O's.

Statement of miles traveled by railway postal clerks, etc.—Contirued.

SEVENTH DIVISION—Continued.

Railway post-office.	Distance from register to register.	No. of round trips per week.	No. of clerks at work on line.	Annual distance traveled by clerks.	Average annual distance traveled by clerks.	Remarks.
	Miles.			*Miles.*	*Miles.*	
Fort Smith, Ark., and Leland, Miss.:						
Fort Smith to Little Rock .	168.00	7	4	169,531	42,383	1 helper runs 46,555 miles.
Little Rock to Leland	137.70	7	3	100,796	33,599	
Fort Smith and Mansfield, Ark.	32.32	7	1	3,943	3,943	Established May 1, 1888.
Fort Worth and Guide, Tex ...	53.78	7	.1	39,367	39,367	
Gainesvile and Galveston, Tex.	411.65	7	7	356,622	50,946	1 helper runs 55,293 miles.
Girard and Galena, Kans	47.68	7	1	34,902	34,902	
Golddust and Memphis, Tenn..	106.50	3	1	33,228	33,228	River service.
Great Bend and Scott, Kans ...	121.12	7	2	80,752	40,376	Great Bend and Ness City R. P. O. extended Sept. 10, 1887. to Scott, Kans.; increase 55.69 miles.
Greely and Denver, Colo	98.43	7	2	72,634	36,817	La Salle (n. o.) and Denver R. P. O. curtailed Sept. 1, 1887; decrease 4.70 miles.
Greenville and Dallas, Tex	54.64	7	1	39,996	39,996	
Gurdon and Camden, Ark......	37.07	6	1	23,280	23,280	
Hannibal and Gilmore, Mo....	86.41	6	2	54,265	27,132	
Hannibal and Sedalia, Mo......	143.35	7	4	64,539	16,135	Established Jan. 23, 1888; 1 helper runs 18,667 miles.
Helena and Clarendon, Ark...	48.77	6	1	30,628	30,628	
Hempstead and Austin, Tex...	115.16	7	2	84,297	42,149	
Henrietta and Dallas, Tex	159.23	7	2	116,556	58,278	
Henry and Saint Joseph, Mo.:						
Day line	73.48	7	1	53,787	53,787	[1]6 round trips per week from July 1, 1887, to Apr. 30, 1888.
Night line	73.48	[1]7	1	[1]47,321	47,321	
Herington and Dodge City, Kans.	203.19	7	3	71,236	23,745	Herington and Pratt R. P. O. (127.15 miles) established Oct. 17, 1887; extended May 25, 1888, to Dodge City, Kans.
Holden, Mo., and Coffeyville, Kans.	201.58	7	3	144,426	48,142	Holden and Independence R. P. O. (183.51 miles), July 1 to Oct. 22, 1887; Kansas City and Independence R. P. O. (206.51 miles), Oct. 23, 1887, to May 12, 1888; Holden and Independence R. P. O. (183.51 miles), May 13 to June 9, 1888; Holden and Coffeyville R. P. O., June 10 to 30, 1888.
Houston and Eagle Pass, Tex.:						
Houston to San Antonio ...	218.01	7	4	234,731	58,183	1 helper runs 65,148 miles.
San Antonio to Eagle Pass.	168.69	7	3	125,733	41,911	San Antonio to Del Rio (172.22 miles), July 1, 1887, to May 14, 1888, and San Antonio to Eagle Pass, May 15 to June 30, 1888.
Houston and Galveston, Tex.:						
Day line	51.40	7	1	37,625	37,625	
Night line	51.40	7	1	37,625	37,625	
Hutchinson and Kinsley, Kans.	84.20	7	1	61,634	61,634	
Independence and Cedar Vale, Kans.	56.12	7	1	49,867	49,867	Chanute and Cedar Vale R. P. O. (95 miles), July 1 to Oct. 21, 1887.
Jacksonport and Brinkley, Ark.	60.90	6	1	38,245	38,245	
Jefferson City and Bagnell, Mo.	45.71	6	1	28,706	28,706	
Jefferson and McKinney, Tex..	155.46	7	3	113,797	37,932	
Julesburgh and Denver, Colo ..	197.88	7	3	144,848	48,282	
Junction City and Parsons, Kans.	157.15	7	3	115,034	38,345	
Kansas City, Mo., and Denver, Colo.:						
Kansas City to Denver	641.02	7	[1]13	995,539	76,580	[1]1 acting clerk additional. 1 helper runs 57,085 miles.
Kansas City to Wallace....	420.40	7	11	631,728	57,429	Kansas City to Ellis (302 miles), July 1, 1887, to Apr. 16, 1888. 1 helper runs 54,080 miles.
Kansas City and Joplin, Mo...	169.25	7	3	123,891	41,297	

Statement of miles traveled by railway postal clerks, etc.—Continued.

SEVENTH DIVISION—Continued.

Railway post-office.	Distance from register to register.	No. of round trips per week.	No. of clerks at work on line.	Annual distance traveled by clerks.	Average annual distance traveled by clerks.	Remarks.
	Miles.			*Miles.*	*Miles.*	
Kansas City and Joplin, Mo. (helpers' run).	180.70	7	¹3	132,272	44,091	Helpers run from Kansas City to Chetopa, Kans., over Kansas City and Joplin to Nevada, and thence over Nevada and Chetopa R. P. O. ¹ Includes the clerk appointed to Nevada and Chetopa R. P. O.
Kansas City, Mo., and Memphis, Tenn.:						
Kansas City to Memphis ..	487.29	7	10	713,892	71,319	
Kansas City to Springfield.	202.63	7	6	296,650	49,442	
Kansas City, Mo., and Pueblo, Colo.:						
Kansas City to Dodge City—						
Day line	382.64	7	18	1,226,581	68,143	2 helpers run 147,205 miles.
Night line	368.64	7	16	1,079,376	67,461	
Dodge City to Pueblo—						
Day line	267.91	7	6	392,220	65,370	
Night line	267.91	7	6	392,220	65,370	
Kansas City, Mo., and Seneca, Kans.	117.64	7	2	25,410	12,705	Established Mar. 15, 1888.
Kansas City, Mo., Salina, Kans., and Pueblo, Colo.	640.83	7	9	333,398	37,044	Osawatomie and McCracken R. P. O. (287.78 miles), July 1 to Dec. 4, 1887; Osawatomie and Horace R. P. O. (413.84 miles), Dec. 5, 1887, to Feb. 28, 1888; Osawatomie and Pueblo R. P. O. (578 miles), Feb. 29 to May 13, 1888; Kansas City, Salina and Pueblo R. P. O., May 14 to June 30, 1888; 1 helper runs 23,685 miles.
Kansas City, Mo., and Wellington, Kans.:						
Day line	270.09	7	5	213,051	42,610	Kansas City and Wellington, July 1 to October 21, 1887; Kansas City and Independence (166.16 miles), Oct. 22, 1887, to Mar. 24, 1888; Kansas City and Longton (190.62 miles), Mar. 25 to June 15, '888; Kansas City and Wellington, June 16 to 30, 1888; 1 helper runs 60,756 miles.
Night line	251.19	7	8	423.072	52,884	Kansas City and Kiowa (338 miles), July 1 to Oct. 14, 1887; Kansas City and Wellington (via Cherry Vale), Oct. 15, 1887, to June 15, 1888; Kansas City and Wellington (via Chanute and Longton), June 16 to 30, 1888.
Kenedy and Corpus Christi, Tex.	89	6	1	59,379	59,379	San Antonio and Corpus Christi R. P. O. (156.06), July 1 to 31, 1887.
Keystone and Barnard, Kans ..	43.23	7	1	4,507	4,507	Established Mar. 26, 1888.
Kincaid and Coffeyville, Kans..	85,59	7	1	35,224	35,224	Morantown and Coffeyville R. P. O. (73.64 miles) established Oct. 24, 1887; extended to Kincaid May 10, 1888; clerk runs only between Coffeyville and Parsons (31.27 miles) on Sundays.
Knobel and Helena, Ark	140.65	7	3	102,956	34,319	
La Junta, Colo., and Albuquerque, N. Mex.	348.22	7	6	270,953	45,159	One helper runs 16,050 miles.
Larned and Jetmore, Kans.....	46.84	7	1	20,703	20,703	Established Nov. 23, 1887.
Lawrence and Gridley, Kans...	83.67	6	2	47,632	23,816	Lawrence and Burlington R. P. O. extended May 5, 1888, to Gridley; increase 9.27 miles.
Leadville and Aspen, Colo	137.82	7	2	58,272	29,136	Leadville and Glenwood Springs R. P. O. established Nov. 27, 1887; extended Dec. 15, 1887, to Aspen, Colo.; increase 42.84 miles.

Statement of miles traveled by railway postal clerks, etc.—Continued.

SEVENTH DIVISION—Continued.

Railway post-office.	Distance from register to register.	No. of round trips per week.	No. of clerks at work on line.	Annual distance traveled by clerks.	Average annual distance traveled by clerks.	Remarks.
	Miles.			*Miles.*	*Miles.*	
Leavenworth and Lawrence, Kans.	34.95	7	1	25,583	25,583	
Leavenworth and Miltonvale, Kans.	166.18	6	3	104,361	34,787	
Leavenworth and Topeka, Kans	57.	7	1	42,222	42,222	
McFarland and Belleville, Kans	104.	7	2	17,393	8,697	Established April 9, 1888.
McPherson and El Dorado, Kans	62.	7	1	45,506	45,506	
Madison and Benedict, Kans...	45.68	7	1	19,082	19,082	Established Dec. 5, 1887.
Manhattan and Burlingame, Kans.	57.99	6	1	35,966	35,966	
Memphis, Tenn., and Little Rock, Ark.	136.00	7	3	99,552	33,184	
Mexico and Cedar City, Mo....	50.34	6	1	31,614	31,614	
Monett, Mo., and Paris, Tex.:						
Monett to Fort Smith......	133.44	7	3	105,109	35,036	Pierce City to Fort Smith (139.88 miles), July 1 to 3, 1887. One helper runs 7,405 miles.
Monett to Paris............	302.07	7	4	207,490	51,873	Monett and Fort Smith night line established Nov. 27, 1887; extended Feb. 5, 1888, to Paris, Tex.
Monett, Mo., and Vinita, Ind. T	77.74	7	1	56,137	56,137	Pierce City and Vinita, R. P. O. (73.66 miles), July 1 to Oct. 1, 1887.
Mount Pleasant and Sherman, Tex.	110.10	7	2	64,519	32,260	Established Sept. 12, 1887.
Mulvane and Englewood, Kans	166.79	7	2	93,111	46,556	Mulvane and Spivey R. P. O. (51.67 miles), July 1 to Oct. 16, 1887; Mulvane and Ashland R. P. O. (151.67 miles), Oct. 17, 1887, to Feb. 29, 1888.
Nashville and Hope, Ark.:						
A. M. line	27.53	7	1	20,152	40,084	Double daily service from July 5, 1887.
P. M. line	27.53	7	....	19,932	....	
Newport and Cushman, Ark...	40.57	7	1	26,374	26,374	Newport and Batesville R. P. O. (28.95 miles), July 1 to Nov. 30, 1887.
Newton, Kans., and Gainesville, Tex.	338.61	7	4	160,177	40,044	Newton and Arkansas City R. P. O. (78.81 miles), July 1, 1887, to June 16, 1888. Purcell and Gainesville R. P. O. (105.73 miles), established Sept. 11, 1887, to Mar. 31, 1888; Florence and Gainesville R. P. O. (346.02 miles), April 1 to June 16, 1888.
Newton and Kiowa, Kans......	127.85	7	3	167,346	55,782	Newton and Caldwell (81.09 miles), July 1, to Oct. 14, 1887. Clerks separate at Attica, one going to Medicine Lodge, performing service on Attica and Medicine Lodge R. P. O.
Olathe, Kans., and Ash Grove, Mo.	155.89	7	3	114,111	38,037	
Omaha, Nebr., and Kansas City, Mo.	216.65	7	4	128,334	32,084	Omaha and Atchison R. P. O. (166.42 miles), July 1, to Nov. 30, 1887; Omaha and Atchison (via Nebraska City, 169.81 miles), Dec. 1, 1887, to June 11, 1888. 1 helper runs 3,290 miles.
Ottawa and Emporia, Kans	56.85	6	1	35,702	35,702	
Ottumwa, Iowa, and Moberly, Mo.:						
Day line	131.54	6	2	82,607	41,304	
Night line	131.54	7	2	96,287	48,144	
Palestine and Laredo, Tex.:						
Palestine to San Antonio...	262.72	7	5	196,800	39,360	1 helper runs 4,489 miles.
San Antonio to Laredo.....	155.53	7	3	113,848	37,949	
Paris and Dallas, Tex..........	98.57	7	2	72,153	36,077	
Pittsburgh and Chanute, Kans.	54.89	6	1	32,711	32,711	Girard and Chanute R. P. O. (41.36 miles), July 1, 1887, to April 1, 1888.

Statement of miles traveled by railway postal clerks, etc.—Continued.

SEVENTH DIVISION—Continued.

Railway post-office.	Distance from register to register.	No. of round trips per week.	No. of clerks at work on line.	Annual distance traveled by clerks.	Average annual distance traveled by clerks.	Remarks.
	Miles.			*Miles.*	*Miles.*	
Pratt and Liberal, Kans.......	136. 23	7	2	12, 805	6, 403	Established May 15, 1888.
Pueblo ai d Silverton, Colo ...	376. 55	7	6	250, 081	41, 680	
Quincy, Ill., and Kansas City, Mo.:						
Day line	225. 92	7	8	330, 746	41, 343	
Day line (helper's run)	124. 44	7	2	91, 090	45, 545	Helpers run from Brookfield, Mo., to Atchison, Kans., over Quincy and Kansas City R. P. O. to Cameron, and thence over Cameron and Atchison R. P. O. 1 helper runs 76,123 miles.
Night line	225. 92	7	9	406, 874	45, 208	
Quincy, Ill., and Trenton, Mo ..	137. 10	6	2	86, 099	43, 050	
Rincon and Silver City, N. Mex	101. 12	7	2	64, 573	32, 287	Rincon and Deming R. P. O. (58.41 miles), July 1, to Oct. 7, 1887.
Rockland and Beaumont, Tex..	73. 52	7	1	53, 817	53, 817	
Rosenberg and Cuero, Tex....	130. 29	7	2	88, 052	44, 026	
Saint Joseph, Mo., and Cald-well, Kans.	295. 55	7	4	182, 691	45, 673	Saint Joseph and Alma R. P. O. (126.45 miles), July 1 to 20, 1887; Saint Joseph and Herington R. P. O. (171.74 miles), July 21, to Sept. 23, 1887; Saint Joseph and Wichita R. P. O. (246.09 miles), Sept. 24 to Oct. 26, 1887.
Saint Joseph, Mo., and Grand Island, Nebr.	252. 54	6	4	158, 595	39, 649	
Saint Joseph, Mo., and Nelson, Nebr.	208. 43	7	3	150, 806	50, 269	Saint Joseph and Hebron R. P. O. (180.74 miles), July 1 to 15, 1887; Saint Joseph and Nora R. P. O. (201.94 miles), July 16 to Sept. 25, 1887.
Saint Louis and Kansas City, Mo.:						
Fast mail..................	283. 00	7	[1]26	1, 518, 900	58, 419	6 helpers run 483,120 miles. [1]Four of these clerks are acting clerks additional.
Day line	283. 00	7	17	893, 572	52, 563	1 helper run 64.948 miles.
Night line	283. 00	7	20	1, 127, 207	56, 360	4 helpers run 298,583 miles.
Saint Louis, Mo., and Colum-bus, Ky.	195. 65	7	4	182, 122	45, 531	1 helper run 38.906 miles.
Saint Louis, Mo., and Halstead, Kans:						
Saint Louis to Monett—						
Day line...............	282. 12	7	8	413, 024	51, 628	
Night line	282. 12	7	8	413, 024	51, 628	
Monett to Halstead—						
Day line...............	248. 02	7	4	181, 551	45, 388	
Night line	222. 60	7	4	32, 054	8, 014	Monett to Wichita; service established April 20, 1888.
Saint Louis, Louisiana, and Kansas City, Mo.	323. 39	7	[1]6	375, 989	53, 713	3 helpers run 139,628 miles. [1]Services of 1 helper discontinued June 24, 1888, and not included in this number.
Saint Louis, Moberly, and Kansas City, Mo.:						
Day line....................	276. 80	7	7	474, 316	67, 759	1 helper run 69,080 miles.
Night line	276. 80	7	10	513, 772	51, 377	3 helpers run 108 536 miles.
Saint Louis, Mo., and Texar-kana, Ark.:						
Saint Louis to Little Rock—						
Day line...............	346. 00	7	17	924, 516	54, 383	2 helpers run 164,700 miles.
Night line	346. 00	7	17	924, 516	54, 383	2 helpers run 164,700 miles.
Little Rock to Texarkana—						
Day line	145. 72	7	10	213, 334	42, 667	Five crews of 2 each perform service on both lines.
Night line	145. 72	7	...	213, 334	......	
Saint Louis and Union, Mo ..	59. 91	7	1	40, 968	40, 968	Established July 25, 1887.
Salina and Luray, Kans.......	67. 07	6	2	33, 630	16, 815	Salina and Lincoln R. P. O. (86.12 miles) ; July 1, 1887, to Jan. 16, 1888.
Salina and McPherson, Kans ..	36. 78	7	1	26, 923	26, 923	
San Antonio and Kerrville, Tex	71. 75	6	1	32, 001	32, 001	Established Oct. 15, 1887.

Statement of miles traveled by railway postal clerks, etc.—Continued.

SEVENTH DIVISION—Continued.

Railway post-office.	Distance from register to register.	No. of round trips per week.	No. of clerks at work on line.	Annual distance traveled by clerks.	Average annual distance traveled by clerks.	Remarks.
	Miles.			*Miles.*	*Miles.*	
Sedalia, Mo., and Denison, Tex.:						
Trains 501 and 506 ...-.....	433.13	7	12	731,094	60,925	Hannibal to Denison (575.11 miles), July 1, 1887, to Jan. 22, 1888.
Trains 507 and 504	433.13	7	18	951,153	52,842	
Helpers run	244.70	7	8	36,216	12,072	Helpers commenced service April 18, 1888.
Sedalia and Kansas City, Mo.:						
Day line	99.35	7	8	72,724	48,483	} 2 crews on both lines.
Night line	99.35	7	....	72,724	....	
Sedalia and Warsaw, Mo.......	43.16	6	1	27,104	27,104	
Shreveport, La., and Houston, Tex.	234.26	7	4	171,478	42,870	
Springfield and Chadwick, Mo.	35.63	7	1	26,061	26,061	
Taylor and La Grange, Tex	70.02	7	¹2	29,268	14,634	Established Dec. 5, 1887. ¹1 clerk is acting additional.
Temple and Ballinger, Tex.....	191.41	7	3	140,112	46,704	
Texarkana, Ark., and El Paso, Tex.:						
Texarkana to Fort Worth .	254.17	7	4	186,052	46,513	
Texarkana to Dallas.......	221.83	7	7	324,760	46,394	3 helpers run 162,380 miles.
Dallas to El Paso	647.39	7	10	581,493	58,149	2 helpers run 107,604 miles.
Texarkana, Ark., and Gatesville, Tex.	305.39	7	4	192,464	48,116	Texarkana and Waco R. P. O. (259 miles), July 1, 1887, to May 30, 1888.
Texarkana, Ark., and Houston, Tex.	330.49	7	5	241,919	48,384	
Texarkana, Ark., and Whitesborough, Tex.	173.74	7	¹3	127,178	42,726	¹1 acting clerk additional.
Topeka and Fort Scott, Kans ..	130.79	7	2	95,738	47,869	
Trenton, Mo., and Leavenworth, Kans.	103.56	7	4	156,355	39,089	2 helpers run 80,549 miles; from Trenton, Mo., to Atchison, Kans., over Trenton and Leavenworth R. P. O. to Atchison Junction, Mo., and thence over Atchison Junction and Atchison R. P. O.
Tyler and Lufkin, Tex.........	89.61	7	2	65,595	32,798	
Wallis and San Antonio, Tex ..	200.58	7	3	126,478	42,159	Hallettsville and San Antonio R. P. O. (137.80 miles), established Aug. 1, 1887; extended Oct. 3, 1887, to begin at Wallis.
West Point and Yoakum, Tex .	50.20	7	1	6,024	6,024	Established May 2, 1888.
Wichita and Mullinville, Kans.	121.58	6	2	70,644	35,322	Wichita and Cullison R. P. O. (96.41 miles), July 1 to Aug. 7, 1887; Wichita and Greensburgh R. P. O. (121.58 miles), Aug. 8, 1887, to Mar. 18, 1888.
Wichita and Kanopolis, Kans..	102.19	7	1	68,031	31,064	Wichita and Geneseo R. P. O. (87.72 miles), July 1, 1887, to Feb. 19, 1888; 3 clerks performed all service on this line and Ellsworth and Wichita R. P. O., the two lines being operated in connection with each other.
Yates Center and Sedan, Kans	76.59	7	1	19,700	34,143	Sidell and Sedan R. P. O. (58.63 miles), established Jan. 28, 1888; extended Feb. 21, 1888, to Yates Center. 4 clerks performed all service on this line, Arcadia and Cherry Vale, and Fort Scott and Webb City R. P. O's.

Statement of miles traveled by railway postal clerks, etc.—Continued.

EIGHTH DIVISION.

Railway post-office.	Distance from register to register.	No. of round trips per week.	No. of clerks at work on line.	Annual distance traveled by clerks.	Average annual distance traveled by clerks.	Remarks.
	Miles.			*Miles.*	*Miles.*	
Albuquerque and Los Angeles.	888. 66	7	12	650, 499	74, 930	8 clerks on through run.
	....	6	....	39, 546	....	1 clerk short run.
				203, 125	....	3 helpers at Albuquerque, N.Mex.
Benson and Nogales	88. 50	7	2	64, 782	32, 391	
Butte City and Ogden	416. 95	7	6	305, 207	50, 867	
Calistoga and Vallejo Junction.	43. 88	12	1	55, 113	55, 113	
Cloverdale and San Francisco..	85. 46	7	2	62, 557	31, 278	
Dayton and Umatilla	97. 85	7	2	71, 626	35, 813	
Deming and Los Angeles	715. 96	7	8	524, 083	65, 510	
Dundee Junction and Airlie ...	52. 86	6	1	33, 196	33, 196	
Garrison and Butte City	52. 14	7	1	38, 166	38, 166	
Helena and Portland..	932. 36	7	15	682, 488	45, 499	
Huntington and Portland......	405. 60	7	5	296, 890	60, 239	
	....		¹1	64, 535	....	¹City distributer for Portland, Oregon.
Ingrams and San Francisco...	87. 25	6	2	54, 793	27, 396	
Ketchum and Shoshone........	70. 34	6	1	44, 174	44, 174	
Los Angeles and Santa Ana ...	35. 60	7	1	26, 059	26, 059	
Los Angeles and Santa Barbara	111. 20	7	2	81, 398	40, 699	
Milton and Stockton.........	30. 09	6	1	18, 897	18, 897	
Moscow and Connell..........	117. 30	6	2	73, 664	36, 832	
Mound House and Keeler......	160. 72	7	3	117, 647	40, 409	7 trips per week Mound House to Candelaria.
	141. 00	3	1	43, 992	....	3 round trips per week, Belleville Junction. Nev., to Keeler, Cal.
Ogden and San Francisco	834. 65	7	20	310, 964	47, 415	20 through clerks, 10 crews.
	....	7	2	66, 385	....	
	....	....	2	128, 100	....	2 clerks short run San Francisco to Sacramento; 2 helpers at Ogden, Utah, and 4 city distributers San Francisco,
	....	....	4	348, 022		
Ogden and Salt Lake	38. 73	14	1	56, 701	56, 701	
Portland and Coburg	123. 38	7	2	77, 483	38, 741	
Portland and Corvallis........	97. 99	6	2	61, 538	30, 769	
Port Harford and Los Olivos...	79. 50	6	1	49, 926	49, 926	
Placerville and Sacramento....	64. 25	6	1	40, 349	40, 349	
Portland and Sacramento......	684. 54	7	12	501, 083	44, 052	12 clerks on through run.
	....	....	2	115, 656	....	2 helpers out of Portland, Oregon.
Redding and Sacramento	171. 41	7	3	125, 472	41, 824	
Reno and Virginia City........	53. 06	7	1	38, 855	38, 855	
Sacramento and San Francisco.	140. 90	7	3	103, 139	34, 379	
Salt Lake and Juab	105. 03	7	2	76, 892	38, 441	
San Bernardino and National City.	132. 81	7	2	97, 217	48, 608	
San Francisco and Los Angeles.	482. 71	14	13	706, 687	53, 426	Double daily service; 13 clerks.
	....	....	2	94, 706	....	2 helpers at San Francisco.
San Francisco and Templeton..	222. 34	7	3	163, 485	54, 485	
San Francisco and Santa Cruz	83. 35	6	1	52, 344	52, 344	

NINTH DIVISION.

Adrian, Mich., and Fayette, Ohio.	33. 26	6	1	20, 887	20, 887	
Ashtabula and Youngstown, Ohio.	64. 70	6	1	40, 632	40, 632	
Alpena and Alger, Mich.......	104. 50	6	2	65, 626	32, 813	
Ashley and Muskegon, Mich..	96. 24	6	2	18, 478	9, 239	Service commenced on this line Mar. 12, 1888.
Baldwin and Grand Rapids, Mich.	74. 70	6	1	46, 912	46, 912	
Bay City and Jackson, Mich...	115. 00	12	4	144, 440	36, 110	
Bay City, Wayne, and Detroit, Mich.	121. 41	6	2	76, 215	38, 122	
Bad Axe and East Saginaw, Mich.	68. 23	6	1	42, 848	42, 848	
Big Rapids and Detroit, Mich..	190. 70	6	3	119, 760	39, 920	
Big Rapids and Holland, Mich.	91. 00	6	2	57, 148	28, 574	

Statement of miles traveled by railway postal clerks, etc.—Continued.

NINTH DIVISION—Continued.

Railway post-office.	Distance from register to register.	No. of round trips per week.	No. of clerks at work on line.	Annual distance traveled by clerks.	Average annual distance traveled by clerks.	Remarks.
	Miles.			*Miles.*	*Miles.*	
Cadillac, Mich., and Ft. Wayne, Ind.	240.76	6	4	151,197	37,799	
Caseville and Pontiac, Mich....	100.73	6	1	63,258	63,258	
Cleveland, Ohio, Fort Wayne, Ind., and Chicago, Ill.	340.50	6	4	213,834	53,458	
Cleveland and Toledo, Ohio....	113.37	12	4	142,393	35,598	
Detroit, Mich., and Chicago, Ill.:						
Day line ,...................	286.69	6	10	449,196	44,919	2 clerks assigned as helpers between Chicago and Kalamazoo.
Night line	286.69	7	18	927,707	51,539	2 clerks assigned as helpers between Detroit and Battle Creek.
Detroit and Grand Haven, Mich.	188.94	6	4	118,654	29,664	
Detroit and Grand Haven, Mich. (short run).	157.50	6	3	140,986	46,995	1 clerk assigned as helper between Detroit and Durand.
Detroit and Grand Rapids, Mich.	170.65	6	3	107,168	35,723	
Detroit and Grand Rapids (short run).	94.72	6	2	59,484	29,742	
Detroit, Mich., and Logansport, Ind.	204.36	6	3	128,338	42,779	
Detroit, Three Rivers, Mich., and Chicago, Ill.	274.49	6	4	172,380	43,095	
Detroit, Mich., and Toledo, Ohio:						
Day line....................	60.50	6	1	37,994	37,994	
Night line	65.90	6	1	41,385	41,385	
East Saginaw and Howard City, Mich.	81.51	6	1	51,188	38,391	1 clerk appointed to the Ludington and Toledo R. P. O. alternates between this line and the Manistee and East Saginaw R. P. O.
East Saginaw and Port Huron, Mich.	92.06	6	2	57,814	43,360	1 clerk appointed to this line alternates between the East Saginaw and Port Huron, Fort Gratiot and Detroit, and the Port Austin and Port Huron R. P. O.
Fort Gratiot, Mich., and Chicago, Ill.	337.73	6	5	295,484	59,097	1 clerk assigned as helper between Fort Gratiot and Battle Creek.
Fort Gratiot and Detroit, Mich.	61.34	6	1	38,521	28,891	This clerk has relief every fourth week.
Grand Rapids, Mich., and Elkhart, Ind.	115.02	12	4	144,465	36,116	
Grand Rapids, Mich., and Lacrosse, Ind.	154.54	6	3	97,051	32,350	
Howard City and Detroit, Mich.	161.22	6	3	128,129	42,709	One of these clerks runs as helper between Detroit and Howell.
Jackson and Adrian, Mich .	47.55	6	1	29,861	29,861	
Jackson and Hillsdale, Mich., and Fort Wayne, Ind.	99.26	6	2	62,335	31,147	
Kalamazoo and South Haven, Mich.	40.20	6	1	25,246	25,246	
Lansing and Hillsdale, Mich....	65.68	6	1	41,247	41,247	
Lenox and Jackson, Mich	106.68	6	2	66,995	33,498	
Ludington, Mich., and Toledo, Ohio.	278.59	6	4	174,954	43,738	
Mackinaw City and Detroit, Mich.	291.23	6	4	182,892	45,723	
Mackinaw City and Detroit, Mich. (short run).	108.00	7	2	79,056	39,528	
Mackinaw City and Grand Rapids, Mich.	226.30	6	4	142,116	35,529	
Manistee and East Saginaw, Mich.	148.13	6	3	93,026	31,009	
Monroe and Adrian, Mich	34.29	6	1	21,534	21,534	
Muskegon and Allegan, Mich..	60.06	6	1	37,718	37,718	
Mount Pleasant, Mich., and Toledo, Ohio.	171.82	6	3	107,903	35,968	

Statement of miles traveled by railway postal-clerks, etc.—Continued.

NINTH DIVISION—Continued.

Railway post-office.	Distance from register to register.	No. of round trips per week.	No. of clerks at work on line.	Annual distance traveled by clerks.	Average annual distance traveled by clerks.	Remarks.
New York, N. Y., and Chicago, Ill.: *						
East division:						
Trains 21 and 12	*Miles.* 289.50	7	42	*Miles.* 2,315,015	*Miles.* 55,167	8 clerks run as helpers between New York and Fonda, and 2 clerks assigned as helpers between Utica and Buffalo, N. Y.
Trains 23 and 2	289.50	6	14	635,048	45,575	2 clerks assigned as helpers between Albany and Syracuse, N. Y.
Trains 11 and 16	289.50	7	56	2,944,792	52,586	6 clerks assigned as helpers between Albany and Syracuse, N. Y.; 1 clerk assigned as helper between New York and Albany, N. Y.; 1 clerk assigned as helper between Syracuse and Buffalo, N. Y.
Middle division:						
Trains 1 and 12	336.26	7	32	1,953,095	61,034	4 clerks assigned as helpers between Buffalo, N. Y., and Cleveland, Ohio.
Trains 3 and 2	336.26	6	36	2,074,410	57,623	4 clerks assigned as helpers between Buffalo, N. Y., and Toledo, Ohio.
Trains 11 and 8	336.26	7	41	2,677,264	65,299	4 clerks assigned as helpers between Buffalo, N. Y., and Toledo, Ohio; 1 clerk assigned as helper between Buffalo, N. Y., and Cleveland, Ohio.
West division:						
Trains 1 and 12	356.61	7	23	1,426,385	62,016	3 clerks assigned as helpers between Toledo, Ohio, and Chicago, Ill.
Trains 3 and 2	356.61	6	28	1,506,233	53,794	2 clerks assigned as helpers between Cleveland and Toledo, Ohio; 2 clerks assigned as helpers between Cleveland and Wauseon, Ohio.
Trains 11 and 8	356.61	7	36	2,306,360	64,065	
Oil City, Pa., and Ashtabula, Ohio.	88.10	6	2	55,327	27,663	
Pentwater and Muskegon, Mich.	45.13	6	1	28,342	28,342	
Port Austin and Port Huron, Mich.	87.71	6	1	55,083	41,312	This clerk has relief every fourth week.
Toledo, Ohio, and Allegan, Mich.	157.42	6	2	98,860	49,430	
Toledo, Ohio, and Chicago, Ill..	244.99	6	8	397,707	49,713	
Trenton and Adrian, Mich.....	49.60	6	1	31,149	31,149	
Ypsilanti and Hillsdale, Mich..	62.14	6	1	39,024	39,024	

* This line is divided into three divisions, viz: East division, New York to Syracuse, N. Y.; middle division, Syracuse, N. Y., to Cleveland, Ohio; west division, Cleveland, Ohio, to Chicago, Ill.

Statement of miles traveled by railway postal clerks, etc.—Continued.

RECAPITULATION.

Division.	Distance from register to register on R. P. O. lines.	Number of clerks at work on lines.	Annual distance traveled by clerks.	Annual average distance traveled by clerks.	Average distance run daily (general average being 326 trips per annum).
	Miles.		*Miles.*	*Miles.*	*Miles.*
First	9,876.25	364	12,947,694	35,668	105.53
Second	14,662.64	574	23,908,755	41,652	128.23
Third	7,190.93	247	10,543,847	42,687	126.29
Fourth	17,303.02	355	16,015,626	45,114	133.47
Fifth	21,730.74	777	36,224,933	46,622	137.90
Sixth	43,302.96	1,050	46,184,090	43,984	130.11
Seventh	32,475.00	717	33,775,125	47,106	139.36
Eighth	7,849.39	148	6,773,440	45,766	135.40
Ninth	9,908.95	453	23,811,579	52,564	155.50
Total	164,289.88	*14,685	210,185,089	44,574	132.09

* Including 11 acting clerks in all. † Including 83 clerks on steamboat R. P. O's.

Statement of pieces of mail separated for city delivery for the fiscal year ended June 30, 1888.

City for which separation was made.	Railway post-office making the separation.	Division to which R. P. O. is assigned.	Packages distributed.	Packages undistributed.	Incorrect slips.	Errors.	Letters distributed (75 to the package).
Boston, Mass	Boston, Springfield, and New York.	First	205,441	*4,971	75	124	15,406,075
New York, N. Y.	Boston and New York.	..do	11,394	*44	719	1,462	854,550
	Boston, Providence, and New York.	..do	24,280	*10	418	654	1,821,009
	Boston, Springfield, and New York.	..do	107,317	*88	670	1,125	8,048,775
	New York and Chicago.	Ninth	234,617	*403	2,708	4,656	17,596,275
	New York and Dunkirk.	Second	53,491	*1,232	599	1,099	4,161,825
	New York and Pittsburgh.	do	254,583	*4,078	2,972	4,051	19,091,400
	New York and Rochester.	..do	33,154	*194	497	717	2,486,350
	New York and Washington.	..do	134,515	*5,840	1,685	2,884	10,088,625
Pittsburgh, Pa†	New York and Pittsburgh.	..do	3,530				†264,750
Philadelphia, Pa	......do	..do	118,113	*1,449			8,858,475
	New York and Philadelphia.	..do	11,805	*23			885,375
	New York and Washington.	..do	22,235	*579			1,669,125
Washington, D. C	Baltimore and Grafton.	Third	30,658	*45	56	86	2,299,350
	Chicago and Cincinnati.‡	Fifth	8,674		44	55	630,550
	Cincinnati and Nashville.‡	..do	6,910		33	41	518,250
	......do§	..do	9,258		41	52	694,350
	Cincinnati and Saint Louis.‡	..do	13,905		52	90	1,042,875
	......do§	..do	23,582		64	104	1,768,650
	Grafton and Cincinnati.‡	..do	18,611		49	62	1,396,825
	......do§	..do	29,624		52	69	2,221,800
	New York and Pittsburgh.	Second	17,512	*117	141	167	1,313,400

* Short of clerks. Heavy delayed mail. † From February 15, 1888, to June 30, 1888.
‡ Day line. § Night line.

Statement of pieces of mail separated for city delivery, etc.—Continued.

City for which separation was made.	Railway post-office making the separation.	Division to which R. P. O. is assigned.	Packages distributed.	Packages undistributed.	Incorrect slips.	Errors.	Letters dis- tributed (75 to the pack- age).
Washington, D. C .	New York and Wash- ington.	Second..	12,446	*167	81	109	933,450
	Washington and Char- lotte.	Third...	30,961	....	43	61	2,322,075
	Washington and Wil- mington.	..do	30,888	....	58	84	2,316,600
	Williamsport and Bal- timore.	Second..	13,060	....	74	83	1,129,500
Saint Paul, Minn...	Chicago and Minne- apolis.	Sixth ...	36,027	....	....	136	†2,702,025
Minneapolis, Minn.	......do	..do	74,518	....	....	4,601	5,588,800
Saint Louis, Mo	Saint Louis and Hal- stead.	Seventh	15,798	....	....	....	1,184,850
	Saint Louis and Kan- sas City.	..do	53,567	....	....	....	4,017,525
	Saint Louis, Moberly, and Kansas City.	..do	19,246	....	....	....	1,443,450
	Saint Louis and Tex- arkana.	..do	9,577	....	....	....	718,275
Portland, Oregon..	Helena and Portland..	Eighth .	26,510	*85	10	36	1,988,250
San Francisco, Cal..	Ogden and San Fran- cisco.	..do	208,094	*602	201	261	15,607,050
	Total................	....	1,907,800	19,927	11,342	23,559	143,091,750

* Short clerks. Heavy delayed mail. † In addition there were 19,575 pieces of paper mail.

Statement of leaves of absence, with pay, granted to railway postal clerks injured while on duty, together with the amount paid acting clerks during the fiscal year ending June 30, 1888.

Name.	Railway post-office line.	Date of in- jury.	Days leave.	Days acting clerk was em ployed.	Amount paid act- ing clerk.
J. L. Killian	Charlotte and Atlanta.	Oct. 20, 1887	254	254	$558.74
J. B. Jones.............	Cairo and West Point................	Sept. 20, 1887	60	17	39.96
C. F. Coyle.............	New Haven and New York.........	Feb. 17, 1888	23	15	33.33
W. R. Wilson..........	Charlotte and Atlanta...............	Oct. 20, 1887	252	252	554.34
James Devine	Salamanca and Kent.................	Mar. 23, 1887	266	266	581.58
C. E. Minor............	Cleveland and Toledo...............	Nov. 19, 1887	30	30	65.22
J. R. Dutcher..........	Rochester and Elmira ....-......	Jan. 17, 1888	36	36	80.00
W. T. Roberts.	Cincinnati and Chattanooga.....	Dec. 31, 1887	182	182	400.00
J. B. Owens	......do............................	Apr. 3, 1888	81	54	118.68
G. V. Tatum	Cincinnati and Nashville	May 5, 1888	11	5	10.99
Orlow A. Evarts	Ashland and Abbetsford...........	Jan. 11, 1888	156	131	289.19
H. P. Goodwin........	Cartersville and Talladega	Mar. 23, 1888	30	30	66.67
Geo. H. Baker.........	Zanesville and Columbus.........	Oct. 1, 1887	21	17	36.96
Frank McNulty	Atchison and Lenora................	Apr. 7, 1887	96	96	208.70
M. Brenneman........	Kansas City and Pueblo...........	Oct. 15, 1887	37	28	60.87
H. M. Bubb............	Saint Louis and Halstead..........	Jan. 17, 1888	120	120	266.68
Frank A. Beebe.......	Saint Louis and Atchison	Nov. 27, 1886	189	150	330.38
A. H. Johnson........	Nashville and Hope.................	Oct. 15, 1887	40	40	76.09
Lord Harleston.......	Cairo and Texarkana...............	Apr. 1, 1888	90	81	178.01
E. L. Landrum........	Atlanta and Montgomery	July 27, 1887	60	60	130.44
James E. Hurley......	Chicago, McGregor, and Saint Paul ..	Sept. 19, 1887	284	284	622.50
John H. Black.........	Calmar and Davenport............	Dec. 21, 1887	173	143	315.54
W. A. Tilley..........	San Francisco and Los Angeles.....	Jan. 2, 1888	15	15	33.34
Geo. B. Clark	Chicago and Burlington...........	Feb. 27, 1888	125	125	277.00
I. N. Merrill	Ogden and San Francisco	Apr. 5, 1888	30	30	65.93
W. H. Miller..........	Dallas and Kemp........	Apr. 9, 1888	8	7	15.38
J. M. Bennett	Boston, Providence, and New York ..	Apr. 12, 1888	14	14	30.77
Chas. Keenan.........	Larabee and Clermont	Apr. 28, 1888	60	60	132.60
E. E. Fowler..........	Pittsburgh and Cincinnati	July 4, 1887	36	36	78.12
W. T. Treleaven	Kansas City and Pueblo...........	Aug. 15, 1887	152	129	279.93
J. B. Wallace	Terre Haute and Evansville	Dec. 31, 1887	12	7	15.22
C. H. Hooten	Baltimore and Grafton.............	Aug. 17, 1887	10	10	21.98
F. A. Robertson.......	New York and Chicago	Aug. 24, 1887	30	13	28.26
James Ryan	Chicago and Cincinnati	Nov. 28, 1887	14	14	30.42
W. F. Stenson..........	Chicago and Burlington.............	Feb. 27, 1888	120	119	262,99

Statement of leaves of absence with pay granted to railway postal clerks, etc.—Continued.

Name.	Railway post-office line.	Date of injury.	Days leave.	Days acting clerk was employed.	Amount paid acting clerk.
Wm. D. Brown	Racine and Rock Island	Feb. 27, 1888	90	90	$198.90
H. D. Burkhimer	Washington and Wilmington	June 16, 1888	14	8	17.58
R. L. Hargrove	Cincinnati and Chattanooga	June 26, 1888	4	4	8.79
W. H. Wiley	Baltimore and Grafton	June 22, 1887	15	9	19.78
J. M. Decker	Williamsport and Reading	Jun. 1, 1887	62	62	137.64
John Kemp	Jefferson and McKinney	Jan. 16, 1888	44	25	55.56
Wales Wasson	Buffalo and Emporium	Apr. 30, 1888	60	60	131.86
W. L. Pollock	Albuquerque and Los Angeles	Dec. 2, 1887	60	60	131.86
H. L. Coleman	Wilkes Barre and Pottsville	May 23, 1888	30	30	65.93
Chas. M. Harriman	Chicago and Cincinnati	June 2, 1888	56	21	46.15
W. P. Colton	Sedalia and Denison	June 15, 1888	30	25	54.95
S. L. Simons, jr	Wilmington and Jacksonville	Dec. 25, 1887	60	60	131.86
John Dundon	Boston, Springfield, and New York	Apr. 16, 1888	75	75	165.00
McC. A. Phillips	Nordmont and Hartley Hall	June 15, 1888	15	15	32.97
W. F. J. Comly	Omaha and McCook	Apr. 27, 1888	64	57	125.40
F. A. Holmes	Syracuse and Rochester	Mar. 16, 1887	13	13	28.89
C. H. Hoyt	Kansas City and Denver	Oct. 19, 1887	150	142	312.40
S. Z. Ettinger	Saint Louis, Moberly, and Kansas City	Dec. 31, 1887	58	55	122.10
James R. Polk	Quincy and Kansas City	Feb. 28, 1887	50	46	102.12
M. B. Domer	Baltimore and Grafton	June 22, 1887	31	29	64.44
E. L. Pippin	Albuquerque and Los Angeles	Feb. 26, 1887	116	116	256.36
S. N. Dykeman	Charlotte and Atlanta	Oct. 20, 1887	236	236	509.20
H. P. Adams	Dallas and Cleburne	Jan. 21, 1888	60	35	121.55
J. W. Dibrell	Houston and Galveston	Jan. 4, 1888	90	85	187.85
W. A. Ramplin	Burlington and Council Bluffs	Sept. 7, 1887	53	53	115.01
F. J. Allen	Atlanta and Montgomery	July 27, 1887	240	233	507.94
R. O'Connor	Chicago and Minneapolis	Dec. 30, 1887	183	183	404.43
G. B. Barham	Deming and Los Angeles	Sept. 10, 1887	30	30	65.22
J. J. McLean	Albany and Rochester	Apr. 12, 1887	100	100	220.00
J. C. Bierce	Kansas City and Pueblo	Oct. 15, 1887	150	132	290.40
H. W. Hetzel	Pittsburgh and Cincinnati	Feb. 20, 1888	30	30	66.67
G. W. Smith	Syracuse, Auburn, and Rochester	Mar. 6, 1887	245	245	536.55
D. J. Whaley	Butte City and Ogden	Sept. —, 1887	60	60	131.86
B. G. Caldwell	New York and Pittsburgh	Mar. 16, 1888	18	18	39.56
B. M. Rigney	Saint Louis and Texarkana	May 24, 1888	4	4	8.79
O. P. Mellor	Saint Louis and Atchison	Nov. 27, 1886	161	161	354.20
P. E. Grimes	Cincinnati and Saint Louis	July 29, 1887	209	205	446.90
W. H. Spaulding	Omaha and Ogden	July 22, 1887	21	21	45.65
J. T. Holtzclaw	Goodwater and Columbus	Sept. 17, 1887	30	30	65.22
John Durkin	Chicago and Burlington	Feb. 27, 1888	41	41	91.02
F. M. Johnson	Macon and Opelika	Jan. 1, 1887	23	22	48.35
Total			6,182	5,816	12,763.12

CASUALTIES.

July 5, 1887.—Bangor and Boston R. P. O. collided with train No. 16 on the Maine Central Railroad at Farmingdale Siding, Me., demolishing 20 feet of postal car. Clerks H. S. French, V. H. Sprague, G. W. Soper, and R. E. Deasey were slightly injured. No mail lost or damaged.

July 7, 1887.—New York and Dunkirk R. P. O., train No. 3, collided with a freight train 3 miles east of Waverly, N. Y., delaying train three hours. No injury to clerks or damage to mails.

July 11, 1887.—Memphis and New Orleans R. P. O., train No. 4, ran over a horse at Cottonville, La., throwing engine-tender, baggage, mail, and express off the track. The mail was scattered upon the floor and slightly damaged by oil and coal, but none lost or destroyed. No one hurt.

July 13, 1887.—Cincinnati and Livingston R. P. O. was run into by a "wild" engine and completely wrecked near Robertson, Ky., and Postal Clerk M. J. Hall seriously injured. The postal car was totally destroyed, though no mails were lost or damaged.

July 14, 1887.—Baltimore and Grafton R. P. O., train No. 6, collided with Baltimore and Grafton R. P. O., train No. 1, at Gaithersburgh, Md., badly wrecking postal car on No. 6. No injury to clerks or loss or damage to mails.

July 18, 1887.—Albuquerque and Los Angeles R. P. O., train No. 52, collided with east-bound freight at Peach Springs (n. o.), Ark., completely wrecking postal car and badly bruising Acting Clerk F. H. Snowden. Mails transferred to express car without loss or damage.

July 22, 1887.—Cairo and New Orleans R. P. O., train No. 4, engine and postal car left the track near Winona, Miss., and went down an embankment. The postal car was considerably damaged, the front trucks having been torn away. Postal Clerk F. J. Snow slightly bruised.. No mail lost or damaged.

July 27, 1887.—Macon and Montgomery R. P. O., train No. 3, was wrecked 8 miles south of Eufaula, Ala. The front end of postal car was telescoped by tender of engine and completely demolished. No mail lost or damaged and clerks uninjured.

July 27, 1887.—Atlanta and Montgomery R. P. O., train No. 52, jumped the track near Opelika, Ala., slightly injuring postal clerk. All mail recovered without serious damage.

July 29, 1887.—Grand Rapids and La Crosse R. P. O., train No. 4, ran through an open switch at Hoppertown, Mich. Mail apartment car slightly damaged. No injury to clerks, or loss or damage to mails.

July 29, 1887.—Cincinnati and St. Louis R. P. O., train No. 2, while descending a grade 3 miles west of Aurora, Ind., at a speed of 40 miles an hour, the axle on the tender broke, derailing entire train. The postal car, being the first to leave the track, was thrown into the ditch, and, being struck by the baggage-car, was completely demolished. Postal Clerks R. E. Baker and P. E. Grimes were precipitated beneath the front trucks of the parlor car. Baker was instantly killed. When his body was recovered (four hours after the accident) his head and breast were fearfully mangled. Grimes was seriously injured in the shoulder and otherwise bruised, being incapacitated for duty two hundred and ten days. Clerks John C. Clark and N. C. Yelton were also considerably bruised and incapacitated for duty. The mail, which was considerably damaged by dirt and torn, was picked up and turned into the Cincin-

nati post-office, and all forwarded to destination except a few pieces
upon which the address could not be found. All registered matter
saved except package No. 3698, from St. Louis, Mo., July 29, 1887, for
Aurora, Ind.

July 30, 1887.—Lancaster and Boston R. P. O. ran into an open switch
near Hooksett, N. H., derailing train and badly wrecking postal car
No. 56. Clerks unhurt. No mails lost or damaged.

July 30, 1887.—Cairo and New Orleans R. P. O., car No. 123, was
thrown from the track at Water Valley, Miss., and, turning on its side,
was badly damaged. The mail was thrown from letter-case and some
damaged by oil from lamps. None lost, and no one hurt.

July 30, 1887.—Jefferson and McKinney R. P. O., train No. 141, was
wrecked 5 miles west of Farmersville, Tex., by mail-apartment car
jumping the track and falling 10 feet down an embankment. Postal
Clerk A. Rowell sustained several severe cuts and bruises, incapacitating him for duty twenty days. All mails recovered, but portion considerably damaged by oil.

August 4, 1887.—Ogdensburgh and Utica R. P. O. ran over an open
switch at Morristown, N. Y., and was derailed. No injury to clerk or
loss or damage to mails. Delayed six hours.

August 10, 1887.—Deming and Los Angeles R. P. O., train No. 20, was
held up by robbers 8 miles west of Pantano, Ariz. The engine and mail
car were derailed. The robbers forced Postal Clerk John Grattan to
leave his car. They then blew a hole in the side of the express car
with giant powder, compelled Grattan to enter it, while they closely followed; forcing the express messenger to open the safe, they robbed it
of its contents and left without molesting the mail car. Train arrived
at Los Angeles thirteen hours late.

August 16, 1887.—Kansas City and Pueblo R. P. O., train No. 6, was
wrecked by a wash-out at Medway Station, 7 miles east of Coolidge,
Kans. Engine and postal car left the rails, the trucks of the former
being forced through the floor of the latter, where Postal Clerk C. L.
Burge was distributing mail. He was violently thrown against the
paper-rack, seriously bruising his hips and shoulders. The stanchions
holding the mail broke and fell across the hips and back of Clerk W.
T. Treleaven. This, with the mail, held him to the floor, seriously bruising his back. Both men were incapacitated for duty. No mails were
lost, but a portion damaged by oil and dirt.

August 17, 1887.—Baltimore and Grafton R. P. O., train No. 4, running at a high rate of speed, left the track inside the Washington City
limits, at a point known as the "Y," caused by air-brakes failing to
work. The entire train was completely wrecked, the engineer killed,
and the fireman and several passengers seriously injured. Although
postal car No. 31 was smashed to pieces, Clerks C. J. Hooton, J. H.
Brown, and S. C. Marlow were only slightly injured. Entire mail saved,
but a portion saturated with oil.

August 20, 1887.—Gainesville and Galveston R. P. O., train No. 1,
was wrecked by cattle near Clifton, Tex., derailing mail-apartment car
and tearing it to pieces. Postal Clerk R. J. Wilson considerably bruised
and disabled for eight days. Mails badly damaged by water and steam
and from oil, but none lost.

August 21, 1887.—Los Angeles and Santa Barbara R. P. O., train No.
38, mail, baggage, and express, and three passenger coaches were derailed near Saugus Junction, Cal., by spreading of the track. Mails
considerably damaged by oil and water, but none lost. Clerk unhurt.

August 23, 1887.—Pittsburgh and Cincinnati R. P. O., second section of train No. 6, left the track at Creswell, Ohio, caused by spreading of the rails. Paper car No. 9 and storage car No. 53 were badly damaged. No injury to clerks or loss or damage to mails.

August 23, 1887.—Washington and Charlotte R. P. O., train No. 53, collided with a freight train one-half mile north of Orange Court-House, Va. The mail-car was telescoped by tender of engine and flooded with water, badly damaging the letter mail. The car was badly wrecked and Substitute Clerk John H. Lane was injured in the back and breast. Clerk J. Y. Weddington was also injured, having his ankle sprained. No mail lost.

August 24, 1887.—Missouri Valley and Rapid City R. P. O., train No. 4, was wrecked and postal car demolished between Wood Lake and Johnstown, Nebr. Mails transferred to way car without loss or damage. Fireman killed, but postal clerk received no injury.

August 24, 1887.—Rome and Gadsden R. P. O. (steamboat service) mail steamer *J. J. Leay* was destroyed by fire at Cedar Bluff, Ala. All mail (except the registered), together with pouches, canvas, and locks, were destroyed. No one injured.

August 30, 1887.—Cairo and New Orleans R. P. O., train No. 5, wrecked 2 miles east of Jackson, Miss., and postal car completely demolished. No injury to clerk or loss or damage to the mails.

August 30, 1887.—Chicago and West Liberty R. P. O. While train was running at a high rate of speed Postal Clerk H. S. Morgridge fell out of the car door near Bird's Bridge, a few miles from Joliet, Ill., and was instantly killed. When found, the back of his head was crushed and his neck dislocated. Near him was a car chair, which was also crushed to pieces. It is supposed Morgridge was sitting in the chair near the door, or in the act of sitting down, when a sudden lurch of the car threw him into the door-way, so far out that he was unable to recover his balance, and that he clung to side of the door for a moment and fell so near the car that he was struck in the head by the rear steps, since, upon the latter, blood and brains were found.

September 1, 1887.—New Orleans and Marshall R. P. O., train No. 51, was wrecked near Rosedale, La. Mail badly damaged, but none lost, and clerk unhurt.

September 2, 1887.—Denver and Pueblo R. P. O., train No. 4, was wrecked by rocks falling on a bridge and breaking it down, 25 miles west of Pueblo, Colo. The engineer and one other person were killed. Postal Clerk G. W. Meldrum badly bruised. No mail lost or damaged.

September 4, 1887.—Baltimore and Freeport R. P. O. (steamboat service). The steamer *Avalon*, together with all the property of the Department, also 25 letters and 4 bundles of papers, were destroyed by fire. The accident occurred at night and Postal Clerk J. R. Maccubbin, who was asleep in his berth, barely had time to escape through the window of his state-room.

September 7, 1887.—Burlington and Council Bluffs R. P. O., train No. 7 (fast mail), collided with train No. 3, near Afton, Iowa, and Postal Clerk W. A. Ramplin was seriously injured and incapacitated for duty sixty days. No mails lost or damaged.

September 10, 1887.—Baltimore and Lexington R. P. O., train No. 10, was wrecked at Timberville, Va. Three cars left the track, and mail car No. 76 turned on its side and was slightly damaged. Postal Clerks J. A. Bartlett and J. H. White slightly injured. All mails saved and transferred to car No. 77.

September 12, 1887.—Baltimore and Grafton R. P. O., train No. 2, was wrecked at Sleepy Creek Bridge, W. Va. Entire train derailed and cars badly damaged. Mails saved and transferred to postal car of train No. 5. No one injured.

September 15, 1887.—Nashville and Hope R. P. O., train No. 3, was wrecked between Ozan and Washington, Ark., by spreading of the rails. Passenger coach and mail apartment car derailed; the latter badly damaged and mails scattered, but none lost or materially damaged. Clerk A. H. Johnson sustained severe injuries, and was incapacitated for duty thirty days.

September 15, 1887.—Cairo and Texarkana R. P. O., train No. 2, was wrecked 2 miles north of Nolton, Ark., caused by a broken fish-plate. Engine was a complete wreck, and postal car thrown down an embankment on its side. Fireman jumped from the engine, and being caught under postal car, was killed. Clerk L. H. Lohr escaped with a few slight bruises on head and back. No mail lost or damaged. Delayed ten hours.

September 17, 1887.—Tacoma and Portland R. P. O., train No. 2, while halting to investigate the cause of a torpedo signal, was run into by a special freight. Letter mail was thrown from cases and water-tank upset upon the paper mail. Railroad Post-Office Clerk McKinney (of Saint Paul and Mandan R. P. O.), who was riding with Acting Clerk D. N. Burwell, was thrown violently to the floor, and his arm severely bruised. Some mail damaged by water, but none lost.

September 19, 1887.—Chicago, McGregor and Saint Paul R. P. O., train No. 3 (west bound), collided with train No. 4, 2 miles north of Dubuque, Iowa. Mail car left the track and rolled over twice, taking fire from the lamps. Before it could be extinguished 200 letters were destroyed and a number damaged. One of the clerks, James Hurley, sustained injuries to his lower limbs and back. Damaged mail taken to Dubuque, Iowa, post-office, separated, and all that could be was forwarded to destination and the remainder to Dead Letter Office.

September 19, 1887.—Dallas and El Paso R. P. O., train No. 4, was stopped by masked men a short distance east of Denver, Tex., who boarded the train and robbed the mail car of 10 registered packages.

September 22, 1887.—Pittsburgh and Chicago R. P. O. was wrecked at Elida, Ohio, being run into by train No. 5. The tender of engine telescoped postal car No. 82, completely wrecking it, the postal clerks miraculously escaping death by jumping from the car. Much mail badly damaged by water and dirt, the address on many pieces being entirely illegible.

September 23, 1887.—Streator and Fairbury R. P. O., train No. 253, was thrown from the track 1½ miles north of Fairbury, Ill., ditching mail car, passenger coach, and freight car. No injury to clerk, or loss or damage to mail.

September 23, 1887.—Denver and Pueblo R. P. O., train No. 1, was wrecked 2 miles east of Elizabeth Station, Colo., by the breaking of flange on car wheel. The engine fell a distance of 100 feet down an embankment, the mail and baggage car following. Mail was scattered about the car, and the oil-stove, which had just been lighted, overturning, a large portion was scorched and saturated with oil, but not sufficient to prevent forwarding to destination. Postal Clerk James M. Rand miraculously escaped death.

September 27, 1887.—Cairo and West Point R. P. O., train No. 2, was wrecked by bad track 3 miles south of Jackson, Tenn., seriously injuring thirty people, among whom was Postal Clerk J. B. Jones, whose shoulder was so badly hurt he was sixty days incapacitated for duty. Postal car completely demolished and mails badly damaged.

September 27, 1887.—Texarkana and El Paso R. P. O., train No. 4, collided with west-bound freight train near Odessa, Tex., demolishing engine, tender, express car, and slightly damaging mail apartment. No mail lost or damaged, and clerk unhurt. Delayed twelve hours.

September 29, 1887.—Closed pouch, from West Bay City, Mich., to Detroit, Mich., was destroyed by fire with a baggage car on the Bay City Division of the Michigan Central Railroad at Carrolton, Mich. Pouch supposed to have contained sixty or seventy letters for Detroit, Mich., Ohio, Eastern States, and Canada, money-orders and advices No. 19097 on Detroit, No. 19098 on Buffalo, and international money-order No. 1262 on Park Hill, Ontario; also a letter containing $2.

September 30, 1887.—Texarkana and El Paso R. P. O., train No. 302, ran through an open switch 3 miles east of Woodlawn, Tex., wrecking engine, mail and express cars, and seriously injuring fireman. No mails lost or destroyed, and clerk unhurt.

October 6, 1887.—Deming and Los Angeles R. P. O., train No. 20, was wrecked at Mammoth Tank, about 20 miles east of Glamis, Cal. The postal car was badly wrecked and considerable mail damaged, but none lost. Postal Clerk J. W. Winston slightly bruised. Arrived at Deming, N. Mex., twenty-six hours late.

October 8, 1887.—Marshalltown and Storey City R. P. O., train No. 35, was wrecked by misplaced switch at Saint Anthony, Iowa. No injury to clerk or loss or damage to mails.

October 9, 1887.—Cairo and Texarkana R. P. O., train No. 1, was wrecked 6 miles south of Fisher, Ark., and mail and express cars turned on their sides. Portion of mail badly damaged by oil from broken lamps. No one hurt.

October 10, 1887.—Marion and Chicago R. P. O. (night express), while stopping near Kout, Ind., to repair engine, was run into by a freight train. The passenger train took fire, destroying pouches from Chicago, Ill., for Akron, Ohio, and Marion, Ohio. These were closed pouches in baggage car, no postal clerk being on train.

October 12, 1887.—Houston and Galveston R. P. O., train No. 451, was wrecked 4 miles south of Harrisburgh, Tex. No mails lost or damaged. Postal Clerk E. H. Sieling had his hand cut, but was not disabled.

October 13, 1887.—Memphis and Little Rock R. P. O., train No. 2, was wrecked one-half mile west of Madison, Ark. Engine, mail, and 4 passenger coaches left the track. Mail car badly damaged. No mails lost and no one injured except baggageman. Delayed twelve hours.

October 13, 1887.—Albuquerque and Los Angeles R. P. O., train No. 52, was derailed between Seligman and Ash Fork, Ariz., by spreading of the rails. Mail car slightly damaged. No injury to clerk or loss or damage to mails. Twenty-eight hours late.

October 18, 1887.—New York and Hackettstown R. P. O., train No. 22, left the track at Hopatcong, N. J. No injury to clerk or mails. Delayed one and one-half hours.

October 19, 1887.—Charlotte and Atlanta R. P. O., train No. 51, collided with freight train 3 miles south of Greer's, S. C., completely demolishing mail car No. 122, and seriously injuring postal clerks, S. N. Dykeman, J. L. Killian, and W. R. Wilson. Dykeman was injured in the back and hips, and badly bruised about the body. He has never resumed duty. Killian was injured internally, and has never resumed duty. Wilson had his head cut and foot mashed, and was incapacitated for duty one hundred and one days. No mails lost or destroyed, but were considerably damaged.

October 23, 1887.—Saint Louis, Moberly and Kansas City R. P. O., train No. 5, ran into a washout near Missouri City, Mo., and badly damaged postal car. No mails lost or damaged. Postal Clerk C. M. Black received a severe cut on the head and was disabled.

October 24, 1887.—Pueblo and Silverton R. P. O., train No. 11, was wrecked near La Veta, Colo., and forward end of car crushed in. Mail transferred, without loss or damage, to box car. No one hurt.

October 26, 1887.—Huntington and Portland R. P. O., train No. 1, was wrecked near Rufus, Oregon, by the ditching of two baggage cars. The rear one contained the through paper mail for Portland, Oregon, which was transferred to passenger coach, arriving eleven hours late. No injury to clerk or loss or damage to mails.

October 27, 1887.—Ottumwa and Moberly R. P. O., train No. 3, collided with a freight train at Macon City, Mo., smashing both engines and breaking off front platform of mail car. No mails lost or damaged. Clerk W. O. Hathaway slightly bruised.

November 1, 1887.—Cincinnati and Chattanooga R. P. O. (night line) ran into a freight train at Kismet, Tenn. The postal car was telescoped by tender of engine, shattering letter case. Four hundred or more letters damaged by water and fire grenades; 25 letters partially or entirely destroyed by fire. Clerk H. M. Brown slightly hurt in his side and breast.

November 3, 1887.—Denver and Ogden R. P. O., train No. 8, was stopped 5 miles east of Grand Junction, Colo., and the mail apartment entered by disguised robbers, who secured 17 registered packages.

November 6, 1887.—Charlotte and Augusta R. P. O., train No. 52, was derailed near Ridge Springs, S. C. The mail car took fire, consuming 1 pouch of letters and 1 registered package; 15 empty canvas sacks and 3 leather pouches were rendered useless; 12 sacks of paper mail and 30 packages of letters were more or less damaged, but were forwarded to destination. Through registered pouch (New York to Augusta) was badly burnt and contents injured. Clerk W. H. Witherspoon slightly bruised.

November 7, 1887.—Kansas City and Joplin R. P. O., train No. 302, was wrecked near Independence, Mo., by the breaking of an axle on front truck of car. Considerable mail damaged by oil from lamps, but not sufficient to prevent forwarding to destination. Clerks unhurt.

November 14, 1887.—Texarkana and Waco R. P. O., train No. 1, stopped at Maginnis, Tex., to take water when a freight train backed into rear end, throwing train off the track and disabling mail car. Mails transferred to another car without loss or damage. Clerks unhurt.

November 22, 1887.—Green River and Huntington R. P. O. was run into the Omaha and Ogden passenger train at Green River, Oregon, by the switch engine. Mail car was turned over and a large portion of letter mail damaged by oil from lamps. No one injured.

November 23, 1887.—Washington and Charlotte R. P. O., train No. 51, and the Danville and Stewart R. P. O., train No. 2, collided 1 mile south of Danville, Va., considerably damaging the latter line. No injury to clerks or loss or damage to mails.

November 24, 1887.—Albuquerque and Los Angeles R. P. O., train No. 1, was stopped by a freight wreck 7 miles north of San Bernardino, Cal. Engine, mail car, and two coaches were taken to a side track 2 miles distant. Upon reaching the switch the engine turned over breaking coupling between it and mail car. The latter ran over the cylinder and telescoped forward coach, wrecking both. Postal Clerk A. D. Gogin had his left shoulder severely wrenched but was able to take his run the next trip. No mail lost or damaged—delayed twenty and one-half hours.

November 25, 1887.—Denison and San Antonio R. P. O., train No. 504, was wrecked by a misplaced switch at Denton, Tex. The front platform and one corner of mail car were badly damaged, necessitating transfer of mails to baggage car. No mails lost or damaged and clerks uninjured.

November 27, 1887.—Williamsport and Baltimore R. P. O., train No. 4, owing to fog, ran into the rear of a freight train near Etters, Pa., wrecking mail car No. 185, but clerks escaped injury. No mail lost or damaged.

November 28, 1887.—Green River and Huntington R. P. O., train No. 501, ran into a drove of cattle near Glenn's Ferry, Idaho, and was wrecked. Mails transferred to express car without loss or damage. No one hurt.

November 28, 1887.—Sedalia and Denison R. P. O., trains No. 501 and No. 506, collided at Osage Mission, Kans. Postal Clerk R. J. Elliott received several wounds and bruises, incapacitating him for duty.

November 29, 1887.—Tyler and Lufkin R. P. O., train No. 101, was derailed 1 mile north of Jacksonville, Tex. The track was badly torn up and train had to be abandoned. No mails lost or damaged, and no one hurt.

December 3, 1887.—Kansas City and Joplin R. P. O., train No. 301, collided with a freight train at Nevada, Mo., and the engine, tender, and front truck of mail apartment were derailed. Clerks L. F. Larkin and J. F. O'Brien slightly bruised. No mail lost or damaged.

December 3, 1887.—Denison and San Antonio R. P. O., train No. 652, ran into a drove of cattle 2 miles south of Kyle, Tex., overturning engine, killing the engineer, seriously wounding fireman, and considerably bruising Postal Clerk S. T. Carroll, incapacitating him for duty. Mail apartment was overturned and disabled and mails damaged by oil, but none lost.

December 4, 1887.—Tracy and Pierre R. P. O., train No. 1, ran into Oakes and Hawarden R. P. O., train No. 41, 2 miles east of Iroquois, Dak. Mail car No. 1096, on train No. 1, was badly wrecked and had to be ditched and mail was transferred to caboose. No mails lost or damaged and clerks unhurt.

December 4, 1887.—Helena and Portland R. P. O., train No. 2, was ditched at Lake, a station 8 miles west of Connell, Wash. The mail car and six coaches left the track, the former turning over, and Postal Clerk Thron Thronson was considerably bruised. All letter mail and registers were thrown out upon the floor, a number falling in the mud through the open door, and, being mixed with water and oil, the greater portion was damaged.

December 7, 1887.—Council Bluffs and Kansas City R. P. O., train No. 4, while standing on main track at Percival, Iowa, doctoring a hot box, was run into from the rear by freight train and wrecked. The front platform of mail car was broken off. Mail transferred without loss or damage to another car. Clerks unhurt.

December 7, 1887.—Delaware and Hudson Canal Company's Railroad. A wreck occurred on the above road near Whallonsburgh, Pa., involving train which left New York 6.30 p. m. previous day for Montreal. Paper mail for Plattsburgh, N. Y., and pouch from Troy for Keeseville, N. Y., were destroyed. Pouch from Albany for Rouse's Point, N. Y., lost. There was no postal car on this train, the mail being carried in baggage car.

December 8, 1887.—Portland and Coburgh R. P. O., train No. 2, was wrecked by spreading of the rails near Brownsville, Oregon. Postal Clerk B. F. Watkins took the mail upon a hand car and traveled 20 miles to the bridge at Thomas Creek, 3 miles south of Scio. One section of the bridge had washed away. After crossing creek mail was placed in postal car in waiting. None lost or damaged. Clerk unhurt.

December 8, 1887.—Charlotte and Atlanta R. P. O., train No. 53, was wrecked 200 yards south of Charlotte, N. C., depot, derailing engine and mail car, the latter being considerably damaged. Postal Clerk F. R. Barford had his right leg severely hurt. No mail lost or damaged.

December 9, 1887.—Cairo and Texarkana R. P. O., train No. 2, was attacked by masked men at Genoa, Ark., and the express car robbed of $10,000. The robbers then proceeded to the mail car, but after a suggestion from Postal Clerk R. P. Johnson that they had secured enough booty, they concluded not to molest the mails.

December 10, 1887.—Dallas and Kemp R. P. O., train No. 2, was derailed 1 mile south of Kaufman, Tex., by the spreading of the rails. No injury to clerk or loss or damage to mails.

December 16, 1887.—Rockland and Beaumont R. P. O., train No. 102, was derailed 3 miles south of Rockland, Tex., and was delayed until the next morning. No mails lost or damaged, and clerk unhurt.

December 16, 1887.—Wallis and San Antonio R. P. O., train No. 2, was derailed 3 miles west of Cuero, Tex. No mails lost or damaged, and clerk unhurt. Delayed eight and one-half hours.

December 19, 1887.—Cairo and Texarkana R. P. O., train No. 1, collided with a freight train near the depot platform at Kingsland, Ark. Postal Clerk S. N. Givens jumped from the car and escaped with slight bruises on his body. No mails lost or damaged.

December 20, 1887.—Cairo and Texarkana R. P. O., train No. 1, was wrecked at Francis, Ark., by an open switch. Engine and two express cars left the track. No injury to mail apartment or mails. Clerk unhurt. Delayed fourteen hours.

December 21, 1887.—Calmar and Davenport R. P. O., train No. 1, was wrecked 2 miles west of Calmar, Iowa. The tender of engine was forced through mail apartment, seriously injuring Clerk J. H. Black, incapacitating him for duty. No mails lost or damaged.

December 21, 1887.—Baltimore and Grafton R. P. O., train No. 1, was derailed at Altamont, Md., and postal car damaged to such an extent as to be unfit for further service. Mails transferred without loss or damage to baggage car. No injury to clerks.

December 21, 1887.—Gurdon and Camden R. P. O., train No. 898, was wrecked 2½ miles north of Camden, Ark. No injury to clerk or loss or damage to mails.

December 22, 1887.—Gurdon and Camden R. P. O., train No. 897, was wrecked near depot at Camden, Ark. No injury to clerk or loss or damage to mails.

December 22, 1887.—Saint Louis and Atchison R. P. O., train No. 2, collided with a branch train of the Jefferson City and Bagnell line at Jefferson City, Mo., badly damaging both engines and resulting in a delay of six hours. No injury to clerks or damage to postal car or mails.

December 22, 1887.—Langdon and Larimore R. P. O., train No. 82, left the track near Park River, Dak. Postal car unfit for service and mails were transferred, without loss or damage, to box car. No one hurt.

December 23, 1887.—Green River and Huntington R. P. O., on leaving Huntington, Oregon, engine ran into mail car No. 1171, smashing end of same and necessitating transfer to baggage car. No mail lost or damaged, and no one hurt.

December 24, 1887.—Sedalia and Denison, train No. 507, was attacked by robbers between Stringtown and Atoka, Ind. T., who fired several shots through the doors of the mail apartment. The clerks were ordered to open the door, which they refused to do, and the robbers finally left without doing any damage. Clerks W. W. Glover, J. H. Armstrong, and C. F. Poffenbach were on duty.

December 24, 1887.—Charlotte and Atlanta R. P. O., train No. 52, ran into an open switch 7 miles north of Atlanta, Ga., and collided with freight cars. Postal car was badly damaged and Clerk G. D. Hall was slightly injured. No mail lost or damaged. Delayed twelve hours.

December 24, 1887.—Tyler and Lufkin R. P. O., train No. 101, was wrecked 4 miles south of Rusk, Tex. Engine and tender left the track and train was delayed twenty-four hours. No injury to clerk or loss or damage to mails.

December 25, 1887.—Deming and Los Angeles R. P. O., train No. 19, left the track 10 miles west of Deming, N. Mex., completely wrecking mail car and slightly injuring Postal Clerk C. B. McKenzie. No mails lost or damaged.

December 25, 1887.—Denison and Troup R. P. O., train No. 658, was wrecked 3 miles north of Troup, Tex., and Postal Clerk W. O. Kretsinger slightly bruised. No mails lost, but a portion damaged by oil.

December 27, 1887.—Kansas City and Oxford R. P. O., train No. 39, while running at the rate of 40 miles per hour, ran into a freight train at Dawson Nebr., owing to an open switch. The mail car was wrecked, but the mails were transferred, without loss or damage, to flat car and transported to Wymore, Nebr., where baggage car was secured and trip finished. No one injured.

December 27, 1887.—Omaha and Atchison R. P. O., train No. 4, was derailed near Hiawatha, Kans. Mails safe and clerk unhurt. Delayed four hours.

December 27, 1887.—Pacific Junction and McCook R. P. O., train No. 4, was wrecked near Plattsmouth, Nebr., and postal car No. 48 thrown from the track. Mails transferred, without loss or damage, to baggage car. No one hurt.

December 28, 1887.—Washington and Round Hill R. P. O., train No. 141, was derailed at Washington and Ohio Junction, 2 miles north of Alexandria, Va. Postal car badly damaged and unfit for service. Mails transferred, without loss or damage, to passenger-coach. Clerk uninjured.

December 30, 1887.—Rockland and Beaumont R. P. O., train No. 103, was wrecked at Rockland, Tex., and mail apartment demolished. No loss or damage to mails. Clerk unhurt. Return trip made in passenger coach.

December 30, 1887.—Chicago and Minneapolis R. P. O., train No. 3, collided with a freight train at Shermerville, Ills., wrecking mail car and injuring Postal Clerk R. O'Connor seriously and George M. Benedict slightly. No loss or damage to mails.

December 31, 1887.—Saint Louis, Moberly, and Kansas City R. P. O., train No. 5, was wrecked at Hull's Point, Mo., by colliding with a

freight car which had been blown off side-track. Engine and postal
car turned over and Clerk S. Z. Ettinger was seriously injured and incapacitated for duty fifty-eight days. The car took fire from the coals
which fell from the heater, but was promptly extinguished. No mails
lost, but a portion damaged by oil.

December 31, 1887.—Cincinnati and Chattanooga R, P. O., train No. 1,
(bound south), collided with train No. 2 (bound north) near Green-
wood, Ky. Postal Clerk James Severance was fatally injured and died
the following day. Clerk W. T. Roberts was badly injured, having his
left arm broken near the elbow, his left leg broken. at the ankle, one
bone of right leg fractured below the knee, and several bruises on other
parts of the body. He has never been able to resume duty. The mail
and car of train No. 1 were consumed by fire. No loss or damage to
mail on train No. 2.

January 1, 1888.—Portland and Ashland R. P. O., train No. 1, ran
into a landslide 6 miles south of Riddles, Oregon. The engine was
overturned and fireman instantly killed. Forward end of postal car
smashed. No injury to clerk or loss or damage to mails. Delayed
eighteen hours.

January 2, 1888.—San Francisco and Los Angeles R. P. O., train No.
18, collided with a freight train at Athlone, Cal., wrecking engines of
both trains, several freight cars, and postal car. The latter was telescoped by passenger engine, and Postal Clerk W. A. Tilley considerably injured. His helper, Luke Fay, was pinned down by the tender
of engine, the débris keeping it from crushing him to death. Tilley
succeeded in freeing himself, and with the aid of a passenger cut Fay
out. All mails saved, but a large portion damaged by water and oil.
Arrived at San Francisco eighteen hours late.

January 2, 1888.—Dallas and Kemp R. P. O., train No. 2, was wrecked
at Kaufman, Tex., and train abandoned. No one hurt nor mails lost
or damaged.

January 2, 1888.—Gurdon and Camden R. P. O., train No. 897, was
wrecked 1 mile north of Wheelen Springs, Ark. No one injured nor
loss or damage to mails.

January 2, 1888.—Louisville and Evansville R. P. O. (steam-boat
service). The steamer *William Porter* of the above line took fire 20
miles below Louisville, Ky., where she was ice-bound, and was burned.
A few empty pouches and canvas were consumed. The mails were
saved by Clerk F. J. Muhlhausen, who took them and walked 7 miles
to Muldrough and came in on the Louisville and Paducah R. P. O.

January 4, 1888.—Houston and Galveston R. P. O., train No. 662,
collided with express train 665 of same line three-quarters mile north
of Harrisburgh, Tex. The mail apartment was totally wrecked and
Postal Clerk J. W. Dibrell was severely injured about the head, face,
and left shoulder, and was incapacitated for duty ninety days. All
mails saved.

January 4, 1888.—Toledo and Marietta R. P. O. was derailed between
Marietta and Caywood, Ohio, and postal car badly demolished. Mails
transferred without loss or damage to passenger car. Clerk unhurt.

January 4, 1888.—Huntington and Portland R. P. O., train No. 5,
ran into train No. 15 near Kamela, Oregon. Engine of mail train ran
through caboose and eight freight cars of No. 15, all being completely
wrecked. Mails thrown out of cases but none lost or damaged. Postal
Clerk Frank Button slightly bruised. Mail transferred around wreck
the following day, reaching Portland seventeen hours late.

January 4, 1888.—Albuquerque and El Paso R. P. O., train No. 3, was wrecked 5 miles south of La Joya and near Rio Salida, N. Mex. Engine thrown from track and rolled 15 feet down an embankment. Postal car badly damaged. Mails transferred to freight cars without loss or damage, arriving at El Paso, Tex., fifteen hours late. Clerk unhurt.

January 6, 1888.—Peoria and Evansville R. P. O., train No. 2. Engine and postal car wrecked 2½ miles north of Olney, Ill., by displaced rail. No injury to clerk or loss or damage to mails.

January 8, 1888.—Springfield and Chadwick R. P. O., train No. 43, was wrecked 3 miles from Chadwick, Mo., on account of the breaking of switch lever. Engine and three cars derailed and turned over in the ditch. Mails transferred without loss or damage to hand-car and arrived at Chadwick ten hours late. No one hurt.

January 9, 1888.—Omaha and Ogden R.P.O., train No. 1, was wrecked 1 mile east of Edson, Wyo. No injury to clerk, postal car, or mails.

January 9, 1888.—Albuquerque and Los Angeles R. P. O., train No. 2, was derailed by snow-drifts at Bellemont, Ariz., without damage. Train was again derailed 23 miles south of same point, badly wrecking coach and seriously injuring several passengers. Mail car kept track and escaped injury, and was taken to Winslow, Ariz., and held until wreck was cleared, arriving at Albuquerque, N. Mex., fifty-four and a half hours late.

January 9, 1888.—La Fayette and Quincy R. P. O., train No. 45, collided with a freight train 1 mile west of West Lebanon, Ind., the tender of engine going into mail car No. 245 its full length. Postal Clerk E. M. Helm had his left ankle and right knee badly sprained and received a slight scalp wound. No mail lost or damaged.

January 9, 1888.—East Lynne and Brownington R. P. O., train No. 1, was wrecked 6 miles north of Clinton, Mo., and train had to be abandoned. No mails lost or damaged, and clerk unhurt.

January 9, 1888.—Kansas City and Pueblo R. P. O., train No. 6, collided with train No. 5 at Wakarusa, Kans., badly wrecking both engines. Front end of postal car was raised off of trucks, the draw-head broken, and otherwise damaged. Postal Clerk W. H. Randall slightly injured. No mails lost or damaged.

January 10, 1888.—Albuquerque and Los Angeles R. P. O., train No. 1, was delayed four days at Williams, Ariz., by snow and wrecks. Left Williams on 14th, and collided with a freight train at Halleck, Cal., badly wrecking engine and seriously damaging mail car. Postal Clerk A. D. Gogin slightly injured. No mail lost or damaged. Arrived at Los Angeles four days and twenty hours late.

January 11, 1888.—Ashland and Abbotsford R. P. O., train No. 6, left the track, throwing mail car over on its side. Three or four letters partially burned and one torn to pieces. Clerk O. A. Everts had his right foot considerably bruised.

January 11, 1888.—Lenoir and Lancaster R. P. O. was wrecked 2 miles north of Hickory, N. C., and postal car burned. Postal Clerk John T. Grist slightly injured. No mails lost or damaged.

January 12, 1888.—Denver and Pueblo R. P. O., train No. 1, was derailed at Piñon, 15 miles east of Pueblo, Colo. Postal Clerk J. M. Rand saved himself by jumping from his car. Mails transferred to caboose without loss or damage.

January 13, 1888.—Shabbona and Sterling R. P. O. Train left the track 4 miles west of Harmon, Ill., caused by a broken rail. Mails transferred to engine without loss or damage. No one injured.

January 13, 1888.—Clifton Forge and Ashland R. P. O. was struck by a shifting-engine in the yard at Ashland, Ky., caused by misplaced switch. Apartment car No. 18 slightly damaged and Clerk S. E. McCoy was badly cut about the head and had one of his fingers broken. No mails lost or damaged.

January 13, 1888.—Cincinnati and Chattanooga R. P. O. Train collided with a freight train at Oneida, Tenn., damaging the mail car and scattering the mails. One hundred letters damaged by oil. Clerks unhurt.

January 14, 1888.—Wichita and Greensburgh R. P. O., train No. 1, collided with rear end of freight train just after leaving Wichita, Kans. The draw-head on postal car was broken and car changed to rear of 'train. No injury to clerk or loss or damage to mails.

January 15, 1888.—Larned and Jetmore R. P. O., train No. 584, was derailed one-half mile from Larned, Kans., while crossing bridge over Pawnee Creek. No injury to clerk or loss or damage to mails.

January 16, 1888.—Jefferson and McKinney R. P. O., train No. 622, was derailed one-quarter of a mile east of Pickton, Tex., caused by spreading of rails. Entire train went down an embankment and Postal Clerk John Kemp was severely injured and incapacitated for duty. No mails lost, but a portion damaged by oil.

January 16, 1888.—New York and Chicago R. P. O., train No. 12, ran through an open switch and collided with a freight train at Springfield, Pa. The storage end of car was badly broken, being telescoped by United States express car. Mails slightly damaged. Clerks unhurt.

January 17, 1888.—Saint Louis and Halstead R. P. O., train No. 4, collided with a switch-engine at Newburgh, Mo., caused by a misplaced switch. Postal Clerk H. M. Bubb, sustained a dislocation of two knuckle joints of right hand and injury to his back, incapacitating him for duty. No mails lost or damaged.

January 17, 1888.—Rochester and Elmira R. P. O., train No. 107, collided with express train 1 mile south of Avoca, N. Y., killing engineer and seriously injuring Postal Clerk J. R. Dutcher, who saved his life by jumping from the car just as the collision occurred. He was struck by pieces of the broken engine and badly bruised about the back and limbs. The tender was driven through the mail apartment and struck the counter of paper-case. The stove was broken and fire strewn about the car, but was extinguished by water from the broken tender. No mail lost.

January 18, 1888.—Ottumwa and Moberly R. P. O., train No. 2, was wrecked by a broken rail 4 miles north of Coatsville, Mo., and coach and sleeper turned over and rolled down an embankment. A few papers and one registered package slightly damaged by oil. Clerk unhurt.

January 19, 1888.—Cairo and Poplar Bluff R. P. O., train No. 802, collided with switch-engine at Poplar Bluff, Mo. No injury to clerk or damage to mails.

January 20, 1888.—Neche and Saint Paul R. P. O., train No. 10, left the track near Donnelly, Minn., on account of broken rail. Letter mail thrown on the floor and portion damaged by oil, but none lost. Clerk unhurt.

January 21, 1888.—Bangor and Boston R. P. O. (day line), train No. 11, ran off track at Augusta, Me., causing three hours' delay. Mail car slightly damaged. No injury to clerk or mails.

January 21, 1888.—Beatrice and Manhattan R. P. O., train No. 252, was derailed 1¾ miles north of Oketo, Kans., and all cars, including one

.with mail apartment, turned over. Postal Clerk A. T. Nichols slightly bruised. No mails lost or damaged.

January 21, 1888.—Dallas and Cleburne R. P. O. Postal Clerk H. P. Adams was seriously injured and incapacitated for duty ninety-seven days by falling from mail wagon between post-office and depot at Dallas, Tex., having been dragged some considerable distance, the wagon finally passing over him.

January 23, 1888.—Rutland and Troy R. P. O. ran off track between Salem and Shushan, N. Y.; the mail-apartment car turning over into the ditch. No injury to clerk or loss or damage to mails.

January 24, 1888.—Quanah and Fort Worth R. P. O., train No. 1, was wrecked 6 miles north of Decatur, Tex. No injury to clerk or loss or damage to mails. Delayed eight hours and fifty minutes.

January 26, 1888.—Boston and Albany R. P. O., train No. 1, collided with a passenger train on the Troy and Albany Belt Line, at Greenbush, N. Y., throwing two cars of the Troy train from track and injuring brakeman. No damage to postal car, clerk, or mails.

January 27, 1888.—Minneapolis and Oakes R. P. O., train No. 66, collided with a snow-plow one-half mile east of Lowry, Minn., delaying train three days. No injury to clerk or loss or damage to mails.

January 28, 1888.—Pottsville, Tamaqua, and Herndon R. P. O., train No. 3, left the track 3 miles west of Tamaqua, Pa., owing to broken frog. Mail car badly damaged and Postal Clerk W. F. Rahn slightly injured in shoulder. Mails safe.

January 29, 1888.—Neche and Saint Paul R. P. O., train No. 9, left the track 8 miles north of Breckenridge, Minn., and delayed six hours, when postal car was replaced on track and run as far as Barnesville, Minn., where car became too much disabled to proceed. Remainder of trip made in baggage-car.

January 30, 1888.—Canastota and Elmira R. P. O., train No. 4, jumped the track at White Church, N. Y. Mails thrown from case and strewn upon the floor, a portion being soiled with oil and dirt. Clerk J. W. Hunt slightly injured.

January 31, 1888.—Texarkana and El Paso R. P. O., train No. 2, was wrecked 3 miles west of Hallsville, Tex., at Lansing Switch. No injury to clerk or loss or damage to mails.

January 31, 1888.—Richland and Niagara Falls R. P. O., train No. 113, left the track and was wrecked at Barkers, N. Y., and express messenger killed. Postal car turned over and mails thrown out of case. None lost or damaged and clerk unhurt. Delayed six hours.

January 31, 1888.—Pittsburgh and Saint Louis R. P. O., train No. 7, ran into an open switch at Urbana, Ohio., and collided with a switch-engine and freight cars. The roadmaster, engineer, and fireman were killed. Postal clerks A. J. Ball, T. W. Smith, M. H. Bradley, William Temman, W. W. Medill, and A. N. Davis, all slightly injured. All mails saved, but a portion slightly damaged.

February 2, 1888.—Gurdon and Camden R. P. O., train No. 898, was wrecked 4 miles south of Gurdon, Ark. No mails lost or damaged. Clerk unhurt.

February 3, 1888.—Dallas and Kemp R. P. O., train No. 2, was wrecked 3 miles south of Kaufman, Tex. No injury to clerk or loss or damage to mails.

February 3, 1888.—Albuquerque and Los Angeles R. P. O., train No. 2, was derailed 12 miles east of Seligman, Ariz., mail, express, and four baggage cars going into the ditch. The letter-case was torn loose from fastening and mail strewn about the floor; none, however, lost or damaged, nor was the clerk injured. Arrived at Los Angeles seventeen hours late.

February 3, 1888.—Portland and Worcester R. P. O. (S. R.) on approaching Lancaster, Mass., ran off track, on account of broken wheel on engine. Forward trucks were torn from under postal car, necessitating transfer of mails to another car. Clerk unhurt.

February 4, 1888.—Bowie and Pope's Creek R. P. O., train No. 195, while standing at Brandywine, Md., the mail-apartment car, which was attached to rear of train, was run into by a construction train and completely demolished. J. W. Ryon, clerk on duty, escaped by jumping from the car. All mails saved and forwarded to destination.

February 5, 1888.—Osawatomie and Pueblo R. P. O., train No. 202, was derailed at Hoisington, Kans., and letter mail thrown out of case and scattered. None lost, and clerk escaped injury.

February 6, 1888.—Ogden and San Francisco R. P. O., train No. 2, collided with freight train No. 23 at a point one-fourth of a mile west of Gold Run, Cal. The mail car was completely demolished and one fireman and an engineer killed. Clerk C. W. Gurney was thrown violently against the stove and had his side badly bruised. Clerk J. W. Stevenson, who was asleep, was thrown against the partition of the car and badly bruised. City distributor A. O. Doe was thrown upon the letter-rack and sustained several bruises. The tender of engine telescoped the "through" end of the mail car, burying the majority of mail, together with three through registered pouches. The working end of mail car was telescoped by express car and completely demolished. No mail lost; but a few letters and papers damaged by water.

February 6, 1888.—Boston and Troy R. P. O., train No. 54, collided with a freight train near Hoosac Falls, N. Y., demolishing the front platform of postal car No. 335, and throwing letters out of case to the floor. Postal Clerk W. W. Carpenter had his wrist and arm badly burned. Clerk B. H. Flaherty jumped from car and escaped injury. No mails lost or damaged. Arrived at Troy, N. Y., at 4.45. p. m., having missed southern and western connections.

February 9, 1888.—Hannibal and Gilmore R. P. O., train No. 1, was wrecked between Frankfort and Bowling Green, Mo. Postal car disabled, and trip completed in baggage car. Mails slightly damaged by oil. Clerk unhurt.

February 11, 1888.—Helena and Portland R. P. O., train No. 1, ran into a rock-slide near Rosa (n. o.), Wash., derailing engine, mail, and baggage car. Clerk-in-charge S. L. Short immediately left his car to go forward to ascertain the cause of the accident. He had barely reached the end of his car when another slide came down the mountain, completely demolishing and burying the mail car and smashing one end of baggage car. Had Clerk Short remained in his car a few seconds longer he would have been crushed to death. The slide consisted principally of large bowlders that had to be blasted with dynamite before they could be removed. Upon reaching the mails it was found that those in the pouches and sacks had escaped injury; but the letters from the cases were scattered throughout the debris and were more or less damaged. As fast as recovered it was dispatched on regular trains. Superintendent Prowell, who had charge of wrecking crew, estimated that there were 1,620 tons of rock on what remained of the mail car. Every precaution was used to protect and find the mail—each shovelfull of rock being examined. Clerk remained with wreck until debris was cleared away and arrived at Portland, Oregon, February 14, with balance of mail.

February 11, 1888.—Dallas and Kemp R. P. O., train No. 2, was wrecked 3 miles north of Kaufman, Tex. No mails lost or damaged. Clerk unhurt. Delayed seventeen hours.

February 13, 1888.—Texarkana and El Paso R. P. O., train No. 4, collided with a freight train between Pecos and Truehart, Tex. No injury to clerk, or loss or damage to the mails. Delayed twelve hours.

February 13, 1888.—Saint Albans and Boston R. P. O., postal car No. 48, jumped the track 3 miles south of Franklin, N. H., caused by a broken wheel. Delayed six hours. No injury to clerks or mails.

February 14, 1888.—Williamsburgh and New Haven R. P. O., train No. 651, was derailed between Northampton and Easthampton, Mass., delaying train two and one-half hours. No injury to clerk, or loss or damage to mails.

February 16, 1888.—Norwood and Rome R. P. O., while waiting near Canton, N. Y., for repairs, was struck by a freight train, killing one passenger and injuring several. Clerks G. H. Sampson and W. McCreary escaped by jumping from the car just before the collision. Postal car badly damaged, but mails uninjured. Delayed several hours.

February 17, 1888.—Denison and Taylor R. P. O., train No. 507, was derailed and wrecked by spreading of the track at Argyle, Tex. Engine and postal car thrown off the track. Mails scattered about car and a portion damaged by oil, but none lost. Clerk unhurt.

February 17, 1888.—Kane and Callery R. P. O., met with an accident, one of the axles of tender having broken, nearly throwing the train from a trestle 100 feet high. Also, when one-half mile south of Petersburgh, Pa., the front end of engine was thrown from the track by an iron nut which had, apparently, been placed on the track for a malicious purpose. No injury to clerk or mails.

February 18, 1888.—Council Bluffs and Moberly R. P. O., train No. 8, collided with a freight train 4 miles east of Salisbury, Mo., damaging mail car. Mails transferred without loss or damage to baggage-car. Clerk uninjured.

February 19, 1888.—Paris and Dallas R. P. O., train No. 18, was wrecked 1 mile south of Farmersville, Tex. Delayed eighteen hours, arriving at Dallas, Tex., next day. No injury to clerk, or loss or damage to mails.

February 20, 1888.—Tyler and Lufkin R. P. O., train No. 101, was wrecked between Tyler and Jacksonville, Tex., considerably damaging postal car. No injury to clerk or mails.

February 20, 1888.—Chicago and Cedar Rapids R. P. O., train No. 6, collided with freight train while in the act of side-tracking at Elburn, Ill. One end of mail car stove in. Mails transferred without loss or damage to No. 4. Clerk uninjured.

February 20, 1888.—Portland and Swanton R. P. O., train No. 2, collided with a log train one-half mile west of Fabyans, N. H., demolishing postal car No. 3, and necessitating its abandonment. Mails transferred to car No. 75 without loss or damage. Clerk uninjured.

February 23, 1888.—Dallas and Kemp R. P. O., train No. 1, was wrecked 6 miles south of Dallas, Tex. Mails transferred without loss or damage from mail apartment to box car. Clerk unhurt.

February 25, 1888.—Omaha and Ogden line express train No. 4, east bound, collided with a freight train at Colton, Nebr. The train took fire from an oil car and 1,120 pounds of mail from Ogden, and all the mails from the Green River and Huntington R. P. O., Rawlins, Laramie, Cheyenne, Wyo., and Sidney, Nebr., were burned.

February 27, 1888.—Chicago and Burlington R. P. O., train No. 2, left Galesburgh, Ill., six hours late on account of the strike of the loco.

motive engineers. At 2.45 train arrived at Naperville, at which point train was obliged to stop for want of steam. The engine was detached from train and run ahead for the purpose of facilitating the raising of steam, and in backing up the engineer lost control of the locomotive and struck the mail-car while running at a speed of 35 miles an hour. The tender was forced back into mail-car 40 feet, completely demolishing the storage end.   Postal Clerks W. F. Stenson and George B. Clark were caught and buried under wreck, and deluged with cold water from the tender.   Clark was rescued first and was found to be seriously injured in the face, hands, and back.   It took one and one-half hours to get Stenson out from under the tender.   His left foot was badly injured and his great toe broken.   Clerk John T. Durkin injured his knee in jumping out of the car.   Clerk John E. Dooley had his shoulder sprained.   Clerk L. A. Goss received a slight cut on his arm.   Clerk-in-charge A. H. Rice escaped without injury.   About 50 letters and a few papers were damaged by water.   Six registered pouches, 1 pouch for Chicago, 1 pouch for New York and Chicago R. P. O., and 50 sacks of papers, all of which were buried under the tender, were recovered and forwarded to Chicago the following day.

February 27, 1888.—Racine and Rock Island R. P. O., train No. 1, was run into at Fulton, Ill., by the Mendota and Fulton R. P. O., train No. 95, wrecking both postal cars and injuring Clerk William D. Brown of the former line, he having received a cut on the knee and was severely bruised on the back and legs.   All mails saved, but a portion damaged by oil.

February 28, 1888.—Cedar Rapids and Council Bluffs R. P. O., Railway Postal Clerk J. H. Murphy reports that 6 empty tie sacks and one-third sack of paper mail were injured by fire and water, and 6 pieces of paper mail destroyed by fire, owing to the falling of a lamp in his car.

March 1, 1888.—New York and Pittsburgh R. P. O., train No. 6. Postal car No. 19 collided with some projection of a passing freight train, bending the platform irons and crushing in end of car.   No injury to clerks or mails.

March 2, 1888.—West Liberty and Council Bluffs R. P. O. delayed at Newton, Iowa, on account of wreck blocking the track at Colfax. While trying to get around via Monroe the engine and front trucks of postal car were derailed by passing over misplaced switch.   No injury to clerk or mails.

March 2, 1888.—Nebraska City and Broken Bow R. P. O.   While at Ravenna, Nebr., engineer lost control of engine in endeavoring to make connection, resulting in a collision with postal car and breaking in the front end.   Delayed six hours.   No injury to clerk or mails.

March 3, 1888.—Palestine and Laredo R. P. O., train No. 652, was wrecked at Cactus, Tex., by a broken rail.   No injury to clerk or mails. Delayed twelve hours.

March 5, 1888.—Denison and San Antonio R. P. O., train No. 7.   Paper mails for the connecting lines and through points, which were in storage end of car, caught fire, and 22 sacks of paper mail were damaged and 10 sacks destroyed.   Mails were piled too near the stove, which was thought to have had no fire in it.   Damaged mail taken to Taylor, Tex., and all forwarded to destination, except 7 sacks, which were sent to Dead-Letter Office.

March 5, 1888.—Texarkana and Fort Worth R. P. O., train No. 1, ran through an open switch at Sherman, Tex., and collided with an empty passenger train. The postal car was disabled, necessitating transfer of mails to baggage car. No injury to clerk or loss or damage to mails.

March 6, 1888.—Council Bluffs and Kansas City R. P. O., train No. 2, collided with a freight train near Hamburgh, Iowa. No injury to clerks, car, or mails.

March 8, 1888.—Kansas City and 'Red Cloud R. P. O., train No. 15, collided with train No. 72 of the Columbus and Atchison R. P. O. at Humboldt, Nebr., on account of brakeman failing to turn switch in time. Some letters thrown from cases and damaged by water, but none lost. Clerks unhurt.

March 11, 1888.—Cincinnati and Chattanooga R. P. O. (night line), train No. 5, was wrecked near Burnside, Ky., and postal car had portion of floor torn up and steps broken off. No clerks hurt. Mails, badly scattered and slightly damaged by oil, were transferred to baggage car.

March 12, 1888.—Palatka and Punta Gorda R. P. O., train No. 19, collided with freight train at Webster, Fla., killing engineer and slightly injuring mail weigher. No injury to clerk or mails.

March 14, 1888.—Pacific Junction and McCook R. P. O. (east bound). Train took the side track at Atlanta, Nebr., to wait for the passing of a freight train. The engineer discovered that he was nearly out of water, and uncoupled his locomotive in order to run to Holdredge, Nebr., for a supply. Returning swiftly, the engine struck the train with considerable force, damaging the mail car and throwing a lot of letters from the cases to the floor, where a portion was damaged by oil. Clerks uninjured.

March 14, 1888.—Denver and Ogden R. P. O., train No. 8, was wrecked 1 mile east of Montrose, Colo., ditching two coaches and completely telescoping postal car. Mails thrown upon the floor, but recovered without loss or damage and transferred to express car. Railway Postal Clerk W. T. Newton considerably bruised.

March 14, 1888.—East Lynne and Browningtou R. P. O., train No. 1, was wrecked one-half mile south of Clinton, Mo., the engine, mail car, and one coach leaving the track. No injury to clerk or mails.

March 14, 1888.—Williamsport and Port Clinton R. P. O., train No. 4, left the track 1 mile north of Port Clinton, Pa., damaging postal car and considerably bruising Clerk J. M. Decker. This is the last of a number of accidents in which Clerk Decker has been involved, and nearly always with injury to himself. No mails lost or damaged.

March 16, 1888.—Omaha and Ogden R. P. O., train No. 1, collided with a freight train at Bronson, Nebr., necessitating transfer of mails to express car. No injury to clerk or loss or damage to mails.

March 16, 1888.—New York and Pittsburgh R. P. O., train No. 8. As above R. P. O. was leaving the Broad Street Station at Philadelphia, Pa., it was run into by an engine which broke in the end of letter car No. 21, seriously injuring Postal Clerk R. G. Caldwell, and slightly injuring clerks T. A. Warlow and J. R. McCoy. Considerable mails damaged by water, but none lost.

March 17, 1888.—Monett and Halstead R. P. O., train No. 3, was wrecked near Brooks Station, Kans., caused by spreading of the rails. Engine and mail apartment derailed, the latter turned on its side and so disabled that mails were transferred, without loss or damage, to caboose. Clerk unhurt.

March 23, 1888.—Cartersville and Talladega R. P. O., train No. 1, telescoped freight car near Lampa, Ala., wrecking postal car, and slightly injuring Railway Postal Clerk H. B. Goodwin. No mails lost, damaged, or destroyed.

March 24, 1888.—Harrisburg and Martinsburgh R. P. O., train No. 1, ran through an open switch into freight cars standing on side-track near Gettysburgh Junction, Pa. Postal car slightly damaged. One sack of paper mail for Chambersburgh, Pa., damaged by water. Postal Clerks C. W. Boyer and H. Brinkman escaped—the former slightly bruised.

March 24, 1888.—Grafton and Chicago R. P. O. (E..D.), train No. 6, collided with a freight train at Littleton, W. Va. The postal car was badly damaged, necessitating transfer of mails to baggage car. No injury to clerks or loss or damaged to mails.

March 26, 1888.—Omaha and Ogden R. P. O., train No. 4, ran through an open switch at South Omaha, Nebr., breaking the front platform and roof of postal car No. 1160. Postal clerks escaped injury, except A. G. R. Calhoun, who was slightly injured by being thrown partly through the glass in the door. No mails lost or damaged.

March 28, 1888.—Boonville and Versailles R. P. O., train No. 184, was wrecked 8 miles north of Tipton, Mo. Mails transferred to box car without loss, a portion being slightly damaged by oil. No one hurt.

March 28, 1888.—Portland and Nazareth R. P. O., train No. 2, while rounding a curve near Penn Argyle, Pa., the mail apartment end of car No. 13 left the track over a 3-foot embankment and ran 100 feet. Letters were thrown out of case and somewhat damaged by oil, but none lost or destroyed. Clerk unhurt. Almost precisely the same accident occurred the following day (29th) to the same train and car.

March 31, 1888 —Grafton and Cincinnati R. P. O., train No. 4, ran through an open switch at Centre Belpre, Ohio, resulting in slight damage to postal car, but no injury to clerk or mails. The latter transferred to baggage car.

April 1, 1888.—Cairo and Texarkana R. P. O. As Postal Clerk Lord Harleston went to the car door for the purpose of delivering pouch to what he supposed was Macon post-office, the car lurched to the left side, and the lower door, having a defective bolt, flew open with the force of the motion of the car; the reverse side motion threw him through the open doorway and out against a bank, thereby causing concussion of the spine from which he has never recovered. Train was moving at the rate of 20 miles an hour at the time.

April 4, 1888.—Branch Junction and Pittsburgh R. P. O., train No. 3, ran into a land-slide west of Selina, Pa., throwing engine and postal car off the track. Mails delayed three hours, but not damaged. Clerk unhurt.

April 5. 1888.—Calmar and Chamberlain R. P. O., train No. 1, went through a bridge near New Hampton, Iowa. The express mails in baggage car were immersed in water and, when recovered, were removed to Sanborn, Iowa, opened and examined by railway postal clerks. They were found to be thoroughly water-soaked and in very bad condition. The letter mail and a small portion of paper mail (after they had been dried) were forwarded to destination. Six and one-quarter tie sacks of paper mail, from which the wrappers had been washed, could not be forwarded. The amount of mail involved consisted of thirteen pouches of letter mail and ten tie sacks of paper mail.

April 5, 1888.—Denison and Taylor R. P. O., train No. 506, ran over a horse 2 miles north of Wautaga, Tex., and was wrecked. No injury to clerks or loss or damage to mails. Delayed nine hours.

April 5, 1888.—Pinckneyville and Marion R. P. O., train No. 22, was derailed 1½ miles north of Creal Springs, Ill. No injury to clerk or mails.

. *April* 6, 1888.—Texarkana and El Paso R. P. O., train No. 4, was wrecked by a broken wheel under postal car 4 miles east of El Paso, Tex. Returned to El Paso and substituted car No. 304 for disabled one. No mails lost, but a portion damaged by oil. Clerk unhurt.

April 6, 1888.—Essex Junction and Boston R. P. O. Five pouches and 5 sacks of mail were burned on express train No. 52 at Bartonsville, Vt.

April 7, 1888.—Council Bluffs and Kansas City R. P. O., train No. 3, collided with freight-train No. 18, at Hall's Station, Mo. No injury to clerk or loss or damage to mails.

April 9, 1888.—Dallas and Kemp R. P. O., train No. 1, was derailed and wrecked 1 mile south of Crandall, Tex. R. P. Clerk W. H. Miller received a severe cut in the face, injury to the spine, a hurt on the knee, and a fracture of the nose, being totally incapacitated for duty. No loss or damage to the mails.

April 10, 1888.—Columbus and Albion R. P. O., train No. 69, was derailed 5 miles west of Genoa, Nebr., caused by spreading of the rails. Postal Clerk G. G. Whitmore slightly bruised. No loss or damage to mails.

April 10, 1888.—Helena and Portland R. P. O., train No. 2, ran into a drove of cattle at Lake, Wash., derailing several cars and tearing up 100 feet of track. No injury to postal-car clerk or mails. Arrived at Spokane Falls sixteen hours late.

April 11, 1888.—Kankakee and Seneca R. P. O., train No. 72, was wrecked between Wauponsee and Seneca, Ill. No injury to clerk or mails.

April 12, 1888.—Monett and Paris R. P. O., train No. 2, collided at Tuskahoma, Ind. T., with two flat cars, which were pushed on main track, where they ran down grade, causing the collision. No mails lost, but a few letters soiled by water. Clerk unhurt. Delayed twelve hours.

April 12, 1888.—Boston, Springfield and New York R. P. O. (night line), and Boston, Providence and New York R. P. O. While mail cars for above R. P. O.'s were being switched in yard of the Grand Central depot in New York, N. Y., they were thrown into depot without a brakeman, and, colliding with a train, postal car No. 58, of the former line, was damaged and mails thrown out of case. J. P. O'Neil, city distributor, had an arm wrenched, head bruised, and was incapacitated for duty. J. M. Bennett, of the latter line, was cut over the eye and had his hip bruised. P. H. O'Neil, also of the latter line, had his back badly bruised. No mails lost or damaged.

April 14, 1888.—Burlington and Council Bluffs R. P. O., train No. 5, collided with a freight train 1½ miles west of Creston, Iowa. Forward postal car was completely wrecked, and, immediately taking fire, was destroyed with all mail therein except 1 pouch of letter mail for Nebraska City, Nebr. The through-registered pouch—Chicago, Ill., to Council Bluffs, Iowa—was destroyed. Storage car, also, was burned, but all mail therein saved. W. W. Dungan, clerk in charge, reports loss of registry-receipt book, all schemes, and clerks' effects. No one injured.

April 15, 1888.—Kansas City and Oxford R. P. O. collided with a freight train at Kesterson, Nebr., and was wrecked, which necessitated transfer of mails to box car. No one injured nor mails lost or damaged.

April 15, 1888.—Pacific Junction and McCook R. P. O., train No. 4, while standing at Dorchester, Nebr., was run into by a backing engine. Water tank of the latter burst, flooding the postal car. Activity on the part of the clerks succeeded in saving the mail, with but a small portion damaged by water. No one injured.

April 15, 1888.—Chetopa and Larned R. P. O. train, No. 481, was derailed near Winfield, Kans. Postal car turned on its side and a portion of the mail damaged by oil, but none lost. Postal clerk unhurt.

April 15, 1888.—Fernandina and Orlando R. P. O. train, No. 8, was derailed near Bryceville, Fla., and Postal Clerk J. C. McKay slightly injured. Mails scattered, but none lost or damaged. Delayed one day.

April 15, 1888.—New York and Pittsburgh R. P. O., express train (P. R. R.) No. 37, collided with an engine near Thirtieth street, Philadelphia, Pa. Baggage car, containing closed mails, was overturned, and pouches for Philadelphia and Lancaster, which were piled near the door ready for delivery, were thrown against the stove and badly damaged by fire and water, but contents were forwarded to destination. About 2 sacks of paper mail from New York for Philadelphia were so damaged they could not be delivered.

April 17, 1888.—Rochester and Punxsutawney R. P. O. collided with freight train at Crawford Junction, Pa., badly damaging apartment car. Mails transferred without loss or damage to baggage car. No one hurt.

April 21, 1888.—New York and Dunkirk R. P. O., train No. 13, while running at a high rate of speed, engine left the track in consequence of a disabled wheel, completely wrecking it, together with six cars, and injuring engineer and fireman. Fortunately the postal car, by request, was on the rear of train and escaped injury.

April 27, 1888.—Omaha and McCook R. P. O., train No. 16, went through a bridge between Orleans and Alma, Nebr., precipitating the postal, baggage, express cars, and one passenger coach into the stream. Clerk-in-Charge James B. Martin escaped without injury. Clerk W. F. J. Comley had two ribs broken. Two persons were killed. The cars took fire, but Clerks Martin and Comley worked hard and succeeded in securing all mail, excepting about 100 letters and one-third of tie sack of papers. Several registered letters were lost. Accident caused by supports to bridge being washed out by heavy rains.

April 28, 1888.—Buffalo and Emporium R. P. O. train was wrecked one-half mile south of Portville, N. Y., caused by spreading of rails. No mails lost or damaged, but Postal Clerk Wales Wasson and Helper Charles Keenan were both seriously injured, the former being cut and burned on the head, left shoulder and side bruised, left arm and hand burned, with other slight bruises and cuts on his face and body. Keenan had his left shoulder-blade broken. The postal car was the first to leave the track, going over an embankment 15 feet high, making a complete revolution. The trucks were torn off when the car turned. Clerk Wasson, notwithstanding his injuries, made up his mail to go south in locked pouches and forwarded them in care of baggage-men.

May 2, 1888.—Deming and Los Angeles R. P. O., train No. 19, collided with a freight train at White Water Station (n. o.), Cal. When tender of engine telescoped postal car 5 feet, entirely demolishing it. Some mail damaged by water, but all forwarded to destination, reaching Deming, N. Mex., four hours late. Clerk unhurt.

May 10, 1888.—Lyons and Sayre R. P. O., train No. 9, was run into by a coal train 1½ miles south of Ithaca, N. Y., wrecking engines, two coaches, postal, and baggage cars. Mail and supplies badly mixed, but none lost or damaged, nor was clerk injured. Accident caused by breaking of hose connecting air-brakes, thus stopping mail train. The freight followed behind, and could not be checked in time to avoid the casualty.

May 11, 1888.—Denver and Ogden R. P. O., train No. 7, was ditched 6 miles east of Delta, Colo. No injury to clerk. Mails transferred without loss or damage to express car.

May 11, 1888.—Rutland, Bennington and Troy R. P. O. train ran off track at Danby, Vt., considerably injuring R. P. Clerk J. P. Fonda. Mails somewhat damaged by oil, but none lost or destroyed.

May 14, 1888.—Atchison and Lenora R. P. O., train No. 401, was wrecked 10 miles east of Concordia, Kans. No injury to clerk nor loss or damage to mails.

May 14, 1888.—Express train No. 7, Atchison, Topeka and Santa Fé R. R., collided with two "wild" freight cars (loaded with naphtha and gunpowder) at Fountain, Colo. Six persons were killed, a number seriously wounded, and the depot and adjacent buildings blown to pieces. The mails were in charge of train baggage-man. The car was entirely consumed, but the pouches and nearly all the canvas mails were saved, but 2 or 3 sacks of papers being destroyed.

May 15, 1888.—Columbus and Atchison R. P. O., train No. 72, was wrecked one-half mile north of Elk Creek, Nebr. No injury to clerk or loss or damage to mails.

May 16, 1888.—Express train No. 3, Denver and Rio Grande Railway, wrecked near Salida, Colo., smashing baggage car. No loss or damage to mails.

May 16, 1888.—The wharf-boat at Moscow, Ohio, in which the mail from steamer *Bonanza* was locked, was destroyed by fire and a small amount of letter and paper mail was consumed.

May 21, 1888.—Jacksonville and Pensacola R. P. O., train No. 2, wrecked 6 miles east of Tallahasse, Fla., seriously injuring Postal Clerk J. C. Gregory and badly damaging the mails.

May 23, 1888.—Denver and Ogden R. P. O., train No. 7, caught fire from mattresses which were being taken over the road in the baggage end of car. The car was side-tracked at Nada, Colo., and allowed to burn up, after all efforts to extinguish the fire were found useless. All mail saved in good condition.

May 28, 1888.—Kane and Callery R. P. O., train No. 18, ran into a cyclone 1 mile west of Lucinda, Pa. The terrible wind and rain storm brought the train to a stand on account of flying boards, fence-rails, etc., when the cyclone lifted the engine, from the track and threw it on its side. About thirty people were injured, but none seriously. Mail car fell on right side, and letter mail remained in case and protected from the rain by sacks with which Clerk W. S. Copley covered it. Some paper mail wet, but none seriously damaged. After several hours' delay, clerk, mail, and passengers were transferred to baggage car. An additional delay was caused by the necessity for removing trees that had fallen across the track, over one hundred being removed in less than 6 miles. Reached Kane at 7 a. m., 29th, a delay of fifteen hours.

May 29, 1888.—Lynchburgh and Pocahontas R. P. O. car, while standing on side-track at Bonsacks, Va., was run into by a coal train and so damaged as to be unfit for further service. Most of the mail was thrown from case, and a portion slightly damaged by oil, but none lost or destroyed. E. S. Dennis, postal clerk, slightly injured.

May 30, 1888.—Tyler and Lufkin R. P. O., train No. 100, wrecked between Alto and Forest, Tex. Postal car badly disabled and abandoned. Trip completed in box car. Clerk uninjured. No mails lost or damaged.

May 30, 1888.—Henrietta and Dallas R. P. O., train No. 552, was wrecked near Pilot Point, Tex., caused by the breaking of axle under tender. No mail lost or damaged, and no one injured. Delayed six hours.

June 4, 1888.—Arkansas City and Warren R. P. O., train No. 558, was wrecked 5 miles east of Warren, Ark., turning over postal car. No injury to clerk or loss or damage to mails.

June 8, 1888.—The express pouch from Sterling to Denver, Colo. (U. P. Rwy. train No. 306), and which was in charge of train baggage-man, fell upon the stove and was considerably burned. Letters not badly damaged and were all forwarded to destination, with explanation to addressees.

June 13, 1888.—Herington and Dodge City R. P. O., train No. 21, ran into an open switch near Dodge City, Kans., wrecking engine and delaying departure of train No. 22. No injury to clerk or mails.

June 15, 1888.—Sedalia and Denison R. P. O., train No. 507, was attacked by robbers near Muscogee, Ind. T. Clerk-in-Charge W. P. Colton went to the door of the car, when the train came to a sudden stop, and was commanded to "Get back, or I'll shoot your head off!" A shot followed this order before he could change his position, taking effect in his left arm. Two robbers then entered the car; finding that it was not the express car, they compelled Clerk J. W. Jenks, of the crew, to accompany them to the express car, ordering him to enter it while they followed. After robbing it, they took Mr. Jenks some distance up the track and told him to return to his car. In consequence of the wound, Mr. Colton was incapacitated for duty sixty days.

June 16, 1888.—Washington and Wilmington R. P. O., train No. 23, collided with a freight train at Laurel Station, 8 miles north of Richmond, Va. Postal car badly damaged and rendered unfit for service. No mail lost and all clerks escaped injury except H. D. Burkhimer, who jumped from the train and fractured his right leg between the knee and thigh. Accident caused by failure of engineer of mail train to see the flagman on account of the smoke.

June 16, 1888.—Nordmont and Hartley Hall R. P. O., train No. 4, was wrecked between Mawr Glen and Muncy Valley, Pa. No injury to mails, though postal car was badly damaged. Clerk M. A. Phillips was considerably hurt, but took the mail in a conveyance to Valley P. O., from which it was forwarded to Laporte.

June 16, 1888.—Oswego and Binghamton R. P. O., train No. 4, ran onto an open switch at Homer, N. Y., and collided with a coal "gondola," killing one man. Postal Clerk R. F. Randall jumped from the train and was seriously bruised about the body, and had his left wrist sprained. No mails lost, but 1 sack damaged by water.

June 22, 1888.—Buffalo and Youngstown R. P. O., train No. 3, collided with gravel train at Miller's Station, Pa., demolishing engine and nine flat cars. Postal Clerks G. W. Moore and F. A. McCullough were thrown on the floor by the collision, but escaped injury. A few papers damaged by water. Delayed four hours.

June 25, 1888.—Dallas and Kemp R. P. O., train No. 1, was wrecked on a bridge 1 mile south of Kleburgh, Tex., throwing mail apartment into the stream. Postal clerk uninjured. Mail considerably damaged by water and some lost. Trip completed in flat car.

June 26, 1888.—Kansas City and Pueblo R. P. O., train No. 6, collided with rear end of express train No. 2, at Kinsley, Kans., disabling postal car of the former and two sleeping coaches of the latter. Six sacks of mail damaged. Some paper mail, of which no description can be given, was buried under the cars and could not be taken out by clerks. Accident caused by train No. 6 being late and running at a high rate of speed; the air brakes failed to work when applied.

June 26, 1888.—Montgomery and New Orleans R. P. O., train No. 3, was wrecked near Tensaw, Ala. R. P. O. Clerk A. F. Davis was mortally injured, dying of his wounds the next day. Clerk T. O. Luckie was slightly bruised. Mail car demolished and 1 pouch of letter mail lost.

Recapitulation of casualties in the Railway Mail Service from 1875 to 1888.

Year ended June 30—	Total number of clerks.	Number of casualties.	Clerks killed.	Clerks seriously injured.	Clerks slightly injured.
1875	2,238	(*)	1	(*)	(*)
1876	2,415	(*)	1	(*)	(*)
1877	2,500	27	2	10	4
1878	2,608	36	2	15	3
1879	2,609	35	3	14	13
1880	2,946	26	......	14	15
1881	3,177	62	7	15	22
1882	3,570	63	3	16	20
1883	3,855	114	1	35	42
1884	3,963	154	7	28	60
1885	4,387	102	2	35	65
1886	4,573	211	......	56	60
1887	4,851	244	5	45	72
1888	5,094	248	4	63	45

* Not reported.

REPORT

OF THE

THIRD ASSISTANT POSTMASTER-GENERAL

TO THE

POSTMASTER-GENERAL

FOR THE

FISCAL YEAR ENDING JUNE 30, 1888.

REPORT

OF THE

THIRD ASSISTANT POSTMASTER-GENERAL.

POST-OFFICE DEPARTMENT,
OFFICE OF THIRD ASSISTANT POSTMASTER-GENERAL,
Washington, D. C., November 9, 1888.

SIR: I have the honor to submit the following report, with accompanying papers, showing the operations of this office for the year ending June 30, 1888. The appended papers, which are worthy of careful examination, are as follows:

No. 1. Explanation of estimates of appropriations for the office of the Third Assistant Postmaster-General for the fiscal year ending June 30, 1890.

No. 2. Statement showing itemized appropriations for the service of the Post-Office Department for the fiscal year ending June 30, 1888, and the expenditures made out of the same.

No. 3. Statement exhibiting the receipts and expenditures, under appropriate heads, by quarters, for the fiscal year ending June 30, 1888, compared with the receipts and expenditures of the fiscal years ending June 30, 1886, and June 30, 1887.

No. 4. Statement showing receipts and disbursements at Treasury depositories during the fiscal year ending June 30, 1888.

No. 5. Statement showing the issue in detail of all the several kinds of adhesive postage-stamps, stamped envelopes, newspaper wrappers, and postal cards for the fiscal year ending June 30, 1888.

No. 6. Statement showing the issue of postage-stamps, stamped envelopes, newspaper wrappers, and postal cards, by denominations, for the fiscal year ending June 30, 1888.

No. 7. Statement showing the increase in the issues of postage-stamps, stamped envelopes, newspaper wrappers, and postal cards for the year ending June 30, 1888, as compared with those of the previous year.

No. 8. Value of postage-stamps issued, by fiscal years, from their introduction to June 30, 1888.

No. 9. Statement, by fiscal years, of the issues of stamped envelopes from their introduction to June 30, 1888.

No. 10. Statement, by fiscal years, of the number of postal-cards issued from their introduction to June 30, 1888.

No. 11. Comparative statement of second-class matter mailed at first-class post-offices, 1886–'87 and 1887–'88.

No. 12. Statement showing the number of registered letters and parcels transmitted through the mails from each of the several States and Territories in the United States during the fiscal year ending June·30, 1888.

No. 13. Statement showing the increase of registered letters and parcels upon which fees were collected at thirty of the leading cities during the fiscal year ending June 30, 1888, over the number registered during the preceding year.

No. 14. Statement showing the operations of the registry system at the cities of New York, Philadelphia, Chicago, Saint Louis, and Washington during the fiscal year ending June 30, 1888.

No. 15. Statement showing the number and value of registered letters and parcels carried for the several executive departments during the fiscal year ending June 30, 1888.

No. 16. Statement showing the operations of the special-delivery system at letter-carrier offices during the year ending September 30, 1888.

No. 17. Calculations showing the number of letters, postal-cards, newspapers and periodicals, and pieces of third and fourth-class matter, mailed in the United States during the fiscal year ending June 30, 1888.

No. 18. Abstract of laws relating to the postal service from 1639 to the present time (November, 1888.)

No. 19. Table of postal statistics from 1789 to 1888.

No. 20. Contract for furnishing registered-package, tag, official, and dead-letter envelopes, during the fiscal year ending June 30, 1889.

STATEMENTS OF FINANCIAL OPERATIONS.

In continuation of the plan adopted in my last annual report, I present the following condensed statements of the revenue, expenditure, and cost of the postal service for the fiscal years ending June 30, 1886, 1887, and 1888, charging to the two former years whatever expenditures have been made on account thereof since their termination, and to all three their estimated liabilities, respectively, now outstanding, as well as the amounts earned by the Pacific railroad companies and credited to them on the books of the Treasury Department as provided by law:

FISCAL YEAR ENDING JUNE 30, 1886.

REVENUE.

1. Ordinary postal revenue		$43,597,871.08
2. Revenue from money-order business		350,551.87
Total gross receipts		43,948,422.95
Deduct amount charged to bad debts		12,174.25
Leaves total revenue		43,936,248.70

EXPENDITURES AND LIABILITIES.

Expenditures:			
From July 1, 1885, to September 30, 1886	$50,627,553.37		
From October 1, 1886, to September 30, 1887	211,881.50		
From October 1, 1887, to September 30, 1888	• 12,020.34		
		50,851,455.21	
Liabilities:			
Estimated amount of outstanding indebtedness for various objects on account of the year	$286.40		
Amount due for transportation on Pacific railroads, for which no appropriation was made	251,101.61		
		251,388.01	
			51,102,843.22
Deficiency in revenue			7,166,594.52

COST OF POSTAL SERVICE.

Amount of expenditures and liabilities as above		$51,102,843.22
Amount certified to the Secretary of the Treasury for credit to Pacific railroads, from July 1, 1885, to September 30, 1886	$1,112,138.40	
From October 1, 1886, to September 30, 1887	391.22	
From October 1, 1887, to September 30, 1888	142.38	
Total amount certified		1,112,672.00
Total cost of the service		52,215,515.22
Excess of total cost of postal service over revenue		8,279,266.52

The receipts were $7,166,594.52, or 14 per cent., less than the expenditures and outstanding obligations, and $8,279,266.52, or 15.8 per cent., less than the total cost of the postal service, inclusive of the amount certified to the Secretary of the Treasury for transportation of the mail on Pacific railroads.

Compared with the previous fiscal year, there was an increase of $1,375,404.87, or 3.2 per cent., in the revenue; an increase of $1,320,224.13, or 2.6 per cent., in the expenditures and liabilities; and an increase, also, of $1,335,974.47, or 2.6 per cent., in the estimated total cost of the service.

FISCAL YEAR ENDING JUNE 30, 1887.

REVENUE.

1. Ordinary postal revenue	$48,118,273.94
2. Receipts from money-order business	719,335.45
Gross revenue	48,837,609.39

EXPENDITURES AND LIABILITIES.

Expenditures:		
From July 1, 1886, to September 30, 1887	$52,391,677.43	
From October 1, 1887, to September 30, 1888	368,160.40	
		52,759,837.83
Liabilities:		
Amount of outstanding liabilities for various objects on account of the year	$75,000.00	
Estimated amount due for transportation on Pacific railroads, for which no appropriation was made	300,009.87	
		375,009.87
Total actual and estimated expenditures for the service of the year		53,134,847.70
Deficiency in revenue		4,297,238.31

COST OF POSTAL SERVICE.

Amount of actual and estimated expenditures, as shown above		$53,134,847.70
Amount certified to Secretary of the Treasury by the Auditor for transportation of the mails on the Pacific railroads, and by law not charged to the appropriations for the postal service, from July 1, 1886, to September 30, 1887	$1,187,027.33	
From October 1, 1887, to September 30, 1888	11,241.72	
		1,198,269.05
Total cost of the service		54,333,116.75
Excess of total cost of service over amount of revenue		5,495,507.36

The receipts were $4,297,238.31, or 8 per cent., less than the expenditures and outstanding obligations, and $5,495,507.36, or 10 per cent., less than the total cost of the postal service, inclusive of the amount certified to the Secretary of the Treasury for transportation of the mail on Pacific railroads.

Compared with the previous fiscal year, there was an increase of $4,889,186.44, or 11.1 per cent., in the gross revenue; an increase of $2,032,004.48, or 3.9 per cent., in the expenditures and liabilities; and an increase, also, of $2,117,601.53, or 4 per cent., in the estimated total cost of the service.

FISCAL YEAR ENDING JUNE 30, 1888.

REVENUE.

1. Ordinary postal revenue	$51,896,858.96
2. Receipts from money order business....., ...	798,317.83
Gross revenue	52,695,176.79

EXPENDITURES AND LIABILITIES.

Expenditures:
　Amount expended to September 30, 1888, on ac-
　count of the year ending June 30, 1888......... $55,795,357.84
Liabilities:
　Amount of indebtedness for various ob-
　jects certified to Auditor and not yet
　reported for payment (partly esti-
　mated) $375,000.00
　Estimated amount of indebtedness not
　yet reported to Auditor (railroad
　service)............................. 404,830.25
　Estimated amount due for transporta-
　tion on Pacific railroads, for which
　no appropriation was made........ 307,215.75
　Estimated amount of indebtedness in-
　curred, for which appropriation will
　be asked of Congress.............. 3,000.00
　　　　　　　　　　　　　　　　　　 ————————— 1,090,046.00

Total actual and estimated expenditures for the service of the year..	56,885,403.84
Estimated amount of deficiency of revenue to be supplied out of the general Treasury on account of the service of the year............	4,190,227.05

COST OF POSTAL SERVICE.

Amount of actual and estimated expenditures, as shown above......	$56,885,403.84
Amount certified to the Secretary of the Treasury by the Auditor for transportation of the mails on the Pacific railroads, and by law not charged to the appropriation for the postal service................	1,240,600.83
Total estimated cost of the postal service for the year.........	58,126,004.79
Deduct amount of gross revenue, as shown above.................	52,695,176.79
Leaves excess of estimated cost of service over amount of revenue...	5,430,827.88

The gross receipts of the fiscal year just ended were $3,100,181.05, or 5.5 per cent., less than the disbursements on account of the year; $4,190,227.05, or 7.3 per cent., less than the disbursements and out-standing obligations; and $5,430,827.88, or 9.3 per cent., less than the estimated total cost of the postal service, inclusive of the amount certi-fied to the Secretary of the Treasury for mail transportation on the Pacific railroads.

Compared with the previous year there was an increase of $3,857,567.40, or 7.9 per cent., in the revenue; an increase of $3,750,556.14, or 7.5 per cent., in the expenditures and liabilities; and an increase also of $3,792,887.92, or 6.9 per cent., in the estimated total cost of the service.

The increase in the principal items of revenue over the previous fiscal year was $3,873,288.88 from the sale of postage-stamps, stamped envel-opes, newspaper-wrappers, letter-sheets, and postal-cards; $78,982.38 in revenue from the money-order business; and $14,784.07 from box rents. There was a decrease of $31,874.47 in letter-postage paid in money, and a decrease, also, of $75,905.03 in miscellaneous receipts.

In addition to the $55,795,357.84 expended as above for service of the year, the sum of $469,044.60 was paid on account of previous years, making the total disbursement during the year $56,264,402.44. Of the disbursements on account of previous years, $206.66 was for a claim under a special act of Congress; $12,020.34 was for 1886; $88,657.20 was for compensation to postmasters readjusted under the act of March 3, 1883; and $368.160.40 was for various objects for 1887.

The increase in expenditure for the free - delivery system was $803,697.37, or 17.4 per cent.; for railroad transportation it was $1,083,559.57, or 7.3 per cent.; and for compensation of postmasters, it was $660,287.25, or 5.5 per cent.

Table No. 3, accompanying this report, gives a comparative statement of receipts and expenditures for the past three years.

The amount of expenditure authorized by the post-office appropriation bill was $55,840,650.15, to which should be added $109,015.64 for the special-delivery service, which does not require a specific appropriation, being paid from the fees; and $578,482, provided for by the act of Congress approved October 19, 1888, for transportation of the mail on railroads, and for foreign mails, making the total sum appropriated $56,528,147.79. In the item for compensation to postmasters, the expenditure was $12,589,768.66, or $889,768.66 in excess of the amount appropriated, for which a deficiency appropriation will have to be made by Congress. The expenditure under this head is always beyond the control of the Department, postmasters under the law being authorized to retain their compensation from the general postal receipts.

The unexpended balances of all the items of appropriation amounted to $1,622,558.61.

In Table No. 2 will be found in detail a statement of the appropriations and expenditures.

REVENUE FOR THE FISCAL YEARS ENDING JUNE 30, 1889 AND 1890.

The increase in the ordinary postal revenue (excluding revenue from money-order business) for the fiscal year ending June 30, 1887, was at the rate of 10.3 per cent. over the revenue of the previous year, and the increase for the year ending June 30, 1888, was at the rate of 7.9 per cent. The receipts for the quarter ending June 30—the last quarter of the past year—were somewhat smaller than had been estimated by the Department, but this unexpected falling off in business it is thought will not continue during the present year, for special returns already received by the Department from thirty of the larger cities for the quarter ending September 30 show an increase of over 9 per cent. In estimating, therefore, for the current and coming years, it is not unreasonable to assume that an increase of 9 per cent. for each year will be maintained. Upon this basis the gross revenue for the years ending June 30, 1889 and 1890, is estimated at $57,392,576.26 and $62,508,658.12, respectively, as appears from the following statements:

FISCAL YEAR ENDING JUNE 30, 1889.

Amount of ordinary postal revenue for the fiscal year ending June 30, 1888	$51,896,858.96
Add 9 per cent. for increase	4,670,717.30
Gives estimated amount of ordinary postal revenue for the fiscal year ending June 30, 1889	56,567,576.26
Amount of estimated revenue from money-order business	825,000.00
Total estimated gross receipts for the year ending June 30, 1889.	57,392,576.26

The amount appropriated for service of this year is $60,860,233.74, or an excess over the amount of revenue estimated above of $3,467,657.48, which will be drawn from the general Treasury should the total amount appropriated be needed.

Estimated amount of ordinary postal revenue for the fiscal year ending June 30, 1889	$56,567,576.26
Add 9 per cent. for increase	5,091,081.86
Gives estimated amount of ordinary revenue for the fiscal year ending June 30, 1890	61,658,658.12
Amount of estimated revenue from money-order business	850,000.00
Total estimated gross receipts for the year ending June 30, 1890.	62,508,658.12

The probable amount of expenditure to be made in carrying on the business of the postal service for the year ending June 30, 1890, as shown by your estimates submitted to the Secretary of the Treasury, is $66,812,073.02. The deficiency to be supplied from the general Treasury is therefore $4,303,414.90.

NEARNESS TO A SELF-SUSTAINING CONDITION.

From the foregoing statements it is seen that the revenue of the Department for the last fiscal year was not enough to meet its expenses by quite a large sum, and that the revenue of the current and the coming year will also be insufficient—a fact which is somewhat surprising, and in some respects to be regretted. But taking everything into consideration—notably, the immensity of the business of the Post-Office Department, now the greatest in the world, the radical reductions for several years past in the rates of postage, the large but necessary extension of the railway mail service, which is reaching nearly every nook and corner of the land, the unusual increase of free-delivery offices, at present numbering nearly 400, and the very liberal rates of compensation to postmasters, constituting, with the exception of railroad transportation, the greatest item of postal expenditure—I do not think that this condition of affairs is discouraging. On the contrary, there can be seen through it the certainty that before long, unless additional changes should be made in the rates of postage, the service will be in a self-supporting condition.

It should not be forgotten, either, that the Department is now annually transporting and handling, with precisely the same trouble and at the same expense as are involved in its other business, but without the slightest compensation therefor, millions of pounds of matter for Congress and the various other branches of the Government, for agricultural colleges and experiment stations, and for newspaper publishers throughout the country within their respective counties of publication. If the value of all this service could be added to the postal revenue, the balance-sheet of the Department would show but a small deficit for the past and the current fiscal year, or for the year to come; and that credit for this service *should* be given to the Department, I think no one will deny.

I am disposed to think, however, that so long as strict economy of administration continues to be the policy of the Post-Office Department —so long as its wants are supplied by Congress with the same liberal spirit that has been manifested for some years past—so long as the postal service faithfully fulfills, as it has, its high obligations to the people, it is of but little moment whether its revenue is adequate or not to fully satisfy its requirements. The following passage from the works of the celebrated Dr. Channing is so fairly expressive of the high mission of the Post-Office Department, its great value to the Union, and the general policy that should govern its administration, that I can not forbear applying it to the present condition of things:

It does much towards making us one by admitting free communication between distant parts of the country which no other channel of intercourse could bring together. It binds the whole country in a chain of sympathies, and makes it in truth one great neighborhood. It promotes a kind of society between the sea-shore and the mountains. It perpetuates friendships between those who are never to meet again. It binds the family in the new settlement and the half-cleared forest to the cultivated spot from which it emigrated. It facilitates beyond calculation commercial connections and the interchange of products. On this account we always grieve to see a statement of the revenue accruing to government from the post-office. It ought not to yield a cent to the Treasury; it should simply support itself. Such importance do we attach to the freest communication between all parts of the country, so much do we desire that the poor as well as rich may enjoy the means of intercourse, that we would sooner have the post-office a tax on the revenue than one of its sources.

AMOUNTS DRAWN FROM THE GENERAL TREASURY.

In addition to the receipts referred to in table No. 3, there were drawn from the general Treasury within the year the following amounts, on account of special and deficiency appropriations, viz:

For deficiency in the postal revenues for the year ending June 30, 1888, under the act approved March 3, 1887, Stats., vol. 24, chap. 388, page 570	$2,564,221.27
For deficiency in the postal revenues for 1885 and prior years, under the act approved February 1, 1888, Public No. 4, page 31 (compensation of postmasters re-adjusted under act approved March 3, 1883)..	160,286.05
For deficiency in the postal revenues for 1885 and prior years, under act approved February 1, 1888, Public No. 4, page 31 (claims)	49,854.79
For deficiency in the postal revenues for 1885 and prior years, under act approved March 30, 1888, Public No. 27, page 17 (compensation of postmasters re-adjusted under act approved March 3, 1883)	380,321.44
For deficiency in the postal revenues for 1885 and prior years, under the act approved March 30, 1888, Public No. 27, pages 18, 25, and 26 (claims)	6,136.92
Total drawn during the year	3,160,820.47

TRANSACTIONS AT TREASURY DEPOSITORIES.

The accounts during the year show the following receipts and disbursements at Treasury depositories, viz:

Balance subject to draft June 30, 1887		$6,516,674.40
Amount of outstanding warrants June 30, 1887.....................		82,237.64
Deposits:		
On account of postal revenues...................	$22,877,485.05	
On account of grants from the general Treasury .	3,160,820.47	
		26,038,305.52
		32,637,217.56
Amount of warrants paid during the year ending June 30, 1888......		26,542,398.14
Balance at depositories June 30, 1888		6,094,819.42
Outstanding warrants June 30, 1888		111,102.56
Balance subject to draft June 30, 1888		5,983,716.86

Of the $22,877,485.05 of postal revenue, $22,156.54 was deposited through national-bank depositories. The balance on hand June 30, 1888, in national-bank depositories, was $5,935.11.

SUSPENSE AND COMPROMISE ACCOUNTS AND BAD DEBTS.

As appears by the following statement, taken from the report of the Auditor, the postal revenue has gained $672.38 during the last fiscal year from the balancing of what are known as the suspense and the compromise and bad-debt accounts:

Amount credited to the postal revenue on suspense account	$4,049.85
Amount due the Government from late postmasters and charged against the revenue on compromise and bad-debt account......................	3,377.47
Gain by suspense...	672.38

The following extract from the report of this office for the fiscal year ending June 30, 1885, clearly explains the principle upon which the Government either gains or loses by the above-named accounts:

The Post-Office Department is accountable for the postal revenues as soon as they are realized at the post-offices, and they are entered into the accounts as reported quarterly by postmasters, the system differing in this respect from that of the general Treasury, which acknowledges only revenue that has actually been deposited. Out of this feature of the postal system grow bad debts, compromise and suspense accounts. To bad debts are charged balances due by late postmasters and uncollectible, resulting of course in a reduction of the amount of revenue reported. A like result follows in the case of suspended accounts, in which the balances due the Government are found too small (usually less than $1) to justify unusual efforts for collection after failure by the ordinary means. On the other hand, the Government derives the benefit from small balances (also usually less than $1) found due late postmasters and not paid to them. Compromise accounts, of course, always result in a loss to the Government. The effects in all these cases are felt upon the revenues for the year in which the accounts are closed.

NEW FORM OF QUARTERLY POSTAL ACCOUNT.

As a matter indirectly connected with the affairs of this office, I take pleasure in reporting that the use by postmasters of the new form of quarterly postal account and the record of postal business, adopted shortly after the commencement of the last fiscal year, has been satisfactory, both as regards the transaction of business at post-offices and the examination and audit of accounts in the office of the Auditor. I understand that fewer delinquencies as to the prompt and correct rendition of accounts by postmasters have occurred during the year than was formerly the case, and that the Auditor has been able to settle accounts with greater exactness and with fewer outstanding cases at the end of each quarter than ever before. As time goes on, the new system will probably work still more satisfactorily.

APPROPRIATIONS, EXPENDITURES, AND ESTIMATES FOR THE SERVICE OF THIS OFFICE.

The appropriations for the service of this office during the fiscal year amounted to $1,242,900, of which $75,872.09 remains unexpended. The only obligation unpaid is a small sum due for letter-sheet envelopes for the six months ending June 30, 1888, the bill for which has not been rendered.

The expenditure for this office for the service of the fiscal year was $1,167,027.91, or $90,527.82 more than for the preceding year. The principal items of increase were $62,147.15 for manufacture of stamped envelopes, $17,680.23 for manufacture of postal-cards, and $8,826.55 for manufacture of adhesive postage-stamps.

The amount expended under each item will be found in Table No. 3, accompanying this report.

The amount required for service of this office for the fiscal year ending June 30, 1890, is estimated at $1,385,051, an increase of $131,095, or 10.4 per cent., over the amount appropriated for the current year. Full explanation of these estimates will be found in Table No. 1, hereto appended.

WORK OF THE FINANCE DIVISION.

The work of the finance division of this office for the fiscal year may be briefly stated as follows:

There were 4,454 contracts for mail service received during the year from the office of the Second Assistant Postmaster-General, and 21,529 orders of the Postmaster-General, recognizing mail service not under contract, curtailing or extending service, or modifying previous orders, all of which contracts and orders were entered upon the books of the division for reference when acting upon certificates of the Auditor of the Treasury for the Post-Office Department for payment of mail contractors and other creditors of the Department.

The number of certificates received from the Auditor and acted upon was 92,570, an increase of 10,067 over the number received for the previous fiscal year.

In addition to the above there were 7,387 certificates received from the Auditor, upon which 7,387 transfer drafts, covering the sum of $817,051.44, were drawn against postmasters having a surplus of postal revenue in favor of late postmasters, or postmasters whose revenues were insufficient to meet the demands upon their offices for payment of railway postal-clerks, rent, and other authorized expenses.

Accounts were kept with the Treasury, nine subtreasuries, and forty-one designated depositories, involving, with the amount on hand subject to draft at the beginning of the year, the sum of $32,554,979.92, against which 92,570 warrants were issued, aggregating $26,571,263.00.

The number of post-office warrants and transfer drafts drawn, and the number of certificates of deposit received, entered, and passed to the Auditor, during the year, compared with the number for the previous year, are shown by the following table:

	Fiscal year ending June 30, 1887.	Fiscal year ending June 30, 1888.	Increase.
Number of warrants	82,503	92,570	10,067
Number of transfer drafts	8,371	7,387	*984
Number of certificates of deposit	211,400	236,729	25,329
Total	302,274	336,686	34,412

* Decrease.

The number of accounts of contractors on the books of the division on June 30, 1888, was as follows, viz:

Railroads	1,995
Mail contractors, star service	14,146
Sub-contractors, star service	9,444
Mail contractors, steamboat service	127
Sub-contractors, steamboat service	10
Mail messengers	5,906
Carriers at offices supplied by a special carrier	2,695

Total number of accounts, requiring the same number of quarterly payments 34,323

This is an increase over the preceding year of 10,004.

There were also prepared and forwarded 3,774 letters relating to the business of the division, 92,570 circulars relating to the issue of warrants, 54,470 circulars instructing postmasters as to their duties in depositing postal balances, and demanding balances on postal account, etc.

CASES FOR INVESTIGATION BY THE CHIEF POST-OFFICE INSPECTOR.

The number of cases made up in the finance division during the fiscal year and referred to the chief post-office inspector for investigation into the accounts of postmasters or late postmasters, for withholding postal funds from deposit, for improper use of postage-stamps, for rendering false vouchers for clerk-hire or rent, and for fraudulent returns of stamps canceled, was 607, or 414 less than were given out in the previous year. The number of such cases prepared after reports of investigation had been received, for the final action of the Department, was 96, in all of which cases the Auditor was requested, through formal orders of the Postmaster-General, to charge the postal accounts of the offending officials, under the provisions of the act of Congress approved June 17, 1878, to the amount of $40,991.23, or $86,066.54 less than for the previous year.

The inspection of the accounts of postmasters, under the general system inaugurated some time since, has been of great benefit to the postal service, as is now being seen in the promptitude with which accounts are rendered and deposits of postal balances made.

The number of general inspection reports received from the chief post-office inspector during the year was 24,845, the summary of postal account in every one of these cases being carefully examined and verified.

ACCOUNTABILITY FOR KEY DEPOSITS.

Several of the cases referred to in the foregoing paragraph comprehend an offense which, though not occurring very often, is yet frequent enough to justify a remedy through the enactment of a special law— the only thorough remedy, indeed, that can be applied. I allude to the appropriation by postmasters, for private use, of what is known as the "key-deposit fund." Under the postal regulations every renter of a post-office lock-box in any building owned or leased by the Government is required to make a deposit of 50 cents with the postmaster upon being furnished with a box key, in order to insure its return when the rental ceases, or to indemnify the Government in case the key is lost. Moneys thus received, called the "key-deposit fund," are simply held by the postmaster in trust, to be returned to the depositors, respectively, upon the surrender of their keys, or, in the event of the postmaster's retirement from office, to his successor.

As long as a postmaster remains in office there is little or no trouble experienced by depositors in securing the return of their money whenever demanded; for the great majority of postmasters are by character honest and faithful, and most of those who are otherwise inclined are restrained from default in so small a matter as this by the fear of consequent removal from office. But when a postmaster has defaulted in some other branch of his official business, or goes out of office in debt to the Government, it is too often the case that the key-deposit fund is appropriated to his own use, in which event the depositor has no means of recovery except to bring an action at law against the appropriator; for the money thus appropriated is not a part of the postal revenue, is never paid into the Treasury, and there is no authority of law for any expenditure out of legitimate postal receipts to reimburse the loser. Of course, whenever any such default occurs, the depositor is subjected in nine cases out of ten to absolute loss; for the amount involved is so trifling, individually considered, that a lawsuit for recovery would be altogether injudicious and probably unavailing.

Although the propriety of making deposits so made to postmasters a part of the postal revenue is somewhat doubtful, owing to questions of ownership in cases where the boxes and keys of post-offices are furnished by the Treasury Department, or in cases where the same thing is done by proprietors of post-office buildings leased by the Government, I am satisfied that some means should be adopted whereby indemnity can be made to all key depositors in case of failure to return the deposits on demand. The best way, perhaps, to accomplish this is in every case to make the sureties of a postmaster liable for moneys received by him in trust under the postal regulations from time to time promulgated, and to authorize the restoration of such moneys as a proper postal expenditure. If this can not be done except under special law, I respectfully recommend that the matter be brought to the attention of Congress.

DEAD-LETTER FUND.

The money taken from dead letters for which no owners could be found, and that realized from the auction sale of unclaimed articles accumulated in the Dead Letter Office, which was turned over to the finance division during the fiscal year, was $10,534.79.

This money was disposed of as follows, viz:

Amount received		$10,534 79
Amount of current funds deposited in the Treasury at Washington, D. C..	$10 253.81	
Amount realized from sale of foreign and uncurrent funds by the postmaster at New York and deposited with the Assistant Treasurer at New York................................	256.77	
Total amount deposited................................	10,510.58	
Amount of loss sustained from sale of uncurrent funds, from counterfeits, and from mutilated minor coins..............	24.21	
		10,534,79

The report of the Auditor states the receipts from dead letters for the year to have been $9,117.72, or $1,392.86 less than shown above. This is explained by the fact that in his previous annual report the Auditor included this $1,392.86 as part of the revenue of the year ending June 30, 1887, it being in reality, however, the receipts for July and August of the fiscal year following.

WORK OF SIGNING WARRANTS AND DRAFTS.

The work of signing warrants drawn in payment of money due mail contractors and other creditors of the Department has grown to such proportions as to be now a very great burden upon the Third Assistant Postmaster-General, who has, under the provisions of the act of Congress approved February 25, 1882, been specially delegated by the Postmaster-General to perform this duty.

Prior to 1882 most of the payments on account of the postal service were made through postmasters in cash, the payments being subject, of course, to examination and audit in their accounts. There were consequently but a limited number of warrants drawn. Since 1882, however, the principle of paying postal indebtedness directly out of the Treasury or sub-treasuries, by warrants drawn thereon, has been considered a safer method of disbursement, and it has been therefore very greatly extended. The following table will show the number of warrants drawn on postal account and the amounts covered thereby since 1873:

Fiscal years.	No. of warrants.	Amount.	Fiscal years.	No. of warrants.	Amount.
1873	8,005	$9,709,737.85	1881	14,712	$13,748,297.25
1874	10,049	11,559,441.06	1882	38,851	19,072,353.51
1875	12,278	11,918,751.15	1883	45,278	20,243,516.32
1876	13,456	11,113,493.59	1884	70,408	22,012,487.96
1877	12,593	11,100,126.57	1885	74,659	24,641,848.23
1878	11,466	9,923,171.72	1886	72,999	24,308,814.69
1879	12,718	9,908,271.89	1887	82,503	25,525,706.96
1880	13,940	9,926,268.29	1888	92,570	26,571,263.06

Including transfer and collection drafts, the number of these papers signed during the past fiscal year amounts to about one hundred thousand. As this duty is performed almost wholly by the Third Assistant Postmaster-General, who can not, under the interpretation heretofore put upon the law, delegate it or any part of it to another, it will be seen that whenever payments are certified by the Auditor in very large numbers, which happens for about two months in every quarter, the time of the Third Assistant Postmaster-General must be almost exclusively taken up in going through this work. The effect is, of course, to prevent him from giving that close and intelligent attention to other branches of his duty which their great importance demands, and which, if not attended to, may at any time subject him to censure.

As an illustration of the demands upon my time made by this exacting work, I may mention that ever since my appointment to the office of Third Assistant Postmaster-General I have been desirous of giving to the affairs of the postage-stamp agency, and the other agencies for the distribution of stamped paper, an exhaustive personal examination; but up to this time, principally for the reason mentioned, I have not been able to carry this wish into effect. I feel that some relief from so continuous and confining a duty ought to be provided; and as the work involved in it is merely mechanical, or in other words does not admit of any examination into the correctness of the warrants to be signed, I can not see any serious objection to the delegation by the Third Assistant Postmaster-General of at least a part of the duty to some official subordinate, or at any rate to the authorization of the acting head of the office to sign these warrants whenever the Third Assistant Postmaster-General may be absent. Indeed, such a delegation of authority might be absolutely necessary in case of illness of the Third Assistant Postmaster-General, or in case of any protracted vacancy in the office.

In view of the above, I urgently recommend that Congress be requested to amend the law above referred to, so as to admit of the signing of warrants, when necessary, by any officer of the Department who may be acting as Third Assistant Postmaster-General, or who, in great pressure of business, may be specially assigned to this duty.

THE SPECIAL-DELIVERY SYSTEM.

The special-delivery system has met with a reasonable amount of patronage during the past fiscal year, and has, I am persuaded, been conducted by postmasters generally with increased efficiency. I present the following statement of the year's business:

For the whole country the Auditor reports that the amount of fees allowed in postmasters' accounts during the year for special delivery is $109,015.64. Allowing for cases where no fees were paid—as, for example, in cases of delivery by letter-carriers or other salaried employés of post-offices—these figures would indicate a total of about 1,434,400 special-delivery letters received during the year at all offices, the special-delivery stamps on which would amount to $143,440. Deducting from this the amount allowed postmasters, and there is left a total profit to the Government on the year's business of over $34,424.

At the letter-carrier offices, from which exact returns have been received, the business of the year will appear from the following statement (see table No. 16):

1. The total number of pieces of all matter received for special delivery at all the letter-carrier offices was 1,220,276, of which 899,494, or nearly 74 per cent., came through the mails from other than the offices of delivery, and 320,782, or 26 per cent., were of local origin.

2. The total number of pieces delivered by the regular messengers was 1,164,668, or over 95 per cent. of the whole, leaving 55,608, or less than 5 per cent., as the number delivered by letter-carriers or other salaried employés, including the few where delivery was impossible.

3. The value of the special-delivery stamps on the pieces received was $122,027.00. The amount of special-delivery stamps sold at the letter-carrier offices, ascertained from returns made by postmasters to this office, aggregates $92,149.20.

4. The average number of messengers employed during each month of the year was 768.

5. The average time consumed in the delivery of matter after reaching the respective offices of destination was 21 minutes.

Statistics in detail of the business at each of the letter-carrier offices in existence on the 1st of July, 1888, are given in Table No. 16 of this report.

I renew the recommendation made in my last annual report concerning the establishment of the pneumatic-tube system, or some equivalent underground means of rapid transit, for special-delivery messages at a few of the prominent cities of the country. I have received information in various ways during the year which convinces me that at least some investigation of the matter is desirable.

DIVISION OF POSTAGE-STAMPS, STAMPED ENVELOPES, AND POSTAL-CARDS.

During the year there were issued to postmasters, through the work of this division, of the various kinds and denominations of stamped paper 2,700,635,170 pieces, valued at $50,636,321.84, as against a total of 2,503,170,139 pieces, valued at $46,619,680 65, for the preceding year, an increase of 7.89 per cent. in number and 8.62 per cent. in value.

The several issues, by aggregates, are as follows:

	Number.	Value.
Ordinary adhesive postage-stamps	1,867,173,140	$36,293,183.00
Special delivery stamps	1,331,790	133,179.00
Newspaper and periodical stamps	3,464,418	1,588,425.00
Postage-due stamps	10,805,572	283,954.00
Stamped envelopes, plain	186,741,000	3,634,508.44
Stamped envelopes, printed request	196,635,250	4,242,611.90
Newspaper wrappers	50,260,500	584,804.50
Letter-sheet envelopes	2,427,000	55,821.00
Postal-cards	381,797,500	3,819,835.00
Total	2,700,635,170	50,636,321.84

Tables showing the separate issues of stamped paper will be found at the end of this report, marked Nos. 5, 6, and 7.

Adhesive stamps.—Of ordinary postage-stamps issued during the year there was an increase over the issues of the previous year of 120,187,620, or 6.88 per cent., in number, and of $2,519,027, or 7.46 per cent., in value; of special-delivery stamps, an increase of 85,850, or 6.89 per cent., in number, and $8,585, in value; of newspaper and periodical stamps, an increase of 432,823, or 14.28 per cent., in number, and $224,011.20, or 16.42 per cent., in value; of postage-due stamps, an increase of 2,559,038, or 31 per cent., in number, and $48,818, or 20.76 per cent., in value.

Stamped envelopes and newspaper wrappers.—Of ordinary stamped envelopes issued during the year there was an increase over the issues of the previous year of 22,439,550, or 13.66 per cent., in number, and $437,687.04, or 13.69 per cent., in value; of special-request envelopes, an increase of 25,521,250, or 14.92 per cent., in number, and $543,451.80, or 14.69 per cent., in value; of newspaper wrappers, an increase of 4,063,650, or 8.79 per cent., in number, and $47,940, or 8.93 per cent., in value.

Letter-sheet envelopes.—Of letter-sheet envelopes, of which only one denomination is issued, there has been a decrease as compared with the issue of the previous year of 2,683,000, or 5.25 per cent., in number, and $61,709 in value. This result, considered in connection with the issues of letter-sheet envelopes for the previous year, seems to indicate that there is no great popular demand for them. Out of a total of 7,536,500 letter-sheets issued to postmasters from the date of their introduction to June 30 last, 5,249,233 have been reported to be sold, leaving 2,287,267 as unsold stock still on hand.

Postal-cards.—Of postal-cards issued to postmasters during the year there was an increase over the issues of the previous year of 24,858,250, or 6.96 per cent., in number, and $248,830, or 6.97 per cent., in value. The number of postal-cards issued, as shown in the tables appended to this report (Nos. 5, 6, 7, and 10), do not include supplies sent to stock the distributing subagencies at Chicago and Saint Louis.

Past issues of postage-stamps, etc.—Tables showing the issues of stamped paper of the several kinds since the dates of their introduction—being a continuation of similar tables included in my last report—will be found hereto appended, marked Nos. 8, 9, and 10.

Registered-package, tag, official and dead-letter envelopes, etc.—In addition to the supplies above enumerated, there were issued for the use of the postal service 11,627,400 registered-package envelopes, 1,341,000 registered tag envelopes, 2,228,500 envelopes for returning dead letters, 31,671,250 official envelopes for postmasters and other postal officials, and 4,378 newspaper and periodical stub-books.

These figures show an increase of 625,450, or 5 per cent., in registered-package and tag envelopes; of 847,800, or 2.5 per cent., in dead-letter and official envelopes; and of 1,473,250, or 3 per cent., in all kinds, over the issues of the preceding year.

REQUISITIONS.

The following statement shows the number of requisitions from postmasters upon which the several kinds of supplies were furnished:

For ordinary postage-stamps 169,185
For postage-due stamps 14,906
For newspaper and periodical stamps... 10,600
For stamped envelopes, plain... 90,037
For stamped envelopes, request 133,452
For postal-cards 76,670

For registered-package envelopes.................................... 61,575
For tag envelopes.. 11,778
For official envelopes... 35,874
For newspaper and periodical receipt books......................... 2,681
For letter-sheet envelopes... 1,573

　　　Total 608,340

PARCELS.

The number of separate parcels in which these supplies were put up and forwarded to postmasters was as follows, viz:

Ordinary postage-stamps.. 174,017
Newspaper and periodical stamps.................................... 10,609
Postage-due stamps... 15,018
Stamped envelopes, plain... 128,486
Stamped envelopes, printed request 98,728
Postal-cards 85,006
Registered-package envelopes....................................... 61,805
Tag envelopes for registered parcels 90,920
Official envelopes 36,120
Newspaper and periodical receipt books 4,386
Letter sheets 1,583

　　　Total.. 706,678

REDEMPTION OF SPOILED STAMPS AND STAMPED ENVELOPES.

The value of spoiled, unserviceable, and unsalable stamps and stamped envelopes received from postmasters and redeemed during the past fiscal year is $135,264.38, for which credits in favor of the remitting postmasters were duly reported to the Auditor. The number of cases comprehended in these and similar credits since 1885 is shown in the following statement:

Year ending June 30—
1885 7,411
1886 13,952
1887 20,602
1888 11,367

Making due allowance for an abnormal increase during the years 1886 and 1887, due to the redemption of 3 and 6 cent stamps and stamped envelopes which by reason of the reduction in the letter rate of postage had become practically useless, this business has increased from 1885 to 1888 at the rate of about 15 per cent. a year. This is very much more than it should be. The ratio of increase in spoiled or unserviceable stamped paper redeemed from year to year, if nothing unusual occurs—such as a change in the rates of postage, for example —ought to diminish rather than increase. At any rate, it should not increase at a greater ratio than the general business of the whole postal service increases, which, on an average, is much less than 15 per cent. It is hoped that in future this work will show a falling off, rather than an increase.

POSTAGE ON SECOND-CLASS MATTER.

The weight of second-class matter sent in the mails during the fiscal year ended June 30, 1888, not including matter circulated free within the county of publication, was 143,662,918 pounds, or over 71,831 tons, and the amount of postage collected was $1,436,629.18. This is an increase of 13.8 per cent., as compared with the business of 1887.

The number of post-offices at which second-class matter was mailed is 7,463, an increase over the previous year of 463, or 6.6 per cent. The number of new publications admitted to the mails during the year is 3,076.

Collections were made during the year to the amount of $4,954.09, from publishers and news agents, for matter mailed at the second-class rate of postage which should have been charged at a higher rate. This is an increase of $1,831.72 over the amount collected for like irregularities during the preceding year.

Attention is invited to Table No. 11, appended to this report, showing the collections of second-class postage at all first-class post-offices during the year, in comparison with the collections of the previous year.

INCREASED USE OF STAMPED ENVELOPES.

It is quite gratifying to notice that the use of stamped envelopes, particularly special-request envelopes, is, so far as the issues to postmasters are an indication, increasing. The percentage of increase during the year of the former is 13.6 over the issue of the previous year; of special-request envelopes the percentage of increase is 14.9. These rates of increase are far beyond the average rates.

Upon the supposition that the prominence given to the subject of stamped envelopes in my last annual report has had something to do with this unusual increase in their issues, and in the hope of a still further increase, I think it not improper to extract from that report the following statement of some of the advantages attending the use of stamped envelopes over that of adhesive postage-stamps:

There are many advantages resulting from the use of stamped envelopes, both to the consumer and to the Department, which should always give them preference, wherever they can be conveniently used, over the adhesive stamps. In the hope that it will encourage the use of stamped envelopes, particularly the special-request envelopes, I avail myself of this opportunity to present a statement of some of the advantages referred to:

1. In case of the non-delivery of letters inclosed in special-request envelopes, they are returned direct to the senders. The long delay and uncertainty incident to the return of ordinary undelivered letters—to say nothing of the necessary invasion of their privacy in the Dead Letter Office—are thus avoided.

2. Where stamped envelopes are used to inclose letters there is never any detention of them for lack of postage, the reverse of which is the case where, when other envelopes are used, an insufficient amount of postage in adhesive stamps is applied. Detention of letters for this reason is not infrequent.

3. Stamped envelopes are very cheap. One of the kinds most commonly used—the No. 4½ first quality—is sold at the rate of only $1.80 a thousand, in addition to the postage, while the third quality of the same size is sold at $1 a thousand, or ten for a cent.

4. The quality of all the stamped envelopes is excellent. The first quality is of finely finished paper, the second quality is the same except that the paper is a trifle lighter, and the third quality—a manilla paper, of smooth finish and good writing surface—is of great strength and durability. They may therefore be sent long distances in the mails without injury.

5. In case stamped envelopes are spoiled by their owners in printing or misdirecting them, they are redeemable at the post-office, at their postage value, in postage-stamps or other envelopes. In similar cases where adhesive stamps are used, the stamps, to be of value, must be detached from the envelopes and regummed.

The advantages to the Government from the use of stamped envelopes are quite as important, comprehending the facility for handling and distributing in the mails the letters inclosed in them, owing to their similarity in size and shape, the fixation of the stamp in the most convenient place for canceling, the impossibility of their being cleansed of their canceling marks and used a second time, and, where special-request envelopes are used to inclose letters, the saving of labor in post-offices and the Dead-Letter Office in cases where the letters are found to be undeliverable.

The following table, giving the number of stamped newspaper wrap-pers, of plain stamped envelopes, and of special-request envelopes is-sued annually from 1877 to the close of the fiscal year 1888, shows the gradually increasing popularity of the request over the plain form of stamped envelope:

Year ended June 30.	Newspaper wrappers issued.	Plain envelopes issued.	Special-re-quest envel-opes issued.	Total.	Per cent. of request envelopes.
1877	21,901,250	84,285,700	64,374,500	170,631,450	37.72
1878	27,200,500	83,514,000	67,845,250	181,580,350	36.96
1879	29,697,000	80,806,700	67,058,258	177,561,950	37.77
1880	31,685,500	98,610,000	76,825,500	207,187,000	37.09
1881	35,751,750	100,291,300	85,024,000	227,067,050	37.44
1882	41,056,500	114,774,700	100,704,250	256,565,450	39.25
1883	44,436,250	114,251,950	100,578,250	259,266,450	38.79
1884	45,490,750	147,225,400	129,515,800	322,232,050	40.19
1885	43,582,500	142,372,150	136,796,750	322,751,400	42.38
1886	45,872,000	155,393,830	152,742,250	354,008,100	43.14
1887	46,205,850	161,301,450	171,104,000	381,011,300	44.84
1888	50,209,500	183,741,000	196,685,250	433,635,750	45.34

REDUCTION IN COST OF STAMPED ENVELOPES.

The present contract for supplying the Department with stamped envelopes and newspaper wrappers was made in 1886, the contract term beginning on the 1st of October of that year. The amount saved under this contract as compared with the prices of the previous con-tract, for the nine months ending June 30, 1887, was shown by my last annual report to be $119,488.77; the amount similarly saved during the fiscal year ending June 30, 1888, is $163,475.60, making a total saving since the beginning of the contract of $282,964.37. The items of saving during the past year are shown by the following table:

Quality.	Number of envelopes.	Cost under contract of—		Saving.	
		1882.	1886.	Amount.	Per cent.
First	328,048,600	$733,585.90	$594,823.09	$138,762.81	18.9
Second	12,554,100	25,738.94	18,683.06	7,055.88	27.4
Third	4,729,500	8,217.08	4,918.89	3,298.19	40.1
Circulars	33,487,500	45,927.41	37,098.33	8,829.08	19.2
Newspaper wrappers	50,269,500	49,760.80	44,237.16	5,520.64	11.1
Total	*429,089,200	863,236.13	699,760.53	163,475.60	18.9

* Four million five hundred and nine thousand and fifty envelopes, costing $8,240, were issued dur-ing the year, for which no corresponding style was issued under the contract of 1882.

STAMP, ENVELOPE, AND POSTAL-CARD AGENCIES.

The work at the several agencies for the distribution of postage-stamps, stamped envelopes, and postal-cards has been conducted satis-factorily throughout the year. Only three packages during the entire year were lost in transmission—two from the postage-stamp agency and one from the stamped-envelope agency—and these were of inconsider-able value.

The standing force of the several agencies during the year was as follows:

Postage-stamp agency:

One agent at a salary of..	$2,500
One clerk at a salary of..	1,500
Four clerks, each at a salary of $720	2,880
One laborer at a salary of..	680
Making a total for salaries of...	7,560

Stamped-envelope agency:[*]

One agent at a salary of..	2,500
One clerk at a salary of..	1,800
Seven clerks, each at a salary of $1,200	8,400
One clerk at a salary of..	1,000
Two laborers, at salaries amounting to.................................	1,500
Making a total for salaries of...	15,200

Postal-card agency:

One agent at a salary of..	2,500
One clerk at a salary of..	1,600
One clerk at a salary of..	1,400
Two clerks, each at a salary of $1,200	2,400
One clerk at a salary of..	1,000
One clerk at a salary of..	900
Making a total for salaries of...	9,800

The force of the postal-card agency was reduced on the 1st of July last one clerk of the $1,000 grade, so that the amount applicable to compensation of employés during the current fiscal year is $8,800. This decrease of force was made on account of the reduction of work at the agency caused by the establishment of a subagency for the distribution of cards at Saint Louis, Mo., allusion to which is hereinafter made.

It will be noticed in the above statements that most of the employés at the postage-stamp agency are given a smaller compensation than those at either of the other agencies—a discrimination that is unfair, and that I can attribute to no other cause than oversight in the preparation and submission of the annual estimates of appropriations. It is certainly not due to any lack of efficiency among the employés at the postage-stamp agency, or to any less requirement from them in the matter of careful, or continuous, or responsible work. They are justly entitled, in my opinion, to higher compensation than they now receive. I take pleasure, therefore, in recommending that at the end of the present fiscal year a small addition to the pay of five of these employés be made, sufficient to increase the annual compensation of each to $900 per annum. This will necessitate an enlargement of the appropriation for the expenses of the agency to the amount of about $1,000, provision for which I have ventured to make in the table of estimates hereto annexed.

SUBAGENCY FOR DISTRIBUTION OF POSTAL CARDS AT CHICAGO.

The subagency at Chicago, Ill., for the distribution of postal-cards, a detailed account of the establishment and advantages of which was given in my last annual report, has been operated during the year with

---

[*] The statement here given covers the present standing force of the agency, but it is not quite exact as to the entire force employed during the year. The total expenditure for employés, including the agent, and temporary clerks whose occasional employment is absolutely necessary, was $15,806.58.

entire satisfaction. It has not materially interfered with the usual business of the post-office, it has not caused any additional expense to the government, and, as has been heretofore demonstrated, it will eventually save a great deal of money. The number of cards sent to this subagency since its establishment and the issues to postmasters up to June 30, 1888, are shown in the following statement:

Number of cards shipped to subagency up to June 30, 1888 150,000,000
Number of cards issued by subagency to June 30, 1888 117,800,500

Number on hand July 1, 1888... 32,199,500

SUBAGENCY AT SAINT LOUIS, MO.

In addition to the subagency at Chicago, Ill., referred to above, there was established a short time prior to the close of the fiscal year ending June 30, 1888, an agency for a like purpose at Saint Louis, Mo. This agency is under the immediate direction of the postmaster, is situated in the post-office building, is governed by precisely the same rules as those which prevail at Chicago, and is, to a proportionate extent, attended with the same advantages to the postal service. Up to this time over 19,000,000 cards have been sent to this subagency, most of which have been distributed to postmasters. The field of distribution for the agency is comprehended within the States of Arkansas, Colorado, Kansas, Kentucky, Missouri, and Texas, and the Territories of Arizona, Indian, and New Mexico. The first issue of cards from the agency was made on an order sent from the Department on the 15th of June, 1888.

PROPOSED SUBAGENCY AT ATLANTA, GA.

The proposed establishment of a subagency at Atlanta, Ga., for the distribution of postal cards and stamped envelopes, allusion to which was made in my last annual report, has been found to be not yet expedient—first, because of the lack of room in the present post-office building necessary for the purposes of the agency ; and, secondly, because, without considerable expense, proper safeguards could not be given in this building to the storage of such a large amount of stamped paper as would be required to make the agency of any advantage to the service. When the post-office building at Atlanta is enlarged (an act authorizing which was, I understand, passed at the late session of Congress), there will be no impediment in the way of establishing the contemplated agency. The field of its distribution will probably comprise the States of Virginia, North and South Carolina, Georgia, Florida, Alabama, Mississippi, Louisiana, and Tennessee.

ENVELOPE-MACHINE AT CINCINNATI EXPOSITION.

Just prior to the close of the fiscal year arrangements were made by your direction with the stamped-envelope contractors, by which one of their most improved envelope-machines was erected at the Centennial Exposition of the Ohio Valley and Central States, which began on the 4th of July, 1888, at Cincinnati, Ohio, and by which it has since been operated as a part of the display made by the Post-Office Department under authority of the act of Congress approved May 28, 1888. Up to the present time, in the operation of this machine, 1,408,500 first-quality stamped envelopes of the No. 4½ size have been made, 850,000 of which have been sent to postmasters, and the remainder of which will be disposed of in the same way. These envelopes have all been made under the same safeguards as surround the manufacture of stamped envelopes at the regular manufactory at Hartford, Conn., and of course have been or will be paid for as they are issued upon the terms of manufacture prescribed by the standing contract with the Department. I understand that the operation of this machine has proved to be a very interesting feature of the postal exhibit at the exposition.

CONTRACT FOR LETTER-SHEET ENVELOPES.

I think it proper to call your special attention to the contract under which letter-sheet envelopes are now furnished to the Department, the following account of which contract was given in the report of this office for the year ending June 30, 1886:

Upon representations that there was a public demand for articles of this character, it was early determined by you to carry the law into operation under such conditions as should involve the Government in no risk or expense. A proposition satisfying these conditions was made by the United States Sealed Postal Card Company of New York, the owners, through letters-patent, of a device that seemed to possess more than ordinary merit. The proposition was accepted, and articles of contract were entered into under date of October 24, 1885. The contract provided that the contractor should bear all the cost connected with the manufacture and issue of the envelopes; the dies and plates to be used for printing the stamps were to be engraved and furnished at the expense of the contractor, subject to the approval of the Postmaster-General, and by such parties as should be satisfactory to him, and they were to become the absolute property of the United States as soon as made, and to be at all times subject to the order and control of the Department. All the work was to be done under the supervision of an agent of the Department, and subject to the approval of the Postmaster-General or his duly authorized representative. A bond, in the sum of $20,000, with approved sureties, was exacted to protect the interests of the Government and to insure the faithful performance of the contract. By a supplemental contract, executed on the 12th day of August, 1886, the contractor was also required to provide for the transportation of the envelopes to all post-offices where the Postmaster-General should decide to place them on sale, the carriers employed to do the work to be subject to the approval of the Postmaster-General. The safe delivery of the envelopes to the points of destination was guarantied by a bond of $50,000. The consideration to be paid the contractor was at the rate of $2.85 per 1,000 for such envelopes as should actually be sold, payments to be made quarterly upon reports from the postmasters through whose offices the sales were effected. In the event that the envelopes should prove unsalable, they were to be destroyed without compensation to the contractor. The right was reserved to the Postmaster-General to annul the contract at his discretion. The price fixed for the sale of the sheets was at the rate of $3 per 1,000, in addition to the postage, an increase of 15 cents over the cost of manufacture having been made to cover the clerical expenses of sale at the post-offices. In short, no chance was left through which the Government might become a loser through the effort to introduce the letter-sheet envelopes. On the contrary, all the contingencies of profit or loss are in favor of the Government.

Under this contract issues of letter-sheet envelopes were begun on the 18th of August, 1885, to a few of the larger post-offices; subsequently the issues were extended to all first and second class offices; and since June 20, 1887, every Presidential office the postmaster at which had made requisition for them has been supplied. Full information concerning these envelopes has been given to postmasters and the public, no unusual delay has occurred in supplying them as ordered, and every opportunity has been offered by the Department to have their utility and convenience thoroughly tested. The public, however, as may be inferred from the following statement of the quarterly sales of the envelopes since their introduction, does not seem to desire them:

Number sold during quarter ending—

September 30, 1886	1,122,457
December 31, 1886	1,185,976
March 31, 1887	751,057

Number sold during quarter ending—

June 30, 1887	421,563
September 30, 1887	475,436
December 31, 1887	536,630
March 31, 1888	401,586
June 30, 1888	354,528

From the above it is seen that there has been a declining demand for these letter-sheet envelopes ever since their introduction. I do not think this can be due to any radical fault in the envelope itself, for it is of very simple and convenient form, and it is made of fairly good paper. It can hardly be due either to the price of the envelopes, for they are sold at only $3 a thousand, in addition to the postage value, or at the rate of three for a cent, a not unreasonable price; nor can it be because the public has not had a full opportunity to purchase them, for, as before said, they have for more than a year past been obtainable at every place in the country of any considerable population. No matter, however, from what cause their unpopularity springs, it is plain that people do not want them to any considerable extent, so that I am inclined to doubt whether the Department will be justified in further continuing their issue.

If they could be comprehended in the regular contract for other stamped envelopes, thus enabling the Department to have the benefit of public competition in furnishing them, I should see no objection to the continuance of their issue, even though there might never be any great demand for them. But it must be remembered that the design of these letter sheets is patented, and that if they are to be furnished at all, they can only be obtained from the present contractors, giving them a monopoly—though it may be an unremunerative one—which is in opposition to the spirit of the law at least. Besides this, it is a labor of no small magnitude every quarter to ascertain the sales of these letter sheets at the several offices to which they have been supplied—a labor which is absolutely necessary under the contract.

I may add that if it be deemed desirable to terminate the contract it can be done without any difficulty or loss to the Government, the Postmaster-General having the right to end the contract at any time he may think it proper to do so, and to withdraw from post-offices all the sheets that may remain unsold. The following clause of the contract covers this latter point:

4. That the Postmaster-General shall have the right, whenever, in his opinion, there shall be an insufficient public demand for the letter-sheet envelopes herein provided for, to withdraw from sale all of them that may be outstanding in any of the post-offices to which they have been furnished, and to cancel them in any manner that he may deem proper; in which event, the contractor shall be allowed for the sheets so canceled only such amount as they may be sold for as waste paper.

NEW CONTRACT FOR REGISTERED PACKAGE AND OTHER OFFICIAL ENVELOPES.

During the year a new contract was entered into by the Department with the Plimpton Manufacturing Company and the Morgan Envelope Company, doing business together at Hartford, Conn., for the supply of registered package, tag, dead-letter, and official envelopes for the present fiscal year. A copy of this contract is hereto appended, marked No. 20. Its specifications and conditions are substantially the same as those of the contract for the preceding year, but the prices are somewhat higher, and there are two additional sizes of envelopes called for by it. The following statement exhibits the prices under the two contracts:

Kinds.	Per thousand under old contract.	Per thousand under present contract.	Kinds.	Per thousand under old contract.	Per thousand under present contract.
No. 1	$0.78	$0.82	No. 9	$3.25	$3.30
No. 2	.96	.95	No. 10	3.72	4.00
No. 3	1.22	1.30	No. 11	4.43	4.50
No. 4	1.70	1.80	No. 12*		4.75
No. 5	1.94	2.05	No. 13*		5.00
No. 6	2.28	2.35	No. 14*	4.75	5.50
No. 7	4.13	4.25	No. 15*	7.70	7.75
No. 8	2.12	2.25			

* Nos. 12 and 13 of the present contract are sizes not included in the former contract. Nos. 14 and 15 are what have heretofore been known as Nos. 12 and 13, respectively.

On the estimated number of the several kinds of envelopes to be required under and during the term of this new contract, the aggregate increase of cost to the Government over what would have been paid at the prices of the old contract will amount to about $3,500. This, it can be truly said, is an inconsiderable increase, which may have been due to higher prices prevailing generally in the envelope trade, to higher prices of paper, or to some other legitimate cause. It has been suspected, however, that the increase resulted from an understanding among leading envelope makers, or at least among those who were apparent competitors for the contract. If this suspicion be correct, the future contracts to be made by the Department for similar articles will probably be controlled by similar combinations of bidders—a contingency that may well excite some alarm. Whether it be correct or not, however, I am thoroughly persuaded that such a combination is in its nature sufficiently adverse to the interests of the Government to justify its prohibition by law. It is therefore a question that may without impropriety be brought to the attention of Congress.

MANUFACTURE OF STAMPED PAPER BY THE GOVERNMENT.

Before the present fiscal year expires the Department will be compelled to advertise for proposals for manufacturing adhesive postage-stamps and postal-cards for the contract term beginning July 1, 1889, and ending June 30, 1893. It is not inappropriate, therefore, at this time to consider whether the system under which the Department now procures its supplies of these articles, or, for that matter, of any kind of the stamped paper used in the postal service, is the best; or, to put the case to a plain issue, whether, instead of relying upon private enterprise to furnish these representatives of value, amounting now to the enormous sum of nearly $50,000,000 a year, it is not much better that the Government itself shall make them, under somewhat the same system, and by the same establishment—namely, the Bureau of Engraving and Printing of the Treasury Department—which now produces the bonds, Treasury notes, internal-revenue stamps, and all other kinds of public securities. For my part I do not hesitate to declare it to be my conviction, after having given the subject mature consideration, that the Government ought to take upon itself the manufacture of every kind of stamped paper used in the payment of postage—adhesive stamps, stamped envelopes, letter-sheets, and postal-cards—just as soon as the necessary arrangements to that end can be completed. The reasons upon which my conviction rests are these:

1. It is fair to presume that the Government can make its postage-stamps and postal-cards, and probably its stamped envelopes, as cheaply as they can be procured from private establishments. When the last

postage-stamp contract was about being let, the Bureau of Engraving and Printing submitted an estimate upon which it proposed to do the work at but a trifle more than the rates bid by the company to whom the contract was awarded; and it is not unlikely that the Bureau could have taken the work even at these rates without loss. Whether this be so or not, it is not perhaps unsafe to say that the Bureau would now undertake to do the work, if required by law to do so, upon a like condition to that which I think was prescribed when the work of printing Treasury notes was originally transferred to it—namely, that it shall not cost any more than the Government now pays for it.

2. As intimated in a previous paragraph of this report, in connection with the manufacture of registered package and other official envelopes, there is now—in this era of trusts and combinations—a perpetual danger of exorbitant prices for articles furnished the Government, through a secret understanding among bidders. In the matter of furnishing stamps and stamped envelopes, this is particularly to be apprehended, inasmuch as there are but few establishments throughout the whole country that have the facilities for doing the work, and the arrangement of a combination would be therefore comparatively easy. I do not think it necessary to discuss the question as to whether combinations among manufacturers or dealers to exact higher prices for their goods from the public is right or wrong; but I have no doubt, so far as concerns supplies to the Government, which is but the representative of all the people, that either there should be perfectly free and genuine competition amongst the persons who are invited to furnish such supplies, or the Government, as far as is practicable, should protect the public interests by itself making the goods. In the long run, economy and convenience would probably be subserved by the latter course.

3. The manufacture of public securities or representatives of value by private establishments is always, I think, attended with more risks to the public interests than where the work is done directly by the Government. In the latter case, at any rate, there would be no division of responsibility for correct management between the Government and any private institution. If it should be determined to have stamped paper made in this way, every detail of the work could be under the eyes of Government officers, selected with especial reference to their capacity and honesty; the system under which the work should be done would be the Government's own devising, to be prescribed, if thought necessary, by law; and the vast values produced, instead of being kept in private vaults and under private control, would be in the permanent custody of public officers, behind the locks and bars of the public Treasury. I speak of this matter, of course, abstractly, and without any special reference to the contractors who are now furnishing the Government with stamped paper: their reputation is deservedly high, and it gives me pleasure to state that their obligations under their contracts with the Department, so far as my observation extends, have been uniformly met with honorable exactness and promptitude.

In accordance with the foregoing views, I recommend that Congress be requested to insert some such provision as the following in the next act making appropriations for the postal service:

That upon the expiration of the present contracts for the manufacture of adhesive stamps and other stamped paper issued under the direction of the Post-Office Department, the work of making such stamped paper shall, if before that time considered advisable by the Postmaster-General and the Secretary of the Treasury, be performed by the Bureau of Engraving and Printing of the Treasury Department, under such regulations as the said officers shall jointly prescribe, the cost of the work to be relatively no greater than the cost under existing contracts, including the expenses of the several agencies: *Provided*, That the stamped paper hereinabove referred to shall always be supplied in sufficient quantities and kinds to meet the wants of the Post-Office Department, to be from time to time made known by the Postmaster-General or any proper official under him, and shall be turned over to that Department promptly as called for, and issued by its designated officials under methods of distribution similar to those now in operation. And payment for the stamped paper thus issued shall be made by warrants on the Treasurer of the United States in favor of the Bureau of Engraving and Printing, payable out of the appropriations now and to be hereafter made for the purpose, the bills to be rendered monthly by such Bureau, and to be regularly audited by the Sixth Auditor in the same manner as other bills for the postal service are audited: *And provided further*, That the Secretary of the Treasury is hereby authorized to provide whatever facilities are needed in the way of machinery, paper, gum, and other supplies to carry the above provision into effect.

I may add that in the furnishing of adhesive stamps and postal-cards there will probably be but little inconvenience in transferring the work of manufacture to the Bureau of Engraving and Printing, as this work is directly in the line of what is now done in that establishment. In the manufacture of stamped envelopes, there will be more or less of inconvenience and difficulty; but I do not doubt that if the necessary authority be given, the transfer can be made so as eventually, if not at once, to work to the advantage of the Department.

DIVISION OF REGISTRATION.

The fees collected on registry business during the year ending June 30, 1888, amounted to $1,125,154.40, which shows an increase of $90,477.60, or 8.7 per cent., over the amount collected during the previous year. Everything considered, this is a gratifying increase.

The classification and number of pieces of matter registered during the year are as follows:

Domestic letters		9,465,414
Domestic parcels		1,066,572
Total domestic		10,531,986
Foreign letters	674,607	
Foreign parcels	44,951	
Total foreign		719,558
Letters and parcels free—on Government business		2,425,625
Aggregate		13,677,169

Statistics of registry business in greater detail will be found in Tables Nos. 12, 13, 14, and 15.

LOSSES.

As appears by statistics kept by the chief post-office inspector, the total number of reported losses of registered matter during the fiscal year ending June 30, 1888, was 4,820, of which 3,978 were fully investigated and reports thereon made. From these reports the following results are ascertained:

Number of cases in which the complaints of loss were found to be groundless		2,700
Number of cases in which articles lost were recovered or made good to the owners		713
Total cases in which no loss was sustained		3,413
Number of cases where loss occurred through burning of post-offices and postal cars, wrecking of postal cars, and other unavoidable accidents	224	
Number of cases of loss in which the cause was not ascertained	128	
Number of cases of loss through fault or criminality of postal employés	213	
		565
Total investigated cases		3,978

If we assume that of the investigated cases, one-third will turn out to be actual losses (and this has been the estimated proportion for five years past), we have 845 cases of loss which occurred or were reported during the year, or one in every 15,334 domestic letters and parcels registered. This is a very marked improvement on the record of the preceding year—an improvement attributable to two general causes : one, the increased efficiency of postal officials, as shown by the fact that with nearly 9 per cent. more registration business than in the year preceding, the total number of reported losses was about 10 per cent. less ; another, the prompt and energetic methods that are now pursued in the investigation of irregularities, as shown by the fact that with 10 per cent. less cases of reported loss, there were 23 per cent. more recoveries. In connection with this latter fact, I take a great deal of pleasure in bearing testimony to the intelligent, zealous, and unremitting efforts of the chief post-office inspector and his corps of assistants in looking after business relating to the registry system. Their work is to a great extent brought directly to the attention of this office for review, or opinion, or for other action, giving me ample opportunity to see the thoroughness with which it is generally done, and justifying unstinted commendation therefor.

I respectfully refer to the report of the chief inspector for fuller details of the investigation of registration losses than are here given.

IMPROVED SYSTEM IN REGISTRY DIVISIONS OF LARGE POST-OFFICES.

The work of systematizing the office methods of large post-offices in registration business has been continued, and fifteen of the thirty leading cities have now been provided with special registration blanks and records, in the use of which they have been specially instructed. Some of these offices have had necessary architectural and mechanical changes introduced, thus giving them in all respects a consistent plan for working registered mail in masses, with checks and balances of such a character that innocent officials may be better protected and the field of investigation narrowed in all cases of presumed or actual loss. This work is to be continued until the registry divisions of all the more important offices are brought into practical uniformity.

· As showing how great a proportion of the immense registration values of the country is handled, at some stage of working, at the thirty most important registration centers, the statistics for the last fiscal year are given as follows :

At all post-offices (57,376) the number of pieces of matter registered was . 13,677,169
Out of this total, the thirty leading cities registered 2,769,149
They also delivered 7,432,320
And they handled in transit.. 6,438,307

MORE SPACE AND BETTER MECHANICAL ARRANGEMENTS NEEDED FOR REGISTRY DIVISIONS IN GOVERNMENT BUILDINGS.

The recommendation of the Postmaster-General in his last annual report, that the Department be provided with an architect thoroughly familiar with post-office requirements to design the interior space and fixtures of post-offices, either under construction or to be leased, applies with especial force to the handling of registered matter in large post-offices. The custody and manipulation of the immense values involved, and the different duties of recording, enveloping, sorting, pouching, checking, and receipting inward and outward with postal clerks, carriers, and the

public, so that all transfers may be made without objectionable contact and without danger, require much planning and forethought. In
but few of the new post-office buildings have the best results been obtained in the adaptation of the architect's plans to the prosecution of
post-office business, so that the work has frequently to be performed
with surroundings far from safe or convenient, requiring more clerical
labor and involving greater delays to the service and to the public.
With correct plans, based on a broad experience, far better provision
could have been made without added expense in the buildings. As far
as it has been possible with such means as I could command, I have
endeavored to remedy some of these defects by making and devising
designs for registry space and fixtures at different' post offices; but so
far as concerns new post-office buildings to be erected, to say nothing
of the large number of new buildings to be leased, it will be impossible
for me to give any such full attention to the plans, so far as they affect
the registry service, as an architect could give who had familiarized
himself with the needs of the different branches of post office work.

As showing the great importance of perfecting and improving the registry system from a Government standpoint, attention is called to Table
No. 15, appended to this report, which gives the Government values in
the registered mail for the fiscal year as aggregating over $911,000,000.

INTERNATIONAL REGISTERED POUCH EXCHANGES.

No extension of this system has been made during the year, although
some additional advantages have been gained through correspondence
in perfecting the system as it has heretofore existed.

Registration losses, which were formerly of frequent occurrence on
the New Brunswick border, have entirely ceased since the establishment last year of through pouches for registered matter exchanged with
that province and the province of Nova Scotia.

Correspondence with the Mexican post-office department for the establishment of through exchanges of registered pouches has been continued, but, owing to questions at issue with respect to the locks to be
used, no positive arrangements have so far been agreed upon; but as
the completion of another great section of the Mexican railway system
has effected a saving of twenty-four hours in the dispatch of registered
matter between the greater portion of the United States and the Mexican States, and as another great extension of railway, now about completed, will make a still further saving of time, it is manifest that some
satisfactory through-pouch system will at no distant day be established
between the two countries.

A through registered pouch exchange has been established between
New York and Eagle Pass, Tex., which up to the Mexican border gives
greater expedition and security to the valuable registered matter passing by the route already completed.   Soon, however, this exchange
will be abandoned for a more advantageous one with Laredo, Tex., to
connect with the new railway extension above alluded to.

IMPROVED FOREIGN REGISTERED-LETTER BILL.

In 1885 a memorandum was prepared for the use of the United States
representatives at the Universal Postal Union Convention at Lisbon,
advocating the adoption of a manifold bill with coupon receipt to super-
sede the less convenient standard form of foreign registered-letter bill
prescribed for countries of the Postal Union; but as the proposed im-

provement was not presented to the Postal Congress by our representatives, no action was taken on the subject.   An arrangement, however,
has been made with the postal administration of the United Kingdom
for the use of such a bill in transmitting registered matter to Great
Britain, under which perfectly satisfactory results have been realized.
Correspondence has been opened, too, during the year, with the postal
departments of five transpacific countries to secure the adoption of a
similar form of bill in dispatches of registered matter from San Francisco.   The Hawaiian postmaster-general has favorably responded; so
have the postmasters-general of New South Wales, Victoria, and
Queensland.

Among the great advantages gained by the use of this bill may be
named, more and better spaces for description of registered articles;
the saving of labor which the manifold process does; and the later
closing of registered bags.   The latter advantage is very important at
San Francisco, where the time between arrival of overland trains and
the sailing of steamers is very short.   The chief advantage of the manifold bill, however, is its coupon feature, securing a direct receipt for
all registered pieces from the postmaster at the foreign exchange office,
and thus enabling our own exchange postmasters to furnish positive
answers to inquiries concerning the safety of individual registered
pieces thus dispatched.

DOMESTIC EXCHANGES OF THROUGH REGISTERED MATTER.

The number of exchanges for registered matter in the domestic mails,
under the through-pouch, inner-sack, and brass-lock systems, the workings of which have several times been described in previous annual reports of this office, has increased considerably during the year.   The
following are the numbers of these exchanges in existence June 30, 1888:

Through registered-pouch exchanges 422
Inner-sack exchanges 410
Brass-lock exchanges... 222

    Total 1,054

DIVISION OF FILES, RECORDS, AND MAILS.

The total number of letters and parcels received, opened, and examined during the year in this division was 1,220,000, an increase of 34,740
over the number of the previous year.

Among these letters and parcels, 492 contained money, and 11,367
contained stamps, stamped envelopes, and postal-cards returned to the
Department by postmasters for redemption.   The number of registered
letters received was 13,142.

Of the letters received, 17,875 were briefed and recorded, and filed
after final action was taken upon them.   The number of letters written
and copied in the office, and mailed, was 30,163.   This does not include
circular letters and short communications with regard to routine matters not sufficiently important to require more formal action.

MAILING OF BOOKS AS SECOND-CLASS MATTER.

I respectfully renew the recommendation made in my last annual report, that books, falsely represented to be periodicals, and now going
through the mails at the pound rate of postage, be charged the same

as other third-class matter; and I repeat here the statements I made in support of this recommendation:

Under the law the conditions upon which a publication shall be admitted to the second class of mail matter are as follows:

1. It must regularly be issued at stated intervals, as frequently as four times a year, and bear a date of issue, and be numbered consecutively.

2. It must be issued from a known office of publication.

3. It must be formed of printed sheets, without board, cloth, leather, or other substantial binding, such as distinguish printed books for preservation from periodical publications.

4. It must be originated and published for the dissemination of information of a public character, or devoted to literature, the sciences, arts, or some special industry, and having a legitimate list of subscribers: *Provided, however,* That nothing herein contained shall be so construed as to admit to the second-class rate regular publications designed primarily for advertising purposes, or for free circulation, or for circulation at nominal rates. (Act of March 3, 1879, section 14, 20 Stats., 359.)

Under these conditions—which were intended to distinguish what are generally known as newspapers and periodicals from books—it may be demonstrated that almost anything in the nature of a book, provided it be without board, cloth, leather, or other substantial binding, may be brought within the privileges of the second-class rate of postage, and the object of the law accordingly defeated.

Let it be supposed, for example, that a publisher wishes to issue the works of Shakspeare in such a way as to secure the privilege of the pound rate of postage when the book is sent in the mails. Every one knows that such a publication is a book, no matter how it may be published; it is certainly not a newspaper or a periodical in the universally accepted sense of these words. The publisher, however, means to have it admitted as such, so he arranges to issue it monthly, giving each part a number and a date, places upon the title page a statement of the place of publication, and binds the parts in paper covers. He thus easily complies with three of the above-mentioned conditions. Next, he publishes a prospectus in which the publication is claimed to be devoted to literature, and he secures through his agents subscribers to the work, in this way complying with the fourth condition of the law.

It must not be supposed that this is merely a hypothetical case. Instances of this exact character have occurred. The postmaster at New York has called attention to the fact that a dictionary—nothing more nor less—issued in this way, was passed through the mails at the pound rate of postage. Not only this, but tons upon tons of books—called "Libraries" or "Series"—being purely and simply paper-covered books or reprints of books, having, probably, no list of subscribers other than booksellers, who buy them just as they buy other books—are every day going through the mails as second-class matter. And the number is constantly on the increase. Unless a check is put to this abuse there is no telling to what extent it will go. Already the mailing of matter of this character, together with pretended sample copies of publications, reference to which is made hereafter, has become so great that the intelligent and careful handling of it at many offices is impossible; so that there is little doubt that a great deal of matter unquestionably subject to a higher rate of postage is constantly smuggled through the mails as second-class matter.

I can not believe that the law was ever intended to allow this class of literature—some of it of very questionable value—to go through the mails at the rate of a cent a pound, while the Bible, the school-book—every other good book that reputable publishers issue under its true character—has to bear postage at the rate of 8 cents a pound.

As a remedy for the evil I suggest the passage by Congress of the following:

"That hereafter no publications shall be admitted to the mails as second-class matter that are but books or reprints of books, whether they be issued complete or in parts, whether they be bound or unbound, or whether they be sold by subscription or otherwise."

A bill embodying the above recommendation was during the last session of Congress introduced into the House of Representatives, and passed without serious objection, but it was not favorably acted on by the Senate.

SAMPLE COPIES OF NEWSPAPERS.

Elsewhere in this report I have urged, in case the letter rate of postage should be reduced, that other changes of postage be also made. Among these changes it was suggested that the rate of postage on sample copies of newspapers and periodicals, which are in the nature of advertisements or business circulars, should be charged the same rate of postage as third-class matter. The following extract from my last annual report may show good reasons for this suggestion:

Under the law as it now stands, publishers and news agents have the right to mail sample copies of their publications at the same rate as for copies to actual subscribers; and as no limit to this privilege is prescribed, postmasters are bound to receive, in every case where a publication is legitimate, any number of sample copies that may be offered. The result is that in many cases publications intended primarily for advertising purposes, and for free circulation, or circulation at nominal rates, originally presented under the guise of bona fide publications, and purporting to have legitimate lists of subscribers, obtain the privilege of admission to the second class, and almost immediately afterwards their publishers flood the mails with sample copies, or copies gratuitously issued. Many cases have come to my notice where there is reason to believe that immense editions of such publications are sent through the mails in accordance with previous guaranties to advertisers; that is to say, the publishers have not aimed to obtain subscribers, but simply to issue their periodicals as advertising sheets with a guaranty to their patrons of a large circulation. It is not an exaggeration to say that in some of these cases the sample copies are perhaps a hundred-fold the edition to bona fide subscribers.

It may be said that in all such cases as these the character of the publication is manifest, and that the postmaster has it in his power to make the facts known to the Department, so that the evil may be corrected. But the difficulty is, as before intimated, that the publication when admitted has all the characteristics of second-class matter, and being thus admitted, the publisher has the right to mail unlimited quantities of it; in the second place, it is not always possible for the postmaster or the Department, without a special investigation, to determine whether the publication is being issued gratuitously or not; and, thirdly, when the publication is discovered to be merely for advertising purposes, it is only after millions of copies have been circulated at the pound rate.

Aside from cases of this kind, it is perhaps a common thing for even legitimate periodicals to begin business with a merely nominal list of subscribers, depending mainly upon the continuous issue of specimen copies to build up a profitable subscription list.

It seems to me that the law was never intended to give to enterprises of the foregoing character the privileges they are now enjoying; and it never could have been foreseen that the very liberal rate of postage on legitimate newspapers and periodicals would be taken advantage of by the publishers of mere rubbish, to the injury of genuine publications.

A remedy for the wrong might, perhaps, be secured by limiting the number of sample copies to a reasonable proportion of the actual subscription list, and to require that every copy sent out as a sample copy should be marked as such under penalty; and never to permit the mailing, except at third-class rates, of even this proportion of sample copies without permission previously obtained from the Department.

DEFECTIVE METHOD OF PAYING NEWSPAPER POSTAGE.

The experience of another year has served to deepen my conviction that the method now in operation under which publishers pay postage on second-class matter is improper, and ought to be changed. I therefore think it advisable to renew my recommendation on this subject, as shown in the following extract from my last annual report:

One of the defects referred to lies in the peculiar method of paying and receiving postage on this class of matter. Instead of being required to place upon the matter mailed postage-stamps in appropriate amounts to pay the postage, as is the rule with all other classes of mail matter, publishers are permitted to bring their publications in bulk to the post-office, and there pay the necessary amount of postage in money, the postmaster giving a receipt therefor, made out on a blank taken from a book of forms kept for the purpose, and attaching to the retained stub of the receipt a corresponding amount of postage-stamps from the stock in his hands, which stamps he is expected to cancel. Quarterly reports of the amounts thus collected are required to be made to the Department, accompanied with the stubs containing the canceled stamps.

Under such a system it seems to me that fraud against the Government is comparatively easy. If, for example, the postmaster should fail to receipt to the publisher when matter is mailed (and this has frequently occurred, whether by design or not is immaterial) it is next to impossible to ascertain whether the necessary stamps have been attached to the stub of the receipt book or not; and so long as the postmaster may attach in any such case as small an amount of stamps as may suit his purposes, he may, of course, retain the surplus in money without fear of detection. The chance of discovering such a fraud, if the publisher should lose his receipt when one is given—another thing of common occurrence—is equally remote. In passing, it may be remarked that the failure of the publisher to take a receipt, or his loss of it after he gets it, should not excite surprise; for, as the law requires postage to be paid at the time of mailing—or, in other words, as the postmaster is forbidden to give credit for postage—the actual mailing of the matter is prima facie evidence of the payment of the postage. So that receipts, except as mere memorandums of mailing, are valueless, and publishers as a rule are probably careless about demanding or retaining them. But even if the postmaster should give the receipt in every case, and the publisher should safely keep it, the Department still may be easily defrauded, for, except in cases where postmasters are suspected of fraud and special investigations are thereupon made, the receipts are never called in and examined; indeed the verification of postmasters' returns by a comparison with these receipts would, owing to the immense number of them, be impracticable without a large increase of the force of the Department; so that in actual practice, the postmaster's return, if it agrees with the amount of stamps found attached to the accompanying stubs, is accepted unquestioningly, without knowing whether it is fraudulent or not.

A case of fraud of this character which occurred about a year ago in the Chicago post-office, where a subordinate of the postmaster was by chance found to have been for years in the habit of retaining large sums of money derived from second-class postage—the returns made to the Department not giving the slightest indication of the fraud—is an illustration of how easily the thing may be done. Besides these opportunities for fraud, there is the further one for collusion with the publisher, in which event nothing can be done to prevent or detect the cheat, unless either the publisher or the postmaster should voluntarily confess it. The opportunity is still better where the postmaster, as is sometimes the case, is also the publisher. I do not mean to be understood as intimating that frauds of this character exist; my purpose is simply to show that the system admits of their ready perpetration.

Besides the above objections to the system, there is the additional one that, from the absence of stamps on matter mailed as second-class, the fact of prepayment of the postage is in very many cases of necessity a matter of doubt to the delivering postmaster. There being on the matter no evidence whatever of prepayment, not even at times a printed statement that the publication has been regularly entered as second-class matter, the delivering postmaster can not, in any case where his doubts may be excited, protect the Government against wrong without delaying the matter and making special inquiry of the Department or the sending postmaster. In the great majority of cases he must simply take it for granted that everything is right and deliver the matter without inquiry. I have reason to believe that a great deal of this matter goes through the mails either without prepayment at all or paid at a lower rate of postage than is required by the law and the regulations. In fact, the quantity of second-class matter that, by reason of the low rate of postage, is now going through the mails is so great that proper examination, even at the mailing offices, is often impossible.

Again, this peculiar system of paying postage necessitates the examination of postmasters' books and returns at the Department, a corps of clerks being usually kept busy on this work. Every quarter tons of the stubs, containing the canceled newspaper stamps, are sent to the Department for comparison with postmasters' reports, and although this work is but of small importance as a means of detecting fraud, it is of value in correcting mistakes that now very frequently occur, but which would not occur under a different system.

It is hardly necessary to state, that if publishers were required to purchase stamps of suitable denominations, running, say, from a minimum value of one-eighth of a cent to any required value above that, or what, perhaps, would be better, to use stamped bands or labels so made that their use would necessitate their cancellation, and to attach such stamps or bands to the matter mailed, in every instance of separate address, similarly to what is done with all other classes of matter, all opportunity for fraud or abuse, as above indicated, and all cumbrous and unnecessary machinery in the collection of postage and the examination of returns, would disappear.

Without being prepared at this time to go into particulars, I think it only necessary to say that I am strongly inclined to believe that if the necessary authority were given by an amendment of the present law, a new system embodying such a change could be devised which would not materially interfere with the convenience of publishers—except to require them to perform labor that is properly their own—and without interfering with the present rate of newspaper and periodical postage, except, perhaps, where single copies of papers might be mailed, in which event a slight excess over an exact fraction of the pound rate would be necessary.

A similar case of defalcation to that which is referred to in the above extract, as having occurred at Chicago, was discovered during the past year at the post-office in this city, the delinquent being a trusted official who was able to carry on his thieving for years without giving rise to suspicion. The amount lost to the Government through him is not positively known, but is probably $4,000 or $5,000. The import-ance of the case, however, is not so much in the amount of money lost as in the fact that the system will permit of just the same thing any-where else.

CONTRAST WITH THE POSTAL SERVICE OF OTHER NATIONS.

Dating from the adoption of the Federal Constitution, the postal serv-ice of the United States is now in the one-hundredth year of its exist-ence, a peculiarly appropriate time, it would seem, for some one to give an account of its humble beginning and wonderful growth. With this idea, I have several times intended to prepare a historical sketch of the Department as a part of the report of this office; but I regret to say that so far I have not been able to see my way clear to the satisfactory performance of such a task. I have, however, collected some interest-ing statistics showing in tabular form the growth of several branches of the postal service, being mainly an extension of a similar table pre-pared some years ago by a very intelligent officer of the Department, and I have had made an abstract, as nearly complete as the time at my disposal would allow, of the most important of existing and former laws relating to the postal service, going back even to colonial times, which two papers I have ventured to add to this report as a part of the ap-pendix (see papers Nos. 18 and 19).

I have also been able to gather some interesting statistics of the postal business of several countries of the Universal Postal Union, which af-ford such an excellent means of contrasting the service of the United States with that of other great nations that I think it entirely proper to introduce them here. From these figures it will be seen that in nearly every item of its vast postal business the United States of America, though commencing its career just a century ago with but seventy-five post-offices and a gross annual postal revenue scarcely more than double the daily receipts now of only one of its great offices, stands conspicuously ahead of every other nation in the world. These statistics are, I believe, the latest that are obtainable, those for Great Britain being mostly taken from the report of the postmaster-general for the year ending March 31, 1888, and those for Germany and France from the last tabulation pub-lished by the International Postal Bureau at Berne, Switzerland. Those which give the number of letters and other pieces of matter transmitted in the mails of the United States are of especial interest, as they are the first accurate statistics of that character ever published.

Beginning with the number of post-offices in operation, we find that the United States stands first among the nations. The figures, in con-trast with those for Germany, Great Britain, and France, the three next great countries of the Postal Union, are as follows:

United States, June 30, 1888 57,376
Germany, December 31, 1886 18,688
Great Britain, March 31, 1888 17,587
France, December 31, 1886 7,296

Excluding Germany, the United States has about as many post-offices as all the countries of Europe combined, and it is adding to the num-ber at the rate of over 2,000 a year. In this feature of its administra-tion it manifests a liberality beyond that of any other great nation; for while the establishment of every new office adds immediately to the cost of the service, the receipts are not correspondingly increased. In fact, the question of revenue in the establishment of new offices is never taken into consideration, the aim of the administration being to give to every community as soon as possible the means of postal intercourse with other places.   The liberality of its policy in this respect is forcibly illustrated by contrasting it with that of Russia, which, with more than twice the extent of territory and nearly double the population of the United States, has not one-tenth the number of post-offices.

In gross postal revenue the United States stands first, also, among nations, as is shown by the following statement:

United States—year ending June 30, 1888................................ $52,695,176.79
Germany*—year ending March 31, 1888 (the amount being ascertained
  by adding 5 per cent. to the amount reported by the International
  Bureau for the preceding year).. 45,194,357.00
Great Britain*—year ending March 31, 1888.......................... 42,362,346.00
France*—year ending December 31, 1887 (the amount being ascer-
  tained by adding 5 per cent. to the amount reported by the Interna-
  tional Bureau for the preceding year).................................... 28,779,301.00

Allowing for a reasonable increase of receipts in Germany, Great Britain, and France (5 per cent. is above their average annual increase), so that their business may be brought down to June 30, 1888, will still leave the United States greatly in the lead ; and this, too, be it remembered, notwithstanding its rates of postage, from which the bulk of all postal revenue is derived, are, everything considered, lower than those of the other countries.

In the total length of mail routes the United States is vastly ahead of all other countries.   The following are the respective lengths, those for Great Britain being ascertained by adding 10 per cent. to an estimate furnished in 1886 by the secretary of the General Post-Office at London:

Routes.	United States (year ending June 30, 1888).	Germany (year ending Dec. 31, 1886).	Great Britain (year ending Mar. 21, 1888).	France (year ending Dec. 31, 1886).
	Miles.	Miles.	Miles.	Miles.
Railroad......................	143,713	23,066	19,525	26,957
Steamboat..................	11,058	1,372	2,750	198
All other	*249,205	61,447	22,000	44,179
Total	403,976	85,885	44,275	65,334

* Not including carrier routes in cities.

The length of mail routes of all kinds in the United States probably now exceeds that of the whole of Europe, omitting France and Russia.

In the mileage of mail service annually performed the United States is immeasurably ahead of all other nations, the contrast with the three countries above named being shown in the following figures :

Kind of service.	United States (year ending June 30, 1888).	Germany (year ending Dec. 31, 1886).	Great Britain† (year ending Mar. 31, 1888).	France (year ending Dec. 31, 1886).*
	Miles.	Miles.	Miles.	Miles
Railroad service performed......	185,485,783	80,863,160	35,619,584	56,999,566
Steamboat service performed	3,216,036	655,818	1,100,000	138,802
All other service performed	‡98,549,226	50,492,717	15,950,000	33,842,435
Total................	287,251,045	132,011,695	52,669,584	90,980,803

*In giving the revenue of Great Britain and France the income from the telegraph service is omitted; in the case of Germany the income from the telegraphs is also left out, together with that arising from the service of couriers and the transportation of travelers—none of these branches of business being comprehended in the postal system of the United States.
† The amounts for Great Britain are ascertained by adding 10 per cent. to an estimate furnished two years ago by the secretary of the general post-office in London.
‡ Not including carrier service in cities.

Coming now to what is the best criterion of the magnitude of the postal service proper—the number of pieces of matter transmitted in the mails—we find that the United States is greatly in advance of the other nations. The following are the statistics :

United States (year ending June 30, 1888) :

Letters mailed, not including free letters on Government business.	1,769,800,000
Postal-cards mailed	370,300,000
Newspapers and periodicals mailed (second-class matter)	1,063,100,000
Pieces of third and fourth class matter mailed (books, circulars, parcels of merchandise, etc.)	372,900,000
Total	3,576,100,000

(The calculations upon which the above statistics are obtained will be found in paper No. 17, appended to this report.)

Great Britain (year ending March 31, 1888) :

Letters delivered, not including free letters on Government business	1,512,200,000
Postal-cards delivered	188,800,000
Book packets and circulars delivered	389,500,000
Newspapers delivered	152,300,000
Parcels delivered	36,732,000
Total	2,279,532,000

Germany (year ending December 31, 1886) :

Letters, not including free letters on Government business	720,497,240
Postal-cards	245,282,540
Newspapers and periodicals sent to subscribers	523,873,340
Miscellaneous articles of printed matter	210,108,220
Samples of merchandise and parcels	116,305,050
Total	1,816,066,390

France (year ending December 31, 1886) :

Letters, not including free letters on Government business	591,451,811
Postal-cards	35,923,379
Newspapers and periodicals sent to subscribers	92,957,793
Miscellaneous articles of printed matter	713,962,439
Samples of merchandise and parcels	28,953,858
Total	1,463,249,280

The average number of pieces of mail matter to every inhabitant of the several countries named, taking the last census as the basis of the calculation, is now about as follows :

United States	pieces per capita..	71
Great Britain	do....	61
Germany	do....	41
France	do....	37

As may be inferred from the foregoing, the postal expenditure of the United States is larger than that of any other country, a fact which should not, however, carry with it the idea that the postal service here is otherwise than economically conducted. The gross amount of expenditures of each of the several nations before named is as follows :

United States, year ending June 30, 1888	$55,795,357.84
Germany, year ending March 31, 1888 (amount being ascertained by adding 5 per cent. to the amount reported by the International Bureau at Berne for the preceding year)	*44,348,939.00
Great Britain, year ending March 31, 1888	†28,876,935.00
France, year ending December 31, 1887 (amount being ascertained by adding 5 per cent. to amount reported by the International Bureau for the preceding year)	*28,327,666.00

* These amounts take in the cost of the telegraph service and all other expenses of the postal service.
† This amount does not include expenses of the telegraph service.

In the cheapness of postage on letters, cards, and newspapers, the United States is also at the head of the world. The following statement will demonstrate this:

United States—
    Rate on letters............................... 2 cents an ounce.
    Rate on newspapers........................... 1 cent a pound.
    Rate on postal-cards........ .... 1 cent each.
Great Britain *—
    Rate on letters............................... 2 cents an ounce.
    Rate on newspapers........................... 1 cent each.
    Rate on postal-cards.............. .... 1 cent each.
Germany—
    Rate on letters............................... 2½ cents a half ounce.
    Rate on newspapers........................... ¼ cent each (not over 1¾ ounces).
    Rate-on postal cards........ .... 1¼ cent each.
France—
    Rate on letters............................... 3 cents a half ounce.
    Rate on newspapers........................... ½ cent per copy.
    Rate on postal cards .... 2 cents each.

ONE-CENT RATE OF POSTAGE.

As some attempt has already been made in Congress to reduce the letter rate of postage to one cent an ounce—a bill to that end having been referred to the Senate Committee on Post-Offices and Post-Roads on the 11th of October of this year—it is not unlikely that this important question will be further agitated during the coming session of Congress, and, it may be, pressed to an affirmative decision. If this action should hereafter appear to be impending (I express no opinion as to the present expediency of such a reduction), I respectfully urge that the following general schedule of postage rates be recommended to Congress:

1. What is now called the letter rate to be 1 cent for every 2 ounces, instead of 1 cent for every ounce as proposed.

2. The newspaper and periodical rate to be the same as now—1 cent a pound.

3. What is called the third-class rate to be the same as now—1 cent for every 2 ounces.

4. What is called the fourth-class rate to be 1 cent for every 2 ounces, instead of 1 cent an ounce as at present.

5. The rate on transient newspapers to be 1 cent for every 2 ounces, instead of 1 cent for every 4 ounces as at present.

6. All serial paper-covered books now going through the mails under the guise of periodicals to be charged 1 cent for every 2 ounces.

7. All sample copies of newspapers and periodicals to be charged 1 cent for every 2 ounces.

Concerning the first of these suggestions, it may be said that an increase merely in the unit of weight of letters, from 1 ounce to 2 ounces, would not materially add to the weight of the mails; that is to say, the average weight of letters, which is now less than half an ounce, would not be perceptibly increased by increasing the permissible weight for a single rate. Consequently, the postal revenue would not be materially affected by such a change.

As to the suggested change in the unit of weight of fourth-class matter from one ounce to two ounces, I apprehend that few persons will see any reasonable ground for objecting to it. The present discrimination against fourth-class matter is not just in itself; or, in other words, it is

---

* For letters above one ounce in weight, the rates of postage in Great Britain are fixed upon a descending scale from the unit rate here given.

not just that a discrimination should be made as between this and the third class of matter; and if so radical a change in the rates of postage as a reduction from two cents to one cent on letters is to be made, surely the postal revenue can stand the removal of the distinction in postage now made between books and merchandise.

So with regard to the change suggested in the rate of postage on transient newspapers. No one can see any just reason for admitting this class of printed matter to the mails at a less rate than that for books or merchandise; and as no hardship would be imposed on anybody by reducing the standard of weight from four to two ounces, that should be done at least for the sake of uniformity.

As to books that are falsely claimed to be periodicals, and as to sample copies of newspapers and periodicals now burdening the mails at the pound rate of postage (most of them being in reality not genuine sample copies), I refer to previous paragraphs in this report for reasons why the rate of postage on them should be increased.

If the above suggestions were adopted, we should have but two classes of mail matter—the first class consisting of letters and miscellaneous matter, at the rate of a cent for two ounces, and the second class consisting of newspapers and periodicals sent by publishers and news agents, at the rate of a cent a pound. Except as to second-class matter, all the present distinctions—many of them unnecessary and unreasonable—between the several kinds of mail matter, in the way of postage, nature of the matter, manner of wrapping, permissible writing, etc., would be wiped out; and with them would be removed the temptation to petty fraud, now so often yielded to by people using the mails, in concealing written matter in matter of a lower class; the annoyance that so often occurs from the detention of matter for insufficient postage; the public dissatisfaction growing out of strictness in rulings as to classification of matter, and to differences in such rulings; the necessity for requiring that any matter should be subject to examination; and the liability of miscarriage to letters which now so often occurs by the accidental concealment of them in unsealed envelopes or parcels of other matter.

ABUSE OF THE FRANKING PRIVILEGE.

Within the past two or three months a number of cases have been brought to my attention involving gross abuse of the franking privilege, in one instance the frank of a member of Congress having been forged upon envelopes bearing unfrankable matter, and in the other cases the genuine franks of Senators and members of Congress having been used by some unknown persons to convey through the mails political pamphlets and other campaign literature in no sense entitled to free transmission; and the circumstances surrounding these cases rather justify the belief that large quantities of unfrankable matter have been thus unlawfully transmitted. There is no reason for believing that any of the gentlemen whose franks have been so misused were guilty of any impropriety in the matter themselves; the wrong in most of the cases has resulted from the delegation of authority to frank, the persons so delegated either directly abusing it or by carelessness permitting others to do so. It would not seem of much importance, however, to ascertain just how the thing occurred. The law has been grossly violated, the postal revenue to more or less extent has been invaded, and the same or other parties may again at any time pursue the practice.

The exercise of the franking privilege has, throughout the entire history of the Department, been attended with constant abuse; indeed, this seems to be almost inseparable from the granting of the privilege. Under the present law, at any rate, offenses against it are so easy of perpetration that they are almost invited; for, in the first place, the delegation of authority to frank may be to as many persons as may be deemed necessary by the franking official, who is not personally responsible for the wrongful exercise of such authority; in the second place, the frank may be put on the matter to be mailed with a hand-stamp, in the custody of which the parties employed to use it may be careless, or which anybody may easily imitate; in the third place, no postmaster can possibly distinguish between a genuine and a forged frank; and finally, even if the abuse is manifest, it is almost impossible to ascertain the perpetrator, and even if he could be discovered there is, strange to say, no punishment prescribed by statute for the offense.

It seems to me that the principle of franking matter by the signature, either written or stamped, of public officials is wrong and ought to be discontinued. I am clearly of the opinion that Senators and Members of Congress should not be required to pay postage on official matter sent by them to their constituents or others. Indeed, I am satisfied that much of their private correspondence partakes somewhat of the nature of public business, and therefore should not be a source of expense to them for postage. But instead of permitting such matter to go through the mails free under the signature of the official who sends it, I think it would be far better to have the postage paid, as in the case of private matter, by the attachment of stamps, which could be bought by the official out of a regular allowance to be made to him for the purpose. I accordingly respectfully recommend that Congress be urged to abolish the franking privilege so far as it applies to Members and Senators, and that a regular yearly allowance for the purchase of postage-stamps be made to them instead. By such a plan every Senator and Member would be placed upon an exact equality. No one could make use of the mails beyond his own allowance unless he paid therefor out of his own pocket; no misuse of the allowance could possibly occur any more than occurs in using the allowance now made to Senators and Members for stationery; no unauthorized persons could make use of the mails to carry free unofficial matter as is now done; and the postal service would get a considerable addition to its revenue for service which is now entirely unpaid for.

The franking privilege as it is now enjoyed by agricultural colleges and agricultural experiment stations should, I think, be also abolished; but as the free use of the mails by these institutions is an entirely proper thing, they might be furnished through the Department of Agriculture with such free penalty-envelopes and labels as would be necessary for their use.

ORGANIZATION.

' The organization of this office is as follows:

Office proper of Third Assistant Postmaster-General:

Third Assistant Postmaster-General	1
Chief clerk	1
Clerks	2
Assistant messenger	1
Finance division:	
Chief of division	1
Clerks	17

Stamp division :
    Chief of division 1
    Clerks 45
    Assistant messenger.. 1
    Laborers... 6
Registration division:
    Clerks... 7
Division of files and mails :
    Clerks... 5

        Total... 88

The classification of the above force is as follows :

Third Assistant Postmaster-General... 1
Chief clerk... 1
Chiefs of division 2
Clerks of class 4 4
Clerks of class 3... 16
Clerks of class 2... 21
Clerks of class 1... 26
Clerks of class $1,000 7
Clerks of class $900.. 2
Assistant messengers 2
Laborers 6

        Total... 88

EFFICIENCY OF OFFICE FORCE.

It is hardly necessary to say, in conclusion, that the work of the office, in all its branches, during the year, has been promptly and satisfactorily performed. No errors of any moment have been made, no failure to fully meet the requirements of the service has occurred, and I have had no occasion at any time to censure a single employé for official or personal misbehavior. On the contrary, I have had cause to congratulate myself and the Department upon the uniform good conduct and efficiency of the entire force—a fact which I take great pleasure in bringing to your notice.

Yours, very respectfully,

                                        H. R. HARRIS,
                            Third Assistant Postmaster-General.
Hon. DON M. DICKINSON,
        Postmaster-General.

No. 1.—*Explanation of estimates of appropriations for the office of the Third Assistant Postmaster-General for the fiscal year ending June 30, 1890.*

                            POST-OFFICE DEPARTMENT,
            OFFICE OF THIRD ASSISTANT POSTMASTER-GENERAL,
                            Washington, D. C., November 9, 1888.

SIR: I have the honor to submit the following estimates of appropriations for the service of this office for the fiscal year ending June 30, 1890 :

1. For manufacture of adhesive postage and special-delivery stamps $155,874
   For pay of agent and assistants to distribute stamps, and expenses of agency 9,000
2. For manufacture of stamped envelopes, newspaper wrappers, and letter-sheets 852,351
3. For pay of agents and assistants to distribute stamped envelopes, newspaper wrappers, and letter-sheets, and expenses of agency................................... 16,000
5. For manufacture of postal-cards 228,781
6. For pay of agent and assistants to distribute postal-cards, and expenses of agency 7,800
7. For registered-package, tag, official, and dead-letter envelopes 109,745
8. For ship, steam-boat, and way letters... 2,500
9. For engraving, printing, and binding drafts and warrants.............................. 3,000
10. For miscellaneous items 1,000

    Total.. 1,386,051

The following statements will explain, the manner in which the above amounts are obtained:

ADHESIVE POSTAGE-STAMPS.

It is assumed that the ratio of increase in expenditure for the manufacture of adhesive stamps during the current over the past fiscal year will be 8 per cent., which is somewhat less than the increase of postal revenue for the past over the preceding year. It is further assumed that for the year ending June 30, 1890, the ratio of increase over the current year will be 9 per cent., which may be a little more than the ratio of increase in the revenue, but which it is deemed prudent to allow. Upon this basis the amount of appropriation required is shown by the following calculation:

Expenditure for stamps issued during the fiscal year ending June 30, 1888	$132,411.00
Add 8 per cent. for increase	10,592.88
Gives estimated amount of expenditure for fiscal year ending June 30, 1889	143,003.88
Add 9 per cent for increase	12,870.35
Gives estimated cost for the fiscal year ending June 30, 1890	155,874.23

The contract now in force for the manufacture of adhesive stamps will expire on the 30th of June, 1889; but although the rates fixed by it are very low, it is not expected that they will be increased under a new contract.

The current appropriation for adhesive stamps is $144,148.

STAMPED ENVELOPES, NEWSPAPER WRAPPERS, AND LETTER SHEETS.

Owing to the fact that greater fluctuations in the issues of stamped envelopes are more likely than in the case of adhesive stamps, a higher ratio of increase is taken as the basis of the estimate for these articles—9 per cent. being thought reasonable for the current over the past fiscal year, and 10 per cent. for the next over the current year. The amount of the appropriation required is therefore as follows:

Cost of stamped envelopes, newspaper wrappers, and letter sheets issued during the fiscal year ending June 30, 1888	$710,884.93
Add 9 per cent. for increase	63,979.64
Gives estimated cost for the year ending June 30, 1889	774,864.57
Add 10 per cent. for increase	77,486.45
Gives estimated cost for the fiscal year ending June 30, 1890	852,351.02

As the present contract for stamped envelopes will not expire until September 30, 1890, no change of prices will occur until then.

The appropriation for the present year is $756,687.

POSTAL CARDS.

As the ratio of increase in the issues of postal-cards for the past year has not been as great as that for either adhesive stamps or stamped envelopes, it is not thought necessary to take so high a ratio as the basis for the next appropriation. Seven per cent. increase for the current over the past, and the same for the next over the current year, is probably sufficient. At this rate the appropriation needed will be as follows:

Cost of postal-cards issued to postmasters and subagencies for the fiscal year ending June 30, 1888	$199,826.50
Add 7 per cent. for increase	13,987.85
Gives estimated sum required for year ending June 30, 1889	213,814.35
Add 7 per cent. for increase as before..	14,967.00
Gives estimated amount for year ending June 30, 1890	228,781.35

The present contract for the manufacture of postal-cards will expire on the 30th of June, 1889; but it is not likely that the charges for manufacture will be increased under a new contract.

The appropriation for the present fiscal year is $212,455.

REGISTERED PACKAGE, TAG, OFFICIAL, AND DEAD-LETTER ENVELOPES.

The cost of the registered package, tag, official, and dead-letter envelopes, issued during the past year, was $87,488.60, or $2,475.11 more than for the previous fiscal year. A much greater increase may be expected for the current and the next fiscal year, both by reason of an increase of prices for the envelopes as shown by the new contract now in force, which will very likely be greater under the next contract, and by a probable increase in the number of envelopes to be issued. It is hardly thought safe to estimate upon a lower basis of increase than 12 per cent. for each year.

The following calculation shows the amount required upon this basis:

Amount of expenditure for the fiscal year ending June 30, 1888	$87,488.60
Add 12 per cent. for increase	10,498.63
Gives amount required for current fiscal year	97,987.23
Add 12 per cent. for increase as before	11,758.47
Gives amount required for year ending June 30, 1890	109,745.70

The present appropriation is $102,865.

The contract for the above-described envelopes is made yearly. The present contract will expire June 30, 1889.

POSTAGE-STAMP, STAMPED-ENVELOPE, AND POSTAL-CARD AGENCIES.

For conducting the business of the several agencies, it is estimated that the following sums will be required, viz:

For the postage-stamp agency	$9,000
For the stamped-envelope agency	16,000
For the postal-card agency	7,800

These amounts correspond with the appropriations for the present fiscal year, except in the case of the postage-stamp agency, the estimate for which is increased $1,000. This is done for the purpose of increasing the pay of five employés, four of whom now get but $720 a year and one but $680. As these clerks are usefully and constantly employed on the same character of work as at the other agencies, it is thought to be but fair that they should have their pay increased to at least $900 per annum, which would bring about something like equality.

SHIP, STEAMBOAT, AND WAY LETTERS.

Under the law, owners or masters of vessels not regularly engaged in the transportation of the mails are entitled to compensation on their arrival in port for letters brought and delivered by them to post-offices for transmission to destination. In every case the amount thus paid the owner or master of a vessel is collected by the postmaster at the office of delivery, in addition to the regular postage, which amount is therefore made good to the Government.

The appropriation for the current year is $2,500, which is estimated to be sufficient for the coming year.

ENGRAVING, PRINTING, AND BINDING DRAFTS AND WARRANTS.

This appropriation is for the purchase of drafts and warrants used for payment to creditors, transfers of funds to and from postmasters, and collection of balances due the Department. The drafts and warrants are prepared and furnished by the Bureau of Engraving and Printing of the Treasury Department.

The expenditure for the fiscal year ending June 30, 1888, was $2,445.50; but as the number of warrants and drafts used will be increased somewhat during the present and next fiscal years, I think it prudent to increase the usual estimate. For the year ending June 30, 1890, the amount required will be $3,000.

MISCELLANEOUS.

The amount of appropriation for miscellaneous expenditures for this office is estimated at $1,000, which is the amount that has been appropriated for several years past. The entire sum is never expended; but as many contingencies that can not be foreseen may at any time occur, it is deemed proper to ask for the usual amount.

The increase of the estimates for the next fiscal year over the expenditures for the last fiscal year is shown in the following tabular statement:

Items.	Expenditure year ending June 30, 1888.	Estimates of appropriation year ending June 30, 1890.	Increase of estimates for the year 1890 over expenditures for the year 1888.	
			Amount.	Per cent.
Adhesive postage and special-delivery stamps.....	$122, 411. 00	$155, 874. 00	$33, 463. 00	17. 7+
Postage-stamp agency............................	7, 558. 04	8, 000. 00	· 441. 96	5. 8+
Stamped envelopes, newspaper wrappers, and let-ter-sheets...	710, 884. 93	852, 351. 00	141, 466. 07	19. 9–
Stamped envelope agency..........................	15, 859. 03	16, 000. 00	140. 97	0. 8+
Postal-cards......................................	199, 826. 50	228, 781. 00	28, 954. 50	14. 4+
Postal-card agency................................	8, 915. 50	7, 800. 00	*1, 115. 50	*12. 5+
Registered package, tag, official and dead-letter envelopes...	87, 488. 60	109, 745. 00	22, 256. 40	25. 4+
Ship, steam-boat, and way letters	1, 428. 71	2, 500. 00	1, 071. 29	74. 9
Engraving, printing, and binding drafts and war-rants..............................	2, 445. 50	3, 000. 00	554. 50	22. 6+
Miscellaneous items..............................	210. 10	1, 000. 00	789. 90	375. 9+
Total..	1, 167, 027. 91	1, 385, 051. 00	218, 023. 09	18. 6

* Decrease.

The excess of the above estimates over the present appropriations is shown in the following table:

Items.	Appropria-tions year ending June 30, 1889.	Estimates, year ending June 30, 1890.	Increase of estimates for the year 1890 over appropriations for year 1889.	
			Amount.	Per cent.
Adhesive postage and special-delivery stamps	$144, 148. 00	$155, 874. 00	$11, 726. 00	8. 0+
Postage-stamp agency	8, 000. 00	8, 000. 00	....	....
Stamped envelopes, newspaper wrappers, and let-ter-sheets	756, 687. 00	852, 351. 00	95, 664. 00	12. 6+
Stamped envelope agency..........................	16, 000. 00	16, 000. 00	....	....
Postal-cards	212, 455. 00	228, 781. 00	16, 326. 00	7. 6+
Postal-card agency	7, 800. 00	7, 800. 00	....	....
Registered package, tag, official and dead-letter en-velopes	102, 866. 00	109, 745. 00	6, 879. 00	6. 6+
Ship, steam-boat, and way letters.................	2, 500. 00	2, 500. 00	....	....
Engraving, printing, and binding drafts and war-rants	2, 500. 00	3, 000. 00	500. 00	20. 0
Miscellaneous items	1, 000. 00	1, 000. 00	....	....
Total	1, 253, 956. 00	1, 385, 051. 00	131, 095. 00	10. 4+

Yours, very respectfully,

H. R. HARRIS,
Third Assistant Postmaster-General.

Hon. DON M. DICKINSON,
Postmaster-General.

No. 2.—*Statement showing appropriations and expenditures for the year ending June 30, 1888.*

Items.	Amount of appropria-tions.	By accounts up to September 30.		
		Amount of expenditures.	Balance unexpended.	Excess of expenditures.
Office of the Postmaster-General.				
For mail depredations and post-office inspectors, and fees to United States marshals, attorneys, etc.	$309,000.00	$290,934.35	$9,065.65	....
For advertising	20,000.00	13,058.41	6,941.59	....
For miscellaneous items in the office of the Postmaster-General	1,500.00	192.05	1,307.95	....
Office of the First Assistant Postmaster-General.				
For compensation to postmasters	11,790,000.00	12,589,768.66	....	$889,768.66
For compensation to clerks in post-offices	5,550,000.00	5,505,519.07	44,480.93	....
For rent, fuel, and light	520,000.00	503,111.39	16,888.61	....
For office furniture	25,000.00	19,025.02	5,974.98	....
For miscellaneous and incidental items	70,000.00	57,955.63	12,044.37	....
For free-delivery service	5,522,500.00	5,422,379.42	100,120.58	....
For stationery in post-offices	50,000.00	49,868.55	131.45	....
For twine	80,000.00	71,175.77	8,824.23	....
For wrapping paper	44,000.00	43,997.55	2.45	....
For letter-balances, scales, and test-weights	17,000.00	16,999.92	.08	....
For postmarking and rating stamps, and ink and pads for canceling and stamping purposes	30,000.00	29,999.71	.29	....
For rent of building for use of the Washington City post-office	5,000.00	5,000.00	....	....
Office of the Second Assistant Postmaster-General.				
For inland mail transportation by star routes	5,400,000.00	5,015,178.22	384,821.78	....
For inland mail transportation by steamboat routes	450,000.00	409,872.56	40,127.44	....
For mail-messenger service	900,000.00	851,709.39	48,290.61	....
For mail-bags and mail-bag catchers	275,000.00	246,592.67	28,407.33	....
For mail locks and keys	23,000.00	22,500.54	499.46	....
For inland mail transportation by railroad routes	*16,430,444.00	15,790,841.51	639,602.49	....
For railway post-office car service	1,934,560.00	1,822,964.37	111,595.63	....
For railway postal clerks	4,990,240.62	4,967,302.17	22,938.45	....
For necessary and special facilities on trunk lines	295,987.53	293,299.16	2,688.37	....
For miscellaneous items	1,000.00	294.50	705.50	....
Office of the Third Assistant Postmaster-General.				
For manufacture of adhesive postage and special-delivery stamps	135,000.00	132,411.00	2,589.00	....
For postage-stamp agency	8,100.00	7,558.04	541.96	....
For manufacture of stamped envelopes, newspaper-wrappers, and letter-sheets	720,000.00	710,884.93	9,115.07	....
For stamped envelope agency	16,000.00	15,859.03	140.97	....
For manufacture of postal-cards	200,000.00	199,826.50	173.50	....
For postal-card agency	10,300.00	8,915.50	1,384.50	....
For registered-package, tag, official and dead-letter envelopes	87,500.00	87,488.60	11.40	....
For ship, steamboat, and way letters	2,500.00	1,428.71	1,071.29	....
For engraving, printing, and binding drafts and warrants	2,500.00	2,445.50	54.50	....
For miscellaneous items	1,000.00	210.10	789.90	....
For special-delivery service	109,015.64	109,015.64	....	....
Office of the Superintendent of Foreign Mails.				
For transportation of foreign mails	†466,000.00	448,365.51	17,634.49	....
For balances due foreign countries	75,000.00	31,408.19	43,591.81	....
Total	56,528,147.79	55,795,357.84	1,622,558.61	889,768.66

* Including the $562,432 appropriated October 19, 1888, for inland mail transportation by railroad routes.
† Including the $16,000 appropriated October 19, 1888, for transportation of foreign mails.

No. 3.—*Statement exhibiting the receipts and expenditures, under appropriate heads,* by
30, 1887,

RECEIPTS.

	Quarter ending September 30, 1887.	Quarter ending December 31, 1887.	Quarter ending March 31, 1888.	Quarter ending June 30, 1888.
Letter postage paid in money²	$26,443.86	$25.47	$5,747.93	$29,696.12
Box rents and branch offices	541,801.16	537,151.61	513,569.38	550,761.90
Fines and penalties	6,197.68	4,090.04	6,425.40	2,870.64
Postage-stamps, stamped envelopes, newspaper wrappers, and postal-cards	11,301,020.73	12,345,111.92	12,158,509.20	12,239,630.87
Dead letters	3,999.89	1,994.77	3,123.06	
Revenue from money-order business	168,266.61	238,879.44	210,494.15	180,677.63
Miscellaneous	31,887.54	26,708.39	12,293.93	17,807.45
	12,079,617.49	13,653,961.64	13,940,163.05	13,021,434.61

Comparison, including revenue from money-order business:
   Increase of receipts over year ending June 30, 1887, $3,837,567.40, or 7.9 + per cent.
   Increase of receipts over year ending June 30, 1886, $8,746,753.84, or 19.9 + per cent.

EXPENDITURES.

Compensation of postmasters	$3,012,459.26	$3,130,275.60	$3,266,035.76	$3,180,996.04
Compensation of clerks for post-offices	1,350,264.76	1,354,806.69	1,378,665.27	1,421,782.35
Compensation of letter-carriers and incidental expenses	1,332,942.58	1,323,670.04	1,346,726.81	1,416,039.99
Wrapping paper	18,633.64	2,493.94	12,114.71	10,750.26
Twine	21,755.34	12,212.77	17,340.16	19,867.50
Postmarking and canceling stamps	6,724.94	9,048.55	10,771.60	3,454.63
Letter-balances and test weights	8,107.53	1,892.25	4,176.33	2,823.81
Rent, light, and fuel for post-offices of the third class	117,718.77	119,965.16	130,532.09	134,875.37
Stationery	17,903.51	13,688.89	5,705.87	12,570.28
Furniture for post-offices	2,031.93	5,368.53	4,703.80	6,920.76
Miscellaneous, Office of First Assistant Postmaster-General	14,330.81	12,893.82	13,263.52	17,447.45
Inland mail transportation, railroad	3,854,863.30	3,866,766.92	3,960,338.09	4,108,873.20
Inland mail transportation, star	1,267,478.93	1,264,010.55	1,228,414.51	1,255,274.23
Inland mail transportation, steamboat	110,383.92	98,640.02	96,688.91	104,159.71
Transportation by postal cars	450,287.11	454,332.48	454,124.90	464,219.58
Special and necessary facilities railroad trunk lines	73,996.86	73,996.86	71,581.80	73,723.64
Compensation of railway postal clerks	1,213,031.73	1,230,115.03	1,250,798.19	1,272,707.22
Compensation of mail messengers	200,511.93	211,257.27	214,075.22	219,864.97
Mail locks and keys	16,040.00	2,600.00	1,750.00	2,110.54
Mail bags and catchers	87,723.22	82,957.26	58,564.38	17,347.81
Mail depredations, post-office inspectors, fees to United States marshals, attorneys, clerks of court, and counsel	66,404.69	67,664.36	76,250.81	80,614.49
Postage-stamps	28,040.47	34,019.85	36,665.68	33,605.50
Distribution of postage-stamps	1,890.00	1,888.04	1,890.00	1,890.90
Stamped envelopes and newspaper wrappers, and letter-sheets	155,754.11	179,918.39	183,176.25	192,036.18
Distribution of stamped envelopes and newspaper wrappers	3,951.64	3,956.64	3,953.30	3,997.45
Postal-cards	44,427.55	43,187.57	62,323.83	49,888.05
Distribution of postal-cards	2,304.73	2,317.70	2,193.20	2,199.87
Registered-package envelopes, tag, official, and dead-letter envelopes	20,181.62	22,425.60	23,833.44	21,527.94
Ship, steamboat, and way letters	418.42	428.27	245.28	336.74
Engraving, printing, and binding drafts and warrants	1,772.50	235.00	90.00	348.00
Advertising	2,603.36	2,971.03	4,340.16	3,143.86
Miscellaneous, Office of Postmaster-General	20.75	21.70	48.50	101.10
Foreign-mail transportation	106,211.26	128,007.89	116,391.78	97,754.58
Balances due foreign countries		674.28	11,146.74	19,587.17
Miscellaneous, Second Assistant Postmaster-General		100.00	79.00	115.50
Miscellaneous, Third Assistant Postmaster-General				210.10

* The bulk of this item consists of balances paid the United States by other countries.

quarters, for the fiscal year ending June 30, 1888, compared with fiscal years ending June and 1886.

RECEIPTS.

Total year ending June 30, 1888.	Total expenditures on account of previous fiscal years.	Total year ending June 30, 1887.	Comparison with year ending June 30, 1887.		Total year ending June 30, 1886.	Comparison with year ending June 30, 1886.	
			Increase.	Decrease.		Increase.	Decrease.
$61,903.40	....	$93,777.87		$31,874.47	$60,004.80	$1,898.60	....
2,173,284.05	....	2,158,499.96	$14,784.07		2,018,048.04	155,236.01	....
19,583.76	....	19,433.56	150.20	....	13,472.35	6,111.41	....
49,544,272.72	....	45,670,963.84	3,873,288.88		41,447,095.88	8,097,176.84	....
9,117.72	....	10,976.35		1,858.63	8,858.33	259.39	....
798,317.83	....	719,335.45	78,982.38	....	350,551.87	447,765.96	....
88,697.31	....	164,602.34		75,905.03	50,391.68	38,305.63	....
52,695,176.79	....	48,837,609.89	3,967,203.53	100,638.13	43,948,422.95	8,746,753.84	....
48,837,609.39	....	....	109,638.13		52,695,176.79		
3,857,567.40	....	....	3,857,567.40	....	8,746,753.84	....	

Comparison, excluding revenue from money-order business:
Increase of receipts over year ending June 30, 1887, $3,778,585.02, or 7.8 + per cent.
Increase of receipts over year ending June 30, 1886, $8,298,987.88, or 19 + per cent.

EXPENDITURES.

$12,589,768.66	$17,657.80	$11,929,481.41	$660,287.25	....	$11,348,178.17	$1,241,590.49	....
5,505,519.07	3,226.88	5,385,812.74	119,706.33	....	4,977,663.47	527,855.60	....
5,422,379.42	134.40	4,618,682.05	803,697.37	....	4,312,296.70	1,110,082.72	....
43,907.55	2,193.95	29,971.82	14,025.73	....	28,766.49	15,231.06	....
71,175.77	....	65,160.79	6,014.98	....	69,192.35	1,983.42	....
29,999.71	125.00	21,005.48	8,994.23	....	16,812.37	13,187.34	....
16,999.72	....	1,091.62	15,908.30	....	1,172.50	15,827.42	....
503,111.39	4,523.51	471,333.23	31,778.16	....	468,932.57	34,178.82	....
49,868.55	1,723.51	45,692.43	4,176.12	....	36,030.10	13,838.45	....
19,025.02	3,028.96	20,470.88	....	$1,445.86	11,214.06	7,810.96	....
57,935.63	592.03	57,775.46	180.17	....	53,498.30	4,457.33	....
15,790,841.51	149,053.11	14,707,281.94	1,083,559.57	....	14,149,401.85	1,641,439.66	....
5,015,178.23	28,046.74	5,119,649.30	....	104,471.08	5,452,456.19	....	$437,277.97
409,872.56	641.75	421,370.24	....	11,497.68	471,447.26	....	61,574.70
1,822,964.37	10,090.68	1,713,391.92	109,572.45	....	1,691,447.80	181,516.57	....
293,299.16	....	285,372.81	7,926.35	....	251,540.82	41,758.34	....
4,967,302.17	3,924.69	4,693,381.91	273,920.26	....	4,467,778.08	499,524.09	....
851,709.39	5,034.40	825,338.17	26,371.22	....	833,968.38	17,741.01	....
22,500.54	....	19,522.00	2,978.54	....	19,995.80	2,504.74	....
246,592.67	9,498.61	245,798.33	794.34	....	215,202.80	31,389.87	....
290,934.35	1,815.17	197,706.08	93,228.27	....	194,435.00	96,499.35	....
132,411.00	6,884.45	116,700.00	15,711.00	....	114,969.09	17,441.91	....
7,558.04	....	7,522.40	35.64	....	6,837.00	721.04	....
710,884.93	65,237.78	583,500.00	127,384.93	....	692,435.04	18,449.89	....
15,859.03	38.00	15,945.07	....	86.04	15,372.09	486.94	....
199,826.50	....	182,146.27	17,680.23	....	168,826.06	31,000.44	....
8,915.50	....	9,970.80	....	1,055.30	7,008.90	1,906.60	....
87,488.60	17,812.49	67,200.00	20,288.60	....	72,366.21	15,122.39	....
1,428.71	....	1,505.58	....	76.87	2,050.83	....	622.12
2,445.50	....	1,959.50	486.00	....	1,984.75	460.75	....
13,058.41	370.40	12,554.75	503.66	....	14,624.66	....	1,566.25
192.05	11.45	106.00	86.05	....	149.71	42.34	....
448,365.51	99,029.52	369,981.52	78,883.99	....	358,929.87	89,435.64	....
31,408.19	....	54,286.86	....	22,878.67	31,927.09	....	518.90
294.50	....	166.90	127.60	....	619.65	....	325.15
210.10	....	114.75	95.35	....	369.22	....	159.12

No. 3.—*Statement exhibiting the receipts and expenditures, under appropriate*

EXPENDITURES—Continued.

	Quarter ending September 30, 1887.	Quarter ending December 31, 1887.	Quarter ending March 31, 1888.	Quarter ending June 30, 1888.
Special-delivery service..........................	$25,007.50	$28,497.16	$26,845.84	$28,605.08
Rent of Washington City post-office.........	....	2,500.00	1,250.00	1,250.00
Compensation of postmasters re-adjusted....	....	....	....	....
Claim, Samuel H. Fleming	....	....	....	....
	13,642,838.76	13,791,780.61	14,076,625.23	14,283,113.24

Total expenditures for transportation of the domestic mails for year ending June 30, 1888.$23,332,155.82
Total expenditures for transportation of the domestic mails for year ending June 30, 1887. 22,247,066.21

    Increase over 1887... 1,085,089.61
                                                                                or 4.8 + per cent.
Increase of expenditures over June 30, 1887, $3,403,689.41, or 6.4 + per cent.

heads, by quarters, for the fiscal year ending June 30, 1888, *etc.*—Continued.

. EXPENDITURES—Continued.

Total year ending June 30, 1888.	Total expenditures on account of previous fiscal years.	Total year ending June 30, 1887.	Comparison with year ending June 30, 1887.		Total year ending June 30, 1886.	Comparison with year ending June 30, 1886.	
			Increase.	Decrease.		Increase.	Decrease.
$109,015.64	$69.28	$92,726.42	$16,289.22	....	$67,652.14	$41,363.50	....
5,000.00	5,000.00	....	5,000.00	....	....	5,000.00	....
....	236,965.16	....	....	....	....	....	....
....	206.06	....	....	....	....	....	....
55,795,357.84	672,067.36	52,391,677.43	3,545,191.91	$141,511.50	50,627,553.37	5,660,848.68	$502,044.21
52,391,677.43	....	....	141,511.50	....	55,795,357.84	502,044.21	....
3,403,680.41	....	....	3,403,680.41	....	5,167,804.47	5,167,801.47	....

Total expenditures for transportation of the domestic mails for year ending June 30, 1888 $23,332,155.82
Total expenditures for transportation of the domestic mails for year ending June 30, 1886. 22,016,293.02

Increase over 1886... 1,315,861.90
or 5.9 + per cent.
Increase of expenditures over June 30, 1886, $5,167,804.47, or 19.2 + per cent.

No. 4.—*Receipts and disbursements at Treasury depositories during the fiscal year ending June 30, 1888.*

Depositories.	Deposits.	Grants from the Treasury.	By transfer.	Aggregate accumulation.	Aggregate receipts.	Increase of receipts over 1887.	Decrease of receipts from 1887.	Warrants drawn.
Treasurer United States, Washington, D. C.	$494,260.85	$3,160,830.47	$18,901.04	$3,673,682.36	$494,260.85	$159,657.38		$525,419.00
Assistant treasurer United States, Baltimore, Md	297,124.54		500,000.00	797,124.54	297,124.54		980.61	671,729.01
Assistant treasurer United States, Boston, Mass	2,407,094.89			2,407,094.89	2,407,094.89	122,434.94		1,753,574.60
Assistant treasurer United States, Chicago, Ill	4,077,676.29		2,200,000.00	6,277,676.29	4,077,676.29	573,885.57		5,848,460.09
Assistant treasurer United States, Cincinnati, Ohio	1,679,599.86		100,000.00	1,779,599.86	1,679,599.86	232,149.26		1,775,58.94
Assistant treasurer United States, New Orleans, La	680,357.31		200,000.00	880,357.31	680,357.31	80,255.12		936,455.00
Assistant treasurer United States, New York, N. Y.	8,405,495.95		800,000.00	9,205,495.95	8,405,495.95	1,336,709.08		9,357,270.57
Assistant treasurer United States, Philadelphia, Pa.	2,160,347.76		200,000.00	2,360,347.76	2,160,347.76	205,135.84		2,504,229.51
Assistant treasurer United States, San Francisco, Cal.	1,032,540.84			1,032,540.84	1,032,540.84	205,241.11		921,184.42
Assistant treasurer United States, Saint Louis, Mo	1,640,830.22		600,000.00	2,240,830.22	1,640,830.22	212,666.98		2,119,482.34
First National Bank, Concord, N. H. Mex	65.46			65.46	65.46	65.46		
First National Bank, Concord, N. H	1,582.23			1,582.23	1,582.23		10.00	
First National Bank, Deadwood, Dak	744.47			744.47	744.47		7,781.61	
First National Bank, Denver, Colo							67.03	
First National Bank, Kansas City, Mo							24.00	
First National Bank, Leavenworth, Kans	2,738.70			2,738.70	2,738.70	2,307.70		
First National Bank of Los Angeles, Los Angeles, Cal.	500.00			500.00	500.00	500.00		
First National Bank, Madison, Wis	500.00			500.00	500.00		5,137.80	
First National Bank, Montgomery, Ala							88.95	
First National Bank, Portland, Oregon	10.00			10.00	10.00	10.00		
First National Bank, Portsmouth, N. H	110.00			110.00	110.00		60.00	
First National Bank, Santa Fé, N. Mex.							30.00	
First National Bank,							660.00	
First National Bank,							64.93	
First National Bank,							472.50	
Second National Bank of Wilmington, Wilmington, Del	135.07			135.07	135.07			
Second National Bank, Saint Paul, Minn	243.25			243.25	243.25	243.25	589.50	
Third National Bank, Utica, N. Y	100.00			100.00	100.00		625.00	
Third National Bank, Buffalo, N. Y	725.00			725.00	725.00	785.00		
Mercantile National Bank, Cleveland, Ohio							639.96	
Merchants' National Bank, Burlington, Vt.	99.00			99.00	99.00	99.00		
Merchants' National Bank, Portland, Me.	200.00			200.00	200.00		541.91	
Merchants' National Bank, Savannah, Ga							150.00	
American National Bank, Dallas, Tex	100.00			100.00	100.00	90.00		
Charter Oak National Bank, Hartford, Conn	1,261.00			1,261.00	1,261.00	661.00		
Citizens' National Bank, Davenport, Iowa	110.00			110.00	110.00	110.00		
Citizens' National Bank, Des Moines, Iowa							1,784.52	
Commercial National Bank, Detroit, Minn	125.00			125.00	125.00		125.00	
Commercial National Bank, Knoxville, Tenn	98.06			98.06	98.06	98.06		
Indianapolis National Bank, Indianapolis, Ind.	780.00			780.00	780.00		.34	
Gate City National Bank, Atlanta, Ga	500.00			500.00	500.00	278.00		
German National Bank, Little Rock, Ark	746.45			746.45	746.45		58.00	

Kentucky National Bank, Louisville, Ky	1,277.87			1,277.87	1,277.87	967.82		
Leavenworth National Bank, Leavenworth, Kans.	281.85			281.85	281.85	281.85		
Nassau National Bank, Brooklyn, N. Y.	176.18			176.18	176.16	51.16		
National Bank of Commerce, Cleveland, Ohio	350.00			350.00	350.00	350.00		
National City Bank, Grand Rapids, Mich.	785.00			785.00	785.00	785.00		
National Bank of Huntsville, Huntsville, Ala	100.00			100.00	100.00	100.00		
National Bank of the Republic, Washington, D. C.	105.00			105.00	105.00	105.00		
National Bank of Raleigh, Raleigh, N. C.							78.60	
National Bank State of Florida, Jacksonville, Fla.	20.00			20.00	20.00	20.00		
National Bank of Virginia, Richmond, Va.	552.37			552.37	552.37	552.37		
Northern National Bank, Toledo, Ohio	44.82			44.82	44.82	44.82		
Omaha National Bank, Omaha, Nebr	573.10			573.10	573.10	425.55		
People's National Bank, Charleston, S. C.	87.98			87.98	87.98		37,706.15	
Planters' National Bank, Danville, Va.							268.02	
Planters' National Bank, Richmond, Va.							270.00	
Saint Louis National Bank, Saint Louis, Mo.	250.00			250.00	250.00	250.00		
San Antonio National Bank, San Antonio, Tex	1,601.00			1,601.00	1,601.00	1,601.00	292.62	
Sioux National Bank, Sioux City, Iowa	523.85			523.85	253.85	163.85		
State National Bank, El Paso, Tex	253.96			253.96	253.96		7,613.60	
State National Bank, Memphis, Tenn	897.77			897.77	897.77	464.90		
State National Bank, Springfield, Ill	2,446.11			2,446.11	2,446.11	1,435.70		
Tradesmen's National Bank, Pittsburgh, Pa.	638.49			638.49	638.49	566.49		
Union National Bank, Salt Lake City, Utah							165.49	
Valley National Bank, Staunton, Va.							257.18	
Assistant Treasurer United States, New Orleans, La.*								
United States depository, Little Rock, Ark.*								
United States depository, Merchants' Bank, Savannah, Ga.*								
United States depository, Galveston, Tex.*								
Total	22,877,485.65	3,160,689.47	4,618,691.04	30,654,906.56	22,877,485.65	3,191,699.24	65,472.91	26,671,283.06
						65,472.91		
						3,124,226.33		

* Old accounts.

No. 4.—*Receipts and disbursements at Treasury depositories during the fiscal year ending June 30, 1883—Continued.*

Depositories.	Increase over 1887.	Decrease from 1887.	Transfer account. From—	Transfer account. To—	Warrants paid.	Outstanding warrants June 30, 1887.	Balances, as per transcripts, June 30, 1888.	Outstanding warrants June 30, 1888.	Balances subject to draft June 30, 1888.
Treasurer United States, Washington, D. C.	$242,792.99	$312,213.89	$3,100,000.00	$18,601.04	$398,280.35	$1,790.96	$253,247.08	$1,575.14	$251,771.94
Assistant treasurer United States, Baltimore, Md.	170,314.96			500,000.00	673,481.50	3,116.35	250,194.11	1,333.86	248,810.25
Assistant treasurer United States, Boston, Mass.	708,604.31		700,000.00		1,780,755.74	1,870.40	590,610.88	4,717.00	594,993.89
Assistant treasurer United States, Chicago, Ill.				2,200,060.00	5,845,666.31	13,965.87	977,783.89	16,562.29	961,211.51
Assistant treasurer United States, Cincinnati, Ohio.	113,658.44			100,000.00	1,769,141.84	6,279.88	547,834.82	10,597.38	537,237.44
Assistant treasurer United States, New Orleans, La.	81,533.86			200,000.00	926,175.68	5,206.96	213,060.22	5,362.37	208,577.85
Assistant treasurer United States, New York, N. Y.		499,915.98	800,000.00	200,000.00	9,515,801.18	28,755.31	1,781,389.58	50,097.69	1,731,291.89
Assistant treasurer United States, Philadelphia, Pa.	146,656.35			800,000.00	3,504,462.95	6,146.52	514,407.61	5,599.08	508,508.53
Assistant treasurer United States, San Francisco, Cal.	82,628.15			200,000.00	920,280.18	6,825.20	484,190.35	7,549.73	410,640.62
Assistant treasurer United States, Saint Louis, Mo.	307,097.91		65.46	600,000.00	2,120,414.46	8,290.08	488,878.82	7,347.96	481,530.86
First National bank, Albuquerque, N. Mex.									
First National Bank, Concord, N. H.									
First National Bank, Deadwood, Dak.									
First National Bank, Denver, Colo.			2,006.24						
First National Bank, Kansas City, Mo.			1,316.00						
First National Bank, Leavenworth, Kans.									
First National Bank of Los Angeles, Los Angeles, Cal.			1,784.07				954.63		954.63
First National Bank, Madison, Wis.			500.00				500.00		500.00
First National Bank, Montgomery, Ala.									
First National Bank, Nashville, Tenn.			10.00				100.00		100.00
First National Bank, Portland, Oregon.			10.00						
First National Bank, Portsmouth, N. H.							50.00		50.00
First National Bank, Santa Fé, N. Mex.									
First National Bank, Toledo, Ohio.			85.07						
First National Bank, Trenton, N. J.									
First National Bank of Wilmington, Wilmington, Del.			213.25				100.00		100.00
Second National Bank, Saint Paul, Minn.									
Second National Bank, Utica, N. Y.			425.00				100.00		300.00
Third National Bank, Buffalo, N. Y.							300.00		
Mercantile National Bank, Cleveland, Ohio.									
Merchants' National Bank, Burlington, Vt.			99.00						
Merchants' National Bank, Portland, Me.			300.00						
Merchants' National Bank, Savannah, Ga.									
American National Bank, Dallas, Tex.							100.00		100.00

	Payments	Balances
Charter Oak National Bank, Hartford, Conn	511.00	750.00
Citizens' National Bank, Davenport, Iowa	110.00	
Citizens' National Bank, Des Moines, Iowa		
Commercial National Bank, Detroit, Mich	76.00	100.00
East Tennessee National Bank, Knoxville, Tenn	98.06	200.00
Indianapolis National Bank, Indianapolis, Ind	710.00	
Gate City National Bank, Atlanta, Ga	500.00	
German National Bank, Little Rock, Ark	772.20	148.95
Kentucky National Bank, Louisville, Ky	1,128.62	281.85
Leavenworth National Bank, Leavenworth, Kans		176.16
Nassau National Bank, Brooklyn, N.Y.	350.00	
National Bank of Commerce, Cleveland, Ohio	775.00	20.00
National City Bank, Grand Rapids, Mich		100.00
National Bank of Huntsville, Huntsville, Ala	103.00	
National Bank of the Republic, Washington, D.C.		20.00
National Bank of Raleigh, Raleigh, N.C.		
National Bank State of Florida, Jacksonville, Fla	555.37	
National Bank of Virginia, Richmond, Va	44.32	
Northern National Bank, Toledo, Ohio	572.10	
Omaha National Bank, Omaha, Nebr	37.88	
People's National Bank, Charleston, S.C		
Planters' National Bank, Danville, Va	250.00	1,561.00
Planters' National Bank, Richmond, Va	100.00	
Saint Louis National Bank, Saint Louis, Mo		
San Antonio National Bank, San Antonio, Tex	283.85	
Sioux National Bank, Sioux City, Iowa	831.43	
State National Bank, El Paso, Tex	620.15	77.63
State National Bank, Memphis, Tenn	2,490.48	454.90
State National Bank, Springfield, Ill	518.49	
Tradesmen's National Bank, Pittsburgh, Pa		
Union National Bank, Salt Lake City, Utah		
Valley National Bank, Staunton, Va		
Assistant treasurer United States, New Orleans, La.*		31,164.44
United States depository, Little Rock, Ark.*		5,823.50
United States depository, Merchants' Bank, Savannah, Ga.*		205.76
United States depository, Galveston, Tex.*		83.36
Total	4,618,001.04	6,983,716.80
	1,857,665.97	
	812,129.87	
	1,645,536.10	

*Old accounts.

No. 4.—Receipts and expenditures at Treasury depositories, etc.—Continued.

COMPARATIVE STATEMENT BETWEEN FISCAL YEARS 1887 AND 1888, AT TREASURY DEPOSITORIES.

Deposits for fiscal year 1888...	$22,877,485.05
Deposits for fiscal year 1887...	19,751,258.72
Increase of deposits for 1888...	3,126,226.33
Grants from the Treasury, 1887...	$6,969,138.98
Grants from the Treasury, 1888...	3,160,820.47
Decrease of grants from 1887...	3,808,318.51
Increase of receipts over 1887...	$3,191,699.24
Decrease of receipts from 1887...	65,472.91
Increase for 1888, as shown above.....................................	3,126,226.33
Warrants drawn for 1888...	26,571,263.06
Warrants drawn for 1887...	25,525,706.96
Increase for 1888...	1,045,556.10
Balance subject to draft June 30, 1887................................	6,516,674.40
Balance subject to draft June 30, 1888................................	5,983,716.86
Decrease from 1887...	532,957.54
Total number of warrants issued during fiscal year 1888.........	92,570.00
Total number of warrants issued during fiscal year 1887.........	82,503.00
Increase for 1888...	10,067.00

No. 5.—*Postage-stamps, stamped envelopes, newspaper wrappers, letter-sheet envelopes, and postal-cards issued during fiscal year ending June 30, 1888.*

ORDINARY AND SPECIAL DELIVERY STAMPS.

Denominations.	Quarter ending Sept. 30, 1887.	Quarter ending Dec. 31, 1887.	Quarter ending Mar. 31, 1888.	Quarter ending June 30, 1888.	Total.
1-cent............	83,936,700	113,015,900	125,318,700	121,718,200	443,989,500
2-cent............	296,217,000	348,012,100	368,931,300	334,520,200	1,347,680,600
3-cent............	101,500	604,100	1,884,700	1,441,100	4,031,400
4-cent............	2,976,250	3,750,700	3,924,675	3,592,125	14,243,750
5-cent............	7,704,880	8,718,160	10,740,620	9,045,560	36,209,220
6-cent............	61,000	....	100,000	5,600	166,600
10-cent...........	4,320,780	5,239,780	5,699,870	4,671,230	19,931,660
15-cent...........	277,020	451,560	357,640	336,940	1,423,160
30-cent...........	67,370	181,120	98,480	95,760	442,730
90-cent...........	5,920	11,490	18,990	18,120	54,520
10-cent special delivery...........	329,970	393,810	311,670	296,340	1,331,790
Total.........	295,998,390	480,378,720	517,386,645	475,741,175	1,869,504,930
Value.........	$7,806,673	$9,390,230	$10,089,807	$9,139,452	$36,426,362

NEWSPAPER AND PERIODICAL STAMPS.

1-cent............	161,580	162,960	169,090	180,840	674,470
2-cent............	137,190	136,645	132,966	134,430	540,570
3-cent............	68,780	64,910	56,570	60,650	252,910
4-cent............	98,960	94,615	99,610	97,025	390,210
6-cent............	57,615	56,630	59,825	60,240	234,710
8-cent............	44,140	41,200	41,690	49,780	176,870
10-cent...........	107,735	102,470	101,920	109,825	421,450
12-cent...........	37,115	41,640	37,670	48,125	164,550
24-cent...........	39,120	37,155	34,530	40,655	151,460
36-cent...........	17,275	17,935	18,650	19,935	73,795
48-cent...........	13,785	13,880	12,440	17,050	57,155
60-cent...........	12,855	12,170	14,530	15,800	55,355
72-cent...........	7,385	7,630	8,890	11,225	35,130
84-cent...........	7,830	7,880	8,250	8,350	32,310
96-cent...........	14,565	16,610	16,675	20,845	68,695

No. 5.—*Postage-stamps, stamped envelopes, newspaper wrappers, letter-sheet envelopes, and postal-cards issued, etc.*—Continued.

NEWSPAPER AND PERIODICAL STAMPS—Continued.

Denominations.	Quarter ending Sept. 30, 1887.	Quarter ending Dec. 31, 1887.	Quarter ending Mar. 31, 1888.	Quarter ending June 30, 1888.	Total.
$1.92	10,150	11,005	10,775	12,810	44,740
$3	7,436	7,460	8,756	8,488	32,140
$6	4,572	3,477	4,715	4,698	17,462
$9	3,010	2,217	3,113	3,486	11,826
$12	2,777	2,466	3,742	3,573	12,558
$24	752	446	1,313	1,712	4,223
$36	616	173	481	735	2,005
$48	420	100	505	626	1,651
$60	790	1,720	2,103	2,360	6,973
Total	856,593	843,654	851,408	912,763	3,464,418
Value	$325,848	$328,294	$438,383	$495,900	$1,588,425

POSTAGE-DUE STAMPS.

Denominations	Quarter ending Sept. 30, 1887.	Quarter ending Dec. 31, 1887.	Quarter ending Mar. 31, 1888.	Quarter ending June 30, 1888.	Total.
1-cent	936,600	1,403,900	1,868,600	1,312,500	5,521,600
2-cent	705,950	992,500	970,800	661,650	3,330,900
3-cent	60,000	12,500	60,200	4,400	137,100
5-cent	83,800	160,440	215,440	120,780	580,460
10-cent	212,300	320,740	435,160	246,340	1,214,540
30-cent		3,300	10,900	580	14,780
50-cent		24	5,350	818	6,192
Total	1,998,650	2,893,404	3,566,450	2,347,068	10,803,572
Value	$50,705	$75,362	$100,141	$57,746	$283,954

STAMPED ENVELOPES.

Denominations	Quarter ending Sept. 30, 1887.	Quarter ending Dec. 31, 1887.	Quarter ending Mar. 31, 1888.	Quarter ending June 30, 1888.	Total.
1-cent	7,652,250	10,716,000	10,815,000	14,356,500	43,539,750
2-cent	29,558,900	37,017,450	36,213,950	40,054,800	142,845,100
4-cent	16,600	16,250	24,000	29,700	96,550
5-cent	60,500	46,250	99,250	36,250	242,250
10-cent	4,000		1,000	4,650	9,650
30-cent	4,000	1,000		1,150	6,150
90-cent	1,000			550	1,550
Wrappers, 1-cent	10,918,000	10,852,000	11,312,500	14,902,000	47,085,500
Wrappers, 2-cent	558,500	747,000	984,500	894,000	3,184,000
Total	47,873,750	59,395,950	59,461,200	70,279,600	237,010,500
Value	$860,576.55	$1,068,360.76	$1,065,593.95	1,224,781.68	$4,219,312.94

STAMPED ENVELOPES BEARING REQUEST TO RETURN.

Denominations	Quarter ending Sept. 30, 1887.	Quarter ending Dec. 31, 1887.	Quarter ending Mar. 31, 1888.	Quarter ending June 30, 1888.	Total.
1-cent	1,680,250	1,819,000	2,014,000	1,668,500	7,181,750
2-cent	44,277,500	48,328,250	49,097,750	47,562,500	189,266,000
4-cent	16,500	26,500	33,000	13,500	89,500
5-cent	23,000	19,500	29,000	16,500	88,000
Total	45,997,250	50,193,250	51,173,750	49,261,000	196,625,250
Value	$992,257.50	$1,083,101.40	$1,103,220.30	$1,064,032.70	$4,242,611.90

2-CENT LETTER-SHEET ENVELOPES.

	Quarter ending Sept. 30, 1887.	Quarter ending Dec. 31, 1887.	Quarter ending Mar. 31, 1888.	Quarter ending June 30, 1888.	Total.
Total	1,100,000	680,000	345,000	302,000	2,427,000
Value	$25,300	$15,640	$7,935	$6,946	$55,821

No. 5 —*Postage-stamps, stamped envelopes, newspaper wrappers, 'letter-sheet envelopes, and postal-cards issued, etc.*—Continued.

POSTAL CARDS.*

Denominations.	Quarter ending Sept. 30, 1887.	Quarter ending Dec. 31, 1887.	Quarter ending Mar. 31, 1888.	Quarter ending June 30, 1888.	Total.
1-cent	87, 455, 000	98, 239, 000	99, 687, 500	96, 290, 000	381, 671, 500
2-cent	27, 500	20, 250	35, 750	42, 500	126, 000
Total	87, 481, 500	98, 259, 250	99, 723, 250	96, 322, 500	381, 797, 50
Value ...:....	$875, 100	$982, 705	$997, 590	$903, 750	$3, 819, 235

* Shipments to subagencies are not considered in this table.

RECAPITULATION.

Articles issued.	Number.	Amount.
Ordinary postage-stamps	1, 567, 172, 140	$36, 293, 183. 00
Special-delivery stamps	1, 331, 790	133, 179. 00
Newspaper and periodical stamps..........................	3, 464, 418	1, 588, 425. 00
Postage-due stamps	10, 805, 572	283, 954. 00
Ordinary stamped envelopes, plain	186, 741, 000	3, 634, 598. 44
Stamped envelopes, request	196, 625, 250	4, 342, 611. 00
Newspaper wrappers	50, 269, 500	584, 804. 50
Letter-sheet envelopes	2, 427, 000	55, 821. 00
Postal-cards	381, 797, 500	3, 819, 235. 00
Aggregate	2, 700, 635, 170	50, 635, 721. 84

No. 6.—*Issue of postage-stamps, stamped envelopes, newspaper wrappers, letter-sheet envelopes, and postal-cards, by denominations, for fiscal year ending June 30, 1888.*

Denominations.	Ordinary, special delivery, and postage-due stamps.	Stamped envelopes, newspaper wrappers, and letter-sheet envelopes.	Postal-cards, not including those shipped to subagencies.	Newspaper and periodical stamps.	Total.
1-cent	449, 511, 100	97, 807, 000	381, 671, 500	674, 470	929, 664, 070
2-cent	1, 351, 011, 500	337, 722, 100	126, 000	540, 570	1, 689, 406, 170
3-cent	4, 168, 500	....	....	253, 910	4, 432, 410
4-cent	14, 243, 750	186, 050	....	390, 210	14, 830, 010
5-cent	36, 789, 680	330, 250	....	....	37, 119, 930
6-cent	166, 600	....	....	234, 710	410, 310
8-cent	....	....	....	176, 870	176, 870
10-cent	22, 477, 900	9, 650	....	421, 450	22, 909, 050
12-cent	....	....	....	164, 550	164, 550
15-cent	1, 423, 160	....	....	....	1, 423, 160
24-cent	....	....	....	151, 460	151, 460
30-cent	457, 510	6, 150	....	....	463, 600
36-cent	....	....	....	78, 795	78, 795
48-cent	....	....	....	57, 155	57, 155
50-cent	6, 192	....	....	....	6, 192
60-cent	....	....	....	55, 355	55, 355
72-cent	....	....	....	35, 130	35, 130
84-cent	....	....	....	32, 310	32, 310
90-cent	54, 520	1, 550	....	....	56, 070
96-cent	....	....	....	68, 895	68, 895
$1.92	....	....	....	44, 740	44, 740
$3	....	....	....	32, 140	32, 140
$6	....	....	....	17, 462	17, 462
$9	....	....	....	11, 826	11, 826
$12	....	....	....	12, 558	12, 558
$24	....	....	....	4, 223	4, 223
$36	....	....	....	2, 005	2, 005
$48	....	....	....	1, 651	1, 651
$60	....	....	....	6, 973	6, 973
Aggregate	1, 880, 310, 502	436, 062, 750	381, 797, 500	3, 464, 418	2, 701, 635, 170
Value	$36, 710, 316. 00	$8, 517, 745. 84	$3, 819, 235. 00	$1, 588, 425. 00	$50, 635, 721. 84

No. 7.—Table showing the increase and decrease in the issue of postage-stamps, stamped envelopes, newspaper wrappers, letter-sheet envelopes, and postal-cards for the fiscal year ending June 30, 1888, as compared with the issue of the preceding year.

Articles issued.	1887.		1888.		Increase.		Per cent. increase.	
	Number.	Amount.	Number.	Amount.	Number.	Amount.	Number.	Amount.
Ordinary postage-stamps	1,746,985,520	$33,774,156.00	1,867,173,140	$36,293,183.00	120,187,620	$2,519,027.00	6.88	7.46
Special-delivery stamps	1,245,940	124,594.00	1,331,790	133,179.00	85,850	8,585.00	6.89	6.89
Newspaper and periodical stamps	3,031,595	1,364,413.30	3,464,418	1,588,425.00	432,823	224,011.20	14.28	16.42
Postage-due stamps	8,246,534	223,138.00	10,806,572	283,934.00	2,550,038	48,818.00	31.63	21.70
Stamped envelopes, plain	164,301,450	3,196,821.40	186,741,000	3,634,508.44	22,439,550	437,687.04	13.66	13.69
Stamped envelopes, request	171,104,000	3,699,194.10	196,625,250	4,242,611.90	25,521,250	543,431.80	14.92	14.69
Newspaper wrappers	46,205,850	526,884.25	50,269,540	564,984.50	4,063,650	47,940.15	8.79	8.99
Letter-sheet envelopes	5,110,000	117,530.00	2,427,000	55,831.00	*2,683,000	*61,709.10	*52.50	*52.50
Postal-cards	356,939,250	8,571,003.00	381,797,500	8,819,835.00	24,864,250	248,830.00	6.96	6.97
Total of all issues	2,563,170,139	46,619,680.05	2,700,635,170	50,636,321.84	197,465,031	4,016,641.19	7.89	8.63

*Decrease.

No. 8.—*Value of postage-stamps issued, by fiscal years, from their introduction, July 1, 1847, to June 30, 1888.*

Year.	Ordinary.	Official.	Newspaper and periodical.	Postage-due.	Special-delivery.	Total.
1847						
1848						
1849	$274,710.00	....	....	....	....	$274,710.00
1850						
1851						
1852	1,525,638.51	....	....	....	....	1,535,638.51
1853	1,608,792.91	....	....	....	....	1,608,792.91
1854	1,520,300.00	....	....	....	....	1,520,200.00
185 5	2,056,127.00	....	....	....	....	2,056,127.00
1856	3,611,274.40	....	....	....	....	3,611,274.40
1857	4,337,135.20	....	....	....	....	4,337,135.20
1858	4,945,874.35	....	....	....	....	4,945,374.35
1859	5,279,405.00	....	....	....	....	5,279,405.00
1860	5,920,939.00	....	....	....	....	5,920,939.00
1861	5,908,522.60	....	....	....	....	5,908,522.60
1862	7,078,188.00	....	....	....	....	7,078,188.00
1863	9,683,394.00	....	....	....	....	9,683,394.00
1864	10,177,327.00	....	....	....	....	10,177,327.00
1865	12,099,987.50	....	....	....	....	12,099,987.50
1866	10,816,661.00	....	....	....	....	10,816,661.00
1867	11,578,607.00	....	....	....	....	11,578,607.00
1868	11,751,014.00	....	....	....	....	11,751,014.00
1869	12,722,568.00	....	....	....	....	12,722,568.00
1870	13,976,768.00	....	....	....	....	13,976,768.00
1871	14,630,715.00	....	....	....	....	14,630,715.00
1872	15,840,649.00	....	....	....	....	15,840,649.00
1873	16,681,199.00	$494,974.70	....	....	....	17,176,163.70
1874	17,275,242.00	1,415,845.20	....	....	....	18,691,087.20
1875	18,271,479.00	834,970.25	$815,902.47	....	....	19,922,351.72
1876	18,773,454.00	663,831.50	945,254.75	....	....	20,382,540.25
1877	18,181,676.00	614,107.20	1,000,605.10	....	....	19,796,388.30
1878	19,468,618.00	618,004.60	1,093,845.30	....	....	21,180,557.90
1879	20,117,259.00	624,999.95	1,088,412.16	$365,957.00	....	22,106,628.11
1880	22,414,928.00	140,199.08	1,254,903.30	251,836.00	....	24,059,866.38
1881	24,040,627.00	107,777.32	1,398,674.00	254,393.00	....	25,801,471.32
1882	28,679,528.00	139,991.75	1,602,069.70	352,170.00	....	30,773,759.45
1883	30,307,179.00	125,830.20	1,752,564.50	404,915.90	....	32,590,498.60
1884	29,077,444.00	140,040.00	1,923,217.80	353,611.00	....	31,494,312.80
1885	28,429,628.00	....	2,047,268.50	308,492.00	....	30,785,388.50
1886	31,172,364.00	....	*1,097,390.00	†150,949.00	6908,956	32,709,609.00
1887	33,774,156.00	....	1,364,413.80	235,126.00	124,594	35,498,299.80
1888	36,293,183.00	....	1,588,426.00	283,954.00	133,179	38,298,741.00

* Postage on second-class matter was reduced from 2 cents to 1 cent a pound July 1, 1885.
† The standard of weight was increased from ½ to 1 ounce for 2 cents, on first-class matter, July 1, 1885.

No. 9.—*Statement by fiscal years of the issues of stamped envelopes, from the date of their first issue, June 27, 1853, to June 30, 1888, with percentages of issues of special-request envelopes, from the date of their first issue, May, 1865.*

Year ending—	Plain envelopes, including wrappers.	Special-request envelopes.	Total.	Percentage of request envelopes.
une 30—				
1853	5,000,000	....	5,000,000	....
1854	21,384,100	....	21,384,100	....
1855	23,451,725	....	23,451,725	....
1856	33,764,050	....	23,764,050	....
1857	33,063,400	....	33,063,400	....
1858	30,971,375	....	30,971,375	....
1859	30,280,300	....	30,280,300	....
1860	29,280,025	....	29,280,025	....
1861	26,027,300	....	26,027,300	....
1862	27,234,150	....	27,234,150	....
1863	25,518,750	....	25,518,750	....
1864	28,218,800	....	28,218,800	....
1865	25,456,175	750,000	26,206,175	2.86
1866	30,386,200	8,708,525	39,094,725	22.28
1867	46,421,400	16,665,250	64,086,650	26.42
1868	47,894,900	25,469,750	73,364,650	34.72
1869	49,851,000	31,824,100	81,675,100	38.97
1870	49,951,500	39,338,000	89,289,500	42.12
1871	56,563,625	48,111,650	101,675,275	45.97
1872	67,100,750	46,825,000	113,925,750	41.10
1873	78,971,350	52,201,250	131,172,600	39.80
1874	84,478,250	51,940,250	136,418,500	38.08
1875	95,135,400	54,631,000	149,766,400	36.48
1876	100,965,750	64,554,500	165,520,250	39.00
1877	106,276,950	64,374,500	170,651,450	37.72
1878	115,715,100	67,815,250	183,560,350	36.96
1879	110,503,700	67,058,250	177,561,950	37.77
1880	130,301,500	76,835,500	207,137,000	37.09
1881	142,043,050	85,024,000	227,067,050	37.44
1882	155,861,200	100,704,250	256,565,450	39.25
1883	158,688,200	100,578,250	259,266,450	38.79
1884	192,716,550	129,515,500	322,232,050	40.19
1885	185,954,650	136,796,750	322,751,400	42.38
1886	201,265,850	152,742,250	354,008,100	43.14
1887	210,507,300	171,104,000	381,611,300	44.84
1888	237,010,500	196,625,250	433,635,750	45.34

No. 10.—*Statement by fiscal years of the number of postal-cards supplied postmasters, from the date of their first issue, May 1, 1873, to June 30, 1888.*

Year.	1-cent.	2-cent.	Total.	Year.	1-cent.	2-cent.	Total.
June 30—				June 30—			
1873	*31,094,000	....	31,094,000	1881	308,412,500	124,000	308,536,500
1874	91,079,000	....	91,079,000	1882	351,394,500	103,500	351,498,000
1875	107,616,000	....	107,616,000	1883	379,424,500	92,250	379,516,750
1876	150,815,000	....	150,815,000	1884	362,789,500	87,250	362,876,750
1877	170,015,500	....	170,015,500	1885	339,336,500	80,000	339,416,500
1878	200,630,000	....	200,630,000	1886	355,499,000	149,000	355,648,000
1879	221,797,000	....	221,797,000	1887	356,778,000	161,250	356,939,250
1880	269,754,000	2,796,500	272,550,500	1888	381,671,500	126,000	381,797,500

* Two months only.

No. 11.—*Comparative statement of second-class matter mailed at post-offices of the first class during the past two fiscal years.*

Post-offices.	Year ending June 30, 1887.		Year ending June 30, 1888.		Increase for 1888.		Increase.	Per cent. of total amount collected in United States.
	Weight.	Postage collected.	Weight.	Postage collected.	Weight.	Postage.		
	Pounds.		*Pounds.*		*Pounds.*		*P. ct.*	
New York, N. Y...	30,359,504	$303,595.04	34,233,441	$342,234.41	3,863,937	$38,639.37	12.73	23.82
Chicago, Ill	12,280,863	122,806.63	14,378,609	143,786.69	2,097,806	20,978.06	17.06	10.10
Boston, Mass	7,689,340	76,893.40	8,978,773	89,787.73	1,289,433	12,894.33	16.60	6.25
Philadelphia, Pa ...	7,268,954	72,689.54	8,215,520	83,155.20	1,046,566	10,465.66	14.40	5.79
Saint Louis, Mo....	5,227,331	52,273.31	6,143,669	61,436.69	916,338	9,163.34	17.53	4.27
Cincinnati, Ohio ..	3,565,859	35,658.59	3,631,324	36,313.24	65,465	654.65	.18	2.53
San Francisco, Cal.	2,198,591	21,988.91	2,723,785	27,237.85	524,894	5,248.94	23.87	1.96
Detroit, Mich	1,894,161	18,941.61	1,914,350	19,143.50	20,189	201.89	1.06	1.33
Milwaukee, Wis...	1,864,355	18,643.55	1,969,612	19,696.12	105,257	1,052.57	5.64	1.37
Saint Paul, Minn..	1,765,921	17,659.21	1,810,909	18,109.09	44,988	449.88	2.54	1.26
Washington, D. C..	1,444,802	14,448.02	1,613,516	16,135.16	168,714	1,687.14	11.67	1.12
Kansas City, Mo...	1,376,783	13,767.83	1,489,535	14,895.35	112,752	1,127.52	8.19	1.04
Louisville, Ky	1,341,727	13,417.27	1,424,417	14,244.17	82,690	826.90	6.16	1.00
Cleveland, Ohio....	1,337,327	13,373.27	1,480,144	14,801.44	142,817	1,428.17	10.68	1.03
Augusta, Mo.	1,327,868	13,278.68	1,702,413	17,024.13	374,545	3,745.45	28.27	1.19
Rochester, N. Y...	1,317,087	13,170.87	1,372,518	13,725.18	*71,609	710.09	5.75	.87
Pittsburgh, Pa.....	1,241,467	12,414.67	1,493,571	14,935.71	131,051	1,310.51	10.55	.97
Atlanta, Ga	1,201,892	12,018.92	1,559,233	15,592.33	291,672	2,916.79	24.27	1.05
Minneapolis, Minn	1,181,363	11,813.63	1,374,362	13,723.62	377,870	3,778.70	31.99	1.08
Omaha, Nebr	1,169,758	11,697.58	1,281,421	12,824.21	202,604	2,036.04	17.32	.96
Baltimore, Md	1,118,221	11,182.21	1,102,461	11,024.61	164,200	1,642.00	14.68	.89
Elgin, Ill..........	1,078,049	10,780.49	1,106,539	11,065.39	24,412	244.12	2.26	.77
Toledo, Ohio	1,074,764	10,747.64	1,122,299	11,222.99	175,824	1,758.24	18.56	.77
New Orleans, La...	946,475	9,464.75	1,192,195	11,921.95	252,045	2,520.45	26.81	.73
Nashville, Tenn...	940,150	9,401.50	907,738	9,077.38	58,562	585.62	6.90	.83
Springfield, Mass ..	849,176	8,491.76	946,538	9,465.38	207,636	2,076.36	28.11	.63
Denver, Colo	738,902	7,389.02	873,543	8,735.43	192,224	1,922.24	28.21	.66
Springfield, Ohio..	681,319	6,813.19	731,143	7,311.43	55,617	556.17	8.23	.60
Indianapolis, Ind..	675,526	6,755.26	771,982	7,719.82	113,570	1,135.70	15.73	.51
Des Moines, Iowa..	658,412	6,584.12	615,818	6,158.18	29,353	293.53	5.01	.54
Albany, N. Y	586,465	5,864.65	509,322	5,093.22	26,050	260.50	5.39	.43
Buffalo, N. Y	483,272	4,832.72	493,007	4,930.07	26,327	263.27	5.64	.35
Richmond, Va.....	466,680	4,666.80	644,807	6,418.07	194,458	1,944.58	43.18	.34
Utica, N. Y	450,349	4,503.49	924,154	5,241.54	87,014	870.14	19.90	.45
Columbus, Ohio....	437,140	4,371.40	441,941	4,419.41	63,712	637.12	16.84	.36
Dayton, Ohio	378,229	3,782.29	268,702	2,687.03	*4,825	48.25	1.78	.37
Elmira, N. Y	273,527	2,735.27	343,725	3,437.23	72,820	728.20	26.88	.19
Portland, Oregon..	270,899	2,699.80	295,606	2,956.06	26,220	262.26	9.74	.24
Portland, Me	268,380	2,693.80	454,693	4,546.93	185,726	1,837.26	60.05	.21
Dallas, Tex........	268,967	2,689.67	195,757	1,957.57	*64,035	643.35	24.65	.32
Galveston, Tex	259,792	2,597.92	274,268	2,742.68	23,538	235.38	9.39	.14
Syracuse, N. Y	250,730	2,507.30	304,603	3,030.03	68,206	682.96	29.02	.19
Topeka, Kans......	235,307	2,353.07	191,904	1,939.04	*32,246	322.46	14.26	.21
Providence, R. I...	226,150	2,261.50	248,913	2,489.13	31,847	318.47	14.67	.14
Brooklyn, N. Y....	217,066	2,10 0.66	261,820	2,618.20	57,139	571.39	27.92	.17
Memphis, Tenn ...	204,681	3,046.81	220,462	2,204.62	20,319	203.19	10.15	.18
Saint Joseph, Mo..	200,143	2,001.43	219,945	2,199.45	20,359	203.59	10.21	.15
Grand Rapids, Mich	190,586	1,995.86	217,473	2,174.73	18,003	180.03	9.03	.15
Hartford, Conn....	199,470	1,994.70	138,215	1,382.15	*51,022	510 22	26.96	.15
Harrisburgh, Pa....	189,237	1,892.37	217,712	2,177.12	33,766	337.66	18.36	.10
Charleston, S. C ...	183,946	1,839.46	193,248	1,932.48	22,547	225.47	13.21	.15
Dubuque, Iowa.....	170,701	1,707.01	229,413	2,294.13	59,915	599.15	35.35	.14
Jacksonville, Fla..	169,408	1,694.98	161,977	1,619.77	*6,942	69.42	4.11	.16
Savannah, Ga.....	168,919	1,689.19	170,979	1,709.79	11,936	119.36	7.50	.11
Troy, N. Y........	159,043	1,590.43	168,861	1,688.61	27,606	276.05	19.54	.12
Lincoln, Nebr......	141,256	1,412.56	165,218	1,652.18	26,652	256.52	18.00	.12
Peoria, Ill.........	130,566	1,395.66	125,315	1,25 1.35	1,944	19.44	1.52	.09
Sacramento, Cal...	123,391	1,233.91	113,617	1,136.17	*5,052	50.52	4.76	.08
Burlington, Iowa..	118,669	1,186.69	124,764	1,247.64	7,458	74.58	6.36	.09
Oakland, Cal	117,306	1,173.06	114,516	1,145.16	11,935	119.35	11.63	.08
Quincy, Ill........	102,581	1,025.81	137,038	1,370.38	42,708	427.08	45.52	.10
Los Angeles, Cal...	94,330	943.30	112,551	1,125.51	29,211	292.11	35.05	.08
New Haven, Conn.	83,340	843.40	90,934	909.34	9,033	90.33	11.03	.06
Reading, Pa.......	81,901	819.01	95,984	959.88	18,233	182.33	23.51	.07
Newark, N. J......	77,755	777.55	42,547	425.47	*22,411	224.11	34.50	.03
Bridgeport, Conn...	64,958	649.58	184,014	1,810.14	124,059	1,240.59	204.88	.13
Lynn, Mass........	60,555	605.55	58,164	581.64	1,589	15.89	2.81	.04
Wilmington, Del..	56,575	565.75	66,050	660.50	12,411	124.11	22.31	.04
Trenton, N. J......	55,639	556.39	69,543	695.43	16,412	164.12	20.89	.04
Worcester, Mass...	53,131	531.31	54,273	543.73	7,106	71.06	15.07	.04
Lowell, Mass......	47,167	471.67	52,120	521.20	52,97	52.97	11.31	.04
Binghamton, N.Y..	46,823	468.23	38,116	381.16	1,405	14.05	3.83	.03
Norfolk, Va	36,711	367.11						

* Decrease.

No.11.—*Comparative statement of second-class matter mailed at post-offices, etc.*—Cont'd.

Post-offices.	Year ending June 30, 1887.		Year ending June 30, 1888.		Increase for 1888.		Increase.	Per cent. of total amount collected in United States.
	Weight.	Postage collected.	Weight.	Postage collected.	Weight.	Postage.		
	Pounds.		*Pounds.*		*Pounds.*		*P. ct.*	
New Bedford. Mass.	31,346	$343.46	37,472	$374.72	3,126	$31.26	9.10	.03
Jersey City, N. J...	27,780	277.80	23,558	235.56	*4,222	42.22	15.20	.02
Allegheny, Pa....	18,316	133.46	36,736	367.36	23,390	233.90	175.26	.03
Bangor, Me	91,413	914.13	115,549	1,155.49	24,136	241.36	26.40	.09
Chattanooga, Tenn	150,087	1,500.87	169,194	1,691.94	19,107	191.07	12.73	.11
Davenport, Iowa...	79,092	790.92	74,354	743.54	*4,738	47.3-	5.99	.05
Erie, Pa	47,484	474.84	41,248	412.48	*6,236	62.36	13.13	.03
Rockford, Ill	67,024	670.24	76,819	708.19	9,795	97.95	14.61	.05
Scranton, Pa......	32,647	316.67	40,973	409.73	8,306	81.06	25.43	.03
Wheeling, W. Va..	87,702	877.02	102,163	1,021.63	14,461	144.61	16.49	.07
Total	104,868,019	1,048,680.19	119,2538.77	1,192,538.77	14,385,858	143,858.58	13.72	82.71

* Decrease.

No. 12.—*Number of registered letters and parcels transmitted through the mails from*

States and Territories.	Quarter ending September 30, 1887.				
	Domestic.		Foreign.		Free.
	Letters.	Parcels.	Letters.	Parcels.	
Alabama	23,777	1,734	617	32	6,387
Arkansas	33,002	1,214	123	7	7,227
California	52,895	11,548	8,074	590	9,650
Colorado	34,067	4,235	1,560	114	4,418
Connecticut	80,754	9,288	2,823	53	56,603
Delaware	4,000	96	131	4	648
Florida	25,168	1,569	619	27	6,292
Georgia	87,261	1,001	210	22	8,0.9
Illinois	115,742	19,058	10,547	386	82,420
Indiana	59,603	1,909	713	27	17,143
Iowa	53,976	2,564	1,503	57	24,844
Kansas	68,257	3,778	1,070	39	22,365
Kentucky	45,696	5,617	364	31	6,645
Louisiana	41,900	3,596	1,509	50	5,214
Maine	40,772	1,250	3,401	83	5,433
Maryland	30,000	1,478	1,112	54	3,458
Massachusetts	72,402	9,391	14,729	220	9,081
Michigan	65,218	3,093	7,044	139	18,530
Minnesota	38,010	2,304	3,969	88	9,551
Mississippi	26,396	2,071	124	11	7,342
Missouri	86,378	10,060	2,138	118	19,940
Nebraska	38,270	1,681	1,580	60	9,843
Nevada	5,379	385	838	14	1,094
New Hampshire	17,299	623	1,669	16	3,561
New Jersey	43,468	1,492	4,831	63	4,785
New York	230,150	63,211	44,036	4,407	71,664
North Carolina	85,149	1,487	86	11	8,960
Ohio	101,831	6,227	3,740	140	25,959
Oregon	20,895	1,797	1,331	71	3,833
Pennsylvania	177,206	8,945	17,858	506	23,942
Rhode Island	11,434	1,626	1,633	57	1,148
South Carolina	20,060	904	142	46	4,453
Tennessee	41,672	1,799	353	46	7,198
Texas	52,673	4,102	2,180	314	18,030
Vermont	13,961	823	867	13	2,106
Virginia	52,093	3,135	346	64	6,768
West Virginia	29,840	474	102	3	3,748
Wisconsin	49,013	2,175	2,849	128	13,357
Alaska	304	71	13	8	6
Arizona	7,555	758	209	2	921
Dakota	85,375	1,134	1,315	55	6,562
District of Columbia	9,704	1,034	457	48	48,229
Idaho	12,140	997	232	6	1,186
Indian Territory	8,107	381	48	3	665
Montana	17,716	1,482	1,332	56	1,735
New Mexico	9,075	1,590	244	22	1,703
Utah	11,167	1,257	463	83	1,278
Washington	18,274	677	832	55	2,301
Wyoming	7,626	766	216	24	816
Total	2,073,574	209,706	151,764	8,466	558,471

each State and Territory in the United States during the fiscal year ending June 30, 1888.

Quarter ending December 31, 1887.					Quarter ending March 31, 1868.				
Domestic.		Foreign.		Free.	Domestic.		Foreign.		Free.
Letters.	Parcels.	Letters.	Parcels.		Letters.	Parcels.	Letters.	Parcels.	
45,249	2,164	328	26	7,096	49,790	1,612	362	35	7,205
47,012	1,987	199	8	8,104	49,376	1,395	201	8	7,757
67,512	27,865	11,864	1,142	9,925	62,177	13,205	9,368	882	10,429
38,475	9,430	2,377	264	5,018	39,322	4,496	2,099	200	4,884
35,478	12,463	3,931	141	63,368	35,011	11,114	3,260	110	66,594
4,508	189	175	5	828	4,510	119	153	1	742
29,895	2,891	701	55	6,563	33,739	2,494	790	62	5,591
40,049	2,640	365	20	8,667	52,077	2,106	395	16	8,602
137,364	31,774	13,169	586	35,188	142,267	23,530	13,236	492	35,386
72,511	3,696	1,032	73	18,573	81,113	2,689	900	58	18,334
62,609	5,965	2,462	290	26,890	65,058	3,375	2,431	226	27,700
75,143	7,743	1,253	114	23,567	74,598	4,101	1,503	76	23,339
50,640	7,612	534	49	7,000	00,063	7,231	479	58	7,093
53,736	5,306	2,030	103	5,427	36,302	4,246	2,197	120	5,759
45,414	3,182	3,334	42	6,034	42,502	1,741	2,923	37	5,649
34,877	2,330	1,420	63	3,723	56,089	1,604	1,328	51	4,011
42,671	17,220	17,660	480	9,466	72,074	11,793	14,099	883	9,635
78,351	6,044	8,671	1,772	20,363	78,210	4,449	8,369	123	21,178
53,842	4,624	5,163	256	10,944	49,390	3,129	5,609	112	10,553
39,772	3,166	202	75	8,480	45,664	2,604	199	3	8,417
107,524	16,438	2,983	529	22,079	115,284	12,106	2,381	242	22,249
47,570	3,994	2,148	234	10,968	47,226	2,314	2,001	60	11,443
6,153	945	485	45	1,134	5,203	481	308	20	1,000
18,912	983	1,925	40	4,022	19,678	539	1,750	9	4,005
41,744	8,505	6,994	160	4,985	40,061	1,776	5,153	101	4,988
256,674	93,483	55,587	6,314	81,762	238,569	67,011	50,050	4,449	90,229
46,300	2,373	131	9	9,327	49,935	1,830	106	6	9,316
125,400	12,146	4,448	308	27,297	135,027	9,052	4,991	201	29,435
27,801	2,909	1,717	511	4,326	27,261	1,081	1,322	182	4,224
189,594	20,608	16,259	877	25,577	199,890	10,737	20,222	540	26,152
11,833	2,130	2,230	40	1,332	11,468	1,655	2,016	18	1,384
33,781	1,188	233	23	4,746	31,614	1,349	208	8	4,562
52,133	2,932	456	32	7,607	56,729	2,068	449	16	7,364
76,814	6,791	2,833	495	19,975	78,251	5,679	2,689	503	19,904
16,703	1,356	1,146	24	8,135	16,584	1,292	1,076	41	8,562
62,803	4,326	394	68	7,283	64,401	3,081	325	44	7,891
83,713	632	774	21	4,468	65,381	448	150	10	4,295
63,043	4,036	2,586	220	15,935	60,074	2,555	3,312	115	15,765
407	126	25	7	10	363	54	12	2	13
8,788	1,327	170	14	1,121	9,221	1,010	204	7	1,068
46,750	2,953	2,343	44	7,762	37,019	1,565	2,351	37	7,106
11,346	2,722	702	96	50,076	19,781	1,679	615	85	55,974
13,901	1,481	229	9	1,259	12,120	795	209	28	1,289
9,965	506	106	6	682	11,683	438	131	....	774
21,787	2,870	1,394	134	1,710	18,971	2,028	1,281	94	1,633
10,551	1,682	364	40	1,973	10,138	1,083	321	20	1,875
12,689	1,808	550	103	1,698	12,838	1,328	499	43	1,631
23,651	1,743	1,487	120	2,709	23,593	1,121	2,299	54	1,493
8,295	1,395	278	31	748	7,997	853	233	25	661
2,493,129	958,189	186,447	16,120	611,020	2,556,285	244,143	176,935	10,024	630,178

No. 12.—*Number of registered letters and parcels transmitted through the*

[States and Territories.	Quarter ending June 30, 1888.					Total.	
	Domestic.		Foreign.		Free.	Domestic.	
	Letters.	Parcels.	Letters.	Parcels.		Letters.	Parcels.
Alabama	44,708	1,669	249	16	7,142	172,524	7,179
Arkansas	43,179	1,281	155	15	7,587	172,579	8,877
California	58,745	14,902	9,501	1,043	9,954	241,329	87,529
Colorado	38,664	3,173	1,813	108	4,961	150,528	21,334
Connecticut	83,741	9,270	3,089	258	61,307	134,088	42,135
Delaware	8,370	82	141	1	714	16,388	486
Florida	31,416	2,197	759	46	5,976	12,218	9,151
Georgia	46,415	2,334	274	10	8,405	183,702	8,941
Illinois	119,570	24,218	11,343	440	84,491	514,943	98,580
Indiana	67,521	2,293	726	27	17,923	280,748	16,627
Iowa	55,087	3,011	1,750	142	27,2 8	2,6,790	14,915
Kansas	63,963	3,523	1,147	37	23,265	281,961	19,145
Kentucky	52,805	7,219	343	37	7,512	209,844	27,679
Louisiana	53,334	4,301	2,006	126	5,653	204,672	17,539
Maine	44,961	1,545	3,012	20	6,019	173,649	7,927
Maryland	84,111	1,543	1,046	121	3,941	135,137	7,044
Massachusetts	76,984	11,162	15,082	389	9,486	311,131	49,516
Michigan	70,814	3,757	7,251	1:0	21,027	292,503	17,334
Minnesota	45,522	2,810	4,285	157	10,238	184,764	12,963
Mississippi	39,617	2,357	163	6	8,480	151,449	10,198
Missouri	99,775	12,431	1,992	404	21,893	408,961	51,617
Nebraska	43,247	1,751	1,640	48	10,915	176,313	9,740
Nevada	5,302	433	377	9	1,098	22,037	2,244
New Hampshire	18,684	516	1,609	15	4,147	74,573	2,661
New Jersey	48,161	1,559	6,303	77	7,628	173,434	8,332
New York	240,403	79,445	48,603	4,398	83,936	963,796	303,150
North Carolina	47,879	1,720	89	6	9,590	178,263	7,410
Ohio	115,240	8,464	4,391	259	27,786	477,498	35,849
Oregon	23,167	2,148	1,300	119	4,478	99,124	8,065
Pennsylvania	199,677	15,296	13,304	729	26,448	766,687	56,656
Rhode Island	11,156	1,822	2,033	22	1,196	45,891	7,233
South Carolina	27,062	3,165	167	30	4,799	113,117	4,606
Tennessee	63,510	1,864	302	15	7,939	218,044	8,653
Texas	64,163	6,533	2,487	454	20,834	272,124	22,105
Vermont	16,168	1,263	1,031	20	3,268	64,506	4,844
Virginia	50,037	3,441	386	25	7,610	238,424	13,983
West Virginia	33,483	517	102	....	3,955	162,417	2,311
Wisconsin	56,340	1,604	2,928	168	15,581	229,970	10,460
Alaska	307	93	14	5	12	1,381	44
Arizona	8,604	726	277	20	1,009	34,258	3,821
Dakota	33,985	1,314	1,755	58	7,478	153,165	6,860
District of Columbia	10,568	1,563	585	55	61,549	42,399	6,998
Idaho	12,070	872	179	13	1,368	50,240	4,145
Indian Territory	9,563	388	135	3	777	89,318	1,11
Montana	18,341	2,157	1,152	70	1,981	76,815	8,537
New Mexico	10,361	953	312	36	2,046	40,125	5,307
Utah	11,164	871	633	35	1,829	47,858	5,321
Washington	23,236	1,110	521	51	2,509	88,754	4,651
Wyoming	7,107	643	460	12	922	31,025	3,657
Total	2,342,426	254,534	159,461	10,341	625,961	9,465,414	1,068,572

mails from each State and Territory in the United States, etc.—Continued.

Total.			Grand total of letters and parcels registered for year ending June 30, 1888.	Fees. received.	Increase.			
Foreign.		Free.			Letters and parcels.	Fees.	Per cent.	
Letters.	Parcels.						Letters and parcels.	Fees.
1,556	109	27,830	210,196	$18,236.80	33,140	$2,990.10	18.71	19.63
678	38	30,675	209,847	17,917.20	23,441	1,982.20	12.57	12.43
38,807	3,657	39,958	301,271	35,131.30	60,383	5,680.40	18.24	19.20
8,089	746	19,311	204,008	18,080.70	31,371	2,868.60	18.60	18.87
13,113	562	247,874	438,072	19,079.80	18,623	1,396.00	4.43	7.89
600	11	2,932	20,417	1,748.50	763	35.60	3.83	2.07
2,860	190	24,702	157,190	13,242.80	2,645	*33.00	1.64	*.24
1,244	68	33,803	249,794	19,590.50	20,120	1,849.00	9.59	10.42
48,205	1,994	137,485	801,207	64,372.20	48,368	3,471.10	6.42	5.51
3,371	185	71,973	366,901	29,493.10	14,765	685.70	4.19	2.88
8,148	715	106,682	307,250	26,076.80	20,770	1,071.10	5.99	4.28
4,973	266	92,576	208,881	30,614.56	*1,621	*1,517.70	*.40	*4.95
1,840	175	28,250	267,828	23,907.80	15,963	1,496.10	6.33	6.63
7,742	309	22,083	252,435	23,035.20	34,181	3,354.40	15.66	17.04
12,670	182	23,135	217,563	10,442.80	23,434	2,026.40	11.84	11.64
4,946	299	15,133	102,549	14,741.60	10,758	934.50	7.08	6.76
61,870	1,472	37,668	461,357	42,368.90	36,340	3,167.60	8.55	8.08
31,355	2,154	81,116	421,854	34,373.60	31,240	2,122.50	7.93	6.58
19,026	615	41,826	260,604	21,936.80	10,826	706.10	4.33	3.77
668	95	32,719	193,140	16,243.00	32,323	2,799.70	19.83	20.81
9,494	1,293	86,161	557,516	47,138.50	46,874	3,178.80	9.10	7.22
7,838	392	43,171	236,954	19,378.30	10,066	541.90	4.43	2.87
1,508	88	4,446	30,343	2,593.70	1,545	113.50	5.32	4.57
7,003	80	15,735	100,052	8,431.70	4,603	268.70	4.82	3.29
22,401	401	22,786	226,654	20,426.80	31,200	2,615.80	15.96	14.68
196,376	19,568	827,595	1,814,485	148,609.00	104,218	7,411.90	6.19	5.24
412	32	37,213	224,330	18,711.70	19,962	1,510.60	9.76	8.78
17,570	908	110,477	642,342	53,180.50	77,104	5,940.50	13.64	12.57
5,670	883	16,861	130,603	11,374.20	18,906	1,749.80	16.08	18.18
67,643	2,751	102,119	904,776	89,205.70	135,694	12,265.50	15.79	15.92
7,912	137	5,060	66,233	6,117.80	7,362	721.20	12.50	13.36
750	69	18,540	137,082	11,874.20	13,845	1,245.80	11.23	11.74
1,620	109	30,108	256,534	22,642.60	48,570	4,670.60	23.30	25.96
10,189	1,766	78,793	884,977	30,618.40	30,443	1,928.60	8.58	6.72
4,120	96	12,873	85,441	7,256.80	5,546	528.10	6.94	7.84
1,451	201	29,052	283,111	25,405.10	*19,103	*1,417.80	*6.32	*5.28
528	34	16,466	181,756	16,529.40	46,431	4,502.40	34.33	37.43
11,675	631	60,658	313,394	25,273.00	11,363	702.40	3.76	2.85
64	22	41	1,852	181.10	480	46.60	34.98	34.64
950	49	4,179	43,257	3,907.00	*2,511	*304.40	*5.48	*7.22
7,764	194	29,368	197,397	16,608.90	12,422	822.10	6.71	5.14
2,839	284	215,628	267,848	5,202.00	34,472	457.00	14.77	9.64
849	56	5,102	60,392	5,529.00	1,755	65.10	2.09	1.19
420	12	2,806	44,861	4,533.30	8,505	786.60	23.71	22.68
5,179	858	7,059	97,948	9,088.90	9,473	829.40	10.70	10.04
1,271	118	7,597	54,418	4,682.10	3,277	176.30	6.40	3.91
2,115	213	6,527	62,067	5,534.00	107	*102.90	.17	*1.81
5,139	280	9,072	107,896	9,882.40	22,771	2,182.70	26.75	28.34
1,187	92	3,147	39,108	3,596.10	*69	*86.30	*.17	*2.34
674,607	44,951	2,425,625	13,677,169	1,125,154.40	1,152,748	90,477.60	9.20	8.74

* Decrease.

RECAPITULATION.

Total domestic letters	9,465,414	10,531,986
Total domestic parcels	1,066,572	
Total foreign letters	674,607	719,558
Total foreign parcels	44,951	
Free		2,425,625
Grand total		13,677,169
Fees received		$1,125,154.40

No. 13.—*Table showing increase in the number of registered letters and parcels upon which fees were collected at the thirty leading cities in the country during the fiscal year ending June 30, 1888, over the number for the preceding year.*

Cities.	Year ending June 30, 1887.				Year ending June 30, 1888.				Increase.				Per cent.		
	Letters.	Parcels	Total.	Fees.	Letters.	Parcels.	Total.	Fees.	Letters.	Parcels	Total.	Fees.	Letters.	Parcels	Total and Fees.
New York, N.Y.	490,139	285,836	776,975	$77,697.50	538,233	286,729	804,961	$99,406.10	48,098	*20,107	27,986	$2,798.60	9.81	*7.00	8.60
Chicago, Ill.	175,810	69,756	245,566	24,554.00	201,864	79,974	281,128	28,182.80	26,054	10,218	36,272	3,627.20	1.48	14.04	14.77
Philadelphia, Pa.	146,830	41,013	187,843	18,734.30	156,501	41,566	198,067	19,806.70	9,671	553	10,524	1,052.40	6.80	1.84	5.61
Boston, Mass.	118,885	28,322	147,207	14,720.70	120,389	28,663	159,052	15,905.20	11,464	341	11,845	1,184.50	9.65	1.27	8.04
San Francisco, Cal.	67,518	31,028	98,546	9,854.60	79,897	34,143	113,540	11,354.00	11,679	8,081	14,960	1,490.00	17.39	9.91	15.17
Saint Louis, Mo.	56,879	34,168	98,546	8,964.60	58,414	31,608	93,017	9,301.70	8,158	435	8,471	347.10	5.48	1.27	3.17
New Orleans, La.	65,483	11,768	77,260	7,725.00	81,217	11,343	92,553	9,256.00	15,735	*425	15,310	1,531.00	24.62	*3.61	19.81
Brooklyn, N.Y.	54,469	15,181	69,650	6,945.00	63,361	16,492	78,853	7,885.30	7,892	1,311	9,203	920.30	14.48	8.63	13.21
Baltimore, Md.	43,440	5,774	49,214	4,921.40	49,945	4,856	54,892	5,489.20	6,504	*918	5,588	556.80	14.97	*13.89	11.35
Cincinnati, Ohio	37,052	9,066	46,118	4,611.80	39,859	11,285	51,144	5,114.40	2,807	2,219	5,026	502.60	7.67	24.47	10.89
Washington, D.C.	39,761	6,691	46,452	4,645.20	43,494	7,264	50,758	5,075.80	3,733	573	4,306	430.60	9.38	8.56	9.27
Louisville, Ky.	15,548	20,975	36,223	3,622.30	17,214	21,443	38,657	8,465.70	2,726	1,976	4,633	443.40	8.81	8.24	8.71
Kansas City, Mo.	25,777	4,631	30,408	3,040.80	29,468	4,601	34,041	5,041.70	3,693	*420	*181	563.10	14.21	42.53	18.52
Cleveland, Ohio	27,237	4,636	32,277	3,227.70	27,488	4,007	32,110	3,211.00	259	*591	4,544	*16.10	.96	*8.31	*.49
Denver, Colo.	18,616	7,438	26,433	2,713.40	27,971	6,752	81,220	3,167.80	3,378	1,171	1,083	434.40	17.12	15.74	16.74
Pittsburgh, Pa.	23,004	5,429	28,433	2,843.20	27,468	4,591	80,990	3,122.00	3,654	*591	4,528	106.30	7.65	*10.19	3.62
Buffalo, N.Y.	18,000	6,727	24,748	2,474.80	21,230	7,392	28,513	3,052.00	3,586	965	3,769	462.80	15.49	28.00	17.13
Detroit, Mich.	29,411	4,937	34,448	2,444.80	24,218	7,056	28,173	2,817.30	8,294	545	8,725	370.90	17.00	8.08	15.23
Minneapolis, Minn.	2,981	25,549	29,520	2,952.00	4,574	23,591	28,165	2,816.50	897	*82	*1,055	872.50	18.05	*2.03	16.22
Waterbury, Conn.	29,708	2,946	32,644	2,364.80	23,307	4,011	87,946	2,794.80	890	*1,508	4,300	*160.50	24.26	36.15	18.16
Saint Paul, Minn.	19,762	4,040	23,307	2,881.60	20,069	6,186	28,267	2,826.70	802	2,138	4,300	290.00	15.63	*3.16	12.70
Providence, R.I.	22,066	8,100	25,274	2,627.60	22,897	8,020	28,028	2,992.00	801	161	650	65.00	3.62	*4.74	2.57
Milwaukee, Wis.	11,443	4,005	16,448	1,962.50	18,600	5,214	22,583	2,986.50	7,166	1,210	8,415	841.50	62.03	81.18	54.47
Newark, N.J.	18,303	1,821	19,625	2,181.90	21,378	1,348	22,621	2,382.10	3,110	*500	2,790	273.00	17.08	*20.42	*4.23
Los Angeles, Cal.	16,673	2,069	21,819	1,934.70	19,971	1,320	20,886	2,063.10	2,609	*749	*324	*22.40	12.54	*28.85	6.94
Des Moines, Iowa	15,894	1,933	19,347	1,934.70	17,292	1,692	20,491	2,024.00	1,848	113	1,344	124.40	10.94	4.04	4.94
Omaha, Nebr.	15,110	1,729	15,800	1,580.00	18,371	2,446	20,360	2,011.60	2,198	*91	2,060	206.10	12.69	8.78	11.25
New Haven, Conn.	13,405	4,081	17,486	1,743.80	17,292	1,706	2N,116	2,011.80	2,771	*799	8,207	820.70	21.82	*5.06	18.90
Memphis, Tenn.					18,176	8,282	19,458	1,918.80			1,972	197.20	20.07	*10.07	11.27
Rochester, N.Y.															
	1,644,816	650,702	2,296,518	229,651.90	1,840,924	652,335	2,492,259	249,225.90	194,108	1,633	195,741	19,574.10	11.79	.25	8.03

* Decrease.

No. 14.—*Statement showing the operations of the registry system at the cities of New York, N. Y., Chicago, Ill , Washington, D. C., Saint Louis, Mo., Boston, Mass., and Philadelphia, Pa., during the fiscal year ending June 30, 1888.*

Description.	New York.	Chicago.	Washington.	Saint Louis.	Boston.	Philadelphia.
Letters registered	551, 817	210, 748	239, 298	62, 122	132, 435	160, 674
Third and fourth class parcels registered	226, 729	79, 974	7, 264	34, 603	28, 683	41, 566
Registered letters received for delivery	*1, 270, 704	590, 928	637, 602	291, 455	313, 865	339, 363
Registered third and fourth class parcels received for delivery....	....	37, 223	14, 408	9, 609	12, 111	17, 360
Registered letters and parcels received for distribution....... ..	1, 328, 072	52, 644	2, 028	7. 495	95, 170	3, 125
Registered packages received......	1, 002, 454	541, 906	589, 437	262, 935	279, 378	270, 729
Registered packages made up and mailed	876, 018	236, 506	168, 450	86, 817	112, 146	124, 289
Registered packages in transit received	794, 047	1, 033, 405	250, 882	844, 911	402, 586	227, 663
Through registered pouches and inner registered sacks received	39, 688	38, 515	22, 091	37, 988	32, 544	17, 483
Through registered pouches and inner registered sacks made up and dispatched	43, 607	36, 973	22, 091	38, 068	31, 343	17, 762
Through registered pouches and inner registered sacks in transit received	12, 596	6, 672	519	447	1, 533	470
Internal revenue through registered pouches dispatched	....	....	9, 336	....	....	....
Internal revenue through registered pouches returned	....	....	9, 214	....	....	....
Postal-note packages made up and mailed	11, 883	....	....	....	....	....
Postage-stamp packages made up and mailed	199, 620	....	....	....	....	....
Total number of articles handled..................	6, 457, 235	2, 885, 495	1, 992, 620	1, 676, 470	1, 441, 794	1, 220, 684

* Includes third and fourth class parcels.

No. 15.—*Statement showing the number and value of registered letters and parcels forwarded during the fiscal year ending June 30, 1888, for the Post Office and Treasury Departments.*

Description.	Number of packages.	Value.
Postage stamps from the New York agency...............................	199, 644	$38, 298, 741. 00
Letter sheet envelopes from the New York agency......	1, 583	58, 821. 00
Stamped envelopes and newspaper wrappers from the Hartford agency..	227, 214	8, 461. 9. 4. 84
Postal-cards from the Castleton agency	85, 006	3, 819, 835 00
Registered packages containing paid money-orders and postal-notes.....	....	136, 055, 662. 42
Surplus money-order funds remitted for deposit by registered mail	....	80, 387, 152 04
Money-order funds remitted by draft in the registered mail	....	*24, 600, 000. 00
Total for the Post-Office Department..................	513, 447	297, 662, 136. 30
Secretary of the Treasury received and sent...............................	3, 667	30, 645, 785. 55
Register of the Treasury received and sent	8, 901	136, 650, 350. 00
United States Treasurer received bonds and coupons, silver certificates, currency, including legal-tender national-bank notes, fractional currency, and coins	18, 063	49, 895, 310. 45
United States Treasurer sent	5, 389	1, 658, 063. 72
Comptroller of the Currency sent United States bonds, incomplete currency, and national bank notes	1, 064	9, 298, 390. 00
Comptroller of the Currency received	656	8, 786, 092. 50
Internal-revenue stamps sent	42, 521	138, 274, 892. 40
Internal-revenue stamps received	5, 075	13, 856, 073. 81
Sixth Auditor received and sent	13, 805	14, 266. 81
Assistant Treasurer of the United States sent	†6, 071	†108, 592, 618. 34
Assistant Treasurer of the United States received......................	‡29, 668	‡14, 638, 106. 01
Internal-revenue collectors received and sent......................	§63, 734	§101, 921, 241. 91
Total for the Treasury Department	228, 614	613, 531, 196. 50
Aggregate.................................	742, 061	911, 193, 332. 80

* Partially and safely estimated.
† Four out of 9 offices estimated by doubling returns for 5½ months.
‡ Reports received from 6 out of 9 offices.
§ Reports received from 57 out of 63 collection districts; 6 districts safely estimated on partial statistics.

16.—*Statement showing the operations of the special-delivery system at all the free-delivery post-offices during the fiscal year ending June 30, 1888.*

Post-office.	Quarter ending Sept. 30, 1887.			Quarter ending Dec. 31, 1887.			Quarter ending Mar. 31, 1888.			Quarter ending June 30, 1888.			Total—12 months ending June 30, 1888.		
	Special-delivery letters and parcels arriving from other places.	Special-delivery letters and parcels deposited for local delivery.	Total special-delivery letters and parcels.	Special-delivery letters and parcels arriving from other places.	Special-delivery letters and parcels deposited for local delivery.	Total special-delivery letters and parcels.	Special-delivery letters and parcels arriving from other places.	Special-delivery letters and parcels deposited for local delivery.	Total special-delivery letters and parcels.	Special-delivery letters and parcels arriving from other places.	Special-delivery letters and parcels deposited for local delivery.	Total special-delivery letters and parcels.	Special-delivery letters and parcels arriving from other places.	Special-delivery letters and parcels deposited for local delivery.	Total special-delivery letters and parcels.
Abilene, Kans	63	4	67	78		78	24	5	29	35	0	35	59	5	64
Adrian, Mich	284	46	330	288	56	344	61	8	69	78	3	81	275	20	295
Akron, Ohio	1,546	145	1,691	1,702	210	1,912	1,571	161	1,732	247	81	328	1,063	251	1,334
Albany, N.Y.				108		172	167		190	1,748	180	202	6,557	696	7,253
Alexandria, Va.	2									8.5		8.5		10	565
Allegheny, Pa.	1,850	881	2,781	1,161	5	3,184	1,694	1,217	2,911	694	1,131		7,211	4,300	11,xxx
Allentown, Pa.	108	7	165	168	5	170	131	10	141	200	25	218	598	24	652
Altoona, Pa	140	51	191	159	55	214	174	51	225	144	156	156	633	213	818
Amsterdam, N.Y.	70	8	78	80	8	88	78	4	82	162	10	106	324	31	355
Annapolis, Md.	60	0	60	63	0	63	152	0	152	90	1	94	365	1	366
Ann Arbor, Mich	125	8	126	172	14	195	146	17	163	179	16	194	625	14	679
Ansonia, Conn	38	1	39	47	8	50	46	6	52	60	2	101	191	12	203
Appleton, Wis							41	1	42	61	0	61	102	1	163
Asbury Park, N.J				77	2	79	47	1	48	108	4	112	111	7	239
Ashland, Wis							53	0	53	61	1	62	111	1	115
Atchison, Kans	100	8	103	145	1	146	141	10	151	108	8	116	494	22	616
Atlanta, Ga.	1,443	121	1,564	1,494	186	2,090	1,527	127	1,654	1,568	114	1,62	6,372	548	6,920
Atlantic City, N.J.	711	21	732	85	2	87	174	6	174	359	6	363	1,327	29	1,558
Auburn, Me.	61	6	67	65	4	69	66	2	72	61		69	255	22	277
Auburn, N.Y.	303	41	344	290	31	320	267	28	295	380	10	246	1,005	110	1,206
Augusta, Ga.	119	8	188	474	20	494	414	16	430	380	21	401	1,407	61	1,672
Augusta, Me.	114	14	140	138	47	127	108	83	189	122	19	141	564	113	540
Aurora, Ill	291	41	242	90	17	153	113	29	143	315	44	143	604	140	584
Austin, Tex.	6,778	1,373	8,151	5,916	1,619	7,565	4,483	1,862	6,345	5,943	1,747	263	24,120	6,631	1,160
Baltimore, Md	588	138	520	868	167	525	296	165	461	295	128	7,090	1,331	100	30,751
Bangor, Me.	86		98	92		90	102		109	87		433	380		1,929
Bath, Me	88	6	88	78	4	90	49	7	74	11	7	98	275	604	340
Battle Creek, Mich	75	13	187	73	17	184	116	23	121	145	19	97	260	74	397
Bay City, Mich		6		174	10	29	26	5	37	50	14	61	102	35	801
Beatrice, Nebr.	131			27	0		20	2	108	92	4	98		5	107
Beaver Falls, Pa.	92	2	94	107		107	101	4		52	4		392	10	402

Place																
Belleville, Ill.																
Bethlehem, Pa.																
Binghamton, N.Y.																
Birmingham, Ala.																
Birmingham, Conn.																
Bloomington, Ill.																
Boston, Mass.																
Bradford, Pa.																
Brattleborough, Vt.																
Bridgeport, Conn.																
Bridgeton, N.J.																
Brockton, Mass.																
Brooklyn, N.Y.																
Buffalo, N.Y.																
Burlington, Iowa.																
Burlington, Vt.																
Cairo, Ill.																
Camden, N.J.																
Canton, Ohio.																
Carlisle, Pa.																
Carthage, Mo.																
Cedar Rapids, Iowa.																
Chambersburgh, Pa.																
Champaign, Ill.																
Charleston, S.C.																
Charleston, W.Va.																
Charlotte, N.C.																
Chattanooga, Tenn.																
Chester, Pa.																
Cheyenne, Wyo.																
Chicago, Ill.																
Chillicothe, Ohio.																
Cincinnati, Ohio.																
Cleveland, Ohio.																
Clinton, Iowa.																
Clinton, N.Y.																
Colorado Springs, Colo.																
Columbia, N.C.																
Columbus, Ga.																
Columbus, Ohio.																
Concord, N.H.																
Corning, N.Y.																
Cortland, N.Y.																
Council Bluffs, Iowa.																
Covington, Ky.																
Cumberland, Md.																
Dallas, Tex.																
Danbury, Conn.																
Danville, Ill.																
Danville, Va.																
Davenport, Iowa.																
Dayton, Ohio.																

No. 16.—Statement showing the operations of the special-delivery system at all the free-delivery post-offices, etc.—Continued.

Post-office.	Quarter ending Sept. 30, 1887. Special-delivery letters and parcels arriving from other places.	Quarter ending Sept. 30, 1887. Special-delivery letters and parcels deposited for local delivery.	Quarter ending Sept. 30, 1887. Total special-delivery letters and parcels.	Quarter ending Dec. 31, 1887. Special-delivery letters and parcels arriving from other places.	Quarter ending Dec. 31, 1887. Special-delivery letters and parcels deposited for local delivery.	Quarter ending Dec. 31, 1887. Total special-delivery letters and parcels.	Quarter ending Mar. 31, 1888. Special-delivery letters and parcels arriving from other places.	Quarter ending Mar. 31, 1888. Special-delivery letters and parcels deposited for local delivery.	Quarter ending Mar. 31, 1888. Total special-delivery letters and parcels.	Quarter ending June 30, 1888. Special-delivery letters and parcels arriving from other places.	Quarter ending June 30, 1888. Special-delivery letters and parcels deposited for local delivery.	Quarter ending June 30, 1888. Total special-delivery letters and parcels.	Total—12 months ending June 30, 1888. Special-delivery letters and parcels arriving from other places.	Total—12 months ending June 30, 1888. Special-delivery letters deposited and parcels for local delivery.	Total—12 months ending June 30, 1888. Total special-delivery letters and parcels.
Decatur, Ill	164	24	178	112	19	164	147	35	182	177	22	199	623	100	723
Delaware, Ohio							70	15	85	91	3	94	161	18	179
Denison, Tex.							38	0	38	32	1	33	70	1	71
Denver, Colo.	2,372	793	3,165	2,270	805	3,270	2,316	878	3,194	2,901	794	3,695	9,859	3,474	13,333
Des Moines, Iowa	2,546	98	645	673		673	546	91	597	543	55	538	2,163	310	2,472
Detroit, Mich.	2,331	1,213	3,544	2,564	1,324	3,888	2,127	1,295	3,422	2,851	1,564	3,935	9,373	5,418	14,749
Dover, N.H.	130	1	131	111	2	113	112	6	118	208	24	230	475	20	485
Dubuque, Iowa	180	18	208	213	16	229	182	24	206	206	8	230	791	8	873
Duluth, Minn	136	50	158	141	36	177	89	31	120	195	34	195	637	121	848
Dunkirk, N.Y.	49	1	60	64	8	72	44	3	47	49	1	50	216	11	2.9
Easton, Pa.	223	39	282	111	78	292	229	56	285	240	40	280	931	294	1,149
East Orange, N.J.	162	9	168	167	33	202	183	10	193	241	17	258	771	46	819
East Saginaw, Mich.	257	27	293	211	11	271	216	50	296	222	43	265	906	161	1,047
Eau Claire, Wis	181	50	298	174	40	199	157	16	173	175	20	195	687	88	775
Elgin, Ill	86	38	136	110	23	188	77	29	106	83	21	104	356	156	514
Elizabeth, N.J.	258	33	291	334	63	396	363	45	418	386	51	449	1,352	205	1,557
Elkhart, Ind	50	9	63	65	13	78	84	1	83	88	5	93	287	32	319
Elmira, N.Y.	470	18	518	416	46	463	363	45	436	88	44	537	1,781	174	1,855
El Paso, Tex.	15	2	20	31	13	45	62	25	65	77	0	92	148	19	165
Emporia, Kan	79	18	97	150	11	110	76	5	101	45	15	62	327	73	400
Englewood, Ill	124	68	128	359	40	134	346	45	43	136	2	138	453	8	461
Erie, Pa	374	79	442	90	11	899	81	25	409	327	82	417	1,464	203	1,667
Evanston, Ill	93	5	98	431	22	101	349	10	363	108	16	122	972	41	413
Evansville, Ind.	467	24	491	380	73	433	361	44	405	414	67	451	1,661	67	1,758
Fall River, Mass	342	65	397				43	18	65	64	85	480	1,473	247	1,725
Fargo, Dak							189	19	208	56	10	60	99	24	122
Fitchburg, Mass	224	10	244	520	31	251	189	11	208	233	9	243	843	69	913
Flint, Mich.	81	3	84	71	7	76	65	0	70	80	7	87	298	27	325
Fond du Lac, Wis	64	2	66	63	0	63	56	0	56	211	2	58	211	2	243
Fort Scott, Kans	71	0	73	62	9	62	41	1	41	105	0	105	281	0	281
Fort Smith, Ark	40	2	51	67	4	71	79	1	80	80	1	80	254	8	263

Fort Wayne, Ind
Fort Worth, Tex
Frankfort, Ky
Frederick, Md
Freeport, Ill
Galesburgh, Ill
Galveston, Tex
Glens Falls, N. Y
Gloucester, Mass
Gloversville, N. Y
Grand Island, Nebr
Grand Rapids, Mich
Hagerstown, Md
Hamilton, Ohio
Hannibal, Mo
Harrisburg, Pa
Hartford, Conn
Hastings, Nebr
Haverhill, Mass
Helena, Mont
Hoboken, N. J
Holyoke, Mass
Hornellsville, N. Y
Hot Springs, Ark
Houston, Tex
Hudson, N. Y
Huntingdon, Pa
Huron, Dak
Hutchinson, Kans
Indianapolis, Ind
Iowa City, Ia. w.
Jackson, Mich
Jackson, Miss
Jacksonville, Fla
Jacksonville, Ill
Jamestown, N. Y
Janesville, Wis
Jersey City, N. J
Johnstown, Pa
Joliet, Ill
Kalamazoo, Mich
Kansas City, Kans
Kansas City, Mo
Keene, N. H
Keokuk, Iowa
Knoxville, Tenn
La Crosse, Wis
La Fayette, Ind
Lancaster, Pa
Lansing, Mich
Lawrence, Kans
Lawrence, Mass

No. 16.—*Statement showing the operations of the special-delivery system at all the free-delivery post-offices, etc.*—Continued.

Post-office.	Quarter ending Sept. 30, 1887.			Quarter ending Dec. 31, 1887.			Quarter ending Mar. 31, 1888.			Quarter ending June 30, 1888.			Total—12 months ending June 30.		
	Special-delivery letters and parcels arriving from other places.	Special-delivery letters and parcels deposited for local delivery.	Total special-delivery letters and parcels.	Special-delivery letters and parcels arriving from other places.	Special-delivery letters and parcels deposited for local delivery.	Total special-delivery letters and parcels.	Special-delivery letters and parcels arriving from other places.	Special-delivery letters and parcels deposited for local delivery.	Total special-delivery letters and parcels.	Special-delivery letters and parcels arriving from other places.	Special-delivery letters and parcels deposited for local delivery.	Total special-delivery letters and parcels.	Special-delivery letters and parcels arriving from other places.	Special-delivery letters and parcels deposited for local delivery.	Total special-delivery letters and parcels.
Leadville, Colo	245	61	309	313	85	398	277	77	354	295	65	360	1,130	291	1,421
Leavenworth, Kans	170	11	181	234	13	247	169	28	169	184	10	194	757	60	817
—, Pa										101	16	117	163	22	168
Lewiston, M	167	28	165	162	27	209	62	6	68	101	13	118	651	79	740
Lexington, Ky	356	15	371	356	23	379	138	11	144	169	20	180	1,457	40	1,560
Lima, Ohio	100	3	149	30	0	30	343	43	388	40	29	120	306	40	306
—, Nebr	511	7	548	570	19	649	116	30	131	472	20	492	1,906	76	2,062
Little Falls, N. Y	46	1	47	65	4	69	383	61	413	104	4	53	198	13	291
Little —, Ark	342	25	367	377	32	409	38	9	40	51	51	399	356	101	1,537
Lockport, N. Y	149	33	182	128	29	157	321	20	382	348	19	141	527	101	628
Logansport, Ind	150	13	163	122	7	129	126	20	118	122	11	122	553	51	553
Long Island City, N. Y							121		141	169	0	68	642	0	68
Los Angeles, Cal	87	275			297	126	792	167	960	489	311	815	2,963	959	4,902
Louisville, Ky	1,836	622	2,192	2,175	692	2,378	1,966	704	2,670	2,246	746	3,044	8,243	2,716	10,539
Lowell, Mass	1,007	236	1,243	388	388	631	940	389	1,309	1,046	324	1,370	4,924	1,297	5,221
Lynchburgh, Va	26	20		50	12		118	16	134	291	16	310	1,078	70	1,148
Lynn, Mass	956	266	1,142	1,046	239		881	196	1,077	1,045	216	1,291	3,908	846	4,756
McKeesport, Pa										154	19	173	154	19	173
Marion, Ohio	461	81	406	614	59	673	500	65	566	490	68	553	2,068	216	2,284
Madison, Wis	180	9	196	170	18	198	153	15	168	196	15	181	678	57	765
Malden, Mass	278	25	303	321	27	348	384	31	385	530	24	347	1,290	107	1,398
Manchester, N. H	507	58	565	485	50	645	461	21	522	14	30	75	961	908	169
Manistee, Mich							11	2	13	21	1	21	65	8	22
Mankato, Minn	118	21	139	151	18	167	40	7	47	201	1	285	164	14	132
Mansfield, Ohio							147	10	157	65		65	677	63	720
M—sea, Ohio										58	1	58	204	1	57
Marlborough, —	68	2	70	75	4		68	3	71	97	3	97	204	3	317
Marquette, Mich							28	0	28	67	4	71	94	2	68
Marshalltown, Iowa	58	8	66	84	9		43	8	53	69	4	69	254	28	282
Martin, Ohio							44		73	71		73	138	12	144
Meadville, Pa	110	25	135	167	52	199	151	60	211	188	61	249	576	218	794

Office																	
Memphis, Tenn																	
Meridian, Miss … 4in																	
McMillan, Miss … 4in																	
Middletown, N. Y																	
Middletown, Ohio																	
Milwaukee, Wis																	
Minneapolis, Minn																	
M tale, Ala																	
Moline, Ill																	
Montgomery, Ala																	
Mr. Vt																	
Mu… ka… Iwa																	
Muskegon, Mich																	
Nashua, N. H																	
… Tenn																	
Newark, May, Ind																	
Newark, N. J																	
… Ohio																	
New Bedford, Mass																	
New Britain, Conn																	
New Brunswick, N. J																	
Newburgh, N. Y																	
Newburyport, Mass																	
New Castle, Pa																	
New … Conn																	
New Orleans, La																	
Newport, Ky																	
Newport, R. I																	
… Kans																	
New York, N. Y																	
Norfolk, Va																	
Norristown, Pa																	
North Adams, Mass																	
… Mass																	
Norwalk, Ohio																	
Norwich … 4in																	
Ogdensburgh, N. Y																	
Omaha, Nebr																	
Oneonta, N. Y																	
Orange, N. J																	
Oshkosh, Wis																	
Oskaloosa, Iowa																	
O… L.																	
Oswego, N. Y																	
O… Ill																	
… Kans																	
Ottumwa, Iowa																	
Owego, N. Y																	
Paducah, Ky																	
Parkersburgh, W. Va																	

No. 16.—*Statement showing the operations of the special-delivery system at all the free-delivery post-offices, etc.—Continued.*

Post-office.	Quarter ending Sept. 3, 1887. Special-delivery letters and parcels arriving from other places.	Special-delivery letters and parcels deposited for local delivery.	Total special-delivery letters and parcels.	Quarter ending Dec. 31, 1887. Special-delivery letters and parcels arriving from other places.	Special-delivery letters and parcels deposited for local delivery.	Total special-delivery letters and parcels.	Quarter ending Mar. 31, 1888. Special-delivery letters and parcels arriving from other places.	Special-delivery letters and parcels deposited for local delivery.	Total special-delivery letters and parcels.	Quarter ending June 30, 1888. Special-delivery letters and parcels arriving from other places.	Special-delivery letters and parcels deposited for local delivery.	Total special-delivery letters and parcels.	Total—12 months ending June 30, 1888. Special-delivery letters and parcels arriving from other places.	Special-delivery letters and parcels deposited for local delivery.	Total special-delivery letters and parcels.
Paterson, N.J	315	29	344	357	36	393	388	46	434	417	39	456	1,477	150	1,627
Pawtucket, R.I	222	7	229	201	10	211	192	15	207	158	24	182	773	56	829
Pekin, Ill	27	5	32	34	9	43	39	7	46	34	6	21	57	18	70
Pensacola, Fla.	65	148	773	519	165	724	500	152	652	84	112	38	120	24	144
Peoria, Ill	172	11	183	188	10	198	158	7	165	194	22	701	712	577	853
Petersburgh, Va.	12,441	2,357	14,792	13,262	4,514	17,806	12,516	4,674	17,190	13,687	5,739	19,426	17,896	17,384	729
Philadelphia, Pa.	51	6	50	39	42	41	59	54	6	82	13	181	13	226	118
Piqua, Ohio	4,787	5,445	10,232	4,753	7,072	11,825	4,312	6,509	10,821	4,840	6,675	11,515	18,692	25,701	44,393
Pittsburgh, Pa.	174	21	195	176	4	183	125	17	142	74	16	82	649	61	718
Pittsfield, Mass.	78	3	81	67	4	171	171	171	81	74	9	82	277	20	297
Port Huron, Mich	931	324	1,255	938	289	1,227	755	280	1,035	970	246	1,216	3,594	1,139	4,733
Portland, Me.	1,418	184	1,602	1,416	203	1,609	967	160	1,147	1,113	157	1,270	4,994	724	5,618
Portland, Oregon	143	1	144	158	2	160	113	6	119	74	10	137	541	19	560
Portsmouth, N.H	68	2	70	32	1	83	25	1	26	52	2	54	177	6	183
Portsmouth, Ohio	63	4	67	60	10	70	41	3	44	60	3	63	224	20	244
Portsmouth, Va.	120	26	146	124	52	188	106	37	143	118	20	138	478	135	613
Pottsville, Pa	275	28	303	381	27	466	316	19	335	258	22	274	1,331	98	1,429
Poughkeepsie, N.Y	1,912	490	2,402	2,075	543	2,818	2,000	604	2,604	2,296	536	2,832	8,283	2,173	10,456
Providence, R.I	38	2	40	12	12	12	14	19	16	18	0	18	3	3	4
Pueblo, Colo	281	146	457	318	141	459	220	127	347	271	117	388	1,100	531	1,631
Quincy, Ill	163	16	179	145	28	173	108	24	131	108	24	160	552	81	635
Racine, Wis	163	9	460	427	6	39	152	4	156	210	2	212	715	21	736
Raleigh, N.C.	365	124	489	265	106	633	280	113	393	383	106	490	1,505	449	1,954
Reading, Pa	192	18	210	245	13	218	162	179	341	162	22	230	757	72	829
Richmond, Ind.	1,116	133	1,249	1,304	220	1,604	1,256	179	2,239	1,330	154	1,484	5,092	685	5,777
Richmond, Va.	1,855	2,565	4,440	1,200	1,682	3,882	2,239	1,510	3,749	1,853	2,183	4,038	6,147	7,962	15,109
Rochester, N.Y.	160	24	192	179	39	218	159	48	207	185	47	232	692	158	824
Rockford, Ill	81	6	87	60	4	64	56	6	51	63	11	74	251	27	274
Rock Island, Ill								130	148	80	0	80	136	130	266
Rome, Ga.	70	2	72	63	0	63	62	0	62	63	0	63	258	2	260
Rome, N.Y.															

Rutland, Vt.
Sacramento, Cal.
Saginaw, Mich.
Saint Joseph, Mo.
Saint Louis, Mo.
Saint Paul, Minn.
Salem, Mass.
Salem, Ohio
Salina, Kans.
Salt Lake City, Utah
San Antonio, Tex.
San Diego, Cal.
Sandusky, Ohio
San Francisco, Cal.
San José, Cal.
Saratoga Springs, N. Y.
Savannah, Ga.
Schenectady, N. Y.
Scranton, Pa.
Seattle, Wash.
Sedalia, Mo.
Selma, Ala.
Sheboygan, Wis.
Sherman, Tex.
Shreveport, La.
Sioux City, Iowa
Sioux Falls, Dak.
South Bend, Ind.
Springfield, Ill.
Springfield, Mass.
Springfield, Mo.
Springfield, Ohio
Stamford, Conn.
Staunton, Va.
Sterling, Ill.
Steubenville, Ohio
Stillwater, Minn.
Stockton, Cal.
Streator, Ill.
Syracuse, N. Y.
Tacoma, Wash.
Taunton, Mass.
Terre Haute, Ind.
Tiffin, Ohio
Titusville, Pa.
Toledo, Ohio
Topeka, Kans.
Trenton, N. J.
Troy, N. Y.
Utica, N. Y.
Vicksburg, Miss.

No. 16.—*Statement showing the operations of the special-delivery system at all the free-delivery post-offices, etc.*—Continued.

Post-office.	Quarter ending Sept. 30887. Special-delivery letters and parcels arriving from other places.	Special-delivery letters and parcels deposited for local delivery.	Total special-delivery letters and parcels.	Quarter ending Dec. 31, 1887. Special-delivery letters and parcels arriving from other places.	Special-delivery letters and parcels deposited for local delivery.	Total special-delivery letters and parcels.	Quarter ending Mar. 31, 1888. Special-delivery letters and parcels arriving from other places.	Special-delivery letters and parcels deposited for local delivery.	Total special-delivery letters and parcels.	Quarter ending June 30, 1888. Special-delivery letters and parcels arriving from other places.	Special-delivery letters and parcels deposited for local delivery.	Total special-delivery letters and parcels.	Total—12 months ending June 30, 1888. Special-delivery letters and parcels arriving from other places.	Special-delivery letters and parcels deposited for local delivery.	Total special-delivery letters and parcels.
Sinoa, Ind	101	22	123	91	25	116	97	21	118	88	19	105	875	87	463
Waltham, Mass	270	5	275	382	12	394	278	25	303	321	18	339	1,251	60	1,311
Warren, Pa	44	1	45	38	0	38	39	0	38	57	0	57	177	1	178
Washington, D. C.	4,046	3,303	7,349	5,270	4,299	9,569	6,991	5,111	11,292	5,830	4,727	10,557	21,237	17,430	38,667
Waterbury, Conn	235	5	230	216	8	224	260	15	275	299	19	318	1,000	47	1,047
Waterloo, Iowa	40	6	46	46	4	50	38	2	40	47	2	49	171	14	85
West ... , N.Y	167	33	200	151	43	194	123	57	180	153	20	173	574	153	727
Wellington, Kans	14	0	14	49	0	60	15	2	17	49	0	49	2	2	85
West Chester, Pa	53	4	57	90	5	95	103	8	111	4	0	4	383	21	414
Westerly, R. I	59	12	71	49	8	57	51	1	61	212	21	121	232	21	253
W...ing, W. Va	497	36	533	530	28	558	442	37	470	440	33	473	1,909	134	2,043
W...ta, Kan	528	15	543	384	10	394	408	20	428	330	18	348	1,619	63	1,713
Wilkes Barre, Pa	210	22	232	270	39	315	296	18	314	313	34	347	1,085	123	1,208
Williamsport, Pa	243	20	263	216	14	229	239	8	247	190	8	198	897	50	807
Wilmi..., Del	411	56	467	495	77	572	430	62	492	528	65	613	1,884	280	2,144
Wilmington, N. C	115	4	115	153	5	158	117	9	126	96	9	105	481	23	504
Winfield, Kans	88	4	42	48	12	60	44	19	63	62	46	98	183	81	283
Winona, Minn	111	27	138	155	29	184	127	39	188	130	47	188	532	144	676
Woonsocket, R. I	63	4	67	70	7	83	56	6	65	69	6	78	261	27	591
..., Mo	64	6	70	67	5	72	68	5	40	75	6	81	274	29	349
..., Mo	1,604	753	2,357	2,441	675	3,116	1,506	810	2,316	1,761	758	2,519	7,312	2,996	10,308
Xenia, Ohio	61	3	64	70	4	74	54	8	54	57	4	61	220	14	253
York, N. Y	228	22	250	158	20	172	271	28	156	299	33	332	1,061	112	1,173
York, Pa	157	30	187	156	16	172	141	15	141	164	16	180	568	77	675
Youngstown, Ohio	259	51	310	298	98	384	249	83	333	247	73	320	1,041	305	1,346
Zanesville, Ohio	330	21	372	323	12	365	280	37	317	283	41	323	1,216	142	1,377
Total	207,066	64,457	271,523	236,064	85,505	322,389	217,036	86,474	303,510	238,698	84,256	322,954	899,494	320,783	1,220,287

No. 17.—*Calculations showing the number of letters, postal-cards, newspapers and periodicals, and pieces of third and fourth class matter, mailed at all the post-offices of the United States during the year ending June 30, 1888.*

LETTERS.

Estimate based on the number of stamps issued :

The number of adhesive postage-stamps issued during the year, exclusive of postage-due, special-delivery, and newspaper and periodical stamps, is	1,867,173,140
Deduct the number probably used to pay fees on registered matter (the actual number of private pieces of matter registered being 11,251,514)	18,000,000
Leaves as the number of adhesive stamps issued usable for postage on all classes of matter except newspapers and periodicals, for which special stamps are required	1,854,173,140
Deduct again for cases where more than a single stamp was used to pay postage on a single piece of matter, say 2 per cent. of the whole number (see Note 1 below).	37,083,462
Leaves as the number of adhesive stamps that may be said to represent separate pieces of mail matter	1,817,089,678
To get at the number of letters represented by these figures, deduct the number of stamps probably used on third and fourth class matter (circulars, miscellaneous printed matter, and merchandise), say 20 per cent of the whole (see Note 2 below)	363,417,935
Leaves the number of adhesive stamps that represent letters	1,453,671,743
Add to this the number of stamped envelopes and letter-sheets issued, not including stamped newspaper wrappers and ungummed stamped envelopes used for circulars.	352,315,750
Makes an aggregate of	1,805,987,493
Deduct from this the probable number of stamps (adhesive and embossed) issued in excess of the number actually sold and used, say 2 per cent. (see Note 3 below)	36,119,750
Net remainder representing an equivalent number of letters mailed during the year..	1,769,867,743

Or, in round numbers, 1,769,800,000.

The following estimate, based upon postmasters' returns of letters collected by carriers at all the free-delivery post-offices, produces substantially the same result as the foregoing, and therefore tends to establish its correctness :

Number of letters collected by carriers at all the free-delivery post-offices during the fiscal year ending June 30, 1888, as reported by postmasters	760,113,963
Deduct for possible errors in the reports of postmasters, say 5 per cent.	38,005,698
Leaves probably correct number collected by carriers	722,108,265
Assuming that the carriers collect 80 per cent of all letters mailed in the free-delivery cities, one-fourth of the above number should be added to it as representing the 20 per cent. mailed directly at the post-offices and stations	180,527,066
Total number of letters mailed at free-delivery offices	904,635,331
As the free-delivery offices collect about 51 per cent. of the postal revenue derived from letters, it is assumed that the above represents that percentage of all the letters mailed in the whole country. Add, therefore, for the 49 per cent. mailed at other than free-delivery offices	867,236,868
Total letters mailed at all post-offices during the year	1,769,872,199

Or, in round numbers, 1,769,800,000.

NOTE 1.—From statistics published in the Report of the Third Assistant Postmaster-General for 1886, it appears that the proportion of letters weighing over a single unit of weight, or 1 ounce each, was about 1½ per cent of the entire number mailed during two given periods at twenty of the leading post-offices. Taking the whole country, the percentage would not be far from this. Two per cent., assumed in the above estimate, is not excessive.

NOTE 2.—From the statistics referred to in the preceding note it would seem that of the entire number of pieces of matter mailed at twenty of the leading post-offices, about 40 per cent. were unsealed parcels and circulars. It is a well-known fact, however, that the great commercial cities of the country—making up these twenty offices—mail a vastly greater proportion of parcels and circulars than do the smaller places—so much greater that, massing the whole country, probably not 20 per cent. of the pieces of matter mailed, other than postal-card and second-class matter, consists of parcels and circulars. This is indicated by the fact that of the entire number of stamped enveloped issued, not more than 19 per cent. are made up of newspaper wrappers and ungummed envelopes used for circulars, of which at least three-fourths go to the very large cities. It is further indicated by the fact that, as shown by exact statistics published in this report, the proportion of parcels to letters registered is about 1 to 9, or say 12 per cent. A further slight indication is afforded by the statistics of undelivered matter sent to the Dead Letter Office—only about 2 per cent. of such matter consisting of parcels. The assumption that 20 per cent. of the adhesive stamps issued are used for third and fourth class matter is about fair.

NOTE 3.—The difference between the value of stamps issued and stamps sold will not average 2 per cent. annually.

POSTAL-CARDS.

Estimate based on the issue of cards :

Number of postal-cards actually issued to postmasters during the fiscal year ending June 30, 1888	381,797,500
Deduct 3 per cent. for excess of cards issued over the number sold and used (the percentage of difference being probably slightly greater than in the case of adhesive stamps and stamped envelopes)	11,453,925
Leaves as the number which may be said to have been mailed during the year	270,343,575

Or, in round numbers, 370,300,000.

NEWSPAPERS AND PERIODICALS (SECOND-CLASS MATTER).

Estimate based on postmasters' returns:

The actual weight of newspapers and periodicals mailed by publishers and news agents during the fiscal year ending June 30, 1848, as shown by reports made to the Third Assistant Postmaster-General, and verified in his office, was 143 662,918 pounds, which, at the rate of six pieces to the pound, will give as the total number of pieces mailed .. 861, 977, 502

Add for newspapers mailed free by publishers in the county of publication, say one-tenth of the above number of pounds, at the rate of 1½ papers to the pound 201, 128, 085

Gives as the total number mailed ....:... 1, 063, 105, 587
Or, in round numbers, 1,063,100,000 pieces.

THIRD AND FOURTH CLASS MATTER (BOOKS, MERCHANDISE, ETC.)

Estimate based on issues of stamps:

In the calculation showing the number of letters mailed it was estimated that there were used on third and fourth class matter during the fiscal year ending June 30, 1-88, adhesive postage-stamps to the number of 363,613,935. On an average of 1¼ stamps to every piece of such matter mailed the total number of pieces represented by this number of stamps would be 290, 891, 148

Add to this the number of stamped newspaper wrappers and ungummed stamped envelopes for circulars issued, less 2 per cent. for excess of number issued over number sold and used... 82, 081, 860

Total, representing the number of pieces of third and fourth class matter mailed during the year ... ...•................... 372, 973, 008
Or, in round numbers, 372,900,000 pieces.

RECAPITULATION.

Letters mailed during the year...... .... 1, 769, 800, 000
Postal-cards mailed 370, 300, 000
Newspapers and periodicals mailed by publishers and news agents...................... 1, 063, 100, 000
Pieces of third and fourth class matter mailed.. 372, 900, 000

Aggregate.. 3, 576, 100, 000

VERIFICATION OF ABOVE ESTIMATES.

The foregoing estimates are verified by their substantial agreement with the amount of revenue derived from the sale of postage-stamps, etc., as reported by the auditor. The following calculation will demonstrate this:

1,769,800,000 letters mailed, averaging in the amount of postage, say, 2 ⁴⁄₁₀ cents apiece*.... $36, 280, 909
1,063,100,000 newspapers, etc., postage on which, from verified reports, was 1, 436, 629
370,300,000 postal-cards, amounting to 3, 703, 000
372 900,000 pieces of third and fourth class matter, postage on which, at an average of 1½ cents each,† was 6, 711, 400
Add for value of stamps used to pay registry fees‡............................... 1, 125, 154
Add for value of special-delivery stamps,‡ say 125, 000
Add for value of postage-due stamps used,‡ say................................... 175, 000

Total 49, 557, 063
Amount realized during the year from the sale of stamps, as reported by the auditor, which substantially agrees with the above 49, 544, 272

No. 18.—*Abstract of laws relating to the postal service in the United States from the year 1639 to the present time.*

COLONIAL PERIOD.

Massachusetts.—Order of the general court, 1639.—"It is ordered that notice be given that Richard Fairbanks his house in Boston is the place appointed for all letters which are brought from beyond the seas, or are to be sent thither to be left with him, and he is to take care that they are to be delivered or sent according to the direction. And he is allowed for every letter a penny, and must answer all miscarriages through his own neglect in this kind."

---

* In estimating the average postage to a letter, allowance must be made for the fact that a large number, known as drop letters, are mailed at other than free-delivery offices at only a cent apiece.
† Out of the total number of pieces of matter of these classes mailed, it must be remembered that over 82,000,000, as shown in a preceding calculation, are positively known to be only 1 cent each, consisting of 1-cent newspaper wrappers and ungummed 1-cent envelopes.
‡ These items all enter into the auditor's aggregate of stamps sold.

Massachusetts.—May, 1677.—Mr. John Hayward appointed by the court "to take in and convey letters according to their direction."

Virginia.—Act of assembly, March 13, 1657.—"That all letters superscribed for the public service shall be immediately conveyed from plantation to plantation to the place and person directed, under a penalty of 1 hogshead of tobacco for each default; and if any extraordinary charge arise thereby, the commissioners of each county are hereby authorized to judge thereof and levy payment of the same. These superscriptions are to be signed by the governor, council, or secretary, or any commission of the quorum, or any of the committee appointed for the militia."

Virginia.—Act of assembly, March 23, 1661.—Provides that all letters superscribed for the service of his majesty or the public service shall be immediately conveyed from plantation to plantation to the place and person directed under a penalty of 350 pounds of tobacco for each default. "If there is any person in the family where the said letters come as can write, such person is required to indorse the day and hour he received them, that the neglect or contempt of any person stopping them may be better known and punished accordingly."

Virginia.— Act of assembly, March 16, 1692.—For encouraging the erection of a post-office under letters patent granted to Thomas Neale, dated February 17, 1692. · (This act was conditional, and was never carried into effect.)

*New York.—*1672.—Establishment of a "post to go monthly from New York to Boston :" postage to be prepaid.

New York.—December 6, 1702.—The Postmaster-General ordered that the post between Boston and New York should set out once a fortnight during the months of December, January, and February.

Pennsylvania.—Act of provincial assembly, March, 1683.—"Every justice of the peace, sheriff, or constable within the respective counties of this province and territories thereof, to whose hands or knowledge any letter or letters shall come directed to or from the governor, shall dispatch them within three hours at the furthest after the receipt or knowledge thereof, to the next sheriff or constable, and so forwards as the letters direct, upon the penalty of 20 shillings for every hour's delay. And in such cases, all justices of the peace, sheriffs, or constables are herewith empowered to press either man or horse for that purpose, allowing for a horse or man 2 pence a mile, to be paid out of the public stock."

Pennsylvania.—Act of general assembly, May, 1693.—"To the end that mutual correspondences may be maintained, and that letters may speedily and safely be dispatched from place to place: Be it enacted by the authority aforesaid, that a general post-office may be erected by Andrew Hamilton, at Philadelphia, from whence all letters and packets may be with all expedition sent into any of the parts of New England and other the adjacent colonies in these parts of America, at which said office all returns and answers may be received.

"And be it further enacted by the authority aforesaid, that it shall be lawful for the said Andrew Hamilton, or some other as shall be appointed by the King, to be Postmaster-General in these parts, and his deputy or deputies in that office, to demand, receive, and take for the postage of all such letters so by him conveyed or sent by post, as follows:

"All foreign letters from Europe, the West Indies, or any part beyond the seas, 2 pence each single letter which is to be accounted such, although it contain bills of lading, invoices, gazettes, etc., and for each packet of letters, 4 pence. And if packets of letters lie at the office unclaimed for the space of forty-eight hours, the postmasters then sending them forthwith to the respective houses of the persons to whom they are directed, 1 penny more for every such letter or packet. And for all foreign letters outward bound there shall be delivered into the post-office 2 pence each letter or packet. The port or inland letters to or from New York to Philadelphia, 4 pence half penny ; to or from Philadelphia to Connecticut, 9 pence; to or from Philadelphia to Rhode Island, 12 pence ; to or from Philadelphia to Boston, 15 pence ; to or from Philadelphia to the eastern parts of New England beyond Boston, 19 pence; to or from Philadelphia to Lewis, Maryland, and Virginia, 9 pence ; to and from every place within 80 miles of Philadelphia, 4½ pence. All letters belonging to the public to be received and dispatched free of all charges, and the post to pass ferriage free at all ferries within this province, town of New Castle, and country depending. Provided always, that the said Andrew Hamilton shall within three months next ensuing prefix certain days of his setting forth and return, and shall continue constant posts to pass from Philadelphia to New York, and from Philadelphia to New Castle."

Pennsylvania.—Act of assembly, May, 1697.—Increasing the rates of postage, and paying the postmaster £20 a year for three years.

South Carolina.—Ordinance ratified September 10, 1702.—Whereas several foreign letters are imported into this part of the province, therefore, for the maintenance of mutual correspondence and prevention of many inconveniences that may happen from miscarriages of the same, and that an office may be managed so that safe dispatch may be had, which is most likely to be effected by erecting one general post-office for that purpose:

Be it therefore enacted by his Excellency John Granvill, esq., palatine, etc., that every master of a ship shall deliver all letters in his custody to Mr. Edward Bourne, and to no other person, and he is required to make an exact list of such letters which shall be fixed in some public place in the house of the said Bourne, there to remain thirty days; and on delivery of each letter he shall write opposite the name of the person addressed the name of the person to whom the letter is delivered; and the said Bourne shall receive for each and every packet or letter received and delivered one-half royal and no more. If he refuses to perform all or every of these particulars, be shall forfeit for each offense the sum of 40 shillings. And the said Bourne is hereby appointed postmaster to receive all such letters as aforesaid, and no other person whatsoever, anything in the act for raising a public store of powder for the defense of this province, ratified October 8, 1694, contained to the contrary notwithstanding. (Repealed by act of September 17, 1703.)

South Carolina.—Ordinance ratified March 28, 1778.—An act for the erecting of a post-office within the State of South Carolina.

Regulations for the post-offices within the State, in addition to such as are already made by the honorable Continental Congress:

As soon as public offices are established within this State commanders of vessels must deposit all letters addressed to persons within this State, or to any of the United States of America, in the nearest post-office. The master of a vessel delivering such letters shall be entitled to receive from the deputy postmaster of such office 1 shilling and 3 pence currency for every letter so delivered, and the person addressed shall pay to the deputy postmaster 2 shillings and 6 pence for each letter. If letters are not called for within twenty-four hours, the postmaster of the town shall send the letter to the person addressed, and may demand 1 shilling and 3 pence for his trouble more than if the letter were delivered at the post-office. If the addressee can not be found, the postmaster shall advertise it if not called for within twenty days, and shall be allowed the expense of advertising. The postmaster shall keep his office open from 9 until 1, and from 5 to 7, excepting Sundays in the morning. Postmasters are exempt from militia duty. Post riders shall have preference in crossing ferries. As soon as post-offices are established in this State by the Continental Congress, or the laws of the State, it shall not be lawful for any person to ride post on any public post-road for the carriage of more than ten letters on any private account, under a penalty of £20.

Act of Parliament, 9th Queen Anne (1710), *chapter x.*—Provides that a postmaster-general shall be appointed for North America from and after June 11, 1711; that a chief letter office be erected at New York; and establishes rates of postage as follows:

All letters and packets from London to New York, in North America, and thence to London: Single, 1 shilling; double, 2 shillings; treble, 3 shillings; ounce, 4 shillings.

All letters, etc., from any part of the West Indies to New York: Single, 4 pence; double, 8 pence; treble, 1 shilling; ounce, 1 shilling and 4 pence.

All letters from New York to Charleston, the chief office in North and South Carolina, and from Charleston to New York: Single, 1 shilling 6 pence; double, 3 shillings; treble, 4 shillings 6 pence; ounce, 6 shillings.

All letters, etc., from Charleston aforesaid, to any place not exceeding 60 English miles: Single, 4 pence; double, 8 pence; treble, 1 shilling; ounce, 1 shilling 4 pence.

All letters, etc., from Charleston aforesaid, to any place not exceeding 100 English miles: Single, 6 pence; double, 1 shilling; treble, 1 shilling 6 pence; ounce, 2 shillings.

Places where posts are not yet settled to pay according to these rates.

The charge for every person riding post to be 3 pence for every horse-hire or postage for every English mile, and 4 pence for the person riding as guide for every stage; each person being entitled to carry a bundle of goods weighing less than 80 pounds free, the same "to be laid on the horse rid by the guide"

Only the postmaster-general and his deputies to provide horses or furniture for persons riding post.

If the postmaster fail to furnish horses, etc., to any person riding post within half an hour after demand, conveyance may be obtained elsewhere, and the postmaster shall forfeit the sum of £5.

Debts for postage not exceeding £5 are to be recovered as small tithes are.

Act of Parliament, 4th George III (1763), *chapter xxiv.*—Allows letters on the public service sent to and from the public officials of the higher ranks to pass through the mails free of postage; and empowers the postmaster-general to authorize certain persons to indorse upon such letters and packets the fact that they are on public business; printed votes, proceedings in Parliament, and newspapers sent without covers, or in covers open at the side, to go free.

Act of Parliament, 5th *George III* (1765), *chapter xxr.*—Repeals the act of 1710, fixing the rates of postage of letters between London and the British dominions in America and places within the said dominions, and establishes the following rates to take effect October 10, 1765:

For all letters and packets passing from London to any port within the British dominions in America, and from any such port unto London: For every single letter, 1 shilling; double, 2 shillings; treble, 3 shillings; ounce, 4 shillings.

For all letters and packets conveyed by sea from any port in the British dominions in America, to any other port within the said dominions: Single, 4 pence; double, 8 pence; treble, 1 shilling; ounce, 1 shilling 4 pence; and so in proportion for every package of deeds, writs, and other things.

For the inland conveyance of all letters and packets to or from any chief post-office within the British dominions in America from or to any other part of the said dominions, not exceeding 60 British miles: Single, 4 pence; double, 8 pence; treble, 1 shilling; ounce, 1 shilling 4 pence.

And being upwards of 60 such miles, and not exceeding 100 miles: single, 6 pence; double, 1 shilling; treble, 1 shilling 6 pence; ounce, 2 shillings.

All letters, etc., from New York to any place within 60 English miles thereof, and thence back to New York: Single, 4 pence; double, 8 pence; treble, 1 shilling; ounce, 1 shilling 4 pence.

All letters, etc., from New York to Perth Amboy, the chief town in West New Jersey, and from each of those places back to New York, to any place not exceeding 100 English miles, and from each of those places to New York: Single, 6 pence; double, 1 shilling; treble, 1 shilling 6 pence; ounce, 2 shillings.

All letters and packets from Perth Amboy and Bridlington to any place not exceeding 60 English miles, and thence back again: Single, 4 pence; double, 8 pence; treble, 1 shilling; ounce, 1 shilling 4 pence.

All letters and packets from Perth Amboy and Bridlington to any place not exceeding 100 English miles, and thence back again: Single, 6 pence; double, 1 shilling; treble, 1 shilling 6 pence; ounce, 2 shillings.

All letters, etc., from New York to New London, the chief town in Connecticut, in New England, and to Philadelphia, the chief town in Pennsylvania, and from those places back to New York: Single, 9 pence; double, 1 shilling 6 pence; treble, 2 shillings 3 pence; ounce, 3 shillings.

All letters and packets from New London and Philadelphia to any place not exceeding 60 English miles, and thence back again: Single, 4 pence; double, 8 pence; treble, 1 shilling; ounce, 1 shilling 4 pence.

All letters, etc., from New London and Philadelphia to any place not exceeding 100 English miles, and so back again: Single, 6 pence; double, 1 shilling; treble, 1 shilling 6 pence; ounce, 2 shillings.

All letters and packets from New York to Newport, the chief town in Rhode Island and Providence Plantation in New England, and to Boston, the chief town in Massachusetts Bay in New England, and to Portsmouth, the chief town in New Hampshire, New England, and to Annapolis, the chief town in Maryland, and from every of those places to New York: Single, 1 shilling; double, 2 shillings; treble, 3 shillings; ounce, 4 shillings.

All letters and packets from Newport, Boston, Portsmouth, and Annapolis, to any place not exceeding 60 English miles, and thence back again: Single, 4 pence; double, 8 pence; treble, 1 shilling; ounce, 1 shilling 4 pence.

All letters, etc., from Newport, Boston, Portsmouth and Annapolis, to any place not exceeding 100 English miles: Single, 6 pence; double, 1 shilling; treble, 1 shilling 6 pence; ounce, 2 shillings.

All letters and packets from New York to the chief offices in Salem and Ipswich, and to the chief office in Piscataway, and to Williamsburgh, the chief office in Virginia, and from every of those offices to New York: Single, 1 shilling 3 pence; double, 2 shillings 6 pence; treble, 3 shillings 9 pence; ounce, 5 shillings.

All letters, etc., from the chief offices in Salem, Ipswich, Piscataway, and Williamsburgh, to any place not exceeding 60 English miles: Single, 4 pence; double, 8 pence; treble, 1 shilling; ounce, 1 shilling 4 pence.

All letters, etc., from the chief offices in Salem, Ipswich, Piscataway, and Williamsburgh, to any place not exceeding 100 English miles: Single, 6 pence; double, 8 pence; treble, 1 shilling; ounce, 2 shillings.

And being upwards of 100 miles and not over 200 miles: Single, 8 pence; double, 1 shilling 4 pence; treble, 2 shillings; ounce, 2 shillings 8 pence.

And for every distance not exceeding 100 miles beyond such 200 miles, and for every such farther distance: Single, 2 pence; double, 6 pence; treble, 8 pence; and so in proportion for every packet of deeds, writs, etc

Authorizes the appointment of surveyors in the chief post-offices in America.

Empowers the Postmaster-General to establish penny-post offices in America.

Limits the weight of packets sent by penny-post to 4 ounces.

Authorizes the Postmaster-General to demand prepayment of postage on all letters sent out of Great Britain.

Fixes penalties for embezzling any letter, etc.; for robbing the mails; for misapplying postage money; and for advancing rates and not accounting for same.

PERIOD OF THE CONFEDERATION.

Resolution of Congress, May 29, 1775.—Naming a committee to consider the best means of establishing posts throughout the continent.

Act of July 26, 1775.—Provides for the appointment of a Postmaster-General for the United Colonies, whose office shall be at Philadelphia, his salary to be $1,000 per annum, and that of secretary and comptroller $340; that a line of posts be established from Falmouth, New England, to Savannah, Ga.; that deputies shall receive as compensation 20 per cent. on amount collected when said amount does not exceed $1,000, and 10 per cent. for all sums above $1,000 a year; that deputy postmasters account quarterly with the General Post-Office, and the Postmaster-General annually with the continental treasurers, paying to said treasurers the profits of the post-office; if the expense should exceed the profits, the deficiency to be made good by the United Colonies and paid to the Postmaster-General by the continental treasurers.

Resolution of July 26, 1775.—Recommending that the Postmaster-General establish a weekly post to South Carolina; that it be left to the Postmaster-General to appoint a secretary and comptroller.

July 26, 1775.—Benjamin Franklin unanimously chosen Postmaster-General for one year, and until another is appointed.

Resolution of Congress, November 8, 1775.—That all letters to and from delegates of the United Colonies, during sessions of Congress, be carried free of postage.

Resolution of Congress, January 9, 1776.—That letters to and from private soldiers in actual service be carried free of postage.

Resolution of Congress, April 9, 1776.—That letters directed to any general in the Continental service be carried free of postage.

Resolution of Congress, April 16, 1776.—That only the committee of safety in each colony shall stop the post, open the mail, or detain letters therefrom.

Resolution of Congress July 8, 1776.—That postmasters be excused from military duty.

Resolution of Congress, August 8, 1776.—That post-riders be exempt from military duty.

Resolution of Congress, August 30, 1776.—That there be employed on the public post-roads a rider for every 25 or 30 miles, who shall set out three times a week on receipt of mail, and travel night and day, until it is delivered to next rider.

Resolution of Congress, September 7, 1776.—That letters to and from the Board of War and Ordnance, or secretary of the same, be carried free of postage.

Resolution of Congress, November 5, 1776.—That the Postmaster-General be authorized to employ additional riders between Philadelphia and headquarters of armies; that ferry-keepers shall expedite travel of such riders; and that the deputy postmaster at the headquarters of the Army be allowed four rations per day for subsistence of himself, his riders, and servant.

Resolution of Congress, November 7, 1776.—That Richard Bache be appointed Postmaster-General in place of Dr. Franklin, who is absent.

Act of Congress, January 11, 1777.—That the Postmaster-General be directed to furnish a list of names of disaffected deputy postmasters, and that he assign reasons why the late resolves of Congress for regulating the post-office are not carried into execution.

Act of Congress, February 17, 1777.—Committee appointed to revise regulations of post-office.

Act of Congress, April 12, 1777.—That the Postmaster-General be authorized to increase compensation of postmasters to any sum not exceeding $200, when necessary; that $2,000 be advanced to the Postmaster-General, he to be accountable.

Resolution of Congress, May 12, 17.7.—That postmasters, post-riders, and persons connected with the post-office ought to be exempted from military duty.

Resolution of Congress, August 1, 1777.—That the commanding officer in the State of Georgia be directed to establish a post in the southern part of said State.

Resolution of Congress, August 6, 1777.—That $2,000 be advanced to Richard Bache, Postmaster General, he to be accountable.

Resolution of Congress, October 17, 1777.—That the Postmaster-General be authorized to appoint two additional surveyors of the post-office; and that all surveyors be allowed $6 a day each for all expenses, and in place of all other allowance. That the tour be as follows: One from Casco Bay to Philadelphia, or while that city is in possession of the enemy, to Lancaster; one from Philadelphia or Lancaster to Edentown, N. C.; and the third from Edentown to Savannah, Ga.

That an inspector of dead letters be appointed, with a salary of $100 a year, to examine dead letters, to communicate to Congress such as contain inimical schemes or intelligence, to preserve letters containing valuable articles, and not to divulge the contents of letters to any but Congress.

That the rate of postage be increased 50 per cent.

That an allowance be made to the present surveyor of the post-office for past extraordinary service.

Resolution of Congress, November 4, 1777.—That $3,000 be advanced to Richard Bache, Postmaster-General.

Articles of Confederation, Article IX.—Ratified July 9, 1778.—Gives to Congress the sole and exclusive right and power of establishing and regulating post-offices in the United States, and exacting "such postage as may be necessary to defray the expenses of the said office."

Resolution of Congress, April 16, 1779.—That $11,967½ be advanced to the Postmaster-General to pay debts.

That the present rate of postage shall be doubled.

That the annual salary of the Postmaster-General for the future shall be $2,000.

That the pay of surveyors and comptroller shall be doubled.

Resolution of Congress, December 1, 1779.—That accounts of the Postmaster-General be referred to board of the treasury for adjustment and liquidation.

That the salary of the Postmaster-General be increased to $3,500 per annum, from September 1, 1778.

That the comptroller's salary be increased to $2,500 per annum, from September 1, 1778.

Resolution of Congress, December 27, 1779.—That the post shall set out and arrive at the places where Congress shall be sitting twice each week, to go as far as Boston, State of Massachusetts Bay, and to Charleston, S. C.

That no express riders shall be maintained at public expense.

That the three surveyors of the post-office shall be allowed the sum of $40 a day.

That the pay of the Postmaster-General be increased to $5,000, and that of the comptroller to $4,000.

Resolution of Congress, December 28, 1779.—That the rate of postage, until further order of Congress, be 20 prices upon the sums paid in the year 1775.

That single letters directed to any officer of the line, and all letters directed to general officers, or to officers commanding in a separate department, and all letters to and from the ministers, commissioners, and secretaries of the United States at foreign courts, be free.

Resolution of May 5, 1780.—That the present rates of postage be doubled.

That masters of vessels be required to put in the post-office all letters brought by them from abroad.

Resolution of June 30, 1780.—Ordering the committee on the post-office to direct the Postmaster-General to make arrangements by which the southern post-riders shall arrive at the place where Congress is sitting only once a week, while the express line established by Governor Jefferson between the southern and northern armies is kept up.

Resolution of September 13, 1780.—Allows the Postmaster-General $1,000 a year salary, to be paid quarterly.

Resolution of December 12, 1780.—Fixes the rate of postage on letters at half the rates paid at the commencement of the present war.

Resolution of August 1, 1781.—Appoints a committee to report the state of the present expenses of the post-office, and a system for regulating the same in future.

Resolution of October 19, 1781.—Changes postage to what it was at the commencement of the war; authorizes the Postmaster-General to allow such commissions as he shall think proper, not exceeding 20 per cent. (to take effect December 1, 1781). Salary of the Postmaster-General to be $1,250; that of Assistant Postmaster-General, $850.

Resolution of January 28, 1782.—Ebenezer Hazard, inspector of dead letters, elected Postmaster-General; James Bryson, Assistant Postmaster-General.

Act of Congress, October 18, 1782.—1. Continued communication by post shall exist from New Hampshire to Georgia.

2. The Postmaster-General shall superintend the appointment of assistants, etc.

3. The Postmaster-General and his assistants shall not open, detain, delay, secrete, embezzle, or destroy, any letter, packet, or dispatch, except by consent of the person to whom the same may be addressed, or by an express warrant under the hand of the President of Congress of the United States, or, in time of war, of the commanding officer of a separate army, or of the chief executive officer of one of the said States. No franked letter shall be opened by any military officer.

4. The Postmaster-General shall take the oath of office, and forfeit $1,000 for violating it.

5 and 6. Only the Postmaster-General and his deputies shall carry mail-matter.

7. Mail shall be carried at least once a week.

8. List of undelivered letters to be published quarterly by postmasters, and at the expiration of the succeeding quarter to be sent to the Dead-Letter Office.

9. Extra post-riders may be employed when necessary.

10. Postage rates shall be as follows, in pennyweights and grains of silver, estimating each pennyweight as five-ninetieths of a dollar: Any distance not exceeding 60 miles, 1 pennyweight, 8 grains; upwards of 60 miles and not exceeding 100, 2 pennyweights; upwards of 100 miles and not exceeding 200, 2 pennyweights 16 grains; and so on, 16 grains advance for every 100 miles; and for single letters to or from Europe, 4 pennyweights; double, treble, etc., for increased sizes. And all letters except dead letters shall remain in the office until postage is paid.

11. Post-riders may be licensed to carry newspapers at such rates as the Postmaster-General may establish.

12. Surplus of income over expenditures to be applied to payment of advances heretofore made to the Postmaster General; after payment of which, surplus to be devoted to establishment of new offices and routes; if expenses exceed income, the deficiency to be supplied by the superintendent of finance on warrants of the Postmaster General.

13. Salary of the Postmaster General to be $1,500; salary of Assistant Postmaster-General to be $1,000.

14. The franking privilege granted to members of Congress and chief officers of the government.

Act of December 24, 1782.—Modification of post-office law; no important changes.

Act of February 28, 1783.—Official letters to be sent free.

Act of November 1, 1783.—The Postmaster-General directed to cause an extra post to be furnished whenever required by the President.

Resolution of April 6, 1784.—Directing the Postmaster-General to discharge account of Jonathan Deare and Joseph Olden, amounting to £4 16s., for disbursements and services in case of robbery of mail at Princeton.

Resolution of April 28, 1784.—That letters and packets to and from the Commander-in-Chief of the United States armies shall be carried postage free, and the Postmaster-General is directed to refund to the late commander-in-chief all money paid by him for postage since the time of his resignation.

Resolution of May 11, 1784.—The postmaster at Princeton exonerated from blame in case of the robbery at his office.

Resolution of February 7, 1785.—The Postmaster-General to remove the department to New York on or before the 1st of March next.

Resolution of June 30, 1785.—The Postmaster-General to inquire and report as to best terms for carrying the mails.

Resolution of September 7, 1785.—The Postmaster-General authorized to make contracts for carrying mail.

Resolution of October 5, 1785.—The Postmaster-General authorized to establish cross-posts.

Resolution of June 21, 1786.—That the Postmaster-General be informed that Congress approves his conduct in directing deputy postmasters not to receive the paper money of any State for postage on letters.

Resolution of September 4, 1786.—The Postmaster-General authorized to contract for transportation of the mail, and for establishing cross-posts.

Resolution of September —, 1786.—Directing the Postmaster-General to instruct postmasters to receive no other money than specie in payment of postage.

Authorizing the Postmaster-General to demand postage at the time letters are put into the office.

Resolution of October 23, 1786.—Authorizing the Secretary of the United States of America for the Department of Foreign Affairs to inspect any letters in any of the post-offices when, in his judgment, the safety or interest of the government requires it, except letters franked by or addressed to members of Congress.

Resolution of February 17, 1787.—Authorizing the Postmaster-General to grant, for a term not exceeding seven years, the privilege of carrying letters and packages upon the cross-roads in Virginia, from Richmond to Staunton, and from Winchester to Staunton.

Resolution of October 20, 1787.—Postage rates reduced 25 per cent. The Postmaster-General authorized to fix rates of postage for carriage of large packets in the mails.

Resolution of January 2, 1788.—Post-office continued on old establishment until February next.

Resolution of May 20, 1788.—That mail be regularly transported once a fortnight between Philadelphia and Pittsburgh, Pa., via Lancaster, York, Carlisle, Jamestown, and Bedford.

Resolution of June 11, 1788.—Instructing the Postmaster-General to deliver any letters or packets that may be found in examining dead letters, directed to any officer of the United States on public business, to such officer free of postage charge.

Resolution of August 29, 1788.—Authorizing the Postmaster-General to establish a weekly post from Wilmington to Dover, Del.

PERIOD OF THE CONSTITUTION.

Act September 22, 1789.—For the temporary establishment of the post-office, to continue in force until the end of the next session of Congress, and no longer.

Act August 4, 1790.—Continues in force the act of September 22, 1789, until the end of the next Congress, and no longer.

Act March 3, 1791.—Continues in force the act of September 22, 1789, until the end of the next Congress, and no longer.

This act (March 3, 1791) provides that all letters to and from the Treasurer, Comptroller, and Auditor of the Treasury, and the Assistant to the Secretary of the Treasury, on public service, shall be received and conveyed by the post free of postage.

Act February 20, 1792.—Continues in force the act of March 3, 1791, until the 1st of June, 1792, and no longer, and provides that *his* act (February 20, 1792) shall continue in force for the term of two years from June 1, 1792, and no longer.

By this act the Postmaster-General authorized to appoint one Assistant Postmaster-General.

This act (February 20, 1792) was the first act subsequent to the adoption of the Constitution fixing rates of postage on domestic letters. It established the following rates, to take effect June 1, 1792:

For every single letter not exceeding 30 miles, 6 cents.

For every single letter over 30 miles, and not exceeding 60 miles, 8 cents.

For every single letter over 60 miles, and not exceeding 100 miles, 10 cents.

For every single letter over 100 miles, and not exceeding 150 miles, 12½ cents.

For every single letter over 150 miles, and not exceeding 200 miles, 15 cents.

For every single letter over 200 miles, and not exceeding 250 miles, 17 cents.

For every single letter over 250 miles, and not exceeding 350 miles, 20 cents.

For every single letter over 350 miles, and not exceeding 450 miles, 22 cents.

For every single letter over 450 miles, 25 cents.

For every double letter, double the said rates.

For every triple letter, triple the said rates.

For every packet weighing 1 ounce avoirdupois, to pay at the rate of four single letters for each ounce, and in that proportion for any greater weight.

Act February 20, 1792, *section* 10.—Letters and packets passing by sea to and from the United States, or from one port to another therein, in packet-boats or vessels, the property of or provided by the United States, shall be rated and charged as follows:

For every single letter, 8 cents.

For every double letter, 16 cents.

For every triple letter or packet, 24 cents.

For every letter or packet brought into the United States, or carried from one port therein to another by sea, in any private ship or vessel, 4 cents, if delivered at the place where the same shall arrive; and if directed to be delivered at any other place, with the addition of the like postage as on domestic letters.

Act February 20, 1792, *section* 13.—The postmasters to whom such letters may be delivered shall pay to the master, commander, or other person delivering the same, except the commanders of foreign packets, 2 cents for every such letter or packet.

Act February 20, 1792, *section* 19.—Letters and packets to be received and conveyed by post, free of postage, under certain restrictions:

All letters or packets to or from the President of the United States and the Vice-President of the United States.

All letters or packets, not exceeding 2 ounces in weight, to or from Senators, Representatives, Secretary of the Senate, and Clerk of the House of Representatives, during their actual attendance in any session of Congress and twenty days after such session.

All letters to or from the Secretary of the Treasury, Assistant Secretary of the Treasury, Comptroller, Register, Auditor, Treasurer, Secretary of State, Secretary of War, commissioners for settling accounts between the United States and individual States, Postmaster-General, and Assistant Postmaster-General.

Provided, No person shall frank or inclose any letter or packet not his own; but public letters or packets, from the Treasury Department, may be franked by the Secretary, Assistant Secretary, Comptroller, Register, Auditor, or Treasurer.

Each person shall deliver to post-office every letter or packet inclosed to him for other persons, that postage may be charged.

Act February 20, 1792, *section* 21.—Printers of newspapers authorized to send one paper to every other printer of newspaper in the United States, free of postage, under regulations of the Postmaster-General.

All newspapers conveyed by mail for any distance not more than 100 miles, 1 cent; and over 100 miles, 1½ cents; if any other matter or thing be inclosed, it is subject to letter rates of postage.

Act February 20, 1792, section 26.—Postmaster-General to make provision for receipt of letters and packets, to be conveyed beyond the sea, or from one port to another in the United States; and for every letter so received, a postage of 1 cent shall be paid.

Act May 8, 1794.—To take effect June 1, 1794, without limit as to time. Establishes a General Post-Office. Sections 9, 10, and 13 of this act re-enact sections 9, 10, and 13 of act of February 20, 1792.

Section 19 of this act re-enacts section 19 of act of February 20, 1792, except that it omits the Assistant Secretary of the Treasury and commissioners for settling accounts between the United States and individual States, and adds the Commissioner of the Revenue and postmasters; the letters and packets of postmasters not to exceed one-half ounce in weight.

Section 26 of this act re-enacts section 26 of act of February 20, 1792.

Act December 3, 1794.—Confers franking privilege on James White, delegate to Congress from the territory of the United States south of the river Ohio.

Act February 25, 1795.—Confers franking privilege on purveyor of public supplies, as to letters to or from.

Act March 3, 1797.—That all letters or packets to George Washington, now President of the United States, after the expiration of his term of office, and during his life, shall be received and conveyed by post free of postage.

Act June 22, 1798.—Extends the privilege of franking letters and packets to the Secretary of the Navy, under like restrictions and limitations as are provided in act May ~, 1794, section 19.

Act March 2, 1799, section 7.—Establishes a General Post-Office at the seat of government of the United States.

For every letter composed of single sheet of paper conveyed not exceeding 40 miles, 8 cents; over 40 miles and not exceeding 90 miles, 10 cents; over 90 miles and not exceeding 150 miles, 12½ cents; over 150 miles and not exceeding 300 miles, 17 cents; over 300 miles and not exceeding 500 miles, 20 cents; over 500 miles, 25 cents.

Double letter or two pieces of paper, double rates.

Triple letter or three pieces of paper, triple rates; and for every packet composed of four or more pieces of paper, or other thing, and weighing 1 ounce avoirdupois, quadruple rate, and in same proportion for greater weights: *Provided*, No packet of letters conveyed by the water-mails shall be charged more than quadruple postage, unless containing more than four distinct letters; no package to be received weighing more than 3 pounds.

Act March 2, 1799, section 8.—Every packet or letter brought in the United States, or carried from one port to another in private ship or vessel, 6 cents, if delivered in office where received; if to be conveyed by post, 2 cents added to ordinary postage.

Act March 2, 1799, section 11.—Authorizes postmasters to whom letters may be delivered by masters or commanders of any ship or vessel arriving at any port within the United States, where a post-office is established, except foreign packets, to pay 2 cents for each letter or packet.

Act March 2, 1799, section 13.—Postmasters authorized to pay mail-carriers 1 cent for each way-letter delivered to them, also mail-carriers authorized to demand and receive 2 cents in addition to the ordinary postage, for every letter delivered by them to persons living between post-offices on their route.

Act March 2, 1799, section 17.—Letters and packets to be conveyed free to and from the following:

Postmasters—not exceeding one-half ounce in weight.

Senators, Representatives, Secretary of the Senate, Clerk of the House—not exceeding 2 ounces in weight, during actual attendance in any session of Congress, and twenty days after such session.

All letters and packets to and from the President of the United States, Vice-President of the United States, Secretary of the Treasury, Comptroller of the Treasury, Auditor of the Treasury, Register of the Treasury, Treasurer of the United States, Commissioner of the Revenue, supervisors of the revenue, inspectors of the revenue, Commissioners, Purveyor, Secretary of War, accountant of War Office, Secretary of State, Secretary of Navy, accountant of Navy, Postmaster-General, and Assistant Postmaster-General.

All may receive their newspapers free of postage: *Provided*, Senators, Representatives, Secretary of Senate, and Clerk of the House shall receive newspapers free during session of Congress, and twenty days after.

Letters or packets from any public officer to be franked by person sending.

All letters and packets to and from George Washington, late President, to be received and conveyed free.

Act March 2, 1799, *section* 19.—Re-enacts section 21 of act February 20, 1792.

Act March 2, 1799, *section* 20.—Fixes postage on newspapers at 1 cent each for not more than 100 miles, and 1½ cents for any greater distance. Single newspapers from one place to another in the same State shall not exceed 1 cent.

Concealing a letter, or other thing, or any memorandum in writing in a newspaper, subjects each article in packet to a single-letter postage.

Magazines and pamphlets, 1 cent a sheet, for not exceeding 50 miles; 1½ cents for over 50 miles, and not exceeding 100 miles; and 2 cents for any greater distance.

Act March 2, 1799, *section* 25.—Postmaster-General authorized to provide for receipt of letters or packets, to be conveyed by sea to any foreign port or home port. Every letter or packet so received, subject to a postage of 1 cent.

Act January 2, 1800, *section* 1.—Confers franking privilege on William Henry Harrison, delegate to Congress from territory northwest of the Ohio River, to send and receive letters free of postage.

Act April 3, 1800.—Confers franking privilege upon Martha Washington, to send and receive letters and packages free of postage during her life.

Act December 15, 1800, *section* 1.—Confers franking privilege on delegate from territory northwest of the Ohio River, to send and receive letters free of postage.

Act February 25, 1801.—Confers franking privilege on John Adams, President of the United States, after the expiration of his term of office, and during his life, on all letters and packets to him.

Act February 18, 1802.—Confers privilege of franking and receiving letters free of postage to any person admitted, or to be admitted, to take a seat in Congress as a delegate.

Act May 3, 1802, *section* 4, *vol.* 2, *page* 191.—None but free white persons shall be employed in carrying the mails.

Act May 3, 1802, *section* 5.—Franking privilege extended to the Attorney-General, to send and receive all letters, packets, and newspapers free of postage.

Act March 26, 1804, *section* 3.—Letters, returns, and other papers on public service, sent by mail to or from offices of inspector and paymaster of the army, to be received and conveyed free of postage.

Act June 28, 1809.—Letters and packets from Thomas Jefferson, late President of the United States, to be received and conveyed by post free of postage during his life.

Act April 30, 1810, *section* 1, *vol.* 2, *page* 592.—Establishes a General Post-Office at the seat of Government. *Postmaster-General shall appoint two Assistant Postmasters-General.*

Act April 30, 1810, *section* 11.—Rates of postage on letters and packets:

Single sheet of paper—	Cents.
Less than 40 miles	8
40 to 90 miles	10
90 to 150 miles	12½
150 to 300 miles	17
300 to 500 miles	20
Over 500 miles	25

Double letters or two pieces of paper, double rates; triple letters or three pieces of paper, triple rates; every packet composed of four or more pieces of paper or other thing, and weighing 1 ounce avoirdupois, quadruple rate; and in same proportion for greater weight: *Provided*, No packet of letters conveyed by the water-mails shall be charged more than quadruple postage, unless containing more than four distinct letters. Weight of packet limited to 3 pounds.

Act April 30, 1810, *section* 12.—Letters or packets brought into the United States, or carried from one port therein to another, shall be charged 6 cents, if delivered at the post-office where the same shall arrive; and if to be conveyed by post to any other place, with 2 cents added to the ordinary rates of postage.

Act April 30, 1810, *section* 15.—Postmasters authorized, on the receipt of letters from any ship or vessel arriving at any port within the United States where a post-office is established, to pay to the master, commander, or other person delivering the same, except the commanders of foreign packets, 2 cents for every letter or packet.

Act April 30, 1810, *section* 17.—Postmasters authorized to pay mail-carrier 1 cent for every letter brought into their offices; also mail-carrier authorized to demand and receive 2 cents, in addition to the ordinary postage, for every letter delivered by him to persons living between post-offices on his route.

Act April 30, 1810, *section* 19.—Provides that any person convicted of robbing the mail shall be sentenced to ten years' imprisonment, and upon conviction a second time for such offense, shall be punished with death.

Act April 30, 1810, *section* 24.—Letters and packets to and from the following officers of the United States to be received and conveyed through the mails free of postage: Postmasters, not exceeding one-half ounce in weight.

Senators, Members, Delegates, Secretary of the Senate, and Clerk of the House, limited to 2 ounces in weight, and during their actual attendance in any session of Congress and twenty days thereafter; excess of weight to be paid for.

All letters and packets to and from the President of the United States, Vice-President of the United States, Secretary of State, Secretary of Treasury, Secretary of War, Secretary of the Navy, Attorney-General, Comptroller, Treasurer, Auditor, Register, supervisor of direct tax of district of South Carolina, superintendent of Indian trade, purveyor, inspector and paymaster of the army, accountants of War and Navy Departments, Postmaster-General, Assistant Postmasters-General, John Adams, and Thomas Jefferson,

All may receive their newspapers free of postage.

Senators, Representatives, Secretary of the Senate, and Clerk of the House of Representatives shall receive their newspapers free of postage only during any session of Congress and twenty days thereafter.

Act April 30, 1810, *section* 25.—Secretaries of the Treasury, State, War, Navy, and Postmaster-General authorized to frank letters or packets on official business, prepared in any other public office, in the absence of the principal thereof.

Act April 30, 1810, *section* 26.—Printers of newspapers authorized to exchange one copy free of newspapers, under regulations of the Postmaster-General.

Act April 30, 1810, *section* 27.—Newspapers by mail, 1 cent each for not more than 100 miles; 1½ cents for any greater distance. Single newspapers, from one place to another in the same State, not to exceed 1 cent.

Act April 30, 1810, *section* 32.—Postmaster-General authorized to provide for the receipt and transmission of letters and packets beyond sea, or from any port in the United States to any other port therein; every letter or packet so received subject to a postage of 1 cent.

Act April 30, 1810, *section* 31.—Drop or local letters, 1 cent each.

Act April 30, 1810, *sec ion* 39.—Adjutant-general of the militia of each State and Territory has the right to receive by mail, free of postage, from any major or brigadier-general thereof, and to transmit to said generals, any letter or packet relating solely to the militia of such State or Territory, under certain restrictions.

Act April 18, 1814, *section* 4.—Secretary of State authorized to transmit by mail, free of postage, one copy of documents ordered to be printed by either House of Congress—namely, of communications, with accompanying documents, made by the President to Congress or either House thereof; of reports made by the Secretary of State, Treasury, War, Navy, Postmaster General, or commissioners of the sinking-fund, to Congress, or either House thereof, in pursuance of any law or resolution of either House; affirmative reports on subjects of a general nature made to Congress, or either House thereof, by any committee, respectively—for each of the judges of the Supreme Court, of the district courts, and of the Territories of the United States, to any post-office within the United States they may respectively designate.

Act December 23, 1814, *section* 2.—From and after February 1, 1815, there shall be added to the rates of postage established by law 50 per centum on the amount of such rates respectively.

Act February 1, 1816.—Repeals so much of act of December 23, 1814, as imposes 50 per centum additional postage.

Act April 9, 1816, *section* 1.—Rates of postage after May 1, 1816:

	Cents
Every letter composed of a single sheet of paper—	
Less than 30 miles	6
Over 30 miles and not exceeding 80 miles	10
Over 80 miles and not exceeding 150 miles	12¼
Over 150 miles and not exceeding 400 miles	18¾
Over 400 miles	25

Every double letter or two pieces of paper, double rates.

Every triple letter or three pieces of paper, triple rates.

Every packet containing four or more pieces of paper or one or more other articles, and weighing 1 ounce avoirdupois, quadruple these rates, and in that proportion for all greater rates. No packet of letters conveyed by water-mails to be charged with more than quadruple postage, unless the same shall contain more than four distinct letters.

Any memorandum written on a newspaper or other printed paper, and transmitted by mail, to be charged with letter postage.

Act April 9, 1816, *section* 3.—Letters and packets to and from Senators, Members, and Delegates of the House, Secretary of the Senate, and Clerk of the House, to be conveyed free of postage for thirty days previous to each session of Congress and for thirty days after the termination thereof; limited to 2 ounces in weight; excess to be paid for.

Act March 1, 1817.—Letters and packets to and from James Madison, President of the United States, after the expiration of his term of office and during his life, to be carried by mail free of postage.

Act March 3, 1825.—An act to reduce into one the several acts regulating the Post-Office Department.

Section 1 establishes at the seat of government a general post direction of the Postmaster-General.

Act March 3, 1825, section 5.—Authorises the Postmaster-General to ... ried by any steamboat or other vessel which shall be used as a ... of the United States, on such terms and conditions as shall be con... *Provided,* That he does not pay more than 3 cents for each letter, ... half a cent for each newspaper.

Act March 3, 1825, section 6.—Master or manager of any steamboat ... port or place to another port or place in the United States, where a ... tablished, to deliver all letters or packets addressed to such port or ... master there, for which he shall receive of such postmaster 2 cents ... or packet so delivered, unless the same shall be conveyed under co... Postmaster-General.

Act March 3, 1825, section 7.—No other than a free white person shall ... in conveying the mail; and any contractor who shall for every such offense incu... a free white person to convey the mail shall employ or permit ... $20.

Act March 3, 1825, section 13.—Rates of postage on letters and packets ... the mail of the United States:

For every letter of a single sheet of paper conveyed—

Not exceeding 30 miles ....
Over 30 miles and not exceeding 80 miles .....
Over 80 miles and not exceeding 150 miles ....
Over 150 miles and not exceeding 400 miles ...
Over 400 miles ....

Every double letter or two pieces of paper, double these rates; every triple ... three pieces of paper, triple these rates; every packet of four or more pieces o... or one or more other articles, and weighing 1 ounce avoirdupois, quadrup... rates; and in that proportion for all greater weights: *Provided,* That no pac... letters conveyed by the water-mails shall be charged more than quadruple po... unless the same shall contain more than four distinct letters; weight of packe... ited to 3 pounds.

Unbound journals of legislatures of the several States liable to same postag... pamphlets.

Memorandum written on a newspaper or other printed paper, pamphlet, or ma... zine, and transmitted by mail, to be charged with letter postage.

Act March 3, 1825, section 15.—Every letter or package brought into the Unit... States, or carried from one point therein to another, in any private ship or vessel, ... be charged 6 cents, if delivered at the post-office where the same shall arrive; an... if destined to be conveyed by post to any other place, with 2 cents added to th... ordinary rates of postage.

Act March 3, 1825, section 18.—Postmasters authorized to pay to the master or com... mander of any vessel, except the commanders of foreign packets, arriving at any port... in the United States where a post-office is established, 2 cents for every letter or... packet delivered by him to the postmaster.

Act March 3, 1825, section 27.—Letters and packets to be conveyed ...
of postage to and from the following:
Members, Senators, Delegates, Secretary of ...
Postmasters—limited to one-half ounce in weight.
Congress), and during th... (excep...
days before and ...
All letters ...

Act March 3, 1825, *section* 28.—Secretaries of Treasury, State, War, Navy, and the Postmaster-General may frank letters and packets on official business prepared in any other public office in the absence of the principal thereof.

Act March 3, 1825, *section* 29.—Printers of newspapers authorized to exchange one paper free of postage, under regulations by Postmaster-General.

Act March 3, 1825, *section* 30.—Newspapers conveyed by mail, 1 cent for any distance not more than 100 miles; 1½ cents for any greater distance. Single newspapers from one place to another in the same State, 1 cent.

Inclosing or concealing a letter or other thing, or any memorandum in writing, in a newspaper, pamphlet, or magazine, subjects it to single-letter postage for each article of which the package is composed.

When mode of conveyance and size of mail will admit, magazines and pamphlets published periodically may be transported in the mail to subscribers, at 1½ cents a sheet for any distance not exceeding 100 miles, and 2½ cents for any greater distance. And such magazines and pamphlets as are not published periodically, if sent in the mail, shall be charged 4 cents on each sheet for any distance not exceeding 100 miles, and 6 cents for any greater distance. (Section 13 of this act defines a sheet to be four folio pages, 8 quarto pages, 16 octavo pages, or 24 duodecimo pages, or pages less than that of a pamphlet size or magazine, whatever be the size of the paper of which it is formed. The surplus pages of any pamphlet or magazine shall also be considered a sheet.)

Act March 3, 1825, *section* 34.—Postmaster-General authorized to make provision for the receipt of letters and packets to be conveyed by any vessel beyond sea, or from one port to another in the United States; and the postmaster receiving the same at the port to which such vessel shall be bound shall be entitled to a postage of 1 cent on each letter or packet received.

Act March 3, 1825, *section* 36.—Drop or local letters delivered at the post-office, 1 cent each.

Act March 3, 1825, *section* 36.—Authorizes the Postmaster-General to employ letter-carriers at such post-offices as he may designate, for the delivery of letters; and the carrier may receive from the person to whom the letter is delivered 2 cents.

Act March 3, 1825, *section* 40.—The adjutant-general of the militia of each State and Territory authorized to receive by mail, free of postage, from any major-general or brigadier-general thereof, and to transmit to said generals, any letter or packet relating solely to the militia of such State or Territory, under certain conditions.

Act March 3, 1825, *section* 46.—Repeals all acts and parts of acts which have been passed for the establishment and regulation of the general post-office.

Act March 2, 1827.—Increases the salary of the Postmaster-General $2,000 over the present amount.

Act March 2, 1827, *section* 2.—One cent to be allowed each postmaster for every letter received from any ship or vessel and mailed by him.

Act March 2, 1827, *section* 4.—Authority to frank and receive letters and packets free of postage extended to the commissioners of the navy-board, Adjutant-General, Commissary-General, Inspector-General, Quartermaster-General, Paymaster-General, Secretary of the Senate, Clerk of the House, Superintendent of the Patent-Office.

No other person or officer except those enumerated herein and in the act of March 3, 1825, shall be authorized to frank or receive letters by mail free of postage.

Act March 2, 1827, *section* 5.—One or more pieces of paper mailed as a letter and weighing 1 ounce avoirdupois, shall be charged with quadruple postage, and at the same rate should the weight be greater. Packages containing four pieces of paper, quadruple rates.

Every printed pamphlet or magazine containing more than twenty-four pages on a royal sheet, or any sheet of less dimensions, shall be charged by the sheet; and small pamphlets printed on a half or quarter sheet of royal, or less size, shall be charged with one-half the amount of postage on a full sheet. Double postage shall be charged, unless there shall be printed or written on one of the outer pages of all pamphlets and magazines the number of sheets they contain.

Act June 30, 1834.—Governors of the several States authorized to transmit by mail free of postage all laws and reports, bound or unbound, and all records and documents of their respective States, which may be directed by the several legislatures of the States to be transmitted to the executives of other States.

Act July 2, 1836, *section* 8.—President authorized to appoint an Auditor of the Treasury for the Post-Office Department, who is authorized to frank and receive, free of postage, letters and packets, under regulations provided by law for other officers of the government.

Act July 2, 1836, *section* 8.—All letters or packets to or from the Chief Engineer, which may relate to the business of his office, free of postage.

Act July 2, 1836, *section* 20.—*Postmaster-General authorized to employ a Third Assistant Postmaster-General, who may receive and send letters free of postage.*

Act July 2, 1836, section 36.—No postmaster shall receive free of postage or frank any letter or packet composed of or containing anything other than money or paper.

All letters and packets to and from Dolly P. Madison, relict of the late James Madison, shall be received and conveyed by post free of postage for and during her life.

Act July 4, 1836, section 1.—Patent-Office established and the Commissioner entitled to receive and send letters and packages by mail relating to the business of his Office free of postage.

Act July 7, 1838.—Every railroad built or to be built declared a post-road, over which the Postmaster-General shall cause the mails to be transported, if the cost thereof be not more than 25 per cent. over the cost of similar service in post-coaches.

Act January 25, 1839.—Postmaster-General not to allow to any railroad company for carrying the mails more than $300 per mile per annum.

Act September 9, 1841.—All letters and packets carried by post to Mrs. Harrison, relict of the late William Henry Harrison, to be conveyed free of postage during her life.

Act January 20, 1843, section 3.—Commissioner of Pensions authorized to send and receive letters and packets by mail free of postage.

Act February 15, 1843, section 1.—Authorizes the chief clerk of the office of Secretary of State to frank all public and official documents sent from that office.

Act March 3, 1843.—*Appropriation for testing the capacity and usefulness of the magnetic telegraph by constructing a line of telegraphs between such points as will determine its practicability.* [Under this act a line of telegraphs was constructed by the Government between Washington and Baltimore.]

Act March 3, 1845, section 1, *vol.* 5, *page* 732.—After July 1, 1845, Members of Congress and Delegates from Territories may receive letters not exceeding 2 ounces in weight free of postage during the recess of Congress, anything to the contrary in this act notwithstanding; and the same franking privilege which is granted by this act to the members of the two houses of Congress is hereby extended to the Vice-President of the United States.

Postage on letters.—For every single letter in manuscript, or marks and signs, by mail, under 300 miles, 5 cents, over 300 miles, 10 cents; double letter, double rates; treble letter, treble rates; quadruple letter, quadruple rates; and every letter or parcel not exceeding one-half ounce in weight shall be deemed a single letter, and every additional weight of one-half ounce or less shall be charged with an additional single postage. Drop or local letters shall be charged a postage rate of 2 cents each.

Act March 3, 1845, section 2.—*Postage on newspapers.*—Newspapers of not more than 1,900 square inches in size may be transmitted through the mails by the editors or publishers thereof to subscribers or other persons, within 30 miles of the city, town, or place in which the paper is printed, free of postage. Newspapers of less size, conveyed by mail beyond 30 miles from the place at which they are printed, shall be subject to the rates of postage chargeable under the thirtieth section, act March 3, 1825. Newspapers of greater size than 1,900 square inches subject to same rates of postage as are prescribed by this act on magazines and pamphlets.

Act March 3, 1845, section 3.—Printed or lithograph circulars, hand-bills, or advertisements, printed or lithographed on quarto-post or single-cap paper, or paper not larger than single-cap paper, unsealed, shall be charged with postage at the rate of 2 cents for each sheet, without regard to distance. Pamphlets, magazines, periodicals, and all other printed or other matter (except newspapers) unconnected with any writing, shall be charged with postage at the rate of 2½ cents for each copy sent, not exceeding 1 ounce in weight, and 1 cent additional for each additional ounce, without regard to distance; and any fractional excess of not less than one-half ounce above 1 or more ounces shall be charged for as if said excess amounted to a full ounce.

Bound books not to be admitted under foregoing provisions.

Act March 3, 1845, section 5.—Repeals all acts and parts of acts conferring upon any person the right or privilege to receive and transmit through the mail free of postage letters, packets, newspapers, periodicals, or other matter.

Act March 3, 1845, section 6.—All officers of the government of the United States, heretofore having the franking privilege, shall be allowed and paid quarterly all postage on official letters, packages, or other matter received by mail.

Postage upon official letters, packages, or other matter received by the three Assistant Postmasters-General shall be remitted, and they shall be authorized to transmit by mail free of postage official letters, packages, or other matter under certain regulations.

Deputy postmasters allowed all postage which they may have paid or have had charged to them for official letters, packages, or other matters, and they are authorized to send by mail free of postage official letters and packets, under certain regulations.

Act March 3, 1845, section 7.—Continues in force act of June 30, 1834, authorizing the governors of the several States to transmit by mail certain books and documents, and authorizes Members and Delegates, Secretary of the Senate and Clerk of the House to transmit by mail free of postage any documents printed by order of either house of Congress.

Act March 3, 1845, section 8.—Senators, Members, Delegates, Secretary of Senate, and Clerk of the House, authorized, during each session of Congress and for thirty days before and after every session of Congress, to send and receive through the mail free of postage any letter, newspaper, or packet, not exceeding 2 ounces in weight. Postage charge for excess of weight on official letters, packages, etc., received during any session of Congress, to be paid out of the contingent fund of the house of which the person may be a member. Authorized to frank written letters from themselves during the whole year, etc.

Act March 3, 1845, section 13.—Transmission of letters by steamboats, under act of March 3, 1825, section 6, not prohibited: *Provided,* That the requirements of said sixth section shall be strictly complied with by the delivery of all letters so conveyed, not relating to the cargo or some part thereof, to the postmaster or agent of the Post-Office Department at the port to which said letters may be delivered ; and the postmaster or agent shall collect upon all letters or other mailable matter so delivered to him, except newspapers, pamphlets, magazines, and periodicals, the same rates of postage as would have been charged upon said letters had they been transmitted by mail from the port at which they were placed on board the steamboat from which they were received; weight of packet limited to 3 pounds.

Act March 3, 1845, section 15.—*Mailable matter defined.*—Letters, newspapers, magazines, and pamphlets periodically published or published in regular series, or in successive numbers, under the same title, though at irregular intervals, and all other written or printed matter, whereof each copy or number shall not exceed eight ounces in weight, except bank-notes sent in packages or bundles, without written letters accompanying them. Bound books not to be included within the meaning of these terms.

Act March 3, 1845, section 16.—*Newspapers defined.*—Any printed publication issued in numbers, consisting of not more than two sheets and published at short stated intervals of not more than one month, conveying intelligence of passing events, and bona-fide extras and supplements of any such publications.

Free exchange of newspapers between publishers as provided for by act of March 3, 1825, section 29, not prohibited.

Act March 3, 1845, section 23.—Franking privilege conferred by former acts on the President of the United States when in office, and to all ex-Presidents, and to the widows of the former Presidents, Madison and Harrison, continued in force.

Act March 3, 1845, section 19, volume 5, page 738.—Railroad transportation of the mails divided into three classes, with varying rates of compensation therefor.

Joint resolution of February 20, 1845.—Postmaster-General authorized to contract with railroads for carrying the mails without advertising for bids.

Joint resolution of March 3, 1845.—Provides that act of March 3, 1845, shall go into effect on and after July 1, 1845.

Act May 29, 1846, section 3.—Same rates of postage to be charged in Texas as in other States of the United States.

Act June 19, 1846.—Appropriation made for defraying expenses of magnetic telegraph from Washington to Baltimore: "*Provided,* That the Postmaster-General be, and he is hereby, authorized to let, for a limited time, the aforesaid telegraph to any person who will keep it in operation for its earnings ; or he may, under the direction of the President of the United States, sell the same."

Act August 10, 1846.—"That the proceeds of the telegraph between Washington City and Baltimore be, and the same are hereby, directed to be placed in the Treasury of the United States, for the benefit of the Post-Office Department, in the same manner as other revenues from postages."

Act August 6, 1846, section 18.—On and after January 1, 1847, postage shall be paid in gold and silver only, or in Treasury notes of the United States.

Act March 1, 1847, section 3.—Members and Delegates in Congress, Vice-President of the United States, Secretary of the Senate, and Clerk of the House to have power to send and receive public documents during their term of office and up to the first Monday of December following the expiration of their term of office.

Act March 1, 1847, section 4.—Secretary of the Senate and Clerk of the House to receive and send all letters and packages free of postage during their term of office ; limited to two ounces.

Act March 1, 1847, section 5.—Members of Congress to receive and send all letters and packages free of postage, up to the first Monday in December following the expiration of their term of office.

Act March 2, 1847, section 1.—Every postmaster whose compensation for the last preceding year did not exceed $200 to send all letters written by himself and receive all addressed to himself, on his private business, free of postage ; limited to one-half ounce in weight.

Act March 3, 1847, *section* 4.—Letters, newspapers, and packets, not exceeding one ounce in weight, directed to any officer, musician, or private of the army of the United States in Mexico, or at any place on the frontier of the United States bordering on Mexico, shall be conveyed in the mail free of postage.

Act March 3, 1847, *section* 5.—Continues in force section 4 of this act during the present war and three months thereafter.

Act March 3, 1847, *section* 7.—Postmaster-General authorized to establish a post-office at Astoria, and other places on the Pacific.

	Cents.
All letters conveyed to or from Chagres	20
All letters conveyed to or from Havana	12½
All letters conveyed to or from Panama	30
All letters conveyed to or from Astoria	40
All letters conveyed to or from any other place on the Pacific	40

Act March 3, 1847, *section* 11.—*Authorizes the Postmaster-General to prepare postage-stamps, which, when attached to any letter or packet, shall be evidence of the payment of postage chargeable therefor.*

Act March 3, 1847, *section* 12.—Repeals so much of section 6 of act March 3, 1845, as requires postage to be paid on free matter from the contingent fund of the two Houses of Congress and the other departments of the government, and in lieu thereof provides for an annual appropriation of $200,000, to be paid to the Post-Office Department.

Act March 3, 1847, *section* 13.—Newspapers by mail (except exchanges between publishers), except such as are franked by those enjoying the franking privilege, and newspapers not sent from the office of publication, and handbills or circulars printed or lithographed, not exceeding one sheet, shall be subject to 3 cents prepaid postage each. Postmaster-General authorized to pay not exceeding 2 cents each for all letters or packets conveyed in any vessel not employed in carrying the mail from one place to another in the United States, under such regulations as he may provide.

Publications or books published, procured, or purchased by either House of Congress shall be considered public documents and entitled to be franked as such.

Act March 3, 1847, *section* 14.—Repeals so much of act of March 3, 1845, and of all other acts relating to the Post-Office Department, as is inconsistent with this act.

Act March 9, 1848.—Letters and packets by mail to and from Louisa Catherine Adams, widow of the late John Quincy Adams, to be free of postage during her life.

Act May 27, 1848, *section* 4.—Commissioner of Patents authorized to send by mail free of postage the annual reports of the Patent Office.

Act June 27, 1848, *section* 1.—Postmaster-General authorized to charge and collect upon all letters and other mailable matter carried in foreign packets the same rate of postage which the governments to which such foreign packets belong impose upon letters, etc., carried in American packets.

Act June 27, 1848, *section* 2.—All letters and other mailable matter conveyed by any foreign ship to or from any port of the United States, to be subject to postage charged as in above section, except letters relating to the vessel or cargo.

Act August 14, 1848, *section* 3.—Postmaster-General authorized to establish a post-office at San Diego, Monterey, San Francisco, and other places on the Pacific, in California, and all letters conveyed to or from any of the above places on the Pacific, from or to any place on the Atlantic, to be charged 40 cents postage; all letters conveyed from one to any other of said places on the Pacific, 12½ cents.

Act March 3, 1849, *section* 1.—Rates on letters transported under the postal treaty with Great Britain:

Letters not exceeding one-half ounce, one rate of postage.

Letters exceeding one-half ounce avoirdupois, and not exceeding 1 ounce, two rates of postage.

Letters exceeding 1 ounce avoirdupois, and not exceeding 2 ounces, four rates of postage.

Letters exceeding 2 ounces avoirdupois, and not exceeding 3 ounces, six rates of postage.

Letters exceeding 3 ounces avoirdupois, and not exceeding 4 ounces, eight rates of postage.

And in like progression for each additional ounce or fraction of an ounce. Newspapers not sent from the office of publication to be charged with the same rates of postage as other papers; to be prepaid.

Act January 10, 1850.—Franking privilege granted Sarah Polk, relict of the late James K. Polk, during her life; to cover all letters and packages to and from.

Act May 23, 1850, *section* 17.—Marshals and their assistants authorized to transmit papers and documents relating to the census through the post-office free.

Act March 23, 1850, *section* 19.—Secretary of the Interior required to appoint a clerk to superintend the census, who shall have the privilege of franking and receiving free of charge all official documents and letters connected therewith.

Act July 18, 1850.—Franking'privilege granted to Margaret Smith Taylor, relict of Zachary Taylor, same as granted to widows of deceased Presidents.

Act September 27, 1850.—Third section act of August 14, 1848, extended to Territories of Utah and New Mexico, and Postmaster-General authorized to establish such rates of postage in said Territories as may to him seem proper, not to exceed those authorized in said act.

Act March 3, 1851, *section* 1.—*Rates of postage on letters.*—From and after June 30, 1851, in lieu of rates of postage now fixed by law, there shall be charged the following rates: Every single letter, in writing, marks, or signs, by mail, not exceeding 3,000 miles, prepaid postage, 3 cents; not prepaid, 5 cents; for any greater distance, double these rates.

Every single letter or paper conveyed wholly or in part by sea, and to or from a foreign country over 2,500 miles, 20 cents; under 2,500 miles, 10 cents (excepting rates fixed by postal treaty); double letter, double rates; triple letter, triple rates; and every letter or parcel not exceeding one-half ounce in weight shall be deemed a single letter, and every additional weight of one-half ounce or less shall be charged with an additional rate. Drop or local letters, 1 cent each. Letters uncalled for and advertised, to be charged 1 cent in addition to the regular postage.

Act March 3, 1851, *section* 2.—Newspapers not exceeding 3 ounces in weight sent from the office of publication to bona fide subscribers shall be charged with postage as follows:

Weekly newspapers free, within the county where published; and for not exceeding 50 miles out of the county where published, 5 cents per quarter; exceeding 50 miles, and not exceeding 300 miles, 10 cents per quarter; exceeding 300 miles, and not exceeding 1,000 miles, 15 cents per quarter; exceeding 1,000 miles, and not exceeding 2,000 miles, 20 cents per quarter; exceeding 2,000 miles, and not exceeding 4,000 miles, 25 cents per quarter; exceeding 4,000 miles, 30 cents per quarter.

Newspapers published monthly, sent to bona fide subscribers, one-quarter of the foregoing rates; published semi-monthly, one-half of the foregoing rates; published semi-weekly, double the foregoing rates; published tri-weekly, treble the foregoing rates; and oftener than tri-weekly, five times the foregoing rates. On other papers, unsealed circulars, handbills, engravings, pamphlets, periodicals, magazines, books, and all other printed matter, unconnected with written matter, of not more than one ounce in weight, and. not exceeding 500 miles, one cent; and for each additional ounce or fraction thereof, one cent; exceeding 500 miles, and not exceeding 1,500 miles, double these rates; exceeding 1,500 miles, and not exceeding 2,500 miles, treble these rates; exceeding 2,500 miles, and not exceeding 3,500 miles, four times these rates; exceeding 3,500 miles, five times these rates.

Subscribers to periodicals required to pay one quarter's postage in advance; postage one-half the foregoing rates.

Bound books and parcels of printed matter, not over thirty ounces, made mailable matter.

Postage on printed matter, other than newspapers, and periodicals published at intervals not exceeding three months and sent from office of publication to bona fide subscribers, to be prepaid.

When printed matter on which postage is required by this section to be prepaid, shall be sent without prepayment, the same shall be charged with double the prepaid rate.

Nothing in this act shall subject to postage any matter exempted from postage by existing law.

Publishers of pamphlets, periodicals, magazines, and newspapers which shall not exceed 16 ounces in weight, allowed to interchange their publications free, confined to a single copy of each publication. Publishers allowed to inclose in their publications bills for subscription without additional postage. Newspapers not containing more than 300 square inches may be transmitted to bona fide subscribers at one-fourth the rates fixed by this act.

Act March 3, 1851, *section* 8.—Provides for the annual appropriation of $500,000 to the Post-Office Department for mail service for the two houses of Congress, and other departments and officers of the government, in the transportation of free matter.

Act August 30, 1852, *section* 1, *vol.* 10, *page* 38.—*Rates of postage on printed matter.*—From and after September 30, 1852, postage on all printed matter passing by mail, instead of the rates now charged, shall be as follows: Each newspaper, periodical, unsealed circular, or other article of printed matter, not exceeding 3 ounces in weight, to any part of the United States, 1 cent; and for every additional ounce or fraction thereof 1 cent additional.

Postage on any newspapers or periodicals paid quarterly or yearly in advance at the office of delivery, or at the office of mailing, one-half of said rates only shall be charged.

Newspapers and periodicals not weighing over 1½ ounces, when circulated State where published, one-half of the rates before mentioned.

Small newspapers and periodicals, published monthly or oftener, and pamp not more than sixteen octavo pages, sent in single packages weighing at least eight ounces to one address, and prepaid by postage-stamps affixed, only one-half cent for each ounce or fraction of an ounce.

Postage on all transient matter shall be prepaid or charged double the rates first above mentioned.

Act August 30, 1852, *section* 2.—*Postage on books.*—Books, bound or unbound, not weighing more than four pounds, will be deemed mailable matter and subject to postage at 1 cent an ounce for all distances under 3,000 miles; 2 cents for all distances over 3,000 miles; to which 50 per cent. shall be added unless prepaid.

Publishers of newspapers and periodicals may exchange free of postage one copy of each publication, and may send to actual subscribers, in their publications, bills and receipts for the same free. Publishers of weekly newspapers may send to each actual subscriber within the county where their papers are printed and published one copy free of postage, under certain conditions.

Act August 30, 1852, *section* 3.—Prescribes certain conditions which if not complied with subject printed matter to letter-postage.

Matter sent by mail from one part of the United States to another, the postage of which is not fixed by this act, shall, unless entitled to be sent free, be charged with letter-postage.

Act August 30, 1852, *section* 5.—Repeals so much of the second section of act of March 3, 1851, as relates to the postage or free circulation of newspapers, periodicals, and other printed matter, and all other provisions of law inconsistent with this act.

Act August 31, 1852, *section* 8, vol. 10, *page* 141.—*Postmaster-General authorized to provide stamped letter envelopes.* Letters when inclosed in such envelopes (with stamps thereon equal in amount to the postage to which such letters would be liable if sent by mail) may be sent and delivered otherwise than by mail under certain conditions.

Act March 3, 1853, *section* 5.—Assistant Postmasters-General to be in future appointed by President and confirmed by Senate.

Act March 3, 1853.—Increases the salary of the Postmaster-General to $8,000 per annum.

Act February 2, 1854.—The Superintendent of the Coast Survey and the assistant in charge of the Office of the Coast Survey authorized to transmit free of postage, by the mails, all letters and documents in relation to their public duties.

Act March 3, 1855, *section* 1.—In lieu of the rates of postage now fixed by law, there shall be charged the following rates:

For every single letter, in manuscript or paper of any kind, in writing, marks, or signs, conveyed in the mail between places in the United States not exceeding 3,000 miles, 3 cents; and for any greater distance, 10 cents; for a double letter, double rates; treble letter, treble rates; quadruple letter, quadruple rates; every letter or parcel not exceeding one-half ounce in weight shall be deemed a single letter, and every additional weight of one-half ounce or less shall be charged an additional rate; the foregoing rates to be prepaid on domestic letters, except on letters and packages to officers of the Government on official business, and except on letters to or from a foreign country.

Postage on drop or local letters, 1 cent each.

Nothing in this act to alter the laws in relation to the franking privilege.

The foregoing section was the first provision of law making the prepayment of postage on domestic letters compulsory.

Act March 3, 1855, *section* 3.—*Authorizes the Postmaster-General to establish a system for registration of valuable letters, and to require prepayment of postage on such letters, as well as of a registration fee of* 5 *cents; the Post-Office Department not to be liable for the loss of such letters or packets.*

Act March 3, 1855, *section* 4.—Franking privilege of Vice-Presidents continued to those who have held or shall hold that office, during life.

Act March 3, 1855, *section* 5.—Books, maps, charts, or other publications, entered by copyright, and which, under act of August 10, 1846, are required to be deposited in the Library of Congress and in the Smithsonian Institution, may be sent by mail free of postage, under regulations to be prescribed by the Postmaster-General.

Act January 2, 1857.—Repeals the provision in the act of August 30, 1852, permitting transient printed matter to be sent through the mail without prepayment of postage; the postage on all such matter shall be paid by stamps or otherwise, as the Postmaster General may direct.

Act April 3, 1860, *section* 1.—Modifies second clause, section 3, of act August 30, 1852, establishing the rates of postage on printed matter, so as to allow only the name, the date when the subscription expires, and the address of the person to whom sent.

Act April 3, 1860, *section* 2.—Postage on drop or local letters delivered by carriers, 1 cent each.

*Act Febru*_____ *section* 2, vol. 12, *page* 167.—*Stamped letter-sheets and newspaper wrappers*____

Act February 27, 1851, *section* 8.—That upon all letters returned from the dead-letter office there shall be paid the usual rate of postage; to be paid on delivery.

Act February 27, 1861, *section* 9.—That upon every letter or packet brought into the United States, or carried from one port therein to another in any private ship or vessel, 5 cents if delivered at the post-office where the same shall arrive, and if destined to be conveyed by post, 2 cents shall be added to the ordinary postage: *Provided,* That upon all letters or packets conveyed in whole or in part by steamers over any route upon which the mail is regularly conveyed in vessels under contract with the Post-Office Department, the same charge shall be levied, with the addition of 2 cents a letter or packet on the domestic rate.

Act February 27, 1861, *section* 10.—Repeals all acts or parts of acts inconsistent with section 9 of this act.

Act February 27, 1861, *section* 12.—That maps, engravings, lithographs, or photographic prints, on rollers or in paper covers, books, bound or unbound, phonographic paper, and letter envelopes, shall be deemed mailable matter, and charged with postage by weight, not to exceed 4 pounds, at the rate of 1 cent an ounce, or fraction of an ounce, to any place in the United States under 1,500 miles; 2 cents an ounce or fraction of an ounce over 1,500 miles, to be prepaid by postage-stamps.

Act February 27, 1861, *section* 13.—That cards, blank or printed, blanks in packages weighing at least 8 ounces, and seeds or cuttings in packages not exceeding 8 ounces, shall also be deemed mailable matter, and charged with postage at the rate of 1 cent an ounce, or fraction thereof, to any place in the United States under 1,500 miles, and 2 cents an ounce, or fraction thereof, over 1,500 miles, to be prepaid by postage-stamps.

The foregoing sections were the first provisions of law that authorized the introduction of merchandise into the mails.

Act February 27, 1861, *section* 14.—Modifies the act of March 3, 1855, so as to require the 10-cent rate of postage to be prepaid on letters conveyed in the mail from any point in the United States east of the Rocky Mountains to any State or Territory on the Pacific, and *vice versa.*

Drop-letters shall be prepaid by postage-stamps.

Act February 27, 1861, *section* 16.—The postage over the overland route, between any State or Territory east of the Rocky Mountains to any State or Territory on the Pacific, on each newspaper, periodical, unsealed circular, or other article of printed matter not exceeding 3 ounces in weight, shall be 1 cent, and every additional ounce, or fraction thereof, 1 cent additional.

Act February 27, 1861, *section* 17.—Rate of letter-postage between any State or Territory east of the Rocky Mountains and any State or Territory on the Pacific, 10 cents for every half ounce.

Act March 2, 1861, *section* 9.—Contractors on overland routes to San Francisco required to run a pony-express during the continuance of their contract or until the completion of the overland telegraph, at certain times, carrying for the government free of charge 5 pounds of mail matter, with the liberty of charging the public for transportation of letters by said express, not exceeding $1 for one-half ounce; to commence before the 25th day of March, 1862 and expire July 1, 1864.

Act July 22, 1861, *section* 11.—Letters written by soldiers in the service of the United States may be transmitted by mail without prepayment of postage, under regulations of the Post-Office Department; postage to be paid by the party receiving.

Act July 24, 1861.—Prepaid letters to soldiers in the service of the United States, and directed to a point where they have been stationed, may be forwarded without further charge.

Act January 21, 1862, *section* 1.—Postmaster-General authorized to return all dead letters to writers, except those containing circulars and other worthless matter. Valuable letters to be charged treble, and all others double the ordinary rates of postage, to be collected from the writers.

Provisions of act of July 2, 1861, section 11, extended to sailors and marines in the service of the United States.

Act April 16, 1862, *section* 1.—Postmaster-General authorized to establish branch post-offices in cities, and to charge 1 cent in addition to the regular postage for every letter deposited in them to be forwarded by mail, to be prepaid by stamps; and 1 cent for every letter delivered at such branch office, to be paid on delivery.

Act May 15, 1862, *section* 1.—Establishes the Department of Agriculture.

Act May 15, 1862, *section* 2.—Provides for the appointment of a Commissioner of Agriculture, and confers franking privilege on said Commissioner to send and receive by mail free of postage all communications and other matter pertaining to the business of his Department; weight limited to 32 ounces.

Act July 1, 1862, *section* 1.—Creates the office of Commissioner of Internal Revenue and confers on the Commissioner the privilege of franking all letters and documents pertaining to the duties of his office, and of receiving free all such letters and documents.

Act July 5, 1862, *section* 6.—Chiefs of the bureaus of the Navy Department authorized to frank all communications from their respective bureaus, and all communications to their bureaus on the business thereof shall be free of postage.

Act July 17, 1862.—Postage stamps to be used as currency in sums less than $5.

Act March 3, 1863, *section* 11, *vol.* 12, *page* 703.—*That letter-carriers shall be employed at such post-offices as the Postmaster-General shall direct for the delivery of letters in the places respectively where such post-offices are established; and for their services they shall severally receive a salary, to be prescribed by the Postmaster-General, not exceeding $800 per annum.*

Act March 3, 1863, *section* 16.—Postmasters of any office where letter-carriers are employed authorized to contract with publishers of newspapers, periodicals, and circulars for delivery by carrier of any such publications not received by mail, at rates and terms to be agreed upon. Contracts have no force until approved by the Postmaster-General.

Postmaster-General authorized to provide for delivery by carrier of small packets, other than letters or papers, and not exceeding the maximum weight of mailable packages; such packages to be prepaid by postage-stamps at the rate of 2 cents for each 4 ounces or fraction thereof.

Act March 3, 1863, *section* 16.—Limits weight to 4 pounds, except books published or circulated by order of Congress.

Act March 3, 1863, *section* 19.—Divides mailable matter into three classes. First class, letters; second class, regular printed matter; third class, miscellaneous matter.

Act March 3, 1863, *section* 20.—First class embraces all correspondence wholly or partly in writing, except that mentioned in the third class.

Second class embraces all mailable matter exclusively in print and regularly issued at stated periods, without addition by writing, mark, or sign.

Third class embraces all other matter which is or may hereafter be by law declared mailable.

Act March 3, 1863, *section* 21.—Fixes the maximum standard weight for the single rate of letter-postage at one-half ounce avoirdupois.

Act March 3, 1863, *section* 22.—Fixes the rate of postage on domestic letters not exceeding one-half ounce in weight at 3 cents, and 3 cents additional for each additional half-ounce or fraction thereof, to be prepaid by postage-stamps affixed.

This was the first law which established a uniform rate of postage on letters regardless of distance to which matter was to be transmitted.

Act March 3, 1863, *section* 23.—Fixes the rate of postage on drop-letters not exceeding one-half ounce in weight at 2 cents, and 2 cents added for each additional half-ounce or fraction thereof, to be prepaid by postage-stamps affixed; "but no extra postage or carriers' fee shall hereafter be charged or collected upon letters delivered by carriers, nor upon letters collected by them for mailing or delivery."

Act March 3, 1863, *section* 24.—Mailable matter wholly or partly in writing, or so marked as to convey further information than is conveyed by the original print in case of printed matter, or sent in violation of law or regulations touching the inclosure of matter which may be sent at less than letter rates, and all matter on which no different rate is provided by law, subject to letter postage: *Provided,* That book-manuscript and corrected proof, passing between author and publisher, may pass at the rate of printed matter: *And provided,* That the publishers of newspapers and periodicals may print or write upon their publications sent to subscribers the address and the date when the subscription expires, and may inclose receipt for payment and bills for subscription.

Act March 3, 1863, *section* 25.—All matter not enumerated as mailable, and to which no specific rates of postage are assigned, subject to letter postage.

Act March 3, 1863, *section* 26.—Double rates of postage to be collected on delivery on any matter on which postage is required to be prepaid at the mailing office: *Provided,* Such matter reaches its destination without such prepayment.

Act March 3, 1863, *section* 27.—Postmaster-General authorized to provide for transmitting unpaid and duly-certified letters of soldiers, sailors, and marines, and all other letters which, from accident, appear to have been deposited without prepayment of postage; but in all cases of letters not prepaid, except certified soldiers' and naval letters, the same shall be charged with double rates of postage, to be collected on delivery.

Act March 3, 1863, *section* 28.—*That when any writer of a letter on which the postage is prepaid shall indorse in writing or in print thereon upon the outside thereof his name and address with the request that the same be returned to him if not called for or delivered within any number of days (not to exceed 30 days), any such letter shall not be advertised nor treated as a dead letter, but shall be returned direct, etc.*

By virtue of this law special-request envelopes were subsequently introduced.

Act March 3, 1863, *section* 29.—Postage on return dead letters, not registered as valuable, 3 cents for the single rate; registered as valuable, double rates.

Act March 3, 1863, section 30.—Letters may be forwarded from office of destination to any other office, with additional charge of postage therefor.

Act March 3, 1863, section 31.—Postmaster-General authorized to pay 2 cents each for all letters conveyed in any vessel not employed in carrying the mail from one place to another in the United States, or from any foreign port to any port within the United States and deposited in the post-office at the port of arrival. If for delivery within the United States, double rates of postage.

Act March 3, 1863, section 32.—Provides that fee on registered letters shall not exceed 20 cents.

Act March 3, 1863, section 33.—Fixes the maximum standard rate for the single rate of postage on printed matter, and also on miscellaneous matter, at 4 ounces avoirdupois, subject to the exception in the next section.

Act March 3, 1863, section 34.—The rate of postage on transient matter of the second class, and on miscellaneous matter of the third class (except circulars and books), shall be 2 cents for each 4 ounces or fraction thereof on one package to one address, to be prepaid by stamps affixed; double these rates for books. Unsealed circulars, not exceeding three in number, 2 cents, adding one rate for three additional circulars or less number to one address.

Act March 3, 1863, section 35.—Postage on matter of the second class, issued once a week or more frequently, from a known office of publication, and sent to regular subscribers, shall be as follows: For newspapers and other periodical publications, not exceeding 4 ounces, and passing through the mails or post-offices of the United States, the rate for each quarter shall be, for publications issued once a week, 5 cents; twice a week, 10 cents; three times a week, 15 cents; six times a week, 30 cents; seven times a week, 35 cents; and in that proportion, adding one rate for each issue more frequent than once a week. For weight exceeding 4 ounces and not exceeding 8 ounces, an additional rate, and an additional rate for each additional 4 ounces or fraction thereof; postage to be prepaid for not less than one quarter nor more than one year, at either the office of mailing or delivery, at the option of the subscriber.

Weekly newspapers, to each subscriber within the county where the same are printed and published, one copy free of postage.

Act March 3, 1863, section 36.—Postage on mailable matter of the second class, issued less frequently than once a week, from a known office of publication, and sent to subscribers, shall be as follows: Upon newspapers, magazines, and other periodical publications, not exceeding 4 ounces, passing through the mails or post-offices of the United States, the rate for each such paper or periodical shall be 1 cent, and an additional rate of 1 cent for each additional 4 ounces or fraction thereof: *Provided,* That the Postmaster-General may provide for the transportation of *small* newspapers in packages at the same rate by weight when sent to one address; postage must be prepaid at office of mailing or delivery, at option of subscriber, for not less than one quarter nor more than one year.

Act March 3, 1863, section 37.—Publishers may inclose in their publications to subscribers bills for subscription, and may write or print on their publications or their wrappers name and address of subscribers and the date when subscription expires; but any other inclosure or addition in writing or in print shall subject the same to letter postage.

Act March 3, 1863, section 39.—Postmaster-General authorized to prescribe the manner of wrapping all matter not charged with letter postage nor lawfully franked; if not so wrapped and secured, the same shall be subject to letter postage.

Act March 3, 1863, section 42.—Confers the franking privilege upon and limits it to the following persons: President of the United States; Vice-President of the United States; the chiefs of the several executive departments; the heads of bureaus or chief clerks of executive departments, to be used only for official communications; Senators, Representatives, and Delegates in Congress, Secretary of the Senate, and Clerk of the House; to cover correspondence to and from them, and all printed matter issued by authority of Congress, and all speeches, proceedings, and debates in Congress, and all printed matter sent to them; to commence with the term for which they are elected, and to expire on the first Monday in December following the expiration of such term; all official communications to any of the executive departments, by an officer responsible to that department, the envelope to be marked "official," with the signature of the officer thereon; postmasters, for their official communications to other postmasters, the envelope to be marked "official," with the signature of the postmaster thereon.

Petitions to either house of Congress, free.

The franking privilege granted by this act limited to four ounces, except petitions to Congress, congressional or executive documents, and publications or books published, procured, or purchased by order of either house of Congress, or joint resolution of both Houses, which shall be considered as public documents, and entitled to be franked as such; and except, also, seeds, cuttings, roots, and scions, the weight of packages to be fixed by regulation of the Postmaster-General.

Act March 3, 1863, *section* 43.—Publishers of periodicals, magazines, and newspapers allowed to exchange their publications free of postage; confined to a single copy, and not to exceed sixteen ounces in weight.

This act to take effect June 30, 1863.

Act March 3, 1863, *section* 45.—Repeals all acts and parts of acts inconsistent with the provisions of this act.

Act January 22, 1864.—Clothing of wool, cotton, or linen, in packages not exceeding two pounds each, addressed to any non-commissioned officer or private in the Army, may be transmitted by mail at the rate of 8 cents for every four ounces or fraction thereof under regulations of the Postmaster-General; postage to be prepaid.

Act March 16, 1864.—The franking privilege of the President and Vice-President shall extend to and cover all mail-matter sent from or directed to either of them.

Act March 25, 1864, *section* 4.—Mailable matter conveyed by mail westward of the western boundary of Kansas, and eastward of the eastern boundary of California, subject to prepaid letter rates, except newspapers sent from a known office of publication to subscribers, not exceeding one copy to each, and franked matter to and from the intermediate points between the boundaries named, which shall be at the usual rate.

Act June 1, 1864.—Official communications to heads of departments or heads of bureaus or chief clerks or one duly authorized by the Postmaster-General to frank official matter, shall be received and conveyed by mail free of postage, without being indorsed, "official business," or with the name of the writer.

Act May 17, 1864, *section* 1.—*Authorizes the Postmaster-General to establish a uniform money-order system at such post-offices as he may deem suitable therefor, and which shall be designated as money-order offices.*

Act May 17, 1864, *section* 3.—Provides that no money order shall be issued for less than $1 or more than $30, and that the fees shall be as follows: Upon an order for $1 and not more than $10, 10 cents; upon an order exceeding $10 and not exceeding $20, 15 cents; upon an order exceeding $20, 20 cents.

Act May 17, 1864, *section* 13.—Provides for the appointment of a Superintendent of the Money-Order System.

Act June 30, 1864, *section* 1.—The franking privilege to the Commissioner of Internal Revenue extended to letters and documents pertaining to the duties of his office and to receiving free of postage all such letters and documents.

Act June 30, 1864, *section* 3.—Confers on the Deputy Commissioner of Internal Revenue the privilege of franking all letters and documents pertaining to the office of internal revenue.

Act July 1, 1864, *section* 8.—The rates of postage on letters and other mailable matter addressed to or received from foreign countries and carried by vessels regularly employed in transportation of the mails shall be as follows: Ten cents for one-half ounce or under, on letters; two cents on each newspaper, and the established domestic rates on pamphlets, periodicals, and other articles of printed matter, to be prepaid on matter sent, and collected on matter received; subject to rates established or to be established by international postal convention.

Act January 20, 1865.—Amends section 4 of act March 25, 1864, so as to insert in the proviso in said section after the word "newspapers," the words "periodicals, magazines, and exchanges."

Act March 3, 1865, *section* 1, *vol.* 13, *page* 515.—Chief clerk authorized for each of the Assistant Postmasters-General, at a salary of $2,000 a year.

Act March 3, 1865, *section* 1, *vol.* 13, *page* 504.—All domestic letters except those franked, and letters of soldiers and sailors, deposited for mailing wholly unpaid, shall be sent to the Dead-Letter Office; those paid only in part to be forwarded to destination and unpaid rate collected on delivery.

Act March 3, 1865, *section* 20, *vol.* 13, *page* 487.—Privilege of franking letters and documents pertaining to the duties of the office of internal revenue, and of receiving free of postage all such letters and documents, is extended to the Commissioner of that office.

Act March 3, 1865, *section* 15, *vol.* 13, *page* 507.—Fixes the prepaid postage on drop letters, at all offices except free delivery, at 1 cent.

Act March 3, 1865, *section* 15, *vol.* 13, *page* 507.—System of free delivery shall be established at every place having a population of 50,000.

Act February 10, 1866.—Confers franking privilege on Mary Lincoln, widow of the late Abraham Lincoln, to cover all letters and packets by mail to and from.

Act June 12, 1866, *section* 1.—Provides for the forwarding of prepaid and free letters at the request of the party addressed, from one post-office to another, without additional postage and the return of dead letters to the writers free of postage.

Act June 12, 1866, *section* 2.—Request letters to be returned to the writers without additional postage.

Act June 12, 1866, *section* 3.—Forbids the issue of money-orders for any sum over $50 and fixes the following fees: Upon an order for any sum not exceeding $20, 10 cents; upon an order exceeding $20, 20 cents.

Act July 13, 1866, *section* 65.—That all official communications made by assessors to collectors, assessors to assessors, collectors to collectors, collectors to assessors, assessors to assistant assessors, assistant assessors to assessors, collectors to their deputies, or deputy collectors to collectors, may be officially franked by the writers thereof and transmitted by mail free of postage.

Act July 13, 1866, *section* 66.—Authorizes the Secretary of the Treasury to appoint a special commissioner of the revenue; and all letters and documents to and from said commissioner relating to the duties and business of his office shall be transmitted by mail free of postage.

Act July 28, 1866, *section* 13.—Establishes the Bureau of Statistics, and authorizes the Secretary of the Treasury to appoint a director to superintend the business of said bureau, and provides for the transmission by mail free of postage of all letters and documents to and from him relating to the business of his office.

Act March 2, 1868.—The adjutants-general of the States and Territories authorized to transmit by mail free of postage any medals, certificates of thanks, or other testimonials awarded, or that may be awarded, by the legislatures of said States and Territories, to the soldiers thereof, under regulations to be prescribed by the Postmaster-General.

Act March 9, 1868, *section* 3.—Letters and documents to and from the Congressional Printer relating to the business of his office shall be transmitted by mail free of postage, under regulations to be prescribed by the Postmaster-General.

Act June 25, 1868.—That the operations of section 4, act of March 25, 1864, shall cease on and after September 30, 1868.

Act July 27, 1868, *section* 1.—Prepaid letters having the name and address of the writer in writing or in print on the outside, after remaining uncalled for at the post-office to which directed 30 days, or the time the writer may direct, shall be returned to the writer without additional postage.

Act July 27, 1868, *section* 2.—Changes the fee on money-orders as follows: For any sum not exceeding $20, 10 cents; for any sum exceeding $20 and not exceeding $30, 15 cents; for any sum exceeding $30 and not exceeding $40, 20 cents; for any sum exceeding $40 and not exceeding $50, 25 cents.

Act July 27, 1868, *section* 8.—Authorizes the Postmaster-General to appoint a superintendent of foreign mails.

Act July 27, 1868, *section* 3.—Weekly newspapers, sent to subscribers in the county where printed and published, to be delivered free of postage when deposited in the office nearest the office of publication; but they shall not be distributed by letter-carriers unless postage is prepaid thereon at the rate of 5 cents per quarter for not less than one quarter nor more than one year, at the office of mailing or delivery, at the option of the subscriber.

Act March 1, 1869.—Requires the franking privilege to be exercised by persons entitled to it by the written autograph signature upon the matter franked; letters or other mail-matter not thus franked to be charged with postage.

Act July 8, 1870, *section* 8.—Provides that the Commissioner of Patents may send and receive by mail free of postage letters, printed matter, and packages relating to the business of his office, including Patent-Office Reports.

Act July 8, 1870, *section* 95.—Any copyright book or other article may be sent to the Librarian of Congress by mail free of postage: *Provided*, The words "copyright matter" are plainly written or printed on the outside of the package.

Act June 1, 1872, *section* 4.—Repeals section 12, act March 3, 1847, and section 8, act March 3, 1851, so far as said sections provide for specific permanent appropriations for carrying free matter in the mails for the several departments and members of Congress; hereafter payment for carrying such matter shall be made out of the annual appropriations.

Act June 8, 1872, *section* 30.—Authorizes the Postmaster-General to establish a blank agency for the Post-Office Department, to be located at Washington, D. C.

Act June 8, 1872, *section* 99.—The rate of postage on newspapers (excepting weeklies), periodicals not exceeding 2 ounces in weight, and circulars, when deposited in a letter-carrier office for delivery by the office or its carriers, shall be uniform at 1 cent each; but periodicals weighing more than 2 ounces shall be subject to a postage of 2 cents each; these rates to be prepaid by stamps.

Act June 8, 1872, *section* 107.—Provides that no money-order shall be issued for more than $50, and establishes the following fees: For any amount not exceeding $10, 5 cents; for any amount exceeding $10 and not exceeding $20, 10 cents; for any amount exceeding $20 and not exceeding $30, 15 cents; for any amount exceeding $30 and not exceeding $40, 20 cents; for any amount exceeding $40, 25 cents.

Act June 8, 1872, *section* 127.—Letters upon the official business of the Post-Office Department may be registered free of charge and pass by mail free of charge.

Act June 8, 1872, *section* 127.—Provides that the fee for registering valuable letters shall not exceed 20 cents in addition to the regular postage, and must be prepaid. Letters upon official business of the Post-Office Department may be registered free of charge and pass through the mails free of charge.

Act June 8, 1872, *section* 130.—Divides mailable matter into three classes: First class, letters ; second class, regular printed matter; third class, miscellaneous matter.

Act June 8, 1872, *section* 131.—Mailable matter of the first class shall embrace all correspondence wholly or partly in writing, except book manuscript and corrected proofs passing between authors and publishers.

Act June 8, 1872, *section* 132.—Second class, to embrace all matter exclusively in print and regularly issued at stated periods from a known office of publication, without addition by writing, mark, or sign.

Act June 8, 1872, *section* 133.—Third class, to embrace all other mailable matter. Matter of this class except books and other printed matter, book-manuscripts, proof-sheets and corrected proof-sheets, shall not exceed 12 ounces in weight. Samples of metals, ores, and mineralogical specimens, limited to 12 ounces.

Act June 8, 1872, *section* 134.—Limits weight of packages to 4 pounds, except books published or circulated by order of Congress.

Act June 8, 1872, *section* 136.—Matter not charged with letter postage, nor lawfully franked, subject to letter-postage, unless wrapped in accordance with regulations of the Postmaster-General.

Act June 8, 1872, *section* 141.—Publishers of newspapers or periodicals may print or write upon their publications to regular subscribers the address, the date when the subscription expires, and may inclose therein bills and receipts for subscription, without extra postage.

Act June 8, 1872, *section* 142.—To inclose or cancel any letter, memorandum, or other thing in any mail-matter not charged with letter-postage, or to write thereon, subjects such matter to letter-postage.

Act June 8, 1872, *section* 150.—Requires that the postage on all mail-matter, except as hereinafter provided, must be prepaid at the time of mailing.

Act June 8, 1872, *section* 151.—Permits mail-matter on which one full rate has been prepaid to be forwarded to its destination, and the unpaid rate collected on delivery.

Act June 8, 1872, *section* 152.—Mail-matter on which postage is required to be prepaid, reaching its destination, by inadvertence, without such prepayment, shall be subject to double the prepaid rates.

Act June 8, 1872, *section* 156.—That on all matter wholly or partly in writing, except book-manuscripts and corrected proofs passing between author and publisher, and local drop letters ; on all printed matter, so marked as to convey any other information than is conveyed by the original print, except the correction of a mere typographical error ; on all matter sent in violation of law or regulations respecting inclosures ; and on all matter to which no specific rate of postage is assigned, postage shall be 3 cents the half ounce or fraction thereof.

Act June 8, 1872, *section* 157.—Fixes the postage on drop or local letters at letter-carrier offices at 2 cents the half ounce or fraction thereof, and 1 cent the half ounce or fraction thereof at all other offices.

Act June 8, 1872, *section* 158.—Quarterly postage on newspapers and other periodical publications, not exceeding 4 ounces in weight, sent to subscribers, shall be at the following rates: On publications issued less frequently than once a week, 1 cent for each issue; issued once a week, 5 cents ; and 5 cents additional for each issue more frequent than once a week ; an additional rate shall be charged for each additional 4 ounces or fraction thereof.

Act June 8, 1872, *section* 160.—Small newspapers issued less frequently than once a week, in packages to one address, to subscribers, 1 cent for each 4 ounces or fraction thereof.

Act June 8, 1872, *section* 161.—Regular dealers in newspapers and periodicals may receive and transmit by mail such quantities of either as they may require, and pay the postage as received, at the same rates as subscribers who pay quarterly in advance.

Act June 8, 1872, *section* 163.—Postage on mailable matter of the third class shall be at the rate of 1 cent for each 2 ounces or fraction thereof, except that double these rates shall be charged for books, samples of metals, ores, minerals, and merchandise.

Act June 8, 1872, *section* 164.—Packages of woolen, cotton, or linen clothing, in packages not exceeding 2 pounds, may be sent by mail to any non-commissioned officer or private in the army, if prepaid, 1 cent each ounce or fraction thereof.

Act June 8, 1872, *section* 166.—Letters conveyed in vessels not regularly employed in carrying the mail shall, if for delivery in the United States, be rated with double postage.

Act June 8, 1872, *section* 170.—*Provides for the issue and transmission by mail of postal-cards at 1 cent each.*

Act June 8, 1872, *section* 180.—Confers the franking privilege upon and limits it to the following named persons:

' First. The President, by himself or private secretary, to cover all mail-matter.

Second. Vice-President, to cover all mail-matter.

Third. The chiefs of the several executive departments.

Fourth. Senators, Representatives, Delegates, Secretary of the Senate, and Clerk of the House—to cover their correspondence, all printed matter issued by authority of Congress, and all speeches, proceedings, and debates in Congress.

Fifth. Such heads of bureaus or chief clerks as the Postmaster-General may designate, to cover official communications only.

Sixth. Postmasters, to cover official communications to other postmasters only.

Written autograph signatures, of all persons entitled to frank, required; mail-matter not thus franked to be charged with postage.

Act June 8, 1872, section 181.—The franking privilege of Senators, Representatives, Delegates, Secretary of the Senate, and Clerk of the House, to commence with the term for which they are elected and to expire the first Monday in December following such term.

Act June 8, 1672, section 182.—Books or publications procured or published by order of Congress, to be public documents, and may be franked as such.

Act June 8, 1872, section 183.—Maximum weight for franked and free matter shall be 4 pounds, except petitions to Congress, congressional and executive public documents, periodical publications interchanged between publishers, and packages of seeds, cuttings, roots, and scions, the weight of which latter may be fixed by the Postmaster-General.

Act June 8, 1872, section 184.—Free mail-matter.—The following mail-matter shall be allowed to pass free in the mail:

First. All mail-matter sent to the President or Vice-President.

Second. Official communications to chiefs, heads of bureaus, chief clerks, or franking-officer of any of the executive departments.

Third. Letters and printed matter sent to Senators, Representatives, Delegates, Secretary of the Senate, and Clerk of the House.

Fourth. Petitions to Congress.

Fifth. Copyright matter to the Librarian of Congress, if marked "copyright matter."

Sixth. Publications sent and received by the Smithsonian Institution, if marked "Smithsonian exchange."

Seventh. Newspapers, periodicals, and magazines exchanged between publishers, not exceeding 16 ounces in weight.

Eighth. Weekly newspapers, one copy to each subscriber within the county where the same is printed and published.

Ninth. Notice to the publishers of the refusal or neglect of subscribers to take newspapers, magazines, or other periodicals from the post-office.

Tenth. Dead-letters returned to the writers.

Eleventh. Medals, certificates of thanks, or other testimonials awarded by the legislatures of States and Territories to the soldiers thereof.

Act June 8, 1872, section 185.—All mail-matter to or from Mary Lincoln, widow of late President Lincoln.

Act June 8, 1872, section 199.—Prepaid and free letters shall be forwarded from one post-office to another at request of the person addressed, without additional charge for postage.

Act January 9, 1873.—Amends section 133 of act of June 8, 1872, so as to authorize the transmission by mail of packages of seeds, cuttings, bulbs, roots, and scions, of any weight. For each package not exceeding 4 pounds, the postage shall be 1 cent for each 2 ounces or fraction of an ounce; to be prepaid in full.

Act January 31, 1873.—Abolishes the franking privilege from and after July 1, 1873.

Act March 3, 1873.—Repeals, from and after June 30, 1873, all laws and parts of laws permitting the transmission by mail of any free matter whatever.

Act March 3, 1873.—Authorizes the use of official postage stamps and stamped envelopes for payment of postage on official matter of executive departments.

Act March 3, 1873, section 1, volume 17, page 486.—Salary of the Postmaster-General increased to $10,000 per annum.

Act January 20, 1874.—Reduces the salary of the Postmaster-General to $8,000.

Act June 23, 1874, section 5.—On and after January 1, 1875, on all newspapers and periodical publications mailed from a known office of publication or news agency, and addressed to regular subscribers or news agents, postage shall be charged at the following rates: On newspapers and periodical publications issued weekly and more frequently, 2 cents a pound or fraction thereof; and on those issued less frequently than once a week, 3 cents a pound or fraction thereof: *Provided,* That nothing in this act shall be held to change section 99 of the act of June 8, 1872.

Newspaper and periodical stamps were introduced under this act.

Act June 23, 1874, section 7.—Newspapers, one copy to each subscriber residing in the county where same are printed in whole or in part, and published, shall go free in the mails; but they shall not be delivered at letter-carrier offices or be distributed by carriers unless postage is paid thereon.

Act June 23, 1874, section 8.—Mailable matter of the third class referred to in section 133 of act of June 8, 1872, may weigh not exceeding 4 pounds to each package, and postage shall be charged thereon at the rate of 1 cent for each 2 ounces or fraction thereof.

Act June 23, 1874, section 13.—Fixes the postage on public documents mailed by any member of Congress, the President or head of any executive department, at 10 cents for each bound volume, and unbound documents the same rate as that on newspapers mailed from a known office of publication to subscribers; and the postage on the daily Congressional Record, mailed from the city of Washington as transient matter, at 1 cent.

Act March 3, 1875, section 3.—Extends the provisions of section 13 of act of June 23, 1874, to ex-Members of Congress and ex-Delegates, for nine months after the expiration of their terms; and postage on public documents mailed by them shall be as provided in such section.

Act March 3, 1875, section 5.—The Congressional Record, or any part thereof, or speeches or reports therein, shall, under the frank of a Member or Delegate, written by himself, be carried in the mail free of postage ; and public documents printed or ordered to be printed for the use of either house of Congress may pass free by mail upon the frank of any Member or Delegate of the present Congress, written by himself, until the first day of December, 1875.

Act March 3, 1875, section 7.—Seeds transmitted by the Commissioner of Agriculture, or by any Member or Delegate receiving them for distribution from said department, together with the Agricultural Reports, shall pass free in the mails under regulations of the Postmaster-General; and the provisions of this section shall apply to ex-Members and ex-Delegates for the period of nine months after the expiration of their term.

Act March 3, 1875, volume 18, page 377.—Amends section 8 of act of June 23, 1874, by inserting the word "ounce" in lieu of the words "two ounces."

Act July 12, 1876, section 15, volume 19, page 82.—Rates on all printed matter of the third class, except unsealed circulars, fixed at 1 cent for 2 ounces. Permits limited inscriptions and addresses on third-class matter.

Act March 3, 1877, sections 5 and 6, volume 19, page 335.—Provides for official penalty envelopes and free transmission of same in mails when sent by executive departments and containing inclosures relating to government business.

Act March 3, 1879, section 29, volume 20, page 362.—The provisions of the preceding act extended to the Smithsonian Institution and to all government officers.

Act March 3, 1879, sections 7–27, volume 20, pages 358–362.—General act repealing all former laws relating to classification of mail-matter and rates of postages. Makes four classes of mail-matter, to wit: First-class, written matter, at 3 cents each half ounce ; second class, periodical publications regularly issued for general information, at 2 cents per pound, including sample copies ; third class, miscellaneous printed matter, at 1 cent for each 2 ounces ; and fourth class, merchandise, all matter not included in the other three classes, at 1 cent each ounce. Liberalizes the provisions of former laws respecting written inscriptions on printed matter, and defines printed matter generally.

Act March 3, 1879, section 32, volume 20, page 362.—Authorizes the Postmaster-General to introduce letter-sheet envelopes and double postal-cards.

Act March 3, 1883, section 1, volume 22, page 455.—Reduces the postage on first-class matter to 2 cents a half ounce on and after October 1, 1883.

Act March 3, 1883, section 1, volume 22, page 526.—The Postmaster-General may authorize postmasters at money-order offices to issue money-orders for small sums under $5, without corresponding advices, to be designated as "*postal notes*," the fee therefor to be 3 cents, and the note to be payable to bearer.

Act March 3, 1883, section 3, volume 22, page 527.—Forbids the issue of a money-order for more than $100, and fixes the fees as follows : For any sum not exceeding $10, 8 cents ; for any sum exceeding $10 and not exceeding $15, 10 cents ; for any sum exceeding $15 and not exceeding $30, 15 cents ; for any sum exceeding $30 and not exceeding $40, 20 cents ; for any sum exceeding $40 and not exceeding $50, 25 cents ; for any sum exceeding $50 and not exceeding $60, 30 cents; for any sum exceeding $60 and not exceeding $70, 35 cents ; for any sum exceeding $70 and not exceeding $80, 40 cents ; for any sum exceeding $80 and not exceeding $100, 45 cents.

Act June 19, 1884, volume 23, page 40.—Rate of postage on newspapers and periodicals sent by other than the publishers fixed at 1 cent for every 4 ounces or fraction thereof.

Act March 3, 1885, section 1, volume 23, page 387.—Reduces postage on first-class matter to 2 cents an ounce or fraction thereof ; the postage on drop letters to be 2 cents an ounce or fraction thereof, including delivery at letter-carrier offices, and 1 cent at non-carrier offices. Reduces the postage on second-class matter sent by publishers to 1 cent a pound or fraction thereof.

Act March 3, 1885, section 3, volume 23, page 387.—Special-delivery system authorized at all places having a population of 4,000 or more. Special stamp authorized to secure immediate delivery, which on arrival of letter at such place is to be performed by special messengers at a fee of 8 cents for each letter.

Act June 29, 1886, section 1, volume 24, page 86.—Reduces the fee on domestic money-orders for less than $5, from 8 cents to 5 cents.

Act August 4, 1886, section 1, volume 24, page 220.—Special-delivery system extended to all post-offices.

Act January 3, 1887, section 1, volume 24, page 355.—Extends the free-delivery service to all cities having not less than 10,000 inhabitants, or at any post-office the gross annual revenue of which is $10,000.

Act March 3, 1887, section 1, volume 24, page 354.—Authorizes the Postmaster-General to designate other than money-order offices to issue postal-notes for sums under $5, fee 3 cents.

Act July 24, 1888.—Rate of postage on seeds, scions, bulbs, cuttings, roots, and plants reduced to 1 cent for every 2 ounces or fraction thereof.

No. 19.—*Statement of postal statistics from 1789 to the close of the fiscal year ending June 30, 1888.*

Years.	Post-offices.	Post routes.	Mail service performed.	Gross revenue of Department.	Gross expenditure of Department.	Paid as compensation of postmasters.	Ordinary postage stamps issued.	Stamped envelopes and wrappers issued.	Postal-cards issued.	Letters, etc., registered.	Dead letters received.	Realized from dead letters.	Domestic money-orders issued.	International money-orders issued.
		Miles.	*Miles.*											
1789	75	2,875	------	*$7,510	*$7,560	*$1,657	------	------	------	------	------	------	------	------
1790	75	1,875	------	37,850	33,110	8,196	------	------	------	------	------	------	------	------
1791	89	1,905	------	46,294	36,687	10,313	------	------	------	------	------	------	------	------
1792	195	5,642	------	67,443	64,530	15,517	------	------	------	------	------	------	------	------
1793	209	5,642	845,468	104,746	72,039	21,645	------	------	------	------	------	------	------	------
1794	450	11,984	------	128,947	89,972	27,155	------	------	------	------	------	------	------	------
1795	453	13,207	------	160,620	117,903	30,272	------	------	------	------	------	------	------	------
1796	468	13,207	------	195,069	131,571	35,729	------	------	------	------	------	------	------	------
1797	554	16,180	1,799,720	213,998	150,114	47,169	------	------	------	------	------	------	------	------
1798	639	16,180	------	232,977	169,084	56,038	------	------	------	------	------	------	------	------
1799	677	16,180	1,900,000	264,846	188,037	63,967	------	------	------	------	------	------	------	------
1800	903	20,817	------	280,804	213,994	68,242	------	------	------	------	------	------	------	------
1801	1,025	22,309	3,057,964	320,442	231,348	78,227	------	------	------	------	------	------	------	------
1802	1,114	25,315	------	327,044	260,866	83,588	------	------	------	------	------	------	------	------
1803	1,258	25,315	3,504,900	351,822	396,866	93,158	------	------	------	------	------	------	------	------
1804	1,405	27,055	------	389,449	337,042	107,713	------	------	------	------	------	------	------	------
1805	1,558	31,076	------	421,373	377,367	115,761	------	------	------	------	------	------	------	------
1806	1,710	33,431	------	446,105	412,223	119,784	------	------	------	------	------	------	------	------
1807	1,848	33,783	------	478,763	453,885	129,041	------	------	------	------	------	------	------	------
1808	2,012	34,035	------	490,504	462,528	126,653	------	------	------	------	------	------	------	------
1809	2,300	34,035	------	509,832	468,412	141,579	------	------	------	------	------	------	------	------
1810	2,403	36,406	5,900,000	552,285	495,969	149,438	------	------	------	------	------	------	------	------
1811	2,610	36,406	------	587,246	499,098	159,244	------	------	------	------	------	------	------	------
1812	------	39,378	------	649,206	540,165	177,452	------	------	------	------	------	------	------	------
1813	------	39,540	------	703,154	681,011	221,849	------	------	------	------	------	------	------	------
1814	2,670	41,738	------	730,370	727,126	234,354	------	------	------	------	------	------	------	------
1815	3,000	43,748	------	961,086	748,121	241,901	------	------	------	------	------	------	------	------
1816	3,260	48,673	------	961,782	804,422	265,944	------	------	------	------	------	------	------	------
1817	3,459	52,089	------	1,002,973	916,515	303,918	------	------	------	------	------	------	------	------
1818	3,618	57,673	------	1,130,235	1,035,832	346,629	------	------	------	------	------	------	------	------
1819	4,000	67,586	------	1,204,737	1,117,861	375,536	------	------	------	------	------	------	------	------
1820	4,500	72,492	------	1,111,927	1,160,926	352,286	------	------	------	------	------	------	------	------
1821	4,650	78,808	------	1,059,087	1,184,283	357,609	------	------	------	------	------	------	------	------
1822	4,709	82,763	------	1,117,490	1,167,572	355,299	------	------	------	------	------	------	------	------
1823	5,043	84,860	10,160,346	1,130,115	1,156,995	380,462	------	------	------	------	------	------	------	------
1824	5,182	84,860	10,505,386	1,197,758	1,188,019	383,804	------	------	------	------	------	------	------	------
1825	5,677	85,053	11,629,061	1,306,625	1,229,043	411,189	------	------	------	------	------	------	------	------
1826	6,150	84,063	11,967,638	1,447,703	1,366,712	447,737	------	------	------	------	------	------	------	‡

* Three months only—October 5, 1789, to January 5, 1790.

No. 19—*Statement of postal statistics from 1789 to the close of the fiscal year ending June 30, 1888—Continued.*

Years.	Post-offices.	Post routes.	Mail service performed.	Gross revenue of Department.	Gross expenditure of Department.	Paid as compensation of postmasters.	Ordinary postage stamps issued.	Stamped envelopes and wrappers issued.	Postal-cards issued.	Letters, etc., registered.	Dead letters received.	Realized from dead letters.	Domestic money-orders issued. Value.	International money-orders issued. Value.
		Miles.	*Miles.*	*Miles.*										
1827	7,003	105,336	12,872,831	$1,524,633.00	$1,465,969.00	$486,411.00								
1828	7,530	105,336	13,709,089	1,659,915.00	1,680,945.00	514,240.00								
1829	8,004	115,000	13,700,000	1,707,418.00	1,782,132.00	534,257.00								
1830	8,450	115,176	13,500,000	1,850,583.00	1,933,768.00	556,234.00								
1831	8,686	114,488	15,488,692	1,997,811.00	1,938,122.00	635,028.00								
1832	9,205	104,466	23,625,021	2,258,570.00	2,266,171.00	715,481.00								
1833	10,127	119,916	28,854,455	2,617,011.00	2,930,414.00	825,253.00								
1834	10,693	119,916	25,500,000	2,823,749.00	2,910,605.00	897,317.00								
1835	10,770	112,774	25,869,486	2,992,354.00	2,757,350.00	945,418.00								
1836	11,091	118,264	27,573,620	3,408,323.00	3,841,766.00	812,263.00								
1837	11,767	141,242	32,697,005	4,226,779.00	3,544,630.00	891,332.00						$12,080.00		
1838	12,519	118,264	34,580,202	4,238,733.00	4,430,662.00	963,348.00								
1839	12,780	133,999	34,496,878	4,484,657.00	4,718,235.00	960,900.00								
1840	13,468	155,739	34,035,025	4,543,522.00	4,718,654.00	1,013,654.00								
1841	13,778	155,026	34,086,686	4,407,726.00	4,497,632.00	1,147,258.00								
1842	13,733	149,732	34,852,981	4,546,246.00	4,374,754.00	1,426,394.00								
1843	13,814	142,295	35,409,634	4,296,225.00	4,374,311.00	1,383,318.00						2,668.00		
1844	14,104	144,687	35,409,634	4,237,288.00	4,296,511.00	1,409,875.00						20.00		
1845	14,183	143,940	35,634,369	4,289,841.00	4,320,732.00	1,042,079.00						1,192.00		
1846	14,601	152,965	37,396,414	3,487,199.00	4,084,297.00	1,060,228.00						1,824.00		
1847	15,146	153,818	38,887,699	3,955,868.00	3,979,570.00						900,000	187.00		
1848	16,159	163,208	41,012,579	4,371,077.00	4,326,850.00							1,286.00		
1849	16,749	163,703	42,544,000	4,905,176.00	4,479,049.00							99.00		
1850	18,417	178,672	46,541,423	5,552,971.00	5,213,953.00	1,220,621.00						1,743.00		
1851	19,796	196,290	53,272,252	6,727,867.00	5,276,402.00	1,781,986.00	4,663,200				1,800,000	1,675.00		
1852	20,901	214,294	58,965,728	6,925,971.00	7,108,459.00	1,526,765.00	54,126,319	$1,000,000		629,332		283.00		
1853	22,320	217,785	61,882,542	5,940,725.00	7,982,957.00	1,405,477.00	56,344,005	21,484,725		717,537		1,284.00		
1854	23,548	219,936	63,387,065	6,255,586.00	8,577,424.00	1,707,708.00	55,380,000	33,724,400		682,903		1,340.00		
1855	24,410	227,986	67,401,821	7,342,135.00	9,968,342.00	2,133,045.00	72,477,300	30,971,873		501,659	2,600,000	475.00		
1856	25,565	229,681	71,906,491	7,620,822.00	10,405,286.00	2,288,610.00	128,729,465	33,784,400		800,774	2,283,000	383.00		
1857	25,588	240,908	74,786,402	8,183,780.00	11,508,058.00	2,395,010.00	178,781,835	39,280,200		802,967	2,550,000	758.00		
1858	27,977	290,002	72,308,402	8,186,793.00	12,722,470.00	2,355,016.00	192,391,920	39,971,875		868,113	2,656,416	410.00		
1859	28,539	290,994	74,724,776	8,664,484.00	15,754,000.00	2,458,904.00	216,870,640	30,280,200		898,113	2,656,416	3,134.00		
1860	28,498	240,594	74,794,776	8,518,067.00	19,170,610.00	2,662,868.00	218,870,640	39,027,300		802,967	2,283,000	903.00		
1861	28,586	140,139	74,455,451	8,349,296.00	13,606,759.00	2,614,157.00	211,788,518	26,027,300		386,113	2,283,000			
1862	28,875	140,019	63,452,526	8,299,820.00	11,125,384.00	2,340,767.00	251,807,105	27,234,150		802,967	2,550,000	1,052.00		
1863	29,047	139,048	56,225,015	11,163,790.00	11,314,207.00	2,870,903.00	338,340,388	25,648,750	2,100,000	872,885	2,656,416			
1864	28,878	139,171	56,315,357	12,438,254.00	12,644,786.00	3,174,236.00	384,064,610	28,218,800		359,786	3,505,525	5,222.00		
1865	20,550	142,940	57,963,404	14,565,159.00	13,694,728.00	3,363,862.00	387,419,455	28,200,175		362,533	4,365,078	18,863.00	$1,360,122.00	
1866	23,828	180,021	71,887,914	14,386,986.00	15,352,079.00	3,464,677.00	347,734,825	39,004,725		375,108	5,196,905		3,977,208.00	

				12,759.00	117,329 406.00		6,566,514.00
				9,019.00	121 261.00		7,717,832.00
349,416,500	11,049,515	4,564,451		12,097.00	117,858,921.00		7,688,776 00
855,643,000	11,045,256	4,708,246		8,858.00	113,819,521.00		6,849,358 00
854,939,250	11,644,297	4,791,698		10,976.00	117,402,660.00		7,178,798.00
861,797,500	12,524,421	5,335,953		9,117.72	119,649,064.98		9,655,630.00
	12,677,169	6,317,876					11,393,870.05

5,795,557.84 12,569,768.06 1,867,173,140 433,635,750

354,608,100 1,746,945,526 381,611,300

1 Returned to writers.
2 From 1789 to 1838.
3 From June 30, 1847, to June 30, 1851. Postage stamps first issued, under act of March 3, 1847.
4 Special-request envelopes first issued in 1865.
5 From November 1, 1864, to June 30, 1866. Money-order system went into operation November 1, 1864.
6 From September 1,

No. 20.—*Contract for furnishing registered-package, tag, official, and dead-letter envelopes during the fiscal year ending June 30, 1889.*

This contract, made this 14th day of May, one thousand eight hundred and eighty-eight, and executed in quadruplicate, between the United States of America, acting by Don M. Dickinson, Postmaster-General, of the first part, and the Plimpton Manufacturing Company (a corporation duly created, organized, and doing business under and by virtue of the laws of the State of Connecticut), by L. B. Plimpton, its president, and the Morgan Envelope Company (also a corporation duly created, organized, and doing business under and by virtue of the laws of the State of Massachusetts), by Elisha Morgan, its president, as principals (said corporations being jointly engaged in the manufacture of envelopes), and Henry S. Dickinson, of Springfield, Mass., and M. S. Chapman, of Hartford Conn., as sureties, of the second part, witnesseth:

Whereas the Postmaster-General, in compliance with law, caused an advertisement, bearing date the 9th day of March, 1888, to be published in certain newspapers in the United States, inviting proposals for furnishing, in accordance with the specifications prepared under his directions, such registered-package, tag, official, and dead-letter envelopes as might be ordered for the use of the Department, postmasters, and the postal service during the fiscal year beginning on the 1st day of July, 1888, a printed copy of which advertisement and specifications is hereunto annexed and made a part hereof, as follows:

"PROPOSALS FOR REGISTERED-PACKAGE, TAG, OFFICIAL, AND DEAD-LETTER ENVELOPES.

[Advertisement.]

"POST-OFFICE DEPARTMENT,
"*Washington, D. C., March* 9, 1888.

"Sealed proposals will be received at this Department until 12 m. on Thursday, the 12th day of April, 1888, for furnishing such registered-package, tag, official, and dead-letter envelopes as may be ordered for the use of the Department, postmasters, and the postal service during the fiscal year commencing on the 1st day of July, 1888.

"Samples of the envelopes for which proposals are invited, showing the different sizes and qualities required, with blank forms of bids, and specifications giving full information, may be had on application to the Third Assistant Postmaster-General, Washington, D. C.

"DON M. DICKINSON,
"*Postmaster-General.*

"SPECIFICATIONS FOR FURNISHING REGISTERED-PACKAGE, TAG, OFFICAL, AND DEAD-LETTER ENVELOPES.

"DESIGNATION AND SIZES OF ENVELOPES.

"The designation and sizes of the envelopes referred to in the foregoing advertisement are as follows:

No. 1.—3⅜ by 5⅜ inches.	No. 6.—4⅞ by 9⅜ inches.	No. 11.—6⅜ by 10⅜ inches.
No. 2.—3⅜ by 6⅜ inches.	No. 7.—5 by 10½ inches.	No. 12.—7½ by 10 inches.
No. 3.—3⅜ by 8⅜ inches.	No. 8.—3⅜ by 5⅜ inches.	No. 13.—7¼ by 11 inches.
No. 4.—4½ by 6⅜ inches.	No. 9.—5⅜ by 7⅜ inches.	No. 14.—9 by 13½ inches.
No. 5.—4⅜ by 9½ inches.	No. 10.—6 by 9 inches.	No. 15.—12 by 15 inches.

"Sizes may be slightly larger than called for above, but no smaller.

"COMPOSITION AND QUALITY OF PAPER.

"The paper from which the Nos. 1, 2, 3, and 4 envelopes are manufactured must be composed in the proportion of 95 per cent. of jute butts and 5 per cent. of South Carolina clay (excluding all other material except the necessary coloring matter), and must weigh 34½ pounds per ream of 500 sheets measuring 22½ by 30 inches, or in that proportion. In the process of manufacture the jute butts must be washed four hours in the washing-engines and beaten eight hours in the beating-engines, and the stock passed through a Jordan engine. The paper must be rosin-sized in the engine and made on a Fourdrinier machine. It must also be well calendered and finished, and the same in color, quality, tensile strength, and in all other respects, as the paper in the sample envelopes furnished to bidders and to be made a part of the contract.

"The paper from which the Nos. 5, 6, 7, 9, 10, 11, 12, 13, 14, and 15 envelopes are manufactured must be composed in the proportion of 30 per cent. of No. 1 rope manila, 30 per cent. of No. 2 rope (consisting of about equal parts of manila, hemp, and sisal), 30 per cent of jute butts, and 10 per cent. of South Carolina clay, excluding all other material except the necessary coloring matter, and must weigh 47 pounds per ream of 500 sheets measuring 22½ by 30 inches, or in that proportion. In the process of manufacture the rope and jute butts must be washed six hours in the washing-engines and beaten nine hours in the beating-engines, and the ingredients passed through a Jordan engine. The paper must be rosin-sized in the engine, and made on a Fourdrinier machine. It must be well calendered and finished, and the same in color, quality, tensile strength, and in all other respects, as the sample envelopes furnished to bidders and to be made a part of the contract.

"The paper from which the tag envelopes for registered packages (No. 8) are to be manufactured must be composed wholly of jute butts (except the necessary coloring matter), and must weigh 90 pounds per ream of 500 sheets measuring 22½ by 30 inches, or in that proportion. In the process of manufacture the jute must be washed four hours in the washing-engines, and beaten five hours in the beating-engines and passed through a Jordan engine. The paper must be rosin-sized in the engine. It must be well calendered and finished, and the same in color, quality, tensile strength, and in all other respects, as the sample envelopes furnished to bidders and to be made part of the contract.

"All or any of the different papers used may be required to be water-marked with such designs as may be approved by the Postmaster-General. All paper furnished or used shall be subject to the supervision and approval of the Postmaster-General or his authorized agent before and after being manufactured into envelopes.

"The Postmaster-General shall have the right to cause inspection to be made, when and in such manner as he may desire it, of the process of manufacturing the paper in all its several stages, and of stationing an agent, for the purpose of inspection, at the mill or mills where the paper is made; in which latter case the contractor will be required to furnish such agent with a properly furnished room in the mill without charge, and give him every needful facility for carrying out his duty.

"Water-marked paper for any of the envelopes that may be spoiled in process of manufacture, or condemned as unfit for use, shall not be used or sold by the contractor in its manufactured state, but shall be reduced to pulp, or otherwise destroyed, without cost to the Government.

"Such spoiled or rejected paper shall not be made over for use in registered package or official envelopes.

"STYLE OF MANUFACTURE.

"The envelopes must be made in the most thorough and workmanlike manner, after the styles and of the cuts shown by the samples furnished to bidders; the joints to be well and securely fastened and with such quality of gum, free from offensive odor, as will secure perfect and permanent adhesion of the paper, and the flaps to be thoroughly gummed with the same or other equally suitable material. The envelopes shall be in all respects subject to the approval of the Postmaster-General or his duly authorized agent.

"PRINTING.

"The envelopes must bear such printing as the Postmaster-General may direct, and the registered package and tag envelopes (Nos. 7 and 8) will be required to be printed in vermilion or some other approved brilliant color, equal to that on the sample. All of the other envelopes must have printed on them the name of the Department, the words "Official Business," and the penalty provided by law for their misuse, besides such other printing as the Postmaster-General may at any time direct. When ordered in separate quantities of 500 of the Nos. 1, 2, and 4 sizes, or of 250 of the Nos. 3, 5, and 6 sizes, or in larger quantities, for the use of postmasters, they will, in addition to the foregoing printing, bear also the name of the post-office for whose use they are intended; when ordered in less quantities, they will bear, in addition to the other printing, the words, "Post-Office at," with a blank space for the name of the post-office to be written in. The printing on the samples is intended to show in a general way some of the forms that will be required.

"PACKING, ETC.

"The envelopes must be banded in parcels of twenty-five, packed in strong pasteboard or straw boxes (not inferior to No. 50 unlined western straw-board), securely bound with linen or cotton cloth on the corners and edges, and of such weight, quality, and construction as shall be approved by the Postmaster-General; and when intended to be sent direct to postmasters, each box shall contain not less than 100 of the Nos. 7 and 8 sizes and not less than 250 of the Nos. 1, 2, 3, 4, 5, and 6, or larger quantities as may be ordered for the principal post-offices; the boxes to be well and securely wrapped in strong manila paper and properly sealed, so as to bear safe transportation by mail. But when required to be sent to the Post-Office Department, each box may contain not less than 500 of any one size and style of printing, in which case the wrapping may be dispensed with, in the discretion of the Postmaster-General.

"When 4,000 or more envelopes of the Nos. 1, 2, 3, and 4, and 2,000 or more of the other numbers, are required to fill the order of a postmaster, or when larger lots of any kind are ordered to be sent to the Department, they must be packed in strong wooden cases and properly addressed ; no case shall contain more than 25,000 of the Nos. 1, 2, 3, and 4, nor more than 10,000 of the other sizes ; but when less than 4,000 are required to be sent to a postmaster, a proper label of direction must be placed on each package, all of which shall be done and furnished by the contractor without additional charge.

"The sizes designated as Nos. 1, 3, 4, 5, 6, 7, and 8 are used mainly by postmasters, and sizes Nos. 2, 9, 10, 11, 12, 13, 14, and 15, mainly in the Post-Office Department; but the right is reserved to order any or all of the different sizes for use of the Post-Office Department, of postmasters, and of postal officers generally.

"STOCK ON HAND.

"The contractor shall at all times keep on hand a stock of the several kinds of envelopes sufficient to promptly meet all orders of the Department, and to provide against any and all contingencies that may be likely to occur during the existence of the contract ; and said envelopes shall be held subject to the control of the Postmaster-General or his duly authorized agent or agents ; and the Postmaster-General shall have the right to require the contractor, at any time during the existence of the contract, to provide an extra quantity of envelopes, not exceeding a supply for three months.

"The Postmaster-General reserves the right to impose a fine upon the contractor, in such sum as he may deem proper, to be deducted in the settlement of accounts, for the failure to have on hand at any time a sufficient supply of envelopes with which to promptly meet all just requirements of the Department.

"In the event that the exigencies of the public service shall require the acceptance by the Department of any envelopes which, in the opinion of the Postmaster-General or of his duly authorized agent, are inferior in any respect to the requirements of the contract, the right is reserved to the Postmaster-General absolutely to fix the price thereof, and to pay for such inferior envelopes any compensation less than the regular price fixed by the contract that may seem to him just and reasonable under all the circumstances, which shall be a complete discharge of all liability on the part of the Government for such envelopes.

"On failure to promptly furnish any article or articles specified in the contract, the Postmaster-General reserves the right to purchase such article or articles in the open market ; and if a greater price be paid than that prescribed by the contract for like articles, the difference shall be charged to the contractor. Failure to furnish any articles within a reasonable time after the same shall have been ordered may be regarded by the Postmaster-General as a sufficient cause for the annulment of the contract.

"AGENT—OFFICE ROOM—INSPECTION.

"An agent of the Department will have supervision of the manufacture, storage, and issue of the envelopes, and he shall, at all times, have full and free access to the apartments where they (or anything entering into their construction) are manufactured and stored, for the purpose of inspecting the same.

"The contractor shall furnish the resident agent of the Department and his clerks suitable and properly furnished office rooms connected with the premises on which the envelopes are made, for the transaction of the business of the agency, without cost to the Government; also a properly furnished room for the use of the post-office in mailing the envelopes, if the same should be required by the Postmaster-General.

"The contractor, his employés and agents, shall conform to such regulations as the Department may from time to time adopt for the security of the Government in any respect.

"DELIVERY.

"The contractor must be ready to commence the delivery of the envelopes on the 1st day of July, 1888; when the contract term begins; and thereafter they must be promptly furnished and delivered, complete in all respects, in such quantities as may be required to fill the orders of the Department. The envelopes may be required to be delivered in separate packages, as above provided for, at the post-office, or at the agency at the place where the same are manufactured, or at the nearest adjacent large post-office with adequate facilities for handling and mailing the envelopes, or at a railway post-office, or at the Post-Office Department, at Washington, D. C., in the discretion of the Postmaster-General; or deliveries may be required to be made at any of the places mentioned in the foregoing, and also at the Post-Office Department, at Washington, D. C., as may be directed by the Postmaster-General.

"STOCK ON HAND AT EXPIRATION OF CONTRACT.

"The contractor may be required, in the discretion of the Postmaster-General, to continue the issue until the same shall be exhausted, of the envelopes that may remain on hand at the expiration of the contract term, at the prices and upon the conditions prevailing while the contract is in force. The right is also reserved to the Postmaster-General to authorize the issue by the present contractors of such envelopes as may remain in their hands at the close of their contract term, and the new contractor shall not be entitled to damages on account of such issues during the new contract term.

"AWARD.

"The contract will be awarded on the basis of the probable number of each of the several kinds of envelopes to be required, as determined by the issues for the year ended December 31, 1887, as follows:

No. 1	18,011,700	No. 6	1,737,500	No. 11	7,500
No. 2	2,647,500	No. 7	11,908,150	No. 12	15,000
No. 3	11,129,450	No. 8	1,447,400	No. 13	15,000
No. 4	305,250	No. 9	1,000	No. 14	7,750
No. 5	1,675,500	No. 10	5,000	No. 15	250

"Bids must be made separately for each item in the foregoing list, the bidders stating in their proposals the price per thousand envelopes, including everything to be done or furnished as set forth in these specifications; and the contract may be awarded, in the discretion of the Postmaster-General, item by item to different bidders, or as a whole to the lowest responsible bidder in the aggregate, the amount of a bid to be ascertained by extending the above issues at the prices bid respectively, and then aggregating the amounts of the several items.

"It must be understood, however, that the proposals made under this advertisement and these specifications shall impose the obligation to furnish at the prices bid all the envelopes ordered by the Department during the contract term, without reference to the numbers above stated, subject to the provision as to those on hand at the termination of the present contract. Should the use of any of the above kinds of envelopes be discontinued during the contract term, the contractor will not be entitled to any compensation for damages on account of such discontinuance.

"Each bid must include all the different items designated in the foregoing.

"The contractor will not be required to pay royalty on envelopes manufactured from samples furnished by the Department.

"PROPOSALS—AGREEMENT—BOND.

"Each proposal must be signed by the person, partnership, or corporation making it, and when made by a partnership the name of each partner thereof must be disclosed; and if the proposal be made by a corporation, the Department must be informed of its name, place of business, object of organization, and business, and the names of the officer authorized to bind it by contract; and it must be accompanied with a guaranty, signed by at least two responsible guarantors, that the bidder shall, within ten days after being called upon to do so, execute a contract, with at least two good and sufficient sureties of the character and to be certified as hereinafter required, to furnish promptly, and in quantities as ordered, the article or articles to be furnished by him, and faithfully and diligently to keep, perform, and abide by each and every of the requirements, provisions, and terms of such contract, and these specifications to be thereto annexed, the responsibility and sufficiency of the signers to such guaranty to be certified to by the postmaster or United States district attorney where the bidder resides; and by such contract the contractor and his sureties shall covenant and agree that in case the said contractor shall fail to do or perform all or any of the covenants, stipulations, and agreements of said contract on the part of the said contractor to be performed, as therein set forth, the said contractor and his sureties shall forfeit and pay to the United States of America the sum of twenty thousand dollars, for which full and absolute sum the said contractor and his sureties shall be jointly and severally liable, as fixed, settled, and liquidated damages, and not as a penalty, to be sued for in the name of the United States. Such sureties shall justify their responsibility by affidavit, showing that they severally own and possess property of the clear value in the aggregate of $40,000 over and above all debts and liabilities and all property by law exempt from execution, to be sworn to before a district or circuit judge of the United States and to be approved by him.

" If the bidder to whom the first award may be made should fail to enter into a contract, as herein provided, then the award may be annulled, and the contract let to another or other bidders under these specifications, and so on until the required contract is executed ; and such next accepted bidder shall be required to fulfill every stipulation embraced herein as if he were the original party to whom the contract was awarded.

" The contract will also provide that if at any time during its continuance the sureties, or either of them, shall die, or become irresponsible, the Postmaster-General shall have the right to require additional and sufficient sureties, which the contractor shall furnish to the acceptance of the Postmaster-General within ten days after notice ; and in default thereof, the contract may be annulled.

" The contract may be required to be executed in quadruplicate.

" RESERVATIONS.

" The Postmaster-General reserves the right to reject any and all bids if, in his judgment, the interest of the Government shall require it ; also the right to annul the contract if, in his opinion, there shall be a failure at any time to perform faithfully any of its stipulations, or in case of a willful attempt to impose upon the Department envelopes inferior to those required by the contract.

" PAYMENTS.

" Payments for envelopes actually issued and delivered to postmasters will be made monthly, after proper examination and verification of accounts, and promptly upon the fulfillment of orders for envelopes sent to the Post-Office Department. Accounts shall be kept and rendered in such manner and form as the Postmaster-General may prescribe.

" Payments may be withheld by the Postmaster-General if it shall appear to his satisfaction that the contract has not been complied with in any particular.

" CONTRACT NOT ASSIGNABLE.

" The contract can not, in any case, be lawfully transferred or assigned.

" EXTENSION.

" Should the interest of the Government require, the contract may be extended beyond the time named, not exceeding three months, by order of the Postmaster-General, and the contract prices and all conditions herein set forth shall govern in such extended contract.

" BLANK FORMS—SAMPLES—ADDRESS OF PROPOSALS.

" Blank forms for bids, with samples attached, showing sizes, style of manufacture and quality of the paper, will be furnished upon application ; and all proposals must be made upon these blank forms, securely enveloped and sealed, marked on the envelope " Proposals for Registered Package and Official Envelopes, " and addressed to the Third Assistant Postmaster-General, Washington, D. C.

" DON M. DICKINSON,
" *Postmaster-General.*

" POST-OFFICE DEPARTMENT,
" *Washington, D. C., March 9, 1888.* "

Whereas upon the opening in public on the 12th day of April, 1888, of the proposals received in answer to said advertisement of March 9th, 1888, it appeared that there were three proposals, the names of the bidders and the amounts of their respective bids, based on the actual numbers of envelopes issued during the year ended March 31, 1888, being as follows:

1. The Whitcomb Envelope Company, of Worcester, Mass................................ $96,058.38
2. The White, Corbin and Company, of Rockville, Conn 95,778.96
3. The Plimpton Manufacturing Company and Morgan Envelope Company, of Hartford, Conn 94,395.73

Whereas it appeared that the proposal of the Plimpton Manufacturing Company and Morgan Envelope Company was the lowest in the aggregate for all the envelopes called for, being $1,484.23 less than the bid of the White, Corbin and Company, the next lowest bidder;

And whereas the Postmaster-General, by an order dated the 14th day of April, 1888, awarded the contract for furnishing said envelopes to the said Plimpton Manufacturing Company and Morgan Envelope Company, which order was duly recorded in the Official Journal of the Post-Office Department, and numbered 78:

Now, therefore, in consideration of the premises and of the stipulations hereinafter set forth, the said Plimpton Manufacturing Company and Morgan Envelope Company, contractors, and their sureties, parties of the second part, do hereby jointly and severally undertake, covenant, and agree to and with the United States of America, and do bind themselves in manner following, to wit:

First. That the said contractors shall furnish and deliver promptly and in quantities as ordered, and subject to the approval of the Postmaster-General in all respects, all the registered package, tag, official, and dead-letter envelopes, of the sizes and kinds called for in the specifications, that they may be called upon to furnish during the fiscal year beginning on the 1st day of July, 1888.

Second. That the paper for the several kinds of envelopes to be furnished, as numbered in the specifications, shall be made of the materials, in the manner, and according to the conditions following, that is to say:

The paper from which the Nos. 1, 2, 3, and 4 envelopes are to be manufactured shall be composed in the proportion of 95 per cent. of jute butts and 5 per cent. of South Carolina clay (excluding all other materials except the necessary coloring matter) and shall weigh 34½ pounds per ream of 500 sheets measuring 22½ by 30 inches, or in that proportion. In the process of manufacture, the jute butts shall be washed four hours in the washing engines, and beaten eight hours in the beating engines, and the stock passed through a Jordan engine. The paper shall be rosin-sized in the engine and made on a Fourdrinier machine; it shall also be well calendered and finished, and the same in color, quality, tensile strength, and in all other respects, as the paper in the samples attached to and made a part of this contract.

The paper from which the Nos. 5, 6, 7, 9, 10, 11, 12, 13, 14, and 15 envelopes are to be manufactured shall be composed in the proportion of 30 per cent. of No. 1 rope manila, 30 per cent. of No. 2 rope (consisting of about equal parts of manila, hemp, and sisal), 30 per cent. of jute butts, and 10 per cent. of South Carolina clay, excluding all other material except the necessary coloring matter, and shall weigh 47 pounds per ream of 500 sheets measuring 22½ by 30 inches, or in that proportion; in the process of manufacture the rope and jute butts shall be washed six hours in the washing engines and beaten nine hours in the beating engines, and the ingredients passed through a Jordan engine; the paper shall be rosin-sized in the engine, and made on a Fourdrinier machine; it shall be well calendered and finished, and the same in color, quality, tensile strength, and in all other respects, as the paper in the samples attached to and made a part of this contract.

The paper from which tag envelopes for registered packages (No. 8) are to be manufactured shall be composed wholly of jute butts (except the necessary coloring matter), and shall weigh 90 pounds per ream of 500 sheets measuring 22½ by 30 inches, or in that proportion. In the process of manufacture the jute shall be washed four hours in the washing engines and beaten five hours in the beating engines and passed through a Jordan engine. The paper shall be rosin-sized in the engine. It shall be well calenderd and finished, and the same in color, quality, tensile strength, and in all other respects, as the paper in the sample attached to and made a part of this contract.

All or any of the different papers used shall be water-marked with such designs as may be approved by the Postmaster-General; and all paper furnished or used shall be subject to the supervision and approval of the Postmaster-General or his authorized agent before and after being manufactured into envelopes.

Water-marked paper for any of the envelopes that may be spoiled in the process of manufacture, or condemned as unfit for use, shall not be used or sold by the contractors in its manufactured state, but shall be reduced to pulp, or otherwise destroyed, without cost to the Government; and that such spoiled or rejected paper shall not be made over for use in registered package or official envelopes.

Third. That the envelopes shall be made in the most thorough and workmanlike manner, after the styles and of the cuts shown by the samples hereto attached and made a part hereof; the joints to be well and securely fastened, and with such quality of gum, free from offensive odor, as will secure perfect and permanent adhesion of the paper, and the flaps to be thoroughly gummed with the same or other equally suitable material; and they shall be fully equal in quality and style of manufacture to the samples hereto attached, and shall be subject in all respects to the approval of the Postmaster-General or of his duly authorized agent.

Fourth. That the envelopes shall bear such printing as the Postmaster-General shall direct, and the registered package and tag envelopes (Nos. 7 and 8) shall be printed in vermilion or some other approved brilliant color equal to that on the sample; that all of the other envelopes shall have printed on them the name of the Department, the words "Official Business," and the penalty provided by law for their misuse, beside such other printing as the Postmaster-General may at any time direct; that when ordered in separate quantities of 500 of the Nos. 1, 2, and 4 sizes, or of 250 of the Nos. 3, 5, and 6 sizes, or in larger quantities, for the use of postmasters, they shall, in addition to the foregoing printing, bear also the name of the post-office for whose use they are intended; that when ordered in less quantities they shall bear, in addition to the other printing, the words "Post-office at," with a blank space for the name of the post-office to be written in.

Fifth. That the envelopes shall be banded in parcels of 25, packed in strong pasteboard or straw boxes (not inferior to No. 50 unlined Western straw-board), securely bound with linen or cotton cloth on the corners and edges, and of such weight, quality, and construction as shall be approved by the Postmaster-General; that when intended to be sent direct to postmasters, each box shall contain not less than 100 of the Nos. 7 and 8 sizes, and not less than 250 of the Nos. 1, 2, 3, 4, 5, and 6 sizes, or larger quantities as may be ordered for the principal post-offices; that the boxes shall be well and securely wrapped in strong manilla paper and properly sealed, so as to bear safe transportation by mail; but when required to be sent to the Post-Office Department, each box may contain not less than 500 of any one size and style of printing, in which case the wrapping may be dispensed with, in the discretion of the Postmaster-General; that when 4,000 or more envelopes of the sizes Nos. 1, 2, 3, and 4, and 2,000 or more of the other numbers, are required to fill the order of a postmaster, or when larger lots of any kind are ordered to be sent to the Post-Office Department, they shall be packed in strong wooden cases and properly addressed, no case to contain more than 25,000 of the Nos. 1, 2, 3, and 4, nor more than 10,000 of the other sizes; that when less than 4,000 are required to be sent to a postmaster, a proper label of direction shall be placed on each package, all of which shall be done and furnished by the contractors without additional charge.

Sixth. That the contractors shall at all times keep on hand a stock of the several kinds of envelopes sufficient to promptly meet all orders of the Department, and to provide against any and all contingencies that may be likely to occur during the existence of this contract; that the said envelopes shall be held subject to the control of the Postmaster-General or his duly authorized agent or agents; and that the contractors shall also, at any time during the existence of this contract that they may be called upon by the Postmaster-General to do so, provide an extra quantity of envelopes, not exceeding a supply for three months.

Seventh. That the contractors shall be ready to begin the delivery of the envelopes on the 1st day of July, 1888, when the term of this contract begins; and thereafter they shall be promptly furnished and delivered, complete in all respects, in such quantities as may be required to fill the orders of the Department; that the envelopes after being inspected and prepared for mailing under the direction of the agent of the Department shall be delivered to the railway post-office or post-offices or postal cars in the city of Hartford, Connecticut, in such manner, in such quantities, at such times, and under such regulations as may be prescribed at any time by the Postmaster-General or his duly authorized agent; and that the Postmaster-General shall have the right, at any time during the existence of this contract, to require the delivery of the envelopes, or any portion of them, to be made either at the post-office or at the agency in the city of Hartford, Connecticut, or at the nearest large adjacent post-office with adequate facilities for handling and mailing them, or at the Post-Office Department at Washington, D. C., in such quantities as he may prescribe.

Eighth. That this contract shall not be transferred or assigned.

Ninth. That accounts of envelopes furnished and delivered shall be kept and rendered in such manner and form as the Postmaster-General may prescribe.

And the United States of America, party of the first part, hereby contracts and agrees:

1st. To pay the said Plimpton Manufacturing Company and Morgan Envelope Company for envelopes delivered and accepted in pursuance of this contract, and subject to all its conditions, at the following rates specified in their proposals, viz:

	Per 1,000.		Per 1,000.
For No. 1.—3½ by 5⅞	$0.82	For No. 9.—5½ by 7½	$3.30
For No. 2.—3½ by 6¼	.95	For No. 10.—6 by 9	4.00
For No. 3.—3½ by 8½	1.30	For No. 11.—6½ by 10½	4.50
For No. 4.—4½ by 6	1.80	For No. 12.—7½ by 10	4.75
For No. 5.—4½ by 9½	2.05	For No. 13.—7½ by 11	5.00
For No. 6.—4⅜ by 9⅜	2.35	For No. 14.—9 by 13½	5.50
For No. 7.—5 by 10½	4.25	For No. 15.—12 by 15	7.75
For No. 8.—3½ by 5½	2.25		

2d. That the said prices shall be full compensation for everything required to be done or furnished as herein set forth—payment for envelopes actually issued and delivered to postmasters to be made monthly after proper examination and adjustment of accounts, and promptly upon the fulfillment of orders for envelopes sent to the Post-Office Department.

3d. That the contractors shall not be required to pay royalty on envelopes manufactured and furnished under this contract.

It is further stipulated and agreed by and between the contracting parties:

1st. That a resident agent of the Department shall have supervision of the manufacture, storage, and issue of the envelopes, and that he shall at all times have full and free access to the apartments where they, or anything entering into their construction, are manufactured and stored for the purpose of inspecting the same; that such agent and his clerks shall be provided by the contractors with suitable and properly furnished office rooms, connected with the premises on which the envelopes are made, for the transaction of the business of the agency, without cost to the Government; also with a properly furnished room for the use of the post-office in mailing the envelopes, if the same shall be required by the Postmaster-General; and that the contractors, their employés and agents, shall conform to such regulations as the Department may from time to time adopt for the security of the Government in any respect.

2d. That the Postmaster-General shall have the right to cause inspection to be made, when and in such manner as he may desire it, of the process of manufacturing the paper in all its several stages, and of stationing an agent, for the purpose of inspection, at the mill or mills where the paper is made; in which latter case the contractors shall furnish such agent with a properly furnished room in the mill without charge, and give him every needful facility for carrying out his duty.

3d. That the Postmaster-General shall have the right to impose a fine upon the contractors, in such sum as he may deem proper, to be deducted in the settlement of accounts, for the failure to have on hand at any time a sufficient supply of envelopes with which to promptly meet all just requirements of the Department.

4th. That in the event that the exigencies of the public service shall require the acceptance by the Department of any envelopes which, in the opinion of the Postmaster-General or his duly authorized agent, are inferior in any respect to the requirements of the contract, the right is reserved to the Postmaster-General absolutely to fix the price thereof, and to pay for such inferior envelopes any compensation less than the regular price fixed by the contract that may seem to him just and reasonable under all the circumstances, which shall be a complete discharge of all liability on the part of the Government for such envelopes.

5th. That on failure of the contractors to promptly furnish any article or articles specified in this contract, the Postmaster-General shall have the right to purchase such article or articles in the open market; and if a greater price be paid than that prescribed by the contract for like articles, the difference shall be charged to the contractors; and if there shall be a failure to furnish any articles within a reasonable time after the same shall have been ordered, it may be regarded as a sufficient cause for the annulment of this contract.

6th. That if at any time during the continuance of this contract the sureties or either of them shall die, or become irresponsible, the Postmaster-General shall have the right to require additional and sufficient sureties, which the contractors shall furnish to the acceptance of the Postmaster-General within ten days after notice; and in default thereof this contract may be annulled.

7th. That in case of failure by the contractors to do or perform all or any of the covenants, stipulations, and agreements of this contract on the part of the said contractors to be performed, as herein set forth, the said parties of the second part shall forfeit and pay to the United States of America the sum of twenty thousand dollars, for which full and absolute sum they shall be jointly and severally liable, as fixed, settled, and liquidated damages, and not as a penalty, to be sued for in the name of the United States.

8th. That in addition to the forfeiture covenanted and agreed to in the foregoing paragraph, the Postmaster-General shall have the right to annul this contract if, in his opinion, there shall be a failure at any time to perform faithfully any of its stipulations, or in case of a willful attempt to impose upon the Department envelopes inferior to those required by this contract. He shall also have the right to withhold payments for envelopes furnished if it shall appear to his satisfaction that this contract has not been complied with in any particular.

9th. That should the interest of the Government require, this contract may be extended beyond the time named, not exceeding three months, by order of the Postmaster-General, and the contract prices and all conditions herein set forth shall govern in such extended contract.

10th. That the contractors may be required, in the discretion of the Postmaster-General, to continue the issue until the same shall be exhausted, of the envelopes that may remain on hand at the expiration of the term of this contract, at the prices and upon the conditions prevailing while in force. That the Postmaster-General shall have the right to authorize the issue by the present contractor, the Holyoke Envelope Company, of such envelopes as may remain in its hands at the close of its contract term, and the contractors herein shall not be entitled to damages on account of such issues made during their contract term.

11th. That no member of or delegate to Congress shall be admitted to any share or part of this contract, as provided by sections 3739, 3740, and 3741 of the Revised Statutes of the United States; and each and all of the provisions in said sections shall be deemed a part of this contract.

And for the faithful and diligent keeping, performing, and abiding by each and every of the requirements, provisions, and terms of this contract, and of the specifications hereto annexed and made part hereof, the said parties of the second part do hereby bind themselves, and each of them, their and his heirs, executors, and administrators.

In witness whereof, the said Postmaster-General has caused the seal of the Post-Office Department of the United States of America to be hereunto affixed, and has attested the same by his signature, and the said parties of the second part, the said corporations, have hereunto set their corporate seals by the hands of their respective presidents and caused these presents to be subscribed by said presidents, and said sureties of the parties of the second part have hereunto set their hands and seals on and as the day hereinbefore written.

[SEAL.]   DON M. DICKINSON,
                 Postmaster-General.

Attest:
  HENRY R. HARRIS,
   Third Assistant Postmaster-General.

         The PLIMPTON MANUFACTURING COMPANY,
[SEAL.]   By L. B. PLIMPTON, *President.*
Attest:
  F. PLIMPTON.

         The MORGAN ENVELOPE COMPANY,
[SEAL.]   By E. MORGAN, *President.*
Attest:
  R. W. DAY.

       (Surety.) HENRY L. DICKINSON. [SEAL.]

Attest:
  R. W. DAY.

       (Surety.) M. S. CHAPMAN. [SEAL.]

Attest:
  N. SHIPMAN.

STATE OF CONNECTICUT,
  County of Hartford, ss:

Henry S. Dickinson, one of the sureties in the foregoing contract of the Plimpton Manufacturing Company and Morgan Envelope Company, being by me duly sworn, upon oath says that he is a resident and freeholder of the State of Massachusetts, and that he is worth the sum of forty thousand dollars, over and above all his debts and liabilities, and exclusive of property exempt from execution.

                HENRY L. DICKINSON.

Subscribed and sworn to before me this third day of May, one thousand eight hundred and eighty-eight, and by me approved.

                N. SHIPMAN,
                 District Judge.

I certify that to the best of my knowledge and belief Henry S. Dickinson, of Springfield, Mass., one of the sureties in the foregoing contract between the United States of America and the Plimpton Manufacturing Company and Morgan Envelope Company, of Hartford, Conn., for furnishing registered package, tag, official, and dead-letter envelopes during the fiscal year beginning July 1st, 1888, is worth the sum of forty thousand dollars, over and above all liabilities and encumbrances whatever.

                JNO. L. RICE,
             Postmaster at Springfield, Mass.

STATE OF CONNECTICUT.
  County of Hartford, ss:

Maro S. Chapman, one of the sureties of the foregoing contract of the Plimpton Manufacturing Company and Morgan Envelope Company, being by me duly sworn, upon oath says that he is a resident and freeholder of the State of Connecticut, and

that he is worth the sum of forty thous:
liabilities, and exclusive of property exe.

Subscribed and sworn to before me thi:
dred and eighty-eight, and by me approv

I certify that to the best of my knowle
ford, Conn., one of the sureties in the f
of America and the Plimpton Manufact
pany of Hartford, Conn., for furnishing
letter envelopes during the fiscal year b
forty thousand dollars, over and above a:

The foregoing contract approved as to

REPORT

OF THE

SUPERINTENDENT OF THE DEAD-LETTER OFFICE

TO THE

POSTMASTER-GENERAL

FOR

THE YEAR ENDED JUNE 30, 1888.

REPORT

OF THE

SUPERINTENDENT OF THE DEAD-LETTER OFFICE.

POST-OFFICE DEPARTMENT,
DEAD-LETTER OFFICE,
Washington, D. C., October 1, 1888.

SIR: I have the honor to submit herewith my report of the operations of the Dead-Letter Office for the fiscal year ended June 30, 1888, the details of which are fully set forth in the several tables embodied in this report.

There were received during the year 6,217,876 pieces of original dead mail matter, an increase of 882,513 pieces, or about 16.5 per cent., over the number received during the fiscal year ended June 30, 1887. In addition to this number, there were also received 237,869 letters without valuable inclosures which had been returned to the writers, but failing of delivery, were again sent to the Dead-Letter Office. These, together with 222 "held-for-postage" letters and 8,903 letters of foreign origin on hand and undisposed of on July 1, 1887, make the total number of pieces treated during the year 6,464,870, which were classified, treated, and disposed of as follows:

1. Domestic mailable letters:
   - (a) Ordinary unclaimed letters 4,670,547
   - (b) Letters returned from hotels 130,068
   - (c) Letters bearing fictitious addresses 18,947
   - (d) Letters returned from foreign countries 173,728
   - (e) Ordinary letters without inclosures sent to writers and returned on failure to deliver 237,869
   - 5,231,159

2. Domestic unmailable letters:
   - (a) Letters containing unmailable articles 1,646
   - (b) Letters held for postage 120,992
   - (c) Letters misdirected or only partially addressed 435,416
   - (d) Letters without address 18,895
   - 576,949

3. Domestic parcels of third and fourth class matter 74,648
4. Letters mailed in foreign countries 499,881
5. Printed matter, samples, etc., mailed in foreign countries and returnable. 60,121
6. Registered articles:
   - (a) Of domestic origin 6,311
   - (b) Of foreign origin 15,801
   - 22,112

   Total as before 6,464,870

769

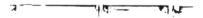

The mail matter treated during the year was disposed of as follows:

Domestic mailable letters:
Card and request letters delivered unopened 77,007
Letters opened (disposed of as detailed below)........................ 4,918,414
Ordinary letters without valuable inclosures sent to writers and re-
turned on account of failure to deliver, and subsequently destroyed. 237,869

Domestic unmailable letters:
Held-for-postage letters forwarded unopened to addresses on receipt of
postage... 3,733
Held-for-postage letters forwarded to officials unopened.............. 251
Held-for-postage letters opened (disposed of as below) 115,785
Held-for-postage letters on hand at close of year..................... 230
Misdirected letters forwarded unopened after correction of addresses.. 100,389
Misdirected letters opened (disposed of as below)..................... 333,889
Letters without address opened (disposed of as below)................. 18,895
Letters containing unmailable articles opened (disposed of as below).. 1,646

Domestic third and fourth class matter :
Parcels opened and disposed of as below............................... 74,648

Foreign matter:
Letters returned to country of origin or delivered to ad-
dresses... 490,048
Letters on hand at close of year 9,833
Parcels of printed matter, samples, etc., returned unopened
or delivered to addresses 60,121
                                                                        560,002

Registered articles:
Domestic—
Of domestic origin, delivered unopened 2,546
Of domestic origin, opened............................. 3,765
                                                                        6,311

Foreign—
Returned to country of origin, or delivered to addressees. 15,420
On hand at close of year 381
                                                                        15,801

Total 6,464,870

The following was the disposition of mail matter opened in the Dead-Letter Office :

Delivered:
Letters containing money 13,830
Letters containing drafts, money-orders, notes, etc 23,589
Letters containing postal-notes 3,259
Letters containing miscellaneous papers, etc................ 36,397
Letters containing postages-stamps 111,623
Letters containing nothing of value......................... 1,527,291
Photographs... 35,183
Parcels of merchandise, books, etc.......................... 36,366
                                                                        1,787,538

Returned to owners and awaiting evidence of delivery :
Letters containing money 1,265
Letters containing drafts, notes, etc 930
Letters containing postal-notes 202
Registered parcels of merchandise, books, etc 46
                                                                        2,443

Under treatment, looking to delivery :
Letters containing money 2,077
Letters containing postal-notes............................. 13
Letters without inclosures.................................. 225,500
                                                                        227,590

Filed upon failure to deliver, subject to reclamation :
Letters containing money 5,540
Letters containing drafts, notes, etc 1,433
Letters containing postal-notes............................. 223
Letters containing miscellaneous papers etc................. 1,222
Letters containing postage-stamps........................... 3,130
Photographs... 5,148
Parcels of merchandise, books, etc.......................... 43,122
Unmailable letters (Section 379, Postal Laws and Regulations) 4,568
                                                                        64,386

Destroyed:
  Letters without inclosures which could not be returned to
    writers 3,413,882
  Parcels containing pamphlets, fruit, seeds, medicine, etc...   14,314
  Letters containing postage-stamps...........................   4,493
                                                        3,432,689

    Grand total... 5,514,646

FOREIGN DEAD MAIL MATTER.

Returned to country of origin:
  Registered articles...   15,015
  Ordinary letters.. 477,508
  Parcels of printed matter, samples, etc.......................   52,872
                                                        545,395

Delivered to addressees on application:
  Registered articles...   210
  Ordinary letters   201
  Parcels or printed matter, samples, etc   556
                                                            967

Misdirected matter forwarded to corrected addresses:
  Registered articles...   195
  Ordinary letters..   12,339
  Parcels of printed matter, samples, etc.......................   6,693
                                                         19,227

On hand under treatment at close of year:
  Registered articles...   381
  Ordinary letters   9,833
                                                         10,214

    Grand total... 575,803

MATTER RETURNED FROM FOREIGN COUNTRIES.

The number of pieces of mail matter originating in the United States and returned to Dead-Letter Office as undeliverable were classified as follows:

Registered articles... 1,795
Ordinary letters (including postal-cards) 180,011
Parcels of printed matter, samples, etc.............................. 45,322
                                                    ——————
    Total 227,128

DEAD REGISTERED MATTER.

Of the 22,112 unclaimed registered letters and parcels received, there were—

Delivered to addressees or restored to senders........................ 20,846
Returned to postmasters for delivery and awaiting receipt.............   151
Filed upon failure to discover ownership and awaiting reclamation.......... 1,115
    Total 22,112

VALUE OF INCLOSURES IN MAIL MATTER RESTORED TO OWNERS.

The following shows the number of letters restored to owners or in course of restoration, with the character and value of contents:

Description.	Number.	Value.
Letters containing money restored to owners	13,830	$24,117.15
Letters containing money outstanding in the hands of postmasters for restoration to owners..	1,265	4,019.76
Number of letters containing drafts, checks, notes, money-orders, etc., restored to owners...	23,589	1,529,970.69
Number of letters containing drafts, notes, checks, money-orders, etc., outstanding in the hands of postmasters for restoration to owners	930	88,111.92
Number of letters containing postal-notes restored to owners	3,259	5,034.78
Number of letters containing postal-notes outstanding in the hands of postmasters for restoration to owners	202	341.45

REVENUE DERIVED FROM DEAD MAIL MATTER.

The amount of revenue derived from dead matter during the year and delivered to Third Assistant Postmaster-General for deposit in the Treasury is shown by the following statement:

Amount separated from dead letters that could not be restored to owners..	$8,511.44
Amount realized from auction sale in December, 1887, of parcels of merchandise which could not be restored to owners.........................	2,023.35
Total ....:.............................	10,534.79

POSTAGE-STAMPS.

The following amounts of postage-stamps were received in the Dead Letter Office from the several sources named and were destroyed under proper supervision:

Separated from dead letters for which no owner could be found...........	$551.37
Found loose in the mails and sent to Dead-Letter Office by postmasters...	498.66
Received for payment of postage on held-for-postage matter forwarded to destination, and parcels of third and fourth class matter returned to senders (sent out from Dead-Letter Office under an official envelope)........	650.47
Received from postal administration of Canada, United States postage-stamps accepted by that administration in payment of postage on matter held for postage in Canada in accordance with the agreement between the two countries..	170.13
Total value of stamps destroyed................:..................	1,870.63

In addition to the above, postage-stamps to the value of $1,280.05 have been received and affixed to parcels of matter addressed to foreign countries not transmissible in the mails unless prepaid at letter rates of postage.

In the exchange of postage-stamps mutually accepted by the United States and Canada in the payment of postage on short-paid matter addressed to either country, there have been received from the Canadian administration United States postage-stamps to the amount of $170.13; there were returned to Canada by this office Canadian postage-stamps amounting to $95.95, leaving a balance due the Canadian administration of $74.18, which has been duly reported for payment.

DEAD MATTER GIVEN TO CHARITABLE INSTITUTIONS.

During the year 12,667 magazines, illustrated papers, picture cards, etc., which could not be restored to the owners were distributed among the inmates of the various hospitals, asylums, and other charitable institutions in the District of Columbia as heretofore by order of the Postmaster-General.

The following shows the number and the character of the matter distributed:

Magazines	911
Pamphlets, etc...	2,991
Illustrated papers	3,439
Picture cards, valentines, etc.....................................	5,326
Total..	12,667

CORRESPONDENCE.

During the year there were received 18,589 inquiries for alleged missing mail matter, which were duly examined and the results reported to the applicants. In a large percentage of these inquiries it was found upon examination that the alleged missing mail matter had been properly delivered by the postal service. Where this was not the fact, and no trace of the missing matter was found upon the records of this office, the cases were duly reported to the chief post-office inspector for further investigation. There were also written 4,239 special communications, in answer to inquiries from postmasters and others, relating to postal matters connected with this office.

Comparative statement of mail matter received and treated in dead-letter office for the fiscal years ended June 30, 1887 and 1888.

Received.	1887.	1888.	Increase.	Decrease.
			Per cent.	*Per cent.*
Domestic mailable letters:				
Ordinary unclaimed letters....................	3,981,420	4,670,547	17.3	....
Letters returned from hotels..................	118,445	130,068	9.8	....
Letters with fictitious addresses.............	21,504	18,947	....	11.9
Letters returned from foreign countries....	161,392	173,728	7.6	....
Ordinary dead letters returned to writers but undelivered................................	239,816	237,869	....	0.8
Total	4,522,577	5,231,159	15.6	....
Domestic unmailable letters:				
Containing unmailable articles...............	2,155	1,646	....	23.6
Held for postage.............................	128,732	120,992	....	6.0
Misdirected	377,997	435,416	15.2	....
Without address..............................	19,110	18,895	....	1.1
Total	527,994	576,949	9.3	....
Domestic parcels of third and fourth class matter.	67,823	74,648	10.1	....
Foreign letters, etc.:				
Letters mailed in foreign countries	412,196	499,881	21.2	....
Printed matter, samples, etc., foreign, mailed.	30,672	60,121	96.0	....
Total	442,868	560,002	26.4	....
Registered articles:				
Of domestic origin...........................	4,888	6,311	43.8	....
Of foreign origin	13,315	15,801	18.7	....
Total	17,703	21,112	24.9	....
Grand total.................................	5,578,965	6,464,870	15.9	....

Treatment and disposition of mail matter received and on hand.

	1887.	1888.	Increase.	Decrease.
			Per cent.	*Per cent.*
Domestic mailable matter:				
Card and request letters delivered unopened.	70,712	77,007	8.9	....
Ordinary letters opened	4,212,049	4,918,414	16.8	....
Returned dead letters without inclosures destroyed	239,816	237,869	....	0.9
Domestic unmailable matter:				
Held-for-postage letters forwarded...........	4,514	3,733	....	17.3
Forwarded to Executive Departments........	....	251	....	....
Held-for-postage letters opened..............	123,996	115,785	....	6.6
On hand at close of year.....................	222	230	3.6	....
Misdirected letters forwarded to corrected addresses.................................	83,702	100,389	19.9	....
Misdirected letters opened...................	294,295	333,889	13.5	....
Letters without address opened..............	19,110	18,895	....	1.1
Letters containing unmailable articles opened...................................	2,155	1,646	....	23.6
Domestic third and fourth class matter:				
Parcels opened and disposed of	67,823	74,648	10.1	....
Foreign mailable matter:				
Letters delivered to addresses or returned to country of origin	403,605	490,048	21.1	....
On hand at close of year.....................	8,591	9,833	14.5	....
Printed matter, samples, etc., returned to country of origin	30,672	60,121	96.0	....

Treatment and disposition of mail matter received and on hand—Continued.

	1887.	1888.	Increase.	Decrease
			Per cent.	*Per cent.*
Registered articles:				
Domestic, delivered unopened	2, 250	2, 546	13. 2	....
Domestic, opened	2, 138	3, 765	76. 1	....
Of foreign origin, delivered or returned to country of origin.............................	13, 003	15, 420	18. 3	....
On hand at close of year....................	312	381	22. 1	....
Total	5, 578, 965	6, 464, 870	15. 9	....
Disposition of matter opened.				
Delivered:				
Letters containing money...................	12, 725	13, 830	8. 7	....
Letters containing drafts, notes, money-orders, etc	21, 868	23, 589	7. 9	....
Letters containing postal-notes	....	3, 259	....	....
Letters containing receipts, paid notes, etc...	31, 230	36, 397	16. 5	....
Letters containing postage-stamps	93, 129	111, 623	19. 6	....
Letters containing nothing of value..........	1, 937, 926	1, 527, 291	....	21.
Photographs..............................	29, 497	35, 183	18. 9	....
Parcels of merchandise, books, etc..........	32, 039	36, 366	13. 5	....
Total	2, 163, 414	1, 787, 538	....	17 (
Outstanding in hands of postmasters:				
Letters containing money	906	1, 265	39. 6	......
Letters containing drafts, notes, etc.........	2, 314	930	....	5(
Letters containing postal notes.............	....	202	....	......
Registered parcels, merchandise, books, etc..	37	46	24. 3	......
Total	3, 257	2, 443	....	21)
Under treatment looking to delivery:				
Letters containing money...................	1, 369	2, 077	51. 7	....
Letters containing drafts, notes, money-orders, etc	....	13	....	....
Letters containing postal-notes	....	13	....	....
Letters without inclosures..................	42, 978	225, 500	424. 6	....
Total	44, 347	227, 590	412. 9	......
Filed upon failure to deliver, subject to reclamation:				
Letters containing money...................	4, 498	5, 540	23. 2	....
Letters containing drafts, notes, money-orders, etc	1, 371	1, 433	4. 5	....
Letters containing postal-notes	....	223	....	6.
Letters containing receipts, paid notes, etc...	3, 329	1, 222	....	4 (
Letters containing postage-stamps...........	5, 649	3, 130	....	1(
Photographs	5, 753	5, 148	....	......
Parcels of merchandise, books, etc	39, 601	43, 122	8. 9	......
Unmailable letters (section 379 Postal Laws and Regulations)...........................	....	4, 568	....	......
Total	60, 201	64, 386	6. 9	....
Destroyed:				
Letters without inclosures which could not be returned to writers	2, 464, 760	3, 413, 882	38. 5	....
Parcels containing pamphlets, fruit, seeds, etc	9, 887	14, 314	44. 8	....
Letters containing postage-stamps...........	....	4, 493	....	....
Total	2, 474, 647	3, 432, 689	38. 7	... .
Grand total.............................	4, 745, 866	5, 514, 646	16. 2	... .
Foreign dead mail matter.				
Returned to country of origin:				
Registered articles........................	12, 596	15, 015	19. 2	.. ..
Ordinary letters..........................	391, 990	477, 508	21. 8	....
Printed matter, samples, etc...............	24, 944	52, 872	111. 9	....
Total	429, 530	545, 395	26. 9	....
Delivered to addresses upon application:				
Registered articles........................	183	210	14. 8	 1
Ordinary letters..........................	203	201	....	111. 0 ....
Printed matter, samples, etc................	263	556	111. 0	....
Total	649	967	49. 0	....

Treatment and disposition of mail matter received and on hand—Continued.

	1887.	1888.	Increase.	Decrease.
Foreign dead mail matter—Continued.				
Misdirected matter forwarded to corrected addresses:			*Per cent.*	*Per cent.*
Registered articles..........................	224	195	....	12. 9
Ordinary letters............................	11, 412	12, 339	8. 0	....
Printed matter, samples, etc.................	5, 465	6, 693	22. 5	....
Total	17, 101	19, 227	12. 4	....
On hand under treatment at close of year :				
Registered articles..........................	312	381	22. 1	....
Ordinary letters............................	8, 591	9, 833	14. 5	....
Total	8, 903	10, 214	14. 7	....
Grand total.............................	456, 183	575, 803	26. 2	....
Matter returned from foreign countries:				
Registered articles..........................	1, 832	1, 795	....	2. 0
Ordinary letters............................	161, 392	173, 728	7. 6	....
Postal-cards	12, 642	6, 283	....	49. 7
Printed matter, samples, etc.................	37, 451	45, 322	21. 0	....
Total	213, 317	227, 128	6. 5	....
Dead registered matter:				
Delivered to addressees or restored to senders.	16, 661	20, 846	25. 1	....
Sent to postmasters and awaiting receipts ...	88	151	71. 6	....
Filed, awaiting reclamation..................	954	1, 115	16. 9	....
Total	17, 703	22, 112	24. 9	....
Letters containing money and negotiable paper.				
Value of inclosures in matter opened :				
Number of letters containing money........	17, 745	20, 437	15. 2	....
Amount of money contained therein........	$29, 687. 10	$35, 245. 38	18. 7	....
Number of letters containing notes, drafts, money-orders, etc	23, 226	23, 638	1. 7	....
Value contained therein	$7, 644, 486. 56	$1, 343, 519. 52	....	82. 3
Number of letters containing postal-notes....	....	3, 697	....	....
Value contained therein	....	$5, 798. 31	....	....
Value of inclosures in matter restored to owners:				
Number of letters containing money restored to owners	12, 725	13, 830	8. 7	....
Amount of money inclosed therein	$22, 639. 12	$24, 117. 15	6. 5	....
Number of letters in hands of postmasters for restoration to owners..........	906	1, 265	38. 2	....
Amount of money contained therein	$2, 744. 27	$4, 019. 76	46. 5	....
Letters on hand and filed on failure to discover owners	5, 867	5, 540	....	5. 4
Amount of money contained therein........	$8, 915. 32	$8, 817. 34	....	1. 1
Number of letters containing notes, drafts, money-orders, etc., restored to owners. ...	21, 868	23, 589	7. 8	....
Value contained therein	$7, 581, 761. 10	$1, 529, 970. 69	....	78. 5
Number in hands of postmasters for restoration to owners	2, 814	930	....	59. 8
Value contained therein	$304, 079. 57	$88, 111. 92	....	71. 0
Number filed on failure to discover owners.	1, 371	1, 433	4. 5	....
Value contained therein	$92, 742. 47	$39, 516. 48	....	68. 4
Number of letters containing postal-notes restored to owners	....	3, 259	....	....
Value contained therein	....	$5. 034. 78	....	....
Number in hands of postmasters for restoration to owners	....	202	....	....
Value contained therein	....	$341. 45	....	....
Number filed on failure to discover owners	....	223	....	....
Value contained therein	....	$393. 77	....	....

Statement showing number of pieces of dead mail matter treated in Dead-Letter Office during the fiscal year ended June 30, 1888.

Class.		Number.
Domestic mailable letters:		
Received during the year	4,993,290	
Returned on failure to deliver to writers (without inclosures)	237,869	
		5,231,159
Domestic unmailable letters		
Held for postage—		
From last fiscal year	222	
Received during the year	120,770	
		120,992
Containing unmailable articles		1,646
Misdirected		435,416
Blanks (without address)		18,895
		576,949
Domestic third and fourth class matter (parcels)		74,648
Foreign matter:		
From last fiscal year	8,591	
Received during the year	491,290	
Printed matter, samples, etc.	60,121	
		560,002
Registered matter:		
Domestic mailed	6,311	
Foreign mailed, on hand, and received	15,801	
		22,112
Grand total		6,464,870

Class.	Delivered unopened.	Opened.	On hand.
Domestic mailable letters	74,876	4,918,414	
Domestic unmailable letters:			
Held for postage	4,977	115,785	230
Containing unmailable articles		1,646	
Misdirected	101,527	333,889	
Without address		18,895	
Registered letters	2,546	3,765	
Domestic third and fourth class matter (parcels)		74,648	
Foreign matter:			
Ordinary letters	490,048		9,833
Registered letters	15,420		381
Printed matter, samples, etc.	60,121		
Total	749,515	5,467,042	10,444
Total			6,227,001
Letters without inclosures returned on failure to deliver to writers and destroyed			237,869
Grand total			6,464,870

Statement showing the disposition of mail matter opened in the Dead-Letter Office during the fiscal year ended June 30, 1888.

	Containing money.		Containing drafts, checks, notes, etc.		Containing postal notes.		Containing merchandise, books, etc.	Containing receipts, paid notes, etc.	Containing photographs.	Containing postage-stamps.	Containing nothing of value.	Total.	
	Number.	Value.	Number.	Value.	Number.	Value.	Number.	Number.	Number.	Number.	Number.	Number.	Value.
RECEIVED.													
Outstanding in the hands of postmasters at close of last fiscal year	906	$2,744.27	2,814	$304,078.57			37					3,257	$306,823.84
On hand undisposed of at Dead-Letter Office at the close of last fiscal year	1,389	2,242.78									42,978	44,347	3,242.78
Received during the year	20,437	35,245.38	22,638	1,343,519.83	3,697	$5,798.81	93,811	37,619	40,381	119,246	5,158,263	5,467,042	1,384,563.21
Total	22,712	40,232.43	25,952	1,647,599.09	3,697	5,798.81	93,848	37,619	40,381	119,246	5,171,241	5,514,646	1,693,629.83
DISPOSITION.													
Delivered to owners	13,830	24,117.15	22,589	1,529,970.69	3,259	5,034.78	36,366	36,397	35,188	111,623	1,627,291	1,787,538	1,569,132.62
Filed in Dead-Letter Office on failure to deliver to owners	5,540	8,817.34	1,433	29,516.48	228	893.77	43,122	1,222	5,148	3,130	4,568	64,396	38,727.59
Destroyed on failure to deliver to owners							14,814			4,493	3,413,883	3,432,689	
On hand in Dead-Letter Office undisposed of	3,077	8,278.18			13	28.31					225,500	227,590	8,306.49
Outstanding in the hands of postmasters for restoration to owners	1,265	4,019.76	920	88,111.92	202	841.45	46					2,443	92,478.13
Total	22,712	40,232.43	25,952	1,647,599.09	3,697	5,798.81	93,848	37,619	40,381	119,246	5,171,241	5,514,646	1,693,629.83

Statement of unmailable, hotel, and fictitious matter received at the Dead-Letter Office during the fiscal year ended June 30, 1888.

Received.		Number.	Disposition.		Number.	Total.
Held for postage:			Held for postage:			
Foreign address	16,004		Foreign address—circulars sent to collect postage		4,964	
Domestic address	104,766	120,770	Official forwarded		251	
			Returned to card address		993	
Misdirected:			Opened		114,562	120,770
Ordinary		479,509				
Blanks		18,895	Misdirected:			
Unmailable, coin, etc.		1,646	Turned over to foreign division		61,971	
Hotel		139,229	Address corrected and forwarded		100,399	
Fictitious		19,322	Returned to card address		1,138	
Returned misdirected		17,818	Opened		316,671	479,509
						18,895
			Without address, opened		....	
			Unmailable (containing coin, etc.), opened		....	1,646
			Hotel:			
			Turned over to foreign division		9,171	
			Opened		129,501	
			Returned to card address		597	139,229
			Fictitious:			
			Turned over to foreign division		375	
			Opened		18,947	19,322
			Returned, misdirected, opened		....	17,818
Total		797,259	Total		....	797,259
Parcels:			Parcels:			
Held for postage		4,900	Examined and turned over to other divisions			43,557
Misdirected		9,665				
Without address		16,264				
Containing unmailable articles		11,689				
Excess of weight and measure		1,039				
Total		43,557	Total		....	43,557
Grand total		840,816	Grand total		....	840,816

Statement showing dead mail matter of foreign origin received and disposed of during the fiscal year ended June 30, 1888.

Received.			Disposition.				
Class.		Number.	Class.	Returned to country of origin.	Delivered to addresses.	Misdirected letters forwarded to corrected address.	On hand.
Registered letters—			Registered letters.	15,015	210	195	381
On hand July 1, 1887	312						
Received during the year	15,489	15,801					
Ordinary letters—			Ordinary letters	477,508	201	13,229	9,633
On hand July 1, 1887	8,591						
Received during the year	491,290	499,881					
Parcels and printed matter		60,121	Parcels and printed matter.	52,872	556	6,693	
Total		575,803	Total	545,395	967	19,227	10,214

Statement showing the number of letters originating in the United States and returned by foreign countries as undeliverable during the fiscal year ended June 30, 1888.

Class.	Number
Registered letters	1,795
Ordinary letters	180,011
Parcels and printed matter	45,322
Total	227,128

Table showing class and number of pieces of undelivered matter returned to and received from the following foreign countries.

Countries.	Returned to—				Received from—			
	Registered.	Ordinary.	Parcels, etc.	Total.	Registered.	Ordinary.	Parcels, etc.	Total.
Antigua	1	50		51		137	9	146
Argentine Republic	42	439	43	524		1,672	67	1,739
Austria-Hungary	3,420	22,567	1,426	27,413				
Bahamas	8	269	1	278		343		343
Bangkok, Siam	1	8		9				
Barbadoes	3	164	2	169		205	33	238
Belgium	86	2,048	6,799	8,933				
Bermuda	5	242	7	254		244	14	258
Bolivia		10		10	7	36	3	46
Brazil	35	491	15	541				
British Guiana	4	90	1	95		84	104	188
British Honduras	7	48	1	56	2	31		33
British India	17	632	74	723				
Bulgaria	4	20		24				
Canada	1,504	110,976	19,218	131,698	522	61,437	9,708	71,667
Ceylon		25		25				
Chili	29	245	23	297		345	1,069	1,414
Colombia, Republic of	13	513	10	536		877		877
Costa Rica	1	102		103				
Cuba	52	1,095	44	1,191		1,069	763	1,832
Danish West Indies		142		142		187	30	217
Denmark	61	5,583	291	5,935				
Dominica		10		10		2	2	4
Ecuador	8	65	3	73	1	9		10
Egypt	15	190	3	208				
France	395	8,943	9,938	19,276		5,021	3,414	8,435
French West Indies	1	40	12	53				
Germany	3,106	73,768	3,263	80,137				
Gibraltar	3	138	1	17		27	7	34
Great Britain	1,418	108,701	3,046	113,165	633	49,908	5,808	56,349
Greece	34	387	10	431		32		32
Grenada		9		9				
Guatemala	7	110	4	121	1	131		132
Hawaii	14	614	11	639		426		426
Hayti	3	82	3	88				
Honduras, Republic of		88		88		6		6
Hong Kong	9	293	3	305		258	1	259
Italy	1,434	45,762	4,294	51,490	137	2,728	2,596	5,461
Jamaica	5	270	10	285	2	261		263
Japan	45	614	95	754		229	87	316
Java, Netherlands Indies	5	48	1	54		40	23	63
Liberia	1	29		30				
Luxemburg	35	508	12	555				
Malta	7	77		84				
Mauritius	3	28		31				
Mexico	97	5,228	75	5,400	341	4,860	43	5,244
Monaco	2	12		14				
Montserrat		4		4				
Netherlands	30	2,225	1,046	3,301				
Netherlands, West Indies	3	75	4	82				
Nevis		3		3				
Newfoundland	10	611	7	628		1,855		1,855
New South Wales	25	862	43	930	26	1,037	14	1,089
New Zealand	11	547	28	586	10	422	701	1,133
Nicaragua		80	3	83		109	1	110
Norway	123	13,634	555	14,312				
Paraguay	1	2		3				
Persia	3	5		8				

Table showing class and number of pieces of undelivered matter, etc.—Continued.

Countries.	Returned to—				Received from—			
	Registered.	Ordinary.	Parcels, etc.	Total.	Registered.	Ordinary.	Parcels, etc.	Total.
Peru	5	150	1	156	12	188	89	289
Philippines	1	45		46		28		28
Porto Rico	2	128		130				
Portugal	142	2,785	100	3,027	19	363	365	747
Queensland	9	353	10	372	10	390	8	408
Roumania	55	1,121	20	1,196				
Russia	1,980	19,977	325	22,282				
Saint Christopher		67	1	68		8		8
Saint Lucia		14	1	15		35	4	39
Saint Vincent		31		31		6		6
Salvador, Republic of	4	33	2	39		2		2
Santo Domingo	2	63	2	67	1	136		137
Servia	4	5		9				
Shanghai, China, United States postal agency	1	4		5				
Society Islands		5		5				
Spain	57	840	874	1,771	28	485	654	1,167
Straits Settlements	4	35		39		41		41
Surinam	2	11		13				
Sweden	272	36,137	721	37,130				
Switzerland	272	4,582	340	5,194				
Tasmania	1	49		50		45		45
Tobago		4		4				
Trinidad		83	2	85		91	4	95
Turkey	23	263	12	298				
Turk's Islands		26		26				
Uruguay	13	117	2	132		739		739
Venezuela	1	130	12	143	4	73	1	78
Victoria	5	638	25	668	12	1,055	176	1,243
Postal Union					17	41,218	19,519	60,754
Miscellaneous					8	1,700	5	1,713
Total	15,015	477,508	52,872	545,395	1,795	180,011	45,322	227,128

Statement showing the number, classification, and disposition of dead registered letters received at the Dead-Letter Office during the fiscal year ended June 30, 1888.

Class.	Number.	Disposition.	Number.
Domestic:		Delivered without being opened :	
Official	18	To foreign division	15,489
Ordinary	2,546	To Executive Departments	18
Request	2,690	Card and request	2,690
Miscellaneous	1,057	Miscellaneous	1,057
Foreign	15,489	Opened	2,546
Total	21,800	Total	21,800

Contents of letters opened.	Number.	Disposition of letters opened.				
		Delivered.	Filed.		Outstanding.	Total.
			At once.	Returned and filed.		
Money	594	353	46	150	45	594
Postal notes	11	9		2		11
Drafts, money-orders, checks, etc	146	121		14	11	146
Photographs, receipts, stamps, etc	213	180	33			213
Merchandise	531	436		49	46	531
Nothing of value	1,051	181	746	75	49	1,051
Total	2,546	1,280	825	290	151	2,546

It will be observed from the comparative statement of mail matter received and treated that the greater increase is in the items " ordinary unclaimed letters" and " letters mailed in foreign countries." This may be accounted for by the fact that in the revised postal laws and regulations which went into operation September last a change was made shortening the time of holding advertised letters from four to two weeks, thus causing additional returns to be sent to the Dead-Letter Office during the last year, which, under the old regulations, would not have been sent in until the succeeding year. Had it not been for this change the percentage of increase would have been about the same as that shown in my report for 1887, and would probably approximate the actual growth of the postal service.

Free-delivery offices are required to make their returns of dead matter by registered mail, and a large number of other offices adopt the same rule. The whole number of registered parcels of this character received during the fiscal year, the contents of which were distributed among the several divisions of the office for treatment, was 40,129. The number received during the preceding year was 27,659, showing an increase during the last year of 12,470. A very large proportion of this increase was undoubtedly the result of recent legislation increasing the number of free-delivery offices; but the figures will show how much the work of this division of the office has been added to by the legislation referred to. This work will, of course, steadily increase in future by reason of the increasing number of offices which will become entitled to free-delivery service.

The increase of matter sent to the Dead-Letter Office without corresponding increase in the number of employés necessitated such a distribution of the force as would enable matter containing valuable inclosures to be treated as specifically required by the regulations; that is, to be made matter of record; thereby reducing the force available for the treatment of letters which did not contain valuable inclosures below the number of persons required to return everything possible to be returned. While the average number returned by individual employés exceeds the average of any previous year, the aggregate number is therefore less. Another reason for this decrease is found in the constantly increasing amount of printed matter, advertising circulars, etc., manifestly intended for general distribution and not desired to be returned, sent out under the reduced rate for letter postage, sealed and therefore classed in the report as " letters received."

It is not only gratifying but just to the chief clerk, the clerks in charge of the several divisions, and all the employés of the office that I should testify to the fidelity and zeal with which they have performed their duties. It would otherwise have been impossible to properly dispose of the work which devolved upon the office.

Very respectfully, your obedient servant,

JNO. B. BAIRD,
Superintendent.

REPORT

OF THE

SUPERINTENDENT OF THE POSTAL MONEY-ORDER SYSTEM

FOR THE

FISCAL YEAR ENDED JUNE 30, 1888.

783

REPORT

OF THE

SUPERINTENDENT OF THE POSTAL MONEY-ORDER SYSTEM.

POST-OFFICE DEPARTMENT,
OFFICE OF SUPERINTENDENT OF MONEY-ORDER SYSTEM,
Washington, D. C., November 13, 1888.

SIR: I have the honor to submit the following report of the operations of the Postal Money-Order System for the fiscal year ended June 30, 1888, which continue to manifest the confidence reposed by the public in its methods, and which are evidence, to some extent, of increased activity in business.

The total amount of domestic money-order transactions for each fiscal year from the inception of the system until the close of the term to which this report relates will be found in Statement A, of the Appendix.

NUMBER OF MONEY-ORDER OFFICES.

On June 30, 1887, the domestic money-order offices in operation numbered 7,853, and during the year ended June 30, 1888, 410 new offices were established, and 22 offices were discontinued; on June 30, 1888, therefore, the total number of domestic money-order offices was 8,241. Since that date the money-order business has been withdrawn from 2 offices, and on the 1st of October the system was extended to 493 additional offices, so that on the latter date there were in operation 8,732 such offices.

NUMBER OF POSTAL-NOTE OFFICES.

At the date of the last report there were in existence 229 postal note offices, which were empowered to issue, but not to pay, postal-notes only, under the authority of the act of Congress approved January 3, 1887. This number was increased during the course of the year just closed to 315, while 4 offices were discontinued, leaving 311 in operation at the close of the year.

Two hundred and fifty additional postal-note offices have been established since that time, 1 has been discontinued, and 22 have been transferred to the list of money-order offices. The total number of postal-note offices on October 1, 1888, was 538.

11843—P M G 88——50

785

ISSUES AND PAYMENTS OF DOMESTIC MONEY-ORDERS.

The number of domestic money-orders issued during the year was
9,959,207, aggregating in amount............................... $119,649,064.9*
And the number of such orders paid during the same
period was 9,866,060 of the value of.......... .... $118,832,330. 01
In addition to which money-orders were repaid to
the number of 78,983, amounting to............. 911,015. 24

Making the total amount of payments and repayments............. 119,743,345. 2

And the excess of payments and repayments over issues...... 94,280.2*

The gross amount of the fees received by postmasters from the public for the issue of domestic money-orders was................... 946,961.12

Comparison with the figures of the preceding year shows an increase
in the number of orders issued of 727,030, or 7.87 per cent.; in the number of orders paid of 726,498, or 7.94 per cent., and in the number of or
ders repaid of 7,718, or 10.83 per cent.

It likewise exhibits an increase in the amount of orders issued of
$2,186,404.09, or 1.86 per cent.; of $2,426,000.63, or 2.08 per cent., in the
amount of orders paid, and of $53,317.96, or 6.21 per cent., in the amount
of orders repaid.

The average amount of the orders issued was $12.01, or 71 cents less
than the average of the year ended June 30, 1887.

The increase in the gross amount of fees received was $34,084.72, and
the average fee was 9.51 cents, being .37 of a cent less than that of the
previous year.

ISSUES AND PAYMENTS OF POSTAL-NOTES.

The number of postal-notes issued during the year was 6,668,006, of the
total value of... $12,134,459.04
And the number of notes paid during the same time
was 6,544,865, amounting to......................... $11,934,759. 13
While the notes repaid at the offices of issue numbered
87,125, and aggregated 170,122. 42

Making the total amount of payments and repayments 12,104,881.55

And the excess of issues over payments and repayments........ 29,577.49

The aggregate amount of fees received from the public was......, ... 200,341.6*

There was consequently an increase in the number of postal-notes issued of 360,454, or 5.71 per cent., and in the amount thereof of $365,634.23,
or 3.10 per cent.; an increase in the number of postal-notes paid of
340,412, or 5.48 per cent., and in the amount thereof of $362,677.86, or
3.13 per cent.

There was likewise an increase in the number of postal-notes repaid, or paid at the office of issue, of 5,572, or 6.83 per cent.; and in the
amount thereof of $15,436.18, or 9.98 per cent.

The average amount of the postal-notes issued was $1.82, or 5 cents
less than the average of the preceding year.

WAR CLAIMS.

In continuation of the custom of former years, the Paymaster-General of the United States Army employed the money-order system for
the purpose of paying the claims of colored soldiers for services in the
late war. The total amount of the money-orders issued to that end for
bounty and back pay during the fiscal year was $1,539.13. The money-

orders in such cases are transmitted through this office—not directly from the War Department to the payees—and are accompanied with specific instructions to the respective postmasters on whom they are drawn enjoining that great care be taken to identify the payees.

DUPLICATE MONEY-ORDERS.

Statement B, appended hereto, shows the number of duplicate money-orders issued by this office during the last fiscal year to have been 21,656, an increase of 2,310 over the preceding year. The number of duplicate postal-notes issued was 6,436, an increase of 1,921 over the year 1886–'87.

Provision is made by law for the issue of duplicate money-orders in case of the loss or destruction of the originals, and when the latter are not paid within one year from the date of their issue, or have received more than one indorsement; likewise, when the originals are drawn for payment to concerns which the Postmaster-General, under authority of section 4041 of the Revised Statutes, has pronounced fraudulent, the money is returned to the remitter by means of duplicate orders.

Duplicate postal-notes are drawn in lieu of notes which have not been paid within a period of three months from the last day of the month of issue, that being the term of validity fixed by law for postal-notes.

DRAFTS AND TRANSFERS.

Every available means is adopted to guard against delay in the payment of money-orders, and to that end postmasters are required, when it becomes necessary, to employ the postal funds in their hands, and to make transfers of such amounts as may be required from the postal to the money-order account. Occasionally, also, it is convenient to transfer sums of money-order funds to the postal account., Notice of every such transfer is transmitted to the Department; an account thereof is kept; and as soon as practicable after the close of each quarter, upon report from the auditor, the balance remaining due to the postal account is repaid by the deposit of an equivalent sum with the Assistant Treasurer of the United States at New York, N. Y., to the credit of the Treasurer of the United States for the service of the Post-Office Department. The amounts of such transfers for the four quarters of the last fiscal year, and the respective dates on which the balances due were paid to the postal fund, were as follows :

Quarter ended—	From postal to money-order funds.	From money-order to postal funds.	Balance due postal funds.	Paid by deposit in sub-treasury at New York, N. Y.
September 30, 1887	$158,019.99	$14,862.38	$143,157.61	May 5, 1888.
December 31, 1887	180,731.72	5,343.21	175,388.51	June 15, 1888.
March 31, 1888	191,188.08	5,897.94	185,290.14	August 24, 1888.
June 30, 1888	153,348.81	3,714.07	149,634.74	November 13, 1888.
Total	683,288.60	29,817.60	653,471.00	

It frequently happens, particularly in the case of the larger offices which are located at the centers of trade, that the receipts from the issue of money-orders are not sufficient to pay the money-orders presented, while the postal funds are required for other legitimate expenditures of the office. In such case, if the deficiency in the money-order funds be on occasional or temporary one, the postmaster is furnished by this office, upon his application, with a draft upon the postmaster at New York, N. Y. If the deficiency is continuous and considerable he is supplied with a book of such drafts and a convenient sum is placed to his credit with the postmaster at New York upon which he may draw by installments. Both the credit and the supply of drafts may be renewed as occasion requires.

The total amount of such drafts paid by the postmaster at New York during the last fiscal year was $12,470,601.89.

Inasmuch as great delay would ensue if postmasters in the extreme Western States and Territories were required to obtain supplies of funds from Washington, arrangement is made for furnishing them with the requisite funds from the post-offices of San Francisco, Cal., and Portland, Oregon, the former of which transmitted to neighboring offices during the fiscal year ended June 30, 1888, the sum of $135,756, and the latter the sum of $91,686.

REMITTANCES OF SURPLUS MONEY-ORDER FUNDS.

It is essential to the success of the money-order system that the funds received from the issue of orders at offices where the payments are few shall as quickly as possible be transmitted to those offices where the payments are more numerous and larger in amount than the issues, and accordingly every postmaster is required by regulation to make daily remittances to some post office, designated as a depository, of all his surplus money order funds. He is allowed to retain, if his business is fluctuating, a small fixed sum termed a "reserve," but at the majority of offices postmasters are required to transmit daily every dollar in excess of the aggregate amount of the unpaid advices which have been in their hands not exceeding two weeks. The remittances of this kind, made in currency by registered mail, or by means of national bank drafts in ordinary mail, aggregated during the fiscal year just closed $103,129,930.74.

LOST REMITTANCES.

Notwithstanding the vast number and very considerable amount of these remittances, only 91 cases of loss were reported during the year, and of these eleven were cases of remittances alleged to have been forwarded during the preceding year. All of these cases, aggregating in amount $6,368.43, were referred, as they were brought to notice, to the Assistant Attorney-General for the Post-Office Department, he being the officer designated to adjudicate postmasters' claims for losses of money-order funds in transit under authority of the act of March 17, 1882, which empowers the Postmaster-General to allow credit, if the loss occurred without fault or negligence upon the part of the remitting postmaster. A description of the remittances above-mentioned will be found in Statement C, of the Appendix.

ERRONEOUS PAYMENT OF MONEY-ORDERS.

During the fiscal year 1887-'88, 61 money-orders were reported as having been improperly paid, or in the ratio of 1 to every 161,739 orders paid. These are described in Statement D, of the appendix, which contains also the particulars of 75 other money-orders alleged to have been erroneously paid; the total amount of the whole number being $3,472.94. They include 35 orders, amounting to $992.35, the inquiry in regard to which had not been concluded at the close of the previous fiscal year; and 40 orders, aggregating $1,018.97, issued prior to July 1, 1887, but in regard to which no claim was made upon the Department until after the commencement of the last fiscal year. As shown by the tabular statement, inspectors of the Department, in the course of their investigations, recovered the amounts of 31 orders and paid the money, in all $845.13, to the true payees.

In 10 cases, in which the orders aggregated $126.50, it was ascertained that the claims were not well founded, the orders having been properly paid in the first instance.

Postmasters were required to make good to the owners the amounts of 41 orders, in all $1,078.45, for failure to exercise the degree of precaution enjoined by the regulations in making payment, and in 1 case, amounting to $4.50, the evidence was not sufficient to fix the responsibility for wrong payment either upon the postmasters or upon the remitters or payees, and the Department, therefore, assumed the loss. The payees themselves, on account of contributory negligence, were required to sustain the loss in 2 cases, involving $12, and the remitter in 1 case, the amount of the order being $11, while the investigation in regard to 50 orders, of the total value of $1,395.36, had not been concluded at the close of the year.

REVENUES AND EXPENSES.

The revenues and expenses of the domestic money-order system for the year to which this report relates are reported by the Auditor as follows:

RECEIPTS.

Amount received for fees on orders issued	$946,961.12
Amount of gain	136.01
Amount of premiums, etc.	219.43
Total	947,316.56

EXPENDITURES.

Amount allowed postmasters for commissions	$317,064.29	
Incidental expenses	84,479.92	
Lost remittances, burglaries, etc.	4,499.58	
		406,043.79
Excess of receipts over expenditures, being gross revenue		541,272.77

Included in the item of "incidental expenses" above mentioned is the cost of blanks, blank books, and printed matter used in the money-order business, and of stationery used exclusively for this business in post-offices, as well as of money-order dating-stamps, stamp-ribbons, numbering machines, etc.

The total cost of blanks, blank books, etc., for domestic and international money-order business and for postal-note business, purchased under contract by authority of special law was $47,597.72, and of this sum $8,666.39 were paid for work ordered on requisitions of the previous year. The cost of such blanks and books for domestic money-order business alone was $42,525.03, including $8,233.40 paid on account of requisitions of the preceding year.

The receipts and expenditures of the postal-note business have been reported by the Auditor as follows:

RECEIPTS.

Amount received for fees on notes issued...................................... $200,341.68

EXPENDITURES.

Amount allowed postmasters:
    For commissions $55,701.39
    Incidental expenses 26,754.91
                                                82,456.30

Excess of receipts over expenditures, being gross revenue........ 117,885.38

The item of "incidental expenses" includes the cost of the blank engraved postal-note forms, amounting to $20,683.69.

THE INTERNATIONAL MONEY-ORDER BUSINESS.

Money-order business was commenced with the Kingdom of Denmark on the 1st of January, 1888, a convention for the purpose, a copy of which is hereto annexed, having been duly concluded with that country. At the close of the fiscal year 1886-'87, 1,642 of the money-order offices were specially authorized to transact international money-order business. Facilities for making remittances to foreign countries were extended to 60 additional offices during the last year, and 1 office was discontinued; so that on June 30, 1888, the number of such offices was 1,701. This number has been still further increased since the close of the year by the addition of 77 international money-order offices, and therefore at date of this report there are 1,778 offices authorized to conduct both international and domestic money-order business.

STATISTICS OF THE INTERNATIONAL MONEY-ORDER BUSINESS.

In the following statement are shown, in detail, the number and amount of the money-order transactions with each of twenty-three foreign countries. The statement also contains an interesting comparison of the figures of last year with those of the previous year, exhibiting the amount as well as the percentage of increase or decrease in every case.

Nationality.	No. of orders issued.	Amount of orders issued.	No. of orders paid.	Amount of orders paid.	No. of orders repaid.	Amount of orders repaid.	Amount of fees received.
Canadian..........	75,526	$1,305,881.54	107,457	$1,309,397.92	538	$8,321.23	$15,678.75
British	371,604	4,826,557.85	49,333	735,421.27	966	11,627.09	61,870.50
German	187,095	2,633,528.27	48,416	1,391,758.93	704	9,510.69	33,250.15
Swiss	32,184	554,933.46	7,163	201,970.63	133	1,981.40	6,558.85
Italian	32,868	868,208.07	1,355	35,907.27	105	2,048.75	9,296.80
French	15,757	234,162.90	4,393	77,343.16	179	2,362.71	2,820.00
Jamaica	167	2,721.89	2,219	64,715.79	4	50.76	33.34
New Zealand	402	8,432.48	1,966	24,254.75	....	....	97.80
New South Wales..	425	10,568.57	1,497	27,056.75	6	74.81	118.30
Victoria............	361	7,464.23	1,305	19,123.81	4	17.33	87.30
Belgian	2,749	47,795.47	1,308	84,841.83	16	196.10	565.95
Portuguese	387	7,138.29	885	14,174.16	8	60.90	63.05
Swedish............	24,059	479,850.26	1,886	52,879.99	53	977.35	5,572.29
Tasmania	23	460.94	318	3,145.22	1	4.00	5.29
Windward Islands.	203	3,526.18	1,702	59,621.93	1	.67	42.50
Japanese	391	6,592.46	852	19,365.20	4	62.10	96.65
Cape Colony	55	1,000.43	237	3,441.62	2	10.50	12.10
Hawaiian	220	4,508.29	1,899	23,684.88	4	75.95	53.78
Queensland	60	1,081.92	353	5,127.93	2	78.60	13.46
Leeward Islands ..	61	703.66	193	4,420.23	2	5.33	8.74
Norway............	10,894	225,500.35	872	20,885.35	5	93.62	2,577.55
Netherlands.......	2,308	27,921.47	1,234	22,579.21	13	182.50	380.04
Denmark	1,837	33,326.05	649	16,568.37	2	7.40	204.55
Total	759,636	11,293,870.05	236,902	4,160,675.64	2,747	37,759.98	138,511.10

Nationality.	Amount of increase or decrease in orders issued as compared with 86 -'87.	Percentage of increase or decrease in issues.	Amount of increase or decrease in orders paid as compared with 86 -'87.	Percentage of increase or decrease in payments.	Amount of increase or decrease in fees received as compared with 1886-'87.	Percentage of increase or decrease in fees.
Canadian	$193,327.59	17.91	$42,130.17	8.32	$2,342.60	17.58
British	1,007,617.26	26.38	60,758.59	9.01	12,835.55	26.08
German	185,175.04	7.56	*58,985.66	*4.07	2,287.40	7.38
Swiss	117,682.75	26.90	21,493.22	11.91	1,365.60	26.80
Italian	165,654.57	23.58	*1,741.94	*4.63	1,730.35	22.87
French	43,021.12	22.51	1,983.17	2.63	532.16	22.28
Jamaica	*313.82	*10.34	4,336.25	7.16	*4.10	*10.90
New Zealand	1,449.35	20.75	2,019.02	9.08	17.05	21.11
New South Wales	4,214.26	66.32	5,047.32	12.69	48.30	68.03
Victoria	916.00	13.99	2,035.91	11.91	11.90	15.78
Belgian	16,706.96	53.74	790.68	2.32	191.45	51.12
Portuguese	*1,952.36	*21.48	*5,383.23	*27.53	*18.20	*17.98
Swedish	263,365.37	121.66	9,029.36	20.59	3,027.10	118.94
Tasmania	338.92	277.76	1,010.67	47.35	3.40	188.88
Windward Islands	1,389.66	65.04	11,930.90	25.02	15.50	58.05
Japanese	2,152.37	33.42	6,686.74	52.78	23.40	32.21
Cape Colony	1.51	.15	91.61	2.73	.30	2.54
Hawaiian	1,857.18	43.07	*4,550.04	*15.05	14.80	88.05
Queensland	482.07	80.37	*414.70	*7.48	5.80	76.32
Leeward Islands	*283.00	*28.68	1,133.34	34.48	*4.20	*30.22

* Decrease. Each amount not marked with an asterisk represents an increase.

Norway exchange did not go into operation until April 1, 1887.
Netherlands exchange did not go into operation until April 1, 1887.
Denmark exchange did not go into operation until January 1, 1888.

This table exhibits an increase in the number of international money-orders issued of 144,231, or 23.43 per cent.; in the amount of such orders issued of $2,258,339.74, or 24.99 per cent.; in the number of international orders paid and repaid, of 15,219, or 6.77 per cent.; and in the amount of such orders paid and repaid of $158,179.68, or 3.91 per cent.

It likewise shows an increase in the amount of fees received of $27,417.80, or 24.45 per cent.

The average amount of the international orders issued was $14.87, the same being 19 cents greater than the average of the preceding year; and the average amount of the international orders paid was $17.61, or 48 cents less than the average of the preceding year.

The increase in the total volume of the international money-order business, including orders issued, paid, and repaid, was $2,416,519.42, or 18.46 per cent.; and the number of transactions increased by 159,450, or 18.98 per cent.

REVENUE FROM INTERNATIONAL MONEY-ORDER BUSINESS.

The gross revenue from the respective international systems for the last fiscal year is reported by the Auditor for this Department to be as follows:

From the Canadian business	$14,636.82	From the Queensland business	$51.99
From the British business	36,934.61	From the Cape Colony business	19.18
From the German business	41,048.89	From the Windward Islands business	462.92
From the Swiss business	12,228.12	From the Japanese business	168.61
From the Italian business	25,286.02	From the Leeward Islands business	24.90
From the French business	5,492.02	From the Norwegian business	101.70
From the Jamaica business	462.86	From the Netherlands business	314.66
From the New Zealand business	245.75	From the Danish business	150.15
From the New South Wales business	254.94		
From the Victoria business	231.69	Total	139,280.94
From the Belgian business	697.11	Less from Swedish business	130.26
From the Portuguese business	142.59		
From the Tasmania business	37.95	Total international revenue	139,159.68
From the Hawaiian business	296.96		

GENERAL FINANCIAL RESULTS.

The total volume of business of all kinds, including domestic and international money-orders and postal-notes, consisted for the year of transactions numbering 17,386,849, and amounting to $143,077,394.07 in issues, and numbering 16,816,772 and amounting to $136,055,662.42 in payments and repayments; and the aggregate amount of all the fees received from the public was $1,286,813.90.

These figures exhibit an increase in issues in the number of transactions of 1,231,715, or 7.62 per cent., and in the amount thereof of $4,810,378.06, or 3.48 per cent.

In compliance with the provisions of section 4050 of the Revised Statutes the gross revenues from all branches of the money-order and postal-note business were deposited quarterly, as soon as they were reported by the Auditor, with the Assistant Treasurer of the United States at New York, N. Y., to the credit of the Treasurer of the United States for the service of the Post-Office Department. These revenues by quarters and the dates of the respective deposits are shown in the subjoined statement:

Quarter ended—	Amount.	Deposited—
September 30, 1887	$163 266. 61	May 5. 1888
December 31 1887	238, 870. 44	June 13, 1888
March 31. 1888	210, 494. 15	August 24, 1888
June 30, 1888	180, 077. 63	November 13, 1888
Total	798, 317. 83	

In accordance with the practice of the Department, there are annually taken into account, for the purpose of making an exact statement of net revenue, all such items of expense as, though paid from appropriations made by Congress, are a legitimate charge upon the money-order system. These expenditures for the last fiscal year were the following:

Salaries to forty-nine employés in the Superintendent's office........... $63,200.00
Salaries to the employés in the Money-Order Division of the Auditor's office 233,500.00
Stationery furnished for use in the Superintendent's office 620.00
Books, blanks, printing, and stationery furnished for use in the Money-Order Division of the Auditor's office 9,392.25
One-half of salaries of employés in the Money-Order building, under the supervision of the Superintendent of the Post-Office Department building... 4,250.00
One-half rent of the Money-Order building 4,000.00
Estimated cost of furniture and miscellaneous expenses of same......... 2,000.00
Rent of building known as Marini's Hall................................... 4,500.00
Salaries of watchmen, laborers, and of incidental and miscellaneous expenses of said building.. 8,100.00
To these sums must be added the total amount of the allowances to postmasters at first and second class post-offices for clerk hire in the money-order business, which, under the act of June 29, 1886, have been paid since July 1, 1887, out of appropriations instead of from the proceeds of the money-order business, the said amount as reported by the First Assistant Postmaster-General being 424,200.00

Total.. 755,301.12

It will thus be seen that the anticipation of last year that the money-order business would, notwithstanding the reduction of the fee for small money-orders from 8 cents to 5 cents, become entirely self-sustaining, has been realized; for, after deduction of the amount of the above mentioned expenses from the amount of the gross revenue, there remains an absolute net profit of $43,016.21.

The advantageous printing contracts made by the Department during the summer of 1887 have contributed largely to this satisfactory result.

It is probable that this profit will be somewhat increased during the current fiscal year by reason of additional conventions concluded, at the instance of this Department, with the postal administrations of nearly all the foreign countries with which it maintains an exchange of money-orders, which additional conventions reduced from three-fourths of 1 per cent. to one half of 1 per cent. the rate of commission to be paid by each country to the other upon money-orders issued; such commissions being the compensation of the country of destination for the labor and outlay incidental to the payment of money-orders.

Such conventions have been duly signed to take effect in the case of Portugal on October 1, 1887; in the case of Great Britain on the 1st of April, 1888; in the case of Italy, Sweden, the Hawaiian Kingdom, and the Leeward Islands on the 1st of July, 1888; and in the case of New Zealand, Japan, the Cape Colony, and Queensland, on the 1st of October, 1888. A similar convention has been executed with the French Government, but has not yet been ratified by that Government.

Negotiations for a like purpose are being conducted with Germany, Switzerland, and Victoria, while in the case of Canada, Norway, the Netherlands, and Denmark, the rate of commission was originally fixed at one-half of 1 per cent., and therefore required no modification.

The net profit to the United States by the reductions already conceded, and entirely agreed to, is estimated at over $9,500 per annum, and the additional profit, if the pending negotiations above mentioned are concluded to the satisfaction of this Department, will amount to about $3,300 per annum.

In conclusion, I have the honor to recommend that legislation be requested to authorize the increase of the maximum amount of a single international money-order from $50 to $100. Such a change would produce uniformity, in respect to the maximum amount, between the domestic and international money orders, and would besides tend to reduce the expenses of the international money-order systems, inasmuch as for sums from $50 to $100 a single order would be required in lieu of two as at present. Since the postmasters and clerks who issue the orders, and the exchange offices which certify them, are compensated for their labor not upon the basis of the amounts of the orders, but upon that of the number of transactions at a fixed rate per transaction, the lessening of expense in the item of clerk-hire in post-offices would be by no means inconsiderable.

I am, sir, very respectfully, your obedient servant,

C. F. MACDONALD,
Superintendent of Money-Order System.

Hon. DON M. DICKINSON,
Postmaster-General.

APPENDIX.

A.—*Tabular statement showing operations of the domestic money-order system during each year since its establishment November 1, 1864, up to June 30, 1888.*

Fiscal year ended—	Number of money-order offices in operation.	Amount of orders issued.	Amount of orders paid and repaid.	Amount of fees received.	Amount of expenses.	Amount of deficit.	Amount of surplus.
June 30, 1865....	419	$1, 360, 122. 52	$1, 313, 577. 08	$11, 536. 40	$18, 584. 37	$7, 047. 97	....
June 30, 1866....	766	3, 977, 259. 28	3, 003, 890. 22	35, 803. 06	28, 664. 27	....	$7, 138. 79
June 30, 1867....	1, 224	9, 229, 327. 72	9, 071, 240. 73	70, 889. 57	44, 628. 96	....	26, 260. 61
June 30, 1868....	1, 468	16, 197, 858. 47	16, 118, 537. 03	124, 503. 19	70, 345. 04	....	54, 158. 15
June 30, 1869....	1, 645	24, 815, 068. 93	24, 654, 123. 46	176, 247. 87	110, 694. 00	....	65, 553. 87
June 30, 1870....	2, 076	34, 054, 184. 71	33, 927, 924. 79	235, 557. 05	145, 382. 42	....	90, 174. 63
June 30, 1871....	2, 452	42, 164, 118. 03	42, 027, 336. 31	295, 563. 38	194, 381. 60	....	101, 181. 78
June 30, 1872....	2, 775	48, 515, 532. 72	48, 419, 644. 97	350, 499. 40	244, 521. 63	....	105, 977. 77
June 30, 1873....	3, 069	57, 516, 216. 69	57, 295, 012. 27	354, 816. 66	286, 232. 66	....	68, 584. 00
June 30, 1874....	3, 404	74, 424, 854. 71	74, 210, 156. 25	462, 238. 54	357, 040. 42	....	105, 198. 12
June 30, 1875 ...	3, 401	77, 431, 251. 58	77, 361, 690. 75	494, 717. 27	374, 575. 18	....	120, 142. 09
June 30, 1876 ...	3, 697	77, 035, 972. 78	77, 106, 334. 85	647, 021. 52	456, 250. 68	....	190, 770. 84
June 30, 1877 ...	3, 686	72, 820, 509. 70	72, 908, 475. 25	624, 409. 66	524, 478. 47	....	99, 931. 19
June 30, 1878 ...	4, 143	81, 442, 364. 87	81, 279, 910. 80	716, 638. 96	513, 686. 61	....	202, 952. 37
June 30, 1879 ...	4, 512	88, 254, 641. 02	88, 006, 200. 20	799, 347. 09	575, 386. 32	....	223, 960. 77
June 30, 1880 ...	4, 829	100, 353, 818. 83	100, 165, 982. 78	917, 091. 58	659, 516. 50	....	257, 575. 08
June 30, 1881 ...	5, 163	105, 075, 769. 35	104, 924, 853. 61	967, 772. 93	715, 458. 29	....	252, 314. 64
June 30, 1882 ...	5, 491	113, 400, 118. 21	113, 388, 301. 90	1, 054, 538. 62	774, 197. 45	....	280, 341. 17
June 30, 1883 ...	5, 927	117, 329, 406. 31	117, 344, 281. 78	1, 102, 838. 42	791, 133. 75	....	311, 704. 67
June 30, 1884 ...	6, 310	122, 121, 201. 98	121, 971, 083. 80	956, 473. 39	702, 603. 80	....	247, 875. 59
June 30, 1885 ...	7, 056	117, 858, 921. 27	117, 996, 205. 06	925, 125. 03	681, 150. 06	....	243, 974. 97
June 30, 1886 ...	7, 357	113, 819, 521. 21	113, 885, 453. 04	922, 781. 97	689, 758. 38	....	233, 023. 59
June 30, 1887 ...	7, 853	117, 463, 660. 89	117, 264, 026. 66	914, 076. 57	402, 458. 59	....	511, 617. 98
June 30, 1888 ...	8, 241	119, 649, 064. 98	119, 743, 345. 33	947, 316. 56	406, 043. 79	....	541, 272. 77
Total....	....	1, 736, 341, 816. 76	1, 734, 287, 602. 84	....	....	....	....

B.—*Statement of duplicate money-orders issued by the Department during the fiscal year ended June 30, 1888.*

	Number.	Remarks.
I.—In lieu of money-orders lost in transit	21, 033	Being 3,265 more than during the preceding year.
II.—In lieu of money-orders, payment of which had been prohibited in pursuance of section 4041 of the Revised Statutes of the United States.	60	Being 251 less than during the preceding year.
III.—In lieu of money-orders lost by the payees, remitters, or indorsees.	185	Being 225 less than during the preceding year.
IV.—In lieu of money-orders mutilated or destroyed while in the hands of the payees, remitters, or indorsees.	77	Being 209 less than during the preceding year.
V.—In lieu of money-orders invalidated by reason of having received more than one indorsement, in violation of section 4037 of the Revised Statutes of the United States.	27	Being 43 less than during the preceding year.
VI.—In lieu of money-orders invalidated by reason of not having been presented for payment within one year after the date of their issue.	274	Being 227 less than during the preceding year.
Total	21, 656	
Duplicate postal-notes issued during the same year ...	6, 436	Being 1,921 more than during the preceding year.

C.—Statement of money-order funds lost in transmission, through the mails, or otherwise, during the fiscal year ended June 30, 1888.

Summary.	Number of cases.	Amount.	Total amount.
I.—Whole number of cases of lost remittances reported and referred to Assistant Attorney General for the Post-Office Department	91		$6, 368. 43
(a) Cases which occurred prior to July 1, 1887.	11	$836. 00	
(b) Cases which occurred after June 30, 1887	80	5, 532. 43	
Total	91		6, 368. 43

I.—REFERRED TO ASSISTANT ATTORNEY-GENERAL FOR THE POST-OFFICE DEPARTMENT FOR HIS CONSIDERATION, UNDER THE PROVISIONS OF THE ACT OF MARCH 17, 1882.

Office of mailing.*	Date of mailing.	Amount.	Office of mailing.	Date of mailing.	Amount.
(a) Cases which occurred prior to July 1, 1887.			**(b) Cases which occurred after June 30, 1887—Con'd.**		
Butler, Ga	May 3, 1887	$2. 00	Spencer, W. Va	Oct. 2, 1887	$160. 43
Carlisle, Ind	May 26, 1887	*20. 00	Clinton, Ark	Jan. 8, 1888	18. 00
Fonda, Iowa	Jan. 24, 1887	30. 00	Leesburgh, Ga	Jan. 12, 1888	20. 00
La Fontaine, Ind	Mar. 15, 1887	15. 00	Chloride, N. Mex.	Dec. 24, 1887	5. 00
Navoy, Tex	June 16, 1887	38. 00	Eastman. Ga	Jan. 7, 1888	123. 80
Bell's, Tex	June 17, 1887	78. 00	Springville, Ariz	Oct. 27, 1887	5. 00
Covington, La	June 30, 1887	106. 00	Sevierville, Tenn	Jan. 20, 1888	21. 00
Big Spring, Tex	Jan. 22, 1887	220. 00	Brandon, Miss	Feb. 24, 1888	90. 00
Warsaw, Va	June 25, 1887	26. 00	Somerset, Ohio	Feb. 29, 1888	210. 00
Spencer, Tenn	May 3, 1887	90. 00	Belmont, Ohio	Feb. 27, 1888	110. 00
Cooper, Tex	June 16, 1887	8. 00	Plainfield, Ohio	Feb. 29, 1888	5. 00
Adamsville, Tenn	May 23, 1887	203. 00	Loveland, Ohio	do	31. 00
			Frazeysburgh, Ohio	do	20. 00
11 cases		836. 00	Chesterville, Ohio	Feb. 28, 1888	81. 00
			Shepherd, Mich	Mar. 15, 1888	100. 00
(b) Cases which occurred after June 30, 1887.			Adeline, Ill	Feb. 25, 1888	6. 00
			Golconda, Ill	Dec. 16, 1887	90. 00
			Myers, Fla	Feb. 24, 1888	10. 00
Payne, Ohio	July 16, 1887	104. 00	Millersville, Ohio	Feb. 28, 1888	174. 00
Cross Pl ins, Ala	do	160. 00	Elmo, Mo	Mar. 3, 1888	285. 00
Arnold, Nebr	July 8, 1887	804. 00	Guntersville, Ala	Apr. 20, 1888	183. 00
Greenleaf, Kans	July 27, 1887	170. 00	McFall, Mo	Mar. 16, 1888	22. 00
Murphy, N. C	July 4, 1887	10. 00	Marquette, Nebr	May 8, 1888	10. 00
Deshler, Ohio	July 14, 1887	74. 00	Myers, Fla	Mar. 27, 1888	20. 00
North Hector, N. Y	Aug. 15, 1887	40. 00	Webster, N. C	do	5. 00
Perrysburgh, Ohio	July 23, 1887	205. 00	Do	Mar. 28, 1888	75. 00
Pacific Junction, Iowa	Aug. 31, 1887	†20. 00	Do	Mar. 29, 1888	16. 00
Judsonia, Ark	Sept. 20, 1887	20. 00	Hennepin. Ill	May 7, 1888	70. 00
Morocco, Ind	Sept. 14, 1887	1. 00	Dallas, Ark	May 5, 1888	30. 00
Lake George, N. Y	Sept. 27, 1887	43. 00	Park City, Mont	May 11, 1888	1. 00
Pemberville, Ohio		142. 00	Leakville, N. C	May 3, 1888	90. 00
Runnels, Tex	Sept. 26, 1887	11. 00	Do	May 9, 1888	90. 00
San Angelo, Tex	Sept. 29, 1887	67. 00	Dallas, Ark	May 7, 1888	55. 00
Woodbine, Iowa	Oct. 6 1887	1. 00	New Burlington, Ohio	Feb. 29, 1888	2. 00
Do	Oct. 5, 1887	19. 00	Marquette, Nebr	May 12, 1888	5. 00
Pemberville, Ohio	Oct. 26, 1887	154. 00	Kincaid, Kans	Apr. 16, 1888	14. 00
Covelo, Cal	Oct. 14, 1887	‡45. 00	Haynesville, La	{ Oct. 7, 1887 Apr. 9, 1888 May 21, 1888 May 23, 1888 May 26, 1888 }	§34. 00
Corinth, Iowa	Aug. 27, 1887	3. 00			
Corfu, N. Y	Aug. 23, 1887	20. 00			
Rolling Forks, Miss	Aug. 31, 1887	10. 00			
Wheatland, Cal	Nov. 7, 1887	40. 00			
Rural Retreat, Va	Dec. 3, 1887	46. 00	Centre, Ala	Apr. 12, 1888	68. 00
Saugatuck, Mich	Oct. 14, 1887	20. 00	Donaldsonville, La	May 5, 1888	515. 00
Pemberville, Ohio	Nov. 18, 1887	267. 00	Ellisville Depot, Miss.	June 7, 1888	69. 00
Ogden, Kans	do	111. 00	Haynesville, La.		20. 00
Morrison, Colo	Dec. 13, 1887	182. 00	Hico, Tex	June 16, 1888	44. 00
Port Clinton, Ohio	Jan. 3, 1888	55. 00	Thornville, Ohio	Feb. 29, 1888	13. 90
New Rockford, Dak	Dec. 27, 1887	20. 00			
Rockmart, Ga	Dec. 31, 1887	146. 00	80 cases		5, 532. 43
Saint Anthony Park, Minn.	Dec. 30, 1887	5. 00			
Homer, La	Dec. 31, 1887	3. 03	Total, 91 cases		6, 368. 43

* Part of $112.   † Part of $43.   ‡ Part of $491.   § Parts of five remittances.

D.—*Statement of money-orders improperly paid, on a forged signature or otherwise, during the fiscal year ended June 30, 1888.*

Summary.	Number of cases.	Amount.	Total amount.
Whole number of orders improperly paid	136		$3,472.94
(a) Orders issued prior to July 1, 1887	75	$2,011.82	
(b) Orders issued after June 30, 1887, and prior to July 1, 1888	61	1,461.62	
I. Recovered	31		$45.13
(a) Orders issued prior to July 1, 1887	12	383.18	
(b) Orders issued after June 30, 1887, and prior to July 1, 1888	19	461.95	
II. Paid to the proper payee	10		126.50
(a) Orders issued prior to July 1, 1887	4	56.00	
(b) Orders issued after June 30, 1887, and prior to July 1, 1888	6	70.50	
III. Charged to paying postmaster	41		1,078.45
(a) Orders issued prior to July 1, 1887	28	768.13	
(b) Order issued after June 30, 1887, and prior to July 1, 1888	13	310.32	
IV. Charged to Department	1		4.50
(a) Order issued prior to July 1, 1887	1	4.50	
V. Charged to payee of order	2		12.00
(b) Orders issued after June 30, 1887, and prior to July 1, 1888	2	12.00	
VI. Charged to remitter	1		11.00
(a) Order issued prior to July 1, 1887	1	11.00	
VII. Unsettled	50		1,395.36
(a) Orders issued prior to July 1, 1887	29	788.51	
(b) Orders issued after June 30, 1887, and prior to July 1, 1888	21	606.85	
Total	136		3,472.94

L—RECOVERED.

(a) *Orders issued prior to July 1, 1887.*

Number of order.	Name of issuing office.	State.	Date of issue.	Name of paying office.	State.	Date of payment.	Amount of order.
Swe. 4690 99972 99973 99974 99975	Omaha	Nebr	Sept. 7, 1885	Strump, Malmö	Sweden		¹$17.42
	Washington*	D.C	Mar. 17, 1887	Natchez	Miss	Mar. 24, 1887	²$204.00
7688	Graham*	N.C	Sept. 6, 1886	Suffolk	Va	Oct. 19, 1886	9.90
33593	New York*	N.Y	Jan 8, 1884	Cullman	Ga	Jan. 19, 1887	20.59
33504	do*	do	.. do	.. do	.. do	.. do	50.00
Dup. 24-60	Augusta*	Ga	Mar. 27, 1887	Kansas City	Mo	Apr. 28, 1887	25.00
B. gifts 5229	Ballybeg*	Ireland	June 27, 1887	Boston	Mass	July 12, 1887	19.48
	New York*	N.Y	May 13, 1887	Fair Haven	Vt	May 16, 1887	18.70
83860	San José*	Cal	June 1, 1887	San Francisco	Cal	June 3, 1887	20.00
12 cases							383.18

(b) *Orders issued after June 30, 1887.*

Number of order.	Name of issuing office.	State.	Date of issue.	Name of paying office.	State.	Date of payment.	Amount of order.
50444	Rome	Ga	July 15, 1887	Atlanta	Ga	July 18, 1887	$20.00
G. 22412	Mullheim	Ger	Sept. 29, 1887	Brooklyn	N.Y	Oct. 15, 1887	4.00
19865	Washington	D.C	Dec. 20, 1887	Saratoga Springs	do	Dec. 21, 1887	10.00
17991	Panora	Iowa	Dec. 16, 1887	North Topeka Sta., Topeka	Kans	Dec. 23, 1887	8.00
3937	Snohomish	Wash	Jan. 23, 1888	Seattle	Wash	Jan. 28, 1888	15.55
18351	Jacksonville	Fla	Nov. 27, 1887	Toledo	Ohio		50.00
26998 27384 27895 2420 3639 4967 5824 6533 8735	Hoboken	N.J		Trenton	N.J		344.23
	New Haven	Conn					
13636	Sation F, Frankfort, Phila.	Pa					
12 039	Station R, New York.	N.Y					
54208	Station B New York.	..do					
3501	Whatcom	Wash	Feb 13, 1888	Seattle	Wash	April 14, 1888	15.17
19 cases							461.95
Total, 31 cases							845.13

¹(Part of the amount of order. (See 3, next page.)   ²Parts of the amounts of orders. (See 4, next page.)

REPORT OF THE POSTMASTER-GENERAL.

D.—*Statement of money-orders improperly paid, etc.*—Continued.

II.—PAID TO PROPER PAYEE.

(a.) *Orders issued prior to July 1, 1887.*

Number of order.	Name of issuing office.	State.	Date of issue.	Name of paying office.	State.	Date of payment.	Amount of order.
23701	Troy *	N. Y..	Jan. 27, 1887	Amsterdam	N. Y..	Jan. 28, 1887	$5. 00
96582	Lebanon *	Pa ..	May 23, 1887	Chester	Pa...	May 23, 1887	25. 00
9654	Breckenridge* .	Ky ...	Aug. 23, 1886	Denver	Colo .	Aug. 30, 1886	20. 00
19623	Covington *	Ga ..	May 2, 1885	Chattanooga ...	Tenn .	May 7, 1885	6. 00
	4 cases						56. 00

(b.) *Orders issued after June 30, 1887.*

13953	Darien	Ga	Oct. 24, 1887	Milledgeville....	Ga....	Oct. 28, 1887	$10. 50
37627	Lebanon	Pa...	July 8, 1887	Chester	Pa...	July 14, 1887	25. 00
17125	Jacksonville...	Fla ...	Sept. 16, 1887	Toledo	Ohio ..	Sept. 22, 1887	10. 00
17126	.....do	.do ...	Sept. 17, 1887	.....do	.do ...	Sept. 26, 1887	10. 90
17354	.....do	.do ...	Sept. 27, 1887	.....do	.do ...	Oct. 2, 1887	10. 00
25278	Laredo	Tex...	Jan 17, 1888	San Antonio ...	Tex...	Feb. 6, 1888	5. 00
	6 cases						70. 50
	Total, 10 cases.						126. 50

III.—CHARGED TO PAYING POSTMASTER.

(a) *Orders issued prior to July 1, 1887.*

	Number of order.	Name of issuing office.	State.	Date of issue.	Name of paying office.	State.	Date of payment.	Amount of order.
Swe.	4690	Omaha	Nebr..	Sept. 7, 1885	Strump, Malmö.	Sweden		*$32. 58
	6500	Gardner	Kans.	Dec. 28, 1886	Durango	Colo ..	Jan. 17, 1887	65. 00
	26286	Summit	Miss..	Apr. 3, 1886	Starkville	Miss..	Apr.14, 1886	10. 00
	45643	Greenville	.do ...	Oct. 14, 1886	Greenville	.do ..	Nov. 5, 1886	5. 00
	25030	South Div. Sta., Chicago.	Ill	Apr. 1, 1886	Arcata	Cal ...	May 5, 1886	50. 00
	13112	Lanesboro*	Minn .	Jan. 4, 1887	Saint Paul	Minn .	Jan. 6, 1887	3. 93
	13276	....do*	.do ...	Feb. 22, 1887	....do	.do ...	Feb. 25, 1887	11. 90
	30090	Los Angeles,...	Cal ...	Mar. 4, 1887	San Francisco..	Cal ...	Mar.26, 1887	50. 00
	40124	Wyandotte	Kans .	Aug.22, 1886	Nevada	Mo ...	Aug. 4, 1896	4. 00
	2771	Sewickley*	Pa	May 28, 1887	Station F, New York.	N. Y..	May 31, 1887	39. 00
	99972 99973 99974 99975	Washington* ...	D. C ..	Mar.17, 1887	Natchez	Miss...	Mar.24, 1887	*140. 84
	53375	Montpelier*	Vt ...	June 30, 1887	New York	N. Y..	July 2, 1887	6. 00
	62502	Fall River*	Mass .	June 15, 1887	Chelsea Station, Boston.	Mass .	June 16, 1887	25. 00
	51087	Tyler*	Tex..	June 11, 1887	Temple	Tex. ..	June 22, 1887	50. 00
	96431	Oakland*	Cal ...	Jan. 15, 1887	Marysville	Cal ...	Jan. 18, 1887	10. 00
	9504	Maiden Rock*..	Wis ..	May 16, 1887	Manitowoc	Wis ?.	June 3, 1887	50. 00
	26685	Golden*	Colo ..	Dec. 27, 1886	New York	N. Y..	Mar. 19, 1887	20. 00
	36570	Brookfield*	Mo ...	Apr. 23, 1887	Kansas City	Mo ...	Apr. 26, 1887	30. 00
	8235	Challis*	Idaho	Sept. 15, 1886	Morris	Ill ...	Dec. 3, 1886	25. 00
	4567	Lost Nation*	Iowa.	June 9, 1887	Des Moines	Iowa.	June 10, 1887	4. 00
	9048	Manning*	.do ...	Dec. 17, 1886	Clinton	.do ...	Dec. 18, 1886	9. 50
	43171	Liberty Hill*	Tex. .	May 5, 1887	Liberty Hill	Tex. .	June 28, 1887	25. 00
Ger.	20161	New York*	N. Y..		New York	N. Y..	Nov. 1, 1887	23. 58
	7085	Eddyville*	Ky ..	May 9, 1887	Louisville	Ky ..	May 11, 1887	10. 50
	33202	Jonesborough* .	Tenn	May 20, 1886	Cedar Rapids ...	Nebr .	May 27, 1886	76. 00
		28 cases ...						768. 12

* Part of the amount of order. (See 1, preceding page.)   * Parts of the amounts of orders. (See 2, preceding page.)

sment of money-orde

CHARGED TO PAY

(b) Orders iss

·ing	State.	Date of
...	Ger...	Sept. 29
...	N. Y..	Nov. 9,
...	Tenn .	Nov. 12,
...	Pa ..	Feb. 4,
..	Ind ...	Oct. 3,
..	Pa	Oct. 29,
..	Ohio ..	Jan. 13,
..	Mich .	Mar. 14,
;	Fr	Dec. 6,
.	..do ...	....do ..
.	..do ...	....do ..
	N. Y..	Jan. 2,
	..do ...	....do ..
	....	....
	....	....

V.—CHARGED

(a) Order issued

'a	Oct. 11, 1(
.....	....

CHARGED TO

) Orders issue

...	July 15, 1(
...	Aug. 8, 1(
...	....

—CHARGE1

rder issued

Oct. 4, 188:
....

D.—*Statement of money-orders improperly paid, etc.*—Continued

VII.—UNSETTLED.

(a) *Orders issued prior to July* 1, 1887.

Number of order.	Name of issuing office.	State.	Date of issue.	Name of paying office.	State.	Date of payment.	Amount of order.
4450	Dundalk	Ontario	Apr. 11, 1877	Louisville	Ky	Apr. 18, 1877	$42.35
4451	...do	..do	...do	...do	..do	....do	42.35
4452	...do	..do	...do	...do	..do	....do	30.50
16092	Bodie	Cal	Dec. 21, 1883	Virginia City	Nev	Dec. 22, 1883	11.00
C. 11½	Port Arthur	Ontario	Nov. 6, 1883	Port Huron	Mich	Nov. 17, 1883	25.00
12349	Chestertown	Md	June 14, 1882	Buffalo	N.Y.	July 21, 188:	20.00
11087	Lawler	Iowa	July 7, 1884	Jersey City	N J	July 11, 1884	30.00
996	Morton	Ill	Jan. 10, 1885	Chicago	Ill	Feb. 6, 1>85	16.00
742	Central City	Dak	Jan. 8, 1881	Detroit	Mich	Feb. 2, 1881	29.00
L. 4512	New York	N.Y.	Oct. 2, 1885	New York	N.Y.	Dec. 17, 1885	47.70
L. 4812	...do	..do	Nov. 23, 1885	...do	..do	Dec. 10, 1885	47.70
L. 4813	...do	..do	...do	...do	..do	....do	28.62
41183	Cedar Falls	Iowa	June 1, 1886	Kimball	Dak	June 7, 1886	6.00
9300	Clinton	Ky	Oct 31, 1883	Frankfort	Ky	Nov. 2, 1883	1.90
3168	Angus	Iowa	June 22, 1886	Poplar Bluff	Mo	Aug. 2, 18-6	9.90
31592	Station C, Washington.	D.C	Aug. 25, 1886	Atlantic City	N.J	Aug. 26, 18-6	10.00
37096	Boulder	Colo	July 23, 1886	Denver	Colo	July 30, 1886	4.75
16940	Silverton	..do	Feb. 24, 1886	Durango	..do	....do	9.10
15606	Ennis	Tex	Feb. 8, 1883	Colman	Tex	Feb. 13, 1883	50.00
Ger. 93044	New York	N.Y.	Mar. 9, 1885	New York	N.Y.	Mar. 13, 1185	8.47
10971	Boston	Mass	Aug. 15, 1867	New Brunswick	N.J	Aug. 17, 1867	50.00
19107	Woodland	Cal	Feb. 21, 1887	Sacramento	Cal	Feb. 21, 1887	100.00
68375	Key West	Fla	Nov. 5, 1886	Monticello	N.Y.	Dec. 20, 1886	10.00
5300	Louisville	Nebr	Jan. 20, 1887	Kansas City	Mo	Jan. 21, 1887	100.00
17241	New York	N.Y.	Aug. 28, 1885	N. D. Station, Chicago.	Ill	Apr. 14, 1886	18.00
B. 41½½	Glasgow	Scot	June 2, 1886	Philadelphia	Pa	July 21, 1886	14.61
10901	Rockwood *	Tenn	May 12, 1887	Chattanooga	Tenn	May 17, 1887	2.25
G. 78007	New York *	N.Y.	Nov. 15, 1886	New York	N.Y.	Dec. 10, 1886	22.41
92055	....do *	..do	May 12, 1887	Philadelphia	Pa	May 13, 1887	10.00
	29 cases						788.51

(b) *Orders issued after June* 30, 1887.

Number of order.	Name of issuing office.	State.	Date of issue.	Name of paying office.	State.	Date of payment.	Amount of order.
68863	Leadville	Colo	Aug. 6, 1887	Pittston	Pa	Aug. 15, 1887	$20.00
41600	Danville	Va	Sept. 5, 1887	Winston	N.C	Sept. 6, 1887	5.15
42763	Station L, New York.	N.Y.		Rochester	N.Y.		13.00
1123	Portland	Dak	Oct. 13, 1887	Red Lake Falls	Minn	Oct. 25, 1887	46.00
73949	Philadelphia	Pa	Feb. 4, 1884	Columbia	Tenn	Feb. 7, 1888	100.00
28803	El Dorado	Ill	Dec. 30, 1887	Trinidad	Colo	Jan. 9, 1888	10.00
22224	South Saint Louis Station, Saint Louis.	Mo	Dec. 24, 1887	Johnstown	Pa		20.00
30582	Waseca	Minn	Aug. 6, 1887	Red Lake Falls	Minn	Aug. 18, 1887	76.00
36765	Port Gibson	Miss	Jan. 4, 1888	Dallas	Tex	Jan. 23, 1888	75.00
10486	Abilene	Tex	Dec. 27, 1887	Gainesville	..do	Jan. 7, 1888	25.00
18649	Florence	Kans	Jan. 14, 1888	Lyons	Kans	Jan. 16, 1888	1.95
23701	Troy	N.Y.	Jan. 27, 1887	Amsterdam	N.Y.	Jan. 28, 1888	5.00
20039	Great Bend	Kans	July 30, 1887	Chattanooga	Tenn	Aug. 23, 1887	9.00
23902	Aspen	Colo	July 19, 1887	Springfield	Mo	Aug. 1, 1887	25.00
720	Augusta	Mont	Dec. 14, 1887	Helena	Mont	Dec 16, 1887	75.00
107	Saint Anthony Park.	Minn	Nov. 16, 1887	Grand Rapids	Mich	Nov. 19, 1887	14.50
38074	Galvin	Ohio	Feb. 6, 1888	Lima	Ohio	Feb. 8, 1888	10.00
12430	Fort Recovery	..do	Mar. 5, 1888	Cincinnati	..do	Mar. 7, 1888	30.00
45560	San Francisco	Cal	Mar. 14, 1888	Newark	N.J	Apr. 16, 1888	20.00
4495	Saint Helena	Nebr	Feb. 10, 1888	Des Moines	Iowa	Feb. 13, 1888	31.25
24260	Clifton Springs	N.Y.	Apr. 14, 1888	Canfield	Ohio	Apr. 30, 1888	1.00
	21 cases						606.85
	Total, 50 cases						1,395.36

* These 40 cases, aggregating $1,018.97, alleged to have occurred prior to July 1, 1887, were not brought to the notice of the Department until after that date.

CONVENTION FOR AN EXCHANGE OF MONEY-ORDERS BETWEEN THE UNITED STATES OF NORTH AMERICA AND DENMARK.

ARTICLE 1.

Exchange of Money Orders.

Between Denmark and the United States of North America there shall be a regular exchange of money-orders.

ARTICLE 2.

Offices of Exchange.

1. The money-order service between the two countries shall be performed exclusively by means of offices of exchange designated for the purpose.

2. The office of exchange on the part of Denmark shall be Korsör, and on the part of the United States of North America, New York, N. Y.

ARTICLE 3.

Maximum amount of orders.

1. The maximum amount for which a money-order may be drawn in Denmark upon the United States shall be one hundred and eighty-six (186) kroner, 50 öre, and the maximum amount for which a money-order may be drawn in the United States upon Denmark shall be fifty dollars, ($50.)

2. This maximum amount of 186 kroner, 50 öre, or 50 Dollars, may, however, be increased by mutual agreement between the Post Office Departments of the two countries to three hundred and seventy three (373) kroner, or 100 Dollars, provided the Post Office Department of the United States of North America is authorized by law to assent to such an increase.

ARTICLE 4.

Payment in gold coin.

Payment, in either country, shall be made in gold coin, or its equivalent in other current money.

ARTIKEL 1.

Udvexling af Postanvisninger.

Mellem Danmark og de Forenede Stater i Nord-Amerika skal der finde en regelmæssig Udvexling af Postanvisninger Sted.

ARTIKEL 2.

Udvexlingsposttkontorer.

1. Udvexlingen af Postanvisninger imellem de to Lande skal udelukkende ske gjennem dertil bestemte Udvexlingskontorer.

2. Korsör Postkontor er Udvexlingskontor for Danmarks Vedkommende og New York, N. Y., for de Forenede Stater i Nord-Amerika.

ARTIKEL 3.

Maximumsbelöb for Postanvisninger.

1. Det höjeste Belöb for Postanvisninger fra Danmark til de Forenede Stater er Et Hundrede Sex og Firsindstyve (186) kroner 50 Øre og det höjeste Belöb for Postanvisninger fra de Forenede Stater til Danmark er Halftresindstyve (50) Dollars.

2. Disse maximumsbelöb, 186 kroner, 50 Øre, respektive 50 Dollars, kunne imidlertid efter Overenskomst mellem begge Landes Postbestyreler forhöjes til Tre hundrede Tre og Halvfjerdsindstyve (373) Kroner, respektive 100 Dollars forudsat, at Postdepartementet et i de Forenede Stater i Nord-Amerika, ved Lov bemyndiges til at indgaa paa en saadau Forhöjelse.

ARTIKEL 4.

Udbetaling i Guldmönt.

Udbetalingen skal i hvert af Landene ske i Guldmönt eller med tilsvarende Voerdi i anden gangbar Mönt.

11843—P M G 88——51

ARTICLE 5.

Commission.

1. The Post Office Departments of the respective countries shall have power to fix the rates of commission which at different times shall be paid by remitters on money orders issued in the respective countries.

2. This commission shall belong to the country of issue, but the Danish post office shall pay to the post office of the United States one-half of one per cent. on the total amount of all money-orders issued in Denmark for payment in the United States, and the post office of the United States shall make a like payment on the money-orders issued in the United States for payment in Denmark.

3. Such payments to be calculated on the totals of the Lists (A) exchanged every quarter by the two countries.

ARTICLE 6.

Rate of Exchange.

1. The conversion of the money of the one country into that of the other shall be effected in accordance with an average rate of exchange, which is fixed at 3 kroner, 73 öre = 1 dollar in gold.

2. The two offices are, however, authorized to fix, by common agreement, another rate of conversion should the course of exchange between the two countries render such a step necessary.

3. No account will be taken of fractions of a cent, or of four öre.

ARTICLE 7.

Special particulars.

1. Every money-order shall give, in full, the surname and at least the initial of one christian name both of the remitter and of the payee; if the remitter or the payee is a firm or company, the name of such firm or company shall be given. Further, the money-order shall contain the address of the remitter, together with the exact address of the person or firm to whom the money is to be paid.

2. The post office address shall be given with the greatest possible accuracy, and in the case of money-orders upon the United States, the name of the State, and, if possible, of the County in which the post office is situated shall be indicated.

ARTICLE 8.

Duplicate orders.

1. If a money-order is lost or missent a duplicate thereof may be issued upon the written application of the addressee,

ARTIKEL 5.

Postanvisningsafgift.

1. Hver af de to Landes Postbestyrelser skal for sit Vedkommende have Ret til at fastsætte den Afgift, der til de forskjellige Tider skal erlœgges af Afsendere af de i vedkommende Land udstedte Anvisninger.

2. Denne Afgift tilfalder det Land, som har udstedt Auvisningen, men det danske Postvoesen skal til de Forenede Staters Postvoesen betale en halv procent af det sammenlagte Belöb af de Postanvisninger som udstedes i Danmark for at udbetales i de Forenede Stater, og de Forenede Staters Postvoesen skal erlœgge en tilsvarende Betaling for de Postanvisninger, der udstedes i de Forenede Stater for at udbetales i Danmark.

3. Disse Betalinger beregnes efter Hovedsummerne af de Fortegnelser (A) der hvert Kvartal udvexles mellem de 2 Lande.

ARTIKEL 6.

Omsoetningsforholdet.

1. Omsoetningen fra det ene Lands Mönt til det andets skal ske efter en Gjennemsnitskurs, der er fastsat til 3 Kroner 73 Øre = 1 Dollar i Guld.

2. Begge Postbestyrelser ere imidlertid berettigede til efter foelles Overenskomst at fastsœtte et andet Omsœtningsforhold, naar Vexelkursen mellem de 2 Lande skulde gjöre et saadant Skridt fornödent.

3. Brökdele af en cent eller Belöb under 4 Øre tages ikke i Betragtning.

ARTIKEL 7.

Soerlige Forskrifter.

1. Enhver Anvisning skal saavel for Afsenderens som for Adressatens Vedkommende angive det fulde Efternavn og i det mindste Begyndelsesbogstavet til et af den Paagjoeldendes Fornavne; er Afsenderen, henholdsvis Adressaten, et firma eller Selskab, skal detten Navn vœre angivet. Tillige skal Anvisningen indeholde en Angivelse, saavel af Afsenderens Adresse som af den Person eller det Firmas nöjaktige Addresse, til hvem Anvisningen skal betales.

2. Bestemmelsesposthuset skal angives med störst mulig Nöjagtighed, og ved Postanvisninger til de Forenede Stater tillige Navnet paa den Stat og om muligt paa den Kreds ("county"), hvori Bestemmelsesposthuset er beliggende.

ARTIKEL 8.

Duplikatanvisninger.

1. Naar en Postanvisning bortkommer ved Fejlsendelse eller paa anden Maade, skal der paa derom indgiven skriftlig

and such duplicate order shall be issued by the Chief Office of the country of payment.

2. Upon the receipt of such an application from the payee, measures shall be taken to prevent payment of the original order.

ARTICLE 9.

Correction of errors in names of payees.

Correction of errors in names of payees shall be made at the request of the remitters by the Exchange Office of the country of origin.

ARTICLE 10.

Repayment of orders.

1. Repayment of a money order shall in no case be made until the Chief Office of the country of payment shall have reported that the order remains unpaid.

2. At the close of each Quarter each Postal Administration shall draw up, in conformity with Form B, annexed, a List showing the particulars of all orders which it has been authorized to repay to the remitters. The total amount of such list, which is to be transmitted to the 2nd Revisions Department, shall be entered to the credit of such Administration in the account mentioned in Article 17.

ARTICLE 11.

Unpaid money-orders.

1. Money-orders which remain unpaid during twelve calendar months from the month of issue shall become void. The amounts of such money-orders shall accrue to and be at the disposal of the country of origin.

2. The Danish Office shall, therefore enter in the quarterly account, (Article XVII) to the credit of the United States, all money-orders entered in the Lists received from the United States which remain unpaid at the expiration of the period specified.

3. On the other hand, the Post Office Department of the United States shall, at the close of each quarter, transmit to the Danish Office, for entry in the quarterly account, a detailed statement of all orders included in the Lists dispatched from the Danish Office which under this Article become void.

Begjoering fra adressaten kunne udstedes Duplikat af Anvisningen, hvilket Duplikat udfoerdiges af Udvexlingskontoret i Bestemmelseslandet.

2. Naar en saadan Begjoering fremsoettes af Adressaten, skal der gives Ørdre til, at den originale Postanvisning ikke maa udbetales.

ARTIKEL 9.

Rettelser af Fejl i Adressaters Navne.

Rettelser af Fejl i Adressaters Navne skulle paa Afsenderens Begjoering foretages af Udvexlingskontoret i Udstedelseslandet.

ARTIKEL 10.

Tilbagebetaling af Anvisninger.

.1. Tilbagebetaling af en Postanvisning kan aldrig finde Sted, uden at der fra Udvexlingskontoret i det Land, hvar Anvisningen er betalbar, foreligger Meddelelse om, at Anvisningen ikke er bleven udbetalt.

2. Efter hvert Kvartals Udlöb skal hver af de 2 Postbestyrelser affatte en i Overensstemmelse med vedföjede Formular B, udfoerdiget detailleret Fortegnelse over alle de Anvisninger, som den er bleven bemyndiget til at tilbagebetale til Afsenderne. Hoved summen af denne Fortegnelse, der indsendes til 2det Revisionsdepartement, krediteres vedkommende Postvoesen i den i Artikel 17 ommeldte Afregning.

ARTIKEL 11.

Uanbringelige Postanvisninger.

1. Anvisninger, der ikke ere udbetalte inden Udlöbet af 12 Kalendermaaneder efter den Maaned, hvori de ere udstedte, ere ugyldige. Belöbet af saadanne Anvisninger godskrives Afsendelseslandet og staar til dettes Disposition.

2. Den danske Postbestyrelse skal derfor i Kvartalaafregningen (Artikel 17.) kreditere de Forenede Stater Belöbet af alle de Postanvisninger, som findes opförtes paa Fortegnelserne fra de Forenede Stater som uindläte ved Udgangen af vedkommende Tidsperiode.

3. Paa den anden Side skal de Forenede Staters Postdepartement ved Slutningen af hvert Kvartal oversende den danske Postbestyrelse til Optagelse i Kvartals-Afregningen en specificeret Opgjörelse over alle de Postanvisninger, der i Henhold til denne Artikel ere opförte som ikke udbetalte paa de fra det danske Postvoesen modtagne Fortegnelser.

List of money-orders.

1. The two Offices of Exchange shall forward to each other by every mail a statement of the money-orders issued in the one country for payment in the other. Such statements are to be made out on Lists similar to Form A, annexed.

2. Money Orders issued in Denmark towards the end of June, and in the United States towards the end of March, and which are not received at the respective Offices of Exchange before the beginning of the following month, shall be entered and advised to the Office of Exchange of the country to which they are sent, on separate Lists dated the last day of the month in which the amounts were received.

3. When no money order amounts are received, a blank List shall be transmitted.

ARTICLE 13.

International numbers.

Every money-order or amount of a money-order, entered upon the Lists shall bear a number, to be called the "International number" commencing each month with No. 1.

ARTICLE 14.

Acknowledgment of receipt of Lists and duplicates of the same.

1. The receipt of each List shall be acknowledged, on either side, by means of the first subsequent List dispatched in the opposite direction; should a List fail to be received, the Exchange Office to which it should have been sent, shall immediately give notice thereof.
2. In such case the dispatching office of exchange, shall forward to the receiving office, without delay, a duplicate List duly certified as such.

ARTICLE 15.
Verification of Lists.

1. The Lists shall be examined by the receiving office of exchange, which shall correct them when they contain manifest errors.

2. The dispatching office of exchange shall be notified of the corrections made in the acknowledgment of the receipt of the corrected List.

Postanvisningsfortegnelser.

1. De to Udvexlingskontorer skulle med hver afgaaende Post gjensidig tiltille hinanden Opgjörelser over de i hvert Land indbetalte til Udbetaling i det andet Land bestemte Postanvisninger. Hertil benyttes Fortegnelser, udfærdigede i Overensstemmelse med vedföjede Formular A.
2. Postanvisninger, der udstedes i Danmark henimod Slutningen af Juni Maaned og i de Forenede Stater henimod Slutningen af Marts Maaned og som ikke indgaa til de vedkommende Udvexlingskontoret förend de förste Dage i den följende Maaned skulle optages i og meddeles Udvexlingskontoret i det Land, til hvilke de sendes, ved særskilte Tillægsfortegnelser med Datum efter den sidste Dag i den Maaned, i hvilken Anvisningerne ere indbetalte.
3. Naar intet Anvisningsbelöb er indbetalt, afsendes en Vacat-Fortegnelse.

ARTIKEL 13.

Internationalt Nummer.

Enhver Postanvisning saavelsom ethvert paa Fortegnelserne opfört Postanvisningsbelöb, skal forsynes med it Lösenummer, der benævnes "Internationalt Nummer." For hver Maaned begynder med No. 1.

ARTIKEL 14.

Anerkjendelse for Modtagelse af Fortegnelser samt Duplikater af disse.

1. Anerkjendelse for hver Fortegnelses Modtagelse skal fra hvert Lands Side meddeles paa den förste derefter i modsat Retning afsendte Fortegnelse; udebliver Fortegnelse, skal det Udvexlingskontor til hvilket den var bestemt, strax give Anmeldelse derom.
2. I saadant Fald skal Afsenderlandets Udvexlingskontor, uopholdelig tilstille Udvexlingskontoret i Bestemmelseslandet en Duplikatfortegnelse, der udtrykkelig betegnes som saadan.

ARTIKEL 15.
Fortegnelsernes Revision.

1. Fortegnelserne skulle gjennemgaa omhyggelig t af det modtagende Udvexlingskontor, som har at rette dem, saafremt de maatte indeholde aabenbare Fejl.
2. Rettelserne skulle bringes til det afsendende Udvexlingskontors Kundskab samtidig med, at der meddeles Anerkjendelse for Modtagelsen af den rettede Fortegnelse.

3. Should the List contain other irregularities, the receiving exchange office shall demand an explanation from the dispatching exchange office, which shall furnish the same as speedily as possible.

4. Inland orders corresponding to the money-orders in which errors have been discovered shall not be issued until the errors have been corrected.

ARTICLE 16.

Issue of inland orders.

So soon as a money order List shall have been received at the Exchange Office of the country of payment, that Office shall issue inland orders in favor of the payees, and for the amounts specified in the Lists, and shall forward such orders to the paying offices, or the payees, in conformity with the regulations in force in each country for the payment of inland orders.

ARTICLE 17.

1. The Danish Office shall at the close of each quarter prepare an account showing:

1. The totals of the Lists which have been exchanged during the quarter between the two countries (Article 12) with the addition of the commission mentioned in Article 5.

2. The totals of the lists of money-orders which the post office of the country of origin has been authorized to repay to the remitters (Article 10).

3. The totals of the money-orders which in each country have remained unpaid (Article 11).

4. The balance, which the account shows in favor of the one or the other country.

2. Such account, which shall be drawn up in conformity with Form C, annexed, shall be transmitted, in duplicate, by the Danish Post Department to the Post Office Department of the United States, which shall return one copy duly accepted.

ARTICLE 18.

Payment of balance.

1. When the quarterly account shows a balance in favor of the Danish office, the Post Office Department of the United States shall, within 14 days after the receipt of such account, and after the same

---

3. Skulde Fortegnelsen indeholde andre Uregelmæssigheder, skal det modtagende Udvexlingskontor forlange en Erklæring af det afsendende Udvexlingskontor, hvilken dette har at afgive saa hurtigt som muligt.

4. For de Anvisningers Vedkommende med Hensyn til hvilke der findes Fejl i Angivelserne, paa Fortegnelserne, udfærdiges de tilsvarende indenlandske Anvisninger förat, naar Fejlene ere rettede.

ARTIKEL 16.

Udfærdigelsen af indenlandske Postanvisninger.

Saasnart en Postanvisningsfortegnelse indgaar til Udvexlingskontoret i Bestemmelseslandet, udsteder dette Kontor indenlandske Postanvisninger til Adressaterne, lydende paa de paa Fortegnelsen opförte Belöb, hvilke Anvisninger tilstilles Adressaterne eller vedkommende Bestemmelsesposthus efter de Regler, der gjælde i hvert af de 2 Lande for Besörgelsen af indenlandske Postanvisninger.

ARTIKEL 17.

Afregninger.

1. Det danske Postvæsen skal ved hvert Kvartals Slutning udfærdige en Afregning der angiver:
1. Hovedsummerne af de Fortegnelser, der i Kvartalets Löb ere blevne udvexlede mellem begge Lande (Artikel 12) med Tillæg af den ovenfor i Artikel 5 nævnte Afgift.

2. Hovedsummerne af Fortegnelserne over de Postanvisninger, som Afsendelseslandets Postvæsen er bleven bemyndiget til at tilbagebetale til Afsenderne. (Artikel 10.)

3. Hovedsummerne af de Postanvisninger, der i hvert af Landene henstaa som ikke udbetalte. (Artikel 11.)

4. Den Saldo, som Afregningen udviser for det ene eller det andet af de to Landes Postvæsen.

2. Denne Afregning, der udfærdiges i Overensstemmelse med ved hæftede Formular C, sendes i 2 Exemplarer af det danske Postvæsen til Postdepartementet for de Forenede Stater, der tilbagesender det ene Exemplar forsynet med behörig Anerkjendelse.

ARTIKEL 18.

Afregningernes Saldering.

1. Naar den fjerdingaarlige Afregning udviser en Fordring for det danske Postvæsen skal de nord-amerikanske Fristaters Postbestyrelse senest 14 Dage efter Afregningens Modtagelse og, efterat den

has been duly examined and accepted, return one copy, and at the same time transmit to the Director General of the Danish Post Department a draft for the amount of the balance due, payable at Copenhagen. Receipt of such draft shall be acknowledged.

2. Should the quarterly account show a balance in favor of the Post Office Department of the United States, the latter, after proper examination and acceptance thereof, shall return one copy. Within 14 days after the receipt of such copy by the Danish Office it shall forward to the Post Office Department of the United States, a draft for the balance due, drawn in favor of the Postmaster-General, and payable at New York. Receipt of such draft shall be acknowledged.

3. The payment of the balance shall be always made in the money of the creditor country and without deduction, and all expenses in the matter shall be at the charge of the debtor country.

4. Should at any time, one of the Post Offices be the creditor of the other for paid money orders amounting to a total exceeding 20,000 kroner, the creditor office shall have the right to demand a provisional payment amounting to three-fourths of the sum due. In such case the payment shall take place immediately.

5. In the event of the balance of an account not being paid within the period specified under paragraphs 1 and 2 above, the amount of such balance shall be chargeable, with interest, from the date of such period, until the day of the transmission of the amount due. Such interest shall be computed at the rate of 5 per cent. per annum, and is to be entered in the accounts next following as a debit against the dilatory Administration.

ARTICLE 19.

Additional rules.

1. The Director General of Posts of each country shall have power to adopt additional rules for the greater security against fraud, or for the better working of the system generally, provided they do not conflict with any of the foregoing provisions.
2. All such additional rules, however, must be communicated to the Postmaster General of other country.

ARTICLE 20.

Power to increase commission, or to suspend issue of orders.

Should it appear that money-orders are used by merchants or other persons in

er bleven behörig prövet og godkjendt, tibagesende det ene Exemplar af den og samtidig oversende en paa Saldobelöbet lydende, til det danske Postvæsens Overbestyrelse betalbar Vexel paa Kjöbenhavn. Herefter tilstiller nævnte Overbestyrelse de nord-amerikanske Fristaters Postbestyrelse en Anerkjendelse for Vexlens Modtagelse.

2. Udviser Afregningen en Fordring for de nord-amerikanske Fristaters Postbestyrelse, tilbagesender denne, efter forudgaat behörig Prövelse og Godkjendelse af Afregningen, det ene Exemplar af denne. Senest 14 Dage efterat dette Exemplar er modtaget af den danske Postbestyrelse, skal denne tilstille de nord-amerikanske Fristaters Postbestyrelse en paa Saldobelöbet lydende, til den nord-amerikanske General-Postmester betalbar Vexel paa New York, for hvis Modtagelse Anerkjendelse udstedes.

3. Saldoen skal altid uden Afkortning erlægges i det betalingsberettigede Lands Mönt, og alle Udgifter i den Anledning blive at udrede af det betalingspligtige Land.

4. Skule nogensinde det ene Postvæsens Tilgodehavende hos det andet for udbetalte Postanvisninger overskride et Belöb af 20,000 Kroner, er det vedkommende Postvæsen berettiget til at fordre en Afbetaling eller en midlertidig Saldering af indtil Tre Fjerdedele af det skyldige Belöb. I dette Tilfælde skal Betalingen strax finde Sted.

5. Hvis Betalingen af en Afregnings-Saldo ikke sker inden Belöbet af de oven for under 1 og 2 angivne Frister, skal Saldobelöbet forrentes fra den nævnte Tid indtil den Dag da det skyldidge Belöb sendes. Denne Rentes beregnes efter en Rentefod af 5 procent pro anno og debiteras i den nærmest fölgende Afregning det Postvæsen, der ikke har erlagt Betalingen i rette Tid.

ARTIKEL 19.

Tillægsbestemmelser.

1. Chefen for hvert Lands Postbestyrelse har Ret til, for at tilvejebringe större Sikkerhed med Besvigelser eller för at lette Gjennemförelsen af Systemet i Almindelighed, at fastsætte Tillægsbestemmelser, der dog ikke maa stride mod oven staaende Bestemmelser.
2. Chefen for det andet Lands Postvæsens skal dog have Underretning om, at saadanne Tillægsbestemmelser ere givne.

ARTIKEL 20.

Ret til at forhöje Postanvisningsafgiften og til at suspendere Udstedelsen af Postanvisninger.

Skulde det vise sig, at Postanvisninger benyttes af Handlende eller andre Per-

Denmark, or the United States, for the transmission of large sums of money, the Danish Office, or the Post Office Department of the United States as the case may be, may increase the commission upon money-orders, and shall have power to suspend for a time, or even wholly, the issue of money-orders.

soner i Danmark eller i de Forenede Stater til Forsendelse af större Summer skal henholdsvis den danske Postbestyrelse eller de Forenede Staters Postdepartement kunne forhöje Postanvisningsafgiften og have Ret til for en Tid endog helt at suspendere Udstedelsen af Postanvisninger.

ARTICLE 21.

Commencement and termination of Convention.

This Convention shall come into operation on the 1st of January 1888, and shall be terminable on a notice, by either party, of six calendar months.

Done in duplicate and signed at Washington, the eleventh day of November, 1887, and at Copenhagen, the twenty-ninth day of November 1887.

(signed)   WM. F. VILAS,
*Postmaster General
of the United States.*

[Seal of the Post-Office Department of the United States.]

ARTIKEL 21.

Konventionens Ikrafttræden og Varighed.

Denne Konvention træder i Kraft den 1ste Januar, 1888, og ophörer at gjælde, naar den fra en af Siderne opsiges med 6 Kalendermaaneders Varsel.

Udfærdiget i 2 Exemplarer og underskrevet i Washington, den Ellente i November, 1887, og i Kjöbenhavn, den ni og tyvende November, 1887.

(signed)   LUND,
*Chefen for det danske
Postvæsens Overbestyrelse.*

[Seal of the Director-General of Posts, Denmark.]

NOTE.—The following changes in the foregoing Convention have been mutually agreed to by the Postal Administrations of the two countries, by means of correspondence. [Letter from Copenhagen July 9th, 1888; reply from Washington, July 27th, 1888.]

In the English text.

Art. 12, par. 1.—Between the words "statement" and "of" insert the words "in duplicate."

Art. 14, par. 1.—Change as follows: "Acknowledgment of the receipt of each "list shall be made by each country by "means of one of the copies received, at "the same time with the dispatch of the "next list forwarded in the opposite di-"rection; should a list fail to be received, "the Exchange Office to which it should "have been sent shall immediately give "notice thereof."

In the Danish text.

Art. 12, par. 1.—Between the words "opgjörelser" and "over" insert the words "i 2 exemplarer."

Art. 14, par. 1.—Change as follows: "Anerkjendelse for hver Fortegnelses "Modtagelse skal fra hvert Lands Side "meddeles paa det ene af de modtagne "Exemplarer samtidig med Afsendelsen "af den förste Fortegnelse i modsat Ret-"ning; udebliver en Fortegnelse, skal "det Udvexlingskontor, til hvilket den "er bestemt, strax gjöre Anmeldelse de-"rom."

A.

KORSÖR POST OFFICE,
———, ———, 188-.

To the Post Office, New York, N. Y.:

I have received your List of the ———, 188-, relative to orders drawn in the United States, Nos. ———, to ———, and payable to persons residing in Denmark.

The examination which has taken place has proved the correctness of the totals, viz: Kr. ——— öre., or ——— dollars ——— cents.

In return, I transmit to you, herewith, a detailed account of the amounts received in Denmark for orders payable in the United States, the particulars of which have reached this office since the dispatch of my last List, No. ———.

Your obedient servant,

———————.

A.

KORSÖR POSTKONTOR,
den ———, ———, 188-,

Til Postkontoret i New York:

Jeg har modtaget Deres Fortegnelse af den 188- over Postanvisninger, udstedte i de Forenede Stater No. ———, til ——— og betalbare til Adressater i Danmark.

Den stedfundne Revision har godtgjort Rigtigheden af Fortegnelsens Hovedsummer, nemlig Kr.———, øre ———, eller $———.

Paa min Side tilstiller jeg Dem herved en specificeret Fortegnelse over de i Danmark indbetalte, og i de Forenede Stater betalbare Postanvisningsbeløb, over hvilke Opgjörelser ere indkomne hertil eftre Afsendelsen af min sidste Fortegnelse No. ———.

Ærbödigst,

B.

—— Quarter, 188—.

List of money-orders from Denmark to the United States of North America which the country of origin has been authorized to repay to the remitter.

Date.	International number.	Original number.	Issuing office.	Amount in United States money.		Amount in Danish money.	
				Dollars.	Cts.	Kr.	Öre.
			Total.......................				

A.

FORTEGNELSE No. ——.

┌─────────────┐
│ Postkontorets │
│ stempel. │
└─────────────┘

Daglig Fortegnelse over Postanvisninger, udfærdigede i Danmark og betal-
bare i de Forenede Stater i Nord-Amerika.

Anvisningens dato.	Internationalt No.	Udstedelses No.	Indbetalings posthuset.	Afsenderens navn und adresse.	Modtagerens fulde navn.	Modtagerens fuldstændige adresse.			Det i Danmark indbetalte Beløb.		Anvisningen udbetales i de forenede Stater med.		Anmærkninger.
						Posthus.	Stat.	County.	Kr.	Øre.	Dolls.	Cts.	

B.

— *Quarter, 188—.*

List of money-orders from Denmark to the United States of North America which the country of origin has been authorized to repay to the remitter.

Date.	International number.	Original number.	Issuing office.	Amount in United States money.		Amount in Danish money.	
				Dollars.	*Cts.*	*Kr.*	*Öre.*
			Total				

B.

—— Kvartal, 188—.

Fortegnelse over Postanvisninger fra Danmark til de Forenede Stater i Nord-Amerika, hvilke Afsendelseslandet er blevet bemyndiget til at tilbagebetale til Afsenderne.

Dato.	Internationalt Nummer.	Udstedelses Nummer.	Indbetalingskontoret.	Belöbet i amerikansk Mönt.		Belöbet i dansk Mönt.	
				Dollars.	Cts.	Kr.	Öre.
			Summa				

REPORT

OF THE

SUPERINTENDENT OF FOREIGN MAILS

TO THE

POSTMASTER-GENERAL

FOR

1888.

Weights and percentages of the mails dispatched to foreign countries—Continued.

TRANSPACIFIC AND MISCELLANEOUS SERVICE.

Countries.	Letters and post-cards.	Per cent.	Other articles.	Per cent.
	Grams.		*Grams.*	
Cuba	3, 205, 686	11. 31	30, 030, 773	8. 67
Porto Rico (direct)	168, 330	....	1, 181, 460	....
Bermuda	780, 685	....	7, 413, 270	....
Windward Islands	1, 307, 540	....	11, 919, 562	....
Jamaica	581, 515	....	6, 336, 240	....
Hayti	406, 150	....	4, 398, 420	....
Bahamas	262, 520	.92	3, 051, 749	.88
St. Thomas and Porto Rico (via Cuba)	187, 999	....	2, 801, 789	....
San Domingo	169, 320	....	2, 519, 100	....
Curaçoa	299, 245	....	1, 362, 220	....
Turk's Island	59, 635	....	456, 725	....
St. Thomas (direct)	2, 231	....	27, 470	....
Hawaiian Kingdom	1, 711, 751	....	21, 068, 887	....
Japan	2, 703, 883	....	27, 465, 617	....
Hong-Kong	1, 473, 636	....	4, 872, 839	....
Tahiti	74, 889	....	1, 364, 683	....
Java	7, 877	....	51, 782	....
Manilla	67, 410	.20	901, 998	.26
Siam	5, 781	....	125, 720	....
Singapore	16, 022	....	256, 065	....
New Caledonia	8, 644	....	121, 492	....
Cochin China	5, 682	....	45, 499	....
United States Consul, Shanghai	595, 056	....	9, 649, 729	....
Marquesas Islands	4, 942	....	113, 107	....
United States of Colombia	1, 687, 453	5. 95	19, 073, 424	5. 51
Guatemala	608, 348	....	7, 212, 119	....
Republic of Honduras	385, 308	....	4, 305, 974	....
Nicaragua	394, 398	1. 39	4, 808, 373	1. 34
Costa Rica	431, 184	....	4, 813, 440	....
Salvador	308, 545	....	3, 678, 945	....
Brazil	1, 177, 626	....	15, 099, 780	....
Argentine Republic	578, 351	....	10, 991, 226	....
Uruguay	151, 700	....	2, 965, 602	....
Paraguay	6, 070	....	144, 520	....
Chili	478, 248	1. 68	13, 388, 531	3. 86
Peru	525, 822	....	10, 423, 101	....
Venezuela	922, 070	....	10, 356, 445	....
Ecuador	304, 366	....	3, 600, 131	....
Bolivia	47, 925	....	1, 465, 420	....
Mexico	928, 572	3. 27	10, 357, 180	2. 99
Newfoundland	25, 215	....	198, 555	....
St. Pierre and Miquelon	3, 715	.01	12, 545	....
Australia	2, 734, 444	....	82, 776, 689	....
Nova Scotia	526, 638	....		....
British Columbia	1, 569, 842	....	1, 768, 505	....
British Honduras	212, 170	....	1, 290, 045	....
From United States Consul at Shanghai	256, 569	....	459, 170	....
Martinque and Guadaloupe	7, 040	....	65, 019	....
Total	:28, 337, 078	....	§346, 083, 996	....

* Or 581,130 pounds.   † Or 2,259,877 pounds.   ‡ Or 62,483 pounds.   §Or 763,115 pounds.

Total weight of mail in grams:
Letters and post-cards 291, 888, 622
Other articles 1, 376, 971, 363
Total weight of mail in pounds:
Letters and post-cards 643, 616
Other articles 3, 022, 992

FOREIGN MAIL STATISTICS.

Estimate of the amount of mail matter exchanged with all foreign countries (including Mexico and Canada by rail and sea) during the fiscal year ended June 30, 1888, based upon the count of such matter exchanged during seven days of October, 1887, and seven days of April, 1888, as made at United States exchanging post-offices in pursuance of the Postmaster-General's order of September 11, 1885.

	Sent.	Received.	Total.	Excess of sent over received.	Excess of received over sent.
Number of prepaid letters	42,785,942	36,758,676	79,544,618	6,027,266	....
Number of unpaid and insufficiently prepaid letters........................	724,094	1,692,688	2,416,782	....	968,594
Number of postal-cards	1,860,924	1,803,616	3,664,540	57,308	....
Number of postal-cards with paid reply..	....	36,992	36,992	....	....
Number of articles of printed matter..	43,229,744	35,322,868	78,552,612	7,906,876	....
Number of commercial papers	102,232	18,278	120,510	83,954	....
Number of packages of samples of merchandise	375,638	868,042	1,243,680	....	502,404
Number of letters free of postage	139,338	119,984	159,322	19,354	....
Number of other articles free of postage	9,022	8,924	17,946	98	....
Total number of articles	89,226,934	76,630,068	165,857,002	12,596,866	....
Number of registered letters..........	696,064	754,880	1,450,944	....	58,816
Number of other articles registered ..	65,176	104,890	170,066	....	39,714
Number of demands for return receipts	26,120	24,496	50,616	1,624	....
Prepaid postages on letters	$1,728,658.99	....	....	....	....
Prepaid postages on postal-cards......	20,699.60	....	....	....	....
Prepaid postages on other articles ...	379,284.79	....	....	....	....
Unpaid postages on letters	36,754.60	$164,689.50	$201,446.10	....	$127,932.90
Unpaid postages on other articles	2,332.20	1,852.62	4,184.82	$179.58	....

COST OF THE SERVICE.

The sums reported on account of the Shanghai and Panama Postal Agencies, the Panama Railway, and the sea-transportation of the United States mails, including "open and closed mail matter" from foreign countries, dispatched from the United States (and including also the inward service on mails from non-convention countries) during the fiscal year ended June 30, 1888, amounted to $464,910.70, distributed as follows:

For Shanghai Agency	$1,534.14
For Panama Agency	856.44
For Panama Railway transit	6,618.16
For Transatlantic service	353,262.08
For Transpacific service..	42,593.13
For West Indian, Mexican, Canadian, Newfoundland, and Central and South American service	58,553.61
	463,417.56
The sums reported for payment on account of transportation of mails of foreign origin during the fiscal year ended June 30, 1888, was.........	26,649.73
Total cost of service	490,067.29
From the above must be deducted the amount of mail matter conveyed by foreign steam-ship companies under subvention and settled for in account of balances due foreign countries............................	25,156.59
	464,910.70
Estimate made in 1886 for fiscal year ended June 30, 1888..............	465,000.00
Cost of service in 1887...	350,882.13
Estimate in 1885 for fiscal year ended June 30, 1887	350,000.00

The following foreign postal agencies were maintained by the United States during the fiscal year ended June 30, 1888: (1) Shanghai, China ; (2) Panama, Republic of Colombia.

As the account of the postal agent at Shanghai for the fourth quarter of the fiscal year ended June 30, 1888, had not reached this office when this report was closed, the amount for that quarter has been estimated on the average of the three preceding quarters.

(1) Shanghai:
  Expenditure:

Clerk-hire	$1,200.00
Messenger and other labor	512.13
Rent	200.00
Gas and fuel	27.65
Miscellaneous	90.36
Total	1,830.14

Income:

Box rents	296.00
Net cost of agency	1,534.14

(2) Panama:
  Expenditure:

Clerk-hire	600.00
Transportation of mails	180.00
Porterage of mails	60.00
Cable messages	16.44
Total	856.44
Net cost of both agencies	2,390.58

Transatlantic service.

[2.205 lbs. =1 kilogram ; 5 francs per kilogram = about 44 cents per pound ; 50 centimes per kilogram = about 4½ cents per pound.]

Name of steam-ship line.	Letters.	Prints.	Compensation.*
	Grams.	*Grams.*	
North German Lloyd	130,274,844	500,597,483	$174,622.80
Cunard (from New York)	66,003,150	255,876,778	88,385.17
White Star	11,568,421	31,515,410	14,204.76
Liverpool and Great Western	20,848,242	86,910,796	28,505.44
Anchor	3,850,262	14,199,070	5,094.40
Hamburg-American	10,672,685	44,806,521	14,628.76
American †	15,758	146,372	81.46
Inman	856,848	4,529,223	1,263.44
Cunard (from Boston)	1,263,200	7,171,340	1,911.03
Thingvalla	3,070	18,411	4.72
Steamer *Cumbrian* (to Africa)	1,365	22,890	3.47
General Transatlantic ‡	18,170,966	78,750,009	23,134.53
Red Star ‡	9,279	1,075	18.93
Netherlands Steam Navigation Company ‡	4,345	283,490	3.13
Total	263,550,944	1,024,866,367	353,282.08

* At the rate of 5 francs per kilogram of letters and 50 centimes per kilogram of prints.
† American Steam-ship Company : Letters, $1.50 per pound ; prints, 8 cents per pound.
‡ Settled for in account of balances due foreign countries.

Transpacific service.

VESSELS OF AMERICAN REGISTER.

Name of steam-ship line.	Letters.	Prints.	Compensation.
	Pounds.	*Pounds.*	
Pacific Mail : San Francisco to Japan...............................	5,920	53,040	$13,715.41
Occidental and Oriental : San Francisco to Japan.................	1,274	12,462	3,045.79
Oceanic * : San Francisco to Australian colonies.................	7,599	202,393	20,000.00
Pacific Mail : Inward service	247	436	430.65
Occidental and Oriental : Inward service	70	101	121.01
Total...	15,110	268,432	37,302.86

Note.— Compensation at the rate of $1.60 per pound of letters and 8 cents per pound of prints.
* Contract service at $20,000 per year.

VESSELS OF FOREIGN REGISTER.

	Grams.	*Grams.*	
Oceanic : San Francisco to Hawaii.................................	917,094	10,356,599	$1,699.15
Occidental and Oriental : San Francisco to Japan.................	1,705,613	15,259,342	3,118.44
Canadian Pacific: San Francisco to Japan	7,457	27,633	9.86
Occidental and Oriental : Inward service..........................	112,393	215,342	129.24
Oceanic : † Inward service...	250,185	....	333.58
Total...	2,992,742	25,858,916	5,290.27
Total cost of transpacific service..............................	....	....	42,593.13

Note.—Compensation at the rate of 5 francs per kilogram of letters and 50 centimes per kilogram of prints.
† Paid at the rate of 2 cents per letter of 15 grams.

Miscellaneous service.

VESSELS OF AMERICAN REGISTER.

Name of steamship lines.	Destination.	Letters.	Prints.	Compensation.
		Pounds.	*Pounds.*	
Pacific Mail (from New York)	United States of Colombia..	7,132	109,276	$20,153.09
Pacific Mail (from San Francisco)......	......do	1,216½	7,360	2,535.13
New York and Cuba Mail.............	Cuba......................	107½	296	195.42
Steamer *Haytien Republic*.............	Hayti and Turk's Islands...	195½	1,788	307.57
Lord & Austin.........................	......do	54	918	175.95
Clyde.................................	Hayti and San Domingo	426½	5,529	1,124.73
Red "D"...............................	Venezuela and Curacoa......	2,593½	24,180	6,084.14
Winchester & Co	Porto Rico.................	26½	84	49.22
New York, Havana and Mexican.......	Mexico	282½	2,656	664.73
Royal Mail	Central America............	1,583	17,013	3,893.51
Do................................	Cuba......................	76½	432	156.61
Do................................	Mexico	39½	19	64.58
Do................................	Central America............	218	1,673	483.39
Oteri's Pioneer	Honduras and Guatamala ..	128	1,950	380.67
United States and Brasil Mail........	Brasil and Windward Islands.	4,128	64,113	11,733.44
New Orleans and Colombia	United States of Colombia..	9	6	14.89
Pacific Mail*.........................	Inward service	79	....	76.38
Pacific Coast†........................	British Columbia	331	3,877	112.36
Oregon Railway and Navigation Company.†	......do	3,130	....	1,321.36
Total		21,675	241,123	49,506.19

Note.—Compensation at the rate of $1.60 per pound of letters and 8 cents per pound of prints.
* Paid for at 2 cents a letter.   † Paid for at 1 cent per letter.

Miscellaneous service—Continued.

VESSELS OF FOREIGN REGISTER.

Name of steamship lines.	Destination.	Letters.	Prints.	Compensation.
		Grams.	*Grams.*	
New York and Cuba	Bahamas	243,715	2,969,045	$521.70
Thomas Ross & Co	West Indies and Venezuela.	23,715	338,530	55.55
George Christals	do	2,870	57,050	8.27
Red Cross	Brazil, etc	107,496	885,838	189.20
Atlantic and West India	Windward Islands	265,500	2,419,717	489.71
W. W. Hurlburt & Co	Central America	1,035	8,830	1.85
Theband Brothers	Venezuela	19,650	231,650	35.89
Do	Mexico	10,105	88,290	23.71
Dominican	Haytì and San Domingo	41,010	534,960	91.20
Williams & Rankine	Central America	158,760	1,681,485	315.47
Perkins & Welsh	Porto Rico	30,860	193,820	48.49
Quebec	Bermuda	760,685	7,413,270	1,419.44
Do	West Indies	662,515	5,974,835	1,213.89
Booth	Brazil	76,075	379,520	110.03
New York and Jamaica	Jamaica	27,525	273,725	52.94
Atlas	Haytì, Jamaica, etc	1,095,625	11,301,895	2,147.92
Winchester & Company	Brazil, Uruguay, etc	18,493	364,797	53.05
Earn Line	Cuba and the West Indies	14,013	110,166	24.16
Funch Edye & Company	Porto Rico	7,505	22,790	9.44
New York and Yucatan	Mexico	1,750	23,555	3.96
Costa Rica and Honduras	Central America	183,530	1,980,105	309.15
Harrison's	United States of Columbia	6,120	10,740	6.94
Oteri's Pioneer	Central America	27,675	276,855	53.42
New Orleans and Central American	Central America	13,230	87,225	21.19
Steamer *Alejandro*	Mexico	2,575	48,951	7.21
Del Campo	Central America	39,352	350,884	71.83
Diamond	Haytì	2,800	73,630	9.81
Coleman	Bahamas	6,845	2,235	6.34
Cush & Curry	Bahamas	4,560	4,334	4.82
F. H. Rohr	Porto Rico	16,315	51,640	20.73
Taurus	Porto Rico	17,395	58,750	22.44
Royal Dutch West India Mail*	Haytì, etc	11,000	18,285	12.38
Steamer *Kiel*	Argentine Republic, etc	43,715	635,085	105.40
Hammonia	Brazil, etc	325,747	7,327,461	1,021.44
Leaycraft & Company	West Indies	1,240	10,775	2.62
Yarmouth†	Nova Scotia	328,428		310.84
Boston, Halifax, and Prince Edward Island‡	Nova Scotia	198,210		152.73
Total		§4,797,259	§46,245,763	9,047.42

* Settled for in account of balances due foreign countries.
† One cent per letter.
‡ Or 10,577 pounds.
§ Or 101,972 pounds.
NOTE—Compensation at the rate of 5 francs per kilogram of letters, and 50 centimes per kilogram of prints.

Foreign closed-mail serv

TRANSATLANTIC SERVICE.

Name of line.	Letters.	Prints.	Compensation.
	Grams.	*Grams.*	
North German Lloyds	11,489,328	29,816,981	$13,964.55
Cunard	4,820,211	11,360,414	5,747.79
Guion	2,189,884	5,426,630	2,636.90
White Star	1,154,134	3,176,144	1,430.24
Anchor	525,314	1,241,468	626.73
Hamburg-American	374,360	911,031	449.17
Inman	28,171	58,583	32.84
General Transatlantic	758,693	2,625,313	965.49
Total	*21,340,095	†54,616,564	25,863.71

* Or 47,055 pounds. † Or 120,430 pounds.

Foreign closed-mail service—Continued.

MISCELLANEOUS SERVICE.

Name of line.	Letters.	Prints.	Compensation.
	Grams.	*Grams.*	
Quebec	19,704	202,173	38.52
United States and Brazil	2,385	77,530	9.78
New York and Cuba	147,590	2,538,416	387.32
New York and Jamaica	1,701	2,035	1.84
Atlas	17,531	85,100	25.13
Atlantic and West India	487	21,809	2.57
Clyde	15,500	201,741	34.43
Dominican	2,314	46,773	6.77
Pacific Mail	41,422	1,112,525	147.32
Red " D "	51,628	472,961	95.47
Williams & Rankine	980	27,006	3.56
Steamer *Haytien Republic*	3,141	82,559	11.00
Steamer *Alert*	9,832	117,324	20.81
Steamer *Thames*	1,297	1,971	1.44
Total	*315,532	†4,969,988	786.02

* Or 696 pounds. † Or 11,003 pounds.

ESTIMATES FOR THE FISCAL YEAR ENDING JUNE 30, 1890.

The amount estimated as necessary to be appropriated for the foreign mail service for the fiscal year ending June 30, 1890, is $760,000.

This sum is composed of the following items, viz: For the transportation of mails of United States origin, including open mail matter of foreign origin, $613,738.97; closed mails of foreign origin, $30,000; railway transit across the Isthmus of Panama, $7,000; maintenance of the United States postal agencies at Panama and Shanghai, $2,500; contingencies, $1,761.03; for balances due foreign countries for intermediary transit, the United States portion of the expenses of the International Bureau of the Universal Postal Union, and the subscription of this Department to the monthly journal (l'Union Postale) of that Bureau, $100,000; and the expenses of the United States delegates to the Vienna postal congress of 1890, $5,000.

There may be an increase during the next fiscal year in the balances due foreign countries, but this Department has no basis on which to estimate this increase, as the next statistical period does not take place till May, 1890.

The cost of the sea conveyance of the United States mails in 1887 and 1888 exceeded that for 1886 and 1887 as follows, viz: Weight of the mails conveyed to ports to which American vessels do not ply was:

	Letters.	Prints.
Fiscal year ended June 30 :	*Pounds.*	*Pounds.*
1887	513,533	2,045,772
1886	464,360	1,930,817
Increase	49,173	114,955
1888	581,130	2,259,877
1887	513,533	2,045,772
Increase	67,597	214,105
Percentage of increase :		
1886-'87	10.59	5.95
1887-'88	13.15	10.46
	23.74	16.41
Average	11.87	8.20

At this rate of increase, 11.87 per cent. for letters, and 8.20 for printed matter, the weights for the fiscal year ending June 30, 1890, will give:

Letters :

	Pounds.
Fiscal year ended June 30, 1888	581,130
Add 11.87 per cent. increase	68,980
Weight in 1889	650,110
Add 11.87 per cent. increase	77,168
Weight in 1890	727,278

Prints :

	Pounds.
Fiscal year ended June 30, 1888	2,259,877
Add 8.20 per cent. increase	185,309
Weight in 1889	2,445,186
Add 8.20 per cent. increase	200,505
Weight in 1890	2,645,691

The cost of conveying the above amount of mail, at 5 francs per kilogram of letters and post-cards (44 cents per pound), and 50 centimes per kilogram for printed matter (4½ cents per pound), will make the total cost of this service—

For letters and post-cards	$320,002.32
For printed matter	119,056.09
Total	439,058.41

The weight of the mails conveyed to ports to which American vessels ply was :

	Letters.	Prints.
	Pounds	*Pounds.*
Fiscal year ended June 30—		
1886	50,299	489,618
1887	48,053	589,959
Decrease	2,246	....
Increase		100,341
1888	55,020	688,229
1887	48,053	589,959
Increase	6,967	98,270
Percentage of decrease 1886–'87	4.67	....
Percentage of increase 1886–'87	....	20.48
Percentage of increase 1887–'88	14.49	16.65
	9.82	37.13
Average percentage	4.91	18.56

At this rate of increase, 4.91 per cent. for letters and 18.56 for printed matter, the weights for the fiscal year ending June 30, 1890, will give:

Letters :

	Pounds.
Fiscal year ended June 30, 1888	55,020
Add 4.91 per cent. increase	2,701
Weight in 1889	57,721
Add 4.91 per cent. increase	2,834
Weight in 1890	60,555

Pounds.

Prints:

Fiscal year ended June 30, 1888.. 688. 229
Add 18.56 per cent. increase 127, 735

Weight in 1889 .... 815, 964
Add 18.56 per cent. increase 156, 443

Weight, in 1890 .... 972, 407

The cost of conveying the above amount of mail, at the sea and inland postage ($1.60 per pound of letters and post-cards, and 8 cents per pound of printed matter), will be:

For letters and post-cards $96, 888. 00
For printed matter 77, 792. 56

Total 174, 680. 56

Add the amounts, viz:

For conveyance of mails to ports to which American vessels do not ply.. 439, 058. 41
For conveyance of mails to ports to which American vessels ply 174, 680. 56
Balances due foreign countries 100, 000. 00
Closed mails 30, 000. 00
Isthmus transit 7, 000. 00
Shanghai and Panama postal agencies 2, 500. 00
Vienna Congress of 1890 .... 5, 000. 00
Contingencies 1, 761. 03

Total 760, 000. 00

Number of sailings annually, for a period of six years (from July 1, 1882, to June 30, 1888), of steamers from New York, New Orleans, and San Francisco to the West Indies, and to the Central and South American States.

Year ended June 30—	From New York.	From New Orleans.	From San Francisco.	Total.
1883..	416	114	30	560
1884..	413	116	36	565
1885..	471	164	36	671
1886..	470	199	43	712
1887..	545	231	55	831
1888..	540	278	43	861

TRANSATLANTIC STEAM-SHIP SERVICE.

Most of the countries of Europe dispatch their mails for the United States by the fastest steamers offered, without regard to the register or flag of the vessel. Great Britain, however, continues to confine the dispatch of all its regular mails to the vessels of the Cunard and White Star (English) Lines, the vessels sailing from Queenstown.

The time required for the conveyance of mails from London to Queenstown is eighteen hours and thirty-five minutes; and from London to Southampton, two hours and forty-five minutes. The vessels of the North German Lloyd Steamship Line sail from Southampton the same day that the White Star vessels sail from Queenstown, and arrive at the port of New York at about the same time, as will be seen from the following tables, Nos. 1 and 2. If the German vessels were allowed to convey from Southampton the mails that accumulate after the departure from London of the mails for dispatch by the Cunard or White Star vessels sailing from Queenstown, it would save not only the difference in the time required to convey the mails from London to Queenstown, and South-

ampton, but advance the dispatch of said mails, now delayed by being
held for dispatch by the next Cunard or White Star steamer sailing
from Queenstown two days after the German vessel sails from Southampton. Therefore, the mails that accumulate before the departure of
the German vessels are always delayed from one to three days.

It will be seen from Table No. 1, " From London to New York," that
in one month the regular mails were subjected to nine delays, amounting
in all to twenty-two days, six hours, and fifty-two minutes; while
from Table No. 2, " From New York to London," it will be observed
that in every instance the steamer to which the mails were awarded delivered them earlier than they would have been delivered had they been
conveyed by any other steamer tendered to this Department. In this
connection it may be well to state that the British mails represent 44 per
cent. of all the mails exchanged between the United States and European
countries. While the country of origin, by treaty stipulation, has absolute control of the dispatch of its mails by whatever route it may
deem proper, in view of the important business relations existing between the two countries, it is to be regretted that the correspondence
exchanged between them should be made to pay tribute to methods
local.

The commercial and manufacturing interests of the country petitioned
your predecessor to use his good offices with the transatlantic Governments to secure the adoption on their part of a policy similar to that
enforced by this Department in dispatching the mails by the fastest
vessel, without regard to the registry or flag of the vessel. This peti-
tion was signed by gentlemen representing hundreds of millions of capital, and largely engaged in international business enterprises between
the United States and Europe, and was transmitted through the State
Department to all the Governments of Europe.

Great Britain replied through her prime minister as follows:

I have the honor to inform you that Her Majesty's postmaster-general has had
under his consideration the representation of the United States Postmaster-General,
copy of which was inclosed in your note of the 7th ultimo, respecting the postal communication from Europe to the United States.

In reply to your above-mentioned note, I beg to assure you that the influentially
signed expression of opinion inclosed therein will not be lost sight of when an opportunity occurs for reconsidering the arrangements now in force for the conveyance of
the mails from this country to New York, but as you are doubtless aware the efforts
which Her Majesty's postmaster-general has from time to time made to adopt the
American transatlantic system have not received so much support in this country as
would at present warrant a disturbance of existing arrangements.

The rates of compensation for sea conveyance of mails to foreign
countries paid by Great Britain, Germany, and the United States, to
national and foreign steamship companies, are shown in the following
table:

Countries.	To national steamers.		To foreign steamers.	
	Letters per pound.	Prints, etc., per pound.	Letters, per pound.	Prints, etc., per pound.
	Cents.	Cents.	Cents.	Cents.
Great Britain	72	6⅓	44	4⅓
Germany	56½	4.3	41	4½
United States	100	8	44	4½

The postal contract of Great Britain with the Cunard Steamship
Company is separate and distinct from the contract of the company

with the Admiralty. The postal contract is for a term of three years and provides for the conveyance of the mails as cargo at so much a pound, as shown in the above table. The Admiralty contract is for a period of five years, with a subvention at so much per registered ton, per annum.

The system of paying for the mails as cargo, at so much a pound, has proved so advantageous that it is hoped there will be no return to the old method, involving the payment of subsidies for the mail service.

If it should be the pleasure of Congress to make an appropriation to aid American steamers plying in trade with foreign ports, it would be a detriment to the efficiency of the foreign mail service to charge it with the administration of such an appropriation.

The wonderful advancement being made in naval architecture, so far as speed of the vessels is concerned, makes it questionable to tie the Post-Office Department in long contracts to certain lines of vessels which may be considered fast to-day but very slow to-morrow; and the policy of dispatching the mails by the fastest steamers tendered, has met with so much favor with all classes of people, that if at this late day they were deprived of the privilege of dispatching their letters by the quickest possible route it would undoubtedly create much dissatisfaction.

As to the system of dispatch of the mails by the fastest steamers, and obtaining the data for such dispatch, I have to say that the Department requires the various exchange offices dispatching the mails from the United States to foreign countries by sea, to make report of the hour and minute that the mails are received by the steamer, and requires the steamer to report the day, hour, and minute that the mails are delivered at the port of destination.

In the case of the transatlantic mails, the London office reports once a week to this Department the day, hour, and minute that the mails are received at the office from each steamer.

From these various reports of the time occupied in the transit of the mails to the office of destination, the mails are awarded, on the 15th of each month, for the next calendar month, to the steamers which show the greatest average speed for the three trips immediately preceding the award; and under this system the mails have been materially expedited, in some instances more than a business day.

In several instances the transatlantic mails have been awarded to steamers in competition, wherein the steamer obtaining the mails earned the award by a difference in time of from one to five minutes; the steamer that delivers the mails the quickest, whether it be one minute, one hour, or one day, having invariably secured the award of the mails without regard to the registry or the flag of the vessel; and the records of this office show that in hardly a single instance during the past fiscal year have the mails been wrongfully awarded; and when such instances have occurred the delay has been caused by some unavoidable detention of the vessel at sea.

It will be observed from the table accompanying this report, showing the time occupied by the steamers of the different transatlantic steamship companies in conveying the United States mails from New York to London and to Paris, that a number of the steamers have not varied in their time in transit more than from one to five hours for the entire fiscal year, a record that is hardly equaled in point of regularity and efficiency in the transportation of the mails over our long domestic railway routes.

No. 1.—*Table showing the dispatches for the month of May, 1888, by steamers of the White Star, Cunard, and North German Lloyd lines, of the regular mails from Great Britain to the United States, and the delays sustained by portions of said mails by being dispatched exclusively by vessels of the White Star and Cunard lines.*

FROM LONDON TO NEW YORK.

Steamer.	Line.	Departure.		Mails recived at New York post-office.	Delay.*
		Port.	Date.		
					d. h. m.
Celtic........	White Star	Queenstown ..	May 3, 5.30 p. m.	May 12, 11.15 a. m.	
Aller	North German Lloyd.	Southampton .	May 3, 7.00 p. m.	May 11, 6.00 p. m.	2 16
Servia	Cunard	Queenstown ..	May 6, 1.40 p. m.	May 14, 10.00 a. m.	
Eider	North German Lloyd.	Southampton .	May 7, 4.20 p. m.	May 16, 3.50 a. m.	2 4 40
Germanic.....	White Star	Queenstown ..	May 10, 1.47 p. m.	May 18, 8.30 a. m.	
Saale	North German Lloyd.	Southampton .	May 10, 5.00 p. m.	May 18, 11.45 a. m.	1 8 45
Umbria.......	Cunard	Queenstown ..	May 13, 1.17 p. m.	May 19, 8.30 p. m.	
Fulda........	North German Lloyd.	Southampton .	May 13, 8.05 p. m.	May 21, 4.05 p. m.	3 22 45
Adriatic	White Star	Queenstown ..	May 17, 1.43 p. m.	May 25, 3.30 p. m.	
Trave	North German Lloyd.	Southampton .	May 17, 7.20 p. m.	May 25, 2.25 p. m.	2 8 50
Aurania	Cunard	Queenstown ..	May 20, 1.12 p. m.	May 27, 11.15 p. m.	
Elbe.	North German Lloyd.	Southampton .	May 20, 9.15 p. m.	May 29, 1.48 p. m.	2 20 50
Britannic	White Star	Queenstown ..	May 24, 1.58 p. m.	June 1, 10.38 a. m.	
Lahn	North German Lloyd.	Southampton .	May 24, 5.45 p. m.	June 1, 9.35 a. m.	1 5 37
Etruria	Cunard	Queenstown ..	May 27, 1.05 p. m.	June 2, 3.12 p. m.	
Werra	North German Lloyd.	Southampton .	May 27, 7.00 p. m.	June 5, 7.05 a. m.	3 10 50
Celtic........	White Star	Queenstown ..	May 31, 2.00 p. m.	June 8, 8.55 p. m.	
Aller	North German Lloyd.	Southampton .	May 31, 8.00 p. m.	June 6, 4.55 p. m.	2 4 35
Servia	Cunard	Queenstown ..	June 3, 12.55 p. m.	June 10, 9.30 p. m.	

* Delay sustained by mails that could have been dispatched by North German Lloyd steamer, but were held over for Cunard or White Star steamer.

No. 2.—*Table showing, for the month of May, 1888, the dispatches of the regular mails from the United States to Great Britain, and the time saved to correspondence by dispatching the mails by vessels that deliver them at the earliest date possible.*

FROM NEW YORK TO LONDON.

Steamer.	Line.	Departure.		Mails received at London post-office.	Time saved to correspondence.
		Port.	Date.		
					d. h. m.
Trave *	North German Lloyd.	New York	May 2, 11.00 a. m.	May 10, 2.53 p. m.	1 5 20
Adriatic	White Star	...do	May 2, 10.38 a. m.	May 11, 6.13 p. m.	
Wieland*....	Hamburg-American ..	...do	May 3, 11.30 a. m.	May 13, 11.05 p. m.	17 36
Aurania *....	Cunard	...do	May 5, 1.31 p. m.	May 14, 6.41 a. m.	10 37
Elbe.........	North German Lloyd	...do	May 5, 2.00 p. m.	May 14, 5.18 p. m.	
Lahn *.......	...do	...do	May 9, 5.00 a. m.	May 17, 12.54 p. m.	5 19
Arizona	Guion	...do	May 8, 6.30 a. m.	May 17, 6.13 p. m.	
Britannic * ..	White Star	...do	May 9, 4 00 p. m.	May 18, 7.15 p. m.	2 6 18
Etruria*.....	Cunard	...do	May 12, 5.10 a. m.	May 21, 7.33 a. m.	3 6
Gellert......	Hamburg-American ..	...do	May 10, 5.00 a. m.	May 21, 4.39 a. m.	
Werra	North German Lloyd.	...do	May 12, 6.30 a. m.	May 21, 12.54 p. m.	
Aller *.......	...do	...do	May 16, 8.33 a. m.	May 24, 7.42 p. m.	8 42
City of Rome.	Anchor	...do	May 16, 10.20 a. m.	May 25, 4.24 a. m.	
Lessing*	Hamburg-American ..	...do	May 17, 9.15 a. m.	May 27, 4.58 p. m.	11 27
Eider*.	North German Lloyd	...do	May 19, 11 30 a. m.	May 28, 4.25 a. m.	2 21
Servia	Cunard	...do	May 19, 10.47 a. m.	May 28, 6.46 a. m.	
Ems*........	North German Lloyd	...do	May 22, 3.00 p. m.	May 30, 10.24 p. m.	23 53
Saale *.......	...do.....	...do	May 23, 4.00 p. m.	May 31, 10.17 p. m.	1 0 37
Germanic....	White Star	...do	May 23, 3.30 p. m.	June 1, 10 54 p. m.	
Umbria *	Cunard	...do	May 26, 6 00 a. m.	June 3, 6.58 a. m.	1 3 7
Fulda	North German Lloyd	...do	May 26, 6.30 a. m.	June 4, 10.05 a. m.	
Alaska*.....	Guion	...do	May 29, 8 00 a. m.	June 7, 4.33 a. m.	13 9
Trave *......	North German Lloyd	...do	May 30, 9.00 a. m.	June 7, 5.42 p. m.	1 13 8
Adriatic	White Star	...do	May 30, 9.02 a. m.	June 9, 6.50 a. m.	
Hammonia *	Hamburg-American ..	...do	May 31, 10.15 a. m.	June 9, 11.08 p. m.	1 7 27
Aurania *....	Cunard ....,......	...do	June 2, 11.55 a. m.	June 11, 6.45 a. m.	

NOTE.—Steamers marked * carried the regular mails; other steamers carried specially-addressed correspondence.

Number of trips per quarter and year, the average apparent time in hours, per trip, per quarter, and year, occupied by the steamers of the transatlantic steam-ship companies in conveying the United States mails from New York to London and to Paris, and the quickest trip made by each steamer during the fiscal year ended June 30, 1888, as shown from the records of this office.

Lines and steamers.	First quarter.		Second quarter.		Third quarter.		Fourth quarter.		Total.		Quickest trip.
	Trips.	Average time occupied per trip.	Trips.	Average time occupied per trip.	Trips.	Average time occupied per trip.	Trips.	Average time occupied per trip.	Trips.	Average time occupied per trip.	
		Hrs.		*Hrs.*		*Hrs.*		*Hrs.*		*Hrs.*	*Hrs.*
Cunard (New York to London via Queenstown):											
Umbria	3	184.8	4	187.1	3	184.5	3	188.2	13	186.2	179.7
Etruria	3	187.8	3	184.7	3	188.3	3	185.9	12	186.7	178.5
Aurania	4	210.2	3	208	2	208.5	4	207.1	13	208.5	200.9
Servia	3	212.4	3	221.8	3	212.4	3	208.8	12	213.8	200.3
North German Lloyd (New York to London via Southampton):											
Lahn					2	195.2	2	188.3	4	191.7	188
Trave	3	195.5	3	201.8	1	216.5	4	195.5	11	199.1	190.6
Aller	2	194.7	4	200.3	1	209.2	3	199.9	10	199.9	186.2
Saale	3	204.6	2	198.5	3	203.2	3	201.3	11	202.2	198.3
Elder	3	198.5	3	202	3	205.4	3	205.4	12	202.8	195
Ems	3	201	3	203.5	2	208	3	202.2	11	203.3	196.2
Fulda	3	203.6	2	201	2	210.4	4	206.6	11	205.4	199.3
Werra	3	207	3	211.8	3	206.3	3	210	12	208.8	202.5
Elbe	2	209.7	2	213.5	3	215.1	4	216.7	11	214.4	207.4
Anchor (New York to London via Queenstown):											
City of Rome	3	206.4	1	209.2	...	....	3	204.9	7	207.6	200.2
Guion (New York to London via Queenstown):											
Alaska	3	204.2	2	212.4	1	213.7	2	210.0	8	208.9	199.7
Arizona	2	217.6	3	227.3	...	....	3	216.1	8	220.7	212.3
Wyoming	...	....	...	....	...	....	2	245.9	2	245.9	237.7
Wisconsin	...	....	1	261.0	2	252.2	...	....	3	255.1	242.2
White Star (New York to London via Queenstown):											
Britannic	3	213	4	222.7	1	202.3	3	215.1	11	216.1	202.3
Germanic	2	213.5	2	222	4	223.8	3	225	11	221.9	211.9
Celtic	1	230.8	2	231	2	240	...	....	5	234.6	223.3
Adriatic	4	236.8	3	239	2	232.5	3	229.2	12	234.7	223.6
Republic	...	....	1	241.8	3	253.4	1	235.1	5	247.4	232.4
Hamburg-American (New York to London via Plymouth):											
Hammonio	2	234.1	1	249.1	...	....	2	229.1	5	235.1	228.9
Lessing	2	239.8	1	237	...	....	1	247.7	4	241.1	237
Wielaud	2	243.4	1	250.6	...	....	2	238.0	5	242.7	224.8
Gellert	2	257.6	...	....	...	....	2	256.4	4	257	249.1
Rugia	1	252.9	...	....	...	....	2	272.6	3	266	252.9
Inman (New York to London via Queenstown):											
City of Chicago	1	230	...	...	1	242.3	...	....	2	236.1	230
City of Richmond	...	....	2	248.8	2	250.3	...	....	4	249.5	243.4
General Transatlantic (New York to Paris via Havre):											
La Champagne	3	198.4	3	202.4	2	200.7	3	200	11	200.3	189
La Bretagne	2	203.7	3	201.6	2	199.3	3	199.4	10	200.9	191.3
La Bourgogne	2	196.2	3	202.7	3	202.5	3	203.2	11	201.7	186.2
La Gascogne	3	201.7	3	201.8	3	206.4	2	210.6	11	205.2	189
La Normandie	3	215.4	2	226.1	3	238.8	3	233.7	11	229.7	208.5

POSTAL CONVENTION WITH THE DOMINION OF CANADA.

On the 12th of January there was signed at Washington, and on the 19th of January at Ottawa, a postal convention between the United States and the Dominion of Canada, abrogating the special postal con-

vention between the two countries of 1875. The new convention, which
went into operation on the 1st of March, 1888, virtually makes one postal territory of the United States and Canada. Under the old convention, which had already established uniformity of postage rates, there
was still this restriction, that no merchandise of any kind could be sent
from the United States to Canada, not even at letter rates of postage.
This restriction has now been removed, and merchandise, with the exception of certain articles specially prohibited by the convention, can
now be sent to Canada at the rates of postage applicable to fourth-class
matter in the United States, subject, however, to such regulations as
will protect the customs revenues.

Owing to the fact that the Canadian domestic rates of postage on
seeds, etc., was 1 cent for each 4 ounces, whilst the United States
domestic rates of postage on the same kind of articles was 1 cent for an
ounce or fraction of an ounce, thus creating a distinction in favor of
Canadian seedsmen, the postal convention above referred to was, by
special agreement between the United States Post-Office Department
and the post-office department of Canada, modified so as to make the
rates of postage charged in the United States and Canada uniform as
regards all third-class matter, viz, 1 cent for 2 ounces, and on all fourth-
class matter (including seeds), viz, 1 cent for each ounce or fraction of
an ounce.

Since the inauguration of the conventions with Mexico and Canada,
thousands of packages of merchandise have been transmitted through
the mails exchanged between the United States and those countries,
which under the old method were absolutely excluded therefrom.

From information derived from accurate sources I am enabled to say
that about 90 per cent. of the packages of merchandise exchanged between the United States and those countries originate in this country,
which fully demonstrates the value of these conventions to our merchants.

I append a copy of the recent postal convention with Canada, and of
the modification referred to, marked Appendix A.

PARCEL POST.

The first parcel-post convention between the United States and any
foreign country was that concluded with Jamaica, and which went into
operation October 1st, 1887; and since then parcel-post conventions
have been concluded between the United States and the following
countries:

	Went into operation.
Barbadoes	Dec. 1, 1887.
The Bahamas	Feb. 1, 1888.
British Honduras	Mar. 1, 1888.
Mexico	July 1, 1888.

The provisions of these different parcel post conventions are substantially the same. The greatest weight of a parcel for any of these countries is 11 pounds; for Mexico the greatest length allowed for a parcel is 2
feet, and the greatest girth is 4 feet; for Jamaica, the Bahamas, Barbadoes, and British Honduras the greatest length allowed for a parcel
is 3 feet 6 inches, and the greatest length and girth combined is 6 feet.

The parcel-post rates to all these countries are the same, viz, 12 cents per pound or fraction of a pound; in addition to this, a charge for interior service and delivery may be collected from the addressee in the country of destination; this charge is 5 cents on each single parcel of whatever weight, and if the weight exceed 1 pound, 1 cent for each 4 ounces or fraction of 4 ounces. The highest possible charge for a parcel weighing 11 pounds sent from the United States to any of the above-mentioned countries, by parcel mail, will therefore be $1.76, of which amount the sender will have to pay $1.32, and the addressee 44 cents. These charges will certainly compare favorably with the charges of foreign express companies; the principal advantage of the new system, however, which has made it so exceedingly popular is, that it does away with the former slow and expensive method of meeting the custom-house requirements.

Prior to the conclusion of the convention with Mexico, July 1, 1887, it was forbidden to send through the mails exchanged between the United States and any foreign country, any article of merchandise having a merchantable value. The effect of these conventions, herein referred to, has been to remove the restrictions which previously existed on the transmission by mail of this class of mail matter, and there can be no doubt that it has and will continue to augment largely the trade relations with those countries without imposing additional burdens on the postal revenue of the United States, as the postage collected on such matter dispatched will more than equal the expenditure.

The conclusion of a parcel-post convention with Mexico is of special importance, as that country with its large population and with rapidly-developing industries, naturally looks to the United States for extending every possible aid in strengthening the bonds of commercial relations between the two great "sister Republics," whose interests are the same, and it will be found that new and hitherto almost inaccessible markets have been opened out to American merchants.

Parcel-post conventions are now pending with all the Central and South American States, and it is hoped that the time is not far distant when the "Three Americas" will be embraced in one grand parcel-post union, which will in its way aid this country in fulfilling its eventual mission, viz, to control the markets of this hemisphere and become the leader in its industrial and commercial progress.

THE UNIVERSAL POSTAL UNION DURING 1888.

During the fiscal year ended June 30, 1888, there have been the following additions to the Universal Postal Union:

	To take effect—
German protectorate:	
Territory of the New Guinea Company..	Jan. 1, 1888
Territory of Togo, Western Africa	June 1, 1888
Territory of Southwest Africa	July 1, 1888
Territory of the Marshall Islands, in the Pacific	Oct. 1, 1888
Regency of Tunis	July 1, 1888

The German Empire has established a German post-office at Apia, Samoan Islands, thus virtually bringing these islands into the postal union.

The only new provision of interest is the following:
Paragraph 5, of Article XV, of the revised postal-union regulations has been modified as follows:

(5) With the exception of stamps for prepayment, and a label with the printed address of the addressee, which is to be pasted on the address side, and the dimensions of which must not exceed 5 centimeters by 6 centimeters, it is forbidden to join or to attach to postal-cards any articles whatsoever.

STATISTICS OF THE POSTAL SERVICE IN THE PRINCIPAL COUNTRIES OF THE UNIVERSAL POSTAL UNION.

The following statistics, like those in last year's report, have been taken from "General Statistics of the Postal Service," published by the International Bureau, Berne, Switzerland. The statistics cover the year 1886, and were published in 1888.

Countries.	Railroads.	All other routes.
1.—Length of postal routes.	*Miles.*	*Miles.*
United States	164,661	245,165
Germany	23,209	63,186
France	21,080	44,510
Russia	17,494	86,806
British India	11,936	92,635
Italy	8,582	50,686
Austria	8,535	37,574
All other countries reported (21)	36,096	....
All other countries reported (24)	....	263,936
2.—Annual transportation.		
United States	166,672,758	86,852,536
Germany	61,336,807	51,447,341
France	57,332,553	35,429,753
Austria	23,211,868	32,921,692
Italy	19,148,196	22,712,230
Russia	17,855,909	23,821,896
British India	14,547,075	14,547,675
All other countries reported (21)	71,479,338	102,110,688

3.—*Articles of mail matter dispatched in the international mails.*

Countries.	Letters.	Postal-cards.	Prints.	Samples.	Parcels of merchandise.
Germany	53,151,430	8,838,740	19,317,720	1,992,320	3,395,376
Great Britain	44,190,756	2,735,992	42,051,042	2,974,720	242,864
Austria	42,025,300	6,875,900	8,763,806	1,979,400	894,560
United States	36,811,079	1,780,967	47,049,064	283,194	
France	35,158,945	1,632,094	16,868,735	1,165,357	1,485,891
Italy	18,351,605	2,219,936	7,934,449	528,150	215,322
Russia	9,166,869	1,361,481	3,060,521	....	6,141
British India	3,727,749		1,331,860		42,902
All other countries reported (24)	64,726,792	12,690,770	26,766,223	3,625,674	1,253,161

4.—*Postal income and expenditure.*

Countries.	Income.	Countries.	Expenditure.
1. Germany	$48,816,200.33	1. United States	$51,018,243.79
2. United States	45,948,422.94	2. Germany	42,237,084.91
3. Great Britain	40,873,530.35	3. Great Britain	28,371,680.32
4. France	33,378,564.11	4. France	27,136,034.27
5. Russia	13,065,041.58	5. Russia	17,905,084.78
6. Austria	12,722,127.19	6. Austria	10,352,726.99
7. Italy	7,743,708.08	7. Italy	5,573,299.92
8. British India	5,618,635.30	8. British India	5,314,492.39
9. Hungary	4,378,133.29	9. Switzerland	3,575,785.42
10. Switzerland	3,881,230.12	10. Hungary	3,548,0.13.02
11. Spain	3,199,521.64	11. Brasil	2,419,828.62
12. Belgium	2,869,892.96	12. Belgium	1,891,346.15
13. Netherlands	2,350,107.70	13. Spain	1,836,485.32
14. Sweden	1,674,178.50	14. Netherlands	1,797,653.76
15. Denmark	1,214,415.46	15. Sweden	1,618,729.60
16. Brazil	916,381.09	16. Denmark	1,171,419.27
17. Roumania	874,380.43	17. Portugal	873,564.35
18. Portugal	871,363.07	18. Roumania	621,688.87
19. Norway	605,520.36	19. Norway	619,278.78
20. Egypt	571,944.86	20. Japan	563,130.56
21. Japan	458,758.78	21. Chili	526,079.49
22. Chili	441,394.84	22. Egypt	454,973.47
23. Greece	211,673.75	23. Bulgaria	297,243.51
24. Uruguay	186,646.64	24. Greece	243,982.49
25. Peru	143,119.43	25. Uruguay	190,191.39
26. Luxemburg	99,816.83	26. Peru	154,202.40
27. Bulgaria	97,212.87	27. Luxemburg	97,481.86
28. Hayti	13,355.60	28. Siam	30,461.96
29. Paraguay	7,537.25	29. Hayti	26,482.63
30. Dominican Republic	7,070.06	30. Dominican Republic	17,012.95
31. Siam	6,615.46	31. Paraguay	13,920.99
32. Congo	3,794.87		

5.—*Postal surplus and deficiency.*

Countries.	Surplus.	Countries.	Deficiency.
1. Great Britain	$12,501,850.03	1. United States	$5,069,820.85
2. Germany	6,579,112.42	2. Brasil	1,543,447.53
3. France	6,241,529.84	3. Bulgaria	200,030.64
4. Austria	2,369,400.20	4. Japan	104,371.78
5. Spain	2,363,036.32	5. Chili	84,685.15
6. Italy	2,169,508.16	6. Portugal	52,201.28
7. Belgium	978,546.81	7. Greece	32,308.74
8. Hungary	830,130.27	8. Siam	23,846.50
9. Netherlands	552,453.54	9. Norway	13,758.42
10. Switzerland	305,444.70	10. Hayti	13,127.08
11. British India	304,142.91	11. Peru	11,082.97
12. Roumania	152,691.56	12. Dominican Republic	10,032.89
13. Egypt	116,970.89	13. Paraguay	6,383.74
14. Sweden			
15. Denmark	42,996.19		
16. Luxemburg	2,364.97		

6.—*Subsidies paid to steam-ship companies.*

Countries.	Amount of subsidy paid per annum.	Countries.	Amount of subsidy paid per annum.
1. France	$5,154,330.61	9. Greece	$105,185.00
2. Great Britain	3,024,334.12	10. Chili	48,250.00
3. Italy	1,732,876.74	11. Denmark	35,340.26
4. Brasil	1,295,416.00	12. Austria	33,619.41
5. Spain	436,180.00	13. Peru	3,868.39
6. British India	281,149.85	14. Uruguay	2,500.00
7. Belgium	161,734.00	15. Roumania	1,171.36
8. Netherlands	106,966.27	16. Siam	261.70

INTERNATIONAL POSTAL CONGRESS OF VIENNA IN 1890.

So far three international postal congresses have been held: The first at Berne, Switzerland, in 1873, which created the General Postal Union; the second at Paris, in 1878, which created the Universal Postal Union, and the third at Lisbon, Portugal, in 1885, which in several respects modified the Paris Convention of 1878. Before the Lisbon Congress adjourned it resolved to meet again at Vienna, Austria, in 1890. The United States has been represented at each of the three congresses, and will, doubtless, also send delegates to the Vienna Congress, which promises to be one of unusual interest, in view of the many important questions—among the rest, that of doing away with all transit charges—which will come up for discussion. In the estimate for the fiscal year ending June 30, 1890, I have asked for an appropriation of $5,000 to defray the expenses of the United States delegates, the same amount which was allowed for the delegates to the Lisbon Congress, and would suggest that our delegates be instructed to introduce a resolution before the Vienna Congress that the next International Postal Congress, probably to meet in 1895, be requested to meet at Washington.

SPECIAL SERVICES MAINTAINED BY FOREIGN COUNTRIES.

In my report for 1886 I briefly referred to the collection service maintained by a great many countries belonging to the Universal Postal Union. In view of the possible introduction, at some future time, of this important service in the American postal system, I have deemed it proper to give below a detailed description of this service in Belgium, where it was first established, and where it has reached a high degree of development; and the latest statistics obtainable of this service in Belgium, France, and Germany.

COLLECTION SERVICE.

The first country to introduce the collection service was Belgium, where it has been in existence since 1842, and where it has reached a high degree of perfection. Germany introduced the system in 1871; Switzerland in 1875; France in 1879; and Austria in 1882. The system has been introduced in several other European countries, and has met with universal favor, as is shown by the large number of collections made and the large amount of money collected.   .

BELGIUM.—REGULATIONS GOVERNING THE COLLECTION SERVICE.

COLLECTION OF BILLS (RECEIPTS, QUITTANCES).

The post-office will collect bills, the charges for such services being as follows :

For each bill not exceeding 20 francs ($3.86), 10 centimes (2 cents).

For each bill exceeding 20 francs and up to 50 francs ($9.65), 20 centimes (4 cents).

For each bill exceeding 50 francs and up to 100 francs ($19.30), 30 centimes (6 cents).

For all bills exceeding 100 francs, an additional charge of 20 centimes (4 cents) is made for every 100 francs or fraction of 100 francs. These charges are paid by postage-stamps affixed to the bills by the senders.

The bills to be collected must be accompanied by a memorandum showing the names of the debtors and the amount of each bill. Forms for such memoranda are furnished to the senders free of charge. Private individuals are at liberty to print and sell such forms, provided they are entirely like those issued by the postal administration.

No bill is presented to the debtor more than twice. The second presentation can only be made twety-four hours after the first, unless the debtor has manifested a desire to pay the bill sooner.

In case of non-payment at the second presentation, a notice is left at the residence of the debtor, requesting him to pay the bill at the post-office within twenty-four hours. After that time has elapsed the bill is considered uncollectible, and is returned to the sender. Bills are also returned which can not be collected owing to wrong indications, or to a change of residence of the debtors.

Bills which, for some cause, have not been collected can again be sent for collection, on payment of half of the charges given above. This privilege, however, only extends to the second presentation. All subsequent presentations are liable to the full charges. These presentations, consequently, give rise alternately to the full or the half-charge. The third presentation is assimilated with the first by a new bill; the fourth to the second, and so on, alternating the full and half charges. Bills which are again presented for collection, and the amount of which has been changed, only give rise to half the original charges at the second presentation, if the changed amount of the bill does not exceed the limit fixed for the levying of this charge. When the original charge does no longer correspond to the amount of the changed bill, it becomes liable to half of said charge, and in addition, to a charge calculated on the amount exceeding the maximum limit of the first charge. In case the amount of the bill is diminished, the half-charge is calculated on the new amount of the bill. The above mode of procedure, as regards subsequent presentations, is applicable to bills whose amount has been diminished.

ARTICLES SENT FOR COLLECTION ON DELIVERY.

There may be forwarded through the mails to destinations in Belgium, letters, newspapers, prints or business papers, to be delivered to the addressee on payment of a bill accompanying such articles. These articles must be prepaid, according to their different rates. Samples or small articles of merchandise, are admitted on the same conditions, if placed in sealed envelopes, or tightly packed. They must be prepaid at the letter rate of postage. All values to be collected (checks, receipts by an agent, protested drafts, returned, etc.) joined to a bill are only admitted as C. O. D. articles, if placed in a sealed envelope, and prepaid at letter rates of postage. All these articles can be registered, but they can only be insured if they consist of sealed letters. Registration and insurance are subject to the general postal regulations in this respect. The insured value need not necessarily correspond with the sum to be collected. The administration of posts is liable to the

same provisions of responsibility as those in force in the general
postal service. Senders may demand delivery at the residence, by paying the charges for the special messenger. These articles must bear
the address of the sender, as well as that of the addressee, and an indication of the amount to be collected.

All articles mentioned in one and the same bill must be put up in
one package, but it is not permitted to comprise in this package articles
for which there is no combined rate, e. g., a letter and a book. No more
than one bill can be joined to one and the same article. O. O. D. articles
are subject to the general prohibitory conditions, viz, the exclusion of
articles which, on account of their nature, are a cause of danger to the
postal employés, or to the correspondence; the prohibition to insert in
articles which have neither been registered nor insured, values on bearer
exceeding 5 francs (96½ cents) or pieces of coin; the prohibition to forward by mail gold or silver substances, jewelry, or other precious
articles.

C. O. D. articles are mailed at the post office windows, accompanied
by a memorandum on which they are entered in detail. As regards bills,
the address of the sender and of the addressee must be given, and mention must be made that payment is made on delivery of the article.
Such payment is proof of the receipt of the article by the addressee.
Each bill is attached to the article to which it relates. When this article is a non-registered article of printed matter, the bill may be written
below the address. The articles are sorted, and put up in bundles by
the office of destination, and are entered in the same order on the list.
Registered, insured, special-delivery, and "poste restante" articles are
entered on special lists. Bills must be prepaid singly by means of postage-stamps, at the ordinary rates of postage for bills, but at the minimum rate of 15 centimes (3 cents).

Forms are furnished free of charge by the post-offices. The office of
mailing gives the sender a receipt. Articles which are neither registered
nor insured are delivered on payment of the bill. If the article is either
registered or insured, the addressee must sign a receipt for it in the
letter-carrier's book. Articles which, after having been presented twice
to the addressee, have not been accepted by him, and are not claimed
within forty-eight hours, are considered as refused. "Poste restante"
articles, however, are kept at the disposal of the addressee for one
month, unless the sender has, on the address, given a shorter period of
retention. Articles whose addressees have changed their residence, or
whose address is incorrect, are considered as undeliverable. All articles
which, for some reason, can not be delivered, are returned to the sender
as soon as possible. He may again mail them for collection, after having
corrected the address, if necessary, on prepayment for the second presentation of half the postage-rates for bills (the minimum being 10
centimes, equal 2 cents), and another complete prepayment of the article
in question. The settling of the account with the sender is done by the
postmaster of the office of mailing, who pays the entire amount of the
collected bills, and delivers returned articles and bills.

BILLS OF EXCHANGE, ETC.

(1) Acceptance of bills.

The administration of posts undertakes to present, in all places in the
Kingdom of Belgium, bills of exchange, etc., at the acceptance of the
drawees or persons indicated to accept in behalf of the drawees.

The administration also undertakes to prepare protests in case of non-acceptance, and the documents proving acceptance, or refusal of acceptance by intervention. Bills are not presented to third parties except in the place where the drawee resides, or in a place within the district served by one and the same post-office.

The rate is 20 centimes (4 cents) for each bill. This charge must be paid by means of postage stamps affixed to the bills by the senders.

Bills originating in foreign countries, to be presented for acceptance, must, as a general rule, when mailed, have attached to them adhesive stamps representing the charge to be levied in Belgium. If this has not been done, the amount of this charge is collected from the drawee, previous to affixing his signature for acceptance In case of refusal to accept by the drawee, for the sole reason that he does not intend to pay the stamp charge, the sender is immediately informed, and the bill can only be protested after having this stamp affixed, or an indorsement for this stamp put on it. Bills must comply with the conditions fixed by the laws and regulations governing such papers.

Bills can not be accompanied by any other article but the list of the bills, unless the accompanying articles are regularly prepaid at the rates of postage applicable to them. Bills sent for acceptance can be mailed at any post-office, at the latest a fortnight before the date of maturity. They can also be mailed on a provisional receipt at postal agencies; but in that case the bills and the general list must be placed by the sender in a sealed envelope addressed to the postmaster of the post-office to which the postal agency is subordinate, their conveyance to such postmaster being free of charge. In mailing bills to be presented for acceptance senders must observe the following rules: Bills must be classified by destinations of collection; for each destination a list is prepared, on which the bills are entered in detail; those which are to be protested in case of non-acceptance must be marked in the list with the letter "P;" bills destined for localities in which there is no post-office must be comprised in the collection list of the post-office by which these localities are served.

Bills to be accepted, if necessary, by a third party, are entered in the list separately, after the other bills. The names of the third parties must be given after the names of the drawees. The bills and the list are placed in a sealed envelope with the heading "bills for acceptance," and bearing the name of the destination of collection, and the signature or printed fac-simile of the signature of the sender, or the impression of a stamp bearing his name. All the articles are then repeated in a re-capitulatory list, which alone must positively bear the manuscript signature of the sender. The list and the recapitulatory list must be furnished by the senders, and must be in conformity with the models published by the administration. The postmaster, after verifying the bills, gives to the sender a receipt showing the number of articles received.

The postmaster of the office of destination immediately informs the sender, by mail, of any difference which he may have discovered as regards the number of bills, and of any errors in the indications of the list.

Bills which have gone astray, irregular or insufficiently prepaid bills, are at once returned to the sender, by mail. Such bills may again be presented, after the error has been corrected, without any additional charge.

Bills are always presented for acceptance at the residence of the drawee; if he personally makes the request, the bill may be left in his hands (on signing a receipt) for twenty-four hours. Bills are only presented once. If the drawee is not at home, or if from some other cause the bill could not be presented to him, the postmaster sends a notice to the residence of the drawee, asking him to give his acceptance at the post-office within twenty-four hours.

If the drawee refuses to accept a protested bill, or if he accepts it irregularly, the fact is recorded by an act of protest. If the person to whom the bill is presented for acceptance refuses to return it, no protest is prepared. In that case the receipt for the bill is sent to the remitter.

The bill which has been refused by the drawee is, after due notice of the protest, if necessary, immediately presented to all the persons indicated for acceptance in case of need. There is prepared for each one of the persons, as the case may be, an act of intervention, or a protest in default of acceptance. These acts are thereupon, on payment of the expenses, transmitted to the intervening party, who effects most discharges, and who alone is permitted to enter his acceptance on the bill.

It is prohibited under penalty of the law to cover the impression of the stamp with writing.

Accepted bills, and those which have been refused acceptance, are returned as soon as possible, with the acts of protest if necessary, to the postmaster of the office of mailing, to be delivered by him to the sender, on payment of the expenses, and of the fee for a money-order intended to transit the amount expended to the postmaster who has advanced the money.

(2) Cashing of bills of exchange.

The administration of posts admits for cashing, on the part of any establishment and any person, bills, with or without protest, on all places in the kingdom.

Bills which have become due, that is to say, where the legal date of their being due has passed, are admitted and considered payable on sight. Bills to be cashed can be mailed at any post-office.

The fees for cashing are as follows: Ten centimes (2 cents) for 100 francs ($19.30) or fraction of 100 francs, up to 1,000 francs ($193), but not less than 25 centimes (5 cents). For bills above 1,000 francs a charge of 50 centimes (10 cents) is made for every 1,000 francs or fraction of 1,000 francs. These fees or charges must be paid by postage-stamps affixed by the senders to the back of the bills before they are mailed, care being taken not to cover the impression of the stamp with writing.

Under the generic name of commercial papers, the law which authorizes the cashing of these papers by mail comprises not only bills of exchange or orders, and bills payable to order, but also promissory notes, bonds received by intervention, checks, letters of credit, etc.

To be admitted for cashing these papers must (1) comply with the conditions of form, etc., required by the laws and regulations on the subject, and must particularly bear a stamp, if necessary; (2) express in Belgian currency the amount of the bill or note, whenever that amount is given in a foreign currency; (3) they must have the receipt of the bearer (i. e. the person who holds the papers in the last place, and who mails them for cashing), or of his attorney; as the administration simply acts as collector, bills cannot be indorsed to its agents; (4) not bear any other writing than what is required in the ordinary forms for such papers, and not be accompanied by any other paper but by a duplicate, which eventually may be joined to it, to justify acceptance by the debtor or payment of stamp-dues. The bearer, however, may, if he deems proper, inclose with the bill other papers on condition of placing them under an addressed band or in an addressed envelope, and prepaying them at the ordinary rates of postage. Bills payable by intervention are only admitted when the persons indicated to pay, in case of need, live in the same borough as the drawee, or debtor, or within a district served by the same post-office.

There are subject to proportional stamp-dues: Negotiable or commercial bills, non-negotiable notes and bonds, and orders on account or from place to place. These dues are as follows: For bills, etc., of 200 francs ($38.60) and below, 10 centimes (2 cents); 200 francs up to 500 francs ($96.50), 25 centimes (5 cents); 500 francs up to 1,000 francs ($193), 50 centimes (10 cents); 1,000 francs up to 2,000 francs ($386), 1 franc (19.3 cents); and above that sum, 50 centimes for every 1,000 francs.

Non-negotiable papers, i. e., papers by which a person directs another person to pay to his order a certain fixed sum, and signs a receipt, without indorsing to a third person, are subject to the stamp dues required by the dimension of the paper used. They are also admitted when on paper to which the proportional stamp is affixed. The administration, however, assumes no responsibility for any fines to which such papers may become liable, in case of protest, for violating the stamp laws.

The proportional dues are likewise applicable to negotiable papers originating abroad and payable in Belgium. These dues may be paid by pasting an adhesive stamp on the back of the paper, or on the first place on the front not covered by writing. The duty to affix the adhesive stamp devolves on the first person in Belgium who affixes his signature to a paper originating abroad.. The stamp must be canceled by writing across it the date and signature, or by impressing a printed fac-simile of the signature. Each stamp must be canceled in this manner. Checks, clearing orders, letters of credit, bank bills to order, and all other bills payable on account, or on sight, from disposable funds, are exempt from stamp dues. There are also exempt from stamp dues second, third, fourth, etc., bills of exchange, when the first is drawn on stamped paper, or indorsed for a stamp, or furnished with an adhesive stamp. In that case, it is indispensable that the first should be joined to the one which is put in circulation and is intended to receive indorsements, acceptances, guaranties, or receipts.

A check and its similars, issued payable at a fixed date, are subject to the proportional stamp dues. An originally regular check loses the benefit of exemption from stamp dues if it forms the subject of an indorsement in favor of the bearer who affixes to it his signature of receipt, and then becomes a non-negotiable bill.

Receipts by intervention, implying a negotiation between signers, are subject to the proportional stamp dues. When papers of this kind only bear the signature of the person issuing the paper, without the intervention of the designated third party for indorsement or receipt, they retain the character of simple receipts.

Persons mailing bills to be cashed must observe the following rules: The papers must be classified by offices of destination, and must be entered on a separate list for each office. Bills becoming due on different days of one and the same month, as well as bills due and payable on sight, may be mailed at the same time and entered on the same list.

Bills which are due or payable on sight, mailed in the course of one month, can not be comprised in the same list with bills, etc., becoming due the next month. The senders must indicate at the head of the lists the different dates when the different bills become due; they are

entered in the accompanying lists, by order of date when becoming
due, commencing with the nearest date. Bills, etc., which have become
due, or payable on sight, are entered separately after the others.
Senders must indicate in the lists by the letter "P" the papers which
should be protested in case of non payment. The officers of the cashing post-office will strictly follow these indications. Bills payable by
intervention in case of need must be mentioned as such, in a separate
column of the lists, the names of the third parties or the acceptors
being entered after the name of the drawee or debtor. The bills, etc.,
for one and.the same office, accompanied by their lists, are placed in a
gummed envelope, left open, which must bear as a heading the word
"encaissement"—cashing—the name of post-office of destination, and
the signature, or printed fac-simile of the signature of the sender.

All the articles sent at one time by one and the same person are re-
capitulated in a general list, to be made out in duplicate, on which list
the sender obligates himself to pay all the expenses of protest and registration, as well as any fines to which these papers may give rise. Only
this list must positively bear the manuscript signature of the sender.
The subdivision by dates of falling due is not made in the recapitulatory
lists where, without regard to date, the bills are entered by offices of
destination. Commercial papers to be cashed should be mailed, at the
earliest, fifteen days, and, at latest, four days, before they become due.
After that period has elapsed they are still received, but the administration does not guaranty to perform in proper time the services of
collection and protest. The post-office likewise undertakes, at the request of the senders and at their risk, to ascertain the non-payment of
bills which have become due and which have been delivered too late to
allow of the protest being made within the period allowed by law. Bills,
etc., to be cashed in a district having only a postal agency, or in places
where there is no post-office, must be addressed to the post-office serving such district or place; and they are entered on the list intended for
that post-office. The lists referred to are furnished by the persons interested, and must conform to the models provided by the administra-
tration of posts.

The postmaster, after having verified and, if necessary, corrected the
lists handed him by the sender, furnishes him with a receipt, giving
the number of articles, the dates when the papers become due, the
total amount of the sums to be cashed, and the date of mailing. Bills
which are in any way irregular or incorrect are taken off the lists and
returned to sender.

When bills are mailed at a postal agency, the sender must place the
bills and the general lists in a sealed envelope addressed to the postmaster of the post-office serving the agency. The agent gives a provisional receipt for the article, which is considered as a registered letter.
and the postmaster of the post-office serving the agency will transmit
to the sender an acknowledgment made out in due form.

Irregular bills, or bills which having gone astray have escaped the
verification of the office of mailing, are immediately returned by the
office of destination and delivered to the sender on his giving a receipt
therefor. The sender may, after correcting the bill, and at his risk,
send it as a supplementary article to the cashing office, up to the evening of the day preceding the date when it becomes due, without having
to pay another fee for cashing. In this case it becomes necessary to
prepare new lists.

Bills, etc., to be cashed are presented to the debtors when they fall
due, and those payable on sight or which have become due, as soon as

possible. Postmasters are only obliged to present them once. Postmasters must accept partial payments offered on the amount of bills of exchange, orders, bills to order, and checks. They must cause these bills, if necessary, to be protested for the remainder. The amount of a bill which has been paid can not, on any pretext whatever, be refunded to the debtor. Liquidation, however, is deferred if the person interested causes opposition to be made by means of an attachment in accordance with the prescribed forms.

If the debtor is not at home, or if for some reason the bill is not paid on presentation, the letter-carrier leaves at the residence of the debtor a notice requesting him to come to the post-office and pay the bill there. Bills which have not been paid, if indicated as subject to protest, necessitate the notification to the drawee of an act of protest.

If a bill refused by the drawee indicates the persons charged to pay in case of need, it is presented to all these persons. If the bill is subject to protest, there is prepared for every person interested either an act of intervention or a protest on account of refusal. After having been duly recorded all the papers and the bill are delivered, on payment of the principal and all the expenses, to the one of the intervening persons who effects most discharges. A protested bill can be paid by any person (even one not designated on the bill) who offers to intervene for the drawee or one of the indorsers; but in that case an act of intervention is only prepared if the party interested requests it. Payment by a third party of a bill, the debtor of which is not known in the place indicated by the drawee, is only accepted after protest.

Postmasters are not authorized to receive funds transmitted to them direct for paying a bill cashed by them. A bill mailed for cashing can only be returned to the sender after having been protested to the debtor and to the persons indicated for paying if need be, and in case of non-payment, after having been protested, if necessary. The only exception from this rule is made in case the debtor has failed or died, or in case of a non-negotiable paper, a bill to order, or a promissory note which has not been indorsed by any one.

The drawee reserves to himself the right to discharge the debt, after protest has been prepared, as long as this protest has not been returned to the sender, but on the express condition that he will pay the expenses occasioned by the protest. If necessary, the postmaster of the office of mailing is notified of payment. Bills which have not been paid are, after having gone through all the prescribed formalities, returned as soon as possible with the protests and refusals of intervention, if necessary, to the office of mailing. This office delivers all the papers to the sender, on payment of the expenses, including the money-order fee for transmitting the amount to the office which has advanced it.

Settlement of accounts with the senders is made exclusively by the second direction of posts, which makes out, as soon as possible, on the duplicate general lists furnished by the senders, the total amount of the sums cashed.

If senders request it, a portion of the amount of the sums to be cashed on bills sent for collection by mail is paid to them on account. This request must be entered on the recapitulatory list in the column of "observations." Payments on account are made in round figures (hundreds of francs), and can not be less than 1,000 francs. Such payments are generally comprised in the liquidations made by the administration of posts on the third day after maturity. Payments of 1,000 francs and more are made by letters of credit on one of the agencies of the national bank to be designated beforehand. . Payments of sums less than 1,000 francs are made by money-orders issued in favor of the senders. Persons living in a place where there is no agency of the national bank can get letters of credit cashed at the post-office where the bills, etc., have been mailed, but only to such an extent as the condition of the funds of the post-office will permit. Letters of credit, or orders issued in payment of commercial papers, are only paid on the receipt of the person in whose favor they are drawn, or his attorney.

3. *Protests.*

Bills which are to be protested owing to their not having been accepted or paid are delivered in due time to a sheriff. In places where there is no sheriff, or if the sheriff residing in the place is from some cause prevented, protests are delivered by a postal employé. Non negotiable values can only be protested by the sheriff. The postal agent or the sheriff who prepares an act of protest leaves at the residence of the person interested a notice giving the name and residence of the bearer who has requested the protest, the name of the postal agent or the sheriff, and the amount of the protested bill. The administration of posts does not accept a simple declaration in place of a protest.
Postal employés receive (1) for a simple protest, or for the first protest, francs 1.50 (28.9 cents). (2) For other acts relating to one and the same bill, 1 franc (19.3 cents) per act, and per residence where delivered.

COLLECTION OF DIVIDEND COUPONS OF THE PUBLIC DEBT, AND CASHING OF COUPONS OF ALL KINDS PAYABLE IN BELGIUM.

This new service is established by royal ordinance, dated 23d September, 1883. The following are the regulations governing it:
(1) The postal administration shall pay on presentation, during the hours the post-offices are open to the public, and free of charge, the dividend coupons of the ordinary public debt of the state, when due.
There shall be paid, on the same conditions, but with application of the fee fixed by article 4 (see below) the coupons of bonds of the "*Caisse des Annuities*" due by the state; the coupons of preference shares and bonds of the "*Grande Compagnie du Luxembourg*," and the coupons of bonds of the "*Crédit Communal.*" These payments shall be effected, within the limits of the funds in hands, by all the first and second class post-offices in the kingdom. The inhabitants of rural communes shall be allowed to avail themselves of the medium of the rural messengers for these collections.
(2) The postal administration shall effect, for the account of the bearers, the collection of dividend and interest coupons on various shares and bonds, as well as of the redeemable securities, which are payable in Belgium.
(3) With the exception of the coupons of the ordinary public debt, all coupons and securities presented for payment or collection must be accompanied by a descriptive list, the form of which shall be furnished by the administration; it shall bear the engagement undertaken by the depositor to reimburse the amount of the coupons which may have been paid wrongly, should such a case occur. A separate list shall be drawn up for each kind of security or coupon, and for each due-date. The articles shall be received for collection at any time, but not earlier than fifteen days previous to their due-dates. The list of paid coupons shall be kept at the disposal of the parties interested during a delay of one year.

.(4) The coupons of all kinds, except those of the ordinary debt of the state, presented for payment or collection shall be subject to the following fees: (a) A fixed fee of 2 centimes per coupon; (b) a proportional fee calculated on the total amount of each list, at the rate of 2 centimes per 10 francs or fraction of 10 francs. These combined fees shall be rounded off per 5 centimes by raising the fractions; they shall be paid in advance by means of postage-stamps, and shall be in no case returned. The securities deposited for redemption shall be subject, as far as the fee is concerned, to the same conditions as the bills of exchange deposited for collection.

(5) The postal administration shall be empowered to receive as deposits in the post-office savings-bank, without charging any commission, certain coupons, to be designated in concert with the administration of the bank in question.

(6) The administration shall be responsible, except in the case of "force majeure," for the value of the coupons and securities deposited in its offices for collection in the regular course of business.

(7) The minister of public works shall take the necessary measures to insure the carrying out of the present ordinance, which shall come into force on the 1st October, 1883.

The principal object kept in view by the Belgian administration in organizing the collection of coupons, and in thus affording to the owners of stocks the greatest facilities for the collection of their income at any place, was to promote the investment of money in securities among all classes of society.

In Belgium there are bonds of the debt of the state of the value of 100 francs, and a considerable number of city bonds (about 5,000,000), likewise of 100 francs, bearing an interest of 3 per cent. and redeemable at a premium.

All these securities, which are an excellent investment for people of small income, ought to be made particularly popular, so as to serve as the complement of the post-office savings-bank; and we have no doubt that this measure will have a considerable effect on the welfare of the masses and the important interests of society.

Statistics of the collection service in Germany (1886), Belgium (1886), and France (1883).

Countries.	Bills mailed for collection.		Bills which could not be collected.			Revenue to the post-office.
	Number.	Value.	Number.	Value.	Per cent.	
Germany	4,362,027	$87,550,220.66	1,206,886	$22,651,258.72	28.5	$288,717.80
Belgium	4,391,263	66,949,312.34	....	....	......	176,840.40
France	5,777,541	70,254,946.73	1,941,494	20,246,677.45	33.6	688,178.39

Nicholas M. Bell

Superintendent of Foreign Mails.

APPENDIX A.

Postal convention between the United States of America and the Dominion of Canada.

For the purpose of making better postal arrangements between the United States of America and the Dominion of Canada, the undersigned William F. Vilas, Postmaster-General of the United States of America, and Archibald Woodbury McLelan, Postmaster-General of the Dominion of Canada, by virtue of authority vested in them by law, have agreed upon the following articles:

ARTICLE 1.

(a) Articles of every kind or nature, which are admitted to the domestic mails of either country, except as herein prohibited, shall be admitted to the mails exchanged under this Convention; subject however to such regulations as the postal administration of the country of destination may deem necessary to protect its custom revenues. But articles other than letters in their usual and ordinary form, must never be closed against inspection but must be so wrapped or inclosed that they may be readily and thoroughly examined by postmasters or customs officers.

The following articles are prohibited admission to the mails exchanged under this Convention:

Publications which violate the copy-right laws of the country of destination; packets, except single volumes of printed books, the weight of which exceeds two kilograms; liquids, poisons, explosive or inflammable substances, fatty substances, those which easily liquefy, live or dead animals (not dried), insects and reptiles, confections, pastes, fruits and vegetables which will easily decompose, and substances which exhale a bad odor, lottery tickets or circulars, all obscene and immoral articles, other articles which may destroy or in any way damage the mails, or injure the persons handling them.

(b) Except as required by the regulations of the country of destination for the collection of its custom duties, all admissible matter mailed in one country for the other, or received in one country from the other, whether by land or sea conveyance, shall be free from any detention or inspection whatever, and shall in the first case be forwarded by the most speedy means to its destination, and in the latter be promptly delivered to the respective persons to whom it is addressed, being subject in its transmission to the laws and regulations of each country respectively.

(c) The classification of, and the rates of postage and the registration fee to be levied and collected upon mail matter originating in either country and addressed to the other, shall be in accordance with the domestic laws and regulations of the country of origin; provided that the rates of postage and registration fees so levied shall not exceed in either country the minimum rates of postage and registration fee prescribed for articles of a like nature by articles 5 and 6 of the Universal Postal Union Convention of Paris of June, 1878, as amended by the additional act of Lisbon of March 21, 1885.

ARTICLE 2.

(a) Each administration shall retain to its own use the whole of the postages and registration fees it collects on postal articles exchanged with the other, including deficient postage. Consequently, there will be no postage accounts between the two countries.

(b) Full prepayment of postage shall be required in both countries upon correspondence of all kinds, except letters upon which prepayment of at least one full rate shall be compulsory. Payment of postage and registration fees shall be certified by affixing the appropriate stamps of the country of origin.

(c) Each insufficiently prepaid letter shall have stamped on its cover the capital letter T, and shall have indicated plainly thereon, in figures, on the upper left-hand corner of the address, by the postal officials of the country of origin, the amount of the deficient postage, and only the amount so indicated shall be collected of addressees on delivery, except in cases of obvious error.

ARTICLE 3.

No postage charges shall be levied in either country on fully prepaid correspondence originating in the other, nor shall any charge be made in the country of destination upon official correspondence which under the postal regulations of the country of origin is entitled to freedom from postage ; but the country of destination will receive, forward, and deliver the same free of charge.

ARTICLE 4.

In case any correspondence is tendered for mailing in either country obviously with the intention to evade the higher postage rates applicable to it in the other country, it shall be refused, unless payment be made of such higher rates.

ARTICLE 5.

(a) Exchanges of mails under this convention, whether by sea or overland, shall be effected through the post-offices of both countries already designated as exchange post-offices, or through such others as may be hereafter agreed upon, under such regulations relative to the details of the exchanges as may be mutually determined to be essential to the security and expedition of the mails and the protection of the customs revenues.

(b) Each country shall provide for and bear the expense of the conveyance of its mails to the other ; or if by agreement the conveyance in both directions in overland exchanges, other than by railway, is provided by one of them, the expense of transportation shall be shared between them in proportion to the distance traveled over the territory of each.

ARTICLE 6.

The United States of America and the Dominion of Canada each grants to the other, free of any charges, detention, or examination whatsoever, the transit across its territory, of the *closed* mails made up by any authorized exchange office of either country, addressed to any other exchange office of the same country, or to any exchange office of the other country.

ARTICLE 7.

(a) Any packet of mailable correspondence may be registered upon payment of the rate of postage and the registration fee applicable thereto in the country of origin.

(b) An acknowledgment of the delivery of a registered article shall be returned to the sender when requested ; but either country may require of the sender prepayment of a fee therefor not exceeding five cents.

ARTICLE 8.

(a) Overland exchanges of ordinary international correspondence may be effected without the use of letter-bills, but registered correspondence must be accompanied by a descriptive list thereof, by means of which the registered articles may be identified for the purpose of acknowledgment by the receiving offices.

(b) If a registered article advised shall not be found in the mails by the receiving office its absence shall be immediately reported by the receiving to the sending office.

ARTICLE 9.

Ordinary and registered exchanges, unless the latter be made in through registered pouches, shall be effected in properly sealed sacks.

ARTICLE 10.

(a) All registered articles, ordinary letters, postal cards, and other manuscript matter, business or commercial papers, books (bound or stitched), proofs of printing, engravings, photographs, drawings, maps, and other articles manifestly of value to the sender, which are not delivered from any cause, shall be reciprocally returned monthly without charge, through the central administrations of the two countries, in special packets or sacks marked "Rebuts," after the expiration of the period for their retention required by the laws or regulations of the country of destination ; the returned registered articles to be accompanied by a descriptive list, and the special packets or sacks used for returning undelivered matter to be forwarded under registration when registered articles are returned in them.

(b) Fully prepaid letters which bear requests by the senders for their return in case of non-delivery by a certain date, or within a specified time, shall be reciprocally returned, without charge, directly to the despatching exchange office, at the expiration of the period for their retention indicated in the requests.

(c) Fully prepaid letters bearing on the covers the business cards, the names and addresses of the senders or designation of places to which they may be returned, as post-office box, street and number, &c., without requests for their return in case of non-delivery within a specified time, shall be reciprocally returned without charge directly to the despatching exchange office, at the expiration of thirty days from the date of their receipt at the office of destination.

ARTICLE 11.

All matters connected with the exchange of mails between the two countries, which are not herein provided for, shall be governed by the provisions of the Universal Postal Union Convention and Regulations now in force, or which may hereafter be enacted, for the governance of such matters in the exchanges of mails between countries of the Universal Postal Union generally, so far as the articles of such Universal Postal Union Convention shall be obligatory upon both of the contracting parties.

ARTICLE 12.

The Postmaster-General of the United States of America, and the Postmaster-General of the Dominion of Canada, shall have authority to jointly make such further regulations of order and detail as may be found necessary to carry out the present Convention from time to time; and may by agreement prescribe conditions for the admission to the mails of any of the articles prohibited by Article 1.

ARTICLE 13.

This Convention abrogates the special postal convention between the two countries signed at the city of Washington the first day of February, 1875, and at Ottawa the twenty-seventh day of January, 1875. It shall be ratified by the contracting countries in accordance with their respective laws, and its ratification shall be exchanged at the city of Washington as early as possible, not later than one month from this date. It shall take effect on the first day of March, 1888, and shall continue in force until terminated by mutual agreement, or annulled at the instance of the Post-Office Department of either country, upon six months previous notice given to the other.

Done in duplicate and signed at Washington the twelfth day of January, one thousand eight hundred and eighty-eight, and at Ottawa the nineteenth day of January, 1888.

[SEAL.]

WM. F. VILAS,
Postmaster-General of the United States of America.
A. W. McLELAN,
Postmaster-General of the Dominion of Canada.

The foregoing Convention between the United States of America and the Dominion of Canada has been negotiated and concluded with my advice and consent, and is hereby approved and ratified.

In testimony whereof, I have caused the Great Seal of the United States to be hereunto affixed.

[SEAL.]

GROVER CLEVELAND.

By the President:
T. F. BAYARD,
Secretary of State,
Washington, January 26, 1888.

AMENDMENT TO POSTAL CONVENTION BETWEEN THE UNITED STATES AND CANADA OF JANUARY, 1888.

For the purpose of establishing a uniform rate of postage upon certain mail-matter exchanged between the United States of America and the Dominion of Canada, the undersigned, Don M. Dickinson, Postmaster-General of the United States of America, and Archibald Woodbury McLelan, Postmaster-General of the Dominion of Canada, by virtue of authority vested in them by law, have agreed upon the following amendment to the Postal Convention between the two contracting countries signed at Washington the 12th day of January, 1888, and at Ottawa the 19th day of January, 1888.

ARTICLE 1.

Amend article 1, paragraph C, of the above referred-to convention, so as to establish a uniform rate of postage of 1 cent per ounce upon all merchandise, and 1 cent per 2 ounces upon all books, pamphlets, occasional publications, printed circulars, price-currents, hand-bills, book and newspaper manuscript, printer's proof-sheets (whether corrected or not), maps, prints, advertising sheets, drawings, engravings, lithographs, photographs, sheet music (whether printed or written), documents wholly or partly printed or written, such as deeds, insurance policies, or other documents of like nature exchanged in the mails between the two contracting countries; and to establish that the registration charge, in addition to postage on correspondence passing between the United States and Canada, shall be a rate of not less than 5 cents and not exceeding 10 cents in either country.

ARTICLE 2.

This arrangement shall take effect upon the 1st day of May, 1888, and shall continue in force until terminated by mutual agreement, or annulled at the instance of the Post-Office Department of either country upon six months' previous notice given to the other.

Done in duplicate and signed in Washington, April 27, 1888, and in Ottawa April 25, 1888.

[SEAL.]
                    DON M. DICKINSON,
          Postmaster-General of the United States of America.
[SEAL.]
                    A. W. McLELAN,
          Postmaster-General of the Dominion of Canada.

I hereby approve the foregoing amended article, and in testimony thereof I have caused the seal of the United States to be affixed hereto.

[SEAL.]   GROVER CLEVELAND.

By the President:
  T. F. BAYARD,
      Secretary of State.
WASHINGTON, D. C., *April 30, 1888.*

APPENDIX B.

Postal convention between Jamaica and the United States of America.

For the purpose of making better postal arrangements between Jamaica and the United States of America, the undersigned, Sir Henry Wylie Norman, G. C. B., G. C. M. G., C. I. E., governor of Jamaica, and William F. Vilas, Postmaster-General of the United States of America, by virtue of authority vested in them by law, have agreed upon the following articles for the establishment of a parcels-post system of exchanges between the two countries.

ARTICLE I.

The provisions of this Convention relate only to parcels of mail matter to be exchanged by the system herein provided for, and do not affect the arrangements now existing under the Universal Postal Union Convention, which will continue as heretofore; and all the agreements hereinafter contained apply exclusively to mails exchanged under these articles, *directly* between the office of New York, in the State of New York, and such other offices within the United States as may be hereafter designated by the Postmaster-General of the United States, and the office of Kingston, Jamaica, and such other offices within the Island of Jamaica as may be hereafter designated by the Postmaster of Jamaica; such matters to be admitted to the mails under these articles as shall be sent through such exchange offices from any place in either country to any place in the other.

ARTICLE II.

There shall be admitted to the mails exchanged under this Convention, articles of merchandise and mail matter except letters, post-cards, and written matter of all kinds that are admitted under any conditions to the domestic mails of the country of origin, except that no packet must exceed 11 pounds (or 5 kilograms) in weight, nor the following dimensions: Greatest length in any direction, 2 feet; greatest girth, 4 feet; and must be so wrapped or inclosed as to permit their contents to be easily examined by postmasters and customs officers; and except that the following articles are prohibited:

Publications which violate the copyright laws of the country of destination; poisons, and explosive or inflammable substances; fatty substances, liquids, and those which easily liquify, confections and pastes; live or dead animals, except dead insects and reptiles when thoroughly dried; fruits and vegetables, and substances which exhale a bad odor; lottery tickets, lottery advertisements, or lottery circulars; all obscene or immoral articles; articles which may in any way damage or destroy the mails, or injure the persons handling them.

ARTICLE III.

A letter or communication of the nature of personal correspondence must not accompany, be written on, or inclosed with any parcel.

If such be found, the letter will be placed in the mails if separable, and if the communication be inseparably attached, the whole package will be rejected. If, however, any such should inadvertently be forwarded, the country of destination will collect double rates of postage according to the Universal Postal Union Convention.

No parcel may contain parcels intended for delivery at an address other than that borne by the parcel itself. If such inclosed parcels be detected, they must be sent forward singly, charged with new and distinct parcel-post rates,

ARTICLE IV.

The packages in question shall be subject in the country of destination to all customs duties and all customs regulations in force in that country for the protection of its customs revenues, and to the following rates of postage, which shall in all cases be required to be fully prepaid with postage-stamps of the country of origin, viz:

In the United States, for a parcel not exceeding 1 pound in weight, 12 cents; and for each additional pound, or fraction of a pound, 12 cents.

In Jamaica, for a parcel not exceeding 1 pound in weight, 6 pence, and for each additional pound, or fraction of a pound, 6 pence.

ARTICLE V.

The sender of each package must make a *Customs Declaration*, pasted upon or attached to the package, upon a special form provided for the purpose (see Model 1, "A," annexed hereto), giving a general description of the parcel, an accurate statement of the contents and value, date of mailing, and the sender's signature and place of residence, and place of address.

The sender will, at the time of mailing the package, receive a certificate of mailing from the post-office where the package is mailed, on a form like Model 2, annexed hereto.

The sender of a package may obtain a return receipt for the same by paying in the United States a fee of 5 cents, and in Jamaica 2 pence, in addition to the postage on each packet, to be affixed to the packet in stamps of the country of origin.

The sender of a package may have the same registered by paying the registration fee required for registered articles in the country of origin, and will receive the return receipt without special charge therefor.

ARTICLE VI.

The addressees of registered articles shall be advised of the arrival of a package addressed to them, by a notice from the post-office of destination.

The packages shall be delivered to addressees in the country of destination free of charge *for postage;* but the customs duties properly chargeable thereon shall be collected on delivery in accordance with the customs regulations of the country of destination; and the country of destination may, at its option, levy and collect from the addressee for interior service and delivery a charge not exceeding 5 cents in the United States and 2½ pence in Jamaica on each single parcel of whatever weight; and if the weight exceeds 1 pound, a charge equal to 1 cent or 1 half-penny for each 4 ounces of weight or fraction thereof.

ARTICLE VII.

The packages shall be considered as a component part of the mails exchanged direct between the United States and Jamaica, to be dispatched by the country of origin to the other at its cost and by such means as it provides, but must be forwarded, at the option of the dispatching office, either in boxes prepared expressly for the purpose or in ordinary mail sacks, to be marked "Parcel post," and not to contain any other articles of mail matter, and to be securely sealed with wax, or otherwise, as may be mutually provided by regulations hereunder.

Each country shall promptly return *empty* to the dispatching office by next mail, all such bags and boxes, but subject to other regulations between the two administrations.

Although articles admitted under this convention will be transmitted as aforesaid between the exchange offices, they should be so carefully packed as to be safely transmitted in the open mails of either country, both in going to the exchange office in the country of origin and to the office of address in the country of destination.

Each dispatch of a parcel-post mail must be accompanied by a descriptive list, in duplicate, of all the packages sent, showing distinctly the list number of each parcel, the name of the sender, the name of the addressee with address of destination, and the declared contents and value; and must be inclosed in one of the boxes or sacks of such dispatch. (See Model 3 annexed hereto.)

ARTICLE VIII.

As soon as the mail shall have reached the office of destination, that office shall check the contents of the mail.

In the event of the parcel bill not having been received, a substitute should be at once prepared.

Any errors in the entries on the parcel bill which may be discovered, should, after verification by a second officer, be corrected and noted for report to the dispatching office on a form, "Verification certificate," which should be sent in the special envelope.

If a parcel advised on the bill be not received, after the non-receipt has been verified by a second officer, the entry on the bill should be canceled and the fact reported at once.

If a parcel be observed to be insufficiently prepaid, it must not be taxed with deficient postage, but the circumstance must be reported on the verification certificate form.

Should a parcel be received in a damaged or imperfect condition, full particulars should be reported on the same form.

If no verification certificate or note of error be received, a parcel mail shall be considered as duly delivered, having been found on examination correct in all respects.

ARTICLE IX.

If a package can not be delivered as addressed, or is refused, the sender will be communicated with through the central administration of the office of destination, as to the manner in which he desires the package to be disposed of, and if no reply is received from him within a period of three months from the date of the notice, the package may be sold for the benefit of whom it may concern.

An order for redirection or reforwarding must be accompanied by the amount due for postage necessary for the return of the article to the office of origin, at the ordinary parcel rates.

When the contents of a parcel which can not be delivered are liable to deterioration or corruption, they may be destroyed at once, if necessary, or if expedient, sold, without previous notice or judicial formality, for the benefit of the right person, the particulars of each sale being noticed by one post-office to the other.

ARTICLE X.

The Post-Office Department of either of the contracting countries will not be responsible for the loss or damage of any package, and no indemnity can consequently be claimed by the sender or addressee in either country.

ARTICLE XI.

Each country shall retain to its own use the whole of the postages, registration and delivery fees, it collects on said packages; consequently, this convention will give rise to no separate accounts between the two countries.

ARTICLE XII.

The Postmaster-General of the United States of America, and the Postmaster of Jamaica, shall have authority to jointly make such further regulations of order and detail as may be found necessary to carry out the present convention from time to time; and may, by agreement, prescribe conditions for the admission in packages exchanged under this convention of any of the articles prohibited by Article II.

ARTICLE XIII.

This convention shall take effect and operations thereunder shall begin on the first day of October, 1887, and shall continue in force until terminated by mutual agreement, but may be annulled at the desire of either Department, upon six months' previous notice given to the other.

Done in duplicate, and signed at Washington the twenty-second day of July, 1887, and at Kingston the third day of September, 1887.

H. W. NORMAN,
Governor of Jamaica.

[Seal of Post-Office Dep't of U. S.]

WM. F. VILAS,
Postmaster-General of the United States.

The foregoing parcel post convention between Jamaica and the United States of America, has been negotiated and concluded with my advice and consent, and is hereby approved and ratified.

In testimony whereof I have caused the Great Seal of the United States to be hereunto affixed.

GROVER CLEVELAND.

By the President:
    T. F. BAYARD,
        Secretary of State.
WASHINGTON, *September 15th,* 1887.

[Great Seal of U. S.]

A.

FORM 1.

Parcel Post between the United States and Jamaica.

Date. Stamp.	FORM OF CUSTOMS DECLARATION.	Place to which the parcel is addressed.

Description of parcel: [State whether box, basket, bag, etc.]	Contents.	Value.	Per cent.	Total customs charges.
		$		$
Total.		$		$

Date of posting: ...., 18..; signature and address of sender { ....

☞ For use of Post-Office only, and to be filled up at the office of exchange.

Parcel Bill No. .... ; No. of rates prepaid .... ; Entry No. ....

B.

Parcel Post from Jamaica.

The import duty assessed by an officer of customs on contents of this parcel amounts to $......, which must be paid before the parcel is delivered.

Date

Stamp.

.... *Customs Officer.*

C.

Parcel Post from Jamaica.

This parcel has been passed by an officer of customs and must be delivered FREE OF CHARGE.

Date

Stamp.

.... *Postmaster-General.*

FORM 2.

Parcel Post.

A parcel addressed as under has been posted here this day.

Office stamp.	....
	....
	....

This certificate is given to inform the sender of the posting of a parcel, and does not indicate that any liability in respect of such parcel attaches to the Postmaster-General.

FORM 3.

| Date stamp of the United States Post-Office. | *Parcels from the United States to Jamaica.* | Date stamp of the Jamaica Post-Office. |

Parcel Bill No......, dated...... 18..; per S. S. "......."

* Sheet No. ....

Entry No.	Origin of parcel.	Name of addressee.	Address of parcel.	Declared contents.	Declared value.	Number of rates prepaid to	Remarks.
					$		
			Totals..	$			

When more than one sheet is required for the entry of the parcels sent by the mail, it will be sufficient if the undermentioned particulars are entered on the last sheet of the Parcel Bill.

lbs.

* Total number of parcels sent by the mail to Jamaica......................
* Total weight of mail...........................

* Number of boxes or other receptacles forming the mail...................
* Deduct weight of receptacles...................

Signature of dispatching officer at New York Post-Office...........................
Net weight of parcels.......................

Signature of receiving officer, Post-Office Kingston, Jamaica.
....

APPENDIX C.

Postal convention between Barbados and the United States of America.

For the purpose of making better postal arrangements between Barbados and the United States of America, the undersigned, Sir Charles Cameron Lees, K. C. M. G., Governor of Barbados, and William F. Vilas, Postmaster-General of the United States of America, by virtue of authority vested in them by law, have agreed upon the following articles for the establishment of a parcels post system of exchanges between the two countries.

ARTICLE I.

The provisions of this Convention relate only to parcels of mail matter to be exchanged by the system herein provided for, and do not affect the arrangements now existing under the Universal Postal Union Convention, which will continue as heretofore; and all the agreements hereinafter contained apply exclusively to mails exchanged under these articles, *directly* between the office of New York, in the State of New York, and such other offices within the United States as may be hereafter designated by the Postmaster-General of the United States, and the office of Bridgetown, Barbados, and such other offices within the Island of Barbados, as may hereafter be designated by the Postmaster of Barbados; such matter to be admitted to the mails under these articles as shall be sent through such exchange offices from any place in either country to any place in the other.

ARTICLE II.

There shall be admitted to the mails exchanged under this Convention, articles of merchandise and mail matter, except letters, post cards, and written matter of all kinds that are admitted under any conditions to the domestic mails of the country of origin, except that no packet must exceed 11 pounds (or 5 kilograms) in weight, nor the following dimensions: Greatest length in any direction, three feet six inches; greatest length and girth combined, six feet; and must be so wrapped or inclosed as to permit their contents to be easily examined by postmasters and customs officers; and except that the following articles are prohibited:

Publications which violate the copyright laws of the country of destination; poisons, and explosive or inflammable substances; fatty substances, liquids, and those which easily liquefy, confections and pastes; live or dead animals, except dead insects and reptiles when thoroughly dried; fruits and vegetables, and substances which exhale a bad odor; lottery tickets, lottery advertisements or lottery circulars; all obscene or immoral articles; articles which may in any way damage or destroy the mails, or injure the persons handling them.

ARTICLE III.

A letter or communication of the nature of personal correspondence must not accompany, be written on, or inclosed with any parcel.

If such be found, the letter will be placed in the mails if separable, and if the communication be inseparably attached, the whole package will be rejected. If, however, any such should inadvertently be forwarded, the country of destination will collect double rates of postage according to the Universal Postal Union Convention.

No parcel may contain parcels intended for delivery at an address other than that borne by the parcel itself. If such inclosed parcels be detected, they must be sent forward singly, charged with new and distinct parcel-post rates.

ARTICLE IV.

The packages in question shall be subject in the country of destination to all customs duties and all customs regulations in force in that country for the protection of its customs revenues, and to the following rates of postage, which shall in all cases be required to be FULLY PREPAID with postage stamps of the country of origin, viz :

In the United States, for a parcel not exceeding one pound in weight, 12 cents ; and for each additional pound, or fraction of a pound, 12 cents.

In Barbados, for a parcel not exceeding one pound in weight, six pence, and for each additional pound, or fraction of a pound, six pence.

ARTICLE V.

The sender of each package must make a *Customs Declaration*, pasted upon or attached to the package, upon a special form provided for the purpose (see Model 1, annexed hereto), giving a general description of the parcel, an accurate statement of the contents and value, date of mailing, and the sender's signature and place of residence, and place of address.

The sender will, at the time of mailing the package, receive a certificate of mailing from the post-office where the package is mailed, on a form like Model 2, annexed hereto.

The sender of a package may obtain a return receipt for the same by paying in the United States a fee of five cents, and in Barbados two and a half pence, in addition to the postage on each packet, to be affixed to the packet in stamps of the country of origin.

ARTICLE VI.

The packages shall be delivered to addressees in the country of destination free of charge *for postage ;* but the customs duties properly chargeable thereon shall be collected on delivery in accordance with the customs regulations of the country of destination ; and the country of destination may, at its option, levy and collect from the addressee for interior service and delivery a charge not exceeding five cents in the United States and two and a half pence in Barbados on each single parcel of whatever weight ; and if the weight exceeds one pound, a charge equal to one cent or one half-penny for each four ounces of weight or fraction thereof.

ARTICLE VII.

The packages shall be considered as a component part of the mails exchanged direct between the United States and Barbados, to be dispatched by the country of origin to the other at its cost and by such means as it provides, but must be forwarded, at the option of the dispatching office, either in boxes prepared expressly for the purpose or in ordinary mail sacks, these boxes or sacks to be marked "Parcel post," and not to contain any other articles of mail matter, and to be securely sealed with wax, or otherwise, as may be mutually provided by regulations hereunder.

Each country shall promptly return *empty* to the dispatching office by next mail, all such bags and boxes, but subject to other regulations between the two administrations.

Although articles admitted under this Convention will be transmitted as aforesaid between the exchange offices, they should be so carefully packed as to be safely transmitted in the open mails of either country, both in going to the exchange office in the country of origin and to the office of address in the country of destination.

Each dispatch of a parcel post mail must be accompanied by a descriptive list, in duplicate, of all the packages sent, showing distinctly the list number of each parcel, the name of the sender, the name of the addressee with address of destination, and the declared contents and value ; and must be inclosed in one of the boxes or sacks of such dispatch. (See Model 3 annexed hereto.)

ARTICLE VIII.

As soon as the mail shall have reached the office of destination, that office shall check the contents of the mail.

In the event of the parcel bill not having been received, a substitute should be at once prepared.

Any errors in the entries on the parcel bill which may be discovered, should, after verification by a second officer, be corrected and noted for report to the dispatching office on a form, "Verification certificate," which should be sent in the special envelope.

If a parcel advised on the bill be not received, after the non-receipt has been verified by a second officer, the entry on the bill should be canceled and the fact reported at once.

If a parcel be observed to be insufficiently prepaid, it must not be taxed with deficient postage, but the circumstance must be reported on the verification certificate form.

Should a parcel be received in a damaged or imperfect condition, full particulars should be reported on the same form.

If no verification certificate or note of error be received, a parcel mail shall be considered as duly delivered, having been found on examination correct in all respects.

ARTICLE IX.

If a package can not be delivered as addressed, or is refused, the sender will be communicated with through the central administration of the office of destination, as to the manner in which he desires the package to be disposed of, and if no reply is received from him within a period of three months from the date of the notice, the package may be sold for the benefit of whom it may concern.

An order for redirection or reforwarding must be accompanied by the amount due for postage necessary for the return of the article to the office of origin, at the ordinary parcel rates.

When the contents of a parcel which can not be delivered are liable to deterioration or corruption, they may be destroyed at once, if necessary, or if expedient, sold, without previous notice or judicial formality, for the benefit of the right person, the particulars of each sale being noticed by one post-office to the other.

ARTICLE X.

The Post-Office Department of either of the contracting countries will not be responsible for the loss or damage of any package, and no indemnity can consequently be claimed by the sender or addressee in either country.

ARTICLE XI.

Each country shall retain to its own use the whole of the postages and delivery fees, it collects on said packages; consequently, this Convention will give rise to no separate accounts between the two countries.

ARTICLE XII.

The Postmaster-General of the United States of America, and the Postmaster of Barbados, shall have authority to jointly make such further regulations of order and detail as may be found necessary to carry out the present Convention from time to time; and may, by mutual agreement, prescribe conditions for the admission in packages exchanged under this Convention of any of the articles prohibited by Article II.

ARTICLE XIII.

This Convention shall take effect and operations thereunder shall begin on the first day of December, 1887, and shall continue in force until terminated by mutual agreement, but may be annulled at the desire of either Department, upon six months' previous notice given to the other.

Done in duplicate, and signed at Washington the tenth day of November, 1887, and at Bridgetown, the twenty-ninth day of October, 1887.

C. C. LEES,
Governor of Barbados.

[Seal of Post-Office Dept. of U. S.]

WM. F. VILAS,
Postmaster-General of the United States.

The foregoing Parcel Post Convention between Barbados and the United States of America, has been negotiated and concluded with my advice and consent, and is hereby approved and ratified.

In testimony whereof I have caused the Great Seal of the United to be hereunto affixed.

GROVER CLEVELAND.

By the President:

[Great Seal of U. S.]

T. F. BAYARD,
Secretary of State.

WASHINGTON, *November* 10th, 1887.

FORM 1.

Parcel Post between the United States and Barbados.

Date. Stamp.	FORM OF CUSTOMS DECLARATION.			Place to which the parcel is addressed.
Description of parcel; [State whether box, basket, bag, etc.]	Contents.	Value.	Per cent.	Total customs charges.
		$		$
Total.		$		$

Date of posting:.............., 18..; signature and address of sender $\{$ ....

☞ For use of Post-Office only, and to be filled up at the office of exchange.
Parcel Bill No..............; No. of rates prepaid..............; Entry No...........

Parcel Post from..................
The import duty assessed by an officer of customs on contents of this parcel amounts to $......; which must be paid before the package is delivered.

Date.

Stamp.

....
Postmaster-General.

Parcel Post from..............
This parcel has been passed by an officer of customs and must be delivered FREE OF CHARGE.

Date.

Stamp.

....
Postmaster-General.

FORM 2.

Parcel Post.

A parcel addressed as under has been posted here this day.

Office stamp.	....
	....
	....

This certificate is given to inform the sender of the posting of a parcel, and does not indicate that any liability in respect of such parcel attaches to the Postmaster-General.

FORM 3.

| Date stamp of the United States Post-Office. | *Parcels from the United States to Barbados.* | Date stamp of the Barbados Post-Office. |

Parcel Bill No....., dated...... 18.. ; per S. S. "...."

*Sheet No......

Entry No.	Origin of parcel.	Name of addressee.	Address of parcel.	Declared contents.	Declared value.	Number of rates prepaid to Barbados.	Remarks.
					$		
				Totals ..	$		

When more than one sheet is required for the entry of the parcels sent by the mail, it will be sufficient if the undermentioned particulars are entered on the last sheet of the Parcel Bill.

lbs.

*Total number of parcels sent by the mail to Barbados ... .
*Number of boxes or other receptacles forming the mail ....
Signature of dispatching officer at New York Office..............................

*Total weight of mail..
*Deduct weight of receptacles.................
*Net weight of parcels......................

Signature of receiving officer, Post-Office Bridgetown, Barbados.
....

APPENDIX D.

Postal Convention between the United States of America and the Bahamas.

For the purpose of making better postal arrangements between the United States of America and the Bahamas, the undersigned, William F. Vilas, Postmaster-General of the United States of America, and Sir Ambrose Shea, K. C. M. G., governor of the Bahamas, by virtue of authority vested in them by law, have agreed upon the following articles for the establishment of a parcel-post system of exchanges between the two countries.

ARTICLE I.

The provisions of this Convention relate only to parcels of mail matter to be exchanged by the system herein provided for, and do not affect the arrangements now existing under the Universal Postal Union Convention, which will continue as heretofore; and all the agreements hereinafter contained apply exclusively to mails exchanged under these articles, *directly* between the office of New York, in the State of New York, and such other offices within the United States as may be hereafter designated by the Postmaster-General of the United States, and the office of Nassau, N. P., Bahamas, and such other offices within the Bahamas as may be hereafter designated by the Postmaster of the Bahamas; such matter to be admitted to the mails under these articles as shall be sent through such exchange offices from any place in either country to any place in the other.

ARTICLE II.

There shall be admitted to the mails exchanged under this Convention, articles of merchandise and mail matter except letters, post-cards, and written matter of all kinds that are admitted under any conditions to the domestic mails of the country of origin, except that no packet must exceed 11 pounds (or 5 kilograms) in weight, nor the following dimensions: Greatest length in any direction 3 feet 6 inches; greatest length and girth combined, 6 feet; and must be so wrapped or inclosed as to permit their contents to be easily examined by postmasters and customs officers; and except that the following articles are prohibited:

Publications which violate the copyright laws of the country of destination; poisons, and explosive or inflammable substances; fatty substances, liquids, and those which easily liquify, confections and pastes; live or dead animals, except dead insects and reptiles when thoroughly dried; fruits and vegetables, and substances which exhale a bad odor; lottery tickets, lottery advertisements, or lottery circulars; all obscene or immoral articles; articles which may in any way damage or destroy the mails, or injure the persons handling them.

ARTICLE III.

A letter or communication of the nature of personal correspondence must not accompany, be written on, or inclosed with any parcel.

If such be found, the letter will be placed in the mails, if separable, and if the communication be inseparably attached, the whole package will be rejected. If, however, any such should inadvertently be forwarded, the country of destination will collect double rates of postage according to the Universal Postal Union Convention.

No parcel may contain parcels intended for delivery at an address other than that borne by the parcel itself. If such inclosed parcels be detected, they must be sent forward singly, charged with new and distinct parcel-post rates.

ARTICLE IV.

The packages in question shall be subject in the country of destination to all customs duties and all customs regulations in force in that country for the protection of its customs revenues, and to the following rates of postage, which shall in all cases be required to be FULLY PREPAID with postage stamps of the country of origin, viz:

In the United States, for a parcel not exceeding one pound in weight, 12 cents; and for each additional pound, or fraction of a pound, 12 cents.

In the Bahamas, for a parcel not exceeding one pound in weight, 6 pence; and for each additional pound, or fraction of a pound, 6 pence.

ARTICLE V.

The sender of each package must make a *customs declaration*, pasted upon or attached to the package, upon a special form provided for the purpose (see Model I, "A,"annexed hereto), giving a general description of the parcel, an accurate statement of the contents and value, date of mailing, and the sender's signature and place of residence, and place of address.

The sender will, at the time of mailing the package, receive a certificate of mailing from the post-office where the package is mailed, on a form like Model 2, annexed hereto.

The sender of a package may obtain a return receipt for the same by paying in the United States a fee of 5 cents, and in the Bahamas 2 pence, in addition to the postage on each packet, to be affixed to the packet in stamps of the country of origin.

The sender of a package may have the same registered by paying the registration fee required for registered articles in the country of origin, and will receive the return receipt without special charge therefor.

ARTICLE VI.

The addressees of registered articles shall be advised of the arrival of a package addressed to them, by a notice from the post-office of destination.

The packages shall be delivered to addressees in the country of destination free of charge *for postage;* but the customs duties properly chargeable thereon shall be collected on delivery in accordance with the customs regulations of the country of destination; and the country of destination may, at its option, levy and collect from the addressee for interior service and delivery a charge not exceeding 5 cents in the United States and 2½ pence in the Bahamas on each single parcel of whatever weight; and if the weight exceeds 1 pound, a charge equal to 1 cent or one half-penny for each 4 ounces of weight or fraction thereof.

ARTICLE VII.

The packages shall be considered as a component part of the mails exchanged direct between the United States and the Bahamas, to be dispatched by the country of origin to the other at its cost and by such means as it provides, but must be forwarded, at the option of the dispatching office, either in boxes prepared expressly for the purpose or in ordinary mail sacks, to be marked "Parcel post," and not to contain any other articles of mail matter, and to be securely sealed with wax, or otherwise, as may be mutually provided by regulations hereunder.

Each country shall promptly return *empty* to the dispatching office by next mail, all such bags and boxes, but subject to other regulations between the two administrations.

Although articles admitted under this Convention will be transmitted as aforesaid between the exchange offices, they should be so carefully packed as to be safely transmitted in the open mails of either country, both in going to the exchange office in the country of origin and to the office of address in the country of destination.

Each dispatch of a parcel post mail must be accompanied by a descriptive list, in duplicate, of all the packages sent, showing distinctly the list number of each parcel, the name of the sender, the name of the addressee with address of destination, and the declared contents and value; and must be inclosed in one of the boxes or sacks of such dispatch. (See Model 3 annexed hereto.)

ARTICLE VIII.

As soon as the mail shall have reached the office of destination, that office shall check the contents of the mail.

In the event of the parcel bill not having been received, a substitute should be at once prepared.

Any errors in the entries on the parcel bill which may be discovered, should, after verification by a second officer, be corrected and noted for report to the dispatching office on a form, "Verification certificate," which should be sent in the special envelope.

If a parcel advised on the bill be not received, after the non-receipt has been verified by a second officer, the entry on the bill should be canceled and the fact reported at once.

If a parcel be observed to be insufficiently prepaid, it must not be taxed with deficient postage, but the circumstance must be reported on the verification certificate form.

Should a parcel be received in a damaged or imperfect condition, full particulars should be reported on the same form.

If no verification certificate or note of error be received, a parcel mail shall be considered as duly delivered, having been found on examination correct in all respects.

ARTICLE IX.

If a package can not be delivered as addressed, or is refused, the sender will be communicated with through the central administration of the office of destination, as to the manner in which he desires the package to be disposed of, and if no reply is received from him within a period of three months from the date of the notice, the package may be sold for the benefit of whom it may concern.

An order for redirection or reforwarding must be accompanied by the amount due for postage necessary for the return of the article to the office of origin, at the ordinary parcel rates.

When the contents of a parcel which can not be delivered are liable to deterioration or corruption, they may be destroyed at once, if necessary, or if expedient, sold, without previous notice or judicial formality, for the benefit of the right person, the particulars of each sale being noticed by one post-office to the other.

ARTICLE X.

The Post-Office Department of either of the contracting countries will not be responsible for the loss or damage of any package, and no indemnity can consequently be claimed by the sender or addressee in either country.

ARTICLE XI.

Each country shall retain to its own use the whole of the postages, registration and delivery fees, it collects on said packages; consequently, this Convention will give rise to no separate accounts between the two countries.

ARTICLE XII.

The Postmaster-General of the United States of America, and the Postmaster of the Bahamas, shall have authority to jointly make such further regulations of order and detail as may be found necessary to carry out the present Convention from time to time; and may, by agreement, prescribe conditions for the admission in packages exchanged under this Convention of any of the articles prohibited by Article II.

ARTICLE XIII.

This Convention shall take effect and operations thereunder shall begin on the first day of February, 1888, and shall continue in force until terminated by mutual agreement, but may be annulled at the desire of either Department upon six months' previous notice given to the other.

Done in duplicate, and signed at Washington the twentieth day of December, 1887. and at Nassau, N. P., the ninth day of January, 1888.

[Seal of Post-Office Dep't of U. S.]　　　　　　　　WM. F. VILAS,
　　　　　　　　　　　　　　　　　　Postmaster-General of the United States.
　　　　　　　　　　　　　　　　　　A. SHEA,
　　　　　　　　　　　　　　　　　　Governor of the Bahamas.

The foregoing Parcel Post Convention between the United States of America and the Bahamas has been negotiated and concluded with my advice and consent, and is hereby approved and ratified.

In testimony whereof I have caused the Great Seal of the United States to be hereunto affixed.

[Great seal of U. S.]　　　　　　　　　　　　　GROVER CLEVELAND.

By the President:
　　T. F. BAYARD,
　　　　Secretary of State.

WASHINGTON, *January 16th,* 1888.

A.

FORM 1.

Parcel Post between the United States and the Bahamas.

Date. Stamp.	FORM OF CUSTOMS DECLARATION.	Place to which the parcel is addressed.

Description of parcel: [State whether box, basket, bag, &c.]	Contents.	Value.	Per cent.	Total customs charges.
		$		$
	Total.	$		$

Date of posting: ...., 18.. ; signature and address of sender { ....

☞ For use of Post-Office only, and to be filled up at the office of exchange.

Parcel Bill No.............; No. of rates prepaid.............; Entry No.............

B.

Parcel Post from ....

The import duty assessed by an officer of customs on contents of this parcel amounts to $.:...., which must be paid before the parcel is delivered.

Date Stamp.

....
Postmaster-General.

C.

Parcel Post from ....

This parcel has been passed by an officer of customs and must be delivered

FREE OF CHARGE.

Date Stamp.

....
Postmaster-General

FORM 2.

Parcel Post.

A parcel addressed as under has been posted here this day.

| Office stamp. | .... |

This certificate is given to inform the sender of the posting of a parcel, and does not indicate that any liability in respect of such parcel attaches to the Postmaster-General.

FORM 3.

Date stamp of the United States Post-Office.

Parcels from the United States to the Bahamas.

Date stamp of the Bahamas Post-Office.

Parcel Bill No. ...., dated .... 18.. ; per S. S. "...."

* Sheet No. ....

Entry No.	Origin of parcel.	Name of addressee.	Address of parcel.	Declared contents.	Declared value.	Number of rates prepaid to the Bahamas.	Remarks.
					$		
				Totals..	$		

When more than one sheet is required for the entry of the parcels sent by the mail, it will be sufficient if the undermentioned particulars are entered on the last sheet of the Parcel Bill.

* Total number of parcels sent by the mail to the Bahamas........................

* Number of boxes or other receptacles forming the mail....................

Signature of dispatching officer at New York Post-Office............................

* Total weight of mail................................

* Deduct weight of receptacles....................

* Net weight of parcels........................

Signature of receiving officer, Post-Office, Bahamas.

....

Ap1

Postal convention between the Un;

For the purpose of making better p(
of America and British Honduras, the
General of the United States of Ameri
of British Honduras, by virtue of auth
the following articles for the establisl
between the two countries.

A

The provisions of this Convention n
changed by the system herein provided
existing under the Universal Postal U1
tofore; and all the agreements herein:
changed under these articles, *directly* 1
other offices within the United States
master-General of the United States, a
within British Honduras, as may be be
ish Honduras; such matter to be admi
be sent through such exchange offices
in the other.

Ar

There shall be admitted to the mail
merchandise and mail matter except
all kinds that are admitted under any
try of origin, except that no packet mu:
nor the following dimensions: Greatest
greatest length and girth combined, si>
to permit their contents to be easily o:
and except that the following articles :
    Publications which violate the cop;
poisons, and explosive or inflammabl:
those which easily liquefy, confections
insects and reptiles when thoroughly (
which exhale a bad odor; lottery ticket;
all obscene or immoral articles; article:
the mails, or injure the persons handlin;

Ar:

A letter or communication of the na'
company, be written on, or inclosed wi:
    If such be found, the letter will be pl:
munication be inseparably attached, th
ever, any such should inadvertently be
collect double rates of postage accordin
    No parcel may contain parcels inteud:
borne by the parcel itself. If such incl
forward singly, charged with new and (

ARTICLE IV.

The packages in question shall be subject in the country of destination to all customs duties and all customs regulations in force in that country for the protection of its customs revenues, and to the following rates of postage, which shall in all cases be required to be FULLY PREPAID with postage stamps of the country of origin, viz:

In the United States, for a parcel not exceeding one pound in weight, 12 cents; and for each additional pound, or fraction of a pound, 12 cents.

In British Honduras, for a parcel not exceeding one pound in weight, six pence; and for each additional pound, or fraction of a pound, six pence.

ARTICLE V.

The sender of each package must make a *Customs Declaration*, pasted upon or attached to the package, upon a special form provided for the purpose (see Model 1, "A," annexed hereto), giving a general description of the parcel, an accurate statement of the contents and value, date of mailing, and the sender's signature and place of residence, and place of address.

The sender will, at the time of mailing the package, receive a certificate of mailing from the post-office where the package is mailed, on a form like Model 2, annexed hereto.

The sender of a package may obtain a return receipt for the same by paying in the United States a fee of five cents, and in British Honduras two pence, in addition to the postage on each packet, to be affixed to the packet in stamps of the country of origin.

The sender of a package may have the same registered by paying the registration fee required for registered articles in the country of origin, and will receive the return receipt without special charge therefor.

ARTICLE VI.

The addressees of registered articles shall be advised of the arrival of a package addressed to them, by a notice from the post-office of destination.

The packages shall be delivered to addressees in the country of destination free of charge *for postage;* but the customs duties properly chargeable thereon shall be collected on delivery in accordance with the customs regulations of the country of destination; and the country of destination may, at its option, levy and collect from the addressee for interior service and delivery a charge not exceeding five cents in the United States and two and a half pence in the British Honduras on each single parcel of whatever weight; and if the weight exceeds one pound, a charge equal to one cent or one-half penny for each four ounces of weight or fraction therof.

ARTICLE VII.

The packages shall be considered as a component part of the mails exchanged direct between the United States and British Honduras, to be dispatched by the country of origin to the other at its cost and by such means as it provides, but must be forwarded, at the option of the dispatching office, either in boxes prepared expressly for the purpose or in ordinary mail sacks, to be marked " Parcel post," and not to contain any other articles of mail matter, and to be securely sealed with wax, or otherwise, as may be mutually provided by regulations hereunder.

Each country shall promptly return *empty* to the dispatching office by next mail, all such bags and boxes, but subject to other regulations between the two administrations.

Although articles admitted under this Convention will be transmitted as aforesaid between the exchange offices, they should be so carefully packed as to be safely transmitted in the open mails of either country, both in going to the exchange office in the country of origin and to the office of address in the country of destination.

Each dispatch of a parcel post mail must be accompanied by a descriptive list, in duplicate, of all the packages sent, showing distinctly the list number of each parcel, the name of the sender, the name of the addressee with address of destination, and the declared contents and value; and must be inclosed in one of the boxes or sacks of such dispatch. (See Model 3 annexed hereto.)

ARTICLE VIII.

As soon as the mail shall have reached the office of destination, that office shall check the contents of the mail.

In the event of the parcel bill not having been received a substitute should be at once prepared.

Any errors in the entries on the parcel bill which may be discovered, should, after verification by a second officer, be corrected and noted for report to the dispatching office on a form, "Verification certificate," which should be sent in the special envelope.

If a parcel advised on the bill be not received, after the non-receipt has been verified by a second officer, the entry on the bill should be canceled and the fact reported at once.

If a parcel be observed to be insufficiently prepaid, it must not be taxed with deficient postage, but the circumstance must be reported on the verification certificate form.

Should a parcel be received in a damaged or imperfect condition, full particulars should be reported on the same form.

If no verification certificate or note of error be received, a parcel mail shall be considered as duly delivered, having been found on examination correct in all respects.

ARTICLE IX.

If a package cannot be delivered as addressed, or is refused, the sender will be communicated with through the central administration of the office of destination, as to the manner in which he desires the package to be disposed of, and if no reply is received from him within a period of three months from the date of the notice, the package may be sold for the benefit of whom it may concern.

An order for redirection or reforwarding must be accompanied by the amount due for postage necessary for the return of the article to the office of origin, at the ordinary parcel rates.

When the contents of a parcel which cannot be delivered are liable to deterioration or corruption, they may be destroyed at once, if necessary, or if expedient, sold, without previous notice or judicial formality, for the benefit of the right person, the particulars of each sale being noticed by one post-office to the other.

ARTICLE X.

The Post-Office Department of either of the contracting countries will not be responsible for the loss or damage of any package, and no indemnity can consequently be claimed by the sender or addressee in either country.

ARTICLE XI.

Each country shall retain to its own use the whole of the postages, registration and delivery fees, it collects on said packages; consequently, this Convention will give rise to no separate accounts between the two countries.

ARTICLE XII.

The Postmaster-General of the United States of America, and the Postmaster of British Honduras, shall have authority to jointly make such further regulations of order and detail as may be found necessary to carry out the present Convention from time to time; and may, by agreement, prescribe conditions for the admission in packages exchanged under this Convention of any of the articles prohibited by Article II

ARTICLE XIII.

This Convention shall take effect and operations thereunder shall begin on the first day of March, 1888, and shall continue in force until terminated by mutual agreement, but may be annulled at the desire of either Department, upon six months' previous notice given to the other.

Done in duplicate, and signed at Washington, the twenty-third day of January, 1888, and at Belize, the tenth day of February, 1888.

[Seal of Post-Office Dep't of U. S.]

DON M. DICKINSON,
Postmaster-General of the United States.
W. J. McKINNEY,
Postmaster of British Honduras.

The foregoing Parcel Post Convention between the United States of America and British Honduras has been negotiated and concluded with my advice and consent, and is hereby approved and ratified.

In testimony whereof I have caused the Great Seal of the United States to be hereunto affixed.

[Great Seal of U. S.]
GROVER CLEVELAND.

By the President:
    T. F. BAYARD,
        Secretary of State.
WASHINGTON, *March 20th*, 1888.

FORM 1.

Parcel Post between the United States and British Honduras.

Date. Stamp.	FORM OF CUSTOMS DECLARATION.	Place to which the parcel is addressed.

Description of parcel: [State whether box, basket, bag, &c.]	Contents.	Value.	Per cent.	Total customs charges.
		$		$
	Total.	$		$

Date of posting: ...., 18..; signature and address of sender { ....
 ....

☞ For use of Post-Office only, and to be filled up at the office of exchange.
Parcel Bill No ....; No. of rates prepaid ....; Entry No ....

B.

Parcel Post from British Honduras.
The import duty assessed by an officer of customs on contents of this parcel amounts
to $......, which must be paid before the parcel is delivered.

Date Stamp.

....
Customs Officer.

C.

Parcel Post from British Honduras.
This parcel has been passed by an officer of customs and must be delivered
FREE OF CHARGE.

Date Stamp.

....
Postmaster-General.

FORM 2.

Parcel Post.

A parcel addressed as under has been posted here this day.

Office stamp.	....
	....
	....

This certificate is given to inform the sender of the posting of a parcel, and does not indicate that any liability in respect of such parcel attaches to the Postmaster-General.

FORM 3.

Date stamp of the United States Post-Office.	*Parcels from the United States to British Honduras.*	Date stamp of the British Honduras Post-Office.
	Parcel Bill No...., dated....18.. ; per S. S."...."	
* Sheet No......		

Entry No.	Origin of parcel.	Name of addressee.	Address of parcel.	Declared contents.	Declared value.	Number of rates prepaid. British Honduras.	Remarks.
					$		
				Totals..	$		

When more than one sheet is required for the entry of the parcels sent by the mail, it will be sufficient if the undermentioned particulars are entered on the last sheet of the Parcel Bill.

lbs.

*Total number of parcels sent by the mail to British Honduras................... * Total weight of mail.............................

* Number of boxes or other receptacles forming the mail..................... * Deduct weight of receptacles ....

Signature of dispatching officer at New Orleans Post-Office....................... * Net weight of parcels.......................

Signature of receiving officer, Post-Office, British Honduras.

....

APPENDIX F.

Parcels post convention between the United States of America and Mexico.

For the purpose of making better postal arrangements between the United States of America, and the United Mexican States, the undersigned, Don M. Dickinson, Postmaster General of the United States of America, by virtue of authority vested in him by law, and Matias Romero, Envoy Extraordinary and Minister Plenipotentiary of the United Mexican States at Washington, duly empowered thereto by the President of the United Mexican States, have agreed upon the following articles for the establishment of a parcels post system of exchanges between the two countries.

Con objeto de establecer mejores arreglos postales entre los Estados Unidos de America y los Estados Unidos Mexicanos, los infrascritos, Don M. Dickinson, Administrator General de Correos de los Estados Unidos de America, en ejercicio de las facultades que le concede la Ley, y Matias Romero, Enviado Extraordinario y Ministro Plenipotenciario de los Estados Unidos Mexicanos en Washington, debidamente autorizado para ello por el Presidente de dichos Estados Unidos Mexicanos, han convenido en los siguientes artículos para el establecimiento de un sistema de Paquetes Postales, entre los dos países.

ARTICLE I.

The provisions of this Convention relate only to parcels of mail matter to be exchanged by the system herein provided for, and affect the arrangements now existing only so far as they relate to merchandise parcels as provided for under the Convention between the two contracting countries signed on the 4th of April, 1887; and all other arrangements therein contained will continue as heretofore; and all the arrangements hereinafter contained apply exclusively to merchandise parcels mails exchanged under these articles.

ARTICULO I.

Las estipulaciones de esta Convencion se refieren tan solo á los paquetes de objetos enviados por el correo, que se cambien por el sistema que ella establece, y afectan solamente en lo que se relaciona con los paquetes de mercancias, los arreglos que ahora existen conforme á la Convencion Postal de 4 de Abril de 1887, y todas las demas estipulaciones de dicha Convencion continuaran vijentes como lo estan ahora; y todas las estipulaciones contenidas en la presente Convencion se applicaran exclusivamente á las balijas de paquetes de mercancias que ce cambien conforme á estos artículos.

ARTICLE II.

1. There shall be admitted to the mails exchanged under this Convention, articles of merchandise and mail matter, except letters, post-cards, and written matter, of all kinds that are admitted under any conditions to the domestic mails of the country of origin, except that no packet must exceed five kilograms or eleven pounds in weight, nor the following dimensions: Greatest length in any direction sixty centimeters, or two feet; greatest girth one hundred and twenty centimeters or four feet; and must be so wrapped or enclosed as to permit their

ARTICULO II.

1. Se admitiran en las balijas que se cambien conforme á esta Convencion, mercancias y objetos trasmisibles por el correo, de cualquiera género que sean, exceptuando cartas, tarjetas postales y todo papel escrito, que se admitan conforme á los reglamentos que rijen respecto de las balijas domesticas del pais de origen, con tal de que ningun paquete exceda de cinco kilogramos ú once libras de peso, ni de las dimensiones siguientes: maximo de largo en cualquiera direccion, sesenta centimetros ó dos pies; máximo de perimetro, un metro veinte centimetros ó

54

contents to be easily examined by postmasters and customs officers; and except the articles mentioned in Article I, paragraph "a", of the Postal Convention between the two contracting countries of April 4, 1887, which are hereby prohibited.

2. All admissible articles of merchandise mailed in one country for the other, or received in one country from the other, whether by land or sea conveyance, shall be free from any detention or inspection whatever, except such as is required for collection of customs duties, and shall be forwarded by the most speedy means to their destination, being subject in their transmission to the laws and regulations of each country respectively.

ARTICLE III.

1. A letter or communication of the nature of personal correspondence must not accompany, be written on, or enclosed with any parcel.

2. If such be found, the letter will be placed in the mails if separable, and if inseparably attached, the whole package will be rejected. If, however, any such should inadvertently be forwarded, the country of destination will collect double rates of postage according to the Universal Postal Union Convention.

3. No parcel may contain parcels intended for delivery at an address other than the one borne by the parcel itself. If such inclosed parcels be detected, they must be sent forward singly, charged with new and distinct parcel post rates.

ARTICLE IV.

1. The following rates of postage shall in all cases be required to be fully prepaid with postage stamps of the country of origin, viz:

2. For a parcel not exceeding four hundred and sixty grams or one pound in weight, twelve cents; and for each additional four hundred and sixty grams or one pound, or fraction thereof, twelve cents.

3. The packages shall be promptly delivered to addressees at the post offices of address in the country of destination, free of charge for postage; but the country of destination may at its option, levy and collect from the addressee for interior service and delivery a charge not exceeding five cents on each single parcel of whatever weight; and if the weight ex-

---

cuatro pies; y deberá envolverse ó cubrirse de manera que permita que su contenido sea facilmente examinado por los empleados del correo y de la aduana; prohibiendose por el presente la admision en las balijas que se cambien entre los dos paises, conforme á esta Convencion, de los objetos, mencionados en el Articulo I, parrafo a, de la Convencion Postal entre los dos paises contratantes de 4 de Abril de 1887.

2. Todos los paquetes de mercancias admisibles que se depositen en el correo de un pais con destino al otro, ó que se reciban en un pais precedentes del otro, ya sea que se trasmitan por tierra ó por mar, seran libres de toda detencion ó inspeccion de cualquiera género que sea, exceptuando solamente la que fuere necesaria para cobrar los derechos aduanales, y se despacharan á su destino por la via mas rapida, quedando sujetos en su trasmision á las leyes y reglamentos de cada pais respectivamente.

ARTICULO III.

1. Ninguna carta ó comunicacion que tenga el caracter de correspondencia personal, podra acompañar al paquete, ya sea que este escrita sobre el, ó incluida en el mismo.

2. Si se encontrare alguna carta, se pondrá en el correo, si pudiere separarse, y s estuviere adherida de manera que no se pueda separar, se desechará el paquete entero. Sin embargo, si alguna carta fuere enviada inadvertidamente, el pais de destino cobrará doble porte por ella, conforme á la convencion de la Union Postal Universal.

3. Ningun paquete podrá contener bultos que tengan que entregarse á una direccion diferente de la que aparezca sobre el mismo paquete. Si se descubrieren tales bultos, se enviaran uno por uno, cobrandose nuevo y distinto porte por cada uno de ellos.

ARTICULO IV.

1. Se pagaran previamente y en su totalidad, en todo caso, los siguientes portes de correo en estampillas del correo del pais de origen, á saber:

2. Por un paquete que no exceda del peso de cuatrocientos sesenta gramos, ó una libra, doce centavos, y por cada cuatrocientos sesenta gramos, ó una libra, adicionales, ó fraccion de este peso, doce centavos.

3. Los paquetes que se entregaran prontamente á las personas á quienes se dirijan, en la oficina de Correos de su direccion, en el pais de su destino, libres de todo recargo por porte de correo; pero el pais del destino puede, á su opcion, imponer y cobrar á la persona á quien se dirija el paquete, y en compensacion del servicio interior y de entrega, un recargo que no ex-

ceeds four hundred and sixty grams or one pound, a charge equal to one cent for each one hundred and fifteen grams, or four ounces, of weight, or fraction thereof.

ceda de cinco centavos por cada paquete que no pase de cuatrocientos sesenta gramos, ó una libra, y si el paquete excedirse de ese peso, se cobrará un centavo por cada ciento quince gramos, ó cuatro onzas de peso, ó fraccion de ese peso.

ARTICLE V.

1. The sender will, at the time of mailing the package, receive a receipt of mailing from the post office where the package is mailed, on a form like Model I, annexed hereto.

2. The sender of a package may have the same registered by paying the registration fee required for registered articles in the country of origin.

3. An acknowledgment of the delivery of a registered article shall be returned to the sender when requested; but either country may require of the sender prepayment of a fee therefor not exceeding five cents.

4. The addressees of registered articles shall be advised of the arrival of a package addressed to them, by a notice from the post office of destination.

ARTICULO V.

1. Al depositar en el correo un paquete, se entregará al remitente un recibo que acredite su entrega en la oficina de correo que lo recibió conforme al modelo anexo No. I.

2. El remitente de un paquete podrá certificarlo, pagando el derecho de certificacion que se cobre en el pais de su origen.

3. Se enviará al remitente cuando asi lo solicite, un documento que justifique la entrega de un objeto certificado; pero cada pais puede exigir del remitente el pago previo de un derecho por ese servicio, que no exceda de cinco centavos.

4. Se informará á las personas á quienes se dirijan articulos certificados de la llegada de un paquete dirigido á ellas, por la oficina de correos de destino.

ARTICLE VI.

1. The sender of each package shall make a Customs Declaration, pasted upon or attached to the package, upon a special Form provided for the purpose (see Model 2 annexed hereto) giving a general description of the parcel, an accurate statement of the contents and value, date of mailing, and the sender's signature and place of residence, and place of address. The Customs Declaration herein provided shall be omitted in the country of origin during such period as the Postmaster General of the country of destination shall request such omission.

2. The packages in question shall be subject in the country of destination to all customs duties and all customs regulations in force in that country for the protection of its Customs Revenues; and the customs duties properly chargeable thereon shall be collected on delivery, in accordance with the customs regulations of the country of destination.

ARTICULO VI.

1. El remitente de cada paquete hará una declaracion aduanal que se pegara ó agregará al paquete, segun una formula especial que se le facilitará para ese objeto, (Véase el modelo anexo No. 2) que contenga una descripcion general del paquete, una manifestacion exacta de su contenido y valor, fecha del envio, fecha y lugar de residencia del remitente y lugar de su destino. Esta declaracion aduanal se omitirá en el pais de origen, durante el tiempo que asi lo solicite el Administrador General de Correos del pais de destino.

2. Estos paquetes quedaran sujetos en el pais de su destino á todos los reglamentos y derechos aduanales que estuvieren vigentes en el mismo pais, para protejer las rentas de sus aduanas; los derechos aduanales que debidamente corresponda cobrar sobre los mismos paquetes, seran cobrados al entregarse estos, de acuerdo con los reglamentos aduanales del pais de destino.

ARTICLE VII.

Each country shall retain to its own use, the whole of the postages, registration, and delivery fees it collects on said packages; consequently, this Convention will give rise to no separate accounts between the two countries.

ARTICULO VII.

Cada pais retendrá para su propio uso, el total del porte de correo, de los derechos de certificacion y de entrega que colecte sobre dichos paquetes; y en consecuencia, esta Convencion no motivará cuentas separadas entre los dos paises.

ARTICLE VIII.

1. The packages shall be considered as a component part of the mails exchanged

ARTICULO VIII.

1. Los paquetes se consideraran como parte componente de las balijas cambiadas

direct between the United States of America and Mexico, to be despatched by the country of origin to the other at its cost and by such means as it provides, in ordinary mail sacks to be marked " Parcels Post." and to be securely sealed with wax or otherwise as may be mutually provided by regulations hereunder.

2. Registered packages shall be exchanged in separate and distinct sacks marked " Registered Parcels Post."

3. Each country shall return to the despatching office by next mail, all bags or sacks used in the exchange of parcels.

4. Although articles admitted under this Convention will be transmitted as aforesaid between the exchange offices, they should be so carefully packed as to be safely transmitted in the open mails of either country, both in going to the exchange office in the country of origin and to the office of address in the country of destination.

5. Each despatch of a parcel post mail must be accompanied by a descriptive list in duplicate, of all the packages sent, showing distinctly the list number of each parcel, the name of the sender, the name of the addressee with address of destination; and must be enclosed in one of the sacks of such despatch under the Form of Model 3, annexed hereto.

ARTICLE IX.

Exchanges of mails under this Convention from any place in either country to any place in the other, whether by sea or overland, shall be effected through the post offices of both countries already designated as Exchange Post Offices, or through such others as may be hereafter agreed upon, under such regulations relative to the details of the exchanges, as may be mutually determined to be essential to the security and expedition of the mails and the protection of the Customs Revenues.

ARTICLE X.

1. As soon as the mail shall have reached the exchange office of destination, that office shall check the contents of the mail.

2. In the event of the Parcel Bill not having been received, a substitute should at once be prepared.

3. Any errors in the entries on the Parcel Bill which may be discovered, shall, after verification by a scond officer, be corrected and noted for report to the despatching office on a Form, " Verification Certifi-

---

directamente entre los Estados Unidos de America y Mexico, y seran despachados por el pais de su origen al otro, á su costo y por los medios que el provea, en sacos ordinarios de correspondencia que se n arcaran : "Paquetes Postales " y se sellaran con la seguridad debida, con lacre, ó de alguna otra manera que se determine mutuamente por los reglamentos respectivos.

2. Los paquetes certificados se cambiaran en sacos separados y distintos marcados: "Paquetes Postales Certificados."

3. Cada pais devolverá á la oficina de correo que los despache, por el próximo correo, todos los sacos usados en el cambio de paquetes.

4. Aunque los objetos admitidos conforme á esta Convencion se trasmitiran en la forma designada, entre las oficinas de cambio, deberan empacarse cuidadosamente, á fin de que puedan, trasmitirse en balijas abiertas de un pais, tanto á la oficina de correos de cambio en el pais de su origen, como á la oficina de correos á donde se dirijan, en el pais de su destino.

5. Cada envio de paquetes postales irá acompañado de una, lista descriptiva, hecha por duplicado, de todos los paquetes enviados, que demuestre distintamente el número de lista de cada paquete, el nombre del remitente, el nombre de la persona á quien se dirije con la direccion de su destino, y deberá incluirse en uno de los sacos del mismo envio, de acuerdo con el modelo numero 3, anexo á esta Convencion.

ARTICULO IX.

El cambio de balijas conforme á esta Convencion, de cualquiera lugar de un pais á cualquiera lugar del otro, ya sea por mar ó por tierra, se verificará por las oficinas de correos de ambos paises, ya designadas como oficinas de correos de cambio, ó por aquellas otras que pueda convenirse mas adelante, conforme con los reglamentos relativos á los detalles de los cambios que se acuerden mutuamente como esenciales á la seguridad y celeridad de las balijas y á la proteccion de los derechos aduanales.

ARTICULO X.

1. La oficina de correos del pais del destino, anotará el contenido de la balija, tan luego como la reciba.

2. En el caso de que no se recibiere una lista de los paquetes enviados por el correo, se hará desde luego una que la sustituya.

3. Los errores que puedan haberse cometido y se descubrieren en la lista de los paquetes enviados por el correo, se corregiran despues de haber sido rectificados por un segundo empleado, y se comuni-

cute," which shall be sent in the special envelope.

4. If a parcel advised on the bill be not received, after the non-receipt has been verified by a second officer, the entry on the bill should be canceled and the fact reported at once.

5. Should a parcel be received in a damaged or imperfect condition, full particulars shall be reported on the same form.

6. If no Verification Certificate or note of error be received, a parcel mail shall be considered as duly delivered, having been found on examination correct in all respects.

ARTICLE XI.

If the packages can not be delivered as addressed, or if they are refused, they should be reciprocally returned without charge, directly to the dispatching office of exchange, at the expiration of thirty days from their receipt at the office of destination, and the country of origin may collect from the sender for the return of the parcel, a sum equal to the postage when first mailed.

ARTICLE XII.

The Post Office Department of either of the contracting countries will not be responsible for the loss or damage of any package, and no indemnity can consequently be claimed by the sender or addressee in either country.

ARTICLE XIII

The Postmaster-General of the United States of America, and the Director General of Posts of the United Mexican States, may by agreement, exempt on account of insecurity in the conveyance, or other causes, certain post offices in either country, from receiving or despatching packages of merchandise weighing from two to five kilograms as provided for by this Convention, and shall have authority to jointly make such further regulations of order and detail, as may be found necessary to carry out the present Convention from time to time; and may by agreement prescribe conditions for the admission to the mails of any of the articles prohibited by Article I of the Postal Convention of the 4th of April, 1887.

caran á la oficina que envio los paquetes, en la forma de "Certificado de Comprobacion," que se enviará en cubierta especial.

4. Si no se recibiere algun paquete de los contenidos en la lista, despues de haberse certificado este hecho por un segundo empleado, se cancelará la anotacion respectiva de la lista, y se dará cuenta de este hecho desde luego.

5. Cuando se recibiere un paquete averiado ó en un estado imperfecto, se comunicaran en la misma forma detalles completos sobre su estado.

6. Si no se recibiere "Certificado de Comprobacion," ó noticia de error, se considerará que la balija de paquetes fué debidamente recibida y que habiendo sido examinada, se encontro exacta bajo todos aspectos.

ARTICULO XI.

Si no pudiere entregarse un paquete á la persona á quien se dirije, ó si esta se rehusare á recibirlo, se devolverá reciprocamente, sin recargo, y directamente á la oficina que lo despachó, à la espiracion de treinta dias contados desde su recibo, por la oficina de destino, y el pais de origen puede cobrar al remitente por la devolucion del paquete, una suma igual al porte que causó cuando se puso por primera vez en el correo.

ARTICULO XII.

El Departamento de Correos de cada uno de los paises contratantes, no será responsable por la pérdida ó averia que sufra algun paquete, y no podrá reclamarse, por lo mismo, en ninguno de los dos paises, indemnizacion alguna por quien lo envie, ni por la persona á quien vaya dirigido.

ARTICULO XIII.

El Administrador general de Correos de los Estados Unidos de América y el Administrador general de Correos de los Estados Unidos Mexicanos podran, por convenio, exceptuar, por motivo de inseguridad en la conduccion ó por otras causas, á ciertas oficinas de correo de cada pais, del recibo ó despacho de paquetes de mercancias que pesen de dos á cinco kilogramos, estipulado en esta Convencion; quedan autorizados para hacer de tiempo en tiempo y de comun acuerdo, los reglamentos posteriores de órden y detalle que consideren necesarios para poner en ejecucion esta Convencion, y podran, por mutuo consentimiento, establecer condiciones para la admision en las balijas de cualquiera de los objetos prohibidos por el Articulo I, de la Convencion Postal de Abril de 1887.

ARTICLE XIV.

This Convention shall be ratified by the contracting countries in accordance with their respective laws, and its ratification shall be exchanged at the City of Washington as early as possible. Once ratified, and its ratifications exchanged, it shall take effect, and operations thereunder shall begin on the 1st day of July, 1888, and shall continue in force until terminated by mutual agreement, but may be annulled at the desire of either Department, upon six months' previous notice given to the other.

Done in duplicate, and signed at Washington the 28th day of April, one thousand eight hundred and eighty-eight.

[L. S.] (Signed) DON M. DICKINSON,
Postmaster-General of the
United States of America.

ARTICULO XIV.

Esta convencion se ratificará por los paises contratantes de acuerdo con sus respectivas leyes, y sus ratificaciones se canjearan en la ciudad de Washington, lo mas pronto que fuere posible. Una vez ratificada y canjeadas sus ratificaciones, comenzará á tener efecto el 1 de Julio de 1888, y continuará en vigor hasta que se termine por consentimiento mutuo; pero podrá anularse, con la notificacion de uno de los Departamentos de Correos hecha al otro, con seis mesis de anticipacion.

Hecho por duplicado y firmado en Washington el 28 de Abril de mil ochocientos ochenta y ocho.

[L. S.] (Signed) M. ROMERO,
Envoy Extraordinary and Minister
Plenipotentiary of the
United Mexican States.

The foregoing Parcels Post Convention between the United States of America and the United Mexican States has been negotiated and concluded with my advice and consent, and is hereby approved and ratified.

In testimony whereof I have caused the Great Seal of the United States to be hereunto affixed.

[Great Seal of U. S.]

GROVER CLEVELAND.

By the President:
T. F. BAYARD,
Secretary of State.

WASHINGTON, D. C., *June* , 1888.

FORM No. 1.

Parcel Post.

Office stamp.	A parcel addressed as under has been posted here this day. ....

This certificate is given to inform the sender of the posting of a parcel, and does not indicate that any liability in respect of such parcel attaches to the Postmaster-General.

FORM No. 2.

Parcel post between the United States and Mexico.

Date. Stamp.	FORM OF CUSTOMS DECLARATION.	Place to which the parcel is addressed.

Description of parcel: [State whether box, basket, bag, etc.]	Contents	Value.	Per cent.	Total customs charges.
		$		$
	Total.	$		$

Date of posting:................, 18..; signature and address of sender { ....
....

☞ For use of Post-Office only, and to be filled up at the office of exchange.
Parcel Bill No. ....; No. of rates prepaid ....; Entry No. ....

FORM No. 3.

Date stamp of the United States Post-Office.		Parcels from the United States for Mexico.		Date stamp of the Mexican Post-Office.
		Parcel Bill No. ...., dated ...... 18..; by "........"		
*Sheet No.				

Entry No.	Origin of parcel.	Name of addressee.	Address of parcel.	Remarks.

When more than one sheet is required for the entry of the parcels sent by the mail, it will be sufficient if the undermentioned particulars are entered on the last sheet of the Parcel Bill.

lbs.

*Total number of parcels sent by the mail to Mexico............................   *Total weight of mail......................

*Number of boxes or other receptacles forming the mail ....   *Deduct weight of receptacles ....

Signature of dispatching officer at the United States Post-Office................   *Net weight of parcels............. ....

Signature of receiving officer at Mexican Post-Office.

....

The undersigned, Don M. Dickinson, Postmaster General of the United States of America, and Matias Romero, Envoy Extraordinary and Minister Plenipotentiary of the United Mexican States at Washington, having met together in the Post office Department for the purpose of exchanging the ratifications of the Parcels Post Convention concluded between the United States of America, and the United Mexican States, and signed at Washington on the 28th day of April 1888, and having carefully compared the ratifications of said Convention, and found them exactly conformable to each other, the exchange took place this day in the usual form.

In witness whereof they have signed the present protocol of exchange, and have affixed thereto the seals of their arms.

Done at Washington this twenty-second day of June, one thousand eight hundred and eighty eight.

[Seal of Post office Dep. of U S.] DON M. DICKINSON,
Postmaster General of the United States of America.

Habiendose reunido los infrascritos, Don M. Dickinson, Administrador General de Correos de los Estados Unidos de America, y Matias Romero, Enviado Extraordinario y Ministro Plenipotenciario de los Estados Unidos Mexicanos en Washington, en la Administracion General de Correos, con objeto de canjear las ratificaciones de la Convencion de paquetes postales celebrada entre las Estados Unidos de America y los Estados Unidos Mexicanos, firmada en Washington el dia 2ª de Abril de 1888, y habiendo comparado ciudadosamente las ratificaciones de dicha Convencion y encontrandolas exactas la una con la otra, tuvo lugar el canje on la forma usual.

En testimonio de lo cual han firmado el presente protocolo y lo han sellado con sus respectivos sellos de armas.

Hecho en la ciudad de Washington el dia veintidos de Junio de mil ochocientos ochenta y ocho.

[Seal of Mexican Legation.] M. ROMERO,
Enviado Extraordinario y Ministro Plenipotenciario de los Estados Unidos Mexicanos.

ANNUAL REPORT

OF THE

AUDITOR OF THE TREASURY

FOR THE

POST-OFFICE DEPARTMENT

FOR THE

FISCAL YEAR ENDED JUNE 30, 1888.

REPORT

AUDITOR OF THE TREASURY FOR THE POST-OFFICE DEPARTMENT.

OFFICE OF THE AUDITOR OF THE TREASURY
FOR THE POST-OFFICE DEPARTMENT,
Washington, D. C., November 27, 1888.

SIR: I have the honor to submit herewith the annual report of receipts and expenditures of the Post-Office Department, as shown by the accounts of this office, for the fiscal year ended June 30, 1888. All expenditures on account of service of last and prior fiscal years are stated to September 30, 1888, as in former reports.

REVENUE ACCOUNT OF THE POST-OFFICE DEPARTMENT.

Service of the fiscal year 1888.

Postal revenues of the year ended June 30, 1888		$52,695,176.79
Expenditures to September 30, 1888		55,795,357.84
Excess of expenditures over all revenues......................		3,100,181.05
Amount placed with the Treasurer to the credit of the Department, being grants from the general Treasury in aid of the postal revenues under section 2 of the act approved March 3, 1887 (Statutes, Vol. 24, page 570).....................................		2,564,221.27
Excess of expenditures over grants.........................		535,959.78
Amount of balances due late postmasters on accounts closed by "suspense"..............................	$4,049.85	
Amount of balances due from late postmasters charged to "bad debt" and "compromise" accounts..........	3,377.47	
Net gain by "suspense".................		672.38
Amount to be placed with the Treasurer....................		535,287.40

Service of the fiscal year 1887.

Balance available October 1, 1887..............................	748,835.74
Expended from October 1, 1887, to September 30, 1888.........,.....	368,160.40
Balance available on account of fiscal year 1887..............	380,675.34

Service of the fiscal year 1886.

Amount expended as per report of 1887	$211, 881. 50
Amount expended from October 1, 1887, to September 30, 1888	12, 020. 34
Total	223, 901. 84
Amount placed with the Treasurer to the credit of the Department, being grants from the general Treasury in aid of the postal revenues under section 2 act approved March 3, 1885 (Statutes, vol. 23, page 385)	225, 621. 23
Balance to be placed in the general Treasury	1, 719. 31

Service of the fiscal year 1885.

Balance available October 1, 1887, certified to the general Treasury.	104, 783. 34

Claims, 1885 and prior years.

Amount expended from October 1, 1887, to September 30, 1888		55, 811. 46
Amount placed with the Treasurer to the credit of the Department, being grants from the general Treasury in aid of the postal revenues under act—		
February 1, 1888, section 3, public No. 4, page 31 ...	$49, 854. 79	
March 30, 1888, section 2, public No. 27, page 18	3, 382. 43	
March 30, 1888, section 3, public No. 27, page 25	1, 348. 29	
March 30, 1888, section 4, public No. 27, page 28	1, 406. 20	
		55, 991. 71
Balance available for claims October 1, 1888		180. 25
Compensation of postmasters and late postmasters re-adjusted and allowed under act March 3, 1883:		
Expended from October 1, 1887 to September 30, 1888		236, 965. 16
Amount available October 1, 1887	$3, 274. 23	
Amount placed with the Treasurer in aid of the postal revenues, being grants from the general Treasury under act—		
February 1, 1888, section 3, public No. 4, page 31.	160, 286. 05	
March 30, 1888, section 2, public No. 27, page 17.	380, 321. 44	
		543, 881. 72
Available		306, 916. 56

GENERAL REVENUE ACCOUNT.

Postal revenues for the year ended June 30, 1888		$52, 695, 176. 79
Expenditures for the service of 1888 ....$55, 795, 357. 84		
Expenditures for the service of 1887	368, 160. 40	
Expenditures for the service of 1886	12, 020. 34	
Expenditures for the service of 1885 and prior years (claims)	55, 811. 46	
Expenditures for the service of 1885 and prior years for salaries of postmasters and late postmasters, re-adjusted under act of March 3, 1883	236, 965. 16	
Total expenditures to September 30, 1888		56, 468, 315. 20
Excess of expenditures over revenue		3, 773, 138. 41
Amount due late postmasters on accounts closed by suspense	$4, 049. 85	
Amount of balance due from late postmasters on accounts closed by bad debt and compromise	3, 377. 47	
Net gain by suspense		672. 38
Excess of expenditures		⌒ 3, 772, 466. 03

Grants from the general Treasury.

Under act of—

March 3, 1887	$2,564,221.27
March 3, 1885	225,621.23
February 1, 1888	210,140.84
March 30, 1888	386,458.36

Total grants $3,386,441.70

Excess of expenditures over grants 386,024.33
Amount of grant to the general Treasury, to repay of the postal deficiency appropriation for 1885 the sum drawn in excess of actual deficiency (paid to the Treasurer by warrant No. 2234, dated January 19, 1888) 104,783.34

Total excess of expenditures over receipts 490,807.67
The balance standing to the credit of the general revenue account
September 30, 1887 .... 4,078,156.82

The balance standing to the credit of the general revenue account
September 30, 1888 .... 3,587,349.15
Of which there was due by late postmasters, in suit, $250,355.28.

POSTMASTERS' QUARTERLY ACCOUNTS CURRENT.

The net revenues of the Department from postages, being aggregate revenues at post-offices for the fiscal year, less the compensation of postmasters and clerks, and the contingent office expenses, were:

For the quarter ended—

September 30, 1887	$7,297,667.82
December 31, 1887	8,729,620.45
March 31, 1888	8,874,718.08
June 30, 1888	8,035,493.94

Total 32,937,500.29

The number of quarterly returns of postmasters received and audited, on which the above sum was found due the United States, was:

For the quarter ended—

September 30, 1887	$56,806
December 31, 1887	56,678
March 31, 1888	57,613
June 30, 1888	58,517

Total 229,614

STAMPS SOLD.

The amount of stamps, stamped envelopes, newspaper wrappers, and letter-sheets and postal-cards sold was:

For the quarter ended—

September 30, 1887	$11,301,020.73
December 31, 1887	12,845,111.92
March 31, 1888	13,158,509.20
June 30, 1888	12,239,630.87

Total 49,544,272.72

LETTER POSTAGES.

The amount of postage paid in money was $61,903.40
Included in the above amount are the following sums paid by foreign countries in the adjustment of their accounts:

Kingdom of Great Britain and Ireland	$36,530.24
Kingdom of Spain	5,071.34
Republic of Chili	1,708.68
Republic of Venezuela	861.91

Republic of Mexico............. .... $11,070.96
Republic of Switzerland...... .... 1,075.68
Republic of Honduras.................................. 700.00
Republic of Salvador......,.. .... 1,006.93
Postal administration of—
    Barbadoes........ .... 15.26
    Costa Rica... 493.50
    Curaçoa.................................. .... 382.68
    Hawaii... 500.00
    New South Wales..................................... 526.66
    New Zealand... 1,618.34
    Saint Lucia... 4.04
    Straits Settlement.................................... .95
    Trinidad 10.59
    Victoria 224.72
    ————— $61,802.48

Balance collected by postmasters..................................... 100.92

The following balances were paid and charged to the appropriation for balances due foreign countries:

International bureau, Berne, Switzerland.............................. $674.25
Kingdom of Belgium.. 7,020.40
Kingdom of Denmark... 15,447.17
Kingdom of Great Britain and Ireland..................................... 4,126.34
Kingdom of Norway 510.13
Kingdom of the Netherlands.. 1,694.94
Dominion of Canada.... .... 74.18
Postal administration of Newfoundland 1,860.75

    Total for fiscal year 1888... 31,408.19

MAIL TRANSPORTATION.

The amount charged to "transportation accrued" and placed to the credit of mail contractors and others for mail transportation during the fiscal year was:

For the regular supply of mail routes................................ $25,233,324.85
For the supply of special offices 51,319.23
For the supply of mail-messenger offices........................... 851,759.37
For the salaries of railway postal clerks............................. 4,966,760.12
For the salaries and expenses of the superintendents of the railway-
    mail service 42,374.92

    Total.. 31,145,538.49

FOREIGN-MAIL TRANSPORTATION.

New York, Great Britain and Ireland, and countries
    beyond, via Great Britain $147,932.44
New York, Great Britain and Germany, and countries
    beyond 203,055.37
Philadelphia, Great Britain and Ireland 81.40
Boston, Great Britain and Ireland..................... 1,911.03
New York, Baltimore, Philadelphia, Boston, Key West,
    New Orleans, and San Francisco, West Indies, Central
    and South America, Mexico, etc 64,191.13
Boston and Nova Scotia............................. 463.57
Upper Pacific coast................................. 1,433.74
San Francisco, China, Japan, Farther India, Australia,
    and South Sea Islands 42,593.13
Boston and West Coast of Africa 3.47
Expenses of Government mail agent at Panama......... 856.44
Expenses of Government mail agent at Shanghai...... 3,018.00

    Total foreign mail... 465,539.72

    Total transportation accrued 31,611,078.21

The amount credited to "transportation accrued" and charged to mail contractors for over-credits, being fines and deductions, was.............................. $373,379.23
The amount of fines and deductions remitted was...... 90,889.27

Net amount of fines and deductions $282,489.96

Net amount of "transportation accrued"....................... 31,328,588.25
The amount paid during the year was............................ 29,599,532.89

Excess of "transportation accrued"............................ 1,729,055.36

PACIFIC RAILROAD SERVICE.

Included in the above amount of "transportation accrued" are the following balances for the transportation of the mails over Pacific railroads, which have been certified to the Register of the Treasury. The amount is not charged to the appropriation for "inland transportation railroads," and is not, therefore, included in the total of transportation paid:

Regular service, 1888.

Union Pacific Railway Company (old U. P. R. R. line) aided	$417,120.82	
Union Pacific Railway Company (old Kansas Pacific line), aided portion	69,726.67	
Lines operated, leased, or controlled by the Union Pacific Railway Company, non-aided portion....................	320,043.35	
Central Pacific Railroad Company, aided portion.........	296,845.79	
Sioux City and Pacific Railroad Company, aided portion..	18,902.00	
Lines operated, leased, or controlled by the Sioux City and Pacific Railroad Company, non-aided..................	1,265.48	$1,123,904.11

Use of postal cars, 1888.

Union Pacific Railway Company (old U. P. R. R. line), aided	70,412.96	
Lines operated, leased, or controlled by the Union Pacific Railway Company, non-aided..........................	6,220.08	
Central Pacific Railroad Company, aided	37,407.72	
Sioux City and Pacific Railroad Company, aided.........	2,372.21	
Lines operated, leased, or controlled by Sioux City and Pacific Railroad Company, non-aided....................	283.75	116,696.72

Regular service, previous years.

Union Pacific Railway Company (old U. P. R. R. line), aided, 1887...................................	1,009.59	
Lines operated, leased, or controlled by the Union Pacific Railway Company, non-aided, 1887	2,799.71	
Central Pacific Railroad Company, aided, 1887............	53.84	
Sioux City and Pacific Railroad Company, aided, 1887....	25.62	
Lines operated, leased, and controlled by the Sioux City and Pacific Railroad Company, non-aided, 1887.	1.87	
Union Pacific Railway Company (old U. P. R. R. line), aided, 1886......................................	42.37	
Union Pacific Railway Company (old Kansas line), aided, 1886	78.71	
Lines operated, leased, or controlled by the Union Pacific Railway Company, non-aided........................	21.30	4,033.01

Use of postal cars, previous years.

Union Pacific Railway Company (old U. P. R. R. line), aided, 1887...............................	4,514.58	
Lines operated, leased, or controlled by the Union Pacific Railway Company, non-aided, 1887	2,830.43	
Sioux City and Pacific Railroad Company, aided, 1887....	5.57	
Lines operated, leased, or controlled by the Sioux City and Pacific Railroad Company, 1887.....................	.51	7,351.09

Total Pacific Railroad service not paid............. 1,251,984.93

STATEMENT OF PAYMENTS TO AND COLLECTIONS FROM LATE POST-MASTERS.

Amount collected during the year from late postmasters ...	\$125,932.98	
Amount charged to suspense	8,042.69	
Amount charged to bad and compromise debts	4,362.17	
		\$138,337.84
Amount paid during the year to late postmasters	166,847.24	
Amount credited to suspense	12,092.54	
Amount credited to bad and compromise debts	984.70	
		179,924.48
Amount remaining due postmasters becoming late during the fiscal year ended June 30, 1888		49,064.54

STATEMENT OF POSTAL ACCOUNTS OF LATE POSTMASTERS IN SUIT ON JUNE 30, 1888.

Amount of postal accounts of late postmasters in suit on June 30, 1887	\$238,702.88	
Amount of postal accounts of late postmasters submitted for suit during the fiscal year ended June 30, 1888	28,564.00	
		\$267,266.88
Amount of postal accounts of late postmasters collected during the fiscal year ended June 30, 1888	16,277.80	
Amount of postal accounts of late postmasters otherwise settled during the fiscal year ended June 30, 1888	633.80	
		16,911.60
Balance of postal accounts of late postmasters remaining in suit on June 30, 1888		250,355.28
Amount of interest and costs collected in suits against late postmasters and sureties on postal accounts during the fiscal year ended June 30, 1888		4,803.22

The tables accompanying this report, numbered as follows, show in detail the transactions of the fiscal year:

No. 1.—Statement exhibiting quarterly the receipts of the Post-Office Department under their several heads for the fiscal year ended June 30, 1888.

No. 2.—Statement exhibiting quarterly the expenditures of the Post-Office Department under their several heads for the fiscal year ended June 30, 1888.

No. 3.—Statement, by States, of the postal receipts and expenditures of the United States for the fiscal year ended June 30, 1888.

No. 4.—Statement showing the condition of the account with each item of the appropriation for the service of the Post-Office Department for the fiscal year ended June 30, 1888.

No. 5.—Statement in detail of miscellaneous payments made by the Post-Office Department during the fiscal year ended June 30, 1888, and charged to "miscellaneous items, office of the Postmaster-General."

No. 6.—Statement in detail of miscellaneous payments made by the Post-Office Department during the fiscal year ended June 30, 1888, and charged to "miscellaneous expenses, office of the First Assistant Postmaster-General."

No. 7.—Statement in detail of miscellaneous payments made by the Post-Office Department during the fiscal year ended June 30, 1888, and charged to "miscellaneous items, Second Assistant Postmaster-General."

No. 8.—Statement in detail of miscellaneous payments made by the Post-Office Department during the fiscal year ended June 30, 1888, and charged to "miscellaneous items, office of the Third Assistant Postmaster-General."

No. 9.—Comparative statement of the receipts and expenditures of the Post-Office Department from July 1, 1836, to June 30, 1888.

No. 10.—Gross receipts, expenses, and net revenue of Presidential post-offices for the fiscal year ended June 30, 1888.

No. 11.—Statement showing the transactions of the money-order offices of the United States for the fiscal year ended June 30, 1888.

No. 12.—Statement showing the number and amount of international money-orders issued, paid, and repaid, and fees collected during the fiscal year ended June 30, 1888.

No. 13.—Statement showing the receipts and disbursements of the money-order offices of the United States during the fiscal year ended June 30, 1888.

No. 14.—Statement showing the transfers to and from the money-order account during the fiscal year ended June 30, 1888.

No. 15.—Statement showing the money-order transactions with the Assistant United States Treasurer at New York, N. Y., during the fiscal year ended June 30, 1888.

No. 16.—Statement showing the revenue which accrued on money-order and postal-note transactions for the fiscal year ended June 30, 1888.

No. 17.—Recapitulation of net revenue for the fiscal year ended June 30, 1888

No. 18.—Statement of assets and liabilities June 30, 1888.

No. 19.—Statement showing the principal international money-order transactions during the fiscal year ended June 30, 1888.

No. 20.—Weight of letters, newspapers, etc., sent by sea from the United States to European countries during the fiscal year ended June 30, 1888.

No. 21.—Weight of letters, newspapers, etc., sent by sea from the United States to countries and colonies other than European of the Universal Postal Union during the fiscal year ended June 30, 1888.

No. 22.—Weights of re-transported foreign closed mails and cost of carriage of same by steam-ship companies.

. Very respectfully,

D. McCONVILLE,
Auditor.

Hon. DON M. DICKINSON,
Postmaster-General.

No. 1.—*Statement exhibiting quarterly the receipts of the Post-Office Department, under their several heads, for the fiscal year ended June 30, 1888.*

Accounts.	Quarter ended September 30, 1887.	Quarter ended December 31, 1887.	Quarter ended March 31, 1888.	Quarter ended June 30, 1888.	Aggregate.
Letter postage................	$26,443.86	$25.47	$5,747.93	$29,686.12	$61,903.40
Box-rents and branch offices ..	511,901.16	537,151.61	543,509.88	550,761.90	2,173,284.05
Fines and penalties ...:......	6,197.68	4,090.04	6,425.40	2,870.64	19,583.76
Postage-stamps, stamped envelopes, letter-sheets, wrappers, and postal-cards.......	11,301,020.73	12,845,111.92	13,158,509.20	12,239,630.87	49,544,272.72
Dead letters....................	3,999.89	1,994.77	3,123.06	....	9,117.72
Revenue from money-order business	188,266.61	238,879.44	210,494.15	180,677.63	798,317.83
Miscellaneous..................	31,887.54	26,708.39	12,293.93	17,807.45	88,697.31
Total receipts...........	12,079,617.49	13,653,961.64	13,940,163.05	13,021,434.61	52,695,176.79

No. 2.—*Statement exhibiting quarterly the expenditures of the Post-Office Department under their several heads for the fiscal year ended June 30, 1888.*

Appropriations.	Quarter ended September 30, 1887.	Quarter ended December 31, 1887.	Quarter ended March 31, 1888.	Quarter ended June 30, 1888.	Total expended on account of 1888.	Expended on account of previous years.	Aggregate expenditures.
Compensation to postmasters	$3,012,459.28	$3,130,275.90	$3,266,035.78	$3,180,968.04	$12,869,768.06	$17,657.80	$12,907,428.48
Compensation to clerks in post-offices	1,350,264.76	1,354,805.60	1,378,665.27	1,421,782.85	5,505,619.07	3,225.88	4,508,745.95
Compensation to letter carriers and incidental expenses	1,338,942.58	1,325,670.04	1,345,728.81	1,416,639.99	5,422,370.43	134.40	4,422,513.83
Wrapping paper	18,683.64	2,498.94	12,114.71	10,750.26	43,997.55	2,193.95	46,191.50
Wrapping twine	21,755.34	12,212.77	17,340.16	19,867.50	71,175.77		71,175.77
Postmarking and rating stamps, and ink and pads for stamping and canceling purposes	6,724.94	9,018.55	10,771.00	3,454.63	29,999.71	125.00	30,124.71
Letter-balances, scales, and test-weights	8,107.53	2,492.25	4,176.33	2,823.81	16,999.92		16,999.92
Rent, fuel, and light	117,718.77	119,985.10	130,632.09	134,675.87	503,111.89	4,523.51	507,634.06
Stationery in post-office	17,963.51	13,888.89	5,765.87	12,570.28	49,863.55	1,723.51	51,592.06
Office furniture	3,031.93	5,366.63	4,703.80	6,929.78	19,025.02	3,023.96	22,083.98
Miscellaneous and incidental items, office of the First Assistant Postmaster-General	14,330.84	12,893.83	13,283.52	17,447.45	57,965.63	592.03	58,547.06
Inland mail transportation—railroad routes	3,851,665.30	3,866,726.92	3,960,338.09	4,108,873.20	15,790,811.51	149,053.11	15,939,864.62
Inland mail transportation—necessary and special facilities	73,996.86	73,996.86	71,581.80	73,723.64	293,299.16		293,299.16
Inland mail transportation—star	1,207,478.93	1,264,010.55	1,228,414.51	1,255,274.23	5,015,178.22	28,046.74	5,043,224.96
Inland mail transportation—steam-boats	110,383.92	98,640.02	96,688.91	104,159.71	409,872.56	641.75	410,514.81
Post-office car service	450,287.11	454,222.48	454,124.90	464,319.88	1,822,964.37	10,090.66	1,834,055.03
Compensation to railway post-office clerks	1,213,631.73	1,220,163.03	1,220,768.19	1,272,967.22	4,967,302.17	3,924.69	4,971,226.86
Compensation to mail messengers	206,611.93	211,257.27	214,075.23	219,864.97	851,709.39	856,743.79	
Mail locks and keys	16,040.00	2,600.30	1,750.00	2,110.54	22,500.84	6,034.40	22,500.54
Mail-bags and mail bag catchers	57,721.22	82,967.26	68,561.38	17,347.81	246,592.67	9,468.61	256,061.28
Miscellaneous items, office of the Second Assistant Postmaster-General		100.00	73.00	115.50	294.50		294.50
Mail depredations and post-office inspectors, and fees to United States marshals, attorneys, and the necessary incidental expenses connected therewith	68,404.09	67,664.36	76,290.81	80,614.49	290,934.35	1,815.17	292,749.52
Postage and special-delivery stamps	28,940.47	34,019.35	38,655.68	33,695.50	132,411.00	6,884.45	139,295.45
Agents and assistance to distribute postage stamps, and expenses of agency	1,890.00	1,848.04	1,890.00	1,880.00	7,558.01		7,558.04
Stamped envelopes, newspaper wrappers, and letter sheets	155,764.11	170,918.39	183,176.25	192,058.18	710,684.98	65,297.78	776,122.71
Agents and assistants to distribute stamped envelopes, newspaper wrappers, and letter sheets, and expenses of agency	3,971.64	3,956.04	3,053.30	3,907.45	15,539.03	38.00	15,897.03
Postal-cards	41,427.55	43,187.57	62,323.33	40,888.05	199,826.50		199,826.50
Agents and assistants to distribute postal-cards, and expenses of agency	2,301.73	2,211.70	3,193.70	2,109.87	8,915.50	17,812.49	8,915.50
Registered-package, tag, official, and dead-letter envelopes	20,181.69	25,425.60	23,333.44	21,527.94	87,468.60		105,392.09
Ship, steam-boat and way letters	118.42	425.27	243.28	836.74	1,428.71		1,428.71
Engraving, printing, and binding drafts and warrants	1,772.50	235.00	90.00	348.00	2,445.50		2,445.50
Miscellaneous items, office of the Third Assistant Postmaster-General							
Advertising	2,603.36	2,071.00	4,340.16	210.10	210.10	370.40	210.10
Miscellaneous, office of the Postmaster-General	20.75	21.70	48.50	3,143.96	13,658.41	11.45	13,428.81
Transportation of foreign mails	108,211.29	124,967.84	110,391.78	101.10	102.05		203.50
			07,724.68	448,265.51	80,069.52	547,906.03	

Balance due foreign countries	....	674.28	11,146.74	19,587.17	31,408.19	....	31,408.19
Rent of Washington City post-office	....	2,500.00	1,250.00	1,250.00	5,000.00	5,000.00	10,000.00
Special delivery	25,067.56	28,497.16	28,845.84	28,605.08	109,015.64	89.28	109,104.02
Compensation of postmasters re-adjusted under act of March 3, 1883	....	....	....	....	....	226,905.16	226,905.16
Claim of Samuel H. Flemming, act of Congress February 21, 1887, chapter 104	....	....	....	....	....	206.66	206.66
Total expenditures	13,642,688.76	13,701,780.61	14,076,625.23	14,283,118.24	55,785,857.84	672,957.36	54,468,815.20

No. 3.—*Statement of the postal receipts and expenditures of the United States for the fiscal year ended June 30, 18-8.*

States and Territories.	Receipts					Expenditures							Excess of expenditures over receipts.	Excess of receipts over expenditures.
	Letter postage.	Waste paper and twine.	Box rents and branch offices.	Postage-stamps, stamped envelopes, and postal-cards.	Total receipts.	Compensation of postmasters.	Clerks for offices, rent, light, and fuel and incidental expenses of post-offices.	Compensation of letter-carriers.	Compensation of postal railway clerks and mail messengers.	Transportation by States.	Total expenditures.			
Alabama		$85.37	$30,565.38	$419,080.63	$439,661.38	$179,965.00	$34,553.02	$18,784.89	$34,671.96	$404,623.78	$673,533.66	$223,991.29		
Alaska		10.15	1,110.00	1,411.42	1,530.57	1,691.00			4.96	13,817.65	14,843.91	13,312.34		
Arizona		10.43	7,157.94	90,061.00	96,261.37	33,702.91	4,173.73	11,532.61	8,846.83	215,251.83	210,204.76	142,943.41		
Arkansas		55.27	15,756.29	323,909.37	329,720.93	167,962.58	27,060.82		40,901.18	324,275.33	467,453.42	147,782.49		
California		337.44	97,970.74	1,528,915.36	1,626,893.54	842,797.33	227,178.85	964,890.33	117,003.78	929,471.89	1,705,021.10			
Colorado		50.80	44,588.72	490,670.73	541,310.25	150,766.19	57,196.89	34,023.36	51,979.31	410,663.27	704,032.62	162,722.37		
Connecticut		311.71	55,544.09	879,490.11	935,354.91	218,530.45	105,901.94	98,412.68	65,467.67	396,825.76	785,567.60			$149,797.11
Dakota		18.86	40,728.74	449,216.18	489,971.78	229,862.53	28,504.26	4,843.07	33,065.63	309,567.90	604,391.79			
Delaware		11.92	2,461.45	108,401.62	110,877.42	34,659.51	9,587.67	13,476.82	65,467.97	785,357.90	785,567.60	116,422.61		
District of Columbia		3,147.38	5,080.40	345,877.52	354,105.28	6,487.76	188,165.75	87,460.87	7,623.70	300,567.90	466,094.59	112,650.81		8,385.48
Florida		19.41	17,539.11	284,850.62	302,409.14	135,227.94	21,568.17	9,633.33	184,941.71	283,210.05	602,179.34	169,776.30		
Georgia		541.92	18,085.34	616,003.54	634,630.80	208,045.98	61,949.28	49,344.66	147,163.68	945,520.97	1,049,124.52	314,412.12		
Idaho		8.80	6,854.29	73,592.75	80,456.84	43,675.69	2,355.99		2,616.52	98,228.96	145,670.21	66,433.43		$487,282.05
Illinois		3,061.61	147,855.42	4,243,567.33	4,394,484.36	753,784.86	634,410.28	573,621.81	648,931.25	842,627.00	2,424,283.35			
Indiana		680.51	68,763.10	1,479,616.31	1,549,061.12	842,797.33	122,167.05	964,890.33	124,873.38	942,627.71	1,424,284.81	385,404.07		
Indian Territory		8.35	1,263.10	47,503.07	48,766.47	1	1,016.92	104,273.38	123,473.47	42,616.67	51,518.07	31,518.07		
Iowa		431.74	111,548.20	1,302,852.97	1,414,392.97	606,470.07	122,944.44	86,567.22	263,738.75	1,042,053.09	1,078,291.98	59,384.41		
Kansas		297.49	91,396.64	1,172,402.88	1,264,396.59	608,226.90	84,729.11	57,735.90	169,108.03	915,125.83	1,715,092.68	451,372.90		
Kentucky		100.98	29,254.53	724,340.76	750,767.67	535,219.80	75,171.16	70,922.81	57,701.76	519,644.01	973,688.04	227,901.37		
Louisiana		83.96	17,994.63	474,760.90	492,538.70	116,020.96	70,270.94	61,065.92	51,452.90	208,110.43	567,831.17	14,992.47		
Maine		372.82	83,880.02	612,410.32	646,363.07	251,526.69	60,433.21	31,018.63	56,730.33	267,407.71	657,450.46	11,067.59		
Maryland		1,283.74	150,443.903	3,265,690.382	3,417,417.92	455,372.44	462,384.22	151,624.90	841,817.44	470,597.512	1,683,803.82	246,906.79		
Massachusetts		707.22	203,621.624	3,624,688.851	3,417,417.92	623,770.13	135,900.52	402,371.50	160,685.88	644,360.191	1,683,235.973			183,444.50
Michigan		385.69	67,313.701	1,103,960.793	1,101,013.99	108,861.95	137,882.02	118,159.27	155,740.63	924,852.614	1,601,288.34	127,420.38		
Minnesota		35.19	64,003.602	901,051.423	926,082.68	154,862.68	108,861.95	6,459.51	34,912.93	375,096.69	226,728.18	443,977.90		
Mississippi		18.09	64,180.692	727,991.942	746,951.16	464,665.77	284,166.84	259,585.60	472,439.34	375,096.69	228,632.692			
Missouri		4.15	35,114.74	93,984.75	947,220.69	478,606.31	51,764.32	3,557.10	472,433.901	102,144.30	204,643.09	619,634.62		
Montana		4.16	1,728.81	94,270.34	947,220.69	31,178.31	4,900.59	3,557.10	4,419.38	934,482.591	123,952.46	634,521.59		
Nebraska		245.44	21,989.89	1,064,629.021	1,120,380.85	290,320.11	94,900.06	26,176.06	20,781.63	101,670.87	142,082.74			
Nevada		18.25	9,063.54	81,522.17	90,612.06	44,486.53	5,699.598	151,069.64	34,063.81	131,947.37	858,851.34	70,865.84		30,878.91
New Mexico				81,022.17	90,612.06	44,486.53			17,531.06	539,178.30	894,881.34			231,514.61
New York		5,916.80	217,815.270	6,046,019.129	270,160.801	1,044,800.221	1,533,900.171	275,846.82	610,941.291	753,135.874	3,129,222.87	140,883.26		3,140,027.73
North Carolina		243.27	14,046.07	591,522.04	606,178.16	304,865.09	20,172.60	11,139.79	27,790.84	960,723.63	640,742.63	231,641.48		

Ohio	1,766.97	124,351.51	3,026,180.06	3,152,298.54	336,911.81	315,174.13	761,790.86	2,525,813.60	4,691,997.46	1,330,698.92		
Oregon	69.34	19,562.08	257,740.52	277,372.54	19,805.74	10,758.78	35,838.66	261,341.71	427,337.69	149,965.15		
Pennsylvania	1,749.59	135,467.59	4,505,963.08	4,643,220.26	569,185.48	664,976.57	427,876.22	206,766.92	3,895,988.64			817,231.62
Rhode Island	128.11	21,259.91	341,570.88	362,958.90	40,367.10	65,788.91	10,330.57	57,318.62	2,27,558.45			135,400.45
South Carolina	41.01	9,939.17	276,507.21	286,487.39	20,186.50	14,414.76	290,350.71	508,063.87	221,663.48		
Tennessee	251.90	16,390.14	650,051.69	666,695.73	65,205.22	46,298.06	123,657.74	292,958.69	741,117.14	74,421.41		
Texas	200.84	61,570.18	918,647.66	1,010,418.68	95,125.08	56,632.26	142,008.42	916,343.68	1,612,966.89	632,545.21		
Utah	44.73	8,314.05	119,636.19	127,994.97	44,210.01	6,234.83	21,789.12	166,391.68	251,293.88	123,384.91		
Vermont	62.15	16,195.53	234,330.69	251,387.79	154,363.46	14,851.00	20,528.03	192,637.62	361,142.17	9,734.28		
Virginia	103.38	18,465.81	729,282.69	748,674.78	66,384.68	52,901.79	63,647.41	713,962.22	262,195.23	454,121.43		
Washington	11.36	13,465.62	181,932.14	197,411.61	14,131.80	4,074.45	5,809.94	231,063.78	348,186.23	110,774.62		
West Virginia	75.36	9,463.65	281,788.83	294,927.24	19,394.26	12,642.12	30,463.78	182,066.95	385,697.96	91,770.72		
Wisconsin	270.85	65,469.96	1,125,252.34	1,190,993.45	108,653.73	97,418.69	90,144.68	713,414.76	1,391,347.53	290,549.08		
Wyoming	1.25	7,012.07	62,378.07	69,391.39	3,911.61	1,569.65	477.25	145,561.14	181,847.26	112,455.97		
Total	24,682.92	2,166,836.34	19,554,120.07	51,747,638.64	6,263,333.75	5,407,200.16	5,818,519.49	25,233,269.40	55,307,866.39	9,872,011.77	6,311,781.02	
Deduct miscellaneous items			9,847.33	5,298.72				1,943,488.50	1,877,179.26	1,877,179.26	5,298.72	
Add miscellaneous items	100.92		4,417.71	4,225.97	46,412.84	15,170.26	492.97					
Grand total	100.92	24,682.92	2,173,284.05	40,544,272.72	51,742,339.92	12,589,768.66	6,309,746,505	6,422,379.42	5,819,011.56	23,289,780.96	53,430,687.13	7,994,822.51	6,306,485.30

Items of expenditure of a general nature not embraced in statement by States.

Amount paid for foreign mails and expenses of Government agents	$418,365.51
Balances paid foreign countries	31,408.19
Ship, steam-boat, and way letters	1,458.71
Wrapping-paper	43,997.55
Twine	71,175.57
Engraving, printing, and binding drafts and warrants	2,445.50
Advertising	2,285.70
Mail bags and catchers	192,114.00
Salary and expenses of assistant superintendents of the railway mail service	42,374.92
Mail locks and keys	22,590.54
Postmarking and canceling stamps	29,999.71
Mail depredations and post-office inspectors	290,634.35
Letter-balances	16,999.93
Expenses of postage-stamps, stamped envelopes, wrappers, and cards	1,015,455.00
Dead-letter, official, and registered package envelopes	87,488.60
Sundry and miscellaneous payments	6,696.65
Excess of expenses brought down	1,688,347.21
	4,033,017.92

Items of receipt of a general nature not embraced in statement by States.

Receipts on account of dead letters	$9,117.72
Receipts on account of fines and penalties	19,583.70
Receipts on account of miscellaneous	61,015.68
Revenue for money-order business	788,317.83
Letter postage	61,802.48
Excess of expenditures over receipts	3,100,181.05
	4,053,017.92

No. 4.—*Statement showing the condition of the account with each item of the appropriation for the service of the Post-Office Department for the fiscal year ended June 30, 1888.*

Title of appropriation.	Amount appropriated (including special acts and deficiencies).	Expended.	Balance unexpended.	Excess of expenditures.
Compensation to postmasters..................	$11,700,000.00	$12,589,768.66	....	$889,768.66
Compensation to clerks in post-offices..........	5,550,000.00	5,505,519.07	$44,480.93	....
Compensation to letter-carriers and incidental expenses......................	5,522,500.00	5,422,379.42	100,120.58	....
Wrapping paper.........................	44,000.00	43,997.55	2.45	....
Wrapping twine.........................	80,000.00	71,175.77	8,824.23	....
Postmarking and rating stamps, and ink and pads for stamping and canceling purposes ...	30,000.00	29,999.71	.29	....
Letter balances, scales, and test-weights	17,000.00	16,909.92	.08	....
Rent, fuel, and light.....................	520,000.00	503,111.39	16,888.61	....
Stationery in post-offices....................	50,000.00	49,868.55	131.45	....
Office furniture........	25,000.00	19,025.02	5,974.98	....
Miscellaneous and incidental items, office of the First Assistant Postmaster-General.....	70,000.00	57,955.63	12,044.37	....
Inland mail transportation, railroad routes	15,867,962.00	15,790,841.51	639,602.49	....
Inland mail transportation, necessary and special facilities.....................	295,987.53	293,299.16	2,688.37	....
Inland mail transportation, star	5,400,000.00	5,015,178.22	384,821.78	....
Inland mail transportation, steam-boats	450,000.00	409,872.56	40,127.44	....
Post-office car service	1,934,560.00	1,822,964.37	111,595.63	....
Compensation to railway post-office clerks......	4,990,240.62	4,967,302.17	22,938.45	....
Compensation to mail messengers	900,000.00	851,709.39	48,290.61	....
Mail locks and keys.....................	23,000.00	22,500.54	499.46	....
Mail-bags and mail-bag catchers..........	275,000.00	246,592.67	28,407.33	....
Miscellaneous items, office of the Second Assistant Postmaster-General..........	1,000.00	294.50	705.50	....
Mail depredations and post-office inspectors, and fees to United States marshals, and the necessary incidental expenses connected therewith	300,000.00	290,934.35	9,065.65	....
Postage and special-delivery stamps	135,000.00	132,411.00	2,589.00	....
Agents and assistants to distribute stamps, and expenses of agency	8,100.00	7,558.04	541.96	....
Stamped envelopes, newspaper wrappers, and letter sheets.....................	780,000.00	710,884.93	69,115.07	....
Agents and assistants to distribute stamped envelopes, newspaper wrappers, and letter sheets, and expenses of agency..............	16,000.00	15,859.03	140.97	....
Postal-cards.........................	200,000.00	199,826.50	173.50	....
Agents and assistants to distribute postal-cards, and expenses of agency.........	10,300.00	8,915.50	1,384.50	....
Registered packages, tag, official, and dead-letter envelopes	87,500.00	87,488.60	11.40	....
Ship, steam-boat, and way letters	2,500.00	1,428.71	1,071.29	....
Engraving, printing, and binding drafts and warrants	2,500.00	2,445.50	54.50	....
Miscellaneous items, office of the Third Assistant Postmaster-General	1,000.00	210.10	789.90	....
Advertising	20,000.00	13,058.41	6,941.59	....
Miscellaneous, office of the Postmaster-General	1,500.00	192.05	1,307.95	....
Transportation of foreign mails................	450,000.00	448,365.51	17,634.49	....
Balance due foreign countries...............	75,000.00	31,408.19	43,591.81	....
Rent of Washington City post-office	5,000.00	5,000.00	....	....
Special delivery	109,015.64	109,015.64	....	....
Compensation of postmasters re-adjusted under act of March 3, 1888..................	540,607.49	236,965.16	303,642.33	....

No. 5.—*Statement in detail of miscellaneous payments made by the Post-Office Department during the fiscal year ended June 30, 1888, and charged to "Miscellaneous items, office of the Postmaster-General."*

AMOUNT PAID BY WARRANT.

Date.	To whom allowed.	For what object.	Amount.
1887. Sept. 13	Nicholas M. Bell, Superintendent Foreign Mails.	For expenses incurred while traveling upon official business per order of the Postmaster-General dated September 3, 1887.	$13.26
Nov. 16	David M. Stone......................	For subscription to the Journal of Commerce from May 11, 1887, to November 11, 1887.	7.50
Nov. 18	M. Kraus	For subscription to the Daily Journal, Milwaukee, Wis., from March 16, 1885, to June 30, 1887.	11.45
Dec. 28	Nicholas M. Bell, Superintendent Foreign Mails.	For expenses incurred while traveling on official business per order of the Postmaster-General dated December 21, 1887.	18.95
1888. Feb. 14	Ellis B. Usher	For subscription to the La Crosse Morning Chronicle from December 18, 1885, to January 18, 1888.	15.00
Mar. 21	Michael Kraus	For subscriptions to the Daily Journal, Milwaukee, Wis., from July 1, 1887, to January 23, 1888.	2.75
Apr. 13	Nicholas M. Bell, Superintendent Foreign Mails.	For actual and necessary expenses incurred while traveling on the business of the Post-Office Department during the period from February 25, 1888, to March 12, 1888, per order of the Postmaster-General dated April 7, 1888.	26.00
May 3	Nicholas M. Bell, Superintendent Foreign Mails.	For expenses incurred while traveling on official business to Canada from April 22, to April 27, 1888, under order of the Postmaster-General dated May 11, 1888.	46.40
May 16	David M. Stone......................	For subscription for Superintendent of Foreign Mails to the Journal of Commerce, from November 11, 1887, to May 11, 1888.	7.50
July 10	T. & J. W. Johnson & Co	For one Patterson's Federal Restraints and postage for the office of the Assistant Attorney General, Post-Office Department.	3.70
July 12	Little, Brown & Co	For books furnished to Assistant Attorney-General for the Post-Office Department, as follows: One U. S. Digest, N. S., vol. 18 ....$5.00 One Sawyer's Reports, vol. 11..... 6.50 One Blatchford's Reports, vols. 23 and 24 ....12.00 One Brightly's N. Y. Digest (3 vols.)...................... ....20.00	43.50
Aug. 1	Gardiner G. Howland, treasurer	For subscription, New York Herald, from June 30, 1887, to June 30, 1888.	7.50
	Total paid by warrant	....	203.50

No. 6.—*Statement in detail of miscellaneous payments made by the Post-Office Department during the fiscal year ended June 30, 1888, and charged to miscellaneous items office of the First Assistant Postmaster-General.*

AMOUNT PAID BY WARRANT.

Date.	To whom allowed.	For what object.	Amount.
1887. Aug. 17	Henry G. Pearson, postmaster, New York, N. Y.	For expenses incurred in attendance at Washington, D. C., by direction of the Postmaster-General, dated July 12, 1887.	$21. 85
Aug. 19	Edward W. Alexander..................	For expenses incurred while traveling as a member of a commission appointed by the Postmaster-General, per order No. 89, dated May 8, 1887, for the purpose of reorganization of first and second class post-offices.	83. 05
Aug. 19	Reading Stoddart....................	For expenses incurred while traveling on official business, as stenographer to the commission appointed by the Postmaster-General, per order No. 89, dated May 8, 1887, for the purpose of reorganization of first and second class post-offices.	76. 15
Sept. 1	......do	......do...........................	29. 10
Sept. 2	Edward W. Alexander..................	For expenses incurred while traveling as a member of a commission appointed by the Postmaster-General, per order No. 89, dated May 8, 1887, for the purpose of reorganization of first and second class post-offices.	65. 47
Oct. 3	......do	......do...........................	65. 60
Nov. 1	......do	......do...........................	50. 65
1888. Mar. 5	John M. Hinkle	For packing boxes necessary for shipment of supplies of stationery.	97. 50
Apr. 9	John R. Mahoney......................	For three barrels of paste furnished on order of February 8, 1888.	18. 75
Apr. 10	Reading Stoddart..............	For expenses incurred while acting as stenographer and type-writer to the commission investigating the Chicago post-office.	71. 84
Apr. 10	W. B. Cooley	For special expenses incurred as a member of the commission designated by the Postmaster-General in order No. 72, dated March 23, 1888, to investigate the Chicago post-office.	67. 70
Apr. 10	George W. Wells.....................	......do...........................	80. 25
June 9	John R. Mahoney...............:.	For three barrels of paste furnished on order of April 23, 1888, and June 1, 1888.	18. 75
	Total paid by warrant	....	765. 06

AMOUNTS CREDITED ON GENERAL ACCOUNTS.

Date.	To whom allowed.	For what object.	Amount.
1887. Oct. 14	C. C. Young, jr., postmaster, Pensacola, Fla.	Miscellaneous expenditures, second quarter, 1887.	$40. 70
	J. M. Gilbert, postmaster, Syracuse, N. Y.	......do.............................	3. 00
Nov. 8	J. D. Thompson, postmaster, Mount Vernon, Ohio.	......do	7. 50
	David Day, postmaster, Saint Paul, Minn.	......do.............................	17. 50
1888. Mar. 16	C. N. Wilson, late postmaster, Savannah, Ga.	Miscellaneous expenditures, first quarter, 1888.	6. 00
June 5	J. A. Thompson, late postmaster, Manistee, Mich.	Miscellaneous expenditures, fourth quarter, 1886.	5. 00
July 20	G. Washington, postmaster, Bay City, Mich.	......do.............................	9. 50
	Total paid	....	89. 20

RECAPITULATION.

Amount allowed to postmasters at the principal post-offices, credited in quarterly accounts current for incidental office expenses, such as repairs, gas-fixtures, telegrams, etc.:

Third quarter, 1887	$14,464.11
Fourth quarter, 1887	12,838.51
First quarter, 1888	12,941.48
Second quarter, 1888	17,453.70
Total	57,697.80
Amount paid by warrant	$765.66
Amount credited on general accounts	89.20
Total	854.86
Less amount counter-entry post-office inspectors' fares	5.00
Total	849.86
Amount paid and charged "Miscellaneous, office First Assistant Postmaster-General"	56,547.66

No. 7.—*Statement in detail of miscellaneous payments made by the Post-Office Department during the fiscal year ended June 30, 1888, and charged to "Miscellaneous items, office of the Second Assistant Postmaster-General."*

AMOUNT PAID BY WARRANT.

Date.	To whom allowed.	For what object.	Amount.
1887. Dec. 21	E. M. Rosafy	For plates of horse and pony regulation mail-wagons.	$100.00
1888. Jan. 23	Mary Lee Dant	For services in opening and in marking proposals under advertisement of September 15, 1887, by authority of the Postmaster-General dated January 3, 1888.	24.00
	Clarence E. Dawson	do	24.00
Mar. 13	E. O. Graves	For two (2) brass dies for the Post-Office Department, for marking proposals for carrying the mail.	81.00
Apr. 17	Mary Lee Dant	For services in opening and marking bids from April 18 to April 20, 1888, both inclusive.	6.00
	Francis L. McKenna	do	6.00
May 19	R. D. S. Tyler	For expenses incurred for self and W. F. McMurray while on an official visit to New York to inspect stock on hand in the mail-bag-repair shop.	31.75
July 3	George F. Stone	For expenses as a witness in cases of the United States vs. J. N. Brafford, tried in the United States district court at Louisville, Ky., March 7, 1888.	71.75
	Total paid by warrant		294.50

No. 8.—*Statement in detail of miscellaneous payments made by the Post-Office Department for the fiscal year ended June 30, 1888, and charged to "Miscellaneous items, office of the Third Assistant Postmaster-General."*

AMOUNT PAID BY WARRANT.

Date.	To whom allowed.	For what object.	Amount.
1888. May 10	Charles F. Lewis	For expenses incurred in visiting the postage-stamp, stamped-envelope, and postal-card agencies at New York, Hartford, and Castleton by direction of the Postmaster-General, as per letter dated April 27, 1888.	$26.50
June 2	E. O. Graves, Chief of Bureau of Engraving and Printing.	For engraving, printing, numbering, and binding Post-Office Department warrants.	183.60
	Total paid by warrant		210.10

No. 9.—*Comparative statement of receipts and expenditures of the Post-Office Department from July 1, 1836, to June 30, 1888.*

Year.	Receipts.			Expenditures.
	Revenue.	Treasury grants.	Total.	
1837	$4, 945, 668. 21		$4, 945, 668. 21	$3, 288, 319. 03
1838	4, 238, 733. 46		4, 238, 733. 46	4, 430, 662. 21
1839	4, 484, 656. 70		4, 484, 656. 70	4, 636, 536. 31
1840	4, 543, 521. 92		4, 543, 521. 92	4, 718, 235. 64
1841	4, 407, 726. 27	$482, 657. 00	4, 890, 383. 27	4, 499, 527. 61
1842	4, 546, 849. 65		4, 546, 849. 65	5, 674, 751. 80
1843	4, 296, 225. 43		4, 296, 225. 43	4, 874, 753. 71
1844	4, 237, 287. 83		4, 237, 287. 83	4, 296, 512. 70
1845	4, 289, 841. 80		4, 289, 811. 80	4, 320, 731. 99
1846	3, 487, 199. 35	750, 000. 00	4, 237, 199. 35	4, 076, 036. 91
1847	3, 880, 309. 23	12, 500. 00	3, 892, 809. 23	3, 979, 542. 10
1848	4, 555, 211. 10	125, 000. 00	4, 680, 211. 10	4, 326, 850. 27
1849	4, 705, 176. 28		4, 705, 176. 28	4, 479, 049. 12
1850	5, 499, 984. 86		5, 499, 984. 86	5, 212, 953. 43
1851	6, 410, 604. 33		6, 410, 604. 33	6, 278, 401. 68
1852	5, 184, 526. 84	1, 741, 444. 44	6, 925, 971. 28	7, 108, 450. 04
1853	5, 240, 724. 70	2, 225, 000. 00	7, 495, 724. 70	7, 982, 756. 59
1854	6, 255, 586. 22	2, 736, 748. 96	8, 992, 335. 18	8, 577, 424. 12
1855	6, 642, 136. 13	3, 114, 542. 26	9, 756, 678. 39	9, 968, 342. 29
1856	6, 920, 821. 66	3, 748, 881. 56	10, 669, 703. 22	10, 405, 286. 36
1857	7, 333, 951. 76	4, 528, 004. 67	11, 881, 956. 43	11, 508, 057. 93
1858	·7, 486, 792. 86	4, 679, 270. 71	12, 166, 063. 57	12, 722, 470. 01
1859	7, 968, 484. 07	3, 915, 946. 49	11, 884, 430. 56	11, 458, 083. 63
1860	8, 518, 067. 40	11, 154, 167. 54	19, 672, 234. 94	19, 170, 609. 89
1861	8, 349, 296. 40	4, 639, 806. 53	12, 989, 102. 93	13, 606, 759. 11
1862	8, 299, 820. 90	2, 598, 953. 71	10, 898, 774. 61	11, 125, 364. 12
1863	11, 163, 780. 59	1, 007, 848. 72	12, 171, 638. 31	11, 314, 207. 64
1864	12, 438, 253. 78	749, 980. 00	13, 188, 233. 78	12, 644, 786. 20
1865	14, 556, 158. 70	3, 968. 46	14, 560, 127. 16	13, 694, 728. 28
1866	14, 436, 986. 21		14, 436, 986. 31	15, 352, 079. 30
1867	15, 297, 026. 87	3, 991, 666. 67	19, 288, 693. 54	19, 235, 483. 48
1868	16, 292, 600. 80	5, 696, 525. 00	21, 989, 125. 80	22, 730, 592. 65
1869	18, 344, 570. 72	5, 707, 115. 30	24, 051, 626. 02	23, 698, 131. 56
1870	19, 772, 220. 65	4, 022, 140. 85	23, 794, 361. 50	23, 998, 837. 63
1871	20, 037, 045. 42	4, 126, 200. 00	24, 163, 245. 42	24, 390, 104. 06
1872	21, 915, 426. 37	4, 933, 750. 00	26, 909, 176. 37	26, 658, 192. 31
1873	23, 996, 741. 57	5, 690, 475. 00	28, 987, 216. 57	29, 084, 945. 67
1874	26, 471, 071. 82	5, 922, 433. 55	32, 393, 505. 37	32, 126, 414. 58
1875	26, 791, 360. 59	6, 704, 646. 96	33, 496, 007. 55	33, 611, 309. 45
1876	28, 634, 197. 50	5, 088, 583. 03	33, 722, 780. 53	33, 263, 457. 58
1877	27, 531, 585. 26	7, 013, 300. 00	34, 544, 885. 26	33, 486, 322. 44
1878	29, 277, 516. 95	5, 307, 752. 82	34, 585, 169. 77	34, 165, 084. 49
1879	30, 041, 982. 86	3, 297, 965. 25	33, 330, 948. 11	33, 449, 899. 45
1880	33, 315, 479. 34	3, 597, 717. 20	36, 913, 196. 54	36, 542, 803. 68
1881	36, 785, 297. 97	3, 297, 921. 46	40, 083, 319. 43	39, 592, 506. 22
1882	41, 876, 410. 15	6, 595. 12	41, 883, 005. 27	40, 482, 021. 23
1883	45, 508, 692. 61	21, 416. 85	45, 520, 109. 46	43, 282, 944. 43
1884	43, 335, 958. 81	140, 690. 79	43, 466, 649. 60	47, 224, 500. 27
1885	42, 500, 843. 83	6, 066, 473. 00	48, 627, 316. 83	50, 046, 225. 21
1886	43, 948, 422. 95	8, 751, 070. 73	52, 699, 493. 68	51, 004, 742. 80
1887	48, 837, 606. 39	4, 746, 167. 06	53, 583, 776. 45	53, 006, 194. 39
1888	52, 695, 176. 79	3, 386, 441. 70	56, 081, 618. 49	56, 468, 315. 20

No. 10.—*Gross receipts, expenses, and net revenue of Presidential post-offices for the fiscal year ended June 30, 1868.*

[This table shows the actual amounts charged and credited at each office, and when full returns have not been received and audited, or an office has become Presidential during the year, the amount of salary reported may be less than the annual salary as stated in the Official Register. An salaries of Presidential offices are based on the gross receipts of the previous year, the amount allowed at offices where the revenues have fallen off will in some instances be found largely in excess of the receipts for the year. Allowance for clerk-hire at offices of the first and second classes are based on the revenues of such offices, but such allowances are made to third-class offices for the distribution of the mails where diverging star routes are supplied at the same time the local mail is distributed to the public. As all clerk-hire is paid from one appropriation, the expenditures are necessarily taken up on the quarterly returns of all postmasters, as office expenses, and are so reported here. The basis of allowance being different, no comparison should be made between the percentage of expenses of third-class offices and those of the first and second classes.]

ALABAMA.

Office.	Class.	Gross receipts.	Salary.	Clerk hire.	Rent, light, and fuel.	Other incidental expenses.	Free delivery.	Total expenses.	Net revenue.	Per cent expenses to gross receipts.	Remarks.
Anniston	3	$9,482.05	$1,600.00	$225.00		$12.90		$1,837.90	$7,644.09	19	
Birmingham	2	65,876.21	2,900.00	6,562.01	$1,766.4?	139.50	$6,211.36	16,719.54	39,155.77	30	
Eufaula	3	5,381.53	2,700.00	616.66		6.54		2,322.20	3,059.33	43	
Florence	3	3,759.58	1,300.00	150.00		2.02		1,452.03	2,304.56	39	
Gadsden	3	4,157.65	1,400.00	157.44		7.04		1,564.48	2,593.17	38	
Greensborough	3	2,624.20	1,100.00			1.20		1,101.20	1,523.00	42	
Greenville	3	3,261.57	1,400.00	190.74		2.10		1,601.84	1,659.72	49	
Huntsville	3	7,919.50	1,750.00	245.92		16.69		2,012.51	5,906.98	25	
Marion	3	2,970.72	1,400.00	78.00		.96		1,478.96	1,491.78	50	
Mobile	2	43,109.79	2,900.00	8,540.00		307.41	7,244.51	19,091.92	24,017.87	44	In Government building.
Montgomery	2	32,664.46	2,590.00	4,545.15		118.52	4,587.59	17,052.47	20,611.99	37	Do.
Opelika	2	4,232.55	1,690.00	253.04		4.98		1,758.90	2,473.65	42	
Selma	2	16,566.44	2,400.00	2,550.00	1,000.00	43.78	1,651.22	7,705.00	8,703.44	47	
Talladega	3	4,061.41	1,500.00	532.93		5.76		1,038.08	3,023.38	50	
Troy	3	2,918.11	1,200.00	500.00		8.09		1,703.00	1,215.03	58	
Tuscaloosa	3	6,478.19	1,600.00	454.00		3.20		2,053.20	4,424.90	32	
Tuscumbia	3	2,695.39	1,000.00	300.00		2.64		1,302.64	1,392.75	48	
Tuskegee	3	2,212.39	1,000.00			2.51		1,002.51	1,209.88	45	
Union Springs	3	2,255.52	1,000.00	200.00		1.12		1,201.12	1,054.40	53	
Total		212,568.30	31,450.00	24,048.18	2,825.67	680.91	18,794.89	80,000.65	132,557.65	53	

ARIZONA.

Office.	Class.	Gross receipts.	Salary.	Clerk hire.	Rent, light, and fuel.	Other incidental expenses.	Free delivery.	Total expenses.	Net revenue.	Per cent expenses to gross receipts.	Remarks.
Phoenix	3	7,634.00	1,675.00	208.33		4.32		1,887.65	5,146.35	26	
Prescott	3	4,786.19	1,700.00	608.38		3.60		2,311.93	2,474.26	55	
Tombstone	3	4,510.18	1,700.00	316.85		8.20		2,020.05	2,490.13	45	
Tucson	2	7,131.12	2,000.00	1,413.42	480.93	10.75		3,905.12	3,226.00	55	
Total		23,401.49	7,075.00	2,546.93	480.95	21.87		10,124.75	13,336.74	43	

No. 10.—*Gross receipts, expenses, and net revenue of Presidential post-offices for the fiscal year ended June 30, 1888—Continued.*

ARKANSAS.

Office	Class	Gross receipts	Salary	Clerk hire	Rent, light, and fuel	Other incidental expenses	Free delivery	Total expenses	Net revenue	Per cent expenses to gross receipts	Remarks
Arkadelphia	3	$3,151.60	$1,200.00	$162.00		$4.83		$1,366.83	$1,785.38	43	
Batesville	3	2,469.53	1,200.00	400.00		3.04		1,603.04	866.49	65	
Bentonville	3	2,227.23	825.00	150.00		1.84		976.84	1,250.39	44	
Camden	3	2,971.58	1,200.00	416.78		3.20		1,620.03	1,351.28	51	Presidential from October 1, 1887.
Eureka Springs	3	5,062.80	1,600.00	900.00		9.52		2,509.52	3,473.88	42	
Fayetteville	3	4,006.29	1,600.00	500.00		4.96		2,104.96	2,001.33	51	
Fort Smith	2	14,790.23	2,300.00	2,253.15	$954.00	2.90	$3,286.65	7,485.10	7,285.13	44	
Helena	2	5,128.41	1,700.00	575.00		1.95		2,292.98	2,857.05	53	
Hope	3	2,995.67	1,300.00	600.00		1.99		1,901.95	1,297.11	56	
Hot Springs	2	15,607.06	2,300.00	2,162.30	1,150.00	8.90	2,240.90	8,275.99	6,811.67	49	
Jonesborough	3	2,653.06	1,300.00	165.00		8.00		1,303.64	1,349.46	45	In Government building.
Little Rock	2	39,665.23	2,300.00	8,100.00		128.56	7,006.16	18,142.73	21,532.50	55	Presidential from April 1, 1888.
Malvern	3	651.85	350.00	50.00		.40		300.40	250.95	53	
Newport	3	2,697.43	1,300.00	198.92		2.88		1,501.59	1,385.63	55	
Pine Bluff	3	11,012.02	2,040.00	1,200.00	645.65	48.71		3,884.36	7,119.26	50	
Prescott	3	2,985.88	2,100.00	162.50		1.52		1,984.02	1,022.86	42	
Searcy	3	7,080.69	1,000.00	154.13		1.28		1,155.40	1,181.53	42	
Texarkana	3	7,080.69	3,900.00	1,050.00		8.08		9,955.08	4,132.61	42	
Van Buren	3	3,576.24	1,360.00	208.38		6.14		1,511.47	2,081.77	47	
Total		131,798.11	28,175.00	19,462.98	3,449.65	240.12	11,532.61	61,980.36	60,925.75	47	

CALIFORNIA.

Office	Class	Gross receipts	Salary	Clerk hire	Rent, light, and fuel	Other incidental expenses	Free delivery	Total expenses	Net revenue	Per cent expenses to gross receipts	Remarks
Alameda	3	6,182.46	1,600.00			42.96		1,642.96	4,499.38	37	
Arcata	3	1,364.08	665.78			1.60		676.88	684.63	49	
Anaheim	3	1,762.57	666.56		12.50	.54		686.63	1,086.03	38	
Auburn	3	3,371.93	1,500.00	186.00		5.63		1,405.88	3,188.00	44	
Bakersfield	3	3,733.88	1,400.00			4.16		1,421.14	2,343.00	37	
Benicia	3	4,940.43	1,400.00	208.53		12.89		1,512.90	2,828.08	58	
Berkeley	3	1,706.45	1,000.00			.24		316.91	389.54	77	
Bodie	3	2,294.07	1,000.00	316.67		1.76		1,301.76	992.01	57	
Calistoga	3	2,675.37	1,700.00	300.00				1,700.00	2,073.97	38	
Chico	3	3,633.37	1,466.00			3.48		1,810.83	1,819.50	38	
Colton	3	990.12	1,300.00	408.34		.24		658.67	940.45	46	
Colusa	3	3,778.72	1,900.00	258.43		2.40		1,302.40	1,477.31	47	
Dixon	3	6,100.17	1,700.00	300.00		11.96		2,011.96	4,157.61	25	

No. 10.—*Gross receipts, expenses, and net revenue of Presidential post-offices for the fiscal year ended June 30, 1898.*

[This table shows the actual amounts charged and credited at each office, and when full returns have not been received and audited, or an office has become Presidential during the year, the amount of salary reported may be less than the annual salary as stated in the Official Register. As salaries of Presidential offices are based on the gross receipts of the previous year, the amounts allowed at offices where the revenues have fallen off will in some instances be found largely in excess of the receipts for the year. Allowances for clerk hire at offices of the first and second classes are based on the revenues of such offices, but such allowances are made to third-class offices for the distribution of the mails where divergiug star routes are supplied at the same time the local mail is distributed to the public. As all clerk hire is paid from one appropriation, no distinction of the mails where divergiug star routes are supplied at the same time the local mail is distributed to the public. As all clerk hire is paid from one appropriation, no expenditures are necessarily taken up on tly returns of all postmasters as office expenses, and are no reported here. The basis of allowance being different, no comparisons should be made between the of expenses of third-class offices and those of the first and second classes.]

ALABAMA.

Office.	Class.	Gross receipts.	Salary.	Clerk hire.	Rent, light, and fuel.	Other incidental expenses.	Free delivery.	Total expenses.	Net revenue.	Per cent. expenses to gross receipts.	Remarks.
Anniston	3	$9,482.05	$1,600.00	$225.00		$12.96		$1,837.96	$7,644.09	19	
Birmingham	2	65,875.31	2,900.00	6,562.01	$1,765.63	359.50	$3,211.36	16,719.54	39,155.77	30	
Eufaula	3	5,381.53	1,700.00	616.00		6.54		2,332.30	3,059.33	43	
Florence	3	4,756.58	1,300.00	150.00		2.02		1,452.03	3,304.56	30	
Gadsden	3	4,157.65	1,400.00	157.44		7.04		1,564.48	2,593.17	38	
Greensborough	3	2,624.20	1,100.00			1.20		1,101.20	1,523.00	42	
Greenville	3	3,261.57	1,600.00			2.10		1,601.84	1,659.73	49	
Huntsville	3	7,919.50	1,750.00	190.74		16.60		2,012.51	5,905.98	25	
Marion	3	2,970.72	1,400.00	245.92		.96		1,478.96	1,491.76	50	
Mobile	2	43,109.79	2,900.00	78.00		307.41	7,344.51	19,001.92	24,017.87	44	In Governme.t building.
Montgomery	2	32,064.44	2,400.00	8,540.00		118.52	4,587.60	12,052.47	20,611.99	37	Do.
Opelika	3	4,232.55	1,800.00	4,548.15		4.96		1,788.90	2,473.65	42	
Selma	2	16,560.44	2,400.00	253.94	$1,060.00	43.78	1,651.22	8,793.44	8,793.44	47	
Talladega	3	4,061.41	1,500.00	532.32		8.70		2,023.38	2,023.38	50	
Troy	3	2,918.11	1,200.00	550.00		3.09		1,703.09	1,215.02	58	
Tuscaloosa	3	6,478.10	1,600.00	500.00		3.20		2,053.20	4,424.90	32	
Tuscumbia	3	2,695.39	1,000.00	450.00		2.64		1,302.64	1,392.75	48	
Tuskegee	3	2,212.39	1,000.00	300.00		2.51		1,002.51	1,200.88	45	
Union Springs	3	2,255.52	1,040.00	200.00		1.12		1,201.12	1,054.40	53	
Total		212,558.30	31,450.00	28,048.18	2,825.67	280.91	18,794.89	80,000.65	132,557.65	33	

ARIZONA.

Office.	Class.	Gross receipts.	Salary.	Clerk hire.	Rent, light, and fuel.	Other incidental expenses.	Free delivery.	Total expenses.	Net revenue.	Per cent. expenses to gross receipts.	Remarks.
Phœnix	3	7,034.00	1,675.00	208.33		4.32		1,887.65	5,146.35	28	
Prescott	3	4,786.19	1,700.00	608.33		3.60		2,311.93	2,474.26	55	
Tombstone	3	4,510.18	1,700.00	316.85		3.29		2,020.06	2,490.13	45	
Tucson	2	7,131.12	2,000.00	1,413.42	480.93	10.75		3,905.12	3,226.00	55	

No. 10.—*Gross receipts, expenses, and net revenue of Presidential post-offices for the fiscal year ended June 30, 1888—Continued.*

ARKANSAS.

Office.	Class.	Gross receipts.	Salary.	Clerk hire.	Rent, light, and fuel.	Other incidental expenses.	Free delivery.	Total expenses.	Net revenue.	Per cent. expenses to gross receipts.	Remarks.
Arkadelphia	3	$3,181.60	$1,200.00	$162.00		$4.82		$1,366.82	$1,785.38	43	Presidential from October 1, 1887.
Batesville	3	2,469.53	1,200.00	400.00		3.04		1,603.04	866.49	65	
Bentonville	3	2,237.23	825.00	150.00		1.84		976.84	1,260.39	44	
Camden	3	2,971.88	1,200.00	416.78		3.26		1,620.02	1,351.86	51	
Eureka Springs	3	5,982.90	1,600.00	900.00		9.52		2,509.52	3,473.38	42	
Fayetteville	3	5,006.29	1,600.00	500.00		4.96		2,104.96	2,901.33	42	
Fort Smith	2	14,780.22	2,300.00	2,253.15	$654.00	2.30	$3,286.65	7,495.10	7,285.13	51	
Helena	3	5,189.41	1,700.00	676.00		7.36		2,383.36	2,807.06	44	
Hope	3	2,898.47	1,300.00	300.00		1.86		1,601.86	811.67	55	
Hot Springs	2	15,087.06	2,300.00	2,182.29	1,150.00	8.00	2,340.80	8,371.99	6,818.40	55	
Jonesborough	3	2,653.06	1,200.00	600.00		3.86		1,803.60	849.46	49	In Government building. Presidential from April 1, 1888.
Little Rock	2	39,665.22	2,200.00	8,305.00		126.58	7,506.16	18,142.73	21,532.50	45	
Malvern	3	531.35	300.00	50.00		2.68		601.50	350.95	65	
Newport	3	2,897.43	1,300.00	198.97		2.88		1,601.50	1,295.63	52	
Pine Bluff	3	11,013.62	2,000.00	1,200.00	645.65	48.71		3,894.96	7,119.26	35	
Prescott	3	2,981.88	1,100.00	162.50		1.52		1,264.02	1,022.86	50	
Searcy	3	2,338.93	1,000.00	154.12		1.28		1,155.40	1,181.53	50	
Texarkana	3	7,090.69	3,900.00	1,650.00		8.08		2,955.08	4,132.61	42	
Van Buren	3	3,576.24	1,300.00	208.33		6.14		1,514.47	2,061.77	43	
Total		131,786.11	28,175.00	19,462.98	2,449.65	240.13	11,532.61	61,860.36	69,925.75	47	

CALIFORNIA.

Alameda	3	6,132.46	1,600.00		12.50	42.08		1,642.08	4,490.38	27	Presidential from November 1, 1887. Presidential from November 28, 1887.
Arcata	3	1,384.68	665.76			1.00		676.76	684.82	49	
Anaheim	3	1,753.67	665.58			.24		666.58	1,086.05	38	
Auburn	3	3,871.22	1,500.00	180.00		5.53		1,685.53	2,186.50	44	
Bakersfield	3	3,745.97	1,400.00			2.98		1,402.98	2,243.16	57	
Benicia	3	2,733.63	1,200.00	908.83		4.16		1,612.99	1,221.14	56	
Berkeley	3	4,340.85	1,500.00			12.59		1,512.59	2,828.64	77	
Bodie	3	1,706.45	1,000.00	316.67		1.76		1,301.76	395.54	77	
Calistoga	3	1,294.37	1,000.00	300.00				1,300.00	992.61	67	
Chico	3	4,678.97	1,700.00			1.76		1,700.00	2,973.97	36	
Colton	3	2,630.12	1,400.00	408.34		2.48		1,810.82	819.50	50	
Colusa	3	1,692.30	1,300.00	358.43		.24		1,658.67	1,000.43	43	
Dixon	3	2,778.73	1,500.00			2.40		1,502.40	1,477.51	47	
Eureka	3	8,169.17	1,700.00	300.10		11.36		2,011.36	6,157.81	25	

Presidential from June 16, 1888.

Fresno City	2	15,845.99	2,300.00	1,250.00	70.00		77.61	3,697.51	11,848.48	24
Gilroy	3	3,281.08	1,400.00				4.24	1,464.24	1,857.42	43
Grass Valley	3	3,422.43	1,900.00	280.00			1.60	1,801.60	3,620.83	38
Hanford	3	2,631.98	1,200.00				.96	1,200.00	1,430.97	47
Hayward	3	4,125.87	1,400.00				3.84	1,503.84	1,721.58	37
Healdsburgh	3	4,482.16	1,500.00				3.44	1,500.61	2,570.52	37
Hollister	3	3,913.97	1,300.00				.84	1,303.84	1,081.52	43
Livermore	1						8.84		1,610.13	46
Los Angeles	3	118,313.91	3,500.00	21,797.70	468.65	$18,471.29	2,470.06	44,389.70	69,114.12	39
Los Gatos	3	3,266.09	1,100.00				5.06	1,105.06	2,141.01	39
Martinez	2	3,504.62	1,100.00	62.64			2.06	1,164.72	1,380.90	47
Marysville	3	4,871.56	2,000.00	968.75	439.04		16.02	3,458.81	5,417.75	39
Merced	3	6,134.30	1,500.00	268.38			8.38	1,663.38	2,975.43	33
Modesto	3	3,760.31	1,700.00				7.60	1,915.98	4,318.87	31
Monterey	3	4,929.81	2,000.00	1,000.00	313.70		57.40	1,402.06	1,267.23	37
Napa City	3	4,985.65	1,100.00	815.68			8.05	3,371.10	6,568.31	38
Nevada City	1	68,777.64	8,100.00	10,288.00	1,025.00	16,916.60	828.46	33,085.35	2,546.34	45
Oakland	3	69.36	43.46					46.45	84,722.80	48
Orange	3	4,701.18	1,500.00	258.46			4.06	48.91	19.91	73
Oroville	3	18,611.80	2,000.00	3,075.27			290.90	2,858.64	2,858.64	39
Pasadena										

No. 10.—*Gross receipts, expenses, and net revenue of Presidential post-offices for the fiscal year ended June 30, 1888*—Continued.

CONNECTICUT—Continued.

Office.	Class.	Gross receipts.	Salary.	Clerk hire.	Rent, light, and fuel.	Other incidental expenses.	Free delivery.	Total expenses.	Net revenue.	Per cent. expenses to gross receipts.	Remarks.
South Norwalk	2	$11,182.25	$2,100.00	$1,000.00	$407.45	$1.73		$3,509.18	$7,672.07	31	
Stanford Springs	3	3,616.12	1,500.00	200.00		4.04		704.18	2,912.04	47	
Stamford	2	18,551.71	2,500.04	1,849.99	1,197.00	35.44	$2,320.09	7,902.52	10,619.19	42	
Stonington	3	3,258.71	1,400.00			4.08		1,404.08	1,854.63	43	
Thomaston	3	4,234.05	1,500.00			4.00		1,504.00	2,730.05	36	
Thompsonville	3	3,676.01	1,400.00	316.85		4.80		1,401.80	2,274.61	35	
Torrington	3	5,704.78	1,700.00			6.00		2,022.85	3,681.93	35	
Unionville	3	3,087.60	1,400.00			2.88		1,402.88	1,644.72	45	
Wallingford	3	10,834.50	2,100.00	1,200.60	2,140.75	17.20	6,528.68	9,757.95	1,076.55	35	
Waterbury	2	35,728.03	2,600.00	4,973.80	2,142.50	97.59		15,296.67	20,423.46	43	
Westport	3	2,364.86	1,100.00			3.04		1,103.04	261.32	47	
West Winsted	2	4,917.73	1,600.00	1,620.00	100.00	4.24		1,604.24	2,313.14	33	
Willimantic	3	10,214.60	1,800.00			13.28		3,833.28	6,381.32	38	
Windsor Locks	3	2,969.15	1,200.00			2.80		1,202.80	1,766.35	41	
Winsted	3	6,208.12	1,600.00	290.00		5.92		1,805.92	4,312.20	31	
Total		747,848.03	97,068.72	84,574.87	17,868.90	2,670.47	87,030.84	289,153.40	458,692.63	39	

DAKOTA.

Office.	Class.	Gross receipts.	Salary.	Clerk hire.	Rent, light, and fuel.	Other incidental expenses.	Free delivery.	Total expenses.	Net revenue.	Per cent. expenses to gross receipts.	Remarks.
Aberdeen	3	12,231.45	2,100.00	1,200.00	480.36	17.08		3,797.44	8,434.01	31	
Alexandria	3	940.02	900.00			.48		1,030.48	909.54	52	
Ashton	3	923.10	900.00			.08		1,000.08	923.02	50	
Bismarck	2	7,111.90	1,800.00	1,070.76		9.04		2,879.80	4,231.80	70	
Blunt	3	1,550.98	1,100.00	187.50		.40		1,227.90	322.08	38	
Brookings	3	3,200.41	1,200.00			1.28		1,201.28	1,999.13	43	
Canton	3	3,548.03	1,400.00	108.43		.48		1,508.91	2,040.12	41	
Casselton	3	3,408.58	1,400.00	216.50		1.04		1,401.04	2,006.54	46	
Chamberlain	3	3,443.99	1,200.00	100.00		1.52		1,418.12	1,024.87	49	
Clark	3	2,657.37	1,200.00	158.83		.34		1,300.34	1,357.11	50	
Columbia	3	494.55	900.00	1,200.00		.66		1,435.88	976.89	56	
Deadwood	2	8,653.67	900.00					8,626.99	8,626.99	84	Presidential from June 6, 1888.
Dell Rapids	3	2,149.89	75.00					75.85	65.84	44	
De Smet	3	2,461.38	1,100.00	262.27		4.48		1,909.75	1,907.98	41	
Devil's Lake	3	4,662.00	1,100.00	298.42		1.12		1,909.54	2,789.81	41	
Ellendale	3	2,744.40	1,400.00	4,073.90	1,177.82	89.07	1,214.13	10,085.62	1,138.95	49	
Fargo	2	21,143.66	2,500.00	193.90		1.41		1,695.40	11,083.04	43	
Grafton	3	3,081.64	1,500.00						2,283.64		

											Remarks
Telluride	3	2,517.31	1,100.00	700.00		.48		1,100.48	1,416.83	44	
Trumbull	3	10,721.72	1,700.00			9.04		2,403.04	8,312.68	22	
Total		376,603.68	48,688.86	50,018.41	2,607.09	1,934.91	34,444.11	137,673.98	229,100.70	87	

CONNECTICUT.

											Remarks
Ansonia	2	13,515.33	2,300.00		905.99	14.09	2,049.73	7,068.88	6,426.45	52	
Bethel	3	2,555.40	1,900.00			2.32		1,602.32	1,553.08	39	
Birmingham	3	12,131.12	2,300.00	1,278.00	1,153.70	23.04	2,598.85	7,353.59	4,777.53	61	
Branford	3	2,064.84	1,300.00			1.84		1,301.81	1,663.04	44	
Bridgeport	1	50,374.21	3,101.00	8,250.51	3,622.58	332.18	12,153.95	27,460.22	31,913.99	22	
Bristol	3	8,727.76	1,900.00			18.50		1,918.50	6,808.96	46	
Colchester	3	1,491.56	687.50			2.10		689.68	801.90	43	
Collinsville	3	2,545.63	1,100.00			1.01		1,101.04	1,444.59	43	
Danbury	2	17,744.78	2,500.00	2,200.00	460.05	81.40	3,383.70	8,625.15	9,119.63	48	Presidential from October 24, 1887.
Danielsonville	3	5,074.71	1,600.00	302.02		7.04		1,909.14	3,165.65	36	
Deep River	3	2,766.88	1,600.00			3.04		1,603.61	1,663.84	39	
East Haddam	3	2,470.12	1,200.00	100.00		1.20		1,301.20	1,162.94	53	
East Hampton	3	1,593.84	819.02			.61		819.69	774.18	51	Presidential from October 3, 1887.
Essex	3	1,785.79	1,300.00			2.48		1,302.48	1,453.31	47	
Greenwich	3	674.21	1,550.00	16.66		6.80		1,523.46	1,1.0.78	23	
Guilford	3	2,353.53	1,100.00			3.20		1,103.20	1,420.33	44	
Hartford	1	140,750.70	3,400.00	20,248.67	1,566.00	632.91	17,671.49	41,953.07	98,896.69	29	In Government building.
Litchfield	3	3,783.40	1,500.00			6.40		1,506.40	2,277.00	50	
Meriden	2	34,139.58	2,700.00	4,001.15		75.54	6,285.45	14,578.14	19,561.44	38	
Middletown	2	20,696.97	2,500.00	2,692.76		49.84	2,633.33	7,875.93	12,821.01	38	Do.
Milford	3	3,537.34	1,400.00			1.68		1,401.68	2,135.66	37	
Moodus	3	4,106.79	1,500.00			1.92		1,501.92	2,601.87	28	
Mystic Bridge	3	4,302.84	1,100.00	16.67		6.48		1,123.15	3,203.60	26	
Naugatuck	3	5,964.10	1,640.10			6.90		1,606.90	4,357.14	45	
New Britain	2	21,408.33	2,400.00	2,600.00	1,174.90	2.24	3,322.41	9,497.31	11,811.01	49	
New Canaan	3	472.40	302.20			.64		302.84	271.54		
New Hartford	1	617.66	302.20			2.24		302.84	314.22		Presidential from March 12, 1888.
New Haven	1	127,056.14	3,008.14	21,448.06	2,078.48	791.59	24,142.86	49,783.49	77,272.65	49	In Government building.
New London	2	22,771.24	2,600.00	3,550.00		90.73		8,320.21	14,451.03	37	Do.
New Milford	3	5,508.63	1,700.00	290.00		8.52		1,903.52	3,603.11	35	
Northford	3	6,191.18	2,200.00	299.45				2,499.45	3,691.73	40	
Norwalk	2	10,187.00	2,000.00	850.00	415.00	25.56		3,290.56	6,846.44	33	
Norwich	2	28,902.14	2,700.00	3,500.00	2,204.50	225.28	4,574.31	13,204.09	15,698.05	48	
Plainville	3	2,689.92	1,200.00			6.00		1,206.00	1,492.92	45	
Plantsville	3	2,220.03	1,100.00			2.48		1,102.48	1,127.55	50	
Portland	3	3,321.36	1,400.00	468.33		2.72		1,402.72	1,918.64	42	
Putnam	3	6,053.28	1,700.00			7.84		2,116.17	3,937.11	35	
Rockville	3	7,488.21	1,800.00			8.40		1,868.40	3,819.10	48	
Seymour	3	227.76	1,400.00			2.40		1,302.40	2,162.82	47	
Southington	3	4,295.01	1,600.00			4.56		1,601.56	2,090.48	37	
South Manchester	3	4,464.56	1,080.00			5.82		1,605.92	2,638.66	36	

No. 10.—*Gross receipts, expenses, and net revenue of Presidential post-offices for the fiscal year ended June 30, 1888—Continued.*

DISTRICT OF COLUMBIA.

Office	Class	Gross receipts.	Salary.	Clerk hire.	Rent, light, and fuel.	Other incidental expenses.	Free delivery.	Total expenses.	Net revenue.	Per cent. expenses to gross receipts.	Remarks.
Washington	1	$312,645.76	$5,000.00	$158,353.15	$9,651.64	$21,462.04	$67,469.37	$261,918.40	$70,127.36	80	Includes $14,969.32 expenses of mail bags repair depot.

FLORIDA.

Office	Class	Gross receipts.	Salary.	Clerk hire.	Rent, light, and fuel.	Other incidental expenses.	Free delivery.	Total expenses.	Net revenue.	Per cent. expenses to gross receipts.	Remarks.
Bartow	3	2,998.62	1,300.00	250.00		3.68		1,553.08	1,444.94	52	
De Land	3	3,779.18	1,500.00			1.81		1,501.84	2,277.29	40	
Eustis	3	2,276.69	1,300.00	16.85		1.81		1,318.09	968.00	58	
Fernandina	3	3,927.97	1,500.00	160.99		4.16		1,665.15	2,262.53	42	
Gainesville	3	6,821.06	1,700.00	416.67		9.28		2,125.95	3,695.11	37	
Jacksonville	1	60,035.88	3,100.00	10,935.99	2,933.80	314.91	6,994.21	24,278.91	25,756.97	36	
Key West	3	9,387.10	1,900.00	425.00		103.40		2,428.40	6,958.70	26	
Kissimmee	3	2,350.18	1,300.00			1.78		1,101.78	1,448.42	48	
Leesburg	3	2,468.78	1,197.29			8.84		1,206.13	1,477.65	48	
Ocala	3	5,773.79	1,700.00	200.00		6.82		1,956.72	3,817.07	34	
Orlando	2	9,303.69	2,100.00	1,200.00	307.56	74.82		3,483.83	5,623.51	39	
Palatka	2	7,965.28	2,100.00	1,000.00	410.00	44.63		3,554.83	4,440.65	45	
Pensacola	2	12,723.46	2,000.00	1,516.78		1.81		6,447.72	6,275.74	51	
Saint Augustine	2	11,807.47	2,000.00	2,154.00		25.28	2,629.12	4,170.28	7,628.19	35	In Government building.
Sanford	3	6,543.83	1,800.00	554.61		10.39		2,364.10	4,136.92	36	Do.
Tallahassee	3	5,331.59	1,600.00	408.42		7.68		2,016.10	3,315.49	38	
Tampa	3	6,158.61	1,800.00	800.00		71.96		2,071.96	3,486.05	43	
Total		148,846.83	30,047.29	20,039.29	3,651.36	688.94	9,623.33	64,060.21	84,786.12	43	

GEORGIA.

Office	Class	Gross receipts.	Salary.	Clerk hire.	Rent, light, and fuel.	Other incidental expenses.	Free delivery.	Total expenses.	Net revenue.	Per cent. expenses to gross receipts.	Remarks.
Albany	3	5,141.03	1,700.00	300.00		15.81		2,015.84	3,125.19	39	
Americus	3	5,870.85	1,600.00	300.00		9.81		2,509.84	3,361.01	43	
Athens	3	10,093.72	1,800.00	808.43		9.76		2,618.19	7,531.99	32	
Atlanta	1	124,914.82	3,800.00	19,645.19	1,190.29	592.18	16,588.13	40,950.59	84,025.32	40	In Government building.
Augusta	2	89,096.86	2,800.00	5,100.00		223.40	9,611.85	18,924.95	20,981.81	45	
Bainbridge	3	3,821.90	1,400.00	300.00		1.04		1,701.04	2,120.86	61	
Barnesville	3	2,149.40	1,100.00	200.00		2.16		1,302.16	847.24	61	
Brunswick	3	6,046.22	1,800.00	300.00		11.12		2,111.12	6,029.10	23	

Grand Forks	2	11,530.37	2,100.00	1,200.00	577.09		12.32	8,899.82	7,040.85	34	Presidential from March 11, 1888.
Groton	3	2,794.15	2,400.00					1,400.73	1,383.43	50
Hillsboro	3	2,605.25	1,100.00				.12	1,100.32	1,044.88	43
Huron	3	11,824.68	2,300.00	1,635.55	368.68		6.65	6,485.06	6,321.80	47
Ipswich	3	4,004.04	1,400.00	16.85				567.19	567.19	85
Jamestown	3	6,363.18	1,800.00	402.42			6.92	214.84	4,053.84	61
Kimball	3	2,115.45	1,200.00	91.66			.88	1,292.54	822.91	61
Le Moore	3	1,679.84	1,000.00				.32	1,000.32	678.53	49
Larimore	3	2,471.65	850.04	208.83			.56	1,062.67	437.66	48
Lead City	3	702.90	1,400.00	216.88			.08	356.12	1,630.01	50
Lisbon	3	3,248.14	1,400.00	100.00			1.28	1,618.13	2,182.62	41
Madison	3	3,686.96	1,200.00				1.36	1,501.96	1,433.77	50
Mandan	3	2,640.53	1,100.00				.56	1,200.56	1,189.38	43
Mayville	3	2,996.52	1,400.00	280.00			1.20	1,101.20	1,044.22	57
Milbank	3	3,616.02	1,200.00	207.00	352.00		1.86	1,886.27	1,714.98	43
Miller	3	2,455.69	1,200.00	108.33			8.38	1,383.84	1,044.22	57
Mitchell	3	8,600.88	2,000.00				.64	1,204.40	1,183.54	66
Parker	3	2,477.03	1,200.00				1.96	789.70	492.32	49
Park River	3	2,892.72	1,200.00	458.34			.40	708.26	431.21	43
Pierre	3	4,534.33	1,500.00	208.36			1.36	1,708.36	824.07	38
Plankinton	3	2,156.93	2,000.00	1,200.00	225.00		8.87	3,438.37	2,727.56	55
Rapid City	3	3,512.09	1,400.00	208.42			1.84	1,610.26	1,901.83	44
Redfield	2	17,468.15	2,400.00	1,081.25	1,138.95	1,865.71	1.98	7,174.89	10,314.28	56
Sioux Falls	3	3,192.00	1,400.00					1,400.00	1,792.00	44
Valley City	3	4,241.11	1,100.00	290.00			1.68	1,301.68	1,351.68	40
Vermillion	3	4,537.00	1,000.00	98.78			8.12	1,702.90	2,688.21	40
Wahpeton	3	157.42	71.42	500.70			7.28	1,407.28	150.82	39
Watertown	3	2,576.01	1,200.00	20.00				62.17	65.25	28
Webster	2	8,783.94	2,000.00	290.00	284.00		.73	1,460.73	1,175.39	50
Woonsocket				1,500.00			91.46	3,943.46	4,523.88	41
Yankton										45
Total		225,538.84	68,603.01	21,592.04	4,559.23	4,343.07	283.47	99,360.81	126,168.03	44

DELAWARE.

Dover	3	6,088.04	1,800.00				4.86	1,804.86	4,283.16	30	In Government building.
Middletown	3	3,061.05	1,800.00				2.16	1,562.16	1,538.89	50
Milford	3	3,429.25	1,800.00	200.00			2.56	1,802.56	2,126.70	58
Newark	3	2,707.31	483.80				.72	1,400.72	1,305.50	58
New Castle	3	1,837.55	433.90	200.00			.96	454.26	463.29	48
Seaford	3	188.88	90.00					90.66	98.03	43	Presidential from June 4, 1888.
Smyrna	3	3,822.49	1,460.00			2.60		1,402.60	1,960.40	47
Wilmington	1	55,675.56	3,100.00	6,720.00		13,476.82	190.67	24,487.49	30,188.07		In Government building.
Total		75,419.95	10,643.96	9,130.00		13,476.82	203.96	33,445.73	41,975.22	44

No. 10.—*Gross receipts, expenses, and net revenue of Presidential post-offices for the fiscal year ended June 30, 1889*—Continued.

DISTRICT OF COLUMBIA.

Office	Class	Gross receipts.	Salary.	Clerk hire.	Rent, light, and fuel.	Other incidental expenses.	Free delivery.	Total expenses.	Net revenue.	Per cent. expenses to gross receipts.	Remarks.
Washington	1	$252,045.78	$5,000.00	$158,353.15	$9,093.84	$21,402.04	$97,469.97	$291,918.40	$70,127.38	80	Includes $14,969.33 expenses of mail-bags repair depot.

FLORIDA.

Office	Class	Gross receipts.	Salary.	Clerk hire.	Rent, light, and fuel.	Other incidental expenses.	Free delivery.	Total expenses.	Net revenue.	Per cent. expenses to gross receipts.	Remarks.
Bartow	3	2,968.62	1,300.00	250.00		3.68		1,553.68	1,444.94	52	
De Land	3	3,170.18	1,500.00			1.84		1,501.84	2,571.29	40	
Eustis	3	3,276.60	1,300.00	10.85		1.61		1,318.46	958.00	43	
Fernandina	3	3,927.97	1,500.00	180.99		4.16		1,685.15	2,262.52	37	
Gainesville	1	5,821.06	1,700.00	418.67		9.28		2,125.95	3,695.11	36	
Jacksonville	3	50,035.88	3,100.00	10,935.99	2,933.80	314.91	6,994.21	24,278.91	23,756.97	48	
Key West	3	9,387.10	1,900.00	435.00		103.40		9,428.40	4,938.70	47	
Kissimmee	3	2,550.18	1,100.00			1.76		1,101.76	1,448.42	43	
Leesburg	3	2,498.78	1,197.29			2.84		1,201.13	1,257.65	48	
Ocala	3	5,773.79	1,750.00	200.00		6.72		1,954.72	3,817.07	34	
Orlando	3	9,306.80	2,100.00	1,200.00		75.62		3,683.88	3,622.51	45	
Palatka	2	7,995.29	2,100.00	1,000.00	397.55	44.63		3,554.63	4,410.65	44	
Pensacola	2	12,722.46	2,300.00	1,816.76	410.00	1.84	2,639.12	6,447.72	7,275.74	51	In Government building.
Saint Augustine	2	11,807.47	1,800.00	2,154.00		25.28		4,179.28	7,628.19	35	Do.
Sanford	3	6,503.83	1,600.00	454.61		10.39		2,064.91	1,328.82	38	
Tallahassee	3	4,158.61	1,500.00	405.43		7.66		2,016.10	3,816.49	38	
Tampa	3			800.00		71.96		2,671.96	3,486.65	43	
Total		148,846.33	30,047.29	20,039.29	3,651.86	668.94	9,633.33	64,060.21	84,706.13	43	

GEORGIA.

Office	Class	Gross receipts.	Salary.	Clerk hire.	Rent, light, and fuel.	Other incidental expenses.	Free delivery.	Total expenses.	Net revenue.	Per cent. expenses to gross receipts.	Remarks.
Albany	3	5,141.03	1,700.00	300.00		15.81		2,015.84	3,125.19	39	
Americus	3	5,870.85	1,600.00	900.00		9.84		2,509.84	3,361.01	43	
Athens	3	10,089.78	1,900.00	308.43		9.76		2,218.19	7,821.59	22	
Atlanta	1	124,914.82	3,200.00	19,645.19	1,190.20	592.18	14,852.13	40,389.59	84,525.32	32	In Government building.
Augusta	2	39,006.86	2,900.00	5,100.00		225.49	9,611.25	18,924.96	20,081.91	48	
Bainbridge	3	2,821.90	1,400.00	300.00		1.04		1,701.04	1,120.96	45	
Barnesville	3	2,149.40	1,100.00	200.00		2.16		1,302.16	847.24	61	
Brunswick	3	9,040.22	1,800.00	300.00		11.13		2,111.13	6,929.10	23	

Cartersville	3	3,040.60	1,300.00	200.00	1,075.00	3.20	3,134.79	1,563.20	1,537.40	49
Columbus	2	18,043.13	2,500.00	1,920.11		81.24		8,711.14	9,331.99	48
Cuthbert	3	2,253.78	1,200.00	67.50		.88		1,283.38	985.40	56
Dalton	3	3,692.26	1,400.00	200.00		4.00		1,694.00	1,996.26	45
Gainesville	3	4,201.61	1,500.00	504.43		6.56		2,014.99	2,186.85	45
Griffin	3	4,706.51	1,600.00	277.50		7.60		1,885.10	2,011.61	39
Hawkinsville	3	3,017.29	1,600.00	250.00		2.99		1,552.96	1,464.24	51
La Grange	2	3,295.22	1,400.00	200.00		2.84		1,602.84	1,681.38	49
Macon	2	35,709.42	2,800.00	5,500.00	1,236.75	378.33	8,748.27	18,601.25	17,648.07	63
Madison	3	2,415.70	1,300.00			.60		1,302.00	1,113.70	54
Marietta	3	5,623.27	1,600.00			10.98		1,818.68	3,817.59	52
Milledgeville	3	3,704.18	1,400.00	200.00		4.36		1,403.36	2,300.82	38
Newnan	3	3,321.13	1,400.00			4.08		1,404.08	1,920.05	43
Quitman	3	2,304.59	1,040.00			1.44		1,151.44	1,155.15	50
Rome	3	12,559.37	2,100.00	150.00	561.15	509.21	1,070.17	5,425.31	7,134.06	88
Savannah	1	72,246.88	3,200.00	10,596.29	2,211.84	361.31	9,927.95	26,297.39	45,949.49	80
Thomasville	3	6,706.85	1,700.00	308.43		11.20		2,019.63	4,686.22	60
Valdosta	3	3,070.38	1,200.00	200.00		4.56		1,404.56	1,665.83	43
Washington	3	2,962.05	1,200.00	100.00		.68		1,300.88	1,601.17	47
Way Cross	3	2,561.12	1,100.00	100.00		2.64		1,202.64	1,358.48	53
West Point	3	2,440.12	1,100.00	199.92		.48		1,300.40	1,139.88	
Total		397,819.62	49,000.00	49,216.58	6,274.94	2,264.09	49,244.66	156,000.27	241,819.35	89

IDAHO.

Boisé City	3	6,098.56	1,700.00	515.08		1.36		2,216.44	3,882.12	36
Eagle Rock	3	1,415.68	1,100.00			.80		2,100.00	315.68	77
Hailey	3	3,591.86	1,500.00	216.85				1,716.85	1,875.01	48
Ketchum	3	1,610.73	978.74	100.00		5.43		1,076.74	533.99	67
Lewiston	3	2,881.63	1,200.00	400.00		.38		1,605.43	1,276.20	56
Murray	3	1,920.92	1,200.00					1,200.33	720.00	63
Total		17,519.38	7,678.74	1,231.93		7.11		8,915.78	8,603.60	51

ILLINOIS.

Abington	3	2,570.79	1,200.00	200.00		.96		1,200.96	1,360.83	47
Aledo	3	3,125.57	1,300.00		610.00	.80		1,500.80	1,624.77	48
Alton	2	11,375.59	2,100.00	1,200.00		14.56		3,924.56	7,451.03	36
Amboy	3	3,501.28	1,400.00	200.00		1.13		1,601.13	1,908.16	41
Anna	3	3,380.63	1,400.00			.72		1,400.72	1,988.91	39
Arcola	3	3,082.84	1,300.00	200.00		1.92		1,501.92	1,580.84	49
Atlanta	3	2,257.67	1,100.00			1.76		1,101.76	1,155.91	40
Auburn	3	1,673.50	1,000.00			1.08		1,000.08	673.42	60
Aurora	2	20,281.61	2,500.00	2,300.00	1,169.42	46.16	6,164.70	12,180.28	8,101.83	50

No. 10.—Gross receipts, expenses, and net revenue of Presidential post-offices for the fiscal year ended June 30, 1888—Continued.

ILLINOIS—Continued.

Office.	Class.	Gross receipts.	Salary.	Clerk hire.	Rent, light, and fuel.	Other incidental expenses.	Free delivery.	Total expenses.	Net revenue.	Per cent expenses to gross receipts.	Remarks.
Barry	3	$2,049.64	$1,000.00			$1.80		$1,001.80	$1,048.04	49	
Batavia	3	7,853.13	1,900.00			3.12		1,903.12	2,650.61	24	
Beardstown	3	2,765.17	1,400.00			1.92		1,401.92	1,401.92	37	
Belleville	2	9,296.30	2,000.00	$1,200.00	$500.00	42.64	$3,120.10	6,052.74	2,343.50	75	
Belvidere	2	6,040.81	1,700.00	200.00		4.60		1,904.60	4,136.51	83	
Bement	3	2,114.29	1,000.00			.48		1,000.48	1,113.81	47	
Bloomington	2	27,462.57	2,900.00	6,800.00	1,602.65	118.55	7,781.56	19,202.76	18,259.81	61	
Braidwood	3	2,650.27	1,300.00			.88		1,300.88	1,349.39	49	
Bunker Hill	3	2,440.40	1,200.10			1.04		1,201.04	1,239.36	57	
Bushnell	3	4,693.74	1,500.00	200.00		5.30		1,705.30	2,538.05	38	
Cairo	2	16,624.83	2,400.00	3,404.87		28.06	2,609.22	8,434.15	8,190.68	51	In Government building.
Cambridge	3	2,612.12	1,200.00	100.00		.72		1,300.72	1,311.40	50	
Canton	3	9,517.73	1,900.00	208.43		3.92		2,212.35	7,205.38	23	
Carbondale	3	3,548.89	1,500.00	200.00		1.80		1,701.80	1,817.29	48	
Carlinville	3	5,088.65	1,600.00	100.00		2.64		1,702.64	3,386.01	33	
Carmi	3	4,154.30	1,500.00	200.00		2.80		1,702.80	2,451.50	41	
Carrollton	3	4,218.14	1,500.00	208.42		2.16		1,710.68	2,507.56	41	
Carthage	3	3,420.77	1,400.00	208.33		1.77		1,610.10	1,810.67	47	
Centralia	3	5,531.63	1,700.00	354.22		2.80		2,057.02	3,474.61	37	
Champaign	2	10,861.58	2,200.00	1,686.06	661.92	.82	1,925.19	6,674.50	4,986.99	54	
Charleston	3	5,222.97	1,600.00	254.13		.44		1,857.57	3,365.30	36	
Chenoa	3	2,025.69	1,600.00			2.40		1,600.40	1,025.29	80	
Chester	3	2,597.19	1,200.00	162.00		2.61		1,364.61	1,412.78	49	
Chicago	1	2,469,611.42	6,000.00	462,264.86	11,410.44	25,279.43	364,256.49	869,151.04	1,600,680.38	35	In Government building. Includes $9,753.64 expenses of mail-bag repair depot.
Clinton	3	8,964.83	1,500.00	200.00		2.64		1,702.64	2,262.29	43	
Collinsville	3	3,034.12	1,200.00			1.36		1,201.36	1,832.76	40	
Danville	2	15,281.34	2,400.00	2,700.00	740.00	209.34	2,671.99	8,771.25	6,510.11	57	
Decatur	2	28,625.79	2,700.00	3,125.00	960.00	62.48	4,358.02	11,205.50	17,320.29	39	
DeKalb	3	7,431.50	1,700.00			8.80		1,708.80	5,712.70	23	
Delavan	3	3,046.31	1,300.00			1.12		1,301.12	1,745.19	43	
Dixon	2	9,789.55	2,000.00	1,000.00	267.28	496.09		3,763.37	6,026.18	38	
Duquoin	3	3,844.49	1,600.00	300.00		2.16		1,902.16	2,242.33	49	
Elgin	3	3,832.51	1,700.00			2.84		1,702.84	2,260.59	43	
Earlville	3	5,611.47	1,700.00			2.94		1,902.94	3,722.80	34	
East Saint Louis	3	4,186.11	1,400.00	174.73		13.84		1,588.67	165.17	50	
Edwardsville	3	4,220.60	1,700.00	200.00		8.76		1,917.10	722.80	50	
Effingham	3	8,329.27	1,400.00	500.00		4.48		1,704.48	1,615.79	51	
Elgin	1	22,682.29	2,800.00	8,000.00	1,699.62	41.12	4,229.68	11,770.42	20,911.87	58	
Elmhurst	3	2,633.50	1,100.00			1.99		1,100.99	1,553.54	41	

Post-office							In Government building.
Elmwood	3	2,119.42	1,000.00	25.00		.64	49
El Paso	3	2,637.36	1,200.00	104.42		1.38	51
Englewood	3	14,627.03	2,400.00	1,428.49	448.10	30.48	44
Eureka	3	2,700.46	1,200.00			2.32	38
Evanston	3	12,276.75	2,300.00	1,068.42	959.00	56.12	38
Fairbury	3	3,881.28	1,540.00			1.28	44
Fairfield	3	8,145.97	1,300.00	100.00		2.72	40
Farmer City	3	2,705.47	1,200.00			.80	40
Forn	3	2,473.36	1,100.00	100.00		1.60	31
Franklin Grove	2	1,564.19	1,100.00				44
Freeport	3	21,218.30	2,600.00	2,266.58	840.00	2.00	47
Fulton	3	3,186.54	1,300.00	100.00		.72	33
Galena	3	7,639.28	1,900.00	400.00		12.80	43
Galesburgh	3	27,881.40	2,600.00	4,182.57	1,213.75	69.92	51
Galva	3	3,356.21	1,600.00	800.00		1.84	61
Geneseo	3	3,970.58	1,800.00	800.00		2.56	34
Geneva	3	2,835.93	1,200.00			1.36	40
Gibson City	3	2,850.58	1,200.00	254.16		.32	43
Girard	3	2,373.87	1,000.00	100.00		2.48	44
Grand Crossing	3	4,445.51	1,500.00			1.60	44
Grayville	3	2,046.23	1,000.00	280.00		2.08	50
Greenville	3	3,301.26	1,400.00			.24	43
Grigsville	2	2,227.39	1,100.00			1.04	48
Harvard	3	2,637.66	1,400.00	90.00		1.52	44
Henry	3	3,299.25	1,300.00	212.54		1.20	20
Highland	3	2,978.40	1,300.00			1.92	43
Hillsborough	3	2,901.55	1,000.00			2.00	43
Hoopeston	3	6,256.40	1,600.00	108.13	777.83	34.24	58
Hyde Park	3	16,988.52	2,500.00	2,500.00		4.48	55
Jacksonville	3	6,068.95	1,600.00	600.00	810.97	16.80	38
Jerseyville	3	22,857.08	2,100.00	3,072.00	275.00	29.02	44
Joliet	3	10,856.96	1,800.00	1,000.00		2.64	44
Kankakee	3	6,488.62	1,200.00			1.13	27
Kewanee	2	2,728.12	1,200.00			.72	41
Knoxville	3	2,636.12	1,100.00	100.00		2.40	38
Lacon	3	681.80	1,400.00	1,000.00		.56	47
Lake Forest	3	664.83	1,000.00			7.20	47
Lanark	3	444.96	1,000.00			.48	47
La Salle	3	2,108.50	1,000.00	150.00		1.38	51
Lemont	3	2,535.64	1,400.00	1,104.12		2.16	54
Lena	2	3,022.11	2,000.00	208.15		12.71	35
Lewistown	3	8,810.27	1,700.00			7.36	38
Lincoln	3	5,572.17	1,200.00			.72	40
Litchfield	3	3,011.45	1,700.00	100.00		8.84	43
Lockport	3	5,491.84	1,300.00			1.88	42
Macomb	3	3,060.58	1,400.00	160.00		1.60	44
Marengo	2	2,791.96	1,300.00			3.68	40
Marseilles	3	2,617.55	1,300.00			8.68	43
Mason City	3	2,713.61	1,200.00			1.04	44
Mattoon	2	8,641.24	2,000.00	997.23	467.03	12.40	40

No. 10.—*Gross receipts, expenses, and net revenue of Presidential post-offices for the fiscal year ended June 30, 1888*—Continued.

ILLINOIS—Continued.

Office.	Class.	Gross receipts.	Salary.	Clerk hire.	Rent, light, and fuel.	Other incidental expenses.	Free delivery.	Total expenses.	Net revenue.	Per cent. expenses to gross receipts.	Remarks.
Maywood	3	$2,942.44	$1,300.00			$2.80		$1,302.80	$1,640.44	44	
McLeansborough	3	2,247.85	1,000.00	$300.00		1.70		1,001.70	1,245.65	45	
Me dota	3	2,108.54	1,800.00	300.00		6.08		2,106.08	4,003.48	34	
Minonk	3	2,364.19	1,300.00	100.00		1.04		2,401.04	1,863.65	49	
Moline	2	16,574.19	2,500.00	2,000.00	$925.00	1.52	$2,773.66	8,203.14	8,531.01	37	
Monmouth	2	10,577.92	2,100.00	1,199.59	543.00	17.21		3,862.10	6,715.82	48	
Monticello	3	2,909.53	1,300.00	100.00		1.68		1,401.68	1,507.85	48	
Morris	3	4,516.15	1,700.00	8.43		3.12		1,711.54	2,801.61	38	
Morrison	3	4,482.64	1,500.00	100.00		1.84		1,601.84	2,881.80	41	
Mount Carmel	3	4,150.98	1,400.00	300.00		4.48		1,704.48	2,446.50	42	
Mount Carroll	3	2,121.92	1,300.00	300.00		2.88		1,702.88	1,476.63	43	
the Morris	3	2,776.63	1,000.00			1.20		1,001.20	1,120.72	47	
Mount ᵗ ski	3	2,776.08	1,200.00	100.00		2.44		1,302.44	1,472.64	47	
Mount ᵗ lng	3	839.06	1,500.00	300.00		2.15		1,801.60	8,677.46	37	
Mount Vernon	3	89.14	1,400.00	200.00		1.90		1,502.19	1,777.98	40	
Murphysborough	3	2,262.21	1,400.00			1.60		1,401.60	1,880.81	43	
Naperville	3	3,340.04	1,400.00			2.68		1,622.06	1,737.96	48	
Nellie	3	10,113.26	2,200.00	266.00		3.28		8,103.28	7,049.98	31	
ᵗ Stock Yards	3	2,144.07	1,000.00	900.00		1.00		1,001.00	1,142.47	47	
ᵗ bn	3	2,257.81	0.00			.32		1,000.32	1,257.49	44	
Nokomis	3	6,268.27	1,600.00	300.00		3.92		1,903.92	4,364.18	31	
Normal	3	12,021.76	2,200.00	905.00	400.00	15.08		3,680.08	8,444.18	30	
Oak ᵗᵏ	3	3,200.58	1,100.10			.08		1,100.08	2,109.48	35	
Odll	3	5,214.57	1,600.00	234.21		8.96		1,963.17	3,251.40	38	
Olney	3	2,584.68				.43		1,100.43	1,484.20	43	
Omaga	2	13,273.40	2,400.00	150.00		2.56		1,552.56	11,720.90	53	
Oregon	3	4,501.35	2,400.00	1,800.00	171.90	65.96	2,618.63	7,073.50	6,441.83	38	
Ottawa	3	2,497.58	1,000.00	251.17		8.16		1,857.13	2,091.72	88	
Pana	3	3,941.32	1,000.00	600.00		9.06		2,408.16	4,889.53	88	
Paris	3	70.61	500.00			.40		1,509.06	2,440.82	88	
Paxton	3	12,298.68	52.30			25.48	1,035.99	62.30	27.41	66	
Pecatonica	1	80,402.53	8,200.00	1,100.00	200.00	355.61	11,247.87	4,301.47	7,877.11	81	
Pekin	3	4,177.78	7,470.00	3,113.90		2.72		25,386.88	65,015.64	34	
Peoria	3	2,782.64	12.50			.83		415.23	2,762.56	45	
Peru	3	4,053.94	1,400.00	300.00				1,700.83	2,083.22	44	
Rarebargh	3	2,644.31	1,400.00	400.00		1.20		1,800.00	2,393.94	41	
Pittsfield	3	703.00	1,100.00			.82		1,101.20	1,543.11	43	
Plano	3	5,232.81	1,700.00	162.23		2.56		1,862.55	3,500.25	88	Presidential from June 12, 1888.
Polo	3	7,561.25	1,900.00	400.00		8.02		2,703.22	5,258.78	90	

Presidential from June 7, 1888.

Presidential from June 1, 1888.

Kendallville	3	4,821.15	1,600.00	293.63	6.68			1,802.30	3,011.85	57
Knightstown	3	2,845.97	1,200.00		4.64		468.33	1,201.84	1,641.33	42
Kokomo	3	7,719.75	1,800.00		10.08		3,900.00	16,023.87	5,581.34	59
La Fayette	2	27,981.82	2,700.00	1,850.00	125.17	8,051.50		1,391.44	11,854.15	57
La Porte	3	3,030.47	2,200.00		1.44		800.00	1,013.97	1,735.03	43
La Porte	3	10,028.60	1,500.00	1,000.00	13.97			4,013.97	1,912.63	57
Lawrenceburgh	3	3,940.15		300.00	8.40			1,908.10	2,181.75	48
Lebanon	3	3,747.52	1,400.00	100.00	8.24			1,506.24	2,291.28	46
Liberty	3	2,560.83	1,100.00	78.00	1.76			1,177.76	1,393.07	43
Ligonier	3	3,688.14	1,400.00	100.00	3.86			1,503.86	2,182.76	41
Logansport	3	14,322.16	2,400.00	2,440.00	72.55	3,320.88	1,059.21	9,252.64	5,069.53	63
Madison	3	9,095.64	2,000.00	1,140.00	19.84		860.00	3,839.84	5,285.80	43
Marion	3	8,088.50	1,800.00	614.17	9.86			2,431.03	5,664.47	50
Martinsville	3	2,555.20	1,200.00	200.00	2.48			1,402.48	1,152.72	52
Michigan City	3	7,061.61	1,000.00	618.85	4.48			1,623.96	5,029.66	30
Mishawaka	3	2,310.33	1,100.00		1.28			1,301.28	458.71	28
Mitchell	3	3,033.99	1,200.00	200.00	4.80			1,404.80	1,000.96	25
Monticello	3	4,363.52	1,500.00	140.00	8.90			1,698.90	1,629.19	49
Mount Vernon	3	10,838.67	1,500.00	612.50	18.01		178.84	2,809.35	2,774.56	57
Muncie	3	12,407.08	2,800.00	1,890.00	58.52	4,042.52	818.00	8,909.04	8,049.32	51
New Albany	3	4,708.01	1,000.00	254.17	2.44			1,357.61	2,850.40	43
New Castle	3	3,746.81	1,400.00		8.92			1,403.92	2,343.89	43
Noblesville	3	3,191.20	1,300.00	100.00	1.68			1,401.68	1,788.52	50
North Manchester	3	2,702.00	1,100.00	243.00	2.88			1,345.88	1,356.12	35
Notre Dame	3	4,434.41	2,000.00		.96			1,000.96	3,433.45	34
Peru	3	8,719.37	2,000.00	860.00	1.04		655.69	3,455.73	5,263.64	50
Plymouth	3	4,485.90	1,800.00		4.73			1,804.73	2,681.27	46
Portland	3	2,794.05	1,500.00	388.53	5.38			1,893.91	892.45	48
Princeton	3	3,524.02	1,400.00	200.00	4.40			1,604.40	1,918.62	61
Rensselaer	3	3,513.45	1,100.00		2.16			1,102.16	1,411.29	49
Richmond	2	27,295.89	2,700.00	3,600.00	98.15	7,197.45	1,428.16	15,023.77	12,272.12	37
Rochester	3	3,644.41	1,400.00	154.16	2.16	.72		1,557.04	2,027.87	58
Rockport	3	2,572.80	1,200.00	90.00	.72	.48		1,291.20	1,281.60	52
Rockville	3	2,731.81	1,200.00	160.00	3.12			1,363.12	1,368.19	35
Rushville	3	3,524.99	1,700.00	208.34	5.24			1,913.58	3,611.41	53
Salem	3	197.69	72.53		.08			65.08	34
Seymour	3	6,626.61	1,700.00	200.00	5.20		72.61	1,905.20	3,721.41	37
Shelbyville	3	6,523.17	2,200.00	243.00	7.64		1,500.00	2,050.04	4,473.13	48
South Bend	2	30,015.16	2,700.00	3,173.49	188.84	7,057.63		14,469.96	10,145.20	61
Sullivan	3	4,466.30	1,800.00	154.16	2.64		1,460.00	1,956.80	1,849.50	51
Terre Haute	2	40,528.00	3,000.00	6,390.00	311.64	9,965.05		20,666.67	19,721.93	49
Tipton	3	2,951.81	1,800.00	114.22	14.00			1,457.66	1,483.95	87
Union City	3	4,922.97	1,300.00	293.62	4.27			1,807.62	3,125.35	38
Valparaiso	3	10,785.38	1,300.00	1,200.00	479.00	11.44		3,890.44	6,894.84	59
Vevay	3	2,700.40	1,300.00	400.00	4.77			1,604.27	1,096.13	63
Vincennes	3	10,753.58	2,200.00	1,550.00	82.83	2,270.99	545.47	6,048.99	4,104.59	52
Wabash	3	7,660.33	1,900.00	508.02	9.86			2,417.88	5,242.85	34
Washington	3	5,570.59	1,700.00	298.43	10.16			1,918.58	3,651.94	37
Waterloo	3	134.06	82.43	150.00	.40			82.82	61.24	60

No. 10.—Gross receipts, expenses, and net revenue of Presidential post-offices for the fiscal year ended June 30, 1888—Continued.

INDIANA—Continued.

Office.	Class.	Gross receipts.	Salary.	Clerk hire.	Rent, light, and fuel.	Other incidental expenses.	Free delivery.	Total expenses.	Net revenue.	Per cent expenses to gross receipts.	Remarks.
Winamac	3	$2,061.43	$1,000.00			$0.96		$1,000.96	$1,060.47	49	
Winchester	3	3,893.02	1,500.00	$240.00		2.60		1,742.60	2,150.22	48	
Grand total		823,115.41	145,194.79	95,425.43	$12,624.94	10,467.63	$104,285.72	388,000.51	463,114.90	44	

IOWA.

Office.	Class.	Gross receipts.	Salary.	Clerk hire.	Rent, light, and fuel.	Other incidental expenses.	Free delivery.	Total expenses.	Net revenue.	Per cent expenses to gross receipts.	Remarks.
Ackley	3	2,494.39	1,200.00	200.00		1.20		1,401.20	1,062.19	56	
Afton	3	2,555.51	1,100.00			.82		1,100.82	1,455.19	43	
Albia	3	3,802.92	1,500.00	300.00		2.56		1,802.56	2,000.36	47	
Algona	3	4,348.61	1,500.00	142.00		2.00		1,815.00	2,503.01	43	
Alta	3	2,490.85	1,400.00	100.00		1.36		1,501.36	1,980.40	43	
Anamosa	3	3,903.13	1,500.00	200.00		1.13		1,701.13	1,701.12	44	
Atlantic	2	8,210.90	2,000.00	1,000.00	200.00	82.03		3,282.03	4,923.87	40	
Audubon	3	3,577.54	1,400.00	56.72		.40		1,457.12	2,120.43	41	
Avoca	3	3,059.02	1,400.00	154.16		1.44		1,556.60	1,503.42	51	
Bedford	3	2,465.60	1,400.00	204.16		.96		1,605.12	861.48	46	
Belle Plaine	3	3,176.20	1,300.00	200.00		.80		1,800.80	875.40	41	
Bellevue	3	3,369.70	1,100.00	200.00		.56		1,300.56	873.38	60	
Bloomfield	3	3,173.94	1,400.00	420.83		1.65		1,601.68	1,708.02	41	
Boone	3	7,204.67	1,800.00			6.26		2,226.19	4,978.48	31	
Brooklyn	3	2,554.98	1,100.00			.72		1,100.72	1,451.14	43	
Burlington	1	42,012.03	3,000.00	7,160.90	8,157.18	172.98	8,386.50	22,426.66	19,585.37	53	
Carroll City	3	4,863.34	1,600.00	150.00		4.32		1,754.32	3,049.03	37	
Cedar Falls	3	5,228.21	1,600.00	300.00		3.92		2,203.92	3,024.53	54	
Cedar Rapids	2	40,306.54	2,900.00	4,267.82	1,653.14	392.78	5,773.10	14,912.64	25,237.90	37	
Centreville	3	4,853.76	1,500.00	368.43		3.44		1,811.87	2,741.69	40	
Chariton	3	5,650.53	1,700.00	400.00		4.96		2,104.96	3,545.67	37	
Charles City	3	5,963.29	1,700.00	216.07		2.88		2,018.55	3,076.74	40	
Cherokee	3	3,141.38	1,600.00	158.36		1.78		1,780.14	881.12	29	
Clarinda	3	4,869.88	1,700.00	656.33		5.04		2,983.87	2,536.01	48	
Clear Lake	3	2,718.66	1,300.00			1.12		1,301.12	1,417.54	41	
Clinton	2	17,282.20	2,500.00	1,991.84	1,177.28	.56	8,386.99	9,000.67	8,261.58	53	
Colfax	3	2,544.59	1,100.00			.10		1,100.16	1,444.23	51	
Columbus Junction	3	1,946.05	1,100.00	75.00		5.07		1,080.07	865.88	57	
Correctionville	3	326.48	187.50			.08		187.03	180.57	51	
Corning	3	5,962.49	1,700.00	450.00		1.92		2,102.92	3,886.57	51	Presidential from May 1, 1888.
Council Bluffs	2	43,997.43	2,900.00	6,840.38	1,275.00	61.35	7,054.98	16,841.71	28,125.71	39	In Government building.

Presidential from April 22, 1882.

Do.

Do.

Office								
Cresco	3	3,573.49	1,410.00	300.00		.24	1,700.24	1,873.25	47
Creston	2	9,925.15	2,100.00	1,307.61	762.66	28.51	4,198.78	5,726.37	43
Davenport	2	10,782.26	2,000.00	673.22	2,250.00	178.00	19,143.65	21,038.71	47
Decorah	2	9,068.57	910.00	568.42		4.00	2,412.42	6,657.16	27
Denison	3	4,181.32	1,603.00	300.00		3.28	1,003.28	2,278.64	45
Des Moines	1	10,615.96	2,500.00	13,216.23	2,106.60	271.00	35,818.69	60,796.97	35
De Witt	2	2,545.16	1,200.00			123.30	1,200.40	1,344.70	47
Dubuque	1	44,845.66	3,000.00	7,576.10		.64	19,702.98	25,672.63	44
Dunlap	3	2,810.78	1,500.00	100.00		.88	1,300.64	1,510.14	46
Eagle Grove	3	2,573.83	1,100.00	200.00		2.08	1,200.78	1,372.95	47
Eldora	3	3,335.70	900.00	243.00		1.20	1,402.06	1,733.63	48
Elkader	3	1,832.27	1,000.00	108.85		3.28	1,244.20	588.07	68
Emmetsburgh	3	2,511.75	1,000.00	511.61		3.84	815.13	708.02	33
Fairfield	3	6,813.20	1,400.00	275.00		35.28	815.45	94.75	34
Fort Dodge	3	8,227.73	1,400.00	1,001.00	349.80	7.16	3,385.69	4,942.65	41
Fort Madison	3	8,426.89	840.00	154.35		2.36	1,961.51	6,485.38	23
Glenwood	3	3,287.65	1,400.00			2.36	1,402.36	985.29	41
Gold	3	394.23	1.00	16.66		1.20	1,147.86	1,276.47	47
Grinnell	3	7,90.16	1,900.00	500.00		2.56	2,402.56	5,297.60	31
Grundy Centre	3	3,053.18	1,300.00	180.00		.56	1,480.56	1,574.63	48
Ida Centre	3	2,224.85	1,100.00	300.00		.96	1,400.96	823.89	63
Hamburgh	3	2,976.85	1,200.00	275.00		2.61	1,477.61	1,308.61	51
Hampton	3	3,522.25	1,500.00	200.00		.56	1,700.56	1,821.69	48
Harlan	3	4,290.03	1,500.00	205.84		.12	1,706.96	2,583.79	40
Ida Grove	3	3,648.30	1,400.00			.48	1,401.68	571.45	41
Independence	3	7,698.72	1,400.00	308.34		1.08	1,401.08	988.07	38
Indianola	3	3,657.11	1,500.00	33.33		4.32	2,112.66	2,022.18	55
Iowa City	2	13,160.91	2,400.00	1,792.18	1,460.00	1.60	1,534.93	5,830.33	43
Iowa Falls	3	3,976.50	1,500.00	200.00		1.76	1,701.76	2,277.74	43
Jefferson	3	3,444.43	1,400.00	150.00		1.44	1,551.44	1,806.99	41
Kingsley	2	25,687.82	2,600.00	3,539.42	1,225.00	93.24	13,411.07	12,276.75	50
Knoxville	3	4,458.19	208.52	18.89			227.41	220.78	54
Lansing	3	4,065.50	1,500.00	708.42		8.13	2,211.56	1,853.96	49
Laporte City	3	2,627.04	1,100.00	180.00		1.60	1,281.60	1,346.44	42
Le Mars	3	2,651.81	1,100.00		235.00	.20	1,101.20	1,550.10	37
Leon	3	96.91	2,000.00	1,100.00		1.78	1,610.81	980.10	52
Logan	3	2,027.42	1,200.00	200.00		.08	1,401.78	1,290.66	51
Lyons	3	2,477.55	1,100.00	250.00		.40	1,250.08	1,177.47	33
McGregor	3	6,773.83	700.00	35.00		2.16	1,904.40	867.43	39
Malvern	3	68.77	1,000.00	800.00		2.16	2,002.16	3,167.61	62
Manchester	3	3,953.70	1,000.00	200.00		.24	1,200.24	735.46	37
Manning	3	3,703.53	1,700.00	461.16		2.32	2,348	3,657.05	51
Maquoketa	3	1,997.01	1,000.00			.56	1,000.56	965.45	53
Mapleton	3	1,977.59	1,100.00			1.68	1,100.00	977.39	84
Marengo	3	5,066.47	1,500.00	96.20		1.04	1,697.88	3,369.59	47
Marion	3	4,366.36	1,400.00	180.00		1.04	1,581.04	1,785.32	48
Marshalltown	3	5,121.39	1,800.00	500.00	1,364.96	3.68	2,303.68	2,817.91	31
Mason City	2	17,822.38	2,500.00	2,500.00		8.38	8,565.98	9,255.40	44
Mt Valley	3	6,804.70	1,800.00	299.73		2.56	2,102.20	4,702.41	45
Monticello	3	3,143.73	1,400.00	243.00		.98	1,613.98	1,490.85	52

No. 10.—*Gross receipts, expenses, and net revenue of Presidential post-offices for the fiscal year ended June 30, 1888*—Continued.

IOWA—Continued.

Office.	Class.	Gross receipts.	Salary.	Clerk hire.	Rent, light, and fuel.	Other incidental expenses.	Free delivery.	Total expenses.	Net revenue.	Per cent. expenses to gross receipts.	Remarks.
Mount Ayr	3	$2,832.77	$1,200.00	$161.71	$101.71	$1.44		$1,363.15	$1,469.62	48	
Mount Pleasant	3	9,627.95	2,000.00	1,000.00		5.28		3,111.97	6,515.98	31	
Mount Vernon	3	3,183.92	1,200.00			.96		1,200.96	1,982.96	41	
Muscatine	2	15,139.70	2,400.00	1,800.00	1,179.25	5.21	$2,683.93	8,068.39	7,071.31	53	
Nashua	3	2,632.28	1,200.00			.82		1,200.82	1,431.96	48	
Nevada	3	2,124.95	1,400.00			.96		1,400.96	722.99	48	
New Hampton	3	2,883.71	1,400.00	200.00		1.20		1,401.20	1,482.51	48	
Newton	3	5,517.40	1,700.00	254.17		4.48		1,958.65	3,558.75	45	
Do	3	2,667.68	1,200.00					1,200.00	1,467.68	45	
Onawa	3	2,265.80	1,100.00	90.00		1.71		1,165.71	1,072.09	53	
Orange City	3	903.88	825.16	50.00		.08		385.24	548.64	41	
Do	3	4,543.57	1,600.00	500.00		1.60		3,101.60	2,441.97	46	
Osceola	3	3,785.49	1,700.00		625.50	2.32		1,702.32	2,033.17	54	
Ottumwa	2	11,663.19	2,300.00	1,640.00	723.10	91.96	1,797.50	6,294.96	5,368.63	54	
Pella	3	23,239.18	2,300.00	3,250.00	35.00	66.03	5,256.81	11,890.84	2,633.79	51	
Perry	3	4,271.62	1,800.00	150.00		1.84		1,751.84	2,518.78	41	
Red Oak	3	7,102.98	1,900.00	408.43		5.44		2,313.86	4,789.12	33	
Rock Rapids	3	2,772.10	1,100.00			.08		1,100.08	1,672.02	40	
Sac City	3	2,578.02	1,200.00	135.00		.24		1,335.24	1,242.78	45	
Sanborn	3	2,106.38	1,000.00	120.00				1,120.00	986.38	53	
Sheldon	3	3,649.10	1,400.00	200.00		.48		1,400.48	2,248.62	38	
Shenandoah	3	5,715.80	1,700.00	150.00		.64		2,000.64	3,715.16	35	
Sibley	3	3,088.81	1,300.00	150.00		1.44		1,451.44	1,637.37	47	
Sigourney	3	3,040.46	1,300.00	294.21		1.84		1,600.05	1,434.41	50	
Sioux City	1	60,777.81	3,400.00	5,064.98	3,200.00	57.94	6,197.12	16,419.92	44,357.89	32	
Spencer	3	3,990.05	1,500.00	262.48		1.68		1,764.16	2,125.89	45	
Spirit Lake	3	3,610.17	1,700.00	106.34		1.24		1,700.57	3,800.60	38	
Stuart	3	3,645.08	1,400.00	138.34		2.24		1,540.58	3,683.40	43	
Tama City	3	2,791.85	1,200.00	200.00		2.00		1,402.00	1,389.85	50	
Tipton	3	2,963.32	1,400.00	250.00		.96		1,650.96	1,712.36	49	
Toledo	3	3,517.81	1,600.00			1.76		1,601.76	2,915.55	49	
Tracy	3	2,871.03	1,100.00			.32		1,100.32	1,770.71	38	
Villisca	3	3,442.66	1,400.00	16.85		1.28		1,418.13	2,024.53	41	
Vinton	3	5,814.10	1,700.00	200.00		4.24		1,904.24	3,409.86	36	
Washington	3	13,366.81	1,700.00	400.00	417.50	2.64	1,987.73	4,102.64	8,610.48	37	
Waterloo	3	3,550.59	2,300.00	199.84		167.89		6,042.95	6,424.28	37	
Waukon	3	3,558.01	1,200.00	208.15		2.15		451.30	1,157.49	33	
Waverly	3	4,936.09	1,600.00	243.56		3.88		1,812.43	3,910.48	45	
Webster City	3	4,900.77	1,300.19	201.21		1.04		1,810.68	2,769.31	47	
West Liberty	3							1,645.25	1,445.62	51	Presidential from March 1, 1888.

No. 10.—*Gross receipts, expenses, and net revenue of Presidential post-offices for the fiscal year ended June 30, 1888*—Continued.

IOWA—Continued.

Office.	Class.	Gross receipts.	Salary.	Clerk hire.	Rent, light, and fuel.	Other incidental expenses.	Free delivery.	Total expenses.	Net revenue.	Per cent expenses to gross receipts.	Remarks.
Mount Ayr	3	$2,852.77	$1,200.00	$161.71	$104.71	$1.44		$1,463.15	$1,469.62	43	
Mount Pleasant	3	9,627.95	2,000.00	1,000.00		5.26		3,111.97	6,515.98	31	
Mount Vernon	3	3,183.92	1,500.00			5.98		1,360.96	1,862.96	41	
Muscatine	2	15,139.70	2,400.00	1,800.00	1,178.25	5.21	$3,663.93	9,200.39	5,938.31	63	
Nashua	3	3,632.28	1,200.00			32		1,400.06	431.96	42	
Nevada	3	3,124.95	1,400.00			98		1,401.00	1,723.99	44	
New Hampton	3	2,883.71	1,400.00	200.00		1.20		1,401.20	1,482.51	48	
Newton	3	5,517.40	1,700.00	254.17		4.48		1,958.65	3,568.75	36	
Odeboldt	3	2,667.68	1,200.00					1,200.00	1,467.68	45	
Onawa	3	2,255.80	1,100.00	90.00		1.71		1,183.71	1,072.09	52	
Orange City	3	933.88	335.16	50.00		.08		385.24	548.64	41	
Osage	3	4,543.67	1,500.00	540.00		1.60		2,101.60	2,441.97	46	
Osceola	3	3,735.49	1,300.00		635.50	2.33		1,702.33	2,033.17	46	
Oskaloosa	3	11,663.59	2,340.00	1,640.00	723.10	91.96	1,797.50	6,294.96	5,368.63	54	
Ottumwa	2	23,239.18	2,300.00	3,250.00		66.93	5,256.81	11,896.84	11,342.34	51	
Pella	3	3,550.39	1,500.00	25.00		1.60		1,728.60	1,823.79	47	
Perry	3	4,271.62	1,600.00	150.00		1.84		1,751.84	2,519.78	41	
Red Oak	3	7,102.98	1,900.00	468.43		5.44		2,373.84	4,729.12	33	
Rock Rapids	3	1,772.10	1,100.00			.08		1,100.08	672.02	62	
Sac City	3	2,878.02	1,200.00	185.00		.24		1,385.24	1,242.78	48	
Sanborn	3	2,108.33	1,000.00	120.00				1,120.00	998.38	53	
Sheldon	3	3,649.10	1,400.00			.48		1,400.48	2,248.62	38	
Shenandoah	3	5,715.80	1,700.00	300.00		.64		2,000.64	3,715.16	35	
Sibley	3	3,088.81	1,300.00	150.00		1.44		1,451.44	1,637.37	47	
Sigourney	3	3,040.46	1,400.00	294.21		1.84		1,696.05	1,434.41	56	
Sioux City	2	60,777.31	2,900.00	6,994.96	2,300.00	57.94	6,410.92	16,410.92	44,357.89	27	
Spencer	3	3,890.03	1,600.00	282.48		1.68		1,704.16	2,125.89	45	
Storm Lake	3	3,810.17	1,400.00	106.33		1.24		1,702.57	2,800.60	43	
Tama City	3	3,446.98	1,200.00	138.24		2.00		1,460.56	2,985.40	50	
Tipton	3	2,791.85	1,400.00	290.00		.96		1,454.96	1,380.85	52	
Toledo	3	3,363.32	1,600.00	250.00		1.78		1,601.78	1,713.26	48	
Traer	3	4,517.81	1,100.00			.33		1,100.32	2,915.85	39	
Villisca	3	3,442.66	1,400.00	16.85		1.28		1,418.13	2,024.58	41	
Vinton	3	5,814.10	1,700.00	200.00		4.24		1,904.24	3,909.86	33	
Washington	3	5,719.12	1,700.00	400.00	417.50	2.64		3,102.64	2,616.48	53	
Waterloo	2	13,366.81	2,400.00	2,000.00		167.82	1,957.73	6,942.55	6,424.26	52	
Waukon	3	2,559.59	1,200.00	199.84		2.16		1,402.00	1,157.59	55	
Waverly	3	4,890.91	1,600.00	208.15		8.28		1,811.43	2,040.48	37	
Webster City	3	4,604.99	1,600.00	243.00		8.68		1,848.68	2,760.31	40	
West Liberty	3	2,950.77	1,300.00	294.21		1.04		1,595.25	1,445.52	51	

Remarks: Presidential from March 1, 1888.

No. 10.—*Gross receipts, expenses, and net revenue of Presidential post-offices for the fiscal year ended June 30, 1888—Continued.*

KANSAS—Continued.

Office.	Class.	Gross receipts.	Salary.	Clerk hire.	Rent, light, and fuel.	Other incidental expenses.	Free delivery.	Total expenses.	Net revenue.	Per cent. expenses to gross receipts.	Remarks.
Garden City	3	$10,603.21	$2,200.00	$1,400.00	$375.00	$42.60		$4,017.60	$6,585.61	38	
Garnett	3	4,736.42	1,600.00	300.00		3.04		1,903.04	2,833.38	40	
Girard	3	4,622.20	1,600.00	300.00		4.32		1,904.32	2,718.88	41	
Great Bend	3	6,244.13	1,800.00	204.21		4.40		2,008.61	4,235.52	32	
Greenleaf	3	110.25	57.42	6.50				62.92	47.33	57	
Greensburgh	3	2,463.15	1,023.37	76.00		2.00		1,100.37	1,367.78	45	Presidential from June 12, 1888.
Halstead	3	4,295.63	1,100.00	214.67		1.56		1,100.56	1,194.47	41	Presidential from October 8, 1887.
Harper	3	4,631.19	1,700.00	98.00		1.52		1,917.87	3,113.25	46	
Hays City	3	3,369.61	1,400.00	221.32		2.88		1,500.52	1,858.99	45	
Hiawatha	3	6,559.32	1,800.00	250.00		3.36		2,036.21	4,523.11	31	
Holton	3	5,101.22	1,500.00	150.00		.32		753.36	4,347.96	31	
Howard	3	3,099.78	1,300.00	300.00		1.44		1,450.32	1,619.46	47	
Humboldt	3	3,064.41	1,400.00	300.00		7.38		1,701.44	1,362.97	56	
Hutchinson	3	13,954.20	2,200.00	1,700.00	80.25	281.96	$1,300.91	5,662.12	8,292.08	41	
Independence	3	6,742.62	1,800.00	403.00		1.76		2,207.36	4,535.26	33	
Iola	3	3,248.71	1,400.00	250.00		.32		1,651.76	1,596.95	51	
Jewell	3	2,104.17	1,100.00	100.00		6.32		1,200.32	864.32	58	
Junction City	3	7,069.40	1,800.00	400.00		5.66		2,206.32	4,897.85	32	
Kingman	3	6,063.86	1,600.00	600.00		.99		2,505.66	4,553.72	35	
Kinsley	3	2,818.67	1,400.00	360.00		.88		971.92	4,792.64	35	
Kirwin	3	2,258.15	1,465.10			.48		1,460.88	417.99	59	
La Cygne	3	7,413.72	1,100.00	200.00		1.36		1,500.48	1,107.90	57	
Larned	3	24,575.12	1,900.00	294.16		9.60		1,365.52	952.82	48	
Lawrence	2	28,820.61	2,700.00	508.33	1,200.00	86.39	5,182.00	2,417.93	4,996.80	51	
Leavenworth	2	3,641.94	2,700.00	3,550.00	840.00	69.04	7,189.10	12,718.48	11,855.04	53	
Lincoln	3	2,315.42	1,400.00	250.00		1.52		15,078.14	13,742.47	44	
Lindsborg	3	6,008.95	1,100.00	100.00		.48		1,651.52	2,190.63	47	
Lyons	3	9,281.28	1,500.00	500.00		1.60		1,001.60	1,214.94	31	
McPherson	3	7,402.63	1,900.00	288.42		10.14		2,410.14	6,861.14	26	
Manhattan	3	3,411.90	1,900.00	200.00		5.44		2,113.98	5,290.07	28	
Mankato	3	3,965.76	1,500.00			2.00		1,502.00	1,909.90	44	
Marion	3	3,794.88	865.49	200.00		1.24		1,066.24	3,660.50	29	
Marysville	3	4,475.03	1,900.00	66.67		1.52		1,903.64	1,962.24	43	
Meade Center	3	4,462.87	1,700.00	200.00		.98		1,900.88	1,141.86	45	Presidential from November 1, 1887.
Medicine Lodge	3	5,735.88	1,900.00	208.42		2.00		1,910.42	661.99	53	
Minneapolis	3	3,055.78	1,000.00			1.20		1,025.40	825.40	33	
Mound City	3	2,188.39	1,000.00			1.20		1,001.20	1,053.56	49	
Neodesha	3	2,273.12	981.96	57.73		10.12		1,001.20	1,187.19	46	
Ness City	2	10,124.64	2,500.00	1,824.00	800.00	17.56	1,942.66	5,784.41	4,339.03	57	Presidential from November 2, 1887.

LOUISIANA.

Office										Remarks
Alexandria	3	3,465.94	1,100.00	800.00		5.25		1,405.25	$1,003.60	30	
Baton Rouge	3	3,060.54	1,000.00	864.00		27.82		2,281.23	5,706.32	28	
Donaldsonville	3	2,831.09	1,000.00			1.66		381.36	1,023.12	43	
Franklin	3	2,194.31	1,200.00			1.66		1,193.06	1,602.13	38	
Lake Charles	3	4,433.95	1,800.00	162.50		4.04		785.64	2,401.12	41	
Monroe	3	3,695.95	1,600.00	300.00		4.84		804.00	629.95	38	
New Iberia	3	3,628.43	1,500.00	300.00				905.84	2,122.58	44	
New Orleans	1	368,749.19	5,700.00	63,540.94		1,949.15	58,989.99	128,190.06	180,559.11	41	In Government building.
Opelousas	3	2,264.31	1,200.00			2.96		1,002.96	1,201.36	44	
Plaquemine	3	2,325.76	1,200.00	150.00	27.00	2.96		1,252.06	1,473.08	44	Do.
Shreveport	3	11,872.77	1,100.00	1,337.50		8.78	1,880.04	5,443.30	6,434.47	45	
Thibodeaux	3	2,365.35	1,100.00	60.00		2.40		1,182.40	1,313.86	53	
Total		355,182.09	19,200.00	66,684.94	27.00	2,009.24	60,880.03	148,651.21	206,480.88	43	

MAINE.

Office										Remarks
Auburn	3	12,658.77	3,300.00	1,008.00	520.00	.66	3,575.07	6,706.33	5,947.43	44	In Government building.
Augusta	1	38,920.64	8,000.00	11,581.41	2,446.13	.66	4,250.95	21,081.07	17,843.67	28	
Bangor	1	61,124.31	8,000.00	7,946.73		172.64	4,290.01	14,613.38	36,710.87	37	
Bar Harbor	3	7,124.44	1,200.00			32.21		918.44	4,383.29	57	
Bath	3	10,473.32	1,700.00	1,450.00		9.78	3,067.94	2,999.79	4,162.44	38	
Belfast	3	10,066.88	2,100.00	1,400.00	345.00	28.44		3,874.44	5,992.38	44	
Biddeford	3	8,901.18	1,000.00			1.60		1,001.60	1,350.02	43	
Bridgton	3	2,851.62	1,800.00	400.00		15.52		2,215.52	4,065.06	43	
Brunswick	3	2,623.40	1,100.00	300.00		2.96		1,402.96	1,130.44	48	
Bucksport	3	5,441.63	1,700.00	700.00		4.88		2,404.88	3,604.75	43	
Calais	3	8,367.99	1,400.00	200.00		5.53		1,602.88	1,402.47	44	
Camden	3	3,284.09	1,400.00	400.00		2.86		1,802.98	1,491.21	45	
Dexter	3	6,697.41	1,600.00	400.88		8.44		2,311.43	689.64	40	
Ellsworth	3	3,669.74	1,000.00	766.33		4.13		1,906.64	5,226.18	44	
Fairfield	3	2,446.11	1,400.00			4.04		1,896.04	1,982.92	44	
Farmington	3	1,857.50	714.85	400.00		1.92		743.77	818.72	48	
Gardiner	3	3,805.69	1,905.00	298.24		21.36		2,129.00	6,176.09	40	
Hallowell	3	3,792.56	1,600.00			5.13		1,505.13	2,287.44	41	
Houlton	3	4,697.87	1,600.00	300.00		2.66		1,903.66	2,784.19	42	
Kennebunk	3	2,451.70	1,100.00			8.84		1,108.84	1,347.86	53	In Government building.
Lewiston	1	29,095.61	2,600.00	2,200.00	1,408.30	63.24	4,367.99	10,628.49	9,569.08	48	
Machias	3	2,178.69	1,000.00	200.00		1.28		1,201.28	977.41	53	
Mechanic's Falls	3	2,533.57	1,200.00	162.00		3.04		1,365.04	1,405.83	48	
Norway	3	3,200.86	1,100.00	284.17		7.12		1,011.29	1,589.67	34	Presidential from October 4, 1887.
Oakland	3	584.32	417.58			1.03		413.10	475.23	47	Presidential from January 31, 1888.

No. 10.—*Gross receipts, expenses, and net revenue of Presidential post-offices for the fiscal year ended June 30, 1888*—Continued.

MAINE—Continued.

Office.	Class.	Gross receipts.	Salary.	Clerk hire.	Rent, lights, and fuel.	Other incidental expenses.	Free delivery.	Total expenses.	Net revenue.	Per cent expenses to gross receipts.	Remarks.
Pittsfield	3	$2,986.69	$1,100.00			92.88		$1,102.88	$1,683.71	42	
Portland	1	100,284.02	3,300.00	$20,161.00		413.59	$13,432.16	37,385.06	62,928.97	37	In Government building.
Richmond	3	2,467.48	1,600.00			3.86				36	
Rockland	2	10,417.06	2,100.00	1,162.50		24.08		8,285.58	2,564.18	80	
Searsport	3	2,073.55	1,300.00			4.89		1,204.80	1,180.48	57	
Saco	3	5,225.70	1,600.00	300.00		14.89		1,914.89	3,314.99	36	
Stonington	3	6,202.58	1,700.00	342.00		8.73		1,831.72	4,360.61	31	
South Berwick	3	2,365.98	1,100.00					1,100.00	1,166.98	48	Do.
Thomaston	3	2,204.36	1,200.00	180.00		4.05		1,304.05	900.37	59	
Waldoborough	3	2,191.06	1,100.00	150.00		3.29		1,163.29	977.65	44	Do.
Waterville	2	9,097.61	1,000.00	744.50	$900.00	15.26		3,084.86	6,032.76	33	
Winthrop	3	2,872.89	1,100.00			3.40		1,102.40	1,770.10	38	
Total		377,682.69	63,169.43	52,667.29	6,132.88	913.20	31,048.02	153,910.97	223,612.02	61	

MARYLAND.

Office.	Class.	Gross receipts.	Salary.	Clerk hire.	Rent, lights, and fuel.	Other incidental expenses.	Free delivery.	Total expenses.	Net revenue.	Per cent expenses to gross receipts.	Remarks.
Annapolis	2	11,649.11	1,900.00	1,850.00	500.00	5,000.70	1,942.09	6,192.09	5,357.02	54	
Baltimore	1	531,095.78	5,000.00	108,995.81	3,650.00		144,326.53	290,962.53	234,113.25	45	In Government building.
Bel Air	3	3,122.45	1,600.00	100.00		6.16		1,700.16	716.29	50	
Cambridge	3	3,014.87	1,500.00	200.00		1.86		1,701.86	1,708.80	47	
Centreville	3	2,169.00	1,300.00	300.00		8.56		1,906.86	1,513.51	47	
Chestertown	3	12,695.05	1,700.00	1,680.00	651.31	45.47	3,675.66	7,625.31	969.88	43	
Cumberland	3	4,344.69	1,600.00	460.00		4.13		2,104.13	5,570.64	43	
Easton	3	2,932.64	1,600.00	300.00		4.89		1,904.89	2,740.47	43	
Elkton	3	2,784.16	1,000.00			2.73		1,302.73	1,847.74	43	
Ellicott City	3	1,678.36	1,000.00			1.60		1,001.60	1,861.43	43	
Emmitsburg	3	11,464.97	1,000.00	1,184.00	1,000.00	10.21	1,563.29	3,004.43	176.95	43	
Frederick	2	6,073.10	2,300.00	395.00		59.89		6,061.89	5,130.24	42	
Havre de Grace	3	12,171.15	2,300.00	1,467.59	613.44	484.19	715.56	5,452.72	3,372.44	38	
Hagerstown	3	2,849.98	1,300.00	148.85		2.86		1,951.71	1,928.17	38	
Lonaconing	3	184.58	182.76			.34		183.10	50.84	44	
Port Deposit	3	2,382.68	1,100.00			2.00		1,102.00	1,279.68	46	Presidential from May 1, 1888.
Salisbury	3	2,525.19	1,500.00	97.50		.48		1,597.98	2,327.21	43	
Towson	3	2,282.22	1,000.00			2.56		1,002.56	1,279.66	44	
Westminster	3	4,680.44	1,500.00	513.50		4.64		2,017.14	2,683.30	43	
Total		643,314.09	32,102.75	117,578.96	6,457.60	5,609.41	151,624.88	313,373.86	331,940.74	48	

LOUISIANA.

Office								Remarks
Alexandria	3	2,468.94	1,100.00	300.00	5.25	1,405.25	50	In Government building.
Baton Rouge	3	8,060.54	1,400.00	364.00	27.83	2,291.32	28	Do.
Donaldsonville	3	2,831.09	1,300.00		1.98	1,301.98	43	
Franklin	3	2,104.21	1,000.00	162.50	2.08	1,102.08	41	
Lake Charles	3	4,256.08	1,600.00	300.00	3.04	1,795.54	52	
Monroe	3	3,423.95	1,500.00	300.00	4.00	1,804.00	41	
New Iberia	1	3,926.42	1,500.00	200.00	4.84	1,905.84	41	
New Orleans	1	308,740.19	8,700.00	68,540.94	1,949.15	128,190.08	44	
Opelousas	3	2,294.21	1,200.00		2.96	1,202.96	43	
Plaquemine	3	1,925.76	1,300.00	150.00	2.08	1,352.08	45	
Shreveport	3	11,673.77	1,300.00	1,337.50	8.76	5,445.30		
Thibodeaux	3	1,966.25	1,100.00	80.00	2.40	1,183.40	43	
Total		355,123.00	19,290.00	66,934.94	27.00	148,651.21	208,430.58	

MAINE.

Office								Remarks
Auburn	2	12,653.77	2,300.00	1,000.00	630.00	.68	6,700.85	5,947.43	54	In Government building.
Augusta	1	38,939.64	3,100.00	11,281.41	3,449.13	.68	21,091.07	17,848.57	54	Do.
Bangor	1	61,250.36	3,000.00	17,046.73	172.64	14,518.98	36,740.98	28	Do.
Bar Harbor	3	7,154.31	1,700.00	299.00	12.44	14,518.44	1,210.87	57	
Bath	2	10,125.44	2,300.00	1,466.00	32.31	6,740.16	4,382.29	88	
Belfast	3	6,473.68	2,100.00	485.00	9.78	3,399.78	4,163.44	44	
Biddeford	2	10,065.63	2,100.00	1,400.00	29.44	4,374.44	4,692.30	35	
Bridgton	3	2,901.18	1,800.00	400.00	1.00	4,091.60	1,350.03	44	
Brunswick	3	2,503.40	1,800.00	800.00	16.52	2,215.52	4,086.05	44	
Buckport	3	5,441.63	1,700.00	700.00	2.96	1,402.96	1,130.44	45	
Calais	3	2,907.99	1,200.00	200.00	4.88	2,404.88	3,036.75	35	
Camden	3	3,007.41	1,400.00	400.00	6.58	2,466.58	1,492.41	44	
Dexter	3	3,557.99	1,400.00	400.00	3.88	1,902.98	1,481.81	45	
Eastport	3	4,441.63	1,500.00	400.33	3.44	2,313.45	1,385.64	44	
Ellsworth	3	2,900.74	1,000.00	705.33	5.13	1,905.53	1,528.18	54	
Fairfield	3	8,845.13	1,400.00	400.00	6.64	1,908.64	1,687.59	44	
Farmington	3	1,957.00	1,400.00		6.64	745.77	1,528.49	48	Presidential from October 4, 1897.
Foxcraft	3	3,865.99	1,500.00	714.83	21.38	2,129.00	811.00	29	
Gardiner	2	4,702.87	1,500.00	206.84	4.12	1,905.12	6,176.00	40	
Hallowell	3	4,451.70	1,100.00	365.00	8.84	1,103.84	2,794.19	41	
Houlton	2	20,066.61	2,100.00		63.24	10,520.43	1,347.86	45	In Government building.
Kennebunk	3		1,000.00	2,200.00	1,468.29	1.28	10,529.43	9,569.00	35	
Lewiston	3	2,178.69	1,000.00	200.00	2.04	1,291.29	977.41	55	
Machias	3	2,823.87	1,200.00	162.00	7.13	1,365.04	1,466.83	46	
Mechanic's Falls	3	3,200.86	1,400.00	204.17	1.08	1,611.29	1,960.57	54	Presidential from January 31, 1898.
Norway	3	894.33	1,100.00	417.58	1.00	102.04	272.11	47	
...kland					4,867.99		413.10	473.33		
...Town									

No. 10.—*Gross receipts, expenses, and net revenue of Presidential post-offices for the fiscal year ended June 30, 1888—Continued.*

MAINE—Continued.

Office.	Class.	Gross receipts.	Salary.	Clerk hire.	Rent, light, and fuel.	Other incidental expenses.	Free delivery.	Total expenses.	Net revenue.	Per cent. expenses to gross receipts.	Remarks.
Pittsfield	3	$2,568.59	$1,100.00	$20,122.00		$2.88		$1,102.88	$1,465.71	43	
Portland	1	100,364.02	3,300.00			421.88	$13,461.16	17,265.05	63,088.97	17	In Government building.
Richmond	3	3,407.43	1,400.00			1.88		1,408.88	2,564.13	28	
Rockland	3	10,411.00	3,100.00	1,162.50		24.00		3,336.50	7,130.43	33	Do.
Saccarappa	3	2,673.55	1,200.00			4.00		1,204.00	1,472.75	31	
Saco	3	5,225.79	1,300.00	200.00		14.00		1,514.00	3,814.80	31	
Skowhegan	3	4,202.38	1,700.00	343.00		8.73		1,951.73	4,360.61	43	Do.
South Berwick	3	2,295.88	1,100.00					1,100.00	1,155.88	48	
Thomaston	3	2,044.35	1,200.00	100.00		4.06		1,304.06	900.27	64	
Waldoborough	3	2,131.06	1,000.00	150.00		3.20		1,153.20	977.85	64	
Waterville	2	9,387.61	2,000.00	748.58	$900.00	15.25		3,964.88	6,022.75	35	
Winthrop	3	2,872.59	1,100.00			2.40		1,102.40	1,770.19	38	
Total		377,632.99	63,100.43	52,667.29	6,123.22	913.20	31,046.62	153,910.97	222,613.02	41	

MARYLAND.

Office.	Class.	Gross receipts.	Salary.	Clerk hire.	Rent, light, and fuel.	Other incidental expenses.	Free delivery.	Total expenses.	Net revenue.	Per cent. expenses to gross receipts.	Remarks.
Annapolis	3	11,649.11	1,900.00	1,850.00	500.00	5,900.70	1,942.08	6,192.02	5,457.09	54	
Baltimore	1	561,005.78	5,000.00	108,995.31	3,650.00	6.16	144,320.52	206,962.59	354,113.25	43	In Government building.
Bel Air	3	3,407.00	1,200.00	200.00		8.15		1,400.15	1,716.29	50	
Cambridge	3	3,014.57	1,300.00	200.00		1.28		1,301.26	1,708.30	40	
Centreville	3	3,109.07	1,300.00			18.81		1,318.81	1,611.61	47	
Chestertown	3	12,090.00	1,300.00	280.00	621.21	65.67	5,473.68	7,623.31	6,370.64	45	
Cumberland	3	4,944.89	1,700.00	480.00		4.15		2,184.15	2,744.47	43	
Easton	3	3,552.54	1,400.00	300.00		4.50		1,804.50	1,947.74	49	
Elkton	3	2,734.14	1,300.00			2.72		1,302.72	1,581.42	47	
Ellicott City	3	11,672.28	1,000.00			1.60		1,001.60	774.05	48	
Emmittsburgh	3	2,390.00	2,000.00	1,184.00	1,000.00	10.31	1,966.32	6,344.43	5,130.24	45	
Frederick	2	2,073.10	1,300.00	200.00		480.19		3,400.86	1,873.14	43	
Frostburgh	3	13,171.15	2,200.00	1,487.80	613.44	2.98	713.86	5,012.71	7,584.44	38	
Hagerstown	3	3,646.99	1,800.00	149.83		.24		1,462.72	1,362.17	38	
Havre de Grace	3		102.78					102.80	90.84	43	
Lonaconing	3	3,285.03	1,100.00	97.90		.45		1,197.95	1,377.01	44	
Port Deposit	3	3,362.19	1,100.00			.61		1,697.96	2,237.21	44	
Salisbury	3	4,690.44	1,500.00	512.50		4.64		2,017.14	2,653.30	43	Presidential from May 1, 1888.
Towson											
Westminster											
Total		645,214.00	32,102.75	117,578.06	6,457.65	6,609.41	151,624.86	313,373.85	331,940.74	43	

MASSACHUSETTS.

Office									Remarks
Abington	3	2,683.36	1,100.00			8.94		1,579.59	1,168.34	41
Adams	3	6,039.36	1,700.00			4.90		4,384.40	1,704.96	38
Amesbury	3	9,563.06	2,000.00			12.00		6,461.06	2,182.00	35
Amherst	2	9,730.38	2,100.00		750.00	570.00	22.88	4,911.99	2,418.87	38
Andover	3	7,209.20	1,500.00		900.00	395.49	52.24	5,076.96	2,612.63	38
Arlington	3	4,575.19	1,500.00		300.00		12.82	3,002.87	1,612.82	40
Ashland	3	2,190.74	1,100.00				5.03	1,065.22	1,065.62	39
Athol	3	5,988.80	1,700.00		400.00		6.72	4,282.08	2,106.72	35
Attleborough	3	6,278.22	1,700.00				13.80	4,667.24	1,713.80	37
Auburndale	3	4,138.56	1,400.00				20.80	2,615.76	1,420.80	43
Ayer	3	3,967.18	1,400.00				4.24	1,992.84	1,430.24	48
Bath	3	2,277.10	1,100.00				2.40	1,176.63	1,102.43	51
Beverly	2	11,006.04	4,100.00		706.66	690.00	47.00	7,551.58	3,444.46	31
Boston	1	1,724,068.12		18,280.23	316,771.95	13,382.53		1,041,959.06	663,949.66	40
Bradford	3	3,460.21	1,100.00				7.70	1,188.00	1,107.70	49
Bridgewater	3	27,568.61	1,100.00				6.00	1,500.08	1,500.08	43
Brockton	2		2,700.00		2,250.00	1,462.78	77.00	14,611.74	12,991.87	47
Brookfield	3	973.04	832.86				1.00	564.98	394.46	50
Campello	3	6,002.86	1,600.00				8.90	3,543.56	1,568.90	48
Canton	3	5,255.40	1,700.00		88.50		7.04	1,755.99	1,464.54	49
Chicopee	2	6,671.60	1,700.00		250.00		12.66	4,066.78	1,912.66	37
Chicopee Falls	3	4,427.63	2,000.00		771.00	285.00	6.00	2,958.49	2,006.00	38
Clinton	2	6,686.31	2,000.00				23.96	3,967.66	2,171.96	43
Cottage City	3	2,534.90	1,000.00		156.00		11.35	1,283.04	1,207.91	54
Dalton	3	4,451.41	1,100.00				6.90	2,944.86	1,160.90	35
Danvers	3	4,901.53	1,400.00		200.00		28.38	3,175.14	1,738.38	38
Dedham	3	5,502.80	1,600.00		208.33		28.96	3,584.86	1,818.34	41
Easthampton	3	3,425.84	1,400.00				4.90	2,020.86	1,404.90	38
East Weymouth	3	3,356.73	1,100.00				4.00	1,985.56	1,104.00	47
Everett	2	35,079.91	2,800.00		4,890.00		149.97	16,787.74	18,392.12	63
Fairhaven	3	29,174.65	2,000.00		2,623.96	1,666.50	73.15	14,382.97	11,681.08	45
Fall River	2	3,523.04	1,400.00				6.63	1,616.80	1,400.80	49
Fitchburg	3	3,482.06	1,800.00				8.17	1,804.61	1,166.87	44
Florence	3	3,026.06	1,400.00				7.96	1,491.70	1,407.96	46
Foxborough	3	6,063.70	1,600.00		16.67		4.56	477.23	1,004.56	34
Framingham	2	28,896.89	2,600.00		2,380.00		6.43	10,443.58	10,443.51	55
Franklin	3	6,682.34	1,700.00				7.64	3,925.20	1,707.04	39
Gardner	2	13,449.06	2,400.00	5,584.89	1,700.00	710.00	30.22	8,002.87	4,844.52	36
Georgetown	3	28,543.87	2,700.00	7,150.66	4,228.50	1,486.00	30.40	13,028.89	15,514.96	64
Gloucester	3	2,858.14	1,100.00		296.23		6.40	1,543.41	1,314.78	45
Great Barrington	3	2,290.06	1,100.00				2.40	1,182.40	1,102.40	48
Greenfield	2	31,191.94	2,900.00	6,453.64	8,108.00	1,300.00	121.52	17,495.98	13,784.66	45
Haverhill	2	4,800.49	1,600.00		590.00	171.55	6.60	3,283.58	1,504.96	45
Hingham										
Holliston										
Holyoke	3	10,621.47	2,100.00				63.70	3,700.23	2,625.25	17
Hudson										
Hyde Park										

In Government building.

Presidential from February 9, 1888.

In Government building.

Presidential from February 1, 1888. In Government building.

No. 10.—*Gross receipts, expenses, and net revenue of Presidential post-offices for the fiscal year ended June 30, 1888—Continued.*

MASSACHUSETTS—Continued.

Office.	Class.	Gross receipts.	Salary.	Clerk hire.	Rent, light, and fuel.	Other incidental expenses.	Free delivery.	Total expenses.	Net revenue.	Per cent. expenses to gross receipts.	Remarks.
Ipswich	3	$3,844.77	$1,500.00			$7.83		$1,507.83	$2,336.94	39	
Lawrence	2	32,525.64	2,700.00	$4,197.91	$4,560.59	218.46	$10,972.38	19,606.12	12,916.50	60	
Lee	3	4,464.84	1,600.00			2.88		1,602.88	2,861.96	35	
Lenox	3	3,069.87	1,500.00			5.68		1,505.68	2,163.69	41	
Leominster	3	8,074.25	1,800.00	100.00		13.66		1,913.66	6,160.57	23	
Lexington	3	658.53	304.95			2.72		307.67	351.86	47	
Lowell	1	85,347.79	3,200.00	7,099.30	3,450.00	454.32	16,435.26	30,548.91	54,798.88	36	Presidential from March 12, 1888.
Lynn	2	55,610.82	2,100.00	5,527.63	3,020.00	851.92	14,360.81	25,969.36	29,741.46	47	
Malden	2	13,752.19	2,300.00	1,211.57	990.00	109.94	3,565.09	8,076.64	5,653.55	58	Presidential from October 5, 1887.
Manchester	3	1,288.55	813.04			4.24		817.28	471.27	63	
Mansfield	3	2,884.16	1,200.00	216.67		6.76		1,265.70	1,678.40	46	
Marblehead	3	7,144.40	1,800.00	945.00	817.00	21.86		2,038.03	5,106.43	28	
Marlborough	3	10,416.64	2,200.00			35.22	1,386.89	4,724.11	5,692.53	45	Presidential from January 1, 1888.
Hayward	3	1,045.40	500.00			.56		500.56	544.90	36	
Medford	3	6,415.55	1,700.00	485.00	528.55	84.90		1,784.96	4,630.64	28	
Melrose	3	17,974.10	2,100.00			83.09		2,183.68	15,625.64	28	
Merrimac	3	3,280.85	1,300.00			6.66		1,306.86	1,734.18	43	
Methuen	3	2,643.00	1,300.00	856.00	396.00	11.68		1,911.68	1,783.08	25	
Middleborough	3	8,664.76	2,000.00			27.62		2,267.62	5,983.96	28	
Milford	3	9,221.57	1,400.00			4.56		1,404.56	3,329.50	38	
Millbury	3	3,621.90	943.90			14.24		943.90	2,278.50	29	
Milton	3	3,185.50	1,400.00			5.12		1,405.12	1,780.38	42	
Monson	3	802.12	1,700.00			5.12		1,705.12	4,097.00	29	
Nantucket	3	8,962.63	1,900.00	400.00		27.44		2,827.44	6,685.88	45	
Natick	1	40,885.59	2,500.00	4,429.21	1,078.44	167.11	10,783.60	18,540.04	22,555.67	33	In Government building.
New Bedford	2	17,366.96	2,100.00	3,200.00	971.67	77.73	3,291.87	9,163.04	6,420.92	38	
Newburyport	3	11,535.45	1,500.00	517.75		18.46		2,013.44	6,017.86	38	
Newton	2	8,960.93	2,500.00			19.44		1,783.44	6,477.49	21	
Newton Centre	3	6,627.00	1,500.00			25.44		2,914.13	16,922.56	38	
Newtonville	3	23,256.71	2,500.00	1,813.59	849.87	943.00	3,262.55	7,057.00	11,071.13	39	
North Adams	2	18,128.18	2,100.00	1,500.00	793.76	92.64	3,163.27	7,116.34	11,422.78	38	
Northampton	2	18,538.12	1,900.00	266.42		2.84		1,102.64	975.81	34	
North Attleborough	3	7,078.45	1,900.00			7.76		1,907.76	6,992.68	43	
Northborough	3	610.44	1,000.00			4.82		1,104.32	1,425.00	43	
North Brookfield	3	520.88	1,100.00			8.44		1,108.44	1,002.19	68	
North Easton	3	2,463.03	1,100.00			1.68		1,001.68	605.21	23	
Northfield	3	1,605.89	1,000.00			7.28		1,107.28	1,730.24	25	
Norwood	3	3,827.52	1,000.00	253.91		6.20		1,005.20	101.24	40	
Orange	3	5,705.44	1,600.00			14.96		1,068.67	2,449.21		
Palmer	3	4,718.08	1,600.00								

Presidential from March 7, 1888.

								Presidential from March 7, 1888.
Peabody	3	7,972.60	1,900.00			23.76		5,183.85	2,090.25	37
Pittsfield	2	22,723.82	2,100.00			69.31		11,793.15	11,020.37	49
Plymouth	2	9,048.40	2,144.00	260.40	1,148.30	1.41	4,880.80	6,037.00	1,594.00	38
Provincetown	2	8,965.71	1,500.00	2,782.87	290.00	4.00		3,261.47	2,991.41	39
Quincy	3	8,222.35	1,800.00	600.00		29.28		1,899.70	2,025.88	29
Randolph	2	3,100.15	1,200.00	200.00		9.28		2,872.28	1,209.28	33
Reading	2	4,382.24	1,400.00			9.36		229.93	1,400.36	37
Rockland	2	4,734.81	1,600.00			4.88		240.40	1,504.88	56
Rockport	2	560.02	318.68			.88		319.56	310.56	48
Salem	3	30,344.73	2,700.00	4,500.00	3,395.00	261.44	8,673.35	13,202.94	17,161.70	39
Sandwich	2	3,745.19	1,800.00			5.44		1,439.75	1,805.44	41
Shelburne Falls	2	3,868.88	1,800.00			6.44		381.44	1,805.44	43
Southbridge	2	4,020.01	1,800.00	150.40	625.00	28.53		363.60	655.00	27
South Framingham	3	6,180.73	1,600.00	1,050.00		5.80		454.20	3,705.63	47
Spencer	2	3,353.36	1,700.00			10.72		627.64	1,718.72	31
Springfield	1	92,132.04	3,800.00	9,361.26	3,000.00	604.20	11,662.97	64,202.62	27,929.43	37
Stockbridge	2	3,814.40	1,400.00			4.72		1,404.72	1,404.72	33
Stoneham	2	3,498.12	1,700.00			22.48		1,767.65	1,722.48	34
Stoughton	2	3,225.03	1,400.00			6.00		1,819.03	1,406.00	40
Taunton	3	24,620.84	2,600.00	8,100.00	1,508.00	132.54	6,904.11	10,284.19	14,284.65	28
Turner's Falls	2	4,252.90	1,500.00			7.28		2,745.62	1,607.28	29
Uxbridge	2	2,141.37	1,000.00	253.33		2.88		1,138.39	1,002.88	38
Wakefield	3	3,942.00	1,800.00			22.88		4,765.85	2,078.31	47
Walpole	2	2,466.35	1,140.00	1,176.00	1,976.74	6.92	3,481.73	3,982.43	1,105.92	31
Ware	2	10,530.63	2,500.00			42.64		7,964.58	8,575.10	81
Warren	2	6,022.57	1,100.00			8.00		290.60	1,465.00	10
Watertown	3	6,132.83	1,400.00	800.00		10.64		414.27	1,460.00	37
Webster	2	5,172.71	1,700.00	200.00		20.66		782.07	1,910.64	33
Wellesley	2	2,459.50	1,500.00			13.76		738.28	1,720.66	34
Westborough	2	6,875.01	1,800.00			39.48		3,162.25	1,813.76	40
Westfield	2	30,843.25	2,500.00	1,500.00	870.38	4.43		15,432.44	4,909.81	29
West Gardner	2	4,561.06	1,400.00					2,176.50	1,444.49	35
West Newton	3	4,854.67	1,700.00			80.24		124.29	1,730.24	38
Weymouth	3	2,811.60	1,200.00			7.66		1,644.12	1,207.66	38
Whitinsville	2	2,750.49	2,100.00			3.76		1,644.72	1,103.76	40
Whitman	3	3,973.68	1,400.00			8.12		2,170.56	1,408.12	35
Williamstown	2	4,314.53	1,200.00	264.17		7.78		490.81	1,207.78	23
Winchendon	2	5,429.70	1,700.00			4.72		480.81	1,632.48	24
Winchester	2	6,638.08	1,700.00	254.37		52.68		318.00	1,194.43	19
Woburn	2	11,195.31	1,900.00	253.37	3,850.00	40.16		9,060.75	3,154.43	35
Worcester	1	110,190.56	3,900.00	13,820.00		2.73		71,650.39	25,512.37	39
Total		3,063,682.66	237,064.27	413,611.21	48,782.89	20,070.00	491,373.23	3,883,561.99	1,200,470.09	39

No. 10.—*Gross receipts, expenses, and net revenue of Presidential post-offices for the fiscal year ended June 30, 1888—Continued.*

MICHIGAN.

Office.	Class.	Gross receipts.	Salary.	Clerk hire.	Rent, light, and fuel.	Other incidental expenses.	Free delivery.	Total expenses.	Net revenue.	Per cent. expenses to gross receipts.	Remarks.
Adrian	2	$14,199.29	$2,400.00	$6,000.80	$940.00	$98.44	$2,723.08	$6,528.47	$6,372.52	35	
Albion	3	9,006.22	1,900.00	216.55		6.00		2,022.55	6,982.97	22	
Allegan	3	5,625.17	1,700.00	200.00		1.12		1,901.12	3,723.15	34	
Alma	3	2,388.45	944.40			1.29		945.69	1,429.77	40	Presidential from October 4, 1887.
Alpena	3	6,847.26	1,800.00	385.00		6.26		2,190.26	4,454.96	32	
Ann Arbor	3	21,657.35	2,600.00	3,728.00	1,850.00	105.25	2,670.22	10,654.47	11,002.88	49	
Battle Creek	2	22,980.46	2,600.00	3,040.00	1,152.00	489.56	4,970.59	12,212.77	11,067.69	51	
Bay City	2	22,888.02	2,700.00	3,360.00	1,100.00	65.78	6,439.93	13,645.71	9,182.31	60	
Benton Harbor	3	5,861.99	1,700.00	369.00		8.44		1,908.44	3,948.45	30	
Berrien Springs	3	3,424.11	1,600.00			1.44		1,601.44	1,822.67	58	
Bessemer	3	4,615.64	1,500.00	1,000.00		2.72		2,502.72	2,112.92	55	
Big Rapids	3	9,874.43	1,600.00		397.35	10.49		2,408.14	5,966.40	36	
Buchanan	3	3,905.69	1,640.00			2.00		1,902.00	2,100.59	41	
Cadillac	3	6,588.92	1,700.00	466.25		4.03		2,133.95	4,481.67	32	
Calumet	3	3,410.04	1,600.00	6.53		1.84		1,410.17	1,999.97	41	
Caro	3	1,297.71	1,100.00			.80		1,100.80	1,196.91	80	
Cassopolis	3	1,354.02	1,600.00			.16		985.82	868.77	44	Presidential from November 1, 1887.
Charlevoix	3	2,418.37	1,200.00	1,200.00	480.00	4.59		3,885.53	4,532.85	27	
Charlotte	3	6,408.79	1,700.00			4.00		1,704.00	4,705.79	36	
Cheboygan	3	3,202.50	1,100.00			.94		1,100.90	1,101.54	39	
Chelsea	3	10,441.04	2,300.00	1,400.00	888.00	13.78		4,468.78	5,942.98	43	
Coldwater	3	4,922.39	1,200.00			.88		1,200.88	3,721.41	24	
Constantine	3	1,177.50	417.50			.86		417.59	759.47	41	
Corunna	3	144.30	185.77			.16		105.93	38.27	74	Presidential from February 14, 1888.
Crystal Falls	3	3,421.97	1,200.00			.40		1,200.40	1,221.57	49	Presidential from May 27, 1888.
Decatur	1	350,243.08	3,700.00	44,765.30		1,391.02	61,476.94	110,338.92	239,911.76	31	
Detroit	2	4,528.90	1,600.00			1.92		1,601.92	2,926.88	35	In Government building.
Dowagiac	3	37,362.95	2,800.00	3,466.96	1,560.00	97.45	8,251.24	16,188.70	21,064.25	43	
East Saginaw	3	148.16	60.44			.16		60.60	65.56	40	
East Tawas	3	3,972.02	1,800.00	100.00		2.64		1,804.64	3,370.35	39	
Escanaba	3	6,184.00	1,300.00	186.00		4.00		1,854.06	6,300.64	28	
Evart	3	3,013.18	1,200.00			1.12		1,201.12	1,813.06	40	
Fenton	3	4,975.17	1,300.00			1.36		1,501.36	2,573.81	30	
Flint	2	14,182.82	4,460.00	1,800.00	977.70	5.04	3,062.29	7,365.07	6,917.75	51	
Fort Gratiot	3	704.98	357.14			.00		357.34	437.34	45	Presidential from February 22, 1888.
Fremont	3	1,205.89	76.92			.96		1,000.98	954.73	51	Presidential from June 6, 1888.
Grand Haven	2	5,784.10	1,700.00	466.00		6.24		76.24	59.64	58	
Grand Ledge	3	2,422.14	1,300.00			462.64		2,166.24	3,447.87	77	In Government building.
Greenville	2	6,724.98	1,800.00	12,947.77		2.13	19,387.96	62,883.38	62,853.38	41	
			1,800.00	350.00				2,002.50	4,722.44	30	

Presidential from June 8, 1888.

Presidential from March 22, 1888.

Presidential from June 18, 1888.

Presidential from March 20, 1888.

Presidential from November 1, 1887.

Hancock
Hart
Hastings
Hillsdale
Holland
Holly
Homer
Houghton
Howell
Hudson
Imlay City
Ionia
Iron Mountain
Iron River
Ishpeming
Ithaca
Jackson
Jonesville
Kalamazoo
Lake Linden
Lansing
Lapeer
L'Anse
Lowell
Ludington
Manistee
Manistique
Marine City
Marquette
Marshall
Mason
Mendon
Menominee
Midland
Monroe
Morenci
Mount Clemens
Mount Pleasant
Muskegon
Negaunee
Niles
Northville
Oscoda
Otsego
Ovid
Owosso
Paw Paw
Pearl Water
Petoskey
Plymouth
Pontiac

No. 10.—*Gross receipts, expenses, and net revenue of Presidential post-offices for the fiscal year ended June 30, 1888—Continued.*

MICHIGAN—Continued.

Office.	Class.	Gross receipts.	Salary.	Clerk hire.	Rent, light, and fuel.	Other incidental expenses.	Free delivery.	Total expenses.	Net revenue.	Per cent expenses to gross receipts.	Remarks.
Port Huron	2	$15,396.69	$2,400.00	$2,071.51		$26.56	$2,086.36	$4,984.43	$9,655.27	41	In Government building.
Portland	3	3,128.94	1,300.00	200.00		.40		1,500.40	1,625.54	48	
Portsmouth	3	2,466.25	1,200.00			.40		1,309.40	1,367.58	49	
Quincy	3	2,566.49	1,500.00	8.97		.08		1,508.43	1,056.04	42	
Reading	3	1,920.56	1,100.00			.08		1,100.56	629.10	57	
Red Jacket	3	1,378.11	454.97					455.58	923.28	33	
Reed City	3	2,843.51	1,400.00			2.84		1,402.64	2,440.87	36	Presidential from February 14, 1888.
Republic	3	352.88	57.43					57.43	295.48	16	
Romeo	3	3,381.99	1,400.00			.96		1,400.96	1,981.03	42	Presidential from June 12, 1888.
Saginaw	2	12,252.97	2,300.00	1,000.00	$452.34	20.55	3,064.52	6,857.41	5,385.46	55	
Saint Clair	3	3,567.67	1,300.00	200.00		1.20		1,501.20	2,066.47	43	
Saint Ignace	3	4,235.94	1,200.00	400.00		1.44		1,601.44	2,634.50	38	
Saint John's	3	5,527.81	1,700.00	400.00		2.96		2,102.96	3,424.85	38	
Saint Joseph	3	4,886.94	1,700.00			2.24		1,702.24	3,184.70	34	
Saint Louis	3	3,861.82	1,500.00	408.43		2.88		1,911.30	1,950.52	49	
Sault de Ste. Marie	3	6,957.55	1,400.00	174.97		.67		1,574.97	5,382.58	23	
South Haven	3	2,518.49	1,400.00			.68		1,400.68	1,118.87	40	
Stanton	3	4,252.98	1,400.00	162.00		1.12		1,461.12	2,588.86	35	
Sturgis	3	4,597.70	1,500.00			2.72		1,452.72	2,905.68	35	
Tecumseh	3	262.86	90.68			2.16		1,692.16	171.92	85	
Three Oaks	3	6,732.00	1,800.00			.08		1,892.80	4,938.20	27	Presidential from June 1, 1888.
Three Rivers	3	6,804.44	1,900.00	424.99		2.82		2,227.31	4,577.13	27	
Traverse City	3	2,564.13	1,200.00			.08		1,260.68	1,963.25	47	
Union City	3	2,753.72	1,200.00	200.00		1.44		1,401.44	1,352.28	51	
Vassar	3	6,726.28	1,700.00	500.00		4.72		2,204.72	4,521.54	38	
West Bay City	3	2,377.92	1,100.00			1.12		1,101.12	1,276.99	46	
Whitehall	3	1,787.81	1,000.00			.98		1,000.98	786.93	47	
White Pigeon	3										
Williamstown	2	10,470.84	2,100.00	1,160.00	402.50	14.40		3,666.90	6,803.94	85	
Ypsilanti											
Total		1,213,725.88	186,233.46	112,760.65	17,850.00	3,185.95	187,870.13	456,466.18	757,317.70	36	

MINNESOTA.

Office.	Class.	Gross receipts.	Salary.	Clerk hire.	Rent, light, and fuel.	Other incidental expenses.	Free delivery.	Total expenses.	Net revenue.	Per cent expenses to gross receipts.	Remarks.
Ada	3	2,108.48	1,100.00	264.21				1,100.00	1,008.48	57	
Albert Lea	3	6,537.45	1,700.00	100.00		2.46		1,966.60	4,560.70	30	
Alexandria	3	3,478.22	1,400.00	163.06		1.12		1,501.12	1,977.20	43	
Anoka	3	4,870.07	1,800.00	300.00		4.80		1,758.78	3,111.31	36	
Austin	3	5,988.70	1,600.00	150.00		5.60		1,905.60	3,083.10	32	
Blue Earth City	3	2,468.30	1,000.00			.88		1,160.68	1,305.62	47	

No. 10.—*Gross receipts, expenses, and net revenue of Presidential post-offices for the fiscal year ended June 30, 1888—Continued.*

MISSISSIPPI.

Office.	Class.	Gross receipts.	Salary.	Clerk hire.	Rent, light, and fuel.	Other incidental expenses.	Free delivery.	Total expenses.	Net revenue.	Per cent expenses to gross receipts.	Remarks.
Aberdeen	3	4,297.79	1,500.00	250.00		3.46		1,753.46	2,544.33	41	In Government-building.
Brookhaven	3	2,716.17	1,100.00	208.33		2.79		1,313.12	1,404.05	48	
Canton	3	3,450.10	1,400.00	200.00		2.96		1,602.96	1,847.14	46	
Columbus	3	3,853.29	1,200.00	568.42		7.28		2,315.70	1,637.59	60	
Corinth	3	2,859.63	1,200.00	360.00		2.08		1,562.08	1,357.54	55	
Greenville	3	2,563.43	1,300.00	200.00		4.08		1,504.08	6,758.35	31	
Grenada	3	2,288.27	1,300.00	250.00		1.26		1,561.26	1,697.00	43	De.
Hazlehurst	3	2,590.31	1,000.00			.24		1,000.24	1,771.68	44	
Holly Springs	2	11,402.47	1,460.00	360.00		18.64	4,976.10	6,886.74	5,873.40	53	
Jackson	2	2,391.48	1,200.00	1,790.00		.57		4,564.73	5,800.75	60	
Kosciusko	3	2,986.76	1,040.00	464.18		5.00		1,018.90	1,305.37	45	
Macon	3	13,797.66	1,100.00	1,500.00	340.00	14.40	3,568.32	7,013.90	4,784.47	41	
Meridian	2	11,285.66	2,200.00	1,000.00	581.65	84.72	1,210.52	4,973.99	4,276.16	44	De.
Natchez	3	2,388.77	1,100.00	100.00		.73		1,200.00	1,198.72	45	
Okolona	3	2,498.74	1,294.61	188.72				1,519.96	1,373.47	48	
Oxford	3	2,682.40	1,100.00	5.43		2.48		1,110.00	1,314.94	45	
Port Gibson	3	2,331.91	2,500.00	100.00		1.00		1,201.00	1,481.90	55	
Starkville	2	10,102.06		3,000.00		77.40	3,711.60	10,512.00	8,569.13	44	
Vicksburg	3	2,296.49	1,100.00			.10		1,100.10	1,431.76	43	
Water Valley	3	3,431.85	1,100.00	262.50		.24		1,100.24	1,196.28	45	
Weneca	3	3,428.28	1,400.00	185.00		8.43		1,005.92	1,700.37	48	
West Point	3	4,318.00	1,500.00	380.00		13.76		1,813.76	1,205.33	42	
Winona	3										
Yazoo City	3										
Total		123,381.25	34,330.61	10,960.85	2,366.00	266.39	9,450.51	57,384.56	65,976.09	44	

MISSOURI.

Office.	Class.	Gross receipts.	Salary.	Clerk hire.	Rent, light, and fuel.	Other incidental expenses.	Free delivery.	Total expenses.	Net revenue.	Per cent expenses to gross receipts.	Remarks.
Albany	3	1,961.90	1,000.00	250.00		0.98		1,250.98	710.92	64	
Appleton City	3	2,164.65	1,100.00	100.00		2.08		1,202.08	962.57	55	
Bethany	3	2,432.49	1,100.00	184.67		2.21		1,286.88	1,163.49	53	
Bolivar	3	3,298.05	1,100.00	394.12		2.38		1,896.46	6,3.59	38	
Booneville	3	5,514.64	1,600.00	450.00		4.00		2,054.00	3,360.81	34	
Bowling Green	3	4,843.97	1,200.00	180.00		3.40		1,382.40	1,162.24	81	
Brookfield	3	2,094.70	1,100.00			2.72		1,552.72	3,301.25	67	
Brunswick	3	2,094.70	1,100.00	100.00		.98		1,200.98	1,423.98	52	
Butler	3	4,427.01	1,100.00	200.00		2.80		1,082.80	3,024.21	57	
California	3	3,476.28	1,100.00	149.91		1.20		1,251.11	1,425.12	67	

Presidential from February 20, 1888.

In Government building.

Presidential from May 28, 1888.

| Cameron |
| Canton |
| Cape Girardeau |
| Carrollton |
| Carthage |
| Charleston |
| Chillicothe |
| Clarksville |
| Clinton |
| Columbia |
| De Soto |
| Edina |
| Fayette |
| Fulton |
| Gallatin |
| Glasgow |
| Hamilton |
| Harrisonville |
| Higginsville |
| Holden |
| Huntsville |
| Independence |
| Jefferson City |
| Joplin |
| Kansas City |
| Kirksville |
| Kirkwood |
| Lamar |
| Lebanon |
| Lexington |
| Liberty |
| Louisiana |
| Macon City |
| Marshall |
| Maryville |
| Memphis |
| Mexico |
| Moberly |
| Monroe City |
| Montgomery City |
| Neosho |
| Nevada |
| North Springfield |
| Palmyra |
| Paris |
| Pierce City |
| Plattsburg |
| Pleasant Hill |
| Poplar Bluff |
| Rich Hill |
| Richmond |

No. 10.—*Gross receipts, expenses, and net revenue of Presidential post-offices for the fiscal year ended June 30, 1888—Continued.*

MISSOURI—Continued.

Office.	Class.	Gross receipts.	Salary.	Clerk hire.	Rent, light, and fuel.	Other incidental expenses.	Free delivery.	Total expenses.	Net revenue.	Per cent expenses to gross receipts.	Remarks.
Rolla	3	2,810.54	1,200.00	258.33		92.48		1,550.81	1,259.73	55	
Saint Charles	3	5,576.98	1,600.00			4.52		1,605.52	3,971.38	29	
Saint Joseph	1	48,873.77	3,200.00	12,382.70	1,478.90	223.60	13,565.41	30,922.30	18,177.97	35	In Government building. Includes $2,974.52 expenses of mail-bags repair depot.
Saint Louis	1	930,970.35	6,000.00	174,200.30	1,411.70	7,963.23	184,100.74	373,575.97	656,394.48	40	
Sedalia	2	18,944.98	2,500.00	2,709.13	554.50	41.92	6,155.52	11,961.07	6,983.81	63	
Shelbina	3	2,499.25	1,100.00	100.00		.96		1,200.96	1,298.29	48	
Slater	3	2,623.58	1,100.00			1.44		1,101.44	1,522.14	42	
Springfield	2	22,467.28	2,500.00	8,350.00	1,650.00	32.64	2,371.61	9,707.25	12,760.03	43	
Stanberry	3	2,473.02	1,300.00	108.25		.48		1,408.73	2,264.29	38	
Sweet Springs	3	2,403.20	1,100.00			1.36		1,101.36	1,301.84	46	Name changed from Brownsville September 14, 1887.
Trenton	3	4,216.43	1,600.00	300.00		6.08		1,904.08	2,310.35	37	
Troy	3	2,551.58	1,100.00			1.30		1,101.30	1,450.28	43	
Warrensburgh	3	5,718.18	1,700.00	324.00		3.60		2,027.60	3,690.58	35	
Washington	3	2,505.23	1,100.00	250.00		2.49		1,352.49	1,152.83	54	
West Plains	3	2,028.75	1,300.00	460.00		1.12		1,761.12	1,325.63	56	
Windsor	3	2,068.69	1,000.00	100.00		1.20		1,101.20	1,067.39	51	
Total		1,741,792.62	119,024.72	209,438.74	6,783.81	19,708.25	259,185.50	655,189.07	1,086,563.00	38	

MONTANA.

Office.	Class.	Gross receipts.	Salary.	Clerk hire.	Rent, light, and fuel.	Other incidental expenses.	Free delivery.	Total expenses.	Net revenue.	Per cent expenses to gross receipts.	Remarks.
Anaconda	3	5,080.62	1,600.00	408.43		.88		1,600.88	3,459.74	63	
Billings	3	2,999.16	1,500.00	616.85		1.60		1,910.02	2,089.14	55	
Bozeman	3	6,524.07	1,700.00	4,100.00		4.64		3,521.49	3,002.58	73	
Butte City	2	24,281.39	2,600.00			.94		18,022.55	17,258.84	81	
Deer Lodge City	3	3,733.92	1,500.00	300.00		1.76		1,800.76	1,933.16	48	
Dillon	3	2,867.67	1,500.00	100.00				1,300.00	1,567.87	44	
Fort Benton	3	30,378.67	2,400.00	4,565.84	1,531.00	34.63	2,665.40	11,737.65	18,841.32	47	
Helena	2	8,908.41	2,400.00	516.84		2.96		919.80	1,988.62	50	
Livingston	3	1,068.61	597.04			.10		597.30	941.41	37	
Marysville	3	4,202.76	1,700.00	500.00		1.68		2,201.68	2,001.08	47	
Miles City	3	6,114.75	1,600.00	500.00		18.96		2,116.96	3,997.79	35	
Missoula	3	3,139.68	1,000.00			2.00		1,002.00	1,187.68	47	
White Sulphur Springs	3										Presidential from March 1, 1888.
Total		96,992.25	20,276.04	12,008.84	1,531.00	68.10	2,665.40	34,480.18	60,512.06	38	

NEBRASKA.

Ainsworth	3	2,318.98	1,100.00	100.00		.16	1,200.10	1,118.73	80
Albion	3	2,931.06	1,300.00	110.65		1.20	1,417.85	1,683.21	43
Alma	3	2,486.85	1,100.00	22.91		.64	1,123.55	1,343.90	43
Arapahoe	3	2,673.04	1,100.00			.40	1,100.40	1,477.64	49
Ashland	3	2,591.52	1,400.00	25.00		1.04	1,426.04	2,165.28	48
Atkinson	3	2,628.07	1,300.00	100.00		.64	1,300.64	1,537.43	38
Auburn	3	3,272.18	1,500.00			.08	1,500.08	1,272.10	48
Aurora	3	4,467.21	1,500.00	268.33	818.24	1.36	1,769.69	4,947.45	49
Beatrice	3	13,784.10	2,401.00	1,633.52		10.29	6,840.65	367.89	56
Benkleman	3	685.06	417.03	50.00		.16	467.19	3,652.31	40
Blair	3	4,234.13	1,500.00	290.00		1.92	1,701.92	941.06	65
Blue Hill	3	1,941.90	1,200.00			2.00	1,200.23	692.10	41
Broken Bow	3	1,410.65	1,000.00	316.66		2.50	1,018.55	776.10	59
Cambridge	3	1,770.66	1,000.00			1.84	652.84	2,996.71	35
Central City	3	649.67	1,000.00	150.00		1.94	1,701.84	3,631.58	29
Chadron	3	1,521.96	1,700.00			8.80	1,948.80	3,065.52	35
Columbus	3	624.32	1,700.00	250.00		.18	1,400.18	1,140.41	90
Creighton	3	544.97	1,100.00	900.00		2.50	1,982.56	4,215.03	55
Crete	3	618.19	1,700.00	100.00					90
Culbertson	3	1,089.21	640.00	80.00		.80	538.41		
David City	3	3,583.24	1,400.00	158.42		2.00	1,560.42	2,023.82	41
Edgar	3	2,174.23	1,200.00	150.00		.16	1,350.16	924.07	63
Fairbury	3	5,270.21	1,300.00	75.80		2.96	1,678.76	3,691.45	31
Fairfield	3	2,518.03	1,200.00		430.75	1.36	1,201.36	1,814.67	48
Fairmont	3	2,898.56	1,300.00	100.00		.96	1,440.96	1,497.66	48
Falls City	3	4,027.38	1,500.00	150.00			1,650.00	3,077.98	40
Fremont	3	14,780.62	2,100.00	900.00		.25	3,000.64	11,070.63	25
Friend	3	2,566.34	1,100.00			.64	1,100.64	1,465.70	44
Fullerton	3	2,534.16	1,100.00	180.00	285.90	1.12	1,100.90	1,145.16	43
Geneva	3	568.82	1,200.00	1,250.00		20.36	251.12	1,357.90	44
Grand Island	3	12,141.95	2,390.00			.80	6,383.13	4,313.07	48
Harvard	3	2,737.21	1,200.00	1,725.84	797.61	42.77	1,300.80	458.41	40
Hastings	3	17,422.17	2,400.00	25.00		2,078.03	2,568.80	10,128.57	57
Hay Springs	3	708.40	373.63				386.63	907.88	57
Hebron	3	2,844.77	1,400.00	100.00		2,399.96	1,612.10	1,223.67	34
Holdrege	3	4,824.09	1,400.00	268.42		8.88	2,001.55	3,632.64	48
Humboldt	3	2,465.47	1,200.00	400.00		1.55	1,200.33	1,295.15	59
Indianola	3	2,635.91	1,300.00			.82	1,650.40	1,085.51	34
Kearney	1	10,194.01	2,000.00	250.00	383.83	6.79	8,452.11	6,701.90	31
Lincoln	1	61,832.38	8,108.00	1,200.90		228.88	10,559.86	42,897.67	83
Loup City	3	2,510.00	1,100.00	6,777.70		.64	1,900.64	1,200.45	34
McCook	3	3,311.81	1,100.00	200.00		8.65	1,703.68	1,607.83	58
Madison	3	2,186.51	1,000.00			.24	1,000.24	1,194.97	

Presidential February 14, 1888.
Presidential February 29, 1888.
Presidential February 16, 1888.
In Government building.

No. 10.—*Gross receipts, expenses, and net revenue of Presidential post-offices for the fiscal year ended June 30, 1888—Continued.*

NEBRASKA—Continued.

Office.	Class.	Gross receipts.	Salary.	Clerk hire.	Rent, light, and fuel.	Other incidental expenses.	Free delivery.	Total expenses.	Net revenue.	Per cent. expenses to gross receipts.	Remarks.
Norfolk	3	$5,407.60	$1,600.00	$150.00		$8.56		$1,758.56	$3,648.04	32	
North Bend	3	2,180.49	1,200.00	250.00		.64		1,450.64	729.85	67	
North Platte	3	4,685.07	1,413.73	179.12		.46		1,598.30	3,085.77	34	
Ogallala	3	2,297.35	1,100.00					1,100.00	1,197.35	48	
Omaha	1	196,229.79	3,500.00	24,281.11	$3,786.33	504.90	$23,784.69	51,900.59	144,348.20	26	In Government building.
O'Neill	3	3,233.74	1,400.00	250.00				1,650.00	1,978.74	50	
Ord	3	2,902.92	1,100.00	150.00		1.52		1,251.52	1,751.40	43	
Orleans City	3	2,766.15	1,500.00			1.13		1,501.13	1,618.15	35	
Plattsmouth	3	3,903.36	1,900.00	108.43		3.72		1,915.15	2,461.24	34	
Plum Creek	3	7,628.98	1,500.00	394.16		.92		1,904.46	6,027.23	31	
Red Cloud	3	3,540.51	1,900.10	315.85		3.64		1,920.39	1,784.09	48	
Saint Paul	3	4,163.00	1,500.00	206.83				1,706.83	2,455.97	41	
Schuyler	3	4,273.48	1,500.00	250.00		2.48		1,758.00	2,523.48	38	
Sidney	3	5,013.21	1,496.00	150.00		1.04		1,652.48	3,360.73	33	
Seward	3	3,528.87	1,400.00	100.00		5.92		1,501.04	2,027.38	42	
South Omaha	3	7,628.90	492.88	200.00		.31		664.78	6,925.13	10	
Sterling	3	3,965.70	1,100.00			.08		1,100.24	565.46	48	
Stromsburgh	3	2,645.69	1,200.00	60.00		1.98		1,288.06	1,365.52	48	
Superior	3	3,060.90	1,300.00	11.36		.72		1,314.23	1,782.71	43	
Sutton	3	2,664.21	1,200.00					1,200.73	1,465.49	44	
Syracuse	3	2,281.66	1,600.00	200.00		.80		1,100.80	1,680.76	49	
Tecumseh	3	3,731.86	1,100.00			.24		1,100.24	1,630.84	45	
Valentine	3	1,496.15	1,100.00	160.00		1.79		1,100.56	795.95	58	
Wahoo	3	4,642.75	1,700.00	313.64		2.88		2,015.62	2,628.12	43	
Wayne	3	2,442.78	1,100.00			.56		1,100.56	1,342.22	45	
Weeping Water	3	3,097.09	1,100.00			1.28		1,101.28	1,926.81	36	
West Point	3	2,356.70	1,200.00	304.19		1.52		1,505.71	1,850.99	38	
Wilber	3	3,438.64	1,200.00			.56		1,200.56	1,828.08	38	
Wymore	3	3,168.13	1,460.00	150.00		2.00		1,562.00	1,617.13	48	
York	3	7,669.62	1,800.00	241.67		3.04		2,044.71	5,764.91	30	Presidential February 14, 1888.
Total		578,228.59	110,663.71	47,046.09	3,786.33	926.71	36,557.10	200,990.04	374,968.55	39	

NEVADA.

Office								Presidential March 9, 1888.
Austin	3	1,834.17	1,000.00	256.42		1,258.42	675.75	65
Carson City	3	5,869.18	1,700.00	748.42		2,413.70	3,454.78	42
Elko	3	2,114.40	1,700.00	243.40	6.28	1,343.32	841.48	61
Eureka	3	30,178.77	1,400.00	1,400.00	.32	2,402.72	866.49	74
Reno	3	7,524.34	1,400.00	666.85	2.72	2,468.59	5,056.65	33
Virginia City	3	8,214.40	1,900.00	918.85	1.44	2,725.81	5,4?8.59	60
Winnemucca	3	2,165.16	1,100.00	260.00	8.16	1,300.56	864.60	
					.56			
Total		31,162.06	10,000.00	3,893.54	19.28	13,912.82	17,249.24	43

NEW HAMPSHIRE.

Office								Presidential March 9, 1888.	In Government building.
Antrim	3	680.35	344.51	300.00	.08	344.59	335.78	51	
Bristol	3	2,122.78	1,000.00	112.50	1.84	1,361.84	820.94	30	
Claremont	2	6,307.66	1,800.00	1,670.00	8.08	1,920.58	4,387.08	44	
Concord	2	30,178.77	2,700.00	881.80	128.05	13,133.27	17,045.50	69	5,037.22
Dover	2	12,755.49	2,300.00	3,640.00	3.38	8,550.80	4,204.69	31	3,363.62
Exeter	3	6,819.52	1,500.00	270.00	16.06	2,086.08	4,733.44	46	
Farmington	3	5,080.81	1,500.00	100.00	2.72	1,964.40	1,665.25	65	
Franklin Falls	3	3,588.26	1,500.00		1.4	1,292.72	2,385.27	39	
Great Falls	3	3,889.97	1,500.00	150.00	4	1,545.40	3,011.29	37	
Hanover	3	4,773.83	1,604.10		11.04	1,761.04	824.29	35	
Hinsdale	3	4,227.41	1,100.00		2.12	1,563.12	1,155.30	49	1,006.00
Keene	2	2,256.10	1,100.00	1,125.00	2.80	1,162.80	9,071.65	36	
Laconia	3	14,218.28	2,400.00	?	15.84	5,146.83	5,181.18	28	
Lake Village	3	6,990.22	1,800.00	600.00	9.04	1,869.04	1,703.12	43	
Lancaster	3	3,106.08	1,400.00		2.98	1,402.90	2,773.09	35	
Lebanon	3	4,278.05	1,500.00		4.96	1,504.96	2,884.54	40	
Littleton	3	4,806.95	1,600.00	398.33	3.28	1,912.41	3,017.94	37	
Manchester	2	4,801.92	1,500.00	250.00	183.58	1,753.28	18,070.90	51	10,063.30
Meredith Village	3	36,750.74	1,000.00	3,960.96	1.62	1,001.53	486.97	53	
Milford	3	1,868.49	1,400.00		4.64	1,404.64	272.90	41	
Nashua	2	20,388.74	2,100.00	2,600.10	70.50	10,242.24	10,212.80	50	3,853.34
New Market	3	2,585.13	1,200.00	400.00	2.24	1,102.24	490.89	43	
Newport	3	2,565.19	1,100.00		2.45	1,602.48	962.54	62	
Penacook	3	2,552.86	1,200.00		3.44	1,103.44	1,448.92	43	
Peterborough	3	8,429.58	1,400.00	150.00	2.96	1,404.28	2,025.34	41	
Pittsfield	2	8,674.85	1,200.00		4.28	1,359.96	1,321.39	51	
Plymouth	3	3,743.12	2,400.00	2,900.00	86.60	7,985.15	2,337.81	38	
Portsmouth	3	15,388.32	2,400.00	400.00	15.20	2,115.20	7,393.17	82	2,608.55
Rochester	2	5,842.16	1,700.00		2.32	1,002.32	3,726.96	36	
Suncook	2	1,999.76	1,000.00	1,000.00	2.89	1,002.89	997.44	50	
Tilton	8	3,688.35	1,400.00	130.00	4.34	1,824.24	2,114.11	42	

No. 10.—Gross receipts, expenses, and net revenue of Presidential post-offices for the fiscal year ended June 30, 1888—Continued.

NEW HAMPSHIRE—Continued.

Office.	Class.	Gross receipts.	Salary.	Clerk hire.	Rent, light, and fuel.	Other incidental expenses.	Free delivery.	Total expenses.	Net revenue.	Per cent expenses to gross receipts.	Remarks.
West Lebanon	3	$1,801.26	$1,000.00			$0.80		$1,000.80	$800.46	56	Presidential from April 1, 1888.
Wilton	3	1,020.10	500.00			1.04		501.04	519.06	49	
Wolfsborough	3	579.76	250.00	$25.00		.64		275.64	304.12	48	
Total		227,972.02	51,804.51	18,901.79	$5,976.76	624.73	$25,922.12	103,219.91	124,752.16	40	

NEW JERSEY.

Office.	Class.	Gross receipts.	Salary.	Clerk hire.	Rent, light, and fuel.	Other incidental expenses.	Free delivery.	Total expenses.	Net revenue.	Per cent expenses to gross receipts.	Remarks.
Asbury Park	2	13,692.16	2,800.00	1,230.00	450.00	86.88	1,099.60	5,116.48	8,575.68	46	
Atlantic City	2	20,551.01	2,500.00	2,788.00	598.29	224.23	3,785.11	9,903.63	10,647.38	48	
Belvidere	3	3,096.46	1,300.00			2.64		1,362.64	1,793.82	42	
Bergen Point	3	3,821.83	1,400.00	308.43		9.36		1,717.79	2,104.04	47	
Beverly	3	3,225.83	1,100.00			2.72		1,102.72	2,123.16	33	
Bloomfield	3	4,727.83	1,200.00			13.16		1,213.16	3,016.16	43	
Boonton	3	2,816.10	1,200.00			8.66		1,208.12	1,298.98	43	
Bordentown	3	4,000.80	1,200.00	400.35	418.34	8.66		2,108.02	1,901.22	45	
Bridgeton	3	11,625.78	2,100.00	990.35		384.02	1,475.21	5,275.59	6,350.81	45	
Burlington	3	7,866.51	1,900.00	380.00		12.48		2,372.48	5,626.08	30	
Camden	2	36,382.29	2,600.00	3,890.00	1,525.00	178.06	14,010.96	22,312.04	16,071.25	58	
Cape May	3	4,945.83	1,600.00	91.20		10.48		1,701.68	3,244.95	34	
Dover	3	5,585.20	1,700.00	200.00		7.80		1,907.80	3,677.00	34	
East Orange	3	26,100.10	2,500.00	1,560.00	476.92	519.73	3,310.95	8,367.59	17,782.51	32	
Elizabeth	2	27,348.61	2,700.00	3,700.00	1,115.20	121.60	8,756.63	16,393.43	10,855.06	60	
Englewood	3	4,659.07	1,600.00			6.64		1,606.64	3,022.43	35	
Freehold	3	4,126.54	1,500.00	200.00		2.16		1,702.16	2,424.38	41	
Gloucester City	3	5,797.77	1,700.00	308.75		6.68		2,015.63	3,721.74	35	Presidential from June 7, 1888.
Hackensack	3	146.01	65.88			.64		66.57	78.44	46	
Hackettstown	3	7,966.27	1,700.00			8.18		1,708.53	6,257.11	21	
Haddonfield	3	3,754.67	1,500.00	250.00		3.68		1,753.53	2,001.15	47	
Hammonton	3	2,697.24	1,100.00			1.76		1,203.60	1,163.23	50	
Hightstown	3	2,687.36	1,100.00			8.36		1,101.76	1,485.48	43	
Hoboken	2	21,481.08	1,400.00			89.44	6,708.98	12,563.77	8,925.49	40	
Jersey City	1	85,277.52	2,800.00	10,004.00	965.40	668.44	40,195.85	84,658.29	619.43	64	In Government building.
Keyport	3	3,383.89	1,200.00			4.72		1,304.72	2,079.11	37	
Lakewood	3	3,948.13	1,400.00			8.00		1,408.00	2,550.15	38	
Lambertville	3	4,186.80	1,700.00	500.00		4.10		1,804.10	2,381.04	38	
Long Branch	3	4,186.80	1,700.00			18.86		1,718.86	4,438.01	38	

No. 10.—*Gross receipts, expenses, and net revenue of Presidential post offices for the fiscal year ended June 30, 1888*—Continued.

NEW MEXICO—Continued.

Office.	Class	Gross receipts.	Salary.	Clerk hire.	Rent, light, and fuel.	Other incidental expenses.	Free delivery.	Total expenses.	Net revenue.	Per cent. expenses to gross receipts.	Remarks.
Silver City	3	$4,384.00	$1,600.00	$333.43		$4.60		$1,937.03	$2,446.97	44	
Socorro	3	3,863.75	1,500.00			1.12		1,561.12	2,302.63	39	
Total		43,274.90	13,850.00	4,197.31	9071.70	26.00		18,745.01	24,529.80	43	

NEW YORK.

Office.	Class	Gross receipts.	Salary.	Clerk hire.	Rent, light, and fuel.	Other incidental expenses.	Free delivery.	Total expenses.	Net revenue.	Per cent.	Remarks.
adas	3	2, 56.97	1,200.00	162.50		1.28		1,363.78	1,204.19	53	
.....	3	4,470.59	1,506.00	280.00		5.04		1,765.04	63.56	42	
Albany	1	174,222.52	3,500.00	36,400.00		2,141.31	$2,860.19	74, 69.15	99,263.37	43	In Government building.
Albion	3	6,611.35	1,800.00	500.00	58.65	8.61		2,346.64	4,304.71	35	
Alfred Centre	3	2,967.75	1,100.00			.40		1,08.40	1,597.35	61	
aany	3	1,844.92	1,100.00			1.40		80.82	843.22	51	
Amsterdam	3	16,532.22	1,900.00	1,980.00	774.56	65.74	3,024.52	8,490.82	8, 65.4+	49	
Atp	3	2,498.43	1,190.00	150.00		.98		1,100.86	1, 8.47	44	
Attica	2	3,880.96	1,540.00			2.18		652.16	2,228.79	43	
Auburn	3	35,225.99	2,800.00	4,640.00	1,897.54	172.89	7,092.61	17,202.84	18,023.15	49	
Avon	3	2,572.87	1,200.00	200.00		1.80		1,401.80	1,172.27	54	
Babylon	3	2,218.21	1,400.00			6.08		1,406.08	812.13	44	
Bainbridge	3	2, 96.40	1,300.00	150.00		.40		1,450.40	1,455.00	50	
Baldwinsville	3	4,410.38	1,600.00	200.00		4.88		1,704.88	2,705.50	39	
aia	3	6, 62.48	1,700.00	300.00	1,100.00	7.04		2,007.04	4,153.44	33	
Batavia	3	13,101.26	2,400.00	1,800.00	560.00	28.88		5,329.88	7,772.38	41	
Bath	3	7, 08.95	2,000.00	1,100.00		2.72		3,602.72	4,307.23	46	Presidential from October 4, 1887.
Bay Shore	3	1,823.48	816.63			3.28		819.31	1,004.15	45	
Bel mt	1	2,155.38	1,000.00	6,481.18	1,280.00	1.20	4,470.29	17,001.20	1,154.18	46	
Binghamton	3	55,010.87	3,100.00			325.90		7,200.24	373.31	33	
Bolivar	3	2, 98.23		243.00		1.12		1,744.12	946.99	54	
Boonville	3	2,562.64	1,500.00			1.76		1,201.76	1,817.92	49	
Brewster	3	2,922.86	1,200.00			1.78		1,201.78	1,721.10	41	
Brighton	3	6,172.01	1,500.00			1.04		1,501.61	5,670.97	29	
Brockport	3	8,971.23	2,000.00	800.00	301.10	10.41		8,111.51	5,869.72	35	
Brooklyn	1	97,770.55	4,000.00	89,630.37	17,277.34	7,398.12	244,795.68	363,031.51	234,748.04	60	In Government building.
Buffalo	3	8,065.20	1,800.00	49,742.06	100.00	1,650.87	73,494.90	129,771.70	257,863.42	33	
Cambridge	3	4,213.43	1,800.00			8.86		1,503.68	2,709.76	36	
Camden	3	2,800.41	1,400.00	200.00		1.84		1,401.84	28-.57	34	
ghamto	3	2,537.40	1,700.00			9.28		1,909.28	3,424.12	38	Do.
Canandaigua	2	10,313.85	2,200.00	1,800.00		22.31		4,022.31	6,7103.54	37	

No. 10.—*Gross receipts, expenses, and net revenue of Presidential post-offices for the fiscal year ended June 30, 1888*—Continued.

NEW YORK—Continued.

Office.	Class.	Gross receipts.	Salary.	Clerk hire.	Rent, light, and fuel.	Other incidental expenses.	Free delivery.	Total expenses.	Net revenue.	Per cent expenses to gross receipts.	Remarks.
Greenwich	3	$3,297.82	$1,400.00			$2.40		$1,402.40	$1,895.42	43	
Groton	3	2,222.88	1,100.00			.16		1,100.16	1,122.72	38	
Hamilton	3	4,635.69	1,600.00			2.16		1,602.16	3,033.53	35	
Hammondsport	3	2,107.09	1,100.00	$250.00		1.12		1,351.12	755.97	64	
Havana	3	2,047.85	1,000.00			1.36		1,001.36	1,046.59	49	
Haverstraw	3	3,906.22	1,400.00	150.00		3.52		1,553.52	2,352.70	40	
Hempstead	3	3,668.95	1,400.00			6.08		1,406.08	2,262.87	38	
Herkimer	3	4,890.06	1,600.00	200.00		6.48		1,806.48	3,083.58	37	
Holley	3	765.59	381.67	12.86		.80		382.67	402.61	49	Presidential from February 7, 1888.
Homer	3	4,290.08	1,800.00			2.88		1,518.24	2,774.42	35	
Hoosick Falls	3	7,853.70	1,800.00	1,400.73		10.24		1,810.24	6,048.46	23	
Hornellsville	2	13,146.23	2,400.00		$1,200.00	30.75	$2,662.83	7,694.31	5,451.92	39	
Horseheads	3	2,609.63	1,200.00			3.52		1,203.52	1,406.11	46	
Hudson	2	14,700.64	2,400.00	1,900.00	1,087.45	61.13	1,808.71	7,247.29	7,352.75	50	
Huntington	3	4,358.01	1,400.00	33.70		.64		1,400.64	2,957.37	32	
Ilion	3	5,090.54	1,700.00			5.28		1,738.98	3,351.56	34	
Irvington	3	2,740.39	1,000.00			4.24		1,004.24	1,726.15	37	
Ithaca	2	8,157.63	1,200.00	3,830.00	1,750.54	4.00		1,204.00	1,953.63	33	
Jamaica	3	24,624.51	1,500.00	155.00		62.32		1,660.32	16,649.40	34	
Jamestown	2	9,237.66	2,000.00	900.00	1,470.05	84.53	4,706.78	11,651.36	12,973.15	48	
Johnstown	3	716.60	370.88		458.35	13.16		371.51	896.15	37	
Jordan	3	2,180.02	1,000.00			1.00		372.06	341.72	82	
Katonah	3	3,013.79	1,000.00	250.00		1.76		1,072.02	1,462.03	51	
Keeseville	3	12,092.44	2,000.00	1,400.00	735.00	133.99		4,468.99	7,623.45	51	
Kingston	3	8,645.00	2,000.00	1,000.00	322.10	4.00		3,226.10	5,318.90	37	
Le Roy	3	8,131.53	1,000.00			1.04		1,130.29		38	
Lima	2	12,641.09	2,300.00	1,600.00	818.75	57.85	2,671.13	11,447.73	8,193.36	47	
Little Falls	3	20,442.70	2,000.00	3,167.86	1,130.80	132.18	4,788.70	11,819.94	8,623.45	59	
Lockport	3	7,534.83	1,700.00	891.85		15.92	1,064.45	8,172.22	4,362.61	42	
Long Island City	3	5,411.00	1,600.00	300.50		4.00		1,904.50	3,506.50	35	
Lowville	3	6,110.72	1,700.00	368.42	398.40	7.44		2,015.86	4,094.86	33	
Lyons	3	5,170.75	2,000.00	800.00		6.72		2,205.12	4,974.63	39	
Malone	3	4,060.98	1,300.00			8.28		1,303.28	4,172.03	47	
Mamaroneck	3	2,180.84	1,500.00	200.00		5.84		1,705.84	2,854.53	43	
Mattewan	3	2,078.67	1,190.00	32.61		1.81		1,324.43	845.99	50	
Mayville	3	6,457.91	1,192.25	145.62		.84		1,338.06	1,728.91	44	
Mechanicsville	3	6,437.68	1,900.00	100.00		.64		1,994.64	4,553.00	29	
Medina	3	3,096.28	1,208.00	50.00		1.26		1,251.28	1,836.00	41	
Mexico	3										
Middletown	2	17,412.35	2,400.00	1,900.00	1,100.00	30.72	1,895.47	7,332.10	10,110.18	42	Presidential from February 14, 1888.

No. 10.—Gross receipts, expenses, and net revenue of Presidential post-offices for the fiscal year ended June 30, 1888—Continued.

NEW YORK—Continued.

Office.	Class.	Gross receipts.	Salary.	Clerk hire.	Rent, light, and fuel.	Other incidental expenses.	Free delivery.	Total expenses.	Net revenue.	Per cent. expenses to gross receipts.	Remarks.
Rondout	2	$11,491.19	$2,200.00	$1,446.70	$525.00	$23.70		$4,195.40	$7,295.79	37	
Rye	3	2,945.93	1,200.00			1.52		1,201.52	1,744.41	41	
Sag Harbor	3	3,603.10	1,400.00	208.42		3.68		1,612.10	2,081.00	44	
Salamanca	3	3,908.99	1,600.00	150.00		4.96		1,754.96	2,154.03	44	
Salem	3	3,139.33	1,300.00			2.24		1,302.24	1,837.09	41	
Sandy Hill	3	4,297.83	1,500.00			3.68		1,503.68	2,794.15	35	
Saratoga Springs	2	26,448.01	2,700.00	3,086.61	1,735.52	227.44	5,477.77	13,227.37	13,220.64	50	In Government building.
Schenectady	2	5,212.81	2,400.00	350.00		5.84		2,955.84	3,256.97	38	
Schoharie	2	18,248.89	2,400.00	2,184.73	1,228.00	75.48	2,940.68	8,968.89	9,280.09	49	
Seneca Falls	3	4,095.97	2,100.00	1,316.00	715.50	1.30		4,109.20	986.77	53	
Sherburne	3	1,086.48	1,200.00			32.63		210.32	1,309.33	32	
Silver Creek	3	4,835.80	1,200.00	16.55		.32		618.29	1,217.31	43	
Sing Sing	2	10,766.64	2,200.00	1,000.00	556.25	1.44		3,780.09	9,540.35	44	
Skaneateles	3	3,542.49	1,500.00			23.84		1,501.52	2,040.97	35	
Springville	3	3,282.54	1,300.00	200.00		1.68		1,501.68	1,780.16	42	
Stapleton	3	4,498.61	1,600.00			13.12		1,613.12	3,885.49	29	
Suspension Bridge	1	137,396.46	1,900.00	1,710.00	4,974.59	5.52		3,215.52	1,299.78	72	
Syracuse	3	7,282.47	1,900.00	16,085.00		844.54	23,276.80	48,581.83	8,814.63	35	In Government building.
Tarrytown	3	8,082.40	1,300.00			28.84		1,928.64	5,353.83	42	
Ticonderoga	3	10,066.28	1,300.00	809.80		1.28		1,301.28	1,781.21	44	
Tompkinsville	3	871.45	1,100.00			9.44		1,296.44	1,696.84	37	
Tonawanda	3	2,729.66	1,100.00		454.77	455.28		6,619.84	6,692.23	49	
Troy	1	100,312.15	3,400.00	16,892.57	3,637.80	1,077.28	22,624.47	48,632.17	51,474.66	49	
Trumansburgh	3	1,401.60	1,100.00			1.60		1,401.60	1,468.06	40	
Unadilla	3	2,154.78	1,100.00			1.12		1,101.12	619.54	51	
Union Springs	3	1,053.66	1,100.00			1.12		1,101.12	1,053.66	46	
Utica	1	61,151.47	3,100.00	9,895.00		225.84	15,173.67	28,394.81	23,756.96	44	
Walden	3	2,493.50	1,200.00	200.00		1.68		1,291.68	1,291.91	41	
Walton	3	3,874.58	1,400.00			2.40		1,600.00	2,274.58	41	
Wappinger's Falls	3	3,778.81	1,500.00	300.00		2.96		1,502.40	2,276.41	31	
Warsaw	3	6,229.49	1,800.00	300.00		1.52		2,102.96	4,129.52	44	
Warwick	3	3,378.83	1,400.00	100.00		8.84		1,501.52	1,877.41	34	
Waterford	3	8,841.38	1,400.00			6.56		1,406.84	2,437.84	37	
Waterloo	3	7,185.78	1,900.00	108.33	1,256.04	189.00		2,014.90	6,120.89	26	
Watertown	2	23,325.85	2,100.00	3,500.00		2.48	5,680.91	13,224.04	10,001.51	57	In Government building.
Waterville	3	3,922.73	1,500.00			6.82		1,502.48	3,430.20	38	
Watkins	3	4,670.15	2,000.00	243.00	499.99	2.48		1,440.87	2,720.83	40	
Waverly	3	4,450.87	2,000.00	683.00		13.44		3,178.43	6,272.44	38	
Weedsport	3	3,902.40	1,400.00			2.04		1,402.84	2,400.82	87	
Wellsville	3	6,076.20	1,700.00	400.00		4.61		2,104.04	3,971.05	15	

No. 10.—*Gross receipts, expenses, and net revenue of Presidential post-offices for the fiscal year ended June 30, 1888—Continued.*

OHIO—Continued.

Office.	Class.	Gross receipts.	Salary.	Clerk hire.	Rent, light, and fuel.	Other incidental expenses.	Free delivery.	Total expenses.	Net revenue.	Per cent. expenses to gross receipts.	Remarks.
Ashland	3	$6,319.14	$1,700.00	$405.00		$4.80		$2,109.80	$4,209.34	33	
Ashtabula	3	8,305.59	1,900.00	408.42		10.40		2,318.82	5,986.77	28	
Athens	3	6,044.69	1,700.00	508.33		8.80		2,217.13	3,827.56	37	
Barnesville	3	3,972.81	1,500.00	360.00		5.98		1,905.98	2,167.45	48	Presidential from May 22, 1888.
Batavia	3	193.37	107.14	7.50		.16		114.80	78.57	59	
Bellaire	2	9,497.97	2,000.00	1,060.00	$496.90	2.66		3,499.56	5,998.41	37	
Bellefontaine	3	6,807.99	1,840.00	800.00		8.48		2,648.48	4,199.51	38	
Bellevue	3	4,770.55	1,640.00	208.33		4.56		1,812.69	2,957.86	37	
Berea	3	3,865.36	1,500.00			4.56		1,504.56	2,360.80	39	
Bowling Green	3	4,294.24	1,300.00	209.00		2.80		1,502.80	2,791.44	35	
Bridgeport	3	3,621.74	1,400.00	204.21		5.12		1,609.33	2,012.41	44	
Bryan	3	5,175.67	1,600.00	250.00		4.88		1,854.88	3,320.59	35	
Bucyrus	3	4,481.61	1,400.00	500.00		9.04		1,909.04	2,572.57	42	
Cadiz	3	4,918.67	1,400.00	308.24		2.48		1,710.72	3,208.15	35	
Cambridge	3	5,956.18	1,700.00	347.50		10.40		2,057.90	3,898.28	35	
Camal Dover	3	8,290.96	1,300.00	150.00		3.36		1,453.36	1,827.00	44	
Canton	2	32,750.33	2,700.00	2,649.72	1,141.11	122.88	$5,967.73	12,081.44	20,148.89	38	
Cardington	3	3,105.03	1,400.00			1.12		1,401.12	1,703.91	45	
Celina	3	2,745.66	1,200.00			1.44		1,201.44	1,544.22	44	
Chagrin Falls	3	2,451.61	1,000.00	200.00		2.56		1,202.56	1,249.05	49	
Chardon	3	2,335.82	1,160.00	100.00		1.36		1,201.36	1,134.46	51	
Chillicothe	2	14,973.00	2,400.00	2,040.00	1,060.00	21.31	727.21	6,148.52	8,824.48	41	
Cincinnati	1	693,872.81	6,000.00	120,030.13		5,021.51	114,851.05	246,725.42	447,147.39	35	In Government building.
Circleville	3	7,478.19	1,900.00	500.00	822.73	17.84		2,417.84	5,060.35	32	
Cleveland	1	266,646.89	3,400.00	52,943.04	14.96	1,906.98	68,611.06	127,281.03	239,365.86	48	Do.
Clyde	3	3,471.38	1,600.00	290.00		4.08		1,894.08	1,577.30	54	
Columbiana	3	2,338.25	1,400.00	60.00		4.08		1,483.64	1,883.64	34	
Columbus	1	140,399.42	4,000.00	29,125.40	1,102.90	733.15	21,837.65	47,302.88	93,096.17	34	Do.
Columbus Grove	3	2,182.05	1,500.00	66.00		2.08		1,568.08	613.17	72	
Conneaut	3	4,547.40	1,500.00	350.00		6.44		1,856.44	2,693.41	41	
Coshocton	3	5,109.73	1,600.00	99.45		1.20		1,700.65	3,154.29	33	
Covington	3	2,242.88	1,000.00			1.30		1,100.65	1,141.72	49	
Crestline	3	2,812.66	1,200.00	350.00		3.04		1,553.04	1,259.62	55	
Cuyahoga Falls	3	4,004.88	1,400.00			1.92		1,401.92	2,602.94	35	
Dayton	1	82,773.00	3,200.00	9,849.45	3,251.91	382.58	13,418.67	30,102.51	52,670.49	38	
Defiance	3	8,761.70	1,900.00	408.32		14.72		2,323.04	6,441.66	27	
Delaware	2	12,721.49	2,300.00	1,600.00	675.00	26.40	900.92	5,502.32	7,219.17	43	
Delphos	3	4,082.43	1,300.00	250.00		4.72		1,784.72	2,327.71	43	
East Liverpool	2	10,176.23	2,100.00	960.00	724.02	404.60		4,219.52	5,946.71	41	
Eaton	3	3,611.40	1,500.00	200.00		3.68		1,703.68	1,907.72	47	
Elyria	2	10,292.31	2,100.00	900.00	656.00	17.27		3,667.27	6,625.04	36	

No. 10.—*Gross receipts, expenses, and net revenue of Presidential post-offices for the fiscal year ended June 30, 1888*—Continued.

OHIO—Continued.

Office	Class	Gross receipts.	Salary.	Clerk hire.	Rent, light, and fuel.	Other incidental expenses.	Free delivery.	Total expenses.	Net revenue.	Per cent expenses to gross receipts.	Remarks.
Niles	3	$2,279.04	$1,210.00		$706.85	$5.84		$1,205.84	$1,773.20	40	
Norwalk	2	10,693.42	2,100.00	$1,300.00	420.00	16.90	$269.19	4,691.94	6,048.48	44	
Oberlin	2	10,298.79	2,100.00	925.00		12.48		3,457.88	6,810.91	34	
Orrville	3	2,532.49	1,100.00			2.08		1,102.08	1,430.41	44	
Ottawa	3	3,278.31	1,400.00	200.00		3.84		1,603.84	1,674.47	49	
Oxford	3	3,699.75	1,500.00			4.00		1,504.00	2,395.75	39	
Painesville	2	15,147.21	2,400.00	1,072.50	397.36	496.70	1,883.51	6,210.15	10,818.65	41	
Piqua	2	13,285.60	2,300.00	1,200.00	810.00	16.64		6,210.15	7,015.45	47	
Pomeroy	3	2,935.91	1,500.00	190.00		2.56		1,692.56	2,253.35	43	
Portsmouth	3	12,673.75	2,300.00	1,500.00	371.25	25.00	2,625.01	6,821.26	5,857.49	54	
Ravenna	3	4,976.69	1,600.00	458.42		7.92		2,216.34	4,762.85	32	
Richwood	3	2,446.09	1,100.00			1.01		1,100.60	1,465.65	41	
Ripley	3	2,653.74	1,100.00	190.00	66.18	2.16		1,292.16	1,457.24	47	
Saint Clairsville	3	2,718.40	1,100.00	200.00		1.36		1,401.36	1,342.69	51	In Government building.
Saint Mary's	2	2,744.05	1,200.00	200.00				1,200.00	9,160.35	29	
Salem	3	12,689.17	2,300.00	800.00			532.64	3,719.82	7,317.78	59	
Sandusky	2	18,247.33	2,500.00	3,394.00	505.00	88.44	4,947.11	10,929.55	7,317.78	44	
Shelby	3	3,220.72	1,400.00			3.60		1,403.60	1,816.62	44	
Sidney	3	9,175.63	2,000.00	950.00		8.80		8,463.80	5,711.83	38	
Springfield	1	57,652.68	3,200.00	8,070.00	2,444.65	220.81	9,672.73	27,918.19	44,634.49	52	
Steubenville	2	14,886.69	3,000.00	1,250.00	1,068.75	12.48	3,225.72	7,991.85	6,094.74	56	
Tiffin	2	11,022.15	2,200.00	1,300.00	625.00	23.49	1,976.39	6,118.88	4,903.27	56	
Toledo	1	130,641.27	3,400.00	21,842.00	2,978.11	865.60	22,601.97	51,902.74	78,818.53	39	
Troy	3	9,468.48	2,100.00	1,040.00	500.00	11.32		3,711.32	5,758.16	40	
Urbana	3	2,975.77	1,200.00	162.00		8.78		1,365.76	1,611.01	46	
Upper Sandusky	3	4,783.93	1,100.00	200.00		6.92		1,906.51	2,878.51	38	
Van Wert	3	10,842.23	2,100.00	1,500.00	380.95	10.36		2,216.66	6,533.59	40	
Wapakoneta	3	7,407.25	1,500.00	408.42		3.28		1,963.28	2,544.97	31	
Warren	3	11,253.97	2,100.00	988.93	637.53	8.28		3,588.17	7,665.50	41	
Washington C. H	3	9,440.69	1,900.00	508.41		41.95		2,428.17	7,012.72	26	
Wauseon	3	3,627.04	1,400.00			19.76		1,400.00	2,227.04	39	
Waverly	3	2,205.61	1,000.00	200.00		2.33		1,202.33	1,003.29	55	
Wellington	2	5,010.50	1,700.00	205.83		2.80		1,908.63	3,101.87	38	
Wellston	3	3,192.28	1,200.00	149.85		1.66		1,351.61	1,840.77	42	
Wellsville	2	5,386.29	1,600.00		717.00	13.28		1,613.28	3,773.01	28	
Westerville	3	2,573.80	1,200.00	100.00		1.12		1,201.12	1,278.27	47	
West Liberty	3	4,104.00	1,400.00			.16		1,500.16	2,603.84	37	
Willoughby	3	2,417.90	1,200.00			2.80		1,202.80	1,624.70	43	
Wilmington	2	5,311.74	1,800.00	225.00		6.24		1,831.24	3,480.50	34	
Wooster	2	11,124.87	2,300.00	1,125.00	717.00	44.10	1,890.50	6,076.02	5,048.85	55	

Xenia	2	10,561.25	2,300.00	1,400.00	545.00	6.29	1,968.44	6,239.73	4,321.52	59
Youngstown	2	25,947.39	2,640.00	2,862.50	1,560.00	597.03	6,031.18	13,500.71	12,356.68	52
Zanesville	2	30,583.30	2,700.00	3,066.36	995.38	88.04	5,034.74	11,914.52	18,666.78	39
Total		2,442,240.99	213,819.23	307,480.30	34,179.29	12,178.62	314,574.13	912,531.77	1,529,918.82	37

OREGON.

Albany	3	5,082.02	1,500.00	208.33		7.04		1,715.37	3,366.65	34
Ashland	3	2,866.41	1,000.00	216.66		2.24		1,218.90	1,647.51	42
Astoria	3	8,154.60	1,900.00	708.33		8.90		2,617.29	2,540.71	31	In Government building.
Baker City	3	4,119.85	1,500.00	499.85		2.72		2,092.27	2,117.48	40
Corvallis	3	3,371.67	1,400.00	299.73		4.08		1,703.81	1,667.86	35
East Portland	3	4,907.50	1,500.00	216.85		11.76		1,729.61	3,178.89	37
Eugene City	2	4,352.96	1,500.00	110.00		2.88		1,602.58	2,750.08	73
Jacksonville	3	1,503.63	1,000.00	99.97		.32		1,100.59	402.74	42
La Grand	3	872.25	368.12			.72		368.85	503.40	29
McMinnville	3	1,654.81	301.50			1.13		303.32	731.49	58
Oregon City	3	2,340.03	1,200.00	100.00		3.64		1,303.64	926.59	33
Pendleton	1	5,663.00	1,200.00	450.00		11.06	9,565.33	1,961.06	8,991.64	29
Portland	3	91,413.61	2,200.00	13,205.00		561.06		28,221.40	65,092.11	56
Roseburg	3	2,207.56	1,190.00					1,300.00	1,007.56	42
Salem	2	11,524.43	2,340.00	1,340.00	1.00	2.83	1,253.45	4,876.78	6,617.05	42
The Dalles	3	6,597.85	1,700.00	341.86		8.88		2,050.54	4,547.31	31
Total		156,314.88	22,970.33	17,766.19	1.00	678.51	10,758.78	52,174.81	104,140.07	42

PENNSYLVANIA.

Allegheny	1	60,506.90	3,100.00	5,567.63	1,480.00	977.11	17,943.71	29,067.85	31,529.05	48
Allentown	2	26,252.64	2,800.00	3,005.83	1,380.00	67.80	6,174.93	13,169.65	13,082.99	50
Altoona	2	21,240.38	2,500.00	2,357.04	1,075.00	76.62	6,421.31	13,439.97	10,850.39	53
Ashland	3	4,534.67	1,620.00			5.36		1,605.36	2,929.61	43
Athens	3	3,817.01	1,500.00	100.00		3.30		1,603.20	2,243.84	49
Bangor	3	2,443.32	1,200.00			8.96		1,198.96	1,240.84	43
Beaver Falls	2	2,048.61	1,140.00	850.00	433.97	21.96	2,345.85	1,208.48	1,430.66	53
Bedford	3	4,749.07	1,200.00	162.00		6.52		1,767.52	2,981.55	37
Bellefonte	3	4,462.07	1,940.00	225.00		8.16		2,133.16	2,328.87	25
Berwick	3	3,101.35	1,300.00			2.72		1,302.72	1,798.63	42
Bethlehem	2	12,785.78	2,300.00	1,210.00	780.00	23.85	1,648.40	1,435.60	6,822.84	47
Blairsville	3	3,055.09	1,300.00	150.00		5.00		1,455.00	1,599.49	41
Bloomsburgh	3	6,196.43	1,860.00	243.00		7.76		2,050.76	4,115.67	33
Blossburgh	3	2,369.00	1,080.00	200.00		1.70		1,201.70	1,167.84	50
Braddock	3	4,461.23	1,618.00			19.20		1,619.20	2,842.03	36

Presidential from February 18, 1868.
Presidential from March 13, 1868.

In Government building.

No. 10.—*Gross receipts, expenses, and net revenue of Presidential post-offices for the fiscal year ended June 30, 188-—Continued.*

PENNSYLVANIA—Continued.

Office.	Class.	Gross receipts.	Salary.	Clerk hire.	Rent, light, and fuel.	Other incidental expenses.	Free delivery.	Total expenses.	Net revenue.	Per cent. expenses to gross receipts.	Remarks.
Bradford	2	$9,329.48	$2,600.00	$3,060.27	$724.32	$30.76	$4,029.11	$10,474.66	$9,854.82	52	
Bristol	3	5,969.56	1,700.00	180.10		0.52		882.59	4,100.04	32	
Brookville	3	6,310.12	1,600.00	508.42		0.35		2,117.78	4,192.34	31	
Brownsville	3	3,420.88	1,400.00			10.72		1,410.72	2,010.16	41	
Bryn Mawr	3	2,905.02	1,400.00			7.84		1,407.84	1,497.18	37	
Butler	3	7,897.90	1,890.00	268.39		17.44		2,125.83	5,771.47	27	
Cannonsburgh	3	1,633.29	1,100.00			4.56		1,104.56	528.73	42	
Canton	3	2,862.90	1,100.00			0.90		1,290.50	1,052.00	43	
Carbondale	3	8,40.52	1,400.00	254.21	331.31	9.12		1,963.33	4,857.19	29	
Carlisle	2	10,966.13	2,200.00	1,420.99		28.74	1,940.42	6,000.46	4,605.67	57	
Catasauqua	2	3,888.35	2,000.00			4.64		1,491.61	2,463.71	38	
Chambersburgh	2	11,287.01	2,400.00	1,500.60	490.00	50.67		5,453.99	5,313.62	53	
Chester	2	17,084.81	2,000.00	2,425.00	626.00	0.64	3,231.90	8,453.70	8,631.05	49	
Clarion	3	4,243.67	1,400.00	162.00		0.64		1,563.64	2,680.03	37	
Clearfield	3	6,044.40	1,700.00	150.00		4.00		1,166.00	3,110.40	37	
Coatesville	3	5,294.21	1,700.00	200.00		16.00		2,716.96	3,310.21	38	
Columbia	3	8,137.34	1,740.00	690.00		12.96		2,021.90	5,430.38	35	
Connellsville	3	6,850.91	1,700.10	84.43		1.04		922.74	3,820.52	45	
Conneautville	3	1,027.77	837.81	62.70		6.99		1,710.25	1,105.03	45	
Conshohocken	3	7,06.37	1,400.00	212.33		5.99		1,710.25	2,073.12	39	
Corry	2	854.04	2,100.00	1,200.00	437.39	17.88		3,755.27	6,098.77	51	
Coudersport	3	2,066.12	1,200.00	102.00		1.12		1,253.12	1,363.01	53	
Curwensville	3	2,686.64	1,100.00	250.00		0.98		1,350.96	1,294.68	40	
Danville	2	8,566.53	2,100.00	900.00	431.25	1.56		3,332.81	5,233.72	40	
Downingtown	3	2,987.15	1,200.00	200.00		2.65		1,402.45	2,164.67	33	
Doylestown	3	6,715.79	1,600.00	300.00		5.76		1,905.76	3,810.03	38	
Du Bois	3	5,880.88	2,600.00	819.00		0.98		3,439.61	3,426.70	38	
Easton	2	23,888.05	2,600.00	2,563.79	1,304.95	178.27	6,672.50	13,380.61	9,513.44	49	
Ebensburgh	3	2,453.30	1,100.00	100.00		4.48		1,204.48	1,258.82	50	
Edinborough	3	1,188.61	1,100.00			0.90		1,100.10	1,068.01	45	
Eldred	3	2,240.42	1,100.00			1.36		1,101.36	1,239.06	48	
Emlenton	3	2,422.88	1,100.10	90.00		2.08		1,192.08	1,206.99	48	
Emporium	3	1,040.01	450.37			2.96		1,102.96	1,320.92	50	
Ephrata	3	1,940.00	450.37			0.72		450.89	589.02	43	
Erie	2	46,904.00	3,000.00	6,500.60	1,281.89	266.13	12,256.03	23,396.66	23,396.44	50	Presidential from February 2, 1888.
Everett	3	2,387.64	1,000.00	100.00	1.36			1,101.36	1,226.18	47	
Franklin	2	10,604.87	2,200.00	1,200.10	415.63	20.06		3,838.01	6,629.36	38	
Freeland	3	97.77	65.93		4.48	0.08		66.01	81.76	80	Presidential from June 7, 1888.
Freeport	3	2,171.29	1,110.00			7.60		1,066.91	1,081.91	44	
Gettysburgh	3	5,741.18	1,700.00	800.00				3,607.60	2,232.58	47	
Greencastle	3	2,146.36	1,000.00			2.96		1,002.96	1,143.40	47	

No. 10.—*Gross receipts, expenses, and net revenue of Presidential post-offices for the fiscal year ended June 30, 1888—Continued.*

PENNSYLVANIA—Continued.

Office.	Class.	Gross receipts.	Salary.	Clerk hire.	Rent, light, and fuel.	Other incidental expenses.	Free delivery.	Total expenses.	Net revenue.	Per cent. expenses to gross receipts.	Remarks.
Nanticoke	3	$4,324.89	$1,500.00	$82.15		63.76		$1,586.91	$2,787.68	87	
New Brighton	3	5,445.25	1,600.00			15.20		615.20	3,830.05	30	
New Castle	2	14,632.47	2,400.00	2,000.00	$700.00	43.52	$2,445.91	7,591.43	6,461.04	54	Presidential from February 5, 1888.
Newport	3	2,341.75	1,200.00	314.00		2.98		1,502.98	1,338.79	53	
Newtown	3	288.71	600.00	110.00		1.08		1,101.08	1,187.08	48	
Neville	3	940.17	462.85	121.10		.40		526.35	423.83	55	
No return	3	14,796.73	2,400.00	1,200.00	1,000.00	37.24	3,232.25	7,809.49	6,927.28	53	
North East	3	3,625.00	1,300.00			1.42		1,301.92	2,827.68	36	
Northumberland	2	3,643.42	1,100.00			8.04		1,103.04	940.39	34	
Oil City	2	14,185.20	2,400.00	2,000.90	518.00	23.44		4,923.64	9,221.78	35	
Oxford	3	3,412.07	362.64	180.00		2.42		1,582.42	1,829.65	46	
Parker's Landing	3	68.91						983.00	818.31	53	
Philadelphia	1	1,671,868.23	6,000.00	315,745.44	5,361.63	10,076.35	444,984.34	782,189.76	1,089,699.47	43	Presidential from February 20, 1888. In Government building.
Phillipsburg	3	7,114.29	1,700.00	198.44		6.70		1,905.22	5,309.07	26	
Phoenixville	2	7,427.72	1,700.00	300.10	927.00	10.16		2,110.16	5,317.56	29	Do.
Pittsburgh	1	412,666.21	3,800.00	68,694.50	630.00	22.89	80,899.76	158,550.29	254,115.92	38	
Pittston	3	12,131.43	2,300.00	1,175.60				4,148.89	7,982.63	34	
Plymouth	3	6,441.24	1,000.00			6.98		1,605.98	4,835.98	25	
Pottstown	2	11,241.87	2,100.00	740.90	178.70	25.87		9,045.63	8,196.24	27	
Pottsville	2	10,357.53	2,400.00	1,937.50	768.00	55.96	3,924.12	9,077.80	7,279.93	56	
Punxsutawney	3	2,791.79	1,000.00	161.00		2.83		1,102.33	2,689.47	29	
Reading	1	50,010.89	3,100.00	7,200.00	1,576.00	193.15	12,401.61	24,495.47	25,644.43	49	
Renovo	3	3,915.38	1,000.00			4.82		1,604.82	2,411.04	38	
Reynoldsville	3	2,960.40	1,200.00			2.10		1,262.10	1,407.24	47	
Ridgway	3	3,535.40	1,572.00	190.00		14.66		1,422.06	1,759.12	47	
Rochester	3	3,025.40	1,140.00	7.10		1.50		1,140.30	2,206.34	48	
Saint Mary's	3	2,317.70	1,100.00	164.59				1,149.99	1,218.50	57	
Sayre	3	1,031.68	444.36			1.00		445.85	857.58	43	
Scotdale	2	3,787.32	2,404.00	7,015.74	2,856.10	161.99	17,075.30	29,677.93	2,380.70	43	Presidential from February 5, 1888.
Scranton	3	51,945.26	1,100.00			7.12		1,407.12	22,367.92	57	
Selin's Grove	2	2,221.08	1,100.00			8.84		1,103.84	1,117.24	50	
Sewickley	3	3,101.49	1,400.00			13.92		1,413.92	1,747.57	46	
Shamokin	3	8,406.55	1,900.00	533.15		10.40		2,916.40	6,492.95	29	
Sharon	2	7,617.31	1,900.00			10.24		2,363.39	5,573.92	43	
Sharpsburgh	3	2,563.04	1,100.00			12.60		1,112.60	1,461.64	43	
Sharpsville	3	1,656.40	807.07			8.16		967.85	628.55	61	Presidential from October 7, 1887.
Sheffield	3	562.23	397.80					397.85	194.88	21	Presidential from March 11, 1888.
Shenandoah	3	8,583.44	1,600.00	500.00		6.98		1,606.98	6,724.56	44	
Shippensburgh	3	4,007.78	1,600.00			4.29		1,803.56	3,204.56	45	
Slatington	3	2,472.45	1,100.00			2.43		1,192.43	1,380.97	45	

No. 10.—*Gross receipts, expenses, and net revenue of Presidential post-offices for the fiscal year ended June 30, 1889*—Continued.

SOUTH CAROLINA.

Office.	Class.	Gross receipts.	Salary.	Clerk hire.	Rent, light, and fuel.	Other incidental expenses.	Free delivery.	Total expenses.	Net revenue.	Per cent expenses to gross receipts.	Remarks.
Aiken	3	$4,514.93	$1,500.00	$316.95		$5.44		$1,822.10	$2,691.93	40	
Anderson C. H.	3	3,695.66	1,500.00	200.00		1.52		1,701.52	1,994.14	46	
Beaufort	3	3,591.85	1,500.00	200.00		3.60		1,703.00	1,888.25	47	Presidential from June 1, 1888.
Bennetsville	3	140.04	82.42			.08		82.50	67.54	59	
Camden	3	2,760.05	1,200.00	160.00		1.92		1,361.92	1,458.13	47	
Charleston	1	66,221.74	3,200.00	11,345.50		250.18	$13,336.65	27,132.83	39,089.41	40	In Government building.
Chester	3	4,125.40	1,300.00	150.00		2.34		1,452.34	2,673.06	35	
Columbia	2	17,840.26	2,600.00	2,500.00		39.18	2,078.15	7,117.33	10,722.93	40	Do.
Darlington C. H.	3	2,631.29	1,000.00			1.12		1,001.12	1,630.17	38	
Florence	3	2,597.52	1,200.00	150.00		2.24		1,352.24	1,245.58	52	
Georgetown	3	2,301.88	1,100.00	104.12		4.08		1,208.20	1,093.63	52	
Greenville C. H.	3	10,980.08	1,100.00	946.00		19.54		3,174.69	6,985.68	53	
Marion	3	2,150.00	1,500.00	100.00	$402.00	1.60		1,101.60	1,048.48	51	
Newberry C. H.	3	4,081.94	1,300.00	210.00		2.40		1,702.40	2,279.54	43	
Orangeburgh C. H.	3	2,819.38	1,100.00	162.37		8.24		1,100.00	1,578.12	44	
Rock Hill	3	5,841.73	1,700.00					1,465.61	1,519.39	43	
Spartanburgh C. H.	3	5,590.44	1,100.00	600.00		8.84		2,305.84	3,284.60	41	
Sumter C. H.	3	4,601.11	1,600.00	208.42		8.04		1,711.46	2,889.65	37	
Winnsborough	3	2,368.05	1,100.00	76.00		1.92		1,177.92	1,060.12	51	Presidential from June 20, 1888.
Yorkville	3	70.00	13.74	25.00		.53		39.25	30.74	56	
Total		145,468.07	27,366.16	17,384.16	402.00	349.80	14,414.80	59,853.98	85,549.12	41	

TENNESSEE.

Office.	Class.	Gross receipts.	Salary.	Clerk hire.	Rent, light, and fuel.	Other incidental expenses.	Free delivery.	Total expenses.	Net revenue.	Per cent expenses to gross receipts.	Remarks.
Bristol	3	5,637.43	1,600.00	216.67		5.76		1,822.43	3,805.00	32	
Brownsville	3	3,079.66	1,200.00	360.00		2.72		1,662.72	1,476.84	52	
Chattanooga	2	53,215.79	3,000.00	9,929.97		390.14	6,823.66	17,768.77	35,457.02	32	
Clarksville	3	9,625.65	2,000.00	751.32	$625.00	11.92		3,652.44	6,873.21	45	
Cleveland	3	3,467.05	1,300.00	250.00	290.20	6.64		1,556.64	1,930.41	32	
Columbia	3	7,492.64	1,900.00	617.69		6.16		2,423.85	5,068.79	32	
Dayton	3	1,035.71	425.10			.64		425.74	606.97	41	Presidential from February 11, 1888.
Dyersburg	3	2,444.54	1,100.00	300.00		1.20		1,101.20	1,343.34	45	
Fayetteville	3	2,513.13	1,100.00	290.03		2.64		1,402.61	1,102.43	50	
Franklin	3	3,098.43	1,300.00			2.40		1,602.40	1,584.03	49	
Gallatin	3	3,807.51	1,300.00	248.85		2.40		1,551.25	1,756.23	47	
Greenville	3	2,372.46	1,100.00	200.00		3.12		1,302.12	1,069.34	55	
Jackson	3	8,040.44	1,900.00	1,000.00		13.44		2,913.44	5,127.00	36	In Government building.

Office								Remarks
Johnson City	3	1,191.57	472.29	......	......	75.00	1.66	548.97	642.90	48	Presidential from October 27, 1887.
Knoxville	3	46,873.48	2,960.00	5,095.00	129.54	15,366.10	80,217.88	24	In Government building.
Lebanon	3	3,719.06	1,400.00	450.00	2.88	1,962.88	960.47	51	
McMinnville	3	2,884.97	1,580.00	300.00	1.16	1,462.18	616.41	59	Do.
Memphis	1	116,680.47	3,383.00	16,685.00	373.19	96,145.00	80,610.71	59	
Morristown	3	3,231.45	1,800.00	350.00	2.66	1,611.07	699.59	52	Do.
Murfreesborough	3	6,002.45	1,800.00	350.00	2.66	1,961.68	3,126.77	48	
Nashville	1	112,862.12	3,900.00	19,857.99	518.13	89,696.95	72,702.48	44	
Paris	3	2,701.29	1,100.00	......	1.52	1,851.53	1,438.77	48	
Pulaski	3	3,605.66	1,460.00	350.00	3.44	1,782.44	1,966.07	47	
Shelbyville	3	3,789.99	1,400.00	350.00	3.92	1,708.93	1,277.01	49	
Trenton	3	2,679.10	1,100.00	......	2.19	1,430.60	1,652.01	57	
Tullahoma	3	3,162.61	1,800.00	117.00	2.60	1,706.50	2,905.49	45	
Union City	3	4,012.99	1,800.00	293.63	4.56	1,102.20	2,905.33	44	
Winchester	3	2,468.68	1,100.00	......	3.20			35	
Total		418,761.96	43,066.39	55,101.90	914.90	1,611.68	147,434.36	271,487.00		

TEXAS.

Office								Remarks
Abilene	3	4,311.11	1,700.00	394.30	......	2.56	2,066.76	2,204.35	46	Presidential from June 26, 1888.
Albany	3	1,672.50	1,100.00	50.00	......	.96	1,150.96	721.54	61	In Government building.
Alvarado	3	168.78	16.11	......	......	......	16.11	143.67	10	
Austin	3	31,680.48	2,900.00	7,646.45	6,466.43	146.81	17,046.19	14,612.36	64	
Beaumont	3	4,244.86	1,400.00	300.00	......	1.66	1,701.60	2,548.36	40	
Belton	3	4,094.10	1,700.00	406.83	......	4.34	2,113.67	2,671.53	56	
Bonham	3	4,637.20	1,600.00	520.60	......	4.44	1,495.94	3,125.72	51	
Brackettville	3	5,198.11	1,700.00	82.16	......	8.16	1,692.72	1,116.67	44	
Brenham	3	4,922.25	1,490.00	575.16	......	8.23	810.47	1,311.78	43	
Brownsville	3	3,168.09	1,600.00	205.15	......	1.66	1,801.66	1,366.40	87	
Brownwood	3	4,347.08	1,900.00	150.00	......	2.04	1,782.04	484.04	44	
Bryan	3	2,986.01	1,300.00	400.00	......	2.64	1,692.66	682.88	70	
Burnet	3	2,983.37	821.43	......	......	.96	371.76	178.61	41	
Calvert	3	550.96	1,800.00	50.00	......	.66	1,560.66	1,382.73	39	
Cameron	3	2,782.80	2,111.00	250.00	......	8.20	2,111.89	2,169.19	55	
Clarksville	3	5,370.71	1,700.00	466.82	......		1,190.66	1,653.66	61	
Cleburne	3	2,158.66	1,100.00	......	......		1,100.00	1,632.66	40	
Colorado	3	4,385.19	1,700.00	300.00	......	2.65	1,702.66	464.97	56	
Columbus	3	4,976.15	1,100.00	215.15	......	1.13	1,447.13	461.66	37	
Corpus Christi	3	10,476.15	1,800.00	600.00	......	7.66	2,308.66	7,197.77	44	
Corsicana	1	3,436.37	1,900.00	......	......	8.92	1,952.92	1,905.85	39	
Cuero	3	93,385.39	8,100.00	10,648.98	1,011.99	264.04	23,964.52	42,966.74	62	
Dallas	3	2,653.99	1,300.00	385.00	......	1.44	1,651.44	1,402.35	63	Presidential from March 6, 1888.
Decatur	3	12,444.34	1,300.00	2,655.66	224.33	71.17	6,090.13	5,945.22	44	
Denison City	3	4,130.30	1,500.00	900.00	......	3.80	90.69	2,829.00	38	
Denton	3	5,049.06	1,052.50	100.97	......	.99	1,162.37	1,946.78		

No. 10.—*Gross receipts, expenses, and net revenue of Presidential post-offices for the fiscal year ended June 30, 1888*—Continued.

TEXAS—Continued.

Office	Class	Gross receipts.	Salary.	Clerk hire.	Rent, light, and fuel.	Other incidental expenses.	Free delivery.	Total expenses.	Net revenue.	Per cent. expenses to gross receipts.	Remarks.
El Paso	2	$14,241.57	$2,400.00	$2,500.00	$697.00	$161.87	$2,091.24	$7,849.72	96,891.84	44	
Ennis	3	3,491.43	2,400.00			1.68		2,401.68	2,089.75	40	
Fort Worth	2	29,440.49	2,700.00	5,900.00	371.35	107.49	6,853.12	14,831.88	14,608.61	50	
Gainesville	1	55,166.98	2,000.00	920.00	74.09	7.12		3,010.21	6,540.99	32	
Galveston	1	2,372.23	3,200.00	10,777.14		122.36	9,478.06	23,487.56	31,673.77	43	In Government building.
Gatesville	3	2,440.72	1,200.00	200.00		1.52		1,400.00	972.22	49	
Georgetown	3	2,434.05	1,500.00	175.00				1,676.53	1,764.20	49	
Gonzales	3	2,434.05	1,100.00	250.00		1.38		1,351.38	1,081.68	55	
Greenville	3	6,176.78	1,200.00	350.00		5.92		1,955.92	4,220.88	32	
Hempstead	3	3,230.34	1,200.00	108.33		.72		1,309.05	921.29	58	
Henderson	3	1,887.48	1,000.00	450.00		.16		1,450.16	437.32	78	
Henrietta	3	3,268.43	1,200.00	230.89		2.40		1,432.29	835.13	64	
Hillsborough	3	2,998.73	1,200.00	25.00		2.83		1,227.83	2,353.41	49	
Honey Grove	3	4,092.21	1,400.00	154.21		2.74		1,556.95	2,476.81	32	
Houston	2	26,308.64	2,500.00	9,140.00	1,359.70	272.96	8,626.35	22,186.91	14,110.08	61	
Huntsville	3	3,566.35	1,400.00	60.00		1.13		1,661.12	228.61	40	
Jefferson	3	3,892.13	1,400.00	208.35		4.90		1,612.35	2,245.00	43	
La Grange	3	4,333.88	1,400.00	350.00		2.66		1,955.36	1,039.46	57	
Lampasas	3	3,055.35	1,700.00	250.00		5.36		1,955.36	2,878.53	45	
Laredo	3	6,086.16	1,700.00	742.12		6.06		2,448.20	4,859.96	37	
Longview	3	3,055.35	1,300.00	312.64		2.32		1,614.96	1,440.39	37	
Luling	3	2,047.19	1,100.00	90.00		1.92		1,191.92	865.77	58	
McKinney	3	4,913.61	1,500.00	125.00		4.14		1,629.14	3,284.47	34	
Marlin	3	1,243.66	1,200.00			.48		1,200.48	1,043.18	34	
Marshall	3	9,072.18	2,000.00	1,275.83		7.52		3,283.34	5,688.84	37	
Mexia	3	2,106.63	1,357.69	800.00		1.28		2,158.97	1,447.85	50	
Mineola	3	3,144.43	1,200.00	200.00		1.16		1,301.82	1,302.56	50	
Navasota	3	108.98	53.43					53.43	77.26	76	
Orange	3	3,274.60	1,300.00	208.43		3.00		1,513.42	1,464.18	30	
Palestine	3	5,799.13	1,100.00	700.00	243.60	2.98		2,100.00	1,700.57	32	
Paris	2	10,708.27	1,700.00	1,253.52		10.24		2,403.92	3,865.20	42	
Rockdale	3	1,667.19	1,200.00	103.50		.88		1,304.38	662.81	66	
San Angelo	3	3,905.71	2,000.00	104.15		2.40		1,606.56	2,200.15	43	
San Antonio	2	36,029.64	2,800.00	6,909.00	1,683.12	416.00	9,325.44	21,123.61	10,405.03	58	
San Marcos	3	3,146.01	1,400.00	160.00		1.44		1,561.44	1,047.57	47	
Sherman	2	12,296.84	2,300.00	1,500.00	411.27	11.45	3,672.96	6,825.68	6,211.26	50	Presidential from June 1, 1888.
Sulphur Springs	3	3,263.43	1,100.00	200.00		2.54		1,102.56	2,160.86	34	
Tyler	3	3,691.05	1,400.00	150.00		1.28		1,601.28	1,990.07	43	
Temple	3	4,323.08	1,600.00	90.00		6.08		1,766.08	2,449.00	41	
Terrell	3	5,352.36	1,800.00			9.84		1,709.83	3,646.53	32	

Office									Remarks
Texarkana	3	3,151.40	964.40	425.28	5.04	999.44	3,191.96	31	Presidential from October 4, 1887.
Tyler	3	7,824.17	1,800.00	100.00	10.16	2,235.43	8,068.76	21	
Uvalde	3	1,757.84	1,000.00	460.00	.48	1,100.48	657.86	32	In Government building.
Victoria	3	3,791.95	1,500.00	460.00	7.76	1,907.76	1,883.90	58	
Waco	2	22,269.67	2,600.00	4,000.00	32.54	7,432.49	14,880.18	33	In Government building.
Waxahachie	3	4,547.33	1,500.00	560.00		2,000.00	2,547.33	44	
Weatherford	3	5,782.05	1,650.00	575.00	2.82	2,547.83	3,354.73	38	
Wichita Falls	3	3,493.97	1,200.00	250.00	1.28	1,431.28	3,963.69	38	
Total		577,582.92	117,062.25	79,431.46	1,881.32	262,259.39	315,363.53	45	

UTAH.

Office									Remarks
Logan	3	2,768.87	1,100.00	180.00	2.64	1,282.64	1,485.73	46	
Ogden City	3	16,060.59	2,500.00	2,900.00	88.46	5,932.46	10,032.13	37	
Park City	3	3,018.20	1,500.00	166.43	1.95	1,910.11	1,986.09	41	
Provo City	3	3,065.85	2,000.00			1,163.36	2,984.99	30	
Salt Lake City	2	43,634.94		1,200.00	156.15	17,146.23	25,488.71	40	
Total		68,396.45	9,000.00	6,200.00	197.29	27,197.80	41,198.65	41	

VERMONT.

Office									Remarks
Barre	3	6,042.34	1,600.00	280.00	8.13	1,863.12	4,339.12	30	
Bellows Falls	3	8,269.28	1,800.00	610.00	.92	2,418.92	5,840.36	29	
Bennington	3	8,451.01	1,500.00	250.00	.80	2,036.80	6,304.21	24	
Bradford	3	1,977.15	1,500.00	61.17	.88	1,585.05	391.10	53	
Brandon	3	2,111.90	1,400.00	280.00	4.40	1,704.40	407.50	30	
Brattleborough	3	15,666.30	1,400.00	1,000.00	1.30	7,718.40	7,942.90	29	
Burlington	2	41,685.11	2,500.00	3,366.00	68.93	12,350.28	29,342.83	28	
Fair Haven	3	3,250.57	1,100.00		8.13	1,503.12	2,490.40	49	
Ludlow	3	4,782.55	1,100.00	500.00	.88	1,100.88	1,148.99	49	
Middlebury	3	10,858.08	2,300.00	1,360.00	2.40	2,162.40	2,690.15	38	In Government building.
Montpelier	3	8,685.89	2,300.00		1.02	6,421.18	4,336.90	38	
Newport	3	2,430.91	1,100.00	950.00	1.68	1,401.66	2,385.71	40	
Northfield	3	561.17	1,400.00		.16	1,100.16	1,380.76	43	
Poultney	3	17,772.63	2,500.00	2,800.00	2.00	1,402.00	2,159.27	54	
Rutland	2	10,560.22	2,100.00	485.00	56.17	4,380.00	8,174.85	28	
Saint Albans	3	7,906.01	2,100.00		16.76	8,737.66	6,131.22	41	In Government building.
Saint Johnsbury	3	3,431.41	1,100.00	625.90	2.64	1,130.72	6,058.35	40	Do.
Springfield	3	3,428.50	1,400.00	90.00	1.72	1,400.01	1,524.21	44	
Swanton	3	2,992.40	1,300.00	203.57	.14	1,300.98	1,044.48	44	
Waterbury	3	2,772.24	1,400.00	209.00	.88	1,601.76	1,691.58	44	
West Randolph	3	3,925.97	1,300.00	208.42	1.78	1,601.78	2,270.48	44	
White River Junction	3				2.90	1,511.23	2,014.75	43	

No. 10.—*Gross receipts, expenses, and net revenue of Presidential post-offices for the fiscal year ended June 30, 1888*—Continued.

VERMONT—Continued.

Office.	Class.	Gross receipts.	Salary.	Clerk hire.	Rent, light, and fuel.	Other incidental expenses.	Free delivery.	Total expenses.	Net revenue.	Per cent. expenses to gross receipts.	Remarks.
						$3.02		$1,653.92	$1,587.51	51	In Government building. Presidential from February 14, 1888.
						.91		250.21	312.79	44	
								1 704.50	1,751.20	49	

Suffolk	3	4,015.43	1,400.00	200.00		5.92		1,603.02	2,400.51	40
University of Virginia	3	3,716.92	1,400.00			12.08		1,412.08	2,304.84	58
Warrenton	8	7,784.13	1,500.00	350.00		8.76		853.76	1,920.36	49
Winchester	8	7,532.82	1,900.00	1,000.00		14.24		2,914.24	4,618.58	39
Woodstock	8	3,036.95	1,200.00	150.00		1.84		1,151.84	885.11	67
Wytheville	8	4,162.87	1,400.00	350.00		4.00		1,754.00	2,408.87	42
Total		398,693.37	56,525.81	56,526.94	2,040.00	1,558.39	53,031.44	169,652.64	229,040.73	43

WASHINGTON TERRITORY.

Cheney	8	1,869.20	1,100.00	204.09		0.56		1,301.65	554.55	71
Colfax	8	5,822.66	1,900.00	960.00		0.72		2,360.72	3,115.91	58
Dayton	3	3,685.67	1,400.00	300.00		1.63		1,701.52	1,985.35	53
Ellensburgh	3	4,270.67	1,500.00	8.33		1.36		1,509.69	860.98	68
North Yakima	3	2,858.58	1,000.00	500.00		.88		1,500.88	857.70	42
Olympia	3	4,963.96	1,600.00	533.82		4.58		2,027.88	925.98	59
Port Townsend	3	4,015.17	1,400.00	610.00		.86		2,010.88	1,055.29	52
Seattle	3	18,384.58	2,100.00	2,162.50	572.86	22.16	1,494.93	6,281.42	12,832.04	23
Spokane Falls	3	19,455.87	2,100.00	2,706.62	641.70	64.96	768.15	6,053.54	12,175.45	22
Sprague	3	3,060.46	2,100.00			.96		1,200.96	1,897.53	39
Vancouver	2	19,283.83	1,200.00	1,421.43	360.00	8.40		5,607.20	13,456.63	51
Walla Walla	2	10,667.18	2,100.00	1,500.00	620.00	11.28	1,810.37	4,231.28	6,435.90	40
Total		100,412.23	20,000.00	10,753.29	2,194.65	126.55	4,073.45	37,147.94	63,264.29	37	In Government building.

WEST VIRGINIA.

Charleston	2	13,592.26	2,300.00	1,344.57		14.37	1,491.49	5,150.43	8,441.83	38	
Charlestown	3	3,242.53	1,500.00	108.43		3.86		1,611.78	630.74	58	
Clarksburgh	3	4,778.44	1,600.00	408.43		9.86		2,017.78	2,746.66	42	
Fairmont	3	3,294.98	1,200.00	250.00		8.92		1,454.56	2,370.43	50	
Grafton	3	6,745.18	1,400.00	203.38				1,614.70	2,129.05	31	
Huntington	3	6,745.19	1,400.00	491.21		14.40		2,101.21	643.97	31	
Martinsburgh	3	6,675.87	1,800.00	359.37		3.04		2,164.67	4,360.88	85	
Morgantown	3	2,773.95	1,200.00	150.00		3.60		1,253.64	1,4.30.83	47	
Moundsville	3	14,918.54	2,400.00	2,230.00		88.16	1,928.18	6,614.34	8,362.20	44	Do.
Parkersburgh	3	2,968.50	1,800.00	8.42		8.28		1,311.70	1,656.80	44	
Piedmont	3	2,898.09	1,000.00	150.00		3.68		1,183.68	1,653.31	41	
Point Pleasant	3	2,925.17	1,300.00			3.52		1,303.62	1,619.65	45	
Wallaburgh	2	2,686.71	1,100.00	181.00		8.20		1,287.20	1,399.51	47	Do.
Weston	2	2,686.71	3,000.00	9,400.00		224.68	9,222.45	21,847.13	21,966.22	50	
Wheeling	2	43,833.35									
Total		118,039.77	23,900.00	15,211.70		335.53	12,642.12	52,089.35	65,050.42	43	

No. 10.—Gross receipts, expenses, and net revenue of Presidential post-offices for the fiscal year ended June 30, 1888—Continued.

WISCONSIN.

Office.	Class.	Gross receipts.	Salary.	Clerk hire.	Rent, light, and fuel.	Other incidental expenses.	Free delivery.	Total expenses.	Net revenue.	Per cent expenses to gross receipts.	Remarks.
Antigo	3	$4,292.50	$1,400.00	$290.00		$2.72		$1,692.72	$2,599.78	39	
Appleton	2	13,733.48	2,200.00	1,615.00	$960.00	5.81	$1,206.94	4,147.75	7,590.73	45	
Ashland	2	14,665.10	2,000.00	1,700.00	568.99	18.98	1,651.15	6,585.61	8,565.81	41	
Augusta	3	2,216.14	1,000.00			.64		1,000.64	1,215.50	44	
Baraboo	3	6,183.93	1,600.00	506.43		3.76		2,112.19	4,071.74	33	
Beaver Dam	3	4,996.06	1,600.00			1.92		1,601.92	3,394.13	32	
Beloit	3	10,558.64	1,600.00	1,232.21	940.00	12.96		4,397.27	6,166.37	41	
Berlin	3	4,363.40	616.80	162.00		2.64		1,784.64	2,598.76	43	
Black River Falls	3	4,172.10	1,980.00	300.00		2.23		1,892.23	2,378.18	53	
Boscobel	3	2,288.17	1,100.00	100.00		.21		1,200.21	1,087.96	52	
Brodhead	3	2,763.31	1,200.00	154.17		1.12		1,355.29	1,533.02	49	
Burlington	3	2,857.85	1,200.00			1.60		1,201.60	1,656.25	42	
Chippewa Falls	2	10,024.60	2,000.00	1,200.00	446.00	192.29		3,838.29	6,186.31	38	
Clinton	3	2,208.85	1,180.00	154.17		.72		1,334.89	931.96	59	
Columbus	3	6,466.74	1,690.00			2.66		1,692.66	4,964.08	26	
Darlington	3	3,882.12	1,500.00	25.00		1.88		1,531.88	1,610.49	39	
Delavan	3	3,055.18	1,300.00			.64		1,300.64	1,674.54	43	
De Pere	3	1,563.86	1,100.00	80.00		.83		1,180.64	1,302.54	45	
Dodgeville	3	18,718.22	1,100.00	100.00		90.00	5,296.25	11,600.63	7,198.60	62	
Eau Claire	3	2,966.57	1,100.00	2,272.74	1,512.64	.48		1,900.43	966.60	57	
Edgerton	3	2,822.00	1,100.00	262.00		1.68		1,101.68	1,721.22	39	
Elkhorn	3	2,910.50	1,300.00			1.38		1,301.38	1,709.44	43	
Evansville	3	125.43	82.43			.16		82.58	43.85	43	Presidential from June 1, 1888.
Florence	2	14,513.77	2,400.00	2,800.00	1,469.23	2.21	2,649.47	9,451.91	5,061.86	65	
Fond du Lac	2	6,283.65	1,600.00	250.00		1.76		1,851.78	4,432.87	30	
Fort Atkinson	3	2,310.75	1,100.00	568.43		3.28		1,611.71	699.04	70	
Fort Howard	3	2,308.47	1,100.00	105.10	467.92	1.60		1,106.70	1,201.71	48	
Grand Rapids	3	11,317.19	2,200.00	1,369.98		14.24		4,052.04	7,265.15	36	
Green Bay	3	352.08	168.79			.84		169.10	142.94	48	
Hayward	3	4,512.92	1,600.00	161.00	1,358.89	7.04	3,128.87	1,090.81	2,124.09	37	Presidential from May 29, 1888.
Hudson	3	17,067.28	2,000.00	2,500.00		3.60		8,472.29	3,124.98	48	
Janesville	3	3,928.96	2,000.00			3.49		1,963.60	3,426.26	32	
Jefferson	3	4,381.16	1,600.00	206.13		8.43		2,016.81	2,344.85	52	Presidential from February 13, 1888.
Kenosha	3	793.67	581.62			.16		264.79	810.00	55	
Kilbourn City	3	30,257.50	2,700.00	3,000.97	1,829.97	138.20	7,787.91	16,056.96	14,201.54	53	
La Crosse	3	4,438.89	2,000.00	75.00		2.96		1,578.96	2,860.90	35	
Lake Geneva	3	2,781.82	1,980.00	100.00		1.90		1,481.90	1,300.82	46	
Lancaster	3	20,432.68	1,960.00	5,249.89		84.77	6,626.01	13,062.77	17,390.03	43	
Madison	3	7,131.60	1,600.00	900.00		7.84		3,107.61	6,022.70	43	
Manitowoc	3	8,783.94	1,600.00			5.90		2,865.90	6,917.68	30	In Government building.
Marshfield	3	2,923.67	1,100.00	100.00		1.64		1,201.44	1,728.63	41	

De.

Mauston	3	4,925.03					1.60	1,401.60		2,622.40	35
Medford	3	1,951.47	1,400.00				1.44	1,001.44	960.03	51
Menasha	3	3,513.24	1,400.00				2.64	1,802.64	1,710.00	41
Menomonee	3	5,101.32	1,000.00				4.00	2,104.00	3,000.32	29
Merrill	3	6,344.64	1,000.00	225.00			4.00	1,829.00	4,515.64	38
Milwaukee	1	297,148.96	8,700.00	44,642.86	1,564.16	65,816.07	1,672.89	106,896.18	190,252.68	49
Mineral Point	3	3,180.72	1,400.00	160.00			1.60	1,541.60	1,639.12	38
Monroe	3	6,448.37	1,600.00	300.00			5.92	1,905.92	2,542.45	30
Neenah	3	6,200.48	1,700.00	162.50			5.28	1,862.78	4,335.70	39
Neillsville	3	3,324.54	1,400.00	250.00			1.78	1,651.78	1,672.78	48
New London	3	2,890.22	1,100.00	7.50			1.60	1,109.10	1,191.12	45
New Richmond	3	2,818.47	1,200.00	65.45			2.56	1,269.03	1,549.45	45
Oconomowoc	3	3,770.73	1,500.00	208.33			4.08	1,712.41	2,058.32	45
Oconto	3	4,827.87	1,500.00	160.00			1.84	1,661.84	3,165.63	48
Oshkosh	2	25,078.27	2,000.00	3,100.00	1,615.96	6,920.78	82.44	14,319.17	10,757.10	57
Plattsville	3	3,609.82	1,400.00	90.00			1.13	1,491.13	2,116.70	41
Platteville	3	6,001.80	1,700.00	500.00			8.68	2,208.68	3,793.22	57
Portage	3	3,652.98	1,300.00	234.20			8.86	1,677.06	1,325.43	53
Prairie du Chien	2	29,062.44	2,200.00	8,847.84	1,466.44	7,962.86	160.51	14,670.80	14,391.64	51
Racine	3	2,081.77	1,200.00				.86	1,400.86	1,026.64	49
Richland Centre	3	1,165.95	1,000.00	160.00			.72	1,160.72	045.64	41
Ripon	3	3,129.07	1,400.00	503.83			1.83	1,901.83	1,991.50	43
River Falls	3	3,368.13	1,600.00		780.00		12.56	1,100.72	1,844.08	55
Sheboygan	3	11,001.42	2,100.00	1,117.50		2,138.86	3.63	945.77	951.58	39
Sheboygan Falls	3	2,401.80	1,700.00	241.83			4.30	2,117.83	3,114.46	38
Sparta	3	4,997.85	1,800.00	313.33			2.64	1,562.64	2,361.76	47
Stevens Point	3	7,221.99	1,800.00				1.23	1,401.23	676.63	38
Stoughton	3	3,864.34	1,640.00	460.00			1.98	1,102.08	1,399.94	45
Sturgeon Bay	3	2,077.98	1,100.00				1.98	1,601.98	1,646.07	67
Superior	3	3,890.33	1,400.00	300.00			.96	1,404.96	1,705.56	43
Tomah	3	2,450.46	2,000.00	1,800.00	625.08		13.54	3,863.84	4,718.08	85
Viroqua	3	6,545.52	2,000.00		590.00		14.54	2,454.54	2,038.63	41
Watertown	3	4,948.61	1,700.00	150.00			.32	1,502.32	1,154.80	41
Waukesha	3	3,655.13	1,500.00				4.40	1,900.82	2,154.80	30
Waupaca	3	8,453.03	1,900.00	616.83			5.60	2,521.25	5,931.78	24
Waupun										
Wausau										
White Water	3	7,192.87						1,905.60	5,887.97	
Total		798,862.51	124,675.83	87,375.64	15,926.22	97,418.69	2,512.82	228,060.20	470,862.31	41

Buffalo	3	2,405.75	1,200.00					1,200.00	1,205.75	49
Cheyenne City	3	14,981.74	2,500.00	2,349.00	4.00	1,569.65	23.24	6,446.89	8,484.85	43
Evanston	3	3,637.06	1,000.00	460.00	4.00		3.36	1,900.00	1,457.06	26
Laramie City	3	6,985.55	1,500.00	250.00			3.63	1,301.36	5,624.19	45
Rawlins	3	3,788.17						1,753.53	2,034.65	47
Total		33,778.27	8,600.00	3,999.00	8.00	1,562.65	40.18	13,307.77	90,578.50	38

No. 11.—*Statement showing the transactions of the money-order offices of the United States for the fiscal year ended June 30, 1888.*

States and Territories.	Balance from last year.	Domestic money-orders issued.			Postal-notes issued.		
		Number.	Amount.	Fees.	Number.	Amount.	Fees.
Alabama	$21,874.93	170,671	$2,270,773.84	$17,216.11	69,307	$125,787.21	$2,081.10
Arizona	10,167.62	32,762	636,222.42	4,162.93	13,808	27,816.62	415.0s
Arkansas	32,401.38	158,463	2,2?2,830.58	27,145.56	84,917	154,328.37	2,549.8?
California	110,705.80	385,507	5,560,335.94	40,491.22	177,252	349,133.39	5,521 52
Colorado	60,498.15	191,173	2,790,311.64	20,233.40	100,941	191,004.22	3,032.16
Connecticut	11,729.95	121,475	1,339,538.01	10,993.07	92,883	171,810.92	2,7⁹0 ⁸1
Dakota	23,741.50	97,618	1,115,729.51	9,054.09	117,708	207,911.42	3,537.45
Delaware	2,669.06	13,804	15?,272.55	1,249.11	14,266	27,461.34	422.22
District of Columbia	15,186.16	49,839	7?4,053.08	5,244.24	25,1?0	49,640.18	736 ?9
Florida	19,205.4?	107,433	1,290,472.70	10,222.78	61,1?9	111,790.41	1,8⁹ 5⁴
Georgia	31,932.00	181,251	2,36?,055.80	18,125.93	110,604.	211,045.11	3,321.12
Idaho	37,298.20	28,949	535,950.50	3,57⁴.93	15,706	30,054.67	471.⁸1
Illinois	89,612.19	753,4??	7,905,855.50	66,565.50	494,716	899,758.60	14,886.15
Indiana	38,203.60	401,449	4,131,506.14	35,244.48	265,107	475,502.34	7,96⁴ 09
Indian Territory	1,075.53	8,922	148,219.9?	1,028 8?	6,005	11,809.28	181 6?
Iowa	6?,784.74	503,278	4,858,70?.03	42,764.40	488,783	825,075.46	14,67? ??
Kansas	67,750.26	504,975	4,896,700.75	43,081.57	39?,009	672,787.34	11,86? 9?
Kentucky	13,580.41	137,631	1,461,210.21	1?,228.99	7?,917	130,565.5?	2,19⁰ 1?
Louisiana	65,424.18	139,6?0	2,474,039.61	16,779.6?	31,845	57,842.34	956 7⁰
Maine	14,900.48	98,385	1,263,780.33	9,742.89	76,624	143,086.68	2,30?.?⁰
Maryland	8,417.94	69,407	944,?72.18	7,119.89	6?,3?6	124,451,36?	1,⁰?? ⁴⁵
Massachusetts	23,?74.60	304,154	3,637,959.55	28,837.3?	234,127	415,016.49	7,0?? 5?
Michigan	70,725.60	463,961	4,968,140.2??	41,437.15	336,851	606,024.61	10,11? 4?
Minnesota	45,979.21	231,860	2,525,617.4?	20,872.36	174,919?	31?,585.39	5,?5?.9⁶
Mississippi	24,900.94	195,969	2,593,058.83	19,806.8?	56,?96	100,604.50?	1,71?.0⁶
Missouri	71,151.78	445,191	5,155,3?5.9?	41,492.46	297,3?6	536,453.16	8,8?0 ??
Montana	32,755.95	53,268	924,390.91	6,282.31	35,789	70,983.18.	1,0?? 4?
Nebraska	41,321.03	203,820	1,979,685.74	17,278.97	207,371?	347,?05.77?	?,??? 6⁹
Nevada	10,858.93	32,637	583,8⁰0.0?	3,957.71	11,59?	24,533.9?	34?.0⁹
New Hampshire	7,358.96	61,55?	661,433.0?	5,528.46	64,245	122,59⁰.2?	1,9⁵0 ⁰.
New Jersey	10,777.46	114,857	1,484,406.80	11,380.6?	71,600	130,068.76	2,15⁰ ??
New Mexico	16,895.13	34,144	495,740.4?	3,6?2.1?	19,?96	37,239.76.	58⁴ 6?
New York	66,120.92	699,293	8,540,666.94	66,904.19	498,691	939,372.5⁴	14,59? ??
North Carolina	2?,586.08	142,65?	1,763,141.8?	13,8?0.74	84,316	162,919.0?	2,53? 4?
Ohio	56,646.6?	625,299	6,414,377.20	54,592.88	445,952	803,531.3?	13,39? 5⁴
Oregon	65,074.86	90,236	1,556,528.47	10,700.01	51,018	93,271.7??	1,53?.5?
Pennsylvania	78,060.72	537,348	6,238,768.50	5?,080.6?	426,543	797,770.7?	12,81?.9?
Rhode Island	5,122.99	39,607	482,333.8?	3,779.99	22,325	40,213.7?	67?.9?
South Carolina	17,493.60	109,434	1,291,346.64	10,341.9?	51,363	99,469.1?	1,5⁴?.4?
Tennessee	28,591.56	173,722	2,194,180.30	17,013.07?	76,384	188,714.50	2,?9? 1?
Texas	138,771.39	548,354	8,418,102.0?	60,184.26	244,91?	430,454.30	7,3?5 8⁴
Utah	18,637.74	31,843	520,027.66	2,614.47	16,585	34,491.6?	43? 5?
Vermont	8,032.13	56,090	544,396.66	4,718.41	51,24?	92,609.35	1,53? 5?
Virginia	21,940.95	128,051	1,479,037.69	11,922.6?	82,044	158,733.70.	2,46?.6??
Washington	16,155.04	75,848	1,273,162.70	8,780.78	40,728	76,016.56	1,??? 0⁶
West Virginia	7,301.90	56,579	578,347.84	4,890.4?	44,498	81,794.07.	1,336 ?⁹
Wisconsin	47,496.07	324,223	3,694,131.3?	30,075.38	230,59?	425,009.0??	6,9??.??
Wyoming	7,397.48	24,720	39?,016.95	2,768.42	13,59?	26,325.8?	40?.2?
Total	1,699,808.6??	9,959,207	119,649,064.98	946,961.1??	6,668,006	12,134,45?.0⁴	2⁰⁰,341.6?

No. 11.—*Statement showing the transactions of the money-order offices, etc.*—Continued.

States and Territories.	International money-orders issued.			Number of certificates of deposit.	Deposits received from postmasters.	Drafts on postmasters at New York.
	Number.	Amount.	Fees.			
Alabama	2,228	$38,604.19	$455.30	12,393	$1,160,874.68	$40,930.00
Arizona	367	9,445.04	101.90	....	22,845.00	....
Arkansas	998	15,169.66	186.40	13,470	1,184,155.46	63,235.00
California	39,407	772,628.14	8,837.55	22,833	4,543,377.63	41,100.00
Colorado	18,775	437,557.00	4,527.15	13,189	1,924,690.64	23,725.00
Connecticut	20,951	287,904.83	8,615.40	6,694	448,037.86	217,077.00
Dakota	5,059	68,242.57	724.05	1,529	110,327.43	135,964.00
Delaware	2,108	29,502.93	970.40			7,190.00
District of Columbia	8,263	126,593.90	2,296.00	6,081	1,187,034.24	8,713.82
Florida	1,787	86,807.36	423.55	7,633	470,283.01	25,257.78
Georgia	2,828	63,019.14	715.40	25,351	1,762,161.23	292,020.00
Idaho	335	7,455.40	85.90	647	109,10.71	5,283.00
Illinois	63,042	919,871.09	11,451.45	103,549	8,263,184.59	1,634,445.20
Indiana	7,942	160,899.09	1,821.00	25,907	1,504,181.07	875,303.00
Indian Territory	18	339.76	3.90			305.00
Iowa	7,756	95,202.93	1,275.35	52,143	2,079,934.01	967,033.00
Kansas	4,291	56,816.30	767.45	6,025	324,336.74	785,340.00
Kentucky	3,619	52,326.71	650.35	10,785	653,604.00	317,000.00
Louisiana	6,331	134,781.44	1,517.70	25,647	3,987,060.35	4,415.00
Maine	5,495	88,522.18	1,080.20	11,935	905,771.18	91,470.00
Maryland	8,127	113,202.80	1,428.45	13,974	953,581.92	92,415.00
Massachusetts	81,805	1,150,019.21	14,425.85	30,399	2,495,808.63	423,069.00
Michigan	31,120	448,144.40	5,633.66	38,577	2,015,068.53	756,170.00
Minnesota	12,491	193,926.76	2,895.50	35,784	1,941,512.72	211,789.00
Mississippi	477	8,558.69	99.30			87,535.00
Missouri	16,972	276,058.19	3,840.60	130,892	7,932,975.98	417,870.00
Montana	7,537	173,428.81	1,900.55	5,536	721,879.82	2,300.00
Nebraska	4,426	61,308.01	776.35	23,776	1,559,107.19	157,675.95
Nevada	1,396	28,391.12	326.70		1,195.00	
New Hampshire	4,814	66,452.15	836.55			77,025.00
New Jersey	40,057	521,237.78	6,650.70	1,674	79,762.44	318,232.00
New Mexico	635	14,066.59	160.00	4,910	341,684.03	30,030.00
New York	187,785	2,546,360.82	32,131.30	81,975	32,143,269.51	3,512,203.16
North Carolina	950	20,697.62	239.00	5,592	338,097.18	121,060.00
Ohio	32,898	435,322.72	5,593.90	68,031	3,305,192.76	1,114,411.00
Oregon	8,869	79,584.63	909.60	15,044	1,819,945.58	45,000.00
Pennsylvania	73,660	960,736.24	12,346.95	68,849	5,189,567.08	566,641.93
Rhode Island	11,734	156,032.77	1,995.10	2,647	176,803.75	2,320.00
South Carolina	1,201	26,895.59	305.50	11,466	749,421.56	75,890.00
Tennessee	2,478	37,543.97	461.90	24,523	1,748,353.54	117,380.65
Texas	6,834	113,071.10	1,361.15	49,299	4,680,544.49	277,239.50
Utah	2,578	38,026.51	481.20	4,292	460,581.78	67,560.00
Vermont	3,326	54,582.86	659.45			126,386.06
Virginia	2,734	50,815.03	604.45	19,061	1,385,172.66	280,561.00
Washington	3,595	77,571.32	873.20		27,613.00	
West Virginia	876	11,571.86	148.25			88,385.00
Wisconsin	14,592	186,505.71	2,454.05	34,763	2,464,019.88	388,950.00
Wyoming	1,200	22,915.19	263.00			75.00
Total	759,636	11,293,870.05	139,511.10	1,012,075	103,129,930.74	14,884,075.05

States and Territories.	Transferred from postage fund.	Gain.	Premium.	Balance due postmasters.	Domestic money-orders.			
					Paid.		Repaid.	
					No.	Amount.	No.	Amount.
Alabama	$2,670.20	$0.96		$243.93	80,184	$1,223,898.97	1,504	$17,290.00
Arizona	75.01			2.12	7,706	220,674.96	379	8,270.61
Arkansas	284.90			103.07	68,458	1,101,286.72	1,715	21,921.33
California	24,971.10	12.76		196.39	289,429	5,199,092.95	3,463	48,357.13
Colorado	6,138.01	4.51		45.30	96,653	1,703,006.19	1,826	35,383.77
Connecticut	6,605.56			128.01	126,128	1,353,025.09	704	6,724.55
Dakota	6,019.20	9.33		178.89	39,449	661,007.64	950	16,485.92
Delaware	1,543.81		$45.11	3.65	8,096	113,815.40	74	1,022.85
District of Columbia					77,794	846,652.14	335	5,489.84
Florida	5,108.89		2.12	79.86	54,207	816,152.71	1,026	13,429.49
Georgia	2,578.94			91.72	161,746	2,115,726.02	1,967	14,135.62
Idaho	1,139.98		96.00	10.03	6,940	109,228.80	231	4,485.51
Illinois	57,239.32			823.27	1,229,034	11,972,212.71	5,930	63,531.04
Indiana	14,831.33			629.94	320,174	3,709,684.79	2,701	26,450.27
Indian Territory					1,471	29,122.42	93	1,063.38
Iowa	26,620.79	1.58		652.51	339,717	4,001,678.48	3,998	36,179.47
Kansas	45,700.44		56.98	417.60	269,873	3,812,818.55	5,062	47,155.06
Kentucky	7,425.82	.15		169.31	140,496	1,709,245.83	1,162	10,722.23
Louisiana	1,660.55	.75		109.83	177,356	2,014,006.05	949	14,519.50
Maine	7,093.86	.53		150.36	99,376	1,219,028.06	523	8,462.51
Maryland	5,557.88			124.99	111,277	1,571,717.47	506	6,493.65
Massachusetts	25,314.41		3.12	487.98	504,756	5,015,221.68	1,794	21,897.96
Michigan	29,125.63			476.88	339,877	4,184,871.88	3,468	36,724.73
Minnesota	175,686.49			309.06	178,615	2,210,928.41	1,873	29,764.22
Mississippi	1,861.54		16.10	206.22	66,707	919,113.61	1,568	16,350.18
Missouri	22,915.47	2.69		481.77	610,305	8,234,144.28	3,781	46,145.23
Montana	302.51			151.89	18,374	248,909.94	463	7,892.57
Nebraska	13,376.72			791.97	113,740	1,559,864.97	1,937	19,392.61
Nevada	120.31			17.92	7,340	151,361.44	289	4,607.56
New Hampshire	7,348.10			102.99	38,672	518,367.72	386	3,265.38
New Jersey	9,150.39	.10		107.53	95,605	1,471,305.30	832	8,907.44
New Mexico	582.67			28.67	9,825	206,481.99	342	4,043.62
New York	52,312.68	85.34		995.22	1,573,161	15,351,401.87	5,063	63,601.13
North Carolina	4,207.81			87.55	67,953	936,600.53	1,012	9,969.50
Ohio	26,997.49			990.65	692,498	7,456,673.01	4,218	41,456.43
Oregon	1,322.64			55.98	52,320	1,297,536.61	966	16,951.73
Pennsylvania	26,710.73	5.42		832.08	674,739	6,891,640.99	4,035	46,372.11
Rhode Island	530.27			3.85	26,397	361,568.32	225	2,604.15
South Carolina	2,126.12			55.24	51,960	670,131.46	656	6,403.96
Tennessee	11,265.84			114.48	175,266	2,536,990.85	1,371	14,891.84
Texas	14,246.38	10.21		848.69	311,495	5,615,980.81	4,896	60,641.85
Utah	1,876.41			9.39	21,083	452,354.17	313	4,732.68
Vermont	5,021.68			173.47	37,403	485,544.47	378	3,391.60
Virginia	7,951.14	.04		238.98	106,812	1,501,416.71	963	8,889.11
Washington	5,257.33	.73		.11	25,441	610,223.11	809	14,518.72
West Virginia	2,678.84			891.28	27,356	366,402.77	428	4,965.60
Wisconsin	12,087.28	.89		540.36	240,661	3,091,606.36	2,223	24,382.73
Wyoming	232.73				5,520	109,519.28	195	3,680.37
Total	683,288.60	156.01	219.43	13,140.30	9,866,060	118,832,230.01	78,962	911,815.34

No. 11.—*Statement showing the transactions of the money-order offices, etc.*—Continued.

States and Territories.	Postal-notes.				International money-orders.			
	Paid.		Repaid.		Paid.		Repaid.	
	No.	Amount.	No.	Amount.	No.	Amount.	No.	Amount.
Alabama.	27,272	$55,596.60	799	$1,482.03	254	$5,814.19	9	$75.56
Arizona	2,809	6,542.68	148	309.60	57	2,276.52	2	9.50
Arkansas	31,576	64,913.20	843	1,622.37	399	12,255.40	5	50.58
California	118,703	265,112.01	2,331	5,061.71	10,671	236,616.00	195	2,763.27
Colorado	44,763	92,055.92	1,596	3,343.43	1,369	49,852.89	47	909.22
Connecticut	121,332	174,391.05	1,277	2,830.55	5,060	62,813.65	66	279.31
Dakota	31,163	56,667.15	1,591	3,529.68	1,511	45,006.11	22	271.50
Delaware	4,675	10,322.55	170	337.77	168	3,295.07	5	60.01
District of Columbia.	76,491	117,818.92	501	971.11	3,998	32,919.58	35	884.81
Florida	26,881	52,198.14	963	1,878.75	877	19,175.97	9	154.27
Georgia	83,245	164,642.57	1,625	3,174.19	379	8,008.85	9	260.29
Idaho	2,535	5,721.25	143	286.32	126	4,736.66	2	62.00
Illinois	853,453	1,523,183.24	5,853	10,550.30	22,425	392,912.94	230	2,881.58
Indiana	160,377	331,394.63	2,463	4,736.95	2,943	62,607.54	37	322.73
Indian Territory	581	1,182.77	62	157.63	3	109.80		
Iowa	233,074	458,213.07	4,596	8,027.17	3,587	90,885.15	41	607.64
Kansas	149,326	278,157.34	4,687	8,414.20	2,047	55,242.12	32	370.06
Kentucky	60,843	112,733.58	835	1,514.15	1,075	24,498.97	13	191.07
Louisiana	257,815	438,066.90	561	1,075.71	2,053	88,953.46	20	304.82
Maine	71,192	115,381.75	678	1,291.41	4,783	57,102.24	22	288.06
Maryland	67,943	138,379.31	1,200	2,802.22	2,129	42,022.18	25	219.76
Massachusetts	450,258	794,892.02	5,796	12,039.20	21,800	307,721.32	263	3,518.91
Michigan	220,677	420,490.13	3,921	7,237.12	10,268	206,010.16	176	2,772.07
Minnesota	122,346	235,275.84	2,548	4,922.99	5,633	152,000.89	71	744.74
Mississippi	18,453	37,149.75	983	1,768.65	101	2,284.15	2	5.00
Missouri	379,067	729,697.00	3,720	7,175.30	5,048	113,601.68	61	738.50
Montana	8,162	17,721.34	407	874.34	392	12,306.01	16	358.62
Nebraska	87,834	168,818.73	2,439	4,550.40	2,552	79,392.96	20	306.33
Nevada	2,318	5,410.66	96	200.22	90	2,476.12	8	239.25
New Hampshire	32,294	65,858.42	488	977.13	642	12,398.11	20	392.42
New Jersey	54,478	94,647.52	1,032	2,136.09	6,094	117,999.54	95	1,306.27
New Mexico	4,066	8,715.26	233	455.99	100	2,486.24	2	22.25
New York	1,165,360	2,042,487.60	9,379	19,608.08	73,800	1,046,261.34	610	9,007.78
North Carolina	38,783	82,651.22	1,108	2,090.43	144	2,769.71	1	5.00
Ohio	404,530	868,971.12	4,895	9,235.19	9,245	179,163.21	113	951.31
Oregon	23,533	48,386.29	847	1,573.67	1,302	31,992.78	19	448.16
Pennsylvania	512,949	890,471.27	6,833	13,881.15	19,722	298,212.05	241	2,750.27
Rhode Island	16,082	30,493.98	530	1,072.03	1,496	25,871.78	29	240.48
South Carolina	23,682	48,948.87	597	1,200.48	142	3,426.39	1	10.00
Tennessee	73,206	136,676.12	882	1,670.67	609	13,268.32	18	179.80
Texas	113,949	220,350.18	3,059	5,671.06	2,337	61,575.68	36	620.07
Utah	8,113	18,731.35	138	290.35	349	8,086.45	10	65.50
Vermont	25,898	50,070.76	575	1,062.57	935	17,002.68	11	100.57
Virginia	49,460	109,342.13	937	1,836.01	730	12,609.32	10	249.44
Washington	9,715	20,800.16	532	1,087.88	1,202	32,162.58	7	142.24
West Virginia	15,377	32,912.91	457	829.72	152	3,810.36	3	68.44
Wisconsin	141,334	286,812.54	2,121	3,921.85	6,128	166,781.93	73	854.71
Wyoming	2,450	5,359.33	160	347.60	115	3,538.58	5	56.60
Total	6,544,865	11,934,759.13	87,125	170,122.42	236,992	4,169,675.64	2,747	37,759.96

No. 11.—*Statement showing the transactions of the money-order offices, etc.*—Continued.

States and Territories.	Drafts paid by postmaster, New York, N. Y.	Deposited at first-class offices.	Transferred to postage fund.	Loss.	Expense.
Alabama		$2,347,416.26	$301.07	$244.08	$7.65
Arizona		459,454.21	22.00		10.00
Arkansas		2,544,419.55	499.63	119.00	222.65
California		5,570,908.52	796.31	.40	3,636.68
Colorado		3,500,667.01	759.34	126.13	3,604.66
Connecticut		883,771.88	207.27		
Dakota		876,926.28	1,190.11		18.97
Delaware		90,899.25	678.75		2.09
District of Columbia		1,158,049.00			11,259.06
Florida		1,052,899.82	669.95	5.29	4.09
Georgia		2,409,934.57	334.27		3,838.97
Idaho		482,398.74	891.00	142.61	4.30
Illinois		5,795,535.08	1,213.85	480.07	9,853.36
Indiana		2,931,504.09	1,679.62	273.32	674.49
Indian Territory		129,905.24			
Iowa		4,283,285.02	1,765.59	106.90	22.39
Kansas		3,608,940.24	2,319.91	315.22	50.54
Kentucky		714,698.36	670.72	20.00	2.45
Louisiana		3,595,547.33	436.86	.02	3.25
Maine		1,075,454.62	227.00		12.61
Maryland		481,359.02	228.12		
Massachusetts		2,035,404.96	1,135.93	3.16	148.67
Michigan		4,908,941.80	350.03	207.63	14.45
Minnesota		2,761,196.15	725.18	77.38	21.74
Mississippi		1,827,256.26	288.02	50.05	14.90
Missouri		5,251,768.82	1,412.77	83.21	6,352.09
Montana		1,574,111.02	5.09		4.00
Nebraska		2,314,592.10	1,338.67	250.97	2.65
Nevada		481,355.00	425.00		
New Hampshire		339,928.74	164.07		7.30
New Jersey		862,423.98	18.00	.05	.80
New Mexico		696,954.48	189.00		
New York	$14,891,691.05	13,699,737.77	588,218.47	87.72	47,860.02
North Carolina		1,387,829.68	201.00		8.35
Ohio		3,501,162.85	1,860.00	208.41	3,143.73
Oregon		2,162,934.80	651.00		3,273.06
Pennsylvania		5,666,647.87	1,907.92	84.80	20,854.90
Rhode Island		441,007.76			18.57
South Carolina		1,521,234.68	211.00		24.15
Tennessee		1,560,156.74	202.98	26.66	3,744.62
Texas		8,044,412.94	1,125.97	1,339.06	762.44
Utah		638,504.50	88.90		2.59
Vermont		272,192.82	44.00		42.43
Virginia		1,748,572.72	920.90	122.90	.25
Washington		783,672.05	48.00		2.65
West Virginia		360,682.64	42.00	201.54	88.34
Wisconsin		3,623,847.27	842.22	49.68	
Wyoming		324,263.54			
Total	14,891,691.05	110,967,152.04	617,415.49	4,499.58	115,754.76

States and Territories.	Canada.			Great Britain and Ireland.		
	No. of orders issued.	Amount of orders issued.	Fees.	No. of orders issued.	Amount of orders issued.	Fees.
Alabama	186	$3,715.72	$43.50	1,242	$29,460.27	$348.60
Arizona	56	1,716.99	18.10	117	2,668.85	29.00
Arkansas	69	892.35	13.00	314	5,614.28	67.40
California	4,353	99,285.37	1,113.40	14,119	248,361.36	2,926.05
Colorado	1,977	50,318.41	550.50	10,652	210,068.41	2,396.65
Connecticut	1,356	24,236.49	286.90	11,370	126,196.71	1,692.85
Dakota	529	9,709.24	117.25	1,663	36,436.12	410.30
Delaware	76	1,477.93	17.40	1,335	16,141.98	211.00
District of Columbia	325	4,272.27	55.90	3,666	84,097.31	987.98
Florida	202	3,349.11	41.50	693	12,484.70	150.75
Georgia	325	7,461.43	82.80	1,349	29,945.31	340.70
Idaho	87	1,677.75	11.90	213	4,644.43	54.00
Illinois	3,792	61,723.71	758.55	22,428	281,509.64	3,684.15
Indiana	550	5,651.90	84.65	2,791	32,387.72	430.10
Indian Territory	7	108.77	1.30	3	17.29	.30
Iowa	539	5,006.09	78.95	2,955	34,776.79	465.25
Kansas	409	3,840.90	59.85	1,790	23,962.06	315.70
Kentucky	173	2,268.05	30.30	1,326	17,166.61	217.30
Louisiana	224	4,470.22	52.90	918	17,004.61	201.80
Maine	2,082	36,950.60	442.05	2,556	32,577.08	430.70
Maryland	256	3,700.53	47.90	2,875	38,885.72	497.20
Massachusetts	20,002	356,675.30	4,172.70	44,886	497,159.99	6,543.68
Michigan	8,104	124,631.50	1,549.85	12,140	152,569.13	1,971.10
Minnesota	3,038	57,571.20	681.30	3,798	51,575.75	685.15
Mississippi	35	205.01	4.75	130	2,452.35	28.30
Missouri	1,017	15,038.32	190.80	6,457	96,217.74	1,189.80
Montana	927	24,471.24	265.95	5,510	122,675.46	1,341.50
Nebraska	376	5,062.71	67.00	1,765	23,412.18	299.90
Nevada	179	3,932.45	44.60	871	17,876.52	290.50
New Hampshire	1,232	19,981.52	244.80	3,080	37,688.17	484.40
New Jersey	1,141	19,449.86	232.35	23,309	257,927.64	3,453.60
New Mexico	79	1,309.77	17.10	276	6,628.41	74.15
New York	10,980	168,491.94	2,094.15	96,427	1,195,322.59	15,403.95
North Carolina	63	972.34	12.30	376	6,573.47	82.30
Ohio	2,234	29,848.38	386.00	15,970	189,096.51	2,495.10
Oregon	456	8,887.87	104.80	1,325	25,296.98	296.25
Pennsylvania	2,493	39,945.45	500.20	48,539	550,672.86	7,253.50
Rhode Island	1,480	24,896.96	303.40	8,028	90,798.41	1,219.30
South Carolina	88	1,709.26	19.90	409	8,506.87	100.10
Tennessee	193	2,669.66	34.80	1,083	15,537.16	195.00
Texas	347	4,695.97	60.65	2,144	34,238.06	419.30
Utah	144	2,492.43	31.30	1,785	24,319.94	313.80
Vermont	694	8,510.15	116.60	2,332	39,046.06	464.15
Virginia	351	5,205.51	65.20	1,383	25,812.65	308.60
Washington	996	23,687.65	255.30	1,288	24,501.05	282.10
West Virginia	29	241.13	4.00	432	4,682.38	64.65
Wisconsin	1,242	23,049.40	278.25	2,743	33,533.06	446.50
Wyoming	103	1,919.91	22.70	791	14,611.79	162.10
Total	75,526	1,365,881.54	15,670.75	371,694	4,626,557.86	61,676.50

sued, paid, and repaid, and fees collected during the fiscal year ended June 30, 1888.

German Empire.			Switzerland.			Italy.		
No. of orders issued.	Amount of orders issued.	Fees.	No. of orders issued.	Amount of orders issued.	Fees.	No. of orders issued.	Amount of orders issued.	
536	$8,819.29	$106.25	42	$462.70	$6.00	105	$2,868.50	
128	3,105.26	34.20	29	1,171.00	11.90	10	246.38	
388	6,654.54	73.90	72	749.44	10.30	52	911.91	
10,966	198,031.56	2,299.25	3,103	43,099.50	481.25	1,919	50,902.84	
1,661	30,781.54	357.50	1,665	56,301.19	583.60	1,632	34,019.82	
3,201	40,529.89	530.95	335	5,349.45	64.40	2,942	61,703.35	
402	6,842.10	82.40	63	1,166.50	13.50	42	1,047.00	
378	4,846.06	62.70	63	1,216.43	13.80	175	4,904.25	
2,595	68,532.82	777.00	394	11,313.68	126.00	403	7,281.23	
280	4,739.26	50.90	14	285.12	3.30	210	6,519.94	
781	16,634.27	190.30	29	509.46	6.30	197	3,261.17	
52	983.80	11.40	6	25.25	.60	10	819.52	
21,331	270,909.88	3,513.20	5,616	84,607.02	1,051.60	3,393	104,734.67	1,
3,355	39,219.03	530.95	287	5,544.61	64.60	175	5,514.15	
1	30.00	.30	4	153.00	1.60	1	15.10	
2,810	35,209.29	466.45	257	3,665.23	46.60	94	2,962.34	
1,161	14,618.15	192.85	216	4,232.83	50.05	132	3,264.72	
1,481	19,355.20	249.75	243	4,447.99	51.20	287	7,651.92	
1,074	19,220.13	224.70	201	4,203.51	47.50	3,002	74,577.71	
333	7,012.24	81.50	30	397.85	4.90	121	2,934.08	
3,445	44,234.61	572.50	575	7,909.34	99.90	601	11,393.04	
6,039	89,027.33	1,123.70	965	16,136.22	192.00	3,844	104,762.20	1,
5,527	64,365.04	870.95	719	14,116.79	163.70	819	23,144.25	
3,241	39,706.07	585.10	307	3,939.94	50.80	363	9,804.68	
190	3,209.12	86.45	3	53.00	.60	79	2,009.16	
5,725	75,368.30	971.10	1,123	19,736.42	229.70	1,751	55,296.23	
559	11,192.29	126.06	74	2,358.32	24.60	158	5,146.71	
1,588	20,635.49	266.00	139	1,479.43	19.80	176	4,380.09	
143	3,485.64	38.60	37	451.50	10.00	71	2,261.40	
294	3,920.22	50.80	31	467.69	5.75	69	1,781.26	
10,063	133,398.09	1,705.00	1,409	24,493.33	286.95	1,780	44,068.96	
173	3,904.89	43.60	30	578.06	6.50	47	961.81	
57,268	802,553.23	10,097.55	8,307	123,523.30	1,489.40	2,679	57,701.82	
377	10,005.16	110.60	6	51.06	.90	32	968.68	
10,372	135,819.03	1,768.50	1,870	22,886.92	363.50	1,461	39,456.01	
1,012	19,668.92	227.10	228	4,978.23	54.70	77	2,016.10	
13,799	184,678.46	2,392.25	2,555	49,752.50	570.70	2,902	82,188.25	
720	10,003.48	127.60	98	2,221.44	24.40	245	5,041.03	
473	12,103.75	133.40	13	349.67	3.90	58	904.01	
520	7,432.90	93.30	227	4,656.50	56.50	275	6,195.66	
2,782	44,234.68	538.05	505	8,909.66	105.00	503	11,126.19	
218	3,705.87	45.00	61	822.63	10.70	26	740.87	
95	1,651.03	20.20	28	544.39	6.50	104	3,342.45	
576	10,433.18	123.50	13	292.72	3.50	195	4,469.05	
544	9,624.26	112.30	36	925.58	9.70	79	2,920.76	
300	3,641.57	47.00	47	1,171.33	12.80	49	1,564.00	
8,003	87,992.94	1,214.85	974	12,137.41	160.25	201	5,076.45	
135	2,060.27	23.30	45	1,462.03	15.20	12	388.00	
187,095	2,633,528.27	33,250.15	32,184	554,938.46	6,556.85	32,868	866,208.07	9,

No. 12.—*Statement showing the number and amount of international money-*

States and Territories.	France.			Sweden.		
	No. of orders issued.	Amount of orders issued.	Fees.	No. of orders issued.	Amount of orders issued.	Fees.
Alabama	58	$707.04	$9.00	33	$1,062.10	$11.10
Arizona	28	275.76	4.40	1	42.00	.50
Arkansas	27	762.17	8.50	9	100.00	1.20
California	1,609	24,173.86	291.50	2,178	57,308.36	619.90
Colorado	170	3,233.71	37.00	1,497	45,914.20	490.60
Connecticut	239	3,493.32	42.80	1,171	21,357.64	233.00
Dakota	24	313.84	4.00	196	4,903.21	53.20
Delaware	36	443.16	5.50	14	221.60	2.70
District of Columbia	503	12,015.76	138.10	116	3,554.18	38.80
Florida	108	3,025.45	32.20	61	1,519.65	16.40
Georgia	49	444.88	6.50	43	1,005.23	11.20
Idaho	8	257.92	2.60	......	....	....
Illinois	632	8,617.15	112.40	3,561	66,556.25	787.95
Indiana	148	1,963.71	26.00	433	7,496.43	89.90
Indian Territory	2	15.60	.20	......	....	....
Iowa	124	1,103.16	17.50	500	7,449.51	94.60
Kansas	95	981.40	14.80	397	6,061.38	76.90
Kentucky	85	767.24	11.30	1	15.00	.20
Louisiana	779	12,102.93	146.90	85	1,004.31	10.90
Maine	54	754.46	10.20	51	1,074.54	12.20
Maryland	196	2,421.25	32.25	42	931.23	10.60
Massachusetts	1,062	13,286.09	179.30	3,643	58,193.06	719.00
Michigan	179	2,584.22	33.30	2,047	46,198.47	523.30
Minnesota	160	2,301.70	29.30	1,052	17,977.58	219.45
Mississippi	24	312.00	3.60	9	104.50	1.40
Missouri	237	3,158.01	41.80	341	4,970.09	62.40
Montana	49	725.77	8.60	163	4,413.73	47.00
Nebraska	37	334.21	4.80	290	4,852.48	50.05
Nevada	10	209.13	2.30	3	25.00	.30
New Hampshire	38	615.13	7.00	92	1,404.36	17.20
New Jersey	651	10,344.27	125.65	401	6,927.22	82.90
New Mexico	25	527.25	6.20	1	50.00	75
New York	5,799	83,044.18	1,058.90	2,429	43,639.26	515.35
North Carolina	18	381.31	4.40	13	238.78	2.50
Ohio	448	6,998.71	89.90	119	2,165.31	25.20
Oregon	84	844.34	11.70	323	8,455.62	91.10
Pennsylvania	1,063	14,295.57	185.80	1,201	21,124.11	252.50
Rhode Island	238	3,340.68	41.60	611	12,513.59	142.20
South Carolina	50	771.19	10.00	38	851.85	9.50
Tennessee	53	628.35	6.70	9	148.66	1.80
Texas	278	4,939.28	56.30	89	1,994.96	16.15
Utah	12	265.00	3.20	132	1,923.80	24.30
Vermont	33	516.78	6.10	41	713.00	8.30
Virginia	65	817.68	11.30	28	700.00	7.90
Washington	80	1,310.45	15.50	259	6,584.57	72.20
West Virginia	16	235.26	3.00	......	....	....
Wisconsin	81	1,015.94	13.70	304	5,924.37	69.65
Wyoming	13	454.44	4.70	68	1,875.07	20.30
Total	15,757	234,162.90	2,920.60	24,059	479,850.26	5,572.25

orders issued, paid, and repaid, and fees collected, etc.—Continued.

Norway			Belgium			Portugal			Netherlands		
No. of orders issued.	Amount of orders issued.	Fees.	No. of orders issued.	Amount of orders issued.	Fees.	No. of orders issued.	Amount of orders issued.	Fees.	No. of orders issued.	Amount of orders issued.	Fees.
21	$463.73	$5.20	1	$5.00	$0.10						
2	8.40	.20	1	10.00	.10	3	$118.80	$1.20			
900	24,946.53	266.60	162	2,809.14	32.80	101	2,230.78	24.40	43	$643.95	$8.10
42	1,120.82	12.20	8	128.20	1.50	1	30.00	.30	4	117.50	1.40
76	1,432.73	16.80	30	354.78	4.90	1	6.00	.10	14	119.61	1.70
138	2,582.86	30.50									
10	182.50	2.20	5	25.00	.50						
68	1,977.57	21.90	44	1,214.74	13.50	5	18.93	.50	32	896.86	10.10
183	3,721.40	41.90	7	235.20	2.50				9	325.00	3.30
136	3,667.27	40.70				1	15.12	.20			
			2	54.38	.60						
1,339	26,484.91	310.20	359	6,249.21	74.00	8	30.62	.80	224	2,865.39	36.70
15	124.20	1.90	154	2,443.73	28.20				17	145.45	2.20
119	1,788.46	22.70	84	1,041.70	14.20				191	1,423.97	26.00
5	48.25	.60	68	1,690.73	18.80				2	26.00	.30
			16	325.42	3.80				8	267.64	2.80
40	831.00	9.60	31	840.96	9.30				7	35.32	.70
218	4,583.43	52.80	4	112.37	1.20	1	9.90	.10	4	44.00	.50
77	1,648.61	18.10	11	221.69	2.50	1	31.67	.40	17	362.45	4.10
847	15,534.51	180.55	70	972.49	12.50	156	2,586.25	31.40	49	743.45	9.20
391	6,981.92	83.50	170	3,440.00	40.20				905	8,662.35	131.00
423	6,356.95	79.85	20	239.44	3.30				23	712.40	7.40
			7	131.55	1.50						
17	208.41	2.70	209	4,388.72	50.70	3	37.68	.50	25	262.22	3.60
67	2,081.28	22.20	14	409.90	5.50						
11	84.16	1.40	10	141.02	1.80	2	100.00	1.00			
						1	30.00	.30			
15	355.00	4.00	1	20.00	.20						
826	17,050.42	196.00	70	1,103.29	13.05				245	3,161.23	42.40
			3	23.40	.40						
2,261	44,538.43	508.70	523	7,860.37	96.50	46	514.92	6.55	291	4,424.28	54.10
53	973.61	11.30	2	3.96	.20				2	40.01	.50
289	7,114.39	77.50	29	395.04	4.80				47	627.34	8.10
277	7,366.48	79.40	15	317.52	3.40	13	518.72	5.50	4	49.95	.70
435	8,485.16	96.00	442	6,406.65	77.80	4	26.57	.40	44	723.46	9.00
175	3,954.86	44.30	73	2,245.13	23.70	34	635.95	7.30	9	115.22	1.40
60	1,391.00	14.90							2	30.00	.40
2	42.00	.50	8	76.50	.90				4	95.00	1.00
107	2,284.06	25.70	18	453.05	5.00				5	70.50	.80
74	1,058.06	14.00							7	107.65	1.30
2	19.00	.30	2	23.00	.30	5	185.00	1.90			
67	1,757.88	19.60	4	117.04	1.30				1	10.60	.20
244	6,834.96	73.40	15	353.76	3.60	1	11.00	.20	1	25.06	.30
			3	36.19	.50						
857	15,555.51	184.85	54	815.20	10.40				72	785.67	10.75
4	61.63	.80									
10,894	225,500.35	2,577.55	2,749	47,795.47	565.95	387	7,138.29	83.05	2,308	27,921.47	380.05

No. 12.—*Statement showing the number and amount of international money-*

States and Territories.	New South Wales.			Victoria.		
	No. of orders issued.	Amount of orders issued.	Fees.	No. of orders issued.	Amount of orders issued.	Fees.
Alabama						
Arizona						
Arkansas						
California	127	$2,771.40	$32.70	99	$2,177.19	$24.60
Colorado	13	436.62	4.70	6	94.97	1.20
Connecticut	32	250.02	4.40	62	498.88	8.30
Dakota	1	50.00	.50	1	48.70	.50
Delaware						
District of Columbia	10	373.47	4.10	33	1,036.04	11.40
Florida						
Georgia						
Idaho						
Illinois	16	273.94	3.20	15	460.08	5.30
Indiana						
Indian Territory				2	.24	.20
Iowa						
Kansas	1	9.90	.10			
Kentucky	1	48.70	.50	1	25.08	.30
Louisiana						
Maine	20	875.99	9.10			
Maryland	15	746.69	7.50	8	289.60	4.00
Massachusetts	18	301.48	3.60	21	484.46	5.50
Michigan	9	151.84	1.90	7	103.73	1.30
Minnesota				3	53.57	.60
Mississippi						
Missouri	1	10.00	.10	6	89.03	1.00
Montana	4	143.37	1.50			
Nebraska						
Nevada	1	4.99	.10	7	146.31	1.50
New Hampshire	1	14.61	.20			
New Jersey	8	299.81	3.20	1	10.00	.10
New Mexico						
New York	88	2,229.60	24.50	62	1,234.30	14.50
North Carolina						
Ohio	5	68.44	.90	5	27.84	.63
Oregon	9	340.20	3.60	1	19.48	.20
Pennsylvania	25	478.57	5.70	11	253.24	3.00
Rhode Island	1	4.99	.10	3	32.29	.40
South Carolina						
Tennessee	2	34.09	.40			
Texas						
Utah	1	14.61	.20	5	224.35	2.30
Vermont						
Virginia						
Washington	13	572.64	5.80	3	54.85	.60
West Virginia						
Wisconsin	3	62.70	.70			
Wyoming						
Total	425	10,568.57	119.30	361	7,464.23	87.30

orders issued, paid, and repaid, and fees collected, etc.—Continued.

Japan.			New Zealand.			Hawaiian Kingdom.			Jamaica.		
No. of orders issued.	Amount of orders issued.	Fees.	No. of orders issued.	Amount of orders issued.	Fees.	No. of orders issued.	Amount of orders issued.	Fees.	No. of orders issued.	Amount of orders issued.	Fees.
1	$2.25	$0.15	1	$25.00	$0.30	1	$0.60	$0.10			
....	....	......	2	28.57	.40	....	....	......			
150	2,989.01	33.30	139	2,912.73	33.30	119	2,621.69	30.20	20	$235.42	$3.00
1	1.00	.10							1	48.70	.50
29	1,264.20	12.90	28	201.93	3.30	4	66.00	.50			
						1	7.00	.10			
13	480.20	5.10	8	171.87	2.00	8	267.76	3.00			
									2	35.00	.40
2	24.00	.40									
....	....	......	6	77.35	1.10	....	....	......			
7	68.00	1.00	38	1,428.92	14.90	16	308.60	3.80	3	9.81	.30
3	44.01	.60									
1	14.61	.20							3	32.22	.50
4	26.00	.40	1	4.87	.10	1	6.00	.10	1	8.99	.10
1	50.00	.50				1	3.00	.10	6	140.01	1.70
1	35.00	.40	1	10.00	.15	1	1.91	.10	2	23.86	.30
2	60.00	.60							2	8.37	.20
26	382.51	4.90	13	174.72	2.30	25	613.17	7.30	5	25.74	.50
3	9.00	.35	4	52.17	.70	1	2.00	.10	1	2.50	.10
			4	40.00	.40	1	40.00	.40			
9	220.00	2.30	0	249.20	2.60	1	4.15	.10			
			4	171.10	1.80	1	13.00	.20			
1	50.00	.50	1	48.69	.50	1	5.85	.10			
			2	68.18	.70	2	60.00	.60			
6	162.61	1.80									
5	89.74	1.10	20	602.34	6.50	1	50.00	.50	3	15.99	.30
						1	15.60	.20			
50	823.75	9.55	42	713.35	8.90	22	300.71	4.30	70	1,297.79	15.50
2	38.00	.40									
9	172.30	2.00	3	76.81	.90	3	26.00	.40	3	13.97	.30
2	20.60	.20	2	19.48	.25	3	49.00	.60			
37	808.64	9.40	16	290.07	3.70	2	13.00	.20	9	64.97	1.00
						2	9.85	.20	2	45.00	.50
									1	2.50	.10
1	20.00	.20	49	735.55	9.30	1	10.00	.10	33	705.21	7.90
4	35.65	.50									
19	687.00	7.00	6	249.49	2.60	1	5.00	.10			
2	15.00	.20	5	54.49	.80				1	5.84	.10
			1	25.00	.30						
391	8,592.48	96.05	402	8,432.48	97.80	220	4,506.29	53.70	167	2,721.89	33.30

No. 12.—*Statement showing the number and amount of international money-*

States and Territories.	Cape Colony.			Windward Islands.			Leeward Islands.		
	No. of orders issued.	Amount of orders issued.	Fees.	No. of orders issued.	Amount of orders issued.	Fees.	No. of orders issued.	Amount of orders issued.	Fees.
Alabama				1	$11.99	$0.20			
Arizona									
Arkansas									
California	3	$109.50	$1.10	3	29.49	.40			
Colorado									
Connecticut				2	11.01	.20			
Dakota									
Delaware									
District of Columbia				4	127.03	1.40			
Florida				11	391.29	4.30			
Georgia									
Idaho									
Illinois	3	11.98	.40	2	17.35	.30			
Indiana									
Indian Territory									
Iowa									
Kansas									
Kentucky									
Louisiana	1	4.87	.10	2	14.87	.20			
Maine	1	1.71	.10	5	40.29	.60	1	$15.00	$0.20
Maryland				3	24.87	.30	4	32.87	.60
Massachusetts	14	175.45	2.40	35	594.12	7.40	7	67.43	1.00
Michigan				1	19.99	.20			
Minnesota									
Mississippi									
Missouri									
Montana	1	9.74	.10						
Nebraska									
Nevada									
New Hampshire									
New Jersey	2	58.44	.60	8	97.98	1.20			
New Mexico									
New York	21	437.31	5.10	85	1,411.56	16.90	40	542.29	6.90
North Carolina				2	58.81	.70			
Ohio	1	9.74	.10	1	9.74	.10	1	3.90	.10
Oregon									
Pennsylvania	7	146.69	1.70	18	295.10	3.70	7	41.05	.80
Rhode Island				4	49.99	.50			
South Carolina				1	19.99	.20			
Tennessee	1	35.00	.40						
Texas									
Utah									
Vermont									
Virginia				10	237.97	2.50			
Washington				1	10.00	.10			
West Virginia									
Wisconsin				4	52.74	.80	1	1.22	.10
Wyoming									
Total	55	1,090.43	12.10	203	3,526.18	42.20	61	703.66	9.70

orders issued, paid, and repaid, and fees collected, etc.—Continued.

Tasmania.			Queensland.			Denmark.			Totals.		
No. of orders issued.	Amount of orders issued.	Fees.	No. of orders issued.	Amount of orders issued.	Fees.	No. of orders issued.	Amount of orders issued.	Fees.	No. of orders issued.	Amount of orders issued.	Fees.
									2,228	$38,604.19	$455.30
									367	9,445.04	101.90
						2	$18.00	$0.30	938	15,109.66	186.40
3	$108.77	$1.10	10	$219.26	$2.60	281	6,680.43	72.70	39,407	772,628.14	8,837.55
						44	961.91	10.80	18,775	437,557.00	4,827.15
5	86.87	1.00	10	136.11	2.00	44	617.84	8.30	20,951	287,904.83	3,815.40
						4	93.00	1.00	3,059	63,242.57	724.05
						15	127.00	2.00	2,108	29,592.93	370.40
			2	43.67	.50	34	1,158.51	12.50	8,263	198,835.80	2,298.00
						7	176.22	1.90	1,787	36,807.86	423.55
						6	151.00	1.60	2,828	63,019.14	715.40
						1	15.00	.20	835	7,455.40	85.80
1	10.00	.10	7	87.92	1.20	251	3,608.84	45.50	63,043	919,871.09	11,451.45
						16	342.14	4.10	7,942	100,899.09	1,321.00
									18	339.76	3.90
						79	1,385.45	16.30	7,758	95,202.95	1,275.35
						15	50.96	1.70	4,291	58,816.30	767.45
									3,619	52,326.71	650.35
						9	258.00	2.80	6,341	134,761.44	1,517.70
						9	68.08	1.10	5,495	88,522.18	1,080.20
						8	112.45	1.40	8,127	113,202.80	1,428.45
			6	165.70	1.80	72	1,157.55	13.90	81,803	1,159,019.21	14,425.85
			1	.51	.10	92	1,108.90	15.00	31,120	448,144.40	5,633.65
						50	587.55	8.55	12,491	193,926.78	2,395.50
									477	8,558.69	99.30
2	18.73	.30	2	9.74	.20	40	775.20	8.90	16,972	276,058.19	3,340.60
						6	157.00	1.70	7,587	173,428.81	1,900.55
						31	501.70	6.20	4,428	61,108.01	776.35
						9	340.00	3.50	1,336	29,391.12	326.70
						5	69.58	1.00	4,814	66,482.15	836.55
1	2.44	.10				113	2,100.73	24.70	40,057	521,237.78	6,650.70
									835	14,086.59	160.00
7	117.11	1.30	10	243.17	2.60	268	4,385.95	52.50	187,785	2,546,360.82	32,131.30
						4	90.43	1.10	950	20,697.62	239.60
						33	513.34	6.30	32,893	435,322.72	5,593.90
			1	63.46	.90	24	670.40	7.30	2,869	79,584.63	909.60
			4	71.23	.90	47	673.71	8.30	73,650	960,776.24	12,346.95
1	.24	.10	3	36.16	.50	7	84.50	1.10	11,734	156,032.77	1,995.10
						9	254.00	2.70	1,201	26,895.59	305.50
									2,478	37,543.97	461.90
1	19.48	.20				14	190.00	2.50	6,824	113,071.10	1,361.15
						63	1,576.75	17.90	2,578	38,026.51	481.20
									3,326	54,552.86	659.45
2	97.40	1.00				87	925.10	10.40	2,734	50,815.03	604.45
						7	116.00	1.40	3,595	77,571.32	873.20
									876	11,571.86	148.25
			1	4.99	.10	44	622.78	8.00	14,592	186,505.71	2,454.05
						28	657.05	7.40	1,200	22,915.19	263.00
23	469.94	5.20	60	1,081.92	18.40	1,837	33,326.05	394.55	759,636	11,299,870.05	139,511.10

No. 12.—*Statement showing the number and amount of international mone:-*

States and Terri- tories.	Canada.				Great Britain and Ireland.			
	No. of orders paid.	Amount of orders paid.	No. of orders repaid.	Amount of orders repaid.	No. of orders paid.	Amount of orders paid.	No. of orders repaid.	Amount of orders repaid
Alabama	46	$1,054.70	1	$1.00	87	$1,460.65	3	$31.62
Arizona	9	286.58			20	758.75		
Arkansas	52	1,227.84			48	903.13	2	24.84
California	3,689	80,662.12	85	647.78	2,136	38,285.20	57	662.45
Colorado	697	16,966.86	10	227.50	647	14,695.24	14	235.17
Connecticut	3,260	24,810.42	13	147.01	876	13,212.84	26	304.27
Dakota	484	13,633.16	7	99.00	224	4,162.57	3	19.62
Delaware	43	564.15			73	1,163.14	3	30.61
District of Columbia	1,499	14,783.84			1,631	7,089.11	15	332.94
Florida	190	4,270.61	1	15.00	501	9,468.90	2	8.26
Georgia	100	1,630.54			124	2,140.42	5	178.49
Idaho	15	580.00			57	2,312.14	1	50.00
Illinois	10,939	105,387.24	80	833.70	3,308	52,804.75	72	853.20
Indiana	1,254	19,775.47	5	48.18	402	5,323.52	9	81.25
Indian Territory	1	48.00						
Iowa	781	9,391.70	2	77.50	631	11,543.45	21	373.70
Kansas	279	5,900.83	6	73.46	548	11,188.67	6	33.26
Kentucky	250	3,318.43			193	3,265.04	6	60.07
Louisiana	761	5,240.28			806	7,234.96	4	34.96
Maine	2,850	39,694.42	9	43.60	450	4,530.60	8	116.46
Maryland	630	8,920.14	1	9.64	510	8,831.44	10	82.34
Massachusetts	15,518	203,647.33	109	1,765.13	4,070	57,143.40	105	1,000.70
Michigan	6,601	110,286.04	81	1,364.37	1,213	20,919.73	28	401.58
Minnesota	1,875	36,513.59	17	299.55	710	12,709.53	21	148.03
Mississippi	13	432.00	2	5.00	33	468.77		
Missouri	1,024	16,117.91	5	80.50	958	17,123.41	26	265.05
Montana	195	5,888.56	8	224.50	90	2,574.41	7	129.12
Nebraska	255	6,762.03	2	16.50	568	14,398.87	3	4.73
Nevada	41	1,028.00	2	22.25	24	784.80		
New Hampshire	447	8,404.49	14	355.94	157	3,033.97	5	34.46
New Jersey	1,311	18,987.00	6	96.50	1,994	29,731.12	43	422.76
New Mexico	22	550.35			38	708.00		
New York	35,689	328,889.74	89	935.41	15,473	193,187.37	235	3,515.02
North Carolina	23	442.55			60	1,166.30		
Ohio	3,500	44,385.80	9	166.25	1,844	31,931.90	52	279.31
Oregon	746	15,019.49	4	60.18	190	3,508.68	7	364.94
Pennsylvania	8,018	69,791.71	27	412.32	6,012	87,990.80	112	1,097.38
Rhode Island	740	11,450.83	4	54.00	593	10,517.58	19	163.14
South Carolina	17	385.37			61	1,340.66		
Tennessee	203	2,382.54	4	45.75	158	3,429.54	4	29.89
Texas	129	2,674.28	4	80.00	685	13,110.00	11	144.18
Utah	33	917.87			230	4,716.67	5	33.21
Vermont	751	18,820.16	7	66.70	95	1,593.54	3	18.87
Virginia	160	1,794.81	1	50.00	431	7,686.77	3	44.50
Washington	809	19,349.43	4	124.25	153	4,061.67	1	4.99
West Virginia	18	417.02			100	819.64	2	58.44
Wisconsin	1,346	23,570.08	17	837.18	597	9,425.38	6	61.71
Wyoming	40	1,283.90	2	82.56	43	1,027.27	1	1.54
Total	107,457	1,308,397.92	538	8,821.23	49,333	735,421.27	966	11,627.09

orders issued, paid, and repaid, and fees collected, etc.—Continued.

German Empire.				Switzerland.			
No. of orders paid.	Amount of orders paid.	No. of orders repaid.	Amount of orders repaid.	No. of orders paid.	Amount of orders paid.	No. of orders repaid.	Amount of orders repaid.
91	$2,389.69	3	$24.70	19	$582.18	1	$5.00
22	1,022.50	....	....				
218	7,372.39	1	15.00	38	1,178.06	....	....
1,516	51,721.68	56	844.14	281	8,507.38	7	120.56
323	11,786.28	4	83.00	112	3,963.20	6	71.45
529	14,198.61	10	121.20	54	1,622.70		
608	21,787.67	7	121.49	68	2,168.76	1	2.40
32	1,012.53	2	39.00	11	296.67		
491	5,759.14	15	466.30	102	2,434.38	1	15.00
121	3,582.59	3	105.00	9	412.46		
83	2,581.47			16	467.55	1	14.80
33	999.94	1	12.00	13	529.04		
5,898	179,799.27	77	942.62	691	21,151.59	18	186.12
980	30,065.57	23	189.69	100	2,779.35		
1,670	56,522.15	14	132.36	186	5,508.12	1	5.00
821	26,629.61	10	67.21	201	6,132.61	2	6.91
417	11,863.11	6	111.00	104	3,147.91		
312	8,754.30	7	150.00	59	1,873.02		
20	479.75	1	30.00	6	276.22		
781	19,628.04	10	116.91	65	1,832.00	2	9.60
717	17,286.08	24	408.57	133	2,267.35	2	54.75
1,619	50,963.51	31	436.69	134	3,918.52	3	58.35
1,956	67,349.67	22	178.73	354	11,615.10	1	1 91
39	1,003.25			1	8.00		
2,311	66,629.24	15	160.26	389	11,660.68	6	106.06
48	1,809.37	1	5.09	41	1,339.17		
1,189	40,207.14	13	246.10	293	10,191.75	1	80.00
12	340.03	3	127.00				
24	701.34	1	3.00				
1,948	49,760.81	20	238.42	248	7,078.78	13	299.05
25	753.90	2	32.25	3	29.38		
11,748	288,714.01	163	2,337.97	1,533	34,417.76	30	419.98
30	784.30	1	5 00	4	82.32		
2,873	78,395.61	32	347.93	491	14,051.98	7	69.32
252	9,766.38			40	1,883.48	1	20.00
3,750	101,572.24	64	635.96	530	13,380.49	18	404.68
56	1,368.50			8	265.80	1	4.90
54	1,449.13	1	10.00	3	62.95		
102	2,939.86	3	59.70	82	2,834.33	1	10.00
1,115	34,302.15	10	189.63	224	6,503.77	4	18.20
36	1,053.32	3	11.30	12	403.57	1	20.00
45	680.47			15	500.42		
47	841.83	4	135.71	11	321.21		
153	5,760.91			23	635.08		
70	2,069.66			10	119.16		
3,268	106,169.90	37	355.35	445	13,593.64	4	27.30
26	1,107.77	2	22.50	2	52.92		
48,416	1,391,758.93	704	9,510.69	7,163	201,970.63	133	1,961.40

No. 12.—*Statement showing the number and amount of international money*

States and Territories.	Italy.				France.			
	No. of orders paid.	Amount of orders paid.	No. of orders repaid.	Amount of orders repaid.	No. of orders paid.	Amount of orders paid.	No. of orders repaid.	Amount of orders repaid.
Alabama	1	$38.16			2	$19.04	1	$9.44
Arizona	4	176.12					1	1.50
Arkansas	1	4.77	1	$10.00	7	142.90	1	.50
California	51	1,530.10	9	98.38	253	6,508.53	16	157.86
Colorado	6	183.94	7	122.00	15	471.07	2	29.06
Connecticut	21	747.55	12	249.00	41	738.59	2	8.40
Dakota	3	114.00			3	84.89	2	14.25
Delaware	1	38.16			1	3.80		
District of Columbia	22	149.15	1	35.60	113	1,319.15	2	39.66
Florida	16	535.67	1	20.00	12	316.01	2	5.99
Georgia	2	4.86			14	279.26	1	26.00
Idaho								
Illinois	90	3,667.27	14	277.00	221	4,024.35	6	56.38
Indiana	4	33.83			39	580.54	1	2.00
Indian Territory					2	61.50		
Iowa	4	57.04			34	500.53	2	19.00
Kansas	2	20.03			23	564.66	3	72.00
Kentucky	3	81.09	1	20.00	21	498.76		
Louisiana	161	5,361.42	3	33.80	316	7,260.08	6	86.00
Maine					10	130.26	1	25.00
Maryland	17	368.06	2	21.27	38	571.16		
Massachusetts	72	1,597.84	7	184.06	233	2,290.32	8	26.90
Michigan	13	316.38	7	155.25	64	1,813.84	6	68.84
Minnesota	6	107.93	2	25.00	61	1,909.00	7	42.51
Mississippi	1	7.63			4	61.54		
Missouri	27	857.99	4	104.38	103	1,816.23	4	14.25
Montana					1	.50		
Nebraska	1	5.72			25	875.55		
Nevada	2	76.32	1	25.00				
New Hampshire	2	38.16			3	42.06		
New Jersey	60	1,891.53	5	147.00	160	3,299.58	5	44.54
New Mexico	3	95.31			4	120.54		
New York	547	12,008.07	12	313.07	1,879	27,099.74	60	1,264.86
North Carolina					16	156.12		
Ohio	32	878.86	5	70.00	146	3,922.80	7	17.51
Oregon	1	26.71			16	400.27	5	72.34
Pennsylvania	106	2,947.73	8	118.00	280	3,969.55	6	38.63
Rhode Island	18	574.90			30	555.95	4	8.44
South Carolina	2	66.78			2	35.45		
Tennessee	12	444.97	2	14.00	17	448.02	4	20.46
Texas	16	423.94	1	6.00	78	2,098.01	5	175.00
Utah	2	44.89			3	20.37		
Vermont	3	15.61			5	66.01		
Virginia	8	253.15			30	912.13	2	19.21
Washington					18	608.26	2	13.10
West Virginia	3	112.58			7	90.93		
Wisconsin					41	613.21	4	12.87
Wyoming								
Total	1,355	35,907.27	105	2,048.75	4,393	77,343.16	179	2,382.71

orders issued, paid, and repaid, and fees collected, etc.—Continued.

Sweden.				Norway.			
No. of orders paid.	Amount of orders paid.	No. of orders repaid.	Amount of orders repaid.	No. of orders paid.	Amount of orders paid.	No. of orders repaid.	Amount of orders repaid.
2	$53.61						
	571.26	1	$8.00				
12	571.26						
50	1,863.69	6	105.71	31	$1,152.72		
19	560.84	1	35.00		32.97		
13	442.31	2	35.00	3	970.30	1	$5.00
30	807.71			41	100.00		
3	54.86			2	165.69		
61	290.60			36	43.21		
1	50.00			3	11.00		
1	2.68	2	56.00	1			
344	9,377.44	7	124.47	202	4,365.66	3	68.62
7	155.74			3	14.00		
59	1,749.30			29	817.67		
57	1,950.50	4	107.50	4	44.79		
3	34.10						
4	11.74						
2	26.80			9	333.11		
102	2,373.35	3	12.76	22	402.57		
98	3,306.91	7	159.05	17	545.79	1	20.00
396	12,960.41	1	48.00	137	3,476.16		
2	53.80						
21	639.43	1	5.00	3	76.61		
2	80.28			13	610.72		
86	2,618.45	1	7.00	13	500.58		
1	24.76	2	65.00				
21	602.36	1	45.00	9	352.23		
261	5,986.80	6	35.47	168	3,571.39		
9	192.06			9	241.63		
9	252.62	1	25.00	12	402.92		
90	2,209.76	1	11.00	20	385.38		
19	564.29	1	10.00	2	29.00		
3	83.10						
21	736.33			3	36.24		
13	434.70	1	.99	2	65.69		
		1	15.00				
9	270.66			6	184.42		
54	1,665.50	3	56.30	71	1,872.90		
1	41.37						
1,896	52,879.92	53	977.25	872	20,865.35	5	93.62

No. 12.—*Statement showing the number and amount of international mon-*

States and Territories.	Belgium.				Portugal.			
	No. of orders paid.	Amount of orders paid.	No. of orders repaid.	Amount of orders repaid.	No. of orders paid.	Amount of orders paid.	No. of orders repaid.	Amount of orders repaid.
Alabama	4	$147.61						
Arizona	2	32.57						
Arkansas	16	723.30						
California	56	2,190.93	1	$30.00	55	$2,089.75		
Colorado	17	695.96	2	65.00				
Connecticut	13	235.95			13	587.10	1	$15.00
Dakota	10	392.11			1	10.50		
Delaware	2	27.80						
District of Columbia	14	104.63	1	5.00	2	15.70		
Florida	3	41.88						
Georgia	6	238.06						
Idaho	7	300.96						
Illinois	77	2,202.26	1	5.00	5	118.82		
Indiana	54	2,162.02			6	21.00		
Indian Territory								
Iowa	8	267.13						
Kansas	37	1,164.44						
Kentucky	13	396.23			1	10.00		
Louisiana	35	1,098.92						
Maine	2	15.09	1	30.00	1	1.00		
Maryland	13	281.99			5	19.18		
Massachusetts	41	628.70			219	10,082.57	1	35.20
Michigan	64	2,097.76	1	4.94	2	10.51		
Minnesota	29	1,031.41						
Mississippi	5	161.88						
Missouri	26	702.80			3	48.19		
Montana								
Nebraska	16	434.86						
Nevada	1	9.52			2	58.00		
New Hampshire	38	733.13						
New Jersey	2	56.14						
New Mexico	324	5,245.50	3	15.26	62	927.96	1	10.00
New York	2	45.00						
North Carolina	52	1,609.32						
Ohio	3	135.70						
Oregon	147	2,923.22	5	32.90	4	62.56		
Pennsylvania	1	50.00			3	111.00		
Rhode Island								
South Carolina	3	114.27						
Tennessee	15	467.88						
Texas								
Utah	2	8.39						
Vermont	7	161.62						
Virginia	5	132.21						
Washington	1	4.76	1	10.00				
West Virginia	135	5,355.92			1	7.30		
Wisconsin								
Wyoming								
Total	1,308	34,841.82	16	196.10	385	14,174.16	3	60.20

No. 12.—*Statement showing the number and amount of international money-*

States and Territories.	Victoria.				Japan.			
	No. of orders paid.	Amount of orders paid.	No. of orders repaid.	Amount of orders repaid.	No. of orders paid.	Amount of orders paid.	No. of orders repaid.	Amount of orders repaid.
Alabama								
Arizona								
Arkansas								
California	168	83,474.84	3	$16.94	309	$6,421.60		
Colorado	8	135.01			1	7.31		
Connecticut	17	239.83			20	649.04		
Dakota								
Delaware								
District of Columbia	7	100.48			18	83.74		
Florida					1	1.00		
Georgia					15	351.91		
Idaho								
Illinois	35	376.30	1	.30	23	486.48		
Indiana	25	512.76			4	63.92		
Indian Territory								
Iowa	23	743.35			2	59.20		
Kansas	1	24.85			6	49.06		
Kentucky	21	855.17			3	32.50		
Louisiana	5	74.90			1	85.00		
Maine	283	2,697.60			5	75.00	1	35.00
Maryland					11	124.79		
Massachusetts	59	777.86			32	251.43		
Michigan	9	209.40			83	2,855.20		
Minnesota	8	58.95			1	1.20		
Mississippi								
Missouri	34	692.29			7	165.92		
Montana								
Nebraska	1	24.35						
Nevada	1	9.74						
New Hampshire	2	48.70			1	1.50		
New Jersey	16	249.51			17	214.68		
New Mexico								
New York	452	5,781.51			221	3,273.43	1	5.00
North Carolina					8	80.00		
Ohio	30	282.14			16	320.22		
Oregon							1	21.70
Pennsylvania	63	813.30			29	385.13		
Rhode Island	2	69.39			1	2.80		
South Carolina	1	48.70						
Tennessee	3	15.84			4	79.13		
Texas					2	18.00		
Utah								
Vermont								
Virginia	8	123.05			6	94.00		
Washington	13	628.23			1	25.00		
West Virginia					3	110.00		
Wisconsin	15	405.17			1	25.00	1	.40
Wyoming								
Total	1,305	19,123.31	4	17.33	852	19,355.20	4	62.10

No. 12.—*Statement showing the number and amount of international money-*

States and Territories.	Windward Islands.				Leeward Islands.			
	No. of orders paid.	Amount of orders paid.	No. of orders repaid.	Amount of orders repaid.	No. of orders paid.	Amount of orders paid.	No. of orders repaid.	Amount of orders repaid.
Alabama								
Arizona								
Arkansas								
California	3	$107.14						
Colorado								
Connecticut	7	66.45			1	$14.44		
Dakota								
Delaware								
District of Columbia	5	56.15			1	.95		
Florida	3	48.70						
Georgia								
Idaho								
Illinois	16	191.84			1	.84		
Indiana								
Indian Territory								
Iowa	10	383.30						
Kansas	8	215.46						
Kentucky	2	90.87						
Louisiana	7	18.64			3	20.14		
Maine	43	207.92			7	23.01		
Maryland	4	119.16			1	47.52		
Massachusetts	75	2,422.80	1	$0.57	10	165.15	1	$0.32
Michigan								
Minnesota	1	15.01						
Mississippi								
Missouri								
Montana								
Nebraska								
Nevada								
New Hampshire					1	14.61		
New Jersey	23	621.48						
New Mexico								
New York	1,380	52,661.30			153	3,842.99	1	5.01
North Carolina								
Ohio	9	313.13						
Oregon								
Pennsylvania	94	3,082.04			15	291.08		
Rhode Island								
South Carolina								
Tennessee	2	42.20						
Texas	4	35.21						
Utah								
Vermont								
Virginia								
Washington								
West Virginia								
Wisconsin	1	2.53						
Wyoming								
Total	1,702	59,621.93	1	.57	193	4,420.23	2	3.33

orders issued, paid, and repaid, and fees collected, etc.—Continued.

	Jamaica.				Cape Colony.		
No. of orders paid.	Amount of orders paid.	No. of orders repaid.	Amount of orders repaid.	No. of orders paid.	Amount of orders paid.	No. of orders repaid.	Amount of orders repaid.
12	$109.42			4	$14.61	1	$2.30
1	.97			4	91.92		
17	29.92			6	90.82		
3	2.69			2	2.80		
5	198.41						
4	194.80						
33	611.46			20	332.49		
16	496.90						
6	180.14						
1	20.00						
3	54.87			1	18.48		
46	1,450.18			4	14.00		
64	407.75			38	337.41	1	8.00
33	942.09			4	68.21		
70	1,367.44			16	209.76		
5	209.27			1	5.47		
7	86.50			2	8.76		
25	1,348.55			12	366.73		
33	862.95			13	224.18		
1,633	52,489.48	3	$52.76	89	1,121.99		
11	110.01			3	46.88		
125	2,721.10			13	176.21		
7	46.72						
1	2.01			7	219.15		
13	360.38	1	7.00				
6	292.20						
9	158.10						
1	16.01						
2	19.48						
2,219	64,715.79	4	59.76	237	3,441.62	2	10.50

States and Territories.	Tasmania.				Queensland.			
	No. of orders paid.	Amount of orders paid.	No. of orders repaid.	Amount of orders repaid.	No. of orders paid.	Amount of orders paid.	No. of orders repaid.	Amount of orders repaid.
Alabama								
Arizona								
Arkansas								
California	27	$720.16			32	$958.93		
Colorado					1	4.87	1	$48.70
Connecticut	2	23.13			4	110.78		
Dakota								
Delaware								
District of Columbia					3	5.51		
Florida	1	9.74						
Georgia								
Idaho								
Illinois	9	47.47			27	343.01	1	29.99
Indiana	3	97.40			2	7.05		
Indian Territory								
Iowa								
Kansas					1	6.00		
Kentucky					1	2.67		
Louisiana								
Maine	164	1,209.64			48	378.80		
Maryland	1	34.09			2	14.61		
Massachusetts	17	138.89			16	215.32		
Michigan	1	4.87			3	27.20		
Minnesota								
Mississippi								
Missouri	1	20.45			8	187.49		
Montana								
Nebraska								
Nevada								
New Hampshire								
New Jersey	1	4.26			10	228.40		
New Mexico								
New York	65	524.81	1	$4.00	149	1,839.26		
North Carolina								
Ohio	8	80.60			20	384.23		
Oregon					3	102.27		
Pennsylvania	9	114.37			17	223.23		
Rhode Island	2	48.56			1	.60		
South Carolina								
Tennessee	1	17.05			1	9.74		
Texas								
Utah								
Vermont	1	.06			1	2.41		
Virginia	4	47.73						
Washington								
West Virginia								
Wisconsin	1	2.44			3	75.48		
Wyoming								
Total	318	3,145.22	1	4.00	353	5,127.93	2	78.69

orders issued, paid, and repaid, and fees collected, etc.—Continued.

	Denmark.				Totals.		
No. of orders paid.	Amount of orders paid.	No. of orders repaid.	Amount of orders repaid.	No. of orders paid.	Amount of orders paid.	No. of orders repaid.	Amount of orders repaid.
				254	$5,814.19	9	$75.56
				57	2,276.52	2	9.50
				399	12,255.40	5	50.58
30	$1,133.60			10,071	236,616.00	196	2,762.27
1	5.36			1,840	49,852.89	47	909.92
9	214.85			5,060	82,813.65	66	879.81
15	410.71			1,511	45,006.11	22	271.50
				168	3,265.07	5	60.01
11	16.43			3,998	32,919.58	35	884.81
1	2.50			877	19,175.97	9	154.27
2	53.62			379	8,008.83	9	269.29
				126	4,736.66	2	62.00
96	2,255.97			22,425	392,912.94	230	2,881.58
1	1.00			2,943	62,607.54	87	322.72
				3	109.80		
43	1,082.63			3,587	90,885.15	41	607.64
12	318.61			2,037	55,242.12	32	370.08
				1,075	24,498.97	13	191.07
1	2.68			2,053	38,953.46	20	804.82
3	72.38			4,783	57,102.24	22	288.06
2	22.72			2,180	42,620.18	25	239.76
12	96.12			21,800	307,721.82	263	3,518.91
39	1,265.88			10,268	206,010.16	176	2,772.07
47	1,166.82			5,633	152,000.80	71	744.74
				101	2,284.15	2	75.00
5	127.97			5,048	119,601.68	61	738.50
				392	12,306.01	16	858.62
79	2,821.95			2,552	70,382.98	20	306.33
3	118.99			90	2,476.12	8	239.25
				642	12,308.11	20	392.42
23	450.75	1	$5.00	6,094	117,999.54	95	1,306.27
1	2.54			100	2,488.24	2	32.25
90	1,728.24	1	2.40	73,800	1,046,261.34	610	9,007.78
				144	2,769.71	1	5.00
4	111.47			9,245	179,902.21	113	951.31
11	377.85			1,302	31,092.73	19	448.16
11	230.31			19,722	298,212.05	241	2,750.27
2	21.85			1,496	25,871.78	29	240.48
				142	3,426.39	1	10.00
2	98.93			609	13,268.32	18	179.80
4	42.89			2,337	61,575.68	36	620.07
11	253.15			349	8,086.48	10	65.50
				935	17,002.68	11	100.57
				730	12,600.32	10	249.44
6	187.67			1,202	32,103.59	7	142.24
				152	3,810.36	3	68.44
71	1,847.58			6,126	166,781.93	75	861.71
1	25.35			115	3,538.58	5	56.60
649	16,568.37	2	7.40	236,992	4,169,675.64	2,747	37,759.96

No. 13.—*Statement showing the receipts and disbursements of the money-order offices of the United States during the fiscal year ended June 30, 1888.*

RECEIPTS.

Balance in the hands of postmasters June 30, 1887...................		$1,699,808.63
Amount received for domestic money-orders issued..	$119,649,064.98	
Amount received for postal-notes issued.............	12,134,459.04	
Amount received for international money-orders issued	11,293,870.05	
Total issued		143,077,394.07
Amount received for fees on domestic money-orders issued	946,961.12	
Amount received for fees on postal-notes issued	200,341.68	
Amount received for fees on international money-orders issued....................................	139,511.10	
Total fees...		1,286,813.90
Amount of deposits received from postmasters	103,129,930.74	
Amount of drafts drawn on postmaster at New York, N. Y......................................	14,884,075.05	
Amount transferred from postage fund.............	683,288.60	
Amount of gain	136.01	
Amount of premium	219.43	
Balance due postmasters	13,140.39	
		118,710,790.22
Total receipts....................................		264,774,806.87

DISBURSEMENTS.

Amount of domestic money-orders paid	118,832,330.01	
Amount of postal-notes paid.......................	11,934,759.13	
Amount of international money-orders paid.......	4,169,675.64	
Total paid..		134,936,764.78
Amount of domestic money-orders repaid..........	911,015.24	
Amount of postal-notes repaid....................	170,122.42	
Amount of international money-orders repaid......	37,759.98	
Total repaid......................................		1,118,897.64
Amount of drafts paid by postmaster at New York..	14,891,691.05	
Amount deposited at first-class offices..............	110,967,152.04	
Amount transferred to postage fund................	617,415.49	
Amount of expense................................	115,754.76	
Amount of loss	4,499.58	
Amount paid for commissions on money-orders......	322,020.00	
Amount paid for commissions on postal-notes.......	55,701.39	
Miscellaneous items...............................	22,550.09	
Balance in the hands of postmasters June 30, 1888..	1,722,350.05	
		128,719,144.45
Total disbursements		264,774,806.87

No. 14.—*Statement showing the transfers to and from the money-order account during the fiscal year ended June 30, 1888.*

Amount transferred to money-order account............	$683,288.60	
Balance due postal account, June 30, 1887..............	269,051.77	
		$952,340.37
Amount transferred from money-order account.........	617,415.49	
Balance due postal account June 30, 1888..............	334,924.88	
		952,340.37

No. 15.—*Statement showing the money-order transactions with the United States assistant treasurer at New York, N. Y., during the fiscal year ended June 30, 1888.*

Balance in the hands of the assistant treasurer June 30, 1887	$2,615,968.31	
Amount deposited with assistant treasurer	2,421,089.16	
		$5,037,057.47
Amount of drafts paid by the assistant treasurer	2,336,951.43	
Balance in the hands of assistant treasurer June 30, 1888	2,700,106.04	
		5,037,057.47

No. 16.—*Statement showing the revenue which accrued on domestic money-order transactions during the fiscal year ended June 30, 1888.*

Amount received for fees on money-orders issued	$946,961.12	
Amount of gain	136.01	
Amount of premium	219.43	
		$947,316.56
Amount allowed postmasters:		
For commissions on money-orders	317,064.29	
For incidental expenses	84,479.92	
For lost remittances and burglaries	4,499.58	
Net revenue	541,272.77	
		947,316.56

Statement showing the revenue which accrued on postal note transactions during the fiscal year ended June 30, 1888.

Amount received for fees on postal-notes issued		$200,341.68
Amount allowed postmasters:		
For commissions on postal-notes	$55,701.39	
For incidental expenses	26,754.91	
Net revenue	117,885.38	
		200,341.68

INTERNATIONAL.

Statement showing the revenue which accrued on international money-order transactions during the fiscal year ended June 30, 1888.

CANADA.

Amount received for fees on orders issued	$15,670.75	
Excess of commissions received	184.83	
		$15,855.58
Amount allowed postmasters:		
For commissions	778.06	
For incidental expenses	441.20	
Net revenue	14,636.32	
		15,855.58

GREAT BRITAIN AND IRELAND.

Amount received for fees on orders issued	61,670.50	
Amount of gain on exchange	7,563.36	
		69,233.86
Amount allowed postmasters:		
For commissions	2,377.42	
For incidental expenses	1,737.68	
		4,115.10
Amount paid Great Britain:		
For excess of commissions	28,086.50	
For incidental expenses	97.65	
		28,184.15
Net revenue		36,934.61
		69,233.86

GERMANY.

Amount received for fees on orders issued...............	$33,250.15	
Amount gained on exchange.................	19,428.36	
		$52,678.51
Amount allowed postmasters:		
For commissions.................................	1,001.00	
For incidental expenses...........................	1,319.82	
		2,320.82
Amount paid Germany:		
For excess of commissions........................	9,208.22	
For incidental expenses..........................	100.58	
		9,308.80
Net revenue ....•.........		41,048.89
		52,678.51

SWITZERLAND.

Amount received for fees on orders issued............	6,558.85	
Amount gained on exchange...........................	8,967.51	
		15,526.36
Amount allowed postmasters:		
For commissions	171.76	
For incidental expenses	250.21	
		421.97
Amount paid Switzerland for excess of commissions..................		2,876.37
Net revenue		12,228.18
		15,526.36

ITALY.

Amount received for fees on orders issued..............	9,296.80	
Amount gained on exchange......................	22,631.60	
		31,928.40
Amount allowed postmasters:		
For commissions	182.29	
For incidental expenses	201.08	
		383.37
Amount paid Italy for excess of commissions		6,259.01
Net revenue		25,286.02
		31,928.40

FRANCE.

Amount received for fees on orders issued	2,920.60	
Amount gained on exchange	3,847.97	
		6,768.57
Amount allowed postmasters:		
For commissions	63.35	
For incidental expenses	83.39	
		146.74
Amount paid France for excess of commissions........................		1,129.81
Net revenue...		5,492.02
		6,768.57

JAMAICA.

Amount received for fees on orders issued............	$33.30	
Excess of commissions received.......................	464.75	
		$498.05
Amount allowed postmasters:		
For commissions	2.21	
For incidental expenses	32.98	
		35.19
Net revenue..		402. ~5
		498.05

NEW ZEALAND.

Amount received for fees on orders issued..............	97.80	
Excess of commissions received.....................	155.25	
		253.05
Amount allowed postmasters:		
For commissions	3.39	
For incidental expenses	3.91	
		7.30
Net revenue		245.75
		253.05

NEW SOUTH WALES.

Amount received for fees on orders issued............	119.30	
Excess of commissions received..........	142.86	
		262.16
Amount allowed postmasters:		
For commissions......................................	3.79	
For incidental expenses...........................	3.43	
		7.22
Net revenue		254.94
		262.16

VICTORIA.

Amount received for fees on orders issued..............	87.30	
Excess of commissions received	150.03	
		237.33
Amount allowed postmasters:		
For commissions	2.31	
For incidental expenses...........................	3.33	
		5.64
Net revenue		231.69
		237.33

BELGIUM.

Amount received for fees on orders issued..............	565.95	
Amount of gain on exchange	296.82	
		862.77
Amount allowed postmasters:		
For commissions	28.06	
For incidental expenses	43.19	
		71.25
Amount paid Belgium for excess of commissions		94.41
Net revenue		697.11
		862.77

Amount received for fees on orders issued..............	$83, 05	
Excess of commissions received	106. 07	
		$189. 12
Amount allowed postmasters:		
For commissions	6. 37	
For incidental expenses	40. 16	
		46. 53
Net revenue		142. 59
		189. 12

SWEDEN.

Amount received for fees on orders issued	5, 572. 25	
Loss	130. 26	
		5, 702. 51
Amount allowed postmasters:		
For commissions	220. 88	
For incidental expenses	118. 18	
		339. 06
Amount paid Sweden:		
For loss on exchange...........................	2, 241. 96	
For excess of commissions.....................	3, 121. 49	
		5, 363. 45
		5, 702. 51

TASMANIA.

Amount received for fees on orders issued..............	5. 20	
Excess of commissions received.........................	33. 83	
		39. 03
Amount allowed postmasters:		
For commissions................................	. 35	
For incidental expenses	. 73	
		1. 08
Net revenue		37. 95
		39. 03

WINDWARD ISLANDS.

Amount received for fees on orders issued	42. 20	
Excess of commissions received	441. 02	
		483. 22
Amount allowed postmasters:		
For commissions................................	1. 14	
For incidental expenses	19. 16	
		20. 30
Net revenue		462. 92
		483. 22

JAPAN.

Amount received for fees on orders issued..............	96. 05	
Excess of commissions received	81. 04	
		177. 09
Amount allowed postmasters:		
For commissions	1. 68	
For incidental expenses.............	6. 80	
		8. 48
Net revenue		168. 61
		177. 09

orders issued, paid, and repaid, and fees collected, etc.—Continued.

New Zealand.				Hawaiian Kingdom.			
No. of orders paid.	Amount of orders paid.	No. of orders repaid.	Amount of orders repaid.	No. of orders paid.	Amount of orders paid.	No. of orders repaid.	Amount of orders repaid.
1	$48.70						
				2	$4.75		
278	5,926.62			819	13,453.95	4	$75.95
				3	20.43		
23	273.78			11	92.38		
				1	6.00		
11	119.90			15	148.10		
5	73.05			2	75.00		
1	4.87			1	12.00		
1	14.61						
93	1,159.86			90	1,124.96		
16	84.08			7	121.25		
1	1.46			13	214.00		
13	392.01			1	50.00		
11	383.75			25	314.60		
425	3,407.33			18	242.75		
5	157.45			20	208.45		
137	1,665.86			148	1,586.12		
24	228.12			30	412.89		
5	82.79			7	41.30		
11	142.79			31	331.02		
				2	53.00		
6	267.85			5	24.25		
2	19.48			2	16.00		
				3	101.50		
21	252.76			24	191.65		
673	7,488.39			442	4,650.52		
57	443.34			54	801.15		
4	170.45			7	182.00		
117	1,180.98			92	873.90		
6	87.17			3	22.00		
1	1.25			5	60.05		
8	74.99			1	20.00		
				5	136.75		
1	1.46			3	10.00		
1	24.35			4	62.91		
				1	10.00		
8	116.25			2	9.25		
1,966	24,254.75			1,899	25,684.88	4	75.95

No. 12.—*Statement showing the number and amount of international money-*

States and Territories.	Windward Islands.				Leeward Islands.			
	No. of orders paid.	Amount of orders paid.	No. of orders repaid.	Amount of orders repaid.	No. of orders paid.	Amount of orders paid.	No. of orders repaid.	Amount of orders repaid.
Alabama								
Arizona								
Arkansas								
California	3	$107.14						
Colorado								
Connecticut	7	66.45			1	$14.44		
Dakota								
Delaware								
District of Columbia	5	56.15			1	.95		
Florida	3	48.70						
Georgia								
Idaho								
Illinois	16	191.84			1	.84		
Indiana								
Indian Territory								
Iowa	10	333.30						
Kansas	8	215.46						
Kentucky	2	60.87						
Louisiana	7	18.64			3	20.14		
Maine	43	207.92			7	23.01		
Maryland	4	119.16			1	47.52		
Massachusetts	75	2,422.80	1	$0.57	10	165.15	1	$0.32
Michigan								
Minnesota	1	15.01						
Mississippi								
Missouri								
Montana								
Nebraska								
Nevada								
New Hampshire					1	14.61		
New Jersey	23	621.48						
New Mexico								
New York	1,386	52,661.30			153	3,842.99	1	5.01
North Carolina								
Ohio	9	313.13						
Oregon								
Pennsylvania	94	2,082.64			15	291.06		
Rhode Island								
South Carolina								
Tennessee	2	42.20						
Texas	4	35.91						
Utah								
Vermont								
Virginia								
Washington								
West Virginia								
Wisconsin	1	2.53						
Wyoming								
Total	1,702	59,621.93	1	.57	193	4,420.23	2	5.33

orders issued, paid, and repaid, and fees collected, etc.—Continued.

	Jamaica.				Cape Colony.		
No. of orders paid.	Amount of orders paid.	No. of orders repaid.	Amount of orders repaid.	No. of orders paid.	Amount of orders paid.	No. of orders repaid.	Amount of orders repaid.
....	....	....	....	....	....	....	....
....	....	....	....	....	....	....	....
12	$109.42	....	....	4	$14.61	1	$2.50
1	.97	....	....	4	91.93	....	....
10	29.93	....	....	6	90.82	....	....
....	....	....	....	....	....	....	....
3	2.68	....	....	2	2.95	....	....
5	198.31	....	....	....	....	....	....
4	194.80	....	....	....	....	....	....
33	611.46	....	....	20	832.49	....	....
16	496.00	....	....	....	....	....	....
6	189.14	....	....	....	....	....	....
1	20.00	....	....	....	....	....	....
3	54.87	....	....	1	19.48	....	....
46	1,430.18	....	....	4	14.80	....	....
68	405.75	....	....	38	837.41	1	8.00
33	962.09	....	....	4	68.21	....	....
70	1,367.44	....	....	16	299.76	....	....
5	209.27	....	....	1	5.47	....	....
7	86.50	....	....	3	8.76	....	....
35	1,248.55	....	....	12	366.73	....	....
....	....	....	....	....	....	....	....
....	....	....	....	....	....	....	....
....	....	....	....	....	....	....	....
33	862.95	....	....	12	224.18	....	....
1,633	52,489.48	3	$52.76	89	1,121.99	....	....
11	110.01	....	....	3	46.88	....	....
125	2,721.10	....	....	12	176.21	....	....
7	46.72	....	....	....	....	....	....
1	2.01	....	....	7	219.15	....	....
13	360.38	1	7.00	....	....	....	....
6	292.20	....	....	....	....	....	....
9	158.10	....	....	....	....	....	....
1	16.01	....	....	....	....	....	....
2	19.48	....	....	....	....	....	....
....	....	....	....	....	....	....	....
2,219	64,715.79	4	59.76	287	3,441.62	2	10.50

No. 12.—*Statement showing the number and amount of international money-*

States and Territories.	Tasmania.				Queensland.			
	No. of orders paid.	Amount of orders paid.	No. of orders repaid.	Amount of orders repaid.	No. of orders paid.	Amount of orders paid.	No. of orders repaid.	Amount of orders repaid.
Alabama								
Arizona								
Arkansas								
California	27	$720.16			32	$958.93		
Colorado					1	4.87	1	$48.70
Connecticut	2	23.13			4	110.78		
Dakota								
Delaware								
District of Columbia					3	5.51		
Florida	1	9.74						
Georgia								
Idaho								
Illinois	9	47.47			27	343.01	1	29.99
Indiana	3	97.40			2	7.05		
Indian Territory								
Iowa								
Kansas					1	0.00		
Kentucky					1	2.67		
Louisiana								
Maine	164	1,209.64			48	378.80		
Maryland	1	34.09			2	14.61		
Massachusetts	17	138.89			16	215.32		
Michigan	1	4.87			3	27.20		
Minnesota								
Mississippi								
Missouri	1	29.45			8	187.49		
Montana								
Nebraska								
Nevada								
New Hampshire								
New Jersey	1	4.26			10	228.40		
New Mexico								
New York	65	524.31	1	$4.00	149	1,839.36		
North Carolina								
Ohio	8	80.60			20	384.27		
Oregon					3	102.27		
Pennsylvania	9	114.37			17	223.24		
Rhode Island	2	48.56			1	.60		
South Carolina								
Tennessee	1	17.05			1	9.74		
Texas								
Utah								
Vermont	1	.06			1	2.41		
Virginia	4	47.73						
Washington								
West Virginia								
Wisconsin	1	2.44			3	75.48		
Wyoming								
Total	318	3,145.22	1	4.00	353	5,127.93	2	78.69

orders issued, paid, and repaid, and fees collected, etc.—Continued.

	Denmark.				Totals.		
No. of orders paid.	Amount of orders paid.	No. of orders repaid.	Amount of orders repaid.	No. of orders paid.	Amount of orders paid.	No. of orders repaid.	Amount of orders repaid.
....	....	....	....	254	$5,814.19	9	$75.56
....	....	....	....	57	2,276.52	2	9.50
....	....	....	....	399	12,255.40	5	50.58
30	$1,133.60	....	....	10,071·	236,616.00	195	2,762.27
1	5.36	....	....	1,889	49,852.89	47	909.92
9	214.85	....	....	5,090	62,813.65	66	879.81
15	410.71	....	....	1,511	45,006.11	22	271.50
....	....	....	....	168	3,265.07	5	60.01
11	16.43	....	....	3,998	32,919.58	35	884.81
1	2.50	....	....	877	19,175.97	9	154.27
2	53.62	....	....	370	8,008.85	9	269.29
....	....	....	....	126	4,736.66	2	62.00
96	2,255.97	....	....	22,425	392,912.94	230	2,881.58
1	1.00	....	....	2,943	62,607.54	37	322.72
....	....	....	....	3	109.80	....	....
43	1,082.63	....	....	3,587	90,885.15	41	607.64
12	318.61	....	....	2,037	55,242.12	32	370.08
....	....	....	....	1,075	24,498.97	13	191.07
1	2.68	....	....	2,053	38,953.46	20	304.82
3	72.38	....	....	4,783	57,102.24	22	288.06
2	22.72	....	....	2,189	42,630.18	25	239.76
12	96.12	....	....	21,800	307,721.82	263	3,518.91
39	1,265.88	....	....	10,268	206,010.16	176	2,772.07
47	1,166.82	....	....	5,633	152,000.89	71	744.74
....	....	....	....	101	2,284.15	2	5.00
5	127.97	....	....	5,048	119,601.68	61	738.50
....	....	....	....	392	12,806.01	16	358.62
79	2,821.95	....	....	2,552	70,382.98	20	306.33
3	118.99	....	....	90	2,476.12	8	239.25
....	....	....	....	642	12,398.11	20	892.42
23	450.75	1	$5.00	6,094	117,099.54	95	1,306.27
1	2.54	....	....	100	2,486.24	2	32.25
90	1,728.24	1	2.40	73,840	1,046,261.34	610	9,007.78
....	....	....	....	144	2,769.71	1	5.00
4	111.47	....	....	9,245	179,962.21	113	951.31
11	377.35	....	....	1,302	31,992.73	19	448.16
11	230.31	....	....	19,722	298,212.05	241	2,750.27·
2	21.85	....	....	1,496	25,871.78	29	240.48
....	....	....	....	142	3,426.39	1	10.00
2	98.93	....	....	609	13,268.32	18	179.80
4	42.89	....	....	2,337	61,575.68	36	620.07
11	253.15	....	....	349	8,086.48	10	65.50
....	....	....	....	935	17,002.68	11	100.57
....	....	....	....	730	12,609.32	10	249.44
6	187.67	....	....	1,202	32,163.59	7	142.24
....	....	....	....	152	3,810.36	3	68.44
71	1,847.58	....	....	6,128	166,781.93	75	851.71
1	25.35	....	....	115	3,538.58	5	56.60
649	16,568.37	2	7.40	236,992	4,169,675.64	2,747	37,759.98

No. 20. — *Weight of letters, newspapers, etc., sent from the United States, etc —Continued.*

Steam-ship lines.	Sweden.		Switzerland		Turkey.	
	Letters.	Papers.	Letters.	Papers.	Letters.	Papers.
	Grams.	*Grams.*	*Grams.*	*Grams.*	*Grams.*	*Grams.*
North German Lloyd	11, 656, 735	29, 197, 189	2, 009, 535	8, 875, 690	418, 310	4, 680, 560
Cunard, limited (New York)	3, 393, 830	6, 100, 140	334, 845	914, 800	118, 495	1, 188, 845
Liverpool and Great Western	929, 515	1, 721, 270	377, 410	1, 856, 515	32, 655	296, 033
General Transatlantic	421, 290	1, 079, 170	1, 910, 195	10, 100, 982	15, 845	181, 405
White Star	156, 145	168, 215	74, 740	241, 470	7, 470	63, 563
Hamburg-American	1, 095, 660	2, 636, 267	160, 870	926, 455	42, 135	409, 935
Anchor	603		78, 130	381, 420	5, 920	43, 175
Cunard, limited (Boston)						
Inman	47, 625	102, 115	13, 325	106, 140	2, 390	14, 495
American						
Thingvalla						
Red Star						
Netherland Steam Navigation						
Total	17, 701, 405	41, 004, 366	4, 959, 050	23, 404, 472	643, 220	6, 268. 035
Increase, compared with last year	4, 784, 570	3, 621, 512	301, 150	2, 559, 852	120, 425	396, 555

West Coast of Africa, steamer Cumbrian:
Letters 1, 365
Papers 22, 390

RECAPITULATION BY STEAM-SHIP LINES.

Steam-ship lines.	Letters.	Papers.
	Grams.	*Grams.*
North German Lloyd	130, 274, 844	500, 597, 483
Cunard, limited (New York)	66, 003, 159	255, 876, 778
Liverpool and Great Western	20, 848, 242	86, 910, 796
General Transatlantic	18, 170, 966	78, 750, 009
White Star	11, 568, 421	31, 515, 410
Hamburg-American	10, 672, 685	44, 866, 521
Anchor	3, 859, 582	14, 199, 070
Cunard, limited (Boston)	1, 264, 200	7, 171, 340
Inman	856, 348	4, 529, 222
American	15, 758	146, 372
Thingvalla	3, 070	18, 411
Red Star	9, 279	1, 075
Netherland Steam Navigation	4, 345	282, 490
Steamer Cumbrian	1, 365	22, 390
Grand total	263, 550, 944	1, 024, 887, 367

RECAPITULATION BY COUNTRIES.

Countries.	Letters.	Papers.
	Grams.	*Grams.*
England	114, 061, 185	525, 061, 865
Austria	10, 122, 840	22, 351, 846
Belgium	2, 970, 032	15, 918, 495
Denmark	4, 042, 754	7, 812. 188
France	16, 665, 796	77, 942, 840
Germany	56, 428, 283	207, 816, 360
Italy	13, 173, 610	45, 265, 960
Netherlands	2, 923, 705	11, 210, 440
Norway	8, 764, 830	14, 835, 636
Portugal	851, 639	2, 272, 045
Russia	7, 975, 980	9, 950, 450
Spain	2, 345, 170	13, 754, 895
Sweden	17, 701, 405	41, 004, 366
Switzerland	4, 959, 050	23, 404, 472
Turkey	643, 220	6, 268, 035
West Coast of Africa	1, 365	22, 390
Total	263, 550, 944	1, 024, 887. 367
Increase, compared with last fiscal year	30, 656, 215	97, 099, 502

No. 22.—*Statement showing the weight of foreign closed mails retransported by sea, and the amounts accruing to steam-ship companies for their carriage, during the fiscal year ending June 30, 1888.*

Steam-ship lines.	Letters.	Papers.	Amount.
	Grams.	*Grams.*	*Dollars*
North German Lloyd	11, 489, 328	29, 816, 981	13, 964. 55
Cunard (limited)	4, 820, 211	11, 360, 414	5, 747. 79
Hamburg American	374. 360	911, 081	449. 17
White Star	1, 154, 134	3, 176, 144	1, 420. 24
Liverpool and Great Western	2, 189, 884	5, 426, 630	2, 636. 90
Anchor	525, 314	1, 241, 463	626. 73
Inman	28, 171	56, 583	32. 84
New York and Cuba	147, 590	3, 536, 416	387. 38
Red D	51, 628	472, 961	95. 47
Clyde	15, 500	201, 741	34. 43
Quebec	19, 704	202, 173	38. 53
Atlas	17, 531	85, 100	25. 13
Haytien Republic	3, 141	82, 559	11. 09
Alert	9, 832	117, 324	20. 81
New York and Jamaica	1, 701	2, 635	1. 84
Dominican	2, 394	46, 778	6. 77
United States and Brazil	2, 385	77, 590	9. 78
Atlantic and West India	457	21, 396	2. 57
Pacific Mail	41, 422	1, 112, 535	147. 32
Thames	1, 397	1, 971	1. 44
Honduras and Central American	960	27, 668	3. 56
Plant Investment Company (contract)	1, 190, 987	11, 749, 786	....
Total	23, 087, 921	68, 731, 025	25, 664. 24

INDEX.

o

9 780331 513301